THE FIFTEENTH MENTAL
MEASUREMENTS YEARBOOK

EARLIER PUBLICATIONS IN THIS SERIES

THE FIFTEENTH MENTAL MEASUREMENTS YEARBOOK

BARBARA S. PLAKE, JAMES C. IMPARA,
and
ROBERT A. SPIES

Editors

LINDA L. MURPHY
Managing Editor

The Buros Institute of Mental Measurements
The University of Nebraska-Lincoln
Lincoln, Nebraska

2003
Distributed by The University of Nebraska Press

Note to Users

To

the memory of

ANNE ANASTASI

(1908-2001)

This Yearbook is dedicated to the memory of Anne Anastasi in recognition of her devotion to tests and testing procedures. Dr. Anastasi reviewed in each successive *Yearbook* from *The 1938 Mental Measurements Yearbook* through *The Eleventh Mental Measurements Yearbook* (1992).

TABLE OF CONTENTS

INTRODUCTION

Publication of *The Fifteenth Mental Measurements Yearbook* (*15th MMY*) continues the long-standing history of this unique series originally begun by Oscar K. Buros with *The 1938 Mental Measurements Yearbook*. Criteria for inclusion in this edition of the *MMY* are that a test be (a) new or revised since last reviewed in the *MMY* series, (b) commercially available, (c) available in the English language, and (d) published with adequate developmental or technical documentation.

THE FIFTEENTH MENTAL MEASUREMENTS YEARBOOK

The *15th MMY* contains reviews of tests that are new or significantly revised since the publication of the *14th MMY* in 2001. Reviews, descriptions, and references associated with many older tests can be located in other Buros publications: previous *MMY*s and *Tests in Print VI*.

Content. The contents of the *15th MMY* include: (a) a bibliography of 286 commercially available tests, new or revised, published as separates for use with English-speaking individuals; (b) 508 critical test reviews from specialists selected by the editors on the basis of their expertise in measurement and, often, the content of the test being reviewed; (c) a test title index with appropriate cross-references; (d) a classified subject index; (e) a publishers directory and index, including publisher addresses and other contact information with test listings by publisher; (f) a name index including the names of authors of all tests, reviews, or references included in this *MMY*; (g) an index of acronyms for easy reference when only a test acronym is known; and (h) a score index to identify for users test scores of potential interest.

Appendix. Three separate listings appear in the *15th MMY* for users requiring additional information when a specific test cannot be otherwise located in the *Mental Measurements Yearbook* series. Beginning with the *14th MMY*, a test qualifying for review must provide either an adequate developmental history or sufficient evidence describing the instrument's technical properties. Not all tests submitted for evaluation meet one of these two criteria for review in the *MMY* series. A listing of tests received (but not reviewed) is included to make users aware of the availability of these tests, albeit without supporting documentation or reviews. The Appendix also provides a list of tests that meet review criteria but were received too late for review in this volume. These tests (plus additional tests received in following months) will be reviewed in *The Sixteenth Mental Measurements Yearbook*. Test reviews that are completed prior to publication of the *16th MMY* are available electronically for a small fee on our web-based service Test Reviews Online (http://www.unl.edu/buros). A third list in the Appendix includes titles of tests requested from publishers but not yet received as of this volume's publication. This listing includes tests for which publishers refuse to allow their tests to be reviewed as well as those who routinely make their instruments available for review but who have failed at this point to provide a new or revised test for evaluation.

Organization. The current *MMY* series is organized like an encyclopedia, with tests being ordered alphabetically by title. If the title of a test is known, the reader can locate the test immediately without having to consult the Index of Titles.

The page headings reflect the encyclopedic organization. The page heading of the left-hand page cites the number and title of the first test listed on that page, and the page heading of the right-hand page cites the number and title of the last test listed on that page. All numbers presented in the various indexes are test numbers, not page numbers. Page numbers are important only for the Table of Contents and are located at the bottom of each page.

TESTS AND REVIEWS

The *15th MMY* contains descriptive information on 286 tests as well as 508 test reviews by 305 different authors. Statistics on the number and percentage of tests in each of 18 major classifications are contained in Table 1.

The percentage of new and revised or supplemented tests according to major classifications are contained in Table 2. Overall, 207 of the tests included in the *15th MMY* are new and have not been listed in a previous *MMY* although many descriptions were included in *Tests in Print VI* (*TIP VI*; 2002). The Index of Titles may be consulted to determine if a test is new or revised.

Test Selection. A new policy for selecting tests for review became effective with the *14th MMY*. This new policy for selecting tests for review requires at least minimal information be available regarding test development. The requirement that tests have such minimal information does not assure the quality of the test; it simply provides reviewers with a minimum basis for critically evaluating the quality of the test. We select our reviewers carefully and let them and well-informed readers decide for themselves about the

TABLE 1
TESTS BY MAJOR CLASSIFICATIONS

Classification	Number	Percentage
Personality	78	27.3
Vocations	40	13.9
Miscellaneous	26	9.1
Behavior Assessment	22	7.7
Neuropsychological	20	7.0
Developmental	17	5.9
Intelligence and General		
Aptitude	15	5.3
Reading	15	5.3
English and Language	12	4.2
Education	10	3.5
Achievement	9	3.1
Speech and Hearing	7	2.4
Mathematics	7	2.4
Sensory-Motor	5	1.7
Foreign Languages	1	.4
Fine Arts	1	.4
Social Studies	1	.4
Science	0	.0
Total	286	100.0

TABLE 2
NEW AND REVISED OR SUPPLEMENTED TESTS BY MAJOR CLASSIFICATION

Classification	Number of Tests	Percentage New	Percentage Revised
Achievement	9	44.4	55.6
Behavior Assessment	22	81.8	18.2
Developmental	17	76.5	24.5
Education	10	80.0	20.0
English and Language	12	58.3	41.7
Fine Arts	1	100.0	0.0
Foreign Languages	1	0.0	100.0
Intelligence and General Aptitude	15	46.7	53.3
Mathematics	7	42.9	57.1
Miscellaneous	26	84.6	15.4
Neuropsychological	20	85.0	15.0
Personality	78	76.9	23.1
Reading	15	60.0	40.0
Science	0	0.0	0.0
Sensory-Motor	5	80.0	20.0
Social Studies	1	0.0	100.0
Speech and Hearing	7	57.1	42.9
Vocations	40	75.0	25.0
Total	286	72.4	27.6

essential features needed to assure the appropriate use of a test. Some new or revised tests are not included because they were received too late to undergo the review process and still permit timely publication, or because some reviewers did not meet their commitment to review the test. A list of these tests is included in the Appendix and every effort will be made to have them reviewed for *The Sixteenth Mental Measurements Yearbook*, and included before then through our web-based service Test Reviews Online (TROL).

There are some new or revised tests for which there will be no reviews although these tests are described in *Tests in Print VI*. The absence of reviews occurred for a variety of reasons including: We could not identify qualified reviewers, the test materials were incomplete so reviews were not possible, the tests were sufficiently obscure that reviews were deemed unnecessary, the publisher advised us the test is now out-of-print before reviews were completed, or the test did not meet our criterion for documentation. Descriptions of all these tests still in print were published in *TIP VI* and are included in the Test Reviews Online database.

Reviewer Selection. The selection of reviewers was done with great care. The objective was to secure measurement and subject specialists who would be independent and represent a variety of different viewpoints. It was also important to find individuals who would write critical reviews competently, judiciously, fairly, and in a timely manner. Reviewers were identified by means of extensive searches of the professional literature, attendance at professional meetings, and recommendations from leaders in various professional fields. Perusal of reviews in this volume will also reveal that reviewers work in and represent a cross-section of the places in which testing is taught and tests are used: universities, public schools, businesses, and community agencies. These reviewers represent an outstanding array of professional talent, and their contributions are obviously of primary importance in making this Yearbook a valuable resource. A list of the individuals reviewing in this volume is included at the beginning of the Index section.

Readers of test reviews in the *15th MMY* are encouraged to exercise an active, analytical, and evaluative perspective in reading the reviews. Just as one would evaluate a test, the readers should evaluate critically the reviewer's comments about the test. The reviewers selected are competent professionals in their respective fields, but it is inevitable that their reviews also reflect their individual perspectives. *The Mental Measurements Yearbook* series was developed to stimulate critical thinking and assist in the selection of the best available test for a given purpose, not to promote the passive acceptance of reviewer judgment. Active, evaluative reading is the key to the most effective use of the professional expertise offered in each of the reviews.

INDEXES

As mentioned above, the *15th MMY* includes six indexes invaluable as aids to effective use: (a) Index of Titles, (b) Index of Acronyms, (c) Classified Subject Index, (d) Publishers Directory and Index, (e) Index of Names, and (f) Score Index. Additional comment on these indexes is presented below.

Index of Titles. Because the organization of the *15th MMY* is encyclopedic in nature, with the tests ordered alphabetically by title throughout the volume, the test title index does not have to be consulted to find a test if the title is known. However, the title index has some features that make it useful beyond its function as a complete title listing. First, it includes cross-reference information useful for tests with superseded or alternative titles or tests commonly (and sometimes inaccurately) known by multiple titles. Second, it identifies tests that are new or revised. Third, it may cue the user to other tests with similar titles that may be useful. Titles for the 76 tests not reviewed because of insufficient technical documentation are included in the Index of Titles. It is important to keep in mind that the numbers in this index, like those for all *MMY* indexes, are test numbers and not page numbers.

Because no *MMY* includes reviews of all tests currently in print, a particular test of interest may not be reviewed in this volume. To learn if a commercially published test has been reviewed in this or an earlier volume of the *MMY*, users may access the Buros page on the World Wide Web (www.unl.edu/buros). A search on Test Reviews Online (TROL) will indicate if a test has been reviewed and will include the *MMY* in which the review can be found. TROL also provides electronic access to reviews provided in recent *MMY*s (most current reviews only) and test reviews that have been finalized since the publication of the most recent *MMY*. Therefore, TROL provides ready access, for a small fee, to the majority of tests that have been reviewed in *The Mental Measurements Yearbooks*. As an alternative, *Tests in Print VI* can be consulted. This volume provides a cross-reference to reviews of still-in-print tests in the *MMY* series.

Index of Acronyms. Some tests seem to be better known by their acronyms than by their full titles. The Index of Acronyms can help in these instances; it refers the reader to the full title of the test and to the relevant descriptive information and reviews.

Classified Subject Index. The Classified Subject Index classifies all tests listed in the *15th MMY* into 17 of 18 major categories: Achievement, Behavior Assessment, Developmental, Education, English and Language, Fine Arts, Foreign Languages, Intelligence and General Aptitude, Mathematics, Miscellaneous, Neuropsychological, Personality, Reading, Science, Sensory-Motor, Social Studies, Speech and Hearing, and Vocations. (No tests in the Science category are reviewed in the *15ᵗʰ MMY*.) Each test entry in this index includes test title, population for which the test is intended, and test number. The Classified Subject Index is of great help to readers who seek a listing of tests in given subject areas. The Classified Subject Index represents a starting point for readers who know their area of interest but do not know how to further focus that interest in order to identify the best test(s) for their particular purposes.

Publishers Directory and Index. The Publishers Directory and Index includes the names and addresses of the publishers of all tests included in the *15ᵗʰ MMY* plus a listing of test numbers for each individual publisher. Also included are the telephone and FAX numbers, and email and Web addresses for those publishers who responded to our request for this information. This index can be particularly useful in obtaining addresses for specimen sets or catalogs after the test reviews have been read and evaluated. It can also be useful when a reader knows the publisher of a certain test but is uncertain about the test title, or when a reader is interested in the range of tests published by a given publisher.

Index of Names. The Index of Names provides a comprehensive list of names, indicating authorship of a test, test review, or reviewer's reference.

Score Index. The Score Index is a listing of the scored parts of all tests reviewed in the *15ᵗʰ MMY*. Test titles are sometimes misleading or ambiguous, and test content may be difficult to define with precision. But test scores often represent operational definitions of the variables the test author is trying to measure, and as such they can define test purpose and content more adequately than other descriptive information. A search for a particular test is most often a search for a test that measures some specific variable(s). Test scores and their associated labels can often be the best definitions of the variable(s) of interest. The Score Index is a detailed subject index based on the most critical operational features of any test—the scores and their associated labels.

HOW TO USE THIS YEARBOOK

A reference work like *The Fifteenth Mental Measurements Yearbook* can be of far greater benefit to a reader if some time is taken to become familiar with what it has to offer and how it might be used most effectively to obtain the information wanted.

Step 1: Read the Introduction to the *15ᵗʰ MMY* in its entirety.

Step 2: Become familiar with the six indexes and particularly with the instructions preceding each index listing.

Step 3: Use the book by looking up needed information. This step is simple if one keeps in mind the following procedures:

1. Go directly to the test entry using the alphabetical page headings if you know the title of the test.

2. Consult the Index of Titles for possible variants of the title or consult the appropriate subject area of the Classified Subject Index for other possible leads or for similar or related tests in the same area, if you do not know, cannot find, or are unsure of the title of a test. (Other uses for both of these indexes were described above.)

3. Consult the Index of Names if you know the author of a test but not the title or publisher. Look up the author's titles until you find the test you want.

4. Consult the Publishers Directory and Index if you know the test publisher but not the title or author. Look up the publisher's titles until you find the test you want.

5. Consult the Score Index and locate the test or tests that include the score variable of interest if you are looking for a test that yields a particular kind of test score.

6. If after following the above steps you are not able to find a review of the test you want, consult the Appendix for a list of tests that are not reviewed. Reasons tests are not reviewed include (a) they did not meet our selection criteria, (b) the reviews were not completed in time for publication in this volume, or (c) the publisher failed to respond in a timely manner to our request for testing materials. You also can look in *TIP VI* or visit the Buros web page (www.unl.edu/buros) and use the Test Reviews Online service (TROL) to identify the *MMY* that contains the description and any available reviews for a test of interest.

7. Once you have found the test or tests you are looking for, read the descriptive entries for these tests carefully so that you can take advantage of the information provided. A description of the information in these test entries is presented later in this section.

8. Read the test reviews carefully and analytically, as suggested above. The information and evaluations contained in these reviews are meant to assist test consumers in making well-informed decisions about the choice and applications of tests.

9. Once you have read the descriptive information and test reviews, you may want to contact the publisher to order a specimen set for a particular test so that you can examine it firsthand. The Publishers Directory and Index has the address information needed to obtain specimen sets or catalogs.

Making Effective Use of the Test Entries. The test entries include extensive information. For each test, descriptive information is presented in the following order:

a) TITLES. Test titles are printed in boldface type. Secondary or series titles are set off from main titles by a colon.

b) PURPOSE. For each test there is a brief, clear statement describing the purpose of the test. Often these statements are quotations from the test manual.

c) POPULATION. This describes the groups for which the test is intended. The grade, chronological age, semester range, or employment category is usually given. For example, "Grades 1.5–2.5, 2–3, 4–12, 13–17" means that there are four test booklets: a booklet for the middle of first grade through the middle of the second grade, a booklet for the beginning of the second grade through the end of third grade, a booklet for grades 4 through 12 inclusive, and a booklet for undergraduate and graduate students in colleges and universities.

d) PUBLICATION DATE. The inclusive range of publication dates for the various forms, accessories, and editions of a test is reported.

e) ACRONYM. When a test is often referred to by an acronym, the acronym is given in the test entry immediately following the publication date.

f) SCORES. The number of part scores is presented along with their titles or descriptions of what they are intended to represent or measure.

g) ADMINISTRATION. Individual or group administration is indicated. A test is considered a group test unless it may be administered only individually.

h) FORMS, PARTS, AND LEVELS. All available forms, parts, and levels are listed.

i) MANUAL. Notation is made if no manual is available. All other manual information is included under Price Data.

j) RESTRICTED DISTRIBUTION. This is noted only for tests that are made available to a special market by the publisher. Educational and psychological restrictions are not noted (unless a special training course is required for use).

k) PRICE DATA. Price information is reported for test packages (usually 20 to 35 tests), answer sheets, all other accessories, and specimen sets. The statement "$17.50 per 35 tests" means that all accessories are included unless otherwise indicated by the reporting of separate prices for accessories. The statement also means 35 tests of one level, one edition, or one part unless stated otherwise. Because test prices can change very quickly, the year that the listed test prices were obtained is also given. Foreign currency is assigned the appropriate symbol. When prices are given in foreign dollars, a qualifying symbol is added (e.g., A$16.50 refers to 16 dollars and 50 cents in Australian currency). Along with cost, the publication date and number of pages on which print occurs is reported for manuals and technical reports (e.g., 1999, 102 pages). All types of machine-scorable answer sheets available for use with a specific test are also reported in the descriptive entry. Scoring and reporting services provided by publishers are reported along with information on costs. In a few cases, special computerized scoring and interpretation services are noted at the end of the price information.

l) FOREIGN LANGUAGE AND OTHER SPECIAL EDITIONS. This section concerns foreign language editions published by the same publisher who sells the English-language edition. It also indicates special editions (e.g., Braille, large type) available from the same or a different publisher.

m) TIME. The number of minutes of actual working time allowed examinees and the approximate length of time needed for administering a test are reported whenever obtainable. The latter figure is always enclosed in parentheses. Thus, "50(60) minutes" indicates that the examinees are allowed 50 minutes of working time and that a total of 60 minutes is needed to administer the test. A time of "40–50 minutes" indicates an untimed test that takes approximately 45 minutes to administer, or—in a few instances—a test so timed that working time and administration time are very difficult to disentangle. When the time necessary to administer a test is not reported or suggested in the test materials but has been obtained from a catalog or through correspondence with the test publisher or author, the time is enclosed in brackets.

n) COMMENTS. Some entries contain special notations, such as: "for research use only"; "revision of the ABC Test"; "tests administered monthly at centers throughout the United States"; "subtests available as separates"; and "verbal creativity." A statement such as "verbal creativity" is intended to further describe what the test claims to measure. Some of the test entries include factual statements that imply criticism of the test, such as "1999 test identical with test copyrighted 1980."

o) AUTHOR. For most tests, all authors are reported. In the case of tests that appear in a new form each year, only authors of the most recent forms are listed. Names are reported exactly as printed on test booklets. Names of editors generally are not reported.

p) PUBLISHER. The name of the publisher or distributor is reported for each test. Foreign publishers are identified by listing the country in brackets immediately following the name of the publisher. The Publishers Directory and Index must be consulted for a publisher's address and other contact information.

q) FOREIGN ADAPTATIONS. Revisions and adaptations of tests for foreign use are listed in a separate paragraph following the original edition.

r) SUBLISTINGS. Levels, editions, subtests, or parts of a test available in separate booklets are sometimes presented as sublistings with titles set in small capitals. Sub-sublistings are indented and titles are set in italic type.

s) CROSS REFERENCES. For tests that have been listed previously in a Buros Institute of Mental Measurements publication, a test entry includes—if relevant—a final item containing cross references to the reviews, excerpts, and references for that test in those volumes. In the cross references, "T6:467" refers to test 467 in *Tests in Print VI*, "14:121" refers to test 121 in *The Fourteenth Mental Measurements Yearbook*, "8:1023" refers to test 1023 in *The Eighth Mental Measurements Yearbook*, "T3:144" refers to test 144 in *Tests in Print III*, "7:637" refers to test 637 in *The Seventh Mental Measurements Yearbook*, "P:262" refers to test 262 in *Personality Tests and Reviews*, "2:1427" refers to test 1427 in *The 1940 Yearbook*, and "1:1110" refers to test 1110 in *The 1938 Yearbook*. In the case of batteries and programs, the paragraph also includes cross references—from the battery to the separately listed subtests and vice versa—to entries in this volume and to entries and reviews in earlier *Yearbooks*. Test numbers not preceded by a colon refer to tests in this *Yearbook*; for example, "see 45" refers to test 45 in this Yearbook.

ACKNOWLEDGMENTS

This Yearbook is dedicated to the memory of Anne Anastasi (1908—2001) in recognition of her devotion to tests and testing procedures. Dr. Anastasi reviewed in each successive *Yearbook* from the *1938 Yearbook* through *The Eleventh Mental Measurements Yearbook*.

The publication of the *14th Mental Measurements Yearbook* could not have been accomplished without the contributions of many individuals. The editors acknowledge gratefully the talent, expertise, and dedication of all those who have assisted in the publication process.

Linda Murphy, Managing Editor, is a critical member of the Buros team. In addition to her strong work ethic, she provides a historical base and a knowledge level that keeps us from making many errors we might make without her wise counsel. She makes our job as editors much more palatable than it would otherwise be. Nor would the publication of this volume be possible without the efforts of Gary Anderson, Assistant Editor, and Rosemary Sieck, Clerical Assistant. As always, their efforts go far beyond that required as part of normal job responsibilities. Rasma Strautkalns, Institute Secretary, is also recognized for her important contributions to the success of our efforts. We appreciate all the efforts of these permanent staff, each of whom contributes more than their share to the development and production of all of the Buros Institute's products.

This volume would not exist without the substantial efforts of the test reviewers. We are very grateful to the many reviewers who have prepared test reviews for the Buros Institute of Mental Measurements. The willingness of these reviewers to take time from their busy professional schedules to share their expertise in the form of thoughtful test reviews is appreciated. *The Mental Measurements Yearbook* would not exist were it not for their efforts.

The work of many graduate students helps make possible the quality of this volume. Their efforts have included writing test descriptions, fact checking reviews, looking for test references, and innumerable other tasks. We thank Rene Ayers, Wei Huang, Michael Lemberger, Brad Merker, Rhonda Turner, and Georgette Yetter for their assistance.

Appreciation is also extended to the members of our National Advisory Committee for their willingness to assist in the operation of the Buros Institute of Mental Measurements and for their thought-provoking suggestions for improving the *MMY* series and other publications of the Institute. During the period in which this volume was prepared the National Advisory Committee has included Jane Close Conoley, Gail Latta, Lawrence Rudner, Paul Sackett, and Jeffrey Smith.

The Buros Institute of Mental Measurements is part of the Department of Educational Psychology of the University of Nebraska-Lincoln and we have benefited from the many departmental colleagues who have contributed to this work. We are also grateful for the contribution of the University of Nebraska Press, which provides expert consultation and serves as distributor of the *MMY* series.

SUMMARY

The *MMY* series is a valuable resource for people interested in studying or using tests. Once the process of using the series is understood, a reader can gain rapid access to a wealth of information. Our hope is that with the publication of the *15th MMY*, test authors and publishers will consider carefully the comments made by the reviewers and continue to refine and perfect their assessment products.

Barbara S. Plake
James C. Impara
Robert A. Spies
April 2003

Tests and Reviews

[1]

Academic Perceptions Inventory [2000 Revision].

Purpose: "Developed to assess a profile of the academic self in various classrooms and in the learning environment ... with perceptions of the self as a person, as a student, and at school."

Population: Grades K–16.

Publication Dates: 1979–2000.

Acronym: API.

Administration: Group.

Price Data, 2002: $20 per packet of 25 scales (specify level); $25 per test manual (specify Primary Level [2000, 83 pages], Intermediate Level [2000, 76 pages], Advanced Level [2000, 79 pages], or College Level [2000, 73 pages]); $40 per composite test manual (2000, 146 pages); $.40 per answer sheet; $.30 per scale for scoring.

Foreign Language Editions: Also available in Spanish, Italian, and French.

Time: (5–20) minutes per test.

Comments: Ratings by self and others; previous edition entitled The Affective Perception Inventory.

Authors: Louise M. Soares and Anthony T. Soares.

Publisher: SOARES Associates.

a) PRIMARY LEVEL.
Population: Grades K–3.
Scores: 9 Scales: Self Concept, Student Self, School, Reading, Social Studies, Science, Arithmetic, Fine Arts, Sports and Games.

b) INTERMEDIATE LEVEL.
Population: Grades 4–8.
Scores: 11 Scales: Self Concept, Student Self, School, Language Arts, Reading, Foreign Languages, History and Geography, Science, Mathematics, Fine Arts, Physical Education.

c) ADVANCED LEVEL.
Population: Grades 9–12.
Scores: 13 Scales: Self Concept, Student Self, School, English, Foreign Languages, American History, Mathematics, Biology, Chemistry, Earth Sciences, Physics, Fine Arts, Sports.

d) COLLEGE LEVEL.
Population: Grades 13–16.
Scores: 15 Scales: Self Concept, Student Self, Campus, English, Foreign Languages, World History, Political Science, Business, Mathematics, Biology, Chemistry, Physics, Humanities, Fine Arts, Sports.

Cross References: See T4:130 (3 references); for reviews by Rosa A. Hagin and Gerald R. Smith of The Affective Perception Inventory, see 9:59.

Review of the Academic Perceptions Inventory [2000 Revision] by CAROL E. KESSLER, Assistant Professor of Education, Cabrini College, Radnor, PA:

DESCRIPTION. The Academic Perceptions Inventory (API) is suitable for students from kindergarten through college. The authors developed this inventory for the purpose of "1) describing the present affective dimension of students and interpersonal perceptions in regard to educational experiences, 2) determining the perceptions of self as a person, self as a student, self in various classrooms, self in the school/college setting, 3) comparing the degree of congruence or divergence of self-ratings and others-ratings, 4) obtaining an indirect measure of needs-assessment programs, and 5) for dimensionalizing the construct of self" (Composite Test Manual, p. 1).

The test has four different levels: Primary (Grades K–3), Intermediate (Grades 4–8), Advanced (Grades 9–12), and College (Grades 13–16). All four levels use a 4-point response scale. The number of items for each scale (e.g., Self Concept, Reading) vary except for the primary level where each scale has the same number of items: 18 pairs of interest and ability self-descriptors. The total number of items for the primary level is 115, for the Intermediate level it is 152, for the Advanced level it is 192, and for the College level it is 255. The inventory is a paper-and-

pencil, forced-choice format and can be administered, scored, and interpreted by nonclinical staff.
All four scales are scored in the same manner.
Each item is scored separately (from +2 to −2) and
the algebraic sum of these scored items yields an
index score for the scale. The authors state that
scores falling between the fourth and sixth stanine
evidence moderate perceptions. The total or composite score for each student reveals an overall
view in regard to the degree of negative or positive
perceptions or feelings received or expressed from
the self in a school setting. The major objective of
this inventory is to ascertain the affective development of students in the same fashion examiners
measure students' cognitive development. The examiner could use the results diagnostically in identifying problem areas for the student, class, or school
system. Thus, a group profile can also be obtained.
Scores should not be used for high stakes testing,
rather they should be interpreted in a judicious
and reasonable fashion. There is great stability in
self-perceptions; however, self-reported responses
should not be considered definitive measures because people are rarely so simplistic or transparent.

DEVELOPMENT. The API is the latest
version (copyright 2000) of an assessment device that
has been undergoing development since 1973. Comprehensive information is provided regarding the
initial test development. Likewise, the authors include an excellent review on the theoretical foundation of the concepts underlying this instrument.
The definitions offered for each scale are adequate
and clear.

TECHNICAL. Copious information is included in the various manuals regarding standardization, reliability, and validity. A summary of the
results follows: (a) internal consistency on all scales,
(b) respectable convergent validity between self
and peers and also between self and teachers (the
rater impact was greater for the former), (c) differential discriminant validity (the three varied pictures are detailed in the composite manual), and
(d) varying self-pictures developing from individualized configurations of the encoding process
in the brain. The tables and interpretive remarks
are extensive and valuable, especially in addressing
the critical features of the API inventory and
verify the technical adequacy of this instrument.

COMMENTARY. The presentation and organization of this inventory is very poor and not
manageable. The pages are not numbered and the

booklets are not bound properly. All of the manuals examined fell apart, regardless of the amount of
care given by the reviewer. No tabs were used to
separate topics or sections. Also, different fonts
were used throughout the manuals. Obviously, it
can be assumed from the type-face employed that
much of this information was not updated or
reformatted. Yet, the last page of each booklet
contains an advertisement regarding the consulting services the authors are able to provide, so one
must assume that they do have the capability to
present the inventories in a more understandable,
visually appealing, and organized manner (in the
same technically superior mode).

Further, the original information regarding
this inventory was mixed in with the 2000 revision. It is imperative that the previous manuals
and protocols should be in a separate booklet to
alleviate any confusion for the examiner.

In addition, some issues of concern pertain
to the protocol and directions of the Primary
scales. Reading of the items could be difficult for
some second graders and impossible for most
kindergarten children. Therefore, the inventory
would have to be individually administered and
this would be very time-consuming and probably
defeat the purpose of the test. The size of the type
is small, which is especially problematic for the
younger child who is learning to read and who
might point to the word while decoding. Moreover, the directions are not always consistent with
the required tasks. The heading (example) does
not follow onto the back page. This is confusing
for youngsters. It is not clear that changing to a
continuum (4-point scale) from a bipolar approach
really helps children understand the questions better. Some of the concepts, such as changing water
into steam, might be very difficult for the lower
grades. Also, some of the young children being
tested might not have had exposure to the activities in question (e.g., visiting a museum or skating—Is this item referring to figure skating or
roller-skating?). These practices do not reflect a
true developmentally appropriate understanding.
Currently, most elementary school teachers use a
thematic unit approach in their teaching; therefore, the response to asking primary students
whether or not they like history might be a blank
stare because our children are more familiar with
an integrated curriculum, rather than a discrete
subject matter approach.

For items on the intermediate level, I noticed some questioning regarding use of foreign languages. Many students do not have these experiences or opportunities in elementary school. As far as the Advanced and College level scales are concerned, they seem to be developmentally appropriate and relevant to the experiences that students encounter in high school and college.

Thoughtful and careful consideration of these recommendations might be warranted in order for the inventories to be chosen for assessment purposes by professionals. Reading these materials was so laborious and unwieldy that I would definitely consider them as a last-choice option. These inventories could be very useful for students and the educational professionals whose responsibility it is to enhance their growth and development. The technical aspects seem to be thoroughly considered and addressed appropriately. Moreover, the theoretical constructs are well researched, analyzed, and make logical sense. This assessment tool, in regard to these aforementioned positive aspects, should be rated as very superior but, unfortunately, it is overshadowed by the careless presentation. Except for the comments regarding the Primary level scales, my recommendations could be easily addressed and these problems could be rectified with the proper clerical help.

SUMMARY. To the credit of the authors, they have produced an exceptional instrument that can be administered, scored, and interpreted in a very cost-effective and efficient fashion. I am concerned that the differential impact of ethnicity was not addressed. The inventories appear to be technically adequate and, therefore, it should be concluded that the measurements obtained accurately and consistently represent the proposed constructs. However, these tests are not useable in their present form. With major organizational reform, I believe that these instruments will provide a significant contribution to the field of academic perceptions. Finally, attending to the issues mentioned regarding the Primary level would greatly help in making this protocol developmentally appropriate and useable with younger children.

Review of the Academic Perceptions Inventory [2000 Revision] by AIMIN WANG, Associate Professor of Educational Psychology, Miami University, Oxford, OH:

DESCRIPTION. The revised Academic Perceptions Inventory (API, originally called Affective Perceptions Inventory) is a group administered rating scale that measures feelings about education-related abilities and interests of the self as a person and a student in general and in specific subject areas. The API consists of four sets of forms for four grade levels: Primary (Grades K–3), Intermediate (Grades 4–8), Advanced (Grades 9–12) and College, with 9, 11, 13, and 15 forms for these four levels, respectively. The contents measured by these forms reflect classroom standards from major associations in the corresponding subject areas. The authors indicate that the forms are available for others such as peers, teachers, and parents to rate the individual although these forms are not included for review. Each form takes about 5 minutes to complete and the entire set takes about 1 hour to complete, depending on the age group and reading ability of the participants.

The purpose of the API is to describe students' perceptions of educational experiences. It can also be used, according to the authors, to compare the congruence or divergence of self-ratings and ratings from others, obtain an indirect measure of needs-assessment programs, and dimensionalize the construct of self.

DEVELOPMENT. The items in the API were generalized to measure the identified traits. The initial trait pool was from the work of Cattell, Guilford, Eysenck, etc., with additional traits from another measurement instrument (i.e., Self-Perceptions Inventory; 226) developed by the authors of the API, from measurement experts after defining trait factors empirically, and from field groups such as students, teachers, school administrators, college educators, supervisors, and psychologists. Educators, psychologists, and counselors then evaluated these traits on their appropriateness for the purpose of the API.

A pair of opposite traits is presented at each end of a 4-point continuous dimension. Pilot testing of the API (except the College set) was conducted on 509 student self-raters, 119 student peer raters, and 70 teachers who rated their students.

TECHNICAL. Manuals for both the previous version and the revised version are packed together for each grade level and the manuals for the revised version are add-ons to the ones for the previous version. The norms are reported in the form of stanine profile scores and corresponding raw scores on different areas for each form in each grade level. The distribution of the raw scores is negatively skewed on all the measures and the authors concluded that the participants commonly perceive themselves positively. However, the authors described the general tendencies from their research findings and reported that (a) the self-perceptions of younger children are higher than those of older ones; (b) the self-perceptions of males are higher than those of females; (c) self-evaluations are higher than evaluations by others such as peers or teachers, although gender and grade within a grade level are not separately reported in the norms.

The norms of others' evaluations are not provided. The authors indicate that the ratings from parents resemble self-ratings most closely. Ratings from peers deviate the most from self-ratings. Ratings from teachers fall between these two groups. Although these findings are very likely to be true, they are based on the data collected with previous versions.

Item development and item selection are not mentioned in the test manual except for the College level. It seems that the items were developed along with the identification of the traits as described above with each item measuring two opposite traits. An item pool was developed for the college forms and rated by undergraduate students of different majors and different types of colleges such as junior colleges, technical colleges, and 4-year colleges. The items were also evaluated by graduate students of different majors, specialists in corresponding subject areas, college instructors and department chairs, and psychologists. However, there is no further information regarding how many people from the above categories rated the items in the item pool. How these ratings were used to select or revise items is not reported either.

Test-retest (8-week administration interval) reliability ranges from .59 to .91 for the forms of Primary level, .65 to .83 for the Intermediate level, .68 to .93 for the Advanced level, and .71 to .94 for the College level. There is no information about the participants' age, gender, race, and how many people participated in the test-retest of the API.

Construct-related validity and discriminant functions analyses were reported in the manuals for the previous version as validity measures. Self-evaluation was also validated through correlating self-ratings with the ratings from teachers, peers, etc. The discriminant functions were able to cor-rectly classify raters' gender identities at above 80% accuracy, but the validity indexes measured by correlating self-rating with others' rating vary in a wide range from .38 to .76. However, these validities are not reported in the manuals for this revision.

COMMENTARY. The authors report that there is a difference in the responses of students of different genders and different ages. Other research results concurred with these findings and revealed other variables such as race, social economic status, and cultural backgrounds make differences in how students evaluate themselves (e.g., Harter, 1983). The manuals provide only the overall measures of all the students in each of the four grade levels. More accurate interpretations of the scores could be achieved if the norms and profiles were separately reported according to these variables.

The authors indicate that forms for others' evaluations are available and propose that one of the purposes for using the API is to compare the congruence or divergence of self-ratings and ratings from others. However, the forms for others' evaluation are not provided. The norms or the profiles do not include information from others' evaluation either.

Another purpose of the API is to provide indirect needs-assessment information. The forms cannot accomplish that purpose due to the fact that there are no forms that measure the needs of the students. There are no forms to measure the ideal levels of self or expected self such as those in the Self-Perceptions Inventory (SPI, Soares & Soares, 1999; 226) that allow the comparison between actual self and ideal self to indirectly assess the needs of the self.

The last purpose is to dimensionalize the construct of self. Although this purpose is more promising using the SPI, the API does not collect much information that can be analyzed to study the construct of self, given the fact that the forms in the API are consistent with the subject areas of school curricula.

SUMMARY. The API covers a large range of traits in many academic areas that correspond to the grade levels. It is easy to administer, easy to score, and easy to complete. Test administrators can start to administer the API with limited training. Students in any grade can quickly answer the questions although the questions may need to be read to students of younger ages. The API provides descriptions of students' self-perceptions on school-related ability and interests, but it does not appear to be able to accomplish other intended purposes such as needs-assessment or to dimensionalize the construct of self-concept. The purpose of comparing students' self-evaluations with others' evaluations to study the congruence or divergence of these ratings can be accomplished if the norms of others' ratings are provided.

REVIEWER'S REFERENCES

Harter, S. (1983). Developmental perspectives on the self-system. In E. M. Hetherington (Ed.), *Handbook of child psychology: Socialization, personality, and social development* (4th ed., Vol. 4, pp. 275–385). New York: John Wiley & Sons.
Soares, L. M., & Soares, A. T. (1999). Self-Perceptions Inventory (Revision). Trumbull, CT: SOARES Associates.

[2]

ACER Mechanical Reasoning Test [Revised 1997].

Purpose: "Designed to assess a person's aptitude for solving problems requiring the understanding of mechanical ideas."
Population: Ages 15 and over.
Publication Dates: 1951–1997.
Scores: Total score only.
Administration: Group.
Forms, 2: Parallel Forms A and B.
Price Data, 2002: A$10.45 per test booklet; A$8.25 per scoring key; A$17.05 per 10 answer sheets; A$50.59 per manual (1997, 58 pages); A$89.20 per specimen set.
Time: 20(25) minutes.
Comments: Abbreviated adaptation of ACER Mechanical Comprehension Test (T6:29).
Author: Australian Council for Educational Research Ltd.
Publisher: Australian Council for Educational Research Ltd. [Australia].
Cross References: See T2:2238 (3 references); for reviews by John R. Jennings and Hayden S. Williams of an earlier edition, see 5:875.

Review of the ACER Mechanical Reasoning Test [Revised 1997] by GERALD R. SCHNECK, Professor of Rehabilitation Counseling, Minnesota State University, Mankato, MN:

DESCRIPTION. The ACER Mechanical Reasoning Test [Revised 1997] was developed and published by the Australian Council for Educational Research, Ltd., to replace its predecessors, the ACER Mechanical Comprehension Test and the ACER Mechanical Reasoning Test—Revised. The ACER Mechanical Comprehension Test, a 45-item battery with a 30-minute time

limit, was originally developed during World War II to assist in identifying and assigning Australian Army personnel who possessed an understanding of mechanical and physical system operations into those positions that required these skills. The ACER Mechanical Reasoning Test was developed at the request of the Queensland Department of Public Instruction, which desired a shorter instrument in both time and length, that would measure these same abilities within secondary school-age students.

The parallel forms (Forms A and B) that make up this recent revision of the ACER Mechanical Reasoning Test consist of: (a) selected items taken from both of the earlier tests, which have been combined, modified, and/or revised prior to inclusion; and (b) several newly developed items, which have been included in each of the two parallel forms. A total of 32 items are included in each of the parallel forms. Each test item presents four short questions, a drawing that includes mechanical components and operations, and four response alternatives (A, B, C, and D). Each test form (A and B) is structured with a brief introduction and several test item samples, followed by four test items that are included on each of the multiple pages of the booklets. Item content is stated by the authors as being "wide ranging," covering "wheels, gears, clamps, levers, sliding rods, shafts, pulleys, weights, conveyor belts, fixed and non-fixed pivots, and springs" (manual, p. 1). Some of the items include "objects such as cylinders, crowbars or other devices" (manual, p. 1). Printed text and drawings throughout each test booklet are in two-color format using orange and purple ink, the latter of which is used in varying shades within the drawing provided for each item. Test takers are required to complete the 32 items included in each form of the test within a 20-minute time limit. Test items are presented in separate reusable 8 1/2-inch x 11-inch booklets. Separate "optical mark recognition (OMR)" answer sheets can either be scored by hand with a transparent overlay scoring key or by using an OMR scoring machine.

DEVELOPMENT. The ACER Mechanical Reasoning Test is a group-administered test that is aimed at assessing the ability of test takers to "perceive and understand relationships between components within a mechanism" (manual, p. 1). The developers state that the rationale behind use of "idiosyncratic" (not able to be tied to a particular machine, device, or application) rather than "real-life mechanisms" was to reduce the benefit that some candidates might have through greater familiarity with certain devices and technical terminology than others. In order to achieve performance that was independent of individual reading ability, minimal written text was included within the test.

The main uses of the ACER Mechanical Reasoning Test were stated as being: "1) (s)election of apprentices, trainees, technical and trades personnel, and others involved in work of a mechanical nature; 2) (c)ounseling of individuals, such as school-leavers or mature-age job changers, who aspire to occupations requiring mechanical reasoning ability" (manual, p. 2).

Test authors stated that this instrument can be used within a broader battery of test instruments that are used in "assessing people's aptitude for designing, developing, building, repairing or servicing machinery" (manual, p. 2), but that it "has also been found useful as part of selection and assessment batteries designed for assessing aspirants to professional careers such as airline pilots and others of an engineering-based nature" (manual, p. 2).

TECHNICAL. Testing of trial forms was completed within three technical schools in Melbourne (AU), with a sample of 220 Year 10 and 11 students (mainly 15- and 16-year-olds), 187 of whom had disclosed their gender (85% of the sample), with 139 (74.3%) of them being male and 48 (25.7%) being female. Four pilot formats were included in the trial, with a 30-minute time limitation for completion being used. Within the stated instrument development procedures, items were discarded if the "facility level was higher than 95 per cent [*sic*] or lower than 25 per cent [*sic*]" (the degree of difficulty level for the item) or if the "point-biserial correlation (r_{pb}) fell below .20" (extent of correlation with other items included in the test). Those distracters ("incorrect response alternatives") that had a positive (r_{pb}) were revised to enable them to be "more clearly incorrect." Distracters that were not initially selected were restated, if possible, to increase their "plausibility" (manual, p. 4).

Within their final form, assignment of items to each were matched as closely as possible, based upon "specific content, mean item facility level,

mean item (r_{rb}), and the number of items (32 per form)," with arrangement of these items approximately in decreasing order of item difficulty level.

Standardization was accomplished using a target sample (from ACER's 1994 school sampling frame) of 900 students (Years 10 and 11) at schools located within the five most populous states in Australia (New South Wales, Victoria, Queensland, South Australia, and Western Australia), with proportional representation based on the school population of each state. "State, Catholic, and other Independent schools were included in the sampling frame," with selection based on a "probability proportional to their representation in the target population" (manual, p. 22). Details pertaining to the standardization study and the actual participation of schools and individuals, are provided within the test manual. No replacement of schools that had been selected but that could not participate for various reasons was made, and "this may have introduced a selective bias in the sample of schools included in the study" (manual, p. 22), according to the authors. Detailed data and discussion were presented regarding the standardization process and comparison between current and previous results with the particular sample groups that participated.

Only a "moderate" degree of correlation ($r = .57$) between the two forms was achieved, with Form A (Mean = 15.81, *SD* = 4.81) being somewhat easier than Form B (Mean = 14.12 and *SD* = 4.84). These results indicated, as the authors state, that "the objective of creating a parallel or interchangeable forms has not been successfully achieved," or "that the ACER Mechanical Reasoning Test is not a satisfactory measure for use with secondary school students" (manual, p. 27). However, for the trial sample that was composed of technical school students "there is convincing evidence that Form A and Form B are equivalent" (manual, p. 27), based upon the correlation between forms being reasonably strong ($r = .75$), the means being virtually identical (Mean $_{Form A}$ = 15.32; Mean $_{Form B}$ = 15.54), and their standard deviations also being relatively close (SD $_{Form A}$ = 5.70; Form $_{Form B}$ = 6.15).

The importance of reliability (r) and standard error of measurement (*SEM*) to the test is discussed by the authors, with results for the ACER Mechanical Reasoning Test (Second Revision) being provided for both the secondary school student standardization sample (N = approximately 550) and the trial sample of technical students (N = 220). Reliability estimates are presented as they address alternate forms reliability and internal consistency reliability (using Kuder-Richardson Formula 20 [KR_{21}]), for the full sample and six school subsamples and a small set of secondary students who had indicated some interest in applying for an apprenticeship. Internal consistency reliability coefficients on Forms A and B, ranged from .58 to .77 for secondary school student sample and subsamples and .73 to .75 for the technical school student samples.

Standard error of measurement (SE_m) ranged from 2.36 to 2.57 for the secondary school students and 3.0 to 3.1 for the technical school students. Internal consistency results were stated as being satisfactory for the full samples of secondary and technical school students, and "reasonably satisfactory" for most of the secondary school subsamples, excepting Year 10 females, due to their performance being only marginally reliable (KR_{21} = 0.58) on Form A.

Alternate forms reliability estimates (based on correlation between Form A and B) were deemed "unsatisfactory for the secondary school student subsamples," but "in line with expectation" (manual, p. 29) for technical school students.

The impact of practice effect was also addressed within data and discussion provided in the manual. Relatively small gains were identified, indicating that some practice effect was present.

Through the use of t-tests, the relationship between gender and test performance on both test forms was completed. Results showed that "males achieve significantly higher mean test scores than females on both forms of the ACER Mechanical Reasoning Test" (manual, p. 30). Analysis of variance (ANOVA) results suggest that "gender plays a greater role than either [school] Year level or the order in which the test was taken (Form A first or second) in accounting for individual differences in level of test performance" (manual, p. 30). The relationship between test performance, gender, and stated level of interest in mechanical activities showed that males performed significantly higher than females, regardless of the level of interest stated. Moderate correlation was shown between level of stated interest and level of stated opportunity to develop skills (males and females: r = .49; males: r = .47; females: r = .31). Because stated

levels of interest and opportunity to develop and practice mechanical skills were based upon the subjective judgment of individuals, a cautionary note was provided regarding the meanings and reference points that were present in deriving these ratings.

Both concurrent validity (correlations with other tests) and criterion-related validity evidence were presented as estimates of the degree to which the ACER Mechanical Reasoning Test would generalize to external measures or criteria. In evaluating the concurrent validity for the test, correlations were calculated between the ACER Mechanical Reasoning Test, the Differential Aptitude Test of Space Relations (spatial visualization) and the ACER Word Knowledge Test. Stronger relationship was shown between the ACER Mechanical Reasoning Test and performance on the DAT Space Relations (spatial visualization) test than with that on the ACER Word Knowledge; however, this difference was slight. All correlations provided ranged from a low of .30 to .68 for secondary school students, and between .44 and .64 for technical school students.

Only a preliminary investigation of criterion-related validity was done, according to the manual, and no measures of either concurrent nor predictive validity were provided. A brief discussion of validity of an earlier edition of the test was provided, indicating that the authors believe that the current test would have validity coefficients relatively similar to those shown with a mathematics test (r = .40) and a measure of general reasoning ability (r = .54), due to approximately one-third of the items being taken from these earlier editions. Users were encouraged to monitor the outcomes of administrations of the current test revision in order to add to the data that could be utilized in a future revision of the instrument.

COMMENTARY. The current revision increases the number of test items to 32, from the 24 included in the previous edition. Equivalent (parallel) forms of the test instrument are also provided with the current version, addressing the requests of many end-users who are involved in the guidance and selection of students for technical training, apprentices, and other occupations in which mechanical reasoning would be required. The manual, test forms, scoring keys, and answer sheets are adequate in material presentation, are relatively easy to use, and are fairly similar in cost to other tests of mechanical comprehension or reasoning. Test forms are quite similar to other more well known instruments, such as the Bennett Mechanical Comprehension Test (T6:305); however, the developers continue to place more emphasis on mechanisms and their operation, rather than on the theories and principles underlying the operation of the mechanisms.

Although reliability and validity data are provided and discussed within the test manual, the test continues to suffer from the limitations of sample size, selection criteria for inclusion in the samples, and presentation of concurrent and criterion-related validity evidence in relation to other measures.

SUMMARY. Although the development of a test of mechanical reasoning was justified by the needs of the military and education sectors within Australia, the extent to which it has evolved is questionable. The current parallel form version of the ACER Mechanical Reasoning Test continues to suffer from some of the same deficits that have been identified with earlier editions, particularly with regard to the size of the samples included in the norm groups, the adequacy of item coverage in each form, and with respect to the concurrent validity and predictive validity evidence for the instrument. Without further efforts to adequately provide evidence of the concurrent and predictive validity for this test, there is a question of appropriateness for its use in assisting with the provision of vocational guidance for individuals desiring to pursue training and employment, or for selection of appropriate candidates for apprenticeship or employment in areas that require mechanical reasoning or comprehension.

[3]
ACER Test of Employment Entry Mathematics.

Purpose: "A group test of basic mathematical ability … used for the selection of apprentices, trainees, and any other technical and trades personnel."
Population: Apprentice, trainee, technical and trade applicants.
Publication Date: 1992.
Acronym: TEEM.
Score: Total score only.
Administration: Group.
Price Data, 2002: A$6.59 per test booklet; A$5.50 per score key; A$7.69 per 10 answer sheets; A$67.09 per specimen set.

Time: 25 (40) minutes.
Comments: Can be hand scored or scored by testing service.
Authors: John Izard, Ian Woff, and Brian Doig.
Publisher: Australian Council for Educational Research Ltd. [Australia].

Review of the ACER Test of Employment Entry Mathematics by JAY R. STEWART, Associate Professor and Director, Rehabilitation Counseling Program, Bowling Green State University, Bowling Green, OH:

DESCRIPTION. The ACER Test of Employment Entry Mathematics (TEEM) is a group test that measures basic mathematical ability. The TEEM was developed by the Australian Council for Educational Research Limited (ACER) to aid in the selection of apprentices, trainees, and other trades persons whose intended employment involves basic mathematics.

The TEEM contains 32 items and begins with relatively easy numerical problems then progresses through more difficult numerical, geometry, visual-spatial, and short story problems. All problems have four multiple-choice answers. The test items measure common mathematic skills, including division, percentages, rounding off, and fractions. Understanding of mathematical terms is required to complete the test accurately.

Administration and scoring. The TEEM, a paper-and-pencil test, can be administered individually up to and including large groups. The test is designed to be taken with a 25-minute time limit. Administration of the test takes about 15 minutes, including the completion of two practice problems. The answers are recorded on a bubble-sheet, which can be scored by computer or by hand. ACER Test Scoring Service does the computer scoring, with a promised 5-day turnaround from receipt of answer sheets by mail. Hand scoring is done with a clear acetate transparency overlay key. The number of correct answers is the only raw score to be determined.

DEVELOPMENT. The TEEM was intended to replace the British Assessment Performance Unit (APU), which was designed to assess achievement in a number of areas including math (Marjoram, 1978). It appears that the TEEM was intended to be more specifically attuned to the education attributes and vocational needs of Australian work trainees. The TEEM items were obtained from items in other ACER tests of mathematical ability, which were designed to measure mathematical ability in Australian secondary and post secondary students. A sample of 1,836 apprenticeship applicants were administered 47 items selected from ACER tests. The sample was predominantly male. Item analysis was performed on the results. Items that were either too easy or too hard were discarded, resulting in 32 items in the final form.

TECHNICAL. The raw scores obtained on the TEEM can be easily converted to percentile rank, stanine, and T-scores. Norm group data were obtained from 3,267 Australian apprenticeship applicants. The results were compiled into a table of raw, percentile rank, stanine, and T-scores, which may be used to interpret TEEM test results.

Test characteristics. A 1,832 apprenticeship sample was used to determine test reliability of the TEEM. Kuder-Richardson formula 20 (KR-20) (Kuder & Richardson, 1937), used to analyze the results, produced a reliability coefficient of .80. A sample of 96 Year 10 technical school students (67% male) took the TEEM and yielded a KR-20 reliability coefficient of .85. However, professional literature (Walsh & Betz, 1985) suggested that the KR-20 only be used for dichotomously scored items and should not be used in time-limited tests. The standard error of measurement was found to be 2.3 for the apprenticeship group and 2.4 for the technical school student group. Test scores were also analyzed by age and results indicate a significant improvement in scores from 15 through 40 years of age. To date, the only type of validity for the TEEM that has been investigated is construct validity. An analysis of the scores of students who took both the APU Arithmetic Test and the TEEM revealed a high correlation, which is important because the TEEM was intended to replace the APU in Australia. The TEEM correlated moderately high with components of an Australian adaptation of the General Aptitude Test Battery (U.S. Department of Labor, 1979) and ACER Mechanical Reasoning Test, indicating a moderately high relationship between TEEM scores and reading ability, mechanical reasoning, and spatial ability. A search of American academic literature has failed to produce any articles investigating TEEM test characteristics.

COMMENTARY AND SUMMARY. The TEEM has a rather narrowly defined purpose: to assess persons who are applying for Australian apprenticeships and technical jobs. Test reliability needs to be more adequately assessed. Predictive validity has not been examined, but appears promising because of the correlations with similar assessment instruments that have evaluated predictive validity. The TEEM may have value because of the great advances in technologies that require math skills and the shortage of trained personnel in those newer technologies. Not having many women, persons with disabilities, or other minority groups in the norm sample is a serious limitation for areas that are attempting to recruit and train those individuals.

REVIEWER'S REFERENCES
Kuder, G. F., & Richardson, M. W. (1937). The theory of the estimation of test reliability. *Psychometrika, 2,* 151–160.
Marjoram, D. T. E. (1978). The APU and assessment in the middle years. *Education 3–13, 6*(2), 31–36.
U.S. Department of Labor. (1979). *Guide to the use of the General Aptitude Test Battery.* Washington, DC: U.S. Government Printing Office.
Walsh, W. B., & Betz, N. E. (1985). *Tests and assessment.* Englewood Cliffs, NJ: Prentice-Hall.

Review of the ACER Test of Employment Entry Mathematics by PATRICIA H. WHEELER, President and Principal Researcher, EREAPA Associates, Livermore, CA:

DESCRIPTION. The ACER Test of Employment Entry Mathematics (TEEM) is a 32-item, multiple-choice test of basic mathematical abilities for use with technical and trade apprentices, trainees, and employees. The TEEM can be used for counseling or in conjunction with other data for selection.

The TEEM is a group-administered test with a 25-minute time limit. The test package consists of a reusable test booklet, an optical mark recognition answer sheet, a transparent overlay score key, and a manual. The answer sheets can be hand scored or machine scored. The publisher offers a 5-work-day turnaround scoring service.

The 32 items each have four choices, A through D. Test results are reported as a total raw score (number right). Individual percentile ranks, stanines, descriptive ratings, and T-scores are provided as well.

DEVELOPMENT. The TEEM was developed to provide a new test of basic mathematical ability for use by apprentice trainers in Australia. Many had been using the British APU Arithmetic Test or personnel selection tests.

To develop the test, 47 math ability items were selected from secure ACER tests. A trial administration of these 47 items was given to 1,836 apprenticeship applicants. The group was primarily male test takers, and they were given 45 minutes for the 47-item trial version of the TEEM.

Analyses were performed on these 47 items and 15 were discarded, either because they were too easy or too hard, or because they had a low point-biserial correlation (below .20). The final version of 32 items was compiled, with items arranged in order of increasing difficulty.

TECHNICAL. The manual contains clear summaries of the technical analyses undertaken on the TEEM and displays the results in tables. These include tables showing, for each raw score value, the percentile rank, stanines, descriptive rating, T-score, and the equivalent APU Arithmetic Test raw score. The normative data are based on administrations in 1988–1990 to 3,267 apprenticeship applicants for private and public sector employers, primarily males. The descriptive ratings are linked to the stanines: high (9), above average (7–8), average (4–6), below average (2–3), and low (1). The authors encourage the use of T-scores when using the TEEM scores with other data available in T-score format.

The equivalency study between the TEEM and the APU Arithmetic Test is based on a study with 96 students from three technical schools in Melbourne. About two-thirds of these students were male and one-third were female.

Additional technical data include the mean (20.3), standard deviation (5.2), standard error of measurement (2.3), and KR20 (.80). These reported statistics are said to be based on both the reference group of apprenticeship applicants used for the norming (N = 3,267) and the technical school students used for the equivalence study (N = 96). The manual provides clear explanations of the meaning of these various statistics and scores, and provides references for those seeking additional information on interpreting test scores.

The validation study consisted of correlating the TEEM with the APU Arithmetic Test. The Pearson product-moment correlation was reported as .83. This was based on the 96 technical school students. Correlation coefficients with seven other tests are also provided. They included tests of reading ability, mechanical reasoning, spatial ability, perceptual aptitude, and motor coordination. Correlation coefficients ranged from .12 for the GATB Mark Making to .64 for the ACER Ap-

plied Reading Test. These coefficients were based on samples of 535 to 3,439 apprenticeship applicants tested in 1988–1991. The authors encourage users to undertake their own predictive validity studies.

The authors reported the findings of a study on practice effect. Seventy-three of the 96 technical school students retook the TEEM 2 weeks after the administration for the equivalency study. They obtained the same mean (19.6) with a slightly larger standard deviation on the second administration (6.8 versus 5.8). They cautioned that this is based on a small sample of students and may not apply to adults, especially adults with little recent experience in taking tests.

The authors also examined age and gender differences. The older test takers tended to have higher scores, as did males compared to females. Again, the authors caution against generalizing from the results of these two studies.

COMMENTARY. The overall packaging and presentation of the TEEM is attractive and professional. The manual contains a useful checklist for test administrators. However, the directions for completing the answer sheet do not correspond to the answer sheet provided to the reviewer. For example, the directions say to provide address and age. The answer sheet asks for "school/ organisation" and does not ask for age. Perhaps the manual (1992) reflects an earlier answer sheet than the 1995 version provided. Revised directions should be inserted in the manual to reduce confusion during the test administration.

The description of the equivalence study between the TEEM and APU Arithmetic Test does not explain how the tests were administered to address the issues of practice effect and fatigue.

Item level data would be useful. This should include not only p values and point-biserial correlation coefficients but also the description of the type of item. The TEEM includes far more than arithmetic items (e.g., geometry, spatial, problem solving). It would help the user better ascertain if the TEEM covers the variety of mathematical skills that they need to assess in their applicants.

SUMMARY. Overall, the TEEM appears to be a useful and technically sound test for measuring entry-level mathematical skills of trade and technical program candidates. The materials appear professional and are comprehensive. Appropriate precautions are provided to users on the limitations of the TEEM.

[4]
ACER Tests of Basic Skills—Orchid Series.

Purpose: Developed to assess skills in literacy and numeracy.

Population: Students, year 4 to 6 in Australian school system.

Publication Dates: 1990–1997.

Administration: Group.

Price Data, 2002: A$26.40 per 10 nonreusable Level A & B test booklets for Literacy; A$30.80 per 10 nonreusable Level A & B test booklets with press-out shapes and tiles for Numeracy; A$33 per stimulus material; A$22 per audio tape; A$66 per Level A manual (1997, 73 pages); A$66 per Level B manual (1997, 82 pages); A$93.50 per specimen set; A$26.40 per nonreusable Level C test booklets for Literacy; A$30,80 per 10 nonreusable Level C test booklets with press-out shape and tiles for Numeracy; A$33 per stimulus material; A$66 per Level C manual (1997, 60 pages); A$71.50 per specimen set.

Comments: Earlier versions called Blue and Green Series; requires a cassette tape player.

Authors: Australian Council for Educational Research, Joy McQueen, and Brian Doig.

Publisher: Australian Council for Educational Research Ltd. [Australia].

a) LEVEL A.

Scores, 6: Aspects of Literacy (Reading, Proofreading and Editing, Listening, Writing), Aspects of Numeracy (Number, Measurement and Space).

Time: (222–245) minutes.

b) LEVEL B.

Scores, 6: Same as Level A.

Time: (248–271) minutes.

c) LEVEL C.

Scores, 4: Aspects of Literacy (Reading and Viewing, Proofreading and Editing, Writing), Aspects of Numeracy (Number/Measurement/Space).

Time: (165–181) minutes.

Cross References: For reviews by Lewis R. Aiken and Delwyn L. Harnisch of an earlier edition, see 12:88.

Review of the ACER Tests of Basic Skills— Orchid Series by LISA F. SMITH, Associate Professor, Psychology Department, Kean University, Union, NJ:

DESCRIPTION. The ACER Tests of Basic Skills—Orchid Series is a curriculum-based assessment of literacy and number skills for Australian primary school students. As stated in the teacher's manual, the purpose of the ACER Tests of Basic Skills is to "offer teachers a valuable resource to assist in their assessments of the literacy and numeracy of primary students" (p. 1). The authors are to be commended for developing a testing series that reflects the Australian English and Mathematics Curriculum Profiles and makes use of innovative item formats and a performance assessment component.

The Orchid Series is presented as three kits labeled Level A, Level B, and Level C, corresponding to the fourth, fifth, and sixth years of primary school. Levels A and B include tests of Reading, Proofreading and Editing, Listening, Writing, Number, and Measurement and Space. Level C includes tests of Reading and Viewing, Proofreading and Editing, Writing, Number, Measurement, and Space. Materials for most parts of the tests are provided, including punch-out shapes and simulated magazines. However, the examiner must prepare additional materials in the form of five containers of specific weights for a performance task that is part of Levels A and B. This does not seem too difficult, as detailed instructions for this activity along with suggested common grocery items that meet the weight requirements are given in the teacher's manual. Matchsticks and plasticine (a type of fun tack) are needed for the Levels A and B Measurement and Space tests. Writing prompts are also generated by the examiner, according to guidelines provided in the teacher's manuals.

The items represent a wide variety of response formats. In addition to multiple choice, examinees are asked to write in answers, construct three-dimensional models, draw picture completions, underline errors, look for clues in the simulated magazines, create their own stories, respond to items based on audiotape conversations (Levels A and B), and use a calculator (Level C). The tests are interesting and require the examinee to interact with the test to apply skills learned. Levels A and B share a total of 36 common items (10 Number test items, 2 Measurement and Space items, 11 Reading items, and 13 Listening items) as well as similar Writing tasks. There may be the potential for carry-over effects here, but the ability to evaluate development over time most likely outweighs any problem with this.

There is some flexibility in timing the tests. In general, the examiner is allowed to add a discretionary 5 minutes per test. For the Measurement and Space tests, approximate time estimates for each item are provided. One concern with the test administration is that assistance given by the test examiner may not be standard. For example, for all levels of the Number tests, the examiner may read words, phrases, or entire questions to the whole class or to individual students. Clarification of response modes may be given as needed. The subjectivity associated with what constitutes appropriate clarification could affect scores for individual examinees or between classes.

Scoring may be problematical for some individual items. For example, in the Level A Measurement and Space test, examinees must construct a model of the Three Bears' house using matchsticks and plasticine, based on a drawing in the test booklet. The teacher's manual provides 10 possible models to guide scoring. However, as the manual states, "The constructions are delicate and will not last long" (p. 13). The potential problems in rapidly evaluating 30 or so constructions are obvious. Another item in the Levels A and B Measurement and Space tests asks the examinee to choose a shape from the shapes sheet, punch out eight copies of the chosen shape, and use those shapes to cover a mark so that none of the mark is visible. The answer key shows the correct solution as using only six copies of the shape. Incorrect solutions use up to eight copies. This hardly seems fair. In the Level C Numeracy test, Item 33 states, "subtract 134 from 327" (Level C Numeracy test, p. 18). A correct answer of 193 earns 2 points, but an answer of 213, where each smaller digit is subtracted from each corresponding larger digit, earns 1 point. All other responses earn no points. The rationale for the 1-point response is not given; it is not clear why this is an acceptable answer. Scoring for the Writing tests, although time-consuming, is explained well, with rubrics and examples provided.

At the end of each teacher's manual, student record sheets with room for item-by-item scores for 30 students are provided and may be photocopied. These sheets should facilitate the calculation of final scores as well as provide a method of checking performance of a group on individual items. The individual student profile sheet, also provided, summarizes each student's overall performance and should be useful in communicating personal results. In addition, a Diagnostic Map (DIAMAP) may be constructed for each student.

The DIAMAP is based on arranging scores for a given test in a vertical column according to their difficulty. No information is provided on how the difficulty levels were determined. The result is intended to be a diagnostic guide indicating strengths and weaknesses as demonstrated by the student's performance on the individual items. Instructions for constructing the DIAMAP and reading the results are clear. Examples are given on how to make inferences from the data, with appropriate cautions to gather more evidence before firmly establishing a student's profile.

DEVELOPMENT. The ACER Tests of Basic Skills is in its third series. The original tests for Levels A and B were developed in 1995 for Victoria's Learning Assessment Project; Level C for the 1995 Queensland Year Six Test. The current materials were cross referenced with the English and Mathematics Curriculum Profiles in Australia.

TECHNICAL. Clearly, the weakest aspect of the ACER Tests of Basic Skills lies in the lack of technical data supporting the reliability and validity of the test scores. Level A lists reliability coefficients based on approximately 43,000 students as .80 for Number, .90 for Measurement and Space, .90 for Reading, .68 for Listening, and .76 for Proofreading and Editing. For Level B, the corresponding reliability coefficients were based on approximately 45,000 students, and were listed as .83 for Number, .83 for Measurement and Space, .88 for Reading, .64 for Listening, and .78 for Proofreading and Editing. For Level C, reliability coefficients were based on approximately 36,000 students, and were listed as .90 for Numeracy, .90 for Reading, and .73 for Proofreading and Editing. No information is given about the norming samples or standardization procedures. A statement is made that "extensive consultation with reference groups established by the education bodies originally responsible for the tests in Victoria and Queensland" (p. 3 of each teacher's manual) is offered as evidence of content validity.

COMMENTARY AND SUMMARY. Overall, the ACER Tests of Basic Skills are engaging and, although absent sufficient psychometric support, certainly seem to address their purpose of assessing number and literacy skills. The items on the tests address skills needed for learning in school and applications in life. The simulated magazines and performance assessment tasks are well thought out, appealing, and interesting. The use of the metric system for the numeracy tests, certain spellings (e.g., "colour"), words and phrases (e.g., "please ring me," "gumnuts," "mum," "dearest" for "expensive"), the Australian accents on the audiotapes, and even some of the content in the simulated magazines (e.g., a story about a baby goanna) might limit the use of this series outside of Australia. The teacher's manual states that these tests are being made more widely available; if so, evidence of validity will need to be provided to ensure proper use and interpretation of results.

[5]

Ackerman-Banks Neuropsychological Rehabilitation Battery.

Purpose: Designed as "a comprehensive screening instrument for the rehabilitation setting."
Population: Patients referred for psychological or neuropsychological assessment and/or cognitive rehabilitation.
Publication Dates: 1991–2000.
Acronym: A-BNRB.
Scores, 43: Alertness Scale (Attention/Concentration), Prosody Scales (Receptive Prosody, Expressive Prosody), Memory Scales (Long-Term Memory, Short-Term Interference Memory, Short-Term Input Memory, Short-Term Retrieval Memory), Sensorimotor Scales (Auditory Input, Auditory Discrimination, Tactile Input, Tactile Output, Visual Input, Visual Discrimination, Visual-Spatial Construction, Proprioception, Motor Quality, Motor Writing), Speech Scales (Speech Production, Dysarthria, Dysnomia/Neologisms, Confabulation, Perseveration, Lisping), Academic Abilities Scales (Mathematics, Reading, Writing), Cognitive Problem Solving Scales (Concreteness, Integration, Judgment, Speed), Organic Emotions Scales (Depression, Anxiety, Impulsivity), Laterality Scales (Left-Right Confusion, Left-Brain Controlled Balance, Right-Brain Controlled Balance, Left Hemisphere, Right Hemisphere, Neuropsychological Status), Treatment Problem Scales (Peripheral Damage, Awareness of Deficits, Socially Appropriate Comments, Frustration Tolerance).
Administration: Individual.
Price Data, 2002: $600 per complete kit including professional manual (1994, 206 pages), stimulus card book, 10 administration protocols, 10 response booklets, 10 scoring forms, and processing fee for web-based, mail-in, or faxed computer score submission; $450 per administration package including 10 administration protocols, 10 response booklets, 10 scoring forms, and processing fee for web-based, mail-in, or faxed

computer score submission; $200 per professional manual; $125 per student training manual (2000, 85 pages); student, volume, and research discounts available.
Time: (45–120) minutes.
Authors: Rosalie J. Ackerman and Martha E. Banks.
Publisher: ABackans DCP, Inc.

Review of the Ackerman-Banks Neuropsychological Rehabilitation Battery by SURENDRA P. SINGH, Clinical Neuropsychologist, Professor Learning & Behavior Disorders, College of Education, University of South Florida, Tampa, FL:

DESCRIPTION. In accordance with the test developers "The 85-item Ackerman-Bank Neuropsychological Rehabilitation Battery was developed to provide a valid, efficacious screening instrument for the rehabilitation setting, with minimum assessment time (45 to 90 minutes) and cost for patients" (manual, p. 8). The utilitarian philosophy to keep the cost and the assessment time at a minimum level has its merits, yet these considerations must not be the paramount reasons for developing instruments. It is sufficient to say that the Ackerman-Banks Neuropsychological Rehabilitation Battery (A-BNRB) is a screening device with all the pluses of a screening device (minimum cost and time) and the minuses (validity limited to the purpose, i.e., screening). The test developers have used the 85 items to assess 39 neurpsychological domains and to recommend four treatment plans—a daunting goal.

DEVELOPMENT. The test developers have followed some of the required protocol used by other test developers such as Reitan and Wolfson (1985), Ross (1986), Nelson et al. (1989), and the administration of tests on brain-damaged populations to establish the normative data. The neuropsychological test developers such as Reitan (Reitan & Wolfson, 1985) have used a minimum of four sets of test data collection strategies (i.e., the comparative level of performance [interindividual inference data], the intraindividual comparison data, the use of simple test items sensitive to assess exclusively brain-damaged persons, and the comparison of motor and sensory-perceptual bilateral performances). Each of these strategies has limitations and any of these strategies alone may not yield reliable and valid information. The A-BNRB primarily uses the intraindividual performance strategies, thus making the instrument not as robust as the test developers have wished it to be.

The test developers' philosophy, beliefs, assumptions, and the concept of psychometric tests and testing, at times, are not congruent. The test developers have made some philosophical assumptive claims such as "rehabilitation treatment staff compare current patients to past patients in order to assess the performance and prognosis" (manual, p. 9). First, making impressionistic judgment has limitations. Second, the rehabilitation treatment staffs do not necessarily represent a homogeneous group of individuals; therefore there are no assurances that all treatment staff will do what the test developers' treatment staff might have done.

In all fairness, the test developers indeed have included in the test manual some positive points such as the features of the test battery (p. 9), the professional qualifications (p. 10), making the test easy to administer (p. 13), providing statements of caution such as "Caution should be used in making diagnoses based on the scale score" (p. 120), and statements regarding limitations on interpretation (p. 122).

TECHNICAL. The test developers have conducted six sets of discriminant analyses during pilot validity studies. Some good results are suggested: the Rehabilitation Battery correctly identified the treatment status of 90.7% of the patients at the time of evaluation and some limited predictors such as the summary scales Attention/Concentration, Left Hemisphere, Right Hemisphere, and Neuropsychological Status ranged in predictive accuracy from 20.1% to 53.3% (manual, p. 126). Discriminant analyses were also conducted with a normative population of 300 patients and test developers have rightfully pointed out the limitations of such findings. Split group reliability and the estimates of reliability were calculated by using Cronbach's alpha. The alpha levels range from a low of .48 to a high of .97. Efforts were made to conduct the test-retest reliability study with a small sample of 6. Significant differences are reported on the Depression and Awareness of Deficits scales. Due to the limited control study presented by the test developers, and in the presence of no blind or double blind study standards used, the findings regarding the reliability and validity as presented by the test developers must be cautiously interpreted.

Taking into consideration the complex variabilities of neuropsychological behaviors, the margin of error may be small, speaking statistically. Yet the margin of error, speaking diagnostically and prognostically, must not be minimized.

COMMENTARY. At the outset, the reviewer would like to stress that once one gets past the contradictory, fallacious, and politically motivated professional debate by the test developers, the battery has potential. Because the philosophical statements are included in the test manual, the reviewer is compelled to review them. It is pivotal to address the guiding premise shaping a testing instrument. The reviewer considers some of the philosophical statements reflecting the premise in the test manual may be well-intentioned in part, yet they divert the focus to subjects perhaps best suited for a seminar, colloquium, think tank, or in a psychotherapeutic context. For example, it is troubling that the test developers engage in platitudes for their instrument in stating their philosophy of rehabilitation neuropsychology when they state that "Rehabilitation neuropsychology has a positive focus on diagnosis and treatment, using the philosophy that patients with neuropsychological impairments can benefit from treatment, have strengths and weaknesses, and have varying levels of impairment in several areas. This is in contrast to the psychiatric medical model" (manual, p. 8). It is not clear what message the test developers are trying to convey to their audience, and with which psychiatric model the test developers are comparing and contrasting the Rehabilitation neuropsychology philosophy. Does this mean that the mysterious psychiatric medical model, which the test developers have failed to identify, has no positive focus on diagnosis and treatment? Does this mean that the philosophy of the Psychiatric medical model, whichever psychiatric model the test developers have in mind, is that patients with neuropsychological impairments cannot benefit from treatment, or the test developers are trying to convey to their audience their worst presumption that the psychiatric medical model does not support belief in "the strengths and the weaknesses or in varying levels of impairment in several areas" (manual, p. 2) (whatever the strengths and weaknesses or in varying levels of impairment means).

The test developers have demonstrated a pattern of choosing the politically correct lexicographical terminology and euphemistic solutions to compare their so-called philosophy and the instrument against the other so-called tests. For example, the test developers state that "There is a strong emphasis on assessing the abilities of the patient, with a focus away from the deficit model that is the foundation of many psychological tests" (manual, p. 8). This is done without specificity and citations. Should there be any need to compare the A-BNRB with other psychometric instruments or with any particular philosophy, the test developers must at least name the test and specify the model with which they intend to compare their instrument and provide the citations as needed to substantiate their argument. There are philosophical contradictions and contrasts regarding the concept of rehabilitation itself such as the test developers' belief that "The range of abilities of people without known brain injury adds little to the information about the widely diverse brain injured populations" (manual, p. 9). It is advised that the test developers limit their debates around the psychometric properties of their instrument rather than engaging themselves in a contradictory, fallacious, and politically motivated debate.

The test developers may consider addressing and accentuating the following issues and test limitations as appropriate during their next revision of the A-BNRB:

1. The hypertext software has potential. The success, however, of any software lies in the extent to which it is successful in simplifying the complex phenomenon without becoming simplistic.

2. State with clarity that it is difficult to establish population validity evidence regarding descriptive versus inferential validity due to plausible cohort changes.

3. Test limitations to include: Assessing too many neuropsychological and clinical psychological functions among varied population with varied Central Nervous System (CNS) conditions with a small number of test items creates too many assessment issues including the floor and the ceiling effects.

4. Identify and provide citations for test items and test constructs borrowed from various instruments such as Bender, Wechsler, Wisconsin Card Sort, Rey Auditory Verbal Learning Test.

5. Conduct a study to look into the consequential validity.

6. Incorporate concepts developed long ago by Babcock (1930) for interindividual inferential and intraindividual model.

7. The use of Angoff's (1971, 1982) statistical methodology and determination of the "fit"

items to the Rasch-Wright one-parameter latent trait model and consult Wright (1968), Wright and Douglas (1977), and Wright, Mead, and Bell (1979) in improving the technical quality of the instrument.

SUMMARY. The A-BNRB has potential. It is advised that in the present form the instrument should be used as a guiding device.

REVIEWER'S REFERENCES

Angoff, W. H. (1971). Norms, scales, and equivalent scores. In R. L. Thorndike (Ed.), *Educational measurement* (2nd ed.). Washington, DC: American Council on Education.

Angoff, W. H. (1982). Uses of difficulty and discrimination indices for detecting item bias. In R. A. Berk (Ed.), *Handbook of methods for detecting item bias.* Baltimore: Johns Hopkins University Press.

Babcock, H. (1930). An experiment in the measurement of mental deterioration. *Archives of Psychology, 117*, 4–105.

Nelson, L. D., Satz, P., Mitrushina, M., Van Gorp, W., Cicchetti, D., Lewis, R., & Van Lancker, D. (1989). Development and validation of the Neuropsychology Behavior and Affect Profile. *Psychological Assessment, 1*, 266–272.

Reitan, R. M., & Wolfson, D. (1985). *The Halstead-Reitan Neuropsychological Test Battery: Theory and clinical interpretation.* Tucson, AZ: Neuropsychology Press.

Ross, D. G. (1986). Ross Information Processing Assessment. Austin, TX: PRO-ED.

Wright, B. D. (1968). Sample free test calibration and person measurement. *Proceedings of the 1967 Invitational Conference on Testing Problems.* Princeton, NJ: Educational Testing Service.

Wright, B. D., & Douglas, G. A. (1977). Conditional versus unconditional procedures for sample-free item analysis. *Educational and Psychological Measurement, 37*, 47–60.

Wright, B. D., Mead, R., & Bell, S. (1979). *BICAL: Calibrating items with the Rasch model.* Statistical Laboratory Department of Education RM 23b). Chicago: University of Chicago.

Review of the Ackerman-Banks Neuropsychological Rehabilitation Battery by WILFRED G. VAN GORP, Associate Professor of Psychology in Psychiatry, and Director, Neuropsychology Assessment Program, Weill Medical College of Cornell University, and COLLEEN A. EWING, Postdoctoral Fellow, Weill Medical College of Cornell University, New York, NY:

DESCRIPTION. The Ackerman-Banks Neuropsychological Rehabilitation Battery (A-BNRB) is an 85-item measure developed for use in rehabilitation settings. The A-BNRB was designed to be administered to individuals with suspected or diagnosed neurological and/or neuropsychological impairment. The measure is intended to assess an individual's cognitive strengths and weaknesses, rather than to determine the "presence and/or actual site of brain injury" (manual, p. 8). Specifically, the A-BNRB was developed to determine the individual's current level of functioning, aid in treatment recommendations, and monitor progress in a treatment program. It takes approximately 45–90 minutes to administer and can be given by trained technicians under the supervision of a clinical neuropsychologist or psychologist.

The A-BNRB comprises an interview designed to obtain demographic and medical information and 43 clinical scales that are grouped into broad categories. These categories include Alertness, Prosody, Memory, Sensorimotor, Speech, Academic Abilities, Cognitive Problem Solving, Organic Emotions, Laterality, and Treatment Problems. Although these clinical scales are not designed to give an overall score for all dimensions of neuropsychological functioning, they do provide "a multiple sampling of behavior across an interval of test time" (manual, p. 9).

The testing kit consists of a manual, administration booklet, stimulus care book, and the patient response booklet. The manual is well written and contains all of the test items in the same format as they appear on the protocol. For each item, there is a brief description of the scoring criteria and specific examples of possible responses. The test stimuli appear to be appropriate and well designed. The developers used large print and enlarged visual stimuli, which is especially appropriate for the assessment of geriatric patients. The protocol appears to be easily administered and provides alternative modes of providing instruction. Due to the complexity of the scoring system, computer software has been developed to give a summation of the results and generate specific treatment recommendations.

DEVELOPMENT. The A-BNRB is the latest version (copyright 1994) of a test that has been under development since 1991. The materials provided by the developers offer minimal information regarding initial test development. The definitions offered for each of the 43 clinical scales are good. However, the constructs underlying several scales appear to overlap and little has been done to discriminate theoretically or empirically among them.

TECHNICAL. Information about the psychometric properties of the A-BNRB is very limited and vague. Much of the standardization, reliability, and validity data are based on pilot studies. Although extensive demographic information about the standardization sample was provided, no information was provided on presenting neurological and neuropsychological impairments. Estimates of reliability were made by calculating Cronbach's alpha for the entire battery. High reliability was found using all 43 clinical scales to determine test performance (alpha = .95) and 39 of the clinical scales excluding Attention/Concentration, Left Hemisphere, Right Hemisphere, and Neuropsy-

chological Status (alpha = .97). Test-retest reliability (2-week administration interval) was also impressive (alpha = .86), but negated by the extremely small sample size ($n = 6$). Information was not given concerning the individual test-retest reliability for each clinical scale. Rather, the developers reported that significant differences were found for two of the scales, Depression and Awareness of Deficits.

With regard to validity, the developers reported that in a preliminary validity study, the A-BNRB had over a 90% accuracy rate in distinguishing between four groups of individuals: normal individuals, individuals diagnosed with a left hemisphere cardiovascular accident, right hemisphere cardiovascular accident, or diffuse closed head injury. The developers reported that four distinct profiles emerged for each group. Although they reported that statistically significant profiles emerged for each of the aforementioned groups, they did not report what those profiles were. Further, they reported that only 39 of the 43 scales were used to obtain the profiles without indicating why 4 scales were excluded. In a second study using 150 patients, a correct classification level of 91% was achieved using rehabilitation, psychiatric, and medical patients. All 43 of the scales were used. However, there is no indication as to what significant profiles emerged for each group and why all 43 scales were used rather than the 39 scales used in the previous study. Additionally, there is an excessive ratio of variables to subjects, with there being 43 scales to only 150 subjects. The developers also cite several other validity studies that provide support for the utility of this battery with a variety of individuals (e.g., low education, older individuals).

COMMENTARY. Developers must address several issues before psychometric confidence can be bestowed upon this measure. First, an empirical or theoretical rationale as to how the 43 scales are discriminated from each other would be helpful. Secondly, more information about test development would be critical to judge the instrument as psychologically sound. The developers could do a better job of providing information about the test's standardization, reliability, and validity. The developers need to conduct more research concerning the psychometric properties of this test.

SUMMARY. The A-BNRB as a measure to assess an individual's strengths and weaknesses in a rehabilitation setting has good promise. The developers have produced a measure that can be easily administered in a rehabilitation setting and have considered both physical and psychological issues that are important when making treatment recommendations. However, the A-BNRB falls short of the mark. Significant overlap between the clinical scales with no rationale on how to discriminate between them and insufficient reliability and validity data seriously restricts the use of this measure. Until these shortcomings have been addressed, one cannot interpret the test results with certainty, making it necessary to rely on other methods of assessment.

[6]

Adaptive Behavior Assessment System.

Purpose: "Measures adaptive skills in multiple environments including home, school, community, and work."

Population: Ages 5–21; 16–89.

Publication Date: 2000.

Acronym: ABAS.

Scores, 11: 10 Adaptive Skill Areas (Communication, Community Use, Functional Academics, Home/School Living, Health and Safety, Leisure, Self-Care, Self-Direction, Social, Work), General Adaptive Composite (GAC).

Administration: Individual.

Forms, 3: Teacher, Parent, Adult.

Price Data, 2002: $150 per School kit including manual (2000, 196 pages), 25 Teacher Forms, and 25 Parent Forms; $100 per Adult kit including manual and 25 Adult Forms; $43 per 25 Parent, Teacher, or Adult Forms (quantity discounts available); $195 per Scoring Assistant and PDA Application Complete kit including ABAS PDA Application preloaded with 10 e-record form Credits, and ABAS Scoring Assistant CD-ROM; $79 per ABAS for Palm OS CD-ROM; $153 per ABAS Scoring Assistant (CD-ROM or disk version); $41 per 25 e-record form Credits for PDA Application (Teacher, Parent, and/or Adult).

Time: (15–20) minutes.

Comments: Completed by adult informants (teacher, parent) for children aged 5–21; completed by self or informants for ages 16–89; consistent with both AAMR (1992) and DSM-IV definitions of mental retardation and with the IDEA (1997) special education and disability classification system; Scoring Assistant software scores responses, analyzes strengths and weaknesses, plots Skill Area Profile; Scoring Assistant system requirements: Windows 95/98/2000/NT 4.0, 100 MHz processor, 16 MB RAM, 2 MB video card, 800 x 600 resolution (256 colors), 20 MB free hard disk space,

floppy drive; paper-and-pencil or electronic administration available using ABAS Personal Digital Assistant software; PDA system requirements: Palm OS version 3.0, 2 MB total RAM, 96K dynamic heap, Motorola Dragonball or Dragonball EZ chip, conduit software, cradle; desktop Scoring Assistant required to operate PDA application.

Authors: Patti L. Harrison and Thomas Oakland.

Publisher: The Psychological Corporation.

Review of the Adaptive Behavior Assessment System by JAMES K. BENISH, School Psychologist, Helena Public Schools, Adjunct Professor of Special Education, Carroll College, Helena, MT:

DESCRIPTION. The Adaptive Behavior Assessment System (ABAS), published by The Psychological Corporation, is an effort to offer another choice in the area of assessment of adaptive skills. Measuring or targeting an individual's adaptive skills allows for diagnosing strengths and weaknesses, and for establishing a baseline to compare growth after certain interventions. Adaptive behavior skills are one component necessary in the identification process of individuals as defined by the American Association on Mental Retardation (AAMR, 1992) as mentally retarded. The ABAS includes a Parent Form and a Teacher Form, with age ranges of 5 to 21 years. An Adult Form allows assessment for individuals aged 16–89. Each form can be completed by the rater in approximately 15–20 minutes. The Adult Form may be completed by relatives or other caregivers, or in certain cases, by the target individual. Like other adaptive behavior scales, scoring provides an overall composite score (General Adaptive Composite). Standard scores are compiled through the use of scaled score tables and percentile rankings. Strengths and weaknesses are analyzed via confidence levels and differences from the mean. Standard errors of measurement are used to compute confidence levels. Additionally, age equivalent scores may be computed from raw scores for each adaptive skill area. Defined by both AAMR and the DSM-IV (American Psychiatric Association) these 10 adaptive skill areas include: Communication, Community Use, Functional Academics, School Living, Health and Safety, Leisure, Self-Care, Self-Direction, Social, and Work.

DEVELOPMENT. The ABAS was developed and standardized nationally using samples stratified across the country by "sex, race/ethnicity, and educational level parameters according to the

1999 census data" (manual, p. 41). After determining geographic regions, all three ABAS forms were selected to have representation from all the above mentioned areas. Test items were developed for readability at the fifth grade reading level.

A national "tryout" study along with a pilot study were the basis for gathering information used in item development. The ABAS manual contains comprehensive tables alluding to the standardization samples for age, sex, and education, and for age, sex, and race ethnicity. Test developers sought to study item guessing, item bias, appropriateness of instructions, and the applicability of using the ABAS for clinical studies. Sampling occurred in 107 cities in the United States from December 1998 to December 1999. Population recruitment for the sampling came from random phone calls and flyers to various community organizations including schools and churches. This reviewer found this method of sampling and norms development a strength for the ABAS. The manual presents test development in a well-organized style.

Standardization was accomplished by converting raw scores into percentile ranks, and then into scaled scores with the expected mean of 10 and standard deviation of 3. After utilizing a frequency distribution, each ABAS skill area scaled score was calculated and any needed smoothing of minor irregularities was carried out. As mentioned earlier, item guessing was studied, and tables were presented that listed the mean and *SEM* for each ABAS skill area.

Development of the General Adaptive Composite (GAC) score was accomplished via summing scaled scores and converting them into a mean of 100 with a standard deviation of 15. Once again, adjustments (smoothing) took place in order to allow tables to be presented in as realistic, yet as concise a manner as possible. Limiting the total GAC was necessary depending on the age group.

TECHNICAL. Coefficient alpha reliability coefficients ranged from .86 to .97 across age groups for skill areas in all three forms of the ABAS. Similarly, the reliability coefficients for GAC scores were also high with ranges from .98 to .99 for all age groups. Tables presented reliability coefficients for age and performance sampling, and include relationships by clinical sampling. Sampling included groups diagnosed as ADHD, Learning Disabled, and Mentally Retarded for all

three forms, along with Alzheimer's and other Neuropsychological Disorders for the Adult Form. Tables included number of individuals assessed, and the mean and standard error of measurement.

Standard error of measurement was low for each skills area according to tables presented in the manual. A description of how standard error of measurement was obtained, and how confidence levels were determined was presented for each test form. Test-retest reliability (1–2-week interval) was estimated using Pearson's product moment correlation coefficient. Once again, results showed a high GAC correlation (all in .90s), with the skill areas ranging in a most respectable .80 to .90 range. These tables, along with reported interrater reliability tables, were well organized.

Validity studies sought to demonstrate the usefulness of the ABAS. A test may be valid only if it is also reliable. The test content of the ABAS manual notes the relationship of the 10 skill areas addressed by AAMR's 1992 statement to the usefulness of its system. The authors appeared to have demonstrated high reliability coefficients with all ABAS forms. By applying the premise that often there is more than one rater per form, the authors further underscored significant interrater agreement. Because most response items represent observable behaviors, it would appear that the characterization of an individual by a teacher, parent, or other adult supports test findings. Further, those findings relate to entitlement decisions such as eligibility for special education services (e.g., classification of mental retardation). The ABAS manual presents a stratification by age, sex, race/ethnicity, and education for clinical samples that include degrees of mental retardation, ADD/ADHD, behavior disorders, learning disabilities, hearing impairments, emotional disturbance, physical impairments, and autism. It was noted that the samples were not randomly selected, but presented just as examples of the usefulness of this assessment tool. The authors further offer a precaution that professionals who use the ABAS must also apply their own judgment as to the consequences of its use.

COMMENTARY. The ABAS was developed after considerable research and trial. Its design came about with the assistance of almost 200 standardization examiners, research coordinators, reviewers, and consultants. Clear, straightforward statistical tables, presented in a helpful manner, strengthen its credibility and application for professional use. Like other adaptive behavior scales, the ABAS serves to apply recognized skill areas in the decision-making process. Unlike some adaptive behavior scales, the ABAS has a larger age range, with the flexibility to have certain adults rate themselves.

Unfortunately, some of the norm samples seem relatively small considering the development of this product. Standardizing a test requires considerable investment, both monetarily and professionally. It would be helpful if the authors of the ABAS continue to study its application through further research.

SUMMARY. The ABAS is designed to provide a system to assess adaptive skills for a wide range of ages (5–89 years). Utilizing definitions from AAMR and the DSM-IV, an overall General Adaptive Composite score can be gleaned from the 10 commonly identified skill areas. Entitlement decisions are among the intended outcomes of the ABAS. Research and presentation of material is well thought out. Reliability appears to be high, and validity appears to be well represented. The authors offer suggestions and precautions for professionals interested in using the ABAS. This generally well-normed, well-thought-out system should be given serious consideration. This reviewer would not hesitate to use this test.

REVIEWER'S REFERENCE

American Association on Mental Retardation. (1992). *Mental retardation: Definition, classification, and systems of supports* (9th ed.). Washington, DC: The author.

[7]
ADHD Rating Scale-IV.

Purpose: Designed to help identify the frequency of ADHD symptoms of a child as reported by a parent or educator.
Population: Ages 5–18 years.
Publication Date: 1998.
Scores, 3: Inattention, Hyperactivity-Impulsivity, Total.
Administration: Individual.
Forms, 2: Home, School.
Price Data, 2001: $29.75 per scale including manual (79 pages) and photocopiable scales.
Foreign Language Edition: Spanish questionnaires available.
Time: Administration time not reported.
Comments: Symptom criteria based on the DSM-IV; 18-item rating scale.
Authors: George J. DuPaul, Thomas J. Power, Arthur D. Anastopolous, and Robert Reid.
Publisher: Guilford Publications, Inc.

Review of the ADHD Rating Scale-IV by JILL ANN JENKINS, Consultant Child & School Psychologist, Barcelona, Spain:

DESCRIPTION. The ADHD Rating Scale-IV is an 18-item, paper-and-pencil questionnaire, which aims to identify behaviors that would be suggestive of Attention Deficit Hyperactivity Disorder (ADHD), in children ages 5 to 18 years. There are two versions of the test, the ADHD Rating Scale-IV: Home Version and the ADHD Rating Scale: School Version. The ADHD Rating Scale-IV: Home Version is available in Spanish as well as English, and the ADHD Rating Scale-IV: School Version is available in English only.

The ADHD Rating Scale-IV questionnaires, which are to be completed by teachers and parents, use a 4-point Likert rating scale of 0 (*never or rarely*) to 3 (*very often*) to describe the frequency of different characteristics of ADHD. Nine of the 18 questions seek to investigate symptoms suggestive of "inattention" and the other 9 measure "hyperactivity-impulsivity." The questions are presented in an alternating symptom style ("inattention" are odd-numbered items and "hyperactivity-impulsivity" are even-numbered items). Three raw scores are derived from each version, including "Inattention" (the sum of odd-numbered items), "Hyperactivity-Impulsivity" (the sum of even-numbered items), and "Total" (the sum of all items). The questionnaire takes approximately 10 minutes for parents or teachers to complete. Extreme caution in test interpretation is indicated when 3 or more items are left unanswered. Raw scores are converted to percentiles based on the child's gender and age.

The ADHD Rating Scale-IV is intended to be used as a tool for screening for ADHD, as a part of a thorough evaluation of ADHD (in addition to use with direct observations of school behavior and clinic-based testing), and as a method of evaluating the progress of ADHD symptoms pending treatment. The questionnaires and scoring sheets are included in the manual and the test purchaser is given permission to photocopy them for personal use only.

DEVELOPMENT. The ADHD Rating Scale-IV was developed specifically to obtain parent and teacher ratings of ADHD symptoms based on the DSM-IV criteria. The DSM-IV criteria organizes ADHD into three subtypes: Attention-Deficit/Hyperactivity Disorder, Combined Type

(314.01); Attention-Deficit/ Hyperactivity Disorder, Predominantly Inattentive Type (314.00); and Attention-Deficit/Hyperactivity Disorder, Predominantly Hyperactive-Impulsive Type (314.01) (American Psychiatric Association, 1994). The ADHD-Rating Scale IV has two domain scores, "Inattention" and "Hyperactivity-Impulsivity," resulting in three scores ("Inattention," "Hyperactivity-Impulsivity," and "Total").

The test authors state that the 18 scale items were written, "to reflect the DSM-IV criteria as closely as possible while maintaining brevity" (manual, p. 2). With the exception of 3 of the 18 questions, the test does appear to have achieved this goal. There are nuances in 3 questions that could skew the interpretation. The characteristic in Number 6 on the questionnaire, "Runs about or climbs excessively in situations in which it is inappropriate" omits the DSM-IV qualifier that in adolescents this may be limited to subjective feelings of restlessness. The characteristic in Number 7 "does not follow through on instructions and fails to finish work" has left out "or chores" (indicated in the DSM-IV), which could be quite significant for the Home Version of the scale. Finally, Number 11 of the questionnaire "Avoids tasks (e.g., schoolwork, homework) that require sustained mental effort," has been changed from the DSM-IV description of "avoids, dislikes, or is reluctant to engage in tasks that require sustained mental effort (i.e., such as schoolwork or homework)." Certainly there could be children who do not avoid a task, such as homework, because they feel a sense of duty (or fear of punishment), but complete this task with great reluctance or dislike (which, according to the DSM-IV, would then qualify them for this criteria).

The ADHD Rating Scale-IV: Home Version (Spanish) has two items that are not tightly translated. Number 11, "Avoids tasks (e.g., schoolwork, homework) that require sustained mental effort" is translated as "Evita tareas (trabajo de la escuela) que requieran un ezfuerzo mental continuo." This translation only includes "schoolwork" and does not include "homework," and considering that this is the Home Version of the test, such a detail may be significant. For the detail-oriented examiner, the misspelling of "ezfuerzo" (correct spelling "esfuerzo") should also be noted. In Number 8, "Has difficulty playing or engaging in leisure activities quietly" has been translated to "Tiene dificultad jugando o envolviéndose calládamente en actividades recreativas o de descanso." In this translation, the translators have literally stated that the child "has difficulty in playing or involving themselves quietly in recreational activities or relaxation activities." The criterion probably stands best translated by simply eliminating "o de descanso" ("relaxation activities"), which is not necessary ("actividades recreativas" is already a fair translation of "leisure activities") and adds a confusing element to the question, where "actividades de descanso" is linguistically incorrect in most Spanish languages. Again, for the detail-oriented "calladamente" has been misspelled (accent over first "a"). Two other misspellings were additionally observed in the text of the Spanish version. Overall, the Spanish version is in need of good Spanish editing and a simple spell check. As it stands, using the tool as is should be done with caution. It would be hard for a native Spanish speaker to take it very seriously considering very basic spelling errors and linguistic oddities.

TECHNICAL.

Standardization of ADHD Rating Scale-IV: Home Version. A normative sample of $N = 2,000$ participants was used for the standardization of the ADHD Rating Scale-IV: Home Version ($n = 1,043$ girls, $n = 930$ boys, and $n = 27$ unspecified). Participants attended kindergarten through 12th grade ($M = 4.21$, $SD = 3.46$) and were between the ages of 4 and 20 years ($M = 9.63$, $SD = 3.53$). The sample was selected to approximate the 1990 U.S. Census data distributions for ethnic group and region. Overall, the test appears to have collected an acceptable sample size and have well represented various ethnic groups according to the Census. Of course, if using this test outside of the United States of America, one would need to very carefully interpret test results.

Parent/guardian respondents ranged in age from 19 to 80 years ($M = 37.12$ and $SD = 6.35$). Of the $N = 2,000$ respondents, $n = 1,753$ were female, $n = 244$ were male, and $n = 3$ were unspecified. Most of the respondents were mothers ($n = 1,711$; 85%) and most were Caucasian ($n = 1,470$; 73.5%). Families were mostly living in middle-class socioeconomic circumstances. Despite the fact that the sample appears to have well represented the U.S. population, one must take caution when interpreting test results that the normative sample then represents, for the greatest part, White middle-class mothers' interpretations of their children's behaviors.

The Spanish Version of the ADHD Rating Scale: Home Version was not standardized. Considering this, and the fact that two of the questions appear changed through translation, applying the Spanish Version to the norms should be done with caution.

Standardization of the ADHD Rating Scale-IV: School Version. Participants in the normative sample of N = 2,000 included n = 1,040 boys, n = 948 girls, and n = 12 unspecified. Again, the sample was randomly selected to represent the 1990 U.S. Census. Participants ranged from ages 4 to 19 years (M = 10.6, SD = 3.6) and attended kindergarten through 12th grade (M = 5.1, SD = 3.5). Overall, the test appears to have collected an acceptable sample size and have well represented various ethnic groups according to the U.S. Census. As in the Home Version, if using this test outside of the United States of America, one would need to very carefully interpret test results.

A total of N = 1,001 teachers completed the ratings (n = 793 female, n = 194 male, and n = 14 unspecified). Teachers were predominantly Caucasian (n = 902; 90.2%).

Normative data for both the ADHD Rating Scale-IV: Home and School Version were then created by dividing the total participants into two groups depending on gender, and four subgroups depending on age. In total there were eight groups, consisting of boys and girls placed into the following age groups: 5–7 years, 8–10 years, 11–13 years, and 14–18 years. The groups were approximately evenly distributed in the number of children represented. Children aged 4 and 19 were not included because there were very few cases available. Grouping children with such a large gap of 3 years may surely have influenced the normative data. According to Barkley (1990), many researchers have noted the developmental influence on attention and impulsivity. It may, therefore, have been better to develop narrower age groupings.

Reliability. Test-retest reliability, internal consistency, and criterion-related reliability were estimated using a much smaller sample of N = 71 students from a limited geographic area (Pennsylvania and New Jersey). Despite acceptable levels of reliability reported, there is great caution given in generalizing these results from such a limited representation of the standardization sample.

Test-retest reliability for both the School and Home Version of the ADHD Rating Scale-IV was significant. The School Version test-retest reliability was based on teacher ratings 4 weeks apart. Pearson product-moment correlation coefficients were as follows: Total score = .90, Inattention = .89, and Hyperactivity-Impulsivity = .88. For the Home Version, parent ratings 4 weeks apart resulted in the following Pearson product-moment correlation coefficients: Total score = .85, Inattention = .78, and Hyperactivity-Impulsivity = .86.

Interrater agreement between parents and teachers was low, with correlation coefficients between parents and teachers as follows; Total score: = .41, Inattention = .45, and Hyperactivity-Impulsivity = .40. The lack of consistency between respondents does not necessarily prove a problem with regard to the integrity of this test. Children with difficulties in ADHD may display their symptoms quite differently depending on the context that they are in (home vs. school), the task that is required of them, or the time of day (Barkley, 1990). In addition, this may be related to different degrees of familiarity with the child according to Achenbach, McConaughy, and Howell (1987), who noted a lack of agreement in reports between parents and teachers with regard to child behaviors.

Internal consistency. Alpha coefficients for both the Home and School Versions were very acceptable, respectively reported as Total (Home Version = .92, School Version = .94), Inattention (Home Version = .86, School Version = .96), and Hyperactivity-Impulsivity (Home Version = .88, School Version = .88).

Criterion-related validity. The authors used the Conners' Teacher Rating Scale and Conners' Parent Rating Scale to analyze criterion validity. The Conners' Scales look at hyperactivity and impulsivity (CTRS Hyperactivity score), as well as other emotional and behavioral factors. For the ADHD-IV School Version, the CRTS Hyperactivity Score had a significant Pearson product-moment correlation with the Inattention score, Hyperactivity-Impulsivity score, and Total score (respectively .73, .79, and .86). Similarly, statistical significance was indicated between the CTRS Hyperactivity Score and the ADHD-IV: Home Version, with Pearson product-moment correlation scores of .61 for the Inattention score, .81 for the Hyperactivity-Impulsivity score, and .80 for Total score.

chose an equal number of items for each scale. The authors used both exploratory and confirmatory factor analysis with national populations in excess of 4,000 to determine if "these scales would conform to the bidimensional structure of the diagnostic criteria" (manual, p. 5) for both the Home and School scales, and concluded that the scale items align with both a one- or two-factor (IA, HI) model.

TECHNICAL. This instrument was normed by using the information obtained from the above-mentioned populations used for the factor analysis studies. Random selection was used to select cases from the factor analytic sample; however, the authors state that this process was "constrained to conform with proportions of regional and ethnic distribution" (manual, p. 15). The overall population varies somewhat from the 1990 U.S. Census. The Home Version of the scale slightly underrepresented the South and overrepresented the North, and African Americans were slightly overrepresented. On the School Version, which also overrepresented African Americans, the Midwest was overrepresented, and the West underrepresented.

For the School Version of the ADHD Rating Scale-IV, internal consistency reliability was measured with a coefficient alpha. The coefficients were: Total score = .94, Inattention = .96, and Hyperactivity-Impulsivity = .88. Test-retest reliability for this version was conducted 4 weeks apart yielding Pearson product-moment correlations of: Total score = .90, Inattention = .89, and Hyperactivity-Impulsivity = .88.

The Home Version of the scale had alpha coefficients of: Total score = .92, Inattention = .86, and Hyperactivity-Impulsivity = .88. The test-retest reliability Pearson product-moment correlations were: .85, .78, and .86, respectively. Additional interrater agreement between parents and teachers was moderate, with correlations as follows: Total score = .41, Inattention = .45, and Hyperactivity-Impulsivity = .40.

There was significant variability in both parent and teacher ratings with regard to gender, age, and ethnicity. Younger children and African American children were rated as having more ADHD-type behaviors than Caucasian or Asian children. In addition, boys were rated as having more instances of Inattentive and Hyperactive-Impulsive behaviors than girls. As a result of these

data, norm tables are separate for boys and girls. The size of the population within groups would not permit separate tables for ethnicity, making more difficult the interpretation of scores for African Americans.

To examine criterion validity issues, the authors compared the ADHD Rating Scale-IV: School Version with areas of the Conners' Teacher Rating Scale-39 (CTRS-39). The absolute values for the Pearson coefficients ranged from .22 to .88. As expected, ADHD symptoms as measured with the ADHD Rating Scale-IV and the CTRS-39 measures of Hyperactivity and Hyperactivity Index shared between 53% and 77% of the variance. The same examination of areas of the Conners' Parent Rating Scale-48 and the Home Version of the ADHD Rating Scale-IV showed 15 of 18 contrasts as significant; with a Bonferroni correction, 12 were significant.

The authors looked at school and clinic-based populations to see if the instrument would predict children with ADHD. The results are complex, and any user would be well advised to consult the manual before interpretation of scores. For instance, when predictions are made on the basis of the Inattention scale, both teachers and parents made an equal contribution, but in looking at Hyperactivity-Impulsivity, the parent ratings are more accurate than teacher ratings. Furthermore, according to the authors, prevalence studies show that this instrument tends to overselect, especially in the School Version (21%). This certainly surpasses the 3 to 5% rate found in the DSM-IV. The authors feel that this may be due to using a single informant who produces a frequency count of symptoms, and they conclude that caution must be used in interpretation.

Additional data are presented on the instrument's Positive Predictive Power (PPP), and Negative Predictive Power (NPP). This refers to the statistical power of the instrument to "rule in" as well as "rule out" ADHD. There is evidence this instrument can be used to indicate absence of ADHD as well.

COMMENTARY. The authors state that, "When used as part of a comprehensive assessment battery that included diagnostic interviews, behavior observations, and related measures, the ADHD Rating Scale-IV can provide reliable and valid data regarding the frequency of ADHD symptoms" (manual, p. 42). This reviewer agrees, but there are a few concerns about significant overidentification when using the School Version of this scale. The 21% prevalence rate detected seems to raise questions about the efficiency of the scale.

Furthermore, the problems inherent in the apparent overselection of boys and African Americans continues (this instrument identified 2:1 African American to Caucasian). This is unfortunately characteristic of many of this type of instrument, and may be reflective of broader cultural bias. The authors responsibly caution careful and conservative interpretation when this instrument is used with African Americans. The authors are thorough and forthright in the presentation of descriptions of the instrument, procedures, and supporting statistics. The manual is helpful, and even has a chapter on using the scales for diagnosis and screening. Procedures for determining screening and diagnostic cutoff scores are discussed, and case studies are presented for demonstration purposes. Furthermore, the alignment of the DSM-IV criteria may not be entirely relevant to the school setting. Many children with attention problems do well in the school setting, which underscores the necessity of multisourced assessment and, of course, cautious and conservative interpretation of results.

CONCLUSIONS. The authors have done a creditable job of creating an instrument that aligns with the diagnostic criteria for ADHD found in the DSM-IV. The statistical analysis of the pilot study, and the norm data pulled from the original group were impressive and thorough. There is evidence of reliability, validity, and the instrument's ability to discriminate among subtypes. The ADHD Rating Scale-IV is very easy to use and score, and the manual presented data from both clinical and school settings. The scores are expressed as percentile ranks, which is surprising given the complexity of analysis of supporting data. There are minor misalignments in the norming, but the differences are not sufficient to conclude the instrument would be nonrepresentative of a national sample. As stated above, the School Version of the instrument will undoubtedly result in a number of false positives, given the prevalence rate of the authors' studies.

The two versions, School and Home (the Home Version has a Spanish translation), will no doubt be of interest to those in the schools or clinical settings who would conduct research concerning ADHD characteristics. This instrument will also be of interest to those seeking a screening tool. The individual diagnosis of ADHD will, however, continue to require thorough and multiply sourced data collection. Use of the ADHD Rating Scale-IV in that context would require significant familiarity with the nuances of this instrument and their implications for interpretation.

REVIEWER'S REFERENCE

American Psychiatric Association. (1994). *Diagnostic and statistical manual of mental disorders* (4th ed.). Washington, DC: Author.

[8]
ADHD Symptom Checklist—4.

Purpose: Designed as "a screening instrument for the behavioral symptoms of attention-deficit/hyperactivity disorder (AD/HD) and oppositional defiant disorder (ODD)."
Population: Ages 3–18.
Publication Date: 1997.
Acronym: ADHD-SC4.
Scores, 3: Screening Cutoff, Symptom Count, Symptom Criterion.
Administration: Individual.
Forms, 1: Same checklist completed by parent and teacher.
Price Data, 2001: $52 per kit including 50 checklists, 50 symptom count score sheets, 50 symptom severity profile score sheets, and manual (200 pages).
Time: (5) minutes.
Authors: Kenneth D. Gadow and Joyce Sprafkin.
Publisher: Checkmate Plus, Ltd.

Review of the ADHD Symptom Checklist—4 by ROBERT J. VOLPE, Doctoral Candidate, School Psychology Program, Lehigh University, and JAMES C. DiPERNA, Assistant Professor, School Psychology Program, Lehigh University, Bethlehem, PA:

DESCRIPTION. The ADHD-Symptom Checklist-4 (ADHD-SC4) is a 50-item norm-referenced rating scale designed to assess attention-deficit/hyperactivity disorder (AD/HD), oppositional defiant disorder (ODD), aggression toward peers, and side-effects associated with the use of stimulant medication. According to its authors, the ADHD-SC4 was developed for several uses. First, the ADHD-SC4 was designed as a screening instrument for the most common causes of referral to child psychiatric clinics (disruptive child behavior). Second, the ADHD-SC4 was designed to monitor changes in symptoms during treatment. Third, given the prescription rate of psychostimulants in children exhibiting disruptive behavior, the ADHD-SC4 includes scales to measure observable side effects (Mood, Attention-Arousal, and Physical Complaints) of stimulant medication.

Checklists, Score Summary Records, and Score Sheets may be obtained with the manual as a kit, and purchased separately thereafter. Identical checklists may be used for parents and teachers, and both parent and teacher scores can be recorded on the same Score Summary Record. There are also separate Score Sheets for parent- and teacher-completed checklists that present male and female scoring information (e.g., raw scores and corresponding T-scores and percentile scores) on either side of the form.

The 50-item ADHD-SC4 typically requires less than 10–15 minutes to complete, and contains cells for recording raw category scores. The authors of the ADHD-SC4 advocate two methods of scoring: the screening cutoff score method or the symptom severity score method. The screening cutoff method provides an indication if the number of symptoms should be of concern. The symptom severity score provides a score that can be compared to normative data.

DEVELOPMENT. The items comprising the AD/HD and ODD scales are identical or similar to items of the Early Childhood Inventory—4 (ECI-4; Sprafkin & Gadow, 1996), the Child Symptom Inventory (CSI-4; Gadow & Sprafkin, 1994), and the Adolescent Symptom Inventory (ASI-4; Gadow & Sprafkin, 1997), which are broader rating scales designed to assess psychiatric symptoms in preschoolers, school-aged children, and adolescents, respectively. Although these items are highly consistent with the symptom criteria of the DSM-IV (American Psychiatric Association, 1994), they have not been subjected to recommended methods of item development (e.g., content analyses, expert review). Items of the Stimulant Side-effects Checklist were generated from a review of the stimulant medication evaluation literature that sought to identify signs of stimulant side-effects observable to adults (e.g., unusually talkative, lethargic, drowsy). The items of the peer conflict scale were generated to match the behavior categories of the ADHD School Observation Code (SOC; Gadow, Sprafkin, & Nolan, 1996), which was also used in medication evaluation studies. In sum, although the items of the DSM-IV-based scales closely approximate the symptom criteria set forth in the DSM-IV, additional analysis of item content and properties would further strengthen the evidence to support the use of this instrument.

TECHNICAL. The normative data for the ADHD-SC4 were recently expanded (Gadow & Sprafkin, 1999). According to the authors, T-scores between old and new samples are very similar; however, some differences may be noted between the 1997 ADHD-SC4 manual and the revised Score Sheets. It should be noted that normative data for the ADHD-SC4 scales of AD/HD and ODD were, with few exceptions, generated from the standardization data of other instruments (CSI-4, ECI-4, and ASI-4). Individual items are identical across these measures with the exception of a small number that were revised (i.e., shortened) for the ADHD-SC4. The impact of revising these items appears negligible (Sprafkin, Gadow, & Nolan, 2001).

Normative data were collected in several cohorts and varied in methodology depending on the age group (e.g., preschool, school-age, adolescent) and informant in question. Sample sizes were 929 for preschoolers (531 parent, 398 teacher), 1,875 for school-aged children (552 parent, 1,323 teacher), and 1,755 for adolescents (761 parent, 994 teacher). In several cases, the original and the updated normative data were gathered across multiple geographic regions. However, the updated normative data for the teacher ratings of preschoolers and parent ratings of both 6–12-year-olds and adolescents, were collected in one area of suburban New York, which limits the utility of the ADHD-SC4 with populations that do not approximate this narrow sample. Of additional concern, children of minority status were underrepresented in the teacher ratings of school-aged children and adolescents as well as the parent ratings of adolescents. Hence, it is essential that this be taken into consideration in the use of the ADHD-SC4 with children of minority status. Also, with the exception of the preschool age range, the normative samples were smaller for the Peer Conflict scale. Finally, no normative data are available for the Stimulant Side-Effects Checklist; however, this appears appropriate given the purpose of this scale.

No internal consistency data are reported in the technical manual; however, Sprafkin et al. (2001) recently reported internal consistency coefficients for a clinical sample of 103 children and adolescents between the ages of 5 and 17. Coefficient alphas were high, ranging between .92 and .95 for the Peer Conflict- and DSM-IV-based-scales respectively. Coefficient alphas were also high for the Attention-Arousal index of the Stimulant Side-effects Checklist for parent- ($r = .78$) and teacher-completed ratings ($r = .89$). Alphas for the remaining indices of the Stimulant Side-effects Checklist ranged from .46 to .65 for parents and between .46 and .58 for teachers. In sum, internal consistency coefficients were generally high for both the parent- and teacher-completed ADHD-SC4.

The authors report several studies of the test-retest and interrater reliability of the ADHD-SC4 in the manual. Intervals for test-retest varied from 2 days to repeated tests over several months. In general, adequate test-retest reliability coefficients were reported for the DSM-IV-based scales, but coefficients were substantially lower for the parent-completed Peer Conflict Scale ($r = .35$) in a group of 3–5-year-olds and for the AD/HD: Hyperactive Impulsive category ($r = .38$) in a sample of 4- to 17-year-olds who were being evaluated for treatment with stimulant medication. The interrater reliability of ADHD-SC4 ratings was recently reported in a sample of 103, 5- to 17-year-olds (Sprafkin et al., 2001). Interrater reliability correlations ranged from low (.23) to moderate (.51) across ADHD-SC4 scales; however, these were consistent with previous research concerning agreement between ratings of different informants (e.g., Achenbach, McConaughy, & Howell, 1987).

A variety of evidence is presented in the technical manual to support the validity and clinical utility of the ADHD-SC4 scores. The scales of the ADHD-SC4 correlate well with other rating scales commonly used in the assessment of AD/HD. Specifically, moderate to large positive correlations (.44–.81) were found between the parent-completed ADHD-SC4 and relevant subscales of the Child Behavior Checklist (Achenbach, 1991a) and the Mothers' Method for Subgrouping (Loney, 1984). Similarly, moderate to large positive correlations (.45–.88) were found between relevant subscales of the Teacher's Report Form (Achenbach, 1991b) and the IOWA Conners' Teacher's Rating Scale (Loney & Milich, 1982) and the teacher-completed ADHD-SC4. Partici-

pants of these studies consisted of children and youth referred to a university-based outpatient psychiatric clinic. Although the data presented here may be relevant to such referrals, given the stated purpose of the ADHD-SC4 as a screening instrument, further research with school and community samples is warranted.

Criterion-related validity data for teacher- and parent-completed checklists are available in the ADHD-SC4 manual. Scores on parent- and teacher-completed AD/HD-Inattentive, AD/HD-Combined Type, ODD, and Peer Conflict scales were significantly different between outpatient clinic and normal school samples across age groups. Differences between groups on the AD/HD-Hyperactive-Impulsive category, although significant for males across age groups, were not significant for teacher reports of elementary school-aged females or parent reports of adolescent females (Sprafkin & Gadow, 1996).

An investigation of the diagnostic utility of the ADHD-SC4 was investigated for three age groups (preschool, elementary, and adolescent) by comparing clinic diagnoses to screening cutoff scores on the AD/HD and ODD scales of the ADHD-SC4. Agreement between the ADHD-SC4 and clinic diagnosis appeared to vary by age group, category, and informant. As expected, combining data from both informants markedly improved sensitivity, but at the expense of accuracy in specificity.

Several studies also have investigated the treatment sensitivity of the ADHD-SC4 scales (e.g., Gadow, Nolan, Sverd, Sprafkin, & Paolicelli, 1990; Gadow, Sverd, Sprafkin, Nolan, & Ezor, 1995; Sverd, Gadow, & Paolicelli, 1989). The results of these studies are mixed.

One significant limitation to the validity evidence for the ADHD-SC4 is a lack of factor analytic data to verify the internal structure of the ADHD-SC4 in its current state. Replication of predictive and concurrent validity studies also is necessary to provide evidence of the generalizability of the findings reported in the manual. Further, item analyses, especially for the Peer Conflict and Side-Effect Checklist are needed to identify any items that may be in need of revision or elimination.

COMMENTARY AND SUMMARY. According to the authors, the ADHD-SC4 was designed for screening the behavioral symptoms of AD/HD and ODD, and to systematize the exchange of information between care providers concerning behavioral changes in children with AD/HD resulting from behavioral interventions and/or pharmacotherapy. Although the ADHD-SC4 is a relatively new rating scale, the development of its components began over a decade ago. Because several scales of the ADHD-SC4 were developed separately, the reliability and validity data presented in the manual, with few exceptions, are based on results from studies of *other* instruments. The vast majority of items contained in the ADHD-SC4 are identical to the items on these other instruments; however, some of the AD/HD items were shortened in the ADHD-SC4. In addition, although the AD/HD and ODD items appear first in both the broadband measures (e.g., CSI-4) and ADHD-SC4, the remaining items of the ADHD-SC4 were presented to informants on separate checklists during development. Although a recent study (Sprafkin et al., 2001) reported quite high correlations between the ADHD-SC4 and CSI-4 AD/HD items ($r = .93$), this only partially addresses the issue of scale equivalence. In addition, the clinical sample examined in the Sprafkin et al. study was an aggregate of preschoolers, school-aged children, and adolescents. Hence, information specific to a particular age group is not available at this time. The ADHD-SC4 shows promise as both a screening instrument and a progress monitoring measure. However, further research is needed before the ADHD-SC4 can be used with confidence for these purposes with populations outside of the suburban New York area.

REVIEWERS' REFERENCES

Achenbach, T. M. (1991a). *Manual for the Child Behavior Checklist/4-18 and 1991 Profile.* Burlington, VT: University of Vermont Department of Psychiatry.

Achenbach, T. M. (1991b). *Manual for the Teacher's Report Form and 1991 Profile.* Burlington, VT: University of Vermont Department of Psychiatry.

Achenbach, T. M., McConaughy, S. H., & Howell, C. T. (1987). Child/adolescent behavioral and emotional problems: Implications of cross-informant correlations for situational specificity. *Psychological Bulletin, 101,* 213–232.

American Psychiatric Association. (1994). *Diagnostic and Statistical manual of mental disorders* (4th ed.). Washington, DC: Author.

Gadow, K. D., & Sprafkin, J. (1994). *Child Symptom Inventories manual.* Stony Brook, NY: Checkmate Plus.

Gadow, K. D., & Sprafkin, J. (1997). *Adolescent Symptom Inventory—4.* Stony Brook, NY: Checkmate Plus.

Gadow, K. D., Sprafkin, J., & Nolan, E. E. (1996). ADHD School Observation Code. Stony Brook, NY: Checkmate Plus.

Gadow, K. D., & Sprafkin, J. (1999). *1999 Revised Norms: ADHD-SC4.* Stony Brook, NY: Checkmate Plus Ltd.

Gadow, K. D., Nolan, E. E., Sverd, J., Sprafkin, J., & Paolicelli, L. (1990). Methylphenidate in aggressive-hyperactive boys: I. Effects on peer aggression in public school settings. *Journal of the American Academy of Child and Adolescent Psychiatry, 29,* 710–718.

Gadow, K. D., Sverd, J., Sprafkin, J., Nolan, E. E., & Ezor, S. N. (1995). Efficacy of methylphenidate for attention-deficit hyperactivity disorder in children with tic disorder. *Archives of General Psychiatry, 52,* 444–455.

Loney, J. (1984, August). *A short parent scale for subgrouping childhood hyperactivity and aggression.* Paper presented at the meeting of the American Psychological Association, Toronto.

Loney, J., & Milich, R. (1982). Hyperactivity, inattention, and aggression in clinical practice. In M. Wolraich & D. K. Routh (Eds.), *Advances in developmental and behavioral pediatrics* (Vol. 3, pp. 113–147). Greenwich, CT: JAI Press.

Sprafkin, J., & Gadow, K. D. (1996). *The Early Childhood Inventories manual.* Stony Brook, NY: Checkmate Plus.

Sprafkin, J., Gadow, K. D., & Nolan, E. E. (2001). The utility of a DSM-IV-referenced screening instrument for attention-deficit/hyperactivity disorder. *Journal of Emotional and Behavioral Disorders, 9,* 182–191.

Sverd, J., Gadow, K. D., & Paolicelli, L. M. (1989). Methylphenidate treatment of attention deficit hyperactivity disorder in boys with Tourette's syndrome. *Journal of the American Academy of Child and Adolescent Psychiatry, 28,* 574–579.

Review of the ADHD Symptom Checklist—4 by CYNTHIA A. ROHRBECK, Associate Professor of Psychology, The George Washington University, Washington, DC:

DESCRIPTION. The ADHD Symptom Checklist—4 (ADHD-SC4), developed by K. D. Gadow and J. Sprafkin, is designed to screen for symptoms of attention-deficit hyperactivity disorder (ADHD) and oppositional defiant disorder (ODD) in children ages 3–18 years. It is a 50-item paper-and-pencil test that uses a 4-point Likert scale and can be completed by parents and/or teachers in approximately 5 minutes. In addition to ADHD and ODD Scales, the test includes a Peer Conflict Scale (measuring peer aggression) and a Stimulant Side Effects Checklist (to monitor potential side effects of stimulant medication often administered to children with ADHD).

ADHD-SC4 items can be scored by using screening cutoffs or by examining symptom severity. For the first approach, a Score Summary Record form can be used to compare the Symptom Count (the number of symptoms for a specific disorder) with the Symptom Criteria score (the minimum number of symptoms necessary for diagnosis of a disorder) to determine whether or not a child should be further evaluated. For Symptom Severity, items are added based on the response rate with 0 = *never,* 1 = *sometimes,* 2 = *often,* and 3 = *very often.* Separate teacher and parent Symptom Severity Profiles are provided to indicate whether the total value represents low, medium or high severity depending upon the child or adolescent's age and gender. Both approaches break down ADHD symptoms to reflect ADHD Inattentive Type, ADHD Hyperactive-Impulsive Type, and ADHD Combined Type, in addition to Oppositional Defiant Disorder.

DEVELOPMENT. Items were developed based on the symptoms for ADHD and ODD in DSM-IV, and were reworded slightly to be more easily understood. Items were also reworded to better assess observable behavior, and were stripped of frequency indicators (e.g., "often") because the ADHD-SC4 includes a measure of frequency embedded in the 4-point response format.

The items for the ADHD and ODD scales are essentially identical to items from the authors' previously developed Symptom Inventories (e.g., Gadow & Sprafkin, 1994). The authors had also previously developed the Peer Conflict Scale (Gadow, 1986a) to measure peer aggression, and the Stimulant Side Effects Checklist (Gadow, 1986b) to measure the effects of medication treatment studies of children with ADHD. These two scales became part of a school-based medication evaluation (SBME) procedure (Gadow, 1993). Eventually, that procedure became the Stimulant Medication Checklist (Gadow, 1994), which also contained the ADHD and ODD categories from the Child Symptom Inventory-4. This measure was then modified so that all items used the same response choices (*never, sometimes, often,* and *very often*) and the title was changed to the ADHD-Symptom Checklist-4.

The authors included the ADHD and ODD Scales in one measure (the ADHD-SC4) because ADHD and ODD are two of the most frequently diagnosed disorders in children and adolescents. These two scales are intended for screening and for measuring behavior change following interventions. Items for the Peer Conflict Scale were designed to measure physical and nonphysical aggression toward other children. Items on the Stimulant Side Effects Checklist were designed to measure responses to treatment, given that stimulant medication is a widely used treatment intervention for ADHD. It is not clear in the ADHD-SC4 manual if there was pilot testing of items or any evaluation of content validity for these additional subscales.

TECHNICAL. The most recent norms (revised in 1999; not included in the manual, but a separate handout) for parent ratings were based on ratings of over 1,800 children and adolescents ranging from ages 3 to 18. Norms for teacher ratings were based on ratings of over 2,700 children and adolescents from age 3 to 18. It should be noted that samples were drawn from different populations for the parent and teacher norms, and for different age groups of children and adolescents. For the preschool sample (ages 3–5), data were collected from pediatrician offices, preschools, and day cares. The ethnic distribution of the norm sample approximated U.S. population estimates based on the 1990 Census, although participating preschools were all from Long Island, NY. No children in this subsample had received special education services or medication for behavioral disorders. For 6–12-year-olds, parent norm data were collected from pediatricians and elementary schools on Long Island, NY. This sample was mostly Caucasian. For 13–18-year-olds, the parent sample was drawn from two school districts in Long Island and was also primarily Caucasian. Teacher norms for the adolescent subsample were from public schools in Missouri, Wisconsin, and New York with primarily Caucasian students.

The ADHD-SC4 manual provides detailed information about a number of studies with different ages and populations (outpatient clinic samples, medication evaluation samples, and norms samples) that indicate support for the measure's reliability and validity. There were two test-retest reliability studies that included the ADHD, ODD, and Peer Conflict subscales of the Parent Checklist of the ADHD-SC4. Test-retest reliabilities (using a 6-week administration interval) for the ADHD and ODD have been above .60 and .70; in contrast, the test-retest reliability for the Peer Conflict Scale was $r = .35$ (3-week administration interval). On the Teacher Checklist, test-retest reliabilities ranged from .38 (6-week administration interval) for the hyperactivity/impulsive type of symptoms of the ADHD Scale to .90 (1-week administration interval) for a study using the Peer Conflict Scale.

With regard to content validity, the ADHD and ODD subscales should be similar to the DSM IV classification system. The Checklist as a whole shows a type of predictive validity, correlating with psychiatric diagnoses, in addition to concurrent validity, as demonstrated by correlations between both the Parent Checklist and the Teacher Checklist with other relevant rating scales (e.g., moderate correlations with attention, aggression, and delinquency subscale on the Child Behavior Checklist). The ADHD-SC4 also shows discriminant validity, by differentiating between clinical outpatients and the norms samples.

Studies summarized in the manual suggest slight evidence of discriminant validity for the Parent Checklist Peer Conflict Scale; that scale differentiated between preschoolers receiving special education services and preschoolers in regular education classes. In addition, the Teacher Check-

than including more constructs with fewer devoted items. To some extent, however, the more in-depth assessment consists of asking a few questions in many different ways. For example, there are six items related to whether a child has difficulty remaining seated. If this were a face-to-face interview with a parent, asking him or her to evaluate "rocks in seat," then "moves about while seated," then "shifts position in seat" would be repetitive to the point of rudeness. Redundancy achieves internal consistency, but not necessarily depth, as indicated by the limited amount of variance explained by the two factors (36%). More importantly, this isolated focus limits the scale's autonomy by decontextualizing assessment with regard to other potential problem areas, such as social relations and academic skills. The authors advocate for additional assessment of other variables, but how "comprehensive" is the ADHD-SRS if other diagnostic methods are needed?

The authors' claim that the ADHD-SRS "identifies children with ADHD more effectively" (manual, p. 8) will likely provoke a large audience. The tricky part would be proving that a child is "with ADHD," but leaving this issue aside, the minimum requirements for any effective identification process would be decision reliability and validity (Barnett, Lentz, & Macmann, 2000). There is sufficient evidence, for example, of the high internal consistency and test-retest reliability of the ADHD-SRS subscale and total scores, and that these scores differentiate the group means of children identified with ADHD versus the general population. In practice, however, the scale is used to make relatively permanent and high-stakes clinical decisions (i.e., diagnosis, medication changes). Decision reliability requires evidence that significant subscale differences and "at-risk" or "high risk" status are stable across two testing intervals. Decision validity requires evidence that the scale differentiates among clinical populations, reduces the number of necessary diagnostic methods, or leads to beneficial outcomes for the client. These clinical decisions reflect how the ADHD-SRS and similar instruments are used in practice, and they should be validated for these purposes (American Educational Research Association, American Psychological Association, & National Council on Measurement in Education, 1999).

SUMMARY. The psychometric structure of ADHD is a continuing saga (Barkley, 1997) and the American Psychiatric Association has had considerable difficulty remaining seated in one position. The ADHD-SRS will facilitate the diagnosis of subtypes consistent with the most recent edition of the DSM-IV (American Psychiatric Association, 1994). Users should not assume this instrument will enhance the technical qualities of clinical practice more effectively than its competitors.

REVIEWER'S REFERENCES

American Psychiatric Association. (1994). *Diagnostic and statistical manual for mental disorders* (4ᵗʰ ed.). Washington, DC: Author.

American Educational Research Association, American Psychological Association, & National Council on Measurement in Education. (1999). *Standards for educational and psychological testing*. Washington, DC: American Educational Research Association.

Barkley, R. A. (1997). Behavioral inhibition, sustained attention, and executive functions: Constructing a unifying theory of ADHD. *Psychological Bulletin, 121,* 65–94.

Barnett, D. W., Lentz, F. E., Jr., & Macmann, G. (2000). Psychometric qualities of professional practice. In E. S. Shapiro & T. R. Kratochwill (Eds.), *Behavioral assessment in schools: Theory, research, and clinical foundations* (2ⁿᵈ ed., pp. 355–386). New York: Guilford.

Review of the ADHD Symptoms Rating Scale by RONALD A. MADLE, School Psychologist, Shikellamy School District, Sunbury, PA and Adjunct Associate Professor of School Psychology, The Pennsylvania State University, University Park, PA:

DESCRIPTION. The ADHD Symptoms Rating Scale (ADHD-SRS) is a standardized, norm-referenced rating scale designed to assess ADHD symptoms of children and adolescents ages 5 to 18 years of age. Its stated purpose is to assist in symptom identification, diagnosis, and treatment planning and monitoring for children and adolescents with ADHD. The test kit consists of a manual and rating forms. The manual is well written and covers scale development and standardization; the psychometric properties of the scale; directions for administering, scoring, and interpreting the ADHD-SRS; and the norms tables. The 56-item Rating Form is available in both English and Spanish versions. Examination of the items shows comprehensive coverage of each DSM-IV diagnostic criterion.

The administration section of the manual is complete, including information on preparation, routine administration and scoring, and permissible accommodations for raters. Raters may be selected from home, school, or community settings. Items are rated using a five choice Likert-type scale that uses frequency-based anchor points. About 10 to 15 minutes are needed to complete the ratings. A Total Score and two subscales—Hyperactive-Impulsive (HI) and Inattentive (IN)—are tallied from the item scores. The raw scores are converted to interpretable derived scores that include linear T Scores, confidence intervals, and percentile ranks. Separate norm tables are provided for ages 5–11 and 12–18 and for home and school raters. General (combined sex) norms are recommended for interpretation to prevent masking of the well-established gender differences that occur naturally in the population. Separate norms that can be used for special interpretive purposes are presented for males and females. Descriptive categories have been based on the estimated prevalence rates for ADHD among school-aged children. The highest 6% of the population is considered as "High Risk," with the next 10% designated as "At Risk." The remaining descriptors are "Normal Risk" and "Low Risk."

Although the scale is easily scored by hand, an IBM-compatible computer-scoring program is available. The program will accept either items or hand-computed raw scores and prints reports containing the item scores, all derived scores, and T score profiles plotted against Risk Levels.

DEVELOPMENT. A systematic rational-theoretical approach was used to develop the ADHD-SRS. After symptom descriptors had been developed from a comprehensive literature search, items were written and evaluated as to content representativeness. This resulted in the final 56 items, with 2 to 5 items for each of the 18 DSM-IV ADHD symptoms.

Parent and teacher input was obtained about both a traditional Likert-type scale and a frequency of behavior rating scale to determine the most useful rating format. Data obtained from 753 children and adolescents during the initial item tryout showed strong support for the items and for the rating scale's structure.

Normalized T scores were judged inappropriate because, as with many behavior rating scales, the raw score distributions for all scales were positively skewed. Therefore, linear T scores were developed for standard scores. This requires, of course, that interpretation be based on percentile ranks because there is no consistent correspondence of the T Scores with the percentiles.

TECHNICAL. The ADHD-SRS General norms are based on a national sample of 2,832 children and adolescents designed to approximate the 1998 U.S. Census on gender, race/ethnicity, geographic region, and special education classification. Norming occurred in two phases. Initially 1,089 parent and teacher ratings were obtained

from six school districts located in five states. The standardization program was completed with an additional 1,743 parent and teacher ratings from a variety of U.S. sites. Because the actual percentages of individuals on several variables deviated from the Census targets, the cases were statistically weighted to better approximate the gender and race/ethnicity distributions, a procedure that also brought geographic region into alignment. The percentage of students in the special education categories approximates national rates.

The manual provides strong evidence that scores are highly homogeneous measures of the constructs and are stable over the short term. Coefficient alpha reliability estimates for both subscales and Total Score are quite high, ranging from .92 to .99. The median values for the single ages ranged from .97 to .99. This level of reliability held for home and school raters, for males and females, and for ages 5–11 and 12–18. The test-retest reliability, based on 78 teacher ratings over a 2-week time interval, was uniformly high, ranging from .93 to .98.

Cross-informant correlations across teacher and parent ratings of the same child for 76 adolescents showed correlations between .14 and .35 for T scores. These are comparable to the typical correlations found in cross-informant research.

Several types of validity information are presented in the manual in addition to the content and social validity information collected during development. After exploring the scale structure using several factor analytic models, a principal components two-factor specified oblique rotation resulted in the fewest number of item double loadings. This model also was the most clinically interpretable because it was similar to the DSM-IV diagnostic categories. The Hyperactive-Impulsive factor, consisting of 35 items, accounted for 29.3% of the variance. A 29-item Inattentive factor accounted for 27.7% of the variance. Eight double-loaded items were assigned based on clinical judgment, which also was consistent with the higher factor loading. Item placement based on factor analysis agreed 100% with DSM-IV classification. As would be expected, a moderate correlation of .69 was found between the two factors.

Additional construct validity evidence was provided by examining raw score differences between groups of children known to differ on ADHD constructs. As anticipated, males obtained significantly higher raw scores than females and the average scores decreased with age. A clinical validity study also showed significant differences between the mean ADHD-SRS ratings given by both teachers and parents for children diagnosed with ADHD when compared with undiagnosed children.

Convergent construct validity was examined by correlating the ADHD-SRS with three established ADHD rating scales (Attention Deficit Disorders Evaluation Scale; the Conners' Teacher Rating Scale; and the ADHD Rating Scale-IV) using samples ranging from 63 to 129 children. Across the studies the correlations for like-construct subscales ranged from .90 to .96, providing strong support for the convergent construct validity. Correlations were .85 to .95 for the Total Scale. Lower correlations with non-ADHD scales on the Connors also provided some limited evidence for discriminant validity.

COMMENTARY. In addition to being a carefully developed scale with strong evidence supporting score reliability and validity, the ADHD-SRS has several strong points compared to many other scales used to assess ADHD symptomatology. Its coverage of ADHD symptoms is excellent. Many scales either rely solely on single items for each of the 18 DSM-IV descriptors or do not comprehensively cover each of the 18 descriptors. The ADHD-SRS approach should result in more complete ratings less influenced by construct underrepresentation. A second desirable aspect would appear to be the use of frequency-based ratings rather than traditional anchors such as "seldom" or "often." The latter are highly susceptible to bias based on the raters' internal norms. Another strength is the clear statement by the authors that ADHD cannot be diagnosed solely on results of a scale such as the ADHD-SRS, recognizing the need for a thorough, multisource evaluation. Some scales do not make explicit this appropriate caution.

A few areas of concern should be noted. One is the need to statistically adjust the norms to approximate the U.S. Census, especially on race/ethnicity. It is unfortunate, but not unusual, that a truly representative sample could not be obtained and no information was presented on possible subgroup differences that might impact on this. An associated caution relates to the availability of a Spanish version of the Rating Form. Translation

does not ensure that the scale is culturally fair. Some users may believe using this form will adjust for any cultural differences in the behaviors being rated. Although not a shortcoming of the scale itself, the use of linear T Scores may present interpretive problems for users who expect a direct relationship between T Scores and percentile ranks. Finally, the use of the highest 6% to denote "High Risk" seems somewhat liberal based on the typical 3–5% estimates of ADHD prevalence.

SUMMARY. The available information indicates that the ADHD-SRS is a well-designed and psychometrically sound measure that should be a valuable tool in assessing ADHD in children and adolescents. Its focus on measuring ADHD symptoms through multiple items, with an emphasis on frequency-based ratings, make it potentially one of the most suitable scales available for use in ADHD evaluations. The presence of separate Hyperactive-Impulsive and Inattentive subscales should provide useful information for differentiating subtypes of ADHD and developing treatment plans that target specific symptom patterns. As with all rating scales, as the authors caution, it would need to be used as part of a comprehensive evaluation that includes a thorough history and interviews, observations, and broadband scales to assess for other types of symptomatology that need to be looked at for comorbid (or alternative) disorders such as oppositional defiant disorder or depression. Overall the ADHD-SRS is likely to become one of the best tools available for ADHD assessments.

[10]

Adolescent Anger Rating Scale.

Purpose: Developed "to measure anger expression and specially differentiate among instrumental anger, reactive anger, and anger control."
Population: Ages 11–19.
Publication Date: 2001.
Acronym: AARS.
Scores, 4: Instrumental Anger, Reactive Anger, Anger Control, Total Anger.
Administration: Individual or group.
Price Data: Available from publisher for kit including professional manual (69 pages) and 50 test booklets.
Time: (5–10) minutes for individuals; (10–20) minutes per group.
Comments: Self-rating scale.
Author: DeAnna McKinnie Burney.
Publisher: Psychological Assessment Resources, Inc.

Review of the Adolescent Anger Rating Scale by CARLEN HENINGTON, *Associate Professor of Educational and School Psychology, Mississippi State University, Mississippi State, MS:*

DESCRIPTION. The Adolescent Anger Rating Scale (AARS) is a 41-item self-report measure intended to assess anger and control of anger response in adolescents, age 11 to 19 years. The instrument has a fourth-grade reading level. Items can be read to the respondent. A 4-point Likert-type scale (1 = *Hardly Ever* to 4 = *Very Often* assesses three anger-related behaviors. Twenty items measure Instrumental Anger (IA), a delayed, possibly covert, goal-related response (revenge and/or retaliation) that may include threatening and bullying. Eight items measure Reactive Anger (RA), an immediate response to events perceived as negative, threatening, or fear provoking. Thirteen items measure Anger Control (AC), a proactive cognitive-behavioral anger-management response (higher scores indicate greater control). Total Anger, a general index of anger expression, is determined using the three scale scores. The author indicates the AARS can also screen for social maladjustment and determine treatment effectiveness.

Adolescents are asked to provide typical demographic information and grade average, number of friends, friends' behavior, and living arrangements. The rationale for these questions is that these characteristics may be etiological factors of anger.

The AARS can be administered in individual or group format by professionals with formal psychometric training. Administration time is brief and varies only slightly by format. Scoring involves simple mathematical calculations and can be completed quickly. Raw scores are transformed into *T* scores and percentiles using one of four norms tables (i.e., younger boys, younger girls, older boys, older girls).

DEVELOPMENT. The professional manual furnished by the developer includes information on the conceptualization of the instrument: test development; psychometric properties; clinical and research application; administration, scoring, and interpretive guidelines; and conversion tables. The theoretical background for this instrument is cognitive-behavioral with responses to a provoking event described as a product of appraisal and attributions including cue detection and interpre-

tation, experiences and expectations, belief systems, and physiological arousal. Response to either type of anger (instrumental or reactive) differs in timing, intensity, and frequency (none specifically measured) and is mitigated by level of anger control.

Development of the AARS consisted of five stages: (a) rationale development and content validity check of 106 items by a panel of experts with revision, elimination, and addition of items; (b) initial pilot study examining internal consistency and factor structure; (c) evaluation of reliability and validity with revisions yielding the final 41 items; (d) validity and reliability evaluation of the instrument; and (e) normative data collection. Burney and Kromrey (2001) provide additional instrument development information.

TECHNICAL. Norms were obtained on adolescents from inner city, urban, and suburban settings. The sample consists of 4,187 adolescents divided into middle school (Grades 6 to 8, ages 11 to 14) and high school participants (Grades 9 to 12, ages 14 to 19) from across the U.S. Ethnic representations are identified separately for boys and girls as follows: Caucasian (61.3% and 59.1%), African-American (20.9% and 24.6%), Hispanic (8.2% and 8.0%), Asian (3.5% and 3.3%), Other/Multi-ethnic (4.9% and 4.1%), and undetermined (1.4% and .9%). No indication of socioeconomic status was provided.

Rationale provided in the manual for dividing the respondents into the two groups based on grade level is that expressions of anger are variable throughout adolescent development. The author states that young adolescents are likely to exhibit "higher rates of anger reactions, which tend to decrease as they matriculate through middle school" (professional manual, p. 16), whereas older individuals exhibit "increased anger as the adolescent enters high school; anger declines again at higher grade levels" (p. 16). However, this statement is supported only by results found in the initial instrument development (Burney & Kromrey, 2001) and are not necessarily supported by other empirical studies.

Adherence to the directions and inclusion of a discussion about the purpose for assessment (e.g., assist the adolescent in resolving their difficulties) is imperative. This discussion is important because, although the author states that unusually high AC or low anger scale scores may indicate a "fake good" response set, there is no validity or lie scale in the instrument, making reliance on honesty critical. Each of the four response choices is quantified (e.g., *Sometimes* "means that you behave this way one to three times a month"). This "concreteness" is most likely a strength of this measure.

Coefficient alpha was used to estimate internal consistency. Alphas ranged from .81 to .92 for the total standardization sample. RA obtained lower correlations across gender and grade, with younger girls having lowest alpha (.80). IA obtained the highest values across gender and grades, with older boys having highest (.94). Item-total correlations ranged from .42 to .69 for IA items, .37 to .64 for RA items, and .34 to .65 for AC items. Two-week test-retest using 175 respondents showed correlations from .71 to .79.

Content validity was assessed using an expert panel (e.g., school psychologists, school personnel, clinicians). Criterion validity analyses using conduct referrals (instrumental type and reactive type) yielded positive correlations, indicating relationships described by the authors as "strong" between matched score and referral type. Notably, the strongest matched anger score to referral type was found between RA score to IA type referral (.22). Negative correlations were found between both types of referral and AC scores. Factor analyses used as evidence of construct validity supported the three scales. Convergent comparisons were made between the AARS and the Conners-Wells' Adolescent Self-Report Scales-Long (CASS-L; Conners, 1997). Positive correlations were found between similar scale scores (AARS scores and Conduct Problems) ranging from .35 to .61 and negative correlations were found between divergent scales (AC and Anger Control Problems and Conduct Problems). Discriminant comparisons were made between the AARS and the Multidimensional Anger Inventory (MAI; Siegal, 1986). Rationale for this comparison was that the two instruments measure different aspects of anger. The correlations between the MAI and the IA and RA scales are described as moderately low (.46 and .44, respectively).

To bolster the validity evidence of the AARS, the author provides information on the relationship between the AARS and a number of variables. For example: (a) boys obtained higher anger scores than girls, (b) little difference was found in

anger scales across ethnicity (multi-ethnic individuals scored higher than the other groups and Asian individuals scored higher on AC than the other groups), (c) differences in scale scores were dependent upon emotional functioning (how functioning was measured was not described), (d) differences in AC scores were dependent upon grade average, (e) individuals with the highest suspension rates obtained the highest anger scores and lowest AC scores, (f) having no friends is related to higher anger scores and lower AC scores, and (g) friends' negative behavior was related to higher anger scores and lower AC scores.

COMMENTARY. The AARS is a useful tool to identify individuals with anger-related difficulties and is likely to assist in intervention design. Careful consideration was given to the development of this instrument and the author is to be commended. However, the author does overstate some of the validity data.

Of concern is the issue of the etiology of anger and its relationship to a number of demographic variables. Researchers have found that anger and behavior problems such as conduct disorder, oppositional defiance, and attention deficit disorder are related to, rather than caused by, these characteristics. It cannot be stated strongly enough that the relationship between variables such as family composition and functioning, school performance, and peer rejection has not been established as a cause of anger and aggression. The author indicates that the instrument can be used to assess treatment effectiveness; however, this remains to be determined. It is unknown whether this instrument has sufficient sensitivity to evaluate change over time, especially cognitive and behavioral change. Finally, as a self-report measure with no validity or "lie" scale, it is unknown if responses will be altered to achieve social acceptance of those who have access to the information provided by the adolescent. It is believed that the value of this instrument is likely to outweigh the concerns established in this review.

SUMMARY. The AARS provides relatively reliable and valid scores; it is easy to administer, score, and interpret. It can be used with adolescents in Grades 6 through 12 with adequate norms established. It yields three scale scores, Instrumental Anger, Reactive Anger, and Anger Control, and a Total Anger score. A strength is that it can be used to distinguish between skill deficits (e.g., impulse or self-control, problem solving, social skills) or skill dysfunction (e.g., attributional bias). As such, its usefulness is likely as a tool for treatment planning rather than as an identification or treatment effectiveness measure.

REVIEWER'S REFERENCES

Burney, D. M., & Kromrey, J. (2001). Initial development and score validation of the adolescent anger ranting scale. *Educational and Psychological Measurement, 61*, 446–460.
Conners, K. C. (1997). Conners' Rating Scales—Revised. North Tonawanda, NY: Multi-Health Systems.
Siegal, J. M. (1986). Multidimensional Anger Inventory. *Journal of Personality and Social Psychology, 51*, 191–200.

Review of the Adolescent Anger Rating Scale by HUGH STEPHENSON, *Assistant Professor of Psychology, Ithaca College, Ithaca, NY:*

DESCRIPTION. The Adolescent Anger Rating Scale (AARS) is a 41-item self-rating paper-and-pencil test. The test is suitable for use by those with graduate level training in psychology or social work. The response format is Likert-type and the administration takes 5–10 minutes for individuals or 10–20 minutes for groups. Respondents are asked how often they engage in specific anger- and control-related behaviors on a 4-point scale ranging from *hardly ever* to *very often*. The scale is designed for use with populations aged 11–19.

Scoring is facilitated by the scoring key attached to the underside of the response pages that can be torn off after administration for easy computation of raw scores. *T*-score and percentile conversion tables are provided in the manual along with interpretive guidelines.

The scale total (Total Anger) is computed from the addition of the two subscale scores, Instrumental Anger (IA) and Reactive Anger (RA), and the subtraction of the subscale Anger Control (AC). The information derived from the test may be used to determine the overall level of anger and anger mitigating behavior as well as to differentiate between anger types for the purposes of treatment planning. However, no suggestions are offered or principles for different treatments outlined.

DEVELOPMENT. The 61-page test booklet provides a comprehensive overview of the development process. The Constructs employed in this test include: Instrumental Anger (IA), measuring anger that results in a desired and planned goal of revenge or retaliation; Reactive Anger (RA), anger that is immediately expressed when an event is perceived as negative, threatening, or fearful; and Anger Control (AC), the propensity

to proactively resolve the instrumental or reactive responses to anger.

The subscale descriptions state that each subscale measures the rate and intensity of each behavioral construct. However, because only one score is available for each subscale, rate and intensity are collapsed into a single metric. The authors state that the AARS is the first test to include all three constructs in a single instrument.

The Instrumental Anger subscale contains many items that speak directly to the intent to harm others. The Anger Control subscale may also be construed as an ego strength scale or self-control scale. The Reactive Anger subscale contains items that appear closely related to impulse control (e.g., "When I am angry I talk too much").

The scales RA and IA were rationally developed. An initial pool of 106 items was generated by an expert panel and subsequently reduced to 51 items based on consensus in assignment to the IA and RA scales. A subsequent factor analysis suggested a third scale, which appears to be the negatively keyed items and is here operationalized as the Anger Control (AC) scale. The factor analysis also pointed to the removal of 10 items that did not load on any of three factors to form the final 41-item scale. The three subscales are IA (20 items), RA (8 items), and AC (13 items).

TECHNICAL. Internal consistency reliability was estimated by Cronbach's alphas ranging from .81 to .92 for the subscales and scale total in different male and female samples for two different grade bands. Test-retest reliability was examined using 175 pairs of AARS scores over a 2-week interval. Test-retest correlations ranged from .71 for the IA and RA subscales to .79 for Total Anger.

The AARS is certainly face valid; this may pose a serious limitation for its use in the identification of high levels of anger in some instances. The purpose of the test is immediately obvious to the taker and self-presentation is one of many factors that may result in underreporting or overreporting of anger levels. Many of the items in the IA subscale specifically address the intent to harm others. Future revisions of the test that include an item analysis for social desirability will improve the scale.

In terms of construct validity the authors provide convergent validity information between the AARS and the Conners-Wells subscales

psychological practitioners, who indicated which APS scales would be most useful to include in a short form. The 10 highest ranking scales were chosen for the short form, along with two new scales that assess Anger/Violence Proneness and Academic Problems.

TECHNICAL. A total development sample (n = 3,340), consisting of school (n = 2,834) and clinical (n = 506) samples, provided the basis from which standardization (n = 1,827), school (n = 2,834), combined standardization and clinical (n = 2,333), clinical (n = 384), test-retest reliability (n = 64), school validity (n = 486), several clinic-based validity ($n ≤ 191$), and clinical discriminant validity (n = 162) samples were derived. Each of the individual samples formed for various purposes is described in the test manual using demographic characteristics of age, grade, ethnicity, socioeconomic status, and residence location. Although comparison figures from the U.S. Census Bureau are not presented, the test author states that data from the 1990 U.S. Census Bureau report were used to select a standardization sample that mirrored the population proportions of gender and ethnicity. Norms are presented for the total standardization sample and separately for males and females, and for younger (ages 12 to 14) and older (ages 15 to 19) adolescents. Comparisons of scale means across gender and age produced occasional differences, many of which appear consistent with what is known about differential symptom pictures for these groups. However, "[s]ignificant ethnic differences in scale means were found on a majority of scales" (professional manual, p. 21), prompting a determination of effect sizes for these groups. Effect sizes were found to be relatively small from a statistical standpoint. Examination of the differences reveals that some highly significant (i.e., $p <$ .001) mean score differences among the groups occurred when numerical mean scores differed by as little as 3 or 4 points.

Internal consistency reliability evidence is presented for the total standardization sample, and separately for males and females, as well as for younger and older adolescent subgroups. A parallel presentation of internal consistency reliability evidence is presented for the clinical sample. On balance, the alpha coefficients generally range in the .80s for all groups on the clinical scales. As expected, the validity scales were markedly less internally consistent, typically demonstrating co-efficients in the .40s. Item-with-total scale correlations and interitem correlation coefficients also are included in the tabulated presentation. In addition, respective standard errors of measurement are provided for all groups and subgroups. *SEM*s were in the 3.00 to 4.50 range on the clinical scales for the total standardization sample.

Test-retest reliability was assessed using a sample of 64 adolescents recruited from a single high school who completed the APS-SF on two occasions, separated by a 2-week interval. Reliability coefficients were generally .80 or higher. As a clinical measure that involves psychological trait and state constructs, the APS-SF should not be expected to demonstrate exceptionally high temporal stability. Thus, the reliability coefficients obtained are quite good.

The test author notes that interpretation of APS-SF profiles must be completed by qualified professionals, although administration and scoring may be accomplished by technicians and other personnel with proper training. At the outset of interpretation, customary precautions should be applied to the APS-SF protocol to ensure that responses are complete and appear to be accurate (e.g., the examiner should attempt to discern whether there are unusual or unlikely patterns of responses).

Following the evaluation of the validity scales, scores on the clinical scales are compared to normative data, with scores below 60 interpreted as within normal limits. Scores from 60 to 64 fall in the "subclinical symptom range," those from 65 to 69 are in the "mild clinical symptom range," those from 70 to 79 are in the "moderate clinical symptom range," and scores above 80 indicate "severe clinical" symptoms. To aid the interpretive process, the test manual provides considerably more detail on each clinical scale and anchors many of the key diagnostic features to extant research and to specific APS-SF items. Two case illustrations provide a clear model of the interpretive process, using cases that demonstrate familiar adolescent difficulties. The 26 items designated as Critical Items may provide meaningful data for individual respondents when interpreted qualitatively and in the context of a particular respondent. The test author offers appropriate caveats in the manual concerning these items, including the need to consider individual item content and to use information from Critical Items to guide clinical inquiry and, possibly, additional data gathering.

Validation evidence for the APS-SF is provided in the test manual with attention to content, criterion-related, and construct validity. The test author asserts content validity using item-with-total scale correlation coefficients, with the argument that a large portion of content validity for a clinical measure such as the APS-SF relates to the adequacy of symptom sampling. The extent to which items co-vary with their respective scale provides important evidence of the scales' content validity. The author acknowledges, however, that this approach does not address the extent to which the domain itself has been sampled adequately.

As expected, comparison of APS-SF scales with their corresponding APS scales yielded very high correlation coefficients (11 of 12 clinical scales correlated at the .90 level or higher). Criterion-related validation efforts also involved the use of subsamples of the clinical sample who took the Minnesota Multiphasic Personality Inventory (MMPI), Reynolds Adolescent Depression Scale (RADS), Beck Depression Inventory (BDI), or the Suicidal Ideation Questionnaire (SIQ), in addition to the APS-SF. An examination of the comparisons, all of which are presented in the test manual, reveals that related MMPI scale scores, as well as RADS, BDI, and SIQ total scores, demonstrate moderately high coefficients of correlation.

Similar findings emerged using the school sample, where a subsample (n = 486) provided data on the APS-SF, the RADS, Hamilton Depression Rating Scale (HDRS), Revised Children's Manifest Anxiety Scale (RCMAS), SIQ, Suicidal Behaviors Inventory (SBI), and the Rosenberg Self-Esteem Scale (RSES). A pattern of correlation coefficients emerged that support criterion-related validation. For example, the highest correlation coefficient for the RSES (-.63) occurred in its association with the APS-SF Self-Concept scale, and the SBI and SIQ demonstrated their highest values (.64 for each) when compared to the APS-SF Suicide scale.

Construct validity was assessed using (a) intercorrelations among APS-SF scales, (b) evidence of discriminant validity, (c) evidence of contrasted groups validity, and (d) factor analyses. Moderate to high coefficients were expected and demonstrated in both the standardization and clinical samples between pairs of phenomenologically similar disorders and between pairs of disorders where substantial comorbidity occurs. A few

scales—notably, Interpersonal Problems (IPP), Academic Problems (ADP), and Posttraumatic Stress (PTS)—demonstrated sizable correlation coefficients with the majority of other scales. For the most part, however, the APS-SF appears to assess distinct areas of psychopathology, more so than nonspecific general psychological distress; some scales do this better than others.

Discriminant validity measures employed included measures of general cognitive ability and a short form of the Marlowe-Crowne Social Desirability Scale. In addition, academic achievement was evaluated using grade point average as the metric, with the expectation that this measure would demonstrate convergence rather than divergence. Findings supported discriminant validity, as near-zero coefficients were observed for the measures of cognitive ability, and low negative correlations characterized the relationship between the clinical scales and the measure of social desirability. Grade point averages and APS-SF scales demonstrated moderately low negative coefficients, with the (expected) exception of ADP, where the coefficient was in the moderate range (.53).

Selected APS-SF clinical scales discriminated significantly (p < .0001) a subsample of individuals in the clinical sample with specific diagnoses that have base rates sufficiently high to justify the analyses—Conduct Disorder, Major Depression, and Substance Abuse Disorder. Further, all clinical scales discriminated the clinical group from the standardization group at p < .0001, a finding that supports the contrasted groups validity of the APS-SF.

Factor analytic procedures yielded a two-factor solution consistent with the conceptual understanding of adolescent psychopathology grouped as internalizing and externalizing disorders. The test manual also presents factor analytic results for each of the 12 clinical scales, together with a discussion of these findings and, in many cases, relates the findings to DSM IV diagnostic features.

COMMENTARY. The APS-SF demonstrates many strengths as a measure of adolescent psychopathology. As a short form of the parent version, the APS-SF is responsive particularly to the needs of school-based professionals. Evaluations in school settings often include domains that are central to the educational process that may not be assessed in clinical settings (e.g., academic achievement) and may consume considerable time.

adolescence is extremely important (Pfeiffer & Reddy, 1998). The APS-SF is commended for attempting to serve as a *"pre-referral evaluation (measure) of students"* (Professional manual, p. 1) [italics added].

The technical manual is clearly written and well organized. The flexible response format that conforms to DSM-IV symptom criteria is unique and a noteworthy strength. The use of the DSM-IV makes the APS-SF, similar to the Devereux Scales of Mental Disorders (Naglieri, LeBuffe, & Pfeiffer, 1994)—an adolescent rating scale that is aligned with the most widely used diagnostic model of developmental psychopathology. Another noteworthy feature of the APS-SF is the 26 items designated as Critical Items. Practitioners will appreciate this feature, which is based on item content and/or the ability of the item to differentiate clinical from nonclinical adolescents.

One would be remiss not to identify weaknesses with the APS-SF. One, the manual states that the purpose of the instrument is to serve as, "an excellent measure in the *pre-referral evaluation* of students who, based on the results of this evaluation, may be considered for more comprehensive evaluation with the APS" (p. 1) [italics added]. Prereferral suggests screening prior to parental notification and consent. However, it would be unethical for a clinical instrument such as the APS-SF to be used with minors, without first obtaining the informed consent of the parent.

Two, and related to the first concern, many of the items are highly personal and emotionally charged. It is unlikely that a nonreferred, adolescent school population would be inclined to willingly complete the APS-SF without some assurance about the anonymity and confidentiality of their responses. It is the rare adolescent who would disclose to an unfamiliar individual information about their drug use, violent behavior, or eating problems. Most schools would be disinclined to permit its use as a screening instrument because of the likely adverse reaction from the student body (and parents).

A third concern is the proportion of the standardization sample that falls within the mild clinical symptom range on the clinical scales. Assuming a normal distribution, the percentage of adolescents in the standardization sample with T scores between 65 and 69 on the 12 clinical scales appears to range from 2% to 6%, together totaling 52%. Even with a high degree of comorbidity within the standardization sample, it is problematic that the calibration of cutoff scores creates such a large proportion of the standardization group with a significant level of clinical pathology. Six percent of the standardization sample falls within the mild clinical symptom range on CND, DEP, SCP, and IPP, and 4% on OPD, AVP, ADD, PTS, and EAT.

A fourth concern is the questionable representativeness of the standardization. The manual notes that the sample was selected to correspond to the 1990 U.S. Census. However, the sample departs significantly from the present representativeness of the population in the United States. For example, the APS-SF Hispanic sample is 6.4%, which is almost one-half the present proportion in the United States (U.S. Census Bureau, 2000). The APS-SF standardization consists of 10.9% living in urban settings, which is approximately one-third of the present proportion of citizens residing in urban environments (Council on Environmental Quality, 1999). Almost 62% of the APS-SF standardization sample live with both parents, which is almost double the national figure (U.S. Census Bureau, 2000). Finally, the necessity of computer scoring is a limitation, particularly if the APS-SF is used as a screening device in the schools.

SUMMARY. The author, to his credit, has taken on the important task of developing a self-report screening test to measure psychopathology among adolescents. The APS-SF is linked to the DSM-IV and covers the most frequent psychological problems likely to be found in an adolescent population. On balance, however, the APS-SF falls short of its goal of serving as a prereferral screening instrument that complements its parent test, the APS. APS-SF items are too provocative and clinical to be used in the schools as a prereferral measure. Readers seeking an alternate self-report screening instrument may wish to consider the Behavior Assessment System for Children (T6:280; Reynolds & Kamphaus, 1992).

REVIEWER'S REFERENCES

Council on Environmental Quality. (1999). *U. S. population in urban, suburban, and rural areas, 1950–1996.* Retrieved July 31, 2001, from http://web.lexisnexis.com/statuniv/

Naglieri, J. A., LeBuffe, P. A., & Pfeiffer, S. I. (1994). *Devereux Scales of Mental Disorders: Manual.* San Antonio: The Psychological Corporation.

Pfeiffer, S. I., & Reddy, L. A. (1998). School-based mental health programs in the United States: Present status and a blueprint for the future. *School Psychology Review, 27,* 84–96.

Reynolds, C. R., & Kamphaus, R. W. (1992). *Behavioral Assessment System for Children (BASC) manual.* Circle Pines, MN: American Guidance Service.

Reynolds, W. M. (1998*). Adolescent psychopathology scale: Administration and interpretation manual*. Odessa, FL: Psychological Assessment Resources.

United States Census Bureau. (2000). Census 2000: Profile of general demographic characteristics. Retrieved July 31, 2001, from http://www.census.gov

[12]

Adolescent Symptom Inventory-4.

Purpose: Designed as a "screening instrument for the behavioral, affective, and cognitive symptoms of a variety of adolescent psychiatric disorders."

Population: Ages 12–18.

Publication Dates: 1997–1998.

Acronym: ASI-4.

Scores, 15: 11 scores shared on both Parent and Teacher Forms: AD/HD Inattentive, Hyperactive-Impulsive, Combined, Conduct Disorder, Oppositional Defiant, Generalized Anxiety Disorder, Schizoid Personality, Schizophrenia, Major Depressive Disorder, Dysthymic Disorder, Bipolar Disorder; 4 additional scores on the Parent Form: Antisocial Personality Disorder, Separation Anxiety, Anorexia Nervosa, Bulimia Nervosa.

Administration: Individual.

Forms, 2: Teacher Checklist, Parent Checklist.

Price Data, 2001: $102 per deluxe kit including 25 parent checklists, 25 teacher checklists, 50 symptom count score sheets, 50 parent and teacher symptom severity profile score sheets, screening manual (1997, 145 pages), and norms manual (1998, 168 pages); $52 per 50 parent checklists; $38 per 50 teacher checklists.

Time: [10–15] minutes.

Comments: Checklists completed by teachers and caregivers about adolescents; scores are not intended for diagnostic purposes, only screening purposes.

Authors: Kenneth D. Gadow and Joyce Sprafkin.

Publisher: Checkmate Plus, Ltd.

Review of the Adolescent Symptom Inventory—4 by STEPHEN N. AXFORD, Psychologist/Assistant Director of Special Education, Pueblo School District No. Sixty, Pueblo, CO:

DESCRIPTION AND DEVELOPMENT. The Adolescent Symptom Inventory—4 (ASI-4) is a screening instrument for adolescent (ages 12 to 18 years) emotional and behavioral disorders. ASI-4 items are aligned to *Diagnostic and Statistical Manual of Mental Disorders* (*DSM-IV*) criteria and related educational disabilities as specified in the Individuals with Disabilities Education Act (IDEA). As such, the ASI-4 potentially has utility for both mental health clinicians (i.e., psychiatrists, clinical psychologists, and clinical social workers) and school personnel such as school psychologists, school social workers, and school counselors. The authors caution that clinical diagnosis can be made only by "qualified clinicians," but that school personnel should find the ASI-4 helpful in determining need for referral for further clinical assessment. The ASI-4 may also have utility in screening (e.g., prereferral) for emotionally or behaviorally based educational disabilities (for an individualized Education Plan, for example) as related to IDEA, Section 504 of the Rehabilitation Act, and the Americans with Disabilities Act (ADA). The ASI-4 consists of two "checklists" utilizing a combination of Likert-type scales (i.e., "never, sometimes, often, very often"; "poor, below average, average, above average, superior") and dichotomous rated (i.e., yes/no) items. The ASI screening manual notes there is both a "parent" and "teacher" version of the checklist. The actual scoring protocol for the teacher checklist is clearly indicated. The "parent version" of the ASI-4 checklist is actually intended to be used by practically any sufficiently familiar rater. The parent version consists of 120 rated items. The teacher checklist consists of 106 rated items. According to the authors, the teacher checklist differs from the parent version in three ways: (a) it focuses on educational setting and academic performance; (b) it excludes certain items about which the teacher is unlikely to have sufficient knowledge (e.g., sleep patterns), and (c) it "does not include specific disorders that are characterized by behaviors that are problematic primarily in the home setting (e.g., separation anxiety)" (p. 12).

Despite being aligned with *DSM-IV* diagnostic criteria, the ASI-4 is written in nontechnical, easy-to-understand language. As stated by the authors, "items were rephrased replacing psychiatric jargon with more easily understood (user friendly) terminology" (screening manual, p. 12).

Two types of scoring sheets are provided for the ASI-4: the Symptom Count score sheet, a criterion-referenced approach using cutoff scores corresponding to 28 *DSM-IV* disorders; and the Symptom Severity Profile, a norm-referenced approach providing separate scores for males and females. With the criterion-referenced approach, "Rule Outs" are provided when item summations equal or exceed criterion scores. Essentially, this involves alternative diagnoses to rule out. Of course, this potentially provides a useful tool for differential diagnosis, a critical aspect for a screening instrument. In addition, the Symptom Count score sheet provides columns for recording parent,

ASI-4 note that when confronted with discrepant parent-completed and teacher ASI-4 data, decisions will have to be made as to the more credible source. In addition, as the authors note (Quick Guide to Using the Symptom Inventories, p. 2), there is the added factor of behaviors differing in different settings.

COMMENTARY. The authors clearly emphasize that multiple sources of information are required for making a clinical diagnosis. The ASI-4 thus serves as a method for expeditiously gathering information to be used in combination with other information to guide further assessment or referral. To further assure appropriate use of the ASI-4, the authors devote several chapters and appendixes in the screening manual and norms manual to issues related to data interpretation and clinical application. Numerous examples are provided.

In regard to the parent checklist, the authors made reasonable attempts to ensure a representative norm sample in terms of a number of critical demographic variables. Nevertheless, future efforts to norm the ASI should focus on ensuring representation from different regions of the country, as this instrument surely is being marketed and used outside the Long Island, New York area. In addition, a larger norm sample would ensure more adequate representation of minority groups. Although the authors ensured appropriate proportionate minority representation relative to census data, the total sample is small such that few minorities were actually represented in the study.

SUMMARY. The ASI-4 offers an efficient method for screening adolescents in making decisions about further clinical assessment or referral. The authors are careful in clarifying that ASI-4 Screening Cutoff scores/norms should not be used in verifying the presence or absence of specific disorders. In addition, the authors provide useful guidelines and examples for appropriate screening using the ASI-4, as an initial step in differential diagnosis. Although the ASI-4 would benefit from additional validation and development of norms using larger and demographically more representative samples, it is sufficiently developed to be strictly used as a screening instrument. In addition, the ASI-4 manuals, survey forms, and scoring sheets are user friendly and professional in quality. Clinicians and special educators (e.g., school psychologists) should find the ASI-4 to be useful as a screening instrument.

REVIEWER'S REFERENCES

Achenbach, T. M. (1991). *Manual for the Teacher's Report Form and 1991 Profile.* Burlington, VT: University of Vermont, Department of Psychiatry.
Gadow, K. D., & Sprafkin, J. (1997). *Quick guide to using the Youth's Inventory—4 screening kit.* Stony Brook, NY: Checkmate Plus.

Review of the Adolescent Symptom Inventory— 4 by PATTI L. HARRISON, Professor of School Psychology, The University of Alabama, Tuscaloosa, AL:

DESCRIPTION. The Adolescent Symptom Inventory-4 (ASI-4), a behavior rating scale completed by parents and teachers of adolescents aged 12 to 18 years, was designed to provide a brief screening of a number of disorders in the fourth edition of the *Diagnostic and Statistical Manual of Mental Disorders* (*DSM-IV*; American Psychiatric Association, 1994). The authors of the ASI-4 also publish the Child Symptom Inventory-4 (CSI-4; 47) for younger children. The current versions of the adolescent and child instruments are revisions of similar instruments (CSI-3, CSI-3R, ASI-3R) that corresponded to earlier editions of the *DSM*. The parent checklist of the ASI-4 contains 120 items, and the teacher checklist contains 79 items and excludes items about which teachers have little knowledge or that measure disorders problematic in a home setting. Each item represents a specific symptom found in the criteria for a number of mental disorders in *DSM-IV*. Parents and teachers are instructed to rate each item according to the adolescent's overall behavior and may choose one of four possible ratings: *never, sometimes, often,* and *very often.*

The ASI-4 has two scoring systems. The Screening Cutoff score method, or Symptom Count, includes 29 disorders on the parent checklist and 22 disorders on the teacher checklist. Some disorders are characterized by only one or two symptoms and, thus, have only one or two items on the ASI-4. Most items are assigned quantitative values of 0 (for ratings of *never* or *sometimes*) or 1 (for ratings of *often* or *very often*) to indicate the absence or presence of a *DSM-IV* symptom.

Using the Symptom Count score sheet for the Screening Cutoff method, the professional calculates the total item score, or number of symptoms present, for each disorder. A criterion score is based on the number of symptoms required for a *DSM-IV* diagnosis and, thus, indicates an ASI-4 screening cutoff. If an adolescent meets the screening cutoff for a disorder, additional comprehensive evaluation is recommended. For example, the criterion score for the disorder of AD/HD Inattentive is 6; if an adolescent is rated as having six or more symptoms for this disorder, or a total score of 6 or higher on the nine items, then he or she is recommended for additional evaluation. The score sheet for the Screening Cutoff method also identifies "rule outs" for each disorder, or other disorders that must be considered when conducting a comprehensive clinical evaluation to determine if alternative disorders can account for the adolescent's problems.

The Symptom Severity scores of the ASI-4 are available for fewer disorders than the Screening Cutoff score method. The 12 disorders for the parent checklist and 11 disorders for the teacher checklist each have 3–15 items. The Symptom Severity scores are based on different numerical values for item ratings than the Screening Cutoff method: *never* = 0, *sometimes* = 1, *often* = 2, and *very often* = 3. The professional user sums scores for each disorder and, using a symptom severity profile, converts the sums of item scores to norm-referenced *T* scores (M = 50, SD = 10). *T* scores of 70 or higher are classified as high severity, 60–69 as moderate severity, and 59 or below as low severity. As is true for most problem behavior rating scales, the score distribution is skewed because very few children obtained high scores. Because normative data suggested significant differences by gender, separate norms are available for males and females, but not by age group. The authors note that scores in the moderate and high severity range may indicate the need for additional, more thorough evaluation. Also, the authors caution that the Screening Cutoff and Symptom Severity scoring methods do not have perfect agreement, given the different methods of obtaining scores and the skewed distribution for normative scores. For example, it is possible an adolescent may not meet the screening cutoff for a disorder, but may have a *T* score in the high severity range.

DEVELOPMENT. The ASI-4 screening manual, published in 1997, contains a detailed description of item development and focuses on the Screening Cutoff score method. Specific symptoms listed in the *DSM-IV* formed the basis of items but symptoms were rewritten to be more understandable by parents and teachers, to reflect observable behaviors, and to delete examples or

other details judged to be superfluous or unnecessary by the authors. The manual provides tables that list the *DSM-IV* symptoms and corresponding ASI-4 items. The detailed information about revision of the symptoms into items for the ASI-4 is informative. However, a few ASI-4 items seem different from and may not measure exactly the same constructs or behaviors described in the *DSM-IV* criteria. For example, a *DSM-IV* criterion describes difficulty in sustaining attention, but the ASI-4 item states only, "has difficulty paying attention to tasks" (screening manual, p. 23). The authors provide no information about evaluation of items by other professionals during the item development process; such a review would provide assurance to ASI-4 users that the items have been judged to provide the best possible measures of the *DSM-IV* criteria.

A separate manual, the norms manual, was published in 1998 and focuses on the Symptom Severity scoring method. The authors state that the Screening Cutoff score method provides the easiest method of interpretation and that they had been content with the Screening Cutoff method. However, they recognized that a norm-referenced system would allow a comparison with other adolescents and provide important interpretive information for users.

TECHNICAL. The ASI-4 manuals provide quite comprehensive reliability and validity data, although the data suggest only limited support for the technical adequacy of the instrument. Test-retest reliability data, with ratings 6 weeks apart, are reported only for the CSI-4 parent checklist, not the ASI-4, and were obtained from a study of children with AD/HD. Test-retest correlations for the symptom counts of the Screening Cutoff score method range from .02 to .72 and for the Symptom Severity scores range from .37 to .82. For the teacher checklist, test-retest reliability data are reported only for the AD/HD and Oppositional Defiant Disorder categories with a sample of children rated during baseline and treatment for a stimulant medication evaluation. Test-retest coefficients (with ratings 1–2 week apart) range from .62 to .90, with one exception of a coefficient of .38.

The parent and teacher checklists were used in a predictive validity study of 144 referrals to an outpatient service. The ASI-4 Screening Cutoff scores were compared to actual diagnoses of disorders made by child psychiatrists after comprehensive evaluation. The manual reports both sensitivity rates, or percentages of adolescents correctly identified by the ASI-4 as having the disorder, and specificity rates, or percentages of adolescents correctly identified by the ASI-4 as not having the disorder. For some disorders such as AD/HD, Conduct Disorders, and Oppositional Defiant Disorders, the sensitivity and specificity rates were quite high and the ASI-4 correctly identified 60% to 80% of the sample. Sensitivity and specificity rates for other disorders were often lower. Rates for the parent checklist were generally higher than those for the teacher checklist. The authors also present data to demonstrate that sensitivity and specificity increased for some disorders when both parent and teacher checklists were used and an adolescent met the screening cutoff on either checklist.

Although the data suggest that the ASI-4 may be accurate in screening for some disorders, the predictive validity study had some methodological problems and the data should be interpreted with caution. There is the possibility of criterion contamination because the child psychiatrists used the ASI-4 scores, along with other evaluations, to determine the actual diagnoses for children; thus, the criterion—the actual diagnosis—was not independent of the screening measure. Another problem is that some disorders (e.g., Separation Anxiety Disorder, Posttraumatic Stress Disorder) were not diagnosed at all in the sample or had very few study participants with the diagnosis; thus, the validity of the ASI-4 in identifying children with these disorders could not be investigated.

The predictive validity sample of 144 referred children also was used to investigate the concurrent validity between the Symptom Severity scores of the ASI-4 parent and teacher checklists and the Child Behavior Checklist for parents and its corresponding Teacher Report Form. Generally, the pattern of correlations suggested that ASI-4 disorders had their highest correlations with comparable scales on the Child Behavior Checklist and Teacher Report Form. The validity study sample also was used to investigate the agreement between scores on the parent and teacher checklist. The correlations are generally low. The predictive validity study sample and the normative samples were used to calculate intercorrelations between Symptom Severity Scores for categories. The correlations suggest moderate to strong relationships between some categories; the authors

interpret this finding to confirm the similarity in symptoms for some disorders.

The norm samples on which the norm-referenced T-scores of the ASI-4 Symptom Severity scoring method are based are very restricted and not representative of the U.S. population. The parent checklist was normed with 824 adolescents in two Long Island, New York school districts, and over 90% of the sample was in a school district described as suburban, middle class. As a result, the sample was 92% Caucasian with a socioeconomic status representation of 5% in the lower group, 44% in the middle group, and 51% in the higher group. The teacher checklist was normed with 1072 adolescents in one school district each in Missouri, Wisconsin, and New York, and the sample was over 90% Caucasian. Each teacher evaluated up to 15 students per class, a data collection method that can impact the independence of a teacher's independent ratings across students.

COMMENTARY. The ASI-4 has a number of positive features. The manuals include comprehensive information and details, especially to establish a foundation for assessing mental disorders in adolescents and to link the ASI-4 to the *DSM-IV*. Administration is relatively straightforward, although scoring and transferring item data to the score summaries could be time-consuming and tedious. Both manuals provide detailed presentations of technical data and comprehensive guidelines for interpretation. The manuals include useful appendixes with frequency data indicating the percentage of children in the clinical and normative samples that received each possible rating on each item. Most importantly, the authors provide clear and repeated instructions to use the ASI-4 only for the purpose it is intended, screening of adolescents for additional needed evaluation, and emphasize that the ASI-4 should not be used for comprehensive diagnoses of mental disorders.

Unfortunately, the technical properties of the ASI-4 are problematic. The parent reliability data are based on the CSI-4, and the teacher reliability data are limited to a couple of disorders with a sample of children in an AD/HD medication study. The predictive validity study is flawed by criterion contamination and the small sample does not allow evaluation of the ASI-4's use with all disorders. For the Symptom Severity scoring method, norms samples are not representative of the population of children with whom the ASI-4 may be used.

The authors do not provide a strong rationale for including the Symptom Severity scoring system with the ASI-4, in addition to the Screening Cutoff system. The potential for inconsistent results across the two systems is of concern, and different results could be confusing for users. The manual for the Symptom Severity scoring system contains much information that is repetitive with the screening manual. Throughout the manual, the authors present the Symptom Severity scoring almost as an afterthought in their development of the instrument, do not appear supportive of its use, and appear to emphasize the Screening Cutoff system.

SUMMARY. In spite of the positive characteristics of the ASI-4, the limitations in its psychometric properties greatly decrease the value of its use. The norms for the Symptom Severity scoring method are based on unrepresentative samples and, thus, would not be appropriate for most children. The reliability data provide almost no information to support the instrument. The validity data, although reported in detail by the authors, have potential flaws and do not address all disorders. Perhaps the limited validity data led the authors to recommend the use of the ASI-4 to only a few disorders, as stated in the screening manual: "Research suggests that the ASI-4 serves as an effective screening instrument for the following disorders: AD/HD, oppositional defiant disorder, conduct disorder, obsessive-compulsive disorder, and tic disorders" (p. 122). The ASI-4 seems to have promise, and it is hoped that the collection of additional reliability, validity, and normative data will be undertaken to provide more support for its technical properties. Until then, instruments such as the Child Behavior Checklist (Achenbach, 1991a), Teacher Report Form (Achenbach, 1991b), and Behavior Assessment System for Children (Reynolds & Kamphaus, 1992), which have a wealth of research and technical data to support their use, will provide useful alternatives for professionals.

REVIEWER'S REFERENCES

Achenbach, T. M. (1991a). *Manual for the Child Behavior Checklist/4-18 and 1991 Profile*. Burlington, VT: Child Behavior Checklist.
Achenbach, T. M. (1991b). *Manual for the Teacher's Report Form and 1991 Profile*. Burlington, VT: Child Behavior Checklist.
American Psychiatric Association. (1994). *Diagnostic and statistical manual of mental disorders* (4th ed.). Washington, DC: Author.
Reynolds, C. R., & Kamphaus, R. W. (1992). Behavior Assessment System for Children. Circle Pines, MN: American Guidance Service.

[13]
Aggression Questionnaire.

Purpose: Designed to aid in evaluating an individual's aggressive responses and ability to channel those responses in a safe and constructive manner.

Population: Ages 9–88.

Publication Date: 2000.

Scores, 7: Physical Aggression, Verbal Aggression, Anger, Hostility, Indirect Aggression, Inconsistent Responding, Total Score.

Administration: Individual or group.

Price Data, 2002: $92.50 per complete kit; $32.50 per 25 AutoScore™ answer forms; $164 per computer disk; $15 per 100 answer sheets; $48 per manual (2000, 95 pages).

Time: (10) minutes.

Comments: Updated version of the Buss-Durkee Hostility Inventory; computer scoring is available from publisher.

Authors: Arnold H. Buss and W. L. Warren.

Publisher: Western Psychological Services.

Review of the Aggression Questionnaire by JOHNNIE A. BROWN, Administrator, Clinician and Adjunct Professor, University of Maryland University College, Adelphi, MD:

DESCRIPTION. The Aggression Questionnaire (AQ) is an instrument for assessing anger and aggression. The AQ is an updated version of the Buss-Durkee Hostility Inventory (BDHI) (Buss & Durkee, 1957).

This version of the AQ is a 34-item instrument. Each AQ item describes a characteristic related to aggression. The respondent rates the description on an intensity scale ranging from 1 to 5. The two poles are: 1, indicating *Not at all like me* to 5, indicating *Completely like me*.

The 34-item instrument is intended to sufficiently cover the following five scales: Physical Aggression (PHY), Verbal Aggression (VER), Anger (ANG), Hostility (HOS), and Indirect Aggression (IND). The total AQ score is a summary measure of the overall level of anger and aggression expressed by the respondent. The process provides for the conversion of the AQ total and raw scores to *T*-scores.

The AQ was normed on a cross section of individuals from various locations within the continental United States of America. The standardization sample consisted of 2,138 individuals, ranging in age from prepubescence to octogenarian.

The test can be administered to respondents individually or in groups. For research and comparable purposes, administration can be limited to the first 15 items of the inventory, and short versions of each scale can be scored.

On the average, the entire AQ can be administered in approximately 23 minutes by a trained technician. Both administration and scoring can be accomplished manually or by using a personal computer (PC).

The computerization option lends itself to the scoring of large numbers of tests efficiently, the program works on a standard operating system, which enables the transfer of data to other programs for the purpose of information/data management, presentation, technical reporting, and statistical analyses.

DEVELOPMENT. The AQ is the latest version of an instrument that was developed over 40 years ago, beginning with the BDHI (Buss & Durkee, 1957), followed by the first version of the AQ (Buss & Perry, 1992), then to the most recent version, the AQ (Buss & Warren, 2000).

Each successive version provides greater utility, in terms of readability and ease of administration. Historically, the respective authors sought to word their queries in such a way as to minimize untrue answers from some respondents; in particular, diction was used to ward off defensive or socially acceptable (but untrue) answers from the respondents.

Additionally, this version of the AQ has a provision that can alert the examiner to inconsistencies in a respondent's answers. The provision is called the Inconsistent Responding (INC) index. The score that is derived from this index can be an indicant of validity or the lack thereof.

TECHNICAL. The information describing the norming process is lucid, if not downright instructive, in terms of the model, methodology, and quality of the research work it presents.

Future research is aided by a technical chapter on the psychometric properties of the AQ, as well as appendices and bibliographical listings. The "Topical Listing of Published Studies Using the BDHI or the AQ" and the "References" provide a quickly accessible list of useful scholarly references by topic or by alphabetized names of authors.

The demographic characteristics of the AQ standardization sample entail the following features: 2,138 individuals, consist of 880 males, and 1,252 females. Ethnic characteristics of this sample included 18 Asians, 320 Blacks, 165 Hispanics, 12 Native Americans, and 1,547 Whites. The age range for the members of the standardization was 9 to 88 years, and they came from the four geographical regions in the USA.

The instrumentation provides for the conversion of the AQ total and raw scores to T scores.

In terms of reliability and validity (Downie & Heath, 1983), by all available statistical work and allied indicators, the AQ is a stable instrument that tends to sufficiently gauge anger and aggression when it is properly administered, truthfully answered, and professionally interpreted.

Hence, the AQ represents a balance between power and efficiency in assessing anger and aggression. In this sense, it meets the criteria of parsimony (Babbie, 1979).

COMMENTARY. In this reviewer's estimation, this is an excellent instrument—excellent, in that it is likely to continue moving research and clinic work forward to greater understanding and better applications.

SUMMARY. The Aggression Questionnaire (AQ) is an instrument for assessing anger and aggression. The AQ is an updated version of the BDHI (Buss & Durkee, 1957).

The five case examples are illustrative. They show, unequivocally, how the AQ can be used singularly, or in conjunction with other instruments and professional clinical judgment for assessing a respondent or client.

Buss and Warren have presented an enhanced instrument for assessing anger and aggression. The AQ can be administered, scored, and interpreted relatively efficiently and economically.

REVIEWER'S REFERENCES
Babbie, E. R. (1979). *The practice of social research.* Belmont, CA: Wadsworth Publishing Company, Inc.
Buss, A. H., & Durkee, A. (1957). An inventory for assessing different kinds of hostility. *Journal of Consulting Psychology, 21,* 343–349.
Buss, A. H., & Perry, M. (1992). The Aggression Questionnaire. *Journal of Personality and Social Psychology, 63,* 452–459.
Buss, A. H., & Warren, W. L. (2000). *Aggression Questionnaire Manual.* Los Angeles, CA: Western Psychological Services.

Review of the Aggression Questionnaire by MARY LOU KELLEY, Professor of Psychology, Louisiana State University, Baton Rouge, LA:

DESCRIPTION. The Aggression Questionnaire (AQ) consists of 34 items scored on five scales: Physical Aggression (PHY), Verbal Aggression (VER), Anger (ANG), Hostility (HOS), and Indirect Aggression (IND). In addition, the scale yields a Total score and a validity measure of Inconsistent Responding (INC). The AQ is described as an updated version of the Buss-Durkee Hostility Inventory (BDHI; Buss & Durkee), 1957). The PHY scale contains 8 items and measures the use of physical force when expressing anger. VER consist of 5 items pertaining to hostile speech. ANG is a 7-item scale that focuses on emotional arousal and irritability. According to the authors the HOS scale is the one most associated with severe pathology and consists of 8 items repressing attitudes of bitterness, social alienation, and paranoia. The 6-item IND scale measures the tendency to express anger in actions that avoid direct confrontation.

The AQ is a self-report measure for use with individuals age 9 and older. Each item of the AQ is rated on a 5-point scale with 1 = *Not at all like me* to 5 = *Completely like me*. The authors report that the items can be easily read and understood by anyone with a third grade reading ability. The AQ can be administered individually or in groups and can be completed in a short period of time. The authors state that the first 15 items can be completed only for research purposes. The short version has some items from each scale of the AQ.

The AQ can be administered on paper for hand scoring using an AutoScore™ system or by computer with computer scoring. The AutoScore™ requires the respondent to firmly circle a response for each item. Scores are transferred to the appropriate scale columns and added to produce a scale raw score. Raw scores are plotted on a Profile Sheet. There are three sets of norms with corresponding profile sheets. Youth (ages 9–18), Young Adult (ages 19–39), and Older Adults (ages 40 and above).

DEVELOPMENT. The AQ is a revised version of the BDHI and contains some similar items but new items were added. The Guilt factor of the BDHI was deleted from the current instrument. The items appear logically placed on the various factors. The factor structure was based on three independent samples of college students. A nice feature of the AQ is the INC scale in which items are paired due to similar content and scores are compared for discrepant responding. The manual that accompanies the test is clear and adequately detailed with regard to administration, standardization, and psychometric properties. The authors appropriately indicated that the instrument should be used only by a professional trained in the use of psychological tests. The authors discuss in great deal profile interpretation and presents a number of case examples. This discussion often goes beyond the data and does not appear to have adequate psychometric support for scale interpretation.

TECHNICAL. The AQ was standardized using a sample of 2,138. The sample suffers from underrepresentation of minorities and young adults. Separate norms for males and females are present for the PA, VA and Total Score scales. Overall, the standardization sample appears small given the age range for which the scale is intended. The addition of norms for different ethnic groups would be useful.

Internal consistency coefficients were barely adequate for the individual scales with alphas at about the .70 level. Reliability estimates for the PA scale and the Total Score scale were higher with estimates for the Total Scale .90 and above. The lowest reliability estimates were for the Indirect Aggression (IND) scale and ranged from .65–.71 across the age groupings. The alpha coefficients for children, especially the 9–10-year-olds, were inadequate for all scales with the exception of the Total Score scale. The authors caution against scale interpretation with young children. Test-retest reliability was adequate.

The concurrent validity of the AQ was assessed by correlating AQ scores with scores from related measures. The correlations between the AQ and the Novaco Anger Scale and the Provocation Inventory were moderate to good. However, the correlations between the AQ and the Children's Inventory of Anger and the Attitudes Toward Guns and Violence Questionnaire were low. A number of studies assessing AQ scores in clinical samples were conducted and the results were mixed. Also, correlations between the AQ and other measures of pathology were not consistently obtained but generally were in the expected direction and at times were highly correlated with related measures.

COMMENTARY. The AQ is a promising measure for assessing anger and aggression in children, adolescents, and adults. The manual is well written and the authors discuss limitations of the measure. However, my biggest concern is with the interpretation of the scale and the suggested profiles. There does not appear to be adequate validity data to support profile interpretations. Further, the use of the measure with young children appears questionable given the relatively poor internal consistency of the scales with the exception of the Physical Aggression and Total Score scales. It may be that children lack the ability to assess and report on some aspects of anger and aggression. Finally, there are few data on the validity of the information reported by children. For example, correlations between children's self-report and that of their parents or teachers might be very informative regarding the nature of children's self-report.

SUMMARY. The Aggression Questionnaire is a brief measure for assessing anger and aggression. The scale is a revised version of the Buss-Durkee Hostility Inventory. The manual is well organized and well written. Reliability is generally adequate and the items are worded in a clear, specific manner. Validity studies show some support for the measure but additional studies are needed. Finally, the standardization sample was underrepresented by minorities, which limits its use with these populations. Overall, the AQ is a suitable measure for assessing anger. However, the limitations of the standardization process and reliability and validity must be given appropriate consideration in use of the test. I recommend that the Total Score rather than the individual scales be emphasized along with review of individual items endorsed by clients.

REVIEWER'S REFERENCE

Buss, A. H., & Durkee, A. (1957). An inventory for assessing different kinds of hostility. *Journal of Consulting Psychology, 21,* 343–349.

[14]

Analytical Aptitude Skills Evaluation.

Purpose: To evaluate aptitude and potential for analyzing business problems.
Population: Entry-level and experienced candidates for positions requiring the ability to analyze business problems.
Publication Date: 1993.
Acronym: AASE.
Scores: Total Score, Narrative Evaluation, Rating, Recommendation.
Administration: Group.
Price Data, 2001: $235 per candidate; quantity discounts available.
Foreign Language Edition: French version available.
Time: (60) minutes.
Comments: Scored by publisher; must be proctored.
Author: Bruce A. Winrow.
Publisher: Walden Personnel Performance, Inc.

Review of the Analytical Aptitude Skills Evaluation by JOHN S. GEISLER, Professor of Counselor Education and Counseling Psychology, Western Michigan University, Kalamazoo, MI:

DESCRIPTION. The Analytical Aptitude Skills Evaluation (AASE) is a two-problem, five-page, paper-and-pencil-administered instrument that appears to assess business logic, business mathematics, business processes, and the translation of business solutions into symbolic logic. Problem 1 (25 minutes) has six questions that have five multiple-choice answers dealing with business transactions (purchases, interest calculations, discounts on merchandise, balance sheets, etc.). Problem 2 (35 minutes) measures both the ability to solve logistical problems associated with business operations when constraints are imposed (10 potential answers) and locating and correcting two logistical errors in a six-set array of symbolic instructions (4 answers).

It would appear that there are 20 potential answers (6 in Part 1, 14 in Part 2). The publisher reports that the potential number of correct points is 36 (18 for Part 1, 18 for Part 2) although no information is provided as to the number of points for each correct answer (it is reasonable to assume that there are 3 points awarded for each correct answer in Part 1; 3 x 6 = 18). The answers are recorded in the test booklet and are then sent (via mail, fax, or telephone) to the scoring service (there is an extra charge for the answers that are phoned in or faxed).

The score report consists of three sections: (a) the percent of correct responses, (b) a plot of the score on a continuum (Below Average, Average, Above Average), and (c) an overall employment rating that falls into one of four categories depending upon the percent of correct answers (0—57% Not Recommended, 58—64% Recommended for Limited Use, 65—79% Recommended, 80—100% Strongly Recommended). Each category has descriptions about the likelihood for success (e.g., Not Recommended—We DO NOT recommend this individual for a career as an analyst).

DEVELOPMENT. No information is available on the development, history, or rationale for the AASE. No information is available regarding the justification for the four-classification rating scheme.

TECHNICAL. No validity or reliability data are available for the AASE. The normative data

(N = 200) are very vague and incomplete. No demographic data are reported on the normative group. The mean, median, mode, standard deviation, variance, range, and the total sum of scores are reported. It is clear that the computations on these data were computed on the percent correct scores, not on the raw scores (maximum raw score = 36). Because percent scores are neither interval nor ratio data some of the data reported are not appropriate (means, standard deviations, etc.).

Data on males (n = 106) and females (n = 57) are reported (means and standard deviations), but no statistical difference tests were performed. It is interesting to note that the table containing these data also reported the total sample to be 200, yet the combined male and female participant total is 163.

COMMENTARY. The utility of the AASE is highly questionable and has little or no value for potential employers. Reliability and validity data are nonexistent. There is no information on the rationale, history, or development of the instrument and precious little data on the reference group. The statistical information is suspect and no rationale is provided for the distribution of the four score categories.

SUMMARY. The developers have published a unique, expensive ($235/person), and easy-to-administer instrument that is seriously lacking in terms of reliability, validity, and norm group data. No development information is available. No theoretical or empirical data are available to justify its use. The data that are provided are suspect and the justification for the classification system that is employed is absent. Use of this instrument for employee selection is not recommended.

[15]

Apraxia Battery for Adults, Second Edition.

Purpose: Designed to "verify the presence of apraxia in the adult patient and to estimate the severity of the disorder."
Population: Adults.
Publication Dates: 1979–2000.
Acronym: ABA-2.
Scores: 6 subtests: Diadochokinetic Rate, Increasing Word Length, Limb Apraxia and Oral Apraxia, Latency Time and Utterance Time for Polysyllabic Words, Repeated Trials, Inventory of Articulation Characteristics of Apraxia.
Administration: Individual.

Price Data, 2003: $123 per complete kit including 25 profile/examiner record forms, picture book, and manual (2000, 46 pages); $41 per 25 profile/examiner record forms; $45 per examiner's manual; $36 per picture book.
Time: (20) minutes.
Comments: Publisher states that the "vocabulary and conceptual structure of the six subtests allows administration of the battery to adolescents and children down to about age 9"; however, the norming group included only adults.
Author: Barbara L. Dabul.
Publisher: PRO-ED.
Cross References: See T5:163 (3 references) and T4:179 (4 references); for a review by Norma Cooke of an earlier edition, see 9:77 (1 reference).

Review of the Apraxia Battery for Adults, Second Edition by ELAINE CLARK, Professor of Educational Psychology, University of Utah, Salt Lake City, UT:

DESCRIPTION. The Apraxia Battery for Adults, Second Edition (ABA-2) was developed to identify apraxia, assess its severity, and direct treatment. According to the author, Barbara Dabul, the ABA-2 is the only test available to assess adult apraxia. The test, however, is only to be used with individuals who are English speaking due to the phonemic structure and format of the test. It is not entirely clear from the examiner's manual who is supposed to administer the ABA-2. The test appears most suited to speech and language pathologists. Other professionals who work with patients who have communication problems as a result of neurologic insult, however, may appreciate some of the features of the ABA-2 (e.g., neuropsychologists). Six subtests are included in the test and assess a number of communication functions involving voluntary motor movement: phoneme production (Diadochokinetic Rate), phoneme sequencing and articulation agility (Increasing Word Length), speech and nonspeech motor coordination (Limb and Oral Apraxia), confrontation naming (Latency Time and Utterance Time for Polysyllabic Words), consecutive repetition (Repeated Trials), and speech errors (Inventory of Articulation Characteristics of Apraxia). There is no total score that indicates an apraxic condition, only cutoff scores indicating level of impairment. According to the manual, "the examiner must use additional information concerning the examinee in order to make general assumptions about the presence or absence of apraxia" (p. 28).

DEVELOPMENT. The ABA was first developed by Dabul at the Veterans Administration (VA) Outpatient Clinic in Los Angeles in the late 1970s. According to the manual, an eight-subtest measure was pilot tested with 40 male patients at the VA and later revised for publication in 1979 as a six-subtest version. The first test lacked appropriate norms and the author failed to report reliability and validity data in the manual. Despite this, Cooke (1985) described the ABA as useful in designing treatments for apraxic patients. The ABA was also the only test of its kind. When revised for publication in 2000, new norms were collected (i.e., in 1998 and 1999), several items were added and/or replaced, and psychometric studies were included in the examiner's manual.

TECHNICAL. Despite reported improvements in the test, the norms for the ABA-2 remain limited. Only 40 apraxic adults and 49 nonapraxic adults (between the ages of 30 and 93) were included in the standardization. Participants were apparently selected by speech and language pathologists who served as examiners at rehabilitation hospitals across the country. There is no indication that the examiners had any prior experience with the ABA as all were randomly selected. Because no procedures to prepare examiners to administer the test were included in the manual, and no interrater reliability data were reported, it is not clear what, if anything, was done to insure that the testing of the norming sample was done using standardized administration procedures.

The only reliability data reported in the manual pertain to internal consistency (i.e., alternative-form reliability and Cronbach alphas). Coefficients for individual subtests ranged from .83 to .97, indicating that items are measuring similar constructs. According to the author, test-retest reliability studies were not considered appropriate given the fact examinees may improve in response to treatment. However, improvement would be expected for all from the first to second testing; therefore, the rank ordering of items would remain essentially the same (supporting the meaningfulness of the stability coefficients).

Although validity data are provided in the manual, the data are limited by the sample studied. With only one exception, the validity studies with the ABA-2 were conducted using the norming sample. That one study, however, involved a very small (i.e., five aphasics and seven dysarthric patients) or unspecified sample (apraxic and normal speech). The results of the validity studies reported in the manual indicate that the ABA-2 is useful in discriminating individuals with apraxia from those who do not have apraxic conditions, and items are sufficiently powerful to discriminate the performance of apraxic subjects (i.e., item discrimination indexes ranged from .52 to .84). The lowest discrimination index, in fact, was for the subtest, Inventory of Articulation Characteristics of Apraxia, a measure that describes characteristics of apraxia rather than identifying the condition.

COMMENTARY. Dabul has developed a very user-friendly measure of apraxia, possibly the only one. Ease of use, however, is no substitute for psychometric soundness and numerous unanswered questions remain about the standardization process and empirical support. The ABA-2 may actually be a better test than what appears on paper; however, potential users will be left to make the decision to select the test based on limited data. This starts with limited normative data. It is rather surprising that the test author made the effort to gather a national sample yet settled on the same number of apraxic participants she did 20 years ago, and in one site, the VA Clinic in Los Angeles. Although data from the 40 apraxic participants were sufficient to show a significant difference between patients in the standardization group who had apraxia from those who did not, the question remains as to whether these values are reasonable (and generalizable) for the broader population. The same can be said of the validity data that were collected and included in the manual. Although the construct, and structure of the test itself, is supported by the data, the ability of the test to discriminate among groups independent of the standardization sample has yet to be demonstrated. Similarly, the stability of the test has not been shown and users should rightfully question how the test would perform on a different population. This is not to say that the ABA-2 is unsound, but the soundness of the ABA-2 is not adequately supported by the data provided. It is not clear if the author stopped short of demonstrating the improvements that were actually made with the revised test, or the test falls short of being a significant improvement over its predecessor, the ABA. Despite this, the test may still be useful in developing treatment plans for apraxic patients, and evaluating progress. However, whether the test is worth the time it takes to administer in a standardized manner, and scored according to specific criteria remains to be answered.

SUMMARY. Perhaps the greatest value of the ABA-2 has to do with the stimuli the test provides, and the setting occasioned for observation purposes. Clearly, the value of the test lies beyond the data provided in the manual. Professionals looking for a tool to use with patients who have voluntary motor problems may not have to look further; however, they may want to consider spending time looking for ways to make better use of the tests they have, including the ABA-2.

REVIEWER'S REFERENCE

Cooke, N. (1985). [Review of the Apraxia Battery for Adults.] In J. V. Mitchell, Jr. (Ed.), *The ninth mental measurements yearbook* (p. 80). Lincoln, NE: Buros Institute of Mental Measurements.

Review of the Apraxia Battery for Adults, Second Edition by RAYMOND S. DEAN, George and Frances Ball Distinguished Professor of Neuropsychology, Neuropsychology Laboratory, Ball State University, and JOHN J. BRINKMAN, JR., Associate Director, Neuropsychology Laboratory, Ball State University, Muncie, IN:

DESCRIPTION. The Apraxia Battery for Adults, Second Edition (ABA-2) written by Barbara Dabul is an individually administered test of speech apraxia. It was designed to guide the treatment of expressive language impairments. Though the intent of the original Apraxia Battery for Adults (ABA) (1979) was to screen for speech apraxia in adults, the present edition purports to allow for the assessment of adolescents and children down to 9 years of age.

The test administration is in English and takes approximately 20 minutes to complete. English is the focus because the phonemes used in the ABA-2 do not necessarily translate directly to other languages. The test is broken down into six subtests each addressing different aspects of speech with the last subtest designed to guide treatment interventions. The first subtest, Diadochokinetic Rate, addresses volitional control and agility of articulation. This purports to measure how quickly the examinee is able to repeat syllable combinations in a given time period (i.e., 3 and 5 seconds for two-syllable and three-syllable combinations respectively). The second subtest, Increasing Word Length, also attempts to measure agility of articulation along with the ability to sequence phonemes. This is attempted through the repetition of words with increasing numbers of syllables

(e.g., thick, thicken, thickening). The third subtest, Limb Apraxia and Oral Apraxia, considers oral instruction with the upper limbs and structures of the mouth. It requires the examinee to produce specific movements in response to oral directions (e.g., "make a fist" or "stick out your tongue"). The fourth subtest, Latency Time and Utterance Time for Polysyllabic Words, involves a timed test of the confrontational naming and addresses the examinee's ability to initiate a word from a picture that is presented and assesses length of time it takes to pronounce the word once it has been initiated. The fifth subtest, Repeated Trials, assesses the change in speech production of particular words. This subtest requires the examinee to repeat polysyllabic words (e.g., telephone) over three successive trials. The sixth subtest, Inventory of Articulation Characteristics of Apraxia, was designed to guide treatment of the examinee's speech behavior. Speech behavior is assessed through spontaneous speech, reading, and automatic speech.

Scoring is done by hand. Scores for Subtest 1 represent the number of correct repetitions for each trial. Scores for Subtests 2 and 3 are assigned a number based on the examinee's ability to perform a task (e.g., "2 = The examinee performs correctly after demonstration" for limb and oral apraxia). Scores for Subtest 4 record the number of seconds for latency and utterance times. Scores for Subtest 5 represent the number of errors produced over each trial with a summation of "0," "+," or "-" to describe the changes over Trials 1, 2 and 3. Scoring for Subtest 6 is based on observation and is done by placing a check mark next to the noted behaviors. A summary of raw scores and levels of impairment is completed on the profile/examiner record form. There are four levels of impairment: None, Mild, Moderate, and Severe. These levels were based on the norm sample performance of individuals with normal speech and individuals with speech apraxia. Cutoff scores for each level were determined by dividing scores into quartiles based on "discrete observations." None represented the first quartile with the lower limit being set one standard deviation below the speech sample mean of normal individuals, Mild represented the second quartile, Moderate represented the third quartile, and Severe represented the lowest quartile.

DEVELOPMENT. The original Apraxia Battery for Adults was developed at the Veterans

Administration Outpatient Clinic in Los Angeles and first published by C.C. Publications in 1979, and then republished in 1986 by PRO-ED. According to Dabul, the test author, the revision of the ABA-2 was prompted by Neeley's (1980) master's thesis project, the experiences of clinicians using the ABA, and the review of the ABA by Cooke (1985). The ABA-2 revision includes updated norms from 1998 and 1999; the adjustment of items to raise the ceiling on Subtests 1 and 2; and item revisions to update pictures and gestures, and to identify speech apraxia based on current research.

TECHNICAL. The ABA-2 was normed on a sample of 89 adults with 40 people identified with speech apraxia and 49 people identified with normal speech. No information was provided on the definition or identification process of individuals described to have "normal speech" (examiner's manual, p. 27). The norming sample was collected from 10 states across the country to include: Arizona, Connecticut, Florida, Kansas, Missouri, New Hampshire, North Carolina, Ohio, Texas, and Virginia. The sample identified with speech apraxia included 16 women and 24 men ranging in age from 33 to 93 years of age. The sample identified with normal speech included 32 women and 17 men ranging in age from 30 to 90 years of age. There was no information on the performance of individual ethnic or cultural groups.

Reliability was estimated using both alternate form and internal consistency. The reliability for Subtest 1, Diadochokinetic Rate, ($r = .95$) was estimated using alternate form reliability. The alternate form was described as "three trials of the same task were given during one testing session; the correlation between Trial 1 and Trial 3 is the reliability index that was used to estimate content sampling error" (examiner's manual, p. 29). The internal consistency reliability for Subtests 2 through 6 was estimated using coefficient alpha. The following internal consistency reliability estimates were obtained: Subtest 2, Increasing Word Length—Part A, ($r = .97$); Subtest 2, Increasing Word Length—Part B, ($r = .99$); Subtest 3, Limb Apraxia—Part A, ($r = .90$); Subtest 3, Oral Apraxia—Part B, ($r = .89$); Subtest 4, Latency Time for Polysyllabic Words, ($r = .94$); Subtest 4, Utterance Time for Polysyllabic Words, ($r = .95$); Subtest 5, Repeated Trials, ($r = .97$); Subtest 6, Inventory of Articulation Characteristics of Apraxia, ($r = .83$).

Validity evidence for the ABA-2 involved using content description, criterion prediction, and construct identification. The content description validity evidence was provided by 40 individuals identified to have speech dyspraxia. This study used both a qualitative and a quantitative approach. First, a qualitative description for an ability was defined (e.g., Subtest 1, Diadochokinetic Rate, assesses volitional control and agility of articulation). Then, the specific ability (e.g., Subtest 1, repeating syllable combinations in a given time period) is quantified and evaluated using item discrimination. Median discriminating powers among test items for the group with apraxia were as follows: 1, Diadochokinetic Rate, (.77); 2, Increasing Word Length—Part A, (.72); 2, Increasing Word Length—Part B, (.84); 3, Limb Apraxia, (.67); 3, Oral Apraxia, (.61); 4, Latency Time for Polysyllabic Words, (.73); 4, Utterance Time for Polysyllabic Words, (.81); 5, Repeated Trials, (.71); 6, Inventory of Articulation Characteristics of Apraxia, (.52).

The criterion-related validity evidence was provided by Neeley (1980). In this study 25 patients with speech dyspraxia were compared using the ABA with the Porch Index of Communicative Ability (PICA). Though the PICA is used to assess aphasia, by evaluating verbal, gestural, and graphic abilities, it is the only other test able to characterize speech apraxia by identifying a significant gap between the Verbal and Gestural subtest scores. Results indicated that the PICA was able to identify severe speech apraxia, with the ABA being able to distinguish apraxia more accurately.

Construct identification validity evidence was obtained by looking at four variables: differentiation between groups with speech apraxia and groups with normal speech; differentiation among groups with impaired speech; the interrelationships among subtests and composites; and item validity. Differentiation between groups with speech apraxia and groups with normal speech was demonstrated by computing a t-test. Means, standard deviations, t-ratios, and probability levels were reported for the two groups. Results indicated that the group with speech apraxia had lower means for Subtests 1, 3, and 5 and higher means for Subtests 2, 4, and 6, demonstrating significance at the .006 level. Differentiation among groups with impaired speech was demonstrated by comparing means and standard deviations for four groups: normal speech, apraxia, aphasia, and dysarthria. Though differences were reported, the results must be interpreted with caution because the number of individuals in groups with aphasia ($n = 5$) and dysarthria ($n = 7$) were relatively small (examiner's manual, p. 35). The interrelationships among subtests and composites were established by intercorrelating groups of individuals with apraxia and individuals with normal speech. The correlation coefficients and the probability levels among the ABA-2 subtests were reported. Results indicated that all of the coefficients exceeded positive or negative .55, and this can be accepted as evidence to support the validity of individual subtests. Item validity was demonstrated by item discrimination discussed above with construct identification.

COMMENTARY. The ABA-2 is a quick clinical test that has been offered to assess speech apraxia by identifying several different characteristics of the disorder. Dabul presents a thorough definition and description including the mechanisms involved for normal speech and apraxic speech. The updated norm group is simply not large enough. Although the adjustment of items to raise the ceiling and item revisions have all improved the test, more data are necessary on reliability and validity. The ABA-2 offers many well-designed studies in an effort to validate the concept of speech apraxia. The ABA-2 also outlines treatment planning that is specific to each subtest, thus allowing for the identification and intervention of specific characteristics of speech apraxia. However, no studies were provided on the utility of the ABA-2 in the treatment of patients with speech apraxia. The use of the ABA-2 should be interpreted with caution based on the lack of standardization and reliability.

Standardization utilized small groups, there was no information provided on male versus female differences, ethnic group performance, or the performance of children. Further, no children were a part of the standardization process even though the manual suggests that the ABA-2 can be administered to children down to 9 years of age. Reliability studies should have employed interrater studies. The ABA-2 may be seen more as a clinical measure, but with little important psychometric evidence.

SUMMARY. The ABA-2 is a measure to assess the presence and severity of speech impairment. Further it may be a useful clinical tool to plan for the treatment of individuals with different aspects of apraxic speech. The measure lacks persuasive reliability evidence, but has well-designed validity studies. The standardization groups are small, which may rely more upon the skill of the examiner than the measure as a psychometric test.

REVIEWER'S REFERENCES

Cooke, N. (1985). [Review of the Apraxia Battery for Adults.] In J. V. Mitchell, Jr. (Ed.), *The ninth mental measurements yearbook* (p. 80). Lincoln, NE: Buros Institute of Mental Measurements.
Neeley, V. L. (1980). *Performance of apraxic and non-apraxic examinees on the Apraxia Battery for Adults.* Unpublished master's thesis, University of La Verne, La Verne, CA.

[16]

Aptitude Profile Test Series.

Purpose: Designed to assess a range of core cognitive abilities relevant to and known to predict success in many occupations and areas of study.

Population: Years 9–11 in Australian school system to adults.

Publication Date: 2000.

Acronyms: APTS and APTS-E.

Scores, 4: Abstract Reasoning, Quantitative Reasoning, Spatial-Visual Reasoning, Verbal Reasoning.

Administration: Individual or group.

Price Data, 2002: A\$19.80 per Verbal Reasoning test book; A\$19.80 per Quantitative Reasoning test book; A\$19.80 per Abstract Reasoning test book; A\$19.80 per Spatial Reasoning test book; A\$13.20 per 10 answer sheets; A\$25.29 per score keys; A\$119.90 per manual; A\$225.50 per specimen set.

Time: 30(45) minutes per test.

Authors: George Morgan, Andrew Stephanou, and Brian Simpson.

Publisher: Australian Council for Educational Research Ltd. [Australia].

a) APTITUDE PROFILE TEST SERIES.

Purpose: "Developed for use … with assessing people's abilities in relation to employment and to occupational needs of organisations and industry."

Population: Adults.

Acronym: APTS.

b) APTITUDE PROFILE TEST SERIES—EDUCATIONAL.

Purpose: "Developed for … assessing students' abilities in an educational context."

Population: Years 9–11 in Australian school system.

Acronym: APTS-E.

Price Data: A\$7.70 per Verbal Reasoning test book; A\$7.70 per Quantitative Reasoning test book; A\$8.80 per Abstract Reasoning test book; A\$9.90 per Spatial Reasoning test book; A\$10.89 per 10 answer sheets; A\$105 per manual including score keys; A\$137.50 per specimen set.

example, the proverbs task of the fourth Verbal Reasoning subtest is similar to items found in the old Comprehensive Ability Battery but not encountered elsewhere. Also, the items in the Spatial-Visual Reasoning test are different from those found in most widely used American instruments measuring spatial abilities. It might be worthwhile to combine some of these item forms with other, more widely used item types to examine their properties and potential usefulness, but there is insufficient linkage to other tests to permit their ready interpretation. One feature that I found disturbing in Parts 1 and 3 of the Spatial-Visual Reasoning test was that the format of the items changed in the middle of a timed section. Examinees are required to read and decode new directions as part of the test itself.

SUMMARY. These new tests have some potentially interesting features, but until there is a lot more evidence about their properties and permissible interpretations and much more adequate normative data, there is no justification for using them in an applied setting. The use of British or Australian spelling and metric units could also cause some problems for American examinees. This test is not a serious contender to replace its American counterparts in the U.S.

[17]

Asperger Syndrome Diagnostic Scale.

Purpose: "Designed to assess individuals who manifest the characteristics of Asperger syndrome."
Population: Ages 5–18.
Publication Date: 2001.
Acronym: ASDS.
Scores, 6: Language, Social, Maladaptive, Cognitive, Sensorimotor, Total.
Administration: Individual.
Price Data, 2003: $94 per complete kit including 50 summary/response forms, and examiner's manual (39 pages); $41 per 50 summary response forms; $55 per examiner's manual.
Time: (10–15) minutes.
Comments: Ratings by parents, teachers, and professionals at home and school.
Authors: Brenda Smith Myles, Stacey Jones Bock, and Richard L. Simpson.
Publisher: PRO-ED.

Review of the Asperger Syndrome Diagnostic Scale by KIMBERLY ANN BLAIR, Assistant Professor of Education, Duquesne University, Pittsburgh, PA:

DESCRIPTION. The Asperger Syndrome Diagnostic Scale (ASDS) is recommended primarily for use as a diagnostic instrument for identifying Asperger syndrome (AS) in individuals aged 5 through 18 years. Other suggested uses include documenting the progress made in intervention programs, developing intervention goals for the individual's Individual Education Plan, and assessing AS for research programs.

The ASDS is a 50-item behavior rating scale that can be completed in approximately 10 to 15 minutes by an individual who has had close contact with the referred individual for at least 2 weeks. All test items are selection-type, requiring the respondent to indicate whether specific behaviors have been observed or not observed in the referred individual. Observed behaviors receive a rating of 1 and unobserved behaviors receive a 0. All test items are used to provide the Asperger Syndrome Quotient (ASQ), which is the only score suggested to be used in the diagnosis of AS. The 50 items are also categorized into five subscales: Language, Social, Maladaptive, Cognitive, and Sensorimotor. Although these five subscales are not recommended for use in identifying AS, it is argued that the subscales provide the examiner with information of clinical interest that can assist in treatment planning for an individual.

The ASDS provides percentiles and standard scores for each subscale, in addition to the quotient score. Test items are arranged on the response form according to subscales. Raw scores for subscales are obtained by adding ratings for each item within a subscale and the total raw score is the total of subscale raw scores. Tables are provided in the appendix of the ASDS examiner's manual to convert raw scores to percentiles, standard scores, and the quotient score (with a mean of 100 and standard deviation of 15). Guidelines for identifying the likelihood for AS based on a comparison to the normative sample are provided on the Summary/Response Form and in the ASDS examiner's manual. The ASQ is reported as reflecting the probability of AS as being very likely, likely, possibly, unlikely, and very unlikely.

In addition to test items, the ASDS Summary/Response Form provides sections for identifying information, interpretation guide, score summary and profile of scores, a list of key questions that may elicit additional information useful in diagnosing AS, space for examiner's interpretations and recommendations, and a description of the characteristics of the ASDS.

DEVELOPMENT. *The Diagnostic and Statistical Manual of Mental Disorders: Fourth Edition* (DSM-IV; American Psychiatric Association, 1994), the *International Classification of Diseases—Tenth Edition* (ICD-10; World Health Organization, 1992), a review of all recent published literature on AS, and Hans Asperger's original research served as the reference base for item development. Based on a comprehensive review of the above sources, the authors developed a checklist of behavioral characteristics of AS that was then organized into six categories that became the five ASDS subscales (Language, Social, Maladaptive, Cognitive, and Sensorimotor). From this list, a total of 50 items were written. An item analysis on the entire normative sample was performed to demonstrate the items on the ASDS were satisfactory. Each item correlated significantly with the ASQ, indicating a strong contribution to the measured construct. The ASDS examiner's manual provides a brief summary of the research supporting the use of the identified categories and gives a brief description of the subscales.

TECHNICAL. Information is provided in the ASDS examiner's manual regarding standardization practices including participant selection, demographic characteristics of normative group, and the development of normative scores. Parents, teachers, educational diagnosticians, psychologists, and other school district personnel were solicited to complete the ASDS on students diagnosed as having AS. No details regarding the respondents' qualifications and training for completing the ASDS were reported in the manual.

The normative group comprised 115 children, ages 5 through 18, from 21 states across the U.S. Participants were previously diagnosed with AS. No information is provided regarding how participants were diagnosed and no verification of the diagnosis of the participants was completed. Therefore, there is no way to confirm the appropriateness of participants selected for the norm group. As the manual correctly points out, this is a low-incidence disorder, with little known information regarding the demographic characteristics of individuals with AS. The normative sample generally matches what is known regarding the demographic characteristics of individuals with AS and the school-age population in general with regards to gender and ethnicity. Information is provided in the manual regarding the geographic distribution of participants, but no information is provided regarding socioeconomic status.

The ASDS demonstrates moderate to good reliability estimates. A study of internal consistency yielded a coefficient alpha of .83 for the ASQ and a range from .64 to .83 for ASDS subscale coefficients. Due to lower reliability coefficients, it is recommended in the manual that subscales be used only for determining individual strengths and weaknesses and not for diagnosing individuals as having AS. A study conducted to examine interrater reliability of the ASQ utilized a small sample of participants rated by parents and teachers. The resulting correlation coefficient between the parent-reported mean ASQ and teacher-reported mean ASQ was .93, indicating strong interrater reliability. No test-retest reliability studies were reported.

Validity evidence for the ASDS was provided in a variety of ways. Median item discrimination coefficients for the five subscales on the ASDS ranged from .47 to .67, offering some moderate support for interpreting the scale's scores relative to the content. In addition to the normative sample, data were collected during standardization for 177 individuals with other exceptionalities, including autism, behavior disorders, attention deficit/hyperactivity disorder, and learning disabilities. A discriminant analysis study of these two groups found the ASDS ASQ correctly differentiated the AS sample from the non-AS sample at an 85% accuracy rate. However, as with the original participants previously identified as having AS, the non-AS sample's diagnoses were not confirmed.

The validity of each of the ASDS's basic constructs was addressed in the examiner's manual. Correlation coefficients of ASDS raw scores with age on the original normative sample were not significant, supporting the presumption that the behaviors typical of AS are not related to age. Each item on the ASDS was significantly correlated to the ASQ, providing support for the second construct that all items should correlate with the total test score, as all items on the ASDS describe traits characteristic of AS. In another test of the ASDS's construct validity, the ASDS standard scores were correlated with the Gilliam Autism Rating Scale (GARS). The ASQ was correlated with the total score of the GARS, yielding a moderate but not significant correlation coefficient. This finding was used to provide support for the construct interpretation of scores because the ASDS measures behaviors characteristic of AS; therefore, it should not be correlated with a scale measuring autistic behaviors. Not addressed was the relationship between AS and autism and the continued controversy about whether AS represents a distinct disorder or is part of a continuum of a single autism spectrum disorder. It is therefore unclear whether comparing the ASDS to the GARS in this manner is an appropriate way to provide evidence of construct validity. Scores on the ASDS for the norm sample were compared to scores on the ASDS for four other diagnostic groups, including autism, behavior disorders, attention-deficit/hyperactivity disorder, and learning disabilities. On each ASQ, the AS group performed significantly higher than the other diagnostic groups, providing additional evidence support of construct validity because the ASDS measures behaviors characteristic of AS. Therefore, results should differentiate individuals with AS from individuals with other known disorders. However, the problems with confirmation of diagnoses and comparisons of individuals with AS to individuals with autism described above remain.

COMMENTARY. There is relatively little research on AS as compared to many other disorders. Although the ASDS makes a good effort at filling a void in the current research, it has several limitations. Technically, there are concerns as noted above regarding the selection of participants for norm and comparison groups. There was no confirmation of diagnosis for the participants and, therefore, no guarantee of the appropriateness of including them in specific diagnostic groups. Although the ASDS attempts to provide a measure that can be used both diagnostically and for treatment planning and monitoring, there is little information in the examiner's manual on the use of the ASDS for anything other than as a diagnostic instrument for AS. Theoretically, the relationship between AS and autism and the continued controversy about whether AS represents a distinct disorder or is part of a continuum of a single autism spectrum disorder is not addressed. This has direct implications for the ASDS both in terms of its technical merits and as a diagnostic tool in general.

SUMMARY. There is clearly a need for a well-constructed instrument that can be used to assist professionals in diagnosing Asperger syndrome. The ASDS appears to be a useful addition to the instrumentation available to professionals in diagnosing Asperger syndrome. There is also some utility for it to be used as a means of developing and monitoring intervention programs. It is apparent that considerable effort was made in developing a relatively well-written and well-constructed diagnostic instrument. As with any assessment instrument, clinicians are advised to use multiple sources of data to complete a thorough and comprehensive assessment.

REVIEWER'S REFERENCES

American Psychiatric Association. (1994). *Diagnostic and statistical manual of mental disorders* (4th ed.). Washington, DC: Author.
World Health Organization. (1992). *International classification of diseases and related health problems* (10th ed.). Geneva, Switzerland: Author.

Review of the Asperger Syndrome Diagnostic Scale (ASDS) by PAT MIRENDA, Associate Professor, Faculty of Education, University of British Columbia, Vancouver, British Columbia, Canada:

DESCRIPTION. The Asperger Syndrome Diagnostic Scale (ASDS) is a 50-item scale arranged in five subscales (Language, Social, Maladaptive Behavior, Cognitive, and Sensorimotor) that can be used in the diagnosis of Asperger's syndrome (AS), one of the pervasive developmental disorders. The scale is appropriate for use with persons ages 5 through 18 and can be completed in 10—15 minutes by an individual who knows the focus person well and/or has an opportunity to observe him or her over a period a time (e.g., parent, teacher). Items are scored simply as *observed* or *not observed,* and the sum of the raw scores for each subscale is converted into a Quotient Score (the Asperger Syndrome Quotient or ASQ) that is then normalized into a standard score distribution with a mean of 100 and a standard deviation of 15. The larger the ASQ, the greater the probability the individual has AS.

DEVELOPMENT. The items in the ASDS were drawn from the work of Hans Asperger (1944), who first described the syndrome, as well as from recent research and current definitions of AS found in the *Diagnostic and Statistical Manual of Mental Disorders*, 4th edition (*DSM-IV*; American Psychiatric Association, 1994) and the *International Classification of Diseases and Related Health Problems*, 10th edition (*ICD-10*; World Health Organization, 1992). In addition, the ASDS authors conducted a review of the literature on AS from 1975–1999, using the ERIC and PsychInfo databases. The manual offers a reference list of the articles upon which the items were based; the articles range in date from 1944 (Asperger's original article) to 1999, with most of them published in the mid 1980s-mid 1990s.

TECHNICAL. The ASDS was normed on a sample of 115 children and adolescents between the ages of 5 and 18 (M = 10.42, SD = 3.44) who had been diagnosed with AS and who lived in 21 states in the United States of America. Although predominantly of European background (n = 75), they also included African American (n = 10), Hispanic American (n = 10), and Asian American (n = 5) individuals. The sample consisted of 83 males and 17 females, which approximates the gender ratio of 4:1 (males:females) reported in the literature. Given that the population of persons with AS is quite small, the normative sample seems appropriate and reasonable in both size and composition.

The test manual reports data for both reliability and validity. With regard to the former, the internal consistency of the ASDS was measured using Cronbach's coefficient alpha, which was found to be .83 across all 50 items (range = .64–.83 for individual subscales). This suggests that the total score on the ASDS is sufficiently reliable for contributing to important diagnostic decisions, but that the subscales should not be used separately in this regard. In addition, the interrater reliability of the ASDS was examined with a sample of 14 individuals who were rated by both their parents and teachers. The resulting coefficient was r = .93 (p < .01), indicating that different examiners who know the person well can use the ASDS and be confident that their ratings will be similar.

The validity evidence for the ASDS was measured in several ways, First, content-description validity is evident by the manner in which the authors developed the scale, namely, by using well-respected sources such as the *DSM-IV* and the *ICD-10*, in addition to the article by Asperger (1944) and a review of recent literature. In addition, an item analysis was conducted on all cases from the normative sample, resulting in median item discrimination coefficients of .55 (Language), .59 (Social), .57 (Maladaptive), .47 (Cognitive), and .67 (Sensorimotor). These coefficients are

well beyond the minimum criterion of .35 that is considered desirable (Ebel, 1972; Pyrczak, 1973).

Second, criterion-prediction validity, the ability of the ASDS to differentiate between individuals with AS and those with other disabilities, was assessed using the normative sample (N = 115) and a second sample consisting of 177 individuals with autism (n = 92), behavior disorders (n = 28), ADHD (n = 31), and learning disabilities (n = 26). A discriminant analysis on the ASQs of the two groups (i.e., AS vs. non-AS) revealed a significant difference between the mean ASQ of the AS sample and that of the non-AS sample (p < .01), with correct identification of AS versus non-AS occurring for 85% of the participants. This suggests a high degree of accuracy with regard to the diagnosis of AS using the scale.

Third, construct-identification validity, the extent to which a test actually measures what it purports to measure, was evaluated in four ways. First, the correlation between age and ASQ was calculated, with resulting r = .14. This is congruent with the construct that age and ASQ should not be related. Second, the item-total correlation was measured using the point-biserial method to determine the extent to which each of the items on the scale measures the same construct. All items were significant at p < .01, suggesting strong construct validity. Third, both the ASDS and the Gilliam Autism Rating Scale (GARS; Gilliam, 1995), an instrument commonly used to measure autism, were administered to 16 individuals with AS. The ASQ was correlated with the total score from the GARS. Because these two scales were designed to measure different disorders, the authors hypothesized that the ASQs and the GARs scores should not be significantly correlated and, in fact, they were not (r = .46, p > .05). This suggests that the ASDS does, indeed, measure a disorder other than autism.

Finally, the mean subscale scores on the ASDS were compared for the AS and non-AS groups used for the discriminant analysis described previously. For all five subscales, the AS group received significantly higher scores than the non-AS group (p > .05), providing additional evidence that the ASDS can be used differentiate individuals with AS from those in other diagnostic groups.

COMMENTARY. Overall, this instrument presents as a well-constructed collection of test items based on both classic and recent research on

Asperger's syndrome. It provides a profile of behaviors in five areas that are related to AS as well as standard scores, percentiles, and a total quotient score, the ASQ. It has good to excellent psychometric properties, and can probably be used with confidence as one component in the diagnosis of persons with AS. In addition, it may be useful for targeting intervention goals, documenting progress as a result of intervention, and measuring AS in research projects.

REVIEWER'S REFERENCES

American Psychiatric Association. (1994). *Diagnostic and Statistical Manual of Mental Disorders* (4th ed.). Washington, DC: Author.

Asperger, H. (1944). Die 'Autistichen Psychopathen' im Kindersalter. *Archiv für Psychiatrie und Nervenkrankheiten, 117*, 76-136.

Ebel, R. L. (1972). *Essentials of educational measurement* (2nd ed.). Englewood Cliffs, NJ: Prentice Hall.

Gilliam, J. E. (1995). Gilliam Autism Rating Scale. Austin, TX: PRO-ED.

Pyrczak, F. (1973). Validity of the discrimination index as a measure of item quality. *Journal of Educational Measurement, 10*, 227-231.

World Health Organization (1992). *ICD-10: International classification of diseases and related health problems*, (10th rev.). Geneva, Switzerland: Author.

[18]

Assessment for Persons Profoundly or Severely Impaired.

Purpose: Designed to measure the responsiveness of a preverbal individual's communicative functioning.

Population: Infants through adults who are preverbal and functioning with a mental age between approximately 0 and 8 months.

Publication Dates: 1984–1998.

Acronym: APPSI.

Administration: Individual.

Price Data, 2003: $153 per complete kit including examiner's manual (1998, 31 pages), 25 record booklets, 25 profile/summary forms, set of cards, and other manipulatives; $45 per examiner's manual; $45 per 25 record booklets; $25 per 25 profile/summary forms; $45 per object kit.

Time: Untimed.

Comments: A revision of the Preverbal Assessment—Intervention Profile (T4:2093).

Authors: Patricia Connard and Sharon Bradley-Johnson.

Publisher: PRO-ED.

a) STAGE I.

Population: Mental age 0–1 month.

Scores: 4 domains: Visual Responsiveness, Auditory Responsiveness, Tactile Responsiveness, Interaction with Others.

b) STAGE II.

Population: Mental age 1–4 months.

Scores: Same as *a* above.

c) STAGE III.

Population: Mental age 4–8 months.

Scores: 2 domains: Responsiveness to Objects, Interaction with Others.

Cross References: For reviews by Karen T. Carey and Joe Olmi of the earlier edition, see 11:301.

Review of the Assessment for Persons Profoundly or Severely Impaired by CAROLYN MITCHELL-PERSON, Associate Professor in the Special Education Department and Director of the Research Roundtable (Title III) at Southern University, Baton Rouge, LA:

DESCRIPTION. The purpose of the Assessment for Persons Profoundly or Severely Impaired (APPSI) is to provide assessment results relevant to planning effective intervention for individuals functioning at the lowest levels of mental development, regardless of the definition employed to classify their condition (examiner's manual, p. 1). It is a revision of the Preverbal Assessment-Intervention Profile (PAIP). The authors stated that the APPSI is consistent with and undergirded by the 1992 definition of mental retardation put forth by the American Association on Mental Retardation (AAMR). This definition differs from earlier ones because it represents a significant change in the way those with mental retardation are viewed. Rather than describing mental retardation as a state of global incompetence, the new definition refers to a pattern of limitations, looking at how people function in various contexts of everyday life (Hawkins-Shepard, 1994). One of the contexts defined in the AAMR definition is communicative behavior. The APPSI is designed to evaluate the communicative behavior of an individual who is functioning in Piaget's sensorimotor Stage IV with the following components: color/pattern cards (solid yellow, black-and-white checked, and pastel checked), a horn, maraca, squeaky toy, and objects to try for spectacle. Several additional objects in which the examinee has shown an interest are also needed. These items should be appropriate for waving, banging, and producing sound. The APPSI communicative domains are Visual, Auditory, and Tactile Responsiveness, as well as Responsiveness to Objects and Interactions with Others. The APPSI is not presented as a diagnostic instrument but as a tool to delineate intervention. The authors state that it provides information that should assist in planning individualized intervention programs, developing Individualized Education Programs (IEPs), and in planning and implementing IEP objectives.

DEVELOPMENT. During test validation, the samples used must be of adequate size and of sufficient representativeness to substantiate validity statements, to establish appropriate norms, and to support conclusions regarding the use of the instrument for the intended purpose. The APPSI, as a revision of the Preverbal Assessment-Intervention Profile (PAIP), resulted from organizational and clarification changes to the PAIP. Additionally, test materials and items were added and the separate motor skills domain was eliminated. The APPSI was piloted in three states with 39 individuals with severe and profound impairments. The sample consisted of 13 males and 19 females between the ages of 2 and 24 years. The individuals included in the sample had severe cognitive impairments and many had additional sensory impairments. Trained school psychologists tested each individual in her or his educational setting. The authors acknowledge that individuals with severe and profound impairments represent a relatively small population. No other specific demographic characteristics are given for the individuals included in the sample.

TECHNICAL. Fundamental to the evaluation of any instrument is the degree to which test scores are free from measurement error and are consistent from one occasion to another when the test is used with a target group (Rudner, 1994). Sources of measurement error, which include content sampling, contribute to an individual's score and lower a test's reliability. The authors state that content sampling reflects the degree of homogeneity among items within a test and that to determine the homogeneity, the internal consistency of the items must be studied. They used Cronbach's coefficient alpha method to study internal consistency. Cronbach's coefficients are reported for percentage scores for visual, auditory, and tactile responsiveness, and for the composite of the three. The scores resulted from responses to items that were scored dichotomously (i.e., *yes, a response occurred* or *no, a response did not occur*). In all sections of the test, individuals received a score of 1 for a response or 0 for no response. Cronbach's alpha is generally used for measures where participants respond to questions on a scale. The authors state that reliability coefficients must approximate or exceed .80 in magnitude for the test to be minimally reliable and that coefficients must be .90 or above to be considered most desirable. They report the alphas for the sensory modes and composite as highly acceptable; however, the magni-

tudes for the coefficients were computed and shown as .88 (Visual Responsiveness), .86 (Auditory Responsiveness), and .76 (Tactile Responsiveness). The magnitude of the composite is shown as .92.

The first important characteristic of a good test is adequate reliability. The second characteristic a test must have is validity. Validity is the relation between the trait and some important behavior that the investigator hopes to predict. The authors do not provide a discussion of validity.

Only professionals with graduate training in individual assessment should administer the APPSI. Examiners should understand both theory and research in tests and measurement, child development, educational psychology, and mental retardation, with further experience in working with individuals who are profoundly or severely mentally handicapped or multiply handicapped, including systematically observing their behavior.

Scoring of the APPSI is complex. The authors recommend that the manual be read several times before the initial administration of the test. Additionally, they recommend that the reader practice the test at least three times prior to the initial administration. The examiner is required to report both qualitative and quantitative information about the examinee's interactions with others, and her or his visual, auditory, and tactile responsiveness. During the administration the examiner must also consider the materials used, the length of exposure, distance at which the stimuli are presented, and the number of times the stimuli are presented. A record booklet is provided in which scores are to be placed. As stated above, if a response is made to a specific stimulus a score of 1 is awarded. If not, a score of 0 is awarded. Percentages are to be calculated by dividing the number of responses (represented by the score 1) by the total number of trials (number of times the stimuli are presented).

The authors provide detailed information about interpreting the results of the APPSI and provide good information about how to use the results in designing and implementing objectives for therapy. They also provide cautions for interpreting the results by stating that the assessment of individuals with severe and profound impairments is a complex task requiring knowledge of cognitive functioning and psychometrics, as well as experience working with individuals with severe/profound impairments. Although comprehensive in tapping crucial components of sensory modality responsiveness and preverbal communication skills, the APPSI is not recommended as an exhaustive measure of preverbal communication. The authors also caution that observation over time may be needed to provide enough information for conclusions about levels of functioning and skills that should be targeted for instruction.

COMMENTARY. After reviewing the APPSI, the reviewer had several concerns. First, even though the authors state that the requirement for administration of the APPSI is that examinees (newborn through adults) must be functioning in Piaget's sensorimotor Stage IV, there is no discussion of this stage or its characteristics. It appears to be assumed that the users of the APPSI will have previous knowledge of Piaget's stages and know that the sensorimotor stage is generally divided in six stages and that in Stage IV individuals generally exhibit the first clear evidence of thought (Owens, 2001). In Stage IV, individuals are capable of demonstrating imitation behaviors including facial imitation, manual searching for objects, the realization that objects can cause action, and the establishment of a goal prior to the initiation of an activity. Additionally, individuals in Stage IV generally demonstrate anticipation of outcomes. Neither Stage IV nor the two higher Piagetian stages (Stage V or VI) are evaluated. Only the lower stages (Stages I-III) are assessed. It would appear that because it is important to elicit an examinee's highest level of performance, all levels would be assessed. Additionally, essential information about the construction of developmental objectives would be provided to those responsible for designing and implementing intervention.

Second, the reviewer has concerns regarding the lack of demographic information about the subjects. The sample was described as having "*many* had additional sensory impairments" (examiner's manual, p. 25); however, there are no data nor is there a discussion of the type of sensory impairment or of the number who had sensory impairments. Three types of sensory responsiveness (visual, auditory, and tactile) provide the foundation of the APPSI. It would be beneficial if the authors provided a discussion of how and to what degree the sensory responsiveness of individuals with cognitive and sensory impairments was impacted and to what degree their responsiveness differed from those individuals with cognitive impairments only.

Third, concerns exist about the administration and scoring of the APPSI. The reviewer found the very detailed scoring and administration guidelines somewhat confusing and difficult to follow. For example, the instructions state that two 5-minute observations should be carried out during feeding and two during socialization/play. There is space provided on the record sheet to record scores and calculate percentages for these two observations; however, there are no instructions about how to include the two percentages in the total percentage count for the two observations.

Fourth, the *Code of Fair Testing Practices in Education* (Joint Committee on Testing Practices, 1988) specifies that test developers should identify and eliminate biased instruments and strive to make tests that are as fair as possible for test takers of different races, gender, ethnicity, or handicapping conditions. There is no discussion about whether or not the authors took steps during test development, validation, and norming to minimize the influence of ethnolinguistic factors on individual test scores.

SUMMARY. The APPSI was developed to provide information to use in the intervention for communicative functioning impairment of individuals with severe/profound impairments. The authors defined what the test measures and for what it is to be used. The reviewer applauds the effort of the authors to provide information about intervention planning for a population that is not easy to work with even though there are no clear statements about the specific characteristics of the population, how the sample was chosen, the identification and elimination of bias, nor about validity. As one part of an extensive intervention protocol for individuals with severe and profound impairments that must include obtaining pre-intervention baselines, consideration of ethnolinguistic diversity, the systematic use of specific stimulus-response-consequence procedures, the use of basic training techniques to facilitate learning, the organization and implementation of teaching sessions, and the systematic measurement of client performance and treatment efficacy, the APPSI can yield valuable information that contributes to effective and efficient intervention planning.

REVIEWER'S REFERENCES

Hawkins-Shepard, C. (1994). *Mental retardation.* Retrieved July 17, 2001 from the World Wide Web: http://ericec.org/digests/e528.html

Joint Committee on Testing Practices. (1988). *Code of fair testing practices.* Washington, DC: National Council on Measurement in Education.

Owens, R. E. (2001). *Language development: An introduction* (5th ed.). Boston: Allyn and Bacon.

Rudner, L. (1994). *Questions to ask when evaluating tests.* Retrieved July 17, 2001 from the World Wide Web: http://www.ed.gov/databases/ERIC_Digests/ed385607.html

Review of the Assessment for Persons Profoundly or Severely Impaired by LAWRENCE J. RYAN, California Licensed Psychologist, and Vice President and Academic Dean, St. John's Seminary College, Camarillo, CA, and Core Faculty Member, The Union Institute and University, Cincinnati, OH:

DESCRIPTION. The Assessment for Persons Profoundly or Severely Impaired (APPSI) is an untimed individual test designed to measure the responsiveness of a preverbal individual's communicative functioning. The APPSI is applicable for preverbal infants through adults with a mental age of approximately 0 to 8 months. The data that emerge from the APPSI are intended to assist in planning effective interventions. The test includes three stages (0–1 month, 1–4 months, and 4–8 months). At the first two stages four domains are measured (Visual Responsiveness, Auditory Responsiveness, Tactile Responsiveness, and Interaction with Others). At the third stage there are two domains (Responsiveness to Objects and Interactions with Others). At all stages the Interaction with Others domain items are derived from systematic observations of the examinee with his or her caregiver. One of the domain subtests includes the presentation of colorful and highly auditory stimulus objects such as a maraca, horn, plastic "Slinky," bells, and a squeaking rubber duck. All of these objects are highly attractive, and are delivered with the test kit inside a handy white mesh bag that helps the examiner to manage these materials. Scoring of the APPSI is based on observations of interactions between the caregiver and the examinee or between the examiner and the examinee. Response data are entered into a well-organized record booklet form and later transferred to a Profile/Summary Form. Scoring the APPSI requires the computation of a series of percentage scores for the various domain areas.

DEVELOPMENT. The APPSI is a revision and refinement of the Preverbal Assessment Intervention Profile (PAIP) (Connard, 1984). The research that constituted the basis for the PAIP and the APPSI emerged after the authors surveyed 26 measures employed to assess profoundly or severely mentally impaired individuals and observed only one instrument designed specifically for use with preverbal individuals. With its emphasis on the assessment of communication potential, the APPSI does not purport to assess any aspect of motor skills. The authors defer the evaluation of motor functions to the expertise of physical or occupational therapists. The APPSI is grounded in the Piagetian sensorimotor framework with particular focus on the communication of awareness, attending, and orienting behaviors as prerequisites to the development of functional language.

TECHNICAL. The standardization data for the APPSI are described as a pilot sample. The sample includes 32 individuals (13 males and 19 females) between the ages of 2 and 24 years with severe cognitive impairment. No information is offered regarding the geographic distribution or other demographic data regarding the members of the pilot sample. Testing was accomplished in an educational setting by trained school psychologists. The authors address reliability via the report of coefficient alpha internal consistency scores ranging from .76 to .88 for the APPSI domains, and .92 for the composite score. No validity data are reported in the manual.

COMMENTARY. The APPSI is an instrument that will have appropriate clinical application in specialized settings that provide evaluative services for profoundly impaired individuals. It is an instrument that requires considerable training and a strong background in developmental theory to administer. Effective administration and interpretation of the APPSI is likely to require considerable experience with the instrument as well as extensive background in observing and interacting with preverbal profoundly impaired individuals. Although the APPSI is an instrument with an acceptable level of face validity, other more specific validity data are not reported in the manual. Additionally, only minimal reliability data are presented. Because the APPSI administration procedures rely heavily on initiation activities of the examinee's caregiver, there is a high probability of variation in the standardized instructions. Although the APPSI administration instructions are clearly stated, precise scoring directions and standards are less discernible in the manual. In spite of its psychometric weaknesses, the APPSI provides a useful structure interactive observation framework that could result in meaningful recommendations for programming and care for profoundly impaired individuals.

SUMMARY. The APPSI is an individually administered instrument designed to assess indicators of communicative functioning in profoundly impaired individuals. Requiring considerable administrative and interpretive skill, the APPSI and its manual manifest some psychometric gaps in terms of its standardization sample, reliability, and validity data as well as in regard to scoring standards. The potential of the APPSI appears to lie in its potential use as a structured framework for observing and interacting with nonverbal and profoundly impaired individuals.

REVIEWER'S REFERENCE

Connard, P. (1984). The Preverbal Assessment-Intervention Profile. Austin, TX: PRO-ED.

[19]

Assessment of Language-Related Functional Activities.

Purpose: Designed to answer the question, "Despite this person's impairment, is he or she able to integrate skills adequately to perform selected functional daily activities?"
Population: People with suspected language or cognitive compromise, aged 16 to 95.
Publication Date: 1999.
Acronym: ALFA.
Scores, 10: Telling Time, Counting Money, Addressing an Envelope, Solving Daily Math Problems, Writing a Check and Balancing a Checkbook, Understanding Medicine Labels, Using a Calendar, Reading Instructions, Using the Telephone, Writing a Phone Message.
Administration: Individual.
Price Data, 2003: $159 per complete kit including 25 profile/examiner record forms, picture book, examiner's manual (39 pages), and an additional materials kit; $35 per materials kit including 10 tokens, clock, medicine chart, and 25 envelopes; $27 per 25 profile/examiner record forms; $56 per picture book; $45 per examiner's manual.
Time: (30–120) minutes.
Authors: Kathleen Anderson Baines, Heidi McMartin Heeringa, and Ann W. Martin.
Publisher: PRO-ED.

Review of the Assessment of Language-Related Functional Activities by STEVEN R. SHAW, Lead School Psychologist, Department of Developmental Pediatrics, The Children's Hospital, Greenville, SC, and Associate Professor of Pediatrics (Greenville), Medical University of South Carolina, Greenville, SC:

DESCRIPTION. The Assessment of Language-Related Functional Activities (ALFA) is a measure of functional skills on a set of language-related tasks. The ALFA is designed for persons between the ages of 16 and 95 who can understand the directions of the subtests, who are able to formulate the necessary responses, and who have some familiarity with the functional areas assessed. According to the authors, the purpose of the ALFA is to answer the following question, "Despite this person's impairment, is he or she able to integrate skills adequately to perform selected functional daily activities?" The 10 activities are: Telling Time, Counting Money, Addressing an Envelope, Solving Daily Math Problems, Writing a Check and Balancing a Checkbook, Understanding Medicine Labels, Using a Calendar, Reading Instructions, Using the Telephone, and Writing a Message.

DEVELOPMENT. Most clinicians are accustomed to impairment-centered tasks (i.e., measures that break down skills into component parts and processes, and then are analyzed). Traditional assessment focuses on impaired constructs (e.g., attention, pragmatic language, abstract reasoning, semantic language skills, and so on). In contrast to impairment-centered tasks, the ALFA provides a functional measure of language skills. Very likely, tests such as the ALFA will start to enjoy wider use due to requirements from several relevant organizations that require functional assessment of patients' skills. Medicare, Medicaid, managed care organizations, and private insurance organizations are all requiring evidence of positive outcomes of rehabilitation programs. Information from functional assessments is also critical in discharge planning, program development, and program evaluation.

TECHNICAL.

Reliability. Coefficient alpha provides evidence of internal consistency. For the normative sample, coefficients for the 10 subtests ranged from .80 to .88. Coefficient alphas for six clinical subgroups ranged from .73 to .93. That the six clinical subgroups had similar reliability coefficients was taken as evidence that the ALFA contains little or no bias relative to these groups. Although certainly a necessary condition, similar reliabilities are not adequate evidence supporting a claim of no bias.

Interscorer reliability was assessed with two staff people rescoring 30 protocols. Correlations between the examiners' scoring for the 10 subtests was $r = .99$.

For a test with potential utility for assessing change over time due to either recovery or rehabilitation, assessment of stability would appear to be essential. No studies of stability in absence of treatment, also known as test-retest reliability, appear in the manual. Without test-retest reliability data it is not possible to know if change over time is due to real change or the instability of the test.

Validity. The ALFA manual does not present adequate validity studies to allow judgment. The validity chapter of the manual provides a detailed content description of each subtest and the rationale for including the subtest in the ALFA. A study of 103 patients involved administration of the Reading Comprehension Battery for Aphasia and the ALFA. Correlations between these two measures were moderate (range = .43 to .71). However, the variance in cognitive ability in the sample of patients taking the test is unknown. This study was the only concurrent validity study reported in the manual. There is evidence that the ALFA scores increase as a result of therapy. A study of 41 patients receiving therapy improved dramatically on the ALFA. However, it is unclear whether this increase is due to test instability, practice effects, or therapy efficacy. Comparing mean scores of the normal sample and the clinical sample showed statistically significant differences on all 10 subtests of the ALFA.

Normative sample. The normative sample consisted of 150 normally functioning adults and 495 patients with clinical issues. The clinical population consisted of persons with the following diagnoses: first incidence right CVA, first incidence left CVA, multiple CVA, traumatic brain injury, dementia, and post surgical confusion or other events. The sample is consistent with the 2000 U.S. Census. The normal population is slightly overrepresented by females and whites. Although the ALFA is for persons ages 16 to 95, there are extremely few younger participants in the normative sample. Only 7% of the clinical group ($N = 34$) is 54 or younger. Only 14% of the normally functioning sample ($N = 21$) is 54 or younger. Because of the underrepresentation of

younger participants, the ALFA can be recommended only for persons 55 years of age and older.

The scoring system is derived from the normative sample. For each subtest, raw scores are converted into an independent functioning rating. These ratings are a 1, 2, or 3. A rating of 1 consists of the top 84% of the population and means that there is a high probability that the patient can function independently on the task. A rating of 2 consists of the patients from the 6th to 15th percentile. This rating means that the patients will need some level of assistance on the task. A rating of 3 is the lowest 5% of the population. This rating means that there is a high probability that the patient cannot function independently on the task.

COMMENTARY. Although the movement toward functional assessment rather than impairment-centered assessment is certain to be welcome by many clinicians, the ALFA has some technical weakness, and in some areas there is inadequate technical information provided in the manual. For example, when a test claims to be unbiased there should be some evidence that bias was appropriately investigated.

The ALFA has some strengths. Specifically, the collection of important daily living tasks are among tasks that many rehabilitation professionals will find are assessed more conveniently than by direct observation or by using homemade functional activities. A minor quibble, however, is there might be other functional language tasks that have been assessed and are frequent targets of rehabilitation such as social communication, understanding road signs, and describing physical symptoms to physicians. Although there are clearly some technical problems, the ALFA provides a rapid, easy, and practical method of assessment of functional activities of language.

SUMMARY. The ALFA assesses the ability of adults to integrate language skills to perform a variety of important functional activities. The ALFA is a rapid, easy-to-administer, easy-to-score, and flexible measure. There are some technical weaknesses including normative sample selection, lack of reported validity studies, lack of support for the claim that the ALFA is an unbiased test, and lack of reported reliability data. Future research may support the reliability, validity, and claim of unbiased testing, but the data presented in the manual are not adequate. Despite these weaknesses, the ALFA presents a much needed advance in functional assessment of important language-based skills. As such it is certain to find a niche in the assessment market.

Review of the Assessment of Language-Related Functional Activities by T. STEUART WATSON, Professor of Educational Psychology, and R. ANTHONY DOGGETT, Assistant Professor of Educational Psychology, Mississippi State University, Starkville, MS:

DESCRIPTION. The Assessment of Language-Related Functional Activities (ALFA) is designed to assess language-related functional skill levels in patients with acquired brain injury, including right hemispheric, left hemispheric, and subcortical cerebral vascular accidents (CVAs), traumatic brain injury, and progressive neurological diseases, and for use within the general geriatric population. The ALFA can be administered to individuals between the ages of 16-0 and 95-0. The ALFA can be used in a variety of patient settings: in- and outpatient rehabilitation programs, subacute rehabilitation programs, foster care homes, nursing homes, home health care, and other settings. The authors assert that the instrument is designed to provide physicians, family members, and other professional personnel with an objective assessment of functional language and cognitive skills that can be directly linked to treatment and aide in placement decisions as well as discharge plans. Furthermore, the authors indicate that the ALFA is designed to provide an objective evaluation of the treatment efficacy often required by third-party payors. Finally, the test constructors suggest that the speed and ease with which the ALFA can be administered facilitates its use in research with patients who have language or cognitive compromise and who cannot participate in lengthy neuropsychological evaluations for research purposes.

The ALFA contains 10 subtests: Telling Time, Counting Money, Addressing an Envelope, Solving Daily Math Problems, Writing a Check and Balancing a Checkbook, Understanding Medicine Labels, Using a Calendar, Reading Instructions, Using a Telephone, and Writing a Phone Message. Subtests 1, 2, 3 and 4 are timed. The first 9 subtests contain 10 questions each and the final subtest contains 5 questions. Total testing time ranges from approximately 30 minutes to 2 hours. The test can be given in its entirety or by selection of subtests that are directly relevant to patient needs. The ALFA is administered from a durable easel-bound picture book. The specific materials needed, subtest directions, and scoring guidelines are reported at the beginning of each subtest in the stimulus book. Answers are recorded in a dichotomous fashion, with the examiner recording a "1" for correct responses and a "0" for incorrect responses. The correct answers are included in the stimulus book and on the protocol form. The examiner's manual also includes additional instructions and examples for scoring Subtests 3, 5, and 10 as these subtests require written responses and may be harder to score. ALFA subtest results are recorded in numeric form as raw scores, percentages correct, and finally as Independent Functioning Ratings on the protocol form. The Independent Functioning Ratings serve as cut-off scores across three levels of ratings and allow the examiner to compare the degree to which the examinee can complete the specific task relative to the sample patient population.

All materials come in a cardboard box that is easily transportable. In addition to the easel-bound picture book and protocol forms, the kit also contains a wooden clock with metal hands, envelopes, plastic "pills," and a medicine chart. The examiner will need to supply a stopwatch, working telephone, local phone book, money, paper, and pen. Functional adaptive devices such as a calculator or magnifying glass may also be required, but not supplied, for some subtest items. Finally, the test manual competently provides additional information pertaining to examiner qualifications, building rapport, and minimizing error during test administration.

DEVELOPMENT. The rationale provided by the authors for developing the ALFA is the lack of psychometrically sound instruments specifically designed to assess multiple language-related functional activities as a whole, across language modalities, and the integrated functional skill level. The test developers further indicate that the skills assessed by the ALFA have traditionally been evaluated in a nonstandardized format making the outcome measures subjective and inappropriate for comparison within and between patient populations. The constructors of the ALFA also report that the objective and quantitative properties of the test minimize examiner bias often associated with nonstandardized measures of functional abilities. Finally, the test authors maintain that the ALFA was specifically designed to assist with all levels of patient programming including initial evaluation, goal setting, therapy activity planning, periodic progress assessment, discharge planning, and measurement of functional outcomes.

STANDARDIZATION. Participation was requested from a random sample of speech pathologists working in rehabilitation hospitals from all 50 states. Practitioners from 32 states responded and administered the ALFA to 10 to 20 patients who had experienced a first or multiple CVAs, TBI, or who were suffering from dementia, postsurgical confusion, or other relevant events. The examiners also administered the test to 1 to 5 normally functioning adults. As a result, 495 patients with neurologic traumas and 150 normally functioning adults served as the standardization sample. The demographic characteristics of the patients and normally functioning adults were based on population projections for the year 2000 by geographic region, gender, race, ethnicity, educational attainment, and age. Ninety-two percent of the patient population was 55 years or older and 86% of the normally functioning adult population was 55 years or older.

RELIABILITY. Two types of reliability were assessed: internal consistency and interrater. The authors provide two easy-to-read tables summarizing internal consistency reliability across two age groups, four patient subgroups, and gender. Average coefficient alphas for the subtests ranged from .80 to .88 across the two age groups. Coefficient alphas ranged from .73 to .93 across the four patient groups and from .77 to .92 across gender. Interrater reliability was assessed from 30 completed protocols on a sample ranging from 30-4 through 77-6 years in age. Interrater reliability was .99 across all 10 subtests. Test-retest reliability was not examined in the ALFA. This is a bit unfortunate as low test-retest coefficients would be further evidence that the ALFA is sensitive to treatment effects, as it is designed to be.

VALIDITY. Three types of validity were assessed: content validity, criterion-related validity, and construct validity. Content validity of the ALFA was addressed qualitatively through presentation of a detailed rationale for the formats and items of each subtest and quantitatively through use of the item-total-score Pearson correlation index. Discrimination coefficients ranged from .42 to .70 across two age levels. Criterion-related validity was assessed by correlating raw scores from the ALFA with another language-related test, the Reading Comprehension Battery for Aphasia (RCBA; LaPointe & Horner, 1979) while partialing for age. Correlations between nine subtests on the ALFA (Subtest 10 was dropped as it was only administered to a few participants) and the RCBA ranged from .43 to .71. Finally, five basic constructs thought to underlie the ALFA were tested to provide a measure of construct validity. The mean raw scores for the normally functioning sample used to standardize the ALFA were compared to the mean raw scores for three patient groups (right CVAs, left CVAs, and multiple CVAs) in order to test the hypothesis that the patient subgroups should perform lower on language-related tasks. Results revealed that raw score means for the three patient subgroups were 2 to 3 points below the normally functioning group's mean on most subtests. Second, three subtests (Telling Time, Counting Money, Solving Daily Math Problems) were used to determine the degree to which the ALFA could detect changes over time in patients receiving treatment, given that this is one of the reported purposes of the test. Statistically significant improvement was evidenced across all three tests. Third, patients suffering from a neurologic trauma scored significantly lower than normally functioning adults. Fourth, the ALFA subtests for the entire normative sample were intercorrelated to provide additional evidence of construct validity. All coefficients were statistically significant at or beyond the .0001 level. The final evaluation of construct validity was examined by correlating performance on the items with the total score on the ALFA. Resulting coefficients ranged from .42 to .70. All validity coefficients were presented in easy-to-read tables.

SUMMARY AND CONCLUSIONS. Overall, the ALFA appears to be a theoretically and psychometrically sound instrument for assessing language-related functional daily tasks in patients suffering from neurologic trauma and who are 55 years of age and older. Further research needs to be conducted for persons age 16-0 to 54-11 to demonstrate the usefulness of the instrument with this population whose functional language tasks are likely to be much different than those in the 55 and older age categories. With respect to its stated purposes, the ALFA appears to be appropriate as an assessment tool for assessing pretreatment functioning, planning therapy goals, and perhaps for evaluating treatment outcomes. The manual is written in a clear manner and the materials are user-friendly. Finally, the strengths of the ALFA include its adequate norm sample of patients ages 55 and older and normally functioning adults, brevity of administration, reliance on direct measures of behavior, assessment of relevant functional activities, linkage of assessment outcomes to intervention, and easy-to-understand results, all of which make it well suited for assessment and treatment evaluation.

REVIEWER'S REFERENCE

LaPointe, L. L., & Horner, J. (1979). Reading Comprehension Battery for Aphasia. Austin, TX: PRO-ED.

[20]

Assessment of Practices in Early Elementary Classrooms.

Purpose: "Designed to evaluate the use of developmentally appropriate practices in early elementary classrooms . . . that include children with disabilities."

Population: Kindergarten through Grade 3 classrooms.

Publication Date: 2001.

Acronym: APEEC.

Scores: Total score only.

Administration: Group or individual.

Manual: No manual.

Price Data, 2002: $11.95 per booklet (39 pages).

Time: Administration time not reported.

Comments: Assesses three domains of classroom practices: physical environment, curriculum and instruction, social context.

Authors: Mary Louise Hemmeter, Kelly L. Maxwell, Melinda Jones Ault, and John W. Schuster.

Publisher: Teachers College Press.

Review of the Assessment of Practices in Early Elementary Classrooms by EDWARD J. DALY III, Associate Professor of School Psychology, University of Nebraska—Lincoln, and MICHAEL PERSAMPIERI, Doctoral Student, University of Nebraska—Lincoln, Lincoln, NE:

DESCRIPTION. The Assessment of Practices in Early Elementary Classrooms (APEEC) is a 16-item test, administered through direct observation of the classroom and teacher interview. The examiner is to spend a day in the classroom, observing the items sampled by the test. Next, the examiner conducts a 20- to 30-minute interview with the teacher using suggested interview questions provided on the score sheet. All items are rated on a 7-point Likert-type scale with higher scores presumably representing the extent to which the classroom effectively uses developmentally appropriate practices. Individual items are scored according to descriptors that characterize the classroom setting and instructional practices. Scoring is largely subjective and conducted on a single day. The interview is not standardized and is made up of suggested, open-ended, and nonleading questions. Scoring examples are given only as a starting point and adjectives such as "few," "some," and "many" are left purposefully undefined, requiring users to exercise their own judgment relative to local circumstances.

Item scores are summed and the result is divided by the total number of items administered to produce a total score. The authors state, "Higher scores on the APEEC items are intended to reflect higher quality classrooms, which should be associated with positive child outcomes" (p. 1). Besides a general statement that the test can serve as a tool for "both practitioners and researchers who want to understand elementary school practices (K–3) in general education classrooms serving children with and without disabilities" (p. 1), no mention is made of specific uses of the test, types of decisions for which the test is appropriate, or how the scores can be used to improve classrooms. The classroom and not the student is the unit of analysis. However, given the diversity of disabilities that teachers are likely to encounter (e.g., a child with a mild learning disability versus a child with cerebral palsy), the lack of specificity of objectives and justified appropriate uses is especially problematic. Educators who are knowledgeable about developmentally appropriate practices, instruction in the early elementary grades, and special education would be most qualified to administer the APEEC.

DEVELOPMENT. It appears that the test was developed out of a perceived, pragmatic need for evaluation tools for developmentally appropriate practices in early elementary classrooms. Based on a review of the research literature, the position statement of the National Association for the Education of Young Children, and their collective professional experiences, the authors identified a number of potential items within a largely atheoretical model of three broad domains of classroom practices—physical environment, curriculum (exclusive of specific instructional content), and social context. Through a process of expert review, item try-out, analysis of interrater agreement, and subsequent item revision, the authors refined and reduced the number of items to 16. The items were field tested by the authors before publication.

Unfortunately, no empirical research is cited in support of how the items collectively represent the broad construct of developmentally appropriate practice. The authors also provide no empirical support or even a stated rationale for the 16 items on the test, leading us to question the relative importance of items such as Display of Child Products as compared to Instructional Methods, for example. The descriptors are often vague and no theoretical or empirical justification is provided for the ordering of descriptors (which is critical to the ratings that are given).

TECHNICAL. Although the authors report field-testing at two locations, they provide no details about the classrooms in which it was done and no standardization data are reported. Furthermore, the lack of standardization in the administration procedures coupled with the absence of objective scoring criteria only compound difficulties with interpretation of scores. As a result, there is simply no comparative index for establishing what the scores mean.

Several types of reliability data are reported. Interrater agreement (based on observations in 59 classrooms) was calculated for descriptors (the criteria that determine rankings for items) and items (both exact agreement and agreement within 1 point). Average interrater agreement for descriptors is .86 (range = .76 to .93); average interrater agreement for items is .58 (range = .31 to .81) for exact agreement and .81 (range = .5 to 1.0) for agreement within 1 point. The obtained median weighted Kappa is .59, and the measure of internal consistency, based on intraclass correlations, is .86.

Validity data are based on correlations with three other measures—the Assessment Profile for Early Childhood Programs (ABECP), the Teacher Beliefs and Practices Scale (TBPS), and the Caregiver Interaction Scale (CIS). Acknowledging that the ABECP was actually designed for use in preschool settings and not elementary school settings, the authors felt justified using it as a criterion measure because, "it had recently been used in elementary grades as well" (p. 2). Based on

data gathered in 69 classrooms, correlations with the APECP and CIS were .67 and .61, respectively. The TBPS yields two scores, one for Developmentally Appropriate Practices and one for Developmentally Inappropriate Practices. Correlations of the APEEC with these scales were .55 and -.28, respectively. The authors conclude, "Overall, the interrater agreement and validity data for the APEEC suggest that it is a valid, reliable tool for measuring individualized and developmentally appropriate practices in K–3 classrooms. Additional research is needed to understand further its psychometric properties" (p. 2).

COMMENTARY. We wish to state emphatically that we are sympathetic to efforts to develop scales that evaluate more than just child characteristics. The APEEC represents an attempt to assess the context in which students with disabilities are expected to learn and grow academically and socially, and for this we applaud the authors. From a psychometric perspective and, more importantly, from an educational decision-making standpoint, however, the result is quite disappointing. In addition to the ambiguity of test score meaning noted above, there are a number of other problems. The test suffers as a result of an antiquated notion of psychometric adequacy on the part of the authors; this notion is evidenced in their blanket endorsement of the test as a "valid, reliable tool." *The Standards for Educational and Psychological Testing* (American Educational Research Association, American Psychological Association, & National Council on Measurement in Education, 1999) clearly indicate that test validation is relative to specific decisions. Beyond scoring considerations, decision making is virtually ignored throughout the test. There is no guidance in appropriate uses and limitations of the test. Practitioners and researchers are not likely to find the test helpful for making determinations about developmentally appropriate practices.

We disagree with the authors that a few correlations adequately substantiate construct validity, and caution possible test users against naïve and narrow conceptualizations of construct validity. A stronger empirical rationale (e.g., factor analysis and other data analytic techniques) and theoretical and rational justification are needed to substantiate that the items adequately represent the construct of developmentally appropriate practices. Indeed, in its current form the test holds real potential for distracting educators from examining more robust and functionally relevant variables that are not included in the test. One can easily imagine a situation in which an examiner spends time evaluating whether displays of child products include three-dimensional pieces and whether hands-on materials are used for the majority of the day rather than evaluating whether instructional materials are of appropriate difficulty level and quality for teaching the curriculum (factors not examined by the test). A test of this type should be guided by considerations of *academic* and *social outcomes* for students, which represents the ultimate criterion of developmental appropriateness. This issue is not dealt with at all.

We were less impressed than the authors with the reliability data. Interrater agreement provides an upper-bound reliability estimate. Because examiners will interpret a *score* and not a range of scores, exact agreement is the appropriate metric for evaluating this form of interrater agreement. The subjective nature of the items and the poor interrater agreement suggest that results will probably not be reliable. There is also good reason to be concerned about other aspects that impact the decision reliability of the test. The test recommends that observations be conducted on 1 day only. Anyone associated with education knows how variable classrooms are from day to day. The lack of test-retest reliability and a format that encourages error prone practice are especially problematic. Finally, although the implicit purpose is to help make teachers deliver more developmentally appropriate educational experiences for children with disabilities, the test is completely devoid of when or how treatment plans should be formulated based on the results and facilitated by an independent party. Changing instructional practices of teachers involves a complex social influence process for a consultant or administrator (Erchul & Martens, 2002). A subjective observational tool that produces questionable results and offers no guidance in this process is not likely to contribute in a constructive way to increasing developmentally appropriate practices in classrooms.

SUMMARY. The test's acronym provides a suitable description of what it produces (i.e., "a peek"). Unfortunately, in view of the complexity involved in educating a child with disabilities with developmentally appropriate practices, the peek one gets is akin to looking through a door's peep hole. Because this population is vulnerable, greater psychometric rigor should be expected of tests that affect in any way these students' educational opportunities. Educators should require more than a peek at the weighty issues of decision reliability, construct validity, and treatment utility. If readers are interested in a test that permits careful examination of the instructional context and the appropriateness of instruction, The Instructional Environment System-II (Ysseldyke & Christenson, 1993; T6:1223) is a much stronger instrument by virtue of the careful, systematic development of domains and how results can be translated into instructional recommendations.

REVIEWERS' REFERENCES

American Educational Research Association, American Psychological Association, & National Council on Measurement in Education. (1999). *Standards for educational and psychological testing.* Washington, DC: American Psychological Association.
Erchul, W. P., & Martens, B. K. (2002). *School consultation: Conceptual and empirical bases of practice* (2nd ed.). New York: Plenum Press.
Ysseldyke, J., & Christenson, S. (1993). *The Instructional Environment System-II.* Longmont, CO: Sopris West, Inc.

Review of the Assessment of Practices in Early Elementary Classrooms by KATHLEEN A. DOLGOS, Professor of Education, Kutztown University of Pennsylvania, Kutztown, PA:

DESCRIPTION. The Assessment of Practices in Early Elementary Classrooms (APEEC) was developed to provide a tool for understanding elementary school practices in K–3 classrooms serving children with and without disabilities. It does not measure curricular content or in-depth teacher-child interactions. It also does not focus on the broader school environment or special subject classes.

The 16 items on the APEEC are grouped in three categories: Physical Environment (4), Instructional Context (6), and Social Context (6). Each item consist of several descriptors. There is a total of 135 descriptors across the 16 items. Physical Environment includes descriptors such as room arrangement and health and classroom safety. Instructional Context descriptors include use of materials and instructional methods. Social Context includes children's role in decision making and diversity.

Items are scored on a continuum of "1" to "7" (where 1 is inadequate and 7 is excellent), which represents the degree to which developmentally appropriate practices are used in the classroom. Each item is based on the rating of the observer who decides if the descriptors are true (T), not true (NT), or not applicable (NA). Descriptors also fall in the category of observation only, observation and interview, and interview only. If an interview is involved, suggested questions are included and 20–30 minutes need to be allotted to interview the teacher about classroom practices. Observations can be done in 1 full day.

Two different scoring methods can be used with the APEEC. The first method requires the observer to rate only those descriptors required to obtain an item-level score. The second scoring method is to use the APEEC as a checklist, scoring each of the 135 descriptors. The score sheet has space for descriptor-level scores, item-level scores, and observer notes. Interview questions are included where appropriate and space is provided for responses. A total APEEC score is found by totaling the item scores and dividing by the total number of items administered.

DEVELOPMENT. A multistep process was used to develop the APEEC. After a review of pertinent literature on early childhood and the insights drawn from the experiences of the authors, three domains of classroom practices were delineated. The domains were physical environment, curriculum and instruction, and social context. Forty items were developed using a 7-point response scale. The authors then sought the expertise of practitioners and researchers in the field. Sixty professionals were involved in the review process. Thirty were university faculty or employees of research institutions and 30 were practitioners. The authors revised the APEEC based on the reviewers' feedback and reduced the number of items to 22. After using the items in the classroom, the items were reduced to 16. Two of the authors pilot-tested the APEEC in the classroom again and then the authors field-tested the 16-item measure in 69 classrooms in the spring of 1998. The data from the field-test suggested that the APEEC is internally consistent, has good interrater agreement, and is a valid measure of developmentally appropriate practices.

TECHNICAL. In the 1998 field test, the interrater agreement and validity data were gathered from 69 classrooms, Grades K–3, in North Carolina and Kentucky. Interrater agreement was high at the descriptor level, item level, and total score level. At the descriptor level, the percentage agreement among two observers across the 135 descriptors averaged 86% with a range of 76% to 93%. At the item level, the average exact percent-

age of agreement was 58%, ranging from 31% to 81%. A Kappa statistic, which accounts for chance agreement and the degree of disagreement between observers, was calculated. Kappas of .50 or higher are considered to be acceptable levels of agreement. Of the 16 items of the APEEC, 12 items were .50 or higher. Two items fell below .47. The median weighted Kappa was .59.

Internal consistency was also measured. The interclass correlation between the two observers' ratings was .86. Due to the resulting Kappas and the high correlation, it was suggested that a high level of interrater agreement occurs with the APEEC.

Construct validity evidence was provided by comparing the APEEC to two other measures of developmentally appropriate practices. It was compared to the Assessment Profile for Early Childhood Programs (Abbott-Shim & Sibley, 1988) and the Teacher Beliefs and Practices Scale (Buchanan, Burts, Bidner, White, & Charlesworth, 1998; Charlesworth et al., 1993). To measure teacher-child interaction, the APEEC was compared to the Caregiver Interaction Scale (Arnett, 1989). The Pearson correlations between the APEEC and the three measures mentioned ranged from .55 to .67. Overall, the data suggest that the APEEC provides valid and reliable scores for measuring developmentally appropriate practices in K–3 classrooms.

COMMENTARY. The authors emphasize that to use the APEEC successfully, the observer must be knowledgeable about developmentally appropriate practices, early elementary classrooms, and special education practices. The vocabulary of the items reflects the profession and would be clear to an experienced educator.

The score sheet is separate from the written items/descriptors to be observed. This going back and forth from statements and numbers to the scoring sheet adds one more layer of converting the scores to a final score. The written item, numbers (1–7), and interview questions should all be on one page for reading ease. Determining the item-level score can also be a challenge. Observers need to be well trained in understanding how the 1–7 scores are obtained.

In looking at the two possible scoring methods suggested, I recommend using the entire APEEC as a checklist, scoring each of the 135 descriptors. The results will give a better overall look at the use of developmentally appropriate practices in a particular classroom.

SUMMARY. The authors have developed the APEEC to be used in Grades K–3 to determine if developmentally appropriate practices are being used in the classroom. The item descriptors do reflect the philosophy of the early childhood classroom, special education practices, and developmentally appropriate practice. The interrater agreement and validity data for the APEEC suggest that it provides valid and reliable scores that measure the teaching strategies used in the K–3 classroom. Training in the use of the scoring sheet is a must to insure consistency among observers.

REVIEWER'S REFERENCES

Abbott-Shim, M., & Sibley, A. (1988). Assessment Profile for Early Childhood Programs. Atlanta, GA: Quality Assist.

Arnett, J. (1989). Caregivers in day-care centers: Does training matter? *Journal of Applied Developmental Psychology, 10*, 541–552.

Buchanan, T. K., Burts, D. C., Bidner, J., White, V. F., & Charlesworth, R. (1998). Predictors of the developmental appropriateness of the beliefs and practices of first, second, and third grade teachers. *Early Childhood Research Quarterly, 13*, 459–483.

Charlesworth, R., Hart, C. H., Burts, D. C., Thomasson, R. H., Mosley, J., & Fleege, P. O. (1993). Measuring the developmental appropriateness of kindergarten teachers. *Early Childhood Research Quarterly, 8*, 255–276.

[21]
Attitudes Toward Industrialization.

Purpose: Designed to measure "desire for industrialization (versus status quo or retention of agrarian situation) of a region or community."
Population: College-age students.
Publication Date: No date.
Scores: Total score only.
Administration: Individual.
Price Data, 2001: $2 per specimen set.
Time: (10) minutes.
Author: Donald E. Kaldenberg.
Publisher: Psychometric Affiliates.

Review of the Attitudes Toward Industrialization by L. CAROLYN PEARSON, Professor of Education, University of West Florida, Pensacola, FL and TREY MARTINDALE, Assistant Professor, East Carolina University, Greenville, NC:

DESCRIPTION. Attitudes Towards Industrialization was designed as a short instrument to aid community groups that are considering industrial expansion. The author states that attitude towards industrialization is a one-dimensional construct that constitutes a continuum of underlying variables, yet the variables are never identified. The individual version of the instrument consists of 18 items that can be self-scored using a 5-point Likert scale with values that range from *strongly agree* to *strongly disagree*. The instrument requires approximately 10 minutes to complete. The directions briefly state what is being measured and that there are no right or wrong choices; however, there is no indication of exactly how responses should be marked. A key is included, which is simply a scoring matrix indicating which items should be reverse-scaled when totaling the items. The instrument needs to be reformatted and the items revised for clarity. For example, instead of stating "New younger people will bring 'wider' interests to our region," a better statement would be "An influx of young people will bring diverse interests to our region." Many of the statements are either grammatically poor, unnecessarily complex (containing more than one idea), and/or are regionally specific (e.g., rolling hills, farmland). A manual of instructions is included that provides minimal information on item construction and refinement, evidence of reliability and validity, and normative data.

DEVELOPMENT. The author derived an initial pool of 97 items by developing attitude statements from nine 1-hour taped interviews from an unknown number of Iowa State University students enrolled in industrial and agricultural courses. Based on the agreement of four out of five raters, 69 of the initial 97 items were retained. The 69 items were then administered to 110 students using the same 5-point Likert scale as the final version. The total score distribution was then obtained for the upper and lower 27% of the respondents to determine the respective discrimination of high and low groups. Due to nonnormality of the total score distribution, appropriate nonparametric analyses were used to examine the internal consistency of the responses. These analyses led to a further reduction, resulting in 43 items. A criterion measure was also developed based on eight objective background items: father's occupation, size of high school from which graduated, high school subjects elected, population of home community, part of newspaper usually read first, occupational field believed to offer the most opportunity today, present major field, and desire to complete a major in another field, and if so, what field. The high and low groupings were analyzed using the same technique that determined internal consistency. Using the results from both methods, the final instrument was composed of 18 items.

TECHNICAL. Information describing the norming process was not included in the instructional manual. The manual did include raw score totals and their corresponding percentile ranks from a sample of 110 Iowa State students and 100 Northwestern University and Illinois Institute of Technology engineering students. The author gave no explanation for the selected sample, which led us to assume it was a convenience sample. The author investigated gender differences and found that males exhibited significantly more favorable and less diverse attitudes toward industrialization than females. No other variables (e.g., ethnicity, age, education) were investigated in the norming process.

Internal consistency reliability, estimated from the original sample on the final 18-item version, was .80 when corrected for length. No other estimates to support reliability were provided. Evidence to support validity was also weak. Total scores on the final 18-item version were positively correlated with total scores of the 8-item background criterion (r = .55). In examining concurrent validity, there was also a low correlation between the attitude scores and intelligence scores (r = .12 with ACE L, and r = .16 with Q score). The author does not provide any rationale for why a positive correlation with intelligence scores provides support of validity. Graphs of the distributions of scores representing the high and low criterion groups were presented, but the author did not explain how the 6-point classification scale was derived, or what the graphs mean.

COMMENTARY. The lack of norming data and limited evidence of reliability and validity severely compromise the value of the instrument as a measure of attitudes towards industrialization. The items were never grounded in a solid conceptual framework, and they need substantial revision. The entire form appears dated and needs reformatting. The author provides no rationale or theoretical framework for the statements that are used as the items. The author also provides weak documentation of the logical analysis of how the items were developed, pre-tested, and selected. Ultimately the user of the instrument must determine if attitudes towards industrialization are really being measured.

Unfortunately, some of the items also address contexts that may not be appropriate for the user's environment. Also, it appears that the au-thor did not conduct any additional empirical studies to build a case for reliability and validity of scores from the instrument. There is also no evidence of research to determine if the items are free of bias. Therefore, this attitude measure is probably only suitable for facilitating discussion among community groups.

SUMMARY. The Attitudes Toward Industrialization instrument is completely lacking in a conceptual framework for item construction and is based on weak empirical evidence. We doubt that this instrument is capable of providing any useful information concerning attitudes towards industrialization. Further studies that gather empirical evidence about the instrument's reliability, validity, and biases have yet to be provided. We cannot recommend this instrument as a measure of attitudes towards industrialization.

[22]

Attitudes Towards Guns and Violence Questionnaire.

Purpose: Designed to measure "attitudes concerning guns, physical aggression, and interpersonal conflict."
Population: Ages 6–29.
Publication Date: 2000.
Acronym: AGVQ.
Scores, 6: Total (Favorable or Unfavorable to Violence and Guns), Inconsistent Responding, Aggressive Response to Shame, Comfort with Aggression, Excitement, Power/Safety.
Administration: Group.
Price Data, 2002: $86 per kit including 25 score forms, manual, computer disk for on-site scoring, 2 PC answer sheets, 50 Aggressive Behavior checklists (25 teacher forms and 25 student forms); $32.50 per 25 answer forms; $39.50 per manual; $19.95 per 100 Aggressive Behavior checklists (teacher or student form); $85 per Windows scoring computer disk (good for 50 uses); $125 per Windows screening computer disk (good for 100 uses); $15 per 100 PC answer sheets.
Time: (5–10) minutes.
Author: Jeremy P. Shapiro.
Publisher: Western Psychological Services.

Review of the Attitudes Towards Guns and Violence Questionnaire by STEPHEN E. TROTTER, Associate Professor, Department of Psychology, Tennessee State University, Nashville, TN:

DESCRIPTION. The Attitudes Towards Guns and Violence Questionnaire (AGVQ) is a 26-item checklist utilizing a pencil-and-paper carbonless autoscore process or scored via a computer program. The test takes approximately 5–10 minutes to complete and reportedly requires a third grade reading threshold. The respondent is asked to rate statements along a 3-point Likert continuum consisting of *agree, not sure, disagree.* The test yields an overall score, four subtest scores, and a validity scale for a total of six scores. The test is described as appropriate for ages 6–29 with at least third grade reading ability. The test may be administered by a wide variety of staff but the interpretation of the results of the instrument requires the supervision of a psychologist or like trained individual. The manual (p. 2) identifies uses of the AGVQ as clinical, research and program evaluation.

The author clearly states the objective is an attitudinal not behavioral measure and as such addresses motivational and cognitive factors that may influence behavior. The manual provides clear directions for hand scoring the protocol. The manual also provides a scale-by-scale listing of items (p. 15). Of particular interest to users is a section on "Implications for prevention and treatment" (pp. 19–23).

DEVELOPMENT. Part II of the manual provides background data on the development and standardization of the AGVQ. The instrument is new (copyright 2000) and is no doubt a result of a felt need regarding perceived increases in violence in general and particularly school student on student or student on teacher violence utilizing hand guns. It should be noted that the highly publicized cases in Stockton, California, Santee, California, and Colorado involved a variety of weapons including but not limited to hand guns. The manual cites compelling data addressing the increase in homicide rate involving handguns. In addition, research is cited for the relationship between handguns and violent crime. The standardization population is reported in the manual and is fairly representative of the recent Census figures for the United States, with gender balancing, ethnic representation and geographical representation all within appropriate parameters. The normative group may be somewhat more educated than the general population with 17% of the heads of household reporting postgraduate degrees.

TECHNICAL. The factor structure of the instrument (i.e., four scales) appears well supported by the factor analysis results using varimax and promax rotation to arrive at an oblique solution resulting in congruency coefficients ranging from 97 to 98. Factor loadings are reported as a function of SES, gender, age, ethnicity, and geographic region.

The validity section includes data on construct, criterion, concurrent, and discriminant validity. Construct correlations were reported as statistically significant but appeared generally very low, ranging from .17 to .30 on the Devereux Behavior Rating Scale—Teacher Report. Significant relationships between self-esteem measures (Piers-Harris Children's Self-Concept Scale) and the AGVQ subscales were near zero in keeping with some theorists' positions regarding the independence of the two variables.

Criterion validity presents a conundrum. Despite assurances to the contrary, a clear distinction is not made in the mind of this reviewer that "Gun" is clearly understood to stand for handgun and not a class of weapons. The instructions, sample items, and test items never specify to the reader that a rifle is not a part of the class of weapons referred to as "guns" on the scale. Therefore, items addressing "gun" ownership may be misconstrued to include rifles. The developmental sample provided the basis for this supporting evidence and was composed exclusively of metropolitan Cleveland youths. It is also noted that only 55 individuals self-identified as gun owners. It may well be that gun ownership in rural areas of the United States or in the general norming population might have generated different outcomes.

Discriminant validity based on research with adjudicated youths aged between 12–17 resulted in mixed findings. Those youths identified as current violent offenders were lower or equal on all scales when compared to nonviolent offenders. This may well highlight the danger of impression management endemic to self-report rather than reflect on the lack of discriminatory power of the AGVQ.

COMMENTARY. The instrument no doubt comes at a time when concerns regarding youth violence in schools are at a high point. In addition, the terrorist attacks of 9-11-01 in the United States have increased gun sales. This event and its fallout may well present a threat to the validity of this instrument and its research regarding the relationship of gun ownership and the propensity for violence. In addition, despite claims to the contrary, a clear distinction is not made on the test form in regard to rifle versus handgun. Paraphrasing an item "I'd like to own a gun" may be open to a wide variety of interpretations of weapon type by individuals aged 6–29. The test instructions do not instruct individuals that gun is to be construed as limited to handgun and not rifle. This is further compounded by much of the AGVQ validity research being based on the urban developmental sample rather than a mix of urban and rural participants.

With these caveats in mind the instrument remains useful for a wide variety of its intended uses. The Aggressive Behavior Checklist (ABC) is included in the manual to assess the behavioral component of violence. The combined use of the two allows for the foundation of a multiple gating approach that may prove fruitful in identifying psychopathology or precursors to violent behaviors (Loeber, Dishion, & Patterson, 1984). The reviewer believes it would be very useful as a pre and post measure to a variety of treatment and educational programs. As a predictor or profiler of violent tendencies it is obviously limited as are most self-report measures. As a screener for suspected at-risk students it may serve well as a step in secondary prevention (Kauffman, 1989).

SUMMARY. Its strengths lie in its brevity, ease of administration and scoring (both hand and computer), and its relative low cost. The inclusion the Aggressive Behavior Checklists is also helpful in identifying those clients who have acted upon their aggressive belief systems. It might well provide a basis for discussion in both group and individual therapy of youthful offenders. The factors (aggressive response to shame, comfort with aggression, excitement, and power/safety) all are issues that may arise in clinical work with youths and young adults.

REVIEWER'S REFERENCES

Kauffman, J. M. (1989). *Characteristics of behavior disorders of children and youth* (4th ed.). Columbus, OH: Merrill Publishing.

Loeber, R., Dishion, T. J., & Patterson, G. R. (1984). Multiple gating: A multistage assessment procedure for identifying youths at risk for delinquency. *Journal of Research in Crime and Delinquency, 21,* 7–32.

Review of the Attitudes Toward Guns and Violence Questionnaire by DELORES D. WALCOTT, Associate Professor, Western Michigan University, University Counseling and Testing Center, Kalamazoo, MI:

DESCRIPTION. The Attitudes Toward Guns and Violence Questionnaire (AGVQ) is a 26-item, self-report questionnaire that can be administered to either an individual or a group. The AGVQ was designed to measure attitudes concerning guns, physical aggression, and interpersonal conflicts. The AGVQ can be used with delinquent and psychiatric populations when involvement with guns and violence is of concern. Each item is a statement related to some aspect of violence, guns, or conflict behavior. The AGVQ is appropriate for children and adolescents aged 6–18, as well as young adults aged 19–29. Six scores are obtained on the AGVQ: the Total Score, the Inconsistent Responding Score, and four subscale scores: Aggressive Response to Shame Score, Comfort With Aggression Score, Excitement Score, and Power/Safety Score. These factor-based scores assess attitudinal components of overall attraction to guns and violence. Interpretation is based on validity indicators, *T*-score elevation, content interpretation, and subscale comparison. The Inconsistent Responding Score, which is the validity indicator, is meant to measure whether an individual's item responses appear to be unrelated to the item content. Raw Score obtained for the Total Score and the four subscales are converted to *T*-scores and percentiles scores, which are stratified by age and gender subgroupings. The questionnaire has clinical application in mental health facilities and juvenile justices, as well as school and counseling settings. As a research tool, the AGVQ can be used to investigate variables associated with violence-related tendencies.

The AGVQ can be scored either by computer or by hand. The manual includes a separate chapter for computer scoring. The questionnaire is easily administered, which makes it an attractive choice. The AGVQ was written so that it can be read by anyone with at least a third grade reading level. The manual also indicates that younger individuals may need to have the items read to them. Instructions for administering the questionnaire, which are detailed in the manual, are clear and explicit. The AGVQ test form, "What's Your Opinion?" can be administered in just 5–10 minutes. There are two versions of the test form, the AGVQ AutoScore form for hand scoring and the computer-scored AGVQ PC answer sheet. The AGVQ questionnaire can be administered and scored by paraprofessionals with adequate training. However, appropriate use and interpretation of the instrument requires supervision of a psychologist or other professionals with appropriate training. As in the case of most questionnaires, the AGVQ Scores must be interpreted cautiously and in conjunction with information from other sources. Included in the AGVQ test kit is the Aggressive Behavior Checklist, which measures actual aggressive and violent behavior with children between the ages of 11 and 13. The student and/or teacher using the appropriate form can complete the Aggressive Behavior Checklist by rating the student's actual aggression or violent behavior. This instrument was included and referenced in the AGVQ manual in an effort to complement results obtained from the AGVQ.

DEVELOPMENT. The Attitudes Toward Guns and Violence Questionnaire (AGVQ) comprises a 3-point Likert-type scale with response options of Agree, Not Sure, and Disagree. Items involving antiviolence statements are reverse-scored, so that high scores always indicate violence proneness. The AGVQ was developed to measure specific attitudes toward guns, particularly handguns, because they play an important role in the problem of youth violence today. In essence, the AGVQ is an attitudinal measure that looks at beliefs, motives and emotional concerns, aggression, and conflict. It should be noted that the author made a distinction between users of rifles for hunting and those with a specific interest in guns for use against people.

The AGVQ manual makes reference to the AGVQ being developed over the course of several studies. Initially, a pilot version of the measure for the purpose of determining the instrument's psychometric properties was administered to 451 fifth, seventh, and ninth grade students in an urban (Cleveland) public school system. Responses to the items were inspected to identify the best set of original items to retain in the final instrument. Of the 79 candidate items, 61 exhibited adequate correlations. Factor analysis revealed four major factors, which make up the current four subscales. A second study (1997) of 1,619 students, also drawn from students in the Cleveland area, included 930 boys and 680 girls from diverse ethnic backgrounds. In the second study, 52 of the 61 items meet the criteria for item retention. In order to shorten the test it was decided to remove items with secondary loading or marginal primary loading resulting in the author retaining 23 items. Several analyses were performed to determine if decreasing the items compromised the internal

consistency and validity of scores from the test. Cronbach's alpha for the 23 items yields a measure of .88, compared to .94 for the 52 items. The correlation between Total Score on the shortened version of the tests and validation items was .65 compared to .63 for the 52 items. For both the 61-item and the 23-item versions of the tests, the mean score for gun owners (only 5% of the sample) was approximately 1% *SD* greater than the mean score for nonowners. These results suggested that shortening the instrument did not reduce its utility. Two other analyses were carried out to assess the stability of the AGVQ factor structure across the long and shortened version of the test. These findings indicated a high degree of stability for the AGVQ's factor structure. In the final form, the AGVQ yielded four subscales made up of 23 items and 3 additional items, which make up the Inconsistent Responding Scale.

TECHNICAL. Normative data were collected from 1,508 children ages 6–18, and young adults ages 19–29. Reportedly, the sample was ethnically and socioeconomically diverse, and was drawn from major geographical regions of the United States. Socioeconomic was defined in terms of head of household's years of education. Follow-up studies revealed that boys obtained higher scores than girls on the Aggressive Response to Shame, the Excitement, the Comfort with Aggression, and the Power/Safety subscales. Although these group differences are not large, it was decided to provide separate norms based on gender. AGVQ score differences related to age were substantial, therefore aged-based norms were also provided.

Reliability was estimated by Cronbach's alpha. Reportedly, reliabilities on each of the subscales obtained by the standardization sample were .87 for the Total Score, .84 for Aggressive Response to Shame, .81 for Comfort With Aggression, .82 for Excitement, and .73 for Power/Safety. Although these numbers are impressive as indicated in the manual, the alpha statistic is technically a measure or scale of homogeneity and is believed to mark the lower boundaries of reliability.

The correlations of Total Score with subscale scores were reported to be high, with low to moderate correlations among subscales. Moderating demographic variables in the form of *T*-scores revealed information about the relationship between geographic, ethnicity, socioeconomic status, age, grade, and gender. There were no interregional differences noted of significance. Meaningful group differences were observed for the Native American group, but the small number of respondents makes it impossible for realistic comment. There were also significant group differences indicated for the White and Other groups and between the White and Black groups. Reportedly, the actual size of the differences associated with ethnicity was relatively small. Socioeconomic (SES) status showed notable difference between Aggressive Response to Shame Score for the two highest and two lowest SES groups. Boys obtained higher scores than girls on Aggressive Response to Shame, Excitement, Comfort with Aggression, and Power/Safety scales. Likewise, large score differences related to age were obtained. Therefore, it was decided to have separate norms based on gender and age.

Two subscales of the Devereux Behavior Rating Scale, School Form, were used to provide construct validity. When compared to the teachers' reported Devereux subscales, the AGVQ Total Scores showed correlations of .27 with Interpersonal problems and .29 with Inappropriate Behavior and Feelings. When the AGVQ subscales were examined separately, correlations were significantly different for Aggressive Response to Shame, Comfort with Aggressive, and Excitement scores, but not for Power/Safety scores. It should be noted that a self-report adaptation of the Devereux was constructed for this study, which leads the reviewer to question the validity of using this measure to examined construct validity. Construct validity of the AGVQ was also based on a large study that examined the relationship between students' ratings of their own behavior, teachers' ratings of students' behavior, and AGVQ Total Score. The correlation between students' self-report of their aggressive behavior and their attitudes reflected by the AGVQ Total scores was low (.27).

Self-reported gun ownership was used to assess criterion validity. Findings obtained from the development sample indicated that AGVQ scores for gun owners and for those who denied ownership had a mean of 25.89 and 13.15, respectively. Discriminate Validity was examined by administering the AGVQ to 66 residents of a juvenile correctional faculty (50 males and 16 females). Subscales to Total Score correlations were high and intersubscale corrections were in the low to moderate range.

COMMENTARY. The author has produced a questionnaire that can be administered, scored, and interpreted in a relatively efficient and cost/effective manner. The manual is easy to follow and the figures and instruction in the manual help ease scoring. Practice questions on the questionnaire are particularly helpful. Figures used to assist in scoring instructions helped ease the process of scoring. In general, the entire manual contains enough information for a qualified user or reviewer of a test to evaluate the appropriateness of the test. However, the value of the AGVQ as a measure of adolescents' attitudes toward violence and aggression seems compromised. It is a known fact that self-reporting questionnaires are vulnerable to underreporting, distortions due to response style bias, inaccurate reporting, defensiveness, and denial. This is true with most self-reporting measures. This is particularly true given the nature of the attributes being assessed with the AGVQ. Adolescents tend to be concerned about self-presentation to others; therefore, they may be reluctant to reveal their true feelings regarding guns and violence. The author acknowledges that the test items are intrusive (e.g., "I'd like to have a gun so that people would look up to me," "carrying a gun makes people feel powerful and strong"), and that adolescents are likely to minimize or underreport their involvement with guns and aggressive behavior. The inclusion of the Inconsistent Responding Scale to address this concern is noted. However, the reliability of scores from the test remains a concern. As a clinical instrument, the AGVQ questionnaire seems suspect when evaluating adolescents given the domain being measured. Therefore, if used as a clinical tool, other assessment sources are indicated. However, as a research tool the anonymous nature of data collection information can add to a much-needed area of study.

This reviewer's major reservation is a question of validity as normative data were collected on a restricted population. The instrument was developed and standardized primarily with public schools and a few private schools across the United States. The developer does not state how the norm group compares to the United States population in general. To assume that norms of the volunteer group can be generalized to schools in general is erroneous. To the author's credit, a series of studies specifically designed to objectively evaluate the reliability and validity of the revised version of the

Attitudes Toward Guns and Violence Questionnaire was included.

SUMMARY. Although the Attitudes Toward Guns and Violence Questionnaire is available as a clinical tool and as a research tool, caution must be emphasized. Tests users should proceed with caution when interpreting AGVQ test results. Although self-reports have clear limitations, they have some validity related to standardization, economics, limited training required for administration, and administration time. Perhaps using the scale as a quick screen or as a way to elicit further information in an interview may be appropriate. Additional research on the technical quality of the test, using larger samples that include sufficient numbers in varying ethnic and educational background, is also needed. These concerns should be addressed in future publications of this questionnaire.

[23]
Australian Developmental Screening Checklist.

Purpose: Designed to "identify children who display signs of early developmental delay."
Population: Ages 3–60 months.
Publication Dates: 1968–1994.
Acronym: ADSC.
Scores, 5: Personal/Social, Language, Cognition, Fine Motor, Gross Motor.
Administration: Individual.
Price Data: Available from publisher.
Time: (10–15) minutes.
Author: Barry Burdon.
Publisher: The Psychological Corporation [Australia].

Review of the Australian Developmental Screening Checklist by JAMES A. ATHANASOU, Associate Professor, Faculty of Education, University of Technology, Sydney, Australia:

DESCRIPTION. The purpose of the Australian Developmental Screening Checklist (ADSC) is to identify children who display signs of early developmental delay (examiner's manual, p. 3). The aim is to provide assistance or interventions that overcome the delay as early as possible. The target population for the test is children from 6 to 60 months of age. The checklist is not designed for diagnosis, rather it aims to identify a need for more detailed assessment if a delay is indicated as a result of the ADSC. It is an indi-

vidually administered checklist that takes around 10–15 minutes and is designed for a range of users, such as early childhood teachers. Information for the checklist is obtained from persons who are well acquainted with the child or from personal observations of the child through informal interactions.

The checklist contains 180 items and yields five scores in the Personal-Social, Language, Cognition, Fine Motor, and Gross Motor domains. Users are required to establish a basal level and then record any item delays in development. Assessment continues until a ceiling level is reached, where failure occurs on three consecutive items. Performance is judged relative to chronological age. Children are classified as *well above* (2 or more months above the chronological age), *satisfactory* (at or 1 month above the chronological age), *slightly below* (1–2 months below the chronological age), or *well below* (more than 2 months below the chronological age). Overall developmental status is classified as "Assessment recommended," "Monitor," or "No delay" on the basis of a number of criteria. For instance, one of the three criteria for "Assessment recommended" is "one domain with more than two item delays" (p. 33).

DEVELOPMENT. Work on the checklist commenced as early as 1973 and the first version was prepared in 1985. The revision of earlier materials for the ADSC commenced in 1989. The checklist contains items that focus on responses that occur in everyday contexts and behaviors that are observable. Items are structured to reflect developmental progress. A pool of some 1,000 items was obtained from existing instruments and a review of the literature on age-related behaviors. A reduced pool of items was then piloted with child care staff and observations were made to determine the age-related occurrence of the items and their ease of assessment. Items were assigned to age groups based on the criterion that 90% of children in the norm group passed that item. The procedures for the refinement of items are not spelled out clearly in the manual. The ADSC has items arranged in five descriptive developmental domains but makes no claim to assess these domains as constructs. The criteria for the allocation of an item to a domain is not outlined but is described as being made on the basis of consultations with professionals.

TECHNICAL. The ADSC was standardized on a metropolitan sample of 127 children in

South Australia and renormed in 1992 on a sample of 436 children. Tables are provided that show the occupation of parents, birthplace of parents, and their socioeconomic status, but no statistical comparison is made with census data. Available evidence indicates effects of race and maternal formal education on early screening profiles of 2–6-year-olds in the U.S. (e.g., Ittenbach & Harrison, 1990). It is not possible, however, to determine the appropriateness of these norms or performance on the ADSC for socioeconomic, gender, indigenous, or ethnic groups or for different geographical locations throughout Australia.

Test-retest reliability was examined for a group of 32 children across a period of no longer than 3 weeks. Reliability was determined using kappa (K = .84) together with interrater reliability (K = .83). The sample was dominated by children who had no delay. Furthermore, reliability estimates of the scores within each of the five domains are also required for an objective evaluation of the ADSC because these domains are listed on the record form. Finally, the interrater reliability is really an indication of validity of results rather than an estimate of the stability of a child's behavior.

Classification scores on the ADSC correlated .82 (N = 74) with its predecessor, the Australian Developmental Record for Infants and Young Children; however, a product-moment correlation may not be appropriate given the skewed and nonnormal distribution of classifications listed. The ADSC classified correctly 14 children who had been identified as having some developmental delay as "Assessment Recommended." The specificity of the classifications of the ASDC was also compared against its predecessor using the data in the criterion-related validity but other useful comparisons such as with parental concern might also be investigated. McGinty (2000) reported a significant association between parental concern for language development and pass/failure on screening measures.

COMMENTARY. The 34–39 items that constitute each domain reflect a useful developmental sequence and address the assessment task directly. An underlying assumption is that development within each domain is orderly and structured. The ASDC offers a coherent and structured checklist of behaviors in a helpful and easy-to-use format that will appeal to a wide range of professional groups. It builds upon a considerable pedi-gree of experience and research in the area of developmental assessment in Australia and should find wide application in clinics and preschool settings. Further psychometric evidence of validity and reliability of results, together with support for the constructs (e.g., the five domains lend themselves readily amenable to Rasch analysis), as well as external evidence of its sensitivity and specificity are required.

SUMMARY. Screening is an important and first step in identifying developmental problems and current opinion confirms the value of early intervention. The ASDC is recommended as a basis for developmental screening and one means of identifying young children in Australia who may display signs of early developmental delay.

REVIEWER'S REFERENCES

Ittenbach, R. F., & Harrison, P. L. (1990). Race, gender and maternal education differences on three measures of the Early screening Profiles. *Educational and Psychological Measurement, 50,* 931–942.

McGinty, C. (2000). An investigation into aspects of the Mayo early language screening test. *Child, Care, Health & Development, 26,* 111–128.

[24]

Australian Developmental Screening Test.

Purpose: Designed to provide a brief screening measure of early developmental delay.

Population: Ages 6–60 months.

Publication Date: 1993.

Acronym: ADST.

Scores, 5: Personal-Social, Language, Cognitive, Fine Motor, Gross Motor.

Administration: Individual.

Price Data, 2001: A$539.19 per complete kit including manual (135 pages), stimulus cards, 25 record forms, and a set of toys; A$91.51 per 25 record forms.

Time: (15–20) minutes.

Author: Barry Burdon.

Publisher: The Psychological Corporation [Australia].

Review of the Australian Developmental Screening Test by KORESSA KUTSICK MALCOLM, School Psychologist, Augusta County Public Schools, and Adjunct Faculty Member, Mary Baldwin College, Staunton, VA:

DESCRIPTION. The Australian Developmental Screening Test (ADST) is an individually administered early childhood screening procedure. It was specifically designed to provide medical and education personnel in Australia a screening test that was normed for children in that nation.

The ADST can be administered to children ages 3 to 60 months of age. The test is composed of 150 items that are arranged in five traditional functional domains. These domains include Personal-Social, Language, Cognitive, Fine Motor, and Gross Motor skill areas. The ADST takes 15 to 20 minutes to administer. Items are scored based on results of direct administration, observational data, or parent/caregiver report. Age equivalent scores in developmental indexes are obtained for each of the five domains. Examiners plot these domain age scores and compare them to the child's chronological age to determine when noted delays warrant follow-up.

DEVELOPMENT. A comprehensive overview of the developmental process of the ADST is provided in its manual. In many ways, the ADST is an extension of the Australian Developmental Record for Infants and Young Children (ADRIYC). The ADRIYC was a parent/caregiver report inventory used in Australia to identify children who were showing indicators of early developmental delay. The ADRIYC had been found to be a valuable screening procedure when examiners were familiar with a child (i.e., when the examiner was a day care provider). The interview format of the ADRIYC did not lend itself well to single session evaluations conducted in various clinical settings when examiners did not have regular contact with the child. Given this situation, the need for a screening procedure that utilized a direct assessment was noted. This need led to the conceptualization of the ADST.

Item selection for the ADST began with a review of the items of the ADRIYC. Items that were not readily translated to a direct assessment format were removed from the item pool. A review of other preschool assessment instruments was then undertaken to find items that could be added to the item pool. Through several stages of review, these items were eventually reduced to the 150 that comprise the ADST. These final items were reported to reflect several criteria, including developmental appropriateness, reflection of developmental theory, and an "economy of materials." This latter criterion involved finding items that would minimize the numbers of materials an examiner needed to manipulate in the screening process.

TECHNICAL. The standardization and norming processes of the ADST are fully described in its manual. Recognized sampling procedures were utilized to find children to participate in the standardization and norming of this test.

Children were selected to fit the major demographic categories of metropolitan Adelaide (a large city in Australia). Children from other parts of the nation, including those of more rural areas, were not included in the developmental processes of this test. Socioeconomic status for children in the standardization and norming samples were determined by parent occupation and stratified to reflect the distribution of adult occupational roles in Adelaide. No breakdown of race or ethnicity was specifically provided. This variable was discussed in terms of birth nation of the children's parents.

Reliability of the ADST was examined by a review of studies conducted on data obtained during the development process of this test. Although the number of these studies, as well as the sample sizes of some of them, was small, the results were promising. The standard error of measurement reported for the ADST was less than one point for most age levels. Test-retest (interval of no more than 3 weeks) and interrater reliability studies yielded strong positive correlations (.77 to .86 range).

Validity information provided for the ADST is somewhat limited and much of it has been conducted by the author of the test. The ADST was not designed to be a test of particular constructs, but rather of developmental skills at particular age levels. As such, it is difficult to evaluate the construct validity of this test. The organization of the ADST, however, does reflect its focus on various developmental skills at age-appropriate levels. Support for the content validity of the ADST can be found in the process of review that was undertaken to select items for this test. In one study conducted with only 18 children, some support of the discriminate validity of the ADST was found. In this study, all 18 of the children had been found to exhibit developmental delays in previous evaluations. Results of the ADST indicated all would have been identified as needing additional evaluations. The manual cited just one study where results of the ADST were compared to those of another test. Because that other test was the ADRIYC, the test that formed the basis of the ADST, it is not surprising that the two instruments yielded similar results.

COMMENTARY. The Australian Developmental Screening Test is a promising assessment procedure for use in its intended nation of Australia. There are many developmental screening instruments on the market, but few with a norm base in that particular country. The ADST taps the major domains typically assessed in a preschool screening. It does so in an efficient manner. The test materials are well organized. The effort made to minimize challenges to the examiner in limiting the number of manipulative needed to administer this test is applauded. Many preschool tests are quite cumbersome given the number of materials they involve and the physical weight of their kits. These properties are not an issue for the ADST.

A comprehensive plan was followed in the development of the ADST. The process of item review should have ensured a collection of assessment tasks that would tap a large number of skill areas.

Some of the weaknesses of the ADST are found in its standardization and norming procedures. Although it was contended that the standardization and norming samples were reflective of the nation's demographic variables, this might not be the case. It would have been better to have administered this test to children from areas throughout Australia, rather that in just one metropolitan area. Inclusion of children from rural settings as well as from different regions of the nation would have strengthened the generalizability of this test for use in these areas.

As with most new tests, additional reliability and validity studies need to be conducted to verify the value of the ADST as a preschool screening instrument. The author has been conducting research in these areas with good results.

For a test that was designed to be a direct assessment instrument, the ADST relies on parent/caregiver report for many of items items. Inclusion of report options is necessary for work with very young children; however, it seems more of the items of the ADST should first be directly administered, and then follow-up allowed if the child would not perform the item.

The administration and scoring procedures of the ADST are straightforward. Adequate explanations for following basal and ceiling rules are provided. The directions for administering the items of the ADST are somewhat difficult to follow given the print organization in the manual. Some form of highlighting would have been helpful to set directions off from descriptors of the tasks. Each task can be administered with relative ease. The process of converting raw scores to age scores is clearly defined. Some challenges are found

in following the interpretation guidelines for the ADST. The decision points for classification of scores into one of three options (Assessment Recommended, Monitor, and No Delay) could be refined. For example, it would seem that the criteria of a 3- or 4-month delay could hold different predictive value for a 10-month-old child than for a 45-month-old child.

SUMMARY. The ADST shows promise as a useful early childhood screening instrument for children in Australia. Additional work needs to be conducted to add to data of the reliability and validity of the test. This is especially true in terms of the value of this instrument in correctly identifying children who might be demonstrating developmental delays and need further evaluation. In addition, data supporting the validity of scores from the ADST for children who live outside of the metropolitan Adelaide area need to be gathered. A refining of the process of score interpretation might also add to the utility of this test. As a screening instrument, the ADST is an easy-to-administer test that has good predictive potential for identifying possible developmental delays in young children. It should prove to be a useful tool for early childhood specialists working in Australia.

[25]

The Autistic Continuum: An Assessment and Intervention Schedule.

Purpose: Designed to indicate the presence of autistic features and to aid in developing educational and therapeutic programs.
Population: Ages 2–8.
Publication Dates: 1987–1992.
Scores: Item scores only in 8 areas: General Observations, Attention Control, Sensory Function, Non-Verbal Symbolic Function, Concept Formation, Sequencing and Rhythmic Abilities, Speech and Language, Educational Attainments and Intelligence.
Administration: Individual.
Price Data, 1998: £60 per manual (1992, 78 pages) incorporating schedule; sample sheets are free.
Time: Untimed.
Comments: Revision of Is This Autism? A Checklist of Behaviours and Skills for Children Showing Autistic Features.
Authors: Maureen Aarons and Tessa Gittens.
Publisher: NFER-Nelson Publishing Co., Ltd. [England].
Cross References: For reviews by William M. Bart and Doreen Ward Fairbank of the earlier edition, see 12:197.

Review of The Autistic Continuum: An Assessment and Intervention Schedule by DOREEN W. FAIRBANK, Associate Professor of Psychology, Meredith College, Raleigh, NC:

DESCRIPTION. The Autistic Continuum: An Assessment and Intervention Schedule is a revision of Is This Autism? A Checklist of Behaviours and Skills for Children Showing Autistic Features, originally published in 1987. The authors, who are speech and language therapists, originally developed the instrument for speech and language therapists but have expanded the interest of the test to include other professionals working with children with autism. According to the authors, a primary purpose for this revision was to update the test items to follow the philosophy that autism exists on a continuum and can no longer be regarded as a disorder with definite characteristics or boundaries. This revised edition was designed to reflect this variability and continuum structure.

The Autistic Continuum: An Assessment and Intervention Schedule was designed to provide a framework for gathering information on children ages 2–8 years with suspected autistic characteristics. The information provided from this test should help the assessor to interpret the child's present level of functioning and how to best develop a program for educational or therapeutic interventions. The test does not provide an overall comprehensive scoring procedure and, therefore, is not designed for diagnostic purposes. The scoring guide for several areas is based on a 1–3 scale with 1 "shows some idea of how to tackle the task, but is unable to proceed very far"; 2 "makes a good attempt at the task, with some success"; and 3 "completes the task successfully." The Schedule provides space for observations, notes, and planning at the end of each section. The Schedule is completed using several techniques: interviewing the parents, direct observation of the child, and administering test items to the child directly. The manual does not discuss the qualifications needed to administer The Autistic Continuum: An Assessment and Intervention Schedule.

The Autistic Continuum: An Assessment and Intervention Schedule consists of a manual and a reproducible Schedule. The Schedule is divided into eight sections that are intended to represent a developmental approach and order: General Observations, Attention Control, Sensory Function, Non-Verbal Symbolic Function, Concept Formation, Sequencing and Rhythmic Abilities, Communication Development, and Educational Attainments and Psychometric Assessment. The manual is cross-referenced to the items in the Schedule and provides information on research findings, theoretical concepts, and clinical observations underlying the questions asked or items given in each section of the Schedule. It also gives the assessor background information on why that idea is important. However, the material/equipment needed to complete each section is not provided to the assessor. The manual provides a list of places where one can purchase the materials but this may pose a problem to the assessor.

DEVELOPMENT. The Autistic Continuum: An Assessment and Intervention Schedule is the latest revision of Is This Autism? A Checklist of Behaviours and Skills for Children Showing Autistic Features. The original test was published in 1987. The manual discusses a short history of autism, definitions of autism, and diagnostic issues relating to autism. The manual also provides information on recent research findings, theoretical concepts, and clinical observation underlying the philosophy and development of the manual and the Schedule. The authors have based their revisions for this edition on the information provided in the above-mentioned sections and the current concept that autism exists on a continuum of severity. However, the manual does not discuss or give any further information on how the test was developed, piloted, revised, or generally standardized. Several sections of this test are based on other instruments and the manual states that the assessor needs to be familiar with these other instruments. For example, Section II: Attention Control and Section IV: Non-Verbal Symbolic Function are taken from relevant sections of *Helping Language Development* by Cooper, Moodley, and Reynell (1978).

TECHNICAL. The manual does not provide any technical information regarding standardization, reliability, and validity. The Autistic Continuum: An Assessment and Intervention Schedule intends to provide a pattern of relative strengths and weaknesses rather than a statistical comparison with typically developing peers. The manual states, "children with autism may develop skills unevenly, omit some stages or appear not to follow the usual developmental order. It is the unstable area of emerging skills and the relationship between the various aspects of development that must be identified" (p. viii).

COMMENTARY. The Autistic Continuum: An Assessment and Intervention Schedule provides an interesting approach to assessing the strengths and weaknesses for a child with autism. The information from a completed Schedule would enable the professional working with a child with autism to provide a relevant teaching or therapy program. The Schedule would also provide a means to monitor progress and make the appropriate changes as the child develops.

However, the test does contain several limitations. Although the test is based on a continuum structure and measures strengths and weaknesses, it would be a benefit to the assessor to have the technical information regarding standardization, reliability, and validity as well as more specific information on test development. Another major limitation is that the test does not provide all the information and materials necessary for administration. Several additional instruments and texts are needed to administer the Schedule. The instrument also does not contain the necessary equipment to correctly administer the test. The manual lists all the materials needed; however, the suppliers are all located in Great Britain and may be of limited accessibility to some potential users in North America. Collecting all the necessary materials may also be a time-consuming process for the assessor. In general, the Schedule could serve as a useful starting point for developing a comprehensive needs assessment.

SUMMARY. The Autistic Continuum: An Assessment and Intervention Schedule is a qualitative instrument intended for use with children with autism, ages 2–8 years. The instrument is completed through parent interview, observation of the child, and direct administration of test items to the child. The test is not self-contained and the assessors need to gather the necessary materials before administering the test. The manual does not contain any information regarding standardization, reliability, validity, or specific scoring criteria and, therefore, the instrument should not be used as a diagnostic tool, but rather as an instrument for monitoring behavior and education/communication progress. The instrument provides a systematic method to collect and organize information across areas of social, educational, and language development and to enhance program development for children with autism.

REVIEWER'S REFERENCE
Cooper, J., Moodley, M., & Reynell, J. (1978). *Helping language development*. London: Edward Arnold.

Review of The Autistic Continuum: An Assessment and Intervention Schedule by PAT MIRENDA, Associate Professor, University of British Columbia, Vancouver, British Columbia, Canada:

DESCRIPTION. This British assessment tool consists of a manual and photocopiable Schedule (i.e., test record form) that is designed "to provide a framework for gathering information relevant to the understanding of children with a spectrum of autistic or autistic-like difficulties" (manual, p. viii). The authors imply that the Schedule may be used by professionals such as "teachers, clinical psychologists, and speech language therapists" (p. 11) to diagnose autism spectrum disorders. They provide a rationale for its use in this regard within the British context: The medical profession is not in a position to make a diagnosis satisfactorily because the training of doctors is unlikely to include anything but an overview of what is essentially a disorder of social development—rather than a disease. At the same time, the authors encourage use of the Schedule as a "clinical or teaching tool" (manual, p. viii) for intervention planning and for monitoring children's progress over time. The fact is that diagnosis, intervention planning, and monitoring progress over time are three related but distinct enterprises, and it is difficult to imagine a tool that would be equally useful for all three purposes. The lack of clarity and specificity about the purpose of the Schedule and its accompanying documentation is a major weakness.

The basis of the Schedule is a conflation of developmental tests and assessments that the authors themselves (both speech-language pathologists) have found useful in working with children (ages 2–8) with autism. Thus, the Schedule requires that additional measures (or sections thereof) also be administered, including the Symbolic Play Test (Lowe & Costello, 1988), the Derbyshire Language Scheme (Knowles & Masidlover, 1980), the Reynell Developmental Language Scales (Reynell, 1985), the Test for Reception of Grammar (Bishop, 1983), the Action Picture Test and The Bus Story (Renfrew, 1989), and the Pragmatics Profile of Early Communication Skills (Dewart & Summers, 1988). Some of these measures (e.g., the Reynell Scales) are standardized and readily available, whereas others are not; for example, the

TECHNICAL. The 60-item scale was normed using 9,172 children and adolescents, 7 to 18 years of age, who attended regular classes in the U.S. and Canada. No special education students were included. Roughly equal numbers of males and females were included in each age group. The self-identified ethnic composition included 50% Caucasian/White, 35% Hispanic, and less than 4% each of other ethnic groups. Norms were calculated separately by age and gender.

On both the long and the short forms, internal reliability (Cronbach's alpha) was acceptable for all domain scales (.65 to .90), with the lowest reliability coefficients for the six-item Intrapersonal Scale. Mean correlations of items within scales were low to moderate for each scale (.14 to .55). Test-retest reliability at 3 weeks was moderate to high for each scale (.77 to .89), but the sample for this analysis included only 60 children.

Factorial analysis of validity revealed that the 40 items from the domain scales produced a four-factor solution, with each item loading at least moderately on their matching factors and only slightly with other factors. Intercorrelations of domain scores were low to moderate (.16 to .72), suggesting relatively distinct factors. Correlations between matching scales on the long and short forms were high, which is not surprising given that short-form scales are subsets of items from the long form. Correlations of the EQ-i:YV with the Children's Depression Inventory (CDI), the NEO-Five Factor Inventory (NEO-FFI), the Conners-Wells Adolescent Self-Report Scale (CASS), and the Conners Parent Rating Scale—Revised, Short Form (CPRS-R:S) were moderate and negative. The highest correlations (.85) were between the EQ-i:YV Stress Management scale and the Anger Control Problems of the CASS, which contain very similar items.

COMMENTARY. The BarOn Emotional Quotient Inventory: Youth Version (EQ-i:YV) is an interesting test of an important construct, but its usefulness may be limited by several factors, including (a) guidelines for administration and interpretation, (b) differences between long and short versions, (c) issues regarding development and standardization, (d) developmental appropriateness, and (e) theoretical foundations.

Oral administration is suggested for respondents with reading difficulties or a non-English first language. This procedure may be advisable for many children with beginning reading skills. However, such procedures were not tested during standardization, and effects of administration procedures on responses cannot be ruled out. Empirical comparison of oral and silent reading administration is needed. Similarly, the authors suggest that the inventory can be administered remotely (by phone) or in groups, but these conditions were not tested during standardization.

The basic guide for interpreting scores is vague. In general, high scores indicate better functioning, whereas low scores suggest a "need to improve." However, interpretative guidelines suggest that scores more than 1.5 standard deviations above the mean could indicate well-developed functioning, "atypically well-developed" capacity, social desirability response sets, or failure to understand directions. Substantial clinical judgment therefore may be required to interpret high scores. Similarly, markedly low scores may indicate impaired emotional/social competencies, but may also result from depressed mood or current life stressors. Given the need for clinical interpretation of extreme scores, the test is at risk of becoming a projective technique. Furthermore, use of assessment in treatment planning is not adequately described.

The long and short versions differ somewhat in the wording of scale anchors. No rationale is given for this difference. The short version also is printed in larger font. These differences suggest that the short form may be more appropriate for younger children. However, this use is not stated by the authors, and correlations between long and short forms are not provided separately for each age group.

Test development issues include questions about the standardization sample. No information was provided on the types of schools from which participants were recruited. Ethnicity percentages are given, but no information on percentages in each age and gender group. The adult form was tested extensively for cross-cultural differences, but only U.S. and Canadian participants were used in developing the youth forms. Finally, no children from special education classes were included. Norms on this group are important given that the test may be used primarily for children with problems.

Age, gender, and ethnicity effects were evaluated using several series of Factorial and Oneway ANOVAs. It is unclear why MANOVAs were not used. The authors decided to compute separate age and gender norms on the basis of several significant effects, although eta^2 was less than .01 for all but two of the significant effects of age (General Mood, eta^2 = .02; Positive Impression, eta^2 = .12). In comparison, separate norms were not computed for ethnic groups, although several significant effects also were found in these analyses, and eta^2 values were not appreciably smaller than those for age and gender. It was unclear why the authors decided to provide separate age and gender, but not ethnicity norms.

The total standardization sample was quite large (N = 9,172), but inadequate sample sizes were used for some of the reliability analyses. Specifically, only 60 children participated in test-retest reliability estimates, and the number in each age group was not provided. Similarly, only 49 participants, females only, were used to obtain correlations of the youth version and adult version in 17- to 18-year-olds. Concurrent validity studies included adequate sample sizes.

Perhaps the most important considerations involve developmental and theoretical issues. First, the test may not be developmentally appropriate for the wide age range of 7 to 18. The fourth-grade reading level suggests that younger children will have difficulty reading and understanding the items. The authors note that younger children are likely to respond in ways that put them in a favorable light, and correction procedures are suggested to compensate for this difference. However, other cognitive differences between younger and older children are not addressed. More abstract concepts are likely to be difficult for children under age 9 or 10, and word meanings may differ (e.g., "seldom"). Children also show a normal developmental progression in the ability to think realistically about the self.

From a theoretical perspective, it is not clear that the items on the test are a satisfactory sample of the constructs of interest. For example, the intrapersonal dimension of emotional intelligence theoretically includes five sets of abilities: recognizing and understanding one's own feelings; expressing feelings, beliefs, and thoughts; appraising oneself accurately; realizing one's potential; and thinking and acting in self-controlled and self-directed ways. However, all six items of the Intrapersonal Scale are concerned with expressing one's feelings to others (e.g., "I have trouble telling others about my feelings"). Similarly, the Stress

Management scale primarily contains items concerning anger expression. Other scales also have a limited range of content, particularly on the short form.

Other construct validity measures are needed, particularly to determine the degree of overlap of domain scales with tests of other constructs (e.g., self-esteem, anger, anxiety, depression). Many of the items on the test are quite similar to these tests, and it remains to be seen whether the EQ-i:YV provides different information.

Using self-report to assess "emotional intelligence" seems limited. People with poor insight into their own feelings or their interactions with the world are unlikely to provide useful information in this format. To measure this multifaceted construct adequately, greater emphasis on use of supporting evaluation is needed. For example, equivalent inventories for parent, teacher, and other informant ratings may provide useful comparisons to self ratings, as may behavior observations in simulations or in real-life settings.

SUMMARY. The Bar-On Emotional Quotient Inventory, Youth Version (EQ-i:YV) is a newly developed test that was carefully constructed using both rational and empirical procedures. It is intended as a measure of emotional intelligence in children and adolescents ages 7 to 18. Evaluation of reliability and validity was adequate, although not as extensive as that of the original adult version. Norms for special education, ethnic, and cross-cultural groups are needed. Further evaluation of predictive, divergent, and discriminant validity is needed. The inventory may prove useful for screening and for research purposes, but its use in clinical treatment planning is unclear. Further research is needed to determine the adequacy of the inventory, or of any self-report instrument, in measuring the theoretical components of emotional intelligence.

REVIEWER'S REFERENCES

Cox, A. A. (2001). [Review of the BarOn Emotional Quotient Inventory]. In B. S. Plake & J. C. Impara (Eds.), *The fourteenth mental measurements yearbook* (pp. 106–108). Lincoln, NE: Buros Institute of Mental Measurements.
Guion, R. M. (2001). [Review of the BarOn Emotional Quotient Inventory]. In B. S. Plake & J. C. Impara (Eds.), *The fourteenth mental measurements yearbook* (pp. 108–109). Lincoln, NE: Buros Institute of Mental Measurements.

Review of the BarOn Emotional Quotient Inventory: Youth Version by FREDERICK T. L. LEONG, Professor of Psychology, The Ohio State University at Columbus, Columbus, OH:

DESCRIPTION. For almost two decades, Gardner (1983) has argued cogently that, despite the dominance of "g" or general intelligence, there are multiple intelligences such as musical or spatial intelligence. Similarly, Sternberg (1996) has proposed that practical intelligence is more important than "inert" or academic-related intelligence and needs to be distinguished from the latter. More recently, the concept of emotional intelligence or EQ was made popular by Daniel Goleman, New York Times Science reporter in his bestseller, *Emotional Intelligence* (Goleman, 1995). Since then, various tests that measure this type of intelligence have also begun to attract attention from more and more social scientists. The BarOn Emotional Quotient Inventory: Youth Version (EQ-i:YV) is one of these recently developed measures of emotional intelligence.

The EQ-i:YV is designed for persons from ages 7–18 years. It is an extension of the adult version of the EQ-i that was published in 1997 (Bar-On, 1997; T6:244). The EQ-i:YV consists of 60 items that measure the following dimensions of emotional intelligence: (a) Intrapersonal, (b) Interpersonal, (c) Adaptability, (d) Stress Management, and (e) General Mood. In addition to these five primary scales, the EQ-i:YV also consists of two additional "validity" scales, namely the Inconsistency scale (measure of random responding) and Positive Impression scale (measure of attempts to "fake good"). There is also a short form of the EQ-i:YV consisting of 30 items.

DEVELOPMENT. The EQ-i was developed using a combined rational and empirical strategy. It was based on Bar-On's model that defined emotional intelligence as "an array of emotional, personal, and interpersonal abilities that influence one's overall ability to cope with environmental demands and pressures" (technical manual, p. 33). The EQ-i:YV, as a youth edition of the adult EQ-i, was developed following the same rationale and procedures. However, it went through several stages of development in order to identify and refine a set of items appropriate for children and young persons. The set of items was also subjected to both exploratory and confirmatory factor analyses in order to check their conformity to the five dimensions of emotional intelligence found in the adult EQ-i.

TECHNICAL. In general, the EQ-i:YV is a psychometrically sound instrument with good psychometric properties. In terms of reliability, the internal consistency estimates for the various subscales range from .65 to .90 with most of them in the .80 range. The stability of the subscale

scores is also supported by the mean interitem correlations presented by the test authors. Test/retest reliability (3 weeks) was also quite good with correlations ranging from .77 to .88. The test-retest correlation for the total EQ-i was .89 for the regular version and .88 for the short version. It would have been good to provide an additional estimate of the test-retest estimates with a longer period such as several months and not just weeks. The internal consistency, mean interitem, and test-retest reliability scores for the short form were comparable to the regular version although somewhat lower as would be expected given the fewer items. The correlations between the regular and short forms were also very good with estimates ranging from .92 to .97. There is also a good set of normative data for the EQ-i:YV.

It is generally accepted that the accumulation of evidence for the validity of a test is usually open-ended as compared to that for reliability. The latter tends to have a more finite number of indices that demonstrate the stability and consistency of a test across time. Validity, on the other hand, is more open-ended and requires an ongoing accumulation of evidence in order to build that "nomological net" of theoretically expected relations that underlie construct validity (Cronbach & Meehl, 1955). In this perspective, the evidence for the validity of the EQ-i:YV has a good start but is not quite "there." The authors of the EQ-i:YV have conducted many of the usual studies to demonstrate validity but there are still a few missing elements.

In terms of validity, Bar-On and Parker have conducted most of the standard evaluation "tests" for the validity of the EQ-i:YV. For example, they have carried out factor analyses to determine the factorial validity of the inventory. As expected, they were able to capture the five subscales with the items loading moderately well in their matched factors and no major problems with cross-loadings across factors. They also found evidence for concurrent validity when they correlated the EQ-i:YV with the original adult version of the EQ-i. However, it should be noted that among the correlations between these two versions, the correlations for the Intrapersonal ($r = .56$) and Adaptability ($r = .63$) subscales were somewhat lower than desirable and suggest some caution when using these subscales with the younger population of the EQ-i:YV. In an effort to examine convergent and divergent validity, the authors also correlated the EQ-i:YV with the NEO Personality Inventory using the short form, the NEO-FFI (Costa & McCrae, 1992). In general, theoretically expected relationships were found such as negative correlations between the NEO-PI Neuroticism and EQ-i:YV Adaptability ($r = -.31$) and Stress Management ($r = -.43$) subscales. Similar patterns of results were found when the authors correlated the EQ-i:YV with the Children's Depression Inventory (CDI; Kovacs, 1992), Conners-Wells Adolescent Self-Report Scale (CASS; Conners, 1997), and Conners Parent Rating Scale—Revised (Connors, 1997).

COMMENTARY. Whereas many of the standard "tests" of the validity of an inventory have been conducted for the EQ-i:YV, there are a few important missing elements. In examining the validity of the EQ-i:YV, Bar-On and Parker did not provide much evidence regarding its concurrent validity. For example, it would have been useful to examine how the EQ-i:YV relates to other existing measures of emotional intelligence. This is also important because different theorists have proposed different dimensions (operationalized as subscales in EQ measures) underlying the construct of emotional intelligence. Such comparative analyses would also provide information about possible differences in incremental validity. For example, does the EQ-i:YV measure additional variance above and beyond other measures of emotional intelligence or does it measure essentially the same variance? Also lacking are any analyses of the relationships between the EQ-i:YV and measures of IQ. Theoretically, it would be important to demonstrate that a measure of emotional intelligence does not share a significant amount of variance with traditional measures of intelligence. This is also relevant to the issue of discriminant validity.

Another element missing is any evidence for the predictive or criterion-related validity of the EQ-i:YV. Besides convergent and divergent validity to mental health measures such as the CDI and the CASS, it would be important to demonstrate that the EQ-i:YV can predict actual *behavioral* differences in the emotional domain. For example, young people scoring higher on the EQ-i:YV should be able to manage frustrations, stressful situations, and interpersonal conflicts better than those scoring lower. Behavioral measures of

these outcomes should be devised and scores on the EQ-i:YV be used to predict scores on these outcome measures.

SUMMARY. In conclusion, the EQ-i:YV is a well-developed and psychometrically sound measure of emotional intelligence for young persons. It is a downward extension of the EQ-i for adults and possesses many of the same excellent psychometric qualities. Nevertheless, there are still a few missing elements in the demonstration of the validity of the EQ-i:YV. These missing elements include concurrent validity tests with other existing measures of emotional intelligence as well as relationships to traditional measures of IQ. There is also a lack of sufficient evidence for the predictive or criterion-related validity of the EQ-i:YV. However, it should be noted that demonstration of the construct validity of a test is complex and an ongoing process. There will be opportunities for the authors of this measure or other scientists to take on these remaining validity issues.

REVIEWER'S REFERENCES

Bar-On, R. (1997). BarOn Emotional Quotient Inventory. Toronto, Ontario, Canada: Multi-Health Systems, Inc.
Conners, C. K. (1997). *Conners' Rating Scales–Revised: Technical manual.* Toronto, Ontario, Canada: Multi-Health Systems Inc.
Costa, P. T., Jr., & McCrae, R. R. (1992). *Revised NEO Personality Inventory (NEO-PI-R) and NEO Five-Factor Inventory (NEO-FFI) professional manual.* Odessa, FL: Psychological Assessment Resources, Inc.
Cronbach, L. J., & Meehl, P. E (1955). Construct validity in psychological tests. *Psychological Bulletin, 52,* 281–302.
Gardner, H. (1983). *Frames of mind: The theory of multiple intelligences.* New York: Basic Books.
Goleman, D. (1995). *Emotional Intelligence.* New York: Bantam Books.
Kovacs, M. (1992). *Children's Depression Inventory (CDI): Manual.* Toronto, Ontario, Canada: Multi-Health Systems Inc.
Sternberg, R. J. (1996). Successful intelligence: How practical and creative intelligence determine success in life. New York: Simon & Schuster.

[27]

Basic Number Diagnostic Test [2001 Revision].

Purpose: Designed to "show what a child can do (and cannot do) so that teaching objectives for that child can be determined."

Population: Ages 5–7.

Publication Dates: 1980–2001.

Scores, 13: Reciting Numbers, Naming Numerals, Copying Over Numerals, Copying Underneath Numerals, Counting Bricks, Selecting Bricks, Writing Numerals in Sequence, Writing Numerals to Dictation, Addition with Objects, Addition with Numerals, Subtraction with Objects, Subtraction with Numerals, Total.

Administration: Individual.

Forms, 2: A, B.

Price Data, 2002: £8.99 per set of 10 copies; £13.99 per manual (2001, 30 pages); £14.99 per specimen set.

Time: (15–25) minutes.
Comments: "Criterion-referenced."
Author: Bill Gillham.
Publisher: Hodder & Stoughton Educational [England].
Cross References: For a review by Mary Montgomery Lindquist of an earlier edition, see 9:117.

Review of the Basic Number Diagnostic Test [2001 Revision] by CLEBORNE D. MADDUX, Professor of Counseling and Educational Psychology, University of Nevada, Reno, NV:

DESCRIPTION. The Basic Number Diagnostic Test is a 50-item, individually administered, criterion-referenced test for children from 5 to 7 years of age. The 15- to 25-minute test is organized around 12 sections intended to measure fundamentals of using the number system. Each section yields a separate subtest score. The 12 sections are Reciting Numbers, Naming Numerals, Copying Over Numerals, Copying Underneath Numerals, Counting Bricks, Selecting Bricks, Writing Numerals in Sequence, Writing Numerals to Dictation, Addition with Objects, Addition with Numerals, Subtraction with Objects, and Subtraction With Numerals. A total score can also be calculated (50 points are possible). Alternate items are provided for use in retesting, but only for the four addition and subtraction sections.

The test booklet contains both directions for administering each item and space for the child to record answers, when appropriate. After administering the test, results in each of the 12 sections are summarized on the first page of the booklet, as is the child's number age and whether or not the total score reflects performance below the 20th percentile.

The manual provides seven score ranges for conversion to seven number ages from 5 years to more than 7 years, with half-year increments in number age at each successive score range excluding the lowest. The manual contains directions for filling out the graphical profile reflecting performance, as well as how to indicate 3-month objectives on the profile.

Although the test items and norms are unchanged in this revision, the mathematical vocabulary and follow-up activities were revised to be more consistent with national standards. Also new are supplementary norms to determine whether or not a child falls into the bottom 20% of his or her age group.

The test includes approximate norms (score ranges only), but the manual states that the main purpose is to determine what a child can and cannot do with respect to fundamentals of using the number system, and to help teachers determine specific objectives for that child. Specific teaching suggestions are provided in the manual. Although the manual suggests that the test is appropriate for screening all children who are in the first 2 years of primary school, it goes on to suggest that the test be used in conjunction with The Basic Number Screening Test. When this procedure is followed, The Basic Number Diagnostic Test is to be given only to children with a number age of 7 years and 6 months or less.

DEVELOPMENT. Published in Great Britain, this revision of the original test was carried out to make it consistent with the National Curriculum of England and Wales—specifically the key elements of the National Numeracy Strategy from Reception through Year Two. The test requires only a pencil, an eraser, the test booklet, the teacher's manual, and 30 plastic bricks 1 centimeter in size. The bricks are not included in the test materials, however, although an address in Great Britain is provided where users can order a set. Any small, plastic objects could probably be substituted, but it is unfortunate that the developers chose not to supply them as part of the materials.

No information is provided on how the test was developed, other than statements that it is consistent with the National Numeracy Strategy from Reception through Year Two. There is no discussion of item development.

TECHNICAL. The test was standardized with 292 students from 5 to 7 years of age in 24 primary and infant schools in a single English city. This is an unacceptably limited sample in geographic terms, and because there are no data on ethnicity or socioeconomic status of children in the sample, use of the norms with children outside the single city in England, or with ethnically diverse students, is not advisable.

The manual provides only two sentences devoted to reliability. The only reliability statistic reported is a Spearman rho of .93, calculated after a split-half study of the tests of 32 children in three schools who took the regular test items and the retest items. There is no information on the demographics of these students or how they were chosen, and the adequacy of the other research procedures cannot be judged from the scant description of the study, beyond the observation that there were not enough subjects included. There are no data on test-retest or alternate form reliability, even though the manual suggests that the instrument be used on a test-retest basis, and retest items are included for some test sections. Likewise, there are no data on interrater reliability, even though the manual suggests that the test can be administered by teachers and does not suggest that special training is needed. Because of the inadequacies of the manual on this subject, the best that can be said about the reliability of the instrument is that it is unknown.

There are no reported validity data. This is particularly unfortunate because a critical issue in criterion-referenced instruments is content validity. Yet, this is never mentioned, and the user has no way to assess whether or not items included are truly representative of the specified skill. Validity of the test is unknown.

COMMENTARY. The test is easy to administer and the directions are clear and complete. The test booklet is well-designed and easy to understand and use. The test could be quite useful as a diagnostic tool in the hands of an experienced teacher of young children. The lack of data on content validity is a serious weakness and makes it difficult to know whether the test adequately samples the domains it purports to measure. The test does seem to overemphasize writing ability, and some areas seem to be missing. For instance, there are no items to assess a child's understanding of "more-than" or "less-than" concepts, and no items assessing the understanding of place value concepts.

The main problem with the test, however, is in the inclusion of norms. The inclusion of a number age derived from very gross score ranges, coupled with inadequate technical information makes such scores practically useless. So long as the diagnostic nature of the test is kept firmly in mind, and comparisons of number ages across students avoided, the test could be an inexpensive and valuable addition to the teaching tools of primary teachers.

SUMMARY. The Basic Number Diagnostic Test is an inexpensive, easy-to-administer and score, diagnostic instrument for assessing fundamental number skills in children 5 to 7 years of age. It could be useful in compiling diagnostic information about children experiencing difficulty with number skills and concepts. If the developers had refrained from including aspects of norm-referenced tests, and concentrated instead on refining the instrument as a criterion-referenced instrument, users would have been far better served. As it is, reliability data are inadequate, and no data on validity are provided. Until these deficiencies are rectified, particularly with respect to documenting content validity, the test must be considered a promising, but wholly experimental and incomplete instrument.

Review of the Basic Number Diagnostic Test [2001 Revision] by JEFFREY K. SMITH, Professor and Chair, Department of Educational Psychology, Rutgers, The State University of New Jersey, New Brunswick, NJ:

DESCRIPTION. The Basic Number Diagnostic Test [2001 Revision] is a diagnostic assessment of children's basic understanding of numbers and rudimentary addition and subtraction. It is based on the British National Numeracy Strategy. It is designed to be administered individually to students by classroom teachers or educational psychologists. The purpose of the test is to determine what children can and cannot do with regard to basic number skills. Because the test can be administered by the classroom teacher, and because diagnostic interpretation of the child's approach to responding to the tasks is encouraged, the test also provides information to the teacher on the nature of the difficulties the child encounters. The test is designed to take 15–25 minutes to administer. Two forms of the test are provided in the booklet designed for student administration. The teacher's manual for the test provides information on how to interpret specific behaviors exhibited by children on the test and makes suggestions on how to remediate difficulties.

Although the author describes the test as being fundamentally criterion-referenced in nature (and indeed it appears to be such), some basic norming information is provided in the teacher's manual. The norms are based on the performance of a small sample of British school children. The test is designed for use with children between the ages of 5 and 7, and is intended to be a complement to the Basic Number Screening Test (28), which is designed for use with children ages 7–12.

DEVELOPMENT. The 2001 edition of the test is the third edition, with previous editions being published in 1980 and 1996. The new edi-

these age-to-score relationships had changed in the past 25 years, yet there is no evidence provided that is related to the stability of the norms over this period. The development of the age norms was not described in the manual and so it is difficult to assess their quality.

The two forms are claimed to be parallel and a reading of the task descriptions of the two sets of items does lend credence to this assertion. However, a comparison of item level statistics would help in establishing this claim.

The directions to teachers imply that the latter part of the test is more difficult than the earlier sections. A presentation of item difficulty indices would be useful in supporting this inference and also help those teachers who want to know more about individual item functioning.

SUMMARY. As noted, the Basic Number Screening Test is a small test aimed at the specific classroom function of identifying those students who may be likely to have problems in mathematics. It is easy to administer and score. The age norms are potentially useful but their relevance to contemporary students is not established. Those wishing to use the test would be well advised to develop local norms in order to interpret test scores for classification purposes.

Review of the Basic Number Screening Test [1996 Edition] by SUZANNE LANE, Professor, Research Methodology Program, University of Pittsburgh, Pittsburgh, PA:

The Basic Number Screening Test [1996 Edition] is designed to provide a quick assessment of number concepts and number skills. It was developed for children ranging from 7–12 years, but the authors indicate that it may be appropriate for older, less able children. The intended purpose is to identify children whose knowledge of number concepts and number skills is poor for their age or who are not making progress in these areas. The author indicates that children who perform poorly, those who receive a number age of 8 years or less, can be given the linked Basic Number Diagnostic Test (27). This suggestion may be reasonable for children who are between the ages of 9 and 10 years, but is questionable for children who are 7 or 8 years of age.

TEST CONTENT AND DEVELOPMENT. The authors indicate that the Basic Number Screening Test assesses one part of the primary mathematics syllabus defined in England's National Curriculum: basic principles underlying the number system and computation processes. The authors further state that the content "has been determined by our understanding of the development of children's number concepts, an appreciation of the changing nature of mathematics in schools, but above all by practical experience and detailed discussion with class-teachers" (manual, p. 5). However, no additional information on how the content was selected is provided in the manual. Given the authors' statement that the nature of mathematics in schools may change, it seems ironic that test content and items have not been revised since 1976.

The authors indicate that two parallel forms were developed (Forms A and B). Each form consists of 30 items: 15 number concept items and 15 number skill items. They further indicate that the items that assess number concepts focus on place value, series, grouping, and conservation and the items that assess number skills "are designed to sample the understanding of the processes involved in basic computation rather than the ability to do complicated 'sums'" (manual, p. 5). However, the authors do not provide test specifications, which would allow for the evaluation of the content of each form and the similarity of the content across forms. In addition, the item parameter estimates, means, standard deviations, and internal consistency reliability coefficients for each form are not reported. Without such information it is difficult to evaluate the extent to which the forms are parallel.

The authors indicate that the items on the two forms represent a "minute fraction of those used during item try-outs in schools" (manual, p. 5) and that both teacher and student feedback was a major consideration in item selection. No additional information, however, on the piloting of the items nor the procedures for obtaining teacher and student feedback regarding the items is provided.

TEST ADMINISTRATION AND SCORING. The manual indicates that the test can be individually or group administered. The reported testing time for the individual administration is approximately 20 minutes and for group administration it is approximately 30 to 35 minutes. The authors provide stopping guidelines for children who are 7 to 8 years of age so they do not receive items that are too advanced. Suggestions are provided to help eliminate children copying from one another, including giving the parallel forms to alternate children in a classroom. Both the group and individual administration directions to the children are clear and appear to be as concise as possible. The directions for scoring as well as the scoring key are clear and should be easy to follow for teachers and other school personnel.

NORMS. The norm group consisted of 3,042 children ranging from 7 years 6 months to 11 years 6 months in the city area of Nottingham, England. The norm data were obtained at the end of February and the beginning of March in 1976, which was at the midpoint of the school year. Number age norms are provided, which range from 7 years 0 months to 12 years 0 months. It was reported that the two number ages at either end of the scales were obtained by extrapolation. The extent to which the norm group is representative of all children in England is questionable. Further, the norms are outdated.

RELIABILITY. An alternate form reliability coefficient was obtained by administering the two forms, Form A and Form B, 1 week apart. The reported Pearson product-moment correlation coefficient is .93. There is no indication if all 3,042 children were used to obtain this estimate or if a subset of the children were used. Also, there was no indication if a counterbalanced design was implemented.

VALIDITY. The authors state that "since the test directly samples the attainment it is measuring (i.e., it does not presume to be measuring a hypothetical 'ability'), validity is assumed not to be a serious problem" (manual, p. 13). As indicated previously, the authors do not provide test specifications for the test nor any evidence to demonstrate the link between the content of the test and the part of the national curriculum that it is intended to assess. Thus, there is little content validity evidence provided that would facilitate in the evaluation of the content of the test. The validity evidence that is provided is the relationship between teachers' ratings, using a 7-point scale, of the children in their class before the administration of the test and the test scores for those children. These data were obtained from one school. The reported average Spearman's *rho* between the ratings and the test scores for that school is .82.

SUMMARY. The lack of validity evidence for the Basic Number Screening Test is of concern. Further, both the test and norms, which were not representative of children in England, have not been revised since 1976. Given these major shortcomings, I cannot recommend the use of this test for identifying children with basic mathematics difficulties.

[29]

Basic Reading Inventory, Eighth Edition.

Purpose: Designed as an informal measure of students' reading behavior.

Population: Pre-primer through Grade 12.

Publication Dates: 1978–2001.

Scores, 9–16: 3 reading scores (Independent, Instructional, Frustration, Word Recognition in Isolation, Word Recognition in Context, Comprehension—Oral, Comprehension—Silent, Listening Level); Rate of Reading (Optional); 9 informal Early Literacy Assessment ratings (Alphabet Knowledge, Writing, Literacy Knowledge, Wordless Picture Reading, Caption Reading, Auditory Discrimination, Phoneme Awareness, Phoneme Segmentation, Basic Word Knowledge).

Administration: Individual.

Levels, 2: Pre-primer through Grade 12; Grades 3–12.

Forms, 6: A, B, C, D, LN, LE.

Price Data: Price data available from publisher for manual with paper-and-pencil materials (2001, 472 pages), including CD-ROM (with videos, Performance Booklets, and Record Booklet, and demo disk for recording and tracking software); a training video is available to train administrators.

Time: [20] minutes.

Comments: Optional Basic Reading Inventory Tracking Software available to assist with advanced qualitative analysis available from publisher. System requirements: Windows or Macintosh, CD-ROM drive, 20 MB RAM, 20 MB hard drive, sound and video options.

Author: Jerry L. Johns.

Publisher: Kendall/Hunt Publishing Company.

Cross References: For reviews by Michael Harwell and Steven A. Stahl of the seventh edition, see 14:34 (6 references); see also T5:257 (4 references); for reviews by Jerrilyn V. Andrews and Robert T. Williams of the fifth edition, see 12:43 (3 references); see also T4:255 (4 references); for a review by Gus Plessas of the second edition, see 9:119.

Review of the Basic Reading Inventory, Eighth Edition by MATTHEW K. BURNS, Assistant Professor of Special Education, Central Michigan University, Mt. Pleasant, MI:

DESCRIPTION. The eighth edition of the Basic Reading Inventory (BRI) marks the 30th anniversary of this widely used and pioneering informal reading inventory (IRI). Like most assessment tools generated from the IRI paradigm, the BRI is an individually administered reading tool used to estimate a child's instructional level. The current edition contains six forms including word lists for levels ranging from pre-primer to Grade 12, oral reading passages including comprehension questions for pre-primer to 8th grade and 3rd to 12th grade, and silent-reading passages for pre-primer to Grade 8. All of the forms result in estimates of Independent, Instructional, and Frustrational levels, but a reading rate can also be computed. Also included in the current edition are measurements of various early literacy skills for emergent readers such as Alphabet Knowledge, Literacy Knowledge, Auditory Discrimination, Phoneme Awareness, and Phoneme Segmentation.

DEVELOPMENT. The manual provides information about the development of the graded word lists, which involved comparing words from the Reading Core Vocabulary and the Basic Skills Words Lists. Although the process of including only words that are assigned to the same grade on each list is a sound approach, the lists were most recently published in 1979 and 1980, respectively.

Little information is presented about the development of the reading passages. Forms A, C, and D used the same passages as in the Seventh Edition, and new passages were developed for the Forms B, LN, and LE. The manual stated that the "Passages in the *Basic Reading Inventory* were evaluated by one or more readability formulas," (p. 116) but never discusses the results of these evaluations. Furthermore, it was mentioned that input from various sources was gathered to revise the grade passages, but no data were presented and no indication of the revisions was included. In fact, the description of the supposed revisions and development of the new Form B comprised only two paragraphs in the manual.

To the developers' credit, two additional forms were added to the inventory to allow for more pre- and posttesting of reading skills, and the passages were field tested with 537 students with below average reading skills from Grades 3 through 8. However, the results of the field testing and a discussion of the resulting revisions were not included. Much more information about the field

testing is needed, including demographics of the participants and how "below average" reading skills were defined. The only information provided was that the field testing occurred in Illinois, Missouri, and Michigan, which is a sample that lacks national representativeness, and the number of students who read each form. Forty to 55 students each read the various graded passages for Forms LN and LE, which is a small sample even though the total number of participants was over 500.

Also to the developers' credit, assessments of various emergent skills were included in the current manual, but no information about the development of these measures was included. Therefore, although there is a need to assess these readiness skills of emergent literacy, use of these tools is not recommended.

Each graded reading passage includes a total of 10 comprehension questions across five formats: fact, topic, evaluation, inference, and vocabulary. Because there are five formats and 10 questions each, there are frequently 2 or less questions from some formats. This is too limited of a sample to make conclusions about these skills. Furthermore, no information was provided about how these comprehension questions were developed.

TECHNICAL. As far as can be determined from the manual, the BRI is almost completely devoid of standardization. For example, the manual suggests use of normative data about oral reading fluency provided by Hasbrouck and Tindal (1992), but does not provide guidance on how to do so, does not provide information about that norm group, and does not discuss purposes for this comparison. In fact, use of these norms is recommended to be conducted "informally" (manual, p. 38).

There also appears to be a lack of standardization of administration procedures as well. Test examiners are advised to rate the background knowledge of the student subjectively while assessing comprehension, but only a subjective and extremely minimal rubric (high to low) is included. The only guidance that resembles a ceiling or discontinue rule is the advice to discontinue when frustration is apparent, but frustration is not operationally defined. Examiners are told to "omit [comprehension] questions to shorten the administration time" (manual, p. 43) without guidance as to how or what to omit. There is a lack of consistency for telling students unknown words because the manual suggests that "Some students may need to be told a word if they pause for ten or fifteen seconds" (p. 27). However, whether a student consistently has to wait 10 or 15 seconds to receive the word can impact both the fluency score and comprehension (Burns et al., in press). Finally, the manual suggests that "Some teachers find a practice passage helpful" (p. 24) and provides some warm-up passages in the appendix. However, whether or not these warm-up passages are used could impact the score, and therefore, consistency of use would strengthen confidence in results.

Reliability and validity. During the discussion of establishing rapport, the manual suggests that "If the reading inventory is to yield valid, reliable, and useful results, it is necessary to obtain the student's cooperation" (p. 20). This is the only line in the manual that addresses reliability and validity. No data to support the consistency, validity, or instructional utility of the results are presented in the manual, which has been a longstanding criticism of this and other IRI measures. In fact, the manual does not even present a rationale for not presenting this information.

COMMENTARY. Most IRIs, including the BRI, are based on Betts's (1946) classic theory of instructional, independent, and frustrational levels, which is a sound theory with practical implications. However, assessing Betts's levels with the BRI cannot be recommended due to difficulties with standardization that could impact scores, and a complete lack of psychometric data. Professionals interested in using an IRI to measure pre- to postintervention progress could examine more psychometrically sound tools such as the Standardized Reading Inventory (2nd ed.; Newcomer, 1999; T6:2354) or the Gray Oral Reading Test (4th ed.; Wiederholt & Bryant, 2001; 111). Use of the BRI for pre- and posttesting cannot be recommended until alternate form, test-retest, and/or delayed-alternative form reliability estimates are conducted in order to assure that changes in scores are due to growth in achievement and not test error.

The most important issue for the BRI, or any other IRI, when using the data to determine instructional placement is content validity. In other words, how well does the assessment instrument match the student's reading curriculum? The BRI manual indicates that the reading passages were compared to one or more readability formulae, but does not provide information about what those formulae determined, and there was no mention

of how these passages compared to various reading curricula. Professionals interested in determining instructional placements may wish to consult Gickling's (Gickling & Rosenfield, 1995) version of curriculum-based assessment (CBA), which interprets and assesses Bett's model using the child's reading curriculum. This not only assures a match between assessment and curriculum, but data also exist to support the reliability (Burns, Tucker, Frame, Foley, & Hauser, 2000) and instructional validity (Shapiro, 1992) of CBA results.

SUMMARY. The Basic Reading Inventory is one of the oldest and most widely used IRIs. The eighth edition includes two additional forms and an appendix containing readiness assessments for emergent literacy students. However, several significant concerns pointed out in previous reviews, centered mostly on a lack of psychometric data, still exist. Additionally, the word lists are dated, administration procedures are poorly standardized and could impact results, some comprehension formats are inadequately sampled, no data are provided to support any of the purported uses of the test data, and the level of match between passages and common reading curricula is unknown.

Previous reviews of the BRI are largely negative because of this lack of psychometric data, yet the test is in its 30th year. However, the *Standards for Educational and Psychological Testing* (American Educational Research Association, American Psychological Association, & National Council on Measurement in Education, 1999) calls for data to support the stability and usefulness of results. Therefore, use of the BRI is not recommended until additional data are provided.

REVIEWER'S REFERENCES

American Educational Research Association, American Psychological Association, & National Council on Measurement in Education. (1999). *Standards for educational and psychological testing.* Washington, DC: American Educational Research Association.

Betts, E. A. (1946). *Foundations of reading instruction, with emphasis on differential guidance.* New York: American Book Company.

Burns, M. K., Tucker, J. A., Frame, J., Foley, S., & Hauser, A. (2000). Interscorer, alternate-form, internal consistency, and test-retest reliability of Gickling's model of curriculum-based assessment for reading. *Journal of Psychoeducational Assessment, 18,* 353–360.

Burns, M. K., Tucker, J. A., Hauser, A., Thelen, R., Holmes, K., & White, K. (in press). The minimum fluency rate necessary for comprehension: A potential criterion for curriculum-based assessments. *Assessment for Effective Intervention.*

Gickling, E., & Rosenfield, S. (1995). Best practices in curriculum-based assessment. In A. Thomas & J. Grimes (Eds.), *Best practices in school psychology* (3rd ed., pp. 587–595). Washington, DC: National Association of School Psychologists.

Hasbrouch, J. E., & Tindal, G. (1992). Curriculum-based oral reading fluency norms for students in grades 2 through 5. *Teaching Exceptional Children, 24*(3), 41–44.

Newcomer, P. L. (1999). The Standardized Reading Inventory (2nd ed.). Austin, TX: PRO-ED.

Shapiro, E. S. (1992). Use of Gickling's model of curriculum-based assessment to improve reading in elementary age students. *School Psychology Review, 21,* 168–176.

Wiederholt, J. L., & Bryant, B. R. (2001). Gray Oral Reading Test (4th ed.). Austin, TX: PRO-ED.

Review of the Basic Reading Inventory, Eighth Edition by ZANDRA S. GRATZ, Associate Professor of Psychology, Kean University, Union, NJ:

DESCRIPTION AND DEVELOPMENT. The Basic Reading Inventory (BRI) is an individually administered measure used to establish a youngster's Frustration, Independent, and Instructional reading levels. This is accomplished through the use of graded word lists and comprehension passages; six forms are provided. Materials range from pre-primer through Grade 12. Additional early assessments are provided. Designed to be used by teachers, the BRI offers suggestions for both quantitative and qualitative inferences.

Graded word lists are administered to establish the level at which to begin the graded reading passages and to garner information relative to the youngster's word identification strategies. Administration of the reading passages during oral reading yields scores on miscues as well as comprehension. Miscue analysis, in context, is a new feature to the current edition. Three procedures for interpreting miscues are offered. The first involves the overall count of miscues, the second involves the type miscue (substitution, insertion, omission, and reversal), and the third is a qualitative analysis of miscues involving such elements as graphic similarity. Several strategies for scoring Comprehension are offered. These include asking the BRI-supplied comprehension questions, which include topic, evaluation, inference and vocabulary items; assessing engagement (congruity of wrong answers to the test); asking the test taker to retell the story; and combining retelling with questions. Other scores including Reading Rate, Listening Level, and Silent Reading Comprehension are available. No estimate of the time needed to administer the BRI is offered.

The manual is 475 pages in length and at first glance is overwhelming. However, only the first 117 pages present information relative to the development, administration, and use of the BRI. The remaining pages, the bulk of the manual, contain the actual test material and evaluation forms. Icons appear in the margins of the manual to alert the reader to cautionary statements, administration tips, or segments demonstrated in the companion CD. The CD provides video presentations of youngsters being administered the BRI and forms for use when administering the BRI. Although some difficulty was met when downloading the necessary software to view the CD (particularly the video), once accomplished, the downloads were helpful. Throughout the manual, the reader is referred to a variety of reading resources that may be used in concert with the BRI. Although the manual is clear and easy to read, the various forms, levels, and alternate scoring procedures are somewhat cumbersome to maneuver through.

TECHNICAL. The manual cautions the BRI user to establish rapport with the test taker and to completely and accurately record the student's reading behavior in order for the BRI to "yield valid, reliable, and useful results" (p. 20). However, the manual provides no information as to the psychometric properties of the BRI. That is, the manual offers no information as to the level of score reliability or validity that can be achieved if administration and scoring procedures are followed. Beyond this, the manual indicates "you can probably omit one question without changing the scoring guide at the bottom of every passage" (p. 43). The word "probably" does not engender confidence in the efficacy of the scores when different users can omit different items.

A review of the literature located a reliability study of an earlier version of the BRI in which Pearson estimates of alternate form reliability ranged from .64 to .73 (Helgren-Lempesis & Mangru, 1986). Although these coefficients are moderate at best, some suggest this level of reliability is sufficient in that differences in passage content across and within forms interact with test takers' attention, understanding, and recall of material (Bader & Wisendanger, 1989). This attitude toward informal reading inventories may explain the paucity of available reliability data. The manual offers many references that articulate the conceptual basis of the BRI. To some extent, these citations are suggestive of the construct validity of the BRI. However, no information is provided to support the contention that the BRI actualizes the theoretical constructs that underpin it.

The BRI provides reading rate normative data based on a study wherein the method for computing reading rate was not consistent with that recommended in the BRI. Although the manual suggest the user exercise caution in using the data, one wonders why the data were included in the manual. No information is offered as to how to take into account the different scoring methods. The manual indicates that the numerical criteria for the establishment of levels does not represent absolute standards. Despite this, use of alternate form reading passages is suggested as a means of measuring change over time. The manual also provides equivalency data between BRI levels and other reading programs such as Reading Recovery; however, no data are offered that delineate the manner in which these comparisons were made.

COMMENTARY. As noted in earlier reviews (e.g., Harwell, 2001), the usefulness of the BRI rests on whether it is viewed as an assessment tool or as an ancillary to instruction. If the user's primary interest is in using the BRI to assess youngsters' instructional, frustration, and independent reading levels, other measures (e.g., Degrees of Reading Power; T6:753) exist that provide acceptable psychometric evidence and linkages to instructional material. The many scores provided by the BRI may be considered by some as providing a rich picture of the reading ability of a youngster. However, the current reviewer has concerns about the meaning of the scores generated and the inferences that can be drawn from examining the pattern across scores. The absence of psychometric data precludes confidence in classifications based on BRI results.

The primary advantage of the BRI appears to be that of an ancillary to instruction rather than a means of assessment. In such a use, it is up to the potential user to examine carefully the content validity of the BRI. This would require an analysis of the extent to which the BRI passages, scores, and interpretations are likely to support a particular instructional program. The manual cautions the reader to use BRI results in conjunction with observation, student records, and other test data; otherwise errors could result. Although a reasonable caution, no information is provided as to how to integrate BRI results with the other data consulted, nor does the manual describe how to resolve conflicts. Beyond this, no data are provided to suggest that the BRI provides information that goes beyond that accessible from other sources.

The BRI's potential rests in its ability to develop a detailed profile of reading behavior. However, to make use of the myriad of scoring schemes offered by the BRI, considerable expertise in reading is necessary. For example, there are four ways of scoring the Comprehension questions; to do this successfully, and make credible, useful diagnostic decisions, considerable knowledge of the psychology of reading and reading pedagogies is necessary. For this reason, the BRI may be more appropriate for use by a reading specialist than a classroom teacher.

SUMMARY. The BRI used by a trained reading clinician offers a means to develop a profile of reading behavior and instructional interventions. As an assessment tool, to classify students by reading ability, the BRI lacks psychometric evidence to support its use.

REVIEWER'S REFERENCES
Bader, L. A., & Wiesenger, K. D. (1989). Realizing the potential of informal reading inventories. *Journal of Reading, 32,* 402–408.
Harwell, M. (2001). [Review of the Basic Reading Inventory, Seventh Edition.] In B. Plake & J. Impara (Eds.), *The fourteenth mental measurements yearbook* (pp. 112–113). Lincoln, NE: Buros Institute of Mental Measurements.
Helgren-Lempesis, V., & Mangrum, C. T. (1986). An analysis of alternate-form reliability of three commercially-prepared informal reading inventories. *Reading Research Quarterly, 21,* 209–215.

[30]

Basic Skills Locater Test.

Purpose: "Designed to assess a person's functional skill levels in math and language."

Population: Ages 15 to adult who are functioning below a 12th grade level.

Publication Date: 1998.

Scores, 2: Language, Math.

Administration: Group or individual.

Price Data, 2002: $195 per Basic Skills Locater Test (software version) including 1 guide, 1 reproducible test master, and software; $195 per Basic Skills Locater Test (print version) including 1 user's guide, 10 reusable test booklets, 100 answer sheets, 1 test key, and a Windows scoring disk; $995 per Network Version.

Time: (30–60) minutes.

Comments: Test results place test-takers into four levels corresponding to GED and grade levels: GED Level 1 (grades 1–3); GED Level 2 (grades 4–6); GED Level 3 (grades 7–8) and GED Level 4 (grades 9–12). Bar graphs representing competency in each level in the two domains of Language and Math yield 8 levels of competency for each test-taker.

Author: Helena Hendrix-Frye.

Publisher: Piney Mountain Press, Inc.

Review of the Basic Skills Locater Test by HOI K. SUEN, Professor of Educational Psychology, Pennsylvania State University, University Park, PA:

DESCRIPTION. The Basic Skills Locater Test (BSLT) is a 72-item multiple-choice test. The intended purpose of the test is to provide a quick and simple method of obtaining GED/grade levels for individuals in the areas of Language and Math usage. Of the 72 items, 36 were designed to address Language usage and the re-

little evidence is provided. The little evidence provided is neither adequate nor appropriate. The use of the BSLT for educational and counseling purposes is not recommended until appropriate and better evidence to support its scoring, reliability, and validity are gathered.

[31]

Beck Youth Inventories of Emotional & Social Impairment.

Purpose: To "evaluate children's emotional and social impairment."
Population: Ages 7–14.
Publication Date: 2001.
Forms, 5: Beck Depression Inventory for Youth, Beck Anxiety Inventory for Youth, Beck Anger Inventory for Youth, Beck Disruptive Behavior Inventory for Youth, Beck Self-Concept Inventory for Youth.
Administration: Group or individual.
Price Data, 2001: $108 per starter kit including manual (59 pages) and 25 combination inventory booklets: $70 per combination inventory including 25 booklets (quantity discounts available); $34.50 per 25 inventories (specify BDI-Y, BAI-Y, BANI-Y, BDBI-Y, or BSCI-Y) (quantity discounts available); $54 per manual.
Time: (5–10) minutes per inventory.
Comments: Brief self-report measures of behavior, cognitions, and feelings; consistent with IDEA requirements; inventories can be administered alone or in combination.
Authors: Judith S. Beck (tests and manual) and Aaron T. Beck (tests and manual) with John Jolly (manual).
Publisher: The Psychological Corporation.
a) BECK DEPRESSION INVENTORY FOR YOUTH.
Acronym: BDI-Y.
Score: Total.
Comments: Consistent with DSM-IV depression criteria.
b) BECK ANXIETY INVENTORY FOR YOUTH.
Acronym: BAI-Y.
Score: Total.
Comments: Reflects specific worries about school performance, the future, others' negative reactions; fears; physiological symptoms.
c) BECK ANGER INVENTORY FOR YOUTH.
Acronym: BANI-Y.
Score: Total.
Comments: Evaluates thoughts of being treated unfairly by others; feelings of anger, hatred.
d) BECK DISRUPTIVE BEHAVIOR INVENTORY FOR YOUTH.
Acronym: BDBI-Y.
Score: Total.

Comments: Identifies thoughts and behaviors associated with conduct disorder, oppositional-defiant behavior.
e) BECK SELF-CONCEPT INVENTORY FOR YOUTH.
Acronym: BSCI-Y.
Score: Total.
Comments: Taps cognitions of competence, potency, positive self-worth.

Review of the Beck Youth Inventories of Emotional & Social Impairment by MIKE BONNER, Assistant Professor in School Psychology, University of Nebraska at Omaha, Omaha, NE:

DESCRIPTION. The Beck Youth Inventories of Emotional & Social Impairment (BYI) is a set of five self-report rating scales for use separately or in various combinations for children ages 7 to 14. The five inventories, separately named, address five areas of emotional and behavioral disturbance: the Beck Depression Inventory for Youth (BDI-Y), Beck Anxiety Inventory for Youth (BAI-Y), Beck Anger Inventory for Youth (BANI-Y), Beck Disruptive Behavior for Youth (BDBI-Y), and Beck Self-Concept Inventory for Youth (BSCI-Y). A combination form is also available that includes all five scales.

Each inventory contains 20 statements for which the child indicates the frequency in which he or she experiences having that thought, feeling, or behavior. In the Combination Form, the items are numbered consecutively on continuous pages to facilitate separate scoring, yet appear as one instrument. Scores are reported in *T*-Scores, with cumulative percentages for each norm group also available. Norms are available for males and females in age groups 7–10 and 11–14 years. The time required to complete each of the inventories is reported to range from 5–10 minutes whereas the complete set requires 30 minutes to 1 hour, depending upon the child's reading ability or other circumstances.

According to the manual, the inventories have been written at approximately a second grade level, meaning most children covered by the norm group should be able to read the items and instructions. However, this needs to be verified for individual children, particularly those who are younger or with language- and reading-related difficulties. The manual states that "significant variability was encountered in the reading level" (p. 9) for younger children. If necessary the inventories can be read to children. Administration procedures are for the examiner to read the instructions to the child, after introducing the general task demands to the child. Essentially, the child is asked to rate statements related to how often they think or feel consistent with the item, "especially in the past two weeks" (manual, p. 10).

DEVELOPMENT. The manual describes the development of the inventories as following pilot studies for initial item selection in clinical settings, apparently generated from statements children provided in therapy. Item selection is not described in great detail, but yielded 25 items. These items were further reduced to the published 20 items by four criteria: low item to total correlation, higher inventory alpha with item deleted, clinical judgment, and nonsignificant factor loading across or within inventory factor analyses.

The final norm group of 800 was drawn from an initial ("community") sample of 1,100 children aged 7 to 14 from "Northeast, South, North Central, and West" (manual, p. 25) regions of the United States. Development of the norm group is generally well described. Significant recruitment and screening effort went into ensuring that participants met demographic criteria. Unfortunately, they do not detail these "varied demographic characteristics" (manual, p. 25). Additional inclusion criteria of regular school attendance, first language of English, second grade reading level, and no severe physical or mental condition were screened by telephone interviewers from a pool selected for the community sample.

Methodology employed during the standardization across the 800 children at 30 plus sites in each region are also fairly well described. Assigning children to one of five possible test sequences controlled for order effect with the various inventories. Four hundred children also received a second instrument for use in validity studies. These instruments varied and will be further reviewed in the Technical section below.

The final standardization sample was stratified from the community sample described above. The sample was stratified to match U.S. Census for ethnicity, parent education level, ages 7–10, ages 11–14, and gender. For this limited stratification, the sample was able to very closely match 1999 Census data, although there is some variation within specific demographic variables. For example, White boys aged 7–10 were matched

63.39% (census) to 63.82% (sample), whereas African American boys were slightly less represented in the sample (17.25% to 15.58%) and Hispanic boys were slightly overrepresented (14.77% to 16.08%). The community sample is reported to contain 5% of children reported to be receiving special education services, which is less than the national rate of 8.6% for special education placement (1998 U.S. Department of Education, cited in the manual). Unfortunately, the percentage of the final sample receiving special education services is not reported.

TECHNICAL. Internal consistency was computed for each of the five inventories across the gender/age norm group stratification. Cronbach's alpha coefficients are generally consistent, hovering around .9, with the Disruptive scale for 7–10 years being the lowest (.86 and .87 for girls and boys, respectively). The Depression and Anger scale coefficients were the strongest (.91 and .92 for girls and boys). Test-retest was calculated using a subsample of 105 children and a median retest interval of 7 days. No further information is reported on the methodology. Corrected correlations for the younger children (7–10 years) ranged from .74 to .90 and for the older children (11–14 years) ranged from .84 to .93. Although these are respectable coefficients for a self-report scale with children, the reader is cautioned that these are limited data (sample size, only one study) with which to fully consider reliability. Examining the coefficients for the individual scales shows they are variable across age and gender.

Intercorrelations among the five inventories were computed to argue for the validity of the internal structure of the inventories. Not surprisingly, there were high correlations found between the Depression, Anxiety, and Anger scales. The Anger and Disruptive Behavior scales also were highly correlated among the standardization norm group. This evidence should provide caution to practitioners when interpreting findings from the various scales as pure measures of the construct described by the inventory name.

Four concurrent validity studies were reported in the manual, conducted concurrently with standardization and norm development. The inventories were correlated with the Children's Depression Inventory (CDI), Revised Children's Manifest Anxiety Scale (RCMAS), Conners-Wells' Adolescent Self-Report Scale: Short Form

(CASS:S), and the Piers-Harris Children's Self-Concept Scale (PHCSCS). In general, correlations are consistent with expected patterns, but these data also support cautious interpretation. For example, although the Anxiety scale correlated highest with the RCMAS (.70), Anger and Depression were also highly correlated (.60 for each), suggesting that measuring anxiety, or any of these constructs in isolation is a risky proposition. The CASS:S Conduct Problems scale correlated highest with the Disruptive Behavior inventory (.69), but similar or higher correlations were obtained between the Anger inventory and the Hyperactive-Impulsive subscale (.68) and the AD/HD Index (.73) of the CASS:S. To complicate matters further, the Depression inventory correlated .69 with the AD/HD Index as well.

Criterion validity was presented by describing BYI scores of children receiving special education services and another set of children who were referred for clinical outpatient treatment. It was hypothesized that these two groups of children would express generally higher levels of distress on the inventories compared to matched control groups. In fact, mean differences were reported for all scales, although they were more significant in the special education-control comparison. Less robust differences were reported for the clinical-control comparisons, except for the Self-Concept inventory.

Discriminant validity was argued for by presenting data comparing scores of the clinical sample with various diagnoses. The manual appropriately cautions that results reported on differences between diagnostic groups "are preliminary and should be viewed with caution" (p. 40). One published study is available, providing additional preliminary construct validity evidence (Steer, Kumar, Beck, & Beck, 2001). This study showed scores for a sample of 100 children from a clinical outpatient setting correlated with the CDI and the Conners' Parent Rating Scale-Revised: Short Form. These data were supportive, consistent with preliminary data reported in the manual.

COMMENTARY AND SUMMARY. The BYI is a new set of self-report rating scales for use with school-aged children who have at least a second grade reading ability. The inventories are likely to be popular among school and clinical professionals due to their brevity, flexibility, and purported construct measures.

Although evidence supporting the psychometric technical adequacy of these scales is generally positive, it is preliminary. As a result, interpreting these scales as direct evidence of single constructs presented is not warranted. An even larger problem, and one that these scales share with all rating scales, is the undetermined reliability and validity associated with decisions practitioners will make regarding differential diagnosis, treatment, screening, or evaluation using data generated from these (or any) scales. Traditional psychometric analyses of reliability and validity are optimistic in relation to the decision reliability and incremental validity (Barnett, Lentz, & Macmann, 2000).

Despite this, use of rating scales such as these to guide diagnostic decision making remains popular. I expect applied practitioners will quickly add these scales to their repertoire and assess the added utility of these scales in the context of their clinical experience. Concurrently, I expect that these scales will be popular with researchers, which should add to the understanding of the technical properties, including decision reliability and incremental validity, of these measures.

REVIEWER'S REFERENCES

Barnett, D. W., Lentz, F. E., Jr., & Macmann, G. (2000). Psychometric qualities of professional practice. In E. S. Shapiro & T. R. Kratochwill (Eds.), *Behavioral assessment in schools: Theory, research, and clinical foundations* (2nd ed., pp. 355–386). New York: Guilford.

Steer, R. A., Kumar, G., Beck, J. S., & Beck, A. T. (2001). Evidence for the construct validities of the Beck Youth Inventories with child psychiatric outpatients. *Psychological Reports, 89*, 559–565.

Review of the Beck Youth Inventories of Emotional & Social Impairment by HUGH STEPHENSON, Assistant Professor of Psychology, Ithaca College, Ithaca, NY:

DESCRIPTION. The Beck Youth Inventories are five self-report paper-and-pencil measures that assess a broad range of behavioral and emotional concerns for children aged 7–14. They are intended to be brief screening questionnaires. The inventories can be used singly or together to assess Depression (BDI-Y), Anxiety (BAI-Y), Anger (BANI-Y), Disruptive Behavior (BDBI-Y), and Self-Concept (BSCI-Y).

Each scale contains 20 items. The response format is Likert type with respondents asked to indicate how frequently they have certain behaviors, thoughts, and emotions. Raw score totals are calculated in the test booklet and transferred to the profile sheet. The child's raw score can be converted to *T*-scores and percentile ranks. *T*-

score conversions are provided for two age bands and separately for males and females.

The authors recommend the scale for use in schools, outpatient, forensic, residential managed care, and medical settings. The manual states that the administration of the inventories may be conducted by a variety of people under supervision, but the individual responsible for the overall administration and interpretation of the inventories should be trained in clinical assessment procedures.

DEVELOPMENT. The manual provides a broad overview of scale development. Initial item selection was based on the verbal reports of children in therapy. The authors do not say how these reports were collected. In some cases items were chosen on their ability to predict clinical criteria. The final inventories were based on responses to 25-item inventories from which 5 items were dropped during pilot studies. The authors state that items were dropped for a number of psychometric reasons including low item-total correlations and failure to load on relevant factors in a factor analysis. The fact that exactly 5 items were dropped from each scale suggests elegance was also a criterion.

The community sample used for development included 1,100 children aged 7–14. Participants were recruited from different regions of the country by phone and their parents received payment for participation. The order of test administration was varied to control for sequence effects.

TECHNICAL. The normative standardization sample includes 800 children stratified to match the 1999 U.S. Census for ethnicity and parent education level. The normative reference groups for *T*-score conversions are males and females aged 1–10, and 11–14. According to the authors these four normative samples capture most of the significant differences in the variability of inventory scores.

In terms of internal consistency, the alpha values for each scale range from .86 to .92. Test-retest coefficients on a subsample of 105 individuals (corrected for variability on the first testing) range from .74 to .93 for the five scales. The median time between testing is reported as 7 days.

Intercorrelations between the Beck Youth Inventory scales range from -.23 between Self-Concept and Anxiety for males aged 7–10 to .81 between Anger and Depression for males 11–14. The weakest relationships generally exist between Self-Concept and the other scales, which is what one would expect as Self-Concept is conceptually distinct from Anger, Depression, Disruptive Behavior, and Anxiety. Disruptive Behavior also has lower correlations with other scales except Anger.

The manual also reports convergent validity studies that examine the relationship between the Beck Youth Inventories and other measures of related constructs. The correlation between the Depression scale and the Children's Depression Inventory (CDI) is .72, higher than any other correlation between the Beck Youth Inventories and the CDI. However, the correlation between the Anger and Depression scales of the Beck Youth Inventories in the male 11–14-year-old group is .81 and .78 for females in the same age group. This suggests that the BDI-Y operationalization of depression taps elements of anger that the CDI does not, or that the Depression scale of the Beck Youth Inventories is not sufficiently differentiated from Anger.

The Anxiety scale is reported as having a correlation of .70 with the Revised Children's Manifest Anxiety Scale.

The correlation between the Disruptive Behavior scale and the Conduct Problems subscale of the Conners-Wells' Adolescent Self-Report Scale: Short Form is reported as .69. There are also high correlations between the Anger scale and the Conners-Wells' Hyperactive Impulsive scale (r = .68) and AD/HD Index (r = .73), which suggests poor differentiation between anger and ADHD.

Concurrent validity of the Self-Concept scale is also addressed in a study that examined its relationship with the Piers-Harris Children's Self-Concept Scale. Although the Self-Concept scale has a correlation of .61 with the Piers-Harris, the Depression scale and Anxiety scale have stronger relationships, being .67 and .63, respectively. The authors suggest this may be due to elements of negative affect that are tapped by the PHSCSC but not by the Self-Concept scale. It also may indicate problems with the Self-Concept scale itself.

In addition to the standardization sample, the developers examined response patterns of both a special education and a clinical sample. The special education sample includes 89 children between 8–12 years of age. Fifty percent of this sample is white with 63% being male. Sixty-one percent of the sample received special education services for less than half of the day. A comparison of this sample and a sample matched for age, gender, and ethnicity shows effect sizes for differences between the mean T scores in the order of .50 to .57. These effect sizes indicate that the typical T-score for a student in the special education sample is approximately half a standard deviation higher than the mean for the matched controls.

The clinical sample is predominantly white (83%) and male (70%) with ADHD being the most common diagnosis. The authors describe the sample as mostly in the 7–10-year-old range. Some categories are not well represented (i.e., females with mood disorders account for just 6.54% of the total sample). Surprisingly, no significant differences exist between the clinical sample and matched controls on the Anxiety or Depression scales. Small to moderate effect sizes exist for the Anger, Disruptive Behavior and Self-Concept scales. This may be due to the fact that almost 40% of this clinical sample has an ADHD diagnosis as opposed to mood on anxiety diagnosis. When specific diagnostic groups are isolated, more meaningful differences emerge. The mean T-score for Depression of those in the clinical group who had a diagnosis of mood disorder is 63.82, significantly higher than other diagnostic groups. Low Self-Concept scores are also associated with a diagnosis of mood disorder.

The manual provides guidelines for clinical application and interpretation. Although detailed discussions of the assessment of Anxiety and Depression are included, the manual notes that the scales should not be used for diagnosis. The manual provides less guidance for the interpretation of Disruptive Behavior, Anger, and Self-Concept.

The authors suggest interpretations for specific T-score ranges. A T-score of 55–59 is described as a mild elevation, and 60–69 as moderate elevation. Thus, a child with a score of 55 on the Depression scale would be described as having a mild elevation on depression. This might be a bit misleading as it puts the child in the 73rd percentile of the normal population. More than one in four children will have mild elevations on this scale. Because the mean Depression score for those identified with a mood disorder was 63.82, which corresponds to the 91st percentile of the normal population, higher cutoffs might be more reasonable.

COMMENTARY. The BYI is a brief screening tool that can assess a variety of childhood concerns within the normal population of children aged 7–14. It is suitable for use in a wide range of settings for both group and individual administra-

tion. There is some evidence that the high scores on the Depression and Self-Concept scales call for further assessment, but more research is needed and, as the authors note, additional assessments are needed to make a diagnosis.

The intercorrelations of the BYI scales and their relationships with other instruments suggest that some of the measures may tap related constructs. The Anger and Depression scales may be insufficiently differentiated. In addition, the Anger scale seems closely related to external measures of ADHD, and Self-Concept has not been demonstrated to be closely related to an independent measure of that construct. The instrument will benefit greatly from further research that helps elaborate the construct validity of each scale.

The manual states that each scale may be read to respondents but provides no relevant normative or validity data to support this use. It is reasonable to assume that responses may change when a child is read an item such as "I wish I were dead" or "I like being mean to others" and asked to respond to it versus reading it.

Several typographical errors are noted in the manual. On page 11, for instance, the acronym for the disruptive behavior scale is identified as the BDBI-I when it should be the BDBI-Y. This adds to the confusion of distinguishing the five scales at a glance because they are named BSCI-Y, BAI-Y, BDI-Y, BANI-Y, and BDBI-Y. Another error noted is on page 34. Here it is stated that the correlation between the Conners-Wells' Conduct Problems score and the BDBI-Y is .70. It is reported in the table (5.6), however, as .69.

SUMMARY. The BYI is a brief screening instrument for use in a variety of settings. It elicits self-reports of Depression, Anxiety, Anger, Self-Concept, and Disruptive Behavior in 7–14-year-old children. It provides valuable information in addition to parent reports and other sources of information. It should not be used in isolation to make a diagnosis or treatment decision. It can provide an indicator of which children may benefit from further assessment.

[32]

Behavior Rating Inventory of Executive Function.

Purpose: Designed to assess impairment of executive function behaviors in the home and school environments.

Population: Ages 5–18.
Publication Dates: 1996–2000.
Acronym: BRIEF.
Administration: Individual or group.
Scores, 11: Inhibit, Shift, Emotional Control, Behavioral Regulation Index, Initiate, Working Memory, Plan/Organize, Organization of Materials, Monitor, Metacognition Index, Global Executive Composite.
Forms, 2: Parent Form, Teacher Form.
Price Data: Available from publisher for introductory kit including professional manual, 25 Parent Form Questionnaires, 25 Teacher Form Questionnaires, 50 Parent Form Scoring Summary/Profile Forms, and 50 Teacher Form Scoring Summary/Profile Forms.
Time: (10–15) minutes.
Comments: Ratings by teachers, parents, or guardians.
Authors: Gerard A. Gioia, Peter K. Isquith, Steven C. Guy, and Lauren Kenworthy.
Publisher: Psychological Assessment Resources, Inc.

Review of the Behavior Rating Inventory of Executive Function by CORINE FITZPATRICK, Associate Professor and Acting Advisor, Counseling Psychology, Manhattan College, Riverdale, NY:

DESCRIPTION. "The Behavior Rating Inventory of Executive Function (BRIEF) is a questionnaire for parents and teachers of school age children that enables professionals to assess executive function behaviors in the home and school environment" (professional manual, p. 1). Designed for a broad range of children, ages 5 to 18 years, it includes those with learning disabilities, attentional disorders, traumatic brain injuries, lead exposure, pervasive developmental disorders, depression, and other developmental, neurological, psychiatric, and medical conditions. It includes a teacher form and a parent form, each containing 86 items within eight clinical scales that measure different aspects of executive functioning: Inhibit, Shift, Emotional Control, Initiate, Working Memory, Plan/Organize, Organization of Materials, and Monitor. "The clinical scales form two broader indexes, Behavioral Regulation and Metacognition, and an overall score, the Global Executive Composite" (professional manual, p. 1). The focus is on executive functions, which are a set of processes responsible for guiding, directing, and managing cognitive, emotional, and behavioral functions, particularly during active, novel problem solving. It is one of the first systems of this sort and represents a significant advance in the assessment of children.

The parent form and the teacher form yield scores in *T*-score units and percentiles based on either a national norm group or by gender in the norm group. "The BRIEF was standardized and validated for use with boys and girls, ages 5 through 18" (professional manual, p. 5). The BRIEF can be administered and scored by individuals who do not have formal training in neuropsychology, school psychology, counseling psychology, or related fields. The BRIEF parent form is designed to be completed by the parent or guardian and it is recommended that both parents complete the ratings if possible. "The BRIEF teacher form is designed to be completed by any adult who has had extended contact with the child in an academic setting" (professional manual, p. 6). The authors note that it is important for this person to have had a considerable amount of contact with the child (e.g., 1 month of daily contact would be sufficient). The form takes 10–15 minutes to complete. Calculation of raw score totals for the eight clinical scales is easily done on the attached carbonless scoring sheet. Scoring also includes a negativity scale and an inconsistency scale. *T*-scores and percentile ranks are then obtained using the normative table. The Behavior Regulation Index (BRI), the Metacognition Index (MI), and the Global Executive Composite (GEC), which is the sum of the other two indexes, are then calculated. Profile forms are available for interpretation.

TEST DEVELOPMENT AND THEORY. The BRIEF has been carefully developed and represents a synthesis of what is known about the brain basis of executive functions and the role of developmental factors. The authors reject the notion that organization of the executive functions is seated solely in the prefrontal region. Rather, they contend that executive dysfunction can arise from damage to prefrontal regions as well as damage to the densely interconnected posterior or subcortical areas. Their review of the literature on metacognition is focused on development, in particular in relation to learning disabilities.

The items for many of the components have been derived from a review of the relevant literature and clinical experience, including clinical interviews by the authors. Each of the clinical scales has established constructs and items with high content validity. Item content was further refined by comparison to other well-known behavior rating scales (e.g., the Child Behavior Checklist; the

Shift (switching to a new task or activity), and Emotional Control (modulate emotional responses). The Metacognition Index scales include Initiate (initiating tasks and activities), Working Memory (manipulating information in memory), Plan/Organize (manage task demands), Organization of Materials (orderliness of work and play areas), and Monitor (self-assessments).

The BRIEF takes roughly 15 minutes to administer. The Parent and Teacher versions each include 86 items, although both versions use different items. Nevertheless, both versions measure the eight scales described above. Parents or teachers rate the individual on 86 behaviors such as "is fidgety" and "makes careless errors" by indicating whether the behavior occurs *never, sometimes,* or *often.* Ratings can be administered individually (e.g., one parent) or in groups (e.g., all family members or a group of teachers). Scale scores are computed by summing the weighted individual items on that scale, where a rating of *never* receives a score of 1, a rating of *sometimes* receives a score of 2, and a rating of *often* receives a score of 3. For example, 5 items with a score of 3 would yield a score of 15.

The BRIEF is accompanied by a 150-page manual, complete with information about administration, scoring, reliability and validity, interpretation, development, and standardization of the instruments. Six case illustrations are included as well that are helpful guides to interpretation. The manual is clearly written and concise. However, one problem is that the manual is too brief in places, including the rationale for the BRIEF, as well as a discussion of why the authors included the present scales. Much more could be said about the controversial topic of executive functions and how they are related to one another in the cognitive system (Butler & Winne, 1995). In addition, a more thorough description of each subscale would help the novice examiner interpret the scales, and the test as a whole, more accurately.

At present, it is somewhat unclear how one might interpret the BRIEF because there are three distinct "levels of interpretation" (professional manual, p. 20). One option is the combined score based on 86 items, which the manual refers to as the Global Executive Composite. This score provides a measure of "the child's executive dysfunction level" (professional manual, p. 21). A second option is to use two index scores referred to as the Behavioral Regulation Index and the

Metacognition Index. The former provides a measure of "the child's ability to switch mental set"; whereas the latter measures "the child's ability to initiate, plan, organize, and sustain future-oriented problem solving" (professional manual, p. 20). A third option is to use each of the eight scales that comprise the BRIEF. The authors recommend using the eight individual scales, in part, because they can be charted and visually inspected.

TECHNICAL. The BRIEF has been standardized on a sample of 1,419 parents and 720 teachers. Samples matched key demographic variables of the United States population. Approximately equal numbers of males and females were used across five ethnic categories. The manual presents scores from the standardization sample broken down by gender, age, ethnicity, and SES.

The manual provides a concise but thorough discussion of reliability and validity. Reliability for each of the eight scales is approximately .90 using Cronbach's alpha. The Global Executive Composite reliability is .97. Test-retest reliability at 3 weeks was .91 for the global executive composite, and approximately .80 for the individual scales. However, in contrast to the generally high intra- and interscale reliability, interrater reliability for parents and teachers rating the same child was .50 or below.

Construct validity was assessed in two ways. The first was to perform an exploratory factor analysis of the full scale using an oblique rotation. This yielded two factors that explained 75% of variation in the sample data. The two factors corresponded to the Behavioral Regulation and the Metacognition Indices described above. The factor analyses indicated a correlation of .65 between the factors. The second way construct validity was assessed was to correlate the scales with a variety of outcome measures such as the Child Behavior Checklist (Achenbach, 1991) and the Behavior Assessment System for Children-Parent Rating Scales (Reynolds & Kamphaus, 1992). Generally speaking, the individual scales and global executive composite scores correlated with aggressive behavior in the .50–.80 range, with attention problems in the .6–.90 range, with delinquency in the .40–.60 range, with hyperactivity in the .30–.60 range, and with depression in the .30–.50 range. In addition, the Working Memory and Inhibit scales were used to detect differences in different diagnostic groups of individuals with ADHD. These scales typically yielded an 80% prediction accuracy, demonstrating a reasonable degree of predictive validity.

COMMENTARY. The strengths of the BRIEF include (a) easy administration and scoring, (b) alternative forms suitable for parents and teachers, (c) a thorough standardization sample, (d) a well-written manual, (e) high reliability and construct validity, and (f) reasonable predictive validity. Weaknesses include (a) use of subjective ratings, (b) that scores depend in large part on how well the rater knows the child, (c) the relatively low interrater reliability between parents and teachers.

SUMMARY. Overall, the BRIEF provides a quick and efficient measure of executive dysfunction. It provides specific information about two major subscales, the Behavioral Regulation Index and the Metacognition Index. These indices provide useful information about the child's ability to control and switch behavior, and effective planning and problem solving. The BRIEF probably is most valid and useful when interpretations are based on the eight scales, each having a narrow interpretation.

REVIEWER'S REFERENCES

Achenbach, T. M. (1991). *Manual for the Child Behavior Checklist and 1991 Profile.* Burlington, VT: Department of Psychiatry, University of Vermont.
Butler, D. L., & Winne, P. H. (1995). Feedback and self-regulated learning: A theoretical synthesis. *Review of Educational Research, 65,* 245–281.
Reynolds, C. R., & Kamphaus, R. W. (1992). Behavior Assessment System for Children. Circle Pines, MN: American Guidance Service.

[33]
Behavioral Objective Sequence.

Purpose: Designed to "assist special educators and other professionals assess behavioral competencies of students with emotional and behavioral disorders."

Population: Students (preschool through high school) with emotional and behavioral disorders.

Publication Date: 1998.

Acronym: BOS.

Scores, 6: Adaptive Behaviors, Self-Management Behaviors, Communication Behaviors, Interpersonal Behaviors, Task Behaviors, Personal Behaviors.

Administration: Individual.

Price Data, 2001: $39.95 per manual (1998, 104 pages), recording forms, and test.

Time: Administration time not reported.

Comments: "Can be used as a bank of (behavioral) objectives, as a rating scale, or as a structured observational system"; completed by educational/psychological professionals about a student; software program available.

Authors: Sheldon Braaten (test and software program) and John B. Merbler (software program).

Publisher: Research Press.

Review of the Behavioral Objective Sequence by M. DAVID MILLER, Professor of Educational Psychology, University of Florida, Gainesville, FL:

DESCRIPTION. The Behavioral Objective Sequence (BOS) is an instrument intended to help special educators and other educational professionals to assess the behavioral competencies of students with serious emotional and behavioral disorders (EBD). These behavioral competencies would identify developmentally appropriate strengths and deficits of students with EBD to allow development of realistic goals and interventions based on specific behavioral objectives. Consequently, the BOS would be used to prepare an Individual Education Plan (IEP) or an intervention for a student with EBD. The manual also suggests that it could be used with other primary disabilities or any student exhibiting challenging behaviors.

The BOS can be used for individual assessment or program evaluation. For individual assessments, the BOS can help to inform appropriate placement options for students with EBD or can be used to develop specific and targeted interventions for the students. To assist the user in developing interventions, the manual includes Individual Intervention Plan Forms that can be used to target short-term goals and objectives. The manual has a wide array of tools to use the instrument for planning interventions, monitoring changes, and interpreting results.

DEVELOPMENT. The original BOS was completed in 1976. Ongoing development, including reliability and validity studies, led to the current version of the BOS. The BOS was developed using behavioral and developmental concepts in Wood's model of Developmental Therapy. Individual items were generated through an analysis of the development literature and a task analysis.

The instrument consists of 233 items on six domains. The six subscales are: Adaptive Behaviors, Self-Management Behaviors, Communication Behaviors, Interpersonal Behaviors, Task Behaviors, and Personal Behaviors. Each of the items is an observable behavior that can be scored through a team or an individual observer. Each item includes a behavioral statement with multiple specific examples for raters to include in rating the student. Mastery criteria for the objectives are arbitrary and determined by the user. Consequently, they will vary by rater. The BOS suggests that high mastery standards should be set and frequent observations can lead to more confidence in the ratings.

The behaviors within each subscale are divided into three levels based on the developmental age associated with the behaviors. Level 3 skills are based on very young children (before Grade 1) without disabilities. Level 2 are skills that are generally mastered in the elementary school years. Level 1 skills are generally mastered in adolescence or as young adults. Consequently, skills and behaviors are identified in six areas that show a student's approximate developmental level in the absence of disabilities. The behavioral objectives are also placed in sequence for examining the developmental level of the student.

The list of skills are not considered to be exhaustive and do not contain academic skills or specific career/vocational skills. However, the skills are broad enough to use in preparing an IEP. The BOS can be used to set relevant goals and objectives as well as suggesting interventions. On the other hand, the authors caution that this instrument should be part of a larger and more comprehensive assessment process that should include a variety of instruments and other information.

TECHNICAL. Little information is given on the technical quality of the BOS. According to the manual, "limited data exists which does indicate that the BOS has strong characteristics for use as a rating scale and predictive potential for assisting in making placement decisions" (p. 24). A single, unpublished study was completed to examine the reliability and validity of scores from the instrument. The study was completed over a 2-year period with about 300 students with EBD or other disabilities and ranging in age from kindergarten through high school. Although no data are included in the manual, the manual reports a study that does include reliability estimates (interrater and test-retest) and several indicators of validity including content validity, factor analysis and correlations with the Child Behavior Checklist. Because specific data are not included in the manual nor in any published report, the technical quality of the BOS remains questionable. This reinforces the author's assertion that the instrument should only be used in conjunction with other sources of information in planning interventions or placements for students with EBD or any other disability.

SUMMARY. The Behavioral Objective Sequence provides important information about students with EBD with regard to development on behavioral objectives over a broad range of areas and a wide range of ages. Although the technical information on the BOS is limited, the manual contains the necessary cautions for using the instrument. That is, the instrument should not be used for high stakes decisions in the absence of other information and mastery criteria would need to be more clearly defined. However, in conjunction with other assessments and a clearer definition of the mastery criteria, the BOS can be useful in planning IEPs and interventions for students having behavioral problems, particularly students with EBD.

Review of the Behavioral Objective Sequence by STEPHANIE STEIN, Professor of Psychology, Central Washington University, Ellensburg, WA:

DESCRIPTION. The Behavioral Objective Sequence (BOS) is intended to be a task-analyzed sequence of 233 behavioral objectives or skills "that are essential to the success of children and youth in social and school context" (manual, p. 2). The items are divided into six different subscales: Adaptive Behaviors, Self-Management Behaviors, Communication Behaviors, Interpersonal Behaviors, Task Behaviors, and Personal Behaviors. Within each subscale are further "sub-subscales" of goals and objectives hierarchically arranged across three levels of functioning.

The skills presented in the BOS are divided into three different levels. The Level 3 skills (also referred to as the 300-level) represent basic skills that are typically mastered by young children without disabilities prior to Grade 1. The Level 2 skills (200-level) are those skills typically mastered by elementary school age children. Finally, the Level 1 skills (100-level) are the more advanced skills typically mastered during adolescence and early adulthood.

Each numbered behavioral objective is positively phrased in terms of desirable, prosocial behaviors. Following each objective is a list of behavioral examples that can be used to determine whether the student has met that objective. The 233 behavioral objectives across the six subscales and the three levels of functioning are intended to serve as a scope and sequence of the non-academic skills necessary for success in school.

In addition to the list of skills and objectives, the BOS includes guidelines on selecting goals and objectives, establishing mastery criteria, using the BOS current performance form, making placement decisions with the BOS, using the BOS as a curriculum for inclusion, using the intervention plan forms, intervention planning, and conducting individual and program evaluation with the BOS. The appendix includes a plethora of forms including a Current Performance Form (which can be used with a 4-point rating scale), Baseline Recording Forms for each level, a Target Objective Functional Analysis Planning Worksheet, a Functional Analysis Planning Worksheet Summary, an Individual Intervention Plan Form, a Daily Monitoring Record, a form for Team Meeting Notes, a School-Community Agency Coordinated Intervention Plan, a form for Interagency Meeting Notes, Target Behavior Performance Charts, a Behavioral Progress Report, and an Annual Progress Summary Form. Finally, an optional software package is available that includes all of the behavioral objectives and forms.

DEVELOPMENT. Limited information is available on the development of the BOS. According to the manual, "each subscale is a domain of related and sequenced skills derived from task analysis, deductive logic, and child and adolescent development literature" (p. 2). In particular, the Developmental Therapy model by M. M. Wood (Wood, 1981; Wood, Davis, Swindle, & Quirk, 1996) was cited as a theoretical influence in the development of the BOS. No further information regarding development of the instrument is available in the manual.

TECHNICAL. According to the manual, research was conducted on the BOS with approximately 300 kindergarten through high school age students. About 200 students in the sample were apparently identified with emotional and behavioral disorders. The remaining 100 students were identified with learning disabilities. No further information about the subject pool is provided.

The BOS manual further reports that research studies have been conducted on the statistical properties of the BOS in relation to "interrater reliability, test-retest reliability, content validity, sequence validity, factor analysis" (manual, p. 24), and correlations with the Child Behavior Checklist. However, no specific data are provided in the manual.

The developer of the BOS concludes that the research results "indicate acceptable to high reliability levels across the subscales and predictive potential for identifying appropriate service settings" (manual, p. 24). He goes on to report correlations of around .90 (or higher) between the rating scale procedures of the BOS with direct daily observation procedures. Again, no specific studies or data are provided in support of these claims. Email correspondence with the BOS developer confirms that research has been conducted on the BOS, but the format and results of that research have not been provided.

COMMENTARY. It is clear how the BOS could have seductive appeal for school districts searching for ways to manage the Individual Education Plan (IEP) process for students with emotional or behavioral problems. The extensive list of objectives along with preprinted forms for any conceivable special education purpose make an attractive package that promises an easy way of designing developmentally appropriate behavior plans for students of any age. Whether the BOS actually delivers what it promises is unclear.

The significant weaknesses of the BOS are the lack of available normative data and technical or statistical research data to support the reliability and the validity of the scores. The manual makes brief reference to statistical research on the BOS but the only source provided is to a grant report that is not in wide circulation.

If the BOS is going to provide six subscales (as opposed to descriptive categories), then there should be evidence that these subscales (and their items) are based on something more than just deductive logic. Furthermore, there should be some evidence that the items in each level actually differentiate elementary-age students from younger or older students.

One of the primary tenets of the BOS is that it provides a list of behavioral skills that are essential for school success. However, no evidence is provided that successful students possess all or even most of these skills, nor is there evidence that unsuccessful students lack these skills. In fact, it is not even clear what is meant by an "unsuccessful" or a "successful" student, though one can surmise from the emphasis in the introduction that the developer is referring to students with and without emotional and behavioral disorders.

Several aspects of the BOS are also potentially confusing to users. Among these confusing aspects is the use of an optional rating scale that leads one to expect that some sort of summative or normative conclusion can be drawn about a student's functioning. However, the ratings are only intended to be rough indicators of frequency of the behavior, not normative indicators. In addition, the practice of labeling the more basic skills as Level 3 skills and the more advanced skills as Level 1 skills appears to be counterintuitive.

As for the strengths of the BOS, the objectives themselves appear to be clearly written in observable terms and represent desirable prosocial skills. The BOS does an admirable job of providing an extensive bank of possible behavioral objectives for inclusion in IEPs. The manual also recognizes that the list of objectives is not exhaustive and makes it possible for users to customize and add additional behavioral objectives.

SUMMARY. The decision to recommend or not recommend the BOS depends on what users are expecting from this instrument. If all that is needed is a bank of behavioral objectives for educators to use in developing IEPs, then the BOS appears to be a potentially quite useful and time-saving resource. However, users who are seeking an empirically supported system of hierarchical skills, divided by subscale and developmental level, should exercise extreme caution when considering the BOS. There are no empirical data in the manual to support the selection of the items, the development of the subscales, or the validity of the levels. Through email correspondence, the BOS developer reported that research on the instrument is currently underway and that an international research network on the BOS has been established. It is hoped that additional research data on the BOS will be included in a revision of the manual in the near future.

REVIEWER REFERENCES

Wood, M. M. (1981). *Developmental therapy source books* (Vols. 1 & 2). Austin, TX: PRO-ED.
Wood, M. M., Davis, K. R., Swindle, F. L., & Quirk, C. (1996). *Developmental therapy-Developmental teaching: Fostering social-emotional competence in troubled children and youth* (3rd ed.). Austin, TX: PRO-ED.

[34]

Behaviors and Experiences Inventory.

Purpose: "An initial screen for Attention-Deficit/Hyperactivity Disorder (ADHD), Conduct Disorder (CD), and Antisocial Personality Disorder (ASPD)."

Population: Adults.

Publication Dates: 1998–1999.

Acronym: BEI.

Scores, 24: ADHD: Inattention (Difficulty Sustaining Attention, Fails to Finish Assignments, Inattention to Details/Careless, Difficulty Organizing Tasks/Activities, Tendency to Lose Things, Distractible), Hyperactivity, Impulsivity, Conduct Disorder as a Child/Adolescent (Aggression, Destruction of Property, Deceitfulness or Theft, Serious Violation of Rules, Cruelty to Animals and Fire-Setting), Antisocial Personality Disorder (Failure to Conform to Social Norms, Deceitfulness, Impulsivity, Irritability/Aggressiveness, Reckless Disregard for Safety, Irresponsibility, Lack of Remorse), History of Abuse as a Child/Adolescent (Physical, Sexual, Emotional).

Administration: Individual.

Price Data: Available from publisher.

Time: (15–20) minutes.

Comments: Can be administered as paper-and-pencil questionnaire or as a structured interview; screens for DSM-IV diagnostic criteria, providing an estimate of the likelihood that an individual meets the criteria for ADHD, CD, and ASPD; covers current problems only.

Authors: Norman G. Hoffmann, David Mee-Lee, and Gerald D. Shulman.

Publisher: Evince Clinical Assessments.

Review of the Behaviors and Experiences Inventory by MARK R. COOPER, School Psychologist, Howard County Public Schools, Ellicott City, MD:

DESCRIPTION. The Behaviors and Experiences Inventory (BEI) is a 50-item instrument designed to screen for behavioral and personality disorders including reading difficulties/dyslexia, abuse victimization, Attention-Deficit/Hyperactivity Disorder (ADHD), Conduct Disorder, and Antisocial Personality Disorder. The BEI can be self-administered as a paper-and-pencil questionnaire or as a brief structured interview. All items are selection type (Yes/No). The authors recommend that the examiner determine if the respondent can read the questions before administering the BEI in a questionnaire format. If the examiner suspects reading difficulties, the respondent's reading ability can be verified by orally administering the second item first, which inquires about past reading problems. If the respondent has reading difficulties, then test items can be administered orally.

The BEI should only be administered, scored, and interpreted by qualified, licensed professionals with training and experience in diagnosing and treating addictions or mental health conditions (e.g., psychologists, psychiatrists, addictions counselors, and social workers). A scoring template is provided to assist the examiner in organizing responses and making interpretations. Items are grouped with each associated condition on the scoring template. The examiner can mark on the scoring template the items that the respondent answers affirmatively. The developers indicate that the BEI is not a diagnostic instrument. BEI results should only be used in conjunction with other information when making diagnostic decisions.

Items for ADHD, Conduct Disorder, and Antisocial Personality Disorder are based on symptoms listed in the *Diagnostic and Statistical Manual of Mental Disorders—Fourth Edition* (DSM-IV; American Psychiatric Association, 1994). The test manual provides information on the DSM-IV criteria for each of these three disorders and the corresponding items that attempt to measure each symptom. However, items on the BEI do not address each specific symptom, but rather attempt to capture the general intent of the symptoms. Furthermore, items on the BEI do not cover every DSM-IV symptom and qualifier. For example, the DSM-IV states a diagnosis of ADHD should only be made if an individual exhibits six or more symptoms of inattention or hyperactivity-impulsivity. The BEI only addresses six of the nine possible symptoms of inattention and not all of the nine hyperactivity-impulsivity symptoms listed in the DSM-IV. The BEI also does not include the required DSM-IV time and impact qualifiers, which state that symptoms of inattention and/or hyperactivity-impulsivity "have persisted for at least 6 months to a degree that is maladaptive and inconsistent with developmental level" (American Psychiatric Association, 1994, p. 83). The time qualifiers and impact criteria are also not addressed for Conduct Disorder or Antisocial Personality Disorder.

The BEI also contains items that require the respondent to provide information on reading difficulties and history of physical, sexual, and emotional abuse victimization and perpetration. Definitions of physical, sexual, and emotional abuse are provided in the test manual. Only one item on the BEI addresses reading difficulties.

DEVELOPMENT. The BEI is in its first edition (copyright, 1999). The development of the BEI was based upon data collected from a group of 244 males ranging in age from 17 to 36. These individuals were receiving treatment in an aftercare program for persons convicted of nonviolent drug-related offenses. The developers report that the pilot sample was predominantly Hispanic and African American, although demographic information was not collected on the initial version of the BEI. Items on the BEI reflect problems and disorders that are prevalent in a correctional population. Demographic items were added to the initial version of the BEI. The wording of several items was also altered in order to make them more socially desirable. The manual contains tables indicating the frequencies of positive responses from the pilot sample.

TECHNICAL. The BEI is not a norm-referenced test and does not yield standard scores. The pilot sample was used to modify test items and collect reliability and validity data. The BEI manual reports internal-consistency reliability coefficients. Cronbach alpha coefficients range from .74 for the Antisocial Personality Disorder index to .84 for the questions covering Conduct Disorder. Some items were excluded in the reliability analysis but were not omitted on the test. Therefore, these coefficients do not accurately reflect the internal consistency of all of the items associated with each disorder.

Validity data were not collected on the BEI. The authors mention that the BEI has high face validity, which is highly subjective and not a technically adequate determinant of validity. The manual states that the BEI is useful for identifying ADHD and Antisocial Personality Disorder in individuals entering treatment programs. However, no criterion-related validity evidence was gathered to measure the BEI's usefulness in identifying these disorders.

COMMENTARY. The utility of the BEI as a screening instrument for mental disorders, reading difficulties, and abuse cannot be determined given its psychometric inadequacies. No attempt was made to collect construct or criterion-related validity data. The developers point to the high frequency of positive items in their pilot sample as evidence of the instrument's usefulness. However, no attempt was made to compare the pilot sample of a correctional population with a sample of the general population.

Internal-consistency reliability coefficients are modest even for a screening instrument. In addition, the reliability data that were reported did not measure internal-consistency for all items in a given category. Items were excluded from the reliability analysis if they did not correlate highly with other items within the scale but were not eliminated from the test. Nevertheless, it is noteworthy that reliability coefficients were moderate given that there are relatively few items per scale. Internal consistency reliability was not estimated for the abuse and reading problem areas. Reading problems are assessed solely on the basis of the examinee's response to one item.

The BEI is easy to administer and score. Findings should be interpreted with caution given the limitations previously discussed. Attempts were made to make several items more socially desirable. However, social desirability may be even more problematic when using this instrument with individuals who are not being treated in correctional facilities. Further research on the effects of social desirability on respondent's selection of items is needed.

SUMMARY. The BEI is a screening instrument for selected behavioral and personality disorders that are prevalent in the addictions and correctional populations. Administration and scoring procedures are simple and time-efficient. Attempts were made to develop items that address DSM-IV criteria for several disorders. However, not all DSM-IV criteria for the disorders are reflected in the items. Construct, content, and criterion-related validity evidence was not determined. The reliability estimates for scores from the BEI are also questionable given the procedures used to determine internal consistency and the lack of test-retest reliability data. Readers are cautioned against making diagnostic decisions based upon the results of the BEI. More psychometrically sound tests of mental disorders should be used in conjunction with, or in lieu of, the BEI such as the Minnesota Multiphasic Personality Inventory—Second Edition (MMPI-2; T6:1623). Although the MMPI-2 is more time-consuming than a screening test, there is strong evidence to support its utility in diagnosing personality and mental disorders in adults (Nichols, 1992).

REVIEWER'S REFERENCES

American Psychiatric Association. (1994). *Diagnostic and statistical manual of mental disorders* (4th ed.). Washington, DC: American Psychiatric Association.
Nichols, D. (1992). [Review of the Minnesota Multiphasic Personality Inventory-2]. In J. J. Kramer & J. C. Conoley (Eds.), *The eleventh mental measurements yearbook* (pp. 562–565). Lincoln, NE: Buros Institute of Mental Measurements.

[35]

Benchmarks [Revised].

Purpose: "Assesses skills and perspectives that leaders can learn from experience; also, potential flaws that can derail a career."

Population: Middle- to upper-level managers and executives with at least 3–5 years of managerial experience.

Publication Dates: 1990–2001.

Scores, 21: 3 Skill Areas: Meeting Job Challenges (Resourcefulness, Doing Whatever It Takes, Being A Quick Study, Decisiveness), Leading People (Leading Employees, Confronting Problem Employees, Participative Management, Change Management), Respecting Self and Others (Building And Mending Relationships, Compassion And Sensitivity, Straightforwardness And Composure, Balance Between Personal Life And Work, Self-Awareness, Putting People At Ease, Differences Matter, Career Management), Potential for Derailment (Problems With Interpersonal Relationships, Difficulty Building And Leading A Team, Difficulty Changing Or Adapting, Failure To Meet Business Objectives, Too Narrow Functional Orientation).

Administration: Group.

Restricted Distribution: The publisher requires a 2-day certification program for those who wish to give feedback from Benchmarks in their own organization or as a consultant.

Price Data, 2002: $275 per set including 12 survey questionnaires, scoring of surveys, Feedback Reports, Developmental Learning Guides (paper-and-pencil or online version); $40 handling fee charged per set; quantity discounts available.

Foreign Language Editions: Available in French, French-Canadian, Dutch, French, German, Italian, and Spanish; document assisting non-English-speaking raters to complete the English observer form available in Dutch, French, French-Canadian, German, Italian, and Spanish; normative comparisons available for Canada, and the United Kingdom.

Time: (30–40) minutes.

Comments: Available in paper-and-pencil and online formats; hard copy Feedback Report is generated providing mean scores and normative comparisons for all items and the 21 scores as rated by all observers, self, boss, superior, peer, direct report, other; Developmental Learning Guide "suggests strategies for change" including exercises to help analyze feedback, presentation of "tactics and strategies."

Authors: Michael Lombardo, Cynthia McCauley, Diana McDonald-Mann, and Jean Brittain Leslie.

Publisher: Center for Creative Leadership.

   a) BENCHMARKS GROUP PROFILE.

   Purpose: "To assess the caliber and potential of management to fulfill … objectives, and to develop more appropriate and effective management and organizational development strategies."

   Price Data: $275 per group profile.

   Comments: Provides group-level mean scores and normative comparisons for the 21 scores as rated by all observers, self, boss/superior, peer, direct report, other.

Cross References: For a review by Sheldon Zedeck of an earlier edition, see 12:50.

Review of the Benchmarks [Revised] by HEIDI M. CARTY, Associate Director, Student Research & Information, University of California—San Diego, La Jolla, CA:

DESCRIPTION. The Benchmarks revised edition (version 2.0) is a refinement of the Benchmarks first published in 1990. The Benchmarks was designed as a 360-degree feedback instrument and process, providing managers or work groups with information regarding management development. In identifying strengths and developmental needs, Benchmarks provides managers with a so-called benchmark of how they or their organization are doing from the perspective of their superiors, peers, other observers, direct reports, and a self-assessment. The Benchmarks has two general functions: It is a confidential tool for individual development and a profiling instrument for work groups. The Benchmarks focuses on what a person has learned from past experiences, skills they have gained, what perspectives and values have been learned, and potential threats to development or derailment. The developers include a cautionary note, that the Benchmarks "is designed for developmental purposes and not designed for selection, compensation, or performance appraisal purposes" (facilitator's guide, p. 5–3).

The revised Benchmarks consists of 148 items focusing on three major sections, including leadership skills and perspectives (16 scales, 106 items), potential problems (6 scales, 26 items), and the ability to handle different challenging assignments (16 items), administered either by paper-and-pencil or computer. The developers of the Benchmarks complete the scoring of the instrument and provide a 39-page comprehensive feedback report and Development Learning Guide to each manager. Once Benchmarks has been administered and scored, a certified feedback facilitator can conduct a Benchmarks workshop for the managers receiving the feedback. Feedback is an integral component to the success and usefulness of the Benchmarks. Feedback can only be provided to participants via training programs or one-to-one sessions from certified trainers. To receive the most complete feedback, the developers recommend that the survey be completed by the participant, at least three peers, three direct observers, an immediate supervisor, and at least one superior. As written in the administration section of the facilitators manual, the Benchmarks requires a minimum of 8 weeks to complete the process. New to this version, the total Benchmarks package is available in a variety of languages, including Dutch, French, French Canadian, German, Italian, Spanish, and Spanish for Mexico.

The materials provided by the developers, including a facilitator's manual, a sample survey, and a sample feedback report, are quite thorough. Included in the facilitator's manual are sections describing the theoretical framework underlying the process, development of the instrument, directions and guidelines for administering the instrument, how to interpret the results, provide feedback, and prepare a development plan, along with the psychometric properties of the instrument. The developers recommend consulting the Development Learning Guide for more assistance in analyzing results and in creating a comprehensive plan for development. Included in the Development Learning Guide are a number of useful exercises to assist respondents in analyzing their own results. More specifically, these exercises allow respondents to see how they "measure up," how others view them, and their strengths and weaknesses. The development plan can be created alone or with the assistance of a facilitator. The feedback report is divided into two sections: the leadership skills and perspectives section, discussing 16 success factors essential to management and executive roles, and the problems that can stall a career section, discussing five problem areas that may lead to derailment. New to this version of the facilitator's manual is the inclusion of a section discussing how to use the Benchmarks internationally.

DEVELOPMENT. As discussed in a prior review by Sheldon Zedeck (Zedeck, 1995) the research underlying the development of the Benchmarks is impressive. The one concern was the overrepresentation of white males used in creating the instrument. The developers responded to this concern and have refined the Benchmarks to be a more valid assessment for multicultural groups. However, the only racial and ethnic minority group taken into consideration with the revised edition was African Americans. In addition, the developers do not mention gender differences with regard to instrument construction nor do they discuss representation of women in the samples used for various psychometric studies. Larger numbers of ethnic minorities and females, representative of the U.S. population, need to be included in the database and examined.

TECHNICAL. According to the facilitator's manual, "in order to provide norm group comparisons, data are collected from Benchmarks users on a continuous basis" (pp. 2–15). The normative data are updated approximately every 2 years. In addition, norms data are kept current to reflect recent skill levels and behaviors by removing the "oldest" data once new data are generated. The only concern is that norm group data are derived from a sample of convenience and therefore may not be generalizable to the entire population of managers in U.S. organizations. One other weakness is that only 30% of the 3,449 norm group is female. The developers include the results of one study discussing the norm differences by gender. No normative data exist for racial and ethnic minorities. New to this version, the developers have generated normative data for Canadian participants.

With regard to evidence in support of reliability and validity, the revised Benchmarks meets the minimum accepted psychometric standards for substantiating reliability and validity evidence established in the *Standards for Educational and Psychological Testing* (AERA, APA, & NCME, 1999). Measures of internal consistency (alphas) are generally high for each scale of the instrument ranging from .79 to .95. The developers indicate that as additional data are collected, other measures of reliability, such as test-retest and interrater reliability, will be examined. Both content and criterion-related validity studies were used to develop the revised Benchmarks. Using IRT-DFIT to eliminate biased items ($n = 4$), the developers found a high degree of measurement equivalence for Caucasian Americans and African Americans. It would be useful for the developers to focus some attention on measuring construct validity and other forms of validity with the revised Benchmarks. It would also prove useful to examine validity differences with respect to other ethnic minorities and gender. Although the developers include an informative annotated bibliography section sighting several validity studies utilizing the Benchmarks, the majority of the studies appear to be based on the original Benchmarks, not the revised edition.

Two areas that continue to remain unanswered with the revised Benchmarks, as written in the first published review (Zedeck, 1995), are how effectively the developmental process works and what are the long-term effects as a result of participating in this process. Do the managers who participate in this process become more effective leaders? Are they promoted to higher level positions at a higher rate compared to those managers who do not participate? Long-term effects as a result of participating in the Benchmarks process needs to be addressed.

COMMENTARY. The theoretical framework underlying the Benchmarks, based on key events research and occupational derailment research, appears well grounded. The developers present an extensive listing of studies examining the relationship between the Benchmarks and various criterion-related variables and other measures (e.g., MBTI and BarOn EQ-i). It is unclear whether the majority of these studies were utilizing the original Benchmarks or the revised version.

The revised edition includes additional items added to the Leadership Skills and Perspective section in four scales: Change Management, Participative Management, Differences Matter, and Career Management. Other than citing the elimination of biased items toward African Americans, the developers need to address how these changes have improved the instrument. For example, how have these new items improved the instrument in regard to content validity?

As stated above, more validity studies utilizing the revised Benchmarks need to be conducted. These studies need to take into account possible differences by gender and race.

SUMMARY. Overall, the revised Benchmarks continues to be a very useful multirater instrument in providing meaningful information about the skills and perspectives reflective of successful executives. The revised Benchmarks has been designed to eliminate bias with regard to multicultural differences, specifically with regard to African Americans. More validity studies need to be conducted addressing gender differences and other ethnic minorities. Also, it would be useful to provide norms for racial and ethnic minorities. Finally, it would be useful to assess the long-term effects of the program.

REVIEWER'S REFERENCES

American Educational Research Association, American Psychological Association, & National Council on Measurement in Education. (1999). *Standards for educational and psychological testing.* Washington, DC: American Educational Research Association.

Zedeck, S. (1995). [Review of the Benchmarks]. In. J. C. Conoley & J. C. Impara (Eds.), *The twelfth mental measurements yearbook* (pp.128–129). Lincoln, NE: Buros Institute of Mental Measurements.

Review of the Benchmarks [Revised] by MICHAEL SPANGLER, Dean of Business and Technology, Highland Community College, Freeport, IL:

DESCRIPTION. Benchmarks is an instrument to develop, according to the authors, "360-degree-feedback" for managers' assessment of their strengths and areas for improvement. The survey feedback can be used for individual development or for identifying characteristics of work groups. Managers rate themselves and receive feedback from superiors, peers, subordinates, and other observers. Additional feedback is generated by comparison with a suitable norm group. The Benchmarks survey is constructed to apprehend the experience and skill of mid-level to senior executive management. Additionally, the feedback is useful in identifying behaviors that lead to professional career blocks or executive "derailment." The instrument is designed for developmental purposes and is not intended for selection or performance appraisal.

The survey form is presented in four sections using a paper form or an online format. Sections 1 and 2 of the survey comprise the 155 items that are included in the feedback report. Sections 3 and 4 contain 24 items for research only and are not included in the participant's feedback report. The participant is instructed to complete her or his survey and distribute surveys to at least three peers, at least three immediate reports, their immediate supervisor, and at least one superior.

The publisher scores the instrument and furnishes a 39-page individual Feedback Report. Scaled values for Section 1 describe the participant's Leadership Skills and Perspectives. Included are average scores, norm group comparisons, and identification of which of the 16 scales the participant and observers considered "Most Important." Section 2 of the feedback report contains five scales for identifying "Problems That Can Stall A Career." The information in the feedback report is used in conjunction with workshops or with direct interaction with certified trainers.

A facilitators manual explains in considerable detail the rationale, administration, research foundations, and interpretation of Benchmarks.

The Development Learning Guide is designed to help the participant reflect on the feedback, identify growth areas, and decide on behaviors to address the feedback.

DEVELOPMENT. Benchmarks is based on two research areas, Key Events and Executive Derailment. Studies in Key Events seek to identify how executives learn and grow over their careers. Foundation research, conducted in 1987 by Lindsey, Homes, and McCall and by Morrison, White, and VanVelsor, examined through in-depth interviews the characteristics of successful men and women executives in Fortune 100 corporations. Further studies through 2000 have continued to refine traits measured by the Benchmarks survey. Executive Derailment research studies compared successful executives with those who derailed to determine the kind of development needed for ascension to senior positions. Initial research (McCall & Lombardo, 1983) was conducted to examine "fatal flaws" or reasons for derailment. Continuing studies have refined the data and addressed concerns for international (U.S. and Europe) application of the research.

TECHNICAL. Information describing the norming process is comprehensive. Sampling methods are sound and differential validity was assessed across various ethnicities and nationalities. The instrument has been examined through multiple studies for content validity. Reliability is well examined. Scale internal consistencies (alphas) for Section 1 ranged from .93 to .79 and in Section 2 from .95 to .87. The facilitators manual includes results from a considerable number of validity studies. Included in the research report are correlations among Benchmarks scales and several management success criteria as identified by participant supervisors. Additional correlations among the 21 Benchmarks scales and the Myers-Briggs Type Indicator are reported, as are correlations with the BarOn Emotional Quotient Inventory.

COMMENTARY. Particularly noteworthy is the package that accompanies the Benchmarks survey. The Feedback Report is informative with distinct graphics, the facilitators manual is comprehensive and expertly presented, and the Development Learning Guide affords a ready focus for the user.

The only serious concern by this reviewer was also noted by Sheldon Zedeck (1995) in the previous *Mental Measurements Yearbook* review:

What is not known (at least not presented in the manual), however, is how well the developmental process works. That is, after completing the instrument, obtaining feedback, and constructing and implementing a developmental plan, is there a long-term effect such that the respondents improve, become more effective managers, and/or achieve higher level jobs? This question is directed toward the influence of the feedback and the developmental plan. (p. 129)

SUMMARY. Benchmarks is useful for self-appraisal of a manager's strengths and weaknesses as well as a tool for building group profiles. The package is complete, easily administered, and readily comprehended. The feedback skills needed by the facilitator are easily attainable through workshops and the manual. Again this reviewer concurs with the previous review, "The question to be answered concerns its long-term usefulness—does participation in the process make a difference?"

REVIEWER'S REFERENCES
Lindsey, E. H., Homes, V., & McCall, M. W., Jr. (1987) *Key events in executives' lives.* Greensboro, NC: Center for Creative Leadership.
McCall, M. W., Jr., & Lombardo, M. M. (1983, February). What makes a top executive? *Psychology Today,* pp. 26–31.
Morrison, A. M., White, R. P., & VanVelsor, E. (1989). *Breaking the glass ceiling: Can womem reach the top in America's largest corporations?* Reading, MA: Addison-Wesley.
Zedeck, S. (1995). [Review of the Benchmarks.] In J. C. Conoley & J. C. Impara (Eds.), *The twelfth mental measurements yearbook* (pp. 128–129). Lincoln, NE: Buros Institute of Mental Measurements.

[36]
Birth to Three Assessment and Intervention System, Second Edition.

Purpose: Designed to "identify children who are developmentally at risk in the areas of language and learning."
Population: Birth to 3 years.
Publication Dates: 1986–2000.
Acronym: BTAIS-2.
Scores, 5: Language Comprehension, Language Expression, Nonverbal Thinking, Social/Personal Behaviors, Motor Behaviors.
Administration: Individual.
Price Data, 2003: $246 per complete kit including screening test kit, comprehensive test kit, and teaching manual (2000, 163 pages); $71 per teaching manual.
Time: Untimed.
Authors: Jerome J. Ammer and Tina E. Bangs.
Publisher: PRO-ED.
  a) SCREENING TEST OF DEVELOPMENTAL ABILITIES.
  Purpose: Designed "to identify young children who may have developmental delays."
  Price Data: $81 per complete screening test kit including manual (2000, 93 pages) and 25 record forms; $59 per manual; $25 per 25 record forms.
  b) COMPREHENSIVE TEST OF DEVELOPMENTAL ABILITIES.
  Purpose: Designed "to identify each child's specific strengths and weaknesses and to guide the preparation of instructional plans."
  Price Data: $101 per complete comprehensive test kit including manual (2000, 107 pages) and 25 record forms; $59 per manual; $45 per 25 record forms.

Cross References: See T5:315; for a review by Donna Spiker of an earlier edition, see 11:45; for a review by Bonnie W. Camp of an earlier edition, see 9:152.

Review of the Birth to Three Assessment and Intervention System, Second Edition by KIMBERLY A. BLAIR, Assistant Professor of Education, Duquesne University, Pittsburgh, PA:

DESCRIPTION. The Birth to Three Assessment and Intervention System, Second Edition (BTAIS-2) was developed to assist in the screening, program planning, and monitoring developmental progress of at-risk or developmentally delayed children under 3 years of age. The BTAIS-2 is nearly identical to the first edition. The BTAIS-2 comprises the Screening Test of Developmental Abilities (B-3 STDA), the Comprehensive Test of Developmental Abilities (B-3 CTDA), and the Manual for Teaching Developmental Abilities (B-3 MTDA). The B-3 STDA is a screening tool for identifying infants and toddlers who are at risk for language and learning difficulties. The B-3 CTDA is a criterion-referenced test intended to facilitate the development of Individual Family Support Plans. The B-3 MTDA is designed to provide interventions based on B-3 CTDA test results.

The B-3 STDA is recommended for use by in-home care providers and professional and paraprofessional service providers for monitoring of continuing child development, assessing the need of a child for intervention or further evaluation, identifying parents in need of parent skills training, and planning instructional programs. There are 85 items across five subtests on the B-3 STDA including Language Comprehension, Language Expression, Nonverbal Thinking, Social/Personal Behaviors, and Motor Behaviors. Test materials include a four-page record form and an examiner's manual, which contains two forms in the appendix that can be copied by the examiner. The Extended Observation Guidesheet is available to assist in the completion of test items that require extended or multiple observations. The Related Factors Form aids the examiner in analyzing the environmental context in which the child is evaluated. Standard materials for test items are not provided and although the manual contains lists of needed materials, this limits the standardization required to confidently compare scores from different children. For each scale, administration starts with the first item, regardless of the child's age, and testing is discontinued when five items are missed in a row. Items are scored as observed, emerging, and not observed. An observed behavior receives a score of 1 and raw scores are calculated by adding all the observed behaviors for each subtest. No credit is given for emerging behaviors. Detailed information is provided in the manual or on the record form for each item as to needed materials, procedure, number of trials required, and scoring requirements. Raw scores on the B-3 STDA can be converted to *T*-scores, stanines, and percentiles for each subtest for ages 4 to 36 months. No global score for overall development is used.

The identified uses and characteristics of the B-3 CTDA are similar to those for the B-3 STDA. The B-3 CTDA consists of 240 items on the same subtest dimensions as the screener and is recommended for use as a criterion-referenced test to facilitate the development of intervention programs. The B-3 CTDA record form contains more items than the screener and each subtest is divided into 6-month intervals. When administering the test, the examiner is directed to start with the first item appropriate to the child's chronological age. Basal level is established when the child passes all 8 items in an age interval. Testing should then be discontinued when a child fails all 8 items of an interval. Items are scored in the same manner as with the B-3 STDA. Raw scores for each subtest include credit given for all items falling before the basal. Developmental age scores are calculated for each subtest by multiplying the raw score by .75 as each item is proposed to represent 3/4 month.

The third component of the system, the B-3 MTDA, is an intervention manual for use in developing early intervention programs based on the results from the other BTAIS-2 assessments. The manual provides an overview of developing intervention plans and general suggestions for interventions, information on team building, example activity plans, and a number of blank forms to assist in data collection.

DEVELOPMENT. The BTAIS-2 is the latest revision of what initially was titled the Birth to Three Developmental Scale. Little information is provided in any of the manuals regarding any changes to the previous editions for the second edition. Changes discussed primarily involve an increased emphasis on the use of the measure in

home and community settings. The wording of test items, materials, examples, and forms has been rewritten to support this focus. Administration and scoring procedures have been clarified.

TECHNICAL. Data presented regarding standardization, reliability, and validity appear essentially the same as the previous edition and are subject to many of the same concerns outlined in Spiker's (1992) review of the first edition. The information provided regarding the standardization sample in the second edition appears identical to what was reported in the second edition. Although some changes have been made in the current edition, as outlined above, it appears that a new standardization was not completed. Little information is provided regarding the demographics of the norm sample. Information is provided regarding age, gender, and community residence (urban or rural) but no data are presented regarding ethnic backgrounds and socioeconomic status. Only students who were deemed to be developing normally were used in the norm sample; therefore, the utility of making decisions on delayed children is limited.

Issues of reliability and validity have not been significantly improved since the previous version (see Spiker, 1992). Interrater reliability for the screener was reported to be between .88 and .99. No other reliability data are presented. Although information is provided in the manual describing test development and item selection to support construct and content validity, few statistical data regarding criterion, content, or construct validity are presented.

Other than a basic overview of theory, no specific information is provided on the construction of the B-3 CTDA. Raw scores are converted to developmental age scores; however, the theoretical basis for the method used in calculating the developmental age score on this criterion-referenced measure is not clear. Some useful information is provided in the manual on interpreting test results for educational purposes and making the next step to intervention.

COMMENTARY. The BTAIS-2 demonstrates some utility for developing intervention plans and monitoring the development of infants and toddlers. However, there are some technical issues that detract from its overall quality. The standardization sample used for the B-3 STDA and B-3 CTDA included only normally developed children and includes no ethnic and SES information. Although test content on face value seems based on solid developmental theory, validity and reliability do not meet accepted psychometric standards as established in the *Standards for Educational and Psychological Testing* (AERA, APA, & NCME, 1999) and therefore are not confirmed. The lack of standardized testing materials limits the ability of the user to make comparisons between children. The intervention manual provides a good foundation for developing interventions for at-risk or delayed children, but could be improved with more specific information on direct intervention and how to assist children in developing the skills that are not achieved, as indicated on the screener and criterion-referenced measures.

SUMMARY. The Birth to Three Assessment and Intervention System, Second Edition was developed to assist in the screening, program planning, and monitoring developmental progress of at-risk or developmentally delayed children for children from birth to 3 years of age. The system contains three components: a screening test, a criterion-referenced checklist, and an intervention-planning manual. Although the measure has face validity based on solid developmental theory, it lacks sufficient reliability and validity data. The system is useful as a screener for at-risk children and identifying specific skill areas that need remediation. However, if a standardized measure is needed for diagnostic purposes, users should look to other measures such as the Bayley Scales of Infant Development, Second Edition (Bayley, 1993; T6:271).

REVIEWER'S REFERENCES
American Educational Research Association, American Psychological Association, & National Council on Measurement in Education. (1999). *Standards for educational and psychological testing.* Washington, DC: American Educational Research Association.
Bayley, N. (1993). Bayley Scales of Infant Development, Second Edition. San Antonio: TX: The Psychological Corporation.
Spiker, D. (1992). [Review of the Birth to Three Assessment and Intervention System.] In J. J. Kramer & J. C. Conoley (Eds.), *The eleventh mental measurements yearbook* (pp. 110–112). Lincoln, NE: Buros Institute of Mental Measurements.

Review of the Birth to Three Assessment and Intervention System, Second Edition by LEAH M. NELLIS, Assistant Professor of Educational and Counseling Psychology, University of Kentucky, Lexington, KY:

DESCRIPTION. The Birth to Three Assessment and Intervention System (BTAIS-2) is a three-component system that was designed to assist early childhood professionals meet the developmental needs of children under the age of 3. The first component, the Birth to Three Assess-

ment and Intervention System: Screening Test of Developmental Abilities (B-3 STDA), is a norm-referenced screening instrument intended for use with children who are at high risk for developmental delays. According to the authors, the instrument can be used to identify the need for further evaluation; monitor ongoing child development; and assist in special education decision making, parent training, and instructional decision making. The B-3 STDA purportedly can be used both with children suspected of developmental delay and those who are developing ahead of their peers. In addition, the screener can be adapted for usage with children who are nonverbal, use sign language, or use communication devices. The B-3 STDA manual states that administration can be done "by any person who can reliably observe and evaluate a child's behavior" (p. 11). Such "nontraditional examiners" should first receive appropriate training from a qualified examiner. Although administration can be completed by paraprofessionals, it is stated that scoring and administration should be conducted by only qualified examiners.

The B-3 STDA is composed of 85 items organized into 5 subtests: Language Comprehension, Language Expression, Nonverbal Thinking, Social/Personal Behaviors, and Motor Behaviors. The items are untimed and require specific materials to be selected by the user so that they fit naturally into the child's environment. Administration follows specified entry, ceiling, and wait time rules with procedures clearly explained in the manual. In addition, some items require ongoing parental observations conducted according to instructions provided by the examiner. Many items consist of multiple trials and all are scored as observed, emerging, or not observed. Raw scores for each subtest are converted to T-scores, stanines, and percentiles. Although the raw scores are whole numbers, the norms are presented in tenths and contain multiple entries for some raw scores. The explanation in the manual is unclear in stating that this occurrence is due to the sensitivity of the items. An averaging method is explained but does not adequately address the issue. Test authors identify the range of scores between 35 and 65 as average with scores below 35 as the criterion for a referral for additional evaluation.

The second component of the system is the Birth to Three Assessment and Intervention System: Comprehensive Test of Developmental Abilities (B-3 CTDA). The B-3 CTDA is a criterion-referenced assessment of essential language and learning skills for children from birth to 3 years. Intended uses of the B-3 CTDA include assessing developmental skills, monitoring ongoing development in response to intervention, identifying areas for parent training, and facilitating instructional planning. The B-3 CTDA is similar to the B-3 STDA in terms of intended population and users.

The B-3 CTDA consists of 240 items organized into the same five subtests represented on the screening instrument. Each subtest is divided into six 8-item sets that correspond to a 6-month age interval. Procedures for administration and scoring are clearly outlined in the manual and are similar to those discussed previously for the screening tool. The B-3 CTDA Record Form provides space for repeated administration of the items for use in monitoring developmental progression. Developmental age scores are computed for each subtest by summing the items scored as "Observed" and then applying a formula that accounts for each item being equivalent to three quarters of a month of developmental growth. Developmental ages are interpreted in the context of intervention planning and performance monitoring.

The third component of the system, Birth to Three Assessment and Intervention System: Manual for Teaching Developmental Abilities (B-3 MTDA), was intended as an instructional guide for early childhood professionals working with children with developmental delays. The B-3 MTDA provides an overview of the development of language and learning skills, a rationale for early childhood assessment and intervention, guidelines for intervention planning, and teaching strategies within a context that emphasizes parent partnership and natural environment intervention.

DEVELOPMENT. The Birth to Three Assessment and Intervention System, Second Edition is the revision of a previous system originally based upon the language and learning research conducted by Tina Bangs over the last 20 years. In general, the BTAIS-2 was revised to facilitate implementation of Part C of the 1997 reauthorization of IDEA. Specifically the items, forms, examples, and wording of administration and scoring procedures of the B-3 STDA were revised to increase clarity and more fully accommodate home and community service settings. Changes to the B-3 CTDA focused on the instrument's role in

monitoring developmental progress as well as a family-centered perspective of assessment. As such, materials, prompts, examples, forms, and wording were revised. Further, the revised B-3 MDTA outlines a systematic early intervention program that moves from assessment and identification to intervention.

TECHNICAL. The norms for the B-3 STDA are based upon 357 children from the states of California, Tennessee, and Utah. Participants ranged in age from 4 to 36 months with 60 children in each of the following age groups: 4–6, 10–12, 16–18, 22–24, 28–30, and 34–36 months. The manual does not clearly state when the standardization data were collected; however, a prior review conducted by Spiker (1992) noted that the data were based upon an earlier 1979 study by Bangs. The current revision did not mention the inclusion of a normative update. No updated reliability evidence was provided, as the sole study presented was one conducted in 1986 in which interrater reliabilities for scoring procedures were between .88 and .99 for pairs of raters consisting of the test author, a nurse, and speech pathologist. The manual does not provide evidence of concurrent, predictive, or discriminant validity. The B-3 CTDA contains no information regarding reliability or validity.

COMMENTARY. The comprehensive nature of the BTAIS-2 provides a valuable resource to the field of early intervention. Specifically, the attempt to link assessment with intervention in a manner that facilitates ongoing monitoring of developmental progression is critical for early intervention programming. Further, the emphasis on assessment and intervention in home and community settings is in spirit with recognized best practice in the field. The two assessment components entail several noteworthy features such as the use of multiple trials, observations over time, flexibility in material selection, and a scoring option for emergent skills.

However, general concerns exist regarding the stated examiner qualifications and attention given to cultural diversity and fairness. Both assessment component manuals address fairness by highlighting examiner selection of materials and prompts as well as the importance of establishing rapport, familiarity, and professional communication with families. Research regarding the topic of test fairness would be beneficial.

Numerous technical flaws limit the utility of the B-3 STDA as a norm-referenced instrument. For example, although characteristics of the standardization sample remain unclear, it appears as though the normative data are extremely outdated and not based upon the current version of the instrument. Additional limitations associated with the sample include a restricted age range with the lack of any child under the age of 4 months, which seriously limits its use with the stated population of children from birth to 3 years. Further, there is no explanation about how norms were generated for children whose chronological age group was not part of the standardization sample. For example, although there were no children aged 13 months in the sample, there is a corresponding norm table for this age group. In addition, possible T-scores range from 34 to 66 for all ages and subtests. Although the instrument is only intended for screening purposes, the range of possible derived scores should extend beyond approximately 1.5 standard deviations from the mean. This concern is highlighted by the lack of information about how the criterion score ($T<35$) was established. It is not supported by the research presented. Additionally, the use of the instrument for screening developmentally advanced children is not justified given the restricted range of scores. In general, the presented reliability and validity evidence limits the use of the B-3 STDA as a norm-referenced instrument.

Similarly, the lack of reliability and validity data for the B-3 CTDA limits its usage and interpretation. This concern could be addressed with the inclusion of research that investigates the use of the instrument for the intended purposes of assessment, developmental monitoring, and instructional planning. Although expanded upon in the current version, the B-3 CTDA manual would benefit from increased attention to interpretative uses and procedures.

The B-3 MTDA provides adequate coverage of issues relevant to early childhood intervention. Although learning strategies and planning forms are provided, the system is not comprehensive enough to support its use as a curriculum or program in early intervention.

SUMMARY. The Birth to Three Assessment and Intervention System, Second Edition (BTAIS-2) presents an assessment, intervention, and monitoring package for use in early intervention. The system has potential for making a significant impact on the provision of services for children below the age of 3 years. However, concerns exist regarding the technical properties of the screening instrument. Specifically, its use as a norm-referenced instrument is limited by inadequate standardization data and evidence for reliability and validity. In addition, due to the lack of reliability and validity support for the criterion-referenced instrument, caution should be used in interpreting results. These concerns could be addressed with additional research into these psychometric issues, which could provide the necessary support for the use of the BTAIS-2 as a valuable tool in early intervention.

REVIEWER'S REFERENCE

Spiker, D. (1992). [Review of the Birth to Three Assessment and Intervention System.] In J. J. Kramer & J. C. Conoley (Eds.), *The eleventh mental measurements yearbook* (pp. 110–112). Lincoln, NE: Buros Institute of Mental Measurements.

[37]

The Boston Qualitative Scoring System for the Rey-Osterrieth Complex Figure.

Purpose: Designed as a quantifiable approach to rating the qualitative features of the ROCF (which was designed to assess visuoconstructional ability and visual memory performance in brain-impaired patients).

Population: Ages 18–94.

Publication Dates: 1994–1999.

Acronym: BQSS.

Scores, 23: Qualitative (Configural Presence, Configural Accuracy, Cluster Presence, Cluster Accuracy, Cluster Placement, Detail Presence, Detail Placement, Fragmentation, Planning, Neatness, Vertical Expansion, Horizontal Expansion, Reduction, Rotation, Perseveration, Confabulation, Asymmetry), Summary (Copy Presence and Accuracy, Immediate Presence and Accuracy, Delayed Presence and Accuracy, Immediate Retention, Delayed Retention, Organization).

Administration: Individual.

Price Data: Available from publisher.

Time: (45) minutes, including a (20–30) minute delay interval.

Authors: Robert A. Stern, Debbie J. Javorsky, Elizabeth A. Singer, Naomi G. Singer Harris, Jessica A. Somerville, Lisa M. Duke, Jodi A. Thompson, and Edith Kaplan.

Publisher: Psychological Assessment Resources, Inc.

Review of The Boston Qualitative Scoring System for the Rey-Osterrieth Complex Figure by D. ASHLEY COHEN, Clinical Neuropsychologist, CogniMetrix, San Jose, CA:

DESCRIPTION. The Boston Qualitative Scoring System for the Rey-Osterrieth Complex Figure (BQSS) is an individually administered neuropsychological test designed for persons ages 18–94. Examinees must have sufficient vision to see the stimulus (a geometric line-drawing taking up most of a sheet of standard-sized paper), and adequate motor ability to hold a writing instrument and control its application to paper.

The original Rey-Osterrieth Complex Figure Test (ROCF) was itself designed to measure visual-constructive ability and visual memory capacity. The BQSS is meant to enable quantifiable measurement of the qualitative aspects of the ROCF. Neuropsychologists have been using qualitative data from the ROCF for many years, but without an agreed upon scoring system, or normative data to which to compare their observations. The purpose of the BQSS is to provide such a standard method of recording qualitative aspects of the test and of comparing those observations to an established normative base.

The first portion of the test (Copy Condition) involves presenting the examinee with a line-drawing, black on white paper, of a large rectangle with many linear and geometric details attached to the outside and contained within. The individual being tested is instructed to copy the figure as accurately as possible, with the understanding that time is not a factor. The examiner is required to keep track of the order in which the individual produces elements of the drawing. There are two means of doing this, either handing the examinee a different colored marker at "critical transition points," or recording the process on a flowchart supplied with the testing materials. In some previous versions of the ROCF, examiners were instructed to switch colors or markers at intervals, such as every 30 seconds. In the BQSS, there is a discussion of seven types of "critical transition points" in drawing the figure, and the examiner is instructed to switch colors of pens at these points. It is cautioned that one must study the scoring criteria in detail before attempting to determine when a critical point has been reached. These critical points are not particularly intuitive, but are clearly defined. One can reasonably wonder whether the typical examiner will successfully memorize and consistently apply these seven critical points. When the copy trial is completed, the time to completion is recorded and the stimulus card is removed, as is the examinee's drawing.

At this point the Immediate Recall Condition begins. The examinee is given a blank sheet of paper, and is told to reproduce the same figure that was copied, but this time from memory. Again the production is timed, and the examiner records the process either with switching colored markers, or with a second flowchart. The BQSS manual does not make this caution, but it would not be advisable to administer another visual task immediately after this trial. After 20–30 minutes, the Delayed Recall Condition takes place. The examinee is once again asked to draw the figure from memory, is timed, and the same procedure (switching colors of pens or using a third flowchart) as before is used to keep track of the order in which configural elements were produced.

The BQSS divides the ROCF into sets of three elements: Configural Elements, Clusters, and Details. When completed, the test yields 23 separate scores relating to aspects of the examinee's qualitative production. Among these are 17 Qualitative Scores that are then reduced to 6 Summary Scores. The Qualitative Scores cover aspects of the drawing such as whether there is size distortion of the figure in the horizontal or vertical directions, rotations, perseverations, confabulations, fragmentation, or asymmetry. They also measure more global aspects such as accuracy, planning, and neatness. The Summary Scores are determined by calculating the means of several of the previous measures, determining the overall presence of and accuracy of aspects of the drawing, organization, and both immediate and delayed retention.

A one-page Quick Scoring Guide was developed to enable those familiar with the BQSS to score ROCF drawings when faced with significant time constraints. Using this sheet, accomplished BQSS users can score a series of drawings in less than five minutes.

All six Summary Scores may be converted to T scores, and guidelines are provided for rating the obtained T scores as to range of performance. Six ranges are delineated, from Superior to Severely Impaired.

DEVELOPMENT. The BQSS is based on the Boston Process Approach to neuropsychological assessment, as conceived by Edith Kaplan. A central tenet of this approach is analysis of the quality and process of the examinee's test behavior and production, not simple derivation of a summary score or rating. The authors of the BQSS felt the existing 36-point system used in the ROCF failed to record important qualitative detail and process features of the examinee's drawings. Previous attempts by others at developing a qualitative scoring system focused on only a few aspects of the drawings. Some of the BQSS features came from the Boston Process Approach theory. In addition, test authors interviewed experienced neuropsychologists who were using previous versions of the ROCF to determine which types of qualitative data they felt to be important, and many of those were incorporated into the test.

This measure has been undergoing successive revisions over the past 8 years. Changes were made following interrater reliability studies, feedback from users of initial versions of the instrument, input from research assistants who were serving as scorers, and preliminary validation studies. Several revisions were needed to maximize the clarity of the scoring criteria, so all users would be likely to obtain the same score for the same drawing after studying the manual. Further changes were undertaken to normalize frequency distributions for scores of nonimpaired persons. For impaired persons taking the test, their scores were checked against ratings made by a single, (though very experienced) neuropsychologist, and then further adjusted.

TECHNICAL.

Standardization. There were a total of 433 individuals of both genders in the standardization sample, ranging in age from 18 to 94 years. They were predominantly white, and all lived in the Northeastern region of the United States or parts of Canada. Potential participants were excluded if they had any neurological, psychiatric, developmental, or substance abuse condition. Most were of middle to upper-middle SES, and lived in urban or suburban areas. Age and gender were found to be significant variables in BQSS test performance, with older age and female gender predicting worse performance overall. There was no interaction effect for age by gender, and no significant effect for educational level.

Reliability. Two types of reliability studies were reported in the test manual. Perhaps the most important for a test of this type is interrater reliability, and this was examined in detail by several methods. The majority of the scores derived had excellent reliability, several had good, and only two had fair reliability. Test-retest reliability for any version of the ROCF is of suspect validity, as pointed out by the test authors, as once the examinees have seen and copied the figure, they are no longer naïve to the task. The authors carried out a 1-year test-retest reliability study with HIV patients. Reliability coefficients obtained were only moderate.

Validity. Test authors conducted several discriminant validity studies, using separate patient groups such as those with traumatic brain injury, dementia, HIV, ADHD, and some who were substance abusers. The manual offers sensitivity and specificity figures for differentiation of four pairings of participant groups: TBI versus controls, Alzheimer's versus vascular dementia, HIV+ versus HIV- persons, and ADHD adults versus controls. Unfortunately, the numbers in these groups were all quite small (ranging between 16 and 33).

To examine convergent validity, test developers compared the BQSS with those from other neuropsychological tests designed to measure executive functioning. The other tests were Trail Making Test (Part B), Wisconsin Card Sorting Test, Controlled Oral Word Association, and the Wechsler Adult Intelligence Test—Revised (WAIS-R) Similarities subtest. A matrix of correlations was obtained between aspects of the BQSS and various scores of each of the other neuropsychological tests. In general the correlations among the other neuropsychological tests themselves were comparable to correlations between some of those tests and specific variables of the BQSS.

The only data offered in the manual concerning ecological validity is a study based on an older version of the BQSS, that found differences between schizophrenics and normals. The schizophrenics had poorer performances on the BQSS, and were rated lower on an assessment of activities of daily living. These sorts of data need to be established, but are hardly surprising, and it appears much more work is needed in order to say the ROCF and the BQSS are of use in predicting functioning in daily life.

Exaggeration of Deficits. As with ecological validity, the topic of malingering is being considered more often in test development and during neuropsychological assessments. The developers performed one study using 89 undergraduates, in an analogue malingering paradigm, using both Coached and Uncoached simulators of deficit. Using four variables of the BQSS, an overall 84% correct classification rate was obtained.

COMMENTARY. As might be expected given the complexity and breadth of the scoring system, over half (61%) of the 209-page manual is devoted to teaching the scoring system and illustrating the scoring criteria. By contrast, a scant 10 pages (<5%) are devoted to interpretation, including three case examples. It is certainly not urged that less space be given to learning the scoring system; however, more could have been done to assist examiners in making use of the scores they eventually obtain. A frequent failing of neuropsychological reports is the listing of many T scores or percentiles, with a dearth of information on what this means for the real world functioning or the prognosis of the individual who was examined. Similarly, only six pages of the manual were devoted to reliability and validity studies, many of which used either very small Ns, or earlier versions of the BQSS. Mention is made that the ROCF is believed related to executive functioning, but this idea is not further developed in the manual, nor is there a discussion of the theoretical underpinnings of the BQSS, as conceived by the test authors.

Because the ROCF has typically been used in the examination of individuals with confirmed or suspected neuropsychological disorders, it would have been desirable to have some additional norms or tables for comparison of some of the major disorders commonly seen in clinical practice. As it is, the obtained scores can be compared to normals and rated as deficient compared to expected normal performance, but it would be useful to be able to compare scores to determine if a middle stage Alzheimer's patient is performing better or worse than others in that group. A listing of specific pathognomonic signs by disorder, if such exist, would also be helpful.

The strength of this test is the strength of every Boston Process related test—the amount of detail that can be gleaned from a protocol is astounding. For those doing research in which this test could factor, a plethora of variables exist. The weakness of this test is also that of process instruments—considerable study and practice are required to learn the complex scoring system, each protocol takes an extended amount of time to score, and a bewildering number of data points are yielded. The paradox is that a clinician would not likely be proficient (let alone efficient) scoring the BQSS until he or she has administered many of these tests, yet in many settings the test will not be used with all or most patients because of the time needed to learn the system and calculate the scores. This is unfortunate, as for cases in which the examiner requires this level of detailed analysis, there is probably nothing better.

SUMMARY. As noted just above, in the opinion of this reviewer there is no better single test than the BQSS for measuring every conceivable aspect of visual-spatial production and two-dimensional visual-spatial learning and retention. It provides a remarkable amount of data on how examinees approach such tasks, where they focus, what they ignore, what they find easy or difficult, and how they organize a somewhat complicated production. Those needing this level of detailed information in their clinical or research setting are well advised to obtain the BQSS. For neuropsychologists who currently administer the ROCF only occasionally, the necessary time spent learning the system and actually scoring the test will probably not seem worthwhile. Clearly, this is another test in the mold of other Boston Process Approach instruments, with all the sometimes mind-numbing detail that inheres in those tests, and all of the splendid data.

Review of the Boston Qualitative Scoring System for the Rey-Osterrieth Complex Figure by ROBERT A. LEARK, Associate Professor, Pacific Christian College, Fullerton, CA:

DESCRIPTION. The Boston Qualitative Scoring System for the Rey-Osterrieth Complex Figure (BQSS) is not a test; rather, it is a scoring method for a previously developed test, the Rey-Osterrieth Complex Figure (ROCF). The BQSS presents a standardized administration procedure coupled with three scoring methods: Comprehensive Scoring Method (CSM), Quick Scoring Guide (QSG), and a combination method utilizing both the CSM and the QSG. The CSM relies upon specific scoring criteria developed by the BQSS authors. According to the authors, the CSM is "warranted in situations when scoring must be *exact* [italics by BQSS authors], such as in (a) clinical cases when diagnostic issues are in question or when there is litigation involved, (b) research, or (c) other circumstances when interrater agreement is critical" (professional manual, p. 14). The authors described the QSG for use when clinicians otherwise might "not score the ROCF productions with any scoring method because of time constraints" (professional manual, p. 14).

The standardized administration developed by the authors includes oral instructions given to the examinee for each of the three standardized trial conditions. The trial conditions are the Copy, Immediate Recall, and the Delayed Recall (20 to 30 minutes). In addition, the examiner is required to track the order of the pen strokes in which the respondent draws each of the trial conditions. To assist with this, the authors have recommended use of colored pens or use of a flowchart developed for the examiner.

The BQSS divides the ROCF into three hierarchically arranged sets of elements: Configurable Elements, Clusters and Details. The BQSS provides a template reference guide to assist the clinician in locating each of these domains. Then, the BQSS provides scores for 17 qualitative scales over each of the three trial conditions (51 scales in all). The qualitative scales are: Configural Presence, Configural Accuracy, Cluster Presence, Cluster Accuracy, Cluster Placement, Detail Presence, Detail Placement, Fragmentation, Planning, Neatness, Vertical Expansion, Horizontal Expansion, Reduction, Rotation, Perseveration, Confabulation and Asymmetry. Each scale is based upon ordinal scale rating of the subject's drawing. The scores range from 0 (*extremely poor planning, extremely messy*) to 4 (*good planning, very neat*). The examiner is guided in choosing the most appropriate rating by examples for each score. The manual provides over 100 pages of examples for each of the scores possible. The qualitative scales are scored for raw total then converted into cumulative percentage.

These 17 qualitative scales merge into six summary scales: Copy Presence and Accuracy, Immediate Presence and Accuracy, Delayed Presence and Accuracy, Immediate Retention, Delayed Retention, and Organization. The manual provides data tables for converting these into summary scores, T scores and percentiles. Interpretation guidelines for the T scores are based upon range of T-score value.

DEVELOPMENT. The ROCF is a widely used complex geometric figure originally published by Andre Rey (1941) designed to measure visuoconstructional ability and visual memory. Several years later, Osterrieth (1944) developed a standardized administration, added normative data, and created a scoring system for the ROCF. As the authors of the BQSS point out, the use of the

ROCF is compounded by multiple administrative procedures, differing stimulus qualities for the figure itself, and differing scoring systems. The BQSS rests heavily upon the Boston process approach (Kaplan, 1988) wherein the neuropsychologist evaluates the quality of a subject's behavior rather than relying upon a standardized or summarized score. The authors' goal was to "produce a reliable, valid, and *quantifiable* [author italics] set of scores that depict a large number of the *qualitative* [author italics] features observed in ROCF productions" (professional manual, p. 167). Eight years of investigation have gone into the development of the current BQSS. The authors used experienced clinicians (presumably experienced in the Boston process approach, although this is not clear) initially to describe observed features in their scoring of the ROCF. These observations led to the initial scoring system. Further, conversion charts were developed to assess accuracy and placement of the ROCF elements for cases where the drawing is incomplete or disproportionate. The authors used feedback from other uses as well as data from reliability and frequency distributions of the BQSS variables to monitor and evaluate the efficacy of the scoring system. Relying upon data from an initial interrater reliability study (Stern et al., 1994), a final modification to the scoring system was made, yielding the current criteria and procedures. This final revision highlighted a serious data problem—"a large proportion of healthy participants were in the *impaired* [author italics] range on a few Qualitative scores" (professional manual, p. 168). Thus, the final revision accounts for adjustments made in the scoring system (although these are not discussed) to decrease the rates of false positive scores.

TECHNICAL. The BQSS standardization sample was derived from a convenience sample of 433 subjects (257 females/176 males), ages ranging from 18 to 94 years. The sample was primarily Caucasian of middle to upper-middle class from urban or suburban areas. Exclusion criteria were established to restrict the sample to fairly typical subjects free from brain or medical injury, learning disabilities, ADD, other psychiatric diseases, substance abuse, or alcoholism. Age groupings are used to provide summary data (18–39, 40–59, 60–69, 70–79 and 80–94). Gender differences were found on most BQSS summary scales with females performing significantly poorer than males.

The manual provides data on two distinct reliability studies, interrater reliability and test-retest reliability. No data are provided for internal consistency reliability of scales. The BQSS is reported to have Kappa coefficients ranging from .53 (Cluster Placement) through 1.0 (Configural Presence, Cluster Presence, Reduction, Vertical Expansion) for the Copy condition. The summary scores for the Copy condition ranged from .77 (Delayed Retention) to .93 (Copy Presence and Accuracy, Delayed Recall Presence and Accuracy). No interrater reliability data are presented for either the Immediate Recall or the Delayed Recall.

Test-retest reliability data are presented in the manual. One problem in the investigation of test-retest reliability is the fact that subjects are no longer naïve to the task, which may inflate coefficient values. The authors chose a one-year interval, using 29 healthy males (mean age = 30.2 years, standard deviation = 6.1) to assess temporal stability of the scores. The authors indicate "Because of the lack of variability among the individual Qualitative scores, only the Presence and Accuracy Summary scores for each of the three conditions were examined for test-retest reliability (professional manual, p. 170). The results were Copy Presence and Accuracy, .50, Immediate Presence and Accuracy, .66, and Delay Presence and Accuracy, .68.

Validity data for the BQSS scoring system were evaluated by using a series of studies with various clinical populations to control subjects. A multivariate logistic regression analysis was conducted to examine the ability of the BQSS to correctly classify the clinical subjects (sensitivity) and the control subjects (specificity). The regression yielded the following sensitivity/specificity data: traumatic brain injury vs. controls (81%/82%), Alzheimer's disease vs. ischemic vascular dementia (75%/75%), asymptomatic HIV vs. HIV-controls (72%/76%), and ADHD adults vs. controls (78%/72%).

Convergent validity data were assessed by using a different scoring system (Duley et al., 1993). The same patient data (as cited above) were rescored using this model. However, only the Copy Presence and Accuracy summary score was evaluated. The Pearson correlation was .95. A second investigation of the convergent validity compared three qualitative scores plus the Organization Summary score to other neuropsychological measures of executive functioning. Correlation coefficients

obtained between the Wisconsin Card Sorting Test—Perseverative Responses ranged from −.29 to −.39 ($p < .001$). Although statistically significant, these values are far from robust, indicating about 16% shared variance at best. Similar coefficients were obtained when comparing the Controlled Oral Word Association Test (.33 to .49).

COMMENTARY. The scoring system was derived from a convenient sample of primarily Caucasian subjects from the middle to upper-middle class. This is a serious limitation to the use of the system. The normative data do not reflect U.S. Census data, nor do the normative data meet recommended guidelines for test development (AERA, APA, & NCME, 1999). Use of the BQSS with subjects outside of the normative base should be with extreme caution. Reliability data on the Immediate Recall and the Delayed Recall are lacking. Comparative data between the three trial conditions are lacking and may be helpful towards understanding individual performance. The test-retest data are confusing, as it seems only a few of the many scale variables are reported.

The relationship of the BQSS to measures of executive functioning (Wisconsin Card Sort Test—Perseverative Responses, Total Correct and Categories Completed) reported in the manual, although statistically significant, is not robust. Using these coefficients, it is evident that only a small percentage of shared variance is related to the overall executive function domain (16%). This should not be surprising, or unexpected, given that the ROCF (either with or without the BQSS) is a measure of visuoconstructional ability and visual memory. It would have been helpful to see an investigation into similar measures of visual memory, but these are not reported in the manual.

It should also be noted that use of the BQSS might result in about 25% of normal subjects being classified as impaired. Further, about 20% of the traumatic brain-injured (TBI) subjects were misclassified. This may have been due to the type of injury, location of injury, or the severity of the TBI, as the manual does not provide such information.

The 100+ pages of information describing each category and ordinal equivalent are overwhelming. The authors have done an extensive job in providing details to their scoring system.

SUMMARY. The BQSS is an attempt to integrate quantitative scoring along with qualitative observation. The authors must be credited for their work in attempting to integrate the two models. They have looked at a variety of possible drawing responses and provided categorical definitions for these. They have made an earnest attempt to create a normative process for their system.

The BQSS is an important and necessary step toward the use of the ROCF in clinical practice. It does represent the most comprehensive approach available as of this review. Yet, there are some inherent difficulties. The BQSS is not consistent with test standards in that it utilizes a convenient sample with little variation in SES and of primarily a Caucasian background. Generalizing results to other ethnic subjects or subjects in lower SES is not recommended due to the lack of empirical evidence for this.

REVIEWER'S REFERENCES

American Educational Research Association, American Psychological Association & National Council on Measurement in Education. (1999). *Standards for educational and psychological testing.* Washington, DC: American Educational Research Association

Duley, J. F., Wilkins, J. W., Hamby, S. L., Hopkins, D. G., Burwell, R. D., & Barry, N. S. (1993). Explicit scoring criteria for the Rey-Osterrieth and Taylor complex figures. *The Clinical Neuropsychologist, 7,* 29–38.

Kaplan, E. (1988). A process approach to neuropsychological assessment. In T. Boll & B. K. Bryant (Eds.), *Clinical neuropsychology and brain function: Research, measurement, and practice.* Washington, DC: American Psychological Association.

Osterrieth, P. A. (1944). Le test de copie d'une figure complexe: Contribution a l'etude de la perception et de la memoire [The Complex Figure Test: Contribution to the study of perception and memory]. *Archives de Psychologie, 30,* 206–356.

Rey, A. (1941). L'examen psychologique dans les cas d'encephalopathie traumatique (Les problems.) [Psychological examination of traumatic encephalopathy problems.] *Archives de Psychologie, 28,* 215–285.

Stern, R. A., Singer, E. A., Duke, L. M., Singer, N. G., Morey, C. E., Daughtrey, E. W., & Kaplan, E. (1994). The Boston Qualitative Scoring System for the Rey-Osterrieth Complex Figure: Description and interrater reliability. *The Clinical Neuropsychologist, 8,* 309–322.

[38]

Brief Symptom Inventory 18.

Purpose: Designed to "screen for psychological distress and psychiatric disorders in medical and community populations."

Population: Age 18 and older.

Publication Dates: 2000–2001.

Acronym: BSI 18.

Scores, 4: Somatization, Depression, Anxiety, Total (General Severity Index).

Administration: Individual or group.

Price Data, 2002: $37 per preview package with profile reports including manual (2001, 54 pages), answer sheets with test items, and all materials necessary to conduct 3 assessments and receive profile reports using MICROTEST Q Assessment System software; $19 per 25 answer sheets (English or Hispanic); $3.65 per profile report (quantity discounts available); $86 per hand-scoring starter kit including manual, 50 answer sheets, and 50 profile forms (specify community or oncology norms); $41 per 50 answer sheets (English or Hispanic); $22.25 per 50 profile forms (community or oncology norms); $30 per manual.

Time: (4) minutes.

Comments: Abbreviated adaptation of Brief Symptom Inventory (T6:335); self-report; may be administered in paper-and-pencil format or online.

Author: Leonard R. Derogatis.

Publisher: NCS Assessments [Minnetonka].

Cross References: For information on the Brief Symptom Inventory, see T5:337 (198 references); for reviews by Bert C. Cundick and Charles A. Peterson, see 10:35 (7 references); see also 9:160 (1 reference).

Review of the Brief Symptom Inventory 18 by ROGER A. BOOTHROYD, Associate Professor, Department of Mental Health Law and Policy, Louis de la Parte Florida Mental Health Institute, University of South Florida, Tampa, FL:

DESCRIPTION. The Brief Symptom Inventory 18 (BSI 18), as its name implies, is an 18-item "self-report symptom inventory designed to serve as a screen for psychological distress and psychiatric disorders" (manual, p. 1). According to the administration manual the measure was designed for use "with a broad spectrum of adult medical patients 18 or older and adult individuals in the community who are not currently assigned patient status" (p. 3). Patients rate their level of distress during the past week on each of the 18 symptoms using a 5-point Likert-type scale ranging from 0 (*not at all*) to 4 (*extremely*). The author indicates that the items assess three symptom dimensions: Somatization (6 items), Depression (6 items), and Anxiety (6 items), as well as a Global Severity Index (GSI) based on all 18 items. The BSI 18 is recommended for use by health and behavioral health professionals as a psychological screen, to support clinical decisions, for monitoring treatment progress, and to assess treatment outcomes. The BSI can be completed by most respondents in 4 minutes and is purportedly written at a sixth grade reading level.

DEVELOPMENT. The BSI 18 has an extensive developmental history. It is a reduced version of the 53-item Brief Symptom Inventory (BSI; Derogatis & Melisaratos, 1983) that was developed from the Symptom Checklist-90 (SCL-90; Derogatis, Rickels, & Rock, 1976) that originally evolved from the Hopkins Symptoms Checklist (HSCL; Derogatis, Lipman, Rickels, Uhlenhuth, & Covi, 1974). The BSI 18 focuses on three symptom dimensions in contrast to the nine dimensions assessed by its predecessors. The author indicates that the three symptom dimensions of the BSI 18 were selected because they represent about 80% of the psychiatric disorders that occur in primary care practice. The author also states that although multiple criteria were used to determine which items to retain, the high prevalence of the specific symptoms in clinical disorders was the most significant selection factor.

TECHNICAL.

Scoring and standardization. In the absence of missing responses, raw scores are simply the sum of the item responses within a symptom domain. The manual includes scoring instructions for dealing with missing responses. Raw scores are converted to standardized *T* scores using the norm tables provided. Gender specific normative data are provided on two samples: a community sample of 1,134 adults and an oncology sample of 1,543 adults being treated for cancer. Although the age distributions of these samples are provided, no information is presented regarding the racial/ethnic composition of either sample, raising some question about the ethnic/racial diversity of the norming samples. Scores can then be plotted on the appropriate profile sheet. Computerized scoring is available through the purchase of *MICROTEST Q* 5.04 Assessment System from NCS Assessments. The software supports scoring of the BSI 18 and other NCS assessments, reporting results, and storing and exporting data. Optical scanning is also available; however, the time and effort required for hand scoring and interpretation is minimal.

Reliability. Internal consistency reliability estimates were derived from the community sample. Alpha coefficients for the three symptom dimensions and GSI are .74 (Somatization), .84 (Depression), .79 (Anxiety), and .89 (GSI), and are certainly very acceptable. Additionally, these reliability estimates compare favorably with those derived from the longer BSI on a sample of 719 psychiatric outpatients. Although no test-retest reliability studies are reported on the BSI 18, the author provides test-retest estimates ranging from .68 to .84 on the symptom dimensions over an unspecified time interval based on a sample of 60 nonpatients who completed the BSI. GSI test-retest estimate was .90.

Validity. As with many newly developed measures, evidence of validity is limited. The construct validity of the BSI 18 was assessed by correlating the three symptom dimension scores

and GSI with the corresponding scores on the SCL-90-R. All correlations were high ranging from .91 on the Somatization dimension to .96 on Anxiety (Depression and GSI were both .93) suggesting little information was lost with the reduced number of items.

The factor structure of the BSI 18 was examined using data from the community sample as a means of validating the hypothesized symptom dimensions. Although the results of a principal component analysis support a four-factor solution, the author argues that the findings are not "fundamentally inconsistent with the hypothesized structure of the BSI 18 test" (manual, p. 14). His rationale is that the items loading on the fourth factor, representing panic, are subsumed under anxiety disorders in the DSM-IV (American Psychiatric Association, 1994).

Although no specific studies using the BSI 18 are reported, evidence of the measure's convergent-discriminant validity and criterion-related validity is inferred on the basis of studies conducted with its predecessors the BSI and SCL-90.

COMMENTARY. The BSI 18 is the newest incarnation of the Hopkins Symptoms Checklist that has been evolving over a span of nearly 30 years. The measurement foundation of the BSI 18 is quite strong even though the psychometric properties of this specific rendition are not well understood. The measure is brief and easy to score. The three symptom dimensions of the BSI 18 should identify individuals with the most common mental health problems. The dimensions are highly correlated to those in the more extensive SCL-90-R, supporting the validity of scores from the BSI 18. However, it would be a worthwhile effort to compare scores from the BSI 18 to other independently developed brief patient self-report symptomatology measures such as the Colorado Symptom Index (Shern, et al., 1994) as was done with the BSI by Conrad et al. (2001). This would provide additional validity evidence for the BSI 18. The administration manual is well written and contains information frequently omitted such as how to treat missing data in scoring. Over a quarter of the manual is devoted to "Specific Application of the BSI 18 Test" (p. 15); however, all of the studies summarized in this section were conducted using the longer 53-item BSI.

In Peterson's (1989) review of the BSI, he questioned whether the reduction in administration time from 15–20 minutes for the SCL-90 to the 7–10 minutes of the BSI was meaningful in light of the potential loss of clinical sensitivity. His concern certainly remains apropos with the BSI 18 given the number of symptom domains has been reduced from nine to three and that administration time is now a mere 4 minutes. Perhaps as Peterson suggested the time is approaching when we will just ask people "Do you feel depressed?"

SUMMARY. The BSI 18 appears to be a useful measure for assessing anxiety, depression, and somatization as well as for obtaining an overall level of psychological distress. Although few studies have been conducted assessing the psychometric properties of the BSI 18, it is an abbreviated version of a frequently used and psychometrically tested measure of mental health symptomatology.

REVIEWER'S REFERENCES

American Psychiatric Association. (1994). *Diagnostic and statistical manual of mental disorders* (4th ed.). Washington, DC: Author.

Conrad, K. J., Yagelka, J. R., Matters, M. D., Rich, A. R., Williams, V., & Buchanan, M. (2001). Reliability and validity of a modified Colorado Symptom Index in a national homeless sample. *Mental Health Services Research, 3,* 141–153.

Derogatis, L. R., & Melisaratos, N. (1983). The Brief Symptom Inventory: An introductory report. *Psychological Medicine, 13,* 595–605.

Derogatis, L. R., Rickels, K., & Rock, A. (1976). The SCL-90 and the MMPI: A step in the validation of a new self-report scale. *British Journal of Psychiatry, 128,* 280–289.

Derogatis, L. R., Lipman, R. S., Rickels, K., Uhlenhuth, E. H., & Covi, L. (1974). The Hopkins Symptom Checklist (HSCL): A measure of primary symptom dimensions. In P. Pichot (Ed.), *Psychological measurement in psychopharmacology* (pp. 79–111). Basel, Switzerland: Karger.

Peterson, C. A. (1989). [Review of the Brief Symptom Inventory.] In J. Close Conoley & J. J. Kramer (Eds.), *The tenth mental measurement yearbook* (pp. 112–113). Lincoln, NE: Buros Institute of Mental Measurements.

Shern, D. L., Wilson, N. Z., Coen, A. S., Patrick, D. C. et al. (1994). Client outcomes II: Longitudinal client data from the Colorado Treatment Outcome Study. *Milbank Quarterly, 72,* 123–148.

Review of the Brief Symptom Inventory 18 by WILLIAM E. HANSON, Assistant Professor, Department of Educational Psychology, University of Nebraska-Lincoln, Lincoln, NE:

DESCRIPTION. The Brief Symptom Inventory 18 (BSI 18) is a norm-referenced, self-report instrument composed of, as its namesake suggests, 18 items. According to the manual, it is first and foremost a screening instrument, "developed primarily as a highly sensitive screen for psychiatric disorders and psychological disintegration and secondarily as an instrument to measure treatment outcomes" (administration, scoring, and procedures manual, p. 1). The manual indicates that it may be useful in most clinical and research settings and may be used with a wide range of medical and community populations, including, to name a few, people (18 years old or older) who have been diagnosed with cancer, who have a

compromised immune system (e.g., HIV/AIDS), and/or who are experiencing chronic pain or sexual difficulties. The manual did not, however, indicate the minimum reading level required to complete the instrument.

DEVELOPMENT. The BSI 18 is the fourth iteration in a family of well-known and widely used symptom-based instruments. Its parent instrument, the Brief Symptom Inventory (BSI; Derogatis, 1993; Derogatis & Spencer, 1982), is a derivative of the Symptom Checklist-90—Revised (SCL-90—R; Derogatis, 1977, 1994), which, in turn, is a derivative of the Hopkins Symptom Checklist (HSCL; Derogatis, Lipman, Rickels, Uhlenhuth, & Covi, 1974). It was developed with the following considerations/assumptions in mind: Mood and anxiety disorders are common, though difficult to detect/diagnose appropriately, especially in medical and community settings; somatic symptoms co-occur frequently with Mood and anxiety disorders, further complicating the diagnostic picture; and administration and scoring of the instrument should be brief (<4–5 minutes), straightforward, and cost-effective.

The instrument has 18 nonoverlapping items, all of which were taken directly from the BSI (Derogatis, 1993; Derogatis & Spencer, 1982). They were selected based on "multiple considerations, including prevalence of the symptom, item analysis characteristics, and loading saturations in factor analyses of the BSI and SCL-90—R" (manual, p. 2). No other details related to the development of the instrument were reported (e.g., specific results of item analyses, factor loadings, or pilot testing). It is difficult, therefore, to evaluate the appropriateness of the selection criteria and the decision rules that were used to choose the 18 items.

Nevertheless, the BSI 18 has three, six-item subscales: Somatization (SOM), Depression (DEP), and Anxiety (ANX); and a Total, or Global Severity Index (GSI), score. The subscale and total scores measure constructs identical to the like-named BSI scores (Derogatis, 1993; Derogatis & Spencer, 1982). Specifically, the SOM subscale score measures "distress caused by the perception of bodily dysfunction, focusing on symptoms arising from cardiovascular, gastrointestinal, and other physiologic systems" (manual, p. 5). The DEP subscale score measures "core symptoms of various syndromes of clinical depression" (e.g., disaffection, dysphoric mood, suicidal ideation; manual,

p. 5). The ANX subscale score measures "symptoms that are prevalent in most major anxiety disorders" (e.g., nervousness, tension, apprehension; manual, p. 5). The GSI score is a composite measure of psychological distress and is "the single best indicator of the respondent's overall emotional adjustment and psychopathologic status" (manual, p. 6). Each subscale is scored on a 5-point Likert-type scale, ranging from 0 *not at all* to 4 *extremely*. Subscale scores can range from 0–24 and can, if desired, be summed to obtain a total score, which can range from 0–72.

TECHNICAL INFORMATION.

Standardization procedures: Norming. Normative information is available for two separate samples: an adult nonclient, or "community" sample; and an adult nonclient "oncology" sample. The community sample consisted of 1,134 adult employees (605 men and 517 women; 12 did not report their sex) of an unspecified U.S. corporation. The employees were of diverse age (reported range: 18–69), with the majority being between the ages of 40–59. No other characteristics of this sample were reported (e.g., race/ethnicity, education level, or SES), making it difficult to determine its representativeness. Details related to how these individuals were identified and/or recruited to participate in the original norming study were also not reported.

The oncology sample consisted of 1,543 adults (802 men and 741 women) who had been diagnosed with cancer and who were patients at an unspecified U.S. east coast cancer center. The adult cancer patients were of diverse age (reported range: <30–80+), with the majority being between the ages of 50–69. At least 20 different types/manifestations of cancer were represented. Similar to the community sample, no other characteristics of this sample were reported.

Of note, both the community and the oncology norms are gender-keyed. Separate norms are available for men and women. Combined norms are also available. However, test users are "strongly recommended" to use the separate, gender-keyed norms (manual, p. 37).

Administration and scoring. Administration and scoring procedures are straightforward and easy to understand. The BSI 18 may be administered by hand or by computer. It may also be scored by hand, using a preprinted scoring sheet that includes detailed scoring directions, or by computer, using scoring software that may be purchased from the publisher. Computer-based progress reports are also available for purchase. The availability of progress reports is appealing and, if used, may prove to be a useful feature of the scoring software.

If administered by hand, the instructions, a sample test item, and the 18 test items are printed on one side of a single sheet of paper. Test takers are instructed to read a list of "problems," or symptoms, and to indicate how much each symptom has distressed or bothered them over the past week (i.e., "the past 7 days including today").

If scored by hand, the scoring directions and either a community- or oncology-based blank profile graph (one for men and one for women) are printed on one side of a single sheet of paper. Nine specific, step-by-step scoring directions are provided, including directions for determining a profile's validity, for calculating estimated values of omitted items, and for plotting raw score totals on the blank profile graph. As a general rule of thumb, a test taker may omit two items per subscale without jeopardizing the validity of the BSI 18's scores. If, however, three or more items are omitted from any of the three subscales, the scores should be considered invalid. Also, test users are reminded to always calculate estimated values of omitted items, as these estimates are included in raw score totals.

Interpretation. To facilitate interpretation, raw score totals are converted to area, or uniform, *T*-scores, with a mean of 50 and a standard deviation of 10. Conversion tables for the two normative samples (community and oncology) are in the manual. Percentile rank equivalents of the raw scores are also in the manual.

The manual recommends that interpretation of the BSI 18 occur at three interrelated levels: the global level; the dimensional level; and the symptom, or item, level. Basically, it involves three steps. The first step occurs at the global level. It involves determining "caseness" (manual, p. 23), that is, whether or not the test taker's scores meet predetermined, empirically based criteria for identification/positive risk of psychological distress—stated differently, that they fall within the clinical range. If so, then the test user is encouraged to evaluate the test taker further.

The second step occurs at the dimensional level. It involves considering each BSI 18 subscale score independently, in the following recommended order: DEP, ANX, and SOM. If any of these subscale scores fall within the clinical range (T score >63), then the test user is also encouraged to evaluate the test taker further.

The third and final step occurs at the symptom, or item, level. It involves considering individual BSI 18 items. For example, Item 17 (an item related to suicidal ideation) and Items 9, 12, and 18 (items related to panic attacks) should be examined closely to determine if further evaluation is necessary in these clinically important areas. Test users are referred to Derogatis and Savitz (1999) for additional information related to interpretation.

RELIABILITY AND VALIDITY. Reliability estimates of the BSI 18 subscale and total scores are, based on the adult nonclient "community" sample mentioned earlier, satisfactory and meet traditional professional standards of acceptability. Estimates of internal consistency range, in this sample, from "fair" (Somatization [.74], Anxiety [.79]) to "good" (Depression [.84], Total [.89]; cf. Cicchetti, 1994). Test-retest reliability estimates are not reported. However, test-retest reliability estimates of the BSI (Derogatis, 1993; Derogatis & Spencer, 1982) are reported. These estimates range, in a different sample of 60 nonpatients, from .68 (Somatization) to .90 (Total). By reporting these estimates, it appears that the author is relying on reliability induction, whereby test-retest reliability of the subscale and total scores is generalized from one sample (and, in this case, a different test, the BSI) and assumed to be an appropriate estimate for another sample (and the BSI 18). BSI 18 test users are, therefore, encouraged to compute reliability estimates, including estimates of internal consistency and test-retest reliability, for their "data in hand."

Standard error of measurement (*SEM*), a common method of estimating the reliability of a test taker's score, is also not reported for the BSI 18 subscale or total scores. Subscale and total score intercorrelations are not reported either, which limits appropriate and responsible interpretation of the subscale and total scores and precludes profile interpretation altogether (Anastasi, 1985).

Preliminary evidence of equivalence, or correspondence, between BSI 18 scores and SCL-90—R scores is provided in the manual. These correlations, which are based on the community sample, ranged from .91 (SOM) to .96 (ANX). The manual states that "basic considerations concerning such issues as face and content validity have been addressed previously in the context of the development of the parent instrument" (pp. 13–14). Preliminary evidence of criterion-related validity of BSI 18 scores is also provided in the manual. This evidence is based on a selective review of published studies that used the BSI—not the BSI 18. The studies were related to eight different clinical areas: screening studies, cancer populations, pain assessment/management, military populations, HIV/AIDS research, immune system functioning, human sexuality, and medical and law students.

Finally, preliminary evidence of construct validity, in particular, convergent validity, is provided in the manual. This evidence is based on correlations between BSI and SCL-90—R scores and MMPI clinical, content, and Tryon cluster scores that measure similar constructs. Reported correlation coefficients ranged from .40–.72 and were generally in the expected direction. Specific evidence of discriminant validity was not reported. Of relevance here, factor analyses of the BSI 18 resulted in a four-factor solution that accounted for a respectable 57.2% of the total variance. The four identified factors and corresponding item loadings are more-or-less consistent with the author's hypothesized, a priori dimensional structure of the instrument and its scores.

CONCLUSIONS AND RECOMMENDATIONS. The BSI 18 is an intriguing new, commercially available screening instrument. Given the popularity and track records of its parent instruments (e.g., BSI, SCL-90—R), it likely has a promising future. Because of how it was developed, its overall strengths and weaknesses parallel those of its predecessors (for *MMY* reviews of the BSI, see Cundick, 1989, and Peterson, 1989; for *MMY* reviews of the SCL-90—R, see Pauker, 1985, and Payne, 1985). Its most obvious strengths include: professionally developed, user-friendly testing materials and scoring software; brevity; straightforward administration, scoring, and interpretation procedures; availability of computer-based progress reports; and acceptable estimates of internal consistency. Its most obvious weaknesses include: limited normative, reliability, and validity data, including data related to score sensitivity and specificity; lack of profile interpretation capabilities; and, similar to other brief, self-report instruments, susceptibility to distortion and "faking" of responses.

That said, the manual, in its current form, makes it virtually impossible to determine the BSI 18's true merits. Though well organized and well written, it is largely uninformative. Too few details are included. Test users who refer to it for information regarding: the reading level required to complete the instrument; specific details related to how/why the test items were chosen; characteristics of the two normative samples; test-retest reliability estimates; *SEM* estimates; subscale and total score intercorrelations; and, perhaps most importantly, adequate evidence of construct and predictive validity, will be disappointed. The omission of these types of details is significant and, in this reviewer's opinion, should be addressed in future editions of the manual.

All things considered, use of the BSI 18 may, quite frankly, be premature. Clearly, additional normative, reliability, and validity data are needed *on the BSI 18* to justify its use, especially for clinical purposes. Until that occurs, it is recommended that the BSI 18 be used only for research purposes and as an adjunct, or supplement, to traditional, more well-established screening instruments/interview methods in clinical applications and settings. Also, it is recommend that, at this time, only the Total, or GSI, score be used.

Prospective test users looking for a suitable, though slightly longer, alternative to the BSI 18 may find the OQ—45.2 (Lambert et al., 1996) to be a potentially satisfactory, psychometrically sound option.

REVIEWER'S REFERENCES

Anastasi, A. (1985). Interpreting results from multiscore batteries. *Journal of Counseling and Development, 64,* 84–86.

Cicchetti, D. V. (1994). Guidelines, criteria, and rules of thumb for evaluating normed and standardized assessment instruments in psychology. *Psychological Assessment, 6,* 284–290.

Cundick, B. P. (1989). [Review of the Brief Symptom Inventory]. In J. C. Conoley & J. J. Kramer (Eds.), *The tenth mental measurements yearbook* (pp. 111–112). Lincoln, NE: Buros Institute of Mental Measurements.

Derogatis, L. R. (1977). *Symptom Checklist-90—R (SCL-90—R) administration, scoring, and procedures manual I.* Baltimore, MD: Clinical Psychometric Research.

Derogatis, L. R. (1993). *Brief Symptom Inventory (BSI) administration, scoring, and procedures manual* (3rd ed.). Minneapolis: NCS Pearson, Inc.

Derogatis, L. R. (1994). *Symptom Checklist—90—R (SCL-90—R) administration, scoring, and procedures manual* (3rd ed.). Minneapolis: NCS Pearson, Inc.

Derogatis, L. R., Lipman, R. S., Rickels, K., Uhlenhuth, E. H., & Covi, L. (1974). The Hopkins Symptom Checklist (HSCL): A measure of primary symptom dimensions. In P. Pichot (Ed.), *Psychological measurements in psychopharmacology* (pp. 79–111). Basel, Switzerland: Karger.

Derogatis, L. R., & Savitz, K. L. (1999). The SCL-90—R, Brief Symptom Inventory, and matching clinical ratings scales. In M. E. Maruish (Ed.), The use of psychological testing for treatment planning and outcomes assessment (2nd ed.; pp. 679–724). Mahwah, NJ: Lawrence Erlbaum Associates.

Derogatis, L. R., & Spencer, P. (1982). *Brief Symptom Inventory (BSI) administration, scoring, and procedures manual I.* Baltimore, MD: Clinical Psychometric Research.

Lambert, M. J., Hansen, N. B., Umphress, V., Lunnen, K., Okiishi, J., Burlingame, G. M., & Reisinger, C. W. (1996). *Administration and scoring manual for the OQ-45.2.* Stevenson, MD: American Professional Credentialing Services LLC.

Pauker, J. D. (1985). [Review of the SCL-90-R]. In J. V. Mitchell, Jr. (Ed.), *The ninth mental measurements yearbook* (pp. 1325–1326). Lincoln, NE: Buros Institute of Mental Measurements.

Payne, R. W. (1985). [Review of the SCL-90-R]. In J. V. Mitchell, Jr. (Ed.), *The ninth mental measurements yearbook* (pp. 1326–1329). Lincoln, NE: Buros Institute of Mental Measurements.

Peterson, C. D. (1989). [Review of the Brief Symptom Inventory]. In J. C. Conoley & J. J. Kramer (Eds.), *The tenth mental measurements yearbook* (pp. 112–113). Lincoln, NE: Buros Institute of Mental Measurements.

[39]

Brief Test of Attention.

Purpose: Designed "to assess the severity of attentional impairment among nonaphasic hearing adult patients."
Population: Ages 17–82.
Publication Date: 1997.
Acronym: BTA.
Scores: Total score only.
Administration: Individual.
Forms, 2: N (Numbers), L (Letters).
Price Data: Available from publisher for kit including manual (34 pages), and 50 scoring forms, and for audio tape.
Time: (10) minutes.
Author: David Schretlen.
Publisher: Psychological Assessment Resources, Inc.

Review of the Brief Test of Attention by ELIZABETH KELLEY BOYLES, Assistant Professor of School Psychology at Marshall University Graduate College, South Charleston, WV:

DESCRIPTION. The Brief Test of Attention (BTA) is a test of divided auditory attention. It takes less than 10 minutes to administer and is administered through the use of an auditory cassette tape. Form N consists of a voice reciting lists of letters and numbers. The examinee must specify how many numbers were read aloud, disregarding their value. In Form L, the test taker must listen to the lists and specify the quantity of letters that were read. It is recommended that those taking the test be given both forms of the measure although individuals with extremely poor performance on the first form may omit the second form. The test is designed to be used with individuals aged 17 to 82 who are nonaphasic. Potential examinees must be able to hear and comprehend the difference between auditorially presented numbers and letters. Scoring consists of summing the examinee's correct responses and referring to a chart in the manual that provides percentile ranks by age group.

DEVELOPMENT. The BTA was developed based on the work of Cooley and Morris (1990) in the area of selective attention (Schretlen, Bobholz, & Brandt, 1996). Their goal was to "devise a brief, relatively simple and easily administered test of auditory divided attention that would be sensitive to subtle attentional impairments" and "to reduce confounding task demands such as psychomotor speed or conceptual reasoning" (Schretlen, Bobholz, & Brandt, 1996, p. 81)." The BTA audiotape consists of a female broadcaster reading the lists at one letter or number per second with 5 seconds between trials. The tape was remastered to filter out extraneous noise.

TECHNICAL. The BTA norm group consisted of 74 children between the ages of 6 and 14 (who all attended the same elementary school) and 667 adults from ages 17 to 82. All individuals in the norm group were recruited in Baltimore, Maryland or Buffalo, New York and were "screened to eliminate individuals with dementia, severe psychiatric disorders, or current substance dependence" (manual, p. 11). The test manual does not elaborate on these screening or exclusionary procedures. Later, 587 adult patients from Johns Hopkins were selected to serve as a "clinical sample" (manual, p. 11). These individuals provided small cells of patients in several diagnostic categories, with nearly 20% having their diagnosis "not recorded" (manual, p. 12). When a stepwise multiple regression was calculated using the normative factors recorded (age, race, education level, and gender), a model was formed in which these four factors accounted for 17.5% of the variance in test scores. Age accounted for the greatest portion of the variance (8.7%), followed closely by ethnicity (5.0%) and education level (4.0%), and finally by gender (.8%). The authors chose to calculate a single normative table providing scores in 13 age groups [Editor's Note: Page 12 of the manual indicates 14 age groups but the publisher advises this was a typo].

The test authors chose to examine reliability through measures of internal consistency, form equivalence, and test-retest performance. Measures of internal consistency were calculated for the entire normal sample (.80 for the complete test, .69 for Form L, and .65 for Form N) as well as the normal sample combined with a subset of 490 patients from the clinical sample "for whom item scores were recorded" (.90 for the complete test, .82 for Form L, and .81 for Form N) (manual, p. 13). The between form correlation for Forms L and N for the full standardization sample was .65.

When the results of the clinical sample were included, the correlation was .79. Two test-retest studies are cited in the manual. In the first, otherwise healthy senior adults with hypertension were retested from 6 to 12 months after their initial evaluation yielding a correlation of .70. The second study of 78 teenage girls included a retest interval of 3 months and yielded a correlation between scores of .45.

Validity studies compared BTA results for subsamples of the normal and clinical groups to the Wechsler Digit Span subtest (.53 for backward and .43 for forward), the Trail Making Test (Part B -.55, Part A -.48), and the Stroop Color and Word Test (Word Reading .66, Color Naming .68, Color-Word Naming .67). A study of 27 patients with Huntington's Disease found they had significantly lower BTA scores than normal adults (Schretlen, Brandt, & Bobholz, 1996). Ten patients with amnesia had BTA scores consistent with matched controls (Schretlen, Brandt, & Bobholz, 1996). BTA scores were found to explain a significant portion (39%) of the outcome differences in a study of 45 adults recovering from closed head injury. Driving histories for elderly drivers were compared to their BTA scores, indicating a nonsignificant difference in favor of individuals with fewer accidents having higher BTA scores.

COMMENTARY. The BTA is an application of the theoretical approach of Cooley and Morris (1990). The task and directions are clear and the procedures for making the tape appear excellent. The validation studies indicating poor BTA scores in those with known attentional impairments and relatively normal scores in those with amnesia are promising.

Given the group with which the test is most likely to prove useful (the elderly), hearing status may be a significant concern to examiners. It would have been helpful to have had data on the degree of hearing acuity necessary for valid administration.

The standardization included a small norm group that was limited geographically. Although the manual mentions that those in the initial standardization group were screened to eliminate those with certain disabilities, there is no mention of how this was done or what the criteria were for removal. Sadly, given the importance of this domain for children's learning and school performance, the children's standardization group was so limited as to be of no use in establishing norms for those under age 17. Given these limitations, it is difficult to understand why the children's scores were included in the calculations of reliability.

Finally, there are some concerns with the norm calculations. Given the impact of demographic factors beyond age (such as education level) on scores, norms tables that provided score conversions accounting for these criteria would have proven useful. Finally, the choice of percentile ranks as the sole means of communicating the individual's relative standing on the test is a poor one. The inclusion of standard scores would have been psychometrically more clear and useful.

SUMMARY. The BTA is a brief measure of divided auditory attention that may prove useful in screening hearing adults for selective attention difficulties. It is not appropriate for use with those with hearing problems, aphasia, or those under age 17. Although further study is needed, it appears to differentiate between older adults with known attention difficulties and to be relatively unaffected by the presence of amnesia.

REVIEWER'S REFERENCES

Cooley, E. L., & Morris, R. D. (1990). Attention in children: A neuropsychologically based model for assessment. *Developmental Neuropsychology, 6,* 239–274.

Schretlen, D., Bobholz, J. H., & Brandt, J. (1996). Development and psychometric properties of the Brief Test of Attention. *Clinical Neuropsychologist, 10,* 80–89.

Schretlen, D., Brandt, J., & Bobholz, J. H. (1996). Validation of the Brief Test of Attention in patients with Huntington's disease and amnesia. *Clinical Neuropsychologist, 10,* 90–95.

Review of the Brief Test of Attention by STEVEN R. SHAW, Lead School Psychologist, Department of Developmental Pediatrics, The Children's Hospital, Greenville, SC, and Associate Professor of Pediatrics (Greenville), Medical University of South Carolina, Greenville, SC:

DESCRIPTION. The Brief Test of Attention (BTA) is a brief measure of divided auditory attention. The BTA is designed for nonaphasic hearing persons aged 17 to 82. Administration of the BTA consists of a recorded voice reading a list of letters and numbers. The task is for the examinee to tell the examiner how many numbers he or she heard (Form N) or how many letters he or she heard (Form L). Each form consists of two examples and 10 items. The stimuli presented on Form L and Form N are identical. Both forms are administered. The estimated time to administer both forms is 8 minutes. Raw scores are reported as correct or incorrect. Raw scores range from 0 to 20. Percentile ranks corresponding to each raw score by age group are provided in a table in the manual. The BTA is designed to identify impairments in the ability to divide attention between simultaneously presented stimuli.

DEVELOPMENT. The goal for developing the BTA was to develop a simple test of auditory divided attention that is sensitive to subtle impairments in attention. A secondary goal was to reduce confounding task demands such as conceptual reasoning, previous knowledge, and psychomotor speed from the measure of attention.

TECHNICAL.

Reliability. The BTA manual provides information on internal consistency, form equivalence, and stability. Internal consistency, estimated by coefficient alpha, is .80 for the BTA, .69 for Form L, and .65 for Form N. The manual also provides additional coefficient alphas when the (N = 490) clinical sample is combined with the (N = 741) normative sample. Of course, this artificially increases the variance and creates inflated coefficient alphas. Between-form correlations, not surprisingly, are quite high. Data are provided showing minimal score differences between forms and minimal impact of order of administration. Stability was investigated by two studies. Study 1 consisted of 60 adults (mean age was 66.2 years) assessed an average of 9 months apart, resulting in Pearson correlation of .70. Study 2 consisted of 78 adolescent girls tested 3 months apart. Pearson correlation from that study was r_{tt} = .45. Study 2 resulted in a lower stability coefficient because the adolescent girl sample scored higher with a more restricted range of results than did the 60- to 80-year-old adults from Study 1. Overall, reliability estimates are adequate for a brief test.

Validity. There are several studies demonstrating the validity of the BTA in the assessment of attention. Positive and significant correlations are reports between the BTA and Digit Span, Trail Making Test, and the Stroop Color Word Test. A factor analysis of the BTA in a battery of psychometric tests with a sample of 107 psychiatric patients was conducted. The BTA showed modest loading on the first factor, which reflects general and verbal mental ability. The BTA had significant loading on the second factor, reflecting attentional ability. And just as importantly, the BTA had low to moderate loading on the third factor, which reflected psychomotor speed and perceptual skills.

Several clinical studies also helped to examine validity of the BTA. A sample of 27 patients with Huntington's Disease was administered the BTA along with 27 control individuals matched on age and results of the Mini Mental State Examination. Huntington's Disease is well known to have severe effects on attention. The Huntington's group scored significantly lower than the control group. Another study includes a clinical sample of adults (N = 10) with anterograde and retrograde amnesia and an age-matched control group. This clinical population had demonstrated impaired learning and memory skills. However, the BTA showed no differences between groups. This supports the claim that the BTA measures attention, but relies little on learning and memory skills. The BTA was also found to yield low scores in samples of persons with several mental illnesses and closed head injury. BTA results also are associated with risk of motor vehicle accidents in an elderly population. The BTA was also associated with gray matter volume in an MRI study of 100 normal participants. Overall, the validity evidence of the BTA is very strong based on the information presented in the manual.

Normative Sample. The normative sample consists of 667 adults (M = 47.5 and age range = 17–82) and 74 children (M = 10.1 and age range 6–14) from either Buffalo, New York or Baltimore, Maryland. Over 63% of the normative sample was female. Race and ethnicity were not recorded for 40 adults. The remainder of the sample was 81.7% white, 18.0% African American, and .3% Other. The children were from second, fifth, and eighth grade classrooms. Over 51% were male. In the sample of children, 94.6% were white with the remainder being African American. It is interesting that the sample of children were documented in the manual because the test is described as being for adults aged 17 to 82 years. There is no child information in the provided scoring table. For the child sample, the BTA was correlated with age and education. Also boys scored significantly lower than girls. These gender differences also existed in the adult samples. However, there are not different scoring tables for males and females. There were 587 participants in the patient sample. The patients were drawn from clinics at Johns Hopkins University. Their diagnoses included schizophrenia, mental retardation, dementia, affective disorders, substance dependence, eating disorder, brain injury, adrenaleukodystrophy, and sexual disorders.

COMMENTARY. The BTA is a brief test with a limited domain. In most practices there are few occasions to assess auditory selective and divided attention in adults. However, this test is well executed and well supported by validity data in the manual. Reliability is lower than acceptable for most individual tests. However, given the brevity of the BTA, reliability data are adequate. There are clearly limitations in the gender and geographic aspects of the normative sample. However, these are fairly minor quibbles for most clinical purposes. I would recommend and will use the BTA in my own clinical practice.

SUMMARY. The Brief Test of Attention is a measure of selective and divided auditory attention. The Brief Test of Attention is notable for an impressive reporting of validity studies and a well-written manual. Although there are minor weaknesses in standardization sample and the scope of this test is quite narrow, the Brief Test of Attention certainly can be an excellent addition to a test battery focusing on components of attention.

[40]

Brief Visuospatial Memory Test—Revised.

Purpose: Designed as an equivalent, multiple-test form assessment of visual memory.
Population: Ages 18–79.
Publication Dates: 1988–1997.
Acronym: BVMT-R.
Scores, 12: Trial 1, Trial 2, Trial 3, Total Recall, Learning, Delayed Recall, Percent Retained, Recognition Hits, Recognition False Alarms, Recognition Discrimination Index, Recognition Response Bias, Copy (Optional).
Administration: Individual.
Forms, 6: 1, 2, 3, 4, 5, 6.
Price Data: Available from publisher for kit including manual (1997, 131 pages), recognition stimulus booklet, recall stimulus booklet, and 10 response forms.
Time: (45) minutes including 25-minute delay.
Comments: Can be administered bed-side by appropriately trained personnel.
Author: Ralph H. B. Benedict.
Publisher: Psychological Assessment Resources, Inc.

Review of the Brief Visuospatial Memory Test—Revised by ANITA M. HUBLEY, Associate Professor of Measurement, Evaluation, and Research Methodology, University of British Columbia, Vancouver, British Columbia, Canada:

DESCRIPTION. The Brief Visuospatial Memory Test—Revised (BVMT-R) measures visuospatial learning and memory in adults. Six forms of the BVMT-R are available, which is useful for multiple testing purposes. Respondents are asked to reproduce an array of six figures that is presented to them for 10 seconds. Each form of the test consists of three learning trials, a delayed recall trial, a recognition trial, and an optional copy trial. Twelve scores are obtained from the BVMT-R and are described in detail in the manual.

Test administration may be conducted by anyone with a background in psychological testing who has been trained on the BVMT-R by a qualified psychologist. The administration instructions are very clear as are the scoring instructions. How each of the various scores are computed and what they are meant to measure is clearly laid out. Specific steps are provided to aid in the scoring. Separate appendices provide examples for scoring accuracy and location. The scoring worksheet and record form (provided on the response form) are very clear and easy to use. Clinical interpretation must be made by a qualified psychologist with professional training and expertise in clinical psychology and/or neuropsychology.

DEVELOPMENT. The original BVMT (1988) consisted of two trials: immediate recall and a 25-minute delayed recall. Scoring consisted of awarding one point per figure for accuracy and an additional bonus point if all figures were located correctly. Explicit rules were established for developing figures in each position in a 2 x 3 array so that alternate forms with designs matching in general format, complexity, and difficulty could be created. Fourteen alternate BVMT forms originally were developed; subsequent research, which is described in detail in the manual, resulted in six equivalent forms.

The BVMT was revised to (a) increase the range of scores, (b) assess learning and reduce the susceptibility of the initial trial scores to momentary fluctuations in attention, and (c) assess recognition memory, which is less reliant on graphomotor performance. The revised scoring system is similar to that used with the Rey-Osterrieth Complex Figure and increases the range of scores by giving equal weight to the location of figures (not just their accuracy). No rationale is provided for the use of a 25-minute delay interval except to reference the (30-minute) delay interval of the

Wechsler Memory Scale—Revised (WMS-R) Visual Reproduction subtest. A much shorter delay interval (e.g., 10 minutes) might have been sufficient for this brief test. The manual does not report how long the BVMT-R takes to administer.

The development of the original alternate forms and the recognition task are detailed in the manual and seem appropriate. A missing piece of information is why Figure F in each form of the BVMT-R is designed to be more difficult than the other figures in both its design and in its discriminability from nontargets. Further research needs to examine whether targets (or nontargets) show an equal likelihood of being selected across forms in the recognition task. Finally, because the original equivalence studies were conducted with college students only, further research needs to establish that equivalent total score performance on the various forms is obtained with other adult age groups.

TECHNICAL. Normative data, based on 588 normal participants, are provided for adults aged 18–79 years. An analysis showed that BVMT-R scores were affected by age, but not by gender or education. Thus, demographically corrected normative data are presented in separate tables for 28 age groups using the method of overlapping midpoint age cells (e.g., 18–22 years, 20–24 years, 22–26 years). In addition, separate norms are presented for a subset of the normative sample ($n = 377$) that was selected to reflect the age distribution of the projected U.S. Census for 2000. These norms are presented in a single table and are not age-graded. The author does not provide a rationale for presenting two sets of norms; nor does he provide any information in this section about which form(s) of the BVMT-R were used. Norms for Trials 1, 2, and 3, Total Recall, Learning, and Delayed Recall are reported using percentiles and linear T-scores whereas Percent Retained, Recognition Hits, Recognition False Alarms, Recognition Discrimination Index, and Recognition Response Bias norms are reported using percentile categories because these scores tended to be highly skewed and restricted in range.

Scoring of the figures requires considerable subjective judgment. Interrater reliability was estimated using the figures from 282 clinical and nonclinical participants. All Pearson r coefficients were over .97, suggesting a high level of interrater reliability. It is recommended that the author also report a measure that considers absolute agreement among raters rather than just consistency (i.e., an intraclass correlation of absolute agreement; see McGraw & Wong, 1996).

A key benefit of the BVMT-R is the existence of multiple forms. Interform reliability was estimated in two well-designed and described studies. No significant differences were found among the forms in either study. The means-level data provided for the first study are quite impressive. The reporting of test-retest reliabilities using the same form from test to retest, however, is problematic. Reliabilities, with all forms combined, ranged from .60 for Trial 1 to .84 for Trial 3. However, the sample sizes for each form are quite small (ranging from 11 to 13), the test-retest interval could only be reported as an average (M = 55.6 days, s = 10 days), and this type of reliability estimate does not seem appropriate given the participants' extensive exposure to the test stimuli.

The validity of interpreting the BVMT-R scores as a measure of visuospatial memory was examined in three ways. First, the BVMT-R scores were correlated with scores from a number of theoretically convergent measures (i.e., other visuospatial memory tests) and discriminant measures (i.e., language tests) in a clinical sample. The pattern of correlations found supports the intended interpretation of the BVMT-R. Second, scores obtained from a clinical sample on a number of tests were submitted to a principal components analysis with varimax rotation. The results showed that the visuospatial memory items (including the BVMT-R) clustered together and were separate from verbal learning and memory, general cognitive processing, and response bias factors.

Third, performance on the BVMT-R was examined in a series of studies using contrasted or known groups. BVMT-R measures (except Response Bias) were able to discriminate between (a) HIV-1 seropositive patients with documented cognitive impairment and age and education matched controls as well as between HIV patients with dementia versus minor cognitive/motor disorder; (b) individuals with dementia (Alzheimer's disease and vascular dementia patients) and age and education matched controls, although not between the two dementia groups; and (c) focal and severe anterograde amnesia patients and participants from the standardization sample who were matched approximately on age and education.

Interpretive information is provided for a variety of BVMT-R measures with specific comments devoted to base rate comparisons. In addition, guidelines are suggested for the clinical interpretation of T-scores and percentiles. Further information on the interpretation of "lower" and "higher" Recognition Response Bias scores and how to apply this information would be beneficial.

COMMENTARY. The BVMT-R is a highly promising measure of visuospatial memory. Its two key strengths are that (a) there are multiple forms of the test which is ideal when repeated testing is needed; and (b) it appears to be a brief, original approach to visuospatial learning and memory assessment. The procedure for developing multiple forms and the interform reliability results are impressive, although further research is needed to establish comparability among forms in older age groups. Also, the author needs to address whether or not practice effects are evident when the different forms are used in repeated measures studies.

The BVMT-R is a considerable improvement over the original version of this test. The manual is well written and organized. Particular attention has been paid to the scoring of the figures with numerous examples provided. Interrater reliability is high. The validation research conducted thus far is very promising; further validation work needs to consider other clinical samples as well as focus on cognitively intact adults. The addition of case studies that demonstrate the pattern of learning and memory deficits that one might expect to find with particular disorders (e.g., Alzheimer's Disease, Korsakoff's syndrome, stroke, traumatic brain injury) would be a strong addition to the manual.

Finally, there are some lingering questions, such as why so many age groupings were selected in the norms, why Figure F is designed to be more difficult than the other figures, and when one should use the U.S. Census norms rather than the age norms.

SUMMARY. The BVMT-R is recommended as a brief and original approach to assessing visuospatial learning and memory in adults. A particular strength of this test is that it consists of six forms that can be used for multiple testing purposes, although further evidence is needed to establish the comparability of forms for specific age groups (e.g., older adults). Test development, administration, scoring, and interpretive information is clearly presented in the manual. Interrater reliability is high, interform reliability appears strong, and the validity evidence presented is very promising. Further validation work will only strengthen the utility of the BVMT-R.

REVIEWER'S REFERENCE

McGraw, K. O., & Wong, S. P. (1996). Forming inferences about some intraclass correlation coefficients. *Psychological Methods, 1,* 30–46.

Review of the Brief Visuospatial Memory Test— Revised by TERRY A. STINNETT, Professor, School of Applied Health and Educational Psychology, Oklahoma State University, Stillwater, OK:

DESCRIPTION. The Brief Visuospatial Memory Test—Revised (BVMT-R) is an individually administered, short measure of immediate and delayed visual-spatial memory. The instrument was originally developed to serve as an alternative to existing memory scales because there was a dearth of commercially available instruments that had alternate forms. Clinicians working with patients in the area of cognitive rehabilitation needed alternate-form memory tests, otherwise their frequent multiple assessments of memory in their patients were confounded by error associated with practice effects.

The BVMT-R measures only immediate and delayed memory and recognition of figural stimuli, which can be considered to contribute to the broader construct of Visual Processing (*Gv,* see Carroll, 1997; McGrew & Flanagan, 1998). There are six equivalent forms (Form 1 through Form 6). The instrument is appropriate for those aged from 18 years through 79 years and it is likely to be used with those who have suffered neurological insult or brain damage.

Each of the forms contains 6 items (figural stimuli) presented in a 2-by-3 matrix array. The examinee is exposed to all items on the selected form simultaneously for exactly 10 seconds, the stimuli are removed, and the examinee is then instructed to draw as many of the figures he or she can remember in their correct location on the Response Form. The Delayed Recall Trial follows Trial 3 and a 25-minute delay. Immediately after Delayed Recall is the Recognition Trial (12 recognition items). There is an optional Copy Trial that can be administered after the Recognition Trial.

Scores. Twelve scores can be calculated based on an examinee's performance. The scoring procedures for each are clearly described in the professional manual. Raw scores for Trials 1, 2, and 3 are calculated based on accuracy and location of the drawing and these are converted to linear *T*-scores ($M = 50$, $SD = 10$) and percentile ranks. The Total Recall score is indicated to be the most sensitive indicator of overall visuospatial memory capacity provided by this test. A Learning score can be calculated and it reflects the amount of learning across the three trials. There is also a Delayed Recall score and a Percent Retained score. Delayed Recall measures long-term visuospatial memory and retrieval skill, whereas the Percent Retained score represents long-term memory based on the amount of information that was initially learned. Other scores include the Recognition Hits (the number of correct yes responses to target items) and Recognition False Alarms (number of incorrect yes responses to foil items), which are based on the examinee's performance during the delayed recognition trial. Additional measures include the Recognition Discrimination Index (ability to discriminate previously presented target stimuli from nontarget stimuli) and the Recognition Response Bias (the tendency to answer yes to recognition items regardless of whether they were target stimuli or not) scores. All of the recognition scores can be converted only to percentile ranks. The Copy score is a raw score only and is used to determine if the examinee has copying deficits rather than memory deficits.

TECHNICAL.

Standardization. The normative sample ($N = 588$) is a weakness for this test. The sample is geographically restricted to the northeast region of the United States, more highly educated as compared to the average level reported in a U.S. Census report (U.S. Department of Commerce, 1994), mostly white (82%), mostly women (64%), and small in size. Handedness is the only other demographic variable reported in the manual (61.9% right handed, 6.3% left handed, 31.3% unreported). The sampling design included "normal" participants and consisted of college students ($n = 171$) drawn from a northeastern university and community volunteers ($n = 417$) who responded to a newspaper advertisement. The effects of age, gender, and educational level on BVMT-R performance of the participants were examined as part of the development of the normative sample. Hierarchical regression models indicated significant linear effects for age on all BVMT-R variables except for Learning (variance accounted for ranged from 1% to 24%). Years of education and gender were not significant predictors of BVMT-R performance. Thus, the author chose to develop demographically corrected norms based on age. There are 28 separate overlapping midpoint age group tables in the norms. The overlapping midpoint procedure serves to increase the number of participants who comprise the norms in each age-group table. Each age-group interval is based on 4 years, 2 above the midpoint age and 2 below (e.g., the midpoint age of 20 years includes participants aged 18–22) except for the last group (midpoint 75 years). For the midpoint age of 75 years, the interval ranged from 72 through 79 years. Even after using the overlapping midpoint procedure, the ns for each age group are a concern. All of the age groups are small, except for the 18–22-year group, which is based on 178 participants. The median n per interval is 39 (ns range from 26–178). The problem of small sample size is especially noted at the elder age groups; most of these have fewer than 40 subjects for a 4-year age interval.

There are interpretive descriptors for both normative and individual comparison standards. The normative standards range from Very Superior to Very Inferior, the individual comparison standards from Normal to Severely Impaired. Both the normative and individual comparison standards are based on T-scores and percentile ranks.

If there was no measurement of the examinee prior to a neurological insult, the test author recommends estimating the level of premorbid functioning that would have been expected. No direction is offered for this in the manual so users of this instrument should use this procedure with caution.

A subset of the overall sample ($n = 377$) was selected to match the U.S. Census (U.S. Department of Commerce, 1994) 2000 middle series projections for age and does closely approximate the projected percentages expected in the U.S. population. This subset was used to develop a U.S. Census Age-Matched normative table, which allows users of the test to compare an examinee's performance to a group taken as a whole as well as to his or her specific age group. It is unfortunate that none of the other reported sample demographics mirror the U.S. Census.

A very helpful interpretive feature included in the manual is base rate data for normal and various neurologic groups. This base rate information allows users to compare the performance of an examinee to people with no cognitive impairments as well as to the various clinical groups reported in the table.

Reliability. For estimating interrater reliability, the test author and two advanced undergraduate research assistants judged 282 protocols of randomly selected participants drawn from normal and patient groups. Interrater reliabilities for Trials 1, 2, 3, Total Recall, and Delayed Recall were excellent (rs were all .97 or .98).

All six forms of the BVMT-R were evaluated for temporal consistency (Trials 1, 2, 3, Total Recall, and Delayed Recall). Seventy-one participants in different age groups were administered the same form they had taken earlier. These were extremely small groups (ns ranged from 11–13 for each form). The time interval between test and retest was adequate and averaged 55.6 days. The separate form test-retest coefficients are disappointing. For Total Recall only Form 1 (.86), Form 2 (.92), Form 3 (.82), and Form 5 had adequate temporal stability. For Delayed Recall Form 1 (.87) and Form 2 (.91) were adequate. Test-retest reliability is also marginal when the data are considered across all forms and based on the entire 71 participants (rs: Trial 1 = .60, Trial 2 = .70, Trial 3 = .84, Total Recall = .80, and Delayed Recall = .79). Reliability coefficients of at least .90 have been recommended as the lowest acceptable for individual diagnostic purposes (Salvia & Ysseldyke, 1998). One procedural safeguard to this reliability problem would be to use the standard errors of measurement when describing an examinee's obtained score. The standard errors of measurement are omitted in the BVMT-R. Given that the reliabilities (test-retest) are marginal and that error is likely in the obtained scores, this is an important oversight.

Between groups interform reliability was evaluated based on the test performance of 600 normal participants enrolled in the standardization study. No significant differences were indicated across forms for the recall or recognition measures. Interform reliability was also evaluated with a within subjects design. Eighteen college students took each of the six forms in six separate sessions with 1-week intervals between each administration. No significant effects were noted for form. These studies support that the BVMT-R has six alternate and equivalent forms.

Validity. The relationships of BVMT-R scores with a variety of other visual memory tests and expressive language tests were examined in a group of neurologic and psychiatric patients (see Benedict, Schretlen, Groninger, Dobraski, & Sphritz, 1996). The BVMT-R was more highly correlated with the other visuospatial memory and visuospatial construction tests than with the expressive language tests. It is somewhat surprising that the test author did not include a table in the manual reporting the intercorrelations among each BVMT-R form and the others.

Another sample of 138 neurologic patients completed a brief neuropsychological battery that included the BVMT-R, the Trail Making Test (Reitan, 1958), Controlled Oral Word Association Test (Benton & Hamsher, 1983), the Developmental Test of Visual-Motor Integration (Beery & Buktenica, 1982), and the Hopkins Verbal Learning Test (Brandt, 1991). Principal components analysis indicated that the BVMT-R variables loaded on two components, a visual memory component that included Trials 1, 2, 3, and the Delayed Recall variable and a response bias component that includes the BVMT-R Response Bias variable and the Hopkins Verbal Learning Test Response Bias variable (Benedict et al., 1996). This demonstrates that the underlying structure of the BVMT-R is as expected and is evidence of the instrument's construct validity.

A series of contrasted groups studies are also reported in the manual to support the test's validity (Benedict et al., 1996). The BVMT-R was effective in discriminating between normal control individuals and patients with HIV-1 minor cognitive/motor disorder, HIV-1 patients with associated dementia complex, with primary progressive dementia (Alzheimer's dementia, vascular or mixed dementia), and anterograde amnesia. There were significant differences between the groups on BVMT-R measures and they were in the direction expected. These studies combined indicate that the BVMT-R has utility for discriminating a variety of impaired clinical groups from normal control groups.

COMMENTARY AND SUMMARY. The BVMT-R test-retest reliability was marginal. Temporal stability is critical for all tests but particularly for a test like the BVMT-R that is designed to be used repeatedly with one examinee in serial fashion. The omission of standard errors of measurement is annoying because users will have to calculate them by hand as needed to construct confidence intervals. The standardization sample is small and unrepresentative of the U.S. population. In the separate age tables there are very small numbers of participants at the elder age ranges. This is a problem because many elderly are likely to be assessed for stroke, dementia, and other age-related cognitive impairments.

The BVMT-R fares better in terms of validity. A variety of methods and studies demonstrated aspects of the test's criterion and construct-related validity. To date, the test's author and his colleagues have done most of these studies. Overall, the test shows good promise for research and clinical application. It certainly could be included as a narrow band measure of *Gv* in a cross battery assessment (see McGrew & Flanagan, 1998). The instrument is recommended for research and clinical application as part of a multifactored assessment protocol, but not as the main device for diagnostic purposes. If a multiconstruct (auditory and visual) memory assessment is needed, the Wechsler Memory Scale—III (T6:2695; Wechsler, 1997) might be considered instead.

REVIEWER'S REFERENCES

Beery, K. E., & Buktenica, N. A. (1982). *Revised administration, scoring, and teaching manual for the Developmental Test of Visual-Motor Integration.* Cleveland, OH: Modern Curriculum Press.

Benedict, R. H. B., Schretlen, D., Groninger, L., Dobraski, M., & Sphritz, B. (1996). Revision of the Brief Visuospatial Memory Test: Studies of normal performance, reliability and validity. *Psychological Assessment, 8,* 145–153.

Benton, A. L., & Hamsher, K. (1983). Multilingual Aphasia Examination. Iowa City, IA: AJA Associates.

Brandt, J. (1991). The Hopkins Verbal Learning Test: Development of a new memory test with six equivalent forms. *The Clinical Neuropsychologist, 5,* 125–142.

Carroll, J. B. (1997). The three-stratum theory of cognitive abilities. In D. P. Flanagan, J. L. Genshaft, & P. L. Harrison (Eds.), *Contemporary intellectual assessment: Theories, tests, and issues* (pp. 122–130). New York: The Guilford Press.

McGrew, K. S. & Flanagan, D. P. (1998). *The intelligence test desk reference (ITDR): Gf-Gc cross-battery assessment.* Boston: Allyn and Bacon.

Reitan, R. M. (1958). Validity of the Trail Making Test as an indicator of organic brain damage. *Perceptual and Motor Skills, 8,* 271–276.

Salvia, J., & Ysseldyke, J. E. (1998). *Assessment* (7th ed.). Boston, MA: Houghton Mifflin Company.

U.S. Department of Commerce, Bureau of the Census. (1994). *Statistical abstract of the United States: 1994* (114th ed.). Washington, DC: U.S. Government Printing Office.

Wechsler, D. (1997). Wechsler Memory Scale—III. San Antonio, TX: The Psychological Corporation.

[41]

BRIGANCE® Infant & Toddler Screen.

Purpose: Designed to obtain a broad sampling of a *very young child's development and skills; ... enables* professionals to monitor children's developmental progress, advise parents on how to promote a child's development, initiate individualized instruction, and recommend special services to facilitate learning needs and/or family adjustments.

Population: Infants (birth through 11 months) and toddlers (12 months through 23 months).

Publication Date: 2002.

Administration: Individual or group.

Price Data, 2002: $110 per manual (89 pages); $31 per 30 Infant or Toddler data sheets (English or Spanish), volume discounts available; $39.90 per 10 Infant or Toddler record folders (English or Spanish); $59.95 per box of materials; $49 per technical report (232 pages); $29.95 per Screens Scoring Software; $15.95 per Screens Inservice Video (20 minutes) and Facilitator's Guide.

Time: (15) minutes.

Comments: Screens Scoring Software provides percentile ranks, standard scores, and age equivalent scores; includes directions in Spanish.

Authors: Albert H. Brigance (Screen) and Frances Page Glascoe (Screen and Technical Report).

Publisher: Curriculum Associates, Inc.

> *a*) INFANT.
> **Scores, 7:** Fine-Motor Skills, Receptive Language Skills, Expressive Language Skills, Gross Motor Skills, Self-Help Skills, Social-Emotional Skills, Total Score.
> *b*) TODDLER.
> **Scores, 12:** Fine-Motor Skills, Receptive Language Skills—General, Receptive Language Skills—Body Parts, Receptive Language Skills—Picture Naming, Receptive Language Skills—Environmental Sounds, Expressive Language Skills—General, Expressive Language Skills—Object Naming, Expressive Language Skills—Phrases, Gross Motor Skills, Self-Help Skills, Social-Emotional Skills, Total Score.

Review of the BRIGANCE® Infant & Toddler Screen by THERESA GRAHAM, Adjunct Faculty, University of Nebraska—Lincoln, Lincoln, NE:

DESCRIPTION. The BRIGANCE® Infant & Toddler Screen is a criterion-referenced and norm-referenced screening assessment designed to assess general development across a range of skills in children from birth to 23 months of age. There are two basic assessments within the BRIGANCE® Infant & Toddler Screen: Infant (for children from birth through 11 months) and Toddler (for children from 12 months through 23 months). Skills within the screen include: Fine Motor, Gross Motor, Expressive Language, Receptive Language, Self-Help, and Social and Emotional skills. The Infant & Toddler Screen is appropriate for use with all children to identify children who may need to be referred for a more comprehensive evaluation, to ascertain placement within a program or a group, or to facilitate program planning for individual needs. The screen

takes about 10 to 20 minutes to administer and can be administered either by observing children, directly eliciting skills from children, or by parental report.

The manual is extremely helpful in describing the appropriate administration of specific items and in providing directions for completing and scoring the data sheet. Within each skill area there is a range of items to be assessed. For each item, the manual describes what the examiner should do with the infant or toddler and the criteria the examiner should use to give credit for the response. In addition, specific verbal instructions are provided if the skill is assessed through parental report. Because there is a significant range of abilities within the first 2 years, there is a suggested start point for different ages of children. Once three consecutive correct responses have been provided, credit is given for the lower items within the skill area. Items are discontinued within a skill area when an infant or toddler fails on three consecutive items.

Initial scoring is easily accomplished using the data sheets. Skills within each area are numerically organized. The examiner circles correct responses and places a slash through skills not demonstrated. Subtest scores are then calculated by adding all of the circled responses (including the lower level skills not assessed) and multiplying the sum by the point value for the particular subtest. Subtest scores are then added together to provide the total score. Total scores are evaluated on the basis of cutoff scores. For the Infant Screen, cutoff scores are provided according the age of the infant in 1-month increments (e.g., 1 month, 2 month). For the Toddler Screen, cutoff scores are provided according to the age of the toddler in 2-month increments. Cutoff scores are used to determine whether an examiner recommends further evaluation or referral. In addition, risk factors such as parental education or parental employment may also be considered in evaluating the results of the screen.

DEVELOPMENT. The BRIGANCE® Infant & Toddler Screen is based on a number of developmental principles including the ideas that development is malleable, transactional, and age-related. Moreover, the authors note that although it is important to sample a number of developmental domains, certain domains are better at predicting school success (e.g., self-help and motor have low relationship to academic achievement, whereas language development is significantly related). Given this fact, the authors weight different subskill areas accordingly in the scoring.

Because the BRIGANCE® Screens were derived from more extensive assessment (i.e., most of the items from the BRIGANCE® Infant & Toddler Screen were taken from the Inventory of Early Development—Revised [IED-R]), little information is provided on item development. There was no discussion about the appropriateness of any specific items or on how items were selected from the IED-R. There are only five new items included in the screen that were not taken from the IED-R (one new item on the Infant Screen; four new items on the Toddler Screen).

TECHNICAL. The technical report includes information on all of the BRIGANCE® Screens (Infant & Toddler, Early Preschool, Preschool, and K & 1 Screens). Thus, much of the information provided within the report is not relevant to the reliability or validity of scores from the Infant & Toddler Screen. For example, the authors cite the first standardization of the Inventory of Early Development. However, this assessment was standardized on children ranging in age from 1 year 1 month to beyond 6 years, which does not include the population of infants. Moreover, the items included in the Infant & Toddler Screen come directly from the IED-R and not the IED. No reliability or validity data are provided explicitly for the IED-R, nor is it clear how closely related the IED-R and the IED are to one another. Finally, although prior research was cited to support the standardization of the screens, none of the studies cited were relevant for the Infant & Toddler Screen.

The Infant & Toddler Screen was normed on a population of infants and toddlers recruited from 29 sites, including pediatric offices, child find programs, child care and preschool programs, and university-affiliated clinics in 21 states. Although the authors provide general information on the demographics of the sample used (e.g., ethnicity, parental education, gender), it is impossible to determine whether the data for the infants and toddlers are nationally representative because the authors collapsed the demographic data across all of the different age groups (birth to 6 years). For example, it is not known how many infants and toddlers were cared for in child care settings or how many parents completed Grade 12. Moreover, the authors report the performance on the Infant & Toddler Screen according to ethnic group, parental education, and other demographic data. However, they provide the total N of the sample (all of the age groups) and not the N for the infant and toddler sample.

Internal consistency was high with a Guttman scalability coefficient of .97 for the Infant Screen and .94 for the Toddler Screen and a Standard Error of Measurement of .86 and 1.01, respectively.

Test-retest reliability was assessed by having one examiner retest 34 children within 1 week of the original testing. For both the Infant and Toddler Screens, the test-retest reliability was within acceptable ranges. Fine Motor and Receptive Language were somewhat lower, in part because motor skills are more likely to be inconsistently expressed in young children and many of the receptive language items relied upon motor skills (e.g., wave bye bye, give block on command). Interrater reliability was also acceptable. It was assessed by having a second examiner retest 36 children within 1 week.

The authors state that the test covers areas generally important to infant and toddler development. Content validity was based on the fact that scores increased as age increased. Prior research was cited to support the content validity of the BRIGANCE® Screens. However, the research cited was not relevant to the infant and toddler population.

Intercorrelations among the skills on the BRIGANCE® Screens demonstrate that there is considerable overlap across the skill areas. Factor analyses on the data revealed a two-factor solution that accounted for 63% of the variance in scores. The first factor is Non-Verbal and includes Fine Motor, Gross Motor, Self-Help, and Social-Emotional skills. The second factor is Communication and includes the two language subtests.

Concurrent validity was assessed by comparing the Infant & Toddler Screen with a number of different measures including the Mental Development Index, the Infant Behavior Record of the Bayley Scales of Infant Development, the Cattell Infant Intelligence Test, the Rosetti Infant Toddler Scale, and the Vineland Adaptive Behavior Scales. Results indicate that total scores on the Infant & Toddler Screen were significantly correlated with criterion measures.

To assess sensitivity and specificity, children were categorized according to the presence and absence of developmental delays. Cutoff scores for each of the Basic Assessments were determined to best identify children with disabilities. Given the range of abilities for infants and toddlers, cutoff scores were provided for each month in the Infant Screen and for each 2-month interval for the Toddler Screen. Eighty-six percent of the infants and 85% of the toddlers were correctly specified as absent disability. Seventy-seven percent and 76%, respectively, were correctly identified with the presence of disability. In addition, the authors note that the BRIGANCE® Infant & Toddler Screen is designed to identify giftedness as well. However, the reader is cautioned about using any measure to identify giftedness at such an early age and instead it is suggested that infants and toddlers who score above a specific cutoff score are demonstrating a significant strength and not necessarily giftedness.

COMMENTARY AND SUMMARY. In general, the BRIGANCE® Infant & Toddler Screen succeeds in accomplishing its primary goal: to quickly assess a broad range of skills in infants and toddlers to identify strengths and weaknesses that may require further evaluation. However, the success of that goal is tempered by a number of issues: (a) It is difficult to assess the sample that was used to norm the data because specific demographic data were not provided for the infant and toddler sample; (b) users are encouraged to use parental report to gather data. However, no information is provided regarding the reliability of those data versus those obtained by an independent examiner; (c) most of the items used in the screen were taken from the IED-R. However, there is no psychometric information provided for the IED-R. Moreover, given that few items were new for the screen, little information is provided regarding specific item development. Although there are some cautionary issues, the Screen is related to other relevant measures of infant and toddler development. Thus, the BRIGANCE® Infant & Toddler Screen is an appropriate initial way to assess children's early development.

Review of the BRIGANCE® Infant & Toddler Screen by LORAINE J. SPENCINER, Professor of Special Education, University of Maine at Farmington, Farmington, ME:

DESCRIPTION. The BRIGANCE® Infant & Toddler Screen is a screening instrument designed for children, birth through 23 months of age. The screening materials include the screening easel, data recording sheets, and a summary record (for early care or intervention programs). A box of toys and other materials used in some of the test items may be purchased separately from the publisher. Two forms of data sheets are included: one for infants from birth through 11 months and one for toddlers from 12 months through 23 months. The forms are color-coded for ease of use and are available in English or Spanish. Optional forms for the examiner's and teacher's observations and a parent-child interaction rating compiled by the examiner are included in the screening easel.

Both the infant form and the toddler form include a number of test items to assess fine and gross motor skills, receptive and expressive language skills, self-help skills, and social-emotional skills. Many of the test items include pictures that illustrate positioning of the child. The examiner's screening easel includes information about how to check functional hearing and vision and suggestions for observing possible hearing or vision problems.

The data sheets indicate entry points to begin screening and basal levels (three in a row correct). Each section also indicates the ceiling point at which the examiner stops (three consecutive failures or misses). Correct responses are recorded on the data sheet. Some item areas (receptive language skills for both infants and toddlers and expressive language skills–phrases for toddlers) are weighted more than other areas. The total possible score for both infants and toddlers is 100 points. Cutoff scores are provided for each month of age for infants and for 2-month ranges for toddlers.

For children who were born 4 or more weeks premature, the examiner's easel provides a chart to adjust chronological age. The adjusted chronological age is used when comparing a child's score with cutoff scores. Children whose scores fall below the cutoff scores are referred for further assessment.

The publisher does not assign specific educational requirements for administering this instrument. According to the examiner's screening easel, training in test administration is helpful but not required to administer the Infant & Toddler Screen. Examiners, including educators, therapists, nurses, physicians, or paraprofessionals, can conduct screenings but they must be familiar with the directions and procedures for scoring.

This instrument is part of the BRIGANCE® System of screening instruments and diagnostic inventories for children and youth. The BRIGANCE® Infant & Toddler Screen consists of skills also included in the BRIGANCE® Diagnostic Inventory of Early Development—Revised (Birth–7 years), a criterion-referenced instrument often used to monitor children's progress. Thus, for programs using this criterion-referenced instrument, screening information could be recorded in the Developmental Record Book, avoiding duplication of assessment.

DEVELOPMENT. Development, standardization, and validation of the BRIGANCE® Infant & Toddler Screen was completed from 1998–2001. A total of 203 infants and 179 toddlers from 29 sites participated in the standardization sample including pediatric offices, public health clinics, child-find programs, child care and preschool programs, and university-affiliated assessment clinics in 21 states. Infants and toddlers whose primary language was Spanish were tested in Spanish and their parents were interviewed with Spanish versions of the demographics questionnaire and other materials. Additional demographic information is not available for this particular screen as the *Technical Report for the Brigance® Screens* (Glascoe, 2002) summarizes demographic information across BRIGANCE® Screens.

TECHNICAL. The *Technical Report for the Brigance® Screens* reports several types of reliability but, again summarizes much of the information across the BRIGANCE® Screens. Because some of the data are collapsed, information about a specific screening instrument is difficult to identify. The following information was available for the BRIGANCE® Infant & Toddler Screen.

Internal consistency and test-retest reliabilities were reported. The Internal consistency (using the Guttman lambda coefficient) was .97 for infants and .94 for toddlers with standard error of measurement of .86 and 1.01, respectively. A small study of 34 children found very high test-retest reliability using the same examiner within 1 week of the original testing. For infants, test-retest total score reliability estimate was .98 with subtests ranging from .86 (Social-Emotional Skills) to .99 (Gross Motor Skills). For toddlers, the test-retest total score reliability estimate was .99. Two subtests had reliability estimates that were below .80 (Receptive Language Skills—General with a

correlation of .70 and Fine Motor Skills with a correlation of .74). Other subtests ranged from .85 to .99. In a second small study involving 36 children, interrater reliability between two different examiners for infants was .98 (total score) with subtests ranging from .90 to .99. For toddlers, interrater reliability was .99 (total score) with subtests ranging from a low of .69 (Fine Motor Skills) to a high of .99 (Receptive Language Skills—Environmental Sounds, Expressive Language Skills—Phrases, and Total Expressive Language).

The *Technical Report for the BRIGANCE® Screens* reports evidence of content, construct, and concurrent validity. The Report also includes a table indicating specificity and sensitivity of the screen for infants and toddlers. These two terms are important when evaluating a screening instrument. Sensitivity refers to the instrument's ability to select children who should be referred for further assessment; whereas, specificity refers to the instrument's capacity to accurately select children who should not be identified. For infants, 77% of the children who were identified for further assessment should have been identified. For toddlers, 76% of the children who were identified for further assessment should have been identified.

COMMENTARY. Screening and assessing young children's development involves looking at the five developmental domains: communication, adaptive (self-help), physical (including fine and gross motor, vision, and hearing), social emotional, and cognitive skills. Federally mandated ChildFind procedures involve screening each developmental domain. Unfortunately, the BRIGANCE® Infant & Toddler Screen assesses skills in only the first four domains, making it necessary for practitioners to include an additional screening measure.

Aside from this major omission, the instrument appears easy to use and the technical report provides evidence of technical adequacy. Both the examiner's screening easel and the technical report are well-written and contain valuable information for the examiner. For example, the screening easel contains general recommendations for screening and suggestions to consider when a child receives a low score. The technical report presents technical information in a readable format as well as providing valuable information. This manual contains suggestions for building rapport with very young children, common errors in administration and rapport, and interpreting results. Several case studies (profiles of children) are included to illustrate interpretations and recommendations. Included in the technical report appendices is a set of valuable information sheets for parents, Websites, and other useful parent resources. The technical report does not indicate whether or not these may be duplicated.

The instrument does not include a parent report form, although some BRIGANCE® screening instruments do provide a parent report (e.g., the Parent's Rating Form for Two-year Old Children and higher). Gathering information from the parent's perspective about their child's development provides another critical piece of information during screening and assessment procedures. One would hope that such a form will be included in the Infant & Toddler Screen in the future.

This instrument uses an age adjustment for prematurity. By adjusting for prematurity, do we fail to identify children who may be at risk for disability? Wilson (1987) provides a rationale for the use of age adjustment; yet little research has been completed to support the technique. Siegel (1983) found that adjusting for prematurity appears to be appropriate in the first few months but in older infants slightly more accurate predictions were obtained by using the uncorrected scores. Aylward, Verhulst, and Colliver (1986) found that the use of an adjusted age did not appear to "cover up" dysfunction in infants at 9 and 18 months.

SUMMARY. The BRIGANCE® Infant & Toddler Screen meets many criteria for a screening instrument for very young children, birth through 23 months of age. The instrument is brief, inexpensive, technically adequate, and easy to score. The instrument covers four of the five developmental domains. The Infant & Toddler Screen could be improved by including a parent report that is completed by the child's parents regarding any questions or concerns that they may have about their child's development. Helpful ancillary materials for both examiners and parents are included in the examiner's screening easel and in the technical report.

REVIEWER'S REFERENCES

Aylward, G. P., Verhulst, S. J., & Colliver, J. A. (1986, August). *To correct or not to correct: Age adjustment for prematurity.* (ERIC Document Reproduction Service No. ED 280 609) Paper presented at the annual meeting of the American Psychological Association, Washington, DC.

Glascoe, F. P. (2002). *Technical report for the Brigance® screens.* North Billerica, MA: Curriculum Associates®, Inc.

Siegel, L. S. (1983). Correction for prematurity and its consequences for the assessment of the very low birth weight infant. *Child Development, 54,* 1176–1188.

Wilson, W. M. (1987). Age adjustment in psychological assessment of children born prematurely. *Journal of Pediatric Psychology, 12,* 445–450.

[42]

Brown Attention-Deficit Disorder Scales for Children and Adolescents.

Purpose: "Designed to elicit … [information] that may indicate impairment in executive functions related to Attention-Deficit/Hyperactivity Disorders (AD/HD)."

Population: Ages 3–18.

Publication Date: 2001.

Acronym: Brown ADD Scales for Children.

Scores, 7: 6 cluster scores (Organizing/Prioritizing/ and Activating to Work, Focusing/Sustaining/and Shifting Attention to Tasks, Regulating Alertness/Sustaining Effort/and Processing Speed, Managing Frustration and Modulating Emotions, Utilizing Working Memory and Accessing Recall, Monitoring and Self-Regulating Action), Total Score.

Administration: Group or individual.

Price Data, 2001: $270 per complete kit including manual (149 pages), 25 each Ready Score Parent Forms and Teacher Forms (ages 3–7), 25 each Ready Score Parent Forms, Teacher Forms, and Self-Report Forms (ages 8–12), 25 Ready Score Answer Documents (ages 12–18), and 10 each Child Diagnostic Forms (ages 3–12) and Adolescent Diagnostic Forms (ages 12–18); $79 per manual; $10 per 25 Ready Score Parent Forms (ages 3–7 or 8–12); $40 per 25 Ready Score Teacher Forms (ages 3–7 or 8–12); $40 per 25 Ready Score Self-Report Forms/Answer Documents (child, ages 8–12; or adolescent, ages 12–18); $20 per 10 Diagnostic Forms (child, ages 3–12; or adolescent, ages 12–18); $350 per Scoring Assistant kit including manual, 25 each Parent Forms (ages 3–7 and 8–12), 25 each Teacher Forms (ages 3–7 and 8–12), 25 each Self-Report Forms (ages 8–12 and 12–18), Brown ADD Scoring Assistant CD-ROM (3.5-inch diskette version available); $40 per 25 Parent or Teacher Forms (ages 3–7 or 8–12); $40 per 25 Self-Report Forms/Answer Documents (child, ages 8–12; or adolescent, ages 12–18).

Time: (10–20) minutes.

Comments: Downward extension of the Brown Attention Deficit Disorder Scales for Adolescents and Adults (T6:352); describes cognitive, affective, behavioral symptoms beyond DSM-IV diagnostic criteria to assess executive function impairments; optional Brown ADD Scales Scoring Assistant software scores, analyzes results, maintains records, generates graphical and narrative reports; system requirements: Windows 95/98/2000/ME/NT 4.0, 100 MHz Pentium processor, 32 MB RAM, 2 MB video card capable of 800 x 600 resolution (256 colors), 20 MB free hard disk space, 3.5-inch floppy drive, 50 MB temporary disk space.

Author: Thomas E. Brown.

Publisher: The Psychological Corporation.

a) PRIMARY/PRESCHOOL LEVEL.

Population: Ages 3–7.

Forms, 2: Parent Form, Teacher Form.
Comments: Elicits parent and teacher reports of symptoms.
b) SCHOOL-AGE LEVEL.
Population: Ages 8–12.
Forms, 3: Self-Report Form, Parent Form, Teacher Form.
Comments: Elicits parent, teacher and self-reports of symptoms.
c) ADOLESCENT LEVEL.
Population: Ages 13–18.
Form, 1: Ready-Score Answer Document.
Comments: Elicits parent and self-reports of symptoms.

Review of the Brown Attention Deficit Disorder Scales for Children and Adolescents by KAREN E. JENNINGS, Clinical Psychologist, LaMora Psychological Associates, Nashua, NH:

DESCRIPTION. The Brown Attention-Deficit Disorder Scales for Children and Adolescents is a multicomponent assessment device designed as an initial screening device and/or a comprehensive component of a multidimensional battery. In addition to the parent, teacher, and child questionnaires, there is a diagnostic formulation booklet. The diagnostic booklets contain semi-structured clinical interview questions, developmental history queries, diagnostic rule-out information, and quantitative summary charts (Total Raw Score grid, Cluster Score Graph, Multi-evaluator rating summary sheet, and a worksheet for inter- and intra-IQ discrepancy analysis). The scales yield a profile of patient's developmental abilities/impairments in attention, working memory, executive functions, cognition, affect, and behavior.

DEVELOPMENT. The Brown ADD Scales were developed for adolescents and adults in 1996. Brown extended the age range down to 3 years of age and added items for the 2001 edition. The author designed these scales in response to his observations of children who demonstrated learning problems in the absence of a frank learning disability. The author conceptualized ADHD as a multidimensional disorder that requires a multidimensional diagnostic process. Brown operationalized the multidimensional nature of ADD via the six nonorthogonal clusters of the scales. Items were designed to assess one of the six clusters.

Brown devised a model for his scale on the basis of his synthesis of literature on the varied manifestations of attention deficit disorders. His model is similar to other researchers' perspectives on the central role of executive deficit in the combined type of ADHD (Barkley, 1997; Nigg, 2001). The author suggested that executive function impairments were sin qua non of Attention Deficit disorders. He incorporated an assessment of executive deficits within the clusters of the scale.

Pilot studies were conducted to assess the readability and comparability of versions of the scales. The tryout studies were performed to assess item selection and to discern the relative efficacy of individual or group administration. The author decided to administer the scale individually based upon the results of these preliminary studies. He did not discuss the findings of these tryout studies or the decision rules he incorporated in making these choices.

TECHNICAL.
Standardization. The Brown ADD Scales child normative sample was standardized on a stratified sample of 800 children aged from 3–12 years. Two hundred participants were selected from each of four geographic regions of the United States. The author selected a sample stratified by race and parental education. The sample replicated the distribution reported in the 1999 U.S. Census. The manual did not discuss whether the participant selection was based on the principle of randomness. The initial selection of participants for the child normative sample excluded children diagnosed with a psychiatric disorder or learning disability. Thirty-three children previously diagnosed with ADHD were added to this normative sample after it was collected. The author desired to ensure the representativeness of the sample to the population through incorporating this procedure because this number of cases represents the prevalence of ADHD in the population. Unfortunately, this decision may have added error variance in these norms. The author did not discuss the implications of this sampling procedure and the potential bias created by this procedure.

The child clinical sample consisted of 240 children who were clients in the practices of multidisciplinary clinicians. Two hundred eight, of the original 240, were diagnosed with an attention deficit disorder based on DSM-IV criteria, clinical interviews with the child and his of her parents, teacher reports and standardized psychological testing. These children were selected as the clinical normative group. The author did not discuss the sampling techniques utilized in collecting this sample nor the characteristics of the children who did not complete the study. Limited data are provided on the standardization and clinical samples for adolescents. More details about these samples may be found in the previous (1996) manual.

Reliability. The author collected internal consistency, test-retest reliability, and interrater reliability information for the child scales. Internal consistency (coefficient alpha) data were strong for clusters, total inattention scores, and total combined scores (e.g., cluster coefficients ranged from .73 to .91). Test-retest reliability (time interval from 1–4 weeks) data were generally strong. The test-retest coefficients (corrected coefficients) for teacher ratings of children aged 3–7 ranged from .78 to .89. For children aged 8–12, parent and teacher corrected test-retest reliability coefficients ranged from .84 to .92 and .84 to .93, respectively. The test-retest reliabilities for the child self-report ranged from .45 to .69. Interrater reliability coefficients ranged from .39 to .58 for ages 3–7, and from .46 to .57 for ages 8–12. The author attributed the lower rater correspondence to the differences in perspective.

Validity. The author presented three types of information in support of the validity of scores from this scale: internal structure, criterion-related evidence, and convergent evidence of validity. The intercorrelation matrices of cluster and total scores presented strong evidence of validity. Cluster score coefficients ranged from .62 to .84. Cluster-total score coefficients ranged from .81 to .96.

Brown presented criterion-related evidence for validity by comparing the performance of individuals previously diagnosed with ADHD and matched nonclinical individuals on the Brown scales. The author indicated that the Brown scales discriminated the control groups from the ADHD samples to statistically significant levels across age groups. Estimates of the practical significance of these statistically significant findings would further elucidate the robustness/power of the group differences.

Brown presented intermeasure correlations as evidence for convergent and divergent validity. The comparability of the Brown scale to Achenbach's Child Behavior Checklist (CBCL), Behavior Assessment System for Children (BASC), and Conners' Rating Scales was assessed. These measures have been widely used and are highly respected in the assessment of attention deficit

disorders. The CBCL assesses a wide variety of possible pediatric behavioral problems. The BASC and Conners' Scale measure manifestations of attention deficit disorders.

As expected, the Brown Scales demonstrated stronger correlations with attention specific subtests than other behavioral categories on the CBCL. The coefficients for the parent version of the Brown Scales and CBCL ranged from -.25 (for CBCL Somatic Complaints and Brown's cluster 5 score) to .69 (for CBCL Attention Problems and Brown's cluster 6-Memory) for the ages 4–7. Correlation coefficients for the clinical sample aged 8–12 ranged from -.05 (for CBCL Somatic Complaints and cluster 6) to .70 (for CBCL Attention Problems and cluster 2-attention). These data support the premise that the Brown scales measure behavioral dimensions similar to and distinct from aspects of child behavior measured by the CBCL.

The data for the BASC, Conners' Rating Scales and Brown cluster correlation coefficients provided evidence for the convergent validity of this scale. BASC Teacher ratings of attention problems demonstrated a strong relationship to the Brown Scales cluster scores (coefficients ranging from .50 to .91). The Brown Scales demonstrated a strong correlation to the Conners' Parent and Teacher Rating Scales. The Conners' Scales AD/HD index demonstrated a moderately high correlation with both the Inattention and Combined Totals scores for the clinical samples within the 3–7 and 8–12 age groups (coefficients ranged from .68 to .82). The Conners' Hyperactivity Scale demonstrated a moderately high correlation to the Brown Scales Monitoring and Self-regulation cluster (coefficients were .55 for 3–7-year-olds and .79 for 8–12-year-olds). These findings illustrate the similarity amongst the Conners' Rating Scales and the Brown Scales for measuring aspects of attention deficit disorders.

COMMENTARY. The Brown Scales for Children and Adolescents are an important and valuable contribution to the ongoing theoretical debate about the nature of ADHD. The breadth of coverage of the theoretically based elements of executive functions dovetails with contemporary discussions about the nature of primary, secondary, and tertiary deficits of ADHD (Barkley, 1997; Nigg, 2001). The incorporation of subtests that operationalize and measure elements of these neurocognitive functions is a strong asset to the empirical investigation of these functions. These scales would be useful in the comprehensive evaluation of a child with suspected attention, behavioral disinhibition, and/or learning problems. The Brown Scales contribute a plethora of important information for the evaluator of a child with suspected learning difficulties.

The potential vulnerabilities of the Brown Scales for Children lie in some of its sampling procedures. The standardization sample was selected to parallel the U.S. Census in its representativeness. Unfortunately, the absence of a discussion of the incorporation of the principal of randomization may result in sampling error, increased risk for bias, and decreased generalizability of findings. Most likely the author instituted safeguards for minimizing these possibilities. A discussion of these safeguards would be helpful for the test user.

SUMMARY. The Brown Scales for Children and Adolescents are important tools in the multidimensional assessment of children struggling to learn. The handouts and organizational materials are very useful to performing a complete profile analysis of the multiple aspects assessed by this measure. Ongoing assessment of the psychometric implications of possible sampling error, limits in generalizability, and continued elucidation of the underlying dimensions of the constructs of this measure will mostly be an ongoing and important process. However, these scales are very useful, convenient, informative, and user-friendly measures necessary to the comprehensive evaluation to rule out attention deficit disorders.

REVIEWER'S REFERENCES

Barkley, R. (1997). Behavioral inhibition, sustained attention, and executive functions constructing a unifying theory of ADHD. *Psychological Bulletin, 121*, 65–94.

Nigg, J. T. (2001). Is ADHD a disinhibitory disorder? *Psychological Bulletin, 127*, 571–598.

Review of the Brown Attention-Deficit Disorder Scales for Children and Adolescents by WILLIAM K. WILKINSON, Consulting Educational Psychologist, Boleybeg, Barna, County Galway, Republic of Ireland:

DESCRIPTION. The Brown Attention-Deficit Disorder Scales for Children and Adolescents (Brown ADD Scales) is a downward extension of a pre-existing measure known as the Brown Attention Deficit Disorder Scales for Adolescents and Adults (T6:352). The author notes that the purpose of the test is to "elicit parent and teacher observations of symptoms in 3- to 12-year-olds and to elicit self-report from children ages 8 years and older that may indicate impairment in executive functions related to Attention Deficit/Hyperactivity Disorders" (manual, p. 5). Towards this end, the test includes five rating forms: Parent Form age 3–7, Parent Form 8–12, Teacher Form 3–7, Teacher Form 8–12, and Self-Report Form (children 8 to 12). Test materials also include a Diagnostic Form that can be used for gathering developmental history, reviewing DSM-IV symptoms of AD/HD, and summarizing rating results as well as cognitive test scores (e.g., ability and achievement).

Further, the test package includes a revised Diagnostic Form for Adolescents and a rating scale for this same age group. The manual includes a conversion table for the 12- to 18-year age group, so the Brown ADD Scales effectively covers an age range from 3 to 18 years.

The rating forms are clearly presented and easy to use. The Parent and Teacher Forms (ages 3 to 12) can be completed independently by these raters. The Child Self-Report Form is completed in an interview method (to insure the child understands the items and the assessor understands the child's responses). There are 40 to 50 items, depending on the form. The author recommends that the Adolescent Form be completed in a joint interview situation. This seems wise, because the Adolescent rating form has two number scales (e.g., 0 = *Never*; 1 = *Once or Twice a Week*; 2 = *Twice a Week*; and 3 = *Almost Daily*) for each item. If the adolescent were to complete the form independently, and it was then given to a parent, the parent could see the adolescent's self-report and this could influence the parent assessment. It should be noted that the Adolescent scale does not have a corresponding teacher version. Although the author discusses why this is so, this is a disadvantage, because it reduces the numerical/objective quantification of AD/HD-type behaviors beyond the home environment. Generalizability of AD/HD-type problems across settings is alluded to in DSM-IV, although how this is done remains "nonstandardized" and variable across clinicians. This is why a Teacher Form for the Adolescent age group would be useful.

The forms are easy to score. One simply tears the perforated form and transforms item ratings to cluster and total scores (converted to *T*-scores). The following scores are obtained for the

Child Version: Activation, Focus, Effort, Emotion, Memory, with the total of these five clusters yielding a Total inattention score. This score is then added to the final cluster, Action, and all scores are summed to obtain an ADD Combined Total score. An optional CD-ROM Scoring Assistant is available.

DEVELOPMENT. One of the most positive aspects of the Brown Scales is the theoretical base for item development. Rather than delimit itself to the DSM-IV description of Inattention and Impulsivity/Hyperactivity, the author has expanded the item pool based on more recent theoretical developments, namely "executive functions" (manual, p. 10). In this regard, the six cluster scores relate to theory, yet realistically cover the "true" problems related to AD/HD. Take for example the Cluster score, Emotion. Experts widely agree that negative emotions abound in children and adults with AD/HD. Yet, it is never clear whether these emotions play a secondary role (as most AD/HD experts suggest) to AD/HD, or whether these emotional states play a fundamental role in creating/maintaining AD/HD-type behavior. By allowing for a separate cluster score in this area, and others, the user of the Brown ADD Scales will have a more refined and accurate clinical picture. From a technical standpoint, I would like to know the empirical base for the clusters (e.g., how did these clusters emerge from initial item sets?). There is significant overlap among the clusters, but it is the author's contention that the clusters are related, but not synonymous.

TECHNICAL. The author presents a well-organized and reasonably thorough discussion of the standardization and psychometric properties of the scale. The standardization sample of 800 children follows U.S. Census data. Raw score transformation tables are provided for different raters and the different forms. The author notes the raw scores were "skewed" and that the conversion to "standardized scores" was used because of the nonnormal distribution. I wish the author had engaged in speculation about the reasons for the skewness. And the implications of the nonnormal distribution are readily apparent when the author discusses T-score threshold interpretation. For example, in the Diagnostic form, the T-scale is given and a T score of 45–54 is considered "Average range; possibly significant concern"; T score of 55 to 59 is "Somewhat Atypical; probably a significant concern." Yet, in a "normal" distribution,

we are still less than one standard deviation above the mean when we get to a T-score of 59. Obviously, the raw score distribution packed up in the lower raw score ranges, and the conversion to a standardized t-distribution will not fix this. I would warn potential users to be aware of this issue and ask, "why the skew?" I would also suggest that test users adopt a T-score threshold of 60 or above before considering the relevance of cluster scores or total AD/HD.

Reliability evidence is thorough and meets acceptable standards. Of particular interest are the test-retest reliability data (retest interval 1–4 weeks) for the child group (ages 8 to 12). Here the stability coefficients drop well below .80. It should be noted that the retest sample consisted of 43 children from the standardization sample and that of this sample, maybe 1 to 3 children were "clinical" (diagnosed with AD/HD). Therefore, the reliability data reported reflects a predominately "nonclinical" population. However, if one were to assess a purely "clinical" group, consisting of children who meet guidelines for AD/HD, my guess is the reliability coefficients would be considerably lower (knowing that children with AD/HD are notoriously poor in self-awareness).

Validity evidence is very thorough. The author covers factorial validity, differential population validity (raters score the AD/HD sample and non-AD/HD sample significantly different on clusters and total scores), and convergent validity (the Brown Scale correlates with other scales measuring similar constructs).

COMMENTARY. The Brown ADD Scales represent a significant advance related to previous instrumentation regarding adult ratings of AD/HD. Existing measures are confined to DSM-IV symptoms and minimal elaboration of these symptoms in behavioral terms. By contrast, Brown follows more recent theoretical advances related to AD/HD, with much of this theorizing on "executive functions." Items were developed with these functions in mind. And the reliability and validity evidence suggests that the scales measure these functions.

There are additional strengths of the Brown ADD Scales. First, the forms are well presented and easy to administer and score. The addition of a self-report form for children is an important extension, although the data derived from a young child's self-report should be viewed cautiously.

The diagnostic form is also a convenient summarizing form and clinicians should find it very useful in the overall evaluation of AD/HD.

The significant caution is the "Threshold Interpretation" the author recommends, specifically the *T*-score cutoff points. In this regard, we have to consider the positive skew. However, even if no skew were reported, I would question how one could say that a *T*-score of between 45 and 54 can be interpreted as "Average range, possibly significant concern" (manual, p. 41). We should not forget that the mean of the *T* distribution is 50, so that the author risks identifying at least 50% of the population as having some type of ADD-type difficulty (or concern). The potential implication is a significant increase in "false positives" (e.g., considering that children have an ADD-related problem when in fact they do not). I strongly suggest that test users review this information and make appropriate adjustments.

A related point is that when scores surpass certain threshold levels, the author says a "diagnosis" of ADD is "strongly suggest[ed]" (manual, p. 40). Again, given the concern about the threshold cutoffs, this interpretation should be carefully reviewed. And, as the author notes, the most prudent way to view the overall diagnosis of ADD is to place rating data in the context of all other data obtained, especially clinical interview, behavior observations (e.g., at home school, during standardized testing), and other test outcomes.

SUMMARY. The Brown ADD Scales represent significant advancements in the measurement of adult perceptions of a child's AD/HD-related difficulties. The scales follow theoretical advancements related to AD/HD as opposed to a limited set of "atheoretical" psychiatric symptoms. The forms are relatively easy to administer and score. In addition, there is adequate technical support related to the normative sample, reliability, and validity. The one important caveat is that potential users reconsider the author's interpretation of the scale scores (e.g., Threshold Interpretation) to more prudent, realistic, and appropriate levels.

[43]
California Psychological Inventory™, Third Edition.

Purpose: Designed to assess personality characteristics and to predict what people will say and do in specified contexts.

Population: Ages 13 years and over.
Publication Dates: 1956–1996.
Acronym: CPI.
Scores, 36: 20 Folk Scales: Dominance (Do), Capacity for Status (Cs), Sociability (Sy), Social Presence (Sp), Self-Acceptance (Sa), Independence (In), Empathy (Em), Responsibility (Re), Socialization (So), Self-Control (Sc), Good Impression (Gi), Communality (Cm), Well-Being (Wb), Tolerance (To), Achievement via Conformance (Ac), Achievement via Independence (Ai), Intellectual Efficiency (Ie), Psychological-Mindedness (Py), Flexibility (Fx), Femininity/Masculinity (Fm); 3 Vector Scales: v. 1 (Internality/Externality), v. 2 (Norm Questioning/Norm Favoring), v. 3 (Self-Realization), plus 13 Special Purpose scales: Managerial Potential, Work Orientation, Creative Temperament, Leadership, Amicability, Law Enforcement Orientation, Tough-mindedness, Baucom Scale for Masculinity, Baucom Scale for Femininity, Leventhal Scale for Anxiety, Wink-Gough Scale for Narcissism, Dicken Scale for Social Desirability, Dicken Scale for Aquiescence.
Administration: Group.
Price Data, 2001: $18.50 per preview kit including prepaid answer sheet and item booklet; $70 per 25 reusable item booklets; $176.50 per 10 prepaid answer sheets (for mail-in scoring, for use with item booklets); $16.50 per 25 scannable answer sheets (specify for use with NCS Sentry 300 scanner or Scantron 8000 series scanners); $76 per manual (1996, 431 pages); $60.10 per A Practical Guide to CPI Interpretation, Third Edition.
Foreign Language Editions: French, German, Italian, and Spanish editions available in an earlier edition.
Time: (45–60) minutes.
Comments: Previous edition still available; 1 form; reports available: Narrative, Configural Analysis; Scoring Options: Prepaid (mail-in), CPP Software System, skillsone.com
Authors: Harrison G. Gough and Pamela Bradley (manual).
Publisher: Consulting Psychologists Press, Inc.
Cross References: See T5:372 (118 references) and T4:361 (57 references); for reviews by Brian Bolton and George Engelhard, Jr., see 11:54 (108 references); for reviews by Donald H. Baucom and H. J. Eysenck, see 9:182 (61 references); see also T3:354 (195 references); for a review by Malcolm D. Gynther, see 8:514 (452 references); see also T2:1121 (166 references); for reviews by Lewis R. Goldberg and James A. Walsh and an excerpted review by John O. Crites, see 7:49 (370 references); see also P:27 (249 references); for a review by E. Lowell Kelly, see 6:71 (116 references); for reviews by Lee J. Cronbach and Robert L. Thorndike and an excerpted review by Laurance F. Shaffer, see 5:37 (33 references).

Review of the California Psychological Inventory™, Third Edition by MARK J. ATKINSON, Adjunct Associate Professor, Department of Psychiatry, University of Calgary, Calgary, Alberta, Canada:

DESCRIPTION. The current version of the California Psychological Inventory™ (CPI) contains 434 items that make up 20 Folk Scales (Dominance, Capacity for Status, Sociability, Social Presence, Self-Acceptance, Independence, Empathy, Responsibility, Socialization, Self-Control, Good Impression, Communality, Well-Being, Tolerance, Achievement via Conformity, Achievement via Independence, Intellectual Efficiency, Psychological-Mindedness, Flexibility, and Femininity/Masculinity), as well as three Vector scales (Internality-Externality, Norm-Questioning/Favoring, and Self-Realization), and 13 Special Purpose scales. Cut scores on the three Vector scales form the basis of a cuboidal personality typology, which is used to classify individuals into four categories. Scoring guides are provided to help administrators assess the validity of respondent profiles including the identification of faking bad, faking good, and random responding.

The CPI is self-administered using either pencil-and-paper or computer methods. Scannable forms are available for automated data entry. The typical administration time is 45–60 minutes and the requirements for testing conditions are minimal. Items are written at the fifth grade level and it is recommended that respondents be at least 13 years of age. Computer scoring programs are available that provide automated scoring and interpretation for the basic profile and special scales, as well as configural analyses across scales and various special purpose reports.

DEVELOPMENT. The stated intents of the CPI are (a) to predict how people will behave in specific contexts, and (b) to identify the significant ways that individuals are described or evaluated by those around them. The author notes that these objectives are consistent with an instrumental view of personality measurement (i.e., to assess the ways in which individuals are socially described as having certain characteristics). It is argued that an instrumental approach allows for a greater degree of criterion relevance than would be the case if a measure were developed using only factor analytic approaches to personality trait definition. This said, the results of a principal axis factoring of the CPI scale scores presented in the manual (Five factors: extraversion, personal integrity, conventionality, flexibility, and emotionality) are quite similar to the general five-factor model of personality found using factorial approaches (Compton, 1998; Marshall, Wortman, Vickers, Kusulas, & Hervig, 1994; Briggs, 1992).

Of the 434 items on the CPI, 171 were originally taken from the Minnesota Multiphasic Personality Inventory (MMPI). The authors report that 13 of the Folk Scales were developed by comparison against external or nontest criteria using empirical methods, 4 by internal consistency methods, and 3 by a mixture of strategies. The test construction process and external criteria used during the development of the Folk, Vector, and Specialty scales are presented in the score interpretation sections of the manual.

TECHNICAL.

Standardization. Arguably, the norm reference scaling used on the Profile Report form is more suited for the evaluation of profiles of high school and university-aged respondents, because the most recent norming sample (3,000 of each gender) is heavily weighted by high school (50%) and undergraduate (16.7%) students. As a result, use of normed scale scores should be supplemented by a comparison of respondents' raw scores with those of other similar reference groups. The CPI manual provides extensive reference tables for such comparative purposes.

Reliability. Using the norming sample, the internal consistency estimates (Cronbach's alpha) reported on the 20 Folk Scales range from .43 to .85 (median .76), 4 were below the commonly accepted minimum .7 standard. The internal consistency estimates of the three Vector scales were somewhat higher (.77–.88). Similarly, Cronbach's alphas for the 13 specialty scales ranged from a low of .45 to a high of .88, with 4 scales below .70.

The 1-year, 5-year, and 25-year duration between subsequent assessments for the reported test-retest reliability coefficients are too long to provide an estimation of short term scale reliability. The vast majority of test-retest reliability estimates among high school students were quite high (between .6 and .8 for a 1-year period). Among adults, the estimates for the longer time frames are between .4 and .8.

Validity. Extensive empirical evidence is presented regarding the validity and interpretive meaning of the Folk Scales, the Vector scales, the cuboidal classification scheme, and to some degree the Specialty scales. In general, the construct validity of the Folk and Vector scales has been quite thoroughly explored, with moderate to strong correlations (.4–.8) between CPI scales and measures of similar constructs from well-known and well-validated personality instruments. Although personality constructs, including those measured by the CPI, are demonstrated, the predictive power of these with respect to individual behavior in any particular situational or observational context is consistent but relatively weak.

Two related sets of criterion measures were used to assess the performance of CPI scales regarding their primary purpose, namely to assess how most people would describe respondents' behavior. First, trained observers used the (personality or interpersonal) California Q-Sets to rate respondents according to their behavioral characteristics (Block, 1961). Across all CPI scales (the Specialty scales were not included in this set of analyses), significant low to moderate correlations (.1 to .4) were observed between Q-Set results and CPI scale scores.

A second method was also used to examine the validity of some scales; people (i.e., spouse, peers, and staff) who knew respondents well rated them using various forms of an Adjective Check List (ACL). The point-biserial correlations between relevant adjectives and CPI scale scores were also low to moderate (.1–.4). These correlations using the four cuboidal classes were lower (.1–.2).

COMMENTARY. Given variation in the psychometric performance across scales, researchers, educators, and clinicians are encouraged to evaluate the CPI on the specific dimensions of interest. Some scales are psychometrically stronger with respect to the degree of internal consistency, score stability, and the quality of validation support. The CPI manual (3rd ed.) contains extensive information to serve as a guide.

The CPI can assist in the description of individuals' personal and interpersonal characteristics associated with stable dimensions of personality. Given the relatively weak correlations between scale scores and single descriptive items the CPI results are only suggestive and descriptive classification requires careful cross-validation with other sources of corroborating information. Moreover, one might expect descriptive results to be subject to the effects of social and cultural context.

The authors themselves recognize this as an area in need of further research.

SUMMARY. Over the nearly five decades since the creation of the CPI, an extensive body of research has formed that examines its performance in diverse assessment populations and age groups. This body of knowledge provides a wealth of comparative reference materials. The CPI provides a substantiated method to aid in the consensual description of difference between individuals and groups across many substantiated dimensions of personality. Since its inception, the CPI has been quite successful in its groundbreaking attempt to describe a broad array of fairly robust personality characteristics across a wide cross-section of society.

REVIEWER'S REFERENCES

Block, J. (1961). *The Q-sort method in personality assessment and psychiatric research.* Springfield, IL: Charles C. Thomas.
Briggs, S. R. (1992). Assessing the five-factor model of personality description. *Journal of Personality, 60,* 253–293.
Compton, W. C. (1998). Measures of mental health and a five factor theory of personality. *Psychological Reports, 83,* 371–381.
Marshall, G. N., Wortman, C. B., Vickers, R. R., Jr., Kusulas, J. W., & Hervig, L. K. (1994). The five-factor model of personality as a framework for personality-health research. *Journal of Personality & Social Psychology, 67,* 278–286.

Review of the California Psychological Inventory™, Third Edition by KEITH HATTRUP, Associate Professor of Psychology, San Diego State University, San Diego, CA:

DESCRIPTION. The California Psychological Inventory™ (CPI) is a self-report measure of dimensions of normal personality, administered by paper and pencil or computer. The purposes of the CPI are to identify how examinees might be described by others, and to predict how examinees will behave in specified contexts. It is recommended that interpretation of CPI scores be done only by persons who have received sufficient training in the measure. The manual provides considerable detail about relationships observed between CPI scores and specific behaviors, and includes references to a substantial number of published works that can assist in interpretation of CPI scores.

The latest revision of the CPI, Form 434, includes all but 28 of the items in the earlier version, Form 462, which were dropped because they contained objectionable or unlawful content. Thus, Form 434 provides scores on the same 20 Folk Concept scales and 3 Vector scales that were included in Form 462. Form 434 also provides scores on 13 Special Purpose scales; five of these are new for Form 434, including Leadership, Amicability, Law Enforcement Orientation,

Toughmindedness, and Narcissism. Given that a small number of items were added to and deleted in each of the 20 scales, correlations between the old and new scales ranged between .96 and 1.00. The revisions to the Third Edition of the CPI are limited enough that many of the observations about the measure that have been made by previous reviewers are still true today.

New normative data are provided for Form 434, based on samples of 3,000 males and 3,000 females. Unfortunately, the large norm samples cannot be considered random or representative (e.g., adults working in professional occupations are underrepresented). Information about the ethnic and racial background, geographic location, and socioeconomic background of respondents is still lacking. However, the manual includes new norms for 52 samples of males and 42 samples of females, including graduate students in various fields, college majors, members of different occupations, and so on. Comparisons of examinees' scores with these norms can facilitate interpretation of observed scores.

DEVELOPMENT AND TECHNICAL CHARACTERISTICS. The CPI is often cited as a textbook example of the use of empirical keying methods in scale construction. Of the 20 Folk Scales, 13 were developed using pure empirical methods, 4 used a rational approach, and 3 used a combination of rational and empirical item selection procedures. Evidence of the reliability and construct validity of the CPI must be interpreted in light of the methods of scale construction that were utilized. Empirical keying results in scales that share many of the distributional characteristics, and sources of variance, that are present in the criterion measure. So, it is not surprising that the alpha reliabilities of the CPI scales range from .62 to .84 in the total sample, with a median of .77. When criteria used for empirical keying are factorially complex, scales developed for predicting these criteria will also be low in internal consistency. However, several of the scales with the lowest alphas were developed using a rational approach.

Retest reliabilities are based on samples of 108 males and 129 females who were retested after a 1-year interval, and samples of 91 females and 44 males who were retested after 5- and 25-year intervals, respectively. For the 1-year retest, reliabilities range from .51 to .84, with a median of .68. For the 5-year and 25-year retest, reliabilities ranged from .36 to .73, and from .37 to .84, respectively. The low retest reliabilities for some scales are not surprising given the substantial amount of time between retests. Unfortunately, the manual does not report standard errors of measurement (*SEM*s) for the scales, which can facilitate interpretation of differences among examinees' scores.

COMMENTARY. Much has been written about the methods of scale construction used in developing and validating the CPI. A common criticism is that the development of the CPI was not driven by theory. Instead, Gough's goal was to identify scales that could predict practically or theoretically important criteria. As a consequence, several of the Folk and Special Purpose scales correlate substantially with each other (as high as r = .82 for males, and .84 for females), and hence, as reviewers have noted, the CPI fails to provide a clear, parsimonious, and theoretically compelling summary description of the normal personality (e.g., Eysenck, 1985; Thorndike, 1959). Gough argues that the CPI measures concepts of personality used by lay persons; therefore, if folk concepts are correlated in the minds of lay persons, CPI scales should be similarly correlated. Furthermore, Gough argues that subtle differences in the interpretations of scores on related scales justifies keeping them separated despite high collinearity. Unfortunately, empirical evidence of differential prediction of the scales, or of interactions among the scales implied by Gough's cuboid model, is not presented. There are several additional limitations to the evidence of construct validity presented for the CPI.

First, despite the fact that the pragmatic goal of the CPI is to predict various criteria, considerable effort has gone into naming the scales and invoking trait-like constructs when interpreting scores on the CPI scales. Empirical keying means that scales containing items that were validated against other existing measures, or other factorially simple criteria, are easier to describe in trait-like terms than scales that are developed from items that correlate with behaviorally complex criteria. In the latter case, it is probably not theoretically defensible to describe a complex set of criterion correlates with a simple trait label. An alternative approach would involve theoretical explication of the trait determinants of criterion variance, and then development of multiple factorially pure scales to predict the criterion using multivariate methods. This latter approach contributes more to our theoretical understanding of the determinants behavior, and thereby facilitates the practical use of multiple predictor measures, compared to the factorially complex scales that emerged from Gough's empirical approach.

A second limitation is the lack of justification of the criteria used in developing the Folk Scales. Evidently, there were 20 criteria of interest to Gough, including delinquency, high school and college grades, income, and so on; and hence, 20 Folk Concepts are assumed to be necessary in describing personality. Thirteen Special Purpose scales were developed for predicting other criteria, but these are not considered basic folk concepts. The lack of theoretical explication of the criterion domain is troubling. Gough notes that the CPI was developed on the basis of an "open system," which means that new scales can be developed any time a new criterion is to be predicted. Unfortunately, there may be no limit to the number of criteria that might be used in developing CPI scales, many of the criteria are likely to be empirically redundant, and many of the criteria lack any clear psychological meaning. Further, it is unclear why scales that were designed to predict certain criteria (e.g., success as a Psychologist [Py]) are more basic, or deserving of status as folk concepts, than scales that are labeled "special purpose" (e.g., anxiety, work orientation, creative temperament).

Finally, the factor analyses that are described in the manual for Form 434 do not contribute much to the construct validity evidence for the CPI. Earlier versions of the CPI were criticized for failing to base decisions about scale construction and interpretation on factor analytic methods. Gough argues that factor analysis is inconsistent with the goals of the CPI, which include measuring folk concepts. It is regrettable, but not surprising, that the CPI manual fails to discuss alternative models of personality that have emerged from studies of the natural languages, but have been developed using factor analytic methods. Goldberg (1981) concluded in a review of the lexical approach to personality measurement that most existing measures mapped on to five factors, which have come to be known as the Five Factor Model (FFM). The manual for Form 434 of the CPI now reports factor analyses of items within each of the 20 Folk Scales. As would be expected, these analyses show that most of the 20 Folk Scales are factorially complex, as were the criteria. The Vector scales and cuboid model are based on smallest space analyses of the 20 Folk Scales, and a factor analysis of the 20 Folk Scales extracted five factors that are similar, but not identical to the FFM. The problem with analyses of the relationships of the 20 Folk Scales is that the scales are themselves factorially complex. As a consequence, the factors that emerge are composites of complex components, and hence, are more difficult to interpret than factors that emerge from analysis at the item level.

SUMMARY. The Third Edition of the CPI is a minor change from the previous version. Hence, most of the issues described in previous reviews about scale construction and construct validity are still true of Form 434. If the goal is to predict criteria like those described in the CPI manual, the CPI probably has considerable practical value. But, if the goal includes understanding of the trait-like constructs that contribute to variance in valued criteria, then other measures, such as the Revised NEO Personality Inventory (T6:2110) or the Hogan Personality Inventory [Revised] (T6:1159), provide scores on a parsimonious and empirically validated taxonomy of the dimensions of personality. Complex combinations of factorially pure dimensions of personality might be used to predict complex criteria, thereby contributing more to our theoretical understanding of personality, and of relevant criteria, than can be obtained from the CPI's factorially complex scales. Certainly, measures of the FFM have attracted much more attention in the recent scholarly literature on the prediction of job performance criteria than has the CPI.

REVIEWER'S REFERENCES

Eysenck, H. J. (1985). [Review of the California Psychological Inventory.] In J. V. Mitchell, Jr. (Ed.), *The ninth mental measurements yearbook* (pp. 252–253). Lincoln, NE: Buros Institute of Mental Measurements.
Goldberg, L. R. (1981). Language and individual differences: The search for universals in personality lexicons. In L. Wheeler (Ed.), *Review of personality and social psychology: 2* (pp. 141–165). Beverly Hills, CA: Sage.
Thorndike, R. L. (1959). [Review of the California Psychological Inventory.] In O. K. Buros (Ed.), *The fifth mental measurements yearbook* (pp. 97–99). Highland Park, NJ: The Gryphon Press.

[44]

Career Planning Survey.

Purpose: Intended "to help students in grades 8–10 identify and explore personally relevant occupations and high school courses ... to provide students with a general sense of direction for career exploration ... show students how occupations relate to each other, thus providing them with a context in which to explore their career options."

Population: Grades 8–10.
Publication Dates: 1997–2001.
Scores, 4: (UNIACT) Interest Inventory, Inventory of Work-Relevant Abilities, and 2 ability measures (Reading Skills, Numerical Skills).
Administration: Group.
Price Data, 2001: $3.80 per Assessment Set Option A (with ability measures); $3.25 per Assessment Set Option B (without ability measures) (each set includes an answer sheet [scored by ACT], a student guidebook, prepaid scoring, and two copies of the student report); $12.50 per examination kit (with detailed information and sample materials for the preview of Career Planning Survey, including test booklet, Directions for Administration, Counselor's Manual [2001, 48 pages], and student guidebook [2001, 24 pages]); $.65 per reusable test booklet; $8.25 per Counselor's Manual; $2.25 per Directions for Administration; volume discounts available.
Time: (90) minutes (Option A); (45) minutes (Option B).
Author: ACT, Inc.
Publisher: ACT, Inc.

Review of the Career Planning Survey by SANDRA A. LOEW, Assistant Professor of Counselor Education, University of North Alabama, Florence, AL:

DESCRIPTION. The Career Planning Survey is a computer scored paper-and-pencil test for 8th through 10th graders. It is used to assist them in exploring career options. The test consists of a list of 90 activities that students mark with *like* (L), *dislike* (D), or *indifference* (I). There are self-ratings of work-related abilities in 15 areas such as "meeting people" or "organization" that students complete as part of the exploration. There is an optional reading and mathematics test that increases the time required from 45 to 90 minutes.

The developers state in the Counselor's Manual that "two bipolar dimensions of work tasks and work task preferences—data/ideas and people/things—underlie Holland's (1997) hexagon" (p. 4). They have used these dimensions to construct a World of Work Map that is part of the report students receive. This map is divided into 12 regions that represent combinations of the data, ideas, people, and things work tasks dimensions. This map suggests that a student whose interests indicate a preference for working with people and data might explore marketing and sales or social and government services as career possibilities. Students also receive a Career Planning

Guide that provides information on finding more resources. Included in this booklet is a section that lists activities common to certain careers that are arranged according to the career clusters. Students indicate the number of times they have done the activity so that they become aware of the tasks common to various work settings, and some of the experiences they may have already had relative to the world of work. Overall, the booklet provides students the opportunity to explore their interests, abilities, and experiences and gives them new information to consider in career exploration.

DEVELOPMENT. The Career Planning Survey was developed to assist counselors in providing course planning and career exploration in a group setting. It is part of a comprehensive guidance program that encourages students to investigate career options several times during middle and high school. The premise is that the world of work is very complex and students may not have an awareness of various occupations or what is required in those occupations. This program assesses students in such a way that they learn about career options and about themselves in relation to those career options. According to the developers, self-concept plays a large role in the choice of a career and this assessment takes that factor into consideration.

TECHNICAL. The Interest Inventory section of the Career Planning Survey was normed in 1992 with over 4,000 students in each of 8th, 10th, and 12th grades (total is over 13,000 students). This sample was generally representative of the population for gender and race and slightly less so for geographic region. The work-related abilities portion and the math and reading abilities tests were normed in 1997 with over 8,000 each of 8th and 10th grade students (a total of over 16,000 students). This sample was generally representative of the population for all demographic characteristics.

The developers of the Career Planning Survey use the "wideband approach" to assessment that uses a number of different types of brief measures. This approach provides a reasonable testing time but does limit accuracy. Because this measure is for career exploration and is designed to be used on an ongoing basis with learning occurring as part of the process, that limitation is not a major concern.

Internal consistency reliability estimates for the Interest Inventory range from .84 to .91 for

Grade 8 and .86 to .92 for Grade 10. Test-retest reliability coefficients for the Interest Inventory ranged from .68 to .78 for males and .69 to .82 for females. Test-retest interval ranges from 3 weeks to 4 years. Because this measure is an exercise in exploration and learning, these coefficients are more than adequate.

Test-retest reliability coefficients for the work-related abilities section of the Career Planning Survey were .71 to .78 for Grade 9 and .69 to .78 for Grade 11. Because this section is so brief, the reliability coefficients are quite impressive. The internal consistency reliability estimates of the ability tests range from .80 to .88. The work-related experiences list has an internal consistency reliability estimate ranging from .61 to .87.

Studies provide content-related evidence of validity of the scores from the Interest Inventory of the Career Planning Survey, and there is extensive evidence of criterion-related validity based on the interests of people in the criterion groups. This assessment seems to match similar career exploration inventories. The developers have been particularly concerned with the use of the scales with racial/ethnic minorities and they conducted several studies to confirm that the test is appropriate to use with those populations.

COMMENTARY. The ability portion of this instrument tests only Reading and Mathematics skills and ignores other areas such as Science. Scores would give an incomplete picture of students' abilities and would not be very useful in career exploration or course placement. Most school systems have achievement testing in place and those results could be used to complement the Career Planning Survey.

This assessment, used as part of a comprehensive guidance program, would be very helpful for students in their career exploration. Because the test must be sent away to be computer scored, more than one class period is required to use the instrument effectively. Ideally, it should be given to students in Grades 8, 9, and 10 with several class periods set aside each year to explore careers and students' choices. Although an inexperienced test administrator could easily follow the directions and administer this test to groups of students, it requires a counselor to help students interpret the results and use them in meaningful career exploration.

The Counselor's Manual provides an excellent overview of the theory behind the development of the Career Planning Survey and much of that information would be a review of career counseling courses taken in graduate school.

SUMMARY. The Career Planning Survey is a well-designed measure that, when used as part of a comprehensive guidance program, can assist students in career exploration and preparation. The reliability and validity estimates are acceptable and appropriate for this type of assessment. Based on sound career development theory, this instrument will be familiar to counselors and a valuable device for students to begin to think of themselves in the world of work. The ability section of the test would be inadequate and redundant in most school districts, and not recommended. The comprehensive materials are well-written and easy to understand and use. Overall, this is a very useful tool for school counselors.

[45]
Career Transitions Inventory.

Purpose: Designed "to assess the resources and barriers" experienced "in making a career transition."
Population: Adults.
Publication Date: 1991.
Acronym: CTI.
Scores, 5: Readiness, Confidence, Personal Control, Support, Independence.
Administration: Group.
Manual: No manual.
Price Data: Available from author.
Time: Administration time not reported.
Author: Mary J. Heppner.
Publisher: Mary J. Heppner (the author).

Review of the Career Transitions Inventory by ROBERT J. DRUMMOND, *Professor of Counselor Education, University of North Florida, Jacksonville, FL:*

DESCRIPTION. The Career Transitions Inventory (CTI), a 40-item test that measures dimensions of career transition, can be individually or group administered. The test contains 40 Likert-type items. The test taker responds to each item on a 6-point scale ranging from (1) *Strongly agree* to (6) *Strongly disagree*. There is no middle category such as "not sure." There are five scales having eight items each and labeled Readiness, Confidence, Personal Control, Support, and Independence.

The CTI is designed to assess the resources and barriers the counselees may experience in making a career transition. Career transition is defined by the author as any of the following three types of change: (a) task change—a shift from one set of tasks to another; (b) position change—a shift in jobs, same employer or different; and (c) occupational change—a transition from one set of duties to another set.

DEVELOPMENT. The development of the Career Transition Inventory was influenced by the theory of Schlossberg who stresses the influence of how the individual perceives that transition, the characteristics of the individual, the psychosocial competencies, role identification, and the pre and post environments. The intent of the CTI was to develop a multidimensional scale that would be economical and would include a number of constructs in one instrument. The purpose of the instrument is to help individuals and counselors understand the psychological factors that might be affecting the career transition process, to present a common shared vocabulary for both counselors and client, and to assist clients in making targeted interventions.

TECHNICAL. Primarily, the author of the test presents basic validity and reliability evidence. Construct validity of the scales was examined by factor analysis. A 5-factor solution was extracted and accounted for 44.5% of the variance. Reliability studies were also conducted by use of Cronbach's alpha. The author reported a Cronbach's alpha of .85 for the whole test. The individual factors ranged from a low of .66 to a high of .87 for Readiness. Heppner (the author) also reported a test-retest coefficient of .84 with 3 weeks between testing. The CTI provided the user with some basic strategies regarding how to interpret the data with individuals in transition. Besides these guidelines, one case study was included in the technical literature provided. There are technical data that are not presented in the supplementary documentation that would be helpful to counselors. The norming group is not described in detail. It would be interesting and valuable if age, gender, diversity, and educational level were presented. The matrix of correlations between the five scales would aid the counselor in test interpretation.

COMMENTARY. The author did not report some data that would have helped in using the test (e.g., the means and standard deviations and the standard errors of the five scales as well as the correlations between the scales). One also might consider evaluating the reading level of the test. The author might want to develop norms for different groups of individuals in transition such as age norms, ethnicity, and educational level. Additional validity studies would provide additional insight into the construct validity of the CTI such as comparing the CTI with the Career Attitudes and Strategies Inventory (13:47). Criterion-related studies could compare the CTI and rating of counselors with clients in transition.

SUMMARY. The CTI shows promise as a scale to use for working with individuals in career transition. Preliminary data indicate that the test has construct validity and is fairly reliable. Additional studies would enhance the technical soundness of the CTI and aid the counselor in working with clients in transition.

Review of the Career Transitions Inventory by JEAN POWELL KIRNAN, Associate Professor of Psychology, The College of New Jersey, Ewing, NJ:

[The reviewer wishes to acknowledge the contributions of Lauren Muller. Her diligent research and keen insights contributed greatly to this review.]

The Career Transitions Inventory (CTI) is designed for use with adult clients who are contemplating or currently engaged in a career change. The instrument assesses the resources and barriers a client will face during a career transition. Although traditionally career and vocational counseling have emphasized the measurement of client interests and abilities and matched these with job positions, this instrument is designed to assess barriers to an effective transition. It should be noted that the results of this test are to be used in conjunction with counseling. The CTI thus presents an integration of career and personal issues, venturing into a previously uncharted area of counseling. With the increasing number of individuals experiencing both voluntary and involuntary job changes, the CTI's introduction is timely indeed.

DESCRIPTION. The CTI contains 40 statements to which the respondent expresses their level of agreement or disagreement using a 6-point Likert scale. It can be given to clients in a group setting, is self-administered, and does not require a trained administrator. Even though support materials are available, there is no formal manual for this test. The test authors are strongly urged to provide users with a formal manual to answer questions regarding cost, reliability, validity, administration, and scoring.

The physical format of the answer sheet has several characteristics that are confusing and may lead to errors on the part of the respondent. The Likert scale options are printed at the top of the answer sheet as: 1 = *strongly agree* (SA), 2 = *moderately agree* (MA), 3 = *slightly agree* (SA), 4 = *slightly disagree* (SD), 5 = *moderately disagree* (MD), and 6 = *strongly disagree* (SD). The remainder of the answer sheet contains 40 numbered rows, one for each item, with three columns each. However, for any given row the numerical Likert scale appears in only one column. For example, in Row 5 the numerical scale appears in the third column, in Row 6, it appears in the second column, and in Row 7 it is back in the third column. As respondents move from one statement to another, they must search for the proper column in which to record their responses.

Additionally, at the top of each of three columns, the abbreviations, SA through SD, appear again. However, the section in each row where answers are recorded lists only the numerical scale, forcing the client to continuously reference the column headings on top of the page. This extra effort could be avoided by having the response section contain actual abbreviations, rather than their numerical equivalents. Furthermore, the abbreviations printed at the top of each column are redundant, SA refers to both *strongly agree* and *slightly agree* and SD refers to both *strongly disagree* and *slightly disagree*. Different wording and abbreviations could reduce confusion.

To score the test, the answer sheet that contains the original answers is peeled away leaving two separate sheets each with three columns, one column for each of the five scales: Readiness, Confidence, Personal Control, Support, and Independence. The numbers that are calculated for each scale are then converted to a ranking of high, medium, or low.

The apparently haphazard placement of the response scales in the three different columns facilitates scoring, but at the expense of ease in responding. The authors should consider streamlining the answer sheet and using templates for scoring the different scales. Alternatively, the CTI might be adapted for a computerized administration and scoring.

As with many personality measures, several of the questions appear transparent. Consequentially, the accuracy and ultimate utility of the instrument depends on the client's honesty in responding. Some items are also worded poorly, which may affect the validity of responses. A few statements have conditional phrases that pose a problem if the respondent agrees with the first part, but not the second. Other items present situations that may not have been encountered by all the respondents. Without a neutral option, the individual is forced to choose between some form of agreeing or disagreeing.

DEVELOPMENT. The CTI was originally designed to measure six constructs of the career transition that had been identified in the literature and also through the author's experiences as a career counselor. These constructs included: self-efficacy, self vs. relational focus, motivation, rational beliefs, risk-taking, and control. Initially, 12 items (6 positively worded and 6 negatively worded) were drafted for each of the six constructs. These 72 items were subjected to a pilot review by a small group of counselors and adults in career transition. Items were rewritten for clarity. Subject matter experts sorted the revised questions into the six constructs. An initial rate of agreement that ranged from 77% to 92% was improved to 100% with some additional rewording of the items.

A sample of 300 adults in career transition were administered the 72-item CTI and their responses were used in a principal components analysis. The 72 items were reduced to 40 by eliminating items that failed to load on a factor or loaded on more than one factor. The number of constructs was reduced from 6 to 5 and they were renamed to more accurately reflect their item composition: Readiness, Confidence, Control, Perceived Support, and Independence.

TECHNICAL. The instrument reports more than adequate evidence of reliability using both internal and test-retest techniques. Cronbach's coefficient alpha was calculated on a sample of 300 subjects for each of the subscales and the total score as Readiness, .87; Confidence, .83; Control, .69; Perceived Support, .66; Independence, .67; and Total, .90. Although the internal stability of Control, Perceived Support, and Independence are relatively low, this is not unusual for measures of personality and attitudes. A test-retest study using a sample of 43 graduate students tested over a 3-week interval also showed acceptable stability. The stability over time yielded coefficients of Readiness, .74; Confidence, .79; Control, .55;

Perceived Support, .77; Independence, .83; and Total, .84. The repeated weakness in the Control scale (low on both measures of reliability) suggests that this scale be reviewed for possible improvement or modification. Three of the scales have few items (Control = 6, Support = 5, and Independence = 5) that may contribute to low reliability estimates.

Validity. Construct validity was demonstrated by correlating the CTI with several demographic variables (sex, education, type of transition, marital status). Generally speaking, the results were in the expected directions. As expected, younger respondents scored higher on Readiness, Control, and Support, but in a later sample only differed on Control. Married individuals also scored higher on Support. An additional sample of 104 adults in career transition were used to demonstrate construct validity. In addition to the CTI, this sample responded to The Hope Scale and My Vocational Situation (MVS). Again, there was general agreement in the expected directions.

COMMENTARY. The development of the CTI was grounded in theory, and utilized outside experts and statistical analysis to derive the final wording and reduction to 40 statements measuring five constructs of career transition. Acceptable reliability and demonstrated construct validity add to the psychometric value of this instrument. The response format is awkward, but easily remedied. The main weakness, which the authors recognize, is a developmental one of a small, homogenous (ethnically and geographically) normative group. The few other instruments that measure vocational barriers such as the My Vocational Situation (MVS; Holland, Daiger, & Power, 1988; reviewed by Lunneborg, 1985; Westbrook, 1985) are not as well developed and fail to demonstrate adequate validity and reliability.

SUMMARY. The CTI is not a diagnostic tool but rather a self-exploratory instrument, used with a counselor as a facilitator. A refreshing new instrument, the CTI taps into a previously ignored area of concern, the resources and barriers affecting successful career transitions. The authors used sound psychometric techniques and were cautious in their recommendations for use. This instrument can serve well for its intended purpose as a source of clues into barriers and resources for career transition.

REVIEWER'S REFERENCES

Holland, J. L., Daiger, D. C., & Power, P. G. (1980). *My Vocational Situation.* Palo Alto, CA: Consulting Psychologist Press.

Lunneborg, P. W. (1985). [Review of My Vocational Situation.] In James V. Mitchell, Jr. (ED.), *The ninth mental measurements yearbook* (pp. 1026–1027). Lincoln, NE: Buros Institute of Mental Measurements.

Westbrook, B. W. (1985). [Review of My Vocational Situation.] In James V. Mitchell, Jr. (ED.), *The ninth mental measurements yearbook* (pp. 1027–1029). Lincoln, NE: Buros Institute of Mental Measurements.

[46]

Child and Adolescent Adjustment Profile [Revised].

Purpose: Designed to "measure five factor-analyzed areas of adjustment."

Population: Children and adolescents seen in mental health programs, outpatient and inpatient, health care programs, and schools.

Publication Dates: 1977–1998.

Acronym: CAAP Scale.

Scores, 5: Dependency, Hostility, Peer Relations, Productivity, Withdrawal.

Administration: Individual.

Price Data, 2002: $10 per 25 scales; $5 per 25 profiles; $25 per manual (1998, 28 pages).

Time: (10) minutes.

Comments: Pre- and posttreatment ratings by parents, teachers, and counselors.

Authors: Robert B. Ellsworth and Shanae L. Ellsworth.

Publisher: Ellsworth Krebs Incorporated.

Cross References: See T5:449 (4 references) and T4:430 (1 reference); for reviews by Robert H. Deluty and David R. Wilson of an earlier edition, see 9:211.

Review of the Child and Adolescent Adjustment Profile [Revised] by SHERI BAUMAN, Assistant Professor, Department of Educational Psychology, University of Arizona, Tucson, AZ:

DESCRIPTION. The Child and Adolescent Adjustment Profile (CAAP) is a 20-item rating scale for assessing psychosocial development. Respondents rate the child of interest on a series of behavioral descriptions, using a 4-point Likert-type scale. The scale can be completed in approximately 10 minutes by parents, teachers, counselors, or others involved with the youth, who rate behaviors observed in the previous month. Areas of adjustment, each assessed by four items on the scale, are (a) Peer Relations, (b) Dependency, (c) Hostility, (d) Productivity, and (e) Withdrawal. No overall adjustment level is given.

Scoring is done on the completed rating forms. Values assigned each rating are added to obtain a sum for each factor; instructions are provided to manage subscales with missing data. Scores are transferred to one of two CAAP Profiles (Home and Community Adjustment or School

Adjustment), on which individual results are plotted. Scores are ordered such that higher scores represent a more desirable trait, presumably indicative of better adjustment. The profile sheet gives approximate *T*-scores, and indicates which scores fall in the range of below average or above average adjustment. Separate norms for males and females, or by age group, are not provided. The profile includes space to record pre- and post-ratings if the scale is to be used to evaluate progress in treatment or the effectiveness of an intervention.

DEVELOPMENT. The revised version of the CAAP (copyright, 1997, 1998) offers formatting and wording changes to the 1977 version of the rating scale and to the manual, but no additional psychometric data were obtained or reported. The manual does not describe the theoretical basis for the construct of adjustment that the scales are purported to measure.

Development of the initial version of the scale began with 292 items derived from a literature review and expert input. This version was administered to 262 children with an average age of 11.2. Mothers represented 89% of raters. Fifty-six percent of the children in the sample had been referred for mental health services. The manual indicates that males comprised 57% of the sample, but other demographic information (race, ethnicity, community type, etc.) is not available. Factor analysis yielded six meaningful factors. Data on each item were examined to determine whether the item differentiated between referred and nonreferred participants, had high factor loadings on only one factor, and were judged by experts to be relevant to the constructs being measured. No information is provided on number or qualifications of the judges, who are only identified as treatment staff.

Items that met the three criteria were retained in the next version, a 55-item scale then used to rate 248 participants with a mean age of 13.8. Parents completed the scale on 65% of the sample, whereas 20% were completed by probation officers, and 15% by teachers. Analysis of these data resulted in the deletion of items that were not consistent for both genders, were not sensitive to change over time, or did not differentiate between groups expected to differ. One factor found on the initial version (Anxiety Depression) was deleted because it did not meet these criteria.

The final scale, published in 1977, is composed of 20 items that were administered to 430 children who had not been referred for mental health or learning problems. This sample was subdivided into a home and community sample (203 children, average age 9.6, 54% male, and 65% rated by a parent, 90% of whom were mothers), whose results were used to establish the Home and Community Adjustment norms. Ratings on the remaining 227 participants (average age 13.7, 57% male, all ̲ated by teachers in seven public schools) were the normative data for School Adjustment.

Neither the manual nor the first author of the manual (S. Ellsworth, personal communication, November 2002) provided important demographic information about the samples used to develop the instrument. The norms were established more than 25 years ago on a sample for which characteristics are only vaguely described. No updating of these norms has been attempted. Several studies were published that used the CAAP, or portions of it, in research, but none reported reliability or validity analyses.

TECHNICAL. Reliability for the scale was examined on the first edition, published in 1977. Coefficient alpha was used to estimate internal consistency reliability of each factor, which was found to be high (.80 to .90). The sample size used in calculating this coefficient was 157, with no information provided as to the selection of this subsample. Test-retest reliability was calculated on re-ratings completed by 105 parents, teachers, and probation officers (no breakdown provided) in 1-week intervals, which resulted in correlations of between .78 and .89. Again, no information is provided about the sample used in these calculations.

The authors used several methods of gathering the validity evidence for this instrument. According to the manual, discriminant validity was calculated using a combination of parent ratings from the Phase Two sample, using only items that were retained on the final version of the scale, and ratings obtained from the normative sample. However, total number of cases reported does not equal the total of the groups from which the subsample was drawn, indicating that some protocols were omitted. No explanation of this discrepancy is provided. The authors do not provide any explanation of the lack of validity data using the teacher or probation officer ratings. Differences among age groups were tested using the data from the normative sample. The manual does not indicate whether all protocols were used in these calculations. Further, although the manual states the oldest group differed in expected directions from the youngest group on the Dependency and Productivity factors, the actual values are not reported, and the manual does not clearly indicate whether the difference was statistically significant. Gender and grade level differences were found on Peers Relations and Productivity, which the manual states are statistically significant, but again actual values are not provided. Further evidence of discriminant validity is presented, noting that expected differences were found between teacher and parent ratings. Although the authors indicated that different raters are expected to provide different ratings, they nevertheless compared ratings of parents and probationers ($N = 25$) and parents and teachers ($N = 18$), and found some evidence of agreement on some scales. Again, no information was provided regarding the subsamples used for the analysis. Evidence that the scale is valid for assessing progress in treatment was provided using results of t-tests for correlated means on pre- and posttreatment scores. Statistical significance was found on all but the Peer Relations factors. No information about the type and duration of treatment was provided. No attempt to examine concurrent validity was reported.

COMMENTARY. The CAAP has the advantages of brevity and ease of scoring, and the factor structure is robust. However, inadequate reliability and validity data render the measure of questionable utility. The psychometric properties described in the manual are based on outdated and imprecisely reported data. Little is known about the development and normative samples in terms of geography, race, ethnicity, community type, etc., so potential users of the scale are not able to make an informed decision about the applicability of the normative group to their own clientele. The absence of updated norms and independent validity studies in the revised edition diminishes the practical application of this measure.

A second limitation of this scale relates to the interpretive procedures. First, the profile sheet identifies scores as either "below average" or "above average." The absence of an "average" range contradicts what is known about the normal distribution of most traits. One would expect a range of scores (approximately 68%) to be in the average range. This omission could lead to misinterpreta-

tion of results. Further, without norms for different age groups, it is difficult to utilize the below and above average adjustment comparisons, which are based on group mean scores. The authors report in the manual that average scores differed on most factors by age group. However, apparently only the mean of all normative participants was used to develop the profile sheet. Is it reasonable to interpret a 16-year-old's rating as "above average adjustment" when compared to a normative group with a mean age of 9.6?

The authors suggest using the rating scale as a measure of change over time. However, there was no control group with which to compare the observed changes in the development sample, which could be a consequence of maturation rather than treatment effect. Further, the lack of information about the treatments administered makes the data problematic at best.

A potential user might wish to obtain the references cited in the bibliography included in the manual in order to become better informed about the scale. Unfortunately, the bibliography is replete with errors, which does not speak well for the attention to detail necessary for developing an assessment instrument. In addition to several typographical errors, a journal was incorrectly named in two citations, and another reference listed the incorrect year of publication. Bibliography format was inconsistent.

SUMMARY. The CAAP is a brief, easy-to-use rating scale that has undergone only cosmetic changes in the revised edition. It is disappointing that the concerns mentioned in an earlier review of the scale (Wilson, 1985) have never been addressed, and that no research has been published testing the scale on other samples. No studies were found to have examined the concurrent validity of the scale, and the validity studies cited in the manual are inadequate. Thus, despite the efficiency and cost-effectiveness of using this scale to measure progress in treatment, or to evaluate intervention programs, the reader might be on firmer ground by using one of the more technically adequate behavior rating scales for children and adolescents, albeit longer and with more complex scoring procedures. The other alternative is for users to conduct their own reliability and validity studies in the settings in which the CAAP would be used.

REVIEWER'S REFERENCE

Wilson, D. R. (1985). [Review of Child and Adolescent Adjustment Profile]. In J. V. Mitchell, Jr. (Ed.), *The ninth mental measurements yearbook* (pp. 296–297). Lincoln, NE: Buros Institute of Mental Measurements.

Review of the Child and Adolescent Adjustment Profile [Revised] by MARK R. COOPER, School Psychologist, Howard County Public Schools, Ellicott City, MD:

DESCRIPTION. The Child and Adolescent Adjustment Profile [Revised] (CAAP) is a 20-item paper-and-pencil questionnaire that is completed by parents, teachers, counselors, and others to assess psychosocial adjustment of youth. The test yields five adjustment factors: Peer Relations, Dependency, Hostility, Productivity, and Withdrawal. The developers report that the test can be used to assess the efficacy of interventions, identify problems in adjustment, and screen for childhood adjustment problems.

Because the CAAP is not intended to be used as a diagnostic instrument, nonclinical staff can administer and score the test. However, interpretation of the test does require some background knowledge of tests and measurements. Instructions are clear and written on the report form. Respondents rate the frequency of each behavior using a Likert-type rating scale. Scoring instructions in the test manual are easy to follow. Examiners are given instructions on how to score missing values. Once the CAAP is scored, the raw score sums for each adjustment area are transferred to a CAAP Profile Form. The Profile Form provides a visual representation of the level of adjustment for each area and assists with interpretation. Cutoff points for above and below average adjustment are clearly marked on the Profile Form. Each adjustment scale yields standard scores based on a mean of 50 and a standard deviation of 10. The CAAP Profile also permits the comparison of scores for different groups or for the same individual over time using pretest and posttest scores.

DEVELOPMENT. The CAAP (1978, revised 1997, 1998) has been revised several times under different names. The CAAP is based upon a similar scale, known as the Personal Adjustment and Role Skills (PARS), which was developed to evaluate the efficacy of mental health programs through the assessment adult adjustment (Ellsworth, 1970, 1973, 1975, 1978, 1979a, 1979b; Ellsworth, Foster, Childers, Arthur, & Kroker, 1968; Ellsworth et al., 1979). What is currently known as the CAAP went through three phases of revision and was previously known as the Children's PARS, PARS II, and PARS III.

The initial version of the CAAP consisted of 292 items measuring the adjustment of children and adolescents. Item content was based upon previous studies, other tests, and input from clinicians. A pilot study of 147 youth was conducted and items were retained if they demonstrating the ability to differentiate children who were referred versus those that were not referred for mental health services. The test developers also based their retention decisions on the opinions of clinicians. Of the total 292 items, 69 items were determined to be highly relevant. These 69 items were factor analyzed and 55 were found to load highly on the six adjustment dimensions.

A larger sample of children (*N* = 248) was used for the second phase of analysis. Ratings of children were collected from a more representative sample of adults (parents, teachers, and probation officers). Items were selected based upon their ability to differentiate children across gender and age groups and those who were sensitive from pretest to posttest (intake versus follow-up). The final selection of items was determined by their factor loading, test-retest reliability results, and internal consistency evidence. The result was a 20-item scale that consisted of five adjustment factors. The manual does not specify what changes, if any, were made to the CAAP when it was revised for the most recent edition. Concerns surrounding previous editions of the CAAP (1977–1981) included unclear sampling procedures used for determining reliability and validity (Deluty, 1985) and inadequate norms (Wilson, 1985).

TECHNICAL. The norm group for the final version of the CAAP consisted of 430 children and adolescents ranging in age from 3–19, who were not being seen for emotional or learning problems. The norm group was representative based upon gender (54% were male). Information was not provided on the ethnic and racial composition of the standardization sample. The test manual does not provide separate norms by age or gender. Differences in scores between these various groups were not reported. The authors did attempt to address differences between subgroups by only selecting those items that were consistent across age and gender groups.

The CAAP does provide separate norms for teacher and parent ratings through separate scoring profiles. The norms for the School Adjustment Profile were based exclusively on 227 teacher ratings of 356 children. Attempts were made to randomly select students for this normative group. The Home and Community Profile was based on 203 parent ratings. Sampling procedures for the Home and Community Profile were not reported.

Internal consistency and test-retest reliability studies were conducted. Coefficient alphas ranged from .80 to .90 for the CAAP Adjustment Scales. Test-retest coefficients for the Adjustment Scales (1-week interval between administrations) were in the .78 to .89 range. Multiple methods were used to evaluate the validity of the CAAP. Validity was examined by comparing probation and normal groups using parent ratings. F ratios were significant for all groups. Significant differences were also found between pretreatment and treated groups (3 months following treatment) for all scales except Peer Relations. However, the mean differences between probation and normal groups were relatively small and ranged from 3.41 to .55. Hit and miss rates for the identification of clinical groups were not reported (e.g., percentages of false positives, true positives, false negatives).

Differences between rater groups were also found. Ratings of the same group of children by probation officers and teachers were significantly different from ratings of parents on several scales. The low to moderate agreement between ratings of parents and teachers was expected and has been noted in the research literature (Kratochwill & Sheridan, 1990). Differences were also found between pre- and postmeasures for treatment groups, although the specifics of the intervention, characteristics of the treatment groups, and the amount of control incorporated into the research design were not reported. Factor loadings for each of the five Adjustment Factors ranged from .53 to .85. Correlations between scales were low providing evidence of their independence. Teacher ratings yielded higher intercorrelations than parent ratings.

COMMENTARY. The CAAP has undergone several revisions, which has resulted in the selection of items that have high correlations with the constructs that they measure. The test-retest and internal consistency reliabilities of the CAAP are impressive given that it consists of only 20 items. Criterion-related validity is questionable based upon the statistically significant but relatively small mean differences between normal and treatment groups.

The racial, ethnic, and geographical representation of the norm group cannot be established because these data were not published in the manual. Although score differences were found between age and gender groups, no attempt was made to provide separate norms for these groups. School and Home/Community profiles offer separate norms for parent and teacher ratings. However, both parent and teacher reports should be collected when feasible. Research has supported the incremental utility of combing both parent and teacher behavior ratings scales (Power et al., 1998)

The CAAP may be particularly useful for monitoring the effectiveness of interventions. Behavior rating scales, such as the CAAP, provide a useful and objective measure for pre- and posttest evaluation of intervention programs. However, it is important to note that behavior ratings are not completely objective accounts, are an indirect method of assessment, and are not necessarily reflective of actual occurrences of the behaviors in the natural environment (Kratochwill & Sheridan, 1990).

SUMMARY. The CAAP is a 20-item paper-and-pencil questionnaire that measures the psychosocial adjustment of youth. Administration, scoring, and interpretation are simple and clear. The generalizability of the test to various ethnic, racial, and geographic groups cannot be determined due to the lack of information on the relative composition of the standardization sample. The reliability and construct validity evidence for scores from the CAAP is moderate to strong. The five CAAP adjustment factors appear to be internally consistent and have adequate convergent and discriminate validity. The ability of the CAAP to differentiate among treatment and normal groups is questionable given the small mean group differences and the lack of information on positive and negative identification rates. In light of the questionable diagnostic utility of the CAAP, the reader is cautioned when using it to screen for or identify adjustment problems in youth. There is a paucity of tests, such as the CAAP, designed to evaluate and monitor children's adaptive coping skills and prosocial behaviors. Despite its psychometric limitations, the CAAP shows promise as a tool to assess the effectiveness of interventions.

REVIEWER'S REFERENCES
Deluty, R. H. (1985). [Review of Child and Adolescent Adjustment Profile]. In J. V. Mitchell, Jr. (Ed.), *The ninth mental measurements yearbook* (pp. 294–295). Lincoln, NE: Buros Institute of Mental Measurements.

Ellsworth, R. B. (1970). Upgrading treatment effeciveness through measurement and feedback of clinical outcomes. *Hospital and Community Psychiatry, 21,* 115–117.

Ellsworth, R. B. (1973). Feedback: Asset or liability in improving treatment effectiveness? *Journal of Consulting and Clinical Psychology, 40,* 383–393.

Ellsworth, R. B. (1975). Consumer feedback in measuring the effectiveness of mental health programs. In M. Guttentag & E. L. Struening (Eds.), *Handbook of evaluation research* (Vol. 2, pp. 239–274). Beverly Hills, CA: Sage Publications.

Ellsworth, R. B. (1978). *The CAAP Scale: The measurement of child and adolescent development.* Roanoke, VA: Institute for Program Evaluation.

Ellsworth, R. B. (1979a). *The PAL-H Scale: Profile of adaptation to life: Holistic scale manual.* Roanoke, VA: Institute for Program Evaluation.

Ellsworth, R.B. (1979b). *The PARS Scale: A measure of personal adjustment and role skills.* Roanoke, VA: Institute for Program Evaluation.

Ellsworth, R., Foster, L., Childers, B., Arthur, G., & Kroker, D. (1968). Hospital and community adjustment as perceived by psychiatric patients, their families, and staff. *Journal of Counseling & Clinical Psychology, 32,* 1–4.

Kratochwill, T. R., & Sheridan, S. M. (1990). Advances in behavioral assessment. In T. B. Gutkin & C. R. Reynolds (Eds.), *The handbook of school psychology* (2nd ed., pp. 328–364). New York: Wiley & Sons.

Power, T. J., Andrews, T. J., Eiraldi, R. B., Doherty, B. J., Ikeda, M. J., DuPaul, G. J., & Landua, S. (1998). Evaluating attention deficit hyperactivity disorder using multiple informants: The incremental utility of combining teacher and parent reports. *Psychological Assessment, 10,* 250–260.

Wilson, D. R. (1985). [Review of Child and Adolescent Adjustment Profile]. In J. V. Mitchell, Jr. (Ed.), *The ninth mental measurements yearbook* (pp. 296–297). Lincoln, NE: Buros Institute of Mental Measurements.

[47]
Child Symptom Inventory 4.

Purpose: Designed as a "screening instrument for the behavioral affective, and cognitive symptoms" of childhood psychiatric disorders.

Population: Ages 5–12.

Publication Dates: 1994–2002.

Acronym: CSI-4.

Scores, 13: AD/HD Inattentive, AD/HD Hyperimpulsive, AD/HD Combined, Oppositional Defiant Disorder, Conduct Disorder, Generalized Anxiety Disorder, Schizophrenia, Major Depressive Disorder, Dysthymic Disorder, Autistic Disorder, Asperger's Disorder, Social Phobia, Separation Anxiety Disorder.

Administration: Individual.

Forms, 2: Parent Checklist, Teacher Checklist.

Price Data, 2002: $98 per deluxe kit including screening and norms manual (2002, 179 pages), 25 parent checklists, 25 teacher checklists, 50 symptom count score sheets, and 50 symptom severity profile score sheets; $22 per screening manual or norms manual; $32 per 50 parent checklists; $60 per 100 parent checklists; $20 per 25 Spanish parent checklists; $32 per 50 teacher checklists; $60 per 100 teacher checklists; $13 per 50 profiles for parent or teacher checklists; $225 per computer scoring and report writing software.

Time: [10–15] minutes.

Comments: Instrument is designed to correspond to the DSM-IV classification system.

Authors: Kenneth D. Gadow and Joyce Sprafkin.

Publisher: Checkmate Plus Ltd.

[Note: The following reviews are based on an earlier version of the manual for this test. Reviews based on the new 2002 manual and recent articles supporting reliability and validity will be included in a future *Mental Measurements Yearbook.*]

Review of the Child Symptom Inventory 4 by JAMES C. DiPERNA, Assistant Professor, and ROBERT J. VOLPE, Doctoral Candidate, School Psychology Program, Lehigh University, Bethlehem, PA:

DESCRIPTION. The authors of the Child Symptom Inventory 4 (CSI-4) report that it is intended to serve as a screening instrument for behavioral, affective, and cognitive symptoms of approximately 20 different DSM-IV-based (American Psychiatric Association, 1994) childhood disorders. The instrument was developed for use in clinical settings as an alternative to time-consuming screening interviews. In addition, the authors wanted to create a rating scale that yielded results consistent with DSM-IV diagnostic criteria to facilitate identification of children in need of a comprehensive assessment for a specific psychiatric disorder. The CSI-4 is appropriate for students in Grades K–6, and both parent (97 items) and teacher (87 items) forms are available. Downward (Early Childhood Inventory-4; Sprafkin & Gadow, 1996; T6:858) and upward (Adolescent Symptom Inventory-4; Gadow & Sprafkin, 1995; 12) extensions of the CSI-4 are available; however, these instruments are published separately and not included in the current review.

Both forms of the CSI-4 require approximately 10–15 minutes to complete. Although directions for respondents are brief and straightforward, some items are unnecessarily long (e.g., "has stolen things when others aren't looking") or are compounds (e.g., "feels worthless or guilty") that may create some difficulty for respondents.

The authors of the CSI-4 have developed two methods of scoring (Symptom Severity and Screening Cutoff) that are used for different purposes. As its name suggests, the Symptom Severity method is used to establish the overall severity of symptoms that the child is demonstrating at the time of assessment. Under this scoring method, individual items are scored using a 4-point Likert scale reflecting frequency (e.g., *never* = 0 and *very often* = 3). Item scores from each category are summed to obtain raw total scores that can be converted to norm-referenced scores (*T*-scores and percentiles) if desired. The Symptom Cutoff scoring method is used to determine if the child demonstrates a sufficient number of symptoms to be considered for a comprehensive assessment of a DSM-IV childhood disorder. Under this method, items are scored dichotomously (*never* or *sometimes* = 0, *often* or *very often* = 1). Although both methods are conceptually straightforward, scoring can be somewhat cumbersome in practice because item scores must be summed and transferred to a separate scoring form, and the user must select the appropriate form based on the checklist type (teacher or parent), sex of the child, and method used.

DEVELOPMENT. The CSI-4 was developed to assess a variety of childhood disorders in the *Diagnostic and Statistical Manual of Mental Disorders* (4th ed.) (DSM-IV). Predecessors to this instrument corresponded with the DSM-III (American Psychiatric Association, 1980) and the DSM-IIIR (American Psychiatric Association, 1987) and included the Sprafkin, Loney, und Gadow Checklist (SLUG), Stony Brook Child Symptom Inventory-3 (CSI-3), and Child Symptom Inventory-3R (CSI-3R). Because the CSI-4 reflects DSM-IV symptom criteria, scales on the CSI-4 are explicitly linked to specific disorders such as attention-deficit/hyperactivity disorder (AD/HD), oppositional defiant disorder (ODD), etc., and items within these scales closely correspond with symptom criteria specified in the DSM-IV. Aside from a detailed explanation of the relationships between CSI-4 items and DSM-IV diagnostic criteria, limited information is provided regarding development, revision, and retention of items for the final versions of the parent and teacher rating scales.

TECHNICAL.

Standardization. The authors explicitly state that the CSI-4 was developed to serve as a screening instrument for a clinic-referred population rather than the general population. In addition, the primary scoring method (Symptom Cutoff) is based on a criterion-referenced decision rather than norm-referenced methods. Thus, although the authors do report normative data for both the parent and teacher forms of the CSI-4, they emphasize that this information is of secondary importance. Revised and expanded in 1999, normative data for the parent ratings are based on a moderate sized sample that is approximately evenly distributed across grade and sex. Significant limitations of this sample include that it is primarily (approximately 75% of the participants) from one state (New York) and disproportionately Caucasian (86% of the participants). The normative data for the teacher ratings are based on a large student

sample (*n* = 1,520) that also is relatively evenly distributed across grade and sex. Like the parent sample, however, the teacher sample was collected across a small number of states (New York, Missouri, and Wisconsin), and Caucasians are disproportionately represented (95% of the total sample). Thus, neither the parent nor teacher normative data can be considered representative of a national sample of children in Grades K–6.

Reliability. Reliability evidence for the CSI-4 primarily consists of test-retest coefficients. For the parent form, test-retest coefficients (6-week interval) were reported for a sample (*n* = 75) of boys, and moderate coefficients were observed for all scales except Schizophrenia. Teacher test-retest coefficients were calculated using biweekly ratings collected during a study of the effectiveness of stimulant medication for students with AD/HD. Correlations between teacher ratings (AD/HD and ODD scales only) ranged from moderate to large. Interrater reliability coefficients based on ratings between parents and teachers were calculated for a sample of children (*n* = 101) with clinical diagnoses. These correlations ranged from low to moderate as would be expected based on other cross-informant studies with rating scales (e.g., Achenbach, McConaughy, & Howell, 1987). No internal consistency estimates of reliability are reported.

Validity. The authors report several forms of validity evidence to justify the primary use of the CSI-4 with its target population (i.e., children referred to a clinic for assessment and intervention). Specifically, the authors explore predictive validity through an analysis of sensitivity and specificity of symptom severity scores from the CSI-4 (parent and teacher forms) for the childhood disorders it assesses. Overall, the CSI-4 scales displayed moderate to large sensitivity and specificity coefficients for identification of individuals with diagnosed disorders; however, the anxiety scales appear to be somewhat less sensitive in the identification of individuals with anxiety disorders. One limitation of the sensitivity and specificity analyses is that they are based on a single sample (*n* = 101) with consecutive referrals to a child psychiatry outpatient clinic. An additional limitation of this sample is that sample sizes varied significantly across types of disorders. These limitations, in turn, limit the generalizability of the results.

Concurrent validity for the Parent form of the CSI-4 was explored through an analysis of the relationships between ratings on CSI-4 scales and ratings on the Child Behavior Checklist (CBCL; Achenbach, 1991a). Similarly, scores on the Teacher form of the CSI-4 were compared to scores on the Teacher Report Form (TRF; Achenbach, 1991b). As expected, scales measuring similar constructs demonstrated the largest correlations in both of these analyses. Additional validity evidence was presented using comparisons of prevalence rates and severity scores across known groups (clinic-referred and normal samples). Consistent with the authors' expectations, prevalence rates and severity scores were significantly higher in the clinic-referred samples.

COMMENTARY. The CSI-4 has been developed to provide a screening assessment for children ages 5–12 who are suspected of having a behavioral, emotional, or cognitive disorder. Although initial reliability and validity evidence demonstrates support for this purpose, the reported evidence has limitations that must be addressed before the instrument can be recommended for use outside of the specific setting in which reliability and validity data were collected. Specifically, additional studies using samples representative of the target examinee population are necessary to provide adequate evidence of reliability. Additional validity studies with representative clinic-referred samples are necessary to explore the generalizability of initial findings reported in the CSI-4 manuals (i.e., patterns of relationships with other instruments, differences between known groups, and predictive validity of subsequent diagnoses). New validity studies also are needed to confirm the internal structure of the CSI-4 when used with the target examinee population.

SUMMARY. The CSI-4 demonstrates potential for addressing the need for an instrument to screen students suspected of having a DSM-IV disorder. Further reliability and validity evidence is necessary, however, before the CSI-4 can be recommended for use in childhood clinic settings. In addition, although it is not a primary use of the instrument, the authors have provided normative data for interpretation of individual child ratings relative to the general population. The samples used to generate these norms are not representative of the general student population. Thus, a norm-referenced approach to score interpretation is not recommended until new data are available that reflect the current student population ages 5-12.

REVIEWERS' REFERENCES

Achenbach, T. M. (1991a). *Manual for the Child Behavior Checklist/4–18 and the 1991 Profile*. Burlington, VT: University of Vermont Department of Psychiatry.

Achenbach, T. M. (1991b). *Manual for the Teacher's Report Form and 1991 Profile*. Burlington, VT: University of Vermont Department of Psychiatry.

Achenbach, T. M., McConaughy, S. H., & Howell, C. T. (1987). Child/adolescent behavioral and emotional problems: Implications of cross-informant correlations for situational specificity. *Psychological Bulletin, 101*, 213–232.

American Psychiatric Association. (1980). *Diagnostic and statistical manual of mental disorders* (3rd ed.). Washington, DC: Author.

American Psychiatric Association. (1987). *Diagnostic and statistical manual of mental disorders* (3rd ed., rev.). Washington, DC: Author.

American Psychiatric Association. (1994). *Diagnostic and statistical manual of mental disorders* (4th ed.). Washington, DC: Author.

Gadow, K. D., & Sprafkin, J. (1995). *Adolescent supplement to the Child Symptom Inventories manual*. Stony Brook, NY: Checkmate Plus.

Sprafkin, J., & Gadow, K. D. (1996). *The Early Childhood Inventories manual*. Stony Brook, NY: Checkmate Plus.

Review of the Child Symptom Inventory 4 by ROSEMARY FLANAGAN, Director of the Masters Program in School Psychology/Assistant Professor, Derner Institute of Advanced Psychological Studies, Adelphi University, Garden City, NY:

DESCRIPTION. The Child Symptom Inventory 4 (CSI-4) is a screening instrument that includes the affective, behavioral, and cognitive symptoms of childhood psychiatric disorders. The test kit contains separate Parent and Teacher checklists, a test manual, a norms manual and supplementary norms and scoring guides. The supplementary norms demonstrate the continued refinement of the inventory, as these were published subsequent to the scale. The items were based on the diagnostic criteria specified in the *Diagnostic and Statistical Manual of Mental Disorders* (4th ed.; DSM-IV; American Psychiatric Association, 1994), and should be useful in assessment planning.

The selection of disorders was based on those that are commonly seen in clinical and school settings. Among the disorders included are: Attention Deficit Hyperactivity Disorder, Oppositional Defiant Disorder, Conduct Disorder, Generalized Anxiety Disorder, Specific Phobia, Obsessive Compulsive Disorder, Posttraumatic Stress Disorder, Depressive Disorder, Tic Disorders, Schizophrenia, the Pervasive Developmental Disorders spectrum, Social Phobia, Separation Anxiety Disorder, Enuresis, and Encopresis. Respondents mark their responses on the questionnaire.

All items are rated on a 4-point scale: *never* = 0, *sometimes* = 1, *often* = 2, *very often* = 3. Scoring is available according to Symptom Counts (clinical cutoff) on a 2-point scale that collapses the four response options into two: *never* and *sometimes*, which become the "no" category, and *often* and *very often* which become the "yes" category. Symptom Severity is scored according to *T*-scores and percentile ranks, on the 4-point scale as presented. Scoring is readily accomplished by summing the ratings within each category of symptoms for both Symptom Counts and Symptom Severity and comparing to norms. A scoring guide, separate from the manual, is provided, with detailed stepwise directions for scoring, interpretation, and further assessment. The authors repeatedly state that use of the CSI-4 is not a substitute for a clinical interview and should not be used to make a diagnosis. Its use may be greatest when informants are limited in some manner (e.g., ability), when the clinician is encountering a disorder not commonly seen in his or her practice, or when comorbid diagnoses are being ruled in or out.

DEVELOPMENT. The authors developed the scale to facilitate information gathering in clinical settings from both parents and teachers, and to systematize the information exchange between the clinician and the school, which permits comparison of ratings by respondent and setting. The symptom descriptions provided in the DSM were rewritten for the parent and teacher respondents; this resulted in the items being more understandable for respondents.

As the name implies, there were several forerunners of the current instrument, beginning in 1984. Initially, the effort began as a child psychiatry checklist for several externalizing disorders that was completed by parents and teachers. Expanded inventories were then developed according to the current versions of the DSM, which resulted in two inventories. This was followed by the current version of the inventory, corresponding with the latest revision of the DSM (American Psychiatric Association, 1994). Similar inventories have also been developed for adolescents and young children.

TECHNICAL. Numerous studies examining the psychometric properties of the CSI-4 are reported in the manual and norms supplement. The norm sample for the Parent Checklist was composed of 129 girls and 134 boys aged 5–12 years. The sample was drawn from seven states, and is consequently limited in terms of racial-ethnic diversity. Composition of the sample was 86% White, 10% Black, 3% Hispanic, and 1% Other. Children placed in special education as well as those with neurologically based or chronic medical conditions were excluded from the sample. The norm sample for the Teacher Checklist was larger, being composed of 662 boys and 661 girls, but was even less diverse in terms of the number of states sampled and its racial-ethnic composition. An additional clinic sample was composed of 441 boys and 149 girls referred to a university-based outpatient clinic; over 90% of these youngsters were also rated by their teachers, and were the source of the majority of reliability and validity data. The racial-ethnic distribution of the outpatient clinic sample was 85.4% White, 8.8% Black, 4.1% Hispanic, and 1.7% Other. The most common diagnoses were Attention Deficit Hyperactivity Disorder (ADHD) and Oppositional Defiant Disorder; anxiety and mood disorders were also prevalent, either as the sole problem or comorbid with another disorder. Frequency data for different samples and different raters are provided in the manual by response, allowing the test user to make his/her own evaluation as to the representativeness of the sample.

A study of test-retest reliability of the Parent Checklist used the clinic sample at a 6-week interval. The results indicate correlations for the Symptom count ranging generally from .02 to .72, with 9 of 11 values of at least .50. These values for the Symptom Severity Scores ranged from .37 to .82, with only one value below .50. Noteworthy is that the highest values were obtained for ratings of externalizing disorders, such as ADHD. Parallel data for the Teacher Checklist were obtained within the context of a medication trial, and are, therefore, not comparable. Other correlations among scales on both the Parent and Teacher Checklists are expectable, given comorbidity rates (e.g., Brady & Kendall, 1992); for example, Generalized Anxiety Disorder Scores correlate with those for Depressive Disorder.

Prevalence data, taken to be indicative of predictive validity, are reported according to gender for the Parent and Teacher Checklists. Similar to other multiple rater assessments (e.g., Reynolds & Kamphaus, 1992), parent and teacher ratings do not always agree. The data suggestive of clinical utility are stronger for the Teacher Checklist, in that more categories are distinguished at a statistically significant level; this may reflect the differences in the samples according to size and composition. More importantly, data presented in the manual indicate that the accuracy of diagnosis increases when both parent and teacher data are considered in view of data-based psychiatric diagnoses (multiple methods and multiple raters), as this process minimizes both false positives and false negatives. For the clinic-referred sample, the false positives generally met the criteria for *some* DSM diagnosis, suggesting that the referral was appropriate in the first place. Important is the possible utility of the CSI-4 in schools with the population referred for psychoeducational evaluations in assisting in the identification of comorbid psychiatric diagnoses. Finally, data and procedures are outlined in the manual indicating the manner in which items were refined to increase specificity and sensitivity, which was more problematic for internalizing disorders.

COMMENTARY. Application in practice is discussed. Regardless of the setting in which the instrument is used, it is important to note that it is a screening device and it should not be used as the sole determinant of a DSM diagnosis. The authors state this important point repeatedly. By using the criterion scores for Symptom Sensitivity and Symptom Specificity for both the parent and teacher forms, and by considering the rule-outs (which are listed on the form) of comorbid problems, the need for further assessment can be readily determined. In addition, it is explained in the manual how to use the specificity and sensitivity indices together to limit the number of either false positives or false negatives. Given the time constraints imposed by managed care and the mandated time lines under which school psychologists must complete their work, such a tool is valuable, as most current tools available are not keyed to the DSM criteria. To the credit of the authors, sections of the manual describe the application of the CSI-4 to each of the DSM diagnostic categories screened for by the instrument.

SUMMARY. Overall, the CSI-4 is a promising tool that is novel. Limitations include the sampling used to provide reliability and validity data, as the samples do not approximate census tract data, although sampling was conducted in various locales. An additional limitation is the need for frequent updates in order to keep pace with anticipated revisions of the DSM. Should individuals become dedicated test users, it is likely that there will be a time period during which the data obtained will be of limited diagnostic useful-

ness, although the data should remain clinically useful. Nevertheless, the inventories should have a place in practice and in research. Studies are needed to establish the research utility of the inventories, which may be of considerable potential. The authors do not discuss this use of their instrument in the manual.

REVIEWER'S REFERENCES

American Psychiatric Association. (1994). *Diagnostic and statistical manual of mental disorders* (4th ed.). Washington, DC: Author.
Brady, E. U., & Kendall, P. C. (1992). Comorbidity of anxiety and depression in children and adolescents. *Psychological Bulletin, 111,* 244–255.
Reynolds, C. R., & Kamphaus, R. W. (1992). *Manual for the Behavior Assessment System for Children.* Circle Pines, MN: American Guidance Service.

[48]

Children's Interview for Psychiatric Syndromes.

Purpose: Deisgned to identify "symptoms of 20 common Axis I psychiatric disorders in children and adolescents."

Population: Ages 6–18.

Publication Date: 1999.

Acronym: ChIPS.

Scores, 20: Attention-Deficit/Hyperactivity Disorder, Oppositional Defiant Disorder, Conduct Disorder, Substance Abuse, Specific Phobia, Social Phobia, Separation Anxiety Disorder, Generalized Anxiety Disorder, Obsessive-Compulsive Disorder, Acute Stress Disorder, Posttraumatic Stress Disorder, Anorexia, Bulimia, Depressive Episode, Dysthymic Disorder, Manic Episode, Hypomanic Episode, Enuresis, Encopresis, Schizophrenia/Psychosis.

Administration: Individual.

Price Data, 2002: $44.95 per interview administration booklet (1999, 32 pages).

Time: Administration time not reported.

Authors: Marijo Teare Rooney, Mary A. Fristad, Elizabeth B. Weller, and Ronald A. Weller.

Publisher: American Psychiatric Publishing, Inc.

Review of the Children's Interview for Psychiatric Syndromes by JANET F. CARLSON, Professor and Department Head, Department of General Academics, Texas A&M University at Galveston, Galveston, TX:

DESCRIPTION. The Children's Interview for Psychiatric Syndromes (ChIPS) is a recently revised, highly structured interview designed to screen for symptoms of 20 DSM-IV Axis I disorders in children and adolescents from 6 to 18 years of age. It is intended to provide an indication of psychiatric diagnosis, per DSM-IV taxonomy (American Psychiatric Association, 1994). The parent version (P-ChIPS) is identical in content to the ChIPS, except that the phrasing of questions has been modified for third-party reporting. Although the ChIPS is strongly related to the DSM-IV, the test authors advise potential users that it is a screening instrument and, as such, it will overidentify potential problem areas. It is intended to be used in conjunction with other information that can provide an integrated, clinically sound picture of the individual interviewee.

Questions on the ChIPS are close-ended and mirror very closely specific clinical symptoms presented in the DSM-IV. Almost all questions require a simple "yes" or "no" answer. Responses must be evaluated continuously in order to follow the correct question sequence and minimize the amount of time required to complete the interview. The earliest portion of the interview gathers general and background information about the child as well as his or her understanding of the nature of his or her difficulties. The "branching" format used in the symptom review portion of the interview provides for particular responses to be followed by related questions, whereas other responses allow the interviewer to skip ahead to another section of the interview. The closing section of the interview focuses on other stressors that the child may be experiencing. Total responses are evaluated in terms of whether the respondent has: (a) demonstrated symptoms associated with any of the 20 specific diagnoses covered by the ChIPS, (b) met the DSM-IV diagnostic criteria for any diagnosis (or diagnoses), and (c) met the symptom duration specifications to warrant a DSM-IV diagnosis on Axis I.

To administer the ChIPS, it appears that at least the spiral-bound interview book and the ChIPS scoring form are needed. An "optional" ChIPS report form also is available. The test authors suggest that the report form "may be used to easily document endorsements made by a child or parent on the ChIPS or P-ChIPS" (manual, p. 16), a claim that appears somewhat contradictory to an earlier declaration (manual, p. 13) about "ample space on the scoring form to record the child's responses." Guidelines for administration are provided in the ChIPS manual. The final chapter of the manual presents a five-step training procedure, through which professionals and paraprofessionals may be trained to administer the ChIPS. The test authors suggest that a "clinician" should retain oversight of training processes. Total administration time varies depending largely on

the characteristics of the test taker with regard to how many of the 303 questions contained on the interview actually will be administered. For clinical samples, administration time tends to run about 45 minutes, according to the test manual.

DEVELOPMENT. The current version of the ChIPS has evolved since 1985, when the initial version was developed following a review of existing structured diagnostic interviews for children and adolescents. Some of the questions derived from these sources served as the basis for modified questions to be developed, although the test manual states that most questions were newly written by the test authors. The test authors report that they attended to word selection, question length, and comprehensibility when developing potential questions. However, no evidence is cited in the test manual to corroborate that the reading level is appropriate for the entire age range targeted. In several instances, wording of questions appears to exceed the comprehension abilities of children from the youngest age groups. In addition, the group of children used to check comprehensibility was quite small and nonrepresentative, consisting of 23 psychiatrically hospitalized children ranging in age from 6 to 11 years.

Since its inception, the ChIPS has been revised to reflect modifications in nosology and diagnostic criteria that have accompanied each DSM revision. The current version of the ChIPS aligns with DSM-IV criteria. During the revision process, "[o]ld questions were kept whenever possible and realigned to fit the new disorders" (manual, p. 11). The term, *realigned*, is not explained in the test manual.

TECHNICAL. Internal consistency reliability and test-retest reliability were not assessed. Only interrater reliability was evaluated, with results of these comparisons briefly noted in the test manual. Near the end of training, trainees scored videotaped interviews that had been conducted and scored by an experienced interviewer. When trainees began interviewing children, the trainer observed and scored an unspecified number of interviews conducted by the trainee. Interrater reliabilities were computed from these data and are reported as .90 or better for individual questions and the diagnoses. An unspecified number of random reliability checks reportedly occurred occasionally as well, but these were not planned or executed systematically. Nonetheless, the test authors state that these reliability coefficients were at least .90 as well.

The test authors note that interpretation of ChIPS data must be completed by a qualified clinician, although administration and scoring may be accomplished by technicians and other personnel with proper training. The chapter on interpretation consists of seven case reports, which present narrative write-ups only, as no accompanying scoring or report forms are reproduced. Three of the case reports have little value as they simply present a final report and have no "Comment" section. Without access to any data, there is little gain from reading these three case reports. The commentary sections in the remaining four cases may help clinicians understand how to use the ChiPS as a screening instrument, and illustrate how clinical judgment is not circumvented by its use.

The test authors note that validation studies with the ChIPS "have been conducted only in English-speaking populations, and the demographic distribution of the study samples was largely Caucasian" (manual, p. 2). Thus, the validity evidence for the ChIPS has not been gathered for use with children from ethnically or linguistically diverse backgrounds. Apart from age ranges used, the test manual presents no further demographic information about participants in the validation studies.

The test manual reports results from a series of five studies to support validity. Two of the studies appear to focus on the current DSM-IV version of the ChIPS, one appears to concern either the current or just-previous P-ChIPS, and the other two use older versions of the ChIPS and other structured interviews (e.g., the DSM-III-R-Revised Diagnostic Interview for Children and Adolescents by Reich & Welner, 1988) to assess the extent of diagnostic agreement. None of the clinical samples used children from the entire age range for which the ChIPS claims to be valid, with the widest age range sampled being from 6 to 18 years. Consistently, sample sizes were small, comprising groups of 36, 40, 42, 47, and 71. It appears that clinician-derived diagnoses also were available for some studies and typically were used to derive standard or rare kappa coefficients and percent agreements. Given the extremely low base rates observed in the groups used in the validation studies, percent agreement data are likely to be misleading. All five validation studies have a reference date of 1998, so it is not clear from the information provided in the test manual exactly when various data were collected.

Apart from agreement data described above, no other forms of validity are expressly addressed in the test manual. For example, the extent to which items co-vary with their respective syndrome could be used to provide evidence of content validity. More importantly for an instrument of this type, the ability of the ChIPS to discriminate a clinical sample from a nonclinical one should be readily demonstrable.

COMMENTARY. The ChIPS appears to be used most appropriately in clinical settings where diagnosis and documentation are central concerns. Perhaps one day the conceptual clarity of how to classify disorders will improve to such an extent that continual revisions to DSM taxonomy no longer will be needed. Until then, structured interviews that link to DSM criteria are subject to the same criticisms levied at the current edition of DSM regarding diagnostic validity. In situations where there is a need for understanding the nature of a child's difficulties or appreciating the various types of problems a given child may experience, the ChIPS would be of little use because of its heavy diagnostic emphasis.

In using positive wording, such that an affirmative response denotes pathology, the ChIPS may promote faking or malingering on the part of the interviewee to a greater extent than is desirable. Indeed, it may be preferable to use positive wording consistently in an effort to avoid confusing respondents, but it also would behoove the test authors to address the issue of faking in a more forthright manner than they do in the current test manual. Prospective users should be apprised of these possibilities, beyond the dismissive remark on page 2 of the test manual that "the information obtained is only as reliable as the informant from whom it comes." Given that the ChIPS has no "validity scales," it would be helpful to have explicit guidelines about how to detect or when to suspect that information obtained may be inaccurate.

Much of the information provided in the test manual is vague or not sufficiently specific to permit potential users to evaluate its appropriateness for use in a given setting. Some claims made in the test manual are not supported adequately by evidence. For example, the suggestion on page 2 of the test manual that a "more detailed discussion" of inaccurate self-reporting occurs in the chapter on interpretation appears unfounded. None of the case reports presented in the chapter on interpretation mention questionable veracity of the self-report. As another example, the test authors suggest more than once that the ChIPS requires shorter administration times than comparable instruments. In making these claims, however, they sometimes use a nontraditional level of statistical significance and fail to mention that some differences do not amount to much from a pragmatic standpoint. For instance, a statistically significant, but practically meaningless, difference was observed for mean administration times of 21.3 minutes and 24.3 minutes ($p<.02$). Similarly, 48.9 minutes emerged as shorter than 53.5 minutes ($p<.08$).

SUMMARY. The ChIPS is a relatively recently revised instrument, intended to be used and integrated with other information, to document symptom endorsements and suggest diagnoses among children and adolescents. Its applicability is restricted to clinical diagnostic purposes and, perhaps, related research. The exclusive relationship between the ChIPS and the taxonomic system of DSM-IV makes it more viable in clinical than in school or other applied settings. Sparse psychometric evidence, vague indicators of test development procedures, and lack of validation for use with individuals with any measure of demographic diversity greatly limit its appeal. The Adolescent Psychopathology Scale—Short Form (APS-SF; 11) offers a more practical, brief, and psychometrically sound method to gain information similar to that sought by the ChIPS.

REVIEWER'S REFERENCE

American Psychiatric Association. (1994). *Diagnostic and statistical manual of mental disorders* (4ᵗʰ ed.). Washington, DC: Author.

Review of the Children's Interview for Psychiatric Syndromes by R. JOEL FARRELL II, Associate Professor of Marriage and Family, Faulkner University, Montgomery, AL:

DESCRIPTION. The Children's Interview for Psychiatric Syndromes (ChIPS) is a highly structured diagnostic interview. The ChIPS utilizes a self-report format to screen for the presence of the 20 most common childhood psychiatric disorders based upon the DSM-IV's diagnostic criteria. The 20 disorders are scored in 21 categories with schizophrenia and psychosis being separated on the scoring form/profile sheet. The 21 categories evaluated for diagnosis are Attention-Deficit/Hyperactivity Disorder (ADHD), Oppositional Defiant Disorder (ODD), Conduct Disorder (CD), Substance Abuse (SUBAB), Specific Phobia (PHO), Social Phobia (SOCPHO), Separation Anxiety Disorder (SEPANX), Generalized Anxiety Disorder (GENANX), Obsessive-Compulsive Disorder (OCD), Acute Stress Disorder (ASD), Posttraumatic Stress Disorder (PTSD), Anorexia (ANO), Bulimia (BUL), Depressive Episode (DEP), Dysthymic Disorder (DYS), Manic Episode (MAN), Hypomanic Episode (HYPOMAN), Enuresis (ENU), Encopresis (ENC), Schizophrenia (SCZ), and Psychosis (PSY). The interview also contains items that screen for common psychosocial stressors including child abuse and neglect.

The ChIPS is designed for use in any setting—clinical, educational, or research—where a psychiatric diagnosis is desired. The ChIPS can be administered by trained lay interviewers. The administration manual for the ChIPS contains the training procedure to be followed in preparing mental health professionals and paraprofessionals. The training, under the guidance of a competent clinician, consists of a working knowledge of childhood psychopathology, interviewing procedures, and the 20 disorders addressed by the ChIPS. The recommended training process includes observation of interviews and in vivo supervised practice.

The ChIPS is designed for administration to children ages 6 to 18. Because the interview requires self-report, the interviewee must have adequate receptive and expressive language abilities. Thus, the interview is not recommended for administration to psychologically/medically incapacitated, mentally retarded, or reticent individuals. The validation and reliability studies were conducted in English with a largely Caucasian population; thus, users must be sensitive to cultural, ethnic, and language influences when interpreting results.

The interview is divided into 21 sections—1 per disorder and 1 for psychosocial stressors. The questions utilize a hierarchical branching format where the first few items in the section screen for the presence of the disorder. If the interviewee provides a positive response, then the remaining questions for the disorder are used. If the interviewee provides a negative response, then the interviewer may move on to the next disorder. At the conclusion of all the questions for a disorder, the interviewer inquires about symptom onset, duration, and impairment. A scoring form and an optional report form are provided to document the child's responses to the interview items.

The administration manual does not list specific time parameters for the interview. The interviewer is instructed to monitor the child's focus on the questions. If the child is not focused, then brief—5 to 10 minutes—breaks may be required. The interview may also be administered in separate sessions on the same day or consecutive days. However, any extended time lapse may effect the results because of a change in symptomology. In the five studies conducted by the developers, the average administration time was 49 minutes for inpatients, 36 minutes for outpatients, and 21 minutes for community samples. In general, the child's age, cognitive functioning, verbal ability, and symptom complexity will determine the speed and duration of the interview.

DEVELOPMENT. The ChIPS is the first published edition (copyright, 1999) of an instrument that has been under development since 1985. The developers began ChIPS as a new diagnostic interview rather than a modification or adaptation of preexisting interviews. The goal was to create a brief, easy to administer interview that utilized the criteria of the DSM. The developers selected the structured interview format as a means to increase the reliability of the diagnostic assessment process.

The interview began development under the DSM-III and was adjusted for the DSM-III-R and DSM-IV. The interview is based upon the fields of psychodiagnostics and psychopathology. The interview uses the theoretical frame of the medical model applied to psychodiagnostics. The interview uses a hierarchical decision-making model based upon the DMS-IV criteria for diagnosis.

The ChIPS initially began development in four phases, but extended to six phases as a result of the DSM revisions. The first phase of development was a review of the existing diagnostic interviews for childhood populations. The developers reviewed the Schedule for Affective Disorders and Schizophrenia for School-Aged Children (Kiddie-SADS), the Interview for Children (ISC), the Children's Assessment Schedule (CAS), the Diagnostic Interview for Children and Adolescents (DICA), and the Diagnostic Interview Schedule for Children (DISC). The second phase of development was the creation of a question pool. Al-though some questions from the review phase were modified, most questions were newly written based on appropriate word selection, sentence length, and comprehensibility. The third phase established the format of the interview. The syndromes order of presentation was based on epidemiology estimates with the most common disorder listed first. The questions for each section were listed in a progression from global to specific criteria. The fourth phase was the completion of reliability and validity studies. Phases 5 and 6 were the revision of the interview for the DSM-III-R and DSM-IV. These phases also required conducting further reliability and validity studies. During Phase 5, a parent version of the ChIPS was developed. The parent version is identical to the ChIPS except the text of the questions was changed to third person.

TECHNICAL. The manual contains adequate information regarding research and evaluation of the ChIPS. A discussion and summary tables for each study conducted are provided. Because the ChIPS is not a normative instrument, but a criterion-based diagnostic instrument, the evaluation process focused on interrater reliability, kappa coefficient, and concordance of diagnosis, sensitivity, and specificity. The interview was evaluated in comparison to the DICA, DICA-R-C, and actual clinical diagnoses. A posttraining interrater reliability coefficient of .90 was obtained and maintained throughout the research process. A significant level of agreement ($p < .05$) was found between the ChIPS and the two versions of DICA across three nonoverlapping population groups—inpatient, outpatient, and community-based. The overall technical performance of the ChIPS was equal to or greater than the DICA and DICA-R-C. The ChIPS also performed adequately in comparison to actual clinical diagnosis with the main area of disagreement being the greater specificity of the ChIPS.

COMMENTARY. The ChIPS can serve as a valuable diagnostic tool in a variety of settings. This instrument is based on theory, is technically adequate, and is time efficient. The revisions of the DSM have forced the developers to revise and re-evaluate the interview twice. Overall, this is a well-developed instrument for diagnostic purposes.

However, the interview does have two areas of concern. As previously mentioned, the instrument has not been evaluated for use with different cultural, ethnic, or language groups. Some potential users of the ChIPS may work with population groups whose culture, ethnicity or language does not fit this instrument. The second area of concern is the use of trained lay interviewers. Although a training program is outlined for mental health professionals and paraprofessionals, the manual does not provide enough specificity for the qualifications of the paraprofessionals. The user can deduce from the reported research studies that graduate students, advanced undergraduate honor students, medical students, and other medical personnel (only staff nurses and child psychiatrists are identified) are qualified to be trained. The concern is that in many mental health settings, individuals with minimal education and training are considered paraprofessionals and could be trained to administer this interview. Although, this may be ethically questionable, the manual does not explicitly prohibit this application.

SUMMARY. The ChIPS provides accurate diagnosis according to DSM-IV criteria in a convenient, brief, and efficient format. When used as designed, the ChIPS is effective as an independent measure of psychopathology. The ChIPS can be utilized with clinical populations (inpatient and outpatient) and community populations. The ChIPS can serve as a valuable tool for research or training involving diagnosis. Overall, the ChIPS is a quality instrument that is comparable to other childhood diagnostic interviews, such as the Schedule for Affective Disorders and Schizophrenia for School-Aged Children (Kiddie-SADS), the Interview for Children (ISC), the Children's Assessment Schedule (CAS), the Diagnostic Interview for Children and Adolescents (DICA), and the Diagnostic Interview Schedule for Children (DISC).

[49]
Children's Inventory of Anger.

Purpose: Designed "to measure aspects of a youngster's experience of anger."
Population: Ages 6–16.
Publication Date: 2000.
Acronym: ChIA.
Scores, 5: Frustration, Physical Aggression, Peer Relationship, Authority Relations, Total.
Administration: Group or individual.
Price Data, 2002: $82.50 per kit including 25 AutoScore' answer forms, manual (51 pages), 2-use disk for on-site computer scoring, and 2 PC answer sheets; $32.50 per 25 AutoScore' answer forms; $45 per manual; $85 per 25-uses scoring disk (PC with Microsoft Windows); $15 per 100 PC answer sheets.
Time: (10–15) minutes.
Comments: Self-report inventory.
Authors: W. Michael Nelson III and A. J. Finch, Jr.
Publisher: Western Psychological Services.

Review of the Children's Inventory of Anger by THERESA VOLPE-JOHNSTONE, *Clinical and School Psychologist, Pleasanton, CA:*

DESCRIPTION. The Children's Inventory of Anger (ChIA) is a 39-item, self-report measure. It is designed to evaluate the subjective intensity of anger experienced in response to a variety of potential anger-arousing situations and is modeled after the initial Children's Inventory of Anger (CIA; 1978) and the Novaco Anger Inventory (NAI; Novaco, 1975). It is targeted to assess children and adolescents ages 6 through 16. A third-grade reading level (Flesch-Kincaid readability level) is recommended but the test can be read to any examinee with reading difficulties. The ChIA items are responded to on a 4-point Likert scale that is coupled with representative pictures that facilitate the child's awareness of his or her experience of anger. The resultant profile yields T scores and percentile ranks for a Total Score and the subareas of Frustration, Physical Aggression, Peer Relationships, and Authority Relations. An Inconsistent Responding Index (INC) is the validity check that must be examined before interpretation and assumes specific item pairs should be similarly rated. When they are not, they are considered to be inconsistent and the profile would not be valid.

The ChIA can be used as a screening test to help determine a child's needs or as a repeated measure to denote treatment progress/outcome. It is not a diagnostic tool but should be used in conjunction with other appropriate measures and clinical judgement.

The ChIA can be administered through many agencies including schools, hospitals, clinics, or theological enterprises. However, only trained personnel can interpret the results. Administration time is approximately 10 to 15 minutes. It can be given in individual or group format, and requires examinees to rate their subjective anger in situations presented in statement format. The child's age must be known or appropriate scores cannot be obtained.

There are two forms of scoring, hand score (the manual refers to an AutoScore form) and computerized scoring. The computer score program is PC-based and responses can be input by the examinee at the time of administration or by the examiner at a later date from a specialized answer sheet. A two-page scoring profile is generated giving T-scores and percentiles.

DEVELOPMENT. The ChIA is modeled after the Novaco Anger Inventory (NAI; Novaco, 1975) and is a redevelopment of the Children's Inventory of Anger (CIA). Both the CIA and the ChIA are an attempt to measure the construct of anger in children and were developed "by generating a range of problem situations that were thought to evoke angry responses in children and adolescents" (manual, p. 25). These provoking situations are placed in statement format with Likert-type choices of increasing intensity paired with pictorial representations. The items for the ChIA were chosen from the CIA's 71-item format. A decision to keep an item was dependent upon initial factor analytic studies demonstrating its contribution to a distinct factor forming the subscales. If an item was kept, it was evaluated for its readability. Initial studies used responses of children without diagnosed disabilities and those with emotional disturbance. Four subscales were developed for the ChIA by what is described as rational inspection of item groupings. Additional factor analytic studies have also been conducted that found the four groupings to account for 45% of the variance in item responses. The final factor structure did not vary by gender or age-based groupings. Pairs of items that were highly correlated contributed to the Inconsistent Responding Index (INC). In the standardization sample, it was found to be unusual if more than five item pairs differed by more than 1 point on the INC. When compared to randomly generated responses, the probability of random responses rose incrementally with each differing pair above five.

TECHNICAL. The standardization sample included 1,604 children, ages 6 through 16, drawn from urban and suburban public school settings. Specific locations were not indicated but demographic data indicate four regions: south, north, west, and northeast. Ethnic background of the subjects was fairly consistent with U.S. population demographics but with a slightly higher socioeconomic level. Reliability was investigated by internal consistency and test-retest methods. The authors examined reliability for the entire standardization sample and for children 6 and 7 years of age separately. Their rationale was determined by the notion of "young children [being] notoriously unreliable reporters" (manual, p. 33). The alpha coefficient was .95 for the total sample and the young group and considered excellent. Test-retest correlations (1-week interval) were adequate for both groups with the entire sample obtaining a correlation of .75 and the younger children obtaining a correlation of .66.

Reliability studies were conducted on the 1978 CIA with clinical and nonclinical samples. It was determined by the authors that because the ChIA items are a subset of the 1978 CIA, the dated research of the CIA applies to the ChIA. All studies referenced demonstrated adequate reliability but two studies stood out. In one study, when the ChIA was used as a repeated measure for children 7 to 12 years of age in a public school setting every 2 weeks for four administrations, the Total score declined significantly. It would be expected that no change should occur as these children were all assumed to be "anger-healthy" and were not in a treatment model. Second, when administered to emotionally disturbed children at Day 3 and 30 following admission to inpatient services, split-half correlation coefficients for first-second half reliability and for odd-even reliability were .93 and .96, respectively. Test-retest was .49 suggesting the respondents answered differently across occasions. To this reviewer, these relationships would demonstrate efficacious treatment.

Individual test items were designed to be specific to three dimensions of anger: setting, person, and external events. Factor analytic studies verified subscale discrimination, and content validity was further examined by receiving feedback from child psychologists working with children directly and with the 1978 CIA for readability and content. A range of situations for anger arousal, the type of situation likely to arouse that anger, and the magnitude of proneness to provocation within those settings was thus elucidated.

Construct validity evidence is directed at measuring how well the instrument assesses the trait it is meant to examine. For the ChIA, anger in particular (Total score) and specific facets (sub-areas) of anger are hypothesized constructs. One method of evaluating construct validity is by assessing convergent and divergent validity using a multitrait-multimethod matrix and factor analysis.

The authors utilized a concurrent validity strategy by examining correlations with other measures of anger and aggression with the ChIA and previously, a multimethod assessment utilizing a variety of self-report and significant other rating scales with the CIA. Results indicated that anger as measured was more closely related to depression and anxiety than to aggressive tendencies. These findings compromise the construct to the degree that anger is associated with aggression. The authors astutely point out, however, that this association is a mistaken tendency. Based on the studies provided, this reviewer agrees with this conclusion. Correlations with the ChIA and a variety of rating scales found weak relationships between the experience of anger and the expression of aggression and negligible correlations between the ChIA and self-concept measures. The CIA did not significantly correlate with peer ratings of anger or teacher ratings of anger but consistently and significantly correlated with measures of depression and anxiety.

The ability of the ChIA to discriminate between clinical and nonclinical children was assessed. Results indicated that the ChIA's ability to discriminate among samples was gender specific. Boys in correction centers or residential homes had scores that were significantly higher than girls in similar situations and from the standardization group as a whole. Effect sizes were large ranging from .71 to .93 for the scales and Total score, meaning that the groups differed by 7 to 9 T-score units. The evidence from the validity studies does not support a strong construct of anger as operationally defined. However, it does appear to support a construct of anger relative to an individual's state of subjective well-being. This is probably why the test-retest of normal elementary school children demonstrated significant declines in anger score, although research is needed in this area.

COMMENTARY. The strengths of the ChIA are in its brevity, its ease of administration, and its computer scoring. It is also a noble approach to a difficult construct that by nature is highly variable. Individual test items quickly offer a clinician valuable information with which to begin to formulate hypotheses. It can be used effectively as a repeated measure to document change and progress within a therapeutic environment. The pictorial format and flexibility in administration are assets. The ChIA's weaknesses include the elusiveness of the construct of anger itself. The validity studies did not strongly correlate subjective anger and overt behavior. Further research is needed, particularly on the internal expression of anger, as the external expression of anger and the ChIA have low correlations. Another drawback of the ChIA is that the AutoScore system can be confusing.

SUMMARY. The ChIA is a tool that can be useful in treatment settings for identifying hypothesized factors of anger along with other measures to assure convergent validity. It is easy to administer, fairly easy to score, and the item composition has good content validity. Further research is needed in defining anger.

REVIEWER'S REFERENCE

Novaco, R. W. (1975). *Anger control: The development and education of an experimental treatment.* Lexington, MA: Lexington.

Review of the Children's Inventory of Anger by DELORES D. WALCOTT, *Associate Professor, Western Michigan University, University Counseling and Testing Center, Kalamazoo, MI:*

DESCRIPTION. The Children's Inventory of Anger (ChIA) is a 39-item, self-report inventory that can be administered to either an individual or a group. The ChIA was designed to identify a range of anger provocations, to identify individuals whom a child might view as a provocateur of his or her aggressive behavior, and to pinpoint events that evoke the anger response for a given child. Pictorial representation of a 4-point Likert-type response scale was employed; the authors' previous research had shown that impulsive/aggressive children are more likely to think in pictures than in words. The test was designed to be self-administered by individuals with at least a third grade reading level. A reading ease index was employed, placing the ChIA in the Very Easy range. There are no time limits but the inventory typically requires 15 minutes. The instrument yields a Total Score; an Inconsistent Responding Validity Index (INC); and four subscale scores: Frustration (FRUST), Physical Aggression (PHYS), Peer Relationships (PEER), and Authority Relations (AUTH). The child completes the inventory by indicating the degree of anger he or she would experience if the incident described by the item happened. The choices on the scale represent increasing intensities of anger (I don't care, That bothers me, I'm really angry, and I can't stand that).

The ChIA is easily administered and cost-effective, which makes it an attractive choice. The

ChIA can be scored either by computer or by hand. There are three scoring options: the ChIA AutoScore for hand scoring, the on-screen PC-based scoring, and the ChIA PC Answer Sheet in which the responses can be entered into the computer and then scored. The scoring program for the PC-based scoring includes a user guide that contains hardware and software requirements. The program is equipped with online help and provides step-by-step instructions. The ChIA computer program allows you to save a file for the printing of an unlimited number of reports. Also the ChIA results from a number of clients can be saved to a single file to be used for conducting group statistical analyses.

DEVELOPMENT. The Children's Inventory of Anger (ChIA) was developed specifically to assess the subjective feelings of anger in children. A range of problem situations that evoke anger responses in children and adolescents make up the instrument. The original Children's Inventory of Anger (CIA) consisted of 71 items, describing provocative incidents indicating the degree of anger one would experience if the incident described actually happened. One of the primary drawbacks of the original CIA was its length, which was problematic with a young child with emotional or behavior problems. The wordings of some of the items were also awkward. In developing the current version of the ChIA, the original 71 items were revalidated for readability and distinct factors, which form the four subscales of the test. Some of the items retained from the original CIA were reworded to eliminate passive constructions and to shorten sentences. The readability of the item set was reduced from a fourth-grade level to a third-grade level.

TECHNICAL. The ChIA standardization sample consisted of 1,604 children (796 males and 785 females) ages 6 through 16. The sample was drawn primarily from public school settings and a few private schools across the country. They were selected from both urban and rural areas. According to the manual, the sample represented a cross section of socioeconomic and ethnic diverse groups, who were in Grades 4 through 7. Socioeconomic status was based on head of household's level of education. Average ChIA's T-scores for males and females revealed that all but one of the scores were significantly different, with girls obtaining lower scores than boys.

Sample subgrouping of children with Native American, Asian, and Other ethnic background were too small to provide useful information. When the effects of age and race were taken into account with Blacks, Hispanics, and Whites, none of the T-scores represented either clinical or statistically significant difference from the T-scores obtained by full sample size. Average scores for younger and other children varied considerably; therefore, it was decided to stratify the standardization sample into three combined age groups. The reliability of ChIA scores was examined on the entire standardization sample and separately for children 6 and 7 years old, because younger children are considered unreliable reporters. The alpha coefficient for ChIA Total score is .98 for both groups. Subscale alpha coefficient ranged from .85 to .86 for the full sample and from .85 to .87 for the younger children. Test and retest estimates for ChIA for a sample of 87 children age 6–11 with one-week interval yield a correlation of .75 for the entire sample. Estimates for 24 children who were 6–7 years old revealed a correlation of .66, for subscales test-retest correlations ranged from .65 to .75 for the full sample and .48 to .75 for the younger sample.

The manual reported on two forms of validity studies: discriminant and concurrent. Each type provided information on how well the ChIA measures the construct of interest. The ChIA was cross validated against other self-reports: the Attitude Towards Gun and Violence Questionnaire (AGVQ), the Aggression Questionnaire, Novaco Anger Scale and Provocation Inventory, and Piers-Harris Children's Self-Concept Scale. The 362 children who completed the ChIA and the AGVQ revealed a weak correlation. The highest correlation was between ChIA Frustration Score and the AGVQ's Aggressive Response Score. The correlation between the ChIA and Aggression Questionnaire (AQ) was moderate (.44). The correlation between the ChIA and Novaco Anger Scale and Provocation Inventory ranged from weak to moderate. The correlation between ChIA and the Piers-Harris Children's Self-Concept Scale was negligible. To determine the ChIA discriminate validity, the ChIA's ability to identify children in correctional and clinical settings was evaluated. Children in correctional settings were found to have higher ChIA scores than those in the standardization sample.

COMMENTARY. The manual is impressive. I found it to be well organized and complete. The manual is divided into Part I and Part II. Part I covers administration scoring and interpretation and Part II contains the technical components. The entire manual contains enough information for a qualified user or reviewer of a test to evaluate the appropriateness and technical adequacy of the test. There is a separate section at the end of the manual that covers computerized services for the ChIA. User qualifications, administration, and scoring are clearly described in the manual. The reviewer was equally impressed with the scoring form. The hand-scoring form contains scoring aids that were designed to make scoring rapid, while eliminating the potential for key error. Responses are transferred through to underlying pages where the administrator can follow steps for scoring. If the client fails to press hard and/or if the examinee did not indicate a response for a particular item, the examiner can utilize a median response value system based on age. In the manual there is a large body of research literature attesting to the validity of the original CIA test in a variety of contexts. However, additional research attesting to the validity of the current ChIA is warranted.

SUMMARY. The ChIA is an excellent test for assessing feelings of anger in children. However, it is a known fact that self-reporting is vulnerable to underreporting, inaccurate reporting, and denial. This is particularly true with younger children. Therefore, as with most self-reporting inventories, the ChIA should be used in conjunction with other sources to insure a comprehensive assessment. This is true with most self-reporting measures. The data reviewed in the manual demonstrated the reliability and validity properties of the ChIA. The discriminative ability of the ChIA in differentiating children in correctional and clinical settings was reported. Future studies on the ChIA and/or continued use of the ChIA should afford the developers the opportunity to check for group differences with larger samples and to investigate whether or not these differences indicate test bias.

[50]

Children's Inventory of Self-Esteem, Second Edition.

Purpose: "Provides ... a quick way to assess the relative strength of a child's self-worth."

Population: Ages 5–12.
Publication Dates: 1987–2001.
Acronym: CISE.
Scores, 7: 4 components of self-esteem: Belonging (B), Purpose (P), Control (C), Self (S); Total (T); 2 favored coping styles: Defensive (TD), Aggressive (TA).
Administration: Group.
Price Data, 2001: $99 per an individual lifetime license for individuals, including examiner's manual (2001, 24 pages), CISE for girls, CISE for boys, answer form, Exploring Your Child's Self-Esteem form, Your Child's Sense of Self form, Your Child's Sense of Purpose form, Your Child's Sense of Control form, Your Child's Sense of Belonging form (all forms personalized with unlimited copying privileges); $125 per school or agency lifetime license; $110 per lifetime license for each school when purchased by school district (minimum 2 schools); $4.95 shipping/handling fee.
Time: (10) minutes.
Comments: 64-item behavior rating scale completed by parents and teachers of child; provides strategies for helping improve self-esteem.
Author: Richard A. Campbell.
Publisher: Brougham Press.
Cross References: For reviews by Kathy E. Green and Nicholas A. Vacc of a previous edition, see 12:78.

Review of the Children's Inventory of Self-Esteem, Second Edition by R. JOEL FARRELL II, Associate Professor of Marriage and Family, Faulkner University, Montgomery, AL:

DESCRIPTION. The Children's Inventory of Self-Esteem (CISE) is a 64-item inventory administered by paper and pencil. All the items require true/false responses. The items describe 32 defensive and 32 aggressive behaviors. The inventory measures the inferred self-esteem of a child between the ages of 5 and 12 based on the child's behaviors as reported by the significant adults involved with the child—parents, guardians, teachers, caregivers, etc. The inventory compares the relative strengths and weakness for four self-esteem component scales—Belonging (B), Purpose (P), Control (C), Self (S); a composite self-esteem scale, Total (T); and two coping styles scales, Defensive (TD) and Aggressive (TA). The CISE measures the inferred self-esteem on these scales based on the responses of adults.

The CISE is designed for use by school and mental health counselors, school and clinical psychologists, social workers, psychiatrists, and other qualified helping professionals. The minimum criterion to be an examiner for this inventory is a graduate degree or status as a graduate student in counseling, psychology, social work, educational testing, psychological testing, or a related field. According to the CISE's manual, the qualified helping professional can administer this inventory to (a) measure children's inferred self-esteem on the scales, (b) develop strategies for counseling, (c) focus parent and teacher consultations, (d) evaluate the effectiveness of self-esteem programs and counseling, (e) develop counseling goals and strategies, and (f) identify coping strategies. The CISE is designed as a practical tool for the helping professional to use in the clinical process. The inventory should be used in conjunction with interviews of the child and the significant adults, in particular, parents. The CISE is not designed as a normative instrument, thus normative data are not provided. The scores for the CISE are to be used according to the clinical judgment of the examiner.

The CISE can be administered in 10 minutes and scored in 5 minutes. The inventory may be administered individually, in groups, in the office, or outside the office. The CISE can be administered in any situation where concern is expressed about an elementary-aged child. The administrator selects the appropriate gender forms for completion by the significant adult(s). The gender-specific behavior descriptions are identical except for insertion of the appropriate pronoun—he or she. The 64 behavioral descriptions are contained on two sheets of paper. The respondent is provided with an item response form that is designed to facilitate quick scoring. The respondent is instructed to respond based on his or her first impression of the behavior described as it pertains to the reference child.

The administrator scores the inventory and completes the report forms for self-esteem component scales and the composite self-esteem scale. A separate form is provided for each of the four scales (B, P, C, and S) and the composite scale (T) to facilitate feedback with the respondent. The inventory has been designed so that "true" responses are inappropriate behaviors—Items 1–32 describe Defensive behaviors and Items 33–64 describe Aggressive behaviors. The response form has been designed so that each column measures a single component of self-esteem. The response sheet is numbered horizontally in four columns. The examiner counts the "true" responses in each column for Defensive and Aggressive behaviors to obtain the child's score for a component scale. The scores for the Total self-esteem scale T is obtained by summing the four component scale scores. The coping styles composite scales, TD and TA, are obtained by summing either the Defensive scores or the Aggressive scores on each component scale.

DEVELOPMENT. The CISE is the second edition (copyright, 2001) of an instrument based on the belief that the observable behaviors of children provide adults insight into the child's self-esteem. The second edition of the CISE report forms have been modified so that each component is placed on a separate page. The report forms have been updated and modified to provide more information on strategies. The score sheet was modified to increase usability. In addition, the second edition has been evaluated to determine its effectiveness in distinguishing between children who exhibit a healthy self-esteem and those who exhibit an impaired self-esteem. The second edition is also being published as a licensed instrument in order to lower user costs.

The CISE's examiner's manual provides very minimal information on the development of the instrument in general or the component scales. According to the manual, the instrument and the component scales were derived from a review of the literature since the late 1970s and the clinical observations of the instrument's author. The manual does not provide a summary, rationale, or relevant citations for the component scales, the 64 behavioral items, or the overall instrument. The manual does not provide any information regarding the CISE in comparison to other published self-esteem instruments.

The CISE's examiner's manual provides the user with strategies for using the CISE results. The user is provided with strategies for parents, teachers, and children. The manual also provides examples of several interventions based on the CISE results.

TECHNICAL. Because the CISE is not a normative instrument, the inventory has not undergone a standardization process. However, as stated previously, the inventory's ability to discriminate between individuals with healthy and impaired self-esteem has been evaluated. This evaluation involved the distribution of 600 inventories to counselors. The counselors then identified two equal size groups of children—a healthy group and an impaired group. The inventories were then provided to the parents and teachers of these children. A total of 492 usable inventories were available for analysis (healthy group $n = 246$; lowered group $n = 207$; inflated group $n = 39$). The manual only indicates that the "normative instrument" was analyzed by a descriptive comparison of group means. The manual provides means for the three analysis groups, for gender, and for two childhood grade groups (Grades K–3 and 4–6). The manual does not provide or indicate that any other analysis was conducted such as a test for randomness, significance, etc.

The manual describes an alternate form method for evaluating the reliability of the instrument. The alternate form method was used to determine if individuals were consistent in their responses to the items. The manual states that a reliability coefficient of .93 was obtained; however, neither data nor details are provided on the statistical methods or sample used. The manual does not indicate that any reliability analysis of the scales was conducted.

The manual also does not provide statistical information regarding the validity evidence of the CISE. The manual does describe the process used to examine the construct validity of scores from the inventory, but data from the item analysis are not provided.

COMMENTARY. The value of the CISE as an independent measure of inferred self-esteem is limited. The instrument appears to be a product of the author's clinical experiences and review of the literature. The theoretical model used for this instrument is not detailed or evaluated. The author does not define or establish the existence of the concepts for Self-Esteem, Belonging, Purpose, Control, Self, Defensive, and Aggressive except through the summary of the literature review. Overall, evidence of the CISE's technical quality is minimal. The instrument and the scales involved have not been adequately analyzed.

However, the CISE does have value as a clinical tool for discussion of a child's self-esteem in relation to defensive and aggressive behaviors. As the manual states, this inventory is a tool for clinicians to use in conjunction with interviews of children and parents (this reviewer would suggest that each respondent—parents, guardians, teachers, caregivers, etc.—should be interviewed). The danger in utilizing this instrument is the tendency to view the obtained scores as diagnostic labels. Because the CISE is not normative, the clinician must guard against improper applications.

SUMMARY. The CISE is a convenient, simple, and inexpensive means of gathering information on a child's behavior. As an independent measure of self-esteem, the CISE falls short on technical adequacy. Although the examples and applications provided in the manual seem to be based on normative assumptions, the CISE is not a normative instrument and should not be viewed as such. The CISE has a very inexpensive lifetime license that may be reflected in the technical quality of the instrument and the overall quality of the manual. Overall, in the hands of an experienced clinician, this inventory can be a valuable, inexpensive, and efficient means of communicating to parents, teachers, and others involved with children. Clinicians seeking a more rigorous diagnostic instrument should consider other instruments.

Review of the Children's Inventory of Self-Esteem, Second Edition by JACQUELINE JOHNSON, Research Scientist, New York State Office of Mental Health, Albany, NY:

DESCRIPTION. The Children's Inventory of Self-Esteem (CISE) is a 64-item, paper-and-pencil, criterion-referenced inventory administered to teachers and/or caregivers of children, ages 5 to 12. The CISE consists of separate Forms SM and SF for boys and girls, respectively, which contain identical items, except for pronoun use (he/she) in the sentences. The respondent of the CISE supplies true/false responses to all 64-items and is asked to provide an estimate of the child's overall sense of worth from four choices: "healthy," "lowered," "inflated," or "sense of worth changes often." According to the user's manual, the CISE takes less than 10 minutes to administer.

The CISE score sheet involves reverse scoring of "true" items (i.e., all "true" responses are scored as behaviorally inappropriate), which are easily tallied from four separate columns, each containing 16 items from the total response set. These columns are divided into upper and lower sections. The upper section contains the first 32 items of the inventory and is assumed to describe "defensive" (D) behavior. The lower portion of the score sheet contains the last 32 items of the inventory and is assumed to describe "aggressive" (A) behavior. The column layout of the score sheet allows the scorer to quickly calculate the sum of items and record sums next to each D or A under every column. These D and A subscores are added and their sum creates a Component score for each of the following scales: Belonging (B) scale, Control (C) scale, Purpose (P) scale, and Self (S) scale. Component scale scores are assumed to represent elements of self-esteem that can be inferred from the child's behavior. A Total (T) scale score is obtained through the sum of the four Component scores. As a check, the total of D (TD) added to the total A (TA) equals the Total scale score. Only true responses, assigned a numerical value of 1, are calculated. A higher numerical score for an individual component indicates a greater "need" for intervention in that specific component of self-esteem. Each component score ranges from 0 to 16. The CISE Total score ranges from 0 to 64. Although the CISE numerical system is easy to use, it is difficult to determine what numerical value above zero would constitute an elevated score. Likewise, any behaviors that are developmentally, culturally, or gender linked would be difficult to discern without a norm reference group.

To report results to informants, a record form, SY500, is available. The form describes the construct of self-esteem, describes what the CISE measures, and provides a table and graph, which when completed by the test administrator, demonstrates comparisons across respondents (e.g., mother, father, teacher) for each Component score and CISE Total. Separate forms are available to describe individual Component scores (i.e., Self, Purpose, Control, and Belonging), with a list of strategies to use to target weakness identified by the CISE.

DEVELOPMENT. The construction of the CISE (2001) is based on clinical observations of the test developer and the opinions of "authors, experts, and practicing counselors, psychologists, and social workers." The developer's collection and integration of observations and opinions resulted in identification of four conditions of self-esteem. A total of 143 specific behaviors that demonstrate conditions of poor self-esteem were then identified through clinical observation, studies, and other pertinent literature. The developer created an inventory composed of items related to the 143 behaviors, and administered the inventory to teachers and parents of referred children over a 24-month period. Reasons for referral were not reported in the manual nor were the characteristics of the students referred. The 20 most frequently observed behaviors of referred children were selected to form an 80-item instrument. School counselors administered the 80-item inventory over a 12-month period, and based on a second frequency count, the developer reduced the number of items to 16 questions per each hypothesized component of self-esteem.

The examiner's manual provides adequate definitions of the hypothesized individual components of self-esteem. However, any relationship across hypothesized constructs is not discussed and no empirical support is cited to demonstrate how these components are associated with the underlying construct of global self-esteem. The developer cites no empirical literature nor statistical analyses to support the four domains (factors) of self-esteem measured. Nor are data given to demonstrate the overlap and distinctiveness of these separate constructs. Additionally, any variation by ethnicity, age, and/or gender that might exist in the expression or development of self-esteem is unreported. Differences in child temperament or individual child characteristics that may account for variation in self-esteem scores similarly are not discussed. Situational factors, if any, that are involved in self-esteem are lacking from the developer's summary of healthy versus unhealthy sense of self-worth. Although suggestions to parents are abundant, the CISE handouts list interventions that implicate environment as a causal link to self-esteem and may wrongly imply parental blame.

TECHNICAL. Development of the CISE relied heavily upon self-help literature and anecdotal information. Analysis of internal consistency of the CISE occurred through use of an alternative form that consisted of the original instrument plus two repeated items selected randomly from each of the four CISE subscales. These eight items were compared for item response consistency, resulting in a Pearson product-moment correlation coefficient of .93. Analyses of consistency over time or between raters were not reported. To determine how well the CISE distinguishes between children with healthy self-esteem from children who exhibit impaired self-esteem, the developer instructed counselors to distribute the measure to parents and teachers of an equal number of children suspected of having impaired self-esteem and healthy self-esteem. A total of 492 completed inventories were analyzed based on the range, median, and means of scores. The mean score of children suspected of having healthy self-esteem was comparably smaller than scores of those suspected of having impaired self-esteem. However, statistical significance was not reported. A third group of children described as having "inflated" self-esteem were categorized as part of the sample. The construct, however, was not defined in relation to healthy and impaired self-esteem, and more importantly, the implications of this identification on intervention were not provided. The developer cautions that the CISE is not intended to label or categorize children. Evidence to support the validity of the CISE is limited.

COMMENTARY. The CISE, as a criterion measure of self-esteem, is easy to administer and supplies multiple interventions to offer parents and teachers of children with identified behavior weaknesses hypothesized to be related to self-esteem. Items of the CISE are straightforward; however, they may correlate not only with inferred self-esteem, but also with serious childhood adjustment difficulties, such as Depression or Anxiety. For this reason, the clinical utility of the CISE is vague. It seems necessary to caution the user of the CISE that further exploration, rather than interpretation, of a child's emotional and behavioral health is indicated when elevated scores exist. Whether the CISE provides incremental validity above parent, teacher, or counselor observation is debatable. Also, the exclusion of written or verbal self-report limits a clinical understanding of the child's perspective regarding the observable behaviors. Again, further exploration appears necessary when using the CISE.

SUMMARY. The usefulness of the CISE is limited at best. Affirmative responses to items may indicate serious clinical concerns that require further assessment. The test developer should specify this caution in the user's manual. Furthermore, the CISE measures an informant's observation of seemingly negative behaviors. This instrument does not measure the presence of strengths and competencies that contribute to the development of self-esteem, which when pinpointed, help in the creation of targeted intervention. Overall, the CISE is a narrow screening tool with too few domains to measure more specific behavioral or emotional difficulties of children.

[51]

Clinical Assessment Scales for the Elderly and Clinical Assessment Scales for the Elderly—Short Form.

Population: Ages 55–90.

Publication Dates: 1999–2001.
Scores, 10: Anxiety, Cognitive Competence, Depression, Fear of Aging, Mania, Obsessive-Compulsive, Paranoia, Psychoticism, Somatization, Substance Abuse.
Administration: Group.
Forms, 2: R (caregiver rating), S (self-rating).
Price Data, 2001: $235 per combination kit including professional manual (2001, 140 pages), 25 Short Form R test booklets, 25 Short Form S test booklets, 25 Form R item booklets, 25 Form S item booklets, 25 Form R hand-scorable answer sheets, 25 Form S hand-scorable answer sheets, and 100 profile forms; $20 per 50 profile forms; $40 per professional manual.
Comments: Addresses selected DSM-IV Axis I disorders.
Authors: Cecil R. Reynolds (test and manual) and Erin D. Bigler (test).
Publisher: Psychological Assessment Resources, Inc.
   a) CLINICAL ASSESSMENT SCALES FOR THE ELDERLY.
   Purpose: "A comprehensive measure of acute psychopathology in the elderly."
   Acronym: CASE.
   Price Data: $150 per introductory kit including professional manual (2001, 140 pages), 25 Form R item booklets, 25 Form S item booklets, 25 Form R hand-scorable answer sheets, 25 Form S hand-scorable answer sheets, and 50 profile forms; $20 per 25 reusable item booklets (Form R or S); $39 per 25 hand-scorable answer sheets (Form R or S) (discount available for 50 or more).
   Time: 20–40 (30–50) minutes.
   b) CLINICAL ASSESSMENT SCALES FOR THE ELDERLY—SHORT FORM.
   Purpose: To "screen for acute psychopathology in the elderly."
   Acronym: CASE-SF.
   Price Data: $110 per Short Form introductory kit including professional manual (2001, 140 pages), 25 Form R item booklets, 25 Form S item booklets, and 50 profile forms; $39 per 25 test booklets (Forms R or S) (discount available for 50 or more).
   Time: 10–20 (20–30) minutes.

Review of the Clinical Assessment Scales for the Elderly and Clinical Assessment for the Elderly–Short Form by STEPHEN J. DePAOLA, Assistant Professor of Psychology, Auburn University Montgomery, Montgomery, AL:

DESCRIPTION. The Clinical Assessment Scales for the Elderly (CASE) is composed of four instruments used for measuring Axis I disorders in individuals from 55 to 90 years of age according to the criteria of the *Diagnostic and Statistical Manual of*

Mental Disorders (DSM-IV). Research indicates that Axis I disorders have a higher probability of being diagnosed and treated in older adults than Axis II personality disorders. In addition, Axis I disorders have the potential to become exacerbated with age. The complete version of the instrument contains the CASE Form S (Self) and a behavior rating scale labeled the CASE Form R (Other rater). Any individual who is familiar with the person being assessed can respond to the questions contained in the CASE Form R. Form S contains 199 items and Form R contains 190 items. The response options provided for the respondent are *daily or always, weekly, monthly, once a year or less,* and *never.* The full version of the CASE includes 13 scales (3 validity scales and 10 clinical scales). The 10 clinical subscales are as follows: Anxiety, Cognitive Competence, Depression, Fear of Aging, Mania, Obsessive-Compulsive, Paranoia, Psychoticism, Somatization, and Substance Abuse. The 3 validity scales comprise a Lie (L) or social desirability scale, an Infrequency (F) Scale, and a Validity (V) scale containing items structured to determine indiscriminate or disingenuous answering. In addition, a shortened version of the self-report and a brief screening version of the behavior rating scale are also available. The short forms can be used to assist the clinician in deciding if more detailed testing is required. According to the authors, both full-length forms can be completed in 30 minutes or less. The short forms take 15 minutes to finish. The authors also employed large print with the CASE to ensure it can be used with older adults. The manual provides clear instructions for administration and scoring, which is readily accomplished by hand. In addition, the manual includes procedures for prorating incomplete protocols. Raw scores are converted into *T* scores and then a profile is computed for each individual. Finally, profile forms are provided that enable the clinician a brief and efficient method for obtaining the *T* scores for each CASE scale.

DEVELOPMENT. The items for the CASE were written based on the clinical definitions for each subscale, along with diagnostic criteria employed in the DSM-IV. The initial item pool contained roughly 1,000 test items. Rational, actuarial, and construct validation procedures guided the item selection process. The initial 1,000 test items were then reviewed by another expert panel and items were eliminated. The remaining items were split into two forms and 200–300 older adults completed the forms during an item tryout. Based on an item analysis some items were eliminated. The remaining items were compared to diagnostic criteria and a final set of 300 items remained. The 300-item versions of Forms S and R were then standardized. Samples of 1,000 older adults (aged 55 to 90) completed Forms S and R, and items were dropped that correlated the greatest among multiple scales.

STANDARDIZATION. The CASE was standardized on 2,000 participants ranging in age from 55 years to 90 years. The sample is well represented with respect to geographic region, gender, and race. Population-proportionate sampling with a designated stratification plan was used to obtain the sample. The stratification plan was developed to correspond to the U.S. Bureau of Census Statistical Abstracts of the United States population projection published in 1998. The manual provides comprehensive descriptions and analyses of sample demographics.

RELIABILITY. Both measures of internal consistency and test-retest reliability are reported in the CASE manual. The median alpha coefficient for the 10 clinical subscales on Form S is .90. The lowest alpha coefficient reported for the clinical subscales is .82. The median alpha coefficient for the Form R scores is .90, and the lowest alpha coefficient is .83. Test-retest reliability at a 30-day interval for the Form S clinical scales ranges from .56 to .75. In contrast, the Form R test-retest coefficients indicated greater stability over time. The Form R correlations for the clinical subscales ranged from .62 to .83. Alpha coefficients for the validity scales are mixed. The median alpha coefficient for the F scale is .87 (Form S), and the median value for Form R is .93. In contrast, the median alpha coefficient for the L scale is .52 and .58 for Form S and Form R, respectively. Alpha coefficients are not reported for the V scale because it was devised to test for invalid response sets. Consequently, the V scale should not display a high degree of internal consistency.

VALIDITY. The manual provides clear and comprehensive summaries of validation data. The authors have stressed the importance of validity throughout the development of the CASE. For example, definitions were written that reflected the content of the diagnosis criteria and discussions contained in the DSM-IV. In addition, the CASE Form S subscales correlate with the Beck Depression Inventory and the Beck Hopelessness

Scale. Another group of older adults completed the CASE and the State-Trait Anxiety Inventory (STAI). Only the Cognitive Competence and Fear of Aging subscales were significantly associated with both the State and Trait anxiety scores of the STAI. Only the Depression subscale was significantly associated with the STAI Trait anxiety scale. Interestingly, the correlation between the CASE anxiety subscales and the STAI scales was not significant. The authors also report a study examining the CASE Form S with the MMPI-2, and the overall pattern of correlations is supportive of the CASE subscales. The Cognitive Behavior Rating Scale (CBRS), which assesses a variety of cognitive symptoms and depression in older adults, was also correlated with the CASE Form R. Both convergent and divergent validity was suggested by the results. For example, the Cognitive Competence (COG) scale is significantly associated with every CBRS scale except the Agitation and Depression scales. These findings are consistent with the authors' goals of having the CASE COG scale assess a variety of cognitive symptoms in older adults. Results are also reported that indicate the usefulness of the CASE Form R in identifying cognitive problems in dementia patients and accompanying psychopathology. Finally, a group of clinicians completed the CASE Form S protocols along with assigning a DSM-IV diagnosis to a group of older adults. The results provide further support for the validity of the CASE Form S scales.

COMMENTARY AND SUMMARY. The CASE provides a reliable, valid, and needed assessment instrument for identifying AXIS I disorders in individuals from 55 to 90 years of age. The manual is well written and provides helpful information regarding the development of the scale. There is a clear need for assessment devices for older adults and very little attention has been given to the development of reliable and valid instruments. As the authors point out, the older population is the fastest growing segment of the United States population. A major strength of the CASE Form R is that it can be used with nursing staff who are working with the frail elderly in nursing homes. Additionally, Form R allows caregivers to provide their observations of the examinee's behavior. Ultimately, the data from Form R can provide the clinician with another perspective on the individual's behavior.

Review of the Clinical Assessment Scales for the Elderly and Clinical Assessment Scales for the Elderly—Short Form by IRIS PHILLIPS, Assistant Professor of Social Work, University of Southern Indiana, Evansville, IN:

DESCRIPTION. Clinical Assessment Scales for the Elderly (CASE) consists of four instruments to assess clinical disorders based on the fourth edition of the *Diagnostic and Statistical Manual of Mental Disorders* (DSM-IV) in individuals 55–90 years of age. The CASE provides an assessment tool for Axis I clinical disorders specifically for this age population. The two full-length self-report and behavior rating instruments contain 13-scales, 10 clinical and 3 validity. Clinical subscales include: Anxiety, Cognitive Competence, Depression, Fear of Aging, Mania, Obsessive-Compulsive, Paranoia, Psychoticism, Somatization, and Substance Abuse. Validity subscales consist of Infrequency, Lie, and Validity. The two CASE Short Forms (CASE-SF) include all 10 clinical subscales and two of the validity subscales (Infrequency omitted).

The CASE Form S (self-administered) booklet has 199 items with Likert-type response choices: *daily or always, weekly, monthly, once a year or less,* and *never.* The CASE-SF Form S consists of 100 items using the same response options. Items on the self-administered portion of the assessment require a reading ability of a 3.5 grade level. The CASE Form R (other rater) booklet has 190 items for a spouse, family member, caregiver, or anyone with sufficient knowledge concerning the patient to complete. The CASE-SF Form R consists of 88 items using the same response options. Form R requires a reading ability of 3.3 grade level.

Trained staff may administer and score the CASE; however, interpretation requires a clinician trained in psychopathology, psychometrics, and assessment and diagnosis. Each assessment instrument includes a reusable item booklet, carbonless answer sheet, and a profile form. The profile form allows a quick summary of each CASE form. Charting multiple CASE performance scores on the Profile form allows for tracking profiles.

DEVELOPMENT. The authors, with 40 years of clinical experiences and a review of relevant literature, determined the constructs associated with clinical disorders prior to instrument development. They determined that the lengths of the instruments were not to exceed 200 items based upon issues related to fatigue, attention, and concentration. Clinical psychologists, clinical neuropsychologist, and measurement psychologists generated the initial pool of 1,000 items. Elimination of 100 items occurred during the initial review process. The remaining items comprised two separate forms for a trial with individuals 55 years of age. Analysis of the item trial narrowed the item pool to 300. Two thousand individuals completed the 300-item version of the CASE. Data analysis eliminated items through average correlation across all clinical scales compared to the item-total correlations for the item's assigned scale.

Researchers determined that the CASE-SF should consist of no more than 100 items from the full-length version. The development process of the SF began with items ranked by their correlation with the total score on their assigned scale. Items' ability to predict scores on the full-length version of CASE guided their inclusion to the SF. No correlation between CASE-SF and CASE could be less than .90.

TECHNICAL. One hundred individuals in 30 states contributed to standardization of CASE Forms S and R. The sample consisted of 2,000 English-speaking U.S. residents 55 to 90 years of age, stratified by age, educational level, ethnicity, gender, geographical location, type of residence, and employment history. These 2,000 individuals provide the normative base for the instrument; however, participants have a higher mean of educational achievement than Census data for the same age populations.

Of the 10 clinical scales median alpha coefficients estimate reliability for the seven age categories, five subscales were .90 and higher, whereas the lowest coefficient is .82. Reliability estimates of Form R for 7 of the 10 subscales were at or above .90 and the other three were .83, .88, and .88. Alpha coefficients for the Lie subscale within the validity subscale range from .60 to .45 in Form S and .40 to .67 in Form R.

Individuals completed Form S twice within 30 days to evaluate stability over time. The clinical subscales test-retest coefficients ranged from .56 to .75. Another group of individuals completed Form R twice in a 30-day period. The test-retest coefficients of Form R were higher on 12 of 13 subscales, ranging from .62 to .83. Again, the validity subscales had lower stability coefficients on both Form S and Form R.

Validity began with the development of the constructs within CASE. Subscales in the CASE correlate well with other tests such as the Beck Depression Inventory (BDI), Beck Hopelessness Scale (BHS), State-Trait Anxiety Inventory (STAI), Cognitive Behavior Rating Scales (CBRS), and the Minnesota Multiphasic Personality Inventory-2. The manual provides details and tables illustrating the subscales' correlation with these instruments. Clinical trials evaluated score interpretation in clinical groups. Data were collected on individuals with a preexisting diagnosis established prior to the CASE administration and a control group. CASE performed well in the clinical trials as documented in the manual.

COMMENTARY. Although the answer sheet provides easy scoring, it appears to be a bit difficult for participants to complete easily. Normative data reflect higher than average educational levels represented among the same age populations. Some differences were noted in raw scores based upon gender and ethnicity, as documented in the manual. Relevant literature on clinical application, discriminate and predictive abilities, and populations will develop with use.

SUMMARY. The CASE is designed to meet the assessment needs for clinical disorders among individuals ages 55–90. Normative data from a large representative sample of individuals took into account factors such as race, gender, educational level, ethnicity, living arrangement, and geography. Initial reliability and validity of the clinical subscales was demonstrated in alpha values, test-retest studies, and clinical case studies.

[52]

Coddington Life Events Scales.

Purpose: Designed "to assess the influence of life events and change in a young person's life, and help determine how these events affect their personal growth and ability to adjust."

Population: Ages 5 and under, ages 6–11, ages 12–19.

Publication Dates: 1981–1999.

Acronym: CLES.

Scores: Total Life Change Unit score only.

Administration: Group.

Forms, 3: Preschool (CLES-P), Child (CLES-C), Adolescent (CLES-A).

Price Data, 2002: $114 per complete kit including technical manual (1999, 58 pages) and 25 Quikscore forms for the CLES-P, CLES-C, and CLES-A; $30 per 25 Quikscore forms (specify CLES-P, CLES-C, or CLES-A); $38 per specimen set including technical manual and 3 of each Quikscore form for the CLES-P, CLES-C, and CLES-A.

Time: (15) minutes.

Comments: Self-report, assisted self-report.

Author: R. Dean Coddington.

Publisher: Multi-Health Systems, Inc.

Cross References: See T5:557 (7 references) and T4:1453 (3 references).

Review of the Coddington Life Events Scales by JAMES A. ATHANASOU, Associate Professor, Faculty of Education, University of Technology, Sydney, Australia:

DESCRIPTION. The Coddington Life Events Scales (CLES) were published from 1981 to 1999 and their purpose is to link problems of adjustment or health with any stressful changes in a young person's life. Another aim of the CLES is to identify children who may be at risk for illness, injury, depression, or behavioral problems as a result of difficult life circumstances. The CLES may be used by medical, social welfare, psychological, and educational professionals as a standard screening assessment. There are three target populations: (a) children under 6 years of age for the 30-item Preschool version (CLES-P); (b) children aged 6–10 are the target population for the 36-item Child version (CLES-C); and (c) ages 11–19 for the 50-item Adolescent version (CLES-A).

The CLES is designed as a self-report form or interview form for younger children. Administration time is around 10 minutes and it may be administered individually or as a group assessment. The respondent is required to indicate whether he or she has experienced a significant life event such as the death of a parent, a major decrease in parent's income, or breaking up with a boy/girlfriend. In the case of the Preschool and the Child versions the CLES forms may be completed separately by a parent or by a professional in conjunction with the child.

The CLES contains positive events such as being recognized for excellence in a sport or other activity or getting a first permanent job as well as negative events. The majority of the life events, however, are negative (e.g., around 82% on the Preschool form could be perceived as negative). The respondent indicates how many times the event has occurred and whether it occurred 0–3 months ago, 4–6 months ago, 7–9 months ago, or

10–12 months ago. The reading grade level for the items is around the fourth grade level. The scoring uses well-designed QuikScore forms and is relatively straightforward. QuikScore forms use a carbon copy impression that does not require reference to separate norm tables or the use of scoring templates.

The CLES produces Life Change Unit (LCU) scores for the last 3 months, 6 months, 9 months, and year. Each event is rated in terms of life change units that reflect the amount of personal and social adjustment that is required of a child. In the Adolescent version, events are rated from a maximum of 108 for the death of a parent 0–3 months ago down to 5 for being invited to join a social organization or beginning the first year of high school 10–12 months ago. These scores are doubled if the event occurred two or more times. The recency of an event is taken into account. For example, being hospitalized for illness or injury (Item 6) or the birth of a brother or sister (Item 8) are rated as 50 if they occurred 0–3 months ago, or 38 if they occurred 4–6 months ago, 25 for 7–9 months ago, and 13 for 10–12 months ago.

The scoring of all the scales is similar; it is quite easy and self-explanatory. The CLES comes in a multiform answer sheet containing the scoring and interpretive guidelines that are separated after completion of the questionnaire. The 75th percentile is used as a cutoff point for identifying any children who might be at risk for physical or emotional consequences. This point is listed neatly on the multiform scoring sheet in a table of interpretive guidelines for each age. The cutoff points do not increase across the age group 3 to 5 years; they remain constant for the ages 6–10 years but increase for 11- and 12-year-olds; whereas for adolescents there is a monotonic increase from 13 to 17 years where the cutoff points reach a maximum.

The test results are interpeted in a six-step sequence that involves consideration of contextual factors, the appropriateness of the items for the person, the overall LCU score, examination of the individual life events, integration of the information from the CLES with other data, and determination of an intervention strategy. The manual stressed (p. 12) that individual life events should be considered in further detail and chapter four of the manual offered four illustrative case studies to guide users.

DEVELOPMENT. The scale was based on Holmes and Rahe's (1967) well-known Social Readjustment Scale for adults. Four questionnaires were developed initially for different age groups but the details leading to the current three versions are not outlined.

The key assumptions underlying the CLES are: (a) a causative model of human behavior, namely, that a clearly defined set of life events is likely to influence adjustment; (b) the range of life events requiring adjustment responses increases with age; (c) the effects of life events at any age can be quantified; (d) the effects of different events are additive; (e) effects can be expressed in a common metric; and (f) the effect of all events diminishes over time in a regular fashion (three-quarters for 4–6 months ago, half for 7–9 months ago, and one-quarter for 10–12 months ago).

Items describing a range of events were obtained from previous studies and from clinical observations. An unstated number of pediatricians, teachers, and mental health workers were asked to rate the amount of adjustment needed for someone encountering each event. It is not clear how items were then selected from the initial pool of items. Probably an a priori classification and/or an analysis of the frequency of responding might have been used although some type of empirical keying might have been appropriate.

The three questionnaires reflect an underlying conception about the extent to which situations require personal or social adjustment. The ratings for similar items across the three versions appear to increase or decrease in a relevant manner both in absolute and relative terms. The "death of a brother or sister" is rated as 59 in the Preschool version increasing to 86 for the Child version and remaining relatively stable at around 88 for the Adolescent version, whereas "hospitalization of a parent" remains fairly stable with ratings of 51, 52, and 52, respectively; and "marital separation of parents" decreases in value across the three versions from 74 down to 66 and 62, respectively.

TECHNICAL. The CLES was normed on 3,526 children drawn from samples of convenience (e.g., at swimming pools, community centers, day care centers, county fairs) and house-to-house surveys in Columbus, Ohio. It is stated (p. 19) that the sample was demographically representative and it seems reasonable to consider that the sample matches the intended population for the CLES in terms of age, gender, and social class. It cannot be said, however, that all ethnic and minority groups are represented. Some items in the CLES, especially the adolescent version, would not be relevant to other cultures (e.g., dating).

The evidence for score consistency is limited and probably underestimates the score reliability of the scales. Test-retest reliablity was based on a sample of 120 high school football players completing the questionnaire on three occasions 3, 7, and 11 months). The test-retest correlation at 3 months was cited as .69. Interrater reliability between 30 parents and adolescents for the total score was only .45. This may be partly understandable in that some aspects of adolescent lives might not be apparent to all parents. Evidence from this analysis is also cited in support of validity. Recently, Sandberg, Rutter, Pickles, McGuiness, & Angold (2001) noted that parent-reported events failed to relate to onset of psychiatric disorder in children.

A helpful table of test-retest correlation coefficients for items over a 3-month period produced some consistent findings but there were some perplexing results also, such as the test-retest correlation of .08 for the "death of a grandparent." Evidence is required of the test-retest stability for all three scales across the four time periods used in the CLES. Moreover, the low reported levels of reliability may reflect problems of sample selection as well as inconsistencies in self-reporting and recall under conditions that do not reflect the actual use of the CLES.

Content validity evidence for the CLES-C was determined by the coverage of items for a sample of parents and children. Concurrent validity evidence was obtained by comparisons of events reported by 84 fourth-grade children with the reports of their parents but the overall correlation was only .27. Strong evidence of predictive validity for experiencing behavioral problems was provided for the same fourth-grade sample when it was divided into those encountering high versus low levels of change. Although the results are reported as chi-square, when converted to effect sizes, the value for Cohen's d is .4. The manual includes an annotated bibliography of some 50 studies that provides a rich resource of validity data for both researchers and practitioners.

COMMENTARY. The major strength of the CLES is that it offers an easy-to-use, standardized, and brief assessment of events that may influence the adjustment or potential adjustment of a person in terms of health and/or behavioral problems. It ensures that key events are not overlooked. A weakness of the CLES lies in the extent of the technical data relating to reliability and validity of the results. Furthermore, the quantification of events may not be valid unless it can be demonstrated that there really is a common metric of adjustment response to events. Nevertheless, the items do appear to be adequate for assessing exposure to a range of life stressors.

SUMMARY. The CLES will find ready application in child and adolescent clinics. It supplements psychological assessments with helpful information that may not always be obtained in interviews and is supported by a range of studies. The psychometric details of the scales are not as comprehensive as one might desire in such an established and commercial questionnaire but there is substantial support for links between responses to the scale and health consequences, injury, or behavioral difficulties in children and adolescents to warrant its use.

REVIEWER'S REFERENCES

Holmes, T. H., & Rahe, R. H. (1967). The social readjustment rating scale. *Journal of Psychosomatic Research, 11*, 213–218.
Sandberg, S., Rutter, M., Pickles, A., McGuiness, D., & Angold, A. (2001). Do high-threat life events really provoke the onset of psychiatric disorder in children? *Journal of Child Psychology & Psychiatry & Allied Disciplines, 42*, 523–532.

Review of the Coddington Life Events Scales by HOWARD M. KNOFF, Professor of School Psychology, University of South Florida, Tampa, FL:

DESCRIPTION. The Coddington Life Events Scales (CLES) consist of three versions of a self-report (or interview for younger children) scale designed to identify the number and recency of numerous life events (e.g., the death or hospitalization of a parent or sibling, a move to a new home, the loss of a job by a parent) that preschoolers through adolescents have experienced over the past year. Organized into a 30-item version for preschool children under the age of 6 (CLES-PS), a 36-item version for children from 6 to 10 years old (CLES-C), and a 50-item version for adolescents from 11 to 19 years old (CLES-A), the scales purport to "determine what events the respondent has experienced and how these events may contribute to both psychological and physical illness" (manual, p. 11). It is based on a normative sample of 3,617 children and parents who were said to demographically represent the state of Ohio (Coddington, 1972, quoted in manual). The CLES manual was published in 1999, and yet much of the research cited occurred or was published in the early 1990s or before.

In an attempt to provide a rationale for these scales, the author makes a number of assertions throughout the manual that are rarely validated either through data collected using the CLES or through research involving others' work. For example, a major theme cited throughout the manual is that "it has long been believed that experiencing traumatic events is associated with the etiology of disease" (manual, p. 1). Clearly invoking a causal medical model, the manual provides an annotated bibliography in its appendices that describes briefly 52 research studies and one book chapter that have used the CLES (or a variation of it) with adolescents or children (no studies were provided at the preschool level). Unfortunately, many of these studies are not cited in the manual-proper, and they are not organized, analyzed, and/or used effectively to validate the above assertion.

Moreover, the manual provides virtually no guidance (beyond six generic steps) as to how a practitioner could functionally use the CLES to either determine or validate its hypothesized "event-disease association," or ways that the CLES could be used to develop a treatment or intervention plan. Although four case studies are provided (chapter 4), they are principally descriptive in nature, they do not model a functional assessment process whereby the CLES is used to link directly to interventions, and they address children or adolescents with fairly extreme psychological concerns (i.e., conduct disorders, depression, and suicide).

Three additional subtle assertions are that (a) "both positive and negative events have been linked to increased risk of physical and emotional problems" (manual, p. 12); (b) the effect of life events diminish over time and in a "straight-line" regression-oriented way (i.e., they are "fully weighted" by the CLES during the first 3 months after their occurrence, 75% weighted after 4 to 6 months, 50% weighted after 7 to 9 months, and 25% weighted after 10 to 12 months); and (c) children and adolescents are equally and functionally "at-risk" when they exceed the 75th percentile of the CLES scores for those individuals in the normative sample. None of these assertions are supported by any research or CLES-specific data in the manual, and the latter assertion contradicts many clinical scales that use a 95th percentile cutoff to determine clinical significance.

Nonetheless, the CLES is described as a self-report scale that can be completed in under 15 minutes by most children or adolescents, and that can be read to a child by a parent or administrator when the individual cannot read, has below a fourth-grade reading level, or their first language is not English. In addition, it is suggested that the CLES could be completed by a parent or administrator if necessary, although the manual does not address whether or not these people would have full knowledge of all of a child's life events in order to accurately complete a scale (e.g., would an administrator know about a parent's job change or about problems between a parent and child; would a parent know about a child's being recognized for an outstanding personal achievement outside of the home or for being told that he or she is attractive?). The manual also does not address or provide data demonstrating that one parent would complete the CLES in the same way as the other parent. Regardless, the CLES is completed by marking on the appropriate Preschool, Child, or Adolescent scale, respectively, the number of times (zero, once, or twice or more) a particular event occurred during each of four time frames (0–3, 4–6, 7–9, and 10–12 months).

Cumulative scores for the CLES are determined using a scoring page that is prepublished immediately under the protocol completed by the child or adolescent. Each life event that has occurred within the past 12 months receives a weighted score relative to its frequency within one of the four time frames and, thus, its recency. The cumulative weighted scores (called Life Change Units—LCUs), calculated for each of the four time frames, then are entered into a normative table that is organized by age and time. From the table and the four respective LCU scores, a child or adolescent is determined to be "at-risk" based on a 75th percentile cutoff generated from the LCU scores of the normative sample. Thus, an "at-risk" designation could occur for events occurring between 0–3, 0–6, 0–9, and 0–12 months, respectively.

The manual notes that the CLES can be fully scored in approximately 10 minutes using the "QuikScore" protocol. Overall, the scoring process is explained in good detail in the manual, and the organization of and directions on the QuikScore protocol is user-friendly and effectively designed.

DEVELOPMENT. Aside from descriptions of the administration and scoring for the CLES, the manual provides a brief chapter (chapter 5) on the normative and psychometric properties of the tool. As noted earlier, the CLES is based on a normative sample of 3,617 children and parents who were said to demographically represent the state of Ohio in the early 1970s (Coddington, 1972, as quoted in the manual). Critically, this sample was not random, demographic information from the sample (e.g., cross-referencing age by gender by race by SES) was missing, and parents were used to collect the elementary school data even though these students now are allowed to complete the CLES independently. Clearly, the use of this sample to make any kind of clinical decision is inappropriate given these concerns, the fact that the normative data now are almost 30 years old, and the absence of any research demonstrating that the norms from this Ohio sample can be generalized to the entire country.

Relative to the broader development of the scale, no construct validity evidence was reported in the manual. Thus, it is not known whether there is a more parsimonious way to score and interpret the CLES (e.g., using smaller and more clinically relevant factors). Two reliability tables are presented that suggest a factor structure (with Family Events, Extrafamilial Events, Desirable and Undesirable Events, and Total score "factors"), but nowhere is the source or validation of this structure presented. The absence of evidence of this scale's construct validity is notable. Without construct validity, there is no way to fully determine if the CLES scores can be interpreted as intended or if the constructs underlying the scale are consistent across age, gender, race, or SES. Beyond this, the norms reported in the manual do not appear to have been generated through a multivariate analysis that differentially evaluated the age data to include other demographic variables.

Relative to the actual items on the scale and the weighted scoring system, the manual states that "mental health professionals consulted during the CLES' development consented that some events would have more impact on an individual's life than others" (manual, p. 4). The manual does not identify these professionals (e.g., who they were, how many were involved, how they were chosen, and what their background expertise was), when and how they were used, how they "consented" to the items and weightings used in the

CLES, and whether their decisions were empirically validated. Moreover, no research was provided to support the fact that the three scales, respectively, contained more negative life events than positive life events (the Preschool scale had 15 negative to 7 positive events; the Children's scale had 21 negative to 11 positive events; and the Adolescent scale had 26 negative to 21 positive events). Finally, no research was presented to support the different rank orders of the most impactful life events across the three scales, or the use of the birth of a sibling item as the "central event" of the scale (it scores 100 points on each scale when it occurs twice or more within the last 3 months of scale completion). Expanding the first point, the "top five" events for each scale had some differences: CLES-Preschool: Death of a Parent, Divorce of Parents, Separation of Parents, Remarriage of Parents, Death of a Sibling; CLES-Childhood: Death of a Parent, Death of a Sibling, Divorce of Parents, Separation of Parents, Death of a Grandparent; CLES-Adolescent: Death of a Parent, Death of a Sibling, Getting Married, Divorce of Parents, Death of a Close Friend.

TECHNICAL. Relative to the reliability and validity data reported in the CLES manual, comprehensive data were not presented for *all three* scales, and some of the studies cited had limited generalizability (e.g., a study using 120 high school football players to demonstrate test-retest reliability). What data *were* provided suggest insufficient reliability, at least relative to the issue of test-retest. Overall, the reliability studies cited in the manual focused more on the completion of the scale and not at all on the reliability of the life events and their differential impact on children and adolescents' lives over time. Moreover, even with the focus provided on the scales' reliability, no internal consistency reliability data were reported.

Relative to validity, the concurrent validity data reported actually appeared to be more about reliability than validity. Beyond this, a number of the predictive and discriminant validity studies were not described in enough detail to allow an independent evaluation; were not in refereed publications; did not specifically report their dependent variables, comparison instruments, or outcome data; and/or used samples that do not generalize easily to broader samples or populations. Finally, once again, no validity studies were provided to support the use of the 75th percentile

cutoff used by the CLES to identify a student as "at risk." In the end, it is difficult to fully evaluate the validity of the CLES scores given the information in the manual. However, the absence of evidence of the scales' construct validity, and research demonstrating the independent validity of all three scales is significant and noteworthy.

SUMMARY. The manual explicitly states that the CLES can be used for both clinical and research purposes in a wide variety of psychologically related settings. Given especially the limited and outdated normative sample, the weak or missing psychometric properties of this tool, and the other concerns noted throughout this review, it is recommended that the CLES be used only as a research scale at the present time. The research and empirical foundation of the CLES critically needs to be revisited, updated, and revalidated. Any clinical use of this tool should come only after a complete restandardization using a random stratified national sample, and the subsequent re-evaluation and satisfactory establishment of the CLES' reliability and validity.

[53]

Cognitive Abilities Scale—Second Edition.

Purpose: Developed to assess the cognitive abilities of infants and young children and to identify children who have delays in cognitive development.

Publication Dates: 1987–2001.

Acronym: CAS-2.

Administration: Individual.

Price Data, 2003: $72 per examiner's manual (2001, 83 pages); $40 per 25 Profile/Examiner Record Booklets (Infant Form); $40 per 25 Profile/Examiner Record Booklets (Preschool Form); $15 per 25 Symbol Reproduction Forms; $40 per 25 Mikey's Favorite Things Book; $29 per Picture Cards; $9 per Ramp; $204 per Manipulatives Kit; $437 per complete kit including examiner's manual, 25 Profile/Examiner Record Booklets (Infant Form), 25 Profile/Examiner Record Booklets (Preschool Form), 25 Symbol Reproduction Forms, 25 copies of "Mikey's Favorite Things," Picture Cards, Ramp, and Manipulatives Kit.

Time: (20–30) minutes.

Authors: Sharon Bradley-Johnson and C. Merle Johnson.

Publisher: PRO-ED.

a) INFANT FORM.

Population: Ages 3–23 months.

Scores, 3: Exploration of Objects, Communication with Others, Initiation and Imitation.

b) PRESCHOOL FORM.

Population: Ages 24–47 months.

Scores, 5: Oral Language, Reading, Math, Writing, Enabling Behaviors.

Cross References: See T5:559 (1 reference); for reviews by A. Dirk Hightower and Gary J. Robertson of the original edition, see 10:65.

Review of the Cognitive Abilities Scale—Second Edition by BERT A. GOLDMAN, Professor, School of Education, University of North Carolina at Greensboro, Greensboro, NC:

DESCRIPTION. The Cognitive Abilities Scale—Second Edition (CAS-2) is a norm-referenced test developed by Sharon Bradley-Johnson and C. Merle Johnson to assess the cognitive ability of infants 3 months of age to children 3 years 11 months while they are engaged in playing with interesting toys. Two forms are available: the Infant Form (3 months through 23 months) and the Preschool Form (24 months through 47 months). Both forms provide a General Cognitive Quotient (GCQ) that represents the child's cognitive ability across all items and a Nonvocal Cognitive Quotient (NCQ) that represents the child's ability excluding performance on the vocal items. This latter quotient provides a measure of cognitive abilities for a child who is shy, has unintelligible speech, or is unwilling or unable to talk. The scale's authors say that their aims are the same as those of Alfred Binet, which were to assess current level of functioning and to identify children who would benefit from special instruction in order to improve their ability. Further, the test can be used to monitor children's progress over time to determine the effectiveness of intervention.

Exploration of Objects, Communication with Others, and Initiation and Imitation are the three areas comprising the Infant Form of the CAS-2. All items are used to determine the GCQ, but the NCQ is based upon the nonvocal items only.

Academic abilities used in the classroom comprise the five areas of Oral Language, Reading, Mathematics, Handwriting, and Enabling Behaviors, all of which are included in the CAS-2 Preschool Form and are used to determine the GCQ whereas only the nonvocal items are used to determine the NCQ.

There are no timed items on either form of the CAS-2, which requires about 20 to 30 minutes to administer by an examiner who has had formal graduate-level, individual assessment instruction.

The CAS-2 reflects the fact that its authors paid attention to previous editions' reviewers' comments as is evidenced by a variety of improvements including extending the test's age range downward to 3 months, collecting all new normative data, providing additional validity and reliability information, including new toys for the youngest children, and making instruments more user-friendly by adding a spiral-bound manual, attaché case, and colored and numbered picture cards.

Directions for administering the instrument as well as those for scoring and interpreting the results are clearly presented. Given the myriad materials comprising the test, administration and scoring require considerable familiarity with the instrument before attempting its use, even though examiners possess formal graduate level, individual assessment instruction.

DEVELOPMENT. Development of the CAS began in 1982 based upon a review of 18 well-known tests relevant for 2- and 3-year-olds and an extensive review of the literature. Test items employing toys rather than pictures were used as much as possible. After field-testing the items on 24 two-year-olds from various socioeconomic levels in urban and rural areas of Michigan, the test for 2-year-olds was revised. A 63-item version for 3-year-olds was developed in 1983 and administered to 21 children from various levels in urban and rural Michigan. Following an evaluation of the data, the test was revised. Then in 1984, the 2-year-old and 3-year-old versions formed the basis of a 109-item CAS administered to 35 Michigan 3-year-olds. Following this administration the test was reduced to 88 items that were field-tested on a national sample of 77 two-year-olds and 99 three-year-olds whose demographic characteristics closely correspond to the 1980 U.S. Census data according to gender, geographic distribution, race, residence, and parental occupation. An analysis indicated that the instrument was ready for normative data to be collected from a representative national sample. This followed and the CAS was published in 1987.

TECHNICAL. The normative sample was selected from the four major geographic regions of the country as designated by the U.S. Bureau of the Census. Representation of the population was addressed in the sample of 1,106 children under the age of 5 from 27 states through demographic stratification, which included geographic area, gender, race, residence, ethnicity, educational attainment of parents, disability status, and age in months. Data from the sample were obtained from October 1997 through August 1999. Quotients, percentiles, and age equivalents are the three types of normative scores provided along with information about them.

Content sampling, time sampling, and interscorer differences are the three forms of reliability evidence provided. Content sampling was addressed by alpha coefficients calculated to estimate the instrument's internal consistency reliability. Approximately two thirds of the coefficients demonstrated a high degree of stability by being in the .90s. The remaining one third tended to show satisfactory stability by being in the .80s. Time sampling was carried out by the test-retest method with a 1- to 2-week interval between testing sessions. Six of the eight correlation coefficients ranged from .90 to .98, suggesting a high degree of stability. The remaining two coefficients demonstrated considerably less stability with values of .79 and .81 for the under 1-year-olds. Interscorer differences were addressed by three scores that produced excellent interscorer reliability with four coefficients ranging from .95 to .99.

The authors gathered content validity, criterion-related validity, and construct validity evidence for their instrument. Three assumptions formed the framework in developing the test: (a) the items should consist of interesting, stimulating toys; (b) no items on CAS-2 are timed; and (c) the items assess important cognitive abilities and academic skills. A narrative provides a description of each area and a detailed rationale for the selection of each area's items. Item analyses were conducted to determine each item's discriminating power. The median discriminating powers presented reveal that of the 22, 10 ranged from a satisfactory .35 to .42 whereas the remaining 12 ranged from .27 to .34. Item-content bias was checked using the logistic regression procedure for detecting differential item functioning. Of the 79 Infant Form items and the 88 Preschool Form items that were checked for bias against male/female, African American/Non-African American, and Hispanic American/Non-Hispanic American groups, the findings reveal that only 6 items were suspect. However, the authors retained all items in the final CAS-2.

Concurrent validity was examined by concurrently administering the CAS-2, the Bayley Scales of Infant Development—Second Edition,

the Pictorial Test of Intelligence—Second Edition, and the Wechsler Preschool and Primary Scale of Intelligence—Revised. High correlations for the NCQ of the CAS-2 with the three intelligence tests ranged from .80 to .87. The GCQ of the CAS-2 Preschool Form produced varied correlations of .67, .77, and .82 with the three intelligence tests. The CAS-2 Infant Form was correlated with only the Bayley Scales and produced the lowest correlations of .62 (NCQ) and .66 (GCQ).

Long-term criterion-prediction validity data were not available for the CAS-2 Infant Form. Also, no long-term criterion-prediction validity data were given for the CAS-2 Preschool Form. Instead, the reader is told to infer such results from two former CAS studies because the CAS and the CAS-2 Preschool Forms have identical items. In the first study, correlations of the CAS with the Stanford-Binet Intelligence Scales—Fourth Edition, the Test of Early Reading Ability—Second Edition, and the Test of Early Mathematics Ability over a time interval ranging from 4.3 to 5.7 years produced less than high coefficients of .66, .52, and .59, respectively. For the second study, correlations of the CAS with the Wechsler Intelligence Scale for Children—Revised and the Reading and Math sections of the Kaufman Test of Educational Achievement, over a time interval ranging from 3.8 to 6.3 years, produced lower coefficients of .63, .52, and .50, respectively, than those of the first study.

The authors cited four basic constructs that they thought underlie the CAS-2. These include: (a) strong correlation with chronological age, (b) differentiation between individuals known to be average and those expected to be low average or below average in cognitive ability, (c) high correlations of the items with the total score, and (d) performance on the CAS-2 should be related to performance on achievement tests.

The correlations between the Infant Form and Age Intervals produced high correlations of .80 and .91. However, the Preschool Form produced considerably lower correlations, both of which were .70.

For the group differentiation, it was expected that individuals with disabilities affecting cognitive skills would do less well than individuals not evidencing such disabilities. This was the case for the mentally impaired whose standard score means ranged from 63 to 71.

The CAS-2 Preschool Form was correlated with the Test of Reading Ability—Second Edition and with the Test of Early Mathematics Ability—Second Edition, which produced high correlations of .84 and .83 for the NCQ, but lower correlations of .71 and .63 for the GCQ.

COMMENTARY. The norm-referenced Cognitive Abilities Scale—Second Edition, so named, in part, as an attempt to avoid the controversial intelligence test label, in general appears to be a well-crafted instrument. Authors Sharon Bradley-Johnson and C. Merle Johnson heeded suggestions from critiques of earlier versions of the instrument and thus made a more user-friendly instrument. Clear directions for administering, scoring and interpreting results are presented in the manual. However, considerable familiarization with the myriad test materials is essential before use. In general, reliability data are excellent for both test forms. Results from a variety of validation techniques are presented. For example, concurrent validity data are strong for the Preschool Form, Nonvocal Cognitive Quotient (NCQ); less so for the Preschool Form, General Cognitive Quotient (GCQ); and weak for both the GCQ and NCQ of the Infant Form. Also, construct validity in the form of correlations with age are good for the Infant Form, but moderate for the Preschool Form. Further, construct validity in the form of differentiation of subgroups indicated that the test differentiated among subgroups as expected. Predictive validity was not presented.

SUMMARY. In conclusion, it appears to this reviewer that one may use the CAS-2 with reasonable confidence. But nonetheless, the test authors should strive to provide additional, improved validity data.

Review of the Cognitive Abilities Scale—Second Edition by JOYCE MEIKAMP, Professor of Special Education, Marshall University Graduate College, South Charleston, WV:

DESCRIPTION. The Cognitive Abilities Scale—Second Edition (CAS-2) is a clinical instrument for assessing the cognitive abilities of infants and young child while engaged in play with toys. Professionals with formal graduate-level training in individual assessment, as well as experience assessing young children, can administer, score, and interpret the instrument. Although the CAS-2 is untimed, total administration time ranges from 20 to 30 minutes. The CAS-2 has two forms, the Infant Form (ages 3 months through 23 months) and the Preschool Form (ages 24 months through 47 months). Two quotients are generated on both forms to estimate children's overall cognitive abilities, the General Cognitive Quotient (GCQ) and the Nonvocal Quotient (NCQ). The child's cognitive ability across all items is measured by the GCQ, whereas the NCQ measures performance excluding the vocal items. Ultimately, the CAS-2 generates raw scores, quotients, percentiles, and age equivalents. The Infant Form consists of three areas and the Preschool Form has five. The Infant Form areas include: Area 1, Exploration of Objects; Area 2, Communication with Others; and Area 3, Initiation and Imitation. According to the CAS-2 developers, Infant Form Area 1 examines the infant's abilities to explore the environment. Area 2 addresses early receptive and expressive abilities, whereas Area 3 assesses abilities enabling the infant to learn. Although the Infant Form has entry points, basals, and ceilings, items may be administered in a flexible order to meet the interests of the child. The profile/examiner record booklet contains this information at the beginning of each area. Items using the same materials are grouped in clusters to facilitate administration. Each item is presented three times and the infant is given a score of 1 when the skill is demonstrated or 0 if it is not.

Academic abilities used in the classroom are addressed on the Preschool Form of the CAS-2 via five areas. The child's ability to understand and use oral language is assessed in Area 1, Oral Language. Area 2, Reading, assesses early reading abilities, whereas Area 3, Mathematics, involves various mathematical skills. Area 4, Handwriting, measures manuscript writing abilities. Finally, Area 5, Enabling Behaviors, examines efficient learning abilities. Unlike the Infant Form, the Preschool Form does not have entry points, basals, or ceilings. For all five areas, children begin with Item 1 and take all of the items. The GCQ is derived from the total points the child earned in all five areas and the NCQ from total points on the nonvocal items only. The CAS-2 examiner's manual suggests several uses. First, the norm-referenced results can be used to help identify children deficient in cognitive ability and in need of special education services. Secondly, specific skill areas for further testing or intervention can be targeted. The CAS-2 reportedly provides a means for integrating assessment and instruction. As such, it can be used to measure and evaluate the effectiveness of intervention. Finally the CAS-2 could potentially be used as a research instrument in the study of cognitive development.

DEVELOPMENT. Under development since 1982, the CAS-2 is the result of a 2001 revision of the CAS, with the addition of an Infant Form. The CAS became the Preschool Form of the CAS-2 and was expanded to include the Infant Form, thereby encompassing an age range of 3 months through 3 years 11 months. Apparently no single theoretical approach was the basis for the development of the CAS-2. Moreover, the examiner's manual indicated no single unifying theory could sufficiently address all aspects of cognitive development in young children. The authors stated, "Information processing theories, Piagetian theory, theories involving visual perception, and learning theories were considered in developing the CAS-2, along with classic and current research on cognitive development of infants, toddlers, and preschoolers" (manual, p. 2). They further acknowledge assessment should be comprehensive and include multiple areas of development with the cognitive area being just one. The CAS-2 was developed to measure current level of functioning and to identify children for intervention. Cognitive abilities addressed include attention, memory, recognition of cause-effect and means-end relationships, and response to novelty. The examiner's manual describes each area of the Infant and Preschool Forms and provides a detailed rationale for selection of each item, as well as research evidence supporting relevance and age appropriateness. However, the process for area or item development and final selection were not addressed. Although the CAS-2 includes an expanded age range, specifics as to area and item identification for the Infant Form were not discussed.

TECHNICAL. Originally standardized in 1987, the CAS-2 contains all new normative data from a sample of 1,106 children in 27 states, ages 3 to 47 months. The sample was keyed to the 1997 U.S. Bureau of the Census data for children under 5 years old. The standardization sample was distributed geographically to be representative of the United States for gender, age, racial and ethnic origin, parental education, and disability. The data reported suggest this is a very representative sample and should insure individual scores can be accurately interpreted for individuals for whom the test is intended.

Estimates of reliability discussed in the examiner's manual suggest a high degree of reliability for the CAS-2. Internal consistency was measured utilizing Cronbach's alpha coefficients based on the entire normative sample, very acceptably ranging from .89 to .94. Cronbach's alpha coefficients for subgroups (i.e., males, females, European Americans, African Americans, Hispanic Americans) ranged from .93 to .98. Test-retest reliability coefficients based on infants for the CAS-2 Infant Form (delay of 1–2 weeks) ranged from .79 to .93. However, the authors caution interpreting results for infants under 12 months due to low stability over time. Moreover, no mention is made as to whether or not these children were randomly selected. Recent test-retest data for the Preschool Form were not provided, with only CAS test-retest coefficients discussed.

Validation evidence for the CAS-2 is provided in the manual, including consideration of content-description validity, criterion-prediction validity, and construct-identification validity. An extensive qualitative description and rationale for each test item was provided. Item analysis of the normative sample revealed discrimination coefficients ranging from .27 to .42. Three studies, with samples of 26 to 37 children, were cited relative to concurrent validity. Correlation coefficients between the CAS-2 and intelligence tests varied from .62 to .87.

No studies were presented relative to criterion-prediction validity for the CAS-2 Infant Form. Two studies of the CAS were presented as predictive validity evidence for the CAS-2 Preschool Form with the rationale they both have identical items and scoring criteria. However, these correlations were done with older versions of tests (e.g., Wechsler Intelligence Scale for Children—Revised [WISC-R]), suggesting comparisons with more recent versions (e.g., Wechsler Intelligence Scale for Children—Third Edition [WISC-III]) are in order.

COMMENTARY. The CAS-2 has strong features making it a desirable instrument for measuring cognitive abilities of infants and young children. First, it is untimed and not complicated to learn to administer. The nature of the test caters to the natural affinity of children for play and toys. Moreover, the order of administration of areas or items can be changed to meet the needs of the child. Directions for administration are clear and straightforward and are contained in the profile/examiner record booklet for ease of administration. The explanation provided in the examiner's manual for scoring a hierarchical item from the Infant Form was confusing. Additional examples might be helpful. The manual lies flat with the spiral binding making it easy to fold back the pages as needed. However, the attaché case is particularly cumbersome to zip shut when all of the manipulatives are placed inside. It was difficult to organize them inside the attaché case with the manipulatives being easily crushed.

Although scores are supported with strong reliability data, the validity of the CAS-2 Infant Form, in particular, has not been firmly examined. Despite this weakness, the CAS-2 covers a broader and younger age range than many other instruments. The CAS-2 developers are to be commended for their candor in the examiner's manual as to the strengths and weaknesses of the instrument. Previous critical reviews are summarized and concerns addressed straightforwardly. The interrelatedness of intelligence, achievement, and cognitive abilities was discussed. Although admittedly the CAS-2 is not based on a particular theoretical approach, a more in-depth discussion of the influence of specific theoretical contributions to area and item development and ultimately construct validity is warranted.

SUMMARY. The CAS-2 is a clinical instrument for assessing cognitive abilities of infants and young children while engaged in play. Both the Infant Form and the Preschool Form of the instrument are untimed with directions for administration clear and straightforward. Although the CAS-2 development meets standards of technical adequacy, the validity of the Infant Form has not been completely addressed.

[54]

Cognitive Distortion Scales.

Purpose: Designed to measure cognitive distortions (dysfunctional thinking patterns).
Population: Ages 18 and over.
Publication Date: 2000.
Acronym: CDS.
Scores, 5: Self-Criticism, Self-Blame, Helplessness, Hopelessness, Preoccupation with Danger.

Administration: Individual or group.
Price Data: Available from publisher for kit including manual (2000, 40 pages), 25 booklets, and 25 profile forms.
Time: (10–15) minutes.
Author: John Briere.
Publisher: Psychological Assessment Resources, Inc.

Review of the Cognitive Distortion Scales by SANDRA D. HAYNES, Interim Associate Dean, School of Professional Studies, Metropolitan State College of Denver, Denver, CO:

DESCRIPTION. The Cognitive Distortion Scales (CDS) is a 40-item pencil-and-paper test that requires approximately 10 to 15 minutes to complete. Scoring the carbonless test booklet can be accomplished in about 5 to 10 minutes. Each item represents a dysfunctional thought or feeling. Persons taking the test are asked to "Mark how often you have had this thought or feeling *in the last month*" on a 5-point scale ranging from *never* (1) to *very often* (5). Results yield scores on five nonredundant scales, each containing 8 items. The scales are Self-Criticism, Self-Blame, Helplessness, Hopelessness, and Preoccupation with Danger.

Nonclinical staff can administer and score the CDS. Only persons with appropriate graduate level training from an accredited college or university should interpret the CDS. The CDS can be administered to individuals or groups. A raw score for each scale is calculated by adding the endorsed value for each item in the scale. The raw score is then converted into a *T* score for purposes of interpretation. The *T* score is a linear transformation of the raw scale scores, "derived so as to have a mean of 50 and a standard deviation of 10" (manual, p. 11). *T* scores at or above 70 are considered clinically significant (2 standard deviations above the mean). *T* scores between 60 and 69 indicate cognitive distortion but below a clinical level.

DEVELOPMENT. The CDS was based on existing literature regarding cognitive distortions; however, references not directly related to assessment tools measuring similar constructs are lacking. From this review, the author identified five types of cognitive distortion: low self-esteem, self-blame, helplessness, hopelessness, and chronic perception of danger in the environment. Eighty-five statements referring to these constructs were presented. The number of items was condensed by clinician consultation for less relevant or potentially confusing items and then by item analysis that identified redundant or weak predictors of their scales. Briefly, the scales measure the extent to which an individual engages in particular cognition distortions as follows: Self-Criticism (SC), tendency to self criticize; Self-Blame (SB), blaming self for unwanted events; Helplessness (HLP), perception of not being able to control important aspects of life; Hopelessness (HOP), belief that the future is bleak; and Preoccupation With Danger (PWD), tendency to view the world as dangerous. The manual contains in-depth descriptions of these scales.

TECHNICAL.

Standardization. Two samples were used in the standardization of the CDS. A stratified, random sample of 541 participants was selected by a national sampling service and an additional 70 participants were selected from a pool of university students. Participants ranged in age from 18–91 with a mean of 47, consistent with the target population of the CDS, ages 18 and over. Although the samples were largely Caucasian, analysis indicated that little variance was accounted for by ethnicity. Participants were relatively evenly divided between genders. Enough variance was accounted for by gender to lead the author to establish a different set of norms for males and females. Such differences are represented on the profile sheet for ease of interpretation.

Normative sample participants were also asked to complete the Detailed Assessment of Posttraumatic States (DAPS), the Inventory of Altered Self Capacities (IASC), and a revised edition of the Traumatic Events Survey (TES). Results from these tests were used in validity analyses of the CDS.

Reliability. Reliability was measured as internal consistency. Internal consistency for the CDS was measured using the normative sample of (n = 611) and a validation sample (n = 108). Alpha values for each sample were consistent and high (normative sample, .89–.97; validation sample, .94–.98). No standard errors of measurement or equivalent statistics were given for the total score, subscale scores, or cutoff scores. Likewise, alternate-form reliability estimates or estimates of stability over time were not conducted. These omissions leave questions as to the overall reliability of the CDS.

Within the reliability section, the author presents data on the factor structure and scale intercorrelations. Factor analysis yielded four factors

with Helplessness and Hopelessness merging as a single factor. Scales were highly intercorrelated (.69–.92).

VALIDITY. Construct, convergent, and discriminant validity were measured on the CDS using a sample of 116 clinical participants. The CDS was administered to all participants; other tests were administered apparently at random without explanation of the selection process.

Construct validity was examined by comparing scores on the CDS with various measures or subscales of these measures designed to assess suicidality, victimization, posttraumatic stress, and depression as these variables are known to correlate with cognitive distortion. Thus, the author predicted that scores on specific subscales of the CDS would be high when scores on corresponding test scales were high. No overt statements were made regarding the usefulness of the CDS in predicting or assessing these conditions.

To assess the relationship between the CDS and suicidality, scores on the CDS were correlated with scores on the Suicidality scale of the DAPS and the Suicidal Ideation scale of the Personality Assessment Inventory (PAI). Scores correlated relatively strongly on the PAI and CDS and less strongly on the DAPS, the authors propose, because the PAI focuses on cognitions and the DAPS focuses on behaviors and not thoughts or self-statements as is the focus of the CDS. Twenty-two highly suicidal individuals were asked to complete the CDS and had substantially higher scores on all scales than those reporting low or no suicidal ideation.

The author's hypothesis that the CDS would predict interpersonal trauma was supported in the MANOVA comparison between the CDS and the DAPS and IASC. Gender was also identified as a main effect. Additionally, results from administration of the TES in the norming sample were correlated with CDS scores to further assess the relationship between victimization and the construct of cognitive distortion. Self-criticism was the only significant predictor of childhood emotional abuse.

The Preoccupation with Danger Scale was hypothesized to correlate with the posttraumatic stress symptom of hypervigilance. To test this presupposition, scores on the CDS were correlated with scores on the DAPS and on the PAI Hypervigilance (PAR-H) subscale. Scores were moderately correlated with the former and more highly correlated with the latter.

Last, comparing CDS scale scores to three measures of depression, the Sad Mood scale of the Multiscore Depression Inventory (MDI), the Depression scale of the PAI, and the Depression scale of the TSI, assessed construct validity. All tests yielded relatively high correlations.

Convergent validity was assessed by correlating scores on the CDS to scores on tests that were most closely designed to assess similar traits, the Beck Hopelessness Scale (BHS), the Multiscore Depression Inventory Cognitive Scales (MDI), and the Traumatic Stress Institute Belief Scales (TSIBS). Scores, as predicted, were moderately correlated.

COMMENTARY. A major strength of the CDS lies in its unique aim. The psychometric qualities of the CDS are sound. Administration and scoring are easy and the ability to administer the CDS in a group is a plus. The manual is likewise well organized and easy to follow with cutoff scores being easily accessible and straightforward. A more in-depth review of the literature leading to the development of such a test and supporting interpretive comments would make the test stronger. Although the author appears well versed in the literature focused on cognitive distortions, few references are given regarding the cognitive distortion literature in general. Additional evidence of reliability needs to be presented and standard errors of measurement provided as mandated by the *Standards for Educational and Psychological Testing* (1999).

A clear statement of purpose would help the user understand the usefulness of the instrument. As it stands, the clinical functions are left strictly to imagination. More research on the value of the CDS in predicting such things as suicidality, victimization, etc., would help in this regard. The manual is frustrating to read at times as measures are sometimes referred to with acronyms without further explanation.

SUMMARY. The CDS is an overall sound measure of cognitive distortions. The norming sample was sufficiently large. Although not wholly representative of the population at large in terms of diversity, steps were taken to assure that such differences did not interfere with test interpretation. The psychometric qualities are acceptable although more research would help solidify this information as well as augment the purpose for administration.

REVIEWER'S REFERENCE

American Educational Research Association, American Psychological Association, & National Council on Measurement in Education. (1999). *Standards for educational and psychological testing.* Washington, DC: American Educational Research Association.

Review of the Cognitive Distortion Scales by *TIMOTHY J. MAKATURA, Clinical Neuropsychologist and Assistant Professor, Department of Physical Medicine and Rehabilitation, University of Pittsburgh Medical Center, Pittsburgh, PA:*

DESCRIPTION AND DEVELOPMENT. The Cognitive Distortions Scales (CDS) was reportedly developed to fill the need created by the "dearth of clinical, standardized multi-scale measures of distorted or negative cognitions" (Briere, 1997). The author argues for the necessity of this type of measurement because these symptoms are associated with a variety of disorders including anxiety, depression, anger and aggression, postvictimization reactions and posttraumatic stress disorder, and personality disorder. The author further points out that currently available tests that measure these particular negative ideations are inherently limited by a number of factors including: age range restrictions, limited number of items, poorly defined constructs, and questionable accuracy in distinguishing between cognitive distortions and mood states.

The CDS is a 40-item measure consisting of five scales with 8 items each. It may be administered in either individual or group testing situations. Each item is scored between 1 and 5 based on the rate of occurrence over the prior month. The scales are named for the construct that is measured and are as follows: Self-Criticism, Self-Blame, Helplessness, Hopelessness, and Preoccupation with Danger. The entire instrument can be completed in 10–15 minutes and scored in approximately 5–10 minutes. Specific administration and scoring instructions are furnished in the manual.

TECHNICAL. Raw scores and standard T scores (Mean = 50, SD = 10) are derived for each of the five scales. These standard scores are then placed on the profile sheet that allows for side-by-side comparison of the five scales on a common metric. Because the raw to standard score conversions occur on the profile form, the risk of errors is minimized.

The normative data for the Cognitive Distortions Scales are based on the performance of 541 randomly selected participants and 70 university students. This sample of randomly selected participants was stratified based on geographical location. The mean age of the overall normative sample of 611 participants is 47 years (*SD* = 17, range 18–91), and predominantly male (53%). The ethnic composition of the sample is as follows: Caucasian (80%), African American (6%), Hispanic (3%), Asian (3%), Native American (1%), and Other/Unspecified (6%). Each participant completed a battery of tests including the Cognitive Distortions Scales (CDS), the Detailed Assessment of Posttraumatic States (DAPS) (Briere, in press-a), the Inventory of Altered Self Capacities (IASC) (Briere, in press-b), and a revised edition of the Traumatic Events Survey (TES) (Elliott, 1992). Approximately 50% of the males and females in the sample reported childhood or adult experiences of interpersonal violence that met DSM-IV criteria for traumatic events or that involved childhood sexual abuse. Noninterpersonal traumas that met DSM-IV criteria were also reported at approximately the same rate. Analysis of the influence of demographic factors on CDS performance revealed gender and age differences. The author reports that females scored higher than men on all except the Helplessness scale and participants under 55 years of age scored higher on the Self-Criticism and Self-Blame scales.

Internal consistency reliability estimates for the five scales ranged from .89 to .97. Exploratory factor analysis revealed a four factor solution with items from the Hopelessness and Helplessness scales forming a single factor. Intercorrelations between scales range from .68 to .92, indicating a high degree of relatedness among the scales.

Validity was examined using a specific sample of 116 participants recruited from the caseloads of 11 clinicians across the United States. This sample was predominantly female (72%) with a mean age of 31 years (*SD* = 11, range is not specified). Ethnic composition of this sample is as follows: Caucasian (70%), Hispanic (14%), African American (5%), Asian (2%), Native American (2%), and Other/Unspecified (7%). Fifty-eight percent of these participants reported experiencing a trauma fulfilling the DSM-IV criteria for Posttraumatic Stress Disorder (PTSD).

Construct validity was examined by comparing performance on the CDS scales with performance on other instruments that measured four variables known to correlate with cognitive symp-

toms. These variables are: suicidality, victimization, posttraumatic stress, and depression. For suicidality, performance on the CDS scales was compared to the Suicidality scale of the DAPS (Briere, in press-a) and the Suicidal Ideation scale of the Personality Assessment Inventory (PAI) (Morey, 1991). Although the correlations between these measures are relatively high, ranging from .41 to .89, the correlations between the PAI Suicidal Ideation Scale and the CDS Hopelessness (.89), Self-Criticism (.84), and Helplessness (.82) scales are particularly high. A subsample of normative participants (*N* = 22) identified as acutely suicidal were also reported to score substantially higher than their peers on all scales of the CDS. The validity of the construct "victimization" was examined by comparing CDS scales with the DAPS and the IASC. It was found that exposure to interpersonal trauma was substantially related to all five CDS scales. The validity of the construct "posttraumatic stress" was examined by correlating the CDS scales with the DAPS PTSD scales and the PAI PAR-H (Hypervigilance) subscale. The predicted correlations between particular scales were confirmed; however, correlations between all scales were noted to be only slightly below the values of the predicted correlations. The validity of the construct "depression" was examined by correlating CDS scale performance with the Traumatic Symptom Inventory (TSI) Depression scale (Briere, 1995), Multiscore Depression Inventory (MDI) Sad Mood scale (Berndt, 1986), and PAI Depression scale. There were generally strong correlations between the CDS scales and these three scales. In addition, CDS scales were correlated as predicted with the Beck Hopelessness Scale (Beck & Steer, 1988), the Multiscore Depression Inventory (Berndt, 1986) Cognitive Scales, and the Traumatic Stress Institute Belief Scales.

SUMMARY. Overall, the Cognitive Distortion Scales is a new instrument that will be of use in the identification and quantification of symptoms associated with anxiety and/or mood disorders. Unfortunately, less than compelling evidence is presented to support the groupings of items into the five specific and mutually exclusive factors. In fact, evidence presented by the author indicates significant overlap among factors. In addition, much of the information that supports the validity of this instrument is based on comparisons with relatively unknown instruments. Therefore, until further evidence is presented, this instrument would be best used as a general measure of distorted ideations.

REVIEWER'S REFERENCES

Beck, A. T., & Steer, R. A. (1988). *Beck Hopelessness Scale manual.* San Antonio, TX: The Psychological Corporation.

Berndt, D. J. (1986). *Multiscore Depression Inventory (MDI) manual.* Los Angeles, CA: Western Psychological Services.

Briere, J. (1995). *Trauma Symptom Inventory professional manual.* Odessa, FL: Psychological Assessment Resources.

Briere, J. (1997). *Psychological assessment of adult posttraumatic states.* Washington, DC: American Psychological Association.

Briere, J. (in press-a). *Detailed Assessment of Posttraumatic States professional manual.* Odessa, FL: Psychological Assessment Resources.

Briere, J. (in press-b). *Inventory of Altered Self Capacities professional manual.* Odessa, FL: Psychological Assessment Resources.

Elliott, D. M. (1992). Traumatic Events Survey (TES). Torrance, CA: Author.

Morey, L. C. (1991). *Personality Assessment Inventory professional manual.* Odessa, FL: Psychological Assessment Resources.

[55]

Cognitive Linguistic Quick Test.

Purpose: "To assess the relative status of five cognitive domains in adults with known or suspected neurological dysfunction."

Population: Adults ages 18–89 with known or suspected acquired neurological dysfunction.

Publication Date: 2001.

Acronym: CLQT.

Scores, 7: 5 Cognitive Domain Scores (Attention, Memory, Language, Executive Functions, Visuospatial Skills), Total Composite Severity Rating, Clock Drawing Severity Rating.

Administration: Individual.

Price Data, 2002: $150 per complete kit including examiner's manual (146 pages), stimulus manual, 15 English record forms, and 15 response forms; $71 per examiner's manual; $61 per stimulus manual; $53 per 25 English record response forms; $32 per 15 Spanish record/response forms.

Foreign Language Editions: Available in English and Spanish versions.

Time: (15–30) minutes.

Comments: Test is composed of 10 tasks (Personal Facts, Symbol Cancellation, Confrontation Naming, Clock Drawing, Story Retelling, Symbol Trails, Generative Naming, Design Memory, Mazes, Design Generation); includes 5 tasks with minimal language demands; hand-scored.

Author: Nancy Helm-Estabrooks.

Publisher: The Psychological Corporation.

Review of the Cognitive Linguistic Quick Test by TONY CELLUCCI, Associate Professor and Director of the Psychology Training Clinic, Idaho State University, Pocatello, ID:

DESCRIPTION. The Cognitive Linguistic Quick Test (CLQT) is a newly published screening measure of adult neuropsychological dysfunction. It is intended to provide an overall estimate of cognitive difficulties for adults ages 18 to 89 with acquired cognitive dysfunction (i.e., CVA, TBI, or dementia). There are 10 CLQT tasks (Personal Facts, Symbol Cancellation, Confrontational Naming, Clock Drawing, Story Retelling, Symbol Trails, Generative Naming, Design Memory, Mazes, and Design Generation). Subtest scores are converted to severity ratings (i.e., within normal limits, mild, moderate, severe) for five cognitive domains, (i.e., Attention, Memory, Language, Executive Functioning, and Visual Spatial) as well as a Total Composite rating. The test can be administered at bedside and administration time is reportedly 15 to 30 minutes depending on the examinee's cognitive and physical abilities. Its primary use would appear to be assessment within rehabilitation settings. A Spanish version is also available.

The test materials include a stimulus manual, record form, subject response booklet, two scoring transparencies, and the examiner's manual. Lynch (2002) has noted that the record form itself is well organized, complete with directions for test administration and useful clinical notes. The examiner manual is also very complete, providing detailed information regarding the administration and interpretation of each task. Five neurologic case profiles including suggested readings add to the manual's value.

DEVELOPMENT. Dr. Helm-Estabrooks brings many years of experience working with neurological cognitive and communication disordered patients to the development of the CLQT. The manual is very professional and thorough in describing the development of the test. The aforementioned cognitive domains are said to be critical to independent adaptive functioning, and are generally interrelated and coordinated in carrying out everyday activities. The initial tasks were developed by reviewing the existing neurological literature on stroke, TBI, and Alzheimer's. Content validity evidence is based on the selection of tasks that tap cognitive and language skills critical to clinical practice. Initial pilot testing of items was used to assure that individuals without neurological dysfunction could correctly respond to the test items. Thereafter, 30 speech and language pathologists and psychologists in 18 states administered the CLQT to assess the performance patterns of 28 patients with known neurological dysfunction and 64 normal examinees matched for age, ethnicity, and education level. The resulting data including clinician observations (e.g., ease of administration, potentially biased items) were used to modify the test (e.g., demonstration item added to Symbol Cancellation, predrawn circle for Clock Drawing, initial Design Generation task deleted). In a second study, 154 nonclinical examinees varying in age and ethnicity were administered the revised instrument and additional changes were made (i.e., Story Retelling and Generative Naming tasks). A new Design Generation task was also added. Finally, a third CLQT study involved testing an additional 119 examinees (38 clinical and 81 nonclinical) and included the reliability and validity studies.

TECHNICAL ASPECTS.

Standardization sample and scoring. The standardization sample for the CLQT is relatively small. The CLQT clinical sample consisted of 38 individuals with one of five types of neurological dysfunctions, (i.e., right CVA, left CVA, bilateral CVA, closed head injury, and Alzheimer's). In keeping with prevalence data, almost all individuals with head injuries fell within the youngest age group. Individuals with a history of mental or psychiatric illness were excluded. The CLQT nonclinical research sample consisted of 170 participants combined from Studies 2 and 3 and stratified by five age categories (18–39 through 80–89). For 7 of the 10 CLQT tasks, U.S. Census data percentages were approximated for sex, race, and educational level. Changes in the tests and study samples precluded matching census data on the remaining three tasks and resulted in a smaller sample (n = 80) for the revised Design Generation task, although the author points out that all scoring is based on criterion cutoffs and not normative scores.

Scoring rules for each of the CLQT tasks were developed to maximize the difference in performance between the clinical and nonclinical samples. Informed by the standardization sample, the author selected task criterion cut scores. Formulas were developed for computing each cognitive domain score based on the percentage each task was viewed as contributing to that domain. Score ranges were then selected to reflect severity ratings and matched with level of clinical performance. The Clock Drawing test does not computationally contribute to any of the cognitive domain scores but is used independently to provide a second screen and qualitative information. Based on age analyses, it was decided to present criterion cutoff scores for two age categories: ages 18–69 and 70–89 years.

Reliability. Some information is presented in the manual regarding reliability of the CLQT. A test-retest study involving examiner retesting of 46 nonclinical examinees after 80–140 days was conducted. The stability coefficients ranged from .61 (Memory) to .90 (Executive Functioning) for the cognitive domain scores. Due to restriction in range and little variability, stability estimates were low or uncalculated for various individual tasks (e.g., Symbol Trails, Confrontational Naming). Absolute score differences, however, were generally small. Two tests, Clock Drawing and Generative Naming, require application of scoring rules; interscorer agreement for the nonclinical sample was reportedly .86 and .99, respectively, for scoring these two tasks. Although the initial estimates of stability are promising, the reliability of the memory domain appears low. Moreover, it would be helpful to have reliability estimates for a clinical sample as well.

Validity. Two major analyses are presented in the manual to support the validity of the CLQT scores. First, confirmatory factor analyses were performed on each of the five cognitive domain subscales to support the hypothesized test structure. Goodness of fit statistics supported one-factor models for each of the separate domains. Second, an analysis of 76 matched examinees indicated that neurological patients have significantly lower performance on each of the CLQT tasks than a nonclinical comparison group. Also, a small scale study involving 13 left hemisphere CVA patients (Helm-Estabrooks, 2002) may be of interest. Among these aphasia patients, little relationship was found between linguistic performance and nonlinguistic tasks on the CLQT, although severe aphasia patients showed greater variability in their nonlinguistic task performance.

Clearly, it would be desirable to have more comprehensive data on the sensitivity and specificity of CLQT scores in detecting cognitive impairment in different populations. It would also be useful to relate CLQT scores not only to other screening instruments (e.g., Cognistat, RBANS), but a complete neurological assessment and eventually rehabilitation outcomes. A current limitation of the test is a lack of information on how CLQT scores might be affected by psychiatric distress.

COMMENTARY. The CLQT is a promising addition to available neurological screening measures (Lynch, 2002). In keeping with the author's background in language disorders, it includes several linguistic tasks useful for describing degree of aphasia and several cognitive tasks that make minimal language demands. The selection and development of the test items was guided by current literature and seemingly involved considerable review and revision. The materials are professionally presented with several cautionary notes regarding interpretation in the examiner's manual.

Perceived weaknesses in the CLQT include a limited standardization sample and few validity studies. For some disorders there are no individuals in some age categories within the clinical sample, and limited information is presented as to the importance of educational background (see Ruchinskas, Repetz, & Singer, 2001). Although useful in assessment and treatment planning in rehabilitation settings, more data on sensitivity and specificity of cutoff scores are needed to recommend its use in detecting neurological problems in a general population. The reliability of the Memory domain score also appears low. Mostly, more research in different settings is needed comparing the CLQT with other measures and focusing on specific neurological groups. Given that psychiatric patients were excluded, the RBANS (Hobart, Goldberg, Bartko, & Gold, 1999; Randolph, Tierney, Mohr, & Chase, 1998) would be a more preferable choice for a neurological screener in psychiatric settings.

SUMMARY. The CLQT is a newly developed test of neurological dysfunction including language and nonlanguage tasks that will be useful in rehabilitation settings and particularly with aphasic patients. Given its short history, further research is needed to validate its clinical and prognostic value.

REVIEWER'S REFERENCES

Helm-Estabrooks, N. (2002). Cognition and aphasia: A discussion and a study. *Journal of Communication Disorders, 35*, 171–186.
Hobart, M. P., Goldberg, R., Bartko, J. J., & Gold, J. M. (1999). Repeatable Battery for the Assessment of Neuropsychological Status as a screening test in schizophrenia: Convergent/discriminant validity and diagnostic group comparisons. *American Journal of Psychiatry, 156*, 1951–1957.
Lynch, W. J. (2002). Assessment of traumatic brain injury: Update on recent developments. *Journal of Head Trauma Rehabilitation, 17*, 66–70.
Randolph, C., Tierney, M. C., Mohr, E., & Chase, T. N. (1998). The Repeatable Battery for the Assessment of Neuropsychological Status (RBANS): Preliminary clinical validity. *Journal of Clinical and Experimental Neuropsychology, 20*, 310–319.
Ruchinskas, R. A., Repetz, N. K., & Singer, H. K. (2001). The use of the Neurobehavioral Cognitive Status Examination with geriatric rehabilitation patients. *Rehabilitation Psychology, 46*, 219–228.

Review of the Cognitive Linguistic Quick Test by THOMAS McKNIGHT, Psychologist, Private Practice, Spokane, WA:

DESCRIPTION. The Cognitive Linguistic Quick Test (CLQT) was designed to allow one to "quickly assess the relative status of five cognitive domains (attention, memory, language, executive functions, and visuospatial skills) in adults with known or suspected neurological dysfunction" (examiner's manual, p. 1). The examiner's manual notes the CLQT is appropriate for English-speaking or Spanish-speaking adults, ages 18–89 and can be administered bedside or while seated at a table, within 15–30 minutes. The only examiner requirements are experience administering cognitive assessment instruments to adults with "acquired neurological dysfunction" and experience evaluating adults with linguistic, cultural, and educational backgrounds similar to the person being tested. Thus, the instrument can be used by nursing personnel, occupational therapists, physical therapists, speech-language pathologists, and psychologists.

The test consists of 10 tasks: personal facts, symbol cancellation, confrontation naming, clock drawing, story retelling, symbol trails, generative naming, design memory, mazes, and design generation. Patients must be able to "manipulate" a pen, with either hand, for 5 of the tasks, and must give a verbal response for 4 of the tasks. With the exception of a stopwatch and felt-tipped pen, all material for administration and scoring is provided. Scores on the 10 tasks are converted to "ranges of severity" of deficit, including: Within Normal Limits (WNL), Mild, Moderate, and Severe. These severity ratings are averaged for a Composite Severity Range Score, also WNL, Mild, Moderate, Severe. Adequate explanations and appropriate examples of scoring procedures are provided in the examiner's manual.

DEVELOPMENT. According to the author, the 10 tasks that make up the Cognitive Linguistic Quick Test were chosen for "their ability to tap specific cognitive skills within a short time period, with relatively simple administration and scoring procedures" (examiner's manual, p. 109). The author notes the initial set of tasks was developed by reviewing "existing standardized and nonstandardized assessments for individuals who have neurological dysfunction" (examiner's manual, p. 109), and published literature and research on stroke, traumatic brain injury, and Alzheimer's disease.

The 10 tasks reportedly evaluate attention, memory, executive functions, language, and visuospatial skills, with each task loading on more than one of the five "cognitive domains." The basis for choosing specific tasks is unclear, other than the author's contention that "research showed that they tapped into" cognitive and language skills and "had proven useful in clinical practice" (examiner's manual, p. 126). After the tasks were selected, there was pilot testing on 13 people with no known neurological disorder, to evaluate clarity of items. The outcome was some unknown revision of test items, format, and directions for administration. Initial field testing involved 92 participants, 28 of whom (clinical sample) had diagnosed neurological problems, including left CVA, right CVA, bilateral CVA, closed head injury, and Alzheimer's disease. There were several changes in the test material based on the initial field-testing and examiner feedback. These changes are described in the manual. Following revisions, there was a second study of 154 nonclinical participants, to evaluate the impact of age on performance. There was a third study of 81 nonclinical participants and 38 clinical participants. Nonclinical cases from the third study and 89 of the 154 nonclinical cases from the second study were combined for a total of 170 cases in the nonclinical research sample. The clinical research sample consisted of only 38 cases.

TECHNICAL. Test-retest reliability is based on the 46 nonclinical cases with intervals of 80 to 140 days. Coefficients ranged from .03 to .81 for the 10 tasks and from .61 to .90 for the cognitive domains. Most of the CLQT tasks are objectively scored and interscorer reliability coefficients for the two tasks requiring clinical judgment were .86 and .99. Although the CLQT is supposed to be a criterion-related instrument, means and standard deviations were calculated for the 10 tasks and the five cognitive domains. Differences between mean scores for the clinical group and the nonclinical group were statistically significant. On the surface, standardization participants reflect the geography, ethnicity, gender, and education reported in 1999 data from the U.S. Bureau of Census. However, the total number of cases is too small and cannot truly represent the population.

COMMENTARY. Directions for administering and scoring the Cognitive Linguistic Quick Test are clear and multiple examples are provided for the two tasks where scoring is more subjective. Thus, interscorer reliability is high. Test-retest reliability is less impressive. Only 1 of the 10 tasks had a coefficient greater than .80 and only two of the five domains had coefficients higher than .80. Information about validity is limited. Although the instrument appears to distinguish between clinical and nonclinical samples, there is no information about false positives and false negatives and the number of cases in the standardization samples is severely limited.

There are no studies comparing this test with other instruments shown to assess domains the CLQT attempts to tap. The manual contains more than one reference to the author's "expert analysis" (p. 121) or "clinical expertise" (p. 119). The episodic shifting from third person to second person in the manual is awkward.

SUMMARY. There are clear shortcomings in the development of this test. Perhaps input from outside consultants and guidance from an experienced project director and development team would have improved this instrument. The ceiling of each task is too low and the range of difficulty too narrow to screen for more subtle cognitive deficits. The Spanish version of this test has all the same limitations. The Cognitive Linguistic Quick Test might find a place in research but should be used with great caution, if at all, when decisions are made about patients' cognitive functioning.

[56]

Color Trails Test.

Purpose: Designed as a test of sustained visual attention and simple sequencing.

Population: Ages 18 and over.

Publication Dates: 1994–1996.

Acronym: CTT.

Scores, 10: Color Trails 1, Color Trails 1 Errors, Color Trails 1 Near-Misses, Color Trails 1 Prompts, Color Trails 2, Color Trails 2 Color Errors, Color Trails 2 Number Errors, Color Trails 2 Near-Misses, Color Trails 2 Prompts, Interference Index.

Administration: Individual.

Forms, 8: Color Trails 1: A, B, C, D; Color Trails 2: A, B, C, D.

Price Data: Available from publisher for kit including manual (1996, 88 pages) and 50 record forms (25 each of Form A for CTT1 and CTT2).

Time: (10) minutes.

Comments: The CTT was developed to be free from the influence of language, and is an analogue of the

Trail Making Test (TMT). Administration instructions in Spanish and English are provided in the manual. Respondents must be able to recognize Arabic numerals 1–25.

Authors: Louis F. D'Elia, Paul Satz, Craig Lyons Uchiyama, and Travis White.

Publisher: Psychological Assessment Resources, Inc.

Review of the Color Trails Test by JAMES C. REED, Chief Psychologist, St. Luke's Hospital, New Bedford, MA:

TEST DESCRIPTION. The Color Trails Test (CTT) materials consist of a manual and CTT Record Form. (Only Form A is reviewed here because the other forms are considered experimental for the present, and only Form A was used in the collection of the data presented in the normative tables in the manual.) Each test form consists of the following: Color Form 1 test sheet (practice trial on one side, test trial on the opposite side); Color Form 2 test sheet (practice trial on one side, test trial on the opposite side). "CTT stimuli consists of circles... with numbers printed inside. Each circle has either a vivid pink or yellow background. (These colors are perceptible to colorblind individuals)" (manual, p. 2). On CTT1 the circles are numbered from 1 to 25, and the task is to draw a line connecting the circles in numerical order regardless of the color of the circle—the odd numbers are in pink circles and the even numbers are in yellow circles. The time score is the number of seconds for completion. On CTT2 each number is presented twice, once in a pink circle and once in a yellow circle. The task is to draw a line connecting the circles in numerical order but by alternating between the yellow and pink circles (pink circle 1 to yellow circle 2, to pink circle 3 to yellow circle 4, etc.). Again, the time score is the number of seconds for completion. The prompt score is the number of prompts given by the examiner. A prompt is allowed if the examinee pauses for 10 seconds or more before proceeding from one circle to the next. The error score is the number of times the examinee moves to a wrong circle. A near miss is when the examinee starts towards a wrong circle but spontaneously self-corrects. The scores of time, error, prompt, and near miss are calculated separately for CTT1 and CTT2. The Interference Index is a ratio score: CTT2 Time minus CTT1 Time divided by CTT1 Time. The directions for administering and scoring the test are clearly presented in the manual, and the test can be administered and scored by a technician. Interpreting the scores requires a professional.

NORMATIVE DATA. The normative data for the CTTs were derived from a total group of 1,528 normal participants collected from several distinct samples. The normative individuals were healthy volunteers without a history of medical, neurological, psychiatric, or psychosocial problems that would interfere with neuropsychological test performances. The Caucasian subsample (n = 1,054) consisted of medically healthy individuals from a variety of settings in diverse regions of the United States. The African American subsample (n = 182) consisted of urban dwelling men without a prior history of neurological or psychiatric problems or illicit drug abuse. They were volunteers who had agreed to serve as normal controls for a larger neuropsychological study. The Hispanic subsample (n = 292) consisted of volunteers from church and community groups in central and eastern Los Angeles County (CA). In sum, subjects were excluded from the normative samples if there was a history of neurological, psychiatric, or medical factors that would interfere with neuropsychological test performance.

The normative sample is subdivided into five age groups (18–29, 30–44, 45–59, 60–74, 75–89 years) and each age group is divided into six educational levels (≤8 years, 9–11, 12, 13–15, 16, 17–21 years) for the purpose of interpreting the test scores. The scores for error, near misses, prompts and the interference index were presented primarily for research purposes. The raw scores (time in seconds for CT1 and CT2) were changed to T scores by linear transformations and were calculated to have a mean of 50 and a standard deviation of 10. Standard scores and percentile ranks were also calculated. The standardized scores were scaled so that the higher scores reflect better performances.

The normative data provide information on how an examinee's performance on the CTT compares with that of individuals in the normal population. The authors wisely remind the clinician that the focus of the interpretation should be the examinee's performance (i.e., the performance may be impaired but not the examinee). Numerical guidelines are presented for rating performances from severely impaired to above average. The severity ratings reflect the performances of normal individuals. The ratings do not indicate degree of neurological impairment. To assist in interpretation, a table shows what percentage of the normal normative population falls into the various severity categories, as well as the percentage from a mildly brain-damaged group (n = 21) and a severely brain-damaged group (n = 15) that also fall into those same classifications.

RELIABILITY and VALIDITY. The temporal stability of the CTT time scores was calculated on the basis of test-retest. The group consisted of 27 healthy volunteers, mean age was 35.4 years (SD = 10 years) and mean education level was 15.1 years (SD = 2.3 years). The average length of time between test administrations was 14 days (SD = .3 days). The values were as follows: CTT1, r = .644; CTT2, r = .787.

The authors also presented temporal stability in terms of diagnostic reliability. They distinguished between psychometric and clinical reliability. On the basis of demographically corrected T scores, they classified the scores as either normal or abnormal. For the time scores, the percentage agreement of clinical interpretation was 100% for both CTT1 and CTT2, a not surprising finding considering the demographic characteristics of the sample. For the qualitative variables the percentage agreements ranged from 77% to 96%. Three of the ratings were <88% and five were ≥ 88%.

Validity evidence is presented in terms of construct validity, convergent validity, factorial validity, and criterion-related validity. Much of the evidence is drawn from studies previously published. Construct validity was analyzed by administering a battery of neuropsychological tests (TMTA, TMTB; Reitan & Wolfson, 1993) to healthy volunteers (students, physicians, or nurses) at four different sites: Bangkok, Kinshasa, Munich, and Naples (n = 30 at each site). The variability across sites was greater for TMTB than for TMTA, CTT1, and CTT2. The authors concluded that the increased variability for TMTB indicated that it was more subject to cultural influences than the other tests. Convergent validity was demonstrated by calculating correlation coefficients between CTT1 and TMTA (r = .41), and between CTT2 and TMTB (r = .50, n = 30), and all participants were healthy volunteers. The coefficients were statistically significant, but the shared variance was no more than modest.

Several factor analytic studies were presented. The factor analysis of the CTT variables for the normative sample yielded four factors named speed of perceptual tracking, susceptibility to interference, simple perceptual sequencing, and impulsivity. Other factor analyses were done but the sample sizes in some of these studies were too small to produce reliable and stable factors (e.g., in one study of what was described as a frontal lobe test battery, n = 22).

Finally, criterion-related validity was studied by (a) comparing a normative group against a brain-injured group (N = 63 in each group) and (b) by researching the sensitivity of the CTT to HIV-1 serostatus. For (a) the findings indicated that the patient group was significantly slower on CTT1 and CTT2 than the normal controls. However, the authors did not indicate the percentage of overlap in the two groups (i.e., what percent of the patients were faster than the mean or median of the controls and what percent of the controls were slower than the mean or median of the patients?).

With respect to serostatus the authors reported an investigation that showed that among 11 neuropsychological test measures, the percentage of symptomatic HIV-1 seropositive patients who showed impairment was highest for the CTT2. Out of an N of 298, 18.3% showed impairment on CTT2, and the percentages varied from 9.8 to 13.5 for the remaining 10 neuropsychological tests. The authors stated that the results support the clinical validity and utility of the CTT. The authors did not report whether out of 11 percentage values the largest value differed significantly from the others or whether, indeed, the differences among the 11 neuropsychological tests were statistically significant at all.

COMMENTARY. The CTT is an analogue to the TMT but an analogue implies similarity only, not equivalency or interchangeability. No studies were presented in the manual to compare the sensitivity and specificity of the two tests in identifying patients with brain dysfunction versus normal controls. Furthermore, patients from different cultures frequently have attitudinal sets toward test taking that differ from the typical American patient. Such cultural variables that may affect test results are not eliminated by replacing letters of an alphabet with colored circles. Hence, the CTT should be viewed cautiously as a diagnostic test. It is impressive to see normative data that cover six age ranges and five educational levels. However, information about the sample size in each of these cells was not provided. I would like to know the number of subjects who have more than 17 years of education and are between the ages of 75 and 89. It is stated that 2.4% of the normative population (.024 x 1528 = 37 persons) fall into the classification of moderate impairment, whereas 4.8% or 1 person in a group of moderate-to-severe brain-injured patients (N = 15) fall into the same category. How stable is that comparison? The authors state that one should not make an interpretation on the basis of a single score, but I do not believe they point out the limitations of their data sufficiently.

The evidence is lacking on whether the CTT is a measure of frontal lobe functions. Results of a factor analysis of an alleged frontal lobe test battery are presented. CTT1 and CTT2 load on the same factor as TMT A and B, but it is not clear that the latter are measures of frontal lobe functions. Furthermore, in the manual, comparisons between groups of patients that had cortical lesions *posterior to* the frontal lobes and groups that had lesions *restricted to* the frontal lobes were not reported.

Finally, for the clinical evaluation of a non-English-speaking patient, how useful is the CTT? How does it compare to the Porteus Maze, which is another minimally language-influenced test that also requires sustained visual attention? The answers are unknown. More research is needed, specifically, more studies with larger numbers of brain-damaged patients. Only then will we know.

SUMMARY. Practicing clinicians should try the test. The clinician should make use of the normative data, recognizing the limitations, and then determine whether or not the referring question can be answered. The research presented in the manual in support of the CTT is greater and better than that of much research behind many neuropsychological tests currently in use. A significant amount of investigation and effort has been put into the development of the CTT. It looks promising but its usefulness in clinical evaluation has yet to be determined.

REVIEWER'S REFERENCE

Reitan, R. M., & Wolfson, D. (1993). The Halstead-Reitan Neuropsychological Test Battery. Tucson, AZ: Reitan Neuropsychology Laboratory.

Review of the Color Trails Test by SURENDRA P. SINGH, Clinical Neuropsychologist, Professor Learning & Behavior Disorders, College of Education, University of South Florida, Tampa, FL:

DESCRIPTION AND DEVELOPMENT. The Color Trails Test (CTT) is a modified version of the Trail Making Test (TMT; currently a component of the Halstead-Reitan Neuropsychological Battery; Reitan & Wolfson, 1993; T6:1114). According to the test developers:

> The Color Trails Test (CTT) arose, in part, from needs expressed by members of the second consultation committee for the World Health Organization (WHO) multicenter study of HIV infection (1990). One of the tasks of this committee was to develop a test similar to the TMT that had the sensitivity and specificity of the standard TMT, but which had broader application in cross-cultural contexts. The goal was to create an analogue of the TMT that was free from the influence of language as possible and, thus, one that corrected for the limitations inherent in the original (e.g., potential flaws in photocopy reproduction). (manual, p. 2)

The test developers' claim that the CTT (which substitutes the use of color rather than English alphabets) retains the same psychometric properties as the standard TMT is justified and well supported by the rationale and continuous research efforts cited in the test manual. At the outset, this reviewer would like to state that the test developers, indeed, have succeeded in creating a test like the TMT, minus the influence of language, with capacity to provide information that may assist in assessing the neuropsychological functional status in a cross-cultural context. The test has excellent potential for use in clinical practice and research.

The test manual provides historic perspective and recognizes the pioneering contribution of John Partington (Partington & Leiter, 1949) and later contributions of Ward Halstead and Ralph Reitan. It was refreshing to read a test manual providing due credits and recognition.

The CTT package consists of a manual, the record form, and four alternate test forms: CTT Forms A, B, C, and D for CTT 1 and 2. The test is designed for individuals 18 years of age and older. The test is easy to administer. The test directions are clear. The test manual provides professional requirements and adheres to the *Standards for Educational and Psychological Testing* (American Educational Research Association, American Psychological Association, & National Council on Measurement in Education,

1999). The test manual includes the Spanish language administration instructions.

TECHNICAL. The test developers developed the normative data from a group of 1,528 consisting of three samples (Caucasian, African American, and Hispanic) of normal individuals with no history of medical, neurological, psychiatric, or psychological conditions. At the present time, the normative data for Form A are available, and Forms B, C, and D are considered experimental (manual, p. 13). The inclusion of four alternate forms is a plus and will assist in conducting longitudinal research. The test manual provides means and standard deviations for the normative and three ethnic subsamples (Caucasian, African American, and Hispanic) by age and education. Selection of normative variables, and the influences of demographic variables, are well documented and supported by research. During the standardization, the tests were administered by trained neuropsychologists rather than technicians, another beginning of a tradition that the test reviewer wishes would become the standard in neuropsychological clinical practice as well as in research.

The test developers provide the guidelines for the test interpretation and have provided base rates for normative participants and brain-injured patients. The interpretation guidelines are supported by case examples. The efforts to improve sensitivity to subtle neurological alterations is appreciated. The manual provides scoring criteria to quantify the cognitive slippage. The interpretive descriptions are concise and complete.

Reliability data provide temporal stability and equivalence of alternate test forms. According to the test developers, "The normative data presented in Appendix B were collected using Form A only, and therefore, Form A is the only form that should be used for clinical evaluation purposes" (manual, p. 33). The provisions to reconcile between psychometric and clinical reliability are presented.

Impressive validity data are presented including a content validity study conducted in different geographic and sociocultural contexts including Bangkok, Thailand; Kinshasa, Zaire; Munich, Germany; and Naples, Italy (Maj et al., 1991, 1994); the study conducted by the WHO multicenter HIV study participants (Maj et al., 1993); the convergent validity information of the CTT (Maj et al., 1993); the factorial validity study (Uchiyama, Mitrushina, D'Elia, Satz, & Mathews, 1994); criterion-related validity data presented on a group of traumatic brain injury patients; and the data on the sensitivity of CTT to HIV-1-associated cognitive impairment.

COMMENTARY. The CTT remarkably conceptualized, standardized, and studied. However, one of the basic premises of all functional predictions based on statistical analysis is based on the laws of probability with all its pluses and minuses. Statistical predictions numerically computed against empirical data are limited to that statistical precision. The decision to use T scores because the clinical conditions/phenomenon are not normative is plausible, yet limiting in its scope. The premise that the clinical conditions are not normative suggests that the clinical conditions are individually varied, thus multiplicity of individual variabilities must be statistically analyzed and correlation coefficients tabulated rather than betting on the simplistic T scores alone. Although the CTT interpretive guideline provides some bases for qualitative interpretation, there is a need for extensive research to develop the qualitative interpretive procedures. The manual has provided some case references clinicians can use as a guideline in making qualitative interpretation.

SUMMARY. The CTT developed by the "Masters of Neuropsychology" backed by impressive study data is an excellent test to be used in conjunction with neuropsychological test batteries.

REVIEWER'S REFERENCES

American Educational Research Association, American Psychological Association, & National Council on Measurement in Education. (1999). *Standards for educational and psychological testing.* Washington, DC: American Educational Research Association.

Maj, M., D'Elia, L. F., Satz, P., Janssen, R., Zaudig, M., Uchiyama, C., Starace, F., Galderisi, S., & Chervinsky, A. (1993). Evaluation of two new neuropsychological tests designed to minimize cultural bias in the assessment of HIV-1 seropositive persons: A WHO study. *Archives of Clinical Neuropsychology, 8,* 123–135.

Maj, M., Janssen, R., Satz, P., Zaudig, M., Starace, F., Boor, D., Sughondhabirom, B., Bing, E., Luabeya, M., Ndetei, D., Reidel, R., Schulte, G., & Sartorius, N. (1991). The World Health Organization's cross-cultural study on neuropsychiatric aspects of infection with the human immunodeficiency virus (HIV-1): Preparation and pilot phase. *British Journal of Psychiatry, 159,* 351–356.

Maj, M., Satz, P., Janssen, R., Zaudig, M., Starace, F., D'Elia, L. F., Sughondhabirom, B., Mussa, M., Naber, D., Ndetei, D., Schulte, G., & Sartorius, N. (1994). WHO neuropsychiatric AIDS study, cross-sectional phase II: Neuropsychological and neurological findings. *Archives of General Psychiatry, 51,* 51–61.

Partington, J. E., & Leiter, R. G. (1949). Partington's Pathways Test. *Psychological Service Center Journal, 1,* 11–20.

Reitan, R. M., & Wolfson, D. (1993). *The Halstead-Reitan Neuropsychological Test Battery: Theory and clinical interpretation.* Tucson, AZ: Neuropsychology Press.

Uchiyama, C. L., Mitrushina, M. N., D'Elia, L. F., Satz, P., & Mathews A. (1994). Frontal lobe functioning in geriatric and nongeriatric samples: An argument for multimodal analyses. *Archives of Clinical Neuropsychology, 9,* 215–227.

[57]

Community Improvement Scale.

Purpose: Designed as "a device for measuring neighborhood morale" and "obtaining a diagnostic analysis of principal areas of neighborhood morale maintenance."
Population: Citizens in a neighborhood.
Publication Date: No date.
Scores: Total score only.
Administration: Individual or group.
Price Data, 2001: $3 per specimen set.
Time: (10) minutes.
Author: Inez Fay Smith.
Publisher: Psychometric Affiliates.

Review of the Community Improvement Scale by JODY L. KULSTAD, Assistant Professor, Professional Psychology and Family Therapy, Seton Hall University, South Orange, NJ:

DESCRIPTION. The Community Improvement Scale (CIS) is a 17-item paper-and-pencil measure designed to gather information on neighborhood morale and key areas of neighborhood morale maintenance. Though the actual date of publication is unclear, it appears that the CIS was developed in the early to mid 1950s. Target respondents include any individual living in the neighborhood or community of interest. Though the manual provides scant information about the rationale for the measure, it appears the instrument was developed in response to the growing urbanization of society in the 1950s and the "need for analysis of the problems of community living" (manual, p. 1).

The instrument measures a person's perceptions or attitudes about a variety of physical and interpersonal aspects of a community or neighborhood. Items address attitudes about such areas as treatment by local business owners, recreation, neighborhood cleanliness and health, public library facilities, property values outlook, security, community services, and friendliness. The questionnaire also includes items related to transportation, distance from elementary school, neighborhood aesthetics, friendliness of neighbors, perception of neighbor's financial status, and gossiping among neighbors.

The CIS can be used to identify community and neighborhood areas that need improvement, from the perspective of area residents. Once gathered, the information can be disseminated to civic organizations, governmental agencies, media outlets, institutional or individual research organizations, and sociological fact-finding services.

TEST INFORMATION AND ADMINISTRATION. The CIS is a 17-item questionnaire that can be individually or group administered to members of a neighborhood or community. The CIS takes approximately 5–10 minutes to complete. No special training or education is needed to administer the measure. The two-page manual suggests withholding the true purpose of the survey (i.e., gathering information on neighborhood morale) from the respondent, assumedly to reduce any potential bias. Although there is no stated age range, the content and wording of some items do not appear appropriate for individuals under the age of 18. Also, as the CIS was developed approximately 5 decades ago, the content and wording are dated and may need modifications for contemporary use.

Items 1–13 ask about aspects of the neighborhood, whereas Items 14–17 gather demographic information. The 13 content items have five choices, specific to the question (e.g., "Recreation of the types desired by most people here is a) not available or too expensive, b) unnecessarily limited, c) available to half the people, d) available to most people, e) inexpensive and available to all"). Items are scored on a 5-point scale ranging from a = 1 to e = 5, with omitted items receiving 3 points. Scores for the 13 items are then summed to obtain a total raw score. Scores can range from 13 to 65, with higher scores indicative of higher neighborhood morale.

DEVELOPMENT. The CIS manual provides minimal information on the development of the CIS. A preliminary scale was developed and piloted using 100 participants from a district in a large urban Midwestern city. There is no indication from where the items were derived, nor how many items were originally developed. After completing the scale, the respondents were asked two questions—whether the instrument was missing any important items and whether any items should be omitted from the instrument. Several modifications were made to the original scale, including the addition of items asking about community services and school convenience. The modified format was then administered to two different communities, one a predominantly African American neighborhood and the other a predominantly upper socioeconomic status neighborhood.

TECHNICAL. Psychometric information available in the manual is derived from the original development of the CIS. The manual provides norms based on the pooling of a random sample of 218 Chicago, Illinois residents (specific date unavailable). The norms are for comparison of individual scores, not for group aggregates. Also, these norms are dated and are not acceptable for today's user. New norms are necessary if the test user is interested in comparing individual or community/neighborhood scores.

There is little evidence to support the reliability of scores from the CIS. Using a random sample of 150 Chicago, Illinois residents (specific date unavailable), split-half reliability (corrected by Spearman-Brown Prophecy formula) was .86. No other reliability information is available.

Evidence supporting the validity of the CIS is generally lacking. Validity was evaluated using evidence of criterion validity. Based on sociological research suggesting improved residential conditions as one moves from the center of the city to the periphery, the developer used "distance from the loop" (in Chicago) as the criterion. The criterion was correlated with the median "neighborhood" CIS score. According to the developer (manual p. 2), neighborhood was "crudely" defined as a Chicago postal zone. Using 36 such neighborhoods, a .67 coefficient was obtained. No other validity information is available.

COMMENTARY. The test developer's goal in developing the CIS was to measure neighborhood morale and those factors that maintain neighborhood morale. The test developer is vague on the theoretical underpinnings of the CIS. Regardless, contemporary understanding about factors that promote, moderate, and weaken neighborhood morale has moved well beyond that of researchers and theorists in the mid 20th century. Furthermore, the rationale for the development is unclear, making the test content questionable. For example, why were certain items included and others omitted? The manual provides scant information about the development of the CIS as well as the psychometric quality of the measure. First, there is little information about the data used for any of the studies. For example, when were they completed? Were they all from the same sampling? Also, it does not appear that any further testing was completed. To be fair, most literature search engines do not reach back to the years immediately following the CIS development, but it appears that the CIS has not been used in contemporary research literature. Also, the test

distributor indicates that several years have passed since anyone ordered the test from their company. What began as a valid line of inquiry into the problems of an increasingly urbanized and suburbanized society, the CIS has rightly faded into the landscape of an even more diverse society.

SUMMARY. It is clear that although the CIS is premised on an interesting idea, that of exploring neighborhood morale and the factors that support it, the measure itself falls far short of realizing this objective in contemporary research and practice. Dated content and wording, vague and incomplete information provided in the manual, and minimal psychometrics caution against the use of this scale. Any future use of this scale would require considerable revision, and interested parties may be better served by starting from scratch. Today's knowledge base and more refined standards of testing could provide for a new scale that would be able to realize the goal of helping contextually based morale problems.

[58]

Comprehensive Assessment of Spoken Language.

Purpose: Designed to measure the processes of comprehension, expression, and retrieval in oral language.
Population: Ages 3–21.
Publication Date: 1999.
Acronym: CASL.
Scores: 15 tests: Basic Concepts, Antonyms, Synonyms, Sentence Completion, Idiomatic Language, Syntax Construction, Paragraph Comprehension, Grammatical Morphemes, Sentence Comprehension, Grammaticality Judgment, Nonliteral Language, Meaning from Context, Inference, Ambiguous Sentences, and Pragmatic Judgment; plus Core Composite scores, Category Index scores (Lexical/Semantic, Syntactic, Supralinguistic); Processing Index scores (Expressive, Receptive).
Forms, 2: 1, 2.
Administration: Individual.
Price Data, 2002: $299.95 per complete kit including manual (164 pages), three test books, 12 record Forms 1 and 2, norms book (168 pages), and carry bag; $20.95 per 12 record Form 1; $26.95 per 12 record Form 2; $199.95 per AGS computer ASSIST™ CD for CASL (Mac/Win).
Author: Elizabeth Carrow-Woolfolk.
Publisher: American Guidance Service, Inc.

Review of the Comprehensive Assessment of Spoken Language by KATHARINE A. SNYDER,

Assistant Professor of Psychology, Shepherd College, Shepherdstown, WV:

DESCRIPTION. The purpose of the Comprehensive Assessment of Spoken Language (CASL) is to assess the oral language skills of children and adolescents between ages 3 and 21. By assessing lexical and syntactic as well as pragmatic and supralinguistic language skills, the CASL provides a means for speech pathologists and psychologists to incorporate greater depth into assessment. Hence, the CASL battery comprises four components, which address each of these types of language skills.

DESCRIPTION/DEVELOPMENT OF LEXICAL AND SYNTACTIC COMPONENTS. Lexical component tests are designed to assess the comprehension of single words or phrases. Tests include the following: Comprehension of Basic Concepts (age 3:0–4:11, Core Test; age 5:0–6:11, Supplemental Test), Antonyms (age 5–12, Core Test, age 13–21, Supplemental Test), Synonyms (age 7–12, Supplemental Test; age 13–21, Core Test), Sentence Completion (age 3–21, Supplemental Test), and Idiomatic Language (age 11–21, Supplemental Test). Comprehension of Basic Concept items require examinees to point to correct responses on picture cards. Antonym items require examinees to say words opposite in meaning to stimulus words, whereas Synonym items require examinees to say the similar word from among four alternative words previously read aloud by the evaluator. Sentence Completion and Idiomatic Language items require examinees to complete sentences with the most appropriate words.

Speech pathologists have historically focused on lexical semantic skills as well as grammar, syntax, and morphology. The Syntactic component of the CASL includes the following measures: Syntax Construction (age 3–10, Core Test; age 11–21, Supplemental Test), Paragraph Comprehension of Syntax (age 5–10, Core Test; ages 3–4 and 11–12, Supplemental Test), Grammatical Morphemes (age 11–12, Core Test; ages 7–10 and 13–21, Supplemental Test), Sentence Comprehension of Syntax (age 11–12, Core Test; age 13–21, Supplemental Test), and Grammaticality Judgment (age 7–12, Supplemental Test; age 13–21, Core Test). Syntax Construction and Paragraph Comprehension of Syntax items require examinees to respond to stimulus items with the correct words, phrases, or sentences that are semantically and grammatically compatible. Grammatical Morphemes items require examinees to complete stimulus sentences with appropriate words (e.g., Example 4 for ages 11–21, "do is to don't as could is to __"). Grammaticality Judgment items require examinees to recognize and correct grammatical errors in stimulus sentences. Sentence Comprehension of Syntax test items have examinees determining whether or not two stimulus sentences refer to the same thing (e.g., Example 1, "the boy watched TV after supper" compared to "after he had watched TV, the boy ate supper").

DESCRIPTION/DEVELOPMENT AND COMMENTARY ON THE SUPRALINGUISTIC AND PRAGMATIC COMPONENTS. Lexical and syntactic components of the CASL represent the first level of analysis. At the second level of analysis, the Supralinguistic and Pragmatic components, examiners can carry out a broader assessment of oral language skills. Supralinguistic component tests include the following: Nonliteral Language (age 7–21, Core Test), Meaning from Context (age 11–12, Supplemental Test; age 13–21, Core Test), Inference (age 7–17, Supplemental Test), and Ambiguous Sentences (age 11–21, Supplemental Test). Nonliteral Language items emphasize the comprehension of figurative speech, indirect requests, and sarcasm. For instance, in Example 1 for ages 7–10, the examiner asks the following: "Jenny said, 'I feel like an ice cube.' What did she mean?" Using a different approach, Meaning from Context items have examinees derive the meaning of stimulus items from the linguistic context. Example 2, for instance, reads as follows: "As they paraded slowly through the extremely narrow streets, the band members were so serried that they could hardly play their instruments next to each other. Explain what serried means." It is claimed that all information needed to solve these problems is provided in the sentences, which is difficult to evaluate. Inference items, however, require examinees to infer the meaning of stimulus words from previously acquired knowledge. For instance, Example 1 for ages 7–10 reads as follows: "Mother called to four year old Sondra, 'Be sure to bring your bathing suit. And don't forget your shovel and bucket.' Where were they going." Ambiguous Sentence items require examinees to come up with two meanings for a stimulus item (e.g., "The cold kept him from going to the party").

Finally, the CASL inventory concludes with the Pragmatic Judgment Test (age 3–21, Core Test) and two observational rating scales. Pragmatic Judgment items assess activities of daily living that require communication. For instance, Example 2 for ages 3–7 is as follows: "Suppose the telephone rings. You pick it up. What do you say?" Researchers assert that the Pragmatic component assesses communicative intent; selecting appropriate topics for conversation; discerning important information for directions or requests; initiating conversation or turn-taking; adjusting communication level to fit the situation; and using language to express appreciation, sadness, and other emotions. Similar to Meaning from Context items, it is difficult to evaluate these assertions. There is no discussion of what factors might lead an examinee to do well on the Pragmatic component, yet still exhibit difficulties with the above mentioned assertions outside of the testing situation. Previous researchers have brought up a similar issue on another test developed by the author of the CASL, the Carrow Elicited Language Inventory (CELI; McDade & Simpson, 1983; T5:430). A broader definition of oral communication is needed; however, this definition should include an assessment of the ability to express and comprehend prosody or tone-of-voice.

TECHNICAL/COMMENTARY. Normed on a nationwide standardization sample of 1,700 examinees, stratified to match U.S. Census data on gender, race/ethnicity, region, and mother's education level, standard scores were developed for the CASL tests and Core Composites. Reliability of scores from the CASL tests and Core Composites was assessed by administering the CASL two times to 148 randomly selected examinees in each of the following age groups: 5-0 through 6-11 (41 cases), 8-0 through 10-11 (38 cases), and 5-0 through 6-14 (69 cases). Intervals between tests ranged from 7 to 109 days, with 6 weeks being the median interval. Test-retest reliabilities ranged from .65 to .95 for the Core Battery scores and .88 to .96 for the Indices. Split-half reliability was assessed using a Rasch model, with item difficulty and examinee ability as factors. The Rasch split-half method yielded reliabilities of .80 to .90. More information is needed to address the question of why the median as opposed to the mean was used. Information on the nature of the distribution and the possible presence of extreme scores would be helpful.

Researchers present a convincing argument, well grounded in theory, about the selection of the four components, but additional information would also be useful in supporting the internal validity of the CASL. For example, information on the extent to which scores on the CASL correlate with other assessments of language (concurrent validity) and more information on the extent to which scores on the CASL allow for the prediction of language skills outside of the evaluation context (predictive validity) would be helpful. Because some states require separate expressive and receptive (comprehension) scores, evaluators need to be cognizant of the fact that the CASL tests do not separate out these factors very well. This reviewer is not convinced that Basic Concepts, Paragraph Comprehension, Synonyms, and Sentence Comprehension rely on receptive aspects more than other tests in the battery.

SUMMARY/COMMENTARY. Numerous features of the CASL will enable the measure to become another useful tool to speech/language pathologists, psychologists, and other professionals. Examiners have the assurance of a well done Core Battery along with the flexibility to use supplemental tests. Standardization of the open-ended verbal response alternatives and the establishment of basal, ceiling, and prompting rules are well done. Another noteworthy feature of the CASL is consideration, albeit limited to observational ratings, of neuropsychological factors affecting performance (e.g., verbal fluency, attention). In sum, the theoretical basis of the CASL is that lexical, syntactic, supralinguistic, and pragmatic semantics play an important role in school functioning. For instance, a student may do well with lexical skills, but have school difficulties because of supralinguistic and pragmatic difficulties. For examiners wishing to assess these four components, the CASL would be a good choice.

REVIEWER'S REFERENCE

McDade, H. L., & Simpson, M. A. (1983). Reply to Carrow-Woolfolk. *Journal of Speech and Hearing Disorders, 48*(3), 334–335.

Review of the Comprehensive Assessment of Spoken Language by GABRIELLE STUTMAN, Adjunct Assistant Professor, CUNY/Bronx Community College, Private Practice, Westchester and New York City, NY:

DESCRIPTION. The Comprehensive Assessment of Spoken Language (CASL) is a norm-referenced, developmentally based battery of oral language tests for ages 3 through 21 years that uses a purely linguistic orientation; there is no need for the subject either to read or to write; only pointing, single word, or open-ended verbal responses are required. Its subtests were specifically designed to assess auditory comprehension, and receptive and expressive spoken English language competence. All subtests were standardized on the same population. The CASL attempts to provide an in-depth evaluation of (a) oral language processing systems (auditory comprehension, oral expression, and word retrieval); (b) the knowledge and use of words and grammatical structures of language; (c) the ability to use language to assist higher level cognitive functions; (d) and the contextual/communicative use of knowledge (pragmatics). The four language categories of the test (Lexical/Semantic, Syntactic, Supralinguistic, and Pragmatic) reflect these goals. All test categories except Pragmatics are divided into subtests. Not all subtests are administered to all ages, and a given subtest may be a "Core" test for one age and a "Supplementary" test for another age. All tests have suggested "age-appropriate" starting points to speed administration. Basal and ceiling rules in each test control administration time.

The Lexical/Semantic category includes the Comprehension of Basic Concepts (auditory comprehension of words), Antonyms, Synonyms, Sentence Completion, and Idiomatic Language. The Syntactic category includes subtests that seek to measure Syntax Construction, Paragraph Comprehension of Syntax, Grammatical Morphemes, Sentence Comprehension of Syntax, and Grammaticality Judgment. The Supralinguistic category includes subtests that seek to assess the domains of Nonliteral Language, Meaning from Context, Inference, and Ambiguous Sentences. The Pragmatic Judgment subtest is the sole test of the Pragmatics category.

The administration of the various subtests depends on the use of three easel test books (one each for the Lexical/Semantic, Syntactic, and Supralinguistic/Pragmatic tests) and two record forms (Form 1 for ages 3–6 and Form 2 for ages 7–21).

DEVELOPMENT. The CASL has its foundation in the Carrow-Woolfolk "Integrative Language Theory" (ILT). Work began on the CASL in 1987. Three pilot studies were completed from 1992 through 1994 and a rhyming subtest was deleted on the basis that it appears not to be a systematic developmental acquisition. Following the pilot studies, a national tryout was conducted to explore optimal scoring criteria, investigate test administration time, obtain statistical information about items and tests, and identify items that demonstrated bias or offensive content. Bias analyses resulted in changing the names in test items to better represent U.S. ethnic diversity. The Word Classification subtest was dropped because it was not a good fit with the assessment model, and Paragraph Comprehension of Syntax was added as an additional measure of syntax for the younger examinees.

TECHNICAL. The National Standardization took place between September 1996 and August 1997, when a representative sample of 2,750 examinees aged 3 to 21 years were tested at 166 sites nationwide. This sample matched the 1994 U.S. Census data and was stratified by gender, race, ethnicity, geographic region, socioeconomic status, and special education categories. The authors have also given clear definitions and explanations of each type of reliability, validity, source of error variance, and the procedures used to gather the evidence. Normative analyses were performed to derive the final basal and ceiling rules for each test. Normative standard scores with a mean of 100 and a standard deviation of 15 were developed for all age intervals, tests, composites, and indexes. Test-age equivalents were also developed. The three factors (category indexes) that were supported are Lexical/Semantic, Syntactic, and Supralinguistic. Factor analysis also supported the Receptive and Expressive categories for the 7- to 10-year age band.

Internal reliability estimates are generally high. Core composite reliabilities are in the .90s and reliabilities for the indexes range from .85 to .96. Standard Errors of Measurement (*SEM*s) for the 12 age groups ranged from 3.6 to 9.0, due to the large variance across different age groups. *SEM*s of the core composites and indexes, however, range only from 2.8 to 5.8. Test-retest reliability coefficients (with an average administration interval of 6 weeks) for the three age samples suggest only a minor practice effect. Content validity, construct validity, and criterion-related validity are all well supported.

COMMENTARY. The Integrative Language Theory, upon which the CASL is based, is a developmental theory that distinguishes separate language domains, differentiates functionally between language knowledge and language performance, and differentiates structurally between form and content. The three language domains, distinct but interactive, are represented on the CASL by the four testing categories previously described. The view that language disorders are best viewed on a continuum is mainstream. By measuring linguistic ability on a continuum, professionals can make their own judgment as to the point of impairment. Distinguishing linguistic performance in terms of the four categories helps to target remediation; a table of test-retest coefficients enables measurement of intervention effectiveness. The experimental research cited is relevant, apparently well conceived, and supports both the theory and the instrument.

Test administration is easy. The instructions, scoring, and right/wrong answers are given in both the easel and record forms, the easel is tabbed, and basal and ceiling rules are consistent across subtests. It is helpful to have two forms as Form 1 has only the five subtests that are administered to the 3- to 6-year-olds, and is much smaller. One scoring inconsistency that may lead to examiner error is the appearance of four 3-point items (#39, 40, 44, and 51) in the midst of a subtest in which all others are 1 point. If these items cannot be dropped, perhaps some kind of highlighting might make error less frequent. The preponderance of short verbal or multiple-choice answers facilitates scoring, yet as linguistic complexity increases, responses approach a naturalistic communication that creates increasing difficulty for scoring. This, however, may be unavoidable in an instrument that seeks to assess the full range of linguistic functioning. Another scoring difficulty is in the "Core vs. Supplementary Subtest" structure of the test. Impaired functioning on a core subtest prompts administration of the supplementary subtests in that domain. It would be helpful if some rule of thumb were given for supplementary subtest administration, rather than having to look up the standard scores. A computer program for scoring that could be used in tandem with the testing would also ease this difficulty. Although the black-and-white drawings are of good quality, they are somewhat outdated because the Wechsler IQ has documented the preferability of drawings in color.

Possible confounds may create difficulty in interpreting the meaning of results from some of the subtests. In the Paragraph Comprehension subtest, the use of a visual multiple-choice format makes scoring easy but may confound complex verbal comprehension with visual acuity. The use of a verbal sentence completion format might be preferable. In the Meaning From Context subtest, a previous knowledge of the word to be understood, rather than the ability to grasp meaning from context, may significantly influence results as the level of difficulty increases.

SUMMARY. The CASL fills an important niche and serves its stated purpose by providing a battery of conormed subtests that require no reading or writing ability. Strengths include ease of administration, well-designed test books and record forms, generally objective scoring, and consistent basal and ceiling rules. Index scores are useful to pinpoint sources of linguistic difficulty and to structure intervention. Test-retest coefficients partial out practice effects when measuring intervention effectiveness. Freedom from bias, generally good subtest reliability, and well-supported validity enhance the examiner's confidence.

Weaknesses include occasional scoring inconsistency, awkwardness in knowing when to administer the supplementary tests, black-and-white drawings, possible confounds in interpreting the Paragraph Comprehension and Meaning from Context subtests, and no option for computer scoring or reports.

[59]

Comprehensive Receptive and Expressive Vocabulary Test—Second Edition.

Purpose: "To identify ... deficiencies in oral vocabulary ... discrepancies between receptive and expressive vocabulary, [and] ... progress in instructional programs."

Population: Ages 4-0 through 89-11 (Receptive Vocabulary), ages 5-0 through 89-11 (Expressive Vocabulary).

Publication Dates: 1994–2002.

Acronym: CREVT-2.

Scores, 3: Receptive Vocabulary, Expressive Vocabulary, General Vocabulary.

Administration: Individual.

Forms, 2: A, B.

Price Data, 2002: $226 per complete kit; $40 per forms (A or B); $78 per photo album picture book; $71 per examiner's manual (2002, 141 pages).

Time: Untimed.

Comments: Combines the CREVT and CREVT-A; old editions still available.

Authors: Gerald Wallace and Donald D. Hammill.
Publisher: PRO-ED.
Cross References: See T5:655 (CREVT, 1 reference) and T5:656 (CREVT); for reviews by Alan S. Kaufman and Mary J. McLellan of the CREVT, see 13:80 (1 reference); for reviews by Margaret E. Malone and Wayne H. Slater of the CREVT-A, see 14:93 (1 reference).

Review of the Comprehensive Receptive and Expressive Vocabulary Test—Second Edition by LUANNE ANDERSSON, Assistant Professor, Department of Speech-Language Pathology and Audiology, Ithaca College, Ithaca, NY:

DESCRIPTION. The Comprehensive Receptive and Expressive Vocabulary Test—Second Edition (CREVT-2) is an untimed, individually administered test composed of one receptive and one expressive subtest. Scores from the Receptive Vocabulary and Expressive Vocabulary subtests are combined to form a total test score, referred to as a General Vocabulary score. Two equivalent forms of the test are available (Form A and Form B). Note that the CREVT-2 is a revised edition that combines items from two existing tests. By combining the CREVT, a test for children, with the CREVT-A, a test for adults, the authors have created a single test that is purportedly suitable for individuals who range in age from 4-0 to 89-11.

The reported purposes of the test are to identify deficiencies in oral vocabulary, identify discrepancies between receptive and expressive vocabulary, document progress in instructional programs, and serve as a research tool. The authors describe the test as a measure of oral vocabulary. This may be confusing to examiners who are speech-language pathologists, because a receptive language task would not typically be included in a test of *oral* language skills. The authors of the CREVT-2 do provide a definition for the term *oral vocabulary;* the meaning of the term as it is used in this test is consistent with the use of the term in the field of psychology.

There are 76 items on the Receptive Vocabulary subtest. The stimuli for this subtest consist of 60 color photographs. Each of the 10 pages of the stimulus manual contains 6 photographs of people or objects; all of the photographs on a single page pertain to a single category (e.g., transportation). The examinee is asked to point to the picture labeled by the examiner; 1 point is received for each item correctly identified. Although most items appear to be straightforward, difficulty is noted with stimulus items that are associated with the pictured person or object, rather than being directly depicted. For example, the stimulus "engineer" refers to a photo of a train in which no engineer is visible and "ailment" refers to a photo of a doctor. Inclusion of at least one associated term within the demonstration items might reduce confusion.

The stimuli for the Expressive Vocabulary subtest consist of 29 single words spoken aloud by the examiner. The examinee is asked to provide a definition for each word presented; 1 point is received for each definition meeting criteria listed in the test booklet. Expressive items reflect the same 10 categories represented in the receptive portion of the test. The examiner is permitted to ask for clarification of some responses; these responses are listed in the record booklet for each test item.

The test yields standard scores (mean = 100, standard deviation = 15) and percentile ranks for each subtest and for the total test. Standard scores and percentile ranks are available for all ages. Age equivalency scores are yielded for each subtest and for the total test. Cautions regarding the use of age equivalency scores are clearly stated in the manual along with appropriate references guiding readers to additional sources for learning more about equivalency scores.

DEVELOPMENT AND TECHNICAL. The normative sample for the CREVT-2 consists of 2,545 persons; however, this sample includes the normative samples for the CREVT (a test for children and adolescents) and the CREVT-A (a test for adults). The number of individuals to whom the final version of the CREVT-2 was administered during the test development process is not clearly stated. The normative sample was closely matched to the general population along the following parameters: geographic region, gender, race, ethnicity, family income, and educational attainment of parents. Children with mental retardation, speech-language disorder, learning disability, and unspecified other handicaps were included in the normative sample. The inclusion of children with disabilities in the normative population is important as this reduces the likelihood of inflation of the mean. Unfortunately, the age ranges for the children with disabilities are not provided in the examiner's manual; thus, it is unclear whether they are equally distributed across the age ranges of the test population. If they are not equally distributed, the mean will be inflated at some age intervals but not at others. An area of concern is that the nature of the "speech-language disorders" and the "learning disabilities" are not specified. It is unclear what proportion of these children had difficulties in the area of language. For example, the "speech-language disorders" group may have included children who stutter but whose vocabulary is developing normally.

Discussion of three types of validity is provided in the examiner's manual: content description, criterion prediction, and construct identification. The item selection process is discussed in the content description validation section. Item difficulty on both subtests is dependent on frequency of occurrence of the word in the English language. The statistical methods used in the item selection process are discussed in detail; however, there is no discussion of the process used to determine acceptability of responses on the Expressive Vocabulary subtest. It is unclear whether acceptability of responses was determined empirically, based on actual responses, or by another method, such as best judgment of the test developers.

Support for criterion prediction validity is provided by comparing scores on the CREVT-2 to scores on tests thought to measure similar abilities. Criterion prediction information was gathered using tests given to individuals ranging from 4 years to 18 years (no single test covered this entire age range). Test results for adults were not used in the criterion prediction process. The total test scores on the CREVT-2 correlate highly with the total test scores of two comprehensive language abilities tests, the Clinical Evaluation of Language Fundamentals—Revised (CELF-R) and the Test of Language Development-2 Primary (TOLD-P:2). These results suggest that all three tests are measuring similar abilities. Correlations are lower for three tests of spoken vocabulary, ranging from ..39 to .75 on the CREVT-2 Forms A and B subtests and from .63 to .75 on the CREVT-2 Forms A and B total test. The strength of the correlations is not consistent with what might be expected. For example, the correlations with the Wechsler Intelligence Scale for Children—Third Edition (WISC-III): Vocabulary subtest (on which children define words) are higher for the Receptive subtest of the CREVT-2 Form B than for the Expressive subtest. Explanations for apparent discrepancies in correlations are not provided.

One procedure used in the construct identification validation process is that of group differentiation. Although the test developers contend that the CREVT-2 can be used to detect deficiencies in oral vocabulary, the average standard score for children with learning disabilities and those with speech-language disorders ranges from 90 to 94 on both subtests of Forms A and B of this test. The average total test scores for these subgroups range from 89 to 92. These scores are well within −1 SD of the mean. Only the subgroup of individuals with mental retardation received average standard scores of more than −1 SD below the mean. Because the average standard score for children with speech/language disorders is in the average range, this test cannot be considered a useful instrument for determining the presence of a language disorder nor for determining a child's eligibility for language intervention. The usefulness of this instrument might be improved if the authors provided more detailed descriptions of the children in the various disabilities groups including age, type of disorder, and severity of disorder.

Five measures of reliability are reported in the examiner's manual. When tests are used to make educational decisions a reliability of ≥.90 is desirable. Coefficient alpha for each subtest was calculated for 18 age intervals and ranged from .78 to .98 on Form A and from .80 to .98 on Form B. The coefficient alpha for the total test for 18 age intervals ranged from .89 to .98 on both forms of the test. Coefficient alpha for selected subgroups (e.g., males) ranged from 91 to 99. Test-retest reliability (with administration intervals of 2 weeks and 2 months) and interscorer reliability were ≥.90. Two measures of alternate form reliability were calculated with averaged subtest reliability coefficients ranging from .88 to .95. Total test reliability coefficients were acceptable for making educational decisions regardless of the measure of reliability.

COMMENTARY AND SUMMARY. This test is easy to administer and score and the reliability is acceptable for making educational decisions. The primary difficulty with this test is that it does not adequately distinguish individuals with language abilities that are above or below the average range. The average subtest and total test standard scores for children with speech-language disorders and learning disabilities are within -1 SD of the mean. As a result, this test has limited usefulness for determining eligibility for language intervention or for determining the presence of a language impairment. The highest standard scores possible are within +1 SD of the mean for at least four of the adult age intervals on both subtests. Thus, for adults with vocabularies in the above average range, this test would not provide an accurate indication of their abilities nor would it be sensitive to deterioration of those abilities if the individual's abilities remained in the above average range.

Review of the Comprehensive Receptive and Expressive Vocabulary Test—Second Edition by GRETCHEN OWENS, Professor of Child Study, St. Joseph's College, Patchoque, NY:

DESCRIPTION. The Comprehensive Receptive and Expressive Vocabulary Test—Second Edition (CREVT-2) has been recently revised and partially renormed. The new version is a combination of the 1994 CREVT for children ages 4–16 and the 1997 CREVT-A for adults. It is designed to assess oral vocabulary in English by looking at both language functions—reception (understanding) and expression (speaking)—in an untimed, individually administered test.

For the Receptive Vocabulary subtest, the examinee looks at a page containing six photographs and points to the one that best depicts the word the examiner says. There are 10 pages, each showing a different category: animals, transportation, occupations, clothing, food, personal grooming, tools, household appliances, recreation, and clerical materials. Examinees of all ages start with the first item. For the 29-item Expressive Vocabulary subtest, the examiner asks the person to define words. Younger children begin with Item 1, 12-year-olds and older with Item 14. Basal and ceiling rules apply. Raw scores are later converted to standard scores (with a mean of 100 and standard deviation of 15), percentiles, and language age equivalents. Standard scores from the two subtests are also combined and converted into a General Vocabulary composite. Norms tables are in 6-month intervals from ages 4-0 to 12-11, 1-year intervals from 13-0 to 17-11, 10-year intervals from 18 to 39-11 (and 80 to 89-11), and 20-year intervals from 40 to 59-11 and 60 to 79-11.

The authors state that the CREVT-2 can be administered by "anyone who is reasonably competent in the administration of tests" (examiner's manual, p. 11). They caution that CREVT-2 results alone should not be used for eligibility decisions; if scores are low, further assessment should be done by those who are experienced in language assessment.

The manual includes directions for conducting an intra-ability discrepancy analysis to see whether there is a significant difference between an individual's receptive and expressive vocabulary skills. Based on the reliability coefficients for the subtests, the authors suggest that a 12-point discrepancy between subtest scores should be considered significant, with 24 points labeled a "severe discrepancy" (examiner's manual, p. 31). Because reliability coefficients (and presumably, intercorrelations between Expressive Vocabulary and Receptive Vocabulary scores) vary at different ages, it would be helpful if the manual provided a table listing the appropriate cutoffs for significance at each age level. The manual should also note that at least one of the two standard scores (i.e., Receptive Vocabulary or Expressive Vocabulary) must be below average to be clinically significant. (For example, having a standard score of 113 for Receptive Vocabulary and 99 for Expressive Vocabulary has no clinical significance, despite the 14-point discrepancy.)

DEVELOPMENT. In this revision, the authors have attempted to directly address criticisms aimed at the 1994 edition of the CREVT. Some have been remedied (such as explicitly informing the examinee that some items will be used more than once in the Receptive Vocabulary subtest), whereas others have been more difficult to correct (e.g., the relative paucity of verbs and adjectives among the stimulus items). Other improvements are mentioned in the technical section below.

The rationale for the development of the original CREVT is described in detail. The authors wanted to provide a vocabulary test that would be convenient and not time-consuming, and that would use the same norm group for both receptive and expressive skills. They based their decision to focus on the semantic aspect of language on past theoretical work suggesting that oral vocabulary knowledge is the best single index of general learning ability and predictor of school success.

They first reviewed intelligence tests, academic achievement tests, and language batteries to determine what aspects of oral language were assessed on each, and followed that up with a study of 109 current oral vocabulary tests to determine the preferred format for assessing receptive (RV) and expressive vocabulary (EV). Next, they located two extensive, full-color photograph collections that had been developed to teach vocabulary to students, and they built picture plates for 15 of the categories depicted. The authors then generated 50 words for each picture plate. From this initial pool of 750 words, they eliminated 250 that were too difficult or too infrequent (based upon appropriate published sources). From the remaining 500 words, they randomly drew 100 words, which were field-tested twice, with some picture plates from the RV subtest and some words from the EV subtest deleted after each field-testing.

The 1997 adult version, the CREVT-A, used 63% of the items from the CREVT and added other higher level words. To build the most recent version, the CREVT-2 (published in 2002), the authors combined items from the CREVT for children with items from the CREVT-A for adults and updated two pictures (the sewing machine and telephone). They then used logistic regression to determine "how an examinee [from the earlier norm groups] would have performed on the items he or she did not take" (examiner's manual, p. 62), which became the person's new raw score. After this, they used conventional item analysis to eliminate 19 items and reorder the remaining items by level of difficulty.

TECHNICAL. The description of the standardization sample is problematic. The norm group participants were mostly obtained by using the PRO-ED customer files. The authors recruited experienced testers who had purchased vocabulary tests in the previous 2 years and asked them to give the tests to students in their schools. Although the authors claim that "the CREVT-2 was normed on a sample of 2,545 persons in 38 states" (examiner's manual, p. 35), in reality the new CREVT-2 was given to only 385 individuals from 14 states, along with 180 students from Hartford, Connecticut, who were unaccountably left out of the final norm group. The remainder of the normative data are from the 1993 and 1996 normings done for the original CREVT and the CREVT-A (for children and adults, respectively). These individuals' scores were not based on exactly the same items as those on the current CREVT-2, and examinees' hypothetical scores for the CREVT-2 were derived statistically rather than through actual test administration.

The most recent samples are inadequately described. Other than giving the sex breakdown and noting that 18% of them had known disabilities (mostly learning or language), no other demographic data are provided for the most recent samples. Instead, the demographic information is for the combined sample from all three tests. In general, these combined data adequately match projections for the year 2000 from the U.S. Bureau of the Census 1998 data, though individuals from moderate- to high-income families are underrepresented (24% of sample vs. 39% of the U.S. population), and those with speech and language disorders are overrepresented (8% of sample vs. 2% of the U.S. population). The adult groups are relatively small: 204 young adults (44% male), 256 middle-aged adults, and 126 elderly adults recruited through senior centers. Norms have been stratified by age, and some additional cross-tabulations have been provided (though others would be helpful for determining the representativeness of the sample, such as educational level x age in the adult group).

Extensive reliability data are presented and are generally good to excellent. Coefficient alpha was computed for both forms at 18 age intervals and for various groups (children with learning disabilities, speech-language disabilities, and mental retardation). Of the resulting coefficients, all were at or above minimal levels except Form A for 5-year-olds. Composites at all age levels were high (above .85). Evidence is provided for test-retest reliability on three samples (12th graders and adults after 2 weeks and kindergartners after 2 months), for interscorer agreement, and for alternate forms reliability, both immediate and delayed. Reliability coefficients were nearly all over .80, with most above .90.

Construct validity data are from the original CREVT. If one accepts the authors' contention that these can be extended to the new CREVT-2, they are acceptable. In the original piloting, the authors conducted conventional item analyses to eliminate items that had inadequate discriminating power and those that were too easy or too difficult. In addition, they applied differential item functioning analysis to detect potential bias. They made 630 comparisons (one for each item on each form for each of three focus groups: males vs. females, African Americans vs. non-African

Americans, Hispanic Americans vs. non-Hispanic Americans). These analyses identified 51 potentially biased items, but only 1 of the 51 showed a moderate to large effect size. This 1 item represents less than 1% of the items on the CREVT. The authors further argue for lack of bias by showing that mean scores for all groups (males and females, African Americans, Hispanic Americans, European Americans) were still within the normal range (mean between 90 and 104 for each group).

Criterion-related validity was examined by correlating scores from the CREVT with scores from three single-skill measures—the Peabody Picture Vocabulary Test—Revised (PPVT-R), the Expressive One-Word Picture Vocabulary Test—Revised (EOWPVT-R), and the Vocabulary subtest of the Wechsler Intelligence Scale for Children (WISC-III)—and two more complete language measures—the Clinical Evaluation of Language Fundamentals—Revised (CELF-R) and the Test of Language Development-2 Primary (TOLD-P:2). The small samples (N = 14 to 41 for each study) were school-age students, almost all of whom had some sort of disability (mostly learning or language), except for the WISC-III study, which employed a mostly nondisabled sample. The correlations between CREVT-2 scores and scores on the PPVT-R, EOWPVT-R, and WISC-III Vocabulary subtest are all statistically significant but lower than expected (.39–.75). The moderate correlations between tests that measure exactly the same skill are especially surprising: the correlations between the WISC-III Vocabulary subtest and the CREVT-2 Expressive Vocabulary subtest are .75 for CREVT Form A and only .59 for Form B, the correlations between the PPVT-R and the CREVT-Receptive .59–.61, and between the EOWPVT-R and CREVT-2 Expressive are only .57 and .39. On the other hand, the overall General Vocabulary scores on the CREVT-2 and total scores from the CELF-R and the TOLD-P:2 are all over .89, which suggests that the test may be measuring a general proficiency in oral language rather than semantic knowledge per se.

Though the authors cite the generally lower mean scores for children with known speech/language disorders as evidence of construct validity, this group's mean scores on all components of the CREVT were still within the normal range (M = 89 to 94), which brings into question the ability of the CREVT-2 to detect those with language deficiencies.

COMMENTARY. One practical problem with the CREVT-2 is that by extending its range to include both children and adults, the risk is that adults may find early items condescending. A different starting point for teenagers and adults might be helpful. A more important drawback is that because the test has been kept short, there are insufficient items for above average adults. Because so many adults attain perfect scores, anyone over age 17 can score no higher than a standard score of 116 on Receptive Vocabulary (no higher than 109 for ages 40–60) and no higher than 118 on Expressive Vocabulary. Even among 12-year-olds, standard scores cannot reach the superior level. This attenuation of the norms table makes the test useless for identifying verbally gifted students after age 11.

On the whole, the authors have done a good job of beginning to deal with criticisms of the earlier edition. They have given information on differential item functioning to address the issue of potential item bias, have changed the instructions to let examinees know that the Receptive Vocabulary pictures may be used more than once, and seem to have added some validity and reliability studies employing clinical populations. On the other hand, the authors have overcompensated for earlier criticism of the lack of individuals with speech/language disorders in the normative sample, and this group is now overrepresented, which presumably lowers average scores and may be part of what is making it difficult to identify those who have language disabilities. However, the mean standard scores for children with known speech/language problems were still 89 and 90 on the two forms of the CREVT-2, which brings the test's discriminant validity into question and places serious limitations on its usefulness for identifying children with language disorders.

SUMMARY. The strengths of the original CREVT remain: The test materials (clear, realistic color photographs) are appealing, and administration and scoring are quick and simple. The shared norm group for the receptive and expressive components makes intra-individual comparisons more valid.

Validity and reliability data range from weak (concurrent validity) to excellent (test-retest reliability, alternate forms reliability, interscorer agreement). One of the CREVT-2's most significant problems is that it employs normative data from previous versions that are up to 10 years old (except for that from a convenience sample of only 385 individuals of unknown demographic characteristics). It is hoped that the authors will be able to renorm this test in the future using the newer version and a larger, more randomly selected, well-described sample. The other significant problem is that of test sensitivity; further studies would help clarify the question of whether the test can accurately discriminate between those with and without language disabilities.

In the meantime, the CREVT-2 should be viewed as a screening instrument that gives a rough measure of English-language vocabulary. As such, it is appropriate for research and possibly for progress evaluation. However, the user should not use the CREVT-2 to determine eligibility for special services, due to concerns about discriminant validity and because it assesses only one of the five components of oral language. Any child being assessed for possible intervention services in the speech-language area should be tested with more comprehensive tools that include measures of phonology, morphology, syntax, and pragmatics, not just semantics.

[60]
Comprehensive Test of Phonological Processing.

Purpose: Designed to measure "phonological awareness, phonological memory, and rapid naming."
Population: Ages 5 to 24.
Publication Date: 1999.
Acronym: CTOPP.
Administration: Individual.
Price Data, 2003: $231 per complete kit including examiner's manual (159 pages), 25 each profile/examiner record booklets for ages 5 to 6 and ages 7 to 24, picture book, and audiocassette; $45 per 25 profile/examiner record booklets for ages 5 to 6; $56 per 25 profile/examiner record booklets for ages 7 to 24; $35 per picture book; $81 per manual; $20 per audiocassette.
Time: (30) minutes.
Authors: Richard K. Wagner, Joseph K. Torgesen, and Carol A. Rashotte.
Publisher: PRO-ED.
   a) 5- AND 6-YEAR-OLD VERSION.
   Population: Ages 5–6.
   Scores, 11: Phonological Awareness (Elision, Blending Words, Sound Matching), Phonological

Memory (Memory for Digits, Nonword Repetition), Rapid Naming (Rapid Color Naming, Rapid Object Naming), Blending Nonwords (Supplemental Subtest).
   b) 7- THROUGH 24-YEAR-OLD VERSION.
   Population: Ages 7–24.
   Scores, 17: Phonological Awareness (Elision, Blending Words), Phonological Memory (Memory for Digits, Nonword Repetition), Rapid Naming (Rapid Digit Naming, Rapid Letter Naming), Alternate Phonological Awareness (Blending Nonwords, Segmenting Nonwords), Alternate Rapid Naming (Rapid Color Naming, Rapid Object Naming), Phoneme Reversal (Supplemental Subtest), Segmenting Words (Supplemental Subtest).

Review of the Comprehensive Test of Phonological Processing by DAVID P. HURFORD, Director of the Center for the Assessment and Remediation of Reading Difficulties and Professor of Psychology and Counseling, Pittsburg State University, Pittsburg, KS:

DESCRIPTION. The Comprehensive Test of Phonological Processing (CTOPP) is a test designed to assess the phonological processing skills of individuals aged 5 through 24 years. Because the test covers a wide range of ages, the authors developed two versions of the CTOPP, the first version of the CTOPP was developed for children aged 5 and 6 years, whereas the second version was developed for individuals between 7 and 24 years of age. Although the CTOPP has no time limits, administration typically is completed within approximately 30 minutes. The CTOPP assesses three components of phonological processing: Phonological Awareness, Phonological Memory, and Rapid Naming.

The authors intend the CTOPP to be used "to identify individuals who are significantly below their peers in important phonological abilities, to determine strengths and weaknesses among developed phonological processes, to document individuals' progress in phonological processing as a consequence of special intervention programs, and to serve as a measurement device in research studies investigating phonological processing" (manual, p. 13).

The items that comprise each subtest were constructed as a function of the use of these tests in published research. Median discriminating coefficients averaged .49 and ranged between .29 (Memory for Digits for 17-year-olds) and .72 (Elision for 13-year-olds). Median item difficulty coefficients averaged .59 and ranged between .03

(Elision for 5-year-olds) and .98 (Elision for 15-year-olds). Generally, item difficulty for an instrument should approximate .50, which is the case for the CTOPP.

TECHNICAL. The CTOPP was standardized with a norming group of 1,656 children from 30 states that included children with learning disabilities, speech and language disorders, and mental retardation. The normative sample was very similar to the demographic characteristics of the population of the United States. The CTOPP provides standard scores, percentiles, and age and grade equivalents.

Reliability was estimated using internal consistency, test-retest reliability, and interrater reliability. Internal consistency was assessed by computing coefficient alphas for each of the subtests at each of the 14 age levels (5, 6, 7, 8, 9, 10, 11, 12, 13, 14, 15, 16, 17, and 18 through 24 years). Coefficient alphas ranged from .70 (for 7-year-olds on the Rapid Letter Naming Test) to .96 (for 12-year-olds on the Rapid Digit Naming) with a mean of .87 when age level and subtest were collapsed. Coefficient alpha was also calculated for males, females, European Americans, African Americans, Hispanic Americans, Asian Americans, children with learning disabilities, and children with speech and language disorders, by subtest. These values were quite similar to those reported above with a range of .68 to .97 and a mean of .89. These values indicate that the CTOPP shows evidence as a reliable measure of phonological processing for individuals 5 through 24 years of age regardless of gender, minority group status, or developmental status.

Test-retest reliability was evaluated by assessing 91 individuals residing in Tallahassee, Florida: 32 children aged 5 through 7 years, 30 children aged 8 through 17 years, and 29 individuals 18 through 24 years. The CTOPP was administered twice with a 2-week interval between the two times of testing. Correlation coefficients ranged between .68 and .97 (mean of .82) for the subtests for the 5- through 7-year-olds, .72 and .93 (mean of .80) for the subtests for the 8- through 17-year-olds, and .67 and .90 (mean of .79) for the subtests for the 18- through 24-year-olds. Although the correlation coefficients are adequate, it is surprising that they are not stronger, particularly at the oldest age levels where one would believe that little development in phonological processing would occur between times of administration.

Interrater reliability was assessed by examining the results of two employees from the publisher's research department who independently scored 30 completed CTOPP protocols for the 5- and 6-years-olds, and 30 completed CTOPP protocols for the 7- through 24-year-olds. Although this method assesses the likelihood of arriving at similar results when the protocols have already been completed, it does not directly assess interrater reliability. To adequately assess this type of reliability requires that two individuals independently administer the CTOPP to the same child, transcribe the responses that the individual provides, and then score the protocol. Although the authors report in the manual that the interrater reliability was .98, this is an incomplete, inadequate, and invalid evaluation of interrater reliability.

Validity was assessed with content validity (including item rationale, item response theory, and differential item functioning analysis), criterion-related validity, and construct validity. With regard to content validity, each of the subtests that comprise the CTOPP has been used in research paradigms examining phonological processing over the past two to three decades. The subtests, therefore, are well established in assessing phonological processing. The manual provides brief and adequate descriptions of the subtests with citations to authors who have used the various subtests in their research examining phonological processing.

To examine the possibility of item bias in the CTOPP, Delta scores were computed between males and females, European Americans and Non-European Americans, African Americans and all other races, and Hispanic Americans and all other ethnic groups. Correlation coefficients for the Delta scores for the various groups named above ranged between .86 and .99 (mean of .98). These values indicate that the relative difficulties for the items were consistent between groups. As a result, differential item functioning was not indicated.

Criterion-related validity was very well evaluated with several studies. The first examined the correlations between the CTOPP Composite Scores and composite scores determined from the Word Identification and Word Analysis subtests of the Woodcock Reading Mastery Test—Revised (WRMT-R). Two hundred and sixteen kindergarten students participated in this study. Correlation coefficients for Phonological Awareness,

Phonological Memory, and Rapid Naming and the WRMT-R composites were .71, .42, and .66 one year after the CTOPP was given in kindergarten. When this same group was assessed in first grade with the CTOPP and then compared to their WRMT-R composites a year later in second grade even better values resulted: .80, .52, and .70, respectively. Another 603 students, 100 students from each grade from kindergarten through fifth grade, were administered the CTOPP and the Word Identification and Word Analysis subtests of the WRMT-R in addition to the Sight Word Efficiency and Phonetic Decoding Efficiency subtests of the Test of Word Reading Efficiency (TOWRE). Correlation coefficients ranged from .25 to .74 (mean of .48). The correlation between the CTOPP and the Word Identification subtest of the WRMT-R assessing 25 students from kindergarten, second grade, fifth grade, and seventh grade 40 students from high school, and 22 college students ranged between .46 and .66 (mean of .57). Concurrent and predictive validity measures examining the CTOPP and the Lindamood Auditory Conceptualization Tests, the WRMT-R, the Gray Oral Reading Test-3, and the Wide Range Achievement Test-3 (WRAT-3) produced concurrent validity coefficients ranging between .00 and .75 (mean of .43) and predictive validity coefficients ranging between .21 and .72 (mean of .46). The normative sample described above was also used to describe the relationship between the CTOPP and the subtests of Sight Word Efficiency, Phonetic Decoding Efficiency, and Total Word Reading Efficiency of the TOWRE for the two versions of the CTOPP. For the 5- and 6-year-old version, the mean correlation coefficient was .45 and ranged from .19 (for Phonetic Decoding Efficiency and Memory for Digits) to .70 (for Blending Nonwords and Sight Word Efficiency, and Blending Nonwords and Total Word Reading Efficiency). For the 7-year-old through 24-year-old version, the mean correlation coefficient was .43 and ranged from .25 (for Segmenting Words and Phonetic Decoding Efficiency) to .61 (for Phoneme Reversal and Sight Word Efficiency).

Finally, construct validity was assessed utilizing confirmatory factor analysis, age differentiation, and group differentiation. The confirmatory analysis of variance provides evidence that the subtests tap the hypothesized abilities measured with the CTOPP, that is, Phonological Awareness, Phonological Memory, and Rapid Naming. For the 5- and 6-year-old version, and the 7- to 24-year-old version similar factor loadings result between the factors and the subtests. All of the factor loadings were above .52.

One statement that the authors make regarding using group differentiation to support construct validity is somewhat inconsistent with their results from the differential item functioning analysis. The Delta scores indicated that there was no item bias for the CTOPP among African American vs. non-African American participants. However, there were differences between the standard scores of African American participants and other participants, some as large as a *SEM* from the mean. The authors claim that "The differences among groups on measures of phonological awareness should not be taken as evidence of test bias, but rather as confirmation of the fact that differences in language experience in the home and neighborhood can have an impact on the development of phonological awareness in children" (manual, p. 103). Although this may be true, the evidence they use to support this claim is based on a study they performed that, most likely, included participants from the norming group. This renders the argument somewhat circular. As the authors note in the manual, the study of validity is a continuous process. This is one aspect of their validity study that warrants further investigation and verification.

COMMENTARY. The case for validity was established. Confirmatory factor analysis demonstrated that the constructs of Phonological Awareness, Phonological Memory, and Rapid Naming are being assessed. Age differentiation data indicated that performance on the CTOPP increased with age, which provides validity given that phonological processing abilities are purported to develop with age. Surprisingly, the case for group differentiation was not as compelling.

The record booklet has sections for identifying information (e.g., name, gender, school, grade, age), recording the scores (e.g., raw scores, age equivalents, grade equivalents, percentile ranks, and standard scores), and score profiles (graphical display of the standard scores and quotients). The subtests along with their brief instructions are contained within the record booklet. The last two pages of the record booklet contain space for the examiner to write interpretations and recommendations.

The manual is concise and complete. The novice user of the CTOPP will not find it difficult to comprehend the administration or scoring procedures, nor the reasons for assessing phonological processing. The first chapter of the manual provides an excellent overview of the CTOPP in addition to a brief, but informative, discussion of phonological processing. One minor criticism of the manual concerns the authors' overly cautious remarks regarding interpretation of the results. This overly cautious attitude is present in several places within the manual. These remarks are most likely related to the authors' backgrounds in research. As researchers, the authors were trained to avoid statements that were not totally grounded in the data and to eschew making Type I errors (indicating there are differences, difficulties, or relationships that do not, in reality, exist). Given the massive amount of research examining the relationship between phonological processing and reading and language difficulties, the cautions are not warranted. Finally, the psychometric properties of the CTOPP are appropriate for making rather strong statements concerning one's phonological processing abilities.

SUMMARY. The CTOPP is a test that assesses the phonological processing abilities of individuals aged 5 to 24. It was developed to identify individuals who are performing poorly on phonological processing, to determine individuals' strengths and weaknesses with regard to phonological processes, to document the progress of interventions in phonological processing, and to be used as a research instrument for studies examining phonological processing abilities. Because the CTOPP does not offer an alternative form, its use in research is somewhat limited. The CTOPP has acceptable psychometric properties, excluding interrater reliability, which was not properly addressed. The CTOPP is a welcomed instrument to assess phonological processing.

Review of the Comprehensive Test of Phonological Processing by CLAUDIA R. WRIGHT, Professor of Educational Psychology, California State University, Long Beach, CA:

DESCRIPTION AND DEVELOPMENT. The Comprehensive Test of Phonological Processing (CTOPP) was designed as an assessment of phonological awareness, phonological memory, and rapid naming for identifying individuals who

perform below their peers in phonological processing ability. Relative strengths and weaknesses among phonological processing skills can be inferred from test scores and can serve to monitor progress or to develop individualized intervention programs. Two versions of the CTOPP have been developed for administration to children, adolescents, and young adults (ages 5-0 to 24-11); one for children between the ages of 5-0 and 6-11, and the second for those between 7-0 and 24-11.

The CTOPP version for children, 5-0 to 6-11, yields 11 possible standard scores derived from seven core subtests that produce three composite scores and one supplementary subtest. The three composite scores are Phonological Awareness (PACS), Phonological Memory (PMCS), and Rapid Naming (RNCS), made up of three, two, and two subtests, respectively. The 60-item PACS is considered relevant to reading instruction and is made up of the standard scores from three core subtests: (a) Elision, a 20-item subtest, requires the examinee to repeat aloud a target word then identify elements of it on demand (e.g., after correctly repeating the target word "bold," the task is to report the sound produced when the /b/ sound is dropped); (b) Blending Words (20 items) involves listening to sounds produced on an audiocassette recording, then combining the phonemic sounds of strings into words; and (c) Sound Matching (20 items) uses initial and final sounds of words as targets for examinees to identify other words with similar initial or final sounds. The 39-item PMCS is made up of standard scores from two of the core subtests: (a) Memory for Digits subtest (21 items) assesses short-term memory recall when presented with a two- to eight-digit number presented on audiocassette; and (b) Nonword Repetition (18 items) requires reproduction of nonwords ranging from 3 to 15 sounds. The 144-item RNCS includes two core subtests: (a) Rapid Color Naming (72 items) measures the speed at which the respondent identifies a series of blocks with different colors; and (b) Rapid Object Naming (72 items) presents a series of six objects, randomly arranged in a 4x9 table, to be named as quickly as possible. The supplementary subtest (not used in any composite score) is an 18-item scale, Blending Nonwords, for assessing one's ability to combine separate sounds into nonwords.

For examinees aged 7-0 to 24-11, the CTOPP yields 17 possible standard scores derived from 12 subtests and five composite scores. Six core subtests produce three of the composite scores (PACS, PMCS, and RNCS); and of six supplemental subtests, four are used to create two composite scores labeled Alternative Phonological Awareness (APACS) and Alternative Rapid Naming (ARNCS). The PACS is a 40-item composite score, also relevant to reading instruction, made up of standard scores from two core subtests: (a) the 20-item Elision subtest and (b) the 20-item Blending Words subtest. Excluded from this composite, compared to the version for younger children, is the Sound Matching subtest. The 39-item PMCS is identical to the version for younger children. However, the 144-item RNCS employs two new speeded core subtests: (a) Rapid Digit Naming (72 items) measures the speed at which the respondent names strings of six digits randomly arranged in a 4x9 table and (b) Rapid Letter Naming (72 items) presents strings of six letters to be reported, randomly arranged in a 4x9 table. The last two composite scores, APACS and ARNCS, are compiled from the supplemental subtests. The 38-item APACS is made up of the 18-item Blending Nonwords subtest used in the previous version and the 20-item subtest, Segmenting Nonwords, which requires the examinee to break nonwords into the corresponding phonemes. The 144-item ARNCS employs the two naming subtests, Rapid Color Naming and Rapid Object Naming. The two supplementary subtests, not used in any composite score, are Phoneme Reversal (18 items), a task to reorder speech sounds to create new words, and Segmenting Words (20 items) that requires the examinee to identify the separate phonemes that make up the target word.

Test administration and scoring. Users of the CTOPP are expected to have extensive training in assessment with special emphasis on phonological ability testing, test statistics, scoring, and interpretation. The CTOPP technical manual provides detailed, step-by-step administration procedures for each subtest including useful scripts for the examiner, practice items, prompts, feedback, and guidelines for "entry" points and "ceilings" for terminating testing.

Clear guidelines are provided for recording, scoring, generating profiles for each examinee, and using conversion tables to transform raw scores to percentiles, standard, age-equivalent, or grade-equivalent scores. Detailed information and guides are provided for interpretation of the various forms

of test scores. Appropriate cautions are included with respect to the reliability estimates of subtests, the limitations that affect interpretation of test scores, and reminders that performance on CTOPP subtests should not be used in isolation when constructing a curriculum for a particular student.

TECHNICAL.

Norming procedures. Normative data were obtained from a sample of 1,656 individuals in 30 states during 1997–1998. Sample sizes for 14 age groups ranged from 76 to 155 (13 samples represented each age, 5 through 17, separately; ages 18 to 24 comprised a single sample of 112 respondents). It appears that respondents were not randomly selected. The test publisher identified psychologists and speech/language pathologists who had previously participated in norming procedures conducted by the company and those who had purchased the Tests of Phonological Awareness (Torgesen & Bryant, 1994) to be invited to participate in the CTOPP norming effort. In addition, the three authors set up data collection sites in Florida, Kansas, and Washington. A comparison to U.S. school population estimates for the targeted year revealed close matches for the resulting percentages of CTOPP examinees across the four regions, gender and age, ethnicity, and other SES indicators.

Reliability of CTOPP scores. Internal-consistency reliability (Cronbach alphas) estimates were reported for all nonspeeded subtest scores; alternate-form reliability estimates for speeded subtest scores were obtained. Across age groups, most subtest scores yielded alphas of .80 or higher with composite scores generally yielding higher estimates than subtest scores; averaged coefficients ranged from .77 to .95 (mdn = .88). Reliability estimates fell below .80 for only 3 of the 21 possible subtest scores: Memory for Digits, Nonword Repetition, and Rapid Object Naming. Analysis of reliability estimates yielded similar results to those observed for the total sample across subgroups including males (n = 823), females (n = 833), four ethnic groups (1,220 European-, 225 African-, 144 Hispanic-, and 52 Asian-American respondents), learning disabilities (n = 67), and speech/language disabilities (n = 60). In general, it appears that the CTOPP scores yield acceptable estimates of internal-consistency reliability. Stability (2-week test-retest) coefficients were obtained for CTOPP subtests with three groups of respondents: (a) ages 5–7 (n = 32), rs ranged from .68 to .97 (mdn = .79); (b) ages 8–17 (n = 30), rs ranged from .72 to .95 (mdn = .80); and (c) 18 and older (n = 29), rs ranged from .67 to .91 (mdn = .80). Finally, interrater reliability estimates were provided by two staff persons who independently scored 30 completed CTOPP batteries for the 5-0 to 6-11 group and 30 batteries for the 7-0 to 24-11 group. For the 11 subtests and composites scored for the first group, interrater reliability estimates ranged from .95 to .99 (mdn = .99); for the 17 possible scores for the second group, the range was .95 to .99 (mdn = .99). Authors provided reasonable cautions regarding the reliability of test scores.

Validity of CTOPP scores. Traditional indicators were provided of item analyses and for content, criterion-related, and construct validities. A logistic regression procedure was employed for nonspeeded test items to examine differential item functioning (DIF) to detect bias for groups (gender and ethnicity) and resulted in the elimination of 25 items from the final version of the CTOPP. A follow-up analysis using 36 Delta subgroup comparisons (male vs. female; European vs. Non-European American, African vs. Non-African American; Hispanic vs. Non-Hispanic American) yielded sufficiently large correlation coefficients ranging from .86 to .99 (mdn = .99) leading to the conclusion that little or no detectable bias was evident among the items. The possible exception was observed for the African vs. Non-African American group comparisons that ranged from .86 (for Sound Matching) to .99 (mdn = .98).

A series of studies was conducted to examine the criterion-predictive and concurrent validity of CTOPP composite and subtest scores. For the first CTOPP version, 216 kindergarten and first-grade students were administered the CTOPP composites (PA, PM, and RN) and, one year later, the Woodcock Reading Mastery Test—Revised (WRMT-R) (see 14:423) (Decoding subtest). Moderate correlations obtained between sets of scores for the kindergarten group (.71, .42, and .66, respectively) and for first graders (.80, .52, and .70, respectively) supported the predictive validity of the CTOPP for these samples.

Concurrent validity for CTOPP scores was demonstrated using partial correlations, controlling for age, for a sample of 603 kindergarten through fifth-grade students. Coefficients were examined between CTOPP core subtests scores

and (a) two WRMT-R subtests (Word Identification and Word Analysis) and (b) two subtests, Sight Word Efficiency and Phonetic Decoding Efficiency, of the Test of Word Reading Efficiency (TOWRE; Torgesen, Wagner, & Rashotte, 1999), a measure of word reading ability. The strongest coefficients, across the four criterion tests, were observed for the Elision subtest (rs, .67 to .74); the lowest coefficients, for Rapid Color Naming (rs, .25 to .33). Concurrent validity coefficients ranged from .46 (Sound Matching) to .66 (Nonword Repetition) (mdn = .57) between CTOPP core subtest scores and the WRMT-R Word Identification subtest for a second sample of 164 students (25 each of kindergarten, Grades 2, 5, and 7; 40 high school; and 22 college students).

For a sample of 73 students with learning disabilities, both concurrent and predictive partial correlations (controlling for age) were examined for six of eight CTOPP core subtests using various measures including the Lindamood Auditory Conceptualization Tests (LACT; Lindamood & Lindamood, 1971), a measure of phonological awareness. The LACT produced statistically significant coefficients across the CTOPP subtests (rs, .41 [Nonword Repetition] to .75 [Elision], mdn = .50; all p<.001). The WRMT-R Word Attack subtest yielded six coefficients ranging from .32 (Blending Words) to .74 (Elision), mdn = .53; all p<.01; and Word Identification generated five significant coefficients, .22 (Nonword Repetition) to .57 (Rapid Digit Naming), mdn = .48; all p<.05. Correlations observed between the WRAT-R and six CTOPP cores ranged from .27 (Blending Words) to .62 (Elision), mdn = .50; all p<.05. Evidence of predictive validity was provided by retesting the same LD sample 6 months later using the same WRMT-R, GORT-3, and WRAT-3 scales cited above. Similar to the previous findings, nearly all low to moderate coefficients were statistically significant, with the Elision (rs, .46 to .72, mdn = .62), Rapid Digit Naming (.55–.66, mdn = .60), and Rapid Letter Naming (.49–.62, mdn = .59) yielding the strongest predictors across all measures.

Finally, a series of studies was conducted to examine the CTOPP scores' ability to differentiate between students with and without various disabilities (speech/learning, language, and reading). Findings revealed that those with learning disabilities (n = 67) tended to score below all other groups (males, females, and ethnic groups) on phonological processing subtests (Elision, Nonword Repetition, Phoneme Reversal, Segmenting Nonwords, and all Rapid Naming tests). Those with speech/language disabilities (n = 60) tended to score slightly higher than those with learning disabilities; with their lowest scores in the areas of Sound Matching, Memory for Digits, and Nonword repetition. College-age examinees identified with reading disabilities (n = 25) produced statistically significant lower CTOPP subtest scores compared to those without reading disabilities (n = 29). Caution is warranted in interpreting these findings as subgroup comparisons were based on small sample sizes.

Construct validity was supported using confirmatory factor analyses. A three-factor solution for the normative sample of 5- and 6-year-olds yielded (a) Phonological Awareness made up of the Elision, Sound Matching, and Blending Words subtests; (b) Phonological Memory, which includes Memory for Digits and Nonword Repetition; and (c) Rapid Naming, Rapid Color Naming, and Rapid Object Naming. Similar patterns were observed for the normative sample of 7- through 24-year-old respondents.

SUMMARY. Test administration instructions are well written with detailed examples. Test materials (book of picture stimuli and technical manual) are sturdy text in glossy, ringed hardback books that will survive continuous use. An audiocassette, for presenting sounds used in the Blending Words and Phonological Memory subtests for both versions of the CTOPP, provides clear, well-articulated speech samples at an easy pace. Overall, CTOPP subtest scores appear to provide reliable and valid indicators of phonological awareness, phonological memory, and rapid naming for individuals of ages 5-0 through 24-11. Additional studies are needed to replicate the observations reported for individuals with learning and speech/language disabilities.

REVIEWER'S REFERENCES

Lindamood, C., & Lindamood, P. (1971). Lindamood Auditory Conceptualization Test. Austin, TX: PRO-ED.
Torgesen, J. K., & Bryant, B. R. (1994). Test of Phonological Awareness. Austin, TX: PRO-ED.
Torgesen, J. K., Wagner, R. K., & Rashotte, C. A. (1999). Test of Word Reading Efficiency. Austin, TX: PRO-ED.

[61]

Comprehensive Trail-Making Test.

Purpose: Developed for the evaluation and diagnosis of brain injury and other forms of central nervous system compromise.

Population: Ages 11 to 74-11.
Publication Date: 2002.
Acronym: CTMT.
Scores, 6: Trail 1, Trail 2, Trail 3, Trail 4, Trail 5, Composite Index.
Administration: Individual.
Price Data, 2002: $87 per complete kit; $40 per 10 record booklets; $49 per examiner's manual (79 pages).
Time: (5–12) minutes.
Author: Cecil R. Reynolds.
Publisher: PRO-ED.

Review of the Comprehensive Trail-Making Test by NORA M. THOMPSON, Psychologist— Learning Disability Specialist, University of Washington, Seattle, WA:

DESCRIPTION. The Comprehensive Trail-Making Test (CTMT) is a brief (5 to 12 minutes) pencil-and-paper, timed, visual search and sequencing test for testing individuals between the ages of 11 and 75 years. The author proposes that the CTMT will be a useful addition to the neuropsychological evaluation to detect brain dysfunction and track progress in rehabilitation. Examiners administering the CTMT should have formal training in assessment. Proper interpretation of the CTMT in the context of a larger assessment battery requires advanced training in functional neuroanatomy and neuropsychology. The examinee completes each of three practice trails and five timed test trails in the record booklet. Detailed instructions for administration and scoring of the test are provided in the test manual. A Composite Index T-score as well as T-scores for each of the five individual trails (Trail 1, Trail 2, etc.) can be derived from the normative tables provided in the manual. A table depicting conversions of T-scores to percentiles, quotient scores, z-scores, and stanines is also provided.

DEVELOPMENT. The CTMT builds upon the longstanding popularity of trail-making tasks as easy and quick ways to administer measures proven sensitive to the effects of brain injury of a variety of etiologies. Developed in 1938 by Partington (Partington & Leiter, 1949), the original Trail-Making Test was later incorporated into the U.S. Army Individual Test Battery in 1944 as well as the neuropsychological test battery pioneered by Halstead (Halstead, 1947; Reitan & Wolfson, 1993). The original Trail-Making Test measures complex visual scanning, motor speed, attention, and executive function, particularly the ability to shift cognitive set (Lezak, 1995; Stuss et al., 2001).

The CTMT was developed to overcome limitations in the normative data available for the original Trail-Making Test (for a further discussion of this topic, see Spreen & Strauss, 1998) as well as to improve sensitivity to brain dysfunction by assessing resistance to distraction and improving reliability for assessing cognitive set-shifting. Trail 1 of the CTMT is similar to Trails A of the original Trail-Making Test. The assessment of attention and resistance to distraction is enhanced by the addition of distractor circles for Trails 2 and 3. Trail 4 assesses the added factor of set-shifting by using numbers in numeric and English word forms (e.g., 1, two, 3, four). Trail 5 mimics the original Trails B with addition of distractor circles. There is no specific rationale offered for the format of the changes made to the original Trail-Making Test beyond the agreement of 10 advanced level neuropsychologists with the author. There is no discussion of pilot studies used in the development of the test.

TECHNICAL. Information describing the norming process is clearly described in the manual and the normative sample of 1,664 individuals closely matches the U.S. population in terms of geographic area, gender, race, ethnicity, family income, parent education, and disability status and is well stratified across demographic characteristics. There appear to be no meaningful differences in Trail scores as a function of gender or ethnicity for European, African, and Hispanic Americans, particularly when relying on the Composite Score.

Internal consistency reliability estimates of each Trail time T-score with a composite including the remaining four Trail times T-scores was calculated on the entire normative sample. The resulting correlations reach or exceed $r = .70$. Similar levels of internal consistency were found when the sample was subgrouped by gender, ethnicity, and broad age group (adolescents and adults). Test-retest reliability was assessed on 30 adults at one test location with a 1-week retest interval. A .3 SD practice effect was found with correlations reaching or exceeding .70.

Analyses conducted on the entire normative sample provide convincing evidence of the CTMT's validity. Principal components analysis yielded a two-factor solution supporting the author's contention that Trails 1, 2, and 3 are distinguished

from Trails 4 and 5. Performance improves with age in adolescence and progressively declines after 30 years of age.

The CTMT was apparently conormed with the Developmental Test of Visual-Perception—Adolescents and Adults (DTVP-A; Reynolds, Pearson, & Voress, 2002) and the Draw-A-Person Intelligence Scoring, the DAP:IQ (Reynolds & Hickman, 2002). In fact, Trail 2 appears on both the CTMT and the DTVP-A. External validity correlations between the CTMT and these tests suggest the presence of common requirements for visual perception and visual-motor skill. A low correlation with the DAP:IQ was found ($r = .16$). The bulk of the support for the validity of the CTMT as a measure of attention and executive function stems from the decades of research on the original Trail-Making Test and the logical similarity between the two tests. Yet surprisingly, there are no data directly comparing the CTMT to the original Trail-Making Test or other well-established measures of executive function such as the Wisconsin Card Sorting Test or the Category Test. Three special populations were studied and included 57 gifted/talented teenagers, 30 teenagers with undefined learning disability, and 28 adults participating in rehabilitation following cerebrovascular accident. Age-corrected mean scores for these groups fall in the expected directions from the mean.

COMMENTARY. The strengths of the CTMT lie in its logical similarity to the original Trail-Making Test and the robust normative data set the author has developed. With regard to the former, the test is brief and easy to administer and score. Because of its long history of use in clinical and research applications, the neuropsychological literature provides more than ample empirical evidence that the original Trail-Making Test is effective in identifying individuals with brain dysfunction. In fact, one might argue whether the Trail-Making Test was originally developed upon theoretical grounds, or whether current theories have grown, in part, to encompass the findings of the Trail-Making Test and other neuropsychological measures.

Nonetheless, there is a great need for improved normative data for neuropsychological tests in general and thus, the CTMT addresses an important gap. The normative data for the CTMT are an asset, reflecting current U.S. population demographics stratified across demographic categories. Internal consistency and factor structure are strong and show virtually no bias from gender or ethnicity when used with European, African, and Hispanic Americans. In addition, the test materials are well laid out and the manual is logically organized and easy to follow.

However, there is not yet convincing evidence upon which the clinician could rely with confidence that the CTMT can replace the original Trail-Making Test in the neuropsychological evaluation process. There has not been a study comparing the CTMT with the original Trail-Making Test; nor has there been evidence of the utility of the CTMT in distinguishing specific diagnostic groups, whether administered in isolation or as part of a larger collection of neuropsychological measures.

SUMMARY. The CTMT addresses an important need in neuropsychological assessment to have assessment instruments with sound psychometric properties. By improving upon a well-established neuropsychological test of attention, visual search, and cognitive set-shifting, the author has set out to refine important aspects of neuropsychological assessment. The CTMT holds promise as an important contribution to neuropsychological research and diagnosis. At this point, however, more research-based evidence supporting the validity of the CTMT in the neuropsychological assessment and diagnostic process is needed before the test can be used clinically with confidence.

REVIEWER'S REFERENCES

Halstead, W. C. (1947). *Brain and intelligence: A quantitative study of the frontal lobes.* Chicago: University of Chicago Press.

Lezak, M. D. (1995). *Neuropsychological assessment* (3rd ed.). Oxford: Oxford University Press.

Partington, J. E., & Leiter, R. G. (1949). Partington's Pathway Test. *The Psychological Service Center Bulletin, 1,* 9–20.

Reitan, R. M., & Wolfson, D. (1993). *The Halstead-Reitan Neuropsychological Test Battery: Theory and clinical interpretation* (2nd ed.). Tucson, AZ: Neuropsychological Press.

Reynolds, C. R., & Hickman, J. A. (2002). *Draw-A-Person intelligence scoring, the DAP:IQ.* Austin, TX: PRO-ED.

Reynolds, C. R., Pearson, N. A., & Voress, J. K. (2002). *Developmental Test of Visual Perception—Adolescent and Adult.* Austin, TX: PRO-ED.

Spreen, O., & Strauss, E. (1998). *A compendium of neuropsychological tests* (2nd ed.). Oxford: Oxford University Press.

Stuss, D., Bisschop, S. M., Alexander, M., Levine, B., Katz, D., & Izukawa, D. (2001). The Trail Making Test: A study in focal lesion patients. *Psychological Assessment, 13,* 230–239.

[62]

The Computer Category Test.

Purpose: Designed for neuropsychological screening via computer.
Population: Ages 9–14, adult.
Publication Dates: 1994–1999.

Acronym: CAT, ACAT.
Scores: Information available from publisher.
Administration: Individual or group.
Levels, 2: Adult, Intermediate.
Price Data, 2002: $360 per MS DOS computer program on 3.5-inch disk including manual (1994, 98 pages); $45 per MS DOS computer program preview (3 uses) on 3.5-inch disk.
Time: (30–40) minutes; up to 90 minutes for impaired patients.
Comments: A computerized version of the Halstead Category Test including the Adaptive Category Test (ACAT); requires MS DOS compatible computer, a graphics card, and a disk drive.
Authors: James Choca, Linda Laatsch, Dan Garside, and Carl Arnemann.
Publisher: Multi-Health Systems, Inc.

Review of The Category Test by ROBERT A. LEARK, Associate Professor, Pacific Christian College, Fullerton, CA:

DESCRIPTION. The Computer Category Test (CAT) is a computer-program version of the Halstead Category Test (HCT) with additional variations. The CAT allows for the standard administration of a computer generated full original HCT, an Adaptive Category Test (ACAT), a Russell Revised Short Form (RRSF), the Intermediate Version (IV) for children 9 to 14, and, finally, a User-defined Version (UDV).

The computer program utilizes the same stimulus as in the original slide version of the HCT for the full version; however, for the IV, there are adaptations of the original IV stimuli. The adapted stimuli maintain the original scoring concept for the HCT but are not always the same in appearance or in test order. The ACAT is an "interactive computer version of the Cat" (Choca, Laatsch, Garside, & Arnemann, 1994, p. 10). The ACAT "uses built-in archival data to compare each subject to statistical 'groupings' [highlight by test author] as they respond to each subtest. The version then uses that group's statistical results to accurately predict the subject's final score" (Choca et al., 1994, p. 10).

The RRSF uses the HCT stimuli selected by Russell & Levy (1987). The RRSF is a modified HCT, using fewer stimuli (95 items grouped into six subtests). The RRSF does not contain the memory subtest from the HCT. The RRSF also reorganizes two subtests, V and VI, into counting and proportional principles (Choca et al., 1994). The UDV allows for the examiner to modify and develop a personalized version with the understanding that no normative data exist for such use.

The authors make note that the original HCT was not standardized using a "strict set of instructions in the manner of, for instance, the Wechsler batteries" (Choca et al., 1994, p. 61). The CAT test authors do elaborate on the necessity for the examiner to make certain that the individual taking the test does indeed understand the instructions. Furthermore, as with the HCT, the examiner may offer encouragement, prompting to task, and even clarifications of instructions to make certain the subject is performing at the best level possible. Subjects are to be prompted to press the key only once and to release the key immediately once pressed. Although there is no time limit to the test (or any of the modified versions) the examiner is encouraged to prompt the subject to move along at a reasonable pace

Scoring of any of the test versions is done automatically by the computer program. The program provides distinct scores for each of the possible tests administered. For the full version of the HCT, the program provides number of errors, number correct, response time in seconds, and average time per response for each subtest. The ACAT provides the examiner similar scores for each subtest as those provided for the full HCT. However, because the ACAT is based upon a predicted full score, there are differences in scoring. For the ACAT, the scores include actual number of errors, a predicted final score, time in seconds, number of items given, and average time per response. The predicted final score is based upon a cluster analysis (Laatsch & Choca, 1994). In addition, each response given for every item administered is provided so that the examiner can do an item analysis. Following each profile score, a brief narrative interpretation is given

The CAT also provides two additional scores not given by the original HCT or any of its modifications. One of these is the Perseveration Index (PI). The PI is the percentage of possible wrong choices consistent with the rule of a previous subtest. The index is the number of such wrong choices made, divided by the total number of such wrong choices possible on that subtest, then multiplied by 100 (Choca et al., 1994). The PI is an experimental index in that little empirical evidence is available to support its validity and interpretation. The Reaction Time (RT) is the other experimental measure. The RT normative population was derived from 99 subjects. As stated in the manual, the data distribution is skewed and the RT lacks normative means and standard deviations. The CAT uses extreme scores as warnings to the examiner.

DEVELOPMENT. According to the manual, the ACAT was developed in seven steps: (a) item analysis to exclude original HCT items that were either too easy or too difficult; (b) HCT items were then rearranged taking into account difficulty indices; (c) use of a cluster analysis of the remaining items within each subtest; (d) use of the cluster-derived data to characterize statistical differences between groupings; (e) development of rules for each subtest to permit the prediction of the entire subtest based upon sample of subtest items; (f) comparison of performance by the archival sample, based upon the rules developed; and, (g) cross validation of the rules.

The item analysis yielded the removal of 29 items from the original HCT item pool. The data from the archival sample were then re-analyzed following the removal of these 29 items from that data. There were no statistical differences between group mean error totals with these items removed (r = .9979). Then, Subtests V and VI were rearranged dependent upon item difficulty indices.

Following this, the authors used cluster groups wherein differing subject groups were characterized based upon their performance on the test. According to the authors, "When a new subject appears to *belong* [italics in original] to one of these statistically different groups, the test or subtest can be discontinued, and the subject given the average score of the group that characterizes his or her performance" (Choca et al., 1994, p. 51). From here, branching points were used to designate 95% confidence ranges and to assure clustered group differences. In all, about 200 branching points were derived and are incorporated into the software-scoring program. Once this was completed, the scoring was cross validated. The cross validation of the branching scoring determination rules for the modified HCT items yielded essentially normal distributions. Correlation between the modified or correct HCT and the ACAT was .96 for Group A and .95 for Group B. Classification analysis yielded 94% for Group A and 91% for Group B. From here the authors have concluded that the ACAT is "essentially identical" (Choca et al., 1994, p. 57) to the HCT.

TECHNICAL. The information on the normative sample used for the derivation of the test is not given in the manual. There is reference to a 46-subject (male inpatients at a VA hospital and private rehabilitation hospital) cross validation study (Choca & Morris, 1992). However, no other information is given concerning the normative sample: age, gender, SES, ethnic composition of sample, etc.

The validity of scores from the ACAT to the HCAT was assessed by examining the similarity of subject scores on both instruments in a validation and cross validation sample. However, little description of the samples is provided in the manual. The authors concluded that the ACAT is essentially the same as the modified HCT. Even though there is correlation cited between the standard HCT and the computerized HCT ($r = .90$) from one study of 46 male inpatient participants, the manual fails to indicate composition of the participant group except for the fact that participants were excluded if they were deemed to be "too cognitively impaired" (Choca et al., 1994, p. 29). In addition, the ACAT was compared to the modified HCT (available in the software). Here the authors indicate that 250 participants were arranged into samples to examine the validity of scores from the ACAT. Again, the description of the sample is lacking, as there is no information on age, gender, SES, ethnicity, or the like. The two samples were found to have correlations of .96 and .95, respectively, when the two samples were compared on the ACAT and the modified HCT.

Reliability data are not provided although item analyses were conducted on the original HCT items. No reliability data were found in the manual to estimate either internal or temporal stability for any of the tests within the software.

COMMENTS. The Computer Category Test is more than a computerized version of Halstead's Category Test. The CAT is a variety of the category test (a derivative). Although the test does allow the examiner to use the original HCT, this application has limited validity or reliability evidence in its current version. The manual provides a historical summary of the development of the HCT, but it leads the reader to believe that the computerized version(s) are exactly the same test. Clearly, there are similarities between the various category tests available, including this one. However, there is little empirical evidence with brain-injured or otherwise impaired individuals, to indicate their use in place of the original HCT. The CAT certainly takes less time to complete than the original HCT, especially the ACAT. The CAT is also much more convenient to use. However, the CAT lacks normative information that would make the instrument a solid replacement. The CAT fails to live up to the standards for test development established by the AERA, APA, and NCME (1999) in that it does not provide information on the normative sample. It also does not provide information on the stratification of the sample with regard to ethnicity, grouping (i.e., normal controls, brain injured, psychiatric, etc.), gender and the like. Furthermore, the manual does not provide evidence of reliability of scores from the instrument. The validity data available in the manual are helpful, but need to be written in a clearer mode.

Multi-Health Systems, Inc. (MHS), the test distributor, has established itself as a leader in test development and distribution of professional products. This manual and product do not meet that expectation. The manual reviewed had numerous spelling errors, was not adequately organized to find information on the samples, and did not provide the reader with examples of scoring supplied by each of the various tests available. It was also confusing in that it was difficult to understand the options available for testing.

SUMMARY. This reviewer recommends use of this test for experimental purposes only, until adequate normative, validity, and reliability data become present. The computer software does present itself as promising, but that promise is not yet fulfilled.

REVIEWERS REFERENCES
American Educational Research Association, American Psychological Association, & National Council on Measurement in Education. (1999). *Standards for educational and psychological testing.* Washington, DC: American Educational Research Association.

Choca J., Laatsch, L., Garside, D., & Arnemann, C. (1994). *CAT: The Category Test computer program.* Toronto, ON, Canada: Multi-Health Systems, Inc.

Choca, J., & Morris, J, (1992). Administering the Category Test by computer: Equivalence of results. *Clinical Neuropsychologist, 6,* 9–15.

Laatsch, L., & Choca, J. (1994). Cluster-branching methodology for adaptive testing and the development of the Adaptive Category Test. *Psychological Assessment, 6,* 345–351.

Russell, E. W., & Levy, M. (1987). Revision of the Halstead Category Test. *Journal of Consulting and Clinical Psychology, 55,* 898–901.

[63]

Computerized Lifestyle Assessment.

Purpose: Designed to identify lifestyle behaviors such as substance use, health maintenance, preventive activities, social issues, and emotional well-being to provide a basis for individuals to discuss their lifestyles with a health professional.

Population: 14 years and older.

Publication Date: 1994.

Scores, 16: Nutrition, Eating Habits, Caffeine Use, Physical Activity, Body Weight, Sleep, Social Relationships, Family Interactions, Tobacco Use, Alcohol Use, Non-Medical Drug Use, Medical/Dental Care, Motor Vehicle Safety, Sexual Activities, Work & Leisure, Emotional Health.

Administration: Individual.

Price Data, 2002: $195 per MS-DOS disk for 100 uses; $895 per MS-DOS disk for 500 uses; $25 per Previous Version MS-DOS for 3 uses.

Time: (20–30) minutes.

Comments: Self-report; designed to run on most IBM-compatible computers; minimum requirements include a color graphics adapter card (CGA, EGA, VGA, or SVGA), DOS ver. 3.3 or later, 640K free RAM, and 2 floppy drives or 1 hard disk and 1 floppy disk drive; registered users receive all program upgrades free for the first year after purchase.

Author: Harvey A. Skinner.

Publisher: Multi-Health Systems, Inc.

Review of the Computerized Lifestyle Assessment by F. FELICIA FERRARA, Adjunct/Associate Professor, Department of Educational Measurement, University of South Florida, St. Petersburg, FL:

DESCRIPTION. The Computerized Lifestyle Assessment (CLA) is a questionnaire consisting of 20 content areas related to health issues and lifestyle patterns, yielding descriptive summations on each of the 20 categories. It can be administered individually or offered via group administration if adequate computer terminals are available. Total administration time should approximate 20–30 minutes, depending on each participant's computer savvy. Confidentiality is assured as only an ID number is used to identify each profile. Reading levels are not provided; it appears that all items are brief and concise. The manual purports that the instrument is appropriate for use in institutional settings, reform schools and jails, hospitals, and numerous other lifestyle counseling or assessment settings. Risk levels and preparedness to change reports are available for each of the 20 areas: Nutrition, Eating Habits, Caffeine Use, Physical Activity, Weight, Sleep, Social Relationships, Family Interactions, Physical Abuse, Use of Cigarettes, Alcohol Use, Drinking Problems, Alcohol Dependence (ADS), Non-Medical Drug Use, Drug Problems (DAST-20), Medical & Dental Care, Motor Vehicle Safety, Sexual Activities, Work & Leisure, and Emotional Health.

The computer program runs an internal scoring system, providing participants with a full report and plotted chart on the obtained results for each scale. The scoring decisions and cutoff scores for each scale are not provided in the manual, and thus are difficult to interpret other than via visual analysis of the graph patterns found on a final printout. Individual item analysis for each participant is not available for each subdomain, thus areas of strengths and weaknesses within each category are not identified for the participant. The manual provides basic descriptions of subdomain scales, Section 12—Alcohol Problems consisting of 15 items; Section 13—Alcohol Dependence (ADS-25 items); and Section 15—Drug Problems (DAST-20 items). The remaining 17 subdomains are not described in terms of item values or response formats for specific scales. According to the test developer, the individualized administration of the test may encourage greater honesty in responding to sensitive topics such as drug use or alcohol abuse versus the traditional paper-pencil test. Not all subdomains need to be administered at one time, so an individualized profile using any amount of subdomains is possible. No reference exists as to what impact this would have on technical properties of the subdomain administered in shorter versions of the CLA, and no overall total score can be obtained using any two or more subscales.

Administrative staff must be familiarized with working within a DOS environment for uploading and administering the test, which is an antiquated method for most users. A floppy disk is provided with the purchase of the test available in three limited administration quantities: (a) a 5-test sample disk; (b) a 100-test disk, and (c) a 500-test disk, each requiring a different purchase price. Renewals will have to be bought when supply diminishes, thus requiring an administrator to track the remaining test applications available for subsequent administrations. Site licenses are also available from MHS Researchers. Users accustomed to working in the Windows environment may find the floppy disk usage in DOS to be awkward and frustrating in use. Although the visual windows initially appear adequate, manipulating throughout the test requires use of tabs and spacebar versus the more familiar use of a mouse.

DEVELOPMENT. The manual supplied with the CLA indicated a 1994 copyright date and is based on earlier research throughout Canada and the United States on lifestyles and longevity based on lifestyle patterns. The CLA was initially pilot-tested in 1980, wherein participants liked the computerized version but staff and administrators were often reticent to use this administration format. Patients surveyed in 1988 indicated they liked the computerized version, but missed the doctor's personal touch in the interview process. Also, persons with good visual-motor skills preferred the computerized format the most, and higher educated and defensive clients liked it least. The manual also reports that clients with a small amount of experience with computers like it least, understandably so. Another study (dated 1982) cited in the manual noted that most patients' first choice was that of an interview process rather than self-administered computerized questionnaire. Given the date of this research, attitudes concerning computerized testing may be quite different in the years 2002 and later. Another study noted in the manual indicated that hospital staff preferred to administer the computerized version as patients responded more freely, thus revealing significant disorders not previously noted, such as suicidal thoughts. The manual did not provide data on how each item and subdomain were developed and pilot tested, other than a review of previous research with emphasis on alcohol and drug dependence areas of concern.

TECHNICAL PROPERTIES. Technical properties were reported for the 25-item Michigan Alcoholism Screening Test, included in the CLA, as an alpha of .90 when administered in 1983. Given the date of administration and lack of demographics on type of participant, it is difficult to assess the generalizability of this scale. However, a subsequent study (cited in the manual as in 1993) yielded a Cronbach's alpha of .99 for both the Drug Abuse Screening Test and the Alcohol Dependence Scale when included in the CLA. Test-retest (average administration interval of 3.3 weeks) analysis using 117 family practice patients yielded median test–retest correlations ranging from .99 to .66 for various subdomains. No detailed results are provided for demographics on the participants in this study. Only seven subdomain reliability coefficients are provided in the manual tables; thus, it is difficult to draw valid conclusions on the reliability of scores for the CLA as an entire test or for the other subdomains that were not reported.

Validity coefficients were not reported for the CLA, other than concurrent validity using a comparison of CLA reports to doctors' reports. A 79% agreement rate was found for subdomains of alcohol and cigarette smoking, and nonmedical drug use at 85% agreement rate. One 1993 study, using a modified version of the CLA, compared results with patient file information. Agreement rates of 77% occurred for substance abuse issues but no other subdomains of the CLA were reportedly used in the study. Discriminant validity was studied in 1989 using the DAST, as included in the CLA, and earned an overall 85% accuracy rate in classifying individuals based on DSM-III diagnosis of drug abuse/dependence and an 88% classification rate for alcohol dependence in accordance with the DSM-III diagnosis for alcohol dependence.

COMMENTARY. Although the CLA shows promise as a health-related questionnaire, the current focus appears to be on subdomains of drug and alcohol use, using scales that were developed earlier by previous researchers. The remaining subdomains of the CLA are not emphasized in the manual and the technical property discussions focus on uses for drug and alcohol abuse identification. Although this questionnaire is entitled Computerized Lifestyle Questionnaire, it appears to emphasize and focus on screening for alcohol and drug use. The manual notes that if sensitive material is embedded in other materials, chances are that honesty in responding will be enhanced. Even if this is true, the benefits and risks of not informing clients of the screening and identification process should be weighed, particularly in consideration of human subject review matters. Other concerns such as reporting findings to courts, program administrators, or authorities, in light of illegal substances and duty to warn, must be considered. Obviously, misuse of the findings from the CLA questionnaire can result in high-risk costs to the participant; therefore, unless all examinees are either assured confidentiality or mandated to submit to all tests from a court order, the embedded scales need to be presented with the client's informed consent.

SUMMARY. Directions should be given for administrators addressing examinees' rights and potential risks if confidentiality is broken to report possession of illegal substances or duty to warn in cases of homicide and/or suicide. If consequences of this questionnaire include removal of children from the client, return to jail for broken probation, or reporting to authorities for use of drugs or alcohol, then the overall disclosure of material to the client needs to be reconsidered. Although no test developer can assure the ethical and moral behavior of the test administrators, directions and protocols presented for new test facilitators may enhance standardized administration as prescribed in the *Standards for Educational and Psychological Testing* (American Educational Research Association, American Psychological Association, & National Council on Measurement in Education, 1999).

Similar recommendations are made for the manual, which provides vague and brief directions for many sections. The software installation section would definitely benefit from more graphics or figures displaying each screen of the installation process. The computerized program is awkward to install in the DOS environment and poses problems for users most familiar with the Windows operating environment. A counter for test administrations remaining may be helpful as well. Essentially, it would appear that the CLA may prove more marketable if it is updated in software applications, refocused to reflect the emphasis on Drug and Alcohol use, and if the remaining subdomains are addressed in the manual. Technical properties of the current instrument need to be acquired and posted in the manual for all subscales in a manner consistent with AERA/APA/NCME (1999) Standards. Although the CLA may prove beneficial for use in the intake process for medical exams for purposes of enhancing diagnostic findings, then used for treatment purposes, an ethical dilemma may arise for the test administrator who must break confidentiality if mandated reporting of drug or alcohol exists in that setting. Further research and development of the CLA would appear warranted to enhance the positive aspects of the CLA.

REVIEWER'S REFERENCE

American Educational Research Association, American Psychological Association, & National Council on Measurement in Education. (1999). *Standards for educational and psychological testing*. Washington, DC: American Educational Research Association.

Review of the Computerized Lifestyle Assessment by CHOCKALINGAM VISWESVARAN, Associate Professor, Florida International University, Miami, FL:

DESCRIPTION. The Computerized Lifestyle Assessment (CLA) is a collection of scales to gather lifestyle information from individuals and to assess their motivation to change their routine. It is a self-report instrument that compares individual responses to standard health conventions (e.g., U.S. Food Guide Pyramid) and provides a summary of strengths and weaknesses of individuals. According to the manual, the CLA can be used in health care settings, schools, the workplace, and the justice system for identifying individuals at risk for serious illness.

The CLA can be administered with any IBM-compatible personal computer with a color graphics adaptor card. It requires 640K of free RAM and a DOS version of 3.3 or higher. Finally, also required are two floppy disks or one floppy disk and hard drive. The instructions for setting up and executing the program are straightforward and clearly explained in the manual. There are also provisions for modifying the program to select specific scales and to customize the report for individuals.

The CLA has a list of 20 scales of which 3 are optional. The 17 scales routinely administered are: Nutrition, Eating Habits, Caffeine Use, Physical Activity, Weight, Sleep, Social relationships, Family Interactions, Physical Abuse, Use of Cigarettes, Alcohol Use, Non-Medical Drug Use, Medical and Dental Care, Motor Vehicle Safety, Sexual Activities, Work and Leisure, and Emotional Health. Three optional scales included in the CLA are: Drinking Problems, Alcohol Dependence, and Drug Problems.

To administer the CLA, the scales to be administered are selected first. The respondent has the option of giving anonymous responses. Once an identification number is provided, the program presents questions for each of the 20 (or preselected) sections. The default is to start with the Nutrition section and proceed through the 17 sections noted above. Respondents can skip any item. At the end of each section a graph is provided indicating how healthy the respondent is in that section. After all sections are completed, an overall assessment is provided. The overall assessment consists of a bar chart with the different sections scored as risk or concern or strength. Finally, the program asks the respondents questions relating to their change intentions. These are also summarized in the overall assessment.

DEVELOPMENT. Items on the 20 scales included in the CLA have high face validity. The manual cites several studies that found positive user reactions. Acceptability is high for both respondents and health care providers. However, no data are presented that indicate that the items cluster together into 20 scales. Moreover, there is some ambiguity as to where the items came from (how many items were in the initial pool, how many were discarded, what type of item analysis was done, etc.). It appears that some of the scales are from pre-existing scales. For example, on page 32 of the manual, it is stated that the Alcohol Dependence scale of the CLA and the Michigan Alcoholism Screening Test (MAST) correlated highly and had comparable predictive validity for screening substance abuse in a clinical sample. However, on page 39, the manual states "the 25-item Michigan Alcoholism Screening Test, included in the CLA, had an internal consistency or reliability of … ." The next revision of the manual should provide some more information of where the items of the 20 scales originated. Finally, although it is obvious that nutrition habits of respondents can be compared to the U.S. Food Guide Pyramid, more information is needed as to how concerns are identified in some of the scales (e.g., Social Relationships). From page 27 it appears that the assessed health of family relationships and other scales are based on single studies. Are these results generalizable?

TECHNICAL. Information on internal consistency reliability reported in the manual is ambiguous. On page 39, the manual claims that a study published in the *Journal of Consulting and Clinical Psychology* found high coefficient alphas for all scales included in the CLA regardless of the format of the administration (computerized, paper and pencil, etc.). More information should be provided in the manual of details such as sample sizes involved. Another study is reported on 117 family practice patients who took the CLA at an average of 3.3 weeks apart. Test-retest reliabilities are provided for 7 of the 20 scales.

Several validation studies are summarized. One study found that a modified version of the CLA agreed with file information in identifying substance abuse 77% of the time in a sample of 100 offenders. Another study reported low correlations between the CLA and self-identified lifestyle concerns in a sample of 600 undergraduate university students. Given that the CLA is a self-report assessment of lifestyle habits, whether these low correlations reflect concurrent validity or

reliability estimates is debatable. The manual also reports on two studies that found evidence of discriminant validity for the substance abuse scales of the CLA. Finally, several studies are reported that found favorable user reactions for the CLA. The authors claim that the computerized assessments of the CLA are more likely to elicit truthful responses, especially in sensitive areas such as substance abuse.

COMMENTARY. The manual states that the CLA can be used in school settings, the workplace, and the judicial system. It is not clear how this assessment will stand motivated distortion in a high stakes testing situation. For example, how many job applicants will admit drug abuse when the CLA is administered? Second, although the items have a high degree of face validity, it is not clear how they were chosen or how they were grouped into scales. This instrument may be useful to individuals to summarize their lifestyle habits and provide a snapshot of problem areas in their lives.

SUMMARY. Overall, the CLA is a cost-effective tool to identify potential patients for serious illnesses. Health promotion and disease prevention are increasingly emphasized, and lifestyle and behavior changes are critical in health promotion. A cost-effective tool such as the CLA that can be used to assess a large number of individuals has an important role to play in this regard. The manual should be revised to indicate clearly how the items were derived, any evidence of the underlying factor structure, what normative data are being used to evaluate the responses (and its generalizability), and clear description of studies that provide evidence of the reliability and validity of the scales.

[64]

Conditional Reasoning Test of Aggression.

Purpose: "To identify people who have a high probability of engaging in aggressive, harmful behavior."
Population: Employees ages 18 and over.
Publication Date: 2000.
Acronym: CRTA.
Scores: Total score only.
Administration: Group or individual.
Price Data, 2003: $165 per complete kit including manual (63 pages), 25 test booklets, answer sheet, scoring key, and score interpretation; $50 per manual; $125 per 25 test booklets, answer sheet, and score interpretation.

Time: (25) minutes.
Comments: Provides an indirect measure of "potential for aggressive tendencies"; paper-and-pencil format only; hand-scored.
Authors: Lawrence R. James and Michael D. McIntyre.
Publisher: The Psychological Corporation.

Review of the Conditional Reasoning Test of Aggression by JAYNE E. STAKE, Professor of Psychology, University of Missouri—St. Louis, St. Louis, MO:

DESCRIPTION. The Conditional Reasoning Test of Aggression (CRTA) is a 25-item multiple-choice test that was designed as an indirect measure of tendencies to engage in aggressive behavior. The test is based on a theoretical model of aggression in which certain cognitive biases (i.e., aggressive reasoning) are thought to underlie and predict acts of aggression. Aggression is defined broadly as any actions that intentionally do harm to persons, organizations, or property. The definition encompasses a wide range of behaviors from violent acts of aggression (e.g., murder) to what may represent covert or passive acts of aggression (e.g., absenteeism). The characteristics of aggressive reasoning intended to be assessed by this measure are: (a) the attribution of malevolent intent to the actions of others, (b) the derogation of targets of aggression, (c) the emphasis of retaliation over reconciliation, (d) the perception of the self as an exploited victim, (e) the framing of interpersonal issues in terms of the strong and the weak, and (f) lack of respect for traditional beliefs and conventions. These cognitive biases are thought to provide justifications to the individual for aggressive behavior.

The CRTA may be administered individually or in a group setting. A seventh-grade reading level is required. To disguise the true intent of the measure from test takers, the title that appears on the test booklet is "IAT Reasoning Test," and the test instructions state that the test measures critical reasoning ability. Each question begins with a set of premises concerning the behavior of one or more individuals. Respondents are asked to study this information and decide which of four conclusions is the most logical based on the information provided. The first two items and Item 6 are critical reasoning items that are not scored. The remaining 22 items include two illogical conclusions, one logical conclusion intended to reflect aggression reasoning, and one logical conclusion intended to reflect nonaggressive reasoning. Ad-

ministration of the test requires a maximum of 25 minutes. Respondents may complete the items with a pen or pencil, and the test is hand-scored. A single score of aggressive reasoning is derived by summing the number of endorsements of aggressive reasoning options. Test results are considered invalid if respondents fail to give logical responses on five or more items.

DEVELOPMENT. Each of the 22 CRTA aggression items was constructed to reflect one or more of the six identified facets of aggressive reasoning listed earlier. Items were evaluated for their face validity as an inductive reasoning task by a logician.

TECHNICAL. The CRTA manual provides information from a standardization sample of 357 employees. In this sample, a score of 2 or less was obtained by 28% of the participants and a score of 8 or higher by 8%. Based on this and other, nonspecified samples, test users are advised to interpret scores of 2 or lower as low aggressive reasoning, scores of 3 to 7 as moderate aggressive reasoning, and scores of 8 or above as high aggressive reasoning. However, separate norms are not provided by gender or ethnic group, and little information is provided to determine for which test takers the norms would be appropriate.

The internal consistency (Kuder-Richardson coefficient) for the CRTA was .76 in a sample of 216 employees. For a subgroup of 12 items, the 2-month test-retest reliability estimate was .82 in a sample of 276 students. A factor analysis of the items for this sample resulted in a nine-factor solution that accounted for 75% of the total variance of the items. The factor analysis was then constrained to a four-factor solution, which accounted for 59% of the total variance. Thus, although the CRTA is designed to yield just one score of aggressive reasoning, the scale appears to be multifactorial. When the four factors were scored as separate subtests, the internal consistency (coefficient alpha) ranged from .84 to .86 for the four factors. The factors appeared to coincide with the following facets of aggressive reasoning: (a) retaliation bias, (b) bias to frame issues in terms of strong versus weak (i.e., potency bias), (c) potency bias and social discounting bias, and (d) a combination of facets related to willingness to justify hostility.

Construct validity (i.e., correlation with behavioral indicators of aggression) was assessed in a series of studies that tested five employee samples and three student samples. A total of approximately 1,000 individuals were included in the validity studies, with approximately equal numbers of men and women. Only a small number of minority groups were in the samples, including 90 African Americans and 25 Hispanics.

The construct validity of the CRTA was tested in two groups of students from upper-level business classes and one group of students from an introductory psychology class. CRTA scores were moderately correlated with indices of irresponsible student behavior, including absenteeism (+.37), lying about extra credit points (+.49), and a combined measure of aggressive and nonaggressive student conduct violations (+.55). In addition, the CRTA was related to poor work performance and conduct in five employee groups. Absenteeism was linked to the CRTA in nuclear plant operators (+.42) and package handlers (+.34). Supervisor ratings of overall job performance were negatively related to CRTA scores in patrol officers (-.49), quitting was linked to the CRTA in restaurant workers (+.32), and unreliable behavior was associated with the CRTA in a group of temporary business workers (+.43).

Although the CRTA appears to involve conceptual reasoning skills, the measure does not correlate with American College Testing (ACT) scores. It is likely that participants with low conceptual reasoning skills would give invalid profiles (i.e., select five or more illogical responses), but information on this relationship is not provided in the test manual. Women students tended to show less aggressive reasoning than men students; gender differences were not found in the employee samples. No differences among ethnic identity groups were found. However, the number of nonwhite participants was quite limited, and it is possible that the meaning of the aggressive reasoning items and normative responding differs among ethnic groups.

COMMENTARY AND SUMMARY. The test developers have provided a clear description of the theoretical model that underlies the test, and the concept of aggressive reasoning holds promise as a means of predicting unsatisfactory performance and deportment at school and in the work place. The validity studies indicate that high scorers on the test are more likely to be unreliable and to violate standards of conduct than low scorers. Particular strengths of the scale are that it has good face validity and is quick to administer and score.

It should be noted, however, that the test developers have provided little evidence that the scale is predictive of those behaviors that are normally included in the domain of aggression. Instead, they have broadened the definition of aggression to include most indices of poor work performance and conduct. The test manual (p. 31) provides a very long list of behaviors that are included in the definition of aggression, and many of them do not normally represent forms of aggression (e.g., "shoddy work, habitual tardiness"). Although the CRTA may be used as a general predictor of poor employee performance and conduct, this test does not provide information about the positive qualities an individual may bring to a position, such as potential for leadership. The California Psychological Inventory (Gough, 1996; 43), which comprises a broad set of subscales relevant to work performance, provides a more comprehensive assessment of an individual's strengths and weaknesses and may therefore be preferable to the CRTA for student and employee selection.

REVIEWER'S REFERENCE

Gough, H. G. (1996). California Psychological Inventory, 3rd Edition. Palo Alto, CA: Consulting Psychologists Press.

[65]

Conners' Adult ADHD Rating Scales.

Purpose: Designed to assess "psychopathology and problem behaviors associated with adult ADHD."
Population: Ages 18 and over.
Publication Date: 1999.
Acronym: CAARS.
Administration: Individual.
Forms, 6: Self-Report: Long (CAARS-S:L); Self-Report: Short (CAARS-S:S); Self-Report: Screening (CAARS-S:SV); Observer: Long (CAARS-O:L); Observer: Short (CAARS-O:S); Observer: Screening (CAARS-O: SV).
Price Data, 2002: $192 per complete kit including manual (144 pages) and 25 QuikScore™ forms for each of the 6 forms; $40 per manual; $29 per 25 QuikScore™ forms for either Long form; $28 per 25 QuikScore™ forms for either Short form or either Screening form; Quantity discounts available; $45 per specimen set including manual, and 1 QuikScore™ form for each of the 6 forms.
Comments: Observer rating and/or self-report.
Authors: C. Keith Conners, Drew Erhardt, and Elizabeth Sparrow.
Publisher: Multi-Health Systems, Inc.

a) CAARS—SELF-REPORT: LONG; CAARS—OBSERVER: LONG.

Scores, 9: Inattention/Memory Problems, Hyperactivity/Restlessness, Impulsivity/Emotional Lability, Problems with Self-Concept, DSM-IV In-

attentive Symptoms, DSM-IV Hyperactive-Impulsive Symptoms, DSM-IV Total ADHD Symptoms, ADHD Index, Inconsistency Index.
Time: (30) minutes.
b) CAARS—SELF-REPORT: SHORT; CAARS—OBSERVER: SHORT.
Scores, 6: Inattentive/Memory Problems, Hyperactivity/Restlessness, Impulsivity/Emotional Lability, Problems with Self-Concept, ADHD Index, Inconsistency Index.
Time: (10) minutes.
c) CAARS—SELF-REPORT: SCREENING; CAARS—OBSERVER: SCREENING.
Scores, 4: DSM-IV Inattentive Symptoms, DSM-IV Hyperactive/Impulsivity Symptoms, DSM-IV Total ADHD Symptoms, ADHD Index.
Time: (10) minutes.

Review of the Conners' Adult ADHD Rating Scales by ANDREW S. DAVIS, Assistant Director of the Neuropsychology Laboratory, University of Northern Colorado and RIK CARL D'AMATO, Assistant Dean, College of Education, M. Lucile Harrison Professor of Excellence, University of Northern Colorado, Greeley, CO:

DESCRIPTION. The Conners' Adult ADHD Rating Scales (CAARS) is a multimodal measure designed to aid in the diagnosis of Attention Deficit Hyperactivity Disorder (ADHD) in adults age 18 and above. There are two sources of information with the CAARS, a Self-Report measure and an Observer checklist, completed by an acquaintance. There are three different versions of the CAARS, a long form, a short form, and a screening form. Information is collected via Likert scale ratings with the participant and the observer rating the participant's behavior on a 4-point scale, ranging from *Not at all, never* to *Very much, very frequently*. On the long form, both the Observer and Self-Report measure contain 66 items and each yields 4-factor derived subscales, three DSM-IV ADHD symptom subscales, an ADHD index, and an Inconsistency index. The four-factor derived subscales are Inattention/Memory Problems, Hyperactivity/Restlessness, Impulsivity/Emotional Lability, and Problems with Self-Concept. The DSM-IV symptom subscales are Inattentive Symptoms, Hyperactive-Impulsive Symptoms, and Total ADHD Symptoms. The ADHD Index aims to identify adults who are likely to be diagnosed with ADHD. The Inconsistency Index measures response irregularities that may be produced by

random responses or noncompliant behavior. The Observer and Self-report short forms have 26 items and contain the four-factor derived subscales, the ADHD Index, and the Inconsistency Index. The Observer and Self-Report screening forms contain 30 items and generate the three DSM-IV Symptom subscales and the ADHD Index.

Scoring and administering of the CAARS is simple and convenient and can be done without the manual. The respondent's answers pass through the top page onto another page from which the conversion and plotting of raw scores to *T*-Scores can take place. Computer administration and a computer-scoring program are also available.

DEVELOPMENT. The CAARS was developed due to the lack of a valid measure for identifying adults with ADHD. The authors constructed a 93-item initial pool that was administered to 839 nonclinical adults. A factor analysis resulted in 66 items being retained using a four-factor derived solution that resulted in creation of the long form. The short form and screening form were created with the items that correspond to their subscales.

The ADHD Index was created by comparing responses from a clinical group of participants ($n = 39$) who met the DSM-IV criteria for ADHD and a matched sample from the normative data. Statistical procedures were used to identify items from the item pool that could differentiate between the two groups. This resulted in 12 items being retained to create the ADHD Index. This small number of items is quite problematic, as is the small sample size.

The Inconsistency Indices consist of eight pairs of congruent responses. The Inconsistency Indices were fashioned by comparing results from randomly selected respondents from the normative data and 100 random sets of numbers.

The DSM-IV Symptom Scales were crafted from the DSM-IV's (APA, 1994) list of 18 symptoms that are categorized into two different clusters: 9 items that assess inattentive symptoms and 9 items that assess hyperactive-impulsive symptoms. The authors adopted items from the widely used Conners' Rating Scales—Revised (Conners, 1997) and modified the items slightly for adult respondents. These 18 items comprise the Inattentive subscale, the Hyperactive Impulsive subscale, and the total DSM-IV Symptom subscale. The Observer scales were created by taking the same questions from the Self-Report scales and modifying them, asking the observer to rate a specific person.

TECHNICAL. The normative data for the CAARS were collected on a large sample of nonclinical adults from the United States and Canada. The norms are broken down in terms of gender and age, with the four age ranges being 18 to 29, 30 to 39, 40 to 49, and 50 years and older. Care should be exercised when using the CAARS with the elderly because the normative sample's age range is overly broad. Unfortunately, some demographic information (e.g., ethnicity or location) was not included in the manual. Thus, it is unclear if the sample is representative of the overall population of the United States or of Canada. The normative sample of the CAARS Self-Report forms consisted of 1,026 adults, and the DSM-IV Symptom subscales were gathered from 144 cases. The Observer forms were collected from 943 adults, and the DSM-IV Symptom subscales were garnered from 150 cases.

The authors do an excellent job providing the available reliability information about the CAARS. There is a detailed table breaking down the internal reliability coefficients for gender and the four age groups. The total sample internal consistency for the Self-Report measures has coefficients ranging from .66 to .90. The internal consistency estimates for the Observer measure's total sample was good, ranging from .81 to .92. The test-retest of the CAARS was examined on the long form with a time interval of 1 month for the Self-Report measure and 2 weeks for the Observer measure. The correlation coefficients were good, but unfortunately, no test-retest studies were conducted for the other two forms. Mean interitem correlations and standard errors of measurement were provided that supported the reliability of scores from the instrument. The test authors also do an outstanding job of providing comprehensive validity information about the CAARS. A confirmatory factor analysis of the CAARS revealed acceptable goodness of fit and indicated no significant differences for men and woman across the age groups. The overall classification result of the ADHD Index was 73%, which led the authors to suggest the ADHD Index could serve as a useful screening measure to aid in the identification of adults who would benefit from further assessment. Given these findings, examiners should be cautious about placing too much

weight on the ADHD Index results. To evaluate the construct validity of the CAARS, the authors reported research that examined the CAARS Self-Report long form as compared to the Wender Utah Rating Scale (WURS; Ward, Wender, & Reimherr, 1993). When they compared this child measure of ADHD to the CAARS, a measure of adult ADHD, they found acceptable correlations.

COMMENTARY. The CAARS appears to be a useful multimodal instrument in the assessment and intervention of adults with ADHD. Indeed, a unique feature of the measure is the Self-Report forms, which can then be compared to the observations of an acquaintance. The test is easy to administer and score, and can be used in an individual or group setting. The manual is not needed to administer or score the test, as all of the information is provided on the forms. Another positive element of the measure is the availability of computerized administration and scoring. The authors have provided the examiner with a variety of choices that can be made via the long form, short form, and screening form of the test, although the long form should be used when possible, as it provides the most information for treatment planning. The Inconsistency Index provides the examiner with an indication of disinterest, malingering, or a pattern of random responses. The four-factor structure of the test facilitates the diagnosis of ADHD, and provides client outcome information. The authors succeeded in creating a DSM-IV ADHD Symptom subscale that closely matches the DSM-IV criteria for the identification of ADHD. However, examiners should be cautious about using the ADHD Index for differential diagnosis.

The number of participants comprising the measure's normative sample was excellent, yet some important demographic information was lacking. The reliability of the CAARS appears to be good, yet more research is needed using various time intervals. The validity of the test seems excellent, yet as with any new measure, more information is needed before the validity of scores from the test can be determined. The lack of a psychometrically sound adult measure for comparison with the CAARS hinders the analysis of construct validity. Additional information regarding the discriminant validity of the test is needed. The CAARS appears to be the most promising measure of adult ADHD at this time.

SUMMARY. The test authors have produced what appears to be a reliable and valid tool to aid in the assessment and intervention of adults with ADHD. The test is easy to administer and score, and requires a minimum of time and materials. The information presented in the manual should leave the examiner comfortable when using this measure. A noteworthy feature is the ecological foundation of the measure, which includes the collection of information from the subject and an independent observer. The long form, short form, and screening form allow the examiner several options for assessing the various components of adults who are likely to be diagnosed with ADHD. This multimodal instrument appears to be a valuable clinical tool that fills a void in the assessment of adults with ADHD and is recommended as the measure of choice for practitioners and researchers alike.

REVIEWERS' REFERENCES

American Psychiatric Association. (1994). *Diagnostic and statistical manual of mental disorders* (4th ed.). Washington, DC: Author.
Conners, C. K. (1997). *Conners' Rating Scales—Revised: Technical manual.* North Tonawanda, NY: Multi-Health Systems, Inc.
Ward, M. F., Wender, P. H., & Reimherr, F. W. (1993). The Wender Utah Rating Scale: An aid in the retrospective diagnosis of childhood attention deficit hyperactivity disorder. *American Journal of Psychiatry, 150,* 885–890.

Review of the Conners' Adult ADHD Rating Scales by RONALD J. GANELLEN, Associate Professor, Department of Psychiatry and Behavioral Sciences, Northwestern Medical School, Chicago, IL:

DESCRIPTION. Knowledge about Attention Deficit/Hyperactivity Disorder has changed during the 1990s. One important development in our understanding of ADHD was the recognition that ADHD does not always involve excessive behavioral activity, but may primarily involve difficulties with sustained attention, distractibility, and difficulties organizing and completing tasks. Another major shift in thinking involves the relatively recent recognition that ADHD is not only a disorder of childhood or early adolescence, but frequently affects adults as well. Generations of researchers and clinicians were trained to believe that children "outgrew" ADHD. The work of Wender (1995) and Barkley (1990), among others, rejected this assumption and showed that symptoms of ADHD may persist into adulthood.

The Conners' Adult ADHD Rating Scales (CAARS) was developed to assess ADHD-related symptoms and behaviors in adults. Parallel forms of the CAARS were developed to be completed in a self-report format and by observers familiar with an individual. Both forms use a 4-point Likert-sytle format to rate behaviors or problems in functioning and contain items that are readable and easily understood. The authors explained that the self-report and observer forms were developed to provide different sources of information about an individual's functioning. The self-report and observer versions contain identical items and yield the same scales to be used in clinical decision making.

The CAARS presents three different versions of self-report and observer ratings: a long form with 66 items that yields scores for nine subscales; a short form with 26 items that yields six subscales; and a screening version with 30 items rating criteria contained in the DSM-IV for ADHD. In other words, when source of informant (self vs. observer) is crossed with version (long form, short form, and screening version), there are six different versions of the CAARS.

All versions of the CAARS contain an ADHD Index, developed to differentiate between an ADHD clinical sample and a nonclinical sample by identifying adults who are likely to be diagnosed with ADHD. In addition, the long and short versions also have an Inconsistency Index, which shows whether or not items were responded to in a consistent manner. An elevated score on the Inconsistency index raises concerns that the respondent had difficulty comprehending the items or answered in a careless, indiscriminate, or random fashion.

DEVELOPMENT. The authors created scales tapping some central features of ADHD using factor analysis and logically developed scales assessing clusters of symptoms of ADHD defined by the DSM-IV (e.g., Inattentive Symptoms, Hyperactive-Impulsive Symptoms, and Combined Symptoms).

The authors generated a pool of 93 items describing different features of ADHD after reviewing literature pertaining to ADHD in adults and adolescents. Based on the results of factor analyses, four scales were defined: Inattention, Hyperactivity, Impulsivity, and Problems with Self-Concept. Items were eliminated if they did not load on any one of the four factors identified in the factor analyses or if they loaded on more than one factor.

It should be noted, however, that the other five CAARS subscales were not developed using factor analysis. For instance, items making up the subscales measuring symptoms contained in the

DSM-IV were written to reflect each symptom. One item was generated for each DSM-IV criterion. Although these items appear to reflect the relevant construct of DSM-IV criterion, no additional validity data for the DSM-IV Symptom scales are contained in the CAARS manual. Thus, it is not clear that these scores on these scales can be interpreted as they are intended to be or that the single items are sufficient to cover each DSM-IV criterion in a comprehensive manner.

Another CAARS scale, the ADHD Index, was developed using a series of *t*-tests and discriminant function analyses to identify items that most effectively discriminated between a nonclinical control group and a group of individuals diagnosed with Adult ADHD. An initial pool of 30 items was reduced using these procedures until 12 items were identified that effectively discriminated between the groups.

Several aspects of the procedure used to develop the ADHD Index are puzzling, however. For instance, although the authors state they performed multiple analyses until 12 items were selected for the ADHD Index, no rationale was provided for having 12 items for this scale as opposed to any other number of items. More important, of the 12 items comprising the ADHD Index, 6 are unique to the ADHD Index; these items do not overlap with any items of the four scales generated through factor analysis or the three scales developed by the authors to assess DSM-IV ADHD criteria.

It is puzzling that the ADHD Index was developed using items not contained in the scales the authors created using empirical methods or by writing items that appear to fit the DSM-IV criteria. Even more perturbing is the finding that of the 42 items contained in the four factor analytically derived scales, only 6 were included in the ADHD Index. None of the items from the DSM-IV symptoms scales appear on the ADHD Index. It is unclear why 6 ADHD Index items were not included on other CAARS scales, even though their content is obviously relevant to ADHD (e.g., "I am always on the go, as if driven by a motor"; "I can't keep my mind on something unless it's really interesting").

TECHNICAL. Six of the nine CAARS scales were normed using a sample of 1,206 adults ranging in age from 18 to 80. The three DSM-IV ADHD Symptom scales were developed using a sample of 226 participants. No information was provided concerning the geographic distribution or ethnic and racial composition of the normative sample. It is, therefore, not clear whether the normative sample is representative of the contemporary population of the U.S.A. and whether the CAARS can be used with members of minority groups.

The CAARS scales have high internal consistency values. Test-retest reliability for both the self-report (1-month interval) and observer (2-week interval) versions of the CAARS over brief periods of time were excellent (e.g., $r = .80-.95$).

Limited data concerning the construct validity of CAARS scales were presented. The available data showed that the four factor analytically derived CAARS scales and the ADHD Index effectively discriminated between clinical and control groups. As noted above, no validity data for the DSM-IV ADHD Symptom Scales were provided.

COMMENTARY. The need for an instrument to identify adults with ADHD and measure the intensity of symptoms associated with ADHD is evident. There are a number of reasons, however, why the CAARS should be viewed with some skepticism. As noted above, the methods used to develop CAARS scales are questionable as some scales were developed empirically and some on the basis of face validity. The rationale guiding development of the ADHD Index is unclear as items appear on the Index that were excluded from other CAARS scales, few items from the factor analytically derived scales are contained in the Index, and none of the items making up the DSM-IV Symptom scales are included in the Index.

The authors acknowledge the need for information other than the CAARS to accurately identify Adult ADHD. Users of the CAARS must recognize that the CAARS alone cannot diagnose Adult ADHD, particularly given the importance of determining whether symptoms of distractibility and/or hyperactivity were present in early childhood. Because the CAARS focuses on aspects of adults' contemporaneous functioning, it does not address childhood behaviors or difficulties.

Another issue that requires further investigation concerns how to integrate information obtained from different sources, the self-report and observer versions of the CAARS, especially should disagreements be found. Although having both perspectives is appealing, the authors provide little guidance as to how to weight and resolve discrepancies provided by different sources. It is not clear, for instance, whether observers should be considered to be more objective than individuals or whether individuals are more aware of their actions, difficulties, and patterns of behaviors than others.

Diagnosis of Adult ADHD can be complicated by other psychological disorders, either because other disorders can produce restless, impulsive, or agitated behavior or disturb the ability to focus and sustain attention. This may be of particular importance when psychological conditions are comorbid with ADHD. Further research is needed to investigate the extent to which CAARS scales may be influenced by other types of psychopathology and whether they aid in differentiating between ADHD and other psychological disorders.

SUMMARY. The authors of the CAARS clearly articulate the rationale for developing an instrument to identify Adult ADHD, measure different aspects of the disorder, and provide a means to objectively gauge the severity of symptoms. As they point out, such a measure has considerable potential to be useful in both clinical and research settings. The CAARS represents a first step in the direction of developing a measure of Adult ADHD, but requires further refinement before it can be used with confidence. Reservations about the CAARS are raised in part because it contains some scales developed using empirical approaches and some scales developed to be face valid. Additional data are needed to provide support for a measure containing scales developed using different approaches and to examine whether CAARS scales are comparable in sensitivity to detecting Adult ADHD and discriminating ADHD from other psychological disorders.

REVIEWER'S REFERENCES

Barkley, R. A. (1990). *Attention Deficit Hyperactivity Disorder: A handbook for diagnosis and treatment.* New York: Guilford.
Wender, P. H. (1995). *Attention-deficit hyperactivity disorder in adults.* Oxford, UK: Oxford University Press.

[66]

Conners' Continuous Performance Test II.

Purpose: A computerized assessment tool used to assess attention problems and to measure treatment effectiveness.

Population: Ages 6 to adult.

Publication Dates: 1992–1996.

Acronym: CPT II.

Scores, 12: Omissions, Commissions, Hit Reaction Time, Hit Reaction Time Standard Error, Variability of Standard Error, Attentiveness (d prime), Perseverations, Hit Reaction Time Block Change (Vigilance Measure), Hit Standard Error Block Change (Vigilance Measure), Hit Reaction Time Inter-Stimulus Interval Change (Adjusting to Presentation Speed), Hit Standard Error Inter-Stimulus Change (Adjusting to Presentation Speed), Confidence Index.

Administration: Individual.

Price Data, 2002: $495 per Psychmanager Lite CD kit and Correction Manager CD kit with manual; $45 per preview version.

Time: (14) minutes.

Comments: Self-completed performance measure; includes CD-ROM and 3.5-inch disk; requires Windows 95 or higher.

Authors: C. Keith Conners and the MHS staff.

Publisher: Multi-Health Systems, Inc.

Cross References: For a review by James Ysseldyke, see 14:97; see also T5:679 (2 references).

Review of the Conners' Continuous Performance Test II by BEVERLY M. KLECKER, Assistant Professor of Education, Morehead State University, Morehead, KY:

DESCRIPTION. The Conners' Continuous Performance Test II (CPT II), is a computerized assessment tool used to assess attention problems and to measure treatment effectiveness. The CPT II is a revision (for Windows) of the CPT 3.0 for DOS. The respondent's continuous performance task is to press the space bar or click the mouse button when any letter except the target letter "X" appears. White letters appear on a black screen at varying Inter-Stimulus Intervals (ISIs) of 1, 2, and 4 seconds with a display time of 250 milliseconds. There are six blocks, with three subblocks, each containing 20-letter presentations. The order of ISIs presentation varies between blocks. The CPT II takes 14 minutes to complete. The age range for this assessment is 6 years through adulthood.

The administration steps delineated in the manual include (a) obtain informed consent, (b) assure confidentiality, (c) administer the practice test, and (d) the protocol for administering the CPT II. The administrator is to be unobtrusively present while the test is administered. "Questions posed by respondents during administration of the CPT II need to be dealt with quickly and accurately since such diversions can affect performance on the task" (technical guide and software manual, p. 15).

The computer program captures response times and records them to the nearest millisecond. Speed and consistency of reactions are measured. Logarithmic transformations are used in all of the computations involving reaction times. The program classifies reaction times less than 100ms as perseverations. In addition to analyzing the response speed, the CPT II also provides measures of the accuracy of responses. Errors fall into two main categories: omission errors (no response after a non-X letter) and commission errors (a response to an X). Scores are calculated by block results (changes in reaction time speed and consistency as the test progresses). Scores are calculated by change in reaction time speed and consistency for different Inter-Stimulus Intervals (ISIs). Signal detection theory statistics are also included in scoring. Scores are presented as *T*-scores and percentiles described in the technical manual and software guide as:

> All of the measures of the CPT II except the Confidence Index and Overall Index (which are readily interpreted without conversion) are converted to *T*-scores and percentiles. *T*-scores represent the score of the individual taking the test relative to the population average. *T*-scores and percentiles compare the respondent to those in the normative group who are of the same gender and who are in the same age group. (technical guide and software manual, p. 22)

The performance assessment can be administered only after preparing a "Patient Profile" with the software. Scores are automatically computed, graphed, and converted to a text explaining the results. In a short preface to "Chapter 3: Interpreting Results," the authors suggest:

> The reader is encouraged to supplement this information with further reading on CPT theory, signal detection theory, and statistical texts. Users generally find the narrative portion of the interpretive report to be helpful, and practitioners are encouraged to routinely refer to these reports to clarify interpretation. (technical guide and software manual, p. 25)

DEVELOPMENT. The authors examined and evaluated existing continuous performance tests and found that the most important deficiency was that commonly used paradigms were based on infrequently occurring targets. The authors reversed the structure of this paradigm to make targets frequent and nontargets rare. One of the first versions of the CPT II was the DOS-based Version 1.0 used to pilot the paradigm. Version 2.0 included clinical normative data for compara-

tive purposes, and Version 3.0 included a full set of both clinical and nonclinical normative data. CPT II was created to make the program available in the Windows platform, to restandardize and expand the norms, to include new computational features, and to expand reporting options.

TECHNICAL. Normative data include a clinical sample of 378 diagnosed ADHD cases (diagnosis methods varied) and 223 adult individuals identified "with some type of neurological impairment" (technical guide and software manual, p. 46). The nonclinical sample included 1,920 individuals from the general population. Normative data are described by age and gender categories. The age and gender breakdowns are separate. There are nine age categories, but the gender breakdowns for each age category are not provided. Gender is described with the dichotomous age categories of "Under 18" and "18+." The "Under 18" category is composed of 52.5% males and 47.5% females. The "18+" category is composed of 28.8% males and 71.2% females. In the ADHD clinical sample of 378, the "Under 18" category is composed of 75.3% males and 24.7% females; the "18+" category is composed of 54.2% males and 45.8% females.

The manual describes a split-half reliability procedure using 520 cases, and the resulting split-half correlations "between the measures computed for the subgroup" (technical guide and software manual, p. 56). The description of the split-half procedure is very difficult to follow and the correlations are nearly impossible to interpret. Internal-consistency reliabilities are reported for the measures of Hit Reaction Time, Commissions, Omissions, Standard Error, Variability, *d* prime, and Beta. It is essential that the measures in this performance test be stable over time because the instrument is used to establish baseline data for individuals in treatment. The authors present test-retest reliability evidence based on 10 participants from the nonclinical group and 13 participants with "a variety of clinical diagnoses" (technical guide and software manual, p. 56). The length of time between test and retest, on average, was 3 months. The test-retest reliabilities range from a low of .05 (Hit SE ISI Change) to a high of .92 (Confidence Index, Neuro).

Discriminant validity and concurrent validity of the CPT II are addressed in 18 pages of research studies in the manual. The authors repeatedly emphasize that the instrument is not to be used alone as a diagnostic tool.

COMMENTARY. In the administration protocol the suggested answer to *questions during the timed administration* (reviewer's italics) is, "I can answer that after you are finished. Please continue" (technical guide and software manual, p. 15). The initial directions should be, "Are the directions clear? I cannot answer any questions until after you have finished the task, which will take about 14 minutes." I took the performance test; it required absolutely focused attention and rapid response. Removing attention from the task to ask a question would totally invalidate the rigorously timed test. Yet, there is no requirement in the administrative instructions that removal of attention must be noted.

The suggestion that the administrator (or reviewer) read extensive outside sources or rely on the graphs, diagrams, and textual interpretation may limit the usefulness of this assessment for many practitioners. These practitioners may not have ready access to these outside sources.

The authors' interpretation of Table 5.8 (technical guide and software manual, p. 79) as presenting consistent results of evidence of correlations between the CPT II and WISC-III ($n = 17$) and CPT II and CAAB ($n = 18$) is not accurate. The authors follow a presentation of simple linear correlations ranging from -.01 to -.20 (*without* the necessary conversion to r^2) with the statement:

> The shared variance exists because attention deficits/capacity can impact cognitive intelligence. This shared variance is properly captured by the low negative correlations between the CPT II and IQ results. A zero correlation would mean that the shared variance is not appropriately captured. If the correlation were too high, then the test becomes a measure of cognitive intelligence. (technical guide and software manual, pp. 79-80)

By squaring the correlation coefficients, we can see that the shared variance between the measures ranges from $[-.01^2 = .0001] = .01\%$ to $[-.20^2 = .0004] = .04\%$.

SUMMARY. There is a concern that permitting interruptions by the administrator to answer examinee questions could impact test scores and therefore invalidate test socre interpretations. Reliability evidence to establish stability of scores across time (test-retest) used too few subjects and the time interval was not sufficiently described. The age-by-gender norms cannot be determined because of the way normative tables are presented, for example, how many individuals are in the normative ADHD category for a 9-year-old female? With whom are her scores being compared? This instrument should be used with caution and a lot of additional, reliable evidence.

Review of the Conners' Continuous Performance Test II by WESLEY E. SIME, Professor of Health and Human Performance, University of Nebraska—Lincoln, Lincoln, NE:

DESCRIPTION AND DEVELOPMENT. The Conners' Continuous Performance Test II (CPT II) was designed to detect attention lapses in individuals with petit mal epilepsy and has since been used in more generalized vigilance studies. The authors suggest that the instrument has been particularly sensitive to drug treatment assessment in hyperactive children. The random appearance of letters of the alphabet onto the computer screen requiring quick reaction on the space bar is a very boring task wherein children become less efficient as they fail in signal detection or distinction (when the "X" comes up, reaction to it is an error). Essentially, the test identifies difficulty in processing information fast enough because of "mind wandering." Anticipatory mistakes (impulsivity) are also detected in the test. The authors suggest that it may be used as a relatively quick screening device for monitoring the effects of treatment, and for research efforts related to vigilance, signal detection, or AD/HD. It is not clear how this test differs from the Conners' Adult ADHD Rating Scales (65).

TECHNICAL. Signal detection theory statistics are used in this program to account for response biases and distributional information. Confidence values are compromised when a single administration of the test is used in clinical settings as opposed to multiple administrations for reliability. However, the authors argue that even in single administration, reaction time speed acts as an indicator of the test taker's confidence level and they note 88 of 100 participants would be correctly identified into clinical versus nonclinical cases (88% Confidence Index).

Interpreting the results hinges on several variables beginning with Response Style (Beta Statistic) to evaluate speed/accuracy trade-off.

Higher Beta values indicate cautious responses making sure of the correct decision. Omissions indicate an invalid test, usually due to misunderstanding the instructions. Discriminant function and the confidence index are used to determine clinical diagnosis of an attention deficit. Inattention, impulsivity, and vigilance are the primary categories of distinction. Hit reaction time standard error is used as a measure of "erraticness" (technical guide and software manual, p. 30). Attentiveness is defined as a measure of how well the individual discriminates between targets and nontargets. Perseveration responses are anticipatory guesses as indicated by reaction time less than 100ms following the stimulus, which is beyond neuromuscular transmission capability. Vigilance is determined by a slowing of the reaction time according to slope of responses and/or slope of the standard error thereof. Other variations are noted when the speed of stimulus presentation is changed from quick repetitions to very long periods between stimuli.

The authors have provided substantive normative data analysis on 1,108 nonclinical cases obtained in a multisite study. Cultural studies comparing Asian, African American, and Caucasian populations revealed only marginal differences between the black and white groups on 2 of 14 measures. Test-retest correlation coefficients (3-month interval) were generally high ranging from .55 to .84 for the most relevant outcome measures. The authors suggest that there are no significant practice effects as shown by minimal gains across multiple test sessions. Validity evidence is apparently strong as shown by several research studies on clinical ADHD or ADD populations noting accuracy in differentiating between clinical and nonclinical groups. The authors caution appropriately against using the CPT II independently without corroboration of other interview and testing information to make diagnostic decisions. It appears that the classification accuracy is satisfactory when it is used as a screening instrument and for differentiating age and developmental status. The studies comparing the CPT II with clinical rating scales show only a mild correlation, presumably because they are measuring somewhat different dimensions of the complex construct of attention. The authors acknowledge that more research is needed to determine the relationship between attentional factors and overall cognitive intelligence performance.

COMMENTARY. The test manual furnished by the developer includes sufficient background information and detailed instructions for conducting the testing and interpreting process.

The software is user-friendly for the operator and it is easy for the participant to respond to the test stimuli. Unfortunately, the breadth of content involved in the testing is woefully inadequate in comparison to other similar test instruments such as the Cognameter, the Test of Variables of Attention (TOVA; T6:2566), and the Integrated Visual and Auditory Continuous Performance Test (IVA; T6:1230). Clinicians who offer nonpharmaceutical treatment interventions would be less than enthusiastic about the service provided by this software package.

SUMMARY. The CPT II is a reliable instrument with moderate validity for the populations identified. It is easy to use and can be interpreted adequately in light of other clinical observations and test results. The research to support its efficacy in AD/HD and related populations is adequate. The only serious deficiency lies in the limited breadth of testing variations. Other similar test instruments provide better measures offsetting the boredom issues inherent in this test procedure.

[67]

Constructive Thinking Inventory.

Purpose: "Evaluates an individual's experiential intelligence and coping skills."
Population: Ages 18–81 years.
Publication Date: 2001.
Acronym: CTI.
Scores: Emotional Coping (Self-Acceptance, Absence of Negative Overgeneralization, Nonsensitivity, Absence of Dwelling), Behavioral Coping (Positive Thinking, Action Orientation, Conscientiousness), Personal Superstitious Thinking, Categorical Thinking (Polarized Thinking, Distrust of Others, Intolerance), Esoteric Thinking (Belief in the Unusual, Formal Superstitious Thinking), Naive Optimism (Over-Optimism, Stereotypical Thinking, Polyanna-ish Thinking), Defensiveness, Validity, Global Constructive Thinking.
Administration: Individual or group.
Price Data, 2003: $142 per introductory kit (3.5-inch disk) including scoring program with on-screen user's manual, professional manual (59 pages), 25 test booklets, and 25-use key disk; $33 per professional manual; $109 per 25 test booklets with 25-use key disk.
Time: (15–30) minutes.

Comments: Administered in paper-and-pencil format only; responses are manually entered into scoring program; software generates raw scores, *T*-scores, and profile; system requirements: Windows 95/98/NT/2000/ME/XP; 8 MB hard disk, 16 MB RAM (Windows 95/98/ME) or 24 MB RAM (Windows NT/2000/XP), 3.5-inch disk drive.
Author: Seymour Epstein.
Publisher: Psychological Assessment Resources, Inc.

Review of the Constructive Thinking Inventory by Y. EVIE GARCIA, Assistant Professor, Educational Psychology, Northern Arizona University, Phoenix, AZ:

DESCRIPTION. The Constructive Thinking Inventory (CTI) consists of 108 self-report items, designed for adults 18 years or older. Items are presented in the form of self-statements describing thoughts and behaviors. Respondents rate how well each statement describes them on a scale from 1 (*Definitely False*) to 5 (*Definitely True*). The CTI is a measure of constructive and destructive thinking consisting of nine scales. Five of the scales have two to four subscales. The Personal Superstitious Thinking scale has no subscales. A general scale, called the Global Constructive Thinking scale, includes items from all of the main scales (except for Esoteric Thinking). The Emotional Coping scale assesses the degree to which people cope with frustration based on self-acceptance, not overgeneralizing following adverse outcomes, not being overly sensitive to criticism, and not dwelling on misfortune. The Behavioral Coping scale assesses whether people think in ways that promote effective action by looking at the positive side of things, thinking in ways that lead to effective action, and thinking in ways that promote hard work, planning, and doing one's best. The Personal Superstitious Thinking scale assesses the degree to which people have developed private superstitions (e.g., if something very good happens, it will be countered by something bad happening). The Categorical Thinking scale assesses whether people view the world in black-and-white terms and are distrustful and intolerant of others who are not like themselves. The Esoteric Thinking scale assesses the degree to which people believe in unusual and scientifically questionable phenomena such as conventional superstitions, ghosts, and astrology. The Naïve Optimism scale assesses the degree to which people think in simplistic, stereotypical ways and are unrealistically optimistic.

The test is intended for a broad variety of uses wherever information about an individual's implicit views about themselves and the world may impact behavior. Suggested uses for psychotherapy and counseling, substance abuse, college student selection, personnel selection, and industrial organizational issues are supported, in part, by a rather extensive volume of research using the CTI, in whole or in part, across diverse settings and populations.

The CTI takes about 15–30 minutes to complete and requires a Grade 6.4 reading level. Item responses are then manually entered into the CTI scoring program that generates an item response list and a table and graph of raw and *T*-scores for each scale and subscale. *T*-scores ranging from 45 to 55 are considered average. *T*-scores ranging from 56 to 65 are moderately high. *T*-scores above 65 are considered very high. Conversely, *T*-scores of 35 to 44 are moderately low and *T*-scores below 35 are considered very low. High scores on Global Constructive Thinking, Emotional Coping, and Behavioral Coping and low scores on Personal Superstitious Thinking, Categorical Thinking, Esoteric Thinking, and Naïve Optimism indicate flexible thinking and ability to adjust behavior across situations for adequate adaptation. The manual describes characteristic thinking patterns of individuals who score high or low on the scales.

DEVELOPMENT. The CTI is based on a theory of personality developed by the test's author, Seymour Epstein, called cognitive-experiential self-theory (CEST; Epstein, 1994). The theory, briefly explained in the manual, suggests that people adapt to their environments with the aid of two parallel, interactive processing systems: rational and experiential. The rational system operates via a person's understanding of culturally transmitted rules of reasoning and knowing. The rational system is characterized by slow, effortful, conscious, analytic, affect-free, mostly verbal processing. It is intellectual understanding and reasoning that is measured by intelligence tests.

The experiential system is derived from life experiences. These schemas, or implicit beliefs, provide the basis for a person's understanding and behaving in the world. The experiential system is characterized by "rapid, effortless, preconscious, concrete, holistic, primarily imagistic" (professional manual, p. 1) and affect-associated processing.

Seemingly contradictory use of terms such as "concrete" and "imagistic" to describe the same cognitive process requires clarification not included in the manual. The author states that experiential intelligence may be examined by measuring spontaneous or automatic, constructive and destructive thoughts but fails to make a convincing connection between his theory and the measurement of constructive and destructive thought processes.

The CTI measures statements indicating habitual thinking—both constructive and destructive. These concepts are part of existing cognitive behavioral theory and the usefulness of using constructive and destructive thought processes in predicting adaptation to diverse situations is well established in the literature (see Vernon, 2003 and Kalodner, 2003 for good overviews of cognitive behavioral theory and treatment outcomes). No reference is made in the manual to previous authors and pioneers of cognitive-behavioral theory such as Albert Ellis and Aaron Beck, who have established the importance of constructive and destructive thought processes in a variety of problems such as anxiety, depression, and stress management.

The initial 64-item version of the CTI (Epstein & Meier, 1989) was selected from a 200-item pool derived primarily from daily records over 30 days of students in a class on emotions where the students kept records of their most pleasant and unpleasant experience each day and the constructive and destructive thoughts that preceded those emotions. Items were sorted into constructive and destructive categories then later into 18 categories, further narrowed to six scales and one global scale via factor analytic and reliability procedures. Items were assigned to scales and retained if they loaded more highly on the assigned scale than on other scales, contributed to the internal consistency reliability of the scale, and were conceptually consistent with other items on the scale. A validity scale was constructed and included in the initial version of the test.

Following use of the initial CTI scales to study self-reported success in the workplace, with social relations, and physical and mental well being, the CTI was expanded in 1992 to include additional items from the item pool to strengthen the scales and a Defensiveness scale was added. The resulting version had 108 items and subscales were developed for all of the main scales with the exception of the Personal Superstitious Thinking scale, which seemed its most unstable subscale.

The current 2001 version of the CTI was based on a factor analysis of the results from a college student development sample of 1,500. Like the 1992 version, the current CTI has 108 items and the item structures of all the scales remained the same except that items from the Personal Superstitious Thinking scale, which did not emerge as a separate factor, were distributed into Emotional Coping and Behavioral Coping scales.

TECHNICAL. The author indicates that studies reported in the manual often use earlier versions of the CTI. Thereafter, the studies are listed by topic, such as the relationship between the CTI and other assessment instruments. The reader must look at the date of each study to determine the test version that must have been used for each. The results are confusing and the reader would be better served by studies listed under each version of the test.

Standardization. The current version of the CTI (N = 908) was standardized from data collected over the Internet through a leading market research firm. The firm reportedly maintains a database of potential respondents that exceeds 2 million people. Respondents were initially screened and given the option of participating in the survey. Participants were paid $10 for their participation. Data were collected to reflect the 1998 United States Census for age, education, race/ethnicity, and gender. Regression analyses on the effects of age, education, and gender on CTI data revealed small linear effects for age and education. However, incremental increases in the proportion of variance accounted for by these factors were not considered meaningful. Likewise, effects of gender on several subscales were statistically significant but small, with little practical utility.

Reliability. The author lists only "alpha reliabilities" for the normative sample. Overall, reliability coefficients provided for the main scales appeared satisfactory. Global Constructive Thinking was .92. Reliability coefficients for the other six main scales ranged from .76 (Naïve Optimism) to .94 (Emotional Coping). Subscales, having fewer items, showed lower alpha coefficients ranging from .44 to .86. Subscales with low reliabilities should be interpreted cautiously.

Validity. The manual includes an impressive array of empirical validity studies that comprise exactly half of the manual's content. Studies are usually well described and useful. However, the volume of studies presented is somewhat overwhelming. The author breaks the studies into categories, which, however, are also so numerous as to be daunting. In addition, it is very difficult to tell which studies support which versions of the test. The validity information is difficult to summarize and best used as a reference tool to look up results for specific populations or issues of concern.

Overall, the validity studies indicate evidence for concurrent validity via correlational studies of the CTI scales and a variety of personality tests and CTI scales and measures of emotional and physical well-being. Studies also indicate a strong relationship between school, work, and leadership performance and favorable scores on the CTI. Consistent with the developer's description of theoretical differences between experiential and rational intelligence, measures of potential for success and intelligence test scores did not correlate highly with the CTI. In general, the Global Constructive Thinking, Emotional Coping, and Behavioral Coping scales appeared to be the most commonly cited as having stronger predictive characteristics and higher positive correlations with adaptive measures, and stronger negative correlations with measures of maladaptive behaviors or traits.

Factor analytical studies indicate that five of the six main scales of the CTI are factorially stable, with the exception of Personal Superstitious Thinking. However, the Personal Superstitious Thinking scale has been retained because of intriguing empirical findings regarding items on this scale. In addition, the author reports that the 1992 version of the CTI was translated into German and administered to 439 college students and 187 skin disorder patients and found to demonstrate similar factor loadings and scale correlations as those later found with the American student standardization sample. Likewise, the 1992 version of the CTI was translated into Romanian and administered to a sample of 1,054. Results indicated that subscales distributed themselves as expected with minor exceptions attributed to translation problems.

COMMENTARY. The CTI is a good tool for evaluating constructive and destructive thought processes that influence functioning. The scales are robust, with the exception of Personal Superstitious Thinking, and are descriptive of often hard-to-define thought patterns seen in clients, students, and employees who exhibit limited flexibility across situations and poor adaptation to their environments. Administration is quick and easy and the scoring program is very useful, allowing the scorer to view many items simultaneously and to easily return to previous screens to edit scores. There is a plethora of studies examining the relationship of CTI scales with a very diverse array of tests, situations, and populations. The test would likely be very useful in a variety of situations where thought patterns interfere with daily functioning and may have particular appeal for test users with a cognitive-behavioral bent.

The main problems with the test are the theory behind it and failure to clarify information in the manual. Additional information on the reliability of the measure is also needed. Failure to report test-retest reliability compromises the utility of the test.

Finally, standardizing the test according to U.S. Census Bureau statistics and doing factor analytic studies abroad was a good start. More studies using the CTI with ethnic minority populations, especially in the U.S., would enhance its validity with these populations.

SUMMARY. The CTI is simply a great tool for usefully measuring and describing adaptive and maladaptive thought patterns. The author has done an admirable job selecting items and defining categories of thinking that may be subjectively reported and useful in designing cognitive behavioral interventions. The CTI is easy to administer and to score. The scales are mostly robust with good supporting validity studies. Efforts were made to parallel the 1998 U.S. Census for age, education, race/ethnicity, and gender during standardization, which is a step toward increased sensitivity toward multicultural issues. The CTI would benefit from more information on reliability, better clarification of the attached theory, reorganization of the validity studies to indicate which version of the test was used in each case, and increased studies including multicultural populations in the U.S.

REVIEWER'S REFERENCES

Epstein, S. (1994). Integration of the cognitive and the psychodynamic unconscious. *American Psychologist, 49,* 709–724.
Kalodner, C. R. (2003). Cognitive-behavioral theories. In D. Capuzzi & D. R. Gross (Eds.), *Counseling and psychotherapy: Theories and interventions* (3rd ed., pp. 212–234). Upper Saddle River, NJ: Merrill Prentice Hall.
Vernon, A. (2003). Rational emotive behavior therapy. In D. Capuzzi & D. R. Gross (Eds.), *Counseling and psychotherapy: Theories and interventions* (3rd ed., pp. 212–234). Upper Saddle River, NJ: Merrill Prentice Hall.

Review of the Constructive Thinking Inventory by TIMOTHY Z. KEITH, Professor of Educational Psychology, The University of Texas—Austin, Austin, TX:

DESCRIPTION. The Constructive Thinking Inventory (CTI) is designed to measure constructive and destructive thinking in individuals ages 18 and older. The scale is based on cognitive-experiential self-theory, which posits two "parallel, interactive processing systems, rational and experiential" (professional manual, p. 1). According to the author, each of these systems has it own type of intelligence; traditional intelligence tests measure intelligence for the rational system, whereas the CTI is designed to measure experiential intelligence. Seymour Epstein is the author of both the CTI and the theory from which it is derived.

In its current form, the CTI includes 108 items designed to measure Global Constructive Thinking, as well as several components of constructive thinking (Emotional Coping, Behavioral Coping) and destructive thinking (Personal Superstitious Thinking, Categorical Thinking, Esoteric Thinking, and Naïve Optimism). Most of these scales also include several subscales, and all scales except the Esoteric Thinking scale contribute to the overall score. Many of the subscales include relatively few (3–7) items. There are also short Validity and Defensiveness scales. All raw scores are converted to *T* scores.

The CTI materials include the manual, record forms, and computer disks. Examinee's responses are entered from the paper-and-pencil record forms into the computer scoring program, which produces a score report. The report includes a listing of raw scores and *T* scores, along with a profile of those scores.

DEVELOPMENT. The manual devotes several pages to describing the development of the CTI; the test has expanded from a 64-item version in 1989 to its present form. According to the manual, the CTI scales were developed primarily based on factor analysis and examinations of the contributions of each item to scale reliability. Items were initially placed on scales based on a priori decisions, but the current grouping of scales is based on a series of factor analyses of various samples. It is unclear how closely the factor analytic results matched the a priori groupings. The evidence presented in the manual suggests that most of the CTI scales (except for Personal Super-stitious Thinking) are factorially stable across samples. The manual does not report which items make up each scale and subscale. Although the CTI is based on theory, it is unclear how theory was used in the development of the items, and no evidence is provided that the scale adequately measures the different components of the theory.

TECHNICAL. The CTI was standardized on a sample of 908 individuals ages 18 through 81. Standardization was conducted through the internet by a market research company. The manual does not report when the standardization occurred. Information in the manual does suggest, however, that the sample approximated 1998 U.S. Census data for a number of criteria, including sex, race/ethnicity, and education level. Older, minority individuals were somewhat underrepresented. The manual argues for the equivalence of computer-administered and paper-and-pencil exams, but does not present evidence for the equivalence of the CTI in its standardization (computer) versus normal (paper) methods of administration.

The CTI is scored separately by sex, but not by age. The manual presents evidence that CTI scores are affected by age, sex, and education, but argues that the variance accounted for by these predictors is not "substantial" (p. 16). Norms were separated by sex based on previous research suggesting sex differences in CTI characteristics. Either more evidence needs to be presented supporting the norming decisions or norms should be provided for separate age levels.

Reliability estimates (coefficient alpha) for the standardization sample for the main scales ranged from .76 (Naïve Optimism) to .94 (Emotional Coping). Estimates for the subscale and validity (Defensiveness and Validity) scale scores were generally lower, and ranged from .43 to .86. The alpha coefficient for the global Constructive Thinking composite for the standardization sample was .92. Similar alpha and test-retest estimates were obtained for an often-cited, but poorly defined, sample of 1,500 college students.

There is extensive information in the manual concerning the validity of the CTI scores. As noted above, the CTI items and subscales appear factorially stable. Correlations or joint factor analysis with other measures measuring divergent and convergent characteristics would demonstrate more completely whether the CTI scales measure emotional coping, behavioral coping, and so on, rather than some other characteristics. The manual summarizes a number of studies relating the CTI to a variety of personality, emotional, and academic criteria.

COMMENTARY. I have misgivings about some of the validity data presented. For example, the author makes much of small differences in correlations without any tests of statistical significance, some of the measures and samples are only vaguely defined, studies use samples in research (e.g., high school and junior high school students) for whom the test was not standardized, and one study used college CTI scores to predict previous high school GPA. Despite these concerns, it is obvious that the CTI Constructive Thinking scale, along with some of the other scales, indeed can predict important outcomes, often above and beyond their prediction by more traditional measures.

SUMMARY. The CTI is a short, easily administered test designed to measure constructive versus destructive thinking and, more broadly, experiential intelligence. The CTI appears to assess an important and adaptive constellation of emotional characteristics, characteristics that may help explain important outcomes. Still, further development of the instrument is needed before its results can be interpreted with confidence. The author and publisher should better define the standardization sample. The relation between the theory and the CTI items and scales needs more explanation, and research is needed to demonstrate that the CTI scales measure the characteristics listed rather than other aspects of personality. Future manuals should provide more detail concerning the validity studies reviewed. In the meantime, the CTI may provide a useful adjunct to more traditional measures as well as a promising research instrument.

[68]
Coolidge Assessment Battery.

Purpose: Designed to assess personality disorders and neuropsychological functioning.
Population: Ages 15 and over.
Publication Date: 1999.
Acronym: CAB.
Scores, 46: 7 Axis I scales (Anxiety, Depression, Post-Traumatic Stress, Psychotic Thinking, Schizophrenia, Social Phobia, Withdrawal); 14 Axis II scales (Antisocial, Avoidant, Borderline, Dependent, Depressive, Histrionic, Narcissistic, Obsessive-Compulsive, Paranoid, Passive-Aggressive, Sadistic, Schizoid,

Schizotypal, Self-Defeating); 4 Neuropsychological Dysfunction scales (Overall Neuropsychological, Language Functions, Memory and Concentration, Neurosomatic Functions); 4 Executive Functions of the Frontal Lobe scales (Overall Executive Functions, Decision Difficulty, Planning Problems, Task Completion Difficulty); 5 Personality Change due to Medical Condition scales (Aggression, Apathy, Disinhibition, Emotional Lability, Paranoid); 3 Hostility scales (Anger, Dangerousness, Impulsiveness); 5 Normative scales (Apathy, Emotional Lability, Indecisiveness, Maladjustment, Introversion-Extroversion); 4 Validity scales (Answer Choice Frequency, Random Responding, Tendency to Look Good or Bad, Tendency to Deny Blatant Pathology).
Administration: Group or individual.
Price Data, 2001: $38 per manual (1999, 54 pages); $12 per narrative report (Self Rating or Other Rater); $9 per brief report (Self Rating or Other Rater); $99 per Windows software package including disks, software manual, and test manual.
Time: (40) minutes.
Comments: Originally published as the Coolidge Axis II Inventory (14:102); mail-in or software scoring.
Author: Frederick L. Coolidge.
Publisher: Sigma Assessment Systems, Inc.
Cross References: For reviews by Kevin L. Moreland and Paul Retzlaff of an earlier edition, see 14:102; see also T5:690 (3 references).

Review of the Coolidge Assessment Battery by MARK A. STAAL, Director of Counseling Services and Associate Professor of Behavioral Sciences, Department of Behavioral Sciences and Leadership, United States Air Force Academy, CO:

DESCRIPTION. The Coolidge Assessment Battery (CAB) is a 225-item test, administered either by paper and pencil or computer. All items are answered on a 4-point Likert scale ranging from *Strongly False* to *Strongly True*. The CAB's scales are generally organized around three assessment domains. The first domain consists of clinical syndromes listed on Axis I of the *Diagnostic and Statistical Manual of Mental Disorders* (DSM). The second domain consists of 14 DSM Axis II scales and the third domain concerns neuropsychological dysfunction and consists of four scales.

The CAB augments these larger domains of interest with several additional scales. Included in this list are four scales that assess behaviors involving goals: Overall Executive Functions, Decision Difficulty, Planning Problems, and Task Completion Difficulty; five scales related to personality change due to a medical condition: Aggression,

Apathy, Disinhibition, Emotional Lability, and Paranoid; and three scales related to hostility: Anger, Dangerousness, and Impulsiveness. The CAB also includes a set of five scales termed "Other" and "Normative" scales: Apathy, Emotional Lability, Indecisiveness, Maladjustment, and Introversion-Extroversion; and five scales that are referred to as "Non-Normative Scales" that have been included based on their content: Depersonalization, Drug and Alcohol, Eccentricity, Frustration Tolerance, and Sexuality. Finally, the CAB includes four validity scales.

According to the CAB manual, a doctoral level degree is required to score and interpret the test; however, it notes that, "People with a Master's degree in clinical psychology and with specific course work in psychopathology may in some circumstances be allowed to use the CAB" (manual, p. 2). It does not directly indicate the qualifications of the administrator but does indicate that the overall validity of the test depends on the knowledge of its administrator.

The CAB can be completed directly by the patient (Form S) or by a significant other (Form R). The CAB's administration and scoring options include a paper-and-pencil method (mail-in scoring) and a computer-assisted method. Report options range from a Brief Report (raw scores, percentiles, and T-scores for each scale on a bar graph) to a Narrative Report (the Brief Report plus critical item lists, drug and/or alcohol items, narrative text for each scale beyond normal limits, information on possible therapy issues, and diagnostic possibilities). These options expand slightly with the computer-assisted method to include a Data Report (raw scores on each scale) designed for research purposes and a CAB Score Report with Significant Item and Responses, which appears to be the same information as the Narrative Report without any narrative text or remarks.

DEVELOPMENT. This is the latest version of a test that was previously known as the Coolidge Axis II Inventory (CATI; Coolidge, 1984). It was renamed to better reflect its focus and recent developments to its content.

The manual indicates that the CAB is primarily based on a dimensional approach to personality assessment. However, the CAB's predecessor and much of its content are based on the DSM-III and DSM-III-R criteria used for categorical diagnosis. This apparent contradiction

and its potential implications are not addressed. The CAB asserts that its dimensional approach leads to greater reliability in diagnosis. No data or research are presented in the manual to substantiate this claim. The CAB's developer suggests that this model of assessment (dimensional) relates to the entire test; however, nothing is mentioned further about how this applies to the test's remaining scales.

TECHNICAL. Information describing the CAB's normative data is brief and somewhat vague. The test manual indicates that subjects were gathered by college students from "their friends, relatives and acquaintances. The college students were asked to recruit people whom they deemed normal and psychologically healthy" (manual, p. 23). They were also instructed to avoid individuals who had previously been imprisoned, diagnosed as mentally retarded, or been committed to a psychiatric hospital. No attempt appears to have been made to further screen or evaluate the appropriateness of the subject pool. As the demographic tables suggest, the CAB's normative sample suffers from an overrepresentation of young, single, Caucasian, well-educated individuals.

Internal consistency for the individual scales of the CAB are reported using Cronbach alpha estimates. In general, the CAB's internal scale consistencies fall between the .60s and .80s (ranging from .50 to .92). These values for internal consistency provide very mixed confidence for the CAB and its measures. Although the Axis I and Axis II scales have adequate values (.70s and .80s), many of the remaining scales have questionable reliability (.50s and .60s). A single study ($N = 39$) of test-retest reliability (1-week interval) is added as evidence of the test's stability. It would have been helpful and more convincing to include a readministration of the CAB after 1 month or perhaps longer as little would be expected to change in neuropsychological functioning or Axis II pathology in such a brief period of time.

Evidence to support the validity of scores from the CAB is limited to 2 of the Axis I scales (Anxiety and Depression), all of the Axis II scales, and the 4 Neuropsychological Dysfunction scales. None of the remaining 29 scales are supported in the manual with any reference to their validity. Convergent and face validation support are provided for the Anxiety scale revealing moderate correlations with the Spielberger State-Trait Anxiety Scale and the Minnesota Multiphasic Personality Inventory (MMPI) Anxiety scale. The manual does not indicate whether or not the author is referring to the MMPI's clinical scale, *Psychasthenia* or its content scale, *Anxiety.* Similar data are provided for support of the Depression scale, which also achieved moderate correlations with the MMPI Depression scale and the Beck Depression Inventory (BDI). Validation of the CAB's Axis II scale scores was accomplished through a correlational study examining their relationship to scores on the Millon Clinical Multiaxial Inventory–II (MCMI-II). In this study of only 24 personality disordered patients, the CAB scales' median convergent validity correlation was .58 (ranging from .10 to .87). It should be noted that most of the measures used in the CAB's validation support have been replaced by improved test editions (e.g., BDI-II, MMPI-2, and MCMI-III). This creates the perception that the CAB is a step behind other instruments and is dated in comparison.

Validation support for the Neuropsychological Dysfunction scale scores rests on a discriminant validity study of 17 patients. The scales themselves were derived through a factor analysis of the normal individual's data. As a previous reviewer points out, "a development procedure that used actual patients would have been stronger" (Retzlaff, 1999, p. 348). Confusing this point further is that the three factor structure model that was revealed following the Varimax rotation does not match the structure of the scales outlined by the manual as the Neuropsychological Dysfunction scales. This is not addressed or clarified adequately in the manual.

COMMENTARY. What value the CAB has as a measure of personality disorders, neuropsychological dysfunctioning and psychopathological syndromes is unclear. There are aspects of the test that have solid empirical backing and support whereas other areas seem to lack such enthusiastic endorsement. It is surprising that there is so little empirical research to support many of its scales given the extensive time that Dr. Coolidge has invested in the test. Although a handful of criticisms and recommendations from previous reviewers have been addressed, many have gone unheeded to include: the lack of empirical support, low internal consistency issues, limited validation data for many of the scales reported, and reliance on outdated tests for what little validation work has been conducted.

The CAB's normative sample is adequate, but fails to reflect the significantly diverse population that exists in many communities in the United States. There is significant room for improvement in the test's norming procedures and the sample base from which its limited empirical support is derived.

SUMMARY. The CAB is an ambitious attempt to combine a core group of Axis I and Axis II scales that have adequate empirical support with several neuropsychological dysfunctioning scales and a loosely cohesive grouping of additional scales that have limited, and in some cases insufficient, research support.

The author of the CAB has created a broad assessment tool that has the potential to be a useful instrument once its technical aspects are improved. Several of its scales require further validation and this process should include convergent measures that are current with the latest advances in the field. Given that the competition includes the MCMI-III, the MMPI-2, and various neuropsychological screening questionnaires, the CAB's brevity has promise but its quality has some distance yet to travel.

REVIEWER'S REFERENCES

Coolidge, F. L. (1984). Coolidge Axis II Inventory. Washington, DC: The author.
Retzlaff, P. (1999). [Review of the Coolidge Axis II Inventory]. In B. S. Plake & J. C. Impara (Eds.), *The fourteenth mental measurements yearbook* (p. 348). Lincoln, NE: Buros Institute of Mental Measurements.

Review of the Coolidge Assessment Battery by PETER ZACHAR, *Associate Professor of Psychology, Auburn University Montgomery, Montgomery, AL:*

DESCRIPTION. The Coolidge Assessment Battery (CAB) is a test for measuring *Diagnostic and Statistical Manual* of the American Psychiatric Association (4th ed.; DSM-IV) Axis I syndrome disorders and Axis II personality disorders. It also has scales for the assessment of neuropsychological functioning. It was formerly known as the Coolidge Axis II Inventory, but the name has been changed to better reflect its more global purpose.

The Axis I scales measure psychological states such as depression, anxiety, and psychotic thinking that are associated with syndrome disorders. They also measure particular syndrome disorders such as Schizophrenia, Posttraumatic Stress Disorder, and Social Phobia. The Axis II scales include all 10 of the personality disorders currently listed in the DSM-IV, plus scales for assessing

Depressive, Passive-Aggressive, Sadistic, and Self-Defeating personality disorders.

Three different scales are used to measure problems commonly associated with neuropsychological deficits. The first one is a neuropsychological dysfunction scale composed of 18 pathognomic signs of brain damage. The second scale measures executive function deficits. The third scale measures personality problems that often result from a traumatic brain injury—these are the same traits listed in the DSM-IV: Aggression, Apathy, Disinhibition, Emotional Lability, and Paranoia. The inclusion of neuropsychological scales is a major strength of the Coolidge.

Various items can be used to measure other personality traits that are considered important in psychiatric settings such as Introversion-Extroversion and Indecisiveness. Of special note in the additional scale category is a Hostility scale with subscales such as Anger, Dangerousness, and Impulsiveness.

The Coolidge Assessment Battery is available in both a self-report format and a format for completion by another rater such as the patient's spouse. It also contains validity scales to assess Random Responding, Faking Good, Faking Bad, and the Tendency to Deny Blatant Pathology. There are both paper-and-pencil and computerized versions.

DEVELOPMENT AND TECHNICAL COMMENTARY. The CAB development strategy employed convenience samples of nonpsychiatric individuals (principally undergraduate students) and some small samples of psychiatric patients.

With respect to the reliability data, the manual reports internal consistency coefficients in the form of coefficient alpha. With a few exceptions, these appear to be acceptable. It is not clear when the constructs being measured are homogenous or heterogeneous, so determining what might be considered a reasonable alpha is problematic. For the most part, the coefficients range from the mid .60s to the high .80s. The manual also has some errors (e.g., the reported mean for the schizoid scale is larger than the score someone would get if she or he answered all the questions affirmatively).

The Sadistic and Self-Defeating Personality Disorder scales have alphas below .70, and are probably no longer needed given that they are eliminated from the DSM-IV. The neuropsycho-logical scale alphas are quite high given their number of items. The alphas are less adequate for scales measuring personality traits that might reflect traumatic brain injury. These reliabilities should be higher because they are clearly homogeneous constructs. The alphas on these scales would be better assessed with a sample of patients who have sustained a brain injury. Higher alphas for these personality scales would give the CAB an advantage over some of its competitors because it would aid in making a differential diagnosis between Axis II disorders and a Personality Change Due to a General Medical Condition.

The test-retest reliabilities are inadequately presented. This is a major flaw, especially for the personality disorder scales. The manual claims that the average 1-week test-retest reliability for a sample of 39 college students was .90 for the Axis II scales. Test-retest coefficients for the individual scales are not printed in the manual and the only reference is to a paper presented at a regional conference. These reliabilities should be included in the manual, and they should also be cross-validated with a larger sample. For the Axis II scales, more information about temporal stability needs to be explicitly provided in the manual.

The validity evidence is unsystematic. Some of the studies reviewed have not been published in peer-reviewed journals, especially the studies for the Axis I scales. The validity information for the Axis II and neuropsychological scales is better documented in the literature. A brief PsychInfo search indicated a plethora of studies using the Coolidge Axis II scales.

The manual lacks an index, which is symptomatic of a larger problem involving a deficiency of information. More importantly, it fails to present easily accessible information about the item composition of each scale. One of the best ways to learn what a scale is measuring is to read through all the items on the scale at the same time. The manual devotes several pages of case studies to help clinicians interpret results, but it does not let users see directly what each scale is measuring.

By not providing information about scale composition, users are not provided a scoring key. Although there is an option with the computer program to score and then export data into a statistical package, it would be easier for researchers if they also had the scoring keys. They could then score the programs using SPSS or SAS and compute their own alpha coefficients, assess better and worse performing items, and create latent variables.

The manual is not clear about item overlap between scales. One of the weaknesses of the competitor Millon Clinical Multiaxial Inventory (MCMI) is item overlap. If psychological states such as anxiety and depression are correlated, those correlations should be determined by independent scales, and not artificially as a function of shared items between scales. According to the manual, the Coolidge Axis II scales minimize item overlap, but this strategy was abandoned for the other scales in the battery. There are approximately 36 separate clinical scales, with just over 700 items, but the entire battery has only 225 questions. I believe that is a lot of overlap! Not surprisingly, no scale intercorrelations were presented, nor would I recommend using these scales as predictors in a multiple regression analysis.

The battery's home-spun feel is reflected in its theoretical basis. The manual claims that the test is based on the dimensional model of psychiatric disorders as opposed to the categorical model. Its definition of the categorical model is something of a straw man definition. Obviously, as a psychological test, the Coolidge Assessment Battery is going to suggest that patients can score higher or lower on any scale. That is irrelevant to whether or not something such as Schizophrenia is a dimension on which everyone has a score, or whether it is a category to which people belong or not (Meehl, 1995). Best evidence to date suggests that Depression is more dimensional and Schizophrenia is more categorical (Haslam & Kim, 2001), but either one can be assessed with a psychological test.

A psychiatric taxon still has a range of severity, and that range is what psychological tests are able to describe. Although a disorder such as Borderline Personality appears to be dimensional, suggestions for interpretation of high scores are usually presented in terms of categories. Taking a dimension and talking about high scorers as "types" does not require committing to fixed categorical boundaries (Zachar, 2000). As long as high scorers on a dimension are conceptualized as types, it is important to know when an individual can be reliably assigned the descriptors that are associated with that type.

Therefore, the ability of the CAB to help clinicians make decisions about patients needs to be assessed with a hit rate analysis. It is not adequate to say that hit rates are used to make decisions about category membership and, therefore, not applicable to a psychological test that is based on the dimensional model. Furthermore, cut scores should not be defined only in terms of statistical deviance from the normal population mean, especially when using samples that minimized the presence of psychiatric disorders. The CAB uses one standard deviation above the mean as the cut score for all scales. Establishing a cut score is a scale-specific and, sometimes, population-specific process. The cut score for any scale should be that point at which the clinician is going to be correct most of the time if they decide that the test taker has the disorder measured by the scale.

This recommendation should come as no surprise to the developers. The manual claims that the cut scores on the Tendency to Deny Blatant Pathology validity scale should be different for "normals" than it is for those suspected of having a personality disorder and for persons with Schizophrenia. It also presents evidence that the positive predictive value and the negative predictive value of the Neuropsychological Dysfunction scale is impressive. The cut scores used for the other scales on the CAB deserve the same kind of detailed analysis.

There is some evidence that the strategy of picking one or two standard deviations above the normal population mean as the cut score is comparable to the more sophisticated strategy used by the Millon Clinical Multiaxial Inventory-II (MCMI II) for detecting prevalence rates (Sinha & Watson, 2001). In its favor, the deviation score strategy avoids the headaches associated with computing prevalence rates for different groups. It would still, however, be better to assess the hit rates of the scales using rigorous criteria such as psychiatrists' diagnoses by means of a structured clinical interview.

The computer-generated reports are efficiently organized and easy to navigate. Each type of report organizes information in a slightly different way, but all will be readily understandable by qualified users. These reports are for professionals, not patients. As a result they emphasize statistical information and critical items, plus brief diagnostic and treatment suggestions. In future revisions, the more numerically rich Score Report should provide standard errors of measurement. There is a separate manual for using the SigmaSoft CAB computer program. This manual is well-written and the design of the program makes it easy for both psychologists and their patients to use.

Trusting that the manual is accurately reporting minimal item overlap among the Axis II scales, the developers might want to consider more explicitly mimicking the Minnesota Multiphasic Personality Inventory-2 (MMPI-2; T6:1623) and providing configural interpretations, for example, identifying differences between an elevation on Borderline and Depressive versus an elevation on Borderline and Paranoid—which would be a more complex theory of types.

SUMMARY AND CONCLUSIONS. The Coolidge Assessment Battery manual lacks information that would be needed for a confident recommendation. It does not present enough information for users to fully understand what the scales are measuring, or to assess how independent the scales are from each other. Lack of an available scoring key makes the CAB researcher-unfriendly, which is unfortunate. It is supposed to help clinicians assess the probability that someone has a particular psychiatric disorder, but the cut scores need better validation. The test was originally designed to assess Axis II disorders. Some of the items were understandably reorganized to also assess neuropsychological problems. I believe Professor Coolidge should have limited his test to the Axis II scales, the neuropsychological scales, and probably the hostility scales. The additional scales make the whole thing too crowded.

REVIEWER'S REFERENCES

Haslam, N., & Kim, H. C. (2001). *Categories and continua: A review of taxometric research.* Unpublished manuscript, The New School University, New York.

Meehl, P. E. (1995). Bootstraps taxometrics: Solving the classification problem in psychopathology. *American Psychologist, 50,* 266–275.

Sinha, B. K., & Watson, D. C. (2001). Personality disorder in university students. A multitrait-multimethod matrix study. *Journal of Personality Disorders, 15*(3), 235–244.

Zachar, P. (2000). Psychiatric disorders are not natural kinds. *Philosophy, Psychiatry, & Psychology, 7,* 167–182.

[69]

Coping Inventory for Stressful Situations, Second Edition.

Purpose: Designed as a "scale for measuring coping styles."

Population: Adolescents, Adults.

Publication Dates: 1990–1999.

Acronym: CISS.

Scores, 5: Task, Emotion, Avoidance, Distraction, Social Diversion.

Administration: Individual or group.

Forms, 3: Adult, Adolescent, Situation-Specific.

Price Data, 2002: $45 per complete kit including 25 QuikScore™ forms, and manual (1999, 87 pages) (specify Adult or Adolescent Form); $30 per specimen set including 3 Adult QuikScore™ forms, 3 Adolescent QuikScore™ forms, 3 Situation Specific QuikScore™ forms, and manual; $24 per 25 QuikScore™ forms (specify Adult or Adolescent); $26 per manual.

Foreign Language Editions: French (European), French (Quebec), Arabic, Armenian, Danish, German, Greek, Hebrew, Icelandic, Italian, Japanese, Korean, Malaysian, Norwegian, Polish, Russion, Spanish (U.S.), and Spanish (European) translations available.

Time: (10) minutes.

Comments: Self-report.

Authors: Norman S. Endler and James D. A. Parker.

Publisher: Multi-Health Systems, Inc.

Cross References: For reviews by E. Thomas Dowd and Stephanie Stein, see 14:104, see also T5:696 (2 references).

Review of the Coping Inventory for Stressful Situations by WILLIAM C. TIRRE, Senior Research Psychologist and Research Manager, Career Vision, The Ball Foundation, Glen Ellyn, IL:

DESCRIPTION. The Coping Inventory for Stressful Situations (CISS) is a 48-item paper-and-pencil, self-report instrument available in both adult and adolescent forms. The manual also briefly describes a computer-administered format, and a 21-item Situation-Specific form, but these were not reviewed. The CISS was designed to allow practitioners to investigate three major coping styles in their clients: Task-Oriented, Emotion-Oriented, and Avoidance, each assessed with 16 items. Avoidance is composed of two subscales, Distraction (8 items) and Social Diversion (5 items). To each item on the instrument, the examinee responds using a 5-point frequency scale where 1 is *Not at all* and 5 is *Very Much.* Scoring is accomplished using a scoring grid attached underneath the answer sheet. On the other side of the scoring grid is the profile sheet, which gives standard score (*T* with mean of 50 and standard deviation of 10) and percentile conversions. On the adult form, separate norms are given for males and females within two categories, general population and psychiatric patients. On the adolescent form, separate norms are given for 13-to-15-year-olds and 16-to-18-year-olds. Separate college student norms are printed in the manual.

DEVELOPMENT. The theoretical framework motivating the CISS was the interaction model of anxiety, stress, and coping (Endler, 1988, 1993, 1997), a type of person-situation or interactionist model. The theory is complicated (at least in this reviewer's opinion) and to fully understand it, one would have to read the primary references. The CISS manual probably cannot stand on its own in this regard. Basically, this model says that person variables (e.g., trait anxiety, cognitive style, vulnerability) interact among themselves and with situation variables (e.g., life events, crises, traumas), which can interact among themselves, to produce a subjective perception of danger or threat. This perception of danger or threat, in turn, can affect both person and situation variables and lead to an increase in state anxiety. Reactions to changes in state anxiety include coping responses, defenses, and behavioral, biochemical, and physiological reactions and mental and physical illness. These reactions can also interact among themselves, and affect the person variables and stressors in the situation. In effect, there is a continuous feedback loop in operation. Endler and Parker (the test authors) argue that coping behaviors must be examined within the social and psychological context and not in isolation.

The CISS was designed to measure a person's preferred styles of coping with stressful situations. Although the Endler and Parker model appears to emphasize the person-situation interaction, the authors avoid falling into the trap where situation has stronger influence on behavior than personality. Coping behaviors might change in response to different types of stressors, and this process can be studied in the intraindividual approach. "The interindividual approach to coping, however, utilizes coping scores of the same individuals aggregated over different measurement occasions, or scores collected on a single occasion to represent a stable index of the individual's coping processes or styles" (manual, p. 30). This approach permits one to identify and measure individual differences in coping strategies that a person might use in a variety of stressful situations.

The coping strategies measured in the CISS are either task-oriented and problem focused, or person-oriented and emotion focused. The CISS scales include the following. *Task* involves purposeful behaviors aimed at problem solving, cognitive restructuring, and attempts to alter the situation. Planning and problem solving are emphasized. *Emotion* refers to self-oriented emotional reactions aimed to reduce stress, which are not always effective. Self-blaming, self-preoccupation, and fantasizing are examples. Sometimes this reaction can backfire and actually increase

stress. *Avoidance* refers to behaviors and cognitive changes aimed at avoiding the stressor. Two varieties are *Distraction* in which one attempts to distract oneself with unrelated situations or tasks, and *Social Diversion* in which one takes oneself out of the stressful situation for a time by doing such things as spending time with friends.

These dimensions were not identified a priori but emerged through repeated factor analyses of item data. To develop the initial version of the CISS, psychologists and graduate students generated coping items based on their experience and knowledge of the literature. They also evaluated items from existing coping surveys and research on coping. This resulted in a list of 120 items that were judged to be a comprehensive sampling of coping behaviors. After redundant and biased items were removed, 70 items remained that were administered to a sample of 559 undergraduates. A 5-point Likert scale was used where 1 was *Not at all* and 5 was *Very much*. Principal components analysis with Varimax rotation identified 19 components with eigenvalues of 1 or better. The scree test (Cattell, 1978) identified three factors, which are preserved in the current CISS: Task-Oriented coping (19 items), Emotion-Oriented coping (12), and Avoidance-Oriented coping (13). These factors were replicated in separate analyses of males and females. An additional 40 items were then generated for the Emotion and Avoidance subscales. The 12 Emotion and 10 Avoidance items that survived an interjudge agreement criterion of 80% were then added to the 44 items for a 66-item test, which was administered to 394 undergraduates (275 males, 130 females) and 284 adults (154 males, 130 females). Principal components analysis was applied again, resulting in three factors in both the undergraduate and adult samples. Items that loaded on more than one factor, had a factor loading less than .35, or lacked face validity were omitted, resulting in a 48-item inventory with 16 items per factor. Principal component analysis applied to the individual scales—Task, Emotion, and Avoidance—resulted in a single factor for Task and Emotion, and two for Avoidance. This same factor structure has held up consistently for both sexes, and for distinct population categories (e.g., general population, psychiatric patients, and undergraduates).

The development of the adolescent form of the CISS began in consultation with several teachers and researchers working with adolescents. Six items were simplified. The revised survey was then administered to samples of 13- to 15-year-olds (152 males, 161 females) and 16- to 18-year-olds (270 males, 234 females). Principal components analysis results were virtually identical to those found for the adult, undergraduate, and psychiatric patient samples.

TECHNICAL. The normative samples consist of 537 adults (249 males, 288 females), 1,242 undergraduates (471 males, 771 females), 302 psychiatric patients (164 males, 138 females), 313 13- to 15-year-old adolescents (152 males, 161 females), and 504 16- to 18-year-old adolescents (270 males, 234 females), all English-speaking North Americans. The manual does not report details about how the samples are distributed according to race and ethnicity, age, and location so it is difficult to assess their adequacy.

Two types of reliability estimates are provided in the manual. Internal consistency was assessed with Cronbach's alpha and test-retest reliability was assessed over a 6-week interval. Coefficients alpha estimated and averaged across the normative samples were as follows: Task = .90, Emotion = .86, Avoidance = .82, with subscales Distraction = .75 and Social Diversion = .79. There was little variation across groups. These figures indicate acceptable levels of internal consistency for the scales. Test-retest reliability or score stability was estimated on a sample of 238 undergraduates (74 males, 164 females). Test-retest reliability was for the most part adequate: Task = .73 (males), .72 (females); Emotion = .68 (males), .71 (females); Avoidance = .55 (males), .60 (females); with subscales Distraction = .51 (males), .59 (females); and Social Diversion = .54 (males), .60 (females).

Construct validity evidence was presented in the form of factor analysis, and for the adult form, correlations with (a) social desirability, (b) The ways of Coping Questionnaire (Folkman & Lazarus, 1988), (c) the Basic Personality Inventory (Jackson, 1989), (d) the Minnesota Multiphasic Personality Inventory (MMPI-2) (Hathaway & McKinley, 1989), (e) the Beck Depression Inventory (Beck, 1978), (f) the Eysenck Personality Inventory (EPI; Eysenck & Eysenck, 1975), (g) Endler Multidimensional Anxiety Scale (Endler, Edwards, & Vitelli, 1991), (h) Type A, (i) two measures of somatization, and (j) Absorp-

tion Scale from the Multidimensional Personality Questionnaire (Tellegen, 1982). For the adolescent form, correlations were reported with the Youth Self-Report (Achenbach & Edelbrock, 1987), the Self-Perception Profile for Adolescents (Harter, 1988), and the UCLA Loneliness Scale (Russell, Peplau, & Cutrona, 1980). The factor analytic (actually principal components) results can be summarized briefly: The same three principal components are identified regardless of the form or sample (male vs. female, normal adult vs. psychiatric patient vs. undergraduate). The congruence coefficients all exceed .95, indicating virtual identity of factor structures. In addition, analyses of the Avoidance subscale consistently point to two factors (viz., Distraction and Social Diversion). Correlations with other measures also tell a consistent story. Task-Oriented coping and Avoidance-Oriented coping were consistently either unrelated or negatively related to negative, undesirable behaviors and traits, although Distraction was modestly correlated with anxiety. In contrast, Emotion-Oriented coping was moderately to strongly correlated with psychological distress, psychopathology, and somatization. The most telling correlations in my opinion were with EPI Neuroticism (about .64 with Emotion) and Beck Depression Inventory (about .53 with Emotion).

COMMENTARY AND SUMMARY. The CISS was developed using sound test construction practices, is well grounded in theory, and has been subjected to a fair amount of construct validation that indicates the CISS measures what it is intended to measure. Internal consistency of the subscales is quite good and the test-retest reliability is adequate. For the most part, the manual is easy to read and reports a lot of meaningful and important data. Detracting from this otherwise solid test, we find that the normative samples are not fully described and may not be as representative of North Americans as desirable. With both the U.S. and Canada becoming increasingly multicultural/ multiethnic, it is important to investigate the appropriateness of a test for a cultural subgroup. To their credit, the test authors are careful to point out the limitations of their test in this regard.

Although overall a high quality product, the test manual does have some errors. There were a couple of misspelling or typing errors, but more importantly, I came across a seemingly impossible situation described on page 17 of the manual. R.S.

has a raw score of 32 on Avoidance (*T*-score 44), a 30 on Distraction (*T*-score 72), and a 20 on Social Diversion (*T*-score 65). The sum of the raw scores for Distraction and Social Diversion will be 3 to 15 points less than Avoidance total, because only three items are in Avoidance that are not in Distraction and Social Diversion. Checking with Dr. Endler, he agreed that it was an error and that it would be corrected in the next printing. In conclusion, I would not let the shortcomings of this test prevent me from using the test in research and practice. The good outweighs the bad.

REVIEWER'S REFERENCES

Achenbach, T. M., & Edelbrock, C. (1987). *Manual for the Youth Self-Report and Profile.* Burlington, VT: University of Vermont, Department of Psychiatry.

Beck, A. T. (1978). *Depression Inventory.* Philadelphia: Center for Cognitive Therapy.

Cattell, R. B. (1978). *The scientific use of factor analysis in behavioral life sciences.* New York: Plenum.

Endler, N. S. (1988). Hassles, health, and happiness. In M. P. Janisse (Ed.), *Individual differences, stress, and health psychology* (pp. 24–56). New York: Springer.

Endler, N. S. (1993). Personality: An interactional perspective. P. J. Hettema & I. J. Deary (Eds.), *Foundations of personality* (pp. 251–268). Dordrecht, Netherlands: Kluwer Academic Publishers.

Endler, N. S. (1997). Stress, anxiety, and coping: The multidimensional interaction model. *Canadian Psychology, 38,* 136–153.

Endler, N. S., Edwards, J. M., & Vitelli, R. (1991). *Endler Multidimensional Anxiety Scales: Manual.* Los Angeles: Western Psychological Services.

Eysenck, H. J., & Eysenck, S. B. G. (1975). *The manual of the Eysenck Personality Inventory.* San Diego, CA: Educational and Industrial Testing Service.

Folkman, S., & Lazarus, R. S. (1988). *Manual for the Ways of Coping Questionnaire.* Palo Alto, CA: Consulting Psychologists Press.

Harter, S. (1988). *Manual for the Self-Perception Profile for Adolescents.* Denver, CO: University of Denver.

Hathaway, S. R., & McKinley, J. C. (1989). MMPI-2 (Minnesota Multiphasic Personality Inventory—2). Minneapolis: The University of Minnesota Press.

Jackson, D. N. (1989). *Basic Personality Inventory Manual.* Port Huron, MI: Sigma Assessment Systems, Inc.

Russell, D., Peplau, L. A., & Cutrona, C. E. (1980). The revised UCLA Loneliness Scale: Concurrent and discriminant validity evidence. *Journal of Personality and Social Psychology, 39,* 472–480.

Tellegen, A. (1982). *Brief manual for the Multidimensional Personality Questionnaire.* Minneapolis: University of Minnesota.

[70]

Coping Scale for Adults.

Purpose: Designed as a self-report inventory that examines coping behavior.

Population: Ages 18 and over.

Publication Date: 1997.

Acronym: CSA.

Forms, 2: Short Form, Long Form.

Scores, 19: Seek Social Support, Focus on Solving the Problem, Work Hard, Worry, Improve Relationships, Wishful Thinking, Tension Reduction, Social Action, Ignore the Problem, Self-Blame, Keep to Self, Seek Spiritual Support, Focus on the Positive, Seek Professional Help, Seek Relaxing Diversions, Physical Recreation, Protect Self, Humor, Not Cope.

Administration: Group.

Price Data, 2002: A$121 per complete kit; A$24.70 per 10 short forms; A$24.70 per 10 long forms; A$11.55 per 10 scoring sheets; A$11.55 per 10 profile charts; A$51.80 per manual (60 pages).

Time: Administration time not reported.

Authors: Erica Frydenberg and Ramon Lewis.

Publisher: Australian Council for Educational Research Ltd. [Australia].

Review of the Coping Scale for Adults by PE-TER MILES BERGER, Area Manager, Mental After Care Association, London, U.K.:

DESCRIPTION. The Coping Scale for Adults (CSA) is an instrument designed to measure an individual's coping strategies. The scale has its origin in the Adolescent Coping Scale (ACS; T6:77) published by the same authors in 1993. The full CSA consists of a two-sided, three-page questionnaire. Two parallel scales are included, each using 74 five-point Likert-type items. Separate forms are used to measure "General" and "Specific" coping strategies. A "Short Form" also is offered, comprising "General" and Specific" measurement of 20 items each, directly querying the subjects about their use of the 20 identified coping strategies.

The "Specific" questionnaire allows the individual completing the scale to designate a life event and the coping skills applied to such event. Theoretically, the participant could examine coping strategies related to any number of life events (e.g., work, home-life, parenting).

The stated purpose for the CSA is to function as a research and clinical tool allowing participants to examine how they cope, both generally and in response to certain user-defined life events. The instrument is not standardized in the sense of offering reference groups or normative data, so findings are descriptive, rather than inferential. Although normative data are not provided, the manual offers a very transparent view of the test development process and the underpinning psychometric characteristics.

In reviewing this instrument, I first self-administered the questionnaire, according to instructions in the user manual. I scored the test and profiled the scores by hand, according to the manual's instructions. I then examined my results and interpreted them before considering the instrument from a psychometric viewpoint.

I was pleased and interested in the interpretation of my scores. I felt the resulting profile gave thoughtful suggestions of ways to cope that I had perhaps not considered. Specifically, my findings suggested that I underutilize relationships, social action, spiritual support, physical recreation, and humor as coping strategies, while utilizing problem solving, wishful thinking, and positive focus as primary coping strategies. My "Specific" profile addressing "Social Life and Love" indicated that I use the same overall pattern for coping, although I worry far more, and blame myself more, when considering these specific concerns.

I also tested myself using the CSA Short Form. By comparison with the Long Forms, the constructs considered in these 20 questions eliminated all precision. These forms are better seen as a checklist of proposed strategies that might be considered for group discussion, or to frame a counseling intervention.

As a test consumer, I found the scoring and profiling process uncomfortable and inconvenient. Although the test forms are provided in an optical-scoring format, there is presently no machine-scoring service. To score and profile this test, one must manually transfer 148 scores into 19 rows consisting of 3, 4, or 5 numbered items that appear to be randomly distributed. For example, "Worry" consists of item numbers 7, 24, 37, and 64. Each row score is then multiplied by 3, 5, or 7 to arrive at an adjusted score.

The scoring process is reminiscent of the Wechsler Adult Intelligence Scale (WAIS) Digit Symbol test. Scoring also requires accurate multiplication and the ability to derive a graph from a numerical score. This difficulty would seem a barrier to use of this instrument with less skilled employees and others who may lack the requisite clerical skills. I found hand scoring cumbersome and time-consuming. The manual's estimate of 10 minutes for scoring and profiling is highly optimistic.

Scoring and profiling could be facilitated greatly by an accessible computer-scoring service. Unfortunately, the publisher does not offer a machine-scoring service, and after a thorough search I was unable to locate any computer-scoring service available for the CSA. The publisher should consider offering inexpensive, computer-based scoring and profiling software.

I was satisfied with the overall experience of taking and interpreting the CSA. From the point of view of a test taker, I felt the CSA offered some constructive self-criticism, and a guide to how I might alter my coping patterns to live more effectively.

DEVELOPMENT. The manual offers an informative and thorough explanation of the test's development. Much of the development work originated with the authors' earlier instrument—the Adolescent Coping Scale (ACS; 1993). The manual explains the statistical parameters used to refine a larger item pool that had been accumulated by an open-ended survey of "people working in education, psychology, and community settings" (p. 16)

The work of Lazarus and associates is expressed as the cornerstone for the CSA. The main objectives stated for the CSA are to increase psychosocial competence, to advance research, and to facilitate personal development programs. Suggested applications include self-help, research, clinical practice, cognitive-behavioral change, career plans, and group/team dynamics.

TECHNICAL. The manual illustrates factor loadings and coefficient alpha reliability estimates for the derived scales comprising the precursor instrument (ACS). The factor analysis for the ACS yielded impressive results, with only 5 of 62 items loading ambiguously. Coefficient alpha reliability estimates for the ACS averaged .72.

The manual explains the rationale for item development of the CSA. In addition to items contained in the ACS, additional items were created based on a second open-ended survey of 250 adults. Thus, the original question pool for the CSA consisted of 80 items from the ACS plus 16 items that seemed to add further relevant content. The item pool was refined by eliminating the least reliable items, based on coefficient alpha analyses.

Reliability. Test-retest reliability is reported for a group of 25 respondents who took a second administration of the CSA after 10 to 14 days. Correlations ranged from .11 to .95. Except for 10 items, every test-retest correlation exceeded a .001 probability threshold. The 10 items with lower correlations can be explained by interpreting them as measuring more sensitive *states*. This view is consistent with the authors' approach to using a "Specific" scale in parallel with the "General" scale. Overall, the reported test-retest results are impressive, leaving no cause for concern over the instrument's stability.

Coefficient alpha reliabilities for 18 subscales averaged .80. Sound test development has resulted in excellent overall reliability for the CSA.

Factor structure. The manual presents factor analysis based on a sample of 371 participants. The analysis hypothesized an 18-factor solution derived through prior investigation. Impressively, the analysis accounts for 69% of variance, and factor loadings are nearly all as expected, with only three ambiguous loadings out of 73 items. These results reflect comprehensive and effective development, resulting in 18 clean, crisp, and unambiguous subscales. Each subscale represents 1 of 18 distinctly different approaches to coping.

Validity. The assiduous and comprehensive approach to this instrument's development affords high confidence in the internal validity of the CSA. The distinct and mutually exclusive characteristics of the subscales suggests that the test measures definable constructs.

The manual does not present any concurrent or comparative studies, and does not propose that the CSA predicts any particular outcomes. Thus, it is no surprise that predictive studies are not presented, although they are suggested for future research.

My opinion is that the CSA offers commonsense validity. On face value, the scales *feel* as though they describe distinctly different ways of responding to stressful events.

Norms. Eighteen means and standard deviations, one per factor, are reported for a sample of 369 individuals. Although technically this constitutes a norm table, comparative interpretation is discouraged. Instead, "within subject" interpretation is suggested, so conversion tables and standard scores are superfluous.

COMMENTARY. The CSA is proposed for use "in clinical practice." To clarify, the authors delimit application of the CSA to "counselling" applications where the user can benefit by focusing on coping strategies. Use in psychological, psychiatric, or medical diagnostics is not suggested, although the instrument has obvious value in rehabilitation planning, and as a counseling tool.

The authors propose use of the CSA in developing cognitive behavioral treatment protocols. Although no outcome research is cited to support such use, the instrument's face validity and concreteness logically support this claim. Further research could focus on how behavioral patterns can be changed therapeutically using a coping scale.

The authors propose that the CSA might be used in career planning, based on the supposition that certain coping patterns may be associated with certain career choices. However, without external validation, the matching of coping patterns to career choices is only speculative. Many interacting variables contribute to career choices,

and the contribution of coping paradigms to the effective and appropriate choice of careers is not established.

Finally, the CSA is offered as a tool for "personnel practitioners, to enhance their understanding of an individual's behaviour or that of a team or other work group" (manual, p. 15). With this use of the CSA, managers must remember that coping patterns are as likely a reflection of managerial practice and workplace conditions as they are a reflection of the coping traits of individual workers.

Comparisons. The CSA based its development on the work of Richard S. Lazarus, Ph.D. Because Lazarus himself published a coping questionnaire, entitled "Ways of Coping Questionnaire" (WAYS; Folkman & Lazarus, 1988), this seems a good point of reference.

The 50-item scale of the WAYS measures a domain similar to that measured by the CSA. The WAYS reports eight empirical subscales that look at similar kinds of coping strategies.

Empirical factor analysis of the CSA's subscales reveals a four factor solution: Dealing with the Problem, Not Cope, Optimism, and Sharing the Problem. The WAYS offers eight empirical scales: Confronting, Distancing, Self-Controlling, Social Support, Accepting Responsibility, Avoidance, Planning, and Re-Appraisal. The 18 subscales of the CSA fully include the WAYS domain. Examination of the content of the two instruments leaves little discrepancy, as might be expected given the stated origins of the CSA.

A second instrument used for comparison is the "Coping Orientations to Problems Experienced Scale" (COPE; Carver, 1989). This instrument, in the public domain, is a 60-item Likert-type scale. As with the CSA, a long and a brief version are available. No formal manual is published; however, the instrument's properties are published in a peer-reviewed journal. The COPE's derived subscales, describing its coping strategy constructs, are generally similar to those of the CSA and WAYS.

Comparison of other instruments with the CSA shows remarkable agreement in their content and strategies. Similarities also can be seen in the constructs that emerge in factor and content analyses. These comparisons demonstrate a high level of agreement among researchers, lending credence and validity to the "Coping Strategies" construct.

SUMMARY. The Coping Scales for Adults helps elucidate individuals' strategies for coping. This instrument measures general and situational strategies. The CSA is presented as an exploratory tool to facilitate understanding and self-reflection. I am persuaded that the instrument does a good job for the user, pointing out helpful information that potentially can be a guide toward more effective living.

Although the instrument is not unique in what it measures, and its methodology is not necessarily innovative, psychometric development of the instrument is highly professional, assiduous, and sound. The manual is very well presented and offers a clear explanation of the test's development and psychometric properties. The publishers should offer computer scoring and profiling capability.

What commends this instrument is its thoroughness and integrity of development that should give future researchers a psychometrically sound foundation. The CSA also delivers useful information for individuals to better understand how they cope with stress.

REVIEWER'S REFERENCES

Carver, C. S., Scheier, M. F., & Weintraub, J. K. (1989). Assessing coping strategies: A theoretically based approach. *Journal of Personality and Social Psychology, 56*, 267–283. Retrieved February 8, 2002 from http://www.psy.miami.edu/faculty/ccarver/sclCOPEf.html
Falkman, S., & Lazarus, R. S. (1988). *Manual: Ways of Coping Questionnaire.* Palo Alto, CA: Consulting Psychologists Press.

Review of the Coping Scale for Adults (CSA) Research Edition) by M. ALLAN COOPERSTEIN, Clinical Psychologist & Forensic Examiner, Independent Practice, Willow Grove, PA:

DESCRIPTION. The present Coping Scale for Adults (CSA) is a self-report inventory composed of 74 items. The General Form presents 70 structured items assessing conceptually and empirically distinct coping strategies, 3 items forming an optional "Not Cope" scale, and an open-ended question eliciting coping behaviors beyond those listed. Structured items are rated on a 5-point Likert scale.

The authors' research indicates that some coping behaviors are situation-specific. Consequently, they developed a Specific (long) Form enabling response measurements to self-selected or administrator-selected situations containing the same items but phrased differently. These two forms, the General and Specific, are referred to as the Long Forms of the CSA.

There is also a Short Form composed of 20 items: 19 structured items from the Long Form and an open-ended response question. Research

has demonstrated this to be a useful indication of how respondents will perform on the Long Forms. There are also General and Specific versions of the Short Form.

Long Forms average approximately 10 minutes to complete; Short Forms take 2–3 minutes. Ten to 15 minutes are suggested for dispensing questionnaires, explaining the test purpose, completing demographic information, reading instructions, and answering possible questions.

Test materials include the administrator's manual, non-reusable Long and Short questionnaires, scoring sheets, and profile charts. The forms have been thoughtfully color-coded to reduce confusion and error. Scoring sheets have also been color-coded.

Scoring may be performed manually or by machine, using optical scanning recognition. Hand scoring of the Long Form takes approximately 10 minutes, during which scores are transferred to a profile sheet. The Short Form does not require scoring (because it is composed of one item from each of the scales of the Long Form, the answer sheet also serves as a profile sheet).

In scoring the Long Form, items are tallied on a score sheet and adjusted to produce a final score for each scale. Adjusted scores are transferred to a profile sheet that graphically delineates the individual's use of the 18 coping scales and the 19th, NotCope, scale.

DEVELOPMENT. Described as a research instrument and clinical tool enabling individuals to examine coping behaviors, the CSA was developed to assist those working with adult individuals or organizations requiring clinical, counseling and human resource efforts related to coping and aid in facilitating development of coping strategies.

The authors describe coping as behaviors "akin to adaptation, mastery, defense, or problem solving" (p. 6), the fundamental concepts underlying CSA development originating from the cognitive-phenomenological theories published by Lazarus and his associates who describe coping as adaptive functioning within which the individual and his/her environment operate interactively (Folkman & Lazarus, 1980 Folkman, Lazarus, Dunkel-Schetter, DeLongis, & Gruen, 1986). Coping is thus conceptualized as a "dynamic phenomenon" (p. 7), a set of cognitive and affective positive human "actions which arise in response to a particular concern" (p. 7). Coping represents homeostatic attempts through which individuals attempt to restore equilibrium and/or decrease stress.

Related to coping, the authors cite *stability* (consistent coping behavior over time), *generality* (the assumption that individuals generalized their strategies across situations), and *dimensionality* (a grouping of coping strategies based upon purpose, meaning or functional value). They indicate the need for equilibrium between rational and empirical scale development, pointing out that difficulties arise in evaluating effective and ineffective coping behaviors because effective coping behavior in one context is not necessarily effective in another. Outcome efficacy cannot be readily determined; therefore, the authors assume that a more productive direction is to focus upon examination of the coping process without evaluating outcome.

The CSA yields 18 coping strategies derived empirically via factor analyses: Seek Social Support, Focus on Solving the Problem, Work Hard, Worry, Improve Relationships, Wishful Thinking, Tension Reduction, Social Action, Ignore the Problem, Self-Blame, Keep to Self, Seek Spiritual Support, Focus on the Positive, Seek Professional Help, Seek Relaxing Diversions, Physical Recreation, Protect Self, and Humor. There is also an optional scale, "Not Coping," that detects the inability to cope and occurrence of psychosomatic disorders. Four coping styles are also identified and tentatively labeled as Dealing Independently with the Problem, Non Productive Coping, Optimism and Sharing.

The CSA was developed based upon the Adolescent Coping Scale (ACS) (Frydenberg & Lewis, 1993). Following publication of the ACS, it became apparent that an adult form was needed. The authors examined the empirical structure of the ACS with a sample of 235 adults. Items were analyzed to determine if modifications were needed for adults. Next, adult coping behaviors were solicited from 250 individuals employed in education, psychologym and community settings to evaluate whether additional scales were needed to capture a full range of adult coping strategies. The next step involved a trial coping scale administered to a sample of 371 adults. In sum, 856 adults provided a research population for developing the rudimentary adult coping tool.

TECHNICAL. In the first of two analyses, 235 adults (ages 24–55) were administered the General Form of the ACS, the data analysis was based upon awareness that the factor structure of

the General and Specific scales had sufficient similarity to generalize from one form to the other. Distribution of the sample by gender and occupational status indicated a bias in occupational status towards the upper strata.

Item responses were factor analyzed (oblique with Oblimin rotation) to evaluate the appropriateness of the ACS when used with adults, as it was assumed that scales would not be entirely orthogonal or independent (i.e., the authors hypothesized that some coping strategies would overlap or relate to each other).

Replicating the analyses originally conducted on adolescent responses, items were grouped under scales for which they were written, the groups being randomly assigned to three categories composed of items designated to assess six coping strategies. Three factor analyses were performed on a sample of 235 adults. The results indicated that the 26 items in the six scales loaded significantly on their hypothesized scales, supporting suitability for their use in an adult population.

An examination of item suitability resulted in changes to six items based upon their contribution to alpha coefficients of their respective scales. Exclusion from their scales led to increased magnitude of the alpha coefficients. The authors state a hypothesis that subtle conceptual distinctions are made by adults that are not made by adolescents. A review of the open-ended questions demonstrates that the majority were consistent with the 18 scales, but a need for four additional strategies became apparent: *Thinking through the problem, Humor, Protect sense of self,* and *Plan and prioritize.*

Assessing the stability of item responses over time, 25 respondents repeated the questionnaire, 10–14 days following the first administration. Test-retest correlations were computed and reliable items were those reaching at least .58 or higher. If the correlation was lower, respondents' answers within 1 point of measurement were considered, with the rationale that an item's responses could be poorly correlated over two occasions due to a restricted range of response rather than instability. Items with less than satisfactory test-retest correlations were deemed reliable if at least 80% of respondents provided responses within 1 point of measurement on the two test occasions.

Computing the statistical properties of each scale, each scale had distributions covering virtually the full range of possible raw scores with alpha coefficients now ranging from .69 (Tension Reduction) to .92 (Seek Spiritual Support, Seek Professional Help), indicating strong evidence of reliability.

Examining scale intercorrelations, of 153 correlations between scale pairs, 11% were greater than .4 and less than 3% were greater than .5. No intercorrelations were greater than .6 and scales appeared sufficiently discrete.

Long Form coping styles were further explored by factor analysis. Factor 1 depicted a style encompassing hard work, solving the problem while a social dimension was maintained, and characterized by relaxation, humorous diversions, and physical recreation with improving significant social relations. Factor 2 involved strategies associated with inadequate coping involving worrying, isolation, blaming one's self, wishful thinking, ignoring the problem, and tension reduction. This factor was referred to as Non Productive Coping. Factor 3 is referred to as Optimism and includes strategies such as focusing on the positive, seeking relaxing diversions, seeking spiritual support, and wishful thinking. Factor 4 is referred to as Sharing and involves strategies focusing on seeking professional help, social action, seeking social support, and disclosure of the problem to others.

Examination of coping styles in the Short Form indicated satisfactory discrimination between scales, although reliability was considerably lower than for the Long Form. The authors recommend that coping style dimensions be assessed using the Long Form.

Due to the occasional impracticality of administering a full questionnaire, a shortened form was developed. Nineteen items were selected based upon wording and their relationship to other items comprising the scale from which it was drawn. Intertest correlations are .73 or greater with a mean of .84.

COMMENTARY. The CSA can be used as a self-help instrument through which people can come to understand their own coping behavior and subsequently initiate changes. It can also be used in research, clinical practice, career plans, monitoring cognitive behavioral change, and in personnel work understanding an individual's behavior or that of a team.

There is a high degree of face validity and interpretation is idiographic rather than normative. The issue of construct validity remains to be explored and refined as competing models exist.

It is considered a psychological tool and should be given only by appropriately qualified, licensed, or trained professionals. Proficiency depends upon an understanding of human life-span development as well as the liabilities and assets of psychometric testing in general and limitations of self report inventories in particular. The tool is not restricted to use by psychologists alone.

SUMMARY. Generally, the CSA appears to be a useful supplement to clinical situations, but it still needs further refinement. Although, intuitively, one would expect little difference, corroboration of its generalizability to an American sample is needed, as cross-cultural differences may exist (Sica, Novara, Dorz, & Sanavio, 1997). Criterion-related validity research is also needed to establish normative data in a stratified, American sample and between populations coping with emotional stress, pain, medical illness, etc. The application of the CSA under these circumstances would necessitate normative data and consideration of a response bias scale. Concurrent validity studies comparing individuals' weaknesses in coping strategies and styles to reliable, valid instruments assessing various psychopathologies (and pathological levels) could prove most useful. Overall, the Coping Scale for Adults holds considerable promise for its potential use in a variety of settings. Its development is solidly based upon earlier instruments assessing coping in adolescents and was logically extended, modified, and refined into an adult form. I agree with the authors in their caveat regarding the users' qualifications. The CSA may potentially be misused or misinterpreted when applied in human resource situations and interpreted by unqualified personnel.

REVIEWER'S REFERENCES

Folkman, S., & Lazarus, R. S. (1980). An analysis of coping in a middle-aged community sample. *Journal of Health and Social Behavior, 21,* 219–239.
Folkman, S., Lazarus, R. S., Dunkel-Schetter, C., DeLongis, A., & Gruen, R. J. (1986). Dynamics of a stressful encounter: Cognitive appraisal, coping, and encounter outcomes. *Journal of Personality and Social Psychology, 50,* 992–1003.
Frydenberg, E., & Lewis, R. (1993) *The Adolescent Coping Scale.* Melbourne, Victoria: Australian Council for Educational Research.
Sica, C., Novara, C., Dorz, S., & Sanavio, E. (1997). Coping strategies: Evidence of cross-cultural differences? A preliminary study with the Italian version of coping orientations to problems experienced (COPE). *Personality & Individual Differences, 23*(6) 1025–1029.

[71]

Coping With Health Injuries and Problems.

Purpose: Designed to assess coping with physical health problems.

Population: Adults.

Publication Dates: 1992–2000.

Acronym: CHIP.

Scores: 4 dimensions: Distraction, Palliative, Instrumental, Emotional Preoccupation.

Administration: Group.

Price Data, 2002: $48 per complete kit including technical manual (2000, 76 pages) and 25 QuikScore forms; $24 per 25 QuikScore forms; $86 per 100 QuikScore forms; $30 per technical manual; $32 per specimen set including technical manual and 3 QuikScore forms.

Time: (10) minutes.

Comments: Self-report.

Authors: Norman S. Endler and James D. A. Parker.

Publisher: Multi-Health Systems, Inc.

Review of Coping with Health Injuries and Problems by LINDA K. BUNKER, Professor of Human Services, University of Virginia, Charlottesville, VA:

DESCRIPTION. The Coping with Health Injuries and Problems (CHIP) is a 32-item self-report survey completed by paper-pencil responses to a Likert scale. Items assess a patient's preferred coping strategy from among Distraction, Palliative, Instrumental, and Emotional Preoccupation coping. The CHIP was developed for use with individuals experiencing a diverse set of health problems (both chronic and acute), in order to better understand coping strategies and how they mediate the way an individual reacts to stressful situations.

Administration of the CHIP requires approximately 10 minutes and is easily scored using the QuickScore form provided for each respondent. A fourth-grade reading level is required for this questionnaire, making it suitable for most adults to self-report. Scoring is done on an easy-to-use matrix grid that also allows for the calculation on an Inconsistency Index. The raw scores are then converted into standard scores based on the age and gender of the client.

The use of the results is more complex, and the manual specifies that the interpretation and communication of results must ultimately be assumed by a professional with advanced training in psychological assessment, who adhere to the Ethical Guidelines of the American Psychological Association (APA, 1992). This warning is perhaps appropriate, though the instrument was purported to be useful to any professional dealing with injuries or long term illness.

DEVELOPMENT. This CHIP is the fifth version (copyright 2000) of an instrument that has been under development since 1989. The authors state that the CHIP was developed to address the psychometric and methodological limitations that were associated with previously existing coping measures.

The CHIP is a multidimensional measure of coping strategies for specific illnesses or injuries that probes four concepts or preferences/"preoccupations" for dealing with stress: Distraction, Palliative, Instrumental, and Emotional. It was designed to allow the prediction of preferred coping and patterns of coping reactions. The constructs underlying their description of coping with illness, anxiety, and stress are nicely described in the manual, and the four preferences are defined and theoretically described.

TECHNICAL. Information describing the methodology for developing the CHIP and the norming process seems adequate, though not thoroughly justified. The manual reports that the normative sample included approximately 2,300 individuals, whose data have been normed into three different age groups by gender. The presentation of age-based norms is probably advisable, but there is little justification for the specific determination of 18–29, 30–49, and 50 and over, as appropriate demarcations, especially given the different environments under which individuals completed the questionnaire: 1,312 individually completed it while visiting the Ontario Science Centre, 476 were university students who completed it at the end of a regularly scheduled class, 391 adults seeking medical treatment finished it while in the doctor's waiting room, and 189 older adults living in a retirement community completed it (it is unspecified as to whether they completed the questionnaire individually or in a group session). There is no indication as to why both individual and group administrations were mixed in determining the norms, in spite of the instructions in the manual that specify individual administration is preferred, nor why the specific age ranges were selected.

Norms indicated that women scored significantly higher ($p<.001$) than men on all scales. With no indication of illness or injury severity, it is difficult to interpret the significance of the differences regarding women, or the fact that when age differences were found (for Distraction and Instrumental coping), older individuals always scored higher than younger individuals. Thus, there appears to be missing critical information necessary to interpret the importance or theoretical relevance of these gender and age differences, and no information about other variables such as ethnicity, socioeconomic status, or education that might be important in understanding the coping process and the validity of scores from this instrument and its norms.

The eight items for each preference are distributed within the questionnaire form, and an Inconsistency Index is provided to detect item response consistency (on a 5-point Likert scale ranging from [1] *Not at all* to [5] *Very much*) within the subscales.

The items on the questionnaire have been distributed across the instrument in terms of the subscales, but not in terms of the directionality of the questions. Almost all items are stated in the positive, socially desirable direction and seem quite obviously linked to the relevant coping strategy.

Reliability and internal consistency were extensively reported in the manual for the CHIP. Internal reliability (consistency) was generally in the moderate to high range ($r = .70–.84$) with the one exception for both older females and males on the Palliative scale ($r = .65$ and $.66$, respectively). The authors further suggest that the level of the interitem correlations for the CHIP scales supports the internal stability of the various CHIP scales, though the magnitude of those correlations ($r = .19–.41$) is not particularly strong.

The stability of the ratings over time was reported in terms of test-retest reliability. This element is especially important when proposing that a scale determines a relatively stable preference for one type of coping behavior over another. The only data presented on test-retest reliability were from Endler, Courbasson, and Fillion (1998) on an earlier version of the test over a 2-week interval for men (mean age 66.65 years with prostate cancer) and women (mean age 53.59 years with breast cancer). The reliabilities for this limited, oldest age group were generally very good ($r = .64–.85$), but should be tested and reported across the other age ranges.

Evidence to support the validity of the CHIP is presented in the manual, and reported in terms of three central issues: the multidimensionality (factor structure) of the various CHIP scales, its construct validity, and the criterion validity of the CHIP. The factor structure of the 32 items of the CHIP was investigated using principal components analysis with varimax rotation. All the items loaded at a high level with their coping scale, and had low or very low correlations with other factors. Similarly, the intercorrelations across CHIP scales were low to moderate (all ≤.39), indicating relatively distinct factors (scales).

Construct validity is a more difficult determination in relation to a scale such as the CHIP. In this case, the authors compared scores on the CHIP with other measures of general coping style, many of which had been created in their own laboratories and clinics. In particular, the CHIP and the CISS (Coping Inventory for Stressful Situations) were found to be highly correlated for the CHIP Emotional Preoccupation scale and the CISS Emotion-Oriented scales and moderately correlated between the CHIP Instrumental scale and the CISS Task-Oriented scale, the CHIP Distraction scale and both the CISS Avoidance-Oriented subscales, and the CHIP Palliative scale and CISS Avoidance-Oriented scale and Distraction subscale.

Construct validity was also estimated by comparing the CHIP and basic personality factors assessed by the EPQ (Eysenck Personality Questionnaire) such as neuroticism and extraversion that have been found to have moderate correlations with the CHIP Emotional Preoccupation. Two elements have been shown to be related in women only: Extraversion was positively associated with the CHIP Distraction scale, and Psychoticism was negatively associated with the CHIP Instrumental scale.

Criterion validity is difficult to determine for such instruments, and in this case was compared to the coping behaviors of adults with chronic and acute health problems. In this case, the theoretical underpinnings of the questionnaire were compared to predictions based on logical inferences (Endler, Parker, & Summerfeldt, 1998). For example, it was predicted (and supported) that patients with chronic health problems (such as diabetes) would have higher levels of Instrumental Coping ($p>.001$) because of greater interactions with health care professionals, and would have more susceptibility to emotional problems related to depression, anger, and anxiety (see Taylor, 1999) and thus score higher on the Emotional Preoccupation scale ($p<.001$). (It should be noted that there were no significant main effects related to the Palliative scale or the Distraction scale, though a relationship between the Palliative scale and acute health problems might have been predicted.)

COMMENTARY. The value of the CHIP as a way to detect individual preferences for coping strategies, and the apparent link to stress management abilities when faced with injuries or significant health problems, is based on the assumption that individuals need different coping strategies for different stressors. The manual provides extensive information about reliability, but less about validity—a critical limitation to the present documentation. To the credit of the authors, they invite interested researchers and clinicians to correspond with them to provide further thought, refinements, and improvements regarding the CHIP.

The manual presents one set of sample profiles as a key to the scoring system. The hypothetical client, JD, shows an obviously low level of Palliative coping (*T*-score of 42), with other scores at the above average range (Distraction = 66, Instrumental = 68, and Emotional = 70). The guide to interpreting scores specifies that a *T*-score of >70 is very much above average. In this case, three of four scales are quite high, and there is no indication of the significance of that finding. In contrast, Case Studies 1, 2, and 4 showed marked differences between the high use and low use coping skills. In all three cases, patients scored very low to average in Distraction coping, and no mention was made in the manual as to the importance of this score, or how it might be used in an intervention strategy. In contrast, emphasis was placed on increasing Instrumental (task-oriented) coping. Overall the seven case studies are very interesting and informative, but seem to display a subtle preference on the part of the authors that may reflect their counseling/clinical philosophy for increasing instrumental coping strategies.

Several concerns remain about the original research sample and the norming of this instrument. In particular (a) the norms include no information about the nature of the health problems in the sample (e.g., chronic, acute, injury, disease), (b) no information about other aspects of coping preferences are assessed (e.g., length of illness, socioeconomic status, education, use of medical professionals), (c) the issue of self-disclosure is always present, with some individuals known to underreport or underestimate their preferences and behaviors due to social-desirability factors, whereas some may more negatively depict their thoughts and behaviors in an effort to gain attention or services.

SUMMARY. The CHIP questionnaire is an easily administered and scored instrument to determine the preference for coping strategies by patients with serious health or injury problems. It would be a good descriptive instrument or "interview tool" when talking with clients about coping strategies. However, the overall psychometric methods of development and validity seem weak as an assessment tool.

REVIEWERS REFERENCES

American Educational Research Association, American Psychological Association, & National Council on Measurement in Education. (1999). *Standards for educational and psychological testing*. Washington, DC: American Educational Research Association.
American Psychological Association. (1992). *Ethical guidelines of the American Psychological Association*. Washington, DC: American Psychological Asssociation.
Endler, N. S., Courbasson, C. M. A., & Fillion, L. (1998). Coping with cancer: The evidence for the temporal stability of the French-Canadian version of the Coping with Health Injuries and Problems (CHIP). *Personality and Individual Differences, 25*, 711–717.
Endler, N. S., Parker, J. D. A., & Summerfeldt, L. J. (1998). Coping with health problems: Developing a reliable and valid multidimensional measure. *Psychological Assessment, 10*, 195–205.
Taylor, S. E. (1999). *Health psychology* (4th ed.). Boston: McGraw-Hill.

Review of Coping With Health Injuries and Problems by LEONARD HANDLER, Professor of Psychology, and AMANDA JILL CLEMENCE, Doctoral Graduate Student, University of Tennessee, Knoxville, TN:

DESCRIPTION. The Coping with Health Injuries and Problems (CHIP) is described by the authors as a 32-item multidimensional self-report measure of coping strategies for specific acute or chronic illnesses and injuries. The authors conceptualize the use of the test as an instrument that can "identify an individual's coping responses to a variety of health problems, and that could be administered over the course of the specific health problem to help determine the coping strategies used at different times in the development and/or treatment of the problem" (p. 29). The test measures the variables of Distraction (the extent to which the respondent avoids preoccupation with health problems), Palliative (self-help responses), Instrumental (focus on task-oriented strategies), and Emotional Preoccupation (the extent to which the individual focuses on the emotional consequences of the health problem). The test can be administered either individually or in a group, in about 10 minutes.

The respondent is asked to write in his or her most recent health problem ("illness, sickness, or injury") and is then asked to respond to the test items by circling a number from 1 (*not at all*) to 5 (*very much*) to indicate how much he or she engaged in the specific activity described when they encountered their health problem. An Inconsistency score, to detect noncompliant or unmotivated response approaches, is calculated by comparing differences between each of eight pairs of test questions. Individual responses are transferred to a scoring sheet and subscale totals are calculated by hand. Total scale scores are then transferred to a table by circling each score under the appropriate age and gender column, and the corresponding T-score appears on the same row as the circled raw score. The circled numbers are then connected with straight lines to construct the profile.

The authors describe a step-by-step interpretive procedure in which individual item responses are examined to determine which types of coping strategies are being over- or underutilized by comparing T-scores on each scale. The authors include a table for the interpretation of the T-scores, ranging from "very much below average" ($T<30$) to "very much above average" ($T>70$) in nine steps. The scores can also be interpreted using an analysis of profile pattern that allows the interpreter to compare coping behaviors across different illness situations, or over time in coping with the same illness.

DEVELOPMENT. The authors refer to the method utilized in their assessment of coping strategies as "intraindividual" (p. 26) because it is purported to measure ways in which coping responses may vary from one situation to the next in an individual dealing with health problems. The authors conceptualize "health problems" as "a specific type of stressor that may vary according to duration, degree of chronicity, or amount of personal control" (Endler, Parker, & Summerfeldt, 1998, p. 196). Therefore, this instrument was designed to assess a wide variety of health and illness concerns as opposed to any specific health or medical problem. Furthermore, "coping" is defined as "cognitive and behavioral attempts to change, modify, or regulate internal or external factors (which may be adaptive or maladaptive)" (Endler et al., 1998, p. 196).

Item development began with the creation of 120 items that characterize a variety of techniques and behaviors that may be used to cope with health-related problems. The authors consulted with a variety of professionals in the field to narrow the list to 75 items perceived as generalizable and applicable to a variety of individuals and to a wide range of health problems. These items

were administered to a sample of 532 undergraduate students at an Ontario university. Participants were given the items with similar instructions to those included in the final version of the measure. Six items were omitted due to over- or underendorsement. The remaining 69 items were analyzed using eigenvalue and scree test criteria along with a split-half factor comparabilities method. Furthermore, the use of a principal-components analysis resulted in 45 items that loaded uniquely on each factor in a four-factor model. These factors were labeled: Emotional Preoccupation Coping (15 items), Instrumental Coping (10 items), Distraction Coping (14 items), and Palliative Coping (6 items).

In a second investigation, the authors created 25 new items in an effort to increase the number of items loading onto the Palliative Coping factor and to arrive at a measure that contains an equal number of items on each factor. The new 70-item measure was administered to 598 adult visitors to the Ontario Science Centre. Eight items were dropped due to over- or underendorsement and a principal-components analysis was applied to the remaining items. Items were retained that loaded uniquely above .35 on one of the four factors. To attain an equal number of items on each factor, items with the lowest loadings were removed until each factor contained 8 items.

TECHNICAL. A total of 2,358 individuals make up the normative sample for this measure. The sample consists of 1,312 adult visitors to the Ontario Science Centre, 476 university students, 391 adult patients of four general practitioners, and 189 adults living in a retirement setting. Participants are 945 males and 1,413 females ranging in age from 18 to 96 years. Due to the effects of age and gender on the results of this measure, these factors are accounted for in the norms.

Across studies (normative data and Endler et al., 1998), the coefficient alpha reliability estimates range from .70 to .80 for the Distraction scale, .65 to .82 for the Palliative scale, .73 to .83 for the Instrumental scale, and .82 to .84 for the Emotional Preoccupation scale. These findings suggest adequate internal consistency reliability for the CHIP. Across this same set of participants, mean interitem correlations range from .22 to .34 for the Distraction scale, .19 to .37 for the Palliative scale, .27 to .39 for the Instrumental scale, and .37 to .38 for the Emotional Preoccupation scale.

With correlations in this range, each subscale appears to be measuring related but somewhat distinct aspects of coping with health problems.

In a study of 160 cancer patients (50 males and 110 females) who completed the CHIP on two occasions (2 weeks apart), Endler, Courbasson, and Fillion (1998) found test-retest reliabilities ranging from .75 to .85 across scales for males and from .64 to .82 for females.

VALIDITY. The manual discusses validity by an examination of the factorial validity, the construct validity, and the criterion validity of the CHIP. In a principal-components factor analysis of the normative sample, four factors emerged that closely matched the four coping scales of the CHIP. Low to moderate correlations were found among the four CHIP scales across gender (.13 to .39) and age groups (.17 to .43). Endler et al. (1998) report moderate significant correlations (.42 for males; .35 for females) between the CHIP Instrumental scale and the Task-Oriented scale for the Coping Inventory for Stressful Situations (CISS), with low or nonsignificant correlations between the CISS Task-Oriented scale and the three other CHIP scales. High significant correlations were found between the CHIP Emotional Preoccupation scale and the CISS Emotion-Oriented scale (.61 for males; .60 for females), but not with the other CHIP scales. Summerfeldt and Endler (1998) obtained similar results in a sample of patients seeking treatment at a pain clinic. Endler et al. (1998) found a moderate correlation between the CHIP Instrumental scale and the CSI Problem Solving scale for men (but not for women) and moderate correlations were found between the CHIP Distraction scale and the CSI Seeking Social Support scale. The CSI Avoidance scale was moderately associated with the CHIP Palliative and Emotional Preoccupation scales for women (but not for men). Endler, Parker, and Summerfeldt (1992) found, as predicted, moderate correlations between the CHIP Emotional Preoccupation scale and the Neuroticism scale on the Eysenck Personality Questionnaire (.53 for males, .48 for females). Endler et al. (1998) examined the criterion validity of the CHIP by comparing the coping behaviors of adults with chronic and acute health problems. Their findings were consistent with the research that finds that those with chronic health problems are more susceptible to emotional problems related to depression, an-ger, and anxiety compared with those patients with acute health problems.

COMMENTARY. The manual is clear and well written. It contains case illustrations as well as a description of the authors' model of the relationship between the multidimensional interaction model of stress, anxiety, and coping. The authors report excellent efficiency statistics for the Inconsistency Index, using a cutoff score of 10 (e.g., Sensitivity, 98%; Specificity, 97%; Overall Correct Classification, 98%).

The CHIP has excellent test-retest reliability and good to excellent evidence of validity. It is well standardized and has case study information. However, there are no available data concerning separate racial groups and norms for various socioeconomic subgroups within the North American population. As with all self-report measures, CHIP scores are subject to dissimulation. Therefore, the test might benefit from validity scales in addition to the Inconsistency Index to detect those cases in which the participant wants to present himself or herself in a more favorable or less favorable light.

Additional research is necessary to compare the psychometric properties and the factor structure of the CHIP in those patient populations experiencing more homogeneous medical problems, such as cancer patients compared with cardiac or renal patients. More validity data are needed concerning possible patterns of change in coping over the course of specific illnesses.

SUMMARY. The CHIP has excellent evidence of test-retest reliability and good to excellent validity. Administration and scoring are simple and the measure may be administered quickly and efficiently to groups or on an individual basis. Therefore, the test appears to be quite efficient and useful for research purposes as well as for use with individuals experiencing difficulty managing their reactions to health problems. However, given the lack of separate racial and socioeconomic norms, care should be taken when interpreting results until more comprehensive comparison data are available.

REVIEWERS' REFERENCES

Endler, N. S., Courbasson, C. M. A., & Fillion, L. (1998). Coping with cancer: The evidence for the temporal stability of the French-Canadian version of the Coping with Health Injuries and Problems (CHIP). *Personality and Individual Differences, 25*, 711–717.

Endler, N. S., Parker, J. D. A., & Summerfeldt, L. J. (1992). *Coping with health problems: Developing a reliable and valid multidimensional measure.* Department of Psychology Reports, Number 204, York University, Toronto.

Endler, N. S., Parker, J. D. A., & Summerfeldt, L. J. (1998). Coping with health problems: Developing a reliable and valid multidimensional measure. *Psychological Assessment, 10*, 195–205.

Summerfeldt, L. J., & Endler, N. S. (1998). Coping with chronic pain: Psychological variables, personality, and illness experience and outcome. In J. Bermudez, B. deRaad, J. de Vries, A. M. Perez-Garcia, A. Sanchez-Elvira, & G. L. van Heck (Eds.), *Personality psychology in Europe* (Vol. 6, pp. 409–416). Tilburg: Tilburg University Press.

[72]
Culture-Free Self-Esteem Inventories, Third Edition.

Purpose: "A set of self-report inventories used to determine the level of self-esteem in students ages 6-0 through 18-11."

Population: Ages 6-0 through 18-11.

Publication Dates: 1981-2002.

Acronym: CFSEI-3.

Administration: Group.

Levels, 3: Primary, Intermediate, Adolescent.

Price Data, 2003: $184 per complete kit including manual (2002, 60 pages), 50 primary examiner/record forms, 50 intermediate profile/scoring forms, 50 intermediate student response forms, 50 adolescent profile/scoring forms, and 50 adolescent student response forms in a storage box; $51 per manual.

Time: (15-20) minutes.

Comments: Newly normed revision of Culture-Free Self-Esteem Inventories, Second Edition; all levels include Defensiveness Score (a lie scale); previous editions entitled Culture-Free Self-Esteem Inventories for Children and Adults; derivative entitled North American Depression Inventories for Children and Adults (11:265).

Author: James Battle.

Publisher: PRO-ED.

a) PRIMARY.

Population: Ages 6-8.

Score: Global Self-Esteem Quotient.

Price Data: $28 per 50 primary examiner/record forms.

b) INTERMEDIATE.

Population: Ages 9-12.

Scores, 5: Academic, General, Parental/Home, Social, Global Self-Esteem Quotient.

Price Data: $28 per 50 intermediate profile/scoring forms; $28 per 50 intermediate student response forms.

c) ADOLESCENT.

Population: Ages 13-18.

Scores, 6: Academic, General, parental/Home, Social, Personal, Global Self-Esteem Quotient.

Price Data: $28 per 50 adolescent profile/scoring forms, $28 per 50 adolescent student response forms.

Cross References: See T5:746 (4 references); for reviews by Michael G. Kavan and Michael J. Subkoviak of a previous edition, see 12:100 (7 references); see also T4:700 (9 references); for reviews by Gerald R. Adams and Janet Morgan Riggs of the original edition, see 9:291 (1 reference); see also T3:644 (1 reference). For reviews by Patricia A. Bachelor and Michael G. Kavan of the North American Depression Inventories for Children and Adults, see 11:265 (1 reference).

Review of the Culture-Free Self-Esteem Inventories, Third Edition by BETHANY A. BRUNSMAN, Assessment Specialist, Lincoln Public Schools, Lincoln, NE:

DESCRIPTION. The Culture-Free Self-Esteem Inventories, Third Edition (CFSEI-3) were designed to be norm-referenced culture-fair self-report measures of self-esteem intended for students ages 6 through 18. The three versions of the inventory—Primary (ages 6–8), Intermediate (ages 9–12), and Adolescent (ages 13–18)—consist of 29, 64, and 67 items, respectively. On the Primary and Intermediate forms, the items consist of statements to which students respond "yes" or "no." On the Adolescent form, items are written as questions with "yes" or "no" responses. Each form takes about 15–20 minutes to complete. Scoring requires another 15–20 minutes. The Primary form yields a Global Self-Esteem score. In addition to Global Self-Esteem, the Intermediate and Adolescent forms generate the following subscale scores: Academic, General, Parental/Home, Social, and Personal (Adolescent form only). All three forms also contain items that produce a Defensiveness score, which can be used to invalidate results.

For the Primary Form, the administrator reads the items aloud to the child and records the child's responses on the scoring form. For the Intermediate and Adolescent Forms, the students read the items and record their responses on the response form independently. The CFSEI-3 may be administered individually or in groups. The scoring/profile forms facilitate scoring and interpretation with graphics and graphical representations of scores that may be easily filled in by the test administrator. The manual suggests that appropriate "training in assessment and an understanding of test statistics" (p. 7) are necessary for interpretation of scores. The manual identifies four uses for the CFSEI-3: (a) identification of children in need of psychological assistance, (b) planning of school interventions, (c) identification of areas of difficulty to target in therapy, and (d) for use in research studies in which self-esteem is a variable.

DEVELOPMENT. The CFSEI was first published in 1981. The second version was released in 1992. The CFSEI-3 (2002) is the third version of the inventory. Battle revised some of the items and conducted new norming and validity studies.

The CFSEI-3 is based on Harter's (1998) theoretical framework for self-esteem. The age groups for which each form and corresponding scales are designed are based on Harter's stages. The manual defines self-esteem as "the perception the individual possesses of his or her own worth, which develops gradually and becomes more differentiated with maturity and interaction with significant others" (manual, p. 30). According to Harter's model, self-esteem develops and becomes more complex with age. By middle to late childhood (ages 9–12), children are able to cognitively distinguish among several aspects of self. For this reason, the Intermediate form of the CFSEI-3 contains subscales. Adolescents (ages 13–18) are able to make further differentiations in self-esteem. Consequently, the Adolescent form also contains a personal self-esteem scale.

No theoretical framework for the "culture-fairness" of the CFSEI-3 is provided.

According to Battle, the items on the CFSEI-3 were developed to cover all areas of the construct, based on a review of the self-esteem literature and other self-esteem instruments. The subscales were determined by exploratory factor analysis. Items were selected and revised using discrimination indices and Differential Item Functioning (DIF) analyses.

TECHNICAL. The norm sample, which was collected between fall 1998 and fall 2000, although not a random sample, was relatively representative of students in the United States based on comparison census data. Sample sizes were 359 for the Primary form, 547 for the Intermediate form, and 821 for the Adolescent form. Participation of males and females in the norm group was approximately equal. Only small numbers of non-White students were included, however. Norms are available only for the total group. The table provided for converting standard scores to percentile ranks suggests a ceiling effect for scores. The highest percentile rank possible on the Primary form is 91 and the highest percentile rank for the Intermediate and Adolescent forms is 94.

Separate coefficient alphas were provided for subscale scores of several groups of students, including males, females, European Americans, African Americans, Hispanic Americans, gifted students, and students with learning disabilities in the norm sample. Coefficient alphas and Standard Error of Measurement (SEM) were provided for each of the subscale scores for all ages of students. Reliability data for a group of Canadian students were also included. Test-retest reliability with a 2-week interval was computed for very small groups of students taking each of the forms. The reliability coefficients ranged from .68 to .98 with most of the values in the .75 to .85 range. Reliability coefficients for African American and Hispanic students were slightly lower than for other groups of students.

The manual contains instructions for dealing with missing items, for invalidating results based on Defensiveness scores, and for reading the inventory to students who are reading below a certain grade level, but no theoretical or empirical information was presented to support these instructions. Cut scores are also provided with directions for interpreting scores in relation to the purposes of the inventory. These cut scores seem to be arbitrary and based on the distribution of scores in the norm group.

Battle conducted differential item functioning (DIF) analyses to detect bias based on gender and ethnicity (comparisons of scores of African American and Hispanic students to White students). He examined the effect sizes for items with significant uniform DIF (indicating potential bias). Two items on the Adolescent form exhibited moderate effect sizes and were targeted for replacement. No judgmental bias review procedures were used.

Battle provides several types of evidence for the validity of score interpretations in addition to the careful development and selection of items. Correlations of scores with other measures of self-esteem for small samples of students at some of the ages represented by the scales ranged from .51 to .85 for related subscales and .56 to .90 for global self-esteem scores. Mean scores for different ages and groups of students were relatively similar. Model fit statistics for confirmatory factor analysis indicated close fit.

COMMENTARY. Battle presents sufficient evidence of reliability of scores and some evidence of validity of score interpretation for students similar to the norm group for the CFSEI-3. The norm group also seems to be representative of the school-age population of the United States at the time of the studies. The CFSEI-3 scores show strong relationships with other measures of self-esteem for these groups of students. The validity evidence supporting the purposes of the inventory described in the manual, however, is insufficient. Additional evidence that would strengthen the proposed score interpretations for the CFSEI-3 could include relationships between scores and psychological diagnoses, evidence that scores change with particular interventions or therapy, relationships between scores and other educational outcome measures, and relationships between scores and other characteristics and abilities that have been studied. Some support for the cut scores proposed in the manual would also be critical.

The assertion that the CFSEI-3 is culture-free is not adequately supported. Even Battle's use of the term "culture-fair" is somewhat questionable. Statistical analyses of bias were completed, but the development process did not include any judgmental review of items for bias. Shepard (1982) suggests that both judgmental and statistical methods of bias detection are necessary because statistical methods may not detect aspects of the content or format of items that are offensive to members of some groups. Offensive material can affect both the performance on particular items and performance on the instrument as a whole. Additionally, the norm group contains only small numbers of non-White students. Although it reflects the population in the United States, the numbers of students in other ethnic groups may not be enough to substantiate the validity of the CFSEI-3 for non-White students. Evidence of absence of bias is critical for a culture-fair instrument, but not sufficient to establish culture fairness. It could be argued that the groups of students whose self-esteem educators might be interested in measuring with a culture-fair instrument would include students who are from cultures other than those represented by students in the U.S. Very few if any of these students participated in the norm group and Battle provides no theoretical basis for the cultural fairness of items.

SUMMARY. For students similar to the norm group, the CFSEI-3 should be a reliable measure of self-esteem. Administration and scoring are relatively quick and easy. The manual provides detailed information about administering and scoring all three forms. More data are necessary to determine if the instruments should be used for the purposes proposed by Battle, however. The evidence that the CFSEI-3 is "culture-fair" is also inadequate. Studies with larger numbers of diverse groups of students from other cultures would be necessary to support this claim.

REVIEWER'S REFERENCES

Harter, S. (1998). The development of self-representations. In W. Damon & N. Eisenberg (Eds.), *Handbook of child psychology: Vol. 3. Social, emotional, and personality development* (5th ed., pp. 553–617). New York: Wiley.
Shepard, L. A. (1982). Definitions of bias. In R. A. Berk (Ed.), *Handbook of methods for detecting bias* (pp. 9–30). Baltimore, MD: Johns Hopkins University Press.

Review of the Culture-Free Self-Esteem Inventories, Third Edition by Y. EVIE GARCIA, Assistant Professor, Educational Psychology, Northern Arizona University, Phoenix, AZ:

DESCRIPTION. The Culture-Free Self-Esteem Inventories, Third Edition (CFSEI-3) is a self-report inventory designed to measure self-esteem in children and adolescents ages 6–18 years. There are three age-related forms of the inventory.

The CFSEI-3 inventories may be administered by an examiner or self-administered by children or adolescents with at least a third grade reading level. Items are answered Yes or No. Some Yes answers are scored positively, others are scored negatively. The method used to identify the scoring directions is clear. The inventories for all three age groups yield a general self-esteem raw score obtained by summing the raw scores and then converting them to a quotient called the Global Self-Esteem Quotient (GSEQ). The GSEQ has a mean of 100 and a standard deviation of 15. A Defensiveness score (a lie scale) is also derived for each inventory by summing raw score boxes that are shaded to indicate Defensiveness items.

The Adolescent Form (for students 13–18 years old) has 67 items. In addition to yielding a GSEQ and a Defensiveness score, items are also assigned to one of five subscales: Academic, General, Parental/Home, Social, and Personal, which are summed and converted to standard scores with means of 10 and standard deviations of 3.

The Intermediate Form (for children 9–12 years old) has 64 items across the first four subscales used in the Adolescent Form (no Personal subscale is included for this age group). These scores are derived in the same manner as for the Adolescent Form.

The Primary Form (for children ages 6–8) is not differentiated into subscales. It consists of 29 items yielding a GSEQ and a Defensiveness raw score.

The GSEQ is considered the most useful value. The author indicates that unusually high and low scores that deviate from the norm (e.g., lower than 90 or above 110) should be investigated and some useful examples of implications for very high or low GSEQ scores were provided. The author cautions that "important decisions about diagnosis should rest only on the interpretation of GSEQ scores" (manual, p. 15). Subscale scores should be interpreted only in terms of specific content and may be used for generating hypotheses about why an examinee's GSEQ is high or low.

A table in the manual (Table 3.1, p. 14) provides descriptive categories for both GSEQs and subscales ("Very Low," "Low," "Below Average," "Average," "Above Average," "High," and "Very High" Self-Esteem) with no additional guidance for interpreting the implications for each category.

DEVELOPMENT. The CFSEI-3 is the latest and substantially improved version (copyright 2002) of a test that has been published since 1981. The underlying theory for the test, now based partly on Harter's (1998) neo-Piagetian stages of development of self-esteem, was updated for this edition.

The CFSEI-3 model describes self-esteem as an attitude toward oneself based on one's perception of abilities and limitations, which is thought to correlate with cognitive development. In early or middle childhood (about ages 6–8), self-esteem is thought to begin as a globally positive or negative attitude and develops into increasingly differentiated categories of self-esteem. By ages 9–12, as a child begins to cognitively differentiate aspects of the self, global self-worth differentiates into general, academic, social, and parental/home-related self-esteem. At ages 13–18, adolescents demonstrate increasing cognitive ability to abstract and therefore to view their self-concepts in abstract and sometimes contradictory terms (e.g., the flexible concept of having both introverted and extroverted characteristics). Based upon this assumption, a Personal Self-Esteem subscale was added to the Adolescent Form.

TECHNICAL.

Standardization. The CSFEI-3 was normed on a sample of 1,727 children and adolescents in 17 states, from fall of 1998 through fall of 1999 or fall of 2000 (the author lists different end dates on p. vi and p. 19, respectively) at norming sites in 17 U.S. states. Sample percentages regarding gender, race, ethnicity, rural or urban residence, family income, parents' education, disability, and geographic region approximate percentages projected for school-age children in the year 2000 by the U.S. Bureau of Census (1999). Percentages of Native American, Hispanic American, Asian American, and African American students from the standardization sample were virtually equivalent to U.S. Bureau of Census percentages for school-aged children.

Reliability. Intermediate and Adolescent form GSEQs yielded internal consistency coefficient alphas of .92 or higher. The GSEQ alpha for the Primary Form was lower, but still in the acceptable range at .81. Mean coefficient alphas for each of the subscales exceeded or approached .80.

For a sample of seven selected subgroups taken from the normative sample (male, female, European American, African American, Hispanic American, gifted and talented, and learning disabled) and a separate Canadian sample with a "large" but unspecified aboriginal representation, coefficient alphas were roughly consistent across subgroups. GSEQs for the Intermediate and Adolescent forms were .90 or higher and subscales ranged from .68 to .89. GSEQ for the Primary Form ranged from .70 to 83.

Test-retest reliability (2-week interval) using a smaller, separate sample of 77 children and adolescents yielded satisfactory coefficients for all forms. Specifically, the Adolescent Form yielded the highest GSEQ (.98), the Intermediate Form yielded .86, and the Primary Form yielded .72. Test-retest reliability scores for subscales of the Intermediate and Adolescent Forms range from .70 to .95.

Validity. The structure of the CFSEI-3 follows a theoretical rationale. Items for the CFSEI-3 were developed by reviewing self-esteem literature and examining the content of related instruments. Exploratory factor analyses were used to develop subscales for the CFSEI-3 forms. Consistent with self-esteem development theory, items did not form clear subscales for children ages 6–8. In addition, items formed somewhat different subscales for 9–12-year-olds than for 13–18-year-olds. Therefore, three separate forms were developed. In item analysis, item discrimination coefficients met or exceeded .35, indicating that items differentiated adequately among test-takers of different ages on each form's subscales and on global self-esteem scores.

As one method to examine the validity of the instrument for individuals of diverse cultures, the author explored whether examinees of the same self-esteem level but of different ethnic or gender groups performed differently on the same item. Differential item functioning (DIF or item bias) analysis, using logistic regression, was applied to all unique items on all three forms (a total of 131 items) with the normative sample. Comparisons were made between three dichotomous groups: male/female, African-American/non-African-American, and Hispanic/non-Hispanic. Of the 393 comparisons, 32 were found to be statistically significant at the .001 level. The DIF analysis indicated minimal detectable bias for gender and ethnicity.

Concurrent validity coefficients between the CFSEI-3 and the Self-Esteem Index (SEI; Brown & Alexander, 1991), the Piers-Harris Children's Self-Concept Scale (Piers-Harris; Piers & Harris, 1984), and the Multidimensional Self-Concept Scale (MSCS; Bracken, 1992) were examined. The GSEQ scores on all of the CFSEI-3 forms correlated highly with the total scores of all three criterion measures (median coefficient = .72).

Correlation coefficients between scores on the CFSEI-3 Primary Form, the SEI, and the Piers-Harris were moderate to high (median coefficient = 60). The Primary Form GSEQ correlated most highly with the SEI Self-Esteem Quotient and the Piers-Harris Total score.

The author reported that correlation coefficients between scores on the CFSEI-3 Intermediate Form and "theoretically similar scales" on the SEI and the Piers-Harris ranged from moderate to high (median coefficient = .66). Likewise, the author reported coefficient scores between the Adolescent Form and "theoretically similar scales" (manual, p. 37) on the SEI, the Piers-Harris, and the MSCS ranged from moderate to high (no coefficient provided).

Construct validity evidence was provided in the following ways: First, consistent with current theory that self-esteem is thought not to increase with age, self-esteem scores on the CFSEI-3 were not strongly correlated with age. Second, the CFSEI-3 tended not to discriminate between scores by gender, ethnicity, or nationality similar to the U.S. For example, African American, Hispanic American, disabled, talented/gifted, learning disabled, males, females, and Canadians, all scored in the Average Self-Esteem range. Scores were roughly equivalent to scores of the normative sample as a whole. Third, subscale standard score correlation coefficients ranged between .49 and .63 (≥.0001 level of statistical significance). Therefore, subscale scores appeared to be meaningfully related to the self-esteem construct. Fourth, maximum likelihood confirmatory factor analysis was satisfactory based on three indices of goodness of fit, suggesting that the underlying traits measured by CFSEI-3 items fit reasonably well with the theoretical model on which the inventory is based.

COMMENTARY. The CFSEI-3 is vastly improved over the CFSEI-2 (1992). The author is commended for making many improvements. These improvements include updating the theoretical rationale supporting the development of self-esteem and the need for three age-related forms of the inventory; providing new normative data that approximated the U.S. Bureau of Census (1999) numbers for the entire school-age population; reanalyzing test items to weed out biased items and those that fit poorly with other items; increasing ease of scoring; and conducting additional reliability and validity studies and comparing validity information for some targeted groups.

One problem with the test is the lack of demonstrated validity for the intended uses of the test. For example, the author describes the intended uses of the CFSEI-3: (a) to identify children who may be in need of psychological assistance; (b) to plan academic, personal, or affective interventions; (c) to identify specific areas of difficulty; and (d) to serve as a measurement device in research studies investigating self-esteem and associated constructs. Validity and reliability demonstrated in the manual adequately support the use of the CFSEI-3 to identify specific areas of low self-esteem and for use in research studies of the self-esteem construct. However, almost no theoretical or statistical information is provided to link level of self-esteem to the need for psychological assistance or to plan interventions. For example, the vaguely named Personal Subscale included on the Adolescent Form appears to address emotional issues (e.g., anxiety) associated with self-esteem. However, the manual fails to adequately describe the negative implications of low self-esteem and the benefits of high self-esteem. Additional information on interventions and interpretation based on the underlying theory of self-esteem described at the beginning of the manual might aid interpretation and treatment planning.

Finally, the test author acknowledges that the CFSEI-3 may be better described as "culture-fair" and that the term "culture-free" may be less acceptable today than when the test was first published in 1981. Nonetheless, the term "culture-free" was deliberately maintained for "historical purposes" (manual, p. vi).

A useful chapter on test bias has been added to the CFSEI-3 manual to address the issues of cultural fairness. However, a thoughtful chapter on how self-esteem is experienced in different cultures might also be useful in accurately assessing, diagnosing, and developing treatment plans based on the findings of the CFSEI-3.

SUMMARY. The CFSEI-3 is an easily administered, theory-based instrument useful for a diverse array of children and adolescents. This third version evidences a tremendous amount of work to improve the technical characteristics of the measure and to give attention to eliminating test bias. The test would benefit from additional guidelines for meaningful interpretation and from additional evidence to support its uses in determining psychological need for treatment. Recommendations include changing the name of the test and adding information on the role of culture for self-esteem to avoid misperceptions regarding the role of culture in self-esteem and to aid in designing culturally sensitive interpretations and interventions. Recommended improvements do not preclude the usefulness of this generally sound measure for examining self-esteem in a standardized fashion, if appropriate cautions to explore the cultural aspects of self-esteem are taken.

REVIEWER'S REFERENCES

Bracken, B. (1992). Multidimensional Self-Concept Scale. Austin, TX: PRO-ED.
Brown, L., & Alexander, J. (1991). Self-Esteem Index. Austin, TX: PRO-ED.
Harter, S. (1998). The development of self-representations. In W. Damon (Editor-in-Chief) & N. Eisenberg (Vol. Ed.), *Handbook of child psychology: Social, emotional, and personality development* (5th ed., Vol. 3, pp. 553–617). New York: Wiley.
Piers, E. V., & Harris, D. B. (1984). Piers-Harris Children's Self-Concept Scale. Los Angeles: Western Psychological Services.

[73]

DCS—A Visual Learning and Memory Test for Neuropsychological Assessment.

Purpose: Designed as "a learning and memory test for detecting memory deficits resulting from neurological disorders."
Population: Ages 6–70.

Publication Date: 1998.
Scores: Score information available from publisher.
Administration: Individual.
Price Data, 2001: $89 per complete kit including folder, 50 record and evaluation sheets, 18 test cards, 5 wooden sticks, and manual (48 pages); $15 per 50 record and evaluation sheets; $30 per set of 18 test cards and 5 wooden sticks; $39.50 per manual.
Time: (20–60) minutes.
Authors: Georg Lamberti and Sigrid Weidlich.
Publisher: Hogrefe & Huber Publishers.

Review of the DCS—A Visual Learning and Memory Test for Neuropsychological Assessment by ANDREW S. DAVIS, Assistant Director of the Neuropsychology Laboratory, University of Northern Colorado, and RIK CARL D'AMATO, Assistant Dean, College of Education, M. Lucile Harrison Professor of Excellence, University of Northern Colorado, Greeley, CO:

DESCRIPTION. The DCS—A Visual Learning and Memory Test for Neuropsychological Assessment (DCS) requires the examinee to reproduce visual nonverbal figures from memory. The "DCS" acronym is confusing because it does not relate to the current name or purpose of the instrument. Indeed, the authors retained the DCS name from the original version of the test, which was designed to detect cerebral damage. The evaluation of memory has been an important issue for over a century (Hess & D'Amato, 1998). The purpose of this measure is to assess selective attention, figural perception, storage of figures in memory, and reproduction of figures and sensomotoric transfer. Results of the test produce a Cumulative Reproduction Score, designed to measure the learning process, a Lability Index that examines the rate of forgetting, and qualitative observations of errors. The latest version of the DCS also provides a parallel form, which can be used to reduce test-retest problems in determining recovery from brain impairment. The test should be administered to children age 10 and older and adults under the age of 70.

The standardized instructions are read to the subject. The examinee is shown nine figures on white 9 x 9-centimeter cards, each consisting of five black lines that form a figure on a white card. The subject is allowed to view each card for as long as they desire. Once the subject has been allowed to view all nine cards in order, he or she is required to reproduce as many figures as can be recalled from memory, using five wooden sticks. This procedure is repeated up to six times, with the subject reaching a ceiling when he or she has correctly reproduced all of the figures in a single trial or the six trials have elapsed. Scores obtained from the Cumulative Reproduction Score can be converted into percentile ranges by using one of several different normative tables that are provided in the manual. A Lability Index can also be calculated that "correlates the rate of forgetting to the overall amount of reproductions" (manual, p.7). This is useful in determining the varying stability in the rate of reproduction, as well as an indication of working and long-term memory.

DEVELOPMENT. The DCS is the third version of a test that was originally released in 1972. Although the original DCS served as a screening device, the current instrument is intended to serve "as a test for cerebral (dys)function for the area of visual memory" (manual, p. 2). The current version of the DCS changed from earlier versions mainly in that there are now only six trials presented to the subject, as opposed to an earlier number as high as 15. The test manual does not provide complete information on the evolution of the test from the original version.

TECHNICAL. Information describing the norming process is vague. There is not a clear or detailed explanation of how the information was collected, and the reader must consult the referenced studies to learn important psychometric information. The norms came from a series of studies that were conducted with small samples, by different researchers, in different years, using different versions of the test. The standardization sample and the information provided about the sample is a primary weakness of the DCS. The test authors wrote, "both the original version and the parallel version of the DCS would benefit from a new standardization with a representative sample" (manual, p. 21). The norming tables do not differentiate for gender. The adult norms are not broken down in terms of age; there are separate charts for "high school graduates" and "nonacademic," which is a confusing term that is not explained. The Lability Index information comes from three separate studies, with subject numbers ranging from 15 to 49. Given these numerous problems the accuracy of the overall sample must be called into question.

The reliability evidence for scores from the DCS suffers from similar problems seen in the collection of the standardization sample. The authors present three separate studies from 1969, 1989, and 1991 that examined test-retest reliability, hence there is no overall reliability figure provided. No reliability information is available concerning the most recent revision of the test. Instead, the authors offer studies that were conducted 12 to 32 years ago. The most recent study from 1991 looked at the retest reliability with 45 brain-damaged patients using a 1-week administration interval. The individual Cumulative Reproduction Scores of both the original and parallel versions yielded individual trial test-retest consistencies ranging from $r = .33$ for Trial 1, to $r = .92$ for Trial 6. Again, the biggest problem with the reliability evidence of the test is the lack of information provided.

Studies using past versions of the DCS appeared to differentiate between brain-damaged and non-brain-damaged subjects, and the Lability Index seemed to discriminate between patients with cerebral vascular infarction and non-brain-damaged neurotic patients. Although early studies with older versions of the DCS have suggested that it is valuable for differentiating between brain-damaged and non-brain-damaged subjects, there is not sufficient information provided in the test manual to support its claim of its validity. Moreover, there is no information provided about the validity of scores from the test across gender, racial, ethnic, and/or cultural groups.

COMMENTARY. The value of the most recent version of the DCS as a test of visual learning and memory is questionable at best. This is primarily due to the limited information regarding the validity and reliability of the measure. English speakers may encounter difficulties in evaluating previous studies concerning the instrument because most research appears to be in German. The test suffers from the lack of a cohesive standardization sample. Some of the psychometric data offered comes from two different studies, with the most recent being 25 years old, and using older versions of the measure. The lack of standard scores limits the ability to compare a subject's scores to others in a similar population, rendering normative and ipsative comparisons difficult.

SUMMARY. The authors of the DCS have attempted to create a visual learning and memory test revision based on an earlier version of the test, and a compilation of past research that has used various versions of the DCS. Although the underlying components of the DCS have not changed significantly, a comprehensive, independent, normative sample for this version of the test does not exist. The reliability and validity evidence for the instrument in its current form is dubious. The DCS does not produce standard scores and the conversion of scores into percentile ranges is hampered by multiple difficulties. The authors admit in the manual that the DCS needs a new standardization sample. Based on these problems, individuals who seek to administer learning and memory measures should consider other measures that produce standard scores, have current norms, and have well-established reliability and validity, such as the Test of Memory and Learning (Reynolds & Bigler, 1994; T6:2550) or the Wechsler Memory Scale-III (Wechsler, 1997; T6:2695).

REVIEWER'S REFERENCES

Hess, R. S., & D'Amato, R. C. (1998). Assessment of memory, learning, and special aptitudes. In A. S. Bellack & M. Hersen (Series Eds.) & C. R. Reynolds (Vol. Ed.), *Comprehensive clinical psychology: Volume 4: Assessment* (pp. 239–265). Oxford, England: Elsevier Science Ltd.

Reynolds, C. R., & Bigler, E. D. (1994). Test of Memory and Learning. Austin, TX: PRO-ED.

Wechsler, D. (1997). Wechsler Memory Scale-III. San Antonio: The Psychological Corp.

[74]

Delis-Kaplan Executive Function System.

Purpose: To "comprehensive assess … the key components of executive functions believed to be mediated primarily by the frontal lobe."

Population: 8–89 years.

Publication Date: 2001.

Acronym: D-KEFS.

Scores: 9 tests: Trail Making Test, Verbal Fluency Test, Design Fluency Test, Color-Word Interference Test, Sorting Test, 20 Questions Test, Word Context Test, Tower Test, Proverb Test.

Administration: Individual.

Price Data, 2001: $415 per complete kit in box including manual (388 pages), stimulus booklet, sorting cards (3 sets of 6 cards each), 1 tower stand with 5 color disks, 25 record forms, 25 Design Fluency Response booklets, 25 Trail Making response booklet sets (each set contains 25 response booklets for the 5 Trail Making conditions; $470 per complete kit with soft-side case; $520 per complete kit in box with Scoring Assistant (CD-ROM or diskette, Windows only); $575 per complete kit in a soft-side case with Scoring Assistant; $155 per D-KEFS Scoring Assistant (CD-ROM or diskette); $68 per examiner's and technical manual; $53 per examiner's manual; $42 per technical manual (144 pages); $37 per 25 record forms; $21 per 25 Sorting or Color-Word Interference test record forms; $55 per 25 sets of Trail Making Test response booklets (each set contains 25 different response booklets for the 5 Trail Making conditions); $15 per 25 Trail Making or Design Fluency Test record forms; $22 per 25 Verbal Fluency, 20 Questions, or Word Context test record forms; $18 per 25 Tower or Proverb test record forms; $21 per 25 alternate record forms for Sorting, Verbal Fluency, 20 Questions Tests; $42 per Sorting Test set of cards including 2 sets of standard sorting cards, and 2 practice set; $42 per Sorting Test alternate set of cards including 3 sets of 6 cards each.

Time: (90) minutes for all 9 tests.

Comments: Each test assesses a different executive-function domain; tests may be administered alone or in combination; hand-scorable; D-KEFS Scoring Assistant software available; scoring software generates reports in table or graphical format; for system requirements contact publisher.

Authors: Dean C. Delis, Edith Kaplan, and Joel H. Kramer.

Publisher: The Psychological Corporation.

a) D-KEFS TRAIL MAKING TEST.

Purpose: Assesses "flexibility of thinking on a visual-motor task."

Form, 1: Standard Record Form.

Scores, 6: Visual Scanning, Number Sequencing, Letter Sequencing, Number-Letter Switching, Motor Speed, Composite Score.

b) D-KEFS VERBAL FLUENCY TEST.

Purpose: Assesses "fluent productivity in the verbal domain."

Form, 2: Standard Record Form, Alternate Record Form.

Scores, 3: Letter Fluency, Category Fluency, Category Switching.

c) D-KEFS DESIGN FLUENCY TEST.

Purpose: Assesses "fluent productivity in the spatial domain."

Form, 1: Standard Record Form.

Scores, 3: Filled Dots, Empty Dots Only, Switching.

d) D-KEFS COLOR-WORD INTERFERENCE TEST.

Purpose: Assesses "verbal inhibition."

Form, 1: Standard Record Form.

Scores, 4: Color Naming, Word Reading, Inhibition, Inhibition/Switching.

e) D-KEFS SORTING TEST.

Purpose: Assesses "problem-solving, verbal and spatial concept formation, flexibility of thinking on a conceptual task."

Forms, 2: Standard Record Form, Alternate Record Form.

Scores, 2: Free Sorting, Sort Recognition.

Comments: Alternate set of scoring cards available.

f) D-KEFS TOWER TEST.
Purpose: Assesses "planning and reasoning in the spatial modality [and] impulsivity."
Form, 1: Standard Record Form.
Score: Total Achievement Score.

g) D-KEFS 20 QUESTIONS TEST.
Purpose: Assesses "hypothesis testing, verbal and spatial abstract thinking, [and] impulsivity."
Forms, 2: Standard Record Form, Alternate Record Form.
Score: Initial Abstraction Score.

h) D-KEFS WORD CONTEXT TEST.
Purpose: Assesses "deductive reasoning [and] verbal abstract thinking."
Form, 1: Standard Record Form.
Score: Total Consecutively Correct.

i) D-KEFS PROVERB TEST.
Purpose: Assesses "metaphorical thinking, generating versus comprehending abstract thought."
Form, 1: Standard Record Form.
Scores, 2: Total Achievement scores: Free Inquiry, Multiple Choice.

Review of the Delis–Kaplan Executive Function System by ANTHONY T. DUGBARTEY, Psychologist, Forensic Psychiatric Services Commission, and Adjunct Assistant Professor of Psychology, University of Victoria, Victoria, British Columbia, Canada:

DESCRIPTION. The Delis-Kaplan Executive Function System (D-KEFS) is a neuropsychological test battery that assesses those higher level cognitive abilities typically described as executive control functions (ECF). Each of the nine tests comprising the D-KEFS was developed as a standalone measure that (with the exception of one test) can be administered to individuals from ages 8 to 89 years. The nine tests comprising the D-KEFS are the Trail Making Test, Verbal Fluency Test, Color-Word Interference Test, Sorting Test, Twenty Questions Test, Word Context Test, Design Fluency Test, Tower Test, and Proverb Test.

Scoring and interpretation of the D-KEFS tests is based on the "cognitive-process" theoretical approach to neuropsychological assessment, which disfavors the exclusive reliance upon a single-score method in quantifying neuropsychological test performance. Instead, equal importance is placed on understanding how the examinee attempts to solve the task. Each test of the D-KEFS yields achievement (or aggregate) and process scores. The availability of several ways of scoring the D-KEFS (including response accuracy, error

rates, and response latencies) offer a wide range of options in interpreting examinee performance. Interpretation of the D-KEFS tests is facilitated by conversion of raw scores to age-corrected scale scores with a mean of 10 and standard deviation of 3. The D-KEFS is presented as a neuropsychological instrument that can be employed in assessing children with neurodevelopmental pathologies and adults suffering from a wide variety of cortical and subcortical neurodegenerative disorders and focal frontal brain lesions. Alternate forms are available for three of the D-KEFS tests (the Sorting, Twenty Questions, and Verbal Fluency tests).

DEVELOPMENT. The D-KEFS was developed in response to the need for novel tests of ECFs. The authors point out that the D-KEFS, which took over a decade to develop, includes both new tests and modifications of extant clinical and experimental devices for measuring ECFs. Rather than declaring a specific theory or putative model of frontal lobe functioning as the basis from which the D-KEFS was derived, the authors astutely state that the D-KEFS is empirically based rather than theoretically derived. The authors provide ample relevant information on the background and historical foundations of the tests that make up the D-KEFS. Pilot testing of the D-KEFS was conducted during the mid-1990s, and culminated in a tryout study with over 300 individuals.

TECHNICAL. The scope of items selected for inclusion in the D-KEFS tests cover a broad spectrum of the neurocognitive domains known to be sensitive to executive control dysfunction.

Standardization. The D-KEFS was standardized on a stratified sample of 1,750 individuals. Of this sample, 700 were children whose ages ranged from 8 to 15 years, 700 were between ages 16 and 59 years, and 350 were between ages 60 and 89 years. Information describing the standardization study and norm development process is very clearly and comprehensively described in the D-KEFS technical manual. The test developers were diligent in selecting field examiners and participants in the standardization study. Appropriate data management techniques were applied in the norm development process (especially in dealing with skewed distributions of error rate scores) and in analyzing outlier values. An especially valuable approach in developing the D-KEFS norms was the conversion of raw scores into age-corrected scaled scores with a mean of 10 and standard deviation of 3. This metric is similar to other commonly used standardized cognitive instruments such as the Wechsler scales and the fifth edition of the Stanford-Binet intelligence scales. Normative data are provided for the alternate forms of the D-KEFS with a much smaller sample of 286 individuals ranging in ages from 16 to 89 years. The correlations between the standard and alternate forms of most of the D-KEFS measures are rather modest.

Reliability. Several classes of reliability estimates were employed for the D-KEFS. Internal consistency reliability was generally quite high for composite scores on the Trail Making Test (i.e., from .57 to .81), Verbal Fluency Test (from .32 to .90 across several conditions), Color-Word Interference Test (.62 to .86), but somewhat lower for the Sorting and Twenty Questions Tests, likely because of the high interdependence of the constituent items.

The test-retest reliability estimates of the D-KEFS, obtained based upon an average administration interval of 25 days, although generally impressive, was quite variable across age groupings on a few tests.

Standard errors of measurement were also provided for the D-KEFS tests using test-retest and internal consistency reliability estimates. With the exception of some of the switching measures and a measure on the Twenty Questions Test, the majority of the D-KEFS tests had low standard errors of measurement. On a positive note, the D-KEFS authors included tables that provided information on the confidence interval of the test scores.

In general, the D-KEFS manual provides detailed information to support the view that the reliability of this instrument is generally acceptable.

Validity. The authors, although conceding that they have not conducted factor analytic studies aimed at deriving index scores on the D-KEFS, provide an unconvincing explanation that these data reduction techniques were not performed because each test was designed to be a stand-alone measure.

Adequate data are presented on the intercorrelations of various intratest measures of the D-KEFS. It was especially interesting to find that part-whole correlations were presented for some of the D-KEFS tests (i.e., Sorting Test), which showed some impressive correlation results. Also gratifying were the intertest correlations of the total achievement and process scores of the D-KEFS, which were presented to show the lack of redundancy of the various tests in measuring the multifactorial ECF construct.

Very limited concurrent validity evidence was available comparing the D-KEFS and other neurocognitive tests. The correlations between the D-KEFS and California Verbal Learning Test—Second Edition (CVLT-II) were, not surprisingly, rather low. A correlation study comparing the D-KEFS with the Wisconsin Card Sorting Test (i.e., using number of categories and perseverative responses) using a very small sample of 23 individuals showed that these two measures had shared variance of only 16% to 36%. A significant drawback is the absence of viable predictive validity evidence of the D-KEFS.

COMMENTARY. The D-KEFS is a brave and laudable addition to the repertoire of tests for executive control functions available to clinical and research neuropsychologists. It is quite evident that considerable planning went into the development of this very user-friendly instrument. The layout of the test is attractive and the technical and examiner's manuals provide very detailed information about this instrument.

Unfortunately, no clear rationale is given for the development of alternate forms of only three tests of the D-KEFS. The lack of ecological and predictive validity analyses supporting the utility of the D-KEFS is a serious flaw.

The D-KEFS must necessarily be considered only a partial assessment system of ECF, in that to the extent that personality change is an important consequence of frontal-lobe system impairment, the D-KEFS does not assess the full spectrum of behavioral problems that are encountered in ECF problems.

SUMMARY. In spite of its shortcomings, the D-KEFS sets a high standard in the cognitive assessment of ECFs, and has much to offer clinical practitioners and researchers. Although several of the tests that comprise the D-KEFS appear remarkably similar to existing tests of frontal-lobe functioning, this instrument nevertheless offers a strong advancement in the range of test batteries available for assessment of higher level cognitive functions.

Review of the Delis-Kaplan Executive Function System by PAMILLA RAMSDEN, Senior Lecturer, Bolton Institute, Bolton, Lancashire, England:

DESCRIPTION. The Delis-Kaplan Executive Function System (D-KEFS) consists of nine independent tests that assess a wide spectrum of verbal and nonverbal executive functions. Each test is designed to be an autonomous instrument that can be administered individually or in combination with the other D-KEFS tests. The selection of tests is determined by the provider and is dependent upon the assessment needs of the examinee or the time constraints on the examiner. Each assessment instrument takes approximately 20 minutes to administer and score. The D-KEFS is composed of the following: Word Context test, Sorting Test, Twenty Questions test, Tower test, Color-Word Interference test, Verbal Fluency test, Design Fluency test, Trail Making test, and Proverb test. In addition, alternative versions are available for the Sorting test, Verbal Fluency test, and Twenty Questions test to eliminate practice effects if an individual is to be retested. The D-KEFS contains a large, well-detailed and clearly written manual, a technical manual consisting of standardization sample and reliability/validity studies, and a stimulus booklet.

Word Context test. This assessment is intended to evaluate deductive reasoning and verbal abstract thinking. The task is to discover the meaning of made-up or mystery words based on clues given in the sentence.

Sorting test. This assessment is a modification of a previous version called the California Card Sorting test. It assesses problem solving, verbal, and spatial concept formation and measures an individual's ability to initiate problem-solving behavior. This test requires individuals to sort objects into 16 different sorting concepts across two sets of cards.

Twenty Questions Test. This assessment is a modification of a popular informal game. It assesses visual attention and perception, object recognition, and object naming. The test requires that individuals identify various categories and subcategories represented in the 30 objects and formulate the abstract, yes/no questions that eliminate the maximum number of objects.

Tower test. This assessment is another modification of a popular game. The Tower test is similar to the Towers of Hanoi, London, and Toronto but without the problems of their psychometric properties. The tower measures spatial planning, rule learning, inhibition of impulsive responding, inhibition of perseverative responding, and establishing and maintaining the instructional set. The assessment requires that individuals move disks across three pegs to build a tower in the fewest number of moves possible.

Color-Word Interference test. This is a modified version of the Stroop (1935) test. It measures the inhibition of a more automatic verbal response (reading) in order to generate a conflicting response of naming the dissonant ink colors.

Verbal Fluency test. This is a modified version of the Controlled Oral Word Association Test (1969). This test measures fluent productivity in the verbal domain and is sensitive to frontal involvement in general and left-frontal damage in particular. This assessment requires that the individual generate words in a phonemic format from overlearned concepts.

Design Fluency test. This is a modified version of two types of design tests. This test measures fluent productivity in the spatial domain. The individual is presented with rows of squares, with each square containing five symmetrically placed dots. The individual is then asked to draw figures by connecting the dots.

Trail Making test. This is a modified version of the Trail Making test and consists of five conditions instead of two. This assessment measures flexibility of thinking on a visual-motor task and assesses whether a deficient score on the switching condition is related to a higher level deficit in cognitive flexibility.

Proverb test. This is a modified version of Gorham's (1956) proverb test, modified again for the D-KEFS. The previous modification was called the California Proverb test. This assessment measures the neurocognitive mechanisms underlying poor performance on this verbal abstraction task. This test requires that an individual provide a correct abstract interpretation of a proverb.

The primary objective in designing and compiling this system was to add features or testing conditions that would increase the sensitivity of the tests to mild brain damage, in general, and mild frontal-lobe involvement in particular.

The D-KEFS was nationally normed on a population of over 1,700 children and adults from ages 8 to 89 and matches the demographic characteristics of the United States population. The 2000 U.S. Census figures were used as target values for the composition of the D-KEFS normative sample. Stratification was based on age, sex, race/ethnicity, years of education, and geographic region.

The scoring system for all nine of the assessment instruments is uniform and specific with good explanations of discontinue rules and time limits. Special attention and consideration have been provided in the manual for the scoring of ambiguous but common responses. Raw scores are converted to scaled scores, with a mean of 10 and a standard deviation of 3. There is no overall composite score as each instrument is scored and interpreted separately. There are 16 different age groups and raw scores that have been converted to cumulative percentile ranks and corrected for each of the 16 age groups.

All nine D-KEFS tests are cognitive assessment instruments. Psychologists with formal training and experience in the assessment of intellectual and cognitive functions are qualified to administer and interpret the D-KEFS. The authors suggest that interpretations that address the integrity of brain functions should be made by psychologists who have had adequate training in clinical neuropsychology.

DEVELOPMENT. The test developers have attempted to integrate a theoretical perspective of executive lobe function and consulted with prominent neuropsychologists about the design and makeup of the tests. Executive lobe function presents difficulty in the area of testing and assessment as the precise nature and function in specific regions and subregions of the frontal lobe is still in the early stages of research. Large sets of verbal and nonverbal tasks were selected to provide both "breadth and depth in the assessment of executive functions" (manual, p. 14). The authors either designed new tests or made modifications to traditional clinical tests to enhance the sensitivity of the instruments and incorporate a cognitive-process approach so that the fundamental and higher level components of executive order functions could be quantified. Most of the D-KEFS tests were developed within a 10-year period beginning in 1980. All nine tests were assembled by 1994. Pilot testing occurred between 1994–1995 with both normally functioning examinees and patients with brain damage. A "tryout" study was conducted in 1996 and included over 300 children and adults

and resulted in the final revisions of the tests. The national standardization study was conducted between 1998 and 2000.

TECHNICAL. Each instrument has its own section in the technical handbook and the manual. These sections contain instructions, scoring, interpretation, reliability/validity data, and norms.

Test-retest reliability studies (interval ranged from 9 to 74 days) were conducted with a sample of 101 cases distributed across all of the age groups. Standard errors of measurement and confidence intervals were conducted with all nine tests reporting good values across the age ranges.

Validity studies were conducted only on one assessment: the Sorting test. Research indicated that scores on this particular test were valid but no other validity studies were conducted on the other eight tests of the D-KEFS.

Correlational analyses were conducted on a sample of normal-functioning individuals with the result that many measures loaded on a single factor. The authors caution that the use of correlational or factor-analytic techniques with executive-function tests in normal-functioning or mixed-clinical samples may mask important cognitive distinctions, especially because such tests typically tap multiple fundamental and higher level cognitive skills. Factor-analytic techniques to derive index scores, similar to IQ measures or other factor scores, have not been utilized.

The D-KEFS was compared with performance on two other assessment instruments: the California Verbal Learning Test—Second Edition (CVLT; 2000) and the Wisconsin Card Sorting Test (WCST; 1993). The correlational study with the CVLT involved a sample of 292 individuals. However, the WCST only involved a small sample size of 23. The correlations between the D-KEFS scores and CVLT scores were mostly low positive or unrelated. The WCST scores tended to have moderate correlations with scores on several of the primary measures of the D-KEFS. The perseverative-responses measure of the WCST tended to correlate at somewhat lower levels with key D-KEFS measures.

COMMENTARY. The value of the D-KEFS is its national norms within a broad spectrum of executive lobe functioning assessments. Few assessment instruments have been available to clinicians to measure and diagnose executive functioning. Most of the instruments in current use have been designed in the 1940s with poor norms and psychometric properties. It may be that the field must overcome one obstacle at a time. The test developers have met their main objective of incorporating principles and procedures into a new set of executive-function tests. They have provided clinicians with a comprehensive set of assessment instruments for documenting each patient's profile of spared and impaired executive functions. However, additional research is needed, especially in the psychometric arena. The D-KEFS is a compendium of tests with each instrument being independent of the other. The system does not provide an overall picture; instead, the examiner must sift through the material and make the neurological determination that again is largely dependent upon the examiner's experience and skill. An advantage of the system is that it is designed to be used in a flexible manner, the manual is not needed during administration, and everything is provided in the stimulus booklet or record form. There is a lack of strong statistical data concerning the factors and performance but this may be related in part to the difficulty in understanding the specifics of executive functioning.

SUMMARY. The D-KEFS is a group of nine independent neuro-cognitive assessment instruments designed to comprehensively measure and quantify higher level cognitive functioning in both children and adults. The tests measure a wide spectrum of verbal and nonverbal executive functions. The system has adequate psychometric properties and a strong norming base. The D-KEFS has facilitated the ease of administration of these types of neuropsychological tests with the task instructions and prompts provided in the stimulus booklet and provides specific, uniform scoring guidelines. In general, clinicians will find this system to be very useful.

[75]
Dementia Rating Scale—2.

Purpose: To measure and track "mental status in adults with cognitive impairment."
Population: Adults ages 56–105.
Publication Dates: 1973–2001.
Acronym: DRS-2.
Scores, 6: Attention, Initiation/Perseveration, Construction, Conceptualization, Memory, Total.
Administration: Individual.
Price Data: Available from publisher for introductory kit including professional manual (2001, 47 pages), 50 scoring booklets, and set of 32 stimulus cards.

Time: (15–30) minutes.
Comments: Revised version of the DRS; DRS-2 stimulus cards same as for original DRS; can be administered bedside by appropriately trained personnel.
Authors: Steven Mattis (professional manual, stimulus cards, scoring booklet), Paul J. Jurica, and Christopher L. Leitten (professional manual).
Publisher: Psychological Assessment Resources, Inc.
Cross References: See T5:776 (63 references); for a review by R. A. Bornstein of an earlier edition, see 11:107 (2 references).

Review of the Dementia Rating Scale—2 by IRIS PHILLIPS, Assistant Professor of Social Work, University of Southern Indiana, Evansville, IN:

DESCRIPTION. The Dementia Rating Scale-2 (DRS-2) is a 36-task and 32-stimulus cards instrument designed to assess level of cognitive functioning for individuals with brain dysfunction. The DRS-2 assesses cognitive functioning on five subscales: Attention (ATT, 8 items); Initiation/ Perseveration (I/P, 11 items); Construction (CONST, 6 items); Conceptualization (CONCEPT, 6 items); and Memory (MEM, 5 items). Mental status instruments may exhibit a "floor effect" (professional manual, p. 3), where differences in lower functioning are not discriminated. However, the DRS-2 is sensitive at the lower ends of functioning and differentiating levels of deficits. Conversely, the instrument generally will not discriminate individual functioning in the average or higher range of intelligence due to the design to minimize floor effects of clinically impaired individuals.

The DRS-2 consists of a professional manual, scoring booklets, and 32-stimulus cards. The skip patterns assume that satisfactory performance on the first one or two difficult tasks within a subscale will have similar results on the remaining tasks. Test examiners may score accordingly and proceed with testing, saving time. Ideally, administration of the DRS-2 is in a quiet room, but it is also effective at the participant's bedside. Interpretable results depend on the participant's willingness and ability to work toward item solutions. Test examiners trained and supervised by a qualified psychologist may administer and score the DRS-2. However, clinical interpretation of scores requires professional training and expertise in clinical psychology and/or neuropsychology.

DEVELOPMENT. The Dementia Rating Scale-2 (DRS-2) is an enhanced version of the original DRS (1973) designed to provide standardized, quantitative cognitive functioning assessment in neurologically impaired populations. DRS development drew upon the multidisciplinary tasks used by neuropsychologists, neurologists, and neurosurgeons to assess cognitive functioning over time. The initial pool of items was revised for comprehensive and brief administration, however, allowing for a low floor so that even severely impaired individuals could be evaluated.

The DRS used a single cutoff score for the DRS Total Score regardless of age and education. However, research indicated that age and level of education significantly influenced subscales and total scores. Normative data from the Mayo Older Americans Normative Studies (MOANS) included in the DRS-2 professional manual provide a wider age and education range than the DRS. The DRS-2 age-corrected, scaled and percentile ranks are more sensitive to assessing change in cognitive status. An Age- and Education-Corrected MOANS Scaled Score (AEMSS) conversion provides interpretation of an individual's scores taking into account the effect of age and education.

The original scoring form was intended to improve the ease of administration. There are no changes in the tasks and stimulus cards from the DRS consisting of five subscales designed to assess overall level of cognitive functioning.

TECHNICAL. MOANS provides the normative data for the DRS-2 taken from 623 healthy adults living in community settings from ages 56–105. The professional manual cautions that those in the normative data base were predominately Caucasian adults with higher than average educational levels.

The manual provides a comprehensive literature review of DRS research. Test-retest reliability estimates reported from the original manual were based on 30 patients diagnosed with dementia of the Alzheimer's type (DAT) who were administered the DRS twice within a 1-week interval between administrations. The correlation coefficient for the total DRS was .97, with subscale correlation coefficients ranging from .61 to .94. Twenty-five patients with diagnoses of organic brain syndrome or senile-dementia, aged 65 to 94 years of age, provided the sample used to evaluate internal consistency using a split-half technique yielding a split-half reliability coefficient of .90.

Various research studies using factor analysis provide support for the DRS subscale structure.

Research by Hofer, Piccinin, and Hershey (1996) with Alzheimer, mixed dementia, and control groups resulted in four factors with acceptable alpha coefficients. Colantonio, Becker, and Huff's (1993) research indicated a three-factor model with 219 Alzheimer patients who were administered the DRS. Woodard, Salthouse, Godsall, and Green (1996) confirmed these factors with 171 Alzheimer patients. The Attention-Initiation-Perseveration factor was the least reliable of the subscales.

Construct validity research has used the Mini-Mental State Examination (MMSE), the Wechsler Adult Intelligence Scale (WAIS), and the Paired Associate Learning (PAL) with acceptable correlations. Convergent validity analyses with Parkinson's disease patients found statistically significant correlations with a number of established instruments such as: Wechsler Adult Intelligence Scales Revised, Digits Span Forward; Wisconsin Card Sorting Test, Perseverative Responses; WAIS-R, Similarities; and Wechsler Memory Scale, Immediate Logical Memory.

Clinical validation using a number of dementia populations, such as Dementia of the Alzheimer's type, Vascular dementia, Parkinson's Disease, Huntington's Disease, Mental Retardation, Schizophrenia, HIV and AIDS, Neuronanatomical and physiological correlates, Depression, and Behavioral Correlates is also documented. The clinical research with various populations is extensive and briefly presented in the manual. For more in-depth information regarding specific populations, review of the relevant literature is necessary.

COMMENTARY. The MOANS normative data base addresses criticism of the original DRS for the lack of normative data. However, the score reflects predominately Caucasian adults with higher than average education levels. The professional manual suggests using caution when interpreting scores of non-Caucasians and individuals with less than 8 years of education. Although gender and race do not influence performance on the DRS, language may have an effect on scores. As noted in the manual, individuals for whom English is a second language have higher impairment level scores.

SUMMARY. The DRS-2 is a well-documented instrument designed to assess cognitive impairment over time. The purpose is to be able to discriminate cognitive functioning at lower levels of ability without experiencing floor effects. The professional manual provides clear directions for administering, scoring, and interpreting scores. Documentation of relevant clinical research with a broad range of dementia populations is provided.

REVIEWER'S REFERENCES

Colantonio, A., Becker, J. T., & Huff, F. J. (1993). Factor structure of the Mattis Dementia Rating Scale among patients with probable Alzheimer's disease. *Clinical Neuropsychologist, 7*, 313–318.

Hofer, S. M., Piccinin, A. M., & Hershey, D. (1996). Analysis of structure and discriminative power of the Mattis Dementia Rating Scale. *Journal of Clinical Psychology, 52*, 395–409.

Woodard, J. L., Salthouse, T. A., Godsall, R. E., & Green, R. C. (1996). Confirmatory factor analysis of the Mattis Dementia Rating Scale in patients with Alzheimer's disease. *Psychological Assessment, 8*, 85–91.

Review of the Dementia Rating Scale—2 by PAMILLA RAMSDEN, Senior Lecturer, Bolton Institute, Bolton, Lancashire, England:

DESCRIPTION. The Dementia Rating Scale—2 (DRS-2) is an instrument designed to measure and track "mental status in adults with cognitive impairment" (professional manual, p. 1). This instrument consists of 36 tasks incorporating 32 stimulus cards and takes approximately 30–60 minutes, dependent upon the level of cognitive impairment. The instrument has five subscales that provide information on Attention, Initiation/ Perseveration, Construction, Conceptualization, and Memory.

The DRS-2 requires a high level of professional training and cannot be administered or scored except by a qualified psychologist or an individual who is trained and supervised by the same. This limits the practicality of the instrument, as it is dependent upon the professional's background, knowledge, and experience. Therefore, highly skilled and practiced individuals will have superiority and be better able to utilize the instrument than a novice in the field. The instrument manual acknowledges that utilizing the DRS-2 for clinical or diagnostic purposes "should not be attempted without adequate understanding of brain-behavior relationships" (p. 3). However, "adequate" understanding is too vague in its description in terms of medical and psychological factors involved and what specific level(s) of understanding are required and/or implied.

The DRS-2 tasks are presented in a fixed order corresponding with the subtests. The most difficult items of each subtest are presented first. If the participant performs well on the initial items, subsequent tasks in the subscale are credited with a correct performance and the examiner proceeds to the next subscale. Scoring is generous, especially on the Construction tasks, and instructions can be repeated, amended, and elaborated whenever necessary with the exception of the Attention tasks. The administrative booklet contains easy-to-read directions and scoring criteria. Raw scores are summed across the subscales and then transferred and summed on the summary table in the scoring booklet. The DRS-2 total score is based on raw scores of all subscales. The raw scores are then applied to the corresponding scaled score called the age-corrected AMSS score. The age-corrected scales are located in the manual.

Interpretation can either be based on the age-corrected scores (AMSS) or the percentile range. The manual provides guidelines for the interpretation of the scores and these cutoff scores indicate the degree of impairment. There are three different levels of impairment: mildly impaired, moderately impaired, and severely impaired. The subscales are interpreted on the same scale with the same levels of impairment. The age-corrected scores are based on norms provided on a sample of healthy adults ranging from 56 to 105 years of age.

DEVELOPMENT. The DRS-2 is a revision from the earlier version of the DRS published in 1988. The original instrument was designed "to provide a brief, standardized, quantitative and multifaceted assessment of cognitive functioning in neurologically impaired populations" (professional manual, p. 1) and the revised instrument has maintained that primary objective. Research conducted on the original instrument indicated that both age and level of education contributed significantly to the DRS total and subscale scores, possibly negating their usefulness. Further research on the DRS indicated that this was a major impediment in the interpretation of DRS scores. Therefore, the instrument underwent revision. Age-corrected norms were generated in collaboration with researchers at the Mayo Clinic, which provided the revised version with a larger sample and wider age range than was available with the original DRS. An additional change to the instrument was the revision of the scoring form. The form was improved to facilitate administration and scoring and integrated prompts, examples, and instruction. The tasks and stimulus cards remain unchanged from the original instrument. Item development was designed from a multidisciplinary perspective and incorporated tasks routinely used by neuropsychologists and neurologists. Items were then selected and reviewed for their comprehensiveness, clarity, and brevity by a team of neuroscience professionals. These items/tasks were then combined into the DRS with five subscales. The Attention subscale consists of 8 tasks and contains both auditory-visual and verbal-nonverbal tasks of attention. The Initiation/Perseveration subscale contains 11 tasks and assesses the ability to initiate, switch, and terminate a specific activity with fluency and without perseveration. The Construction subscale consists of 6 tasks and requires reproduction of stimulus designs that vary in difficulty. The Conceptualization subscale contains 6 tasks and assesses the ability to induce similarities and detect differences among verbal and visual stimuli. The Memory subscale contains 5 tasks, both verbal and nonverbal items, which are presented in recall and recognition.

TECHNICAL. The norms for the DRS-2 were amassed in collaboration with the Mayo Clinic and included a total of 623 community-dwelling elderly participants (199 men and 424 women) screened for medical/psychiatric history. These norms are not representative of the general U.S. population as they were predominately Caucasian adults, with a higher than average education level. Research has also indicated that the instrument has a negative relationship with age, indicating that as age increases performance decreases. In addition, there is a positive relationship with education. Additional studies have found that race and gender are not significantly correlated to or predictive of the DRS total score as 40 matched pairs of African American and Caucasian dementia patients were included and no appreciable evidence of test bias was demonstrated. However, language appears to have an effect on DRS scores, yielding higher cognitive impairment ratings among people whose primary language is not English. The DRS-2 uses the previously established reliability and validity scores. A test-retest reliability correlation coefficient was .97 with subscale correlation coefficients ranging from .61 to .94. The DRS was administered twice with a 1-week interval between administrations to a group of 30 patients diagnosed with dementia of the Alzheimer's type. A split-half reliability coefficient was .90, utilizing a sample of 25 patients ages 65 to 94 years who received diagnoses of either organic brain syndrome or senile dementia. A t test indicated no significant differences between scores on the two halves. The alpha coefficients were calculated for four DRS subscales using a combined dementia sample. The alpha coefficients were Attention (.95), Initiation/Perseveration (.87), Conceptualization (.95), and Memory (.75). Five factors were found; however, there is a confound of scoring dependence as patients who score positive on the initial items are given credit for the remaining items on the subtest, which results in an artificial correlation. The DRS-2 was compared with the Mini-Mental State Examination (MMSE), which displayed a significant correlation ($r = .82$) with the DRS-2 showing a greater sensitivity to change than the MMSE in patients with severe dementia. In addition, correlations with the Wechsler Adult Intelligence Scale indicated a correlation of .75 between the WAIS full scale and the DRS-2 total score.

COMMENTARY. Research has been conducted on the clinical usefulness of the DRS-2 in a variety of clinical populations. The test was originally designed to quantitatively assess the status of patients with dementia and track the progression of their disease. In certain populations, the utility of the DRS-2 is clear and the research within these populations indicates that the DRS-2 is very useful in the assessment and progression of dementia of Alzheimer's type, vascular dementia, Parkinson's disease, Huntington's disease, and age-related dementia in mental retardation and Down's syndrome. The progression of these types of clinical groups follow the age-corrected norms established for the instrument and the research indicates that with different dementia types the DRS-2 is able to discriminate and track the progression of dementia. However, the research conducted on Schizophrenia and HIV/AIDS remains unconvincing. More stringent research in these areas is required before statements can be made that this instrument is able to follow objectives for these populations. Another consideration when working with these types of clinical populations is that the average age range of these illnesses is below the established norms for the DRS-2. Three other clinical populations were studied in conjunction with this instrument: neuroanatomical and physiological correlates, depression, and behavioral correlates. Within these three populations, other types of instruments are better utilized than an instrument designed to detect and follow the progression of dementia.

SUMMARY. The DRS-2 measures deficits in a wide range of cortical functions and differentiates deficits of varying levels of severity. It has a higher sensitivity to differences at the lower end of functioning and will not detect impaired cognitive ability in individuals who function in the average or higher range of intelligence. In the hands of an experienced neuropsychologist/clinical psychologist, this is an excellent instrument but it is highly dependent upon qualifications and skill of each individual test user. Its reliability and validity properties are excellent. Within certain clinical populations—Alzheimer's type, vascular dementia, Parkinson's disease, and Huntingdon's disease and age-related dementia in mental retardation and Down's syndrome—this instrument indicates high potential in its ability to detect and follow the progression of dementia and appears to be more comprehensive than the MMSE. The instrument's major limitation is that it may underestimate cognitive ability in individuals whose primary language is not English and care should be utilized when applying the DRS-2 to clinical populations outside of the established norms.

[76]

Derogatis Interview for Sexual Functioning.

Purpose: "A brief semistructured interview designed to provide an estimate of the quality of an individual's current sexual functioning in quantitative terms."
Population: Adults.
Publication Dates: 1987–1989.
Scores, 6: Sexual Cognition/Fantasy, Sexual Arousal, Sexual Behavior/Experience, Orgasm, Sexual Drive/Relationship, Total Score.
Administration: Individual.
Price Data, 2002: $50 per 50 DISF or DISF-SR (specify gender); $25 per 50 DISF or DISF-SR score sheets (specify gender); additional shipping charges apply.
Foreign Language Editions: Danish, Dutch, English, French, German, Italian, Norwegian, and Spanish editions available.
Time: (15–20) minutes for DISF; (10–15) minutes for DISF-SR.
Author: Leonard R. Derogatis.
Publisher: Clinical Psychometric Research, Inc.
    a) DEROGATIS INTERVIEW FOR SEXUAL FUNCTIONING.
    Acronym: DISF.
    Time: (15–20) minutes.

Comments: Semistructured interview format using a 4-point Likert scale.
b) DEROGATIS INTERVIEW FOR SEXUAL FUNCTIONING—SELF REPORT.
Acronym: DISF-SR.
Time: (10–15) minutes.
Comments: Paper-and-pencil format using Likert scales; may be used to gain evaluations of patient's sexual functioning by the patient or the patient's spouse.

Review of the Derogatis Interview for Sexual Functioning by SHERI BAUMAN, Assistant Professor, Department of Educational Psychology, University of Arizona, Tucson, AZ

DESCRIPTION. The Derogatis Interview for Sexual Functioning (DISF/DISF-SR) provides a quantitative measure of an individual's sexual functioning. It is available in both semistructured interview and self-report formats assessing five domains of sexual functioning: Sexual Cognition/Fantasy, Sexual Arousal, Sexual Behavior/Experience, Orgasm, and Sexual Drive/Relationship. Separate gender-keyed versions for males and females are available, and a general version is available using gender-neutral terminology, suitable for use with both homosexual and heterosexual individuals. The 25 Likert-type items use from five to nine response options. Both formats can be completed in 15–20 minutes, although the author cautions that the interview format may involve slightly more time, as individuals may want to elaborate their answers. Scores can be interpreted at the item level, the domain level, or the global level. The scale can be used periodically to evaluate treatment effects, or as a pre- and postintervention measure. The scales can also be given to the patient's spouse in order to evaluate the individual's sexual performance. Raw scores are converted to area T-scores so that performance can be compared across domains within the individual, as well as across respondents. Separate norms are provided for each gender, based on a sample of nonpatient community respondents, and the scale is available in eight languages in addition to English. The scale was developed in response to a perceived need for a scale with applications in both clinical practice and outcomes research.

DEVELOPMENT. The scale is based on Masters and Johnson's (1966, as cited in Synopsis of the Derogatis Interview for Sexual Functioning, undated) construct of the sexual response cycle.

The author presents a clear rationale for constructing a measure of sexual functioning that is gender specific and applicable to both homosexual and heterosexual respondents. He argues that interview and self-report formats each have advantages, and thus the scale is available in both formats. The complex nature of human sexuality argues for a multidimensional scale, with core sexual constructs that are biologically mediated as the most important. However, nowhere in the available documentation is there any description of the process of item selection. It is noted that the interview version was developed first, and that preliminary validation studies were conducted. However, no data about those studies are presented. The self-report version was then developed and items were designed to be equivalent to the interview items. No mention is made of validation studies on this version.

TECHNICAL. The interview version of the scale was standardized on a sample of 122 community members, and the self-report version was standardized on 277 community members. Gender distribution of this sample or other demographic data were not provided. Reliability data on the self-report version include measures of internal consistency and temporal stability. Internal consistency coefficients range from .74 to .80 in each of the five domains. Test-retest coefficients, calculated at 1-week intervals, range from .81 to .90, with a total score coefficient of .86. Interrater reliability data were collected on the interview version. Using "clinical judges" whose qualifications are not described, and a videotaped interview conducted by the scale's author, interrater coefficients were found to be from .84 to .92 on domain scores, with an overall value of .91. Although reliability coefficients for the scale appear respectable, it is unclear how the samples for these analyses were selected.

The author presents several studies that provide evidence of score validity. The dimensional structure was "generally supported" by a factor analysis conducted on data from 252 men with erectile disorder. A six-factor structure emerged, with a factor representing autoeroticism added to the five hypothesized factors. Confirmatory factor analysis is not reported, and the author did not revise the scale or interpretive guidelines to reflect this additional factor. The pattern of correlations among dimension scores and total scores is presented as evidence of validity. Correlations were calculated based on responses of 168 community participants for the self-report version and 26 "sexually dysfunctional women" for the interview version. Correlations among dimensions were low, whereas correlations with the total score were moderate, which is consistent with expectations. Evidence of discriminative validity is found in results of a study of 43 men with prostate cancer. Patients were classified clinically as fully functional, marginally functional, and impotent. The DISF scores of the three groups were ranked as predicted and differences among groups were statistically significant. All of the groups scored in the lower third of the normative distributions. These data were further analyzed to determine sensitivity, specificity, and predictive value of results on this scale. A final validity study was conducted on a preliminary version (not further described) of the scale using a community sample of 82 men and 86 women with a mean age of 33.9. The sample was 94% White, 54% married; 84% had some college education. The DISF-SR scores were used to classify participants as adequate or less than adequate in terms of sexual functioning. The two groups were then compared on well-being scores obtained on the Derogatis Affective Balance Scale, and statistically significant differences in the expected direction were found between the two levels of sexual functioning on well-being.

Area T-scores are used in interpreting the results. This method has several advantages over the more widely used linear transformation (Krus & Krus, 1977), and can be used when the coefficient of skewness is not statistically significant (Area Transformations, 2002). The author does not report this coefficient, so the reader is left to assume that this assumption was met.

COMMENTARY. The author makes a strong case for the need for this scale, and is convincing in his defense of the various parameters that were considered in its design. Only passing mention is made of the theoretical underpinnings of the scale (Masters & Johnson).

Although psychometric data available to date suggest that the instrument produces reliable and valid scores, the absence of complete information on the development of items and dimensions is a concern. The absence of detailed demographic information about the standardization sample and several of the validation studies leaves the reader without a basis to determine the applicability of the sample to a particular population.

The fact that the scale is brief and that it can be administered repeatedly to gauge the effects of treatment are strengths of this measure. The ability to interpret results at item, domain, or global levels, is another useful feature of this measure. The use of area *T*-scores adds to the precision of interpretation. It is advantageous to have both interview and self-report formats available to the user, and users will appreciate gender-specific forms. Although the existence of a general form, suitable for use with both homosexual and heterosexual respondents, is commendable, it appears the examiner would have to be aware of the individual's sexual orientation prior to selecting the version, unless the general form were used routinely.

Research to date using the scale has been supportive of the reliability and validity of the scores, although there are unanswered questions regarding the composition of the samples. In a 1997 publication, the author indicated that the instrument was being used in a number of "substantive clinical trials" (Derogatis, 1997, p. 304). As results of further studies become available, the reader will be in a better position to evaluate the psychometric properties and clinical utility of this scale.

SUMMARY. The Derogatis Interview for Sexual Functioning (DISF/DISF-SR) is a brief (25-item) scale with both interview and self-report formats for assessing sexual functioning. Results can be interpreted globally, in each of the five domains, or on individual items of interest. Evidence exists to support the psychometric soundness of the measure, but adequate information about samples used in these studies was not available. The author indicated (Derogatis, 1997) that the DISF/DISF-SR was employed as an outcome measure in several "substantive" clinical trials. The publication of results of this research will add to the evidence about this instrument. Until that information is available, the reader might wish to compare this scale with similar instruments available for this purpose (see Meston & Derogatis, 2002) to decide which is the most appropriate for the intended purpose and setting.

REVIEWER'S REFERENCES

Area Transformations. Retrieved November 24, 2002 from http://www.public.asu.edu/~pythagor/hoarea.htm.
Derogatis, L. R. (1997). The Derogatis Interview for Sexual Functioning (DISF/DISF-SR): An introductory report. *Journal of Sex & Marital Therapy, 23,* 291–304.
Krus, D. J., & Krus, P. H. (1977). Lost: McCall's T scores: Why? *Educational and Psychological Measurement, 37,* 257–261.

Meston, C. M., & Derogatis, L. R. (2002). Validated instruments for assessing female sexual dysfunction. *Journal of Sex & Marital Therapy, 28,* 155–164.

[77]
Detailed Assessment of Posttraumatic Stress.

Purpose: Designed as a comprehensive diagnostic measure of trauma exposure and posttraumatic stress and associated functions, including dissociative symptoms, substance abuse, and suicidality.

Population: Adults 18 and over who have undergone a significant psychological stressor.

Publication Date: 2001.

Acronym: DAPS.

Scores: 2 validity scales (Positive Bias and Negative Bias) and 11 scales in 3 clusters: Trauma Specification (Relative Trauma Exposure, Peritraumatic Distress, Peritraumatic Dissociation), Posttraumatic Stress (Re-experiencing, Avoidance, Hyperarousal, Posttraumatic Stress—Total, Posttraumatic Impairment), Associated Features (Trauma-Specific Dissociation, Substance Abuse, Suicidality).

Administration: Individual or group.

Price Data: Available from publisher for kit including professional manual (56 pages), 10 item booklets, 50 hand-scorable answer sheets, and 50 male/female profile forms.

Time: (20–30) minutes.

Comments: Self-administered.

Author: John Briere.

Publisher: Psychological Assessment Resources, Inc.

Review of the Detailed Assessment of Posttraumatic Stress by ROGER A. BOOTHROYD, Associate Professor, Department of Mental Health Law and Policy, Louis de la Parte Florida Mental Health Institute, University of South Florida, Tampa, FL:

DESCRIPTION. The Detailed Assessment of Posttraumatic Stress (DAPS) is a 104-item self-report measure assessing exposure to trauma and posttraumatic response. The measure is intended for use with individuals who have undergone a significant psychological stressor. It can be used to assist clinicians in determining the presence or absence of a probable Posttraumatic Stress Disorder (PTSD) or Acute Stress Disorder (ASD) diagnosis. The DAPS can be group or individually administered and scored by individuals with no specialized training. It is appropriate for use with persons 18 years of age and older and requires that respondents have at least a sixth-grade reading level. The measure takes between 20 and 30 minutes to complete and can be scored and profiled in approximately 20 minutes. After reporting their exposure to various potentially traumatic life events, respondents report the severity of the most traumatic experience and the frequency of various symptom clusters using a 5-point scale with varying anchors ranging from a low of 1 to a high of 5.

The DAPS contains 13 scales. It has two validity scales designed to identify respondents who deny or underreport their symptoms (i.e., Positive Bias) as well as those who overreport their symptoms and endorse usual symptoms (i.e., Negative Bias).

Four scales evaluate respondents' lifetime exposure to trauma. The Relative Trauma Exposure scale assesses the extent to which respondents have been exposed to multiple sources of trauma. A single item on the Onset of Exposure scale determines the recency of the traumatic event. The Peritraumatic Distress scale evaluates the severity of the distress respondents experienced at the time the event occurred. The Peritraumatic Dissociation scale determines whether a respondent dissociated during the traumatic event.

Three of the scales relate to common PTSD symptom clusters (i.e., Intrusive Reexperiencing, Avoidance/Numbing, and Autonomic Hyperarousal). Additionally the DAPS contains a summary scale (i.e., Posttraumatic Stress—Total) and a scale to assess impairment of psychosocial functioning (i.e., Posttraumatic Impairment). Finally, the DAPS includes three scales assessing associated features of PTSD (i.e., Trauma-Specific Dissociation, Suicidality, and Substance Abuse).

DEVELOPMENT. Originally the author developed 190 items to examine response validity and to assess the diagnostic criteria set forth for Posttraumatic Stress Disorder (309.81) in the DSM-IV-TR. The items were subsequently reviewed by clinicians experienced in treating PTSD and 59 items were eliminated because of redundancy or inadequacy. The remaining 131 items were administered to 105 individuals to obtain preliminary psychometric information. Based on these results, an additional 27 items were eliminated, resulting in the current 104-item measure.

TECHNICAL.

Scoring & Standardization. In the absence of missing responses, raw scores are simply the sum of the item responses within a symptom domain. The manual includes scoring instructions for handling missing responses, including the number of items that can be missing and still produce a valid score, which differs by subscale. Raw scores are converted to standardized *T* scores by either plotting them on the profile sheets provided or by using the normative conversion tables in the test manual. Normative information was obtained from responses to a stratified (based on geographical location) random sample of adults obtained from a national sampling service. The DAPS and other related materials for assessing its psychometric properties were mailed to an unspecified number of individuals. In addition, 70 college students were administered the same protocol. The author does not provide any information on the response rate for this mailing or the extent to which respondents were representative of the initial sample of individuals to which materials were mailed.

The normative sample included 446 participants who completed and returned the DAPS and who reported at least one DSM-IV-TR level traumatic event. Descriptive data on the age, gender, and racial/ethnic composition of respondents from the normative sample are provided. The effects of these respondent characteristics were examined in relation to scale scores. No age or racial/ethnic differences were found. Gender differences were found on a number of scales. Given this, gender specific profiles and normative tables were developed and are provided in the user manual.

The manual also provides decision rules to assist users in determining the likelihood that a respondent has a PTSD or ASD diagnosis. The decision rules used to establish a probable diagnosis of PTSD employ symptom scale cutoff scores and those used to identify an ASD diagnosis are based on a criterion-based method. Four examples based on the responses of trauma-exposed individuals are provided to assist DAPS users with score interpretation and determining diagnosis.

Reliability. In addition to the normative sample, reliability information is provided based on a combined clinical/community sample and a university sample. Internal consistency reliability in the form of Cronbach's alpha is the only type of reliability information provided. The majority of the 13 multiple-item scales have Cronbach coefficients above .8 across the three samples. The internal consistency estimates on the Positive Bias scale range from .61 to .80 whereas the Negative Bias and Relative Trauma Exposure scales have coefficients in the .49 to .67 range. The author notes that the lower internal consistency reliabilities associated with these two scales is of less concern given that the Negative Bias scale reflects endorsement of unusual symptoms and is not intended to be internally consistent and the Relative Trauma Exposure scale is a count of respondents' exposure to different types of trauma and is not representative of a specific symptom domain.

Validity. Three types of evidence are provided in support of the validity of scores from the DAPS: the relationship of DAPS scores with conceptually important variables, its convergence with similar measures, and its discrimination from less-related measures. In terms of theoretically meaningful variables, DAPS scale scores were correlated with the total number of traumas respondents experienced, the type of trauma experienced (i.e., interpersonal [e.g., rape, physical assault] versus noninterpersonal [e.g., disaster, motor vehicle accident]), and the amount of distress experienced at the time of the trauma, to determine if the scales were associated with these variables in the manner suggested by the existing literature. The number of lifetime traumas experienced (i.e., RTE scale) was significantly correlated with most of the symptom scales. As expected, greater exposure to trauma was associated with increased reporting of distress, reexperiencing, avoidance, hyperarousal, posttraumatic impairment, dissociation, and suicidality. Similarly, respondents' ratings of the level of distress experienced at the time of the trauma were found to be significant predictors of subsequent posttraumatic stress levels. As the literature would suggest, higher levels of distress were associated with higher levels of reexperiencing, avoidance, hyperarousal, and posttraumatic impairment. Finally, as anticipated, respondents who experienced interpersonal trauma reported significantly higher levels of distress, reexperiencing, avoidance, and suicidality than did those who had experienced noninterpersonal trauma.

Convergent and discriminant validity were assessed by correlating the DAPS scales with various other measures. In general, the Positive Bias and Negative Bias scales of the DAPS were significantly correlated in the anticipated direction (in the ± .4 to .5 range) with the validity scales from the Trauma Symptom Inventory (Briere, 1995), the Minnesota Multiphasic Personality Inventory (MMPI-2; Butcher, Dahlstrom, Graham, Tellegen, & Kaemmer, 1989), and the Personality Assessment Inventory (Morey, 1991) indicating good convergent and discriminant validity. Similarly, the DAPS symptom scale scores were also correlated with symptom scales from these other measures as an assessment of convergent validity. Over 92% of these correlations (46 of 51) were above .60 whereas 33% exceeded .70. When the DAPS subscale scores were correlated with scales from less-related measures (as an assessment of discriminant validity) the magnitude of the correlations was less than .5 in 75% of the cases. The same strategy was used to assess the convergent and discriminant validity of the DAPS associated feature scales and produce similar support for the validity of these scales.

The DAPS has also been shown to have a high level of diagnostic agreement (Kappa = .73) with the Clinician-Administered PTSD Scale (CAPS; Blake et al., 1990), a measure that requires nearly three times the amount of time to administer compared to the DAPS. Additionally, the DAPS has been shown to have good sensitivity (.88) and specificity (.86).

COMMENTARY. The DAPS was developed to closely conform to the PTSD diagnostic criteria and includes specific scales for each of the three symptom clusters as well as individual scales for three associated features. Its developer is clearly an expert in the field of PTSD assessment. The manual is well written and contains information of the measure's development, administration, scoring, interpretation, and psychometric properties as well as normative information on nearly 450 trauma-exposed individuals. However, additional information on the norming sample such as the response rate to the mailing and representativeness of respondents to the original sample would have been helpful to include. The data provided on the DAPS to date suggest that it is a psychometrically sound measure of PTSD.

SUMMARY. The DAPS is a promising measure for assessing PTSD and distinguishing it from ASD. Although information on the stability of the measure is lacking, other psychometric properties are quite acceptable.

REVIEWER'S REFERENCES

Blake, D. D., Weather, F. W., Nagy, L. M., Kaloupek, D. G., Klauminzer, G., Charney, D. S., & Keane, T. M. (1990). A clinician rating scale for assessing current and lifetime PTSD: The CAPS-1. *The Behavior Therapist, 13*, 187–188.
Briere, J. (1995). Trauma Symptom Inventory. Odessa, FL: Psychological Assessment Resources, Inc.
Butcher, J. N., Dahlstrom, W. G., Graham, J. R., Tellegen, A., & Kaemmer, B. (1989). *Minnesota Multiphasic Personality Inventory (MMPI-2): Manual for administration and scoring.* Minneapolis: University of Minnesota Press.
Morey, L. C. (1991). *Personality Assessment Inventory: Professional manual.* Odessa, FL: PAR Psychological Assessment Resources, Inc.

Review of the Detailed Assessment of Posttraumatic Stress by LARISSA SMITH, Presley Center for Crime and Justice Studies, University of California, Riverside, CA:

DESCRIPTION. The Detailed Assessment of Posttraumatic Stress (DAPS) is a 104-item, self-report paper-and-pencil inventory measuring extent of trauma exposure and post-traumatic response. Subscales include three trauma-specific subscales (Relative Trauma Exposure, Peritraumatic Distress, Peritraumatic Dissociation), five posttraumatic scales (Reexperiencing, Avoidance, Hyperarousal, Posttraumatic Stress total, Posttraumatic Impairment), three associated features scales (Trauma-Specific Dissociation, Substance Abuse, and Suicidality), and two validity scales (Positive Bias and Negative Bias). Questions are either dichotomous or on a 5-point Likert scale and address experiences and behaviors both during the event and during the month before protocol administration.

The DAPS converts to a scoring sheet designed to facilitate hand-scoring, including a worksheet area for evaluating the extent to which the examinee meets DSM-IV criteria for Post-Traumatic Stress Disorder (PTSD). Profile charts are provided for both men and women, allowing visual comparison to the normative sample using standardized T scores. The test can be administered by nonclinical staff, though the interpretation of scores and profiles requires graduate training in clinical/counseling psychology and in test interpretation. Specific instructions for examinees are included in the manual. The manual also provides guidelines for dealing with missing data, calculating raw scores, and T-score conversion, and provides sample profile interpretation case studies. The test takes approximately 20–30 minutes to complete and requires the equivalent of a sixth-grade reading level.

DEVELOPMENT. An initial pool of 190 items was reduced to 104 through consultation with expert clinicians and through item analysis based upon the first 105 participants in the normative sample.

Scales appear to have been developed based upon DSM-IV criteria and prior research in the field of posttraumatic stress. The manual provides a detailed description of each scale, including item content, characteristics of high scorers, and empirical and/or theoretical basis.

TECHNICAL.

Standardization. The authors employed a national sampling service to construct a stratified random sample of adults from Department of Motor Vehicles registries and telephone books. Participants were mailed the DAPS as part of a battery of instruments assessing trauma-related experience, including a survey specifically designed to evaluate the presence or absence of childhood and adult trauma. Of the participants contacted, 620 completed the protocol (there is no information about what response rate this represents), and 446 of those participants reported having experienced at least one DSM-IV-TR-level incident in the past. In addition, a sample of 70 university students were administered the protocol in order to extend the age range of the sample.

In the trauma-exposed sample, mean age was 45.6 years (range 18–91). Just over half the respondents were men, and the sample was primarily (83.4%) Caucasian. Analyses of this sample showed no age or ethnicity differences in scale scores. Some scales have gender differences; the manual presents norms by gender and separate profile sheets to take those differences into account.

Reliability. When the normative process was complete, further data were collected in a clinical/community sample and an undergraduate sample ($N = 257$) in order to assess reliability and validity. Participants in the undergraduate sample also reported at least one prior traumatic event. The clinical sample ($N = 191$) was recruited by clinicians in various parts of the United States; the community sample ($N = 58$) was recruited through flyers and newspaper advertisements and included participants with at least one prior traumatic event.

The community sample was primarily female (80%) and Caucasian (77%), mean age of 35 years. The university sample was similarly primarily female (74%) and Caucasian (84%), mean age of 19.6 years.

Alpha reliabilities for the scales range from .52 (Negative Bias) to .96 (Posttraumatic Stress—Total) overall, though it should be noted that the Negative Bias scale is intended to detect fake-bad responses based upon endorsement of bizarre or unusual symptoms and is not intended to measure a single construct. Reliabilities were marginally lower in the university sample than in the clinical/community sample. No information on test-retest reliability is provided. Most interscale correlations are above .30.

Validity. The manual provides an impressive amount of validity information. Depending upon the subsample, the DAPS was co-administered with some subset of at least a dozen scales, including the Minnesota Multiphasic Personality Inventory-II (MMPI-2). The DAPS Positive Bias (PB) and Negative Bias (NB) scales correlate substantially, and in the predicted direction, with validity scales from other trauma- and personality-related assessment instruments. Correlations between the symptom scales and symptom scales of other inventories are presented with their associated Ns and are mostly in the .60–.80 range. Correlations with scales measuring antisocial personality, mania, and somatic complaints, theoretically and empirically unrelated to PTSD, were substantially lower, in the .10–.30 range.

Diagnostic utility for PTSD assessment was assessed against the Clinician-Administered PTSD Scale (CAPS). On the basis of the CAPS, a subsample of participants from the clinical sample was categorized as PTSD positive (N = 25) or PTSD negative (N = 44). The DAPS miscategorized only nine of this sample—six false positives and three false negatives—producing a kappa of .73, sensitivity of .88, and specificity of .86. Diagnostic utility for Acute Stress Disorder (ASD) was not assessed due to the recency of the diagnostic category and the paucity of structured clinical interview assessments, and the manual recommends caution in diagnosing ASD solely on the basis of the DAPS decision rules.

COMMENTARY. The DAPS manual presents a very thorough survey of currently used PTSD assessment instruments and makes a well-supported case for the DAPS' contribution over and above existing instruments. There is also an impressive level of detail in the scale descriptions, the administration and scoring instructions, and the profile interpretation examples. Information on the normative sample and the validational process is also presented in considerable detail. With regard to the normative sample itself, a substantial amount of care was taken in the acquisition and composition of traumatized and comparison subsamples. The scales have a higher degree of overlap (as indicated by interscale correlations) than might be considered optimal, but the scale structure is well-grounded in prior literature. Items are for the most part clearly worded and readily understandable, though there is the

occasional digression into the vernacular (e.g., Item 24, "You 'spaced out.'").

The answer sheet is a bit awkward in its flow, but the ease of scoring and diagnosis that it provides outweighs that awkwardness. Profile sheets are easily understood and completed. That the DAPS allows for both scale scoring and profile interpretation is a benefit, especially given the detailed examples and interpretive instructions.

SUMMARY. The DAPS can be administered easily and relatively quickly, and provides a large amount of information. Issues of missing data, response bias, gender effects, and data administration conditions are all adequately addressed in the manual, and evidence for internal consistency reliability and for discriminant, convergent, and predictive validity is fair to good. Scales are well-grounded theoretically and empirically, and the author provides a well-done and detailed placement of the DAPS within the body of already-existing instruments. The bulk of the evidence weighs in favor of the test's utility for its stated purpose.

[78]

Developmental Assessment Resource for Teachers (DART) English.

Purpose: Designed to "assist teachers of upper primary and middle primary in their assessment of students' viewing, reading, listening, speaking and writing skills."

Population: Australian students in years 3–4, 5–6.
Publication Dates: 1994–1997.
Acronym: DART ENGLISH.
Scores, 5: Viewing, Reading, Listening, Speaking, Writing.
Administration: Group.
Forms, 2: Form A, Form B.
Publisher: Australian Council for Educational Research Ltd. [Australia].

a) DART MIDDLE PRIMARY ENGLISH.
Population: Students in years 3–4 in Australian classrooms.
Publication Date: 1997.
Price Data, 2002: A\$132 per specimen set including 1 of each test component; A\$49.50 per manual (1997, 152 pages); A\$18.65 per 10 Viewing answer booklets; A\$53.90 per Viewing video; A\$21.95 per 10 reusable Reading stimulus booklets (specify Form A or Form B); A\$10.95 per 10 Reading answer booklets A; A\$14.25 per 10 Reading answer booklets B; A\$7.65 per 10 Listening answer booklets; A\$14.25 per audio cassette; A\$10.95 per 10 reusable Character Review Speak-

ing Guides; A\$10.95 per 10 Writing answer booklets.

Time: (40–190) minutes per section.

Authors: Wendy Bodey, Lynne Darkin, Margaret Forster, and Geoff Masters.

b) DART UPPER PRIMARY ENGLISH.

Population: Students in years 5–6 in Australian classrooms.

Publication Date: 1994.

Price Data: A\$120 per specimen set including 1 of each test component; A\$45 per manual (1994, 159 pages); A\$16.95 per 10 Viewing answer booklets; A\$49 per Viewing video; A\$5 per Viewing poster; A\$19.95 per 10 reusable Reading stimulus booklets (specify Form A or Form B); A\$9.95 per 10 Reading answer booklets A; A\$12.95 per 10 Reading answer booklets B; A\$6.95 per 10 Listening answer booklets; A\$12.95 per audio cassette; A\$9.95 per 10 reusable Speaking poetry booklets; A\$9.95 per 10 Writing answer booklets; A\$295 per complete package including testing materials for 30 students.

Time: (40–190) minutes per section.

Authors: Margaret Forster, Juliette Mendelovits, and Geoff Masters.

Review of the Developmental Assessment Resource for Teachers (DART) English by VALENTINA McINERNEY, Professor of Educational Psychology, School of Psychology, University of Western Sydney, Sydney, Australia:

DESCRIPTION. DART English (1994) and DART English Middle Primary (1997) comprise integrated packages of classroom activities and assessment tasks for five English literacy strands: Viewing, Reading, Speaking, Listening, and Writing. The target populations for the DART English are upper primary and junior secondary school students (Grades 5, 6, and 7), whereas the DART English Middle Primary is for use with middle primary school students (Grades 3 and 4). As scores for each literacy strand are standardized separately, there is considerable flexibility in the ways that DART English can be used for diagnosis and development of students' literacy skills. The first use is as the basis for an integrated 4- to 6-week program of work around the themes of the tests; the second is as one-off assessments, separate from the ongoing classroom literacy program; and the third is as part of a school's literacy assessment and reporting procedures. For example, students can be pretested on the five strands at the start of a school

year, and then retested after the completion of a school-wide literacy program.

The central component of the DART English package is a video of the Australian drama for children, *Danny's Egg,* to which all the assessment tasks are thematically linked. The content of the DART English Middle Primary is organized around a "myths and legends" theme that includes the video *Why Mosquitoes Buzz in People's Ears.*

Students' scores on DART English (1994) are referenced against Australian norms derived from samples of Year 5 and Year 6 students in 1995, and Year 3 students in 1996 for DART Middle Primary (1997). These norms are broken down into four levels of achievement for each of the five strands, and are presented in an overall profile chart in such a way as to show how numerical scores in each level correspond to one another across the five strands. In this way, a teacher can display a student's scores for Viewing, Reading, Speaking, Listening, and Writing on the one chart, and determine their relative levels of proficiency at a glance. As well as a numerical profile chart, a verbal description of the skills and understandings typically shown by the norming sample at each level is provided for the five literacy strands. This is in line with the goal of the Australian government to identify specific developmental outcomes through which students' progression in literacy can be described, and achievement can be reported comparably across school systems and regions (*National Literacy Benchmarks for Grades 3, 5 & 7;* Curriculum Corporation, Victoria, Australia, 2000; retrieved from http://online.curriculum.edu.au/litbench/intro.asp).

DEVELOPMENT. There is no information given in the teacher's manual about the development of either of the DART English tests, other than the authors' acknowledging a long list of individuals (largely classroom teachers and some "curriculum and assessment specialists") who contributed to "expert panel reviews" and piloting of the early materials. The qualifications of these panels as "experts," the criteria for selecting them (almost exclusively from nongovernment schools), and the procedures used to obtain consensus are not explained, however. In this context, the authors provide no theoretical or empirical justification for the choice of content in terms of level of interest and relevance to potential test takers. This lack of conceptual base may be a function of the need in the mid 1990s to develop a battery of tests for large-scale national and school assessment of key skills and understandings identified in the National English Profile for Australian Schools (*English— A curriculum profile for Australian schools.* Curriculum Corporation, Victoria, Australia, 1994).

TECHNICAL. Norming of DART English (1994) materials took place in 1995 with a "nationally representative and stratified sample" of Grade 5 and 6 students from 70 schools "with the appropriate representation of the government, Catholic, and independent sectors" (technical information, p. 9). Data provided, however, show that schools were largely from the government sector and excluded nongovernment schools from two territories and one state, with no rationales given for the inclusion of particular schools and selection of participating teachers (973 schools were approached to achieve the final sample of 379). Also omitted are important details about the gender, socioeconomic background, ethnicity, and spoken language of students in the sample.

In the case of the DART Middle Primary (1997), norming was conducted in 1996 with a "nationally representative" sample of "almost" 4,000 Grade 3 students from schools that were invited to participate. Again, data are not given to verify the representativeness of the sample and the schools from which they were drawn, nor are explanations given for why many schools chose not to participate or withdrew. In the context of the *Standards for Educational and Psychological Testing* (AERA, APA, & NCME, 1999, Part 1.1), such omissions reduce the validity of the norming process considerably.

The authors offer no related research, technical data, or case study examples to demonstrate that the test offers valid information for making instructional decisions. There is no theoretical model or research evidence to support the choice of test items and activities as valid representations of the five literacy content domains.

The authors talk about their extensive efforts to ensure content validity of the tests. Evidence to support this claim is not provided, however. On close examination of the items and activities in each of the five literacy strands, it is difficult to see how they are fair and accurate measures of the constructs. The descriptive (verbal) reports derived from the English Profiles are intended to assist test users in interpreting students' scores on the DART. In reality, the way in which these are correlated with DART scores could easily lead to meaningless interpretations of a test taker's competence, with potentially inaccurate reports of strengths and weaknesses. For example, on the more difficult Form B of the Reading strand, a score of 24/28 indicates a high level of proficiency, at the top of Level 4, and supposedly demonstrates that the student "Understands the connection between parts of a text." It is not clear, however, how this high level ability is to be differentiated from the low Level 1 where the student "Makes a connection between parts of the text," which corresponds to a poorer score of only 12/28.

The authors acknowledge that the Speaking strand may not be a valid assessment for some students "because they are too shy to speak to a large audience or because they choose not to participate" (DART manual, 1994, p. 75; DART Middle Primary manual, 1997, p. 84). With this in mind, test bias potentially can be avoided against students from cultural backgrounds in which children's "speaking up" to adults or in a formal public setting, and verbosity and elaboration of ideas are neither encouraged nor considered appropriate. Such cautions also need to be borne in mind for test takers from linguistic minority backgrounds who may need more time to process the listening and viewing tasks, and may answer less quickly and accurately than those who are native English speakers. Care needs to be taken in interpreting such students' scores despite the authors' claims that "Reference groups screened all test tasks to ensure that they did not discriminate unfairly against students from different cultural or language backgrounds" (technical information, p. 3). It is difficult to see how many of the test items are fair and accurate measures of the constructs for some students, as DART activities are neither culturally nor linguistically neutral (see Culican, Emmitt, & Oakley, 2001). Familiarity with Anglo-Australian culture—bush lore and outback life—would increase test takers' Reading and Viewing scores with DART English (1994). Similarly, having such "educated" experiences as reading myths, legends, and fables from around the world and watching current affairs television would advantage scores in Speaking within DART Middle Primary (1997).

As far as the writing tasks are concerned, the scoring guide is helpful for analyzing the content and language aspects of the test taker's work, especially as this is accompanied by annotated work samples. The validity of the scoring procedure, however, is diminished when an additional "on-balance" or overall impression mark is to be provided subjectively by the test administrator.

COMMENTARY. Overall, the normative information provided for the DART (1994) is quite dated today, and both DART tests should be restandardized. Given the high stakes, large scale systemic and national literacy testing conducted in Australia using DART English, the consequential validity of test scores in terms of classroom grouping, withdrawal from classes for "remedial" reading, and communications with students' primary caregivers, it is critical that strong validity can be demonstrated empirically. Australian data need to be provided on the differential outcomes of DART English testing for males and females in interaction with ethnicity and language background. In this context, the reliability of scoring DART Reading tasks needs to be questioned.

The claim is made that "All DART materials have been equated" (technical information, p. 4), which is followed by a brief overview of the process adopted for "equating" the eight DART Reading tests over the period May 1994 to May 1997. The limited quantitative information provided does not provide a basis for accepting that these tests (described variously as "harder," "easier," "secure," "released") have been rigorously equated. Strictly speaking, it is not even possible to vertically equate reading (or any literacy) ability characteristics in a way that allows for diagnosis of developmental or educational levels (AERA, APA, & NCME, 1999, Part 1, 4). Rather, scores can be considered "scaled" or "comparable." In light of the *Standards for Educational and Psychological Testing* (AERA, APA, & NCME, 1999, Part 1, 2), these many limitations cause serious doubts about the reliability of the DART English tests scores, about which no estimates are given by the authors for either of the test packages.

An explanation of why the DART English tests are called "developmental" is not provided. Given this title, it is presumed that the primary purpose of the DART is to enable the test user to produce a detailed diagnosis of a student's level of "development" in each of the five areas of literacy against benchmarks set by the National English Profile mentioned above. In this sense, its use by classroom teachers to design interventions for students would be appropriate. Rather than "development," however, the term "achievement" is used exclusively throughout the DART. By providing calibrated criteria for competence at four levels in each of the five strands, it is easy to see why the DART has been adopted in testing entire grades within schools and across school systems in Australia. Of course, the reliability and validity of measuring and comparing test takers' literacy competence on the basis of such a test are highly questionable, especially when the norms are dated. Given the huge variation in student demographics within and between urban and rural schools across Australia's six states and two territories, great caution must be exercized when compiling and publishing reports of student scores on the DART English, especially when such reports may be provided to parents.

The ability to speak confidently and logically in public is an important skill to develop during primary school. In relation to the Speaking component of the DART English Middle Primary, the authors' awareness of the need to process information cognitively before speaking, and the benefits of social interaction to facilitate this, is clear. In this context, opportunities are provided for students to brainstorm and discuss their ideas in a small group and then to rehearse their presentations with a partner before presenting individually. In these ways, possible performance anxiety can be minimized as well as allowing for depth and organization of content to be developed. Even so, it would be helpful for the developers to propose a range of ways of assessing the speaking strand that might be less threatening to some students than an individual oral presentation to the whole class.

SUMMARY. DART English is the only instrument readily available to teachers in Australia that models current practice in literacy teaching and assessment, where literacy skills are seen as an integration of reading, writing, speaking, listening, and viewing. It also provides a developmental framework for focusing on the literacy outcomes that students are achieving at a particular time, rather than on what they are not able to do (Culican, Emmitt, & Oakley, 2001). These tests can provide a general "snapshot" of the specific literacy skills and knowledge identified in Australia's *National Statements and Profiles,* against which they are referenced, with the exception of nonnative and indigenous speakers, for whom no norms are available.

In a world where text is increasingly related to the visual, the auditory, the spatial, and the behavioral, as in the mass media, multimedia, and electronic hypermedia, DART English can offer only limited information to educators and parents. Of greater concern in terms of the rigorous *Standards for Educational and Psychological Testing* (AERA, APA, & NCME, 1999), though, is that the information derived from DART English scores, in the absence of a published technical manual, lacks evidence of psychometric validity and reliability, which casts considerable doubt on the worth of decisions derived from it for educational and policy settings.

REVIEWER'S REFERENCES

American Educational Research Association, American Psychological Association, & National Council on Measurement in Education. (1999). *Standards for educational and psychological testing.* Washington: American Educational Research Association.

Culican, S. J., Emmitt, M., & Oakley, C. (2001). *Literacy and learning in the middle years.* Victoria, Australia: Consultancy and Development Unit, Faculty of Education, Deakin University.

Review of the Developmental Assessment Resource for Teachers (DART) English by GRETCHEN OWENS, Professor of Child Study, St. Joseph's College, Patchogue, NY, and JAN HARTING-McCHESNEY, Assistant Professor of Child Study, St. Joseph's College, Patchogue, NY:

DESCRIPTION. The Developmental Assessment Resource for Teachers (DART) English is an assessment package developed by the Australian Council for Educational Research (ACER). The DART English kits are designed to measure literacy skills as part of ongoing classroom assessment of student achievement, or as part of a school's larger assessment program. The "strands" of the DART cover five aspects of a comprehensive literacy program: Viewing, Reading, Listening, Speaking, and Writing.

Each DART kit contains a variety of appealing materials, including a videotape, an audiotape for the listening tasks, two short "magazines," a colorful trade book, and a speaking guide/graphic organizer for working with a partner and participating in group discussions. Five test booklets also are provided: one each for viewing, listening, and writing, and two forms (easier and harder) for reading. The manual contains instructions for administering and scoring the tests and a set of forms for reporting results. The first report form indicates the specific skills a child with a given raw score is likely

to be able to demonstrate, along with an indication of the Australian level (helpful for showing progress over time). The second presents an item analysis identifying skills on which a student has shown relative strength or weakness, which can be useful for instructional planning. The norms tables allow comparisons of students with others of the same age and grade level, and the teacher can complete a profile form for each student that simultaneously displays his or her performance on all five strands. Class record sheets are included for each strand.

The DART was designed to address learning outcomes described in the *English Profile for Australian Schools,* which sets out national curriculum standards. The content of each DART kit has a distinctively Australian flavor. Following the national curriculum framework, the DART materials are divided into eight levels of mastery rather than according to grade or age levels. The authors assume that in any given grade, students will be working at a variety of levels, so each of the two DART instruments covers four levels, with different content in the two measures but overlap in difficulty levels. DART Middle Primary English (designed for third- and fourth-graders) covers Levels 1–4 (with the majority of the items at Levels 2 and 3). The DART Upper Primary English (designed for fifth- and sixth-graders) covers Levels 2–5 (with the majority of items at Levels 3 and 4). Several optional supplements are provided that assess interactive speaking and listening during small group discussions, along with the ability to write procedural text. Clearly articulated scoring rubrics and record sheets are provided for these activities as well.

DART Middle Primary raw scores can be converted to a scaled score (from the National English Literacy Scale, or NELS) with a mean of 300 and a standard deviation of 100 for third-graders. The means and standard deviations are higher for each subsequent level, but the amount of increase varies between each of the strands, which makes interpretation of NELS scores, especially for older children, challenging. The educator who wishes to determine a child's performance relative to others is largely limited to reporting approximate percentile levels instead of a standard score. (Rather than providing a typical norms table, the manual instead gives box-and-whisker plots indicating the 10th, 20th, 50th, 80th, and 90th percentiles, so these percentile rank conversions are far from exact.)

DEVELOPMENT. In developing the DART tests, the authors took care to include a variety of types of text and tasks at varying levels of difficulty. Items that showed potential cultural bias, those that showed inadequate discriminatory power, and those that failed to fit Rasch test models satisfactorily were omitted from the final version. This resulted in a total of eight DART reading tests (A through H), five of which were then used in various national assessment programs between 1994 and 1997. Data from these trial tests and a special equating study were used to equate statistically the eight reading tests and bring them to a common scale. Thus, high scores on the easier tests produce scores that are equivalent to a lower score on a more difficult test. Unfortunately for users in other countries, the scores that are produced represent the level of literacy proficiency for Australian schools, which does not easily translate to American or British grade equivalents or standard scores.

TECHNICAL. The technical manual for the DART is not yet available in published form, but one of the authors forwarded a summary of the psychometric analyses they have conducted to this point (e-mail correspondence from Margaret Forster, May 22, 2002). In this, the evidence of content validity of the DART is provided by citing extensive review and revision during the development of the materials by panels of experts, aimed at assuring that the skills assessed give an adequate representation of the outcomes specified in the Australian national curricula frameworks. They included text from the 1996 National School English Literacy Survey report listing the 60 learning outcomes covered at Levels 1–5 of the framework and tables that show which of these are addressed by the DART at Years 3 and 5. (A complete table of specifications for all levels, noting which skills are emphasized more at different levels, would be a helpful addition to the eventual manual.) As a further demonstration of the validity of the DART, the authors note that students regularly show increases in performance from one year to the next as a reflection of the number of years of instruction in literacy. In addition, they argue that the Rasch item calibration model they employed assures that the items all indicate "a student's status on a single underlying variable measuring a single trait" (DART technical information, p. 4), thus allowing measurement on the same continuum or scale.

No criterion-related studies designed to demonstrate concurrent validity (correspondence with other established literacy assessment instruments or teacher evaluations of students' abilities) nor the predictive validity of the DART appear to have been conducted as yet.

The ACER norming studies used data from 1,800 students for Form C and 1,500 students for Form D. Later, norms were derived from administration of the tests to national samples of 10 third-graders and 10 fifth-graders selected randomly from the classrooms of teachers in selected classes from each of 379 public and private schools (for a total of nearly 3,800 students). These schools were selected to proportionately represent the populations of the eight Australian states and territories. No information is provided about the demographic characteristics of the norming group other than the geographic locations and the types of schools (government, Catholic, or independent).

Although the authors undertook checks of internal consistency using coefficient alpha with all DART tests (e-mail from Margaret Forster, May 22, 2002), this information is not reported in the draft technical manual. The author stated in her correspondence that the r for the DART Upper Primary Reading is .96.

COMMENTARY. Despite the currently incomplete technical information, the DART has several laudable features. First, the tasks go well beyond the multiple-choice format of many competing group assessment instruments and give opportunities for critical thinking, problem solving, and collaboration. Even the materials themselves (e.g., the audiotapes for the Listening strand and the graphic organizers for the Speaking guide) present models of problem solving and collaboration from which students can learn even as they are being assessed. The implied goal is to show how students actually use language and information in the classroom setting and, by extension, how well they are able to transfer their skills outside the classroom. In these ways, the DART provides a more authentic assessment of literacy skills than most instruments being used currently.

Second, the DART materials are interesting and appealing. One often forgotten guideline for good assessment practices is that those creating a test should consider not only what children *can* do but what they *like* to do. These authors seem to have kept that principle at the forefront. For example, the various DART activities should engage most third-graders' interest as they read an award winning book, write out directions for making a bird mask, take part in a group discussion about the characters in a video they have viewed together, or create their own sketch of a set design while listening to its description in an audiotape.

A third strength of the DART is that it is appropriate for teachers of various levels of experience and proficiency and in an assortment of classroom situations. The manual provides clear directions for what to do for each strand, but also notes options for how and when to administer the various components. The authors suggest that the DART materials and activities can be used as an assessment tool over several days or as the basis for a 4- to 6-week, thematically integrated language arts unit, with other discussions and projects added (and possibly linked to science and math activities as well). This flexibility makes it more likely that the DART can be incorporated into a variety of classroom programs and for diverse populations of students.

A fourth strength is in the directions for scoring. On the objective tests (e.g., Viewing, Reading, and Listening), marking guides list basic criteria for earning credit, accompanied by examples of correct and incorrect answers, which should increase scoring consistency. For Speaking and Writing, clear rubrics are provided, along with explanations and already scored samples of student writing.

Unfortunately, there are also some problems that need to be remedied in order for this very promising instrument to realize its potential. First, if DART is to be purchased for use in the U.S., teachers need to understand that they would have the additional expense of converting the videotapes so that they can be read on U.S. video players. Australia uses a different video system from the U.S. system. Secondly, a complete technical manual is needed to properly evaluate the psychometric adequacy of the measures. If the test is ever to be used as part of the decision-making process about eligibility for special education services, the authors will need to set up a common scale for all grade levels (so performance can be readily interpreted for grades other than third) and to provide a more precise set of norms tables arranged by actual grade placement rather than according to the Australian levels.

The final comments serve more as a caution than a criticism. The accent on the tapes is decidedly Australian, but it is likely that most American children would be able to understand all but an occasional word, which their teacher may have to interpret for them ("spice" means space, a "toadler" is a toddler). In addition, the authors definitely do not talk down to children: The vocabulary is at a higher level than that of most reading materials used in American classrooms, though the majority of the more advanced words are embedded in a context that encourages comprehension. The themes and context as a whole are definitely Australian, and there may well be a more direct match between the language of the DART and that heard in everyday life by Australian children than by American youngsters. If the DART were being used with the Australian norms for identifying major deficiencies in reading or listening comprehension of American students, this could be a problem, but for demonstrating progress or identifying patterns of strengths and weaknesses in the various literacy areas, it should not pose a major impediment.

SUMMARY. The DART English kits provide an integrated package for a comprehensive assessment program in literacy. The well-organized manual and clear scoring system are major strengths. The DART yields information that can be used to evaluate individual students' literacy progress, aid in instructional planning, and determine how students in a particular school or district compare with Australia-wide samples. There are gaps in the psychometric data that should be filled via a complete technical manual so Australian users can place more faith in the results they obtain. With addition of a more complete table of specifications, statistical evaluations of the DART's discriminatory power, and investigations of test-retest reliability and interscorer agreement, the DART promises to be an extremely worthwhile tool for a complete literacy assessment. In addition to the preceding psychometric data, American users would need new national norms for interstudent comparisons, and they cannot expect to use the DART as presently configured for entitlement decisions, but it does provide a promising curriculum-based assessment tool. As such, it provides an excellent model of a flexible, integrated assessment system that is content area driven and embedded in instruction, and an interesting alternative to current assessment techniques.

[79]

Developmental Assessment Resource for Teachers (DART) Mathematics.

Purpose: "Provides an estimate of a student's level of achievement on each of four strands of the [Australian] national mathematics profile ... and on each of three strands of the national benchmark framework."

Population: Australian students in years 5–6.

Publication Date: 1998.

Acronym: DART MATHEMATICS.

Scores, 5: Number, Space, Measurement, Chance and Data, Data Sense.

Administration: Group.

Forms, 2: Form A, Form B.

Price Data, 2002: A$273.90 per kit including video, manual (160 pages), 30 grid sheets, 30 measurement sheets, and photocopy master answer booklet and stimulus for all tests; A$34.95 per manual; A$54.95 per video; A$21.95 per each photocopy master answer booklet and stimulus (specify Number, Space, Measurement, Chance and Data or Data Sense; also specify Form A or Form B); A$14.25 per 30 grid sheets; A$14.25 per 30 measurement sheets.

Time: (60) minutes per section.

Authors: Eve Recht, Margaret Forster, and Geoff Masters.

Publisher: Australian Council for Educational Research Ltd. [Australia].

Review of the Developmental Assessment Resource for Teachers (DART) Mathematics by CARLEN HENINGTON, Associate Professor of Educational and School Psychology, Mississippi State University, Mississippi State, MS:

DESCRIPTION. The Developmental Assessment Resource for Teachers (DART) Mathematics is intended to be used by Australian teachers of upper-elementary and early-secondary students to evaluate and report mathematics achievement in one or more areas. The DART can also be used to evaluate school-wide performance. The instrument assesses five areas or strands identified in the mathematics profile for Australian schools: Number/Number Sense, Space/Spatial Sense, Measurement, Chance and Data, and Data Sense using one of two forms (Form A and Form B). In general, Form B is described as more difficult than Form A. The DART can be used to measure an individual student's or an entire school's performance, to report that performance in relation to the mathematics profile for Australian schools (a "curriculum" standards framework) and to compare levels of achievement with the national numeracy standards (national "performance" standards).

Achievement is evaluated using applied math problems related to activities that might be completed by zoo personnel (e.g., feeding the animals, determining zoo hours, collecting and presenting data on animal behavior). The theme is initially set by a 21-minute video, *Maths at the Zoo*, filmed at the Melbourne Zoo. The assessment kit contains the video, assessment, supporting materials, and manual. The manual provides administration information, answer keys, and reproducible record sheets for both forms of each framework area. The manual also provides guides to interpreting student performance and a description of each task completed in the five strands. Other materials provided in the kit include an answer booklet and supporting materials for tasks to be completed. In some situations the answer booklet provides all the information needed to answer a question. In other cases additional information must be found in the support materials, Zoo Pages. Form A and Form B of each of the five areas assessed has its own answer booklet and Zoo Pages conveniently pre-packaged together in resealable cellophane. These materials are to be photocopied and assembled by the classroom teacher. For some tasks other materials are required and are provided in the "starter kit," but replacements must be purchased from the publisher (i.e., measurement sheets, grid sheet). Additional needed materials not provided but that are usually readily available in classrooms include a calculator, ruler, and string.

Administration information, a list of needed materials, and individual instructions for each of the strands are clearly provided in delineated sections of the manual. Elaborate instructions are also provided for copying and collating the testing materials. Instructions vary from Form A to Form B and include making sure students understand that some questions can be answered from information provided in the answer booklet and that other questions require them to use the Zoo Pages and other materials. Administration requires up to 60 minutes for each strand assessed with 19 to 24 questions. Presentation of the questions is not ordered by difficulty. For example, the Number strand Item 1 (a question assessing skill at the lower end of Level 3 proficiency) is followed by Item 2 (a question assessing a skill at the upper end of Level 4 proficiency). Some questions require a single step, whereas others require several steps or skills.

Using the corresponding report form a teacher can estimate expected level of achievement and, through error analysis, can identify areas of weakness or strength. This analysis would enable a teacher to individualize instruction to either the class or the individual student.

DEVELOPMENT. The DART strands were derived from two frameworks that drive achievement expectations of Australian students: the national mathematics profile framework (Mathematics—a Curriculum Profile for Australian Schools developed by the Curriculum Corporation in 1994) and the Australian national benchmark framework. As such, this instrument can be described as a broad curriculum-based instrument driven by two nationally derived learning outcomes frameworks.

There is some overlap between the two frameworks. Where this is the case, the tasks are the same and the authors indicate that the materials evaluate performance on both frameworks. The national benchmark framework consists of three strands: (a) Number Sense, defined as the ability to manipulate and calculate with numbers; (b) Spatial Sense, defined as the understanding and interpretation of spatial concepts such as location, shape, movement, and orientation; and (c) Data Sense, defined as the ability to measure and use estimation, the understanding of chance variation, and the ability to present and interpret data. The national profiles framework consists of four strands: (a) Number, which overlaps with the benchmark framework strand Number Sense; (b) Space, which overlaps with Spatial Sense; (c) Measurement, defined as the ability to measure and estimate using a variety of units; and (d) Chance and Data, defined as the understanding of chance variation and the ability to present and interpret data (some tasks used to evaluate this strand are also used to evaluate the Data Sense strand from the benchmark framework).

The development of the materials is not further explained in the manual, but the Acknowledgements section indicates that professionals affiliated with the Australian Council for Educational Research (ACER) served as a review panel. The instrument was trial-tested using professionals affiliated with the Australian Capital Territory Department of Education and Training and teachers throughout Australia.

No information is provided in the manual on item development, pilot testing, selection of final items, or evaluation of the appropriateness of individual items for the frameworks.

TECHNICAL. No direct norm data are currently available. To provide data to support the equivalence of DART to the other curriculum measures, the authors report that they administered a combined "set of DART Mathematics items" and a "set of items from the Third International Mathematics and Science Study (TIMSS)" (manual, p. 147) for which national normative information was available. Norms were inferred for DART from the "equating" study, which used a national sample of 300 students. The authors leave it to the consumer to extrapolate the remaining strand scores based on score equivalence of the Number strand to the other strands. No reliability data nor any further validity data are provided.

COMMENTARY. A strength of the DART is its organization along specific math areas (strands) and the relative durability of the materials. Teachers will find the instructions for its use also well organized, making the instrument easy to administer. Students are likely to find most of the tasks on the DART novel and interesting. However, the strong applied problem-solving approach may be unfamiliar to some students. This adds additional, perhaps unintended, components (e.g., task persistence, problem-solving development) to the assessment.

The DART can be compared to curriculum-based measurement (CBM) in that the materials revolve around a defined set of criteria developed for Australian schools. The strengths of CBM are multiple and have been identified by leaders in academic assessment and intervention (Shapiro, 1996; Shinn, 1989). As a curriculum-based instrument, however, the DART does have limitations. The DART Mathematics does not provide adequate theoretical background to readily translate the usefulness of this instrument to curriculum outside Australia. However, using the description of tasks on each strand, any teacher could use this instrument to obtain additional information not normally provided by other standardized, norm-referenced measures, nor many curriculum-based measures. The DART has two forms and, therefore, should only be administered twice to the same student. Finally, some questions require several skills to complete the task, making subskill assessment difficult.

SUMMARY. The developers have produced a mathematics assessment instrument that teachers may find useful if they are looking for a novel approach to evaluate a broad range of skills of an individual or an entire school. The instrument is relatively easy to prepare, administer, score, and interpret. However, the interpretation is based on Australian framework learning outcomes and, as such, teachers from other nations must convert the materials to their own curriculum goals. Information about skills assessed by the DART is provided and the task of converting this information to a curriculum, although difficult, is not impossible. The best use of the DART is as a curriculum-based instrument. However, there are several limitations to its use in this manner outside of the probable mismatch to curriculum. Most notably the instrument cannot be used multiple times to evaluate incremental gains. Individuals wishing to use a novel, well-organized instrument using applied problems to evaluate math abilities may find this instrument an attractive alternative.

REVIEWER'S REFERENCES

Shapiro, E. S. (1996). *Academic skills problems: Direct assessment and intervention* (2nd ed.). New York: Guilford Press.
Shinn, M. R. (Ed.) (1989). *Curriculum-based measurement: Assessing special children.* New York: Guilford Press.

Review of the Developmental Assessment Resource for Teachers (DART) Mathematics by JUDITH A. MONSAAS, Professor of Education, North Georgia College and State University, Dahlonega, GA:

DESCRIPTION. The Developmental Assessment Resource for Teachers (DART) Mathematics: Upper Primary assessment is designed to measure mathematics achievement in five strands: Number/Number Sense, Space/Spatial Sense, Measurement, Chance and Data, and Data Sense for students in upper primary and early secondary levels (Grades 5, 6, and 7 in the Australian system). The assessments were developed and published by the Australian Council for Educational Research. There are two forms (Form A and B) for each strand with Form B being slightly more difficult. A conversion table shows equivalent scores for the two forms.

The forms are organized thematically around the workings and life in a zoo. A 21-minute video is shown prior to administration of the assessments. Each assessment strand takes about 1 hour to administer. The test is designed to be integrated into day-to-day teaching and is aligned with outcomes of the Mathematics Profile for Australian Schools. The materials are attractively packaged and the assessment materials should be attractive to students.

The items on the assessment are primarily supply type where the student must provide a numeric response. There are also multiple-choice items and questions that require students to provide an explanation or interpretation. The metric system is used throughout, which may limit the use of this test in the U.S. or other countries not using the metric system, though most problems can be solved without specific knowledge of the metric system. This would influence student's familiarity with the measures used in the problems, but may not influence their ability to solve the problems.

A very thorough manual is provided with directions for administering and scoring the assessment. Photocopy masters are provided for the student answer booklets and Zoo Pages. Zoo Pages are data/information sheets that students use to answer some of the questions.

Several score reporting formats are provided. A class record sheet may be reproduced and shows, by student, which questions were answered correctly. Student scores can be reported by level using the five levels of the mathematics profile for Australian schools. Individual student profiles are available for each strand. The descriptive report visually shows the level at which the student performed and includes narrative descriptions of what type of problems the student was and was not able to solve. This report would be especially helpful to the classroom teacher. This reporting schema is cited in the National Research Council's summary of research on cognitive psychology and assessment as a "notable attempt to measure growth in competence and to convey the nature of student achievement in ways that can benefit teaching and learning" (National Research Council, 2001, p. 190).

A Diagnostic Report shows the level at which students performed on the subsections of each strand assessment. For example, Form A of Number has four subsections, seal meals, food store costs, admission prices, and gorilla cake. An individual student's profile can be reported for these four sections. This might be more helpful to the classroom teacher if the subsections were reported in terms of the mathematics skills measured by these subsections. For those interested in a normative interpretation of the test scores, the strands have been equated to a national administration of the

Third International Mathematics and Science Study (TIMSS) test. Through this individual test scores can be translated into percentile ranks.

One limitation is the absence of a technical manual that reports validity and reliability evidence. Analysts at the Australian Council for Educational Research (ACER) provided data by email for this review. Nonetheless, if ACER is publishing and marketing this assessment outside of Australia, a technical manual is necessary.

DEVELOPMENT. The assessment materials were developed to address outcomes described in the Australian mathematics profile framework (Curriculum Corporation, 1994). Items were developed to assess attainment level for upper elementary and lower secondary school students. The thematic approach was taken to be consistent with current thinking about best teaching practice and current literature in cognitive psychology. About 200 items were pilot tested on a nonrepresentative sample of students and this item pool was reduced to the final number based on Rasch analysis, which was used to calibrate items and measure fit. The materials were also pilot tested with a sample of teachers to ensure that teachers could manage this integrated approach to assessment. Data on number of teachers and students included in the pilot testing were not provided though the teachers' manual states the items were field tested on a "substantial number of students" (p. 147).

TECHNICAL.

Standardization. The assessment is criterion-referenced to the Australian National Curriculum profiles. Items were developed and field-tested to ensure match to the curriculum framework. To provide national norms, a set of DART Mathematics items was combined with a set of items from the Third International Mathematics and Science Study (TIMSS). This composite test was administered to a national sample of 300 students in an "equating study." A representative sample of 3,325 Year 5 students had taken the TIMSS in 1994 and the DART scores were equated to the TIMSS mathematics scores. Thus, Australian national norms (percentile ranks) are available on the DART assessments.

Reliability. The reliability of person separation coefficient from Rasch analysis is .98, which is comparable to coefficient alpha. Results for the separate strands, levels, or any demographic groups were not provided.

Validity. The evidence provided in the Developmental Assessment Resource for Teachers, on the website, and from personal correspondence supports the validity of the assessment for measuring the Australian mathematics curriculum at Year 5. Rasch analyses support the developmental levels of the assessments. DIF analyses were performed and items were selected to minimize differences between males and females. Given the technical expertise at the Australian Council for Educational Research one can assume that additional analyses were performed in the development of the assessment and to ensure the continued support of this instrument. One can only wish that a technical manual were available to help the user identify additional test uses.

COMMENTARY AND SUMMARY. Overall, this assessment appears to do a good job of assessing the mathematics curriculum in the Australian school systems. It is consistent with the latest research on teaching and learning and is cited as a model of how to integrate teaching and assessment to improve student learning. This test is being marketed outside of Australian and the stakes are now different. A technical manual is critical to assist potential users outside of Australia to determine if the assessment is appropriate for their students and how it might be used with different populations and curricula.

It is suggested that users considering this assessment determine how closely the skills covered in this assessment (and the Australian curriculum) match the skills covered by the user. If there is a match and if the use of the metric system is not a concern, I would recommend local schools and systems conduct their own pilot test of the assessment.

REVIEWER'S REFERENCES

Curriculum Corporation. (1994). Mathematics—a Curriculum Profile for Australian Schools. Australia: Curriculum Corporation.
National Research Council. (2001). *Knowing what students know: The science and design of educational assessment.* Committee on the Foundations of Assessment (J. Pelligrino, N. Chudowsky, and R. Glaser, Eds.). Board on Testing and Assessment, Center for Education, Division of Behavioral and Social Sciences and Education. Washington, DC: National Academy Press.

[80]

Developmental Readiness Scale—Revised.

Purpose: Designed as a screening instrument for school readiness.

Population: Ages 3–6.

Publication Dates: 1982–1993.

Acronym: DRS-R.

Scores, 9: Fine Motor, Visual Motor, Numbers, Concepts, Body Image, Language, Personal-Social, Gross Motor, Reading.
Administration: Individual.
Price Data, 2001: $90 per starter set including manual (1993, 117 pages), test kit, stimulus cards, 25 test forms, and 25 report forms; $30 per manual; $20 per test kit; $16 per set of stimulus cards; $24 per 25 test forms; $24 per 25 report forms; quantity discounts available.
Time: (30–40) minutes.
Author: Barbara Ball.
Publisher: Academic Consulting & Testing Service. [Note: The publisher advises in March 2003 that current studies have been done and are in progress to update norms and provide psychometric evidence of reliability and validity. This information was not available to the reviewers.]

Review of the Developmental Readiness Scale— Revised by HOI K. SUEN, Professor of Educational Psychology, Pennsylvania State University, University Park, PA:

DESCRIPTION. The Developmental Readiness Scale—Revised (DRS-R) is a 56-item individually administered instrument. The test author estimated that administration takes about 25–30 minutes. The purpose is to assess a child's level of readiness for kindergarten. It is not intended to be an academic readiness scale. Rather, it is designed to measure developmental readiness. Although a portion of items are designed to measure academic readiness (e.g., uppercase letter and word recognition), the use of that portion is optional. The core 56 items are divided into eight areas with 7 items each. The eight areas include Fine Motor, Visual Motor, Numbers, Concepts, Body Image, Language, Personal—Social, and Gross Motor Tasks. Each of the 7 items in each of the eight areas corresponds to one of seven developmental age ranges starting from the range of 3.6–3.11 years to the range of 6.6–6.11 years. Based on the common requirement that children enter kindergarten at the chronological age of 5, a child who can successfully complete the item for the 5.0–5.5 range and all of the 3 items below that range for a given area of development is judged to be developmentally ready in that particular area. The author suggested that the DRS-R could be used to aid in educational planning and to identify children in need of extra assistance. Explicit detailed educational implications for low scores are provided in the manual.

DEVELOPMENT. Very little information was provided regarding how the test was developed. The choice of the eight areas (i.e., fine motor, visual motor, etc.) does not appear to be guided by any particular theoretical framework nor by any explicit consensual professional standards. The author alluded to the work of Arnold Gesell and to the Denver Developmental Screening Test, but did not clarify whether the DRS-R is based on either of these two frameworks. It appears that many potential items had been developed for each of the eight areas of interest. The final 56 items were then selected from these items based on four criteria: (a) the behavior must appear at the specified developmental age, (b) the item had to support a hierarchy of development, (c) the task must have "child appeal," and (d) at least 65% of the children at the designated age level must be able to complete the task successfully. No information was provided as to what standards were used to determine if a given item had indeed met any of the first three criteria, nor which particular hierarchy of development was used for the second criterion.

TECHNICAL. To determine the developmental age of each item, a national sample of more than 2,500 children was used. The date of the norming study was not reported but is likely to have been sometime in the 1980s. The sample appears to be representative of the nation in terms of race, gender, and family structure of the time. Based on this sample, the percentage of children in each chronological age category passing each item was calculated. The developmental age of an item is determined/verified by having more than 65% of the children in the corresponding chronological age passing the item.

Reliability of DRS-R scores was estimated based on a test-retest (2-week interval) strategy using a sample of 87 children. However, no conventional reliability coefficient, standard error of measurement, informational function, nor any common indices of individual score precision were reported. Instead, a general group statistic indicating that the percentage of children passing each item in the retest was within 2 points of that of the first test was reported as an estimate of reliability.

No validation study was done specifically for the DRS-R. Three studies based on previous versions of the test were reported. The first two studies were based on the 1970 version of the test and the third study was based on either the 1970 or the 1982 version. The first study was done in 1970–1974 using a sample of more than 1,500 children. From this study, only a single outcome was reported: With the 1970 version, children whose developmental ages were 1 or more years below their chronological ages in at least three areas were considered "high risk." Of the approximately 200 children who fell into the high-risk category, 90 were administered either one of two general intelligence tests. None were found to score above the 50th percentile on the intelligence tests.

A second longitudinal follow-up study was also done by following an unspecified number of children to examine their scores on an achievement test when they were in the third/fourth grade. Again, only a single outcome was reported: Of the children who scored below 1.1 grade level on the Reading Readiness portion of the 1970 version of the scale at the end of their kindergarten year, 92% were found to be 6 months or more behind in the reading portion of the later achievement test.

The author also reported a national study had been done in 1985 involving 1,336 children ages 3.0 to 8.4. Yet no results from this study were reported in the manual. In any event, the 1985 study appears to aim at norming and not validation. The results were used to guide a 1986 expansion of the test. It can also be inferred that the 1985 study was based on the 1982 revised version of the test.

COMMENTARY. Overall, given the information provided in the manual, the DRS-R has yet to meet basic professional standards of quality. The user manual is strong on how to administer the test and weak on why. The content, procedures, scoring, and interpretation appear to represent the personal, albeit professional, opinions of the author, rather than independently verifiable results or professional consensus.

There is no particular theory, consensus, literature, or evidence provided to suggest that the particular eight areas measured are appropriate, meaningful, or useful dimensions of kindergarten readiness. In fact, there is some evidence that the author was inconsistent with the only explicit reference to external considerations discussed. Specifically, the author observed that kindergartens are becoming more academically oriented. Yet, the portion of items in the test devoted to academic readiness was made optional and is not one of the core areas. There was no formal step, either judgmental or statistical, to safeguard that the seven items chosen for each of the eight areas are indeed relevant and representative of that particular area.

The scoring system relies entirely on an age-equivalent score concept. The procedure used to derive age-equivalent scores, however, was not a standard one and appears to be somewhat arbitrary. Specifically, the developmental age of an item is determined by having at least 65% of the children in a particular chronological age category passing the item. Yet the implementation of this criterion is not consistent. For example, 68% of the children with chronological ages of 4.6–4.11 in the sample had passed the item called "visual motor—EACH" and the item was thus given a developmental age-equivalent score of 4.6–4.11. On the other hand, 68% of the children with chronological ages of 3.6-3.11 had passed another item called "fine motor—cuts line." Yet this item was given a developmental age-equivalent score of 4.0–4.5.

No solution or procedural safeguards were offered against the numerous known problems that have plagued age- and grade-equivalent scores for decades. Furthermore, age-equivalent scores are quite sensitive to the representativeness of the norming sample. The date when the norming data were collected was not reported but appears to be in the 1980s. Although the particular sample used might be representative of U.S. population in the 1980 Census, it is unlikely to be representative of children today. For example, 84% of the children in the sample lived in households headed by two parents. According to the 2000 Census, only 24% of U.S. households today consist of children under 18 headed by married couples. Therefore, there is a good chance that the age-equivalent score for each of the items is not consistent with children today.

Some of the scoring schemes are clearly arbitrary and questionable. For example, academic readiness was assigned grade-equivalent scores based on the combined sum of the numbers of upper-case letters and words recognized. Starting from recognizing 1–3 letters/words, which is given a grade-equivalent score of K.1, for each additional 2 letters/words recognized, a child is given an additional month of score. Thus, recognizing 4–5 letters/words would be K.2 and recognizing 6–7 letters/words would be K.3 and so on. This implies an assumption that of the 34 letters/words, a child will learn 2 every month. This is not only arbitrary and inappropriate, but also implies a concept of child development that is linear and uniform along time.

Reliability was estimated using a group statistic that is, in fact, not a measure of reliability at all. The author reported that the percentages of children passing each item did not differ by more than 2% between test and retest. There is no evidence that the same children passed both times. Minimally, a proportion agreement index or a kappa coefficient would have been more informative. As it is, the reliabilities of the scores are in fact unknown.

Very little evidence of validity was offered and the little evidence provided was not relevant to DRS-R. The single result of the first study essentially provided some preliminary support for the utility of the categorization of "high risk." However, the study was based on data obtained using the 1970 version of the test. Further, the categorization of high risk is no longer used in the DRS-R. Thus, the result of this study is not relevant to DRS-R. The single result of the second study provided partial evidence to demonstrate that the Reading Readiness subscale *grade-equivalent* scores based on an earlier version of the test were somewhat predictive of later reading scores on achievement tests. Yet the Reading Readiness score is not used in the DRS-R. Additionally, the results of the second study investigated the predictive power of the grade-equivalent scores. The DRS-R does not use grade-equivalent scores. Therefore, again, this particular study is not relevant to the DRS-R. A third study was mentioned, but the results, which were not reported at all, appear to have been used internally for formative purposes only. No evidence of validity from this study was offered. A new feature in the DRS-R called *QuickScreen* was explicitly described by the author as reliable and valid, yet no evidence of either was offered.

Issues of potential gender, cultural, primary language spoken at home, and other forms of bias were not addressed at all. The test offered no evidence of freedom from bias nor any procedural safeguard against bias. For example, the passing rates for many of the 56 items are drastically different between boys and girls (e.g., 61% vs. 84%). No attempt was made to explain these differences. Are these inherent gender differences or are the items biased? It would have been useful had possible biases along this and other factors

been investigated through at least a sensitivity review, if not formal DIF analyses. As is, we have no idea if the DRS-R leads to biased results at all, although there is clear evidence of adverse impact at least along gender lines.

Finally, the author offered detailed explicit lists of score-based educational implications. These implications suggest diagnostic uses of the screening test. In the absence of any evidence of clinical utility, these implications can only be considered personal opinions of the author based on the author's professional experience. The possible consequences of using these diagnostic implications broadly are unknown.

SUMMARY. In the absence of meaningful evidence, the quality of scores and decisions based on the DRS-R can be described as unknown at best. The test seems to be an expression of the author's personal view, with little external objective corroboration. The use of instruments with unknown qualities is inherently risky, unethical and potentially harmful. The use of the DRS-R for actual screening purposes should await appropriate evidence to support minimally its scoring, reliability, validity and freedom from bias.

Review of the Developmental Readiness Scale— Revised by KATHRYN E. HOFF, Assistant Professor, Department of Psychology, Illinois State University, Normal, IL, and MARK E. SWERDLIK, Professor Department of Psychology, Illinois State University, Normal, IL:

DESCRIPTION. The Developmental Readiness Scale—Revised (DRS-R) is an individual screening instrument designed to evaluate kindergarten entry for children aged 3 to 6. The DRS-R consists of 56 items measuring a child's developmental level in eight areas: Fine Motor, Visual Motor, Numbers, Concepts, Body Image, Language, Personal-Social, and Gross Motor. Also included are an optional "academic readiness" indicator (measuring numeral and letter recognition and word attack skills) and a 24-task Quick Screen (to identify children who need further evaluation). The DRS-R serves multiple purposes. The DRS-R can be used as a screening tool to identify children who require additional assessment, assess the child's "place in the sequence of development" (manual, p. 85), create an educational program at a child's developmental level, and for assessing school readiness.

The DRS-R can be administered and scored by school personnel and takes approximately 30–40 minutes to complete. The test kit is composed of an examiner's manual, individual response form, parent feedback form, and manipulatives. The tasks children are required to complete are similar to those of other developmental assessments; however, some activities rely heavily on motor activities and may not be suitable for children with motor difficulties (e.g., physical disability). Information regarding test administration and scoring is straightforward and easy to follow. In general, the manual is well organized and provides useful scoring examples that assist the examiner in making scoring determinations. The examiner starts with the General Questions, and then assesses one content area at a time (e.g., all Fine Motor). Testing begins "just below" the child's chronological age. If the child does not answer these items correctly, the examiner proceeds in reverse order until the child has passed two consecutive items. If the child answers the initial items correctly, testing is continued until the child fails two consecutive items. Norm tables are included for the total sample and separated by gender. The table includes the percentage of children passing a specific task for a target age, and also the percentage of children passing the task at the next lower and higher age level. The tables extend from age 3.6–6.11.

The author notes that interpretation does not require professional training but the examiner should understand the concept of developmental age. Guidance is not provided for specific interpretation of results; however, the author recommends an analysis of "the child's strengths and weaknesses in order to make realistic recommendations for the child's educational program …. If there are 'gaps' in the child's performance the examiner should determine why" (manual, p. 84). The interpretation section includes possible reasons a child may exhibit a deficit and lists educational implications for delays in the specific content area. These suggestions seem to go beyond the data produced by the DRS-R. The manual includes a checklist of the behaviors for the examiner to look for when screening and useful administration suggestions, such as building rapport, structuring the testing session, and praising the child's effort. Including a brief parent feedback form allows the examiner to easily communicate the results to the school and family.

The primary weakness is the lack of clarity between the assessment guidelines given in the manual and the administration conditions of the norm group. For example, the author states that it is not necessary to administer the eight general areas in the order they appear in the response booklet, and that questions may be "repeated or rephrased" (manual, p. 17) unless there are explicit instructions not to do so. The author also states that a quiet area is essential and that the parent may be in the testing room with the child. In no area is the examiner required to note these changes on the test booklet. Unfortunately, it is not clear under which conditions the standardization sample completed the test. For example, if children in the sample completed the test in a different order with parents there and questions were rephrased, different results may have been obtained. Additionally, there is little information regarding the Quick Screen option, such as under what circumstances should one administer the Quick Screen?

DEVELOPMENT. The development of the DRS-R was guided by needs created for assessing school readiness and education planning. According to the manual, the original Developmental Readiness Scale was created by a school psychologist in 1970 to identify children who are ready to begin school, in need of additional assistance, or require additional in-depth testing. The Developmental Readiness Scale was in part created because many instruments assessing child development at that time were not adequate for use in kindergarten screenings or to assess school readiness. The Developmental Readiness Scale—Revised represents a revision of the original DRS.

Items for the DRS-R are similar to the original DRS; however, the author indicates that some items on the DRS-R were modified from the original Developmental Readiness Scale ("preserve the best features … eliminate those items test users found cumbersome, outdated, or unfair"); however, the author notes that the content is "basically unchanged" (manual, p. 8). The author indicated the criteria for item selection were the following: "developmentally the behavior had to appear at the age specified; the item had to support a hierarchy of development or represent a learned behavior necessary for independent functioning; the tasks had to have 'child appeal to maintain interest while accomplishing the desired result'; and all items had to be passed by 65–75%

of children at the designated age level" (manual, p. 8). No additional information is presented for the selection of items, why certain items were included, who determined the criteria, or the relevancy of items to other indicators. This is a limitation, as the author indicates the eight skill areas represented in the DRS-R are skills "considered necessary for success at the kindergarten level" (manual, p. 5).

TECHNICAL. Information on the standardization sample is limited and the representativeness of the sample cannot be determined. The manual indicates "more than 2500 children" were included in the standardization sample; however, the specific number, ages, or abilities of children (e.g., prior preschool experience or the presence of a disability) included in the sample are not provided. The manual indicates that the racial and geographical distribution of participants reflected the U.S. Census data; however, additional data are needed. For example, the author does not provide data as to how the sample relates to the census data, socioeconomic norms are not included, and the specific number of males or females representing the various ethnic/racial groups is not included. The standardization sample was fairly equally distributed between males and females, and data are included on the family arrangement of participants (number of parents child is living with and placement of the child within the family constellation). The specific methods for standardization are unclear (e.g., recruitment of students, qualifications of the examiners, length of time to administer the test).

Interrater reliability data were collected with a subsample of 87 children; however, specific information regarding the demographics of children in the subsample is lacking and the representativeness of the sample cannot be determined. Students were re-administered the DRS-R 2–4 weeks after initial administration of the DRS-R. The author indicates that the results of the second testing session were within two percentage points of the percentages obtained on the first administration; however, reliability coefficients are not reported. The author purports that the Quick Screen provides a reliable indicator of a child's performance; however, reliability data on the Quick Screen are not provided.

Validity data supporting the use of the DRS-R are not provided. Although the author purports various uses of the DRS-R including screening, educational planning, and assessment of school readiness, there are no data provided for performance on the DRS-R and other indicators (e.g., actual school performance, correlation with school readiness measures). This represents a significant limitation, especially if decisions are to be made concerning whether a child is ready to enter kindergarten. The author does describe the results of comparing the DRS with other measures in the 1970s; however, these data do not pertain to the DRS-R and no equivalency data comparing the DRS and the DRS-R are provided. Validity data supporting the use of the Quick Screen are not presented.

COMMENTARY. The stated purposes for the DRS-R are confusing for a test user, as they are not consistently stated throughout the manual. For example, the author indicates "the purpose of the DRS-R is to find the child's place in the sequence of development, share the results with the parent, and provide meaningful activities appropriate to the maturity of the child" (manual, p. 85). In other places the author discusses using the DRS-R to assess school readiness. For example, school readiness is referred to in the manual and the examiner records what grade the child is "developmentally ready for" on the Developmental Readiness Report, a one-page form used to convey the child's assessment results to his or her parents. This is of concern, as reliability and validity evidence for the various uses of the test scores is not provided. Additionally, limitations of determining developmental age or school readiness are not addressed in the manual; however, the author does provide the examiner some criteria for school readiness. The author states in the manual that school readiness should not be determined based on one subtest of the DRS-R and indicates that a child may still be ready for school despite a low developmental age on the DRS-R.

SUMMARY. The Developmental Readiness Scale—Revised represents an individual measure for assessing kindergarten readiness and educational planning. Although the manual is useful and the test is user-friendly, validity evidence is lacking and the purported uses of this test are unsubstantiated. The standardization sample and the samples on which the conclusion of adequate reliability is based also are limited. Due to poor psychometric properties, the DRS-R is not adequate for decision making or educational planning purposes.

[81]
Devereux Early Childhood Assessment.

Purpose: "To assess preschool children's protective factors and behavioral concerns."
Population: Ages 2–5.
Publication Date: 1999.
Acronym: DECA.
Scores, 5: Initiative, Self-Control, Attachment, Total Protective Factors, Behavioral Concerns.
Administration: Individual.
Price Data, 2002: $199.95 per kit including 40 record forms, user's guide (65 pages), technical manual (42 pages), classroom strategies guide, 20 parent guides, and classroom observation journal in a carrying case.
Foreign Language Edition: Parent guides and record forms also available in Spanish.
Time: (10) minutes.
Comments: Ratings by teachers and parents.
Authors: Paul A. LeBuffe and Jack A. Naglieri.
Publisher: Kaplan Companies, Inc.

Review of the Devereux Early Childhood Assessment by ERIC S. BUHS, Assistant Professor, Educational Psychology, University of Nebraska—Lincoln, Lincoln, NE:

DESCRIPTION. The Devereux Early Childhood Assessment (DECA) is a four-subscale, 37-item observation-based behavior rating instrument intended to assess within-child protective factors in preschool children aged 2 to 5 years. This standardized, norm-referenced paper-and-pencil measure rates children's behavior using parents, family caregivers, and/or early childhood professionals as raters. The stated purposes of the DECA are to identify children who are low on protective factors or exhibiting behavioral concerns so that they may be targeted for interventions, to generate profiles of classroom groups that teachers may use to inform instructional practice, and to assist early childhood programs in measuring progress and performance. Test materials include a list of Head Start Performance Standards that are evaluated by the DECA.

The measure consists of 37 items indexing children's adaptive and problem behaviors. Behaviors are rated on a 5-point frequency scale by observers with "sufficient exposure to the child" (user's guide, p. 9; i.e., a minimum of 2 hours/day, 2 days/week over the preceding 4 weeks). The DECA includes three Protective Factor scales (Initiative, Self-Control, Attachment), as well as a Behavioral Concerns scale. The three Protective Factor scale scores are summed to create an overall score. Interpretive guidelines are provided.

The DECA instrument is part of the Devereux Early Childhood Initiative (DECI) program. An evaluation of the DECI is beyond the scope of this review, but it is important to note that this instrument was developed, in part, to provide practitioners and parents with data that serve as a basis for development of intervention strategies to foster resilience in the home and preschool, and for long-term follow-up of children's social and emotional health.

DEVELOPMENT. The DECA was developed during 1996–98 and the version evaluated here is the first published version (DECA, 1999). As a measure of child protective factors, the DECA is unique as a commercially produced assessment. The conceptual basis of the instrument is rooted in research on children's development that describes protective factors as originating within the child and the surrounding environment (e.g., child X environment models; Garmezy, Masten, & Tellegen, 1984).

The developers drew the initial item pool from the research literature on resilience and from work with focus groups composed of parents and early childhood professionals. In the Protective Factors scales the authors identified groups of items that represent within-child protective characteristics as described by their focus groups and the empirical research. The Behavioral Concerns items were a subset of items from the Devereux Scales of Mental Disorders (Naglieri, LeBuffe, & Pfeiffer, 1994). The pool of items selected was intended to tap directly observable behaviors characteristic of resilient children as well as emotional and behavioral problems.

The developers used exploratory factor analyses to derive the Protective Factor scales from the larger pool of items administered to their standardization samples. Their analyses yielded three factors that they retained, though no indication was given as to the total number of factors initially derived, the precise criteria used for omission of factors from final analyses, the content of discarded factors/items, or the proportion of variance explained by the factors they retained. The three Protective Factors retained were labeled Initiative (11 items), Self-Control (8 items), and Attachment (8 items). The Protective Factor scale descriptions provided are conceptually distinct and the included items seem to address distinct and cohesive sets of behaviors. The 10-item Behavioral Concerns scale was distilled from a pool of 77 items drawn from the Devereux Scales of Mental Disorders (Naglieri, LeBuffe, & Pfeiffer, 1994). The authors state only that items were selected, "based on both their psychometric properties and their representation of a wide range of challenging behaviors" (technical manual, p. 12).

One weakness of the development of the Protective Factors scales was the failure of the developers to list, a priori, the specific target constructs their items were intended to tap. The literature on children's resiliency is well developed and the authors could have provided users with the specific constructs they felt might be key protective factors and described the role these constructs play in children's resilient responses to stress. For example, although the developers provide clear support for the expectation that their attachment construct would be represented in their factors and for the subsequent role they expect attachment to play in their interventions, the initiative and self-control constructs do not receive a similar treatment and thus the factors appeared to be more data driven.

TECHNICAL. The DECA was piloted and normed during 1997 and 1998, using two national samples ($N = 2,000$ and $N = 1,108$) composed of children aged 2 to 6 years. Preschool teachers and parents completed early versions of the DECA containing 130 items. Detailed descriptive/demographic statistics regarding the representativeness of the standardization samples are provided and the sample appeared to be a good fit to the targeted population (i.e., U.S. preschool children). The sample includes children from underrepresented ethnic and racial groups roughly in proportion to the U.S. population.

Reliability. The authors evaluated internal reliability of the scales using Cronbach's alpha and obtained acceptable values from the norming sample data for both parent and teacher raters, ranging from .71 to .94. Test-retest correlations over a 24–72 hour period indicated that teachers were more consistent raters than parents. Teacher ratings on the Protective Factors ranged from .87 to .91, whereas parents' scores ranged from .55 to .80. Correlations for the Behavioral Concerns scale were lower, at .55 for parents and .68 for teacher ratings.

Interrater reliability was also examined on a subsample of children using parent and teacher raters (teacher-teacher, teacher-parent, and parent-parent pairs). Teacher-teacher pairs, rating children at the same time, demonstrated reliability coefficients of .57–.77 on the scale scores. Parent-teacher pairs and parent-parent pairs who did not observe the children at the same time, demonstrated lower values ranging from .19 to .44. These relatively low values for the parent ratings raise the concern that the measure may be functioning more reliably when used as a teacher-rated or school-based assessment. Although lower correlations on the interrater scores are expected when observers evaluate behaviors at different times and in different contexts, the results suggest caution in interpreting the parent-generated scores. Many of the behaviors described by items are likely to occur more frequently in the preschool context (e.g., interactions with peers) and thus may give observers in that setting a more representative sample for their ratings.

Validity. The developers examined the validity of the DECA through criterion- and construct-related evidence. Children from a representative subsample, identified as having emotional or behavioral problems ($N = 95$), scored lower on all Protective Factors scales and higher on the Behavioral Concerns scale than a normative sample ($N = 86$). Additionally, DECA Protective Factor scores correctly predicted individuals' group membership for 67% of the risk group subsample and 71% of the normative subsample. Children's Behavioral Concerns scores correctly predicted sample membership for 78% of the risk group and 65% of the normative subsample. Stress/risk inventories for the validity sample were also completed by parents and these scores were used to examine construct-related validity. Results were consistent with those predicted by resiliency theory (i.e., lower risk/stress and higher protective factor scores were associated with lower Behavioral Concerns scores).

Although the authors imply that protective factors play a causal role in adjustment (i.e., higher levels of protective factors lead to lower behavioral problems) within stressful circumstances, it is important to note that these concurrent analyses cannot rule out other likely possibilities. There is the distinct possibility that levels of behavioral problems may indicate children's existing behavioral orientations that foster or hinder access to social resources or secure attachments that, in turn, support the development of protective factors. The developers also chose to rely on parent ratings for all scores in this set of analyses, thus increasing the probability of shared variance problems.

COMMENTARY. The materials the developers provide present a reasonable level of detail regarding the conceptual and empirical foundations of the DECA. The definitions of the Protective Factor scales describe distinct behavioral categories that have a relatively well-developed level of support within the literature on young children's resiliency and adjustment. Close relationships with adults (Attachment) have generally been viewed as relational contexts that support adjustment and children's self-directed behaviors (Initiative) and emotional or behavior control (Self-Control) are also valued by teachers and other adults as adaptive aspects of children's behavior (e.g., Birch & Ladd, 1997; Wentzel, 1991).

In spite of this level of support for the DECA constructs within the literature, however, the authors do not define the role of their constructs in supporting or hindering adjustment as clearly as they might have. This is a relatively minor point in relation to the overall technical quality of the DECA instrument, but becomes more significant when viewed in relation to the DECI interventions. Models of adaptation, such as those presented by Masten and colleagues (e.g., Masten, Best, & Garmezy, 1991, as cited in the DECA user's guide) stress the interaction of child characteristics with those of the social environment in which they function. The user's guide would benefit from a more precise description of the role the constructs represented by the Protective Factor scales play in shaping these interactions and affecting adjustment outcomes.

SUMMARY. The developers have published a useful behavioral assessment targeted at identifying the strengths or adaptive characteristics of young children. The DECA is quick and reliable for early childhood practitioners to use and requires minimal training to administer and score. Interpretation guidelines are thorough, contain appropriate cautionary language, and seem likely to provide effective means for giving constructive feedback to parents and practitioners. The scores obtained from parent raters (vs. observers in the preschool setting), as the authors note, may require more caution in interpretation and use. In future editions of the DECA, the authors may wish to present a more detailed and explicit model of the role the child characteristics represented by the DECA scales may play in fostering children's adjustment.

REVIEWER'S REFERENCES
Birch, S. H., & Ladd, G. W. (1997). The teacher-child relationship and children's early school adjustment. *Journal of School Psychology, 35,* 61–79.
Garmezy, N., Masten, A. S., & Tellegen, A. (1984). The study of stress and competence in children: A building block for developmental psychopathology. *Child Development, 55,* 97–111.
Masten, A., Best, K., & Garmezy, N. (1991). Resilience and development: Contributions from the study of children who overcome adversity. *Development and Psychopathology, 2,* 425–444.
Naglieri, J. A., LeBuffe, P. A., & Pfeiffer, S. I. (1994). *Devereux Scales of Mental Disorders manual.* San Antonio: The Psychological Corporation.
Wentzel, K. R. (1991). Social competence at school: Relation between responsibility and academic achievement. *Review of Educational Research, 61,* 1–24.

Review of the Devereux Early Childhood Assessment by MARY "RINA" M. CHITTOORAN, Associate Professor of Educational Studies, Saint Louis University, St. Louis, MO:

DESCRIPTION. The Devereux Early Childhood Assessment (DECA) is a standardized, norm-referenced behavior rating scale that uses parent and teacher ratings to evaluate within-child protective factors in preschoolers that are associated with resilience and positive life outcomes. The DECA includes three Protective Factors scales: Initiative, Self-control, and Attachment; an overall Total Protective Factors Scale; and a Behavioral Concerns Scale, which assesses problem behaviors thought to be associated with negative life outcomes. The major purposes of the DECA are to: (a) identify strengths and weaknesses in protective factors within young children, (b) generate classroom profiles of children's strengths prior to instruction, and (c) screen children who exhibit incipient problem behaviors.

The DECA is intended for use by classroom teachers and administrators. Training requirements for administration, scoring, and interpretation are minimal. Ratings can be completed in about 10 minutes by parents and teachers who have a sixth-grade reading level and who "have contact with the child for two or more hours for at least two days per week for a four week period" (user's guide, p. 9). The rater responds to 37 items that evaluate the frequency of 27 positive behaviors and 10 problem behaviors by answering questions such as, "During the past 4 weeks, how often did the child …" "make decisions for himself/herself?" "have temper tantrums?" and by checking options such as *Never, Rarely, Occasionally, Frequently,* or *Very Frequently.*

The protocol includes a detachable, carbon-backed rating form that allows the rater's checkmarks to be transferred automatically to a scoring form beneath. Examiners may plot scores graphically on the individual profile or may use the provided norms tables to convert raw scores to T-scores (Mean = 50; SD = 10) and percentile ranks. Interpretation guidelines suggest that T-scores of 40 and below on the Protective Factors scales indicate a concern, those between 41 and 59 are typical, and those of 60 and above indicate a strength. On the Behavioral Concerns scale, T-scores of 60 and above indicate a concern. The user's manual also addresses advanced interpretive techniques such as cross-scale and cross-rater comparisons as well as longitudinal comparisons on a particular child.

DEVELOPMENT. Initial development of test items occurred through an examination of the literature on resilience and through focus groups with preschool teachers and parents who were asked to identify positive behaviors in children who were doing well or were likely to do well and problem behaviors in children who were likely to have difficulties. Early in 1997, a pilot study of scale items resulted in the development of Form A, with 53 items related to within-child protective factors, and Form B, which included the same 53 items and an additional 77 items related to problem behaviors. An exploratory factor analysis yielded a three-factor solution that best described the data and that corresponded with the three Protective Factors scales.

TECHNICAL. The DECA was standardized during fall 1997 and spring 1998 using two stratified samples that reflected demographic proportions identified in the 1996 U.S. Census; 51% were males and 49% were females, one quarter came from families of low socioeconomic status, and all major ethnic groups were represented. Subjects were tested at 95 sites in 28 states in four geographic regions: Northeast, Midwest, South, and West. Preschool teachers and parents from preschool programs and those who responded to advertisements served as raters during standardization.

The DECA Protective Factors sample consisted of 2,000 children between the ages of 2 and 6 years. Teachers provided ratings on 1,017 children, and parents provided ratings on 983 children. Ratings were obtained on both Forms A and B; however, these were combined into one data set for all analyses as results did not indicate any meaningful age-related changes across the 2- through 6-year age span. The DECA Behavioral Concerns sample consisted of 1,108 children between the ages of 2 and 6 years who were rated on Form B.

The internal consistency of the DECA was measured using Cronbach's alpha. Reliability coefficients ranged from .91 for parent raters to .94 for teacher raters on the Total Protective Factors scale and from .71 for parent raters to .90 for teacher raters on the Behavioral Concerns scale. A median of .80 for parents and .88 for teachers was obtained across all scales. Test-retest reliabilities over a 24–72 hour period were calculated for a group of 26 parents, with coefficients ranging from .55 to .80; reliabilities ranging from .68 to .94 were also calculated for a group of 82 teachers. The interrater reliability of the DECA was established by comparing ratings of children between teacher-teacher aide pairs, parent pairs, and parent-teacher pairs. Correlations ranged from a low of .19 between parent and teacher on the Attachment scale to a high of .77 between teacher and teacher's aide on the Self-control scale. Generally, interrater reliabilities between teachers and their aides were the highest, ranging from a low of .57 to a high of .77, and were significant at the .01 level. Standard errors of measurement ranged from 2.97 for parents on the Total Protective Factors scale to 2.39 for teachers on the same scale; however, an evaluation of standard errors of measurement on individual scales suggests that the test is most reliable when used by teachers and when it is used to assess total protective factors rather than behavioral concerns.

Content validity was established by selecting items for inclusion based on a review of the literature and comments from focus groups of parents and teachers. Criterion-related validity was demonstrated in several ways: The DECA was able to satisfactorily discriminate between the scores of a clinical sample of 95 children and a community sample of 86 children; it did not differentiate between children of different races because this factor is irrelevant to the purpose of the DECA; and finally, it was able to correctly classify 69% of children into clinical or nonreferred groups. Construct validity was explored by comparing scores on the Total Protective Factors scale and the Behavioral Concerns scale; an overall correlation of -.65 was obtained, showing a desirable and expected inverse relationship between protective factors and problem behaviors.

COMMENTARY. The DECA is grounded in the theory on resilience, a relatively new area of study that has engendered considerable interest in the aftermath of increasing accounts of stress among school children. The authors emphasize the critical link between assessment and intervention, stress the importance of primary prevention with young children, and use a holistic, strength-based approach to working with students at risk. The test is also based on developmentally appropriate practices as outlined by the National Association for the Education of Young Children.

Test development, as described in the user's guide and technical manual, appears to have been based on careful forethought and planning. Standardization samples have been systematically selected to conform to the general population, internal consistency is excellent, and test-retest reliability, particularly on the Total Protective Factors scales with teachers, is superior. Interrater reliability is moderately good when the test is used to evaluate protective factors across raters in the same setting (e.g., teachers in the school setting). Content and construct validity appear to be satisfactory and criterion-related validity is superior, particularly as it relates to differentiation between clinical and nonclinical samples. Items on the DECA are generally easy to read and interpret, and examples have been provided in the case of potentially problematic items. Administration, scoring, and interpretation are facilitated by the two-part protocol, the inclusion of a glossary, sample completed protocols, and examples of profile patterns that display varying levels of risk.

Despite these positive features, the following issues are of some concern. The technical manual does not include any mention of exceptional children in either of the standardization samples. Moreover, the use of volunteer parent raters during standardization, although understandable, is problematic. The DECA could also be improved by the addition of a greater number of items addressing each of the protective factors. Interrater reliability across settings is rather low and that between sets of parents is lower still; although such ratings typically show greater variability than those obtained by similar raters in the same setting, they do suggest a need for additional studies in this area, not only by the test authors, but by independent sources. The test protocol is flimsy and likely to tear. It also appears that clarity and readability have been sacrificed for economy on the profile form. Although the authors state that items can be read to raters with limited English proficiency, they do not address the historic difficulty of obtaining oral ratings, in general, or from those who speak minimal English, in particular. Quantifiers could have been provided for ratings such as Occasionally and Frequently, both of which are subject to varying interpretations. Ratings based on children's behaviors in the "past four weeks" may be misleading and may result in false positives as well as false negatives; such inaccuracies may be obviated by repeating ratings on several occasions and by supplementing them, if possible, with independent behavioral observations in both home and school settings. Finally, there is little longitudinal research to support the relationship between protective factors and positive outcomes; it is possible, therefore, that further studies in the area of resilience could significantly influence the utility of the DECA.

SUMMARY. The DECA is the first published measure of its kind and is a useful addition to the growing arsenal of tools available to assess social-behavioral functioning in young children. It is theory-based, psychometrically sound, demands minimal training and time for administration and interpretation, and links assessment to intervention. The DECA probably should not be used for eligibility decisions in special education and caution is suggested with regard to parent ratings of behavioral concerns in their children. On the other hand, it is highly recommended as a measure of protective factors in preschoolers when ratings are made by teachers in school settings, when it is used as an adjunct to other measures of social-behavioral functioning, and when results are used in program planning.

[82]

Diagnostic Achievement Battery, Third Edition.

Purpose: Designed "to assess children's abilities in listening, speaking, reading, writing, and mathematics."
Population: Ages 6-0 to 14-11.
Publication Dates: 1984–2001.
Acronym: DAB-3.
Scores, 22: 14 subtest scores (Story Comprehension, Characteristics, Synonyms, Grammatic Completion, Alphabet/Word Knowledge, Reading Comprehension, Capitalization, Punctuation, Spelling, Writing: Contextual Language, Writing: Story Construction, Mathematics Reasoning, Mathematics Calculation, Phonemic Analysis) and 8 composite scores (Listening,

Speaking, Reading, Writing, Mathematics, Spoken Language, Written Language, Total Achievement).
Administration: Individual.
Price Data, 2003: $251 per complete kit including manual (2001, 152 pages), student booklet, 25 profile/examiner's record booklets, 25 student response booklets, assessment probes, and audiotape; $109 per software kit including manual and CD-ROM; $71 per manual; $40 per 25 student response booklets; $56 per 25 profile/examiner's record booklets; $40 per student booklet; $15 per audiotape; $35 per assessment probes.
Time: (90–120) minutes.
Author: Phyllis Newcomer.
Publisher: PRO-ED.
Cross References: See T5:821 (2 references); for reviews by Jean-Jacques Bernier and Martine Hébert and by Ric Brown of an earlier edition, see 12:114 (2 references); see also T4:774 (1 reference); for a review by William J. Webster of the original edition, see 9:333.

Review of the Diagnostic Achievement Battery, Third Edition by MICHAEL B. BUNCH, Vice President, Measurement Incorporated, Durham, NC:

DESCRIPTION. The Diagnostic Achievement Battery, Third Edition (DAB-3) is a "standardized norm-referenced multi area achievement test with components that are individually administered and some components that may be group administered" (examiner's manual, p. 3). The 14 subtests are grouped into five composites and a Total Achievement score: Listening (Story Comprehension, Characteristics), Speaking (Synonyms, Grammatic Completion), Reading (Alphabet/Word Knowledge, Reading Comprehension), Writing (Capitalization, Punctuation, Spelling, Contextual Language, Story Construction), and Mathematics (Reasoning, Calculation). Listening and Speaking combine to form Spoken Language, and Reading and Writing combine to form Written Language. The Phonemic Analysis subtest is supplemental and is meant to help examiners identify deficits related to children's spoken language and reading problems.

The examiner reads most of the test aloud to an individual child. The examiner simultaneously records responses in a Profile/Examiner Record Booklet. There is a separate Student Response Booklet for the following subtests: Capitalization and Punctuation, Spelling, Contextual Language, Story Construction, and Calculation.

Each subtest consists of 25 to 65 separate short-answer items. However, children do not respond to all the items. Items are arranged in increasing level of difficulty. Children younger than age 9 start at Item 1, whereas children 9 or older start at Item 11 or some other more advanced location. Procedures for establishing floors and ceilings (starting and stopping places) are carefully explained in the examiner's manual. All items below the floor are counted as correct, whereas all items above the ceiling are counted as missed.

Assessment Probes is a supplemental booklet that provides scripts for probing incorrect answers. The scripts are built around questions that are meant to elicit either a correct response or a reason for the incorrect response. For example, if the child states that the mouse is bigger than the cat, the examiner asks, "Why do you think the mouse is big? What makes the mouse bigger?" By probing into the child's comprehension of the task, thought processes, and learning potential, the educator can make better informed recommendations about instruction. The responses to the probes do not affect scores; they are meant only to guide instruction.

The examiner's manual provides not only complete directions for administering and scoring the test but also instructions for interpreting the results. It provides information on norming, reliability, validity, and other technical and practical issues.

DEVELOPMENT. The DAB-3 follows the DAB (1984) and DAB-2 (1990). The original instrument was intended to identify academic achievement and eligibility of school-age children for special education services under the Education for All Handicapped Children Act of 1975 (PL 94-142) and now the Individuals with Disabilities Education Act (IDEA). The original DAB had essentially the same subtests as the DAB-3, except for Phonemic Analysis. The DAB-2 was nearly identical to the DAB except for the addition of the *Assessment Probes*. The DAB-3 follows the same model as the DAB and DAB-2.

The examiner's manual describes in some detail the nature and rationale for item development and selection for each of the 14 subtests and for combining subtest scores into composites. Reading level is controlled by the use of Thorndike and Lorge's (1944) and Wepman and Hass's (1969) graded word lists. Mathematics items are designed to assess standards promulgated by the National Council of Teachers of Mathematics (NCTM, 1995).

TECHNICAL. Norms for the DAB-3 are based on a sample of 1,094 children ranging in age from 6 to 14, typically 115–130 at each age. The sample closely resembles the population of the United States in terms of geography, gender, ethnicity, income, parental education, and disability. Percentile ranks and standard scores are provided for all subtests. Appendices provide conversions of composite scores to percentiles and standard scores and conversions of subtest scores to age and grade equivalents.

Reliability information is provided for all subtests by age and across ages. Total Achievement reliability is quite high, ranging from .98 to .99 for all ages. Few composites have alpha coefficients below .90, and most subtests have alpha coefficients in the low .80s to the mid .90s for every age group. Test-retest reliability coefficients, based on two samples each with 35 children, ranged from the low .70s to high .90s. Composite test-retest reliabilities ranged from .83 for Writing to .99 for Listening.

Validity evidence of several types is provided. Content validity evidence is offered in the form of thorough explanations of the rationale and development process for items in the individual subtests. Information about differential item functioning (DIF) is also offered, and it is quite favorable. Scores on the DAB-3 correlate moderately with their counterparts in the Stanford Achievement Test (Stanford 9) at the subtest level and strongly at the Total Achievement level. As one would expect from a wide-range test, there is a smooth progression of scores on all subtests from age 6 to age 14.

Confirmatory factor analyses support both a one-factor and a four-factor solution. The author treats the two solutions as equally viable. The four-factor solution results in uniformly larger unique subtest variances (i.e., those unaccounted for by the factors) than does the one-factor solution; therefore, the user may favor the one-factor solution.

COMMENTARY. The author and publisher appear to have paid close attention to earlier reviews and have attempted to address issues raised therein. It is therefore surprising, in light of earlier criticisms of sample size, that the DAB-3 has the smallest norming sample of the three editions. The original DAB was normed on a sample of 1,534 children in 13 states; the DAB-2 was normed on a sample of 2,623 children in 40 states. In contrast, the DAB-3 was normed on a sample of 1,094 children in 16 states.

The subtests appear to be valid and reliable measures of the constructs they address, and despite the size of the norming sample, the norms-based scores are reasonable. The DAB-3 seems to do all the things an achievement measure should do and to avoid the pitfalls often associated with such measures.

There is less to recommend the DAB-3 as a diagnostic tool, particularly when one examines closely the procedures involved in identifying strengths and weaknesses. The basic assumption seems to be that strengths and weaknesses are a function of the discrepancy between one subtest score and another. Much of the statistical treatment of difference scores is fairly acrobatic. In particular, the presentation of minimally significant differences between scores on the DAB-3 and scores on other tests is of dubious value, as it relies on an unsupported procedure for estimating the correlation between tests.

Although discrepancy analysis is one of the longest sections of the examiner's manual, no empirical findings are presented there. Given the fact that much of the content of the DAB-3 is identical to that of the DAB-2 and DAB, it would be quite appropriate to have reported results of research studies involving either predecessor as evidence of the efficacy of the score discrepancy approach to diagnosis that the author and publisher promote. A user might be better served by skipping this section of the examiner's manual and giving greater attention to the *Assessment Probes*. The *Probes*, although informal, are quite well constructed and promise to be a great help to classroom teachers and counselors who will ultimately make the diagnoses.

SUMMARY. The DAB-3 is a well-grounded and well-constructed achievement battery for children 6–14 years of age. The subtests have sufficient reliability and validity to give users confidence in the scores. Although the norming sample is quite small, it does appear to be adequate, and the norms smoothing procedures have produced a reasonable score progression across ages. As a diagnostic measure, the DAB-3 has less appeal, relying as it does on questionable statistical procedures and lacking research evidence to support discrepancy analysis. The *Assessment Probes*, intelligently used to supplement the subtests, may be the user's best diagnostic tool.

REVIEWER'S REFERENCES
National Council of Teachers of Mathematics. (1995). *Assessment standards for school mathematics*. Reston, VA: Author.
Thorndike, E. L., & Lorge, I. (1944). *The teacher's word book of 30,000 words.* New York: Teachers College, Columbia University.
Wepman, J. M., & Hass, W. (1969). *A spoken word count: Children—ages 5, 6, and 7.* Chicago: Language Research Associates.

Review of the Diagnostic Achievement Battery, Third Edition by CLEBORNE D. MADDUX, Professor of Counseling and Educational Psychology, University of Nevada, Reno, NV:

DESCRIPTION. The Diagnostic Achievement Battery, Third Edition (DAB-3) is a standardized, individual achievement test for children ages 6-0 through 14-11. The test is designed to measure achievement in Listening, Speaking, Reading, Writing, and Mathematics, the five areas (called "components" in the test) mandated by federal special education law. There are 13 subtests and 1 additional, supplementary test. The 13 subtests are Story Comprehension, Characteristics, Synonyms, Grammatic Completion, Alphabet/Word Knowledge, Reading Comprehension, Capitalization, Punctuation, Spelling, Writing—Contextual Language, Writing—Story Construction, Mathematics Reasoning, and Mathematics Calculation. The supplementary subtest is Phonemic Analysis.

The test is intended for individual administration, although the manual states that the subtests tapping math computation and writing skills can be administered in small groups. If individually administered, testing time is given as 90 to 120 minutes. Test materials furnished in kit form include a student test booklet, a student response booklet, an examiner record booklet, an audiotape, an examiner's manual, and a booklet containing assessment probes. Administration should be limited to those with formal training in assessment, including supervised practice in administering and scoring tests.

According to the examiner's manual, there are four goals for the instrument: (a) to identify students who are significantly below their peers in the areas of spoken language, written language, and mathematics; (b) to identify individual strengths and weaknesses; (c) to evaluate student progress after specific intervention programs; and (d) for use in research projects.

Subtest scores can be combined to produce composite scores for the five components listed above; for the three achievement domains of spoken language, written language, and mathematics; and for total achievement. Six types of scores can

be derived: raw scores; percentile ranks; subtest standard scores (mean of 10, standard deviation of 3); composite quotients (mean of 100, standard deviation of 15); age equivalents; and grade equivalents.

The test involves typical use of entry points, basals, and ceilings, with entry points either determined by the student's age or starting with the first item. Most basals consist of five consecutive correct responses, and ceilings consist of five consecutive errors.

The manual is exceptionally well-written. Every section is clear and complete. Instructions are so well done that they are a pleasure to read, and the entire manual could serve as a model for such publications.

DEVELOPMENT. The first edition of the test was published in 1984, and was followed by a revision in 1990. The current, third edition was published in 2001, and represents a substantial improvement over earlier versions. Major changes from the DAB-2 include addition of the phonemic analysis supplementary subtest; improvements and additions to reliability and validity data; additional normative data to accurately reflect population demographics; the division of the original writing composition subtest into two subtests; inclusion of an audiotape for use in the story comprehension subtest; and improvement of instructions for establishing entry items, basals, and ceilings. Other minor improvements have also been made.

TECHNICAL. The normative sample consisted of 1,094 persons in 16 states. Data were collected from 1997 through 2000. Very complete data on the sample are presented in the manual, including helpful tables comparing the geographic, gender, race, residence, ethnicity, family income, educational attainment, disability status, and age of the normative sample with those same characteristics in the school-age population at large. An additional table shows the demographic information stratified by age. These very complete data adequately demonstrate the representative nature of the normative sample.

Reliability data are presented in a separate chapter of the manual, and are very complete. Internal consistency was studied by calculating coefficient alpha for all subtests and composites at nine age intervals using data from the entire normative sample. Averages for these coefficient alphas are all .80 or higher (about one-third are .90 or higher), with the exception of the Mathematics

Reasoning subtest average, which was .77. To demonstrate reliability for specific subgroups of children, tables of coefficient alpha are presented for all subtests and composites for seven subgroups representing gender, racial, ethnic, linguistic, and disability categories. All are adequate to good. Test-retest reliability (2-week interval) is also presented for all subtests and composites and is also adequate to good, although only two very small samples of 30 and 35 children were used. Not surprisingly, interrater reliability values are excellent, given the objective nature of the test.

The manual includes extensive information relating to validity, beginning with content validity. A separate section in the manual addresses this topic for each subtest. Complete information concerning item analysis is furnished, and tables are included detailing item discrimination coefficients and item difficulties. Item bias was examined through differential item functioning analysis and revealed that less than 1% of the test items were potentially biased in regard to the groups studied. Concurrent validity evidence is provided by correlating subtest and composite scores of the DAB-3 with language, total reading, total math, and abbreviated battery scores of the Stanford Achievement Test—Ninth Edition. For the composite scores of the DAB-3, these correlations range from .49 to .84, with 75% of these coefficients ranging from .60 to .80.

COMMENTARY. This revision of the Diagnostic Achievement Battery represents a substantial improvement over previous editions. The test has been improved in numerous ways, and the normative sample has been brought up to date. Reliability and validity data are extensive, well-presented, and generally acceptable to good.

The manual is superior in every way, and could serve as a model for others developing test manuals. Instructions for administration are clear and concise, and items are engaging for children.

It is difficult to find anything to criticize severely about the DAB-3. One of the few legitimate criticisms of the test is related to its name. It could be argued that the test is not primarily a diagnostic test, but is more accurately a traditional, norm-referenced achievement test. Criterion-referenced tests might more accurately be considered as diagnostic tests. On the other hand, the test kit includes an excellent booklet containing assessment probes for comprehension, thought

processes, and learning potential. This booklet contains extensive probes for all 14 subtests, and an excellent chapter detailing administration procedures, as well as how the probes could be used. Those using the DAB-3 and the assessment probes might very well develop skill at using the instrument for diagnostic purposes.

SUMMARY. The DAB-3 is a well-constructed, impressive achievement battery. The manual is exceptionally complete and well-written, and the assessment probes are an interesting supplement to the test. Reliability and validity data are extensive and acceptable. The DAB-3 has the potential to replace other popular individual achievement tests for elementary-age children.

[83]
Diagnostic English Language Tests.

Purpose: Designed to measure "ability to cope with the English language demands of upper secondary school in Australia."

Population: Non-English-speaking students entering Australian secondary schools at years 10 and 11.

Publication Date: 1994.

Acronym: DELTA.

Scores, 3: Reading, Writing, Listening.

Administration: Group.

Price Data, 2002: A$195 per complete set; A$21.95 per 10 copies Reading Test; A$21.95 per 10 copies Listening Test.

Time: (180) minutes.

Authors: Joy McQueen and Cecily Aldous.

Publisher: Australian Council for Educational Research Ltd. [Australia].

Review of the Diagnostic English Language Tests by ALFRED LONGO, Instructor in Education, Social Science Department, Ocean County College, Toms River, NJ:

DESCRIPTION. The Diagnostic English Language Tests (DELTA) are a series of assessments that assist in the determination of the type of English-as-a-Second-Language support needed for an individual student. The test can assist in class placement. It is designed to have focused utility for secondary school students.

The battery includes Listening, Reading, and Writing tests. The Listening test (41 items) is composed of school announcements, teacher instructions, classroom lessons, and social interactions between students. The Reading test (43 items) contains texts of varying length and difficulty and texts from academic subject areas. The Writing test also features authentic school tasks such as report writing, and the authoring of persuasive essays.

It should be noted that the DELTA is not purported to be an ability or achievement test. The goal of the test battery is to identify students' particular strengths and weaknesses in English language. The results of the battery are intended to be diagnostic and should provide a foundational point from which to begin language instruction and to place ESL or NES students appropriately.

A diagnostic map for both the Reading and Listening tests permits the scorer to see the relative difficulty of test items and an expectation of where an individual might score. Scoring is a five-step process ending with test data being entered onto a student profile that delineates raw score, strengths and weaknesses.

There is some latitude for the acceptance of the test taker's responses. Although this is present in both the Reading and Listening tests, there is more variability in grading the Listening test. A six-step rubric is used to score the Writing test. One to 3 points are awarded for the following: Response to Task, Register (style and tone), Cohesion, Range and Complexity of Structures, Verb Use and Formation, and Vocabulary. Samples of the various score points are given in the administration manual. Readers are untrained beyond the directions given in the manual. Including practice items, the battery takes slightly over three hours to complete.

DEVELOPMENT. A range of educational professionals were consulted in the initial development of the DELTA. Overseas students were observed by teachers and also were asked to outline any particular problems they encountered with English. The two sets of perceptions were then aligned. Out of this alignment came an approximation of the language needs of overseas students. Another broad group of educators from the private and public sectors, language specialists, and those with ESL teaching experience provided direction for the development.

Trial testing of two parallel forms of the Listening and Reading tests was conducted. Eight writing tasks were also produced. The entire battery was administered to 400 students in 12 schools and language training centers in Australia. The results of the trial administrations were analyzed using Rasch item response modeling (Rasch, 1960).

TECHNICAL. An analysis of the trial data using judgment sampling as opposed to random sampling was conducted. The developers felt that this was an appropriate methodology because the goal of the trial was analysis and not norming. Given the purpose of the instrument, this seems to be a fair procedure in the validation process.

The Listening test analysis produced 41 items from the initial selection of 86. The relationship of student ability to test item difficulty seems to be strong. It should be noted that 80% of the variance in student performance is attributed to student ability and not measurement error.

For the Reading test, 43 items were chosen from an initial body of 102 items. Again, percent of student variance with respect to ability stands at 81%.

The writing analysis used a paired correlation between tasks (i.e., according to the authors, "Either of the two report tasks, and either of the two argumentative tasks can be administered, and their performance can be compared directly," manual, p. 44). The results of the correlation of all possible pairs of tasks are .86. Although this correlation is acceptable, one must look at the use of untrained readers with suspicion. Interrater reliability is moderate and less than superior at .66. The variance as noted by the authors ("Differences in overall harshness were apparent," manual, p. 45) between those raters who consistently gave high ratings as opposed to those displaying more "harshness" is not acceptable. Rater training and the refining of their judgments should be conducted prior to final development and should be part of each test administration. This can remedy the low interrater comparability.

The sample size was appropriate and standardization procedures were well matched to the purpose of the instrument. So, too, are the number of initial trial items and the diversity of the educators used as consultants. Validity and reliability will fluctuate slightly, however, because of the discretion given the scorers in evaluating the testtaker's responses. The number of possible ratings a scorer has to choose from will also influence the results, although not significantly for a transactional language test.

The DELTA has a foundation in Bachman's (1990) interpretation of communicative language ability that includes both knowledge of the form and use of language structures. Further, Cummins's (1983) division of language based on its usage for interpersonal or academic purposes is also part of the underpinnings of this test.

As previously mentioned, Rasch item response modeling was utilized to remove "misfitting" items from the instrument and to examine construct validity. Content validity evidence was determined by means of consultation with a number of practitioners in the ESL field. Additionally, a group of Australian assessment materials was referenced in the DELTA's creation. The authors state that "In the interests of authenticity the range of difficulty levels of the reading texts is close to that encountered in the secondary school environment." Although this may be true, the referencing of other second and emerging language tests in English in conjunction with the above should have been completed. Such an initiation may also be fruitful in examining the reliability of the instrument. Reliability, as such, is not mentioned in the "Technical Information" section of the DELTA's administration manual.

COMMENTARY. The DELTA seems to have utility as a means of identifying starting points for language instruction of second language and emerging English language learners. Its reliance on "real world" test items such as school announcements, teacher instructions, and social interactions between students (Listening test) support its purpose. Other academic and transactional items that are in the testing domain include texts relating to school subjects (Reading test) and report writing (Writing test). Again, "world of school" prompts and activities are congruent with the stated goals.

The battery is comprehensive. Directions are clear and all supporting materials are of good quality. The administration manual is complete containing specific directions, practice items, and diagnostic maps. The latter are well constructed and contain skill descriptors that allow the assessor to discriminate levels of difficulty of test items and the relative performance of the test taker. The manual is precise in its directions on interpreting the diagnostic maps.

Test questions are appropriate in difficulty for the target population, middle to upper secondary students. The problem with being more definitive in this regard is that the test has a unique focus on students newly arrived to Australia. This reviewer does not understand the magnitude of this immigration, or the level of expectation of Australian educators. Attempts to get clarification

of these issues were unsuccessful. One of the authors did state that the DELTA has not previously been reviewed publicly and has not been marketed beyond school systems within Australia. Much of the literature in Australia deals with literacy issues of native learners and not with immigrants.

Despite these qualifications, the DELTA can give a rather accurate portrait of the strengths and weaknesses of a given student. This diagnosis sets a course for future study and can aid in placement decisions.

The DELTA is similar in structure and purpose to the IDEA Proficiency Tests (IPT), specifically the IPT III (Grades 7–12) in that the IPT has oral language, reading, and writing tests. In addition, the purpose of that instrument is integrative and pragmatic.

The Language Assessment Scales (LAS) (DeAvila & Duncan, 1991) published by CTB/McGraw Hill generates measures of oral proficiency for individuals in kindergarten through adulthood. Language proficiency as measured by the LAS has been linked with reading achievement as demonstrated by performance on the Comprehensive Test of Basic Skills (CTBS) (DeAvila and Duncan, 1990). This link may allow for a broader view of an examinee's language skills.

SUMMARY. The DELTA is a battery of tests (Listening, Reading, Writing) that judge an examinee's "ability to cope with the English language demands of upper secondary school in Australia" (manual, p. 1). The assessment contains a diagnostic map (Reading test and Listening test) that affords the examiner the opportunity to see the relative difficulty of individual items.

In the development of the DELTA, standardization procedures were matched to the purpose of the instrument. Sample size and trial item numbers were respectable. A broad range of educators were used as consultants in the development process.

There is variability in scoring the Listening test. Untrained readers are used in scoring both the Listening and Writing tests. Some variance in scoring may result from this.

The test manual is clear, comprehensive, and precise. With the exceptions noted above, the authors have been diligent in addressing issues of validity. Based upon the pragmatic use of language ("real-life" uses), the application of the DELTA is limited to Australia.

REVIEWER'S REFERENCES

Bachman, L. F. (1990). Fundamental considerations in language testing. Oxford: Oxford University Press.

Cummins, J. (1983). Language proficiency and academic achievement. In J. W. Oller, Jr. (Ed.), *Issues in language testing research* (pp. 108–130). Rowley, MA: Newbury House.

DeAvila, E. A. & Duncan, S. E. (1990). *LAS, Language Assessment Scales, Oral technical report, English, Forms 1C, 1D, 2C, 2D*. Monterey, CA: CTB MacMillan McGraw-Hill.

DeAvila, E. A., & Duncan, S. E. (1991). Language Assessment Scales (LAS). Monterey, CA: CTB/McGraw-Hill.

Rasch, G. (1960). Studies in Mathematical Psychology: I. Probabilistic models for some intelligence and attainment tests. Copenhagen, Denmark: Nielsen & Lydiche.

[84]

Diagnostic Reading Record, Second Edition.

Purpose: Designed to reveal the child's reading strategies and response to texts.

Population: Ages 4 to adult.

Publication Dates: 1992–1998.

Scores: No scores.

Administration: Individual.

Price Data, 1999: £25.99 per Teacher's Handbook; £6.50 per 20 profiles.

Time: Administration time not reported.

Author: Helen Arnold.

Publisher: Hodder & Stoughton Educational [England].

[Note: The publisher advised in December 2001 that this test is now out of print.]

Review of the Diagnostic Reading Record, Second Edition by THOMAS E. HANCOCK, Associate Professor of Education, George Fox University, Newberg, OR:

DESCRIPTION. The Diagnostic Reading Record provides the materials and methods for assessing an individual's reading development. The focus is on understanding the reader's strategies and responses to text so that reader can be helped toward reading maturity.

Assessment is accomplished first by analyzing oral reading, particularly the miscues, according to inferences about the graphophonic, syntactic, and semantic cueing systems. Secondly, assessment is accomplished by engaging the student to elicit responses along the lines of retelling, seeing relationships, and appreciation/judgment.

All materials are included in the handbook. In this handbook there are the rationale for this type of assessment—miscue analysis; instructions on how to administer the assessment including how to mark and code miscues and how to assess reader's response; and then 24 single-page, photocopiable reading passages.

The passages are fictional, autobiographical, and informational—with readability values ranging from 6 to 12 on the Fry readability scale. The stories do not have illustrations although the informational texts have various captions and diagrams. In each case the passage is not just an excerpt, but is a complete text. The language used is occasionally particularly British: petrol, mum, footballer, eggs and chips for my tea, etc.

The assessment is administered individually. The evaluator tape-records the oral reading from one of the appropriately selected reading passages and marks all miscues. Then the miscues are coded (on a word-within-sentence level and not a letter-within-word level) according to type of miscue: nonresponse or refusal, substitution, omission, insertion, reversal, self-correction, hesitation, and repetition. Also, each miscue is coded as a positive or negative miscue. It is deemed negative if the miscue does not make sense for that passage and positive if the miscues are reasonable and show that the reader is making use of all available information.

The primary purpose for using the Diagnostic Reading Record is not to determine a child's reading level in reference to other children, nor to determine which skills are not in-place, nor to support reading research programs, but simply to help developing readers become mature readers. However, the author does point out that the results can be used to determine whether a child's achievement fits with the National Curriculum Levels in England. Those levels are specified in the handbook.

The particular focus of the first part of the assessment—reading strategies—is to determine the reader's relative balance in using the three cueing systems (graphophonic, syntactic, and semantic). If one system is identified as not being adequately used to create meaning, the instructor would then be empowered to focus any intervention or help directed to where the breakdown seems to be. The purpose of the second part of the assessment, the reader's response, is to make qualitative judgments related to the reader's engagement with the text, including accurate recalling, but also predicting, inferring, appreciating, and evaluating. Those judgments can then be used to guide the reader toward maturity in reading, which would involve full engagement with the text. As the author indicates, once reading maturity is attained the use of the Diagnostic Reading Record is probably not appropriate.

DEVELOPMENT. There is little information on the development of this particular procedure for miscue analysis. The author says that it is based on Kenneth Goodman's Miscue Analysis—but the citation is of another author who reported on Goodman's work (Arnold, 1982). The author of Diagnostic Reading Record does state that Goodman's work has been simplified for classroom use, but does not explicitly specify how.

The underlying assumptions of this approach to assessing reading are discussed above in the Description section.

Related to the reading passages, it is stated in the handbook that they have been specially prepared with miscue analysis in mind. For example, there are no illustrations in the narrative accounts so that miscues can be more confidently related to the linguistic cues in the text. The range of genres provides both for more potential insight into reader's abilities with different texts and also for reflecting the "range of material" specification in the National Curriculum assessment requirements. It is also indicated that the passages were selected to provide "a strong stimulus for discussion … ample opportunities for children to retell, to predict, to go beyond explicit information by means of inference and deduction, and to express opinions. The selections appeal to a wide range of interests. This makes them suitable material for assessing the depth and scope of children's understanding and response" (p. 6). It is stated that criteria for readability included not only the Spache and Fry formula but also difficulty of vocabulary, and complexity of sentence structure. However, there are no details as to how these criteria were applied.

In the acknowledgements section of the handbook, it is noted that some of the passages were tested by teachers and then modified accordingly and also that many of the teachers' suggestions were included in the handbook. Again there are no specifics provided.

TECHNICAL. There is no evidence for standardization or reliability. A few comments indicate that there is anecdotal evidence for validity. The author puts forth her stance toward such technical supports for good testing when she states, "No statistical norms can be deduced, as the trials confirmed that evidence from miscue analysis concerns the individual child, and is not intended to be quantifiable. Teachers did however find trends occurring at certain ages, tending to confirm the findings of existing miscue analysis research" (Acknowledgements section, no page number).

COMMENTARY. The biggest strength of the Diagnostic Reading Record is that it is rooted in what most academics and reading professionals in the world (e.g., both the International Reading Association and the National Council of Teachers of English) know to be the way to approach reading education. The point of reading is to create meaning and to enjoy. The point of reading education is to facilitate that natural process and to encourage its growth into adulthood. It is evident with this assessment tool that those same priorities are in place. Reading assessment, in its most humane form, is for the purpose of helping the developing reader.

This type of assessment is gravely needed, particularly in the United States. In light of the great need for assessments like the Diagnostic Reading Record, it is unfortunate that there are no attempts by the author to satisfy the needs for more valid indicators of reading. The author dismisses such needs with a few sentences. In fact, it would be relatively easy to provide good evidence for validity and reliability. That the instrument is intended for the individual child is as it should be; however, that there is no effort to satisfy the traditional standards of good measurement is denying the needs of the community and ultimately of the students who will suffer if more humane measurement such as this assessment are not implemented on a more widespread basis.

It would have been desirable if the author had more explicitly related her work to this instrument's foundations in Ken Goodman's work and to the miscue research that she mentioned. For example, what was she improving and how does it relate to the literature and needs in the field? In that way, the user could more easily connect the author's thinking to that of the entire community of reading educators and more particularly to the user's own previous experiences and education.

Even though the language is occasionally uniquely British, that should not be a practical problem in assessing the reader's development. However, it may help users feel more comfortable with the tool if the author adjusted vocabulary and certain phraseology for the non-British audience.

The new user should know that to perform miscue analysis confidently will take some time to learn. It would have been helpful if the author provided some more guidelines and suggestions. Although the author has provided some indications about how to use the results of the miscue analysis, more would be better.

SUMMARY. This is an excellent tool for assessing reading development. It can provide specific guidance for the particular help that certain readers may need to be able to use their graphophonic, syntactic, and semantic cueing systems more efficiently. Its focus is not accurate reading, but rather the creation of meaning. The test would be more readily useable if the author were to explain more about the test development and also provide reliability and validity data.

Review of the Diagnostic Reading Record, Second Edition by RONALD A. MADLE, School Psychologist, Shikellamy School District, Sunbury, PA, and Adjunct Associate Professor of School Psychology, The Pennsylvania State University, University Park, PA:

DESCRIPTION. The Diagnostic Reading Record, Second Edition (DRR-2) is an informal technique intended to allow classroom teachers to assess reading development through the observation and analysis of the child reading a short, complete text and then discussing the passage. The components include a teacher's manual and profile forms. The manual contains administration and scoring directions, five case studies, and 24 graded reading passages designed for miscue analysis. At each of eight reading levels there are autobiographical, narrative, and informational passages. Practically, the utility of the instrument would be limited to countries that employ British spellings, as these are quite evident. The DRR-2 is considered appropriate for individuals with reading ages of 6:0 to 11:0 years, regardless of actual age.

DRR-2 administration involves audiotaping the child reading a short passage appropriate to his or her reading level. The teacher then has the child retell and respond to the passage. Open-ended questions can be used to prompt additional information, if needed. After data collection the child's word-level miscues are coded onto a photocopy of the passage using a system presented in the manual. Several types of miscues are coded: nonresponses or refusals, substitutions, omissions, insertions, reversals, self-corrections, hesitations, and repeti-

tions. These are summarized on the profile sheet and several quantitative "scores" then are obtained in addition to the number of each type of miscue. These include the number of miscues, the number of words read correctly, and the number of positive and negative miscues. Each substitution is entered on a Venn diagram to describe the cueing systems involved. Substitutions reflecting the use of two or three cueing systems are positive, whereas the use of a single (or no) system is negative. Finally, the child's hesitations, repetitions, and fluency are rated on 3-point scales. To assess understanding, the reverse of the profile sheet provides 3-point scales for rating the child's response to the passage in the areas of Retelling, Seeing Relationships, and Appreciation and Judgment. Also included are selected descriptors from the Reading portion of the National Curriculum used in the United Kingdom.

DEVELOPMENT. The author states that the DRR-2 is based on Kenneth Goodman's classic work on miscue analysis, although it has been simplified for classroom use. This position treats miscues as reflecting the graphophonic, syntactic, or semantic cueing systems. Miscues are not considered errors because even experienced readers make these deviations when reading aloud—they are signs of the cueing systems being used. The theory suggests that all three cueing systems should be used by readers in a balanced and effective way.

The DRR-2 is an informal assessment and the teacher's manual provides little information on the actual development of the instrument. Discussion mostly focuses on the determination of readability levels. Three types of passages—autobiographical, narrative, and informational—were developed and then graded for readability using both the Spache and Fry formulas. However, the author indicates that the readability criteria also included difficulty of vocabulary, complexity of sentence structure, and the possibility of using inference and deduction and notes that the "passages are not statistically related to reading ages" (p. 6).

There is no information in the manual on developmental testing except for a brief notation in the Acknowledgements that says "a sample of the passages was distributed and trialled by teachers in the Manchester area, and by students working with children at Homerton College, Cambridge. The texts were modified according to their findings, and many of their suggestions have been incorporated in the teacher's manual."

TECHNICAL. Scores obtained from the DRR-2, like other informal reading assessments such as informal reading inventories, are not standardized and yield no normed scores. In fact, the Acknowledgements section states that no "statistical norms can be deduced, as the trials confirmed that evidence from miscue analysis concerns the individual child and is not intended to be quantifiable." Interestingly, a somewhat contradictory statement then is made. "Teachers did however find trends occurring at certain ages, tending to confirm the findings of existing miscue analysis research."

No information regarding any type of reliability or validity studies that have been conducted is presented (or referenced) in the teacher's manual. Even the most basic level of reliability—interscorer agreement—is not reported.

COMMENTARY. Assessing the quality and characteristics of a tool like the DRR-2 is very much dependent upon the viewpoint of the user about assessment. The DRR-2 was developed as an authentic assessment based on a top-down model of reading. Generally these approaches are qualitative and developers disdain traditional psychometric standards and criteria such as norms development, reliability, and classical validity. They advocate criteria such as consequential and instructional validity. Users who adopt this view may find the DRR-2 useful. The DRR-2 appears to be, however, a "hybrid" measure (Murphy, 1998) that to some degree attempts to span both this camp and a more traditional view.

As an informal, diagnostic technique the primary strengths of the DRR-2 are to give some structure to the assessment process by providing prepared passages, scoring methods, a profile form, and several case studies illustrating its use. A number of substantial flaws, however, limit the DRR-2's value, even as an informal instrument. First, the procedure for administering and scoring is time-consuming and complex, a frequent criticism directed at miscue analysis in general. Also, the administration directions are rather vague; often saying the examiner might "say something like…" (p. 8). The manual offers minimal guidance on establishing which passages to use, even though this is stated to be critical for a miscue analysis. Reading specialists with knowledge of

miscue analysis may likely be more appropriate users of the DRR-2 than classroom teachers. Additionally, no information is presented to suggest that this "revised" edition provides anything new over the initial edition. Only two old references are used, with the newer one being published in 1982.

From a psychometric perspective, the DRR-2 is quite flawed. Even authentic assessments should meet basic criteria to make the results useful. The lack of interscorer reliability information is a particularly serious omission given the complex and subjective scoring system. The manual clearly states that judgment about miscues is bound to be subjective to some extent. This raises questions about the replicability across teachers of the information obtained. This is also the case with the various ratings employed, which certainly should be judged by traditional criteria of reliability and validity.

The DRR-2's validity is not supported, either directly or through referencing relevant literature. Even the construct being measured seems unclear. The manual states that positive miscues are reasonable deviations that indicate the reader is making use of available information whereas negative miscues involve deviations that do not make sense. No evidence is provided to show that the coding of positive and negative strategies according to the number of cueing systems being used adequately operationalizes this. Further, the ratings of hesitations, repetitions, and fluency, not to mention the comprehension ratings and their linking to the National Curriculum, beg for information on their construct and concurrent validity. Even by criteria used for instructional or consequential validity the DRR-2 falls quite short. No evidence is presented to support that measuring reading development in the manner presented results in improved instruction or student outcomes.

SUMMARY. The DRR-2 is an authentic assessment consistent with one current view in the field of educational assessment. Although a different theoretical model is used, it is allied with approaches such as informal reading inventories and curriculum-based assessments. In this reviewer's opinion, however, it cannot be recommended for virtually any of its stated purposes. Any of several miscue analysis procedures available in the educational literature would be just as well used. Little information is provided to support its use. The DRR-2 does not present evidence that two users can arrive at similar "scores" or that using the assessment will in any way improve instruction or student outcomes. In fact, many believe the underlying assumptions and procedures behind miscue analysis still need empirical validation after approximately a quarter century. Although a quick computer search on miscue analysis revealed over 200 references, most were case descriptions, procedures to conduct miscue analysis, and formal research on reading development using miscue analysis. Even though literature exists, this second edition provides little support for the technique or for the DRR-2 itself.

REVIEWER'S REFERENCE

Murphy, S. (1998). *Fragile evidence: A critique of reading assessment.* Mahwah, NJ: Lawrence Erlbaum & Associates.

[85]

Differential Aptitude Tests—Australian and New Zealand Editions [Forms V and W].

Purpose: Provides a standardized procedure for measuring the abilities of males and females for the purpose of educational and vocational guidance.
Population: Grades 8–12.
Publication Dates: 1973–1989.
Scores, 9: Verbal Reasoning, Numerical Ability, Abstract Reasoning, Clerical Speed and Accuracy, Mechanical Reasoning, Space Relations, Spelling, Language Use, Verbal Reasoning + Numerical Ability.
Subtests: Available as separates.
Administration: Group.
Price Data, 1999: A$163.95 per 25 Test 1 (Abstract Reasoning, Numerical Reasoning, Abstract Reasoning); $69.95 per 25 Test 2 (Clerical Speed and Accuracy); $142.95 per 25 Test 3 (Mechanical Reasoning); $116.95 per 25 Test 4 (Space Relations); $95.95 per 25 Test 5 (Spelling and Language Usage); $19.95 per score keys; $15 per 10 answer sheets; $59 per exam kit; $84.95 per manual (1989, 160 pages).
Time: (225) minutes for entire battery.
Comments: New Zealand manual information included; Australian manual same as that for the American version of the Differential Aptitude Tests with norms and revisions for the Australian and New Zealand population.
Authors: Marion M. de Lemos (Australian manual), George K. Bennett, Harold G. Seashore, and Alexander G. Wesman.
Publisher: The Psychological Corporation [Australia] and Australian Council for Educational Research Ltd. [Australia].

Review of the Differential Aptitude Tests, Australian and New Zealand Editions, Forms V and W

by LYNN LAKOTA BROWN, Assistant Professor, Educational Psychology, Northern Arizona University, Flagstaff, AZ:

DESCRIPTION. The Differential Aptitude Tests (DAT) is an integrated battery consisting of eight tests measuring various aspects of cognitive aptitudes in adolescents, Grades 8–12. The first three tests: Verbal Ability, Abstract Reasoning, and Numerical Ability are designed to measure general scholastic ability. Tests of Mechanical Reasoning and Space Relations examine the student's ability to work with objects, whereas the final three tests: Clerical Speed and Accuracy, Spelling, and Language Use measure the student's ability to function in the world of office work. General reading level is Grade 6–8 ability based on the Dale-Chall analysis method.

Testing is usually done by a school counselor, assisted by classroom teachers. The tests are designed to be given in two sessions of about 2 hours each. Answers are placed on a separate answer sheet that may be hand or machine scored; test booklets are reusable.

DEVELOPMENT. The DAT was developed in 1947 in the United States, with substantial revisions in 1962 (Forms L and M) and in 1972 (Forms S and T). The current revision (Forms V and W) was completed in 1980 in order to provide gender equality in examples, to convert math problems to metric standards, and to normalize spelling and vocabulary to Australian practices. In addition, some questions were eliminated in the latest version in order to shorten the time needed to take the battery of tests. This Australian version would most likely be used in Year 10 as students are deciding what courses to take for the final 2 years of high school.

Although individual test scores provide useful information, the true power of the DAT is the integrated pattern provided by the entire battery. These scores, taken together with ancillary information such as academic history, family and cultural background, interests and goals, will aid the counselor in guiding the student's future progress.

TECHNICAL. The norming sample for the original (1947) battery was approximately 50,000 students throughout the United States. The sample for the current Australian version comprised approximately 1,500 students in four states: Victoria, South Australia, Western Australia, and Tasmania, who were enrolled in state, Catholic, and independent schools. No gender numbers were given in the narrative; however, from the tables it appears that the numbers of males and females was approximately equal. Additionally, no breakdown of ethnicity of the sample was provided for Australian-born students.

Reliability was measured through internal consistency of the test items using the Kuder-Richardson Formula 20. These coefficients for the Australian data ranged from about .85 to .95 on most tests, slightly lower than the United States data.

Earlier forms of the DAT evaluated concurrent validity of the test through comparison of results from the DAT with various measures of achievement such as grade point averages. The test manual states that the current usage of Forms V and W is for vocational counseling rather than predictive validity of future academic performance. Nonetheless, results from the Australian version of the test were compared to assessments of performance using "other measures of linguistic, quantitative, and school ability" (Australian manual, p. 48). What these measures were or how they were measured is not given in more detail by the test manual.

The test manual recommends that it would be "advisable to conduct preliminary studies on the validity of the test for the specific purpose for which it is to be used" (p. 49). Only one example of research is included in the manual, however, and that is a pilot study of 25 students completed in 1984.

COMMENTARY. The manual is dated and confusing to read. Although complete instructions are provided for administering the test, the manual contains no suggestions for interpretation. No illustrative case studies or indications of the current research direction are provided. Examples of the original normative work in the United States are mixed indiscriminately with those from the Australian sample. In addition to the socioeconomic status based on the father's occupation, it would have been useful to have an ethnic breakdown of the sample on which the Australian test was normed in order to generalize the results to all populations.

SUMMARY. The DAT provides a useful tool, taken in conjunction with other measures of aptitude, for counselors seeking to guide student vocational planning. The Australian Council for Educational Research is to be commended for providing a needed revision of this test battery for the Australian market. Nonetheless, their effort needs to be updated with a more useful manual of instruction for future test administrators.

Review of the Differential Aptitude Tests—Australian and New Zealand Editions [Forms V and W] by JACK F. GEBART-EAGLEMONT, Chief Executive Officer and President, International Institute for Personality Assessment and Therapy, Watsonia, Victoria, Australia:

DESCRIPTION. The Differential Aptitude Tests (DAT) is a battery developed in the United States in 1947 primarily for use in secondary schools. The battery can also be used in the educational and vocational counseling of young adults and in the selection of employees. The battery consists of eight tests devised to measure aptitudes defined as "developed abilities" (Australian manual, p. 11), in the sense that they correspond to the basic set of skills required by the Western educational and vocational systems. The eight tests of the DAT cover the following aptitudes: (a) Verbal Reasoning (a measure of ability to understand concepts framed in words), (b) Numerical Ability (understanding of numerical relationships and facility in handling numerical concepts), (c) Abstract Reasoning (nonverbal measure of the student's reasoning ability), (d) Clerical Speed and Accuracy (speed of response in a simple perceptual task), (e) Mechanical Reasoning (understanding the principles of operation and repair of complex devices), (f) Space Relations (ability to deal with concrete materials through visualization), (g) Spelling (knowledge of English vocabulary and spelling), and (h) Language Use (ability to detect errors in grammar, punctuation, and capitalization).

Students may be tested individually or in groups. The responses are recorded on special purpose answer sheets printed for the DAT by the Australian Council for Educational Research. The answer sheets are devised for computerized scoring. The scoring may be ordered through the Australian Council for Educational Research. The test kit also contains the lists or correct answers that may be used for manual scoring. The individual profiles can be hand plotted or computer produced by test scoring services of the Australian Council for Educational Research.

The Australian manual contains clear and sufficient instructions concerning the scheduling of testing programs, general considerations for administration (such as training the staff, timing, preparing materials, physical conditions), and a good description of steps involved in administering the DAT. The manual also provides some basic information about the history of the test. The larger part of the manual deals with the technical information on the Australian standardization of the DAT, including the standardized scores and norms for age and sex groups. The Australian manual was supplied with the test kit, although the test booklets were marked as "Australian and New Zealand Edition."

DEVELOPMENT. The original United States standardization sample for Forms V and W consisted of more than 61,000 students in Grades 8 through 12 drawn from 64 parochial school systems throughout the United States. The history and development of the original American battery will not be discussed here, because it was widely reported by many sources over a long period of time; this review focuses specifically on the basic aspects of the Australian standardization and normalization. The Australian standardization samples were much smaller than the American ones: $N = 759$ for Form V, and $N = 746$ for Form W. The Australian samples were well balanced in respect to Year Levels (9, 10, 11), state, type of school attended (State, Catholic, other), and sex. Most of the students tested were from an Anglo-Saxon background (83%). Of the remaining students, about 50% came from a Southern European background, with the remaining students coming from Northern European, East European, Middle Eastern, and Asian backgrounds, or from a "mixed non-Anglo-Saxon background" (manual, p. 58). Persons from a Native Australian background were not included, which seems to be typical for most Australian psychological studies.

TECHNICAL. The standardization study investigated the effects of Form V versus W (nonsignificant), and order of presentation (nonsignificant). Differences between sexes were also studied, with results indicating generally no significant differences in scores on Verbal Reasoning, Numerical Ability, and Abstract Reasoning. Concerning other tests, females scored consistently higher on Clerical Speed and Accuracy, Spelling, and Language Use; males scored consistently higher on Mechanical Reasoning. There was also a weak trend for the males to score higher on Space Relations, but the differences were significant mainly at the Grade Level 9. The effects of relative age in grade were nonsignificant.

The effects of ethnic background were demonstrated at different levels of differentiation. At the simplest level of differentiation, the consistent effect was maintained for Verbal Reasoning, Mechanical Reasoning, and Space Relations, with Australians or English-speaking migrants scoring generally higher than non-English-speaking migrants. At the higher level of differentiation, the effect was maintained for Verbal Reasoning, Mechanical Reasoning, and Space Relations, with the specific group of immigrant children (South European) scoring frequently lower than other groups (predominantly English, North European, and East European). The effects of socioeconomic status were more pronounced in the non-English-speaking group (only for some tests). Considering the differences between English and non-English backgrounds at each Occupational level, significant differences were demonstrated for all tests within the Managerial parental occupational group. The effects of type of school attended indicated predominantly higher results obtained by students of the Catholic and other independent schools than by students of the State schools.

Reliability of the DAT was estimated in the Australian sample using the KR-20 formula. The reported reliability coefficients were generally around the 90 level, ranging from about .85 to .95.

Validity evidence for the DAT scores in the Australian sample was provided by correlating the DAT scores with scores on the ACER Higher Tests and on the Otis-Lennon School Ability Test (OLSAT). All correlations were significant at the level of $p < .01$. The relationships between the DAT scores and ratings in school subjects demonstrated predominantly significant correlations, with some exceptions, especially for Physics, Foreign Languages (Asian), and Music. The normative materials are well presented in the manual. The tabulations for each test and for each age group are split by sex and the tables also contain U.S. and N.Z. norms. The tables of standardized scores are presented for each test and each age group, and a table for conversion of standardized scores into corresponding percentile scores and stanine scores is included.

COMMENTARY. The Australian standardization of the DAT demonstrated sufficient reliability levels, comparable with the U.S. standardization. The indices of validity were also satisfactory, which confirms the usefulness of the DAT in the Australian conditions. The manual is written clearly and all instructions are easy to follow. The computerized scoring services provided by the Australian Council for Educational Research make it possible to test larger groups of students or job applicants efficiently.

The supplied test kit did not include any information concerning the New Zealand standardization sample. Although the test booklets are marked "Australian and New Zealand Edition," the manual provided for a review is merely titled "Australian Manual." Appendix II presents tables of norms for Grades 9 to 11. The tables for Grade 9 shows only Australian and U.S. norms, the materials for Grades 10 and 11 include Australian, U.S., and New Zealand norms.

One of the most striking characteristics of the standardization sample is a complete exclusion of the persons from a Native Australian background. Such an exclusion, in my opinion, serves primarily to conceal the various aspects of educational neglect of native populations and secondarily leads to a further discrimination and fostering of the status quo (deprivation of the basic educational and vocational opportunities).

SUMMARY. The Australian standardization of the DAT allows the successful utilization of this useful instrument in Australia, at least with the populations of colonial and immigrant heritage. The test materials provided for a review did not include any standardization data concerning the characteristics of the New Zealand sample. Subsequently, the author of the current review is not in the position to form any opinions concerning standardization processes, reliability, and validity evidence of the DAT in New Zealand's populations.

Concerning the Australian standardization, it should be noted that it would be prudent and fair to secure an adequate representation of the Native Australians in future standardizations of the DAT.

[86]

The Discipline Index.

Purpose: "Systematically obtains information from a child about the child's overall perceptions of each parent's disciplinary practices."
Population: Ages 6–17.

Publication Dates: 1999–2002.
Acronym: DI.
Scores, 6: Mother and Father scores for: Clear Expectations, Effectively Monitors, Consistently Enforces, Fairness, Attunement, Moderates Anger, plus Mother Total, Father Total.
Administration: Individual.
Price Data, 2002: $199 per complete kit including handbook (2000, 140 pages), 8 sets response cards, 8 scoring summaries, stylus-pen, placement dots, updates, and 3-year update service; $99 per 8 response cards with summaries; $159 per 16 response cards with summaries; $199 per 24 response cards with summaries; $198 per computer scoring program (half price when purchased with kit); $129 per handbook.
Time: (35 minutes).
Authors: Anita K. Lampel, Barry Bricklin, and Gail Elliot.
Publisher: Village Publishing.

Review of the Discipline Index by PATTI L. HARRISON, Professor of School Psychology, The University of Alabama, Tuscaloosa, AL:

DESCRIPTION. The Discipline Index is a rating assessment in which a child, aged 6 to midadolescence, provides his or her perceptions about parental discipline, and it includes a comparison between the child's perceptions about their mother's and their father's disciplinary practices. The authors describe a number of situations in which obtaining information about children's perceptions of discipline may be useful, including planning therapeutic interventions, assessing a child for behavioral or emotional problems, assessing the effectiveness of parenting interventions, and developing parenting plans. However, the authors provide little information about using the Discipline Index in these situations.

The Discipline Index has a total of 64 questions, with 32 corresponding items assessing each parent. For example, an item questions how often the mother is fair about disciplining the child when upset with him or her, and a corresponding item asks the same question about the father. Odd numbered items reference the mother, and even numbered items reference the father. However, items are ordered so that mother and father items with the same question are not adjacent and are separated by 32 items. Some items have negative wording, such as "If dad is mad at you, how often does he make sure not to hurt your feelings?" The authors note that indirect wording is used because children are often afraid to report abusive behavior, but the negative wording may be confusing for younger children.

The 32 items per parent are categorized into six scales, with 4–7 items on each scale. The scales measure clear expectations, or how the parent conveys his or her expectations to the child; effectively monitor behavior, or if the parent knows what the child is doing; indicate consistent enforcement, or the parent's use of consistent rules; measure fairness, or the parent's fairness in disciplinary practices; measure attunement, or if the parent knows the child well and moderates anger; or the parent's response to minor matters and use of physical discipline. Total scores for mother and father are also possible.

During administration, a pack of 64 cards, each 3.5 by 8.5 inches in size, is used with each child. The examiner reads from the back of each card, on which the item and a scoring scale of 1-60 is printed. The child sees the front of the card, on which a horizontal line is printed. The horizontal line is anchored with a negative descriptor (e.g., *not so often, not so good*) printed on the left and a positive descriptor (e.g., *very often, very good*) printed on the right. After the examiner reads the item on the back of the card, the child responds by using a stylus to make a pinhole on the horizontal line to indicate where on the line the parent would fall.

Each item on the Discipline Index is scored by examining the scale of 1–60 on the back of the card to determine where the child's puncture is located. Each item score is transferred to a score summary sheet, and item scores are summed to obtain scores for each of the six scales and total score for mother and father. Use of the score summary sheet is quite cumbersome, especially because the order of items on the summary sheet, which pairs the mother and father items on the same topic, is different from the actual order of the item cards. There is a possibility of clerical error when transferring scores from the item cards to the score summary sheet. An accompanying computer-scoring program is helpful, because item scores are entered in the same order they appear on the cards, and provides sums of item scores for the six scales and total scores, as well as the number of items on each scale for which mother scored higher, father scored higher, or mother and father tied.

No normative scores are provided for the Discipline Index. Instead, clinical evaluation of the raw scores and methods for comparing the

child's ratings of mother and father are described briefly in the test handbook. Four case histories are reported in the handbook to assist in clinical interpretation. The authors contrast interpretation of the Discipline Index to that for the Bricklin Perceptual Scales (Bricklin, 1998). They recommend that interpretation of the former should consider interventions based on the child's perception of a parent functioning less than adequately in some areas, whereas the latter focuses on the number of measured areas in which one parent is better than others.

DEVELOPMENT AND TECHNICAL INFORMATION. The handbook provides little information about the development and psychometric properties of the Discipline Index. The authors include short narrative descriptions of the six scales, but provide only limited rationale and conceptual foundations for the content and no empirical basis for the six scales. The handbook has only a brief paragraph about development, which simply notes that items were selected based on research about children's experience with discipline and were reviewed and refined based on professional judgment and feedback during pilot testing and assessment by clinicians. The authors refer the user to research about discipline issues cited in the handbook's reference list.

Although no normative scores are available for the instrument, the authors report preliminary standardization data in the handbook. The Discipline Index was administered to 50 children, ages 6–14 years, from middle socioeconomic status in a clinical sample of children in divorcing families, with about 25% of the sample from minority groups. Average total scores for mothers and fathers are reported in the handbook, and the authors recommend that clinical interpretation of poorer scores should consider the average scores of the norm sample.

Several validity studies are summarized in the handbook, although the samples are small and poorly described. A sample of 40 children was assessed with the Bricklin Perceptual Scales, for which information about preferred parent was obtained, and the Discipline Index; children in the sample selected the preferred parent as the better disciplinarian 70% of the time. A sample of 26 children completed the Discipline Index, and their teachers provided information about a variety of symptoms of externalizing and internalizing disorders. Although the criterion measure for children's problems is not described well, children whose teachers reported problems had greater mean differences between mother's and father's total scores on the Discipline Index than children with no reported problems. Another study compared 30 children's scores on the Discipline Index with parents' scores on two parent stress scales or the Conner's Behavior Rating Scale. Although mothers and fathers differed in their reports of stress, children rated mothers and fathers equally on discipline. In a study with 25 children, pairs of parents rated themselves on a limit-setting inventory and children rated parents with the Discipline Index; parents who rated themselves as having higher limit-setting in the pair had higher discipline scores.

No reliability data are reported. The authors attempt to justify the lack of data with a statement in the handbook that they aimed for a heterogeneous set of items and did not expect a child to answer consistently within a given subcategory.

COMMENTARY. Although the Discipline Index provides a unique assessment of parent discipline practices from the child's perspective, there are a number of shortcomings that seriously compromise its use. The authors provide little justification for use of the instrument and present limited rationale and support for the items and scales. Similarly, the authors provide almost no direction for interpreting the instrument. The handbook has only brief descriptions of the uses, design, interpretation, and psychometric properties of the instrument. In fact, only about one third of the handbook is devoted to the Discipline Index. Most of the handbook consists of an appendix containing excerpts from the manual of the Bricklin Perceptual Scales and other sources; the relationship between these excerpts and the Discipline Index is not readily apparent.

Administration and scoring of the Discipline Index are awkward. Administration requires a fresh set of cards for each child, and the authors do not provide a rationale for using a stylus to puncture the cards over a more typical paper-and-pencil format for a rating scale. Transferring item scores to the score summary sheet could result in clerical error, although the computer-scoring program can reduce some of this error. Interpretation of the scores from hand-scoring and the computer program, which include sums of item scores or

numbers of items for which mother and father score higher or tied, is only addressed briefly in the handbook and is not supported by technical data.

The lack of normative scores to assist in interpretation and failure to report any type of reliability data is of major concern. Although the handbook provides some information from validity studies, the samples and methodology used in the studies are limited and the authors do not integrate the results of the studies with uses and interpretation of the instrument.

SUMMARY. The Discipline Index was clearly intended to be a flexible, clinical instrument. However, all assessment instruments must meet basic technical standards, including adequate psychometric qualities and provision of guidelines to assist professionals with proper use and interpretation. Unfortunately, the Discipline Index has a number of limitations, has cumbersome administration and scoring, and lacks technical support to justify its use.

REVIEWER'S REFERENCE

Bricklin, B. (1998). *Bricklin Perceptual Scales manual.* Furlong, PA: Village Publishing.

Review of the Discipline Index by DARRELL L. SABERS, Professor of Educational Psychology, University of Arizona, Tucson, AZ:

DESCRIPTION. The Discipline Index (DI) contains 64 items administered orally to children aged 6 through 17. The examinee uses a stylus to indicate a response on a continuum anchored on the right end by the perception that the parent does the behavior in question very often (or very well) and on the left end by the perception that the parent does not do the behavior in question very often (or not very well). The examinee indicates the perception by making a point on a line, and the point corresponds to a number from 1 to 60 on the back of the response card. There are 32 items referencing the mother and 32 identical items referencing the father. The responses can be entered into a scoring summary or a computer scoring program to produce the six subscores and total score for each parent.

DEVELOPMENT. The DI is another element in ACCESS—A Comprehensive Custody Evaluation Standard System (T6:15) developed by Barry Bricklin and associates. ACCESS was reviewed in a prior *Mental Measurements Yearbook* (Roberts, 2001) before the DI was produced. The rationale supporting the DI includes the belief of the importance of the parent's role in socializing the child, and the belief that the child's perception of the delivery of discipline is an important factor in the socialization. Consistency in the delivery of discipline is assessed by comparing the scores assigned to the two parents. The authors emphasize the importance of recognizing that discipline is not synonymous with corporal punishment; rather, it is "a dyadic interaction between two people, one of whom is the discipliner and one of whom is the disciplinee" (DI Handbook, p. 7).

Questions were worded carefully to be a bit indirect because children are often reluctant to report abusive parental behaviors directly. Items were developed related to disciplinary practices that fall into six areas, and the resulting category scores are expected to contribute to pattern analysis. However, there are no derived scores and no norms presented to support a profile type of interpretation.

TECHNICAL. There is a dearth of technical information provided for the DI. Very little validity information is presented, and what is presented is not described with sufficient adequacy to allow a judgment of how well the test can be used for the intended purposes. Issues like the effect of the order of presentation of items are left unresolved, posed as intellectual questions rather than as information about the best way to administer the test. There is a suggestion that alternate caregivers may be used as targets of the questions; however, no information is presented to describe the effect of such substitutions. The scoring range for each item is from 1 to 60, but there is no evidence that the responses are precise when using this extended scale. There is a suggestion to tell the examinee to "spread your answers" (p. 16) when it is recognized that responses are consistently extremely positive, but there is no information describing exactly when to give such a direction or what is the effect of the direction.

The authors suggest that the test has a "criterion-referenced format" (p. 18); however, there is no criterion indicated. It is obvious that no normative format is provided for score interpretation, but that is not sufficient to make the format criterion referenced. The instrument is developed to direct the user towards interventions, but there is no validity information to document the effectiveness of that use.

The lack of reliability information is addressed by statements that internal reliability is not desired for questions within a subcategory or between subscales. No other type of reliability is considered. Thus, the only information available to suggest any reliability is found in the limited (validity) data such as differences between average total scores of subgroups of parents or children. Some results of studies are mentioned, but not with sufficient description to support claims of validity. The reporting does not meet accepted psychometric standards for substantiating validity evidence (AERA, APA, & NCME, 1999).

There is so little information about the population of parents and children involved in the pilot study that it is probably most accurate to describe the DI as an instrument that has not yet been developed. No standardization data are provided. This same observation has been made about the ACCESS system in a previous review in *The Fourteenth Mental Measurements Yearbook* (Roberts, 2001).

COMMENTARY. It is not clear why a scoring program is provided for the DI. The scores provided by the program are not what are used by the authors in their description of the case studies intended to illustrate the use of the DI. Four case studies are the only attempt to address the issues of score interpretation, yet two of the cases do not include a mention of even one score (but one of these cases does say the DI revealed differences). The two cases for which scores are provided do not demonstrate that the DI is valid for planning any intervention. For the last case, only the Bricklin Perception of Parents Scales was found useful, and "this case is included to remind the clinician that no scoring system of any test is perfect, nor can a test be a substitute for good clinical practice" (p. 28). Without questioning the correctness of the preceding statement, a reader might still request information on score interpretation to demonstrate how the DI should be used.

The DI Handbook consists of 32 pages relating to the DI and 80 pages on other ACCESS materials. It is clear that the authors intend for the DI to be incorporated into the larger ACCESS system. The lack of detailed information about the DI is so obvious that one wonders why it is marketed as a test. It certainly is not standardized.

SUMMARY. The following comment about ACCESS is relevant and appropriate for the DI. "In summation, the ACCESS system constructed by Bricklin and associates over the past several decades is a fascinating clinical tool that begs for an adequate psychometric foundation. As currently described, ACCESS does not meet minimum standards for test construction, reliability, or validity. The ACCESS system is very expensive and time-consuming. ACCESS is not recommended for use" (Roberts, 2001, p. 4). Incorporating additional tests like the DI will not lead to a recommendation for the use of ACCESS unless a psychometric foundation is provided. The DI is not recommended for use.

REVIEWER'S REFERENCES

American Educational Research Association, American Psychological Association, & National Council on Measurement in Education. (1999). *Standards for educational and psychological testing.* Washington, DC: American Educational Research Association.

Roberts, M. (2001). [Review of ACCESS—A Comprehensive Custody Evaluation Standard System.] In B. S. Plake & J. C. Impara (Eds.), *The fourteenth mental measurements yearbook* (pp. 2–4). Lincoln, NE: The Buros Institute of Mental Measurements.

[87]

d2 Test of Attention.

Purpose: Designed as "a psychodiagnostic instrument for measuring concentration, and in particular visual attention."

Population: Adults.

Publication Date: 1998.

Acronym: d2 Test.

Scores: Score information available from publisher.

Administration: Individual.

Price Data, 2001: $64 per complete test including 20 recording blanks, set of 2 scoring keys, and manual (80 pages); $12.50 per 50 recording blanks; $9.50 per set of 2 scoring keys; $45 per manual.

Time: (8) minutes.

Comments: Originally conceived to assess individuals' suitability for driving, the test has also been used as a part of personnel selection in other workplace environments where high levels of visual attention and concentration are demanded.

Authors: Rolf Brickenkamp and Eric Zillmer.

Publisher: Hogrefe & Huber Publishers.

Review of the d2 Test of Attention by PHILLIP L. ACKERMAN, Professor of Psychology, Georgia Institute of Technology, Atlanta, GA:

DESCRIPTION. The d2 Test of Attention is described by the authors as a measure of selective attention, or more concretely, as a "standardized refinement of the so-called cancellation test" (manual, p. 1). The test is highly speeded, and is made up of a practice set of items, and 14 roughly identical 20-second segments, for a total administration time of about 8 minutes (including instruction time). Numerous measures are collected from the test, including number of items correct, number of errors (omission and commission), and measures of differences between test segments. The test was developed in Germany, and most of the background and validational data are from European samples. Very little published research and application information is available in English. The authors note that although this particular cancellation test was developed to predict driving performance, numerous researchers have investigated the test in the context of "clinical psychology and psychiatry, educational psychology, vocational counseling, industrial psychology, [and] sport psychology" (manual, p. 1). The test is hand-scorable with templates.

DEVELOPMENT. The test is a modification of traditional cancellation tests (first developed in the late 1800s and early 1900s). The test is more complex than simple letter canceling tests, because it requires more specific recognition/counting in order to match the target stimulus to a predetermined rule. The test was originally developed in Germany to "distinguish between 'good' and 'poor' motorists" (manual, p. 4). The test content is virtually unchanged since the original version of 1962, but additional research and norms have been collected in the intervening period.

TECHNICAL.

Reliability/Validity. Extensive reliability data are presented by the authors. As would be expected from most short and highly speeded "perceptual speed" tests (see Ackerman & Cianciolo, 2000 for a review), internal consistency of the number correct scores is relatively high (>.90), especially when using odd-even and split-half computations (which are generally ill-advised for highly speeded tests—see Anastasi & Urbina, 1997). Scores for errors and derived scores have lower reliabilities (as would be expected, in the former case because of highly skewed scores, and in the latter case, given the inherent psychometric limitations of difference scores). Test-retest reliabilities are also reported, but for much smaller sample sizes (fewer than 125 in the largest study). For total scores, test-retest (same-form) reliabilities are quite high within a day (roughly .90), and declining reliabilities with increasing length of time. Test-retest reliabilities of error and derived scores are much lower. Internal test correlations are presented for a U.S. sample of 506 college students. Although several of the measures are confounded, the correlations among the component scores suggest that there is a single underlying factor (though no such analysis is presented) that represents the majority of reliable test variance.

Validity data, though substantial, are far from complete or comprehensive. Most surprising is that relatively few data are presented to evaluate whether the current test is differentiable (in terms of convergent validity) from other cancellation tests, or from other perceptual speed tests. The only data pertaining to this issue are correlations between the d2 and a Symbol-Digit Modalities Test ($r = .47$) for the U.S. college student sample; and correlations between the d2 and a German version of the Digit Symbol test from the Hamburg-Wechsler Intelligence Test for Adults. The latter correlations were for several small samples of clinical patients, and ranged from $r = .28$ to $.60$ for the total test scores. Remaining validity data are reported mostly as significant differences (> 0) between various groups (e.g., clinical vs. normals; pretreatment vs. posttreatment in clinical populations). Although the manual suggests that the test is used in industrial selection applications, no specific data are presented regarding concurrent or predictive validity in such situations.

Norms. The major source of norms is from previous research with German samples (the main sample of 3,132 children and adolescents), the sample of 506 U.S. college students, and small clinical samples of children. The tabled norms for the college students do not appear to agree well with a graph of mean performance by ages from the German samples, so it is not clear how well the norms generalize across language and sample differences. The German data, though, suggest that age group differences are substantial across the range from age 10 to age 60, especially on error rates.

ADMINISTRATION/INTERPRETATION. The administration instructions are concrete and easy to follow. However, there is some lack of standardization in the flexibility recommended for either children or adolescents, or for examinees with lower levels of intelligence. No data are presented to determine the effects of such instructions/modifications. No information is provided to aid in the interpretation of scores. In addition, given the large set of small, but significant correlations with a variety of different contrasts (intelligence, personality, psychopathology, pharmacologic reactions), it seems clear that this test is not likely to yield effective differential diagnoses across such constructs.

SUMMARY. The d2 Test of Attention is a modern instantiation of a procedure (the cancellation test) with a long psychometric history, in terms of assessing perceptual speed and/or attention. From a qualitative taxonomic perspective, the test appears to have much in common with digit-symbol tests (given the memory component), with other Perceptual Speed—Memory tests, and with other Perceptual Speed—Complex ability tests (Ackerman & Cianciolo, 2000), such as the Federal Aviation Administration's Directional Headings Test (e.g., see Ackerman & Kanfer, 1993). However, it remains to be demonstrated that the d2 Test of Attention provides either equivalent validity or incremental predictive validity over other such perceptual speed tests. It is also unclear whether the test shares sufficient common variance with other tests of selective attention, or discriminant validity with tests of other kinds of attention (e.g., focused attention or sustained attention) to provide a univocal classification of the test as one of selective attention. The information presented in the manual does suggest that, like other tests of perceptual speed and attention, the d2 Test is somewhat sensitive to a wide variety of phenomena and clinical syndromes—though it does not differentiate among them.

REVIEWER'S REFERENCES

Ackerman, P. L., & Cianciolo, A. T. (2000). Cognitive, perceptual speed, and psychomotor determinants of individual differences during skill acquisition. *Journal of Experimental Psychology: Applied, 6,* 259–290.
Ackerman, P. L., & Kanfer, R. (1993). Integrating laboratory and field study for improving selection: Development of a battery for predicting air traffic controller success. *Journal of Applied Psychology, 78,* 413–432.
Anastasi, A., & Urbina, S. (1997). *Psychological testing* (7th ed.). New York: Prentice Hall.

Review of the d2 Test of Attention by ELAINE CLARK, Professor of Educational Psychology, University of Utah, Salt Lake City, UT:

DESCRIPTION AND DEVELOPMENT. The d2 Test of Attention (d2 Test) was first published in 1962 in Germany by Rolf Brickenkamp. It was not until 1998, however, that it was published in English (by Brickenkamp and Zillmer). The d2 Test is essentially a letter cancellation task intended to assess selective attention; it also measures sustained attention and speed of processing. The test was initially intended to measure driving ability. It has been used to meet other purposes, including employee selection in industrial settings for jobs requiring a high level of concentration and visual discrimination, in schools to evaluate students' attentional capacity for learning, and in clinical settings where patient response to psychotropic drugs is an important target behavior.

The d2 Test is a simple paper-and-pencil test that requires an examiner have only a stopwatch and the test materials (protocol, scoring transparencies, and d2 Test manual). Examinees are required to cross out all "relevant" or target letters. The target letter is a "d" that appears with two dashes, that is, two dashes above or below the "d," or one dash above and one dash below the letter. The test consists of 14 lines of letters (both target and distractor letters). The authors estimate that it takes about 8 minutes to administer, including time for instructions. Examinees are allowed 20 seconds on each of the 14 lines. After 20 seconds, examinees are instructed to stop and go to the next line. This procedure continues until all 14 lines are completed. There are some exceptions, including the allowance for more or less time to complete the test; however, most examiners will use the 20 second rule since this is the only administration with norms.

Before starting the test, examinees are read rather lengthy instructions. Fortunately, they are also shown an example of what is expected and given an opportunity to practice on one line. Depending on the examinee, the test may take longer than 8 minutes. Examiners are allowed considerable latitude to elaborate on the instructions to insure that examinees understand what they are expected to do. Examinees with significant attention and/or comprehension problems may, therefore, be expected to take longer grasping the instructions. The test can be given in a group setting; however, it is not clear how the examiner would insure that the test is being completed as instructed (i.e., stopping work on a particular line after 20 seconds and going on to the next).

The actual scoring of the test is straightforward. Two transparencies are needed for scoring, and grid marks help to keep the scorer from making mistakes. The instructions for scoring are clear and the two examples included in the manual help a great deal. The test protocol is set up to make it relatively easy to calculate scores quickly. Because some score boxes are located next to the target and distractor letters, some examinees may be distracted. Scores are transcribed to the front of the protocol sheet where percentages, percentile ranks, and standard scores, are recorded.

A number of scores can be computed from the d2 Test. These include scores for Total Number of Items Processed (TN), Errors (E), Percentage of Error (E%), Total Number of Items Processed Minus Errors (TN-E), Concentration Performance (CP), Fluctuation Rate (FR), and Skipping Syndrome (S-Syndrome). TN is a sum of all target and nontarget items processed. It is thought to be a measure of allocation of attentional resources, processing speed, and amount of work completed. The E score is the sum of all mistakes, including omission and commission errors. Omission errors are used to provide information about attentional control, rule compliance, accuracy of scanning, and overall performance quality. Commission errors also help to assess accuracy and rule compliance; however, these errors provide information about likely problems with inhibitory control, cognitive flexibility, and tendency to be careless. The E% score represents the amount of error proportionate to the amount of information processed, essentially a measure of speed-accuracy tradeoff. As expected, E% and E are highly correlated (e.g., .91 and .99).

Further information about speed and accuracy can be obtained from the CP score. This score allows a more accurate estimation of concentration (i.e., without scanning errors). A similar score can be calculated. TN minus E provides a measure of the quantity of information processed without error; unlike the CP it can be skewed by haphazard scanning. The TN-E score and the CP scores are highly correctly reported (e.g., for the U.S. college sample as an average $r = .94$ and for U.S. children $r = .98$).

The FR score is intended to measure performance consistency. This score has been shown to be only moderately correlated with the others (e.g., with TN an $r = .36$, and with E% an $r = .40$). Extremely high scores are suggestive of inconsistent work, and/or poor motivation. Although no score is actually calculated for the S-Syndrome, this is noted when examinees hastily scan the grid and complete a large number of items with a large number of errors. High "skipping" scores may indicate impulsivity and is noted on the face of the protocol form.

TECHNICAL. Norms are provided for a number of scores, including the TN, TN-E, E%, FR, and CP. Because the CP is a relatively new score, only a subset of the original German standardization data were recalculated to obtain this index. The CP norms, however, are based on 900 participants (i.e., participants who range in age from 9 to 59). Only preliminary U.S. norms are available in the d2 Test manual; thus, examiners in the U.S. will likely rely on these and the other German norms for test score interpretation. Although the authors could have described more completely the procedures used to collect the German norming data (e.g., how the participants were selected and how tested), the number of participants included in the normative base is large. A total of 3,000 adults ages 19 to 59-11, and 3,132 children and adolescents, ages 9 to 20, participated in the norming process. Separate norms have been calculated for various age groups (at 2-year intervals) starting at 9 years of age and going up until 19. Above age 19 the age groupings are quite reasonable, 19 to 39-11, 40 to 49-11, and 50 to 59-11. Separate German norms are also included for adolescents attending high school and vocational school, and for male and female children and adolescents. Unlike the adult data that showed no sex effect, there was a sex effect in the child and adolescent data. According to the authors, the adult sample was representative of a wide range of occupational, educational, and economic backgrounds. The data for the adult norming study were collected from clients at the Institute for Safety in Mining, Industry, and Transportation in Germany.

Preliminary U.S. norms have been collected for children, college students, and adults. Brickenkamp and Zillmer also provided norms for a U.S. sample of children. This sample includes a group of 56 "normal" children and 40 children diagnosed with an Attention Deficit Hyperactivity Disorder (ADHD). According to the manual, the "normal" group consisted of 96% Caucasians (unclear who the 4% non-Caucasians were), and 28 males and 26 females.

These norms, for the college population, are for a sample of 506. These college students range in age from 18 to 32 years. The majority are Caucasian (77%), the only minority groups represented were Asian American and African American, 14% and 9%, respectively. Males represent 59% of the group, females 41%. No sex differences were found for this sample; therefore, scores for males and females were combined. The only other adult U.S. norms reported in the manual were those collected in 1989 by Spreen and Strauss (1991) for 80 individuals aged 50 and older. Spreen and Strauss report separate norms for males and females, and for individuals in four different age

groups (50–59, 60–69, 70–79, and 80 and older). Thus some of the mean scores represent as few as 4 individuals. There is a significant gap in the norms for U.S. adults.

RELIABILITY AND VALIDITY. A variety of methods were used to estimate internal consistency of the German data, but for the U.S. sample, only coefficient alpha was used. With the exception of E% coefficients in the .71 to .79 range, all alpha values were .84 or above. Even higher coefficients were found for the U.S. data (e.g., no coefficient below .79). Stability over time has also been examined. Correlation coefficients for test-retest periods, ranging from 5 hours to 40 months, show consistently high values. The only exception is that of coefficients for E% and FR (e.g., E% = .37, and FR = .49). The most stable indicators are TN and CP with reliability coefficients consistently above .88. Some of the adolescent studies, however, showed instability over time, including TN coefficients as low as .24 (with behavioral disturbed) and CP coefficients of .74. Several types of validity evidence are provided for both the German and U.S. data sets. Only the U.S. studies are highlighted in this review. In addition to factor analytic studies that support the underlying notion of each of the measures (e.g., TN, CP, and FR as measures of selective attention and E as a measure of flexibility), several correlational studies have been conducted and shown significant correlations between d2 Test variables, TN-E and CP, and measures of attention and executive functioning. For example, TN-E correlates .47 with the Symbol Digit Modalities Test (SDMT) and .34 with Stroop (both attention measures), and -.34 to -.51 with Tower of London and -.37 with the Computerized Progressive Maze (both referred to as executive measures). The CP index correlated with the Stroop (.34) and SDMT (.47), as well as Trail Making (e.g., -.33 and -.36 with Parts A and B). Studies comparing scores on the d2 Test of Attention and the Wisconsin Card Sorting Test (WCST) have, however, failed to show significant correlations (e.g., .14 with WCST categories and -.24 with perseveration).

COMMENTARY AND SUMMARY. The d2 Test of Attention has a long history of use in Europe, and may well enjoy extended use in the U.S. First, however, more studies need to be conducted with U.S. populations. Without more information about the way in which the test was (and is) being normed, potential users may be discouraged and look for another test. The manual is comprehensive in many ways. For one, excellent instructions are provided on how to give and score the test. Unfortunately, too little detail is provided about the standardization procedure and the individuals who participated in the norming studies (both in Germany and the U.S.). Because the test has been revised seven times in German since 1962, it is possible this information exists somewhere besides in the English manual. However, even the description of the U.S. studies was lacking in detail. More information is clearly needed about the norming sample and procedures and performance data from a more representative U.S. sample are needed. At this point, the norms for U.S. children are based on very small sample sizes (e.g., 28) and the norms for adults are severely restricted (i.e., ages 18 to 32, and college education only). The size of the German standardization group is enviable; however, without further information about the process used to gather the data, and the particular sample, interpreting the test scores will be difficult even knowing that the pattern of test scores (i.e., intercorrelations) is similar for both the U.S. and German samples. The d2 Test has come a long way from a driving measure. It has been used as a test to evaluate the impact of anesthetics and other drugs on performance, and the impact of disease processes, including Alzheimer's, on attentional capacity. It is hoped that with further information forthcoming about the test, and more published studies, researchers in the U.S. will include the d2 Test in their investigations and provide data to argue more forcefully for its use in evaluations. Until then, potential users will have to continue asking themselves what the test will add to the attentional measures they already use.

REVIEWER'S REFERENCE

Spreen, O., & Strauss, E. (1991). *A compendium of neuropsychological tests; Administration, norms, and commentary.* New York: Oxford University Press.

[88]

Dyslexia Early Screening Test.

Purpose: A battery of tests to "provide ... a simple 'at risk' index for dyslexia."
Population: Ages 4-6 to 6-5.
Publication Date: 1996.
Acronym: DEST.
Scores, 11: 2 Tests of Attainment (Digit Naming, Letter Naming), 8 Diagnostic Tests (Rapid Naming, Bead Threading, Phonological Discrimination, Pos-

tural Stability, Rhyme Detection, Forwards Digit Span, Sound Order, Shape Copying), At Risk Quotient.
Administration: Individual.
Price Data, 2002: $119 per complete kit including manual (1996, 65 pages), score keys, subtests, sample permission letter, 50 record forms, blindfold, balance tester, Forwards Digit Span tape, Sound Order test tape, and carrying case; $55 per 50 record forms.
Time: (30) minutes for entire battery.
Comments: Downward extension of the Dyslexia Screening Test (88); normed in the United Kingdom.
Authors: Rod I. Nicolson and Angela J. Fawcett.
Publisher: The Psychological Corporation Europe [United Kingdom]; distributed by The Psychological Corporation.

Review of the Dyslexia Early Screening Test by KATHLEEN M. JOHNSON, Psychologist, Lincoln Public Schools, Lincoln, NE:

DESCRIPTION. The Dyslexia Early Screening Test (DEST) is intended by the authors to be a brief, individually administered screening instrument used to "pick out children who are 'at risk' of reading failure early enough to allow them to be given extra support at school" (manual, p. xi). It was designed for use by school professionals (e.g., teachers, special needs coordinators, nurses) to screen young children in order to determine a child's need for more comprehensive disability assessment, along with identifying a child's strengths, weaknesses, and developmental skills, according to the authors. The DEST is a British product and contains some vocabulary that may cause some confusion in other countries, a heavy emphasis upon diagnosing dyslexia, and specific references to educational regulations in the United Kingdom.

The instrument is designed for children 4 years, 6 months to 6 years, 5 months of age. It is composed of 10 brief subtests that can reportedly be administered in approximately 30 minutes. Most of the materials needed come with the test kit in a handy carrying bag. A stopwatch, a small container to hold beads, an audio cassette player (used for two subtests), pencil, and unlined paper need to be provided by the examiner. The protocol is a two-sided sheet on which the items are marked on one side and the overall scoring is completed on the other side. The subtests are: Rapid Naming (time needed to name one page of line drawings), Bead Threading (number of beads threaded on a string in 30 seconds), Phonological Discrimination (identifying same vs. different for nine pairs of similar words), Postural Stability (four ratings of body balance following physical contacts to the child's back), Rhyme Detection (identifying if eight pairs of items rhyme or not, and 5 items of identifying initial sounds in words), Forwards Digit Span (14 items, up to seven digit sequences), Digit Naming (7 items), Letter Naming (10 lower case items), Sound Order (16 items of identifying which sound came first in a pair of sounds as the time between the sounds gradually decreases), and Shape Copying (7 items). The authors describe Digit Naming and Letter Naming as "tests of attainment" and the other eight as "diagnostic tests" (manual, p. 6).

The 65-page manual contains detailed administration and scoring instructions as well as helpful practice items for most sections. The examiner instructions to the child are highlighted and easy to follow. However, the manual contains some redundancy with a strong focus on the description and administration aspects of the instrument, whereas the available technical and normative data are limited. Scoring for the Postural Stability and Shape Copying subtests is fairly subjective despite the scoring guidelines. A child's raw subtest scores on the DEST are converted to categorical ratings using a scoring key overlay for his or her age level: (—) highly at risk for percentiles 1–10, (-) at risk for percentiles 11–25, (0) normal for percentiles 26–75, (+) above average for percentiles 76–90, and (++) well above average for percentiles 91–99. The authors then devised a method for combining the results of the subtests to obtain a composite "at risk" score (ARQ—At Risk Quotient). This score (along with another more subjective method of determining "at risk" status offered by the authors) basically identifies those who score similar to the bottom 10–11% of children in each age group as "at risk."

DEVELOPMENT. The authors acknowledge that there are few studies and even fewer instruments that assess dyslexia as early as they attempt with the DEST. Nicolson and Fawcett developed and organized this scale primarily on the basis of a study they published in 1995. They report that the results indicated that dyslexia is more than a phonological disability. Additionally, they maintain that by sampling a number of different areas of difficulty (e.g., balance, phonology, speed of processing, memory), dyslexic and nondyslexic children can be differentiated using a simple index representing various measures of those difficulties.

Additionally, the DEST is to some extent a downward revision of the Dyslexia Screening Test (DST; 88), which was also developed by these authors (to screen for characteristics associated with dyslexia in children 6.5 to 16.5 years of age). The specific tasks included in the DEST were gathered by the authors based upon their analysis of the dyslexia literature and "refined such that each test could be undertaken quickly and objectively by the tester without need for extensive training" (manual, p. 9). In the manual, the authors describe how the various tasks relate to the current theories about dyslexia.

With regard to test and item selection, the manual states only that an extensive series of studies, administrations, and revisions took place in designing the subtests and then norms were determined for each test for each age. The norm group is described as including over 1,000 children and having at least 100 children at each 6-month age interval. Details describing the norm group are not available in the manual. No data are included about sample stratification or population representation and, in fact, the authors note that norm testing took place with "whole classes of children at selected schools in Sheffield and throughout England and Wales" (manual, p. 9). The authors describe their use of the At Risk Quotient (ARQ) and descriptive categories as making intuitive sense; the resulting weighted score should not be interpreted as a statistically derived standard score. The authors offer intervention ideas for children scoring "at risk" in the form of a bibliography (chapter 4), consistent with their stated purpose of addressing those in need of more support in reading.

TECHNICAL DATA. The reliability of the test is addressed by only one measure in which 26 children (all 5 years, 5 months to 6 years, 5 months of age) were retested after 1 week. The correlations for the subtests ranged from .625 to .878, which the authors reported to be similar to those for comparable tests. Only two of the subtests had reliability correlations above .85 and the very small number of items in most of the subtests likely contribute to the reliability problems. The authors note that the reliability data could have been improved by retesting more children. No data are presented on the reliability of the at risk composite score. Salvia and Ysseldyke (1998) recommend higher reliability levels than are reported here for tests used to make educational decisions for individual children. It is recommended in the manual that 6 months pass before retesting children with the DEST in applied settings because of practice and training effects. With regard to interrater reliability, the data from another test (the Dyslexia Screening Test) were reported in the manual and the authors asserted that the DEST data were adequate and accurate because "the same scoring system is used" (manual, p. 12). Subtest intercorrelations are reported in the manual but the authors provided no interpretation of the data.

Stating that this is the only test of its kind for young children, the authors asserted that there is no possibility for gathering concurrent validity data. Construct validity was addressed by a brief review of the most common views of dyslexia and by describing how the various subtests reflect the theories (e.g., the Rapid Naming test is based on phonological deficit theory). Nicolson and Fawcett (the authors of the DEST) also note that the DEST has components similar to some lengthy early screening batteries but provide no data about how the test results compare. As a disability screening instrument it would seem essential to examine the adequacy of the DEST with regard to predictive validity, but no data are available on this topic in the manual.

SUMMARY. The DEST is a brief instrument aimed at screening children for early reading difficulties and thereby documenting these difficulties primarily for the purposes of special education referral and intervention. Although the DEST is titled and described as a screening instrument, the authors often refer to the results as providing diagnosis information. The data collected with the DEST are actually fairly limited in scope and some of the skills being assessed are only hypothetically associated with the concept of dyslexia (e.g., validity of the Postural Stability measures) and thus more research is needed. The technical and normative data presented with the instrument are quite limited and indicate needs for additional investigation. It would be important, for example, to examine the relationship between the DEST results and later school performance levels. The instrument could be used, as suggested by the authors, to help justify a referral for a comprehensive assessment of special needs. However, teachers working with young students assess several of these areas within the literacy curriculum (e.g., phonological skills, letter naming) and thus probably do not need a screening device to help identify the students who are at risk for reading failure. The DEST offers little information that skilled teachers could not document through informal and curriculum means as they are working with young children who are struggling with early literacy skills.

REVIEWER'S REFERENCE
Salvia, J., & Ysseldyke, J. (1998). Assessment (7th ed.). New York: Houghton Mifflin.

Review of the Dyslexia Early Screening Test by WILLIAM K. WILKINSON, *Consulting Educational Psychologist, Boleybeg, Barna, County Galway, Republic of Ireland:*

DESCRIPTION. The Dyslexia Early Screening Test (DEST) was designed to fill the significant instrumentation void in the early identification of dyslexia. As the authors note, there is a paradox between the call for early identification of dyslexia and the fact that dyslexia is not formally identified until a child is roughly 8 years of age. The late detection of dyslexia is due to the fact that a child cannot fall significantly behind (e.g., 18–24 months) in reading/spelling/writing attainment, because such delays are not apparent until several years after the child begins formal instruction in reading (normally around age 6).

Thus, the DEST is designed for a 2-year age group between 4.6 and 6.5. The authors of the test also have as their mission the creation of a test that can be used by school professionals (e.g., regular classroom teachers, specialized reading teachers) and one that is enjoyable for young children.

The DEST consists of 10 subtests that are reported to be theoretically/conceptually related to different aspects of dyslexia. The 10 subtests are divided into two "attainment" tests (e.g., early school learning related to naming numbers and letters) and eight "diagnostic" tests. The "diagnostic" tests are a varied set of tasks that relate to phonological processing (e.g., discriminating word sounds, sequencing sounds, sound awareness), motor skills (e.g., threading beads, postural stability, paper-pencil control), and memory related tests (e.g., immediate repetition of increasing number sequences).

The equipment included to administer the 10 subtests are a Rapid Naming card, beads and cord for threading, balance tester and blindfold for Postural Stability subtest, digit and letter cards, shape copying card, and cassette tapes for administration of the Digit Span and Sound Order tests. The test also includes four scoring keys.

In reviewing the manual, and by engaging in practice administrations of the test, this reviewer found the administration and scoring directions simple and relatively straightforward. The tests appear "face valid" with respect to the purposes for which they are intended.

The test is easy to score. The record form allows the user to record item responses within each subtest. On the reverse side, the subtest scores are collated and reduced to an "At Risk" index. The form itself is generally simple and easy to sue. The "At Risk" index is important and requires elaboration.

To simplify interpretation, the authors split the percentile rank distribution into five categories as follows: A percentile rank of 1 to 10 is assigned a mark of —, a percentile rank of 11 to 25 is assigned a mark of -, a percentile rank of 26–75 is assigned a mark of 0, a percentile rank of 76–90 is given a mark of +, and finally, a percentile rank of 91 to 99 is assigned a mark of ++. The four scoring keys, which correspond to four age groups (4.6–5.0; 5.0–5.5; 5.6–5.11; 6.0–6.5), provide the raw score equivalents for each of the 10 subtests that match the above five percentile categories. The result of all this is the "At Risk Quotient," which is defined, on average, as 10 scores marked as - or any combination of subtest totals leading to a total of 10 (e.g., five subtests at or above normal, and five scores in the lowest decile). The authors report that using an ARQ cutoff of 1.0 led to 11% of their standardization sample meeting the "At Risk" cutoff.

DEVELOPMENT. The selection and development of the 10 DEST subtests seems both face and theoretically valid. The theoretical justification for each of the 10 subtests is appropriately delimited in the test manual.

TECHNICAL. Herein lies my greatest concern regarding the DEST. It could be that the authors restricted technical information in the test manual because of the intended audience (one in which it is guessed that technical issues related to test development would not be of primary importance). Nonetheless, there is flimsy and superficial treatment of important test development issues. An example is the standardization sample. All we know is that at least 100 children in the aforementioned four age brackets were sampled in schools in Sheffield and throughout England and Wales. Therefore, caution is needed with regard to the use of this test outside England and Wales (perhaps within England and Wales as well, depending on how geographically representative the sample is of these areas).

This type of simplified technical information continues in other areas as well. For example, the authors provide an interesting intersubtest correlation matrix. However, no discussion of the data is given, even though these data are extremely important in determining conceptual clusters, or symptom groupings. Perusal of a table on page 13 of the manual supports the notion of "attainment" tests in the Letter Naming and Digit Span are correlated .71 (the highest intercorrelation in the table). However, as far as additional groupings, this is the responsibility of the test authors to inform.

Reliability data are provided in test-retest form (approximately 1-week administration interval) and vary from a low .64 for Sound Order to .88 for Letter Naming. Low test-retest reliability estimates would be expected given the young age groups involved. It would be interesting to see test-retest coefficients for the four different age groups.

Validity data (at least in empirical form) are not presented, based on the authors' contention that there are no competitors by which to get convergent validity coefficients. It is unclear why the authors subsequently mention other early screening tests in the manual. In the future, it is suggested that convergent/divergent validity data be considered with respect to these measures.

Finally, the potential user should be aware of restricted score ranges for certain tests at certain ages. For example, for the 6.0 to 6.5 age group, the Letter Naming test has a maximum raw score of 10. A score of 0 to 8 is in the lowest decile, whereas a raw score of 9 is in the next lowest score category, with a maximum score of 10 equaling any of the remaining three percentile ranks divisions. In other words, there is very little score range in this particular test for this age group.

COMMENTARY. The general impression regarding the DEST is that it represents a significant advance in the early measurement of dyslexia. To the credit of the test authors, the term "At Risk" is used, but there is no implication that the child is genuinely "dyslexic." As the authors note, this requires a more specialized assessment that cannot be undertaken until the child is around 8 years of age or older.

Further, one must be circumspect about what the implications of "At Risk" mean. The authors note that young children so identified should receive "extra help." This is a benign consequence and should be advantageous to the child. Individual schools, and perhaps districts, may need to develop specific guidelines about how high the "At Risk" score should be before school resources are deployed to help the child (e.g., resource teaching, learning support).

A final caution regarding the DEST is that children who obtain a significant "at risk" profile are by no means "dyslexic." The DEST cannot be used for the purpose of differential diagnosis, as the authors note. Any of a number of difficulties could account for poor performance. Certainly, specific learning difficulty (dyslexia) is one, but so too are general learning difficulties, speech/language/impairment, dyspraxia, non-verbal learning difficulties, attention problems, and so on. Put in a different perspective, the 11% of the standardization sample considered "at risk" are so identified for any of a number of different learning-type problems. In my opinion, the DEST is a "screen" for a wide range of learning difficulties. Whether any, or which one (or ones) come to fore, requires additional assessment with more formal and specialized evaluation procedures.

SUMMARY. The rationale for the DEST is very compelling, namely that professionals who assist children with specific learning difficulties (such as dyslexia) may be aware of early signs of the problem, but have, heretofore, no formal procedures by which to quantify/identify it. The DEST provides a procedural sequence that fills the gap between informal observation and more formal assessment. In addition, the DEST can be used by teachers, so the information derived could have immediate instructional benefit. Technically, the DEST requires further documentation, especially regarding the reliability and validity evidence. Potential users may wish to develop "local" norms because the normative sample is restricted to several schools in England and Wales.

[89]

The Enright Forgiveness Inventory.

Purpose: "To measure the degree to which one person forgives another who has hurt him or her deeply and unfairly."
Population: High school and college and adults.
Publication Date: 2000.

Acronym: EFI.
Scores, 10: 3 Affect scores (Positive Affect, Negative Affect, Total Affect), 3 Behavior scores (Positive Behavior, Negative Behavior, Total Behavior), 3 Cognition scores (Positive Cognition, Negative Cognition, Total Cognition), Total.
Administration: Group or individual.
Price Data, 2001: $35 per manual (70 pages); $75 copying privileges of less than 100 copies; student discount available; additional price information available at www.forgiveness-institute.org.
Time: (40) minutes.
Authors: Robert D. Enright, Julio Rique, and Catherine T. Coyle.
Publisher: International Forgiveness Institute.

Review of the Enright Forgiveness Inventory by LAURA L. B. BARNES, Associate Professor of Educational Research and Evaluation, Oklahoma State University, Tulsa, OK:

DESCRIPTION. The Enright Forgiveness Inventory (EFI) is a 60-item Likert-scaled paperpencil measure designed to assess the degree to which the respondent forgives another person who has "hurt him or her deeply" (user's manual, p. 5). The scale is intended to measure the cognitive, affective, and behavioral domains of forgiveness. Each item is a word or short phrase that describes the respondent's feelings, thoughts, and behaviors concerning the offending person. For the purposes of this instrument, interpersonal forgiveness is defined as "a willingness to abandon one's right to resentment, negative judgment, and indifferent behavior toward one who unjustly injured us, while fostering the undeserved qualities of compassion, generosity, and even love toward him or her" (user's manual, p. 1).

The instrument yields 10 scores: a total scale score based on all 60 items, three subscale scores—Affective, Behavioral, and Cognitive—composed of 20 items each, three 10-item scales based on the positively worded items from each subscale, and three 10-item scales based on negatively worded items from each subscale. Five additional items that are not part of the forgiveness scales measure pseudo-forgiveness. High scores on this validity scale do not indicate forgiveness, but rather that the respondent may be in denial or is justifying the injury. The authors suggest that, for some research purposes, EFI scores from respondents with high scores on the pseudo-forgiveness scale be eliminated from the data. The front page of the EFI asks respondents several questions regarding the hurtful experience and the offending person and serves as the context for the EFI responses. The very last item on the inventory asks respondents to indicate the degree to which they have forgiven the offender. To avoid creating conceptual biases, this is the only place on the inventory that the authors use the word "forgiveness."

The authors indicate the EFI was developed for use with young adolescents through adults and requires a fifth-grade reading level. It is self-administered and is reported to require about 40 minutes with college students—somewhat longer for high school students. Directions for administering and scoring are quite simple and clear. The authors emphasize two validity issues in administration: (a) the word "forgiveness" should not be used during any instruction for administration—the EFI should be called an attitude scale, and (b) it should be stressed to participants that they be sure to report their current feelings, current thoughts, and current behaviors. The authors note significant differences have been found among the subscales of Affect, Cognition, and Behavior so they caution against the use or interpretation of a single subscale. They suggest that interpretation of change over time should take into consideration both the EFI total score and the pattern of relationship among the subscales, though they do not elaborate on this pattern in this manual. The authors report that language translations of the EFI have been developed and validity studies conducted for several countries including Austria, Brazil, and Israel.

DEVELOPMENT. The EFI is grounded in a four-phase process of model of forgiveness developed by Enright and the Human Development Study Group—a team of University of Wisconsin—Madison researchers and graduate students in psychology, education, and philosophy. The initial pool was 150 items measuring the cognitive, affective, and behavioral domains of forgiveness with both positive and negative characteristics in each domain. These 150 items were administered to 197 college students and their same-sex parents. Items were selected for the final form based on two criteria: (a) a positive correlation over .65 between the item and its respective 50-item subscale score and (b) a correlation below .17 with the Crowne-Marlowe Social Desirability Scale.

TECHNICAL.

Standardization. Norms are reported only for the EFI total score. Separate percentile norms

are reported for college students, adults, and high school students and are reported separately by gender for each group. Normative data were collected in three separate studies published in 1995, 1996, and 1999. The college student sample ($n = 397$) was composed of University of Wisconsin-Madison students; the students' same-sex parents comprised the adult sample ($n = 406$). The high school student sample ($n = 180$) came from a private school in the Midwest. Their same-sex parents ($n = 158$) provided another adult sample for which separate adult norms are reported. The authors provide neither a rationale for maintaining two separate sets of adult norms nor guidance for choosing between them. The only reported difference between the two groups of adults is that the college students' parents were slightly older (mean = 49 years) than the high school students' parents (mean = 43.16 years); however, no other demographic information regarding the latter is provided (though relatively high SES can be inferred because the data came from a private high school). Demographics provided for the college students and their parents describe these samples only with respect to education level, marital status, religiosity, and religion. Neither ethnicity nor socioeconomic status is reported, though again SES of the sample can be inferred from the high percentage of college graduates. Thus, though the sample sizes are generally adequate, the representativeness of the samples is limited.

The manual provides percentile norms for samples of male and female college students and adults in Austria, Israel, and Brazil. The sample sizes range from 29 for Israeli males to 101 for Austrian females. No descriptive information is given for these samples in the manual though readers are invited to contact the International Forgiveness Institute for further information regarding the international forgiveness project.

Reliability. Internal consistency reliabilities computed on scores obtained from portions of the standardization samples are in the upper .90s for all subscales and total score scales for high school students, college students, and adults. Four-week test-retest coefficients for 36 college students ranged from .67 for negative behavior scale scores to .91 for the total cognition scale score with .86 as the stability coefficient for the total EFI scores.

Validity. The results of a principal axis factor analysis with oblique rotation on the EFI were interpreted to support an essentially unidimensional factor structure. This provides supportive validity for interpreting a total scale score. However, the authors caution that patterns of differences among the subscales should be interpreted, and they state "a high score on the subscale of cognition is not necessarily indicative of a high score on the other subscales or of a high total EFI score" (user's manual, p. 10). They report that there are differences in the rates and amounts of change on the subscales, suggesting a dynamic factor structure. Certainly, the forgiveness construct as described by the authors in the manual and elsewhere (e.g., Enright, 2001) is more complex than suggested by the factor analytic results reported in the manual. The authors do not provide correlations among the subscales in the manual; however, Subkoviak et al. (1995) reported interscale correlations ranging from .80 to .87.

Reported correlations with other measures show EFI scores to be related positively to other measures of forgiveness, negatively correlated with state anger, state anxiety, and depression, and not correlated with a social desirability response style. The authors note these negative correlations are stronger within "developmentally appropriate contexts of hurt" (user's manual, p. 35) such as between romantic partners, spouses, or college students and their parents than when the offender is a stranger. An apparently contradictory statement in the manual that "forgiveness has no correlation with depression when a researcher is working with normal samples" (p. 35) is clarified in Subkoviak et al. (1995) who reported this to be a statistical artifact due to range restriction in his nonclinical sample (p. 651).

COMMENTARY. One of the strengths of the EFI is that it was developed from a strong theoretical model of forgiveness that is described fully in the manual and elsewhere in the literature. The authors are very clear on what forgiveness is and what it is not. Thus, the EFI can be subjected to rigorous construct validation. The instrument is supported by a great deal of research. The manual lists references for numerous research studies, both published and unpublished, and a packet of research articles is available from the publisher upon request. Thus, the EFI as a research tool is supported by both theory and research.

Though clinical applications of the EFI are discussed somewhat in the manual, the EFI is probably most highly developed as a research tool

that "serves as a foundation for recommended clinical practice" (Enright, undated). The manual contains little guidance for clinical interpretations of the EFI and lacks some critical supporting information. For example, there are no case studies involving the EFI or suggested score profile interpretations; neither are confidence bands provided for individual score interpretation. Validity evidence supporting its use in clinical settings is not reported in the manual. The standardization sample was not very well described and the norms lack representativeness with respect to geography and likely with respect to other variables such as SES and ethnicity. On the other hand, the manual does provide references for what appear to be clinical studies and an issue of the *World of Forgiveness*, a periodical with a focus on Forgiveness in Therapy and Research, was included with the manual. Clinicians who wish to use the EFI as part of a forgiveness therapy intervention would be advised to refer to these additional references.

SUMMARY. The EFI appears to be a well-developed tool for conducting research on forgiveness. Reported reliability coefficients for scale scores are respectable and the scores generally appear to behave in accordance with theoretical expectations relative to other measures. The shortcomings of the standardization sample, though limiting its usefulness as a reference group, probably will not affect most research applications. The EFI has been translated into other languages and reportedly validated for use with other cultures; readers are reminded that this review pertains only to the American English version.

REVIEWER'S REFERENCES
Enright, R. D. (2001). *Forgiveness is a choice: A step-by-step process for resolving anger and restoring hope.* Washington, DC: American Psychological Association.
Enright, R. D. (undated). Announcement accompanying order form for the EFI. Madison, WI: International Forgiveness Institute, Inc.
Subkoviak, M. J., Enright, R. D., Wu, C., Gassin, E. A., Freedman, S., Olson, L. M., & Sarinopoulos, I. (1995). Measuring interpersonal forgiveness in late adolescence and middle adulthood. *Journal of Adolescence, 18,* 641–655.

Review of the Enright Forgiveness Inventory by JAMES FAUTH, Assistant Professor of Counseling Psychology, and SCOTT T. MEIER, Professor of Counseling Psychology, The State University of New York at Buffalo, Buffalo, NY:

DESCRIPTION. The Enright Forgiveness Inventory (EFI) is a self-report measure designed to assess the degree to which respondents forgive another person who has hurt them deeply and unfairly. The EFI is divided into four sections. First, respondents describe their most recent experience in which they felt unfairly and deeply hurt by another person. Second, they answer the actual EFI items, which ask them about their current positive and negative feelings, behaviors, and thoughts about the person who hurt them. Third, they respond to a Pseudo-Forgiveness scale. Finally, they respond to a one-item Forgiveness scale. Only the items in the second section are used in the actual EFI scores.

The EFI itself contains 60 Likert-type items (1 = *Strongly Disagree*, 6 = *Strongly Agree*) items and three scales (i.e., Affect, Behavior, and Cognition) consisting of 20 orthogonal items each. Further, each scale contains two subscales (i.e., Positive and Negative) consisting of 10 orthogonal items each. For example, an item on the Negative Affect scale is "I feel bitter toward him/her," whereas an item on the Positive Behavior scale is "Regarding the person, I do or would reach out to him/her." The five-item Pseudo-Forgiveness scale is used as a validity check; this scale was designed to detect respondents who are exhibiting psychological defenses such as denial rather than forgiveness. For example, an item on the Pseudo-Forgiveness scale is "My feelings were never hurt." The one-item Forgiveness scale, which directly asks respondents the degree to which they have forgiven the person who hurt them, is included as a "validity check" for EFI scores.

Nonclinical staff can administer, score, and interpret the EFI. The EFI can be administered in individual and group formats. On average, the EFI requires 40 minutes to complete (for adults and college students). The EFI was developed for use with both adolescents and adults; it requires a fifth-grade reading level. Finally, the EFI has been translated into six languages: English, Brazilian-Portuguese, German, Hebrew, Korean, and Taiwanese.

To score the EFI, all of the items on the Negative Affect, Negative Behavior, and Negative Cognition scales are reverse scored. These scores are added to the scores on the Positive Affect, Positive Behavior, and Positive Cognition scales. Thus, the EFI total score ranges from 60 to 360, with higher scores reflecting higher levels of forgiveness. According to the test authors, scores of 20 or higher on the Pseudo-Forgiveness scale reflect an overly defensive response pattern, suggesting that such scores should be discarded.

DEVELOPMENT. The test authors defined forgiveness as "a willingness to abandon one's right to resentment, negative judgment, and indifferent behavior toward one who unjustly injured us, while fostering the undeserved qualities of compassion, generosity and even love toward him or her" (manual, p. 1). They believe that forgiveness is interpersonal in nature and involves affective, behavioral, and cognitive dimensions. Finally, they posit that forgiveness is associated with positive mental health.

McCullough (2001) described forgiveness as "prosocial motivational changes" (p. 194) on the part of a person who has been hurt by another. Thus, someone who forgives another moves from being motivated to seek revenge or avoid the transgressor toward motivation to help that person. Kaminer, Stein, Mbanga, and Zungu-Dirwayi (2000) also noted that theorists agree that forgiveness involves a voluntary choice on the part of the wounded person, much like the cancellation of a debt. Some personality characteristics have also been found to be associated with a tendency to forgive, including agreeableness and emotional stability (McCullough, 2001). Agreeable persons tend to possess more empathy and care for others and thus are more forgiving; similarly, emotionally stable persons also have been found to be more forgiving, perhaps because they ruminate less about the transgression. Thus, theory and research indicate that forgiveness can have affective, cognitive, and behavioral components, identifiable correlates, and potential implications in clinical settings (Sells & Hargrave, 1998).

According to the test authors, the EFI originally consisted of 150 items generated by an interdisciplinary group at the University of Wisconsin-Madison. These items were subsequently administered to 197 college students and 197 of their same-sex parents. Item selection for the final version of the EFI was based on two criteria: (a) a positive and at least "moderate" correlation with its subscale score and (b) minimal correlations with the Crowne-Marlowe Social Desirability scale.

TECHNICAL. The authors offered minimal information about the norming procedure and samples. The EFI was normed on a sample of 180 (108 female, 72 male) adolescents, 397 (248 female, 149 male) college students, and 564 adults (328 female, 236 male) in three separate studies. The adult norm sample consisted of the same-sex parents of the adolescent and college student respondents. A representative norm sample was not achieved. First, the adolescent respondents all attended a single Midwestern high school; similarly, the college respondents attended a single Midwestern university. Second, the norm samples were disproportionately female and religious and homogeneous with regard to educational level and age. No information was given about the ethnicity, race, or socioeconomic status of the respondents. Finally, although norms for Austria, Brazil, and Israel appeared in the user's manual, no information was given about the norming process in these countries; further, these norms are based on fairly small samples.

The internal consistency (Cronbach's alpha) estimates for the EFI total score, scale scores, and subscale scores ranged from .98 to .99, .96 to .98, and .93 to .98, respectively. In addition, four-week test-retest reliabilities from a small sample ($N = 36$) were .86 for the total score and .81, .79, and .91 for the Affect, Behavior, and Cognitive scales, respectively. The results of a Confirmatory Factor Analysis on data from the 394 college students and their same-sex parents revealed a one-factor structure for the EFI (accounting for nearly 50% of the variance), casting doubt as to the utility of the scale scores. Further, the results of the factor analysis may be invalid due to the low sample size relative to the number of items in the EFI and the fact that the student/parent data were nested within family (i.e., non-independent).

As evidence of concurrent validity, the authors reported positive associations between EFI scores and Forgiveness Scale scores (r ranging from .53 to .74) and Wade Forgiveness Scale scores ($r = .79$). In terms of divergent validity, they reported data indicating that EFI scores and Crowne-Marlowe Social Desirability scale scores are not related (r ranging from .00 to .13). In addition, they reported two studies in which the magnitude of the inverse relationship between EFI scores and either the State-Trait Anxiety Inventory and Beck Depression Inventory or State Anger Scale increased in "developmentally appropriate contexts of hurt" (user's manual, p. 35) (i.e., being hurt by a family member rather than a stranger). The change in the association between EFI scores and State Anger Scale scores in different contexts, however, was very small and probably not statistically significant (statistical significance was not reported). Overall, the evidence of validity reported in the manual was weak. Notably, no longitudinal studies were cited to indicate

that changes in EFI scores are related to changes in meaningful behavioral or mental health criterion variables. It would also be useful to demonstrate that EFI scores are not redundant with scores on interpersonal, ego strength, or optimism/pessimism measures. Despite the attention that the test authors gave to the EFI scales and subscales, as well as the Pseudo-Forgiveness and Forgiveness scales, they did not report any evidence of validity for them.

COMMENTARY. The EFI represents an interesting attempt to measure the somewhat complex and vague construct of forgiveness. Currently, however, the utility of the test seems to be limited. First, the test has not been adequately normed on a representative sample. Second, factor analysis failed to support the hypothesized three-factor structure of the EFI. Third, no attempt has been made to differentiate scores on the EFI from measures of potentially similar constructs (e.g., agreeableness, interpersonal style, ego strength). Fourth, the evidence of validity for EFI scores is currently very weak and would profit from longitudinal studies. Finally, no evidence of validity was reported for the Pseudo-Forgiveness and Forgiveness scales.

SUMMARY. The developers have, to their credit, attempted to produce an easily administered instrument capable of measuring the complex construct of forgiveness while attending to denial and the influence of social desirability. Further, the EFI appears to possess excellent internal consistency. Overall, however, the factor analytic work failed to support the hypothesized three-factor structure of the EFI. Further, the evidence supporting the construct validity of the EFI is weak; considerable future research will be necessary to establish the adequacy of the EFI.

REVIEWERS' REFERENCES

Kaminer, D., Stein, D. J., Mbanga, I., & Zungu-Dirwayi, N. (2000). Forgiveness: Toward an integration of theoretical models. *Psychiatry: Interpersonal & Biological Processes, 63*, 344–357.

McCullough, M. E. (2001). Forgiveness: Who does it and how do they do it? *Current Directions in Psychological Science, 10*, 194–197.

Sells, J. N., & Hargrave, T. D. (1998). Forgiveness: A review of the theoretical and empirical literature. *Journal of Family Therapy, 20*, 21–36.

[90]

Essential Skills Assessments: Information Skills.

Purpose: "Broad measures of achievement set within the Essential skills of the New England Curriculum Framework ... [for the purpose of] formative assessment."

Population: *Ages 9–14.*
Publication Date: 2001.
Acronym: ESAs:IS.
Levels, 3: Primary, Intermediate, Secondary.
Administration: Group.
Price Data, 2002: NZ$36 per full specimen set including 1 each of primary, intermediate, and secondary tests, and teacher's manual (71 pages); NZ$22.50 per specimen set including all tests and teacher's manual (primary level); NZ$27 per specimen set including all tests and teacher's manual (intermediate level); NZ$22.95 per specimen set including all tests and teacher's manual (secondary level); NZ$450 per CD-ROM pack including CD-ROM with all tests (PDF format), teacher's manual, 1 set of printed tests, and help sheet; NZ$18 per teacher's manual; NZ$9.90 per 10 Finding Information in Books (all levels, specify level); NZ$9.90 per 10 Finding Information in Graphs and Tables (primary level); NZ$12.60 per 10 Finding Information in Graphs and Tables (intermediate level); NZ$11.70 per 10 Finding Information in Graphs and Tables (secondary level); NZ$9.90 per 10 Finding Information in a Library (primary and intermediate levels, specify level); NZ$12.60 per 10 finding Information in a Library (secondary level); NZ$9.90 per 10 Finding Information in Reference Sources (primary and intermediate levels, specify level); NZ$9.90 per 10 Evaluating Information in Text (intermediate level); NZ12.60 per 10 Evaluating Information in Text (secondary level); NZ$12.60 per 10 finding Information in Prose Text (intermediate and secondary levels, specify level).
Time: (30) minutes per test.
Comments: Replaces the Progressive Achievement Tests of Study Skills (T5:2095); tests include both constructed-response and selected-response format items; normed on children living in New Zealand; available in print or CD-ROM format; CD-ROM system requirements: 600 dpi laser or inkjet printer, Adobe Acrobat reader version 3 or 4.
Authors: Cedric Croft, Karyn Dunn, and Gavin Brown.
Publisher: New Zealand Council for Educational Research [New Zealand].
   a) FINDING INFORMATION IN BOOKS.
   Levels, 2: Primary, Intermediate.
   Scores: Total score only.
   b) FINDING INFORMATION IN GRAPHS AND TABLES.
   Levels, 3: Primary, Intermediate, Secondary.
   Scores: Total score only.
   c) FINDING INFORMATION IN A LIBRARY.
   Levels, 3: Primary, Intermediate, Secondary.
   Scores: Total score only.
   d) FINDING INFORMATION IN PROSE TEXT.
   Levels, 2: Intermediate, Secondary.
   Scores: Total score only.
   e) FINDING INFORMATION IN REFERENCE SOURCES.
   Levels, 2: Primary, Intermediate.
   Scores: Total score only.
   f) FINDING INFORMATION IN TEXT.
   Levels, 2: Intermediate, Secondary.
   Scores: Total score only.
Cross References: See T5:2095 (1 reference); for reviews by Michael D. Hiscox and Ronald C. Rodgers of an earlier edition, see 9:1006; see also T3:1913 (1 reference).

Review of the Essential Skills Assessments: Information Skills by ROBERT L. JOHNSON, Associate Professor, Educational Psychology, University of South Carolina, Columbia, SC:

The Essential Skills Assessments: Information Skills (ESAs:IS) consists of six modules that consist of 14 tests. Each module focuses on the specific information skills identified in its title (i.e., Finding Information in Books, Finding Information in Graphs and Tables, Finding Information in a Library, Finding Information in Prose Text, Finding Information in Reference Sources, and Evaluating Information in Text). Modules are available for three school levels: Primary (Years 5 and 6), Intermediate (Years 7 and 8), and Secondary (Years 9 and 10).

Each test begins with student instructions that state the purpose of the test. Next, two practice items provide examples of the answer formats that are used in the test. Students record their answers in the test booklet. Each test takes approximately 30 minutes to complete.

The publishers indicate that the tests contain constructed-response and multiple-choice items. The constructed-response items, however, typically require only a single word or brief phrase to answer. They may better be described as short-answer or fill-in-the-blank items. Many of the items are interpretive exercises that present information in the form that students "are likely to encounter on a daily basis" (p. 14). Examples of interpretive materials include a table of contents, an index, a dictionary page, graphs, and a timetable. Questions engage students in analysis of the interpretive materials and application of information skills to answer the item. This is consistent with the ESAs:IS framework that "conceptualizes information skills as problem-solving processes" (teacher's manual, p. 3).

Narratives provide another source of interpretive material that students use in answering

Validity of interpretations about student information skills is supported by developers' review of curriculum documents and the current literature on information skills. Also supporting validity is the incorporation of teachers in the review of items and to provide feedback after the pilot test. Internal validity is supported by the intercorrelations of the ESAs:IS tests. Scores correlate from .69 to .80 with the median of .75, providing initial evidence of a common construct. Concurrent validity evidence was collected on four instruments: Richmond Test of Basic Skills, National Education Monitoring Project Tasks, the Progressive Achievement Tests: Reading Comprehension, and the Test of Scholastic Abilities. Correlations with other tests range from .49 to .84 with a median of .71. A description of the content of the criterion measures would assist the reader of the manual in the interpretation of these correlations. Authors did not correlate ESAs:IS scores with any instruments that provide discriminant evidence of validity.

COMMENTARY. A strong component of the ESAs:IS is the evidence supporting the validity of inferences about students' information skills. Contributing evidence includes (a) the development of the instrument based on the New Zealand curriculum standards, (b) the authors' review of the current literature on informational skills to guide the instrument development provides support for validity, and (c) the solicitation and use of teacher feedback in the test development process. Further documentation about these aspects of test development would strengthen the evidence. Inferences about students' information skills appear to be supported by the correlation with criterion measures; however, better descriptions of the criterion measures would allow the reader of the manual to determine if the correlations are to be expected.

Reliability evidence for ESAs:IS is limited. Internal consistency measures show generally acceptable levels of reliability; however, these are the only form of reliability reported. Statements about the role of teacher judgment in the scoring of tests indicate the need for a study of interrater reliability. In addition, the manual presents the possibility of reviewing changes in test means over the course of a program. Such use of scores for program evaluation purposes indicates the need to conduct a study of scores in a test-retest design.

The ESAs:IS uses graphics and narrative to engage students in the problem-solving associated with informational skills. These interpretive materials are presented in a context familiar to students through the use of, for example, people, places, and animals associated with New Zealand. The focus on New Zealand, however, limits the use of the instruments for assessment or research purposes in other countries. The narrative used as interpretive material in the tests lacks the authenticity of works by authors of trade books.

SUMMARY. The ESAs:IS offers a useful set of tests to gauge students' abilities to apply information skills in a New Zealand context. The instrument will benefit from reliability studies as well as improved reporting about the representativeness of the norm group. In subsequent editions, the authors should consider the inclusion of authentic texts for use as interpretive materials.

[91]

Everstine Trauma Response Index.

Purpose: Designed to measure the presence of and extent of psychological trauma.
Population: Adults.
Publication Dates: 1988–1998.
Acronym: ETRI.
Scores, 3: Duration, Intensity, Trauma Response Index.
Administration: Group.
Price Data: Not available.
Time: (15–20) minutes.
Comments: A self-report questionnaire.
Author: Louis Everstine.
Publisher: Behaviordata, Inc.
[Note: The publisher advised in February 2002 that this test is no longer available.]

Review of the Everstine Trauma Response Index by BRIAN F. BOLTON, University Professor of Rehabilitation Education and Research, University of Arkansas, Fayetteville, AR:

DESCRIPTION. The Everstine Trauma Response Index (ETRI) was designed to assess the impact of a traumatic event on an individual who experiences trauma. Examples of traumatic events are rape, bankruptcy, death of a child, burglary, causing injury, and severe illness. The ETRI is a self-report inventory consisting of 35 brief questions that reflect a range of thoughts, feelings, and behaviors.

Respondents to the ETRI record their reactions to a traumatic event by (a) specifying the nature of the subjectively experienced symptomatology, (b) indicating how upsetting the experience was, and (c) reporting the length of time the symptoms were experienced. Basic factual information about the traumatic event is also recorded (i.e., type of event [more than 40 are listed], physical injury, hospitalization, physician care, and counseling received).

The ETRI is self-administered and takes between 15 and 20 minutes to complete for the typical respondent. For each of the 35 symptoms that is affirmed, an Intensity rating (on a scale of 1 to 10) is multiplied by the number of months the symptom was experienced (Duration). These symptom scores are then summed to produce a total score called the Trauma Response Index.

DEVELOPMENT. The conceptual framework on which the ETRI is premised includes three fundamental propositions: (a) Response to trauma is a homeostatic mechanism that restores equilibrium to the victim's life; (b) people respond differently to trauma, evidencing unique reaction styles and coping functions; and (c) reaction patterns constitute important factors in planning therapeutic interventions to foster recovery from trauma.

To operationalize the symptomatology of response to an "extreme traumatic stressor," the diagnostic criteria for posttraumatic stress disorder outlined in the *Diagnostic and Statistical Manual of Mental Disorders, Third Edition, Revised* (DSM-III-R; American Psychiatric Association, 1987) were used as the domain map. The 35 ETRI questions represent four symptom categories (with number of items in parentheses): (a) re-experiencing the traumatic event (4 questions), (b) avoidance of stimuli associated with the trauma (11 questions), (c) symptoms of increased arousal (10 questions), and (d) associated features and disorders (10 questions).

TECHNICAL. One small normative sample consisting of 75 adults who brought lawsuits for personal injuries caused by traumatic events provides the basis for translating ETRI total scores to percentiles. A second sample of 49 parents of spinal cord injured children was available but not tabled. No reliability data are given for the ETRI.

Two types of validity information are reported. The use of *DSM-III-R* diagnostic criteria as the formulation for operationalizing the domain of trauma symptomatology established a reasonable argument for content validity. The only evidence of concurrent validity is a correlation of .39 ($p<.001$) between the ETRI total score and the

PK scale of the Minnesota Multiphasic Personality Inventory for the normative sample. No other data supporting the validity of the ETRI are presented.

COMMENTARY. There are five areas in which problems exist with the ETRI: construction, scoring, interpretation, reliability, and validity. First, the manual does not explain how the *DSM-III-R* diagnostic criteria for posttraumatic stress were translated into ETRI questions. Also, no rationale is given for the distribution of the 35 items across the four categories of diagnostic symptoms. An explicit domain-sampling plan would strengthen the content validity argument for the ETRI.

Second, the manual fails to provide justification for multiplying the Intensity and Duration components in generating trauma scores. The question of how to appropriately combine score elements raises technical scaling issues. Regardless, it is necessary to provide a reason for multiplying the ETRI components to legitimatize the scoring procedure. Also, the huge numbers that result (e.g., the median ETRI total score for the norm group is 2,600) suggest a degree of precision that is not warranted.

Third, strategies and suggestions for interpreting ETRI scores are of questionable value. Descriptive information about the normative sample is not adequate. Specifically, the types of traumatic events experienced by members of the group are not given. Furthermore, the manual recommends various rules of thumb for interpreting ETRI scores that are baseless. For example, it is suggested that endorsing 10 or more of the 35 symptoms "is probably indicative that some form of trauma exists" (Manual for Administration, p. 7). No substantive rationale is provided.

Fourth, because reliability data are not presented, the consistency and stability of ETRI responses and scores are not known. Fifth, validity data are sparse. The main problem with the evidence for content validity was mentioned in the first point above (i.e., the absence of a strategy for systematically representing the *DSM-III-R* diagnostic domain). Finally, the concurrent correlation with the MMPI PK scale is not interpreted in terms of the constructs measured. Also, it would be desirable to table the correlations of the MMPI clinical scales with the ETRI score components separately (i.e., Symptoms Affirmed, Intensity, and Duration).

SUMMARY. The ETRI is premised on a worthwhile concept, which entails the translation of psychiatric diagnostic criteria for posttraumatic stress disorder into a scorable assessment instrument. If ETRI development satisfied accepted measurement standards, the inventory would be helpful to counselors and psychologists who work with trauma victims. Unfortunately, there is insufficient evidence supporting the construction, scoring, interpretation, reliability, and validity of the ETRI to warrant its use as a psychometric questionnaire. [Editor's Note: The publisher advises that a revised manual is in preparation that will provide information on research that reflects positively on reliability and validity of this test. The test will be reviewed again when this is available.] However, the ETRI may have utility when used informally as a self-report symptom checklist with clients who have experienced trauma.

REVIEWER'S REFERENCE

American Psychiatric Association. (1987). Diagnostic and statistical manual of mental disorders (3rd ed. rev.). Washington, DC: Author.

Review of the Everstine Trauma Response Index by HEIDI K. PAA, Senior Researcher, Renaissance Learning, Inc., Madison, WI:

DESCRIPTION. The Everstine Trauma Response Index (ETRI) is a 35-item instrument completed by paper and pencil that is intended to assess reactions to traumatic events. Respondents reply to each item in three ways: whether the item applies to them, how upsetting the experience was for them, and the duration of this upsetting experience. For example, the first item reads, "Did you lose a lot of weight?" Respondents would indicate whether this occurred to them as part of their reaction to a traumatic event, how upset they were by the weight loss, and how long the loss of weight lasted. The instrument also collects demographic information and details about the experienced traumatic event. The ETRI yields three scores: an Intensity score, a Duration score, and a Trauma Response Index, which measures the "relative nature of people's reactions to trauma" (manual, 1993, p. 9).

Although not specified in the manual, it appears that the ETRI is to be administered by mental health clinicians and can be either self-scored or scored by computer. In addition to gaining an understanding of the nature of the respondent's reaction to a traumatic event, the ETRI was constructed to aid in the diagnosis of Post-Traumatic Stress Disorder (PTSD) using DSM-IV criteria. The scoring procedure described in the manual is somewhat confusing. In addition, because the intensity scale uses a 10-point scale and the scoring procedures involve multiplying numbers, the range of scores is quite large. For example, the "Duration Score" is yielded by "multiplying each Intensity rating by the Duration expressed in months" (manual, 1993, p. 8). As a result, the Duration Score can vary from zero to 21,000! The manual fails to provide a rationale for the use of a ten-point scale with two anchors (*not very upsetting* to *extremely upsetting*) for the Intensity ratings, and it is not clear if respondents would be able to differentiate their level of being upset among 10 points.

DEVELOPMENT. The ETRI was developed to fill a void in the assessment of individuals' reactions to traumatic events. Specifically, the author notes that existing instruments measured only whether an event occurred and failed to account for an individual's reaction to that event. Moreover, the ETRI was constructed to align with DSM-IV criteria to assist in the diagnosis of PTSD. Appropriately, the author cautions testusers against relying solely on the ETRI for diagnosis and advocates for its use with other assessment procedures such as a clinical interview.

The DSM-IV criteria for PTSD include the following: one of five symptoms related to re-experiencing the trauma, three of seven symptoms related to avoidance of stimuli, and two of five symptoms related to increased arousal. In contrast, the ETRI includes the following: 4 questions related to re-experiencing the trauma, 11 questions related to avoidance of stimuli, and 10 questions related to increased arousal. Despite the lack of correspondence with the DSM-IV symptoms, the ETRI uses the same minimal criteria for diagnosis: one re-experiencing symptom, three avoidance symptoms, and two increased-arousal symptoms. Given that more questions on the ETRI measure the second two groups, it seems that a positive diagnosis may be more likely with the ETRI versus the DSM-IV criteria. At a minimum, information regarding how the items were written and evaluated is needed in the manual.

TECHNICAL. The norming sample consisted of 75 adults who were involved in litigation for personal injury due to a traumatic event. Data were gathered in five states with most of the respondents residing in Washington and California. About 65% were female, and half were married. Unfortunately, the manual fails to provide information regarding race and/or ethnic background. As a result, clinicians should exercise caution when using the ETRI with minority clients. Moreover, "trauma survivors" represent a relatively large and heterogeneous group. Individuals involved in litigation due to personal injury may not be representative of all trauma survivors. To the extent that this is not the case, the norms for the ETRI may not be representative of all survivors. The author asserts that an individual scoring at the 71st percentile on the ETRI "has suffered more trauma than 70% of the population of similar victims of traumatic events" (manual, p. 10). This appears to be quite a bold claim given the limited norm sample.

No reliability estimates are presented for the ETRI. Instead, the author discusses an examination of the instrument's "internal validity" or its susceptibility to deception. Forty-nine parents of children who had suffered a spinal cord injury and who were not involved in litigation completed the instrument, and their scores were compared to individuals from the norm sample who were involved in litigation for personal injury. An examination of mean differences showed that the parents scored higher on the ETRI than the norm sample; however, no statistical significance tests were conducted. The author argued that because the parents were not involved in litigation, they would have less "incentive" to exaggerate their scores. Although the statistical significance of this finding is uncertain, the parents could also score higher on the instrument because a child's spinal cord injury is inherently more traumatic than a "personal injury" (manual, p. 10).

The manual also describes a concurrent validity study that compared the ETRI to the PK scale of both the MMPI (Minnesota Multiphasic Personality Inventory) and the MMPI-2. Using Spearman's Rho, the correlation between the ETRI and the PK scale of the MMPI was not significant but positive (rho = .24). This sample included only 19 participants. With a sample of 56 participants, the ETRI correlated significantly and positively with the PK scale of the MMPI-2, rho = .41, $p <$ .01. Finally, in a sample of 75 participants, the ETRI correlated significantly and positively with the combined PK scales from both the MMPI and the MMPI-2, rho = .38, $p <$ .01. The author notes that future research investigations, such as a factor analysis of the ETRI, are under consideration.

COMMENTARY. A technically sound instrument designed to assist in the diagnosis and treatment of PTSD would be of great use to both researchers and clinicians. Unfortunately, in its current form, the ETRI cannot be recommended to fulfill this purpose for the following reasons. First, because no clear link exists between scores on the ETRI and a PTSD diagnosis using DSM-IV criteria, future research is needed to establish this connection. Second, the ETRI's scoring procedures are confusing and produce scores with an extremely large range. In addition, the norms are based on a small sample and may not be representative of all trauma survivors. Research with survivors of different traumatic experiences is greatly needed. Finally, evidence for the reliability and validity for scores from the ETRI has not been demonstrated. The manual contains no information regarding reliability estimates, and provides limited information about evidence for validity. Given these concerns, the ETRI should be used only as a research or screening instrument and not for diagnostic purposes.

SUMMARY. Because quantifying reactions to traumatic events is a difficult task, the test author should be given credit for her attempt to capture the varying and complex symptoms associated with PTSD. The strengths of the ETRI lie in its potential use for clinicians and researchers. Given the increasing violent nature of our society and the resulting increased incidence of PTSD, an assessment tool that would help to understand and treat the disorder is sorely needed. However, the ETRI has several limitations that need to be addressed before it can be recommended for this task. Namely, more representative norms are needed, and evidence for reliability and validity should be gathered and presented in the manual. Readers seeking an alternative assessment of PTSD may consider the PK scale of the MMPI-2 (Butcher, Dahlstrom, Graham, Tellegen, & Kaemmer, 1989).

REVIEWER'S REFERENCE

Butcher, J. N., Dahlstrom, W. G., Graham, J., Tellegen, A., & Kaemmer, B. (1989). *MMPI-2: Manual for administration and scoring*. Minneapolis, MN: University of Minnesota Press.

[92]

The Executive Control Battery.

Purpose: "To document the presence and extent of the 'executive dyscontrol' or 'frontal lobe' syndrome."
Population: Adults.
Publication Date: 1999.

Acronym: ECB.

Administration: Individual.

Price Data: Available from publisher.

Comments: Neuropsychological battery; subtests can be administered independently.

Authors: Elkhonon Goldberg, Kenneth Podell, Robert Bilder, and Judith Jaeger.

Publisher: Psych Press [Australia].

    a) THE GRAPHICAL SEQUENCES TEST.

    Purpose: "Designed to elicit perseverations … and various behavioural stereotypies."

    Scores, 7: Hyperkinetic Motor Perseverations (Occurrences), Perseveration of Elements (Occurrences, Repetitions), Perseveration of Features (Occurrences, Repetitions), Perseverations of Activities (Occurrences, Repetitions).

    Time: (15–20) minutes.

    b) COMPETING PROGRAMS TEST.

    Purpose: "Designed to elicit various types of echopraxia, behavioural stereotypies, and disinhibition."

    Scores, 8: Simple Go/No-Go (Random, Simple Stereotype, Alternating Stereotype, Total Errors), Simple Conflict—Visual (Random, Simple Stereotype, Alternating Stereotype, Total Errors).

    Time: (12–15) minutes.

    c) MANUAL POSTURES TEST.

    Purpose: "Designed to elicit various types of echopraxia and 'mirroring'."

    Scores: 3 ratings: Correct, Full Mirroring, Other.

    Time: (10–15) minutes.

    d) MOTOR SEQUENCES TEST.

    Purpose: "Designed to elicit various types of motor perseverations, stereotypies, and other deficits of sequential motor organisation."

    Parts, 2: Dynamic Praxis, Bimanual Coordination.

    Time: (10–15) minutes.

      1) *Dynamic Praxis.*

      Scores, 6: Two Stage Movement (Imitation, Continuation, Without Model), Reversal of Two State Movement (Imitation, Continuation Without Model), Three Stage Movement (Imitation, Continuation Without Model.

      2) *Bimanual Coordination.*

      Scores, 6: Distal (Imitation, Continuation Without Model), Proximal (Imitation, Continuation Without Model), Mixed (Imitation, Continuation Without Model).

Review of The Executive Control Battery by ANTHONY T. DUGBARTEY, Psychologist, Forensic Psychiatric Services Commission, and Adjunct Assistant Professor of Psychology, University of Victoria, Victoria, British Columbia, Canada:

DESCRIPTION. The Executive Control Battery (ECB) comprises four individually administered tests that purport to assess the behavioral and cognitive markers of the dysexecutive (or "frontal lobe") syndrome. Although each of the four tests comprising the ECB can be used as a stand-alone measure, each was nonetheless designed as part of an integral battery that assesses the broad spectrum of executive control functions. The ECB was developed primarily for use with adults.

The following is a description of the ECB tests. The Competing Programs Test (CPT) evaluates movement responses to auditory and visual commands that conflict with those produced by the examiner. The Graphical Sequences Test (GST) probes perseveration in motor control of drawing and writing. The Manual Postures Test (MPT) assesses allocentric and egocentric spatial representation by way of precision of imitation behavior. The Motor Sequences Test (MST) assesses a variety of alternating movement sequences with one or both hands. Although normed on clinical samples with schizophrenia, focal frontal lesions, and traumatic brain injury, the ECB can be administered to patients with a wide variety of anterior cerebral disorders.

The ECB administration time ranges from 60 to 90 minutes for clinical populations, and I have found that it takes approximately 70 minutes for healthy normal individuals to complete. The clinical acumen and extensive training required by the ECB precludes its administration by nonclinical personnel. This exclusion can be extended to otherwise competent clinical neuroscientists who are unfamiliar with the work of Alexander Luria, particularly when administering the MST subtest of the ECB. Scoring the ECB rests very heavily on error analysis. Consequently, precise discernment of both the various error types and Luria's theories of the behavioral expressions of prefrontal lesions are essential for accurate scoring of the ECB. Scoring of the ECB is done manually as no computer scoring of this test battery is available. Percentile ranks can be derived for each of the four ECB tests in comparison to 32 healthy controls and 101 individuals with a variety of neurologic and psychiatric disorders. Appropriate interpretation of the ECB test scores requires advanced knowledge of brain-behavior relationships.

DEVELOPMENT. The ECB, which represents an attempt at providing a standardized and quantifiable way of appraising the various aspects of the dysexecutive syndrome, is based almost exclusively on Luria's theories and conceptual notions of brain function. This is the first version (copyright, 1999) of the ECB, which was originally developed as a novel assessment battery that is sensitive and specific to the frontal lobe syndrome. With the exception of the test developers' assertions that the ECB items emanated from observations of Luria's clinical work with his patients, very limited information is offered in the administration manual regarding the derivation of the tests and items that make up the ECB. Put differently, little information exists concerning the item selection criteria for the tests making up the ECB. Although no reports from a pilot study were provided, the test developers described findings from confirmatory factor analysis showing a dissociation between perseverative and field-dependent domains from the four measures of the ECB.

TECHNICAL. The ECB developers point out the limited utility of traditional psychometric approaches in delineating the subtle and often complex underlying reasons for deficits in scores. Their introduction of error analysis is a welcome addition in the assessment of the dysexecutive syndrome. The test developers fail to provide detailed information on how the healthy controls were selected and considered to be free of cerebral disease. With regard to the clinical group, the individuals comprising the traumatic brain injured group were tested within 48 hours, but no information is provided on the duration between diagnosis and testing of the other clinical populations. Moreover, the schizophrenia group was diagnosed using outdated diagnostic criteria (i.e., DSM-III) that were published almost two decades before the ECB was published. The normative population of healthy controls on which the ECB was standardized is very small (i.e., 23 males and 9 females). Although the scoring systems for the ECB tests are discussed in detail, and the use of copious examples is helpful, a great amount of time and effort is required in order for the examiner to become adept at administering the ECB. Moreover, the examiner with right-left orientation problems would have great difficulty scoring the ECB correctly. As well, the Motor Sequences Test has a complex set of error scoring criteria that could be made more user friendly with the inclusion of a quick reference guide on the scoring sheet.

Interrater reliability estimates for two of the tests of the ECB (i.e., GST and MP) were quite high at .94 and .98, but the test developers acknowledged that the inter-rater reliability for classifying the type of perseveration was lower. No internal consistency reliability data for the individual ECB tests were reported.

No information on ecological validity of the ECB was proffered. In terms of concurrent validity, however, the MP mirroring errors were as accurate as the Wisconsin Card Sorting Test in discriminating healthy controls from clinical populations with executive control impairments.

COMMENTARY. The utility of the ECB as a measure of executive control functions is limited by a number of factors. First, there is no avenue for including collateral information about the patient's daily functioning and adjustment, an important aspect of assessing the dysexecutive syndrome. There is ample empirical evidence supporting the view that personality and social-interpersonal skills are affected by the executive control dysfunctions. A related issue is that the use of the term "Executive Control Battery" to describe this measure is a misnomer because the constituent tests do not assess the full myriad of behavioral and cognitive manifestations of the dysexecutive syndrome.

Second, there are several errors (albeit minor) mostly typographic in nature, that detract from the ease of reading of the ECB administration manual. An erratum to a considerable portion of the ECB manual was issued in September 2001.

Third, in addition to the need for an increase in the size of the normative sample, additional validity and reliability data supporting the ECB are needed.

Finally, it is worth pointing out that no single "gold standard" measure of executive control functions exists at present (see Committee on Research of the American Neuropsychiatric Association, 2002), and this includes the ECB.

SUMMARY. The ECB represents a brave attempt to blend qualitative and quantitative approaches to the assessment of the dysexecutive syndrome and claims the distinction of being one of the few instruments that measures environmental/field dependency. For the most part, however, the ECB is neither a comprehensive measure of executive control function nor does it have adequate validity information to support its widespread clinical use at this time. The relatively low ceiling of most items comprising the ECB limits its application only to patients suffering from severe forms of the dysexecutive syndrome.

REVIEWER'S REFERENCE

Committee on Research of the American Neuropsychiatric Association. (2002). Executive control function: A review of its promise and challenges for clinical research. *Journal of Neuropsychiatry and Clinical Neurosciences, 14*, 377–405.

Review of The Executive Control Battery by SHAWN POWELL, Director, Cadet Counseling and Leadership Development Center, United States Air Force Academy, USAF Academy, CO, and DAVID McCONE, Assistant Professor, Department of Behavioral Sciences and Leadership, United States Air Force Academy, USAF Academy, CO:

DESCRIPTION. The Executive Control Battery (ECB) consists of four independent tests, designed to assess executive deficits resulting from damage to the prefrontal regions. The ECB includes the Graphical Sequences Test, Competing Programs Test, Manual Postures Test, and Motor Sequence Test. The ECB items require different responses depending on the specific test being administered. To complete the ECB, individuals are required to mimic and inhibit motor responses, write, draw, and produce verbalized responses. The ECB requires the coding of behavioral responses into numerous qualitative error categories. Additionally, it was designed to "combine the advantages of qualitative and quantitative approaches" (administration manual, p. 8). Means and standard deviations are provided for three of the ECB's four tests for a nonclinical and three clinical samples: schizophrenia, focal frontal lesions, and traumatic brain injury. The means and standard deviations are listed for the following types of errors: Graphical Sequences Test perseveration errors, Manual Postures mirroring errors, Competing Programs mirroring and perseveration errors. No comparison data are reported for the Motor Sequences Test.

The ECB has to be administered, scored, and interpreted by a qualified professional who is thoroughly trained in behavioral observation. Scoring requires hand coding an individual's responses into one of numerous qualitative categories depending on the test being administered.

DEVELOPMENT. The ECB is designed to determine the existence and severity of "executive dyscontrol or frontal lobe syndrome" (administration manual, p. 8). It is reportedly based on the clinical work of Luria and the primary test author. It was developed to increase the psychometric

qualities of Luria's neuropsychological assessment process, while maintaining the qualitative integrity of Luria's methodology. The ECB is intended to elicit and measure perseveration, inertia, and stereotypies through specific error analysis. The class of behaviors the ECB elicits and assesses is commonly referred to as executive function (Lezak, 1995).

For this review, an administration manual and protocols for the four tests were provided. The administration manual briefly reviews historical advancements in prefrontal lobe injury assessment. However, it does not provide a conceptual framework to explain the relationship of ECB to executive function other than to specify that the four tests are "eliciting the features of the dysexecutive syndrome" (administration manual, p. 9). The definitions and reasons provided for developing an assessment battery from these four tests are extremely limited. Information presented on the different aspects of executive function in the four tests measure is minimal.

TECHNICAL. The normative process used for the development of the ECB is inadequate due to small sample sizes and an inadequate description of the normative process. The sample sizes reported in the administration manual are too small to allow sufficient statistical analysis. The nonclinical population ($n = 32$) included 23 males and 9 females. The focal frontal clinical population ($n = 25$) included 17 males and 8 females divided into three classes: Left Frontal ($n = 11$), Right Frontal ($n = 10$), and Bifrontal ($n = 4$). The schizophrenic clinical population ($n = 29$) consisted of 21 males and 8 females. The Traumatic Brain Injury clinical population ($n = 47$) consisted of 29 males and 18 females. Particularly troublesome for the Traumatic Brain Injury clinical population is the reported Glasgow Coma Score (GCS) range of 5 to 15. This suggests that a wide disparity exists in this subset of the normative sample as these GCS scores indicate mild to severe post injury responsiveness. The small sample sizes and the large standard deviations reveal significant overlap between the healthy control and various clinical groups, reducing the ECB's usefulness to distinguish impaired versus nonimpaired functioning. The administration manual does not present any comparison data to determine if the various group scores are significantly different.

The administration manual does not present original reliability data. The only type of reliability information presented is a 1992 study concerning the interrater reliability of the Graphical Sequences Test and the Manual Postures Test. Although the interrater reliability appears impressive it is provided for only two of the ECB's four tests and appears to have been collected from a relatively small sample.

Regarding test-retest reliability, the test authors wrote, "We believe that the inherent variability in the expression of executive dyscontrol will artificially decrease the correlation and therefore render it meaningless. Also, the possibility of a practice effect is strong" (administration manual, p. 15). Rather than conducting reliability studies, the authors contend such correlations would be meaningless. When individuals with neuropsychological deficits display specific types of errors during an evaluation, it is reasonable to assume they would produce similar errors on subsequent evaluation regardless of repeated assessment exposure. Thus, the lack of adequate reliability data undermines the authors' contention that the ECB was intended as a qualitative and quantitative instrument.

The administration manual lists several validity studies comparing three of the ECB's four specific tests to the Wisconsin Card Sorting Test or the Mattis Dementia Rating Scale. These validity studies did not include each of the tests comprising the ECB, as no comparative studies involving the Motor Sequences Test are offered. Another detriment of the reported validity studies is that they did not involve the ECB's listed normative sample. Due to these limitations, and a lack of reliability information, it is difficult to determine the validity of scores from the ECB.

COMMENTARY. The ECB was designed to assess the behavioral characteristics associated with prefrontal lobe injuries. The ECB was intended to advance Luria's neuropsychological assessment methodology through the combination of a qualitative assessment approach with quantitative rigor. The administration manual does not provide a theoretical or practical rationale for why the tests that comprise the ECB were chosen. It is difficult to comprehend how these four tests were selected for inclusion in this testing battery and how they contribute to each other. There are no provisions given to compare or combine the scores from the four tests. Therefore, the results of the ECB's four tests must be considered independently. Yet, even when considered independently

it is difficult to distinguish clinical from nonclinical functioning based on the ECB results as comparison scores are not provided for each of the tests.

Without repetitive practice the ECB's administration and simultaneous scoring is nearly impossible. What adds to this challenge is the population the test is designed for, namely individuals with prefrontal lobe injuries, many of whom would likely have resulting impatience and a lack of inhibition, which complicates its administration. The majority of the ECB's scoring system is difficult to interpret and is cumbersome to apply in evaluation sessions. To have clinical value the ECB has to be administered, scored, and interpreted by an experienced neuropsychologist thoroughly trained in qualitative behavioral observation.

The ECB's development involved small sample sizes from four separate groups. The total lack of reliability data other than a reference to a former study involving interrater reliability raises serious questions about the ECB's applicability and use. The authors' explicit disregard for reliability studies and the failure to conduct validity studies on the normative sample is concerning given the ECB's description as a test that was developed to combine both qualitative and quantitative aspects. Without adequate psychometric qualities, it is difficult to recommend the use of the ECB as a measure of neuropsychological functioning.

SUMMARY. The authors of the ECB combined four tests developed to elicit and assess behaviors associated with prefrontal lobe injuries. The behaviors the ECB is designed to measure are commonly referred to as executive function (Lezak, 1995). The authors' stated intention was to produce an instrument based on the qualitative approach of Luria and to improve the assessment instrument by increasing its methodological rigor. The administration manual provides little evidence of the success of this endeavor. The ECB lacks conceptual framework and has poor psychometric qualities. The capability to use its results for clinical treatment planning, or to identify an individual with impaired functioning is highly questionable. It may prove useful to a thoroughly trained neuropsychologist as a method to increase the understanding of the behavioral presentation of an individual with a prefrontal lobe injury. Beyond this limited use, the ECB falls short of its intended goal.

REVIEWERS' REFERENCE

Lezak, M.D. (1995). *Neuropsychological assessment* (3rd ed.). New York: Oxford University Press.

[93]

Experience and Background Inventory (Form S).

Purpose: "Provides quantitative measures of past performance and experience."

Population: Adults (Industry).

Publication Dates: 1980–1996.

Acronym: EBI.

Scores: 9 factors: School Achievement, Choice of a College Major, Aspiration Level, Drive/Career Progress, Leadership and Group Participation, Vocational Satisfaction, Financial Responsibility, General Responsibility, Relaxation Pursuits.

Administration: Group.

Price Data, 2002: $102 per start-up kit including 25 test booklets, 25 score sheets, and interpretation and research manual (1996, 15 pages); $54 per 25 test booklets; $32 per 25 score sheets; $28 per interpretation and research manual.

Time: Administration time not reported.

Authors: Melany E. Baehr and Ernest C. Froemel.

Publisher: Reid London House.

Review of the Experience and Background Inventory (Form S) by F. FELICIA FERRARA, Adjunct/Associate Professor, Department of Educational Measurement, University of South Florida, St. Petersburg, FL:

DESCRIPTION. The Experience and Background Inventory (EBI) is a 70-item scale, predominately designed with a 5-point Likert response format. Individual or group administration appears appropriate as the EBI is a self-report survey intended for adult use in various settings within industrial applications, career or counseling exploration, and general populations. Six subscales that represent various aspects of life (biodata) including: Work Experience; Activities and Interests; Educational Experience; Financial Responsibility; Financial Experience; and Leadership and Responsibility. The six subscales are used to report scores on nine dimensions. The nine dimensions (or factors) relate to a range of areas of education, achievement, leadership qualities, financial and general responsibility, and relaxation pursuits.

Response format varies within the nine subscales as well as across subscales including categorical items, yes/no items, and Likert response formats. This varied response format may

be a source of confusion for the examinee. For example, the Work Experience subscale consists of 12 demographic items; Activities and Interests consists of Items 13–17, which are categorical, but then the item response format switches to a Likert scale for items 18–22. The other scales are equally variable in terms of response format, thus responding may be difficult and confusing.

Nor directions for scoring are provided. However, it is assumed that response options selected are summed. Because of the variability of response choice categories, this method of scoring is inconsistent with traditional and acceptable practice. Overall, number scales vary from categorical to interval, which are mixed throughout the measure. I have serious questions about the efficacy of deriving scores by summing across item responses that are on clearly different scales. If the authors redesigned the instrument so that a consistent type of response format and consistent item-types were constructed, this instrument may have potential.

DEVELOPMENT. Although the manual indicates that the EBI is a strong predictor instrument designed to predict performance in 12 key occupational areas for higher level management and professionals, item content is more consistent with that of an interest inventory rather than an aptitude test actually used as a predictor of success on the job. The EBI information guide indicates that research for the manual was provided in a previous manual published in 1986, thus information on how items were developed is not available.

Background research began in 1950 at the Human Resources Center of the University of Chicago. Although the EBI is not occupation specific, the information guide advocates use of biodata items by psychometric clustering or factorial procedures that are said to produce interpretable dimensions of biographical data. However, based on the mixed item content and varied response formats, the process used to determine total scores and cut scores is not rational.

The initial EBI was developed for male employees in high executive positions in the 1950s. Information provided in the information guide was quite limited. Further research conducted in the 1980s was said to have identified 7 of the 9 factors presented in the current version of the EBI.

TECHNICAL. The authors note that a review of item content was conducted concerning EEOC requirements and ADA mandates, but no specifics were provided as to which year or document was used for that review. Also, no mention existed as to adherence to test development procedures and standards in the *Standards for Educational and Psychological Testing* (AERA, APA, & NCME, 1999). However due to the inclusion of items on individual financial details, a sensitive and invasive topic, several items in the earlier version were deleted. A content comparison between earlier and current versions was not available.

Reliability was examined using a sample of 421 in 1995. Coefficient alpha for the revised subscales ranged from .52 to .83 across subscales. Until the data or type of data collected from each item is uniform in response format, internal consistency does not seem to be an appropriate method for estimating score consistency.

Validity was presented using (a) intercorrelation analysis, (b) prediction of selection and promotion, (c) and prediction of earnings. Of the 36 unique intercorrelations, 17 were statistically significant (p <.05), but 6 of the 36 equaled or exceeded .3. This suggests that in general the scores across dimensions are somewhat independent, as would be expected when dimensions are developed using a factor analytic approach. The highest correlation was .63 between Financial Responsibility and General Responsibility subscales, a correlation one might expect when correlating two dimensions of the same factor (responsibility).

Second, validity evidence related to selection and promotion was based on the 1967 sample of 680 males across 10 occupational groups. Although 15 subscales existed in the earlier version, only 9 were retained on the current version. Therefore, the data reported were indeed outdated based on a 30-year-old sample base.

Predictive validity evidence was based on performance criteria from the 1967 study. This raises similar concerns about the utility of the data due to outdated data and inappropriate statistical analysis procedures. In one study of 102 individuals employed in a chemical company, the Human Research Center used 22 possible predictors and five background dimensions against overall indexes of Sales Performance, Service Efficiency, and leisure. Again, although the choice of predictors may be suitable, the same defects in data collection and item and response format may not be suitable indexes in the 2000s.

An ANOVA analysis was conducted to investigate if the EBI could differentiate across various employees at different levels of job assignment (i.e., Line, Professional, Sales, and technical groups) on four hierarchies of factors. Then normal means were reported with significance levels, but no factor values or source table were provided. The authors note that subscales are consistent with McClelland's (1961, 1968) theories of Power Drive.

Construct validity evidence was provided by using nine different test instruments dated from 1959 to 1985, with 22 of 144 coefficients having a value of .20 or greater. Compatibility between chosen instruments to compare against the EBI was not revealed. The information guide did not include specifics of test selection for use in the construct validity studies, the sample size, or demographics, and actual coefficients and degrees of freedom were not provided. These findings do not substantiate use of the EBI based on technical data reports available to this reviewer. Also, studies cited here do not meet psychometric standards for establishing validity evidence as required in the *Standards for Educational and Psychological Testing* (AERA, APA, & NCME, 1999). No reference was made to updated studies in the information guide.

COMMENTARY. The EBI may have potential to establish job candidate attributes, but in its current format it appears that the test developers mixed demographic data and actual scale data in each subtest. Response formats should be separated, perhaps with one preliminary demographic questionnaire and subscales that consist of only perceptual questions. Response formats also should be redesigned for clarity and consistency throughout the instrument.

In its current form, the EBI appears unfocused and the current design may be a source of confusion for the examinee who must alter mindsets across items. Scoring directions need to be provided once the developer identifies proper scaling and organization of items. Theoretical models may also be updated to incorporate more recent theoretical concepts on employee success in higher level management with more female participants included.

SUMMARY. Although the test developer no doubt proceeded with the necessary steps usually expected in analyzing the psychometric properties of an instrument, shortcomings are extensive. Although the test developer addressed EEOC and

ADA guidelines in dealing with human resources in general, no note was made of legislative updates or specifications in precautions during studies to adhere to human subjects review issues or the industry standards cited in the *Standards* (AERA, APA, & NCME, 1999). The appropriateness of combining all nine dimensions, even if modified by separate sections for demographics and perceptual data within each dimension, should be reconsidered so that a summative total scale score might reflect actual abilities within a given dimension. More current research is also needed in the conceptualization of the scale and each dimension. A more complete manual should also be completed in keeping with the *Standards* (AERA, APA, & NCME, 1999). In short, much work is needed to substantiate psychometric properties and format of the EBI in its current form.

REVIEWER'S REFERENCE

American Educational Research Association, American Psychological Association, & National Council on Measurement in Education. (1999). *Standards for educational and psychological testing.* Washington, DC: American Educational Research Association.

Review of the Experience and Background Inventory (Form S) by CHANTALE JEANRIE, Industrial/Organizational Psychologist, Associate Professor of Measurement and Évaluation, Department of Fondements et pratiques en éducation, Faculty of Education, Laval University, Quebec, Canada:

DESCRIPTION. The Experience and Background Inventory (Form S) (EBI) intends to provide quantitative measures of past performance and experience. The authors also associate it to a motivational measure (information guide, p. 7). The purpose of the EBI is to contribute to personnel selection by predicting job performance of men and women in a wide range of higher level occupations. It is not limited to a specific type of industry or job.

DEVELOPMENT AND ACTUAL FORM. The EBI (Form S) was derived from a few former versions. The content of the items is similar to what is usually contained in biodata measures and the Inventory is considered as such by its authors. Items, however, were not empirically keyed but were factor analyzed. No information is provided about the development or the choice of items.

The inventory was first built to screen male applicants for higher level positions (1968). Factor analyses lead to the identification of 16 dimensions. The authors refer the readers to previously published papers for more information. Later, a similar measure was developed for female applicants. Both have now been combined.

Seven of these dimensions were later found to be more predictive of performance in higher level occupations and were retained, and included with two other dimensions, to produce the 1980s EBI. To comply with the Equal Employment Opportunity Commission's Uniform Guidelines on Employee Selection Procedures (1978), and other related state laws, some items from two specific dimensions ("Financial Responsibility" and "General Responsibility") had to be retrieved and replaced (1994). The authors indicate that the new version retained its previous validity for use and refer the reader to a published paper for more information. However, the mere fact that the correlations between the original and the new scales (for both dimensions) are respectively .45 and .54 raises questions about what exactly was maintained.

Item format and content. Item format is that of a self-report multiple-choice scale. Some are objective in content (the response is not necessarily so, however), some others reflect opinions or perceptions. Response choices vary from 1 to 2 or from 1 to 9. Items are easy to read, unambiguous, and clearly linked to the response scale. They should be adequate for the intended populations.

Administration and scoring. Unfortunately, no information about administration or scoring were provided. A note on the test booklet permits one to believe that the test can be scored manually or through a computerized program. Because the singular objective of the EBI is to discriminate between three occupational levels, one would minimally expect norms or cut-scores to be available for each of these three levels.

TECHNICAL.

Reliability. Cronbach's alpha coefficients were calculated in 1995 for a group of higher level employees from various occupational backgrounds ($n = 421$). The mean of the reliability coefficients is .68. When dimensions are, indeed, heterogeneous, high consistency is not expected, so the magnitude of these coefficients can be considered acceptable. However, because relative heterogeneity was to be expected from the items' content, internal consistency does not appear to be the more appropriate reliability index. Test-retest coefficients would have been more valuable information.

Validity. The authors seem to have devoted special care to the evaluation of uses of EBI scores.

Over the years, many validation studies have been conducted. Three categories of studies are presented in the information guide: (a) Correlations between scales and with intellectual, aptitudes, and behavioral measures; (b) analyses of variance among different occupational groups or levels; and (c) concurrent validity studies. Categories are presented and can easily be distinguished. But, although it is clear that not all validity studies can be reproduced in the guide, the lack of details about them restricts the utility of the demonstrations.

Correlational analyses. Many scales are independent, but some correlations as high as $r = .40$, .43, and .63 can yet be found between dimensions. These high correlations suggest that dimensions may not be that well defined. To adequately interpret the correlations between different measures, a priori hypotheses would have been extremely helpful. Even without such hypotheses, however, one clear result can be noted: Four scales present significant and moderate correlations with mental abilities measures. It is important to note that the "School achievement" dimension is not among those four scales.

Analyses of variance. Different concurrent studies are summarized in the information guide. From the results, which are described but not interpreted, it can be observed that the EBI differentiates more easily between the first and the other two occupational levels than between these last two. In some cases distinctions can be made between Levels 2 and 3 but the pictorial format of results only provides rough information about which differences are really significant. From the figures, it seems that the EBI is more effective for two of the four managerial hierarchies presented.

Concurrent validity studies. Two different types of concurrent studies have been conducted. The first ones all originate from studies anterior to 1980, thus before the EBI was restricted to nine dimensions. Results are interesting and reveal acceptable and good validity level. Results from the prediction of earnings study are, on the other hand, quite strong. Validity coefficients (for the total of all dimensions) vary from $r = .51$ to $r = .85$ (before modifications to comply with EEOC's Guidelines). These validity coefficients are higher that those that are usually expected from mental ability measures (Schmidt & Hunter, 1998). Correlations obtained after revision of the two scales are considerably lower but correlations between these two new scales and the other ones are not provided. So it is difficult to evaluate what the new validity coefficients would be. Actually, this appears to this reviewer as being one more evidence that the items do reflect opportunities rather than experience. It is helpful to remember that this is a concurrent and not a predictive study. It is highly likely that higher earnings are indeed obtained by those employees who actually hold a job that provides more opportunities for leadership, financial management, etc., thus highly contaminating the scores obtained on the Inventory. If the items were truly reflecting experience and predicting performance instead of describing opportunities, validity coefficients should *not* be as high because there is more to performance (even measured by earnings) than a quantitative listing of past experiences.

COMMENTS. Actually, although it would have been more interesting to see validation studies based upon the new version, the EBI seems to be a valid predictor of some type of job performance. That it measures experience, however, is still not obvious to this reviewer. In addition to the apparent confusion with experience and opportunities, it would still be important to demonstrate that social desirability is not a major interference because many answers are clearly more acceptable than others.

As mentioned, some items had to be changed to comply with the EEOC's Uniform Guidelines. Remaining items, however, could still be seen as invading privacy or as indirectly bringing up topics restricted by some specific state's or province's legislation. Many items referring to activities or to financial experience could be considered offensive, irrelevant or, in Quebec for example, indirectly pertaining to prohibited grounds of discrimination (Quebec's Charter of Human Rights and Freedom, 1975).

Another concern is raised by the item content. Instead of defining one's type of experience, the EBI attempts to identify situations where people may or may not have gained experience or situations that can reveal past attainments. By so doing, items become more a measure of opportunities to gain experience than of experience itself. The difference may have important consequences on validity and adverse impact issues.

One could object to this review that biodata are not conceptual and serve prediction purposes without pretending to cover the reasons for performance. However, it is the opinion of this reviewer that the sole fact that an inventory uses questions related to past personal situations or attainments is not sufficient for this measure to qualify as a biodata instrument.

SUMMARY. If a potential test user does consider the EBI as being a genuine biodata measure, the criterion validity studies may appear a little outdated but sufficient. However, to one who believes that the Inventory's content may have been wrongly chosen, this reviewer cannot recommend the use of this instrument as a measure of experience and would favor other types of measurement, such as rigorous conceptual or subject matter experts' approaches.

REVIEWER'S REFERENCE

Schmidt, F. L., & Hunter, J. L. (1998). The validity and utility of selection methods in personnel psychology: Practical and theoretical impacts of 85 years of results findings. *Psychological Bulletin, 124,* 262–274.

[94]

EXPLORE.

Purpose: Measures the academic progress of eighth and ninth graders in four areas: English, mathematics, reading, and science reasoning; helps students explore the range of career options; and assists them in developing a high school coursework plan.
Population: Grades 8–9.
Publication Dates: 1995–2000.
Administration: Group.
Price Data, 2001: $52.50 per 30 reusable test booklets; $135 per 30 consumable student assessment sets; volume discounts available.
Time: (120) minutes for four academics tests; (45–60) minutes for interest inventory, plans and background information, and needs assessment.
Comments: The initial component of ACT's Educational Planning and Assessment System (EPAS), which also includes PLAN (T6:1916), the ACT Assessment (T6:57), and Work Keys (T6:2749).
Authors: ACT, Inc.
Publisher: ACT, Inc.

a) EXPLORE ENGLISH TEST.
Purpose: Measures understanding of the conventions of standard written English.
Scores, 3: Usage/Mechanics (Punctuation, Grammar and Usage, Sentence Structure), Rhetorical Skills (Strategy, Organization, Style), Total.
Time: 30 minutes.
b) EXPLORE MATHEMATICS TEST.
Purpose: Measures mathematical reasoning and achievement.
Scores: Total score only.
Time: 30 minutes.

c) EXPLORE READING TEST.
Purpose: Measures reading comprehension as a product of referring and reasoning skills.
Scores: Total score only.
Time: 30 minutes.
d) EXPLORE SCIENCE REASONING TEST.
Purpose: Measures scientific reasoning skills.
Scores: Total score only.
Time: 30 minutes.

Review of EXPLORE by SANDRA A. LOEW, Assistant Professor of Counselor Education, University of North Alabama, Florence, AL:

DESCRIPTION. EXPLORE is a computer-scored, timed, paper-and-pencil test for eighth and ninth graders that measures their academic progress in English, math, reading, and science. Each section takes 30 minutes. There is an interest inventory section in which students indicate whether they like, dislike, or are indifferent to 90 activities. The Student Report generated is used in conjunction with the booklet, *It's Your Future! Student Guide to EXPLORE,* which explains the scores on the Student Report and outlines the World-of-Work Map and its use in career exploration and planning. The booklet lists numerous jobs from the *Occupational Outlook Handbook* and indicates related high school courses. It also lists other resources for students to consult such as books and websites that furnish more in-depth information about jobs, careers, and the outlook for various professions. There is also a coursework planner that shows a connection between trial job choices and courses in high school.

The Student Report produces test scores in English with subscores in Usage/Mechanics and Rhetorical Skills, Mathematics, Reading, and Science Reasoning. The student's scores are on a grid that shows the percentage of students in a national norm group who scored at or below the student's individual score in those areas. A composite score is the average of the four academic test scores. A procedure is suggested to permit students to identify areas of weakness and areas of strength. The scores from the interest inventory are seen as shaded regions on the World of Work Map on the second side of the Student Report.

DEVELOPMENT. Materials furnished by the publisher include a technical manual that explains that EXPLORE is an achievement test that may be used by itself or as the entry point for a program developed by American College Testing

(ACT) that continues with PLAN for 10th graders and ACT Assessment for 11th and 12th graders. EXPLORE is based on the type of content that is typically taught in middle and junior high schools with an emphasis on the ability of students to reason and make judgments. Items for each of the academic tests were developed after careful study of instructional objectives for Grades 6 through 9 from states that had published objectives. State-approved textbooks for Grades 6 through 8 were also reviewed, and educators of Grades 6 through 12 and at the postsecondary level were consulted.

The administrator's manual is well-developed and easy to use. Any test administrator following the directions in this manual will have no difficulties in administering this test. A pamphlet for students and their parents, *Getting Ready for High School and Beyond, Helpful Suggestions for Students and Their Parents,* is included in the packet. This serves as an informational brochure and a reminder of when the test will be administered. The EXPLORE booklet and Instructions for Completing Your Answer Sheet are reusable.

The Program Guide explains what is measured by the test and what each of the scores mean. Basic reporting services that come with the EXPLORE package include a student roster with all students' scores and local norms, two copies of individual student reports, a school summary report, a presentation packet, and early intervention rosters that identify students who have no post high school plans, composite scores below the 10th percentile for the national norm group, and students who expressed a need for help in academic work. There is a section that provides pretest activities for students, parents, school personnel, and the community, as well as a very detailed discussion on how to explain and use the results of the assessment. There is also a "Standards for Transition" section that explains what students are likely to know and be able to do given a certain score on each of the four tests. This provides some meaning for the numerical score.

TECHNICAL. EXPLORE was originally normed in 1992 with over 4,000 eighth grade students. The sample was fairly representative of the national population in terms of gender, with some discrepancy in the demographic characteristics of race and geographic region. In 1995, the assessment was normed on over 14,000 eighth grade students. This sample was stratified using school size, public or private status, and geographic region. Again, there was some discrepancy in the characteristics of race and geographic region. The 1995 sample scored slightly higher than the 1992 sample, which the developers suggest could be due to different cohorts or sampling error. A new set of norms are the result of another study done in 1999 with 4,789 eighth graders and 6,660 ninth graders. The latest study provides three sets of norms for those eighth graders tested in the Fall, those tested in the Spring, and those ninth graders tested in the Fall. Eighth graders were not actually tested in the Spring but the eighth and ninth graders' scores were averaged to determine the norms for a Spring assessment of eighth graders. The same problem of underrepresentation of racial and geographic demographic characteristics is evident in the latest sample, The 1999 sample scored slightly higher than the 1995 sample.

Reliability coefficients for the subtests ranged from .78 on the Science subtest to .88 on the English subtest. There are four forms of the EXPLORE and the reliability coefficient for the composite scores for each of the four forms is .95, with the highest standard error of measurement on Form 3 at 1.03 and the lowest on Form 2 at .93.

The developers of EXPLORE compared students' grades with their test scores expecting a correlation between EXPLORE scores and grades. The correlations range from .39 to .62. The highest composite test score correlation with grades was .66. There is a higher correlation between EXPLORE and PLAN test scores with a range of .58 to .82, showing there is a higher correlation between these two assessments than there is between EXPLORE scores and students' grades.

COMMENTARY. The quality of most of the materials for EXPLORE is exceptional. The testing booklet and materials that students and parents receive are well written and professionally done. EXPLORE is useful in assisting students in determining what classes to take in high school and to recognize any areas needing remediation. The scores from this achievement test might be used to place students in various levels of classes, such as determining which is more appropriate, Pre-algebra or Algebra. If this assessment is used instead of other achievement tests then users must be aware of the low correlation between grades and EXPLORE scores. If it is used in addition to other district-wide achievement testing then it becomes redundant.

The technical manual gives numerous charts concerning reliability and validity but not enough narrative on that information. Thus, the information is less useful than it could be for those using this assessment. It seems that much research has been done, yet the information presented does not accentuate that research.

SUMMARY. Because EXPLORE is a prelude test for the ACT Assessment (T6:57), which is used to measure how well prepared students are for college level study, this assessment may serve as a practice test for the more high-stakes testing that is in the future for many high school students. The interest inventory adds a career exploration dimension but it appears to be an afterthought rather than an important aspect of this assessment.

EXPLORE is a well-made achievement test developed by ACT. It is worth the investment to begin the program with eighth and ninth graders if large numbers of students in a school will be taking the ACT Assessment in the future, especially if it is used instead of, rather than in addition to, other achievement tests that might be given to this age group. The information that is gathered will be useful to assist students academically as they progress through high school and will prepare them well for the ACT Assessment. If the goal is career exploration and planning, then ACT's Career Planning Survey (44) is better suited for exploring career options for all students rather than just the college-bound students. It can also be incorporated into a comprehensive guidance program that would be beneficial to all ages and skill levels.

[95]

Expressive One-Word Picture Vocabulary Test [2000 Edition].

Purpose: Designed to measure an individual's English-speaking vocabulary.
Population: Ages 2–18.
Publication Dates: 1979–2000.
Acronym: EOWPVT.
Scores: Total score only.
Administration: Individual.
Price Data, 2002: $140 per kit including manual (2000, 128 pages), 25 record forms, and test plates in a vinyl portfolio; $75 per test plates; $25 per 25 record forms; $40 per manual.
Time: (10–15) minutes.
Comments: The editor combines the lower and upper levels in previous editions and extends the use of the test through age 18-11.

Authors: 1990 and earlier edition by Morrison F. Gardner; later edition prepared by publisher.
Publisher: Academic Therapy Publications.
Cross References: See T5:994 (53 references) and T4:946 (23 references); for reviews by Gregory J. Cizek and Larry B. Grantham of an earlier edition, see 12:147 (6 references); for reviews by Jack A. Cummings and Gilbert M. Spivak of the Lower Level, see 9:403 (2 references).

Review of the Expressive One-Word Picture Vocabulary Test [2000 Edition] by ALFRED LONGO, Instructor in Education, Social Science Department, Ocean County College, Toms River, NJ:

DESCRIPTION. The Expressive One-Word Picture Vocabulary Test (EOWPVT) [2000 Edition] is an assessment of an individual's English-speaking vocabulary that is individually administered and norm-referenced. The EOWPVT can be used with individuals between 24 months and 18 years, 11 months of age.

The test administrator presents the examinee with a series of illustrations representing objects, concepts, or actions. An approximation is made by the examiner to determine a starting point for the presentations. Testing is concluded when, according to the publisher, the examinee is unable to correctly name a number of consecutive illustrations. As the testing progresses, the difficulty of test items increases. Administration can be completed in less than 20 minutes. Raw scores are then converted to standard scores, percentiles, and age equivalents.

The current edition of the EOWPVT has national norms and was conormed with the Receptive One-Word Picture Vocabulary Test (ROWPVT) and, thus, permits the comparative analysis of both the examinee's ability to use language in speaking and writing (expressive) and the ability to recognize and understand the spoken or written words of others. This latest edition features new test items, the elimination of some test items, full color test items designed to hold interest and elicit more specific responses, and new procedures for administration that allow the examiner to prompt examinees and point them to the "focus" of the test item.

The complete package of the EOWPVT contains a comprehensive manual (directions, technical specifications, conversion charts, etc.), a spiral-bound book with 170 test plates, and record forms.

DEVELOPMENT. A number of items in the current edition of the EOWPVT have been used in previous editions of the test. In the initial development of the EOWPVT, a list of common words children (ages 18 months to 2 years) use was created by means of a questionnaire sent to 435 sets of parents. Some items appearing in previous editions were deleted because they were considered anachronistic or culturally biased. Additional items were selected from a number of vocabulary books/lists. A list of these sources appears in the test manual. Information gleaned from interviews with test administrators of previous editions contributed to changes in the testing domain and in some administration procedures.

A pilot test was conducted in 1998 to establish item difficulty and sequence of their usage. The pilot was given to 154 students ranging in age from 2 to 18. Almost 70% of this sample was Caucasian.

Classical test theory and item response theory were used in the analysis of item data. Item bias was addressed by computing phi coefficients to compare demographic characteristics. After removing some items, a second item analysis was conducted. This analysis indicated that some of the potential bias of the pilot test had been eliminated. In addition, the item analysis, differential item functioning, and qualitative commentary from examiners and members of a cultural review panel were used in the second selection of test items.

The final item analysis considered item difficulty, sequence of prompts, and discrimination by age level. A basal of eight consecutive correct answers and a ceiling of six consecutive inaccurate responses was used. In each age group, high correlations (.93 to .98) validate the strength of the relationship between item order and item difficulty. This is a positive result in terms of reducing the administration time (i.e., large numbers of items that are either too easy or too difficult do not have to be administered).

TECHNICAL. In the standardization of the EOWPVT, an initial pool of 3,661 was pared to 2,327 randomly selected examinees to create a demographic "balance." In contrast to standardization procedures of earlier editions of the EOWPVT, testing was conducted in a wide range of locations (32 states and 220 sites). This increase is a major improvement over previous standardization samples. Although black-and-white test plates were used in most test sites, the test in its final stage uses colored test plates. In addition to conducting their own research showing no significant differences between color and black-and-white plates, the authors cite a study by Husband and Hayden (1996) to support the contention that "no significant difference was found" (manual, page 55) between color and black-and-white plates.

Norms reflect the use of broad demographic characteristics in the standardization sample. The sample stratification resembles the pattern (by age) found in the United States population.

Standard scores, percentiles, and age equivalents were derived from the raw data. Charts in the test manual demonstrate converting standard scores to other useful derived scores. The conversion matrix addressing NCEs, T-scores, scaled scores, and stanines is well presented and is a strong aid in interpretation. In sum, appropriate measures were undertaken to improve the breadth and consistency of administration.

In terms of reliability, coefficient alpha was computed to assess homogeneity of test items. The median coefficient was .96 with a range of .93 to .98. Split-half coefficients reflected a median of .98. These coefficients speak well to the internal consistency of the instrument.

The EOWPVT is consistent over time as demonstrated through test/retest. A 20-day period separated the first and second testing. Although test-retest correlations are strong, the duration of the time between test and retest should be lengthened.

Interrater reliability, so important in a test of this type, was addressed in a straightforward manner as scoring, response evaluation, and consistency of administration were all examined. Results of these examinations were productive and demonstrate a strong confidence level for interrater reliability.

Content, construct, and criterion-related validity are all addressed. With reference to content validity, the simplicity of the test tends to eliminate extraneous assessment of other language skills. If a word could not be illustrated, it cannot appear in the testing domain. Although an effort was made to address item bias and to choose the most discriminating items, the need for illustration may inhibit the full analysis of language proficiency.

The EOWPVT was correlated with 12 other vocabulary measures. Correlations are not overly high (median .79). The authors attribute this to "the wide range of dissimilarity of the task format" (manual, p. 70). This may be true, but potential users should review this statistic and the format of similar instruments carefully before choosing a vocabulary test.

The construct validity evidence is extensive. Correlations between the EOWPVT and various measures of constructs such as cognitive ability and academic achievement are not overly high and suggest the narrow scope of the assessment. There is a stronger relationship between the former and the current edition of the EOWPVT.

COMMENTARY. The most recent version of the EOWPVT remains steadfast in its purpose and has addressed some of the criticism of the earlier editions. Despite an item review and DIF studies to remove problem items including problems due to dialectic variation, the use of dialects present in particular sections of the country are not truly accounted for and variance in scoring may result.

Standardization procedures for the EOWPVT have been enhanced. The increase in the size of the standardization sample, for instance, is most notable. Test-retest studies demonstrate strong consistency over a short time span. The analysis of response evaluations suggests interrater consistency between both experienced and inexperienced examiners.

Further research on the scope of this test is needed. Therefore, the EOWPVT should be used with more global measures of intelligence and/or verbal ability. The EOWPVT has been correlated with other like instruments (e.g., the Peabody Picture Vocabulary Test) and does have criterion validity in these comparisons. It has also been correlated with vocabulary subtests of intelligence tests such as the Weschler Intelligence Scale for Children and the Stanford-Binet Intelligence Scales. Results on the verbal section of the Stanford-Binet Intelligence Scales were compared to the results of the EOWPVT and provide evidence supporting its construct validity. Other than the EOWPVT's provision for quick assessment, it may be more suitable to use more broad based instruments in assessing verbal ability to make placement decisions in schools.

SUMMARY. There have been a number of improvements in the EOWPVT that reflect a positive reaction to criticism of earlier editions. A main virtue of the instrument is the speed of administration. In addition, scores have been correlated with more global measures of intelligence in order to enhance interpretative value.

New test items have been added and several items lacking discrimination have been removed. Standardization procedures and validity and reliability studies suggest that the EOWPVT, within narrow boundaries, has usefulness. The EOWPVT can function as a subtest similar to vocabulary tests found in assessments of cognitive ability. As such, its utilization is recommended.

REVIEWER'S REFERENCE

Husband, T. H., & Hayden, D. C. (1996). Effects of the addition of color to assessment instruments. *Journal of Psychoeducational Assessment, 14,* 147–151.

[96]

Eyberg Child Behavior Inventory and Sutter-Eyberg Student Behavior Inventory—Revised.

Purpose: Designed "to measure conduct problems in children ages 2 through 16 years."
Population: Ages 2–16 years.
Publication Dates: 1978–1999.
Acronym: ECBI; SESBI-R.
Scores, 2: Intensity, Problem.
Administration: Group or individual.
Forms, 2: Eyberg Child Behavior Inventory; Sutter-Eyberg Student Behavior Inventory—Revised.
Price Data: Available from publisher for introductory kit including professional manual (1999, 64 pages), 50 ECBI test sheets, and 50 SESBI-R test sheets.
Time: (10) minutes.
Comments: ECBI is a rating form completed by parents; SESBI-R is a rating form completed by teachers.
Authors: Sheila Eyberg (SESBI-R, ECBI, and professional manual), Joseph Sutter (SESBI-R), and Donna Pincus (professional manual).
Publisher: Psychological Assessment Resources, Inc.
Cross References: For information on the Eyberg Child Behavior Inventory, see T5:997 (30 references) and T4:948 (26 references); for a review by Michael L. Reed of an earlier edition, see 9:404 (6 references); see also T3:858 (2 references). For information on the Sutter-Eyberg Student Behavior Inventory, see T5:2595 (2 references) and T4:2668 (1 reference); for a review by T. Steuart Watson of an earlier edition, see 11:410 (2 references).

Review of the Eyberg Child Behavior Inventory and Sutter-Eyberg Student Behavior Inventory—Revised by JOYCE MEIKAMP, Professor of Special Education, Marshall University Graduate College, South Charleston, WV:

DESCRIPTION. The Eyberg Child Behavior Inventory (ECBI) and Sutter-Eyberg Student Behavior Inventory—Revised (SESBI-R) are paper-and-pencil-administered rating scales, focusing on the measurement of conduct problems in children ages 2 through 16 years. Materials include a professional manual and individual ECBI and SESB-R inventory test sheets. Both the ECBI and the SESBI-R purportedly assess the severity of disruptive behavior and the extent to which parents and teachers find these behaviors problematic. These rating scales are meant to identify children in need of treatment for conduct problems and their accompanying presenting behavior problems.

The ECBI, consisting of 36 items, was designed for completion by parents in clinical settings. Respondents mark their answers directly on the inventory test sheets and circle the responses corresponding to their ratings of each listed behavior. Developed over a 2-year period from case record data, these items represent the most typical behaviors reported by parents of conduct-disordered children.

Created as a companion instrument to the ECBI and similar in format and content, the SESBI-R contains 38 items for teacher completion, of which 13 are completely new from the SESBI. These new items are the result of selection from chart review of problem behaviors most frequently reported by teachers of children referred for treatment of behavior problems. As such, the developers reported they replaced SESBI items not relevant to the school situation.

Both instruments can be administered and scored by individuals without formal training in psychology or related fields. Interpretation assumes formal graduate level training in psychology, counseling, or a related field. The professional manual suggests both instruments are suitable for group administration or via telephone. Thus, administration of both the ECBI and SESBI-R reportedly provides an assessment of behaviors across settings.

On the ECBI, as well as the SESBI-R, respondents rate behaviors on two scales, a 7-point Intensity scale, indicating how often the behaviors currently occur and a Yes-No Problem scale identifying whether or not the child's behavior is problematic. Completion of either the ECBI or SESBI-R requires approximately 10 minutes and scoring an additional 5 minutes.

Both the ECBI and the SESBI-R are hand scored by the examiner with total raw scores being generated for the Intensity and Problem scales. Raw score subtotals are then converted to T-scores for the Intensity and Problem scales. If a T score for either of these scales is greater than 60, it is noted the score "Exceeds Cutoff." A child rated at or above this score should receive additional evaluation for potential psychopathology. Both the Intensity and Problem scales are continuous with a higher score suggesting a greater level of conduct-disordered behavior. These instruments are to be used as the initial step in two-stage diagnostic assessment.

DEVELOPMENT. The ECBI and companion instrument, the SESBI, originally were designed for therapists to assess disruptive behavior. Initially, the 36 behaviors on the ECBI were selected from case record data as the most typical parent-reported problem behaviors of children in treatment for conduct-disordered behavior. The SESBI-R is the result of a 1999 SESBI revision with items not relevant to the school situation replaced by 13 new items, reflecting teacher-reported behaviors and chart review for children referred for treatment of behavior problems.

For item revision of the SESBI, ratings from a sample of 726 students, 5th through 12th grade, were used in the development of the SESBI-R. From the SESBI, eight original items were deleted and replaced with 10 new items. Thus, the SESBI-R replaced the SESBI reportedly for the assessment of disruptive behavior problems in the classroom.

Respondents rate behaviors on the ECBI, as well as the SESBI-R, on two scales, a 7-point Intensity scale, indicating how often the behaviors currently occur, and a Yes-No Problem scale, identifying whether or not the child's behavior is problematic or not. Although the Intensity and Problem scales are central to these two instruments, the professional manual provides very limited definitions for both scales. Limited rationale is provided as to how these two scales fit together to measure conduct disorders. A rationale was not given as to why the Intensity scale is based on 7 points. Moreover, the developers do not provide a theoretical discussion as to the construct of conduct disorder.

TECHNICAL. Originally standardized in 1980, the ECBI was restandardized in 1999 with a sample of 798 children (aged 2 to 16 years), extending its applicability to a variety of social and demographic contexts. The 1999 sample was reportedly representative of the general child and adolescent population in the southeastern U.S., with consideration given to age, gender, ethnicity, rural versus urban status, and socioeconomic status. No mention is made as to why the sample is from the southeastern U.S., or how the sample was selected. Moreover, no mention is made as to how socioeconomic status was determined.

Standardization procedures for the SESBI-R are cause for concern. Only one study was cited regarding SESBI-R standardization, from which a sample of 415 elementary school children from 11 schools in Gainesville, Florida was utilized. Children from kindergarten through fifth grade were rated by 8 African American and 44 Caucasian teachers. Of the 415 children rated, 314 were in regular classes and 101 were in exceptional student education classes for behavioral or emotional problems. Although the SESBI-R's target population is supposed to be children from ages 2 through 16, not all ages were represented in the sample used for standardization. In fact, the children were only described in terms of grade level, regular versus exceptional student education (ESE) classes, sex, and ethnicity. There was no evidence of the age of the child as a variable being taken into account in the standardization process.

The items selected for use in the ECBI/ SESBI-R rating scales are described in the professional manual as using nonpathological and non-age-specific terms for misbehavior (e.g., "Acts bossy with other students," from the SESBI-R, and "Sasses adults," from the ECBI). However, interrater reliability relative to these items being nonpathological or non-age-specific is not addressed.

Internal consistency reliability studies indicated Cronbach alpha values for the ECBI Intensity scale ranging from .98 to .95. Kuder-Richardson 20 values for the ECBI Problem scale were reported to be in the .90s as well. Test-retest reliability (administration intervals of 3 weeks, 12 weeks, and 10 months) ranged between the .80s and .70s for both the ECBI Intensity and Problem scales, depending upon the length between testing. Interrater reliability for parents was reported to range from .86 to .61.

Comparable Cronbach alpha coefficients, ranging from .98 to .96, were reported for the SESBI-R. Test-retest reliability estimates (administration intervals ranged from 1 week to 12 months) were .87 to .93 for children in regular classrooms. The test-retest correlations for special education were less stable, ranging from .64 to .94. Interrater reliability between teachers was not assessed.

Convergent validity of the ECBI against the Child Behavior Checklist and Parenting Stress Index was investigated with resulting correlations ranging from .41 to .75. Discriminate validity was investigated in the ECBI restandardization sample with a comparison between problem behavior and nonproblem children. Significant differences were found between the groups.

The authors cited several studies of the SESBI-R as supportive of convergent and discriminant validity. Correlations with the Revised Edition of the School Observation Scale ranged from .33 to .64. The amount of empirical research supporting discriminate validity of the SESBI-R is limited with significant differences reported between regular and ESE students only on the Intensity scale. The authors acknowledge further study is warranted.

COMMENTARY. The developers acknowledge teacher reports of children's behavior have limitations because they are subjective and may have idiosyncratic interpretations of scale items. Although the rationale supporting the ECBI and SESBI-R seems to have merit, the scales seem to be compromised on several levels. First, how the individual scale items were selected seems to be suspect. Reportedly, the scale items are nonpathological and non-age-specific, but information is not presented about how this was determined.

Moreover, for both instruments raw scores converted to T scores greater than or equal to 60T are reportedly clinically significant, and below 60T are within the normal range and thus holds true for children between 2 and 16. The professional manual indicates the derivation of this cutoff score was based on the frequency distribution in the 1999 normative sample of 798 children. No mention was made as to how the scores for the distributions were determined to be clinically significant. Raw score conversion to T scores across all age groups are identical (e.g., a raw score of 50 converts to a T score of 37 for children from 2 to 16).

SUMMARY. The ECBI and SESBI-R are paper-and-pencil-administered rating scales for the measurement of conduct problems in children. Although it is important to assess behaviors across settings, at best these instruments should be considered initial screening devices for problem behaviors. Although the premise supporting both instruments may be worthwhile, due to technical limitations results should be interpreted with caution.

Review of the Eyberg Child Behavior Inventory and Sutter-Eyberg Student Behavior Inventory—Revised by SUSAN C. WHISTON, Professor of Counseling and Educational Psychology, and JENNIFER C. BOUWKAMP, Doctoral Student, Counseling Psychology, Indiana University, Bloomington, IN:

DESCRIPTION. Both the Eyberg Child Behavior Inventory (ECBI) and the Sutter-Eyberg Student Behavior Inventory—Revised (SESBI-R) are rating scales that measure conduct problems in children ages 2 to 16. The ECBI is completed by parents and attempts to indicate the frequency of disruptive behaviors in the home; whereas, the SESBI-R is completed by teachers and is an assessment of disruptive behaviors in a school setting. Although it is not necessary to use both instruments simultaneously, when used together they are designed to be used in the identification and treatment of children's and adolescents' conduct-disordered behaviors. Both of the assessments measure the severity of conduct-related problems and the extent to which parents or teachers find the behaviors troublesome; however, the instruments were not designed to provide a specific diagnosis.

The ECBI is a 36-item instrument in which parents respond to specific conduct-disordered behaviors in two ways. First, they indicate on a 7-point Intensity scale how often the behavior (e.g., has temper tantrums) currently occurs within a range from *never occurring* to *always occurring*. For the second scale, the parents select either *Yes-No* to identify whether the behavior is currently problematic for them. The SESBI-R is similar; however, teachers respond to 38 items in which they rate the behaviors on a 7-point Intensity scale and indicate Yes-No on the Problem scale. Hence, for both the ECBI and the SESBI-R, there are two scales (i.e., the Intensity scale and the Problem scale), and the raw scores for each scale are converted to *T*-scores. According to the manual, a *T*-score of 60 or above is considered clinically significant, whereas scores less than 60 are within the normal range. Each instrument takes about 10 minutes to complete and is hand scored.

DEVELOPMENT. The 36 behaviors included in the Eyberg Child Behavior Inventory were selected from case records completed over a 2-year period. The original evaluation of the ECBI items was conducted with 512 parents of children seen in a pediatric clinic, and there were significant correlations between each item and the total score. Nevertheless, only a small percentage (6%) of this sample indicated that the reason they were visiting the clinic was for behavioral evaluation of their child. Those who did indicate they were there for behavioral evaluation, however, endorsed the 36 behaviors more often than those parents who visited the clinic for other purposes.

In the original Sutter-Eyberg Student Behavior Inventory, items were developed to reflect the content of the ECBI. Eleven items are identical, another 12 items were slightly altered to reflect a school setting, and an additional 13 items were developed from reviewing charts completed by teachers. The SESBI, however, was revised after a sample of teachers completed the instrument on 726 students from 5th through 12th grade. In this study, 17 non-age-specific criteria from three targeted DSM-III-R disorders were added to the original 36 items. Through a process that was not quite clear, the SESBI-R now consists of 38 items.

As both the ECBI and the SESBI-R are designed to assess children from age 2 through 16, the authors sought to minimize the content of the items that is age-specific. This, however, is a difficult task given the range of developmental levels and the discrepant behaviors associated with age-appropriate behaviors. This uniformity of items is further complicated as there is only one norming group and no differential in item use or weighting depending on the child's age.

TECHNICAL. The norming of the ECBI was restandardized in 1999 on parents from six outpatient pediatric settings in the southeastern United States and involved 798 children between the ages of 2 and 16 years. The sample is 74% Caucasian, 19% African American, 3% Hispanic, 1% Asian, 1% Native American, and 2% other or mixed ethnicity. Although the sample is 52% male and 48% female, there are not separate norms or cutoff scores for males and females. This lack of separate gender norms may be problematic given the trend for boys to exhibit more of the behaviors associated with disorders of interest (i.e., Attention Deficit Hyperactivity Disorder, Conduct Disorder, Oppositional Deviant Disorder) (American Psychiatric Association, 2000). Although Eyberg and Pincus stated in the 1999 manual that they did not find gender differences on Intensity scale scores, they did find a significant gender by age interaction where, at the elementary level, boys had significantly higher Problem scores than girls. Even with this difference, the authors suggest that a single cutoff score is appropriate for the Intensity scale and appropriate for the Problem scale in most situations.

There are also a number of limitations with the SESBI-R as the standardization sample included only 52 teachers who completed the SESBI and the SESBI-R for 415 elementary children. Thus, it was difficult to determine the precise number of students in the sample for the SESBI-R. It should also be noted that the sample was only with elementary children and did not include students older than the fifth grade even though the instrument is designed to be used with children through age 16. Furthermore, there were indications that individual teacher differences may have accounted for as much as 25% of the variance in the SESBI and SESBI-R Intensity scales and about half of the variances in the Problem scales.

Measures of internal consistency provide support for the reliability of scores from both the Intensity scale and Problem scale of the ECBI. For the restandardization sample, the internal consistency coefficients were .95 for the Intensity scale and .93 for the Problem scale. Furthermore, the coefficients were very similar for both males and females and children at different age levels and from different ethnic groups. Test-retest reliability estimates indicated coefficients of .86 and .88 for 3-week intervals, .80 and .85 for 12-week intervals, and .75 and .75 for 10-month intervals for the Intensity and Problem scales, respectively. The internal consistency coefficients for the SESBI-R are also in the .95 to .98 range. With children in regular classrooms, the test-retest coefficients were .87 and .93 for the Intensity and Problem scales. The estimates, however, were not quite as high for children in Exceptional Student Education as the coefficient for the Intensity scale was .64 and .94 for the Problem scale. Further reliability studies are needed with the SESBI-R, as the manual did not provide information on the reliability of the instrument with older children.

Additional validation studies should also be encouraged, as the validation evidence is meager for both the ECBI and SESBI-R. There are indications that the ECBI correlates with other instruments such as the Child Behavior Checklist, the Parenting Stress Index, and the Colorado Child Temperament Inventory. The evidence related to the ECBI ability to discriminate between children with conduct-related problems and normal children is not as compelling; however, there are a few studies with the older standardization group and cutoff score. In our opinions, the authors provide little empirical support for the efficacy of the cutoff score and its clinical importance. Furthermore, there is documentation that the ECBI Problem scale is sensitive to treatment differences, but the studies do not indicate the Intensity scale is sensitive to the effects of treatment. As the authors indicate, there is less empirical evidence for the SESBI-R, and there appear to be few studies that have used the revised edition. There is some evidence that the SESBI-R correlates with the Revised Edition of the School Observation Scale and the teacher form of the Child Behavior Checklist. Although the authors provided some indication that the SESBI could differentiate between nonreferred and referred for treatment preschoolers, only one study (Rayfield, 1998) was discussed related to the ability of the SESBI-R to discriminate, which provided little evidence of the SESBI-R ability to discriminate among children and adolescents. There was, however, a study (Schuhmann, 1999) that found that the SESBI-R scores of elementary children did correlate significantly with times in the next 2 years in which children were suspended from school and referred to the school principal for conduct problems.

COMMENTARY AND SUMMARY. The authors should be commended for designing instruments that measure conduct problems both from the parent's viewpoint and teacher's perspective for children ages 2 to 16. We, however, suggest that clinicians be extremely cautious in using either the ECBI or SESBI-R in assessing and/or diagnosing the severity of the conduct problems. The instruments appear to lack some refinement with little attention given to differences in conduct-related behaviors for children between ages 2 and 16, when indicators of problematic behavior change dramatically as children age and develop. Furthermore, the lack of age-specific norms and dearth of information supporting the cutoff scores on the instruments further limits the utility of both the ECBI and the SESBI-R. Although there are some indications that the SESBI-R has improved psychometric qualities over its predecessor, the SESBI, the lack of children in the norming group who are older than fifth grade is particularly problematic. In conclusion, there are a number of psychometric issues that need to be addressed before these instruments can be used as a sound measure of children's and adolescents' conduct problems.

REVIEWERS' REFERENCES

American Psychiatric Association. (2000). *Diagnostic and statistical manual of mental disorders* (4th ed., text revision). Washington, DC: Author.

Rayfield, A. D. (1998). Concurrent validity of the Sutter-Eyberg Student Behavior with grade school children (Doctoral dissertation, University of Florida, 1998). *Dissertation Abstracts International, 58,* B3932.

Schuhmann, E. M. (1999). *Predictive validity of the Sutter-Eyberg Student Behavior Inventory-Revised and the Teacher Report Form.* Doctoral dissertation, University of Florida, Gainesville.

[97]

Faculty Morale Scale for Institutional Improvement.

Purpose: Designed "as a diagnostic instrument—an attitudinal fact-finding device."
Population: Faculty members.
Publication Date: No date.
Scores: Total score only.
Administration: Group.
Price Data, 2001: $3 per specimen set.
Time: Administration time not reported.
Author: A Local Chapter Committee, American Association of University Professors.
Publisher: Psychometric Affiliates.

Review of the Faculty Morale Scale for Institutional Improvement by KEITH HATTRUP, Associate Professor of Psychology, San Diego State University, San Diego, CA:

DESCRIPTION. The Faculty Morale Scale for Institutional Improvement is a paper-and-pencil measure of faculty members' attitudes towards their jobs and universities. It includes 34 items that are rated with a 5-point Likert scale. As stated in the manual, the goals of the inventory are to provide diagnostic information about faculty attitudes relevant to the design and implementation of institutional changes. The manual does not provide information about the target population; for example, it is not clear whether the measure is relevant for use at any college or university, or with faculty at any level. Information about the administration of the measure is also not provided, and the instrument fails to include instructions to the examinee. Although the basic content of the measure is probably self-evident to most examinees, the manual fails to provide recommendations for communicating to examinees information relevant to the purposes of the measure, what outcomes might result from administering the measure, and how confidentiality and anonymity will be managed. As a consequence, administrators must be knowledgeable about issues relevant to psychological interventions in organizational settings, including survey administration and feedback. Scoring is done by the user, following simple instructions in the manual.

DEVELOPMENT. The Faculty Morale Scale for Institutional Improvement is based on a theoretical model of faculty job satisfaction (i.e., "morale") developed by one of the scale's authors. Respondents rate their satisfaction with 34 job characteristics that were determined by a committee to be relevant to the job of university professor. Item analysis, factor analysis, and internal consistency reliability analyses were not performed to refine the measure. It is unfortunate that the authors chose to develop a new measure of faculty job attitudes rather than use or revise well-known existing measures such as the Job Descriptive Index (JDI; 130). The theoretical model that guided the development of the measure is unique and appears to neglect consideration of a substantial body of theoretical and empirical literature on the nature and measurement of attitudes in organizations (e.g., Cranny, Smith, & Stone, 1992).

TECHNICAL. Norms are provided for each item for a sample of 74 faculty at a private university in the Midwestern United States. Full scale percentile ranks are provided for the sample of 76 faculty at the same university, and an additional sample of 21 respondents from a random mailing to 50 new members of the American Association of University Professors. No information is provided in the manual about respondents' ethnic or racial background, institutional tenure, age, or sex. Generalizability of the norms presented in the manual across universities, disciplines, and demographic groups cannot be assumed.

Reliability evidence consists of a corrected split-half reliability, based on an odd-even split of items, of .94 in the combined norm sample of 97 faculty members. Additional evidence of the instrument's reliability would contribute to supporting inferences about the stability of the measure across time and test content. Standard errors of measurement (SEMs) are not provided in the manual. SEMs assist in the interpretation of differences among scores.

Evidence of validity of the measure is limited to an observed correlation of .15 between the full scale score and a measure of faculty academic rank in a sample of 83 respondents. The authors offer that a low correlation is expected, without explaining why. Much more evidence of reliability and validity must be presented before a clear understanding of the measure is possible.

COMMENTARY AND SUMMARY. The Faculty Morale Scale for Institutional Improvement is a new measure developed on the basis of a unique theoretical model of job satisfaction/morale. Very little normative information is provided, and insufficient evidence of reliability and validity are presented in the manual. Until additional psychometric evidence is made available, the measure can only be recommended for research applications. Users who are interested in evaluating job attitudes among university faculty are encouraged to study the extant theoretical and empirical literature on the nature and measurement of attitudes in organizations, and to consider using the JDI or a related instrument.

REVIEWER'S REFERENCE

Cranny, C. J., Smith, P. C., & Stone, E. F. (1992). Job satisfaction: How people feel about their jobs and how it affects their performance. New York: Lexington.

[98]

Family System Test.

Purpose: Designed "for representing emotional bonds (cohesion) and hierarchical structures in the family or similar social systems."

Population: Individuals and families.

Publication Dates: 1993–1998.

Acronym: FAST.

Scores: Score information available from publisher.

Administration: Individuals or group.

Price Data, 2001: $298 per complete test including 20 recording blanks, board and schematic figures, and manual (1998, 80 pages); $19.50 per 20 recording blanks; $39.50 per manual.

Time: (5–10) minutes for individuals; (10–30) minutes for groups.

Comments: A "figural technique"; "language independent"; authorized English translation of the 1993 German edition "Familiensystemtest" (FAST).

Author: Thomas Gehring; translated from the German edition by Anita Arnone-Reitzle.

Publisher: Hogrefe & Huber Publishers.

Review of the Family System Test by LISA BISCHOFF, Associate Professor, School of Education, Indiana State University, Terre Haute, IN:

DESCRIPTION. The Family System Test (FAST) is designed to provide qualitative and quantitative information regarding family relationships from the perspective of individuals and groups within the family system. Administration of the FAST involves collecting demographic information, asking individuals and/or groups to place wooden figures representing male and female family members on a board to show specific aspects of family relationships, observing behavior of respondents during the procedure, and conducting follow-up interviews with participants.

The FAST can be administered to individuals age 6 years and older and to family groups. Information provided through the FAST may be used to aid the clinician in facilitating discussion among family members and in understanding family networks, constructs, and processes from a systemic perspective. The FAST is not designed to provide a rigid assessment of family functioning and the authors indicate that use of the instrument in this manner would be unethical.

The FAST is a standardized instrument. Detailed instructions are provided for the examiner to facilitate collection of demographic information including family roles, employment and educational history of family members, basic physical and mental health histories of family members, and reason for referral for the family. Information is recorded on the protocol using codes provided in the manual. Standardized instructions are read to the participant(s) to explain the test procedure, to provide context about how the participant(s) should place the figures on the board, and to query the respondent about the representation they have provided using the wooden figures. The manual indicates that instructions may be modified to help respondents understand the procedure, but no specific procedures for modification are provided. Behavioral observations are recorded in brief, narrative format on the test protocol.

The FAST yields both quantitative and qualitative data. Quantitative results are provided in terms of cohesion, hierarchy, flexibility, differences in perceptions, and relational structures. Qualitative results are provided through behavioral observations, verbal responses, and interview responses. Levels of cohesion and hierarchy are categorized as low, medium, or high. Levels are provided for the entire family system as well as for subsystems such as parents and siblings. Flexibility of cohesion and hierarchy are also calculated, resulting in a numerical value purported to be indicative of the degree and direction of change from the ideal or conflict situation to the typical pattern of interaction. Differences in perception are calculated between individual family members and between individual family members and the system as a whole. Differences are reported in numerical values that are intended to illustrate differences in perception within the family system. Finally, the family structure is classified as belonging to one of three groups including "balanced," "labile-balanced," and "unbalanced." Relationship structural patterns may be provided for the entire family system as well as for subsystems with the group. Qualitative results involve integration of observational and interview data with quantitative results. No specific format or procedure is provided to guide the interpretation or reporting of qualitative results.

DEVELOPMENT. The FAST was developed to provide a standardized method of conceptualizing spatial representations of family relationships based on information provided by family members and family systems. Administration of the FAST was pilot-tested at the University of Zurich. In the initial phase, administration and scoring procedures had not been standardized; information obtained in the study related to the viability and clinical validity of the procedure. A single empirical study was cited to illustrate positive clinical results following therapy in which these procedures were used. Following the pilot studies, administration and scoring procedures were standardized and distances between figures and heights of figures were calculated. Following psychometric studies conducted in California with nonclinical samples, scoring procedures were modified and colored figures were introduced into the test. Follow-up questions were added to the test at this time.

TECHNICAL.

Standardization. The FAST was standardized using a sample of 598 nonclinical respondents from middle-class families in San Francisco, California between the years 1985 and 1988. The scoring procedures used in the final version of the FAST were not included in the standardization study as they were not yet developed. Further

studies were conducted through a three-phase process to examine issues of construct validity.

The standardization sample was somewhat diverse with 70% of the respondents being Caucasian, 14% Asian, 10% Hispanic, and 6% African American. Diversity in terms of socioeconomic status, geographic region, and language was not represented in the sample. All families included in the standardization sample had three to six members, with all family members in sixth grade or above. One-third of the families included single parents. Information presented in the manual did not indicate if same-gender parents, blended families, or multi-ethnic families were included in the sample. Although the sample does include ethnic/racial diversity, the lack of socioeconomic and geographic diversity limits the use of this instrument to a narrow population at this time.

Reliability. Test-retest reliability coefficients are provided for representations of children in sixth grade and for adolescents in Grades 9 to 12. Stability of information provided by children was assessed over a 1-week period resulting in coefficients ranging from .47 (cohesion at the dyad level) to .65 (hierarchy at the dyad level). Stability of information provided by adolescents was assessed over a 1-week period resulting in coefficients ranging from .73 (cohesion at the dyad level) to .87 (cohesion at the family level).

Validity. The FAST is designed to provide qualitative and quantitative information regarding family relationships. Results of construct validity studies suggest that FAST results do differentiate between clinical and nonclinical family participants on concepts delineated in structural family theory. Concurrent validity studies were reported using the FAST and two self-report measures including the Family Adaptability and Cohesion Evaluation Scale (FACES III) and the Family Environment Scales (FES). Coefficients from correlation of cohesion and hierarchy scores from the FAST with cohesion/adaptability scores of the FACES III and cohesion/control scores of the FES indicate correlations ranging from .21 to .27 (hierarchy) to .47 to .49 (cohesion.)

Issues of validity were discussed in terms of three criteria including independence of cohesion and hierarchy, family and subsystem representations, and convergent and discriminant diversity. Participant responses overall showed a very low correlation between variables of cohesion and hierarchy dimensions with coefficients ranging from .06 to .17, suggesting that these variables represent independent dimensions of family relationships. Furthermore, participant responses indicated high correlations between cohesion and hierarchy scores of parent-child dyads and average family dyad scores and moderate correlations between parent and sibling dyad and average family dyad scores. This suggests that average family scores reflect primarily parent-child scores, which is consistent with the high number of two-generation dyad included in the sample. As the scoring procedure was modified in the final version of the test, the application of these results to the final version is somewhat questionable.

Interpretation of the FAST for individual families requires that the clinician "integrate information from the representations with the answers provided by the respondent in the follow-up interviews" (manual, p. 36). The process through which such integration occurs is not clearly specified. Furthermore, the authors indicate that families may present an "optimal picture" of their family and the evaluator must determine the extent to which responses are influenced by external factors. Specific methods for determining the effect of external factors on individual responses are not noted in the manual.

Potential uses of the FAST include application in theoretical, research, training, and practice settings. The authors suggest that the FAST may be useful in planning, conducting, and evaluating therapy, yet clear instructions as to how to apply the FAST to these activities are lacking. The FAST manual states that the FAST may be used with "respondents as young as six years," although cautions are provided for interpretation. However, families included in the standardization sample included only children in Grade 6 or above. Furthermore, narrowness of the standardization sample in terms of socioeconomic status, family construction, and geographic location limit the usefulness of this instrument substantially.

COMMENTARY. The FAST is based on theories of structural and developmental family therapy. The instrument is designed to assess important components of family relationships integral to these therapeutic models. The FAST provides a distinctive method for assessing family relationships, thus providing family therapists with an alternative to traditional assessment models.

The FAST involves both quantitative and qualitative results and allows for broad interpretations by the administrators. Construct validity has been demonstrated through a number of studies and concurrent validity studies indicate a moderate to high level of divergent and convergent validity with other measures in the field. Standardization information and reliability estimates are based on a narrow population sample. The psychometric properties of the FAST represent a moderate level of reliability and validity for use in a therapeutic environment. As other figure-placement techniques are somewhat less developed in this area, the FAST may be useful for research and practice in the area of structural and developmental family therapy in combination with other measures.

SUMMARY. Overall, the Family Systems Test provides family-oriented researchers, therapists, and educators an instrument for assessing family structure that is time efficient, useful for individuals across a broad range of ages, and flexible enough to use in a variety of situations. Scoring instructions are specific for quantitative items, yet instructions for interpretation are vague and details regarding application to intervention and therapy are not included. Strengths of the FAST include administration details, focus on psychometric properties, and inclusion of quantitative and qualitative information. However, additional research on the FAST, particularly with a more diverse array of individuals and families is recommended to support use of this instrument in a therapeutic environment.

Review of the Family System Test by RICHARD B. STUART, Program Director, Respecialization in Clinical Psychology, The Fielding Graduate Institute, and Clinical Professor Emeritus, Department of Psychiatry, University of Washington, Seattle, WA:

DESCRIPTION. Drawing on structured family theory, the Family System Test (FAST) employs figure-placement techniques to identify perceptions of family interaction from the perspective of individuals, dyads, subsystems of family members, and/or the family as a whole. A descriptive and metaphorical rather than normative test, its authors believe that it is useful for a wide age spectrum, from preschool to adulthood. Test materials consist of a monochromatic board with 81 squares in a 9 x 9 pattern, six male and six female wooden figures with faces marked by eyes and mouth, one additional male and female figure in each of three colors, and six cylindrical blocks in each of three different heights. A 10-page form is provided for recording responses by each family member. A manual offers detailed instructions for scoring.

After listing present and former members of the family, the test administrator then explains how placing figures in squares on the board and orienting them to face toward or away from each other indicates the closeness of the relationship, and how elevating the figures on cylinders symbolizes the level of power or influence relative to the others. Respondents are asked to represent typical intrafamilial relationships as perceived at present (TR), ideally (IR), and when conflict occurs (CR). After each representation, the examiner asks several predetermined questions that constitute the "inquiry." Respondents are then given an opportunity to replace any of the neutral figures with colored figures to convey other emotions. For example, after representing relationships as they are at present, respondents are asked whether the arrangements apply to a specific event, how long the relationships have existed, how they have changed from the past, what might explain the relationships, and whether the orientation of the faces has meaning. Respondents are also asked to explain their choice of colored replacement figures. In addition to individual administration, all or subsets of members of the family can be asked to collaborate on a single set of representations. The positions and elevation of each figure on the grid, with arrows indicating the direction in which the figure is facing, are recorded for TR, IR, and CR, as are answers to the inquiries.

In addition, the clarity of family structures can be assessed and families can be classified as "balanced," "labile-balanced," or "unbalanced," depending upon their levels of cohesion and hierarchy. Data can also be added from interviews such as respondents' estimates of the stability of the reported relationships and the recurrent subjects of conflict. Information gleaned through interviews is useful in interpreting the meaning of responses. As presented in seven case illustrations, the FAST yields data relevant to planning and evaluating intervention.

TECHNICAL. Information about the validation samples is not as clear as one might wish. A nonclinical sample of 598 respondents was re-cruited through a Stanford University program. Of these, 173 were parents, one third of whom were single parents. However, the total number of families is unknown as the manual does not state whether the 114 who were in two-parent families responded singly or as couples. Nor is information provided about the size of any of the families. Of the children, 41% were sixth graders, 22% were in high school, and 8% were college students. Most (70%) were Caucasian, 14% were Asian, 10% Hispanic, and 6% African American. A second sample of 400 Caucasian children were drawn from schools in Zurich, Switzerland, 280 of whom comprised the "nonclinical" sample, with the rest being clients in outpatient psychiatric clinics. These children were drawn from Grades 1 through 12.

No data on interjudge reliability are reported for either the quantitative or qualitative aspects of the FAST. Because the scoring is not entirely intuitively obvious, it is important to know whether multiple judges would reach similar conclusions if these data are to be used by clinicians other than the examiner. As reported, test-retest reliabilities at 1 week appear to be moderately high among U.S. children in the 6th through 12th grades, but were not reported for either U.S. adults or Swiss children. Discriminant validity was tested in the U.S. sample and revealed that the coherence and hierarchy dimensions are essentially independent. In evaluating convergent validity, the cohesion score on the FAST correlated positively with the cohesion scale of the widely used FACES III (Olson, Portner, & Lavee, 1985), and the Family Environment Scale (Moos & Moos, 1974). Predictive validity was evaluated by showing that children who reported more discordant family ties were more likely to experience higher levels of anxiety, depression, and behavioral problems.

COMMENTARY. Although the authors claim that the FAST can be used with children as young as 6 years, children younger than 8 who were tested for this review had enough difficulty in understanding the instructions to make the validity of their responses questionable. Moreover, no validating data are presented for children younger than first graders. Also, although the manual suggests that the test can be administered to individuals in 5–10 minutes, doing so produced only quantitative data and was quite rushed. To maximize the value of the inquiry and take advantage of potentially valuable qualitative data, 20–30 minutes was more realistic. That would require several hours to test a family of five or more, particularly if coalitions were assessed in addition to individuals.

When respondents are motivated and articulate, the data produced by the FAST are clinically useful and administration of the test itself appears to have therapeutic benefits. The format of the FAST appeared to be a welcome diversion when used as part of a multi-instrument protocol, which consisted of an exploratory interview and a series of pencil-and-paper inventories. However, it was the inquiry phase that seemed to produce the most salient information and the questions that comprise the inquiry could be included in a structured interview without the FAST. Were that done, the FACES III (T6:968), a well-documented 20-item instrument, would usefully quantify respondents' views of family coherence.

SUMMARY. The FAST is not for everyone. It cannot be self-administered or administered in a group. It can be administered quickly only at the loss of valuable information. And it yields information about subjective aspects of family dynamics rather than more tangible data. Therefore, it is best suited for therapists who are not pressed to do brief therapy and who are comfortable with multitextured assessments. Although participants are not asked to write complex answers, they are asked to describe, idealize, and report the history of subtle family relationships, some as participants and others as observers. They are also asked to physically represent and verbally analyze these relationships. None of these is an elementary task. Therefore, the test is best suited for individuals of at least average intelligence who are comfortable with abstract thought. Finally, the FAST should be considered to be a variant of projective testing that is in its developmental stage at present. Where suitable, use of the FAST can enrich family assessment and therapy.

REVIEWER'S REFERENCES

Moos, R., & Moos, B. S. (1974). *Family environment Scale*. Palo Alta, CA: Consulting Psychologists Press.
Olson, D. H., Portner, J., & Lave, Y. (1985). FACES III. In D. H. Olson, H. McCabe, H. Barnes, A. Larsen, M. Mien, & D. H. Wilson (Eds.), *Family inventories* (pp. 7–42). St Paul, MN: Family Social Science, University of Minnesota.

[99]

Fear of Appearing Incompetent Scale.

Purpose: Designed "to identify if individuals are concerned about maintaining or saving face around others to the extent of sacrificing tangible rewards in order to do so."

Population: Adults and college-age.
Publication Date: No date.
Scores: Total score only.
Administration: Group.
Price Data, 2001: $3 per specimen set.
Time: Administration time not reported.
Authors: L. R. Good and K. C. Good.
Publisher: Psychometric Affiliates.

Review of the Fear of Appearing Incompetent Scale by WILLIAM C. TIRRE, Senior Research Psychologist and Research Manager, Career Vision, The Ball Foundation, Glen Ellyn, IL:

DESCRIPTION. The Fear of Appearing Incompetent Scale is a 36-item self-report, true-false instrument designed to measure the "motive to avoid appearing incompetent." The target population is college students and adults. Examinees respond to items by circling T or F for each item. Scoring is accomplished by comparing responses to a paper key. No technical manual was provided, just a four-page description of the instrument, which includes the 36 items as a table. From this description, it can be inferred that the authors intend the instrument for research purposes only.

DEVELOPMENT. The theoretical basis for this instrument is found in the work of B. R. Brown (Brown, 1968, 1970, 1971; Brown & Garland, 1971) and Goffman (1959). Brown used confederates in social psychology experiments to make participants in a game believe they had been made to look foolish or weak before an audience. Then, when given a choice to either retaliate against an exploitive opponent (confederate) or concentrate on their own monetary gain, the exploited participants tended to retaliate even though this resulted in costs to themselves. On the other hand, if the participant had been told he looked good to the audience because he played fair against the opponent, there was less incidence of retaliation against the exploitive opponent. This effect was found especially in the condition where the participant was told the opponent was unaware of the participant's personal costs for retaliation. According to Brown, this was additional evidence that saving face rather than revenge was motivating the participant's behavior. Brown felt that his results were consistent with Goffman's postulated need to save face (i.e., to avoid appearing foolish or incompetent to one's peers) even when this results in some cost to the person.

Good and Good (the authors of this undated scale) decided to develop an individual differences measure of this motive. Forty items were written and pilot-tested on samples of students at Purdue University and Middle Tennessee State University in 1971. The items cover a broad variety of situations in which a person might be concerned about appearing incompetent. Four items were eliminated for either low item-total correlation or low endorsement rate. The final form has 20 items keyed as true and 16 keyed as false.

TECHNICAL. Norm tables were not provided in the four-page test description by Good and Good. The only thing approximating a standardization sample was a sample of 355 Middle Tennessee State University students (185 females, 170 males) enrolled in introductory psychology in 1972. A mean and standard deviation are reported for this sample, but no additional descriptive statistics or demographics are provided. The only reliability information reported was an internal consistency estimate, KR-20. The KR-20 was .89, which indicates that the instrument is quite homogeneous in content. A test-retest (stability) coefficient would be necessary if the authors want to interpret scores as reflecting a stable personality trait. A fatal shortcoming, if this scale is to be used as a psychological test, is that no validity data are presented. At the least, the authors should present correlations of their scale with comprehensive measures of personality such as the California Psychological Inventory (43) or the 16PF (T6:2292). The only attempt at presenting validity data comes in the form of a comparison of men and women on the scale such that women were found to score significantly higher (i.e., have more fears about appearing incompetent). This finding is consistent with Brown and Garland (1971).

COMMENTARY AND SUMMARY. The Fear of Appearing Incompetent Scale is a research instrument with adequate theoretical motivation. It does not have the norms, test-retest reliability data, nor validity data required for a psychological instrument that is to be used in professional practice.

REVIEWER'S REFERENCES

Brown, B. R. (1968). The effects of need to maintain face on interpersonal bargaining. *Journal of Experimental Social Psychology, 4*, 107–122.
Brown, B. R. (1970). Face-saving following experimentally induced embarrassment. *Journal of Experimental Social Psychology, 6*, 255–271.
Brown, B. R. (1971). Saving face. *Psychology Today, 4*(12), 55–59, 86.
Brown, B. R., & Garland, H. (1971). The effects of incompetency, audience acquaintanceship, and anticipated evaluative feedback on face-saving behavior. *Journal of Experimental Social Psychology, 7*, 490–502.
Goffman, E. (1959). *The presentation of self in everyday life.* New York: Doubleday.

[100]
Fear of Powerlessness Scale.

Purpose: Developed as "a self-report measure of the motive to avoid powerlessness."
Population: College-age and adults.
Publication Date: No date.
Scores: Total score only.
Administration: Group.
Price Data, 2001: $3 per specimen set.
Time: Administration time not reported.
Authors: L. R. Good, K. C. Good, and S. B. Golden, Jr.
Publisher: Psychometric Affiliates.

Review of the Fear of Powerlessness Scale by NATHANIEL J. PALLONE, University Distinguished Professor (Psychology), Center of Alcohol Studies, Rutgers University, Piscataway, NJ, and JAMES J. HENNESSY, Professor (Counseling Psychology), Graduate School of Education, Fordham University, New York, NY:

DESCRIPTION. This instrument contains 36 self-relevant statements, each focusing on one or another situation involving control of behavior (e.g., "I sometimes feel I will have insufficient control over what happens to me"; "I am prone to fear that I will be treated unjustly by persons in positions of authority over me"), to which those completing the instrument are asked to respond *True* or *False*. The one-and-a-half-page "manual" contains a scoring key, although the direction in which each item is scored appears to rest entirely on that item's face validity. Among the students in the standardization sample, the mean score was found to be 10.86, with a standard deviation of 6.68; no other normative data are presented. Because several items relate directly to college or university governance and because the only data concerning the meaning of scores (as just recited) derive from a sample of undergraduates, one must conclude that the authors intend that the instrument be used with college students rather than adults or individuals of younger age.

DEVELOPMENT. During the 1971–1972 academic year, 261 undergraduates at a single public university responded to two instruments devised by the authors, one of which (the present instrument) is said to measure fear of powerlessness and the other of which (not otherwise described in the "manual" that accompanies the present instrument) is said to measure "need for social power" (manual, p. 1).

TECHNICAL ISSUES. Reliability and validity evidence for the present instrument reside entirely in the single, sketchily described study just mentioned. At a KR-20 coefficient of .86, reliability seems acceptable; validity is, even in the best light, highly dubious.

According to the authors, validity inheres in coefficients of correlation between scores on this instrument and those on the otherwise not described "need-for-social-power" (manual, p. 2) scale they also constructed. Those coefficients are reported at +.01 for 130 male participants and -.08 for 121 female participants. But it is not self-evident that coefficients of correlation between scores on a fear of powerlessness scale and scores on a need for power scale that hover near zero even begin to demonstrate validity for either instrument.

In terms of formal logic, the perennial distinction between "contraries" and "contradictories" is engaged. It seems equally plausible to believe that, if I fear powerlessness, I shall strive to gain and wield social power (in which case, one should expect to find high positive correlations between the two sets of scores) as to believe that, if I fear powerlessness, I shall shrink from the pursuit of social power (in which case, one should expect high negative correlation between the two sets of scores). The orthogonal logic—that need for social power is not diametrically, but perpendicularly, related to fear of powerlessness—strikes one as genuinely unfathomable, because the only valid conclusion to be drawn is that the two scales measure different things (contraries), not that they measure opposite things (contradictories).

Nor is there evidence adduced to differentiate powerlessness, or fear thereof, from such other psychological traits or characteristics as negative self-assessment, self-abasement, a pervasive sense of external control, or even frank paranoia. Some items seem virtual parodies of the credo of the John Birch Society, then a potent political group centered on the evils of "big government" (e.g., whether the respondent believes that "governmental agencies" are compiling secret dossiers of one or another sort that will ultimately be used "against me in some way at a later time" or are otherwise engaged in activities that "might excessively restrict my freedom" or whether "I fear I will be treated like a pawn in the hands of governmental officials"). As Rokeach (1960) had opined, assent to such items seems indicative of clinical issues of which a generic "fear of powerlessness" may be only symptomatic. Whether that conjecture holds merit might have been assessed through concurrent administration of instruments validated as indices of clinically relevant conditions (e.g., the *Pa* Scale of the Minnesota Multiphasic Personality Inventory [MMPI]), but neither psychometric nor behavioral cross-validation is reported.

The data on which this instrument rests were gathered within a calendar year of the interventions of the National Guard in student anti-Vietnam war protests at Kent State and Jackson State—unprecedented military actions that left a dozen students dead. The summoning of military force to quell campus unrest at those institutions and elsewhere was undoubtedly intended precisely to engender a sense of powerlessness and vulnerability among students. Not long thereafter, the formation of a cartel within the Organization of Petroleum Exporting Countries rapidly inflated the price of oil and triggered a worldwide economic decline that severely affected the job prospects of college students, yielding (or perhaps perpetuating) a widespread sense of powerlessness in its wake. It is, therefore, quite disappointing that, in the final sentences in their manual, the authors candidly admit that:

> Important for the demonstration of construct validity would be behavioral predictions based on fear-of-powerlessness scores in social contexts which arouse such a motive. At this time, unfortunately, the authors have no data of this nature, having not, as yet, been able to think of a good study to do with this scale. (manual, p. 2)

A search of the PsychInfo data base in February 2002 suggests that, three decades later, neither have these authors nor anyone else been able "to think of a good study to do with this scale."

SUMMARY. Clinicians may require a brief, reliable, valid means through which to assess a subjective sense of powerlessness in patients who have been traumatized, criminally victimized, etc. Researchers may wish to assess whether a situationally determined or stimulus-driven experience of vulnerability (i.e., "state" powerlessness) can be psychometrically differentiated from a more pervasive sense of helplessness ("trait" powerlessness, akin to what sociologists term anomia). If either clinician or researcher looks to this instrument for any such purpose, disappointment shall ensue.

Constructed in 1971–1972 but apparently not employed for research purposes since, the Fear of Powerlessness Scale is a 36-item self-report questionnaire of acceptable reliability but dubious validity apparently intended for use with university undergraduates. In the absence either of concurrent psychometric cross-validation, criterion-referencing against independent judgments of fear of powerlessness, or predictive behavioral validation, there is no compelling reason to believe that the instrument measures what it purports to measure. Thirty years after its development, one suspects that this instrument's principal value is as an exemplar of questionable workmanship in test construction. Researchers or clinicians in search of reliable, valid measures of powerlessness are better advised to consult Seeman's (1991) review of standard and experimental instruments for assessing alienation and anomie.

REVIEWERS' REFERENCES

Rokeach, M. (1960). *The open and closed mind.* New York: Ballantine.
Seeman, M. (1991). Alienation and anomie. In J. P. Robinson, P. R. Shaver, & L. S. Wrightsman (Eds.), *Measures of personality and social psychological attitudes* (pp. 291–371). San Diego: Academic Press.

[101]

Fear of Success Scale.

Purpose: Designed as a self-report measure of fear of success.

Population: College students.

Publication Date: No date.

Scores: Total score only.

Administration: Group.

Price Data, 2001: $3 per specimen set.

Time: Administration time not reported.

Authors: L. R. Good and K. C. Good.

Publisher: Psychometric Affiliates.

Review of the Fear of Success Scale by LAURA L. B. BARNES, Associate Professor of Educational Research and Evaluation, Oklahoma State University, Tulsa, OK:

DESCRIPTION. The Fear of Success Scale (FOSS) is a 29-item dichotomously scored, self-report measure that was introduced into the research literature in 1973 (Good & Good, 1973). The authors report that it is grounded in Horner's (1968) work on sex differences in achievement motivation that suggests that "many women may fear social ostracism and loss of femininity should they achieve well in competition with others" (cited in FOSS manual of instructions, p. 1). The items are statements that the respondent is asked to mark true or false; for 23 of the statements, "true" is the keyed response. The items are situation-neutral and could ostensibly apply to a variety of contexts. It appears that each item is worth unit value and the score is the sum of the item scores, with a score range of 0 to 29. The "Manual of Instructions" appears to be a reprint of the 1973 *Psychological Reports* journal article.

DEVELOPMENT. For the purposes of the instrument, the authors write that they defined fear of success as the worry that a superior performance in various activities would antagonize others. They wrote 30 statements requiring a true/false response, which were then administered to 228 psychology students (125 females, 103 males) at Middle Tennessee State University during the 1973 spring semester. One item with a low item-total correlation was eliminated, and the remaining 29 items subjected to further analysis.

TECHNICAL. A KR-20 score reliability computed for the student sample was reported to be .81 and the mean point-biserial r was .40. The female mean score (7.69, $SD = 4.67$) was statistically significantly higher than that for males (mean = 6.11, $SD = 4.16$). Though the authors did not interpret this difference, it appears to be in the expected direction given the theoretical context of the instrument. This is the extent of the information concerning the instrument in the manual of instructions.

A PsychInfo "all fields" search for "Fear of Success Scale" yielded 43 publications since 1973; however, there was more than one scale with the same title. A Social Science Citation search showed that the Good and Good (1973) article was cited 31 times since 1981, though not all those articles reported research in which the FOSS was used. A great deal more effort would be required to enumerate the specific publications in which the Good and Good (1973) Fear of Success Scale was used in research—a task that does not belong to this reviewer. Nevertheless, some additional validity information was gleaned from reading some of the pertinent research articles. Chabassol and Ishiyama (1983) described and examined correlations among three Fear of Success Scales—Good and Good (1973), Zuckerman and Allison (1976), and Pappo (1972). They found concurrent validities with these scales varied by gender of respondent. For women, the correlations were .52 and .44 with the Pappo and the Zuckerman and Allison measures, respectively; but for men, the correlations were .35 and -.08, respectively. Orlofsky (1978) reported correlations between the FOSS and a fear of failure measure of .34 for males and .11 for female college students. Tomkiewicz and Bass (1999), in a study of change in women's fear of success in business settings, reported for a sample of female business majors that FOSS scores were negatively correlated with attitudes toward women ($r = -.42$). The correlation for male business students was -.10. Orlofsky (1978) examined differences in FOSS scores among male and female college students at different stages of identity development. Results supported his hypothesized differences in patterns for males and females depending on developmental stage. It was noted that females' FOSS scores were higher than males' only among those in the moratorium stage, and not significantly so. Chabassol and Ishiyama (1983) found no significant mean score differences between males and females in their study. More recently, Tomkiewicz and Bass (1999) reported no significant FOSS score differences between male and female business students in general; however, progressive female students (so identified based on their "attitude toward women" score) scored lower than either males or traditional female students. These studies indicate the FOSS is still being used in research on achievement motivation. It is related to, but different from, other measures of the same name. The elevation and perhaps the meaning of the scores varies by gender, college major, and developmental stage. Researchers choosing among Fear of Success measures would do well to read Chabassol and Ishiyama's (1983) article that compares the FOSS to two competing measures.

COMMENTARY AND SUMMARY. The information currently provided by the publisher of this test is quite lean with respect to recommended standards for a published test. The test itself may, however, be a reasonable measure of fear of success. Though 30 years old, reports of score reliability suggest good internal consistency. It continues to be used in research and, thus, there exists a rich source of data for evaluating construct validity. My advice to anyone searching for an instrument to measure fear of success would be to begin with a thorough review of the research literature and make their own comparison among the various scales, paying special attention to how the construct is defined and operationalized. The results

of the Chabassol and Ishiyama study suggest some important differences among various fear of success instruments. Nevertheless, if this instrument is to be marketed, the publisher really should update and expand the manual to include current information, particularly with respect to validity.

REVIEWER'S REFERENCES

Chabassol, D. J., & Ishiyama, F. I. (1983). Correlations among three measures of fear of success. *Psychological Reports, 52,* 55–58.
Good, L. R., & Good, K. C. (1973). An objective measure of the motive to avoid success. *Psychological Reports, 33,* 1009–1010.
Orlofsky, J. L. (1978). Identity formation, achievement, and fear of success in college men and women. *Journal of Youth and Adolescence, 7*(1), 49–62.
Pappo, M. (1972). *Fear of success: A theoretical analysis and the construction and validation of a measuring instrument.* Unpublished doctoral dissertation, Teachers' College, Columbia University.
Tomkiewicz, J., & Bass, K. (1999). Changes in women's fear of success and fear of appearing incompetent in business. *Psychological Reports, 85,* 1003–1010.
Zuckerman, M., & Allison, S. N. (1976). An objective measure of fear of success: Construction and validation. *Journal of Personality Assessment, 40,* 422–430.

[102]
Firefighter Learning Simulation.

Purpose: Designed to "simulate the learning process required of entry-level firefighters in Fire Academies."
Population: Applicants for firefighter trainee positions.
Publication Date: 1998.
Acronym: FLS.
Scores: Total score only.
Administration: Group.
Price Data: Price information available from publisher for test material including administration guide and technical manual (11 pages), and training manual (26 pages).
Time: 90 minutes.
Comments: Simulated training manual is provided to examinees in advance of the test.
Author: Psychological Services, Inc.
Publisher: Psychological Services, Inc.

Review of the Firefighter Learning Simulation by JoELLEN V. CARLSON, Measurement and Evaluation Consultant, Washington, DC:

DESCRIPTION. The Firefighter Learning Simulation (FLS) appears to be a course and an end-of-course test. The FLS consists of a training manual, which contains seven lessons, and a 65-item test. The test items, all very short, four-option multiple-choice items, are based directly on the lessons in the training manual. The test yields a number-correct score, which can be compared to the raw-score-to-percentile conversion table provided. The purpose and intended uses of the test are unclear, although the scoring and usage section of the administrator's guide and technical manual offers the publisher's service to score tests, weight portions of the test according to the user's instructions, and produce an eligibility list. Presumably, this "eligibility list" would be used in firefighter selection.

DEVELOPMENT. The only information about the origin of the items in the FLS is that they were selected from 81 items that were originally administered in a "large jurisdiction located in a southwestern state" (manual, p. 8). The items were written to reflect directly the information presented in the lessons of the FLS training manual. The guide/manual says that the lessons were developed to cover the "important work behaviors" composing the "domain of firefighting" (p. 5). No information is given as to how the behaviors were identified, how the lessons relate to the behaviors, or how the items reflect the behaviors. There is no evidence that the work behaviors listed in the guide/manual are important; neither job analysis, validity studies, nor expert review are described. Despite the lack of important types of validity evidence, the manual claims "face validity" because each item is referenced to a specific page in the training manual.

Many of the items appear to be answerable by a naïve person who has neither participated in the training nor read the manual. Item statistics indicate a disproportionate number of very easy items, with 21 (more than 29%) of the items having p-values of .90 and above, and another 26 (more than 38%) between .80 and .89. There is also no evidence that the items measure important content and are not trivial, as many seem to be. All of the items are based on simple recall of information directly from the lessons. No problem solving or other application of knowledge appears to be required. Further, "simulation" seems to be a misnomer for the FLS materials; simulation is not apparent in any of the materials—neither in the training manual nor in the test.

TECHNICAL. Basic item and test statistics are reported—test statistics for 11,186 examinees and item statistics for 11,160 of those examinees. No information is given about these examinees, unless one is to infer from the statement that the items were administered in a southwestern state that these examinees were used to determine the reported item statistics. No research results are reported other than the p-values provided and basic test characteristics: Mean = 54.15, sd = 9.44, sem = 2.60, KR20 = .92. An "adjusted item-total point-biserial correlation" (manual, p. 8) is re-ported for each of the items, although "adjusted" is not defined.

COMMENTARY. Throughout the guide/manual, there are inconsistencies about the intended purpose(s) of this instrument. Although the publisher provides norms and offers to produce an "eligibility list" from the results of the test, there is also emphasis on the direct relationship between the lessons and the test items.

The publisher does not clarify how the training manual and test are to be used. The mention of "eligibility" determination implies that it is intended to be more than an end-of-course or practice test. However, there is no discussion of whether, how, or when the training should be provided relative to administration of the test. There is no discussion of procedures for enhancing fairness or minimizing adverse impact. More space is devoted to steps for administering and timing the test than to important technical information.

One additional area of serious concern is the support for norm-referencing in the presumed application of determining firefighter eligibility. Although it may be customary to norm-reference in this context, it is an inappropriate practice. It is the responsibility of test publishers to advise against such a practice, not to support it.

SUMMARY. As a personnel selection instrument, there is a serious dearth of evidence that this instrument meets legal requirements or professional guidelines. The publisher does not provide direct discussion of the intended use(s) of the instrument or caution about appropriate use of the lessons. There simply is not adequate information regarding development and technical characteristics to support the use of the FLS in selection. Consequently, it would seem that the only apparent utility of the FLS is as a study guide and practice test, assuming an appropriate relationship to a jurisdiction's job analysis. Significant work on the part of each user jurisdiction would be required to establish validity of the instrument for this purpose.

Review of the Firefighter Learning Simulation by JAMES W. PINKNEY, Professor of Counselor and Adult Education, East Carolina University, Greenville, NC:

DESCRIPTION. The Firefighter Learning Simulation Training Test (FLS) is a 65-item instrument intended to assess fire department firefighter trainee applicants' mastery of very basic

Review of the Firefighter Selection Test [Revised] by CHANTALE JEANRIE, Industrial/Organizational Psychologist, Associate Professor of Measurement and Évaluation, Department of Fondements et pratiques en Éducation, Faculty of Education, Laval University, Quebec, Canada:

DESCRIPTION. The Firefighter Selection Test (FST) is intended to measure abilities deemed important to perform satisfactorily in the firefighting job. It is a personnel selection device, especially suited for entry-level personnel.

Item format and content. Each form of the FST comprises 100 items, separated into three subtests. But for some exceptions, Forms A-R and B carry the same number of items for each subtest's components. All items use a multiple-choice response format. Mechanical comprehension items are all accompanied by a figure picturing the problem to solve.

Administration and scoring. The test material includes an administrator guide that is very well organized. It emphasizes standardization and provides detailed information about the necessary steps to conduct a test session.

Scoring can be done either manually or through an automated system. The scoring key was not included so it is not possible to comment on its use. Norms are provided for the total score. The norms are based on a sample of over 2,600 firefighter candidates. No further data are provided about the sample.

In addition, and this is a valuable advantage for the FST, a study guide is provided in order to help applicants prepare for the test. This guide carefully explains how to answer, how to deal with time limits, and how the answers are marked. Practice items are provided for each subtest, and instructions as well as answer keys are included. Items are representative of those contained in both A-R and B forms.

DEVELOPMENT AND PRESENT FORM. The FST as presented today is a second-generation test. The first part of its development was the creation of the Versions A and P. The second generation of this test (Form A-R) was developed to improve the initial version and to produce an equivalent form (Form B), an important asset for a personnel selection device.

The development process of the first versions is not explained except for the facts that three item types were included and that items included in the reading comprehension subtest were extracted from genuine training material. Items were chosen to be job relevant and free of bias against women and ethnic groups. The mechanical systems and reading comprehension tests are divided into a few components (e.g., pulley systems, resolution of forces, rescue procedures, fire spread). Although these components seem appropriate at face value, references to the job content domain should have been presented. Consequently, it is difficult to know if these subtests and components really match what is most important in the job.

Field tests were conducted on a sample of 3,010 firefighter applicants. Diverse analyses provided evidence that the two forms share comparable means and standard deviations. However, the equivalence has to be assumed from the raw data. No statistics (T tests) are presented to support the statistical equivalence of the means.

The development process of Forms A-R and B is not described with more details. Original and reviewed items were used to improve Version A and build Version B. Field tests of Forms A-R and B were conducted on a sample of 90 students or students' friends or relatives. These field tests led to the addition of new items and to the modification of other ones. The mechanical comprehension subtest contains exactly the same items in both Form A-R and B but these are presented in different orders. The reading comprehension and report interpretation subtests are composed of items that are specific to each form. Items of Form B were chosen based on statistical properties in order to equate both forms' means, standard deviations, and standard error of measurement.

The absence of reference to a job analysis appears to be the major shortcoming of this test. The authors assume that the dimensions they have chosen consist of general and sufficient predictors of job performance as a firefighter, without providing any such demonstration. The dimensions that are included do make sense but a content-validation strategy usually requires more than a mere appearance of relevance. Reference to a specification table would have helped to convince readers of the general relevance of this test for firefighter selection and to help them to decide whether other instruments should be included in the selection process.

TECHNICAL.

Reliability. Reliability data are provided for former versions A and P and for the newer A-R and B forms. Internal consistency coefficients

(Kuder-Richardson-20) range from .87 to .92 (original versions: $n = 3,010$, new versions: $n = 90$) and can be considered suitable for this type of test. However, it would have been more appropriate to add a reliability index for each subtest. Because each of them taps a specific knowledge or ability universe, unidimensionality is unlikely, so a general score may alter results interpretation.

The equivalence coefficient of Forms A-R and B is relatively high ($r = .89$), and very high ($r = .98$) when corrected for attenuation. The magnitude of these coefficients fully supports the use of both forms as equivalent versions of the FST.

Validity. Validity studies were conducted on previous A and P versions only. Because the later forms are very closely related to the original ones, validity data from the initial scales are transposed to Forms A-R and B, which seem acceptable. However, because a few items have been modified and the sample used to develop A-R and B forms was not very large and was not composed of job applicants, some further studies on these versions would be required.

Many efforts have been devoted to evaluating validity of the use of the FST's scores. Three different criterion-related validity studies were performed. The first two used various relevant work-related measures from supervisor ratings to job knowledge tests and work samples. Results can be considered as ranging from good to very good (Study 1: $r = .19$ to $r = .55$, median, $r = .31$; Study 2: $r = .55$ and $r = .42$ for training tests and work samples, respectively). The samples were broken down to present the number of job candidates for three different ethnic groups (Black, Hispanic, or nonminority) but results are presented for the whole sample only. The third study describes the success rate in training according to trainees' test results. As one would expect from valid predictors, the rate of applicants who were terminated increases as score levels decline. However, only a very small percentage (4.6%) of candidates were excluded from further training, and this limits the value of this study.

Test scores of different ethnic groups were scrutinized to assess the potential presence of bias. The results obtained in the first two studies were analyzed using a three-step procedure (Gulliksen & Wilks, 1950). The results of these validity analyses indicate the presence of bias for a little more than half the criteria. Standard error of measurement is equivalent in all cases but between-groups differences in regression slope reveal more accurate prediction for Black candidates whereas intercept differences favor Black candidates. It is worthwhile to notice that biases are found on both objective and judgemental criteria. However, as it frequently happens in such comparative studies, subsample sizes are disproportionate, thus suggesting that these results should be interpreted with care. No study was undertaken to determine whether the FST was equally fair to men and women.

COMMENTS. The firefighter selection test is a measurement device that holds paradoxical characteristics. The absence of information about degree of overlap between the content of the test and the major requirements for the job is indeed a serious flaw. However, the test authors have put considerable efforts into the validation of scores from the FST when used to predict relevant criteria. Because results of these studies came out very positively, the relevance of the test for its intended use appears to be supported. It is this reviewer's opinion, however, that more validity studies should be conducted on the new test forms and that a more thorough bias analysis should be completed.

SUMMARY. The Firefighter Selection Test is considered by this reviewer as a very interesting assessment instrument. Although the test development should have been more thoroughly documented, information about the equivalence of forms suggests that the work done on the FST was rather rigorous. Nonetheless, in the absence of job analysis results, it is difficult to conclude that the FST is relevant for every job of firefighter, regardless of the contexts and environments. Consequently, the use of this test is recommended, but it is also suggested that all potential users refer to job analysis data in order to evaluate the appropriateness and fullness of the FST for their personnel selection needs.

REVIEWER'S REFERENCE
Gulliksen, H., & Wilks, S. S. (1950). Regression tests for several samples. *Psychometrika, 15,* 91–144.

Review of the Firefighter Selection Test [Revised] by DENIZ S. ONES, Hellervik Professor of Industrial Psychology, Department of Psychology, University of Minnesota, Minneapolis, MN:

DESCRIPTION. The Firefighter Selection Test is a written selection test, aimed at measuring job relevant cognitive abilities for entry-level firefighters. Two alternate forms of the test are available, Forms A-R and Form B. Form A-R is the revised version of the original published version (Form A). An unpublished form also exists (Form P). Each form contains 100 items aimed at assessing mechanical comprehension, reading comprehension, and report interpretation. Forms A-R and B use the same mechanical comprehension items, presented in different orders. A single score, ranging from 0 to 100, is produced for each test taker by counting the number of correct answers given.

Test-related materials offered by the test publisher include the technical manual (22 pages), administrator's guide (6 pages), and a study guide for job applicants (16 pages). The administration of the test has been standardized. Appropriate instructions and admonishments are provided on test security, test-taking conditions, and special considerations when using alternate forms, answer sheets, and test instructions. The time limit for the test is 2.5 hours. The test is not speeded.

The test can be scored manually or by a scanning machine. The administrative guide states that the Firefighter Selection Test can be used "for ranking, as well as with a cutoff score" (p. 5).

DEVELOPMENT. The technical manual states that items "were developed to have job-relevant content and be free of bias against minorities and women" (p. 1). The mechanical comprehension items were written to measure job-related knowledge rather than physics textbook knowledge. Mechanical principles tested by the items (e.g., hydraulics, center of gravity, resolution of forces, shape and volume) are couched in terms relating to firefighter job duties (e.g., operating pumps, raising and securing ladders, making hose connections). The reading comprehension items were based on actual training materials used by entry-level firefighters. As with traditional reading comprehension items, test takers are presented with reading passages and questions aiming to assess whether the read passage was understood. The report interpretation items were developed to measure the ability to "read charts and reports and correctly interpret the information" (administrative guide, p. 1). Again, the items are contextualized to be fire department relevant.

Items were tested with 3,010 firefighter applicants. Three goals of item selection were (a) to maximize the item-total correlation of the correct answer, (b) to maximize the effects of distractors, and (c) to maintain a moderate level of difficulty.

Items were evaluated for item bias against minorities and women. A procedure proposed by Angoff and Ford (1973) was used in these analyses. Items showing bias were excluded from the final version of the test. Until 1998, only this original version of the test was available (Form A).

Both a revision of Form A and the creation of an equivalent, alternate form was undertaken in 1997. An item pool composed of all Form A items and 70 experimental items culled from previous research were administered to community college students and their friends/relatives in Lorain, Ohio ($N = 90$). The technical manual does not discuss what specific analyses were performed to arrive at a final set of items for the revised version of Form A. However, we are told that four reading comprehension items were replaced. The revised form (Form A-R) now presents the mechanical comprehension, reading comprehension, and report interpretation items in scrambled format. The same is true for Form B. In creating an equivalent, alternate form (Form B), the same mechanical comprehension items as Form A-R were used. For reading comprehension and report interpretation items were selected based on difficulty and item-total correlations. Another goal was to make Form B as similar to Form A-R as possible in terms of statistical properties, content, and length. Forms A-R and B are designed to be classically parallel forms. The new items on Form A-R and Form B do not appear to have been tested for item bias.

TECHNICAL. A single set of test norms are provided for a sample of 2,677 recent firefighter candidates (i.e., separate norms are not provided for the different forms). The demographic characteristics of the normative sample are not described. Current federal laws pertaining to personnel selection prohibit within-group norming. Therefore, separate norms are not provided for women, minorities, and different ethnic groups.

Mean score differences between protected groups (i.e., women, African Americans, Hispanic Americans) are documented in a small sample of firefighter applicants ($Ns = 71, 32, 31$ for Caucasian Americans, African Americans, and Hispanic Americans, respectively). Differences approach 1 standard deviation units, favoring Caucasian Americans. Data for this study were gathered in mid 1970s and may be in need of updating, especially in light of the well-documented Flynn effect (Neisser, 1998)—rising of cognitive ability test scores over time in all groups studied. Potential gender differences are not documented.

The reported internal consistency reliabilities (KR-20) of test forms are .91 (Form A, $N = 3,010$ firefighter applicants), .87 (Form P, $N = 3,010$ firefighter applicants), and .92 (Form A-R; sample size and nature of test takers not reported), and .92 (Form B; sample size and nature of test takers not reported). Using data from the same samples, coefficients of equivalence are as follows: .83 for Forms A and P, .997 for Forms A and A-R, and .89 for Forms A-R and B (recall that Forms A and A-R differ by four items and item order; and Form A-R and B contain the same set of mechanical comprehension items). Evidence has been presented that Forms A-R and B assess the same construct: the alternate form correlation corrected for measurement error using internal consistency reliability estimates is .98. Test-retest reliabilities have not been reported.

Validity data for the test have been reported in three studies. In Study 1, 144 firefighter applicants "took the Firefighter Selection test (Form P), completed fire college, and became firefighter probationers" (technical manual, p. 5). Criterion-related validities were computed for a variety of criteria: work samples and training tests (part of academy training), job knowledge tests, and officers' (supervisors) and firefighters' (peer) ratings (designed to reflect major tasks carried out on the job, based on a job analysis). Work sample tests were standardized measures of ability to carry out critical work behaviors (e.g., hydrant operation, knot tying, hose evolutions). Observed correlations ranged from .19 (for a composite criterion of officers' ratings) and .55 (for training tests). Work sample tests correlated .35 with the Firefighter Selection Test.

A second study augmented the sample from the study described above with other firefighter applicants ($N = 335$). This sample was ethnically diverse (i.e., included 44 African Americans and 39 Hispanic Americans). The validities for training tests and work samples were reported as .55 and .42, respectively.

A third study examined fire college drop out rate as a function of test scores ($N = 336$ firefighter applicants from Study 2). Cross tabulations presented (test score range by termination status [terminated/retained]) suggest some usefulness for the test in predicting dropping out.

A series of analyses, using the samples discussed above, are presented examining test bias (standard error of estimate, regression slope, and intercept differences) for African Americans and Hispanic Americans. These analyses are repeated with the different criteria employed (e.g., work samples, training tests). Despite problems of statistical power (small Ns), some statistically significant results for bias were found in the prediction of work sample, training, and job knowledge tests. However, in all these cases, the detected bias was in favor of the minority groups.

COMMENTARY. Cognitive ability is a necessary but not a sufficient condition for success as a firefighter. The Firefighter Selection Test is an appropriate personnel selection tool that can be used with firefighter candidates. Evidence for its job relatedness has been offered in the form of correlations with work samples, training tests, job knowledge tests, and ratings of job performance. These criterion-related validities were computed on small samples, but perhaps more importantly using Form A of the test. Yet, there is reason to believe that new validity studies, if conducted, would continue supporting the use of the test in firefighter selection. This is because (a) alternate forms of the test appear to be highly correlated (and classically parallel) and, more importantly, (b) voluminous past research with cognitive ability tests has shown them to be good predictors of a variety of work behaviors, including overall job performance (Viswesvaran & Ones, 2002). Another positive feature of the test is the job relevance of its items. Test takers are likely to perceive the instrument as face valid.

The usefulness of the Firefighter Selection Test has not been studied in selection systems including other predictors. It would be valuable for future research to document incremental validity and divergent/convergent validity with other cognitively based tests. Another glaring absence is a discussion of gender differences on the test. Data documenting mean score differences and examinations of test/predictive bias should be reported in the test's technical manual. Traditionally, women have been underrepresented among firefighters and demonstrations of freedom from test bias for this group is particularly important.

As was noted above, the test publishers provide a study guide to be used by test takers. Neither the technical manual nor the administrative guide for the test include any discussion of research pertaining to the effects of test familiarity, self study, and coaching on test scores.

SUMMARY. The constructs assessed by the test have a long, well-established history in predicting performance (Salgado, Viswesvaran, & Ones, 2001). The Firefighter Selection Test [Revised] appears to be a reliable work horse that can be successfully used in firefighter selection. The existence of two classically parallel forms and face validity of the instrument are its strengths. The existing strengths of the test can be enhanced by presenting evidence for (a) the impact of the test for hiring and predicting performance of women firefighters and (b) the impact of test preparation on test scores.

REVIEWER'S REFERENCES

Angoff, W. H., & Ford, S. F. (1973). Item-race interaction on a test of scholastic aptitude. *Journal of Educational Measurement, 10,* 95–106.

Neisser, U. (Ed.). (1998). *The rising curve: Long-term gains in IQ and related measures.* Washington, DC: American Psychological Association.

Salgado, J., Viswesvaran, C., & Ones, D. S. (2001). Predictors used in personnel selection: An overview of constructs, methods and techniques. In N. Anderson, D. S. Ones, H. Sinangil, & C. Viswesvaran (Eds.), *Handbook of industrial, work, and organizational psychology* (Vol. 1, pp. 165–199). London, UK: Sage.

Viswesvaran, C., & Ones, D. S. (2002). Agreements and disagreements on the role of General Mental Ability (GMA) in industrial, work and organizational psychology. *Human Performance, 15,* 211–231.

[104]

FIRO-B™ [Fundamental Interpersonal Relations Orientation–Behavior™].

Purpose: Designed "to measure behavior that derives from interpersonal needs."

Population: Age 13 and over.

Publication Dates: 1957–2000.

Acronym: FIRO-B™.

Scores, 7: 2 Overall Behavior scores (Expressed, Wanted) for each of 3 dimensions (Inclusion, Control, Affection) plus Overall Need score.

Administration: Individual or group.

Price Data, 2001: $60 per 10 FIRO-B™ self-scorable forms; $38 per 10 FIRO-B™ technical guides (2000, 77 pages); $9.35 per Introduction to the FIRO-B™; $160 per 10 prepaid Leadership Reports; $100 per 10 FIRO-B™ Interpretive Reports for Organizations.

Time: (10–15) minutes.

Comments: May be administered via paper-pencil or online at skillsone.com; earlier versions entitled FIRO Awareness Scales.

Authors: Will Schutz (original test), Allen L. Hammer (technical guide), and Eugene R. Schnell (technical guide).

Publisher: Consulting Psychologists Press, Inc.

Cross References: See T5:1036 (13 references) and T4:982 (18 references); for a review by Peter D. Lifton of an earlier edition, see 9:416 (12 references); see also T3:890 (45 references), 8:555 (147 references), and T2:1176 (58 references); for a review by Bruce Bloxom, see 7:78 (70 references); see also P:79 (30 references) and 6:94 (15 references).

Review of the FIRO-B [Fundamental Interpersonal Relations Orientation—Behavior] by MICHELLE ATHANASIOU, *Associate Professor of School Psychology, University of Northern Colorado, Greeley, CO:*

DESCRIPTION. The Fundamental Interpersonal Relations Orientation—Behavior (FIRO-B) is a self-report instrument designed to measure behaviors that derive from interpersonal needs. It is geared toward adolescents and adults who can read and understand both the instrument and interpretive results. The instrument includes 54 items that are rated using two types of 6-point rating scales. It can be administered in individual or group formats, and generally can be completed in 10 to 20 minutes. The instrument can be administered using the self-scoring version, online version, or the computer-scored version, which requires software from the publisher.

The FIRO-B measures three interpersonal needs (Inclusion, Control, and Affection), and the degree to which each of those needs are Wanted and Expressed, resulting in a 2x3 matrix of needs. Expressed needs refer to the extent to which an individual initiates related behaviors. Wanted needs refer to wanting others to initiate such behaviors and wanting to be the recipient of such behaviors. Scores are provided for Overall Need, Total Behavior (Expressed and Wanted), Total Need (Inclusion, Control, and Affection), and individual cell scores (Wanted Inclusion—wI, Expressed Inclusion—eI, Wanted Control—wC, Expressed Control—eC, Wanted Affection—wA, and Expressed Affection—eA).

Although respondents are asked to rate each item on a 6-point scale, each item is scored as either significant or nonsignificant. Significant ratings receive a score of 1, and nonsignificant ratings receive a score of 0. Individual cell score totals range from 0 to 9, Total Need scores can range from 0 to 18, Total Behavior scores range from 0 to 27, and Overall Need scores range from 0 to 54.

The items are relatively straightforward, and were written using a Guttman scale, whereby items with like content are written in increasingly strong language. The assumption is that a respondent who responds in the affirmative to a strongly worded item will also respond affirmatively to less strongly worded items with similar content. Although this method of item construction may enhance instrument validity, it may appear to the respondent that items are redundant. The self-scoring protocol is easy to complete and score; nevertheless, the technical guide that accompanies the instrument is needed to fully interpret scores. Because it is unlikely that all respondents have access to the manual, it might be helpful to have brief interpretative information included directly on the protocol. Also, because item meaning is relatively obvious, test takers could easily present themselves in a favorable way. The authors say that because test takers do not know the cutoffs used to score an item 0 or 1, it is difficult to fake a presentation. However, some type of validity scale or method to disguise items would be helpful.

It is unclear how interpretations for various score ranges were derived. For example, for the Overall Need scale, scores between 0 and 15 are considered Low, scores between 16 and 26 are considered Medium-Low, scores between 27 and 38 are considered Medium-High, and scores above 38 are considered High. Information about how these cutoffs were determined is absent from the technical manual.

DEVELOPMENT. The FIRO-B was developed in 1958 by William Schutz to understand how high performance military teams would work together. The instrument was based on Schutz's theory of interpersonal needs, which states that interpersonal needs can be summarized in three areas. Inclusion refers to "the need to establish and maintain satisfactory interactions and associations with other people" (technical guide, p. 3). Control refers to a person's behavior related to responsibility, power, influence, and decision making. Affection is related to a person's behavior in forming personal relationships with others. Schutz maintained that each of those needs can be either expressed or wanted from others. In other words, people may want to express inclusion, control, and affection behaviors toward others, or they may desire to be the recipient of inclusion, control, and affection behaviors from others. Although the FIRO-B has been available for many years, the current manual provides an update of research on the instrument. No changes to the instrument were made.

TECHNICAL. The current FIRO-B manual updates the technical information on the FIRO-B, and it reports the results of a national study on the instrument that was conducted concurrently with the 1998 revision of the Myers-Briggs Type Indicator (MBTI). This study involved contacting potential participants using random-digit telephone dialing. After receiving information about the project, those who agreed to participate were mailed a survey, and they were asked to return it to the developers. In all, 3,000 adults (over age 18) completed the FIRO-B. Although the sample was similar to the U.S. Census, white females were overrepresented, and black males were underrepresented. The authors note that the FIRO-B items were presented last in a "very long survey" (technical guide, p. 21), and that some participants did not complete the entire survey. Because survey items contained content irrelevant to the FIRO-B, the extent to which FIRO-B responses were tainted by exposure to previously encountered content is unclear.

Reliability of scores from the FIRO-B is presented in the form of reproducibility indices. According to the authors, reproducibility is the appropriate method for determining internal consistency in an instrument using Guttman scaling. This method involves predicting an individual's scores on similar-content items by knowing the person's scale scores. Reproducibility with 90% accuracy was used as the criterion. Reproducibility data were calculated on a sample ($N = 1,543$) of college students and U.S. Air Force personnel. Indices ranged from .93 to .94, suggesting that the FIRO-B is an internally consistent instrument. Test-retest reliability (1–4-week interval) was also examined for junior high students, college students, and adults. Reliability estimates ranged from .71 (eC for adults and wC for college students) to .85 (eA for junior high students). Eight out of 18 correlations meet the accepted .80 standard for subscale reliability.

A large portion of the FIRO-B manual is dedicated to providing validity evidence. The authors draw upon numerous studies conducted by independent researchers. Some of the research presented adds to evidence for the instrument's validity; however, much of what is presented is research using the FIRO-B as an independent or dependent measure. Unfortunately, some of this information is erroneously referred to as evidence for validity. A separate section of the manual should be reserved for such information (e.g., correlations between responses on the FIRO-B and affection for dogs). The volume of research conducted using the instrument is impressive, and users are encouraged to read the literature review in the manual; however, results of the research do little to add to evidence for FIRO-B validity.

There is some legitimate validity information presented in the manual. Among the studies reported, there are several that speak to convergent validity. The authors report intercorrelations among FIRO-B scales, and correlations between scores on the FIRO-B and the MBTI, California Psychological Inventory (CPI), Adjective Checklist instrument, and the Group Embedded Figures Test. It should be noted that although most correlations are in the desired directions and are statistically significant, absolute values of the correlations are very small (i.e., most are below .20). The authors attribute this to restriction of range in possible FIRO-B individual cell scores. Perhaps correlations should be computed using available formulas for correcting for range restriction. In addition, most of these studies were conducted by independent researchers. It is unclear whether the purpose of those studies was to investigate FIRO-B validity, or to use the instrument in a study.

COMMENTARY. The FIRO-B provides a measure of interpersonal needs, organized into six separate subscales based on Schutz's theory. Good evidence for the reproducibility of the instrument is presented; overall, test-retest estimates are lower than would be expected, given the purported trait-like nature of the scales and a retest period ranging from 1 to 4 weeks. Despite the face validity of the instrument, more research on the validity of the FIRO-B is needed. Such evidence might include testing Schutz's theory to provide construct validity evidence. Although correlations presented in the research review generally support the subscales and overall scores, at times many presumptions are made. For example, when comparing FIRO-B scores among various occupational groups, the authors claim that higher scores were found among those in more people-oriented occupations. No support is given for how "people-orientedness" was determined. For example, it is unclear why being a Harvard Business School graduate student is considered more people-oriented than being a Radcliffe freshman, a female high school student, or a Harvard freshman. In addition, several of the comparisons involved correlating FIRO-B scores with single- or several-item survey questions administered as part of the national study. More research is needed comparing the FIRO-B to established and validated measures of similar or dissimilar constructs. A final concern is the lack of information related to determinants of cutoff scores, both for individual items and for qualitative descriptors associated with each scale.

SUMMARY. The FIRO-B provides a brief and straightforward measure of a person's perceived interpersonal needs. Results have many applications, and these are nicely detailed in the manual. Several options for scoring and interpretation are available, and interpretive reports can be purchased. The instrument has solid face validity, although the Guttman scaling procedure results in what appears to be rather homogeneous content for each of the six areas. The instrument has been used internationally in a wide variety of research endeavors, and its results have applications in business, group, individual, and family contexts. Finally, although the instrument is internally consistent, more evidence for the stability of scores, and more solid and theoretically based support for the validity of the Schutz theory and instrument is needed.

REVIEWER'S REFERENCE

Schutz, W. C. (1958). *FIRO™: A three-dimensional theory of interpersonal behavior.* New York: Holt, Rinehart, and Winston.

Review of the FIRO-B [Fundamental Interpersonal Relations Orientation—Behavior] by DONALD OSWALD, Associate Professor of Psychiatry, Virginia Commonwealth University, Richmond, VA:

DESCRIPTION. The Fundamental Interpersonal Relations Orientation—Behavior (FIRO-B) is a self-report instrument focused on the assessment of interpersonal behaviors that are related to successful teamwork, leadership, and individual relationships. The instrument is also intended for use in organizational contexts to help clarify and address corporate culture conflicts.

The FIRO-B is based on a conceptual framework for interpersonal behavior developed by William Schutz, which divides interpersonal needs into three domains: inclusion, control, and affection. Schutz apparently also created the FIRO-B; Hammer and Schnell, the authors of the present FIRO-B manual, do not provide any information about their role in the development or validation of the instrument. The instrument consists of 54 items, each of which is completed using one of two 6-point rating scales. For 24 of the items, the response choices relate to the frequency with which the respondent engages in the behavior (*Never*,

Rarely, Occasionally, etc.); for the remaining 30 items, the response choices describe *with how many people* the respondent engages in the behavior *(Nobody, One or two people, A few people,* etc.). The authors state that the instrument will be completed by most respondents in 10 to 20 minutes.

The FIRO-B employs a self-scorable booklet. For each item, if the response exceeds the designated cutoff on the response continuum, a score of 1 point is given. Item scores are then summed within six scales: Expressed Inclusion, Wanted Inclusion, Expressed Control, Wanted Control, Expressed Affection, and Wanted Affection. Scale scores may be combined to derive Total Need scores for Inclusion, Control, and Affection by adding Expressed and Wanted scores. Total Expressed and Total Wanted scores are derived by adding Inclusion, Control, and Affection scores. Finally, an Overall Need score is obtained by summing all six scale scores.

Each of these scores can be converted to a score category (e.g., Low, Medium-Low, Medium-High, High) by means of a table provided in the manual. Unfortunately, no rationale is offered for the categories. The mean Overall Need score for the standardization sample falls toward the lower end of the "Medium-Low" range and, if the Overall Need scores are normally distributed, almost 40% of the population will fall in the "Low" category. The table also includes a brief description of the meaning of the score; for example, for the Overall Need Score, the Low category is associated with descriptors that include: "Involvement with others is not a primary source of need satisfaction" and "Tend to need privacy to do their best work" (technical guide, p. 15).

DEVELOPMENT. Information in the technical guide about the development of the instrument is rather sparse. The authors note only that a "scale was constructed for each of the six patterns that represent combinations of the three need areas (Inclusion, Control, and Affection) with the two behavioral dimensions (Expressed and Wanted)" (technical guide, p. 19). The authors provide a discussion of Guttman scaling in an effort to clarify why sets of items seem somewhat repetitive with only subtle differences in wording. However, this discussion provides little in the way of elaboration regarding the procedure for developing the item pool or assigning the items to scales. The authors also state that the Guttman scaling technique was used to determine how the items were ordered and where the scoring cutoff was established, but no evidence is offered to support this assertion.

TECHNICAL. Norms reported in the technical guide were based on a "national sample of about 3,000 adults" (p. 21) The sample is said to be a "stratified" sample "based on random-digit dialing of telephone numbers in the United States" (technical guide, p. 21). The authors do not report the nature of the strata nor do they indicate what proportion of individuals so contacted agreed to participate and actually completed the instrument. Although the goal was to have a sample that matched the U.S. Census, in fact, Whites (91.7%) and females (53.7%) are disproportionately represented in the sample.

Tables of scale score means and standard deviations are provided for the entire sample, for Blacks and Hispanics, and for men and women. The authors correctly note that "the sample size for each group [Blacks and Hispanics] is small and probably not representative of the ... population" (technical guide, p. 22). Tables also provide mean scores and standard deviations for the national sample disaggregated by educational level and by age. Finally, scores for samples of managers from 17 countries are reported by country and by organizational level.

Internal consistency reliability estimates for the six FIRO-B scales ranged from .85 to .96. The authors also report on "reproducibility," a construct associated with Guttman scaling said to be "a more stringent criterion than other measures of internal consistency" (technical guide, p. 29). The "usual criterion for reproducibility" is reported to be 90%; reproducibility coefficients for FIRO-B scales ranged from .93 to .94. Test-retest reliability coefficients ranged from .71 to .85; time between tests ranged from 1 week to 4 weeks.

The authors provide some data on the intercorrelation of FIRO-B scale scores. Particularly in the national sample, correlations among Expressed and Wanted scores for Inclusion and Affection are relatively high (.42–.59). Nonetheless, they state that the evidence supports the six FIRO-B scales as "separate and distinct psychological constructs" (technical guide, p. 32). This discussion would benefit from a consideration of how the scales might be expected to relate to one another based on the instrument's conceptual framework.

The technical guide reports a validity study of mean FIRO-B scores for a variety of occupational groups: Traveling salesmen and Harvard Business School graduate students were reported to have the highest Overall Need scores whereas physics majors and creative architects had the lowest. However, the number of individuals included in the occupational groups varies dramatically (from $n = 32$ to $n = 1,488$) and the authors do not report whether the score differences between groups achieve statistical significance.

The technical guide also summarizes validity studies that examined the association of FIRO-B scores with a wide range of constructs including Leadership, Job Satisfaction, Relationship Satisfaction, Leisure Activities, Birth Order, Spirituality, Values, Self-Esteem, and Health, Stress, and Coping. However, these studies are of limited value with respect to the validity of the instrument because of significant methodological problems and the lack of a clear conceptual basis for the relationship of the constructs.

Finally, the authors of the technical guide provide data regarding the relationship between FIRO-B scale scores and scores on a variety of other personality measures including the Myers-Briggs Type Indicator, the Adjective Check List, the California Psychological Inventory, and the Interpersonal Behavior Inventory. The authors conclude that "relationships with other instruments demonstrate the convergent and divergent validity of the FIRO-B scores" (technical guide, p. 61). The absence of a clearly explicated conceptual framework for the instrument, however, makes it difficult predict how the scores *should* be associated and thus, this reviewer is reluctant to endorse that conclusion with confidence.

COMMENTARY. The FIRO-B seeks to quantify interpersonal needs that are thought to be important determinants of interpersonal behavior. Although the instrument is based on William Schutz's theory of interpersonal needs, the documentation that accompanies it fails to provide sufficient information about that theoretical framework. Thus, it is difficult to determine the extent to which the theory offers testable hypotheses or the extent to which the instrument contributes to the testing of those hypotheses.

The FIRO-B is intended mainly for use in organizations and possible applications are described in the manual. The test is relatively short and easy to administer, complete, and score.

The manual is very weak with respect to documentation of the development of the instrument. There is simply not enough information to determine if the author has followed reasonable standards of test development.

Scoring cutoffs are quite varied from one item to the next. For some items, only a rating of "6" is considered item endorsement whereas for other items any rating from "3" through "6" is scored as an endorsement. No convincing rationale is offered for this unusual approach.

Evidence for instrument reliability appears to be adequate but the validity studies are generally quite weak. This limitation is largely due to the fact that the fundamental constructs under consideration are not well defined.

SUMMARY. The FIRO-B is intended to assist individuals and organizations in understanding interpersonal needs and their impact on interpersonal functioning. On balance, the instrument appears to fall short of the mark due to flaws in conceptualization and implementation. For the purposes of supporting group process and interpersonal problem solving and fostering self-awareness, the Myers-Briggs Type Indicator (T6:1678), in spite of its limitations, offers assessment of a broader range of psychological constructs and possesses a more developed research base.

[105]

Fluharty Preschool Speech and Language Screening Test—Second Edition.

Purpose: Designed to identify preschool children whose speech and language skills warrant a comprehensive communication evaluation.
Population: Ages 3-0 to 6-11.
Publication Dates: 1978–2001.
Acronym: FLUHARTY-2.
Scores, 8: Articulation, Repeating Sentences, Following Directives and Answering Questions, Describing Actions, Sequencing Events, Receptive Language, Expressive Language, General Language.
Administration: Individual.
Price Data, 2003: $153 per complete kit including examiner's manual (2001, 65 pages), picture book, 25 profile/examiner record forms, and a set of 12 colored blocks; $30 per 25 profile/examiner record forms; $27 per set of blocks; $51 per picture book; $51 per examiner's manual.
Time: (10) minutes.
Author: Nancy Buono Fluharty.
Publisher: PRO-ED.

Cross References: See T5:1047 (7 references) and T4:993 (2 references); for reviews by Nicholas W. Bankson and Harold A. Peterson of an earlier edition, see 9:422 (1 reference).

Review of the Fluharty Preschool Speech and Language Screening Test—Second Edition by DAVID P. HURFORD, Director of the Center for the Assessment and Remediation of Reading Difficulties and Professor of Psychology and Counseling, Pittsburg State University, Pittsburg, KS:

DESCRIPTION AND DEVELOPMENT. The Fluharty Preschool Speech and Language Screening Test—Second Edition (FLUHARTY-2) is an individually administered screening instrument designed to assess young children's (aged 3 years 0 months to 6 years 11 months) speech and language skills. Its purpose is to identify children who need a more comprehensive diagnostic evaluation of their speech and language skills. Administration of the FLUHARTY-2 typically takes 10 minutes. The FLUHARTY-2 assesses expressive and receptive language abilities and provides a global language quotient.

The FLUHARTY-2 represents the first major revision of the Fluharty Preschool Speech and Language Screening Test (FPSLST; 1978). Past reviewers were very critical of the FPSLST's psychometric properties. Theoretically, the FLUHARTY-2 is built on Foster's (1990) communication model. This model views language as a modular system consisting of phonology (sounds), lexicon (words, word usage, and word changes), semantics (meaning), morphology (the study of the smallest linguistic units with meanings of its own), syntax (rules for combining words into meaningful sentences), and pragmatics (the speaker's purpose for using language).

The FLUHARTY-2 is composed of five subtests: (a) Articulation, which measures the child's ability to articulate single words; (b) Repeating Sentences, which measures the child's ability to recall and reproduce sentence patterns; (c) Following Directives and Answering Questions, which measures the child's ability to comprehend the meaning of statements such that directives could be accomplished and questions answered; (d) Describing Actions, which measures the child's ability to produce complete sentences that describe actions using progressive verb forms; and (e) Sequencing Events, which measures the child's ability to convey information by generating a series of complete sentences.

The Receptive Language Quotient (RLQ) incorporates the standard scores of the Repeating Sentences and Following Directives and Answering Questions subtests. The Expressive Language Quotient (ELQ) incorporates the standard scores of the Describing Actions and Sequencing Events subtests. The General Language Quotient (GLQ) measures the child's general language ability, consists of the standard scores of each of the four subtests, and assesses each of the theoretical modules on which the FLUHARTY-2 is based. The decision to further assess a child with a comprehensive diagnostic device can be based on the RLQ, ELQ, or GLQ.

TECHNICAL. The FLUHARTY-2 was standardized with a norming group of 705 children from 21 states that included children with learning disabilities, speech impairments, and mental retardation (although there were no psychometric analyses that involved the participants who were mentally retarded). The normative sample was very similar to the demographic characteristics of the population of the United States. The FLUHARTY-2 provides standard scores, percentiles, age equivalents, and quotient scores (RLQ, ELQ, and GLQ). Although age equivalents have been extensively criticized, the author of the FLUHARTY-2 reluctantly provides them for administrative purposes of the agencies that use the inventory.

Reliability was assessed with internal consistency, test-retest reliability, and interscorer reliability estimates. Internal consistency was assessed by computing coefficient alphas for each of the subtests at each of the four age levels (3, 4, 5, and 6 years). Coefficient alphas ranged from .70 (for 4-year-olds on the Following Directives and Answering Questions subtest) to .92 (for 4-year-olds on the Describing Actions subtest) with a mean of .82 when age level and subtest were collapsed. Coefficient alpha was also calculated for males, females, European Americans, African Americans, Hispanic Americans, Asian Americans, children with learning disabilities, and children with speech impairments, by subtest. These values were quite similar to those reported above with a range of .72 to .94 and a mean of .85. These values indicate that the FLUHARTY-2 is a reliable screening device for individuals aged 3-0 through 6-11 regardless of gender, minority group status, or developmental status.

Test-retest reliability was evaluated by assessing 30 children (15 three-year-olds and 15 five-year-olds) who resided in Cincinnati, Ohio.

The FLUHARTY-2 was administered twice within a 4-month interval. Correlation coefficients ranged between .77 and .96 (mean of .88) for the subtests for the 3- and 5-year-olds. The typical length of time between administrations for test-retest reliability is 2 weeks. These correlation coefficients are quite good. When one considers the relatively long interval between test administrations, these values are even more impressive, particularly when one considers the possible changes in responses due to language development between the first and second administrations.

Interscorer reliability was assessed by examining the results of two employees from the publisher's research department who independently scored 30 completed FLUHARTY-2 protocols (7 for 3-year-olds, 13 for 4-year-olds, 8 for 5-year-olds, and 2 for 6-year-olds). Although this method assesses the likelihood of arriving at similar results when the protocols have already been completed, it does not directly assess interrater reliability. To adequately assess this type of reliability requires that two individuals independently administer the FLUHARTY-2 to the same child, transcribe the responses that the individual provides, and then score the protocol. The raters' evaluations would then be compared with the use of a correlation coefficient to determine interrater reliability. Although the authors report in the manual that the interrater reliability measures ranged between .95 and .98 (mean of .96), this is an incomplete, inadequate, and invalid evaluation of interrater reliability.

Validity was assessed with content validity (including item rationale, Item Response Theory, and bias), criterion-related validity, and construct validity evidence. With regard to content validity, each of the subtests that comprise the FLUHARTY-2 was developed with reference to Foster's modular model of language, and from a research base evaluating children's language development. The items for each subtest were examined for item discrimination and difficulty. Median discriminating coefficients averaged .30 and ranged between .49 (Following Directives and Answering Questions for 4- and 5-year-olds) and .73 (Describing Actions for 4-year-olds). Median item difficulty coefficients averaged .75 and ranged between .43 (Repeating Sentences for 3-year-olds) and .95 (Articulation for 6-year-olds). Generally, item difficulty for an instrument should approximate .50, which is nearly the case for the FLUHARTY-2.

To examine the possibility of item bias in the FLUHARTY-2, Delta scores were computed between males and females, European Americans and Non-European Americans, African Americans and Non-African Americans, and Hispanic Americans and Non-Hispanic Americans. Correlation coefficients for the Delta scores for the various groups named above ranged between .70 and .99 (mean of .93). The smallest correlation coefficients were for the Delta scores for African American/Non-African American (.76) and Hispanic American/Non-Hispanic American (.70). Nevertheless, these values indicate that the relative difficulties for the items were fairly consistent between groups. As a result, test bias is not indicated.

Criterion-related validity was examined by correlating the scores between the subtest and composite scores of the FLUHARTY-2 and the Test of Language Development-Primary: Third Edition (TOLD-P:3). Both of these tests are purported to measure young children's speech and language abilities. The correlation coefficients for the subtest scores ranged between .54 and .95 (mean of .74). The correlation coefficients for the composite scores ranged between .72 and .91 (mean of .79). These values support criterion-related validity.

Construct validity was assessed utilizing confirmatory factor analysis, age differentiation, and group differentiation. The confirmatory analysis of variance provides evidence that the subtests tap the hypothesized abilities measured with the FLUHARTY-2 (i.e., Expressive and Receptive Language). The factor loadings for Receptive Language were .69 and .78 for Repeating Sentences and Following Directives and Answering Questions, respectively, and the loadings for Expressive Language were .48 and .76 for Describing Actions and Sequencing Events, respectively. The correlation coefficient for the Receptive and Expressive Language factors was .88, which was anticipated given that the subtests measure abilities that cross between the two factors. For example, Describing Actions (which is a measure of expressive language) taps syntax, as does Repeating Sentences (which is a measure of receptive language). Finally, the indices that test the confirmatory factor analysis model's fit to the data were quite good (relative chi-square of 2.16, Tucker and Lewis's index of fit, .99; Browne and Cudeck's root mean square error of approximation, .05).

Age differentiation is another means to examine the validity of a test. Language abilities continue to develop, so that moderate correlation coefficients are expected between the subtests of the FLUHARTY-2 and age. Although, the correlation coefficients are relatively weak, data provided in the manual indicate that the means for the various subtests increase with age, thus supporting validity. Given that the means are well within one standard deviation for the age levels, it is not surprising that the correlation coefficients were not large. In addition, the range of ages was restricted. That is, the range in which the ages fluctuated was between 3 and 6, the ages for which the FLUHARTY-2 was created. In many cases, restricting the range of a variable in a correlational study weakens the resulting coefficient.

Group differentiation can also support validity. If a test of language ability can differentiate between groups of children who are known to have poor language abilities, such as children with learning disabilities and children with speech impairments, validity would be further supported. Children with learning disabilities and children with speech impairments should perform significantly worse than children without disabilities. Data reported in the manual indicate that this was the case. Children with learning disabilities performed the worst on the Repeating Sentences and Following Directives and Answering Questions subtests, which is consistent with learning disabilities. Children with speech impairments performed the worst on Articulation, which would also be expected.

COMMENTARY. The case for validity was strong. Confirmatory factor analysis demonstrated that the constructs of Receptive and Expressive Language are measured. Age differentiation data indicated that performance on the FLUHARTY-2 increased with age, which provides validity given that language abilities in young children continue to develop with age. The correlation coefficient associated with age differentiation was somewhat weak, but the range of ages was restricted and therefore weaker correlation coefficients were expected. Group differentiation indicated that children with learning disabilities and speech impairments performed less well than children without these difficulties.

The record booklet has sections for identifying information (e.g., name, gender, school, grade, age), recording the scores (e.g., raw scores, age equivalents, percentile ranks, and standard scores), and score profiles (graphical display of the standard scores and quotients). The subtests along with their brief instructions are contained within the record booklet. There are boxes to mark regarding the child's voice quality and fluency. The manual is concise and complete. The novice user of the FLUHARTY-2 will not find it difficult to comprehend the administration or scoring procedures. The supplementary materials, the picture book and small blocks, are appropriate for helping the children to generate the desired speech and language responses.

SUMMARY. The FLUHARTY-2 is a screening instrument that assesses the language abilities of children aged 3-0 to 6-11. It was developed to identify children who need a more comprehensive diagnostic evaluation of their speech and language skills. The FLUHARTY-2 has acceptable psychometric properties, excluding interrater reliability, which was not properly addressed. The FLUHARTY-2 appears to have addressed and rectified the criticisms of its earlier version, the Fluharty Preschool Speech and Language Screening Test.

Review of the Fluharty Preschool Speech and Language Screening Test—Second Edition by REBECCA McCAULEY, Professor of Communication Sciences, University of Vermont, Burlington, VT:

DESCRIPTION. The Fluharty Preschool Speech and Language Screening Test—Second Edition (Fluharty-2) represents a substantial revision of an earlier test designed to provide a 10-minute screening of speech and language skills in young children ages 3:0 to 6:11. Its stated purposes are identifying children who require a more comprehensive examination of communication skills, providing tentative suggestions regarding a child's strengths and weaknesses, and providing supplementary information for use in a more complete evaluation. It consists of five subtests: Articulation, Repeating Sentences, Following Directives and Answering Questions, Describing Actions, and Sequencing Events. Directions for administration and scoring are appropriately detailed, but may be a bit complicated in some cases, especially where alternative answers are used to accommodate speakers of differing dialects.

DEVELOPMENT. The revision of the original version of this test included a substantial change in theoretical orientation, the addition of three tasks, and the inclusion of updated norms and new studies concerning reliability and validity.

Whereas the initial version of the test was based on the work of Chomsky, the revision is based on the communication model of Foster (1990). This model is composed of phonology, lexicon, semantics, morphology, syntax—all of which are subsumed under grammar—and pragmatics. Pragmatics is seen as overarching the other five modules. Each of the five subtests is designed to address one or more language component. For example, the subtest Describing Actions is intended to tap the lexicon, morphology, and syntax. There are three predominantly expressive subtests (i.e., Articulation, Sequencing Events, and Describing Actions) and two predominantly receptive subtests (Following Directives and Answering Questions as well as Repeating Sentences). The content areas represented by the tasks are supported by a brief literature review. Items were selected and are scored with attention to dialectal variations.

Analyses of item discrimination and difficulty were conducted to guide the selection of items, although specifics of the item tryout are not discussed. When these analyses were repeated on data from the normative sample for the final items included in the test, median item discrimination was generally good for all subtests at all four ages, but median item difficulties suggested that items may have been relatively easy for all ages, particularly for the Articulation subtest. A lack of item bias was supported through findings of high correlations of a measure of relative item difficulties (Jensen, 1980) between four groups: males versus females, European Americans versus all other races, African Americans versus all other races, and Hispanic Americans versus all other ethnic groups.

In addition to subtest scores, there are three composite scores: the General Language Quotient that is used for identifying children who require additional testing, as well as separate quotients for Receptive Language and Expressive Language. These latter two scores are intended to provide guidance regarding further testing that might follow failure on the overall screening. Subtest and composite scores can be represented as standard scores, percentiles, and age equivalents.

TECHNICAL. Norms were based on data from 705 children who were identified through speech-language pathologists with whom the publisher had a connection. The children came from 21 states. Demographic information regarding them included age, gender, race, residence (urban versus rural), ethnicity, and disability status. Each of the four ages for which sample sizes are given

(ages 3, 4, 5, and 6) is represented by over 100 children. Eighty-two percent of the children tested for the norms were described as having no disabilities and 18% were described as having a learning disability (2%), speech impairment (12%), mental retardation (1%), or other learning disability (3%). Information about the percentage of these characteristics relative to national census data for school-age children (1998) is provided and appears generally consistent. In addition, whereas children with speech impairments make up 12% of the children sampled, they represented only 3% in the census data. This representation of individuals with disorders prevents the possibility of the most extreme scores obtained among the norms nonetheless representing performance within the range of normal performance by virtue of having been obtained from children who seemed to be normally developing (McCauley & Swisher, 1984).

Reliability. Reliability studies examined internal consistency, test-retest reliability, and interscorer reliability. Internal consistency of subtest and composite scores was examined using coefficient alpha for each age group as well as for selected subgroups based on gender, ethnicity, and disability categories. Values fell at generally acceptable to high levels in most cases, with the only exception being the subtest Following Directives and Answering Questions, which had values in the .70s. Results of a test-retest reliability study conducted on a total of 30 children ages 3 and 5 without identified disorders over a 4-month period yielded reliability coefficients that were generally high (.90 and better) for the subtest and composite scores. The exception was a .77 for Sequencing Events and the Expressive Language composite scores. To examine interscorer reliability, 30 randomly selected protocols were independently compared, producing very high reliability coefficients of greater than .95. This finding, however, is a bit difficult to interpret because it was hard to tell if the evaluation of individual responses was included in the process used in the reliability study.

Validity. In addition to the information about content description and item analyses provided in support of validity, the test manual for the Fluharty-2 reports on five lines of evidence. As evidence supporting the validity of the Fluharty-2 as a screening measure, performances for 23 children were compared against their performances on a more comprehensive and generally well-regarded language measure, the Test of Language Development Development—Primary, Third Edition (TOLD-P:3; Newcomer & Hammill, 1997). This measure, which is intended for a slightly older age group (4:0 to 8:11), has received quite positive reviews (Madle, 2001; Stutman, 2001). Correlations between composite scores from the Fluharty-2 with the associated subtest and composites on the TOLD-P:3 were generally moderate to high. Ideally, this study would have been based on larger sample sizes and would have included children with disorders as well as those with normal development. Nonetheless, it represents an important piece of evidence supporting the Fluharty-2's use as a screening tool.

Four studies are reported to demonstrate the relationship of the measure to the underlying constructs on which it is based and information about item content that contributes to judgments of validity. One study employed factor analysis to support the subtest and composite structure of the test. A second found low to moderate correlations between age and subtest scores, confirming the hypothesized developmental nature of test performance. Group differentiation was examined in a third study, which reported—but did not statistically compare—mean standard scores for groups consisting of females, children with European American backgrounds, African American, Hispanic American, and Asian American backgrounds. Mean standard scores were also reported for children with learning disabilities and with speech impairments. The fourth study examined the intercorrelation of subtest scores and found expected patterns of correlations ranging from .08 to .54, with a median of .31. Such slight to moderate correlations provide additional support that the measure is assessing the constructs it is intended to measure. These four studies help support the use of this measure as a means of providing tentative suggestions about a child's strengths and weaknesses, and to a lesser extent, the use of the measure to supplement other testing.

COMMENTARY. A thoughtful revision has strengthened the theoretical foundation and psychometric evidence provided for this brief screening measure. Strong evidence of test-retest reliability was obtained for a small number of children ages 3 and 5, and internal consistent levels appear

adequate—particularly for the overall score that would be used in making screening decisions. In terms of validity, the strongest lines of evidence appear to support the use of the measure as a screening tool, but some evidence is also given for its tasks, thus providing some evidence that it can be used to look at strengths and weaknesses and supplement other test results. A real strength of the measure is its efforts to make the normative sample and scoring more sensitive to children with a range of regional and cultural dialects.

SUMMARY. For readers who are seeking a brief standardized screening tool of language for children between the ages of 3 and 6:11, this measure may serve as a reasonable choice. Although additional evidence regarding the validity of the measure for its intended purposes would be highly desirable, the author has made a reasonable start through the careful planning of this revision and the preliminary evidence provided regarding its psychometric characteristics.

REVIEWER'S REFERENCES

Foster, S. H. (1990). *The communicative competence of young children: A modular approach.* London: Longman.
Jensen, A. R. (1980). *Bias in mental testing.* New York: Free Press.
Madle, R. A. (2001). [Review of Test of Language Development—Primary, Third Edition]. In B. S. Plake & J. C. Impara (Eds.), *The fourteenth mental measurements yearbook* (pp. 1247-1248). Lincoln, NE: Buros Institute of Mental Measurements.
McCauley, R. J., & Swisher, L. (1984). Psychometric review of language and articulation tests for preschool children. *Journal of Speech and Hearing Disorders, 49,* 34–42.
Newcomer, P. L., & Hammill, D. D. (1997). Test of Language Development—Primary, Third Edition. Austin, TX: PRO-ED.
Stutman, G. (2001). [Review of Test of Language Development—Primary, Third Edition]. In B. S. Plake & J. C. Impara (Eds.), *The fourteenth mental measurements yearbook* (pp. 1248-1250). Lincoln, NE: Buros Institute of Mental Measurements.

[106]

Frontal Systems Behavior Scale.

Purpose: "Provides a means ... to quantify behavioral change due to frontal lobe lesions."

Population: Ages 18–95.

Publication Date: 2001.

Acronym: FrSBe.

Scores, 4: Apathy (subscale A), Disinhibition (subscale D), Executive Dysfunction (subscale E), Total Score.

Administration: Individual or group.

Forms, 2: Family Rating Form, Self-Rating Form.

Price Data, 2002: $145 per introductory kit including professional manual (109 pages), 25 handscorable Self-Rating test booklets, 25 hand-scorable Family Rating test booklets, 25 Self-Rating profile forms, and 25 Family Rating profile forms; $40 per professional manual; $49 per 25 hand-scorable test booklets (Self-Rating or Family Rating); $15 per 25 profile forms (Self-Rating or Family Rating).

Time: 10 minutes to administer; 10–15 minutes to score.
Comments: Revision of the Frontal Lobe Personality Scale; available in paper-and-pencil form only; obtains ratings of patients's behavior before and after an injury or illness.
Authors: Janet Grace and Paul F. Malloy.
Publisher: Psychological Assessment Resources, Inc.

Review of the Frontal Systems Behavior Scale by HARRISON D. KANE, Assistant Professor, Western Carolina University, Cullowhee, NC, and SHAWN K. ACHESON, Assistant Professor, Western Carolina University, Cullowhee, NC:

DESCRIPTION. The Frontal Systems Behavior Scale (FrSBe) is a pencil-and-paper rating scale designed to measure and monitor the spectrum of behavioral syndromes associated with frontal lobe damage (e.g., ADHD, stroke, head injury, vascular dementia, Parkinson's disease, and Alzheimer's). Specifically, the authors indicate the FrSBe is intended to (a) provide brief, reliable, and valid measures of behavior; (b) assess pre- and postmorbid behavior; and (c) provide ratings from multiple sources.

As a behavioral rating system, the FrSBe consists of two 46-item forms (i.e., Family Rating Form and Self-Rating Form). Forms are handscorable. These different forms permit comparison of respondents' ratings that assist the clinician in identifying behavioral problems specific to natural settings. An asset of the FrSBe is that each form provides two response scale columns, one for rating behaviors that occurred before illness or injury and one for rating behaviors that were manifested after. Thus, behavioral changes are assessed from an established baseline. The brief length of the scale and reading level of the items permit completion by an adult with few errors. Although the FrSBe may be administered and scored by nonclinical staff, occupational therapists, and speech pathologists, interpretation is advisedly left to individuals with formal training in neurocognitive psychology.

Respondents' ratings produce an overall (or Total) scale score, as well as scores on three subscales corresponding to behavioral syndromes associated with frontal lobe impairment: Apathy (A; 14 items), Disinhibition (D; 15 items), and Executive Dysfunction (E; 17 items). For each of these subscales, the professional manual provides standard scores scaled to a metric with a mean of 50 and standard deviation of 10 (i.e.,

T scores). Subscales are fully described in the professional manual, and the authors offer suitable case studies to guide clinical interpretation.

DEVELOPMENT. The development of the FrSBe is well described in the test manual. The FrSBe is the published revision of the Frontal Lobe Personality Scale (FLOPS; Grace, Stout, & Malloy, 1999), a scale that was used primarily for research. The authors identified the aforementioned behavioral syndromes from a literature review pertaining to frontal lobe insult and injury (e.g., Cicerone & Tannenbaum, 1997). Items were composed and assigned to subscales based on face validity and an independent Q-sort procedure. Review of the items suggests ample specificity and independence in content. For the most part, items are identical across the Self-Report and Family Rating forms, with content reworded appropriately to match the rater. Items follow a Likert rating format. That is, respondents indicate the frequency of observed behaviors before and after impairment (i.e., 1 = *Almost Never*, 2 = *Seldom*, 3 = *Sometimes*, 4 = *Frequently*, and 5 = *Almost Always*). Items are worded in both positive and negative terms, with higher ratings always indicating greater levels of pathology.

TECHNICAL.
Standardization. The standardization sample for the FrSBe contained a total of 436 adults (57% female) from 18 to 95 years of age (*M* = 48.1, *SD* = 18.0). Data were collected through volunteer and community agencies in several Midwestern and Northeastern states. Both group and individual testing were used. All participants were screened for neurological illness, psychiatric disturbance, substance abuse (last 2 years), and current use of psychotropic medications. The mean level of education was 14.2 years (*SD* = 2.4) and participants completed ratings corresponding to the "After" condition only (i.e., present behavior only). Age, education, and gender were all found to be significantly related to the total score and to each of the subscales on both the Family Rating and the Self-Rating forms. The racial composition of the standardization sample was restricted to Whites. In accordance with the literature examining racial differenes in cognitive ability (e.g., Jensen, 1998), clinicians should exercise considerable caution in extending the clinical utility of the FrSBe to other racial/ethinic groups. Essentially, the FrSBe may reveal lower scores for

individuals of Hispanic and African American origin.

Reliability. Using the standardization sample (responses corresponding to present condition only), internal consistency values on the Family Rating form ranged from a low of .78 for the Apathy scale to a high of .92 for the Total scale. Internal consistency values on the Self-Rating form ranged from a low of .72 for the Apathy scale to a high of .88 for the Total scale. Several clinical samples were also used to assess reliability of both "Before" and "After" conditions. In all cases, reliabilities were at least .78 or higher.

Validity. Factor analysis was conducted on a group of 324 neurological patients with pathologies including frontal and nonfrontal stroke, head injury, Alzheimer's, Parkinson's, Huntington's, frontotemporal dementia, Lewy Body Dementia, and vascular dementia. A three-factor solution was specified, consistent with the theoretical model used to develop the FrSBe, and was found to account for only 41% of the item variance. Given the complexity of frontal lobe systems, there may be nascent factors that are not fully illuminated by the relatively small number of FrSBe items. However, the vast majority of items were found to load on the scales to which they had been originally assigned.

Additional studies reported in the manual indicate that the FrSBe is related to some of the same constructs measured by the Neuropsychiatric Inventory (Cummings et al., 1994) and can effectively discriminate Alzheimer's from Huntington's disease patients as well as neurological patients with frontal lobe pathology from those with nonfrontal lobe pathologies. Using the Family Report form, other studies demonstrate that the FrSBe can detect changes in behavior from preinjury to postinjury and that the behavior of frontal-injury patients is markedly different from that of normal controls (e.g., Grace et al., 1999). There is also evidence that the FrSBe can successfully differentiate those with psychiatric disturbances with frontal-like impairments from those patients with true frontal lobe dysfunction.

COMMENTARY. The FrSBe joins a growing number of published rating scales designed to measure behavioral syndromes and change attributable to frontal systems impairment (e.g., Behavioral Rating Inventory of Executive Function, Frontal Behavioral Inventory). The FrSBe holds a number of comparative advantages. First, the FrSBe does not require a trained clinician for administration. Second, the FrSBe renders subscales that assess specific behavioral syndromes. Third, different forms permit behavioral comparisons across observers, settings, and occasions. Fourth, standard scores permit normative comparisons.

SUMMARY. Overall the FrSBe is a sound instrument with acceptable evidence of reliability and validity. The FrSBE's primary value comes from its ability to assess and compare premorbid patterns of behavior to post-injury or impairment patterns of behavior. These ratings, however, should be interpreted cautiously. The assessment of premorbid behavior is done retrospectively and is always subject to various forms of bias. Although reliability estimates for the various scales are reasonably high, such results could also be obtained if observers' ratings were systematically biased. There is also some concern about the overall factor structure of the FrSBe. The three-factor model described in the manual accounts for only 41% of the item variance and there are no model fit statistics reported. Further research should establish the clinical utility of the FrSBe with nonwhite populations.

REVIEWERS' REFERENCES

Cicerone, K., & Tanenbaum, L. N. (1997). Disturbance of social cognition after traumatic orbitofrontal brain injury. *Archives of Clinical Neuropsychology, 12*(2), 173–188.
Cummings, J. L., Mega, M., Gray, K., Rosenberg-Thompson, S., Carusi, D. A., & Gronbeon, J. (1994). The Neuropsychiatric Inventory: Comprehensive assessment of psychopathology in dementia. *Neurology, 44*(12), 2308–2314.
Grace, J., Stout, J. C., & Malloy, P. F. (1999). Assessing frontal lobe behavioral syndromes with the Frontal Lobe Personality Scale. *Assessment 6*(3), 269–284.
Jensen, A. R. (1998). *The g factor: The science of mental ability.* Westport, CT: Praeger.

Review of the Frontal Systems Behavior Scale, by NORA M. THOMPSON, Psychologist—Learning Disability Specialist, University of Washington, Seattle, WA:

DESCRIPTION. The Frontal Systems Behavior Scale (FrSBe) is a 46-item rating scale filled out by the patient (Self-Rating form) and/ or a family member (Family Rating form). Using a 5-point, Likert-type frequency rating, it is designed to measure the behavioral syndromes associated with damage to the frontal lobes and frontal brain systems. The scale is intended to track these behavioral changes over time, including changes before and after brain injury or illness. The FrSBe is designed for use in rehabilitation or outpatient assessment settings with a wide range of adult populations (18–95 years of age), including those with stroke, head injury, brain tumor, dementia, Parkinson's disease and psychiatric disorders. The scale is appropriate for individuals with a sixth grade or higher reading level and takes about 10 minutes for most individuals to complete. Guidelines are provided in the manual for determining whether a neurologically impaired patient is capable of completing the Self-Rating scale reliably. Item responses are tabulated into three subscales: Apathy, Disinhibition, and Executive Dysfunction. T-scores for these subscales, as well as a composite T-score, are then developed from the normative tables. Although training in assessment should be sufficient for administering the FrSBe, professional training in neuropsychology, neurology, or neuropsychiatry is typically required for appropriate interpretation.

DEVELOPMENT. The test was developed in several phases. First, a literature review culminated in the adoption of a theoretical basis outline by Cummings (1993). This model identifies three distinct behavioral syndromes that correspond to the three subscales of the FrSBe. Second, the authors generated a list of behavioral descriptors for each of the behavioral syndromes, resulting in a total of 60 descriptors. This list was reduced to 46 items by eliminating items judged to be redundant, poorly written, or difficult to rate. Items were worded in either positive or negative orientation, but higher ratings always reflect greater behavioral abnormality. Wording was adjusted for the Self-Rating form. The authors sorted items into subscales based on face validity. A Q-sort by an independent expert rater (clinical neuropsychologist) confirmed this structure.

TECHNICAL. The normative sample consists of ratings from 436 individual volunteers recruited from community and volunteer organizations primarily in New England and two Midwestern states. Each volunteer completed a Self-Rating form and had a spouse or significant other complete a Family Rating form. Volunteers were screened for neurological and psychiatric illness, substance abuse, and use of psychotropic medication. Because the subscale scores varied separately with age, education, and gender, the normative sample was stratified by gender and into three age groupings (18 to 39 years, 40 to 59 years, and greater than 59 years) and two education groupings (<12 years and >12 years) for the calculation of normative values. It is important to note that the normative sample is limited to Caucasian men and women and that most volunteers had completed high school.

No information is provided in the manual about the family income level of the volunteers.

Within-scale reliability was tested using the entire normative sample as well as (a) a clinical sample of 39 frontal lobe and stroke patients and (b) a clinical sample of 324 neurological patients. Reliability estimates were stronger for Family Rating forms than Self-Report forms, as would be expected when gathering self-report information from neurologically impaired patients. High within-scale reliability estimates resulted. There was no report of test-retest reliability.

The Family Rating form, but not the Self-Report form, from the clinical sample of 324 neurological patients was also submitted to a factor analysis. The details of this sample are thoroughly described in the test manual. Factor analysis results supported three intercorrelated factors confirming the theoretical foundation for grouping the items into three subscales. Convergent validity was assessed by comparing the FrSBe with the Neuropsychiatric Inventory (NPI; Cummings et al., 1994) in a sample of patients with dementia. A strong positive correlation ($r = .64$, $p < .001$) was found for the total scores. The two corresponding subscales were also positively correlated (Apathy $r = .37$, $p < .05$; Disinhibition $r = .62$, $p < .001$).

Several studies summarized in the manual provide preliminary support for the discriminant validity of the FrSBe, particularly when using the Family Rating form. These included classifying Alzheimer's versus Huntington's disease, fronto-temporal dementia versus mild Alzheimer's or nonfrontal stroke, and Alzheimer's versus Parkinson's disease. The manual also presents some intriguing findings related to the use of the FrSBe for discriminating between patients with frontal lesions and those with bipolar and unipolar depression.

COMMENTARY. The FrSBe addresses an important, yet often elusive, aspect of the neuropsychological evaluation of individuals with frontal lobe dysfunction. It allows measurement of those behavioral syndromes that, although not seen during formal testing, result in serious functional impairment and increased caregiver burden and stress. The FrSBe provides a theoretically sound method for capturing important information in a brief, easy-to-complete format, allowing for multiple points of view of the patient's behaviors. Reliability data are adequate, although additional information about test-retest reliability is needed to support using the FrSBe to evaluate behavioral changes over time. The validity data available at this time support the organization of the scale into three subscales. Notably, the FrSBe holds promise for discriminating between patients with various neurological etiologies as well as between patients with frontal lobe lesions and affective disorder. The potential clinical user is encouraged to track ongoing research with this measure, as current clinical samples are not sufficiently large enough to base differential diagnosis of individual patients.

The main drawback of the FrSBe relates to the limitations of the normative sample. The potential user must be aware of the composition of the normative sample and is cautioned to consider the difficulties inherent in interpreting the FrSBe with non-Caucasian individuals or those with less than 12 years of education. An exploration of cultural factors influencing FrSBe ratings is needed before using this measure with individuals from minority cultures. The Self-Report form is currently less well supported in terms of technical characteristics. Further research into comparisons of the Self-Report form and Family Report form in neurologically impaired populations would enhance the clinical utility of the FrSBe.

SUMMARY. The FrSBe is a theoretically sound and internally consistent rating scale for measuring the behavioral syndromes seen in patients with damage to frontal lobe brain systems. The scale has proven to be reliable for single use with certain populations, specifically Caucasian adults with high school level or greater education. Within these limitations, the FrSBe holds promise for contributing to the differential diagnostic process. Further research is needed to support its use with a broader spectrum of the population and for the purpose of assessing change over time.

REVIEWER'S REFERENCES

Cummings, J. L. (1993). Frontal-subcortical circuits and human behavior. *Archives of Neurology, 50,* 873–880.
Cummings, J. L., Mega, M., Gray, K., Rosenberg-Thompson, S., Carusi, D. A., & Gornbein, J. (1994). The Neuropsychiatric Inventory: Comprehensive assessment of psychopathology in dementia. *Neurology, 44,* 2308–2314.

[107]

Functional Fitness Assessment for Adults Over 60 Years, Second Edition.

Purpose: Developed as a field test to determine the functional capacity of older adults.
Population: Adults over age 60.
Publication Dates: 1990–1996.
Scores, 7: Body Composition (Body Weight, Standing Height Measurement), Flexibility, Agility/Dynamic Balance, Coordination, Strength/Endurance, Endurance.

Administration: Group.
Price Data, 2001: $12 per manual ('96, 60 pages).
Time: Administration time not reported.
Authors: Wayne H. Osness, Marlene Adrian, Bruce Clark, Werner Hoeger, Dianne Raab, and Robert Wiswell.
Publisher: American Association for Active Lifestyles and Fitness.
Cross References: For reviews by Matthew E. Lambert and Cecil R. Reynolds of an earlier edition, see 13:128.

Review of the Functional Fitness Assessment for Adults Over 60 Years, Second Edition by ANITA M. HUBLEY, Associate Professor of Measurement, Evaluation, and Research Methodology, University of British Columbia, Vancouver, British Columbia, Canada:

DESCRIPTION. The Functional Fitness Assessment for Adults Over 60 Years (FFA) was designed so that paraprofessionals could assess functional capacity in men and women over the age of 60 in a practical manner without the need for special facilities or equipment. According to the manual, the test was designed to (a) evaluate change due to intervention strategies, (b) establish an individual's condition prior to designing an exercise program, and (c) provide feedback to an individual about his or her functional capacity.

The FFA assesses body composition, flexibility, agility/dynamic balance, coordination, strength/endurance, and endurance. Body composition is measured using the "ponderal index," which is computed from a person's height and weight and conveniently listed in a table. Flexibility is measured through an exercise of trunk and leg flexibility. Agility and dynamic balance is measured by the time taken for a person to complete a circuit of sitting, raising and lowering feet, standing, walking, and making a change of direction. Coordination is measured by the time taken to complete a "soda pop" coordination task that requires the individual to turn over a number of unopened pop cans with his or her preferred hand along a marked strip of masking tape. Strength and endurance is measured by the number of times a weight is lifted in a specified fashion within 30 seconds. Finally, endurance is measured by time taken to complete an 880-yard walk.

Administration instructions and scoring for the FFA are clearly presented and some measures include diagrams to assist the examiner. However, the authors need to give more stress to the importance of standardization of instructions, measurements, and equipment (e.g., weights) as deviations could lead to considerable errors in measurement. Some clarification is needed (a) on precisely what to measure in the flexibility task, and (b) the impact of reversing the route (but not the numbers) in the coordination task for left handed individuals. No indication is given as to how long it takes to administer the entire series of FFA measures.

DEVELOPMENT. The development of the FFA is very poorly described. Functional fitness is defined in the manual as "the physical capacity of the individual to meet ordinary and unexpected demands of daily life safely and effectively" (manual, p. vi). However, it is not clear how or why the six functional fitness indicators (e.g., Flexibility) or their measures (e.g., sit and reach test) were selected and no reference is made to any research literature. The authors claim that measures were selected or rejected based on redundancy, failure to meet eight guidelines, or on the basis of reliability and validity information, but no details are provided. The eight guidelines are listed, but are not clearly explained (e.g., "2. The test would not relate to follow-up prescriptions at this point in time," p. vi).

Further clarification is needed for (a) use of the preferred hand only in the coordination measure; (b) the selection of 4 lb and 8 lb weights for women and men, respectively, in the strength/ endurance measure; (c) not standardizing the use of a warm-up session for the endurance measure; and (d) use of single versus double trials for different measures.

TECHNICAL. The description of the standardization sample for the FFA is inadequate. The manual states that national age and gender norms have been collected for over 2,000 individuals. No rationale is provided for reporting norms by gender and 5-year age bands. No demographic information is provided (e.g., mean age and education level per group, ethnic composition), no evidence is provided to indicate what makes this a national sample, and no comparison is made to U.S. Census data. Despite the authors' claims, it is not clear how representative each group is of individuals who are "ambulatory and able to complete the test protocols" (p. 25) especially as it is not clear if anyone in the standardization sample was administered all of the FFA measures. Furthermore, because not all individuals were administered all of

the FFA measures, the sample sizes for each measure often differ considerably. Norms are reported using raw scores. Although raw score means and standard deviations are important to report, the norms should be reported using derived scores (e.g., T-scores or percentiles) for comparative purposes.

Only test-retest reliability estimates are reported for the FFA measures. Unfortunately, although these estimates are all reported to be over .80, this information is not interpretable because no indication is given of the length of interval between tests or if the interval was the same for all studies. Six reliability studies are cited, but no references are provided making it unclear whether any of these studies have been published or how they can be accessed. Moreover, no description is given of the samples used in these studies, except to note the gender and the sample sizes, and no study contained all of the FFA measures. Vague reference is also made to other published studies that provide reliability evidence, but no specific studies are cited and no details are provided. Reliability estimates should be used to compute standard errors of measurement for each FFA measure, which then may be used to produce error bands.

The limited validity evidence that is provided in the manual is neither well justified nor adequately reported. For example, the FFA coordination measure is correlated .59 with laboratory reaction time measures and only .40 with hand steadiness and .35 with hand-eye coordination. In addition to not providing a rationale for their choice of measures, the authors do not seem to fully grasp the meaning of their findings (e.g., these results seem to suggest the coordination task might be a better measure of reaction time than of coordination). No information is provided about the samples on which this information is based. With some measures, no validity evidence is provided at all. That is, the authors claim that because the selected body composition, flexibility, and agility/dynamic balance measures do not have a clinical equivalent and "gold standard," "it was necessary for the committee to use its best judgment concerning the validity of these particular items to provide quality data for the given parameter" (p. 21). No other types of validity evidence are provided for FFA measures (e.g., content validity using subject matter experts, "known-groups" validity, criterion-related validity). It is strongly recommended that the authors consult both the validity literature (e.g., Hubley & Zumbo, 1996; Pedhazur & Schmelkin, 1991; Sireci, 1998) and a measurement or test development expert in planning further validation studies.

COMMENTARY. This is the second edition of the FFA; no information is provided about how this 1996 edition differs from the original 1990 edition. On the positive side, the authors have attempted to provide a much-needed test of physical functioning that can be administered in the field without the need for special facilities and equipment. Furthermore, the FFA measures are easy to administer and score. Unfortunately, the weaknesses of this test, as it is currently presented, far outweigh its benefits. The development of the FFA, the rationale for the selection of measures used, the standardization sample, and the reliability evidence are all inadequately described. The validity evidence is limited at best. Based on a prior *Mental Measurements Yearbook* review of the FFA (Lambert, 1998), it appears that at least some promising reliability and validity evidence for the FFA has been published in the research literature although this research is not presented in the manual. The interpretive information provided is simply inadequate. No guidance is provided to the reader about how to use the test information to provide feedback to clients besides use of the labels "average," "above average," and "below average," which are based on cut-offs one standard deviation above and below the mean and which the authors themselves state is an "arbitrary performance evaluation" (p. 25). Case studies and some concrete advice on how to use results from the FFA to establish the baseline condition of a client, evaluate change, and/or provide feedback to the client would be a welcome addition to the manual. It is strongly recommended that the authors consult with a measurement or test development expert to assist them in gathering appropriate psychometric evidence on the FFA.

SUMMARY. The FFA appears to consist of a reasonable series of tasks related to functional fitness in older adults. The key weak point of the FFA is the lack of well-presented reliability, validity, and normative data as established in the *Standards for Educational and Psychological Testing* (AERA, APA, & NCME, 1999). This is followed by an inadequate discussion of (a) proper interpretation and use of the obtained scores, and (b) the rationale for, and development of, the FFA mea-

sures. At this point, the FFA cannot be recommended for use as a measure of functional fitness. Reynolds' (1998) comments from a prior review still apply: the FFA "is likely to result in inappropriate interpretations and potentially harmful recommendations regarding activities for adults over 60 years" (p. 444). Readers might want to consider the Functional Fitness Test for Seniors (Rikli & Jones, 1999) as an alternate measure.

REVIEWER'S REFERENCES

American Educational Research Association, American Psychological Association, & National Council on Measurement in Education (1999). *Standards for educational and psychological testing.* Washington, DC: American Educational Research Association.
Hubley, A. M., & Zumbo, B. D. (1996). A dialectic on validity: Where we have been and where we are going. *Journal of General Psychology, 123,* 207–215.
Lambert, M. E. (1998). [Review of the Functional Fitness Assessment for Adults over 60 Years.] In J. C. Impara & B. S. Plake (Eds.), *The thirteenth mental measurements yearbook* (pp. 442–443). Lincoln, NE: Buros Institute of Mental Measurements.
Pedhazur, E. J., & Schmelkin, L. P. (1991). *Measurement, design, and analysis: An integrated approach.* Hillsdale, NJ: Lawrence Erlbaum Associates.
Reynolds, C. R. (1998). [Review of the Functional Fitness Assessment for Adults over 60 Years.] In J. C. Impara & B. S. Plake (Eds.), *The thirteenth mental measurements yearbook* (pp. 443–444). Lincoln, NE: Buros Institute of Mental Measurements.
Rikli, R. E., & Jones, C. J. (1999). The development and validation of a functional fitness test for community-residing older adults. *Journal of Aging and Physical Activity, 7,* 129–161.
Sireci, S. G. (1998). The construct of content validity. *Social Indicators Research, 45,* 83–117.

Review of the Functional Fitness Assessment for Adults Over 60 Years by ANTHONY M. PAOLO, Research Associate Professor of Psychiatry and Behavioral Sciences, University of Kansas Medical Center, Kansas City, KS:

DESCRIPTION. The Functional Fitness Assessment for Adults Over 60 Years is a field test designed to assess the functional fitness of adults over 60 years of age. The parameters selected for inclusion in the test were; Body Composition, Flexibility, Agility/Dynamic Balance, Coordination, Strength/Endurance, and Endurance.

The Body Composition parameter is calculated using the ponderal index from the subparameters of body weight and standing height. The Flexibility parameter is scored by the number of inches reached in each trial, whereas the Agility/Dynamic Balance, Coordination, and Endurance parameters are scored in terms of the time required to complete test trials. The Strength/Endurance parameter is scored for the number of repetitions completed in a 30-second interval. Average score ranges for each parameter as well as any special considerations for each test are provided in the manual.

The test manual provides detailed instructions for setting up and administering the test items utilizing simple, readily available equipment (i.e., weight scale, tape measure, masking tape, chair, soda

that formed four core subscales" (examiner's manual, p. 29). Item analysis of subscale items yielded the median item discrimination coefficients for Social Interaction, Restricted Patterns of Behavior, Cognitive Patterns, and Pragmatic Skills of between .56 and .68. These data suggest that overall the items show strong associations with their parent subscales but because the range of discrimination coefficients for each item was not provided, it is impossible to determine whether any individual items display relatively poor discrimination.

The eight supplemental items comprising the Early Development subscale were selected from those included in the Gilliam Autism Rating Scale (GARS; Gilliam, 1995), an instrument intended to assist in the diagnosis of Autistic Disorder.

TECHNICAL. The norm sample for the GADS consisted of 371 individuals "previously diagnosed with Asperger's Disorder" (examiner's manual, p. 23). No information regarding verification of diagnosis is provided. Individuals for the sample were recruited through professionals in schools and treatment centers and through parents via the Internet. Most participants came from the U.S. but the sample included a small number (n = 8) from Canada, Great Britain, Mexico, Australia, and from "other countries" (examiner's manual, p. 23). The mean age for participants in the norm sample was 10 years (SD = 4 years; range = 3–22). The sample was disproportionately male (85%) in rough accordance with the literature regarding sex ratio for the disorder. Other sample characteristics matched the U.S. school-age population reasonably well except that Black students and Hispanic American ethnicity students were underrepresented and Other Race students and Other Ethnicity students were overrepresented. The age distribution of the sample is uneven with the largest number of students falling in the range from 5 years to 14 years. Relatively few children under 4 years old (n = 4) and relatively few 18–22 year-olds (n = 14) are included in the sample.

The author provides internal consistency data for the norm sample as well as for several smaller samples (Autistic Disorder, Other Disabilities, No Disability). Coefficient alphas for the norm sample ranged from .68 to .87 for the five subscales and the composite score; coefficient alphas for the other samples tended to be somewhat higher. The author advises that the standard error of measure-

ment for GADS subscales is about 1 and for the Asperger's Disorder Quotient is about 5; this latter statement is slightly discrepant from an earlier report in the manual that the *SEM* for the Asperger's Disorder Quotient is 4.

Test-retest reliability for the Asperger's Disorder Quotient is reported to be .93. For the subscales, test-retest reliability coefficients range from .71 to .77. The stability study, however, was done over a 2-week interval on a very small, homogeneous sample (N = 10) of individuals with Asperger's Disorder. Interrater reliability coefficients ranged from .72 to .92, but again the sample was quite small (N = 16).

Evidence of concurrent validity was provided by examining the relationship between the GADS and the GARS subtests. The hypothesized relationships were generally supported. A contrasted groups study examined differences among a control group and three diagnostic groups (Asperger's Disorder, Autistic Disorder, and Other Disabilities). The Asperger's Disorder group had significantly higher mean scores, compared to the other groups, on each of the core subscales and on the Asperger's Disorder Quotient.

COMMENTARY. The GADS represents an effort to supplement diagnostic assessment of individuals suspected of having Asperger's Disorder through the use of an objective behavior-rating scale. The Asperger's Disorder construct is well defined in the literature and in existing diagnostic manuals.

Sources for the initial pool of items were well chosen. However, the extent to which the wording of the items accurately reflected the meaning and intent of those sources is unknown; a procedure for expert review of items would have increased users' confidence that the items indeed reflect the intended construct. The author implies that final item selection was based on factor analysis but does not offer additional information. Data about the factor analytic procedure and item factor loadings would add to the discussion of test development. The rationale for borrowing selected Early Development subscale items from the GARS is not provided and the psychometric data reported for this subscale are minimal.

Further, the norm table for converting raw scores to standard scores and percentiles (Table A.1) indicates that, for the Early Development subscale, higher raw scores are associated with lower standard scores. According to the conversion table, a raw score of 0 on Early Development (corresponding to the absence of early developmental indicators associated with Asperger's Disorder) yields a standard score of 13, whereas the highest possible raw score (i.e., 8) yields a standard score of 1. The author has indicated (personal communication) that there is, in fact, an inverse relationship between Early Development raw scores and the likelihood of Asperger's Disorder. However, in this reviewer's judgment, the Early Development subscale should be used with caution, pending further psychometric studies.

The instrument is intended to supplement, not replace, clinical diagnostic assessment. However, the author might have provided a stronger, more consistent position regarding the inability of the GADS alone to establish a diagnosis.

The standardization sample is modest but adequate given the state of the field. More vigorous efforts to verify the diagnosis of sample participants would have provided the user with greater assurance that scores reflect a comparison to the intended target population.

The test-retest reliability study reported in the examiner's manual is inadequate due to a small sample and a failure to include non-Asperger's Disorder individuals in the sample. The interrater reliability study is also weak due to a small sample. Additional demonstration of the instrument's reliability is critical if it is to be used widely. Validity studies reported in the manual are adequate for the release of the instrument but further validation with carefully documented diagnostic groups is an important priority.

SUMMARY. The Gilliam Asperger's Disorder Scale is a valuable addition to the tools available to support the diagnosis of Asperger's Disorder. Although diagnosis cannot be established using the GADS alone, it offers an objective, easily administered means of eliciting information about characteristics of Asperger's Disorder from parents and other caregivers. The Early Development subscale should be interpreted with caution, and a conservative position suggests that standard scores for this subscale should not be reported or included in the computation of the Asperger's Disorder Quotient until there is further validation of the subscale. Although the GADS is the most carefully constructed of the currently available Asperger's behavior rating scales and holds excellent promise,

additional psychometric studies are essential if it is to fulfill that promise and to endure as an important component of diagnostic evaluations.

REVIEWER'S REFERENCES

American Psychiatric Association. (2000). *Diagnostic and statistical manual of mental disorders—Fourth edition—Text revision.* Washington, DC: Author.
Gilliam, J. E. (1995). Gilliam Autism Rating Scale. Austin, TX: PRO-ED.
World Health Organization. (1992). *International classification of diseases and related health problems* (10th ed.). Geneva, Switzerland: Author.

Review of the Gilliam Asperger's Disorder Scale by THERESA VOLPE-JOHNSTONE, Clinical and School Psychologist, Pleasanton, CA:

DESCRIPTION. The Gilliam Asperger's Disorder Scale (GADS) is a 40-item behavioral rating scale with four core subscales and an optional developmental subscale. It is designed for five purposes related to behaviors associated with the DSM-IV-TR and the ICD-10 diagnosis of Asperger's Disorder (AD): (a) to identify persons with AD, (b) to assess for unique behavioral problems, (c) to document progress, (d) to target goals, and (e) to conduct research. The age range for the GADS is 3 through 22 years. The manual indicates the GADS is to be given to the rater to complete but this reviewer's experience with the GADS would support an interview format. The GADS's four core subscales comprise 32 questions unequally distributed and are responded to using weighted scores (0–3) asking the rater to describe the frequency of behaviors from their observation of the individual over an average 6-hour period. The frequency ratings are summed and a raw score for each subscale is derived, yielding standard scores (SS) and percentile ranks. The SS have a mean of 10 and a standard deviation of 3. The remaining 8 items comprise the optional Early Developmental Subscale that must be completed by a caregiver and is responded to in a yes/no format. This scale also yields a standard score. The standard scores are then summed and an Asperger's Disorder Quotient (ADQ) is determined from either the four core or all five subscales. This is to determine the likelihood that an individual has AD and the severity of it. The ADQ has a mean of 100, standard deviation of 15. The four core subscales include Social Interaction, Restricted Patterns of Behavior, Cognitive Patterns, and Pragmatic Skills. The GADS can be completed by a classroom teacher, parent, or any individual who has had "regular sustained contact with the subject for at least 2 weeks" (examiner's manual, p 9). However, scoring and interpretation should be conducted by qualified persons, that is, persons trained in psychometrics including test construction and statistical characteristics and who understand the conceptual framework of the instrument. The GADS is untimed but can be completed within 5 to 10 minutes. If given in interview format, as suggested by this reviewer, the completion time lasts from 15 to 25 minutes.

DEVELOPMENT. The GADS was developed as the first standardized norm-referenced instrument for identifying persons with characteristics of Asperger's Disorder (AD). Brief and concise facts relative to characteristics of AD as noted in the literature (American Psychiatric Association, 2000; Asperger, 1944; Klin, Volkmar, & Sparrow, 2000; World Health Organization, 1992) were provided. The author indicated that:

> Items on the subscales have strong face validity because they are based on the diagnostic criteria for Asperger's Disorder published in the *Diagnostic and Statistical Manual of Mental Disorders-Fourth Edition-Text Revision* (DSM-IV-TR ...) and the *International Classification of Diseases and Related Health Problems-Tenth Edition* (ICD-10 ...). (examiner's manual, p. 2)

Information on item selection was not clearly delineated although reference was made to the "examination of the data [revealing] that 32 of the items grouped together in four categories that formed the four core subscales" (examiner's manual, p. 29). This reviewer was unable to find the data referred to but assumed the data were the DSM-IV-TR and ICD-10 diagnostic criteria as well as the disorder descriptions in the literature that first led to a 70-item experimental version of the GADS. Those items were analyzed utilizing a correlational procedure referred to as item discrimination. The discrimination desired would be the presence or absence of the described trait in any of the core subscales that met or exceeded a .05 level of statistical significance and at least half of the coefficients had to reach or exceed .35 in magnitude. Again, not clearly stated but assumed, this procedure removed 38 of the 70 original items and led to the scale and its components as currently reviewed. Items forming the early child development optional scale were borrowed from the author's Autism Rating Scale (Gilliam, 1995) and scored in a reverse direction. That is, the

higher the raw score, the lower the standard score. Although not discussed in the manual, apparently a reverse score is used because the early developmental course of the Asperger child is fairly typical compared to the general population, which is why this disorder is usually diagnosed once the child begins school.

TECHNICAL. The standardization sample included 371 previously diagnosed individuals with Asperger's Disorder, ages 3 through 22. The sample was solicited from school districts and treatment centers from a wide geographic range including 46 states, the District of Columbia (92% overall), Canada, Great Britain, Mexico, and Australia (8%) among others. For the GADS normative sample to be representative of the reference population, it was necessary to use previously diagnosed individuals rather than a nonclinical population. This was an appropriate procedure. Further research is needed to determine if Asperger's Disorder is normally distributed relative to race and ethnicity but the author suggests that there is no reason not to assume this given that contradictions were not found in the literature. A one-way analysis of variance was conducted and there were no differences in gender in the sample suggesting that the same norms would be appropriate for males and females. Gender ratio of the sample (5:1 males: females) was representative of the manifestation of the disorder as featured in the DSM-IV-TR. Separate age norms were not necessary because correlations between raw scores and age were not significant. The relationship between the Restricted Patterns of Behavior subscale and age was significant but considered not to "represent a strong relationship" (examiner's manual, p. 33) but would suggest that age can lead to differences in subscale scores in that domain.

Reliability was investigated by conducting studies of internal consistency, which the author supports with small standard errors of measurement throughout the test, test-retest methods, and interrater agreement. Using Cronbach's coefficient alpha, internal consistency was computed on all the subscales of the GADS and the different diagnostic groups that comprised the sample. This included individuals diagnosed with autistic disorder, individuals with no known disability, and individuals with various disabilities other than Asperger's or autistic disorder. Adequate reliability in this fashion was demonstrated for all groups with coefficients ranging from .70 to .90 for the four core subscales and moderate to strong reliability for the Asperger's Disorder Quotient (ADQ) with coefficients ranging from .87 to .95. Unfortunately, the lowest coefficient alpha and the highest standard error of measurement for the ADQ were for the individuals in the Asperger Disorder group (.87 and 5.41, respectively). This means that the GADS may systematically introduce error into the construct of Asperger characteristics and therefore the ratings were more variable. It did support consistent ratings for the other groups, meaning that the items more consistently contribute to the total scores and would likely discriminate well from these groups. The coefficient of stability, or test-retest reliability, was demonstrated using a small sample ($n = 10$) of identified students with Asperger's Disorder at a 2-week interval. Correlation coefficients ranged from .71 to .77 for the core subscales and .93 for the ADQ representing adequate stability. Using a total sample of 16 individuals with diagnoses of AD ($n = 10$), learning disabilities ($n = 2$), or autism ($n = 4$), interrater reliability, which is needed for observational tools such as the GADS, was strong (r ranged from .72 to .92 for subscales and .89 for the ADQ).

Content validity asks, "does the content of the test cover the behavior domain to be measured?" and was examined through item discrimination and item difficulty analyses. Item discrimination attained statistical significance at the .05 level or beyond with a minimum magnitude of .35. On the subscales, median item difficulty coefficients were .60 for Social Interaction, .56 for Restricted Patterns of Behavior, .68 for Cognitive Patterns, and .61 for Pragmatic Skills. The effectiveness of the GADS in predicting persons who are likely to have AD, that is, criterion-prediction validity (or criterion-related validity), was found when correlations with the Gilliam Autism Rating Scale were positive. Criterion-prediction validity refers to how effective the test is in predicting one's performance in specific domains. Significant relationships were noted in social interaction, restricted patterns of behavior scales, and total scores as would be expected given the similarity of domain functioning. Discriminant analysis found statistically significant differences between the means of an AD versus a non-AD group on subscale and quotient scores. Construct identifica-

tion (or construct validity) asks "to what extent does this test measure the hypothesized theoretical construct or trait?" and was determined based on: (a) the low relationship between results of the GADS and a participant's age (all below .10 except Restricted Patterns of Behavior described elsewhere), (b) the interrelationship among GADS scales (all correlations significant [$p < .01$]) demonstrating that the behavioral characteristics of AD are being measured, (c) subscale items relating to their respective subscale total scores (median correlations all significant at the .01 level ranging from .56 to .68), and (d) the ability of GADS scores to discriminate between AD and other behavior disorder groups (mean scores for four groups indicated that the AD group had significantly higher scores [$p < .01$] than the other three groups).

COMMENTARY. The GADS is a welcome addition to the assessment and identification process of individuals with Asperger's Disorder. It offers the opportunity to attain systematic information from more than one source to help make a difficult diagnosis and can be used to develop long term goals and objectives for treatment. It should not be used as a sole diagnostic tool. The domain item language presents difficult concepts into clear definable behaviors. It is quick to administer, easy to score, and the interpretation guide on the protocol is an added benefit for discussing outcome in understandable terms with a caregiver. In the test construction realm, one weakness of the GADS would be the small sample size. To this reviewer, this is a small matter considering that although within the Asperger group there is great heterogeneity, compared to the general public the group is quite homogeneous, which is shown in the validity studies provided. Item selection procedures were unclear and should have been explained. A significant weakness to this reviewer's view would be in the subscales Cognitive Patterns and Pragmatic Skills for the younger age groups. Coefficient tables by age were not provided but overall coefficients for the subscales were provided for the entire sample. The resultant coefficients were .07 and -.08, respectively, suggesting that differences in subscale scores are not related to age. The negative correlation was not discussed in the manual. When actually administering these subscales to the youngest population for which it is normed, 7 of the 14 items between these scales are either not relevant or not typically displayed by children within those early ages, making responding to those items difficult. Therefore, the ADQ can yield false negatives. The optional Early Development Subscale has the lowest internal consistency coefficients and does not add to the discriminative power of the GADS or to the overall qualitative performance of the AD person. The standard score units should be represented by scaled score units in order to be consistent with other tools that also use a mean of 10, standard deviation of 3. This would be less confusing. Despite these shortcomings, the GADS was developed based on the current understanding of Asperger's Disorder and is a good introduction to caregivers into the nature of the differences in functioning between children with and without this particular cluster of behaviors. It is a good first tool to aid in the possible subsequent diagnosis of Asperger's Disorder.

SUMMARY. The GADS was designed to assess persons with Asperger's Disorder and other severe behavioral disorders. It is norm referenced and subscale items are based on definitions of Asperger's Disorder by the American Psychiatric Association and the World Health Organization. Four core subscales and an optional Early Developmental Subscale yield standard scores that should be defined as scaled scores. When summed, an Asperger's Disorder Quotient is obtained. The GADS was normed on a small sample. Reliability coefficients were strong but most impressive for interrater reliability. Studies demonstrating content, criterion-related, and construct validity were conducted. Administering and scoring are easy. Interpretation ease is dependent upon one's knowledge and background in autistic spectrum disorders. This reviewer would recommend this test for its descriptive value and the ability of the items to help a caregiver understand potential behavioral differences in children with pervasive developmental disorders. Further research is needed on this scale relative to the relationship of age differences at the 3-, 4-, and 5-year levels on the subscales of Cognitive Patterns and Pragmatic Skills and overall on race and ethnicity.

REVIEWER'S REFERENCES

American Psychiatric Association. (2000). *Diagnostic and statistical manual of mental disorders-Fourth Edition-Text revision.* Washington, DC: Author.

Asperger, H. (1944). Die "Autistichen Psychopathen" im Kindersalter. *Archiv für Psychiatrie und Nervenkrankheiten, 117,* 76–136.

Gilliam, J. E. (1995). *Gilliam Autism Rating Scale.* Austin, TX: PRO-ED.

Klin, A., Volkmar, F. R., & Sparrow, S. S. (Eds.). (2000). *Asperger Disorder.* New York: Guilford Press.

World Health Organization (1992). *International classification of diseases and related health problems* (10th ed.). Geneva, Switzerland: Author.

Goldman Fristoe Test of Articulation—Second Edition.

Purpose: Designed as "a systematic means of assessing an individual's articulation of the consonant sounds of Standard American English."
Population: Ages 2–21.
Publication Dates: 1969–2000.
Acronym: GFTA-2.
Scores: 3 subtests: Sounds-in-Words, Sounds-in-Sentences, Stimulability.
Administration: Individual.
Price Data, 2002: $189.95 per complete kit including manual (2000, 146 pages), test easel, 25 response forms, canvas carrying bag, and supplemental developmental norms booklet; $26.95 per 25 response forms; $35.95 per manual.
Time: 5–15 minutes.
Authors: Ronald Goldman and Macalyne Fristoe.
Publisher: American Guidance Service, Inc.
Cross References: See T5:1095 (48 references) and T4:1045 (15 references); for a review by Donald E. Mowrer of an earlier edition, see 10:126 (7 references); see also T3:960 (21 references); for reviews by Margaret C. Byrne and Ralph L. Shelton, and an excerpted review by Dorothy Sherman, see 7:952 (4 references).

Review of the Goldman-Fristoe Test of Articulation—Second Edition by STEVEN LONG, Assistant Professor, Communication Sciences, Case Western Reserve University, Cleveland, OH:

DESCRIPTION. The Goldman-Fristoe Test of Articulation—Second Edition (GFTA-2) is a norm-referenced test of Standard American English consonant articulation that can be administered to individuals 2–21 years of age. The test is divided into three parts—Sounds-in-Words, Sounds-in-Sentences, and Stimulability—that are intended to assess consonant production across different speaking conditions. The subtests can be administered separately and only the Sounds-in-Words subtest is norm referenced. Administration time for the Sounds-in-Words subtest is reported to be 15 minutes or less. No times are reported for the other two subtests.

Test responses can be recorded in two ways, depending on the examiner's level of training. In the first, target phonemes are merely scored as correct or incorrect. In the second, responses are recorded using phonetic symbols, which requires training in phonetic transcription and some knowledge about articulation disorders. The raw score for the Sounds-in-Words subtest is the number of articulation errors produced. The type of error (omission, substitution, distortion) or its developmental commonness (e.g., among children /s/ is more often replaced by [t] rather than [h]) is not considered in scoring.

DEVELOPMENT. The GFTA-2 is the first major revision of the GFTA, a test that was originally published as a criterion-referenced instrument in 1969, with norms added in 1972 and then extended in 1986. The new version differs from the GFTA in three respects. First, the age range and population diversity of the norms has been expanded and the normative data can be expressed in standard score and test-age-equivalent form and as percentile scores. Second, the test items have been edited to remove words (e.g., gun, Christmas tree) and story events (skipping school) that were deemed either offensive or culturally biased. These items have been replaced with others, chosen in such a way that the phonemic balance of the entire test remains intact and some additional consonant clusters are sampled. To achieve all of these aims, the authors increased the number of words in the Sounds-in-Words from 44 in the GFTA to 53 in the GFTA-2. The third major change in the new version is the development of new artwork that is more contemporary (e.g., the rotary telephone picture has been replaced with a push-button model) and balanced in its representation of various ethnic groups.

Overall, the rationale and design features of the GFTA-2 remain essentially the same as with its predecessor. To simplify administration, the test continues to focus exclusively on consonant production and to sample more than one phoneme in most target words. The lack of vowel sampling is justified by statements in the manual that vowels are less likely to be produced in error, are more subject to dialectal variation, and have been found to have lower interlistener reliability than consonants. No research evidence is cited in support of these claims.

The GFTA also continues to use a word model of phonological structure. Thus, any target phoneme that is not in the initial or final position of a word is designated as "medial." This results in a grouping of sounds that vary considerably in their context of occurrence: the [g] in "wagon" occurs intervocalically in a single morpheme; the [m] in "swimming" is also intervocalic but precedes a morphological boundary; the [s] in "pencils" is part of a cluster with the preceding nasal;

the [t] in "bathtub" follows a consonant as well as a morphological boundary; and so forth. In the test manual, the authors briefly discuss the issue of "consonant position designation" (p. 10) and conclude that the word model of structure is justified by speech pathologists' need to communicate with parents and professionals who lack "detailed knowledge of syllabic structures" (p. 10).

TECHNICAL. It is clear that the developers of the GFTA-2 devoted considerable effort to achieving a standardization sample that mirrors the population of North America. The test manual describes in some detail the procedures by which testing sites were identified and operated. A large set of tables indicates how the standardization sample was distributed by age, gender, geographic region, ethnic group, and disability status, and how that distribution compared to recent population data from the U.S. Bureau of the Census and Department of Education. It is important to note that, although the GFTA-2 standardization sample was stratified by region and ethnicity, no attempt was made to ascertain the use of dialect by the speakers tested. It is therefore unknown, for example, how many of the African American children in the sample were speakers of African American English. More importantly, the norms themselves are not tabulated by ethnicity or dialect, making it impossible to compare a dialect speaker to his or her linguistic peers. Thus, the test remains biased against such speakers because no allowance is made in scoring for pronunciations that are acceptable dialectal variations (e.g., "bathtub").

Appendix A of the test manual indicates that the great majority of examiners were speech pathologists and mention is made of practice that was required before participants received their testing assignment lists. It is unclear, however, whether examiners were actually required to demonstrate proficiency in judging the accuracy of children's speech. Though one would like to assume that anyone working as a speech pathologist must possess such skill, previous normative research has not found this to be the case (Smit, Hand, Freilinger, Bernthal, & Bird, 1991). As noted earlier, the GFTA-2 is promoted as being useful at two levels, one that requires training in phonetic transcription and the other that does not. However, all of the standardization testing appears to have been conducted by individuals with professional training. There is no indication how the normative data might have

ment of the GFTA-2 materials, an entirely new standardization sample was needed for the development of new norms. A nationwide sample, stratified with regard to gender, race or ethnic group, geographical region, and mother's education level, matching U.S. Census data (March 1998), led to a sample of 2,350 individuals, aged 2 to 21 years. From this sample, age-based standard scores were derived, representing the difference between an individual's raw score and the mean score for their particular age group. A linear standardization was used, but the assumption of normality was not made. Because very few errors are made within the older age groups, the distribution is skewed with a long right tail. Test-age equivalents represent the age for which an individual's raw score is the median score.

Reliability for the GFTA-2 was assessed by internal consistency, test-retest, and interrater methodologies. With a median interval of 14 days, 53 individuals, ranging in age from 4 years 6 months to 7 years 0 months, were given the test a second time by the same examiner. Test-retest reliability is reportedly quite high, with the median percentages of agreement for the initial, medial, and final sounds being 98%. To examine interrater reliability, 30 individuals were tested twice by two different examiners. Mean percentages of agreement were not unreasonable, with 70% agreement for initial consonant, 73% for the medial consonant, and 73% for the final consonant. However, when using the median percentages of agreement, the rates increased to 93%, 90%, and 90%, respectively. This could be the result of the skewness of the distribution. More information about the distribution and possible presence of extreme scores would be useful. Previous reviewers have mentioned this in reference to the first edition (Mowrer, 1989). The GFTA-2 manual does a good job in providing descriptive data about the samples used for each of these assessments.

Content validity of the GFTA-2, compared to the first edition, is improved, but more information is needed for construct validity. Content validity is the degree to which the content of an assessment represents the content of what is intended to be measured. Because the GFTA-2 assesses 23 of the 25 sounds recognized as Standard English consonants, the content of the GFTA-2 represents the content of Standard English consonants quite well, and is thereby said to

have high content validity. On the other hand, construct validity is the degree to which an operational definition adequately represents the reported construct. It is argued that by showing a developmental progression in articulation errors, with reductions in error occurring as a function of age, construct validity is documented. The researchers develop what is referred to as a mastery age criterion, which is defined as the youngest age for which the percentage of correct productions is .85 or greater for each consonant or consonant cluster. This reportedly reveals "a close match to widely accepted patterns of development and to the historical National Speech and Hearing Survey" (Hull, as cited in manual, p. 56), but more information would be helpful. The manual should mention that the first edition of the GFTA has been utilized in longitudinal investigations (e.g., Roberts, Burchinal, & Footo, 1990).

COMMENTARY. As in the previous edition, there is little discussion of concurrent validity (the degree to which scores on the GFTA-2 correlate with other known measures of articulation) or predictive validity (the degree to which GFTA-2 scores allow for the prediction of actual articulation in context). Nearly all of the discussion of reliability and validity focuses on the Sounds-In-Words component of the GFTA-2. Predictive validity could be addressed in terms of how well performance on the Sounds-In-Words component predicts scores on the Sounds-In-Sentences component. The manual should mention that the first edition of the GFTA has been used previously to establish the predictive validity of other scales (Sommers, Kozarevich, & Michaels, 1994).

The GFTA-2 is a significant revision over the first edition, with the introduction of new testing items, enhanced content validity evidence, and improvements in normative work. The manual does a good job in demonstrating that the scores of individuals taking the GFTA-2 can be compared to norms for representative individuals on the GFTA-2 and does not purport to generalize beyond the actual test given. It is quite possible that the skewed nature of the distribution, which is a product of the phenomenon itself, and the presence of extreme scores is why findings differ when using the mean versus the mode. More attention to this in the manual would be helpful.

SUMMARY. In conclusion, the GFTA-2 represents a significant improvement over the first edition and, like the predecessor, will be a valuable tool for speech pathologists looking for a rapid and easy-to-administer assessment of articulation abilities for comparison to a representative group of individuals' performance on the same measure.

REVIEWER'S REFERENCES

Mowrer, D. E. (1989). [Review of the Goldman Fristoe Test of Articulation.] In J. C. Conoley & J. J. Kramer (Eds.), *The tenth mental measurements yearbook* (pp. 323–325). Lincoln, NE: Buros Institute of Mental Measurements.

Roberts, J. E., Burchinal, M., & Footo, M. M. (1990). Phonological process declines from 2 1/2 to 8 years. *Journal of Communication Disorders, 23*(3), 205–217.

Sommers, R. K., Kozarevich, M. M., & Christine, M. (1994). Word skills of children normal and impaired in communication skills and measures of language and speech development. *Journal of Communication Disorders, 27*(3), 223–240.

[110]

Graded Arithmetic-Mathematics Test.

Purpose: Designed to assess overall mathematical attainment.

Population: Ages 5–12.

Publication Dates: 1949–1998.

Scores: Total score only.

Administration: Group.

Price Data, 1999: £7.99 per 20 tests; £7.50 per manual; £8.99 per specimen set.

Time: (30) minutes.

Comments: Oral administration instructions provided.

Authors: P. E. Vernon and K. M. Miller.

Publisher: Hodder & Stoughton Educational [England].

Cross References: See T3:972 (3 references) and T2:618 (8 references); for a review by Stanley Nisbet of the original edition, see 5:476.

Review of the Graded Arithmetic–Mathematics Test by KEVIN D. CREHAN, Associate Professor of Educational Psychology, University of Nevada, Las Vegas, Las Vegas, NV:

DESCRIPTION. The Graded Arithmetic-Mathematics Test (4th ed.) (GAMT) consists of 70 supply type items that broadly tap a range of achievement from number recognition to pre-algebra. The test claims to yield a useful assessment of overall mathematical attainment for 5- to 12-year-olds. Group, individual, or oral administration allows the student 30 minutes to complete the work. A scoring key is provided for hand scoring. Items predominately measure facts and applications of arithmetic with a sparse scattering of general knowledge, measurement, geometry, and pre-algebra items. Separate norm tables are provided for English, Scottish, and Canadian students to allow converting the single number right score to a mathematics age ranging from 5 to 12. An additional norm table appears to merge the norming data from the three countries. This table allows converting a raw score to a mathematics age, age-based percentile rank, and a mathematics quotient (actually a deviation standard score). The test manual goes into some detail describing the derived scores, but other than the literal interpretation of overall mathematical attainment, does not suggest any additional interpretations, applications, or uses of results.

DEVELOPMENT. The manual gives only very general indications of the test development process. The manual states, "If there is a generally agreed arithmetic-mathematics curriculum, therefore, it is much more straightforward to arrive at a representative sample of items to constitute a reliable test" (p. 2). The quoted sentence causes this reviewer some pause. Its strange construction first questions the existence of a generally agreed curriculum, then seems to conclude one exists. Additionally, it suggests a representative sample of items will yield a reliable test. Although this may be true, some evidence of the correspondence between test items and curriculum would be more interesting and valuable information to potential test users. The manual further states that the "test focuses on primary-age children and comprises six to eight items for each successive year group, with sufficient difficulty items to stretch even bright pupils aged up to 12:0" (p. 3). The methods used for the determination of item-to-year correspondence are omitted and there is no indication of which items are keyed to which years. Other than very broad statements, no test specifications or content description is offered. The manual states that preliminary trials of a much larger number of items (than the 70 in the test) were given to some 3,000 students. Items selected for the test were those that "covered the desired range of ability most evenly, and showed consistent rises with age level" (p. 11). Beyond this statement, no information on item development, selection, or refinement is presented.

TECHNICAL. Following the selection of the 70 items that comprise the test, a standardization sample of 4,247 English, Scottish, and Canadian students was tested in 1975. The manual states that, even though the English samples were drawn from a single county, they are likely to be representative of this country's students. No claim of representation is made for the remaining samples. It appears that the 1975 norming data were used to develop the two tables described above. Apparently the current (1998) edition did not include revisions that would affect the usefulness of the 1975 norms. The data are not disaggregated by gender or ethnicity. However, although the manual states that there were no sex differences below 10:0 years, it reports that males consistently scored higher than females above this age (by as much as one-half standard deviation).

Reliability was estimated by corrected odd-even split-half correlations for students in several classes at various ages above 8:0. These estimates were all greater than .90 and averaged a very respectable .92. A standard error of 4.2 is reported for the mathematics quotient. The mathematics quotient is actually a deviation standard score with a mean of 100 and a standard deviation of 15.

The manual does not provide any evidence for the validity of test score interpretation. According to the manual, the score is a useful assessment of overall mathematical attainment. This claim can be challenged because the degree of correspondence of test content to the extant mathematics curricula of England, Scotland, and Canada is in question.

COMMENTARY. It is difficult to comment favorably on this test. If there is a market for a short, wide-range arithmetic test with questionable curriculum correspondence, perhaps the GAMT might be considered. Test shortcomings are many but the absence of validity evidence to support any interpretations trumps all other weaknesses.

SUMMARY. If this test is to be considered for adoption, the screening process should include an item-by-item review to ascertain the appropriateness of test content to the decision situations to be informed by test results. Alternative assessments should be considered. One that might be considered is the Progressive Achievement Tests in Mathematics—Revised (PATM-R; 199) (Australian Council for Educational Research, 1997). These tests serve as an example of a well-constructed national level mathematics test series. The PATM-R provides evidence to support useful interpretations and a comprehensive individual student report that supports instructional decisions and communicates to students and parents. Because the PATM-R was developed to correspond to Australian curriculum, it may not prove useful in other locales. However, a test adoption or development board would be informed on test potentials by their review.

REVIEWER'S REFERENCE

Australian Council for Educational Research. (1997). *Progressive Achievement Tests in Mathematics—Revised.* Melbourne, Australia: Australian Council for Educational Research Press.

Review of the Graded Arithmetic—Mathematics Test by DELWYN L. HARNISCH, Professor, Department of Curriculum & Instruction, University of Nebraska—Lincoln, Lincoln, NE:

DESCRIPTION. With the need today of improving performance in mathematics, classroom teachers must have access to instruments to help them measure their students' performance against established standards. The test must be easy to administer and allow the teacher to score and evaluate the results without sending it outside for scoring.

The Graded Arithmetic—Mathematics Test addresses these needs. The test was developed in Great Britain and is based on the content of the mathematics curriculum for schools in England and Scotland. The items draw on the students' basic knowledge of a number of different areas of mathematics including number facts, operations, and tables.

The test can be used with children ages 6 through 18+ and takes 30 minutes to administer. For younger children or children who have difficulty reading, there is an oral version of the test that is contained in the administrator's manual. The authors suggest that no time limit should be imposed if the oral version is used.

The test is composed of open-ended questions. Students write the answers next to or below the question. This allows the scorer to see all of the student's work. An answer key is included in the administration manual. The authors suggest that multiple scorers be used to guard against bias. There are also suggestions in the manual for dealing with problems such as illegibility of answers.

TECHNICAL. Although this test appears fairly easy to administer and the reliability estimate reported in the manual is .92, there are several problems with the test that will greatly limit its validity. First, in the manual there is no table of specifications for the test. Although the authors say that the items were based on the "general consensus as to the content of the arithmetic and mathematics curriculum" (manual, p. 2) in schools in England and Scotland, there is no statement regarding the concepts that were being tested. This calls into question the evidence of content validity.

Second, the test was normed in 1975 in England and Wales, Scotland, and Canada. There is little demographic information included in the manual to describe the norm group. For example, the authors state that the Canadian samples came from "urban and rural areas in five provinces" (manual, p. 11). The only other information that appears to be available is age.

Third, the interpretation of the scores is confusing. Although the authors discourage the calculation of a "Mathematics Quotient," which is defined as the "ratio of a pupil's Mathematics Age to his Chronological Age" (manual, p. 11), this method is presented as a possible means of interpretation.

Finally, there is some confusion regarding the administration of the test. The test is designed for ages 6 through 18+. The authors suggest in the manual that the test administrator can decide on an appropriate starting place for the age group being tested. The manual suggests that there are four possible starting points, but it was not clear to this reviewer where those are. Also, there is no information on what the starting point was for the norm group.

COMMENTARY AND SUMMARY. This test has some major flaws that raise serious issues as to the validity of the test scores. Because there is little information regarding the criteria used to select the items, and given the age of the norms, this test has little value to the classroom teacher.

[111]

Gray Oral Reading Tests, Fourth Edition.

Purpose: Designed "to provide a measure of growth in oral reading and an aid in the diagnosis of oral reading difficulties."
Population: Ages 6-0 to 18-11.
Publication Dates: 1967–2001.
Acronym: GORT-4.
Scores, 4: Rate, Accuracy, Fluency, Comprehension.
Forms, 2: A, B.
Administration: Individual.
Price Data, 2003: $189 per complete kit including 25 each of profile/examiner record forms (Form A and Form B), student book, and examiner's manual (2001, 146 pages); $41 per 25 record forms (specify Form A or B); $48 per student book; $72 per examiner's manual.
Time: (20–30) minutes.
Authors: J. Lee Wiederholt and Brian R. Bryant.
Publisher: PRO-ED.
Cross References: See T5:1131 (18 references); for reviews by John D. King and Deborah King Kundert of an earlier edition, see 12:166 (5 references); see also T4:1084 (9 references); for reviews by Julia A. Hickman

and Robert J. Tierney of an earlier edition, see 10:131 (15 references).

Review of the Gray Oral Reading Tests, Fourth Edition by NANCY L. CRUMPTON, Assistant Professor, College of Education, Department of Counseling, Troy State University Montgomery, Montgomery, AL:

DESCRIPTION. The Gray Oral Reading Tests, Fourth Edition (GORT-4) provides an objective measure of oral reading Rate, Accuracy, Fluency, and Comprehension. It provides a determination of the effects of instruction over time on oral reading as well as serves as an aid in the diagnosis of oral reading difficulties. It is intended for children aged 7 years 0 months (7-0) to 18 years 11 months (18-11). Two parallel forms, Form A and Form B, each contain 14 separate stories with five multiple-choice comprehension questions for each story. The GORT-4 was designed to (a) help identify students significantly below level in oral reading ability and who may benefit from additional work; (b) aid in identifying the kinds of strengths and weaknesses the student has; (c) document reading progress as a consequence of reading intervention programs; and (d) serve as a research tool in measuring the reading abilities of school-aged children. The test can be administered in 15–45 minutes.

The GORT-4 also has a system for performing an analysis of the types of reading errors or miscues made in five areas: Meaning Similarity, Function Similarity, Graphic/Phonemic Similarity, Multiple Sources, and Self-Correction. The frequency of each error is reported as a percentage. This information is useful in identifying reading difficulties.

The test includes the Examiner's Manual, Student Book, and Form A and Form B Profile/Examiner's Record Booklet. The manual provides specific description of the test, administration and scoring procedures, interpretation/analysis, and technical characteristics. The student book is reusable. There are separate profile/examiner record booklets for each form in which student responses are recorded and scoring is completed.

DEVELOPMENT. The first edition of the Gray Oral Reading Tests (GORT) was published in 1963 and consisted of four alternative forms. It was a widely used test of oral reading rate, accuracy, and comprehension for approximately 20 years before the first revision was made in 1986

(GORT-R). At that time there were two alternative forms with new or modified story passages. New national norms were developed with updated reliability and validity data as well as a new system for coding reading errors.

The third revision in 1992 (GORT-3) was the result of feedback from test users that the test was difficult to score, particularly in determining basals and ceilings. A review by Salvia and Ysseldyke (1991) discussed the need for a stratified normative sample. The 1992 revision included the same two forms, A and B, but improvements were made in the addition of separate Rate and Accuracy scores, simplified scoring, and a stratified sample comparative to the 1990 U.S. Census data. New reliability and validity analyses were completed. The GORT-3 was well received, but criticism of the technical aspects of the test was made. These areas of criticism involved documentation of the equivalency of Forms A and B, need for more extensive validity data for assessing student progress in reading, socioeconomic description of students in the standardization sample, and the normative data being 15 years old.

The GORT-4 has met the challenge of prior criticism by providing all new normative data that were collected in 2000 and are representative of the current U.S. population as defined by 2000 Census data projections. Normative information is comprehensive and descriptive with stratification of the sample within each descriptor. New reliability and validity studies were completed for subgroups of the normative sample as well as the entire normative group. Documentation of coefficients of equivalence between Form A and B are provided to show evidence of parallel forms. Administration and scoring procedures were rewritten to increase clarity and understanding. One new story was added at the beginning of each form to provide additional information on the reader.

TECHNICAL. Standardization sites for the GORT-4 were in each of the four geographic regions of the U.S. per U.S. Bureau of the Census. Regional testing sites were in Rochester, New York (Northeast); Mandan, North Dakota (Midwest); Brownsville, Texas and Austin, Texas (South); and Bookings, Oregon (West). The normative sample included 1,677 persons in 28 states. The entire sample was collected between Fall 1999 and Fall 2000. All students were enrolled in general classes and students with disabilities who were members of the classes were included in the sample. Demographic characteristics of the sample were defined by geographic area, gender, race, residence (urban or rural), ethnicity, family income, educational attainment of parents, disability status, and age. A comparison of the percentages of the characteristics of the sample to those reported in the *Statistical Abstract of the United States* (U.S. Bureau of the Census, 1997) indicated the sample was representative.

Norms for the four subtests of the GORT-4 are presented in standard scores with a mean of 10 and *SD* of 3. Standard scores for the subtests are presented in tables in Appendixes. For Rate, Accuracy, Fluency, and Comprehension, the standard scores provide intraindividual measures of specific oral reading skills. There are two forms of the test. A linear equating procedure (Kolen & Brennan, 1995) adjusts scores on the two test forms to allow scores on Form A and B to be used interchangeably. The Oral Reading Quotient (ORQ) is the measure of overall reading ability and is determined by combining standard scores for Fluency and Comprehension.

In estimating reliability, three sources of error variance were measured: content sampling, time sampling, and interscorer differences. Coefficient alphas (Cronbach, 1951) were calculated at 13 age intervals using data from the entire norm sample. The average coefficients for the subtests and composite (ORQ) averaged from .91–.97. the large alpha coefficients demonstrated that the GORT-4 is reliable for all subgroups. Content sampling error was determined by correlating Form A and Form B scores obtained during one test session. Both forms of all four subtests have nearly identical means and standard deviations and correlate .85 or better with each other. Test-retest data were obtained on 30 elementary students, 10 middle school students, and 9 high school students. In the sample, ages ranged from 6–18 years; 22 males and 27 females; ethnicity was 78% European American, 16% African American, and 2% other. Test-retest reliability (administration interval not provided) for the four subtests and ORQ ranged from .85 to .95. A random sample of 30 test protocols was independently scored by two members of the PRO-ED research staff. Interscorer differences were minimal with scorer reliability ranging from .94–.99.

The GORT-4 consists of two parallel forms, each containing 14 developmentally sequenced reading passages with five comprehension questions following each story. Vocabulary in the questions was controlled to insure the vocabulary would not be more difficult than that in the stories. Miscues made by readers were analyzed. Item discrimination and item difficulty statistics determined satisfactory passages to be selected for the GORT-R. The GORT-4 contains the same items as the GORT-R except one story was added to each form and the order of stories was changed. Statistical tests for item bias were performed on all 140 comprehension items for both forms of the GORT-4. There were no statistically significant comparisons of bias that had moderate or large effect sizes. Based on Jodoin and Gierl's (2000) criteria, it is reasonable to conclude that the test is nonbiased in regard to gender, race, and ethnicity.

Correlations between the GORT-4 (Form A) and other measures of reading resulted in high coefficients regarding the criterion-prediction validity of the GORT-4 (median correlations of .63–.75, except Reading Comprehension with a score of .45). Results of studies that include those of earlier GORT versions provide evidence that measurement of oral reading performance by the GORT-4 is valid for a range of ages and reading ability.

COMMENTARY. According to the manual, the GORT-4 is almost identical to the GORT-R (Wiederholt & Bryant, 1986) and GORT-3 (Wiederholt & Bryant, 1992). Throughout its use, the GORT has been studied and revised to respond to reviewer and user comments or criticism. The GORT-4 appears to be the most comprehensively revised edition with new stratified normative data and studies completed to indicate the absence of culture, gender, race, and disability bias. Reliability studies included content sampling, time sampling, and interscorer differences (although the sample for interscorer differences was small). The range of coefficients revealed the GORT-4 has little test error and users can be confident that the test is consistent in measuring oral reading ability. New validity studies for content-description, criterion-prediction, and construct identification provide evidence that the GORT-4 is a valid measure of reading performance.

SUMMARY. The GORT-4 has the advantage of being the fourth edition of a test of oral reading that has been extensively used since 1963. The most recent edition has kept the former version format and content of the stories, the

comprehension questions, and scores derived from administration of the test. The updated version has made extensive qualitative changes in normative data, stratification of the sample, studies providing validity, reliability and bias information, and equivalence coefficients that present evidence of parallel forms of the test. Documenting and scoring student responses are clearly presented in the examinee manual; however, considerable practice on the part of the examiner is required to be able to prompt the reader, time the reader's rate, and mark deviations from print in the process of testing. The history of use of the GORT and revision through the years has resulted in an edition that meets technical challenges and provides the test user with information reflecting current theoretical rationale in measuring reading ability.

REVIEWER'S REFERENCES

Cronbach, L. J. (1951). Coefficient alpha and the internal structure of tests. *Psychometrika, 16*, 297–334.
Jodoin, M. G., & Gierl, M. J. (2000, April). *Evaluating Type I error rates using an effect size measure with the logistic regression procedure for DIF detection.* Paper presented at the annual meeting of the American Educational Research Association, New Orleans.
Kolen, M. J., & Brennan, R. L. (1995). *Test equating methods and practices.* New York: Springer.
Salvia, J., & Ysseldyke, J. E. (1991). *Assessment in special and remedial education* (5th ed.). Boston: Houghton Mifflin.
U.S. Bureau of the Census. (1997). *Statistical abstract of the United States: The National data book.* Washington, DC: U.S. Department of Commerce.
Wiederholt, J. L., & Bryant, B. (1986). Gray Oral Reading Tests—Revised. Austin, TX: PRO-ED.
Wiederholt, J. L., & Bryant, B. (1992). Gray Oral Reading Tests—Third Edition. Austin, TX: PRO-ED.

Review of the Gray Oral Reading Tests, Fourth Edition by MARIE MILLER-WHITEHEAD, Director, Tennessee Valley Educators for Excellence (TVEE.ORG), Muscle Shoals, AL:

DESCRIPTION. The Gray Oral Reading Tests, Fourth Edition (GORT-4) is an individually administered norm-referenced analytic assessment that yields scores for Rate, Accuracy, Fluency, Comprehension, and overall reading ability and a scoring rubric for miscue analysis. The test may be administered in from 15 to 45 minutes by an examiner with formal training in assessment and administration of reading tests. Each form consists of 14 progressively difficult reading passages and five multiple choice comprehension questions per story with levels corresponding to reading vocabulary in grades 1 through 12. The test results yield an Oral Reading Quotient (ORQ) score on a seven interval scale ranging from 130 and above (Very Superior) to 70 or less (Very Poor). Documentation includes an Examiner's Manual, Student Book, and Profile/Examiner Record Booklet for the two available forms (A and

B) of the tests. The same administrator's manual and student book may be used for both forms for all levels and ages. The test authors report that the GORT-4 has addressed most if not all of the concerns of users of the earlier versions of the Gray Oral Reading series. These mainly were related to documentation and reporting of the test's psychometric properties such as reliability coefficients for each subgroup of the norming population, equating of Forms A and B, and item bias analysis (Hickman, 1989; King, 1995; Kundert, 1995; Marlow & Edwards, 1998; Radencich, 1986; Tierney, 1989). Although most of the content is unchanged from the GORT-3, the authors updated the test format and added a new story to each form for lower level readers. The manual provides a table for conversion of GORT-4 Oral Reading Quotients to percentiles, NCEs, T-scores, z-scores, standard scores, and stanines (p. 31).

DEVELOPMENT. The GORT-4 is the fourth edition of this standardized oral reading assessment that has a rather lengthy history. The Gray Oral Reading Tests (GORT) was first printed in 1963 with a second printing in 1967, and its 1915 predecessor, the Standardized Oral Reading Paragraphs, was one of the most popular oral reading assessments of its time. In 1986 J. L. Wiederholt and B. R. Bryant produced a substantial revision of the 1963 original, the Gray Oral Reading Tests—Revised (GORT-R), followed in 1992 by the Gray Oral Reading Tests-3 (GORT-3). Although its use has been extended from the original intent, from an historical perspective the original assessment dates to a period of public education when children were expected to demonstrate learning primarily by rapid and fluent recitation, with careful attention paid to the niceties of pronunciation. More recently the GORT-4 has found favor as a diagnostic (not to be confused with the GORT-D or the GDRT-2) to identify students with reading problems and as a pre- and posttest measure of student progress in reading.

TECHNICAL. The test has been renormed using the latest census data drawn from a sample population of 1,677 persons in 28 states. Alpha coefficients for subgroups range from .90 to .99, an indication that the test exhibits consistent internal reliability by gender, ethnicity, and disability; subtest standard scores and Oral Reading Quotient (ORQ) means are provided for the norm population and eight subgroups. There are tables for comparison of

statistically significant and clinically useful quotient scores for several language and intelligence tests. Subscores for fluency and comprehension on the GORT-R had correlations of .60 and .65 with the Wide Range Achievement Test—Revised (WRAT-R) Reading scores, .39 and .44 with the Woodcock Reading Mastery Tests—Revised (WRMT-R) Word Attack scores, and .39 and .45 with the Wechsler Intelligence Scale for Children—Revised (WISC-R) Comprehension scores.

Readability indices based on the Flesch-Kincaid Readability Formula ranged from 0.0 for Story 1 to 12.0 at approximately Story 9 through 14. Alternate forms reliability coefficients were higher for Rate (.82 to .97), Fluency (.84 to .97), and Accuracy (.81 to .97) than for Comprehension (.71 to .86), with Form A and B test-retest (2-week interval) reliability coefficients ranging from .85 to .95 for the total test. Linear equating procedures revealed no significant differences in difficulty between Form A and B of the test.

The Examiner's manual provides recommendations for entry points and detailed instructions for the establishment of the examinee's basal and ceiling oral reading and reading comprehension level. Subtest norms have a mean of 10 and a standard deviation of 3 to correspond to those of the WISC-III, the Wechsler Adult Intelligence Scale—Third Edition (WAIS-III), and the Detroit Tests of Learning Aptitude—Fourth Edition (DTLA-IV). Scores may be reported as standard scores, percentiles, or age or grade equivalents using the tables provided by the publisher, although the authors follow contemporary recommendations and cautions regarding the reporting of age and grade equivalents (Drummond, 2000; Jaeger, 1990; McLean & Lockwood, 1996).

The GORT-4 stories are drawn from widely used reading vocabulary word lists and from grade level subject area texts, an indication of content validity. The authors do not provide a rationale for the method of determining basal and ceiling cut scores, although directions for computing these are quite detailed with ample examples. However, on every test a certain percentage of students will score higher or lower than their true ability (Dwyer, 1996; Impara & Plake, 2000; Jaeger, 1990; McLean & Lockwood, 1996). The authors provide confidence intervals for determining if pre- and posttest student scores in oral reading and reading comprehension can be considered significant after accounting for measurement error.

COMMENTARY. This is a test that places much responsibility on the examiner to minimize scoring error and to assure standardization in administration, testing environment, and scoring, requiring that scorer(s) consistently and accurately complete six steps for each passage read by the examinee. These include accurate timing in seconds of reading time for each passage; marking deviations from print; calculating Rate, Accuracy, Fluency, and Comprehension scores; observing and recording anecdotal data; and counting and recording miscues. The scoring booklet provides a separate section for "summary of other reading behaviors" but because regional pronunciations are not to be marked as deviations, examiner agreement on this point is important, particularly if more than one person will be scoring tests. The test authors indicate interrater reliability ranging from .94 to .99 but as the raters were publishing company researchers results for less highly trained and experienced scorers might not yield the same correlations (Moore & Young, 1997; Myerberg, 1996; Reckase, 1997). Additionally, it is equally important that students be assessed under standardized testing conditions. The series of tests are widely used in the assessment of students with reading and speech difficulties such as dyslexia, attention deficit disorder, and autism (Filippi, 1996; Landa, 1995; Simmons, 2000).

SUMMARY. The GORT-4 will be used to best advantage by examiners who have formal training in reading assessment, and if it is to be used with these populations of students, by examiners who have formal training in assessment of ESL students and students with reading, behavioral, or speech disabilities. District and state guidelines should be considered if results will be used to make decisions about student placement.

REVIEWER'S REFERENCES

Drummond, R. J. (2000). *Appraisal procedures for counselors and helping professionals* (4th ed.). Upper Saddle River, NJ: Merrill.

Dwyer, C. (1996). Cut scores and testing: Statistics, judgment, truth, and error. *Psychological Assessment, 8*(4), 360–362.

Filippi, A. D. (1996). Differences in fixations and latencies of eye movement patterns in reading disabled versus nondisabled children viewing nonreading material. *Dissertation Abstracts International, 57*(1B), 0722. (University Microfilm No. AAM9613853)

Hickman, J. A. (1989). [Review of the Gray Oral Reading Tests, Revised.] In J. C. Conoley & J. J. Kramer (Eds.), *The tenth mental measurements yearbook* (pp. 334–337). Lincoln, NE: Buros Institute of Mental Measurements.

Impara, J. C., & Plake, B. S. (2000). *A comparison of cut scores using multiple standard setting methods.* Paper presented at the annual meeting of the American Educational Research Association, New Orleans. (ERIC Document Reproduction Service No. ED 445012)

Jaeger, R. M. (1990). *Statistics: A spectator sport* (2nd ed.). Newbury Park, CA: Sage.

King, J. D. (1995). [Review of the Gray Oral Reading Tests, Third Edition.] In J. C. Conoley & J. C. Impara (Eds.), *The twelfth mental measurements yearbook* (pp. 422–423). Lincoln, NE: Buros Institute of Mental Measurements.

Kundert, D. K. (1995). [Review of the Gray Oral Reading Tests, Third Edition.] In J. C. Conoley & J. C. Impara (Eds.), *The twelfth mental measurements yearbook* (pp. 423–425). Lincoln, NE: Buros Institute of Mental Measurements.

Landa, M. C. (1995). The relationship of conflicting stimuli, evaluation apprehension, and anxiety with a task of word recognition by children with Attention-Deficit-Hyperactivity Disorder. *Dissertation Abstracts International, 55*(10B), 4607. (University Microfilms No. AAM9507313)

Marlow, A., & Edwards, R. P. (1998). Test review: The Gray Oral Reading Test, Third Edition (GORT-3). *Journal of Psychoeducational Assessment, 16*, 90–94.

McLean, J. E., & Lockwood, R. E. (1996). *Why we assess students–and how: The competing measures of student performance.* Thousand Oaks, CA: Corwin Press.

Moore, A. D., & Young, S. (1997). *Clarifying the blurred image: Estimating the inter-rater reliability of performance assessments.* Paper presented at the annual meeting of the Northern Rocky Mountain Educational Research Association, Jackson, WY. (ERIC Document Reproduction Service No. ED414319)

Myerberg, N. J. (1996, April). *Inter-rater reliability on various types of assessments scored by school district staff.* Paper presented at the annual meeting of the American Educational Research Association, New York. (ERIC Document Reproduction Service No. ED400291)

Radencich, M. C. (1986). Test review: Gray Oral Reading Tests—Revised Formal Reading Inventory. *Journal of Reading, 30*(2), 136–139.

Reckase, M. D. (1997, March). *Statistical test specifications for performance assessments: Is this an oxymoron?* Paper presented at the annual meeting of the National Council on Measurement in Education, Chicago. (ERIC Document Reproduction Service No. ED410283)

Simmons, J. (2000). *You never asked me to read: Useful assessment of reading and writing problems.* Needham Heights, MA: Allyn & Bacon.

Tierney, R. J. (1989). [Review of the Gray Oral Reading Tests, Revised.] In J. C. Conoley & J. J. Kramer (Eds.), *The tenth mental measurements yearbook* (pp. 337–338). Lincoln, NE: Buros Institute of Mental Measurements.

[112]
Gray Silent Reading Tests.

Purpose: "Designed to assess silent reading comprehension."

Population: Ages 7–25.

Publication Date: 2000.

Acronym: GSRT.

Score: Silent Reading Quotient.

Administration: Group.

Forms, 2: A, B.

Price Data, 2003: $138 per complete kit including 25 profile/response forms, 10 each of reading book Forms A and B; and manual (101 pages); $15 per 25 profile/response forms; $29 per 10 reading books (specify Form A or Form B).

Time: (15–30) minutes.

Comments: Developed to be used as an adjunct to the Gray Oral Reading Tests (111) or independently.

Authors: J. Lee Wiederholt and Ginger Blalock.

Publisher: PRO-ED.

Review of the Gray Silent Reading Tests by HAROLD R. KELLER, *Professor and Chair, Department of Psychological and Social Foundations, University of South Florida, Tampa, FL:*

DESCRIPTION. The Gray Silent Reading Tests (GSRT) consist of two parallel forms, each with 13 paragraphs (stories). Each story is followed by five multiple-choice questions designed to assess individuals' comprehension of unfamiliar reading material. The GSRT may be administered individually or in group format, and the required response format is to fill in bubbles on an answer sheet. Administration and scoring require that basal and ceiling levels be determined. The basal is established when all five comprehension questions for a story are answered correctly. The ceiling is attained when three out of five comprehension questions for a story are answered incorrectly. Suggested ranges of stories to be read in a group administration are provided, based upon the norms. Individual follow-up administration is recommended for the few individuals in a group administration for whom a basal and ceiling are not established. Norms are provided for individuals 7 through 25 years of age, yielding standard scores (Silent Reading Quotients, SRQ, with mean of 100 and standard deviation of 15), age equivalents, grade equivalents, and percentiles.

DEVELOPMENT. The GSRT was designed as an ecologically valid measure of reading, which could be used independently or as an adjunct to the Gray Oral Reading Tests—Fourth Edition (GORT-4; Wiederholt & Bryant, 2001; 111) and the Gray Diagnostic Reading Tests—Second Edition (GDRT-2; Bryant, Wiederholt, & Bryant, 2001). The GORT-4 is a similarly designed oral reading test, and the GDRT-2 was designed to assess a variety of skills related to reading development.

Multiple types of comprehension questions (i.e., literal, inferential, critical, and affective) were generated. Attempts were made to create mostly passage dependent questions. Questions have few words in common with the vocabulary used in the stories, to prevent simple word matching as a response approach. Vocabulary difficulty levels in the questions were maintained consistent with difficulty levels in the stories. The above considerations and the application of statistical criteria for test reliability, item discrimination, and item difficulty were used in the final selection of comprehension questions.

TECHNICAL. Normative data were gathered from 1,400 individuals in 32 states. Geographic areas were proportionately represented relative to national data. Males were slightly underrepresented, but were dramatically underrepresented in the 7–8-year range. Overall ethnicity matches relatively well with national data, but at the 7–8-year range, African American and Hispanic groups are underrepresented. Individuals from rural settings were relatively underrepresented, and people from families with income less than $50,000 were overrepresented.

The authors provide an inaccurate and misleading definition of age and grade equivalents in the interpretation section. Specifically, they state that these scores "allow examiners to report that an individual is reading at a particular age or grade level" (examiner's manual, p. 26). Subsequently, the authors state more appropriately that the scores "indicate the age or grade that corresponds to a raw score made by an individual" (examiner's manual, p. 41). The authors acknowledge that authorities in assessment discourage the use of age and grade equivalents. Later they suggest that test users interpret the scores with caution, but the authors never articulate the problems with misinterpretation and misunderstanding that are promoted by their former definition and use in the manual. Provision of age and grade equivalents for the GSRT is justified by the authors because the scores "are an accepted (and often mandated) means of interpreting reading inventories" (examiner's manual, p. 26). Percentiles are accurately defined, and examiners are urged to become familiar with their advantages and disadvantages. No discussion of those advantages and disadvantages is provided. Neutral descriptors for the interpretation of standard score ranges are provided, a laudable improvement over tests that persist in using terms such as borderline defective. The authors also provided a reasonable discussion of statistical significance and severe discrepancies, topics of critical importance when a test such as the GSRT is used in categorical decision making. More emphasis might have been placed on this, given the central role of reading measures in the classification of learning disabilities. Finally, the authors provide a good discussion of standard errors of measurement and data for informed users of the GSRT.

Internal consistency reliability estimates, via coefficient alpha, are .93 and above for each age group, and .97/.98 for gender, ethnicity, and disability groups. Concurrent alternative forms reliabilities were .85 and above, except for ages 11–13 which ranged from .79–.81. Test-retest reliabilities (2-week administration interval), with a sample of 42 children, were .86 and .93 for Forms A and B, respectively, and .83 across alternate forms. Interscorer reliabilities were .97 and .98 for Forms A and B, respectively.

Readability formulas were applied to the GSRT, item discrimination analyses were conducted, and differential item functioning analyses were conducted with gender and ethnicity groups, all sets of analyses providing adequate data for content and item selection. Criterion-related validity was examined in a series of studies that correlated the GSRT alternate forms with various other reading inventories, with all correlations in the acceptable .60s and .70s range. Consistent with the developmental progression of reading skills, the mean scores of the normative sample show a typical age progression. Typical cross-group patterns of scores were obtained, with lower scores for children with disabilities (learning disability, serious emotional disturbance, attention deficit hyperactivity disorder, and poor readers), as identified by participating districts, and higher scores for children identified as gifted and talented.

COMMENTARY. Silent reading is the typical approach to reading for most individuals, and the GSRT appears to assess individuals' silent reading comprehension in a manner that allows normative comparisons. Individuals performing poorly on this measure would require considerably more assessment in order to understand their reading difficulties. The authors have described well how the GSRT might be used within a more comprehensive evaluation of individual reading problems.

SUMMARY. The GSRT appears to be a psychometrically sound measure of silent reading comprehension. It provides one useful piece of information to understanding an individual's reading difficulties. The authors might have omitted the age and grade equivalent scores because of problems with misunderstanding and misinterpretations. At the very minimum, they might have articulated these problems. Elaborated discussion of advantages and disadvantages with the use of percentiles might have been provided as well. Finally, more information might have been supplied on the use and misuse of the GSRT scores in categorical decision making about disabilities.

REVIEWER'S REFERENCES

Bryant, B. R., Wiederholt, J. L., & Bryant, D. (2001). Gray Diagnostic Reading Tests—Second Edition. Austin, TX: PRO-ED.
Wiederholt, J. L., & Bryant, B. R. (2001). Gray Oral Reading Tests—Fourth Edition. Austin, TX: PRO-ED.

Review of the Gray Silent Reading Tests by DARRELL L. SABERS, Professor of Educational Psychology, University of Arizona, Tucson, AZ:

DESCRIPTION. The Gray Silent Reading Tests (GSRT) is a norm-referenced measure of silent reading comprehension intended for individuals aged 7 through 25. The GSRT has two alternate forms each containing 13 separate paragraphs or stories. Each story is followed by five 4-option multiple-choice comprehension items. Basal and ceiling rules are used in scoring, so group administration may be difficult. The raw scores (number of items correct) on each form can be converted to age or grade equivalents, percentile rank, or standard score. The standard score is called a Silent Reading Quotient (SRQ) although the authors acknowledge that the score is not really a quotient.

DEVELOPMENT. The GSRT is one of three tests in a series. The other two tests in the series are the Gray Oral Reading Tests, Fourth Edition (GORT-4; 111) and the Gray Diagnostic Reading Tests—Second Edition. The standardization of the GSRT appears to be separate from the other two tests in the series, and the tests are intended to be used independently or as a battery. The GSRT is intended to measure "the fluent recognition of words and a clear grasp of the meanings implied by the symbols used" (manual, p. 4).

The decision to use the story format for assessing comprehension was based on a desire to match the format used for the Gray Oral Reading Tests. Also, this type of format is commonly used in reading tests and in classroom assessment, and continuous text is common for adult reading. Literal, inferential, critical, and affective questions were drafted for the norming study of the GSRT, and the "best" five of seven items for each story were selected for the published test. More information on development is included in the discussion of validity below.

TECHNICAL. The GSRT was normed on a sample of 1,400 individuals from 32 states, tested between 1996 and 1998. Characteristics of the sample are described and shown to be fairly comparable to the U.S. Census data as reported in 1997. Given that the sample of 1,400 is distributed across 12 age levels, it would not be appropriate to suggest that there should be separate norms for different gender or ethnic groups.

Reliability is best represented for this test by alternate forms coefficients. "Corrected" coefficients reported for the 12 age intervals range from .79 through .89. However, it is not clear why these coefficients were corrected for restricted range (it is appropriate to report these reliability values by age level; this should not be considered as a restricted range) and what the obtained coefficients were prior to correction. Coefficient alphas in the .90s are reported for the separate age groups, but these are likely to be inflated due to the use of basal and ceiling rules in test administration. Stability estimates (test-retest was approximately 2 weeks) were obtained on a sample of 42 examinees ranging in age from 7 through 18 years. The table that reports test-retest and alternate forms reliability presents inflated coefficients rather than obtained data. The desired information for the user would be coefficients that reflect the various sources of error arising when the test scores are used, but what is presented is information separating the error components to produce spurious results.

Validity information includes use of readability formulas and raw scores on the items associated with the passages. The professional writer who wrote the stories "controlled for density of words, length of words and sentences, complexity of sentence structure, structure of sentences, logical connections between sentences and clauses, and coherence of topics" (manual, p. 61). Vocabulary was controlled by use of extensive word lists. Care was taken to ensure that the vocabulary in the items was not more difficult than that used in the stories. Relevant content-related evidence of validity is absent. Although four types of items—literal, inferential, critical, and affective—were originally developed for the tryouts, there is no assurance that all four types remain in the test after standardization. The number of items of each type (perhaps by story) should be reported.

Criterion-related information is presented by reporting the results of two studies, one with 91 examinees ranging in age from 7 to 15 and the other with 66 examinees ranging from age 14 to 17. The tests used in the comparisons were the Standardized Reading Inventory—Second Edition and the Gray Oral Reading Tests, Third Edition. The resulting coefficients, corrected for restricted range when appropriate, ranged from .63 to .72. It is not clear why either of the ranges included in these studies should be considered "restricted" when the information of most use to the potential test user would be based on a give age level.

Age differentiation is shown by reporting average scores (with standard deviations) across the 12 age intervals. Both forms show good age

"growth," especially evident at the early ages. Minor group differences are reported between gender and ethnic groups, supporting the belief that the test is not biased. Greater average differences are found with categories of examinees reported to have learning disabilities, serious emotional disturbance, or ADHD, and between poor readers and students identified as gifted and talented. The data for both forms provide evidence of good differentiation.

COMMENTARY. Four specific purposes are identified: "(a) to identify individuals whose scores are significantly below those of their peers and who might need additional assessment and intervention designed to improve reading comprehension, (b) to determine areas of relative strength and weakness across reading comprehension abilities, (c) to document overall progress in reading development as a consequence of intervention programs, and (d) to serve as a measure for research efforts designed to investigate reading comprehension" (manual, p. 6). It seems appropriate to comment on how each purpose is supported by the data in the manual.

Purpose "a" is likely the most important of the above uses, and is the one best supported by the data. The test is well developed, and the description of content and development should satisfy many potential users. Potential concerns are described later.

Purpose "b" requires a battery of tests, and the other two tests in the series are suggested as necessary for this purpose. Several pages of the manual are devoted to the significance of differences between the GSRT and measures of reading, language, and intelligence. No evidence is given that any of these tests have comparable norms to the GSRT; thus, the evidence that these difference scores have meaning is missing.

Purposes "c" and "d" may be supported after data are gathered from users of the test. If the test is judged satisfactory for purpose "a," then these additional uses are a natural extension. Even if the GSRT is judged to be too unreliable for purposes "a" and "b" for scores on individual students, reliability is less of an issue for purpose "d" and perhaps for purpose "c" where more reliable averages for groups of students might be used.

The major problem with the standardization procedure is that there was not a joint effort to norm both the GSRT and the GORT-4 at the same time. A co-norming would enhance the validity of difference scores that could be used to calculate discrepancies between oral and silent reading performance. A comparability study is needed to support discrepancy analysis if the scores on the two tests are to be compared for profile analysis.

It should be mentioned that the reporting of inflated reliability information is not unique to the GSRT; rather, spurious coefficients are often associated with tests that use basals and ceilings in calculating raw scores, and also are common for tests intended to be used for a wide range of ages.

The test is easy to administer, although the correct responses might have been made more accessible to the examiner who must refer to a table in the manual for the keyed responses. It is not difficult for the examiner to know the answers (or to learn and remember them), but to watch the examinee as the responses are marked to enforce the ceiling rule (only two correct of the five) might require some prior thought to a seating arrangement.

The manual includes a good description of the efforts to ensure that the items are passage dependent; that is, the examinee must read the passage to answer the items correctly. However, the data to support the contention that this dependency was checked are not provided. There are statements that "these questions are all text related in that they can only be answered by reading the text" (manual, p. 62) and "graduate students were given the questions and asked to answer them without reading the stories. Results indicated random guessing" (manual, p. 62). Results obtained by this reviewer were different than that, and on several sets it appears relatively easy to get three items correct (that is enough to pass the ceiling requirement and continued the testing) without reading the passage. The authors could have reported the data to support the contention that their results approach random responses.

No data on individual items are included. This is a major shortcoming, especially when the section on item bias presents a graph of unrelated material to demonstrate the plot of item Delta scores rather than actual data from the GSRT. This reviewer found a suspect item in the test, but was not able to examine any data about the item because the item Delta scores were not reported for the GSRT. Why the actual data are not shown is not explained in the manual. Certainly, there is limited support for the statement that "examiners

can use the GSRT with confidence, especially when assessing individuals for whom most other tests might be biased" (manual, p. 74).

SUMMARY. The GSRT is an attractive package that should appeal to many potential users. The directions for administration and scoring are clear, and the procedures for converting raw scores to derived scores are simple. Cautions against using grade and age equivalent scores are provided, as are recommendations to use additional information in making decisions about students.

If the purpose of the test user is to find a measure that allows comparison of silent reading and oral reading, the GSRT is likely to be satisfactory even with the limitations noted above. The many strengths and potential strengths of the test may be overlooked due to the many shortcomings of the reporting in the manual, and a revised manual with more complete and accurate reporting is desired. When that manual is produced, perhaps the GSRT may be highly recommended.

[113]

Group Reading Assessment and Diagnostic Evaluation.

Purpose: "A diagnostic tool to see what pre-reading or reading skills individuals have and what skills they need to be taught."

Population: Grades Pre-K and higher.

Publication Date: 2001.

Acronym: GRADE.

Administration: Individual or group.

Levels, 11: P (pre-kindergarten and kindergarten), K (kindergarten and first grade), 1 (kindergarten through second grade), 2, 3, 4, 5, 6, M (middle school, grades 5–9), H (high school, grades 9–12), A (grades 11 to postsecondary).

Forms, 2: Form A, Form B.

Price Data, 2002: $899.95 per Elementary Resource Specialist set (Levels P–6) including 10 each of Form A and Form B student booklets per Elementary Level, 1 teacher's administration manual—Form A and B—per Elementary Level (22–81 pages), 1 scoring and interpretative manual per elementary level (59–90 pages), 1 set of hand-scoring templates, and 20 answer sheets for each of Levels 4, 5, and 6; $429.95 per Secondary Resource Specialist set (Levels M—A) including 10 each of Form A and Form B student booklets per Secondary Level, 1 teacher's administration manual per Secondary Level (22–24 pages each), 1 scoring and interpretative manual per Secondary Level (72–90 pages), 1 set of hand-scoring templates, and 20 answer sheets per secondary level; $209.95 per Levels P or K Class-

room Set with Forms A and B including 30 each of Form A and For B student booklets, 1 teacher's administration manual (Forms A and B), and 1 scoring and interpretative manual; $189.95 per Levels 1, 2, or 3 Classroom Set with Forms A and B including 30 each of Form A and Form B student booklets, 1 teacher's administration manual, and 2 scoring and interpretative manual; $279.95 per Levels 4, 5, 6, M, H, or A Classroom Set with Forms A and B including 30 each of Form A and Form B student booklets, 1 teacher's administration manual, 1 scoring and interpretative manual, 1 set of hand-scoring templates, and 60 answer sheets; $122.95 per Levels P, K, 1, 2, or 3 Classroom Set with Form A including 30 of Form A student booklets, 2 teacher's administration manual, and 1 scoring and interpretative manual; $169.95 per Levels 4, 5, 6, M, H, or A Classroom Set with Form A including 30 of Form A student booklets, 1 teacher's administration manual, 1 scoring and interpretative manual, 2 set of hand-scoring templates, and 30 answer sheets; $26.95 per 10 student booklets (all levels); $9.95 per 10 answer sheets (Levels 4–A); $39.95 per Forms a and B hand-scoring templates (each of Levels 4–A); $11.95 per teacher's administration manual (each of Levels P or K); $9.95 per teacher's administration manual (each of Levels 1–A); $39.95 per scoring and interpretative manual (each of Levels P–A); $49.95 per technical manual (Levels P–A); $99.95 per GRADE Resource Library (each of Levels P–A); $299.95 per GRADE Scoring and Reporting Software (single-user version); $9,995 per GRADE Scoring and Reporting Software (network version).
Time: (45–90) minutes.
Comments: May be hand scored or computer scored; scoring system requirements: OS 7.0 or later, 16 MB RAM, 68030 CPU or higher (Macintosh); Microsoft Windows, Version 3.1 or better, 6 MB RAM (Windows), 4 MB hard drive space; computer-generated report options include group and individual score summaries, diagnostic analyses for each subtest, reports to parents and students; networked version of the GRADE scoring software available; GRADE Resource Library (GRL) software on CD-ROM contains teaching activities and reproducible worksheets.
Author: Kathleen T. Williams.
Publisher: American Guidance Service, Inc.
   a) LEVEL P.
   Scores, 8: Picture Matching, Picture Differences, Verbal Concepts, Picture Categories, Sound Matching, Rhyming, Listening Comprehension, Total Score.
   b) LEVEL K.
   Scores, 9: Sound Matching, Rhyming, Print Awareness, Letter Recognition, Same and Different Words, Phoneme-Grapheme Correspondence, Word Reading, Listening Comprehension, Total Score.

   c) LEVEL 1, 2.
   Scores, 6: Word Reading, Word Meaning, Sentence Comprehension, Passage Comprehension, Listening Comprehension, Total Score.
   d) LEVEL 3.
   Scores, 6: Word Reading, Vocabulary, Sentence Comprehension, Passage Comprehension, Listening Comprehension, Total Score.
   e) LEVEL 4–A.
   Scores, 5: Vocabulary, Sentence Comprehension, Passage Comprehension, Listening Comprehension, Total Score.

Review of the Group Reading Assessment and Diagnostic Evaluation by MARK H. FUGATE, Associate Professor, Division of School Psychology, Alfred University, Alfred, NY:

DESCRIPTION. The Group Reading Assessment and Diagnostic Evaluation (GRADE) is a series of group and individually administered emergent literacy and reading tests designed to assess the prereading and reading skills for prekindergarten through young adult students. The GRADE appears to be a well-designed and useful set of assessment measures for assessing prereading and reading skills, and for monitoring reading progress as a student passes from one grade to another in school.

The GRADE is organized into 11 levels of tasks or subtests that are designed to assess reading skill development from prekindergarten through early college. Each subtest is designed to measure skills that are developmentally appropriate for students at that level. Each level contains two equivalent forms to facilitate progress monitoring from fall to spring of each academic year. In addition, a Growth Scale Value (GSV) score is provided to track an individual student's progress across his or her years in school. Each individual GRADE level is designed to assess the reading skills of low-, middle-, and high-performing students at the recommended grade in school. However, guidelines for out-of-level assessment are provided if an individual student is believed to possess reading skills that are remarkably higher or lower than what is typical of students at his or her grade level in school.

Administration, levels, and subtests. The number of subtests varies from a maximum of eight for the kindergarten level (Level K) to a minimum of four subtests in the more advanced levels (Levels 4 through A). The GRADE contains a separate level for each year of school from prekindergarten through sixth grade. Beyond Level 6 there are three additional Levels: (a) Level M for middle school students; (b) Level H for high school students; and (c) Level A for advanced high school and postsecondary students. Directions for administration of the GRADE are easy to follow and are found in the teacher's administration manual for each level. The GRADE is not a timed test and estimates of administration time range from 45 to 90 minutes depending on the level.

The subtests in Level P (prekindergarten) include: (a) tests of phonological awareness (Rhyming and Sound Matching); (b) tests of visual skills (Picture Matching and Picture Differences); (c) a test of basic word meanings (Verbal Concepts); (d) the ability to find a common concept among a group of pictures (Picture Categories); and (e) the ability to understand simple words and phrases (Listening Comprehension). At this level the test is as much a test of cognitive skills more indirectly related to reading development as well as a more direct measure of emergent literacy. The kindergarten level (Level K) is more clearly a measure of emergent literacy. Level K continues with tests of phonological awareness (Sound Matching, Rhyming) and Listening Comprehension. In addition, Level K assesses transitional skills (Print Awareness, Letter Recognition) and early reading skills (Same and Different Words, Phoneme-Grapheme Correspondence, Word Reading). Beginning with Level 1, the GRADE is a test of developing reading skills. All of the levels from 1 through A contain the core subtests of Sentence Comprehension, Passage Comprehension, and Listening Comprehension. Other subtests that are found in some levels include: Word Meaning (Levels 1 and 2); Word Reading (Levels 1, 2, and 3); and Vocabulary (Levels 3 through A).

Scoring and interpretation. Directions for scoring and interpretation can be found in the teacher's scoring and interpretative manual for each level. Scoring for Levels P through 3 will be more time-consuming because the students write their responses in the test booklet. For Levels 4 through A, students fill in a circle on a response sheet. There is a page with a scoring key in the manual; however, hand scoring would be easier if an overlay scoring template was provided. In addition to hand scoring, software is also available for computer scoring of response sheets and interpretation of results.

The GRADE provides two types of scores for the interpretation of test results. Standard scores, percentile ranks, normal curve equivalents (NCE), stanines, and grade equivalent scores are provided for individual subtests, composite scores, and the total test score. In addition to these scores, which are typical of norm-referenced tests (NRT), the GRADE provides a Growth Scale Value (GSV) score. The GSV score is available for the total test scores only, and is an equal interval scale that provides the opportunity to track individual student progress from one year to the next. GSV scores were developed from data obtained in the development and standardization process using a Rasch model of analysis. Given the availability of a score for measuring the individual growth of a student from year to year, as opposed to the in-group comparisons of typical NRT scores, there are a variety of administrative and research uses for the GSV score.

DEVELOPMENT AND TECHNICAL. Information about the structure, reliability, and validity of scores from the GRADE is reported in the technical manual. Development and standardization of the GRADE occurred in two stages. In the tryout phase, four forms of the GRADE were administered to more than 20,000 students in a 4-month period. Data from this sample were used to complete item analysis and determine the final items for each level and form of the GRADE. Standardization of the GRADE was completed in 2000 and included 16,408 students in the spring and 17,024 students in the fall. The tryout and standardization samples include students from 43 states and represent students from urban, suburban, and rural communities. Demographic data presented in the technical manual are extensive and suggest that a nationally representative sample was obtained.

The reliability evidence for the GRADE appears to be adequate. An extensive list of internal consistency (alpha) and split half reliability data is presented. Reliability estimates for the total test score are very strong across all levels of the tests. All of the reliability coefficients for the total test score are .90 or greater with the exception of one alpha, which was .89 (Level K, Form A, spring, given to first grade students). Composite scores demonstrate moderate to strong reliability with coefficients ranging from .50 to .96. Most of the composite scores are quite acceptable, with the lowest scores occurring for Passage Comprehension in late kindergarten and first grade. The reliability coefficients reported for individual subtests are similar to those reported for the composite scores. Overall, as evaluated by internal consistency and split-half reliability, the total test scores are most reliable and coefficients obtained for the higher levels of the test are stronger than those at the lower levels. Older students' performance appears to be measured somewhat more consistently than the performance of younger students.

Reliability was also evaluated by comparing scores on the alternate forms of the GRADE (Forms A and B) and by evaluating the equivalency of both forms. Coefficients for alternate forms reliability range from .81 to .94, and a comparison of the means and standard deviations of both forms supports the equivalence of the forms. Finally, test-retest reliability was measured with a group of 816 students (73.7% Form A; 26.3% Form B). Test-retest reliability coefficients ranged from .77 to .98 with most coefficients (81%) exceeding .87 (administration intervals varied from 3.5 days to 42 days).

A detailed description of the content validity evidence is presented and the GRADE would appear to have well-developed content. However, an important measure of any test's validity is the extent to which that test matches the curriculum of the classroom. Criterion-related concurrent validity is demonstrated by measuring the relation between the GRADE and several group and individually administered reading tests. Correlation coefficients range from .69 to .90 suggesting that the GRADE is measuring similar skills to those of other tests of reading ability. Students involved in these concurrent validity studies ranged in grade from first to eighth. There are no concurrent validity data presented for Levels P, K, H, and A; as a result, the concurrent validity of these levels is unknown. The discriminant validity evidence of the GRADE is demonstrated in two studies with dyslexic and learning disabled (reading) students. In both of these studies the dyslexic and learning disabled students scored significantly lower on the GRADE than students in a matched control group.

COMMENTARY AND SUMMARY. Overall, the GRADE appears to be a very useful test of reading ability. The test can be group or individually administered, and can be used with students from prekindergarten through post-high school. The GRADE is well constructed and reflective of a wide variety of emergent literacy and reading skills. Scoring and interpretation of test scores is generally uncomplicated, although at the early levels (P through 3) scoring requires that the teacher work through the entire response booklet. In addition to the more typical normative comparison scores, the GRADE provides a Growth Scale Value (GSV) score, which is useful for long-term progress monitoring with individual students. However, the instructional relevance of this progress monitoring is quite limited.

Although the GRADE is an appropriate tool for monitoring progress toward broad reading curricular objectives, the fall and spring assessment cycle is not useful for the short-term repeated measurement necessary for monitoring student progress through the instructional curriculum of the classroom. Unfortunately, the GRADE appears to be less relevant for the detailed curriculum-based assessment required to determine the gap between an individual child's reading performance and specific curricular expectation of the classroom. The knowledge gained from curriculum-based, or criterion-referenced, forms of assessment is critical for developing effective academic intervention. As such, the instructional relevance of the GRADE is also limited. In this era of state-mandated "high stakes tests," the GRADE might be useful as a broad-based mechanism for monitoring student progress toward curricular objectives, and monitoring the relative effectiveness of classwide instructional adaptations across the course of a school year. It is important to note that these speculations are only educated guesses. There is no research reported in the various manuals provided with the GRADE regarding the validity of the GRADE for making instructional decisions. Given the recent movement toward evidence-based educational practice, this would be important research to conduct.

The technical qualities of the GRADE appear to be quite good. The standardization sample seems to be representative and more than adequate in size. The reliability estimates for the total test scores, as reported in the technical manual, are more than adequate for educational decision making. Although the reliability estimates of individual subtests and composite scores are generally quite good, there is some variability. It is important to review the reliability tables provided to determine the relative value of a specific subtest score at a specific level. The reported concurrent validity evidence of the GRADE is generally adequate; however, no data are presented for the lowest and highest levels. It is important that additional research be conducted to replicate the results of the research presented in the technical manual and to extend this research into new areas.

Review of the Group Reading Assessment and Diagnostic Evaluation by BETSY B. WATERMAN, Professor, Counseling and Psychological Services Department, State University of New York at Oswego, Oswego, NY:

DESCRIPTION. The Group Reading Assessment and diagnostic Evaluation (GRADE) is a group or individually administered reading measure for which the primary purposes are to determine the prereading and reading skills that students have already acquired, identify those skills that need to be taught, and monitor student progress. The GRADE includes two forms (i.e., A and B) at 11 possible levels (i.e., Pre-K; K; 1; 2; 3; 4; 5; 6; Middle School, M; High School, H; Adult, A). Multiple subtests/skills that are developmentally appropriate to a given grade/age and represent a broad range of difficulty are included at each level, including a measure of Listening Comprehension.

The GRADE is not timed and is reported to take approximately 60 to 90 minutes to administer. Each subtest includes practice items. Items of lesser and greater difficulty are mixed throughout each subtest with easier questions at the beginning and the end to help students feel greater success. Subtest clusters should be given in different sessions that may be administered over several days or all on the same day. Because this is a diagnostic test, students are not encouraged to randomly guess on an item and all items must be administered.

The GRADE can be hand or computer scored. Raw scores for individual subtests are converted to stanines by entering the appropriate norm table. Norms for both spring and fall testing are included for each level. Percentile ranks, grade equivalents, standard scores (Mean = 100; *SD* = 15), and normal curve equivalents (NCE) can be determined for Composite and Total Test raw scores. NCEs are included such that a student's growth can be measured across different GRADE levels. A diagnostic analysis can be performed in

which a child's item-by-item performance can be compared to a national sample or to peers in his or her class. Error patterns can also be determined for the individual child (i.e., specific skill strengths and weaknesses). *P*-values (the probability that a child will answer that particular item correctly) are provided for comparisons with the national sample and instructions are included for developing *p*-values for a specific classroom. A brief discussion of the hypotheses and instructional ideas that may be drawn from an individual student profile are included in the teacher's scoring and interpretive manual.

DEVELOPMENT. A detailed discussion of the test's development was included in the technical manual. The testing content was carefully developed to follow a theoretically sound sequence of skills, from prereading to higher reading skills. Five primary sequential elements were considered as the author identified subareas of the reading process-visual and conceptual knowledge, reading readiness skills, recognition and understanding of words in print, comprehension of sentences and passages, and oral language development. Research was cited that supported the author's choice of item selection and testing format, and interpretive information. The initial version of the GRADE was administered to 800 preschool students and 1600 students. The "tryout" version included 17 total subtests, over 2,500 test items, and four different forms. Items were statistically examined for difficulty, discrimination, and "goodness-of-fit." Items that were confusing, did not discriminate, were a poor fit, or were biased were deleted from the pool. Items were also carefully screened for evidence of gender or cultural bias using both qualitative and quantitative evaluations (differential item functioning analyses and the Rasch scaling method). Over 700 teachers gave input about administration procedures and content of the items. Changes in some of the names used in the text (to capture a broader ethnic mixture), gender references, and artwork were made as an outcome of the preliminary testing. A subtest at the prereading level was also eliminated following trial testing. The final version of the test included 16 subtests and 2,290 items that were assigned to levels and divided into two forms.

TECHNICAL. Standardization of the instrument was conducted in the spring and fall of 2000. The fall testing included students from postsecondary programs that were not a part of the spring testing. The standardization sample included 16,408 students and 17,024 students respectively in spring and fall testing at a total of 134 sites across the U.S. Groups were approximately equal in terms of gender representation and included racial and ethnic groups that closely matched the national population figures. Special education students were also included in the sample if they were mainstreamed into regular classes for a part of the day.

High internal consistency reliability estimates (.89 to .99) were reported. Alternative form reliability ($N = 696$) ranged from .81 to .94. Test-retest reliability (administration interval from 35 to 42 days) ($N = 816$) was reported as ranging from .77 to .98. Equivalency between Forms A and B was reported as adequate (no group differences exceeded that of random sampling error).

Content validity was documented through careful, well-researched test development. Corrected coefficients of Total Reading scores on the Iowa Test of Basic Skills and GRADE suggested concurrent validities that ranged between .69 and .83 ($N = 185$) for Levels 4, 5, and M. Corrected coefficients of Total Reading scores on the California Achievement Test and GRADE ranged from .82 to .87 ($N = 119$) for Levels 1 and 2, and from .86 to .90 using the Gates-MacGinitie Reading Tests ($N = 313$) for Levels 1, 2, 3, 6, and M. Coefficients of Total Reading Scores for the GRADE and the Peabody Individual Achievement Test—Revised ($N = 30$) were reported as .80 (concurrent validity) with a coefficient of .47 reported for the GRADE Comprehension Composite and the PIAT-R General Information subtest (divergent validity). Predictive validity for Levels 2, 4, and 6, was examined by correlating scores earned on the GRADE during fall testing with standard scores earned by these students on the TerraNova, which was administered in the spring ($N = 232$) with coefficients ranging from .76 to .86.

Construct validity was evaluated by correlating scores among subtests of the Iowa Test of Basic Skills and GRADE for a sample of seventh and eighth grade students. Highest correlations were reported on Total Reading scores (.83, .76) whereas the lowest correlations were reported on Math Computation scores on Level M (.58, .55) Growth curves were also presented suggesting that reading performance changes by grade placement and level of experience with reading stimuli. Finally, a comparison of two groups of students who possess a disability (Dyslexia and those with a Learning Disability in Reading) with a control group of students suggested statistically significant differences between those determined to have reading disorders and those who did not ($p < .001$ in most cases).

COMMENTARY. The author of the GRADE has done a laudable job creating a comprehensive reading test that is diagnostic in nature, can track students' reading performances over time, covers a wide spectrum of ages and abilities, has been carefully standardized, and can be administered individually, to small groups, or to whole classes. The inclusion of training items, alternative forms, a broad coverage of reading subskill areas, a listening comprehension subtest, and procedures for item-by-item analyses are all strengths of this assessment. A few small concerns, however, do exist.

First, the hand-scoring method appears quite laborious and would be expected to take considerable teacher time to complete. From the material available for review, it was not possible to see how the computer-scoring version might expedite this process, but the purchaser may want to consider this.

Second, the use of this instrument as a group reading assessment measure appears appropriate for levels 1 to A, but does not appear appropriate for P and K levels without considerable one-on-one help available to students. Although the stimuli/tasks are well matched to these young children, their familiarity with the procedures associated with assessment is very limited. In fact, trial testing by this reviewer with a single, typically developing preschooler suggested that considerable support, particularly early in the assessment process, was necessary for the youngster to follow directions and respond consistently to the "workbook" format. A caution was made by the author about the difficulty using a group administration format with children of this age, but, perhaps, should be more strongly stated.

Third, although the number of items included within individual subtests is generally adequate, the attempt to sample as many subskills as possible (e.g., Print Awareness, Letter Recognition, Same and Different Words) necessitates the restriction in the number of items that may be included in any one area. Information about a child's ability to perform a specific subskill gained from this test, therefore, must be viewed with some caution with greater confidence placed on component rather than subtest scores.

Finally, although the author generally did a good job of examining the reliability and validity of scores from the instrument, very little information about reliability and validity was available for the youngest levels (i.e., P and K). This suggests that information obtained for children at these levels may not share the same psychometric soundness as that at higher levels.

SUMMARY. Overall, the GRADE appears to be a theoretically and psychometrically sound, group or individually administered, reading instrument. It appears to be predicated on sound reading theory with appropriate developmental sequences of skills surveyed at each of the levels. The ability to track students' performance across grades, compare their achievement with both national and local peers, and identify specific reading skill strengths and weakness make this a valuable test. It appears, in fact, to be one of the few group-administered reading measures that offers the kind of specific diagnostic information that can frequently be achieved only through an individually administered reading test. Although some concerns at the youngest ages exist relating to reliability and validity and the appropriateness of group testing with the very young, overall, the GRADE clearly has something to offer educators as a group-administered measure of reading abilities.

[114]

Hanes Sales Selection Inventory [Revised Edition—2001].

Purpose: Designed "to help select potentially successful insurance, printing and closely allied salesmen."
Population: Applicants for sales positions.
Publication Date: 2001.
Scores: Part II, Part III, Drive Score.
Administration: Group.
Price Data: Price data available from publisher.
Time: (30) minutes.
Author: Bernard Hanes.
Publisher: Psychometric Affiliates.

Review of the Hanes Sales Selection Inventory [Revised Edition—2001] by THEODORE L. HAYES, Personnel Research Psychologist, U.S. Immigration & Naturalization Service, Washington, DC:

DESCRIPTION. The Hanes Sales Selection Inventory [Revised Edition—2001] is a 37-item paper/pencil assessment purporting to differentiate between "successful salesmen and general applicants" (manual, p. 1) based on four subtest parts. The first part contains biodata and weighted application blank-type items. The second part contains a combination of vocabulary and general reasoning items. The third and fourth parts, which both contain personality-oriented items, are distinguished by the publisher conceptually but not by item wording or scoring key. The Inventory may be administered untimed, either individually or in a group setting, with scoring performed by a trained clerk. The publisher states that the results are "not fool proof and should only be considered as an aid having statistical backing in the selection of successful salesmen" (manual, p. 1).

DEVELOPMENT. The publisher states that the Inventory was developed to select "successful insurance, printing, and closely allied salesmen from the general run of applicants for such positions" (manual, p. 1). Apparently, the current edition of the inventory is based upon "a two-year follow-up of successful salesmen" (manual, p. 1). Elsewhere, the publisher mentions normative values for steel salesmen, though it is not clear how that sample figured into the development of the Inventory; nor is it made clear how steel sales, insurance sales, and printing sales are similar other than being sales-oriented jobs. No validity transportation studies or validity generalization analyses are presented to support the publisher's contention that this Inventory has been able to identify "successful salesmen" across these industries. The publisher does not provide more qualitative or psychometric detail, published/unpublished references, etc. related to test development.

TECHNICAL. No psychometric data (e.g., reliability, validity, normative data) are provided for the biodata section; the publisher states that it should be considered "in the case of border-line applicants" (manual, p. 3). However, this section contains questions concerning the applicant's health status and age. These questions should be well-known to any test publisher as being clearly inappropriate from the perspectives of both professional practice and civil rights laws. Other biodata questions (number of children, spouse's work status) may distress some applicants. The Inventory's manual and the items in this section seem to have been written with the assumption that the applicant is male.

Part 2 of the Inventory consists of 18 items. Two of these are arithmetic reasoning items, 3 items are verbal analogies, and 13 items are vocabulary/synonyms. The reported split-half reliability for this entire section is .84. Correct responses are weighted 1, 2, or 3 points toward a total score; no rationale is offered for this scoring system. The publisher states that the total score from Part 2 correlated .39, using a Spearman's rho correlation, with "total PMA intelligence" in a group of 30 college graduates who were applying for sales jobs with a steel company. Aside from the obvious cavils one could have about sample size and composition, this reported correlation is curiously low—when corrected generously, the construct-level validity of scores from Part 2 with the external intelligence measure tops out around .46. A review of items in Part 2 indicates no obvious content validation strategy other than an attempt to amass an informal measure of general mental ability. The publisher notes that "men scoring about the 95th percentile on part two tend to talk above the heads of their prospects" (manual, p. 3).

Part 3 is supposed to capture the applicant's overall sales personality whereas Part 4 (the "Drive Score") is an assessment of sales motivation. Both parts are scored using a yes (agree)/no (disagree) format where the "yes" responses may receive between −4 and +3 points (though not zero points; no rationale is offered). It seems that the 50th percentile total score for Part 3 is a negative point total. The publisher does not discuss the implications of amassing a negative personality score. The reported split-half reliability for Part 3 is .89, with no estimate provided for Part 4. Part 4 is supposedly separate from Part 3, but the Inventory's format and scoring guidelines considerably obfuscate the role and use of Part 4.

The publisher states that the applicant must "qualify on EACH PART [i.e., Parts 2 and 3] in order to merit consideration" (manual, p. 3). No rationale is provided for this assertion. The publisher presents two separate contingency tables based on undescribed, independent samples. These tables purport to show that those passing each part are more likely to be "successful salesmen" versus "general applicants." However, the contingency tables do not provide adequate information about sample sizes for each group to determine any correlations between the test parts and even this vague criterion. Finally, no information is provided regarding demographic analyses, cutoff scores, feedback to applicants or management, or any further psychometrics of this Inventory.

COMMENTARY. This Inventory does not seem to be based on any particular sales or personality model. It is sparsely documented, and the available documentation is unprofessional. The Inventory's item content might be unable to withstand legal review.

SUMMARY. Small businesses cannot typically provide the revenue stream that a consulting company needs to make a human resources selection project profitable. The result is what one may refer to as a sort of Gresham's Law of Testing: Better tests that might have been developed by a consulting company are ruled out, which leaves the small business owner to think that tests such as the Hanes Sales Selection Inventory [Revised Edition—2001] are the only recourse for "scientific"/objective selection. However, an HR generalist from a small company would be better served by either buying an off-the-shelf test from a reputable professional test publisher (such as The Psychological Corporation, Psychological Assessment Resources, etc.), or by working with a professor from a local business school who is knowledgeable about selection, or by developing a structured interview using almost any reference on interviewing available at a local book store (e.g., Doverspike & Tuel, 2000). There is no obvious reason to recommend the Hanes Sales Selection Inventory as a viable substitute for these other approaches.

REVIEWER'S REFERENCE

Doverspike, D., & Tuel, R. C. (2000). *The difficult hire: Seven recruitment and selection principles for hard to fill positions.* Manassas Park, VA: Impact Publications.

[115]

HCR-20: Assessing Risk for Violence.

Purpose: Designed as "a broad-band violence risk assessment instrument with potential applicability to a variety of settings."

Population: Adults (Psychiatric and Correctional Settings).

Publication Date: 1997.

Scores, 4: Final Risk Judgment, Historical Items, Clinical Items, Rick Management Items.

Administration: Individual.

Price Data: Available from publisher.

Time: Administration time not reported.

Comments: "Research instrument."

Authors: Christopher D. Webster, Kevin S. Douglas, Derek Eaves, and Stephen D. Hart.

Publisher: Mental Health, Law, and Policy Institute, Simon Fraser University [Canada].

Review of the HCR-20: Assessing Risk for Violence by PAUL A. ARBISI, Staff Psychologist, Minneapolis VA Medical Center, and Assistant Professor, Department of Psychiatry, University of Minnesota, Minneapolis, MN:

DESCRIPTION. The HCR-20: Assessing Risk for Violence is a checklist of risk factors for violent behavior consisting of 20 items subsumed within three categories. The first category details 10 historical factors associated with increased risk for violence including H1: Previous Violence; H2: Young Age at First Violent Incident; H3: Relationship Instability; H4: Employment Problems; H5: Substance Use Problems; H6: Major Mental Illness; H7: Psychopathy; H8: Early Maladjustment; H9: Personality Disorder; and H10: Prior Supervision Failure. The second category details five clinical variables including C1: Lack of Insight; C2: Negative Attitudes; C3: Active Symptoms of Major Mental Illness; C4: Impulsivity; and C5: Unresponsive to Treatment. The final category details future risk management issues including R1: Plans Lack of Feasibility; R2: Exposure to Destabilizers; R3: Lack of Personal Support; R4: Noncompliance with Remediation Attempts; and R5: Stress.

Directions for administration of the HCR-20 are somewhat vague and nonspecific in that the associated risk assessment scheme draws upon a broad range of data sources including file review, interview, and testing. In addition, consultation with colleagues responsible for treatment or community release may be necessary to complete the Risk Management section (manual, p. 17). The manual does not provide clear-cut suggestions for sources of information and it is difficult to determine if traditional measures of reliability are applicable in such a case. Further, the manual is quite vague with regard to user qualifications. The minimal qualifications include expertise in conducting "individual assessment," and "expertise in the study of violence" (manual, p. 17). The authors equivocate a bit with regard to user qualifications and contend that it may be setting specific. That is, if the HCR-20 is to be used to make decisions regarding placement, treatment, or management of an individual, users should have a high level of

expertise. However, if it is to be used for research purposes it may be administered by people who are not "fully qualified" (manual, p. 18). It would seem that this is an ill-advised suggestion. Either the highest level of training and competence is required in the use of the instrument or it is not. Research on the instrument should not be compromised based on less reliable administration of the instrument.

DEVELOPMENT. The HCR-20 is a work in progress that appears to hold some promise as a risk assessment instrument in the prediction of violent behavior. According to the manual, the use of the HCR-20 should be restricted to settings in which there is a high proportion of individuals with histories of violence and mental illness. The aim of the authors was to produce a guide to assess the risk of violence that was based in the scientific literature and was efficient to use. On the whole, the authors appear to have accomplished this goal. The manual provides a rationale for the adoption of the particular risk assessment strategy employed by the HCR-20 and describes the HCR-20 as "a guide to assessment, and not a formal psychological test" (p. 1). The HCR-20 is designed to assist the user in integrating the prediction of violence with clinical assessment and is intended to be used as an "aide memoire" and a research instrument (p. 5) rather than a hard and fast predictor of future violent behavior. The authors hope to develop the checklist into a standardized scale, but according to the manual, this goal is somewhere off in the future.

TECHNICAL. The manual does not report interrater reliabilities for Version 2 of the HCR-20. Most of the data regarding the reliability and predictive validity of the HCR-20 contained in the manual appear to pertain to Version 1. Generally, if there are significant changes in the wording of items or the coding of items from one version of an instrument to another, it is incumbent upon the test authors to report the relevant test statistics for the newer version. In the case of the HCR-20, the coding for 12 out of the 20 variables, factors, or issues was changed from Version 1 to 2. Therefore, reporting the interrater reliabilities from the previous version is insufficient and the interrater reliabilities and item total correlations should be presented for the current version of the HCR-20. Additionally, all studies cited in the manual appear to have been conducted retrospectively from file reviews of patients obtained from correctional, forensic psychiatric, and civil psychiatric settings. From the later setting, interrater reliabilities of what is assumed to be the first version of the HCR-20 were highest for the Historical factors (.89), followed by the Risk Management issues (.82). The lowest interrater reliabilities were for the Clinical variables (.72). Fortunately, interrater reliabilities for Version 2 reported in subsequent papers are quite similar and suggest that the reliabilities cited in the manual for Version 1 are representative of Version 2 (Dernevik, 1998; Douglas, Ogloff, Nicholls, & Grant, 1999).

The HCR-20 Historical, Clinical, and Risk Management items are coded on a 3-point scale according to the rater's confidence that the risk factors are present. A "0" indicates the item does not apply or is not present. A "1" indicates that the risk factor is possibly or partially present, and a "3" indicates that the risk factor is definitely present. An omission or *don't know* response is also permitted if there is insufficient valid information to permit a decision. In examining the actual items and the accompanying scoring scheme in the manual, the authors do not provide behavioral or conceptual anchors for the various responses. Indeed, examples of what might constitute a 0, 1, or 2 ratings would be most welcome. The concepts become quite fuzzy and difficult to define even under the best of circumstances. For example, it is conceivable that a group of forensic examiners could disagree on what behavior would constitute "unresponsiveness to treatment" without reference to specific examples and behavioral anchors that would aid in rating the item. Unfortunately, the manual provides little guidance in rating this item. Examples of unresponsiveness to treatment provided in the manual seemed, at best, tautological. For example, "People who score high may refuse to start treatment, start but stop treatment, 'sham' their way through treatment, or complete treatment but fail to benefit from it" (p. 59). The items or risk factors call for a great deal of subjective judgement on the part of the examiner. Given this level of subjectivity, it is surprising that the interrater reliabilities are as high as they are. One explanation for the relatively robust reliabilities reported in the manual is that the studies from which the reliabilities are derived appear to be have conducted by the authors of the HCR-20 (Douglas et al., 1999). It would be of great interest

to report reliabilities for raters who are not intimately involved with the development of the HCR-20. Such individuals would be much less likely to share a conceptual understanding of the item development and hold common internal anchors for the item ratings.

Regarding the utility of the HCR-20 and the ability of the instrument to predict violence in high-risk groups, the manual offers meager guidance in reaching summary decisions. Again, this appears to be more a factor of lack of data than a failure on the part of the authors to understand the complexity of the risk assessment process. The manual states, "It is not possible to specify a method of reaching a summary or final decision that is appropriate for all situations. For research purposes, it is possible to treat the HCR-20 as an actuarial scale and simply sum the number item codes" (p. 21). On the other hand, for clinical purposes, the authors find that it makes "little sense to sum the number of risk factors present in a given case and then use fixed arbitrary cutoffs to classify the individual as low, moderate, or high risk" (p. 22). No suggestions are made regarding the use of cutoffs or critical items in making clinical decisions. The data contained in the manual regarding predictive validity demonstrate that the H and R scales are consistently related to violence. Correlation with previous violence was .52 for the Historical scale and .31 for the Clinical scale in a correctional setting. In prediction of violent behavior in civil commitment settings, the authors mention that a receiver operating characteristic analysis found effect sizes were moderate to large with the H and R scales most consistently related to violence. However, no data are provided in substantiating this claim. In a subsequent paper, the data related to the ROC analysis is made available and provide reason for optimism given the findings (Douglas et al., 1999). For a cutoff of 20 on the HCR-20 total score, the sensitivity is .70 and the specificity is .72 in the prediction of subsequent violence. More relevant from the practitioner's perspective is that the positive predictive power is .60 and the negative predictive power is .80 for the same cutoff score. These figures suggest that using a cutoff of 20 on the HCR-20, 70% of the individuals who go on to commit violent acts can be identified at a significantly better than chance level with an associated 28 percent rate of false positives.

COMMENTARY. The point prediction of violence is a notoriously sticky psychometric problem in that the actual occurrence of violence remains a relatively rare event even in populations where violence is relatively common. Initially, it was thought that clinicians' ability to predict violence was only accurate 30% of the time (Borum, 1996). However, with a move away from the point prediction of violence and a shift toward a risk assessment approach, the accuracy of prediction has climbed into the moderate range particularly with at risk groups (Borum, 1996; Douglas et al., 1999). Nonetheless, the accurate prediction of rare events remains quite problematic because there is always error involved in prediction and the consequence of such error in the prediction of a rare event is magnified substantially in comparison to prediction of more common events (Meehl & Rosen, 1955). The type and magnitude of acceptable error depends on the setting and the ultimate impact of the decision, both given an accurate judgement and given an inaccurate judgement. Consequently, it may be reasonable if a particular violent act involves the death or serious injury of many people, to erroneously indicate that 40% of a particular group of individuals will commit the violent act in order to prevent 100% of the individuals who will commit the violent act from doing so. Under different circumstances (the violent act is not lethal and does not result in serious injury), this level of inaccuracy would be unacceptable and rightfully condemned as unjustified and unfair.

Unfortunately, the HCR-20 manual does not report the rates or impact of various instrument-based decisions on the subsequent prediction of violence. The sensitivity, specificity, and importantly, positive predictive power and negative predictive power are crucial parameters in making a judgement regarding the impact of a particular clinical decision and the acceptable rate of error given a set of consequences. Therefore, the utility of the instruments, as least as represented in the manual, remains more speculative than tangible.

SUMMARY. The HCR-20 is an instrument that is still in development. Since the publication of the manual, there have been several studies that suggest the instrument has promise and may serve to increase the accuracy of risk assessment in samples prone to violence. However, this information is not contained in the manual and much of the data were accumulated using a Swedish version of the HCR-20 (Belfrage, 1998). Addition of the most recent studies to the manual would be of critical importance in helping the user decide in which clinical settings to apply the instrument and what rate and type of error is acceptable given the consequence of an erroneous judgement in each setting. Further, data indicating the equivalence of various translations of the HCR-20 would also be most welcome. Despite the fact that the HCR-20 shows significant promise as a clinical tool for the risk assessment of violence, until studies conducted by the scale's authors are replicated and the manual revised, the HCR-20 should remain a research instrument.

REVIEWER'S REFERENCES

Belfrage, H. (1998). Implementing the HCR-20 scheme for risk assessment in a forensic psychiatric hospital: Integrating research and clinical practice. *Journal of Forensic Psychiatry, 9,* 328–338.
Borum, R. (1996). Improving the clinical practice of violence risk assessment: Technology, guidelines, and training. *American Psychologist, 51,* 945–956.
Dernevik, M. (1998). Preliminary findings on reliability and validity of the Historical-Clinical-Risk assessment in a forensic psychiatric setting. *Psychology, Crime, and Law, 4,* 127–137.
Douglas, K. S., Ogloff, J. R. P., Nicholls, T. L., & Grant, I. (1999). Assessing risk for violence among psychiatric patients: The HCR-20 violence risk assessment scheme and the Psychopathy Checklist: Screening Version. *Journal of Consulting and Clinical Psychology, 67,* 917–930.
Meehl, P. E., & Rosen, A. (1955). Antecedent probability and the efficiency of psychometric signs, patterns, or cutting scores. *Psychological Bulletin, 52,* 194–216.

Review of the HCR-20: Assessing Risk for Violence by COLIN COOPER, Senior Lecturer, School of Psychology, The Queen's University, Belfast, U.K.:

DESCRIPTION. The HCR-20 is designed to predict violent behavior in offenders and psychiatric patients, such as those diagnosed with personality disorder or schizophrenia. It is based on ratings completed by trained assessors, and consists of 19 items, each of which is rated on a 3-point scale (0, 1, or 2). Nine items assess past behavior (Historical), five measure current (Clinical) characteristics, and five assess Risk factors the person may encounter in the future. The 10th historical HCR-20 "item" is actually the score on a standard checklist assessing psychopathology, the Hare Psychopathy Checklist (Revised) (Hare, 1991) or the screening version of the test (Hart, Cox, & Hare, 1995). The scores on the Hare Checklist are recoded as 0, 1, or 2 when analyzed as part of the HCR-20 so that all items in the HCR-20 carry equal weight.

The items in the HCL-20 represent quite different aspects of behavior, and so this is not a psychological test in the conventional sense of a set of items that form a homogeneous scale. It is instead a scheme for predicting behavior from diverse pieces of information—a list of diverse behaviors each of which should predict violent behavior, but which need not (and for best prediction should not) intercorrelate at all. Thus, it would be inappropriate to study the internal consistency of the items or their factor structure.

DEVELOPMENT. The manual stresses that this is primarily a research instrument, best suited to identification of the potentially most violent individuals within groups (e.g., prisoners) rather than between groups, and that it should be used in conjunction with other information to permit a proper assessment of risk. The underlying theoretical model, the origins of the items, and the differences in theoretical approach, item content, and psychometric properties between the HCR-20 and other instruments such as the Violence Risk Appraisal Guide (Harris, Rice & Quinsey, 1993) are not spelled out.

TECHNICAL. Much of the test manual contains guidance for coding the 19 items involving the rating of behavior, for example clarifying what is meant by "possible/less serious employment problems" (p. 35) or "definite/serious lack of insight" (p. 51). The manual and some later published studies (e.g., Dernevik, 1998) show a generally high degree of correlation between raters, though the most appropriate measure of agreement (kappa) does not appear to have been used. There may occasionally be some opportunity for tightening the wording still further: For example, when coding "active symptoms of major mental illness" (p. 54), the manual is limited to discussing various psychotic symptoms while inferring that raters discount less serious problems, such as anxiety disorders. However, given this scheme it is not at all clear how should one code a clinically depressed prisoner, for example. The manual does not explore issues of bias or group differences, nor is gender viewed as a risk factor for aggressive behavior.

Scores on the HCR-20 do seem to predict violent behavior in both retrospective and predictive studies (e.g., Douglas, Ogloff, Nicholls & Grant, 1999) and the manual reports correlations of between .25 and .52 with a variety of measures of violent behavior. The HCR-20 also shows substantial correlations with other instruments, but it is not obvious whether this is because of shared items. However, there appears to have been no attempt to identify the best-predicting items,

for example by relating each item to the criterion via a *t*-test or correlation. Nor has there been any attempt to use differential weighting to enhance the predictive validity of the instrument. The measurement model also assumes that the items are additive; it is possible that the predictive power of the instrument may be improved if interactions between variables are also considered. Thus the predictive validities quoted in the manual and subsequent literature (e.g., Dernevik, 1998) may well increase if a few more statistical analyses are performed and are found to cross-validate.

COMMENTARY. This instrument also raises the issue of how strong the relationship between predicted and actual violence should be in order for the test to have clinical utility. Given the type of context in which the instrument is likely to be used, the consequences of either a false-positive or a false-negative outcome can be serious for the prisoner or members of the public. Does even a correlation of .5, or an area of .75 under the receiver operating characteristic curve, suffice? That said, it seems clear that scores on the HCR-20 do predict several forms of violent behavior, and so it is likely to be a useful aid for mental health professionals. The HCR-20 has already made an important contribution to the process of risk assessment. Its utility could be further increased by improving its predictive power through differential item weighting, and consideration of what types of evidence should supplement the HCR-20 scores in order to allow a comprehensive assessment of risk in various settings.

SUMMARY. The HCR-20 is designed for one purpose only—to assess the risk of violent behavior within a psychiatric or correctional setting. It is a simple device comprising a checklist of risk factors, together with guidelines for coding them. The literature shows that the total score can be a good predictor of violent behavior in several settings, and so the test deserves to be widely used in strategies for the comprehensive assessment of risk.

REVIEWER'S REFERENCES

Dernevik, M. (1998). Preliminary findings on reliability and validity of the Historical-Clinical-Risk assessment in a forensic psychiatric setting. *Psychology Crime & Law, 4,* 127–137.

Douglas, K. S., Ogloff, J. R. P., Nicholls, T. L., & Grant, I. (1999). Assessing risk for violence among psychiatric patients: The HCR-20 violence risk assessment scheme and the Psychopathy Checklist: Screening Version. *Journal of Consulting and Clinical Psychology, 67,* 917–930.

Hare, R. D. (1991). *Manual for the Hare Psychopathy Checklist—Revised.* Toronto: Multi-Health Systems.

Harris, G. T., Rice, M. E., & Quinsey, V. L. (1993). Violent recidivism of mentally disturbed offenders: the development of a statistical prediction instrument. *Criminal Justice and Behavior, 20,* 315–335.

Hart, S. D., Cox, D., & Hare, R. D. (1995). *Manual for the screening version of the Hare Psychopathy Checklist—Revised (PCL:SV)*. Toronto: Multi-Health Systems.

[116]

Health and Daily Living Form, Second Edition.

Purpose: To examine the influence of extratreatment factors on treatment outcome as well as to explore the social resources and coping processes people use to prevent and adapt to stressful life circumstances.

Publication Dates: 1984-1990.

Acronym: HDLF.

Administration: Group.

Forms, 2: Youth Form, Adult Form B.

Price Data, 2003: $30 per sampler set; $120 per 1-year use permission for up to 150 administrations.

Time: (30-45) minutes.

Comments: May be administered as an interview or as a questionnaire.

Authors: Rudolf H. Moos, Ruth C. Cronkite, and John W. Finney.

Publisher: Mind Garden, Inc.

  a) YOUTH FORM.

  Population: Students ages 12-18.

  Scores: 9 indices: Health-Related (Self-Confidence, Positive Mood, Distressed Mood, Physical Symptoms, Medical Conditions, Health—Risk Behaviors), Social Functioning (Family Activities, Activities with Friends, Social Integration in School).

  b) ADULT FORM B.

  Population: Adults.

  Scores: 41 indices: Health-Related Functioning (Self-Confidence, Physical Symptoms, Medical Conditions, Global Depression, Depressive Mood and Ideation, Endogenous Depression, Depressive Features, Depressed Mood/Past 12 Months, Alcohol Consumption—Quantity, Alcohol Consumption—Quantity/Frequency, Drinking Problems, Smoking Symptoms, Medication Use), Social Functioning and Resources (Social Activities with Friends, Network Contacts, Number of Close Relationships, Quality of Significant Relationship), Family Functioning and Home Environment (Family Social Activities, Family Task Sharing, Tasks Performed by Self, Tasks Performed by Partner, Family Arguments, Negative Home Environment), Children's Health and Functioning (Children's Physical Health Problems, Children's Psychological Health Problems, Children's Total Health Problems, Children's Behavioral Problems, Children's Health—Risk Behaviors), Life Change Events (Negative Life Change Events, Exit Events, Positive Life Change Events), Help-Seeking (Mental Health Professional [past 12 months], Mental Health Professional [ever gone], Non-Mental Health Professional [past 12 months], Non-Mental Health Professional [ever gone]), Family Level Composite (Quality of Conjugal Relationship, Family Social Activities, Family Agreement on Task Sharing, Family Agreement on Household Tasks, Family Arguments, Negative Home Environment).

Cross References: See T5:1181 (28 references) and T4:1135 (19 references); for reviews by Arthur M. Nezu and Steven P. Schinke, see 10:137 (8 references).

Review of the Health and Daily Living Form, Second Edition by SANDRA D. HAYNES, Interim Associate Dean, School of Professional Studies, Metropolitan State College of Denver, Denver, CO:

DESCRIPTION. The Health and Daily Living Form (HDL) is an extensive structured survey designed to assess the influence of extratreatment factors on treatment outcome as well as to explore the social resources and coping processes people use to prevent and adapt to stressful life circumstances. The manual and test protocol forms are provided as a set. Forms are reproducible at a fee to the test user. The HDL can be administered as an interview or questionnaire and to individuals or groups. The authors encourage the use of the HDL with community groups to validate patients' responses or to assess environmental impacts on personal functioning. Persons taking the test are asked to "answer each question as accurately as [they] can by placing an 'X' in the box next to the answer that [they] select or by entering information in the space provided" (Adult Form B). Such generic instructions are necessary as sections and sometimes questions within sections use a different format (e.g., Likert-type scales, yes/no, symptom checklist). There are two forms of the HDL in the second edition, one for adults (Form B that contains revisions from the original Form A) and one for youth. The Youth Form is suitable for adolescents aged 12 to 18.

Results from the Adult Form yield score indices of individual functioning, stressful life circumstances, social network resources, and help seeking. Thirteen scores are related to health-related functioning, the first 8 related to self-confidence and symptoms and the last 5 related to substance use and problems: Self-Confidence, Physical Symptoms, Medical Conditions, Global Depression, Depressive Mood and Ideation, Endogenous Depression, Depressive Features, Depressed Mood, Alcohol Consumption-Quantity, Alcohol Consumption-Quantity/Frequency, Drinking Problems, Smoking Symptoms, and Medication Use. Four scores are related to social functioning and resources: Social Activities with Friends, Number of Social Network Contacts, Number of Close Relationships, and Quality of Significant Relationship. Although the manual states that there are three indices that tap aspects of family functioning, the scoring instructions and statistical tables present five indices. This confusion needs to be clarified. They are: Family Social Activities, Family Task Sharing, Tasks Performed by Self, Tasks Performed by Partner, and Family Arguments. One additional item in this category assesses the quality of physical home environment. Five indices assess the individuals' children's health and functioning: Children's Physical Health Problems, Children's Psychological Health, Children's Total Health Problems, Children's Behavioral Problems, and Children's Health-Risk Behaviors. The next set of indices, life change events, was adapted from the Holmes-Rahe Social Readjustment Rating Scale (1967). Three sets of overall indices are derived in this group with three time frame subsets in each: Negative Life Change Events, Exit Events, and Positive Life Change Events. Finally, for individual users, the HDL measures help-seeking behavior from mental health or non-mental health professionals within specified time frames on four indices: Mental Health Professional (last 12 months), Mental Health Professional (ever), Non-mental Health Professional (last 12 months), Non-mental Health Professional (ever). If the HDL is given to more than one family member, six family level composite indices can be calculated: Quality of Conjugal Relationship, Family Social Activities, Family Agreement on Task Sharing, Family Agreement on Household Tasks, Family Arguments, and Negative Home Environment.

The Youth Form of the HDL is much shorter and contains only two sets of indices: six health-related and three social functioning. The authors caution that, because social functioning in this form includes school functioning, adolescents not in school and in the 16-to 18-year age range should be given the Adult Form B. There are no provisions for younger children not being in school. The health-related indices are: Self-Confidence, Positive Mood, Distressed Mood, Physical Symp-

toms, Medical Conditions, and Health-Risk Behaviors. Indices of social functioning are: Family Activities, Activities with Friends, and Social Integration in School.

No information on the level of training needed to administer, score, or interpret the HDL are given in the manual. Likewise cutoff scores are not provided. Interpretation is based solely on comparison of each index score with means and standard deviations obtained by the authors by comparing a group of depressed patients to a matched community sample. Children were included in this sample in order to assess differences in scores between children of depressed individuals and the community at large on the indices of children's health and functioning. Thus the HDL appears to be useful only for research purposes.

DEVELOPMENT. The HDL was developed to "examine the influence of life context factors on treatment outcome as well as to focus on the social resources people use to prevent and adapt to stressful life circumstances" (manual, p. 8). The notion that such events and circumstances play a role in psychological functioning is indeed an important concept and is imbedded in the *Diagnostic and Statistical Manual-IV-TR* (American Psychiatric Association, 2000) multiaxial system for diagnosis of mental disorders. The research base used to develop the items of the HDL is not reviewed in the manual. Instead, readers are referred to other works for this information. The process of development of the measure itself is likewise not described in detail in the manual. The reader is simply told, "items were chosen on the basis of empirical criteria such as item intercorrelations, item-subscale correlations, and internal consistency analyses" (p. 8). Items needed to be correlated with their own subscale more strongly than with other subscales in the same domain and discriminate among individuals. Items are nonredundant except on the depression scales.

TECHNICAL.

Standardization. Two samples were used in the standardization of the HDL Form B and one sample was used for the Youth Form. A sample of 424 patient participants was selected from depressed persons seeking treatment of one of five psychiatric facilities. Four criteria were required for acceptance: a diagnosis of major or minor depression according to the Research Diagnostic Criteria, depression not related to a neurological or metabolic disorder, no manic symptoms or alcohol abuse in the past 6 months, and 18 years of age or older. The patient group was meticulously matched with 424 control subjects randomly sampled from within the patients' census tract and neighborhood. No exclusion criteria were given for the match comparison group. Additionally, each group had several members whose spouses also took the HDL. The purpose of this additional administration and the use of the additional data were omitted from the manual. It can only be assumed that the matched control group for children of depressed patients was obtained at the same time. The information provided in this regard for the Youth Form was that it was "developed in our research program on depressed patients and their families and matched community controls" (manual, p. 27). Appropriate demographic information is clearly lacking in the manual.

Reliability. A summary of reliability data was strikingly missing in the manual. Alpha scores are presented in each of the summary tables representing internal consistency. Values are generally acceptable to high. A reference to reliability can be found in the validity section where the reader is referred to other research papers for results.

Validity. Face and content validity were built in to the HDL. Construct, discriminative, and criterion-related (both concurrent and predictive) validity were reported to be generally good. As with measures of reliability, the reader is referred to other sources to obtain specific information about validity and the studies supporting it. The authors note that validity "must be considered in relation to specific indices in the HDL and the investigator's purpose" (manual, p. 10).

COMMENTARY. The major strength of the HDL is its attempt to standardize a questionnaire that accesses an often neglected and important feature of diagnosis and treatment. The HDL has been used in several research studies resulting in a rich body of literature regarding its value (more so for Form B than the Youth Form). Administration and scoring are straightforward and the ability to administer the CDSS to individuals, as a questionnaire or an interview, and to groups is a plus.

The manual is not well organized and is difficult to read. The total number of indices is confusing. As it stands, the HDL should only be considered a research tool as clinical utility has not been assessed nor the manual prepared for other purposes. A more in-depth review of the literature leading to the development of this instrument would make the manual and the instrument stronger. Supporting interpretive comments would make the test more useful in clinical situations.

SUMMARY. The HDL appears to be a well-researched measure of psychosocial factors that influence treatment compliance and success. Lacking is a central place describing the test in detail. The HDL does not appear suitable for clinical use in its current condition.

REVIEWER'S REFERENCES
American Psychiatric Association. (2000). *Diagnostic and statistical manual of mental disorders: DSM-IV-TR.* Washington, DC: American Psychiatric Association.
Holmes, T. H., & Rahe, R. H. (1967). The Social Readjustment Rating Scale. *Journal of Psychosomatic Research, 11,* 213–218.

Review of the Health and Daily Living Form by ASHRAF KAGEE, Research Fellow, Department of Psychology, University of Stellenbosch, Maitland, South Africa:

DESCRIPTION. The Health and Daily Living Form (HDL) is a structured assessment procedure intended to determine health-related and social functioning, chronic and acute stressors, social resources, and help-seeking behaviors. The scale may be administered to respondents in either an interview or questionnaire format and is appropriate for use with both patient and community groups. The authors consider the scale to be especially appropriate for users interested in assessing the process of psychosocial adaptation among psychiatric and medical populations.

Part I of the scale addresses the demographic characteristics of the respondent whereas Part II addresses employment history and current status. The remainder of the scale assesses health-related issues in sequential sections: the respondent's health in the last 12 months and in the last month; stressful events in the past year; perceived social support; and issues concerning the respondent's home and children. The scale is presented in a checklist format and appears to require minimal effort on the part of a respondent or interviewer to complete. Most items require a simple "yes/no" response, some are presented in a Likert-type format, and a few require the respondent to write in a number. The coding values and column numbers for entering responses to each item are placed in small print next to each item. The item responses have been numbered so that they may be tallied into a database or scoring sheet. No software is required to score the test, as it is hand scored, and the scoring keys for the various subscales are self-explanatory and easy to follow.

DEVELOPMENT. The second edition of the HDL manual replaces the first edition, which was first published in 1984. The scale's indices were arrived at from data from two samples: 424 persons seeking treatment for major depressive disorder at a psychiatric facility, and a sample of case controls obtained by randomly sampling a household from within each patient's neighborhood and census tract.

The HDL is composed of four indices that measure: (a) individual functioning; (b) stressful life circumstances; (c) social network resources; and (d) help-seeking behavior. The manual offers no theory of how these indices fit together, or what the developers' understanding is of the relationship between health and daily living.

In the manual, the developers state that they formulated definitions of specific constructs (e.g., depression, social activities, and help-seeking), prepared items to reflect the definitions of these constructs, and selected items that were conceptually related to a dimension as agreed upon by independent raters. Items were also chosen on the basis of empirical criteria such as item intercorrelations, item-subscale correlations, and internal consistency analysis. The selection of items was based on positive association with other items on the same subscale, an association with other items on the same subscale that was stronger than that of associations with other subscales, and the ability of items to discriminate among individuals.

TECHNICAL. The HDL includes a set of 12 indices of individual health-related functioning. The first set of 7 of these indices assesses a respondent's Self-Confidence and various aspects of physical and mood-related symptoms such as Physical Symptoms, Medical Conditions, Global Depression, Depressive Mood and Ideation, Endogenous Depression, and Depressive Features. The second set of 5 indices assesses the quantity and frequency of alcohol use, Drinking Problems, Smoking Symptoms, and Medication Use. It is difficult to establish how the construct of Self-Confidence fits in with other subscales on the scale and the authors do not offer a rationale for this inclusion. Moreover, there seems to be some overlap in terms of constructs such as Global Depression, Depressive Mood and Ideation, Endogenous Depression, and Depressive Features. With respect to these depression-related subscales, it is unclear how or why these subscales have been identified as no factor analysis of the HDL is reported or cited. If these indices are to be considered separately, there needs to be a more convincing theoretical rationale for delineating them in their present form.

Several of the items on the scale appear to inadvertently tap physical functioning in addition to their purported purpose of assessing social functioning. For example, items assessing whether the respondent attended a concert, card game, or picnic; went hiking, hunting or fishing, swimming, or played tennis presuppose the functional ability of the person to perform these activities. Yet, these items are listed under the part of the scale entitled "Your friends and family." These items represent an opportunity for the scale to assess more than it claims and the authors might do well to call attention to these possibilities.

The internal consistencies of the Self-Confidence and Symptoms subscales as measured by Cronbach's alpha are generally high, ranging from .77 to .92 for the depressed and community norm groups. However, these high reliability estimates may be explained in part by the similarity of items within each scale (i.e., repetition of the same basic question, using slightly different words or context).

Two alpha coefficients reported for the Substance Use and Problems indices fall below the .70 point: Medication Use ($r = .54$ and .53 for the depressed and community groups, respectively), and Smoking Problems (.69 and .68 for the depressed and community groups, respectively). The authors need to address these relatively low alpha coefficients and explain why the scale might still be used despite these disappointing statistics. Evidence to support the validity of scores from the HDL is limited. No validity data are presented in the manual, although studies showing concurrent validity are included in the reference section.

COMMENTARY. A major advantage of the HDL is its ease of administration and scoring. Presumably for this reason, there are a large number of published studies that use this instrument, especially in its previous form. However, it appears that the scale lacks a clear focus and appears to aspire to measure depressive symptoms despite the availability of far superior measures to accomplish this task. The scale contains a combination of different constructs without a clear rationale for their inclusion. This reviewer has concerns about the individual items and subscales selected for the measure. These concerns include a lack of construct articulation, a lack of construct differentiation, and the homogeneity of item content within the scales.

SUMMARY. The HDL has been designed to determine health-related and social functioning, chronic and acute stressors, social resources, and help-seeking behaviors. Its major advantage is its ease of administration. However, its utility is compromised by its attempt to be too widely encompassing in the constructs it purports to measure. The absence of a theoretical rationale that underpins the scale is a further concern. Thus, despite its apparent benefits, these concerns constitute important limitations to the usefulness of this measure in its present form.

[117]

Health Status Questionnaire 2.0.

Purpose: Designed "to measure physical and social functioning and emotional well-being."
Population: Ages 14 and older.
Publication Date: 1994.
Acronym: HSQ® 2.0.
Scores, 8: Health Perception, Physical Functioning, Role Limitations-Physical, Role Limitations-Emotional, Social Functioning, Mental Health, Bodily Pain, Energy/Fatigue.
Administration: Group.
Price Data, 2002: $19 per 25 answer sheets; $26 per user's guide (48 pages); $1.20 per MICTOTEST Q Assessment System Software single administration report; price data available from publisher for MICROTEST Q Assessment System Software Progress Report.
Time: (5–10) minutes.
Comments: Self-administered; may be administered in paper-and-pencil format or online; contains all items found on the SF-36 Questionnaire (MOS 36-Item Short Form Health Survey; T6:2273) and SF-36 scores are included in the HSQ 2.0 report; scoring via MICROTEST Q Assessment System Software.
Author: Health Outcomes Institute and the RAND Health Services Program.
Publisher: NCS Assessments [Minnetonka].

Review of the Health Status Questionnaire 2.0 by JOHN C. CARUSO, Assistant Professor of Psychology, University of Montana, Missoula, MT:

DESCRIPTION. The Health Status Questionnaire 2.0 (HSQ 2.0) consists primarily of the 36 items of the Short Form Health Survey (SF-36; Stewart, Hays, & Ware, 1988) and the RAND 36-Item Health Survey (RAND Health Sciences Program, 1991). As such, this review draws on research on the 36 items, regardless of which test was administered. The bulk of the validation research has been performed on the SF-36, but applies equally to the HSQ 2.0. The 36 items are combined to form eight nonoverlapping scales with relevance to health issues. The primary difference between the HSQ 2.0 and the SF-36 is that the HSQ 2.0 contains an additional set of items assessing depression (3 items), health status change (1 item), and demographic characteristics (7 items) known to affect functioning and well-being. The HSQ 2.0 facilitates efficiency in that no separate depression inventory is required, and a standardized demographic assessment is included, all on a form that can be processed via optical scanner. The test manual states that the HSQ 2.0 can usually be administered in 10 minutes. Versions of the scale have been published in several languages including Spanish, Chinese (Taiwanese), Hebrew, Swedish, and German, facilitating cross-cultural comparisons.

DEVELOPMENT. The development of the HSQ 2.0 is intertwined with the development of the SF-36, and the interested reader should refer to research and reviews of the SF-36 for additional information. The eight-factor structure of the 36 health status items has some support cross-culturally using both exploratory and confirmatory factor analysis. The 3 additional depression items were selected to be consistent with common diagnostic criteria and to have face validity but were not subjected to psychometric analyses.

TECHNICAL. Three large samples are described in the user's guide with a combined size of 4,198. Unfortunately, the samples were not carefully selected to match any particular population. The use of these samples for comparison therefore requires careful consideration in terms of match between the "normative" data and one's own patients. For the eight main composite scores, the values of internal consistency reliability for the three samples in the test manual ranged from .75 (Social Functioning) to .89 (Physical Functioning) for participants 18–64 years old and from .79 (Mental Health) to .93 (Physical Functioning) for those 65 years old and older. There is some additional evidence of score reliability for the HSQ

2.0, and there have been no negative findings (i.e., samples showing egregiously low score reliability), but more research in this area is required.

The 3 depression items, immediately following the 36 items of the SF-36, are "In the past year, have you had 2 weeks or more during which you felt sad, blue, or depressed; or when you lost all interest or pleasure in things that you usually cared about or enjoyed?" "Have you had 2 years or more in your life when you felt depressed or sad most days, even if you felt okay sometimes?" and "Have you felt depressed or sad much of the time in the past year?" Although the items have face validity and are consistent with common diagnostic criteria, they seem only slightly better than simply asking the respondent if they are depressed. Furthermore, the 3 items are not summed to arrive at a composite score. The user's guide recommends simply examining the scores on the 3 items to determine the need for further evaluation. Clearly, the addition of the depression items was only intended as a very quick screening device.

The other main addition to the SF-36 offered by the HSQ 2.0 is a set of demographic questions included on the scannable form assessing date of birth, gender, race, educational level (highest degree attained), income (grouped by 10K through 80K), and marital status.

COMMENTARY. Issues have been raised in the literature regarding the appropriateness of the SF-36 items for elderly patients (e.g., Lloyd, 2000) but empirical studies have generally supported the scales' validity in this population. The SF-36 items (that compose the bulk of the HSQ 2.0) have compared favorably to competing instruments in terms of scaling (specifically, other measures may be more prone to ceiling effects). There is a need for additional psychometric evaluations of the HSQ 2.0 in diverse populations. There is also a need for psychometric evaluations of the three depression items, even though the test scoring procedure does not recommend forming a composite score. If the items do not correlate strongly or do not produce a reliable score, then their addition to the SF-36 items seems questionable.

SUMMARY. The primary advantage of the HSQ 2.0 seems to be the ability to collect data on the 36 health status items of the SF-36, along with a set of demographic items and a quick depression screener, all on an optically scannable form. However, relatively brief measures of depression that produce reliable and valid scores are readily available (e.g., Beck Depression Inventory; Beck, Steer, & Brown, 1996; T6:273). Researchers and practitioners who have used the SF-36 or the RAND 36-Item Health Survey and wished for a simultaneous demographic assessment or quick depression screener, particularly if a large amount of data are collected and processed via optical scanner, will be those who find the HSQ 2.0 most useful.

REVIEWER'S REFERENCES

Beck, A. T., Steer, R. A., & Brown, G. K. (1996). *Beck Depression Inventory—II manual.* San Antonio, TX: The Psychological Corporation.
Lloyd, A. (1999). "Assessment of the SF-36 version 2 in the United Kingdom": Comment. *Journal of Epidimiology & Community Health, 53,* 651–652.
RAND Health Science Program. (1992). RAND-36 item health Survey 1.0. Santa Monica, CA: Author.
Stewart, A. L., Hays, R. D., & Ware, J. E., Jr. (1988). The MOS Short-Form General health survey—Reliability and validity in a patient population. *Medical Care, 26,* 724–735.

Review of the Health Status Questionnaire 2.0 by THEODORE L. HAYES, Personnel Research Psychologist, U.S. Immigration & Naturalization Service, Washington, DC:

DESCRIPTION. The User's Guide for the Health Status Questionnaire 2.0 (HSQ 2.0) states that the HSQ is a self-administered, standardized measure of a patient's self-perceived health status. The HSQ 2.0 may be completed by those 14 years of age or older in about 10 minutes either on-line, using a machine-scorable form, or presumably as part of a multimodality epidemiological or insurance provider survey. Most of the 39 health-related items refer to the patient's self-perceived functioning over the past 4 weeks prior to instrument completion. Thirty-five of the 39 health-related items are scored to develop the following scale scores: Health Perception, Physical Functioning, Role Limitations-Physical Health, Role Limitations-Emotional Problems, Social Functioning, Mental Health, Bodily Pain, and Energy/Fatigue. The remaining four items include a global health perception question and three others that seem to be included on a trial basis specifically to indicate depression. Output includes a report displaying item responses as well as scale score charts. A progress report may be generated for multiple administrations to the same patient.

DEVELOPMENT. The HSQ 2.0 is a revised version of the SF-36 Health Survey (Kagee, 2001; Pallone & Hennessy, 2001). As Pallone and Hennessy (2001, p. 1125) noted, the SF-36 was designed to differentiate patients and assess use of medical resources. Presumably, the impetus for the SF-36 (and thus the HSQ 2.0) was a shift in medical practice away from remediation of disease and pain, and toward restoration of the patient to desired activities of daily living. The user's guide to the HSQ 2.0 provides no further detail on the rationale or history of the instrument other than to note studies where comparative data were collected. Reviews of the SF-36 (Kagee, 2001; Pallone & Hennessy, 2001) indicated that it had sufficient development documentation. Pallone and Hennessy (2001) previously criticized the SF-36 for not providing a direct diagnosis of a particular mental health condition as opposed to assessing generalized distress. The trial depression items seem to have been included to diagnose this particular affective disorder, though the scale has no current official use in the HSQ 2.0.

TECHNICAL. As a revised instrument, one should expect the HSQ 2.0's publishers to provide adequate psychometric documentation. There should be criterion-oriented evidence that changes in diagnosed health status relate to changes in perceived health status, or even vice-versa. Finally, scale score stability over time (i.e. repeated medical appointments) should be reported. Again, reviews of the SF-36 (Kagee, 2001; Pallone & Hennessy, 2001) noted positive psychometric data for that assessment related to some of these considerations. Unfortunately, psychometric information in the HSQ 2.0 user's guide is disappointing.

The scale scores for the HSQ 2.0 seem to have adequate internal reliability, ranging from .75 to .93, for both younger and older respondents; oddly enough, internal reliability apparently was lower in the SF-36. No data are provided regarding score stability or alternate-forms reliability. In terms of convergent validity, the average interscale obtained correlation presented in the HSQ 2.0 user's guide among younger respondents is .44, and it is .54 among older respondents. Thus, even though the scales may be purported to assess either physical or mental health perceptions, there is a large unidimensional component in scale ratings. This could be due either to common method variance or to transient response error variance, as these are self-reports of perceptions collected in the same modality at a given point in time. Regardless, there is little compelling evidence that there are distinct "physical" and "mental" dimensions. No data are provided regarding correlations to other inventories, so there are no other means to assess convergent and divergent validity.

The HSQ 2.0 guide presents correlational data in tables separated by age group in an attempt to show that the scale scores relate to medical diagnoses. Correlations are presented for combined samples of men and women. These tables seem impressive on the surface, but upon further review they are deeply unsatisfying. Even if one were awed by all the "significant" correlations, the level of correlation is remarkably low. These correlations are not only low, they may be confounded by the gender of the respondent: More positive health perceptions were correlated with being male. The publisher does not note the prevalence of medical condition by gender group, nor the proportion of respondents in either table that are female, and so it is not possible to control the effect of gender on the correlation between scale score and medical condition.

Even if the correlations are taken at face value, they show that people with diagnosed medical conditions report lower self-perceived daily functioning. It is not clear what value this adds to the medical or healing process. It would be more useful in the future for the publisher to report correlations between diagnoses and ratings of specific activities of daily living rather than scale scores.

Finally, no data are presented on expected change scores, correlations between scales and medical intervention, etc. Also, some colloquial item wording may confuse those with limited English-language competence (e.g., "down in the dumps," "full of pep").

COMMENTARY. The HSQ 2.0 guide makes no substantive claims as to the value of the instrument other than suggesting that it is "(A) part of an overall outcomes management system. Other information about clinical outcomes, interventions, and disease-relevant variables should be drawn from patient questionnaires, medical records, or other assessment instruments" (p. 1). The HSQ 2.0 has no obvious diagnostic value; even the publisher suggests that the same (or better?) information "should be drawn" through other means. Presumably a corporate health care sponsor or insurer might wish to gather outcomes-oriented data in a structured, standardized format such as the HSQ 2.0. However, as the instrument assesses only perceived health status, and because there is weak—if any—external criterion-oriented validity data for the HSQ 2.0, it should be considered as only one among many options for corporate sponsors.

SUMMARY. The HSQ 2.0 provides measurements of perceived health status. These measurements have adequate internal reliability. It may be better used as an indicator of the patient's overall emotional well-being at the time of the medical appointment rather than an indicator of physical health status. The instrument may be useful to health care providers who wish to employ a standardized intake interview, or possibly to corporate health survey sponsors who wish to create localized databases of patient perceptions. Further claims as to its diagnostic or predictive value are currently unwarranted, though future research may substantiate them.

REVIEWER'S REFERENCES

Kagee, A. (2001). [Review of the SF-36 Health Survey.] In B. S. Plake & J. C. Impara (Eds.), *The fourteenth mental measurements yearbook* (pp. 1123–1125). Lincoln, NE: Buros Institute of Mental Measurements.
Pallone, N. J., & Hennessy, J. J. (2001). [Review of the SF-36 Health Survey.] In B. S. Plake & J. C. Impara (Eds.), *The fourteenth mental measurements yearbook* (pp. 1125–1126). Lincoln, NE: Buros Institute of Mental Measurements.

[118]
The Hospital Anxiety and Depression Scale with the Irritability-Depression-Anxiety Scale and the Leeds Situational Anxiety Scale.

Purpose: Designed to detect and distinguish "between anxiety and depression and measures the severity of emotional disorder."
Population: Adults.
Publication Date: 1994.
Acronym: HADS.
Scores, 3: Irritability, Anxiety, Depression.
Administration: Group.
Price Data: Available from publisher.
Time: (5) minutes.
Authors: R. P. Snaith and A. S. Zigmond.
Publisher: NFER-Nelson Publishing Co., Ltd. [England].

Review of the Hospital Anxiety and Depression Scale with the Irritability-Depression-Anxiety Scale and the Leeds Situational Anxiety Scale by MICHAEL H. CAMPBELL, Director of Residential Life and Food Service, New College of Florida, Sarasota, FL:

DESCRIPTION. The Hospital Anxiety and Depression Scale (HADS) is a 14-item self-report paper-and-pencil measure designed for use with medical patients whose experience of depression or anxiety should inform the treating clinician. Nonclinical staff can easily be trained in procedures for administration and scoring; the HADS can be administered in a wide variety of settings;

and the questionnaire takes just a few minutes to complete. The Likert-type items are equally divided between subscales for Anxiety and for Depression. Combined raw scores for each scale range from 0 to 21. Scores fall in one of four levels of descriptive interpretation: normal, mild, moderate, and severe. The authors encourage use of the HADS as a repeated measure to obtain an ongoing picture of a patient's health during the course of medical treatment. The items for Depression focus primarily on anhedonic symptoms; the items for Anxiety reflect affective and cognitive more than somatic symptoms. The HADS has been translated into a number of languages; a list of versions is available from the publisher.

The HADS is distributed with two other instruments: The Irritability-Depression-Anxiety Scale (IDAS) and the Leeds Situational Anxiety Scale (LSAS). The IDAS consists of 14 Likert-type self-report items divided into three subscales: Irritability (four items), Depression (five items), and Anxiety (five items). Administration procedures for the IDAS are essentially the same as those recommended for the HADS. Combined raw scores for each scale fall into three interpretive ranges: normal, borderline, and morbid. The authors note that the construct of irritability measured in this second version of the IDAS measures outwardly (rather than inwardly) directed irritability. However, other than this statement, the manual provides no other information on the development or psychometric adequacy of the IDAS.

Information about the LSAS is even more incomplete. The authors describe the LSAS as a "useful checklist to make the clinician aware of particular areas of anxious concern" (manual, p. 15). The checklist takes the form of a list of 24 potentially phobic stimuli or situations (e.g., cats, thunderstorms, walking alone, blood, and eating in the presence of others). Patients rate their anxiety for each item as *no anxiety, mild anxiety,* or *very anxious.* The instrument does not yield any quantitative data; rather, the aim seems to be production of a qualitative catalogue of potential phobias for a given patient. Although this may provide useful data for follow-up, the LSAS does not possess the qualities of a bona fide psychometric instrument. Moreover, the authors provide no information or references regarding development, standardization, or norms.

DEVELOPMENT. The manual provides telegraphic and generally inadequate coverage of test development. The authors state that the HADS was developed "largely for the purpose of screening ... [for the] presence of the mood as a disordered state" (manual, p. 5). Although the manual makes no reference to the demographic characteristics of the normative sample, the original study (Zigmond & Snaith, 1983) states that the HADS was normed on 50 medical patients ranging in age from 16 to 65. In a study conducted after the publication of the manual, White, Leach, Sims, Atkinson, and Cottrell (1999) report norms and suggested cut-off scores for adolescents (ages 12-17). They report significant gender effects, with girls scoring higher than boys on both anxiety and depression subscales, but no age effect. Similarly, Spinhoven, Ormel, Sloekers, and Kempen (1997) report only very small correlations with age in a study with adult and elderly populations.

TECHNICAL. The manual reports limited data regarding the score reliability of the HADS, including item-subscale correlations of .41 and .76 for anxiety and .30 and .60 for depression. Although this is far from convincing evidence of item homogeneity, the manual also reports alpha coefficients of .93 and .90 for Anxiety and Depression, respectively in a study of 568 cancer patients (Moorey, et al., 1991). Additionally, the authors cite unpublished data indicating test-retest (no time interval indicated) reliability coefficients of .92 (Depression) and .89 (Anxiety) for respondents without medical illness.

The manual provides very brief coverage of evidence supporting the validity of the HADS, noting factor analytic support of construct validity for the two scales (Moorey, et al., 1991). The manual cites a few studies purported to demonstrate evidence of concurrent validity, but the results are not summarized or even characterized in basic terms to the reader.

The technical coverage in the manual is clearly insufficient to inform a responsible clinician considering the HADS. Technical coverage for the IDAS and the LSAS is practically nonexistent and certainly does not meet the standards of the *Standards for Educational and Psychological Testing* (AERA, APA, & NCME, 1999). However, considerable research since the manual's publication in 1994 provides additional data in support of the HADS.

For example, Spinhoven (1997) evaluated the HADS using a much larger sample of participants (N = 6,165). They report coefficient alphas

of .80 to .84 for Anxiety and .71 to .86 for Depression, depending on population group. However, the study also emphasized the difficulty of distinguishing between anxiety and depression, given colinearity between the scales. They also note that the HADS has some predictive value for identification of minor psychiatric disorders in medical patients but conclude that the instrument is most appropriately used as a screening (not diagnostic) measure because of low positive predictive value. In a more recent study, White, et al. (1999) support the use of the HADS as a screening instrument for adolescent populations. They report that the HADS distinguishes between adolescents with diagnosed anxiety or depressive disorders and a nonclinical sample.

COMMENTARY. The aims of the HADS are laudable. Anxiety and depression are concomitant of many medical illnesses and are important factors in treatment. Brief and cost-effective screening instruments have tremendous utility in inpatient and outpatient medical settings, where time is limited and formal consults are costly. However, the HADS requires more work to credibly meet its aspirations.

Serious inadequacies of the manual warrant caution when considering use of the HADS. The manual is not well written and provides only telegraphic coverage of important technical data. Moreover, the manual needs revision to incorporate important new research since its publication in 1994. This more recent research would clearly bolster the authors' claims regarding the clinical utility of the HADS. An updated manual with more thorough and more complete coverage of evidence for score reliability and validity would make the HADS a more viable choice for clinicians. This criticism is even more appropriate for the IDAS and the LSAS, for which the manual offers almost no technical data.

SUMMARY. The HADS is a convenient and cost-effective screen for anxiety and depression in medical patients. However, technical data supporting score reliability are limited; the information that does exist is incompletely and unclearly reported in the manual, which is several years out of date. More importantly, the manual provides little justification for the interpretive categories and does not elucidate their clinical implications. Clinicians would be better served at present by brief instruments with more compelling validity evidence and more useful supporting materials (e.g., the Reynolds Depression Screening Inventory, Reynolds & Koback, 1998, T6:2121; the Beck Depression Inventory-II, Beck, Steer, & Brown, 1996, T6:273). However, the HADS shows promise predicated on continuing research and the publication of an improved and up-to-date manual.

REVIEWER'S REFERENCES

American Educational Research Association, American Psychological Association, & National Council on Measurement in Education. (1999). *Standards for educational and psychological testing.* Washington, DC: American Education Research Association.

Beck, A. T., Steer, R. A., & Brown, G. K. (1996). Beck Depression Inventory-II. San Antonio: The Psychological Corporation.

Moorey, S., Greer, S., Watson, M., Gorman, C., Rowden, L., Tunmore, R., Robertson, B., & Bliss, J. (1991). The factor structure and factor stability of the Hospital Anxiety and Depression Scale in patients with cancer. *British Journal of Psychiatry, 158,* 255–259.

Reynolds, W. M. & Koback, K. A. (1998). The Reynolds Depression Screening Inventory. Odessa, FL: Psychological Assessment Resources, Inc.

Spinhoven, P., Ormel, J., Sloekers, P. P. A., & Kempen, G. I. J. M. (1997). A validation study of the Hospital Anxiety and Depression Scale in different groups of Dutch subjects. *Psychological Medicine, 27*(2), 363–370.

White, D., Leach, C., Sims, R., Atkinson, M., & Cottrell, D. (1999). Validation of the Hospital Anxiety and Depression Scale for use with adolescents. *The British Journal of Psychiatry, 175,* 452–454.

Zigmond, A. S. & Snaith, R. P. (1983). The Hospital Anxiety and Depression Scale. *Acta Psychiatrica Scandinavica, 67*(6), 361–370.

Review of The Hospital Anxiety and Depression Scale with the Irritability-Depression Anxiety Scale and the Leeds Situational Anxiety Scale by WILLIAM E. MARTIN, JR., *Professor of Educational Psychology, Northern Arizona University, Flagstaff, AZ:*

DESCRIPTION. The Hospital Anxiety and Depression Scale (HADS) "is a self-administered questionnaire which detects, and distinguishes between anxiety and depression and measures the severity of emotional disorder" (manual, outside back page). The HADS consists of 7 Anxiety items (A-scale) and 7 Depression items (D-scale). The 14 items are presented alternately by the two constructs on a one-page answer sheet. There are 8 negatively stated items such as "I feel as if I am slowed down" and 6 positively stated items including "I feel cheerful." There are four response choices for each item reflecting a summative scale format. Although the four response choices are similar, they are stated differently for each of the 14 items and sometimes reversed in emphasis. For example, the ordered choices for one item are *Nearly all the time, Very often, Sometimes,* and *Not at all* and for another item the choices are *Not at all, Occasionally, Quite often,* and *Very often.* A score is given for a response to each item ranging from 0–3. A higher score reflects greater anxiety or depression. The anxiety and depression subscale scores are found by adding the numbers associated with the 7 items of each subscale. The following guidelines are provided for interpreting the subscale scores for anxiety or depression: 0–7 *normal,* 8–10 *mild,* 11–14 *moderate,* and 15–21 *severe.*

In addition to the HADS, the Irritability-Depression-Anxiety Scale (IDAS) and the Leeds Situational Anxiety Scale (LSAS) are presented in the manual as two previously unpublished scales in "photocopiable" format. The IDAS has four items to measure the outward directed Irritability subscale, five items for the Anxiety subscale, and another five items for the Depression subscale. The items and response format are constructed similar to those of the HADS. The scoring procedure is also like that used for the HADS but the interpretation labels are *normal, borderline,* and *morbid.*

The LSAS is a checklist used to help the clinician become aware of particular anxiety concerns of respondents. There are 24 items listed that reflect situations that might produce anxiety such as "Being alone," "Spiders," and "Air travel." Respondents are asked to circle a response to each item from one of the following choices: 0 = *No anxiety,* 1 = *Mild anxiety,* or 2 = *Very anxious.* No overall score is calculated.

DEVELOPMENT. The HADS was developed in recognition of the emotional component of physical illness. According to the authors, anxiety and depression states associated with somatic symptoms may increase the distress of physical illness or confuse the diagnosis. As such, the HADS should provide the clinician with guidance as to the best therapeutic intervention. Even though there is limited information in the manual about the technical development of the HADS, the authors reported that an item analysis of a longer list of items completed by medical outpatient clients was used to form the test. The separation of the items into the two subscales of the HADS was "based upon their correlation to independent assessment" (p. 5). It appears that interviews were conducted to establish anxiety and depression states.

Information from two previous studies is referenced as an earlier version of the IDAS. The authors report that a 1978 version included both inward and outward irritability subscales but the inward irritability scales were removed as a result of findings from a 1985 study. The current scale of outward irritability items is combined with depression and anxiety items. Unlike the HADS, there is no separation of the depression and anxiety constructs and the authors report that the

IDAS provides less exact indices of these constructs. No information is provided about the development of the LSAS.

TECHNICAL. The HADS, IDAS, and LSAS are not norm-referenced tests so standardization information is not provided. Moreover, there is no detailed information as to how the criteria that are used to interpret the summative subscale scores were developed.

Item-subscale correlations from a study of 50 clients were reported as a measure of internal consistency for the HADS. The correlations ranged from .41–.76 for the A-scale and .30–.60 for the D-scale. Another study of 568 participants resulted in Cronbach's alpha coefficients of .93 for the A-scale and .90 for the D-scale. Test-retest reliability coefficients were reported to be .89 for the A-scale and .92 for the D-scale. No time interval between testing was provided.

A factor analytic study was reported to provide support for the construct validity of the HADS. Two independent factors emerged accounting for 53% of the variance. The manual provided specific data relative to a concurrent validation study comparing the HADS to 5-point psychiatric rating scales of anxiety and depression with 100 medical outpatients. Correlations of .54 for the A-scale and .79 for the D-scale were identified. References to four other concurrent validity studies were provided in the manual but no specific data accompanied the references. Finally, there is a reference to the validity of the separation of the two subscales of the HADS but again no data are given. No reliability or validity information is given for the IDAS or the LSAS.

COMMENTARY. The HADS, IDAS, and LSAS instruments and test documentation reflect considerable limitations. The overriding concern is that the test documents, specifically the manual, do not provide sufficient detail to judge important information about the instruments. References are made to other publications throughout the manual that supposedly provide key information about the tests. The manual and accompanying documents need substantial expansion to provide complete information about the instruments that including relevant information about the tests from other publications. Although most sections of the manual are incomplete, some areas need immediate attention.

The item selection process for all three tests needs elucidation. A detailed description of the origin and rationale underlying the use of the item response format and interpretation "scoring bands" is essential to understand the meaning of respondent scores. Additionally, not enough information is presented in the manual to justify the use of the IDAS and LSAS for reasons other than research.

SUMMARY. Certainly the goal of the HADS, IDAS, and LSAS to assess states of anxiety, depression, and irritability associated with physical illness has utility for clinicians. However, there is not adequate psychometric information available to support their use beyond research purposes. Professional practitioners do have available to them other brief measures that more fully meet the standards for psychological testing. Readers should consider the Beck Anxiety Inventory (reviewed by Dowd, 1998) and the Hamilton Depression Inventory (reviewed by Isenhart, 1998) as alternative tests to the HADS, IDA, and LSAS.

REVIEWER'S REFERENCES

Dowd, E. T. (1998). [Review of the Beck Anxiety Inventory.] In J. C. Impara & B. S. Plake (Eds.), *The thirteenth mental measurements yearbook* (pp. 97–98). Lincoln, NE: Buros Institute of Mental Measurements.
Isenhart, C. (1998). [Review of the Hamilton Depression Inventory.] In J. C. Impara & B. S. Plake (Eds.), *The thirteenth mental measurements yearbook* (pp. 477–480). Lincoln, NE: Buros Institute of Mental Measurements.

[119]

How I Think Questionnaire.

Purpose: Designed to "measure self-serving cognitive distortion."
Population: Ages 12–21.
Publication Date: 2001.
Acronym: HIT.
Scores, 11: Hit Questionnaire, Overt, Covert, Self-Centered, Blaming Others, Minimizing/Mislabeling, Assuming the Worst, Opposition-Defiance, Physical Aggression, Lying, Stealing, Anomalous Responding.
Administration: Group.
Price Data, 2001: $25.95 per 20 questionnaires and manual (46 pages).
Time: (5–15) minutes.
Authors: Alvaro Q. Barriga, John C. Gibbs, Granville Bud Potter, and Albert K. Kiau.
Publisher: Research Press.

Review of the How I Think Questionnaire by JACK E. GEBART-EAGLEMONT, Chief Executive Officer and President, International Institute for Personality Assessment and Therapy, Watsonia, Victoria, Australia:

DESCRIPTION. The How I Think Questionnaire (HIT) is a 54-item test developed to measure cognitive distortions. The authors define cognitive distortions as "inaccurate or biased ways of attending to or conferring meaning upon experiences" (manual, p. 1). The test is based on an assumption that cognitive distortions represent at least a predisposition for psychopathology because the existing research links such types of thinking patterns with emotional and behavioral problems. The HIT is a paper-and-pencil test, and the items are presented in a 6-point Likert-type form (*disagree strongly* to *agree strongly*). The subscales of the HIT are grouped in two main categories: cognitive distortion subscales (Self-Centered, Blaming Others, Minimizing/Mislabeling, Assuming the Worst) and behavioral referent subscales (Opposition-Defiance, Physical Aggression, Lying, Stealing). The results may be presented as scores on the two major scales: Overt scale (Opposition-Defiance and Physical Aggression), Covert scale (Lying and Stealing), and as Overall score (which represents average of all eight subscales).

The scores can be easily calculated using the HIT Questionnaire Computation Form. The Profile Form allows a clear and easily interpretable graphical representation of the eight subscales, plus the Overall score, and the Overt and Covert scales. The process of calculation and plotting is clearly described in the Guidelines for Administering and Scoring the How I Think Questionnaire (HIT), which is supplied with the test package. The plotted results may be interpreted in terms of the symptom severity as Nonclinical (50th to 72nd percentile), Borderline Clinical (74th to 82nd percentile), and Clinical (84th percentile and above).

DEVELOPMENT. The HIT was developed as a measure of self-serving cognitive distortions, and is based on a four-category typology formulated by Gibbs and Potter on the basis of their research on sociomoral development of young people. The categories are defined as (a) Self-Centered: According status to one's own views, expectations, needs, rights, immediate feelings, and desires to such a degree that the legitimate views of others are scarcely considered or are disregarded altogether; (b) Blaming Others: Misattributing blame to outside sources, especially another person, a group, or a momentary aberration (one was drunk, high, in a bad mood, etc.), or misattributing blame for one's victimization or other misfortune to innocent others; (c) Minimizing/Mislabeling: Depicting antisocial behavior as causing no real harm or as being acceptable or even admirable, or referring to others with a belit-

tling or dehumanizing label; (d) Assuming the Worst: Gratuitously attributing hostile intentions to others, considering a worst-case scenario for a social situation as if it were inevitable, or assuming that improvement is impossible in one's own or others' behavior. In terms of social-psychological theories, self-serving cognitive distortions represent egocentric bias and rationalizations that serve to neutralize conscience or guilt.

The authors also added the Behavioral Referent Scale, "in order to provide broad and meaningful content for the cognitive distortions" (manual, p. 6). The items for this scale are derived from the Conduct Disorder and oppositional Defiant Disorder syndromes as defined by the fourth edition of the *Diagnostic and Statistical Manual of Mental Disorders.* The test also contains two nonclinical sets of items: Anomalous Responding and Positive Fillers. The Anomalous Responding scale was designed to screen for disingenuous, incompetent, or otherwise suspect responding (a control scale), and Positive Fillers were included to "encourage full use of the response scale." The current version of the HIT represents a modification and improvement of the first form of the questionnaire, psychometrically analyzed by Barriga and Gibbs in 1996.

TECHNICAL. Readability of the HIT was analyzed using Grammatik (Wampler, 1988). The HIT's linguistic complexity was compared with the Gettysburg Address, a Hemingway short story, and the tax form 1040EZ instructions. The results indicate generally that the readability level of the HIT compares well with the levels that are present in Hemingway's short story.

Reliability of the HIT was assessed by computing coefficient alpha for subscales. These values ranged from .63 to .92; the Overt and Covert scales yielded distinctly higher coefficients ranging from .83 to .94. Internal consistency of the overall scores was very high, ranging from .92 to .96. These results support the use of the overall score in clinical judgments. The subscale scores demonstrated much lower levels of reliability.

Test-retest reliability at a 1-week interval was tested using the 1996 version of the HIT and reported as .91. The authors provided evidence of validity using confirmatory factor analysis. This attempt was misconceived because only two hypothetical structures were compared: a 6-factor solution versus a 3-factor solution. The 1-factor solution, which is clearly suggested by the results of internal consistency analyses, was not included; therefore, the presented approach is theoretically untenable (because all subscales are highly intercorrelated, the 1-factor solution should be included as a hypothesis). Another basic error in these analyses is represented by an inclusion of Anomalous responding and Positive Fillers in the computations. By definition these scales should be theoretically independent from the clinical scales, but their "factors" were still significantly (negatively) correlated with the clinical scales (at the level of $p<.001$). Although the confirmatory factor analysis strategy was incorrect, the authors acknowledge that the high intercorrelations among subscales suggest that "self-serving distortions may be consolidated into a holistic worldview that can be characterized as a 'criminal mind' (cf. Samenow, 1984)" (manual, p. 11). This hypothesis could have been easily tested by an inclusion of a 1-factor model.

Convergent evidence of the HIT's validity was provided analyzing correlations between the HIT scores and the scores obtained from other measures of antisocial behavior. The correlation coefficients between the HIT scores and the Externalizing scale of the Youth Self-Report ranged from .45 to .66. Correlation between the HIT scores and the Self-Report Delinquency Scale was .49. All other reported attempts to assess convergent validity by relating the HIT scores to antisocial behaviors yielded correlation coefficients below .4. This indicates that the HIT scores are more related to the cognitive characteristics than to the actual behaviors, which suggests evidence of validity of HIT scores.

Discriminant validity testing concentrated mainly on calculations of the effects of group, gender, and race using ANOVA in the four validation samples. The reported results are somewhat questionable because in one sample (Sample 2) the effect of race was significant, whereas the effect of group (criterion) was not. It should be noted that the effect of race far exceeded the effect of the criterion in this sample. Moreover, the main effect in Sample 4 is not reported, which leaves us with only three comparisons.

COMMENTARY. The HIT is a short and easy-to-administer measure of self-serving cognitive distortions. The simplicity and the readability of the questionnaire indicates that the instrument can be used adequately with young delinquents, which was the primary objective of the test.

The instrument appears to be a reliable measure, especially if the total score is used for clinical judgment. Validity evidence is somewhat compelling at least in terms of convergent validity, but additional work is required to investigate the contaminating effect of racial differences on the instrument's discriminant validity. The reported results indicated problems in this area, and further research is required in order to define (and possibly eliminate) the source of such contaminations. These problems may be due to the sampling process used in different validation samples.

SUMMARY. The HIT scores reliably indicate the level of self-serving cognitive distortions. The test is based on a sound theory that was developed from pragmatic research in the area. The reliability value of the Overall score is high, but clinicians should be cautious concerning the use of the subscales and the two major scales because their factorial validity has not been demonstrated and the reliability of separate subscales is much lower. The authors concede that the total score's reliability and the substantial intercorrelations among the subscales of the HIT indicate the existence of just one construct, labeled by them as a "criminal mind" dimension. The presented research indicated some convergent validity of this construct, and generally the test can be used as a screening instrument. Because the contaminating effect of racial differences was reported, the use of the HIT as a sole diagnostic instrument should be avoided. Any diagnostic conclusions should be predominantly based on objective behavioral data although the HIT scores may be helpful in providing some insight into the underlying cognitive processes of the client. In research settings, the full scale HIT scores may represent a useful variable in investigations testing the relationships between cognitive characteristics and other social psychological phenomena, such as antisocial behaviors, sociomoral development, social intelligence, and socialization levels.

REVIEWER'S REFERENCES
Barriga, A. Q., & Gibbs, J. C. (1996). Measuring cognitive distortion in antisocial youth: Development and preliminary evaluation of the How I Think Questionnaire. *Aggressive Behaviors, 22*, 333–343.
Wampler, B. E. (1988). *Grammatik.* San Francisco: Reference Software.

Review of the How I Think Questionnaire by JOSEPH C. KUSH, Associate Professor and Coordinator, School Psychology Program, Duquesne University, Pittsburgh, PA:

DESCRIPTION. The How I Think (HIT) Questionnaire is a group-administered, paper-and-pencil measure, designed to assess the cognitive distortions of adolescents. The questionnaire requires a fourth-grade reading level and requires between 5 and 15 minutes to be completed. Questions are presented in a 6-point Likert scale format and the instrument is designed for clinical and research applications.

The rationale underlying the How I Think (HIT) Questionnaire is based on cognitive theories of psychology that suggest individual thoughts contribute to emotional and behavioral responses. More specifically, in the area of psychopathology, cognitive distortions protect the individual from blame or guilt by deflecting or redefining the environmental message, thereby maintaining the integrity of the ego. The importance of cognitive distortions in the development of both internalizing and externalizing disorders has been studied extensively by prominent cognitive theorists including Bandura (1991), Dodge (1991, 1993), and Kendall (1991).

DEVELOPMENT. The development of the HIT Questionnaire was based upon a four-category typology of cognitive distortions including: Self-Centered, Blaming Others, Minimizing/Mislabeling, and Assuming the Worst. These categories are described by the authors as also referring to "one or another of four categories of antisocial behavior derived from the Conduct Disorder and Oppositional Defiant Disorder syndromes listed in the fourth edition of the *Diagnostic and Statistical Manual of Mental Disorders* (DSM-IV)" (manual, p. 6). The original version of the HIT Questionnaire was published in 1996 and contained 52 cognitive distortion items and 8 validity items termed Anomalous Responses. Item analyses, based on the initial scale, were then used to generate the questions included in the current version of the scale. The HIT Questionnaire manual indicates that the selection of final items was subsequently based upon five psychometric criteria: (a) the ability to differentiate criterion groups, (b) correlations with other self-report measures of antisocial behavior, (c), increased correlations with intended item subscales, (d) lack of confoundance with anomalous responses, and (e) improved scale floors and ceilings. As a result, the current version of the scale includes 54 total items: 39 cognitive distortion items, 8 anomalous items, and 7 newly created "positive fillers" (e.g., "When friends need you, you should be there for them"). The role of these anomalous and filler items is designed to control for response biases.

Standardized directions for administration are presented, which direct the test user to administer the questionnaire in a room free from distractions, "individually or in small groups (up to 20 individuals), with appropriate proctoring" (manual, p. 22). Instructions require the examiner to read the directions on the front page of the questionnaire aloud, while the adolescent reads along silently. Scoring is based on a 6-point Likert scale: 1 = *disagree strongly* to 6 = *agree strongly*. The HIT Questionnaire manual indicates that the readability of the scale is at a fourth-grade reading level. Means, standard deviations, standard errors, and percentile ranks are all derived from the normative sample.

TECHNICAL. The standardization sample(s) described in the HIT Questionnaire manual represents one of the greatest limitations of the instrument. The manual indicates that five independent samples were collected, all from the Midwestern region of the United States. One of the samples served as the "Refinement Sample" from which the final version of the instrument was derived and four additional samples served as "validation" samples. The refinement sample consisted of 143 male and female adolescents ages 13 through 19 years of age. Ninety-two of these adolescents were incarcerated at a Department of Youth Services facility and the remaining 51 students came from an urban high school. Three major factors, therefore, significantly limit the generalizability of the instrument given its incomplete standardization procedure. First, all students in the sample were drawn from the Midwestern region of the United States. Second, the ethnic breakdown of the standardization sample does not correspond to the ethnic distribution of the most recent United States Census. Third, no attempt was made to stratify the standardization sample on any type of cognitive/intellectual variable nor on any measure of socioeconomic status.

Subscale and summary norms for the HIT Questionnaire were derived with reference to the nonreferred youth from all five samples. The resulting normative sample included 412 youths 14 to 19 years of age. One hundred ninety three of these participants were college students from validation sample 4. The ethnic breakdown of the normative sample was 65% Caucasian, 22% African American, 9% Asian American, 2% Hispanic, 1% Native American, and 2% who did not report their race.

Additionally, the HIT Questionnaire manual indicates that 527 students were subsequently included as part of four validation samples. The majority of these students came from psychiatric facilities or court-ordered treatment facilities; 193 of these students were enrolled in an introductory psychology course at a large midwestern university. Much like the refinement sample, individuals likely to be experiencing behavioral or mental health disorders are greatly overrepresented in the combined validation sample. Although cognitive distortions are clearly more likely to be related to indices of psychopathology, without an adequate representation of how often cognitive distortions occur in a normal population an adequate base rate can never be established. As a result it is likely that users of the HIT Questionnaire should expect to encounter more false-positives than are likely to exist in a normal population.

The HIT Questionnaire manual does provide basic information describing some of the psychometric characteristics of the instrument. Face validity was examined by asking 10 graduate students in psychology to classify each item, first by cognitive distortion category and then according to DSM behavioral referent category. Judges were reported to be highly accurate in classifying items by cognitive distortion category. Of the 39 items, 16 were accurately classified by 100% of the judges, 13 items by 90% of the judges, and the remaining items by no fewer than 60% of the judges. Similar correct behavioral referent classification was also exhibited by the judges. Construct validity of the HIT Questionnaire was evaluated through confirmatory factor analyses using the four validation samples. Two competing modes were tested: (a) a six-factor solution (four cognitive distortion/behavioral referent categories and two validity categories) and (b) a three-factor solution (one global cognitive distortion/behavioral referent category and two validity categories). Although support for the six-factor model was found, the authors did note a high degree of intercorrelation (many in the .80 range) among subscales. Additionally, many of the factor loading point estimates were lower than would be expected in a more "pure" multifactored model. Specifically, none of the factor loadings exceeded .80, 11 items were in the .70 range, 15 of the items were in the .60 range, 7 of the items were in the .50 range, 3 items were in the .40 range, and 3

items were in the .30 range. Therefore, additional construct validity research must be undertaken before any firm conclusions can be derived supporting either the unitary or multifactored, underlying, nature of the HIT.

Internal consistency estimates of the HIT were assessed using Cronbach's coefficient alpha. Alpha coefficients were generally high with cognitive distortion and behavioral referent subscales producing alphas ranging from .63 to .92. Internal consistency estimates of the overall scale were very high with alphas ranging from .92 to .96.

Unfortunately, the HIT also fails to provide any evidence of interrater or test-retest reliability. Potential users are given insufficient information about what constitutes normal fluctuation across time or across subgroups. In the absence of published reliability data, potential users of the HIT are unable to determine whether changes in scores over time reflect normal fluctuations, possible abnormal etiology, or ratings that are being scored differentially across time by examiners.

A number of studies are reported in the HIT Questionnaire manual examining the convergent and divergent validity of scores from the instrument. For the most part, although statistically significant, these correlations are only moderately large and therefore reflect a relatively small percentage of variance accounted for. For example, correlations between the HIT and the Externalizing Scale of the Youth Self-Report, in each of the five standardization samples range from .45 to .66. A similar correlation (.49) was reported between the HIT and self-reported antisocial behavior as measured by the Self-Report Delinquency Scale. Equally disappointing were correlations (.29 and .32) between the HIT and the Externalizing Scale of Achenbach's Child Behavior Checklist. Finally, HIT scores were found to yield no significant correlations with socioeconomic status, intelligence, academic achievement, or grade-point average.

A series of discriminant validity analyses are also presented in the HIT manual producing somewhat unexpected results. Because of the relatively small numbers of Hispanic, Asian American, and Native American students, only comparisons between Caucasians and African Americans were calculated. A main effect for group was found in three of the four samples, no main effects were found for gender, and a main effect for race was found in one of the five samples. The only significant group x race interaction occurred in the same sample.

The HIT Questionnaire manual also fails to provide evidence of predictive validity for the scale. As a result, clinicians will be severely constrained in their ability to derive even basic diagnostic decisions when utilizing the HIT. Additionally, the test manual provides no evidence of incremental validity, that is, the extent to which information derived from the HIT will increase the accuracy in predictions derived from other sources of information. Multiple regression analyses would help ascertain whether a significant amount of additional variance in diagnostic criteria could be accounted for when the HIT is added to an already established test battery.

Finally, two studies reported in the HIT manual examined clinical outcomes. In the first study, the HIT was used to assess reductions in cognitive distortions of adolescents in a young adult boot camp who were exposed to an intervention utilizing a 12-hour videotape series. The study found no significant differences ($p<.08$) in reduced cognitive distortions between students exposed to the intervention and a control group. In the second study, a significantly greater reduction in HIT scores was found for adult inmates who participated in a program teaching transcendental meditation than for control participants.

SUMMARY. The HIT possesses many psychometric shortcomings that significantly limit the usability of the instrument. The HIT could become a potentially useful instrument for assessing the cognitive distortions of adolescents if more comprehensive norming procedures were undertaken and if additional reliability and validity studies were completed. Until that time, caution should be exercised when using the HIT as a diagnostic instrument. Perhaps this "second generation" of the instrument can evolve into a more psychometrically sound, revised questionnaire with an expanded empirical and research base.

REVIEWER'S REFERENCES

Bandura, A. (1991). Social cognitive theory of moral thought and action. In W. M. Kurtines & J. L. Gewirtz (Eds.), *Handbook of moral behavior and development: Vol. 1. Theory* (pp. 45–103). Hillsdale, NJ: Erlbaum.

Dodge, K. A. (1991). The structure and function of reactive and proactive aggression. In D. J. Pepler & K. H. Rubin (Eds.), *The development and treatment of childhood aggression* (pp. 201–218). Hillsdale, NJ: Erlbaum.

Dodge, K. A. (1993). Social-cognitive mechanisms in the development of conduct disorder and depression. *Annual Review of Psychology, 44,* 559–584.

Kendall, P. C. (1991). Guiding theory for therapy with children and adolescents. In P. C Kendall (Ed.), *Child and adolescent therapy: Cognitive-behavioral procedures* (pp. 3–24). New York: Guilford.

[120]

H.R.R. Pseudoisochromatic Plates for Detecting, Classifying and Estimating the Degree of Defective Color Vision.

Purpose: Designed to test for color vision.
Population: People who may have color vision deficiency.
Publication Date: 1991.
Scores, 3: Normal Color Vision, Defective Color Vision (Red-Green Deficiency, Blue-Yellow Deficiency).
Administration: Individual.
Price Data, 2001: $197 per H.R.R. book including 4 demonstration plates, 20 test pages, and score sheet.
Time: (1–3) minutes.
Authors: Richmond Products, Inc.; LeGrand H. Hardy (manual), Gertrude Rand (manual), and M. Catherine Rittler (manual).
Publisher: Richmond Products, Inc.

Review of the H.R.R. Pseudoisochromatic Plates for Detecting, Classifying and Estimating the Degree of Defective Color Vision by AYRES G. D'COSTA, Associate Professor, Quantitative Research, Evaluation and Measurement in Education, College of Education, The Ohio State University, Columbus, OH:

DESCRIPTION. The H.R.R. Pseudoisochromatic Plates (HRR) test is a color perception test, originally designed in the WWII years by Hardy, Rand, and Rittler (1946), for detecting (screening/identifying) color-vision defective persons, classifying (qualitatively discriminating red-green and blue-yellow defectives), and attempting to provide a quantitative estimate of the severity or degree of color vision defect. The original version of this test was first published in 1955 by the American Optical Company (AO) and was referred to as the AO-HRR test. According to Walls (1959), a second edition was published by AO in 1957. The currently available (1991) H.R.R. test is a republished version marketed by Richmond International, Inc. following the discontinuation of the second edition by AO around 1980. It is simply referred to as H.R.R. Pseudoisochromatic Plates.

The publisher indicated to this reviewer that no changes were made to the AO-HRR (second edition) test, although the color plates are now printed using a more modern printing process, which is health-hazard-free. The new HRR consists of 24 color perception plates (4 demonstration, 6 screening, and 14 diagnostic). The test binder comes with accessories including a pad of

50 scoring sheets, instructions for administration, page numbering labels, and a camel's hair brush. An Easel Illumination Lamp is sold separately.

No technical manual as such is available for the HRR from Richmond International. They provide an eight-page mini-booklet with simple instructions for administration of the test. In this mini-booklet, it is claimed that four of the existing validation studies on the HRR were reviewed by the Subcommittee on Color Blindness Studies of the Inter-Society Color Council (Deane B. Judd, Chair) who concluded that the HRR's validity claims are legitimate.

DEVELOPMENT. Walls (1959) indicated that the HRR Pseudoisochromatic Plates test (HRR) was originally developed during WWII from its Stilling (German) and Ishihara (Japan) counterparts, when these tests became unavailable in the U.S.A. There appears to have been considerable theoretical thinking and research associated with the original development of the HRR. Hardy, Rand, and Rittler (1946) identified four types of plate designs: the *vanishing* design (which screens color defectives), the qualitatively *diagnostic* design (which differentiates red-green defectives as to whether they are protans or deutans), the *transformation* design (which shows two figures, one visible to the normal, the other visible to a defective), and the *hidden digit* design (used in diagnosis of color defects of older patients). The patient is expected to discern, locate, and name embedded symbols made of color spots.

The administration of the HRR is claimed to take a couple of minutes, with special test-takers (e.g., children, the elderly, and those with language problems) taking slightly longer. The procedures and instructions for administration and scoring are very clearly presented in the mini-booklet provided with the HRR.

The administration process is well standardized to ensure precision and reliability of the decisions. The HRR plates are attractively printed and the scoring sheet is clear. A camel's hair brush is given to the patient to use when locating the symbols on the plates in order to protect the plates from dirt and finger oils.

TECHNICAL. The standardization of the HRR is reported in the mini-booklet to have been done by the authors on the first edition using 600 normals and 150 R-G defectives, and on the second edition with 160 normals and 100 defectives. Further work is reported to have been completed by Sloan and Altman (65 defectives), by Schmidt (300 normals, 19 defectives), and by Farnsworth (no figures provided). No research was reported to have been conducted with the rare B-Y defectives because of their unavailability. It is not clear how these samples were selected or whether they are representative.

The reliability of the HRR scores, in terms of their internal consistency or test-retest correlation, has not been reported. All of the studies reported in the literature have focused on decision consistency with the HRR, which is understandable given the criterion-referenced nature of its use. The Cohen's Kappa (1960) formula is used. Pokorny et al. (1981) reported that test reliability (in terms of decision consistency) depends on which type of decision (screening, discrimination, severity) is made with the HRR. For example, based on the original studies by the HRR authors in 1954, reliability indexes of .97, .98, and .79 are reported for screening classification, and severity decisions, respectively. However, Paulson's (1971) reliability studies are reported to be much lower (.38 for discrimination and .53 for severity decisions). No information is provided about sample characteristics in these studies, although it could be presumed that these are clinical cases, and therefore opportunistic.

The content validity evidence for the HRR lies primarily in its theoretical underpinnings. The plates are developed so as to represent special "confusion lines" and to diagnose specific color discrimination problems.

The HRR has been analyzed extensively in terms of its criterion validity. Seventeen validation studies have been reported by Pokorny et al. (1981), including those by Walls (1959) and Voss, Verkaik, and Boogard (1972). In many of these studies, decision comparisons were made with the anomaloscope, which is often used like the "gold standard." Three types of decisions were investigated for criterion validity: screening, discrimination, and severity. The five studies that examined screening validity reported Cohen's Kappa indexes in the .90s, which is very high. The discrimination validity indexes reported by another seven studies averaged in the .70s, although they ranged from the high .50s to the low .80s. The five studies related to severity validity averaged in the .30s, which, of course, is low. All of these studies were reported prior to 1980.

Based on their extensive review of literature, Pokorny et al. (1981) noted that the HRR is 85% to 90% effective as a screening test. However, there appeared several false negatives (but no false positives) when the HRR was used for discriminating color defect type. His Committee found that the HRR's grading of severity is somewhat inaccurate. They concluded that the HRR:

Is useful for rapid screening of red-green and blue-yellow defects. It provides differential diagnosis of protan and deutan, classifies three levels of severity, and provides differentiation of defect. It is especially useful in testing children and others who comprehend geometrical symbols, but not numerals. (p. 44)

COMMENTARY. The HRR is viewed as one of the two or three major color vision tests of its type. Its strength lies in the original research by the authors to ensure its acceptance by the optometry community. However, not much has been done to improve this test since it was first developed into its second edition by the original authors. Richmond International is making this test available following a period of about 15 years when the test became unavailable to new users and requests were made for its republication.

The field of color vision testing has moved well beyond where the HRR test is now. Although confirmed to be suitable for use with normal children (Shute & Westall, 2000), and in certain drug-associated toxicity cases (Vu, Easterbrook, & Hovis, 1999), more needs to be known about the HRR's suitability for use with special clients, such as mentally retarded, congenital night-blind persons, and diabetics. The trend today is to make color-vision testing easy to handle (Cotter, Lee, & French, 1999), including computer administration (Ionica & Gastaud, 1999); Kogure, Iijima, & Tsukahara, 1999) and using color monitors (Regan, Riffin, & Mollon, 1994; Watanabe, Pokorny, & Smith, 1999).

No studies were found that examined the construct validity of scores from the HRR, although the detailed technical evaluations, such as by Lakowski (1966), should make this effort feasible in the future. Construct validity explores the underlying latent traits measured by a test. To do this effectively, one would need to make the HRR scoring more sensitive. This reviewer believes that the traditional scoring process of the HRR is too global to be precise and effective. Much of the information available from patient responses seems to be ignored.

The lack of a formal technical manual is a serious deficiency for the HRR in meeting the professional *Standards for Educational and Psychological Testing* (AERA, APA, & NCME, 1999), and could easily be remedied. Much of the information needed for such a manual is available in the literature, although it is not conveniently accessible nor systematically presented. It appears that optometry practitioners currently tend to seek such information in the textbooks (Birch, 1993; Ekridge, Amos, & Bartlett, 1991) that students use in this field. Clearly, such information needs to be specific, comprehensive, accessible, and up-to-date for use by practitioners. Professional guidelines exist for the needed content of such technical manuals for published tests.

SUMMARY. The HRR is reasonably good within its class of color vision tests for routine screening and simple classification of color vision defectives. It is well known that the HRR lacks sensitivity and is, therefore, not valid for measuring the severity of such problems. Efforts to upgrade the test for modern-day use in computer-based screening might help popularize it. If properly validated, the research based in the development of its plates could be useful in developing modern prototypes. Aside from its older competitors (Ishihara, Farnsworth) this test will now find newer challengers such as the Neitz (Neitz, Summerfelt, & Neitz, 2000), which claims inexpensive and quick testing by teachers in a classroom setting under ordinary lighting conditions. Needless to say, one gets what one pays for.

REVIEWER'S REFERENNCES

American Educational Research Association, American Psychological Association, & National Council on Measurement in Education. (1999). *Standards for educational and psychological testing.* Washington, DC: American Educational Research Association.

Birch, J. (1993). *Diagnosis of defective color vision.* New York, NY: Oxford University Press.

Cohen, J. (1960). A coefficient of agreement for nominal scales. In *Educational and psychological measurement* (2nd ed.). Washington, DC: American Council on Education.

Cotter, S. A., Lee, D. Y., & French, A. L. (1999). Evaluation of a new color vision test: "Color vision testing made easy." *Optometry and Vision Science, 76,* 631–363.

Ekridge, J. B., Amos, J. F., & Bartlett, J. D. (1991). *Clinical procedures in optometry.* Philadelphia: Lippincott.

Hardy, L. H., Rand, G., & Rittler, M. C. (1946). A screening test for defective red-green vision. *Journal of Optometry Society of America, 36,* 610–614.

Ionica, V., & Gastaud, P. (1999 February). Representation of normal and pathologic macular color vision. *Journal Francais d Ophthalmologie, 22,* 53–56.

Kogure, S., Iijima, H., & Tsukahara, S. (1999 April). Assessment of potential macular function using a color saturation discrimination test in eyes with cataract. *Journal of Cataract and Refractive Surgery, 25,* 569–574.

Lakowski, R. (1966). A critical evaluation of color vision tests. *British Journal of Physiological Optics, 23,* 186–209.

Neitz, J., Summerfelt, P., & Neitz, M. (2000). *Neitz Test of Color Vision.* Los Angeles, Western Psychological Services.

Paulson, H. M. (1971). Color vision testing in the United States Navy. In J. R. Pierce & J. R. Levene (Eds.), *Visual science* (pp. 164–176). Bloomington, IN: Indiana University Press.

Pokorny, J. et al. (1981). *Procedures for testing color vision.* Report of Working Group 41, Committee on Vision, National Research Council. Washington, DC: National Academy Press.

Regan, B. C., Reffin, J., & Mollon, J. D. (1994). Luminance noise and the rapid determination of discrimination ellipses in colour deficiency. *Vision Research, 34,* 1279–1299.

Shute, R. H., & Westall, C. A. (2000). Use of the Mollon-Riffin Minimalist color vision test with young children. *Journal of the American Association of Physiological Optics Society, 4*(6), 366–372.

Vos, J. J., Verkaik, W., & Boogard, J. (1972 October). The significance of the TMC and HRR color-vision-tests as to red-green defectiveness. *American Journal of Optometry and Archives of American Academy of Optometry, 49,* 847–859.

Vu, B. L. L., Easterbrook, M., & Hovis, J. K. (1999). Detection of color vision defects in chloroquine retinopathy. *Ophthalmology, 106,* 1799–1803.

Walls, G. L. (1959, April). How good is the H-R-R test for color blindness? *American Journal of Optometry and Archives of American Academy of Optometry* [monograph] 1–25.

Watanabe, A., Pokorny, J., & Smith, V. C. (1999). Measuring short-wavelength-sensitive cone discrimination thresholds using pseudoisochromatic figures displayed on a color monitor. *Japanese Journal of Ophthalmology, 43,* 5–8.

[121]

IDEA Feedback for Department Chairs.

Purpose: Designed to diagnose administrative performance and discover ways to effectively improve it.

Population: College and university department chairpersons.

Publication Dates: 1977–1998.

Scores: 17 scores in 3 areas: Overall Ratings (Summary Judgement, Effectiveness in Performance, Five Types of Administrative Responsibilities); Effectiveness in Performing Twenty Specific Administrative Responsibilities (Administrative Support, Personnel Management, Program Leadership/Support, Building Image/Reputation, Developing Positive Climate); Description of Administrative Methods and Personal Characteristics (Democratic/Humanistic, Goal-Oriented/Structured, Supports Faculty, Promotes Positive Climate, Promotes Department Advancement, Ability to Resolve Issues, Communication Skills, Steadiness, Trustworthiness, Openness).

Administration: Group.

Price Data: Available from publisher.

Time: (15–30) minutes.

Comments: Previous version entitled Departmental Evaluation of Chairperson Activities for Development; publisher scores and generates interpretive reports; online inventory completed by faculty about their department chairs.

Authors: IDEA Center and Donald D. Hoyt (Technical Report, 1998).

Publisher: IDEA Center.

Cross References: See T4:741 (1 reference).

Review of the IDEA Feedback for Department Chairs by JOHN W. FLEENOR, Director of Knowledge Management, Center for Creative Leadership, Greensboro, NC:

DESCRIPTION. According to the manual, IDEA Feedback for Department Chairs provides the only nationally available data-based tool for assessing and developing departmental chairpersons at colleges and universities. Published by the Individual Development and Educational Assessment (IDEA) Center at Kansas State University, this instrument (called a "system" by its authors) is designed to assess the effectiveness of the academic chairperson or department head. IDEA Feedback for Department Chairs is a revision of an earlier IDEA instrument entitled Departmental Evaluation of Chairperson Activities for Development (DECAD). The instrument is based on the idea that effective management depends on setting appropriate goals for the department and successfully meeting those goals.

The IDEA Feedback for Department Chairs system is designed to measure effective management by focusing on the chairperson's success in meeting departmental goals. According to the manual, the system uses ratings by both faculty members and the chairperson to provide feedback that is accurate, reliable, and relevant. The system also provides suggestions on strategies for improving performance to the chairperson, which may help him or her improve administrative effectiveness.

The IDEA Feedback for Department Chairs system consists of two computer-scored survey forms—one completed by faculty members and one completed by the department head. Both forms have six sections. The first section of the faculty form consists of 20 items designed to measure the effectiveness of the department head on the primary responsibilities of the position (e.g., "Guides curriculum development"). On the department head form, the chair rates importance of these same 20 items for his or her job.

The second section of the faculty form contains 10 items on which faculty rate the department head on personal characteristics, such as interpersonal skill and judgment. On the third section of the faculty form, faculty rate how frequently the department head demonstrates 30 administrative behaviors thought to be effective for that position (e.g., "Tries out new ideas with the faculty"). Section 4 consists of five items that measure potential impediments to the chair's effectiveness, such as inadequate facilities, and bureaucratic rules and regulations. Finally, there is a summary judgment item ("I believe the department would be better off if we replaced the current head/chair").

Section 2 of the department head form consists of six items that measure the degree to which the chair emphasizes certain programs, such as undergraduate or graduate programs. The remaining four sections on the department head form each consist of one item that gathers biographic or demographic information.

A one-page guide for administering the IDEA Feedback for Department Chairs system is provided. The completed forms are mailed to the IDEA Center for scoring. The feedback reports are shipped back to the administrator, typically within 20 working days. Each chairperson receives a copy of his or her report. The report provides feedback on performance, administrative behavior, and personal characteristics, as well as statistical detail as to how faculty responded to each item.

DEVELOPMENT. A 57-page manual, published in 1998, describes the development of the instrument. The report is essentially a description of the revision process for the earlier version of the instrument, the DECAD, which was developed in 1977. The purpose of the revision was to (a) update the instrument based on current research, (b) provide an overall measure of effectiveness, (c) cover administrative functions that have been identified as important for effective performance, (d) account for factors that are beyond the department head's control, and (e) reduce the number of items. The result was a revised instrument that consisted of 66 items, 4 fewer than the original version. Overall, 20 new items were added, and 24 old items were deleted in the development of the new version.

TECHNICAL. Norms are based on data from 289 academic departments. All findings in the feedback report are analyzed by type of institution: research university, doctoral-degree granting institution, master's-degree granting institution, health-related institutions, and institutions offering associate degrees. There were not sufficient data to develop norms for bachelor's-degree granting institutions. Over 34% of the institutions in the norm group are located in the Midwestern United States.

Many of the analyses reported in the manual were conducted on data gathered with the earlier version of the instrument. Only those results that are relevant for the revised instrument will be discussed here (i.e., analyses of items that appear on both versions of the instrument). Interrater reliabilities are presented in the manual for the faculty ratings of the effectiveness of the department heads. For the ratings of eight faculty members, these reliabilities ranged from .54 to .76. Reliabilities of the administrative behavior items and the potential impediments items were similar to those of the effectiveness ratings. No internal consistency or split-half reliabilities were reported.

As evidence of validity, the manual reports correlations between each individual item and an aggregate score of the 54 items that made up the effectiveness, administrative behaviors, and limitations sections. These correlations were generally in the .50s and .60s, with a few above .70. The manual also reports similar results, using step-wise regression procedure.

As additional evidence of internal validity, the manual reports a principal components analysis of the faculty ratings of administrative behavior. The results of this analysis indicated that this section consists of two components, which the authors label "Democratic/Humanistic" and "Goal-Oriented/Structured." The items that loaded on these two components were included as scales on the revised instrument.

COMMENTARY. The IDEA Feedback for Department Chairs system seems to have some potential to become a useful instrument. As indicated by the authors, few, if any, similar instruments are available. However, the evidence of reliability and validity as presented in the manual is inadequate; therefore, the instrument cannot be recommended without reservation. As the authors indicate, ratings from at least 12 faculty members are necessary before the instrument will reach an acceptable level of reliability. This does not, however, seem to be an unreasonable number, given the size of most academic departments.

As indicated in this review, the psychometric analyses reported in the manual were conducted using data from an earlier version of the instrument. Additionally, many of the analyses reported are not useful in determining the psychometric quality of the instrument. For example, the practice of correlating individual items with an aggregate score of items from the same instrument provides limited information. At a minimum, evidence of external validity (i.e., correlations with an external criterion) is necessary before the instrument can be recommended for uses other than for research purposes.

The norms are based on a fairly small sample of academic departments, many of which are located in one section of the United States. A larger and more representative sample is necessary before the norms can be used without caution.

The feedback report presents a large amount of data for the department head's consumption. The report is not easy to interpret, however, and it will take a fair amount of time to digest fully. The report could be improved by changing the format and the presentation of the results to make it easier to interpret. Additionally, it is not clear how the feedback report alone can be used for developmental purposes because the tool does not provide specific recommendations for development.

SUMMARY. This instrument cannot be recommended for use as a feedback tool for academic department heads until a comprehensive psychometric study is conducted on a large sample of data collected with the current instrument. Such a study would include complete reliability and validity analyses and the collection of a representative sample of data to develop new norms.

Review of the IDEA Feedback for Department Chairs by M. DAVID MILLER, Professor of Educational Psychology, University of Florida, Gainesville, FL:

DESCRIPTION. The IDEA Feedback for Department Chairs is a revision of the Departmental Evaluation of Chairperson Activities for Development (DECAD) program developed in 1977. The instrument consists of two surveys: a Department Chair survey and a Faculty survey. The Department Chair survey consists of 30 items measuring the importance of administrative responsibilities (20 items), the department emphasis on various functions (6 items), and background information (4 items). The Faculty survey consists of 66 items measuring performance on administrative responsibilities (the same 20 items that department chairs rate for importance), the strengths of the department chair (10 items), the frequency of administrative activities (30 items), impediments to effectiveness (5 items), and a summary rating of the department chair.

According to the manual, the intent of the IDEA Feedback for Department Chairs is to provide evaluative data of department chairs to assist summative and formative evaluation. That is, the data could be used for recommendations regarding merit salary, promotion and other administrative decisions (summative), or for improv-

ing administrative performance (formative). The IDEA Center scores the data and provides an eight page summary report, showing frequencies and means on individual items with accompanying interpretations. On many items, raw means are reported as well as a mean adjusted for department characteristics.

The intended population for this instrument is defined as academic departments in any academic discipline or type of institution. However, the national database upon which comparisons are made has mostly doctoral and master's programs (28.7% and 51.6%, respectively). The sample has smaller numbers of community colleges (4.5%) and health-profession schools (4.5%). This information is especially important for community colleges where the results of the national database show significantly different results from other types of institutions (fewer differences are reported across other types of institutions).

DEVELOPMENT. The IDEA Feedback for Department Chairs is a revision of an instrument developed in 1977. Three reasons led to the revision. First, a substantial literature on the role of department chairs and other administrators in higher education had appeared. Second, a diversity of types of institutions had used the prior instrument leading to questions about norms and item statistics by institution type. Third, there was an interest in adjusting ratings for circumstances beyond the control of the chair that may influence their performance ratings.

On the basis of books published on administration in higher education, the content of the instruments was modified. The primary modifications included items on personal characteristics of the chair that the literature suggested were important to effective functioning, and items to reflect underperformance. Items were developed to distinguish means and ends. The revised instrument included five considerations: (a) maintain the rationale and purpose of the program, (b) add an "overall" measure of effectiveness, (c) cover administrative purposes (i.e., ends) and processes (i.e., means) that are identified in the literature, (d) measure factors that are beyond the control of the chair, and (e) be shorter than the original form.

TECHNICAL. Documentation was not available on the technical characteristics of the modified instrument that is currently being used. Data are reported from the original instrument developed in 1977, which includes many items that are the same. As a result, the technical data only provide a loose fit to the current instrument and clearly draw into question the use of the instrument for anything except exploratory data. That is, evaluation, whether summative or formative, is merely based on the face value of the individual items and their psychometric properties are not yet known. The rest of this section will summarize trends from the earlier version of the instrument.

Standardization. The original instrument was administered to 289 departments from 52 institutions classified by institutional type as Associate of Arts (*n* = 13), Health-Profession Schools (*n* = 13), Master's (*n* = 149), Doctoral (*n* = 83), and Research (*n* = 31). The authors do not describe an approach to sampling and clearly make no claims to the representativeness of the sample. Later analyses show few differences by institution type except that the Associate of Arts programs differ. Clearly, the data do not approximate norms of any type but are informative on their own as a research report. The means from any administration should only be interpreted in a criterion-referenced manner.

Reliability. All data are reported at the item level that leads to lower estimates of reliability. All reliabilities are reported for the department means and not for individual faculty ratings. The moderate to low reliabilities for the group means reported, and discussed, below, suggest that individual ratings are too unreliable to be used. The manual suggests that item means are not reliable with less than 8 faculty. With 8 faculty, the item means show a range of reliabilities from .54 to .70 (median = .59) for faculty ratings of performance on administrative responsibilities. For a sample size of 20, the reliabilities range from .75 to .89. With a target reliability of .70, a minimum sample size of 15 is needed. With a target reliability of .80, even a rating by 20 faculty is too small for many items. Clearly, the reliability of individual items is reasonable only with a large number of faculty completing the survey.

Validity. Validity evidence for the original instrument is based on exploratory factor analyses, correlations, and other statistical measures of the relationships of items within the same instrument, and the relationship of the instrument to institution type. Although each provides valuable information, it should be noted that no validation evidence is reported for the possible evaluation uses suggested (i.e., summative or formative evaluation of department chairs). The exploratory factor analyses also suggest that scales could be created that would lead to more reliable results.

SUMMARY. The IDEA Feedback for Department Chairs purports to measure the effectiveness of department chairs for evaluative purposes. However, there are several problems with this relatively high stakes use of the instrument. First, the items on the instrument are not construct-based or theoretically derived. Second, suggested uses of the instrument are not examined in any systematic way so that the validity of those uses is questionable. Third, the reliability of scores from the instrument can only be realized at the group level with a large number of faculty (*n*>15) completing the survey. Fourth, no data are reported for the current, revised form of the instrument.

Reporting of individual items does provide simpler interpretations but raises other issues. The use of single items in reporting is not consistent with the factor analysis and effectively ignores any larger constructs in the data. The single items are also one reason for the questionable reliability of the results with a smaller number of faculty. Finally, the response options on the items are not consistent with the presentation of data. For example, the options for performance items are: 1 = *Poor,* 2 = *Only So-So,* 3 = *In Between,* 4 = *Good,* and 5 = *Outstanding.* Even if these categories do not overlap, they are clearly not interval and means are not an appropriate summary of the data.

The IDEA Feedback for Department Chairs may provide interesting data for a department administrator, but the instrument needs further work to justify any high, or even moderate, stakes use of the results.

[122]

Illinois Test of Psycholinguistic Abilities, Third Edition.

Purpose: Designed "to help children who have weakness in various linguistic processes including spoke or written language."

Population: Ages 5-0 to 12-11.

Publication Dates: 1961–2001.

Acronym: ITPA-3.

Scores, 12: Spoken Analogies, Spoken Vocabulary, Morphological Closure, Syntactic Sentences, Sound Deletion, Rhyming Sequences, Sentence Sequencing, Written Vocabulary, Sight Decoding, Sound Decoding, Sight Spelling, Sound Spelling.

Administration: Individual.

Price Data, 2003: $164 per kit including 25 profile/examiner record booklets, 25 student response booklets, manual (2001, 165 pages), and an audio cassette; $45 per 25 profile/examiner record booklets; $41 per 25 student response booklets; $71 per examiner's manual; $15 per audio cassette; $109 per software scoring and report system.

Time: (45–60) minutes.

Authors: Donald D. Hammill, Nancy Mather, and Rhia Roberts.

Publisher: PRO-ED.

Cross References: See T5:1240 (51 references), T4:1201 (53 references), 9:496 (37 references), and T3:1126 (145 references); for reviews by James Lumsden and J. Lee Wiederholt of an earlier edition, and an excerpted review by R. P. Waugh, see 8:431 (269 references); see also T2:981 (113 references); for reviews by John B. Carroll and Clinton I. Chase, see 7:442 (239 references); see also 6:549 (22 references).

Review of the Illinois Test of Psycholinguistic Abilities, Third Edition by ROGER L. TOWNE, Associate Professor and Head, Department of Communication Disorders, Northern Michigan University, Marquette, MI:

DESCRIPTION. The Illinois Test of Psycholinguistic Abilities, Third Edition (ITPA-3) is designed to test true psycholinguistic abilities in children between the ages of 5-0 and 12-11 using 12 subtests. These subtests were selected to test function across three levels of organization (reflexive, form, and content), three psycholinguistic processes (reception, expression, and association), two channels of input (auditory and visual) and two channels of output (vocal and manual). The 12 subtests also have been designed and selected to represent three "global" composites: general language, spoken language, and written language. In addition, eight specific composites are sampled across spoken language (semantics, grammar, and phonology) and written language (comprehension, word identification, spelling, sight-symbol processing, and sound symbol processing). It is intended that this organization will enhance the clinical and diagnostic usefulness of the test.

Verbal directions for each subtest, basal and ceiling criteria, and correct responses are all contained in the Profile/Examiner Record Booklet. The front page of this booklet also contains a section for child identification information (name, date of birth, etc.), a section to record subtest performance (raw score, percentile rank, and stan-

dard score), and a section in which to record performance quotients for each of the general and specific composites. The first six subtests are considered to be verbal subtests as they require verbal presentation of each subtest item by the examiner as well as verbal responses from the child. The last six subtests are considered to be written subtests as they consist of either a written presentation of subtest items and/or written responses from the child. Therefore, the stimulus items for these subtests are also contained in a separate Student Response Form from which the child reads and/or records his or her written responses. Only children who are 6-6 or older are administered the six written subtests. The authors suggest that the ITPA-3 can usually be administered in a single 45- to 60-minute session, but, if needed, can be administered in multiple sessions.

According to the authors, the administration and interpretation of the ITPA-3 requires some formal training in assessment with the examiner having some basic understanding of testing statistics, general procedural knowledge about test administration, scoring and interpretation, and specific knowledge regarding the evaluation of cognitive and linguistic abilities. Test scoring is a simple process. Tables are provided that (a) allow raw scores for each subtest to be converted into percentile scores and standard scores within 2-month age ranges, (b) convert the sums of each composite into quotients and percentiles, (c) convert subtest raw scores to age and grade equivalents, and (d) determine the relation of standard scores to percentile ranks and to each other. Guidelines for the interpretation of test results are also provided.

DEVELOPMENT. The ITPA-3 is the third in a series of editions dating back to 1961 and 1968. People familiar with the original experimental version and second edition of the ITPA will still recognize its general format; however, the test has undergone very significant changes. As the authors note "the ITPA was one of the most popular and influential clinical assessment instruments in the United States from 1960 to about 1980" (manual, p. ix) which "is evidenced by the fact that only 10 years after the publication of its 1968 edition, the 1978 *Eighth Mental Measurements Yearbook* (pp. 573–578) listed 381 bibliographic references for the ITPA" (manual, p. ix). Yet despite its popularity and widespread use, the test had many critics who identified four major limitations of the test to be (a) it did not really test psycholinguistic abilities; (b) the norms were not representative of the country's demographics; (c) subtest reliabilities were low; and (d) validity was unsubstantiated, especially relative to instructional relevance. The motivation of the current authors to create a third edition of the ITPA was to rectify these four valid criticisms while retaining the tests' theoretical basis in Osgood's (1957) original communication model.

Test materials include the examiner's manual, the Profile/Examiner Record Booklet, the Student Response Booklet, and a cassette tape for presenting the stimulus items for Subtest 5: Sound Deletion. The examiner's manual is quite extensive and contains information on test development, administration procedures, scoring and interpretation, reliability and validity of test results, and the normative tables.

TECHNICAL. The ITPA-3 was normed on a sample of 1,522 children aged 5 to 12 years in 27 states. Testing sites and participating individuals were selected so the normative sample would be reflective of the nation as a whole with regards to geographic region, gender, race, rural or urban residence, ethnicity, family income, educational attainment of parents, and disability status. These data compare favorably to those projected for the school-age population in the year 2000 by the U.S. Census Bureau, suggesting that the authors met their goal of having a nationally representative sample.

Normative scores provided by the test include standard scores, percentiles, age equivalents, and grade equivalents. Similar to other familiar tests, norms for subtests are presented in standard scores having a mean of 10 and a standard deviation of 3, whereas norms for subtest composites have a mean of 100 and a standard deviation of 15. Derived percentile scores allow one to determine the percentage of normative scores that occur at or below a particular raw score. Percentile scores are provided for individual subtests as well as for subtest composites. Age and grade equivalents were calculated by computing the average scores of all individuals in each age interval between 5-0 and 12-11 and each grade level between kindergarten and eighth grade. The variety of normative scores available provides examiners using the ITPA-3 many means by which the performance of a child can be measured and interpreted.

Test reliability was estimated by measuring three types of possible testing error: content sampling error, time sampling error, and interscorer differences. Content sampling error was assessed by measuring the degree of homogeneity among test items by calculating correlations between subtests across age using the coefficient alpha method. With the exception of one subtest (Rhyming Sequences) average coefficients for individual subtests as well as subtest composites are at .90 or greater, indicative of high reliability. The Rhyming Sequences subtests averaged .79, only slightly below the .80 acceptable criterion level. Time sampling error was measured by calculating test-retest correlations on a sample of 30 children representative of the group as a whole. The interval between testing and retesting was approximately 2 weeks. Test-retest correlations for individual subtests and subtest composites ranged between .86 and .99 with a mean correlation across the test of .95. This degree of correlation between the two test administrations indicates a very low degree of time sampling error and high test-retest reliability. Finally, interscorer differences was measured by having two members of the publisher's research staff independently score a set of 30 randomly selected protocols from the children in the normative sample. Standard score correlations were then computed between the two scorers for the individual subtests and subtest composites. Interscorer correlations ranged between .95 and .99, indicating that scoring a child's performance on the test is highly reliable across different scorers. The reliability data presented are a strong indicator that the ITPA-3 demonstrates a high degree of reliability across all three types of potential error.

Validity of the ITPA-3 was examined by showing evidence of three types of validity: content-description validity, criterion-prediction validity, and construct-identification validity. Content-description validity, or the representative sampling of the behavior to be measured (in this case psycholinguistic ability), is demonstrated five ways. First, the authors provide rationales for the formats and items of each subtest. Second, psychometric and demographic support is given for four clinical groups that were created based on a comparison between a child's Spoken Language Quotients and Written Language Quotient. Third, evidence is presented to validate that the contents of subtests are in basic agreement with the components of Osgood's (1957) communication model. Fourth, conventional item analysis data are presented for median discriminating powers and median item difficulties for the subtests across eight age levels. Fifth, differential item functioning analysis using a logistic regression procedure was done to identify test items presenting bias. This analysis indicated that only 4 of 1,136 comparisons made (less than 1%) had effect sizes that could be described as moderate or large. Based on the information and data presented by the authors, they appear to have gone to great lengths to document the degree of content-description validity of the ITPA-3.

Criterion-prediction validity, the effectiveness of a test in predicting an individual's performance in other activities, was measured by how well the ITPA-3 correlated with other tests that are known or presumed to measure the same ability. Concurrent validation is presented with correlation data comparing performance on the ITPA-3 to the same child's performance on either the Woodcock-Johnson Psycho-Educational Battery—Revised, the Comprehensive Scales of Student Abilities, the Comprehensive Test of Phonological Processing, or the Test of Language Development—Intermediate: Third Edition. Strong criterion-prediction validity is demonstrated by the fact that all but one of the 14 subtests in the General Language Composite demonstrated correlation coefficients of .75 or greater with similar subtests of the comparison tests.

Finally, construct-identification validity, the extent to which a test measures a theoretical construct, was tested by first identifying seven basic constructs thought by the authors to underlie the ITPA-3, and then creating seven related questions that could be tested. Data are presented relative to how the test correlates with children's age, how well it can differentiate between children with different language levels, subtest score intercorrelations, its relationship to school achievement, its relationship to intelligence, the results of a confirmatory factor analysis, and subtests correlation to total test performance. The plethora of data presented provide additional strong evidence to support the authors' contention that "we have provided a respectable amount of evidence to show that the ITPA-3 is a valid measure of spoken and written language and that it can be used with confidence" (manual, p. 89).

COMMENTARY. The authors of the ITPA-3 set out to revise the older version of the ITPA and to fix the four most important weaknesses and limitations of the original versions. To this extent the authors have succeeded and achieved their goal. First, the name of the test now correctly notes that it is indeed a test of psycholinguistic abilities. The authors carefully chose and created subtests that are consistent with the definitions of psycholinguistics, language, and linguistics. In so doing, they constructed a test "that could be used to assess children's performance in spoken and written language that is related to phonologic, morphosyntactic, graphophonemic, orthographic, and semantic competence" (manual, p. 2).

Second, the authors took care to make sure that the ITPA-3 was normed on individuals who would closely reflect the demographics of the country in general and the school-age population in particular. By so doing, examiners can use the test with a high degree of confidence that it is not demographically biased for or against the child being tested. This is an important improvement as the country has experienced a significant increase in the diversity of its population compared to when the earlier versions of the test were created.

Third, test reliability of the ITPA-3 appears to be much improved over the original versions, which were strongly criticized for having low internal consistency and stability. The reliability measures now incorporated into the test indicate that the ITPA-3, when administered correctly, should have low content sampling error, low time sampling error, and small differences between different scorers. Examiners can have considerable confidence that test results are a true reflection of a child's abilities and that the results are repeatable.

Fourth, validity of the ITPA-3 is also much improved over the original versions of the test. In a large part this is due to the careful selection of subtests that are in fact measuring psycholinguistic skills. Test validity is further documented by the inclusion of data from several other measures that provided evidence that the test is inherently a valid instrument. As the authors note, the validity of scores from any test is documented over time through its use and through other validity studies. Therefore, conclusive answers relative to validity will take years of data collection and analysis.

SUMMARY. The ITPA-3 represents a major improvement over previous versions for which use has dwindled over the years. It now appears to be what was always intended, a psychometrically sound measure of children's psycholinguistic abilities. Even though the administration and scoring of the test is relatively simple, examiners need to be aware that accurate and meaningful interpretation of the results requires knowledge and competence in language and psycholinguistics. This is not a test in which the score in and of itself is particularly meaningful. One also needs to keep in mind that the ITPA-3 is not a screening test, and therefore does take an investment of time to administer, especially with younger children. Finally, although the ITPA-3 can be considered a comprehensive assessment tool, it should be remembered that specific constructs are evaluated with only two subtests. Therefore, further testing in specific construct areas should follow with children who demonstrate potential problems in these areas. Readers who used and relied on the older versions of the test should find the ITPA-3 a familiar and much stronger assessment tool. Other readers who have wanted a comprehensive assessment tool for psycholinguistic abilities should also find the ITPA-3 a welcome addition to their inventory of choices.

REVIEWER'S REFERENCE

Osgood, C. E. (1957). A behavioristic analysis of perception and language as cognitive phenomena. In J. S. Bruner, E. Brunswik, L. Festinger, F. Heider, K. F. Muenzinger, C. E. Osgood, & D. Rapaport (Eds.), *Contemporary approaches to cognition: A report of a symposium at the University of Colorado, May 12–14, 1955* (pp. 75–118). Cambridge, MA: Harvard University Press.

[123]

Illness Behaviour Questionnaire, Third Edition.

Purpose: "To record aspects of illness behaviour, particularly those attitudes that suggest or are associated with inappropriate or maladaptive modes of responding to one's state of health."

Population: Pain clinic, psychiatric, and general practice patients.

Publication Dates: 1983–1994.

Acronym: IBQ.

Scores, 9: 7 factors (General Hypochondriasis, Disease Conviction, Psychological vs. Somatic Perception of Illness, Affective Inhibition, Affective Disturbance, Denial, Irritability) and Discriminant Function Score and Whitely Index of Hypochondriasis.

Administration: Individual or group.

Price Data, 1999: $40 per manual ('94, 95 pages) including test.

Time: (10) minutes.

Comments: Self-report instrument; the Discriminant Function Score indicates likelihood of conversion disorder.

Authors: Issy Pilowsky and Neil Spence.

Publisher: I. Pilowsky [South Australia].

Cross References: See T5:1241 (6 references) and T4:1203 (6 references).

Review of the Illness Behaviour Questionnaire, Third Edition by COLIN COOPER, Senior Lecturer, School of Psychology, The Queen's University of Belfast, Belfast, United Kingdom:

DESCRIPTION. The Illness Behaviour Questionnaire (IBQ) is a self-report measure designed to assess several aspects of behavior variously described as somatoform disorder, hypochondriasis, or hysterical conversion in the psychiatric literature. Such patients present with physical symptoms for which the physician can find no organic basis, and these symptoms persist despite reassurance that all is well. The authors of the IBQ view such symptoms as forming a continuous scale, and the items certainly appear to be suitable for use with nonpsychiatric samples. The questionnaire comes in two forms. One (the IBQ) is designed for use with patients, and the other (IBQ Form B) does not assume the presence of illness, and so is more appropriate for nonpatients. Most items are identical in the two forms. The only difference is that items that assume current illness in the IBQ are rephrased in the IBQ Form B. A fictitious example is "does your illness make you feel depressed?" which might be rephrased as "do you feel depressed when you are ill?" Respondents are asked to endorse each of the items "yes" or "no."

DEVELOPMENT. These 62-item scales build on Pilowsky's Whitely Index of Hypochondriasis, and include the 14 items of the Whitely Index. The IBQ was developed as it was recognized that the Whitely scales may not have tapped all relevant variables, and the scales were too short to allow fine discriminations to be made. Thus, a 52-item version of the questionnaire was developed using factor analysis, and an additional 10 items were added to try to ensure that each factor was identified by at least five variables.

The original factor analysis was, however, somewhat esoteric. The criterion for the number of factors to be extracted was such that each factor should have at least two loadings greater than .4. More conventional techniques such as the Scree or MAP Seven factors were extracted and VARIMAX rotated, and 30 of the 52 variables showed loadings above .4 on one of these factors. It is not clear that tetrachoric correlations were calculated.

Two factor analyses of the items in the 62-item scale are also reported in the manual. However, the factors from different studies tend not to resemble each other in either number or nature. Congruence coefficients, which could demonstrate equivalence, are not presented. For example, the strongest factor in the initial study comprised 9 items, and was labelled "general hypochondriasis." When cardiac patients' scores were analyzed, 8 rather than 7 factors emerged. None of these is labelled "general hypochondriasis," although 3 of the hypochondriasis items loaded on a factor called "somatic concern," along with three other variables that had not previously shown large loadings on any factor. Two of the original hypochondriasis variables plus one other formed another factor, named "sick role acceptance," and the remaining 4 items failed to load appreciably on any factors. Another sample of cardiac patients produced 11 factors, which again often failed to resemble any previous analyses. It is not at all clear that the factor structure of the questionnaire has been adequately determined, and without this it is impossible to know how to score it.

The use of VARIMAX rotation is also puzzling, as it assumes that the various measures of hypochondriasis are uncorrelated, which seems a priori somewhat unlikely. Indeed, the manual advocates calculating scores on second-order factors, which is nonsensical if the scales are uncorrelated. (A table showing the correlations between the scales is cited in the text but appears to have been omitted from the manual.) [Editor's Note: Table 4 was missing from Appendix D in the review copies.]

TECHNICAL. Test-retest correlations are reported over an interval of 1–12 weeks, and are commendably high. However, the internal consistency of the scales (coefficient alpha) is not reported. Normative data (by age and sex) are provided.

Studies cited in the manual show good evidence that the scales of the questionnaire discriminate between patients diagnosed with hysteria or who appear to present with no organic illness, and controls, or those who do show organic symptoms. Unfortunately, many of these use discriminant analysis to try to separate the two groups, which will capitalize on chance variations in the data and overestimate the discriminatory power of the test. In addition, it is not always clear that the studies discussed in the manual provide unambiguous evidence for the validity of the scores from the

different scales. For example, why does the finding that those who make claims for whiplash injury following a motor accident have higher scores on some scales provide "strong support for the predictive validity of these scales"? (manual, p. 29). They may have made claims and had higher scores because their necks hurt more and not because of hypochondriasis, because many of the IBQ items ask about the debilitating effects of illness.

COMMENTARY. The key issue is whether hypochondriasis, as measured by these scales, is different from anything assessed by other questionnaires. The manual cites data showing very high correlations between the scales and anxiety, depression, and neuroticism; these range up to .76. It would be useful to determine whether any of the scales have predictive power other than due to the influence of these well-researched traits (e.g., by using partial correlation or analysis of covariance).

SUMMARY. The structure of the IBQ appears to have been determined by a single technically flawed factor analysis. Attempts to replicate the factor structure have failed, and it is not entirely clear that any of the scales measure anything other than anxiety, depression, or neuroticism. One cannot recommend the present form of the test even for research purposes.

Review of the Illness Behaviour Questionnaire, Third Edition by M. ALLAN COOPERSTEIN, Clinical Psychologist & Forensic Examiner, Independent Practice, Willow Grove, PA:

DESCRIPTION. The Illness Behaviour Questionnaire (IBQ) is a systematized, psychometric response to a medical need for a research and clinical tool that could be used as an "objective way of gathering information about ideational and affective aspects of clinical syndromes in essentially non-psychiatric settings such as general practice and general hospitals" (manual, p. 9). It is proposed for use in differentiating between individuals with valid somatic illnesses and those complaining of physical symptoms, but whose clinical presentation and empirical verification do not validate the complaints. More recently, attempts to classify these phenomena have led to the use of terms such as Hypochondriasis, Hysterical Conversion, Somatization Disorder, Conversion Disorder, Pain Disorder, Somatoform Disorder, and Body Dysmorphic Disorder (DSM-IV-TR, American Psychiatric Association, 2000).

The IBQ-62 was developed for clinical settings and is most appropriately administered when given by an individual trusted by the patient to keep information in a confidential manner. Although the IBQ was written in uncomplicated language, there is no indication of its reading level.

The IBQ is considered "only as an aid to interviewing" (manual, p. 17). The authors refer to the IBQ as a catalyst between the physician and patient and as a means suggestive only of the presence of Abnormal Illness Behaviour (AIB), requiring follow-up as needed.

Cutoff scores may vary from one setting to another. Some cutoffs are provided in the manual based on statistical analysis and (unexplained) "clinical experience". However, we are cautioned that other information "is invariably available concerning the patient" (manual, p. 18) and should be taken into account in an overall appraisal.

The IBQ provides 62 yes-no items that are scored using the Illness Behaviour Score Sheets. To these items is added separately the Whiteley Index of Hypochondriasis. Scores are transferred to the Illness Behaviour Questionnaire Report Form where raw scores and scale percentiles may be entered. These, in addition to second order factors, may then be plotted on a graph provided on the same sheet, which also provides the formulae for second order factors and a discriminant function.

Scores may be used in their raw forms, relative to a normative population and also relating to the possible range on a scale. To clarify this matter, I contacted Dr. Pilowsky who informed me that profile sheets provided are to be used in indicating percentiles of scores rather than standardized T scores (I. Pilowsky, personal communication, September 10, 2001). From this profile, attitudes towards illness are interpreted although interpretation guidelines are not detailed or systematized.

DEVELOPMENT. The Illness Behaviour Questionnaire (IBQ) is an extension of the earlier Whiteley Index of Hypochondriasis (WI) (see Pilowsky, 1967) developed as a screening tool for hypochondriasis.

Recognizing the restrictions imposed by the subscales of the WI, the latter's index was developed into a 52-item questionnaire. Other areas of experience were added based upon the research literature, hypotheses, and clinical experience. These included anxiety, depression, tension, irri-

tability, interpersonal friction, the capacity to communicate feelings, and items reflecting current life stresses and attribution of causes. This initial form was administered to 100 patients in a multidisciplinary pain clinic; results were analyzed using a principal component analysis with orthogonal rotation. This resulted in the isolation of seven dimensions: General Hypochondriasis, Disease Conviction, Psychological vs. Somatic Perception of Illness, Affective Inhibition, Affective Disturbance, Denial, and Irritability (see Pilowsky & Spence, 1975).

Following completion of the initial normative study and isolation of the dimensions, the IBQ was administered to a variety of other clinical populations producing differences to a significant level between pain and hospital outpatient groups relative to age. Pain and general practice groups also showed greater discrepancies.

Pilowsky and Spence (1976) also analyzed the scale scores of 100 pain clinic patients in an interesting hierarchical numerical taxonomy in which patient profiles were interrelated to assess which groups were closer to each other among response configurations. Six clusters were identified, illustrating varieties of clinical presentation. Anger was also a factor examined in this group with the pain group reporting greater inhibition in keeping with an earlier psychodynamic perspective.

Deciding that the IBQ could be enhanced with the addition of items so that all scales were composed of at least 5 ITEMS, a 62-item form was developed. The 14 WI items were also incorporated. In addition, an alternative form (B) was developed for a nonpatient population.

TECHNICAL. Numerous studies have been performed using the 62-item questionnaire. Both forms have been examined in three discriminant analyses by groups of pain, general practice, and family practice patients (in Adelaide and Seattle) revealing three separate, similar discriminant functions providing an adequate degree of accuracy in classifying a new group of 50 pain patients (Pilowsky, Murrell, & Gordon, 1979).

There is some evidence for construct, predictive, and concurrent validity. These have included a TMJ population, as well as surgical and neurological patients.

COMMENTARY. The primary author reported (I. Pilowsky, personal communication, September 17, 2001) that the original work was published as a screening test. Response bias for litigating patients has been considered, but he stated that a questionnaire cannot do what a clinical examination cannot achieve.

Thus, the IBQ demonstrates some value as a screening instrument in medical practices and hospitals for which it was developed. However, there remain continuing limitations related to response bias and secondary gain and the development of normative data with larger, more stratified population samples.

SUMMARY. In its present form, the IBQ is easily manipulated by respondents who wish to present themselves in a light consistent with their needs. However, for more complex and robust assessment normed on larger populations and incorporating symptom validity testing, other existing psychometrics (e.g., the Millon Behavioral Health Inventory), more appropriately meet this need.

REVIEWER'S REFERENCES

American Psychiatric Association. (2000). *Diagnostic and statistical manual of mental disorders text revision* (DSM-IV-TR, 4th ed.). Washington, DC: Author.
Pilowsky, I. (1967). Dimensions of hypochondriasis. *British Journal of Psychiatry, 113*, 89–93.
Pilowsky, I., & Spence, N. D. (1975). Patterns of illness behavior in patients with intractable pain. *Journal of Psychosomatic Research, 19*, 279–287.
Pilowsky, I., Murrell, T. G. C., & Gordon, A. (1979). The development of a screening method for abnormal illness behavior. *Journal of Psychosomatic Research, 23*, 203–207.
Pilowsky, I., & Spence, N. D. (1976). Is illness behavior related to chronicity in patients with intractable pain. *Pain, 2*, 167–173.

[124]

Infant Index.

Purpose: Designed as a screening tool "to identify and monitor children at risk of having or developing, special educational needs."
Population: Students entering infant school (ages approximately 4–5 years).
Publication Date: 1995.
Scores, 7: Literacy Skills, Mathematical Skills, Social Behaviour, Independent Learning, Basic Skills Composite Score, Behaviour Composite Score, Total Score.
Administration: Individual.
Price Data: Not available.
Time: Administration time not reported.
Comments: Checklist completed by educator.
Authors: Martin Desforges and Geoff Lindsay.
Publisher: Hodder & Stoughton Educational [England].
[Note: The publisher advised in December 2002 that this test is now out of print.]

Review of the Infant Index by BERT A. GOLDMAN, Professor, School of Education, University of North Carolina at Greensboro, Greensboro, NC:

DESCRIPTION. The Infant Index, developed by Martin Desforges and Geof Lindsay, was standardized on a sample of children ranging in age from 4 years 3 months to 5 years 2 months. This instrument, developed in England, is designed for use toward the end of the first half of the English Infant School. The Index may be used to compare each child with other children, to compare a child's own strengths and weaknesses, and to monitor a child's progress. As such, the Index provides a screening procedure to identify and monitor children at risk of having, or developing, special educational needs.

Fifteen items are grouped into the four subscales of Literacy Skills comprising Reading, Writing, and Spelling; Mathematical Skills comprising Number Skills, Sequencing, Maths, and Sets and Graphs; Social Behaviour comprising Listening Speaking, Peer Relationships, Compliance, and Co-operation; and Independent Learning comprising Concentration/Attention, Independence/Self-Help, and Motivation. In evaluating a child on each item, the teacher selects one of three levels that best reflects the child's performance or attainment in the area covered by the item. Thus, the teacher obtains 15 item scores, 4 subscale scores, and by combining the two subscales of Literacy Skills and Mathematical Skills, a basic Skills Composite score is obtained along with a Behaviour Composite score formed by combining the Social Behaviour and Independent Learning subscales. If a child is unable to perform any of the activities described at each of an item's three levels, the score for that item will be zero. Scores for each item range from 0 to 3. Thus, the maximum score for all 15 items is 45.

DEVELOPMENT. Initial development of the Infant Index began in England when a group of five teachers and two educational psychologists prepared a checklist reflecting important skills necessary for school learning. This checklist was piloted in September 1992 on a sample of infant schools chosen to reflect the full range of communities within one Local Education Authority (LEA) and included schools from large council estates, residential areas, and the inner city. The sample chosen reflected low, medium, and high disadvantage using school meals as an indicator. Also some schools were selected because of their high proportion of children from ethnic minority backgrounds.

The next development phase involved the headteachers of these schools agreeing to allow their reception class teachers to take part by asking them "What ten things do you expect a child to be able to do at school entry in order to be able to reach National Curriculum level 2 at age 7?" (teacher's handbook, p. 27). The purpose was to see what teachers regarded as important. This led to the identification of 15 areas each with three levels of achievement. All of these areas were piloted by 16 schools. However, there is no explanation of "how" or even "if" this phase had any tie to the initial development of the instrument.

A total of more than 900 pupils comprising a 1 in 4 sample from all LEA schools were administered the revised profile in January and September of 1993. Minor modifications were made following an analysis. Finally, in September 1994 every third or fourth child was selected from more than 90% of LEA schools with an infant intake to ensure that the standardization sample reflected the gender, ethnic, and socioeconomic composition of the LEA. However, no other information is provided concerning the actual specific composition of the standardization sample.

TECHNICAL. Norm tables developed from the standardization sample are presented for item, subscale, composite, and total scores. These tables enable teachers to determine easily for any score the percentage of children with equal or lower scores. Ease of score interpretation is provided by exemplar cases.

Interrater reliability was determined using a sample of 74 children from five schools. The class teacher and a nonteaching assistant independently completed the Infant Index in each of four schools involving over 50 pupils, and in one school two job-sharing teachers independently completed the Index. The correlation for the total score was .89. Test-retest reliability (interval = 7–14 days) in two schools involving 28 children produced a correlation coefficient for total scores of .86. The manual indicated that further trials are underway involving larger samples. There is no explanation for not initially using larger samples. These reliability coefficients between raters and those reliability coefficients over a brief period of time indicate reasonable test stability.

High face validity is claimed because items were constructed using the views of involved professionals who selected items that they judged as related to successful school-based learning. Further, evidence of validity is based upon the fact that overall, girls were found to score at higher levels than boys. These two assertions provide weak evidence for validity. The manual indicates that predictive validity studies are planned and that information from such studies will be reported as it becomes available. Until such time, one must conclude that validity remains to be seen.

Results of the standardization sample were factor analyzed. This produced two factors, one of Basic Skills containing seven items and one of Behaviour containing eight items. Factor loadings of .5 or more were chosen to indicate a significant loading, which was the case for all items with the exception of the Speaking item loading at .46 on Basic Skills and at .47 on Behaviour. Concentration/Attention produced significant loadings of .50 (Basic Skills) and .56 (Behaviour), albeit just at or above significance. Overall, there is substantial evidence in support of two factors.

COMMENTARY AND SUMMARY. The Infant Index provides teachers with a simple, easy-to-use screening procedure for identifying the attainment of literacy, mathematics, social behavior, and early independent learning skills of pupils between roughly the ages of 4 and 5 years. Reliability evidence for the instrument appears adequate; however, predictive validity evidence has yet to be gathered. The manual provides easy-to-follow instructions for administering, scoring, and interpreting of results. However, a major limitation of the Index for usc in the United States is the need for norms based upon a representative sample of U.S. pupils. When such a sample is selected, its composition should be completely described. Until predictive validity is examined and appropriate norms are developed, teachers in the United States will have difficulty justifying use of this instrument.

Review of the Infant Index by MARK E. SWERDLIK, Professor of Psychology, Illinois State University, Normal, IL, and KATHY HOFF, Assistant Professor of Psychology, Illinois State University, Normal, IL:

DESCRIPTION. The Infant Index is a 35-item paper-and-pencil teacher-rating scale that provides an assessment of the progress of students in their first year of schooling (approximately ages 4–5 years). All items are forced choice with three behavioral descriptors of behaviors as choices under each item. Ratings for 15 items are completed for items grouped into four areas including Literacy (Reading, Writing, and Spelling); Mathematical Skills (Number Skills, Sequencing, Maths, and Sets and Graphs); Social Behavior (Listening, Speaking, Peer Relationships, Compliance, and Co-operation); and Independent Learning (Concentration/Attention, Independence/Self-Help, and Motivation). Composite scores are yielded for each of the four subscales; Basic Skills (consisting of Literacy and Mathematical Skills subscales) and Behaviour (Social Behaviour and Independent Learning) and an overall total score can be computed.

Uses of the Infant Index include assessing a pupil's relative strengths and weaknesses, identifying targets for intervention; instructional grouping of children at similar levels; screening students who are at-risk of having or developing special education needs necessitating a comprehensive assessment; continuous progress monitoring, providing a baseline against which future progress can be measured; and as part of a district's needs assessment related to such decisions as allocation of funds for special education. As the development of young children is predictable for some but highly unpredictable for others, the authors stress that the Infant Index should be used for continuous monitoring and as a recording system of a child's learning and development.

Teachers rate all of their pupils, after having been enrolled for at least 4 weeks but "before the end of the first half-term." More detailed descriptions of items, from those provided on the record form, are included in the manual. A zero rating, indicating a student is unable to do any of the activities described at any of the three levels, is also available for each of the items. However, there are no response options for the rater to indicate "Don't Know" or "No Opportunity to Observe." Teachers can complete the scale without the child present. However, some items, for particular children, may require additional observation. Instructions to the respondents include rating each area independently reflecting actual behavior/skills observed in the classroom and not what the teacher "thinks" the student "could do." The manual does include more complete descriptions of the various subareas and items. Case studies are provided to aid in interpretation.

The norm tables provide percentages of the standardization sample that were given a rating at a given point, given a lower rating and given a higher rating on each point of the 4-point (0, 1, 2, and 3) scale for each of the 15 items. Similar percentages can be found for the subscales (e.g., Literacy) and for each of the three composite scores.

DEVELOPMENT. The development of the Infant Index was guided by needs created for screening students in the core subjects of the National Curriculum (England). In addition to assessing levels in basic skill areas, the scale includes behaviors thought to be important for independent and group learning within a classroom. The Infant Index was also developed to address school district needs based on England's Code of Practice on the Identification and Assessment of Special Education Needs and Section 167 of the 1993 Education Act of England such as determining the amount of funds allocated for special education and the need for a particular student to be referred for a comprehensive assessment.

Index items were chosen by a seven-member group of experts including a headteacher, deputy headteacher, and two advisory teachers for National Curriculum Assessment (primary), a special needs teacher, and two educational psychologists. The initial test development phase included a simple checklist linked to the National Curriculum and also important skills necessary for school-based learning. The initial checklist was piloted on a sample of infant schools chosen to be geographically, ethnically, and socioeconomically representative of one Local Education Authority (LEA). Headteachers at these schools responded to the question, "What ten things do you expect a child to be able to do at school entry in order to be able to reach National Curriculum level 2 at age 7?" (teacher's handbook, p. 27). The responses were then analyzed according to the National Curriculum and matched against "attainment targets" whenever possible. On the basis on this initial tryout, 15 areas were identified and, for each, 4 levels of skill attainment were created.

The revised checklist was then piloted in 16 schools with teachers in the appropriate grade completing the scale for every fourth child on their "school register." In addition to rating selected students, teachers were asked to comment on individual questions as well as the checklist as a whole. Although there was general support for the profile, revisions were made to clarify some of the items.

TECHNICAL. The standardization sample consisted of "900+ pupils" enrolled in "all schools in the LEA" (teacher's handbook, p. 28). Students were rated after they had been enrolled in the school full-time for at least 4 weeks and before the end of the first half-term (the length of which was not indicated). A request was made for the participating schools to complete a "1 in 4 sample [i.e., random sampling of every fourth child on the school register] of all pupils beginning school in January 1993 and again in September 1993" (teacher's handbook, p. 28). The authors then noted that the "results of this cohort were analyzed … and minor modifications made in the light of this experience, and used on a 1 in 3 [i.e., random sampling of every third child on the school register] sample of children beginning school in September 1994" (teacher's handbook, p. 28).

Pupils comprising the standardization sample ranged in age from 4 years 3 months to 5 years 2 months with the majority being between 4 years 6 months and 4 years 10 months. The authors note it is not possible to give reliable norms for particular ages by months within this range so all of the ages were collapsed together. Although the authors suggest that the sampling method employed insured that the standardization sample reflected the gender, ethnic, and socioeconomic diversity of the LEA, the specific numbers of students at the various age levels, of males or females, and those representing various racial/ethnic groups are not provided. Genders or ethnic/culture specific norms are not provided nor is a rationale provided as to why they are not. No evidence is presented to support collapsing the norms by age or gender. However, the authors do note that girls scored at higher levels than boys although no specific data related to this finding are presented in the manual.

Interrater reliability evidence, based on 74 children from five schools rated by different adults independently, yielded a coefficient of .89 for the total score. Interrater reliability becomes particularly important as a number of the rating scale items appear ambiguous (e.g., can read from a simple story book; generally independent in dressing/undressing). Test-retest reliability evidence, based on 28 pupils from two schools with the same rater completing the Infant Index on the same child at two different times "usually some 7–14 days apart" (teacher's handbook, p. 29), yielded a test-retest reliability coefficient of .86 for the total scores. Total scores are not precisely defined (basic skills, behavior, and/or total score). Subsequent research by Lindsay & Desforges, (1999) further supports the reliability of the Infant Index (coeffi-

cient alpha of .92) based on another cohort of over 5,000 children ages 4 and 5 years from one LEA.

The test user cannot determine the representativeness of the samples on which the reliability evidence is based. In addition, reliability evidence does not appear to exist for the four subareas nor the basic skills or behavior composite scores.

The authors claim face validity (or more accurately content validity) for their rating scale based on the test development process drawing on the expertise of various professionals. However, no specific data related to the alignment of rating scale content with the National Curriculum are provided.

Although a higher level of scores for girls than boys is cited as evidence of construct validity, no specific data are provided. However, subsequent research (Lindsay & Desforges, 1999) supports this finding, for another cohort, with girls being rated as more advanced than boys in literacy and other domains. Significant differences were also reported based on children's ethnic background and home language. Further evidence of the construct validity of the checklist is provided by a factor analysis, based on data from the standardization sample, supporting the two factors of Basic Skills and Behaviour.

Although the authors note that predictive validity research is planned, including follow-up on students from the standardization sample at 7 years of age using the "National Curriculum end-of-key Stage 1 assessment," this criterion measure is not described. Further, validity data supporting the various uses of the Infant Index (e.g., developing effective classroom interventions, screening for the need for more comprehensive assessment) are not available.

COMMENTARY. The Infant Index was developed by researchers in Sheffield, England for apparent use in their country. Many terms, such as the National Curriculum, Infant School, half term, and different types of school personnel (who participated in the norming and technical adequacy research) are not adequately defined or described for test users from other countries, such as the United States, to determine the usefulness of the checklist. However, even for potential users in England, the rating scale lacks an adequate description of the standardization sample and reliability/validity evidence for the various uses of the test.

SUMMARY. The Infant Index represents an easily administered and scored teacher rating scale intended to be used with all students during their first year of school. The checklist is tied to the National Curriculum of England and includes 15 items divided into four areas grouped into basic skills and behavior thought to be critical for success in an infant (elementary) school classroom. Although the manual includes an expanded description of the 15 items on the rating scale and case studies to facilitate interpretation, the standardization sample and the samples on which the conclusion of adequate reliability is based are limited. Validity evidence is also lacking to support the various uses of the Infant Index. At present, this rating scale should be restricted for use only for research purposes in England.

REVIEWERS' REFERENCE

Lindsay, G., & Desforges, M. (1999). The use of the Infant Index/Baseline-PLUS as a baseline assessment measure of literacy. Journal of Research in Reading, 22, 55–66.

[125]
Interference Learning Test.

Purpose: Designed "for detecting and characterizing mild and moderate as well as severe levels of" neuropsychological impairment.
Population: Ages 16–93.
Publication Date: 1999.
Scores: Learning Performance (List 1 Total Recall, Best Recall, List 2 Total Recall, Added Words, Lost Words, Middle Recall, Recency Minus Primary, Subjective Organization, Category Clustering, Seriation, Intertrial Consistency, New Word Priority, Repeats, Source Errors, Confabulations), Delayed Recall Performance (Short Delay Recall, Long Delay Recall, Cued Recall, Retroactive Inhibition, Cueing Facilitation, Encoding, Rebound), Recognition Performance (Recognition Correct, Overlap Correct, Novel Foil Correct, Indirect Correct), Total.
Administration: Individual.
Price Data, 2002: $150 per kit including manual (186 pages), 5 Response Record Forms, a stimulus booklet, 5-use disk for computer scoring and interpretation; $50 per stimulus booklet; $50 per manual; $32.50 per 20 Response Record Forms; $240 per 20-use disk.
Time: (20–30) minutes.
Comments: Computer administration option available.
Authors: Michael M. Schmidt and Frederick L. Coolidge.
Publisher: Western Psychological Services.

Review of the Interference Learning Test by JOAN C. BALLARD, Clinical Neuropsychologist, Associate Professor of Psychology, State University of New York College at Geneseo, Geneseo, NY:

DESCRIPTION. The Interference Learning Test (ILT) is an individually administered verbal learning and memory test that incorporates several types of embedded interference. This interference "taxes source memory, invites intrusion errors, and presents obstacles to the examinee's spontaneous efforts at organizing the words to be learned" (manual, p. 3). The ILT is similar to other verbal list-learning tasks in its basic format. It differs from other such tasks in that it includes ongoing, embedded interference factors; it explicitly measures indirect memory; and it allows differentiation of recall for concrete and abstract nouns. The ILT also was developed using sophisticated conceptual, statistical, and evaluation procedures, and it produces a variety of interpretable scores.

The authors clearly state that the ILT should be administered only to individuals who are alert and cooperative, and who have sufficient reading and language expression skills to indicate their responses. The ILT should be used only with individuals similar to those of the normative sample (ages 16 to 93, 10+ years of education, estimated premorbid IQ≥85). The ILT is not recommended for severely demented or retarded individuals, for basic memory screening, or in situations for which a brief assessment is needed.

Standardized administration procedures are included in the manual. Words are presented on cards in a bound stimulus booklet. Each of 44 words on List 1 is printed on either a white or a blue card. Individuals read each word aloud as it is presented, but they must attempt to recall only the 20 words on the white cards. After each of four trials, individuals report the white-card words they recall. The 16 words on List 2 are printed on white cards only, and the individual must try to recall all of these words on two consecutive trials. Next, subjects are asked to recall the white-card words from List 1 (Short-Delay Recall). After an interval of 30 minutes, during which nonverbal tasks should be administered, individuals are asked to name white-card words from List 1 (Long-Delay Recall). The next trial involves semantic cueing for white-card words in the categories of birds, vegetables, things around the home, and "other" words (abstract nouns). Recognition memory for white-card words is assessed next, followed by a final trial in which the individual is asked to identify *blue*-card words from List 1 (the previously ignored words) that seem familiar. Foils on both the recognition trials include words from List 1, List 2, and novel words.

Scores are counts of correctly recalled words in each phase. A large number of Summary Indices can also be calculated, including learning curves, position effects, organizational techniques, discriminability, response biases, and many others. The authors recommend computer scoring with WPS Test Report software program, although handscoring is possible. The computer print-out of results is a multipage report on responses and performance, including a concise, one-page report that shows numerical data (raw scores and *T*-scores) and an easy-to-read graphical representation of *T*-scores for each Trial Score and Summary Index. Computerized task administration also is possible, but the authors note that this procedure was not used in the norming process.

The ILT manual includes clear and thorough explanations of the method of calculation of summary indices. Interpretation guidelines are quite detailed, and they include a discussion of the possible meaning of high and low scores on each score or summary index, cautions regarding identification of invalid profiles, and the likelihood of at least a few poor scores even among unimpaired individuals. Sixteen clinical case studies are presented in detail to provide illustrations of the clinical uses of the ILT for individuals with various neuropathological conditions.

DEVELOPMENT. The technical portion of the manual begins with a review of empirical evidence that suggests a memory test should include three components: explicit examination of source monitoring deficits, multiple measures of learning, and information needed to perform qualitative analyses. The Interference Learning Test (ILT) was designed to incorporate these features.

Selection of items for the word lists was exceptionally careful. These words were chosen on the basis of their semantic and psychometric properties. Specifically, words were excluded if they were objectionable, negative, evaluative, or ambiguous. Several techniques were used to control other properties of stimulus items. Selected words are short nouns with a moderate to high frequency of occurrence. Selected concrete nouns are rated as highly representative of their respective categories, and abstract nouns are evenly divided among high imagery and low imagery nouns. Word characteristics generally are distributed evenly among se-

mantic categories, although the abstract word category includes more low-frequency words. The number and position of semantic and phonetic foils are carefully balanced across the word lists, and the structure of each list is described in detail in the manual. The authors also found a very low degree of overlap of ILT stimulus items with other list-learning tasks, which makes testing with multiple measures possible in a clinical setting.

TECHNICAL. The standardization sample included 393 nonpatients aged 16 to 93, with a mean IQ in the average range. All were recruited in the states of Colorado and Montana. Compared to U.S. Census statistics, the sample was slightly overrepresentative of females, Whites, and persons with some college education.

Differences in scores across demographic groups were evaluated using correlations and effect sizes. No effects of ethnicity were revealed, although the representation of nonwhite ethnic groups was inadequate in this sample (e.g., only 4 Asian and 16 Black individuals). Gender differences were minimal, as were education effects. IQ and age differences were found on many scores. Adjusted normalized *T*-scores therefore were established by comparing unadjusted *T*-scores to *T*-scores predicted from a regression equation using age and IQ as predictors.

Internal consistency estimates included intertrial, intercategory, odd-even interitem, and Cronbach's alpha, all of which were computed using 382 of the standardization sample and a separate group of 256 subjects from clinical settings. Coefficients ranged from .80 to .96, with comparable values in the clinical and nonclinical samples.

Test-retest reliability was examined in a very small group (*N* = 28) of nonclinical participants from the standardization sample. Intervals ranged from 20 to 514 days. Most scores and indices demonstrated adequate to strong stability, although some, most notably the "Process and Qualitative" measures, were not at all reliable across time. The authors suggest that such indices should be used in the evaluation of performance on a single administration, but should not be used to assume stable characteristics. The authors also point out that scores across test-retest intervals showed substantial practice effects.

Validity was assessed in several ways. Content validity seems adequate. Convergent validity was assessed using comparisons with the Rey

Auditory Verbal Learning Test (RAVLT) and the California Verbal Learning Test (CVLT) for comparable samples of 20- to 29-year-olds. Mean performance was similar on corresponding measures across the three tests, with differences evidently stemming from presentation procedures. ILT performance was less strongly related to Story Learning scores. Divergent validity was suggested by a minimum of significant correlations of adjusted ILT T-scores with IQ, reading achievement (Wide Range Achievement Test—Revised; WRAT-R), and subtests of the Halstead-Reitan Battery.

Discriminant validity was shown by different patterns of response for members of different clinical groups compared to the standardization sample. A substantial number of schizophrenia and stroke patients produced scores in the impaired range. Less consistent impairment was present in about one-third of adult ADHD, multiple sclerosis (MS), mild traumatic brain injury (MTBI), and multiple-diagnoses groups. Factor analysis and cluster analysis were used to further explore clinical and nonclinical group differences.

COMMENTARY. The authors of the Interference Learning Test (ILT) employed a well-conceived and sophisticated approach to test development and standardization. The test is likely to be useful in both clinical and research settings. Further research is needed on some elements of its psychometric properties and interpretation.

First, characteristics of the test should be studied in more broadly representative samples to determine the generalizability of norms to groups from different geographic regions, cultures, socioeconomic levels, and levels of education. The standardization sample was not representative of groups other than Whites (only 24 individuals were Hispanic, and 16 or fewer individuals represented each of other ethnic groups). Generalization to these ethnic groups should not be assumed without further normative work.

Norms should be obtained from a larger clinical sample, perhaps divided into groups by neuropathological status. Independent group comparisons of clinical and nonclinical average scores were included in the standardization procedures. Matched pair comparisons would be helpful to control for individual differences in a variety of characteristics.

Test-retest reliability should be evaluated using larger samples of both clinical and nonclinical

individuals. It will also be helpful to evaluate reliability systematically across different time intervals. Information about changes in test scores after remediation or rehabilitation treatment would be useful, but may not be possible given practice effects.

SUMMARY. The Interference Learning Test (ILT) is a verbal list-learning task for the assessment of memory in adults. It is a well-crafted instrument that will likely be a useful addition to memory assessment techniques in both research and clinical settings. Its unique contribution lies in its systematic incorporation of interference factors designed to tax memory resources. These factors help to approximate the everyday learning conditions in which memory may be disrupted by a variety of external factors. The ILT is conceptually sound, and its psychometric properties are adequate to good. Further research will likely confirm additional psychometric qualities.

Review of the Interference Learning Test by SHAWN POWELL, Director, Cadet Counseling and Leadership Development Center, United States Air Force Academy, USAF Academy, CO:

DESCRIPTION. The Interference Learning Test (ILT) is purported to identify and classify neuropsychological deficits. It measures word recognition, the ability to discriminate between targeted words versus distractors, learning, and memory recall. The ILT was standardized on a sample of individuals ranging in age from 16 to 93, with an estimated premorbid IQ of 85 or higher, and a 10th grade education.

The ILT is composed of word lists. The first list contains 20 target words printed on white cards with 24 distractor words printed on blue cards. The second list is composed of 16 target words, presented without distractors. The lists contain four word categories used for cued recall trials. In completing the ILT, individuals are asked to read presented words aloud, discriminate between target words versus distractors, and then recall them.

The ILT is composed of 11 trials. Trials 1 to 4 assess learning and discrimination. Trials 5 and 6 measure learning. Trial 7 assesses short delay recall and proactive inhibition. Trial 8 evaluates delayed memory. Trial 9 measures delayed cued recall as individuals are asked to recall target words after being cued to a specific word category. Trial 10 evaluates recognition through the presentation of a word set that contains target words intermingled with distractors. Trial 11 assesses recognition memory for distractors from the first list. The ILT produces scores divided into learning, delayed recall, and recognition categories. A validity measure is also provided for individuals being evaluated to determine the presence of a mild traumatic brain injury.

The ILT can be administered by paraprofessionals or computer administered; however, its interpretation requires a trained clinician. It can be manually or computer scored. ILT results are reported as T-scores with five functional descriptive ranges provided: $60T$ and higher suggests above average; $40T$ to $59T$ suggests average; $35T$ to $39T$ suggests mild impairment; $30T$ to $34T$ suggests moderate impairment; and $29T$ and below suggests severe impairment. If an estimate of premorbid IQ is available or concurrently administered, T-scores can be adjusted for age.

DEVELOPMENT. According to the manual, the ILT was developed "for detecting and characterizing mild and moderate as well as severe levels of impairment" (manual, p. 3). Its multiple trial format, involving continuing interference, reportedly increases the ILT's generalizability to interference encountered in routine day-to-day situations. Clinicians are encouraged to administer the ILT as a part of a neuropsychological battery. It differs from other verbal learning and memory tests as its words are read aloud by the individual being evaluated compared to being heard or read silently.

The ILT manual made available for this review provides detailed information on the ILT's administration and scoring. The manual includes 16 case studies and a section on resolving common administration problems. The interpretation chapter is intentionally limited to using ILT scores to determine the existence and severity of neuropsychological learning and memory deficits. A theoretical framework of the relationship between the 11 word trials and the neuropsychological processes they assess are not presented. Likewise, the implication of specific neuropathological conditions accounting for poor performances is not presented. A validity scale is presented to assess the possibility of not putting forth one's best effort. However, this validity scale only applies to individuals being assessed to determine the presence of a mild traumatic brain injury.

TECHNICAL. The authors of the ILT used sound methodology in their selection of words for the test's various word lists. The words used in the ILT were evaluated for inclusion based on multiple criteria such as their frequency of occurrence in the English language, degree of imagery, length, categorical representation, and the ruling out of ambiguous words.

The ILT's normative sample included 393 nonclinical participants, age 16 to 93 years, primarily from Colorado and Montana. The normative sample was intended to reflect 1991 U.S. Census data. Among the sample's participants, 87% had some college or a college degree, compared to 39% of the U.S. population. The limited locations from which the normative sample participants were drawn, the overrepresentative portion of the sample with college experience, and the sample size reduces the generalizability of ILT results. The manual also presents a clinical sample ($n = 256$) composed of 10 impairment categories. The number of participants in the clinical sample's 10 categories (with sample sizes ranging from 9 to 83) is listed. No other descriptive information is provided about the clinical sample.

In estimating the reliability of the ILT, two forms of reliability are offered. The first is internal consistency, which is reported across learning trials, word categories, and individual items. For the nonclinical sample ($n = 382$) the reliability coefficients range from .83 to .90. For the clinical sample ($n = 256$) the reliability coefficients range from .87 to .93. These reliability coefficients suggest the ILT has adequate reliability to be used as a clinical measure. The second type of reliability reported is test-retest. Stability information was collected on a small sample ($n = 28$) with some retest data collected at less than a 1-month interval; other retest data were collected at more than a 17-month interval. The stability study's weaknesses prohibit inferences to be drawn from its results.

The ILT manual presents various forms of validity. Its content validity is attributed to the word selection process the authors used in constructing the ILT's word lists. Convergent validity evidence is provided through comparisons of the ILT to the Rey Auditory Verbal Learning Test (RAVLT) and California Verbal Learning Test (CVLT). In making these comparisons a matching sample approach was used by presenting the means and standard deviations of four separate studies, with four different samples ranging in size from $n = 126$ to $n = 498$. Correlations from these comparisons are not provided and none of the studies used the same participants. This approach diminishes the ability to adequately examine convergent validity.

The manual presents evidence for construct validity through comparison to several measures including the Wechsler Adult Intelligence Scale—Revised (WAIS-R), Halstead-Reitan Battery, Story Learning, and Figure Learning. The comparisons between these measures are presented in a correlational table that only shows significant correlations ($p<.05$) between the measures. The presented significant correlations are low. Other comparison data appear in the form of means, standard deviations, and the number of significant correlations ($p<.05$) between 26 of the ILT scores and over 40 scores from the other measures. No significant correlations exist between the ILT and the memory components of the WAIS-R or the Halstead-Reitan Battery. Additionally, significant correlations between the ILT and the WAIS-R's Digit Symbol subtest and the Halstead-Reitan Battery Finger Tapping suggest the ILT does not measure memory recognition, and learning in a fashion similar to that of other established instruments.

COMMENTARY. As the ILT contains delay recall trials, interference, and recognition learning, it meets the criteria set forth by Lezak (1995) for memory testing procedures. The multiple criteria approach used in the development of its word lists are indicative of a thorough process. However, the ILT has several psychometric deficiencies. The first is the test's normative sample. It included a relatively small number of participants drawn primarily from two western mountain states, and is overly populated with participants who have college experience or a college degree, in comparison to the U.S. Census data. These characteristics reduce the level of confidence that can be placed in generalizing ILT results.

Reliability is a second limitation for the ILT. The ILT's internal consistency reliability is adequate. However, the small sample size, and the span of time during which retest data were collected present insurmountable problems for the stability coefficient study. Thus, the stability of ILT scores is unknown. Third, although there is evidence of encouraging content validity data, the evidence of other forms of validity is incomplete. The few correlations presented suggest the ILT is not measuring memory in the same way as other memory tests. Scoring the ILT to account for age requires an estimated premorbid IQ score.

SUMMARY. The authors of the ILT developed a method for the assessment of memory, recognition, and learning. It assesses the cognitive processes essential for tests measuring memory, recognition, and learning. The ILT's strengths are its administration, standardization, and word selection process. Its weaknesses include the lack of a conceptual framework, not linking poor test performance to specific neuropathological conditions, an insufficient sample, minimal reliability information, and inadequate evidence of validity. These weaknesses reduce the confidence that can be placed in its results.

REVIEWER'S REFERENCE

Lezak, M. D. (1995). *Neuropsychological assessment* (3rd ed.). New York: Oxford University Press.

[126]

International Personality Disorder Examination.

Purpose: To "identify those traits and behaviors that are relevant to an assessment of the criteria for personality disorders in the ICD-10 and DSM-IV classification systems."

Population: Adults

Publication Dates: 1988–1999.

Acronym: IPDEE.

Scores: 11 scores for DSM-IV version: Paranoid, Schizoid, Schizotypal, Antisocial, Borderline, Histrionic, Narcissistic, Avoidant, Dependent, Obsessive-Compulsive, Not Otherwise Specified; 10 scores for ICD-10 version: Paranoid, Schizoid, Dissocial, Emotionally Unstable/Impulsive Type, Emotionally Unstable/Borderline Type, Histrionic, Anankastic, Anxious (Avoidant), Dependent, Unspecified.

Administration: Individual.

Parts, 2: DSM-IV Module, ICD-10 Module.

Price Data: Available from publisher for introductory kit including 25 screening questionnaires (specify for DSM-IV or ICD-10), 15 scoring booklets (specify DSM-IV or ICD-10), and 50 answer sheets (specify DSM-IV or ICD-10), and for manual (1999, 240 pages).

Time: [60–120] minutes.

Comments: Complete administration includes a self-administered questionnaire as well as a clinical interview with client/subject.

Author: Armand W. Loranger.

Publisher: Psychological Assessment Resources, Inc.

Review of the International Personality Disorder Examination by FELITO ALDARONDO, Senior Staff Psychologist, University Counseling and Testing Center, University of Kentucky, Lexington, KY, and KWONG-LIEM KARL KWAN, Associate Professor, Department of Educational Studies, Counseling and Development Program, Purdue University, West Lafayette, IN:

DESCRIPTION. The International Personality Disorder Examination (IPDE) is a two-tiered system of assessment composed of the IPDE screening questionnaire and the IPDE semistructured clinical interview. For each of these components there are two modules, one that corresponds to the DSM-IV personality disorders and another derived from ICD-10 personality disorder classification. The IPDE screening questionnaire is a 77-item, true-false answer format, self-administered, paper-and-pencil test. It can be administered individually or in groups. The IPDE screening questionnaire has multiple purposes; one of the main goals is to assist in determining whether or not to use the longer and more involved semistructured interview. The IPDE semistructured interview contains 99 items, most of which can be asked of the subject as well as an informant. Information gathered from an informant is to be sought in lieu of or outside of the interview with the client. The last 7 items of the interview are based on clinician behavioral observations.

Responses to the interview questions are scored 0 (behaviors/traits are not present or are only infrequently engaged in or endorsed), 1 (behaviors/traits are present, but subthreshold), or 2 (prevalence of behaviors/traits suggestive of pathology). For each question, specific guidelines are provided for scoring. There are also prompts for queries.

Time required for the IPDE screening questionnaire is relatively short. An average of 20 minutes was reported. The reading level for the IPDE screening questionnaire is not specified. It was suggested in the manual that the interview portion of the IPDE takes approximately 1 to 1 1/2 hours to complete.

The DSM-IV version of the IPDE system provides 11 scores in the following diagnostic categories: Paranoid, Schizoid, Schizotypal, Antisocial, Borderline, Histrionic, Narcissistic, Avoidant, Dependent, Obsessive-Compulsive, and Not Otherwise Specified. The ICD-10 version of the IPDE system provides 10 scores in the follow-

ing diagnostic categories: Paranoid, Schizoid, Dissocial, Emotionally Unstable/Impulsive Type, Emotionally Unstable/Borderline Type, Histrionic, Anankastic, Anxious (Avoidant), Dependent, and Unspecified. The primary differences in the two modules are in terminology, although criteria for determining certain diagnoses (depending on the disorder) also differ. Both categorical and dimensional scores are yielded for diagnostic and research purposes.

DEVELOPMENT. Initial development of the IPDE began in 1985 as part of a joint project between the World Health Organization (WHO) and the U.S. National Institutes of Health (NIH). The IPDE is an internationalized extension and modified version of the Personality Disorder Examination. It was originally written in English and later translated into Dutch, French, German, Hindi, Japanese, Kannada, Norwegian, Swahili, Tamil, Danish, Estonian, Greek, Italian, Russian, and Spanish. In the early stages, workshops were conducted in which psychiatric experts from participating countries discussed the PDE-derived item content, interview structure, and scoring. Following subsequent revisions based on the experience of the interviewers and DSM-III-R criteria, a large-scale pilot study was conducted at 14 different treatment centers from 11 countries. After the field trials, further revisions were made to the IPDE.

The IPDE was piloted in 11 countries in various languages, and the interviews were administered by 58 clinical psychologists and psychiatrists. The normative sample was composed of 716 psychiatric patients enrolled in 14 different treatment facilities from 11 countries. However, very limited information regarding the normative sample was reported in the manual. Relevant demographic information of age, gender, race/ethnicity, and socioeconomic status, as well as data pertaining to the means and standard deviations of items and scales were not provided. Details of the international pilot study could be found in Loranger et al. (1994) and Loranger, Janca, and Sartorius (1997), which indicated that there were 364 men and 352 women in the overall sample. Two hundred and ninety-five were inpatients and 421 were outpatients. These patients ranged from 21 to 55 years of age. There was no inclusion of a "normal" comparison group in the field testing process. Additional information regarding the training of the primary investigators who supervised the administrators of the interviews in the pilot study was briefly described.

TECHNICAL.

Reliability. Interrater agreement was determined through subsequent interviews conducted by an independent, silent observer using approximately 20% of the original normative sample. Details about the selection process for this subsample were not discussed in the manual. These normative data were collected using the exam that was based on the DSM-III-R diagnostic system. Temporal stability was examined over a 6-month (average) period when 243 patients were readministered the interview. Interrater reliability was calculated for the number of criteria met, dimensional score, and on diagnoses. The diagnostic category was initially subdivided into the Definite and Probable diagnosis, but later combined for computation of kappa statistics. Thus, the number of cases eligible for determining interrater reliability was inflated. Kappa values were reported to range from .34 to 1.00 for the DSM-IV personality disorders; similar results were found for the ICD-10. It was noted that in 93% of the test-retest cases, both interviews were conducted by the same interviewers (Loranger et al., 1994). The researchers had intended to use the same interviewers in only half of the retest cases and new interviewers for the other half; however, the procedure was abandoned due to logistic constraints. Although the investigators indicated that interviewers were not necessarily interchangeable, it is apparent that subsequent diagnostic ratings by the same interviewers could be biased by knowledge of the first interview and previous diagnostic impressions.

Validity. Significant validity information of the IPDE was lacking in the manual. Some support for the validity can be implied through the procedures used to determine item content, which reflected interpretation of widely accepted diagnostic criteria by "experts" from countries participating in the pilot study. The content of the items was based on the DSM-IV and ICD-10 personality disorder criteria. Therefore, these IPDE items are subjected to the same criticisms for potential validity concerns, especially on the overlap among personality disorders and the lack of cross-cultural and international applicability (Sue, Sue, & Sue, 1997; Tyrer, 1995).

The procedures for examining validity as suggested by the *Standards for Educational and Psychological Testing* (American Educational Research Association, American Psychological Association, & National Council on Measurement in Education, 1999) were not addressed in the manual. The concurrent validity of scores from the IPDE was unclear as there was no report of the correlations of IPDE scores with other established personality disorder assessments and other behavioral indices. The internal validity of the IPDE remains an empirical question as internal structure studies were not reported. Incremental validity, especially on how clinical judgment could be improved, was not addressed. In sum, validity data were virtually not available in the IPDE manual; yet, such validity concerns are also characteristic of other semistructured diagnostic interviews (for a comparison of the IPDE with other personality disorder instruments and interviews, see Zimmerman, 1994).

COMMENTARY. The IPDE is a comprehensive assessment that directly taps the criteria for personality disorder diagnosis based on the DSM-IV and ICD-10. One of the main benefits of this system is that it has been translated into numerous languages, and it has been piloted in several countries. Problems exist, however, on a number of levels. Primary concerns with the IPDE relate to the lack of validity evidence for the examination. Although the assessment is largely based on two widely accepted classification systems, personality disorders as identified by these sources have been questioned in terms of empirical support, problems with overlap, and variations in diagnostic criteria (i.e., some disorders are based more on concrete behaviors and others more on self-appraisals). Reliability of scores from the exam was indicated by interrater agreement. However, it should be noted that some of the kappa values dropped below acceptable standards (e.g., .34). The same is true for data presented on temporal stability, which showed that the dimensional scores fared better with regard to interrater agreement. The primary use of the exam at this point, however, is for diagnostic classification, which is categorical. Temporal stability was also compromised by having the same raters for the test-retest interviews.

A more critical question regarding the conceptual equivalence of the instrument remains: To what extent can the various personality disorders assessed by the IPDE be universally applied? This is a question of the construct validity of the instrument, which is a crucial issue given that the instrument is meant for "international" use.

The IPDE manual provides detailed guidelines on scoring, queries, and sample questions for clarifying duration of traits/behaviors. It also includes a sample interview supplement for gathering relevant background information. One significant criticism of the IPDE is the lack of information included in the manual. Normative sample information is limited with regard to age, gender, race/ethnicity, and socio-economic variables (such as level of education, occupation status). No minimal reading level is specified for the IPDE screening questionnaire. A number of references for the few studies cited in the text are not provided in the manual. Details of the instrument's development reported previously should be included in the manual.

SUMMARY. The IPDE is an assessment system closely aligned with DSM-IV and ICD-10 personality disorder criteria. The exam is unique in its focus on both categorical and dimensional personality disorder scores. Yet, interrater agreement and temporal stability is problematic. No reliability data were provided for some disorders because the base rates (for definite diagnosis) in the normative sample were so low. Validity data are virtually nonexistent. Even though the assessment has many translated versions with established translation equivalence, the cross-cultural applicability of the exam remains an empirical question. Issues of content, conceptual, functional, and scalar equivalence with different populations need to be established. No normative data are presented regarding use with racial and ethnic minorities in the United States or in other countries. In light of the IPDE's questionable validity and reliability evidence, the instrument should be used as a research tool only. Other well-established measures, corroborative information (e.g., family members and close friends, as suggested in the manual), and the normative values of the cultural contexts should be considered in conjunction with the instrument in the assessment and diagnostic process.

REVIEWERS' REFERENCES

American Educational Research Association, American Psychological Association, & National Council on Measurement in Education. (1999). *Standards for educational and psychological testing.* Washington, DC: American Educational Research Association.

Loranger, A. W., Janca, A., & Sartorius, N. (Eds.). (1997). Assessment and diagnosis of personality disorders: The ICD-10 International Personality Disorder Examination. Cambridge, UK: Cambridge University Press.

Loranger, A. W., Sartorius, N., Andreoli, A., Berger, P., Buchheim, P. Channabasanna, S. M., Coid, B., Dahl, A., Diekstra, R. F. W., Ferguson, B., Jacobsberg, L. B., Mombour, W., Pull, C., Ono, Y., & Regier, D. A. (1994). The International Personality Disorder Examination: The World Health Organization/Alcohol, Drug Abuse, and Mental Health Administration international pilot study of personality disorders. *Archives of General Psychiatry, 51,* 215–224.

Sue, D., Sue, D. W., & Sue, S. (1997). *Understanding abnormal behavior* (5th ed.). Boston: Houghton-Mifflin.

Tyrer, P. (1995). Are personality disorders well classified in DSM-IV? In W. J. Livesley (Ed.), *The DSM-IV personality disorders* (pp. 29–42). New York: Guilford.

Zimmerman, M. (1994). Diagnosing personality disorders: A review of issues and research models. *Archives of General Psychiatry, 51,* 225–245.

Review of the International Personality Disorder Examination by GREGORY J. BOYLE, Professor, Department of Psychology, Bond University, Gold Coast, Queensland, Australia, and Visiting Professor, Department of Psychiatry, University of Queensland, Royal Brisbane Hospital, Herston, Australia:

DESCRIPTION AND DEVELOPMENT. The International Personality Disorder Examination (IPDE) is a multidimensional psychometric trait instrument intended for the clinical psychodiagnostic assessment of personality disorders (apparent for at least 5 years) in adults. An extension and refinement of the Personality Disorder Examination (Loranger, 1988), the IPDE comprises both a pencil-and-paper self-report Screening Questionnaire, and a separate semistructured diagnostic Interview rated by the psychiatric or clinical psychological examiner. Separate modules of the IPDE Screening Questionnaire and the IPDE Interview are based on the DSM-IV and the ICD-10 classification systems, respectively.

The Screening Questionnaire test booklet (DSM-IV module) comprises 77 true/false self-report items (ICD-10 module has 59 True/False items), whereas the DSM-IV and ICD-10 Interview modules comprise 99 items and 67 items, respectively. Although keeping the scoring of the Screening Questionnaire items as simple as possible for the patient, the resultant dichotomous data inevitably restrict statistical analyses to those applicable to simple categorical data. For the IPDE Interview, each item is scored on a 3-point scale (0, 1, or 2), along with a "?" category for when the patient is unable to respond with certainty. Seven of the DSM-IV based items, and 10 of the ICD-10 related items also include a not applicable (NA) category. For each module, the IPDE scoring booklet allows for a definite, probable, or negative diagnosis with respect to each personality disorder, along with recording of the number of diagnostic criteria met and a continuous dimensional score (because personality traits are distributed in the population at large, and it is assumed that personality disorders represent the exaggerated extremes of such traits). The two separate IPDE modules have been translated into several foreign languages (including Spanish, French, Italian,

Greek, German, Dutch, Norwegian, Danish, Russian, Estonian, Japanese, Hindi, Swahili, and Tamil), enabling its use internationally and facilitating cross-cultural comparisons of the incidence of personality disorders. Thus, the IPDE goes some way toward fulfilling a major aim of the World Health Organization (WHO) and U.S. National Institutes of Health (NIH) Joint Project on Diagnosis and Classification of Mental Disorders—namely the development of standardized diagnostic assessment instruments for use worldwide (Jablensky, Sartorius, Hirschfeld, & Pardes, 1983).

The IPDE Interview examiner ratings can be based either on the patient's own answers to interview questions (contained in the IPDE manual), or on the responses of an informant familiar with the patient's behaviors. The IPDE also allows a "past personality disorder" diagnosis when an individual previously (prior to the past 12 months) has satisfied the diagnostic criteria (but no longer exhibits the particular traits), as well as a "late onset" diagnosis when the diagnostic criteria have only been met after age 25 years.

The IPDE Interview purports to measure 11 DSM-IV classified personality disorders labelled: Paranoid, Schizoid, Schizotypal, Antisocial, Borderline, Histrionic, Narcissistic, Avoidant, Dependent, Obsessive-Compulsive, Not Otherwise Specified. The ICD-10 personality disorders purported to be measured include: Paranoid, Schizoid, Dissocial, Emotionally Unstable (Impulsive Type), Emotionally Unstable (Borderline Type), Histrionic, Anankastic, Anxious (Avoidant), Dependent, and Unspecified. Use of the Screening Questionnaire alone does not allow clinical diagnosis. However, it can be used to exclude patients who do not exhibit any personality disorders, or any specific personality disorder. The Interview produces a higher proportion of false positives than does the briefer Screening Questionnaire. In general, the test author, Loranger, recommends that if there are any elevated personality disorder scale scores, the Screening Questionnaire should be followed by the Interview. For the Screening Questionnaire, scoring is straightforward, as item scores are reproduced automatically on the score sheet (attached underneath). In regard to scoring the IPDE Interview, detailed instructions are provided in the test manual.

TECHNICAL QUALITY. Interrater reliability estimates range from .71 to .92 (M = .83) for

the number of criteria met, and from .79 to .94 (M = .86) for the dimensional score on each of the DSM-IV and ICD-10 classified personality disorders. Temporal stability coefficients range from .55 to .84 (M = .69) for the number of criteria met, and from .65 to .92 (M = .77) for the dimensional score, respectively. Because the test-retest interval is not designated in the IPDE manual, it is difficult to evaluate the stability estimates. Moreover, the IPDE manual does not report any item homogeneity data (Cronbach alpha coefficients) for the various personality disorder scales. Consequently, the internal consistency and/or item redundancy (Boyle, 1991) of the IPDE scales remains unknown. Construct validity (e.g., factor analytic) evidence is also missing from the test manual. Loranger (manual, p. 213) simply asserted that, "It was the opinion of most of the clinicians who participated in the field trial that the IPDE was a useful and essentially valid method of assessing personality disorders." Nevertheless, subjective speculations and unsupported opinions can never substitute for empirical scientific evidence. Consequently, the psychometric properties of the IPDE need urgent investigation before widespread use of the instrument can be recommended.

Furthermore, differing numbers of items across the personality disorder scales in both the DSM-IV and ICD-10 modules are problematic, causing discrepancies in measurement variance, and invalidating any simple comparison of scale scores—both within and between each module. In addition, the IPDE does not appear to differentiate satisfactorily between state and trait measures of personality disorders (cf. Boyle, 1985), although Loranger et al. (1991) have acknowledged this issue. Finally, the IPDE manual fails to provide any evidence pertaining to item-response characteristics (cf. Boyle, 1987)—a fundamental issue in contemporary psychometric assessment.

COMMENTARY. The use of self-report methodology in the Screening Questionnaire and in the Interview (also ratings by others) is a substantial weakness, not only because of response sets and motivational distortion, but also because patients may not be fully aware of and lack insight into their own personality disorders. Demand characteristics underlying ratings have been pointed out previously (Fernandez & Turk, 1994). Likewise, the serious limitation due to item transparency of self-report personality instruments has been discussed elsewhere (Boyle, 1985). Not only are patients themselves unlikely to have clear insight into their own idiosyncratic personality disorders, but also the ratings of others who may act as informants for the IPDE Interview may be seriously distorted because of their own perceptual biases. For example, it has been shown that schizotypal personality traits are prevalent within the population at large (Boyle, 1998), and it is quite likely that individuals with elevations on such traits may have distorted perceptions of the behaviors of others. This argument can also be extended to a wide range of other personality characteristics that may bias observer ratings. In view of this serious problem, it is especially surprising that there are no validity scales to correct for faking good, faking bad, or other types of motivational distortion. In recognition of this problem of response bias, such correction scales have explicitly been incorporated into the design of many standardized personality instruments (such as the Minnesota Multiphasic Personality Inventory [MMPI] or the Sixteen Personality Factor Questionnaire [16PF]) for decades.

SUMMARY. To his credit, Loranger has devised a creative and novel approach to the clinical assessment of personality disorders that can be administered, scored, and interpreted in a relatively cost-effective manner. Also on the positive side, the IPDE includes relevant items, employs a psychometrically valid quasi-interval response scale (Interview component), and avoids colloquial or slang expressions. The IPDE has been used extensively in a wide range of studies, and there are numerous published reports suggesting its popularity (19 such studies are indexed in the PsycINFO database since 1999). The IPDE appears to make a useful contribution to the clinical diagnosis of personality disorders, and evidently many clinicians intuitively feel that the Screening Questionnaire and Interview are valid and reliable. Nevertheless, subjective impressions can never substitute for empirical evidence. Although the test manual is relatively informative, the inclusion of much further detail is needed, particularly regarding psychometric issues. Clearly, research is urgently needed to refine the factor structure and psychometric properties of the IPDE Screening Questionnaire and the IPDE Interview.

REVIEWER'S REFERENCES

Boyle, G. J. (1985). Self-report measures of depression: Some psychometric considerations. *British Journal of Clinical Psychology, 24,* 45-59.

Boyle, G. J. (1987). Review of the (1985) "Standards for educational and psychological testing: AERA, APA and NCME." *Australian Journal of Psychology, 39,* 235–237.

Boyle, G. J. (1991). Does item homogeneity indicate internal consistency or item redundancy in psychometric scales? *Personality and Individual Differences, 12,* 291–294.

Boyle, G. J. (1998). Schizotypal personality traits: Extension of previous psychometric investigations. *Australian Journal of Psychology, 50,* 114–118.

Fernandez, E., & Turk, D. C. (1994). Demand characteristics underlying differential ratings of sensory versus affective components of pain. *Journal of Behavioral Medicine, 17,* 375–390.

Jablensky, A., Sartorius, N., Hirschfeld, R., & Pardes, H. (1983). Diagnosis and classification of mental disorders and alcohol- and drug-related problems: A research agenda for the 1980s. *Psychological Medicine, 13,* 907–921.

Loranger, A. W. (1988). *Personality Disorder Examination (PDE) manual.* Yonkers, NY: DV Communications.

Loranger, A. W., Lenzenweger, M. F., Gartner, A. F., Lehmann-Susman, V., Herzig, J., Zammit, G. K., Gartner, J. D., Abrams, R. C., & Young, R. C. (1991). Trait-state artifacts and the diagnosis of personality disorders. *Archives of General Psychiatry, 48,* 720–728.

[127]
Inventory of Altered Self-Capacities.

Purpose: Designed to assess difficulties in relatedness, identity, and affect control.
Population: Age 18 and above.
Publication Dates: 1998–2000.
Acronym: IASC.
Scores, 11: Interpersonal Conflicts, Idealization—Disillusionment, Abandonment Concerns, Identity Impairment, Self-Awareness, Identity Diffusion, Susceptibility to Influence, Affect Dysregulation, Affect Skill Deficits, Affect Instability, Tension Reduction Activities.
Administration: Group or individual.
Price Data: Available from publisher for kit including 25 reusable item booklets, 50 hand-scorable answer sheets, 50 profile forms, and professional manual (2000, 49 pages).
Time: [15–20] minutes.
Author: John Briere.
Publisher: Psychological Assessment Resources, Inc.

Review of the Inventory of Altered Self-Capacities by ROSEMARY FLANAGAN, Director of the Masters Program in School Psychology/Assistant Professor, Derner Institute of Advanced Psychological Studies, Adelphi University, Garden City, NY:

DESCRIPTION. The Inventory of Altered Self-Capacities (IASC) is a 63-item questionnaire developed to assess difficulties in affect regulation, relatedness, and identity in individuals who are at least 18 years of age. The IASC consists of seven scales: Interpersonal Conflicts, Abandonment Concerns, Identity Impairment, Susceptibility to Influence, Affect Dysregulation, Idealization-Disillusionment, and Tension Reduction Activities. Two of the scales, Identity Impairment and Affect Dysregulation, contain two subscales. Difficulties in self-regulation may be associated with various psychological difficulties including cognitive distortions, negative mood states, posttraumatic stress, psychosis, and functioning in general. Perhaps more importantly, some of these characteristics are associated with more pervasive difficulties, including the criteria for Borderline Personality Disorder according to the *Diagnostic Manual of Statistical and Mental Disorders, 4th Edition* (DSM-IV; American Psychiatric Association, 1994).

The IASC is a targeted, specific, evaluation tool. Clinicians are otherwise limited to using tools that assess an array of constructs, and only indirectly assess self-capacities such as with the Rorschach, the Minnesota Multiphasic Personality Inventory, Second Edition (Butcher, Dahlstrom, Graham, Tellegen, & Kaemmer, 1989), and the Millon Multiaxial Inventory, Third Edition (Millon, Davis, & Millon, 1997). Materials are generally user-friendly, although the 63 test questions are in an item booklet separate from the answer sheet. Test items are rated on a 5-point scale, with 1 = *never,* and 5 = *very often.* Respondents are instructed to consider only the past 6 months when responding. Scoring is accomplished by separating the carbonized answer sheet, summing the ratings for each scale, and plotting these on the profile form, from which *T*-scores are obtained directly. Specific instructions are provided for addressing missing responses and determining the validity of the profile obtained. The scale takes 15–20 minutes to complete, and approximately 10 minutes to score. The IASC can be administered in either a group or individual format. There are standard instructions to be read to test takers.

The *T*-scores, with a mean of 50 and standard deviation of 10, are considered clinically and statistically significant at *T* = 70, which is two standard deviations above the mean. *T*-scores between 65 and 69 merit attention. An extended discussion of interpretation is in the manual, including the meaning of elevations on individual scales. Elevations on most scales can mean the presence of Borderline Personality Disorder, although such a profile may also be a "cry for help" (Professional manual, p. 9). It is also possible that only some scales will be elevated. The author notes that the data should be interpreted within the context of a comprehensive battery. Nevertheless, data presented in the manual indicate that individuals with a diagnosable clinical disorder tended to score much higher than those with no clinical

disturbance on all IASC scales, suggesting effective discrimination between clinical and nonclinical individuals. For each scale, the mean scores obtained by the clinical sample (*N* = 105) exceeded the mean scores for the normative sample by more than two standard deviations.

DEVELOPMENT. The original item pool for the IASC was 166 items. Omitting items that were redundant, poorly written, or believed to be poor indicators of the particular domain, accomplished an eventual reduction to 63 items.

TECHNICAL. Normative data were obtained using a stratified random sample of registered automobile owners and individuals with listed telephone numbers. The IASC was mailed to these individuals along with three other scales. In order to have more individuals in the lower age ranges, some university students served as participants, bringing the total sample to 620 individuals. The mean age of the normative group was 47 years of age (range = 18–91). Fifty-three percent were men, and 80% of respondents were Caucasian; the sample is not representative of census data. Noteworthy is that women scored slightly higher than men on some IASC scales; these differences are minor.

Internal consistency reliability estimates (coefficient alpha) for the normative sample ranged from .78 to .93, with a mean of .89. Values were comparable for both the clinical sample and a university sample. Exploratory factor analysis was somewhat consistent with the expected structure of the scale in that 10 factors emerged; the difference being that 3 factors emerged within one scale. Three samples (clinical [*N* = 116], university [*N* = 290] and community [*N* = 33]) were used to provide evidence of construct, convergent and discriminant validity. The major concern with the validation data is that some of the measures used to collect validity evidence are unpublished, having been developed by the author of the IASC. Evidence of construct validity includes correlation of the IASC with a history of child abuse, measures of attachment style and interpersonal relations, suicidality and substance abuse in the expected directions for each group, with the strongest relationships demonstrated for the clinical group.

Evidence of concurrent and discriminant validity included positive correlations with measures of trauma, maladaptive object relations, and the Borderline Features scale of the Personality Assessment Inventory (PAI; Morey, 1991) for the clinical sample. Clinician ratings demonstrated positive correlation with IASC scales; few were significant, making interpretation difficult. Examining the correlations between the IASC and several other measures provided evidence of discriminant validity. Significant correlations were demonstrated for measures of trauma and PAI scales that assess borderline features and paranoia. Correlations were not significant for a scale that assesses PTSD as well as the antisocial features scale of the PAI.

COMMENTARY. Although the IASC fills a need for practitioners, the data suggest that the instrument should be used with caution, until additional research data are collected. Preliminary validity data are impressive. One concern is that some unpublished measures were used in the validation studies. An additional concern is that although it is clear that the author obtained a good approximation of a random sample to develop norms, the sample is not sufficiently diverse, and does not reflect census data. Another concern is that it is difficult to evaluate the criteria used to shorten the scale to its present form.

SUMMARY. The IASC should be a useful addition to a practitioner's repertoire, and fills a need for a brief measure of Borderline Personality Disorder. In addition, it is also useful to practitioners to be able to identify those individuals who have comorbid features of Axis-II disorders, when such disorders are not the primary focus of treatment. This will permit practitioners to more readily determine the type of "treatment risk," and will have a psychometric means of documenting the need for additional treatment, as per insurance guidelines.

Despite the limitations noted, the author is to be commended for the clear explanations of the rationale for the decisions made in the development of the instrument, determination of its psychometric properties, and for the extensive data that are in the manual for independent review.

REVIEWER'S REFERENCES

American Psychiatric Association (1994). *Diagnostic manual of statistical and mental disorders* (4th ed.). Washington, DC: Author.

Butcher, J. N., Dahlstrom, W. G., Graham, J. R., Tellegen, A., & Kaemmer, B. (1989). *The Minnesota Multiphasic Personality Inventory, Second Edition.* Minneapolis, MN: University of Minnesota Press.

Millon, T., Davis, R., & Millon, C. (1994). *Millon Multiaxial Clinical Inventory, Third Edition.* Minnetonka, MN: National Computer Systems.

Morey, L. C. (1991). *Personality Assessment Inventory.* Odessa, FL: Psychological Assessment Resources.

[128]
Inventory of Interpersonal Problems.

Purpose: "A self-report instrument that identifies a person's most salient interpersonal problems."
Population: Adults ages 18 and over.
Publication Date: 2000.
Acronym: IIP
Scores, 9: Domineering/Controlling, Vindictive/Self-Centered, Cold/Distant, Socially Inhibited, Nonassertive, Overly Accommodating, Self-Sacrificing, Intrusive/Needy, Total.
Administration: Individual or group.
Price Data, 2002: $111 per complete kit including manual (2000, 98 pages), 25 64-item question sheets, 25 64-item scoring sheets, and 25 32-item question scoring sheets; $48 per manual; $42 per 64-item question/scoring sheet combination including 25 64-item question sheets, and 25 64-item scoring sheets; $33 per 25 32-item question/scoring sheets.
Time: (10–15) minutes for Full Version; (5–10) minutes for Short Version.
Comments: Full version (IIP-64) contains 64 items; short version (IIP-32), intended for screening, contains 32 items.
Authors: Leonard M. Horowitz, Lynn E. Alden, Jerry S. Wiggins, and Aaron L. Pincus.
Publisher: The Psychological Corporation.

Review of the Inventory of Interpersonal Problems by JOSHUA M. GOLD, Associate Professor & Program Coordinator, Counselor Education Program, University of South Carolina, Columbia, SC:

DESCRIPTION. The Inventory of Interpersonal Problems (IIP) focuses on "common interpersonal problems" (manual, p. 1). The IIP is offered in a 32-item format (measuring social inhibition, nonassertiveness, and neediness) and a 64-item format (measuring the three constructs mentioned in the 32-item format plus being domineering/controlling, being vindictive/self-centered, being cold/distant, being overly accommodating, and being self-sacrificing). The response scale on both formats has 5 points (0 = *not at all;* 1 = *a little bit;* 2 = *moderately;* 3 = *quite a lot;* 4 = *extremely*). Both formats are divided into two sections: "things I find hard to do with other people" and "things I do too much." The individual scale scores can be summed to create a score measuring an individual's overall interpersonal distress. Both formats offer paper-and-pencil administration. The manual does not explain the rationale for the development of the 32-item test, nor the process by which certain scales from the 64-item test were included or excluded.

There is no mention of the qualifications of the test administrator. Data can be immediately scored on the accompanying scoring sheets. Instructions clearly direct the scorer on which scale to attribute an item's response in the calculation of raw scores. Raw scores can be added to obtain a total score. T-score conversion is clearly outlined in the manual. This compares the individual to the norming sample. The IIP also generates ipsative scores allowing individuals to compare the relative weight of each problem for that person. Referred to as the "difference score," this process is harder to follow than the use of a normative comparison but can be calculated through careful attention to manual directions. Through these two scoring processes, applicable to both formats, individuals gain a sense of comparison to the nonclinical norming group and also to an individual's other concerns. The scoring procedure can be transposed on a circumplex visualization of the relative immediacy of each issue.

The scoring profiles designate T score equivalents greater than 60 as "above average" and those T scores above 70 as "significant difficulty relative to non-clinical representative US sample" (manual, p. 6). However, there is no equivalent description of those T scores that fall below the T score of 40.

DEVELOPMENT. The IIP (copyright, 2000) reflects the categorization of 200 different problems of clients presenting at the Stanford Psychiatric Clinic. Presenting issues were first grouped into interpersonal concerns or noninterpersonal concerns by "14 naïve judges" (manual, p. 13). The manual does not describe the qualifications of these judges nor the criteria by which complaints were categorized. As the framework for this inventory, this lack of detail may raise questions about the validity of scores from the IIP. The authors claim a theoretical adherence of presenting complaints along interpersonal dimensions of affiliation (hostile to warm) and of dominance (controlling to submissive). The authors then describe a multidimensional scaling process, leading to thematic clusters of problem behaviors around intimacy, socializing, assertiveness, compliance, and independence. Based on the five clusters and two categories of "what I find hard to do" and "what I do too much," 10 combinations emerged.

TECHNICAL. The norming procedures for this test utilized 800 cases representative of U.S. adults aged 18–89. The norming group was stratified according to U.S. Census Bureau categories by gender, age category (18–24, 25–44, 45–64, 65 and over), race/ethnicity (White, African American, Hispanic, other), and education level (12 years or less, 13–15 years, and 16 or more years). Additionally, regional representation was integrated by use of four different regions and selection of one larger and one smaller city within that region. It seems clear that the test developers wanted to ensure a wide usage of their instrument and recognized that care with the norming process would be a valuable step toward that end.

Items selected for inclusion are worded in a colloquial fashion and seem to be easily understood. Scale assignment of answers is appropriately varied through both formats so that respondents' response bias patterns may be alleviated. There is no measure of social desirability in respondents' answers, raising the possibility of respondents minimizing or underreporting their problems.

The internal consistency estimates of the IIP for the individual subscales of each format as reported in the manual seem to be gathered from one study. Cronbach alpha coefficients range from .76 to .88 for the IIP-64 format and from .68 to .87 for the IIP-32. Test-retest reliability coefficients for the IIP-64 are reported between .58 and .84 for a 7-day span; and between .61 and .83 for the IIP-32 over the same time period.

In terms of the IIP, the developers sought evidence of convergent validity with several instruments including the Beck Depression Inventory, the Beck Anxiety Inventory, the Symptomatic Checklist 90-R, and the Social Adjustment Scale. A review of the correlations can best be described as mild-moderate. The developers then attempt to connect high individual T scores (>70) with DSM diagnostic criteria. For example: "people with antisocial personality disorders and people with narcissistic personality disorders obtain high scores on this scale as well as on the Vindictive Self-Centered scale" (manual, p. 38). Such assertions are made for each scale with differing disorders; however, the developers do not document how they arrived at these conclusions, nor do they present evidence of studying populations already with such diagnoses to confirm their hypotheses.

COMMENTARY. The value of the IIP remains in its original intent. If a test user required a measure of interpersonal concern, and could accept the constructs germane to the IIP, then the current test may offer insight for clients. In addition, the behavioral orientation of the scale questions offer direction toward intervention and practice.

However, a potential test user must remember that the norming sample is based in a nonclinical population. The lack of distinction between clients seen in outpatient or inpatient settings leads to questions about the relative weight one can assign to scale scores. Of particular concern is the inclusion of unsupported assertions about the relationship between scale scores and psychopathological diagnosis.

The manual claims a utility of the scale results for clinical intervention. However, in the development of the items, the developers decided that a difficulty in one area of interpersonal functioning (e.g., "saying no to my boss") could be generalized into a difficulty saying no to all people. This "trait"-based approach may be challenged through consideration of the context in which a particular problem is evident. As in the prior example, one may generalize that my difficulty saying no to my boss may epitomize similar patterns with others in authority over my life. However, extrapolating such difficulty to relations with peers or with persons I may consider unequal to me requires substantiation. Potential users of this test must reconcile their beliefs around the trait versus context controversy of interpersonal difficulty in favor of the "trait" belief system for the theme of this instrument to be of value. Were a clinician working from a solution-focused model, the theory behind this test, which assumes that exceptions to the presenting issue do not, in fact, occur in the client's life, may be incompatible with that model of therapy.

SUMMARY. The developers, to their credit, have produced an instrument based in a desire to normalize clients' interpersonal issues. They have prepared representative norming tables and offered the option of considering the scores as an ipsative picture of presenting concerns. Even in that regard, the lack of validity and reliability data raise concerns about the value of the IIP. Moreover, the developers seem to overextend the utility of the test by suggesting its value in psychodiagnostics. If potential users seek only a measure of client self-perception as an opening for issue discussion, the IIP may be a possible choice. However, given the reservations expressed, even those results must be viewed tentatively and any more

extensive or diagnostic use of the results would be very strongly cautioned.

Review of the Inventory of Interpersonal Problems by BRIAN HESS, Director of Test Development & Research, National Commission on Certification of Physician Assistants, Norcross, GA:

DESCRIPTION. The Inventory of Interpersonal Problems (IIP) is a pencil-and-paper self-report instrument that identifies a person's most salient interpersonal difficulties. The full version contains 64 items (IIP-64); the short version contains 32 items (IIP-32) and is intended for screening. In both versions, the items are divided into two sections: One section begins, "The following are things you find to do with other people," and the other section begins, "The following are things that you do too much." A 5-point Likert-type response scale is utilized; response options range from Not at all to Extremely. Apart from a Total Score, eight 8-item scale scores indicate the person's level of difficulty in specific domains of interpersonal functioning: Domineering/Controlling, Vindictive/Self-Centered, Cold/Distant, Socially Inhibited, Nonassertive, Overly Accommodating, Self-Sacrificing, and Intrusive/Needy.

Specific qualifications for administering the IIP are not provided in the manual (albeit it seems very likely it is intended for a trained clinician). Three normative groups (overall, men, and women) are provided for the Total Score and for each of the eight IIP-64 and IIP-32 scale scores. Standard (non-ipsatized) T scores are used for evaluating the person's overall interpersonal difficulty relative to a standardization sample (N = 800) based on the U.S. Census. IIP-64 scores can be used to compare groups of individuals in different settings or a single group before and after clinical treatment; IIP-32 scores can be used particularly to screen if an individual is sufficiently distressed to justify treatment. In addition to traditional scoring, individual-based (ipsatized) T scores for each of the eight scales may also be calculated (these are difference scores, or an individual's Standard T score for each scale minus the Total T score). These allow the clinician to assess an individual's scores on the different scales relative to each other—pinpointing a specific area of interpersonal problems that the person reports is most troubling. Individual-based T scores may be ordered around a circle (circumflex) located on a two-axis graph.

The "X" axis represents an affiliation (friendliness) dimension and the "Y" axis represents a dominance (power) dimension. Theoretical support of this two-dimensional model is provided in the manual. Profiling based on the individual-based circumflex scores may be most beneficial for individual treatment planning.

DEVELOPMENT. This IIP is the first published version (copyright, 2000) of a test that has been under development since 1979. In the early stages of development, a pool of interpersonal problem statements were identified based on a large sample of intake interviews, and their content was studied systematically and eventually formed a 127-item inventory of interpersonal problems. Using Henry Stack Sullivan's theory on interpersonal behavior and problems as a framework, the previous version of the IIP measured the salience of the two interpersonal dimensions (i.e., affiliation and dominance) that were empirically supported using multidimensional scaling and hierarchical clustering methodologies. Later, Alden, Wiggins, and Pincus (1990) applied principal components factor analysis to the original 127-item version to determine each item's factor loading on the two predominant factors. Then they divided this two-axis circumflex space into eight octants and identified the 8 items that were most representative of each octant. This is how the eight 8-item scales comprising the current IIP-64 were derived (the 63 items of the original 127-item version that were not included in the IIP-64 are listed in the manual). Finally, the IIP-32 short version was developed using 4 items of each scale with the highest item-total correlations.

The IIP manual provides fairly good information regarding initial test development. The two-dimensional theoretical model drove development of the IIP, and these two predominant constructs appear to have been supported during each stage of development. However, a theoretical framework for developing the specific eight domains is not provided (it seems the eight domain scales have been only empirically derived). The definitions provided for each scale are, however, cogent and straightforward and in line with the empirical foundations for these scales.

Finally, by using the supplied IIP Question and Scoring Sheets, both the IIP-64 and IIP–32 are very easy to administer and score. Clinical profiling based on individual-based T scores is easily achieved using a graph depicting the two-axis circumflex space with its eight octants.

TECHNICAL. Information describing the norming process is straightforward. A relatively small nonclinical standardization sample of 800 cases (400 men and 400 women) was utilized; the sample was representative of the U.S. population of adults aged 18–89. A U.S.-Census-driven, stratified sampling plan was used to ensure that a sufficient number of men, women, and participants of different ages were represented. An equal number of participants were selected by gender (n = 100) within each age group (18–24, 25–44, 45–64, and 65 and over). Race/ethnicity and education level were stratified within gender group and the overall sample. The developer found only significant gender differences on most IIP scales, and consequently, gender-specific norms were established.

Internal consistency was based on alpha coefficients for the individual IIP-64 scales that were fairly high, ranging from .76 to .88, and its Total Score reliability estimate was very high (.96). Reliability estimates for the IIP-32 scales were also satisfactory, ranging from .68 to .87, and its Total Score reliability estimate was also high (.93). The IIP reliability coefficients are good, considering that eight items comprise each scale with little overlap and most items focus on behaviors that are clearly and directly linked to the content of associated scales (e.g., "I am too aggressive toward other people" from the Domineering/Controlling scale).

Test-retest reliability coefficients for IIP scale T scores were computed using a subsample of 60 individuals from the standardization sample. Retesting occurred after a 7-day interval. Estimates for both the IIP-64 and IIP-32 ranged from the .50s to the low .80s. The stability is somewhat lower than what the developer found from clinical samples, mostly because a nonclinical standardization sample shows a smaller range of scores (i.e., less variability). Test-retest reliability coefficients for IIP individual-based (ipsatized) T scores indicated less stability over time than the norm-based T scores. The developer explains, "this is to be expected because these scores are difference scores (the difference between a total score and a scale score), and difference scores are known to be less reliable" (manual, p. 27).

In general, the studies and methods used in the validation process met accepted psychometric standards for substantiating validity evidence established in the Standards for Educational and Psychological Testing (AERA, APA, & NCME, 1999). Concurrent validity was examined by correlating IIP-64 standard scale scores with scores on other assessments of psychological symptoms, including the Beck Depression Inventory II and the Beck Anxiety Inventory. Correlations between the IIP-64 and both Beck scales ranged from .31 to .48. Correlations between the IIP-64 standard T scores and the Global Severity Index of Derogatis' Brief Symptom Inventory ranged from .57 to .78. Correlations between the IIP-64 scales and the Behavior and Symptom Identification Scale, a measure of general mental health functioning, were also moderate to high, ranging from the .20s to the .60s. In addition, correlations between the IIP-64 and the Social Adjustment Scale—Self Report were mild to moderate (.16–.49)—the Nonassertive and Socially Inhibited scales correlated highest with self-reported role functioning (particularly with regard to social and leisure time).

Construct validity evidence was provided for the two circumflex scales of Affiliation and Dominance. Principal components analysis (with procrustean rotation) indicated that the scales Vindictive/Self-Centered, Cold/Distant, Overly Accommodating, and Self-Sacrificing loaded on the Affiliation factor, whereas the remaining scales appropriately loaded on the Dominance factor. Thus, the principal components analysis supported the theory that affiliation and dominance underlie issues of interpersonal relatedness. The factor structure has been replicated across gender and racial/ethnic groups.

Finally, a number of other studies supporting the clinical applications of the IIP are discussed in the "Score Interpretations and Clinical Applications" section of the manual (it would have been perhaps more appropriate to summarize these studies in the validity chapter). Most of these clinical studies focused on the relationship between certain IIP-64 scales and personality disorders, social phobia, and depression. In short, these studies helped to relate the different interpersonal problem dimensions to different diagnostic categories as well as to different attachment styles.

COMMENTARY. The value of the IIP as a measure of interpersonal problems with a clinical population appears to be both adequate and useful. There is a sense of general construct articulation and differentiation among the eight scales, and little homogeneity of item content within scales. The developer did not acknowledge that clients may be likely to underreport their problems, and thus the use of "truth-corrected" scores cannot be evaluated.

The clinical interpretation of elevated Standard (nonipsatized) T scores is clearly presented and well substantiated based upon numerous resources. T score values of 70 and greater indicate clinical levels. There are, however, no specific treatment recommendations for elevated Total Scale scores or for any of the eight scale scores. The developers point out that "certain types of problems improve more readily than others, and the treatability of a problem may be related to its location in the interpersonal space" (manual, p. 48). Thus, the developers do show, for each of the eight problem domains, how often a patient and his or her therapist agreed that the problem had been discussed in treatment, and then determined the proportion of the problems that were improved.

More evidence is clearly needed to support the validity of the IIP constructs. The developers might have selected a more versatile statistical procedure such as confirmatory factor analysis to examine the factor structure of the IIP scales. Similarly, instead of reporting a "hodge-podge" of correlational studies, it would have proved stronger if a "nomological validation" approach was adopted using theory as a guide. For example, there is some discussion on how specific attachment styles can be determined based on individual profiles of interpersonal problems, and the developers acknowledge that attachment styles may explain the relationship between interpersonal problems and personality disorders. Studying this by modeling these constructs empirically (e.g., using structural equation modeling) might have provided some supportive theory-based nomological evidence for the IIP's constructs.

SUMMARY. The developers have produced a very applicable instrument for identifying a person's interpersonal difficulties. It can be administered, scored, and interpreted in a relatively efficient manner. They have considered a clear, theoretical framework from which to develop the scale, and have considered gender differences (and racial/ethnic and level of education differences, as well) in the norming process. Clinical interpretation of elevated IIP scores is presented and supported. Sufficient reliability or validity evidence exists to assert that the test scores consistently or accurately reflect the associated constructs. However, evidence supporting nomological validity would lend better support to the IIP constructs. Also, specific recommendations for individual treatment based on either standard T scores or the individual-based T scores should have been delineated.

REVIEWER'S REFERENCES

Alden L. E., Wiggins, J. S., & Pincus, A. L. (1990). Construction of circumflex scales for the inventory of interpersonal problems. *Journal of Personality Assessment, 53*, 521–536.

American Educational Research Association, American Psychological Association, & National Council on Measurement in Education. (1999). *Standards for educational and psychological testing.* Washington, DC: American Educational Research Association.

[129]

Jackson Vocational Interest Survey [1999 Revision].

Purpose: "Designed to yield ... a set of scores representing interests and preferences relevant to work ..., conceptualized as work roles and work styles."

Population: High school and above.

Publication Dates: 1977-2000.

Acronym: JVIS.

Scores, 50: 34 Basic Interest Scales (Creative Arts, Performing Arts, Mathematics, Physical Science, Engineering, Life Science, Social Science, Adventure, Nature-Agriculture, Skilled Trades, Personal Service, Family Activity, Medical Service, Dominant Leadership, Job Security, Stamina, Accountability, Teaching, Social Service, Elementary Education, Finance, Business, Office Work, Sales, Supervision, Human Relations Management, Law, Professional Advising, Author-Journalism, Academic Achievement, Technical Writing, Independence, Planfulness, Interpersonal Confidence); 10 General Occupational Themes (Expressive, Logical, Inquiring, Practical, Assertive, Socialized, Helping, Conventional, Enterprising, Communicative); 3 Administrative Indices (Unscorable Responses, Response Consistency Index, Infrequency Index); Academic Satisfaction; Similarity to College Students; Similarity to Occupational Classifications.

Administration: Group.

Price Data, 2002: $79 per examination kit including manual (2000, 149 pages), applications handbook, occupations guide, machine-scorable answer sheet for Extended Report, reusable test booklet, hand-scorable answer and profile sheets, and jvis.com password; $32 per test manual; $36 per applications handbook; $22.95 per Occupations Guide-2000; $34.50 per 25 reusable test booklets, quantity discounts available; $12 per 25 hand-scorable answer sheets, scannable answer sheets, or profile sheets, quantity discounts available; $11 per Extended Report including machine-scorable answer sheet and laser-printed report; $8 per Basic Report including machine-scorable answer sheet; report in duplicate; quantity discounts available on both reports;

$99 per SigmaSoft JVIS for Windows start-up package including disks, software manual, test manual, and 10 coupons; $1.75 per SigmaSoft Coupon, quantity discounts available; cost per report: 2 coupons per Data Report, 4 coupons per Basic Report, 6 coupons per Extended Report.

Foreign Language Editions: Available in Spanish (booklets only) and in French (booklets and extended reports); also, online administration using SigmaSoft JVIS for Windows and reports).

Time: (45)55 minutes.

Comments: Former edition no longer available; available in paper-and-pencil format (hand scoring or mail-in scoring), Basic and Extended Reports online administration and scoring available using SigmaSoft JVIS for Windows software; system requirements: SigmaSoft JVIS for Windows also can be used for scoring data scanned by an optical mark reader using SigmaSoft Scanning Utility; SigmaSoft JVIS for Windows produces Basic Report, Extended Report, and Data Report.

Authors: Douglas N. Jackson and Marc Verhoeve (applications handbook).

Publisher: Sigma Assessment Systems, Inc.

Cross References: See T5:1334 (5 references and T4:1297 (1 reference); for reviews by Douglas T. Brown and John W. Shepard of a previous edition, see 10:158 (1 reference); for reviews by Charles Davidshofer and Ruth G. Thomas, see 9:542; see also T3:1204 (1 reference).

Review of the Jackson Vocational Interest Survey [1999 Revision] by ELEANOR E. SANFORD, Vice-President for Research and Development, MetaMetrics, Inc., Durham, NC:

DESCRIPTION. The Jackson Vocational Interest Survey (JVIS) was developed by Douglas Jackson as a means to describe the vocational interests of males and females across a common set of dimensions during career exploration and planning. The 1999 edition of the JVIS is a result of the following: (a) renorming the instrument, (b) conducting additional studies with the instrument (reliability, validity, and other areas of research), and (c) revising and updating reports and interpretative materials. The JVIS booklet consists of 289 pairs of statements describing occupational activities that are used to represent interests (work roles) and preferences (work styles) relevant to work. The respondent is asked to determine which of the two statements he or she prefers (regardless of ability).

The JVIS reports the following scores: 34 Basic Interest scales that examine work roles and work styles, 10 Occupational Themes, Academic

Satisfaction Scale, similarity to 17 clusters of educational majors, similarity to 32 job groups, and 3 administrative indices (number of unscorable responses, Response Consistency Index, and the Infrequency Index). Once converted to percentile ranks, the scores are used to develop a profile of the respondent's vocational interests and preferences.

ADMINISTRATION. The JVIS can be administered either individually or in a group setting by paper-and-pencil, on the computer (using the *SigmaSoft JVIS for Windows* computer software), and over the Internet. The JVIS will take the respondent about 45–60 minutes to complete, and it may be scored by hand or by computer. If scored by computer, the report contains a comparison of the individual's profile with various educational groups and occupational clusters.

Before interpreting the JVIS profile, the results from the three administrative indices should be examined to determine the validity of the situation and examine the respondent's test-taking behavior. The respondent's profile can be interpreted in relation to combined norms or gender-specific norms. The manual suggests that gender-specific norms are more appropriate for some scales (e.g., Engineering, Elementary Education) because the use of separate norms can encourage the diminishment of traditional occupational roles.

The manual provides extensive information and case studies to help counselors and other test administrators interpret the results of the JVIS. There is a section that describes recurring counseling problems and situations with suggestions and solutions: a flat JVIS Basic Interest profile, measured interests are discrepant with career plans, abilities and interests appear to conflict, low reliability index for an individual machine-scored profile, Basic Interest scales appear to conflict with Similarity to Job Groups, and the client is considering an occupation that appears unrelated to any of the 32 job groups. In addition, the *JVIS Applications Handbook* provides extensive case studies that can be used during training.

DEVELOPMENT. The JVIS has undergone an extensive development process. The conceptual foundation of the JVIS is related to the work of David Campbell with the Strong Vocational Interest Blank (SVIB). The SVIB examined the relationship of vocational interests to specific occupations. Jackson departed from this way of thinking to instead relate vocational interests to

work roles and work styles (occupational clusters). Thus, the focus of the results is more for career exploration and planning (examining many occupations), rather than seeing how well an individual's interests match a specific occupation. Jackson began by identifying a large set of work roles and work styles and then selecting dimensions to measure within these work roles and work styles.

Initially over 3,000 statements were developed and administered in multiple forms to 2,203 respondents. The results were examined by first suppressing response bias resulting from the initial item format (the respondent was asked to indicate whether he or she "liked" or "disliked" the activity in the statement). The residual score matrix was then factor analyzed to identify statements that were related to each of the Basic Interest scale dimensions. Based on these results, the final items were selected for each scale such that the relationship of the item to other items on the scale was maximized and the relationship of the item to other scales for which it was not related was minimized.

The JVIS was renormed in 1999 with 3,500 secondary school students and adults. The sample was equally split between males and females. Raw score means and standard deviations and percentile ranks are provided for each scale for males, females, secondary students, adults, and the combined sample.

TECHNICAL.

Reliability. In the JVIS manual, test-retest (1-week and 4–6-week intervals) and coefficient alpha coefficients are presented for the Basic Interest scales (generally in the mid 70s to low 80s) and for the General Occupational Themes (generally in the mid to upper 80s).

Validity. The internal structure of the JVIS is examined by correlating the scales. Generally, the scales are independent for samples of females and males ($N = 1,250$ in each sample) with the mean interscale correlation coefficient of .28 for males and .24 for females. In another study, a factor analysis was conducted with 1,163 male and 1,292 female high school students. Two conclusions were drawn from the results of the factor analysis: (a) there are characteristic patterns of JVIS scores and the counselor can expect to see these patterns, and (b) the emergence of the patterns permitted the development of the 10 Occupational Themes for reporting results. The manual also contains studies showing how the JVIS can be used in other areas of research: relationship to academic major, genetic and environmental influences on career interests, choice of academic college, classification of occupational groups, structure of interests, and the career assessment of groups of individuals—individuals with disabilities, women, minorities, and different age groups.

COMMENTARY AND SUMMARY. The JVIS takes a different approach to the assessment of vocational interests by examining the relationship of interests and preferences to occupational clusters. By focusing on occupational clusters rather than specific occupations, respondents are more likely to explore careers that they may not have considered previously. The respondent can then take into consideration other information related to career choice: the availability of opportunities, interest in higher education or training, individual abilities and interpersonal skills, and individual values in relation to work satisfactions. The JVIS is a well-developed test for examining occupational interests for career planning and has adequate validity and reliability evidence for this use.

Review of the Jackson Vocational Interest Survey [1999 Revision] by WENDY J. STEINBERG, Assistant Professor of Psychology, Eastern University, St. Davids, PA:

DESCRIPTION. The Jackson Vocational Interest Survey (JVIS) is a measure of vocational interest for use in educational and career counseling and planning. It is a measure of interests, not abilities, values, or opportunities. Thus, for example, a person could be interested in clerical occupations, but lack clerical aptitude.

The JVIS consists of 289 forced-choice pairs of statements describing occupational activities. Examples include: #17 A. Starring in an opera, or B. Typing reports from employees' work records; #208 A. Creating an attractive backyard flower garden, or B. Arranging to have experts testify in court on behalf of a client. Test takers select the activity in each pair in which they have more interest.

The items form 34 Basic Interest Scales, of which 26 scales are for Work Roles and 8 scales are for Work Styles. Work Roles are associated with specific occupations or classes of occupations (e.g., Performing Arts, Engineering, or Medical Service). Work Styles reflect a preference for certain work environments or modes of behavior (e.g., Dominant Leadership, Job Security, or Planfulness.)

The JVIS extended report provides scores on several additional scales, as well as the 34 Basic Interest Scales. The 10 General Occupational Themes reflect "general orientations to the world of work" (manual, p. 34). Examples include Expressive, Enterprising, and Helping. These themes derive from a factor analysis of the 34 scales and, like Holland's six occupational themes, they seem to incorporate personality tendencies. The Academic Satisfaction scale predicts satisfaction in traditional scholarly or scientific activities. The manual points out that this score is useful in choosing between similar career interests requiring different amounts of academic preparation, such as lab technician versus professional chemist. The Similarity to College Students section compares the test taker's interest profile to that of college students in 17 academic clusters. Examples include Food Science, Environmental Resource Management, and Business. The Similarity to Job Groups section compares the test taker's interest profile to that of people working in 32 job groups. Examples include Health Service Workers, Sales Occupations, and Occupations in Entertainment. This section of the report also includes, for the test taker's top three Job Groups, a list of specific occupational titles and their DOT codes. Uniquely, this section also lists suggested readings, activities, and professional organizations for further career information. A Where to Go From Here section provides similar reading, activity, and professional organization information, but for career planning in general.

The JVIS can be administered either in paper-and-pencil format or on-line, and it can be either hand-scored or scored by computer. However, the hand-scored report consists of only the 34 Basic Interest Scales, whereas the computer-scored report gives the extended report.

Taking the test in either paper-and-pencil or computer format is straightforward. Directions are clear. Items are written at a seventh-grade reading level, and all follow the same forced-choice format. Scoring, however, is more troublesome. The 17 x 17 response matrix on the hand-scored answer sheet is faintly printed and neither numbered nor well delineated by columns and rows. Therefore, this reviewer experienced difficulty in both marking and counting responses. Thin bars distinguishing male and female norms are barely discernible after score bars are drawn; neither are they labeled on the profile sheet. An

[130]

Job Descriptive Index (1997 Revision) and The Job in General Scales.

Purpose: Designed as measures of job satisfaction to be useful for diverse organizations and employee groups.
Population: Employees.
Publication Dates: 1969–1997.
Acronym: JDI; JIG.
Scores, 6: Work on Present Job, Pay, Opportunities for Promotion, Supervision, People on Your Present Job, Job in General.
Administration: Group or individual.
Price Data, 2001: $100 per 100 test booklets; $50 per paper user's manual ('97, 275 pages); $40 per electronic manual (pdf format 340 KB).
Time: (60) minutes.
Authors: Patricia C. Smith, Lorne M. Kendall, and Charles L. Hulin (earlier edition); William K. Balzer, Jenifer A. Kihm, Patricia C. Smith, Jennifer L. Irwin, Peter D. Bachiochi, Chet Robie, Evan F. Sinar, and Luis F. Parra.
Publisher: Bowling Green State University, Department of Psychology.
Cross References: See T5:1348 (16 references); for reviews by Charles K. Parsons and Norman D. Sundberg for an earlier edition of the Job Descriptive Index and Retirement Descriptive Index, see 12:199 (33 references); see also T4:1312 (63 references); for reviews by John O. Crites and Barbara A. Kerr of an earlier edition of the Job Descriptive Index, see 9:550 (49 references).

Review of the Job Descriptive Index (1997 Revision) and the Job in General Scales by MICHAEL R. HARWELL, Professor, Program in Research Methodology, Department of Educational Psychology, University of Minnesota, Minneapolis, MN:

DESCRIPTION. The Job Descriptive Index (JDI) is designed to assess various facets of job satisfaction, and the Job In General (JIG) scale is designed to provide an overall evaluation of job satisfaction. The manual contains a clear description of job satisfaction as typically construed in the job satisfaction literature, the need to measure this complex construct, and the rationale that guided the development of the instruments. According to the manual, the JDI can be used to monitor changes in a job situation, diagnose problems, and evaluate the effects of a job improvement program. The JIG provides an overall measure of job satisfaction. These widely used measures of job satisfaction are described as being applicable to diverse companies and organizations, and the availability

of norms means that average responses on these instruments for a company can be compared to those of other workers. Information about the JDI and JIG can be obtained from their website at http://www.bgsu.edu/departments/psych/JDI/.

The JDI and JIG have both been positively reviewed in earlier editions of the *Mental Measurements Yearbook* (e.g., Crites, 1985; Kerr, 1985; Parsons, 1995; Sundberg, 1995). The JDI relies on 72 items to measure five discriminable facets of job satisfaction. The Work on Present Job facet (18 items) focuses on an employee's satisfaction with the job itself, Present Pay (9 items) focuses on an employee's satisfaction with their pay, Opportunities for Promotion (9 items) measures satisfaction with the company's promotion policy and the way that policy is administered, Supervision (18 items) reflects satisfaction with one's supervisor, and People on Your Present Job (18 items) assesses satisfaction with coworkers. The JIG uses 18 items to assess overall satisfaction. The items for these scales consist of a list of short phrases and adjectives of five or less words of low reading difficulty (e.g., boring). Respondents mark Y (Yes), N (No), or ? (Cannot Decide) for each item. A Yes or No is scored 3 or 0 depending on the wording of the item, and a Cannot Decide response is scored 1, the rationale being that a 1 is close to an unfavorable response. The manual also states that companies can include additional items constructed by the company, apparently without damaging the information provided by the JDI and JIG.

Each examinee receives a total score that is obtained by summing their point totals on each facet of the JDI or their points on the JIG. The point totals for the Present Pay and Opportunities for Promotion facets are doubled so that each facet and the JIG share a common score range of 0–54. The scoring is done on-site by the company, although off-site computerized scoring is available. Scores are compared to norms based on fairly large samples of workers. The norms in the manual are broken down by job tenure (five categories based on years in the job), manager status (manager, non-manager), job level (based on response to a 5-point Likert scale from *Lowest* to *Highest*), organization type (governmental organization, for-profit organization, nonprofit organization, self-employed), and age (based on 10 categories). The manual emphasizes that the five facets of the JDI reflect different constructs and warns users against adding facet scores on the JDI to obtain an overall score—that is the purpose of the JIG.

The manual is easy to follow although relatively few details of the development of these scales and their psychometric properties are provided. Instead, users are referred to published and unpublished documents for this information. The manual contains a helpful list of questions for companies considering using the JDI or JIG: (a) What is the scope of the project? (b) Will the JDI and JIG alone provide the necessary information diagnosing/evaluating the job situation? (c) Who should administer the JDI and JIG? (d) How many employees should complete the JDI and JIG? (e) Should demographic information be collected? (f) How should the scales be administered and collected? In each case, the answers to these questions provided in the manual are prudent and reflect the considerable experience of the authors with these instruments.

DEVELOPMENT OF THE JDI. The JDI has a long history in the assessment of job satisfaction literature, with initial validation of the JDI begun in 1959 and the original JDI published in 1969. The first revision was published in 1985 and the second revision of the JDI appeared in 1997. Considerable attention has been paid to psychometric standards such as reliability, validity, and the development of norms.

Norms. In 1996 a pool of 7,000 employees stratified by U.S. state and selected at random was generated based on U.S. Census and Social Security data. The 7,000 employees were asked to respond to the JDI National Norm Survey. Based on the responses of approximately 1,600 (23%) of the employees, norms were developed for several key variables. The manual notes that differences in response rates among certain demographic subgroups emerged, and as a result separate norms were developed for several of these subgroups (e.g., race, gender, job tenure). Apparently, differences among several of these subgroups were slight and only norms for job tenure, manager status, job level, organization type, and age are presented in the manual. However, other norms can be obtained by contacting the authors. Both graphs and numerical tables of norms are provided, allowing the responses of a particular company to be compared against the norms. Specific information about the kinds and frequencies of jobs represented in the sample of workers is not provided.

Reliability. Reliability estimates on each of the five facets in the 1997 revision were computed using the data from approximately 1,600 respondents to the JDI. Cronbach alpha coefficients ranged from .86 to .91.

Validity. Because most of the items on the 1985 and 1997 revisions of the JDI are the same, reported validity evidence for the 1997 revision relies heavily on data collected for the earlier version. In the 1985 revision the authors used a variety of techniques for data collected for 795 employees to examine how items and facets were operating, including correlations with other measures of job satisfaction, factor analyses, and item response theory models. In general, there is strong evidence of construct validity in that the JDI has been shown to correlate with other job satisfaction scales and with various job attitudes and behaviors.

DEVELOPMENT OF THE JIG. Based on theoretical and empirical evidence suggesting that producing an overall job satisfaction score for the JDI was inappropriate, the authors developed an 18-item instrument intended to provide an overall evaluation of how workers feel about their jobs. Initially, responses of 1,149 civil service workers in Florida to 42 items were analyzed using traditional item analysis techniques, factor analysis, and item response theory models. A similar process was followed for other employee samples, including 4,490 employees representing a variety of companies (Ironson, Smith, Brannick, Gibson, & Paul, 1989). Based on these analyses the pool of items was reduced to 18.

Norms. Norms are presented for the JIG for job tenure, manager status, job level (based on response to a 5-point Likert scale from *Lowest* to *Highest*), organization type, and age. The same sample of workers was used to develop the JDI and JIG norms reported in the manual. Specific information about the kinds and frequencies of jobs represented in the sample of workers is not provided.

Reliability. The resulting 18 items showed evidence of high reliability via coefficient alpha (.91) and acceptably small standard errors of measurement.

Validity. Evidence of convergent validity is reported in Ironson et al. (1989), who also reported evidence of the discriminant validity of the JIG. Through a pattern of predictions, Ironson et al. indicated that the JDI and JIG are not assessing the same underlying construct. The JIG has been shown to correlate with other job satisfaction scales and various job attitudes and behaviors.

COMMENTARY AND SUMMARY. The JDI and JIG are widely used tools for assessing job satisfaction that have considerable empirical evidence supporting their psychometric properties. These instruments are also easy to administer and score, and the availability of norms substantially increases their attractiveness. Perhaps the major concern is the absence of specific information about the kinds and frequencies of jobs represented in the sample of workers used to generate the norms. This deficiency could easily be remedied by making this information available to potential users, perhaps on the JDI and JIG website.

REVIEWER'S REFERENCES

Crites, J. O. (1985). [Review of the Job Descriptive Index]. In J. V. Mitchell, Jr. (Ed.), *The ninth mental measurements yearbook* (pp. 753–754). Lincoln, NE: Buros Institute of Mental Measurements.
Ironson, G. H., Smith, P. C., Brannick, M. T., Gibson, W. M., & Paul, K. B. (1989). Construction of a Job in General scale: A comparison of global, composite, and specific measures. *Journal of Applied Psychology, 74,* 193–200.
Kerr, B. A. (1985). [Review of the Job Descriptive Index]. In J. V. Mitchell, Jr. (Ed.), *The ninth mental measurements yearbook* (pp. 754–756). Lincoln, NE: Buros Institute of Mental Measurements.
Parsons, C. K. (1995). [Review of the Job Descriptive Index]. In J. C. Conoley & J. C. Impara (Eds.), *The twelfth mental measurements yearbook* (pp. 514–515). Lincoln, NE: Buros Institute of Mental Measurements.
Sundberg, N. D. (1995). [Review of the Job Descriptive Index]. In J. C. Conoley and J. C. Impara (Eds.), *The twelfth mental measurements yearbook* (pp. 515–516). Lincoln, NE: Buros Institute of Mental Measurements.

[131]
Job Observation and Behavior Scale.

Purpose: Designed as "a work performance evaluation for supported and entry level employees."
Population: Ages 15 and above.
Publication Dates: 1998–2000.
Acronym: JOBS
Scores, 4: Work-Required Daily Living Activities, Work-Required Behavior, Work-Required Job Duties, Quality of Performance Composite/Total.
Administration: Individual.
Price Data, 2001: $75 per complete kit including 25 record forms and manual (1998, 28 pages); $30 per 25 record forms; $50 per job manual.
Time: (30) minutes.
Authors: Howard Rosenberg and Michael Brady.
Publisher: Stoelting Co.

Review of the Job Observation and Behavior Scale by AYRES G. D'COSTA, Associate Professor, Quantitative Research, Evaluation and Measurement in Education, College of Education, The Ohio State University, Columbus, OH:

DESCRIPTION. The Job Observation and Behavior Scale (JOBS) is authored by Howard Rosenberg and Michael Brady, and it is published

by the Stoelting Company. The authors claim it is an employment performance evaluation tool for use with high school and other adults entering the workforce. It was first copyrighted in 1998 and appears appropriate for use for entry-level workers with supported employment needs as in rehabilitation and welfare-to-work programs. The examiner's manual, however, indicates the JOBS is suitable for use with all adults, with or without disabilities and special employment needs. This broad claim does not appear justified.

The JOBS is a rating scale that must be completed by employers or other persons responsible for the supervision or occupational development of a worker needing a supportive work environment. It consists of three subscales: Work-required Daily Living Activities (DLA), Work-required Behavior (BEH), and Work-required Job Duties (JD). The entire scale consists of 30 items claimed to "represent the most critical patterns of behavior needed for obtaining, maintaining and developing employment opportunities" (examiner's manual, p. 5).

The list of DLA items includes commonly recognized job-related expectations such as attendance, personal hygiene, and communication. BEH items include stress tolerance, honesty, and handling criticism. JD items include quality of work, speed of learning new tasks, safety habits, and motivation.

Each of the 30 items is rated by the employer for two aspects: *Quality of Job Performance* (relative to similar workers not receiving supports), and *Type of Support* (received by the worker on the job). Each of these two aspects is rated on its own 5-point rating scale. There is also a third column (Adaptive/Prosthetic, AP) that is checked (X) if an Adaptive or Prosthetic device is used, for each item rated. These two aspect ratings and the AP checks are then summarized by each of the three subscales and totaled for the entire instrument. Each of the three subscale sections allows space for free responses to four questions as follows: Adequacy of job performance quality, Indication/justification for promotion or salary increase, Impact of decrease in current job supports, and Change in type of job support.

This instrument must be completed by employers who are able to observe the worker, and who should have been on the job for at least 1 month. It is claimed that the entire instrument can be typically completed in less than 30 minutes even by evaluators unfamiliar with it, and more experienced evaluators would need substantially less time. An eight-page booklet is provided for each employee evaluation.

The interpretive guide, which is included in the 24-page examiner's manual, recommends both a quantitative and a qualitative analysis of the scale ratings. The quantitative analysis can use normative information such as means, standard deviations, and ranges as provided in the standardization section. These standardization norms are based on 45 high school students, 135 supported adults, and 45 entry-level workers, for a total of 225 employees. These are very small samples for proper norm development. It appears that 9 out of 10 agencies were from Florida, which leads one to question their representativeness and generalizability.

Despite these limitations, the guide is nicely designed to provide effective interpretation using actual case studies as models. The authors follow their own recommended interpretation process and outline the quantitative and qualitative analyses for their cases. Finally, they provide a detailed discussion of "What this means to community employers?" Implicit in all this process is, of course, the benefits accrued by the worker who has been helped through a difficult transition.

DEVELOPMENT. The JOBS examiner's manual presents a literature review based on approximately 45 journal articles mostly from the vocational rehabilitation area. These articles track the history of research associated with "alternative models of employment" for persons with disadvantages. The last decade has highlighted a strong social concern to provide transitional services to employment-challenged persons as they move from high school or sheltered environments to a competitive work environment. Prominent legal mandates for such concerns have been reflected in Section 504 of the *Rehabilitation Act of 1973*, the *Development Disabilities Act of 1984*, the *Rehabilitation Act Amendments of 1986*, and the *Americans with Disabilities Act of 1990*. The JOBS attempts to help disadvantaged persons achieve their vocational promise by providing a simple instrument for employers to objectively evaluate their job performance. It is hoped that this exercise will generate fair attitudes toward disadvantaged persons.

The JOBS is also based on the premise that there are other groups of Americans without the typically identified disabilities who face employment difficulties. These include non-English-speaking persons, new immigrants, and low socio-economic-status persons. These persons also need supported employment programs. The JOBS is designed to serve the needs of all persons who have difficulty in job entry and job success because of these physical, social, or other disadvantages.

The authors claim that the final 30 JOBS items were chosen using a two-step process. First, the professional literature "was reviewed to identify the patterns of behavior which are critical to work adjustment" (examiner's manual, p. 5). Second, employment experts from this rehabilitation field were asked to review the items found from Step 1 and suggest additions or revisions. Finally, the selected items were subjected to a Q-sort process that resulted in the three clusters identified as the subscales of this instrument. The manual does not document the original items culled from the literature, or the expert process. Nor is the Q-sort process documented or referenced.

The standardization process involved three categories of employees as follows: (a) High school students in various types of special needs programs, including special education, vocational education, dropout prevention, ESL, and alternative education; (b) adults with special employment needs, including people with disabilities, history of substance abuse, and on welfare; and (c) general entry-level full or part-time employees without work supports.

TECHNICAL. There is no indication of any systematic sampling process utilized in selecting the 225 persons involved in the standardization process. The groups are mostly from South Florida, with one group from Hartford, Connecticut, suggesting that this was a convenience-based local sample. It is clearly not a national sample. Although attempts have been made to describe the resulting three groups, it is clear that this instrument has limited generalizability.

Both interrater and test-retest reliability indexes are reported separately for the three groups of employees and for the two aspects (*Quality of Performance* and *Type of Support*). All raters were provided a 2-hour training prior to using the instrument. The overall interrater reliability estimate for *Quality of Performance* ratings is .83, with a high estimate (.91) for general adults and a lower estimate (.74) for high school students. The corresponding figures for *Type of Support* are .86, .93, and .82. Test-retest (2-week interval) reliability indexes are also high and at similar levels.

Content validity is claimed on the basis of the relationship of the items to job success criteria found in published research, which is referenced in the manual. Items were included if they appeared in at least 10 articles, over a period of at least 10 years, and in the work of at least five independent investigators.

Concurrent criterion validity was computed using the usual job ratings by the *same* evaluators, raising concerns about potential bias (halo effect) in such studies. Credibility of the raters was established by using only those with relevant job titles and with direct information about the employees evaluated. Criterion validity indexes in the .80s are reported for the three types of groups.

COMMENTARY. The JOBS is clearly a much-needed instrument to help both employers and employees bridge the transition process to a job. Disabled and disadvantaged adults are clearly in need of such an objective process. Finding and retaining the first job is a challenge, especially for persons with poor backgrounds.

This instrument does have some obvious limitations with respect to its development. Although efforts appear to have been made to utilize the special literature in general vocational rehabilitation and special education, it is unclear to this reviewer why the many occupational and employment resources available in the broader occupational analysis domain were not also used. If those with employment challenges are not also oriented to the general expectations of the world of work, then they remain in a sheltered environment, and to that extent unrealistic.

There were no references to any of the national job analyses, worker trait characteristics, and other standard occupational research, such as is published in the *Dictionary of Occupational Titles,* and routinely conducted by the U.S. Employment Services and other Labor organizations. Because employment exchanges routinely utilize these resources, it would be appropriate to examine work performance expectations in the context of what is regularly expected in the real world. There is also no attempt in the JOBS to relate to the many tests and work performance criteria that have been developed and published by personnel/occupational/industrial psychologists. This is a very serious oversight.

The standardization process and the norms presented are somewhat local and limited. Efforts are needed to broaden the use of this instrument to other states and to a broader set of industries to check its relevance and utility. Although the reliability and validity evidence provided is laudable and does accrue psychometric credit to this instrument, the ultimate test of validity for this instrument lies in how well it fulfills its original purpose of providing an effective bridge for these workers. A follow-up study is needed to examine how well these workers were helped by this process.

SUMMARY. The JOBS is a very limited instrument, but it is a reasonably well-designed instrument judging from the processes followed and reported. It is relatively new. Its purpose addresses a need that is critical to the employment challenged, but more importantly, to a nation that prides itself in full employment and equal opportunity for all. The JOBS technique should be of interest to all employers who wish to nurture their employees, whether or not they are in need of adaptive or prosthetic help. In the ultimate analysis, all new employees could use some form of special school-to-work bridging support. Providing such support is another way of showing that the workplace can be a caring environment.

Review of the Job Observation and Behavior Scale by SHELDON ZEDECK, Professor of Psychology, University of California at Berkeley, Berkeley, CA:

DESCRIPTION. The Job Observation and Behavior Scale (JOBS) is used by employers, job coaches, educators, rehabilitation professionals, and others to evaluate the performance of students and adults who are in supported work environments, such as programs for vocational education, special education, rehabilitation, community work-to-welfare, and sheltered workshops. The JOBS is used to evaluate the readiness of individuals to enter the workplace, to assess the need for support, and to compare the performance of these students and adults to workers not receiving supports and who perform the same competitive jobs. It is also used to evaluate the performance of those who are being considered for entry level employment, promotions, job retention, salary increases, probationary-period outcomes, etc.

The JOBS yields scores on three subscales and a composite measure. The first subscale, Work-

Required Daily Living Activities, is composed of 13 items that pertain to patterns of self-care and personal behavior that allow individuals to function within a competitive work environment. Issues addressed are attendance, punctuality, personal hygiene and grooming, personal schedule, self-identification, and other self-items. The second subscale, Work-Required Behavior, is composed of 8 items that represent the interpersonal and social skills needed for employment, such as stress tolerance, interpersonal work interactions, honesty, work initiative, and work endurance. The third subscale, Work-Required Job Duties, is composed of 9 items that pertain to the actual job task functions common to entry-level jobs, such as quality of work, quantity of work, multiple task performance, organization of work tasks, and employee motivation. Three rating categories are relevant to each of the 30 items: (a) the quality of performance, which uses a 5-point scale ranging from "1" or not *acceptable for competitive employment* to "5" or *superior;* (b) the type of support that the employee receives during the shift or work day, another 5-point scale ranging from "1" or *continuous supervision from the job coach or supervisor* to "5" or *no unique supervision or support needed beyond that provided to other workers;* and (c) whether adaptive or prosthetic materials (e.g., written or pictorial instructions) are used by the employee along with support from others (a "yes" or "no" rating). Quality of Performance and Type of Support Composites are formed by adding the scores from the respective rating categories across the 30 items. In addition, there is a count of the number of items to which the respondent indicated that an adaptive or prosthetic device was used.

It usually takes less than 30 minutes to self-administer and score the JOBS. It is recommended that the employee be in the job setting for approximately 1 month prior to being evaluated.

DEVELOPMENT. The underlying focus for the JOBS is the "model of supported employment," which involves the engagement of workers in specific job skills and work-related behaviors and participation in real job tasks as well as integration of workers with unique employment needs into the competitive workforce. Development of the JOBS initially focused on a literature review that examined the link between entry-level job success and worker behaviors and dispositions, with a particular emphasis on identifying the criti-

cal vocational behaviors that all employees must demonstrate to obtain and maintain employment. Experts in business, welfare reform, and human services reviewed the items generated from the literature review, added and deleted items, and based on their professional judgment, identified the final 30 items in the scales. The examiner's manual states that "this pool of items was submitted to a Q-sort process resulting in three clusters which the experts perceived as most closely related to one another" (p. 5). No detail is provided about this process and analysis.

The examiner's manual presents full descriptions and definitions of the 30 items that represent the content and structure of the subscales; the test booklet itself presents only generic titles such as "Attendance," "Verbal Communication," "Stress Tolerance," "Work Initiative," "Quality of Work," and "Speed of Learning."

TECHNICAL. The standardization sample ($N = 225$) consisted of (a) 45 high school students enrolled in various types of special need programs in two counties in Florida; (b) 135 adults with special employment needs (e.g., with disabilities, history of substance abuse, etc.) and who were in full- or part-time supported employment or in sheltered work; and (c) 45 adults who were in full- or part-time employment and were not receiving work supports. Age, gender, and locale data are presented for the three samples. No detailed information or breakdown is presented regarding the work histories, types of jobs engaged in, employment settings, or other demographic and background information for the norm group that would allow comparison of the target group to a standardization sample. The examiner's manual presents means, standard deviations, and ranges for the three samples, for the three subscales, and the composite scores on the JOBS. It is suggested that use of the JOBS allows comparison of an employee's ratings to the appropriate norm sample. Frankly, however, the norm samples are rather small (45 or 135) and the information on which to compare the target and standardization sample is limited (i.e., the employee can only be compared to either high school student, adult supported, or adult, entry level). There is no information to allow one to compare on the basis of gender, race, age, type of work, reason for support need, etc. More data need to be collected to enhance the value of the norm tables.

Interrater and test-retest reliability estimates are reported. Interrater reliability is based on ob-

The subscales appear to be well supported by the factor analyses, with the authors opting for a two-factor solution that serves to create crisp and distinct subscales, even if they do not pick up every scrap of measured variance.

The main method to demonstrate reliability is via internal consistency using coefficient alpha. Alpha reliability scores are consistently in the high 70s to 80s—very acceptable levels indeed. The authors pay very particular attention to internal consistency in their step-by-step approach to instrument development, and their meticulous approach has paid off with clean factor loading and high internal consistency reliability.

Test-retest data are provided in the manual, ranging from .48 to .75 over various time intervals. Although it is always nice to see how stable an instrument acts over different time periods, there is a strong counter-argument with instruments such as the JSS that seek to measure state, rather than trait variables. As work-related stress is a state created mainly by the workplace, stress will vary according to day-to-day, or even momentary, changes in the workplace. For this reason, the test-retest approach is somewhat theoretically inconsistent with this instrument. Split-halves analysis could further strengthen the reliability picture.

Given the objectives of this instrument, the reliability evidence seems entirely adequate. I would not see a need for serious caution as to reliability.

The manual pays extensive attention to validity. Validity evidence was collected throughout the item development process. Original items for the pool were derived from previous research and other instruments, and were then validated on advice from people working in the fields being studied (e.g., police and teachers). This process offers strong assurance of face validity—an excellent starting point.

The original item pool was then subjected to extensive factor analysis to refine the pool based on each item's discriminative power and precision. The final item pool for the JSS apparently went through three rounds of this process to derive the final 30-item pool.

Internal validity of subscales is documented by the technical criteria used for inclusion within a subscale. There are two 10-item subscales in this 30-item instrument. Ten items were rejected for inclusion in subscales. These items were properly excluded as their factor loadings were overly complex. Thus, the authors have provided an empirical basis for the validity of their two subconstructs (i.e., Job Pressure events, and Lack of Organizational Support scales).

Numerous comprehensive, concurrent validity studies are cited in the manual. A large concurrent study compares results of the JSS with Rotter's (1966) Locus of Control scale. A rather convoluted argument is made about correlations between these instruments, supporting a notion that "employees who indicated that they had less control over their work environment reported more occupational stress" (professional manual, p. 33). This particular study does little to inspire or deflate my view of the JSS and might, perhaps, have been more cogently summarized.

A conversely stimulating concurrence study is presented using the Myers-Briggs Type Indicator (MBTI) and the JSS. This study illustrates the importance of taking individual differences into account when measuring constructs such as job stress. This study points out that MBTI personality type often predicted how participants rated job stress events. The study lends strong evidence in favor of the weighted scoring system.

The most compelling concurrence study reported is the simplest. Fifty-five engineers were evaluated for the general score on "Job Satisfaction," the inverse correlation with JSS stress index was -.52 $p<001$. This finding shows that JSS shares 26% common variance with Job Satisfaction (as measured). There is no question that something meaningful and integrally related to job satisfaction is being measured by the JSS.

Norm Tables. Reference tables providing norms for scoring and comparison purposes are provided for all nine JSS scales, typically presented separately for male, female, and mixed group participants. The tables convert raw scores to percentiles. The manual gives norms for 983 Managerial and Professional Employees; 808 Clerical/Skilled-Maintenance Employees; and 358 Senior Military Personnel (males only). Twenty-four female Military Personnel were not considered sufficiently representative to warrant publishing female norms from this group.

COMMENTARY. For the consumer, these norms are a starting point. As other jobs are looked at, different patterns of stress will no doubt be found. For practical purposes, differences within groups in real life work situations will offer far more useful interpretations than those based on the norms alone. Spikes indicating high stress on any JSS item should give rise to the question whether something could be improved.

The JSS is a very easy and user-friendly instrument. In its paper-and-pencil incarnation, administration takes about 15 minutes. Scoring is easy, yet requires some basic Numeracy that may interfere if less numerate individuals are being evaluated. Still, it is an instrument that can be comfortably given and scored in the first hour of a day's seminar. A clear and interpretable graph presents the outcomes, and item feedback is calculated and shown numerically.

The value of the JSS is that, even though it may save organizations very substantial human resources (costs), it offers a vehicle for employers to understand and hear the views of their employees to create the least stressful workplace. It offers employees the opportunity to explore how they fit in the workplace, offering them a guide toward less stressful ways of working, and the chance for better coping.

The JSS is published in Dutch, Flemish, German, Norwegian, and Spanish. The manual cites research showing psychometric properties similar to the original version. I have confidence in the universality of constructs developed in the JSS, so I would feel comfortable recommending this instrument in translation. It would be desirable for foreign language norms to be published as they emerge.

The final, and to me the most important, point of the JSS is the evangelical message to employers—Awake! Job stress is gnawing at your profits and your work force and there is something you can do about it.

SUMMARY. After using this instrument, scoring it both by hand and by computer, and after reviewing the manual, I am strongly of a view that the JSS represents the gold standard of the psychometrist's art. The overwhelming value of this instrument is its simplicity and clarity. What it promises, it delivers, and what it delivers is highly useful and helpful.

REVIEWER'S REFERENCE

Rotter, J. B. (1966). Generalized expectancies for internal versus external control of reinforcement. *Psychological Monographs, 80*(1, Whole No. 609).

Spielberger, C. D., Westberry, L. G., Grier, K. S., & Greenfield, G. (1981). Resources Institute Monograph Series Three, No. 6). Tampa, FL: University of South Florida, College of Social and Behavioral Sciences.

Review of the Job Stress Survey by JAMES W. PINKNEY, Professor of Counselor and Adult Education, East Carolina University, Greenville, NC:

DESCRIPTION. The Job Stress Survey (JSS) consists of 30 items that are generic, job-related events that may result in psychological strain for workers. Each item has two parts to which the worker must respond. The respondent first makes a self-reported estimate of the amount of stress associated with the described event. The respondent is asked to compare each event's stress level to a "standard" event, which is the assignment of disagreeable duties (a stress level of 5 on a 9-point scale). This is followed by a self-report of how often the event occurred during the past 6 months (ranging from 0 to 9+ days).

All 30 items are used to assess the overall level of job stress (Job Stress Index, JS-X) by combining the severity and frequency estimates. The respondent's estimates of perceived severity (Job Stress Severity, JS-S) are used to generate an average estimate of stress. Job Stress Frequency (JS-F) is also an average obtained by summing the self-reported estimates and dividing by 30. The two 10-item subscales of the JSS, Job Pressure (JP) and Lack of Organizational Support (LS), use the same process to provide average estimates. The analogous scores are JP-X, JP-S, JP-F, LS-X, LS-S, and LS-F.

The scoring of the JSS is a matter of straight-forward arithmetic, requiring only addition of the item values and division of the sum to arrive at a mean score for each scale. A software scoring program is available that scores the JSS and provides percentiles and *T*-scores. The manual notes that although administration and scoring of the JSS is easy, the interpretation of the results should only be done by a qualified professional. The usefulness of the results will be directly affected by the training and experience of the interpreter with a background in psychological assessment.

DEVELOPMENT. The current JSS is the second version of the original, 1991 assessment instrument. Both are based on the items used in the 1981 Police Stress Survey (PSS) and the Teach Stress Survey (TSS). The 60 items of the PSS were used in a factor analysis that produced a first factor labeled Administrative and Organizational Pressures. The items from this factor were rotated and produced two correlated components: Job Pressure and Lack of Organizational Support.

A subset of 39 of the PSS's items were considered to be applicable for teachers by exchanging the terms *teacher* for *police* and *school* for *department.* A committee of experienced high school teachers then added 21 items to form the 60-item TSS. Further changes in terminology were made in the wording of the 39 common items to make them more generally suitable for business, managerial, and educational settings. The 30 items of the JSS are based on the authors' judgment that these items are the "best generic measures of occupational stress" (professional manual, p. 28). The manual implies that the item selection process was guided by prior research efforts, but in fact, personal judgment is the basis for using the 30 generic items of the JSS.

The JSS's professional manual states that the items assess generic sources of occupational stress, and the self-estimates of both intensity and frequency for each item address recommendations from the occupational stress literature. Those recommendations suggest that the frequency of an event's occurrence is often overlooked as an important component of perceived stress. The potential consumer would want to consider how relevant each of the generic items is to his or her place of employment as part of a decision to use the JSS. This is important because of an anomaly in how the items are scored and the assumption that frequency of occurrence is important. The respondent is asked to rate unexperienced items based on how stressful the item might be. A number of such items would introduce some degree of "pretend" stress that is not actually part of the job. The frequency of such items would be zero.

TECHNICAL. The JSS manual describes three norm groups with a breakdown by gender. A Managerial/Professional (M/P) group was obtained from two large corporate headquarters and a large, urban university (n = 983), a Clerical/Skilled-Maintenance (C/SM) group was obtained from the same sources (n = 808), and a group of Senior Military Officers (SMO) was used from a program for possible promotion to flag rank (n = 382). The only explanation for the selection of any of the groups is for the SMO. They were included to show that the JSS can assess occupational stress in successful leaders with demanding responsibilities. How similar corporate environments and a university setting are is conjectural. Lumping the two together seems like a questionable way to increase the size of the norm groups.

Tables are provided for percentiles and *T*-scores for all groups and scales with the exception of the female SMO group. This group was considered to be too small (n = 24) to be included in the manual. Item means and standard deviations are also included in the manual, and the authors encourage consumers to include the use of them in the interpretation of the JSS results. No norms are reported for any other occupations or ethnic groups. The authors do note that many work settings would need to supplement the generic items of the JSS with additional items unique to the setting or occupation.

The reported internal consistency measures of reliability for the JSS are quite high with alpha coefficients ranging from .77 to .93 with a median value of .88. The lower coefficients tend to be found with the SMO group. These estimates of reliability may be spuriously high for two reasons, the wording of the items and the restricted nature of the generic item domain. The items deal with the two very restricted areas of perceived support and sources of job pressure. In order to be generic, the wording of the items is somewhat redundant. For example, on the LS scale four of the items start with the word lack and four more start with either poor or inadequate. Test-retest coefficients are much lower and only reported as a range (.48 to .75) with no further details provided by the JSS Manual. This form of coefficient measures score stability over time, and the authors note that it is likely inappropriate for a time-sensitive construct such as job stress. The reviewer agrees and wonders why the range of test-retest coefficients was even included in the manual.

Support for the validity of the JSS is very limited. A 10-year-old study correlated the JSS scales with locus of control and an unspecified measure of job satisfaction. A group of 55 engineers had significant inverse correlations for the JS-X scale (-.52) and the LS-F scale (-.66). Lower levels of reported job satisfaction may be partly explained by higher levels of perceived job stress and a more frequently perceived lack of organizational support. Very modest positive correlations (.16-.18) were reported for internal locus of control and the JS-X, JP-S, and LS-F scales. The only other study reported is confusing. Although it is in the manual's section on validity, the alpha coefficients are reported. The authors then assert that the means for job pressure and lack of organizational support are consistent with undefined expectations of "corporate and university cultures" (professional manual, p. 34).

These two studies offer minimal support for the two primary uses of the JSS suggested by the manual: Determine if job stress is being caused by pressures of the job or by a lack of organizational support, and develop interventions that will reduce job stress. Certainly the second use is beyond the capability of the JSS, especially for jobs or settings that have unique stressors and circumstances.

COMMENTARY. The JSS is an attempt to consider frequency of job stress as well as the severity of that stress for a wide variety of jobs and settings. Several issues severely limit its ability to do that validly. Trying to make the JSS widely viable has left it with generic items that are open to interpretation and confusion. This is compounded by the admission that supplemental items will likely be needed in many job settings. Most job settings can make a case for being unique, especially in terms of stressors and working conditions.

SUMMARY. The JSS attempts a difficult task, to include frequency of occurrence as a part of the construct of job stress. Unfortunately, the attempt to use generic items relevant for a wide variety of settings and jobs leaves the items open to a broad range of unknown interpretations by the respondent. The JSS has a developmental history extending back to 1981, but the available information on reliability and validity is sketchy and unconvincing. A potential user would want to examine carefully the individual items to determine how useful they would be in his or her specific job setting. The decision reached may be to create a setting-specific set of items to answer specific job stress concerns.

[133]
Keynotes Music Evaluation Software Kit.

Purpose: Designed to "provide the classroom teacher with a profile of students' strengths and weaknesses in domains considered to be important for most kinds of music learning" and to provide instrumental music teachers and their students with information that may be used to help student select an instrument.

Population: Ages 9–14.

Publication Date: 2000.

Scores, 3: Pitch Discrimination, Patterns Recognition, Music Reading.

Administration: Individual.

Price Data, 2002: A$199.95 per complete kit; A$99.95 per 5 copies CD-ROM.

Time: Administration time not reported.

Comments: Software does not operate on Macintosh computers; requires Windows 95 or higher.

Authors: Jennifer Bryce and Margaret Wu.

Publisher: Australian Council for Educational Research Ltd. [Australia].

Review of the Keynotes Music Evaluation Software Kit by BETHANY A. BRUNSMAN, Assessment Specialist, Lincoln Public Schools, Lincoln, NE:

DESCRIPTION. The Keynotes Music Evaluation Software Kit is a computer-administered assessment/educational tool consisting of two parts. It was designed for use with intermediate elementary and "lower secondary" (middle school) students ages 9–14. Keynotes Part I measures Pitch Discrimination, Rhythmic and Melodic Patterns Recognition, and Music Reading. Keynotes Part II includes video testimonials by students designed to help students select an instrument to learn. This review will focus on Keynotes Part I.

According to Bryce and Wu, Part I may be used by both classroom music teachers and private music instructors to assess new students' strengths and weaknesses in the areas covered by the tests and to suggest appropriate musical instruments for students to learn. Part I may also be used to select students for music lessons or classroom instruction, but should not be used to exclude students from these activities. The three content areas are covered in separate components of the software and may be administered and scored separately. All of the test items are multiple-choice format. With the use of a desktop computer or laptop and headphones, students can take the tests independently. For each item, the student listens to the appropriate music piece(s) as many times as she or he wants, selects a response to the item, and then selects "Next Question." It is not possible to return to previous questions and change answers. When the student finishes a test, the software generates a scoring report, which lists all of the items, the correct answers, the student's responses, and the number correct. The Pitch Discrimination and Music Reading tests each contain 6 practice items and 20 test items and the Patterns Recognition test consists of 4 practice items and 25 test items. All three tests use traditional Western music notation.

DEVELOPMENT. Keynotes Part I was designed to update and improve the Melbourne Music Evaluation Kit (MEK; Bryce, 1979). Development began in 1993 with comments from seven music teachers and curriculum advisers. Based on the comments, Bryce and Wu narrowed the content of Keynotes Part I to the above-mentioned areas. The results of a survey of secondary school music teachers supported the computer format of the test. No information is provided about the reviews or the survey recipients other than their job titles. Information about how they were selected, their areas of expertise (e.g., voice, instruments), and their years of teaching experience should be included in the manual.

Bryce and Wu developed new items based on the questions from the MEK. Panels of test development experts and classroom and studio music teachers at different levels reviewed and discussed the items. Bryce and Wu tried out the items with two groups of (Year 6–7) students. No information is provided in the manual about how these groups were selected or whether they are representative of the group of students in the age range covered by the tests. All of the students were attending school in Australia. Bryce and Wu used item statistics (difficulty and discrimination) to select items for the final versions of the tests. They provide no rationale for the numbers of each type of item included or the numbers of practice items.

TECHNICAL. The manual provides a sample of each type of item in each test along with item statistics for each of the test items. No information is provided about the reliability of the test scores or relationships among the tests and with other instruments or measures. Information that would be helpful in evaluating the tests could include internal consistency reliability coefficients for scores on each test; standard errors of measurement; comparisons of scores of students who are more and less skilled using computers, males and females, students at different ages within the age range specified for the tests, students of different ethnicities, and students who are known to be more or less knowledgeable and skilled at pitch discrimination, patterns recognition, and music reading; data on the adequacy of practice items; and data (or a research base) on the effect of allowing students to listen to the pieces of music multiple times.

Passing standards or cut scores are not provided. The manual provides no guidance about how to interpret scores.

COMMENTARY. There are several advantages to the computer interface that Bryce and Wu highlight. The computer allowed them to integrate the music and the presentation of items without requiring groups of students to take the tests at the same time or the use of large amounts of paper. The computer format ensures the quality of the recordings over time. It also saves time scoring because score reports can be generated automatically upon completion of a test.

The computer interface could also be a disadvantage, however, if students are not experienced computer users. The practice items seem insufficient for students who have little or no computer experience. They may be sufficient to familiarize students with the item formats, but Bryce and Wu do not provide any evidence of their sufficiency. Technical support for the software is not readily available.

The use of multiple-choice items seems reasonable and efficient. This type of format does not allow students to generate or create their own music, but the format seems consistent with what Bryce and Wu purport to measure. Whether the format is sufficient is difficult to determine without any data supporting relationships among the tests, other similar measures, and music learning outcomes.

No evidence supporting the reliability of or the interpretation of scores as described in the manual is available. The only validity evidence provided consists of a short literature review, a brief description of the process used to select the test format and items, and data on item statistics based on a very small sample of students in Australia.

The brief literature review in the manual provides some support for Bryce and Wu's choices of content areas, but the support is not very strong. For example, the MEK was designed to measure pitch discrimination, length of sounds, volume discrimination, tone color discrimination, patterns recognition, identification of instruments and instrumental groups, and knowledge of musical signs and symbols. It is not clear why Bryce and Wu chose to measure only the three areas included in Keynotes Part I. Bryce and Wu mention "concerns about sufficiently fine reproduction of sounds to test tone colour" (manual, p. 23) as a reason for eliminating three of the areas. They mention the "strengthening of instrumental music in schools since the 1970s" (manual, p. 25) as reason for eliminating several of the content areas, but provide neither a description of what they mean by this statement nor any research evidence to support it.

No data are available to document the appropriateness of the tests for students of different genders, ethnicities, or even for students at all ages within the suggested age range. All of the students who participated in the pilot study lived in Australia. It is unclear if the tests would be appropriate for students in other parts of the world.

The manual is brief and provides little guidance about score interpretation. Teachers often have very little training in assessment. They will need specific advice about how to interpret scores. A standard setting study or studies would be appropriate.

SUMMARY. The tests are easy to administer and quick to score with the right computer equipment, but technical support is not readily available. The tests can be completed independently by students who have sufficient computer experience with minimal teacher supervision. It is unclear, however, if they measure what they were designed to measure and there are no guidelines about how to use the scores. The data collected to document reliability and validity are insufficient. Users should be very cautious about interpreting results, particularly for students who are not similar to those included in the pilot studies.

REVIEWER'S REFERENCE

Bryce, J. (1979). ACER and University of Melbourne Music Evaluation Kit, handbook and report. Hawthorn: The Australian Council for Educational Research.

Review of the Keynotes Music Evaluation Software Kit by CHRISTOPHER JOHNSON, Professor of Music Education and Music Therapy, The University of Kansas, Lawrence, KS:

DESCRIPTION. The Keynotes Music Evaluation Software Kit is a 65-item test administered by an IBM compatible computer. The test is designed for music students between the ages of 9 and 14. The testing portion of the program comes in three sections, which are titled: Patterns Recognition, Pitch Discrimination, and Music Reading component. The fourth section of the program is an introduction and guide to different instruments in the orchestra. All items in the testing portion of the program are multiple choice with four response choices. At the conclusion of each section of the test, the test taker is presented with a score sheet and can elect to print it. The test taker must then reenter the program and select the next section.

Various uses for the test include providing the classroom teacher with a profile of students' overall musical strengths and weaknesses. Other suggested uses include instrumental music teachers assessing what instruments a student should

begin playing, along with suggestions on the development of a music curriculum.

There is no training required to administer the test. It is feasible that students could complete the test-taking task independently. For each type of question, an example is provided so that students understand what they must do for each of the following questions. Before a new type of task is given, a new example is presented to illustrate the modified task.

Results of the test are presented in the form of a single-page report for each section, including a list of items and whether or not the correct answer was given. The administrator can then take those individual scores back to the manual and compare the student against previous performances of trial participants. Data given in the manual include: percent correct, point biserial coefficient statistic for each item, and specific descriptive comments for most items. The manual encourages the administrator to use percentages of correct responses for each section to evaluate the students' performances.

DEVELOPMENT. The specifics of the test development are rather vague and often refer to panels of individuals who used their best judgment in making decisions regarding the construction of this instrument.

This test was created from updating the ACER and University of Melbourne Music Evaluation Kit (MEK). The process began in 1993 with consensus building from Australian music educators and administrators. A model test was developed, and with the general approval of individuals attending music education conferences, impetus for developing the full test was attained.

A test development panel was formed and included test development experts, classroom and studio teachers, a tertiary music education teacher, and a postgraduate student. Items were developed and presented at panel meetings. After approval, "final recordings" were constructed. Two pilot tests were constructed and given. No data were available on how those pilot tests were then used in producing the final test.

TECHNICAL. Information on each question is given in Appendix A of the software manual. Each item lists two statistics (facility, point biserial coefficient), and comments based on the pilot testing. Pilot participants were 169 students for the Pitch Discrimination test, 92 students for the

ciency levels with those of native English speaking students provides sufficient evidence of criterion (or content) validity. Reliability coefficients for parallel forms were consistently above .80, with alphas ranging from .83 to .95 for Listening/Speaking, .77 to .97 for Reading, and .90 to .98 for Writing. However, as many of the LPTS items are grouped as 4- to 8-item testlets, these reliability estimates may be inflated (Lee, Brennan, & Frisbie, 2000; Sireci, Thissen, & Wainer, 1991). Forms were calibrated and equated using anchor items from previous administrations so that "by estimating values for the new items with the anchor test items fixed, difficulty values for the new test items were expressed on the original scale" (manual, p. 10). The manual also provides subscale reliability coefficients. LPTS Listening/Speaking scores were positively correlated with LAS Reading and Writing scores for students who had both scores, with correlations ranging from .17 to .55. Correlations of LPTS scores with Language Assessment Scales (LAS) scores were lower for students in Grades 9–12 than for those at Grade levels K–2, 3–5, and 6–8. Correlations of the LPTS with ITBS-Reading ranged from -.20 (for Grades 9–12) to .28 (for Grades 6–8). LPTS Listening/Speaking scores for students in Grades 9–12 were negatively correlated with scores on the Test of Academic Proficiency (TAP). Scale scores were computed using the one parameter IRT Rasch model, a method commonly used to examine item difficulty and to detect differential item functioning (Camilli & Shepard, 1994; Wainer, Sireci, & Thissen, 1991).

COMMENTARY. The administration and scoring guides for the LPTS provide comprehensive instructions for test examiners, with a materials list, allowable test accommodations (if any), and practice questions for each test. With the exception of the Speaking tests, little is required on the part of the examiner other than the ability to read directions to the students clearly and keep accurate time for the timed tests. However, examiners should have formal training prior to administration of the Speaking tests to assure standardization is maintained, as these tests are scored by the examiners and the administrator's guide allows for some examiner discretion in this area. There are the usual issues of interrater reliability when multiple examiners score multiple students to the same criteria. Research suggests that the rate of

acquisition of L2 is not independent of L1 (Rong & Preissle, 1998). However, the technical manual does not provide disaggregated means for all subgroups of the norming population by demographics such as gender, age, length of time studying English, socioeconomic status, ethnicity, native language, disability, or parents' education level. This lack of demographic data for the norm population may be considered a limitation if the results of the tests are to be used for diagnostic purposes. Although scoring rubrics are descriptive, the manuals do not include a test blueprint that provides linkages of test items to test objectives and curricular standards.

SUMMARY. Graphics and illustrations serve as advance organizers in this test series, particularly at the lower grade levels, providing contextual clues for students who have limited English. The tests for Listening/Speaking, Reading, and Writing may be administered and scored independently or as a battery. Examiners who administer the Speaking tests or who score the Writing tests locally should have training in the assessment of ESL or bilingual students. The manual provides limited background on issues related to second language acquisition and characteristics of ESL students. Information is also rather limited for interpretation of scores, including means for groups of students disaggregated only by proficiency level or placement (no English, limited English, advanced ESL, and general education program) for each of the tests.

REVIEWER'S REFERENCES

Camilli, G., & Shepard, L. A. (1994). *Methods for identifying biased test items. Measurement methods for the social sciences* (Vol. 4). Thousand Oaks, CA: Sage Publications.
Lee, G., Brennan, R.L., & Frisbie, D. A. (2000). Incorporating the testlet concept in test score analysis. *Educational Measurement: Issues and Practice, 19*(4), 9–15.
Rong, X. L., & Preissle, J. (1998). *Educating immigrant children: What we need to know to meet the challenges.* Thousand Oaks, CA: Corwin Press.
Sireci, S. G., Thissen, D., & Wainer, H. (1991). On the reliability of testlet-based tests. *Journal of Educational Measurement, 28,* 237–247.
Wainer, H., Sireci, S. G., & Thissen, D. (1991). Differential testlet functioning: Definitions and detection. *Journal of Educational Measurement, 28,* 197–219.

Review of the Language Proficiency Test Series by JUDITH A. MONSAAS, Professor of Education, North Georgia College and State University, Dahlanega, GA:

DESCRIPTION. The Language Proficiency Test Series (LPTS) is designed to assess English language listening, speaking, reading, and writing skills in students whose skills in these areas are below grade level. It is to be used for placement into and exit from LEP/ESL, special education, and Title I programs. There are three tests (Listening/Speaking, Reading, and Writing) and four grade-level clusters (K–2, 3–5, 6–9, 9–12). There are two parallel forms for each test and level.

The Listening/Speaking test includes selection-type responses (listening) and oral responses (speaking). A rubric and sample responses are provided. The Reading test is thematic with all reading selections (and pictures in some cases) and questions addressing a single theme or topic involving typical school and social situations. Students are asked to read a passage and respond to questions about it. Each question has five response choices and for each response choice, the student must answer yes or no. Yes may be the correct response for up to three of the answer choices, so each response is treated as a separate question. The Writing test requires students to write three extended-response essays: a narrative essay, a persuasive essay, and an expository essay. Each essay is graded on language production, focus, description/elaboration, organization, and mechanics. A 6-point rubric (0–5) is provided for all but the mechanics rating, which is rated using a 3-point rubric.

The manual does not specify who may administer these tests, but a classroom teacher or an aide who speaks standard English could administer them. Scoring the writing section and interpreting the test scores require a teacher or other professional. All but the speaking items of the Listening/Speaking test can be group administered.

Raw scores on the tests are transformed into scale scores and reported in terms of proficiency levels. The Listening/Speaking test is a screening test with two levels: not proficient (Level I) and proficient (Level II). Test administrators should use their professional judgment to determine whether or not to proceed with reading and writing assessments for students at Level I on Listening/Speaking. There are four proficiency levels for the Reading and Writing tests. Students scoring in the Level I proficiency range are demonstrating little or no proficiency relative to that needed to perform in a mainstream classroom with age peers. Level IV students demonstrate skills comparable to those in their grade level.

DEVELOPMENT. An earlier version of the LPTS (called the Illinois Measure of Annual Growth in English—IMAGE) was developed in 1997 to assess the language development of language minority students. The Teachers of English to Speakers of Other Languages (TESOL) ESL

standards guided the development of the LPTS. Focus groups of educators were consulted during the design and development stages; they reviewed all test materials as well.

The three tests appear to have been developed, standardized, and equated separately. Equating procedures are most fully explained for the Reading subtest. Item response theory (IRT) was used to create a scale that spanned three of the test levels (presumably Grades 3–5, 6–8, and 9–12). The one-parameter logistic (Rasch) model was used with the IMAGE test. Later versions of the test have been equated to the original IMAGE assessment program by administering IMAGE and LPTS forms to the same students. The K–2 LPTS Reading test forms were equated using the Chicago norm group, whereas the other three levels were equated using the Minnesota sample. Adequate sample sizes are reported though more explanation would clarify whether the sample numbers reflect the IMAGE norm group, the LPTS norm group, or both.

According to the technical manual, the Listening/Speaking tests were developed in a manner "analogous" (p. 9) to the Reading scale development. No details are provided and it is unclear if the equating samples were based on the Chicago sample or a later Minnesota sample.

The Writing subtest appears to have been developed using a different procedure. The field test was used to select and equate the writing prompts at each grade cluster. It is not clear how vertical equating was conducted. Again, total sample sizes are adequate, but demographic breakdowns are not provided.

Development of the performance standards was based on several sources of data: the relationship between LPTS and statewide student achievement measures, average score gains made by students in bilingual programs, and the relationship between LPTS forms and the Iowa Test of Basic Skills (Chicago group only). These three empirical sources of data were used to develop proficiency categories that represent progress towards proficiency, or likelihood of meeting state language arts standards.

TECHNICAL.

Standardization. The standardization sample included several student populations in the Chicago Public Schools. Norm groups for the three tests ranged from 3,196 valid Listening/Speaking tests to 5,245 Reading tests. Bilingual students in regular education, self-contained and pull-out bilingual programs, mainstream students who had previously been in bilingual programs, and regular education students were included in the sample. The number of students in these categories, as well as gender, SES, and language minority, was not provided. Over 60 language groups were represented. A 1999 statewide pilot test was conducted in Minnesota resulting in 17,888 valid reading protocols in Grades 3–12. Information about listening/speaking and writing was not provided. It is not clear whether these tests were pilot tested in Minnesota. The publishers report that smaller studies have also been conducted. But again, no details or references are provided for these studies.

Reliability. Internal consistency for the three tests was estimated using coefficient alpha for the Listening/Speaking and the Reading tests. Coefficients for the Listening/Speaking were in the .80s and .90s and for Reading were over .90 except for the high school form of the subtest, which was a bit lower. Similar analyses were conducted for the Writing subtest yielding high coefficients (all over .90). Interrater reliability studies were not reported for the Writing test.

Internal consistency estimates were computed for the subscales of the Listening/Speaking and Reading test forms. Generally, the reliability coefficients for the subscales are adequate for tests at Level K–8. The reliabilities for the Grades 9–12 test forms are generally lower, especially for Reading; the manual reports that the sample size for that form was only 33. Routine reporting of sample sizes throughout the manual would have been helpful rather than reporting only as an explanation for low coefficients.

The reliability of the proficiency level classifications was estimated using a procedure recommended by Feldt and Brennan (1989) that estimates the proportion of correct classifications (p) and the proportion of correct classifications corrected for chance (kappa). Consistency reliability is based on the test population of bilingual students participating in the field administration of the test forms. Kappa coefficients for all of the classification are generally in the .70s and above with one exception. The classification reliability of the Grades 9–12 form of the Reading test is low (in the .40s).

Validity. Two types of criterion-related validity evidence were obtained. For one set of analyses, students in the initial equating/validation study were classified into four categories. Participants in bilingual programs were classified into one of three groups—beginning, intermediate, or advanced—with respect to their English language proficiency. General education students represented the fourth group. One-way analysis of variance was performed followed by several planned comparisons. The questions addressed were: Do test scores differ by level of proficiency? Do ESL students differ from the general education population? Do scores for beginning and intermediate ESL students differ from the general population?

The data provided generally support all three questions. In all tests, the mean LPTS scores increased by bilingual classification and almost all of the contrasts were statistically significant. For most tests and forms of the tests, the general education mean was not significantly different from the bilingual mean, though the general education mean was significantly higher than the mean for bilingual students classified as beginning or intermediate. Interestingly, the differences between the advanced bilingual and the general education students varied with the general education mean sometimes being lower, higher, and the same as the advanced bilingual mean. This suggests that although the progression from beginning to advanced levels of LPTS for bilingual students is supported, for some tests and levels, advanced bilingual students' performance is at or above the general population. Again, sample sizes would have facilitated the interpretation of these results.

The second type of criterion-related validity evidence is based on correlations of the LPTS tests and the Language Assessment Series (LAS) reading and writing subtests and the Iowa Test of Basic Skills/Tests of Achievement Proficiency reading scores. Correlations between the Listening/Speaking test and the LAS reading and writing scores were positive and significant with one exception: at Grades 9–12, the correlation between Listening/Speaking and LAS reading was not significant. The correlations between Listening/Speaking and ITBS reading were weak and in the case of Grades 9–12 negative. The authors argue that the ITBS/TAP measures academic reading ability and not listening/speaking proficiency. The correlations between the LPTS Reading and Writing tests and the three criterion measures are all moderately strong, statistically significant, and positive, providing validity evidence for the Reading and Writing tests.

COMMENTARY. These tests appear to be an important contribution to the language proficiency assessment of bilingual student populations. The development procedures are sound and the technical data generally support the claims of the publishers. States that have similar curricula to those of Illinois and Minnesota will find this test useful. Schools and systems in other states interested in using the LPTS tests may want to obtain validity evidence to support the use of the LPTS performance levels to ensure that the proficiency categories match the performance standards on local assessments if these tests are to be used for placement.

The technical manual does not always provide sufficient detail to evaluate the technical characteristics of tests. Is it not always clear which standardization sample, Chicago or Minnesota, is used for the various reliability and validity studies and the data are not disaggregated by race/ethnicity, language group, gender, or SES—a serious limitation for a test designed primarily for minority populations.

The test materials suggest that these tests may be appropriate for placement to and from special education and Title I programs. No evidence is provided for this use of these tests and use of the LPTS should be restricted to placement and exit from bilingual programs until validity evidence is provided for additional uses.

SUMMARY. The LPTS tests are attractive and easy to administer, score, and interpret. They provide a valuable addition to the language proficiency assessment of ESL/LEP students for placement and exit from bilingual programs, with evidence supporting their use strongest at the K–8 levels. Local schools and districts with larger LEP populations would do well to consider these tests for bilingual program placement and exit. Other uses of these tests, for special education and Title I students, must await evidence to support the use of these tests for additional populations.

REVIEWER'S REFERENCE

Feldt, L. S., & Brennan, R. L. (1989). Reliability. In R. L. Linn (Ed.), *Educational measurement* (3rd ed.) (pp. 105–146). New York: Macmillan.

[135]

Leadership Development Report.

Purpose: "An expert system provid[ing] insight into how a manager's personality affects his or her performance and how to modify a manager's behavior within his or her natural limits."

Population: Adults.

Publication Dates: 1996–2000.

Acronym: LDR.

Scores, 34: Impulsivity, Understanding, Complexity, Risk Taking, Breadth of Interests, Innovation, Endurance, Cognitive Structure, Order, Organization, Play, Self-Esteem, Anxiety, Tolerance, Change, Achievement, Aggression, Responsibility, Abasement, Value Orthodoxy, Energy Level, Harm Avoidance, Affiliation, Dominance, Exhibition, Interpersonal Affect, Succorance, Social Participation, Social Adroitness, Conformity, Defendence, Social Recognition, Nurturance, Autonomy.

Administration: Group.

Price Data, 2001: $90 per report including test administration materials and return by courier; volume discounts available.

Time: Untimed.

Comments: Includes items from the Jackson Personality Inventory—Revised (T6:1278), The Personality Research Form (T6:1885), and The Survey of Work Styles (T6:2456) (all still available); answer sheets are faxed to publisher; bound reports returned via courier; email delivery available.

Authors: Richard A. Hagberg, Douglas N. Jackson, and Julie Carswell.

Publisher: Sigma Assessment Systems, Inc.

Review of the Leadership Development Report by MARK A. STAAL, Director of Counseling Services and Associate Professor of Behavioral Sciences, Department of Behavioral Sciences and Leadership, United States Air Force Academy, CO:

DESCRIPTION. The Leadership Development Report (LDR) is a 292-item questionnaire, administered either by paper-and-pencil or computer. All statements are rated on a 5-point Likert scale (*Strongly Disagree* to *Strongly Agree*). The original LDR (1996) was composed of intact scales from the Personality Research Form (PRF; Jackson, 1999) and Jackson Personality Inventory (JPI); however, this more recent revised edition contains original scales and combinations of scales taken from the PRF, Jackson Personality Inventory—Revised (JPI-R; 1994), and Survey of Work Styles (SWS; Jackson & Gray, 1993).

The LDR report provides profile information on individuals across 25 personality characteristics that have been rationally aligned with 13 different leadership dimensions, which comprise five broad leadership orientations.

The manual points out that "advanced knowledge of psychological testing is not required" (p. 7) for the proper administration and scoring of the test. However, it also notes that discussion or interpretation with a counselor or coach can be beneficial. It is recommended that the testing setting be quiet and free from distractions. Although there is no time limit on the test, estimates of completion range from 35 to 45 minutes.

DEVELOPMENT. The LDR is the latest version (copyright, 2002) of a test that was previously published in 1996. The only noticeable differences between the two iterations of the test are the creation of its manual (previously it relied solely upon the JPI and PRF manuals) and its restructuring with the inclusion of scales from the SWS. Most of the test's development and construction rests on the merits of these three instruments. The central purpose of the test has not changed, nor has the majority of its content.

Normative data for the LDR are based on the performances of 227 managers (ranging from supervisors to presidents of companies). Of this sample, 70% of the managers were female and 30% were male. An explanation for this atypical gender composition was not provided.

TECHNICAL. The LDR's manual takes a two-pronged approach in its description of the test's psychometric properties. As much of the test itself is simply a recomposition of the JPI-R, the PRF, and the SWS (previously empirically validated instruments), the LDR manual references these test manuals in lieu of further description of its own psychometric strengths and weaknesses. The implicit assumption is that if the components that make up the LDR are technically sound, this should be extended to the LDR by proxy. This is a reasonable, but insufficient, conclusion about the test's theoretical underpinnings, method of construction, and reliability and validity.

In the manual's second descriptive section, the basic assumptions underlying the LDR, its method of scale construction, and the processes used to further develop and analyze its various scales is provided. Biserial correlations were calculated between each individual item and their respective scale to help determine their goodness-of-fit within various scales. A Differential Reliability Index was used to determine the portion of variance contributed by a given item to its total scale. In addition, Kuder-Richardson Formula 20 and scale intercorrelations were then used to further define the relationship between and within various scales. A focus on removing scales and items that were highly intercorrelated and those that were also highly correlated with social desirability bias was maintained throughout these processes. Final judgments about which items best represented the content of each scale, which remained ambiguous or lacked clarity, and which appeared to lack fit were conducted and further items were eliminated based on this rational approach.

The remaining 41 personality scales were subjected to a principal components factor analysis with orthogonal rotation of axes, which resulted in placement of each of the scales along the 25 a priori components (the final 25 scales). Factor loadings ranged from .34 (the PRF scale of Defendence) to .90 (the SWS scale of Job Satisfaction).

Various measures of scale reliability are not reported in the LDR manual. However, the manual refers users of the test to the respective scale reliabilities contained with the PRF, the JPI-R, and the SWS. A review of these tests and their scale reliabilities leads one to conclude that, in general, they do exhibit reasonable to very good measures of internal consistency and test-retest reliability (Cronbach alpha estimates generally in the .70s to .90s).

Evidence to support the validity of scores from the LDR is somewhat more limited. Information about the relationship between self- and peer-ratings on the JPI-R and PRF measures across 44 different leadership performance indicators (from 360-degree feedback statements) is provided. The LDR manual references an additional study connecting the SWS with performance in stressful work situations, and draws the following conclusion, "All measures show meaningful correlations with executive performance." No empirical data have been provided linking various leadership performance outcomes with the personality scales discussed.

Multiple correlations between various LDR personality scales and the 44 different leadership performance indicators (from 360-degree feedback judgments) are provided. Adjusted multiple correlation coefficients range from .23 to .47 across the indicators. The 44 performance indicators were subjected to a principal components factor analysis, which allowed for the extraction of six components. Canonical correlations between the 25 LDR scales and the 6 managerial performance indicators ranged from .38 to .65. The LDR manual notes that advice generated from the 25 different personality dimensions is "clearly based on empirical evidence, as well as on expert judgment" (manual, p. 33). This concluding statement is somewhat confusing as there is little direct connection drawn between the individual advice statements and the factor analytic procedures presented above.

COMMENTARY. The value of the LDR as a developmental management feedback measure seems to be potentially lacking in only one way. The relationship between the various personality dimensions being measured and leadership or manager competencies remains unclear. Although the developers of the LDR have chosen a rational approach to linking these constructs, they have not provided substantial empirical support for these pairings (the relationship between the various scales, the leader dimensions, and the leader orientations).

As mentioned previously, the LDR manual references a study connecting the SWS with performance in stressful work situations, and draws the following conclusion, "All measures show meaningful correlations with executive performance" (p. 30). This conclusion appears unwarranted given that no empirical data have been provided linking various leadership performance outcomes with the personality scales discussed. In fact, the relationship between JPI-R and PRF scales and the leadership performance indicators mentioned previously appears to be based upon subjective self- and peer-ratings issued by executives. Even though this may provide further information linking popular impressions of personality dimensions and leaders and their behavior, it fails to offer any solid empirical support for these connections.

The LDR manual goes on to state, "As the LDR scales are derived from these three standardized personality questionnaires, one can have confidence that the scales are measuring what they purport to measure" (p. 30). If this statement is accurate, readers are left to assume that the LDR measures personality dimensions (because indeed the three tests used to create the LDR are personality measurements); however, as the name of the test suggests, the test is designed to measure such dimensions as they directly relate to leader and manager outcomes and behaviors. These two assertions are not identical and to conclude that by measuring personality traits you are necessarily measuring leader or manager dimensions may be inaccurate, at a minimum overstating the data presented. To say with some degree of certainty that the dimensions

perceived as relating to leadership are in fact the dimensions that do relate to leadership (based on subjective ratings of executives) may be flawed logic. The realization that this logic rests as the foundation of theory behind the test itself is potentially problematic for obvious reasons.

Beyond this most fundamental consideration, the LDR manual has many strengths and only a few weaknesses. There are detailed accounts and substantial discussion concerning the test's construction and methods used to reduce and refine the item pool. In addition, although a blanket assumption that good tests can be combined and recombined without damage to their overall psychometric strengths is tenuous, most of the properties of the PRF, JPI-R, and SWS are very good. This fact does lend some credibility to the LDR.

SUMMARY. The developers of the LDR have taken three tests of personality and work styles, dismantled these tests, and reconstructed elements from each into a measure of personality that they believe directly relates to leader or manager behavior. This is a very ambitious and interesting approach to manager or leader development. However, there are several potential concerns with this test that the developers should address. It has been assumed that scores from the LDR are valid and reliable based on the fact that the three tests making up the LDR have evidence for valid and reliable scores. Empirical support for this assertion is needed.

The relationship between the various personality dimensions measured by the LDR and their managerial or leader correlates have been established based on the subjective perception of a group of executives. These dimensions should be empirically anchored in specific leader or manager behavioral correlates that have been studied and can be measured, not simply the collective perceptions of experienced executives. There is a substantial extant literature that could contribute to this area and such an addition would lend much greater credibility to the expert system used. The LDR has exciting potential once the empirical links between its assumptions and purposes have been made.

REVIEWER'S REFERENCES

Jackson, D. N. (1994). *Jackson Personality Inventory—Revised: Manual.* Port Huron, MI: Sigma Assessment Systems, Inc.
Jackson, D. N. (1999). *Personality Research Form 3rd edition: Manual.* Port Huron, MI: Sigma Assessment Systems, Inc.
Jackson, D. N., & Gray, A. M. (1993). *Survey of Work Styles Research edition II: Manual.* Port Huron, MI: Sigma Assessment Systems, Inc.

[136]

Learning Style Inventory, Version 3.

Purpose: Designed to describe the ways an individual learns and deals with day-to-day situations.

Population: Ages 18–60.

Publication Dates: 1976–2000.

Acronym: LSI3.

Scores: 4 scores: Concrete Experience, Active Experimentation, Reflective Observation, Abstract Concaeptualization; 4 learning styles: Accommodating, Diverging, Converging, Assimilating.

Administration: Group or individual.

Price Data, 2001: $79 per 10 self-scoring booklets; $50 per facilitator's guide to learning (2000, 81 pages); $38 per 15 transparencies; also available online at $15 per person.

Foreign Language Editions: French and Spanish versions available.

Time: [20–30] minutes.

Author: David A. Kolb.

Publisher: Hay Group.

Cross References: See T5:1469 (13 references) and T4:1438 (12 references); for a review by Noel Gregg of an earlier edition, see 10:173 (17 references); see also 9:607 (7 references).

Review of the Learning Style Inventory, Version 3 by CECIL R. REYNOLDS, Professor of Educational Psychology, Professor of Neuroscience, Distinguished Research Scholar, Texas A&M University, College Station, TX:

DESCRIPTION. The Learning Style Inventory, Version 3 (LSI3) consists of 12 questions presented in a multiple-choice format (four choices per item). The LSI3 is presented as "an improved version of the original Learning Style Inventory" (Facilitator's Guide, p. 65) first published in 1976. The scale was developed based upon a theory of experiential learning that argues that individuals learn as a function of their positions on two continuums: Concrete Experience-Abstract Conceptualization and Active Experimentation-Reflective Observation. The LSI3 is intended to provide measurement of the degree to which individuals display these different learning styles as derived from experiential learning theory. In providing a revision of the LSI, the manual (p. 65) tells us that new features of the LSI3 include an improved 12-item, randomized, self-scoring format, improved internal consistency reliability estimates and score stability, "a normative comparison group that is ethnically diverse, is drawn from a wide range of careers, and has an average educa-

tion of 2 years of college" (p. 65), an opportunity to experience the cycle of learning while taking the instrument, and new application information. Scoring consists of a two-dimensional plot of raw scores on a graph, which examinees are then instructed how to interpret. Examinees are provided with a booklet that explains the interpretive process and recommends a variety of other assistive resources that can be purchased from the publisher of the LSI3. Methods used for determining the cut scores designated on the plot are not described beyond the presentation of percentage markers that represent percentile ranges of raw scores. The score distributions are not described nor can they be derived on the basis of the data provided in the manual.

DEVELOPMENT. A brief description of the development of the 12 LSI questions is provided at various points within the manual and apparently some data analyses were undertaken to derive the specific items from a larger item pool. These analyses are, however, not described beyond very general statements. The criteria for item selection and how items were chosen with regard to these criteria are not described.

The LSI3 was originally developed in 1971 by David Kolb to reflect his finding that people fall into four basic types that predict dominant learning styles. These styles are linked to experiential learning theory. A larger pool of items was initially derived and there are periodic discussions throughout the manual of review and analysis of these items but no where is there a comprehensive description of the development of the LSI or its newer version, the LSI3. In fact, there is much confusion in the manual regarding development in the current version. On page 65 of the manual, we are told that a new feature of the LSI3 (completed in 1999 and published in 2000), is "a normative comparison group that is ethnically diverse, is drawn from a wide range of careers, and has an average education of two years of college." On page 66 of the manual, we are told that "the normative comparison group used in LSI version 3 is the same as the one used in LSI 1985." The LSI3 differs from the LSI 1985 version in that the same items are randomized in the LSI3. The reliability data, we are told, represent improved reliability for the LSI3 but these data come from a version of the LSI evaluated in 1991 that is purportedly identical to the LSI3. No explanation for these discrepancies is provided in any discussion of the development of any of the forms of the scale.

TECHNICAL CHARACTERISTICS. Reviews of validity evidence related to interpretations of the LSI are referenced as having been conducted in 1991 and no studies of the LSI3 are reported. In fact, the validity section consists of a single paragraph stating that the LSI in its various versions has been used in many different countries and that research supports the validity of the Learning Style Inventory.

The LSI3 manual is noted to be substantially inadequate in providing documentation regarding technical or psychometric characteristics of the scale as required by professional standards documents (e.g., American Educational Research Association, American Psychological Association, & National Council on Measurement in Education, 1999). Very little of the standards document referenced above is addressed in any way in the manual.

Data that are provided consist of internal consistency and test-retest reliability coefficients associated with four main scores in the battery and these come from the 1991 article for 91LSI and are purported to be reliability indices for the LSI3. The interpretation of the reliability coefficients given in the manual is also at odds with common interpretations that would be made by psychometricians and most other psychologists. The initial sample internal consistency reliability indices reported for the LSI3, based on a sample of 711, provides some 12 alpha coefficients. All 12 of these are below .80 and are categorized as follows: .70–.79, 3 coefficients; .60–.69, 5 coefficients; .50–.59, 1 coefficient; coefficients below .5, 3. The manual states that reliability coefficients of .43, .45, and .48 represent "very good internal consistency" (p. 69). Additional studies show reliability coefficients ranging from .56 to a high of .78. One is hard pressed to believe that reliability coefficients below .5 can be characterized as anything but quite poor as opposed to the manual's interpretation of them as "very good." In fact, none of the coefficients reached the cutoff of .8 recommended by authors such as Cronbach (1990) as the minimally acceptable level for classification of individuals. The stability coefficients, which were in fact calculated using the same samples as the internal consistency studies, are quite high. The entire section on technical characteristics of the LSI3 is naïve psychometrically and provides little guidance to users that is consistent with requirements of professional standards and other literature.

COMMENTARY. The LSI3 may be a useful instrument. However, based upon the information provided in the manual, one cannot determine that it is, in fact, useful nor can one determine that the interpretations of scores proffered in the manual have any evidence of validity. The LSI3 is presented as a substantially improved version of an earlier instrument, yet no technical data are provided with regard to the new scale. All data presented and referenced in the manual pertain to earlier versions of the LSI. The general description of the development of the scale is inadequate to allow an appraisal of the consistency of the items with the underlying theory. Most aspects of the *Standards of Educational and Psychological Testing* (American Educational Research Association, American Psychological Association, & National Council on Measurement in Education, 1999) are simply ignored in the manual. The validity section deals with none of the 24 standards of validity noted in the standards document and the reliability of scores is dealt with only minimally. A discussion of the nature of the revision and contrasts with earlier versions as requested in the standards (see chapter 3) is virtually ignored throughout the LSI3 manual. Similarly, information regarding scaling, development of scoring, and the requested supporting documentation for tests as indicated in the standards are all virtually ignored in the manual.

The manual states that cross-cultural validity of the LSI3 has been established but cites no specific research on this topic and provides no data in the manual. However, there are indications in the manual of substantial differences in mean scores and classification rates as a function of gender, age, and educational level. Yet, the manual would argue in other places that these variables are irrelevant to the validity of score interpretations. No actual evidence regarding this is provided in the manual. There is no discussion of fairness of testing contained in the manual, nor of the use of the LSI3 with individuals of diverse linguistic backgrounds, or of the testing of individuals with disabilities.

SUMMARY. In short, the manual is woefully inadequate in the information it provides concerning the LSI3 and the scale cannot be recommended for use until such time as these gross deficiencies are remediated.

REVIEWER'S REFERENCES

American Educational Research Association, American Psychological Association, & National Council on Measurement in Education. (1999). *Standards for educational and psychological testing.* Washington, DC: American Educational Research Association.

Cronbach, L. J. (1990). *Essentials of psychological testing* (5th ed.). New York: Harper Collins Publishing.

Review of the Learning Style Inventory, Version 3 by DAVID SHUM, Senior Lecturer of Psychology, Griffith University, Brisbane, Australia:

DESCRIPTION. The Learning Style Inventory, Version 3 (LSI3) is a self-report 12-item test developed by David A. Kolb to help people describe how they learn and to identify their learning style. The test describes a person's learning mode according to two polar dimensions: Concrete Experience (CE) vs. Abstract Conceptualization (AC) and Active Experimentation (AE) vs. Reflective Observation (RO). Based on these descriptions, the person's learning style is classified into one of four basic types: Diverging, Assimilating, Converging, and Accommodating.

The LSI3 is suitable for people between 12 and 60 years of age with a seventh grade reading level or above. No special requirements for the administration, scoring, and interpretation of the test are specified. According to Kolb, the main applications of the LSI3 are self-exploration, self-understanding, and self-development.

The LSI3 was designed in such a way that it can be administered, scored, and interpreted by the test taker. One is required to complete 12 sentences that describe learning by ranking four endings (from 4 to 1 for best description to worst description) that correspond to the four learning modes (viz., CE, AC, AE, RO). The 12 sentences are written in easily understood language and printed on a two-part (answer and score) form. The instructions for the test are well organized and clearly written. The scores for the four learning modes can range from 12 to 48. Given the way the sentences are answered and scored, these scores are ipsative in nature.

To find one's preferred learning mode, a diagram called The Cycle of Learning is used to transform the four raw scores into percentile scores based on a normative group of 1,446 adults. Two combined scores are also obtained by calculating the differences, AC – CE and AE – RO. Finally, one's preferred learning style type is determined by plotting the two difference scores on a Learning Style Type Grid.

DEVELOPMENT. Kolb originally developed the LSI in 1971 based on Experiential Learning Theory, which in turn is based on the Jungian concept of styles or types. The LSI3 is the latest revision of the inventory and there are four main changes. First, in LSI2, the endings that represent the four learning modes were organized in the same order for all 12 sentences to facilitate scoring. To control for possible response bias, the order of the endings is randomized in the LSI3. Second, Kolb modified the wordings of the learning style type in the LSI3 (e.g., Converger to Converging) to address the concern that the old terms might give an impression that learning styles do not change. Third, the response sheet for the LSI3 was changed to a two-part color-coded form and it is produced in such a way that answers written on the first page are automatically transferred to the second page. Fourth, a number of experiential activities and information on career development have been added to a 19-page test booklet. An 81-page *Facilitator's Guide to Learning* was published in 2000 to accompany the test.

TECHNICAL. The technical specifications of the LSI3 are included as a six-page section in the *Facilitator's Guide to Learning*. The normative group for the LSI3 comprised 1,446 adults aged between 18 and 60 years. According to the guide, there were 638 males and 801 females, which for reasons not explained do not total 1,446. Kolb states that this group was ethnically diverse, represented a wide range of career fields, and had an average education of 2 years of college. However, detailed description and breakdown of these demographic variables are not available. The percentile scores for all test takers are based on the average performance of this group. Separate norms for different age and gender groups are not provided. This is a concern because there seem to be age and gender differences on some of the scores (see p. 10 and p. 68 of the guide).

Evidence for the internal consistency and test-retest reliability of the LSI scores is based on the data (initial sample $N = 711$, replication sample $N = 1,052$) collected by Veres, Sims, and Locklear (1991) using a version with randomized sentence endings. Mean coefficient alphas for the four learning modes scores ranged from .53 to .71 in the initial sample and from .58 to .74 in the replication sample. These indices are lower than expected and they are lower than those obtained for the LSI2 (from .82 to .85). The test-retest (8-week interval) reliabilities of the four learning modes scores ranged from .92 to .97 in the initial sample and from .96 to .99 in the replication sample. Similar statistics obtained for the LSI2 were much lower and ranged from .25 to .56. Kappa coefficients were also calculated to examine classification stability for the four learning style types and were generally high, ranging from .71 to .86 for the initial sample and .86 to .93 for the replication sample.

The *Facilitator's Guide to Learning* contains a section that discusses the validity of the LSI3 but it is only 10 lines long. In that section, Kolb directs readers to a bibliography that includes studies that tested the validity and applicability of the LSI. In other parts of the guide, Kolb refers to the validity of the LSI3. For example, on page 41, he states that "research on the LSI has tested the relationship between individual learning styles and the careers people choose, and found a strong correspondence between the two." On page 12, he mentions a number of studies that examined the relationships between performance on the LSI and other instruments (e.g., Myers-Briggs Type Indicator, Learning Style Questionnaire) that measure similar constructs. Nevertheless, these points are not elaborated and the studies are not referenced.

COMMENTARY. The strength of the LSI3 lies in its brevity and its simplicity. It can be administered, scored, and interpreted by most people in a relatively short time. The content and instructions of the test are clearly written, and are easy to follow and understand. The color-coded scoring format facilitates scoring and the extensive use of graphics and diagrams in the test booklet and the guide enhances the test taker's understanding of the theory of learning and its associated constructs.

There is a concern regarding the appropriateness of the norms. According to Kolb, the comparison group used for the LSI3 is the same as the one used in the LSI2. This might not be appropriate given that the formats of the two versions are different. The order of the sentence ending for the four learning modes is the same for the 12 sentences of the LSI2, but the order of the ending of the LSI3 is randomized. Given that this change in format has led to changes in internal consistency and test-retest reliability (Veres et al., 1991) and that the equivalence of the two versions has not been demonstrated, the use of the LSI2 normative comparison group for the LSI3 might not be appropriate.

Changing the order of the sentence ending from fixed to random allows for a more accurate estimation of the internal consistency and test-retest reliability of the LSI. The internal consistency of the latest version is found to be lower than that of the previous version and lower than expected. In contrast, the test-retest reliability of the test is found to be high and better than that of the previous version.

Given that validity was the main concern raised in a review of the LSI2 (Gregg, 1989), it is disappointing to see that very little effort was devoted to addressing the validity of the LSI3. Rather than summarizing and discussing data and evidence that provide support for the various types of validity, Kolb simply refers readers to a bibliography and makes general statements about the validity of the LSI3. This lack of effort is also surprising given that interesting issues have emerged in the literature regarding the psychometric properties of the LSI3, such as whether it is appropriate to use ipsative test scores in a factor analysis to evaluate the construct validity of the LSI (Geiger, Boyle, & Pinto, 1993; Loo, 1999). It is also disappointing to see that Kolb does not clarify in the validity section whether new data have been collected specifically to examine the validity of the LSI3 and whether evidence that supports the validity of earlier versions of the LSI can be used to support the LSI3. Given that the equivalence of the various versions of the LSI has not been demonstrated and that the correlations between these versions are not included in the validity section, it is difficult to evaluate the validity of this latest revision of the LSI.

SUMMARY. The LSI3 is the latest revision of a self-report instrument for describing and identifying one's learning mode and learning style. Although the author has provided evidence to support the reliability of the instrument, he has not provided adequate and suitable evidence to support the validity of this latest version of the instrument. This is disappointing given that the LSI seems to be a popular and promising instrument in the educational and organizational literature.

REVIEWER'S REFERENCES

Geiger, M. A., Boyle, E. J., & Pinto, J. K. (1993). An examination of ipsative and normative versions of Kolb's Revised Learning Style Inventory. *Educational and Psychological Measurement, 53,* 717–726.

Gregg, N. (1989). [Review of the Learning Style Inventory.] In J. C. Conoley & J. J. Kramer (Eds.), *The tenth mental measurements yearbook* (pp. 441–442). Lincoln, Nebraska: Buros Institute of Mental Measurements.

Loo, R. (1999). Confirmatory factor analyses of Kolb's Learning Style Inventory (LSI-1985). *British Journal of Educational Psychology, 69,* 213–219.

Veres, J. G., Sims, R. R., & Locklear, T. S. (1991). Improving the reliability of Kolb's Learning Style Inventory. *Educational and Psychological Measurement, 51,* 143–150.

[137]

Learning Tactics Inventory.

Purpose: "Provides … individuals with information about how they learn and illustrates behaviors that they can adopt to become more versatile learners."

Population: Managers, leaders, executives.

Publication Date: 1999.

Acronym: LTI.

Scores: 4 learning tactics: Action, Thinking, Feeling, Accessing Others.

Administration: Group.

Price Data, 2002: $27 per Facilitator's Guide (41 pages); $14 per Participant's Workbook/Survey; quantity discounts available.

Time: 15 minutes.

Comments: An inventory of the behaviors individuals have reported using when engaged in the task of learning from experience; self-scored; Facilitator's Guide includes details of workshop procedures, reproducible overheads, and handout masters.

Author: Maxine Dalton.

Publisher: Center for Creative Leadership.

Review of the Learning Tactics Inventory by KATHLEEN A. DOLGOS, Professor of Education, Kutztown University of Pennsylvania, Kutztown, PA:

DESCRIPTION. The Learning Tactics Inventory (LTI) was created for people who want to improve their ability to become better at learning from experience. The LTI gives information on how one learns and shows behavioral skills to become a more versatile learner. The tool may be used to introduce the individual to the concept of learning management and leadership skills from work-based experiences. It does not measure personality or information-processing style. It offers an inventory of behaviors shown when engaged in the task of learning from experience.

The LTI materials consist of a participant workbook and a facilitator's guide. The workbook contains a Learning Tactics Inventory Self-Assessment Survey that provides a set of scores that can be compared to the aggregate scores of a reference group. The results can help a person understand how they learn or fail to learn when exposed to a novel or unfamiliar challenge. The LTI is designed to be used for career or management development to help participants become more versatile learners.

The Learning Tactics facilitator's guide provides suggestions for presenting the model along with a sample workshop design and administrative guides.

The facilitator's guide contains a section on the administration of the LTI. It gives a suggested sequence for using the LTI as part of leadership training. The material is offered as a template for delivery. Six overhead masters are included to be used in the proposed 2-hour workshop setting. The authors emphasize that the survey is to be used only to increase self-awareness for personal development.

The LTI is designed to show the behavioral tactics used more often by an individual. The LTI measures four kinds of learning tactics. The four sets of learning tactics are labeled Action (learning from direct experiences), Thinking (learning through symbolic representation), Feeling (learning by managing the anxiety), and Accessing Others (socially transmitted learning). The inventory consists of 32 items (tactics) and takes about 15 minutes to complete. For each item there are five choices, ranging from "I have almost never used this approach" to "I have almost always used this approach." The respondent is asked to think about the times that he or she has been faced with the challenge of an unfamiliar task or experience and circle the number corresponding to the appropriate statement listed.

The LTI is self-scoring and should be administered without an explanation about the four sets of tactics. A separate scoring sheet is completed after all items are answered. The circled answers from the survey are transferred to this scoring sheet. Scales A through D give total raw scores that are then transferred to the "Interpretation Sheet." The four columns reflect percentile rankings for the four learning tactics of Action, Thinking, Feeling, and Accessing. Individuals are asked to mark their raw scores at the appropriate percentile block. The participants do a comparison of their own scores to a normative sample. This normative sample consisted of 188 individuals who were in the Center for Creative Leadership's Leadership Development Program. The mean, standard deviation, and median score are compared to give each of the participants an estimate of the sets of behaviors he or she uses as compared with the normative sample.

Individuals are asked to focus on the scores that fall below the 50th percentile and record the tactics that were 1s or 2s. These are the tactics rarely used. Participants are then asked to reflect on how the failure to use these tactics has influenced the ability to learn from an experience. The same approach is used for tactics that scored 4s or 5s. These are tactics that are used most often.

The scores on the LTI can be used in developing a personal development plan to identify skills needed to meet career goals or to complete organizational goals that are job related. The last part of the "workshop" is to write a draft personal development plan using the results from the LTI.

DEVELOPMENT. Items were developed through conversations with people from the pilot learning study at the Center for Creative Leadership, from anecdotal records of the study, and from the literature on learning. Data to support the internal consistency of the scales were collected over a 2-year period from participants in two courses given by the Center for Creative Leadership and from a military training school over a 1-year period.

Originally 75 items were tested for inclusion in the LTI. Theory and item-to-total scores were used to determine which items aligned stronger with the domains. Items were retained if the item-to-total correlation was .35 or greater. Thirty-two items were retained.

TECHNICAL. All of the scales had a .70 or greater level of internal consistency using coefficient alpha.

Two studies of the construct validity of the instrument were done. In the first study, self-report data were gathered on the LTI and on three of the scales from Prospector, an instrument with similar scales to measure ability and willingness to learn from experience (McCall, Spreitzer, & Mahoney, 1996). The scales used were "seeks opportunities to learn," "seek and uses feedback," and "learns from mistakes." Alpha coefficients for these scales, as reported in the test manual, were .88, .82, and .83, respectively.

The first study involved a group of army captains (n = 274) who took the LTI and the Prospector instruments as part of an off-site training opportunity. The resulting statistics show a correlation of the learning tactics with each of the learning scales. The results of the second study, which involved 36 people attending a university leadership program, focused on the self-reporting on the LTI and the boss ratings on the Prospector learning scales. Due to the small sample size in this study, it was difficult to statistically state

variances of each tactic with the learning scales. Looking at both studies, there was a modest relationship between the tactics and the criterion being measured. Additional statistical information was analyzed focusing on metacognition, relationship to personality, and the relationship to managerial effectiveness.

COMMENTARY. The LTI is an instrument to be used for career or management development when the goal is to help individuals become more aware of how to be versatile learners. The suggested sequence in its administration is easy to follow. Time allotment is noted for pacing of the presentation. The procedure is a good structure for a workshop.

The six overhead masters come with little supporting information or explanations. A definition section should accompany the overheads to help the presenter. Words used on the masters are not on the same level as the actual wording used on the LTI.

SUMMARY. The LTI is a tool that can be used at a leadership workshop for self-reflection concerning a person's strengths and weaknesses when faced with the challenge of an unfamiliar task or experience. The skills of the facilitator can make this tool an effective part of the workshop. Participants can reflect on the results and take away what they need from the findings of the LTI to begin to develop their personal development plan.

REVIEWER'S REFERENCE

McCall, M. W., Jr., Spreitzer, G., & Mahoney, J. J. (1996). Prospector. Greensboro, NC: Center for Creative Leadership.

Review of the Learning Tactics Inventory by **WILLIAM B. MICHAEL**, *Professor of Educational Psychology, University of Southern California, Los Angeles, CA:*

DESCRIPTION. Designed to afford individuals with a clear-cut, flexible sense of behavioral strategies that they are most likely to employ when required to learn in an unfamiliar and challenging situation, The Learning Tactics Inventory (LTI) comprises two major parts: (a) the Learning Tactics Inventory facilitator's guide to assist the facilitator (trainer or mentor) to communicate to the learner the principles or applications of the learning model and (b) the Learning Tactics Inventory participant workbook including a scale of 32 items. The items represent four basic types of learning tactics that are postulated to be Action, Thinking, Feeling, and Accessing Others. In the learning process, Action tactics refer to how high a level of engagement the learner is willing to assume in completing the task at hand, which often occurs in an unfamiliar and challenging situation. Thinking tactics reflect those behaviors that are based on an internal and solitary orientation. Both inductive and deductive problem-solving strategies are likely to be basic components of thinking tactics accompanied by the identification of past parallel or contrasting events. Feeling tactics constitute those behaviors that the respondent would employ to acknowledge and to control feelings of distress or anxiety arising from an encounter with an unfamiliar situation. Tactics of Accessing Others reflect ways in which the learner takes part in desired interpersonal behaviors involving modeling, receiving feedback, and seeking help from others who have been in similar situations. In the facilitator's guide, the implication exists that these four learning tactics are being viewed in the context of a working environment rather than a school environment.

DEVELOPMENT. Items for the inventory were developed from information obtained via communication with research personnel at the Center for Creative Leadership in Greensboro, North Carolina. Helpful in generating items were contributions by many psychologists including Bandura (1977), Kolb (1984), Meichenbaum, Price, Phares, McCormick, and Hyde (1989), and Revans (1990). Nineteen items were created from the neo-analytic literature associated with Horney (1970) pertaining to the ability and willingness of persons to take part in novel and unfamiliar situations.

Within the 32 items are four blocks of 8 items corresponding to the constructs underlying the four learning tactics. Items are interspersed in the inventory such that the item associated with a given learning tactic is separated from the preceding appearance of an item representing the same construct by 3 items belonging to the other three learning tactics. For each item, five response alternatives are presented indicating the frequency with which a given approach in learning has been applied: 1 = *I have almost never used this approach*; 2 = *I have rarely used this approach*; 3 = *I have sometimes used this approach*; 4 = *I have often used this approach*; or 5 = *I have almost always used this approach*. Scoring points assigned to the five alternatives vary from 1 for the least frequently used approach to 5 for the most frequently used approach. Thus, for each of the four subtests of 8 items the score could vary from a minimum of 8 points to a maximum of 40 points with the higher scores indicating a more frequent use of the approach described in the item statement.

TECHNICAL. The psychometric data pertaining to the LTI are somewhat limited in terms of the number of different groups studied and the lack of diversity among them. Far more normative data are required for each of the four subscales of the LTI. The major sample studied, which was not clearly identified, included 274 participants. In addition to the presentation of means and standard deviations for scores earned on the four subscales, intercorrelations of their scores are presented. They varied between .18 and .48 with a median value being .40. Internal-consistency estimates of reliability (coefficient alpha) for scores on the four subscales of tactics in Action, Thinking, Feeling, and Accessing Others were .73, .76, .80, and .76, respectively.

From the standpoint of concurrent validity, correlation coefficients were presented between scores of the four subscales of the LTI and those on each of the three criterion variables taken from the three subscales of the Prospector learning scales often used in a military setting. These criterion measures were identified as Learns from Mistakes, Seeks Opportunities to Learn, and Seeks/Uses Feedback. The resulting 12 coefficients varied between .10 and .30 with a median value of .23. All but one of the coefficients were statistically significant at or beyond the .05 level. Multiple correlation coefficients in the prediction of scores on the three criterion measures from an optimally weighted composite of scores on the four LTI subscales fell between .26 and .36, all of which were statistically significant beyond the .01 level.

Attempts were also undertaken in a military sample of 86 individuals to determine concurrent validity coefficients between each of the four LTI subscales and scores on eight criterion measures afforded by the Myers-Briggs Type Indicator (MBTI). For the most part, the 32 coefficients obtained were not statistically significant, although statistically reliable indices occurred between scores on the Action subscale and those on the Thinking and Feeling subscales of the MBTI and between scores on the LTI Feeling subscale and those on the Thinking and Feeling criterion measures of the MBTI. No coefficient exceeded an absolute value of .25.

Finally, an effort was made to find concurrent validity coefficients between scores on the series of item statements from what was identified as the Benchmarks instrument and those on the four LTI subscales. Although several of these coefficients were statistically significant for the sample of 274 participants, none exceeded .33 in absolute value with most coefficients falling between .21 and .27.

COMMENTARY. It appears evident that a great deal more information is required regarding the psychometric properties of the LTI—especially because of the lack of extensive normative information and the somewhat limited scope of data pertaining to both the reliability and validity of scores on the LTI subscales. Factor analyses of the intercorrelations of scores on the items might lend some empirical support to the validity of the hypothesized constructs for the LTI. Factor analyses might also indicate that additional items are needed for construct clarification. Certainly, the addition of a few well-constructed items might also be expected to enhance the internal consistency reliability of scores in each of the four subscales.

The conceptual framework underlying the LTI, which has been carefully formulated, does appear to make a great deal of intuitive sense. The four constructs proposed would seem to have genuine value in the context of learning and problem solving in unfamiliar situations and to offer a great challenge to both the trainee and the facilitator in the instructional process.

SUMMARY. The LTI represents a conscientious effort to provide for individuals facing a challenging and unfamiliar work assignment four behaviorally oriented strategies or tactics (Action, Thinking, Feeling, and Accessing Others) that can be used in their developmental planning in many problem-solving contexts. The facilitator's guide and the participant workbook describe and illustrate application of theory associated with the four learning tactics in a meaningful, interesting, and appealing way. The acquisition of additional psychometric data could lead to substantial improvements not only in the interpretability of scores but also in their accuracy as reflected by enhanced reliability and validity of scores on the four subscales. Despite its psychometric shortcomings, the LTI offers an instructional-learning package that would appear to be quite helpful to those employees who need to solve challenging problems in an unfamiliar context.

REVIEWER'S REFERENCES

Bandura, A. (1977). *Social learning theory.* Englewood Cliffs, NJ: Prentice Hall.
Horney, K. (1970). *Neurosis and human growth.* New York: Norton.
Kolb, D. (1984). *Experiential learning.* Englewood Cliffs, NJ: Prentice Hall.
Meichenbaum, D., Price, R., Phares, J. E., McCormick, N., & Hyde. J. (1989). *Exploring choices: The psychology of adjustment.* Glenview, IL: Scott, Foresman.
Revans, R. W. (1990). *Action learning.* London: Blond and Briggs.

[138]
Level of Service Inventory—Revised: Screening Version.

Purpose: Designed to provide "a risk/needs assessment important to offender treatment planning."
Population: Ages 16 and older.
Publication Date: 1998.
Acronym: LSI-R:SV.
Scores: Total score only.
Administration: Individual.
Price Data, 2002: $85 per complete kit including 25 interview guides, 25 QuikScore™ forms, and manual (1998, 34 pages); $50 per 25 interview guides/QuikScore™ forms; $22 per 25 interview guides; $37 per 25 QuikScore™ forms; $40 per manual; $45 per specimen set including 3 interview guides, 3 QuikScore™ forms, and manual; computer version also available.
Time: (10–15) minutes.
Authors: Don Andrews and James Bonta.
Publisher: Multi-Health Systems, Inc.

Review of the Level of Service Inventory—Revised: Screening Version by IRA S. KATZ, Clinical Psychologist at California Department of Corrections, Salinas Valley State Prison, Soledad, CA, Soledad Medical Clinic, Soledad, CA, and private practice, Salinas, CA:

DESCRIPTION. The Level of Service Inventory—Revised: Screening Version (LSI-R:SV) is an 8-item screening instrument used to provide a quick and efficient tool for offender treatment planners. It is based on the larger 54-item Level of Service Inventory—Revised (T6:1421). The selected 8 items are supposed to represent an appropriate cross section of the needed risk/needs factors. It is a quick and handy instrument.

The LSI-R:SV, like the full version, samples both risk and needs and the item content reflects the "big four" risk factors of criminal history, criminal attitudes, criminal associates, and antisocial personality patterns. In addition, the LSI-R:SV samples the domains of employment, family, and substance abuse.

The scoring of the instrument is quite innovative and easy to use. After the items have been rated, the responses will transfer to the middle page of the QuikScore form. The LSI-R:SV total score is obtained by adding up the item scores. The screening version should be completed on the basis of both an interview and a review of the criminal history. Collateral information can assist when there is some concern about interview and/or record discrepancies.

TECHNICAL. It is unclear how the norms were obtained for the inmate and probationer populations. And more importantly, it is unclear how they were stratified by gender, ethnicity, and other factors such as prior mental health screening and forms of incarceration and institutionalization.

Psychometrically, this reviewer was mostly satisfied with the reliability and validity properties. A very convincing analysis of face validity and convergent validity was explained and illustrated in the manual.

The most critical psychometric analysis is the relationship between the LSI-R:SV and the LSI-R. The findings indicate a correlation of .85 for male inmates, .68 for female inmates, and .84 for probationers (both genders). Overall the correlations are sizable, ranging from .32 to .85.

Predictive validity may be the most important type of validity. Outcomes predicted by the LSI-R:SV included in-program recidivism (including charges pending and reconvictions), multiple reconvictions, success in correctional halfway houses and misbehaviors while incarcerated. There were also good data for paroling authorities on prediction of parole violations. Finally the LSI-IV also predicted institutional misconduct, which is helpful to correctional staff responsible for the classification and management of prison populations. One interesting data element suggests that low scorers on the LSI-R:SV are more likely to be successful in halfway houses.

Generalizability is a very important empirical concern. The full LSI-R is based on a general theory of criminal behavior (Andrews & Bonta, 1998) and the expectation that there would be few limits on generalizing to other settings and other offender groups. To date the LSI-R:SV has predicted a range of outcomes (e.g., recidivism, halfway house outcome, and prison misconduct) with different offenders (inmates and probationers) across gender. In addition, in a sample of 52 Aboriginal offenders (Bonta, 1989) the correlation between the LSI-R:SV total scores and reincarceration was $r = .35$.

COMMENTARY. As a practitioner in a correctional environment, it seems to me that the "first pass" at the client will usually yield the best unfiltered information. With more questions there is greater opportunity to separate out any instrumental response behavior. This reviewer is unconvinced that less is more. There are other reservations this reviewer has with this instrument.

The manual is handy and easy to understand. It does become a little muddied in the case studies presented. The cases on face are excellent. The end result recommendations are somewhat confusing. The first example shows a "Mr. Brown" who has an LSI-R:SV score of "5," which put him in the medium range indicating the full LSI-R follow-up is strongly recommended. Looking at the percentile distribution it is possible that will not happen even though the client is only slightly below the mandatory range. Perhaps that is just coincidental. The second case study has a "Ms. Lake" scoring "0" out of 8. The QuikScore box indicates that even with a "0" and a cumulative frequency percentage of men and women at 26, an LSI-R follow-up is desirable. Why bother with a screen if even a score of "0" yields a possible full-scale referral.

There is the potential of applications of this unique instrument to several "at-risk" populations such as spousal abusers, jail population, youth authorities, juvenile halls, county probation departments, and for use in training of mental health providers and extenders. It would be helpful to consider both the screening version and the larger instrument in training for correctional officers who often are the best evaluators of offender population behaviors.

SUMMARY. The LSI-R:SV has strengths and limitations. It is user-friendly, quick, and a good pretest. It is not a substitute for the full LSI-R which is an excellent instrument. Perhaps combining the LSI-R interviewer guide with the LSI-R:SV could ameliorate the weakness and uncertainty in predictive validity of the shorter instrument. The LSI-R:SV does have a very good interview guide. But it is limited by design to focus on only the eight selected questions. In this reviewer's opinion, if an institution is going to do a screen anyway, why limit the richness and robustness of the information that can be gathered at the first sort? Efficiency is not always effectiveness.

This reviewer is a fan of the full LSI-R. For over 20 years that instrument has provided a great tool to those of us working with the growing incarcerated populations. The LSI-R's proven validity, reliability, and overall utility are hard to match or replace on any level. This reviewer continues to be impressed with the quality of forensic research and published empirical research literature that supports the LSI-R. We are indebted to the Canadian offender population research and the subsequent psychometric tools that have evolved over the years. Like all new tools, in the spirit of fairness, the jury is still out on the LSI-R:SV. Modifications may ameliorate current shortcoming and build on the clear strengths and utility.

REVIEWER'S REFERENCES

Andrews, D.A., & Bonta, J. (1998). *The psychology of criminal conduct* (2nd ed.). Cincinnati, Ohio: Anderson.
Bonta, J. (1989). Native inmates: Institutional response, risk and needs. *Canadian Journal of Criminology, 31,* 49-62.

Review of the Level of Service Inventory— Revised: Screening Version by KEVIN J. McCARTHY, Clinical Assistant Professor of Psychiatry, Louisiana State University, Health Science Center, New Orleans, LA:

DESCRIPTION. The Level of Service Inventory—Revised: Screening Version (LSI-R:SV) is an 8-item form, drawn from the 54-item Level of Service Inventory—Revised (T6:1421). It has been designed to assess a "cross-section of the risk/needs factors represented on the longer version" and has been offered as "a cost-effective, time-efficient screener for level-of-service-related assessment" (manual, p. 1). Much of the information provided in the manual has been drawn from the original Level of Service Inventory—Revised. Although the current version has been offered under the mantle of credibility associated with the LSI-R, little useable information is available regarding the LSI-R:SV. The authors posit this instrument as an offender risk/needs assessment, yet its brevity and limited scope of assessment precludes its utility in all but the most youthful and inexperienced offender populations.

DEVELOPMENT. The developmental history of the LSI-R:SV is generally parallel with, but later than, the emergence of the longer version Level of Service Inventory—Revised. The authors note that the empirical body of literature and criminogenic theory are generally consistent with the LSI-R. Yet the current expansion of the correctional population argues for a careful and considered assessment process for all convicted offenders, to enhance offender treatment programs and reduce the incidence of recidivism. Reducing the assessment demands through the use of an abbreviated screener is not likely to enhance either the effectiveness of treatment programs or the reduction of recidivism rates. In some legal jurisdictions the courts have mandated the expansion of offender assessment programs, as an essential element in administering custody, care, and control of offender populations. The criminal justice statistics offered as a rationale for use of a brief assessment model (manual, p. 1) actually press the case for a thorough offender evaluation. Although the growing offender population suggests a continuing criminal justice challenge, this fact argues for comprehensive offender assessments to inform policy and practice decisions in terms of treatment and prevention issues.

TECHNICAL. The normative sample came from three databases: probationers, male inmates, and female inmates, all drawn from a provincial Canadian correctional population. The statistical summaries offered in several tables do not lend themselves to easy comparison, with inconsistent use of data on female inmates. The authors posit that the Level of Service Inventory—Revised and the Level of Service Inventory—Revised: Screening Version "share a beginning rooted in professional practice" (manual, p. 18). Reliability and validity data for the LSI-R:SV "are described in the manual for the LSI-R, and the reader is referred to that manual for more detailed information" (manual, p. 17). The LSI-R manual was not provided for review, therefore information about the reliability and validity of the LSI-R:SV was insufficient for adequate review. The authors note in the manual for the brief screening version that "there is no information on test-retest reliability ... there is no empirical data available on interrater reliability" (manual, p. 18). The authors offer a Cronbach's alpha value of .54 for the male inmate and probationer's samples. No information was provided on the female inmate sample, though the 526 females in the group were part of the normative sample (manual, p. 17). Internal consistency data, which were offered, were inadequate to sustain the burden of establishing score reliability. Using a conservative approach to the issue of validity, the reviewer posits that the manual fails to provide sufficient evidence of score validity for several reasons: (a) It is commonly accepted that scores cannot be considered valid without having established score reliability; (b) the brief nature of the instrument as it attempts to span broad, but essential areas of criminogenic interest; (c) the weak statistical support for construct/convergent validity is confounded by the insufficiency of comparison with a wide variety of alternative measures. Correlations offered as evidence of construct/convergent validity "ranged from .18 to .28 and produced a Multiple R of .30" (manual, p. 19). Apart from reference to the construct of antisocial personality, no rationale was offered to support the selection of alternative measures. Although the authors have done various research studies with offender populations, the LSI-R:SV appears to be a retooled LSI-R. "Re-analysis of the authors' data sets finds LSI-R:SV scores to predict a range of outcomes" (manual, p. 20). As mentioned above, data were not presented in a manner that facilitated meaningful comparisons. Information provided was inadequate for a thorough review of the brief screening version. Requests to the publisher for additional information were unsuccessful in producing supplemental documentation.

COMMENTARY AND SUMMARY. The Level of Service Inventory—Revised: Screening Version is a product derived from its predecessor the Level of Service Inventory—Revised for purposes of facilitating brief offender evaluations. It is offered as a brief screening instrument that provides a step-up approach to offender risk/need assessment. For reasons discussed above, brevity may not comport well with the inherent goals mandated by offender treatment and prevention decisions. Making important decisions regarding the future of offenders should not be predicated upon the brevity of review, but rather the depth of knowledge developed about the individual. If the LSI-R:SV is nothing more than a way to organize the acquired data, then it is still seriously flawed by the inadequacy of its reliability and validity. At this time, there is little evidence to establish its value as a useful psychometric instrument, other than serving as a list of possibly pertinent questions.

Criminal justice administrators are frequently faced with managing the demands of a system of competing services. Information is the essential element facilitating the smooth operation of this system. Reduced information demands may satisfy the legal requirement for offender classification procedures, but are likely to miss the target of effective treatment and prevention planning for offender populations. Assessment brevity and effective resource allocation must be balanced with the long-term goals of treatment and prevention programs. The Level of Service Inventory—Revised: Screening Version is probably most suitable for use with a youthful and inexperienced offender population. It provides a narrowly focused approach to the initial task of offender screening, but would not be suitable for use as a sole approach to this type of assessment. Its effectiveness is likely to be contingent upon the experience level of the examiner. The future utility of the LSI-R:SV may be enhanced with additional normative studies to develop its potential usefulness in diverse populations. Particular emphasis should be placed upon the development of instrumentation that has adequate evidence of reliable and valid scores.

[139]
The Listening Skills Test.

Purpose: Designed to measure "comprehension monitoring and message appraisal."
Population: 3 years 6 months to 6 years 11 months.
Publication Date: 2001.
Acronym: LIST.
Scores: 4 subtests: Referent Identification, Message Appraisal, Comprehension of Directions, Verbal Message Evaluation.
Administration: Individual.
Price Data, 2002: $103.98 per complete test kit including record forms, stimulus manual, and manual (101 pages).
Time: (20–30) minutes.
Authors: Peter Lloyd, Ian Peers, and Caroline Foster.
Publisher: The Psychological Corporation Europe [United Kingdom].

Review of The Listening Skills Test by PAM LINDSEY, Associate Professor of Education, Tarleton State University, Stephenville, TX:

DESCRIPTION. The Listening Skills Test (LIST) is a 45-item individually administered instrument used, according to the manual, to assess children's ability to make decisions about verbal information as "they hear it" (p. 1). Specifically, the authors purport that the LIST measures the child's "ability to reflect upon and manipulate the structural features of spoken language" (p. 1). The LIST has four subtests and an Extensions and Follow-up section that suggests follow-up assessments for children who score poorly on one or all of the subtests. The four subtests include Referent Identification (RI), Message Appraisal (MA), Comprehension of Directions (CD), and Verbal Message Evaluation (ME). Three of the subtests evaluate the examinee's evaluation of oral messages in relation to pictorial contexts; the fourth evaluates the examinee's ability to make verbal judgments. Administration takes approximately 7–8 minutes per subtest. The stimulus book uses a wipe-off overlay format for examinees to record their responses.

Professionals who have experience with standardized test administration, scoring, interpretation, and assessing young children (3–7 years old) should administer the LIST. The manual provides standard scores, age equivalent scores, and percentile ranks for each subtest and for the composite score (LIST score). The subtest scaled scores are based on a mean of 10 and a standard deviation (SD) of 3, whereas the LIST composite score is based on a mean of 100 and a standard deviation (SD) of 15. The confidence interval suggested by the authors is at the 68% level. A test taker scoring within one SD of the mean for both subtests and composite scores is considered to be within normal listening skills range. Using the scores and the follow-up suggestions, the examiner can make decisions about the need for further testing in the area of listening comprehension. Although normative data are provided for each subtest, it is suggested that the full battery be administered to provide a complete profile.

DEVELOPMENT. The LIST (copyright, 2001) may be used with young children between the ages of 3 years 6 months and 6 years 11 months and 30 days of age. The LIST is based on the construct of referential communication paradigm, specifically, that much of the "business of the classroom" (p. 1) is conducted through spoken language and that a child's ability to make appropriate decisions about linguistic messages directly impacts his or her school success. The four subtests are designed to assess different, but related, components of listening comprehension and verbal decision making.

The materials provided by the developers include the manual, which provides the rationale and technical and development information as well as detailed descriptions of each subtest. The manual also provides clear administration and scor-

ing directions that are color coded so that the test instructions provided to the examinee are clear. Conversion tables for standard scores, age equivalent scores, and percentile ranks are provided for each subtest and for the overall LIST composite score. The stimulus notebook and protocols are also provided in the test kit along with an eraser rag to clean the overlays. A marker pen is not included in the kit. The kit comes in a soft carrying case.

TECHNICAL. The manual provides pilot phase, standardization, and normative sample data. The standardization sample is described as representative of the population of the United Kingdom and included "in excess" (manual, p. 42) of 50 children in each age range, for a total of 378 in the norming sample. The sample included children between the ages of 3.6 and 7 years and was structured according to age, gender, SES, race/ethnicity, and geographic regions of the United Kingdom. The third author of the test was the primary examiner.

The internal consistency reliability coefficients for the subtests and composite scores ranged across age bands from .42 to .80 for total, with the Verbal Messages (VM) subtest reporting the poorest reliability estimates (range .07–.55). The reported coefficients for VM make it unreliable for measuring the construct. The Comprehension of Directions subtest also had very poor reliability estimates for five of the seven age ranges (.47–.63). The 6.0–6.11 age range had minimally acceptable to reliable ranges (.75–.77). The Referent Identification and Message Appraisal subsets reported the most reliable technical properties. The composite LIST score appeared most reliable for the younger children with the oldest of the seven age bands reporting the lowest reliability (.49–.60).

The authors reported that the test-retest reliability coefficients (2- to 7-week interval) were moderate to good and comparable to other standardized measures. This may be true; however, the LIST composite score appears to be the only one with an acceptable level of reliability. The reported test-retest reliability coefficients for the subtests ranged from .45–.59, which, according to Sattler (2000), would be considered unreliable. However, in fairness, test-retest reliability should not be considered as the determinant of the instrument's reliability as children's behaviors change from one administration to the next.

Discriminant validity studies were conducted by comparing the LIST score to scores on the Wechsler Preschool and Primary Scales of Intelligence—Revised (WPPSI-R) and The Clinical Evaluation of Language Fundamentals (CELF)—Preschool receptive language scores. The correlation between the WPPSI-R is reported as low; however, the two tests do not measure the same construct. Results of the analysis between the LIST and CELF were reported as modest. Overall, the authors conclude that because the LIST measures skills not formally measured by any other instrument, there are none to which it can be truly compared.

Content validity was ambiguously discussed documenting literature sources on which the test items and skills were based. Overall evidence to support the technical quality of the LIST to measure what it purports to measure is limited. The reliability evidence for the instrument is also weak.

COMMENTARY. The LIST is based on a specific paradigm and normed on a specific population, which makes its usefulness very limited. Even being used with children in the U.K. population, it should be considered a screening instrument at best. The Comprehension of Directions subtest is very confusing and would be very difficult to use with young children. This fact probably accounts for the low reliability statistics found at ages 3.6–5.11. The Verbal Messages subtest has the child evaluate a sentence as "good" or "bad" when in actuality the question should be, "does the statement make sense or not."

The language used in the directions of the test is very specifically U.K. oriented. For example, children in the United States would not understand such terms as "tick" for check mark. The Extensions and Follow-up section is fair; its strongest feature is that it directs the examiner to investigate further before making any decisions based on the LIST scores only.

SUMMARY. The test developers have a good idea and an instrument in the making. But it is just not quite finished. Because the ability to listen to and interpret spoken messages is a critical skill for school success, there is certainly a need for a standardized instrument to assess listening abilities in children. However, the LIST needs stronger reliability and item analysis as well as validity studies before it can be used as a viable source of information about a child's listening skills. It may be useful as a screening instrument to determine if more testing is needed for a specific population in the United Kingdom. It has limited if any usefulness as an instrument to be used with any other populations. In addition, scores obtained on the LIST should not be used to make educational decisions about a child's listening skills and abilities.

REVIEWER'S REFERENCE

Sattler, J. (2001). *Assessment of children cognitive applications* (4th ed.). San Diego, CA: Sattler Publishing.

Review of The Listening Skills Test by GENE SCHWARTING, Associate Professor, Education Department, Fontbonne University, St. Louis, MO:

DESCRIPTION. The Listening Skills Test (LIST) is designed to: (a) assess the ability of children ages 3 1/2 to 7 years of age to make decisions about verbal information, (b) measure change in the ability to make independent decisions about language, and (c) focus on the pragmatic aspects of metalinguistic awareness. The LIST may be used by educational psychologists, speech/language pathologists, teachers, and other professionals with experience in test administration and scoring who wish to assess the communication skills of young children. It contains four subtests: Referent Identification (the ability to detect ambiguity in messages), Message Appraisal (the ability to judge statements as true or false), Comprehension of Directions (the ability to follow an extended set of instructions), and Verbal Message Evaluation (the ability to evaluate the content of verbal statements without context cues) as well as producing an overall score.

The test kit includes the examiner's manual and a reusable stimulus manual that includes plastic sheets over each page on which the child uses a provided marker to indicate his or her response. Each subtest begins with sample items that can be used to familiarize the participant with the format for that subtest. It is emphasized that the examiner must speak clearly, but the child need not verbalize, so the test could be used with children with impairments in language. There are no time limits, basals, or ceilings, with testing time estimated as 20 to 30 minutes. The test was developed in the United Kingdom, and some of the vocabulary (e.g., "roundabout" and "petrol") is distinctly British.

Norms tables at 6-month age intervals are used to convert the raw scores to standard scores that have a mean of 10 and standard deviation of 3, with confidence intervals at the 68% and 95%

levels provided. The sum of these subtest standard scores is converted to an overall LIST Total standard score that has a mean of 100 and a standard deviation of 15, with confidence intervals again provided. In addition, tables are provided to convert scores into percentile ranks or age equivalents.

DEVELOPMENT. The LIST was constructed to monitor comprehension and evaluate language, build upon research in referential communication and metapragmatics, and assess language decoding and oral comprehension. In addition, it was designed to be easily administered and scored, and to be attractive and interesting to children ages 3 to 7 years. It connects with the Listening aspect of the Speaking and Listening core component of the U.K. National Curriculum. Piloting of the LIST involved eight studies with over 300 children, resulting in a number of modifications of the original items as well as in the administration and scoring procedures.

TECHNICAL. Norming was conducted in 2000–2001 in 23 schools throughout the United Kingdom, following the identification and training of test administrators. The sample consisted of 378 children, with at least 50 in each of seven 6-month age intervals from 3.6 to 7 years of age. Children who were non-English-language dominant, or who had a known disability, were excluded. The sample was matched with regard to gender, socioeconomic status, race/ethnicity, and region to the 1991 U.K. Census.

Internal consistency reliability, using Cronbach's coefficient alpha, is reported by subtest and age level. Results vary from a low of .07 (Verbal Message with 3.6 to 3.11-year-olds) to a high of .82 (Message Appraisal with 5.6 to 5.11-year-olds). When collapsed across ages, the coefficients vary from .60 in Verbal Message to 0.88 in Referent Identification, whereas the LIST Total score has a coefficient of .88 across all ages. A test-retest reliability study with a sample of 32 children (2–7-week intervals) resulted in subtest coefficients ranging from .45 to .59, whereas the LIST Total score was .71.

Construct validity information notes the intercorrelations of the subtest standard scores range from .26 to .42, indicating a moderate degree of overlap. Criterion-related validity was examined through a study ($n = 27$) involving the Wechsler Preschool and Primary Scale of Intelligence—Revised U.K. (WPPSI-R) and the Clinical Evaluation of Language Fundamentals—Preschool U.K. (CELF). The LIST's correlation with the WPPSI-R performance score was .17, and with the CELF receptive language score was .39.

COMMENTARY. The authors note the importance of listening in school, and emphasize that the skills developed in the home do not necessarily convert to the classroom environment, particularly in lower-income households. The LIST is presented as an instrument to identify children lacking the ability to listen effectively and subsequently to benefit from classroom instruction, and who are therefore in need of intervention. An argument is put forth about the independence of each subtest, but the intercorrelations would seem to indicate that the skills measured are not necessarily discrete. The issues of attending deficits and distractibility, particularly in a classroom setting, would also not necessarily be addressed through an individual assessment like the LIST.

Certainly, the development and norming of the test in the United Kingdom, along with some British vocabulary terms, would raise concern as to the usefulness of the LIST in oher countries. The test items also assume some understanding of basic concepts in position, numbers, and colors that may influence scores. Finally, the reliability and validity data provided are limited.

SUMMARY. The Listening Skills Test is an interesting assessment tool that attempts to provide information useful to teachers of young children. Potential users need to consider the concerns addressed above, and determine whether the information obtained from the LIST justifies the time and cost expended to obtain it until these concerns have been addressed.

[140]
Management Development Questionnaire.

Purpose: A personal competence assessment instrument "designed to help managers identify their weakness and strengths and decide what they need to do to develop themselves."

Population: Managers.

Publication Date: 1997.

Acronym: MDQ.

Scores, 20: Initiative, Risk Taking, Innovation, Flexibility/Adaptability, Analytical Thinking, Decision Making, Planning, Quality Focus, Oral Communication, Sensitivity, Relationships, Teamwork, Achievement, Customer Focus, Business Awareness, Learning

Orientation, Authority/Presence, Motivating Others, Developing People, Resilience.
Administration: Individual.
Price Data, 1998: $20 per assessment and narrative report; $9.95 per questionnaire; $24.45 per user's manual (52 pages).
Time: (35) minutes.
Author: Alan Cameron.
Publisher: Human Resource Development Press.

Review of the Management Development Questionnaire by SAMUEL HINTON, Professor, Educational Studies, Eastern Kentucky University, Richmond, KY:

DESCRIPTION. The Management Development Questionnaire (MDQ) is a 160-item inventory of management competencies and is administered by paper and pencil or by computer. The test taker has the option to select an answer to each item by selecting one of five rating scales— strongly agree, agree, neutral, disagree, and strongly disagree. The test taker is advised to consider each statement quickly, answer all the items, avoid using the neutral rating, and describe self honestly.

The 20 competencies are identified as follows: Initiative, Risk Taking, Innovation, Flexibility/Adaptability, Analytical Thinking, Decision Making, Planning, Quality Focus, Oral Communication, Sensitivity, Relationships, Team work, Achievement, Customer Focus, Business Awareness, Learning Orientation, Authority/Presence, Motivating Others, Developing People, and Resilience. They are arranged under five meta/ global clusters, namely—Managing Change, Planning and Organizing, Interpersonal Skills, Results Orientation, and Leadership.

Managers and professional staff can administer the questionnaire. It is a competence assessment instrument for learning and development, which can be used for selection and recruitment. However, caution is advised when using the instrument for selection and recruitment because the MDQ is not validated for this purpose. The instrument can be used as a candidate self-perception inventory instead of, or alongside, validated personality assessment instruments such as the Sixteen Personality Factor Questionnaire (16PF; T6:2292). The developers claim that it will provide competence information relevant to successful managerial performance.

Materials provided include the main questionnaire, which is printed in reusable booklets.

Instructions for the test taker are provided on the answer sheet. The answer sheet is double paged and the scoring key is on the second page. The instrument is scored on a profile sheet containing a sten scale and brief behavioral descriptions of each of the competencies measured. Reports are provided in a computer generated format. Instructions are provided for persons administering the questionnaire. The administrator must explain in broad terms what the questionnaire measures and why it is being used.

Test takers with guidance from the test administrator can independently score the questionnaire. The answers to items scored on a rating scale of 1–5 are shown on the second page of the second sheet. This information is provided on page 13 of the user's manual.

The scoring key is reversed for negatively phrased questions. Question order follows the sequence of competencies shown on the Profile sheet. For example, the first question measures initiative, the second question measures risk-taking, the third question measures innovation, etc. Each question is phrased differently. For example, the first question is phrased positively, the second negatively, the third negatively, etc. Each page on the questionnaire corresponds to an answer column on the answer sheet, and each row on the answer sheet corresponds to a competence scale. The test developer's advise that information on the scoring system should not be made public to test takers until they have completed the questionnaire.

DEVELOPMENT. The developer stated that a wide-ranging literature search was conducted to identify competence dimensions related to successful management performance. The literature search covered literature in competencies and management textbooks. Usually, a test publisher will provide a bibliography of texts and documents searched. No such bibliography is provided in this publication. According to the test developer, competence dimensions were identified and sorted into groups under labels of frequently occurring competencies. Twenty competencies were selected and then classified into five secondary clusters. The description of the process of competence identification is not well documented.

TECHNICAL. Scoring involves the use of a scoring key, a profile chart, and a norm table. The profile chart is in the user's manual. The norm conversion table is also in the manual. The manual scoring process outlined in the user's manual is very brief and is sometimes unclear. However, the test developers have a software system with a Test Base User Manual that can be ordered separately from the publishers.

Sten scores are "standardized ten" score scales ranging from 1–10, with a mean of 5.5 and a standard deviation of 2. Scores that fall further from the mean in a high or low direction are considered more extreme. Help with sten scale interpretation is provided in the MDQ manual Interpreting MDQ Competencies: A Competency Model For MDQ. Scores are presented in a sten scale, which shows how the test taker compares with other managers. Comparison is based on results from a norm group. Sten scores interpretation is based on which norm group the researcher uses.

Reliability. Internal consistency is stated to be in the .60 to .80 range ($N = 364$). The average scale reliability is .69. The mean standard error of measurement based on raw scores is estimated at 2.23.

Validity. The test developers used exploratory factor analysis to determine the factor structure of the questionnaire. Principal Component Analysis (PCA) was the extraction method used. A factor structure table is provided. Other than stating the independence of the MDQ competence dimensions as appearing in many recently developed company frameworks and in the MCI frameworks, statements of validity of specific scales are vague. The developers admit that there is a need to compare the MDQ results with results of similar instruments. They promise to address this issue in the future.

COMMENTARY. Information from the MDQ is intended to challenge managers' thinking about what they need to develop in their management skills and abilities. Managers and managers in training are expected to complete the inventory and encourage feedback from their colleagues or superiors on specific items. An interpretative report helps the process by presenting a profile of potential strengths, weaknesses, and development points based on the sten profile. Discussion of the profile with peer, supervisors, and professionals will enhance the accuracy of the information and is strongly advised. Test takers who strongly object to the information derived from their test taking are advised to disregard the report. Both the profile chart and the computer-generated report should supplement a feedback discussion conducted by a qualified professional. The test developers describe the inventory as a conceptual, or theoretical model of competence. They concede that it overlapped the "Big Five" theory of personality. However, they did not provide an adequate explanation of how the MDQ competence model is similar to, or is different from, the "Big Five" theory of personality.

SUMMARY. The MDQ is a self-perception inventory. It asks questions about competencies relevant to successful managerial performance. The MDQ competence model measures 20 management competencies, which are dimensions of five global or meta-management competencies. The developer claims that it is a competence assessment instrument for learning and development, which can be used for selection and recruitment. However, it is better to be on the side of caution and use it solely as a professional development instrument. Validity and reliability coefficients were provided but not adequately discussed. When there are wide discrepancies between the report of the assessor and that of the assessed, the test developer advised that the assessed should simply ignore the report. The inventory has not been cross validated with similar instruments for concurrent validity. However, the developer recognized that this must be done in the future.

This inventory was professionally developed. It can be used as a needs assessment instrument. The competency enhancement activities in each of the 20 scales are particularly relevant to the professional development of managers and managers in training. These behavioral competency enhancement activities can assist managers and supervisors to enhance strengths or to develop competencies for which they obtained a low score.

Review of the Management Development Questionnaire by EUGENE P. SHEEHAN, Dean, College of Education, University of Northern Colorado, Greeley, CO:

DESCRIPTION. The Management Development Questionnaire (MDQ) is a learning and development tool aimed at assisting managers and professional staff in identifying their strengths and weaknesses. The authors also suggest that the MDQ can be used in recruitment and selection, although they point out that the instrument has not been validated for this purpose. Specifically, the MDQ purports to measure 20 personal competencies in five competency clusters: Managing Change (Initiative, Risk Taking, Innovation, and Flexibility and Adaptability), Planning and Organizing (Analytical Thinking, Decision Making, Planning, Quality Focus), Interpersonal Skills (Oral Communication, Sensitivity, Relationships, and Teamwork) Results Orientation (Achievement, Customer Focus, Business Awareness, and Learning Orientation), and Leadership (Authority and Presence, Motivating Others, Developing People, and Resilience). The scale consists of 160 items to which respondents indicate their level of agreement on a 5-point, *strongly agree* to *strongly disagree*, scale. Each competency is measured by eight items.

The MDQ is easily administered. Instructions are clear and straightforward. Respondents indicate their answers on a separate sheet. The questionnaire can be self-scored. Scores on each competency are easily converted into sten scores, which can then be plotted on a profile chart.

DEVELOPMENT. The MDQ is based on the premise that competencies are important in determining who will be an effective manager. That is, if one has certain competencies one will be a more effective manager. The competence approach does not, however, consider in any depth the power of the environment in which a manager finds herself or himself. The statement on the positive and negative aspects to both low and high scores could be confusing to some readers. Three approaches to competencies are briefly described in the user's manual: Behavioral, Management Standards, and Meta-Competencies. The explanation for the theoretical model behind the MDQ is far too brief. The reader is left with no understanding of the conceptual groundwork that underlies the instrument.

Information on the development of the MDQ is limited. Beyond saying "The MDQ questionnaire was designed using current best practices in the design of self-perception questionnaires" (user's manual, p. 37), the author provides no information on how items were written or selected for inclusion in the questionnaire. Similarly, there is no information on the population used in the item analysis or norming process. The standard norms "are based on a mixed sample of managers from a range of companies" (user's manual, p. 38).

On the positive side, the user's manual does provide a comprehensive section dealing with the interpretation of the MDQ competencies. This might be the most useful section as it could provoke discussion between trainers and managers as the trainers lead managers through the learning and development process.

TECHNICAL. Only one type of reliability is described—internal consistency reliability. The user's manual contains the internal consistency reliability estimates for the 20 scales. These range from an unacceptable .23 (Motivating Others) to .88 (Oral Communication). One other scale, Flexibility/Adaptability, has an unacceptably low reliability coefficient (.35). The average internal consistency reliability is .69. Although the user's manual indicates that the internal consistency reliabilities are based on a population of 364, no information on the composition (occupation, managerial level, age, gender, or ethnicity) of this group is provided.

Validity is discussed in terms of an exploratory factor analysis. Three factors accounting for 62% of the variance were identified. This three-factor structure does not, however, support the five metacompetency structure upon which the questionnaire is based.

A cross-validation study, using MDQ scale intercorrelations, suggests the competence dimensions in the MDQ are identified in other competency frameworks. Unfortunately, the user's manual contains little information concerning the details of this study. For example, we know neither the size nor the composition of the subject population upon which this study was based.

Information on concurrent and predictive validity is lacking. We do not know how scores for managers were deemed as more effective. Reflecting the relatively recent advent of this questionnaire, the manual does not describe other studies in which the MDQ has been used.

COMMENTARY. Without a solid psychometric foundation, the value of any questionnaire is limited. The above-mentioned paucity of information on item analysis, norming, reliability, and validity leaves the MDQ open to the criticism that we really have little evidence that it accurately identifies valid managerial competencies.

SUMMARY. The MDQ is designed to assess managerial competencies in 20 areas. The questionnaire can be easily and efficiently administered and scored. However, the identified psychometric inadequacies and weaknesses leave one to ponder just what it is that the MDQ actually measures. Incomplete reliability or validity evidence and lack of information on norming procedures do not permit the assertion that the MDQ systematically measures managerial competencies. The section of the user's manual that describes the competencies, including high and low score behaviors, could be used to provoke discussion with managers undergoing professional development.

[141]
Management Team Roles—Indicator.

Purpose: "A team roles model and questionnaire [that] identifies the contribution ... made by each individual to the success of [his or her work] team" and "indicates which [of 8 distinct] Jungian function-attitudes are primarily being used at present."
Population: Adults.
Publication Date: 2000.
Acronym: MTR-i.
Scores: 8 team roles: Coach, Crusader, Explorer, Innovator, Sculptor, Curator, Conductor, Scientist.
Administration: Group.
Price Data, 2001: £49.50 per specimen set including technical manual (2000, 95 pages), question card, answer sheet, report, and 360 Degree feedback form; £35 per 10 self-score answer sheets; £35 per 10 report and 360 Degree feedback forms; £42.50 per technical manual.
Time: (10–15) minutes.
Comments: Can be completed online.
Author: Stephen P. Myers.
Publisher: The Test Agency Limited [England].

Review of the Management Team Roles Indicator by GARY J. DEAN, Professor, Department of Adult and Community Education, Indiana University of Pennsylvania, Indiana, PA:

DESCRIPTION. The Management Team Roles Indicator (MTR-i) is an ipsative instrument designed to identify the types of roles played by members of work teams. The eight roles identified by the instrument are Coach, Crusader, Explorer, Innovator, Sculptor, Curator, Conductor, and Scientist. These roles are based on a product-oriented view of Jung's personality theory. The author states that product orientation refers to the contribution a person makes to a team; their contribution is seen as a product.

The materials received for review included a 95-page manual (version 3), a reusable question card (containing the items to which team members respond), an answer sheet, and a 360 degree feedback form. The question card contains six sets of eight items for a total of 48 items. Respondents are to distribute 12 points among the eight items within each set. The points can be assigned in any manner the respondent desires (for example, all 12 points to one item or a combination of points to any or all of the eight items). There are a total of 72 points for the entire inventory. As respondents complete the answer sheet their point allocation is transferred to a carbonless copy. Respondents then tally their points on the carbonless copy to arrive at a total number of points for each of the eight team roles. Interpretation is accomplished by having the respondents rank their roles from the one receiving the highest score to the lowest. Consistent with ipsative instruments, the scores themselves are to be ignored; only the rankings of the roles are used in interpretation. A person's self-rating can then be compared to ratings from other team members to obtain a 360 degree feedback.

The MTR-i can be used as a stand-alone activity or in conjunction with the Myers-Briggs Type Indicator (MBTI; T6:1678). The eight roles measured by the MTR-i are compared to the personality types identified by Jung and by the personality types measured by the MBTI.

DEVELOPMENT. The development of the MTR-i was accomplished in several stages. Myers cites a need for a team role assessment inventory that is consistent with the MBTI. The author states that both team role assessment and the MBTI have received enduring interest, but previous attempts to compare existing team role assessment inventories with the MBTI have proved less than satisfactory for practitioners. The development of the MTR-i is intended to fill this void by providing a team role assessment inventory that can be used alone or in conjunction with the MBTI.

Myers states that the MTR-i has undergone over 90 revisions prior to being published. The author has attempted to collect data on a large scale by making the inventory available on-line (http://www.mtr-i.com) resulting in over 20,000 responses to various versions of the inventory. A plea is made in the manual for users to forward data collected to the author for continued development of the instrument.

TECHNICAL INFORMATION. The published version of the MTR-i is ipsative. This format was chosen because the author felt that it best reflected the basis of Jungian personality types as identified by the MBTI. A factor analysis was conducted on a nonipsative version of the inventory in which respondents (n = 240) rated each of the 48 items on a scale of 1 to 5 (*never* to *always*). The Kaiser Normalization procedure was used, which resulted in a range of interscale correlation coefficients from -.44 (Crusader to Conductor) to +.37 (Sculptor to Conductor). In addition, alpha coefficients were computed from the same sample and ranged from +.81 (Explorer) to +.92 (Coach and Conductor). Data for these studies were collected by responses to an internet version of the nonipsative format of the MTR-i.

Further investigation attempted to compare the eight team role types of the MTR-i with the personality types measured by the MBTI. These data were also collected via internet and are based on 585 responses to the nonipsative version of the MTR-i. In this study, the respondents self-reported their four-letter MBTI code. These MBTI codes were then matched against the raw scores from the nonipsative version of the MTR-i. A 28% agreement was found between the self-reported MBTI personality types and the measured MTR-i team role. A 78% agreement was found between the MTR-i scores and the self-reported MBTI personality types when only two of the MBTI functions were used.

Further internet studies have focused on application of the MTR-i to various occupations. Respondents completing the internet versions of the MTR-i were asked to give their occupations, which were then classified into groups of occupations. The occupation studies were conducted using a selection ratio, which was calculated according to the following formula: the number of people reporting that team role in that occupation, divided by the number of people reporting that occupation, times the percentage of the team role in that occupation. The result is a list of 35 occupations in which the ratio is defined for each role for each occupation. The ratios range from 0.0 to 4.3. The sample sizes for each occupation ranged from 10 to 138. The resulting selection ratio is intended to provide an understanding of the rate at which the different team roles are found in various occupations.

COMMENTARY. The intended use of the inventory is in work settings to help members of work teams better understand their role on a team and the dynamics of team functioning. The instrument is intended to be used either with the MBTI or alone. The author purports that the eight team roles identified by the MTR-i correspond with the personality types identified by the MBTI. There are several critical comments, however, that can be made about the development of the MTR-i. First, the author is not clear on how the eight team roles were developed with respect to the Jungian personality types and the MBTI. No information is contained in the manual, or on the website, that details this process. Second, although a substantial amount of data were collected by the author in validity and reliability studies, the data appear to have been collected unsystematically, relying on self-report responses to the internet website. Further, no demographic characteristics are provided for the respondents who participated in the various reliability and validity studies. Third, the factor analysis studies to develop validity and reliability were conducted with a version of the MTR-i that is substantially different from the paper version published for general use. These studies were based on a nonipsative version of the inventory whereas the published version is ipsative. This difference calls into question the application of the findings of these studies to the published version. Fourth, the study to relate the MTR-i roles to the personality types of the MBTI is problematic. MBTI types were not measured but self-reported. This procedure makes a weak case, at best, for comparing the findings of the two instruments. Fifth, the attempt to relate the findings of the MTR-i to occupations is conceptually confusing and of limited utility. From a practical standpoint, the selection ratio is not easy to understand or apply in any practical way. The manual and website do not offer any practical or theoretical explanation for the occupational studies. It should be noted as well that all of the occupations listed in the manual are professional; no blue-collar occupations are included. This may be the result of employing self-selected samples.

Recommendations include continued testing of the MTR-i with the MBTI to further substantiate that the team roles measured by the MTR-i are comparable to the personality types measured by the MBTI. In addition, further explanation in the manual of the correlation among Jungian personality theory, the MBTI, and the MTR-i would be helpful to the user. There should also be further studies of the concentrations of team roles in various occupations. The initial studies are interesting but the author does not develop the conceptualization of these studies to explain their theoretical or practical significance. Additional studies of an expanded list of occupations to include blue-collar occupations would also increase the uses of the instrument.

SUMMARY. The manual provided to the reviewer was very thorough. It contained not only administration and technical information, but complete lesson plans and overhead transparency materials for teaching the concepts underlying the MTR-i. The presentation of the inventory and manual is very professional. The inventory itself is well organized and easy to use and understand. Conceptually, the MTR-i team roles are easy to understand and apply in a work setting. The eight team roles identified by the MTR-i would seem to have some usefulness in a work situation to help team members better understand their own roles as well as team dynamics. It appears problematic, however, to assume that the eight team roles measured by the MTR-i can be compared directly with the Jungian personality types measured by the MBTI.

Review of the Management Team Roles Indicator by JOHN TIVENDELL, Professor of Psychology, Université de Moncton, Moncton, New Brunswick, Canada:

DESCRIPTION. The Management Team Roles Indicator (MTR-i) is a recently developed workshop-oriented paper-and-pencil instrument, developed and published by its author, Steve P. Myers. The object of the MTR-i is to identify an individual's own preferred team role and those of his or her colleagues. The test is presented as an alternative to Belbin's popular Team Roles Self-Perception Inventory (T6:299) because it is theoretically linked to and influenced by the Myers-Briggs Type Indicator (MBTI; T6:1678), rather than Raymond B. Cattell's trait theory-based Sixteen Personality Factor Questionnaire (16PF; T6:2292). However, in large part because of its association with the MBTI, the MTR-i suffers some of the same problems.

The MTR-i is presented in a single technical manual that contains little information on the purpose, background, and administration of the measure. The document is primarily aimed at providing workshop organizers with overhead-type material, although it also addresses some

pertinent psychometric questions about its technical features.

The author defines the purpose of the MTR-i in single sentence headings such as: "The MTR-i is a team roles model and questionnaire that can be used in team building—either independently or in conjunction with the MBTI ... that helps individuals and teams recognise the(ir) contributions" (user manual, pp. 5–6). However it is evident that the instrument is to be used as an organization-specific team building exercise. The MTR-i is not a sophisticated diagnostic tool for managers seeking self-improvement but rather a quick way for team members to label themselves and their team mates in terms of roles.

ADMINISTRATION. The MTR-i questionnaire consists of six blocs of eight statements corresponding to the eight distinct team roles. Because the MTR-i is an ipsative measure, the participant is asked to distribute 12 points across each set of eight statements. The participant then transfers his or her answers to the report form, in particular noting his or her rank order for each role. If done as a group exercise, the participant also ranks each other member's roles and receives feedback on his or her own roles as perceived by his or her team mates. The questionnaire is straightforward and simple to use and only requires qualification to the British Psychological Society's Level A standards (Myers, 2002).

DEVELOPMENT. The section on the history of the test's development first explains Jung's original work and how it was used by Katherine Briggs and Isabel Briggs-Myers in the early 1960s. The author then explains and criticizes in more detail the theoretically independent work of Belbin. There is some mention of the Margerison-McCann MBTI based model but it, too, is criticized for not representing teams from the orthodox MBTI perspective. Unfortunately, there are only six very short sentences in five remaining paragraphs telling us when (1990s) the author developed his "100% compatible" (user manual, p. 38) test that measures all the MBTI types. In fact it is in the next section that we learn that over 20,000 people answered one of 90 versions of the questionnaire, mostly via the internet.

TECHNICAL. Like its counterpart by Belbin, the MTR-i is a purely ipsative measure as it requires a fixed number of points to be distributed across the eight roles. The aim of using an ipsative test is usually to control for faking and acquiescence and, arguably, social desirability. Personnel selection and training exercises may be prone to faking but it would seem that team building workshops should rely on trust and openness. The ipsative forced-choice format has often in itself been identified as a source of invalidity, which can be further compounded by weak theoretical or empirical underpinnings (Broucek & Randell, 1996). Good descriptions of the eight roles are provided but there is insufficient information about the process used to develop these. There is no evidence that the author used the ample prior research on teams (Bales, 1950; Cohen, Cohen, Ledford, & Spreitzer, 1996; Medsker & Campion, 2001; Sundstrom, De Meuse, & Futrell, 1990) except for its link to the MBTI. Although some may still argue the pros of type versus trait instruments, one would expect that any new personality dependent measure would be hard pressed not to somehow involve a theoretically and psychometrically valid five factor model.

Nevertheless, the author argues well the necessity of using an ipsative test format in order to match the underlying Jungian theory. He also developed a nonipsative version in order to undertake a confirmatory factor analysis. There was a bias in the sampling procedure used to test this nonipsative version, in order to represent each self-declared personality type in each of the eight roles. He then reports that he further corrected the factor analysis to take into account what he termed a response bias (i.e., because the first analysis produced an unidentifiable g-like factor). Unfortunately, neither the Varimax rotated solution nor any possible error factor is reported. We do have the eigenvalues and Cronbach alpha coefficients for each of the eight reported factors. Finally, some other information is reported: comparing self-declared four letter (MBTI) perceptions with their scores on the nonipsative internet versions of the MTR-i; presenting the ratio of people from different occupations choosing each team role; and some reliability data for the ipsative version of the MTR-i. The author does put out a call for any new independent data that could contribute to the test's validity, as this is a first edition of the MTR-i.

COMMENTARY. The actual manual looks like it was developed for a computer technician helping to prepare a workshop rather than to be read by an expert wanting to learn about and then use a new psychometric test. The table of contents is not well organized, albeit it is arranged into three parts: Using the MTR-i; Background information; and Development, validation, and reliability. Fortunately, the questionnaire itself is very clear and straightforward because the first part of the manual overwhelmingly deals with suggested workshop agendas and overhead-like content. Actual administration and scoring are all but ignored. The second part skims over the test's background and history and concentrates again on describing each team role. The final part of the manual describes the nonipsative version study, presents some data on the ipsative version of the measure and, in lieu of norms, the link between declared occupation and reported team roles. The remaining third of the manual presents still more overheads.

SUMMARY. The Management Team Roles Indicator is primarily designed to be used in a team building type workshop, probably as an adjunct to MBTI exercises. The development of the instrument involved a great number of internet users but their data were not used to query the theoretical underpinnings of the instrument. The instrument can only be recommended for applications where psychometric issues are not important. Additional research is needed for this to be used for any organizational decision making.

REVIEWER'S REFERENCES

Bales, R. F. (1950). A Set of Categories for the Analysis of Small Group Interaction. *American Sociological Review, 16,* 257–263.
Broucek, W. G., & Randell, G. (1996). An assessment of the construct validity of the Belbin Self-Perception Inventory and Observer's Assessment from the perspective of the five-factor model. *Journal of Occupational and Organisational Psychology, 69,* 389–405.
Cohen, S. G., Ledford, G. E., Jr., & Spreitzer, G. M. (1996). A predictive model of self-managing work team effectiveness. *Human Relations, 49,* 643–676.
Medsker, G. J., & Campion, M. A. (2001). Job and team design. In G. V. Salvendy (Ed.), *Handbook of industrial engineering* (3rd ed., pp. 868–898). New York: Wiley.
Myers, S. (2002). MTR-I : A new arena for team roles. *Training Journal* article, January 2002, available from http://www.trainingjournal.co.uk.
Sundstrom, E., De Meuse, K. P., & Futrell, D. (1990). Work teams: Applications and effectiveness. *American Psychologist, 45,* 120–133.

[142]
Managerial Scale for Enterprise Improvement.

Purpose: Designed "to measure management morale."

Population: Managers.

Publication Date: No date.

Scores: Total score only.

Administration: Group.

Price Data, 2001: $2 per specimen set.

Time: (12) minutes.

Author: Herbert A. Kaufman.

Publisher: Psychometric Affiliates.

Review of the Managerial Scale for Enterprise Improvement by NAMBURY S. RAJU, Distinguished Professor, Institute of Psychology, Illinois Institute of Technology, Chicago, IL:

DESCRIPTION. The Managerial Scale for Enterprise Improvement (MSEI) consists of 34 items, with each item having a Likert-type format (*Very Good, Good, Average, Poor,* and *Very Poor*). Each item is scored on a 5-point scale, with a *Very Good* response receiving a score of 5 and a *Very Poor* response, a score of 1. The total score on this scale is simply the sum of item scores. The omitted items are given a score of 3 in arriving at the total score. This scale is designed to measure management morale and to provide a "detailed analysis of an enterprise by anonymous expression of opinions of those persons who should know most about it" (p. 1). It is recommended that the participants or respondents not be told that the MSEI is intended as a measure of morale. The MSEI scale is intended for both individual and group administrations.

DEVELOPMENT. According to the manual, the MSEI items were developed from a detailed and lengthy review of the research literature on morale and from interviews with psychologists and industrial relations and management personnel. Not much additional information was provided in the manual to offer a more detailed account of a description of the content domain, item development, item tryout, and psychometric analysis associated with the item tryout.

TECHNICAL. The manual notes that the split-half reliability of the MSEI is .89, which appears acceptable. No estimates of test-retest or parallel reliability indices were reported.

For validity evidence, the MSEI scores of managers with less than 90 days of management experience (N = 57) were compared with the MSEI scores of managers with more than 90 days of management experience (N = 156). The scores on the MSEI were correlated with the dichotomous variable representing the level of management experience. The resulting correlation of .47, based on a sample of 213 respondents, was statistically significant. No other validity evidence was reported for the MSEI scale. There also was no additional description in the manual about where the sample came from and its representativeness.

Percentile ranks (in 5-point intervals) are reported in the manual, with no specific information on what the standardization sample was or its representativeness.

SUMMARY. The manual for the MSEI scale, as a measure of management morale, offers very limited information about the psychometric properties of this scale and also on how to use this scale in practice. Unless additional technical data are provided to substantiate the psychometric quality of this scale, it is difficult to make a definite recommendation about the use of the MSEI scale for measuring management morale.

[143]
Manifestation of Symptomatology Scale.

Purpose: Designed "to identify problems of children and adolescents."
Population: Ages 11–18.
Publication Date: 1999.
Acronym: MOSS.
Scores, 20: Validity Scores (Inconsistent Responding, Random Responding, Faking Good, Faking Bad), Summary Index (Affective State, Home, Acting Out), Content Scales (Sexual Abuse, Alcohol and Drugs, Suspiciousness, Thought Process, Self-Esteem, Depression, Anxiety, Mother, Father, Home Environment, Impulsivity, School, Compliance).
Administration: Group or individual.
Price Data, 2002: $106 per kit including 25 AutoScore forms, manual (69 pages), 2-use disk and 2 PC answer sheets for on-site computer scoring and interpretation, $42.50 per 25 AutoScore forms; $49.95 per manual.
Time: (15–20) minutes.
Comments: Self-report inventory.
Author: Neil L. Mogge.
Publisher: Western Psychological Services.

Review of the Manifestation of Symptomatology Scale by RONALD A. BERK, Professor of Biostatistics and Measurement, The Johns Hopkins University, Baltimore, MD:

DESCRIPTION. The Manifestation of Symptomatology Scale (MOSS) consists of 124 true-false items (58 negative, 66 positive) that describe a range of behaviors and emotional states. It is designed to identify comprehensively the problems of children and adolescents 11 to 18 years of age. The MOSS could be used as a screening tool and as an assessment instrument. For example, as a brief instrument covering most of the concerns of outpatient therapy, it could serve in the intake process to define treatment needs and as an outcome measure of treatment gains. In the context of a full assessment, it can identify personality dynamics, environment concerns, treatment issues, and placement needs.

The MOSS is partitioned into 17 scales: four validity scales that measure Inconsistent Responding, Random Responding, Faking Good, and Faking Bad, and 13 content scales on the following traits: Sexual Abuse (4 items), Alcohol and Drugs (6 items), Suspiciousness (8 items), Thought Process (10 items), Self-Esteem (9 items), Depression (10 items), Anxiety (10 items), Mother (6 items), Father (6 items), Home Environment (8 items), Impulsivity (11 items), School (10 items), and Compliance (11 items).

A teacher or paraprofessional can administer the MOSS in individual or group format in typically 10–20 minutes. It can be employed in a variety of settings such as juvenile courts and detention centers, custody evaluation sites, regular and special education classrooms, and counseling and psychological services facilities. The scales can easily be scored manually or by computer. The scores should be interpreted by a psychologist, counselor, social worker, or remedial or special education teacher.

The MOSS yields four validity scores, 13 content scores, and three summary indices (Affective State, Home, and Acting Out), which are aggregates of three different content scale scores each. Detailed guidelines are provided for hand scoring to calculate all 20 raw scores plus individual respondent profiles that convert raw scores to standard scores (T-scores). Interpretation considers the validity of the respondent's protocol (four validity scores), individual scores relative to the appropriate normative data by gender, and the pattern of scores in the profile. In addition to lucid descriptions of the meaning of each scale score, several illustrative case study profiles with interpretations are given.

DEVELOPMENT. The items for all of the content scales and of the validity scales were generated from "clinical judgment and the referral questions typically asked by the courts" (manual, p. 33). These questions identified the information needs of therapists who work with difficult youngsters. No formal blueprint or domain specification was mentioned to produce or sample items systematically. Initially, 600 items were written. Extensive readability analyses using three different indices reduced the pool to 271.

A judgmental panel of five licensed mental health professionals then sorted those items into the 15 content areas and reviewed them for clarity, wording, and content. No information was provided on the qualifications of the panel members, the steps for sorting, or the percentage agreement among panelists on the sort of each item. This review reduced the item collection to 160. These items were then piloted-tested with 182 children. No description of the sampling procedures or the sociodemographic characteristics is reported. Item-scale correlations were computed on this sample and those with "low" coefficients were deleted. "Low" was not defined, although among the correlations that were reported for the acceptable items, one was .06 and three others were as low as .28 and .29. That deletion process decreased the number of items to the final 124.

Subsequent to the collection of the normative data, two additional validity indicators were developed: Inconsistent Responding and Faking Bad. The former was based on highly correlated pairs of items, which should not elicit incongruent responses; the latter was constructed from items rarely endorsed in the pathological direction by 45 "at risk" individuals or 713 youths in the normative sample.

TECHNICAL. The norms of the MOSS were derived from a sample of 713 children and adolescents, 11 to 18 years of age, drawn predominantly from the public school settings, but also 50 private schools, in Tennessee, Kentucky, Rhode Island, Iowa, Minnesota, Texas, and Alabama. No scientific sampling methods were described to evaluate the representativeness of the sample and sampling error. The ethnic composition was similar to U.S. Census percentages and the age distribution roughly reflected the distribution of youths who come in contact with the juvenile justice system. The gender distribution was 54.4% females, 45.6% males. Just how the distributions on these three variables emerged is not known. There was no mention of a stratified random sampling design or any other. Separate norms for each gender were generated with substantial positively skewed distributions on all scores.

Evidence of the reliability of the content scale scores and summary indices was obtained from estimates of internal consistency on the norm sample and on a separate sample of 138 adolescents referred for evaluation by the juvenile court system. Stability coefficients based on a test-retest design over a 14-day interval with 53 adolescents were also computed. For scales being used for individual decisions, the magnitude of the coefficients was less than adequate. The majority of alpha coefficients were in the .70s and low .80s with two in the mid .60s for the 13 content scales. The coefficients for the three summary indices ranged from .85 to .92. Split-half Spearman-Brown estimates for the very small adolescent sample were higher. Most were near .80 with two as high as .90 and two as low as .65. The test-retest coefficients on an even smaller sample were even higher; most were in the .80s and low .90s with two in the upper .60s. The summary index coefficients for the two small adolescent samples were in the .80s and .90s.

Validity evidence was reported in terms of the three traditional categories—content, criterion-related, and construct. Beyond the previous description of how the items were selected by the panel of five experts, there was no other independent review for content validity. Sorting items into the 13 categories to create the scales was the only process indicated to infer that the 124 items adequately and representatively characterize the emotional and behavioral problems of children and adolescents referred for treatment.

Criterion-related validity evidence was collected from teacher ratings of 39 adolescents, 20 entering after-school day treatment and 19 attending a school for behaviorally disordered individuals. Correlations between MOSS scale scores and teacher ratings in each of the domains ranged from .40 to .60 for sexual abuse, impulsivity, school problems, compliance, and acting out, and were even lower for the other areas. Criterion-group data were also gathered on five "representative" groups identified among youths most likely to complete the MOSS: Home Problems, Unruly, Alcohol and Drugs, Sexual Abuse, and School Problems. Group sizes ranged from 14 to 30. Average T-scores were computed for all scales by group. In general, it was concluded that the MOSS was differentially sensitive to those five characteristics and useful for identifying individuals who possess them.

Construct validity evidence was presented in four forms: (a) estimates of internal consistency reliability, (b) item-scale correlations, (c) interscale correlations, and (d) correlations with comparable scales from the High School Personality Questionnaire, Suicide Probability Scale, Reynolds Adolescent Depression Scale, Revised Children's Manifest Anxiety Scale, and Children's Depression Inventory. No factor analytic methods were chosen to confirm the scale and index structure of the MOSS. The bulk of the evidence focused on correlations with comparable scales. The sample sizes for the various comparisons ranged from 108 to 144 for all except the last named inventory, which was based on only 44 adolescents. In general, the magnitude of the correlations was low to moderate with the highest ones in the .60s and .70s in the directions expected. Greater than 50% of the variance of the MOSS scales was explained by selected comparable scales from current personality, depression, and anxiety scales.

COMMENTARY. The value of the MOSS as a screening or comprehensive assessment tool for pinpointing the problems of children and adolescents is diminished by the quality of the development procedures, sampling methods and sample sizes upon which the norms and reliability and validity studies were based, and the resulting psychometric characteristics. Given the available psychological research on the constructs being measured by the MOSS, it was disappointing not to find a formal blueprint for building the 13 content scales and systematic procedures for generating items that provide representative samples of the respective constructs. Once the items were sorted into the content categories, no independent judgmental review of those sorts was conducted to verify the degree of match, representativeness of the item coverage, and item quality to furnish content-related validity evidence.

The sampling procedures employed for standardization and norming appear biased. No scientific methods were described for the selection of schools in seven states to establish the representativeness of the sample in relation to some target population of 11- to 18-year-old youths and to estimate the magnitude of sampling error. The samples chosen for the reliability and validity studies appear to have been picked unsystematically or according to ambiguous criteria. Although the gender and ethnic composition was usually reported, the distributions were inconsistent from one sample to another. Finally, the sample sizes were inadequate for the test-retest and split-half reliability estimates, criterion-related validity coefficients and T-scores, and construct validity coefficients with the Children's Depression Inventory.

Many of the reliability and validity coefficients are unsatisfactory considering the use of the scores for individual screening and placement decisions; those that seem acceptable may be inflated due to small sample sizes and/or biased due to sampling methods. These problems render the generalizability of the psychometric properties as questionable. There was also no differential validity evidence by gender even though results are reported and interpreted by gender.

Extreme caution should be exhibited in interpreting scale scores on the MOSS. Its ease of administration and scoring belie the serious psychometric weaknesses noted above and the limitations imposed on score inferences.

SUMMARY. A cursory examination of the MOSS and its technical manual suggests that considerable thought and effort have gone into the design, scoring, and interpretation of the 20 scales. Unfortunately, a more detailed scrutiny reveals serious flaws in the development, norms, and psychometric evidence for the MOSS that underlie its scores and their interpretation. As a screening or total assessment measure, individual scale score and profile analysis could be misleading. Consequently, if the MOSS is used, its score interpretation should be regarded as suggestive and considered in conjunction with other relevant evidence from parent and teacher ratings, clinical observations, and clinical judgment in reaching individual decisions about a child or adolescent.

Review of the Manifestation of Symptomatology Scale by RICHARD B. STUART, Regional Faculty, The Fielding Graduate Institute and Clinical Professor Emeritus, Department of Psychiatry, University of Washington, Seattle, WA:

DESCRIPTION. The Manifestation of Symptomatology Scale (MOSS) is a pencil-and-paper self-report instrument that was developed for use in screening children and adolescents to identify "personality dynamics, environmental concerns, treatment issues and placement needs" (manual, p. 3) at intake, during intervention, and as a means of measuring treatment progress in settings ranging from juvenile courts and detention centers to special education and private practice settings. The instrument can be administered by paraprofessionals, typically within 15–20 minutes, and can be scored by hand or computer. Scoring is straightforward, involving counting

columnar responses on a multipart answer-score sheet. Responses can then be transferred to a profile form for either boys or girls, yielding a visual display that will be familiar to users of standard objective personality measures based on transposition of items as linear T scores. Unfortunately, a 3.5-inch floppy disk (dated 9/11/01) included with the sample program was defective, precluding evaluation of the computer scoring of test results for this review.

The test consists of 124 items, most of which are written at the middle-elementary school level and have face validity. Thirteen content scales are addressed by varying numbers of items as follows: Sexual Abuse, 4 items; Alcohol and Drugs, Mother, and Father, 6 items each; Suspiciousness and Home Environment, 8 items each; Self-esteem, 9 items; Thought Processes, Depression, Anxiety, and School, 10 items each; and Impulsivity and Compliance, 11 items each. Three of these scales (Depression, Anxiety, and Self Esteem—29 items) can be combined to yield an Affective State summary index; three (Mother, Father, and Home—20 items) yield a Home summary index; and three (Impulsivity, School and Compliance—32 items) an Acting Out summary index. In addition, two items ("I would never try to hurt myself" and "I often feel like hurting myself") are offered as a suicide risk indicator. The alpha coefficients for these scales are generally acceptable, although Alcohol and Drug (.64) and Home Environment (.65) are at the lower end of acceptability.

Double-marked responses count as missing, and 13 or more such responses invalidate the protocol, and 3 or more missing or double-marked items invalidate each scale. Four validity scales are included. The Inconsistent Responding scale contains eight pairs of items that should either be answered the same or differently (e.g., "I have lots of friends" and "Not many people like me"). Three or more such inconsistent responses warrant interpreting the test results "with caution," which was necessary with 7% of the validation sample. A score of four or more suggests inattentiveness or reading problems that invalidate the scale. Random Responding is evaluated by eight items (e.g., "Water is wet" and "Most balls are square"), with two or more random answers invalidating the scale. Faking Good and Faking Bad are each assessed with eight items. Those for Faking Good (e.g., "I never think bad thoughts") have much greater face validity than those for Faking Bad (e.g., "When I am at home, I do not feel safe") and one can question the validity of this validity scale. Rather than invalidating the overall protocol, these scales are regarded as manifestations of respondents' defensiveness or potential for malingering.

TECHNICAL. The instrument was standardized with a sample of 713 children drawn from seven states. The participants roughly correspond to the 1990 U.S. Census profile: 84.3% White, 13.9% African American, 8.8% Hispanic, the rest Asian and other. One-third of the sample was 11 to 14 years of age, with the largest segment (47%) being 16 or 17. Although the author stipulates that the test can be used with children from age 11 to 18, normative data for the lower end of that spectrum are tentative at best.

Test-retest reliability was evaluated with readministration of the test over a 14-day period to 53 adolescents, with Suspiciousness (.67) and Alcohol and Drugs (.68) showing the lowest correlations. Split-half reliabilities ranged from .65 for Thought Processes and Compliance to .90 for Sexual Abuse and Mother. These findings, too, are acceptable although not compelling.

The subscales of this instrument intercorrelate at what the author describes as "desirable ... weak to moderate" (manual, p. 38) levels suggesting that they bear some relationship to each other but measure different aspects of the participants' concerns. The scales comprising the summary indices (Affective State, Home, and Acting Out) appear to address a different feature of each variable. However, the Sexual Abuse and Alcohol and Drug scales responses are markedly unrelated to the other scales, a finding that is counter-intuitive.

A subset of children 14 and older in Tennessee was used to evaluate comparisons between this measure and others commonly used with the same population (i.e., the High School Personality Questionnaire, the Suicide Probability Scale, the Reynolds Adolescent Depression Scale, the Children's Depression Inventory, and the Children's Manifest Anxiety Scale). A smaller group of participants was used to contrast responses to this instrument with evaluations by teachers, finding moderate agreement, with similar results when the instrument scores were contrasted with small groups of other children with whom use of the instrument is intended (e.g., court referrals and participants in various problem-focused treatment groups).

COMMENTARY. The extent to which this scale enhances clinical judgment is uncertain. Seven case illustrations are presented in the manual, and in each instance, the test scores coincide with, but do not elaborate, clinicians' description of the respondents. This reviewer administered the MOSS to two clients whose responses did not detect problems that were not otherwise apparent, although they did correspond with clinical observation. This suggests that the present instrument might be more valuable as a screening tool than as an adjunct to individual assessment, and that it might be most appropriate for older adolescents because of the skew in the age range of the validation sample.

SUMMARY. The moderate correlations found in the concurrent validity assessment suggest that this instrument might offer an efficient overview of children's concerns, with specific difficulties evaluated by administration of one of the topic-specific measures. But the fact that correlations were not higher suggests that some children's concerns will not be identified, and the relative weakness of the Alcohol and Drug and Sexual Abuse scales raises the real possibility that children with these serious concerns will be missed. To compensate for this possibility, it might be useful to buffer the responses to the MOSS by also administering instruments such as the Trauma Symptom Checklist for Children (Briere, 1995; 269) and the Alcohol Use Inventory (Horn, Wanberg, & Foster, 1987; T6:139) for older adolescents.

REVIEWER'S REFERENCES
Briere, J. (1995). Trauma Symptom Checklist for Children (TSCC). Lutz, FL: Psychological Assessment Resources.
Horn, J. L., Wanberg, K. W., & Foster, F. M. (1987). Alcohol Use Inventory. Minnetonka, MN: NCS Assessments.

[144]
The Maroondah Assessment Profile for Problem Gambling.

Purpose: Designed as "an instrument that assists counselors in developing treatment intervention for their clients with gambling problems."
Population: People with gambling problems.
Publication Date: 1999.
Acronym: G-MAP.
Scores, 17: Beliefs About Winning (Control, Prophecy, Uninformed), Feelings (Good Feelings, Relaxation, Boredom, Numbness), Situations (Oasis, Transition, Desperation, Mischief), Attitudes to Self (Low Self-Image, "Winner," Entrenchment, Harm to Self), Social (Shyness, Friendship).

Administration: Group or individual.

Price Data, 2002: A\$240.90 per kit including 10 questionnaires, manual (2000, 234 pages), 10 answer sheets, 18 photocopiable action sheet masters, 10 profile sheets, 10 response reports, and computer scoring program disk; A\$60.50 per 10 questionnaires; A\$42.90 per 10 answer sheets; A\$22 per 10 profile sheets; A\$55 per 10 response reports.

Time: (20) minutes.

Comments: Self-report inventory.

Authors: Tim Loughnan, Mark Pierce, and Anastasia Sagris-Desmond.

Publisher: Australian Council for Educational Research Ltd. [Australia].

Review of The Maroondah Assessment Profile for Problem Gambling by GEORGE ENGELHARD, JR., Professor of Educational Measurement and Policy, Emory University, Atlanta, GA:

DESCRIPTION. The purpose of The Maroondah Assessment Profile for Problem Gambling (G-MAP) is to assist counselors in the development of treatment interventions for individuals who have been previously identified as having gambling problems. The G-MAP is not designed to diagnose or identify an individual as a problem gambler. The G-MAP is an 85-item self-report survey designed to assess 17 factors in five groups: Beliefs About Winning (Control, Prophecy, Uninformed), Feelings (Good Feelings, Relaxation, Boredom, Numbness), Situations (Oasis, Transition, Desperation, Mischief), Attitudes to Self (Low Self-Image, Winner, Entrenchment, Harm to Self), and Social (Shyness, Friendship). Although the scales are called factors, they were not developed on the basis of a formal factor analysis. Respondents use 5-point Likert scales (4: *Applies to me very strongly,* 3: *Applies to me strongly,* 2: *Applies to me moderately,* 1: *Applies to me a little,* 0: *Does not apply to me at all*) to respond to the 85 items. The G-MAP is designed for anyone who has a gambling problem. In essence the G-MAP assists counselors in identifying a map of the 17 factors associated with problem gambling—this map provides the framework for discussion and suggestions for the focus of a treatment plan.

DEVELOPMENT. The theoretical and conceptual underpinnings of the G-MAP are based on direct clinical observations and case discussions by three psychologists working exclusively over a 3-year period with problem gamblers. Although the factors are practice-based, the authors also provide a mapping between the major theories of gambling be-

havior and the 17 factors measured by the G-MAP. The instrument is very well developed with an attractive, easy-to-read form that is computer scorable. Computer software is also provided for the administration and scoring of the G-MAP.

TECHNICAL. The technical characteristics of the G-MAP are summarized in a technical supplement included as an appendix to the administrator's manual. The psychometric properties of the five groups and the 17 separate factors were examined using item response theory. All of the analyses are based on a group of 263 individuals who were identified as problem gamblers.

In support of the psychometric quality of the G-MAP, multidimensional rating scale and partial credit Rasch models were used to model a very small data set ($N = 263$). The authors found that the partial credit model provided better model-data fit, and reported item calibrations and fit statistics for this model. The equations reported in the manual reflect unidimensional Rasch models, and it is not clear how a multidimensional model was used. Because typical users of the G-MAP will be counselors, the revised manual should include more detail about the multidimensional model. Weighted and unweighted fit indices are reported (mean squares and standardized t statistics) for combined scales within each of the five groups. Interpretations of individual item fit statistics are provided, but summaries of these fit statistics are not provided. It is not clear how the potential user should interpret the "misfitting items." Summaries of the fit statistics, such as the means and standard deviations for each factor and group, would help the reader evaluate the psychometric quality of the G-MAP.

For each of the 17 factors, two indices of reliability are reported: Person separation index and Cronbach's alpha. The person separation index has a median value of .66 with a range from .09 to .77, whereas Cronbach's alpha has a median of .79 with a range from .54 to .86. For both indices of reliability, the Friendship factor has the lowest reliability coefficient. No evidence is reported regarding the stability of the G-MAP scores over time. The internal consistency of the G-MAP is somewhat on the low side for an assessment designed for individual interpretations, but this is probably due to the small number of items (five per factor) and the homogeneous nature of the sample—the sample is composed of 263 individuals who have been identified a priori to be problem gamblers.

No direct evidence regarding validity is presented in the manual. The authors should minimally include the variable maps for the items calibrated within each group. These data are available in several tables, but users would benefit from a graphical display of the item locations for each construct (group).

Profiles are used to report the scores. These profiles can be generated by hand or by computer. The authors also report Expected a posteriori (EAP) scores generated with dummy data. This is another case where most potential users of the G-MAP will require much more detail and information regarding what these EAP scores mean and how they should be used. No norms are reported for the G-MAP.

COMMENTARY. The accuracy of student self-reports of attitudes and behaviors is always an issue with survey instruments such as the G-MAP. The use of the G-MAP within a clinical context should provide additional opportunities for the counselor to confirm or disconfirm responses. The authors stress the importance of establishing rapport between counselor and client. The authors do a very nice job of stressing the necessary cautions that should be taken when interpreting the G-MAP. They also stress the limitations of this type of self-report inventory.

The psychometric evidence in support of the G-MAP is quite weak due to the small sample size. The use of multidimensional item response theory to model data from 263 examinees seems questionable. Traditional statistics reflecting item means and standard deviations should be added in the future; this type of information is needed by a typical counselor who might need to interpret the G-MAP.

SUMMARY. Overall, the G-MAP is a well-designed instrument that should be of use to trained counselors who provide services to problem gamblers. As pointed out earlier, it is not designed to diagnose someone as a problem gambler. Results from the G-MAP appear to provide a fruitful template for discussions between client and counselor regarding factors that relate to problem gambling. It should be stressed that the use and ultimate value of the G-MAP profiles will depend on the skill and creativity of a trained counselor within a therapeutic setting designed to treat problem gambling.

Review of The Maroondah Assessment Profile for Problem Gambling by MICHAEL G. KAVAN, Associate Dean for Student Affairs and Associate Professor of Family Practice, Creighton University School of Medicine, Omaha, NE:

DESCRIPTION. The Maroondah Assessment Profile for Problem Gambling (G-MAP) is an 85-item self-report instrument that is designed to assess factors that may be associated with or cause problem gambling, not to assess the presence of pathological gambling. The G-MAP purportedly allows a counselor to evaluate the problems associated with excessive gambling, discuss these with the client, and then develop a self-help plan that enables the client to address these issues as they relate to gambling.

The G-MAP is available in paper-and-pen and computer-administered formats. Clients are asked to read and then indicate the degree to which each statement applies to them at the time of administration. Untrained personnel should be readily able to administer and score this instrument. To score the paper-and-pen version, test administrators must calculate points and then transfer these to a response report and then a profile sheet. This is automatically done with the computer scoring software that accompanies the test manual. Total time for administration and scoring is estimated at between 35–40 minutes; less for those using a computer. The authors suggest that the G-MAP should be used only by "appropriately qualified or trained professionals" who have a conceptual understanding of problem gambling, experience working with problem gamblers, and training in crisis management and suicide. They also recommend that it be used only within the context of counseling clients about their problem.

Once scoring is completed, the counselor may compare responses within and between each of the 17 factors that comprise the following five groups: Beliefs about Winning, Feelings, Situations, Attitudes to Self, and Social; note the most striking individual responses and factor scores; and then develop tentative hypotheses about the client and his or her gambling problem. The authors emphasize that the significance of a given score can only be ascertained by an exploration of individual items within each factor. Therefore, the counselor is urged to meet with the client to analyze the profile further and to explore the various factors contributing to the gambling problem more fully. The detail involved in this exploration is considered to be the "key purpose" of the G-MAP. A section entitled "Implications for Treatment" is provided for each factor within the manual. It is recommended that "clients with *numerous high scores* may require immediate assessment of personal safety and level of depression" (Administrator's manual, p. 46).

DEVELOPMENT. The G-MAP is apparently based on themes and issues that emerged from case discussions among three psychologists who worked exclusively for several years with persons who were experiencing problems with gambling. The authors state that although item development was based on direct clinical observations rather than a particular theory about gambling, their theoretical beliefs regarding gambling (i.e., the etiology and maintenance of gambling is usually multifactorial) have shaped their approach to the assessment and treatment of this problem. The manual provides no other information regarding the development of items. The factors that make up the G-MAP are said to be "clinically" versus "statistically" derived; thus, the authors state that the 17 factors or five groupings should not be interpreted as being based on statistical analyses.

TECHNICAL. The psychometric properties of the G-MAP were based on a sample of 263 "problem gamblers" (113 females and 150 males) from several agency sites in Australia. The mean age of this group was 36.51 years and the primary mode of gambling for approximately 80% of the sample was electronic gaming machines. No other descriptive information for this sample is provided within the manual. As mentioned above, the authors have emphasized that the significance of a score can only be ascertained by an exploration of each item and factor with the client as opposed to comparing client results with statistically derived normative data. Therefore, no normative data are provided in the manual.

Reliability data are provided for each of the 17 G-MAP factors. Internal consistencies (Cronbach alpha) range from .54 (Social—Friendship) to .86 (Beliefs About Winning—Uninformed). An IRT reliability index, which is the proportion of the observed person measure variance that is considered true, is also provided for each factor. These range from .09 (Social—Friendship) to .77 (Beliefs About Winning—Uninformed). The rest of the manual includes information on the calibration of items

within each factor and group, confidence intervals, and sex differences. However, no information is provided in the manual that supports the utility of the G-MAP in clinical settings.

COMMENTARY. The authors promote the G-MAP as "primarily a clinical tool" (Administrator's manual, p. 1) that provides the counselor and client with a "map" of factors associated with a client's gambling problem. They continue by stating that the G-MAP should not replace a more extensive clinical evaluation of the client, including an assessment of depression, suicide risk, and personality disorders. Although the G-MAP assesses what would be perceived as intrinsically important areas related to gambling, the fact that no data are provided to support either its clinical utility in the assessment of these issues or the usefulness of the counseling suggestions provided within the manual limits severely the confidence of using the G-MAP for these purposes. Therefore, rather than thinking of the G-MAP as a clinical tool, it should more appropriately be considered a research tool that appears promising if studies can be completed to support its use in these areas. Until then, its use (as the authors suggest) should be limited, at most, to incorporating the G-MAP into a more extensive battery that is meant to more thoroughly explore clients' attitudes and beliefs about their gambling problems.

SUMMARY. The G-MAP is an easy-to-administer, self-report measure designed to investigate problem areas in the lives of persons already determined to have a gambling problem. Items have good face validity; however, no factor analytic studies have been completed on the 17 factors, norms are lacking, and no studies are cited within the manual to support the validity of the G-MAP in clinical or rehabilitation settings. Therefore, although the G-MAP has the potential to be an important addition in the assessment of problems associated with gambling, its present role in the clinical setting should be restricted to a supplemental instrument at best, and possibly, more appropriately, to that of a research tool.

[145]

Matching Assistive Technology & CHild.

Purpose: A series of instruments designed to assess "infants' and children's need for assistive technology" to determine the most appropriate child-technology match.

Population: Children with disabilities, ages 0–5; children older than age 5 depending on developmental level.

Publication Date: 1997.

Acronym: MATCH.

Administration: Individual.

Price Data: Available from publisher.

Time: (120) minutes for entire battery.

Comments: To be used by Early Intervention and Special Education professionals with parents.

Author: Marcia J. Scherer.

Publisher: Institute for Matching Person & Technology, Inc.

a) TECHNOLOGY UTILIZATION WORKSHEET FOR MATCHING ASSISTIVE TECHNOLOGY & CHILD.

Purpose: Designed to "review technologies the child is currently using, has used in the past, and needs."

Scores: No formal scores; examines perceptions in 10 areas: Communication, Mobility/Gross Motor, Vision, Hearing, Fine Motor Skills, Daily Living, Health Maintenance, Play, Self-Care, Learning/Cognition.

Comments: Completed by parent and/or educator.

b) WORKSHEET FOR MATCHING ASSISTIVE TECHNOLOGY & CHILD.

Purpose: Designed to "obtain parent perspectives of a child's particular limitations, goals, and interventions as well as strengths which can be built upon in planning interventions."

Scores: No scores; examines perceptions of 10 areas: Communication, Mobility/Gross Motor, Vision, Hearing, Fine Motor Skills, Daily Living, Health Maintenance, Play, Self-Care, Learning/Cognition.

Comments: Completed by the child's parent.

c) SURVEY OF TECHNOLOGY USE.

Purpose: Designed to "help identify technologies and technology functions/features a child is likely to feel comfortable or successful in using."

Acronym: SOTU.

Scores: No formal scores.

Comments: Completed by educator and/or parent.

d) MATCHING ASSISTIVE TECHNOLOGY & CHILD.

Purpose: Designed to help "select the most appropriate assistive technology for a child's use while pinpointing areas for training and further assessment."

Acronym: MATCH.

Scores: No formal scores.

Comments: Completed by caregiver or educator.

Review of Matching Assistive Technology & CHild by LIBBY G. COHEN, Professor of Special Education, University of Southern Maine, Gorham, ME:

DESCRIPTION. Matching Assistive Technology & CHild (MATCH) is a process that uses four worksheets or instruments that assist in matching children ages 0 through 2 years with appropriate assistive technology. The term "assistive technology" includes a broad range of supportive tools and equipment. Examples of assistive technology include adapted spoons, head mouse, modified or alternate keyboards, switches, voice recognition and text-to-speech software, and high tech systems for environmental controls. According to the Individuals with Disabilities Education Act (IDEA) (1997), the federal special education law, an assistive technology device is "any item, piece of equipment, or product system, whether acquired commercially off the shelf, modified, or customized, that is used to increase, maintain, or improve the functional capabilities of a child with a disability."

The MATCH process and instruments were developed through a collaboration of parents and professionals in the Monroe County (NY) Health Department Early Intervention Program, the Rochester Center for Independent Living/Genesee Finger Lakes Technology Related Assistance for Individuals with Disabilities (TRIAD) Project, and the Institute for Matching Person and Technology, Inc.

The test author's approach was developed to ensure that assistive technology (AT) users are integrally involved in the selection of AT. The process allows AT users, parents, caregivers, and professionals to communicate about AT needs and expectations so that inappropriate AT selections (matches) can be made. The MATCH focuses on three areas: the child and parent, the technology, and the milieu or environment. The MATCH process can be varied depending on a given situation.

The instruments are contained within the 12-page manual. Copies of each of the 2-page instruments can be made. Few directions are provided about how to engage in the MATCH process or the steps needed to complete the worksheets. The MATCH includes the following instruments: The Technology Utilization Worksheet for Matching Assistive Technology and CHild, The Worksheet for Matching Assistive Technology and CHild, The Survey of Technology Use

(SOTU), and the MATCH: Matching Assistive Technology and CHild.

The purpose of the Technology Utilization Worksheet for Matching Assistive Technology and CHild instrument is to review the technologies that the child is currently using, has used, and currently needs. The worksheet has five columns. Areas of difficulty are listed on the column on the extreme left side of the instrument. The areas of difficulty are daily living, health maintenance, play, self-care, learning/cognition, communication, mobility/gross motor, vision, hearing, and fine motor skills. Information about each area of difficulty is provided in the remaining four columns: Name of Technology, Technology(ies) Currently Used, Technology(ies) Used in the Past, and Technology(ies) Needed.

The purpose of the Worksheet for Matching Assistive Technology and CHild is to obtain the parent's overall views of the child's limitations, goals, strengths, and interventions. This worksheet consists of three columns. The first column lists areas of difficulty (e.g., daily living, health maintenance, play, self-care, learning/cognition, communication, mobility/gross motor, vision, hearing, fine motor skills). The middle column includes small spaces to list the child's goals and strategies, and the third column lists examples of technologies and environmental changes (e.g., picture communication board, ramps, adapted tooth brushes, adapted toys). The brief directions for completing this form state, "In which of the following does the child experience difficulty? Check all that apply. Then, for each, indicate goals as well as potentially desirable technologies, environmental accommodations, and other interventions for the child."

The Survey of Technology Use (SOTU) is intended to identify technologies and technology features with which the child will probably be comfortable and successful. This worksheet addresses the technologies and toys the child uses and finds familiar, reactions of the parents and/or caregivers to technology, the child's typical activities, and the child's personality and behavior. Questions on this instrument are cursory in nature. For example, for the category "Your overall reactions to technology as a parent/caregiver," three items are included. These items ask parents/caregivers to use a 5-point Likert scale to rate their comfort, interest, and degree that they encourage their child to use technology. Items included in describing the child's typical activities section include the degree of: engagement, participation in group activities, satisfaction, novelty of activities, and interactions with family, siblings, and friends. No directions are provided on this worksheet.

The MATCH: Matching Assistive Technology and CHild is to be used to identify the most appropriate assistive technology for the child and areas for further assessment and training. The front of the worksheet consists of two checklists relating to satisfaction with child's development and family characteristics. On the reverse of the worksheet, characteristics of several devices that are under consideration are rated on a 5-point Likert scale. Examples of these characteristics include whether: the device can be used with little or no assistance, the device will help the child achieve desired outcomes, training is required, and the device is easy to maintain and repair.

TECHNICAL. The manual does not contain technical information about the process or the instruments. However, the author has written several books that describe the process and articles that provide information concerning validity. In *Evaluating, Selecting, and Using Appropriate Assistive Technology* (Galvin & Scherer, 1996), the author describes the matching person with technology process or MPT. She states that the following steps should be used in the process: "1. Establish goals/expectations. 2. Assess need for no technology, low technology, or high technology device. 3. Match person and technology. 4. Select and fit assistive technology to the person. 5. Train person for assistive technology use. 6. Assess/evaluate outcomes of assistive technology use according to goals/expectations. 7. Return to Number 1" (Galvin & Scherer, 1996, pp. 8–9). Additional publications by Scherer provide some technical information about using the process with adults, but none with young children.

SUMMARY. Matching Assistive Technology & CHild (MATCH) is a process that uses four worksheets that assist in matching children ages 0 through 2 with appropriate assistive technology. The assessment of assistive technology is an emerging area. The manual provides little guidance on how to use the instruments and what to do with the information once it has been collected. Currently, there is no information available on standardization, reliability, and validity.

REVIEWER'S REFERENCES
Galvin, J. C., & Scherer, M. J. (1996). *Evaluating, selecting, and using appropriate assistive technology.* Gaithersburg, MD: Aspen Publishers.
Individuals with Disabilities Education Act Amendments of 1997. (1997). Washington, DC: U.S. Government Publications Office.

Review of Matching Assistive Technology and CHild by T. STEUART WATSON, Professor of Educational Psychology, Mississippi State University, and R. ANTHONY DOGGETT, Assistant Professor of Educational Psychology, Mississippi State University, Starkville, MS:

DESCRIPTION. The Matching Assistive Technology and CHild (MATCH) is not a test in the traditional sense because it does not result in a comparison to either a normative group or a criterion. Nor does it have reliability and validity data. Rather, it is a process that consists of a progressive series of four worksheets that are designed to match the individual needs of the child with specific assistive technology. The author designed this process to take into account three critical components for the successful use of assistive technology: (a) the targets of the technology (i.e., parents and their child), (b) the technology, and (c) the environment in which the user and technology will interface. The "packet" consists of seven stapled sheets that include a cover page, one page of introductory comments, four pages of worksheets, and a blank page at the end. In the introduction, the author provides a brief overview of the worksheets, the rationale behind the process, and appropriate words of caution regarding the process.

Each of the four worksheets has a different purpose. The Technology Utilization Worksheet for Matching Assistive Technology and CHild reviews past and current technology uses and needs in 10 domains (communication, mobility/gross motor, vision, hearing, fine motor skills, daily living, health maintenance, play, self-care, and learning/cognition). The Worksheet for Matching Assistive Technology and CHild is designed to obtain the parent's, as well as the clinician's, perspectives regarding the child's limitations and strengths and their goals and strategies for intervention in each of the 10 domains. The Survey of Technology identifies those technologies that are likely to be successful based on parent report of the child's reactions to common environmental stimuli (e.g., light, sound, textures) and to existing technologies and toys. In addition, the Survey asks questions about the parents' reactions to technol-ogy, the child's typical activities, and the child's behavior and personality. The MATCH: Matching Assistive Technology and CHild is used to select the most appropriate technologies and actual devices based on information gleaned from the first three instruments and the child's skill and development in 20 different skills/areas (e.g., self-feeding, social skills, vision, rate of learning).

DEVELOPMENT. There is no information included in the materials that describes either how the worksheets were developed or how items were chosen for the worksheets. This is a rather significant limitation because the potential user cannot readily discern why particular domains were chosen (although all are very appropriate) nor why others were not included. Perhaps most importantly, the absence of development information precludes one from drawing conclusions about the relationship between worksheet responses and effectiveness of chosen technology.

TECHNICAL. As previously mentioned, there are no "technical" data as part of the packet of materials. This is not to say that reliability and validity data do not apply to this process for surely they do. Rather, the lack of technical data is a serious omission particularly in light of the need to show reliability among respondents and to demonstrate validity for its stated purpose.

COMMENTARY. The worksheets included as part of this package are adequately designed, self-explanatory, and easy to follow. There are some minor flaws in the worksheets including not giving the clinician sufficient space to record responses/information, condensing too much information on a single page, and having unlined rows which makes it difficult to follow across columns.

One particular criticism of the MATCH process is that all the information is gathered via parent report or clinician judgment. Although this is a valuable and necessary part of a technology assessment, more direct measures should be included as part of the assessment process. For instance, presenting the child with stimuli associated with various devices and observing their responses to these stimuli would aid in making more informed, data-driven decisions. As another example, observing the interaction between the parent(s) and child with various types of devices may assist the professional in making more informed decisions about the most appropriate assistive technology for a particular family.

Although the introduction to the material indicates that all of the worksheets can be completed in approximately 2 hours, this seems unlikely, except perhaps for someone who has conducted a number of these assessments and is highly familiar with the materials. The author states that this assessment process is intended for children ages 0–2. It seems plausible, however, given the domains sampled and the lack of age specificity on individual items, that it would be applicable for older children as well. There is no explanation in the material as to why the process is only for children in this age range.

SUMMARY. It appears that the MATCH is a compendium of fairly well-designed structured interviews (i.e., worksheets) that can assist professionals in making better decisions regarding the most appropriate assistive technology for a very young child based on his or her particular strengths and needs. It is not a "test" in any way and will not yield the kind of information one expects of a test. Providing brief information on the development of the instrument and conducting reliability and validity studies on the worksheets could substantially strengthen the materials.

[146]
Measure of Existential Anxiety.

Purpose: Designed as a measure of existential anxiety.
Population: Adults and college-age.
Publication Date: No date.
Scores: Total score only.
Administration: Group.
Price Data, 2001: $3 per specimen set.
Time: Administration time not reported.
Authors: L. R. Good and K. C. Good.
Publisher: Psychometric Affiliates.

Review of the Measure of Existential Anxiety by MATTHEW E. LAMBERT, Clinical Assistant Professor of Neuropsychiatry, Texas Tech University Health Sciences Center, Lubbock, TX:

DESCRIPTION. The Measure of Existential Anxiety is a 32-item, true-false, self-report measure of existential anxiety. Items are listed on a double-sided, single sheet with response area listed to the left side of the items. Individuals completing the instrument circle their responses to each of the items. Instructions for completing the instrument are listed on the top of the item and response sheet.

Scoring is accomplished by lining up a paper scoring key with the responses and counting the number of items keyed in a particular direction. This yields a single measure of overall existential anxiety. No specific training or requirements are necessary for scoring the instrument, nor do there appear to be any specific procedures for interpretation. No cutoff score is listed, nor are there any scoring bands used to discriminate levels of existential anxiety.

A four-page document accompanies the test form and scoring key. The first two pages describe the theoretical underpinnings of the instrument's development and the results from an initial study used to test the instrument's theoretical tenants. This initial study was conducted in 1973. The third page lists the test items and the keyed direction for scoring. The last page lists five references related to the theoretical basis for developing the instrument's items and the two other instruments administered during the initial study. All references are for works published in 1965 or earlier.

DEVELOPMENT. The Measure of Existential Anxiety was developed as a way to measure existential anxiety or neurosis based on the writings of Victor Frankl. According to their theoretical rationale for the instrument's development, the authors (L. R. Good and K. C. Good) suggest that: "Compared with neurotic anxiety, then, existential anxiety in more the product of despair than distress, of alienation than guilt, of emptiness than fear" (p. 1). As such, "The Authors wrote 32 true-false items to comprise the initial form of the existential scale. Frankl's writings provided the primary stimulus for the content of these items" (p. 2). Unfortunately, there is no description of how the authors developed the items or any revisions of the items as they were being developed. Nor was there any indication of from which aspect of Frankl's writings any particular items came or what part of existential anxiety was to be measured. Moreover, there is no indication about why an item was keyed in a particular scoring direction.

A review of the items, however, raises significant questions as to whether existential anxiety or another construct such as depression might have been assessed. Items such as Item 8 "My daily activities mostly seem to be rather pointless" or Item 21 "I feel that my life is of no real importance to anyone" may reflect more simply described depressive symptoms than more ambiguous constructs of existential anxiety.

TECHNICAL. The Measure of Existential Anxiety's entire set of psychometric properties rest on the single page description of a study in which the instrument was administered to 237 undergraduate psychology students at Middle Tennessee State University during one semester in 1973. In that study, the authors hypothesized inverse relationships between scores on the Measure of Existential Anxiety and a 16-item test anxiety scale and a 20-item achievement motivation scale administered at the same time.

The authors report that an item analysis was conducted that revealed a reliability estimate (KR-20) of .89, and all 32 items evidenced moderate item-total correlations, ranging from a low of .22 to a high of .72 with the average point-biserial r being .49. Unfortunately and again, this provides little understanding of the psychometric characteristics of the scale. Certainly, a skewed set of correlations could have resulted in an average r of .49 with the vast majority of items having poor item-total correlations and a few outliers bringing up the average. More appropriately, a listing of the item-correlations for each of the instrument's items would be the starting point for allowing a test user to evaluate the score reliability. Other reliability measures such as test-retest reliability are lacking.

Validity data are presented in relation to the hypotheses posed for the authors' initial study. The Measure of Existential Anxiety was found to be negatively correlated with the achievement measure (r = -.45, p<.001), which was consistent with the hypothesis posed that existential anxiety would be inversely related to achievement motivation. Yet, the Measure of Existential Anxiety was positively correlated (r = .32, p<.001) with the measure of test anxiety, which was contrary to the authors' hypothesis that those suffering existential anxiety are relatively free of more traditional anxiety symptoms. This raises concerns about the construct validity of existential anxiety as a concept that can be measured apart from other aspects of general anxiety or depression. Again and consistent with the concerns about reliability, the lack of any further validity data makes scores from the instrument of questionable meaning as there is no anchor by which to interpret the score produced.

COMMENTARY. The Measure of Existential Anxiety is a poorly designed and inadequately normed measure of a concept related to the existential writings of Victor Frankl. Although it was formulated to measure existential anxiety, it appears to overlap with other more typical measures of anxiety and depression. In that vein, there are a multitude of other more highly developed instruments available. Moreover, one has to question whether the concept of existential anxiety as posed by the authors in 1973 even has any validity in our current world. The advancement in anxiety and depression research of the past 30 years, in many ways, has dramatically changed our perception of those concepts and includes both biological and psychological conceptualizations.

The lack of utility for this instrument is also noted from a recent MEDLINE search conducted using the Boolean term MEASURE+EXISTENTIAL+ANXIETY. The results produced only the original article published to describe the instrument (Good & Good, 1974). No other references were uncovered. Overall, it appears that the Measure of Existential Anxiety has limited value for use as either a clinical or research instrument. Considerable research is needed before it could be considered as a reasonable tool for any purpose.

SUMMARY. The Measure of Existential Anxiety suffers great problems related to evidence of reliability and validity. It has little clinical or research utility. Moreover, the theoretical foundation upon which it is built has questionable validity in our current world. It would probably be best if the Measure of Existential Anxiety would fade into the ethereal world it seeks to measure.

REVIEWER'S REFERENCE

Good, L. R., & Good, K. C. (1974). A preliminary measure of existential anxiety. *Psychological Reports, 34,* 72–74.

[147]

A Measure of Self-Esteem.

Purpose: Designed as a "measure of self-esteem ... that was constructed on the assumption that low self-esteem is indicated when someone feels inferior, inadequate, unworthy, disliked, helpless, etc."
Population: College-age and adults.
Publication Date: No date.
Scores: Total score only.
Administration: Group.
Price Data, 2001: $3 per specimen set.
Time: Administration time not reported.
Authors: L. R. Good and K. C. Good.
Publisher: Psychometric Affiliates.

Review of A Measure of Self-Esteem by JEFFREY A. ATLAS, Clinical Psychologist, St. Chris-

topher-Ottilie Services for Children and Families, Queens, NY:

DESCRIPTION. A Measure of Self-Esteem is a 27-item true/false measure with scattered true or false items identified in a score key to indicate high self-esteem. The scale is aimed at an adult population and is meant to be administered in a group setting, but there is no evident reason it might not be administered individually (e.g., as part of a precounseling, research, or psychological test protocol). Although no examiner qualifications are provided, it would appear that nonclinical staff may administer and score the test. The test authors utilize a definition of low self-esteem as indicated when an individual feels "inferior, inadequate, unworthy, disliked, helpless, etc." (manual, p. 1).

DEVELOPMENT. A Measure of Self-Esteem was developed as an adult model of a measure created by Coopersmith (1967) designed for use with children. The one-and-one-half page "Manual of Instructions" provided by the present authors, along with the scoring key and an answer sheet comprising the specimen set, gives minimal information concerning test development or use. The aggregate of items constituting the measure's construct of "self-esteem" have good face validity, encompassing traditional, and presumably universal, aspects of self-esteem such as body image (e.g., "I do not feel that I weigh more than I should," keyed for "True"), initiative ("I have a high degree of self-confidence": True), and self-worth ("I sometimes feel that I would rather be someone else": False). Initial item analysis resulted in the elimination of items correlating poorly with the total score (3 items) or contributing minimal variance (2 items). Of the remaining 27 items, several have a Western-culture-based slant (e.g., feeling clumsy at parties, having difficulty with school work). Given the small number and restricted age and social class range of the normative sample (83 females and 75 males enrolled in freshman psychology at Middle Tennessee State University), applying the scale to other age groups and to the population at large (i.e., other than freshman psychology students) should be done with caution. The significantly higher mean score for males' self-esteem over females' score may be consistent with patterns in the overall (United States) population, but wider testing across age groups and specified ethnicities would be needed to support this finding.

TECHNICAL. Although face validity and internal consistency of A Measure of Self-Esteem appear adequate, the manual furnishes no data on convergent validity scores that might provide direction regarding contexts in which the scale is to be used. Indeed, within the scale itself there are no cutoffs given for what total score would constitute significantly low or high self-esteem, and how the latter would be understood. In the absence of such guidelines one might employ the respective means and standard deviations for females and males as anchoring points for self-esteem measure, with scores two standard deviations below the means pointing towards significance. For example, in school or counseling settings low scores might suggest intervention strategies for helping individuals better actualize their abilities in work when faced with low self-appraisals in comparison to others. The scale is not designed to measure varied and more in-depth dimensions of self-esteem, such as the Tennessee Self-Concept Scale (T6:2508) domains of Psychosis versus Neurosis, which are more relevant to psychiatric settings.

COMMENTARY. A Measure of Self-Esteem is a quick, simple, inexpensive self-esteem measure that might have been presented more effectively in journal format, wherein questions related to cutoff criteria, validity, and generalizability might have been more adequately addressed. The measure does feature items of sufficient breadth to include both general self-evaluations of worthiness and more specific attributes related to work. This format has the advantage of examining a wide universe of self-appraisals, in aggregate form, without making questionable assumptions about the strength of different contributors or dimensions to self-esteem.

SUMMARY. A Measure of Self-Esteem may prove to be a useful instrument for use with restricted populations (e.g., college students) in assessing self-esteem as this contributes to school or workplace satisfaction. More extended use of the measure might be acceptable after provision of more validity data with different populations. Human-services workers looking for more in-depth instruments relevant to self-esteem measurement in clinical evaluations would be better off looking towards instruments such as the Tennessee Self-Concept Scale (T6:2508; Fitts, 1988).

REVIEWER'S REFERENCES

Coopersmith, S. (1967). *The antecedent of self-esteem.* San Francisco: W. H. Freeman.

Fitts, W. H. (1988). Tennessee Self-Concept Scale—Revised. Los Angeles: Western Psychological Services.

[148]
Measure of Self-Evaluation.

Purpose: Developed to measure an individual's need for self-evaluation.
Population: Adults.
Publication Date: No date.
Scores: Total score only.
Administration: Group.
Price Data, 2001: $3 per specimen set.
Time: Administration time not reported.
Comments: Manual is entitled An Objective Measure of the Self-Evaluation Motive.
Authors: L. R. Good and K. C. Good.
Publisher: Psychometric Affiliates.

Review of the Measure of Self-Evaluation by JODY L. KULSTAD, Assistant Professor, Professional Psychology and Family Therapy, Seton Hall University, South Orange, NJ:

DESCRIPTION. The Measure of Self-Evaluation (MSE) is a 25-item true/false paper-and-pencil instrument designed to assess need for self-evaluation based on Leon Festinger's (1954) theory of social comparison. The MSE is premised on the notion that individual's have a drive to evaluate their opinions and abilities through comparison with others. Items relate to the need for validation from others for one's work, ideas, and personal qualities (e.g., "I am usually very much concerned about how others will react to my opinions") as well as items about confidence in one's own beliefs, activities, and personal development (e.g., "I am mostly interested in taking courses in which I can learn something about myself").

TEST INFORMATION AND ADMINISTRATION. The MSE is a 25-item questionnaire that can be individually or group administered. The MSE takes approximately 5–10 minutes to complete. It does not appear that any special training or education is needed to administer the measure.

With the exception of an insert that indicates whether an item is true or false, there is no information on scoring. The test user is left to assume how to use the "key." For example, one would have to assume that an item marked as true on the key, and marked as true on the respondent's form, would receive a 1. Using this approach, the higher the respondent's score, the greater their need to evaluate their opinions through social comparison.

DEVELOPMENT AND TECHNICAL CHARACTERISTICS. The 38-item preliminary MSE was administered to 214 undergraduate students yielding a KR-20 reliability estimate of .75. Several items were deleted or modified, and a few new ones were written, resulting in a 32-item scale. The new scale was administered to 177 undergraduate students (88 female, 89 male). Several item analyses were performed and the "best" 25 items (those with a point-biserial correlation greater than .31) were retained. Mean scores were 12.35 (*sd* = 4.9), with females scoring slightly higher than males (13.72 vs. 10.98; $p < .001$). Reliability estimates for the 25-item MSE were .79 (KR-20) based on scores from the 177 students. No further reliability information was provided and it does not appear that any further studies have been completed to assess the reliability of the MSE. Also, there is no information available about the validity or standardization of the MSE.

COMMENTARY. The three-page manual, which includes less than one full page of test information, provides no further description of scale purpose or uses. Additionally, the manual includes minimal information about test development and psychometrics. Publication date is not stated; according to the publisher it has been in existence for several decades. It is unclear whether the MSE has ever been revised. It should be noted that the test developer and publisher indicates that though the MSE is still available, there have been no requests for the measure in the last several years. Attempts to locate any studies that have used the MSE, including the original study, were also unsuccessful.

Although the premise of the MSE is interesting and theoretically grounded, the measure itself has no basis for use. The MSE suffers primarily from lack of information. Beyond stating the purpose of the measure, the test developer provides no further clues as to why or how the MSE is used. Furthermore, psychometrics are incomplete and dated. Use of the MSE, in its current state, is not recommended.

SUMMARY. For the reasons stated above, the MSE is not recommended for either clinical or nonclinical use.

REVIEWER'S REFERENCE

Festinger, L. (1954). A theory of social comparison processes. *Human Relations*, 7, 117–140.

[149]

Measure of Vindication.

Purpose: Designed to measure the vindication motive.

Population: College-age and adults.

Publication Date: No date.

Scores: Total score only.

Administration: Group.

Price Data, 2001: $3 per specimen set.

Time: Administration time not reported.

Authors: L. R. Good and K. C. Good.

Publisher: Psychometric Affiliates.

Review of the Measure of Vindication by DENNIS DOVERSPIKE, Professor of Psychology, University of Akron, Akron, OH:

DESCRIPTION. The Measure of Vindication Motive is a 30-item, self-report measure of the vindication motive. It is a paper-and-pencil instrument. All items are of the type commonly found on self-report personality measures, and are responded to using a true-false scale. The test is designed to be a measure of vindication or the vindication motive. The vindication motive can be defined as reflecting one's tendency to seek out or be reinforced by others who have similar attitudes.

The target population is adults, including those in the college age group. No date is given for publication of the test. The manual for the test (*Measure of Vindication Motive: Manual*, Good & Good, no date) is also not dated. The test can be administered to individuals or to groups. Administration does not require any special training or education. Scoring results in a total or overall score; no subscale scores are provided.

It should be noted that this measure could be best described as falling into the general class of measures of specific social psychological attitudes. This measure differs from most such instruments in that it is published and does have a manual, albeit a rather brief manual.

DEVELOPMENT. The concept of *vindication* is related to the social psychology phenomena of attitude similarity-dissimilarity as an explanation for interpersonal attraction. In general, a person should be more attracted to others with similar attitudes. Basically, vindication then is the idea that there are individual differences in the extent to which a person seeks out agreement with others in interpersonal relationships. Vindication would appear to function as a moderator for the relationship between attitude similarity and attraction to another. Thus, a person who is high on vindication would be satisfied being in a relationship with a person with similar attitudes, and, conversely, would be dissatisfied being in a relationship with a person with dissimilar attitudes. However, for the person who scores low on vindication motive, there should be no correlation between attitude similarity and attraction to others. An individual who is highly motivated by vindication should also enjoy seeing their views endorsed and should seek to influence others (Good & Good, 1971, 1972).

Originally, 42 statements were written by the authors and administered to groups of students. Based on an analysis of the 42 items, the measure was reduced to 30 items. The items included appear to be appropriate for measuring the construct of interest.

TECHNICAL. The manual is very brief. The instrument does not require any interpretation by the test administrator nor any subjectivity in scoring.

No real information on norms is provided besides means and standard deviations for one local sample. Data on means and standard deviations by gender are reported, and a study by Good and Good (1972) indicated that the hypothesized effects of vindication occurred only for females. Breakdowns by ethnic group are not provided.

The internal consistency reliability estimate for the test is adequate for such a measure; the manual reports a KR-20 of .81.

No data on validity are reported by the manual, although Good and Good (1972) found that the hypothesized relationships occurred for the vindication motive for males but not for females. No other validity data are reported.

COMMENTARY. As indicated above, although this instrument is published, it would appear to be more similar in its format and style to many unpublished measures found in the social psychological literature. As such, the main question would appear to be, if one were looking for a measure of vindication motive for a social psychological experiment, would there be any advantage to using this instrument versus developing one's own measure.

The obvious advantage in using the Measure of Vindication is that it is published, it appears to be face valid, and there are some psychometric data already available. However, the psychometric data are very limited and fail to answer a basic question-is this instrument different from basic Five Factor Personality dimensions such as agreeableness and/or extroversion, or from other well-established personality measures?

Although the questions appear to measure the construct of vindication, many of the items are written in a manner that can confuse test takers. Many of the items have a *not* in the stem. When combined with a *False* response, this creates a double negative, which can be very confusing to those of limited reading skills.

SUMMARY. The Measure of Vindication is a short, self-report instrument intended to provide a way to operationalize a construct from the social psychological literature on attraction. It would appear to be primarily useful for those seeking such a specialized measure for a research study. However, even those researchers would be well-advised to ask themselves whether they could develop their own measure or rely upon measures of similar traits found in many personality questionnaires.

REVIEWER'S REFERENCES

Good, L. R., & Good, K. C. (1971). An objective measure of the vindication motive. *Psychological Reports, 29*, 983-986.
Good, L. R., & Good, K. C. (1972). Role of vindication motivation in the attitude similarity-attraction relationship. *Psychological Reports, 31*, 769-770.

[150]
Mellenbruch Mechanical Motivation Test.

Purpose: Designed to measure mechanical trainability using "items representing objects commonly seen and used."
Population: Grade 7 and over.
Publication Date: No date.
Scores: Total score only.
Administration: Group.
Price Data, 2001: $4 per specimen set.
Time: (35) minutes.
Author: P. L. Mellenbruch.
Publisher: Psychometric Affiliates.
[Note: The publisher advised in June 2002 that this test is now out of print.]

Review of the Mellenbruch Mechanical Motivation Test by STEPHEN J. FREEMAN, Professor, Counseling and Development, Department of Family Sciences, Texas Woman's University, Denton, TX:

DESCRIPTION. The Mellenbruch Mechanical Motivation Test is designed to measure mechanical trainability using "items from common experience rather than specialized experience" (manual, p. 1). The test consists of 84 numbered pictures, broken into seven groups of 12, that are matched with the corresponding lettered pictures with which they go best. Instructions contained in the test booklet alert the examinee that there are 12 numbered pictures and 14 lettered pictures. The stimulus pictures are black-and-white (pen-and-ink) drawings and are, for this reviewer, difficult to discern accurately. The pictures, besides being somewhat dated, appear to be gender biased. The test has a 35-minute time limit and there are two forms of the test, Form A and Form B.

The manual contains no information on user qualification. Directions for administration are absent in the test manual; however, it does state that "The directions for administration are very simple, in fact, except for the control of the time, the test is almost self-administering. The simple directions and also sample exercises are included on page one of each test booklet" (p. 2). Directions for scoring are also missing from the test manual. The manual does state that "Scoring is completely objective and is accomplished in the minimum of time and with little effort" (p. 2). A scoring key is provided and is the same for both forms of the test. It appears that scores are the sum total of item matches that are correct; however, the manual does not elucidate on scoring protocol. Information is provided on "Suggested Industrial Employment and Placement Use" and is linked to reported scores. Information provided on the use of scores is reportedly based on test results checked against foreman's ratings and actual type of mechanical tasks performed.

DEVELOPMENT. The manual states that the author selected 425 pairs of items representing objects commonly seen and used. The exact methodology used to guide the author in selecting these items is not reported. The items were then arranged in various combinations to form tests of 100 pairs and the tests were administered to 1,000 men and women in shops and training schools. Following this administration, ratings were obtained on examinees from either their teacher or foreman. According to the manual, these ratings were taken into consideration in an evaluation of the separate items and of the test as a whole, resulting in the test's current version.

The description of the test's development provided in the manual is woefully inadequate.

There is no information on the specifications used in selecting the picture items or on the item domain from which they were selected. When raters' judgments (teachers and foreman) are used as criteria, the training and experience of the raters should be described. There is no such information provided in the manual. The author cites no references to current research on evaluating mechanical trainability. Overall, there appears to be a total lack of sound scientific basis for the development of this test, as reported in the manual.

TECHNICAL. Information describing the norms and the norming process is vague to absent. The manual contains tables reporting mean scores for different groups (Academic—Boys and Girls, Women and Men) with the number of reported cases totaling 3,450. Although this would be an acceptable number of participants, there is no information on when and how participants were selected, descriptive statistics, sampling design, or participation rates. Without additional descriptive information on those individuals who happened to take this test, the data reported are of little to no value.

Evidence of internal consistency reliability is provided using the split-halves method and values ranged from .82 to .88. Alternate forms reliability was reported as being .87. No other reliability estimates are provided.

Evidence to support the validity of the instrument is somewhat limited. Criterion-related validity is reported as a correlation ($r = .59$) between the test and teacher rank for a small sample. However, without sufficient information about the rater's education and training, this correlation is meaningless. A correlation ($r = .60$) was also reported for the test and examinee's self-report of experience with mechanical activities (e.g., using a saw and hammer, drilling holes, making clothes, and changing a tire). No theoretical connection is provided between this self-reported experience and mechanical trainability; therefore, nothing can logically be inferred by the correlation. Construct validity of scores from the test was assessed by correlating it with other measures of mechanical aptitude. Moderate to low correlations ($r = .61$, $r = .49$) were reported between the test and two other aptitude tests (Stenquist Mechanical Aptitude Tests and Air Force Mechanical Information Test). No evidence of predictive validity is reported. If the Mellenbruch Mechanical Motivation Test is to be used to select individuals for

employment as stated in the manual (Suggested Industrial Employment and Placement Use), then evidence of predictive validity must be provided. Additionally, correlations were reported between the test and measures of intelligence with low ($r = .29$ to .33) to a very low ($r = .17$) correlation being reported. The manual reports that these correlations are sufficiently low to justify the interpretation that the test is not an intelligence test; however, there is limited evidence to support the author's contention that the test is a measure of mechanical trainability.

The validation process described in the manual is weak at best and does not meet accepted psychometric standards for substantiating validity evidence established in the *Standards for Educational and Psychological Testing* (AERA, APA, & NCME, 1999).

COMMENTARY. The value of the Mellenbruch Mechanical Motivation Test as a measure of mechanical trainability is compromised on a number of levels. First, standardized procedures for the administration, scoring, and interpretation of the instrument are missing from the manual or are inadequate. Second, there are concerns regarding the soundness of scientific principles applied to the development of the instrument. Third, although (minimal) reliability estimates are provided, the validation process does not meet acceptable standards.

SUMMARY. An insufficient foundation has been prepared to bear the weight of a psychometrically sound instrument. Insufficient information is provided on test development. Reliability estimates of the instrument are adequate; however, the only acceptable assessment of validity provided is construct validity, and these correlations are moderate to low. There is an explicit need for evidence supporting criterion-related validity as well as predictive validity.

REVIEWER'S REFERENCE

American Educational Research Association, American Psychological Association, & National Council on Measurement in Education. (1999). *Standards for educational and psychological testing.* Washington, DC: American Educational Research Association.

[151]

Michigan English Language Institute College English Test—Grammar, Cloze, Vocabulary, Reading.

Purpose: "To provide educational institutions and researchers with information about the English language competencies of their own students, employees, or research participants."

Population: Adult nonnative speakers of English.

Publication Date: 2001.

Acronym: MELICET-GCVR.

Scores: Total score only.

Administration: Group.

Forms, 2: AA, BB.

Price Data, 2001: $75 per complete testing package (specify Form AA or BB) including 20 test booklets, 100 answer sheets, stencil, and user's manual (32 pages); $30 per 20 test booklets (specify Form AA or BB); $10 per 100 answer sheets; $10 per plastic scoring stencil (specify Form AA or BB); $25 per user's manual.

Time: 75(90) minutes.

Comments: Consists of retired forms of grammar, cloze, vocabulary, and reading components of the Michigan English Language Assessment Battery, Part 3 (MELAB, see T6:1584); administered and scored by educational institutions or researchers who have purchased the test for use within their institution; test is nonsecure; all items are of multiple-choice format; scoring by punched stencil, purchasers may use their own scannable answer sheets.

Author: The English Language Institute Testing and Certification Division.

Publisher: English Language Institute, The University of Michigan.

Review of the Michigan English Language Institute College English Test—Grammar, Cloze, Vocabulary, Reading by THOMAS P. HOGAN, Professor of Psychology, University of Scranton, Scranton, PA:

DESCRIPTION. The Michigan English Language Institute College English Test—Grammar, Cloze, Vocabulary, Reading, going by the rather awkward acronym MELICET-GCVR, consists of retired forms of Part 3 of the Michigan English Language Assessment Battery (MELAB; English Language Institute, 1994). For this review, we will use the more compact acronym M-G for MELICET-GCVR. Understanding M-G requires a brief description of its parent instrument, MELAB. MELAB contains three standard tests: Composition (a 30-minute written essay scored by trained raters); Listening (answering questions after listening to a tape-recorded presentation); and the Grammar/Cloze/Vocabulary/Reading (GCVR) test. MELAB also has an optional Speaking test administered in a one-on-one interview setting. MELAB is a highly secure test under control of the English Language Institute at the University of Michigan. It is the principal

alternative to the more widely used Test of English as a Foreign Language (TOEFL; 14:94). Like the TOEFL, MELAB is intended for high-stakes testing for admission to educational institutions or for job applications. For further information on MELAB, see http://www.lsa.umich.edu/eli/melabgeninfo.htm. For reviews, see D'Costa (2001) and Garfinkel (2001).

As noted, M-G consists of retired forms of Part 3 only of MELAB. Thus, there are two key differences between M-G and MELAB. First, M-G is not a secure test. It may be purchased, administered, and scored by any educational institution or similar organization. Second, M-G contains only the 100-item GCVR test. There is no Composition, Listening, or Speaking test in M-G. The M-G was first released as a spinoff from MELAB in 2001.

M-G's stated purpose is to assess the ability of nonnative users of English to pursue academic study in an English-language college or university. By extension, it may be used for similar assessment of candidates for professional development programs or employment requiring, in the language of the manual, high-intermediate to advanced levels of academic English-language proficiency. M-G test materials consist of a 12-page reusable test booklet containing the test items, a 1-page hand-scorable answer sheet, an overlay hand-scoring key, and the 32-page user's manual, which contains directions for administering, descriptions of the test and its purpose, and technical information. Item counts by part are: Grammar—30, Cloze—20, Vocabulary—30, and Reading—20. Grammar items require the examinee to insert a word or phrase into a given sentence in grammatically correct fashion. Cloze items require insertion of approximately every seventh word in a continuous narrative passage. Vocabulary items require the examinee to select a synonym for a word underlined in a sentence or to furnish a word left out of a sentence (very much like the cloze procedure). The Reading part consists of several short passages each followed by comprehension items. All items are four-option multiple-choice. There are two forms: AA and BB. The test booklet format is clean and simple. Items appear to be carefully edited for clarity.

Total testing time is 75 minutes; parts are not separately timed. The test yields a single, total score; there are no subscores. Although all items are multiple-choice, there appears to be no provision for machine-scoring the test. It does seem likely that local users, if testing sizeable numbers of examinees, might adapt the test to machine scoring. If that is done, one must at least raise the question about direct comparability of scores arising from the alternate answer media. This reviewer is willing to grant such comparability, especially for the types of examinees involved and the low-stakes nature of testing anticipated for use of the M-G.

TECHNICAL INFORMATION. Regarding scores and norms, the total raw score on the test is first converted to a scaled score, also sometimes referred to in the user's manual as an equated score. The origin and nature of the scaled score are not described, except to note that the scale ranges from 15–100. Scaled scores are converted to percentile ranks. One would expect the two forms to be equated at the point of raw score to scaled score conversion but that is apparently not the case, as the two forms have somewhat different scaled score to percentile rank conversions. Percentile ranks are given in 5-point intervals (5, 10, 15, ...). A more refined table is obviously warranted. For example, on Form AA the norm table calls for converting a scaled score of 57 to a percentile of 15 and a scaled score of 63 to a percentile of 20. Why not fill in the intermediate points? Further, for missing entries (e.g., 59) the reader is not told to read to the next highest number, to the closest number, or to interpolate. The percentile rank norms (Table 4.1 in user's manual) are based on approximately 7,000 cases per form. The manual does not say so but one presumes these are the same cases as those described more fully in Table 5.1, that is, examinees tested with the full MELAB from 1986–1998 (although Tables 4.1 and 5.1 apparently reverse the number of cases per form). These groups are described by gender, age, and first language group later in the manual. Thus, the M-G did not undergo independent norming. Reliance on the norms given for M-G in the manual depends on the assumption of reasonable equivalence in the testing conditions for the full MELAB, with its high-security, high-stakes ambience, and conditions under which M-G might be taken. The M-G user's manual does not present any evidence regarding this assumption; nor does it even raise the issue. This reviewer is willing to grant some indulgence on the point. It seems likely that the MELAB-based norms provide a serviceable basis for interpreting M-G scores.

However, one does need to be aware of the assumption being made about the equivalence of testing conditions.

Apart from percentile norms, the M-G user's manual discusses what it calls criterion-based interpretation. These discussions reference scores to minimum requirements (or guidelines) at one university, one community college, and one state nursing board. The discussions are of some help to the potential user. However, all three sources use the full MELAB. Sorting out requirements for the full MELAB versus just the GCVR test (i.e., M-G) is no simple matter. Further, one would hope to see information for a wider range of institutions.

Probably the most useful information for purposes of interpreting M-G scores is Figure 4.1 in the user's manual showing how M-G scores differentiate among seven groups classified by level of speaking and writing ability, as determined with the full MELAB (including the Speaking test). Oddly, the M-G manual makes little use of this figure, which not only provides a useful interpretive framework but also addresses the validity of the test. One can easily imagine how the full MELAB database could be used to further elaborate this interpretive methodology.

Regarding reliability, the user's manual discusses test-retest, equivalent forms, and internal consistency reliability. A test-retest (1–2-week interval) reliability coefficient of .92 is reported for the total score based on a rather thin $n = 63$. Although a section is labeled "Equivalent Forms Reliability," the manual does not report such reliability. Rather, confusingly, it describes a forms equating study. Even more remarkable is the fact that the MELAB manual *does* report alternate form reliability for the GCVR part of the MELAB. Under internal consistency, the M-G manual reports KR-21 coefficients of .95 and .94 and Cronbach alpha coefficients of .95 and .93 for the two forms, respectively. All of these data seem predictable for a 100-item test of a generally homogenous trait (mostly reading ability) in a heterogeneous population (students from all over the world). It seems safe to declare the M-G provides highly reliable scores. Having said that, one must add two notes. First, it is difficult to understand why anyone in modern psychometric practice would use KR-21, a convenient estimate in the precomputer era but a clearly obsolete method. Second, although subscores

(Grammar, Cloze, Vocabulary, Reading) are not used for any interpretive purpose, the manual reports alpha coefficients for these subscores. That is harmless enough. However, the manual goes on to apply the Spearman-Brown formula to give the reliabilities of each part if it were brought to 100 items. That is a virtually meaningless exercise and potentially mischievous for the unwary user.

Regarding validity, the M-G manual discusses content validity and, as evidence of construct validity, the results of factor analyses. The exceedingly brief section (one paragraph, p. 29) on content validity simply notes that "a systematic procedure was followed in specifying what needed to be tested and in constructing and selecting test items," and that "tests were constructed by test development teams" from the English Language Institute. The treatment is clearly inadequate. To conduct factor analyses, subscores were generated for the Grammar, Cloze, two item types within Vocabulary, and Reading sections. Results are presented separately for 148 cases on Form AA and 196 cases on Form BB. The manual does not say what method was used for the analyses, whether axes were rotated, or how the cases were selected. Thus, one is left rather helpless in trying to evaluate these results. The manual does conclude that the M-G sections all measure a single, common trait. Despite the difficulty in making sense of what the manual reports, the conclusion is, no doubt, correct: The M-G is a unifactor reading test.

Although not discussed under validity in the M-G user's manual, there is further evidence relevant to the M-G's validity both in the M-G manual and in the MELAB manual. First, although the M-G manual seems to studiously avoid discussing the full construct of English language competency among nonnative users, the MELAB manual has extensive discussion of this topic. The discussion helps explicate the content validity of the M-G test. More importantly, the MELAB manual presents correlations among all the parts of the MELAB, as well as factor analyses of the parts. The results provide substantial help in understanding the role that the GCVR section (i.e., M-G) plays in covering the full construct. In addition, the data on group differentiation mentioned earlier, which are not included in the validity section of the M-G manual, actually reflect

very favorably on the test's validity. Thus, this reviewer concludes that there is better evidence for the validity of the M-G than what is presented in the validity section of the M-G manual. The practical question for the user is whether M-G is any more valid for its purposes than is any general purpose reading test. The M-G manual does not address this question—but it should. In this reviewer's opinion, if one simply wants a measure of ability to read in English, any general purpose reading test will do as well as the M-G and will do so in substantially less time. The value of the M-G as a reading test, especially for nonnative users of English, is the potential for tapping into the rich MELAB database, a potential inadequately exploited by the M-G manual.

The M-G manual contains a number of other serious technical flaws. Some of these are just annoying, for example, reporting indices of skewness and kurtosis as measures of central tendency and defining the first quartile as the score "at 25% above the minimum" (p. 20). Others may be misleading for the user as noted previously. Surely, the test's developer can access the technical expertise to produce a substantially improved manual.

SUMMARY. As an offspring of the well-established MELAB, the M-G inherits a rich array of technical and interpretive information. Unfortunately, the M-G manual does a poor job of drawing on this information. The manual omits crucial information that is, in fact, available in the MELAB materials. The manual also fails to present information in an effective manner for the prospective user. The M-G test is potentially a more useful instrument than one would infer from the manual. The publisher should immediately undertake a wholesale revision of the M-G manual. The M-G can be a valuable measure of reading-in-English for users who would find the MELAB database an aid to interpretation. However, the local user must be willing to assume reasonable equivalence in testing conditions between the local situation and the high-stakes, high-security MELAB testing situation.

REVIEWER'S REFERENCES

D'Costa, A. (2001). [Review of the Michigan English Language Assessment Battery]. In B. S. Plake & J. C. Impara (Eds.), *The fourteenth mental measurements yearbook* (pp. 754–756). Lincoln, NE: Buros Institute of Mental Measurements.

English Language Institute (1994). *MELAB technical manual.* Ann Arbor, MI: Author.

Garfinkel, A. (2001). [Review of the Michigan English Language Assessment Battery]. In B. S. Plake & J. C. Impara (Eds.), *The fourteenth mental measurements yearbook* (pp. 756–757). Lincoln, NE: Buros Institute of Mental Measurements.

[152]

Miller Common Sense Scale.

Purpose: Designed to "permit the individual to compare his/her level of common sense with other individuals ... and to determine changes that should be made as a result of this information."

Population: Ages 15 to adult.

Publication Date: 1997.

Scores: Total score only.

Administration: Group.

Price Data, 2001: $35 per administration via webpage (Visa or MasterCard are required to use this test).

Time: (15) minutes.

Comments: Administered and scored on the internet; printout of results is provided. [Editor's Note: Since November 2002, the webpage for administration of this test has been unavailable.]

Author: Harold J. Miller.

Publisher: Meta Development LLC [Canada].

Review of the Miller Common Sense Scale by CARL ISENHART, Coordinator, Addictive Disorders Section, Mental Health Patient Service Line, VA Medical Center, Minneapolis, MN:

DESCRIPTION. The Miller Common Sense Scale is a 26-item, web-page-based assessment instrument that allows individuals to compare their level of "common sense" with others. The results include suggestions for changes that should be considered given an individual's responses to the test items. It is designed for ages 15 to adult and takes about 15 minutes to complete. The respondent logs on to the website and clicks the response that best describes the extent the statements are like him or her using one of these response options: "a lot," "moderately," "somewhat," and "not at all."

The print-out gives the individual score (out of a maximum of 78), lists the items to which the respondent indicated "somewhat" or "not at all," and provides some advice on how to address or rectify those issues (e.g., the importance of balance and the wisdom of using scheduling to better achieve balance). There is also a table with five score ranges and accompanying levels of common sense: from no common sense to having high levels of common sense.

DEVELOPMENT. There is no information about the development of the Miller Common Sense Scale or even how "common sense" is defined. In the "validity" section of the "frequently asked questions" (FAQ) area of the website there is a reference to developing the scale from other individuals' philosophy and research of common sense. However, there is no discussion about what the philosophy is or the research results used to develop the instrument. Also, no references are provided that describe any theoretical background. There is no discussion regarding the rationale for the inclusion of the instrument's items and how the scale was eventually developed and refined (if at all).

TECHNICAL. Very limited technical information was found in the "FAQ" section of the website; there are three sections: description, reliability information, and validity information. There appear to be no other areas to obtain "background" or psychometric information about the instrument that are readily available to anybody interested in using the instrument.

Standardization. There is no information regarding the standardization of this instrument. One stated goal of the test is to compare one's common sense with that of others. However, there is no information as to who those others are; there is no information about sample size, age, gender, education, income or occupational levels, or geographic information.

Reliability. Two types of reliability measures were reported: test-retest and split-half. The author reported a test-retest reliability of .88; however, there was no report of the interval between the administrations and there was no information about the characteristics of the sample or any description of, or references to, any studies. The split-half reliability was reported to be .90; however, again, there was no information about, or references to, any studies from which this result was obtained.

Validity. No information is provided supporting the validity of scores from this instrument. The validity section of the website was peculiar and consisted of an estimated maximum validity coefficient based on the test-retest reliability coefficient (which has nothing to do with the instrument's actual validity), some vague reference to some "research" whereby group differences have been found that support the theory on which the instrument is supposedly based, and there is a frankly odd inclusion and discussion of Taylor-Russell tables. None of this material is pertinent in addressing the major question: Does the Miller measure some concept referred to as common sense? Of particular concern is that in the description of the Miller Common Sense Scale there is a statement about employers using this instrument to assess common sense (presumably in employees or candidates for positions), but there are no data or any information to support that statement. If an employer uses this instrument to assess common sense and make employment decisions, and there is no support for making these kinds of decisions, then the employer is setting himself or herself up to make poor decisions and to be at risk for lawsuits.

COMMENTARY/SUMMARY. The Miller Common Sense Scale is a web-based self-report instrument that is used to assess "common sense." However, there is no information about the scale's development, standardization, and validity; there is some information about reliability, but not enough to make an independent evaluation of reliability. Because these are essential characteristics to evaluate when contemplating the use of an instrument, background and technical information needs to be provided before this instrument can be considered for use.

[153]

Miller Depression Scale.

Purpose: Designed to "measure an individual's depression level."
Population: Ages 15 years and over.
Publication Date: 1997.
Scores: Total score only.
Administration: Individual or group.
Manual: No manual.
Price Data, 2001: $35 per administration via webpage (Visa or MasterCard are required to use this test).
Time: (15) minutes.
Comments: "Designed to be given and scored over the internet"; printout of results provided; can be used to monitor treatment effectiveness. [Editor's Note: Since November 2002, the webpage for administration of this test has been unavailable.]
Author: Harold J. Miller.
Publisher: Meta Development LLC [Canada].

Review of the Miller Depression Scale by CEDERICK O. LINDSKOG, *Professor, Department of Psychology and Counseling, Pittsburg State University, Pittsburg, KS:*

DESCRIPTION. The Miller Depression Scale is a scale available from a website. The test intends to "measure the individual's depression level in persons 15 years and older. It permits one to compare one's level of depression to other

people" (descriptive information sheet from publisher). The 20 items are self-describing (*a lot, moderately, somewhat, not at all like me*). The information provided from the web page indicated scores are provided as percentile ranks falling into one of five levels ranging from minimal to severe depression. The author's statements indicate the scale's intended use is for judging treatment effects and screening for depression.

DEVELOPMENT. This 1997 version is only available by going to the Metadevelopment web site. It is administered and scored for a $35 fee. The author states that the items were developed by using items that are descriptive of individuals experiencing depression and "symptoms described by others working with depressed patients." There was no indication of item alignment with any specific definition or referenced theoretical construct.

TECHNICAL. There was no information provided concerning norming of this instrument, so the scores cannot be evaluated in terms of any "anchor" that might allow interpretation. The only reliability value provided was a test-retest (unknown interval), which suffers the same flaw as the norming because there are no population-specific data. The stand-alone test-retest reliability was reported as .87, again this is of little use without further data upon which to ground an interpretation. The author did cite split-half reliabilities, but only given as if the test were hypothetically doubled in length.

The validity of scores from the test was addressed through discussion of the maximum validity score possible based on the test-retest reliability coefficient. However, because this is true of statistical derivation of validity in general, it is not particularly meaningful to the validity of the Miller Depression Scale. The author cites primary evidence of validity as construct validity. However, the author then explains that the items were obtained by "using items that are consistent with symptoms found in individuals with depression, and from symptoms described by others working with depressed patients." This is merely face validity, because there is no reference to any theoretical structure relevant to the items. The survey items themselves do seem to survey symptomatology associated with depression, but not within any theoretical construct.

COMMENTARY. The Miller Depression Scale has a number of flaws that seriously compromise its use as a measure of depression. Foremost would be the lack of published data regarding the norms, reliability, and validity.

The information provided this reviewer did not address any discussion of a norm group, so the scores, which are presented as percentiles, cannot be anchored to any specific population and are rendered meaningless. Furthermore, there was no justification or rationale for the score levels of depression (minimal to severe).

The reliability cited was test-retest, again with no specific information about the population from which the data were derived. The author cited a split-half reliability study, but did not furnish the coefficient. The author cites the maximum validity that could be derived based on reliability scores. This is a statistical fact, but largely unrelated to the instrument's actual validity, and it is potentially misleading to unsophisticated consumers.

Although the 20 items themselves do appear to be descriptive of behaviors and characteristics often used with reference to persons experiencing depression, there was no rationale given to a construct of depression that might justify the items. No validity statistics were cited, again barring meaningful interpretation. Furthermore, there was no justification for the levels of depression into which the scores might fall.

SUMMARY. The Miller Depression Scale is a web-based scale intended to assess depression in individuals 15 years of age and older. The instrument cannot be recommended for practice or research, as it fails to produce basic data needed for interpretation of results. This is true for the test construct, norms, reliability, and validity. It is laudable to enter the internet with a goal of providing a service to those who might not otherwise have access to this kind of diagnostic, but the author has not provided the necessary information to interpret the results.

Those seeking a depression assessment would benefit from contacting a mental health professional who uses the Beck (T6:273) or Reynolds (T6:2121) Depression Scales, both reviewed in the *Fourteenth Mental Measurements Yearbook.*

[154]

Miller Emotional Maturity Scale.

Purpose: Designed to "measure the individual's emotional maturity."
Population: Adults with reading levels at 7th grade or above.

Publication Date: 1991.
Scores, 8: Secure, Stable, Independent, Optimistic, Responsible, Assertive, Social, Honest.
Administration: Individual or group.
Manual: No manual.
Price Data, 2001: $35 per administration via webpage (Visa or MasterCard are required to use this test).
Time: (30–45) minutes.
Comments: Designed "to be administered and scored on the internet"; printout of results is provided. [Editor's Note: Since November 2002, the webpage for administration of this test has been unavailable.]
Author: Harold J. Miller.
Publisher: Meta Development LLC [Canada].

Review of the Miller Emotional Maturity Scale by ROBERT J. DRUMMOND, Professor of Counselor Education, University of North Florida, Jacksonville, FL:

DESCRIPTION. The Miller Emotional Maturity Scale (MEMS) is a computer-assisted personality inventory designed to measure an individual's emotional maturity. The MEMS provides information on eight dimensions of emotional maturity that are labeled Secure, Stable, Independent, Optimistic, Responsible, Assertive, Social, and Honest. A Likert-type scale ranges from (1) *Very much like me—I always do or feel this way,* (2) *Most like—often like me,* (3) *Somewhat like me,* (4) *A little like me,* (5) *Not very much like me—I rarely do this,* to (6) *This does not apply to me—I never do this.* MEMS contains 160 questions. Individuals taking this test should be able to read at the seventh grade level but the test was primarily developed for use with adults. Each subscale has 20 items.

DEVELOPMENT. The MEMS was designed to be administered and scored on the internet. Because it is computer assisted, it can be administered individually or in groups. The Miller Emotional Maturity Scales is one of the nine scales Dr. Miller has developed in the field of personality development. All these tests were developed to be administered and scored on the internet. No information on the item development or construct validity were included on the web pages on the internet.

TECHNICAL. The test takes 30–45 minutes. The results are available to the test taker on completion of the scale and consists of a six-page report. Miller provides two types of reliability estimates for the MEMS: test-retest and split-half. The test-retest (interval was not indicated) coefficients range from a high of .85 on Secure to a low of .75 on Responsible. Split-half coefficients corrected by the Spearman-Brown Prophecy formula ranged from .67 to .95. The author discusses validity issues but not in the detail that most users would like to have available. He states that the scales were developed from the theory and research proposed by common self-concept theory. Factor analytic studies were not presented to validate the scale structure. The author does report that a concurrent validity study was conducted comparing the MEMS with the 16PF. The author states that there is a need for a large number of additional studies in order to determine the range of usefulness of the MEMS for employee and student selection purposes.

COMMENTARY. The administration and scoring personality inventories on the computer has been of much interest to individuals in the field of testing. The MEMS appears to have a degree of face validity. Using the test for personnel selection raises the issue of consequential validity. Individuals need to be concerned about the privacy issue and whether the test can be interpreted by the test taker and understood without the psychologist being available to answer questions and help in the understanding of the results.

SUMMARY. There are advantages to have tests that are administered and scored on the internet. The Miller Emotional Maturity Scale has potential for use in research and counseling; however, there are a number of concerns that need to be addressed to make it more useful. These are conducting more construct validity studies, especially factor analysis, reporting any gender or age and other diversity results, and re-investigating reading level of the instrument.

Review of the Miller Emotional Maturity Scale by JEFFREY A. JENKINS, Assistant Professor, Roger Williams University, Bristol, RI:

The Miller Emotional Maturity Scale (MEMS) is one of a series of 11 personality scales developed by the publisher that also includes measures of motivation, love, self-concept, psychological independence, stress, marriage satisfaction, depression, common sense, getting along with people, and happiness. The MEMS is a web-based instrument for which the only method of administration and scoring is through the publisher's internet

web site (www.metadevelopment.com). The MEMS provides measures of eight subscales: Social, Secure, Stable, Responsible, Independent, Assertive, Honest, and Optimistic.

No rationale is given for these eight subscales as dimensions of personality, although a broad definition of each of the concepts is given. Each subscale purports to provide a measure of "the degree to which a person": "is confident about themselves" (Secure); "is firm and steadfast in their behavior patterns" (Stable); "is self-governing" (Independent); has a "positive attitude" (Optimistic); has "responsible thoughts and behaviors" (Responsible); "secures their rights without interfering with the legitimate rights of others" (Assertive); is "involved in relating with groups of other people" (Social); "is honest" (Honest). The publisher states that these are based upon "common self-concept theory," but offers no explanation as to why these concepts are included or how they relate to emotional maturity.

After going to the publisher's website and paying the test fee, the user responds by rating each item on a 6-point Likert scale with descriptors ranging from *Very much like me—I always do this* to *This does not apply to me—I never do this*. The website's home page indicates that "administration can be either individual or group," but does not state how group administration is accomplished. Twenty items comprise each subscale, for a total of 160 items in the instrument. The publisher does not report which specific items fall within each subscale, nor is any support given for why particular items are grouped within a given subscale. Although it may be possible to discern the subscale into which certain items would fall (e.g., "I like to spend time with other people" probably falls within the Social subscale), the user should not be left guessing as to how each construct is measured.

Upon completion of the MEMS, total scores and percentile scores are provided immediately. How the scores are computed is unknown; no guidance is given by the publisher about the metric of the total scores (i.e., raw scores, percentages, or some other metric). Further, no information is given about the normative group, making interpretation of the percentile scores impossible. The inability to interpret the scores provided is a serious failure. The publisher makes an attempt to provide interpretive commentary to the test user, but this material consists only of reiterating the items within each subscale corresponding to various score ranges. For example, the commentary for a high Social subscale score includes statements such as "You are quite a friendly person. You hope other people feel at home when they are around you." Two of the MEMS items, presumably part of the Social subscale are Item 28, "I am friendly," and Item 48, "I try to make other people feel at home when they are around me." Thus, the commentary only offers a summary of the actual items rather than a specific interpretation of the scores provided.

The publisher provides little information about the technical characteristics of the MEMS, making a psychiatric evaluation of the instrument difficult. Although website pages are devoted to short sections of material on score reliability and validity, much of the information given is general in nature and not specific to the MEMS. The publisher reports test-retest (the interval is not reported) reliability coefficients for the subscales ranging from .75 to .85. Although these may be acceptable for this type of measure, the sample and manner with which the coefficients were obtained is not reported, other than noting that "a restricted range of individuals were used for the sample." Also reported is a coefficient alpha of .97, presumably for the total scale. A total score for "emotional maturity" is not given or discussed, rendering the reported coefficient alpha meaningless.

The information given on validity has similar shortcomings. First, the publisher reports the square root of the reliability coefficient for each subscale as the "maximum validity possible," implying that this represents the validity of each subscale from which "very useful inferences can be made." This is simply not a demonstration of the validity of scores from the MEMS or its subscales. Further, although the publisher notes the importance of construct validity for such an instrument, the summary states only that research indicated the existence of "subject to subject" as well as group differences that are consistent with "common self-concept theory," and that counseling sessions with clients showed differences in subscale scores. This is not evidence of construct validity. The publisher also suggests that studies have been performed to examine concurrent and predictive validity. Other than noting an "appropriate" correlation with the Career Maturity Inventory and a "predicted relationship" with the 16PF Question-

naire, no further information is given. Whatever research has been done to study the validity of the scores should be reported in detail or, at a minimum, made available to the test user by reference.

As a measure of emotional maturity or any of the aspects of personality the MEMS purports to measure, it cannot be recommended for either clinical or educational purposes. It may have some use in the research setting if minimal levels of score reliability and validity can be obtained by the researcher within the sample under study. The MEMS has a few strengths, however. First is the ease of administration through the website and the immediate scoring provided. Second is the easily understandable items and the simplicity of response required. Unfortunately, these strengths do not offset the serious and fundamental problems with the instrument. The publishers of the MEMS fail to satisfy even minimally the standards set out for such instruments in the *Standards for Educational and Psychological Testing* (AERA, APA, & NCME, 1999). Particularly crucial is the need for evidence of construct validity and a clear explanation of the theoretical basis for both the existence of the concepts measured and the manner of measurement. Until such information is provided, users should be very cautious about drawing any inferences about groups or individuals on the basis of results from the MEMS.

REVIEWER'S REFERENCE

American Educational Research Association, American Psychological Association, & National Council on Measurement in Education. (1999). *Standards for educational and psychological testing.* Washington, DC: American Educational Research Association.

[155]
Miller Forensic Assessment of Symptoms Test.

Purpose: Designed to "provide information regarding the probability that an individual is malingering psychiatric illness."
Population: Ages 18 and over.
Publication Dates: 1995–2001.
Acronym: M-FAST.
Scores, 8: Reported vs. Observed, Extreme Symptomatology, Rare Combinations, Unusual Hallucinations, Unusual Symptom Course, Negative Image, Suggestibility, Total.
Administration: Individual.
Price Data: Available from publisher.
Time: (5–10) minutes.
Author: Holly A. Miller.
Publisher: Psychological Assessment Resources, Inc.

Review of the Miller Forensic Assessment of Symptoms Test by MARC JANOSON, Forensic Psychologist in Independent Practice, Manhattan, NY:

DESCRIPTION. The Miller Forensic Assessment of Symptoms Test (M-FAST) is a screening instrument for the Structured Interview of Reported Symptoms (SIRS; T6:2399). It is a 25-item interview for individuals ages 18 and older. Seven forced-choice items are presented in two parts. After asking each question for Items 1, 7, and 11, the examiner observes the examinee to determine whether the examinee's behavior is consistent with his or her self-report. Item 25, the last item, consists of two alternate follow-up questions to a question asked at the beginning of the interview. The M-FAST provides a quantitative estimate regarding the probability that an individual is malingering psychiatric illness. Interpretation can be made of the Total scale, the scale scores, and individual item responses. The Total score provides an estimate of the likelihood that the respondent is malingering psychopathology. The second level of interpretation involves examination of the scale scores. There are seven scale scores: Reported vs. Observed (RO), Extreme Symptomatology (ES), Rare Combinations (RC), Unusual Hallucinations (UH), Unusual Symptom Course (USC), Negative Image (NI), and Suggestibility (S). Four of the scales (UH, RC, RO, and ES) have been found to consistently differentiate malingerers from honest responders. The examinee's responses to individual items should be examined, as well.

Mental health clinicians with formal training in diagnostic interviewing and forensic psychology or psychiatry can administer and score the M-FAST. Interpretation of the results should be completed by a licensed clinician who is trained to use the instrument. The responses are coded 1 for true or yes and 0 for false or no. Scores are tabulated for each of the seven scales. The Total score is obtained by summing the seven scale scores. The cutoff score selected by the author is 6. Examinees who endorse six or more M-FAST items are deemed to be presenting in a manner highly suggestive of malingering. The clinician is instructed to examine the subject's performance on scales UH, RO, RC, and ES to obtain another estimate regarding the likelihood that the examinee is malingering.

DEVELOPMENT. The development of the M-FAST began in 1995. It was developed to serve as a quick screening interview for malingering. It generally takes approximately 5 to 10 minutes to administer the 25-item structured interview.

TECHNICAL. The author posits that "false positives" are less of a concern with a screening measure because the clinician is strongly advised to obtain corroborating data and to administer the SIRS to all persons who test positive on the M-FAST. Therefore, the cutoff scores were chosen to maximize Negative predictive Power without decreasing the Positive Predictive Power to any considerable extent. For the clinical samples this goal was not fully achieved. Using 6 as the cutoff, the Positive Predictive Power is only .68, whereas for the nonclinical samples it is 1.00. This is a shortcoming of the instrument.

The statistical underpinning of the instrument has weak spots. The reliability for the Reported vs. Observed (RO) scale for the nonclinical sample is .44. Heilbrun (1992) suggested minimal reliability coefficients of .80 or above for tests used in forensic settings. The test-retest reliability of the M-FAST Total score is .92 and clearly meets and passes the Heilbrun .80 benchmark. A significant problem with the demographics of the samples rests with the fact that there were no females in the clinical sample of 280 subjects.

COMMENTARY. The manual provides convergent validity evidence by correlating the M-FAST results with the Minnesota Multiphasic Personality Inventory—2 (MMPI-2) indicators of symptom overreporting. The M-FAST Total and scale scores were compared to MMPI-2 scale F (Infrequency), Fb, and F(p). The highest correlation is between the M-FAST Total score and the MMPI-2 F(p) at .78. Although F(p) is the most sensitive and specific measure for overreporting on the MMPI-2, the manual contains no narrative about this correlation. However, much is made of the correlation between the M-FAST and F and Fb. F also pulls for psychoticism, careless responding, and a need to exaggerate/cry for help and is therefore a far less adequate marker for malingering than F(p).

SUMMARY. The test developer has successfully produced a screening instrument for the malingering of psychiatric illness that can be administered, scored, and interpreted in a relatively efficient and cost-effective manner. Although further validation research with broader samples is needed, the M-FAST is an excellent addition to the armamentarium of the forensic psychologist performing assessment of response bias. The author rightly advises clinicians to follow-up the M-FAST with the longer, more robust SIRS for all who have been designated probable malingerers. The reviewer reminds forensic psychologists that the validity scales of the MMPI-2 stand alone in terms of the variety and usefulness of measures to assess a broad range of dimensions related to response styles, attitudes, and approaches to self-presentation. Clinicians seeking a quick, adjunctive instrument to add to the well-known and well-standardized instruments in the field now have what they have wanted.

REVIEWER'S REFERENCE

Heilbrun, K. (1992). The role of psychological testing in forensic assessment. *Law and Human Behavior, 16*(3), 257–272.

Review of the Miller Forensic Assessment of Symptoms Test by NATHANIEL J. PALLONE, University Distinguished Professor (Psychology), Center of Alcohol Studies, Rutgers University, Piscataway, NJ, and JAMES J. HENNESSY, Professor (Counseling Psychology), Graduate School of Education, Fordham University, New York, NY:

DESCRIPTION. According to its author, "The M-FAST is a structured interview designed to provide information regarding the probability that an individual is malingering psychiatric illness" (professional manual, p. 3). The Miller Forensic Assessment of Symptoms Test (M-FAST) is described as a "25-item screening instrument [that] can be administered in a relatively brief time period (5–10 minutes)" (professional manual, p. 3). In respect to overt content, 11 of the 25 items concern hallucinatory experiences (auditory, visual, tactile, command); 7 concern mood (anxiety, depression, euphoria, bipolar oscillation); 4 concern delusions; and 3 concern depersonalization experiences. Responses are limited to true/false/not applicable or always/sometimes/never, but the author is quite insistent that the items be administered individually by a mental health clinician (rather than be completed by an examinee as a series of self-reports) and that interpretation of scores can be undertaken only by a "licensed clinician" (professional manual, p. 6). Moreover, administration of the instrument "should always be preceded by a clinical interview with the examinee" so as to "gather a full psychiatric and medical history" (professional manual, pp. 6–7). To that extent, the instrument is quasi-actuarial.

SCORES AND THEIR MEANING. In addition to a total score, these 25 items yield scores on no fewer than seven scales, albeit three rest on a single item: Reported vs. Observed Symptomatology, Extreme Symptomatology, Rare Combinations, Unusual Hallucinations, Unusual Symptom Course, Negative Image, and Suggestibility. Still, the total score—derived by summing the seven scale scores—is paramount because "Examinees who endorse six or more M-FAST items are presenting in a manner highly suggestive of malingering" (professional manual, p. 13), a threshold selected so as to "minimize false negatives rather than false positives" (professional manual, p. 11).

DEVELOPMENT AND TECHNICAL. Early versions of this instrument were administered to 280 inpatients in a forensic psychiatric hospital charged with "crimes ranging from trespassing to murder" (professional manual, p. 22) who had uniformly been judicially declared "incompetent to stand trial because of mental illness" (professional manual, p. 22). However, differential diagnoses of the character of the mental illnesses underpinning such judicial determination are not reported. These individuals also completed the Minnesota Multiphasic Personality Inventory-2 (MMPI-2) and the Structured Interview of Reported Symptoms (SIRS) (Rogers, Bagby, & Dickens, 1992). On the basis of SIRS scores, patients were syllabicated as "malingerers" or "honest responders." For comparison purposes, the M-FAST was administered sequentially to groups of 100 and 116 undergraduates, respectively, enrolled in introductory psychology courses. Half the students in each group were asked to role-play malingering as it might be enacted by "people who try to fool mental health professionals (i.e., pretend they have a mental illness) to avoid going to jail for a crime or to gain money from a lawsuit or government benefits" (professional manual, p. 23). For the M-FAST total score, coefficients of correlation are reported at .71 with the F scale of the MMPI-2 and between .58 and .67 on the four principal scales of the SIRS (Rare Symptoms, Improbable or Absurd Symptoms, Symptom Combinations, Reported vs. Observed Symptoms). Reliability for the M-FAST total score is reported by an alpha value of .93 for an independent sample of 50 forensic inpatients.

COMMENTARY. In the raised voice of italics, the author urges caution in the interpretation of "high" scores on the instrument, defined as the endorsement of six or more of the 25 items:

> The examinee's Total Score on the M-FAST was significantly elevated, indicating that this individual may be malingering mental illness. (professional manual, p. 13)

But even so wary a statement appears to exceed what can validly be concluded, for, despite the meticulous craftsmanship with which it has been constructed, through its very title the instrument promises more than it can currently deliver. By the author's own consistent description (professional manual, pp. 3, 5, 10, 13, 21, 31), in the most generous interpretation, what the M-FAST yields is a "probability" of malingering in a quite limited sphere; it is far from a "forensic assessment of symptoms" (professional manual, p. 3).

That limitation inheres in the character of the forensic inpatient sample on which the construction of the instrument pivots. We are told that these individuals had uniformly been found incompetent to stand trial; by implication, none had been found (or at least, not as yet) to be not guilty by reason of insanity. Under convergent guidelines promulgated by the American Law Institute (Stone, 1984; Stone & Stromberg, 1976), the American Psychiatric Association (1984), and the American Bar Association (1989), supported in many jurisdictions by legislative and/or judicial decision, there are but two acceptable bases for either a pleading of nonculpability in a criminal trial or a finding of incompetence to stand trial in a criminal proceeding. Those grounds are, respectively, (a) "significant mental retardation," as indicated by an inventoried intelligence quotient of 55 or below on an instrument like the Wechsler, and (b) "only those severely abnormal mental conditions that grossly and demonstrably impair a person's perception or understanding of reality and are *not* attributable to the voluntary ingestion of alcohol or other psychoactive substances" (American Psychiatric Association, 1984, p. 17). Absent information about differential diagnoses among the inpatients in the forensic psychiatric hospital where the development of the instrument was launched, one should expect only the severely mentally retarded and/or the floridly psychotic in the standardization sample. However, because there are cautions against the use of the M-FAST with patients who "are mentally retarded or of borderline intellectual ability" or "who have profound cognitive impairment" (professional manual, p. 6), especially in consequence of neurological dysfunction, one must assume that individuals with IQs at or below the convergent threshold were eliminated. That leaves the floridly psychotic—and perhaps explains why the overt content of 15 of M-FAST's 25 items deal either with hallucinations or delusions. Accordingly, when the total score reaches or exceeds the M-FAST threshold, only a less expansive conclusion seems justified: "This examinee's Total Score is similar to scores of a group of forensic psychiatric inpatients found incompetent to stand trial who were found through other psychometric instruments to be malingering symptoms of florid psychosis." That is a substantially more modest statement, but it is also much closer to the mark empirically.

The professional manual posits the instrument's utility in civil cases. Yet the bases on which benefits are claimed in disability proceedings or compensation sought in liability cases only rarely invoke mental disorders of the sort found in abundance among people judged incompetent to stand trial. Instead, the disorders prototypically adduced in such cases involve panic, phobia, startle response, persistent sleep disturbance, appetite disturbance, and other indicia of traumata. Such symptoms are notoriously eligible for malingering, distortion, exaggeration, or downright factitiousness, especially when precipitating events or situations do not rise to the level of "catastrophic stress" as defined by DSM-IV. Members of the defense bar especially would thus welcome a reliable methodology to distinguish genuine from feigned symptomatology. But it is not immediately evident that the manner in which the M-FAST has been developed and validated permits any legitimate conclusion about malingering of disorders of the sort generally focal in civil cases.

According to the professional manual, a clinician should "use the individual's performance to determine whether a more comprehensive assessment of malingering ... is warranted" (p. 11). In the two case examples presented in the manual, such "more comprehensive assessment" is undertaken through administration of the SIRS and the MMPI-2. Especially at a time when interpretations of Federal Rule of Evidence 702 in Federal and state courts alike appear uniformly to favor traditional, long-established, and/or "industry-standard" means of adducing evidence, buttressing M-FAST scores in precisely that fashion seems prudent indeed.

SUMMARY. The M-FAST is a recently published, meticulously crafted instrument with a title that promises more than it can presently deliver. The instrument will likely find its most fruitful use as a rapid screen to detect the probability of malingering among criminal defendants pleading incompetence to stand trial. Test-test correlations are marginally sufficient indicators of clinical validity and utility. Doubtless, future research with the instrument will increase its scope to validate utility with criminal defendants pleading insanity, with claimants for disability benefits, and with plaintiffs seeking damage awards in civil cases. Until such time, the instrument will remain a highly reliable correlate of other psychological questionnaires, some of which themselves await validation against non-questionnaire-based judicial and psychiatric judgments.

REVIEWERS' REFERENCES

American Bar Association. (1989). *ABA criminal justice mental health standards.* Washington, DC: The American Bar Association.

American Psychiatric Association. (1984). *Issues in forensic psychiatry: Insanity defense, hospitalization of adults, model civil commitment law, sentencing process, child custody consultation.* Washington, DC: American Psychiatric Press.

Rogers, R., Bagby, R. M., & Dickens, S. S. (1992). *SIRS, Structured Interview of Reported Symptoms: Professional manual.* Odessa, FL: Psychological Assessment Resources.

Stone, A. A., & Stromberg, C. D. (1976). *Mental health and law: A system in transition.* New York: Jason Aronson.

Stone, A. A. (1984). *Law, psychiatry, and morality: Essays and analysis.* Washington, DC: American Psychiatric Press.

[156]
Miller Getting Along With People Scale.

Purpose: "Designed to help individuals determine how well they get along with other people."
Population: Ages 15 to adult.
Publication Date: 1996.
Scores: Total score only.
Administration: Group.
Price Data, 2001: $35 per administration via webpage (Visa or MasterCard are required to use this test).
Time: (15) minutes.
Comments: Administered and scored on the internet; printout of results provided. [Editor's Note: Since November 2002, the webpage for administration of this test has been unavailable.]
Author: Harold J. Miller.
Publisher: Meta Development LLC [Canada].

Review of the Miller Getting Along With People Scale by ALBERT M. BUGAJ, Associate Professor of Psychology, University of Wisconsin—Marinette, Marinette, WI:

The Miller Getting Along With People Scale is a self-report inventory designed by Harold Miller to, as its name indicates, help individuals determine how well they get along with others. Descriptive information found on the test's website further indicates it is useful both for individuals and employers, and that after future research it may be found to be of use during therapy. The test must be taken and scored on the Internet. The test is scored and the feedback returned immediately. The URL for the site opens to the homepage of Meta Development LLC. The user will there find links to 11 tests, including the Getting Along With People Scale. Among other links are also those to a Frequently Asked Questions (FAQs) list, a chat room, and a survey concerning why one did or did not purchase one of the available tests. The website, as well as the links, opens quickly. It is well organized and uncluttered.

Opening the link to the Getting Along With People Scale, one sees brief, straightforward instructions to "Read each statement below. Please click one of the ratings to indicate how much a statement is like you." The directions are followed by the 32 items of the test each contained in its own box in a table. Each item is accompanied by four anchors labeled "A lot," "Moderately," "Somewhat," and "Not at all." Upon submitting one's responses to the items, a web page opens indicating the test taker's score on a scale ranging from zero to 96. Only one score is presented. A score below 19 indicates "You don't get along with people." A score over 77 indicates "You have excellent people skills," whereas scores between 39 and 57 show "You get along with people as well as others you know." Scores between 20 and 38 show one sometimes gets along, whereas those between 58 and 76 show one gets along most of the time.

No interpretation of the scores appeared on the reviewer's screen, although the text on the web page indicated "suggestions are provided for you as possible ways to improve your relationship," and "it is hoped that you will use this information to find creative and effective ways to increase your level of relationship."

The materials provided for review did not include an explanation of how the test taker's score is derived. However, it would seem that a response indicating an item describes oneself "a lot" receives 3 points, "moderately" 2 points, and so forth. Responding "a lot" to all 32 items thus results in the highest possible score of 96. As responding "not at all" receives no points, responding in such a manner to all items would result in a score of zero.

DEVELOPMENT. Information regarding the technical aspects of the Getting Along With People Scale are found by accessing the FAQs pages of the website, which was the sole source of information made available for review. The FAQs page provides no information regarding how items were selected for the test, nor does it indicate if the items were submitted to factor analysis to ascertain if a single component exists, or if subscale scores should be provided. There is also no indication that a normative sample was used to determine the descriptors (e.g., "You don't get along with other people") associated with the scoring key.

Close examination of the test and items and anchors indicates the possibility of two inherent problems. First, the nature of the anchors may not create an equal interval scale in the psychological set of the test-taker. That is, the low end of the scale is anchored by "not at all," an absolute statement. The opposite end is anchored by "a lot." This indicates a high degree of the trait being rated, but may not indicate an absolute amount of the trait. If an equal interval scale does not exist, the apparent scoring procedure may be called into question.

A potentially more serious problem lies with the items themselves. Namely, it is possible that a response bias could easily occur when taking the Getting Along With People Scale. There is no apparent reverse scoring of items, which seem to be positively worded in all cases. Some examples are the first item, "I greet people when they are near," Item 5, "I practice good personal hygiene," and Item 31 "I give and receive compliments." It seems hard to imagine one would indicate "not at all" for such items, or would frequently respond "somewhat." It is also hard to imagine one would also select "not at all" as a response to slightly less powerful items such as "I am happy when other people are successful." Without research indicating otherwise, it is thus likely that the Getting Along With People Scale is susceptible to faking or a less purposeful social desirability bias due to such things as the need to avoid criticism, or to seek social approval (Edwards, 1957; Crown & Marlowe, 1964).

TECHNICAL. The FAQs page for the Getting Along With People Scale indicates a test-retest reliability coefficient of .85 for the test. Unfortunately, the interval between the times at which the test was administered is not indicated. There is also no indication of the nature of the sample used in determining the test-retest reliability of the scale, although the website does refer to the fact the coefficient might have been higher if an extended range of individuals was tested. The size of the group is also not reported. A split-half reliability of .88 is indicated on the web page, speaking somewhat to the internal consistency of the test. However, data on the size and demographics of the sample are again omitted, so the generalizability of the statistic cannot be ascertained.

Less information regarding the validity of the Getting Along With People Scale is provided on its FAQs page. The website does state that the "maximum validity possible is equal to the square root of the reliability coefficient," and then provides a "maximum validity possible" of .94, based on a test-retest coefficient of .89 (which differs from the test-retest reliability indicated earlier on the web page). This validity coefficient is, of course, highly theoretical. One of the Taylor-Russell Tables (1939) for determining the net gain in selection accuracy attributable to tests of given validity coefficents is included on the web page. No full explanation of how the table is to be interpreted is provided.

The website further states that the "primary validity that will be elaborated on is construct validity." It goes on to indicate that the Getting Along With People Scale "was developed from the theory and research proposed by the individual's concern with the construct of getting along with people." It does not identify, however, the theory or the people who developed it. The statement continues, "The resulting research indicated that group differences found from subject to subject differences were consistent with the proposed theory. These results were confirmed during counseling sessions with clients manifesting a variety of differences in the scale score." Unfortunately, neither the nature of the between-subject differences, nor the effects of counseling, are explained. There are also no specifics of the theory mentioned, nor are any statistics presented.

The web page indicates, "Predictive validity studies will vary from application to application." It then goes on to state that a large number of additional studies will be needed to monitor client changes during therapy and for research purposes. It is then asserted that future research will prove the Getting Along With People Scale useful for therapy, research, and some hiring purposes.

CONCLUSION. At present, the Miller Getting Along With People Scale cannot be recommended for use outside that of the most basic research regarding its psychometric properties. In the absence of data regarding the group on whom the reliability of the test was ascertained, and the interval over which testing was performed, its exact reliability cannot be judged. One would hope that a series of studies will be performed to see if the test is reliable over varying intervals of time, and for various groups of subjects. Given the lack of specific information (i.e., reference to theory, and statistical data) regarding the construct validity of the test, its appropriateness is also hard to determine. Research on possible response biases is also needed, especially if the test is to be used for counseling and hiring purposes. Although an inexpensive alternative, the Miller Getting Along With People Scale cannot be recommended when compared to other tests containing subscales that may be theoretically related to what the Getting Along With People Scale is measuring, or intended for the same purposes for which it is proposed. Some of these tests would be the Revised NEO Personality Inventory (Costa & McCrae, 1992, T6:2110), and the Millon Index of Personality Styles (Millon, 1994, T6:1611).

REVIEWER'S REFERENCES

Costa, P. T., Jr., & McCrae, R. R. (1992). Revised NEO Personality Inventory. Odessa, FL: Psychological Assessment Resources.
Crowne, D. P., & Marlowe, D. (1964). *The approval motive: Studies in evaluative dependence.* New York: Wiley.
Edwards, E. P. (1957). *The social desirability variable in personality assessment and research.* New York: Dryden.
Millon, T. (1994). Millon Index of Personality Styles. San Antonio, TX: The Psychological Corporation.
Taylor, H. C., & Russell, J. T. (1939). The relationship of validity coefficients to the practical effectiveness of test selection. Discussion and tables. *Journal of Applied Psychology, 23,* 565–578.

Review of the Miller Getting Along with People Scale by JEAN POWELL KIRNAN, Associate Professor of Psychology, The College of New Jersey, Ewing, NJ:

[The reviewer wishes to acknowledge the contributions of Mollyanne R. Zink. Her tireless efforts and keen insights contributed greatly to this review.]

The Miller Getting Along with People Scale (hereafter referred to as "The Miller") is a self-report inventory designed to assess an individual's ability to "get along with other people." Designed for individuals aged 15 and older, the author claims the test is useful for both individuals and employers. However, there is no indication how one is to use the test in a work setting, whether in selection or in facilitation of work teams.

DESCRIPTION. The Miller is designed to be taken and scored on the Internet using one's home or office computer. Although the test can be administered individually or by group, each person taking the test must use their own computer.

The website is easy to navigate, read, and access. Information about the test, such as reliability and validity, can be found in a section of the website called "Frequently Asked Questions."

The test consists of 32 visually clear and easy-to-follow items. However, some of the statements are ambiguous as the numerous references to "people" and "others" are open to interpretation by the respondent. Are they referring to close friends and family, work and school colleagues, or strangers? There are also a few questions (i.e., "I practice good personal hygiene" and "I focus on the work that needs to be done"), that do not appear to have any relationship to how well one gets along with people.

All items are positively worded, which could lead to a response set. The items are fairly transparent in what is being measured. As with many personality measures, the utility of the instrument relies on honest responses and a genuine interest in self-discovery and development.

The individual rates his or her behavior on a 4-point Likert scale of "A lot," "Moderately," "Somewhat," and "Not at all". Each one of these four choices is printed clearly to the right of each test item. The verbal anchors, however, are not balanced as the phrase "Not at all" is more extreme than its converse "A lot." Additionally, it is difficult to imagine how someone could respond "Not at all" to some of the items. Perhaps changing this anchor to "Rarely" would balance the scale and make this response option more likely to be endorsed.

Upon completing the test, the respondent is brought to a new web page where test results and suggestions to improve one's "getting along with people" skills are provided. When this reviewer took the test, three suggestions were presented in paragraph form. The suggestions were numbered 3, 10, and 30, which corresponded to the three items that were answered in the extreme. It would appear that extreme answers triggered the "suggestions."

Although the website claims that a test score is given as a percentile and one can compare oneself to others, this is not clear in the score report. This reviewer's feedback report stated the score as "78 out of 96," where 96 is the total possible score. Thus, no percentile rank is reported. Instead, scores are placed into one of five intervals ranging from "You don't get along with people" to "You have excellent people skills." The description of the lowest interval seems particularly harsh and might be revised to read "You have a great deal of difficulty in getting along with people." Overall, the feedback report appears programmed with little integration or agreement between the suggestions and total scores. This reviewer's total score fell in the "excellent" interval, yet a suggestion was made that professional counseling may be needed.

DEVELOPMENT. There is no information as to the development of the test except to state it was developed from theory and research. No information on number of individuals writing the items, level of expertise, original pool of items, or pilot testing is provided.

The five scoring categories were determined in an unscientific fashion. Following the second test in the test-retest study, a brief interview was conducted and the respondents rated themselves on a scale of 1 to 5 as to how well they got along with people. These ratings were compared to scores on the test to determine categories. No information was provided as to how clean these categories were—if there was overlap or inconsistencies across the respondents. Self-evaluations taken on the same day are an inappropriate method of determining score intervals.

TECHNICAL. The reliability and validity data reported on the website are insufficient and misleading to a naïve reader. Test-retest reliability is reported as .85. A reference is made to "restricted range" of the sample and the suggestion that the true reliability coefficient is in fact larger, though no information is provided as to why or how the sample is restricted or who is in the sample.

However, in a communication with the author (personal communication, August 20, 2001) it was revealed that the reliability data were based on 200 college students with a test-retest interval of 12 days and 234 adult volunteers recruited via a newspaper advertisement with a test-retest interval of 7 days. These time intervals are considered short and may result in an inflated reliability coefficient. Similarly, a split-half reliability measure of .88 is reported, again with no sample demographics, sample size, or method used for splitting the test in half.

In reporting both reliability and validity data, tables are provided with little relevance to the test. On the reliability page, a table with five different split-half coefficients (.5 through .9) and their corresponding Spearman-Brown (SB) corrections for length are reported. If The Miller has a split-half of .88, why not just report the SB correction for a correlation of .88 which would be .93?

The validity provided on the website is misleading. This section begins with the presentation of a "maximum validity possible" of .94. This is a statistical ceiling based on the reliability obtained. Yet nowhere is there any evidence of statistical validity studies being conducted (criterion-related or construct validity with other instruments). Reporting a large possible correlation, without any basis, is misleading to the naïve reader.

Construct validity is suggested on the basis of score differences being confirmed in counseling sessions with clients. There is no information as to the number of clients, if the counselor was "blind" to The Miller scores, or the level of expertise of the counselor. Construct validity is best demonstrated by an accumulation of evidence. It would be more appropriate to provide correlations of The Miller with external measures such as existing psychological tests that are accepted as measuring the ability to get along with others (i.e., the Sociability scale of the California Psychological Inventory [43]) or counselors/supervisors who could rate the individual on interpersonal/sociability skills.

Curiously, the validity section ends with a table containing a variation of the Taylor-Russell Tables which are often reported in personnel selection literature as a method for determining the incremental percent of individuals successful on a particular job controlling for selection ratios, base rate, and test validity. What this has to do with The Miller test is beyond this reviewer's comprehension. The caption on the table indicates that the measures are of successful students. Who the students are, how they are successful, and what this has to do with "getting along with people" is completely unclear. The Taylor-Russell tables are useless for The Miller because they require a validity coefficient, which was not provided for this test.

SUMMARY. The sparse information provided on the website is misleading and unsubstantiated. One is left wondering why reliability conversion tables, a maximum validity coefficient, and Taylor Russell Tables (that have no relationship to the test under study) are presented. Additional data on the test's development and psychometric properties provided by the author in a personal communication reveal insufficient controls and unscientific methods.

Not only is the instrument poorly developed and documented, the technical information provided is often erroneous, inappropriate, and misleading to a naïve user. It is strongly recommended that the instrument not be used.

[157]
Miller Happiness Scale.

Purpose: "Designed to measure eight areas of an individual's happiness."
Population: Grade 7 reading level or higher.
Publication Date: 1998.
Scores, 8: Personal Happiness, Health Happiness, Spiritual Happiness, Intimate Relationship Happiness, Family Happiness, Friendship Happiness, Work Happiness, Leisure Happiness.
Administration: Group.
Price Data, 2001: $35 per administration via webpage (Visa or MasterCard are required to use this test).
Time: (30–45) minutes.
Comments: Administered and scored on the internet; printout of results is provided. [Editor's Note: Since November 2002, the webpage for administration of this test has been unavailable.]
Author: Harold J. Miller.
Publisher: Meta Development LLC [Canada].

Review of the Miller Happiness Scale by JULIE A. ALLISON, Associate Professor of Psychology, Pittsburg State University, Pittsburg, KS:

DESCRIPTION. The Miller Happiness Scale is designed to measure an individual's happiness. Theoretically, happiness is subdivided into eight separate categories, including Personal Happiness, Health Happiness, Spiritual Happiness, Intimate Relationship Happiness, Family Happiness, Friendship Happiness, Work Happiness, and Leisure Happiness. The Miller Happiness Scale is appropriate for individuals with at least a seventh grade reading level, and can be administered either individually or in group settings. The Miller Happiness Scale may be taken online, where scores are immediately available and may be printed out. There is a $35 charge for taking this assessment,

payable immediately prior to its administration. The scale takes 30–45 minutes to administer. No information is available on the intended uses of this measurement, nor on the scoring system that is used for this scale. It is conceivable that this could be used as part of a screening measure, could be used for measuring the subjective efficacy of treatment, and also could be used for research purposes.

DEVELOPMENT. No information is available about the development of this scale. Dr. Harold Miller has developed several different scales, all of which are available online and deal with personal well-being. Reliability and validity data are available for other scales, but no information about the methodology used to obtain these data are reported.

TECHNICAL. No data on the reliability or validity of this scale are available.

COMMENTARY. Due to lack of available data and related information, no conclusions can be drawn about the utility of this measure. To create a measure that can theoretically tease different types of happiness apart and measure each of these uniquely is conceptually attractive. Such a measure could be used for both clinical and research purposes. At this point, it all seems quite theoretical and lacking in empirical support.

SUMMARY. The Miller Happiness Test is conceptually attractive, but lacking in empirical support. Research needs to be done on this measure.

Review of the Miller Happiness Scale by RAOUL A. ARREOLA, Professor and Director, Educational Evaluation and Development, The University of Tennessee Health Science Center, Memphis, TN:

DESCRIPTION. The Miller Happiness Scale (MHS) is one of 11 instruments constructed by Harold J. Miller and marketed on the Internet under the name of Meta Development LLC. The 11 instruments marketed include the Miller Motivation Scale, the Miller Psychological Independence Scale, the Miller Self-Concept Scale, the Miller Stress Scale, the Miller Emotional Maturity Scale, the Miller Marriage Satisfaction Scale, the Miller Depression Scale, the Miller Common Sense Scale, the Miller Getting Along with People Scale, the Miller Love Scale, and the Miller Happiness Scale. All 11 instruments, which are reviewed separately in this volume, are available online for individual, self-administration at a cost of $35 each.

The purpose of the Miller Happiness Scale is to "measure eight areas of an individual's happiness" and to "enable the individual to quickly find areas of life where improvement is needed." The scale contains eight subscales that purport to measure an individual's happiness in the areas of Personal, Health, Spiritual, Intimate Relationship, Family, Friendship, Work, and Leisure. One-paragraph general definitions of each of these areas of happiness are included in the final scoring report for the MHS. Briefly, however, the Personal subscale "measures one's overall satisfaction with life"; the Health subscale "measures one's happiness with one's health"; the Spiritual subscale "measures your happiness with your relationship with your God or Higher Power"; the Intimate Relationship subscale "measures one's relationship with a girlfriend, partner, or spouse"; the Family subscale "measures one's happiness with your family"; the Friendship subscale "measures your happiness with your friends"; the Work subscale "measures work happiness"; and the Leisure subscale "measures one's level of happiness with one's free time." Each subscale contains 10 items with a total of 80 items for the entire MHS. The instrument is estimated to take 30 to 45 minutes to complete.

Upon completion and submission of the online MHS, a personal report is instantly generated and may be printed out. The report is presented on a dark blue background and is thus a little difficult to read on a computer screen. However, when printed out on a black-and-white printer the report is in standard black ink on white paper. The report contains one-paragraph descriptions of what is measured by each subscale as well as an indication of how each subscale score may be interpreted. The report also includes the individual raw scores and percentile scores for each subscale, as well as a colored graphical representation (bar graph) of the percentile scores.

Finally, a brief report for each subscale result is presented separately. These brief reports are not so much interpretations of the respondent's answers but, rather, composite descriptions of the responses to each subscale.

DEVELOPMENT. Despite repeated requests for information concerning the validity studies or theoretical underpinnings of the Miller Happiness Scale, no information was provided by the developer. Rather, one is simply directed to the web site's FAQ page. The web site through which all the Miller scales may be accessed (www.metadevelopment.com) lists a Frequently Asked Questions (FAQ) page that is supposed to include information on the development, validity, and reliability of the various Miller Scales. However, the FAQ page for the MHS does not provide this information.

TECHNICAL. Neither the Miller Happiness Scale itself, nor the final scoring report, provides any reference to a theoretical or empirical construct on which the instrument may be based. On the surface, however, broad similarities to aspects of Aristotle's Theory of Happiness can, of course, be detected. Between the two major current philosophical theories of *happiness*, *hedonism* and *life satisfaction*, the MHS appears to lean more in the direction of the latter. However, no specific psychological model of happiness or theoretical construct is described, and no information regarding the normative group on which the percentile scores may be properly interpreted is provided.

In terms of the technicalities of item construction, the MHS is seriously flawed. The response scale used is both nonparallel and multibarreled. In addition, the response scale often does not match the item. In the MHS the respondent is asked to indicate how much a given statement (item) is "like" them. The response scale includes the choices *"Very much like me—I always to this"*; *"Mostly like—often like me"*; *"Somewhat like me"*; *"A little like me"*; *"Not very much like me—I never do this"*; and *"This does not apply to me—I never do this."* Thus, the response scale combines both an indication of similarity (like me) with an indication of the frequency of taking an action. In addition, selecting the *"This does not apply to me—I never do this"* option generates a numerical item score that is interpreted in the final report as essentially meaning "Very unlike me." If the "does not apply to me" response is taken to mean the item does not, in fact, apply to the respondent then the data for the item should not be included in computation of the subscale score. On the other hand, if the response is taken to indicate the frequency with which the respondent engages in some behavior ("I never do this"), then the interpretation should be in terms of the frequency of that behavior. However, no item in the MHS describes a behavior. Rather, each item states a positive position on a scale of happiness regarding some specific issue.

Thus, the items as written tend to call for either a *"Strongly Agree—Strongly Disagree"* response scale, an *"I always feel this way—I never feel this way"* response scale, or an *"I often feel this way—I rarely feel this way"* response scale rather than the technically flawed response scale used by the MHS. In the absence of firm validity and reliability data, the technical problems with the items and response scale would suggest that the MHS might be of questionable reliability and validity.

The most objectionable part of the Miller Happiness Scale is the portion of the final report that ostensibly provides interpretations of the subscale scores. Although a separate "interpretive" paragraph is generated for each subscale, the paragraph is composed of nothing more than one reflective statement per item in the scale. For example, if the response *"Very much like me—I always do this or feel this way"* is selected for the item "I have many happy thoughts," the "interpretive" statement printed in the report on this subscale reads "You almost always have happy thoughts." Conversely, if one selects the response *"This does not apply to me—I never do this,"* the "interpretive" statement for the item reads "You almost never have happy thoughts."

Because each subscale is composed of 10 items, each interpretive section of the final report generally contains 10 reflective statements of the type described above. On certain occasions a two-sentence response is reflected for a single item. There are no additional interpretive comments provided.

COMMENTARY. From all appearances the Miller Happiness Scale is simply an online expression of the psychoanalytic technique of reflection used particularly in Carl Rogers' form of "client-centered" therapy. This may be an effective technique in the context of continuing, face-to-face psychotherapy, but it makes no sense as an online, self-administered instrument. Although perhaps constructed and offered with well-intentioned professional objectives, the Miller Happiness Scale has the appearance of simply being an attempt to "cash in" on the Internet. Unfortunately, the Miller Happiness Scale has the potential to do harm. It is hard to imagine that someone with a bipolar disorder, sitting alone in front of a computer screen in a darkened bedroom in a state of depression, looking for help on the Internet, would derive any positive benefit from an official-looking psychological report that simply says "You hate where you live," "You have poor mental health," "You get along with very few people," and "You have little fun in your life."

[158]

Miller Love Scale.

Purpose: "Designed to measure eight areas of love."
Population: Ages 16 to adult.
Publication Date: 1998.
Scores, 8: Self-Love, Love Motivation, Value, Perception of Partner, Love Thoughts, Love Feelings, Love Behavior, Spiritual Love.
Administration: Group.
Price Data, 2001: $35 per administration via webpage (Visa or MasterCard are required to use this test).
Time: (30–45) minutes.
Comments: Administered and scored on the internet; printout of results is provided. [Editor's Note: Since November 2002, the webpage for administration of this test has been unavailable.]
Author: Harold J. Miller.
Publisher: Meta Development LLC [Canada].

Review of the Miller Love Scale by JILL ANN JENKINS, School/Child Psychologist—Private Practice, Barcelona, Spain:

DESCRIPTION. The Miller Love Scale is a 160 item internet-administered questionnaire developed for individuals aged 16 years and over. Examinees must read at or above the seventh grade level to take the questionnaire.

Examinees are required to agree, on a 6-point gradient scale, with the 160 statements related to both their individual sense of self and their relationship with their partner. The statements represent eight areas of love categorized as: Self-Love, Love Motivation, Values, Perception of Partner, Love Thoughts, Love Feelings, Love Behavior, and Spiritual Love.

The Self-Love category measures self-esteem. The Love Motivation subscale looks at the "underlying beliefs or values that the person brings into the relationship." The Values subscale measures "the priorities or areas that the partner considers important." The Perception of Partner subscale measures one's "view of their partner," including their "impression, attitude, or sense of their partner." The Love Thoughts subscale measures "concepts" that one has about their partner. The Love Feelings subscale measures the "affective side" of the examinee's relationship, including emotions, moods, passions, sentiments, and tenderness. The Love Behavior subscale measures what the individual does in the relationship and is related to conduct, manners, actions, and performance. The Spiritual Love subscale measures "some aspects of transcendental parts of love" and attempts to "measure the mystical, godly, holy, idealistic and sacred aspects of one's relationship to each other and to one's God or Higher Power."

The Miller Love Scale is self-administered from the computer, either individually or in a group, and results are given immediately to the examinee in the form of a six-page printout. Test administration takes approximately 30–45 minutes.

Results include total scores for each of the eight love categories and their percentages, as well as a description of the examinee's functioning in the eight areas of love. Each of the eight descriptions simply categorizes the first person statements to which examinees needed to agree by repeating them back to the examinee in third person (i.e., if the examinee responded "Yes" to "I frequently dress well," the feedback to the examinees simply states, "You frequently dress well").

DEVELOPMENT. The Miller Love Scale was published in July 1998. The development of the test, underlying assumptions to the test and its eight categories of love, and information regarding item development are not provided by the examiner on his "frequently asked questions" web page, which is provided to examiners and examinees in lieu of a test manual.

TECHNICAL.

Standardization. Obvious and grave technical problems arise in the area of standardization with the Miller Love Scale because the author of this test has not provided a test manual. Information is not provided regarding test norms or standardization of the Miller Love Scale.

Reliability. Some reliability and validity information was provided by the author on his "frequently asked questions" web page. Test-retest reliability coefficients were reported to range from .85 to .92. Information regarding internal consistency reliability was not provided.

Despite the obviously impressive test-retest reliability coefficients, without knowing anything about the standardization of the Miller Love Scale, one cannot judge the quality and integrity of these values.

Validity. Construct validity was reported to fall between .92 and .96 for the subtests. Again, despite the obviously good construct validity rating, one cannot be sure of the quality and integrity of this score without the standardization information and methodology that contributed to its formation. The test author does not address criterion-related validity, concurrent validity, predictive validity, or content validity of the test.

Item analysis. Because no manual is provided (neither "on-line" nor "off-line"), this reviewer is left only to hypothesize about which of the 160 questions belong to which of the eight categories of love. Some of the questions that were clearly about "Spiritual Love" have serious flaws in that plural statements (i.e. "My partner and I experience God's presence in our relationship") are reflected back to examinees in first person tense. To elaborate on this example, if one of the couple does believe in God's presence, and the other does not (indicating a response such as "This does not apply"), it is reflected back to the examinee in a statement such as "You have no reason to believe that God is present in your relationship" (which would not be the case should the examinee feel this way, but their partner not). This flaw of turning a plural couple statement into a first person attribute occurs on numerous occasions.

COMMENTARY. The Miller Love Scale is a seriously flawed instrument for usage in professional settings, in that the author does not provide a rationale for the test, test development information, item development information, information on the development of the subtests, test norms, or standardization information. In addition, reliability and validity information are sorely lacking. The author does comment on his "frequently asked questions" web page that a "large number of additional studies will be needed to determine the range of usefulness." Knowing about the initial study would, of course, be helpful to further studies. The author additionally states that he believes that future research will prove the scale applicable in the areas of self-help, counseling, and research. At present, I do not see it being applicable to any of those settings. One of the subtests specifically, Spiritual Love, has serious flaws in that it reflects plural couple statements back to the examinee as if they are first person attributes.

In a nonclinical setting, such as for usage over the internet by individual examinees, it could be a "fun" activity that perhaps would provoke conversation between couples. However, it is always prudent to reserve psychological examinations of any sort to usage with a qualified professional, especially when reviewing the results. Because the results of the Miller Love Scale do not give any advice or guidance to the examinee, but rather simply reflect the test taker's answers back to them, I fail to see it being an instrument that would fall into the "self help" realm.

If professionals are looking for tools to assist in counseling and guiding couples, a better bet would be the PREPARE/ENRICH test (Olson, Fournier, Druckman, & Adams, 1998; T6:1954). This test considers the different situations that couples may be in before marrying (i.e. young couples, mature couples, with or without children), allowing a tailored counseling approach. There is a separate questionnaire for couples who have already been married for over 2 years as well.

The Marital Satisfaction Inventory—Revised (Snyder, 1998; T6:1505) is another alternative for counselors seeking to begin therapy. This tool, although intended in its initial format for couples who were married or living together for at least 6 months, now addresses a wide range of couples including same-gender couples, couples in the dating phase, and engaged couples, as well as married couples.

Individual assessment with the Quality of Life Inventory (Frisch, 1994; T6:2045) would prove a more reliable and valid manner of addressing what the author refers to as "quality and satisfaction with life." The 17 scales in this test overlap considerably with Miller's "love" scales and have the added benefit of technical information and research to back it up.

SUMMARY. The Miller Love Scale is a computer-based questionnaire that is intended to assist couples in analyzing the "love" aspects of their relationship. Unfortunately, this test appears to fall short on all of the most important aspects of good professional quality and integrity. Without providing a manual to discuss test development, standardization, reliability, and validity, not to mention item analysis and applications, it is regretfully difficult to categorize the Miller Love Test as anything more then a "pop-psychology" quiz. Readers have been referred to three other standardized and research based tools such as PREPARE/ENRICH, The Marital Satisfaction Inventory, and the Quality of Life Inventory.

REVIEWER'S REFERENCES
Frisch, M. B. (1994). Quality of Life Inventory. Minnetonka, MN: NCS Assessments.
Olson, D. J., Fournier, D. G., Druckman, J. M., & Adams, E. (1998). PREPARE/ENRICH. Minneapolis, MN: Life Innovations, Inc.
Snyder, D. K. (1998). Marital Satisfaction Inventory—Revised. Los Angeles: Western Psychological Services.

Review of the Miller Love Scale by S. ALVIN LEUNG, Professor, Department of Educational Psychology, The Chinese University of Hong Kong, Hong Kong, China:

The Miller Love Scale is a 160-item scale intended to measure eight different domains of love, which are Self-Love, Love Motivation, Values, Perception of Partner, Love Thoughts, Love Feelings, Love Behavior, and Spiritual Love. It is a web-based instrument for which test users have to pay a fee (stated as US$35.00 per use based on information provided on the web) in order to take the test. Upon completion of the items, a test taker receives a computer-generated report. This report provides the test taker with information about the meaning of the scales, test scores and their interpretation.

The only source of information related to the Miller Love Scale is from the website (http://www.metadevelopment.com) where the test can be taken. A search of the PSYCINFO and ERIC databases in the past 5 years yielded no published literature on the Miller Love Scale. The items of the Miller Love Scale were written for individuals age 16 or above with at least a Grade 7 reading level. The test used a 6-point scale that ranges from *very much like me* to *this does not apply to me*. The test is designed for individuals who would like to examine the status of their "love" life, and the results could be used in the contexts of premarriage counseling, marriage counseling, and research.

Brief descriptions of the subscales of the Miller Love Scale, including the meanings of high and low scores, are made available to test takers who took the test on the Miller Love Scale website. According to that description, if a person scored above the 75th percentile on a subscale, it is considered a high score. Conversely, if a person scored below the 25th percentile, it is considered a low score. There is no information on how and what items were assigned to subscales, and what measurement approach was used to construct the test and its items. Similarly, it is not clear how the percentile scores were generated. No information was given about the characteristics of the normative sample and the standardization process.

DEVELOPMENT. It is not clear how the 160 items were constructed. The website where the Miller Love Scale is posted does not provide information regarding how the test items were generated or written. Also, there is no information on steps taken to ensure that test items were generated carefully and systematically, such as through a process of pilot testing the items on specific target populations. There is no information on whether the test was based on any theoretical framework related to love or personality. There is no information on how the narrative reports were written and what decision rules were used to generate different types of reports.

TECHNICAL. There is no normative information available on the Miller Love Scale, including demographic information for the normative group such as gender, age, and ethnic/cultural background.

Very limited information regarding reliability and validity are available from the Miller Love Scale website. The test-retest reliability of the eight subscales ranged between .85 and .92. Information regarding "maximum validity" is also provided, and the range was from .92 to .96. Maximum validity was defined as the square root of the reliability coefficient. However, there is no information on how the test-retest reliability coefficients were generated (e.g., sample size, length of time between pre-test and post-test). Such information is needed to evaluate the merits of the coefficients.

There was no information on internal consistency reliability of the subscales of the Miller Love Scale, nor were there information on content, criterion-related, or construct validity. There is no evidence that a systematic research process has been carried out to examine the reliability and validity of the test.

COMMENTARY. I have three major concerns with the Miller Love Scale. First and foremost, the Miller Love Scale is simply a cluster of test items with no evidence of standardization, reliability, and validity. There is no evidence that the test was constructed through a carefully planned scientific process.

Second, there is no information to support the validity of the narrative report generated from taking the Miller Love Scale. The narrative report given to test takers after taking the test consists of specific comments and description about the individual. Without any research findings to support

their validity, there is a clear danger that these interpretive comments might lead test takers to draw inaccurate conclusions about themselves and their relationships. The danger of misuse becomes greater because the interpretive report is issued directly to the test taker without the help of a professional counselor or psychologist.

Third, whereas the claim was made that the Miller Love Scale could be used in the context of relationship counseling such as premarital and marital counseling, there is no empirical evidence to support the claim that actual clients benefited from the instrument in the process of counseling intervention. In the same way, it was suggested that the Miller Love Scale could be used in research. However, there is no information on what constitutes an appropriate use of the test instrument in a research process, and how test scores should be used and computed (e.g., there is no information on the scoring of the subscales).

CONCLUSION. The Miller Love Scale is a poorly constructed test offered on the internet with no evidence of standardization, reliability, and validity. Test takers have to pay a relatively large sum of money (US$35.00) to take the test on the internet, but there is no credible research evidence to support that what they get in their interpretive reports is valid. In the absence of supportive data related to standardization, reliability, and validity, it does not seem ethical to market such a preliminary version of a test to the general public.

[159]
Miller Marriage Satisfaction Rating Scale.

Purpose: "Designed to compare one's level of marriage satisfaction to the marriage satisfaction of other married people."

Population: Individuals who are dating, living together or who are married.

Publication Date: 1997.

Scores: Total score only.

Administration: Group.

Price Data, 2001: $35 per administration via web page (Visa or MasterCard are required to use this test).

Time: (15) minutes.

Comments: Administered and scored on the internet; online documentation lists as Miller Marriage Satisfaction Scale but test itself is entitled Miller Marriage Satisfaction Rating Scale printout of results is provided. [Editor's Note: Since November 2002, the webpage for administration of this test has been unavailable.]

Author: Harold J. Miller.
Publisher: Meta Development LCC [Canada].

Review of the Miller Marriage Satisfaction Rating Scale by FRANK M. BERNT, Associate Professor of Health Services, St. Joseph's University, Philadelphia, PA:

DESCRIPTION. The Miller Marriage Satisfaction Rating Scale is a 27-item self-report scale designed to measure marital satisfaction. Each item includes a statement about one facet of marriage or family, to which one responds using a 4-point rating scale (*a lot, moderately, somewhat, not at all*). The author proposes that the scale can be used by individuals who are "dating, living together, or who are married." Its apparent appeal is that it is self-administered and provides a nearly instantaneous score to anyone interested; the only requirement is internet access and a valid credit card. The scale yields a single percentile score, indicating one's position relative to other couples who have taken the scale. Who those other couples are is not made clear in any of the materials made available for review.

DEVELOPMENT. No technical manual is available for the scale; instead, a very brief description of the scale is provided on the author's web page. There are no descriptions of item generation and selection, of pilot testing, or of standardization or norm-referencing procedures.

TECHNICAL. Information about the reliability and validity of the scale is presented on the author's web page. Test-retest reliability is reported to be .92; however, the author does not cite studies done, describe samples used, or define the intertest interval. The discussion on the web page seems to suggest that the split-half reliability for the test is less than .70. Given the relatively large number of items on the scale, it would seem that more careful item selection based upon an item analysis would yield a stronger internal consistency estimate. If its original appeal was its availability on the internet, this is overshadowed by the existence of many alternative measures of marital satisfaction now available on the internet that are much less expensive (often free) and in most cases also well-documented with respect to validity and reliability information.

The author's discussion of validity skirts the issue of whether this test has demonstrated validity or not. The author admits that "a large number of additional studies will be needed" to determine the utility of his scale; what is left unsaid is that not a single study is cited in support of the scale's validity. At the same time, he is very optimistic that "future research will prove that the Miller Marriage Satisfaction Scale is useful for therapy, research and personal information" (retrieved September 26, 2001 from www.metadevelopment.com/faq/marriagesatisfaction.html).

COMMENTARY. It is the reviewer's strong opinion that this test, at its present level of development, is not suitable for public use. Reliability and validity information are scant or nonexistent, falling far short of published *Standards for Educational and Psychological Testing* (AERA, APA, & NCME, 1999). The user pays $35 for a computer-administered survey (single-use) and receives in return a percentile score indicating relative position in a norming sample that is completely anonymous and amorphous; the size and demographic characteristics of the sample, as well as the sampling method used, are not available.

SUMMARY. The Miller Marriage Satisfaction Rating Scale, unfortunately, has very little to recommend it. Until the author provides the most basic and fundamental information outlined in the *Standards for Educational and Psychological Testing* (AERA, APA, & NCME, 1999), there are many other scales—for example, the Marital Satisfaction Inventory—Revised, (Snyder, 1998), the Dyadic Adjustment Scale (T6:843; Spanier, 1976), the ENRICH Marital Satisfaction Scale, and the Locke-Wallace Marital Adjustment Scale (Locke & Wallace, 1959)—which are widely used, well-documented, and hence highly recommended over the scale in question.

REVIEWER'S REFERENCES
American Educational Research Association, American Psychological Association, & National Council on Measurement in Education. (1999). *Standards for educational and psychological testing.* Washington, DC: American Educational Research Association.
Locke, H. J., & Wallace, K. M. (1959). Short marital adjustment and prediction tests: Their reliability and validity. *Journal of Marriage and the Family, 21,* 251–255.
Spanier, G. B. (1976). Measuring dyadic adjustment: New scales for assessing the quality of marriage and similar dyads. *Journal of Marriage and the Family, 38,* 15–28.
Snyder, D. (1998). Marital Satisfaction Inventory—Revised. Los Angeles: Western Psychological Services.

Review of the Miller Marriage Satisfaction Rating Scale by CINDY I. CARLSON, Professor of Educational Psychology, University of Texas at Austin, Austin, TX:

DESCRIPTION. The Miller Marriage Satis-faction Rating Scale (MMSRS) is a 27-item test administered by computer. Items are to be answered to indicate how much the statement is characteristic of the respondent. All items have the same four response options: a lot, moderately, somewhat, and not at all. The items form a scale that provides a single score. The score is given as a percentile rank. Respondents may place themselves within four levels of scores that range from minimal marriage satisfac-tion to high marriage satisfaction.

The measure is designed to be completed and scored on the internet: http:// www.metadevelopment.com. Results are immedi-ately available upon completion of the scale on a single-page printout. A Visa or MasterCard is re-quired to use the test. The cost of completing the test is $35.00.

DEVELOPMENT. The MMSRS was pub-lished in May 1997. The author provides no infor-mation about test development on the website. The scale is purportedly developed from theory and research on marital satisfaction; however, the theory is not specified and no references are pro-vided. Neither is information provided regarding pilot testing, test revision, internal consistency of the scale, or the characteristics of sample(s) on which the measure was tested.

The measure lacks a manual and norms. There is no guidance for the user regarding popu-lations for which the measure is appropriate be-yond couples that are dating, living together, or married. It is not clear whether the measure has been used with or would be appropriate for homo-sexual as well as heterosexual couples; nor is there any information about the applicability of the scale to ethnically and socially diverse populations.

Items are concise and clearly written. A review of the items, however, suggests that items tap at least two different perspectives of marriage. Whereas 12 items reflect characteristics of the re-spondent as a partner in the marriage and begin with the pronoun "I," the remainder refer to characteris-tics of the marriage. The response options are more appropriate for the items that reflect characteristics of the respondent as a partner in the marriage, and it is difficult to use the response options with the items that reflect marital quality. For example, the item "Neither partner is romantically involved with another person outside of the marriage" is not easily answered with a lot or moderately.

TECHNICAL. There is no information on standardization of the measure. It is impossible to determine the appropriateness of this scale for different gender, ethnic/culture, or sexual orienta-tion groups.

The author reports a test-retest reliability coefficient of .92, which is very good; however, there is no information regarding the length of time between the test-retest or the sample size. The author provides several split-half reliability coefficients, but information is inadequate to de-termine the usefulness of these values.

No data on internal consistency are provided by the author. This is viewed as a major shortcom-ing of the measure given the obvious variation in item perspective between respondent as a marital partner and the perceived quality of the marriage. Moreover, the lack of internal consistency data is inconsistent with the express purpose of the mea-sure to "permit the individual to look at different areas of their marriage." There is no indication that this measure taps different areas of marriage. Rather it purports to measure a single construct and provides no statistical support for that asser-tion. There is no reported research on the validity of scores from the MMSRS.

COMMENTARY. Strengths of the MMSRS include ease of use, readability, and relatively inex-pensive cost. Weaknesses include the lack of em-pirical support for the psychometric quality and treatment utility of this measure. There is no evidence of adequate test development, appropri-ate norms or standardization, or validity of the measure for its purported purpose.

SUMMARY. The MMSRS may be a very convenient measure for individuals or couples to use to quantify their marital satisfaction. The lack of information on test development and psycho-metric quality suggests that both therapists and researchers would be better served by utilizing marital satisfaction measures that have been more carefully developed and supported by a program of research.

[160]
Miller Motivation Scale.

Purpose: "Designed to measure positive and negative aspects of the individual's motivation."

Population: Individuals who have a grade seven reading level or greater.

Publication Dates: 1986–1988.

Scores, 8: Creative, Innovative, Productive, Cooperative, Attention, Power, Revenge, Give-Up.
Administration: Group.
Price Data, 2001: $35 per administration via webpage (Visa or MasterCard are required to use this test).
Time: (30–45) minutes.
Comments: Administered and scored on the internet; printout of results is provided. [Editor's Note: Since November 2002, the webpage for administration of this test has been unavailable.]
Author: Harold J. Miller.
Publisher: Meta Development LLC [Canada].

Review of the Miller Motivation Scale by MICHAEL J. ROSZKOWSKI, Director of Institutional Research, La Salle University, Philadelphia, PA:

DESCRIPTION. The Miller Motivation Scale (MMS), a 160-item self-report inventory measuring multiple dimensions underlying motivated behavior, is intended to foster self-understanding of the positive and negative aspects of motivation among individuals with at least a seventh grade reading level. Although no time limit is imposed, most persons reportedly complete the MMS within 30 to 45 minutes.

In addition to a web site providing an overview of the test, including its purpose, description of the population appropriate for the test, the publication date, scores produced by the test, price, time requirements, and psychometric properties, a paper manual for the Miller Motivation Scale is also available and it was provided upon request. The web site provides psychometric information through the Frequently Asked Questions section.

The respondent's task is to indicate the extent to which each one of the 160 statements in the inventory is descriptive of his or her behavior, attitudes, feelings about a situation, or reasons for a given behavior. The test taker has six available options to answer how much each statement "is like me." The anchors are phrased in terms of a scale combining degree of descriptiveness and frequency: (a) *Very much like me—I always do this or feel this way,* (b) *Mostly like—often like me,* (c) *Somewhat like me,* (d) *A little like me,* (e) *Not very much like me—I rarely do this,* and (f) *This does not apply to me—I never do this.*

The 160 items fall into eight domains, 20 items per domain, four of which are usually considered positive motivations (Creative, Innovative, Productive, Cooperative) and four that are generally viewed as negative motivations (Attention, Power, Revenge, Give-up). The constellation of thoughts and behaviors encompassed under each domain may be self-evident from the names of the scales, with the exception perhaps of the last one, but Miller does an excellent job of explaining every category and provides concrete examples of each in the paper manual. (The Give-up category is characterized by discouragement, hopelessness and ineffectiveness.)

DEVELOPMENT. These categories were selected based on a review of the literature on motivation. For each domain, four times as many items were written as were eventually retained in the final scale, which suggests that an adequate attempt was made to achieve content validity. The pool of potential items was administered to 195 students enrolled in undergraduate and graduate educational psychology courses and an item analysis was carried out. Retained items were ones that correlated at least .20 with the appropriate domain.

TECHNICAL. The Cronbach alphas (internal consistency reliability) are not reported for the eight individual domains; alphas are reported for only two composites of the eight domains. The alpha for a component made up of the four positive motivations is .87 and the alpha for the component consisting of the four negative motivations equals .77. Because the scores are interpreted and reported at the level of the eight domains, alphas should be provided for them as well.

The intercorrelations among the domains are discussed at length in the manual. An examination of the correlations between the domains shows that the negative domains correlate with the other negative domains at an average of about .60. The degree of intercorrelation among the positive motivation domains is also about .60. The correlation of the negative motivation with the positive motivation scales is markedly lower, around .19. Power is the only negative motivation scale that has substantial correlation with any of the positive motivation scales.

Test-retest reliability is reported, based on 180 education majors who were administered the scale approximately 2 months apart. These reliability coefficients range from .58 (Revenge) to .89 (Innovation), with a median of about .70 and a mean of .66. The positive motivation scales exhibit higher reliabilities than the negative motivation scales (mean correlation coefficients of .81 and .60, respectively).

Evidence regarding construct validity can be inferred from a principal components analysis. Based on the amount of variance explained by each of the eight components, the unrotated solution reported in the manual suggests the presence of two major dimensions in the MMS. It would have been helpful to have access to the rotated solution as well in order to determine how each of the eight domains loaded on these two components. Although a rotated solution is not presented in the manual, it appears that one was conducted, given that the internal consistency reliability discussed previously was based on these two components.

No data on criterion-related validity are reported. Rather, the author provides a table showing what the maximum possible validity coefficient would be if the MMS was correlated with a perfectly reliable criterion. These coefficients are simply the square root of the reliability indexes, and obviously, they cannot serve as a substitute for criterion-related evidence derived on the basis of actual empirical studies.

The MMS is not normed on the general population. Instead, the norms are based on 500 college students from five disciplines. The extent to which these individuals differ in their motivation from the population at large is unknown. Thus, one can be most confident with the results if a college student is the client who is compared to these norms. The test results are reported in a percentile rank format. The following benchmarks are offered: 50th is average, 75th is high, and 25th is low. Pattern-based interpretations are made. Thus, an individual who has average or high scores on the positive motivation domains combined with low scores on the negative motivation scales is assumed to be "functioning effectively." If the scores are equal on the positive and negative motivations, the individual is said to be "a house divided against itself." A profile in which the negative motivations are elevated while the cooperation score is low suggests a "person who needs assistance in dealing with life problems." These interpretations, and others like it, seem sound on an intuitive basis, but documentation should be provided in the manual and the Web page in support of these conclusions.

Finally, it should be noted that the psychometric data on the MMS are for a paper-and-pencil version. A variety of evolving technical and ethical issues arise when a paper-and-pencil test is adapted for use on the Internet (Barak, 1999; Buchanan & Smith, 1999; Kirby; Nickelson, 1998; Sampson, 2000; Sampson & Lumsden, 2000). Although in most instances Internet-based administration will probably not have a significant impact on results, there is the line of thought that one needs to validate a test in the medium for its intended use. If so, then reliability and validity data from Internet-based administrations would be needed.

SUMMARY. The MMS is a pioneering effort to bring legitimate psychological testing to the Internet. Too many of the "tests" currently offered on the Web are just pure "Pop Psychology," created by people who do not even have an appreciation for psychometrics. In contrast, the available data on the MMS suggest that it has a number of desirable qualities, but the database regarding its psychometric properties, especially evidence on validity needs to be expanded considerably.

REVIEWER'S REFERENCES

Barak, A. (1999). Psychological applications on the Internet: a discipline on the threshold of a new millennium. *Applied & Preventive Psychology, 8,* 231–245.

Buchanan, T. S. & Smith, J. L. (1999). Using the Internet for psychological research: Personality testing on the World Wide Web. *British Journal of Psychology, 90,* 125–144.

Nickelson, D. W. (1998). Telehealth and the evolving health care system: Strategic opportunities for professional psychology. *Professional Psychology: Research and Practice, 29,* 527–535.

Sampson, J. P., Jr. (2000). Using the Internet to enhance testing in counseling. *Journal of Counseling & Development, 78,* 348–356.

Sampson, J. P., Jr., & Lumsden, J. A. (2000). Ethical issues in the design and use of internet-based career assessment. *Journal of Career Assessment, 8,* 21–35.

[161]

Miller Psychological Independence Scale.

Purpose: Designed to "measure the individual's psychological independence in a dependent-independent continuum."

Population: High school students and athletes.

Publication Date: 1996.

Scores, 8: Independent Behavior, Independence in Relationships, Perfection, Effectiveness, Egocentric, Independent Thoughts, Independent Feelings, Control.

Administration: Group.

Price Data, 2001: $35 per administration via webpage (Visa or MasterCard are required to use this test).

Time: (30–45) minutes.

Comments: "Designed to be given on the internet"; results immediately available in a six-page printout. [Editor's Note: Since November 2002, the webpage for administration of this test has been unavailable.]

Author: Harold J. Miller.

Publisher: Meta Development LLC [Canada].

Review of the Miller Psychological Independence Scale by BRIAN F. BOLTON, University Professor of Rehabilitation Education and Research, University of Arkansas, Fayetteville, AR:

DESCRIPTION. The Miller Psychological Independence Scale (MPIS) was developed to assess the respondent's psychological independence using a framework of eight scales: Behavior, Relationship, Perfection, Effectiveness, Egocentric, Thoughts, Feelings, and Control.

The MPIS is a self-report inventory consisting of 160 items, almost all of which are simple declarative statements beginning "I am," "I think," "I believe," or with a similar phrase. The response format includes six options ranging from "Very much like me—I always do this" to "This does not apply to me—I never do this."

The MPIS is self-administered on the internet and the results are printed immediately in the form of a five-page report. The questionnaire is advertised as being appropriate for high school students and adults.

The MPIS computer report includes three sections: (a) brief descriptions of the eight scales (2 pages), (b) a presentation of the raw and percentile scores for the scales (1 page), and (c) an individualized summary describing the respondent's status on the eight scales (2 pages). Each scale summary contains 12 to 15 sentences beginning "You almost always," "You usually," "You sometimes," "You seldom," or using similar terms that indicate the degree of the trait expressed.

DEVELOPMENT. The author provides the following information about the construction of the MPIS: "The scales were developed from the theory and research proposed by theory that explores psychological independence. The resulting research indicated that group differences found from subject to subject differences were consistent with the proposed theory. These results were confirmed during counseling sessions with clients manifesting a variety of differences in subscale scores" (p. 3).

TECHNICAL. No information is provided about the MPIS norm group. Reported test/retest reliability coefficients (administration interval not indicated) for the eight scales average .85, with a range from .79 to .91. The author suggests that these are lower-bound estimates, due to a homogeneous and small sample, but no descriptive data are presented.

The square roots of the reliability coefficients are listed and referred to as "maximum possible validity coefficients" for the MPIS scales. The author states that "it is possible that very useful inferences can be made from the Miller Psychological Independence Scale" (p. 3).

The author argues that evidence for construct validity exists, based on the explanation given above in the Development section. Concerning predictive validity, the author asserts that "a large number of additional studies will be needed to determine the range of usefulness of the Miller Psychological Independence Scale for employee or student selection purposes. It seems likely that future research will prove that the Miller Psychological Independence Scale will significantly improve selection procedures for positions that require one to be psychologically independent" (p. 3).

COMMENTARY. The MPIS is seriously deficient in four major psychological assessment areas: development, norms, validity, and reporting of results. First, no information is given about the "theory and research" that supposedly established the foundation for the MPIS. What was the source of the eight scales? How were the constructs defined? How were the items selected for the scales? The vague explanation provided by the author is essentially meaningless.

Second, no information is given about the norm group, which is presumably the basis for deriving the respondent's percentile scores. How large is the normative sample? What is the composition of the norm group with respect to sex, age, and education? Without appropriate descriptive data, it is not possible to know which "high school students and adults" may properly complete the MPIS.

Third, no evidence of any kind is presented that supports the validity of scores from the MPIS. The theory or rationale for the inventory is not given (content validity), no empirical studies of the utility of the MPIS with students or employees are summarized (predictive validity), and no investigations that would help clarify the traits measured by the eight scales are referenced (construct validity). In a nutshell, the author's claims about the potential value of the MPIS are entirely unwarranted.

Fourth, the computer report is virtually worthless. The descriptions of the eight scales state that "ideal scores" are above the 75th percentile (except for Egocentric which is reversed). No justification is given for this arbitrary cutoff. The descriptions are incoherent and contain numerous grammatical errors. The individualized scale summaries consist of 12 to 15 regurgitated items, transformed from the original "I am" format to "you are," with a series of adverbs used to reflect the frequency or intensity of the respondent's choices among the options.

SUMMARY. The MPIS does not even remotely approach the minimum technical standards required for psychological instruments. There is absolutely no evidence that suggests that the MPIS measures psychological independence. The author's pronouncement that the MPIS represents "the very best in psychological testing tools" is clearly false.

[162]

Miller Self-Concept Scale.

Purpose: Designed to "measure components of the individual's self-concept."

Population: Anyone with a seventh-grade or higher reading level.

Publication Date: 1989.

Scores, 8: Intrapsychic, Family, Friendship Self-Concept, Work/School Self-Concept, Locus of Control, Attribution, Courage, Flexibility.

Administration: Group.

Price Data, 2001: $35 per administration via webpage (Visa or MasterCard are required to use this test).

Time: (30–45) minutes.

Comments: "Designed to be given and scored on the internet"; results are immediately available in a six-page printout. [Editor's Note: Since November 2002, the webpage for administration of this test has been unavailable.]

Author: Harold J. Miller.

Publisher: Meta Development LLC [Canada].

Review of the Miller Self-Concept Scale by TRENTON R. FERRO, Associate Professor of Adult and Community Education, Indiana University of Pennsylvania, Indiana, PA:

DESCRIPTION OF INSTRUMENT AND SUPPORTING MATERIALS. The Miller Self-Concept Scale, the purpose of which "is to measure components of the individual's self-concept" (Miller, 1997; all citations not otherwise referenced are to this source), is a self-reporting instrument that is available on-line. The registrant is presented with a series of 160 statements, each of

which has six possible responses from which the registrant selects one: (a) "Very much like me—I always do this or feel this way"; (b) "Mostly like—often like me"; (c) "Somewhat like me"; (d) "A little like me"; (e) "Not very much like me—I rarely do this"; (f) "This does not apply to me—I never do this."

Upon completing the instrument, a process that requires at least 45 minutes, the registrant submits the form electronically and receives quickly a computer-generated results document that (a) describes each of the eight subscales (Intrapsychic, Family, Friendship Self-Concept, Work/School Self-Concept, Locus of Control, Attribution, Courage, and Flexibility); (b) provides the total score obtained by the registrant in each of the eight categories; (c) provides the "corresponding percentile rank scores for each of this [*sic*] subscales"; (d) presents a bar chart (called a "graph" in the report) that depicts the percentile rank score of each subscale in comparison with the maximum score that one could obtain from the scale; and (e) provides descriptions, based on the registrant's own recorded responses to the 160 statements, of the registrant's self-concept, arranged according to the eight subscales.

Also available to the prospective user of the instrument is a list of frequently asked questions (FAQs) that presents an overview of the intended results for those who take the instrument and discusses psychometric properties of the Miller Self-Concept Scale, as well as of its 10 companion scales (although only an overview is available for one of the scales).

ASSESSMENT OF THE MILLER SELF-CONCEPT SCALE.

Results document. It is quite clear that the interpretative responses provided in the results document are restatements of the instrument's original statements; they have been prepared in advance and are already resident in the scoring program so that the results document can be generated immediately. This reviewer submitted three completed instruments: (a) one on which he attempted to respond to each statement honestly according to his own self-perception of his self-concept; (b) one on which he marked the response, "Very much like me—I always do this or feel this way," for all 160 statements; and (c) one on which he marked the response, "This does not apply to me—I never do this," for all 160 statements. In each case the contents of the results document reflect directly the responses selected by the reviewer. However, neither the site nor the computer-generated results document provides any assistance to the user in answering such questions as the following: What do these numbers (both raw and percentile) mean? With what group am I being compared? How homogeneous or heterogeneous is that group? How can I better understand myself as a result of taking this instrument? What do (or can) I do now that I have completed this instrument? How can I make changes in the way I am?

Documentation. Beyond the statement of purpose, no rationale is provided to help prospective users understand why they should complete this instrument. What are they to do with the feedback they receive? How can they enhance their positive characteristics and work on changing or improving those that are less positive? Further, the discussion of reliability and validity for 5 of the 11 scales included in the FAQs, including the Miller Self-Concept Scale, is nearly identical. The only differences between the documentation for the Miller Self-Concept Scale and the Miller Motivation Scale are the names of the subscales; even the coefficients are identical.

TECHNICAL. It is quite unclear for whom the FAQs are written. Professionals and researchers investigating the Miller Self-Concept Scale can question fairly the reported reliability coefficients, ranging from .69 to .84 for the eight subscales (six of them ranging from .71 to .79), and the related validity information because the actual data used to generate the reported statistics are not provided. Also lacking is any information regarding the size of the sample used for collecting data, the manner in which the sample was drawn, and the population from which the sample was drawn and to which inferences might be made. Rather, one finds expressions such as "seem reasonable," "researchers should be confident," and "it is possible that very useful inferences can be made." No mention is made of any research or theory base that might have been used as a basis for constructing the instrument. In addition, this reviewer was not able to find any additional studies that either tested this instrument or used it for collecting data.

On the other hand, if the FAQ is addressed to a more general audience, that audience will likely need more help than is provided to under-

stand how to use, for example, the Taylor-Russell Tables that are included. The use of these tables, intended for application in industrial and organizational settings, requires three important factors: "(a) the correlation between the test score and job performance, (b) the base rate of success on the job, and (c) the selection ratio" (Brannick, n. d.). These tables are of no use to individuals taking the instrument. Persons who might have reason to use the tables, assuming they already have data readily available to determine the desired level of job performance and base rate of success on the job, would still need to administer the instrument to groups of people. However, although the website claims that the scale is capable of both individual and group administration, no further information is provided on how group administration might take place; group scores are to be reported; or group scores might be shared with, and interpreted for, the group that might be taking the instrument.

SUMMARY. If the FAQs are intended for a lay audience, that group would most likely not understand the very brief statistical explanations; if for the researcher, then the information offered on the website is far too scanty. Although these statements give assurances of the trustworthiness of the scale, very few data are provided to back up those assurances.

REVIEWER'S REFERENCES

Brannick, M. T. (n. d.). *Taylor Russell Tables.* Retrieved August 4, 2002, from http://luna.cas.usf.edu/~mbrannic/files/pmet/taylor1.htm
[Miller, H.]. (1997). Miller Self-Concept Scale. Retrieved May 3, 2002, from http://www.metadevelopment.com/faq/selfconcept.html.

Review of the Miller Self-Concept Scale by JUDITH A. REIN, President, Interaction Research of Arizona, Tucson, AZ:

DESCRIPTION. The Miller Self-Concept Scale is a 160-item computer-administered and computer-scored instrument designed to measure eight components (i.e., Intrapsychic, Family, Friendship, Work/School, Locus of Control, Attribution, Courage, Flexibility) of an individual's self-concept. Scores are reported in both raw scores and percentile bands. On-line administration is available for both groups and individuals.

DEVELOPMENT. No information is provided regarding development of the scale.

TECHNICAL. Information regarding score consistency is inadequate. Test-retest (time interval not specified) coefficients for the eight subscales, each composed of 20 items, range from .69 to .84.

The sample is described only as being composed of a restricted range of individuals. Coefficient alpha is estimated to be .92; however, there is no supporting evidence.

Validation information also is inadequate and trivial. Square roots of the reliability estimates for the eight subscales, the maximum theoretically possible, but not actual validity coefficients are cited. The instrument supposedly has construct validity because the test manual states that it does, but the claims are not based on any cited theory or research. Given the facts that no evidence is provided of any predictive validity studies and no actual validity coefficients are available, the inclusion of a Taylor-Russell table is senseless.

No information about item development is provided. A list of items used in 1997 was available. Many of those items are ambiguous, double-barreled, and transparent in meaning. No indication is given if the 1997 items are currently being used. No information about the norm sample is provided.

COMMENTARY. Only weakness can be cited for this instrument. The 1999 administration charge of $5 has increased to $35. No credible information about test development, theoretical models, reliability, validity, item development, samples, pilot testing, norm groups, and scores are available. No test manual or opportunity to take the test on-line was available. [Editor's Note: An opportunity to take the test free of charge was available to reviewers but was apparently not accessible during the time this reviewer tried to do so.] In fact, information for this review came from the Frequently Asked Questions section on the metadevelopment.com website.

SUMMARY. This test is not recommended.

[163]

Miller Stress Scale.

Purpose: "Designed to measure the individual's stress in several areas of the individual's life."

Population: Anyone with reading level at or above the 7ᵗʰ grade.

Publication Date: 1992.

Scores, 8: Stressful Behavior, Relationship Stress, Family Stress, Work Stress, Physical Stress, Stressful Thoughts, Stressful Feelings, Coping.

Administration: Group.

Price Data, 2001: $35 per administration via webpage (Visa or MasterCard are required to use this test).

Time: (30–45) minutes.

Comments: "Designed to be given and scored on the internet"; results are available immediately in a six-page printout. [Editor's Note: Since November 2002, the webpage for administration of this test has been unavailable.]

Author: Harold J. Miller.

Publisher: Meta Development LLC [Canada].

Review of the Miller Stress Scale by MICHAEL J. SCHEEL, Associate Professor, Department of Educational Psychology, University of Nebraska—Lincoln, and BRAD M. MERKER, Graduate Assistant, Buros Institute of Mental Measurements, University of Nebraska—Lincoln, Lincoln, NE:

DESCRIPTION. The Miller Stress Scale is a 160-item test, administered via the internet. The purpose of the test is to "measure the individual's stress in several areas of the individual's life" (p. 1). The test is presented as appropriate for individuals with a minimum of a seventh grade reading level and has been used in the upper elementary grades and with senior adults. No specific age ranges or normative data are presented. Approximate administration time is 30–45 minutes and the test can be administered individually or in groups. Cost of the test is stated as $35 per use and a Visa or MasterCard is required. Test results are immediately available after administration, producing a six-page printout. The form of the report of results was not described in the very brief description of the instrument made available by the test developer for this review.

Individuals completing the test are required to indicate the degree to which a statement is like them using a 6-point Likert-type scale ranging from *very much like me—I always do this or feel this way* to *this does not apply to me—I never do this.* Scores are provided as raw scores and percentiles on eight subscales. The results are "provided in a six page printout" (p. 1). However, at the time of writing this review the test developers webpage and the Miller Stress Scale could no longer be located at the stated web address.

The eight subscales are: Stressful Behavior, Relationship Stress, Family Stress, Work Stress, Physical Stress, Stressful Thoughts, Stressful Feelings, and Coping. No rationale is given for the eight scales that comprise the instrument, and the basis for the item construction within each subscale was also not available. No link was provided in the test manual to the existing literature base on stress, leading one to surmise that there is no empirical or theoretical basis for the subscales.

DEVELOPMENT. Harold J. Miller completed the development of the Miller Stress Scale in July 1992. It is one of nine tests developed by Miller and reported to be available on his website. No information is provided defining the constructs, item development, or test construction. Each subscale is reported to contain 20 items. Several items appear to be measuring other constructs. For example, "I feel panic" (Item 3), more likely measures anxiety, whereas other items appear unrelated to stress at all (e.g., Item 35: "I am mixed up"). The developer cites no references to current research in the area of stress and a search of the PsychInfo database reveals no studies incorporating the Miller Stress Scale.

TECHNICAL. No standardization or normative data are available for the Miller Stress Scale. A reference is made to the use of a "restricted range of individuals" (p. 2) in the sample. No demographic information is provided on this sample. Limited reliability information is provided in the form of test-retest reliability and coefficient alpha. Test-retest reliability over an unspecified time frame ranged from .79 to .91, suggesting that individual subscale scores are relatively consistent over time. A coefficient alpha of .94 is provided as another measure of reliability. The test developer notes that coefficient alpha "may be thought of as the mean of all possible split-half reliability coefficients" (p. 2) and that test users and researchers should be confident in the reliability of the Miller Stress Scale. However, no basis is provided in the test manual for making a judgment about reliability specific to the Miller Stress Scale.

Evidence to support the validity of this instrument is significantly lacking. Only broad, general statements that can be derived from any measurement text are provided as a rationale for validity of the Miller Stress Scale. The test developer attempts to provide construct validity evidence by stating that the "scales were developed from theory and research proposed by stress theorists" (p. 3). However, no further information is provided on this research or the identity of the stress theorists. There is mention of predictive validity and the test developer states "a large number of additional studies will be needed to determine the range of usefulness of the Miller Stress Scale" (p. 3). Specific reference is made to using the Miller Stress Scale as a measure of client change and for research purposes. Yet no information is provided on how one should go about incorporating the

scale in clinical practice. Finally, Taylor-Russell tables are provided with a statement relating to the test's benefit for employee selection. No information, rationale, or means for interpreting these tables is provided.

In summary, no evidence of validity was presented specific to the Miller Stress Scale. Such evidence would require data and analysis of data from validity studies involving the instrument or at the very least, references to citations of investigations of validity. What is presented in the test manual is nonspecific to the Miller Stress Scale and irrelevant to the question of the validity of the instrument.

COMMENTARY. The Miller Stress Scale is purported to be a measure of individual stress. It is severely compromised on a number of levels. First, no information is provided on the underlying construct. Second, normative information is significantly lacking, and third, a paucity of reliability and validity information exists. The usefulness of the Miller Stress Scale for clinical purposes cannot be recommended at this time. Further conceptualization and research on the test is needed. Construct validity evidence has not been provided and would require minimally a definition of the construct based on the existing theoretical and empirical work on stress. The instrument would also benefit from item analysis and factor analysis to clearly understand the nature of the relationship among subscales. Criterion validity and convergent validity evidence is needed to enhance the test user's confidence in this test.

SUMMARY. The Miller Stress Scale is an individually or group administered web-based test stated to be appropriate for individuals with at least a seventh grade reading level. The test consists of 160 items measuring eight stress-related domains. Approximate administration time is 30-45 minutes at a cost of $35 per administration. Test takers are provided a six-page printout listing raw scores and percentile scores. Extremely limited reliability and no validity evidence specific to the instrument are provided. More work must be done on this instrument to establish its credibility as a psychological tool to measure individual stress.

[164]

Millon Behavioral Medicine Diagnostic.

Purpose: Designed to "assess psychological factors that can influence the course of treatment of medically ill patients … especially for patients in which psychosocial factors may play a role in the course of the disease and treatment outcome."

Population: Clinical and rehabilitation patients ages 18–85.

Publication Date: 2001.

Acronym: MBMD.

Scores, 39: Validity Indicator, Response Patterns (Disclosure, Desirability, Debasement), Negative Health Habits (Alcohol, Drug, Eating, Caffeine, Inactivity, Smoking), Psychiatric Indications (Anxiety-Tension, Depression, Cognitive Dysfunction, Emotional Lability, Guardedness), Coping Styles (Introversive, Inhibited, Dejected, Cooperative, Sociable, Confident, Nonconforming, Forceful, Respectful, Oppositional, Denigrated), Stress Moderators (Illness Apprehension, Functional Deficits, Pain Sensitivity, Social Isolation, Future Pessimism, Spiritual Absence), Treatment Prognostics (Interventional Fragility, Medication Abuse, Information Discomfort, Utilization Excess, Problematic Compliance), Management Guides (Adjustment Difficulties, Psych Referral).

Administration: Individual or group.

Price Data, 2002: $298 per hand-scoring starter kit including manual (183 pages), hand-scoring user's guide, 10 test booklets, 50 answer sheets, 50 worksheets, and 50 profile forms and answer keys; $28 per 10 hand-scoring test booklets (English or Hispanic); $100 per MICROTEST Q Assessment System Software starter kit with Interpretive Reports including manual and answer sheets with test items and all materials necessary to conduct 3 assessments and receive interpretive reports using assessment system software; $19 per 25 software answer sheets including test items (English or Hispanic); $22.95 per software interpretive report; $15 per software profile report; $100 per mail-in scoring service starter kit with Interpretive Reports including manual and answer sheets with test items and all materials necessary to conduct 3 assessments and receive interpretive reports using mail-in scoring service; $24.95 per mail-in interpretive report (test items and answer sheets included) (English or Hispanic); $17 per mail-in profile reports (test items and answer sheets included) (English or Hispanic); $48 per manual; $60 per audio-cassette (English or Hispanic); $19 per 25 large print answer sheets; quantity discounts available.

Time: (20–25) minutes.

Comments: Available in Spanish and in large-print paper-and-pencil version; upgrading of the Millon Behavioral Health Inventory (T5:1686); self-administered; may be administered in paper-and pencil format, online, or via audiocassette; interpretive reports with healthcare provider summary and profile available; scoring options include handscoring, mail-in, MICROTEST Q Assessment System software.

Authors: Theodore Millon, Michael Antoni, Carrie Millon, Sarah Meagher, and Seth Grossman.

Publisher: NCS Assessments [Minnetonka].

Cross References: For information regarding the original Millon Behavioral Health Inventory, see T5:1686 (7 references) and T4:1634 (6 references); for reviews of the Millon Behavioral Health Inventory by Mary J. Allen and Richard I. Lanyon, see 9:708 (1 reference).

Review of the Millon Behavioral Medicine Diagnostic by MARK J. ATKINSON, Adjunct Associate Professor, Department of Psychiatry, University of Calgary, Calgary, Alberta, Canada:

DESCRIPTION. The Millon Behavioral Medicine Diagnostic (MBMD) is based on one of the most frequently used health inventories in the United States, the Millon Behavioral Health Inventory (MBHI) (developed between 1974 and 1983). The MBMD is a 165-item self-report inventory composed of 29 clinical scales, three Response Patterns scales, one validity indicator, and six Negative Health Habits indicator scales. It is designed to assess psychological and behavioral factors that influence the course of treatment of medically ill adult patients. The MBMD provides clinicians with information regarding patients' negative health habits, psychiatric status, illness-related coping styles, stress moderators, treatment prognostics, and other potentially problematic psychosocial behaviors and attitudes. The instrument is not intended to suggest medical diagnoses, but rather to provide tentative working hypotheses of a psychosocial nature. Its use is restricted to professionals specializing in the delivery of healthcare services, or students under the supervision of qualified professionals.

The specific domains tapped by the MBMD include the assessments of Response Patterns (Disclosure, Desirability, and Debasement), Negative Health Habits (Alcohol, Drugs, Eating, Caffeine, Inactivity, and Smoking), Psychiatric Indications (Anxiety-Tension, Depression, Cognitive Dysfunction, Emotional Lability, and Guardedness), Coping Styles (Introversive, Inhibited, Dejected, Cooperative, Sociable, Confident, Nonconforming, Forceful, Respectful, Oppositional, and Denigrating), Stress Moderators (Spiritual Absence, Illness Apprehension, Functional Deficits, Pain Sensitivity, Social Isolation, and Future Pessimism), Treatment Prognostics (Interventional Fragility, Medication Abuse, Information Discomfort, Utilization Excess, and Problematic Compliance), and Management Guides (Adjustment Difficulties and Psychiatric/Psychosocial Referral).

A clinically useful Interpretive Report, the Healthcare Provider Summary, includes a one-page narrative review with a single-page tear-off for quick reference. Two computer-generated MBMD reports, a Profile Report and an Interpretive Report, are also available, and provide summary information on Patient's Psychiatric Status, Coping Style, Stress Moderators, Treatment Prognosis, and Management Guides scales.

DEVELOPMENT. The primary goal was to enhance the MBHI by including measures of health-relevant attitudes, behaviors, and concerns of patients in clinical, outpatient, and inpatient settings that were not included in the earlier version. The specific objectives of redevelopment of the MBHI were: (a) to expand the relevance of the instrument to new patient populations and clinical settings (including HIV/AIDS, organ transplant, long-term diabetes, neurologic disorders, oncology, gastroenterology, and HMO and VA programs); (b) to build on the advances made in the understanding of psychological factors affecting medical conditions; (c) to expand and add scales that identify and correct for patient distortion of their problems; and (d) to improve the summary of assessment findings and treatment recommendations within Interpretive Reports.

New items (*n* = 800) were drafted based on a series of surveys and consultations with various groups of health professionals. Items that were conceptually complex, likely to elicit biased responses, or that resulted in poor performance were removed. The remaining pool of items was given to eight health psychologists to classify into the conceptual domains of the MBMD. Items that were correctly classified by a majority of raters were retained, leaving approximately 350 items. After several pilot studies, the number of items that were used to make up the Research Form was further reduced to 299 that were used to make up the Research Form. The Research Form was then administered to over 200 patients stratified by age, gender, and disease state. Results were used to remove those items with excessive ceiling/floor effects or items with low correlation with other items on the particular scale. This resulted in a final set of 165 items. A factor analysis of scale scores of 720 individuals resulted in a five-factor solution that explained 78.7% of the total variance and produced a factor structure that is consistent with the theoretical and conceptual basis of the instrument.

TECHNICAL.

Standardization. The MBMD was standardized using a moderate sized norming sample of patients (n = 720) across six major illness groups (cancer, cardiology, diabetes, HIV, neurology, and pain). The racial mix provided a good representation of African American (16%), Hispanic (19%), and White (61%) respondents. Due to the naturally occurring skew in clinical data, the instrument does not rely on normalized T-scores, but rather Prevalence Scores (PS) that identify the presence of a disorder rather than the position of an individual on a normal curve distribution. An estimation of clinical prevalence of the disorder measured by each scale was gathered from a number of clinicians—this was used to set two PS cutscores for each scale, resulting in three levels for each disorder/characteristic (absent, present, and prominent).

Reliability. The Cronbach's alpha coefficients for most scales were good (.74–.89). Lower coefficients were found on about half of the Coping Style scales (.54–.67), but it should be noted that this is typical for measures that assess complex behavior tendencies. Test-retest coefficients using 7- to 30-day intervals were moderate to strong for every scale (.71–.92, with a median of .83). Only one scale out of 27, Information Discomfort, appeared to lack conceptual coherence (Cronbach's alpha = .47).

Validity. Construct validity for each of the MBMD scales has been examined using similar scales of other measurement devices with well-established validity. The convergent correlations between MBMD scales and standard measures were nearly always moderate to high (.50–.87), with the exception of Problematic Compliance (.38) or Utilization Excess (.39–.52). The authors suggest that the reason for poorer performance on these two dimensions is that patient behavior is causally complex and varies greatly across individuals.

The MBMD manual presents the results from various studies addressing issues of concurrent and predictive validity of MBMD scales. A body of evidence is presented in the manual that the MBMD is able to predict patients' help-seeking behavior, differences in the progression of early neoplastic changes, psychological reactions to news of a life-threatening medical illness and psychological adjustment to chronic disease, ability to make healthy life-style changes, medical adherence, immune mediated changes in the progression of disease, and rate of surgical recovery. For example: cardiac patients classified as belonging to the Angry-Moody and Anxious-Irritable groups by the MBMD have been shown to take significantly longer to seek medical attention following an initial coronary event than those in the Dependent-Agreeable or Confident-Outgoing groups. Significant differences were found between the survival curves of cardiac transplant patients who were more inhibited, more emotionally sensitive, less social, and less respectful compared to those who were not. Moreover, negative stressful life events and psychological outlook have been shown to predict significantly poorer health outcomes later in time among persons with diseases in which illness trajectory is associated with immune function (i.e., cervical neoplasia, HIV, and transplant recovery).

COMMENTARY. The MBMD is one of the first instruments designed for use in healthcare that offers a broad assessment across psychiatric indications, coping styles, psychological dispositions, lifestyle behaviors, and communication styles. The broad basis for the measure offers clinical researchers a unique opportunity to advance understanding of the psychosocial determinants of healthcare outcomes. Overall, the psychometric characteristics of the scales are strong, with only a couple of exceptions (Problematic Compliance and Excess Service Utilization).

Of note, the research evidence provided to support the validity of the MBMD scales often involved quite specific examples of findings from uniquely vulnerable populations; such findings may overstate scale performance. For example, the relationships observed among immunologically challenged or deficient patients may be relatively unimportant to disease progression among persons in other illness populations. Clearly, more research is warranted using the MBMD to understand the complex biological and psychosocial mechanisms of disease states that underlie such observations.

A further concern is regarding the clinical cutscores. Clinicians and clinical researchers using the MBMD should note that the PS levels for any scale are likely to differ across patient populations. However, the Prevalence Score Transformation Tables do not take such differences into account, and specific PS tables for different patient populations have yet to be established. Steps should be taken to assure that the cutscores on any scale correspond to

the prevalence of the disorders or problems among the patient population being treated.

SUMMARY. The MBMD is a novel and well-designed instrument. It possesses both the scope and the psychometric characteristics needed to help advance our understanding of the complex interplay of physiological and psychosocial factors that contribute to the progression, treatment, and management of disease. Moreover, individual Profile Reports provide useful patient information that has the potential to enhance clinical care. The manual and testing materials are very well organized and present a convenient synthesis of over 25 years of research in the field of behavioral health psychology.

Review of the Millon Behavioral Medicine Diagnostic by JOHN C. CARUSO, Assistant Professor of Psychology, University of Montana, Missoula, MT:

DESCRIPTION. The Millon Behavioral Medicine Diagnostic test (MBMD) is a new 165-item (true/false) self-report questionnaire that replaces the Millon Behavioral Health Inventory (MBHI; Millon, Green, & Meagher, 1979). The MBMD provides a variety of scores relevant to the treatment of medical problems. Thirty-nine scales are included covering the domains of Response Patterns (score validity), Psychiatric Indications, Coping Styles, Stress Moderators, Treatment Prognostics, Management Guides, and Negative Health Habits. Intended for use with individuals able to read at the sixth grade level or above, the MBMD takes about 20–25 minutes to complete. The manual is detailed, comprehensive, and quite helpful in understanding the potential utility of the scale. Computer scoring and automated interpretive reports are available from the test publisher.

The MBMD, like the MBHI, was designed for use in medical settings. To facilitate holistic treatment, the MBMD "is designed to provide the critical psychological information doctors need to treat the whole patient" (manual, p. 1). Medical Practitioners who subscribe to such a philosophy may find the MBMD invaluable. There is no shortage of empirical evidence that psychological functioning can affect medical outcomes, and the MBMD allows doctors and other medical workers to integrate these findings into their work.

DEVELOPMENT. The development of the MBMD progressed through three phases: theoretical-substantive, internal-structural, and external-criterion. The theoretical-substantive phase guided item and scale development and was based largely on the work of Millon (1981, 1990), and the input from medical practitioners on the limitations of the MBHI. Over 800 items were initially developed and screened. The internal structural phases consisted of reliability and factor analyses, the results of which are described below. The external-criterion phase consisted of several small sample studies of the validity of the scores in terms of their ability to predict relevant external criteria (e.g., medical procedure outcomes).

One of the primary purposes for the development of the MBMD was to establish relevant normative data for a purely medical population (the MBHI normative sample was a mixed clinical/nonclinical group). The MBMD normative sample consisted of 720 individuals with a variety of medical conditions including cancer (16%), cardiology (11%), diabetes (16%), HIV (10%), neurological (17%), pain (9%), and "other" (20%). The normative sample closely matched census values for marital status and educational level but was, in general, older than the general population (as medical patients tend to be). Additionally, Hispanics and African Americans are somewhat overrepresented (compared to census values) because much of the normative data were gathered at university medical settings and public clinics rather than private practice sites.

TECHNICAL. The reliabilities of scores from the clinical (29) and response pattern (3) scales of the MBMD are highly variable. Scales from the stress moderation domain (Illness Apprehension, Functional Deficits, Pain Sensitivity, Social Isolation, Future Pessimism, and Spiritual Absence) all produced internal consistency (coefficient alpha) reliabilities and estimates greater than or equal to .85 in the normative sample. The psychiatric indications domain also produced reliable scores in the normative sample, with all 5 scales (Anxiety-Tension, Depression, Cognitive Dysfunction, Emotional Lability, and Guardedness) having alpha coefficients greater than .75. On the other end of the continuum is the prognostics domain that produced 2 scales with acceptably reliable scores (Interventional Fragility [.80] and Utilization Excess [.76]) and 3 scales for which scores were not sufficiently reliable (Medication Abuse [.65], Information Discomfort [.47], and Problematic

Compliance [.62]). In all, scores on 8 of the 32 clinical and response pattern scales had reliability estimates less than or equal to .65 (Disclosure, Desirability, Sociable, Confident, Respectful, Medication Abuse, Information Discomfort, and Problematic Compliance). Some of these 8 constructs (e.g., Desirability) have alternatives with better psychometric properties (i.e., the Marlow-Crowne Social Desirability Scale; Crowne & Marlow, 1960) whereas others (e.g., Interventional Fragility) do not. In the former case, it is recommended that the alternatives be used. In the latter case, practitioners have little choice but to avoid interpretation of the scores and interpret them cautiously when necessary. Test-retest estimates of reliability (intervals ranging between 7 and 30 days) were more encouraging, with a range of .71 to .92 for scores from the 32 clinical and response pattern scales in the normative sample. This is not contradictory because internal consistency and test-retest procedures incorporate error from different sources (i.e., coefficient alpha assesses item sampling consistency whereas test-retest correlations assess occasion sampling consistency). The bottom line is that we can be more confident that the scores will remain consistent over time than we can be confident that the items that compose each scale each assess the same construct.

The test authors did not perform item-level factor analyses, which may partially explain the low internal consistency reliability of scores for several of the scales. This is understandable because the inclusion of 165 items in the scale requires an enormous sample to have a reasonable chance of the emergence of a stable factor structure. Results of factor analyses of the 29 clinical scales (excluding the Response Pattern and Negative Health Habits domains), using the normative sample and employing principal component extraction with a varimax rotation, produced an interpretable five-factor structure, but there was little match between the factors and the a priori groupings of scales into the five clinical domains. This is not particularly surprising or problematic because of the nature of the measure: For example, a factor labeled "disregard for the customs of social compliance" consisted of (among other things) a high positive loading for the Problematic Compliance scale of the Treatment Prognostics domain and a high negative loading for the Respectful scale of the Coping Styles domain, a result that is consistent with expectations. The domains were devised to represent different types of information, not different constructs, making the lack of match between the factor analytic results and the domain groupings acceptable.

Many of the scales on the MBMD are holdovers from the MBHI with minor modifications and, as such, much of the existing validation work is still relevant. Various comparisons with other questionnaires (e.g., Beck Depression Inventory, State-Trait Anxiety Inventory, Profile of Mood States) have yielded evidence of the concurrent validity of scores on several of the scales. Predictive validity studies have shown scores on various scales to be valid for predicting likelihood of seeking treatment, reactions to new medical diagnoses, disease adaptations, chronic disease adaptations, and the course of physical disease (e.g., complications, infections, etc.). Nevertheless, several of the scales of the MBMD are substantially revised or entirely new and have not yet been sufficiently justified or validated.

COMMENTARY. The MBMD is an attractive device for those who work in medical settings and wish to expand their assessment to include psychological constructs that may impact treatment options and outcomes. The increased attention this affords medically relevant psychological constructs promotes a holistic treatment process. The MBMD is an improvement over the MBHI in terms of the comprehensiveness with which psychological variables relevant to the treatment and outcome of medical problems are surveyed. In addition to utility in medical practice, researchers who focus on the relationship between psychological constructs such as coping and medical outcomes should find the MBMD useful.

SUMMARY. The MBMD is a well-developed battery with sufficient evidence of validity to be recommended for routine use in medical settings. Scores form some of the scales have questionable reliability, however, and this necessarily limits their validity. Fortunately, it appears that scores from the scales of the Stress Moderation and Psychiatric Indications domains are the most reliable, and these are probably the most important scales for most purposes. Perhaps the most attractive property of the MBMD is the breadth of the constructs assessed, a property that is not matched by any other inventory of its type. Medical practitioners are likely to increase the attention

they pay to psychological functioning in an effort to treat the "whole patient," and the MBMD should assist them in doing so.

REVIEWER'S REFERENCES

Crowne, D. P., & Marlow, D. (1960). A new scale for social desirability independent of psychopathology. *Journal of Consulting Psychology, 24,* 349–354.
Millon, T. (1981). *Disorders of personality: DSM-III Axis II.* New York: Wiley.
Millon, T. (1990). *Toward a new personology.* New York: John Wiley.
Millon, T., Green, C. J., & Meagher, R. B. (1979). The MBHI: A new inventory for the psychodiagnostician in medical settings. *Professional Psychology: Research and Practice, 10,* 529–539.

[165]

Mini Inventory of Right Brain Injury, Second Edition.

Purpose: Designed for "screening neurocognitive deficits associated with right hemisphere lesions."
Population: Ages 20–80.
Publication Dates: 1989–2000.
Acronym: MIRBI-2.
Scores, 10: Visual Scanning, Integrity of Gnosis, Integrity of Body Image, Visuoverbal Processing, Visuosymbolic Processing, Integrity of Visuomotor Praxis, Higher-Level Language Skills, Expressing Emotion, General Affect, General Behavior.
Administration: Individual.
Price Data, 2003: $138 per complete kit; $30 per examiner record booklets; $30 per response forms; $15 per response sheets; $15 per caliper; $56 per manual (2000, 58 pages).
Time: (15–30) minutes.
Authors: Patricia A. Pimental and Jeffrey A. Knight.
Publisher: PRO-ED.
Cross References: For reviews by R. A. Bornstein and by John E. Obrzut and Carol A. Boliek, see 11:242.

Review of the Mini Inventory of Right Brain Injury, Second Edition by DANIEL C. MILLER, Professor, Texas Woman's University, Denton, TX:

DESCRIPTION. The Mini Inventory of Right Brain Injury, Second Edition (MIRBI-2) was designed to screen for right-hemisphere dysfunction in English-speaking adults between the ages of 20 and 80. The authors state in the examiner's manual that the test was developed to serve five purposes: (a) to identify adults who exhibit neurocognitive deficits consistent with known right-hemisphere brain injury; (b) to determine relative severity of changes in neurocognitive processing as a result of the right-brain injury; (c) to identify specific deficit areas according to a classification system developed by Pimental (1987a, 1987b, 1987c); (d) to describe a pattern of strengths and weaknesses that can be used in treatment planning, and (e) to serve as a research tool investigating right-hemisphere brain injuries. Pimental's classification system seeks to categorize all combinations of right-hemisphere dysfunction into seven subsyndromes: disorders of visual processing, disorders of appositional language processing, disorders of general behavior and psychic integrity, disorders of memory processing, disorders of orientation, disorders of emotion and affect, and patterns of disorientation, and disorders of nonverbal processing.

The MIRBI-2 is individually administered and takes less than 30 minutes to administer. "The test consists of 27 items distributed across 10 diagnostic subsections from four general functional domains: (a) Visuoperceptual/Visuospatial and Attentional Processing, (b) Lexical Knowledge Processing, (c) Affective Processing, and (d) General Behavioral Processing" (examiner's manual, p. 6). The instrument also provides a Right-Left Differentiation subscale score, based on 10 items that were shown to discriminate between right- and left-brain-injured patients.

The MIRBI-2 includes an examiner's manual, a set of examiner record booklets, a set of report forms for communicating results, a set of examinee response sheets, and a caliper used for one of the test items. The MIRBI-2 generates a total raw score that is the sum of all 27 items. The manual provides norm tables that convert the total raw score into percentile and stanine scores. A severity index classification is provided on the examiner record booklet that is based on the range of the stanine or percentile scores. The severity index ranges from profound to normal across seven possible categories. Only the total test score yields standardized test scores. The four functional domains and the 10 subsections are summarized based on the percentage correct only and offer no normative comparisons.

DEVELOPMENT. The MIRBI-2 examiner's manual provides a clear review of the development of the pilot version, first edition, and the current second edition of the test. The pilot version of the test contained 63 items. The pilot version was administered to 50 patients with diagnosed right-brain injury across 18 sites. Twenty-seven items were selected from the original pool of 63 that discriminated well the symptoms associated with right hemispheric brain injuries. The first edition of the MIRBI was published in 1989. The MIRBI was standardized on 80 right-brain-injured adults

with additional validity data collected on 13 left-brain-injured patients and 30 normal individuals.
TECHNICAL.

Standardization. The MIRBI-2 was standardized on a sample of 128 right-brain-injured patients drawn from 17 states. Additional validity data were collected from 45 left-brain-injured patients and 78 normal individuals free from any neurological condition. The standardization sample approximates 1997 U.S. Census data in terms of gender and ethnic distributions. Efforts were made to balance patients with known right- and left-brain injuries across 10-year age ranges. The test administration instructions are clear and concise and the record forms are well constructed for ease of use.

Reliability. The coefficient alpha for the MIRBI-2 was .84, which indicates a high degree of internal consistency among the test items. The interrater reliability was calculated using a limited sample of four examiners who independently scored eight patients' MIRBI-2 tests. The total scores were correlated between raters and yielded a coefficient of .98 for the raw scores. One of the major weaknesses of the MIRBI-2 was the lack of test-retest reliability data. From the manual it is possible to conclude that the internal consistency of the test is good but the stability of the test scores over time is unknown.

Validity. The authors have included strong evidence of the validity of the test's scores in the examiner's manual. Discrimination coefficients, which examine the test's content validity, ranged from .37 to .81 across all items. Concurrent validity results looked promising with the MIRBI-2 correlating with other known measures of right-hemispheric functions (e.g., WAIR-R Performance IQ, .78; WMS-R Visual Memory Index, .72; Stroop Color-Word Task, .82). The construct-identification validity was examined by determining how well the MIRBI-2 differentiated between right- and left-brain-injured individuals. The authors reported that "the right brain-injured group scored approximately two standard deviations below the normal control group, and approximately one standard deviation below the left brain-injured group" (examiner's manual, pp. 30–31). Several factor analyses conducted by the authors produced a four-factor solution to the MIRBI-2 (visuoperceptual/visuospatial and attentional processing, lexical knowledge processing, affective processing, and general behavioral processing).

COMMENTARY. The authors have attempted to address some prior test reviewer concerns about the first version of the test in the second edition of the MIRBI. The clinical utility of the test would be strengthened if the four functional domain scores and the individual subtests provided standardized scores rather than just percentages. The standardization sample of the test is strong. The authors have provided good evidence of the validity and internal consistency, but the stability of the test scores was not reported.

SUMMARY. The MIRBI-2 appears to be a useful test for evaluating adults with known or suspected right-hemispheric brain injuries. The total test score and the Right-Left Differentiation subscale score are the most clinically useful scores from the test. The subtest and functional domain scores are not reported as standard scores and the stability of the test scores is unknown.

REVIEWER'S REFERENCES

Pimental, P. A. (1987a, October). *Deficit patterns and lesion site in right brain injured subjects.* Paper presented at the annual meeting of the National Academy of Neuropsychology, Chicago.
Pimental, P. A. (1987b). *The Mini Inventory of Right Brain Injury (MIRBI): Development and standardization of right hemisphere brain injury.* Unpublished dissertation. The Chicago School of Professional Psychology.
Pimental, P. A. (1987c, October). *The MIRBI revisited: The first standardized right brain injury screening.* Paper presented at the annual meeting of the National Academy of Neuropsychology, Chicago.

Review of the Mini Inventory of Right Brain Injury, Second Edition by DAVID SHUM, Senior Lecturer of Psychology, Griffith University, Brisbane, Australia:

DESCRIPTION. The second edition of the Mini Inventory of Right Brain Injury (MIRBI-2) is a 27-item screening test. The uses of the test are: (a) to identify individuals with cognitive deficits associated with right-brain injury; (b) to determine the severity of such deficits; (c) to determine specific areas of deficits; (d) to describe strengths and weaknesses in right-brain functions; and (e) to use in research.

The MIRBI-2 is suitable for individuals aged between 20 and 80 years. It comes with an examiner's manual, an examiner record booklet, a report form, a response sheet, and a pair of calipers (for administering a two-point discrimination item). A quarter (for administering a stereognosis item), a pencil, and a piece of blank paper are also needed for administration. The MIBRI-2 can be administered and scored by most health professionals. Interpretation of test results, however, should be conducted by professionals with advanced and extensive training.

The 27 items of the MIRBI-2 should be administered in the given order and takes 15 to 30 minutes. The test items are organized according to four functional domains: (a) Visuoperceptual/Visuospatial and Attentional Processing; (b) Lexical Knowledge Processing; (c) Affective Processing; and (d) General Behavioral Processing.

All test items are scored as correct, partially correct, or incorrect depending on the point value of the item. The total raw score ranges from 0 to 43. An obtained raw score can be converted into a percentile rank and a stanine score using a norm table. These transformed scores can then be used to determine the severity of injury using a seven-category profile (ranging from profound to normal) on the record form. The raw score of an examinee can also be summarized according to the four functional domains and the Right-Left Differentiation subscale (cutoff score = 7) but norms for these scores are not available.

DEVELOPMENT. Pimental and Kingsbury developed the first edition of the MIRBI because they determined that there were no commercially available standardized instruments designed solely for screening right-brain injury. The MIRBI was based on a seven-component right-hemisphere syndrome classification system developed by Pimental.

A pool of 63 items were originally constructed based on theory and findings in the literature and 27 items were retained based on performances of a group of 50 patients with right-brain injury. The items retained were the ones failed by 50% to 100% of the patients. The same 27 items were used in the MIRBI-2 and the authors of the second edition (Pimental & Knight) justified their retention by the results of an item analysis (item-total correlation) using 128 patients with right-brain injury, 45 patients with left-brain injury, and 78 normal individuals.

A number of changes have been made to the MIRBI-2. First, the size of the standardized sample has increased from 30 to 128 patients with right-brain injury, 13 to 45 patients with left-brain injury, and 30 to 78 normal individuals. Second, a pair of calipers was included in the test to ensure standardized administration of a two-point discrimination item. Third, the manual and record form were revised to include more detailed and objective criteria for scoring responses. Fourth, a separate response sheet is used for administering

DEVELOPMENT. There is no information provided on the development of the MMSE in the User's Guide.

TECHNICAL. A comprehensive review of studies of the MMSE found test-retest reliabilities ranging from .80 to .95 (interval not reported in User's Guide) One statistic often computed to assess the validity of scores from diagnostic tests and exams like the MMSE has been what is termed "sensitivity," the percentage of participants who have a clinically diagnosed medical problem that receive a positive test result (score of 23 or lower on the MMSE.) For the MMSE, these percentages were found to be at least 87% based upon a 1992 review of literature published in the *Journal of the American Geriatrics Society*. Another method of reporting validity is in terms of positive predictive values, the percentage of those with a positive test result who are then found to have a clinically diagnosed cognitive impairment. These percentages were found to be at least 79%. The complement of sensitivity is the false negative rate, which would be at most 13%.

COMMENTARY. The MMSE has been in existence for over 25 years. In that time, it has become a very widely used screening exam for determining if there is reason to believe an individual has a cognitive impairment. The MMSE enables the level of impairment to be quantified. Its brevity and ease of administration as well as its relatively high reliability, sensitivity and positive predictive value combine to make it a very valuable tool for establishing the level of cognitive impairment and determining if further diagnostic testing is needed.

The MMSE has normative data reported according to the maximum education attained and age of the person being evaluated. This helps to provide a better context for interpreting the results than would be the case in applying the universal cutscore of 23 indiscriminately. It has been translated into over 100 languages, although the translations have not been as extensively validated as the English version.

One of the problems in reviewing a test that measures mental status is that it creates insecurities in the reviewer. One gets the feeling that some mornings, especially before the morning coffee, one could qualify as fairly cognitively impaired. The Orientation to Time section asks the examinee for the year, season, month of the year, day of the week, and date. The Orientation to Place asks

the examinee for the state, county, city/town, building, and floor of the building. There are times when one's orientation to time can get lost in the press of things to do. Because the MMSE is undoubtedly used frequently to assess the elderly, it is doubtful that orientation to time gets any better for people when they retire and do not have the demands of work to keep them attuned to the day of the week, etc. Regarding the orientation to place, after traveling for a while, particularly if there are multiple stops, it can be a challenge to figure out where one is for a while. This highlights why it is important for the examiner to be qualified in order to sort out whether the examinee is suffering a cognitive impairment, jet-lag, or is in a pre-coffee coma.

Although there is really little to criticize about the MMSE itself and the research supporting its use, there are things about the User's Guide that could be improved. The instructions for examiners are quite detailed and provide good guidance for atypical examinee responses; however, there is no information about how the instrument was developed and information on the reliability and validity is given with insufficient detail to evaluate their merits.

The lack of any information whatsoever in the User's Guide about how the MMSE was developed is a major omission. Although the test-retest reliabilities are impressive, it would be helpful to report internal consistency reliability estimates to determine to what extent the different tasks provide a cohesive total score. Similarly, factor analysis data would help define the internal structure of the instrument.

Although the test-retest and validity coefficients were impressive, it would be helpful to have a more detailed description of how the reliability and validity values were obtained from at least one of the major studies discussed in the review article. One of the major challenges in computing validity percentages such as sensitivity and positive predictive value is in defining what a "true state" is for the examinee. This often involves giving the assessment to patients who have been diagnosed with a medical problem after receiving a full complement of diagnostic procedures. It helps in interpreting the validity data to know how the true state was established.

Also, when reporting specificity (percentage of examinees who have no clinically determined evidence of cognitive impairment who test negative on the MMSE) and negative predictive values (percentage of those testing negative on the MMSE who have no clinically determined cognitive impairment), they are not reported as numerical values but are referred to descriptively as "moderate-to-high" (User's Guide, p. 10). This is not a very informative description of these statistics. Numerical ranges similar to those reported for sensitivity and positive predictive value would be more informative. Because the false positive rate is the complement of specificity, having numerical values for this index would be especially beneficial.

A final point worth mentioning is that the authors recommend classifying the results into four categories: normal, mild, moderate, and severe cognitive impairment. They present no data to support the validity of these cutoff points. It is not clear what the rate of errors of classification might be. Thus, although this may be a very reliable and valid method of classification, there are neither data nor references in the User's Guide to indicate that this is so.

SUMMARY. The MMSE is a very widely used screening exam for determining if there is reason to believe an individual has a cognitive impairment. The MMSE enables the level of impairment to be quantified. Its brevity and ease of administration as well as its relatively high reliability, sensitivity, and positive predictive value combine to make it a very valuable tool for establishing the level of cognitive impairment and determining if further diagnostic testing is needed. The instructions for examiners are quite detailed and provide good guidance for atypical examinee responses; however, the information in the User's Guide on the development of the MMSE, and reliability and validity of scores, is given with insufficient detail to adequately evaluate their merits.

Review of the Mini-Mental State Examination by SANDRA B. WARD, Associate Professor of Education, The College of William and Mary, Williamsburg, VA:

DESCRIPTION. The Mini-Mental State Examination (MMSE) is a brief, individually administered measure of an adult's mental state. The authors state four primary uses of the MMSE: (a) to detect cognitive impairment, (b) to estimate the severity of cognitive impairment at a given point in time, (c) to follow the course of cognitive changes in a patient over time, and (d) to docu-

ment response to treatment. The authors emphasize that the MMSE should not be used for the diagnosis of dementia nor to discriminate between the forms of dementia. Questions/tasks of the MMSE are grouped into eleven categories: (a) Orientation to Time, (b) Orientation to Place, (c) Registration, (d) Attention and Calculation, (e) Recall, (f) Naming, (g) Repetition, (h) Comprehension, (i) Reading, (j) Writing, and (k) Drawing. The administration time for the MMSE is 5–10 minutes. Administration requires the establishment of rapport and reading the questions and/or directions for each item. Administration procedures are clearly explained.

DEVELOPMENT. Although the authors assert that the MMSE has become one of the most widely used and researched measures of cognitive functioning, no information is provided in the manual about item development and test construction. Thus, beyond direct examination of the items, it is impossible to evaluate the appropriateness of the instrument's items for measuring the identified construct. Furthermore, each of the 11 categories cited above contains between 1–3 items. The low number of items per category raises a concern about adequate coverage.

TECHNICAL. Minimal information is provided in the manual about the norming process for the MMSE. The age range for the instrument is not specified, but the only table in the manual includes ages 18 through 85. This table includes median MMSE scores by age and educational level and refers to a study by Crum, Anthony, Bassett, and Folstein (1993) that developed population-based norms. However, the manual does not provide specific details about the standardization process nor the representativeness of the sample in this study. The scoring of individual items is straightforward. An examinee's raw score is the sum of the items completed correctly. The authors contend that the most widely accepted and frequently used cutoff score for the MMSE is 23, with scores of 23 or lower indicating the presence of cognitive impairment. The authors recommend the following breakdown of scores: 27–30, normal cognitive functioning; 21–26, mild cognitive impairment; 11–20, moderate cognitive impairment; 0–10, severe cognitive impairment. No rationale or justification is provided for the cutoff score of 23 or the breakdown of scores by levels.

Evidence for the reliability and validity of the MMSE is drawn from a study by Tombaugh and McIntyre (1992). Test-retest reliability was reported to range from .80–.95, but no information is provided about the specific study such as the sample, length of time between test administrations, data analysis, or specific results. No information is offered regarding evidence of content or construct validity. In fact, the authors do not define "cognitive mental state." The authors claim that most studies using the cutoff score of 23 have found the MMSE to have a sensitivity of at least 87% and a positive predictive value of at least 79%. However, the authors do not site the specific authors of the studies or the specific details of the studies. Consequently, the test users only receive the authors' interpretations. The manual provides more advice than technical information. It is difficult to ascertain the reliability and the validity of scores from the MMSE based on the information provided in the test manual.

COMMENTARY. The MMSE represents an instrument that does not meet the *Standards for Educational and Psychological Testing* (AERA, APA, & NCME, 1999). Although population-based norms are provided in a table in the manual, there is no explanation of how these norms were derived. The data for reliability and validity are insufficient, and it is impossible to determine whether the test consistently or accurately measures the intended construct. Although the authors contend that the MMSE is one of the most widely used and researched instruments, they fail to provide the necessary information about the MMSE to justify its use. Caution should be exercised in the interpretation of MMSE scores, and MMSE scores alone should not be used to determine an individual's degree of cognitive impairment.

SUMMARY. The MMSE is designed to aid in the clinical examination of an individual's cognitive mental state. However, no theoretical model was articulated by the authors for the instrument's development, and there is no evidence reported in the manual regarding the content or construct validity of scores from the MMSE. Consequently, the extent to which the MMSE satisfies its purpose is questionable. Although the MMSE is easily administered and scored, no rationale is provided for the recommended cutoff score or the described levels of cognitive impairment. Thus, caution in the interpretation of scores is advised.

The MMSE should be used only for research and screening purposes. Most importantly, other data should be used in conjunction with MMSE scores to support any conclusions regarding an individual's cognitive mental state.

REVIEWER'S REFERENCES

American Educational Research Association, American Psychological Association, & National Council on Measurement in Education. (1999). *Standards for educational and psychological testing.* Washington, DC: American Educational Research Association.
Crum, R. M., Anthony, J. C., Bassett, S. S., & Folstein, M. F. (1993). Population-based norms for the Mini-Mental State Examination by age and educational level. *Journal of the American Medical Association, 269*(18), 2386–2391.
Tombaugh, T. N. & McIntyre, N. J. (1992). The Mini-Mental State Examination: A comprehensive review. *Journal of the American Geriatrics Society, 40,* 922–935.

[167]
Motivational Styles Questionnaire.

Purpose: "Designed to define the kind of work situation to which individuals are suited and the way in which they will most willingly exert effort."
Population: Job applicants.
Publication Date: 1998.
Acronym: MSQ.
Scores: 10 scales: Work Style Preferences (Achievement, Independence, Structure, Affiliation, System Power, People Power, Person Power), Work and Life Attitudes (Central Orientation, Medium-term Striving, Short-term Striving).
Administration: Individual.
Price Data: Available from publisher.
Time: [20-30] minutes.
Author: Roland Tarleton.
Publisher: The Psychological Corporation Europe [United Kingdom].

Review of the Motivational Styles Questionnaire by GYPSY M. DENZINE, Associate Professor of Educational Psychology, Northern Arizona University, Flagstaff, AZ:

DESCRIPTION. The Motivational Styles Questionnaire (MSQ) is a 45-item test, either administered by paper-and-pencil or computer. The test can be individual or group administered and takes approximately 25 minutes to complete. The test is separated into two major parts. The first part of the MSQ (referred to as Work Style Preferences, WSP) contains 45 selection type items (ipsative in format), which measures what is most important to the respondent in the work situation. It is designed to define the areas of work one uses to satisfy particular needs. The seven WSP subscales are grouped into three broad dimensions: Achievement, Structure, and Power. The second part of the instrument comprises the three

Work and Life Attitude (WLA) scales: Short-Term Striving, Medium-Term Striving, and General Orientation. The 60 WLA items employ a 5-point Likert-type response scale (disagree/agree) based on a normative scoring format. The first part of the test deals with needs, whereas the second part focuses more on goals. The WLA identifies how individuals function in their careers, the rate at which they will work towards achieving their goals, and the level of work providing the appropriate degree of challenge.

Although not clearly stated in the manual, it appears nonclinical staff can administer, score, and interpret the MSQ. Answers from the paper-and-pencil version are handscored using two scoring keys and a scoring sheet for both the WSP and WLA parts. Scores are summed and a constant is added to obtain a final score for the 10 MSQ scales. The final scoring step involves transferring the scores to a profile chart and plotting the position of each of the 10 scale scores. The MSQ can also be administered and scored using the PC-based software diskette. A respondent can key responses directly into the computerized test version or the test administrator can key in item responses taken from the paper-and-pencil version. Raw and sten scale scores can also be entered into the software package. This reviewer found the paper-and-pencil scoring system to be somewhat cumbersome and the instructions for scoring could be improved. Interested users may want to use the computerized scoring version, which is quite user-friendly.

DEVELOPMENT. Detailed information describing the test development is lacking. In the Background section of the test manual, a theoretical overview of the research underlying the development of the MSQ is provided. At the broadest level, the MSQ is purported to be grounded in three main areas of research (a) self-actualization, (b) level of aspiration, and (c) achievement motivation. A diagram of 11 theorists is visually represented to describe the theoretical orientation underlying the MSQ. For example, the test developer cites the work of Adler, Maslow, Herzberg, Lewin, Murray, Rotter, and others. However, the theorists are merely listed and a detailed analysis of how the perspectives of these theorists relate to the MSQ is missing.

During the main phase of development, the MSQ was administered to 1,269 managers and professionals. Of this group, 74% were between 35–54 years of age and 87% of the group were male. The original Work Style Preferences instrument contained 96 items and three subscales: Achievement, Security, and Power. The original version of the Work and Lifestyles Attitudes questionnaire consisted of 105 items and the same three subscales as in the current version. The results from an exploratory Principal Components Analysis, based on a sample of 300 managers and professionals, led the author to revise the two parts of the test. Beyond stating a Varimax Rotation was employed and "the best items were then selected" (p. 49), the test manual provides insufficient information about the PCA techniques and interpretation. The test manual contains a description of all the subscales; however, the theoretical and empirical evidence to support the constructs underlying the MSQ is minimal. It is difficult to evaluate the internal structure of the test given the limited information provided in the manual. Minimally, the proposed underlying structure of the test needs to be explored with another sample and results from a covariance structure analysis would further strengthen the interpretation of the internal structure of the MSQ.

TECHNICAL. The test developer does not furnish norms for the MSQ. Because the manual states subscale scores at the fifth or sixth point on the sten scale should be considered average, normative data may be useful for profile interpretation purposes. A major strength of this test is the large sample utilized for test development. The test manual could be improved by including more information about the sample selection procedures and the characteristics of the sample ($n = 1,269$) employed for the main test development phase.

No content validity evidence is presented. The test manual contains a section titled "Theoretical Validity," which contains a brief overview of some of the steps the author took in developing the MSQ. The construct validity section does not provide sufficient detail to be able to evaluate this test. For example, the author reports that 10 new items intended to measure aspects of working alone were written to create an independence scale as a separate dimension of the Achievement scales. No information is provided regarding how these items were developed, nor is empirical evidence presented to support the assumption that Independence can be differentiated from Achievement. In the validity section on the second part of the test (WLA), the Short-Term and Medium-Term Striving scales are briefly discussed in relation to particular theorists. The Short-Term Striving scale was adapted from Rosenberg's (1965) Self-Esteem Scale. The test developer retained all of Rosenberg's original 10 self-esteem items but expanded the MSQ by writing "new items that are approximately opposite to Rosenberg's" (manual, p. 50). Empirical evidence to support the contention that this scale is based on a unidimensional construct is lacking. In a similar approach, the author developed the Medium-Term Striving scale based on Rotter's (1966) Internal-External Control Scale. A brief discussion of the test developer's factor analytic procedure is mentioned but this reviewer found the interpretation insufficient for evaluating the construct validity of the Medium-Term Striving scale.

Results from a single study (n = 190) are presented in the reliability section of the manual. The internal consistency coefficients for the MSQ are within reasonable ranges, with most scales in the .60 to .90 range with one scale (Short-Term Striving) greater than .90. The alpha coefficient for the Achievement subscale of the Work Style Preference scale was reported as .48. According to the test author, the low reliability coefficient is because "it must inevitably contain a mix of items such as 'reasonable risk' which may be chosen by default when presented opposite 'high risk' (Systems Power scale) and 'low risk' (Structure Scale)" (manual, p. 51). Unfortunately, this explanation is not further explored either theoretically or empirically.

The author also provides test-retest reliability estimates based on a study involving 44 managers and professionals. Participants in the test-retest study completed the MSQ after a time interval between 6 weeks and 7.5 months, with more than 45% after more than 4.5 months. Test-retest coefficients range from .53 (General Orientation) to .85 (Personal Power). Because of the varying time intervals, specific information about the test-retest coefficients would have been helpful. Moreover, during the first and second testing sessions participants in this study received counseling to help them find another job. More detailed technical information regarding time delays between the first and second testings, and the nature and timing of counseling, would be useful for interpreting the test-retest reliability results.

To further explore the internal structure of the MSQ, the author correlated MSQ scores with two other instruments. In one study, MSQ scores were correlated with 16PF4 scales for a sample of managers and professionals (n = 64). In another study, the author reported correlations between the MSQ and the OPQ® Concept for a sample of 66 managers and professionals. Although the correlation matrices are presented for the two studies, unfortunately very little discussion of validity is provided to help potential users interpret the intercorrelations among the scores of the tests. Furthermore, the sample sizes utilized in these studies are considered to be small given the number of subscales for the various tests (MSQ = 10, 16PF4 = 16, and OPQ® Concept = 30). In another set of studies, the test developer explored validity of MSQ scores by obtaining self- and colleague ratings using adjective and phrase checklists. Results showed many significant correlations between MQ subscales and self- and colleague ratings. More information about the methodological aspects of these studies would have strengthened the interpretation of the results.

COMMENTARY. One of the test developer's primary goals was to develop a test that would go beyond measuring personality or ability measures often found in career tests. The author is commended for intending to measure the motivational aspects of career development. Although the author states the theories underlying the test development, there is a need for an expanded theoretical discussion in the manual. In addition, there is a need for further research to explore the internal structure of the test. The manual could be improved by providing significantly more technical information. To the author's credit, the manual does contain very useful information for the user looking for practical information about score interpretation. Also, the manual contains three concise and well-written case studies, which demonstrate how to interpret an MSQ profile. For the practitioner, the author also provides information about four different training workshops available for users of the MSQ. A major strength of this test is the author's intent to share a practical, user-friendly, and relatively low-cost test. Another strength of this test is that it is targeted for use with a specific population (managers and professionals) rather than a diverse group of workers. The narrow population will be useful should the author continue to gather evidence to support the construct and discriminant validity of the test scores. Unfortunately, the practical implications of the MSQ are compromised by the fact that no references to current research in the field of career development are cited in the manual, which would ground the MSQ into the literature.

SUMMARY. Because of insufficient construct validity evidence, caution should be used in using the MSQ to define the kind of work situation that would be the best for an individual. Regrettably, until further work can be completed on the MSQ, I recommend it for use with reservation. Interested users will need to recognize the limitations of the test and may want to consider other career tests for which information is available through the Buros website and publications.

Review of the Motivational Styles Questionnaire by ROBERT L. JOHNSON, Associate Professor, Educational Psychology, University of South Carolina, Columbia, SC:

DESCRIPTION. The purpose of the Motivational Styles Questionnaire (MSQ) is "to define the kind of work situation to which individuals are best suited by providing a clear insight into the direction and the way in which they will most willingly exert effort" (manual, p. 1). The term "direction" refers to what an individual wants out of a situation, whereas the phrase "way in which" refers to how an individual likes to operate. The underlying assumption of the MSQ is that motivation requires an understanding of the area of work with which individuals will identify and the level of work at which they will encounter an appropriate degree of challenge. The manual contends that individuals without a good match between (a) the direction in which they will exert effort and (b) the way in which they will exert effort will find that "their level of performance, satisfaction, and commitment to the organization will gradually decline" (p. 1).

The first half of the MSQ is titled Work Style Preferences and "assesses what individuals want out of the situation, dealing with areas of work to satisfy particular needs" (manual, p. 1). The second half, Work and Life Attitudes, assesses how individuals "like to operate in their careers generally, dealing with the rate at which they will progress towards achieving their goals" (manual, p. 1). In the Work Styles Preference section, an individual's preferences and needs in various areas of work are characterized by seven

scales: Achievement, Independence, Structure, Affiliation, Systems, People, and Personal Power. The scales are designed to assess the respondent's need for personal achievement, independence, structure, team support, power through organizational systems, power through organizing people, and personal power, respectively.

The items in the Work Styles Preference section require individuals to indicate which of two options is most important to them in the work situation. This section has 45 items that address work preferences along the dimensions defined by the seven scales. For example, one item begins with the stem "I am more likely to …" and is accompanied by a 5-point rating scale with the following descriptors: "ask other people's opinions" or "sort things out for myself." The descriptors define only the endpoints of the scale.

The Work and Life Attitudes section of the instrument addresses the goals set by individuals and the way they choose to operate. This section contains 65 statements that provide scores for three scales: Short-Term Striving, Medium-Term Striving, and General Orientation. Respectively, the scales assess global confidence as demonstrated by a belief in self, internal-external control as indicated by belief in control over situations, and resultant achievement motivation as demonstrated by striving for personal success rather than avoiding operational failure. An example of an item in the Work and Life Attitudes section is "My priority at work is to get jobs out of the way as quickly and efficiently as possible." The 5-point scales for the items are defined by the terms "Disagree" and "Agree" at the endpoints.

Directions indicate that respondents should take approximately 10 minutes to complete the first part of the instrument and 15 minutes to complete the second part. Each section of the assessment has a separate answer sheet that is clearly labeled.

Four clear overlay keys are used to calculate scores for the scales. Two of the keys are used to score Work Style Preferences and the remaining two are used to score Work and Life Attitudes. In each pair, one key is used to generate plus scores and the other minus scores.

Each item is scored first with the overlay for the plus scores. The scores are then summed for each scale. The respondents' answer sheet is then rescored with the overlay for the minus scores. The scores for each scale are then tallied. The score for each scale is recorded on the Motivational Scales Profile and plotted along a continuum in which intervals are defined by score clusters (e.g., scores of 20–23, 24–30, and 31–36). When completed, an individual's profile indicates preferences for the work conditions described by the 10 subscales.

The manual provides guidance in the interpretation of scores. The manual contains a description of each scale and a descriptor for high scorers on the scale. For example, Structure is identified as "need for structure" and higher scores as displaying a preference for "low risk, a well-structured environment, clearly defined targets and objectives, security" (manual, p. 8). In another section, the manual presents implications for average/high, moderately low, and low scorers. An example for the Structure scale indicates that high scorers "like to have clear targets and guidelines so that they know what is expected of them," whereas moderately low scorers "will not want to have targets and objectives set out for them, preferring to devise their own approach to some extent" (manual, pp. 21–22).

Case studies offer additional examples of interpretation. Accompanying each case study is a completed MSQ profile. The author offers interpretations about the individual's work preferences based on the scores for the completed profile.

The author outlines a process for reviewing results with respondents. It is suggested that information about the respondent's career be collected. In preparing to review an individual's scores, the author suggests providing an explanation of the structure of the MSQ and the meaning of each subscale. Finally, the discussion centers on career plans using the scales as a basis of information. The goal of the feedback is that the session should result in "both parties being entirely clear on the kind of work situation to which the individual is best suited" (manual, p. 20).

DEVELOPMENT. The author provides some information about instrument development. The technical documentation links the instrument to the literature on self-actualization, level of aspiration, and achievement motivation. The original version of the Work Style Preferences questionnaire consisted of 96 items and three scales (Achievement, Security, and Power). The responses of over 300 managers and professionals were factor analyzed using a principal components analysis with a varimax rotation. The author states that the solution indicated seven factors; however, no specifics about factor loadings or criteria for determining the number of factors are provided.

The original version of the Work and Life Attitudes questionnaire contained 105 items and the three current scales. The Short-Term Striving scale is based on Rosenberg's (1965) Self Esteem Scale and the Medium-Term Striving scale is based on Rotter's (1966) Internal-External Control Scale. The author mentions the use of factor analyses to determine which items to retain from the original instruments; however, no specifics about the analyses were provided.

TECHNICAL QUALITIES. The author indicates that the basis for the scores is normative; however, information about standardization is sparse. In a section labeled "Normative Data," the author indicates the development of the instrument was based on responses of managers and professionals. Information is reported for 1,269 managers and professionals who completed the instrument during the main development phase. The group was 87% male. Ages span 20 years to 60+ years with 68% of the respondents being 40 years of age or over. A column labeled "Qualifications" is difficult to interpret due to the use of acronyms that are not defined. Another column labeled "Functional areas" lists types of employment, such as technical, commercial, production and distribution, and finance and legal, and confirms the business orientation of the respondents. Salary levels are difficult to interpret because the type of currency (e.g., pounds, euros, or dollars) is not specified. None of the data are accompanied by information that describes the general population of managers and professionals in order to make comparisons with the normative sample; so the representativeness of the normative data cannot be determined.

Reliability of scores for the scales is reported for internal consistency and test-retest. Reliability estimates based on coefficient alpha range from .48 (Achievement) to .92 (Short-Term Striving). Estimates based on test-retest range from .53 (General Orientation) to .85 (Personal Power). The error associated with these reliability estimates means that the scores for an individual are likely to vary substantially across testing situations for some scales, thus the scores from the scales should be treated as informative, but not conclusive. Use of the MSQ for research purposes appears viable because Thorndike, Cunningham, Thorndike, and Hagen (1991) demonstrate that mean scores for groups as small as 25 are stable with a reliability of .70 to .80.

The author reports the results of several validity studies. One method used to investigate validity involved rating the respondents by using an adjectives checklist and a phrases checklist. Examples of terms for the adjectives checklist include "team players," "organizers," "high flyers," "innovative," "cautious," and "leaders." Examples of phrases include "keen to do things their own way," "uncomfortable when on unfamiliar territory," and "at their best when under pressure." In one study, a sample of managers and professionals completed the MSQ and the adjective checklist ($n = 63$) and a phrases checklist ($n = 44$). A subset of their colleagues was asked to complete the phrases checklist ($n = 33$). In the second study, a group of managers and engineers were asked to identify a colleague who they knew well and to complete the adjective checklist ($n = 73$) and phrases checklists ($n = 74$) for that person. The adjective and phrases checklists both used a 5-point scale.

The correlations reported in the manual between the MSQ scales and the items on the checklists were in the expected directions. When negative relationships were expected, correlations ranged from -.25 to -.75. When positive relationships were expected, the lowest reported correlation was .24 and the highest positive correlation was ($r = .69$).

Correlations also were reported for the MSQ scales and the scales for two personality instruments. This information could provide the reader with concurrent validity evidence. However, the author did not describe the instruments or their scales. Without knowing more about the meaning of the scales, the information cannot be interpreted by the reader.

No validity information addresses the issue that the instrument "is designed to define the kind of work situation to which individuals are best suited" (manual, p. 1). A similar statement is offered in the interpretation for respondents who are told the instrument "aims to define the kind of work situation to which you are best suited" (manual, p. 16). No evidence is provided that indicates that respondents' scores on the MSQ are related to job satisfaction or productivity.

COMMENTARY. A strength of the MSQ is its basis in the literature on self-actualization, level of aspiration, and achievement motivation. In addition, the studies of validity support the interpretations of the scales. By describing the personality instruments used as criterion measures, the author will provide the information for the readers of the technical manual to interpret the size and direction of the correlations. In addition, the information in the validity section needs to be summarized and organized in a manner that is more reader friendly.

Reliability estimates are reported for both internal consistency and test-retest. The reliability estimates indicate that enough error is associated with scores such that individuals' scores should be used to frame discussions about work preferences, but should not be used in a conclusive manner. The test-retest reliability of scores for several of the scales approximates .80 and appears to be conducive for research purposes when group means are the focus of the study.

The 5-point rating scales that accompany the items raise a question about the meaning of the midpoint. A midpoint in a rating scale that is defined by descriptors at two extremes may be considered neutral. This especially seems to be the case when the descriptors are "disagree" and "agree" as they are in the Work and Life Attitudes section of the MSQ. When the purpose of an instrument is to gauge preferences or attitudes, the inclusion of a neutral point appears deleterious. The directions for the MSQ advise individuals that in answering they should avoid the middle position—even to the point of stating "preferably not more than five times in the first set of 45 questions" (manual, p. 11). The use of a rating scale with an even number of points appears to be appropriate for the scale.

SUMMARY. The MSQ provides a useful tool to examine work style preferences. However, the instrument should not be relied on for making employment decisions. Although initial validity evidence supports the interpretation of the scales, evidence that supports the utility of the instrument in making employment decisions is lacking. In addition, reliability estimates preclude its use in making employment decisions.

REVIEWER'S REFERENCES

Rosenberg, M. (1965). *Society and the adolescent self-image.* Princeton, NJ: Princeton University Press.

Rotter, J. (1966). Generalized expectancies for internal versus external control of reinforcement. *Psychological Monographs: General and Applied, 80*(1), 1–28.

Thorndike, R., Cunningham, G., Thorndike, R., & Hagen, E. P. (1991). *Measurement and evaluation in psychology and education* (5th ed.). New York: MacMillan Publishing Company.

[168]
Motive to Attain Social Power.

Purpose: Designed to evaluate one's "probable enjoyment or dislike (motivational preference) for a variety of socialized power activities."
Population: Undergraduates.
Publication Date: No date.
Scores: Total score only.
Administration: Group.
Price Data, 2001: $3 per specimen set.
Time: Administration time not reported.
Authors: L. R. Good and K. C. Good.
Publisher: Psychometric Affiliates.

Review of the Motive to Attain Social Power by GARY J. DEAN, Professor, Department of Adult and Community Education, Indiana University of Pennsylvania, Indiana, PA:

DESCRIPTION. The Motive to Attain Social Power is a 28-item true-false inventory that measures one's "probable enjoyment or dislike (motivational preference) for a variety of socialized power activities" (manual of instructions, p. 2). The packet of information obtained for this review included a four-page booklet containing development and technical information about the instrument, a copy of the 28-item inventory, and a scoring key. The instrument is straightforward in design. It consists of 28 statements to which the responses are either "true" or "false." Half of the items are worded in a positive format (e.g., "I would enjoy functioning in a high-level, decision-making capacity," Item 4) and half of the items are worded in a negative format (e.g., "I would dislike having to make the decisions concerning who should be promoted," Item 15).

The scoring key lists the response for each item (true or false), which would indicate one's desire to attain social power. To score the inventory, the responses of the individual are compared to the scoring key and a simple tally of matching responses is made. The tally reflects the number of times the individual's responses agree with the response that represents the desire to attain social power.

DEVELOPMENT. The authors base their instrument on the definition of power developed by McClelland (cited in the manual of instructions), which distinguishes desire for "personal dominance over others" (manual of instructions, p. 4) with the "altruistic exercise of power on behalf of others" (manual of instructions, p. 4). Social power is defined by the authors as the latter form of power. The authors further define their use of social power in this instrument as the "fusion of the achievement, dominance, and social recognition motives" (manual of instructions, p. 4). It is this fusion, or combination, of these motives that the authors speculate is the basis for social power.

The specific development of the instrument occurred in the following manner. Good and Good wrote 44 items. They do not elaborate on the origin of the items, but presumably they were derived from the literature and the authors' experiences. The original 44-item instrument was administered to 316 undergraduate students (163 female and 153 male) at Purdue University in 1971. The KR-20 formula was used to obtain a correlation coefficient of .82 from this initial sample. The instrument was reduced to 26 items by selecting items that had an uncorrected item-total correlation of .25 or higher. In addition, the authors included two new items that were "similar in content to those original items evidencing the highest internal validity" (manual of instructions, p. 2). The resulting 28-item inventory was administered to 174 undergraduate students at Purdue.

TECHNICAL INFORMATION. The KR-20 formula was again used to analyze the second and final validation study reported in the manual. A correlation coefficient of .89 was obtained with a mean score of 16.45 and standard deviation of 6.57. The authors reported that the scores ranged from 0 to 28. The item-total correlations ranged from .23 to .64 for the 28 items. The authors further report that in the second sample, males (n = 89) had a mean score of 18.14 with a standard deviation of 6.42 and females (n = 85) had a mean score of 14.69 with a standard deviation of 6.29. This gender difference was statistically significant (t = 3.58, df = 172, p < .001). The difference is explained as: "This finding was to be expected since the social-power orientation is clearly stronger for the males in our culture than it is for the females notwithstanding the efforts of the Women's Lib movement to elevate the power aspirations of the American female" (manual of instructions, p. 4).

COMMENTARY. In general, the procedure used to develop the instrument appears to be sound. The authors do a good job of explaining the procedure used to develop the instrument despite the brevity of the manual. Several questions, however, should be raised about this instrument. First, why is an instrument that was clearly developed about 1970 being submitted for review in the *Mental Measurements Yearbook* at this time? The manual for the instrument does not reflect any research undertaken in the 30 years since its original development. It may be that the instrument has value in understanding the development of the measurement of social power from a historical viewpoint, but it would hardly seem appropriate to use the instrument for research or assessment at this time.

Further, the authors do not state in a direct manner what they perceive as the value of the instrument. It appears as though the instrument is intended primarily for research purposes rather than for assessment of individuals. No norms are provided in the technical information in the manual for interpreting individual scores. The only benchmark one has for interpreting scores is the means given for the second sample of 174 undergraduate students. Use of this instrument for either research or individual assessment is hindered by the lack of normative data from more recent, larger, and more diverse samples.

SUMMARY. The instrument is simple and easy to administer and take. It only took a few minutes for the reviewer to take and score the instrument. The results were easy to understand as well; they were simply compared to the overall mean and mean score of the appropriate gender group. Beyond that, however, there appears to be limited utility for this instrument due to the lack of development over the last 30 years. The lack of continued testing of the instrument, the lack of more recent and diverse samples, and the lack of norms all limit the usability of the instrument.

[169]

Multidimensional Anxiety Questionnaire.

Purpose: Designed "for the evaluation of anxiety symptoms in adults."
Population: Ages 18–89.
Publication Date: 1999.
Acronym: MAQ.
Scores, 5: Physiological-Panic, Social Phobia, Worry-Fears, Negative Affectivity, Total.
Administration: Group or individual.
Price Data, 2003: $106 per introductory kit including 25 hand-scorable booklets, professional manual (94 pages), and 50 profile forms.
Time: (10) minutes.
Author: William M. Reynolds.
Publisher: Psychological Assessment Resources, Inc.

Review of the Multidimensional Anxiety Questionnaire by STEPHANIE STEIN, Professor of Psychology, Central Washington University, Ellensburg, WA:

DESCRIPTION. The Multidimensional Anxiety Questionnaire (MAQ) is a 40 item self-report pencil-and-paper inventory designed to evaluate the severity of anxiety symptoms in adults, ages 18 to 89. The MAQ yields five T-scores: Total Scale, Physiological-Panic (12 items), Social Phobia (9 items), Worry-Fears (10 items), and Negative Affectivity (9 items). In addition, the MAQ Total Scale provides a cutoff score as an "indicator of a clinically significant level of anxiety that warrants further evaluation" (professional manual, p. 18).

The manual provides specific guidelines for administration and scoring of the MAQ. It reportedly can be used for clinical assessment, research, program evaluation, or evaluation of treatment outcome. The MAQ test materials include a professional manual, two-part carbonless test booklet (designed for hand-scoring using built-in scoring key), and profile sheet. The response format on the MAQ is a 4-point Likert-type scale ranging from 1 (*almost never*) to 4 (*almost all the time*). The inventory requires a fourth grade reading level and takes approximately 10 minutes to administer (either individually or group). Six of the items are reversed key scored to control for response set styles (such as endorsing *almost never* on every item).

DEVELOPMENT. The MAQ was developed to provide a brief, easy-to-use, psychometrically sound measure of clinically relevant anxiety symptoms in adults. The items were designed to address a wide range of anxiety symptoms specified in the *DSM-III-R*, though the author reports that the items are also consistent with the symptoms of anxiety disorders included in the *DSM-IV*. Specifically, the items on the MAQ were developed to address the symptoms of anxiety included in Panic Disorder, Generalized Anxiety Disorder, and Social Phobia, and symptoms that are shared between anxiety disorders and depressive disorders.

The initial item pool of 56 items was field tested with approximately 300 individuals, including nonreferred adult community members, college students, and individuals diagnosed with anxiety disorders. Item analysis and expert review of the items led to a selection of 44 items from the original pool. Four of these items were dropped in the final revision of the 40-item MAQ because they had low item-with-total scale correlation co-efficients when tested on the total adult development sample.

The subscale domains were selected, in part, based on a consensus in the field about the major domains of anxiety—physiological, behavioral, cognitive, and affective. In addition to the theoretical rationale, the subscales were empirically supported through factor analysis. The MAQ Physiological—Panic subscale addresses physiological symptoms of anxiety and panic as well as feelings of panic and agoraphobia. The MAQ Social Phobia subscale addresses symptoms of social phobia and social anxiety, thus focusing more on the behavioral component to anxiety. Fearfulness in daily life situations and generalized worry are assessed through the MAQ Worry—Fears subscale, emphasizing the cognitive components of anxiety. Finally, the MAQ Negative Affectivity subscale includes negative symptoms associated with anxiety that also correspond to symptoms of depressive disorders.

TECHNICAL. The standardization sample for the MAQ is fairly well-described in the manual. Over 2,800 adults between the ages of 18 and 89 (600 nonreferred community members, 407 psychiatric outpatients, and 1,831 college students) served as the development and standardization sample for this measure. Demographic characteristics of the norm group, including age, gender, ethnicity, educational attainment, occupational level, and SES are provided. Both the community standardization sample and the college standardization sample were drawn from the Midwestern region of the United States.

The author found small, but statistically significant, gender differences on the MAQ with females reporting more anxiety symptoms than males. Gender differences were found on the Total MAQ score and all of the subscales except for Social Phobia. Therefore, separate community sample norms are available by gender, though the author recommends using the total community norms for greatest reliability and validity. In addition, some age differences were found, with younger adults generally reporting more symptoms than older adults—especially on the Social Phobia subscale. Furthermore, though most of the investigations of ethnic differences resulted in nonsignificant findings, the author did find a significant ethnic difference on the Social Phobia subscale

with Asians scoring higher than Caucasians and African Americans. Finally, the mean MAQ score for the college sample was higher than the community sample. Therefore, separate norms are provided for the total community sample, community sample (females), community sample (males), and the college sample.

Extensive reliability data are provided in the manual. The internal consistency (coefficient alpha) estimate for the combined total adult community/psychiatric outpatient sample was quite high (.96). The separate gender samples resulted in similarly high coefficients. Additional alpha coefficients for subgroups such as psychiatric outpatients with anxiety disorders, psychiatric outpatients with anxiety disorders and other psychopathology, nonreferred community sample, and college student sample all resulted in high internal consistency correlations (all in the .80s and .90s range).

Test-retest reliability for a mixed community/psychiatric outpatient sample (n = 191) at a 1-week retesting interval was .95 for the total scale (with subscales ranging from .90 to .93). A college sample (n = 205) retested after approximately 2 weeks resulted in a total scale correlation of .89 (with subscales ranging from .81 to .84). As an aid in interpretation, the MAQ manual also reports the standard error of measurement (*SEM*) calculated using the test-retest reliability coefficients. For the combined community/psychiatric sample, the *SEM*s are between 2 to 3 *T*-score points. The *SEM*s for the college sample range from 3 to 4 *T*-score points.

Similarly, different types of validity data are available in the MAQ manual. Item-with-total scale correlations (ranging from .50 to .77, median = .63) are presented as partial evidence for the content validity of the MAQ scores. Evidence for the criterion-related validity of the MAQ scores comes from concurrent validity correlations of the MAQ with the HAS (Hamilton Anxiety Scale, .85).

In addition, evidence is provided for the construct validity of the MAQ scores through both convergent and discriminant validity comparisons. The measures used for examining convergent validity in the total adult development sample were the Beck Anxiety Inventory (.82), the Beck Depression Inventory (.83), the Beck Hopelessness Scale (.67), and the Adult Suicidal Ideation Questionnaire (.59). All correlations were significant at the .001 level. Additional convergent measures were used for the college sample, including the State-Trait Anxiety Inventory—State (.66), the State-Trait Anxiety Inventory—Trait (.81), and the Social Anxiety & Distress Scale (.54). Measures used for examining discriminant validity included the Marlowe-Crowne Social Desirability Questionnaire (-.37 total adult sample, -.30 college sample) and the Social Self-Concept Scale (-.39 college sample only).

The author also discusses the factorial validity of the MAQ by describing the principal axis factor analysis procedure used and the four obtained factors with item-factor loadings of .40 or greater. Finally, the clinical validity of MAQ scores is supported by the use of a cutoff score as a "rough, qualitative threshold of clinically relevant level of anxiety symptoms" (professional manual, p. 63). The clinical efficacy of the MAQ total scale cutoff score was evaluated for sensitivity, specificity, positive predictive value, negative predictive value, hit rate, Chi-square, Phi coefficient, and Kappa coefficient. Despite the strong clinical evidence in support of the MAQ cutoff score, the author repeatedly cautions that the MAQ does *not*, by itself, provide a formal *DSM-IV* diagnosis of anxiety disorder.

COMMENTARY AND SUMMARY. The MAQ appears to be a well-designed and technically viable measure of clinically relevant anxiety symptoms in adults. The manual provides extensive data about the development and standardization of the instrument, as well as guidelines for the clinician in the administration, scoring, and interpretation of the MAQ.

In addition to the Total Scale score for the MAQ (with a cutoff score for indicating significant anxiety symptoms), the subscales of the MAQ provide useful indicators of the types of anxiety symptoms present (physiological, behavioral, cognitive, and affective). Of special note is the Negative Affectivity subscale, which addresses the potential comorbidity of anxiety and depressive disorders.

The brevity of the instrument has its potential advantages and disadvantages. Clearly, the short administration time will make this an attractive measure, from both the perspective of the clinicians and the clients. However, it does limit the utility of the measure for identifying the full range of anxiety symptoms, such as fear of specific objects/situations or anxiety experienced by someone attempting to resist a compulsion. However, the author is refreshingly up front in stressing the limitations of the MAQ, cautioning that the re-

sults are not intended to specify disorders, make differential diagnoses, or predict disorders. Therefore, the instrument must be used in conjunction with a clinical interview, at the very least, when diagnosing an anxiety disorder.

In conclusion, the MAQ is an instrument with many strengths and few, if any, detractors. Aside from the obvious technical strengths of this measure, it should be praised for not making any grandiose claims for utility that it cannot empirically support. If anything, the author appears to be exceptionally conservative in delineating the clinical boundaries of the inventory. It appears to be an excellent choice of a current anxiety assessment tool for clinicians to add to their diagnostic arsenal, as well as an effective measure for researching anxiety symptoms in adults.

Review of the Multidimensional Anxiety Questionnaire by ROBERT E. WALL, Graduate Professor, Department of Reading, Special Education and Instructional Technology, Towson University, Towson, MD:

DESCRIPTION. The Multidimensional Anxiety Questionnaire (MAQ) is a self-report measure designed to evaluate levels of general anxiety in adults. The author's goal in developing the MAQ is to provide clinicians and researchers with psychometrically sound, easy-to-use measures of severity of general anxiety in adults. The participant responds to 40 multiple-choice items in a two-layer, carbon-backed test booklet. The carbon-backed top layer copies the responses to a scoring grid on the lower layer. The clinician can then separate the two parts and quickly compute the subscale and Total scale scores. The scores may then be transferred to the MAQ profile sheet to provide a graphic representation of the scores. The MAQ provides an overall anxiety score as well as scores on four factorially derived anxiety subscales: Physiological-Panic, Social Phobia, Worry-Fears, and Negative Affectivity.

The Physiological-Panic subscale consists of 12 items that deal with physiological symptoms of anxiety including difficulty breathing, heart palpitations, dizziness, perspiration, jumpiness, shaky hands, and feeling flush. Additional items examine feelings of panic and agoraphobia. Physiological symptoms are the major domain of anxiety symptomatology and are cardinal signs of panic attack.

The MAQ Social Phobia subscale examines symptoms of social phobia and social anxiety. The nine items on this scale assess worry about what others think, worry about being anxious in front of other people, performance anxiety in work or school, avoidance of people, difficulty talking to people, and other fears of evaluation or negative evaluation by others.

The MAQ Worry-Fears subscale evaluates aspects of generalized worry and fearfulness in daily situations. The 10 items on this scale include assessment of feeling afraid, worry about the future, fear of dying, worry about being alone, and thoughts of harm or bad things happening. Several items on the subscale relate to obsessive thoughts.

The MAQ Negative Affectivity subscale evaluates affective symptomatology related to anxiety. The nine items on this scale assess a range of symptoms such as general distress, sleep difficulty, irritability, difficulty concerning concentrating, and somatic complaints.

It should be noted that the levels of anxiety on these subscales exhibited by the college sample and the community sample show significant differences. As the manual points out, one should be using the standard community standard norms; however, when dealing with the college populations it is best to look at both norms and work from there.

The MAQ profile sheet allows one to easily chart the individual's levels of anxiety in the four subscale areas and the total level of anxiety. The MAQ uses a cutoff score of approximately 1.5 standard deviations above the mean for that group. Scores above that are considered signs of high anxiety. The higher the score the more severe the anxiety.

DEVELOPMENT. An initial item pool was created based on descriptions of anxiety symptoms across various anxiety disorders as specified in the DSM-III-R (1987). From this pool, a 56-item field test version was administered to approximately 300 individuals including those diagnosed with anxiety disorders, college students, and nonreferred community adults. After item analysis and review of the items by experts in the field of anxiety disorders, the field test version was refined to 44 items which were administered to the adult development sample of 1,007. As a result of this testing, 4 additional items were dropped resulting in the current 40-item version of the MAQ.

In its development, the MAQ was administered to 1,000 adults in community and clinical settings and to 1,800 students in four university settings. Norms for the MAQ were developed from a sample of 600 adults (300 males and 300 females) drawn from the general community of nonreferred individuals. General community norms are available for the entire sample or separately for males and females.

TECHNICAL. Norms were also developed for college students based on the sample of 1,160 students (580 males and 580 females) from the four universities in the Midwest. T-scores were based on the results of these tests. Most of the college students were in their late teens and early twenties. No differences were found between male and female college student total MAQ scores. Therefore, separate gender norms were not computed for them. The community standardization sample represented diversity in socioeconomic status and included adults from urban, suburban, and rural areas. There was a small statistically significant difference between male and female mean total MAQ scores with females having higher scores. When the community standardization sample is compared with national demographic data, college degrees and the professions seem overrepresented. Norm tables were developed for the MAQ Total score and subscale for the total community standardization group and college levels.

The manual presents extensive reliability data for the MAQ. The internal consistency reliability coefficients for the Total scale and subscales range from approximately .81 for the lowest scale for the college group to .96 for the total score for the community standards group. The college sample had lower internal consistency reliability coefficients. In addition to the internal consistency reliability coefficients, test-retest reliability estimates were calculated, which is useful and very important in measuring anxiety or any psychological trait. The test-retest reliabilities (1-week intervals) were high although generally lower than the internal consistency reliabilities.

The MAQ manual presents an extensive chapter on determination of validity. According to the authors, they have evidence of content validity, criterion-related validity in the form of concurrent validity, and construct validity. Construct validity evidence was collected through divergent, convergent discriminate validity, and factorial validity studies. Clinical validity evidence was collected contrasting group studies as well as by looking at the clinical specificity sensitivity and efficacy of the MAQ score cutoff.

COMMENTARY. As befitting a test designed to be used in a clinical setting, much information is provided concerning the correct and ethical use of the test, including application, administration, and interpretation. In interpreting the data, it is important to remember the standard errors of measurement are between 2 and 3 *t*-score points for the community groups and 3 and 4 *t*-score points for the college samples. When scores are near the cutoff point then one has to take into consideration the standard error of measurement and utilize other available information in arriving at a clinical decision.

SUMMARY. The MAQ is a test designed to quickly provide an estimate of an individual's general anxiety level. It does not provide a measure of specific DSM anxiety classifications. The development and determination of the validity and reliability are well documented. It appears to be an easily administered test to be used as a screening device to determine a general level of anxiety. In the clinical setting it is a good starting point; however, other measures must be utilized to make specific determinations.

[170]
Multidimensional Aptitude Battery—II.

Purpose: Designed "to provide a measure of general cognitive ability or intelligence."
Population: Ages 16 and over.
Publication Dates: 1984–1998.
Acronym: MAB-II.
Scores, 13: Verbal (Information, Comprehension, Arithmetic, Similarities, Vocabulary, Total); Performance (Digit Symbol, Picture Completion, Spatial, Picture Arrangement, Object Assembly, Total), Total.
Administration: Group or individual.
Price Data, 2001: $45 per machine scoring examination kit including Verbal and Performance booklets, manual (1998, 107 pages), Verbal and Performance answer sheets, and one coupon for computerized scoring; $62 per hand-scoring examination scoring kit including Verbal and Performance booklets, manual, Verbal and Performance answer sheets, record form, and set of scoring templates; $33 per 10 Verbal or Performance test booklets; $17–$19.50 per 25 Verbal or Performance answer sheets; $10–$12 per 25 record forms.; $24 per scoring templates; $48–$56 (depending on volume) per 10 machine-scorable answer sheets and coupons for extended reports; $83–$92 (depending on volume) per 10 machine-scorable answer sheets and

coupons for clinical reports; $99 per software package including disks, software manual for Windows, test manual, and 10 coupons for computer reports.
Foreign Language Edition: Available in French (hand-scorable answer sheets and booklets).
Time: (100) minutes.
Comments: Paper-and-pencil or computer administration available.
Author: Douglas N. Jackson.
Publisher: Sigma Assessment Systems, Inc.
Cross References: See T5:1731 (3 references), and T4:1678 (13 references); for reviews by Sharon B. Reynolds and Arthur B. Silverstein of an earlier edition, see 10:202 (5 references).

Review of the Multidimensional Aptitude Battery-II by DONALD L. THOMPSON, Professor of Counseling and Psychology, Troy State University Montgomery, Montgomery, AL:

DESCRIPTION. The Multidimensional Aptitude Battery-II (MAB-II) was designed to provide a convenient, objectively scored measure of general cognitive ability (intelligence) in the form of a profile containing Verbal, Performance, and Full Scale scores plus five Verbal and five Performance subtest scores. The original 1984 version of the MAB was developed to serve as a measure that would provide scores that were comparable to the Wechsler Adult Intelligence Scale—Revised (WAIS-R), but that could be administered to groups. The 1984 MAB used a comparison of WAIS-R subscale scores and MAB subscale scores to establish equivalence. However, a communication from the vendor (Paul F. Tremblay, March 16, 2000) indicated that as a result of the renorming of the MAB-II in 1998, "the tie between the norming of the instruments was therefore severed." The test has both paper-and-pencil and computer-administered versions. The MAB-II yields a profile of 10 subtest scores, as well as Verbal, Performance, and Full Scale scores. The five Verbal subscales have a total of 167 multiple-choice items grouped into subtests of Information, Comprehension, Arithmetic, Similarities, and Vocabulary. The Performance subscales have 161 multiple-choice items grouped into subtests of Digit Symbol, Picture Completion, Spatial, Picture Arrangement, and Object Assembly. WAIS-R and WAIS-III users will immediately recognize that nine of the subtests are identically named. Digit Span is missing because technical difficulties make this subtest impossible to administer in a group format, and Spatial replaces the WAIS-R/

III Block Design subtest for similar reasons. The test manual indicates that the MAB-II was designed for ages 16 and up, and assumes language skills necessary to read and understand written directions and to comprehend spoken directions. The test is available in English, French, and Spanish versions and should only be administered to a client in his or her primary language. It can be administered in approximately 100 minutes (50 minutes each for the Verbal and Performance subscales). The manual indicates that the minimum test user qualification is an "advanced level university course in psychological testing at the Master's level, as well as training under the supervision of a qualified psychologist" (p. 21).

DEVELOPMENT. As noted earlier, the MAB-II, published in 1998, is a revision/ restandardization of the 1984 Multidimensional Aptitude Battery. The revision included an updating of all normative data. Because there are no changes in the items or subscales of the test from the MAB to the MAB-II, it is appropriate to refer to the process used in developing the 1984 version when discussing items and scales of the MAB-II. An earlier MMY reviewer (Reynolds, 1989) states, "The description of the item selection and scale construction is preceded by a general discussion of test construction. The procedure for selecting the items was clearly and thoroughly described. The items retained were selected after a series of items analyses. These analyses are described in detail in the manual" (p. 522).

TECHNICAL. The MAB-II test manual indicates that the administrative procedures, test manual, and norms have all been updated from the original MAB; however, all items and subtests remain identical to the 1984 edition. Information contained in the test manual is both abundant and precise regarding the restandardization/renorming. The standardization section of the manual provides information describing how the norm sample matches the intended user population. According to the manual, the norm sample for the MAB-II "consisted of a systematic sampling of nine age groups in the United States and Canada. Individuals were sampled to ensure participation from a diverse sample of the general population in terms of race and ethnicity, and North American geographic regions. The norm sample included equal numbers of males and of females. The nine age groups each contained 200 persons, with the exception of

the two oldest age groups, which contained 100 each" (p. 35). The norm sample also incorporated occupational level with a 50/50 distribution between managerial/professional/specialty; and technical, sales, service, and labor occupations.

Reliability data were generated using a variety of methods. Measures of internal consistency were obtained for the Verbal, Performance, and Full Scale, and the 10 subscales using a sample of adolescents that included 230 males and 285 females ranging in age from 15 to 20. Subscale reliabilities ranged from a low of .70 for 16-year-olds on the Arithmetic subscale to a high of .96 for 19- and 20-year-olds on the Spatial subscale. Full Scale reliabilities ranged from .96 for 16- and 17-year-olds to .98 for 18-, 19-, and 20-year-olds. Split-half coefficients on the 10 subscales ranged from .67 (Spatial) to .90 (Comprehension). Test-retest reliability coefficients for a 45-day period are reported for a sample of 52 young adult psychiatric patients. Coefficients ranged from .83 for the Similarities subscale to .97 for the Information subscale. The Full Scale test-retest reliability was .97 (Verbal, .95; Performance, .96). These data indicate that the MAB-II has solid reliability evidence.

Validity data reported in the test manual describe two factor analyses of the MAB-II that support the factor structure that indicates that the Verbal and Performance Scales are measuring different constructs. Also, a factor analysis of the MAB-II and WAIS-R resulted in well-defined verbal and performance factors, adding additional support to the verbal/performance distinction made in the MAB-II manual. In one of the studies listed in the Selected Research Bibliography in the test manual; however, Kranzler (1991) reported a factor analysis of the MAB-II with university students. He concluded that the verbal/performance factor structure was not supported, and that this might result from the fact that for the performance tests, certain verbal skills are also required (e.g., reading test instructions or following oral directions). Concurrent validity evidence is presented indicating the correlations between the MAB-II and the WAIS-R, using a sample of 145 people. Correlations between comparable subscales on the MAB-II and the WAIS-R ranged from a low of .44 for the Spatial/Block Design subscales to a high of .89 on the Arithmetic and Vocabulary subscales. The Verbal, Performance, and Full Scale correlations were .94, .79, and .91, respectively.

The MAB-II appears to have a high degree of validity in that the test results would appear to provide a good indicator of the constructs the test purports to measure.

COMMENTARY. Unlike the Differential Aptitude Tests (DAT; T6:818), USES General Aptitude Test Battery (GATB; T5:2797), or Armed Services Vocational Aptitude Battery (ASVAB; T6:185), the MAB-II does not address the broader range of aptitudes that are normally used in career counseling or similar situations. It is designed as an assessment of general aptitude and should be used in this context. However, within this context, the original development effort for the MAB and the restandardization incorporated into the MAB-II have resulted in a well-developed and empirically sound instrument. The MAB-II should not be used in situations where the subject's reading level is below ninth grade, or if the subject has a learning disability related to reading comprehension. A positive feature of the MAB-II test manual is that the score profile provides information on occupations that may be related to the strengths displayed on the various subscales. However, the links between aptitude patterns and various occupations are not as extensive as other aptitude batteries such as the DAT and GATB.

SUMMARY. The MAB-II has many positive features. This reviewer finds the test to be a good choice for assessing general aptitude (intelligence) in situations where a group-based, general screening tool is needed. The overall reliability and validity data provide strong empirical support for this instrument when it is used in appropriate situations. The test manual is well written and very comprehensive in detailing the standardization process in addition to the test administration and scoring procedures. The software for computer-based administration and scoring is a major plus. The software works well and provides convenient and readily available results. The computer-generated reports are comprehensive and will be useful in many counseling and placement situations.

As a group-administered measure of general ability, the MAB-II is an excellent choice. However, for career counseling purposes, I believe there are better choices such as the DAT or GATB. The MAB-II should not be used as the sole indicator for diagnostic, classification, or placement for mentally retarded or intellectually gifted students.

REVIEWER'S REFERENCES

Kranzler, J. (1991). The construct validity of the Multidimensional Aptitude Battery: A word of caution. *Journal of Clinical Psychology, 47*, 691–697.
Reynolds, S. (1989). The Multidimensional Aptitude Battery. In J. C. Conoley & J. J. Kramer (Eds.), *The tenth mental measurements yearbook* (pp. 522–523). Lincoln, NE: Buros Institute of Mental Measurements.

Review of the Multidimensional Aptitude Battery-II by KEITH F. WIDAMAN, Professor of Psychology, University of California, Davis, CA:

DESCRIPTION. The Multidimensional Aptitude Battery-II (MAB-II) is a battery of ability tests for adults modeled after the Wechsler Adult Intelligence Scale (WAIS), which in turn followed closely the format of the Army Alpha and Beta tests used in World War I. The 10 MAB-II subtests comprise five Verbal tests—Information, Comprehension, Arithmetic, Similarities, and Vocabulary—and five Performance tests—Digit Symbol, Picture Completion, Spatial, Picture Arrangement, and Object Assembly. Thus, the test names and their division into Verbal and Performance categories tend to mimic closely the format of the WAIS that was, for many years, the standard in the field.

Despite their surface similarities, at least two major distinguishing features separate the MAB-II and the WAIS. First, the MAB-II can be administered in group-testing situations or via computer as well as to individuals, rather than requiring individual administration as does the WAIS. Second, the MAB-II is an objectively scored instrument, rather than requiring scorer interpretation of responses. Both of these goals were accomplished by presenting all items on the MAB-II in multiple-choice format and by giving test takers a set amount of time to work on each test. Because the MAB-II is given in this format, the test may be administered by an adequately trained test proctor, rather than requiring a specially trained professional. However, because of the less intimate relationship between test administrator and test taker, the test should not be used for making important diagnostic decisions, such as deciding whether a person has mental retardation, or with certain clinical groups, such as persons with mental retardation or mental illness (e.g., psychosis).

Test takers are given 7 minutes to work on each of the 10 tests, so the entire battery can be administered in about 1.5 hours, given the need for instructions for each test and any rest breaks. Raw scores on each test can be converted into scaled or standard scores on a T-score metric (M

= 50, *SD* = 10). Test scores may then be combined to yield Verbal IQ, Performance IQ, and Full Scale IQ scores on the standard IQ scale (*M* = 100, *SD* = 15).

DEVELOPMENT. The first edition of the MAB was published in 1984, and the present second edition has a 1998 copyright date. Three principal goals guided the current revision of the MAB-II. The first goal was to develop a measure of general intelligence, or general cognitive ability, that was based on current North American norms. The second goal was to unlink the tie between the norming of the MAB-II and the WAIS, which had previously been closely aligned using statistical equating. The third aim was to announce improved ways of reporting scores using computerized scoring of protocols and reporting of scores.

The ability theory underlying the MAB-II is closely aligned with theoretical positions emphasizing general intelligence. The principal viewpoints discussed are those of Spearman and other proponents of the general factor of intelligence. Despite some discussion of their implications, multiple factor theories are given relatively short shrift. Most importantly, the Horn-Cattell theory of fluid and crystallized intelligence is not mentioned at all. Thus, the MAB-II was developed to be easily administered and yield scores that are no longer linked with those from the WAIS. Whether this restriction will result in the MAB-II becoming increasingly out of step with other major ability batteries will be revealed during the next few years.

During the initial rounds of test development, the MAB was subjected to three independent sets of item analyses to select the best items for inclusion in the scale. For the current revision, no item content was changed. Instead, the test was fully renormed on a new, sample representative of both the U.S. and Canada.

TECHNICAL. The MAB-II was standardized on a normative sample of 1,600 persons in nine age-graded groups: 200 in each of seven groups between 16 and 64 years of age, and 100 in each of two groups between 65 and 74 years of age. The normative sample had equal numbers of males and females, and the ethnic composition was 87% white and 13% other. The mean educational level was one year past high school, and the occupational distribution of persons in the normative sample was equally divided between managerial/professional and technical/service/labor. The

normative sample was drawn in rough proportion to the geographic distribution of residents of the U.S. and Canada.

Several kinds of reliability coefficients were reported for MAB-II test and IQ scores. Internal consistency reliabilities, based on six samples of persons, ranged between .70 and .96 (median of .87) for the 10 MAB-II tests and ranged between .94 and .98 for the Verbal, Performance, and Full Scale IQ scores. Split-half correlations for the 10 MAB-II tests ranged from .55 to .87 (median of .77) and comparable correlations for the Verbal, Performance, and Full Scale IQ scores ranged between .92 and .95. Test-retest reliabilities across a 45-day span ranged between .83 and .97 (median of .92) for the 10 MAB-II tests and between .95 and .97 for the Verbal, Performance, and Full Scale IQ scores. Taken together, all reliability evidence suggests quite high and adequate levels of reliability for test scores and all IQ scores derived from the MAB-II. Two studies of the effects of different time limits on psychometric properties verified that little, if anything, was gained by allowing test takers longer than 7 minutes to work on each test.

Several forms of validity information were also reported; unfortunately, most of these results were based on the original MAB, rather than the renormed MAB-II. In the first type of study, principal component analyses showed that all tests loaded highly (.53 or above) on the first principal component, purportedly demonstrating the "*g* saturation" (manual, p. 42) of each test. A varimax rotation of the first two principal components showed the clear separation of tests onto Verbal and Performance components. Common factor procedures and oblique rotations would have been preferred to those reported, but such procedures would likely have supported similar conclusions. In the second type of study, the correlations of the 10 MAB subtests with corresponding scores from the WAIS-R ranged from .44 to .89 (median of .78), and MAB-WAIS-R correlations for the Verbal, Performance, and Full Scale IQs were .94, .79, and .91, respectively.

A third form of validity information was derived from comparisons of the component structures of the MAB and WAIS-R. After varimax rotations of two components for each instrument, coefficients of congruence were .97 and .96 for the Verbal and Performance components, supporting the separate calculation of Verbal and Performance IQ scores on each instrument. The final study reported the correlations between MAB test scores and scores on the Raven's Advanced Progressive Matrices (RAPM). The correlations of RAPM with MAB verbal tests were rather low (median of .19), but with MAB performance tests were somewhat higher (median of .31).

One aspect of the norming tables deserves mention. The lowest IQ score that can be obtained using the tables is 70; the tables do not allow the assignment of IQ scores below 70. As a result, the MAB-II is not useful for studies of populations having borderline levels of intelligence (IQs between 65 and 80), as the norming process does not allow reliable distinctions among persons at these levels.

COMMENTARY. The MAB-II is a solid battery of ability tests that is modeled closely on the WAIS. As a result, the MAB-II yields Verbal, Performance, and Full Scale IQ scores that are similar in nature to the corresponding scores from the WAIS. Moreover, the relatively high correlations between corresponding scores from the MAB and the WAIS-R demonstrate that the two batteries provide very similar information regarding individual differences on dimensions of intelligence.

The principal advantage of the MAB-II over the WAIS is the ease of administration and scoring of the tests. Because the MAB-II can be administered in group testing settings and via computer and does not require a trained professional for its administration, obtaining scores from the MAB-II is much easier and consumes much less time and effort. Furthermore, the MAB-II yields scores with sufficient quality for many research and applied uses.

The primary concern one might have arises from the admittedly close tie between the MAB-II and the WAIS, which some might view as a strength of the MAB-II. The WAIS was developed with strong interest in composing a multifaceted battery to assess general intelligence, but with little attention paid to whether the battery adequately reflected multiple abilities. However, during the past 10–15 years, the Horn-Cattell theory of fluid and crystallized intelligence has been used increasingly as the accepted taxonomy of intellectual abilities. The Woodcock-Johnson battery was designed around the Horn-Cattell model; the most recent revision of the Stanford-Binet incorporates several aspects of the model; and many other intelligence tests are accommodating to the Horn-Cattell model. If ability batteries continue this trend of aligning with the Horn-Cattell model, the MAB-II may be viewed as anachronistic, with greater concern for test format (e.g., verbal and performance) than the constructs the tests assess.

SUMMARY. The developers of the MAB-II have produced a multidimensional ability battery for individuals ages 16 and over that can be administered and scored in an efficient manner. The scores derived from the MAB-II have very strong psychometric properties and are quite highly correlated with comparable scores from the WAIS. The MAB-II cannot be used in high stakes testing situations, such as determining whether a person has mental retardation. However, if one wished to obtain Verbal, Performance, or Full Scale IQ scores for research or many applied uses, the MAB-II is an easily administered test that yields scores that are comparable to those obtained using the WAIS. For its intended uses, the MAB-II is a clear and valuable alternative to the more complex and time-consuming WAIS.

[171]

Multimedia Learning Styles.

Purpose: Designed to assess students' learning styles.
Population: Students in 7th–9th grades.
Publication Date: 1998.
Scores, 9: Auditory Language, Visual Language, Auditory Numerical, Visual Numerical, Auditory-Visual-Kinesthetic Combination, Individual Learning, Group Learner, Oral Expressive, Written Expressive.
Administration: Individual or group.
Price Data, 1998: $295 per kit including 1 guide, (Windows/CD-ROM), 1 reproducible response form, and 1 site license.
Time: (10–15) minutes.
Comments: A self-paced, computer-administered, scored, and interpreted assessment; program includes feedback for teachers and students on the improvement of learning skills; program title is Multimedia Learning Styles; actual assessment within that program is referred to as the Learning Styles Inventory.
Authors: Piney Mountain Press, Inc., Albert M. Babich (technical report), and Phil Randol (technical report).
Publisher: Piney Mountain Press, Inc.
[Editor's Note: The publisher advised in January 2002 that this test is now out of print.]

Review of the Multimedia Learning Styles by BRUCE G. ROGERS, Professor of Educational Psychology, University of Northern Iowa, Cedar Falls, IA:

DESCRIPTION. The Multimedia Learning Styles is an instrument that reflects a concept of learning styles based on self-reported preferences. It is an adaptation of an instrument formerly known as the Learning Styles Inventory (Piney Mountain Press, Inc.), which was reviewed by both Crehan and Fugate (1995). These reviewers provided excellent descriptions of how the nine purported constructs were developed over time and they also provided technical discussions of the psychometric properties. This reviewer strongly recommends that readers consult those two reviews, because the historical information given will yield useful insights.

The MLS inventory consists of 45 statements, each of which is accompanied with four responses ranging from *most like me* to *least like me.* Originally, the instrument was administered on paper and scored by hand (by the teacher). The resulting scores were then given to the student. This laborious task can now be performed on a computer. A compact disk (CD) can be used to administer the instrument to the student and score the resulting responses. The program also can provide the teacher with suggested activities based on the score results.

The preferences of students are conceptualized into three main areas: oral versus written expressiveness, group versus individual working, and learning style (which is divided into five subtopics involving auditory versus visual versus kinesthetic as applied to language and numerical). This yields a total of nine constructs, each of which is measured by five items.

Instead of the CD administration, the instrument can also be administered on paper and the item scores entered into the computer by the teacher for analysis and a computer-generated report. According to the description in the manual for teachers, the CD presentation provides a "modern nondiscriminatory medium" in a "friendly, multi-sensory format," which yields "insightful applications" for teachers. The manual further states that, as a result of using the inventory, "students will feel better about themselves," "teachers will feel better about students," and "teaching will become easier" (p. 1). These are very desirable goals that describe the potential benefits of using the inventory, but, unfortunately, the manual contains no discussion of the existence of any supporting evidence for any of those statements. The manual for teachers consists of instructions for installing the CD and 18 pages of reproductions of the computer screens describing the nine learning styles.

DEVELOPMENT. The authors of the technical report, Albert Babich and Phil Randol, writing in approximately 1975, state that the "instrument was formulated by teachers" but they do not describe the actual process employed by those teachers. After sets of items were administered by teachers in a single school district, the results were subjected to item analysis. Using these data, the final nine scales, of five items each, were assembled. Some teachers and researchers might appreciate a description of the logic by which the constructs and items were developed. They might also appreciate knowing what developments, if any, have been made since the original constructs and items were first made available.

TECHNICAL.
Normative data. The technical manual reports, for a sample of 2,229 seventh, eighth, and ninth grade students, the mean and standard deviation for the scores on each of the nine constructs. There is no discussion given as to how the construct score for a particular student might be evaluated nor is there any discussion of how the construct score is processed by the computer scoring program to produce teacher feedback. Some teachers and researchers might appreciate a discussion of such issues in order to improve their interpretation of the construct scores.

Reliability. The technical manual reports split-half reliability indices for the original administration of the inventory. Because the inventory is now available to be administered with a computer, it would be very appropriate to again conduct reliability studies. Some users might appreciate seeing values for the internal consistency measure coefficient alpha and values for alternate form reliability. If such studies have already been completed, it would be useful to make the reader aware of their existence. The resulting information could then be applied to create a degree of confidence for the assignment of a student to a particular learning style.

Validity. The technical manual does not mention any evidence of validity for the original instruments nor does the 1998 manual prepared for teachers. Evidence of content validity, provided by experts in learning styles, would be perceived as valuable information by many users. Evidence for construct validity, in the form of correlations with other reputable learning style instruments, would be a positive contribution to this inventory.

As mentioned in the Description section, the 1998 manual (prepared for teachers) makes strong statements about how the instrument can affect students and teachers. It would be very useful if the next manual contained some evidence to indicate changes in student and teacher behavior that occurred subsequent to the employment of the inventory. Such data would certainly add to the evidence for construct validity.

As with reliability, there may already exist data pertaining to validity. If so, the manual should either provide the data or reference the sources in the research literature.

COMMENTARY. This instrument has several positive features. It reflects the input of teachers in its construction. Basic item analysis principles were involved in the selection of the five statements for each of the nine constructs. The vocabulary seems appropriate and it appears to have face validity. The computer screens are attractive and the computer creates feedback for both students and teachers.

On the other hand, the value of this test has been questioned by previous reviewers, yet there is no evidence that the authors of the test have subsequently addressed those questions. Among those concerns was the lack of current evidence relating to norms, reliability, and validity. This reviewer encourages the authors to address those issues.

The compact disk, which is now provided, needs to be carefully examined by prospective users. Unfortunately, this reviewer (and several colleagues) did not find the installation instructions to be user-friendly. Each potential adopter of this inventory should insist on the right to open the package, run the program, and then return it without any questions or stipulations.

Finally, the basic purpose of the test should be examined by potential users. The inventory purports to identify student preferences for learning styles. Should the teacher teach each student according to their preferred learning style or should the teacher help every student to acquire skills to enable them to adapt to each of the learning styles? The manuals for this instrument do not address this type of question, but potential users may wish to consider such an issue as they review the instrument.

SUMMARY. It is clear that this inventory was originally carefully designed with the intent to measure learning styles of middle school students. However, users are likely to desire some reasonably current data, relevant to its psychometric properties, to justify its continued use. Recent data for norms, reliability, and validity would be welcomed by potential users. Until such data are made available, this instrument can only be recommended for research use in carefully controlled situations. Its use by teachers, in practical classroom settings, cannot be recommended until the accompanying manuals present the generally accepted evidence for norms, reliability, and validity, as applied to educational measures.

REVIEWER'S REFERENCES

Babich, A. M. & Randol, P. (Undated). *Learning Styles Inventory technical report.* Cleveland, GA: Piney Mountain Press, Inc.
Crehan, K. D. (1995). [Review of the Learning Styles Inventory.] In J. C. Conoley & J. C. Impara (Eds.). *The twelfth mental yearbook measurements yearbook* (pp. 569–570). Lincoln, NE: Buros Institute of Mental Measurements.
Fugate, M. H. (1995). [Review of the Learning Styles Inventory.] In J. C. Conoley & J. C. Impara (Eds.). *The twelfth mental yearbook measurements yearbook* (pp. 570–571). Lincoln, NE: Buros Institute of Mental Measurements.

Review of the Multimedia Learning Styles by GERALD TINDAL, *Professor in Educational Leadership, College of Education, University of Oregon, Eugene, OR:*

DESCRIPTION. This instrument is packaged in a three-ring binder with 23 pages of screen shots from an electronic program used to administer the inventory and summarize the results, a compact disk with both a tutorial and the inventory itself, and a comb-bound Learning Styles Inventory Technical Report that includes an Appendix. The test user is directed to load the inventory onto a local hard drive.

The purpose of the Multimedia Learning Styles (MLS) is to document a student's preferred manner for learning with three dimensions or ways of: (a) learning, (b) working, and (c) reporting. Ways of learning is further divided into "subtopics" (p. 1): (a) auditory language, (b) visual language, (c) auditory numerical, (d) visual numerical, (e) auditory-visual, kinesthetic. The area of working "considers whether a student likes to work or learn in a group or alone" (three-ring notebook, p. 2). Finally, reporting is described as expressiveness, either oral or written.

The descriptions of these constructs are displayed in the software as well as hard copy screenshots and generally provide commonsense definitions that match their labels. For example, "a visual numerical student has to see numbers, on the board, in a book, or in a paper in order to work with them. You are more likely to remember and understand math facts if you have seen them. You don't seem to need as much oral explanation" (three-ring notebook, p. 9). Individual learners are described as the "student gets more work done alone. You think best, and remember more, when you have learned by yourself. You care more for your own opinions than for the ideas of others. You will not have much trouble over-socializing during class" (Three Ring Notebook, p. 10). All other constructs are defined in a similar manner in terms of content specificity and perspective.

Further screen shots are presented covering a range of topics such as essential facts about learning styles, analyzing teaching styles, and learning styles characteristics.

All pages in the notebook are individual screen shots that are linked in the software, which installation includes both a sampler and the program itself. The sampler provides screen shots and is displayed with music and small-captioned video of classroom interactions. Neither the music nor the video are related to the content. The program itself presents several options for taking the instrument and storing the results, either at an individual level or for a group such as a classroom. The software can be licensed at the site level, presumably allowing schools to use it in a computer lab. The menu bar is relatively simple with few options supporting data entry or display.

The instrument itself consists of 45 statements that the student is directed to rate on a 4-point scale with only the end points marked: (4) *Most like me,* (1) *Least like me.*

DEVELOPMENT. The Learning Styles Inventory (LSI) was initiated "to establish a data base to prescribe instruction for students from the students selected learning preference(s)" (technical manual, no page number provided). Initially 166 junior high school students participated in the first pilot testing. An item pool was developed with 10 items per construct and different student groups took a subset of three of these constructs. This one page report on development is presented in an Appendix and provides no data. Three pages of

tables (presenting point-biserial coefficients of each item with the total) are presented after the profile (see below) and presumably are associated with the Phase 1 Report. These coefficients range from .00 to .89 with most in the low-moderate range.

The Appendix includes three charts of item reliability coefficients and descriptive statistics (means and standard deviations for each of grades 7–9 and forms A, B, and C). A one-page Phase 1 report also is included in the Appendix, followed by all three forms, the final form, an answer sheet, worksheet, and profile.

The charts are computer printouts with no codes to understand the numbers and no interpretations presented with them. The three forms are presented with hand-drawn cartoons. The worksheet lists the survey item numbers within each construct and a formula that multiplies the ratings (of the five-item total) by 2. The profile is a one-page Cartesian graph that is hand drawn. The final entry in the Appendix is an article entitled "Vocational classrooms with style" (Fleming, 1989) published in *Vocational Educational Journal.* The content of the article does not report data on the instrument but presents arguments for the need to assess learning styles.

Three forms of the survey were initially developed from which a final form was made. Some statements were reworded in these three forms, though some of them were exact repetitions. No reason is provided why some of the statements were changed and some remained the same. In the technical manual, Chart 3 consists of a table with columns entitled item number, form, and construct. Though not explicitly articulated, it is apparent that for some items, the same statements were used across forms for the same construct.

TECHNICAL. The MLS inventory technical manual describes an assortment of findings that are very difficult to interpret given the lack of details. For example, all three forms of the survey were given to 2,229 students in Grades 7 through 9 "representing all regular junior high schools in USD #259" (technical manual, p. 2). No other information is provided either about the district or demographics about the students. A study is described as Phase 1 to select reliable items from a pool to develop three forms and then in Phase 2 the most reliable constructs were selected from these three forms. The authors then describe two sets of charts: "Chart 1 was then synthesized into

Chart 2 per construct and per form to select reliable constructs for final subtest contribution … The criterion for construct selection is the internal consistency of the construct" (technical manual, p. 3). Then Chart 3 reports the results of the constructs by item. The charts are presented in an Appendix including correlations or means and standard deviations for items, forms, and constructs. No validation data are presented using predictive or concurrent measures or in terms of decision making and learning outcomes.

Some of the text is nonsensical. For example, "generally, internal consistency of constructs reliability will invluence [sic] item reliability; therefore, the item variability of item reliability between forms" (technical manual, p. 3). The technical manual ends with a discussion and recommendations for more research.

Reliability is reported as the percentage of coefficients at various levels with 67% of them below .70. The authors focus primarily on split-half reliability and acknowledge their efforts to keep the instrument brief. "Hopefully, the usability of the instrument is enhanced by keeping the number of items per construct small to minimize testing fatigue. Validity studies would confirm or deny the adequacy of the item number" (technical manual, p. 5).

Reliability also is reported as the percentage of coefficients that changed (improved) from Phase 1 to Phase 2. Though the authors argue that they improved, fully 18% of the coefficients moved from .80 and above to less than .80 in the transition from Phase 1 to Phase 2.

The authors conclude this section of the technical manual by stating "The instrument reported at the present stage of development is in its infancy. Further studies such as factor analysis of the total instrument, validity studies and control field testing for validity should be considered" (technical manual, p. 6).

COMMENTARY. The Multimedia Learning Styles Inventory is unprofessional in every aspect of its content and format and the authors should be reprimanded for not following basic guidelines and standards adopted by the American Educational Research Association, American Psychological Association, and National Council on Measurement in Education (1999). The best statement that can be made about this instrument is that because of the misspellings, poor format, illogical sequence, and mistakes in grammar, the test administrator is very likely to quickly discern how absolutely unacceptable this inventory is for use in the schools. It is likely, however, that the technical manual is not shipped with the software and three-ring binder.

The problems are numerous. The reliability data presented are unacceptable and misinterpreted. More careful research needs to be conducted with procedures explicitly documented. Though the authors use the word "construct" in their description of the dimensions, no attention is given to construct validity. Certainly, given the complex nature of the construct "learning styles," it is likely that misrepresentation is present in terms of construct representation (Messick, 1989). The items are poorly worded and are unlikely to reflect what they are intended to measure. No relationship is presented between the interventions or prescriptions with the statements used to ascertain learning styles. No theory is used to anchor the constructs and no data are presented to support it. The references in the technical manual are all from the 1960s and are selectively used. The technical manual itself is a workout in logic with strange arguments being made that reflect a complete lack of knowledge of either psychological theory-research or measurement development.

SUMMARY. This instrument should not be used by anyone whether in research or practice. The authors provide a glossy interaction using a compact disk (though the software presents strange music and gratuitous video effects) and a data management system with the technical report presented separately. It is likely, however, most users will not see the technical manual because of this electronic packaging and therefore, will be misled. This product should not be sold as a measurement system.

REVIEWER'S REFERENCES

American Educational Research Association, American Psychological Association, & National Council of Measurement in Education. (1999). *Standards for Educational and Psychological Testing*. Washington, DC: American Educational Research Association.
Messick, S. (1989). Meaning and values in test validation: The science and ethics of assessment. *Educational Researcher, 18*(2), 5–11.

[172]

Myers-Briggs Type Indicator® Step II (Form Q).

Purpose: "Provides an in-depth personalized account of personality preferences."
Population: Ages 18 and over.
Publication Date: 2001.
Acronym: MBTI Step II—Form Q.

Scores, 24: Four dichotomies (Extraversion vs. Introversion, Sensing vs. Intuition, Thinking vs. Feeling, Judging vs. Perceiving), 20 facets: 5 Extraversion—Introversion facets (Initiating—Receiving, Expressive—Contained, Gregarious—Intimate, Active—Reflective, Enthusiastic—Quiet), 5 Sensing—Intuition facets (Concrete—Abstract, Realistic—Imaginative, Practical—Conceptual, Experiential—Theoretical, Traditional—Original), 5 Thinking—Feeling facets (Logical—Empathetic, Reasonable—Compassionate, Questioning—Accommodating, Critical—Accepting, Tough—Tender), 5 Judging—Perceiving facets (Systematic—Casual, Planful—Open-Ended, Early Starting—Pressure-Prompted, Scheduled—Spontaneous, Methodical—Emergent).

Administration: Individual or group.

Price Data, 2001: $85 per preview kit including item booklet, prepaid profile answer sheet, and manual (2001, 202 pages); $97 per interpretive (Form Q) preview kit including item booklet, prepaid interpretive answer sheet, and manual; $50 per 25 item booklets; $150 per 10 profile answer sheets; $110 per 5 interpretive answer sheets; $15 per profile web administration; $22 per interpretive web administration; $65 per manual.

Time: (25–35) minutes.

Comments: Includes all items comprising Step I, Form M of MBTI® (T6:1678); can be used to generate all reports produced by Step I, Form M of MBTI®; provides advice for enhancing communication, conflict and change management, and decision making skills; computer or web-administered scoring available.

Authors: Katharine C. Briggs, Isabel Briggs Myers, Naomi L. Quenk (Profile Form, Interpretive Form, MBTI Step II Manual), Jean Kummerow (Profile Form, Interpretive Form), Allen L. Hammer (MBTI Step II Manual), and Mark S. Major (MBTI Step II Manual).

Publisher: Consulting Psychologists Press, Inc.

Cross References: For information about other components of this program, see T5:1755 (78 references) and T4:1702 (45 references); for reviews by John W. Fleenor and Paul M. Mastrangelo of Form M, see 14:251 (1 reference); for a review by Jerry S. Wiggins, see 10:206 (42 references); for a review by Anthony J. DeVito, see 9:739 (19 references); see also T3:1555 (42 references); for a review by Richard Coan, see 8:630 (115 references); see also T2:1294 (120 references) and P:177 (56 references); for reviews by Gerald A. Mendelsohn and Norman D. Sundberg and an excerpted review by Laurence Siegel, see 6:147 (10 references).

Review of the Myers-Briggs Type Indicator® Step II (Form Q) by ALLEN K. HESS, Professor, Auburn University at Montgomery, Montgomery, AL:

DESCRIPTION. Form Q Step II is the most recent iteration of the Myers-Briggs type Indicator (MBTI). Step II develops the facet approach; uses IRT (item response theory) in selecting items; presents a national normative sample; uses a graphical array to show profile results; and reports results via a four-letter personality typing system.

Recently, personality inventories that take a "basic personality" type or trait approach (e.g., the "Big Five" of the NEO-PI-R) have shredded the basic personality traits or types into components. The Form Q Step II uses the term "facets" to depict these components in the MBTI. Two thinking types might have different item and facet endorsements so we might see one as more logical, reasonable, and questioning, whereas the other is more logical, questioning, and critical. The facet scores allow a sharper definition of personality.

DEVELOPMENT. The Form Q Step II uses 93 items from Form M plus 51 more items to compose the total 144-item pool. This allows for the test user to import much of the interpretive wisdom gathered from prior research in using the current Step II edition. Also, it appears that the Step II items are scored on one and only one scale, as opposed to some inventories that use the same item on several scales. The latter compromises any statistical analyses and aborts differential assessment (i.e., makes it hard to distinguish between types of people). Using the item on one and only one scale is excellent and does not inflate scale-to-scale correlations, as is the case with some other inventories.

TECHNICAL.

Sample. A national sample of 1,380 people is a marked advance for the MBTI. Still, the sample is weighted toward the older, the female, and towards Caucasians. When interpretations are made on the basis of the 16 combinations of the types (e.g., ESFP or Extraverted, Sensing, Feeling, and Perceiving person), the normative sample is decomposed. Thus, the interpretation has a smaller sample base if one considers how many of the 1,380 are ESFP types. Future work establishing a sounder normative sample to use in typal interpretation is needed.

Reliability. Internal consistency, or the degree to which items within a scale adhere to each other, is good, particularly given the small number of items (from 5 to 9) on each facet. Alpha coefficients range from .57 to .85 with a median of .77. Test-retest reliability, or the degree to which scores are stable from time to time, is good. The manual presents a more telling stability measure.

Because the MBTI measures types rather than traits, the degree to which people move from one category to another or remain in the same category was computed. The MBTI demonstrates a comforting degree of stability of classification. Finally, the manual presents a Polarity index or a measure of the degree to which people endorse extremes or central positions on the items, a useful feature in interpreting individual profiles.

Validity. Validity concerns the degree to which interpretations drawn from the test are empirically supported. The manual describes the facet scales as correlating with each other (convergent validity) and not correlating with facet scales (discriminant validity) from other dimensions (e.g., Expressive facet with other Extraversion facet scales and not with Thinking scales). Research on factorial purity of the preference scales (e.g., Extraversion-Introversion) is not presented.

The bulk of the validational studies concerns how the MBTI facet and preference scales correlate with several other personality measures: the California Psychological Inventory (CPI), Fundamental Interpersonal Relations Orientation—Behavior (FIRO-B), Eysenck Personality Questionnaire (EPQ), and the Rotter Locus of Control Scale. Also, research based on observer's descriptions of test takers was correlated with MBTI data. Most of the correlations are in the expected direction, providing some evidence of concurrent validity. One problem with this kind of data is that results in the other direction often can be explained away too facilely. The research reported above was either unpublished or published in only one journal, a journal that is not in the mainstream of personality and assessment venues. Thus, predictive and experimental research replicated by various researchers and published in several of the more recognizable journals should provide the type of validational data comforting to test consumers. Finally, the manual asserts that test-taking set is part of personality. No one approaches a test with a test-neutral attitude. Whether for employment, parole, child custody, or, more prosaically, for self-awareness, the test-taker has various attitudes he or she brings to the test items. No validity scales (e.g., social desirability scales) are included, which does not let the test interpreter know the test-taking set of the person being assessed.

COMMENTARY. The MBTI was originally developed by the mother-daughter team of Katherine Cook Briggs and Isabel B. Myers to measure Jungian types so people could know themselves. As such, the Form Q Step II manual stresses that the MBTI measures types (that takes a categorical or more bipolar approach), as opposed to traits (that take dimensional form). This means that a profile should be interpreted holistically rather than from a discrete trait approach. Simply put, a higher score on trait measures of Introversion means a person will show more introversive traits and behaviors. In the type approach, a higher score on Introversion (assuming it as the *dominant function* or most energized and accessible part of a personality) can only be interpreted in light of the *auxiliary function* (which balances the dominant function), the *tertiary function* (opposite to the auxiliary function), and the *inferior function* (opposite to dominant function and least accessible and least known to the person). For example, a person who is extraverted would manifest this dominant function quite differently if he or she has a thinking versus an intuiting auxiliary function. To be fair, any adept trait-oriented test interpreter would take various intensities of traits into account. But the type approach, and the MBTI in particular, builds this holistic interpretation into the fibers of the process. Quite clearly, the person intending to use the MBTI must be immersed in the Jungian perspective to best use the MBTI. The manual provides a good beginning toward orienting the test user in enough Jungian theory to use the MBTI.

SUMMARY. The MBTI has been useful in counseling and employment settings for a half-century. Much "heuristic" validity accumulates when professionals use a test. As test validity depends on the interpretations drawn from a test, the well-written manual provides ample interpretive wisdom. As the test has been used as a stimulus for dialog in counseling and employment, the MBTI might find a place in such collaborative clinical work as Finn and Tonsager (2002) and Fischer's (2000) approach wherein they openly discuss test findings with clients, blending the assessment and therapeutic functions of the clinician. On the other hand, use of the test in making clinical, employment, or forensic decisions without further validational research, particularly of the predictive kind, might be perilous.

REVIEWER'S REFERENCES

Finn, S. E., & Tonsager, M. E. (2002). How therapeutic assessment became humanistic. *Humanistic Psychologist, 30,* 10–22.
Fischer, C. T. (2000). Collaborative individualized assessment. *Journal of Personality Assessment, 74,* 2–14.

Review of the Myers-Briggs Type Indicator® Step II (Form Q) by KEVIN LANNING, Associate Professor of Psychology, Wilkes Honors College of Florida Atlantic University, Jupiter, FL:

The Myers Briggs Type Indicator® Step II (Form Q) (MBTI Step II—Form Q) represents the latest iteration in the continuing development of the MBTI. The MBTI includes scales that measure the dimensions Extraversion—Introversion (E-I), Sensing—Intuition (S-N), Thinking—Feeling (T-F), and Judging—Perceiving (J-P). These measures are typically treated dichotomously, giving rise to 16 types denoted by acronyms (e.g., ESTJ). The four dimensions and resultant type are scored on all three versions of the MBTI currently available from the test publisher, the 126-item Form G, the 93-item Form M (which supplanted Form G as the standard version of the test in 1998), and the 144-item Form Q presently under review. This review includes a brief discussion of the MBTI typology as well as comments specific to Step II—Form Q.

As a Step II measure of the MBTI, Form Q is the product of a lineage that runs largely parallel to that of the more widely used MBTI Forms G and M. Though Form Q is identical to Form M in the scoring of type, Form Q includes additional items derived from the 1989 Form K and its associated MBTI Expanded Analysis Report which, in 1996, was renamed the Expanded Interpretive Report. The additional items allow the scoring of five subscales ("facets") for each of the four dichotomies, which are reported to users in a brief Step II Profile or a more lengthy Step II Interpretive Report. In principle, the inclusion of the Step II facet scales permits more nuanced interpretation than would be afforded by describing persons in terms of type alone.

The facet scales vary in breadth: For each of the four dichotomies, there is a core facet as well as additional, narrower facets. For Extraversion—Introversion, the core facet is Initiating—Receiving. For the functions of S-N and T-F, the core facets are Concrete—Abstract and Logical—Empathetic, respectively, whereas for J-P, the core is Systematic—Casual. For purposes of interpretation, scores are reduced to three categories: "in-preference" (i.e., in the same direction as the broader dichotomy of which the facet is a part), "midzone," and "out-of-preference." Because in-preference scores are expected given the structure of the instrument, it is the out-of-preference scores that are the main source of interest. These latter scores are used as a supplement to the four-letter type to provide an individualized type description, as, for example, in "Enthusiastic, Questioning, Casual INFJ." In addition to the 20 facets, a largely atheoretical Polarity Index measures the omnibus extremity of the facet scales, or the tendency to respond to each scale in a relatively homogeneous way.

DEVELOPMENT. The facet scales were derived from the administration of items from several prior forms of the test to a national sample of 1,380 adults recruited through random-digit dialing. Although the sample was intended to reflect U.S. Census demographics, the average age of respondents is approximately 50. An initial version of the facets was developed based on confirmatory factor analyses of Form K and other sets of items. From these analyses, items were retained for Form Q based on several criteria, including conceptual fit, the item response theory (IRT) discrimination parameter, and contribution to the internal consistency of the scale. Correlations between the Form Q measures and corresponding earlier Form K measures suggest some substantial changes from the prior measure; these range from .57 to .95 with a median of .82.

TECHNICAL. All 20 of the facets are brief, ranging from five to nine items in length, but are presented to users on an 11-point scale. Because these scores are computed using IRT, no hand-scoring is available. The manual includes descriptive statistics for the facets that are broken down by gender and age. The authors also report the kurtosis of the distribution of facet scores, but are incorrect in their assertion that these values, with a range of .09 to -1.41, support the supposed bimodality of the scales.

The correlational structure of Form Q appears largely appropriate to its intended form. In a confirmatory factor analysis, an adjusted goodness-of-fit index (AGFI) of .95 was found for the four factor by five facet model. Correlations among facet scales associated with different MBTI dichotomies are typically modest (most < |.20|), whereas those between facets within a dichotomy are typically higher (most > .5). For all but one of the facet scales, correlations with the corresponding higher order dichotomy range between .5 and .9; the remaining facet (Questioning-Accommodating) is also the only facet scale that does not share items with its broader dichotomy (Thinking-Feeling). The internal consistencies for the facets, with a median of .77, are generally high given the short length of these measures.

In addition to reliability data for the continuous scales, the manual also provides some information regarding the stability of the tripartite categories of in-preference, midzone, or out-of-preference. Across the 20 facets, the median percentage of adults remaining in the same category over a 1-month span was 73%, with only 3% moving across the two extremes.

Because the Form Q facet scales are new, evidence for their validity remains limited. The manual includes correlations with two other self-report measures, the California Psychological Inventory (CPI) and the Adjective Check List (ACL). These correlations are typically in the expected direction, particularly for the facets of Extraversion-Introversion, but do not yet support a differentiated understanding of the meaning of the facets. Similarly, hierarchical regression analyses were undertaken to assess the incremental contribution of the facets beyond the basic MBTI dimensions in the prediction of consequential outcomes such as reported hypertension and punctuality. These results indicate that the facets, when considered together, contribute to the validity of the test, but they do not speak to the meaning of the individual scales. Finally, the manual also presents correlations between the prior Form K facet scales and observer ratings and additional self-report measures; however, given the apparent differences between the Form K and Q facet scales, these are of uncertain relevance to the present instrument.

COMMENTARY. Reviews of previous versions of the MBTI have taken issue with the position that it is a measure of types rather than a measure of traits (see in particular the reviews by Mendelsohn, 1965; Mastrangelo, 2001; & Wiggins, 1989). Because the manual and interpretive materials continue to stress this point, it is appropriate to briefly consider its conceptual and empirical support.

Evidence supporting a typological interpretation of the MBTI would include, but is not limited to, both multidimensional clustering and interactions between type variables in the predictions of outcomes. The four-dimensional space defined by the E-I, S-N, T-F, and J-P axes would ideally be populated by 16 clusters, each discrete and distant from all four axes, with interactions reflected in different patterns of correlations in different clusters (such that, for example, the meaning of Thinking would effectively be different for Extraverts and Introverts). This is a very strong conception of type, but one that is suggested by the manual in the statement that "scores are expected to be bimodal—few scores at the midpoint," "the numerical portion of MBTI results has no ... diagnostic meaning," and "the four type preferences interact dynamically to form a whole that is different from the sum of the parts" (manual, p. 17).

To those raised on the Central Limit Theorem and the belief that characteristics such as extraversion are the product of polygenes and immeasurable experiences, the a priori likelihood that the distribution of MBTI scores would cleave naturally into 16 roughly equal clusters is certainly small. Unfortunately, the manual does not provide empirical evidence which would reduce skepticism on this point. Empirical support for bimodality in the individual scales is lacking (Bess & Harvey, 2002), as is solid evidence favoring a configural interpretation of the instrument (the MMY review by Mastrangelo, 2001; cf. Reynierese & Harker, 2001). But although there is little support for treating the MBTI types as real entities, there is value in using the types as descriptive labels. The MBTI is now considered the most popular test of personality in history. This popularity stems not only from the attractiveness of Jungian concepts, but also from the appeal and cognitive economy of categories over dimensions. "ENFP" is easier to understand than, for example, t-scores of 65 on Extraversion, 35 on Sensing, 32 on Thinking, and 28 on Judging, and this probably accounts for much of the continuing popularity of the instrument. The value of the MBTI typology to consumers cannot be dismissed, despite the fact that it is the product of arbitrary cutting points rather than Aristotelian essences.

There are costs associated with treating the MBTI measures as dichotomies rather than as continua. For example, the reliabilities of continuous scales overestimate those of corresponding dichotomies by a factor of approximately 1.25 (see MacCallum, Zhang, Preacher, & Rucker, 2002). This problem is ameliorated somewhat by the fact that the interpretive materials accompanying the

MBTI encourage recognition of the fallibility of scores on the instrument. The various profile sheets for the MBTI include bar charts and tables that plainly show the extremity (or "preference clarity") of scores. On the Step II Profile Sheet (though not on the Step II Interpretive Report), users are explicitly told that "The longer the bar ... the more likely it is that the instrument has accurately reflected your preference." On the Report (though not on the Profile Sheet), users are given the option of simply entering the client's "verified type" rather than deriving it from responses to the test.

In the MBTI, the categorization of persons into types is inevitably imperfect. Because most individuals will score near the mean on at least one of the major dimensions of the test, type classification may be unstable, with some one-third of all individuals changing type over a span of 1 month (see the MMY reviews by Fleenor, 2001, and Mastrangelo, 2001).

Though inclusion of the facet scales addresses this problem, it does not solve it. For example, consider a woman whose classification as an ESTJ masks only a slight preference for Sensing over Intuition. An examination of her facet scores might clarify the meaning of the moderate S-N score, reflecting, perhaps, two facets in the Sensing direction (Realistic and Practical), two in the Intuitive direction (Theoretical and Original), and one in the midzone. A problem arises when this pattern is reduced to a summary description. Because her preference for Sensing over Intuition is small, different responses to a mere one or two items could lead her to be classified as an ENTJ rather than an ESTJ. The facet scales that were previously out-of-preference would then become in-preference, and so she would change from being classified as a "Theoretical, Original ESTJ" to an "Realistic, Practical ENTJ."

Recognizing the problem that arises when facets are interpreted in light of type, the manual stresses the importance of verifying a client's type prior to providing a substantive interpretation of facet scores. But the notion of "verification" presupposes that the MBTI types really exist in nature, that there are underlying bifurcations on the major dimensions of the test. The evidence does not, again, support this claim; the world includes ambiverts as well as extraverts and introverts. Unfortunately, the midzone scores that are recognized for the facets are not applied to the higher order measures of the MBTI.

SUMMARY. There is a trade-off between simplicity and accuracy in the description of any person, between comprehensibility and completeness. The standard version of the MBTI has achieved popular success by positioning itself near the first of these poles. MBTI Step II represents a step towards the second pole, towards a more thorough if less simple description of personality. Although there is much that is attractive about this step, time will tell whether this new extension of the test retains the popular success of the prior version, and whether its narrow bandwidth facet scales warrant discrete interpretation.

REVIEWER'S REFERENCES

Bess, T. L., & Harvey, R. J. (2002). Bimodal score distributions and the Myers-Briggs Type Indicator: Fact or artifact? *Journal of Personality Assessment, 78,* 176–186.
Fleenor, J. W. (2001). [Review of the Myers-Briggs Type Indicator, Form M]. In B. S. Plake & J. C. Impara (Eds.), *The fourteenth mental measurements yearbook* (pp. 816–818). Lincoln, NE: Buros Institute of Mental Measurements.
MacCallum, R. C., Zhang, S., Preacher, K. J., & Rucker, D. (2002). On the practice of dichotomization of quantitative variables. *Psychological Methods, 7,* 19–40.
Mastrangelo, P. M. (2001). [Review of the Myers-Briggs Type Indicator, Form M]. In B. S. Plake & J. C. Impara (Eds.), *The fourteenth mental measurements yearbook* (pp. 818–819). Lincoln, NE: Buros Institute of Mental Measurements.
Mendelsohn, G. A. (1965). [Review of the Myers-Briggs Type indicator]. In O. K. Buros (Ed.), *The eighth mental measurements yearbook* (pp. 321–322). Highland Park, NJ: Gryphon Press.
Reynierse, J. H., & Harker, J. B. (2001). The interactive and additive nature of psychological type. *Journal of Psychological Type, 58,* 6–32.
Wiggins, J. S. (1989). [Review of the Myers-Briggs Type Indicator]. In J. C. Conoley & J. J. Kramer (Eds.), *The tenth mental measurements yearbook* (pp. 537–538). Lincoln, NE: Buros Institute of Mental Measurements.

[173]

Neale Analysis of Reading Ability, 3rd Edition [Australian Standardisation].

Purpose: Designed to "assess reading progress objectivity [and] to obtain structured diagnostic observations of an individual's reading behaviour."

Population: Ages 6 to 12.

Publication Dates: 1958–1999.

Scores, 3: Accuracy, Comprehension, Rate.

Administration: Individual.

Forms, 2: 1, 2.

Price Data, 2002: A$35 per test booklet; A$1.50 per individual record standardised test (specify form); A$1.50 per individual record diagnostic tutor (specify form); A$49.50 per manual (1999, 141 pages); A$19.95 per audio cassette tape; A$89 per specimen set including test booklet, 1 each individual record standardised test form 1 and 2, 1 each individual record diagnostic tutor Form A and B, and manual.

Time: Administration time not reported.

Comments: Includes six supplementary diagnostic tests (Discrimination of Initial and Final Sounds, Names and Sounds of the Alphabet, Graded Spelling, Auditory Discrimination and Blending, Word Lists, and Silent Reading/Writing).

Authors: Marie D. Neale, Michael McKay, and John Barnard.

Publisher: Australian Council for Educational Research Ltd. [Australia].

Cross References: For information regarding the British Edition, see T5:1765 (36 references) and T4:1714 (7 references); for reviews by Cleborne D. Maddux and G. Michael Poteat, see 11:257 (41 references); see also T3:1567 (13 references) and T2:1683 (7 references); for reviews by M. Alan Brimer and Magdalen D. Vernon, and an excerpted review, see 6:843.

Review of the Neale Analysis of Reading Ability, 3rd Edition [Australian Standardisation] by VALENTINA McINERNEY, Professor, School of Psychology, University of Western Sydney, Penrith South DC, New South Wales, Australia:

DESCRIPTION. The Neale Analysis of Reading Ability is an individually administered test of oral reading ability that enables the examiner to assess an individual's level of reading attainment against Australian norms. It is claimed that the Neale can be used with readers of any age, including adults, and especially those whose first language is not English. It also has been used for many years by reading specialists and clinicians to test the oral reading ability of those with a range of disabilities that have impeded their reading development.

The Neale consists of a reader (which contains Supplementary Diagnostic Tests), manual, and individual record forms. The reader contains short narratives presented at six levels of increasingly difficult vocabulary and grammar, each with a line drawing on the opposing page. The standardized forms of the narratives are presented in two parallel sets—Forms 1 and 2—to enable retesting of a student's reading to check for consistency. The testing procedure involves establishing a student's basal reading level followed by the student progressively reading passages aloud and orally answering comprehension questions until a specified number of errors have been made. The test administrator records the time taken in seconds (using a stop watch) and errors made during reading on the student's individual record. Upon completion of the test administration an error count of the number and types of errors made (mispronunciations, substitutions, refusals, additions, omissions, and reversals) is recorded. These measures provide three raw scores: Accuracy, Comprehension, and Rate, which can be converted to standardized scores.

In addition to the standardized testing materials of the Reader, two parallel sets of supplementary, nonstandardized passages are included in the Neale—Diagnostic Tutor Forms A and B. These include activities for informal diagnosis of a student's reading behavior in a nontesting situation: cloze exercises, informal reading inventories, criterion-referenced assessment, oral and silent reading comprehension, and finding a student's instructional reading level. No scores are calculated.

DEVELOPMENT. The original Neale Analysis of Reading Ability was published in 1958 with a British standardization. It contained more than 25 narrative passages that were graded for vocabulary, syntactic complexity, and length into six levels suitable for students from Grades 1 to 6 (ages 6 to 12). These narratives were to be read aloud to a teacher who was to score them for Rate, Accuracy, and Comprehension. The second edition of the Neale was published in 1988 and involved a review of the content and structure of the original narratives for their suitability to a new generation of school students, particularly in terms of their vocabulary and themes. British and Australian standardizations were also developed for the 1988 edition. The second revision of the Neale, with grading restandardized for both British and Australian students, was published in 1999. Several reasons given by the developer for the Australian revision include: significant changes in reading and literacy instruction; school curricula; reading standards; demographic/cultural profiles of the community; language usage; and changing knowledge about the reading process and its evaluation. These generalizations, however, are not amplified with specifics about the ways in which such important changes have been addressed in the third edition (1999), nor is a theoretical and pedagogical rationale underpinning them provided.

TECHNICAL. The Neale (1999) was standardized in late 1997 on a random sample of 116 Australian schools, stratified on the basis of socioeconomic status. A total of 1,394 students were finally used in proportion to the number of schools and students in the states and territories. Sex and number of students from each school were kept constant, with only the state/territory and type of school (Independent, Catholic, and Government) used as variables (manual, p. 68). Two boys and two girls were randomly selected from each grade

(K–6). The representation of schools varied from only 2 (Catholic) schools in the Northern Territory and 4 (Government) schools in the Australian Capital Territory, to 36 in New South Wales, with the proportion of Government schools to Catholic Schools being 3:1. Given the uneven population distribution of Australia, and the wide diversity of racial groups from traditional Aboriginal groups on welfare benefits in the Northern Territory, to professional middle class Anglos in the Australian Capital Territory, such a sample seems hardly representative, and even less reliable once averaged.

In Australia, there is considerable variation between different states and territories in the ages for earliest enrollment at school, times of enrollment in the school year, names given to year/grade levels, and ways in which students are grouped for literacy instruction. For this reason, the Neale represents norms for each of the Rate, Accuracy, and Comprehension scores in three ways. The first allows the test user to interpret a raw score in terms of a percentile rank or stanine according to Year of Schooling (YOS)—up to 7 years. The second way is by a "traditional," single Reading Age that represents a predicted age from 6 to 12 years for which a given score is an average accomplishment. Third, it is claimed that Neale raw scores can be interpreted in terms of National Profile Levels that describe "student progression of learning typically achieved during the compulsory years of schooling" (manual, p. 30). This claim does not rest on strong empirical support. The process adopted for linking the Neale to National Profile Levels was to equate its Forms 1 and 2 "through anchoring, calibration, equating and transformation" (manual, p. 31) using the Rasch model. An effort was then made to correlate the Neale with an Australian developmental test of literacy, the Developmental Assessment Resource for Teachers (DART) (Forster, Mendelovits, & Masters, 1994) by having "a number of students" complete Form 2 of the Neale and one Reading form of the DART. The correlation coefficients between the two tests are reported in very general terms only (between .70 and .77). It is important to note that there are two DART Reading Forms, which vary in difficulty and, unlike the Neale's oral reading tests, require silent reading of different text genres and written answers to short questions. Which one of the two DART Forms was used is not mentioned. No theoretical framework is given to argue for its concurrent validity with the DART, yet, it is only on the basis of the correlation with the DART Reading that the author argues that "Neale Raw Scores obtained in Forms 1 and 2 can be linked to National Profile Levels that had been previously related to DART tasks." (manual, p. 31).

Reported correlations of the first edition of the Neale (1958) with other standardized reading tests of the time, such as the Vernon and Schonell Reading Tests are also cited as evidence of concurrent validity by the author, as are those of the second edition (1981–82) with the Schonell Graded Word Reading Test (ranging from .76 to .96 for Forms 1 and 2), and the Vocabulary and Similarities subtests of the Wechsler Intelligence Scale for Children—Revised (WISC-R) (ranging from .41 for Rate vs. Similarities to .68 for Vocabulary vs. Comprehension). As mentioned above, correlations of the current edition (1999) with the DART yielded coefficients ranging from .70 to .77. According to the author, taken together, "these results generally confirm that the subscores of the Neale Analysis do measure discrete components of the reading process" (manual, p. 75). Such evidence does not meet the rigorous psychometric standards for substantiating validity set out in the *Standards for Educational and Psychological Testing* (AERA, APA, & NCME, 1999), however.

In relation to the *Standards*, there are a number of additional areas in which the validity evidence for the Neale is weak. One is the extent that reading experts would agree with the developer about the test resembling "real-life" activity, namely, reading aloud and answering comprehension questions. The constantly evolving definitions of literacy as "multiliteracies" (Cope & Kalantzis, 2000), emerging from the rise of interactive multimedia and electronic hypermedia (New London Group, 1996), create doubt about the extent to which the skills examined in the Neale are as necessary for today's students as they were 40 years ago when the test was first published.

It is also a concern that only the author has chosen and modified the passages for inclusion through all editions of the test, apparently without reference to other reading expert reference groups. Brief mention is made of "a number of informal surveys" of professionals who used the Neale to gauge their reactions to proposed changes, as well as age-level samples of British students being asked to respond to the original and alternative narratives in the 1970s (manual, p. 64).

In the current Australian standardization, only minor modifications to the 1988 version of the passages have been made to reduce perceived sex-role stereotyping of main characters. The rationale given is to maintain comparability of data drawn from research using the British edition. As a consequence, the narratives are dated in their style and remain "British" in content. As such they will hold little appeal or relevance to most students in Australian schools, especially those from indigenous backgrounds and non-English-speaking backgrounds. The author has written new passages for the Diagnostic Tutor of the current Australian edition on topics that she feels are of interest to young people: bushfires, steam trains, global communication, and paradigm shifts in a changing world. Given the high stakes attached to reading test results in Australia in terms of classroom grouping, withdrawal from classes for "remedial" reading, and communications with students' primary caregivers, it is critical that strong validity can be demonstrated empirically. Australian data need to be provided on the differential outcomes of Neale testing for males and females in interaction with ethnicity and language background.

To its credit, many studies have been conducted using earlier versions of the Neale over the last 20 years to investigate correlates of the differences between groups of poor and effective readers. Variables identified in such research include educational programs, language backgrounds, information-processing strategies, physical injuries and impairments, parenting, and peer tutoring. In addition, a Braille version is currently being standardized in Britain for use throughout that country (Greaney, 2002). Such evidence is offered as support for the construct validity of the Neale.

During the 1997 Australian standardization process of the Neale, a number of reliability estimates were calculated. These included parallel forms reliability coefficients of above .90 for whole-year age groups. The sample size on which these were calculated is not reported, however, only that "a number of students" (manual, p. 70) were tested on Form 1 and either Form 2 or Form 3 (Diagnostic Tutor). Internal consistency was calculated using KR20. Whole-year age groups, with Ns of around 140, were employed. These studies provided coefficients of around .95 for Accuracy; Rate around

.94, and Comprehension in the high .80s. Particularly high levels of reliability were obtained for the younger age groups. No reliability data are reported for the supplementary diagnostic components.

Interscorer reliability between classroom teachers and trained assessors on administration and scoring of the Neale, as well as test-retest reliabilities after an 8-week interval between administrations, were carried out with a sample of 100 students in two groups. Correlations were high for the three components: Rate ($r = .95$), Accuracy ($r = .95$), and Comprehension ($r = .93$); however, the procedure for allocating students to groups (randomly, by age, grade, YOS) is not given.

COMMENTARY. The Neale Analysis of Reading Ability (Australian Standardization) is not designed as a large-scale reading assessment tool. Rather, it is an informal test of reading given in a one-to-one situation. What it offers the classroom teacher or reading specialist is an easily administered, scored, and interpreted means of diagnosing a student's competence in specific areas of basic reading skills and translating scores into local norms. As such, its value lies in the specificity of the reading constructs it identifies, providing the practitioner with a framework for developing individualized reading improvement plans for students at risk of not achieving minimum literacy standards (as defined in Australian National Profile Levels). Given the demands of busy classroom teachers, the short time (about 20 minutes) that it takes to administer the Neale contributes to its longstanding popularity. In its most recent form, too many weaknesses in terms of its overall validity remain unresolved, however.

SUMMARY. The Neale Analysis of Reading Ability (Australian Standardization, 1999) has limited usefulness as a general measure of reading ability in the Australian context. Effective literacy has been defined at a National level for the last decade as "intrinsically purposeful, flexible and dynamic ... involving the integration of speaking, listening and critical thinking with reading and writing" (Department of Education Employment Training and Youth Affairs, 1998, p. 7). In keeping with current information-processing theory, Fehring (2001) argues that classroom practitioners need to collect literacy assessment information that is both "multimodal" (multiple modes through which information is processed) and "multidimensional" (examining a range of forms within one category of literacy). In this context, the Neale can provide a snapshot of one dimension of a student's literacy achievement. Depending on the age of the test-takers, readers should consider one of the two Developmental Assessment Resource for Teachers (DART) English tests (Forster, Medelovits, & Masters, 1994; Bodey, Darkin, Forster, & Masters, 1997) as more comprehensive and current alternatives to the Neale, with its limited focus on the mechanical aspects of reading.

REVIEWER'S REFERENCES
American Educational Research Association, American Psychological Association, & National Council on Measurement In Education. (1999). *Standards for educational and psychological testing.* Washington, DC: American Educational Research Association (ACER).

Bodey, W., Darkin, L., Forster, M., & Masters, G. (1997). Developmental Assessment Resource for Teachers (DART) English (Middle Primary). Melbourne: Australian Council for Educational Research.

Cope, B., & Kalantzis, M. (Eds.). (2000). *Multiliteracies: Literacy learning and the design of social futures.* South Yarra, Australia: MacMillan.

Department of Education Employment, Education, Training and Youth Affairs. (1998). *Literacy for all: The challenge for Australian schools. Commonwealth literacy policies for Australian schools.* Canberra, Australian Capital Territory.

Fehring, H. (2001). *Literacy assessment and reporting. 12th European Conference on Reading, RAI Dublin 1st–4th July 2001.* Retrieved November, 2002 from http://sece.eu.rmit.edu.au/staff/fehring/irish.htm/

Forster, M., Mendelovits, J., & Masters, G. (1994). Developmental Assessment Resource for Teachers (DART).English Melbourne: Australian Council for Educational Research (ACER).

Greaney, J. (2002). *The development of a new standardized rest of children's Braille reading abilities in Britain.* Retrieved November 2002 from http://www.braille.org/papers/jvib0696/vb960318.htm

New London Group. (1996), A pedagogy of multiliteracies: Designing social futures. *Harvard Educational Review, 66*(1), 60–92.

Review of the Neale Analysis of Reading Ability, 3rd Edition [Australian Standardisation] by BRUCE G. ROGERS, Professor of Educational Psychology, University of Northern Iowa, Cedar Falls, IA:

DESCRIPTION. The Neale Analysis of Reading Ability, 3rd Edition [Australian Standardisation] was devised as a series of passages of text with controlled vocabulary for the purpose of assessing Accuracy, Rate, and Comprehension of oral reading. The test is designed to be individually administered by an examiner who records responses, requiring approximately 20 minutes for the standardized assessment. A Diagnostic Tutor is also provided, with a similar format. Both have alternate forms.

According to the manual, the test was designed to be administered, scored, and interpreted by a classroom teacher; to "create a bond of trust between teacher administrator and student" (p. 1) and to allow the teacher to "observe and record an individual's reading performance sympathetically yet with scientific rigor" (p. 2). While each passage is being read aloud by the student, the teacher records types of errors (e.g., mispronunciations and omissions) and the time, and subsequently administers eight questions to assess comprehension. After computing total raw scores for Accuracy, Comprehension, and Rate, the teacher is referred to tables to create five converted scores (e.g., percentiles, stanines, and reading age).

A Diagnostic Tutor is also included, which is another set of graded passages. However, no normative data are provided in the manual. Rather, it is said to be a "criterion-referenced test." The manual states that teachers are "to set their own standards for particular students" (p. 35). Some teachers may wish that some guidance had been given in the manual toward the setting of standards.

Both the Standardised Test and the Diagnostic tutor contain a set of six "Supplementary Diagnostic Tests" (e.g., Names and Sounds of the Alphabet and Word Lists). They are not standardized, but are designed to "augment the observations that the examiner has made" (p. 40). Explicit directions for administration are given; however, some teachers may wish that some guidance for interpretation had been given also.

Because each of the above mentioned instruments is provided with an alternate form, the teacher may choose to administer the instrument twice without repetition of the specific content. It is anticipated that the teacher will be able to use the complete profile to develop a program to improve the literacy skill of the pupil.

DEVELOPMENT. The first edition of the Neale Analysiswas published and standardized in Great Britain in 1958 and was subsequently revised while the author was in Australia. The third edition purports to reflect changing standards in reading; however, the norms were collected only in Australian schools. The construction of each passage was guided by controlling the vocabulary and the complexity of the syntax. The theoretical basis, according to the author, was in child development, social psychology, and perceptual psychology, along with research in reading. For each passage, a shaded line drawing has been prepared. They are neatly drawn; however, the manual does not describe the logic on which they were developed. Some teachers and researchers might appreciate such information. Although the test purports to be theoretically based, there is very little information in the manual on the theoretical selection of the types of errors and the justification for creating and interpreting the composite error score. Teachers might also appreciate further discussion on how the comprehension questions were constructed. Although the manual contains a section entitled "theoretical framework" and "rationale for development of the Neale Analysis" (p. 4), the statements appeared to this reviewer to be lacking in developing a coherent plan. For example, the sentence "Rate of reading gives insights into sensory co-ordination" (p. 5) stands alone, without any further explanation of what types of insights might be expected.

In developing the third edition, the author has created an attractive reader bookle, and has penned case studies of five individuals spanning the school-age range. Both of these contribute to the value of the instrument.

TECHNICAL.

Normative data. The norm sample (for the Standardised Test) consisted of 116 schools (of 170 that were invited) in Australia. Each school was instructed to randomly select two girls and two boys at each grade level, 1 through 7. Unfortunately, the manual does not give any evidence to substantiate the extent to which the instructions were actually followed. Some researchers have found, to their dismay, that written directions have not been followed in distant locations. Some evidence to support the compliance in this study would be useful. Furthermore, there is not a breakdown of pupils by grade level. A total of 1,394 students participated, resulting in an average of about 12 students per school. But if there were 4 pupils from each grade level, then only about three grades were represented in each school, on the average. The manual does not discuss this discrepancy. The norm tables run from Years 1 through 7 (of schooling in Australian system), but the number of subjects is not given. Although schools were encouraged to train the teachers prior to the administration of the tests, the manual presents no evidence that such training actually occurred. It appears that it was not the intention of the author for the test to be used outside of Australia, therefore, the application of the norms elsewhere, including the United States, would be a less defensible procedure.

Reliability. The manual reports parallel form reliability, a commendable procedure. For some unexplained reason, the values are reported by age level, instead of by grade level. Because reliability is a property of the scores and not the instrument, it would be appropriate to conclude, from the reported data, that a teacher could be reasonably confident that a set of properly collected scores will have reliability for decision making with either form of the test. However, the reliability values reported for "all groups" are highly inflated because all of the ages were aggregated. A more meaningful value would be the median value for each of the age groups.

Because the test is not composed of dichotomously scored items, KR21 (instead of the more common KR20) was used to estimate internal consistency from the means and standard deviations. However, if the passages are conceived as items, then coefficient alpha would be an appropriate measure of internal consistency. Unfortunately, this approach is not addressed in the manual. The manual reports the KR21 values for years of schooling ranging from 1 to 7. These internal consistency estimates for Comprehension scores generally exceed .85 and for Rate and Accuracy scores exceed .94. Overall, the reliability data for the Third Edition represents an improvement in interpretability from the previous versions of the test.

Validity. The evidence for content validity appears to consist only of the opinion of the authors. This evidence might be improved if tables of specification were shown and judgments of experts were collected. The evidence for criterion-related validity consists of the description of the results of some studies and a table showing correlations with one other reading test and two subscales of the Wechsler Intelligence Scale for Children—Revised (WISC-R). The evidence for construct validity consists of data to show discrimination between age levels, sex differences, and interpretation of published studies using the Neale. In general, the validation process might be improved to the extent that it conformed with the accepted published standards for testing.

COMMENTARY. The value of this test is affirmed in several areas. First, the interesting passages and the controlled vocabulary are likely to enhance the willingness of the student to cooperate in the testing situation. Second, the parallel form reliability gives some assurance of stability of the scores. Third, the Australian norms give the teacher one useful tool for interpreting the scores.

On the other hand, the value of this test is likely to be questioned in several areas. First, the teacher may have difficulty understanding how the written passages actually relate to the theory as stated in the manual. Evidence to substantiate the relationships would be useful. Second, the teacher may find the calculation of the scores to be very tedious. Psychometrically, there is no advantage in subtracting the error scores from an arbitrary constant. Likewise, there does not appear to be any advantage in converting the error scores to percentages. The teachers who participated in the norm sample were asked to administer the tests, but not to score them. Thus, there needs to be evidence on how teachers respond to this time-consuming procedure. Third, the teachers may have concerns about the types of inferences that can be made from the resulting scores. For example, how is the interpretation of the Rate score affected by its correlation with the Comprehension score? Information on the interrelationships of the scores would contribute toward an overall understanding of the reading process.

SUMMARY. The author of the Neale Analysis stated a goal to help build a bond between student and teacher. Although that is one desirable goal, the manual appears to not report evidence relating to that issue. The professional printing of the Reader contributes to the face validity of the instrument. The directions for administering are clear, but the scoring of the test may be perceived by some teachers as requiring excessive computation. The scores appear to be reasonably stable, but the evidence for internal consistency could be improved. The validity evidence could be improved to conform to current professional standards. Researchers might want to investigate the construct validity and the generality of the norms. Teachers may find some of the passages to be helpful in identifying areas of strength and weakness in the reading ability of a student. However, the teacher may wish to first examine other commonly used tests currently on the market to determine if the purposes of the teacher will be best served by the Neale Analysis.

[174]
NSight Aptitude/Personality Questionnaire.

Purpose: A "method for measuring a person's work-related characteristics ... [that can be used] for hiring and promoting people who are similar to those already successful in the job."
Population: Adults.
Publication Dates: 1990–2002.
Acronym: NAPQ.

Scores, 26: 3 Cognitive Characteristics (Verbal Reasoning/Comprehension, Numerical Reasoning, Word Knowledge); 1 Achievement Characteristic (Visual Perception); 19 Personality Characteristics measured along 6 subtopics: Thinking Style (Emotional Decision Maker, Analytical Thinker, Logical Thinker, Practical), Drives (Security Oriented, Cooperative, Rule Bound), Stress (Anxious, Tolerant, Apprehensive), Communication (Serious, Reserved, Assuming), Leadership (Passive, Submissive, Suspicious), Reliability (Indifferent, Changeable, Expedient); 3 Validity Scales (Lie, Faking Bad, Faking Good).
Administration: Group.
Price Data, 2002: $168 per assessment including 11-page report and telephone consultation; quantity discounts available.
Time: (120) minutes for Cognitive Characteristics Inventory; Personality Inventory untimed.
Author: Stephen Overcash.
Publisher: Directional Insight International, Inc.

Review of the NSIGHT Aptitude/Personality Questionnaire by JOHN S. GEISLER, Professor, Department of Counselor Education and Counseling Psychology, Western Michigan University, Kalamazoo, MI:

DESCRIPTION. NSIGHT consists of two instruments: the Aptitude Inventory (AI) and the Personality Inventory (PI). The AI consists of four aptitude measures (Cognitive Characteristics): Verbal Reasoning (30 items, 15 minutes), Numerical Reasoning (15 items, 15 minutes), Vocabulary (25 items, 10 minutes), and Visual Perception (50 items, 3 minutes).

The Personality Inventory (PI) (99 items, untimed) assesses 22 personality characteristics that are grouped into seven categories: (a) Self-Perception (Valid/Invalid Candor, Positive/Negative Self-Esteem, and Low/High Self-Concept), (b) Thinking Style (Emotional/Cognitive Decision Maker, Analytical/Instinctive Thinker, Logical/Imaginative Thinker, Practical, Tough-Minded/Empathetic, Sensitive), (c) Drive (Security/Recognition Oriented, Cooperative/Competitive, Rule Bound/Risk Taker), (d) Stress (Anxious/Steady, Tolerant, Conventional/Intolerant, Unconventional, Apprehensive, Concerned/Confident), (e) Communication (Serious, Reflective/Enthusiastic, Reserved/Self-Disclosing, Assuming, Forthright/Political), (f) Leadership (Passive/Assertive, Submissive/Aggressive, Suspicious, Oppositional/Trusting, Accepting), and (g) Reliability (Indifferent/Committed, Loyal, Changeable/Persistent, High Ego Drive, Expedient, Impulsive/Conscientious). The number of items/scale is not provided nor is there any information about which PI items are associated with which scales.

The scoring profile consists of one page and contains: (a) standard scores for each scale, (b) the location of the standard scores on an 11-point (0–10) scale, and (c) high/low descriptions of what the 22 personality and 4 aptitude (cognitive) subtests purport to measure. Three validity scales have been developed: Lie, Faking Bad, and Faking Good. These scales are the first three PI scales described above as the Self-Perception Scales (Candor, Self-Esteem, and Self-Concept). Evidently, these scales serve two purposes.

Information regarding the derivation and conversion of raw scores into standard scores (11-point scale) is not provided except that the scores are described as either Standard Scores (PI) or Cognitive Scores (AI) on the Profile Sheet. Three tables are presented in the manual. Additional tables are not published and must be secured from the publisher.

DEVELOPMENT. No information is provided regarding the origin, development, history, field testing, underlying assumptions, theory, or rationale for the instruments. The developers of the PI and AI indicate that these instruments have been designed to assist employers in making wise choices when selecting potential employees. They indicate that the instruments demonstrate that "employers can test [sic] select workers who learn faster, are more productive, disciplined, safer, happier and more compatible" (p. 1) with the organizational culture they will enter.

TECHNICAL. The normative reference group members (listed as either $N = 6,000$ or $5,000+$) are described as: (a) being between 17 and 58 years old, (b) having "a fairly equal distribution of men and women" (p. 1), (c) being from 10 states, (d) consisting of a cross section of occupations, (e) being mostly adults, and (f) including some vocational school seniors. The sample is ethnically diverse (Euro-American 68%, Afro-American 15%, Oriental 5%, Hispanic 8%, and others 4%).

An analysis of the reliability data ($N = 1,047$) indicates that the reliability coefficients range from .41 (Expedient/Conscientious) to .83 (Numerical Reasoning). Of the 25 scale coefficients listed, 8 are above .70. Data from a test-retest procedure with a 4- to 8-week interval is reported on the PI only ($N = 587$). The resulting coefficients are summarized as being "in the low .70s" (p. 2). No tabular data are presented to support this claim.

Validity studies were conducted correlating AI scale scores with scores from other instruments: the Crawford Small Parts Test, the Sivaroli Reading Comprehension Test, the Bennett Hand Tool Dexterity Test, the Purdue Pegboard, the Wechsler Adult Intelligence Scale—Revised (WAIS-R), and the Wide Range Achievement Test—Revised (WRAT-R) (Arithmetic). The developers report that the correlations between the AI scale scores and these instruments' scores range from .40 to .63. However, results shown in Table 6 of the documentation provided by the publisher indicate that the actual range is between .47 and .89. It is to be noted that the data in this table indicate that the AI is composed of seven scales, yet the actual instrument has only four scales (Verbal Reasoning, Numerical Reasoning, Vocabulary, and Visual Perception). No explanation for this discrepancy is given. Correlations among WAIS-R scores (listed as Verbal, Performance, Full Scale, and Vocabulary) and the AI Verbal Reasoning, Numerical Reasoning, and Vocabulary scores are reported. The correlations range from .41 to .78. No sample size is reported. "Most importantly, we found that the verbal reasoning and the Verbal IQ of the WAISR [sic], NSIGHT's Numerical Reasoning, Performance IQ and Vocabulary all had significant correlations" (p. 4). NSIGHT does not have a Performance IQ subtest.

Concurrent validity studies were conducted for the PI as well. A matrix of correlations is reported between the PI and the 16 PF scales ($N = 647$). Of the 353 correlations that could be listed, 50 are missing. The developers report that the range of correlation coefficients between appropriate scales ranges between .2 and .84. The correlations between the 16 PF Distortion Scale and the AI Validity Scales are: Lie Scale (.73) and Faking Bad (.61), respectively. The developers claim that the correlations with PI scores are significant for 16 PF scales A, E, G, H, and L with PI scales O, O, S, G, and P, respectively. No correlation coefficients are provided in the text to support this contention and the accompanying table indicates that the following coefficients are missing: 16 PF A with PI O and 16 PF E with PI O. The authors report that there are substantial correlations among the following scales: MMPI

Lie and PI Lie (Candor) .78, MMPI F and PI Faking Bad (Self-Esteem) .69, and MMPI K and PI Faking Good (Self-Concept) .77 (N = 178)

The authors report data (N = 1,290) on the predictive validity of the AI and PI. "The results show that NSIGHT successfully predicted both success and failure in over 86% of the cases stud ied" (p. 4). The developers also report on successful "hit rates" for 10 worker traits (Work Traits, Productivity, Accuracy, Knowledge of Job, Attitude, Dependability, Socialization, Appearance, Leadership, and Customer Interaction). The hit rates ranged from 49% to 87% (N = 945) after a 1-year follow-up, again using supervisors' ratings as the criteria.

The developers report on a predictive validity study conducted by computing single and multiple correlations. Supervisors' ratings, received either after 1 year of employment or 1 year after promotion, served as the criteria. The predictors were: Education; Training and Experience; Interview; Experience; GPA-College; Reference Check; Biographical Data; Job Tryout; PI scores; AI scores; PI and AI scores combined; and PI scores, AI scores, Reference Checks, and Interview results (combined). The correlations range from .10 (Education) to .93 (PI, AI, Reference Checks, and Interview results [combined]).

The developers report that they conducted cross validation studies with new samples (size unknown) and report that the predictor/criterion correlation coefficients were .68 or higher (using job family classifications).

The developers indicate that they conducted a construct validity study of the PI. PI scores were used to differentiate 56 patients who had been diagnosed with certain personality disorders from 27 persons who did not have DSM III-R clinical diagnoses. The researchers report that the PI did "pick up, to a significant extent, the traits that resulted in those individuals being hospitalized" (p. 9). No data on this construct validity study are reported.

COMMENTARY. The value of the PI and AI for use as pre-employment assessment instruments is compromised on several fronts. No information regarding the origin, development, theoretical or empirical underpinnings, history, scale construction, foundation, underlying assumptions, or field testing is presented. It is not known whether any empirical procedures (e.g., factor analysis) or theoretical constructs (e.g., Holland

codes) were employed to guide the development of the instruments.

There are multiple errors in the manual (I. Psychometric Properties of NSIGHT) including, but not limited to: incorrectly reporting data and table references, developing new scale names without explanation, using inaccurate or inconsistent test names, and reporting errors in data analysis. Language, grammar, spelling, and syntax errors are frequent and disturbing. The manual is very difficult to comprehend. There are references to NSIGHT scales (subtests) that do not exist. One table lists seven AI subtests. The AI has only four subtests, only one of which is listed in the list of seven in the table. A correlation matrix lists the 19 PI scales in one column, but the other instrument (with 10 subtests) is not identified. Many of the cells in the matrix are blank. No directions are provided for administration (including timing) and the qualifications of the administrator are not given.

No information on the derivation or interpretation of the scores is provided. There are no raw score/standard score conversion tables or formulas presented. The standard score system (an 11-point scale) is not described. There is no indication that the scores from the normative group are the basis for the standard scores. "National Norms = 40+" (p. 6) is a statement that has no meaning. Information on the number of items/scale and which items are associated with which PI subtest is not provided.

The reliability data are weak. Using 1,047 participants, the alpha coefficients computed on 25 of the 26 combined subtests (no reliability correlation coefficients are reported for the AI Visual Perception subtest) indicate that the three aptitude (AI) coefficients are above .62. Only one (NR) is at an acceptable level (.83). The coefficients for the PI subtests range from .39 to .76. Even allowing for the fact that psychological traits are not as stable as cognitive (aptitude) traits, coefficients below .70 are suspect. Sixteen of the 22 PI alpha coefficients are below .70. It is interesting to note that the test-retest coefficients are much higher. Only two correlation coefficients are below .70 and eight are above .80. Some alpha and test-retest correlation differences (on the same subtests) are striking (e.g., .39 and .79, respectively, on the Logical/Imaginative Thinker subtest).

The validity data are more encouraging, but still lacking in many respects. Two of the AI and

WAIS-R coefficients are acceptable (AI VR and WAIS-R Verbal [.78] and the two Vocabulary subtests [.77]). The other coefficients are below .70. The validity correlation coefficients relative to the AI and the Purdue Pegboard, the Crawford Small Parts Test, the Bennett Test, the Sivaroli Reading Test, and the WRAT-R (Arithmetic) cannot be interpreted because the table lists seven AI subtests in the matrix analysis, but the AI has only four known subtests. This discrepancy is inexplicable.

The predictive validity data are somewhat more encouraging. The developers report that the AI and the PI (combined) can successfully predict success and/or failure at a "hit rate" of 86% accuracy. This is a high value and is commendable. They also report that the AI and PI (combined) are successful in rating worker traits (49% to 87%) although the meaning of these data is not made clear. The same can be said for the multiple correlation coefficients between the combined scores (AI and PI scores, interview data, and reference checks) and successful job placement. What is questionable about these data is that the instrument used to rate the employees' placements utilizes a certain ranking system (Top 10% of all employees, Top 25%, Top 50%, etc.) yet the text indicates that all the rated employees were in the top third of their respective groups. The instrument does not have top, middle, or lower third categories.

In addition to the technical concerns that have been raised, the test questions and answers themselves contain form and grammatical errors.

SUMMARY. Although NSIGHT's PI and AI show some promise in predicting job success (combined with other pre-employment data) the faults associated with these instruments far outweigh their strengths.

A case needs to be made that the instruments are built upon solid foundations and that the subtests have sound rationale and justification as well as empirical and theoretical support. Factor analytical studies could be utilized to provide such a foundation and to reduce the number of PI subtests. More extensive and thorough concurrent, construct, and predictive validity studies need to be conducted in order to demonstrate the effectiveness of the AI and PI. The reliability studies that are reported should be expanded with larger and more well-defined samples. The normative sample needs further development and refinement. The 11-point standard scoring system needs

explication and description. All pertinent reliability and validity data (and associated tables) need to be included in the test manual with attention being paid to thorough descriptions of the procedures, instruments, and methods utilized. The test items, booklets, and, most importantly, the test manual are in need of being overhauled.

[175]
Observational Assessment of Temperament.

Purpose: Assesses temperamental characteristics, primarily in industrial/organizational settings.
Population: Higher level specialized and managerial personnel.
Publication Dates: 1979–1996.
Acronym: OAT.
Scores: 3 behavior factors: Extroversive/Impulsive vs. Introversive/Reserved, Emotional/Responsive vs. Nonemotional/Controlled, Self-Reliant/Individually Oriented vs. Dependent/Group Oriented.
Administration: Group.
Price Data, 2002: $54 per 25 tests (including background research, scoring instructions, and norms).
Time: [10] minutes.
Comments: Can be used as a self-assessment or for the assessment of the observed behavior of others; assesses the three behavior factors measured by the Temperament Comparator (T6:2506).
Author: Melany E. Baehr.
Publisher: Reid London House.

Review of the Observational Assessment of Temperament by STEPHEN J. DePAOLA, Assistant Professor of Psychology, Auburn University Montgomery, Montgomery, AL:

DESCRIPTION. The Observational Assessment of Temperament (OAT) is used to assess temperamental traits that are characteristic and permanent for an individual's behavior. The OAT can be used as a self-report instrument or for the assessment of the observed behavior of other individuals, primarily in industrial/organizational backgrounds. Three behavior characteristics are assessed by the OAT and they are rated on a continuum from one extreme to the other. The three traits assessed are: Extroversive/Impulsive vs. Introversive/Reserved, Emotional/Responsive vs. Nonemotional/Controlled, and Self-Reliant/Individually Oriented vs. Dependent/Group Oriented. According to the author, each of these behavior variables occurs in an individual in vary-

kit 3.5-inch disk (self-administering and scoring), manual, administration rates, and guide to profile interpretation; £23 per replacement disk.

Time: (35–45) minutes.

Author: Alan Brimer.

Publisher: Educational Evaluations [England].

Review of the Occupational Interest Rating Scale by HEIDI M. CARTY, Assistant Director, Student Research and Information, University of California—San Diego, La Jolla, CA:

DESCRIPTION. The Occupational Interest Rating Scale (OIRS) was designed as a two-way classification measure used to identify occupational interests and preferences for modes of interaction with persons, materials, or situations that one may encounter within an occupation. There are two forms of the test included within one booklet. If occupational interest information is desired, then only one form of the test is necessary. If both occupational interest and directions of involvement data are desired, then one must complete both forms. Each form has 53 questions, administered either by paper-and-pencil or computer. Each of the two areas (i.e., Occupational Interests & Directions of Involvement) that the scale measures is divided into multiple subscales. Occupational Interest profiles include: Business, Technical, Care, Aesthetic, Scientific, Numerical, and Field. Directions of Involvement include: Persuasive, Operational, Empathic, Making, and Intellectual. Each question consists of pairs of occupational activities in which a preference from most interested to least interested on a 5-point scale is selected for each activity. A higher score is selected for the activity in which one has the most interest.

In computing raw scores, the developer provides a color-coded stencil key and directions. The raw score can be found by simply summing the various color-coded scores. Once a raw score is determined a corresponding scale score is assigned. There is a table on each form for recording both raw and scale scores. The developer provides useful scale score tables to ease interpretation.

DEVELOPMENT. The OIRS was first published in 2002 in England. Materials provided by the developer, including an administrative manual, a technical manual, and a guide to the interpretation of the OIRS profiles provide minimal information regarding test development. According to the developer, the OIRS is the first interest inventory in which Rasch techniques are employed. The developer does not provide documentary rationale for using the Rasch model with an interest inventory over classical item analysis. No underlying assumptions or theoretical framework supporting the underlying constructs of the scales are provided; the developer cites no research in the area of occupational interests or modes of interaction. The scale definitions are vague and appear to overlap. Some scales were developed using data from either males or females, whereas other scales were developed using the total sample. No rationale is provided to explain why gender differences were found in developing the scales. Test items discuss occupational activities rather than actual jobs. This allows for the possibility of self-report bias and may have influenced the discrepancy with the fit analyses for the scales. It would have been useful for the developer to run an inter-item analysis to see which items correlated highly with the overall total test score and within each scale. It appears in some cases that some items have a similar function and could have loaded on more than one scale.

TECHNICAL. There is no information regarding the standardization of the OIRS. The developer claims that because a sample-free item analysis and test-free ability scale scoring system were used in developing the OIRS, normative data are not necessary. No rationale or documentary evidence to support this claim is provided. The developer investigated and found gender differences on various scales. No norms were developed for each gender. Differences between genders are argued to be true differences. The developer does not report age or ethnic differences.

The developer mentions that evidence for internal consistency and validity of the OIRS was sought amongst two samples of students (technical manual, p. 8). Results from these studies were not provided. Rather, the developer reports results from a subsample of 100 students used to generate intercorrelations between the scales. Intercorrelations between the scales ranged from .25 to .87. Correlations between the two forms show corrected estimates of reliability higher than .98. The developer provides only the corrected estimates.

In regard to evidence in support of validity, the developer indicates that the OIRS was correlated with an achievement test known as the Applied Knowledge Test (AKT), which is no longer in print. No information regarding the AKT is provided. It would have been useful for the developer to correlate the OIRS with another occupational interest inventory. Results from the factor analysis showing factor loadings for the resulting multiple interest scales would be helpful. The studies cited to support the reliability and validity estimates of scores on this measure do not meet accepted psychometric standards for substantiating reliability and validity evidence established in the *Standards for Educational and Psychological Testing* (AERA, APA, & NCME, 1999).

The developer includes a section on measurement error associated with each scale score. The error limits provided are useful for interpreting any significant change in occupational interest over time. There appear to be typographical errors with some of the error limits (i.e., the confidence interval for a raw score of 5 and 6 is equal to the interval for a raw score of 4).

COMMENTARY. The usefulness of the OIRS in providing specific occupational interest information is questionable. The items comprising the test are vague and many could easily be represented on more than one scale. As a result, the scales are rather vague and appear to overlap. The test itself is easy to administer and complete. Each form of the test can be completed within 35—40 minutes. It is not clear if one should take one or two forms of the test. It would be helpful to include a section about the need to take both forms to have a score for the person's direction of involvement in the "How To Do The Test" section. Although the test is easy to score, the directions are somewhat confusing and difficult to follow.

Another weakness of the OIRS is the scale scores are not directly related to a normative population. In the absence of normative data, the developer includes a section discussing relative incidence of various scale scores, making reference to a population of scores. According to the administrative manual, "a scale score above 6 is infrequent; 5 or above is likely to be achieved by about the top 25% of the population. Average scores are likely to be 3 or 4" (p. 5). No description of the population used to generate the relative frequency distribution or average scale scores is provided.

Third, the OIRS does not provide information regarding specific occupations, rather broad areas of interest. The developer cautions test users in interpreting scale scores, stating that not every person will have a clear occupational interest and one's abilities will influence the range of jobs one may realistically attain. At best, this scale provides a tool for offering guidance about a general class of occupations. It is recommended that the OIRS be used in combination with other measures of occupational interest for a more reliable assessment, such as measures of ability, past achievements, autobiographical inventories, and an in-person interview.

Finally, in the technical manual the developer includes a useful section discussing the history of gender bias and occupational interest inventories. However, it is not clear how this research underlies the development of the test items or the scales. The developer writes that the "OIRS has been explicitly designed to avoid conflict with laws governing sex discrimination. Both the item content and the manner of the construction of the test have given equable treatment to the sexes" (technical manual, p. 1). When gender differences were found, the developer did not provide a theoretical model or research to support differences.

SUMMARY. Overall, the OIRS is easy to both administer and score, providing information about occupational interests and preferences for modes of interaction in any given occupation. The OIRS should not be used as a stand-alone measure of occupational interests but rather as a secondary source with other occupational interest inventories (e.g., Strong Interest Inventory; 248), and measures of ability. The OIRS is useful in that it provides information about preferences for a given occupational area as opposed to specific occupations.

In the future it would be beneficial to conduct more extensive reliability and validity studies to provide better evidence of the psychometric properties of this measure. It would also be quite useful to provide norms for particular occupations, occupational levels, and preferences for modes of interaction by gender.

REVIEWER'S REFERENCE

American Educational Research Association, American Psychological Association, & National Council on Measurement in Education. (1999). *Standards for educational and psychological testing.* Washington, DC: American Educational Research Association.

Review of the Occupational Interest Rating Scale by KEVIN R. KELLY, Head, Department of Educational Studies, Purdue University, West Lafayette, IN:

DESCRIPTION. The Occupational Interest Rating Scale (OIRS) is a 106-item interest inventory designed for use with adolescents and adults.

The suggested administration time is 35–40 minutes; there is no time limit. The OIRS provides a two-way classification of interests; it yields measures of occupational interests and of preferred work orientation within occupations. Although the uses of this instrument are not described in the administrative or technical manuals, it can be assumed that the OIRS is designed to help adolescents and adults to determine appropriate educational and career choices.

The OIRS has two test forms consisting of pairs of statements describing various work activities. Respondents begin Form 1 by writing down the work activity in which they are most interested, which is assigned a value of 5. They next report the work activity in which they are least interested, which is assigned a value of 1. The respondent then proceeds to the 53 pairs of activities on Form 1 with the instruction to "consider both activities, decide which you feel most concerns you and write 1, 2, 3, 4, or 5 in the box on the answer sheet to show your level of interest in that activity." Respondents next rate their level of interest in the second activity in the pair and then proceed to the next item pair. Respondents may stop after completing Form 1 or continue by completing the 53 activity item pairs on Form 2. The OIRS is available in paper-and-pencil and computer formats.

The OIRS yields two types of scales. The seven Interest scales reflect occupational content: Business, Technical, Care, Aesthetic, Scientific, Numerical, and Field. The five Direction of Involvement scales reflect a focus on interaction with people, materials, or situations within occupational domains: Persuasive, Operational, Empathic, Making, and Intellectual. The Interest scale scores can be derived from responses to Form 1, Form 2, or a combination of the two forms. Both forms must be completed for calculation of Direction of Involvement scales.

DEVELOPMENT. The OIRS was developed with a sample of 440 adolescent students (211 female, 219 male) from a comprehensive school in England. The Rasch model of item analysis was used to develop 0–10 scales for each Interest and Direction of Involvement. This scaling method purportedly precludes the need to develop norms based on large samples.

TECHNICAL (STANDARDIZATION).

Reliability. The author administered the OIRS to 100 Year 10 students. The correlations between Forms 1 and 2 were in the range of .67 for Intellectual to .81 for Aesthetic. The median correlation was .72. The author stated that "The between-form correlations are high and lead to corrected estimates of reliability higher than 0.98 for the combined forms of all scales" (p. 9). The method for calculating the corrected reliability estimates is not specified. Although the author indicated that this sample was retested following a 1-week interval, retest reliability coefficients were not provided.

Validity. Two forms of validity evidence are provided. First, the OIRS scale scores were correlated with mathematics, English, science, and spatial relationship ability test scores. These correlations were in the range of -.16 to .53 with the following median correlations: .035 for Business, .105 for Technical, .02 for Care, .185 for Aesthetic, .27 for Scientific, .12 for Numerical, .115 for Field, .175 for Persuasive, .115 for Operational, .08 for Empathic, .175 for Making, and .375 for Intellectual. The highest corrections were between the Scientific and Intellectual scales and the ability scales. Otherwise, the OIRS and ability scale scores appear to be independent.

The author also provided some preliminary concurrent validity data by matching scale scores with the type of most preferred work activity recorded by respondents at the beginning of the OIRS. The test developer identified eight discrete work interest areas: Teaching, Business, Financial, Scientific, Outdoor/Active, Leisure/Catering, Art/Design, and Technical. It is not clear why the author did not designate work interest areas that corresponded exactly with the Interest and Direction of Involvement domains for this analysis. Contingency tables were compiled to record the top-ranked Interest and Direction of Involvement scale for each of the eight work activity areas. In general, expressed interests were consistent with the highest ranking Interest and Direction of Involvement scales.

COMMENTARY. The OIRS is an innovative approach to interest measurement. However, the instrument has five limitations that restrict its usefulness. First, the test response procedure is somewhat cumbersome and confusing. Respondents are instructed to read each pair of items, decide which of the two activities is of greatest concern, rate the level of interest for this activity, then rate the level of interest in the remaining item of the pair. It is difficult to see how identifying and rating strongest preferences within each activity pair adds to the value of the test results. Second, it is difficult to score the Directions of Involvement scales. This reviewer was not able to complete scoring of these scales based on the instructions in the administrative manual. Third, the author provided no theoretical or empirical justification for the two-way classification of Directions of Involvement within Interest areas. It is not clear why, for example, there are separate Care (Interest) and Empathic (Direction of Involvement) scales. The validity of the two-way classification is belied by the high correlations between the Interest and Direction of Involvement scales. For example, the Business (Interest) scale had correlations of .79 with both the Persuasive and Making (Direction of Involvement) scales; the Care (Interest) scale had correlations of .80 and .79 with the Persuasive and Empathic (Direction of Involvement) scales. Further, the high correlations among the Directions of Involvement scales (median correlation = .77) suggests that these scales may be reflecting a response style (Anastasi & Urbina, 1997) such as acquiescence rather than a differential focus on people, materials, or situations within occupations. The correlational evidence does not support a two-way classification model. Fourth, the author did not describe the demographic characteristics of the population used to develop the test. It is not possible to evaluate the ethnic, racial, and socioeconomic representativeness of the sample based on the available information. Users cannot be confident that the OIRS is valid for use with diverse populations. Fifth, the validity evidence was meager. Factor analyses were not used in the development of this instrument. As a result, the OIRS appears to include an excess of interest scales.

Application of data reduction techniques may have yielded a more parsimonious interest model. The concurrent validity evidence was also limited; this oversight is difficult to understand when numerous interest inventories were available for calibration of the OIRS validity properties. Further, no predictive validity information was presented. It remains to be demonstrated that the OIRS scale scores are related to meaningful educational and occupational outcomes.

CONCLUSIONS AND RECOMMENDATIONS. The OIRS can be seen as a promising test that is still being developed. Further refinement of

its conceptual basis and demonstration of its measurement and validity properties are required. Use of the OIRS for academic and vocational counseling is not recommended until these refinements have been accomplished.

REVIEWER'S REFERENCE

Anastasi, A., & Urbina, S. (1997). *Psychological testing* (7th ed.). Upper Saddle River, NJ: Prentice-Hall.

[177]

OMNI Personality Inventory and OMNI-IV Personality Disorder Inventory.

Purpose: "Comprehensive self-report instruments for measuring normal and abnormal personality traits."
Population: Ages 18–74 years.
Publication Date: 2001.
Administration: Individual or group.
Price Data, 2003: $255 per OMNI/OMNI-IV combination kit (3.5-inch disk) including professional manual (75 pages), 25 OMNI test booklets, OMNI software system with on-screen manual, 5 free on-screen administrations of OMNI, 25 OMNI-IV test booklets, OMNI-IV software system with on-screen manual, and 5 free on-screen administrations of OMNI-IV.
Comments: Paper-and-pencil and computer administration available; computer-scored only (cannot be hand-scored); scoring software generates interpretive report; system requirements: Windows only, Windows 95/98/NT/2000/ME/XP, 8 MB hard drive, 16 MB RAM (Windows 95/98/ME) or 24 MB RAM (Windows, NT/2000/XP), 3.5-inch floppy disk drive.
Author: Armand W. Loranger.
Publisher: Psychological Assessment Resources, Inc.
a) OMNI PERSONALITY INVENTORY.
Acronym: OMNI.
Scores, 44: 2 Validity Scales: Variable Response Inconsistency (VRIN), Current Distress (CD); 25 Normal Scales: Aestheticism (AE), Ambition (AM), Anxiety (AN), Assertiveness (AS), Conventionality (CO), Depression (DE), Dutifulness (DU), Excitement (EC), Exhibitionism (EH), Energy (EN), Flexibility (FL), Hostility (HS), Impulsiveness (IM), Intellect (IT), Irritability (IR), Modesty (MD), Moodiness (MO), Orderliness (OR), Self-Indulgence (SI), Sincerity (SN), Sociability (SO), Self-Reliance (SR), Tolerance (TO), Trustfulness (TR), Warmth (WR); 10 Personality Disorder Scales: Paranoid (PAR), Schizoid (SCH), Schizotypal (SCT), Antisocial (ANT), Borderline (BOR), Histrionic (HIS) Narcissistic (NAR), Avoidant (AVD), Dependent (DEP), Obsessive-Compulsive (OBC); 7 Personality Factor Scales: Agreeableness (AGRE), Conscientiousness (CONC), Extraversion (EXTR),

Narcissism (NARC), Neuroticism (NEUR), Openness (OPEN), Sensation-Seeking (SENS).

Price Data: $155 per OMNI introductory kit (3.5-inch disk) including professional manual, 25 OMNI test booklets, OMNI software system with on-screen manual, unlimited-use scoring and interpretation, 5 free on-screen administrations of OMNI: $40 per professional manual; $125 per 25 test booklets; $125 per OMNI key disk (25 on-screen administrations).

Time: (60–90) minutes.

Comments: 375-item self-report inventory; measure both normal and abnormal personality traits as specified in DSM-IV.

b) OMNI-IV PERSONALITY DISORDER INVENTORY.

Acronym: OMNI-IV.

Scores, 12: 2 Validity Scales: Variable Response Inconsistency (VRIN), Current Distress (CD); 10 Personality Disorder Scales: Paranoid (PAR), Schizoid (SCH), Schizotypal (SCT), Antisocial (ANT), Borderline (BOR), Histrionic (HIS), Narcissistic (NAR), Avoidant (AVD), Dependent (DEP), Obsessive-Compulsive (OBC).

Price Data: $130 per OMNI-IV introductory kit (3.5-inch disk) including professional manual, 25 OMNI-IV test booklets, OMNI-IV software system with on-screen manual, untimed use scoring and interpretation, 5 free on-screen administrations of OMNI-IV; $100 per 25 OMNI-IV test booklets; $100 per OMNI-IV key disk (25 on-screen administrations).

Time: (35–45) minutes.

Comments: 210 items taken from the OMNI; assesses personality disorders as specified in DSM-IV.

Review of the OMNI Personality Inventory and the OMNI-IV Personality Disorder Inventory by KEVIN LANNING, Associate Professor of Psychology, Wilkes Honors College of Florida Atlantic University, Jupiter, FL:

DESCRIPTION. The OMNI is a new (2001) 375-item personality inventory with measures of 25 personality traits and 10 personality disorders, as well as seven factor scales and two validity scales. The OMNI-IV is a shorter (210-item) form of the test that omits the personality trait and factor scales. These measures are intended for use in a range of applications including clinical psychology, correctional use, and neuropsychological evaluation as well as in research. Although the measures include descriptions of personality disorders and are intended for clinical as well as nonclinical popula-

tions, at this writing they are available to users without advanced degrees (i.e., require only an intermediate level of qualifications for use).

Both the OMNI and the OMNI-IV are administered via a microcomputer running Windows software or paper-and-pencil. Scoring is also achieved via microcomputer, although scoring keys are included in the manual. The items of the OMNI are presented to the respondent in several blocks, with responses to be given on 7-point Likert scales. The first series of items concern self-descriptions ("I am not good at understanding other people's feelings"), the remaining two groups ask for subjective assessments of frequency ranging from *always* to *never* ("I mistake objects or shadows for people"). The last block of items is used to assess current level of distress, which is treated as one of the two validity scales in the instrument (the other is variable response inconsistency or VRIN). The OMNI takes about 90 minutes to complete; the OMNI-IV takes approximately half this time.

DEVELOPMENT. The OMNI was developed with the intention of assessing both clinical and general populations, and was based on the premise of an assumed discontinuity between normal and disordered personality. Consequently, the pools of items that were considered for the trait scales and the measures of psychopathology were largely separate. In the present version of the test, there is some item overlap between these domains, with approximately 15% of the items appearing on both a trait and a personality disorder scale.

The personality disorders to be assessed were chosen based on their inclusion on Axis II in DSM-IV. For these scales, items were explicitly written to assess 79 pertinent DSM-IV diagnostic criteria. The set of normal traits measured in the OMNI was chosen by the author, and then revised on the basis of discussions with members of the Psychiatry Department at Cornell University. This led to a set of 581 items, which was administered to a derivation sample of 1,000 persons. Item analyses of these data led to a reduction to the present 375-item OMNI, which was then administered to a new sample of 872 respondents. Although these samples were not intended to mirror U.S. Census demographics, they nonetheless drew from all 50 states, reflected a wide range of ages (18–74, with a median of approximately 40), and were at least marginally ethnically heterogeneous (approximately 12% of respondents self-identified as non-White).

TECHNICAL. The manual reports internal consistencies as well as test-retest stabilities for the normal, personality disorder, and factor scales. In both the derivation and cross-validational samples, alphas for the normal scales, each of which has eight items, ranged from .53 (Modesty) to .86 (Irritability), with a median of .72. Alphas for the personality disorder scales, intended to measure the occasionally heterogeneous syndromes of Axis II, were understandably lower, with a median of .68. For both sets of scales, 1- to 2-month test-retest reliabilities were higher, with a median of at least .80. There was little evidence of mean changes in scale scores on the retest. Alphas and test-retest coefficients for the factor scales, ranging in length from 32 to 140 items, were typically above .90.

Although the manual does not include the full interscale correlation matrix, it does provide the factor loadings of the 35 basic scales onto seven factors. These factors are variants of the familiar five as well as Narcissism and Sensation Seeking. The factor loadings are not used in the computation of the OMNI factor scales, rather, scores on the factor scales are obtained by summing from 32 to 140 responses at the item level. Perhaps surprisingly, given the unit-weighting of the factor scales, the scoring for the personality disorder scales is relatively complex. For each of these scales, responses to between one and five items are averaged to compute an estimated score for each of seven to nine symptoms (or DSM-IV criteria); these criterion scores are then summed to form a score on the Personality Disorder.

For the normal scales, evidence for validity includes correlations with the NEO PI-R and other self-report measures (N = 238), as well as correlations with ratings made by spouses using a form of the OMNI written for observer ratings. In the two development samples, 636 spouses provided supplementary ratings. Correlations between self-rated and spouse-rated scores on the normal scales ranged widely, from .36 for Dutifulness and .37 for Modesty to .67 for Aestheticism and .80 for Conventionality.

For the personality disorder scales, in addition to the self and observer ratings available for the normal scales, a clinical sample was also examined. Correlations were computed with ratings made by psychiatrists based on a standardized interview for a sample of 122 nonpsychotic patients. Within the clinical sample, self-observer correlations for the personality disorder scales were typically high (median = .67), whereas agreement between spouses on these scales was typically modest (median = .46). Evidently, these differences in agreement may be due to the sample (clinical vs. normal), the raters (psychiatrists vs. spouses), the method of rating (interview vs. OMNI), or all of these. The manual also reports mean differences between different sets of ratings. For example, spouses rate their partners as relatively dependent, and the psychiatric patients score significantly higher than the normative samples on all 10 of the personality disorder scales. Indeed, for all but the Narcissistic and Obsessive-Compulsive scales, these differences in means are large, averaging approximately one standard deviation.

COMMENTARY. As a new test, there are a few quirks in the OMNI. The profile sheet for the normal scales arranges these alphabetically rather than conceptually or factorially, and so obscures the quick synthesis of scores that graphs are intended to provide. Such an arrangement leads most respondents to be characterized by a sawtooth profile, in which both trends and exceptions to trends are hard to discern. This is not a problem for the personality disorders scales, which are smaller in number and are arranged according to their order of presentation in DSM-IV. The factor scales are presented on a third profile sheet, and are also arranged alphabetically. A separate page lists scale scores arranged by the factor structure of the test, but does not, unfortunately, do so graphically.

The interpretive report also includes a page listing responses to 30 critical items. Given the inherent unreliability of single responses, the sensitive content of many of these items, and the fact that the test can be used by individuals without advanced degrees in psychology, the inclusion of this in the interpretive report is troubling.

SUMMARY. The OMNI and OMNI-IV are ambitious measures of personality and personality disorders. Although there are some unfortunate weaknesses with the interpretive materials on which clinicians and (particularly) others will rely, an impressive set of evidence has already been marshaled to suggest the potential value of these tests in a range of settings.

[178]
Outcomes: Planning, Monitoring, Evaluating.

Purpose: "A tool for monitoring student progress toward selected goals."
Population: Grades K–12.
Publication Date: 2002.
Acronym: PME.
Scores: 11 categories: Concern Description, Goals and Benchmarks, Benchmark Sealing, Social-Validation Criteria, Intervention Planning, Progress-Monitoring Procedures, Progress Chart, Progress Analysis, Evaluation of Outcomes, Next-Step Strategies, Special Education Considerations.
Administration: Individual.
Price Data, 2002: $85 per complete kit including manual (2002, 139 pages), binder, and 25 record forms; $50 per manual; $40 per 25 record forms.
Time: Untimed.
Comments: Provides a framework for documenting education professionals' problem-solving efforts; helps identify concerns, describe context of problem, rate baseline performance, operationalize goals, plan intervention, monitor and graph student progress, evaluate intervention outcomes, plan next steps.
Authors: Karen Callan Stoiber and Thomas R. Kratochwill.
Publisher: The Psychological Corporation.

Review of the Outcomes: Planning, Monitoring, Evaluating by GYPSY M. DENZINE, Associate Professor of Educational Psychology, Northern Arizona University, Flagstaff, AZ:

DESCRIPTION. The Outcomes: Planning, Monitoring, Evaluating (PME) is not a test, rather it is a systematic procedure for planning, monitoring, and evaluating the outcomes of an intervention or service-delivery program. It is a tool for educators, health care professionals, school psychologists, special education resource teachers, and parents, who desire a comprehensive structure for integrating assessment and intervention practices. The tool was designed for measuring both academic and social goals.

At the broadest level, the Outcomes: PME is grounded in the scientist-practitioner model (Barlow, Hayes, & Nelson, 1984; Hayes, Barlow, & Nelson-Gray, 1999), meaning the user must be involved in gathering data, use the data to monitor progress, and apply various scientific standards when interpreting data to make decisions in an educational setting. The Outcomes: PME is also conceptually consistent with the outcomes assess-

ment framework for clinical practice outlined by Ogles, Lambert, and Masters (1996). Another perspective that the authors relied upon in their development of this tool was a problem-solving framework. From this perspective, users are required to have knowledge of the applications of the procedures and knowledge of the measurement issues related to its application. Therefore, there needs to be sufficient time for users to learn the process and to practice applying the techniques, and available support systems for application in applied settings. Finally, the Outcomes: PME is conceptually and methodologically based on a Goal-Attainment Scaling (GAS) process. The authors provide clear rationale for their choice of the GAS approach in the manual. They make the assertion that interventions are inherently goal-oriented and can therefore benefit from an explicit methodology for specifying and operationalizing intervention goals. Moreover, a GAS approach is adaptable and flexible and can provide an empirical approach to practice. According to the authors, one of the primary strengths of the GAS approach is that it provides a means for reaching consensus among the intervention team members, the student's family, and often the student who is receiving the service.

The manual describes the Outcomes: PME procedure through six chapters. In the first chapter, the rationale and fundamental components of the procedure are presented. The five steps underlying the process are identified: Step 1—Identify, concern, describe context, and establish baseline; Step 2—Set meaningful goal(s) and benchmarks; Step 3—Plan the intervention and specify progress monitoring procedures; Step 4—Monitor progress and analyze data; and Step 5—Evaluate intervention outcomes and plan next steps. These same steps are used when the Outcomes: PME is applied at the individual, classroom, school, or program level.

In the second chapter, the authors describe their recommended basic baseline-intervention design (A-B design) and provide an overview of how users can analyze data according to two types of criteria: clinical and evidence-based. The clinical criteria require the user to evaluate the goal score by social comparison or normative assessment. The clinical criteria also involve obtaining subjective evaluations by individuals (parents, teachers, school psychologist) to be used in a consensus-building process for the purpose of judging goal progress. The 6-page record form contains a Convergent-Evident Scaling protocol to assist team members in reaching consensus. The second criterion is the visual analysis of the data, which is referred to as the Evidence-Based Criteria. According to the Outcomes PME developers, graphical displays of data are useful because they are easy to construct, can involve a wide range of formats, and provide team members a quick way to draw conclusions about the outcomes.

The remainder of the manual contains information and guidelines for using the Outcomes: PME with individual students and for program evaluation purposes. A useful chapter provides potential users with specific information about using this tool at the early childhood and preschool levels. Using the Outcomes: PME with very young children requires the assessment team to pay close attention to family needs and also key developmental markers in the child's thoughts and behaviors. In addition to very young children, the authors discuss how the Outcomes: PME can be used in making eligibility decisions regarding special education.

DEVELOPMENT. The Outcomes: PME process was developed on evidence-based best practices in the assessment of outcomes in educational and clinical settings. As noted in the final chapter, the authors developed the tool based on the following scientist-practitioner principles: (a) authentic assessment provides the most useful data, measurement is ongoing; (b) data should be gathered across varied settings and task demands; (c) data should be collected and interpreted by a team effort; (d) parents should be involved in the full process as much as possible; and (e) the validity of the data will be enhanced by convergent evidence from multiple data sources.

Regarding establishing and monitoring goals, the Outcomes: PME involves the use of multiple methods including: (a) standardized checklists/rating scales, (b) criterion- and norm-referenced tests, (c) curriculum-based measurements, (d) individualized academic concerns, (e) performance-based assessment, and (f) standards-based assessment. The manual contains a brief, but useful, discussion of the advantages and disadvantages for each approach.

TECHNICAL. In chapter 2 of the manual the authors address the issues of reliability and validity as they relate to goal-attainment scaling.

Although they do not report psychometric data for the Outcomes: PME, they provide a review of the literature on GAS and other progress-monitoring approaches. Specifically, they state the following potential psychometric disadvantages of GAS: (a) low interrater agreement for goal scores and improvement ratings and (b) inappropriate use of rating scales based on a restricted range. In response to these concerns, the Outcomes: PME developers recommend users obtain convergent data from multiple sources and consider using a 7-point scale (ranging from +3 to −3) for measuring goal progress. They also remind users that goal scores are based on relative rather than absolute scales.

Throughout the manual, instructions and guidelines for implementing the Outcomes: PME are presented. For example, the authors suggest baseline data be collected over a 1–2-week time interval with minimally three to five measurement times (and in a variety of settings). In addition, guidelines and recommendations are included for how to graph baseline, trend data, and overlapping scores between adjacent phases in an intervention program. As another example of state recommendations, the authors encourage potential users to include benchmark standards from state, district, and classroom sources if they are using a GAS approach to make decisions about eligibility for special services (tutoring, gifted education, special education).

PROPOSED USE. The authors clearly state the Outcomes: PME is not intended for needs assessment. It can be used in any individual or programmatic situation whereby stated outcomes need to be measured. This tool is a process and is designed for providing evidence for decision making, which differentiates it from a decision-making model based on results from a standardized test administered at one point in time.

COMMENTARY. One of the test developer's primary goals was to develop a systematic procedure that would be convenient, flexible, adaptive, and have ecological validity. Based on a careful review, I would state the authors have met their goals. The manual is very well written and contains excellent case studies, examples, and concrete strategies for how to scale, weight, and operationalize goals. The manual is free from technical jargon and would be appropriate to share with parents and various team members. Potential users will find the protocols, checklists, and appendices to be very useful. It is hoped that a future edition will also contain a computerized record form. Although many of the principles and procedures in the manual may be familiar to some team members (school psychologists), the manual and protocols are useful in that they make the method explicit. The record form helps to clarify roles and will ensure all team members agree upon the most important goal(s) to measure.

One possible limitation of the Outcomes: PME is the lack of research to evaluate the validity of the tool. Future research is needed to evaluate the face validity and content validity of the record form for the various groups who will actually use the protocol. For example, it might be useful to know if a panel of expert teachers and expert school psychologists believe the most important information is contained in the record form. This type of research is needed for the various levels of assessment (individual, classroom, school, or program level).

SUMMARY. The Outcomes: PME is a straightforward and comprehensive approach, which is grounded in best practices. Given the low cost of this tool, and the importance of measuring outcomes, this reviewer recommends every school or school district purchase this valuable resource.

REVIEWER REFERENCES

Barlow, D. H., Hayes, S. C., & Nelson, R. O. (1984). *The scientist-practitioner: Research and accountability in clinical and educational settings.* New York: Pergamon Press.

Hayes, S. C., Barlow, D. H., & Nelson-Gray, R. O. (1999). *The scientist-practitioner: Research and accountability in the age of managed care* (2nd ed.). Boston: Allyn & Bacon.

Ogles, B. M., Lambert, M. J., & Masters, K. S. (1996). *Assessing outcome in clinical practice.* Boston: Allyn & Bacon.

[179]

Panic and Agoraphobia Scale.

Purpose: "Determine[s] the severity of panic disorder with or without agoraphobia and … monitor[s] treatment efficacy."

Population: Age 16 and older.

Publication Dates: 1999–2000.

Acronym: PAS.

Scores, 6: Panic Attacks, Agoraphobic Avoidance, Anticipatory Anxiety, Disability, Worries About Health, Total.

Administration: Group.

Forms, 2: Observer-rated, self-rated.

Price Data, 2001: $79.50 per kit including manual (1999, 88 pages), 50 observer-rated scales, and 50 patient questionnaires; $14.50 per 50 patient questionnaires; $12 per 50 observer-rated scales; $49 per manual; $4 per folder.

Time: (5–10) minutes for observer-rated scale.

Comments: Self-administered; computerized version of self-rated scale in preparation; compatible with DSM-IV and ICD-10 classifications.

Author: Borwin Bandelow.

Publisher: Hogrefe & Huber Publishers.

Review of the Panic and Agoraphobia Scale by C. G. BELLAH, Assistant Professor of Psychology, Northwestern State University, Natchitoches, LA:

DESCRIPTION. The Panic and Agoraphobia Scale (PAS) is a 13-item questionnaire designed to assess the severity of symptomology associated with panic and agoraphobia, and it is primarily used to ascertain the efficacy of treatment. The PAS is available in both observer-rated (PAS-O) and self-report (PAS-P) versions. Items are scored on a range of severity from 0–4, with higher values indicating elevated levels of symptomology. A composite score, which represents overall severity, comprises five subscales that represent different areas of impairment for panic patients: Panic Attacks, Agoraphobic Avoidance, Anticipatory Anxiety, Disability, and Worries about Health. The possible range of scores on the PAS is between 0 and 52. Subscale scores are derived by taking the average rating on each of the five symptomatic areas. Interpretation of summative scores is based on a comparison with a 5-point scale that ranges from *borderline/remission* to *very severe*.

Following a general description of panic and agoraphobia, both observers and patients who are administered the PAS are instructed to rate the severity of symptoms experienced in the past week. In addition to the 13 scored items, the PAS includes one item that asks the rater to indicate the degree of expectancy of the reported panic attack(s). The PAS is appropriate for use by psychologists and is currently available in 17 translations. The time of administration ranges from 5 to 10 minutes for practiced clinicians.

DEVELOPMENT. The PAS was designed to serve as an outcome measure of treatment for patients diagnosed with: Panic Disorder Without Agoraphobia, Panic Disorder With Agoraphobia, and Agoraphobia Without History of Panic Disorder. The content of each PAS item was rationally derived based on the author's experience with panic patients and is said to be compatible with the DSM-IV. An exploratory factor analysis (EFA) of the 13 items was performed separately for the observer- and self-rated versions of the test. Both the PAS-O and PAS-P were analyzed using a principal components extraction with a scree test criterion for factor retention, which resulted in three components being retained for rotation to simple structure. Following varimax (orthogonal) rotation, the resulting factor structure of the PAS consisted of three uncorrelated dimensions for both versions of the test. As reported in the test manual, one factor consisted of a mix of "Agoraphobia" and "Disability" items. Furthermore, a second factor consisted of a mix of items that reflect "Anticipatory Anxiety" and "Assumption of Organic Disease," and a third factor consisted of items that were labeled as indicators of "Panic Attack."

Psychometrically, there are a number of notable limitations to the scale development of the PAS. Perhaps most important is the author's unexplained selection of orthogonal factor rotation, which arbitrarily results in uncorrelated scales. Given average inter-item correlations that range from .31 to .63 for PAS-O and .26 to .67 for PAS-P, it seems apparent that sufficient covariance exists in the factor matrix to warrant an oblique rotation, which allows, but does not force, the scales to be correlated. Moreover, given that panic and agoraphobia are both classified as anxiety disorders in the DSM-IV, the rationale for treating the three derived scales of the PAS as unrelated to each other is largely unsubstantiated.

Secondly, sole use of the scree test as the criterion for factor retention has often been criticized in the literature for its tendency to overestimate the number of stable factors in EFA (Floyd & Widaman, 1995). This criticism is borne out in the current example, in which none of the three factors meet the recommended minimum of seven item loadings necessary to have a stable factor structure. This condition of the factor structure is symptomatic of too many factors being retained in the final solution. Therefore, it is unlikely that this factor structure would be replicated in subsequent analyses. Unfortunately, the author does not report results of any cross-validation efforts using confirmatory factor analysis during scale construction, so the composition and stability of the PAS is ultimately inconclusive. Finally, it is remarkable that the reported three-factor structure of the PAS is not commensurate with the scoring procedures of the instrument, which stipulate the scoring of five scales rather than three. Unfortunately, the rationale of this choice is not provided in the test

manual, which calls into question the veracity of scale norms and recommended scoring procedures.

TECHNICAL. Although demographic data are reported on a sample of 235 inpatients used for scale validation, Table 2 of the test manual seems to indicate that a sample of $N = 452$ was used for investigating the PAS-O and PAS-P. In the manual, the author states, "To confirm the reliability of the results obtained with 235 patients, a further analysis was carried out later when the sample size had increased to 452 patients" (manual, p. 13). Unfortunately, the author does not clearly indicate which sample was used for standardization of the instrument. Nevertheless, gender, average age and diagnostic groups of the original participants ($N = 235$) are the only demographic characteristics provided for the sample(s) ostensibly used in test construction. Therefore, the exact composition of the standardization sample for the PAS remains unclear. This conundrum is further complicated by an absence of norm-referenced comparisons (e.g., gender, ethnicity) in the standardization of the PAS, which precludes comparison of any individual patient to a known reference group. Consequently, potential effects of differential item functioning are undetermined, which necessarily renders the practical utility of the PAS in applied settings questionable in its current form.

Consistent with factor analytic procedures, reliability of the PAS was estimated separately for the PAS-O and PAS-P. The interrater reliability of the PAS-O is reported to be .78, and the test-retest reliability (administration interval not reported) of the PAS-P is estimated to be .73. Additionally, internal consistency of the PAS was estimated using Cronbach's alpha to be .85 (PAS-O) and .86 (PAS-P). Overall, neither version of the PAS is reported to possess the estimated reliability requisite for use in applied settings, although the reported level of internal consistency is sufficient for research purposes (Nunnally & Bernstein, 1994).

Regarding validity of scores from the PAS, the test manual provides a listing of a number of moderate to high correlations between the PAS and a variety of anxiety scales. Unfortunately, the text discussion of these correlations in the test manual does not match information printed in the referenced table, so it is difficult for the reader to arrive at an informed opinion, particularly concerning the construct validity of the PAS. Nevertheless, results of a study of 31 patients undergoing treatment for panic/agoraphobia evinced support for the use of the PAS as an indicator of treatment outcome, and this conclusion was further supported in a double-blind placebo-controlled study of 45 patients being treated for Panic Disorder. In sum, the content validity of scores from the PAS is supported by its correspondence with the diagnostic criteria of the DSM-IV, and preliminary evidence supports use of the PAS as an outcome measure of treatment for panic/agoraphobia. However, evidence of the construct validity of the PAS needs clarification, and external validity of the PAS remains largely unsubstantiated.

COMMENTARY. Results of preliminary studies using the PAS support the conclusion that it is an effective indicator of change that occurs in treatment for panic/agoraphobia. Moreover, preliminary analyses suggest that reliability of scores from the PAS is sufficient for use in laboratory settings. However, the PAS remains underdeveloped in a variety of prominent areas that preclude its use in applied settings at the current time. Most notably, a demonstration of the standardization sample's correspondence with the intended population is of primary importance. Also, disparity between the excepted factor structure of the PAS and the prescribed scoring procedure is a central area that needs clarification. Moreover, in its current form, the factor structure of the PAS has not been tested using confirmatory factor analysis, nor has it been cross-validated on secondary samples or examined for differential item functioning. Therefore, it is recommended that interpretation of test scores using the available norms should be made with caution. Nonetheless, preliminary studies using the PAS as a barometer of treatment efficacy show promise; however, it is recommended that these outcome studies be replicated in larger, more representative samples of diverse populations to substantiate the validity of these findings.

SUMMARY. Overall, the PAS is a psychological test in the early stages of development. It is praiseworthy that the PAS has been designed for both observer- and self-report versions, and its availability in 17 languages is quite unique. Also, its brevity and correspondence with the DSM-IV offers a widespread applicability that would likely make it a popular choice among clinicians. However, the author does not indicate the language version(s) used in test development, so it cannot be determined if the stated norms of the PAS are representative of its multilingual format. If provided and with aforementioned points of clarification, it is reasonable to conclude the PAS has potential as an indicator of treatment efficacy for panic and agoraphobia.

REVIEWER'S REFERENCES

Floyd, F. J., & Widaman, K. F. (1995). Factor analysis in the development and refinement of clinical assessment instruments. *Psychological Assessment, 7*(3), 286–299.

Nunnally, J. C., & Bernstein, I. H. (1994). *Psychometric theory* (3rd ed.). New York: McGraw Hill.

Review of the Panic and Agoraphobia Scale by JAMES DONNELLY, *Assistant Professor, and* SCOTT T. MEIER, *Professor, Department of Counseling, School, and Educational Psychology, SUNY Buffalo, Buffalo, NY:*

DESCRIPTION. Borwin Bandelow of the University of Göttingen, Germany, developed the Panic and Agoraphobia Scale (PAS) to assess the severity of panic disorder symptoms. Not intended for differential diagnosis, this brief measure (13 items) is particularly suited for the assessment of symptom severity in the context of treatment efficacy evaluation in individual patients or clinical trials. There are two versions of the scale, a self-report and an observer report, and they are scored to produce total severity and five subscale scores: panic attacks, agoraphobic avoidance, anticipatory anxiety, restriction of activities and quality of life, and worries about health. The scale items are consistent with definitions of panic and agoraphobia given in the DSM-IV and the ICD-10, but extend the assessment to include impact on quality of life. The scale has been translated into 16 languages including the original German and is suitable for individuals over the age of 15.

Agoraphobia, an individual's fear of public places or of being alone, is an anxiety disorder that may or may not be accompanied by panic attacks. Bekker (1996) noted that although agoraphobia is much more common in women, traditional sex-role stereotypes may make it difficult for men to admit to the disorder; a dependent personality characteristic has also been attributed to some agoraphobics. Thus, gender differences and some personality characteristics are likely to be useful validity indicators for a measure of agoraphobia. Also, several treatment modalities have been found to be effective with agoraphobia; therefore, a measure of this construct should be sensitive to changes resulting from such interventions. Bandelow et al. (1998) did find that scores on the Panic and

Agoraphobia scale evidenced change in a sample of 37 patients treated with imipramine for 8 weeks. This is a potentially important purpose of the scale, given that historically, no standardized instrument has been employed in panic disorder trials (Bandelow et al., 1998).

DEVELOPMENT. The manual provides a brief review of the evolution of diagnostic criteria and measurement issues in panic disorder in the past decade, including the ICD-10 and DSM-IV definitions of panic disorder and agoraphobia. The discussion of the measurement issues highlights problems in research when scales are too general, insensitive, or nonspecific with regard to the phenomenology of panic and agoraphobia, or too long to be practical. The justification for development of a brief, specific, and sensitive measure that is usable in clinical trials and therapy evaluations is indeed compelling.

Three of the subscales assess severity of symptoms and the other two scales assess the impact of the disorder on the person. The symptom severity scales include a Panic Attack scale, an Agoraphobic Avoidance scale, and an Anticipatory Anxiety scale. The Panic Attack scale is supplemented by an item that assesses the degree to which the attacks were expected (in a situation in which they have typically occurred) or spontaneous (in novel situations). This item does not contribute information to the scale or total score but may be considered important in certain therapeutic or research protocols. The PAS also includes two scales to assess the impact of the disorder on patient quality of life. These include a Disability scale (degree of impairment in family, social life, and work) and two items related to worries about the impact of anxiety on health.

TECHNICAL.

Administration. The manual suggests that the self-report may be most applicable in monitoring of treatment progress whereas the observer report is well suited to clinical trials. The observer report is to be completed following an interview with the patient, presumably using the PAS as a guide. The two versions are identical with the exception of the content of one item. On the self-report version, the patient is given 23 kinds of situations that may have been avoided because of anxiety and given room to nominate three other situations. The observer report simply asks the number of situations avoided. There is no com-

ment on why the items are formatted differently, but it may be a wise choice if the concern is improving the accuracy of the self-report by providing the patient with specific situations to judge rather than providing a more global estimate. Subscale scores are obtained by averaging the items. The total score is the sum of the subscales.

Standardization. The two versions of the PAS were standardized using an initial sample of 235 and a total of 452 patients in an anxiety disorders clinic at the University of Göttingen. The manual gives details of the diagnostic breakdown of the initial 235, but not the final 452. Several of the statistical tables do not include sample sizes, so it is unclear how many patients are reflected in some of the analyses. One might assume that the larger sample was used whenever possible, but this should be made explicit in the manual. It should also be noted that the total sample of 452 were assessed with only the PAS, with decreasing numbers of patients available for the various validity comparisons. The manual provides a description of item and scale analyses, including both reliability and validity studies. Although the scale is available in 16 languages, there is no discussion of cross-cultural psychometric studies.

Reliability. Reliability analyses included internal consistency for both versions, and interrater and test-retest studies for the observer version. Descriptive statistics are given for both versions, including item means, standard deviations, difficulties, and a column labeled "Cronbach's a" that actually appears to be item-total correlations. The table for the self-rated version also gives the correlation of each item with its equivalent in the observer version. For the observer version, the overall coefficient alpha was .85 and the item-total correlations range from .34 to .63. The self-report version is reported to have a coefficient alpha of .86 with item-total correlations ranging from .26 to .67. The correlations between the parallel items on the two versions range from .56 to .91. The average of these correlations is .77, which is not reported in the manual but was calculated for this review. Interrater reliability for the observer report was estimated by two independent raters seeing the patient on the same day; the manual indicates that one of the observers was the treating psychiatrist but it is unclear who the other rater was. For the sample of 23 patients who were seen twice, the Spearman correlation between the two observations was .78. In addition, test-retest reliability was assessed when 24 patients were observed 1 week apart. The resulting Spearman correlation was .73.

The alpha coefficients for the subscales are reported as follows: (a) Panic Attacks (.67), (b) Agoraphobic Avoidance (.79), (c) Anticipatory Anxiety (.72), (d) Disability (.82), and (e) Worries About Health (.66). Further studies of the interrater reliability of the observer version with larger samples, and in other settings, would seem to be logical extensions of the existing data. The reliability data presented are satisfactory overall.

Validity. Factor analyses of both versions of the scale are presented with very consistent results in the two analyses. After Varimax rotation, three distinct factors are apparent. For both versions of the PAS, the first factor is composed of the items related to agoraphobia and disability, the second factor includes the three panic attack items, and the third factor includes the remaining two anticipatory anxiety items. The text accompanying this analysis mistakenly calls the second factor the anticipatory anxiety factor and the third the "pure panic" factor, when in fact, the reverse of this is true. There is no explanation on why the agoraphobia and disability items are highly correlated, but it is possible that the degree of impairment in functioning is a result of the degree of phobic avoidance.

The total scores from both versions of the PAS were correlated with several general and specific anxiety scales and patient ratings, and the overall pattern of correlations supports the specificity of the PAS as a measure of panic severity. For example, the PAS is most highly correlated with the indicator purported to be most specific to the disorder (the clinician rating). Lower, but moderate and significant, correlations with more general measures of anxiety suggest some discriminant validity. The results reported in this section of the manual do not include the sample sizes for the correlations and the reader is left to infer from the general accrual table given.

COMMENTARY. The layout of the forms is clear, though two observations may be worth mentioning. First, the manual suggests that the first assessment is begun with an explanation of what is meant by the terms "panic attack" and "agoraphobia." The patient self-report form supports this instruction by providing a definition of panic attacks with a listing of 14 symptoms. The symptom list may be confusing to patients because the symptoms could easily be mistaken for items. Each symptom is accompanied by a small empty circle that is apparently meant as a bullet, but might appear to represent a checklist that is to be completed. Secondly, the language translations should be carefully evaluated in the absence of cross-cultural studies. For example, the concept reflected in the British use of the term "lift" is called "elevator" in the U.S. A future direction for improvement of the scale would be to evaluate the translation of concepts and terms across the many languages available for the PAS.

SUMMARY. Overall, the PAS appears to be a useful and reliable measure of the severity of panic and agoraphobia. The inclusion of two subscales reflecting the quality of life of patients with this disorder adds to its applicability in some kinds of research and most therapy situations. It is quite brief, includes parallel versions for self- and observer-ratings, and is easily scored. At the time the manual was published, a computerized version of the scales was reported to be in development. The test kit includes the manual and 50 copies of the self- and observer-report. It should be noted that there are alternatives to the PAS, and the interested reader is referred to a review by Bouchard, Pelletier, Gauthier, Coté, and LaBerge (1997) and a comprehensive practitioner's guide by Antony, Orsillo, and Roemer (2001).

REVIEWERS' REFERENCES

Antony, M. M., Orsillo, S. M., & Roemer, L. (2001). *Practitioner's guide to empirically based measures of anxiety.* New York: Kluwer.

Bandelow, B., Brunner, E., Broocks, A., Beinroth, D., Hajak, G., Pralle, L., & Ruether, E. (1998). The use of the Panic and Agoraphobia Scale in a clinical trial. *Psychiatry Research, 77,* 43–49.

Bekker, M. H. J. (1996). Agoraphobia and gender: A review. *Clinical Psychology Review, 16,* 129–146.

Bouchard, S., Pelletier, M.-H., Gauthier, J. G., Coté, G. & LaBerge, B. (1997). The assessment of panic using self-report: A comprehensive survey of validated instruments. *Journal of Anxiety Disorders, 11,* 89–111.

[180]

The Parenthood Questionnaire.

Purpose: Designed to obtain information from youth concerning their opinions and knowledge of parenting and child development.

Population: Youth who are prospective parents or who may work with children in the future.

Publication Dates: 1977–1978.

Scores: 9 subsections: Opinions About Marriage and Having Children, Feelings About Parenthood, Feelings About Myself, Opinions About Children, Understanding of Children, Child Care Skills, Before Birth, Family Life Situations, Knowledge and Opinions About Sex.

Administration: Group.

Price Data: Available from publisher.

Foreign Language Edition: Spanish version available.

Time: Administration time not reported.

Comments: Intended for use in parent-training or child care training programs; manual title is Education for Parenthood: A Program, Curriculum, and Evaluation Guide.

Authors: James C. Petersen, Jean M. Baker, Larry A. Morris, and Rachel Burkholder.

Publisher: The Assessment and Development Centre.

Review of The Parenthood Questionnaire by SARAH J. ALLEN, Associate Professor of School Psychology, University of Cincinnati, Cincinnati, OH:

DESCRIPTION. The Parenthood Questionnaire is a brief, self-report measure that was designed to obtain information from youth concerning their knowledge and opinions of parenting and child development. The Questionnaire was developed for use in pre- and posttest comparisons to evaluate the Education for Parenthood Program, which is a nationwide program and curriculum intended to provide teenagers with opportunities to develop more positive attitudes about children and parenting, to improve self-awareness and self-understanding, and to increase knowledge and skills related to child care and development. However, this instrument could be used with other programs of the same nature. Specifically, The Parenthood Questionnaire is an 80-item instrument that assesses participants' knowledge, skills, and attitudes along the dimensions of: (a) the course of child development; (b) the social, medical, and emotional needs of children; (c) the family's role in child development and socialization; (d) important factors in prenatal care and the early months of infancy; (e) child-care career possibilities and requirements; and (f) self-awareness. In either instructional or research settings, potential applications for use of The Parenthood Questionnaire range from providing descriptive information about respondents' characteristics, knowledge, skills, and opinions regarding parenting and child development, to determining the effectiveness of instructional efforts in parent or child-care training programs.

Intended for use with youth who are prospective parents or who may work with children in the future, The Parenthood Questionnaire is administered in a group format both prior to and following a parent-training or child-care training program.

Individual administration also would be possible. If used for program evaluation, it is recommended that the instrument be administered to program participants and a matched-sample comparison group who did not receive the training both prior to and at the conclusion of the training program.

Using paper-and-pencil format, administration of the Questionnaire is quick and easy. Respondents are asked to respond to both forced-choice and Likert-type items. Items are organized into nine subsections: Demographic Information; Opinions about Marriage and Having Children; Feelings about Parenthood; Feelings about Myself; Opinions about Children; Understanding of Children; Child Care Skills; Before Birth (i.e., prenatal development); Family Life Situations; and Knowledge and Opinions about Sex. Items comprising this scale are multifaceted (i.e., respondents are asked to respond to items by selecting from multiple-choice alternatives, rating the extent to which they agree or disagree with a statement using a 5-point Likert-type scale, and reacting to brief scenarios). Some items require accuracy in one's response and others, opinion. Although administration times are not reported, it is estimated that most teenagers could complete the instrument in 20–30 minutes. The manual does not include directions for administration or scoring. Both English and Spanish versions of the instrument are available.

DEVELOPMENT. In 1972, a nationwide program called Education for Parenthood (EfP) was initiated by the National Center for Child Advocacy, Children's Bureau, Office of Child Development, in cooperation with the Office of Education and the National Institute of Mental Health. The purpose of the program was to provide youth with opportunities to develop more positive attitudes about children and parenting, to improve their self-awareness and self-understanding, and to increase their knowledge of child development and related topics. Initially, parenthood education curricula were developed for use in schools with students in Grades 7 through 12. In order to collect information about the EfP Program participants in nonschool settings, the instructional experience (i.e., method of instruction, setting, materials, etc.), and effectiveness of the Program, The Parenthood Questionnaire was developed. The manual contains only an overview of the instrument and its use in evaluation. No information is provided in the manual about instrument development, including construction of the item pool, item selection, piloting of the instrument, or its final composition.

The summary of results obtained from the organizations using the EfP Program reported in the manual indicates that the Questionnaire was administered as a nonrandomized pre- and posttest at over 300 locations of seven national organizations that operated an EfP Program. Respondents included 955 program participants and 776 comparison group members. Descriptive information about participants, trainers, setting, approaches used in training, and instructional goals is reported by organization. Adequacy of the sample as being representative of youth-serving programs is difficult to determine. Results are reported as comparisons both between participants among organizations and across participant organizations relative to the control group based on summary statistics for individual items.

TECHNICAL. A strong conceptual basis and logistical rationale for the EfP Program and others like it was provided. Similarly, in response to needs for accountability, the justification and need for development of an evaluation tool such as The Parenthood Questionnaire is evident. However, the manual provides relatively little information about the development or psychometric properties of the instrument. Information regarding the construction of the item pool, item selection, grouping of items by construct, piloting of the instrument, and so forth is not included in the manual. Further, specific directions for administration, scoring, or interpretation of results are not outlined. No data are provided to establish relevance of this measurement tool to instruction beyond face validity. Psychometric properties of the instrument are not reported.

Although this questionnaire is organized in nine sections, only individual item analysis is discussed. Internal consistency reliability data for the scale or the subsections are not provided. Further, evidence supporting the validity of score interpretations from The Parenthood Questionnaire for evaluation of parent or child-care training programs is not discussed.

COMMENTARY. Developed as an evaluation tool for the Education for Parenthood Program specifically, the Parenthood Questionnaire provides information about the knowledge, skills, and opinions of youth concerning parenting and child development. As such, it represents an assessment tool that can be used to describe respondents' knowledge, opinions, and skills based on self-report information, and in pre- and posttest comparisons for evaluation of parent and child-care training program effectiveness. A review of item content provides face validity for use of test results for these purposes. However, consistent with current measurement standards, it is important that care be taken to limit use of this, and any, instrument to the purpose(s) for which validity evidence is provided. The information presented to describe the development, psychometric properties, administration, and intended function of this instrument is general. Similarly, evidence available to support use and interpretation of this measure is general. As always, caution is advised when interpreting the meaningfulness of data obtained from an instrument in ways that have not been validated.

SUMMARY. The Parenthood Questionnaire is an 80-item self-report measure designed to obtain information from youth concerning their knowledge, skills, and opinions of parenting and child development. The instrument can be used to obtain descriptive information from youth on these topics and/or to evaluate the effectiveness of parent or child-care training programs and curricula using pre- and posttest comparisons. Published 25 years ago, the instrument is available in both English and Spanish versions.

Review of The Parenthood Questionnaire by CYNTHIA A. ROHRBECK, Associate Professor of Psychology, The George Washington University, Washington, DC:

DESCRIPTION. The Parenthood Questionnaire, developed J. C. Peterson, J. M. Baker, L. A. Morris, and R. Burkholder (1978) was designed to assess youths' opinions and knowledge of parenting and child development. It appears to be a revised version of the Education for Parenthood Questionnaire described in the manual, *Education for Parenthood: A Program, Curriculum and Evaluation Guide.* The questionnaire was designed to measure change from pre to post in parent training or child-care training programs and is available in English and Spanish versions.

The Parenthood Questionnaire is an approximately 115-item paper-and-pencil questionnaire that includes several different formats across its nine sections. For example, some sections include both yes/no questions and Likert scale responses up to six choices. Most sections range from a 3-point to a 5-point Likert scale format. One section uses a true/false response format, whereas another presents hypothetical dialogues among friends of a protagonist, and asks the respondent to choose the friend with whom he or she most agrees. The manual does not clarify how items are to be scored. Implicitly, it appears that scores on both individual items and subsection totals or averages could be used to evaluate the effectiveness of parent training programs.

DEVELOPMENT. The manual does not include information about how the items were developed, only that they were developed to evaluate the effectiveness of a particular parenting program. In addition, it should be noted that the items were developed in the late 1970s and may not adequately represent content in more recent parenting programs.

TECHNICAL. Norms are not available for this measure. There is no evidence of content validity; it is not clear whether or not the items represent the domain of parenting knowledge as accurately and fully as possible. There is also no evidence of internal consistency for either the measure as a whole or the various sections. There is also no evidence of test-retest reliability, although participants in the program evaluation for which the questionnaire was designed appear to score similarly from pre to post. There is no evidence presented of concurrent validity; it is not known how this measure compares to other measures of parenting or child development. Based on the one program evaluation, there are some individual items and sections that might show intervention effects; however, the differences between program participants and comparison groups do not appear to be "clinically significant."

COMMENTARY. Given the potential datedness of this measure, and the lack of fundamental information about its psychometric properties, it is probably not the measure of choice to assess knowledge of parenting and/or child development. Unfortunately, there are not many reviewed, well-supported measures of these constructs in the literature. Most measures appear to have been designed with the goal of evaluating a particular idiosyncratic program.

SUMMARY. The Parenthood Questionnaire could presumably be used in order to evaluate the curriculum for which it was designed—the Education for Parenthood program. However, even in that case, there is insufficient information about the content validity and internal consistency of the measure. It would be inappropriate to use it for other purposes without further evidence of its reliability and validity.

[181]
Parenting Alliance Measure.

Purpose: "Measures the strength of the perceived alliance between parents of children ages 1 to 19 years"; and "reflects the parents' ability to cooperate with each other in meeting the needs of the child."
Population: Parents of children ages 1–19 years.
Publication Dates: 1988–1999.
Acronym: PAM.
Scores: Total score only.
Administration: Group.
Price Data: Available from publisher for introductory kit; $30 per 25 test forms; $30 per professional manual (1999, 58 pages).
Time: (5–15) minutes.
Authors: Richard R. Abidin (test) and Timothy R. Konold (manual and test).
Publisher: Psychological Assessment Resources, Inc.

Review of the Parenting Alliance Measure by CINDY I. CARLSON, Professor of Educational Psychology, University of Texas at Austin, Austin, TX:

DESCRIPTION. The Parenting Alliance Measure (PAM) is a 20-item paper-and-pencil, hand-scored test. Parents respond to the items using a 5-point rating scale ranging from strongly agree to strongly disagree. The PAM can be completed in less than 10 minutes. Completion of the PAM requires a third-grade reading level. It is permissible to read the PAM items aloud to parents who have difficulty reading.

The PAM can be administered and scored by individuals who do not have formal training in psychology; however, interpretation of the PAM requires graduate training in psychology or related fields. A PAM raw score is calculated by summing the item scores for all 20 items. Corresponding percentile scores and T-score conversions are provided. As scores between mothers and fathers were found to differ significantly in the normative sample, raw scores, percentile scores, and T-scores conversions are provided separately for mothers and fathers. "The PAM Total score provides an indication of the degree to which parents perceive themselves to be in a cooperative, communicative, and mutually respectful alliance for the care of their children" (professional manual, p. 5). The higher the score, the stronger is the perceived parenting alliance. According to the PAM manual, percentile scores equal to or greater than the 20th percentile are considered within the normal range. Scores below the 20th percentile are interpreted as indicative of a parenting alliance that is marginal (15th–19th percentile), problematic (6th–14th percentile), and dysfunctional (1st–5th percentile).

DEVELOPMENT. According to the PAM manual, the PAM was initially developed by Abidin in 1988 as part of a longitudinal study of family relations. The PAM reflects a substantive-construct approach to test development that was guided by clinical and empirical considerations. Empirical research and clinical models that support the concept of the parenting alliance and the impact of the parental relationship on children's adjustments are cited as the basis for the development of items. The PAM manual provides extensive discussion of the development of the test and the factor analysis of the normative sample.

The PAM was originally called the Parenting Alliance Inventory (PAI) and consisted of 80 items. The items were field tested with parents for readability and clarity. Items were next reviewed by experts who rated the degree to which the items reflected the construct of parenting alliance. This rating was used to reduce the measure to 30 items. The 30-item test was administered to a sample of 512 parents. Based upon the factor loadings, the total number of items was reduced to 20. An extensive exploration of the factor structure of the test was completed separately for fathers and mothers on the normative sample. Although a two-factor solution emerged, for a variety of reasons that are carefully explained in the manual, a single-factor structure was adopted.

TECHNICAL. Information regarding the descriptive characteristics of the normative sample is clearly provided in the PAM manual. Normative data for the PAM were based on a sample of 1,224 parents of children ranging in age from 1 to 19 years selected from various settings and regions of the country. Demographic characteristics of the sample are provided and compared with the 1997 U.S. Census projections. A comparison of these data indicates a respectable approximation of the nation's population characteristics with the exception of Hispanic parents who are underrepresented in the normative sample. As parent gender was determined to be a significant influence, separate norms were calculated for mothers and fathers. Although the manual also cites research finding significant differences in parenting alliance scores for parents based on family structure, no separate norms are provided for married, single parent, and remarried mothers and fathers. No data were provided on ethnic differences in test results.

The internal consistency reliability coefficients, as reported in the manual for mothers and fathers in the normative sample, indicate a high degree of internal consistency (>.95). Test-retest reliability indicated stability of the test over a 4- to 6-week period.

Validation evidence for the PAM includes studies completed on both the original PAI and the PAM. Content validity of scores from the test was examined by expert review as noted above. Criterion-related validity was considered by examining the PAM in relation to parenting stress, marital quality, family functioning, and children's self-esteem and social competence. Consistent with hypotheses, results found the PAM to be significantly negatively correlated with parenting stress and significantly positively correlated with family cohesion, family adaptability, and marital quality. Multiple studies have been conducted examining the relation between PAM scores and children's adjustment with results generally in the direction anticipated by theory or previous research. Discriminant validity of the parenting alliance as a unique component of marital quality was considered in a study examining the independent relationship of the PAM and marital adjustment to child behavior problems. The PAM has been found to be uncorrelated with socially desirable responding in three studies to date.

COMMENTARY. The PAM is a carefully developed test of a theoretically relevant construct, the parenting alliance, which has been largely without adequate measurement in research and clinical practice. The measure is brief and simple to administer and score. The test has modest readability requirements making it useful for a broad range of parental education levels. A comprehensive and clearly written manual provides the test user with appropriate documentation of test development, scoring, score interpretation, and normative data for comparison. The measure does not show evidence of social desirability response bias.

Limitations of the PAM include lack of studies and normative or descriptive data comparing mothers' and fathers' scores as these may vary with ethnicity and family structure, including gay and lesbian parents. The lower percentage of Hispanic parents in the normative sample compared with the U.S. Census suggests that caution may be warranted in using the PAM with this population. Finally, based on research cited in the PAM manual, no predictive validity or clinical utility studies, as yet, have been conducted. These will be a welcome addition to the already strong program of research supporting this test.

SUMMARY. The PAM appears to be a psychometrically sound measure of an important construct, the parenting alliance. The measure is an efficient means to collect information that may not be openly admitted except through a self-report method. The developers have based their measure on relevant theory and research. The measure is brief, requires modest reading level, and is easily administered and scored. The Parenting Alliance Measure: Professional Manual that accompanies the measure provides excellent support for the test user including case studies to assist interpretation of scores. This is a well-developed test that should be of great value to clinicians and researchers concerned broadly with the impact of parenting on children.

Review of the Parenting Alliance Measure by MARY M. CLARE, Professor of Counseling Psychology, Lewis & Clark College, Portland, OR:

DESCRIPTION. The Parenting Alliance Measure (PAM) is a 20-item instrument that uses parents' self-reports to reflect the alliance between parents with regard to caring for their children. The PAM is hand-scorable, uses a 5-point Likert-type scale (*strongly agree* to *strongly disagree*), and is written at a third grade reading level. This measure can be completed by most parents in less than 10 minutes and scored by a clinician in half that time.

Based on the idea of *parenting alliance* developed by Weissman and Cohen (1985), the PAM allows practitioners the opportunity to discern the strength of the working relationship between parents relative to meeting the needs of their child or children. Parents respond to items intended to reflect the four dimensions of positive parenting alliance identified by Weissman and Cohen (1985). These dimensions include the parent's investment

in the child's well-being and her or his assessment of the other parent's involvement in parenting, respect for the other parent's judgment regarding the child, and interest in communicating about the child with the other parent. Given its focus on these dimensions, the PAM is appropriate for use in situations of marital conflict and marital transition (e.g., divorce and the developing joint custody arrangements). This measure can also be applied in working clinically with families that include children ages 1–19, and in conducting research on the relationship between parental behaviors and the experiences and behaviors of children.

The authors emphasize that the PAM is best used as part of a larger assessment battery and is not an instrument for lay use. Although scoring is quick, interpretation requires training in psychology or related fields.

DEVELOPMENT. The PAM is the most recent version of an instrument developed in 1988 for use in a study to develop a model of parenting behavior (Abidin, 1992). The original 80-item instrument (the Parenting Alliance Inventory) was taken through a series of field tests with parents, then reviewed by a panel of professional experts who judged the items' fit with Weissman and Cohen's (1985) four dimensions of positive parenting alliance. This process reduced the instrument's length to 30 items. The final 20-item version reflects subsequent factor analysis of the 30-item PAM that ensured the best representation (seen in a two-factor solution) of mothers' and fathers' responses.

The materials accompanying the PAM provide descriptions of the psychometric properties of the instrument that are thorough, practical, and easily understood. The theory underlying the measure is developed in a way that provides both academic context and practical illustration of how the various interpretations available with the PAM are supported by the knowledge base on parenting. The authors underscore the dynamic nature of parenting and child outcomes by referring to parenting as a primary variable in the "path of influence" (p. 1) between marital conflict and children's lives. The guidance offered in the manual for interpreting responses to the PAM includes three case study presentations that enliven the links between scoring, interpretation, and intervention.

TECHNICAL. The PAM is grounded in a normative sample that was collected in 1997 and included 1,224 parents ages 17–70 from 15 states in the U.S. This sample was developed to be in line with the U.S. Census projections of 1997. The authors report that the median income was between $40,001 and $50,000. There were nearly two times more mothers than fathers in the norm sample.

Reliability was examined with internal consistency reliability alpha coefficients all exceeding .95 and test-retest reliability coefficients at .88 for mothers and .63 for fathers for retesting in 4 to 6 weeks. The authors also derived confidence intervals to assist with the interpretation of raw scores.

The validity of scores from the PAM seems also to be well established. Content validity was made clear with the process described above that was undertaken to develop the scale. The input of parents and professionals indicated the strong link between the items of the PAM and both the professional literature and the experiences of parents and professionals who work with families.

Criterion-related validity was indicated with significant correlations ($p<.05$) in comparisons of PAM scores with the Stress Index for Parents and Adolescents (SIPA), the Dyadic Adjustment Scale (DAS), and the Family Adaptability and Cohesion Evaluation Scales III (FACES-III). Correlations between mother's and father's PAM scores and teacher's ratings of a child's self-esteem also revealed significant results. Relation of the PAM to the teacher's assessment of a child's self-competence was significant only with regard to the father's score. As further evidence of criterion-related validity, the authors compared parents from known groups. They found that married parents reported significantly more positive parenting alliances than separated/divorced parents, parents of children who had no history of receiving mental health services reported significantly stronger alliances than parents of children who had such histories, and parents of children who had engaged in delinquent behaviors had weaker PAM scores than parents of children who had not participated in delinquency. Finally, the authors considered parents of children with and without clinical diagnoses. Parents of children without diagnoses and parents of children with ADHD diagnoses reported stronger alliances than parents of children with oppositional defiant disorder (ODD) or conduct disorder (CD).

Discriminant validity was examined by comparing parents' scores on the Marital Adjustment Test (MAT) with PAM scores and making a similar comparison of PAM scores with children's scores on the Eyberg Child Behavior Inventory (ECBI), a measure of child adjustment. The ECBI was not correlated significantly with the MAT, yet the ECBI and PAM were moderately correlated, and the PAM and MAT were strongly correlated. The authors take this as an indication that the PAM stands as a significant measure of the relationship between parenting during marital stress and children's adjustment experiences.

Finally, the factor analyses referred to above add to the strength of validity claims for the PAM. Extensive consideration by the authors of the most accurate factor solutions yielded two-factor solutions for mothers (Communication and Teamwork for Mothers, Feels Respected by Other Parent) and for fathers (Communication and Teamwork for Fathers, Respects Other Parent's Commitment and Judgment).

COMMENTARY. The PAM is a well-researched and thoughtfully developed assessment tool. There are few weaknesses to this measure. In the opening description of the instrument, the authors indicate parenting alliance as being descriptive of relationships between "married or unmarried parenting couples, separated or divorced parents, and parenting partners in a variety of parenting arrangements" (p. 1). However, earlier in that description and throughout the manual, the authors refer consistently to parenting alliance as part of the marital relationship. Many people parent. Grandparents, friends, older siblings, and gay and lesbian couples are all likely to be in parenting roles. The narrow focus in practice (i.e., given the restrictions of the norm sample) limits the application of the PAM. An additional limitation to this instrument is the seemingly high socioeconomic level represented by the norm sample. The use of this instrument with people from low-income or impoverished situations is also likely to be limited.

SUMMARY. The PAM appears to be an instrument of great potential for clinical and research applications. The authors are to be commended on their thorough and clear grounding of this instrument both theoretically and psychometrically. Extended representation in the norm sample of parents from lower socioeconomic situations and of parents with various nontraditional characteristics (i.e., including nonbiological and homosexual parents) seems important as a next step in the development of the PAM.

REVIEWER'S REFERENCES

Abidin, R. R. (1992). The determinants of parenting behavior. *Journal of Clinical Child Psychology, 21,* 407–412.
Weissman, S. H., & Cohen, R. S. (1985). The parenting alliance and adolescence. *Adolescent Psychiatry, 12,* 24–45.

[182]

PASAT 2000 [Poppleton Allen Sales Aptitude Test].

Purpose: "Designed to measure those personality attributes which have a direct relevance to success in sales roles."
Population: Adults.
Publication Date: 1999.
Acronym: PASAT 2000.
Scores: 11 scales: Motivational, Emotional, Social, Adaptability, Conscientious, Emotional Stability, Social Control, Self-Assurance, Attentive Distortion, Adaptive Distortion, Social Distortion.
Administration: Group.
Price Data: Available from publisher.
Time: (20) minutes.
Authors: Steve Poppleton and Peter Jones.
Publisher: The Test Agency Limited [England].
Cross References: For reviews by Larry Cochran and David O. Herman of an earlier edition of the Poppleton Allen Sales Aptitude Test, see 10:285.

Review of the PASAT 2000 [Poppleton Allen Sales Aptitude Test] by RICHARD E. HARDING, Principal and Director of Research, Kenexa Technology, Lincoln, NE:

DESCRIPTION. The PASAT 2000 consists of 153 statements that are given in a past tense (e.g., "I have found …"). Candidates are asked to respond to these statements using a 5-point scale where 1 is *never or very infrequently,* 2 is *infrequently,* 3 is *sometimes,* 4 is *frequently,* and 5 is *very frequently or always.*

There are eight main scales that are scattered across three major factors. The eight scales are Motivational Adjustment, Emotional Adjustment, Social Adjustment, Adaptability, Conscientiousness, Emotional Stability, Social Control, and Self-Assurance. The first five load on a major group factor that has been labeled overall as Adjustment. Scales 6 and 7 load on a second factor that is called Control Over Others and Self, and the last scale, Self-Assurance, is an independent factor. There are three other scales the authors indicate are "designed to detect attempts to present false impressions" (technical manual, p. 18). These

are Attentive Faking, Adaptive Faking, and Social Faking. Most of the items in these last three scales come from items that are in the first eight scales. The manual states that some items are scored in one direction for the main scale score and in a reversed direction for one of the three faking scales.

Overall, the manual is relatively informative. However, in some sections very little explanation is provided, leading to the possibility of making erroneous assumptions about the development, research, and use of the PASAT. For example, the norm tables are included with limited direction on how to use them and it is not clear which norm table is most appropriate for various sales roles. Moreover, there are many references to past journal articles and books, but they are not included in the brief bibliography provided. On the positive side, the test manual is well laid out and has most of the basics one would look for in a manual. However, the manual is written for a very sophisticated and educated user. Not all people involved in the selection of salespeople would have this level of knowledge.

The PASAT 2000 can be administered via a computer using the provided disk or via the internet. The diskette program was easy to use and follow. The graphics for the statements were excellent and the program was very responsive for the test taker. An autogenerated narrative report is available to download and print. This report covers the scales used in the PASAT 2000 but no scale scores are reported. A description of the candidate's scores are given, such as "a middle score on Emotional Adjustment suggest …." The reader is left to provide the interpretation of what is a low, middle, or high score, presumably by reading the normative tables in the manual. The narrative goes on to list behaviors that the test taker is likely to engage in or not after hiring. The scoring was instantaneous with results available immediately upon conclusion of the test.

DEVELOPMENT. The goal of the PASAT 2000 is to help organizations and individuals improve sales staff selection. As such, the PASAT 2000 is purported to measure factors that only contribute to success in a sales role. Yet, the methodology involved in developing the PASAT 2000, as well as a subsequent study, suggests that the PASAT 2000 could be used in other contexts. The authors indicate that personality can be one of the differentiators between the highest performing salespeople and those who are less successful. One has to read between the lines to ascertain that "highest performing" is most likely designated as upper end criterion attainment. No data are provided as to the range of criterion level variables used, which leads to concerns about the reliability of these criteria.

Five of the eight minor group factors are indicated as being closely related to the "Big Five" personality factors. The authors, however, go on to further indicate that the major group factors were intercorrelated to some degree, which led them to the belief that what they were measuring was an overall "general personality factor" that is related to sales performance.

It is unclear in the test manual provided by the publisher whether or not the Poppleton Allen Sales Aptitude Test 2000 (PASAT 2000) is a completely new instrument or a revision of the earlier PASAT. One statement in the manual indicates that it is a new instrument, whereas another indicates that is a major revision of the earlier test. Overall, the PASAT 2000 has undergone extensive research over the last few years.

To develop this version of the test, the authors reviewed historic classifications of sales jobs. They then invited companies that represented diversity in those sales jobs to participate in the development. The first part of the development centered on interviewing 72 people who represented salespeople, sales managers, and customers for a wide range of sales environments and products. These included financial, retail, pharmaceutical sales, and motor retail and direct sales. These interviews yielded 3,565 behaviors that were coded and categorized. This resulted in 1,523 items being generated.

After several iterations of pilot testing and analysis the final instrument contained 140 items across the three major factors of work adjustment, control, and self-assurance as well as the eight main scales of the instrument.

To develop the faking scales, the authors developed a composite 76-item instrument from the Self-Monitoring scale developed by Snyder (1974), the Self-Presentation scale by Roth, Harris, and Snyder (1988), and the Balanced Inventory of Desirable Responding by Paulhus (1991). [Editor's Note: Although all these instruments were cited in the technical manual, no references were provided.] Further analyses were completed resulting in these three scales.

TECHNICAL.

Reliability. Reliability was estimated using coefficient alpha based on a sample size of 560 people. Coefficients ranged from .48 for Self-Assurance to .87 for Social Control. Three of these coefficients were in the .70 to .79 range. The four alphas below .80 are quite low to be making individual decisions on sales candidates, especially the alpha of .48 for Self-Assurance. The faking scales had alphas of .35 for Attentive Management, .49 for Adaptive, and .72 for Social Impression.

A test-retest methodology was also employed using a group of 16- and 17-year-old students and another sample of public sector employees. The students were tested twice, 4 months apart and the public sector workers had 2 months between tests. For students the reliabilities ranged from .69 for Emotional Stability to .88 for Social Control. With the exception of Emotional Stability, all are above .70. For the public sector workers, the range of test-retest reliability was .77 to .88.

Validity. Several studies were undertaken to provide evidence of validity for the PASAT 2000. Concurrent validity studies were conducted with financial services salespeople, pharmaceutical salespeople, retail salespeople, software salespeople, and fuel/oil salespeople. Most of these studies had criterion measures of performance that ranged from objective (sickness levels, number of days missed in the last year) to subjective ratings such as team work and adaptability ratings. Little detail is provided with regard to the validity coefficients. Many are not statistically significant, but most appear to be in the appropriate direction, that is negative to ranking, and positive to variables such as growth on target. The pattern of the concurrent validity coefficients is typical of studies of this nature where results are mixed, indicating that some of the constructs do an excellent job of predicting performance whereas others are relatively weak.

The manual indicates that the questionnaire may be useful in predicting performance and career progression in jobs other than sales. This assertion comes from a study completed on police officers, sergeants, chief inspectors, and constables in the United Kingdom. Based on this limited evidence it would be wise to proceed cautiously when using the PASAT 2000 to assess non-sales-related positions.

The PASAT 2000 was also studied in relationship to the Eysenck Personality Questionnaire

(EPQ), NEO-PIR, and the Manchester Personality Questionnaire (MPQ). Little explanation is given surrounding this type of validity assessment. It appears that the PASAT 2000 is a relatively robust measure of Conscientiousness as measured by the NEO-PIR. The coefficients provided as evidence of construct validity are typical and hardly surprising.

The interscale correlations are in an acceptable range leading to a conclusion of some scale relationship, hence, the claim that overall the test may measure a positive attitude. The three faking scales were correlated to the various criterion measures.

Assessments are given in the manual with regard to the relationship of the PASAT 2000 to gender, ethnicity, first language, Asian, and Black groups. It is very difficult to ascertain the sample size in each of these. No data are presented on an overall PASAT 2000 score regarding group differences.

However, differences in scores were noted across scales for various ethnic groups. No data are provided regarding disabilities, age, or sexual orientation, all of which are mentioned in the manual as being important.

COMMENTARY. Based on these data, the possibility exists that the use of the PASAT 2000 may result in adverse impact with regard to ethnicity. Care should be taken in the use of the PASAT 2000 regarding ethnicity. The manual further states that older and disabled staff were included in the samples, yet no data are presented.

Another concern about the PASAT 2000 is the authors' contention that the PASAT 2000 "can also be used in training and development, either as a diagnostic tool or possibly as an evaluation method, as the behaviors tested are directly related to sales environments" (technical manual, p. 11). Nowhere in the manual can be found the suggested methodology or uses of this tool in a diagnostic or training and development mode.

Another area of concern is the use of cutoff scores. The scaled scores are put into a table where the resultant score is a sten and all of the scales are scored so that the higher the scale the more positive the behavior. The authors indicate that the PASAT 2000 could be used in an actuarial way, that is using cutoffs or a regression equation, to help assess a candidate, but no assistance is provided in the manual for these fairly complex and sophisticated techniques. It is not clear whether or not there is an overall assessment score available. One has to examine the scoring key to find

the overall score. However, no explanation is given as to interpretation, cutoff, or regression techniques. The user is left to establish their own cutoff scores or to use some sort of regression equation to help screen candidates.

SUMMARY AND CONCLUSION. Overall, the PASAT 2000 should be used to assess candidates to determine their probability for success in a sales role as stated by the authors. However, caution should be used by practitioners in doing this. The authors do recommend that local validation studies be completed to develop company-specific norms. This is difficult unless one has the expertise or can employ the authors or other experts to assist. Another limitation of this suggestion is that few sales organizations have a large enough sales force to warrant this approach. The inconsistencies in the manual, issues about ethnicity, and how the process should be used in an organization leads a practitioner to be very cautious and judicious when using the PASAT 2000.

Review of the PASAT 2000 [Poppleton Allen Sales Aptitude Test] by JOHN TIVENDELL, Professor of Psychology, Université de Moncton, Moncton, New Brunswick, Canada:

DESCRIPTION AND DEVELOPMENT. The PASAT 2000 is an untimed test designed to measure personality traits presumed important to the selection of successful sales personnel. It is a revised version of the Poppleton Allan Sales Aptitude Test (see Cochran, 1989) and is now composed of 153 items rated on 5-point Likert scales. The items are the result of job analyses using 72 semistructured interviews, ranging across sales environments as well as gender, age, and ethnicity, and of content analyses of written materials including training manuals. Although purportedly linked to behaviors distinguishing between effective and noneffective sales personnel, the items are self-assessments of attitudes and preferences as well as of behaviors. They are all worded in the past tense because of the authors' assumption "that past behaviours are the best predictors of future behaviours" (technical manual, p. 10). The test now measures eight factors to which three motivational distortion scales have been added.

TECHNICAL. We are told that the authors have carried out a confirmatory factor analysis ($N = 560$) and that their model now comprises a general factor (positive attitude), three major "group factors," and "eight minor factors." However, there is little way to confirm this because, with the exception of some interscale correlations, data on item loadings and eigenvalues are not provided. The factors are presented in a similar way to the 16PF, with descriptions of high and low scorers and, despite references to the works of Christie (Machiavellianism), Freud, Maslow, McClelland, and Vernon (abilities), they have more in common with the Big Five traits such as emotional stability, openness, and conscientiousness.

The eight factors retained have good internal consistency (with the exception of Self-Assurance and two of the three lie scales) and, although we do not know the number of participants, two other studies show excellent test-retest reliability (administration intervals of 2 and 4 months) for all 11 scales. Results of a number of very small concurrent validity studies (often below $N = 30$) are also presented, correlating the scales with performance ratings, target achievement, and in a couple of cases, actual sales data. Cochran (1989) had noted the low number of participants in an earlier review. The sample sizes for these latter studies could only be deduced from what appear to be Pearson r coefficients, as they were not reported.

Finally, the authors present three construct validity studies using the Eysenck Personality Questionnaire, the NEO-PIR, and the Manchester Personality Questionnaire (MPQ). The reported correlations underline the PASAT 2000's scales' (eight plus three motivational distortion scales) independence with these other personality tests' factors, rather than offering clear support for any of its construct validity. For instance, only one of the PASAT's three motivational distortion scales (i.e., Social Distortion—the only one with a good internal reliability coefficient), correlates with the EPQ's lie scale. Most of the other EPQ, NEO-PIR, and MPQ factors rarely correlate with less than three of the PASAT's scales.

SUMMARY. In general, the strength of the PASAT 2000 is again the construction of its test items (see Cochran, 1989). The manual is systematic and well written, and the authors do a good job introducing psychometric concepts and even socio-legal concerns important in evaluating any predictor being considered. Their bibliography is incomplete, but more important still is that more information is needed about their confirmatory factor analysis and about the nature and construct

validity of these eight traits. It is hoped that the authors and other users of the test will soon increase the number of individuals and organizations participating in their concurrent validity studies and, as Cochran had suggested a decade earlier, that they engage in some predictive studies too. Personnel selection officers wishing to explore the potential usefulness of an easy to use and straightforward measure to forecast performance in sales may consider the PASAT 2000 in their research, albeit to be used in conjunction with other predictors. However, its eight factors may not represent actual personality traits and any interpretation of results needs to be done with caution.

REVIEWER'S REFERENCE

Cochran, L. (1989). [Review of The Poppleton Allan Sales Aptitude Test]. In J. C. Conoley & J. J. Kramer (Eds.), *The tenth mental measurements yearbook* (pp. 642–643). Lincoln, NE: Buros Institute of Mental Measurements.

[183]

Paulhus Deception Scales: Balanced Inventory of Desirable Responding Version 7.

Purpose: Designed to measure the tendency to give socially desirable responses to tests.

Population: Ages 16 and older.

Publication Dates: 1998–1999.

Acronym: PDS.

Scores, 2: Impression Management, Self-Deceptive Enhancement.

Administration: Group.

Price Data, 2002: $50 per complete kit including 25 QuikScore™ forms and manual; $25 per 25 QuikScore™ forms; $30 per manual.

Time: (5–7) minutes.

Comments: Self-report; computerized version for Windows™ available on CD.

Author: Delroy L. Paulhus.

Publisher: Multi-Health Systems, Inc.

Cross References: See T5:1898 (1 reference).

Review of the Paulhus Deception Scales: Balanced Inventory of Desirable Responding Version 7 by KWONG-LIEM KARL KWAN, Associate Professor, Department of Educational Studies, Counseling and Development Program, Purdue University, West Lafayette, IN:

DESCRIPTION. The Paulhus Deception Scales (PDS), also known as Version 7 of the Balanced Inventory of Desirable Responding (BIDR), is designed to assess socially desirable responding. Evolving from earlier development and revisions of the BIDR, the PDS is intended to capture two "principal forms" of socially desirable responding: Impression Management (IM) and Self-Deception Enhancement (SDE). IM purports to indicate hypersensitivity to situational self-presentation demands by inflating self-descriptions and engaging in purposeful faking or lying. SDE purports to indicate tendency to give honest but inflated self-description, and reflects an unconscious favorability bias characterized by a pervasive lack of insight. It is noted that the two subscales are relatively independent and that a qualitatively different approach to interpretation is called for.

The PDS has been applied in clinical and personality diagnosis, instrument development and evaluation, and human resources and educational settings. The instrument is part of the standardized assessment battery administered to inmates entering the correctional system in Ontario, Canada. The PDS could also be integrated as part of a test battery to serve as a validity check. It was cautioned, however, that the instrument not be used as the sole criterion for decision making, assessment, and diagnosis.

The PDS consists of 40 statements to which respondents circle a response using a 5-point rating scale with 1 = Not True and 5 = True. The first 20 items constitute the SDE subscale and the last 20 items the IM subscale. Overall, PDS items were clear and straightforward. Negatively keyed items were included throughout the scale, which enables control of potential confounding effect of response style. The Dale-Chall procedure for determining level of readability was reported, which indicated that a North American fifth-grade reading level was needed for the PDS. The reviewer and two of his faculty colleagues found the item "I never read sexy books or magazines" somewhat ambiguous (i.e., does it refer to reading books or magazines about sex or about pornography?). It was noted that college respondents need 3 to 5 minutes to complete the items. The reviewer administered the PDS to two secretaries (high school and college educated) working in a university department, and three graduate students whose first language is not English (a Chicano, and two international students from Europe and Asia). It took the secretaries between 8 and 10 minutes, and the graduate students between 3 and 7 minutes to complete the items. Respondents who have not traveled overseas were not able to respond to the item "I always declare everything at customs."

A dichotomous scoring procedure is used by which only items that receive extreme responses—

a rating of 1 or 5—are scored. All responses are transferred to another scoring sheet, with 1 point assigned to each item that receives an extreme response (i.e., 1 or 5 on the original answer sheet) in the scored direction (i.e., high SDE or IM) and 0 for all other responses (i.e., 2, 3, or 4 on the original answer sheet) to the item. Thus, the total score for the PDS ranges from 0 to 40, and scores for the respective SDE and IM subscales range from 0 to 20. A profile with more than five missing responses is considered invalid. Specific instructions to adjust for (one to four) missing responses for the total scale and respective subscales are offered (manual, p. 4). In general, the scoring instructions and procedure are clear and easy to follow. It is noted that a 7-point scoring system can also be used to integrate the PDS with other assessments, and that continuous (as opposed to dichotomous) scoring of the PDS can also be used. However, it is recommended that the dichotomous scoring be preferred as high scores are more likely to indicate individuals who give exaggerated responses to items that are already highly desirable (manual, p. 18).

The PDS can also be administered and scored via the computer. The QuikEntry mode allows the administrator or assistant to enter responses from paper-and-pencil PDS results into the computer for scoring and report information. The Online mode allows the PDS to be administered and data to be stored directly in one of the three "platforms": PsychManager, Correction Manager, and PeoplePro. It is noted that PsychManager is most appropriate for mental health practitioners, Correction Manager is more specific to correctional settings, and PeoplePro is ideal for personnel selection and career development settings. The respective platforms integrate the PDS results with patient/respondent/offender and practitioner/consultant/case administrator information.

DEVELOPMENT. The PDS culminates the final version of a series of measures for Self-Deceptive Enhancement and Impression Management, which are concluded as the two distinct forms of social desirability responding (SDR). Self-Deceptive Enhancement and Impression Management subscales evolved from the respective Self-Deception Questionnaire (SDQ) and Other-Deception Questionnaire (ODQ), which was developed in conjunction with the theory of self-deception by Gur and Sackeim (1979) and

Sackeim and Gur (1979). These two forms of SDR were developed and elaborated on in response to the criticisms of the lack of convergence in existing measures of SDR and of the conflicting conclusions about the operation of SDR in a particular domain (manual, p. 21). The SDQ and ODQ were revised and integrated into one inventory known as the Balanced Inventory of Desirability Responding—3 (BIDR-3), with subsequent versions (i.e., BIDR-4, BIDR-5, BIDR-6) revised to culminate the final version of PDS.

According to the theory, self-deception represents an unconscious process to deny psychologically threatening thoughts and feelings reflective of psychoanalytic conflicts, and other-deception represents conscious distortion toward self-enhancement. Item content of the two subscales was rationally composed to reflect and distinguish the two respective biases in self-report. Item content of SDQ and ODQ were substantially revised before being integrated into the BIDR-3, and revisions of items that constituted subsequent versions of the BIDR were guided by of conceptual rationales, and empirical studies, as well as consultation with practitioners. On these bases, it was decided that the enhancement, rather than the denial, component be captured in the Self-Deceptive Enhancement subscale. The manual provides detailed information about the studies, both published and unpublished, that guided the development of the PDS into its most current version.

TECHNICAL. Internal consistency data for the general population, college students, prison entrants, and military recruits from the United States and/or Canada were reported in the manual. Overall, satisfactory internal consistency has been found for the PDS (values ranged from .83 to .85) and its two subscales (values ranged from .70 to .75 for SDE; values ranged from .81 to .84 for IM) for the respective samples. A number of studies of the convergent validity, structural validity, and discriminant validity of the PDS and its subscales were reported in the manual, with some of these studies previously published in refereed journals of social psychology and applied psychology.

COMMENTARY AND SUMMARY. It was cautioned that the PDS not be used as a sole criterion for decision making, assessment, or diagnosis (manual, p. 9). At the same time, the PDS is a culmination of years of research of social desirability. The development, revision, and re-

finement of item content were conceptually and empirically grounded. The PDS continues to generate research into other dimensions of social desirability (e.g., denial) and distinction between response set (i.e., situation-specific) versus response style (i.e., trait-like tendency) that constitute socially desirable responding, as well as further understanding of self-deceptive enhancement. These research directions were noted in the manual.

Despite the validity studies reported, it is not clear how the cutoff scores for determining valid and invalid scales were derived. The adjustment correlates (e.g., self-esteem, anxiety, the Big Five personality factors) of SDE and IM are investigated separately. However, the validity of the combined SDE-IM profiles is not reported. In other words, the indications that narcissistic tendencies are associated with a low IM—high SDE profile, or that a "repressor pattern" is associated with a high IM—high SDE profile, remain an empirical question. Nonetheless, the relationship between the various IM-SDE combinations and the respective response and personality styles generates useful and interesting hypotheses to be tested in research and clinical practice.

REVIEWER'S REFERENCES

Gur, R. C., & Sackeim, H. A. (1979). Self-deception: A concept in search of a phenomenon. *Journal of Personality and Social Psychology, 37,* 147–169.
Sackeim, H. A., & Gur, R. C. (1979). Self-deception, other-deception, and self-reported psychopathology. *Journal of Consulting and Clinical Psychology, 47,* 213–215.

Review of the Paulhus Deception Scales: Balanced Inventory of Desirable Responding Version 7 by ROMEO VITELLI, Staff Psychologist, Millbrook Correctional Centre, Millbrook, Ontario, Canada:

DESCRIPTION. The Paulhus Deception Scales (PDS) is a 40-item test instrument designed to measure socially desirable responding in test participants. It is the seventh and final version of the Balanced Inventory of Desirable Responding (BIDR-7) and was developed to provide professionals with a concise and self-contained test of social desirability for use in clinical assessments, human resources settings, and in test development. The PDS contains two subscales to measure the Self-Deceptive Enhancement (SDE) and Impression Management (IM) aspects of social desirability. It is designed to be administered either individually or in a group testing session. All items are scored on a 5-point Likert scale using a Multi-Health Systems Quik-Score Form for rapid administration and scoring of the results. The test form also includes a profiling sheet for raw score and *T*-score conversions using community-based and forensic population norms. A computerized scoring and interpretation system is also available. Test administration time is 5 to 7 minutes and requires a minimum fifth grade reading level.

The PDS can be administered and scored by nonclinical staff although the manual recommends test interpretation be limited to those individuals with postgraduate training in psychometric assessment and familiarity with professional standards of test usage to ensure appropriate use. Interpretive guidelines and recommended cutoff scores are described in the manual for identifying "fake good" and "fake bad" test profiles. The manual lists two case studies describing the appropriate application of the PDS. The test author cautions against the use of the PDS as a stand-alone criterion for assessment or diagnosis and recommends its use as part of a more comprehensive test battery. A conversion formula is also provided to derive the equivalent score on the Marlowe-Crowne Social Desirability Scale (Crowne & Marlowe, 1960).

DEVELOPMENT. The PDS is the latest version of the BIDR, which was originally developed from two measures of social desirability described by Sackheim and Gur (1979). The original measures, the Self-Deception Questionnaire (SDQ) and the Other-Deception Questionnaire (ODQ) were developed in accordance with the author's two-factor model of social desirability. Paulhus (1984) addressed psychometric concerns about the perceived limitations in the SDQ and ODQ by integrating the two measures into the Balanced Inventory of Desirable Responding (BIDR-3) to provide a balanced assessment of the self-deception and other-deception social desirability constructs. The PDS test manual describes the extensive body of research into socially desirable responding using the BIDR-3 and outlines the development of later versions of the BIDR.

The PDS represents the final version of the BIDR and was developed after extensive revision and the development of new test items in consultation with clinical and research psychologists. The test items were selected through the use of exploratory factor analyses. The test manual provides norms and reliability and validity data, outlines a series of PDS validation studies, and discusses the theoretical basis of the impression management and self-deception test constructs.

TECHNICAL. Information relating to norms and the standardization process is provided in the PDS user's manual. The PDS was standardized using a large adult sample (*n* = 441) from the general population, as well as samples from college student, military, and prison populations collected by the author and other researchers using the PDS. Information on the sample demographics and the sampling techniques used are not provided in the test manual and issues of sex or age differences in socially desirable responding are not addressed.

Coefficient alpha reliability estimates are provided for the PDS subscales and the total PDS score for all four samples. Some disparity is noted with Self-Deception Enhancement coefficients falling in the .70–.75 range and IM and PDS total coefficients falling in the .81–.86 range. The relative difference in reliability estimates between the two subscales may be due to the greater uniformity of IM items. No other reliability estimates are given although the situational aspects of social desirability would rule out the use of test-retest reliability coefficients. Individual item reliability coefficients are not provided although the manual describes a factor-analytic study of the PDS items showing a significant goodness of fit with an orthogonal two-factor model reflecting the PDS factor structure.

The test manual provides convergent validity information on the PDS by showing a strong correlation between PDS subscales and a series of established social desirability measures. The IM was found to correlate highly with the Marlowe-Crowne Social Desirability Scale, the Good Impression scale, and the "lie" scales on the Eysenck Personality Inventory and the Minnesota Multiphasic Personality Inventory (MMPI). Significant correlations have also been found between the SDE and the Edwards Social Desirability Scales, the Personality Research Form Desirability scale, and measures of self-esteem, social anxiety, and extraversion.

In other reported studies, the IM is found to be more sensitive than the SDE to situational influences whereas the SDE is more positively associated with self-distortion factors such as overconfidence and hindsight bias. The test author concludes that these validity data described in the manual serve to validate the theoretical framework of the social desirability theory underlying the development of the PDS. There is a considerable body of literature using the PDS and the BIDR for clinical and forensic purposes that is not described in the manual, which provides additional confirmation of the value of the PDS as a measure of socially desirable responding.

Overall, the studies cited and the validation process meet the psychometric standards for test validation as specified in the *Standards for Educational and Psychological Testing* (AERA, APA, & NCME, 1999).

COMMENTARY. The role of social desirability in psychometric responding and the value of social desirability measures in determining response distortion remains a contentious issue in research. One concern that has been addressed in the literature questions whether social desirability should be regarded as a response bias or as a personality construct in its own right (Ones, Viswesvaran, and Reiss, 1996). This question is briefly addressed in the test manual in discussing the level of covariation between the PDS scales and measures of personality functioning under low- and high-demand test conditions and references to more comprehensive overviews of the issue by the test author. A second concern focuses on the use of social desirability measures to partial out the effects of intentional distortion despite research demonstrating the inadvisability of this approach (Ellingson, Sackett, & Hough, 1999). The use of the PDS in this context is not specifically addressed by the author.

The test author acknowledged the need for further research using the PDS and outlined potential avenues for development, including the expansion of the PDS to assess additional aspects of social desirability. More validation work is also needed with respect to the use of the PDS in areas such as human resource settings and in clinical decision making to address issues of ecological validity.

SUMMARY. The PDS represents the final version of a multidimensional social desirability scale that has already become established as a measure that provides valid and reliable information about social desirability and which provides greater flexibility in use and interpretation than more traditional, unidimensional measures. The test author provides extensive reliability and validation data for the PDS, which emphasizes the usefulness of the test in identifying respondent deception. Some concerns are raised about ongoing controversies in social desirability research and the need for further research to further validate the PDS in forensic and human resources settings. In closing, the PDS should be regarded as a valuable tool to be used in any high-demand testing situation as a check on the validity of self-report test responses.

REVIEWER'S REFERENCES

American Educational Research Association, American Psychological Association, & National Council on Measurement in Education. (1999). *Standards for Educational and Psychological Testing*. Washington, DC: American Educational Research Association.

Crowne, D. P., & Marlowe, D. A. (1960). A new scale of social desirability independent of psychopathology. *Journal of Consulting Psychology, 24*, 349–354.

Ellingson, J. E., Sackett, P. R., & Hough, L. M. (1999). Social desirability corrections in personality measurement: issues of applicant comparison and construct validity. *Journal of Applied Psychology, 84*, 155–166.

Ones, D. S., Viswesvaran, C., & Reiss, A. D. (1996). Role of social desirability in personality testing for personnel selection: The red herring. *Journal of Applied Psychology, 81*, 660–679.

Paulhus, D. L. (1984). Two-component models of socially desirable responding. *Journal of Personality and Social Psychology, 46*, 598–609.

Sackheim, H. A., & Gur, R. C. (1979). Self-deception, other deception, and self-reported psychopathology. *Journal of Consulting and Clinical Psychology, 47*, 213–215.

[184]
Peabody Developmental Motor Scales—Second Edition.

Purpose: Designed "to assess gross motor skills and fine motor skills."
Population: Birth to 72 months.
Publication Dates: 1983–2000.
Acronym: PDMS-2.
Scores, 9: Reflexes, Stationary, Locomotion, Object Manipulation, Grasping, Visual-Motor Integration, Gross Motor, Fine Motor, Total Motor.
Administration: Individual.
Price Data, 2003: $413 per complete kit including examiner's manual (2000, 234 pages), 25 profile/summary forms, 25 examiner record booklets, administration guide, motor activities program manual, black-and-white motor development chart, 25 black-and-white motor development parent charts, and manipulatives; $331 per complete test including everything in complete kit except the motor activities program; $61 per 25 examiner record booklets; $25 per 25 profile/summary forms; $81 per motor activities program; $51 per object kit; $10 per shape cards/BLM kit; $92 per administration guide; $81 per examiner's manual; $15 per 25 black-and-white motor development parent charts; $19 per full-color parent chart; $112 per software CD (PC; Windows 95/98).
Time: (45–60) minutes.
Authors: M. Rhonda Folio and Rebecca R. Fewell.
Publisher: PRO-ED.
Cross References: See T5:1901 (19 references) and T4:1943 (3 references); for a review by Homer B. C. Read, Jr. of an earlier edition, see 9:922.

Review of the Peabody Developmental Motor Scales—Second Edition by LINDA K. BUNKER, Professor of Human Services, University of Virginia,

Charlottesville, VA and PEGGY KELLERS, Associate Professor, School of Kinesiology and Recreational Studies, James Madison University, Harrisonburg, VA:

DESCRIPTION. The Peabody Developmental Motor Scales—Second Edition (PDMS-2) is a motor assessment instrument and accompanying motor development program for children ages 0–72 months (birth–6 years). The norm-referenced assessment consists of three scales: Gross Motor Quotient (GMQ), Fine Motor Quotient (FMQ), and Total Motor Quotient (TMQ). The well-illustrated manual provides detailed descriptions for the administration and scoring of the six subtests: Reflexes, Stationary Measures, Locomotion, Object Manipulation, Grasping, and Visual-Motor Integration for a total of nine norm-referenced measures.

Administration of the PDMS-2 requires approximately 20–30 minutes for each subtest and is easily scored using the criteria provided. It is designed for use by occupational therapists, physical therapists, diagnosticians, early intervention specialists, adapted physical educators, special education teachers, and others who are interested in examining the motor skills of children. It takes no special training because the instructions provided are quite clear and the scoring criteria are very objective. The complete PDMS-2 kit includes the examiner's manual, picture book, profile/summary forms, examiner record booklets, object kit, shape cards, and the computer software needed to efficiently score and report the results of the assessment.

DEVELOPMENT. This is the second edition of the Peabody Developmental Motor Scales and consists of six subtests that measure the interrelated motor abilities that develop early in life.

The Reflex subtest includes 8 items that measure a young (0–11 months only) child's ability to react to environmental events. The Stationary subtest includes 30 items designed to measure the ability to sustain control and maintain equilibrium of the body within its center of gravity. The Locomotion subtest includes 89 items including crawling, walking, running, hopping, and jumping forward. The 24-item Object Manipulation subtest requires the child to manipulate balls by catching, throwing, and kicking and is therefore only used for children 12 months or older. The Grasping subtest includes 26 items that progress from holding an object with one hand to the controlled use of the fingers of both hands. The Visual-Motor Integration subtest includes 72 items to assess perceptual motor functioning, including complex eye-hand coordination tasks such as reaching and grasping for an object, building with blocks, and copying designs.

This new edition provides profile/summary forms that make it possible to display graphically a child's performance. The display also includes normative data for easy comparison on each item mastered and for the three "quotients." The GMQ is a combination of the results of subtests that measure the use of large muscle systems, including Reflexes, Stationary, Locomotion, and Object Manipulation subtests. The FMQ is a combination of subtests that measure the use of the small muscles, including skills such as Grasping and Visual-Motor Integration. The TMQ is a composite of the Gross and Fine Motor scores to measure overall motor skill ability.

Scoring is made easier with the new *Illustrated Guide to Administering and Scoring the PDMS-2 Items* that provides a detailed description of every item. In addition, the examiner record booklet contains all of the items to be administered and can be supplemented by a software kit that includes both a scoring and a reporting system on CD-ROM. Each item is referenced by number within each subtest and specific criteria used to score the items are provided.

Each item description includes the age at which 50% of the children from the normative sample mastered the item. Descriptions also include specific information about the procedure used to administer the item, the desired position of the child, any supplementary equipment or stimuli needed, and an illustration of a child performing the item. In addition there is a new Peabody Motor Development Chart that provides a convenient reference. Each motor skill measured by the PDMS-2 is illustrated and the 50th percentile is identified along with each of the subtests.

TECHNICAL.

Standardization. The normative sample consisted of 2,003 children from 46 states in the United States and British Columbia, Canada. Data were collected in the winter of 1997 and spring of 1998. Norms are stratified by age, and the authors report studies showing the absence of gender and racial bias. It should, however, be noted that this normative sample is mainly of U.S. children.

range of reliability values. Time sampling measures were limited to a 1-week period.

The content of the items on the PDMS-2 were drawn from *A Taxonomy of the Psychomotor Domain* by Harrow (1972). Items were considered to be within a developmental sequence, with fundamental skills progressing towards more integrated skills. A confirmatory factor analysis was conducted to assess the structure of the PDMS-2. A confirmatory model was defined as one that allows the subtest to load only on the factor it represents. Information is provided in the examiner's manual about the factor structure for the PDMS-2 at different age levels. Users of the instrument should review this information carefully. There is support for the various factors within the gross and fine motor areas; however, depending upon the age of the child, some factors may not be as robust or as meaningful as others.

COMMENTARY. The information contained in the PDMS-2 kit is thorough. The user is provided with a kit that contains an examiner's manual, a guide to administration, a motor activities program manual, and profile form summary sheets. Also available is a software scoring and report system. Not all of the items needed for individual item administration are provided. The test kit contains a bag of items such as cubes, pegs, pegboard, forms, lacing cards, and measuring tape. The test manual provides a list of items that the examiner needs to provide. These items include such things as crayons, scissors, balls, rattles, rope, and a soft drink can, among other materials. One caveat is clear. The types of materials used, and the age range of the children tested with the PDMS-2, demand that the examiner is vigilant about children mouthing materials, and that materials are kept clean.

Evaluators who have experience with the Bayley Scales of Infant Development (T6:271) will observe some similarities with the PDMS-2. Each item has information about the position the child should be in for the item. As well, procedures are stated for the examiner for the administration of the item. The scoring criteria are based upon a three level system. If the child does not demonstrate mastery of the item, a score of 0 is assigned. A child can achieve partial credit, for which a score of 1 is assigned. For complete mastery of an item, a child can receive a score of 2.

SUMMARY. The PDMS-2 is designed to be used in the assessment of children in early childhood programs, or those in their first years of formal education. The instrument contains profile and summary forms that enable the examiner to record the child's PDMS-2 results in a way to graphically display the child's performance. This allows the user to examine a child's performance on the items he or she has mastered with that of the normative sample. The instrument can be useful in helping parents and others understand the level of development a child has achieved in his or her motor skills development.

Motor skills development is an important, observable, and measurable aspect of a young child. An instrument such as the PDMS-2 can be an important component for an early childhood services team, as well as a guide for parents for determining age-appropriate activities for their child. The instrument is sound and appropriately standardized. The manuals provided are clear. The major drawback is that the test kit is essentially incomplete. Although elements such as stairs cannot be included in a test kit, other basic materials such as scissors, spoons, and food pellets (cereal) can vary in size or appropriateness, and risk reduction in standardization from one administrator to another.

REVIEWER'S REFERENCE

Harrow, A. J. (1972). A taxonomy of the psychomotor domain: A guide for developing behavioral objectives. New York: David McKay.

[185]

Perceptual Speed (Identical Forms).

Purpose: Designed to assess "the ability to rapidly compare visual configurations and identify two figures as similar or identical or to identify some particular detail that is buried in distracting material."

Population: Visual inspectors, proofreaders, clerical personnel.

Publication Dates: 1984–1996.

Scores: Total score only.

Administration: Group or individual.

Price Data, 2002: $51 per 25 tests; $28 per interpretation and research manual (1959, 10 pages); $20 per score key.

Time: 5 minutes.

Comments: Primarily used in industry and governmental organizations (norms provided for these personnel).

Authors: L. L. Thurstone and T. E. Jeffrey.

Publisher: Reid London House.

Review of Perceptual Speed (Identical Forms) by JOHN W. FLEENOR, Director of Knowledge Management, Center for Creative Leadership, Greensboro, NC:

DESCRIPTION. Perceptual Speed (Identical Forms) is a single test battery designed to measure one of Thurston's (1938) primary mental abilities, perceptual speed. According to Thurston, perceptual speed is the ability to quickly and accurately grasp visual details, similarities, and differences. For example, some individuals are able to locate a particular word in a page of print by using dispersed attention to the page as a whole, whereas others require a systematic search through each successive line of print.

The Perceptual Speed test is a paper-and-pencil measure that can be administered individually or in groups. The test, which is timed, measures the speed with which an individual is able to perceive identities in sets of similar appearing figures. The test booklet contains 140 items, each of which presents a figure that is repeated in a series of five similar figures. The test-taker is required to select the figure in the series that is identical to the original figure. A key is provided for scoring the test and a single total score is produced. According to the manual, the test can be used with test takers of all ages.

DEVELOPMENT. The test was developed by Thurstone, using a series of factor analyses in which he identified perceptual speed as one of seven factors that he designated as primary mental abilities. Thurstone developed the test to measure the ability to rapidly compare visual configurations and to identify two figures as similar or identical. This factor is similar to the speed factor identified by Kelley (1928).

TECHNICAL. The manual, a short technical report published in 1996, reports split-half reliabilities of .98, .92, and .96 for the Perceptual Speed test. It should be noted, however, that split-half reliabilities can be spuriously high for timed tests in which speed is an important factor. Parallel forms reliabilities are reported as .83, .87, and .80 for a sample of 88 industrial workers. No further evidence of reliability is presented in the manual.

The factorial validity of the Perceptual Speed test was investigated in more than 16 different studies, starting with the work of Thurstone. In general, these studies have been supportive of the factorial stability of the test.

The manual suggests that the ability measured by the Perceptual Speed test is related to performance in jobs such as key-punch operator, visual inspector, clerical worker, and proofreader. In a criterion-related validity study with a pat-terned interview as the criterion, validity coefficients of .71 are reported for a sample of inspectors ($n = 69$), and .64 for a sample of arc welders ($n = 97$). These coefficients seem quite high for a criterion-related validity study, suggesting the possibility of criterion-contamination in this study.

A comparison of Perceptual Speed mean scores between top-rated clerical employees and lower-rated employees found that the top-rated employees scored significantly higher on the test. Significant differences also were found between supervisors and nonsupervisory employees, with the supervisors scoring higher. This provides some evidence that higher-performing employees tend to score higher on the Perceptual Speed test.

Construct validity was investigated by correlating scores from the test with the scales of the General Clerical Test. These correlations ranged from .32 with Error Location to .55 with a composite score, providing some evidence of convergent validity for scores from the Perceptual Speed test.

COMMENTARY. The Perceptual Speed test was developed as part of the seminal work by Thurstone on primary mental abilities. It appears to be a useful measure of the ability of perceptual speed, as evidenced by the large number of supportive factorial studies. However, even though these results indicate some potential for the Perceptual Speed test in the selection of clerical employees, the manual recommends that the test be locally validated for the particular groups and organizations for which it is to be used.

The manual presents rather sketchy reliability and validity information about the test—a more comprehensive manual that fully describes the development of the Perceptual Speed test would be more useful for test users.

SUMMARY. This test is recommended for use as a selection tool for clerical jobs and similar positions for which perceptual speed is a job requirement. Because of the limited evidence of criterion-related validity presented in the manual, users may want to conduct a local validation study for the test. It is also recommended that users consult other references, such as Thurstone's original works, in addition to the test manual before using this instrument

REVIEWER'S REFERENCES

Kelley, T. (1928). *Crossroads in the mind of man: a study of differentiable mental abilities.* Stanford, CA: Stanford University Press.
Thurstone, L. L. (1938). Primary mental abilities. *Psychometric Monographs,* No. 1.

scale that appears to be yielded by summing responses across all 37 items.

DEVELOPMENT. The POI was developed using a combination of rational and empirical keying methods. First, after a literature review, 500 "screening questions" were constructed and reviewed by two different panels. The first panel consisted of legal and personnel experts who eliminated questions that might be offensive or inappropriate for preemployment inquiry. The second panel contained personnel experts and industrial psychologists, and the manual does not specify their particular objective. The result was a pool of 319 items that were divided by an unstated method to make Experimental Tests A and B composed of 169 and 150 items, respectively.

Next, either Experimental Test A or Experimental Test B was administered to "newly hired employees in the outlets of two major retail organizations" (information guide, p. 4). The outlets were located primarily in metropolitan cities in the United States with the Midwest being slightly overrepresented. Other than total N's for both instruments (601 and 669 for A and B, respectively), no other information is provided about the sample. As a result, the representativeness of the total sample is unclear. It should also be noted that data collection occurred between 1978 and 1979 for Experimental Test A and between 1980 and 1981 for Experimental Test B. It appears that the test authors used these data to construct norms; therefore, a renorming study should be considered.

After 9 months had elapsed, employees who were terminated for cash theft, merchandise theft, or discount abuse, according to their termination forms, were identified as the "theft group." This included 113 people for Experimental Test A and 195 people for Experimental Test B. The manual initially states that a random sample of employees in good standing were selected to serve as the "non-theft" group, but later reports that the remaining 488 people for Experimental Test A and 474 people for Experimental Test B were classified as the "non-theft" group. Future editions of the test manual should provide more clearly organized demographic information about the total sample and each of the criterion samples.

The manual also states that the theft and nontheft groups for both Experimental Test A and Experimental Test B were divided into thirds for cross validation purposes. After randomly sorting each group, two-thirds of each group was retained as the "validation sample," and the remaining third was designated the "cross validation sample." The responses for the theft and nontheft groups in the validation sample were compared, and using a weighting system, items that differentiated the groups were flagged.

For Experimental Test A, 16 items differentiated between theft and nontheft groups, and 26 items differentiated between the groups for Experimental Test B. The manual fails to describe the procedures, statistical or otherwise, used to make these decisions. Moreover, the manual states that 7 of the selected items appeared on both tests, meaning that 35 items were found to differentiate between the two groups. However, the final instrument contains 37 items, and the manual does not explain how the additional 2 items were selected.

TECHNICAL. The authors present the mean scores on the selected items for both the theft and the nontheft groups for both the validation and the cross validation samples. In each case, the theft group scored lower, and the manual states that the differences between the mean scores was "highly significant." Unfortunately, the manual fails to explain the statistical procedures used or the level of significance that was chosen. In addition, the authors imply that because "highly significant" mean differences were found, the items are "predictive of a person's propensity to steal cash or merchandise from work" (information guide, p. 7). It is erroneous to assume that mean differences enable an instrument to predict future behavior. The instrument's ability to predict propensity to steal should be demonstrated statistically before the authors make such a claim.

In terms of reliability, the manual reports a reliability coefficient of .58. However, this was achieved with a 35-item instrument, not the final 37-item instrument. In addition, the authors fail to state the procedure used to determine this estimate. In the same paragraph, a standard error of measurement of 4.7 is cited, and it is assumed that this is also without the two additional items.

The manual provides limited information regarding the validity for scores from the POI. To provide evidence of operational validity, the authors refer to a study of eight retail stores, four that used the instrument as a pre-employment screening method and four that used a different method. According to the manual, the four stores that used the POI reported a 68% decrease in "negative references" while the four stores that did not use the POI reported a 29% increase in negative references. It is not clear whether these differences are statistically significant. In another study, the authors also present mean scores for employees fired for theft versus all new employees (N is unspecified) and again fail to report any statistical significance data. As final evidence of operational validity, the authors note that the percentage of employees who scored in the "reject" range who were eventually fired for theft was 6%. The percentage in the "questionable range" was 2%, and the percentage in the "acceptable" range was .6%. It is not clear if these differences are statistically significant nor is it evident how these cut scores were determined. In general, the validity data provided in the manual are incomplete and fail to provide evidence that the instrument is indeed measuring propensity to steal or that it can be used accurately to predict such behavior.

COMMENTARY. The authors of the POI state that it is intended to assess "propensity to steal" so that organizations can reduce employee theft. One would assume, then, that the POI would be able to predict, with some statistical accuracy, which employees are most likely to exhibit this behavior. Unfortunately, in its current state, one cannot make such an assumption for a number of reasons. First, the data provided in the manual are dated, incomplete, and confusing, and no administration and scoring guidelines are provided. The authors fail to describe one of the two scales of the instrument and provide "patchy" information for the other. In addition, the number of respondents in the sample as well as the number of items selected for the instruments is reported inconsistently. Second, the authors fail to provide any information related to gender and ethnicity. The ethnic minority samples presented in the manual are very low, and although twice as many females than males were reported in the "total sample," no examination of gender differences was reported. Finally, the operational validity information is incomplete and does not demonstrate the ability of the POI to predict propensity to steal. Until future research addresses these concerns, the POI should be used and interpreted with caution.

SUMMARY. Employee theft is a widespread problem, and ultimately honest consumers are forced to "make up the difference" by paying higher prices for goods. As a result, an instrument that could identify employees who are most likely to steal from an organization would be beneficial on a number of levels. The authors of the POI have attempted to achieve this difficult task. They put considerable effort into the development of the instrument and, since its last review, have attempted to consider response validity by the addition of the V scale. Similar attention is necessary with respect to the administration and scoring and psychometric properties of the POI. Many of the concerns raised in this review were also noted in previous *Mental Measurements Yearbook* reviews (Guion, 1989; Murphy, 1989). Currently, the POI should not be used for hiring decision-making purposes.

REVIEWER'S REFERENCES

American Educational Research Association, American Psychological Association, & National Council on Measurement in Education. (1999). *Standards for Educational and Psychological Testing*. Washington, DC: American Educational Research Association.

Guion, R. M. (1989). [Review of the Personal Outlook Inventory]. In J. C. Conoley & J. J. Kramer (Eds.), *The tenth mental measurements yearbook* (pp. 616-617). Lincoln, NE: Buros Institute of Mental Measurements.

Murphy, K. R. (1989). [Review of the Personal Outlook Inventory]. In J. C. Conoley & J. J. Kramer (Eds.), *The tenth mental measurements yearbook* (pp. 617-619). Lincoln, NE: Buros Institute of Mental Measurements.

Review of the Personal Outlook Inventory by *MICHAEL S. TREVISAN, Associate Professor, Department of Educational Leadership & Counseling Psychology, Washington State University, Pullman, WA:*

DESCRIPTION. Publishers of the Personal Outlook Inventory (POI) offer the instrument as a means to identify potential employees who are prone to stealing. Its use is suggested during the candidate application phase. Estimates of revenue loss among businesses in the United States due to employee theft range from 15 to 25 billion dollars per year (Camara & Schneider, 1994). Thus, it is easy to see why businesses are eager to use instruments like the POI in hopes of protecting themselves from financial loss and ruin.

The instrument contains 37 self-report items that ask a variety of questions about an applicant's relationship with his or her parents, attitude toward school and teachers, general demeanor, and behavior. The publishers now offer two subscale scores, rather than the five previously available. These subscales are referred to as: (a) the V-Scale, which indicates whether or not the test is valid for the individual tested; and (b) the S-Scale, which indicates the probability the individual tested will be fired for theft. As in the previous version, no rationale, descriptive, or analytical information is provided to justify the existence and use of these subscales. Pilot testing of items occurred between 1979 and 1981.

RECOMMENDATIONS FROM PREVIOUS REVIEWERS. The first reviews of the POI were published in 1989 in the *Tenth Mental Measurements Yearbook* (MMY). These reviews were critical of both the POI development and technical evidence provided by the publishers. Unfortunately, it appears that the POI publishers did not heed any of the recommendations from previous reviews. In fact, examination of the technical manual supplied with the review material suggests the publishers of the POI have not made any demonstrable changes to the instrument. As mentioned the number of subscales was reduced from five to two but this information is only available by reading the 1989 *MMY* reviews and comparing this to what is stated in the current POI documentation. No statement in the document refers to a previous version or rationale for reducing the number of subscales, essentially hiding the fact that a modification was made to an earlier edition. Previous criticisms, therefore, remain relevant. Those interested in greater detail are urged to peruse the actual reviews (see Guion, 1989 and Murphy, 1989).

DEVELOPMENT. Two experimental tests, referred to as A and B, were administered at different times to 601 and 669 employees of two retail organizations, respectively. The respondents were new hires obtained from over 150 outlets from these organizations although precise numbers from each are not provided. From these samples, two groups were formed; those who were fired for theft, and those still employed after 9 months. Standard procedures were used for administration of the instrument during the pilot phase. However, no norms are provided. In addition, population subgroups, particularly those for African Americans and Hispanics, are too small to make the case for representativeness. As noted by Guion (1989), a variety of item analyses were conducted, inappropriately employing statistical significance tests, obscuring actual item quality.

TECHNICAL. The test lacks reliability evidence. One reliability coefficient is provided although the type is not specified. Its magnitude is .58, meaning that only 58% of the score variability obtained from the POI is due to systematic differences among respondents. With so little information accounted for with this measure, use of the POI is nearly as likely to falsely identify potential

thieves as it is to properly identify these individuals. Given the difficulty many companies have in finding quality employees, use of the POI ironically may lead to the costly negative outcome of mistakenly eliminating quality applicants from consideration. Using the POI would then increase company expense, rather than guard against loss from theft.

Validity evidence presented for the POI is insufficient and misleading. First, cross-validation groups were obtained by further subdividing the theft and nontheft groups used in the pilot. This procedure guarantees an inflated correlation between total score and group membership, as was the case for the POI (Murphy, 1989). Thus, generalizations can only be made to the sample tested, although the publishers overstate the results suggesting that the high correlation obtained is evidence for generalizations to larger groups. Second, the publishers conducted a small study to provide what they refer to as "operational validity." For this study, records from eight stores were examined; four stores using the POI, and four stores not using the POI. A 68% decrease in the number of "negative references" was observed in stores using the POI, whereas a 29% increase was found in the stores that did not. In addition to the small number of stores in the sample, the publishers did not mention sample sizes or how the instrument was used. Also, the publishers claim a form of predictive validity by computing the percentage of employees terminated for theft, given particular score ranges on the POI. The results show most employees terminated had scores in the 0–15 score range. Unfortunately, given the way the information is presented, an unsophisticated test user might draw the conclusion that a score of 15 should be the cutoff score, although the document does not make an explicit statement about cut scores.

COMMENTARY. The following recommendations are offered. First, because the POI publishers have not made any notable changes to the instrument, criticisms from previous reviewers, even though more than 10 years old, remain relevant and should be taken seriously. The publishers are urged to read and consider these reviews and refine the POI accordingly. Second, the "Information Guide" that accompanies the instrument lacks clarity and sometimes appears purposefully ambiguous. The document can be faulted as much for what it does say, or for what it does not say. This was true in previous reviews of the POI and continues to be the case. The document forms the basis for judgments about the type and quality of the instrument and, therefore, must be sufficiently clear so users can read the document with comprehension and thus, make reasonable conclusions about test quality as well as proper application. Third, the publishers continue to use an empirical approach to validity, as was the case at the time of the original reviews. Given the lack of clarity in the document, it is difficult to follow any line of reasoning or logic for the development of the POI. The instrument lacks a validity argument as recommended by current validity thinkers (e.g., Shepard, 1993). Therefore, the publishers are urged to further define their measured construct and develop a validity argument for the POI, logically connecting all validity studies into a coherent framework. Fourth, the POI is based on self-report by job applicants about their behavior and as such, is dependent on accurate, honest answers from these individuals. It is possible that individuals with work place savvy, particularly when pursuing a new job, could figure out what the employer is after in the POI, and out of self-preservation, answer accordingly. Schwarz (1999) argues that self-report items dealing with behavior are particularly susceptible to this phenomenon and offers recommendations for building items that decrease this problem. The publishers are urged to peruse the Schwarz (1999) article and systematically incorporate these ideas in the POI. Fifth, Camara and Schneider (1994) conducted a review of two national reports dealing with integrity testing and similar measures and made a variety of recommendations for producers of these types of instruments. The recommendations include topics such as the development of constructs, development and use of cut scores, and the need for independent evaluations of instruments by outside researchers. The publishers would do well to follow these recommendations in the refinement of the POI.

SUMMARY. The POI forms the basis for a potentially useful tool for identifying individuals who may steal on the job. Given the heavy loss companies experience each year, an instrument like the POI would be timely and useful. The apparent disregard by the POI publishers for following test industry standards as well as recommendations from previous reviewers is disappoint-ing. Until the publishers have followed the aforementioned suggestions, this reviewer cannot recommend its use.

REVIEWER'S REFERENCES

Camara, W. J., & Schneider, D. L. (1994). Integrity tests: Facts and unresolved issues. *American Psychologist, 49*(2), 112–119.
Guion, R. M. (1989). [Review of the Personal Outlook Inventory]. In J. C. Conoley & J. J. Kramer (Eds.), *The tenth mental measurements yearbook* (pp. 616–617). Lincoln, NE: Buros Institute of Mental Measurements.
Murphy, K. R. (1989). [Review of the Personal Outlook Inventory]. In J. C. Conoley & J. J. Kramer (Eds.), *The tenth mental measurements yearbook* (pp. 617–619). Lincoln, NE: Buros Institute of Mental Measurements.
Shepard, L. A. (1993). Evaluating test validity. In L. Darling-Hammond & J. A. Banks (Eds.), *Review of research in education* (pp. 405–450). Washington, DC: American Educational Research Association.
Schwarz, N. (1999). Self-reports: How the questions shape the answers. *American Psychologist, 54*(2), 93–105.

[187]

Phonemic-Awareness Skills Screening.

Purpose: "The PASS is a quick screening that pinpoints" three "specific areas of phonological weakness": to identify students with problems, to determine strengths and weaknesses, to document progress.
Population: Grades 1–2.
Publication Date: 2000.
Acronym: PASS.
Scores: 8 subtests: Rhyming, Sentence Segmentation, Blending, Syllable Segmentation, Deletion, Phoneme Isolation, Phoneme Segmentation, Substitution, Total.
Administration: Individual.
Price Data, 2003: $30 per complete kit including examiner's manual (16 pages); $20 per 25 record forms; $23 per examiner's manual.
Time: (15) minutes.
Comments: Can be administered by a teacher or assistant, requires "no specialized training in testing"; subtests may be administered separately.
Authors: Linda Crumrine and Helen Lonegan.
Publisher: PRO-ED.

Review of the Phonemic-Awareness Skills Screening by STEVEN LONG, Assistant Professor, Communication Sciences, Case Western Reserve University, Cleveland, OH:

DESCRIPTION. The Phonemic-Awareness Skills Screening (PASS) is a 50-item test administered individually to children in the first or second grade. All items are scored as correct or incorrect. The total test score is calculated by summing the results from eight sections: Rhyme, Sentence Segmentation, Blending, Syllable Segmentation, Deletion, Phoneme Isolation, Phoneme Segmentation, and Phoneme Substitution. Each of these sections contains 6–9 test items. Administration time for the entire test is estimated at 15 minutes.

The PASS requires no specialized training in testing and thus can be administered, scored, and interpreted by any teacher or clinician, or by an assistant to one of those professionals. A four-page individual test booklet contains directions for administration, all test items, and sections for test scoring. The only additional material required for test administration is a single picture, printed in the test manual, that is sometimes used to explain the task of Deletion to test takers. The PASS manual describes the test as criterion-referenced, yet the manual contains means, standard deviations, and recommended cutoff scores for each of the eight subtests and for the test as a whole.

DEVELOPMENT. The PASS appears to be the result of the authors' clinical experience in "conducting screenings for phonological awareness and preliteracy levels since 1993" (manual, p. 12). The test manual states a series of "important facts" about the relationship between phonological awareness and the development of literacy skills but cites no references from the research literature. Among the facts asserted by the authors is that phonemic blending and segmentation "are the most closely associated with reading and spelling" (manual, p. 6). Presumably, this is the rationale for the instrument's focus on these skills. There is, however, no explicit description of how the test was constructed in order to provide an overall index of a child's phonological awareness skills. Further, there is no indication of how the number of test items was determined for each subtest or what principles—phonetic, alphabetic, or other—led to the selection of specific word and sentence stimuli.

TECHNICAL. The information offered about the interpretation of PASS results is confusing. In the manual's description of the test's purpose the PASS is described as criterion referenced, yielding "results that are easily translated into lessons" (p. 4). At the end of the manual, however, three tables are provided with means, cutoff scores, and subtest intercorrelations, indicating that the test is to be used as a norm-referenced screening instrument. Table 1, showing means and standard deviations, has clearly misprinted the standard deviation value for the PASS total score, making it impossible to interpret that value in any norm-referenced comparisons.

Very little information is given about the population from which the reported data were derived. The authors report that 166 students from a series of classrooms in a small school system were tested. No details are provided about the children's age (though they might be assumed to be first graders), ethnicity, socioeconomic status, or any other variable of putative interest. Reliability data for the PASS are not reported.

COMMENTARY. It is unclear whether the PASS was conceived and developed as a criterion-referenced or norm-referenced instrument. Either way, it is a seriously flawed test. Viewed as a criterion-referenced instrument, the PASS lacks a coherent model of the relationship between phonological awareness skills and the development of reading and writing abilities. The selection of the eight tasks contained on the test appears to have been based on the authors' clinical familiarity with those tasks. Although there may be a good rationale for the use of these tasks over others, the authors do not present it and, without that rationale, it would be impossible for test users to interpret results in a way that relates children's difficulties on the test to their problems in the mastery of literacy skills. The claim that PASS results "can be easily translated into lessons" merely invites users into a vicious cycle of testing, teaching the tasks on the test, and then testing again. As the authors themselves note, "phonological awareness is essential, but not sufficient for reading success" (manual, p. 6). Teaching students to perform phonological awareness tasks, and then verifying that ability by re-administering the PASS, is bound to be an inadequate approach to reading mastery.

Considered as a norm-referenced instrument, the PASS falls terribly short of basic psychometric requirements. Given the errors contained in the manual's tables, there is reason to doubt the accuracy of the statistical data presented there. Even if the data were known to be accurate, the lack of information about the population on which they were gathered makes peer comparisons impossible. Without reliability data, clinical use of the test becomes a shot in the dark.

SUMMARY. The relationship between children's phonological awareness and learning to read has been the subject of much recent study. The developers of the PASS have seemingly tried to translate that research into an instrument that can be easily used by educators who work with children's reading problems. The test they have created is indeed simple to understand, to administer, and to score. Unfortunately, the simplicity of the test and its manual is its undoing as a psychometric tool. Without a rationale for its construction, without an adequate description of its normative population, and without any assessment of its reliability, the PASS is simply not ready for clinical or educational use.

Review of the Phonemic-Awareness Skills Screening by VINCENT J. SAMAR, Associate Professor, Department of Research, National Technical Institute for the Deaf, Rochester Institute of Technology, Rochester, NY, and RICKI KOREY BIRNBAUM, Adjunct Assistant Professor, Warner School of Education, University of Rochester, Rochester, NY:

DESCRIPTION. The Phonemic-Awareness Skills Screening (PASS) is a criterion-referenced, quick screening tool designed to pinpoint specific areas of weakness in phonological awareness (PA). It is intended for use in first grade classrooms and first and second grade remedial programs. The manual states that the PASS is intended to be used for three primary purposes: (a) to identify students with reading problems, either because they are performing below the level of their peers or because they could benefit from additional reading instruction; (b) to diagnose students' strengths and weaknesses in order to construct an individualized instructional program; and (c) to document a student's progress over time.

The PASS is administered by a teacher or an assistant with the aid of a four-page form. The manual asserts that no training is necessary for the administrator. There are eight sections that direct the child to perform eight specific tasks to assess distinct aspects of PA. These are the abilities to (a) recognize and produce rhymes; (b) segment sentences into words; (c) blend sounds or syllables into words; (d) segment words into syllables; (e) delete a word, syllable, or phoneme from a given word and produce the resulting smaller word; (f) isolate and identify the initial, medial, or final phoneme in a given word; (g) segment words into all of their constituent phonemes; and (h) substitute a given phoneme for an existing phoneme within a given word in order to produce a new word. With each section containing from 5 to 9 items, the total test administration time is approximately 15 minutes. A child's subtest and total percent correct is recorded on the administration form and these scores can be transferred to a useful

PASS Class Record Form, provided at the back of the manual, to aid in comparing students in order to form instructional subgroups. The administration form is easy to use and provides clear and explicit instructions, for the most part. The manual provides means, standard deviations, and 20% cutoff scores for referral for follow-up services.

DEVELOPMENT. The manual presents a brief overview of the critical factors that influence reading and gives the general rationale for developing the PASS. The manual gives little information about how the specific PA tasks were selected and designed. Nevertheless, the structure of the PASS is well motivated by the now considerable literature on the structure of PA and its central role in the reading acquisition process (see the section on validity below).

TECHNICAL.

Standardization. The standardization sample was composed of 166 school children, 55% male and 45% female, tested in 1999. No information is given in the manual regarding the ages, grades, ethnicities, or geographic demographics of the children. Means, standard deviations, maximum scores, and 20% cutoff scores are reported for the standardization sample for each of the PA subtests and for the total PASS score across subtests. Subtest intercorrelations, along with significance levels, are also reported.

Reliability. No reliability data are provided. However, given the very small number of items on each subtest, the reliability of the subtests is somewhat suspect.

Validity. A large and consistent literature now exists that demonstrates the multifactorial structure of PA and its causal and reciprocal role in reading acquisition (see Stanovitch, 2000, for a current review).

The PASS has clear face validity in that the sorts of tasks chosen are consistent with those generally recommended and previously validated in the literature on PA and in that they span each of the known fundamental dimensions of synthesis, analysis, and rhyme. Therefore, the overall screening profile provided by the PASS, in principle, may be capable of yielding a fairly broad screening of a child's phonological awareness strengths and weaknesses.

However, the PASS does not, as yet, have demonstrated construct validity as a psychometric instrument. The subtests have not been shown to

minutes. The test is a screening device and can be administered to large groups of children, but it must be administered individually as each child's responses to questions and tasks must be recorded on a record form. The subtests can be given in any order but the test authors recommend that the Phoneme Deletion subtest not be given first because it has been identified as the most difficult test. The test's purpose is to help educators identify young children between the ages of 4 and 7 who may be at risk for reading failure. However, although normative information for 4-year-olds is provided in the testing manual, the test's authors do not recommend that this test actually be used as a screening measure to identify 4-year-olds who might have potential reading difficulties.

In scoring the test, the number of correct responses for each subtest and number of words per second for speech rate are placed within a centile column in a chronological age band found in the normative tables in the test manual. There is only one chronological age band for 4-year-olds; the bands for the other age groups (5-year-olds through 7-year-olds) are broken into 6-month intervals. According to the test manual, any examinee who scores below the 10th percentile should be considered as being "within the impaired range" (examiner's manual, p. 24).

The testing materials are in a very sturdy cloth shoulder bag and consist of a stimulus booklet, a pack of cards with the alphabet letters on them, a test manual, and a packet of record forms. The manual includes directions for administration, technical information, normative tables, and profiles of three children with reading difficulties who took the Phonological Abilities Test. The purpose of these profiles is to help the test user understand how to score the test and interpret test results.

DEVELOPMENT. The testing manual offers little information on how the test was developed. The test is based on the theory that "the best predictors of early reading progress are children's phonological skills; in particular their ability to reflect upon and manipulate the sounds of spoken words (phonological awareness and their knowledge of letter names and sounds" (examiner's manual, p. 1).

TECHNICAL. The sample administrations were done by University of York (United Kingdom) undergraduate and graduate students in their hometowns during summer break. A total of 826 students between the ages of 4 years and 0 months

and 7 years and 11 months participated in the sample administrations. All children in the study were native speakers of English; the majority of them lived in Northern England and Scotland.

The test developers attempted to establish internal consistency reliability by doing an item analysis of data collected on 60 children (30 boys and 30 girls) from three different classes of an elementary school in York. Coefficient alpha was calculated for all the subtests except for the Rhyme Production for which the correlation of two items, Day and Bell, was established. The Letter Knowledge subtest was not part of the internal consistency reliability analyses. The reliability coefficients ranged from a low of .67 for Speech Rate to a high of .97 for Phoneme Deletion (Beginning Sounds).

To estimate test-retest reliability, the test developers gave the test on two separate occasions, 3 weeks apart, to a group of 35 children who had a mean age of 5 years and 4 months. The test-retest correlations ranged from a low of .58 on Word Completion-Syllables to a high of .86 on Letter Knowledge. The test-retest correlations were generally acceptable but were rather low. Moreover, it is highly unlikely that on a test of this type (i.e., one that tests very specific skills) a group of school-age children would not make some progress within a 3-week-period.

To provide evidence of construct validity, the developers intercorrelated the subtest scores; intercorrelations were only adequate with correlations ranging from .3–.7. To provide evidence of content validity (according to the test manual, to determine if the test has "a strong concurrent and predictive relationship to reading," p. 39), the scores on the Phonological Abilities Test were correlated with scores on The British Abilities Scales test of Single Word Reading (BAS). Correlations ranged from .66 for the Phoneme Deletion—Beginning Sounds subtest to .37 for the Speech Rate subtest. Multiple regression analyses were then done to assess how well the subtests together predicted examinees' BAS skills. An overall analysis of the sample indicated that the Word Completion—Syllables and the Word Completion—Phonemes subtests were not statistically significant in prediction of reading skills measured by the BAS. All other tests contributed significantly in predicting scores on BAS reading skills tasks.

COMMENTARY. The developers of the Phonological Abilities Test offer little information on how this test was developed or how items were chosen, tested, etc. This test looks like a test that could have been put together quickly by any adequately trained elementary teacher. Except for the subtest of Letter Knowledge, each subtest contains less than 20 items and the Rhyme Production subtest offers children only two stimuli from which to create rhymes.

Although the test is designed to identify children with phonological problems who may be at-risk for reading failure, the authors of the test used a test (BAS READ) for which responses are based less on phonological knowledge and more on visual knowledge (calling single words) to provide evidence of the validity of the Phonological Abilities Test. Neither test is an actual reading test and they do not measure the same skills. Although there were significant correlations between scores on the BAS READ and on most of the subtests of the Phonological Abilities Test, it is a leap in logic to assume that if the BAS READ actually does measure something related to reading (word calling is not actually reading), then so does the Phonological Abilities Test.

SUMMARY. Although there is evidence that many young children who have auditory discrimination and processing problems also have reading difficulties, educational personnel would be ill-advised to use only a phonological test such as the Phonological Abilities Test to predict children who were at-risk for reading problems or to use such a test to attempt to determine the basis for all children's reading difficulties. Aside from auditory problems, children may have information-processing problems, such as sequencing and memory problems, and/or visual-perceptual problems that contribute to reading difficulties. A comprehensive test of all of these types of processing should be used to assess children who are at-risk for reading failure or to determine the basis for individual children's reading difficulties.

If this test is being marketed to American educators, those educators should realize that a few items in the stimulus manual will be a little confusing to American examinees. The very obvious package of McDonald's potatoes would be called a package of "French fries" in the United States, but is called "chips" in the script for the stimulus manual and both the pictures of money and of a bus are not what American children are used to seeing.

Phonological Assessment Battery [Standardised Edition].

Purpose: Designed to identify "those children who need special help by providing an individual assessment of the child's phonological skills."
Population: Ages 6–15.
Publication Date: 1997.
Acronym: PLAB.
Scores: 6 tests: Alliteration, Naming Speed, Rhyme, Spoonerisms, Fluency, Non-Word Reading.
Administration: Individual.
Price Data, 1998: £75 per complete set including 10 record booklets and manual (130 pages); £10 per 10 record booklets; sample sheets are free.
Time: (30–40) minutes.
Comments: Is also appropriate for children whose first language is not English.
Authors: Norah Frederickson, Uta Frith, and Rea Reason.
Publisher: NFER-Nelson Publishing Co., Ltd. [England].

Review of the Phonological Assessment Battery [Standardised Edition] by CLAUDIA R. WRIGHT, Professor Educational Psychology, California State University, Long Beach, CA:

The Phonological Assessment Battery (PhAB) was developed for administration to children and adolescents, ages 6:00 to 14:11, who exhibit low performance on literacy tasks or who are not progressing academically. The PhAB is a collection of six principal scales and one supplementary scale and yields 10 scores designed to provide diagnostic information for identifying and processing sounds (phonemes) produced in spoken English: (a) Alliteration Test—identifying the initial sound(s) in single syllable words; (b) Naming Speed Test has two forms: Picture Naming Test and Digit Naming Test—estimating retrieval speed of phonological coding at the word level for both simple objects and single-digit numbers; (c) Rhyme Test—identifying the same end sounds in single syllable words; (d) Spoonerisms Test—breaking down single syllable words into phonemes for a word pair (e.g., "sad cat"), then exchanging the initial sounds of each word (e.g., "cad sat"); (e) Fluency Test—generating as many words as possible of a given type in 30 seconds and examining the ability to retrieve semantic and phonological information from long-term memory in three areas (semantics, alliteration, and rhyme);

and (f) Non-Word Reading Test—decoding one-syllable and two-syllable letter strings. The Alliteration Test with Pictures is a supplementary form to the Alliteration Test designed for examinees having difficulty with the oral response format.

TEST ADMINISTRATION AND SCORING. The instrument was designed for use by individuals trained in the administration of educational tests and in the interpretation of psychometric and diagnostic information. Thorough and detailed, step-by-step administration procedures are provided for each test including practice items and test instructions that include clear descriptors of starting and discontinuance points. In general, the tests can be administered in any order with some well-documented exceptions to which test administrators are alerted. For the most part, the PhAB is made up of tasks of increasing difficulty. It is recommended that the series of tests end with one that can be successfully completed by the examinee such as the Non-Word Reading Test or the Alliteration Test with Pictures. Thorough instructions to the examiner provide helpful suggestions for encouraging the respondent without commenting directly on his or her test performance.

Clear guidelines are provided for recording and scoring, generating profiles for each examinee, and using conversion tables (from raw score to standardized score). Detailed "case studies" provide interpretative guides for test scores and profiles that will be helpful for those preparing individualized education plans (IEPs). Appropriate cautions are provided for minimizing errors of mistaking test scores at the behavioral level with an inference about ability at the cognitive level.

NORMING PROCEDURES. Normative data for nine age groups (6:00–6:11 through 14:00–14:11) were drawn (sample sizes ranged from 66 to 71) from a larger national British study involving 814 schools in England and Wales (*N* = 4,400; with 2,200 boys and 2,200 girls). The purpose of the larger study was to support the restandardization of the Neale Analysis of Reading Ability—Second Revised British Edition (NARA II; see 11:257), a measure designed to assess reading rate, accuracy, and comprehension. The standardization procedures for the PhAB were carried out during the retesting phase of the British study and capitalized on the concurrent administration of the NARA II and the British Ability Scales II (BAS II; Elliott, 1983) to extend a validity study.

An examination of gender differences on the PhAB revealed no statistically significant differences for the total sample with some minor exceptions for age groups. Girls (6:00 to 7:11) outperformed boys on Naming Speed (Digits). Also, girls (12:00—14:11) scored higher than boys on the Fluency (Rhyme) subscale. The authors concluded that the PhAB scale scores would serve as reliable indicators of phonological processing ability for both boys and girls.

RELIABILITY OF PHAB SCORES. Internal-consistency reliability (alpha coefficients) estimates of test scores were reported for all scales across groups (6:00–7:11; 8:00–9:11; 10:00–11:11; and 12:00–14:11). Alphas ranged from .80 to .96 for all but one scale for two age groups. Reliability estimates for scores on the Alliteration Test with Pictures fell to .67 and .19 for age groups 10:00–11:11 and 12:00–14.11, respectively; reflecting small *SEM*s and ease of this scale for older children.

VALIDITY OF PHAB SCORES. To examine the validity of test scores related to PhAB scales, the authors drew upon traditional indicators of content, construct, and criterion-related validity. Content validation for the PhAB rests on the authors' thorough and detailed review of the literature on issues of literacy, phonological processes, and related competencies. A panel of educational psychologists, educational psychology trainers, and academicians participated in the development of items; piloting items, examining task structure and item response formats over a 2-year period.

Criterion-related validity evidence was provided by intercorrelations between PhAB scale scores and scores on the NARA II (Rate, Accuracy, and Comprehension) and BAS II (cognitive and achievement-related scales)(sample sizes ranged from 464 to around 500). Among 30 possible coefficients between PhAB and NARA II scale scores, low to moderate coefficients were obtained ranging from .24 to .72. The strongest coefficients were moderate and observed between two of three NARA II scales (Accuracy and Comprehension). These findings tend to support moderate levels of shared variance between the PhAB as a test of phonological processing ability and the NARA II, a test of reading ability.

As expected, the strongest relationships were observed between a few PhAB scale scores and the cluster scales for the BAS II scores. Moderate coefficients—between .41 and .45—were observed for several PhAB scale scores and the Verbal cluster scale scores and with the Non-Verbal cluster. These findings tend to support the relationship between phonological processing ability (as measured by PhAB scores) and selected verbal and related cognitive skills assessed by BAS II scores.

Construct validity evidence was demonstrated in three ways: (a) as a "developmental" test, PhAB scale scores were expected to increase with age; (b) children with learning disabilities would obtain lower PhAB scale scores than the standardization sample; and (c) a factor analysis of PhAB, NARA II, and BAS II scale scores would yield interpretable results. Generally speaking, older children outperformed younger children on the PhAB scales and children diagnosed with dyslexia underperformed those without. In a study conducted by the authors and reported in the technical manual, children aged 8:00 to 9:11 classified with dyslexia (N = 52) underperformed the standardization sample (N = 136) on the PhAB Alliteration, Rhyme, Spoonerisms, Non-Word Reading, and Naming Speed for both Digits and Pictures (all $p < .01$), but not on the three Fluency subscales. A similar pattern was observed when comparing children aged 10:00 to 12:11 identified with dyslexia (N = 37) with those in the standardization group (N = 208). The authors interpreted these findings as providing evidence that students diagnosed with dyslexia exhibit a higher incidence of difficulty with phonological tests as measured by the PhAB. Finally, when the 10 PhAB scale scores, 3 NARA II scale scores, and the 10 BAS II scale scores were subjected to an exploratory, principal components analysis, six interpretable factors revealed that the PhAB shared two factors with the NARA II. The manual suggests that the principal components analysis was largely consistent with expectations from the theoretical teamwork on which the PhAB is based.

SUMMARY. A clear research-supported rationale was provided for the development of the PhAB scales and the format of items. The instrument has been thoughtfully constructed and subjected to rigorous psychometric examination with reasonably sound evidence of internal-consistency reliability and criterion- and factorial-related validity. Of additional import is the level of "user friendliness." Test administration instructions and explanations are well written with exceptionally detailed examples. Some consideration given to

the content of some items is warranted, particularly if the test is planned for use in the United States or other English-speaking settings outside of the United Kingdom. For example, with respect to the Alliterations Test with Pictures, corresponding correct responses for a picture sequence that displays a well, a clothes pin, and a pot for a plant are described as a "well," a "peg," and a "pot." The extent that cultural differences influence word selection may reduce the reliability and validity indicators for U.S. examinees.

REVIEWER'S REFERENCE

Elliott, C. D. (1983). *British Ability Scales: Manual 2, technical handbook.* Windsor: NFER-Nelson.

[190]

The Phonological Awareness Skills Program Test.

Purpose: "Designed to provide a means for placing students at the appropriate entry points in the Phonological Awareness Skills Program Curriculum."

Population: Ages 4 to 10.

Publication Date: 1999.

Acronym: PASP Test.

Scores: Total score only.

Administration: Individual.

Price Data, 2003: $79 per complete kit including 25 record forms, curriculum manual, and instrument manual (24 pages); $15 per 25 record forms.

Time: (2-4) minutes.

Author: Jerome Rosner.

Publisher: PRO-ED.

Review of The Phonological Awareness Skills Program Test by JANET NORRIS, Professor, Communication Disorders, Louisiana State University, Baton Rouge, LA:

The Phonological Awareness Skills Program Test (PASP) is a revision of the Test of Auditory Analysis Skills (Rosner, 1975). The PASP is modified to be more comprehensive and to serve as a guide for the accompanying intervention program. The test is not designed for general testing of phonological awareness abilities. Rather, it is to be used to identify children who need further training in the Phonological Awareness Skills Program Curriculum, to place the child at the appropriate entry level of the curriculum, and to determine when the deficits have been remedied and treatment discontinued.

The test comprises 31 test items and 4 demonstration items, 2 given at the beginning of the test and 2 when the task changes prior to Item

26. All of the items are presented auditorily with no picture support, and children respond by saying a word that appropriately modifies the target word. Items 1–17 require the child to omit part of a word, such as a word ending, beginning syllable or phoneme, or medial or end phoneme, to create a second real word (i.e., "clap" without the /k/ says "lap"). Items 18–25 demand further phoneme manipulation, requiring the child to substitute one sound for another in a given word position (i.e., Say "dash," but instead of /a/ say /i/ to result in the word "dish"). The final items, 26–31, require the child to respond to an analogy problem. The child must decide after hearing 2 items what type of phoneme manipulation has been made, and then perform an analogous transformation on a given word. This results in items such as "*Top* goes with *tap* the way *cop* goes with ___ (cap)."

If the child cannot perform a task following the first demonstration item, one attempt is made to teach the task. If the second demonstration item is then responded to correctly, the test is continued. If the second demonstration item is missed, the test is discontinued and a score of 0 is assigned. The test is continued until two successive errors are made. The score is equal to the item number reached immediately prior to the ceiling items. Thus, if two successive errors occur for Items 10 and 11, the raw score is 9 even if single items were missed below that point. Items 26–31 are administered only if a ceiling has not previously been reached.

Raw scores are converted to age equivalents, with no additional standard scores provided. An age equivalent at or above the child's chronological age is interpreted to mean that phonological awareness skills have developed to an age-appropriate level and no further training is needed. An age equivalent below the child's chronological age indicates that the child needs training and should be placed in the PASP Curriculum at an instructional point one level higher than the child's current level.

DEVELOPMENT. The PASP was developed to probe two related basic phonological awareness abilities. The first is the ability to analyze spoken words into their separate structural elements or sounds. Analysis involves separating phonological patterns into their component parts. The second is the ability to organize or assemble spoken words on the basis of their phonological features. These two abilities are viewed as reciprocal, with analysis skills leading to organizational

skills, and better analysis in turn resulting as children organize sounds by increasingly larger patterns (e.g., "an," "and"), which then can be used to analyze new words (e.g., "an" is part of "ran," "can," "fan"; "and" is part of "sand," "hand," "band").

The analytical and organizational phonological skills are viewed as important to reading and spelling, particularly at beginning stages of reading. According to the author, poor phonological awareness interferes with the ability to learn by association and thus each word must be learned and memorized as an individual entity. Children who have good phonological awareness recognize many words inductively as being similar in sound and letter patterns to known words, and thus can learn more independently.

The PASP was developed over a period of 25 years, beginning with the original version named the Auditory Analysis Test (Rosner, 1972). The current version was designed to measure the process of phonological analysis and organization rather than phonological skills, and then to provide a program to remedy the deficit process. No further information is provided about item selection or test development procedures.

TECHNICAL. The age equivalents for the PASP were derived from a small sample of 322 children from 4-0 to 10-11 years, or all of the students from 21 intact classrooms in a single elementary school and one preschool in Texas. The scores for each 6-month age equivalent are therefore based on approximately 20 children, or far fewer than the recommended number for normative data. The participants included a greater percentage of males than found in the general population (57%). Although a wide range of ethnic groups were included in the norms, these percentages do not correspond with the demographic population in the United States. There is no representation from different geographic locations. These problems with the normative population severely limit the generalization of the PASP results, even for its designated use with the companion curriculum.

The derived scores on the PASP are limited to age equivalent scores. The scores in each age interval were averaged, then plotted along a graph and smoothed and interpolated to form a line. Because interpolation, extrapolation, and smoothing were used to create the equivalents, the author appropriately recommends caution when interpreting these scores. Further, age-equivalent scores are generally not considered appropriate scores for reporting test performance. These scores are ordinal rather than equal interval measurements and thus there is not the same amount of growth represented between the age levels. It is also somewhat meaningless to say that the score of a 9-year-old is equivalent to a 6-year-old because there may be very different cognitive and qualitative processes between the two that resulted in the same score. These problems render the scores provided by the PASP of limited utility.

Reliability. A measure of test-retest reliability is an important measure of stability. If the results of a test substantially differ from one administration to the next, then no credibility can be placed on the results. The examiner would be uncertain which, if either, of the scores was the "true" score or measure of the ability tested. The authors did not use a test-retest measure, and therefore the degree to which the test reliably elicits consistent scores from children within and across age levels is unknown.

The authors conducted a measure of internal consistency reliability to test whether items within a subtest are related to each other, thus resulting in greater homogeneity and smaller standard error of measurement. The scores for the entire normative sample were analyzed. Coefficient alphas across the age groups ranged from .80 to .95, exceeding the criterion for acceptable internal consistency reliability.

Interscorer reliability was assessed by rescoring 30 protocols (9% of the normative sample). The resulting coefficient was .98, indicating good reliability of examiner scoring procedures.

Validity. Two measures of content validity are provided. First a rationale for the format and items of the test is presented. This rationale is very general. Thirty-one items are used to assess the phonological awareness abilities of children ages 4 through 10 years. No research is provided to demonstrate that these items are measures of the general phonological process abilities the test purports to measure. Median rather than mean discriminating powers and percentages were used, which is not the statistically most valid choice. The discriminating powers ranging from .36 to .62 are within the acceptable range. The percentage of difficulty, based on the median difficulty of test items, ranged from a low of 11% for 4-year-

olds and increased to 92% for 10-year olds. At no age does the median achieve an average difficulty of 50% as recommended by Anastasi and Urbina (1997).

Construct validity was examined by correlating the relationship between participant age and performance on the PASP. Results showed that the mean score increased with each successive age level, and resulted in an overall correlation between age and test performance of .87. The author concludes that these results demonstrate that the PASP is a valid measure of phonological awareness and can be used to determine entry points into the PASP Curriculum.

No measures of criterion validity were provided, nor were studies conducted to determine whether the PASP accurately discriminated between typically developing children and those with known deficits in phonological awareness. All of the data used to examine validity (as well as reliability) was derived from the original test scores of the small normative population.

COMMENTARY. The PASP is a test of phonological awareness that is primarily intended to identify an entry level for training in the PASP Curriculum. The author uses this limited scope as justification for the small normative population and test construction data. However, because the PASP curriculum is distributed nationally and educational decisions are to be made for children on the basis of this instrument, the PASP test should meet the test construction criteria for a nationally normed test. The existing normative data represent merely a good beginning.

The PASP has the potential for much broader use as an assessment instrument for phonological awareness abilities in school-age children. Most of the currently available instruments measure only early developing phonological awareness skills. The PASP presents tasks that are challenging to older students (i.e., 7–10 years) and can serve to identify phonological awareness deficits in this population. Unfortunately, in its current form the test is not adequately normed and lacks important evidence of reliability and validity.

SUMMARY. The Phonological Awareness Skills Program test is a measure of phonological awareness designed for use with children between 4-0 and 10-11 years. Its primary purpose is to identify an entry level for the accompanying training program. In its current form, the test provides only age-equivalency scores that are derived from a population of 322 students recruited from a single elementary school and one preschool. All measures of reliability and validity are derived from this normative data. Important evaluations of test adequacy, such as test-retest reliability, have not been conducted. The test has potential for much broader use and addresses an age group for which good instruments are lacking. However, severe limitations in test construction and normative data preclude its use for these purposes. These problems also limit the use of the PASP for its stated purpose, because there is no evidence that children beyond the small normative sample would perform similarly on this test and would have a similar entry level on the training program.

REVIEWER'S REFERENCES

Anastasi, A., & Urbina, S. (1997). *Psychological testing* (7th ed.). Upper Saddle River, NJ: Prentice-Hall.

Rosner, J. (1972). The auditory analysis test: An initial report. *Journal of Learning Disability, 4,* 384–392.

Rosner, J. (1975). Testing for teaching in an adaptive educational environment. In W. Hively & M. C. Reynolds (Eds.), *Domain-referenced testing in special education* (pp. 43–76). Reston, VA: Council for Exceptional Children.

[191]

Pictorial Test of Intelligence, Second Edition.

Purpose: Designed to "identify children who are significantly 2below their peers in important abilities and to identify children among these who are physically disabled who are more able to think and reason than their traditional communication skills support."

Population: Ages 3–8.

Publication Dates: 1964–2001.

Acronym: PTI-2.

Scores, 4: Verbal Abstractions, Form Discrimination, Quantitative Concepts, Pictorial Intelligence Quotient.

Administration: Individual.

Price Data, 2003: $143 per kit including examiner's manual (2001, 87 pages), picture book, and 25 profile/examiner record booklets; $40 per 25 record booklets; $45 per manual; $61 per picture book.

Time: (15–30) minutes.

Author: Joseph L. French.

Publisher: PRO-ED.

Cross References: See T3:1823 (3 references); for an excerpted review by Thomas A. Smith, see 8:223 (11 references); see also T2:517 (1 reference); for reviews by Philip Himelstein and T. Ernest Newland, see 7:418 (17 references); see also 6:531 (2 references).

Review of the Pictorial Test of Intelligence, Second Edition by MICHELLE ATHANASIOU, Associate Professor of School Psychology, University of Northern Colorado, Greeley, CO:

DESCRIPTION. The Pictorial Test of Intelligence, Second Edition (PTI-2) is an individually-administered test of intelligence for children ages 3 through 8. It is designed to provide an alternative to traditional intelligence tests that rely on verbal and motor responses, thus making it appropriate for children with physical disabilities. The PTI-2 consists of three subtests. Verbal Abstractions (VA) includes 38 items and measures "auditory, visual, and mental processing related to verbal knowledge, verbal comprehension, and verbal reasoning" (examiner's manual, p. 4). Form Discrimination (FD) consists of 30 items and requires test takers to match forms, discriminate between shapes, identify the completed forms of incomplete pictures, find embedded shapes, and complete analogies of abstract patterns. Quantitative (QC; 30 items) measures size recognition, understanding of number symbols, counting, and simple arithmetic knowledge. The three subtests, each producing standard scores ($M = 10$, $SD = 3$), age equivalents, and percentile ranks, contribute equally to the Pictorial Intelligence Quotient (PIQ; $M = 100$, $SD = 15$).

The PTI-2 contains an examiner's manual, an easel-backed picture book, and a record form. All items use a multiple-choice format, allowing examinees to indicate their choice via pointing or eye gaze. The test can be administered in 15 to 30 minutes. Specific verbal instructions are written both in the picture book and on the record form, making the test easy to administer. Nevertheless, the artwork in the picture book is dull, with all symbols and pictures line drawn in black and white.

Administration and scoring procedures of the PTI-2 are objective and straightforward, but do include some potential problems. First, the author directs examiners to begin with the first item in each subtest for all children. The potential exists for older kids to fatigue before completing more difficult items, given that they must answer all preceding items that, for most children, would be too easy. This likelihood is increased given the monotonous nature of the task. Second, there are high floors on the FD and QC subtests for children under 4 years, 5 months, suggesting that these two subtests are too difficult for younger children. Finally, the PTI-2 norm table uses different age groupings, depending on the age of children. Children ages 3 years, 0 months to 5 years, 11 months are provided norm tables separated in 3-month intervals. The intervals switch to 6 months in span for 6- and 7-year-olds. All 8-year-olds are scored based on the same norm table. The potential effect of this wide interval is to inflate the scores of older 8-year-olds and deflate scores of younger ones.

DEVELOPMENT. The PTI-2 is based on Spearman's theory that intelligence is composed of general and specific abilities. In addition, the author relies on research to suggest that specific abilities often are highly intercorrelated. He justifies the selection of PTI-2 subtests and items by asserting that the ability to learn and understand symbols and their relationships is a commonly accepted indicator of intelligence. Because of the overlap between various specific abilities, the author assumes that competency on the factors measured by the PTI-2 should provide a valid indication of other intellectual competencies. Although speculatively sound, additional evidence pointing to the relative value of the three included factors over the myriad of other potential factors is needed.

The PTI-2 is a revision of the 1964 version of the PTI. The original version consisted of a compilation of items similar to those in existing intelligence scales, but modified for administration in a motor-free format. The instrument was revised to address numerous concerns of PTI reviewers. The revision includes an update of the test's rationale to reflect current theoretical conceptualizations of the intelligence construct; a reduction to one form with three subtests; restandardization; evaluation of item bias; the provision of age-specific *SEM* indices; additional reliability, validity, and bias studies; updated artwork; and modification of test materials to facilitate test administration. The procedures used to develop the final PTI-2 item set are nicely detailed in the test manual.

TECHNICAL. The PTI-2 was standardized on a sample of 970 children in 15 states. The sample was stratified on the base of geographic region, sex, race, residence (rural/urban), parent income level, educational attainment of parents, and disability status. Although the sample was selected to be representative of the U.S. population, underrepresentation occurred for children in the south and west, black children, rural settings, and higher income parents. Additionally, fewer 3- and 8-year-olds were sampled, as compared to 4- through 7-year-olds. Finally, it is unclear as to whether children with physical disabilities were included in the norm sample. Two percent of the norm sample included children with an "other handicap" (p. 32), but no further information about the nature of those handicaps is provided in the manual. Because the test specifically is designed to provide an index of intelligence for children with physical disabilities, such children should have been included in the norm sample at a rate reflective of national demographics.

Internal consistency estimates provided in the PTI-2 manual meet accepted standards for diagnostic purposes (Salvia & Ysseldyke, 1998). Subtest internal consistency exceeds .80 at all ages, and the PIQ exceeds .90. Internal consistency estimates are provided separately for sex, race, and disability status groups. The PTI-2 appears to be reliable for all groups, but estimates for various disability status groups are based on samples consisting of as few as 12 children. Test-retest reliability estimates are provided based on a sample of 27 5- to 8-year-olds over a 2-week retest period. Based on this study, the PIQ appears to be sufficiently stable ($r = .91$), but the subtest indices fall short of the accepted .80. Interrater reliability is satisfactory, based on a random sample of 30 standardization sample protocols independently scored by two PRO-ED staff members. Given the allowance of eye gaze as a response mode, interrater reliability studies investigating examiner agreement on examinees' response choices are needed.

Qualitative and quantitative evidence for content validity is provided in the manual. The latter includes item analysis procedures (item difficulty and item discrimination), as well as differential item functioning (i.e., logistic regression) analyses. Each of these procedures was used to eliminate poor and/or potentially biased items.

Criterion-prediction validity was investigated in two studies correlating scores on the PTI-2 with the Cognitive Ability Scales, Second Edition (CAS-2) and the Wechsler Preschool and Primary Scales of Intelligence, Revised (WPPSI-R), respectively. Strong correlations were produced with the CAS-2, but correlations with the WPPSI-R are moderate. More evidence of the criterion-prediction validity of the PTI-2 is needed. Specifically, the two studies described in the manual were conducted on small samples of 3-year-old children. Additionally, given that the test is purported to be useful for children with physical disabilities, validity studies investigating this presumption are warranted.

consistency reliability coefficients of the PTI-2 subtests were medium to high, ranging from .80 to .92. As expected, the PIQ is the most reliable score that can be obtained on the PTI-2; its reliability coefficients ranged from .92 to .95. Test-retest data were gathered for a sample of 27 students between the ages of 5 and 8 who resided in Casper, Wyoming. The test-retest period was approximately 2 weeks. Stability coefficients were moderate for the subtests (i.e., .57 [FD], .69 [VA], and .76 [QC]) and high for the PIQ (i.e., .91). The utility of the test-retest data is found wanting for the following reasons: (a) the sample size is small; (b) the sample is not representative of the U.S. population; and (c) the sample size contains an insufficient number of participants at each age level for which the test was normed, which makes it impossible to draw inferences about trait stability at any age. Notwithstanding, it is noteworthy that IQ increased more than one half of a standard deviation from Time 1 to Time 2, indicating that practice effects should be considered if the PTI-2 is to be used across time. Interscorer reliability of the PTI-2 was high (i.e., > .95). Based on the three types of reliability data reported for the PTI-2, it can be concluded that the PIQ is highly reliable and that interscorer differences are likely to be negligible. In contrast, the individual subtests of the PTI-2 are generally not sufficiently reliable (i.e., all average reliabilities were < .90) to draw inferences about performance in a given cognitive domain (e.g., visual processing). Therefore, subtest data should be used for screening purposes only (e.g., to determine whether more in-depth assessment in a particular area is warranted).

The examiner's manual includes three types of validity evidence for the PTI-2: content description, criterion-prediction, and construct-identification. Content-description validity for the PTI-2 was offered in the form of qualitative and quantitative evidence. In the latter category, median item discrimination coefficients and item difficulty indices were reported. Although these statistics generally meet accepted standards for adequacy, findings are more consistent at the upper ages of the test. Differential item functioning analysis was used to detect item bias. Results of this analysis led to the elimination of six out of a possible seven items that were found to be suspect.

Criterion-predictive validity evidence for the PTI-2 is lacking. The manual reports a single study in which a small sample (N = 32) of nondisabled 3-year-olds were administered the PTI-2 and the Cognitive Abilities Scale—Second Edition (CAS-2; Bradley-Johnson & Johnson, 2001). Of these participants, 15 were also administered the Wechsler Preschool and Primary Scale of Intelligence—Revised (WPPSI-R; Wechsler, 1989). Correlations between the PTI-2 and CAS-2 were medium to high. Nevertheless, given that the CAS-2 is not a widely accepted and well-validated test of intelligence, these data provide little, if any, validity support for the PTI-2. Although the correlational data reported between the PTI-2 and the WPPSI-R would potentially yield more promising evidence of the PTI-2's validity as a brief measure of general intelligence, the data are largely meaningless due to the fact that the sample was small (N = 15), restricted, and nonrepresentative. Noteworthy is the fact that the manual reports no information about the criterion-prediction validity of the PTI-2 for individuals at most age levels of the test (i.e., 4–8-year-olds).

With regard to the construct-identification validity of the PTI-2, results of a principal components exploratory factor analysis of the standard scores of subjects in the normative sample indicated that the three subtests loaded on a single factor—a finding that was described as providing support for an underlying *g* model. This result is not surprising given the small number of subtests that comprise the PTI-2. Information on age and group differentiation were also reported in an attempt to support the construct-identification validity of the PTI-2. These data show that most subtests appear to be appropriately related to age and that most groups performed within the average range as expected (e.g., males, females, European Americans, African Americans, Hispanic Americans). Interestingly, the gifted group (N = 15) mean for the PIQ was 118.5, which is low for this population. It is likely that this finding reflects a continuing problem with the ceiling of this instrument, particularly as it applies to the VA subtest.

Finally, the PTI-2, Test of Early Reading Ability—Second Edition (TERA-2; Reid, Hresko, & Hammill, 1989), and Test of Early Mathematics Ability—Second Edition (TEMA-2; Ginsburg & Baroody, 1990) were administered to 16 nondisabled 3-year-olds. Correlations between the PTI-2 and these achievement tests (i.e., .64 and .65, respectively) were reported as evidence of the

PTI-2's construct-identification validity. Notwithstanding the obvious methodological problems with this study (see limitations of the criterion-predictive validity study above), when these data are evaluated within the context of the correlational data between the PTI-2 and other "intelligence" tests (i.e., CAS-2 and WPPSI-R) reported above, it is not clear how they support the construct validity of the PTI-2. For example, the PTI-2 correlated more highly with reading (.64) and math (.65) tests than it did with the WPPSI-R Performance IQ (.45) and Full Scale IQ (.54). If the PTI-2 was indeed a valid measure of *g*, then it would be expected to correlate more highly with a commonly accepted *g* index (i.e., a Wechsler Full Scale IQ) than with reading and math scores. Overall, the validity evidence available for the PTI-2 is limited and the correlational studies in particular are weak.

COMMENTARY. Based on the data reported in the examiner's manual, the PTI-2 is described best as a brief measure of general ability that yields a reliable ability estimate (i.e., PIQ) for children ages 3–8. The PTI-2 is perhaps most valuable in research settings as a screening instrument for overall level of ability. However, given its substantial correlations with reading and math measures, it may also be useful in psychoeducational and clinical settings as a screener for children at risk for academic learning difficulties. The PTI-2 should not be used diagnostically nor should it be used in discrepancy formulas, such as those employed routinely in the learning disability determination process.

In light of the recent attention that has been given to the importance of brief measures of intelligence in the field of psychoeducational assessment (e.g., Kaufman & Kaufman, 2001), a likely question is, should the PTI-2 join the ranks of the most popular brief intelligence measures, such as the Wechsler Abbreviated Scale of Intelligence (WASI; Psychological Corporation, 1999) and the Kaufman Brief Intelligence Test (K-BIT; Kaufman & Kaufman, 1990)? In general, the answer to this question is "no." Although the reliability of the PTI-2 is similar to that of the WASI and K-BIT, the latter two measures have standardization sample characteristics that are superior to those of the PTI-2. In addition, the WASI and K-BIT are normed across a much larger age range than the PTI-2 (i.e., 6–89 and 4–90 compared to 3–8). Finally, the criterion-predictive validity of the WASI and K-BIT is superior to that of the PTI-2. Thus, when assessment calls for the use of a brief measure of intelligence, the practitioner would be wise to select the WASI, for example, over the PTI-2. However, in cases where a brief estimate of global ability is needed for individuals with physical disabilities or expressive language impairments, the PTI-2 appears to have an advantage over other measures, particularly for children ages 3–8.

SUMMARY. The PTI-2 is a brief measure of general ability that is perhaps most useful as a screening instrument for young children who are at risk for learning difficulties. It is also useful as a screening measure of general ability for individuals who have physical disabilities or expressive language impairments because the examinee may respond to each item by pointing. The PTI-2 is also easy to administer and score and its general ability quotient (i.e., PIQ) is highly reliable. Despite these strengths, the PTI-2 also has a number of limitations. For example, information about the test's normative sample is not presented in sufficient detail to allow for definitive conclusions to be made regarding its representativeness. The validity evidence for the PTI-2 is weak, as it does little to substantiate the claim that it is a measure of "general intelligence." For these reasons, brief measures of intelligence, such as the WASI (T6:2690), are recommended over the PTI-2 for most purposes.

REVIEWERS' REFERENCES

Bradley-Johnson, S., & Johnson, C. M. (2001). Cognitive Abilities Scale—Second Edition. Austin, TX: PRO-ED.

Carroll, J. B. (1993). *Human cognitive abilities: A survey of factor-analytic studies.* New York: Cambridge University Press.

French, J. L. (1964). Pictorial Test of Intelligence (PTI). Boston: Houghton Mifflin.

Ginsburg, H. P., & Baroody, A. J. (1990). Test of Early Mathematics Ability—Second Edition. Austin, TX: PRO-ED.

Kaufman, A. S., & Kaufman, N. L. (1990). Kaufman Brief Intelligence Test (K-BIT). Circle Pines, MN: American Guidance Service.

Kaufman, J. C., & Kaufman, A. S. (2001). Time for the changing of the guard: A farewell to short forms of intelligence tests. *Journal of Psychoeducational Assessment, 19,* 245–267.

Reid, D. K., Hresko, W. P., & Hammill, D. D. (1989). Test of Early Reading Ability—Second Edition. Austin, TX: PRO-ED.

The Psychological Corporation. (1999). Wechsler Abbreviated Scale of Intelligence (WASI). San Antonio, TX: Author.

U.S. Bureau of the Census. (1997). *Statistical abstract of the United States* (117th ed.). Washington, DC: U.S. Department of Commerce.

Wechsler, D. (1989). Wechsler Preschool and Primary Scale of Intelligence—Revised. San Antonio: Psychological Corp.

[192]

Post-Assault Traumatic Brain Injury Interview and Checklist.

Purpose: "Designed to assist in treatment planning and referral for neuropsychological and neurological evaluation, treatment, and rehabilitation."

Population: Assault victims.

each of the domains, but do not provide any theoretical or empirical rationale on how the scales were developed.

COMMENTARY. The P-TBI-IC as a measure to assess physical and psychological symptoms of assault victims holds promise as a clinical tool, but there are some concerns. First, there is no indication from the developers as to when this measure should be administered to victims of assault. It is not clear whether it should be administered shortly after the assault, within the day, week, month, etc., or if it can be readministered periodically to monitor physical and psychological symptomatology. Secondly, no information is provided on its psychometric properties. Is this a reliable and valid measure? Third, it does not offer any information on how to interpret the information obtained. It is designed to be used for treatment planning and referral for evaluation, treatment, and rehabilitation, but does not provide information on how to use the results for these purposes.

SUMMARY. The developers, to their credit, have developed a measure that may be helpful in assessing physical and psychological symptoms of assault victims. Further, the P-TBI-IC can be administered and scored in a relatively time-efficient and cost-efficient manner. However, the P-TBI-IC falls short of the mark. It would be helpful if the developers provided information concerning the test development and its psychometric properties. Further, a section on how to interpret the information obtained on the P-TBI-IC and several examples of appropriate client referrals and treatment planning options would be appreciated.

[193]
The Power of Influence Test.

Purpose: Designed as an instrument that "records the attitudes of pupils toward each other and tells which pupils have friendship capacity."
Population: Grade 5 and over.
Publication Date: No date.
Scores: Total score only.
Administration: Group.
Price Data: Available from publisher.
Time: (5) minutes.
Comments: Also referred to as The Sociometric Test.
Authors: Roy Cochrane and Wesley Roeder.
Publisher: Psychometric Affiliates.

Review of The Power of Influence Test by SALVADOR HECTOR OCHOA, Associate Professor, Department of Educational Psychology, Texas A&M University, College Station, TX:

DESCRIPTION. The Power of Influence Test (POIT) is a sociometric test. "Sociometry is a procedure for measuring the attraction between individual members of a specified group" (Asher & Hymel, 1981, p. 127). The POIT consists of a seating preference chart. This preference-seating chart has seven seats. Students are instructed to write their name on the seat that is in the center of the chart. Each student is then asked to write the name of a classmate that they would like to have sitting near them in each of the remaining six desks on the chart.

The test manual states that POIT is designed to measure a person's "friendship capacity" (p. 2). For junior high and high school students, the test developers state that the POIT measures "friendship capacity or sales aptitude" (p. 3). The manual fails to state explicitly the intended age groups for this test. Instead, the manual provides percentile norms from 5th to 11th grades. The test is intended to assist school personnel in identifying those students who need remedial help in social interactions with their peers.

With respect to test administration, the test manual provides sufficient instructions that should be read to students in a given class. The instructions are appropriate for school-aged students. The manual recommends that the POIT be given to classes that have at least 24 members. Each student's score is obtained by counting the number of "votes" they received (e.g., the number of times a classmate listed them on their preference seating chart). This scores is then compared to the percentiles provided on page 4 of the test manual. This will enable the examiner "to see how he [the student] ranks among others in friendship capacity" (p. 3).

DEVELOPMENT. The manual fails to provide any information about the theoretical underpinnings of this test. The test authors do not provide sufficient information about the theoretical underpinnings and research associated with sociometrics.

TECHNICAL. The POIT has significant limitations when reviewing its standardization, reliability, and validity. With respect to standardization, the test manual provides a percentile norms table. There is no information in the manual on the sample used to obtain these norms.

The test manual provides limited and vague information regarding reliability. The manual mentions two test-retest reliability studies. Information about the first reliability study is vague. The manual reports that 2,480 scores were used in this 1-week test-retest study. One would assume that the sample size used in the study was 1,240. The manual, however, fails to report a reliability coefficient. The manual also provides vague and insufficient information about a second reliability study. The manual states that 329 ninth graders were first tested in a math class and later in a social studies class. There is no information provided about the length of time between these two testing occasions. Additionally, the manual does not provide a reliability coefficient; rather the following statement is included: "The results showed a pattern of reliability similar to that found in the first test-retest study" (p. 2). It should be noted that the manual does provide one test-retest reliability coefficient several paragraphs later. It is unclear if this coefficient pertains to the two aforementioned studies or to another study. The following statement is in the manual:

> The test-retest coefficient of correlation for reliability is .91 + .01, but this does not accurately describe the amount of reliance one can place on a score in this test. Scores at the top are very reliable. Scores at the bottom may vary from a true measure so greatly that only by repeated testing, or by corroborative evidence can a student be labeled as an isolate. (p. 2)

There is no information about validity reported in the test manual. The test authors acknowledge this limitation by stating the following: "We as yet lack validating data, which would only be obtained by a ten-year follow-up of sociometric scores, but even so, we have no better means of estimating a vocational capacity in the sales area then the sociometric test" (p. 3). The test developers claim that this test has been "used successfully by more than 250 teachers and counselors" (p. 4). They, however, fail to provide any data to support this claim.

Moreover, the test authors make unsupported claims about how test scores can be used and/or interpreted. For example, the manual states that "the high ranking pupils on this test can be assumed to be class leaders," and "the views and opinions expressed by these leaders are the views and opinions of the class" (p. 3).

COMMENTARY. The POIT has many significant limitations. First, the POIT manual fails to provide a theoretical model and empirical research to support its use. Second, the POIT's norms are highly questionable as no information is given about the size and characteristics of the sample. No date is given as to when the sample was obtained. There is no way to determine if the sample is representative of the U.S. school-age population. Third, there is a lack of reliability and validity data to support its use. There are no data provided in the manual to support the POIT's claim that it measures friendship capacity or sales capacity. The manual makes claims that this measure has been used successfully by school personnel. There are no data provided to support this claim.

SUMMARY. Given that the POIT has significant limitations, it should not be used. The test developers need to provide a theoretical background about the importance of using sociomerics to examine peer relationships and a child's social status. There has been a significant amount of research done in this area in the last 20 years. Moreover, test developers need to provide sufficient information regarding reliability and validity. At this point, it is doubtful whether using the percentile norms provided in the manual can provide an accurate picture of a student's "best estimate of friendship percentile" (p. 4).

REVIEWER'S REFERENCE

Asher, S. R., & Hymel, S. (1981). Childrens' social competence in peer relations: Sociomeric and behavioral assessment. In J. D. Wine & M. D. Smye (Eds.), *Social competence* (pp. 125–157). New York: Guilford Press.

Review of The Power of Influence Test by JEFFREY K. SMITH, Professor and Chair, Department of Educational Psychology, Rutgers, The State University of New Jersey, New Brunswick, NJ:

DESCRIPTION. The Power of Influence Test (POIT) is a sociometric measure designed for use from fifth grade through high school. The test can be administered and scored by classroom teachers and takes roughly 5 minutes to give. The POIT consists of asking students to write their name in the center box of a grid of seven boxes representing seats in a classroom. Students then write in the six names of the students they would most like to have sitting next to them. The measure is scored by counting the number of times each student in the class is listed by another student as being a desirable seating neighbor. Raw scores are then transformed into percentiles for Grades 5 through 11. According to the manual provided with the test, the POIT "records the attitudes of pupils toward each other and tells which pupils have friendship capacity" (p. 1). In other places in the manual, the authors suggest that the POIT measures leadership and/or salesmanship, although a rationale for this argument is not given.

In a section called "Recording Test Data," the authors recommend making comments on students' record sheets reflecting the teachers' interpretation of the students' sociometric status. Under "Uses of Test Scores," the authors make suggestions for remedial actions that teachers might take on behalf of students who appear to have few friends.

DEVELOPMENT. Very little information is provided about the development of the POIT except for the discussion of a study of 2,480 students from Tacoma, Washington. This study provided data for a test-retest reliability estimation. The measure is quite simple, consisting of writing in the names of the six classmates a student wants sitting next to him or her, so perhaps there is little to discuss by way of development. The POIT uses a fairly standard sociometric approach. Interestingly, the manual provides the days of the month and the times of the day when the measure in the Washington study was given, but not the year in which it was given.

TECHNICAL. The standardization of the POIT is based upon the study mentioned previously. This study resulted in a set of tables of percentiles for Grades 5 through 11. There is also a set of ranges for percentiles based on raw scores.

A test-retest reliability coefficient is provided, apparently based on all students combined from Grades 5 through 11. Although this coefficient is substantial (.91), there are no coefficients provided for each of the grades, even though the standardization provides percentiles for each grade. A second study involving giving the measure in an algebra class and then a social studies class is discussed, but reliabilities are not given. In the reliability section of the manual, the authors discuss visual examination of scatter plots and distributions, but do not provide the data pertinent to the discussion.

There is no validity evidence given for the POIT. The authors argue that a validity study would require a 10-year follow-up of sociometric scores. They go on to argue that there are "no better means of estimating a vocational capacity in the sales area than the sociometric test" (p. 3).

COMMENTARY. The Power of Influence Test is a straightforward classroom sociometric measure. This type of measure has been used for decades to look at popularity in schools and the nature of classroom relationships. It seems a stretch to call this a measure of leadership, salesmanship, or of the power of influence. The manual for the POIT appears to be quite dated and often inappropriate. For example, all personal pronouns where there is no gender specified in the antecedent use the masculine form. Also, when the authors provide samples of what teachers might record on individual student forms, they use phrases such as, "Judy is an Indian girl," and "He [sic] mother is quite neurotic and calls the school quote [sic] often to complain that Mary does not get along with the other students." At another point in the manual, they say, "When there are moral or sanitary reasons why the child has no friends, it may be possible to refer these things for proper handling" (p. 3).

There are two critical deficiencies in the POIT. The first is that the measure is oversold by the authors. This is a simple measure of popularity or degree of friendship. There is no justification provided to call it a measure of leadership, salesmanship, or influence. This leads to the second critical deficiency. The technical data supporting the measure are sorely deficient. There is not much in the way of reliability data and absolutely no evidence of validity. Furthermore, with no information provided on when the reliability/standardization study was conducted, there is some concern about whether the data presented are still pertinent.

SUMMARY. The Power of Influence Test is a single-item sociometric measure indicating how popular a student is with his or her classmates. It can be administered by a classroom teacher in roughly 5 minutes and is simple to score. If this information is desired by a teacher, then this measure will provide it. There is no evidence provided that the POIT measures what the authors claim it does. The lack of thorough reliability evidence and any validity evidence, combined with the excessive claims for the measure by the authors, precludes a general recommendation for its usage.

[194]

Pre-Kindergarten Screen.

Purpose: Designed "to be a quick screening instrument for children between the ages of 4 years 0 months and 5 years 11 months who may be at risk for early academic difficulty."

Population: Ages 4–6.

Publication Date: 2000.

Acronym: PKS.

Scores, 10: Gross Motor Skills, Fine Motor Skills, Following Directions, Block Tapping, Visual Matching, Visual Memory, Imitation, Basic Academic Skills, Delayed Gratification, Total.

Administration: Individual.

Price Data: $65 per test kit including 50 record forms, test plates, and manual (56 pages); $25 per 50 record forms; $18 per test plates; $22 per manual.

Time: [15] minutes.

Authors: Raymond E. Webster and Angela Matthews.

Publisher: Academic Therapy Publications.

Review of the Pre-Kindergarten Screen by MARY "RINA" M. CHITTOORAN, Associate Professor of Educational Studies, Saint Louis University, St. Louis, MO:

DESCRIPTION. The Pre-Kindergarten Screen (PKS) is a standardized, individually administered screening measure designed to assess school readiness in children between the ages of 4-0 and 5-11 years. The nine subtests of the PKS can be used to assess a variety of skills deemed important for success in kindergarten; these are gross and fine motor skills; following one-, two-, and three-step directions; visual discrimination; visual memory; reproducing motor sequences presented visually; imitation of hand and finger pattern sequences; basic academic skills such as counting, color identification, alphabet recognition and recitation, and writing; and finally, self-restraint.

The PKS can be individually administered in 10 or 15 minutes and is intended for use by early childhood educators and educational diagnosticians with minimal training in test administration. Performance on the PKS can be reported as standard scores (Mean = 100; *SD* = 15) and as percentile ranks; in addition, a cutoff score that corresponds to the 25th percentile can be used to identify children at risk for learning problems. The three classification outcomes described in the manual are: (a) *Age-appropriate,* when standard scores and percentile ranks are higher than 89 and 25, respectively, (b) *Monitor,* when standard scores fall between 82 and 90 and percentile ranks fall between 11 and 25; and (c) *Referral,* when standard scores are lower than 82 and percentile ranks fall between 0 and 10.

DEVELOPMENT. The PKS is based on literature that suggests kindergarten success depends on adequate functioning in selected skill areas and that early assessment and intervention are critical for young children, especially those at risk for developmental delays. The manual does not provide information about how the test items were developed nor whether they were piloted with groups of children; however, the authors state that the "majority of PKS items showed item difficulty indices ranging from 0.40 to 0.99" (manual, p. 28) suggesting that some analyses were completed but not described in the manual.

TECHNICAL. The PKS was administered to 854 children between the ages of 3 1/2 and 6 years, from both urban and rural areas in the Northeast, South and West. The measure was subsequently standardized on 679 children ranging in age from 4-0 to 5-11; 70% of these were Caucasian and 30% represented other ethnicities. Norms tables for conversion of raw scores to standard scores and percentile ranks are provided for 2-month age intervals.

Internal consistency was evaluated using Cronbach's alpha, with obtained coefficients ranging from a low of .68 to a high of .83; corrected split-half reliabilities ranged from a low of .67 to a high of .90. The standard error of measurement, another measure of reliability, ranged from a low of 6.18 to a high of 8.49. Interrater reliability was examined across four raters and 12 children for a total of 48 ratings; a concordance rate of 92% was obtained, with examiners rating 9 of the 12 children in identical fashion. Correlations of .99 to 1.0 were also obtained for all possible pairs of examiner ratings. Test-retest reliability was examined for a group of 58 children, ranging in age from 4-0 to 5-5 years, who were tested on two occasions, with intervals between test administrations ranging from 115 to 135 days. An overall temporal stability coefficient of .78 was obtained. with subtest coefficients ranging from .25 to .89.

Content validity of the PKS was evaluated by a group of 12 experts in preschool assessment and instruction. Construct validity evidence was based on expected increases in PKS scores by age. Discriminative validity evidence was obtained through a comparison of scores obtained by three groups of kindergarten students with varying academic needs; results indicated statistically significant differences among mean scores, indicating that the PKS is able to discriminate adequately between the highest and lowest functioning children as well as between the lowest functioning children and those in early intervention programs.

Finally, the predictive validity of the PKS was examined by comparing children's pre-kindergarten PKS scores to (a) their kindergarten outcomes and (b) their teachers' identification of the highest and lowest performing students. On the first comparison, the PKS was able to accurately classify 98.7% of a group of 392 children, and on the second comparison, it was able to accurately classify 91.2% of 125 students.

COMMENTARY. The PKS authors have significant experience in assessment and instruction of, and research with, special-needs young children. The authors recognize the crucial link between assessment and intervention and stress the importance of primary prevention. Administration, scoring, and interpretation of the PKS are relatively simple and are facilitated by the inclusion of a completed sample protocol and four additional examples of scoring and interpretation for children at varying levels of ability. Further, the cutoff score and classification outcomes provide immediate feedback to an examiner about a particular child's potential for success in kindergarten.

There are several drawbacks to the PKS. The manual provides insufficient information regarding the development and refinement of test items. Several of the subtests seem to tap overlapping skills. It may have been helpful to use factor analyses to examine the underlying factor structure of the PKS with young children. Comprehensive information about standardization is noticeably lacking. Standard scores for the Age Appropriate and Monitor classification outcomes overlap slightly and might confuse the average examiner.

Internal consistency is no more than adequate and the test has an undesirably large standard error of measurement. Interrater reliability is relatively high but was based on a sample of only 12 children. Test-retest reliability is unimpressive, even at the 5-year-old level, when it would be expected to be at its highest. Additional subtest items, and therefore, a longer test, may improve reliability. Construct, discriminative, and predictive validity evidence is encouraging; however, evidence of concurrent validity would have been useful for practitioners, as would more information about the content validation performed by domain experts.

The PKS is marked by several undesirable features related to test administration. An easel-back format for the test plates booklet may have facilitated use with young children and the booklet itself could have been larger. Several pages have a crowded, busy appearance and may be problematic for young children, particularly those with special needs. For example, on the Academic Skills subtest, the placement of 26 letters on one small page is positively dizzying.

The wording of several items may lead to problems in test administration. On the Gross Motor Skills subtest, Item 3 that states "Pick up one foot and stand" is subject to misinterpretation, especially because the examiner is not asked to demonstrate. Perhaps the statement "Lift your foot" may have been easier to understand. Item 4, "Now, pick up your other foot," is equally problematic, given that one foot is already off the ground in response to the preceding item. An informal administration of this subtest to two young children and two adolescents resulted in reactions that ranged from bewilderment to hysterical laughter, as all four attempted to hold one, and then both, of their feet in their hands.

On the Gross Motor subtest, Items 5 and 6, which read "Please hop on one foot like this" and "Please hop on your other foot like this," are accompanied by directions to the examiner to hop three times on the left, and then on the right foot, respectively. Scoring instructions state that the items are scored as 1 if they are completed successfully (presumably the way they were demonstrated); however, given the age of the child and the fact that the examiner is facing the examinee, it is very likely that the child will hop first on the *right* foot and then the left. It is unclear whether these responses should be given credit.

The Fine Motor subtest could have used additional samples of drawing to facilitate scoring. On the Following Directions subtest, scoring directions for Item 4, "Stand up, turn around, and sit down," are enormously confusing, and the explanatory note only serves to further cloud the issue. In the description of the Visual Memory subtest, the word "Matching" is used instead of the word "Memory." Item 3 on the Imitation subtest, "Fold arms together," and item 4, "Twiddle thumbs," may not cause any problems for the individual examiner-examinee pair because the child simply imitates the examiner; however, the words "fold" and "twiddle" can be demonstrated in a number of ways. Such potential for variation is not appropriate in a standardized test.

SUMMARY. The PKS is designed as a screening measure of motor, cognitive, academic, and language functions and of school readiness in children just prior to kindergarten entry. Its strengths lie in its simplicity and its ability to predict subsequent academic performance. However, problems with test administration coupled with concerns regarding its technical adequacy, warrant a cautious recommendation for use with preschool populations, at least in its current form.

Review of the Pre-Kindergarten Screen by MARY LOU KELLEY, Professor of Psychology, Louisiana State University, Baton Rouge, LA:

DESCRIPTION. The Pre-Kindergarten Screen (PKS) assesses children's readiness for kindergarten and is for use with children between the ages of 4 years, 0 months to 5 years, 11 months. The measure is administered just before a child begins kindergarten. The authors' stated purpose is to differentiate between children who are likely to encounter failure during the early school years from those who will not.

There are nine subtests that were based on the synthesis of clinical knowledge and insight of a variety of professionals who work with preschool and elementary school-aged children. The nine subscales include: Gross Motor Skills, Fine Motor Skills, Following Direction, Block Tapping, Visual Matching, Visual Memory, Imitation, Academic Skills, and Delayed Gratification. The Gross Motor Skills subtest consists of six tasks measuring balance and movement. The Fine Motor Skills subtest evaluates the child's hand dominance, pencil grip, and copying skills. Following Directions involves one- to three-step directions stated only once. Block Tapping requires the child to reproduce motor sequences presented visually without language. Visual Matching requires the child to correctly match shapes or letters. Visual Memory involves having the child view visual configurations and then having the child identify the configuration. The Imitation subtest requires the child to mimic several hand and finger patterns. Academic Skills evaluates the child's ability to identify letters and colors, recognize and recite the alphabet, print their name, and count to 40. Delayed Gratification assesses the child's willingness to postpone taking a small treat for an indeterminate period of time with the possibility of receiving more at a later point in time.

The PKS is designed to be administered individually. The test materials consist of a record booklet, test plates presented in a spiral notebook, and the manual, which describes test characteristics, administration instructions, and the instrument's psychometric properties. The authors clearly list additional materials such as 6-foot ribbon and treat for the child that are needed for test administration. The manual contains specific instructions for administering each item of the PKS and specifies scoring criteria. For the most part, the scoring criteria are clear and objective. However, some items have more ambiguous criteria such as when to give 1 versus 2 points for drawing shapes.

Item responses earn 1–4 points depending on the quality of the response or scoring criteria for a specific subtest. It is not clear how the authors generated the scoring criteria or why certain items are awarded more points than other items. Items are summed to yield a total score that is used for test interpretation. Scores are compared to a cutoff score that represents the 25th percentile of children 5 years, 0 months or compared to similarly aged children. The authors suggest that children with scores at or below the 10th percentile relative to similarly aged in the standardization sample should be referred for additional testing. The authors also provide guidelines for cutoff scores at different ages and scores for which the child should be closely monitored.

TECHNICAL. The PKS was normed on 854 children ages 3.5 years through 6 years. Normative data were derived only from the protocols of children 4 years to 5 years, 11 months. The sample consisted of 70% Caucasians and 30% other ethnicities. Other demographic information such as SES were not provided. Item difficulty values range from .40–.99 so that the difficulty level was set at a level that most children with average ability could perform the item. Several forms of reliability were reported. Interrater reliability averaged 92% although this was based on only 12 children. Test-retest reliability was obtained approximately 119 days after the first administration. An overall stability coefficient of .78 was obtained for the total score. Subtest coefficient ranged from .25 to .89. Internal consistency was assessed by obtaining split-half reliability coefficients. The coefficients ranged from .67–.90.

With regard to validity, the authors compared PKS scores of children enrolled in an aca-

score correlations were .79 and above for both forms. The subtest and item descriptive statistics also were highly consistent across the two forms for the total sample, and when segregated by verbal and literacy skills and language background. The levels of reliability reported are commensurate with those found with the previously published version of the test and remarkable given the limited number of items per subtest and the target population.

Validity. The construction of the test was consistent with its intended use. Moreover, the data produced from the standardization sample suggest that the PreLAS 2000 is largely valid for its intended purpose. Both the oral and preliteracy sections of the test were able to separate the sample children according to home language background, age, and grade-level but not gender, indicating that the PreLAS 2000 is discriminative on expected variables. The distributions of the scores for the children from minority language backgrounds were lower and more dispersed than were the scores for the children from English-only language backgrounds. Tests of difference showed that total scores, proficiency level, and subscale scores were significantly lower for the children from minority language backgrounds than from English language backgrounds, although the relationship between oral language and preliteracy skills was more straightforward for the children from English-speaking backgrounds than those from minority language backgrounds. In addition, the younger children produced lower scores and were less proficient than were the older children, and scores and proficiency level increased significantly with grade level. A cautionary note is that concurrent, peer-reviewed, and external measures of validity are lacking for the PreLAS 2000. Data also are absent on the test's ability to accurately predict those children who will exhibit difficulty developing reading and other academic skills due to home language differences. Moreover, the functional reality of the proficiency levels and their corresponding total score intervals was not evident.

COMMENTARY. The PreLAS 2000 appears to be well motivated and its construction and standardization are appropriate. It uses a straightforward and child-friendly approach to assessing oral language and preliteracy skills. The administration and scoring procedures are relatively simple, well-documented, and require limited training

except for the story recall subtest ("Let's Tell Stories"). Although the administration manual provides multiple examples for scoring the story recall subtest, it may require additional training if administered by persons with limited background in language development. Moreover, the recommended reliability procedure for the story recall subtest lacks a gold standard, and therefore, does not ensure accurate judgments. The use of recorded speech stimuli promotes consistency in administration of the oral section of the PreLAS 2000 and allows speakers of nonstandard English to administer it. However, children who respond more poorly to recorded speech than speech presented in person may be disadvantaged by this mode of presentation. Presenting the speech stimuli from cassette tape also is somewhat cumbersome and would be easier if the stimuli were available on compact disk. The overall scoring of the PreLAS 2000 is simple, but the source of the weighting applied to the raw scores is not obvious. In addition, assigning the scores to a limited number of proficiency levels restricts the functionality and interpretability of the test results. However, with some effort, interested parties could derive other metrics from the standardization data presented in the test's technical manual.

SUMMARY. The PreLAS 2000 seems to be a good test for the purposes for which it was constructed. Abundant reliability and validity data are available in the technical manual that accompanies the test but the test lacks published peer-reviewed and external documentation of its usefulness and validity. The lack of peer-reviewed data may be a result of Forms C and D being recent revisions of the test, but earlier forms of the test also lack presence in the scientific literature. The administration and scoring of the PreLAS 2000 are relatively straightforward with the exception of the story recall subtest. The interpretation of the test scores is overly simplified by being restricted to a limited number of proficiency levels.

Review of the PreLAS 2000 by ANNITA MARIE WARD, Associate Professor of Education and TESL, Salem International University, Salem, WV:

DESCRIPTION. The PreLAS 2000 consists of an Oral Language Component, appropriate for use with 4-, 5-, and 6-year-olds and a Pre-Literacy Component, appropriate for use with 5- and

6-year-olds. Results of the assessment are used to place English as a Second Language (ESL) learners in appropriate instructional programs and to determine whether English Only and Language Minority students are ready for literacy instruction. (There is a Spanish language version of PreLAS 2000, but it is not reviewed here.) Each individual subscale of each component is administered to individual children, and administrations are not timed, although the publisher estimates it takes 5 to 10 minutes to administer the Pre-Literacy Component and 10 to 15 minutes to administer the Oral Language Component. The total test does not have to be given during a single session.

The examinee's Oral Language Component score is computed by adding together the weighted scores on a series of subscales designed to assess children's ability to follow simple directions (subscale: Simon Says); to answer questions about everyday pictures (subscale: Art Show); to name the parts of the body (The Human Body); to repeat sentences designed to elicit certain morphological and syntactical structures (e.g., use of "did" to form the emphatic past) (subscale: Say What You Hear); to retell a story (subscale: Story Retelling). After the oral language score is computed, it is placed within a proficiency band, which is determined by using the child's age (two age groups are recognized: 4-year-old and 5- and 6-year-olds) and then comparing the score to the proficiency bands for that particular age. These bands range from Proficiency Level 1, non-English speakers (NES), to Proficiency Level 5, fluent English speakers (FES).

The examinee's Pre-Literacy Component score is computed by adding together the weighted scores on six preliteracy subtests (Letters, Numbers, Colors, Shapes, Reading, and Writing). The examinee's score on the Pre-Literacy Component is placed into one of three bands of scores: low preliteracy scores; mid-level preliteracy scores, and high preliteracy scores.

According to the PreLAS 2000 examiner's manual, the test can be administered and scored by proficient speakers of Standard English who are qualified to work with 4- to 6-year-olds. The manual suggests that test administrators be familiar with test administration, either through a workshop or through "self-instruction." Scorers who holistically evaluate the story retelling section of the Oral Language Component must attain a

certain level of reliability using a scoring rubric before being allowed to score that section.

The PreLAS 2000 has two forms, C and D, as well as the Spanish-language version. According to the PreLAS 2000 technical notes, the Spanish-language version is identical in structure, format, and techniques to the English-language version. However, for linguistic reasons, the tests are not translations of each other and the artwork in the Spanish-language version is not the same as the artwork in the English-language one.

The testing kit is a colorful well-constructed cardboard briefcase containing a Quick Reference Guide, answer sheets, a 79-page examiner's manual, game board (used for preliteracy assessment), cue picture book (used for language proficiency assessment), and a cassette (used for language proficiency assessment).

DEVELOPMENT. The PreLAS 2000 is an updated version of PreLAS English, which was published in 1985. PreLAS English is used only to assess English-language proficiency of ESL children. PreLAS 2000 goes beyond this objective to assess language proficiency and preliteracy skills of both speakers of English as a first language and ESL speakers.

According to the PreLAS 2000 technical report, language proficiency as it is understood by the test's authors refers to "linguistic elements necessary for successful communication within the school environment" (p. 2), and communication consists of "both receptive and productive skills, input and output, information sent and received ... made up of both oral and literacy skills: Listening, Speaking, Reading, and Writing" (p. 2).

PreLAS 2000 test development involved a four-step process:

1. Item writing—According to the technical notes, item development was based on literature reviews related to child language, bilingualism, kindergarten readiness, and assessment of immigrant children.

2. Tryout and field testing—Professional item writers, many of whom were educators of young children, wrote items to be tried out. Items were tested in a pilot study, using a sample of 100 English and language minority children. An items analysis of the pilot data indicated items that were not useful. Tryout data were collected and the items for each subscale were placed in Form C or Form D of the test.

3. Analyses and item selection—Items in the pilot data that had an average P-value of .80 for Fluent English Speakers (FES) were generally retained for the tryout sample although linguistic and cultural factors could affect the decision to retain an item.

4. Final production.

TECHNICAL. Tryout samples were composed of approximately 960 children of whom 251 spoke English only and 712 children whose first language was something other than English; 26 such languages were represented in the sample and for purposes of statistical analyses these subgroups were eventually collapsed into one category, Language Minority. Males and females were equally represented in the test development sample. The language most frequently spoken among these children was Spanish with English being the second most frequent. More than 90% of the sample was over 5 years of age.

The technical notes for the test offer descriptive statistics for each test item as well as for each subscale. These statistics for the subscales are offered in three categories: total population as one category then broken down into Fluent English and Limited English, assumed to be Language Minority. *T*-tests were performed to determine if there were significant differences between the two subgroups' mean scores on the subscales of both the Language Proficiency Component and the Pre-Literacy Component. The English Only group had significantly higher scores than did the Minority Language group.

An analysis of variance of the total test results on the Oral Language Proficiency Component indicated that there were no significant differences between males' and females' performance on that component.

Reliability among subscales for Forms C and D was calculated with Cronbach alpha scores ranging from .76 to .92. Interform subscale correlations ranged from .76 to .99.

Although the test publishers provided a 72-page manual, there is no evidence provided that there was an effort to examine content validity for the Language Proficiency Component as an assessment of language proficiency or to examine content validity for the Pre-literacy Component as an assessment of preliteracy skills. Within the statistical information in the technical notes there is no reference to the issue of validity although in

the discussion that precedes this statistical information it is noted that "every effort was made to meet the criteria for reliability and validity of the American Psychological Association" (p. 4).

In the computation of scores for each component of the PreLAS 2000, subtest scores are weighted, but the test's authors offer no justification for that weighting. For example, story retelling has a weight of four whereas naming parts of the human body has a weight of one. No explanation or justification for this weighting is offered.

No explanation is offered for how the cutoff scores for each proficiency level were determined. What is more, the test scorer must establish a proficiency level based on age level. However, all 4-year-olds, 5-year-olds, etc. are grouped together in establishing proficiency levels.

COMMENTARY. Determining English language proficiency is a very important matter for American schools at this point in history as issues related to teaching English to language minority students are not just educational issues but are also political and social issues. Schools must have good ways to assess proficiency and to determine which students will benefit from ESL instruction.

The PreLAS 2000 purportedly measures English-language proficiency and its scoring procedures offer a ranking system by which examinees can be placed into proficiency bands ranging from Proficiency Level 5 (fluent) to Proficiency Level 1 (non-English). However, the test's authors offer no evidence to support the assertion that this test measures English proficiency. The test also supposedly measures preliteracy skills, but, again, no evidence is offered to support the contention that this test actually does measure those skills. What is more, since the 1990s it has been commonly accepted among reading professionals that tests that measure knowledge of print conventions, phonemic awareness, invented spelling, detection of rhymes, and knowledge of story structure are better predictors of readiness for literacy instruction than are tests measuring knowledge of colors, shapes, etc.

The casual standardization procedures for this test are also of concern. The examiner's manual states that an audiocassette is provided so that the test can be standardized. But, on page 14 of that same manual test administrators are told that use of the audiocassette is optional. If test administrators do not use the tape, a bias can be presented and that bias can affect an examinee's score. Children who complete tasks based on information read or spoken by familiar adults, such as their teachers, are likely to receive higher scores than are children who complete tasks based on information presented on a cassette tape. However, these higher scores may work to the disadvantage of these children as they may be denied services they actually need and would qualify for if they had received a standard administration of the test. As no information on how cutoff scores were determined was offered, we cannot know if cutoff scores were based on a standard administration of the test.

Another issue of standardization relates to the holistic scoring of subscale five, Story Retelling, of the Oral Language Proficiency Component. According to the manual, one criterion for eligibility to score this section is "familiarity with developmental characteristics of young children's language" (p. 25). There is no requirement that a scorer must have any sort of training in linguistics or in teaching English. Yet, the rubric for the various scoring levels for this task includes elements that require linguistic judgments, such as "has no sentence structure" and "response has errors in grammar, syntax, vocabulary, usage not likely to be made by a speaker of Standard American English."

Another criterion for being able to do holistic scoring on these responses is the attainment of at least 90% accuracy on the holistic scoring exercise described in the examiner's manual. However, this score of 90% really has nothing to do with the rater being able to conform to a rubric; rather, potential scorers have to be able to conform to the scoring of another potential scorer. Using the rubric, two potential scorers, A and B, might score the same set of 10 responses. In another, to attain 90% accuracy these scorers A and B must have scored 9 out of the 10 responses the same way. The examiner's manual suggests that in case of disagreement "scorers should discuss the bases [sic] upon which their judgments were made" (p. 59). The very obvious problem is this: If two potential scorers misunderstand the rubric and they misunderstand it in the same way, they may very well achieve 90% reliability in their scoring, but still the samples will be scored incorrectly.

SUMMARY. The game board and picture book that are part of the PreLAS 2000 assessment are very attractive and the assessment tasks would be interesting and highly motivating to young children. But no evidence is presented to assure the user that the Oral Language Component is a valid assessment tool for establishing a student's level of English proficiency. Aside from the fact that the test developers made no effort to examine content validity for the Oral Proficiency Component, they also did not explain how the cutoff scores for each proficiency level were established. In addition, the Pre-Literacy Component of the test presents the same problem that the Oral Language Proficiency Component presents: There is no evidence that this test is a valid measurement of preliteracy skills and the test developers offer no explanation as to how the cutoff scores for the three preliteracy levels were established. What is more, it is generally accepted among reading teachers, reading researchers, etc., that the sorts of concepts tested on the Pre-Literacy Component, such as knowledge of colors and shapes, are not the best predictors of emergent literacy skills. Issues related to standardization of test administration and scoring procedures further cloud the effectiveness of the PreLAS 2000 for use as an English-language assessment tool.

[196]
Pre-Literacy Skills Screening.

Purpose: Provides a quick look at the reading readiness skills of children beginning school.
Population: Kindergarten.
Publication Date: 1999.
Acronym: PLSS.
Scores, 11: Rhyme, Sentence Repetition, Naming Accuracy, Naming Time, Blending, Sentence Segmentation, Letter Naming, Syllable Segmentation, Deletion, Multisyllabic Word Repetition, Overall Score.
Administration: Individual.
Price Data, 2003: $51 per complete kit including 25 record forms, and examiner's manual (30 pages); $20 per 25 record forms; $33 per examiner's manual.
Time: (15) minutes.
Authors: Linda Crumrine and Helen Lonegan.
Publisher: PRO-ED.

Review of the Pre-Literacy Skills Screening by CAROL E. KESSLER, Assistant Professor of Education, Cabrini College, Radnor, PA:

DESCRIPTION. The Pre-Literacy Skills Screening (PLSS) was created to determine reading readiness skills of incoming kindergarten children. This tool examines phonological awareness, letter recognition, and word retrieval. It takes approximately 15 minutes to administer this test individually to each student. The PLSS is a 59-item test with nine subtests: Rhyme, Sentence Repetition, Naming, Blending, Sentence Segmentation, Letter Naming, Syllable Segmentation, Deletion, and Multisyllabic Word Repetition. The sum of all the subtest scores is the Composite score and should be considered an overall measure of a student's preliteracy skills. The Composite score is used to identify students at risk by ranking kindergarten children within each class from highest to lowest. Research has indicated that the lowest 20% will probably find reading acquisition difficult. The student is required to motorically (pointing or clapping) and/or verbally respond to the examiner's requests.

It would be expected that educators and specialists (for example, a speech and language therapist) could easily administer, score, and interpret the PLSS depending on the examiner's familiarity with this tool. The use of a computer to enter, analyze, and rank the data is recommended. The nine scales vary in the number of score points and level of difficulty. The authors state that the number of items is not enough for in-depth diagnostic purposes.

All that is needed to administer the PLSS is the four-page record form and the manual. The stimulus picture used in the administration of the test are included in the latter half of the manual. The 15 stimulus plates are colorful and accurately represented. Four of the subtests employ this stimulus material: Rhyme (Plates 1–4), Word Naming (Plates 5–8) and Word Naming Alternate (Plates 9–12), Letter Naming (Plates 13–14), and Deletion (Plate 15). The remaining subtests require no additional material because they are presented orally. The authors suggest constructing a segmenting board to assist the students with the items on the segmenting subtests. A pattern is provided in the manual. My recommendation would be that a segmenting board be included in the package of test materials. This would further enhance the standardization of the protocol. The diagram used to illustrate how the segmenting board should appear is black and white and the directions require colored circles. The specification of how the examiner should encourage the student are clearly delineated. The record form is easy to understand and is organized in a coherent manner. Additionally, the scoring guidelines are articulated very well. Speed and the accuracy of the response are both factors in the Naming subtest. The tables included in the manual are straightforward and are very helpful in understanding the scores.

DEVELOPMENT. The PLSS was developed after many exchanges between the authors in searching for the connection between reading difficulties and language. According to their comprehensive research, which is well documented, those students who have weak phonological skills also experience difficulty in learning how to read. Word-retrieval speed is further correlated with reading ability. With the knowledge of these predictors, the obvious question surfaced: "Why not use them to identify our kindergarten children who are most at risk for reading failure?" (p. ii) The quest for this answer became the pivotal impetus behind the development of this instrument. The 1999 version includes letter recognition and word retrieval items as well as phonological awareness tasks. This is the extent of the information provided that pertains to the initial test development.

The definitions offered for each subtest are coherently written and should be very helpful to the examiner in understanding the various constructs. The items are developmentally appropriate for kindergarten children and appear to be representative of the constructs that are being measured.

Pilot testing has been conducted since 1993; however, only the data from 1998 are used in determining the mean, standard deviation, minimum, and maximum scores for each measure. The sample used included 74 females and 67 males. A larger sample would provide better standardization of this test instrument. Also, because this sample was drawn from one small school system, the predictive strength of this screening tool is limited. Greater specificity in defining the standardization sample should have been provided.

TECHNICAL. Information that describes the norming process is minimal and vague. These specific details need to be included in the manual. The developers state that the PLSS is a "highly predictive screening tool" (p. iii) but they do not document credible evidence to justify this assumption.

In terms of technical adequacy, reliability and validity issues are not mentioned in the manual. Various types of reliability estimates should have been presented. Further, validity evidence should have been reported, but it is not addressed. It should therefore be concluded that this test may not meet acceptable psychometric standards. Corrective action should be implemented to rectify these deficiencies.

COMMENTARY. There are numerous strengths of this instrument. Specifically, the presentation and organization of the materials makes sense and is appealing. The theoretical model that supports the screening device appears reasonable. The current research that supports the test's assumptions is convincing and comprehensive. The ease in the administration and the scoring of the test items is manageable. The manual is very clear and easy to follow. The stimulus plates used in the various subtests are attractive and helpful. The specificity of the directions assists the students in responding correctly. The record form is easy to follow. The tables in the manual facilitate in tabulating and understanding the scores. The tasks are interesting and therefore motivating for the student. The items are developmentally appropriate for kindergarten children. The administration time is reasonable considering the normal attention span of kindergarten children. Finally, the definitions provided for the chosen constructs are well articulated and useful in helping to understand the various dimensions of reading readiness.

The overall weaknesses of this instrument include the general absence of technical information; the lack of a color segmenting board in the test kit; the absence of information about the differential impact of gender, race, and ethnicity; and the assumption that the test has high predictive value regarding literacy skills especially when the standardization sample is so limited by definition and size.

SUMMARY. The authors have developed a screening instrument that can be administered, scored, and interpreted very efficiently. However, insufficient standardization, reliability, and validity information is provided to assert that the assessment tool consistently and accurately measures the theoretical constructs. If these technical issues (as well as the impact on diverse populations) are addressed adequately, the use of this screening device could be recommended.

Review of the Pre-Literacy Skills Screening by
KORESSA KUTSICK MALCOLM, *School Psychologist, Augusta County Public Schools and Adjunct Professor of Psychology, Mary Baldwin College, Staunton, VA:*

DESCRIPTION. The Pre-Literacy Skills Screening (PLSS) was designed to be a screening instrument useful in the identification of young students who demonstrate weaknesses in the development of their phonological awareness. Students with weaknesses in this area often experience difficulties learning to read printed text. A premise of the PLSS is that students who demonstrate phonological weaknesses must be identified early in their school careers so that supportive instruction can be provided.

It is assumed from general descriptors provided by its authors that the PLSS was designed for kindergarten-aged students. No specific age ranges are provided. The PLSS is divided into nine subtests. Each subtest contains three to eight items. Raw scores are obtained for each subtest and for the test as a whole. Total administration time for the PLSS was noted to be approximately 15 minutes.

The PLSS theoretically taps into nine prereading skills. These include rhyming, sentence memory, picture identification, sound blending, sentence segmentation, letter naming, syllable segmentation, sound deletion, and multiple-syllable word repetition. Items for the various tasks that represent these skills are presented to students via pictures on a small easel or through verbal information given by the examiner. A record booklet is provided that includes directions for administration of each subtest and space to record subjects' responses. Some of the subtests are timed. Examiners must provide their own stopwatches.

There are a variety of tasks children must complete when they are administered the PLSS. Traditional preschool screening activities such as color, shape, letter, and picture identification are included. Children are engaged in various language memory and processing activities such as word and sentence repetition. They also blend or delete sounds and word fragments to form spoken words. Rhyming activities are included.

DEVELOPMENT. The PLSS has been under development since 1993 by the authors who are language and learning specialists working in school settings. Crumrine and Lonegran note they found a need for a screening instrument that would help them identify children who did not have the basic phonological skills necessary for reading acquisition. From their reviews of research in the developmental processes of reading, and

direction. Seven scores are derived, one in each of seven rationally derived domains: Relationship Emphasis, Information Emphasis, Facilitative Focus, Confrontive Focus, Mentor Model, Employee Vision, and Overall. According to the PAMI manual, the purpose of these scores is to allow mentors to locate themselves "on the map of the mentoring landscape" (p. 17). Raw scores only are provided. There are no interpretive guides beyond cut scores for classification on each dimension into one of five categories of effectiveness. Cut scores are provided without reference to how they were derived. Nevertheless, the author states in the manual that professionals "can comfortably use the *Inventory* as a diagnostic instrument" (p. 17).

DEVELOPMENT. The PAMI manual provides scant information about the development of the scale. The PAMI was apparently derived rationally from a review of literature, although there are no citations of literature in the manual and there is no reference list or bibliography in the manual. Development included expert review by what the manual describes as juries of scholars (no further description provided). The items violate most tenets of item writing and responses are difficult to interpret due to the presence of so many compound and complex compound constructions. The items may be difficult for examinees to interpret accurately as well; however, there are no data about the meaning or difficulty of interpretation of the items by the examinee or the examiner. The manual indicates that statistical analysis and scale validation were done but no additional description of method or results is offered.

TECHNICAL CHARACTERISTICS. The PAMI manual provides no information regarding the technical or psychometric characteristics of the PAMI. Neither does the manual provide even one reference to any published or unpublished study of the PAMI. The author claims to have some data, but reveals nothing about it.

COMMENTARY. The manual provides none of the most basic of details about the PAMI or its characteristics as is recommended in the standards of the professions of education, psychology, and measurement (American Educational Research Association, American Psychological Association, & National Council on Measurement in Education, 1999) as expressed in the *Standards for Educational and Psychological Testing*. The PAMI may or may not be a useful

scale and may or may not provide reliable scores with valid interpretations associated with outcomes of adult mentoring. However, the PAMI manual provides no information to allow an informed judgment. Neither does the PAMI manual address additional aspects of the *Standards* such as fairness, linguistic background of the examinee and its potential influence on score reliability and interpretation, consequences of test use, or other areas detailed in the *Standards*. Offering this scale as a diagnostic instrument is in no way supported by the evidence (actually the lack of evidence) in the PAMI manual.

SUMMARY. When the behavior of individuals is to be measured and changes in how they interact with others prescribed on the basis of such measurements, information and evidence about the development, psychometric characteristics, and empirically supported interpretations of the scores must be provided and current professional standards exist that describe the proper means of presentation and the specific areas to be addressed (American Educational Research Association, American Psychological Association, & National Council on Measurement in Education, 1999).

REVIEWER'S REFERENCE

American Educational Research Association, American Psychological Association, & National Council on Measurement in Education (1999). *Standards for educational and psychological testing.* Washington, DC: American Educational Research Association.

[198]

Program Quality Assessment.

Purpose: Designed "to evaluate the quality of early childhood programs and identify staff-training needs."
Population: Early childhood program.
Publication Date: 1998.
Acronym: PQA.
Scores: Total score only.
Administration: Individual.
Price Data, 2001: $22.85 per package including administration manual (11 pages), Head Start user guide (16 pages), and assessment form; $7 per administration manual; $7 per Head Start user guide; $10.85 per assessment form.
Time: Untimed.
Author: High/Scope Educational Research Foundation.
Publisher: High/Scope Educational Research Foundation.

Review of the Program Quality Assessment by MICHAEL B. BUNCH, Vice President, Measurement Incorporated, Durham, NC:

DESCRIPTION. The Program Quality Assessment (PQA) is a 72-item rating form used in the evaluation of Head Start or other preschool programs. It is not a test to be administered to preschool children or their teachers but a form to be used by a trained external evaluator or by a program administrator to rate seven categories of program design and performance: Learning Environment (9 items), Daily Routine (12 items), Adult-Child Interaction (12 items), Curriculum Planning and Assessment (5 items), Parent Involvement and Family Services (10 items), Staff Qualifications and Staff Development (14 items), and Program Management (10 items).

Each item in the PQA consists of a simple statement followed by a 5-point rating scale (with 1 being the lowest score and 5 being the highest). Score points 1, 3, and 5 are described in some detail, and users of the instrument are directed to use score points 2 and 4 to indicate conditions between those described.

After each such item, space is provided for evidence and anecdotes to support the rating. The assessment form is 60 pages long. Most pages have either one or two such items. The final page is a summary sheet on which the person completing the form records all scores and derives the total and average scores. This latter score is considered important because it may not be possible to complete all 72 items for a particular program.

DEVELOPMENT. The PQA succeeds the Program Implementation Profile (PIP), also published by High/Scope. The focus has shifted a bit since the 1989 publication of PIP. The items in the survey are keyed to Head Start Performance Standards (HSPS) and Head Start Performance Measures (HSPM). Specific links between individual items and the associated standards or measures are spelled out in the user guide. The ultimate goal of bringing about a greater degree of social competence in preschool children from low-income families is supported by five objectives ranging from enhancing children's growth and development to ensuring well-managed programs that involve parents in decision making. These five objectives are further defined in a series of specific statements such as the following: "HSPS 1304.22 (d) 1: Agencies must ensure that staff and volunteers can demonstrate safety practices" (user's guide, p. 4).

Each item in the PQA addresses one or more of these statements. The relationship is very straightforward. In some instances, the PQA item simply repeats the HSPS statement; in most instances, the PQA item combines related elements of two or more HSPS statements.

TECHNICAL. The administration manual provides information about instrument reliability and validity. Reliability is expressed in terms of interrater agreement, coefficient alpha, and correlations between ratings of trained evaluators and self-assessments. Exact and adjacent agreements are reported for each of the seven scales and for an average rating across the scales. Exact agreement rates (at the item level) for trained raters range from 75% to 91%, whereas exact plus adjacent agreement rates range from 94% to 100%. These agreement rates are quite high for 5-point rating scales.

An overall alpha coefficient of .95 is reported in the administration manual. However, this coefficient is taken from a program evaluation report for the Michigan School Readiness Program (MSRP; Florian, Schweinhart, & Epstein, 1997) in which a different version of the PQA with different scales and 73 items was used.

Validity information is reported in the administration manual in terms of correlations between PQA scores and scores on other measures, typically those also published by High/Scope for use in Head Start program evaluation. The most supportive validity evidence is found in another MSRP evaluation report (Xiang et al., 2000). That report (also using the Florian et al. version of the PQA) shows that programs with higher overall PQA scores had fewer children being required to repeat first grade.

COMMENTARY. This rating instrument for preschool programs is highly relevant to Head Start programs, having been constructed specifically to adhere to the standards and measures associated with that program. Administrators of Head Start programs and other preschool programs with similar aims would be well served by the instrument, either as a training tool for lead teachers and teachers or as an evaluation instrument. Its contents have high face validity, and its application is straightforward and simple. Results are easy to understand.

Potential users should note that the items reflect a specific program vision: that children learn through active involvement with people, materials, events, and ideas. Acceptance of scores on the instrument requires acceptance of the individual items and scoring rubric of the instrument. Some program administrators, lead teachers, teachers, and parents might find some of the items and score points difficult to accept (e.g., [III-D] "Adults use a variety of strategies to encourage and support child language and communication"). Score point 1 (low) contains the following description: "Adults control or disrupt conversations with children by lecturing to or quizzing them. Adults often question children, asking many leading questions with predetermined correct answers (e.g., 'What color is this circle?'). Children are often told to be quiet so they can listen to adults or follow directions." Programs achieve high scores on this item if adults ask children questions sparingly, avoiding questions that call for predetermined answers.

The preceding description is not meant to disparage the PQA but rather to draw attention to the fact that it is based on a point of view that some may not embrace. If it is possible to conduct a successful preschool program under a different philosophy, then use of this instrument would seriously underestimate the positive effects of such a program. The research behind the instrument and the breadth and depth of the experience of the instrument designers argue strongly for its usefulness. The instrument has evolved in response to research findings and changes in the field. The items are clearly and succinctly worded, and the support documents are very helpful.

SUMMARY. The Program Quality Assessment is a well-designed, research-based evaluation instrument clearly aimed at Head Start and other preschool programs. The face validity of the instrument is clear, and there is ample evidence of reliability and validity for use of the instrument as a program evaluation tool. Potential users would do well to compare the vision that drives their own programs to make sure it aligns with the High/Scope vision of early childhood education. If it does, the PQA would be the instrument to use. One further note to program administrators: A trained evaluator using the PQA would be preferable to a self-assessment; the trained evaluator will provide more accurate (less inflated) scores.

REVIEWER'S REFERENCES

Florian, J. E., Schweinhart, L. J., & Epstein, A. S. (1997). *Early returns: First year report on the Michigan School-Readiness Program Evaluation.* Ypsilanti, MI: High/Scope Educational Research Foundation.

Xiang, Z., Schweinhart, L., Hohmann, C., Smith, C., Storer, E., & Oden, S. (2000). *Points of light: Third rear report of the Michigan School Readiness Evaluation.* Ypsilanti, MI: High/Scope Educational Research Foundation.

Review of the Program Quality Assessment by WILLIAM I. SAUSER, JR., *Associate Dean and Professor, Business and Engineering Outreach, Auburn University, Auburn, AL:*

DESCRIPTION. The High/Scope Program Quality Assessment (PQA): Preschool Version is a well-designed protocol intended to guide reviewers through the observation, interviewing, documentation, and evaluation stages of a comprehensive program review of Head Start and other such center-based preschool and child care settings. "The PQA is a comprehensive tool examining all aspects of program implementation, from the physical characteristics of the setting to the nature of adult-child interaction to program management" (administration manual, p. 1).

Multidimensional in nature, the PQA employs a combination of observation and interview techniques. It is designed for use "by trained independent raters conducting research and evaluation, or ... as a self-assessment by agencies interested in identifying program strengths and areas for improvement" (administration manual, p. 1). The PQA was carefully designed using "current theory, decades of practice, and ongoing research" and "reflects 'best practices' in the early childhood field as a whole" (administration manual, p. 1).

The instrument itself contains 72 items covering seven key dimensions of quality for early childhood programs: Learning Environment (9 items), Daily Routine (12 items), Adult-Child Interaction (12 items), Curriculum Planning and Assessment (5 items), Parent Involvement and Family Services (10 items), Staff Qualifications and Staff Development (14 items), and Program Management (10 items).

> Each item is scored using a five-point rating scale extending from low (1) to a high (5) level of quality. Examples are provided for ratings of 1, 3, and 5; the points in between (2 and 4) give the rater additional flexibility in assigning scores. Below each item, space is provided for recording supporting evidence and anecdotes about the settings, activities, individuals, and interactions assessed. (administration manual, p. 2)

The assessment booklet is well designed for easy use; the scale anchors (tailored for each item) are clear and provide helpful guidance; there is considerable space available for documentation, including diagrams and schedules; and the data summary sheet is straightforward and easy to complete. The manual contains clear directions and helpful suggestions for use of the instrument for several purposes, including preservice and inservice training, self-assessment and monitoring, observation and feedback, research and evaluation, and information documentation and dissemination.

The authors are careful to state in the manual—and appropriately so—that the quality of the assessment process is highly dependent upon the quality and depth of observation and interviewing that the assessor conducts prior to the completion of the 72 items. Users are instructed to spend "at least one full day reviewing a program before completing the ratings, allocating half the day to observing in the classroom … and half to conducting the interviews …. If more than one classroom in a center or agency is to be rated, the rater should observe in each classroom for one-half day … and interview the head teacher in each classroom" (administration manual, p. 4). Obviously, the PQA is designed to produce a thorough program evaluation report, and to rush or skip over any of the observational or interviewing steps prior to filling out the 72 ratings would compromise the integrity of the results.

DEVELOPMENT. The PQA appears to be the result of a very careful and comprehensive instrument development process. The authors grounded the instrument in sound educational theory and practice. "In fact, the revised Head Start Performance Standards (Federal Register, 1996) and the Head Start Performance Measures (U.S. Department of Health and Human Services, 1998) were among the key sources that High/Scope referred to in developing the PQA" (user guide, p. 1). The user guide contains reprints of these standards and measures, plus detailed matrices cross-referencing each item on the instrument to one or more standard and measure. These detailed matrices document fully evidence for the content validity of scores from the instrument: Every standard and every measure is tapped. Assuming that the Head Start standards and measures do indeed reflect "best practices" in early childhood education, then users of the PQA can be confident that they are assessing target programs using an appropriate, content-valid method. The instrument assures assessment on each of five key Head Start objectives: (a) Enhance children's growth and development; (b) strengthen families as the primary nurturers of their children; (c) provide children with educational, health, and nutritional services; (d) link children and families to needed community services; and (e) ensure well-managed programs that involve parents in decision making.

TECHNICAL. In addition to the thorough content validation strategy employed during instrument development, the authors sought to assure the psychometric quality of the PQA by subjecting it to three comprehensive field trials using hundreds of classrooms and children across the United States and throughout the state of Michigan. Results of these studies are impressive. Trained assessors produced exact matching scores in 79.4% of the cases; matching scores within one point were produced for 96.7% of the cases. In another study, Cronbach's alpha coefficient on the PQA items was .952 for 49 independent observations and .956 for 642 teacher self-assessments. The test authors note that self-ratings tend to be inflated compared to independent ratings, but both sets of raters tend to identify similar strengths and areas for improvement. Evidence for construct validity scores from the PQA is also impressive. In one study, the PQA correlated .86 with the Early Childhood Environment Rating Scale; in another, .48 with the Arnett Global Rating Scale. Statistically significant validity coefficients are reported in the manual between PQA scores and a variety of measures of teacher qualifications and child development in preschool and kindergarten programs. The test authors report no normative data in the manual (because the PQA is a criterion-referenced rather than norm-referenced instrument), but cite references to studies conducted using the PQA that could produce helpful comparative information as desired.

COMMENTARY. The PQA is impressive in terms of scope and comprehensiveness, usability, theoretical grounding, and psychometric quality. It would be a valuable tool for anyone seeking to conduct a formative or summative evaluation of a Head Start or other early childhood learning center. It is also a valuable learning instrument: teachers, administrators, policy makers, and parents could use the PQA in a variety of settings to gain information about "best practices" in the field of early childhood education and how these practices are being implemented in local centers, classrooms, and even homes. Assessment results provide "face-valid" (as well as content valid) information that can be used to improve programs and centers.

With an instrument such as the PQA, which requires considerable judgmental skill on the part of the assessor, it is important to provide thorough assessor training in observation, interviewing, and especially consistency in interpreting scale anchors. The manual describes a 3-day program necessary to train raters to acceptable levels of interrater reliability. The program includes an overview of the instrument, the viewing of videotapes and observation of early childhood programs, practice writing supporting evidence and anecdotes, discussion of scoring strategies, practice and score comparison sessions, and interviewing techniques. Obviously, a considerable investment of time is necessary to prepare trained raters to use the PQA for large-scale research projects and program evaluation studies. As has already been noted, time must also be invested in thorough classroom observation, teacher and administrator interviewing, documentation of anecdotes and other evidence, and careful scoring if the PQA is to produce meaningful results.

SUMMARY. Educators, program evaluators, and policy makers who desire a well-designed observation and interview protocol and measurement instrument for research, program review, training, and other such purposes are encouraged to consider using the PQA. It is well grounded in educational theory and "best practices," comprehensive and thorough, easy to use, and easy to interpret. It measures all key aspects of federal standards and measures for quality of Head Start and other such early childhood educational programs. Evidence for the reliability and validity of PQA scores—when the instrument is used properly—is impressive. Users should be aware, however, that the PQA requires an investment in time for training, observation, interviewing, and scoring. Plan on a multi-day training program for users plus at least 1 day of observation and interviewing for each classroom evaluated.

REVIEWER'S REFERENCES

Federal Register. (1996, November 5). *Program Performance Standards for the operation of Head Start programs by grantee and delegate agencies.* Washington, DC: U.S. Government Printing Office, 57210-57227.

U.S. Department of Health and Human Services, Administration on Children, Youth and Families, Research, Demonstration, and Evaluation Branch. (1998, March 18). *Second Head Start Program Performance Measures progress report: Draft.* Washington, DC: Author.

[199]

Progressive Achievement Tests in Mathematics—Revised.

Purpose: Designed "to provide information to teachers about the level of achievement attained by their students in the skills and understanding of mathematics."

Population: Australian students in years 4–9.
Publication Dates: 1983–1998.
Acronym: PATMaths Revised.
Scores: Total score only.
Administration: Group.
Forms, 2: Form A, Form B.
Price Data, 2002: A\$3.90 per test booklet; A\$66 per specimen set including booklet, teacher's manual (1997, 21 pages), answer sheet, and score key; A\$49.95 per teacher's manual; A\$5 per scoring key; A\$7.50 per 10 answer sheets; A\$99.95 per combined specimen set including components from each level plus teacher's manual; price data for norming manual (1998, 18 pages) available from publisher.
Time: (45) minutes.
Author: Australian Council for Educational Research Press.
Publisher: Australian Council for Educational Research Ltd. [Australia].
  a) LEVEL 1.
    Population: Years 4–6.
  b) LEVEL 2.
    Population: Years 6–9.
  c) LEVEL 3.
    Population: Years 7–9.
Cross References: See T5:2091 (5 references); for reviews by James C. Impara and A. Harry Passow of an earlier edition, see 11:309 (2 references). For information on the New Zealand edition, see T3:1911 (1 reference); for additional information and a review by Harold C. Trimble, see 8:288.

Review of the Progressive Achievement Tests in Mathematics—Revised by KEVIN D. CREHAN, Associate Professor of Educational Psychology, University of Nevada, Las Vegas, Las Vegas, NV:

DESCRIPTION. The first Australian edition of the Progressive Achievement Tests in Mathematics (PATMaths) (10:309) were adapted by the Australian Council for Educational Research (ACER) from the New Zealand tests of the same name (8:288) in 1984. The tests are designed to assess mathematics achievement over the School Years 3 through 8 in Australia and are based on a published curriculum known as the National Profiles. The revision was designed to bring the tests in line with extant 1997 curriculum emphases. Both the original and PATMaths Revised consist of two parallel tests at three overlapping levels of difficulty. Tests 1A and 1B have 37 multiple-choice items to measure mathematics achievement over School Years 3 through 5. Tests 2A and 2B have 39 multiple-choice items to measure mathematics achievement over School Years 5 through

8, whereas tests 3A and 3B have 41 multiple-choice items for Years 6 through 8. Levels 1 and 2 assess achievement over four National Profiles strands: number, space, measurement, and chance, and data. Level 3 adds algebra to these four strands with a reduction in the number strand emphasis. Machine scoring is available through ACER and hand-scoring templates are provided. The teacher's manual describes the main functions of the tests as: provide broad estimates of mathematics achievement, assist with goal setting and instructional planning, relate student performance to levels of the National Profiles, identification of extreme low and high student performance to allow alternate programming, and identify class weaknesses and strengths to aid in the assessment of degree of attainment on the objectives of the school mathematics curriculum.

Raw score conversion to Rasch scale scores is provided in the teacher's manual and raw score conversion to percentile rank and stanine is tabled in the accompanying norming manual. A student report form for each level and form of the tests provides a detailed display of performance down to the level of individual item within strand. The left portion of this form has item numbers ordered by Rasch difficulty within each strand. To the right of this display is a vertical raw score scale with accompanying Rasch scale score conversion. Within each strand, item numbers are aligned to the Rasch scale. Moving further to the right is a hierarchically aligned verbal description of what a student is typically able to do at each performance level. At the far right of the form is a simple numeric (1–5) display of the National Profiles Levels. The scored version of this form has a horizontal line drawn through the student's raw score which cuts through the response pattern display with the individual student's success indicated for each item. Inspection of the pattern of successes allows an estimation of the typicality of performance. That is, if successes within each strand are predominately near and below the overall Rasch estimate of the student's achievement (as indicated by the horizontal line) then the pattern would be typical. However, if the pattern reveals several successes above the line in one (or more) strands with few or no successes in other strands, the pattern would be judged atypical. An atypical pattern would limit the interpretability of a student's aggregate performance against the norms, verbal descriptions, and National Profiles.

An examination of the raw score to tabular normative and scale score conversions and the detailed student report form allows assessment of the usefulness of this information to accomplish the stated main functions of these tests. The first of these functions is to provide a broad estimate of the student's mathematics achievement. The information clearly provides the basis for both normative and criterion estimates of student achievement. Additionally, the student report satisfies the function of relating student performance to levels of the National Profiles. Another stated function is to allow goal setting and instructional planning. An instructor may base some instructional decisions on an examination of the student reports for his or her class. For example, if students uniformly display a "typical" pattern, then balanced instruction across the strands might be indicated. Alternatively, if students' uniformly display a similar atypical pattern, then instruction may provide greater emphasis on the strands showing weaker levels of performance. Obviously, the greater the mix of performance patterns (and levels) within the class, the greater the challenge in planning. It follows that the function of identifying extreme low and high student performance (to allow alternate programming) is fulfilled. Also satisfied is the remaining function of the tests, which is to identify class weaknesses and strengths to aid in the assessment of the degree of attainment on the objectives of the school mathematics curriculum.

DEVELOPMENT. As mentioned above, ACER adapted the PATMaths from the New Zealand tests of the same name (8:288) in 1984. Little detail on the nature or extent of the original 1984 modification is provided (see 10:309). There is also little information on the extent of change in the current 1997 revision. It is indicated that the revision was designed to bring the tests in line with extant 1997 curriculum that is based on the National Profiles.

TECHNICAL. Before items were selected for the tests, they were extensively piloted and reviewed for fit to the national mathematics curriculum by ACER staff. Norms are based on a nationally representative sample of 9,623 students. Detailed information of the norming sample is provided in the accompanying norming manual. The norms are not disaggregated by gender or ethnicity. The teacher's manual reports very little difference between males and females by test level or by school year. KR20 reliabilities are in the respectable .90 range for the six tests. Rasch scale score conversions with accompanying standard errors are reported the teacher's manual. The manual also provides an excellent section on the interpretation of the scale scores and error estimates. Raw score to percentile rank and stanine conversions are also provided and explained. The primary concern for validity evidence for these achievement tests is the degree of correspondence of test content to curriculum and instruction. Even though the test developers sought to align the content to the national curriculum, they appropriately guide the teacher to perform his or her own content validity analysis against the local curriculum. Support for a claim of indirect evidence of content validity is provided by mean scores and item difficulties that demonstrate a "regular and marked increase in achievement" (teacher's manual, p. 19) from year to year.

COMMENTARY. The PATMaths series is designed to measure mathematics achievement over a broad range of content for 6 years of school in Australia. The test developers used national curriculum to validate item selection. The degree to which local curriculum matches the national specifications determines the value of the tests to Australian educators. To all appearances the tests are useful for the stated functions. The items are well written and designed to tap knowledge, application, and higher levels of thinking. Given a good fit between local and national curriculum, the student report should prove very useful to the classroom teacher in planning instruction and remediation. However, if hand scoring is necessary, the teacher may find completing the student reports time-consuming.

One potential problem is the multiple-choice format that allows examinees to work backwards (from response) on a few items. Unfortunately, some of these items are the most challenging word problems on the test. Evidence that working backwards may have occurred is observed in noting the lower difficulty level of Item 41 compared to Item 35 for Form 3A. In this reviewer's judgement, Item 41 is conceptually the most challenging item on the test. However, working backward by trying the available answers removes the necessity of constructing the complete solution equation from the information given in the scenario. In comparison, Item 35 is empirically the most difficult item

in the test but involves only addition and division to determine a mean. It might be advisable to change to a supply response format for the few items that allow backward solution.

The norming manual that accompanies the test is detailed, well prepared, and should be easy to use. One suggestion would be to indicate on the norm tables the time of year for which the norms are appropriate. Although it is indicated in the text that the norming sample was tested in October—November, the tables do not include this information.

SUMMARY. The PATMaths Revised appear to be well-developed tests that are appropriate for their intended uses at least to the degree that the local district's mathematics curriculum intersects with the test content. The student report forms are very informative and, in addition to their value to teachers, should be useful for communication to students and parents. The teacher's manual is extremely well prepared and comprehensive in coverage. Due to their Australian curriculum specification, these tests may not export well to other locales. However, those charged with similar test development might wish to use the PATMaths Revised teacher's manual and student report as models to emulate.

Review of Progressive Achievement Tests in Mathematics—Revised by CINDY M. WALKER, Assistant Professor, Department of Educational Psychology—Research & Evaluation, University of Wisconsin—Milwaukee, Milwaukee, WI:

DESCRIPTION. Progressive Achievement Tests in Mathematics—Revised (PATMaths—Revised) are intended to help teachers in Australian schools evaluate the level of mathematics achievement attained by students in Years 3 through 9 in the Australian school system. PATMaths—Revised consists of a package of six paper-and-pencil tests, two parallel tests at three levels of difficulty. Level 1 is the easiest level of the test, whereas Level 3 is the most difficult version of the test. Each test contains between 37 and 41 multiple-choice items with four or five response options per item. Items are arranged on the test in content area groups consisting of number, space, measurement, chance, and data. On the two most difficult parallel tests, the additional content area of algebra is assessed. With the exception of the content strand of number, between 5 and 7 items address each content area on each test. Three times as many items measure the content area of number on each test and students can use calculators on two-thirds of these items.

Teachers can administer, score, and interpret these tests at any time they feel it is appropriate. The tests are to be administered in a standardized manner and can be either hand or machine scored. Raw scores can be converted to scale scores, percentile ranks, and stanine scores. Scale scores are based on the Rasch model. Only overall mathematics achievement, as opposed to strand level of mathematics achievement, is evaluated by the tests. Individual student reports that contain this information can be produced by teachers using duplication masters that are included in the teacher manual. These student reports also include scale descriptors that describe what a student is typically able to do at each of three different points on the scale.

DEVELOPMENT. The PATMaths—Revised tests, a revision of the 1984 versions of the tests, were designed by the measurement division of the Australian Council for Educational Research with the help of school administrators. The tests were revised based on Australia's national profiles that were developed in 1994. However, student performance is only evaluated on the national profile strands of number, space, measurement, chance, and data, with the addition of the national profile strand of algebra on the most difficult level of the test. Furthermore, no statistical evidence (i.e., factor analysis) that items are actually measuring the strands they are purported to be measuring is provided. Changes to the 1984 version of the test were made after a careful review of the items by the test development staff. Items that no longer matched appropriate outcomes in the national profiles were discarded. In addition, some items were modified to more closely reflect the national profiles, and some items were added to ensure that all of the content strands were assessed. This revised set of items was piloted in 10 trial tests with approximately 2,000 students in Victorian schools and then further refined and modified based on information obtained in the pilot study.

TECHNICAL INFORMATION. The six tests in the packet were used in a standardization study between October and November in 1997 to obtain norm referenced scores, specifically percentile ranks and stanines. The norming sample consisted of 100 schools at the primary level and 100 schools at the secondary level in each of the eight states or territories of Australia. These schools were selected using a stratified sampling schema. The number of schools selected was proportional to the number of students in the second to last year of primary school and the first year of secondary school in 1995. Public schools, Catholic schools, and private schools were chosen proportional to the number of students enrolled in each. Modifications to the sample obtained using this schema were made to ensure representation of both metropolitan and rural schools, as well as a range of school sizes. Specific descriptive statistics of the actual norming group used are provided in the norming manual. However, only information regarding the number of students in the norming sample from each state crossed with what type of school they attend (i.e., public, Catholic, or private) is given. Testing was conducted in one class at each year in each of the schools that agreed to participate. The test developers state that "the number of males and females attempting these tests was monitored to ensure that about equal numbers of each were represented in each sector and were attempting each test form" (manual, p. 15). However, no descriptive statistics are provided. Furthermore, no information is provided regarding the ethnic makeup of the norming sample so it is unclear if the published norms are appropriate for all cultural groups.

Only internal reliability estimates are provided for each of the tests and these estimates range from .87 to .92. Other estimates, such as test-retest reliability, are lacking. It is unclear if reliability estimates were obtained from the norming sample, or from another sample. The authors merely state that these estimates come from "students from years 3 to 8 in a variety of schools from the various states and territories" (manual, p. 12).

The validity of the tests is poorly documented. No specific validity studies were conducted for these tests at all. No evidence is provided about differential validity across gender, racial, ethnic, or cultural groups. No evidence about differential item functioning is provided. According to the authors, extensive review and revision by the test developers was done "to ensure that the tests have adequate content validity for the purposes for which they were designed" (manual, p. 14). Furthermore, it is stated that only

scores were determined. Therefore, it is difficult to state the extent to which a student's true score will likely fall within the range represented by the confidence interval.

TECHNICAL INFORMATION. The norm groups for both the Comprehension ($N = 12,597$) and Vocabulary ($N = 6,101$) tests appear to be adequate. Students were drawn from a representative national sample of primary and secondary schools including school districts from seven Australian states and territories (no Northern Territory school took part).

The reliability evidence for scores from the PAT-R appears to be quite adequate. Alpha coefficients range from .88 to .91 across all forms of the Comprehension test and .87 to .90 for the Vocabulary test forms. On the other hand, the information provided in the teacher's manual regarding the validity of the Third Edition of the PAT-R seems to be quite limited. There is a caution given to teachers stating that an important measure of a test's validity is the extent to which it matches the curricular objectives of the classroom. Then a range of criterion-related validity coefficients (.65 to .86) are presented. However, the reference provided for these correlation coefficients leads to a summary of studies completed with the second edition of the PAT-R. As such, the authors provide no information regarding the specific validity of the third edition of the PAT-R.

COMMENTARY AND SUMMARY. Overall, the PAT-R Third Edition appears to be a very useful group-administered test of reading comprehension and vocabulary knowledge. The test is well constructed and the updated materials are reflective of Australian National Standards. Scoring and interpretation of test scores is comparatively simple and straightforward. In addition to the more typical normative comparisons, the PAT-R Measurement Scales provide an opportunity for long-term progress monitoring for individual students. These measurement scales make theoretical and practical sense. However, it will be important to verify their validity through applied research in school settings.

The technical qualities of the PAT-R tests are generally sufficient. For the most part the normative sample appears to be representative and adequate in size. The fact that no schools from the Northern Territory were involved in the standardization of the test may create some difficulty. The

question that needs to be answered is the extent to which this oversight creates a generalization problem when interpreting the norm-referenced scores on the tests (percentile rank and stanine). The standard scores (patc and patv) may be less of a problem as they are not norm-referenced scores but are criterion-referenced scores. Again, some research verifying the generalizability of PAT-R test scores in the Northern Territory would be helpful.

The reliability coefficients reported in the teacher's manual are approximately .90, which suggests that the PAT-R has adequate reliability for making educational decisions about individual students. However, the validity of the PAT-R (Third Edition) is largely unknown. The criterion-related correlation coefficients reported in the manual appear to be from studies completed with the Second Edition of the PAT-R. Therefore, the validity of the PAT-R (Third Edition) is known only to the extent to which we can generalize from the demonstrated validity of the Second Edition. Although this lack of demonstrated validity may not necessarily be a fatal flaw, as there is much overlap between the Second and Third Editions of the PAT-R, it is very important that the validity research with the PAT-R (Third Edition) be completed. The PAT-R is a widely used assessment tool and the teachers who use it should not have to guess its value.

[201]

Psypercept–170.

Purpose: "Designed to measure work-related personality and interest variables among managers."

Population: Managers.

Publication Date: 1996.

Acronym: Psypercept–170.

Scores, 17: Directive, Inclusive, Expressive, Persuasive, Persistent, Accommodating, Calming, Inventive, Discerning, Aspiring, Urgent, Materialistic, Numerical, Altruistic, Technological, Artistic, Procedural.

Administration: Individual or group.

Price Data, 2001: $300 per assessment set including 5 reusable test booklets, 50 answer sheets, 50 data summary sheets, 1 set of hand-scoring keys, and manual (66 pages); $75 per 5 reusable test booklets; $75 per 50 answer sheets; $50 per 50 data summary sheets; $60 per set of hand-scoring keys; $75 per manual.

Time: (35–45) minutes.

Comments: A 170-item self-administered questionnaire; "For use in assessing and developing the talents of executives, managers, and supervisors."

Author: Joseph Hartman.
Publisher: Joseph Hartman Consulting Psychology, Inc.

Review of the Psypercept–170 by PATRICIA A. BACHELOR, Professor of Psychology, California State University, Long Beach, CA:

DESCRIPTION. The Psypercept–170 is a self-report work-related personality and interest inventory designed to assess the talents of managerial personnel. The four management effectiveness domains captured on the Psypercept–170 encompass interpersonal, energy, decision style, and interest variables. Several theoretical models from the industrial/organizational research literature on measuring and cultivating management talent were distilled into the content of the 17 scales on the Psypercept–170. The scales are Directive, Inclusive, Expressive, Persuasive, Persistent, Accommodating, Calming, Inventive, Discerning, Aspiring, Urgent, Materialistic, Numerical, Altruistic, Technological, Artistic, and Procedural. The first 11 scales were designed to tap "personality" domains whereas the remaining 6 scales are considered "interest" domains. Each scale consists of five positively stated items and five negatively stated items using a 5-point item response format. In an additional attempt to reduce response biases, items are randomly arranged except that items on the same scale are not presented sequentially. The Psypercept–170 is a paper-and-pencil instrument that may be administered in a group setting or individually in approximately 35 to 40 minutes. Scoring is done by hand; directions and interpretations are clearly detailed in the test materials accompanying the test.

DEVELOPMENT. The Psypercept–170 was constructed to produce a content valid work-related personality and interest inventory for business professionals. The relevant literature on topics including managerial personality, leadership style, interests, and decision-making style was reviewed and categorized. Two hundred forty-nine managers, executives, supervisors, and other business professionals were surveyed on work-related likes and dislikes, and areas of strengths and weaknesses. In addition, each respondent was interviewed about career-related matters and administered a standardized battery of measures to assess cognitive skills, knowledge of supervisory principles, organizational skills, and work-related interest and personality features. From the pool of 846 items, 10 items for each of the 17 scales on the inventory were selected. The procedure by which items were evaluated for inclusion or deletion was not described.

TECHNICAL. The 249 business professionals who comprised the sample used in the development of the content of the Psypercept–170 had a median age of 39 and median education of 16 years. Ninety-five percent of the respondents were Caucasian, 77% were male, and 86% held management positions. States, as well as the number and type of organizations, were widely represented. The sample used to conduct the analyses of the reliability and the construct validity of the Psypercept–170 was made up of 266 managers who had a median age of 40 and a median of 16 years of education. Eighty-five percent were male, 93% were Caucasian, and 89% held general management positions. Almost 200 organizations were represented across 34 states and Puerto Rico.

The internal consistency reliability of the scales of the Psypercept–170 was assessed by computing Cronbach's alpha using the sample of 266 business persons. The reliability coefficients for the scales ranged from .54 to .90. Eight scales had internal consistency coefficients in the .70s and four scales had coefficients in the .80s. The internal consistency reliabilities for each of the scales were: Directive—.80, Inclusive—.60, Expressive—.78, Persuasive—.66, Persistent—.71, Accommodating—.54, Calming—.69, Inventive—.82, Discerning—.70, Aspiring—.75, Urgent—.71, Materialistic—.74, Numerical—.87, Altruistic—.76, Technological—.90, Artistic—.84, and Procedural—.71. There was no mention of an assessment of the internal consistency of the total score on the Psypercept–170.

Next, in a first step to investigate the construct validity of scores from the Psypercept–170, the author performed item analyses using the data generated from the sample of 266 managers. All item-to-scale correlations were positive and statistically significant. The value of each item-to-scale correlation was artificially inflated as the item score was included in each scale score. (The reader is reminded that each scale consists of only 10 items and the sample size is less than 300.) As a consequence, the aforementioned item analyses can only be taken as support for the homogeneity of the scales' content. Further studies would be needed to support the claim of construct validity.

Factor analysis was performed to detect a factor structure that accounted for a substantial share of variance. Fifty-four percent of the variance was explained with a three-factor, nonorthogonal solution. The first factor (A), with substantial loadings on items from the Accommodating, Inclusiveness, Altruistic, Discerning, Calming, Persistent, and Expression scales, was described as a Humanistic factor. A second factor (B) was portrayed as an Opportunistic factor. It had high loadings on items from the Persuasive, Aspiring, Materialistic, Directive, and Urgent scales. The third factor (C) had high negative loadings with items on the Artistic, Technological, and Procedural scales, and hence, was depicted as an Interest-domain factor. The scales are correlated as are the factors (r_{AB} = -.65, r_{AC} = -.38, and r_{BC} = -.27). Twelve of the 17 scales had intercorrelations exceeding .50. These analyses show modest support for the construct validity of the scales of the Psypercept–170.

Additional correlational analyses were performed to assess associations between management variables (position, level, supervisory knowledge, and team leadership); personality variables; education; income; sales knowledge; cognitive variables (verbal comprehension, verbal and numerical reasoning); and interest variables with the scales of the Psypercept–170. Significant correlations between selected scales on the Psypercept–170 and standardized measures of personality and vocational interest were reported. These findings lend empirical and logical support for the criterion-related (concurrent) validity of these scales. Support for criterion-related (concurrent) validity was also garnered from the relationships detected between scales on the Psypercept–170 and various managerial variables.

COMMENTARY. The Psypercept–170 is well-documented and shows strong evidence for content validity. It was constructed in conformity with standard test development practices. After conducting an extensive review of the research literature and interviews with business professionals, a pool of over 800 items was generated. This pool of items was reduced to 170 items. However, the criteria for item selection and deletion were not described. Clear and comprehensive instructions for test administration, scoring, and score interpretations were also detailed in the test materials.

Ample descriptive information about the business professionals who comprised the norma-tive samples was provided. There was, however, a predominance of Caucasians, men, and college educated managers. Statistically significant differences were found on some of the scales by age, gender, and ethnic group. However, the group sizes were typically very unbalanced; hence, a critical appraisal of these findings is warranted.

Internal consistency reliability assessments were provided for individual scales only. No rationale was given for the omission of an assessment of the internal consistency of the total Psypercept–170. The internal consistency reliability of five scales ranged from .80 to .90. All the other scales had reliability coefficients between .54 and .78. Efforts should be made to modify the items on these scales so that the reliability coefficients attain values in line with current testing practices for interest and personality instruments. Employee assessments, in particular, are expected to have highly dependable scores.

Correlational studies support the claim of criterion-related (concurrent) validity of scores from the Psypercept–170. Factor analysis and item analysis were offered in support of construct validity of the scales. Modest evidence was presented.

SUMMARY. The 17 scales of the Psypercept–170, each of 10 items, assesses work-related personality and interest variables of managers. The content of the scales encompasses business professionals' interpersonal, energy, decision style, and interest variables. The normative samples were described on a variety of relevant demographic and managerial variables. The scales are relatively internally consistent (yet several scales had lower than acceptable internal consistency values) and have generally favorable criterion-related validity. Item analysis revealed that the scales were homogeneous and an oblique three-factor structure was detected in the factor analytic inquiry of the scales. The Psypercept–170 adds to the industrial/organizational assessment literature and promises many valuable applications in the identification and development of managerial talent.

Review of the Psypercept-170 by WILLIAM I. SAUSER, JR., Associate Dean and Professor, Business and Engineering Outreach, Auburn University, Auburn, AL:

DESCRIPTION. Psypercept-170 is a 170-item, self-report instrument "specifically designed to measure work-related personality and interest variables among managers" (manual, p. 1). It can be administered individually or in a small group setting, and is designed for hand scoring. "Psypercept-170 is intended for managers with functional English language skills" (manual, p. 32). The instrument is face-valid and the items are straightforward and easy to understand. Only a few appear "double barreled" or otherwise flawed, and all items were subjected to careful logical and statistical analysis before selection for inclusion. Each item is to be rated by the test taker on a 5-point scale of agreement, ranging from *strongly agree* to *strongly disagree*. The inventory is designed to be completed at a leisurely pace in less than 45 minutes; this reviewer spent about 20 minutes taking the test and another 30 minutes or so scoring it by hand. Note that Psypercept-170 focuses on managerial interests, not abilities.

The author clearly states in the manual that "Psypercept-170 is restricted for usage by professionals who have a doctoral degree in the behavioral sciences, including successful completion of graduate coursework in psychometric principles at an accredited university, and applied experience in the assessment and development of managerial talent, as well as membership in good standing with a professional association" (p. 32). This reviewer applauds the test author's caution in seeing that Psypercept-170 is used only as intended by qualified examiners.

Psypercept-170 was carefully developed by a consulting psychologist over a period of 16 years, and is now available for research use by other professionals. The author notes that "the inventory may be used as part of a multimodal appraisal process in the individualized assessment, description and development of management talent" (manual, p. 32). The author also clearly cautions users of Psypercept-170 that the instrument "is not intended to be used in employment selection systems that apply mechanistic cut-off scores as an effort to predict managerial job performance" (manual, p. 32). Clearly the test author intends for Psypercept-170 to undergo further development and validation studies before it is offered for widespread usage. Again, this reviewer commends the author for appropriate caution.

The test manual is thorough and comprehensive. It describes the theoretical framework for the instrument, presents in detail the steps employed to develop and analyze the items, and includes information on test reliability, construct validity, norms, appropriate cautions for usage, instructions for administration and scoring, detailed appendices, and a helpful listing of references. The test author seeks to disclose both strengths and weaknesses of the instrument, and invites users of Psypercept-170 to share results of further research with the instrument for inclusion in future editions of the test manual.

DEVELOPMENT. Over a period of 4 years, in the course of his consulting practice, the test author collected from 249 executives, managers, supervisors, and other business professionals "self-described work-related strengths and areas for improvement, as well as ... likes and dislikes ... for employment, promotional, or career planning purposes" (manual, p. 4). These responses were reviewed, classified, and developed into items intended to measure 17 "interest or orientation dimensions" (manual, p. 5). A thorough career-oriented interview, bolstered by data from a number of standardized instruments, was also conducted by the test author for each of the 249 test takers during the development phase of the project. The author also conducted a review of leadership literature to guide the conceptualization process. "From a pool of eight hundred and forty-six (846) items created by the author for the Psypercept-170, ten (10) items were selected to comprise each scale of the inventory" (manual, p. 6). These items (five positive, five negative per scale) were arranged "on a modified random basis" (manual, p. 7) in the test booklet, which was then subjected to a series of normative, reliability, and validation studies described in detail in the manual.

TECHNICAL. Psypercept-170, although carefully developed and researched, clearly needs more work before it can be pronounced psychometrically sound. Based on a study of 266 additional managers evaluated by the test author, Cronbach's alpha reliability scores for the 17 scales ranged from .54 to .90, with a median reliability of .74. Furthermore, the scale scores were clearly intercorrelated, with 12 scale intercorrelations exceeding .50. An exploratory factor analysis of the 17 intended dimensions yielded three interpretable factors—termed Humanistic, Opportunistic, and Interest—which accounted for 54% of the total variance. Furthermore, these three factors were also found to be intercorrelated. The test author claims, "In general, the factor analysis results were supportive of the inventory's internal construct validity and congruent with its conceptual framework" (manual, p. 14). This reviewer does not agree. It appears to me that the actual constructs being measured by Psypercept-170 in its present form are not clearly identified. Users should interpret the scale scores with caution.

An impressive array of validation studies is presented in the manual, but again this reviewer did not find evidence of construct validity strong enough to warrant use of Psypercept-170 in its present form for any purpose other than research. The instrument shows promise, but needs more work. One glaring weakness of the validation studies presented in the manual is that they all appear to be based on "samples of convenience" rather than samples representative of a broad base of business managers. The test author notes responsibly that validation data were collected during the course of his consultation work and are not representative of the general populace. It is apparent from the data presented in the manual that women and minorities are underrepresented in the normative and validation studies. Clearly this limits the external validity of the instrument and the usefulness of the interpretive data presented in the manual.

COMMENTARY. The test author is to be commended for a "textbook example" of thorough literature review, scale conceptualization, and item construction and analysis procedures. The author presents validation and normative studies in a straightforward, scientific manner, and does not gloss over the weaknesses of the instrument. Instead, the author invites other responsible behavioral scientists to conduct further research with Psypercept-170 and to share results with himself and other members of the scientific and professional community.

The instrument does show promise for interpretive use, but at present the cautions supplied by the test author appear warranted. Psypercept-170 is not yet ready for use in commercial applications, but may prove to be an intriguing instrument for further research. Can the scales be reworked such that their internal-consistency reliability is improved? Similarly, can the factor structure of the instrument be refined and purified? Will other practitioners find Psypercept-170 useful in their consulting practices? Does the instrument yield useful information beyond that gleaned through such better known instruments as the Gordon Personal Profile-Inventory (T6:1059), the Myers-Briggs Type Indicator (T6:1678), the Self-Directed Search (T6:2238), the Sixteen Personality Factor Questionnaire (T6:2292), or the Strong Interest Inventory (248)? Should Psypercept-170 be included within assessment batteries for certain uses? Is it predictive of managerial choices and behaviors in the broader population? Is Psypercept-170 easily "faked" by test-takers seeking to present themselves in a favorable light? All of these questions are ripe for future research.

SUMMARY. Through the use of data collected during the course of his consulting practice over a number of years, the test author, using sound test-development procedures, has created a self-report instrument intended to measure 17 dimensions of work-related managerial interests and personality characteristics. The instrument is face valid, easy to administer and score, and may prove useful for assessing, coaching, and developing managerial talent. Normative, reliability, and validation research performed to date using Psypercept-170 indicates that it is not yet sound enough psychometrically to be used commercially. The instrument shows potential and is being made available by the test author for responsible use by qualified professionals in the behavioral sciences. Whether it will contribute valuable information beyond that routinely collected through the use of standard individual assessment batteries is an empirical question suitable for further research. The test author is commended for making this instrument available for use by others, and for cautioning potential users regarding its current limitations.

[202]

Reading and Arithmetic Indexes.

Population: Age 14–adult applicants for entry level jobs and special training programs.
Publication Date: 1968–1996.
Administration: Group.
Forms, 2: Reading Index, Arithmetic Index.
Price Data, 1998: $53 per 25 tests (specify Arithmetic Index or Reading Index); $19.75 per examiner's manual.
Comments: Self-scoring booklets.
Author: Science Research Associates.
Publisher: Reid London House.
   a) READING–ARITHMETIC INDEX.
   Purpose: "Measures level of development in reading and math."

Acronym: RAI.

Scores, 11: Reading Index (Picture-Word Association, Word Decoding, Comprehension of Phrases, Comprehension of Sentences, Comprehension of Paragraphs, Total), Arithmetic Index (Addition and Subtraction of Whole Numbers, Multiplication and Division of Whole Numbers, Basic Operations Involving Fractions, Basic Operations Involving Decimals and Percentages, Total).

Time: (25) minutes per Index.

b) READING AND ARITHMETIC INDEXES (12).

Purpose: "Assesses proficiency levels in reading and math."

Acronym: RAI-12.

Scores, 14: Reading Index (Picture-Word Association, Word Decoding, Comprehension of Phrases, Comprehension of Sentences, Comprehension of Paragraphs I, Comprehension of Paragraphs II, Total), Arithmetic Index (Addition and Subtraction of Whole Numbers, Multiplication and Division of Whole Numbers, Basic Operations Involving Fractions, Basic Operations Involving Decimals and Percentages, Basic Operations Involving Square Roots and Powers, Basic Operations Involving Geometry and Word Problems, Total).

Time: (35) minutes per Index.

Cross References: For a review by Dorothy C. Adkins of an earlier edition, see 7:20. See T4:2538 (1 reference) and 8:813 (3 references) for information regarding the Reading Index. See T5:171 (2 references) and 8:307 (3 references) for information regarding the Arithmetic Index.

Review of the Reading and Arithmetic Indexes by D. JOE OLMI, Associate Professor and Clinic Director, School Psychology Program, Department of Psychology, The University of Southern Mississippi, Hattiesburg, MS:

DESCRIPTION. Designed to be used as selection procedures for entry-level jobs or training programs for individuals over 14 years of age who possess suspect basic skills, the SRA Reading and Arithmetic Indexes (RAI) are "tests of general reading and computational achievement" (manual, p. 1) that assess functioning through Grade 9. The SRA Reading and Arithmetic Indexes (12) (RAI-12) are designed to assess functioning through Grade 12. The Reading Index of the RAI contains 60 items within five levels or subtests: Picture-Word Association, Word Decoding, Comprehension of Phrases, Comprehension of Sentences, and Comprehen-

sion of Paragraphs. The Reading Index of the RAI-12 is composed of the same first four subtests with the addition of Comprehension of Paragraphs I and II, for a total of six subtests and 72 items. The Arithmetic Index of the RAI is composed of Addition and Subtraction of Whole Numbers, Multiplication and Division of Whole Numbers, Basic Operations Involving Fractions, and Basic Operations Involving Decimals and Percentages (54 items). The Arithmetic Index of the RAI-12, which contains 70 items, possesses two additional subtests: Basic Operations Involving Square Roots and Powers and Basic Operations Involving Geometry and Word Problems, for a total of six. Proficiency scores are noted for each level of the RAI and RAI-12. The RAI and RAI-12 are competency-based power tests that appear to be designed to simply assess the upper limits of functioning within all mentioned areas or levels. Each index of each test is contained in a self-scoring booklet with easy-to-read instructions and a simple multiple-choice response format.

DEVELOPMENT. The RAI and RAI-12 were developed to address shortcomings of standardized academic assessment strategies where job placement and training were concerned, namely that the content of most standardized tests fails to take into account job requirements and the tendency to eliminate qualified applicants from consideration who might function adequately within a job role. The RAI and RAI-12 are designed to appropriately assess functioning levels in reading and math for job placement purposes and to design teaching sessions based on assessed levels of functioning. Very sketchy item development information was provided in the brief information guides of both the RAI and the RAI-12. Science Research Associates (the authors) would have been well advised to provide more detailed information pertaining to item development and selection.

TECHNICAL. In determining psychometric properties for the RAI Reading Index, "87 males and females enrolled in a combination program of on-the-job training and basic education in Chicago" (manual, p. 3) ranging from 17 to 30 years of age were administered the final form of the test. Split-half reliability was .87. The final form of the Arithmetic Index was administered to 57 job training students from Chicago and 419 students in special education programs in Colorado and South Carolina. Split-half reliability for the Chicago sample

Comments: Revision of Reading-Free Vocational Interest Inventory; earlier edition listed as AAMD-Becker Reading-Free Vocational Interest Inventory; self-administered; hand-scorable only.
Author: Ralph L. Becker.
Publisher: Elbern Publications.
Cross References: For information on an earlier edition, see T4:2177; for a review by Robert J. Miller of an earlier edition, see 11:327; see also T3:1996 (2 references); for reviews by Esther E. Diamond and George Domino of an earlier edition, see 8:988 (6 references).

Review of the Reading-Free Vocational Interest Inventory: 2 by ZANDRA S. GRATZ, Associate Professor of Psychology, Kean University, Union, NJ:
DESCRIPTION. The Reading-Free Vocational Interest Inventory: 2 (R-FVII:2) was designed to measure interest patterns among special needs populations, including those diagnosed with mental retardation or a learning disability, and the disadvantaged. The R-FVII:2 generates 11 interest area scores. Five cluster scores are generated by combining 2 or more interest area scores. A key feature of the R-FVII:2 is that no reading ability is required of the respondent. Despite this, as cautioned in the manual, the potential user of the R-FVII:2 must ensure that the examinee is able to comprehend and interpret the pictures presented. It is considered suitable for persons age 12 to 61. Although there is no time limit, it can be administered individually or in a group setting within a 45-minute class period.

The test booklet presents 55 triads of line-drawn pictures of individuals in job-relevant activities. A forced-choice format requires respondents to circle the picture they like the best. Scoring requires the examiner to transfer respondents' selections to an answer sheet. The layout of the answer sheet facilitates the summing of scores to generate each interest area and cluster score. R-FVII:2 interest area raw scores can be transformed into *T*-scores, percentiles, and descriptive ratings that range from Below Average to Above Average.

Record and profile forms are provided on which to record scores and to support score interpretation. The manual provides extensive information on the standard errors of measurement (*SEM*s) for each interest area score and subpopulation. Also presented in the manual are completed forms and interpretations for four sample clients. The R-FVII:2 companion piece, *The Occupational Title Lists, 2nd ed.* (Becker, 2001), provides a description of each interest area assessed by the R-FVII:2 and over 50 jobs falling within each interest area. Although scoring may be completed by a trained clerk or paraprofessional, interpretation of scores should be done by someone with expertise in guidance or vocational counseling.

DEVELOPMENT. The R-FVII:2 began as a Project on Vocational interest at The Columbus State School and published by the American Association on Mental Deficiency. When published in 1975, separate test booklets were used for males and females. The 1981 revision used one booklet for both genders; effort was made to balance gender across job tasks and vocational interest areas. The most current revision was directed at updating pictures, adding contemporary tasks, and expanding normative data.

TECHNICAL. Over 15,000 examinees participated in the normative sample. Norms are stratified by gender, age (12 to 15, and 16 and over) and classification (mental retardation, learning disabled, regular classroom, adult disadvantaged, and adult sheltered work). The number of examinees in each sample ranged from 765 to 1,140. Although for most categories the sample appears sufficient, some concern is noted for data concerning adult disadvantaged. All adult disadvantaged individuals were from one geographic area (distressed Appalachian counties) and the extent to which the data are applicable to adult disadvantaged of other regions, such as inner cities, is questionable.

Internal consistency reliability estimates are presented for a sample of over 1,600 individuals diagnosed as mentally retarded. The sample, stratified by age and gender, yielded KR_{20} estimates ranging from .72 to .95. Most scales sported reliability estimates of .8 or higher, the exception to this was in Materials Handling for which estimates ranged between .72 and .78. In that the KR_{20} estimates were generated from normative sample data, the lack of KR_{20} coefficients for other subgroups (e.g., learning disabled) is a curiosity.

Test-retest estimates with a 2-week interval were obtained from a subsample of the original standardization sample. Samples stratified by gender, age, and classification were included in the test-retest studies and ranged in size from 41 to 76 individuals. For most samples and scales, test-retest reliability estimates were .8 or higher. The exception to this was Material Handling for which test-retest reliability estimates were between .70 and .84. It is interesting to note that for males, across all samples, test-retest reliability estimates for Automotive and Building Trades were .90 or higher whereas for females, test-retest reliability estimates for these scales ranged between .72 and .86. thus, for traditionally male occupations, female test takers demonstrated less consistency over time than males.

Content validity was first examined rationally and then revised in concert with empirical data. The articulation of jobs and interests for the 1975 edition was based on a guide for jobs for persons with mental retardation (Peterson & Jones, 1964). The manual describes revisions in content for the 1981 version to include jobs appropriate for learning disabled students and for adults in sheltered workshops. Item analysis using the extreme groups method indicated sufficient discrimination of items relative to each interest scale. Extreme groups data were also used to identify items that loaded on more than one scale.

Concurrent criterion-related validity evidence included correlations with the Geist Picture Interest Inventory (Geist, 1988). Stratified by age, gender, and classification, correlations ranged from .07 to .79. With the exception of the Materials handling scale, most correlations were statistically significant. In generating these data, the manner in which scales on the Geist were matched to those of the R-FVII:2 is not clear. Beyond this, the manual's explanation for differences in the magnitude of the correlations across scales, as being the result of group differences, is not persuasive.

Also presented in the manual are the R-FVII:2 scale scores of employed persons with mental retardation. Graphs presented confirm that the mean interest scale standard score was highest for the interest area in which the person worked. However, for a number of occupations several interest area scores appear very close to that of the occupation of the individuals. Neither descriptive nor inferential data are presented to allow for further examination of the distance between interest area scores within each occupation. No criterion-related validity evidence was presented in the manual.

COMMENTARY. The manual reports to "furnish information for individuals engaged in a wide range of occupations and job tasks at the range of occupations and job tasks at the unskilled, semiskilled, and skill levels" (p. 3). The manual

does not present detailed content validity data to assess the extent to which a systematic review of jobs likely to be available to the target population was completed. The extent to which jobs depicted in the R-FVII:2 depict unskilled, and skilled occupations is questionable. Beyond this, the original basis for the development of the R-FVII:2 scales is dated (Peterson & Jones, 1964). For this reason, jobs described within the manual and depicted within the inventory may not do justice to jobs in such areas as information technology that may be suitable for the target populations. This limitation puts more onus on the counselor interpreting the scores to recognize clients whose interests may be in such fields as technology.

Although the psychometric qualities of the R-FVII:2 are substantial, some concerns exist. In particular, relatively low levels of reliability and validity for the Materials Handling interest scale place into question interpretation of this scale to guide vocational choice. In addition, as is typical of many interest inventories, gender differences in scale properties appear to exist and should be examined further. Also, although the manual depicts how to compute cluster scores and the resultant definitions, it does not detail how or why one would use them.

Given that the purpose of an interest inventory is to help in vocational planning, predictive criterion-related validity evidence is important. It is, therefore, a concern that the R-FVII:2 does not provide evidence of predictive validity.

SUMMARY. The R-FVII:2 has a long history of providing data to support its use as a measure of interest for individuals who have limited reading ability. A vocational counselor, knowledgeable in the range of jobs available for persons with disabilities, is likely to find the R-FVII:2 a useful addition to their assessment paradigm.

REVIEWER'S REFERENCES

Becker, R. L. (2001). *Reading-Free Vocational Interest Inventory: 2 occupational title lists* (2nd ed.). Columbus, OH: Elbern Publications.
Geist, H. (1988). Geist Picture Interest Inventory. Los Angeles: Western Psychological Service.
Peterson, R. O., & Jones, E. M. (1964). *Guide to jobs for the mentally retarded.* Pittsburgh: American Institute for Research.

Review of the Reading-Free Vocational Interest Inventory: 2 by MARK POPE, Associate Professor, Division of Counseling & Family Therapy, College of Education, University of Missouri—St. Louis, St. Louis, MO:

DESCRIPTION AND DEVELOPMENT. The Reading-Free Vocational Interest Inventory: 2 (R-FVII:2) is the second edition of a 55-item, nonreading, vocational interest inventory for use with individuals with mental retardation or learning disabilities as well as with individuals who are socioeconomically disadvantaged or who are regular classroom students. The purpose of the instrument is to measure the vocational interests of the special needs student/adult as well as regular classroom students. The nonreading feature of this inventory requires no verbal symbols nor written statements that require interpretation by the examinee. It is important to note here that the 165 line drawings used by the test author do require interpretation by the individual along with written instructions.

The R-FVII:2 is the culmination of work that began in 1967 at the Columbus State School for the Mentally Retarded in Columbus, Ohio, USA. The R-FVII:2 was thoroughly revised under a grant from the U.S. Bureau of Education for Handicapped Children and published in 1975 by the American Association on Mental Deficiency (now the American Association on Mental Retardation). Under pressure from passage of Title IX of the Education Amendment of 1972, which prohibited gender discrimination in education, the R-FVII:2 was further revised in 1981 by collapsing the separate male and female inventory booklets into a single, common booklet, combining separate male and female profile reporting forms into a single profile form for both genders, and revising the item drawings by balancing males and females doing job tasks in all vocational areas. The 2000 revision included a modernizing edit for outmoded content of pictorial artwork and to add contemporary occupational tasks in the inventory booklet. Further, the technical manual's content was given a new format and relevant tables and figures were moved from appendices in the rear of the manual, to be closer to the text that references the table or figure.

The new R-FVII:2 manual has been largely rewritten and the inventory has been renormed using 15,564 individuals of whom 6,505 were persons with mental retardation in 26 states and Puerto Rico. These individuals were attending school, in programs of vocational training, employed in the community in competitive work, or engaged in sheltered work. It would seem that the R-FVII:2 author has made a good faith effort to address issues raised by previous reviewers (Cantwell, 1994; Domino, 1988).

The R-FVII:2 inventory booklet is composed of 55 items, each consisting of three pictures in a row of people working at different jobs. Individuals who are taking the inventory are instructed (using printed words) to make a large circle on the picture they liked best of the three presented for each item. They are further instructed that they may only choose one picture in each triad group. The booklet itself is composed of regular white paper, printed on both sides of the page in landscape mode, and bound with two staples in the fold. Picture panels are black and white line drawings of males (short hair) and females (long hair) doing job tasks such as a hospital orderly helping a person who walks with a cane, a farm worker picking fruit from a tree, a gas station attendant checking the oil, a plumber using a pipe wrench, a gardener planting trees, a nurse shaving a patient, and many others.

The 55 pictorial items are followed by four pages that aid in the scoring and reporting of the responses for the individual. The first page of the four is the answer sheet that is perforated at the binding to allow for removal that is recommended in the technical manual. This page is to be completed by the person scoring the inventory, NOT the test taker. The second page (printed on the back of the first page) is titled "Record of Interest and Cluster Scores" and contains spaces for demographics (name, birth date, age [years/months], gender, location, and norms used). It also allows the scorer to record the raw scores, T scores, percentile scores, and verbal rating for each of the 11 interest areas along with a computation grid to calculate the five cluster scores. The third page is also perforated and titled "Cluster Scores" allowing spaces for the entry of the raw scores, cluster quotient, percentile scores, and verbal rating of each of the five occupational clusters on this inventory along with a large blank area titled "Interpretation/Recommendation" which allows for notes by the clinician. The fourth page is the manual profile report form with space for reporting the T scores for each of the 11 interest areas and the cluster quotient for each of the five clusters.

Scoring is completed by a psychometrician or the inventory administrator who removes the last four pages of the inventory booklet and completes the information on each page including the response sheet; the calculation of raw, T, and percentile scores; and the profile report form. For each of the 11 interest areas (Automotive, Building Trades, Clerical, Animal Care, Food Service, Patient Care, Horticulture, Housekeeping, Personal Service, Laundry Service, or Materials Handling), a frequency count for raw scores for "like" responses is made and then converted to a standard T-score, a percentile score, and a verbal rating. For each of the five cluster areas (Mechanical, Outdoor, Mechanical/Outdoor, Food Service/ Handling Operations, and Clerical/Social Service), raw scores, T-scores, percentile scores, and verbal ratings are also calculated.

TECHNICAL. The R-FVII:2 technical manual is substantially better than previous editions (Thomas, 2001) and is filled with examples, cases, and figures of completed report forms as well as substantial normative data to aid in proper interpretation of the data. There are separate normative tables for females and males, for youth and adults in five categories (mental retardation, learning disability, regular classroom, adult disadvantaged, and adult sheltered work) for all 11 interest areas and five clusters, ranging in sample size from 765 to 1,140.

Kuder-Richardson 20 (internal consistency reliability) scores are reported for interest areas and clusters for younger and older males and females who are mentally retarded and range from .72 to .95 for interest area scores and from .80 to .95 for cluster scores with most of the scores falling into the .80s and .90s. The manual also contains a quite substantial discussion of standard error of measurement and estimate versus true score. This is clear and interesting for users of this inventory.

Test-retest reliability scores range from .72 to .97 for a 2-week interval with relatively small sample sizes ranging from 41 to 76 individuals for the five normative categories. Interest scores are aspects of personality and generally are more stable, especially in post adolescent samples, and these data also substantiate that pattern, even in samples diagnosed as having learning disabilities or mental retardation. Further, cluster score reliabilities were higher than interest areas but that is to be expected as the clusters are combinations of the 11 interest areas; therefore, all cluster scales were substantially longer than interest area scales and the increase in reliability scores may simply be a function of test length.

The technical manual also reports data on three types of validity: content validity, criterion-related validity, and construct validity. Each of these types of validity is explained in the manual and then the properties of each are discussed. For content validity, the author first offers a description of the method for selecting items, which is similar to the method associated with that for developing rationally derived instruments. This is not a strong argument for content validity, but more for "face" validity. No data are offered to substantiate this type of validity. The second method was performing an item analysis using extreme groups to see if each item differentiated between the identified extreme groups. This method is rarely used to present content validity data, which is generally not as important for standardized personality inventories such as career interest inventories.

Criterion-related validity was addressed by comparing responses on the R-FVII:2 to the Geist Picture Interest Inventory and reported as Pearson product-moment correlation coefficients. Statistically significant relationships were reported based on gender and four normative samples for nearly all categories, which provided evidence of criterion-related validity.

Construct validity was examined by presenting data indicating that (a) items and subtest scores correlated highly; (b) incumbent workers engaged in an occupation represented on the R-FVII:2 scored higher on the specific scale that defines their occupation; and (c) scales with similar characteristics but different titles and item content showed large, positive correlations; however, negligible to negative intercorrelations were obtained for scales with dissimilar characteristics. There appears to be substantial evidence supporting the validity of scores from the instrument.

COMMENTARY. The R-FVII:2 has a long and substantial history of measuring the career interest patterns of special needs populations. The current revision includes modifications to the pictures used as items in the inventory booklet and extensive updates to the normative data. Although the technical manual has been improved substantially, the pictures used in the inventory booklet still are not as effective as they might be.

Some of the line drawings used in the inventory booklet continue to be confusing and ambiguous. For example, there is a person who is supposedly making copies at a line drawing that looks like a big box, not at all like a copier. Twenty-four (15.5%) of the line drawings were substantially ambiguous enough to require this reviewer to stop and attempt to determine what the person in the line drawing was actually doing as it was not inherently obvious. Further, very few of the line drawings depict the use of technology (according to Thomas, 2001, only 3 do so), although most workers these days have to interact with technology in some way in the course of their regular work day.

Although the 1981 version of this instrument supposedly updated the R-FVII regarding gender differences, there remains a bias. Of the pictorial triads presented in the inventory booklet, 28 (50.1%) were all male in their depiction of workers, 18 (32.7%) were all female, and 9 (16.4%) were composed of two females and one male. None of the depictions were composed of two males and one female doing their work. Further, when the pictorial triads were analyzed for depicting traditional sex role stereotypes (males doing male work, females doing female work), 15 (27.3%) of the pictorial triads were all gender traditional in their depictions, 24 (43.6%) contained two line drawings that were gender traditional, and 16 (29.0%) contained one line drawing that was gender traditional. None of the triads were composed of all nontraditional gender depictions. Finally, all of the line drawings are narrow culturally and there is no attempt at providing any nondominant cultural depiction in any of the pictures. The effect of these issues on the minority culture client who has been diagnosed with mental retardation or learning disability or is disadvantaged is unknown; however, this certainly does provide fertile ground for researchers. Test developers must be sensitive to these issues as they design their instruments. It is important to at least ask the question somewhere in the technical manual even if there is no satisfactory response.

Further, Miller (1992) identified a continuing issue for the R-FVII:2: "Far too many of the activities pictured are low functioning jobs that seem quite limited and stereotypical of the kinds of activities perceived to be appropriate for special needs populations" (p. 752). Becker (the test author), however, states that one must present the item prompts so as to be understood by the test taker, and responded to this issue in a section in the technical manual titled "Testability of the Subject," as he states "although the handicap of limited reading skills is removed in the R-FVII:2 through the presentation of pictures replacing words, there still remains the question of an examinee's comprehension of what the picture is depicting" (p. 5). The higher the complexity of the activity, the more difficult it is to depict it pictorially so that it can be understood easily by the person who is taking the inventory and for whom this inventory was developed. It is important, however, that individuals who are socioeconomically disadvantaged be exposed especially to a wide variety of occupations at all skill levels, as the nature of their problem lies in the too early narrowing of occupational interests. This is not the same problem for those with mental retardation or learning disabilities.

SUMMARY. The R-FVII:2 is an important tool in the collection of the career counselor and rehabilitation counselor. The picture format is a useful way of presenting the information to students and adults who are mentally retarded, learning disabled, or socioeconomically disadvantaged. The instrument may not be perfect, but it may be effective if used carefully.

REVIEWER'S REFERENCES

Cantwell, Z. C. (1994). Reading-Free Vocational Interest Inventory. In J. T. Kapes, M. M. Mastie, & E. A. Whitfield (Eds.), *A counselor's guide to career assessment instruments* (3rd ed.) (pp. 325–330). Alexandria, VA: National Career Development Association.
Domino, G. (1988). Reading-Free Vocational Interest Inventory. In J. T. Kapes & M. M. Mastie (Eds.), *A counselor's guide to career assessment instruments* (2nd ed.) (pp. 270–274). Alexandria, VA: National Career Development Association.
Miller, R. J. (1992). [Review of the Reading-Free Vocational Interest Inventory—Revised.] In J. J. Kramer & J. C. Conoley (Eds.), *The eleventh mental measurements yearbook* (pp. 752–753). Lincoln, NE: Buros Institute of Mental Measurements.
Thomas, S. W. (2001). Reading-Free Vocational Interest Inventory (2nd ed.). In J. T. Kapes & E. A. Whitfield (Eds.), *A counselor's guide to career assessment instruments* (4th ed.) (pp. 412–417). Tulsa, OK: National Career Development Association.

[204]
Reading-Level Indicator.

Purpose: Designed "to identify individual reading at a second-to-sixth-grade level and functional nonreaders."
Population: Upper elementary to college students.
Publication Date: 2000.
Scores, 5: Sentence Comprehension Score, Vocabulary Score, Total Raw Score, Instructional Reading Level, Independent Reading Level.
Administration: Group or individual.
Forms, 2: Blue Form, Purple Form.
Price Data: Available from publisher.
Time: (4–20) minutes.
Author: Kathleen T. Williams.
Publisher: American Guidance Service, Inc.

Review of the Reading-Level Indicator by
ELIZABETH KELLEY BOYLES, Assistant Pro-

fessor of School Psychology, Marshall University Graduate College, South Charleston, WV:

DESCRIPTION. The Reading-Level Indicator is a brief (40-item) paper-and-pencil group screening measure designed to identify individuals experiencing significant reading difficulties. There are two parallel forms of the test, the Blue Form and the Purple Form. Each form contains 20 items designed to assess Sentence Comprehension and 20 items targeting Vocabulary. Sentence Comprehension items consist of a brief sentence with one missing word. The examinee must select the most appropriate word to complete the sentence from a list of four or five alternatives. Vocabulary items consist of a brief sentence with one highlighted word. The examinee must select the word (or group of words) that has the same meaning as the highlighted word from a list of four or five options. The measure yields two grade-equivalent scores, one for the Instructional Reading Level and one for the Independent Reading Level.

The test can be administered by paraprofessionals but it is recommended that it be interpreted by individuals at the classroom teacher level or above. To score the test, the examiner consults the listing of correct answers provided in the manual for the appropriate test form and then adds up the number of correct responses for both the Sentence Comprehension and Vocabulary sections. The raw scores for the two sections are added together and then the summary raw score is compared to the manual's Reading Levels table. This table provides the Instructional Reading Level and its equivalent Independent Reading Level for each potential raw score value. The resulting reading levels may be used to gauge the test taker's ability to make use of grade level instructional materials.

DEVELOPMENT. The Reading-Level Indicator was developed as a screening measure alongside the development of its "parent" test, the more comprehensive Group Reading and Diagnostic Evaluation (GRADE) (manual, p. iv). According to the test manual, Sentence Comprehension items were written for a variety of grade levels with grade level being determined by the reading level of the highlighted word and the most difficult word in the sentence. Items were varied by the complexity of the sentence and the part of speech of the target word. Vocabulary items were reportedly written to cover words from the first grade to college level. After a

pool of items was written in 1998, the items were submitted to nationwide testing in 1999 with selected items then being used to construct both forms of the Reading-Level Indicator and the GRADE. Statistical analysis of items was conducted to determine poorly discriminating items and those that were "not consistent with others in a particular subtest" (manual, p. 18). Items were analyzed quantitatively for gender and racial bias by examining individual items statistically to determine if they were significantly more difficult for either males or females or whites, or for African American or Hispanic populations. In addition, a panel of consultants reviewed the items to assess their fairness and inclusiveness. Items that were judged as quantitatively or qualitatively biased were deleted from the item pool.

TECHNICAL. The standardization of the Reading-Level Indicator appears to have been a byproduct of the 1999 standardization of the GRADE. A pool of items was administered to 17,727 individuals aged 5 to 21 in Grades 1 through 12 to try out items for the Sentence Comprehension and Vocabulary subtests of the GRADE. Later items for the Reading-Level Indicator were drawn from this same pool of items. The standardization testing was conducted in the classroom setting by "a teacher or administrator familiar to the students" (manual, p. 18). The sample consisted of 32% African Americans, 30% Hispanics, 34% Whites, and 4% Other. Grade equivalents were determined by calculating the median ability level for all items and using this to determine the grade equivalents for the raw scores.

Reliability for the Reading-Level Indicator was estimated using coefficient alpha, split-half, and alternate form methods. In all cases reliability was highest for the youngest examinees, decreasing slowly over the grades. Both forms had an alpha coefficient ranging from .93 for 1st graders to .82 for 12th graders. Corrected split-half reliabilities were similar to the coefficient alpha values. Alternate form reliabilities were .94 for the youngest children and .81 for the oldest.

Validity information on the Reading-Level Indicator is sorely lacking. The manual provides the test's item development and selection criteria as evidence of construct validity. There is no information on the Reading-Level Indicator's criterion or predictive validity. The manual provides no evidence that the scores obtained on the measure correlate with any other measures of reading level performance. The manual itself states that although the test can identify nonreaders, it is really most effective at reading levels from the second to sixth grade, lacking sufficient discrimination above the seventh grade level.

COMMENTARY. The Reading-Level Indicator is a screening measure that appears to have been a byproduct of the development of the more comprehensive Group Reading and Diagnostic Evaluation (GRADE). Although item selection appears strong, the standardization sample large, and the reliability adequate, the absence of any data on criterion or predictive validity is a crucial omission. The examiner has no evidence to determine if the Reading-Level Indicator is of any utility in determining a student's actual reading levels or for making data-based decisions about student instructional modifications. The test is of limited utility in determining reading levels outside of the narrow second- to sixth-grade band of performance.

SUMMARY. The Reading-Level indicator is a group-administered screening measure of reading level that was developed in conjunction with the GRADE. Item selection appears strong and the test developer's efforts to avoid gender and racial bias are commendable. However, the manual's lack of information on validity and the measure's limited range of discriminative ability limit the utility of the instrument.

Review of the Reading-Level Indicator by ROBERT E. WALL, *Graduate Professor, Department of Reading, Special Education and Instructional Technology, Towson University, Towson, MD:*

DESCRIPTION. The Reading-Level Indicator is an untimed group-administered norm-referenced reading screener with two parallel forms. Each form of the Reading-Level Indicator contains 40 items presented as multiple-choice questions. The first 20 questions are Sentence Comprehension items and the second 20 questions are Vocabulary items. For Sentence Comprehension, the student reads a sentence with a missing word, and then chooses the best word to complete the sentence. For the Vocabulary test, the student chooses the word that means the same as the target word printed in either purple or blue.

The author is targeting students who are at middle school, high school, or junior college levels, but reading below the seventh grade level.

According to the author, testing time was found to range from 3 minutes and 20 seconds to 14 minutes and 15 seconds for a small study of 42 students in Grades 4 through 12.

DEVELOPMENT. The Reading-Level Indicator items came from the pool of items developed for the Sentence Comprehension and Vocabulary subtests of the Group Reading and Diagnostic Evaluation test (GRADE). The items were tested with a National pool of approximately 18,000 students from 83 sites in 27 states. The pool of participants ranged from 1st graders to 12th graders with approximately 2,000 students in each of the Grades 1 through 6 and then about 900 in each of the Grades 7 through 12. The sampling was structured to achieve an ethnically diverse sample with approximately 32% of the sample African Americans, 30% Hispanics, and 34% Whites. American Indians, Aleut Eskimos, Asians, Pacific Islanders, and other groups made up the final 4% of the sample. There is approximately a 50% split between males and females in the overall sample. Sampling was done by classroom precluding specific controls for gender.

In terms of the sampling, it would have made a stronger case for the representativeness of the samples if in addition to listing the states in which the testing was done, there was some information concerning what percent of the schools involved were urban, rural, or suburban. It is impossible to tell from the information provided whether any of these categories were over- or under-represented.

TECHNICAL. The normative information is based on approximately 18,000 students from 83 sites in 27 states. The criteria for site selection is somewhat vague. There is no information provided concerning the distribution of urban, suburban and rural settings. The final test items were chosen on the basis of content and difficulty level after screening for bias or offensive content. The Rasch model was used to determine statistically if items were more difficult for one ethnic or gender group than another. The test items chosen were assigned to one of the two equivalent forms (Blue or Purple). They were chosen and distributed between the two forms on the basis of item difficulty and content areas. Based on the evidence in the norming tables, the two forms appear to be equivalent.

The analysis for reliability and validity is particularly strong in terms of reliability analyses.

Alpha, split-half, and alternate form reliabilities were computed by grade levels. Calculated reliabilities ranged from .69 to .94 with a median value .90.

The validity information for the test is not as strong. Essentially, the validity evidence cited focuses only on content validity. The authors claim the kind of skills measured are essential parts of reading ability. The authors claim construct validity evidence is provided by their fairly elaborate criteria for selecting and writing the two item types for the Reading-Level Indicator. There is no evidence that performance on this scale correlates with other tests of reading level. No concurrent validity data were provided.

COMMENTARY. In the layout of the two forms, the vocabulary target words are either blue or purple. Students who are color blind or have visual impairments may have trouble distinguishing the target word from the other words in the stem. The author needs to use another method to distinguish the target words. A suggested addition to the manual would be information on how this test would be adapted for special needs students. In many cases, middle school and high school students who are reading below the seventh grade level, which is the author's target group, would likely include students with special needs.

SUMMARY. Although the Reading-Level Indicator seems to have fairly good internal consistency reliability data, it would be useful if studies were conducted to look at other aspects of reliability such as reliability over time. The Reading-Level Indicator provides a quick reading score based on only sentence completion and vocabulary skills. The reported testing time is approximately 4 to 14 minutes and is targeted at middle school and high school students and perhaps junior/community college students who are reading much below level. The validity data are somewhat sparse, only providing comments about content and construct validity. No concurrent validity data of a quantitative nature are provided. The Reading-Level Indicator appears to be adequate as a screening device. It should not be the sole determinant of reading level placement.

[205]

Receptive One-Word Picture Vocabulary Test [2000 Edition].

Purpose: Designed to assess an individual's English hearing vocabulary.

Population: Ages 2–18.
Publication Dates: 1985–2000.
Acronym: ROWPVT.
Scores: Total score only.
Administration: Individual.
Price Data, 2002: $140 per kit including manual (2000, 110 pages), 25 record forms, and test plates; $25 per 25 record forms; $75 per test plates; $40 per manual.
Time: (10–15) minutes.
Comments: Lower and upper levels have been combined into this edition.
Authors: 1985 edition by Morrison F. Gardner; later edition prepared by publisher.
Publisher: Academic Therapy Publications.
Cross References: See T5:2190 (9 references); T4:2239 (1 reference); for reviews by Janice A. Dole and Janice Santogrossi of an earlier edition, see 10:312; for reviews by Laurie Ford and William D. Schaffer of an earlier edition of the upper level, see 11:329.

Review of the Receptive One-Word Picture Vocabulary Test [2000 Edition] by DOREEN W. FAIRBANK, Associate Professor of Psychology, Meredith College, Raleigh, NC:

DESCRIPTION. The Receptive One-Word Picture Vocabulary Test (ROWPVT) is a 170-item multiple-choice test that assesses an individual's English-hearing vocabulary and, therefore, reflects the extent of their understanding of single words. The test kit contains an examiner's manual, a set of 170 full-color test plates, and a package of record forms. The test plates are presented in a spiral booklet with a flip-out easel and are ordered according to their difficulty level. The ROWPVT is an individually administered, norm-referenced test that can be given to individuals ages 24 months through 18 years 11 months. The test, although not a timed test, can usually be administered and scored in 15 to 20 minutes.

The test is most often administered by speech/language pathologists, psychologists, counselors, learning specialists, physicians, occupational therapists, and other personnel who are under the supervision of a professional familiar with assessment and interpretation. The examiner presents a word verbally to the examinee along with four full-color illustrations from the test plates. The examinee selects the illustration that best depicts the meaning of the word and responds by touching the picture or stating the number of the picture. The examinee does not have to respond verbally to the items. The examiner records the response on the record form. Only a subset of the items, or critical range, is administered. The critical range must be determined for each individual. The range begins with a series of items that are easy for the individual and ends at a point where the responses are consistently incorrect. Eight consecutive correct responses are referred to as the basal. To establish the basal level, the examiner determines the chronological age and then starts either from that point or from a suggested starting point from the table in the manual. If the examiner suspects that the individual is going to experience difficulty, it is recommended that the starting point be at a lower level to allow the examinee to feel a sense of success before moving to more difficult items. The examinee must correctly respond to eight consecutive items to establish the basal. If the basal is not established, the examinee returns to the first administered item and proceeds backwards until the examinee establishes a basal or reaches Item 1. At this point the examinee returns to the original administered item and proceeds in ascending order until a ceiling is reached. A ceiling is obtained when the examinee makes six errors out of eight consecutive items or has reached the last item of the test plates. The ceiling is the last item of the eight consecutive items or the last item so reached. If several basals and ceilings are obtained, the manual states to use the lowest ceiling and the highest basal for determining the raw score. The examinee's raw score is the number of correct responses up to the last item in the ceiling. All responses below the basal are considered correct. Once the raw score is established, it can be converted into a standard score, percentile rank, and age equivalent by using the tables listed in Appendix C of the examiner's manual. The manual also makes available the following derived scores: normal curve equivalent (NCEs), scaled scores, T-scores, and stanines. The manual gives adequate instructions for the conversion of all test scores. The results are then recorded on the ROWPVT record form. A confidence interval is also established on the record form.

The examiner's manual includes a section on the importance of vocabulary assessment and its relationship to a number of component skills and the implication it has regarding an individual's cognitive, language, and academic performance. The manual states that the ROWPVT can be used

to in the following ways: (a) assess the extent of hearing vocabulary, (b) assess cognitive ability, (c) diagnose reading difficulties, (d) diagnose expressive aphasia, (e) screen preschool and kindergarten children, (f) assess vocabulary with a nonverbal response requirement, (g) evaluate an English learner's vocabulary, (h) monitor growth, and (i) evaluate program effectiveness. However, the manual also states that the ROWPVT samples only a limited number of skills from each of the above categories and the results should be used along with other measures to fully understand an individual's profile of abilities. The ROWPVT provides a practical, objective, and efficient starting point for the process of a comprehensive evaluation of language skills.

The ROWPVT, a receptive vocabulary test, is co-normed with the Expressive One-Word Picture Vocabulary Test (EOWPVT; 95). (The EOWPVT is a separate test and is not included in the present review.) The manual discusses that the difference between these two types of vocabulary tests is that the EOWPVT adds the additional task requirement of cognitively gaining access to words and retrieving them from memory. On the EOWPVT, the examinee looks at the illustration and must provide the word that best describes the object, action, or concept shown. In contrast, the ROWPVT only requires the recognition of the meaning of a word. Therefore, an individual's receptive vocabulary typically is larger than their expressive vocabulary. The manual states that individuals should show similar performance on both of these tests when a comparison is made through an age-based performance, such as standard scores. However, obtained differences in performance, when significant, can be diagnostically important. For this reason, the manual presents interpretation of differences between the two test scores and gives the score differences required for significance at several levels of confidence. Appendix C also presents the frequency of occurrence of different discrepancy values with the norms group to determine if the difference is actually a clinical difference. If both tests are administered it is recommended that the expressive test be administered first because learning may occur from the administration of the ROWPVT and affect the accurate score of the EOWPVT.

DEVELOPMENT. The ROWPVT is the second edition (copyright, 2000) of a test that was originally published in 1985. The first edition was developed for children ages 24 months through 11 years and 11 months. The age range was extended up to age 15 years and 11 months in the 1987 publication of the test. The current edition combines the original test and the 1987 upper extension and further extends the age through 18 years and 11 months. The second edition has deleted 11 of the original items and added 32 new items. The new items were added to ensure that the test would assess a wide range of ability. Fourteen of the new items are considered very easy, whereas 14 are very difficult, with the remaining 4 new items being considered at a medium difficulty level. Section five of the examiner's manual provides a detailed description and analysis of the development of the ROWPVT. This section includes information and results for (a) the initial and final item selection procedure; (b) the initial, second, and final item selection procedure; (c) the pilot test; and (d) the item bias studies. The final item selection also is based on comments made by examiners and the members of the cultural review panel. The remaining items in the second edition are considered to be highly discriminating, culturally balanced, and sensitive to a wide range of ability.

TECHNICAL. The standardization of the second edition was based on 3,661 individuals at 220 sites in 117 cities in 32 states. The sites included public, private, and parochial schools, private practices, and the examinee's home. The manual provides a list of examiners and the test sites. There were 245 examiners with a majority of these individuals being speech-language pathologists, school psychologists, educational specialists, and graduate students supervised by an instructor. The examiners were selected from a list of former purchasers of the ROWPVT and the EOWPVT. Both the ROWPVT and the EOWPVT were administered to each examinee.

The norms for the ROWPVT were derived from a random sample of 2,327 of the 3,661 examinees. Only individuals whose primary language at home and school is English were included in the norms group. The manual provides data to show that the sample closely represents the demographic characteristics of the school-age population in the following areas: region of the country, race/ethnicity, gender, parent education level, residence in urban or rural areas, and disability status.

The ROWPVT examiner's manual provides sufficient information regarding the reliability studies completed on this test. To assess the internal consistency of the test items, coefficient alpha was computed at each age level with the range being from .95 to .98. Split-half coefficients ranged from .97 to .99. Both of these analyses demonstrate the internal consistency of this test. Test-retest correlations ranged from .78 to .93 with a coefficient of .84 for the entire sample (the average test-retest interval was 20 days), thus, indicating that the ROWPVT has temporal stability characteristics. Interrater reliability was evaluated by examining the consistency with which examiners are able to follow the scoring procedure after the test has been administered. The results of the analysis showed 100% agreement; however, the sample size was relatively small ($N = 30$).

Three types of validity information are presented in the manual: content validity, criterion-related validity, and construct validity. The ROWPVT was compared to 12 other tests that measure receptive language to provide evidence of criterion-related validity. The corrected coefficients ranged from .44 for the Stanford Achievement Test, Ninth Edition vocabulary section to .97 on the Stanford-Binet-4 vocabulary section. The ROWPVT did very well when compared to standard measures such as the Peabody Picture Vocabulary Test—Revised (PPVT-R) with a coefficient of .64 and the Wechsler Intelligence Scale for Children—Third Edition (WISC-III) Vocabulary with a coefficient of .93. The manual also presents the relationship between the ROWPVT and other broad-based tests of language. Again, the corrected correlations ranged from .45 to .92 with a median of .76. The evidence presented in the manual demonstrated strong support to the overall validity of the ROWPVT scores.

COMMENTARY AND SUMMARY. The ROWPVT appears to be a psychometrically sound instrument for assessing an individual's English-hearing vocabulary. The second edition seems to be well developed in terms of its revisions and norming. The test correlates well with other instruments. Evidence is provided regarding test development and studies are reported that reflect reliability, validity, and standardization. Many clinicians will welcome the speed and ease of the test administration and scoring.

Review of the Receptive One-Word Picture Vocabulary Test [2000 Edition] by SHEILA PRATT, Assistant Professor, Department of Communication Science & Disorders, University of Pittsburgh, Pittsburgh, PA:

DESCRIPTION. The Receptive One-Word Picture Vocabulary Test (2000 Edition) is an auditory test of comprehension of English single-word vocabulary. The target population is English-speaking children aged 2 through 18 years. The test is administered individually with the examiner presenting the children a series of plates with four pictures on each plate. When administering the Receptive One-Word Picture Vocabulary Test [2000 Edition] (ROWPVT) examiners say the target word for each plate and the children are required to point to the picture that corresponds with the word. The items are arranged in increasing difficulty, so the test begins at a suggested age or developmental level for better efficiency. A basal of eight consecutive correct responses is established and the test proceeds until a ceiling of six out of eight incorrect responses is obtained. The ROWPT takes about 10–15 minutes to complete with cooperative children and a few minutes to score. The raw scores can be converted to a number of standard test metrics and also can be compared directly to results from the Expressive One-Word Picture Vocabulary Test [2000 Edition] (EOWPVT; 95). The EOWPVT is a companion test and was normed on the same population as the ROWPVT.

DEVELOPMENT. This edition is a substantive revision of the original ROWPVT (Gardner, 1985). Development began by combining items from both the 1985 version of the ROWPVT and the Receptive One-Word Picture Vocabulary Test—Upper Extension (Brownell, 1987), removing problematic and dated items from the previous version, and adding new items that primarily extended the upper and lower difficulty ranges of the test. New illustrations were constructed for the target items and distractors. The distractor illustrations were selected according to conceptual and physical similarities with the target items. The resulting test items were piloted on 154 children and the results were assessed for difficulty, discriminability, and reliability. The items were rearranged according to difficulty and the standardization form of the test and the EOWPVT were administered to a sample of 3,661 children from across the United States. Item analyses of difficulty, discriminability, reliability, and bias were completed on the results from a subsample (510 children) of the standardization population in order to determine the final item composition for the ROWPVT. These analyses resulted in the elimination of 26 items. Based on the remaining 170 items, norms were then constructed from the test results of 2,327 children who were selected so that the sample demographics conformed to the population characteristics of the United States. In addition, whole test and item analyses were completed on these test data. The results from the remaining children were used to assess a number of validity issues.

TECHNICAL. Test characteristics for the ROWPVT are reported in the administration manual. Peer-reviewed publications regarding the characteristics of the test are not available nor are publisher or independent assessments of the commercial form of this version of the ROWPVT. The reliability reported in the manual indicates high internal consistency (.95 or greater) overall and at all age levels as measured by Cronbach's coefficient alphas and split-half reliability coefficients. Test-retest reliability (average 20-day administration interval) conducted with 226 children and the same examiner resulted in a .81 correlation overall and these values ranged from .73 to .91 across the age groups tested.

The development and standardization procedures used to construct the ROWPVT were consistent with good content representation. Evidence for other forms of validity also was acceptable. The correlations between the ROWPVT and other tests of vocabulary ranged from .44 to .97 with a median of .71. However, the corrected correlation of the ROWPVT with the Peabody Picture Vocabulary Test—III (Dunn & Dunn, 1997), a highly regarded receptive vocabulary test of similarly construction and use, was lower than expected (.71). The ROWPVT appears to be sensitive to vocabulary growth associated with increased age in that the scores from the standardization sample systematically increased with age, and the correlation between age and raw score was .85. Correlations with cognitive development, language skill, and academic achievement were moderate to high depending on the measure. The ROWPVT also appeared sensitive to receptive vocabulary delay. The children in the standardization sample who had identified disabilities commonly associated with vocabulary delay produced standard scores that were significantly lower than the estimated population mean, whereas scores for children whose disabilities were not commonly associated with vocabulary delay were not significantly low.

COMMENTARY. This version of the ROWPVT is a substantial improvement over the original version. The selection and standardization of the items are notable improvements as is the inclusion of new illustrations. The new norms are nationally rather than regionally based and efforts were made to reflect the demographics of the United States and to reduce cultural forms of bias. Further, the ROWPVT was conormed with the EOWPVT allowing for easy comparison between receptive and expressive vocabulary skills. Some concerns with the ROWPVT are with the modifications that were made in the form and administration of the test during and after the standardization process. The ROWPVT is an individually administered test but some of the children in the standardization sample were administered the test in a group. This modification may have introduced some error into the norms despite a lack of significant difference between the results from the two different types of administration. It is expected that the composition of a test administered to a standardization population will differ somewhat from the commercial version of the test, but it is an additional concern that the commercial version of the ROWPVT was not tested against the normative data to determine if the full complement of modifications, such as elimination of items and coloring of the illustrations, altered the psychometrics of the test.

One of the limitations of the ROWPVT (a limitation associated with most single-word vocabulary tests) is that it is a very restrictive means of assessing vocabulary. By assessing vocabulary at the single word level, the role of context, language structure, and paralinguistic cues in word comprehension and use is minimized. Moreover, to be applied to disparate groups, the content of the test has to be mainstream and generic and this may underestimate the size and complexity of children's lexicons from unusual backgrounds.

SUMMARY. The second edition of the ROWPVT appears to be a technically sound measure of single word receptive English vocabulary in children ages 2 through 18. This edition of the test is a notable improvement over the earlier version and includes substantive improvements so that it is more competitive with other receptive vocabulary tests such as the Peabody Picture Vocabulary Test—III (Dunn & Dunn, 1997; T6:1823). However, extent of the modifications makes it difficult to apply previously published data from the early version of the ROWPVT to this new version of the test.

REVIEWER'S REFERENCES

Brownell, R. (1987). *Receptive One-Word Picture Vocabulary Test—Upper Extension.* Novato, CA: Academic Therapy Publications.
Dunn, L., & Dunn, L. (1997). *Peabody Picture Vocabulary Test—Third Edition.* Circle Pines, MN: American Guidance Service.
Gardner, M. (1985). *Receptive One-Word Picture Vocabulary Test.* Novato, CA: Academic Therapy Publications.

[206]
Rehabilitation Checklist.

Purpose: Designed to help determine the needs of clients recovering from serious and soft-tissue physical injuries, cognitive impairment (mild to moderate brain injury), and related psychological adjustment and/or trauma.

Publication Dates: 1998–1999.

Acronym: RCL.

Scores: 7 scales (Physical, Cognitive, Emotional Psychosocial, Employability, Job), plus Total and Total Rehabilitation subscale.

Administration: Group.

Price Data, 2002: $82 per complete kit including 25 QuikScore™ forms and manual; $48 per 25 QuikScore™ forms; $43 per manual (1998, 54 pages).

Time: (15) minutes.

Comments: Self-report.

Author: J. Douglas Salmon, Jr.

Publisher: Multi-Health Systems, Inc.

Review of the Rehabilitation Checklist by MICHAEL G. KAVAN, Associate Dean for Student Affairs and Associate Professor of Family Practice, Creighton University School of Medicine, Omaha, NE:

DESCRIPTION. The Rehabilitation Checklist (RCL) is a self-report instrument designed to assess "clients' schemas, which include perceptions of their current barriers to rehabilitation, the impact of injury upon various life areas or roles, changes in their condition over time, and anticipated changes in the future" (user's manual, p. 1). It is also meant to identify clients who may be in need of further psychological assessment. In essence, the purpose of the RCL is to involve clients more actively in their rehabilitation process by assessing their perceptions of potential barriers to success.

The RCL is designed to be administered to adults in an individual or group format with the test administrator being present during administration. The client is asked to complete five major parts including: the actual checklist, which includes factors that inhibit the client from returning to his or her regular lifestyle; a rating of the importance of these factors; the degree of life-role disability; a rating of the importance of these factors prior to the injury and for the future; and a rating of how one's emotional, physical, and overall condition has changed since the onset of problems. In addition, this last part asks the client to estimate when he or she will be ready to return to normal activities and work. It is estimated that most clients can complete the RCL in less than 15 minutes. Untrained personnel may score the RCL by transferring check marks and by performing simple calculations. Scoring results in a Total Rehabilitation Barriers (Total RB) score, a Part 3 Total score, and raw scores for Emotional, Work Environment, Cognitive, Employment, Physical, and Psychosocial factors that are then converted to percentages.

The test author recommends that only experienced rehabilitation professionals interpret scored information. Interpretation consists of first reviewing general and then primary rehabilitation barriers. This is followed by subscale examination and item analysis. Cutoff scores are provided for the Emotional subscale, which is designed to determine those clients at risk for an emotional disorder, the Total RB score, and the Part 3 Total score, which is purported to measure an "Emotional Risk Factor that should warrant special attention" (user's manual, p. 20). The other subscale scores are used in a subjective and relative manner to determine those areas in which predominant rehabilitation barriers exist. The next steps in the interpretation process entail determining the influence of psychological factors on the rehabilitation process and clarifying clients' perceptions regarding their recovery process to date and into the future. The interpreter may then use critical items and subscales to establish the degree to which clients have maladaptive perceptions of their impairment/disability, report mental health concerns, and/or appear to have exaggerated disability.

The manual includes four case studies that illustrate the use of the RCL in clinical settings and two tables that provide a list of intervention strategies for the rehabilitation and life-role barriers identified by the checklist. However, no data are provided to support their utility in this endeavor.

DEVELOPMENT. The RCL is one of several instruments that comprise a larger test battery known as the Rehabilitation Assessment Series, which is based on the author's Rehabilitation Assessment and Intervention Process Model (Salmon & Celinski, 1990). Items from the first section of the RCL, which forms the basis for this measure, were initially derived from frequently cited symptoms, concerns, and complaints of clients with sustained head/brain and soft-tissue injuries. Other "commonly known" (user's manual, p. 37) psychosocial and vocational influences, risk factors, and items meant to detect self-perceived role disabilities and recovery prognosis were also included on the RCL.

TECHNICAL. A factor analysis resulted in the following four major factors in descending order of total variance explained: (a) Emotional problems, (b) Job-Related difficulties, (c) Cognitive problems, and (d) Employment problems. The Physical problem scale and Psychosocial scale were not derived from factor analysis, but were added to the RCL based on theoretical grounds. One study involving clients who were receiving worker's compensation and another involving clients who were in motor vehicle accidents (no other data are provided on these samples) found interscale correlations for the six scales and the Total RB scale as ranging from .17 (Employment and Cognitive scales) to .86 (Emotional and Total RB). Internal consistency (Cronbach alpha) was determined in a sample of 294 persons (no data are provided on this sample) with ranges from .56 (Psychosocial) to .85 (Total RB). The author indicates that test-retest reliability studies are currently underway.

The author begins the validity section within the manual by stating that one of the initial intents of the RCL was to use it as a predictive measure of rehabilitation outcome. Upon further examination of this issue, it was decided that "institutional policies and practices" (user's manual, p. 39) (e.g., insurance and worker's compensation benefits) make the prediction of rehabilitation outcome difficult. As a result, the author decided instead to focus on "pathology related" versus "outcome-related" (user's manual, p. 39) predictive validity. The manual does contain numerous concurrent validity studies supporting this. Also, scant evidence is provided to support the face validity of the RCL and its ability to identify rehabilitation priorities.

Another major objective of the RCL is for it to be used as a screening mechanism for the presence of psychopathology. As such, the RCL Total RB (Rehabilitation Barriers) score was shown to correlate with various Millon Clinical Multiaxial Inventory (MCMI) scale scores (ranging from .23 for the MCMI Somatoform scale to .54 with the MCMI Major Depression scale). The RCL Emotional scale score correlations fell from .26 (MCMI Somatoform) to .55 (MCMI Depression). The Total RB and Emotional scales also correlated .56 and .53, respectively, with the Beck Depression Inventory in a small sample of clients involved in motor vehicle accidents. Other correlations between the RCL scales and various MCMI scales demonstrate slight to moderate correlations that are, for the most part, in the expected direction.

The RCL Primary and Secondary Life-Role scores (a measure of perceived impairment) were modestly correlated with emotional distress as measured by the MCMI Anxiety, Depressive, and Somatoform scales. In addition, the RCL Overall Disability Rating was found to have correlations ranging from .37 to .46 with the MCMI Dysthymia, Anxiety, and Somatoform scores, whereas the RCL Mean Life Role Disability score correlated from .34 to .39 with these same scales and the Major Depression scale. Client perceptions regarding changes in their physical and emotional status and their relationship to various scales from the MCMI showed mixed results. Ratings of clients' self-prognosis for future improvement were also shown to be related to MCMI scales and the BDI. However, no data are provided to support the relationship between any of these variables and the ultimate predictive validity criterion of rehabilitation outcome.

The RCL Cognitive scale was shown to be related to measures of organic pathology cognitive function as demonstrated by significant correlations between this scale and the General Memory Index (-.13) and the Attention Index (-.23) from the Wechsler Memory Scale—Revised (Wechsler, 1987), as well as with the Wisconsin Card Sort Test Categories (-.21) and Perseverance (.15) subtests.

Convergent and divergent validity evidence is presented in terms of the RCL's ability to correlate favorably with acute pathology or DSM-IV Axis I disorders (convergent validity) versus its ability to correlate with more long-standing character pathology or DSM-IV Axis II disorders (divergent validity). However, correlations between RCL scales and MCMI scales that purport to measure personality disorders are relatively high, at least for the clients receiving worker's compensation (range from .42 to .59).

Finally, the manual provides various cutoff scores for predicting emotional pathology that were "statistically determined" (p. 48). However, no information is given on how these were obtained and with whom. The author is commended for cautioning readers that these cutoff scores are meant for screening only and should not be used to diagnose psychiatric/psychologic disorders.

The only "norms" provided within the manual relate to the above-mentioned, "statistically determined" cutoff scores that are used to screen for psychological problems. Cutoff scores are provided for the Emotional scale, Total RB, and Part 3 Total scores along with the number of clients identified with and without a "diagnosis" (manual, p. 49). No other information is provided in the manual about this group or how investigators determined this diagnosis.

COMMENTARY. In the manual's conclusion, the author states that various forms of validity have been established to support the use of the RCL as a screening instrument for psychopathology, as a method to identify illness/disability recovery schemes in clients, and as an instrument that predicts cognitive problems. Although evidence provided within the RCL manual provides an extensive overview on the relationship between RCL scores and various measures of psychological problems, very limited explanation is provided as to why certain cutoff scores were selected and what they truly mean. Second, although intuitively appealing, no studies have been reported that validate the use of the RCL as a means to identify client schemes that can affect illness/disability recovery. Third, some evidence is provided that supports the relationship between RCL scores and cognitive disturbances. However, no guidance is provided as to what should be used as a meaningful cutoff for determining cognitive problems. Thus, other than using the RCL as a somewhat useful structured questionnaire, additional studies must be conducted before the RCL can be used confidently for the stated purposes within the rehabilitation setting.

SUMMARY. The RCL is an easily administered client self-report questionnaire that is meant to measure client perceptions regarding potential barriers to rehabilitation and to screen for potential psychological and cognitive problems. Although the author should be commended for attempting to address client perceptions within the rehabilitation process, limited data are presented to support its use beyond that of a screening measure for psychological and cognitive problems—and even here, it may be better to use more traditional and well-accepted screening measures such as the Brief Symptom Inventory (T6:335) for psychological problems.

REVIEWER'S REFERENCES

Salmon , J. D., & Celinski, M. (1990, June). *New scales for differential, clinical and neuropsychological assessment and for psychological impact of injury.* Paper presented in symposium: Psychology and compensation: Assessment and treatment issues, Canadian Psychological Association Annual Convention, Ottawa, Ontario.
Wechsler, D. (1987). *Wechsler Memory Scale—Revised manual.* San Antonio, TX: The Psychological Corporation.

Review of the Rehabilitation Checklist by CAROLYN MITCHELL PERSON, Associate Professor in the Special Education Department and Director of the Research Roundtable (Title III) at Southern University, Baton Rouge, LA:

DESCRIPTION. The Rehabilitation Checklist (RCL) is a 50-item checklist accompanied by several rating scales designed to help the user accurately determine the needs of clients recovering from serious physical injuries. It is client-centered and designed to help the user accurately determine the needs of clients recovering from injuries and illness with cognitive, physical, and/or emotional after effects. Clients are involved in several tasks. First, they are required to identify items on the checklist portion of the RCL that discourage them from returning to their regular life roles and then rate the five most important ones by priority. Second, the results are transferred and placed into their respective subscales (Physical, Cognitive, Emotional, Psychosocial, Employability, and Job) where the results are totaled. Third, clients are asked to indicate how much their condition impairs the ability to engage in life roles. Fourth, they are to rate the five most important roles in their lives prior to the onset of the medical condition. Fifth, they are asked to indicate how much emotional and physical conditions

have improved or worsened, and when they expect their life to return to normal.

The RCL was developed as a means of facilitating client-centered rehabilitation and treatment planning and plays a critical role in determining whether a treatment plan is one that may be considered "reasonable and necessary" (user's manual, p. 5). It is one of several measures comprising a broader battery of rehabilitation-oriented instruments entitled the Rehabilitation Assessment Series (RAS). The RCL has been specifically formatted to address the primary issues and barriers to rehabilitation as perceived by the client, determine the life role impact of the barriers from the client's perspective, and gauge the perceived degree of change since the onset of the condition.

Licensed professionals in the areas of psychology, education, medicine, social work, physiotherapy, chiropractic therapy, occupational therapy, speech therapy, vocational rehabilitation, or an allied field are the intended users of the RCL.

DEVELOPMENT. The five-part RCL appears to be built upon a carefully constructed conceptual framework supported by the definitions of impairment, disability, and handicap put forth by the World Health Organization (WHO) and undergirded by the Rehabilitation Assessment and Intervention Process Model (Salmon & Celinski, 1990, as reproduced on page 12 of the user's manual for the RCL). The RCL, as part of the Rehabilitation Assessment Series (RAS), is also based on a detailed theoretical model that serves to foster an understanding of the dynamics and interrelations that are important in the rehabilitation process. A full and clear discussion of the conceptual framework, its relation to the WHO definitions, and the theoretical model is provided in the user's manual.

A stringent procedure was followed for the selection of the RCL items in Part 1 (the checklist). They were derived from a combination of the most frequently cited symptoms, concerns, and complaints from clients who had sustained head/brain and soft tissue injuries. The other items in Parts 2–5 (the rating scales) were designed for the detection of self-perceived role disabilities (handicap) and recovery prognoses, reflecting the Handicap Schema and Recovery Schema, respectively. The RCL items were administered to a sample of 296 individuals who received services at the Downsview Rehabilitation Centre. Their responses were subjected to correlational analysis to answer questions about the relations among variables represented by the checklist items. Intercorrelations between the items of the checklist were found to be of sufficient magnitude to warrant factor analysis. Factor analysis is a statistical method for studying the intercorrelations among a set of scores to determine the number of factors (constructs) needed to account for the intercorrelations. The method also provides information on what factors determine performance on each item as well as the percentage of variance in the scores accounted for by the factors. The intercorrelations indicated which items measured the same factor and to what extent they measured the factor. By examining the content of the items that loaded on the same factor, the author was able to infer the nature of the construct measured. Four of six subscales of Part 2 were derived by factor analysis: The Emotional Scale (accounted for 10% of the total variance), Job Scale (accounted for 9.4% of the total variance), Cognitive Scale (accounted for 8.4% of the total variance), and the Employment Scale (accounted for 7.5% of the total variance). The remaining two subscales (Physical and Psychosocial) were not determined by factor analysis. They were derived on theoretical grounds and because of the practical utility of these two item clusters.

There is no discussion of the identification or elimination of unfairness, bias, or stereotyping; however, the author does acknowledge efforts in seeking further input across cultural/linguistic groups, as well as across diverse clinical populations in order to broaden the application of the RCL.

The materials needed for the administration of the RCL are a copy of an intact form for the client and a soft-lead pencil (preferably without an eraser) or a ballpoint pen. Detailed and easy-to-follow instructions are given for the administration and scoring of the RCL. Additionally, examples of completed RCL forms are provided. In Part 1, clients are instructed to put an "X" beside the main things in Column A preventing or discouraging them from returning to their regular lifestyle. In Part 2, clients are asked to indicate the five most important items from the ones that were previously marked in Part 1. Clients are then requested to transfer each "X" in Column A across the row to the white boxes (the subscales are

associated with the white boxes). Next, they are requested to sum the number of "X"s at the bottom of each column to obtain the totals for each factor. Clients then rate the degree of life-role disability, life-role priorities, and condition change. Several subscales have cutoff scores indicating psychological risk factors.

The reliability and validity of scores from the RCL were investigated and a detailed discussion with unambiguous charts and tables illustrating the results is provided. The internal consistency reliability was estimated using Cronbach's alpha to judge the reliability of scores from the RCL by estimating how well the items that reflected the same construct yielded similar results. Cronbach's alpha is a measure of internal consistency that is generally used for measures where participants respond to questions on a scale. Alpha can range between 0 and 1. If a scale has an alpha above .60, it could be considered to be internally consistent (Trochim, 2001). The internal consistencies of the RCL scales ranged from .56 to .85. Some are illustrated as moderate to strong (.78 and .85, respectively), whereas others are shown as low but still acceptable. A discussion of the alpha magnitudes is provided.

Typically, several types of validity (i.e., face, predictive, concurrent, and discriminant validity) are studied when discussing the quality of measurement (Trochim, 2001). The author of the RCL investigated all of these types. The findings of the intercorrelations of the checklist items of Part 1 contributed to the face validity of the instrument. Correlational analysis and analysis of variance approaches were used to study validity. Clear statements about and tables displaying all results are provided. The types of validity mentioned above were well established.

COMMENTARY. Rating scales and their derivatives—checklists, rankings, inventories, and other psychometric devices and procedures—make the assessment of people, objects, and events more objective and meaningful (Aiken, 1996). Checklists are valuable evaluation devices when carefully developed, validated, and applied. A sound evaluation checklist clarifies the criteria that at least should be considered when evaluating something in a particular area; aids the evaluator in not forgetting important criteria; and enhances the assessment's objectivity, credibility, and reproducibility. The RCL is a significant combination of checklist and rating scales that represents a major step forward in assessment within the rehabilitation community. Having served as a rehabilitation professional, the reviewer is aware of the importance of an instrument such as the RCL that is easy to administer and serves both the clinical and research requirements in rehabilitation settings. The RCL meets the key test evaluation standards presented in the Code of Fair Testing Practices in Education (Joint Committee on Testing Practices, 1988).

SUMMARY. The RCL was developed as a means of facilitating client-centered rehabilitation and treatment planning and plays a critical role in determining whether a treatment plan is one that may be considered "reasonable and necessary" (user's manual, p. 1). As part of the assessment and intervention rehabilitation protocol, this self-report instrument can certainly serve to enhance the rehabilitation process of clients who have suffered physical injuries.

REVIEWER'S REFERENCES

Joint Committee on Testing Practices (1988). *Code of fair testing practices in education.* Washington, DC: National Council on Measurement in Education.
Aiken, L. R. (1996). *Rating scales and checklists: Evaluating behavior, personality and attitudes.* New York: John Wiley.
Trochim, W. (2001). *The research knowledge base* (2nd ed.). Cincinnati, OH: Atomic Dog Publishing.

[207]

Reynolds Adolescent Adjustment Screening Inventory.

Purpose: Designed as "a screening measure of adolescent adjustment."
Population: Ages 12–19.
Publication Dates: 1998–2001.
Acronym: RAASI.
Scores, 5: Antisocial Behavior, Anger Control Problems, Emotional Distress, Positive Self, Adjustment Total Score.
Administration: Individual or group.
Price Data: Available from publisher for kit including 50 test booklets and professional manual (2001, 134 pages).
Time: (5) minutes.
Author: William M. Reynolds.
Publisher: Psychological Assessment Resources, Inc.

Review of the Reynolds Adolescent Adjustment Screening Inventory by LYNN LAKOTA BROWN, Assistant Professor, Educational Psychology, Northern Arizona University, Flagstaff, AZ:

DESCRIPTION. The Reynolds Adolescent Adjustment Screening Inventory (RAASI) is a 32-item self-report measure, taken by paper and pencil with a self-scoring carbon answer sheet inside. All items have three response choices (*never or almost never, sometimes, nearly all the time*) to rate behaviors and attitudes of the adolescent over the past 6-month period. A total adjustment score is derived from four subscales. Two of these scales, Antisocial Behavior (AB) and Anger Control Problems (AC), are external markers of adjustment, and two, Emotional Distress (ED) and Positive Self (PS), measure internal attitudes.

The test takes about 5 minutes to administer and is geared to a third-grade reading level. The questions are derived from the Adolescent Psychopathology Scale (APS; T6:82), and the RAASI is designed to be administered by school psychologists, counselors, and others trained in self-report instruments. For these reasons, the instrument is recommended both as an initial screening tool for individuals and as a quick first look at behaviors in larger group settings. Normalized cutoff scores for adjustment are provided.

The test manual includes tables to convert the raw scores to percentile ranks and T-scales so that comparable scores can be determined. No formal method for determining faking-bad and exaggerating is used, although the manual provides paired-questions to compare responses for inconsistency. The test manual cautions that the RAASI does not measure and is not designed to identify suicidal ideation, but rather, gives a broad overall assessment of current adjustment.

DEVELOPMENT. Externalized acting-out behavior at the upper level of normal may be attributed to the vicissitudes of adolescent development. However, recent theory suggests a comorbidity of internalized distress and disruptive behavior. Thus, when examined together, internal and external signs may signal an early warning of more serious problems.

The primary goal of the RAASI development was to measure four broad constructs of adolescent behavior. Antisocial behavior was measured using self-report on items such as violation of rules, substance use, getting in trouble at school, and other nonsocial behaviors. A second externalizing domain, anger control, was selected because of its early predictability of more serious violent behavior. Indications of anxiety and depression were combined into a third scale, emotional distress. A fourth scale, positive self, was added to allow inclusion of positively worded items.

Using 36 questions drawn from the Adolescent Psychopathology Scale, item-with-total correlations were computed. Items with low correlation were dropped if scale consistency could be maintained; and the final number of items was reduced to 32.

TECHNICAL. Standardization of the RAASI used a sample of 1,827 adolescents from school settings in eight states together with a clinical sample drawn from public and private hospital inpatient and outpatient settings. The standardization sample matched the 1990 U.S. Census proportions: Genders were approximately equal in number, and the ethnic mix showed approximately 28% non-Caucasians.

The Total Adjustment Score (the combined score of all four subscales) showed high internal consistency with a coefficient alpha of .91. Subscore alphas ranged from .81 to .88. Although test-retest procedures were not practical for the clinical population, they were performed with a sample of 64 high school students at a 2-week interval and showed an internal consistency of .89.

Concurrent validity evidence was provided by reporting significant correlations between the RAASI, the Adolescent Psychopathology Scale, and the MMPI. Convergent validity evidence included obtaining correlations between the RAASI and measures of suicidality and depression on the Reynolds Adolescent Depression Scale, the Beck Depression Inventory, and the Suicidal Ideation Questionnaire. Correlation coefficients between the RAASI and these instruments were moderate to high for the ED scale and the PS scale, and low for the AB scale, providing further evidence for discriminate validity.

COMMENTARY. Strengths include thorough grounding in theory and extensive norming. The test manual is well designed, providing a good summary of norming, reliability, and validity evidence. Particularly useful are several complete case studies, including individual histories, sample tests, and interpretive results for typical adolescents.

One weakness is the need to refer to the test manual to obtain T-scale correlations. Scoring large numbers of these tests might prove awkward, so providing this information on the inside score portion of the test, or on a separate pull-out section, would speed scoring. Likewise, a clearer

indication of methods to be followed to detect possible faking bad/good would increase accuracy of scoring.

SUMMARY. The RAASI provides a quick, simple way to screen for early signs of distress in adolescents. By measuring both internal and external symptoms, it enables professionals to detect problems at an early stage. Due to the low number of test items for each scale, highest reliance should be given to the total Adjustment scale.

In addition, as this is a self-report, some bias and inaccuracy may be introduced by temporary mood states of the adolescent. It should also be noted that this is only a screening tool and, as such, is not designed to diagnose major problems or provide indication of suicidality. Nevertheless, the RAASI is a welcome addition to the arsenal of any professional wishing to understand the complexities of adolescent behavior.

Review of the Reynolds Adolescent Adjustment Screening Inventory by KEVIN M. JONES, Assistant Professor, University of Cincinnati, Cincinnati, OH:

DESCRIPTION. The Reynolds Adolescent Adjustment Screening Inventory (RAASI) is a self-report rating form for adolescents ages 12 through 19 years. Informants are required to estimate the frequency of 32 thoughts, feelings, and actions during the past 6 months, according to the following three descriptors: *never or almost never, sometimes,* or *nearly all the time.* All items contribute to one of four scales. An Antisocial Behavior (AB) scale includes 8 items related to substance abuse, delinquency, and conduct problems. An Anger Control Problems (AC) scale includes 8 items that assess aspects of anger and oppositional behavior. An Emotional Distress (ED) scale includes 10 items related to anxiety, mood, and negative affect. A Positive Self scale (PS) includes 6 items related to self-esteem and sociability. All items are written at a third-grade level.

Individual or group administration of the RAASI requires only about 5 minutes. Scale responses are handscored using a built-in scoring key that assigns values to each item that range from 0 (*never or almost never*) to 2 (*nearly all the time*). Raw scores for each domain and an Adjustment Total are quickly converted to linear T scores ($m = 50$, $SD = 10$) and associated percentile ranks using a table based on the total standardization sample (N = 1,827). Additional tables provide norms for gender and two age groups (12 to 14, 15 to 19). Higher raw scores, T scores, and percentile ranks are indicative of greater adjustment problems.

The RAASI is designed as the first step in a multiple-gate process that begins with less intrusive, large group screening and proceeds, for a subset of individuals, to more comprehensive assessments. The self-report format and restricted number of items are not intended to provide sufficient evidence for a formal DSM-IV diagnosis. However, an adolescent's ratings may be used as a broad screening of adjustment problems and symptoms that is accomplished in a relatively short period of time. Using standard scores and associated cutoff scores, the RAASI may identify individuals at-risk for more severe expressions of adjustment problems, such as adolescent violence, self-destructive behaviors, or social withdrawal.

DEVELOPMENT. The RAASI items were selected from the Adolescent Psychopathology Scale (APS; Reynolds, 1998), which is a 346-item measure of adolescent psychopathology that consists of 40 scales. Standardization of the APS included over 3,300 adolescents in school settings and over 500 adolescents in clinical sites. A 115-item shortened version of the APS is also available (Reynolds, 2000). The four RAASI scales were selected because they represented both externalizing (AB, AC) and internalizing (ED, PS) problems, with the number of devoted items (8 to 12) deemed optimal for a screening device. All of the final 32 items achieved high item-with-total correlation coefficients during standardization of the APS, and appeared to represent the content of the four RAASI adjustment domains.

TECHNICAL. The technical properties (norms, reliability, and validity) of the RAASI were derived from standardization of the APS. Internal consistency estimates of the four scales and Adjustment Total across demographic and clinical samples ranged from .68 to .92, with the Positive Self scale consistently below .80. Test-retest reliability and mean differences across a 14-day interval supported the stability of all scales and the Adjustment Total.

The validity of scores from this instrument was supported by high correlations between RAASI items and total scores; high correlations between RAASI scale scores and the scale scores of the APS; correlations at the expected magnitude between RAASI scales scores and the scale scores of other psychopathology rating instruments, IQ, and GPA; modest correlations between RAASI scale scores; and factor analysis of the RAASI that revealed four meaningful and distinct domains of psychological adjustment. Further, differences between the standardization and a large clinical sample on all scales were observed. Approximately 250 correlations in the manual are used to support different types of validity, such as construct, content, and criterion-related. There is no discussion, however, of how high or how low any of these correlations would need to be in order to provide evidence against validity.

COMMENTARY. Ease of administration and scoring will likely produce a large consumer demand for the RAASI, particularly among APS users and advocates. The manual provides strong support for the relationship between the abbreviated form and its parent instrument. It is important to note that the RAASI has "passed" a series of independent technical tests that are clearly described and arranged to accumulate evidence of reliability and validity in a manner familiar to test developers and students enrolled in assessment courses.

It is also important to note that RAASI development has not stepped beyond these tired traditions, either. Like so many of its competitors, the vulnerability of clinical decisions based on the RAASI have not been examined (Barnett, Lentz, & Macmann, 2000). During development, tests of reliability and validity are sequenced and examined independently. In practice, all sources of error are fiercely additive. Modest internal consistency, modest test-retest reliability, and numerous unidentified sources of error (e.g., size of group, examination context) may result in unstable scales, particularly within the range of extreme or "cut off" scores. At a minimum, users need to know the stability of RAASI scale scores that fall above clinically significant levels.

During test development, construct validity is the primary focus. In practice, decision validity is the primary concern. Cutoff scores on the RASSI will be used to identify adolescents who are more likely to proceed through subsequent stages of the multiple-gating process. Profile analysis will be used to aid treatment planning, evaluate treatment effects, and predict risk factors. Studies demonstrating correlations with the APS and other scales do not reveal whether the scale sorts adjustment problems into meaningful categories. In short, the RAASI will be used to make decisions, and should be validated for some specified clinical purpose (AERA, APA, & NCME, 1999).

Of course, clinicians and school personnel should increase their confidence in decision making by devoting much time and attention to many sources of information. In practice, however, we are busy, distracted, and uncertain. Screening decisions often pivot on a single test score, academic indicator, rule violation, or behavioral episode. As such, the outcomes and consequences of screening decisions based on the RAASI should be clear.

SUMMARY. Development of the RAASI suggests that its author has successfully sampled items from the APS to create a brief screening measure that can be swiftly administered and scored. Users of the APS and similar instruments will likely embrace the RAASI as a brief screening for adolescent adjustment problems. The degree to which the RAASI strengthens a multiple-gate process of clinical decision making is not clear.

REVIEWER'S REFERENCES

American Educational Research Association, American Psychological Association, & National Council on Measurement in Education. (1999). *Standards for educational and psychological testing.* Washington, DC: American Educational Research Association.

Barnett, D. W., Lentz, F. E., & Macmann, G. (2000). Psychometric qualities of professional practice. In E. S. Shapiro & T. R. Kratochwill (Eds.), *Behavioral assessment* (2nd ed., pp. 355–386). New York: Guilford.

Reynolds, W. M. (1998). *Adolescent Psychopathology Scale.* Odessa, FL: Psychological Assessment Services.

Reynolds, W. M. (2000). *Adolescent Psychopathology Scale—Short Form: Professional manual.* Odessa, FL: Psychological Assessment Services.

[208]
Ross Information Processing Assessment—Primary.

Purpose: Designed to "assess information processing skills in children ages 5-0 through 12-11 who have acquired or developmental problems involving the brain."

Population: "Ages 5-0 through 12-11 who have acquired or developmental problems involving the brain."

Publication Date: 1999.

Acronym: RIPA-P.

Scores, 12: 8 subtests (Immediate Memory, Recent Memory, Recall of General Information, Spatial Orientation, Temporal Orientation, Organization, Problem Solving, Abstract Reasoning); 4 composite scores (Memory, Orientation, Thinking and Reasoning, Information Processing).

Administration: Individual.

Price Data, 2003: $117 per complete kit including manual (61 pages), 25 record booklets, and 25 profile forms; $56 per manual; $40 per 25 record booklets; $25 per 25 profile forms.

Time: (45) minutes for complete battery.

Comments: Certain subtests not administered to younger children.

Author: Deborah Ross-Swain.

Publisher: PRO-ED.

Review of the Ross Information Processing Assessment—Primary by DAWN P. FLANAGAN, Professor of Psychology, St. John's University, Jamaica, NY, and LEONARD F. CALTABIANO, Research Assistant, St. John's University, Jamaica, NY:

DESCRIPTION. The Ross Information Processing Assessment—Primary (RIPA-P) is an individually administered test that purports to measure various areas of information processing in children between the ages of 5-0 and 12-11 who have either acquired (e.g., traumatic brain injury) or developmental (e.g., learning disability) information-processing deficits. The RIPA-P consists of eight subtests that are based on a verbal response format. The subtests have a mean of 100 and a standard deviation of 15, and combine to yield four composites including an overall Information Processing Quotient (IPQ).

Subtest I of the RIPA-P, Immediate Memory, requires the examinee to repeat a series of numbers, words, and sentences, and to engage in a series of body movements that are verbally presented by the examiner. This subtest measures Short-Term Memory (*Gsm*), particularly Memory Span or an individual's ability to attend to and immediately recall a series of elements in the correct order. Subtest II, Recent Memory, requires the examinee to recall information about his or her immediate environment and daily activities. Subtest III, Recall of General Information, requires the examinee to recall general information about mainstream U.S. culture. According to the author, this information is "in remote memory" (examiner's manual, p. 4) and is typically acquired by age 5 and learned by age 12. Subtests I through III combine to yield a Memory Quotient (MeQ) for children ages 5 to 12-11 years.

Subtest IV and V require the examinee to answer questions related to orientation in space (i.e., Spatial Orientation) and time (i.e., Temporal Orientation), respectively. According to the author, both subtests require the examinee to recall information from both recent and remote memory. These subtests combine to yield an Orientation

pected. However, the diagnostic value of these findings is questionable given that the mean performance of the normal controls fell within the *mild impairment* range on six of the eight RIPA-P subtests. Therefore, despite significant group differences, this study does little to support the construct validity of the RIPA-P.

The majority of subtest intercorrelations exceeded .40, suggesting adequate relationships among these measures. Interestingly, some of the strongest correlations are between subtests that are not included in the same composite. For example, the highest intersubtest correlation (i.e., .69) was between Recent Memory and Temporal Orientation, two measures that are not part of the same composite. Overall, subtest and composite intercorrelations provide construct validity evidence, albeit limited, for the RIPA-P. Finally, the author concluded that the result of a confirmatory factor analysis demonstrated that "the three quotients representing the theoretical composites on the RIPA-P are valid indicators of information processing skills" (examiner's manual, p. 43). Insufficient data are available to make this claim or to draw inferences about the underlying theory of the RIPA-P. At best, the results of the confirmatory factor analysis reported in the manual support a three-factor structure for the RIPA-P.

COMMENTARY/SUMMARY. The RIPA-P is relatively quick and easy to administer and has the potential to reveal important information about an individual's processing strengths and weaknesses. However, there are several limitations of this instrument that suggest extreme caution with regard to its use in clinical practice. First, there is insufficient validity evidence to support the underlying theoretical basis of the RIPA-P, which creates significant ambiguity in interpretation. Second, its psychometric properties, including standardization sample characteristics, reliability, and validity evidence are generally either weak or lacking. As a result, clinicians cannot place much confidence in any interpretations that are drawn from the RIPA-P. Third, the scoring procedures of the RIPA-P are not well articulated and are cumbersome to carry out. As such, a high degree of examiner error is probable. Fourth, the finding that "normal controls" performed in the *mild impairment* range on this instrument, rather than within normal limits, calls into question the construct validity of the RIPA-P, particularly as it

applies to its diagnostic utility. In light of these and other psychometric limitations, the RIPA-P should not be used to make diagnostic decisions. Unless and until additional reliability and validity evidence for the RIPA-P becomes available, it is recommended that this instrument be used only as a screening measure for individuals suspected of having information-processing deficits.

Review of the Ross Information Processing Assessment—Primary by MATTHEW E. LAMBERT, Clinical Assistant Professor of Neuropsychiatry, Texas Tech University Health Sciences Center, Lubbock, TX:

DESCRIPTION. The Ross Information Processing Assessment—Primary (RIPA-P) was developed to assess information processing/cognitive-linguistic deficits in children aged 5-0 to 12-11 years with brain impairments secondary to congenital abnormalities or injury. The instrument consists of eight 15-item subtests: Immediate Memory, Recent Memory, Recall of General Information, Spatial Orientation, Temporal Orientation, Organization, Problem Solving, and Abstract Reasoning yielding scores for each subtest and four composite indices: Memory Quotient, Orientation Quotient, Thinking and Reasoning Quotient, and Information Processing Quotient. The Memory Quotient only can be calculated for children under the age of 8-0 as the Temporal Orientation, Organization, Problem Solving, and Abstract Reasoning subtests are not administered to younger children. The entire instrument can be administered in approximately 45 minutes by individuals with basic training in psychometric testing. No specialized training is necessary for administration, although it is indicated that the instrument should be practiced at least three times prior to using it in a formal assessment. Materials needed for administration and scoring include the test manual, record booklet, profile form, and a timing device measuring in seconds.

Subtest items are scored on a 1 to 5 scale for all but the Immediate Memory subtest. A score of 1 indicates "Error response or denial" whereas a score of 5 indicates "A prompt and accurate response" (examiner's manual, p. 5). No score of 2 can be given for Immediate Memory subtest items. Each subtest administration starts with the first item and continues until three consecutive scores of 1 are obtained. Total scores in each subtest are then obtained and converted to standard scores based on age-related norms. Composite indices are obtained by summing standard scores from the subtests that comprise those scales. Subtest standard scores and composite indices can then be plotted against each other on the Profile/Summary Form both on a general profile page or based on percentiles giving a severity rating profile.

DEVELOPMENT. The RIPA-P was developed to accommodate stage, successive and simultaneous, and hemispheric lateralization theories of information processing in assessing cognitive-linguistic deficits. Subtests I through III are based on a stage model of information processing, whereas Subtests IV and V accommodate a hemispheric theory, and Subtests VI through VIII reflect a simultaneous and successive approach to information processing. Unfortunately, there is no information in the manual that describes the process of selecting for or assigning items to particular subtests. A review of the subtest items, however, reveals strong similarity to items in similar tests of cognitive ability but which may or may not reflect the concepts identified.

Following the RIPA-P's construction it was administered to 114 children aged 5 to 12 years with diagnosed traumatic brain injuries or learning disabilities. Sample participants were obtained by contacting rehabilitation centers and special education schools across the United States, and by contacting professionals drawn from the publisher's test purchasers database. Subtest standard scores were then calculated for each of the eight age groups via a regression analysis using raw and predicted participant scores in order to anchor subtest standard scores. The standard scores are based on a distribution with a mean of 10 and a standard deviation of 3.

TECHNICAL. Content sampling and interscorer reliability are reported in the test manual. Coefficient alphas were calculated to determine the internal consistency of each subtest's items and composite measures for each age range. Approximately 90% of the coefficients reached a criterion of .80 or greater with over 40% of the coefficients reaching .90 or more. No internal consistency coefficient was below .75. Averaging of the coefficients across all age ranges produced alphas greater than .80 for all the subtests and composite measures. From this, there appears to be good internal consistency for the RIPA-P subtests

and composite indices. As well, interrater reliability was found to be .99 for a set of randomly selected protocols from the normative samples and scored by two PRO-ED staff members. Unfortunately, test-retest reliability was not assessed. Good test-retest reliability is especially important because the RIPA-P was designed to aid in identifying deficits and treatment planning; this suggests that serial administrations would occur. Therefore, it would be important to be able to determine stability of deficits over time as well as treatment effects.

Content validation of the RIPA-P was undertaken by having three professional reviewers rate the subtests and composite indices for their representativeness in reflecting brain dysfunction mediated cognitive-linguistic deficits. Although reviewer ratings indicated that the subtests and composite indices were reflective of cognitive-linguistic deficits, it seems that rating the subtests and composites after their development is somewhat of a backward process. It would have been more consistent with typical test development procedures to generate a pool of items and then rate them for subtest inclusion based on predetermined criteria. Rating a test after the fact may lead to bias in the ratings as professionals might be less inclined to rate an instrument negatively that already appears to have gone through a significant development effort.

Item analyses were also completed for each subtest to determine item discriminating powers and difficulty levels. Median discrimination coefficients across the subtests ranged from .36 to .81, which demonstrated acceptable item discrimination ability. Similarly, median item difficulties across the subtests ranged from .14 to .91, which also demonstrated acceptable difficulty levels.

Construct validity was assessed by comparing the normative sample's performance to 70 control participants with no history of brain impairment. No age-matching of control participants to the normative sample was reported and all control participants were drawn from the same geographical location. T-test comparisons of controls versus the normative sample for each subtest revealed significant differences. Even though good discrimination between controls and brain-impaired individuals would suggest construct validity, the restricted nature of the controls limits generalizability and, therefore, validity. Further construct validity analyses were conducted by reviewing subtest intercorrelations

ence in gender but did report differences in educational level, with college graduates producing more unique designs than high school graduates, and age, with a decrease in design rate for each of the age groups represented. The normative population included only "normal" participants and excluded individuals with a history of psychiatric hospitalization, polydrug abuse, and neurological disorders. There was no information provided on ethnic or cultural groups.

Reliability (r = .76) of the measure was estimated using a test-retest format with a 6-month retest interval. The sample size (n = 95) was a representative sample of participants (i.e., age, sex, educational level) from the original 358 volunteers. Total unique designs for the first testing session averaged 100.6 and increased to 108.6 at retesting. Further, total number of perseverations decreased between testing sessions. Thus, the normative population was shown to have an increase in design fluency at retesting. This is an important factor when determining improvement at retesting in clinical populations.

Validity of the RFFT was estimated with both a normative and clinical sample of patients diagnosed with either traumatic brain injury or schizophrenia (n = 100). Validity with the normative sample employed factor analysis using varimax rotated loadings for "complex intelligence," "planning," and "arousal." Total unique designs loaded on arousal and complex intelligence whereas perserverative errors to unique designs loaded on planning. Validity with the clinical sample employed factor analysis using varimax rotated loadings for complex intelligence, planning flexibility, arousal, and planning organization. The RFFT loaded on the planning flexibility factor.

Further studies of the RFFT with children and at the neuropsychological applications have been conducted. A study by Vik and Ruff (1988) considered the use of the RFFT with children. This study divided the population of children (n = 86) into four groups by grade: Grades 1 and 2 (n = 19), 3 and 4 (n = 28), 5 and 6 (n = 23), and 7 and 8 (n = 16). Results indicated that older children applied design strategies more often than younger children. The utility of the RFFT with clinical populations of brain-injured patients and patients with cerebrovascular accidents was investigated. The results demonstrated that the RFFT is sensitive to right frontal dysfunction demonstrated by a reduction in unique designs (Ruff, Allen, Farrow, Niemann, & Wylie, 1994). However, no information was provided on how the RFFT is able to predict right frontal dysfunction over other types of brain damage.

COMMENTARY. The RFFT is a unique and quick (approximately 5 minutes to administer) way of assessing design fluency and right frontal functioning. However, the value of the test to address such functioning must be interpreted with caution. First, it should be noted that this test is specific to only one area of brain function. Other tests may be useful in confirming and/or addressing other areas of right frontal function/dysfunction (e.g., memory, personality, etc.). Thus, the test should be used and interpreted within a battery of tests as with The San Diego Neuropsychological Test Battery (see Baser & Ruff, 1987). Second, a thorough understanding of the test and neuropsychology is necessary before clinical interpretations should be attempted. For example, clinical interpretation is needed to assess production strategies, which provide important information about the patient's initiative and planning ability. Similarly, a decrease in perseverative errors at retesting is a function of normal retesting and may not demonstrate an increase in design fluency but rather learning effects. Third, no information was provided to address how other areas of brain damage or other diagnoses may affect the same types of abilities. Finally, the test that is designed to assess design fluency also is affected by visuospatial integration and fine motor coordination. Though abilities such as memory, visuospatial integration, and motor coordination are discussed in the manual, each ability is seen as a confounding factor that must be considered with each individual test administration. Indeed, further research with the RFFT is called for before its use as a measure of localized functioning.

SUMMARY. The RFFT is a quick way of assessing design fluency. Further, it has been studied and suggested as a way to measure right frontal functioning in clinical populations. The authors have established elementary reliability and validity of scores from the test with normal adults, children, and clinical samples. Assessing individual functions is an important aspect of a neuropsychological evaluation; however, specific localization of dysfunction has become less of an emphasis in neuropsychology. With new scanning devices, a comprehensive neuropsychological evaluation for individual functions becomes more the focus in clinical neuropsychology. Most neuropsychologists suggest assessing all areas with a complete diagnostic battery with "pure" measures of individual functioning.

REVIEWERS' REFERENCES

Baser, C. A., & Ruff, R. M. (1987). Construct validity of the San Diego Neuropsychological Test Battery. *Archives of Clinical Neuropsychology, 2,* 13–32.

Jones-Gotman, M., & Milner, B. (1977). Design fluency: The invention of nonsense drawings after focal cortical lesions. *Neuropsychologia, 15,* 653–674.

Regard, M., Strauss, E., & Knapp, P. (1982). Children's production on verbal and non-verbal fluency tasks. *Perceptual and Motor Skills, 55,* 839–844.

Ruff, R. M., Allen, C. C., Farrow, C. E., Niemann, H., & Wylie, T. (1994). Figural fluency: Differential impairment in patients with left versus right frontal lobe lesions. *Archives of Clinical Neuropsychology, 9,* 41–55.

Ruff, R. M., Light, R. H., & Evans, R. (1987). The Ruff Figural Fluency Test: A normative study with adults. *Developmental Neuropsychology, 3,* 37–51.

Vik, P., & Ruff, R. M. (1988). Children's figural fluency performance: Development of strategy use. *Developmental Neuropsychology, 4,* 63–74.

Review of the Ruff Figural Fluency Test by VINCENT J. SAMAR, Associate Professor, Department of Research, National Technical Institute for the Deaf, Rochester Institute of Technology, Rochester, NY:

DESCRIPTION. The Ruff Figural Fluency Test (RFFT) is a test of nonverbal divergent thinking. Divergent thinking, a construct originally developed in the 1950s by Guilford as a major underpinning of human creativity, refers to the ability to produce a large number of ideas or solutions to a problem in a short time without repeating them excessively. The specific form of divergent thinking assessed by the RFFT is nonverbal design fluency, assessed in this case by the ability to generate rapidly as many unique designs as possible by drawing lines on a response form to connect preprinted dots either with or without the presence of distracting lines or shapes. Impairment of design fluency has been shown to be diagnostic of right frontal and right frontocentral brain lesions. As this neuropsychological correlation suggests, the RFFT is essentially an instrument for assessing nonverbal executive functions, including the ability to (a) think fluidly and flexibly in the visual spatial mode, (b) shift cognitive set, (c) plan strategies, and (d) coordinate these cognitive production processes.

The RFFT is a timed test administered in a booklet format with the aid of a stopwatch. It consists of five parts, each part being based on a specific stimulus pattern. The stimulus patterns in Parts 1, 4, and 5 are squares containing three different arrangements of five dots, respectively. The stimulus patterns in Parts 2 and 3 are squares containing the same five dots as in Part 1, but with distracting diamonds or connecting lines added, respectively. Within each part, the patient has the opportunity to produce up to 35 designs in response to the same stimulus. The patient is given 60 seconds to complete each part for a total test administration time of 5 minutes plus instruction and practice prior to each part. Quantitative scoring is based on the total number of unique patterns and the total number of perseverative errors. Qualitative scoring is based on the identification of production strategies used by the respondent, which are chiefly either pattern rotations or enumerative additions of a line from pattern to pattern. Norms are tabulated in the manual for four age groups—16–24, 25–39, 40–54, 55–70, both for the total number of unique designs (an index of fluidity of complex thinking and arousal) and for the ratio of perseverative errors to the total number of unique designs (the Error Ratio, an index of planning efficiency). In addition, a useful correction for educational level is included in the tabulated norms.

DEVELOPMENT. Research over the past 25 years has demonstrated that verbal fluency and design fluency are distinct dimensions of divergent thinking, lateralized respectively to the left and right frontal lobes. Prior to the development of the RFFT, only *verbal* fluency tests were available to the neuropsychologist. The RFFT was developed as a nonverbal analog to verbal fluency tests to allow complementary assessment of right prefrontal dysfunction. The RFFT was published originally in 1988, based on the normative psychometric studies of Ruff, Light, and Evans (1987). The manual was subsequently revised in 1996 and updated to include results of a few new published validation studies.

TECHNICAL.

Standardization. The standardization sample was composed of volunteers from California (65%), Michigan (30%), and the eastern seaboard (5%). The manual notes that the sample was heterogeneous with respect to age and education, but no information is given regarding ethnicity or cultural diversity. Normative studies of the effects of age, sex, and educational stratification on the total number of unique designs and the number of perseverative errors were conducted. The RFFT was found to be unaffected by sex, but to be sensitive to age and education. Hence, the tabulated norms take these latter variables into ac-

TECHNICAL.

Standardization. There were a total of 307 individuals of both genders and many educational levels in the standardization sample. They were stratified by age, (16–24; 25–39; 40–54; and 55–70 years). Regional distribution was 65% from California, 30% from Michigan, and 5% from the East coast. The participants were excluded if they had significant substance abuse problems, serious psychiatric disorders, or neurological conditions. Cell sizes had a low of 7 persons, to a high of 15.

Education and gender were found to have little effect on test performance. With respect to age, there were no significant differences in learning between the younger age groups; those in the oldest age group of the sample did master the test at a significantly lower rate. Thus, in score interpretation, the only distinction is between examinees below age 54, and those 55–70 years.

Reliability. The test authors state that they used test-retest (no time interval specified) to examine reliability of their measure, through the use of alternate forms (the two stimulus cards). They discovered that the second card was more difficult for almost everyone, and modified that card to make it of equivalent difficulty. They then formed two matched participant groups who were given Stimulus Card #1 followed by #2, or the reverse. They obtained a correlation coefficient value of R = .77.

Concurrent validity. The developers correlated RULIT Total Correct and Total Errors scores with scores from several other visuospatial memory tests. The obtained rs were as high as .36, with 9 of 10 comparisons significant at p<.05 or greater (for Total Correct). Total Errors comparisons had only one significant correlation of the six made. They also performed a multiple regression with Total Correct as the outcome measure and several other similar tests' component scores as predictors. Their analysis demonstrated that the RULIT shares significant variance components with other neuropsychological measures.

Construct validity. To determine the relationship of the RULIT with other neuropsychological measures, the authors calculated correlation coefficients using a comprehensive battery of tests. Tests measuring visual and verbal memory had significant correlations, as did those assessing visual attention and speed of performance. Factors such as verbal attention, executive functioning, and VIQ were not found to be related.

Factorial validity. The developers conducted two factor analysis studies. When using a two component solution they labeled the factors visual learning and memory, and verbal learning and memory. There was a weak intercorrelation between the two. In the next study they added tests of verbal and visuospatial skill and attention, and this yielded four principal components, which accounted for ~65% of the variance.

COMMENTARY. The test developers are correct—there has not, until now, been a widely available and well-standardized neuropsychological measure of visuospatial learning. The need for precise fine-motor control, and other confounding factors, has been minimized in the RULIT. The test is not complicated to administer, performance is fairly easy to record, and scores are readily derived. It is portable, and with the exception of the stimulus cards, there are no small pieces to fear losing. Individuals taking the test do not perceive it as objectionable, and most find it at least somewhat interesting.

Some examiners (particularly those not well above the mean themselves in spatial skills) may have initial difficulty keeping in mind the trail to be taught on the two cards. It is easier to learn the trail as one taking the test than to learn it, hold it in mind, then compare it to an examinee's error-filled attempts, while sitting at various degrees of rotation with respect to the card. The manual contains clear examples of how to record scores, which is quite helpful.

Several clinical studies are reviewed in the manual, illustrating the utility of the test in various patient populations with right-hemisphere involvement. The authors note they are conducting further studies to determine right frontal, temporal, and parietal roles in good or deficient test achievement. In their clinical studies they found using a cutoff score of the 16th percentile yielded maximum diagnostic efficiency in patient groups.

For forensic settings, the specification of average number of step errors across trials will be useful. As shown by their analysis, some steps of a trail yielded very few errors in the normative sample, whereas other steps were associated with the majority of the errors made. The two case studies presented were useful in illustrating how one might think about the test scores obtained in any particular case. A few more of these would be desirable. This reviewer would like to see some discussion of ecological validity. It is clear that a poor performance on the RULIT would indicate lower scores on other tests of visuospatial learning or memory, but it is not clear whether or how this may translate into real world difficulty.

The authors state that one of the most robust findings during their test development was the lower performance of the older age group (55–70). That being the case, an extension of the norms up to age 85 or 90 would be very desirable. As there was little or no performance decline progressing through the three younger age groups, beginning with age 16, one can wonder about the pattern that would be obtained in assessing persons of various older age groups.

SUMMARY. The RULIT is a good test of visuospatial learning, and a welcome addition to the selection available for individual assessment. It is inexpensive, uncomplicated, and relatively unaffected by extraneous factors. It appears to measure what it was designed to measure, and does not measure several other areas at the same time. It yields clear and meaningful scores, but not such a bewildering number of scores that software is required to calculate and interpret them. Some qualitative analyses are available for those wishing to examine a protocol in greater depth.

Review of the Ruff-Light Trail Learning Test by JOSEPH G. LAW, JR., Professor of Behavioral Studies, University of South Alabama, Mobile, AL:

DESCRIPTION. The Ruff-Light Trail Learning Test (RULIT) is a 15-step test of visual learning and memory. There are two stimulus cards. Card 1 has 21 circular stimuli and Card 2 has 18 stimuli. There is a dark circle labeled "Start" and another labeled "End" on each card. Not all circles are part of the correct 15-step trail. The respondent is instructed to trace by finger a trail from "Start" to "End" and is given feedback during the test as to the accuracy of each choice. The examinee has two to five possible choices among the interconnected circles. The examiner administers 10 trials and records the correct responses and the number of errors. The number of steps correctly completed in Trial 2 assesses immediate memory and learning is measured by the number of trials required to master the task and the cumulative errors. The respondent is asked to retrace the trail following a 60-minute delay to assess long-term recall. There is a 2-page front and back fold-out test booklet. A copy of each

stimulus card is printed on the inside of the booklet along with a matrix for recording correct and incorrect responses over 10 trials. It is simple and easy to use. The back of the booklet contains two graphs of the learning curves for two groups: ages 16–54 years and 55–70 years for normative comparisons. There are curves for correct choices at the 5th, 25th, 50th, and 75th percentiles. This facilitates comparing an individual's learning curve to the normative group. The front of the test booklet contains spaces for demographic information and score summaries. Raw scores are transformed to T-scores with a mean of 50 (SD = 10) and percentile ranks using information in the appendix of the manual. The components measured are labeled as Learning, Immediate Memory, and Delayed Memory. The manual notes that the RULIT can be administered by a person with training and background in psychological testing, but cautions that only qualified professionals in clinical psychology or neuropsychology should interpret the test. The authors indicate that the validity of scores from the test is related to a thorough knowledge of the manual contents and the background information of the professional. Presumably, the test authors envision actual testing that can be carried out by a nondoctoral practitioner and interpretation by a doctoral level psychologist, although this is not explicitly stated in the manual.

DEVELOPMENT. The RULIT was intended for assessing visual spatial learning and memory in people aged 16 to 70 years. Any neuropsychological battery of tests should include both verbally mediated and visual spatial tasks. Many tests of visual spatial abilities require drawing skills, good motor control and eyesight, and detailed design discrimination, and lend to evaluate learning based on recognition skills. To improve sensitivity to memory and right-hemisphere deficits, the authors have developed a procedure that measures recall rather than recognition. Although many tests rely on information presented in one trial, the RULIT was designed to measure learning that is defined as acquiring information over repeated presentations. Hence, the respondent is tested repeatedly (10 trials), but does not need to have good motor or drawing skills because he or she only has to trace a trail along circles connected by lines. The RULIT was developed specifically to

neurological disorder. The authors reported that the standardization sample roughly approximates the 1980 U.S. Census data with regard to race but they do not provide a breakdown showing those comparisons. The standardization sample does not approximate Census data in terms of geographic representation because 95% of the entire sample resided in either California or Michigan. Participants in the standardization sample ranged from ages 16 through 70 years. The sample was stratified according to age (four groups), sex (180 men and 180 women), and years of education (≤ 12 years, 13–15 years, and ≥ 16 years).

Analyses of the standardization data revealed that age and educational level influenced 2 & 7 Test performance. Age and educational level were found to impact performance significantly when using multiple regression analyses on the test speed measures. Normalized T scores were generated taking age and educational level into consideration. The manual contains norms (T-scores and percentile ranks) for four age ranges (16–24 years, 25–39 years, 40–54 years, and 55–70 years) by educational level (≤ 12 years, 13–15 years, and ≥ 16 years).

Reliability. In 1986, Ruff, Evans, and Light analyzed a subset ($n = 259$) of the final normative group. Ninety-nine participants from this preliminary norm group were readministered the Ruff 2 & 7 after a 6-month interval. Test-retest reliability coefficients ranged from .84 to .97 across four age ranges. Reliability estimates were calculated for an additional subsample ($n = 120$) of the normative group. Six-month temporal stability coefficients ranged from .76 (Automatic Decision Accuracy) to .93 (Controlled Search Speed). Split-half reliability coefficients and measures of internal consistency were both adequate with the speeded scores yielding higher coefficients than the accuracy scores.

Validity. The construct validity of the Ruff 2 & 7 was evaluated by comparing the test to the San Diego Neuropsychological Test Battery (SDNTB) (Baser & Ruff, 1987; Ruff & Crouch, 1991). The demographically corrected Speed T scores for the Ruff 2 & 7 significantly correlated with only tests of visual learning and visual short-term memory. The Ruff 2 & 7 Speed scores were most highly correlated with the WAIS-R Digit Symbol subtest, because both tasks are visuomotor in nature and require sustained effort. The Speed scores also correlated with the Block Span scores, which measures immediate retention. The demographically

corrected Controlled Search Accuracy T scores for the Ruff 2 & 7 did not correlate as well with measures of attention, learning and memory, but did correlate with tests that tapped visual learning and visual short-term memory. The Controlled Speed Accuracy T scores also correlated significantly with the WAIS R Performance IQ and tasks associated with visuospatial processing such as facial recognition and the Rey complex figure copy.

The factorial validity was evaluated using a principal components analyses (PCA) with an oblique rotation using Controlled Speed Search, Automatic Detection Speed, Controlled Search Accuracy, Automatic Detection Accuracy, Speed Difference, and Speed Accuracy Difference Scores. The PCA produced three factors that accounted for 88% of the total variance. The first factor was labeled Speed of Visual Processing, the second factor was labeled Controlled Processing, and the third factor was labeled Automatic Processing. The PCA supports the Ruff 2 & 7 assessment of visual sustained attention and two mechanisms of selective attention. The factorial validity was further supported by including selective attention tests from the SDNTB.

Several studies that showed the effectiveness of the Ruff 2 & 7 in differentiating clinical populations were included in the manual. The Ruff 2 & 7 was shown to differentiate between anterior and posterior lesions (Ruff, Niemann, Allen, Farrow, & Wylie, 1992); discriminate severe TBI patients from demographically matched control individuals (Allen & Ruff, 1990); show slow visual processing speed but average response accuracy in depressed adults (Allen, Ruff, & Logue, 1996); and AIDS patients had significantly lower Speed scores compared to AIDS-related complex patients (Schmitt et al., 1988). The authors also reported multiple discriminate function analyses that showed how the Ruff 2 & 7 could be used to help classify patients with anterior versus posterior lesions and right versus left hemisphere lesions.

COMMENTARY. The test manual does not describe how the test was originally constructed but does describe adequately how the test is administered and scored. The standardization sample is geographically limited, although adequate reliability and the validity evidence of the scores were provided.

SUMMARY. The Ruff 2 & 7 Selective Attention Test appears to be a psychometrically sound instrument designed to measure sustained and selective visual attention. The test is easy to administer and may provide insight into the general location (anterior—posterior, right—left) of a brain lesion in adolescents and adults.

REVIEWER'S REFERENCES

Allen, C. C., & Ruff, R. M. (1990). Self-rating versus neuropsychological performance in moderate versus severe head injured patients. *Brain Injury, 4,* 7–17.
Allen, C. C., Ruff, R. M., & Logue, P. E. (1996). *Visual attention in major depressed inpatients.* Unpublished manuscript.
Baser, C. A., & Ruff, R. M. (1987). Construct validity of the San Diego Neuropsychological Test Battery. *Archives of Clinical Neuropsychology, 2,* 13–32.
Ruff, R. M., & Crouch, J. A. (1991). Neuropsychological test instruments in clinical trials. In E. Mohr & P. Brouwers (Eds.), *Handbook of clinical trials: The neurobehavioral approach* (pp. 89–119). Lisse, The Netherlands: Swets and Zeitlinger.
Ruff, R. M., Evans, R. W., & Light, R. H. (1986). Automatic detection versus controlled search: A paper and pencil approach. *Perceptual and Motor Skills, 62,* 407–416.
Ruff, R. M., Niemann, H., Allen, C. C., Farrow, C. E., & Wylie, T. (1992). The Ruff 2 & 7 Selective Attention Test: A neuropsychological application. *Perceptual and Motor Skills, 75,* 1311–1319.
Schmitt, F. A., Bigley, J. W., McKinnis, R., Logue, T. E., Evans, R. W., Drucker, J. L., & AZT Corroborative Working Group. (1988). Neuropsychological outcome of zidovudine (AZT) treatment of patients with AIDS and AIDS-related complex. *New England Journal of Medicine, 319,* 1573–1578.

[212]

Sales Aptitude Test.

Purpose: "To measure an individual's sales aptitude."
Population: Sales people and sales managers.
Publication Dates: 1993–1996.
Score: Total score only.
Administration: Group.
Price Data, 2002: $106 per start-up kit including 25 test booklets and examiner's manual; $91 per 25 tests; $28 per examiner's manual; price information available from publisher for Quanta scoring software.
Time: (30) minutes.
Comments: Paper-and-pencil or computer administration available.
Author: Science Research Associates.
Publisher: Reid London House.

Review of the Sales Aptitude Test by DENIZ S. ONES, Hellervik Professor of Industrial Psychology, Department of Psychology, University of Minnesota, Minneapolis, MN:

DESCRIPTION. The Sales Aptitude Test is an instrument intended to measure an individual's sales aptitude, defined as "behavioral and personality characteristics which have been shown to be important to success in sales occupations" (information guide, p. 1). Seven attributes are assessed via self-report: achievement motivation, ego strength, energy, enterprise, persuasiveness, self confidence, and sociability. These theoretically distinct traits all contribute toward a single overall total score on "sales aptitude." There are 86 items on the test, 68 of which are multiple choice and 18

are adjectival in format. The adjectival portion of the test is forced choice: choices between 2 competing adjectives are forced. The test is intended for use in personnel selection and making placement decisions for sales and sales management positions. It is available in paper-and-pencil and computerized administration modes. An assessment report is available that provides percentile rank information for the test taker, indexed to both experienced sales people and experienced retail managers.

The Sales Aptitude Test can be considered to belong to a broader category of tests referred to as "job-focused occupational personality scales" in the employment selection literature (Ones & Viswesvaran, 2001).

DEVELOPMENT. The test was developed based on job analyses conducted on sales jobs in electronics, appliance, and medical supplies retail industries. Three types of information contributed to these job analyses: reviews of previously existing job descriptions, interviews with incumbent sales representatives and managers, and data from a job analysis questionnaire. The test developers do not provide details about the numbers of sales representatives and managers involved in the job analytic efforts nor do they provide details about the job analysis questionnaire used. It is clear that the job analytic methodology utilized must have been trait oriented (as opposed to task oriented) because seven personality traits were identified as important for effective job performance in sales and sales managerial jobs (achievement motivation, ego strength, energy, enterprise, persuasiveness, self confidence, and sociability). The Sales Aptitude Test Information Guide provides a brief description of each of these traits.

Initially, 356 items were written to assess these seven traits. Over a 4-year period, data from four samples, made up of "over 1,000 incumbent sales representatives and retail sales managers" (information guide, p. 2), were gathered. Initial item analyses and validation were carried out on the first sample. Cross validation and item refinement were carried out using the other three samples. The resulting 100-item version of the test was then used in an item bias study. Data were gathered from 265 males, 265 females, 135 Caucasian Americans, and 135 African Americans. This fifth sample included college students and experienced sales personnel (the breakdown of the sample between these two groups was not provided). Item bias analyses resulted in the removal of 14 items from the item pool, resulting in the 86-item instrument.

Potential users should note that even though items were created to assess multiple personality and behavioral domains, a single overall score is obtained from the test. The justification for offering a single score includes a statement by test developers that "Research has shown that the seven characteristics are highly intercorrelated" (information guide, p. 2) and high internal consistency (see below) reliabilities. The technical manual did not include a description and the results of the research referred to by test developers.

TECHNICAL. The only document available on the instrument is an 11-page information guide, summarizing technical information about the test. Descriptive statistics (means and standard deviations), internal consistency reliabilities, and validity information are presented for multiple samples.

No single set of test norms is offered. Instead means and standard deviations are reported for male and female sales people (Ns = 338, 499, respectively), male and female college students (Ns = 62, 137, respectively), African American and Caucasian American sales people (Ns = 45, 746, respectively), African American and Caucasian American college students (Ns = 102, 75, respectively), incumbent sales representatives (two samples, Ns = 373 and 134), and female, incumbent assistant store managers (N = 208), incumbent store managers (N = 227), nonsales personnel (N = 202), and experienced incumbent sales people (N = 1,006).

It is commendable to see that the test developers have gathered data on the basic psychometric properties of their instrument for several different samples. However, one sample missing from this list is an important one: sales representative and sales manager *applicants*. Given that one of the uses of the test is personnel selection, job applicants for sales jobs constitute an important population for which norms are necessary, especially because response distortion in motivated samples affect means and standard deviations of noncognitive measures, such as the Sales Aptitude Test.

The data presented suggest that gender differences on test scores tend to be very small (standardized mean differences range from .17 to .24, slightly favoring males). Mean test scores of African Americans and Caucasian Americans are very similar (standardized mean differences of .01 and .12). Consistent with other research on occupational personality inventories (e.g., Ones & Viswesvaran, 1998), the Sales Aptitude Test is not likely to be the cause of adverse impact on women and African Americans. Future research on the inventory should document scores of other ethnic, minority and cultural groups (e.g., Hispanic Americans, Asian Americans, Native Americans).

Internal consistency reliabilities (coefficient alphas) were computed on four separate samples: 373 sales representatives working for an electronics company, 134 sales representatives working for an appliance manufacturer and distributor, 208 assistant retail store managers, and 227 store managers. The coefficient alphas for these samples were .84, .75, .84 and .83, respectively. No test retest reliabilities were reported.

Multiple types of validity evidence are presented for the test. Concurrent validities were computed on the same samples for which coefficient alphas were presented. Criterion-related validities documented correlations with supervisory ratings of overall performance, assessed both with single overall ratings and by summing the dimension scores from performance appraisal instruments. The observed concurrent validities ranged from .13 (N = 127) to .33 (N = 216). These observed validities suggest that the Sales Aptitude Test can predict job performance for sales representatives and managers. Correlations with ratings of sales performance, customer service and selling skills were .22, .25 and .22, respectively, in an assistant store manager sample (N = 154). Correlations with ratings of sales performance and selling skills were .18 and .18 in a store manager sample (N = 211). In interpreting these findings, it is important to keep in mind that these observed validities are conservative estimates as both range restriction and criterion unreliability may have caused attenuation.

In another study supporting test use for its intended purposes, experienced sales people scored about .30 standard deviations higher than nonsales personnel (Ns = 1,006 and 202, respectively). A study exploring the efficacy of the test in distinguishing between levels of sales management found that district sales managers (N = 95) scored almost a standard deviation higher than assistant store managers (N = 208), and over half a standard deviation higher than store managers (N = 227).

The last set of findings suggests that experience is likely correlated with scores on the Sales Aptitude Test. Test scores can be used in the selection of district managers and in placement decisions for store managers. Yet, there may be implications of these finding when selecting for sales positions from external applicant pools. For example, in future studies, it would be appropriate to show incremental validity for the test over sales experience.

Two contrasted group studies documented test score differences between high and low performing store and assistant store managers in providing customer service, selling, and motivating others. Finally, a convergent and divergent validity study examined the relations between the Sales Aptitude Test score and Occupational Personality Questionnaire (OPQ) test scores. Unfortunately, the interpretation of these convergent and divergent validities are hampered because it is uncertain whether or not the ipsative version of the OPQ was utilized.

No data were presented examining differential validity for the test by gender, race, ethnic and culture groups. However, because there do not appear to be large mean differences on the test between these groups, this issue is less likely to arise in challenges to the test.

COMMENTARY. In general, the Sales Aptitude Test possesses the qualities that one would look for in a test to be used in the selection and placement of sales representatives and sales managers. Its development appears to be sound and the data offered supporting test use is quite extensive (multiple samples and multiples lines of evidence have been utilized).

The potential weaknesses of the test involve the absence of sales job applicant norms, evidence documenting relative stability of test scores, and criterion-related validity evidence from truly predictive validation designs. These potential weaknesses can be relatively easy to remedy with the gathering and presentation of new data. There is no reason to believe that such new data would fail to support this test for its intended purposes.

In designing selection and placement systems for sales personnel, test users should keep in mind that despite its name "Sales Aptitude Test," this is a noncognitive instrument, akin to other job-focused occupational personality scales.

SUMMARY. Personality-based measures are increasingly being used in personnel selection and placement (Hough & Ones, 2001). The availability of this instrument adds to the industrial-organizational psychologists' arsenal of similar tests (e.g., Hogan Personality Inventory's Sales Potential Scale [T6:1159], Personnel Decision International's Sales Potential Inventory). Organizations seeking a measure for use with sales representatives and managers are likely to find decision-making value in the present instrument.

REVIEWER'S REFERENCES

Hough, L. M., & Ones, D. S. (2001). The structure, measurement, validity, and use of personality variables in industrial, work, and organizational psychology. In N. Anderson, D. S. Ones, H. Sinangil, & C. Viswesvaran (Eds.) Handbook of industrial, work, and organizational psychology: vol. 1 (pp. 233–277). London, U.K.: Sage.
Ones, D. S., & Viswesvaran, C. (1998). Gender, age and race differences on overt integrity tests: Analyses across four large-scale applicant data sets. Journal of Applied Psychology, 83, 35–42.
Ones, D. S., & Viswesvaran, C. (2001). Personality at work: Criterion-focused occupational personality scales (COPS) used in personnel selection. In B. Roberts & R. T. Hogan (Eds.), Applied personality psychology (pp. 63–92). Washington, DC: American Psychological Association.

Review of the Sales Aptitude Test by SHELDON ZEDECK, Professor of Psychology, University of California at Berkeley, Berkeley, CA:

DESCRIPTION. The Sales Aptitude Test is an 86-item test that is reported to measure an individual's sales aptitude ("sales aptitude" is not defined). It consists of 68 multiple-choice items that focus on background information, experiences, preferences, interests, values, and other self-report characteristics and 18 adjective descriptive items. The test is purported to be appropriate for the selection and placement of individuals for sales and management positions. The "Information Guide" that accompanies the test does not indicate how much time an individual is allowed to take the test; another one-page accompanying description of the test indicates that it takes 30 minutes, but it is not known if that is the time limit for all candidates or if it is the time it usually takes to complete the test. Though there are two sections in the test booklet, one for the 68 multiple-choice questions and one for the 18 adjectives, only a total score is recorded. The test booklet contains a carbon copy that allows for self-computation of the total score.

DEVELOPMENT. The underlying basis for the test is a job analysis conducted in three sales organizations representative of the electronics, appliance, and medical supplies industries. No information is presented on the number of subject matter experts involved in the job analysis nor is there any information on the number of items, types of response scales, or results for the job analysis. The "Information Guide" states that seven behavioral and personality traits were documented by the job analysis as important characteristics for effective job performance. These seven characteristics are: (a) achievement motivation, (b) ego strength, (c) energy, (d) enterprise, (e) persuasiveness, (f) self confidence, and (g) sociability. Items were initially written for each trait to provide a content basis for the interpretation of the test. The "Information Guide" states that over 1,000 incumbent sales representatives and retail sales managers were involved in the initial version of the test. The guide also states that the seven characteristics are highly correlated, that there was one sample for validation and three samples for cross-validation, and that a college sample and experienced sales personnel sample were used to conduct a study of item bias. No demographics are presented for any of the samples reported as being part of the developmental studies. No correlations or analyses are presented to show how or why only one factor, a sales aptitude factor, is the end product of the developmental research. No information is presented as to whether each or any of the seven characteristics was pertinent to both sales personnel and sales managers.

TECHNICAL. Eight studies are reported in a "Reliability and Validity" section of the guide. Four studies focused on criterion-related validity. Correlations across the studies range from .13 to .33. Criteria ranged from overall and composite performance ratings to ratings of sales performance, ratings of customer service, and ratings of selling skills. No data or results are reported with regard to intercorrelations among performance dimensions or reliability of criteria. Test reliabilities range from .75 to .84, but no information is presented as to what type of reliability was computed (e.g., test-retest, internal consistency, etc.). No information is presented regarding the experience levels of the test takers or the appraisers.

The "Information Guide" states that construct validity can be demonstrated by examining the relationship between the sales aptitude test scores and other measures or constructs, in anticipation of demonstrating convergent and discriminant validity. Only one of four construct validity studies incorporated this design. Three other designs involved (a) comparing SRA Sales Aptitude Test scores for experienced sales personnel to nonsales personnel; (b) comparing scores of re-spondents at different levels of management (assistant store manager, manager, and district manager); and (c) comparing test scores of best versus poorest managers. These latter three designs are not designs that can provide compelling evidence for construct validity for the "sales aptitude" measure. There is no reason why "sales aptitude" should differ at different levels of management. Likewise, if sales and nonsales personnel score differently on the test, that is not sufficient evidence to indicate that the test is measuring "sales aptitude." The study that focused on comparing "best" versus "poorest" managers determined performance based on customer service and selling skills. There is no information about the relevance of customer service and selling skills for assistant managers.

The one study that compared the Sales Aptitude Test to another measure is also somewhat inconclusive. The other measure used is the Occupational Personality Questionnaire (OPQ; no reference is provided for this test). Results show that the Sales Aptitude Test is correlated with 28 out of 31 OPQ subscales. No a priori hypotheses are presented as to which subscales should correlate with the SRA test and which should not correlate.

One section of the "Information Guide" reports analyses pertaining to "adverse impact," an analysis that compares the pass rates of a minority group to a majority group. Reported results indicate that there are no differences in pass rates for males and females and for Caucasians and African Americans at the 30th and 50th percentiles of the test distribution. But no data are presented for any other cut score, thus making it impossible to determine if the test has adverse impact at cut score levels that organizations might use. Another problem is that the data in this section are based only on sales personnel; no information is provided for sales managers.

A copy of an "Assessment Report" accompanies the test and guide. It appears that a test taker's score can be compared to either "experienced salespeople" and/or "experienced retail managers." There is no differentiation in terms of different levels of experience, different types of sales, different types of organizations, and other information that would enhance interpretation of an individual's test score. There also is a section on this report that has a heading "Supplementary Information," but the guide does not indicate what information would be presented in this space or how it would be generated.

COMMENTARY. The "Information Guide" is deficient with respect to presenting information that is needed to evaluate the reported validity and reliability results; it also is deficient with respect to how to interpret the results. The samples on which the test was developed are limited to three types of organizations; there is little information on the types of sales work performed by the developmental samples, either for the sales personnel and sales managers. In summary, there are insufficient data and detail to evaluate the effectiveness of the Sales Aptitude Test.

SUMMARY. As noted above, the deficiencies in reporting data as well as concerns about the designs used to collect and evaluate data suggest that there is no basis for using the Sales Aptitude Test until additional data and results are obtained and subsequently made available to those who want to review the test for possible use.

[213]
SalesMax System Internet Version.

Purpose: Designed as a pre-employment assessment for the selection of top performing sales people for professional, consultative sales positions.
Population: Potential employees for consultative sales positions.
Publication Date: 1998.
Scores, 25: Sales Personality (Energetic, Follows Through, Optimistic, Resilient, Assertive, Social, Expressive, Serious-Minded, Self-Reliant, Accommodating, Positive About People), Sales Knowledge (Prospecting/Pre-qualifying, First Meetings/First Impressions, Probing/Presenting, Overcoming Objections, Influencing/Convincing, Closing), Sales Motivations (Recognition/Attention, Control, Money, Freedom, Developing Expertise, Affiliation, Security/Stability, Achievement).
Administration: Group or individual.
Price Data, 2002: $995 per one-time purchase of the web-based system including units for 10 administrations; subsequent report costs vary from $74 to $98 depending on volume purchase.
Time: (90) minutes.
Comments: Administered via the web.
Author: Bigby, Havis & Associates, Inc.
Publisher: Bigby, Havis & Associates, Inc.

Review of the SalesMax System Internet Version by GERALD R. SCHNECK, Professor of Rehabilitation Counseling, Minnesota State University, Mankato, MN:

DESCRIPTION. The SalesMax System is a computerized testing system designed to assist in the selection of professional sales personnel. The developer is a human resources consulting firm that has provided personnel selection, assessment, and related services to many different employers. Prototype and current versions of the software program for the SalesMax were developed during the mid-1990s, with subsequent initial norming and instrument release occurring in 1998.

The online version of the software, which is being addressed in this review, is also available with the capability of advanced purchasing of assessment reports, with the number purchased being selected by the purchaser and incentive pricing provided for orders of larger numbers of reports.

Test takers respond to 32 items. Scoring results are provided in three primary component areas that relate to the selection and management of potentially successful sales professionals. These areas are: (a) Sales Personality, (b) Sales Knowledge, and (c) Sales Motivations. The first two components focus on the selection of potentially successful sales professionals, whereas the third component provides insights as to best manners of supervision and understanding those motivators that are most attractive and effective with the individual completing the test.

DEVELOPMENT. The test authors constructed a preliminary version of the SalesMax Survey in late 1996, which consisted of 45 sales knowledge items, 28 sales motivations items, and 216 work-related personality items. In addition, self-ratings of sales behaviors, sales effectiveness, and sales performance, along with descriptive information about the respondent's work experience, demographics, and self-reported motivations were included.

A performance evaluation survey was developed at the same time, in order to gather information from sales managers about their ratings of their employees on the same list of sales behaviors, sales effectiveness, and sales performance. These same sales managers also provided information about how familiar they were with the individual's performance.

During 1997, the SalesMax validation packet was distributed to sales professionals and sales managers in three companies, as part of the research/

development project. The results of this project formed the foundation for the SalesMax System.

The manual for the SalesMax System includes more specific information about the development and initial validation of each of the test components—Personality, Knowledge, and Motivations. The three companies that participated in the survey development study were representative of the business products, business services, and home siding sales industries. Packets were mailed to participants and sales managers, with 151 completed packets being returned (which included both survey and performance evaluations). Descriptive data pertaining to the demographics of the development sample showed that the participants were: primarily male (63.6%); heavily weighted regarding ethnicity toward Caucasian (96.0%), with very few African American/Black (2.0%), Asian or Pacific Islander (.7%), or Other (1.3%) participants and no (.0%) American Indian or Hispanic/Latino/Latina participants being included. Age range of participants was heavily concentrated in the 20–29 (27.8%) and 30–39 (44.4%) age groups, with fewer falling within the 40–49 (18.5%), 50–59 (8.6%), 60 or over (.7%), and under 20 (.0%) age groups. Participants were paid primarily through salary and bonus (36.4%) and salary and commission (44.4%) methods, with far fewer being paid a straight salary (.7%), straight commission (5.3%), commission and bonus (1.3%), or Other (6.6%). No answer to the question regarding how the respondent was paid was provided by 5.3% of the participants. Sales experience reported by the respondents ranged from Did Not Answer (3.3%) and "I'm just starting out" (5.3%) to "More experience than my peers" (13.9%), "Some Sales Experience" (19.2%), "Somewhat more experience than my peers" (27.8%), and "As much experience as my peers" (30.5%).

The preliminary research results and the experience of test authors identified in a concurrent validation study that 8 of the personality scales included in the initial survey predicted sales performance. Three other scales were retained in order to provide potentially useful information relevant to the management of a candidate, should he or she be hired. A total of 11 sales personality scales were included in the final version of the instrumentation. As many as 7–10 items typically comprised each scale; however, some scales contained more items.

Study findings indicated that sales personnel had different levels of each of the personality characteristics being measured, but success in sales (measured by the individual being in the top 50% in sales performance) indicated that a minimum of each of the personality characteristics were necessary in order to perform at this level of performance. Desirable ranges (in percentiles) were stated within the manual for each of the Personality scales included. A Personality Index Distribution was developed by measuring the strength of each of the desired personality characteristics and weighting this by the predictive value of the scale for each of the scales that was associated with top sales performance. The measure of suitability for sales was stated as having a range of 045 and a strong correlation with actual sales performance (R = .40). The Sales Personality Index was then categorized into five advice ranges: Avoid, OK, Good, Better, and Best. Personality Index advice range distributions were provided, in which the index score range and percentiles were stated for each level of advice being reported (e.g., Best: Index Score Range of 34–45 and range of 87-99%ile; Better: ISR = 27–33 and 60–86%ile; Good: ISR = 24–26 and 44–59%ile; OK: ISR = 19–23 and 18–43%ile; and Avoid: ISR = 00–18 and 0-17%ile). The results of validation for the development of the Sales Personality Index provided a number of concerns regarding variations being presented between sales territories in terms of the quality and potential for sales in each, type of product being sold, etc., that would not necessarily reflect appropriately upon an individual or small group of salespersons' true performance. A relative measure of sales performance was used, in which study participants were divided into two groups representing the bottom half and the top half of sales performers in their companies. Resulting comparisons indicated that appropriate candidates would or should be selected from the Good, Better, and Best groups, with more careful consideration being devoted where selection would potentially be from the OK group. The avoidance of candidates that fell in the Avoid group (representing those with scores in the bottom range) was specified.

Similar research was conducted in order to develop more fully the Sales Knowledge scales, in which six knowledge areas were ultimately selected for inclusion in the finalized instrument. The developers stated that these areas represent the "key stages" of the "consultative sales process." Descriptive information relating to each of the Sales Knowledge scales was said to be used by organizations as aids in gauging candidate's understanding of the basic strategies that are required to be successful in a consultative sales environment.

Development of the Sales Knowledge scales took place with the inclusion of consultative sales training experts, from which a total of 45 preliminary sales situations were used to measure the knowledge dimensions. For each item, candidates were developed with a particular sales situation and then were requested to rank the four possible action responses provided, from First Choice to Fourth Choice. Content validity for these situational items was said to be examined by having an expert in consultative sales training review each of the 45 situations to ensure that each was content valid (i.e., that each was representative of consultative sales situations and behaviors), to evaluate the effectiveness of each action response by rank ordering the response from best to worst, and to select the best six situations representative of each dimension. From this process, 9 items were removed and the remaining 36 situations were retained for subsequent scoring. Each candidate's top ranked response was compared with the consultative sales expert's rankings, from which an item score was calculated. The top ranked responses were chosen, as the developers felt that they would be most representative of a candidate's actual behavior. When the sales expert's top most effective action response was chosen as the candidate's first choice, then 2 points would be awarded. If the sales expert's second-highest ranked response was the candidate's first choice, 1 point would be awarded. For each of the situations, a range from 0 to 2 points can be awarded. Using the six Sales Knowledge scale scores, the total possible points a candidate could receive would be 12, with a range of 0 to 12 points being possible. Developers stated that for those candidates whose scores fell below 4 out of 12, a formal training program would likely benefit those candidates with limited experience, or require informal coaching or training, which would focus on developmental needs for more experienced candidates.

Developers reviewed existing literature on personal motivations, particularly those for sales personnel, arriving at eight potential motivators that were selected for inclusion in the Sales Motivation scales of the SalesMax System. These eight scales include: Recognition/Attention, Control, Money, Freedom, Developing Expertise, Affiliation, Security/Stability, and Achievement. Further investigation of existing literature on human motivations and values took place. From the list of eight motivation dimensions that were arrived at through this investigation, items were created in which each would present the respondent with the beginning phrase of a sentence and the respondent would then have to choose the three endings (which they would rank as most, second most, or third most) that most closely matched his or her opinions, feelings, or attitudes. Each of the developed endings was associated with a particular motivational dimension (e.g., control, affiliation, or money) according to the developers. Twenty-eight (28) items, each having six possible response endings, were eventually included in this section of the SalesMax survey. Balancing of items and responses took place such that each dimension was represented within 21 of the 28 items. Scoring of this section of the survey included the weighting of the dimension selected as "most like me" being assigned 3 points, the ending selected "second most like me" receiving 2 points, and the third ranked ending receiving a total of 1 point. Scale scores for each of the motivational dimensions were calculated by summing the weighted responses for that dimension. Each motivational scale had a possible score range of 0 to 63 (21 items x 3). The information resulting from this section of the instrument was the candidate's current career stage, level of aspiration or life situation, and the candidate's "fit" with the organization.

TECHNICAL. For the 11 Personality scales, reliability estimates ranged from a coefficient alpha of .42 to .74. Personality scale intercorrelations were provided, which showed limited or no relationship being present between a fairly large number of the identified scales (range between -.134 and +.179, including two scales, Expressive and Energetic showing no correlation being present (.000), whereas several pairings showed relatively strong intercorrelations existing (e.g., Follows Through with Energetic = .401* [*$p < 0.5$]; Resilient with Optimistic = .452*; Assertive with Energetic = .454*; Assertive with Resilient = .419*; Social with Optimistic = .559*; Social with Resilient = .443*; and Social with Assertive = .540*).

Range of scores and mean and standard deviations for each of the six scores in the Sales Knowledge scale are provided. Intercorrelations between the six scales ranged from -.151 to .395* (*p<.05), with approximately half of them falling within the -.036 to .064 range.

Scale reliabilities and scale intercorrelations for the Sales Motivation scale were calculated and included in the manual for the sample used for development of the instrument. Although a theoretical scale score of 63 was possible, actual scores were generally near or below 50 for the developmental sample. With the belief being expressed by the developers that respondents and candidates would generally be represented by more than one motivator, the lack of anyone reaching a scale score of 63 or close to this level is not surprising. Motivation scale reliabilities were calculated and reported using an unequal-length Spearman-Brown reliability coefficient, which was determined using a split-half approach. Reliabilities for the eight scales ranged from .67 to .83. Motivation scale intercorrelations ranged from -.29 to .26. Construct validity for the Motivation scales indicated that the correlations between self-ratings and the identified set of motivations ranged from .10 to .50** (p<.01), with many falling between .31** and .50**. A table of percentile equivalencies was provided for this section of the SalesMax System, for the motivation dimensions.

COMMENTARY. The strength of the current SalesMax System (Version 6.0), in assisting potential employers or human resource consulting firms in selecting viable candidates for sales positions is currently compromised, in this reviewer's opinion, by the limited scope of industries and companies included within the developmental sample group. Representation of single companies in each of the business services, business products, and home siding industries is of particular concern, given the existing breadth of organizations, products, and services that utilize sales professionals. Further, the limited representation of women (although the development group included 36.4% female membership) and underrepresentation or noninclusion of persons of color (e.g., African American/Black, Asian American, American Indian) and especially the absence of representation of the most rapidly developing ethnic group in the nation's population (Hispanic/Latino/

Latina), presents the SalesMax System as being highly questionable in its use as an employment screening/selection device within a rapidly changing, multicultural/culturally plural population such as currently exists in the United States. The reliability and validity data provided for each of the three areas covered by the SalesMax System are relatively marginal or weak, when compared with other selection instruments that have been developed for similar or other occupational groups, at this time. Additional research and refinement of this instrument would likely be of benefit, particularly with inclusion of a more representative membership of persons representing culturally diverse backgrounds, along with a major expansion in the numbers and types of industries represented.

Although the developers of the SalesMax System have a lengthy and successful record in the provision of services to assist employers in the selection of sales personnel, dependence of individual employers and other groups on the SalesMax as a primary tool in their own selection process is not felt to be currently advisable, particularly if a limited amount of experience with sales and sales professionals is present within the group that is making such selections. Further research and major changes in the sampling strategies employed in the development of the scales and standards/criteria being used with this instrument will be necessary for the SalesMax to become an appropriate personnel selection tool for the broad range of organizations that employ such personnel.

SUMMARY. The SalesMax provides a good beginning in the development of a more efficient, usable, and accurate tool to aid business owners, human resources staff, and supervisory personnel in the selection of qualified sales personnel. Further research and development, however, is essential before further expansion in use of the SalesMax as a primary tool in the selection of sales professionals for employment. Limited inclusion of a representative sample of industries and persons involved within diverse sales situations is essential for the SalesMax to be considered as an adequate measure of the viability of candidates for all types of professional sales positions and as one that is unbiased in its assessment of employment candidates who are from culturally diverse backgrounds.

Review of the SalesMax System Internet Version by MICHAEL SPANGLER, Dean of Business and Technology, Highland Community College, Freeport, IL:

DESCRIPTION. SalesMax is a web-based instrument designed to measure three essential traits of salespeople. The three criteria identified by the authors as of most concern to their clients are Sales Personality, Sales Knowledge, and Sales Motivation. The instrument is designed for pre-employment assessment and is intended to assist in selection of high performance sales personnel.

The survey form is presented in multiple pages at the publisher web site. Login requires an Account Name and User ID. The program prompts the user for name, demographic information, and a unique password. The user is then entered in the database for file access by the sponsoring agency or potential employer. The survey consists of three sections each addressing one of the criteria noted above. The complete instrument consists of 213 items with the following distribution: Sales Situation—36 items with 4 responses per item to be prioritized Best (1) to Worst (4); Most Like Me—28 items with 6 responses from which 3 were chosen and prioritized; Agree/Disagree Statements—149 items for which the examinee must choose A or D. All the items are presented with the same background colors. Answers are selected by a single mouse click on a radio button. At the end of each section the user is prompted to submit the items. The availability of a user name and password allows the examinee to leave the web site and return at a later date or time. This also affords a safety feature in case of interrupted transmission or network loss. The file is available for user access for 30 days.

When the test is complete the report is generated and is accessible through another login page at the publisher's web site. The seven-page report is accessible online and in a printable format. The report contains definitions and explanations of the three criteria for which scaled values are generated. Additionally, a "composite" score for Potential Sales Success is reported.

DEVELOPMENT. Foundation research for SalesMax is based on the publisher's industry tenure and professional judgment. "Based on our twenty year experience of assessing salespeople and sales managers for our client companies, we developed SalesMax to measure the three areas of most concern to our sales clients" (manual, p. 1). Research in 1996 resulted in the development of a preliminary version of the SalesMax Survey. No

significant details or further citations on the research are noted in the SalesMax System Version 6.0 technical manual. The survey development sample was selected from three companies representative of the following industries: business products, business services, and home-siding sales.

TECHNICAL. In the technical manual, the survey development sample ($n = 151$) shows a reasonable distribution by age, compensation, and experience. Gender demographics are Male = 63.6% to Female = 36.4%. Ethnic distribution in the sample is seriously skewed. Of the 151 sample members 145 or 96.0% were identified as Caucasian, 3 or 2.0% as African American, 1 or .7% as Asian or Pacific Islander, and 2 or 1.3% as Other. There were no Hispanic or Native American members in the sample. The authors acknowledge that the sample contained too few minorities to evaluate adequately.

Scale internal consistencies (alphas) for Section 1, Sales Personality, ranged from .74 to .42. The Sales Personality Index is quantified as a function of sales income. Probability for success is scaled based on the likelihood of being in the top 50% of sales income. Scale ranges include advice as to the best candidate or the candidate to avoid. No correlations with known personality assessments such as the Myers-Briggs Type Indicator (T6:1678) are reported.

Section 2, Sales Knowledge, uses six scales to establish user knowledge of the sales process. An expert in consultative sales training reviewed the Knowledge scales to examine content validity. Descriptive statistics for development sample Knowledge scores were reported as were scale intercorrelations. Only one of the scale intercorrelations was significant at $p = .05$. The six scale scores range from 0 to 11 with means from 4.81 to 6.86 and standard deviations from 1.42 to 2.37. No information on other quantitative analyses was presented.

Section 3, Sales Motivations, uses eight potential motivators in assessment scales. These were chosen from "review of existing literature on motivators, particularly for sales people" (technical manual, p. 19). Motivations scale reliabilities ranged from .67 to .83. Development study participants were asked to self-rank a set of motivators that correspond to the eight motivations measured by the scales. Construct validity was reported by the correlation of the scale scores with the self-ranking scores.

COMMENTARY. The administration of the instrument is its principal advantage. It is comfortably accessed by the participant (providing that one has internet access), responses are easily entered by pointing and clicking on a simple radio button, and the user interface is foolproof with rapid refreshing of the instructions and the capacity to exit and return using a confidential password. This reviewer thought the legibility of the pages (white on green) to be acceptable but not preferable. Error alerts such as incomplete or duplicated responses were rapid and directly addressed any user difficulties. It may be noted that the use of a computer-based administration rather than paper-based for this assessment affords a level of assurance to the user with regard to accidental or unintended responses, marking errors, or duplicated answers. Site access speed and page display was very good even on slower dial-up internet connections.

There are certain basic item design flaws. One example in the Agree/Disagree items is the use of absolutes such as: "Item 72. Criticism *never* bothers you"; "Item 80. Throughout life, you have *always* made good decisions." Additional reliability and validity studies may be in order. This reviewer considers the use of a single expert to evaluate content validity (Sales Knowledge) to be inadequate. The construct validity study using a set of motivations should have some external validating evidence. There are ample resources for the authors to improve evidence of instrument validity. A comparison to an established personality assessment tool such as the Myers-Briggs Type Indicator may be useful.

The report generated from the instrument is easily accessed and well presented. It includes definitions of the scaled characteristics and explanations of the categorical results. Graphics are easily read and interpreted. Included with the resultant scores is a "composite" for Potential Sales Success. No information in the technical manual describes the development, reliability, or validity of this Sales Personality Index; however, the report indicates that the authors' research shows certain probabilities that the participant's score will indicate potential for sales compensation in the top half. Accompanying the score interval on index is an advice term such as Best, Good, or Avoid. This index is followed by more detailed descriptors of the potential strengths and weaknesses of the candidate. The last component of the report contains suggestions on how one may effectively manage the test taker in a sales staff. Again, no research foundation has been presented to affirm the recommendations in this part of the report.

SUMMARY. The SalesMax System Version 6.0 is an attempt to quantify those traits of personality, knowledge, and motivation that lead to success in consultative sales. In the introductory online page of the survey the authors state:

> While SalesMax is a very useful tool, the results from this assessment are only part of a complete evaluation. Other factors—including your experience, education, and job history—are not evaluated by SalesMax and will be considered along with your SalesMax results in making a final evaluation.

This statement may be indicative of the true utility of the instrument. Given the limited development research, reliability and validity information, and the constraining lack of ethnic diversity of the development sample, one may be hard pressed to depend on this instrument as significant influence on employment decisions.

[214]

SASB [Structural Analysis of Social Behavior] Intrex Questionnaires.

Purpose: Designed to measure the patient's perceptions of self and others, based on trait x state x situational philosophy and Structural Analysis of Social Behavior.

Population: Psychiatric patients and normals.

Publication Dates: 1980–2000.

Acronym: SASB Intrex.

Scores: Pattern Coefficient Scores, cluster profiles, and weighted affiliation and autonomy scores for each of 3 areas: Interpersonal Transitive-Focus on Other, Interpersonal Intransitive-Focus on Self, Intrapsychic Introjection; 3 forms (short, medium, long), 6 subtests: Self (Best, Worst), He/I Present Tense (Best, Worst), She/I Present Tense (Best, Worst), Mother/I Past Tense, Father/I Past Tense, Mother with Father/Father with Mother Past Tense.

Administration: Individual or group.

Price Data, 2000: $120 (research use) or $160 (clinical use) per questionnaire and coding software package including all 3 forms of Intrex questionnaire (short, medium, long), electronic forms, questionnaire user's manual (2000, 56 pages), SASBWorks coding programs (Process, Content, Complex, Markov), and coding reference manual (2000, 59 pages); $80 (re-

search use) or $120 (clinical use) per all 3 forms of Intrex questionnaire with electronic forms and questionnaire user's manual; $80 per all 4 SASBWorks coding programs with coding reference manual; $.20 (research use, $10 minimum) or $2 (clinical use, $20 minimum) royalty fee per administration; $25 per questionnaire user's manual; $15 per coding reference manual; miscellaneous specialized SASB coding programs also available (contact Benjamin@Xmission.com for details). **Time:** (60) minutes for complete battery, short form. **Comments:** PC systems with DOS or Windows 95/98/2000 and Microsoft Access2000, Excel (1997 version or later), and Word necessary to process SASBWorks coding programs.
Author: Lorna Smith Benjamin.
Publisher: University of Utah, Department of Psychology.
Cross References: See T5:1298 (1 reference); for a review by Scott T. Meier, see 12:192; see also T4:1258 (2 references).

Review of the SASB [Structural Analysis of Social Behavior] Intrex Questionnaires by DENNIS DOVERSPIKE, Professor of Psychology, Psychology Department, University of Akron, Akron, OH:

DESCRIPTION. This test is designed to measure the respondent's perceptions of self and others. It is based on a trait-state-situational approach to measurement and a structural analysis of behavior. The target population is psychiatric patients and also those within the normal range of personality. However, even the short form of the SASB is a lengthy instrument, and the long form takes 3 to 6 hours to complete. Thus, it would appear that the individual completing the survey would have to be highly motivated and also possess above average reading skills.

The SASB is more of a system than a single test. The manual is intended for users of the short, medium, and long forms of the questionnaire. A CD-ROM was provided with the system. At the time of this review, the measures could not be administered by CD-ROM. However, scoring was accomplished through programs located on the CD-ROM. There is also a second system that can be used for objective observer coding of videotaped interactions. This review is concerned only with the system based on questionnaires.

This is a complex system to learn and to understand, especially for those encountering the materials for the first time. The SASB is described in the manual as being a measure of what is usually discussed in therapy, and at times the SASB reminds one more of a therapeutic tool than of a test or a measure.

There are two versions of the short form, and the standard version of the short form consists of 176 items. The two versions of the short form can be combined into one standard version of the medium form of 352 items. The standard version of the long form has 792 items. The standard versions can be modified depending upon the issues confronting the client or respondent. The manual strongly recommends the use of at least the medium form.

The individual completing the measure first responds to questions asking about *yourself at your best*. Each item is of the type usually found on personality questionnaires; a hypothetical example would be "I like my self." The test taker responds on a scale anchored from 0, *never*, to 100, *always*. In the standard series, the test taker then responds to questions dealing with yourself (introject) at your best, yourself at your worst, your significant other person at their best, yourself in this relationship, your significant other person at their worst, yourself in the other-worst relationship, your mother when you were age 5 to 10, yourself with your mother when you were 5 to 10, your father when you were 5 to 10, yourself with your father when you were 5 to 10, your mother with your father when you were 5 to 10, and your father with your mother when you were 5 to 10.

According to the manual, the reading level corresponds to the seventh to eighth grade. However, readability indexes may be misleading when applied to short questionnaire items. If respondents know the meaning of words such as "fume" and "sulk," then the SASB is at an appropriate level.

In that the SASB is more of a therapeutic tool than a traditional personality test, the qualifications for use are relatively high. The manual suggests that the clinical user be a licensed psychologist, or similarly qualified licensed individual, in a counseling relationship with a client. In addition, the user should be familiar with the SASB model and have completed a workshop or viewed a workshop videotape. A clinical user must be registered, although special provisions are made for research use.

Scoring is complex and accomplished through the use of the CD-ROM. Scores, or parameters, are generated by the system corresponding to: (a) cluster scores for each domain; (b) pattern coefficients; and (c) weighted affiliation and autonomy scores. A report is generated that can be thought of as a map of the individual's relationships. According to the manual, the analyses should not be used for decision-making purposes in connection with legal issues or eligibility for entitlements.

DEVELOPMENT. Although described above as based on a trait-state-situational approach to measurement and a structural analysis of behavior, the model underlying the SASB is far richer and more complex than stating that it is a *trait-state-situational* approach suggests. The SASB is based on an interpersonal model of behavior that has been developed as a result of a number of years of research and work on the instrument. The model underlying the SASB can be traced back to the work on interpersonal and intrapsychic space conducted by Sullivan, Murray, and Leary. These ideas have been further developed by Lorna Smith Benjamin into the system underlying the SASB. Benjamin and colleagues have directed a great deal of research attention toward refining and applying the SASB model.

This theory is too complex to describe adequately in this review. However, in brief, the SASB model identifies interactions or relationships based on three coding decisions involving: (a) attentional focus; (b) love or hate; and (c) separation or differentiation. Those relationships are evaluated at their worst and at their best, and with multiple people under multiple conditions. The nature of these relationships is then compared to one's self-concept. Thus, the SASB provides a structured method for rating such relationships and their effects on self-concept. This rating can serve as a basis for discussions in the therapeutic relationship and can also be used to track progress during the therapy process.

TECHNICAL. Evaluating the psychometric properties of the SASB is difficult in that both classical and modern psychometrics depend upon the concept of a true score or latent trait, and it is just such a latent trait approach that the SASB rejects. The question then becomes one of how do you evaluate the psychometric properties of a trait-state-situational approach. For an instrument such as the SASB, what constitutes a score and what does a score mean? Nevertheless, the manual does try to present data on traditional psychometric properties; however, deciphering what these results mean or how the analyses were conducted is difficult.

The SASB is a standardized instrument. All scoring is completed by the computer programs. The psychologist or counselor may decide to vary the number and nature of the relationships rated by the client.

Norms are available but are surprisingly limited given the number of studies conducted using the SASB. The norms are based on relatively small samples, 98 to 133 participants depending upon form, and the samples are lacking in diversity in terms of age and race.

Although the SASB now uses a more conventional method of estimating reliability, it is still difficult to determine exactly how reliability estimates are being determined. For the medium form, an average split half of .82 is reported for a sample of 98. Test-retest reliabilities (over intervals of 4–6 weeks) also tend to be above .80, although they vary as a function of the score of interest and the relationship being rated. In general, reliabilities are poorer for ratings of relationships at their worst. The reported internal-consistency and test-retest reliabilities are within, or above, the range typically found for self-report personality or attitude measures.

The SASB does appear to be face valid and its content validity is supported through expert judgments and dimensional ratings. The manual presents the results of factor analytic studies. However, it is difficult to evaluate the meaning or impact of these studies based upon the information provided. Furthermore, it is difficult to understand how performing a simple principal components analysis can be used to support the validity of what is a state-trait-situational measure.

The reported correlations with other measures appear to be lower than desirable. The manual lists a number of studies related to predictive validity, although most of these studies seem to involve success in therapy and the manual does not report correlation coefficients. It would appear that the best indicator of the efficacy of the SASB is not to be found in traditional psychometric criteria, but rather in its usefulness in the therapeutic relationship.

COMMENTARY. The strengths of the SASB are probably also its weaknesses. The SASB is a unique system, more of a therapeutic tool than a traditional test. It is based upon a very specific theory of personality that incorporates a state-trait-situation approach, although it is compatible with a wide range of therapies. This approach is somewhat at odds with both the medical model of psychology and also the traditional latent trait model upon which modern and classical psychometrics are based. Thus, whether one decides to use the SASB will be a function of one's personal philosophies and theories toward models of individual differences and approaches to therapy.

Evaluating the SASB is similar to trying to evaluate the Rorschach or the MMPI. The SASB is more of a system than a test, and it is a complex system with its own terminology and approach. Adequate training is required in order to use the system, and it is probably one of those instruments where a person learns something new every time they administer the SASB.

The SASB is the product of a great deal of effort on the part of Benjamin and colleagues. They are to be commended for attempting to continually update and refine the instrument.

One of the weaknesses of the SASB would appear to be its length and complexity. Despite the manual statement that this is an easy instrument to read, there appear to be a number of words in the instrument that would be unknown to many high school students and even a percentage of college students. In addition, the long form of the questionnaire can take hours to complete even for a speedy reader. Thus, this is an instrument where the client must be motivated to put forth a consistent effort to complete the measure in an accurate fashion. One must wonder how many psychiatric patients possess this type of motivation. Unfortunately, scores are not generated that might be used to detect less than honest responding in either the negative or positive direction, nor other types of biased responding.

The manual does seem to reflect improvements from easier versions. However, the placement of figures and tables at the end of the document makes it difficult to read the manual. This would seem to be a relatively easy problem to fix, and perhaps I received an early version of the most current manual.

It is difficult for a traditionalist to evaluate the psychometric evidence presented, and this is partially due to the format in which it is presented. The SASB is hardly a traditional test, and part of the difficulty is no doubt due to the problems inherent in adapting classical psychometrics to a highly unique instrument. However, this does not explain why adequate normative data are not available, but the manual does suggest that such data are on the way.

SUMMARY. The SASB is designed to measure the respondent's perceptions of self and others based on a trait-state-situational approach. It is more of a system than a test, and it is a system that can be used as a therapeutic tool. In its complexity it can be compared to attempting to use the Rorschach or the MMPI, although the underlying theory is obviously quite different. The target population is psychiatric patients and also those within the normal range of personality. However, this is a lengthy, time-consuming instrument, and the rater completing the SASB should be highly motivated. The SASB can probably be best described as a scored, structured measure of a client's relationship history and there are probably very few instruments to which it can be compared. Thus, one's choice to commit to a system as complex as the SASB will be a function of whether one is willing to devote the time and effort necessary to learn and accept the SASB model.

Review of the SASB [Structural Analysis of Social Behavior] Intrex Questionnaires by THOMAS P. HOGAN, Professor of Psychology, University of Scranton, Scranton, PA:

DESCRIPTION AND DEVELOPMENT. The Intrex Questionnaires are purported to be relatively direct measures of the Structural Analysis of Social Behavior (SASB) model. Benjamin, the Intrex author, has expounded the SASB model in a number of publications generally dated to 1974 (see Benjamin, 1974). SASB is a circumplex model, using 108 points as descriptors in a circular or diamond configuration for the full model and a smaller number of points in what is called the cluster model. According to the Intrex manual, the SASB model deals with interpersonal and intrapsychic space in the traditions of Harry Stack Sullivan, Henry Murray, Freedman, Leary, and Schaefer. Although less prominently mentioned than the latter authors, the influence of Freud and Rogers is also apparent. Nor surprisingly in light of this parentage, the principal focus of attention for the model is psychotherapeutic applications. The terms SASB and Intrex are thoroughly mixed in the manual. Sometimes "SASB" refers to the theoretical model, at other times to the questionnaires. The questionnaires are variously labeled SASB, Intrex, and SASB Intrex. The reader struggles to find consistent reference points to the model versus the instrument. Examination of the literature on the SASB model (e.g., the Special Section on SASB in the *Journal of Consulting and Clinical Psychology*; Benjamin & Newman, 1996) makes it clear that the model has struck a resonant chord with at least some clinicians. However, it is also clear that the model can be applied either with Intrex instruments or with other instruments, hence the need to distinguish between SASB as a model and Intrex as specific instruments. There is also a SASB-based observational coding system that is not covered in the Intrex manual or in this review.

The Intrex Questionnaires comprise three forms: Long, Medium, and Short. The Medium form contains slightly less than half of the items in the Long form; the Short form contains half the items in the Medium form. Each form contains 12 sections such as My Introject at Best, My Introject at Worst, My Significant Other Person with Me at Best. The first 2 sections are referred to as the Introject, a kind of self-concept measure. In the Long Form, the first 2 sections contain 36 items; each of the other sections contains 72 items. The manual notes that the relationships described in the sections (e.g., significant other) can also be applied to other relationships, especially the therapist-client relationship. The manual suggests using the questionnaires at various points in time as therapy evolves.

Typical items are: I comfortably look after my own interests; Is very tense, shaky, wary, fearful, with me; I gently, lovingly stroke and soothe her without asking anything in return. Many of the items are repeated from one section to another but with change in reference point, for example, changing I to her or him to me. Responses are given on 11-point scales, ranging from 0 to 100 in 10-point intervals (0, 10, 20, etc.). Lower scale values carry the verbal label "Never, Not at All." Higher scale values carry the verbal label "Always, Perfectly." The manual does not include any description of the development of these items or any revision of item content based on empirical study of item functioning.

It is difficult to define exactly how many scores the Intrex Questionnaires yield. The manual provides data for each of the sections listed above and for several additional dimensions derived from those sections, including Affiliation, Attack, Au-

tonomy, Control, and Conflict. However, references to such scores are inconsistent in the manual. The Intrex software attempts to place the individual examinee in the circumplex SASB model, as described earlier. Significant portions of the Intrex manual describe the use of this exceedingly complex software, which produces graphical displays of results. Many of the graphs, which are visually appealing, are oriented around the control-emancipate, protect-ignore, blame-affirm, and attack-active love dimensions from the SASB cluster circumplex model. The Intrex manual vacillates between espousing dimensional analysis of traits and eschewing any such approach as entirely inadequate. The manual expresses an explicit preference for a "trait x state x situation" philosophy but much of the discussion reverts to a trait analysis.

TECHNICAL INFORMATION. Presentation of technical information in the user's manual is entirely substandard. Many of the studies are based on very small samples or inadequate description of the samples. For example, Short form test-retest reliability data are based on $N = 12$; even for these cases, the manual provides virtually no description other than that they were "undergraduates." What are purported to be norms are based on 71 and 57 undergraduates for Short forms 1 and 2, respectively, 98 cases for the Medium form, and 133 cases for the Long form. All groups receive minimal description. "Norms" consist of means and standard deviations for cluster scores and for Affiliation and Autonomy. These data provide only the grossest interpretive information.

To the extent that one can draw any conclusions about the data presented on reliability, one notes that the indices vary wildly from high to near zero for various scores. Just as for the normative data, reliability data are based on small, inadequately described samples. Validity data presented in the manual include extensive factor analyses. The analyses treat only subgroups of items (e.g., only the "Introject at Worst" or only the "I reacted to mother" items). Hence, it is difficult to make sense of the overall structure of the entire set of items in the questionnaires. Discussions of concurrent and predictive validity are largely discursive, partly explaining why the concepts are inappropriate for Intrex and partly making indirect reference to other studies. The summary statement on validity asserts that "People shown the [Intrex] output with the guidance described in Part I almost always understand it immediately and affirm that it is accurate" (manual, p. 76). The manual presents no evidence in support of this claim, nor any discussion of a Barnum-effect for the purported agreement. Many of the statements in the manual beg for consequential validity evidence but none is forthcoming. For example, the manual states that "Showing research subjects their individual output can be helpful to their personal growth" and "Repeated references to the Intrex report during therapy can keep therapy on track" (p. 12). There is no attempt to validate these and similar claims.

Meier (1996) reviewed the Intrex Short form described in the 1988 version of the manual. He noted that the manual needed to be reorganized, that sample sizes were inadequate, and that further study of validity was required. All these criticisms still stand. In fact, they need to be emphasized.

SUMMARY. The Intrex Questionnaires are by no means ready for routine use. They are deficient with respect to all three of the traditional pillars of psychometric quality: norms, reliability, and validity. Normative information is almost entirely lacking. Reliability estimates, where they are available, are extremely varied. Validity data are sparse. As a first step in advancing what may, in fact, be a promising set of instruments, the publisher should produce a manual that meets at least minimal standards for contemporary practice. For now, the Intrex questionnaires should be confined to research use.

REVIEWER'S REFERENCES

Benjamin, L. S. (1974). Structural analysis of social behavior. *Psychological Review, 81*, 392–425.
Benjamin, L. S., & Newman, F. L. (Eds.). (1996). Structural analysis of social behavior [Special section]. *Journal of Consulting and Clinical Psychology, 64*, 1203–1275.
Meier, S. T. (1996). [Review of the Intrex Questionanires]. In J. C. Conoley & J. C. Impara (Eds.), *The twelfth mental measurements yearbook* (pp. 498–500). Lincoln, NE: Buros Institute of Mental Measurements.

[215]

Scales for Diagnosing Attention-Deficit/ Hyperactivity Disorder.

Purpose: "To help identify children and adolescents who have attention-deficit/hyperactivity disorder (ADHD)."

Population: Ages 5-0 through 18-11.
Publication Date: 2002.
Acronym: SCALES.
Scores, 4: Inattention, Hyperactivity, Impulsivity, Total.
Administration: Individual
Forms, 2: Summary/School Rating Scale Form (SRS), Home Rating Scale Form (HRS).

Price Data, 2003: $86 per complete kit including examiner's manual (78 pages), 25 summary/school rating forms, and 25 home rating forms; $51 per examiner's manual; $25 per 25 summary/school rating forms; $15 per 25 home rating forms.
Time: 15–20 minutes.
Comments: Completed by parents and teachers of target child; designed as part of a comprehensive ADHD assessment; identifies specific behavioral targets for intervention; allows for ratings on DSM-IV-TR criterion for ADHD.
Authors: Gail Ryser and Kathleen McConnell.
Publisher: PRO-ED.

Review of the Scales for Diagnosing Attention-Deficit/Hyperactivity Disorder by JOSEPH G. LAW, JR., Professor of Behavioral Studies, University of South Alabama, Mobile, AL:

DESCRIPTION. The Scales for Diagnosing Attention-Deficit/Hyperactivity Disorder (SCALES) consists of Summary/School and Home Rating Scale forms. There are summary scores for inattention, Hyperactivity, Impulsivity, and a Total score. The Home Rating Scale (HRS) consists of 39 behavioral items that parents use to rate their child on a 4-point Likert scale. A rating of zero is assigned if the student never exhibits the target behavior or if it never interferes with daily activities. A score of 1 indicates that the behavior is seldom exhibited (or rarely interferes), 2 for occasionally exhibits (or sometimes interferes), and a score of 3 if the behavior is regularly exhibited (or constantly interferes). The 39 items on the Parent and Summary/School Rating form (SRS) are phrased very similarly, with only slight changes to differentiate between home and school environments. Just to the right side of the rater's responses are columns labeled Inattentive, Hyperactive, and Impulsive, which are for the examiner's use only. The test administrator transposes the raw scores (Teacher and Parent ratings) to the appropriate column, then sums each column front and back for a total raw score for each of the three dimensions. The cover sheet of the Summary/School form contains sections for identifying information, score summaries, profiles of scores, DSM-IV-TR criteria, and space for interpretation and recommendations. The back of the SRS contains a listing of SCALES items that directly address DSM-IV-TR ADHD symptoms of inattentiveness, hyperactivity, and impulsivity. There is clear, step-by-step guidance for interpretation of the results. SCALES covers ages ranging from 5 years to 18 years, 11 months. There are 18 items measuring Inattentiveness, 12 items for Hyperactivity, and 9 items for Impulsivity.

DEVELOPMENT. The manual contains a review of basic concepts in defining ADHD, and the causes, prevalence, and educational implications of the disorder. DSM-IV-TR criteria are discussed, as well as guidelines established by the American Academy of Pediatrics. The authors report that their underlying assumptions in constructing the SCALES are that the DSM-IV-TR description of ADHD specifies appropriate diagnostic criteria for the disorder and that the criteria can be accurately and reliably applied to individuals. The authors incorporated into the SCALES the DSM-IV-TR criteria that diagnosis of ADHD (a) required interference with age-appropriate behavior, (b) was pervasive (i.e., in two or more settings), (c) occurred for at least 6 months, and (d) had its onset before 7 years of age. Items from the authors' 54-item criterion-referenced scale were subjected to item analysis and bias studies. Some items were dropped. Items were written so they could be applied to home and school and a separate form developed for parents (HRS) and teachers (SRS), thus meeting the DSM-IV-TR and American Academy of Pediatrics guidelines. Behaviorally stated items from other childhood and adolescent inventories such as the Behavior Assessment System for Children, Conners' Rating Scales—Revised (CRS-R), and McCarney's Attention Deficit Disorders Evaluation Scale were studied. The keyword "interference" was adopted from the DSM-IV-TR and a Likert-type scale was used to assess the degree of severity.

TECHNICAL. SCALES was normed on 3,448 children and adolescents ranging in age from 5 years to 18 years, 11 months. The students were drawn from 26 states in four major geographic regions of the United States as defined by the 1998 Census. Teachers were asked to complete their version on three to five of their students. Parents of those children completed the Home version. The ADHD sample contained 1,379 students aged 5–18 years who had previously been diagnosed with ADHD. There were 2,069 non-ADHD students in the same age range who were also assessed with the SRS and HRS. Eighty-two percent were Caucasian, 13% African American, and 5% of other ethnic origins. Forty-nine percent were female, 51% male.

Reliability. Internal consistency reliability was assessed with Cronbach's coefficient alpha averaging in the high .90s across age groups. Reliability estimates for the SRS on the Inattentive, Hyperactive, and Impulsivity scales averaged in the mid .90s. There were similar results for the HRS. Raw scores are transformed into standard scores with a mean of 100 and a standard deviation of 15. Standard errors of measurement are depicted in tables and were very low across age groups (around 3 points for most). A test-retest study (intervals of 2 weeks or more between administrations) using 30 students ages 7 to 10 years in Austin, Texas is reported in the manual. The students were rated on the SRS by three teachers. Reliability among raters was reported as .91 for Inattentiveness, .95 for Hyperactivity, .95 for Impulsivity, and .96 for the total score. Interscorer differences were minimal.

Validity. Conventional item analysis and differential item function analyses were carried out using logistic regression models and showed the SCALES to be nonbiased in terms of gender, race, and ethnic origin. There was a high correlation between parent and teacher scores on the HRS and SRS. Median correlational coefficients were .63. Comparing the SCALES to the Conners' Rating Scale—Revised resulted in a correlation of .67 for the SRS Inattentive score and the Conners' Cognitive Problems scale. SRS inattentiveness correlated .42 with the Conners' Oppositional scale and was nonsignificant when compared to the Anxious-Shy score on the Conners. Results were similar, though slightly less pronounced using the HRS and Conners. There is a wealth of data in the manual that lend strong support to the reliability and potential validity of the SCALES. Two factor analytic studies using oblique rotation are also reported in the manual, which indicate the SCALES to be a promising instrument.

COMMENTARY. The 78-page SCALES manual is a model of clarity and conciseness, yet contains ample information on the development, scoring, administration, interpretation, reliability, and validity of the instrument. In fact, it would make a good teaching example in a graduate course on tests and measurements to illustrate the proper development and documentation of test instruments. There are three appendices with normative data that allow the examiner to compare an individual child or adolescent's scores to the ADHD and non-ADHD samples. Reliability and validity evidence is excellent and factor analytic studies support the rationale behind item selection. Case studies and interpretative information add to the utility of this instrument. The use of DSM-IV-TR and American Academy of Pediatrics guidelines gives the SCALES a firm empirical foundation. The strengths and limitations of using a rating scale to assess ADHD is well covered in the manual.

Although the SRS protocol is well designed and easy to use, there is one potential minor weakness. It contains four pages (one page on each side of the foldout protocol). The actual ratings are completed on the inside of the protocol and there are three vertical columns for use by the test administrator. The raw scores circled by each respondent are transferred by the administrator to the right-most column (with a short horizontal line for each item placed to fall into Inattentive, Hyperactive, or Impulsive categories). The administrator sums the raw scores, then uses the appendices to transform them into standardized scores. However, this column is not clearly labeled to signify that it is for the administrator's use only. Some respondents may inappropriately believe that they should fill in these blanks with something and try to transfer the scores. This could create some confusion.

It would be interesting to compare the results of various visual and auditory continuous performance tests to the Inattentiveness, Hyperactivity, and Impulsivity scores on SCALES. The instrument might also prove useful in validating research using PET and SPECT scans studies of brain function in ADHD students.

SUMMARY. The SCALES is a well-developed, reliable, and potentially valid instrument for use in assessing attention-deficit/hyperactivity disorder. The authors selected items that are good behavioral descriptors of ADHD symptoms, with a sound theoretical and empirical base. Normative data for a large, representative sample of ADHD and non-ADHD students aged 5 to 18 years are provided, along with ample interpretative guidelines and case studies. The SCALES is an excellent instrument for identifying students with ADHD, selecting potential goals for individualized instruction, measuring and documenting educational progress, and for future research. The instrument should be utilized along with other broad measures of behavior

(i.e., rating scales which assist in identifying oppositional defiant behavior, anxiety, depression, etc.). This well-constructed and normed inventory should prove very useful in the future to clinicians, educators, and researchers.

[216]

The Scenotest: A Practical Technique for Understanding Unconscious Problems and Personality Structure.

Purpose: A projective instrument intended "to help very quickly assess emotional problems in children."
Population: Children and adolescents.
Publication Dates: 1971–1998.
Scores: Score information available from publisher.
Administration: Individual.
Price Data, 2001: $775 per complete test kit and manual (1998, 110 pages).
Time: Administration time not reported.
Comments: Material in the test kit consists of flexible human figures and accessories including animals, trees, symbolic figures, and items from everyday life.
Author: G. von Staabs (original edition) and Joseph A. Smith (translated from the German edition and adapted).
Publisher: Hogrefe & Huber Publishers.

Review of The Scenotest: A Practical Technique for Understanding Unconscious Problems and Personality Structure by JOSEPH C. KUSH, Associate Professor and Coordinator, School Psychology Program, Duquesne University, Pittsburgh, PA:

DESCRIPTION. The Scenotest (translated from the German and adapted by Joseph A. Smith) is a projective measure designed as "a means of studying neurotic children's unconscious relations and problems with their immediate environment" (manual, p. 1). More specifically, the Scenotest attempts to "mobilize repressed drives and allows the patient to act these out in a miniature world" (manual, p. 1) by providing a series of bendable figures that are arranged in "scenes" reflective of the patient's environment and how they react to it both consciously and unconsciously.

The Scenotest was originally published in Germany but was out of print for some time until 1964. The English version of the instrument was subsequently published in 1991. The author of the Scenotest, Gerhild von Staabs, indicates the new edition of the Scenotest: (a) contains new knowledge from experiences of the Scenotest in psychiatry, (b) has an expanded section on the use of the scale in forensic medicine and a new section on capital crimes, (c) better describes the use of the Scenotest in studying child-mother relationships, (d) has an expanded reference section, (e) includes testimonials regarding the instrument from outside German-speaking countries, and (f) contains an expanded description of the materials and observation sheets. Five pages of references are included in the test manual although they are significantly outdated, with the most current citation coming from a 1962 publication.

The author indicates that the Scenotest can be used with "children 3 years and older and for adults of all ages" (manual, p. 2). The materials consist of 16 bendable figures (8 adults and 8 children) varying in size from 7 to 15 centimeters. Each of the figures differs in size, clothing, and facial expression "so that all persons in the subject's environment can be portrayed" (manual, p. 3). Additional materials included in the test case are building blocks and accessory parts designed to allow the examinee to create scenes on the test-lid "stage." Specifically, the 16 figures included in the Scenotest kit are a grandmother and grandfather, 2 mothers and fathers (in dress and leisure clothing), a doctor, maid, 4 children, pink and blue twins, a baby, and a princess. Ethnic diversity is not present in the human characters; all figures are Caucasian. Additional materials include 12 animals, 3 vehicles, trees and garden beds, flowers, fruits, household objects, and three symbolic figures (snowman, dwarf, and angel). Consistent with psychodynamic theory, the test manual indicates the symbolic nature of much of the material. For example, the manual indicates that the baby "may express a desire for a younger sibling, or as an object of jealousy for older siblings" (manual, p. 5). Similarly, the "voracious crocodile, the wily fox, the evil gander all can represent external aggression" (manual, p. 5).

Standardized directions for administration are alarmingly absent; in fact, the test manual avoids the opportunity for consistent administration instructions by writing, "The material and the way in which it is presented usually have sufficient clarity and attractiveness to the subject that only few words are necessary to initiate construction of a scene" (manual, p. 8). Given the lack of invariant administration instructions, it is not surprising that the test manual

makes no mention of any evidence of interrater reliability. The closest the manual does come to standardized directions for administration occurs when the author writes that adults might be directed to "construct something—anything that occurs to them—on the stage, like a director would set up a film scene" (manual, p. 8).

A standardized coding criteria is also lacking in the Scenotest manual; following the presentation of the materials, the only scoring criteria provided for the therapist are that he or she should refrain from making suggestions or questioning the subject. The only exception to this guideline occurs when the Scenotest is used as a therapeutic, rather than a diagnostic, tool. Subsequent to the construction of a scene, the therapist asks the client to explain what he or she has built, again avoiding direct questioning. Additional guidelines direct the examiner to observe facial and nonverbal expressions of the examinee, as well as other qualitative aspects of the scene (e.g., which materials are used/discarded; does the subject handle the figures "hesitantly or decisively"?) in an attempt to collect more interpretative information. At this point, the therapist is instructed to sketch or photograph the Scenotest scene. The test manual indicates that most scenes can be completed within 30 minutes.

The majority of the manual (pages 23 through 97) uses anecdotal, case study information in an attempt to describe the clinical utility of the Scenotest as an assessment, therapeutic, and research tool. Examples are provided for utilizing the Scenotest in short-term psychotherapy and in psychoanalytic treatment. Brief examples of how the Scenotest might be used in applied settings such as in developmental psychology, vocational counseling, or in conjunction with hypnosis are also provided. The possibility of inappropriate interpretation is magnified significantly, however, given the fact that no examiner qualifications are provided. Certainly it would be reasonable to expect differential interpretations among examiners with varying levels of experience and qualifications. As such, interrater reliability is not reported. This criticism is not unique to the Scenotest; it is a limitation of many subjectively based projective techniques. Unless substantial agreement exists among psychologists administering an instrument, there exists only a very small likelihood that the instrument will subsequently produce internal consistency, temporal stability, or extratest correlations.

TECHNICAL. Unfortunately, the scale was developed without the benefit of a standardization sample and in the absence of any psychometric data. The lack of adequate norming stands in direct contrast to one of the basic requisites in test construction provided in the *Standards for Educational and Psychological Testing* (AERA, APA, & NCME, 1999). The clinical utility of the instrument is, therefore, greatly compromised and should be used only with great caution.

In addition to the lack of published interrater reliability data, the Scenotest also fails to provide any evidence of test-retest stability. Potential users are given insufficient information about what constitutes normal fluctuation across time or across subgroups (e.g., children and adults, clinical populations, ethnic groups) and the test manual provides no indication of what changes in scenes one should expect from administration to administration. The test manual does indicated that "the intelligence of the subject may be seen in the overall way in which the subject arranges the individual parts of the materials and uses them to express ideas" (p. 13); however, no data are provided to demonstrate whether more creative individuals will produce more varied scenes across examinations, even in the absence of changes in personality. In the absence of test-retest data, potential users of the Scenotest are unable to determine whether changes in examinee's scenes over time reflect normal creative fluctuations, possible abnormal etiology, or scenes that are being measured differentially across time by the examiner. Especially for children, the normal tendency for personality development is that it becomes increasingly stable during the lifespan yet no longitudinal studies are described in the test manual.

COMMENTARY. Even the most meticulously standardized, highly reliable, and comprehensively normed instrument will have little clinical value unless it can demonstrate substantial correlates. Given a lack of established, or even preliminary validity data, clinicians are severely restricted in the confidence they can derive from even basic decision making when utilizing the Scenotest. Additionally, the test manual provides no evidence (beyond personal testimony) of incremental validity (i.e., the extent to which information derived from the Scenotest will increase the accuracy in predic-

tions derived from other sources of information). Without zero-order correlations, or hit rates, an accurate knowledge of true positives, true negatives, false positives, and false negatives can never be known.

SUMMARY. The Scenotest lacks even basic psychometric properties for standardization, reliability, and validity. Examiner qualifications and training are unspecified, a factor that compounds measurement accuracy given that the scenes are highly subjectively evaluated. The test manual provides absolutely no psychometric evidence to support the notion that individualized interpretations of the Scenotest scenes are valid nor that they provide any additional information beyond what could be obtained from other sources of clinical data. Claims of valid individualized interpretations must be supported by replicated, empirical evidence and not solely by the assertions of esteemed and experienced clinicians. Scenotest stimuli are not culture-free, and cross-cultural and cross-national differences certainly may influence participant responses. An additional shortcoming of the Scenotest is the lack of appropriate normative data for various ethnic groups.

To begin to resolve these uncertainties, the initial stage of a long-term research agenda should begin by attempting to establish basic test-retest reliability of results from the Scenotest. This research should commence by utilizing short test-retest intervals, which maximize the likelihood of minimal environmental or psychological change. Samples should include nonpatient, outpatient, and a variety of inpatient populations. Additionally, the assignment of multiple raters to score scenes will facilitate the elimination of temporal inconsistency resulting from interrater disagreement.

REVIEWER'S REFERENCE

American Educational Research Association, American Psychological Association, & National Council on Measurement in Education. (1999). *Standards for educational and psychological testing.* Washington, DC: American Educational Research Association.

Review of The Scenotest: A Practical Technique for Understanding Unconscious Problems and Personality Structure by PAUL RETZLAFF, Professor of Psychology, University of Northern Colorado, Greeley, CO:

DESCRIPTION. The Scenotest is a projective method utilizing objects, dolls, and figures. The participant is asked to construct a "scene." This scene is then interpreted. The "test" is really two parts. The first part is the materials. The second is the interpretation. The author suggests

5-year levels are newer sections of the test and have not undergone the same analyses that were done with younger age levels. Tables depict the characteristics of the sample group.

A great deal of the reference manual is made up of descriptions of earlier versions of the test along with previous validity and reliability studies. The reliability and validity studies on the present SGS II seem scanty. Internal consistency reliability for individual skill areas, using Cronbach's alpha values, are generally in the .90s, with one at .61 and another at .88. Item reliability analysis for consistency of the Cognitive skill area indicates values generally above .60. There are some values, however, at .20 to .49. Although these weaker items represent areas thought to be consistent with cognitive functioning, no attempt is made to examine this lack of correlation. Intercorrelations at age Levels 1 through 4 appear acceptable but at age 5, intercorrelations are much closer to .00. One explanation for this is that children are scoring toward the maximum possible score.

The discussion of validity is limited to two paragraphs with general references to appendices in the areas of concurrent validity and construct validity. The construct and concurrent validity analyses were done using case studies with the authors determining validity indicators in each case. The British version of the Denver Developmental Screening Test was chosen to use for examining construct validity even though the authors declare that the Denver "is too crude and is intended only for screening purposes and not for providing detailed information" (reference manual, p. 34). A reference is made to an ongoing research study using interrater reliability with the Griffiths Mental Development Scale and the SGS II but no results have been posted.

COMMENTARY. In reviewing the items in this instrument, there appears to be a developmental sequence in the various areas but other aspects of the test cast doubt on its usability and strength. The number of children in the norming group is insufficient, particularly at the 4- and 5-year-old ages. The forms are somewhat difficult to follow due to a numbering system that is not explained in the user's guide. No scoring guide is found, other than some examples. The reference manual is difficult to use due to its organization, and references to appendices are vague due to lack of labeling indicators in the text. The chapter on

the history of the development of the original instrument has twice as many pages as the standardization and commentary on the present instrument. Reliability and validity of the test needs further studies to better define its value and usability. As with many developmental tests, it appears to be lacking in these areas at the 5-year-old level. In most of the skill areas, determination of developmental level for a 12-month age range is based on only one or two items. Another area of concern is the Cognitive Skill area, which seems to be arbitrarily constructed from items within the first nine skill areas. Of particular concern is the knowledge that language and cognition are so closely related in preschool years (Bloom, 1970; Bowerman, 1989), yet there are no items used in the Cognitive area from either of the skill areas involving language development.

The test developers have been quite clear that this assessment tool is to be used as a screening instrument and by health professionals as part of an overall health surveillance program for preschoolers. Ongoing training is also stressed as a highly recommended component of the overall program.

SUMMARY. Including this type of developmental screening instrument with an overall health surveillance system adds an important component to such a program along with encouragement to repeat it at regularly scheduled intervals. The developmental sequences have wide age ranges to avoid false positives for developmental delays, which is appropriate for a screening test. The major drawbacks to this instrument are lack of quality studies of reliability and validity; a cognitive scale that is formulated with little concern for concurrent validity; and usability of the manuals that are confusing and at times vague. This test is standardized in the United Kingdom and would, therefore, be unacceptable for use with children in the United States or other countries.

REVIEWER'S REFERENCES

Bloom, L. (1970). *Language development: Form and function of emerging grammars.* Cambridge, MA: MIT Press.
Bowerman, M. (1989). Learning a semantic system: What role do cognitive prerequisites play? In M. Rice & R. L. Schiefelbusch (Eds.), *The teachability of language* (pp. 133–169). Baltimore: P. H. Brookes Pub. Co.

Review of the Schedule of Growing Skills: Second Edition by LEAH M. NELLIS, Assistant Professor of Educational and Counseling Psychology, University of Kentucky, Lexington, KY:

DESCRIPTION. The Schedule of Growing Skills: Second Edition (SGS-II) is a developmental screening procedure for children ranging in age from birth to 5 years. Developed in the U.K., the SGS-II is intended for use by professionals involved in child health programs, especially health visitors, general practitioners, and pediatricians to identify children for whom a comprehensive developmental assessment is needed. The SGS-II consists of 179 developmentally sequenced items organized into nine skills areas: Passive Postural, Active Postural, Locomotor, Manipulative, Visual, Hearing and Language, Speech and Language, Interactive Social, and Self-Care Social Skills. Each skill area is further divided into skill sets, within which similar items are listed in developmental sequence. For example, the Manipulative Skills Area is divided into the following skill sets: Hand Skills (13 items), Bricks (6 items), Drawing (6 items), and Draw-a-Person Test (3 items). An additional Cognitive Skill Area is available based upon 34 items that are also included in the previously mentioned skill areas.

Designed to be administered in a home or clinic setting, the SGS-II serves as a component of a 20-minute interview/observation session with a child and parent. The authors note that users employ clinical judgment to determine the starting point, order of item administration, and selection of skill areas to be assessed. However, it is noted that two or more skill sets within each skill area must be administered for scoring purposes. Administration and scoring procedures are listed in the user's guide. In some cases, procedures and passing criteria are vague, leaving opportunity for administrator interpretation and error.

Scores are calculated and interpreted using the profile form. For each of the nine skill areas, the score is based upon the sum of the highest scores achieved in each skill set administered. Scoring of the Cognitive Skill Area is based upon an item count of successfully performed tasks; thus, all items within this area must be administered. Transferring scores to the profile form provides developmental age equivalents for each of the nine skill areas and the cognitive skill area and allows for comparison between chronological and developmental ages. Users are encouraged to consider the need for a referral for further evaluation when a child's developmental age is more than one age interval below his or her chronological age. Age intervals vary across the age range with a

minimum interval of 2 months and a maximum interval of 12 months.

DEVELOPMENT. The SGS-II is a revision of the previous Schedule of Growing Skills (1987). The original SGS was based upon a research instrument used with children from birth to 3 years as part of the National Childhood Encephalopathy Study (NCES) during the early 1980s. The NCES schedule, a modification of Mary Sheridan's STYCAR developmental sequences, was found to be suitable as a screening tool and was subsequently expanded to include children to 5 years of age and was renamed the Schedule of Growing Skills (SGS).

Regular users of the SGS provided feedback to the test authors, resulting in the changes reflected in the SGS-II. Although feedback was described as positive, the authors report a significant revision of the items and materials. Specifically, items were reworded, deleted, and re-ordered to fit with clinical experience. The authors report that such changes were subjected to investigation; however, the manual does not provide results of such investigation or discuss details of the changes made. The addition of the Cognitive Skill Area in the SGS-II was in response to users' concerns about the lack of sensitivity to cognitive deficits. Items using materials such as a formboard and peg-board were added and existing items were selected to represent the Cognitive Skill Area.

TECHNICAL. The SGS-II was standardized on 348 children recruited from eight NHS Trusts across England and Wales. Examiners were recruited from professionals familiar with the SGS and were asked to identify children to be screened. According to the manual, children were randomly selected based upon whether they were registered to be screened; thus the developmental status of the children remains unclear. Males and females were equally represented in the standardization sample, which was described as mostly White (78%), English speaking (91%), and from professional households.

In addressing the psychometric properties of the SGS-II, the authors state that several studies have been conducted to address the reliability and validity of the instrument. However, some studies appear to be part of an ongoing study and results were not presented. Evidence of internal consistency was provided with coefficient alphas for the 10 skill areas ranging from .61 for Passive Postural to .97 for Cognitive Skills. A concurrent validity study involved administration of the SGS-II to 11 children previously diagnosed with developmental delay. Results were not summarized but were presented individually as brief case studies. A construct validity study was conducted with 15 children using the Denver II and the SGS-II. Again, results were presented as case studies rather than as quantitative data.

COMMENTARY. The authors of the SGS-II provide a pertinent discussion of the areas of developmental assessment and delay and appropriately identify the utility of the SGS-II as being a screening instrument. Although the SGS-II may facilitate clinical decision making by experienced professionals, concerns regarding scale development, administration, and psychometric properties impact its utility as a standardized instrument. Specifically, although the allowance for clinical judgment and flexibility is heralded, the resultant variations in administration and scoring may introduce a significant degree of error. Research regarding interrater reliability may address this issue but was not provided in the manual. Interpretation of the SGS-II is impacted by the varying age intervals as well as scoring procedures that do not account for instances in which all skill sets within areas were not administered. In addition, the selection process for Cognitive Skill items was not fully explained nor supported by the data provided. For example, during development, four items were described as not correlating highly with the overall Cognitive Skill area but were retained in the area for scoring purposes. Further, the user's guide suggests that the addition of this skill area allows the SGS-II to be compared to the Bayley Scales of Infant Development and the Wechsler Preschool and Primary Scales of Intelligence. This suggestion is not supported by data nor by logic, given the differences in scope of these instruments. As with the previous SGS, evidence of reliability and validity is limited with existing studies that are not fully explained and analyzed.

SUMMARY. The SGS-II is purported to be an accurate and reliable measure of developmental screening for young children. However, the test authors do not provide adequate explanation or evidence regarding psychometric properties such as test-retest reliability, predictive validity, and discriminant validity to support its widespread use as a screening tool. Although the SGS-II might be clinically helpful to trained professionals, further research is needed to support its proposed role in developmental assessment.

[218]

SCID Screen Patient Questionnaire and SCID Screen Patient Questionnaire—Extended.

Purpose: "An Axis I symptoms and disorders screening tool."

Population: Psychiatric or general medical patients ages 18 or older.

Publication Dates: 1991–1999.

Acronym: SSPQ, SSPQ-X.

Scores, 6: Mood Disorders, Anxiety Disorders, Substance Use Disorders, Somatoform Disorders, Eating Disorders, Schizophrenia and Other Psychotic Disorders.

Administration: Individual.

Price Data, 2002: $395 per SCID Screen PQ for Windows including 3 report options: Summary of Responses, Concise Report, Long Report; SCID Screen PQ and SCID Screen PQ Extended Software Manual (1999, 108 pages), and PsychManager Lite CD Kit (PsychManager Lite CD, Quick Start Guide, Key Diskette); $45 per SCID Screen PQ for Windows Preview Version (3 uses); Price data available from publisher for SSPQ-X including 2 report options: Summary of Response, Diagnostic Report.

Time: (20) minutes SSPQ; (30–45) minutes for SSPQ-X.

Comments: SSPQ is an abbreviated computer-administered screening version of the Structured Clinical Interview for DSM-IV (SCID-I) and an adaptation of the MiniSCID for DSM-IIIR; SSPQ-X is an extended adaptation of the SSPQ; System requirements: Pentium, 120 MB hard drive, VGA or SVGA color monitor, 16 MB RAM, 3.5-inch floppy disk drive, CD-ROM drive, Windows 95 or higher.

Authors: Michael B. First, Miriam Gibbon, Janet B. W. Williams, and Robert L. Spitzer.

Publisher: Multi-Health Systems, Inc. and American Psychiatric Association.

Cross References: For reviews by Paul D. Werner and Thomas A. Widiger of the clinician version, see 14:373 (9 references); see also T5:2519 (56 references).

Review of the SCID Screen Patient Questionnaire and SCID Screen Patient Questionnaire—Extended by MARK H. STONE, Professor, Adler School of Professional Psychology, Chicago, IL:

DESCRIPTION AND DEVELOPMENT. The SCID Screen Patient Questionnaire (SSPQ, SSPQ-X) is a computerized screening version of the DSM-IV Structured Clinical Interview. This program inquires of the patient's history and symptoms for individual administration by computer, and is appropriate for general medical patients and psychiatric patients ages 18 and older. It is based upon the Structured Clinical Interview for DSM-IV Axis I Disorders: Clinician Version (1997).

The program is published for use with the PsychManager: Your Professional and Personal Organizer. This combination provides a patient screening routine with a data management program. Time for patient administration is indicated as 20 minutes for the SSPQ, and 30–45 minutes for the SSPQ-X. A patient tutorial assists with administering the questionnaire program.

The SSPQ and the extended version SSPQ-X provide for the assessment of patients in six major areas: (a) Mood, (b) Anxiety, (c) Substance Use, (d) Somatoform, (e) Eating, (f) Schizophrenia and Other Psychotic Disorders. The diagnostic categories cover the standard Axis I DSM-IV categories.

There are three report options available: (a) Summary of Responses, (b) Concise Report, (c) Long Report. A validity check is flagged when a patient has given the same answer to all the questions presented. However, the program only "screens" a patient, and the user is cautioned that this is an initial procedure. A diagnosis should be made only on the basis of an interview and review of the patient's record in company with the SCID.

TECHNICAL.

Reliability. Six studies on reliability were reported. Values of .61 for current and .68 for lifetime diagnoses were reported for test-retest reliability in a sample of 592 persons. Reliability, using percentage of agreement, was 82% for major depression and 86% for generalized anxiety for a sample of 75 patients. Interrater reliability using percentage of agreement for 33 patients was 91% for all diagnoses. Kappa values were .89 for cocaine dependence, and .73 for opioid dependence. Values for lifetime substance abuse were .84 for cocaine and .80 for opioid use. Sample size was not given for these data. There is no clear indication whether the data were produced by a standard interview, or by using the computer version.

Validity. One study on validity, comparing ratings by nurses using the diagnostic interview and medical record review to diagnoses by psychiatrists or psychologists, produced a Kappa value of .77. The sample size was not reported. There is no indication that the computer version was used in this study.

COMMENTARY AND SUMMARY. The software program appears to be an efficient and useful adjunct to a busy clinician or agency. The program worked as indicated. Casual use is not recommended, and the clinician will want to validate any outcomes provided by the computer-generated results to other indicators including a personal interview. The reported reliability and validity studies support the general use of the interview instrument, but there were no specific studies reported about computer-generated diagnoses and their relationship to independent clinical evaluations. This deficiency needs to be addressed.

Two earlier reviews (see reviews by Paul D. Werner and Thomas Widiger, 2001) of the Structured Clinical Interview generally applauded the item development of the instrument and its overall high interrater reliability, but they criticized the lack of normative data and follow-up studies. This deficiency remains. The computer-administered version may facilitate the administration of the instrument, but further studies on validation for using this computer version should be forthcoming in order to support any recommendation for its use.

REVIEWER'S REFERENCES

Werner, P. D. (2001). [Review of the Structured Clinical Interview for DSM-IV Axis I Disorders: Clinician Version]. In B. S. Plake & J. C. Impara (Eds.), *The fourteenth mental measurements yearbook* (pp. 1189–1191). Lincoln, NE: Buros Institute of Mental Measurements.
Widiger, T. A. (2001). [Review of the Structured Clinical Interview for DSM-IV Axis I Disorders: Clinician Version]. In B. S. Plake & J. C. Impara (Eds.), *The fourteenth mental measurements yearbook* (pp. 1191–1193). Lincoln, NE: Buros Institute of Mental Measurements.

Review of the SCID Screen Patient Questionnaire and SCID Screen Patient Questionnaire—Extended by PETER ZACHAR, Associate Professor of Psychology, Auburn University Montgomery, Montgomery, AL:

The SCID Screen Patient Questionnaire (SPPQ) and SCID Screen Patient Questionnaire—Extended (SSPQ-X) for Windows' are diagnostic screening instruments. They are sold separately, but share a single manual. The purpose of each instrument is to alert the clinician to possible Axis I syndromes in the Diagnostic and Statistical Manual of Mental Disorders-IV (DSM-IV). Each instrument represents a brief version of the Structured Clinical Interview for DSM-IV (SCID). The SSPQ was formerly called the MiniSCID for DOS.

DESCRIPTION AND DEVELOPMENT. The Axis I disorders assessed by the SSPQ and

SSPQ-X are Mood Disorders, Anxiety Disorders, Substance Use Disorders, Somataform Disorders, Eating Disorders, and Psychotic Disorders. The SSPQ-X also assesses substance-induced mood, anxiety, and psychotic disorders, plus mood, anxiety, and psychotic disorders due to a general medical condition.

The Structured Clinical Interview for DSM-IV is a method for diagnosing psychiatric disorders. The DSM-IV defines each psychiatric disorder using specific diagnostic criteria, and the SCID systematically assesses patients using these criteria. The structured format standardizes diagnosis across different clinicians, and therefore raises its reliability. Ethically, diagnoses have to conform to American (DSM) or International (ICD) guidelines, and even those clinicians who do not use structured interviews have to base their decisions, at least in part, on the criteria used in the structured interviews.

The SCID is a comprehensive, complicated, and time-consuming interview. It is not necessary to diagnose every patient by administering the entire interview. It is more efficient to ask enough questions to obtain a brief overview of the patient's particular concerns, and then follow up possible problem areas with a more targeted and thorough set of questions. The SCID Screen Patient Questionnaires give their users the brief overview.

The programs provide incomplete information and are not designed to make diagnoses. Specific factors relating to history and client presentation are an important part of adequate decision making, and this kind of information is easier to obtain in a clinical interview. Furthermore, the actual diagnostic criteria are often vague and open to interpretation, and a person's answers also have to be verified face-to-face. The SCID Screen questionnaires are designed only to help professionals make better diagnoses by providing them suggestions about what kinds of questions should be systematically emphasized in a clinical interview.

The SSPQ is the briefer instrument. It asks a total of 76 possible questions. A seventh grade reading level is required. The questions are based on the DSM criteria and reworded for an interview format (e.g., have you ever had a panic attack?). The SSPQ-X asks a possible total of 589 questions and gives a more inclusive overview. It comes very close to providing enough information

regarding symptoms for experienced clinicians to make a diagnosis.

Both instruments use a version of adaptive testing. Each disorder assessed has a diagnostic pathway, which includes a series of questions, but people are only taken down a particular pathway if they affirm questions early in the path. The more often they answer "yes" within a series of questions, the farther down the pathway they are taken. So a person who answers "yes" to questions asking about depressive symptoms would be asked many questions about depression, whereas someone who denies having depressive symptoms would only be asked a few questions about depression. Learning to navigate these diagnostic pathways takes time with the SCID, whereas the computer programs do it automatically.

Once the programs have been installed, the questionnaires are easy to both administer and take. They begin with brief tutorials on using the mouse and the keyboard. After the interview begins, each question appears on the screen in conveniently large letters. Examinees are given a chance to respond "yes," "no," or "not sure." They can also view longer explanations of each question if they are unclear about what is being asked. The longer explanations are very helpful, and their availability should be emphasized to all examinees both verbally and during the automated tutorial because the default questions are open to interpretation. The longer explanations are always displayed if the examinee answers "not sure." The program has an option of automatically displaying the longer explanation with each question, and it is an option that I strongly recommend.

The programs halt as soon as all the questions have been answered and instruct the examinee to inform the administrator that he or she is finished. The administrator then punches in a code to exit the program.

Scoring is done automatically and is error free. Once the instruments are scored, the clinician has the option of printing out different kinds of reports. These reports are meant to be used in follow-up interviews.

Each report includes validity indicators. Answering "yes" to every question is suggestive of confusion or faking bad. Answering "no" to every question would not be unusual in the population as a whole, but it would be unexpected in a psychiatric setting if there is some reason to suspect the presence of an Axis I disorder. The reports also specify the amount of time a person took to complete the questionnaire. The average time is 15 to 45 minutes depending on which program is being used. Very brief and very long completion times should be inquired about in the follow-up interviews.

The SSPQ-X has an additional validity indicator called a clinical time marker. The program measures how long the person took to answer a question, and calculates the average time to answer questions in general. It then flags those questions that, compared to all the other questions, the person took a significantly longer or shorter time to answer. This alerts the clinician to questions that may have had some special meaning for the examinee.

The manual should assess more specifically the value of the validity indicators. It would also be useful for all the validity indicators to be placed in one section at the beginning of each report.

The Summary of Responses Report for the SSPQ and the SSPQ-X provides the questions pertaining to each disorder, along with the person's answer to the questions. The SSPQ version also lists which diagnoses might be suggested, supported, or ruled out. This report would be used to verify the person's answers.

The SSPQ also has the option of generating a Concise Report, which is better organized than the Summary Report. It also suggests the DSM-IV decision trees for making more complete diagnosis, and would be most useful for someone who owns the program DTREE.

The SSPQ has the further option of generating a Long Report. It includes the same diagnostic information included in the Concise Report, and also provides a complete set of DSM diagnostic criteria for each possible diagnosis indicated. This appears to be the most useful of the SSPQ reports for follow-up interviews, but it could be improved by being organized as an interview driver. For example, the criteria could be presented in lists, rather than summarized in a single paragraph.

The SSPQ-X has the option of generating a Diagnostic Report, which is organized like the Concise Report. Because the SSPQ-X includes a larger set of questions, the Diagnostic Report makes some predictions about what diagnoses are likely and unlikely. It also lists supporting evidence and disconfirming evidence for each possible diagnosis. For some reason the explicit DSM

diagnostic criteria are not available in this report. It might be a good idea to make them an option.

I was unable to assess if the two programs are organized in such a way as to encourage people to purchase both of them. Experienced clinicians may prefer the briefer program, whereas training agencies and researchers might prefer the longer program. There are no good clinical reasons for leaving the questions about suicidal and homicidal ideation or the clinical time marker validity indicator off of the SSPQ.

An important addition would be for these reports to alert clinicians specifically to ask about precipitants in order to distinguish a primary psychiatric disorder from an adjustment disorder. Rule outs and preemptive diagnoses could also easily be added. I was unable to find a way to generate a report on a laptop computer and transfer it to a desktop computer—an import flaw. If the programs are going to be used, they should be made as useful as possible.

TECHNICAL AND FURTHER COMMENTARY. Psychometrically, these programs cannot be evaluated independently of the virtues of the SCID itself. The SCID is available in research and clinical versions, as well as face-to-face interview, and computer-assisted formats. The reliability and validity data on the SCID are surprisingly sparse, although Widiger (2001, 14:373) suggests that the authors fail to systematically review all the research that has been done on the SCID's psychometric adequacy. They have not remedied this problem in the SCID Screen manual. Most of the studies reported in the manual assess the interrater reliability of the original SCID. It appears that the Cohen's kappa coefficients are good, generally between .70 and .80. The structured interviews are also complex and convoluted, and interviewer errors may lower reliability. Computer programs should reduce this kind of error. I suspect that the reliability for the SSPQ programs in particular will be higher if the option of always displaying the longer explanation of the questions is selected.

The goal of the SSPQ and the SSPQ-X is to facilitate decisions about whether or not someone has a psychiatric disorder. Evaluating their success in achieving this goal would require a hit rate analysis. Unfortunately, no hit rate analysis seems to have been conducted. The authors believe that the SSPQ questions have a high false positive rate—meaning people are more likely to respond "yes" than they would to more detailed questions. Presumably, the programs are likely to suggest the presence of a disorder where none exists. It would be important to know if the programs have a high false positive rate for a psychiatric population, for the general population, or both. As a rule, these programs will be better at identifying when people have no psychiatric disorder than they are at identifying what disorder they might have. If the information obtained by the programs is supposed to contribute to clinical decision making, future editions of the manual should report the positive predictive value (PPV) and negative predictive value (NPV) for each general family of disorder. In other words, it should report the PPV for the anxiety disorders family, rather than for panic disorder. These statistics should be evaluated using the base rates of each Axis I family for both a psychiatric population and the general population. These are only screening instruments, so the PPV especially does not need to be outstanding, but it is still important to know.

Evaluating whether or not the criteria that indicate the presence of a particular disorder are internally consistent, stable over time, or correlated with related items has not traditionally been a part of syndrome-based classification. Perhaps this is due to a widespread belief among psychiatrists and psychologists that polythetic diagnostic and psychometric approaches are incommensurable. It would not be a betrayal of the medical profession to systematically report internal consistency, test-retest reliability, and concurrent validity coefficients for these programs, as is done in a standard test manual. A psychometric analysis of polythetic diagnostic categories using data gathered on thousands of people might help address some of the validity questions that linger regarding the DSM. Rather than leading to the elimination of syndrome-based classification, psychometric analysis can lead to its refinement. These programs offer an opportunity to make a step in that direction, and they already have the option of exporting data to a statistical package.

The programs may have limited use for persons who lack attentional resources due to significant depression, anxiety, or psychosis. They are going to be more appropriate for persons with mild to moderate levels of dysfunction. Their

range of use would be broadened if the developers added an audio option so that people could both read the questions and hear them read. It would be good to have male and female voice options, and, even better, multilingual versions. Clinicians can always read the questions to an examinee by using the programs as interview drivers, but adding an audio component would make for a much more attractive package.

SUMMARY AND CONCLUSIONS. In conclusion, these may be great programs, but a lack of evidence limits my confidence in that evaluation. They should (in theory) raise interrater reliability without making clinicians use a formal structured interview. They could be useful to staff members of large mental health centers for assessing and prioritizing cases. They could increase interview consistency between the different professional disciplines and levels of training. They might also help neophyte residents, doctoral interns, and practicum students stay tied to DSM diagnostic criteria while learning a more open-ended interview style.

Although expensive when compared to the very affordable research version of the SCID, the SSPQ-X in particular would be a convenient tool for selecting research participants, especially when the statistics require large sample sizes. For a typical university professor's or graduate student's research this might be an efficient method for including or excluding persons with specific kinds of disorders. It is doubly useful because users have the option of choosing which Axis I disorders the program assesses.

REVIEWER'S REFERENCE

Widiger, T. A. (2001). [Review of the Structured Clinical Interview for DSM-IV Axis I Disorders: Clinician Version]. In B. S. Plake & J. C. Impara (Eds.), The fourteenth mental measurements yearbook (pp. 1191-1193). Lincoln, NE: Buros Institute of Mental Measurements.

[219]

Screening Assessment for Gifted Elementary and Middle School Students, Second Edition.

Purpose: "Used to identify students who are gifted in academics and reasoning."
Population: Ages 5–14.
Publication Dates: 1987–2001.
Acronym: SAGES-2.
Scores, 3: Mathematics/Science, Language Arts/Social Studies, Reasoning.
Administration: Group.
Price Data, 2003: $184 per kit including 10 K–3 mathematics/science student response booklets, 10 K–

3 language arts/social studies student response booklets, 10 K–3 reasoning student response booklets, 10 4–8 mathematics/science student response booklets, 10 4–8 language arts/social studies student response booklets, 10 4–8 reasoning response booklets, manual (2001, 128 pages), 50 K–3 profile/scoring sheets, 50 4–8 profile/response sheets, and a 4–8 scoring transparency; $15 per 10 K–3 mathematics/science student response booklets; $15 per 10 K–3 language arts/social studies student response booklets; $15 per 10 K–3 reasoning student response booklets; $15 per 10 4–8 mathematics/science student response booklets; $18 per 10 4–8 language arts/social studies student response booklets; $15 per 10 4–8 reasoning student response booklets; $51 per manual; $25 per 50 K–3 profile/scoring sheets; $4 per 50 4–8 profile/response sheets; $5 per 4–8 scoring transparency.

Time: (30–45) minutes.

Comments: This edition replaces both the earlier Screening Assessment for Gifted Elementary Students (T5:2328) and the Screening Assessment for Gifted Elementary Students—Primary (T5:2329).

Authors: Susan K. Johnsen and Anne L. Corn.

Publisher: PRO-ED.

Cross References: See T5:2328 (1 reference); for reviews by Lewis R. Aiken and Susana Urbina of an earlier edition, see 12:349; for a review by E. Scott Huebner of an earlier edition, see 10:327.

Review of the Screening Assessment for Gifted Elementary and Middle School Students—Second Edition by CAROLYN M. CALLAHAN, Professor, Curry School of Education, University of Virginia, Charlottesville, VA:

DESCRIPTION. The Screening Assessment for Gifted Elementary and Middle School Students—Second Edition (SAGES-2) is a group-administered, multiple-choice instrument divided into two levels, one for Grades K–3 and one for Grades 4–8. Each level is composed of three subtests: Mathematics/Science, Language Arts/ Social Studies, and Reasoning. This edition of SAGES represents a revision and subsequent combination of two earlier tests (Screening Assessment for Gifted Elementary Students [Johnsen & Corn, 1987; T5:2328] and Screening Assessment for Gifted Elementary Students—Primary [Johnsen & Corn, 1992; T5:2329]).

The authors identify four principal uses of the scores from the three subtests. The primary purpose is to identify students for gifted classes that focus on academics and reasoning (also re-ferred to as achievement and intelligence or apti-tude in the examiner's manual). The rationale underlying the inclusion of these two factors is the authors' contention that "Research suggests that this base of intelligence and achievement is neces-sary before talents begin to emerge and is therefore critical in the identification of potentially gifted students (Gagné, 1985; Gardner, 1993)" (cited in examiner's manual, p. 14). Further, the authors note that these two subtests sample the areas of intellectual ability and specific academic ability specified in the most recent definition of gifted-ness provided by the U.S. Department of Educa-tion. Secondary purposes include (a) discriminat-ing among those who are in a group who have been nominated for a gifted program; (b) clinically examining a child's strengths and weaknesses, par-ticularly to identify aptitudes that may be masked by lack of exposure to information necessary for successful performance on achievement tests; and (c) studying behaviors of gifted learners, testing theories of giftedness, measuring the relationship of reasoning and achievement to future perfor-mance and evaluating intervention program.

The newly formed test extends the range of children who can be assessed to ages 5-0 through 14-11. The revised edition also divided the gen-eral information subtests of the original tests into Mathematics/Science and Language Arts/Social Studies subtests and eliminated the Divergent Production subtest. Practice items are included in the directions for each subtest. There are between 30 and 35 items on each subtest in the Grade 4–8 form and between 26 and 30 items on each subtest at the K–3 level.

Although the manual suggests that students can be tested in groups of 30, the recommended number for younger children is 10–15. The direc-tions for administration are clear. A specific order for administering subtests is specified, but individual subtests may be given independent of the other subtests.

SAGES-2 is not timed. The authors esti-mate that each subtest will take between 30 and 45 minutes, with the total time varying from 1 1/2 to 2 1/4 hours, and recommend that individual subtests be administered to younger children on different days. Alternative directions for individual administration include the use of ceilings (ceasing to test when three of five consecutive items are missed) to shorten testing time. These same ceil-ings are applied to scoring the group-administered protocols as well; for example, any correct items after three consecutive missed items do not count in the total score. However, this would not be concluded from reading the scoring explanation in chapter 2 and could lead to incorrect scoring of the tests by examiners who read only this explanation of scoring. No data are provided on the comparability of individual and group administration. Items are scored as correct or incorrect according to a template provided with testing materials. Raw scores are translated into two standard scores (based on 6-month intervals) with a mean of 100 and standard deviation of 15 called quotient scores. The first quotient score is derived from norms based on the general population and the second quotient score reflects the student's standing relative to a gifted sample. Quotient scores are translated into percentile scores for the profile reporting form and into a "probability of giftedness" based on the "normal" normative sample and traditional assumptions about the normal distribution curve.

DEVELOPMENT. The authors selected Mathematics/Science and Language Arts/Social Studies as the four core academic areas. The rationale for combining mathematics and science is that their "foundation is more logical or technical" (examiner's manual, p. 73) than the foundation of language arts or social studies. No rationale is presented for the combination of social studies and language arts. The authors assert that the combined tests reflect the standards put forth in the *Curriculum and Evaluation Standards for School Mathematics, Science Education Standards, National Standards for Civics and Government,* and *Standards for the English Language Arts.* The Reasoning subtest contains items sampling one aspect of intelligence: problem solving using analogical reasoning. Items were reviewed by a panel of university professors, graduate students, teachers of the gifted, gifted students, and other professionals. No criteria for reviewers are specified. The original items were administered to samples of gifted (as identified by local school districts) and "normal" populations (total n = 445). Items that did not meet preset criteria for difficulty and discrimination or that evidenced bias were eliminated to ensure adequate ceilings on the test and enhance reliability. Unfortunately, the authors do not provide a clear specification of content domains or the ways in which simple elimination of items based on difficulty or discrimination indices might

have affected the sampling of the domains measured by the subtests.

TECHNICAL. Norms for the subtests of the SAGES-2 are given for both "normal" and gifted populations. The sample from general population—referred to as the "normal" population—was representative of the U.S. school population on the variables of geographic area, gender, race, urban status, ethnicity, income, and education level of parents. The gifted sample was slightly more Caucasian and had higher proportions of parents with higher levels of education than the general population. There were 1,547 students in the K–3 normative sample of "normal" students and 1,476 in the 4–8 "normal" sample. Eight hundred thirty-six students made up the K–3 gifted sample and 1,454 students made up the 4–8 gifted sample. Gifted designation was again based on local school identification. There are only between 174 and 445 students at each age level (e.g., 5.0–5.11) in the "normal" normative sample and 116 and 402 at each age in the gifted norming sample. The norms are provided for 6-month intervals, which means even fewer students as the basis for each conversion to a standard score, far less than recommended for a normative sample. Norms are not provided for subgroups such as African-American or low-income students. Logistic regression analyses to detect bias were used to eliminate items that discriminated between various subgroups; yet three items (10% of the total items) that differential performance between African American and non-African Americans remain on the Language Arts/Social Studies subtest.

The comparison of students' scores to normal distributions in a general population or a subgroup of gifted students may be useful, but the authors make assumptions about the normality of the sample that are not documented. The conversion tables indicate that the distributions are, in fact, skewed. Further, directions that recommend conversion of other test scores by linear transformations of those scores incorrectly imply comparability of scores without consideration of content and norms of those tests.

Failure to describe the basis on which giftedness was determined for the gifted sample, beyond unspecified local school procedures, makes any comparisons to those groups speculative. Further, the authors do not provide any criterion-related validity evidence regarding the relative performance of these groups to scores on the SAGES-2.

Estimates of internal consistency (coefficient alphas) on the general population range from .77 to .96 with higher coefficients for the gifted sample. The standard errors of measurement, which are presumably derived from these coefficients as they follow immediately, range from 4 to 7 across ages 5 to 9. IRT estimates also indicate that the test is most reliable for those scoring above the mean on the instrument. Test-retest reliability (with a 2-week or less interval between administrations) is computed on quotient rather than raw scores and corrected "for restricted and expanded range of the sample" (examiner's manual, p. 66), with values ranging from .78 (4–8 Reasoning) to .97 (K–3 Mathematics/Science and Language Arts/Social Studies). No uncorrected correlations are provided. Not surprisingly, interrater reliability estimates are all .91 or greater.

Validity evidence is provided only as related to the purpose of identification. The test development process described earlier, item analysis data, and differential item functioning analyses provide only tenuous arguments for the content validity of the instrument—particularly along the achievement dimensions. Criterion validity evidence is provided by small sample studies of correlations with the Otis-Lennon School Ability Test, the Gifted and Talented Evaluation Scales (behavioral checklists of giftedness), the Wechsler Intelligence Scale for Children—Third Edition (WISC-III), and the Stanford Achievement Test, Ninth Edition. The discussion lacks adequate justifications for the measures or scales selected as representing the same construct and fails to provide adequate data for discussion of convergent and discriminant validity. Even though age and gifted/nongifted group data provide correlational evidence of the test's ability to differentiate among gifted and nongifted and younger and older students, no discussion of significance of differences is provided. Evaluation of construct validation is further hampered by vague specification of the dimensions of the construct(s) and expected relationships to others. The authors identify the instrument as useful as a screening instrument for the identification of gifted students, but fail to provide a clear concept of giftedness that can be used to assess the construct validity of the instrument. No validity evidence is provided for other uses of the test.

COMMENTARY AND SUMMARY. Although the SAGES-2 presents adequate reliability evidence and is very brief in administration time, it is more limited in scope and validity evidence than other group achievement tests and aptitude tests. In particular, the achievement measures include only a small sample of items from each of the four domains without clear specification of measured dimensions and the reasoning assessment taps only one dimension of intelligence—nonverbal analogical reasoning. SAGES-2 does provide scales that are less prone to ceiling effects than traditional on-grade-level assessments, but schools that already administer standardized achievement and aptitude batteries would be wise to use out-of-level assessment with more extensive norms and validity evidence. As a tool to add data on nonverbal reasoning ability not tapped by instruments currently in use, the Reasoning subtest of SAGES-2 would be worthy of consideration in a screening battery.

Review of the Screening Assessment for Gifted Elementary and Middle School Students—Second Edition by HOWARD M. KNOFF, Professor of School Psychology, University of South Florida, Tampa, FL:

DESCRIPTION. The Screening Assessment for Gifted Elementary and Middle School Students—Second Edition (SAGES-2) is a combined, updated, and revised version of two earlier tests for identifying gifted elementary and primary students, the Screening Assessment for Gifted Elementary Students (SAGES; Johnson & Corn, 1987) and the Screening Assessment for Gifted Elementary Students—Primary (SAGES-P; Johnson & Corn, 1992), respectively. The authors note that the SAGES-2 now has been combined into one group-administered test with two levels, each with three subtests (Mathematics/Science, Language Arts/Social Studies, Reasoning), covering students from age 5 through 14 with updated (normal and gifted student) norms keyed to 1997 census data, and with special attention to previously missing psychometric data and research.

According to the manual, the SAGES-2 has four principal uses: (a) to identify gifted students in the intellectual and academic ability areas assessed, (b) to screen large groups of students relative to their possible gifted status, (c) to identify evaluated students' strengths and weaknesses in the areas assessed, and (d) to provide a psycho-

validly measures ability for learning disabled students is premature given both the criteria used (mean scores) and the fact that less than 60 learning disabled students were reflected in the kindergarten through 8th grade data reported.

COMMENTARY. Beyond the evaluation of different facets of the SAGES-2 above, two important concerns remain. The first involves the ceiling criterion for each SAGES-2 subtest where the test is discontinued (for individual administrations) or correct responses are not scored (for group administrations) when a student makes three errors within five consecutive items. As ceiling criteria are crucial to accurately calculating the raw scores and then the standard scores for individual student performance, they typically receive special treatment in most test manuals. However, the ceiling criteria in the SAGES-2 manual are not highlighted in any marked way. Moreover, the ceiling criteria are missing entirely from the SAGES-2: 4–8 scoring protocol in the area where test users determine individual student's raw scores. All of this creates or increases the probability of scoring errors on the SAGES-2. In all likelihood, these errors will give students credit for items that should not be counted. These students, then, will receive higher raw and standard scores than they should under standardized procedures.

The second concern relates to the relationship of the SAGES-2 standard score quotients for the normal versus gifted normative samples. Critically, most states use a two standard deviation criterion (i.e., a 130 IQ) to define "giftedness" in the intellectual/cognitive domain. And yet, the SAGES-2 manual, in its discussion on using the test's normal versus gifted norms, states that "(I)n general, a raw score that would convert to a quotient of 100 on the normal norms would convert to a quotient of 85 on the gifted norms. That is, the same raw score when converted to a quotient on the normal norms would convert to a quotient *one standard deviation lower* on the gifted norms" (examiner's manual, p. 48; italics by the reviewer). The authors' criterion is further reinforced when reviewing the standard score means for the SAGES-2 normative samples where the means of the normal versus gifted samples all differ, on all three subtests, by approximately one standard deviation.

At face value, the use and existence of a one standard deviation difference between the normal versus gifted samples, instead of a two standard deviation difference, appears to disregard the traditional "definition" of giftedness. In addition, this potentially decreases the sensitivity of the test, especially as an "identification" tool (see the stated principal uses of the SAGES-2 above) and in the Reasoning area, in discriminating a normal versus possibly gifted student. Somewhere in the manual, the authors should have noted this issue and dealt with it directly. If there was an explicit rationale for using a one standard deviation criterion, it is not specified.

SUMMARY. A number of major concerns remain with this newest version of the SAGES-2 despite the improvements cited by the authors and noted by this reviewer. Revisiting the four principal uses stated in the manual, it appears that the SAGES-2 could be used to screen large groups of students relative to their possible gifted status. Given the one standard deviation criterion discussed above, it does not appear that the SAGES-2 can be used to identify gifted students in the intellectual and academic ability areas assessed, especially given the authors' own definition of "identification." Relative to evaluating students' strengths and weaknesses in the three SAGES-2 areas, sufficient reliability and concurrent validity research still is needed. Finally, to endorse the SAGES-2 as a psychometrically sound tool for research (much less for "practice") cannot be done at this time, especially given the breadth and depth of the research cited in the manual and the absence of any construct validity (i.e., factor analytic) data and research. In the end, the SAGES-2 is much improved but not yet ready to stand on its own. Unlike other tests that need better or updated norms and/or standardizations, the SAGES-2 needs to have its existing norms reviewed, while expanding its psychometric and functional research base.

[220]
Screening Test for Developmental Apraxia of Speech—Second Edition.

Purpose: Developed "to screen for the potential presence of developmental apraxia of speech in children."
Population: Ages 4-0 to 12-11.
Publication Dates: 1980–2001.
Acronym: STDAS-2.
Scores, 3: Prosody, Verbal Sequencing, Articulation.
Administration: Individual.
Price Data, 2003: $89 per complete kit including examiner's manual (2001, 37 pages), and 50 profile/

examiner record forms; $40 per profile/examiner record forms; $51 per examiner's manual.
Time: (10–15) minutes.
Author: Robert W. Blakeley.
Publisher: PRO-ED.
Cross References: See T5:2332 (2 references) and T4:2383 (3 references); for a review by Ronald K. Sommers of an earlier edition, see 11:347.

Review of the Screening Test for Developmental Apraxia of Speech—Second Edition by REBECCA McCAULEY, Professor of Communication Sciences, University of Vermont, Burlington, VT:

DESCRIPTION. The Screening Test for Developmental Apraxia of Speech—Second Edition (STDAS-2) represents a substantial revision of an earlier edition (Blakeley, 1980; 11:347). It is to be used with children for whom developmental apraxia of speech is suspected, and can be administered in about 10 minutes.

Despite its designation as a screening test, the author notes that its intended purposes consist of "identifying those children who are markedly deficient in speech-language skills related to developmental apraxia of speech" (examiner's manual, p. 3), which can lead to trial speech treatment or referral for "more specific speech and neurological evaluation" (examiner's manual, p. 3); periodic re-evaluation of affected children; and as a research tool. Although not specifically listed as an intended use, the test manual includes almost a page of information under the heading "Planning Treatment From The STDAS-2 Results" (examiner's manual, p. 12).

Important changes from the earlier version include a reduction in the number of subtests used from eight to three; the inclusion of data for 49 normally developing children, for 51 children with suspected or documented developmental apraxia of speech, and for 51 children with a variety of other speech and language difficulties; and the provision of internal consistency reliability coefficients. In addition, brief discussions of several lines of evidence regarding validity are also included.

The STDAS-2 consists of a Prescreening Task for Expressive Language Discrepancy and three subtests: (a) Prosody, (b) Verbal Sequencing, and (c) Articulation. In the Prescreening Task for Expressive Language Discrepancy, the examiner uses previous testing to compute an age-equivalent discrepancy between receptive and expressive language. Continued administration of the remainder of the instrument is recommended only in cases where the expressive language age equivalent is 6 or more months below the receptive language age equivalent. In the Prosody subtest, the examiner rates a child's prosody in the production of three imitated sentences as normal or deviant based on observations of "deviance in rate, phonemic spacing, inflection or stress" (examiner's manual, p. 9). In the Verbal Sequencing subtest, the examiner elicits up to five imitated trials for 10 sequences, ranging from a CVCVC to a triplet of CVCVCVs. These productions are rated as 1 if the entire sequence is correctly produced and 0 if any errors in production are made. The rate at which sequences are modeled is described as slow. In the Articulation subtest, the examiner elicits imitations of words designed to assess the correct versus incorrect production of each of 24 consonant phonemes in initial, medial, and final position (as allowed by English phonotactics).

DEVELOPMENT. The reduction in the number of subtests contained within this measure was based on the author's insight that "long-term use has demonstrated that information from four of the original subtests is as effective as using all eight subtests to identifying [sic] children with developmental apraxia of speech" (examiner's manual, p. v). The author also maintains that the revision was designed to include studies supporting the validity of the instrument and to base the instrument on current research. Despite this latter claim, however, the rationales provided for the content of the three main subtests under the heading "Content-Description Validity" draw on articles written entirely before 1990. Although more recent studies are cited at various points in the examiner's manual, the burgeoning recent literature on this topic does not appear to have substantially influenced the content or interpretation of the test.

Although item analysis data are reported in the form of discrimination indexes for a group of children with suspected or documented apraxia, they do not appear to have been used in a developmental process in which items were discarded or modified based on their performance in an item tryout. Rather the discrimination indexes are used to support the final set of items for which construction and selection are virtually undescribed.

TECHNICAL. Normative data are provided for 51 children between the ages of 4 and 12, who were tested by a sample of speech language pathologists in 11 states who were asked to test "children in their schools who were suspected of or identified as having developmental apraxia of speech" (examiner's manual, p. 13). Data are also provided for 49 children with "normal speech" in the same age range. For the sample of children with disordered speech, no information is provided about how many children fell into each of two categories (suspected or identified DAS) or how the categories were defined. Furthermore, no information is given about additional diagnoses nor about the number of children falling into each of the three age groups for which interpretations are encouraged (ages 4 to 5; 6 to 7; and 8 to 12). For the sample of children with normal speech, no information is given about how these children were identified. For both groups of children, over two-thirds were described as Hispanic Americans. The lack of information about the normative samples' speech and language, the methods by which they were categorized, and the predominance of speakers whose phonological system may show a substantial Spanish influence seriously undermine the utility of these data.

Internal consistency reliability data consisting of coefficient alphas are reported for the Verbal Sequencing and Articulation subtests, as are standard errors of measurement. The utility of the internal consistency data can be seriously questioned because they were based on the performances of the same problematic group of children with suspected or identified apraxia of speech used in the norms and in various other data reported for the test.

In addition to attempting to marshal evidence of validity from discussions of test content (including item analyses), the author pursues several other lines of empirical evidence related to age differentiation, differentiation among groups of children who differ with respect to developmental apraxia of speech (DAS), and examination of relationships between pairs of subsets. Although these efforts are laudable, they depend almost entirely upon the problematic group of children with suspected or identified DAS, as well as two other groups of children who are also quite poorly defined (viz., a group of 49 children with "normal speech" and a group of 51 children who appeared to present with a range of "articulation problems,

… speech impairments, … and other language impairments," examiner's manual, p. 16).

COMMENTARY. Because it is clear that the author of this instrument has taken considerable care to improve upon the earlier version of this measure, it is unfortunate that it fails to demonstrate utility for any of the numerous purposes for which its use is stated or implied. In his review of the earlier version of the instrument, Sommers (1992) noted the problematic nature of a screening measure developed prior to the development of a valid criterion measure. Despite increased evidence regarding the nature of developmental apraxia of speech, this basic difficulty remains. It is compounded by the misleading nature of the test's documentation, which may cause some readers to believe that the STDAS-2 can be used not only for screening, but for diagnosis, planning treatment, and assessing progress as well.

Among the many serious limitations of this instrument, two most clearly undermine its claims to validity for any obvious application. First, there is the lack of a reasonable theoretical or empirical foundation for the measure's content. Dramatic changes in structure from the previous version of the instrument appear to have been based on the author's impressions of the value of individual subtests in the STDAS, rather than on careful attention to the growing literature on this topic or the use of a traditional empirical process in item development. Second, arguments suggestive of reliability and validity rely upon empirical data obtained from groups that are very poorly described and, in the case of the group of children with suspected or identified DAS, unlikely to be representative of most children for whom the instrument might be used.

SUMMARY. Despite the absence of a well-developed measure designed for the screening or identification of DAS, this measure cannot be recommended for use for any purpose with children who are suspected of having DAS. The documentation is confusing and likely to mislead many potential users. Further, the measure provides neither theoretical or empirical grounding, nor evidence supporting technical adequacy of any kind. The participant groups for normative and validity studies were so poorly recruited and described as to undermine their value for either type of evidence. Fortunately, numerous measures are available to document the serious phonologic difficulties associated with DAS and several descriptive measures are available that may be considered for use in the examination of behaviors to be targeted in treatment (e.g., Hayden, 1999; Kaufman, 1995).

REVIEWER'S REFERENCES

Hayden, D. (1999). Verbal Motor Production Assessment for Children. San Antonio, TX: Psychological Corporation.
Kaufman, N. (1995). Kaufman Speech Praxis Test for Children. Detroit, MI: Wayne State University Press.
Sommers, R. (1992). [Review of the Screening Test of Developmental Apraxia of Speech.] In J. C. Conoley & J. J. Kramer (Eds.), *The eleventh mental measurements yearbook* (pp. 796-797). Lincoln, NE: Buros Institute of Mental Measurements.

Review of the Screening Test for Developmental Apraxia of Speech—Second Edition by JANET NORRIS, Professor, Communication Disorders, Louisiana State University, Baton Rouge, LA:

DESCRIPTION. The Screening Test for Developmental Apraxia of Speech—Second Edition was developed to screen for the presence of developmental apraxia of speech in children. It is not designed to diagnose or label developmental apraxia. The second edition, or the STDAS-2, was modified to include new normative data, reduce the number of subtests and complexity of scoring, base the subtests on child rather than adult symptoms of apraxia, and to update the theoretical rationale for the test.

The test is composed of three subtests: Prosody, Verbal Sequencing, and Articulation. Prosody refers to the melody pattern of speech, including the rate, smoothness of transitions between sounds, and inflection or stress of speech. This subtest requires a subjective judgment. The child is asked to repeat three simple sentences: one question, one statement, and one emphatic sentence. In addition, the examiner is instructed to consider samples from the child's conversational speech. The child is rated as having "deviant prosody" (examiner's manual, p. 6) if atypical patterns are apparent to the ordinary listener. The subtest is scored as 0 (deviant prosody) or 1 (normal prosody). The second subtest, Verbal Sequencing, requires the child to repeat three-syllable sequences of sounds that require distinct movements of the lips and tongue (as in "putuku"), and then to repeat these syllables three times. The 10 repeated sound sequences are each scored as 0 or 1.

The final Articulation subtest evaluates the child's production of speech sounds, tested in word initial, medial, and final position. Word repetition is used to elicit these productions, which are scored as 0 (i.e., sound substitution, omission, or distortion) or 1 (correct target sound). In addition, the examiner is instructed to administer a standardized test of receptive and expressive language development in order to establish an expressive language delay, one of the primary characteristics of developmental apraxia. If a child meets the criteria of having at least a 6-month expressive language delay, the examiner is to refer to the appropriate age level "Likelihood Tables" (examiner's manual, p. 9) to determine the probability that the child has apraxia. The three subtest scores are weighted, so that a child who receives a raw score of "7" on Subtest II and "62" on Subtest III is judged to be "Very Likely" (p. 26) of having developmental apraxia if prosody on Subtest I was scored as deviant, but "Very Unlikely" if Subtest I was scored as normal. Thus, the child must be severely deviant in two characteristics or show deviance in all three characteristics to be considered "likely" for apraxia. Recommendations for treatment then are provided.

DEVELOPMENT. The first edition of the STDAS was published in 1980, and was the first instrument to screen for developmental apraxia. The first edition had four subtests, including a language screening, and assessments of vowels and diphthongs, oral-motor movements, and transpositions. Four of the subtests, including language and the three remaining subtests, were found to be as effective as all eight. A variety of language tests have been published since the 1980s and are widely available to speech pathologists, so only the speech subtests were retained in the second edition of the STDAS. Improvements in the technical developments of the STDAS were made as a result of reviewers' suggestions.

The actual existence of developmental apraxia as a disorder separate from functional articulation disorders has been controversial since the disorder was originally identified almost 50 years ago. Many researchers do not view apraxia to be a distinct or unique type of speech delay. The author argues the characteristic that is most frequently associated with the disorder is a large discrepancy of 1 year or more between receptive and expressive language in otherwise typically developing children. Developmental apraxia also is linked to other neurologically based language disorders such as childhood aphasia and learning disabilities.

TECHNICAL. The population used to standardize the STDAS-2 was composed of 51 children identified with developmental apraxia and 49 children with typically developing speech between the ages of 4 and 12 years. The population included 38 males and 13 females with apraxia, and 27 males and 22 females without speech disorders identified by speech pathologists in 11 states from various regions in the country. In both subgroups, the majority of the population was Hispanic American (67–78%), with 16–20% European American, and 16% African American. Thus, the normative sample was very small, especially considering the wide age range included in the standardization, and not representative of the population of the United States, unless there is reason to believe that Hispanic Americans would exhibit a disproportionately large number of children with developmental apraxia. This bias in subject selection needs to be supported by research.

The scores on the STDAS-2 are composed of a "Likelihood Level" derived by calculating the probabilities of having apraxia of speech for all score combinations at each age level using a logistic regression technique. Probabilities ranging from .75 to 1.0 were judged "very likely" to have apraxia, .50–.74 "somewhat likely," .25–.49 "unlikely," and .00–.24 "very unlikely." Using these criteria, the STDAS-2 Likelihood Levels accurately classified 84%–90% of the normative population.

Reliability. The authors did not use a test-retest procedure to measure the reliability of this instrument. Their rationale was that the children in their sample were receiving treatment, and thus their scores would be expected to change. Given that the disorder, according to the author, is persistent in nature, requires intense and frequent intervention, and is characterized by slow progress and poor generalization from instructional activities to connected speech, it is unlikely that performance of participants would change notably in short test-retest time frames.

The Cronbach's (1951) coefficient alpha was used to estimate the internal consistency. The magnitudes of the coefficients were large, ranging from .75–.96. Similarly, the standard error of measurement for the STDAS-2 is small at each age level. However, the small variance must be interpreted with caution. The population from which the scores are derived is small and homogeneous, with participants demonstrating either known apraxia or age-appropriate speech produc-

tion. A more diverse population would likely result in more variable performance.

Validity. The author attempted to demonstrate that only children with developmental apraxia would exhibit the expressive language discrepancy by comparing the original normative populations of children with apraxia and those with age-appropriate speech, and a third population of 51 children (aged 4–12 years) with speech impairments. Unfortunately, this critical comparison group is not well defined. Only 53% of the participants showed articulation problems, but the severity of these were not further described. The remaining 47% did not exhibit articulation problems, but rather speech impairments (interpreted to mean stuttering) and language impairments. An appropriate comparison group would be children with a comparable number of articulation errors but without the expressive language discrepancy, because the argument is that children with developmental apraxia can be differentiated from those with functional articulation disorders. Even if the speech-impaired group is accepted as a valid comparison group, the use of the expressive language discrepancy did not reliably differentiate between the groups. Eighteen percent of the children with apraxia, or nearly 1 out of 5 participants, did not show the discrepancy, and 18% of the children without apraxia demonstrated the discrepancy.

COMMENTARY. The internal consistency coefficients suggest that, within the limits of the population tested, items within a subtest are reliably related to each other, but it remains unknown whether the scores themselves are reliable. If the items, the method of administering the items, or the scoring have too much variability from one administration to the next, or from one examiner to the next, then the test is not reliable. The potential for variability is inherent in this instrument. Subtest 1, Prosody, is composed of repetition of only three short sentences: one emphatic, one question, and one statement. The scoring calls for a judgment of correctness. Prosody is scored as 0 if "any deviance in rate, phonemic spacing, inflection, or stress" (examiner's manual, p. 6) is noted. No criteria or even definitions of appropriate rate, phonemic spacing, and so forth are provided. No measures of interrater or intrarater reliability are shown for this scoring to demonstrate that the same response would be rated as "normal" or "deviant" by different judges or by the same judge listening a second time. No practice items are given, so it is entirely possible that a child could produce a sentence inappropriately simply because the nature of the task is not understood.

The existence of developmental apraxia as a disorder of speech separate from other types of articulation delays, such as functional articulation disorder, has been controversial. The research conducted for the test construction of the STDAS-2 could have shed some insights into this debate. Unfortunately, problems with the manner in which participants were selected and comparisons made add no further clarity to this debate, and do not make a convincing argument for the use of the STDAS-2 as a valid and reliable method for identifying children with developmental apraxia. Thus, use of the STDAS-2 for its purported purpose, to screen for the potential presence of developmental apraxia of speech in children, is not supported.

The history of the STDAS-2 can actually be used to argue against the existence of developmental apraxia as a distinct and separate disorder. The original version included subtests designed to measure some of the reportedly unique characteristics of developmental apraxia. These were the subtests that were purposefully eliminated in the revision because they failed to contribute meaningfully to the identification of developmental apraxia. What remains in the test are characteristics of articulation that are common to both functional articulation errors and developmental apraxia. The most discriminating factor appears to be a subjective judgment of appropriate versus deviant speech prosody, which is not well supported by the test construction.

Perhaps most bothersome are the resulting recommendations for treatment proposed by the author. Throughout the discussion of apraxia, the author emphasizes the characteristic most frequently associated with developmental apraxia of speech is the expressive language discrepancy. A 1-year language delay for a young child is a highly significant delay, shown to be consistent with long-term language delays and disorders; delays in written language acquisitions including reading, writing, and spelling; and social-pragmatic disorders of language (Conti-Ramsden & Botting, 1999; Stothard, Snowling, Bishop, Chipchase, & Kaplan, 1998). The purpose of early intervention is to minimize these risks by providing treatment for language during the critical language acquisition stages of development. Yet without research to support his statements, the author claims that "working on language while a child displays unintelligible articulation is time poorly spent" (examiner's manual, p. 12), and goes on to recommend a very discrete-skill articulation treatment program. Similarly, the author cautions against using augmentative communication systems, stating this "may be time poorly invested for the child's future communication" (examiner's manual, p. 12). The few references cited to support this are from the 1970s and early 1980s, with only one of these citations data-based. More recent studies demonstrate that working on severe articulation disorders in context is as or more effective than direct articulation treatment programs (Hoffman, Norris, & Monjure, 1990).

SUMMARY. The Screening Test for Developmental Apraxia of Speech—Second Edition was developed to screen for the presence of developmental apraxia of speech in children. The second edition, or the STDAS-2, was modified to include new normative data, reduce the number of subtests and complexity of scoring, base the subtests on child rather than adult symptoms of apraxia, and to update the theoretical rationale for the test. However, the revised test fell short of many of its goals and may have raised more questions than it answered.

The normative data are based on a very small and nonrepresentative sample of participants. Only data used in establishing the norms were used to test for reliability and validity, and many important steps of test construction were not conducted.

The problems presented by the STDAS-2 are representative of the controversies that have long been discussed in the literature regarding developmental apraxia as a disorder of speech. This revision of the test has done little to settle the controversy. Although the test has several interesting features, at this time it cannot be viewed as a valid and reliable screening tool for developmental apraxia.

REVIEWER'S REFERENCES

Conti-Ramsden, G., & Botting, N. (1999). Classification of children with specific language impairment: Longitudinal considerations. *Journal of Speech, Language, and Hearing Research, 42*, 1195–1204.

Cronbach, L. J. (1951). Coefficient alpha and the internal structure of tests. *Psychometrika, 16*, 297–334.

Hoffman, P. R., Norris, J. A., & Monjure, J. (1990). Comparison of process targeting and whole language treatments for phonologically delayed preschool children. *Language, Speech, and Hearing Services in Schools, 21*, 102–109.

Stothard, S. E., Snowling, M. J., Bishop, D. V. M., Chipchase, B. B., & Kaplan, C. A. (1998). Language-impaired preschoolers: A follow-up into adolescence. *Journal of Speech, Language, and Hearing Research, 41*, 407–418.

[221]

Search Institute Profiles of Student Life: Attitudes and Behaviors.

Purpose: Designed to "assist ... communities in measuring 40 developmental assets related to youth well-being."

Population: Grades 6–12.

Publication Dates: 1989–1996.

Scores: Total score only.

Administration: Group.

Price Data, 2001: $55 per 25 copies of survey; $700 per 80-page report.

Time: [50] minutes.

Author: Search Institute.

Publisher: Search Institute.

Cross References: For reviews by Ernest A. Bauer and Sharon Johnson-Lewis of an earlier edition, see 11:350.

Review of the Search Institute Profiles of Student Life: Attitudes and Behaviors by GEORGE ENGELHARD, JR., Professor of Educational Measurement and Policy, Emory University, Atlanta, GA:

DESCRIPTION. The Search Institute Profiles of Student Life: Attitudes and Behaviors (PSL-AB) is a 156-item self-report survey designed to assess 40 developmental assets (92 items), as well as a set of attitudes and behaviors related to developmental deficits (5 items), thriving indicators (8 items), and risk-taking behaviors (31 items). The remaining 22 items are related to demographic information and other background characteristics. The authors categorize the developmental assets into a set of external assets (support, empowerment, boundaries and expectations, constructive use of time) and internal assets (commitment to learning, positive values, social competencies, and positive identity). The PSL-AB is designed to be appropriate for students in Grades 6–12. The major purpose of the PSL-AB is to provide an "aggregate portrait of adolescents in the community" (technical overview manual, p. 8) so that various sectors of the community can "mobilize efforts to increase developmental assets and decrease risk-taking behaviors in their youth" (p. 8). In essence, the PSL-AB provides a profile of the developmental assets as reported by school children within a particular community. The PSL-AB does not provide individual student level information.

DEVELOPMENT. The theoretical and conceptual underpinnings of the PSL-AB are presented in a set of journal publications that are included with the technical overview. Based on an extensive review and synthesis of the literature, the authors have proposed a framework with 40 developmental assets that define both a theoretical model and a research model. The instrument is very well developed with an attractive, easy-to-read form that is computer scorable. Many of the items are taken from other survey instruments developed by various federal agencies, although the authors never provide a clear indication of which items were borrowed, which items were borrowed and modified, and which items were newly developed for inclusion in the instrument.

TECHNICAL. The technical characteristics of the PSL-AB are summarized in a document called the Technical Overview published by Search Institute in September, 1999. The best source for detailed psychometric information is a journal article rather than the technical overview (Leffert, Benson, Scales, Sharma, Drake, & Blyth, 1998). In evaluating the psychometric quality of this survey, it is important to keep in mind that it is not designed to provide individual level information, but rather to provide a broad profile of aggregate units (e.g., a school district and community). Given the major purpose of the PSL-AB, many of the standard psychometric indices may not provide very useful information, but are still reported by the authors.

The authors report reliability coefficients for several assets that are based on very few items. Out of the 40 asset scales there are 5 four-item scales, 15 three-item scales, 7 two-item scales, and 13 one-item scales. As would be expected given the small number of items, the values for these reliability coefficients are quite low. The median value of the internal consistency coefficients is .67 and values range from .31 (adult role models) to .82 (other adult relationships). Thirteen of the developmental assets are measured by individual survey items (one-item asset scales). The consistency and precision of responses to individual survey items is potentially problematic, although the authors suggest that "the literature supports the conclusion that individual items that make up the categories capture the salient elements of the category" (Leffert et al., 1998, p. 214). The authors report the reliability coefficients for the eight categories as follows: support ($r = .65$), empowerment ($r = .32$), boundaries and expectations ($r = .56$), constructive use of time ($r = .32$), commitment to learning ($r = .55$), positive values ($r = .73$), social competencies ($r = .62$), and positive identity

(r = .70). As pointed out earlier, the use of traditional reliability coefficients within the context of survey research may or may not be meaningful.

In terms of validity evidence, the authors suggest that "a good portion of the established validity ... is content validity in the form of face validity" (technical overview, p. 7). Face validity is not validity evidence, and the authors should consider providing validity evidence from the point of view of survey research. For example, do all of the students understand and respond to the survey questions in the same fashion? Direct evidence regarding content validity could also be collected from focus groups or other panels of experts in development psychology.

Evidence regarding construct validity is discussed from the perspective of an exploratory factor analysis based on the 92 items designed to measure the developmental assets. Little to no information is provided regarding this factor analysis study. This is another case where it seems that traditional psychometric practices really do not provide a useful set of criteria for evaluating whether or not the PSL-AB is useful for its recommended uses. Confirmatory factor analyses may be useful within the context of this type of survey, but it may or may not be helpful in evaluating this type of survey instrument.

The strongest construct validity evidence provided by the authors is based on the relationship between counts of dichotomously scored assets and high-risk behavior patterns. The authors group these counts in terms of the number of developmental assets reported by students (0–10, 11–20, 21–30, 31–40). These four categories are then used to predict self-reports of high-risk behaviors (e.g., alcohol and illicit drugs). Even taking into account the potential problems encountered with self-reports, these cross-tabulations are very compelling and persuasive. Counts of developmental assets are strong predictors of self-reported high-risk behaviors. One possible confounding factor is that the authors have collapsed the data over grades in school. If the relationships shown across grades (6–12), also holds within these grades, then this would be very powerful evidence in support of the PSL-AB.

Results of the PSL-AB are reported at the school and community level. Even though the students respond to survey items with various rating-scale formats (e.g., *strongly agree* to *strongly disagree* and *not important* to *extremely important*), the authors dichotomously score the asset scales.

According to the authors, the reporting and interpretation of the 40 asset scales supports the use of these binary scales. Binary scoring reflects the scoring system that is actually used by stakeholders. The use of binary scoring per se is not particularly troubling, as long as detailed psychometric information is reported based on this scoring system. Unfortunately, many of the analyses are reported based on the rating-scale formats. The authors should include sample score profiles and case studies from some of the more than 200 cities that have used the PSL-AB to illustrate its utility.

No norms are reported for the survey, although results from a large convenience sample based on schools that administered the survey in 1996–1997 are used to define what the authors call an "aggregate sample" (N = 99,462 students in Grades 6–12 from 213 cities). Because this is not a nationally representative sample, users must be very cautious regarding how to interpret this information appropriately.

COMMENTARY. The accuracy of student self-reports of attitudes and behaviors is always an issue with survey instruments like the PSL-AB. The anonymous response format should increase the likelihood of accurate student responses taken as a group, even though individual students may either exaggerate or minimize self-reports of some behaviors. It is not clear how the authors addressed this concern. Some questions, such as "During the last 12 months, how many times have you been a leader in a group or organization?" could be checked with other independent sources.

Much of classical psychometrics was designed to provide evidence regarding the quality of psychological and educational tests where the major purpose is the measurement of individual differences. From a psychometric perspective, it seems that the authors have conducted many of the standard and traditional psychometric analyses. There is a mismatch between some of these analyses that were designed for individual assessments rather than for survey instruments like the PSL-AB. For example, it is not clear what reliability coefficients reported for two-item scales really represent. The authors and potential users of the survey would be better served if evidence typically used to evaluate survey instruments was provided. There are several sources, such as Fowler (1993, 1995), that describe evaluative criteria that potential users of the PSL-AB would find useful. In addition to using survey-based criteria for evaluating the precision, accuracy, and credibility of the results obtained with the instrument, it would also be very helpful to report several case studies illustrating how various communities have used the PSL-AB. According to the authors, the instrument has been used in more than 200 cities, and case and evaluative studies from these applications would help the potential user determine whether or not to select this instrument. Further, the authors have very creatively challenged the current theoretical paradigm in developmental science; perhaps they should also consider using new paradigms available in measurement theory. For example, Embretson and her colleagues have proposed a set of "new rules of measurement" based on IRT (Embretson & Hershberger, 1999) that may provide an alternative psychometric framework that provides a better system for evaluating the PSL-AB.

SUMMARY. Overall, the PSL-AB is a well-designed and theoretically grounded instrument. As pointed out by the authors, "The framework ... of benchmarks for positive child and adolescent development, weaving together in an a priori conceptual model a taxonomy of developmental targets requiring both family and community engagement to ensure their acquisition" (Benson, Leffert, Scales, & Blyth, 1998, p. 143). Results from the PSL-AB appear to provide a fruitful template for school- and community-based discussions regarding developmental assets. Communities that consider using the PSL-AB should contact other communities that have used the survey in the past to obtain suggestions regarding how to make the best use of the results. Because of the ambitious nature of the PSL-AB and its theoretical framework, it is difficult to evaluate based simply on traditional psychometric criteria. Additional evidence should be provided by the authors regarding how clients have used the PSL-AB in the past, as well as evaluative information regarding the community-based results obtained from the more than 200 cities that have used this survey and framework.

REVIEWER'S REFERENCES

Benson, P. L., Leffert, N., Scales, P. C., & Blyth, D. A. (1998). Beyond the "Village" rhetoric: Creating healthy communities for children and adolescents. *Applied Developmental Science, 2*(3), 138–159.

Embretson, S. E., & Hershberger, S. L. (Eds.). (1999). *The new rules of measurement: What every psychologist and educator should know.* Mahwah, NJ: Lawrence Erlbaum Associates.

Fowler, F. J. (1993). Survey research methods (2nd ed.). Newbury Park, CA: Sage Publications, Inc.

Fowler, F. J. (1995). *Improving survey questions: Design and evaluation.* Newbury Park, CA.: Sage Publications, Inc.

Leffert, N., Benson, P. L., Scales, P. C., Sharma, A. R., Drake, D. R., & Blyth, D. A. (1998). Developmental assets: Measurement and prediction of risk behaviors among adolescents. *Applied Developmental Science, 2*(4), 209–230.

Review of the Search Institute Profiles of Student Life: Attitudes and Behaviors by CAROL M. McGREGOR, Associate Professor of Education and Human Development, Brenau University, Gainesville, GA:

DESCRIPTION. The Search Institute Profiles of Student Life: Attitudes and Behaviors (PSL-AB) is a 156-item survey administered by paper and pencil for 6th to 12th grade adolescents to provide data to schools and communities as a framework for collaborative efforts between professionals and systems in order to promote positive human development. The survey is administered anonymously in a classroom setting by school personnel such as teachers and counselors. It is scored by the Search Institute where a report is generated and forwarded to the school of origin. The Search instrument measures 40 developmental assets as well as a set of developmental deficits, thriving indicators, and risk-taking behaviors. The findings of this survey provide data that can indicate the developmental assets as well as risk-taking patterns that portray the youth of the community.

Each student is given an eight-page booklet with statements to which they are to respond. The manner of responding is not consistent throughout. On some items, using a Likert-like scale, students respond using numbers of times a behavior occurs, or using word responses for describing behaviors, ranging from a total negative to a highly positive level of agreement with three to eight possible choices. Other questions require similar responses but are aligned in different formats. The authors describe "data cleaning" (p. 5), which is a procedure where misleading individual surveys are removed from the school district's sample. This would happen for the following reasons: wrong grade reported, reported use of a fictitious drug, inconsistent responses, missing data on 40 or more items, or exaggerated reported drug use.

In the Technical Overview, the authors state that in order to more effectively communicate with diverse audiences, percentages are used to report results of individual assets, deficits, thriving behaviors, and risk-taking behaviors and patterns.

DEVELOPMENT. Although the information is not available in the Technical Overview, the developmental asset framework and terminology was introduced through the Search Institute in 1990 in a report sponsored by Lutheran Brotherhood through its RespecTeen Program. At that time, 30 developmental assets were included. Between 1990 and 1995, more than 600 communities and 350,000 6th–12th graders were surveyed on the developmental assets, deficits, thriving indicators, and risk-taking behaviors. Focus groups were conducted to better understand the basic realities in distressed communities. As a result of ongoing research, the Attitude and Behavior Survey was revised in 1996 to include 40 developmental assets.

Materials for this test are sparse in that they consist of the Technical Overview with the individual student answer booklets. At the end of each section within the Overview are references to articles that support the minimum of information presented. Three relevant articles are attached to the Overview with substantive materials in them regarding background, development, and research supporting the premises of the Survey.

TECHNICAL. The population on which the PSL-AB was standardized is 99,462 6th–12th grade public and alternative school students from 213 U.S. cities and towns. This information was gathered during the 1996-1997 academic school year. All communities that surveyed at least one grade between 6–9 and between 10–12 are included.

Reliability measured by internal consistency, using Cronbach's coefficient alpha, was computed for scales of three or more items. The Spearman-Brown prophecy formula was used for two-item scales. Thirteen assets were measured with single items for which there can be no internal consistency measure. These reliability coefficients of the asset categories are the following: support, .65; empowerment, .32; boundaries and expectations, .56; constructive use of time, .32; commitment to learning, .55; positive values, .73; social competencies, .62; and personal identity, .70. Those areas demonstrating low reliability scores are thought, by the authors, to be areas in which this is expected due to measuring assets across multiple contexts. Validity for the developmental assets is largely content validity evidence in the form of face validity. The authors point to significant amounts of research to support this position. Readers are referred to the extensive review of literature by Scales and Leffert (1999) that supports the asset categories as important aspects of adolescent lives in the promotion of healthy lifestyles. In order to examine construct validity, a factor analysis of the 92 asset items was conducted

using the principal component methods for extraction with varimax rotation. The results identify a 16-factor solution, composed of 89 items, which accounted for 49.6% of the variance. The authors state that a number of methods were used to assess construct validity of the assets with results described but only the factor analysis is reported in the Technical Overview. The authors also indicated that a validity study on risk-taking behaviors would be reported but that, too, is not in this Overview. No other parametric studies are included in reference to deficits, thriving indicators, and risk-taking behaviors.

COMMENTARY. The PSL-AB is a widely used survey and a great deal of research has been done since its conceptualization by Benson in 1990. Throughout the Technical Overview, which is quite short, references are listed to support the aspects of the test being described. This is both helpful and a drawback. Because of the prolific listings of support, the authors have given limited data in describing aspects of the test and the reader is required to search out additional information on all properties of the measuring instrument.

The fact that the Search Institute owns the results limits some of the applications for which a community might use the data. Communities can only compare the results in the report they receive with the aggregate sample done by the Search Institute and cannot manipulate the data for their own purposes unless they purchase their raw data. However, the fact that over 200 communities (Benson, Leffert, Scales, & Blyth, 1998) are using the PSL-AB supports the fact that the information provided in them is worthwhile and descriptive. In the articles attached to the Technical Overview, those involved in the development and monitoring of this instrument are open to discussing not only its strengths but also issues requiring further inquiry. Although there are many other surveys available for measuring attributes of community climate, this is probably the most widely researched instrument based not just on problem behaviors but also on those assets that can be used to build a more positive climate of adolescents.

SUMMARY. The PSL-AB is a group administered assessment instrument for students in Grades 6 through 12 for the purpose of assessing adolescent assets and risk factors that can be used by communities to develop positive support programs. The data produced from the surveys belong

"objective assessment and profile of pupils' skills in reading, mathematics and reasoning at ages 10–13." It goes on to claim that a primary purpose of the SSP is to (a) identify strengths and weaknesses, (b) obtain baseline data that can later be used for comparison purposes, (c) serve as a screening instrument for special education, and (d) aid in monitoring students.

If all three scales are to be administered, the manual states that they should be administered on separate days. Each scale requires approximately 40 minutes to administer, although the Reasoning scale requires the administration of a 20-minute practice test prior to taking a break and administering the Reasoning scale.

Although the manual never states the qualifications necessary to administer the test, it does refer at one point to the "supervising teacher" (p. 10). The manual provides very detailed instructions for test administration, including instructions to the administrator for arranging the room and booklets, and scripted directions for the Reasoning practice test and three scales.

The SSP materials include a test manual and booklets for two forms of each scale. Examinees can mark their answers directly on the booklets. The test manual provides administrators with instructions for scoring, including templates for scoring items as well as tables for obtaining standard scores. The administrator can write the examinee's name, class, school, date of birth, date of testing, age in years and months, number correct, and quotient (standard score; M = 100, SD = 15) directly on the individual booklets for each scale. Instructions for completion and interpretation of the Secondary Screening Profile were provided in the manual, but the Profile Sheet was not included along with the other test materials.

DEVELOPMENT. The underlying assumptions and theory that guided the development of the SSP were not stated in the manual. In fact, very little information was provided regarding test development. However, the manual does state that assistance with test development was provided by several Scottish primary and secondary schools. In addition, several "question-types" were piloted in "three main rounds of trials" (p. 31) in order to "establish validity," ensure equivalent forms, and conduct item analyses in the form of correlations of items with other "modes." Although the manual does not clarify what is meant by the word "modes," it appears that the term refers to the other scales (e.g., Reasoning vs.

Math), because the manual states that the purpose of the item analysis was to make sure that the correlations were not too high.

TECHNICAL. Calibration of profiles was based on the final round of pilot testing on 227 children from three schools in Scotland. The manual does not state how these schools were selected and provides absolutely no data regarding the demographic characteristics (e.g., gender, ethnicity, socioeconomic status, parent education level) of the sample. Thus, it is impossible for the test consumer to assess the representativeness of the sample. The only information that was provided was the age range (10-11 to 12-1), with no further information regarding the numbers of examinees at each age. It also should be noted that the age range for the sample is slightly inconsistent with the age range (10–13) for the target population of examinees. Furthermore, the manual states that the equating studies included only children from "one region of Scotland" (p. 31). The last page of the manual mentions the calculation of the norms, but the explanation is vague and appears to be based on common-person equating of the SSP Reasoning scale with the Moray House Test (no description of this test is provided) on a sample of 800 children, ages 11-0 to 13-0 from five schools in England. Again, the demographic characteristics of the sample are not described. This method was used because it is claimed that obtaining the larger samples needed for more traditional norming methods was not realistic. The "standard scores" provided are not age-based standard scores and do not have a common mean and standard deviation, although these standard scores are converted to the age-based quotients mentioned above. Finally, examination of the norms tables suggests that the distributions for the standard scores may be skewed, and clarification of the normalization procedures for creating the quotients was not provided.

Absolutely no evidence of reliability is provided in the manual. There are some minor references to errors in measurement. Specifically, following the claim that the "true" score is more likely to be closer to a score of 100 than the obtained score, the manual claims that the obtained quotients for each scale may be expected to fluctuate plus or minus 3 points, without stating how often this fluctuation is likely to occur. That is, it is not stated how the number 3 was obtained and whether this number represents one or more standard errors of measurement. Test-retest and internal consistency reliability coefficients were not provided. Equivalent forms reliability coefficients also were left out of the manual, although the manual claims the forms are equivalent by means of Rasch rescaling. It should be noted that no further information is provided concerning the Rasch analyses, including the fit of the Rasch model to the data.

No evidence regarding the validity of scores from the SSP is provided in the manual. Specifically, no evidence of content (e.g., how the "points of view" items were selected as a measure of reading, not reasoning), construct (e.g., factor analytic studies, analyses of contrasting groups, correlation of scores with age, convergent or discriminant validity), concurrent, or predictive validity is provided.

Although the manual encourages the analysis of scale profiles, evidence is not provided concerning the (a) stability of profiles, (b) likelihood of specific discrepancies, or (c) predictive validity of profiles. Furthermore, without normative comparisons available, specific profiles cannot be judged to be unique or different from those expected in the population.

Although the manual claims that Rasch methods were used, specific details concerning the item analyses were not provided. Furthermore, no studies of differential item functioning or test bias were reported. However, the manual does provide instructions for oral administration to students with special needs (e.g., dyslexia), although examinees still must read the response options themselves. No data are provided for any students with any types of special needs to support the appropriateness of the suggested modification.

COMMENTARY. The value of the SSP as a measure of pupils' skills in reading, mathematics and reasoning is highly questionable for several reasons related to the paucity of information provided in the manual. First, the representativeness of the standardization sample cannot be assessed, due to the lack of information regarding the demographic characteristics of the sample. Second, the extent to which scores are influenced by extraneous sources of variance cannot be assessed, because no reliability evidence is provided. Third, not only does the manual leave out an explanation of the theoretical foundations for the SSP, it provides no validity evidence of any type. Fourth, the manual recommends the analysis of scale profiles without any psychometric evidence to support this practice.

SUMMARY. The directions for administering and scoring the SSP are clearly explained in the manual. However, the manual lacks critical information concerning the theoretical rationale for the test, development of the SSP, representativeness of the standardization sample, reliability and validity evidence, and justification for the interpretation of profiles. Because virtually no evidence is provided concerning the psychometric properties, the SSP cannot be recommended.

[223]

Self-Directed Search—Second Australian Edition.

Purpose: Designed as an instrument "for students and adults wishing to explore their career options."
Population: Ages 15 and over.
Publication Dates: 1970–2001.
Acronym: SDS
Scores: 4 scales: Activities, Competencies, Occupations, Summary.
Administration: Group or individual.
Price Data: Available from publisher.
Foreign Language and Other Special Editions: Spanish, Vietnamese, French, and Braille editions available.
Time: (50) minutes.
Authors: John L. Holland, Meredith Shears (Australian Manual), and Adrian Harvey-Beavis (Australian Manual).
Publisher: Australian Council for Educational Research Ltd. [Australia].

Review of the Self-Directed Search—Second Australian Edition by NANCY L. CRUMPTON, Assistant Professor, Counseling, Education and Psychology, Troy State University Montgomery, Montgomery, AL:

DESCRIPTION. The Self-Directed Search—Second Australian Edition is the revision of the 1985 Australian edition, which is an adaptation of Holland's Self-Directed Search—Form R. (Only Form R of the SDS has currently been adapted for use in Australia.) The SDS is a self-administered, self-scored, and potentially self-interpreted vocational interest inventory. As a result, the test provides counselors the opportunity to increase the number of persons served. Career counseling services can be provided to persons who may not have access to a counselor, or need only minimal vocational assistance, allowing counselors to focus their attention on helping those who need more comprehensive assistance.

It is designed for use by adolescents and adults for the purposes of career education and exploration, career counseling, job classification, job placement, and identification of training needs. The SDS has been in use since 1971 and there are numerous versions in addition to the Australian edition.

According to Holland, most people can be categorized according to six personality types: Realistic (R), Artistic (A), Investigative (I), Social (S), Enterprising (E), and Conventional (C). Work environments can also be categorized into these same areas. People tend to seek environments that match the characteristic abilities, values, and interests most prevalent in their particular personality type. A three-letter occupational code is determined from the six personality types. This code is used to identify occupations in which the individual would generally have the highest level of satisfaction.

The SDS—Second Australian Edition consists of the Assessment Booklet, Occupations Finder, Alphabetized Occupations Finder, and You and Your Career. The Occupations Finder contains over 1,000 occupations with the six-digit code from the *Australian Standard Classification of Occupations: Second Edition* (ASCO) and the skill level as specified in ASCO. The ASCO code allows an individual to further explore jobs by referring to the ASCO hard copy and CD-ROM versions. The Second Edition has a complete Australian manual, rather than only a supplement as was provided for the first edition. The manual has detailed chapters describing interpretation of the SDS and its use in career assistance. The information in appendices provides normative data and information about the revision process.

DEVELOPMENT. The Self-Directed Search—Second Australian Edition Form R addresses issues that have ensued since the test was revised in 1985 for the Australian population. With changes in technology that promoted change in occupations, revisions were made to certain test items and occupational information. The occupational information was revised to meet job descriptions in the *Australian Standard Classification of Occupations: Second Edition* (ASCO).

The original Australian adaptation of the SDS Form R was published in 1985 using the 1977 U.S. edition as the basis for the revision. Changes included terminology, vocabulary, and phraseology as well as replacing items considered inappropriate. Career teachers, vocational psychologists, and 9th—10th grade students provided feedback to complete the 1985 revision in areas of the appropriateness or applicability of test items. Occupational titles underwent more changes than other categories of information.

The current Australian edition was published by the Australian Council for Educational Research in 2001. Input for revision was provided by career practitioners in many occupational fields throughout Australia and by 10th grade students. Although overall positive feedback regarding use of the 1985 edition was received, revisions were needed in items that were dated and where gender imbalance existed, particularly in the Realistic scale. Due to the large number of new items added to the test (44%), a pilot study was completed to determine most appropriate items and to ensure psychometric integrity. To refine the scales, data collection using the revised Assessment Booklets was completed. Four schools were selected for the pilot study. There were 183 SDS booklets completed, 81 female and 102 male.

Extensive information is provided in the manual describing revision of the Assessment Booklet (Appendix 1) definition of the type of revision made to specific items in the Assessment Booklet (Appendix 2), and Revision of the Occupations Finder (Appendix 3). Revised items in the Assessment Booklet were reworded, added as new items, or taken from the 1994 U.S. Edition. Some existing items from the Australian 1985 Edition remained. Other information in the appendices defines the revision procedure and normative data. Detailed analyses of individual scales and items are provided in terms of validity, reliability, and bias of the scores.

TECHNICAL. The same number of individuals completing the revised Assessment Booklets was selected from 10th grade students (ages 14–17, 70% being age 15) from Queensland, Victoria, Western Australia, and New South Wales. A standardized sampling method (ACER Sampling Frame) was used to select schools with a probability proportional to the number of schools in the state or sector. Schools were also selected to represent populations of students in government, Catholic, and independent schools. Percentages of male/female respondents were 49%/51%, with 90% of students born in Australia. The distributions in the school sample were considered comparable to the actual percentages of schools and students by state and school sector per the Australian Bureau of statistics (2000).

A small sample of tertiary (college) students from the same states excluding New South Wales was also included in the study. Ages ranged from 17 to over 30 with age 18 representing 40% of respondents. Because the number of responses was lower than expected, this sample was not considered representative of all tertiary students.

The revised Australian edition now contains 11 items per category for the Activities and Competencies scales, which is comparable to the latest U.S. version. Reliability coefficients for the revised version were satisfactory to high for typical measures of affective traits. For Activities, Competencies, and Occupations scales, alpha coefficients ranged from .70 to .89 and for summary scales .85 to .91. The current edition indicated overall higher reliability indices than the earlier edition. The reliability coefficients for the Occupations scales were lower in this revision, but were considered satisfactory (.70–.82). Reliability estimates for summary scores for the Australian edition were slightly lower than the reliability estimates of these subscales in the 1994 U.S. edition.

Concurrent validity evidence was provided by measuring agreement between the first letter in the person's summary code (high point code) and the first letter of the code of the most recent occupational daydream or aspiration. The researchers indicated that a review of validity studies of interest inventories showed rates of agreement of 40% to 55% in a six-category scheme (Holland & Rayman, 1986). In this edition, rates of agreement between the two variables were within the 40–55% range. Tables are provided for review of concurrent validity and percentage of agreement of summary high point code and aspiration for the secondary students. Only distribution tables reflect the tertiary students.

Of interest in this revision was the less stereotypical high point score distribution. The authors suggested this could be indicative of a shift from stereotypical selections of occupations by both genders or lowered gender bias in the revised scales. A significant increase resulted in Enterprising high point scores making the Australian and U.S. percentages almost identical.

COMMENTARY. The SDS is a vocational interest inventory that has an extensive history of use in a variety of settings. The Australian version was initially normed for use in 1985 using Form R

with adaptations reflecting differences in language, vocabulary, and occupations of the Australian population. The current edition has taken feedback from the primary users of the test to more precisely evaluate the relevance, wording, and gender bias of items in the previous edition.

Norm data collection was well designed and interpretation was comprehensive. The pilot study was completed to statistically support decisions for the revision of the items in the Assessment Booklet and Occupations Finder. To the credit of the Australian edition, John Holland's foreword in the manual indicated this manual is the most complete that he knows of. He further states that the SDS—Second Australian Edition will provide Australian users an instrument that meets scientific standards and a manual to provide extensive information for its use. The You and Your Career booklet also provides Australian references to supportive career counseling resources. As discussed in previous reviews, predictive validity evidence of the SDS scores is not provided (i.e., there is no evidence to determine how results of testing agree with a person's actual vocational direction).

SUMMARY. The validity, reliability, and bias evidence for individual scales and items in the SDS—Second Australian Edition has been scientifically and extensively analyzed for the intended Australian population. All of the occupational information in the SDS Form R (U.S. Edition) was revised to meet definitions of occupations as presented in the *Australian Standard Classification of Occupations: Second Edition* (equivalent to the U.S. Department of Labor *Dictionary of Occupational Titles*), which allows standardization of occupational information in any setting (educational, industrial, counseling). Revisions in the Assessment Booklet and Occupations Finder provide users of the SDS with a vocational counseling tool that is appropriate for the population. Software is currently not available for this edition; however, the manual states Australian computer software editions are planned.

REVIEWER'S REFERENCE

Holland, J. L., & Rayman, J. R. (1986). The Self-Directed Search. In W. B. Walsh & S. H. Osipow (Eds.), *Advances in vocational psychology: The assessment of interests.* Hillsdale, NJ: Lawrence Erlbaum Associates.

[224]

The Self Image Profiles.

Purpose: To quickly assess self image and self esteem in children and adolescents.

Publication Date: 2001.
Acronym: SIP.
Administration: Group or individual.
Price Data, 2002: $93.71 per complete kit including Adolescent Profiles, Child Profiles, and manual (43) pages.
Author: Richard J. Butler.
Publisher: The Psychological Corporation Europe [United Kingdom].

> *a)* THE SELF IMAGE PROFILE FOR CHILDREN.
> **Population:** Ages 7–11.
> **Acronym:** SIP-C.
> **Scores, 11:** Positive Self Image, Negative Self Image, Sense of Difference, Self Esteem, Aspects of Self (Behaviour, Social, Emotional, Outgoing, Academic, Resourceful, Appearance).
> **Time:** (12–25) minutes.
> *b)* THE SELF IMAGE PROFILE FOR ADOLESCENTS.
> **Population:** Ages 12–16.
> **Acronym:** SIP-A.
> **Scores, 14:** Positive Self Image, Negative Self Image, Sense of Difference, Self Esteem, Aspects of Self (Expressive, Caring, Outgoing, Academic, Emotional, Hesitant, Feel Different, Inactive, Unease, Resourceful).
> **Time:** (9–17) minutes.

Review of The Self Image Profiles by JAYNE E. STAKE, Professor of Psychology, University of Missouri—St. Louis, St. Louis, MO:

DESCRIPTION. The Self Image Profiles for Children (SIP-C) and Adolescents (SIP-A) are 25-item self-report measures designed to provide information about children's and adolescents' views of themselves and the discrepancy between their self-views and ideal selves. The scales may be used in educational and health care settings by educational psychologists and mental health care providers. The SIP-C is designed for children ages 7 to 11, and the SIP-A for adolescents ages 12 to 16. Information from the SIP is intended to be combined with other information for the purposes of designing and assessing interventions for children and adolescents.

The SIP may be administered in groups or individually. The administration time is 12 to 25 minutes for the SIP-C and 9 to 17 minutes for the SIP-A. The test taker is asked to rate each of 25 self-descriptions on a scale ranging from 0 (*not at all*) to 6 (*very much*). In the standard administration, participants rate: "How I Am" and "How I would like to be." The test manual suggests several other possible forms of instructions for rating the items. Children may be asked to rate: "How im-

portant it is to be like that," "How I ought to be or how I should be," "How my parent thinks about me," "How my teacher thinks of me," "How I was before the problem or how I used to be," and "How I will be without the problem."

Separate scores can be calculated for positive self image items, negative self-image items, and the discrepancy between self-descriptions and ideal self-ratings. In addition, scores for content areas of self-evaluation may be derived. The SIP-C comprises seven content areas: (a) behavior (8 items), (b) social (6 items), (c) emotional (4 items), (d) outgoing (3 items), (e) academic (2 items), (f) resourceful (1 item), and (g) appearance (1 item). The SIP-A comprises 10 content areas of self-evaluation: (a) expressive (7 items), (b) caring (4 items), (c) outgoing (5 items), (d) academic (2 items), (e) emotional (2 items), (f) hesitancy to engage with others (2 items), (g) feeling different from others (1 item), (h) inactive (1 item), (i) unease (1 item), and (j) resourceful (1 item).

DEVELOPMENT. The test author has defined self-image as the descriptive aspect of the self (i.e., how I think about myself) and self-esteem as the evaluative judgment of the self (i.e., the distance between where I am and where I would ideally like to be). The test was developed with the assumption that self-descriptions and evaluations are multidimensional and that these dimensions are linked to developmental stage. Item selection was based on the premise that self-concept measures should reflect the content of children's and adolescents' spontaneous self-descriptions. SIP items were therefore identified by asking children and adolescents to describe themselves. The exact wording of commonly offered self-descriptions was then used to construct the SIP questionnaires.

All participants in the development of the SIP were from a large urban area of the United Kingdom. The child samples were: (a) a clinical population of children, ages 7 to 11, who had been identified as having behavioral, academic, emotional, and/or social problems (*n* unspecified) and (b) 118 primary school children. The adolescent sample comprised 892 secondary school children.

TECHNICAL. Norms for the SIP-C were developed from a sample of 513 primary school children, ages 7 to 11, from five primary schools. Norms for the SIP-A are based on 341 adolescents from three secondary schools. No information is provided about the ethnic composition of the norm groups, but it appears that they are primarily white. A range of social class backgrounds is represented in both standardization groups. Normative information for single items and summary scores are provided in the test manual separately by gender and age. It appears that the norm group serves as an appropriate comparison for white male and female children and adolescents in the U.K. A few items (e.g., cheeky) may not be familiar to students in other countries. The norms may not be appropriate for other ethnic groups.

Exploratory factor analysis of responses from the standardization samples was undertaken for both versions of the SIP. Items from both the SIP-C and SIP-A yielded six factors: 1 SIP-C item and 4 SIP-A items failed to load with other items. The content areas are based on the results of these factor analyses. Internal consistency estimates were calculated separately for the 12 positive and 12 negative self-description items. Coefficient alpha was .69 for both SIP-C item categories; the values were .69 for positive SIP-A items and .79 for negative SIP-A items. These reliability values are at the low end of the acceptable range for use in research but are unacceptable for use in decision making about individuals in applied settings.

In an effort to provide construct validity information for the SIP content scores, these scores were correlated with those of the Self-Perception Profile for Children (SPPPC; Harter, 1985) in the child and adolescent standardization samples. Items with high face validity on the SIP correlated with corresponding scales on the SPPC. For example, the SIP-C item, "Like the way I look" correlated +.51 with the SPPPC Appearance scale. However, some correlations between the SPPC and SIP scales that would be expected to be substantial were low. For example, the SPPC Social and SIP-C Social scores were not strongly related (r = +.10). No other information about the validity of the scale is provided in the manual.

COMMENTARY AND SUMMARY. The SIP represents a strong effort to develop a self-concept scale that is rooted in the phenomenological world of the child and adolescent. All items comprise frequently elicited self-statements in samples of children and adolescents. The reliability estimates for the positive and negative scores are acceptable for research purposes; however, they are too low to justify application to applied settings for decision making about individuals. Fur-

ther, although reliability estimates for the content scales are not provided by the author, some may be particularly unstable because they contain only one or two items. Thus, it appears that the derived scores are not sufficiently reliable to justify their use as a basis for clinical decisions.

In addition to the reliability problems, there is scant information about the validity of the SIP except that young people in the U.K. tend to use the self-description dimensions to describe themselves. Harter's Self-Perception Profile for Children (1985) and Marsh's Self-Description Questionnaires (Marsh, Relich, & Smith, 1983; Marsh & O-Neill, 1984; Marsh, Parker, and Barnes, 1985; T6:2236) are alternative choices for measuring self-concept in children and adolescents for which more reliability, validity, and normative data are available. However, the SIP may prove useful in a clinical setting to begin to explore the self-perceptions of a child or adolescent if combined with other sources of information.

REVIEWER'S REFERENCES

Harter, S. (1985) *The Self-Perception Profile for Children: Manual.* Denver, CO: University of Denver.

Marsh, H. W., & O'Neill, R. (1984). Self-Description Questionnaire III (SDQ III): The construct validity of multidimensional self-concept ratings by late adolescents. *Journal of Educational Measurement, 21,* 153–174.

Marsh, H. W., Parker, J., & Barnes, J. (1985). Multidimensional adolescent self-concept: Their relationship to age, sex, and academic measures. *American Educational Research Journal, 22,* 422–444.

Marsh, H. W., Relich, J. D., & Smith, I. D. (1983). Self-concept: The construct validity of interpretations based upon the SDQ. *Journal of Personality and Social Psychology, 45,* 173–187.

[225]

Self-Interview Inventory.

Purpose: Designed "to measure maladjustment potentials in terms of what individuals declare about their past histories and experiences" for "differentiating relatively healthy persons from emotionally disturbed persons."

Population: Adults.

Publication Dates: 1983–1996.

Scores: Current Complaints, Emotional Insecurity, Guilt Feelings, Prepsychotic or Psychotic, Behavior Problems, Childhood Illness, Lack of Carefulness, Lack of Truthfulness.

Administration: Group.

Price Data, 2001: $4 per specimen set.

Time: Administration time not reported.

Author: H. Birnet Hovey.

Publisher: Psychometric Affiliates.

Review of the Self-Interview Inventory by FELITO ALDARONDO, Assistant Professor, Department of Educational Studies, Counseling and

Development Program, Purdue University, West Lafayette, IN:

DESCRIPTION. The Self-Interview Inventory (S-II) is a 185-item, true-false answer format, self-administered paper-and-pencil test. The test is intended to differentiate "neuropsychiatric patients" from controls based on a number of personal history and past experience items. The test was originally copyrighted in 1983 and underwent a series of revisions leading to another copyright in 1996. It contains the following scales: Current Complaints, Emotional Insecurity, Guilt Feelings, a composite neurotic score, Prepsychotic or Psychotic, Behavior Problems, Childhood Illnesses, a composite maladjustment score, and two validation scores. The composite neurotic scale is derived from the sum of the scales preceding it on the test. The composite maladjustment scale is determined by the sum of all scales minus the two validity scales.

Test takers indicate their answer choices on a single-sided answer sheet by writing a "T" or an "F" by the item number. Items are counted in the sum total of a scale if they are omitted in the stencil blank. When a mark shows through the stencil for a particular scale, a point is not added, and it is to be viewed an indicator of mental health. There are four items, however, that have two holes on the stencil. Leaving the items completely blank adds a point towards maladjustment, but any answer choice made is seen as a positive indicator and is not counted into the scales as a form of psychological disturbance.

Although no approximate time lengths or limits to take this test are suggested in the manual, this author's own investigation found that the time required to complete the S-II ranged from 20–30 minutes. The reading level for the S-II screening questionnaire is not specified in the manual.

DEVELOPMENT. It is unclear when the initial development of the S-II started, or from where the original pool of items came. According to the manual, the previous version of the Inventory contained 573 items. The number of items was reduced based on their ability to discriminate between psychologically healthy, and "emotionally disturbed" individuals. There was an early version of the instrument (or at least of the items) in the works as early as the 1940s (see Hovey, 1947). This 1940s version, which contains at least some of the same items as the most current version, was used in a card sort format with a prison population.

TECHNICAL. According to the manual, portions of the S-II were originally normed on a patient sample of veterans between the ages of 25 and 50. The controls were employees of the Veterans Administration (VA) whose participation was solicited through personal contact. The manual does not provide any detail regarding mean ages of either subsample, nor does it provide description of the sample in terms of gender, SES, or race and ethnicity. Because the patient group sample was composed of veterans, it is assumed that a large percentage of those examined were male. Later in the manual, another sample, or possibly an extension of the original one, of 200 participants is mentioned several times in relation to the cluster analysis. No details are provided regarding this sample.

Reliability. No reliability data are presented in the manual for the S-II, and no references are listed or sources cited that refer to studies establishing such psychometric properties. Although no internal consistency statistics (i.e., Cronbach's alphas) are specifically reported, the author of the manual does describe the correlations among the items for the individual scales. His explanation of the method used to determine inclusion of the items in each scale provides some basis for internal consistency for the different scales on the test.

Validity. The procedures for examining validity as suggested by the *Standards for Educational and Psychological Testing* (AERA, APA & NCME, 1999) are not thoroughly addressed in the manual. The manual is vague about the origin of the items. The scales were empirically derived, but little description and no theoretical base are given regarding the constructs representing each scale. No experts judged the adequacy of the domains sampled by the test. The concurrent validity of scores from the S-II is unclear as there is no report of the correlations of S-II scores with other established psychological assessments or behavioral indices. No data are provided regarding predictive accuracy. The validity of scores from the S-II has some support through report of chi square statistics that differentiate the patient and nonpatient groups, and through a cluster analysis that helped determine the subcategories of clients that comprise the various scales. Additional analyses were conducted with the composite maladjustment scale, which according to the manual correctly identified 73 of the 100 patients and produced only five false positives from the 100 participants in the control group. Thus, there is some discriminative value to the test. Incremental validity, especially in terms of how clinical judgment could be improved, is not addressed.

The S-II has two validity scales: the Carefulness scale and the Lack of Truthfulness scale. The 10 items of the Carefulness scale contain traits or virtues that expert judges determined most individuals would use to characterize themselves. The Carefulness scale can alert the examiner to problematic responding by the examinee. The 10 items on the Lack of Truthfulness scale can alert the examiner of an examinee's attempt to present himself or herself in a favorable or negative light. This scale was developed through the identification of items that discriminated between known groups, those who were unusually honest about themselves versus those who normally refrained from admitting faults. The items from both of these scales are, like the other scales, clustered together, and they are the last 20 items at the end of the test.

COMMENTARY. In many ways, this instrument is intended for use similar to that of the Minnesota Multiphasic Personality Inventory—2 (MMPI-2; T6:1623). Apparently, it was originally conceived in the 1940s (when the MMPI was being developed), and has undergone revisions over the years. One strength of the test is that it is somewhat shorter than other tests with similar purposes. Another is that it has empirically derived scales that do distinguish between meaningful categories of clients. Various problems exist with the test, however, many of which relate to lack of published research on the instrument.

Several problems may exist because of the age of the test. For instance, the wording of items and the terminology in the manual may seem awkward, irrelevant, and outdated. Although the manual mentions the process of modifying the test over time through suggestions for improvement from various mental health professionals and from those taking the test, there is no mention of how systematic, how many times, and when this took place. The other major concern, and most important criticism, is the test's lack of psychometric adequacy. The instrument falls short in terms of reliability data. Furthermore, although some validity data exist, construct validity overall is highly suspect.

The text is not visually pleasing as it is printed with a dot matrix printer, and the manual is printed on plain copy paper in black and white. There are several grammatical errors and typos, and there is one paragraph that is erroneously repeated verbatim. In terms of content, the interpretation guidelines and suggestions are overly brief. For some scales, no more than a sentence is provided for interpretation of low or high scores. The author provides interesting interpretations based on various configurations of scale elevations, but information on how these interpretations were deduced is not described. The table presenting raw scores and the Z score conversions is not ruled with vertical lines. Scoring is somewhat tedious and made more difficult by the confusing dividing lines on the stencil indicating the starting and stopping points for items in the various scales. It would be more helpful to have each section color coded, or to distinguish adjacent scales with gray shading. Additionally, the stencil does not line up exactly with the answer sheet, which makes tallying more time-consuming because of the frequent need to realign the pages.

Much of the item content follows standard questions commonly used in intake interviews. For instance, family history, substance abuse issues, medical problems, head injury, various psychological concerns (e.g., psychotic symptoms, depression, and anxiety), and interpersonal and romantic relationships are explored. Some items are poorly written and/or have grammatical problems (e.g., Item 170: "When a person has trusted me, I have always tried to do the right thing by them."). The items for each scale are clustered together rather than being more randomly interspersed throughout the test. This type of item arrangement could lead to response bias. Especially problematic are the two validity scales, both of which come at the end of the test. Some very similar and exact opposite items are placed next to each other, making the test items appear redundant (e.g., Item 31: "When an infant, I was bottle fed" and Item 32: "When I was an infant, I was breast fed."). The test may not be appropriate for international samples or other diverse groups as it contains colloquial language (e.g., "breath-holding" and "farting"). On the flip side of this concern, because language is so colloquial the test may be used with those with lower reading ability and a more limited vocabulary. A few items may be offensive. Some items contain content that would be better explored in two separate questions (e.g.,

Item 129: "When a child, I was raised in three or more different homes, and by different people."). Some items are dependent on other items preceding them (e.g., "The man who raised me ... was a good man" and "He was law abiding"). There are some items that are not scored at all and it is not clear why they are included.

Although information provided in the manual on the normative sample is limited, we can surmise that it is not very generalizable to the U.S. population today. Early studies were conducted in a correctional facility (see Hovey, 1947). Later, the studies in the manual refer to a veteran patient population and a "normal" control group that was composed of employees of the VA whose participation was solicited in person. The systematic or nonrandom manner in which both patient and control samples were solicited is problematic.

SUMMARY. In conclusion, the S-II is a self-report instrument that has some utility in its ability to distinguish those who have serious psychological concerns from those who do not, and in distinguishing subgroups of psychological concerns such as neuroses, psychoses, and behavior problems. There is little published data on this instrument, and it appears somewhat outdated. It has many shortcomings in terms of established psychometric properties, or the lack thereof. More specifically, the reliability of the test is virtually unknown and the validity is questionable. Furthermore, the lack of information about the normative sample, especially in terms of SES, gender, race, and ethnicity, and concerns about how participation was solicited raise additional concerns about appropriate subjects for the test, and its generalizability to a broader population.

There are other instruments that yield similar types of information to the S-II, and many have greater construct specificity and more established psychometrics. Furthermore, many of these other instruments, such as the MMPI-2, the Millon Clinical Multiaxial Inventory—III (MCMI-III; T6:1610), and the Symptom Checklist-90-Revised (SCL-90-R); T6:2464), have undergone significant revisions in recent years making them more contemporary (with closer alignment with the DSM-IV) and applicable to a larger, more diverse population. It is recommended that other more established instruments be used along with or instead of the S-II.

REVIEWER'S REFERENCES
American Educational Research Association, American Psychological Association, & National Council on Measurement in Education. (1999). *Standards for educational and psychological testing.* Washington, DC: American Educational Research Association.
Hovey, H. B. (1947). A self-interview inventory. *Journal of Clinical Psychology, 3,* 191–193.

Review of the Self-Interview Inventory by ANDREW A. COX, Professor, Counseling and Psychology, Troy State University, Phenix City, AL:

DESCRIPTION. The Self-Interview Inventory is a 185-item paper-pencil self-report inventory. The test is designed to measure maladjustment and potential for maladjustment on the basis of individuals' descriptions of their background and prior experiences. The intent of the inventory is to differentiate relatively healthy individuals from those who would be considered emotionally disturbed.

Respondents indicate "true" or "false" to the inventory's 185-items using a separate answer sheet. A scoring key is used to derive raw scores. Scores are obtained on the basis of failure to answer a specific item in the designated direction indicated on the answer key. Raw scores are obtained for the following eight subtests: Current Complaints, Emotional Insecurity, Guilt Feelings, composite neurotic, Prepsychotic or Psychotic, Behavior Problems, Childhood Illness, and composite maladjustment. Two additional subtests entitled Lack of Carefulness scale and Lack of Truthfulness scale are derived for validity purposes. All raw scores are converted to standard z scores with a mean of 50, standard deviation of 10, using a table in the manual. The manual provides statements pertinent to interpreting z score values.

DEVELOPMENT. An initial inventory of 573 items was compiled that was thought to be useful in differentiating healthy from emotionally unhealthy individuals. This pool of items was modified on the basis of input from various mental health professionals and inventory respondents. The current 185-item instrument was refined from the 573-item pool on the basis of items that were found to be statistically significant through chi square analyses. The 20 response validating items, and 24 current complaint items were retained. The time period or process for item refinement, and the number of mental health professionals or inventory respondents providing input is not described within the manual. Inventory items are worded both in socially desirable and undesirable directions.

Items require the respondent to reflect upon both past and present behavior; social, interpersonal, and environmental situations; attitudes, thoughts, and perceptions.

TECHNICAL. Normative data reported for the inventory include a clinical sample of 50 veterans between 25 and 50 years of age. Most individuals within the normative sample were inpatients in a Veteran's Administration facility but a nonspecified number were involved in outpatient treatment. Fifty Veteran's Administration personnel responding to the inventory on a volunteer basis serve as a nonclinical control sample. Gender or ethnic characteristics, geographical representation, diagnosis, educational or occupational level, or similar details regarding the normative sample are not described.

Cluster analysis data are reported to support the instrument's validation. The manual indicates that five clusters comprise the inventory's construct. Cluster analyses are reported through tetrachoric correlation. The clusters appear to overlap and are not independent. Elaboration of the clusters is not provided within the manual. The composite maladjustment, a total index of pathology, is detailed through biserial and phi coefficient correlation procedures. Coefficients appear to be significant but interpretative details associated with this data are not provided.

There are two inventory validity scales. One of the validity scales used four judges to provide assessments of personal assets associated with test responders. The professional identity or characteristics of these raters is not identified. A second validity scale used California Department of Corrections inmates to reflect upon responding truthfulness. Once again, the number or characteristics of this inmate sample is not described within the manual.

The test author describes the use of critical cutting scores to determine inventory validity. One of the cutting scores was determined through clinical judgment. The second set of cutting scores does not appear to be effectively established through validation procedures.

The test author indicates that the total composite score yields minimal false positives in identifying psychopathology. This is the only reliability evidence described for the inventory.

COMMENTARY. The manual is nonprofessional in appearance. Tables are difficult to read with little discussion or labeling of content provided within tables. Interpretation rules and information for obtained scores are contradictory and need to be simplified in order to make the instrument clinically useful. The test developer tends to rely upon clinical judgment in interpreting clinical and validating scale scores rather than providing empirical evidence of scale discriminating ability derived from instrumentation validation. Information provided through this measure's interpretation process would be of limited usefulness to the practitioner.

The instrument's clinical and nonclinical normative samples are narrow in scope and inadequate for the purposes outlined for the instrument. A broader, more representative normative sample would be essential for this measure to be used in clinical practice.

Technical characteristics for the instrument are weak. Additional research to determine how test items discriminate individuals with psychopathology from those without such pathology is required. The test developer describes cluster analysis research with the instrument. Limited discussion of the relevance of this research to the instrument's validation processes is provided. Validation information is nonexistent relative to commonly reported test validation methods such as concurrent, construct, or predictive validation procedures.

Reliability information for the instrument is limited. Reliability data appear to be reported in terms of the total maladjustment score. Reliability measures commonly established for psychometric instruments are not reported for this measure.

SUMMARY. The test developer is to be commended for efforts to develop a fairly brief, 185-item self-report instrument that would differentiate emotionally dysfunctional individuals from those who are functioning in a relatively effective manner. However, this instrument lacks sufficient normative, validity, reliability, or interpretation viability for use in clinical settings. The manual requires complete revision in order to provide a useful document for the practitioner using the instrument. More extensive normative data, further validation, and reliability refinements are required to elevate this instrument to a level that would be minimally acceptable for use as a psychometric tool. Accordingly, this instrument would not be recommended for use in clinical or research settings. There are other technically more robust instruments for use by clinical practitioners to accomplish the same assessment goals outlined for this measure.

[226]

Self-Perceptions Inventory [1999 Revision].

Purpose: To describe "the present affective dimension of children and adults primarily in regard to themselves and their relationships with others."

Publication Dates: 1965–1999.

Acronym: SPI.

Administration: Group.

Price Data, 2002: $20 per 25 forms; $25 per separate test manual (specify for Student Forms, Adult Forms, Teacher Forms, Nursing Forms, or Educational Leadership Forms [1999, 50 pages each]; $40 per composite manual (1999, 150 pages).

Foreign Language and Other Special Editions: Spanish, Italian, and French Editions available.

Time: (5–20) minutes per test.

Authors: Louise M. Soares and Anthony T. Soares.

Publisher: SOARES Associates.

a) STUDENT FORMS.

Population: Grades 1–12.

Scores: 11 scales: Self Concept, Ideal Concept, Reflected Self/Classmates, Reflected Self/Friends, Reflected Self/Teachers, Reflected Self/Parents, Reflected Self/Others, Perceptions of Others/Males, Perceptions of Others/Females, Student Self, Perceptions of Others/Students.

b) ADULT FORMS.

Population: Grades 9–12 and adults.

Scores: 11 scales: Self Concept ["masculine" first], Self Concept ["feminine" first], Ideal Concept, Reflected Self/Friends, Reflected Self/Teachers/Professors, Reflected Self/Parents, Reflected Self/Partners, Reflected Self/Others, Perceptions of Others, Student Self, Perceptions of Others/Students.

c) TEACHER FORMS.

Population: Student teachers and other instructors.

Scores: 7 scales: Self as a Teacher, Ideal as a Teacher, Self as a College Professor, Self as a Student Teacher, Self as an Intern, Reflected Self, Perceptions of Others/Teachers.

d) NURSING FORMS.

Population: Nurses and nursing students.

Scores: 5 scales: Self Concept, Self as a Nurse, Ideal as a Nurse, Reflected Self, Perceptions of Others/Nurses.

e) EDUCATIONAL LEADERSHIP.

Population: Administrators and Coordinators.

Scores: 9 scales: Self Concept, Self as an Educational Leader, Ideal Educational Leader, Self as an Educational Manager, Reflected Self/Leader, Reflected Self/Manager, Perceptions of Others/Leaders, Perceptions of Others/Managers, Ideal Educational Manager.

Cross References: See T4:2421 (1 reference); for a review by Janet Morgan Riggs of an earlier edition, see 9:1101; for a review by Lorrie Shepard of an earlier edition, see 8:673 (2 references). For reviews by Gerald E. DeMauro and Michael R. Harwell of an earlier edition of the Nursing forms, see 11:356.

Review of the Self-Perceptions Inventory [1999 Revision] by MARY M. CLARE, Professor of Counseling Psychology, Lewis & Clark College, Portland, OR:

DESCRIPTION. The Self-Perception Inventory (SPI) is a collection of five instruments, each designed for use with five different groups: students (Grades 1–college), adults, teachers, nurses, and (as of the most recent revision of these scales [1999]) educational leaders. The SPI is available in English, Spanish, Italian, and French. The forms for younger children contain 20 items and the remaining forms contain 36–40 items each. Items are structured in a forced-choice semantic differential format with four gradations of choice along the continuum of the two anchoring terms. For example, with the semantic differential of "happy/unhappy" the respondent would register a response indicating "very happy, more happy than unhappy, more unhappy than happy, or very unhappy." A slight modification in the student forms presents the differential with opposed traits described in brief complete sentences (e.g., "I do well in school. I do not do well in school"). The scales for each of the five groups allow for assessment of the respondent's sense of self as a person, self in role (e.g., as student, teacher, nurse, educational leader), and reflected self (i.e., the respondent's sense of self as perceived by others in her or his personal or professional life).

According to the authors, self-perception is the reported idea of oneself in relation to one's awareness of distinctive existence. Any professional interested in measuring this construct may administer, score, and interpret the SPI. Folders coded for each of the five forms contain manuals for guiding administration and interpretation. A composite test manual includes information on the collection of scales. Included in each of the five manuals is information on all five forms (including outlines of content), the theoretical foundation of the SPI, the research base of the instrument including psychometric data, and instructions for scoring and interpretation. Each manual also includes a description of the Affective Perceptions Inventory (API; T5:120), a related instrument by the same authors, developed to measure self-perception of ability and interest in a school environment. The API is not included with the SPI materials, and is not reviewed here.

The authors of the SPI indicate that its primary use is for the furtherance of research on the construct of self-perception. They list secondary uses for describing children's and adults' affective sense of self and self in relation with others from the perspective of the individual and from the perceptions of others (although there is no instruction in the manuals for how the perceptions of others might be obtained). The authors also mention the possibility of using the SPI as an indirect needs assessment and as a limited clinical tool. None of the manuals available with the SPI use page numbers so reference to particular pages as related to the comments above is not possible.

DEVELOPMENT. The SPI underwent its most recent revision in 1999. According to the authors, this revision included the addition of some scales (e.g., for the Teacher Forms, additions of scales to measure the self-perception of student teacher and graduate interns), slight changes in format, and some alteration of language. The SPI was first published in 1972 and has been translated since into several different languages.

The theoretical foundation of the SPI seems largely unrevised since its initial publication. The authors mention the research of Cattell, Guilford, and Eysenck but provide no citations or bibliography. They open their description of theoretical bases with a brief and somewhat obtuse commentary justifying the operationalization of the concept of self as "inferred from behavior" and "evolving from experience." These two statements stand as justification for self-perception being a measurable concept. The logic in this assertion was difficult for this reviewer to follow. *Self-perception* remains essentially undefined for these instruments. The authors also make what seems an undeveloped non sequitur in referring to poverty and wealth relative to self-concept. There may be something to this, but the language of the manual failed to link the experience of social class to the hypothetical concept or the measurement of it.

There was no indication in the manual of attention to cultural and other human diversity considerations beyond this reference to social class and a list later in the manual of 23 countries "represented in cross-cultural research" on the SPI. The authors do note the inadequacy of a global view of self and provide a visual diagram of a number of variables that influence individuals' interpretations of and reactions to experiences of living. In a sketchy and weakly focused discussion, the authors imply interpretive linkages between scale scores and neurological conditions. The authors suggest, both in their theoretical discussion and later through comments in their suggestions for interpreting scores, neurological implications that they neither elaborate nor support in the narrative of the manuals.

TECHNICAL. The first publication of the SPI was in 1972. The translations of the SPI were tested in 1979. There is no indication in the manual of any update of the original normative sample. In tabular presentations of the norm groups for the Student Forms, the authors consistently describe the samples in terms of being from urban or suburban areas and further indicate the "advantaged and disadvantaged" numbers within each of those categories. The criteria for determining what qualified a sample as urban/suburban or advantaged/disadvantaged were not provided. For the Student Forms, the authors also listed normative data on children from Norway ($n = 75$), Canada ($n = 54$), Puerto Rico ($n = 128$), and Italy ($n = 338$). The utility of these data for determining generalizability are limited without additional information from the authors on the recency of this sample (i.e., when the SPI was last normed) and the meaning of the categories the authors used for describing the sample.

The manuals provided by the authors describe psychometric data, but present this data in disjointed ways. Early in the manuals there is brief and decontextualized mention of validity and reliability. Later in the manuals there is more specific data including factor analytic findings. The initial brief report made by the authors indicates validity for the Student Forms relative to the Coopersmith Self-Esteem Inventory at .68 and using a multitrain-multimethod matrix at .50 and .74. The Adult Forms are reported to show concurrent validity with the Minnesota Multiphasic Personality Inventory (MMPI) at .72 for Self Concept and at .52 for other measures. The Teacher and Nursing Forms are reported more generically: Teacher Forms concurrent validity .55, predictive validity .59; Nursing Forms criterion validity .63, construct validity .61. Test-retest reliability is reported at .88 and internal consistency reliability at

& NCME, 1999) because this revision was finished in the same year the standards were published. However, it is reasonable to expect the authors of the test to provide more precise, organized, and detailed information about the normative data, and evidence of the validity and reliability of the tests.

Interpreting the SPI scores is a relatively complicated process. A high score or a low score of self-concept does not necessarily indicate a more positive or negative self-concept. An extremely high score is interpreted as defensively denying bad traits, lacking self-awareness, or not being mature or sophisticated enough. An extremely low score is interpreted as a tendency toward maladjustment but according to the authors this interpretation should be made with extreme caution. In addition, scores are typically interpreted in terms of their relationships on the profiles. Scores on self-concept are compared with the scores on ideal self and other measures and interpreted according to the relations among these scores.

SUMMARY. Ease of completion is one of the features that stands out for SPI. It does not take much training for the test administrator to get ready to use the SPI, it does not take much effort for the respondents to learn how to answer the questions and to actually answer them. Another merit is that the SPI measures a wide range of traits. Each item measures a pair of traits and the SPI provides a quick and comprehensive assessment of self-concept by oneself and through the eyes of relevant others. On the other hand, only one item per dimension of self-report is used to generalize one overall score from all the measured traits in each form. The scores reflect an aggregated self-perception but are not trait specific and thus exclude the usage of this instrument for diagnosis or pinpointing specific traits for possible intervention unless the items are further categorized into factors. Most of the intended use of the SPI could be accomplished if there were systematically reported norms and profiles provided along with directions of how to use the norms and profiles. Given the present status of the normative data, the use of the SPI is suitable for research only, as the raw scores are the type of data usually needed in research.

REVIEWER'S REFERENCES

American Educational Research Association, American Psychological Association, & National Council on Measurement in Education. (1999). *Standards for educational and psychological testing.* Washington, DC: American Educational Research Association.

Riggs, J. M. (1992). [Review of Self-Perception Inventory.] In J.V. Mitchell, Jr. (Ed.) *The ninth mental measurements yearbook* (pp. 1350–1351). Lincoln, NE: Buros Institute of Mental Measurements.

[227]

Service Animal Adaptive Intervention Assessment.

Purpose: Constructed for "evaluating predispositions to and outcomes of service animal use."

Population: Occupational, physical, and recreational therapists, assistive technology professionals, and animal assisted therapy specialists.

Publication Date: 1998.

Acronym: SAAIA.

Scores, 5: Knowledge and Experience of Animals, Typical Activities/Skills, Personal/Social Characteristics, Requirements of Service Animal Compared to Resources of Person, Total Predisposition Score.

Administration: Group or individual.

Price Data, 1998: $29.95 per complete kit including all assessments as masters for photocopying and manual (10 pages).

Time: (90–120) minutes.

Comments: Ratings by professionals; also includes qualitative information.

Author: Susan A. Zapf.

Publisher: The Institute for Matching Person & Technology.

Review of the Service Animal Adaptive Intervention Assessment by RONALD A. BERK, Professor of Biostatistics and Measurement, The Johns Hopkins University, Baltimore, MD:

DESCRIPTION. The Service Animal Adaptive Intervention Assessment (SAAIA) measures the quality of the match of person and service animal, targets areas for additional evaluation, and highlights areas where training needs to be emphasized. It is an evaluation process that takes into account the client's functional needs and current goals, knowledge of and experience with animals, activities/skills, and personal/social characteristics.

The assessment consists of three sections: (a) Client's Functional Needs Assessment, (b) Service Animal Predisposition Match, and (c) Treatment Care Plan. The entire assessment takes from 1.5 to 2 hours to complete. The primary therapist (usually the occupational therapist) begins with the first section to determine the client's problem areas and needs towards functional independence. The therapist and client decide if a service animal is an adaptive intervention option that could assist the client in meeting his or her goals. The therapist and client then complete the second section to determine if the service animal and person are an appropriate match as an adaptive intervention. The primary therapist completes the last section to establish the client's goals, objectives, and tasks needed from the service animal. The therapist then contacts the service animal agency to begin the process of acquiring a service animal.

The Client's Functional Needs Assessment measures the client's functional abilities and skills, including functional problem areas, physical and motor skills, level of independence in activities of daily living (ADL), and assistive technologies being used. The items are in checklist or unstructured short-answer format; the ADL rating scale consists of 27 tasks rated on a 7-point scale from "Independent" to "Dependent" and five levels of dependency in between.

The Service Animal Predisposition Match measures the client's knowledge of and experience with animals (8 items), typical activities and skills (6 items), and personal and social characteristics (18 items). The knowledge items actually measure attitude toward certain experiences or interactions with animals using "Positive," "Neutral," and "Negative" response anchors. The two other rating scales are structured in a semantic differential-like format with either bipolar positive and negative sentences or adjectives and a short 3-point rating scale: "I Generally Feel," "Neutral," and "I Generally Feel." These scales are designed to provide a psychological profile of the client that can help determine whether he or she would be a successful candidate for a service animal. A fourth scale to be completed by the primary therapist using the information from the preceding three scales measures the requirements of the service animal compared to the resources of the person. Eight items are rated on a 5-point scale ranging from "A Clear and Obvious Mismatch Exists" to "A Good Match Exists of Service Animal and Person." A Service Animal Predisposition Match Scoring Summary sheet is provided to help the therapist hand score this section and guide the decision about whether a service animal is the appropriate adaptive intervention for the client.

The Treatment Care Plan is completed if a service animal is being considered. It identifies the client's treatment long-term and short-term goals needed to improve functional independence. These goals should lead into developing training tasks for the service animal. Information about the service dog agency is also given.

DEVELOPMENT. The components of the SAAIA were derived from the Occupational Therapy Uniform Terminology, various occupational and physical therapy rehabilitation assessments, the Delta Society Texas Coast Service Dog Questionnaire (Zapf, 1995), and the Matching Person and Technology assessments including the Assistive Technology Device Predisposition Assessment Professional Form (ATD PA) (Scherer, 1994a, 1994b). The researcher was given permission through personal communication to use sections of the ATD PA as part of the SAAIA.

No details were given in the manual to specify a blueprint or domain specification to define what the scales are supposed to measure. Nor were any procedures described for how items were selected and assembled into scales, how the number and format of anchors were determined, and whether the items were field tested before their intended use.

The author does state a disclaimer that may diminish the importance of the information collected on the SAAIA: "The assessments are designed to inform, not to replace professional judgment. They are screening tools whose purpose is to indicate areas in need of further assessment and intervention. The assessments are not meant to predict service animal use; they are designed to identify obstacles to use and reduce user frustration with use" (p. 4).

TECHNICAL. There is no information on a norm sample or even any field-test sample to gauge performance on the assessment and to guide the interpretation of the scores on Section 2, in particular. There is no explanation on how the scoring guidelines for the four subscales were determined to interpret the total predisposition score. Directions for administration are incomplete to assure standardized administration of the instruments to all clients. For example, specific statements of what to say to the clients are not given; only general directions to the primary therapist are provided.

Evidence of reliability and validity was collected based on a "subject group" consisting of occupational, physical, and recreational therapists, assistive technology professionals, and animal assisted therapy specialists. The manual does not report how many were in this group, their specific qualifications, or whether the same group was used for both reliability and validity analyses.

The only evidence of "reliability" reported was interrater agreement percentages on Section 2. It was computed to be .85, although it is not possible to determine on what it was based—the total predisposition score for all 40 items or any of the separate four scales or which and how many members of the subject group above. The percentage agreement for the individual items ranged from .58 for the "physical" item to 1.00 for the "psychosocial and training" item. Presumably these are the "physical demands" and "psychosocial demands" items, but it is difficult to tell from the terminology used.

Content-related validity evidence was gathered in the form of frequency distribution scores. The manual states that "there were 23 questions that analyzed the content validity from the SAAIA … four questions on the SAAIA Survey that analyzed the clinical utility measuring the subject's degree of preference of the SAAIA" (p. 5). These scores indicated percentage of agreement between the subjects in Group 1 that completed the survey. Of the 23 questions, 19 had 88%–99% agreement, 2 had 72%, and 2 had 51%–58%. The latter 4 items (client's employment, the treatment plan, cognitive skills, and previous assistive technology) were revised. The author concluded "Overall the SAAIA had good to high content validity" (p. 5).

COMMENTARY. The need for tools to match a client to the appropriate service animal in order to improve his or her (the client's) functional independence is important to meet the requirements of *The Americans with Disabilities Act of 1990*. Unfortunately, the sparse technical information in the manual and flawed instruments of the SAAIA render it unacceptable for that purpose. It fails to satisfy basic psychometric standards for domain/construct specification, item and scale construction, standardization of administration, sample norms, score interpretation, and appropriate evidence and properly executed studies of reliability and validity.

The current assessment, especially the scales in Section 2, have flawed items, inappropriate anchors, and no field-test item analysis data to evaluate their properties. It is not clear what constructs the scales measure. Several of the items do not have face validity with the name of the respective scale. The score interpretation seems arbitrary and totally judgmental. The percentage agreement statistics used as measures of interrater reliability and content-related validity are inadequate and incorrectly interpreted. The entire description of the content validity analysis is confusing and uninterpretable.

SUMMARY. According to the author, the SAAIA is designed to inform, not to replace professional judgment. The methods by which the SAAIA was developed strongly suggest its results may misinform or mislead a therapist's judgment about a client-service animal match. A serious revision of this assessment along with appropriate technical studies may produce an SAAIA worthy of recommendation. At present, the structural flaws in the instruments and insufficient evidence of reliability and validity indicate the SAAIA should not be used until such revision and studies have been completed.

REVIEWER'S REFERENCES

Scherer, M. J. (1994a). *Matching Person and Technology: Assistive Technology Device Predisposition Assessment and Scoring (Professional Version)*. Webster, NY: The Institute for Matching Person and Technology.
Scherer, M. J. (1994b). *Matching Person and Technology: Survey of Technology Use*. Webster, NY: The Institute for Matching Person and Technology.
Zapf, S. A. (1995). *Delta Society Texas Coast Service Dog Questionnaire*. (no reference information given in test materials.)

Review of the Service Animal Adaptive Intervention Assessment by JUDITH A. REIN, President, Interaction Research of Arizona, Tucson, AZ:

DESCRIPTION. The Service Animal Adaptive Intervention Assessment (SAAIA) is a comprehensive evaluation process designed to assess the quality of the match between a person with disabilities and a service animal, target areas for further evaluation, and draw attention to areas where training needs to be emphasized. It is a series of three paper-and-pencil evaluation tools composed of a checklist, open-ended, fill-in-the-blank, and Likert-like items designed to augment a health care provider's professional judgment of the match between a client and a service animal.

Section A, Client's Functional Needs Assessment, is completed by the health care provider, usually an occupational therapist, in order to assess the client's current functional level and develop ways in which the client can improve functional independence. Client background information gathered includes, for example, the client's major functional problem areas, environment, goals, types of equipment currently used or tested, types of equipment/ adaptive interventions being considered, and physical/motor skills. The health care provider, using a 7-point dependent-to-independent scale, scores the client on a checklist of 27 ADL skills.

Section B, Service Animal Predisposition Match, is subdivided into four parts with a score generated using either a 3-point scale (e.g., positive-neutral-negative) or a 5-point scale (i.e., good match to obvious mismatch) for each part and is completed by the health care provider and client working together. This section assists the health care provider in gathering information about the client's knowledge of and experience with animals (8 items), the client's typical activities and skills (6 items), the client's personal/social characteristics (18 items), and the requirements of the service animal compared to the resources of the person (8 items) in order to determine if the client is a viable candidate for a service animal. Directions are included on scoring and interpreting the four parts. For each part, a mean is calculated and then the means across the four parts are summed. The summed mean is the Total Predisposition Score. Dependent on the magnitude of the predisposition score, the match between client and service animal is characterized along a quasi-continuum from a good match to a mismatch.

The health care professional, using information gained in previous sections, completes Section C, Treatment Care Plans, when a service animal is considered. This establishes a treatment plan for the client and leads into specifying the tasks/skills the service animal must possess (e.g., lifting, sound recognition, pushing). This section also includes a service animal/dog agency history element. There are no scores generated in this section.

DEVELOPMENT. The SAAIA was derived in part from occupational and physical therapy rehabilitation assessments, the Occupational Therapy Uniform Terminology, The Delta Society Texas Coast Service Dog Questionnaire, and various Matching Person and Technology assessments. The SAAIA was developed to fill a void and its need is well documented. According to Zapf and Rough (2002), multiple studies document the health benefits to humans by animal companions. They further note that although there is a 75-year record of service by canines to persons with sight impairment and a 25-year record of service to persons with mobility and hearing impairments, there are no instruments to assess the match between the person and the service animal and the outcomes of service animal use. With the exception that a table of specifications was used to develop the SAAIA sections (Zapf & Rough, 2002) and that four items with fair to poor content validity were re-examined and changed per the

suggestions of expert judges, no other information is available about test development.

TECHNICAL. Limited evidence is cited to support the validity of the use and interpretation of SAAIA scores. Content validity and clinical use of SAAIA scores were examined using ratings from expert judges: 22 occupational therapists, 11 physical therapists, 3 certified therapeutic recreation specialists, 1 animal assisted therapy specialist, and 6 technology specialists (Zapf & Rough, 2002). Content validity was examined using 23 items on an SAAIA survey and the percentage of agreement among judges on those items. High content validity (88% to 99% agreement) was found for 19 items. The four items with poor content validity were changed. Clinical utility (4 items) was measured by the percentage of judges who felt the SAAIA was user-friendly (77%) and efficient (70%), and the percentage that liked the SAAIA (86%) and would use the SAAIA (77%) (Zapf & Rough, 2002). No other validity evidence is presented.

To establish evidence of interrater reliability, 12 expert judges viewed a videotape encounter between a therapist and a client and then completed Section B, Service Animal Predisposition Match, of the SAAIA (Zapf & Rough, 2002). Percentage of agreement among judges was .85. No other evidence for score consistency is presented.

Also of concern are some SAAIA items and the scoring procedure. In Section A, it is unclear why the health care provider rates the client on the ADL skills using the checklist. No score interpretation is provided. In Section B, the interpretability of the middle rating categories and, thus, the mean scores for the Section B parts and the total predisposition score are compromised. For example, one item dealing with the client's knowledge and experience with animals inquires if the client's experiences as a pet owner were *positive* (assigned a value of 3 points), *neutral or uncertain* (2 points), or *negative* (1 point). No category is provided for a *not applicable* answer that by default must go into the *neutral/uncertain* category. No directions are given for scoring omits. A list of 18 bipolar adjective pairs is used to assess the client's personal/social characteristics. Unfortunately, not all the pairs are strictly bipolar (e.g., tolerant-frustrated, empathic-sympathetic). In the part addressing the requirements of the service animal compared to the resources of the client, the middle category is also used for two responses—*neutral* as well as *has not been addressed*. The overall predisposition score is simply the sum of the means from each of the four Section B parts but is not evenly weighted across the parts. Three parts use a 3-point scale, but the service animal requirement/ client resources part uses a 5-point scale. The test manual gives no indication that the one part should contribute more to the predisposition score as currently happens.

Once the predisposition score is calculated, interpretation of the score is unclear due to overlapping categories. Predisposition scores of 12 and above indicate a good match, scores from 9 to 11 indicate a close but not perfect match, scores from 7 to 9 indicate a potential match, scores from 5 to 7 indicate that the person will have difficulty, and scores of 5 and below indicate a mismatch. Scores of 5, 7, and 9 have ambiguous meanings; they fit into two different interpretative categories.

COMMENTARY. The SAAIA systematically and thoroughly gathers and documents information using both health care professional and client input to make an informed decision about the potential benefits of using a service animal as well as the potential match between the service animal and the client. For that use, it performs well and has been used very successfully in one western state, not only for documentation but also to secure funding for clients who would benefit from the use of a service animal (Zapf & Rough, 2002). Unfortunately, most information in the test manual concentrates on the need for the instrument, an overview of the SAAIA, and a description of the sections. Meager reliability and validity evidence are furnished. Directions for scoring and score interpretations are included with the instrument itself. Some items, scores, and score interpretations are problematic. Score interpretation needs to be redone. No rationale is offered as to how the interpretative categories were formed (e.g., 9 to 11 indicates a close but not perfect match) and the overlapping categories made interpretation confusing.

SUMMARY. Because few, if any, instruments exist to assess the match between a person and a service animal, the SAAIA is a needed addition to the field. Although the SAAIA is both a comprehensive and well-organized tool to use when documenting the need for and securing the services of a service animal, sparse validity and reliability evidence and problems with items, scores, and score interpretation currently limit its overall

usefulness. The SAAIA needs to be revised and refined and will most likely improve with the current on-going data collection and analyses being conducted (Zapf & Rough, 2002).

REVIEWER'S REFERENCE

Zapf, S., & Rough, R. (2002). The development of an instrument to match individuals with disabilities and service animals. *Disability and Rehabilitation*, 24,47–58.

[228]
Sexual Violence Risk-20.

Purpose: Designed as a "method" (not a test or scale) of assessing an individual's risk for committing sexual violence.

Population: Individuals suspected to be at-risk for committing sexual violence.

Publication Dates: 1997–1998.

Acronym: SVR-20.

Scores: Not scored; ratings in five areas: Psychosocial Adjustment, Sexual Offenses, Future Plans, Other Considerations, Summary Risk Rating.

Administration: Individual.

Price Data, 1999: $44 per kit including manual (1998, 99 pages) and 50 coding sheets; $32 per manual; $19 per 50 coding sheets.

Time: Administration time not reported.

Comments: "Designed to assist evaluations of risk for sexual violence"; administration and coding by trained professionals only; rating done by the professional about a client/offender.

Authors: Douglas P. Boer, Stephen D. Hart, P. Randall Kropp, and Christopher D. Webster.

Publisher: Psychological Assessment Resources, Inc.

Review of the Sexual Violence Risk-20 by RITA M. BUDRIONIS, Licensed Clinical Psychologist, Licensed Sex Offender Treatment Provider, Director Dominion Sex Offenders Program, Juvenile and Adult, Dominion Psychiatric Associates, Virginia Beach, VA:

DESCRIPTION. The Sexual Violence Risk-20 (SVR-20) is designed to assist in identifying individuals who are at risk to commit sexual violence in the future and to rate their likelihood to offend in the future. This instrument is a 20-item assessment procedure that is intended to be administered by individuals who have a "considerable professional skill and judgment" (manual, p. 29). Minimal requirements for evaluation use include training in test administration and interpretation and expertise in the area of sexual offending or sexual violence. Graduate training and professional/legal certification to conduct sex offender assessments, when used for clinical applications, is recommended. Research use requirements are less rigorous, although professional supervision is recommended. Items are coded after all information is collected. Materials used in the evaluation should include historical data, collateral records such as the police report, interview information, psychophysiological data such as polygraph or penile plethysmographic evaluation reports, and standard clinical assessment data such as psychological testing and substance abuse assessment.

DEVELOPMENT. For the purpose of the SVR-20, authors have defined sexual violence as "actual, attempted, or threatened sexual contact with a person who is non-consenting or unable to give consent" (manual, p. 9). This definition includes a broad range of sexual acts ranging from rape, to exhibitionism, to voyeurism. The victims either do not give consent or are legally or functionally unable to do so because of mental deficiency or age, or unawareness of the crime such as being the victim of a voyeur.

The SVR is an integration of factors that were identified through examination of the available research on sex offenders. The authors identified 20 factors that fell into three general categories: (a) Psychosocial Adjustment (11 items), (b) Sexual Offenses (7 items), and (c) Future Plans (2 items.) An additional discretionary category is labeled Other Considerations. Psychosocial Adjustment and Sexual Offense factors are composed mostly of relatively stable factors such as being a victim of child abuse and history of use of weapons or making death threats in sex offenses. Several items are dynamic in nature such as presence of attitudes that support or condone sexual offending. The category, Future Plans, addresses risk factors that are past and current related.

TECHNICAL. Directions for administering the test are clearly written and generally easy to follow. There is no mention of the estimated time for completion of this procedure, although the data gathering and scoring process could be lengthy. Specialized training is required as the scoring process is based on determining the presence or absence of risk factors and recent (past year) change in the status of that factor. The test manual contains numerous cautions regarding the application of the results of the SVR-20 and a "Summary Risk Rating" of Low, Medium, or High is given. Scoring is completed on a coding sheet that is provided.

No validity or reliability information is available for the instrument as a whole as the SVR-20 is the first step in the development of a more comprehensive instrument. Each of the 20 items is discussed separately in the manual with a summary of validity research data supporting its use in this assessment tool.

COMMENTARY. The SVR is designed to be utilized in a number of settings and populations to include civil commitment, presentence evaluations, and community notification. This assessment tool can be used in an actuarial function when dealing with research data. The developers have produced an instrument that attempts to systemize the collection of data related to the risk of sexual violence using research-based data points from which a professional can make a clinical judgment regarding future risk for sexual violence. The SVR has the potential to make a significant contribution to decision-making procedures that are required in the field of sexual violence and sex offender evaluation and treatment. Although still in the initial stages of development, the SVR-20 is to be considered a significant step beyond unstructured clinical judgment.

The validity of scores from the SVR-20 must be evaluated in light of the need for a considerable follow-up period. Predictive validity regarding sexual violence has yet to be demonstrated.

The drawbacks of this procedure include a lack of empirically based cutoff scores. Low, Medium, or High-Risk determination is based on the evaluator's discretion and clinical acumen with a minimum of guidance from the authors. Also, not all of the 20 items are linked directly to sexual violence. The authors do point out that not all factors are directly linked to sexual violence and at times they qualify the inclusion of an item by stating in the manual that the item is "probably," or "may also be" associated with risk for future sexual violence. There is no selective weighing of individual items that reflect research data nor are there concrete guidelines for cutoff criteria when coding each item.

In spite of these drawbacks, however, the authors are clear with their assertions for this instrument that the SVR-20 is a set of guidelines to assist professional judgement in evaluating risk of sexual violence rather than an actuarial instrument or a psychological test. This tool has the potential for encouraging research data in a number of venues. In addition, this tool is admirable for its adherence to professional guidelines in the sex offender field and is based on the most current and credible recent research in this challenging field.

SUMMARY. The SVR-20 is a promising tool for assisting with assessment of sexual violence risk with a research-based foundation, clear instructions, and applicability in a wide variety of forensic and clinical situations. This type of "structured professional judgment" approach can be useful in gathering research data, assisting with evaluations of sex offenders, and giving information to help in making forensic decisions. The SVR-20 is a formalized research-guided approach to risk assessment, utilized to predict the probability of reoffense sexual violence in the future. This guided assessment based on empirical data is a significant step in developing a comprehensive, empirically based risk assessment procedure in the field of sexual violence.

Review of the Sexual Violence Risk-20 by PAUL RETZLAFF, Professor of Psychology, University of Northern Colorado, Greeley, CO:

DESCRIPTION. The Sexual Violence Risk-20 is a coding procedure reported to assist in the risk assessment of sexual offenders. There are 20 variables coded within five categories. The first category is Psychosocial Adjustment and includes as variables sexual deviation, victim of child abuse, psychopathy, major mental illness, substance use problems, suicidal/homicidal ideation, relationship problems, employment problems, past nonsexual violent offenses, past nonviolent offenses, and past supervision failure. The second category is Sexual Offenses and includes ratings on high density offenses, multiple offense types, physical harm to victim(s), uses weapons or threats of death, escalation in frequency/severity, extreme minimization/denial of offenses, and attitudes that support or condone offenses. The third area is Future Plans and includes lacks realistic plans and negative attitude toward intervention. The fourth category is simply one of an open "Other Considerations" area. Finally, the fifth endorsement block is a single overall Summary Risk Rating of "Risk of sexual violence."

Each of the 20 variables under the first three areas and any "Other Considerations" is rated in two ways. First, the presence of the variable is endorsed as "No," "?," or "Yes." Second, recent change is rated as "-," "0," or "+." Each of the 20 codings is rather nicely explained as to rationale, intent, and example in a section of the manual.

DEVELOPMENT. The authors give a fairly comprehensive explanation of clinical and actuarial prediction in the introduction of the manual. They suggest that solely clinical work is too subjective and that purely actuarial systems are too mechanical. This discussion leads to their scale and work but it is unclear if their intent is to take the best from each of the approaches or simply to ignore both. They link the development of sexual violence prediction to that of other violence prediction. They also do a nice job of, at times, pointing out the difficulty of cross validating existing sexual offense scales. These sections of the manual are of great interest to anyone in the field and an excellent primer.

The development of the Sexual Violence Risk-20 is based upon the authors' clinical experience, prior scales of prediction, and the research.

TECHNICAL. To put it bluntly, there is not one number in the entire manual. There is actually not even a "scoring" procedure. The endorsements of items are not summed in any way. There is nothing even as simple as a "yes" on an item being "worth" one point. As such, there is no way to develop norms, or evidence of reliability or validity.

There should be some "norm" work that presents typical item level and scale level numbers for individuals of known classification. What percent of incarcerated sex offenders have a positive value for each item? What is the sum of positive items for known sex offenders?

What types of reliability evidence can be assembled? In a scale of this type, an interjudge consistency such as a Kappa would be necessary to prove that at the item level judges are able to agree and use the supplied coding guidelines.

Validity is important. Are there differences at the item and scale level between "normals" and incarcerated sex offenders? Are there differences between nonsexual offender prison inmates and sex offender inmates? At a multivariate level, are the items of the scale additive or redundant? What does a multiple regression or a discriminant function analysis result contribute to understanding the effectiveness of the scale? An intercorrelation matrix and a factor analysis would also be useful.

COMMENTARY. The authors suggest that this scale be used to structure and inform decisions. That is quite reasonable. It is not reasonable, however, to present absolutely no data. Without any data, one cannot be certain that the goal can even be accomplished. Further, the area of sexual offense risk is quite mature and there are several algorithms that have been subjected to peer review, published, and reality tested against data. The authors of the Sexual Violence Risk-20 cannot simply claim that numbers and data are unnecessary. In many ways, this manual is like a thesis or dissertation proposal. It is well grounded in the literature and the initial method is well developed. A proposal alone, however, does not earn one a degree. Further, there is not a journal in the area that would publish this in its current state.

SUMMARY. In sum, the Sexual Violence Risk-20 is well rooted in theory and prior research. It is rich. Because it is without any data, however, it is not a test or a scale or even a "method." These authors must prove their method and technique is useable, reliable, and predictive.

[229]
Six Factor Personality Questionnaire.

Purpose: Designed as a measure of six personality dimensions or broad factors.
Population: Adults.
Publication Date: 2000.
Acronym: SFPQ.
Scores, 6: Extraversion, Agreeableness, Independence, Openness to Experience, Methodicalness, Industriousness.
Administration: Individual or group.
Price Data, 2001: $56 per examination kit including manual (2000, 68 pages); $30.50–$34.50 per 25 test booklets; $20–$23 per Quick Answer Score sheets; $10–$12 per 25 profile forms; $34 per manual; $99 per SigmaSoft SFPQ for Windows (software); $48–$56 (depending on volume) per 10 machine-scorable answer sheets and coupons for basic report; $99 per software package including disks, software manual for Windows, test manual, and 10 coupons for computer reports.
Time: (20) minutes.
Authors: Douglas N. Jackson, Sampo V. Paunonen, and Paul F. Tremblay.
Publisher: Sigma Assessment Systems, Inc.

Review of the Six Factor Personality Questionnaire by JEFFREY A. JENKINS, Assistant Professor, Roger Williams University Bristol, RI:

DESCRIPTION. The Six Factor Personality Questionnaire (SFPQ) provides a measure of six dimensions of personality: Extraversion, Agreeableness, Independence, Openness to Experience, Methodicalness, and Industriousness. These personality dimensions represent an extension of the "Big Five" personality dimensions discussed frequently in the psychological literature (e.g., Goldberg, 1990), which encompass Extraversion, Agreeableness, Openness to Experience, Neuroticism, and Conscientiousness. The SFPQ divides Conscientiousness into Methodicalness and Industriousness, and redefines Neuroticism as the opposite pole of the dimension, Independence. The SFPQ is intended to be used as a measure of the most well-accepted aspects of personality in a wide variety of social, educational, and work-related contexts.

DEVELOPMENT. The SFPQ benefits from a rich history of personality research. Considerable work on the structure of personality has focused on the factors underlying personality by performing factor-analytic studies of individual responses to preference items, ratings, and other self-reports. These studies have sought to conceptualize personality in terms of psychological constructs, which reveal themselves through interrelationships among item responses. Thus, the conception of personality found in the SFPQ is based upon the analysis of human responses to thousands of items over many decades. Most directly, the SFPQ items are based on the Personality Research Form (Jackson, 1984), analysis of which has suggested the existence of dimensions of personality beyond the Big Five (Jackson, Paunonen, Fraboni, & Goffin, 1996).

The SFPQ consists of 108 items to which individuals respond using a 5-point Likert scale from *strongly agree* to *strongly disagree*. Respondents mark their rating of each item on a carbonless answer sheet that is well-organized and easy to use. Within each of the six factor scales, the SFPQ identifies three specific facets of personality, which comprise 18 subscales of the instrument. Each of these facets is measured by six items. Thus, the instrument is relatively short and concise, requiring approximately 20 minutes to complete, yet offers a broad range of personality constructs to be measured. The authors estimate the reading level of the items to be fifth grade, and the SFPQ can be administered in either computer or paper-and-pencil format. The subscales within each personality factor, along with a sample item follow: Extraversion (Affiliation—I go out of my way to meet people; Dominance—The ability to be a leader is important to me; Exhibition—I like to be in the spotlight); Agreeableness (Abasement—I avoid letting others take credit for my work; Even-tempered—I rarely get angry at myself or at other people; Good-natured—When people laugh at my errors, so do I); Independence (Autonomy—I could be happy living in a very lonely place; Individualism—It seems foolish to worry about my public image; Self-reliance—I prefer to face problems by myself); Openness to Experience (Change—I am always looking for new routes to take on a trip; Understanding—I like to read several books on one topic at the same time; Breadth of Interest—There are very few topics that bore me); Methodicalness (Cognitive Structure—I start a project only when I know the best way to proceed; Deliberateness—My thinking is usually careful and purposeful; Order—My work is always well organized; Industriousness (Achievement—I am willing to work even while other people are having fun; Endurance—I will keep at a problem for hours until I find a solution; Seriousness—I usually have reason for the things I do other than my own amusement).

The SFPQ is easily handscored using the carbonless answer sheet. Removing the top page on which respondents record their answers reveals a scoring form. Ratings made by respondents are summed to produce facet scores, and the facet scores within each personality factor are summed to provide factor scores. Separate profile sheets for males, females, and combined are also provided, allowing factor and facet scores to be plotted, creating a normative profile showing percentiles based on the publisher's norms.

TECHNICAL. The norm group consists of 483 men and 584 women in the U.S. and Canada, chosen by systematic random sampling. Summary statistics for a sample of 4,040 job applicants are also reported, allowing those who use the SFPQ in the employment setting a further basis for comparison. Procedures used in gathering the norm data demonstrate the publisher's attention to detail in making the SFPQ as useful as possible. A breakdown of the normative sample by demographic characteristics is provided in SFPQ manual, which also offers detailed background on the development of the SFPQ and considerable direction on administration and the interpretation of scores and profiles.

The technical characteristics of the SFPQ are excellent for a personality measure. Internal consistency reliability based on the normative sample yielded Cronbach alpha estimates for the facet subscales from .54 to .84, with a median of .65. Reliability estimates for the factor scales ranged from .76 to .86, with a median of .81. As part of the process of developing the instrument, the convergent and dis-

criminant validity of the SFPQ was examined by creating a multitrait-multimethod matrix of correlations between self-ratings and peer ratings by a sample of 94 undergraduate roommates. The validity coefficients thus produced (correlations between the two rating methods for the same underlying factors) averaged .56, which is quite high for this type of measure. The authors also addressed criterion-related validity relating to differential predictability of the Industriousness and Methodicalness scales that, as noted earlier, constitute a new division of the Big Five Conscientiousness factor. This was accomplished by comparing these two factors in the sample of 94 undergraduate roommates to characteristics such as grade point average, smoking behavior, and selection of liberal arts study. The two factors showed a differential pattern of prediction for these criterion variables, indicating their ability to measure distinct aspects of personality.

In addition to the degree of construct validity provided by the development procedures themselves, the authors report several other research studies that provide evidence of validity. These include a confirmatory factor analysis of the normative sample using a community sample from Oregon, a comparison of the six-factor structure of the SFPQ and the NEO Personality Inventory—Revised, and several demonstrations of convergent validity examining the relationship between the SFPQ and the 16 Personality Factor Questionnaire, the Hogan Personality Inventory, and the Jackson Personality Inventory—Revised. Although to some extent the assessment of validity involves a subjective determination, the evidence presented by these studies clearly supports the six factor model of personality proposed by the authors, as well as the measurement of those factors by the SFPQ.

SUMMARY. As one of many personality measures now available, the SFPQ makes an important contribution to the field of personality assessment while also providing a tool with considerable practical utility in a variety of settings. It offers excellent technical characteristics, is not unduly taxing on individual respondents across a wide spectrum of ages and backgrounds, and is easy to understand and interpret. The manual is easy to read and addresses all aspects of the instrument's development, including theoretical background and item selection, as well as technical characteristics, interpretation, and usefulness. The SFPQ will be particularly beneficial for those requiring a screening tool in the clinical and employment settings.

REVIEWER'S REFERENCES

Goldberg, L. R. (1990). An alternative "description of personality": The Big-Five factor structure. *Journal of Personality and Social Psychology, 59,* 1216–1229.
Jackson, D. N. (1984). *Personality Research Form manual.* Port Huron, MI: Sigma Assessment Systems.
Jackson, D. N., Paunonen, S. V., Fraboni, M., and Goffin, R. D. (1996). A five-factor versus six-factor model of personality structure. *Personality and Individual Differences, 20,* 33–45.

[230]

16PF Adolescent Personality Questionnaire.

Purpose: Designed to "measure normal personality of adolescents, problem-solving abilities, and preferred work activities," and to identify problems in areas known to be problematic to adolescents.

Population: Ages 11–22.

Publication Date: 2001.

Acronym: APQ.

Scores: 21 normal personality scales: Primary Personality Factor Scales (Warmth, Reasoning, Emotional Stability, Dominance, Liveliness, Rule-Consciousness, Social Boldness, Sensitivity, Vigilance, Abstractedness, Privateness, Apprehension, Openness to Change, Self-Reliance, Perfectionism, Tension), Global Factor Scales (Extraversion, Anxiety, Tough-Mindedness, Independence, Self-Control); plus a ranking of Work Activity Preferences (Manual, Scientific, Artistic, Helping, Sales/Management, and Procedural), Personal Discomfort (Discouragement, Worry, Poor Body Image, Overall Discomfort), "Getting in Trouble" (Anger or Aggression, Problems with Authority, Alcohol or Drugs, Overall Trouble), Context (Home or School), Coping/Managing Difficulty, Impression Management, Missing Responses, Central Responses, Predicted Grade Point Average; 10 life's difficulties scales: Discouragement, Worry, Poor Body Image, Overall Discomfort, Anger or Aggression, Problems with Authority, Alcohol or Drugs, Overall Trouble, Problems at Home, Problems at School.

Administration: Group or individual.

Price Data: Available from publisher.

Time: (65) minutes (untimed).

Comments: Computerized scoring and interpretive reports available (APQ Guidance Report and APQ Psychological Report); optional Life's Difficulties section provides an opportunity for the youth to indicate particular problems in areas known to be problematic for adolescents, making the APQ appropriate for screening and for introducing sensitive topics in a counseling setting.

Author: J. M. Schuerger.

Publisher: Institute for Personality and Ability Testing, Inc. (IPAT).

Review of the 16PF Adolescent Personality Questionnaire by WILLIAM M. REYNOLDS, Professor, Department of Psychology, Humboldt State University, Arcata, CA:

DESCRIPTION. The 16PF Adolescent Personality Questionnaire (APQ) is described by its author as appropriate for adolescents ages 11 or 12 to 22 years. There are 147 items on the 16 normal personality (Primary Factor) scales, 15 items on the Work Activities scales, and 43 items on the Life's Difficulties scales. The manual states that the APQ has a reading grade level of around 5.5, although a check indicates that some of the APQ items are written at an eighth and ninth grade reading level.

The APQ evaluates most of the same personality domains as the 14-factor High School Personality Questionnaire (HSPQ; Cattell, Cattell, & Johns, 1984) except for Withdrawal and Demandingness. To make the APQ consistent with the 16PF Questionnaire, which is designed for adults, the author included the four factors of: Vigilance, Abstractedness, Privateness, and Openness to Change that are found on the 16PF Questionnaire. These four along with factors (scales) of Warmth, Reasoning, Emotional Stability, Dominance, Liveliness, Rule-Consciousness, Social Boldness, Sensitivity, Apprehension, Self-Reliance, Perfectionism, and Tension constitute the 16 APQ Primary Factors. Weighted scores on these scales are combined to form five Global Factors of Extraversion, Anxiety, Tough-Mindedness, Independence, and Self-Control. The normal personality scales have between 8 and 12 items each, with 10 of the factors consisting of 8 items each. The normal personality scale of Reasoning is actually a brief measure of general cognitive ability rather than personality, although personality (concrete versus abstract) is inferred from this scale.

In addition to the scales of normal personality, further changes included the addition of the Work Activities component that is reported to measure aspects of Holland's (1973) six career types in the form of: Manual, Scientific, Artistic, Helping, Sales/Management, and Procedural scales. The Life's Difficulties section includes three Personal Discomfort scales (Discouragement, Worry, and Poor Body Image, as well as a total Overall Discomfort scale), three Getting Into Trouble scales (Anger or Aggression, Problems with Authority, and Alcohol or Drugs, as well as a total Overall Trouble score), two Context Scales (Home, School), and a seven-item Coping scale. There are also several validity indicators, including Impression Management, Central Responses (selection of the middle option), and Missing Responses.

Sten scores (standard ten) that are based on a scale of 1 to 10 with a mean of 5.5 and a standard deviation of 2 points are provided for the Global and Primary Factors, with endorsement counts for the Work Activities scales, and percentile ranks for the Life's Difficulties scales.

The test manual suggests that, on average, 15-year-olds can complete the APQ in less than 90 minutes. The items are presented in a 21-page test booklet that can be a bit daunting for some adolescents. Item format varies, with most of the normal personality and Life's Difficulties items using a true/?/false format, with a number of these items including additional descriptors to clarify the meaning of items. The 12 Reasoning items use a three-alternative, multiple-choice format, and include verbal analogies, opposites, and other problems typically found on verbal aptitude scales. The Work Activities scale consists of six statements arranged across 15 items using a forced-choice format, with each of the six statements representing one of Holland's career orientation dimensions. Scores on these scales are the number of times the dimension was endorsed.

The manual describes the various personality factors measured by the APQ and the characteristics of individuals with high and low scores on each factor. Many of the descriptions read more like adults than characteristics of adolescent personality. The Life's Difficulties scales are briefly described, with examples of items provided to illustrate content. Following these descriptions, the manual provides a substantial section on interpretation of APQ scales.

The APQ is scored by computer, either by sending the answer sheet into the publisher for scoring and generating an interpretive report, or scoring only using a scoring program diskette. This latter program generates a list of scores for each of the scales. There are two score reports available from the publisher: the APQ Guidance Report, which consists of scores for the 16 Personality Factors and the Work Activities scales, and the APQ Psychological Report, which also includes the Life's Difficulties scales. The computer scoring provides two forms of the report, one for the adolescent and another for the clinician. The

adolescent form, which provides scores on the Global Factors and Work Activities, is written at comprehension level beyond that of many adolescents. The clinician report provides a summary of the Testing Indices, Global and Primary Factors (sten scores and graphic illustration of scores with low and high score descriptions for each scale), scores on the Work Activities scales, and percentile ranks for scores on the Life's Difficulties scales and the Coping scale. An interpretive summary across the APQ domains is also provided.

DEVELOPMENT. The development of the APQ involved several iterations of item development, rewriting, and field testing. The author provides a brief description of the number of items on these forms and approximate sample sizes. The manual indicates that some of this data may be obtained from the author. Approximately 16% of the items on the normal personality scales were from the HSPQ, 28% from the adult 16PF Fifth Edition, 19% from the author of the APQ, and the remainder written by students and IPAT staff.

The final standardization version of the APQ included 199 items. Scale selection was based on a factor analysis (analysis type not specified) with a Promax rotation of item parcels (two or three related items combined) that resulted in a viable 16-factor solution in which two of the anticipated factors, Emotional Stability and Apprehension, loaded on the same factor. The author notes that a subsequent analysis using a 15-factor solution "was very satisfactory" and it was decided to split the Emotional Stability and Apprehension factor into two factors to make it consistent with the 16PF Questionnaire.

PSYCHOMETRIC INFORMATION.

Standardization. The standardization sample varied for different components of the APQ. For the 16 normal personality factors (Primary Factors) and Work Activities scales, the standardization sample consisted of 1,460 adolescents ages 11 to 22 years. A subsample of 410 adolescents also completed the Life's Difficulties scales, although roughly half of these adolescents (n = 213) were from clinical settings (outpatients, educational referrals, and drug treatment). Norms for the APQ Primary Factors, Work Activities, and Life's Difficulties scales were based on the nonclinical sample of adolescents. In this manner it can be estimated that approximately 1,247 adolescents were the basis for the Primary Factors and Work Activities norms, with the Life's Difficulties scale norms based on approximately

197 adolescents. The majority of the 1,460 adolescents in the development sample (88%) were between the ages of 15 and 18 years, with 47% male and 53% female, with 81% Caucasian, 6% African American, 5% Hispanic, and small percentages of various other ethnicities. The majority of this sample (67%) was from the north central United States. Sample characteristics (age, gender, etc.) of the specific normative groups (1,247 and 197) are not provided.

Reliability. Reliability data are presented in the form of internal consistency reliability (coefficient alpha) for all scales, with a test-retest reliability study reported for the Work Activities scales with a sample of 14 "late adolescents and young adults." The manual claims to present equivalent form reliability with a 3-week interval for the normal personality scales as shown by correlations between the APQ Primary Factors and corresponding scales on the 16PF and HSPQ in a sample of 107 "late adolescents."

Internal consistency reliability of the 16 Primary Factors ranged from .64 to .83, with a median reliability of .72 and only one reliability coefficient above .76. The internal consistency reliability coefficients for the Work Activities scales range from .46 to .75 with a median reliability coefficient of .62. However, as the author correctly notes, these coefficients are problematic because the items on these scales are ipsative. The test-retest reliabilities (several weeks interval between administrations) of the Work Activities scales were similar, ranging from .53 to .74, with a median of .62, suggesting low reliability for these scales. Internal consistency reliabilities of the Life's Difficulties scales are low for most scales, with coefficients ranging from .52 to .65 for the three Personal Discomfort scales, .66 to .77 for the Getting into Trouble scales, .60 and .42 for the Home and School scales, respectively and .74 for the Coping scale. Reliability is not reported for the eight-item Impression Management Scale.

Validity. Validity data are presented in a somewhat haphazard manner, with a mix of results from previous development versions of the APQ interspersed among validation data for the current version. Given that the primary use of the APQ is the assessment of normal personality, one would expect the majority of validity evidence for this new measure to focus on the 16 Primary Factor scales. Unfortunately, there are few studies/data to support validity. The first demonstration of validity of the 16 Primary Factors was a correlational study of these factors and those on the adult 16 PF in what appears to be a college sample (average age of 19 years, 70% women, n = 107). Because the APQ includes items from the 16PF Questionnaire, it is not surprising to find moderate correlations between .53 and .81. In a study of 30 adolescents of unknown age and other characteristics who also completed the HSPQ (also a source for APQ items), correlations of .17 to .74 were found between same factor scales, with half of these coefficients below .50.

Additional evidence for validity of the Primary Factors is suggested in the manual by correlations between these scales and adolescents' grade point average (GPA) in four studies. Two of these studies were done with an early research version of the APQ that differed in items from the current version. Across the four studies, relatively low correlations were reported between Primary Factors and GPA, providing limited support for the validity of a measure of normal personality. The exception to this is the Reasoning scale, which consists of scholastic ability type items. In the two studies that used the final form of the APQ, the correlations between the Reasoning scale and self-reported GPA or counselors' ratings of GPA were .41 and .31, respectively, which are relatively low. Because the items on the Reasoning scale are based on academic ability, unless corrected or normed by age (or grade) these correlations are difficult to interpret. The results of the GPA studies and the 16PF Questionnaire and HSPQ are the extent of the validity evidence for the normal personality scales.

Several studies are reported for the validity of the Work Activities Scales, some conducted prior to the addition of these scales to the APQ, using either the normative sample or a large sample of "premedical college students." These studies included various other vocational measures. In most of these studies, low correlations between Work Activities scales and related measures were reported.

Validity data for the Life's Difficulties are presented with a sample of 44 older adolescents and young adults (college students?) who were administered the MMPI and the Personality Assessment Screener (Morey, 1997). Unfortunately, this study was conducted with a development version of the Life's Difficulties scales, which had items and scales that are different from the current version.

COMMENTARY. The 16PF APQ is one of few measures that purports to measure personality in adolescents as opposed to psychopathology. The APQ manual leaves out a great deal of information, particularly as it relates to the psychometric characteristics of this measure. The standardization sample, although adequate for adolescents ages 15 to 18, is limited for those below and above this age range. The normative sample is inadequate in size and description for the Life's Difficulties Scales. Without a description of the age and gender composition of the approximately 197 who constitute the norm group, it is difficult to interpret the percentile ranks derived from these scales.

The manual is missing some useful information. There are no data pertaining to the means and standard deviations of the APQ scales for the standardization sample. This would be useful when interpreting the results of the Life's Difficulties scales for which only percentile ranks are provided as scores. Noticeably missing from the reliability section is information on the standard error of measurement for the various scales. There are numerous references to other data in the author's possession or outcomes with other samples that are supportive of reliability or validity, but are not described in the manual. The lack of complete data and tables is problematic, as is the suggestion of going to the author for more information.

The reliability of the APQ normal personality scales is low to moderate, but higher than previously reported for the HSPQ. Reliabilities for the other APQ scales are mostly low. The validity data for the APQ with adolescents below age 18 are limited. There is no systematic presentation of forms of validity (construct, criterion, convergent/discriminant, etc.) for the normal personality scales, and validity data for the other domains (e.g. Work, Life's Difficulties) are also limited, with many of the reported correlations providing little support for validity.

SUMMARY. The 16PF APQ draws on a rich historical base, namely the High School Personality Questionnaire and the 16PF Questionnaire, with approximately 44% of its items from these two measures. In addition to the 16 normal personality factors, the APQ provides enhanced content and user value by including two brief additional measures, one of occupational preference and the other a brief screen of adolescent psychopathology. This is a commendable combination of assessment domains, particularly for adolescents. However, because of low reliability and limited evidence for validity of these latter two components, care should be taken in their use and interpretation. The relatively modest levels of reliability reported may not preclude the use of the APQ in some counseling settings where clinical decisions are typically not based upon such results.

The 16PF APQ is one of the few measures designed to assess "personality" of adolescents. A similar measure, the Millon Adolescent Personality Inventory (Millon, 1982), has its own set of problems (Reynolds & Sattler, 2001) and cannot be recommended over the 16PF APQ. In keeping consistent with the previous perspectives of personality that were operationalized by the HSPQ and 16PF Questionnaire, the APQ may have kept itself from a more natural evolution to a more contemporary perspective of personality, such as that reflected by the big five. It may be that further research will lend greater support for the use of this measure.

REVIEWER'S REFERENCES
Cattell, R. B., Cattell, M. D., & Johns, E. (1984). *Manual and norms for the High School Personality Questionnaire.* Champaign, IL: Institute for Personality and Ability Testing.
Holland, J. L. (1973). *Making vocational choices: A theory of careers.* Englewood Cliffs, NJ: Prentice-Hall.
Morey, L. C. (1997). Personality Assessment Screener. Odessa, FL: Psychological Assessment Resources.
Reynolds, W. M., & Sattler, J. M. (2001). Assessment of behavioral, social and emotional competencies in children and adolescents. In J. M. Sattler (Ed.), *Assessment of children: Behavioral and clinical applications,* (4TH Ed., pp. 163–188) Costa Mesa, CA: Jerome Sattler, Pub.

Review of the 16PF Adolescent Personality Questionnaire by SUSAN C. WHISTON, Professor of Counseling and Educational Psychology, and JENNIFER C. BOUWKAMP, Doctoral Student Counseling Psychology, Indiana University, Bloomington, IN:

DESCRIPTION. The 16PF Adolescent Personality Questionnaire (APQ) is a 205-item instrument designed to measure aspects of normal personality in adolescents ages 12 to 22 years. This instrument was designed for use in situations where personality is relevant, such as educational adjustment, personal or social difficulty, and passage through developmental tasks. The APQ includes four sections: (a) Personal Style, (b) Problem Solving, (c) Work Activity Preferences, and (d) Life's Difficulties (optional items concerning matters known to be difficult for adolescents). The first three sections provide valuable information to professionals who counsel adolescents related to personal and family issues and to those who assist adolescents in academic and career decision making. The APQ is also designed to indicate learning styles and provide information that can be used in developing Individualized Education Programs. When the Life's Difficulties section is administered with the three other sections, the APQ is appropriate for screening and addressing sensitive topics in the counseling situation, although results are not intended for diagnosis.

The APQ is easy to administer with all four sections contained in one booklet, and administration time is around 65 minutes for all 205 items. Students indicate their responses on an answer sheet where each item has two or three choices depending on the section. The Life's Difficulties section is set off from the other three by a blank page indicating that the student is not to go on unless directed to do so by the test administrator.

Both computerized scoring and hand scoring using a disk are available. The results using either method are organized into four areas: (a) Testing Indices, (b) Normal Personality and Ability, (c) Work Activities, and (d) Life's Difficulties (if administered). Testing Indices includes Impression Management, Missing Responses, and Central Responses. Normal Personality and Abilities includes the Global Factors of Extraversion, Anxiety, Tough-Mindedness, Independence, and Self-Control, under which the Primary Factors of Warmth, Reasoning, Emotional Stability, Dominance, Liveliness, Rule-Consciousness, Social Boldness, Sensitivity, Vigilance, Abstractedness, Privateness, Apprehension, Openness to Change, Self-Reliance, Perfectionism, and Tension are discussed. The Work Activities provides information ranking the young person's preferences for occupational types using John Holland's (1973) typology of Manual, Scientific, Artistic, Helping, Sales/Management, and Procedural. Life's Difficulties supplies information on Personal Discomfort (Discouragement, Worry, Poor Body Image, and Overall Discomfort), "Getting in Trouble" (Anger or Aggression, Problems with Authority, Alcohol or Drugs, and Overall Trouble), the Context in which difficulties are experienced (Home, and School), and Coping (Social Competence, Task Competence, Problem Solving, Utilizing One's Social Network, Reason of Strong Values, and Attitude Change).

Two computerized reports, with separate sections of feedback for the adolescent and for the professional, are also available from The Institute for Personality and Ability Testing (IPAT): (a) the APQ Guidance Report and (b) the APQ Psychological Report. Both reports provide scores on the normal personality factors and their related Global Factors, as well as the Work Activities scales, and some administrative indices. The Guidance Report does not include information on the Life's Difficulties section and is designed for school counselors or qualified teachers in developing academic or therapeutic strategies. On the other hand, the Psychological Report has the same three sections and the results of the Life's Difficulties items. This report is more appropriate for clinical applications and is based on items addressing sexual matters, violent feelings and actions, serious worry and despondency, and other similar thoughts and behaviors.

DEVELOPMENT. The APQ is one measure in the family of tests originally authored by Raymond B. Cattell and colleagues beginning with the Sixteen Personality Factor Questionnaire (16PF; Cattell, Eber, & Tatsuoka, 1970) for adults. The APQ specifically evolved from the High School Personality Questionnaire (HSPQ; Cattell, Cattell, & Johns, 1984). Cattell used what is often called the domain sampling method, where one starts with a defined domain (e.g., personality) and seeks to identify the number and nature of a relatively few variables that capture the meaning of that domain. Cattell and colleagues would write items to represent the domain of interest and then use factor analysis to discern the number and nature of the variables that define the structure of the domain. Following this method throughout the research phases of the APQ, there were three sequential forms of the instrument: (a) a 240-item research version, (b) a 264-item research version, and (c) a 284-item standardization version.

Before creation of the final version of the APQ, items in the Personality and Ability section had been through several revisions and extensive testing. In the final factor analysis, items were merged into "parcels" of two or three items each, according to item correlations and the manifest content of the items. For the Work Activities section, the items were written to reflect Holland's six-trait model, and factor analyses were performed with a mix of adolescent and adult clients from various settings. The problem content areas for the Life's Difficulties section were based on a review of common content scales among existing pathology instruments, as well as a review of the then current *Diagnostic and Statistical Manual* (American Psychiatric Association, 1987). Data for this section were collected with only 80 normal high school students from Florida and Cleveland, 37 adolescents referred to a mental health center in Illinois, and 29 adolescents referred to school psychologists for a variety of problems. The final review and revision of items on the Life's Difficulties section was conducted by IPAT staff and practitioners familiar with adolescent psychology.

TECHNICAL. There were a total of 1,460 young persons involved in the final standardization sample. Of these, 1,050 completed only the Normal Personality and Ability, and Work Activities sections, and another 410 also completed the Life's Difficulties section. Of these 410 young people, 213 were in clinical settings. In age, roughly 6% were between 11 and 14; 88% between 15 and 18; and another 6% between 19 and 21. There was close to an even split on gender, with 47% male and 53% female. Concerning geographic representation, the preponderance of the sample (67%) was from the north-central section of the United States. Of the other participants, 14% were from the south-central U.S., 7% from the northeast, and 6% from both the southeast and west. No data pertaining to race or ethnicity were mentioned in the description of the standardization sample.

Coefficient alphas for the Normal Personality and Ability section vary from a low of .64 (Openness to Change) to a high of .83 for (Social Boldness), a pattern that matches that of the 16PF Fifth Edition. The average over the 16 factors was .72, with the Global Factors having higher reliabilities than the Primary Factors. Test-retest reliabilities (interval of 1 week) ranged from a low of .44 for Reasoning to a high of .95 for Abstractedness. The Global Factors averaged .91. Stability coefficients for the Work Activities section over a period of 1 week averaged .79 over the six scales, whereas test-retest coefficients for the Life's Difficulties section (interval of 1 week) averaged .77.

Scale validity of the APQ Normal Personality and Ability section was examined through correlations with school achievement. Four sets of data were available to address the issue of personality and school grades with the updated instrument. In particular, the relationship between the Reasoning factor and grades, which one would expect to be high, had a wide range of correlation

coefficients across four studies: .27, .77, .41, and .31 (all significant at the .05 level).

Most validity data on the Work Activities section were from the research prior to its use as part of the APQ and were not discussed in the administration manual provided. The conclusion reached by the authors was that the Work Activities results are similar to those obtained from longer instruments and with similar external validity evidence. However, no compelling evidence was provided to support the use of the Work Activities section of the APQ over these other instruments.

Much of the validation evidence for the Life's Difficulties section involved correlating it with the scales of the Minnesota Multiphasic Personality Inventory (MMPI; Hathaway & McKinley, 1943). In our opinion, stronger evidence could have been provided by correlation of the APQ with the adolescent version of the MMPI (MMPI-A) or at least the more recent MMPI-2. Nevertheless, obtained coefficients were low with an average of .29. Additional evidence included correlations with three other external criteria resulting in coefficients of .41 with the Child Behavior Checklist (Achenbach, 1991), .27 with psychologists' reports, and .23 with counselors' reports. These comparatively low coefficients do not indicate a strong relationship between the problem behaviors assessed by the APQ and other measures of child and adolescent difficulties.

COMMENTARY AND SUMMARY. Overall, the 16PF Adolescent Personality Questionnaire appears to be a decent measure for obtaining a "snapshot" look at the typical American adolescent. Furthermore, the instrument may provide the professional with insights into how to work successfully with specific individuals. However, there are some questions remaining about its factor structure as no strong argument or compelling explanation is provided for the selection and inclusion of the three distinct scales of Normal Personality and Ability, Work Activities, and Life's Difficulties. Some of the reliability coefficients for the Primary Factors are low and indicate that a clinician should be cautious in interpreting these results. With regard to adolescent career exploration, one may consider using instruments that incorporate the more current and widely used version of Holland's (1985, 1997) typology. Although the six types in the 1973 version are similar to the more current version, a significant amount of career information and resources use the more current version rather than the terms Holland used almost 30 years ago. Similarly, although the Life's Difficulties section is well-intentioned as an indicator of adolescent troubles, much of the validation evidence seems somewhat outdated and needs to be more substantial before we could recommend extensive use. A strength of the APQ is that it purports to measure the "Big Five" factors of personality for adolescents; however, its limitation indicates the instrument should be used cautiously and with other clinical measures.

REVIEWERS' REFERENCES

Achenbach, T. M. (1991). *Manual for the Child Behavior Checklist/4-18 and 1991 profile*. Burlington, VT: Department of Psychiatry, University of Vermont.

American Psychiatric Association. (1987). *Diagnostic and statistical manual of mental disorders* (3rd ed., rev.). Washington, DC: Author.

Cattell, R. B., Cattell, M. D., & Johns, E. (1984). *Manual and norms for the High School Personality Questionnaire*. Champaign, IL: Institute for Personality and Ability Testing, Inc.

Cattell, R. B., Eber, H. W., & Tatsuoka, M. M. (1970). *Handbook for the Sixteen Personality Factor Questionnaire (16PF)*. Champaign, IL: Institute for Personality and Ability Testing, Inc.

Hathaway, S. R., & McKinley, J. C. (1943). *The Minnesota Multiphasic Personality Inventory*. Minneapolis: University of Minnesota.

Holland, J. L. (1973). *Making vocational choices: A theory of careers*. Englewood Cliffs, NJ: Prentice-Hall.

Holland, J. L. (1985). *Making vocational choices: A theory of vocational personalities and work environments* (2nd ed.). Englewood Cliffs, NJ: Prentice-Hall.

Holland, J. L. (1997). *Making vocational choices: A theory of vocational personalities and work environments* (3rd ed.). Englewood Cliffs, NJ: Prentice-Hall.

[231]

16PF Select.

Purpose: A shorter version of the 16PF Fifth Edition personality measure, which was designed for personnel selection.

Population: Ages 16 and over.

Publication Dates: 1949–1999.

Acronym: 16PF Select.

Scores, 12: Warmth, Calmness, Dominance, Liveliness, Rule-Consciousness, Social Boldness, Trust, Imagination, Self-Assuredness, Openness, Self-Reliance, Organization.

Administration: Individual or group.

Price Data, 2002: $33 per introductory kit including manual (1999, 75 pages), dimension specification form, questionnaire/answer sheet booklet and prepaid mail-in report processing certificate; $30 per manual; $30 per 10 questionnaire/answer sheet booklets; $15 to $30 per report.

Time: (20) minutes (untimed).

Comments: A shorter version of the 16PF Fifth Edition (T6:2292).

Authors: Raymond B. Cattell, A. Karen S. Cattell, and Heather E. P. Cattell, and Mary L. Kelly.

Publisher: Institute for Personality and Ability Testing, Inc. (IPAT).

Cross References: For information about the complete 16PF see T5:2417 (43 references); for reviews of an earlier edition of the 16PF by Mary J. McLellan and Pamela Carrington Rotto, see 12:354 (38 references); see also T4:2470 (140 references); for reviews by James N. Butcher and Marvin Zuckerman, see 9:1136 (67 references); see also T3:2208 (182 references); for reviews by Bruce M. Bloxam, Brian F. Bolton, and James A. Walsh, see 8:679 (619 references); see also T2:1383 (244 references); for reviews of an earlier edition by Thomas J. Bouchard, Jr. and Leonard G. Rorer, see 7:139 (295 references); see also P:245 (249 references); for a review by Maurice Lorr, see 6:174 (81 references); for a review by C. J. Adcock, see 5:112 (21 references); for reviews by Charles M. Harsh, Ardie Lubin, and J. Richard Wittenborn, see 4:87 (8 references).

Review of the 16PF Select by PAUL A. ARBISI, Minneapolis VA Medical Center, Assistant Professor, Departments of Psychiatry and Psychology, University of Minnesota, Minneapolis, MN:

DESCRIPTION. The 16PF Select is a shortened version of the 16PF Fifth Edition (T6:2292) intended for use in prediction of job performance in selection settings. The goals in the development of the 16PF Select were ease in administration and scoring and the ability to be incorporated into a multimethod selection battery that would tap job-related constructs. From the original 185 items comprising the 16PF Fifth Edition, 107 items comprising 12 personality dimensions and three response style indices were retained. The personality dimensions are as follows: Warmth, Calmness, Dominance, Liveliness, Rule-Consciousness, Social Boldness, Trust, Imagination, Self-Assuredness, Open-Mindedness, Self-Reliance, and Organization. With the exception of the dimensions Calmness and Open Mindedness, which have 9 items, the remaining dimensions all have 8 items. In addition there are three response style indices: Impression Management, 9 items, Infrequency, 17 items, and Acquiescence, 67 items.

The questionnaire can be administered individually or in groups and takes approximately 20 minutes to complete. The overall readability of the items is at the fifth grade level. The response format has three options: true, false, and an option placed between the true and false response in the answer booklet in the form of a question mark indicating that neither the true or false response "is better for you." The question and answer sheet are contained in a single form. As the client completes the questions and turns the pages of the booklet, a new row of questions is revealed, as is a new row of the corresponding response options. This format prevents the client from losing his or her place and inadvertently endorsing the wrong response.

In addition to the examinee completing the questionnaire, the examiner in consultation with the client (presumably the individual interested in hiring the examinee) completes a Dimension Specification Form (DSF). This form allows the examiner, in consultation with the client, to specify which 16PF Select personality dimensions are important for the ideal candidate to possess for a particular position. The examiner utilizes either one of two methods for communicating the personality dimensions that are felt to be important in optimal job performance when completing the DSF. In the "Band Method" the examiner specifies the importance of particular dimensions as well as a range of scores that would be acceptable within that dimension for success within a particular position. The Regression Weights Method assumes that validity studies have been conducted for the particular position and the examiner can specify regression weights for each of the 16PF Select dimensions. The examiner either faxes or mails the DSF along with the detached answer sheet to IPAT where the test is computer scored and a summary report is generated based on the examinee's responses to the 16PF Select within the context of the DSF. The resulting report calculates an overall model similarity by comparing the job candidates' scores in stanines on the various personality dimensions with the ideal sten range and the relative importance of the dimension as specified by the examiner.

DEVELOPMENT. The 16PF Select was developed by examining two sources of information. Results from an ongoing meta-analysis were examined and dimensions that were most significantly predictive across studies were identified. The second source of information was derived through the use of 10 expert psychologists who were asked to estimate the expected correlation between the various 16PF dimensions and job performance for four occupations: police officer, customer service, management, and sales. Using a minimum mean estimated correlation of .15 based on the experts' opinion and combined with the preliminary findings from the meta-analysis, specific dimensions were selected for inclusion in the 16PF Select. This process resulted in the elimination of two dimensions contained in the 16PF

Fifth Edition: Sensitivity and Privateness. In addition, the dimension of Tension was also dropped, as was the Reasoning dimension. Items were selected and retained on the dimensions through a three-step process. First, items were reviewed for content to assure that the items were measuring the breadth of the dimension. Second, items were reviewed to ensure that they would not be perceived as inappropriate in terms of the ADA. Finally, items were retained based on item-scale intercorrelation and reliability analysis. In the final step, the goal was to create scales with a mean internal consistency of approximately .70 and no reliability coefficient below .60. This was generally achieved although coefficient alpha for both Warmth and Openness to Change fell at .59 and .60 respectively. Sten scores were developed by summing all items into raw dimension scores and using the 16PF Fifth Edition normative sample to translate the raw scores into sten scores. This process resulted in a shorter questionnaire that according to the manual is very similar to the 16PF Fifth Edition.

TECHNICAL. The manual contains appropriate reliability data drawn from the 16PF Fifth Edition normative sample of 2,260 and an "Operational sample" of 39,600 individuals. The manual contains no description of either of these samples, although it is assumed that the normative sample is well described in the 16PF Fifth Edition manual (see review by Carrington Rotto, 1995). It is unclear what constitutes the operational sample. The mean coefficient alpha for the 16PF Select dimensions is .68 with a range of .57 to .83. Test-retest reliability obtained from two undescribed samples fell in the moderate to good range. After a 2-week interval, test-retest reliabilities ranged from .70 to .88 with a mean correlation of .81 for all dimensions. After a 5-week interval, the correlations ranged from .71 to .86 with a mean correlation of .80.

The most troubling issue with the 16PF Select is the lack of construct and predictive validity evidence. Virtually no data are presented in the manual that demonstrate the relationship between 16PF Select dimensions and relevant job performance parameters. Indeed the manual states, "The correlations between the two forms of the 16PF Questionnaire were high enough that it was decided not to perform separate construct validity studies on the 16PF Select dimensions" (manual, p. 45). There are several problems with this statement. First, the correlations between the two instruments were reported for "two independent samples of students." There is no further description of the nature of these samples or justification for using students to establish the equivalency of an instrument that is primarily developed for use in personal selection of working adults. In addition, the magnitude of the correlation with the Calmness dimension and the Emotional Stability and Tension parent dimensions from the 16PF indicate that at least with regard to the Calmness dimension, independent validity studies need to be conducted. Finally, the issue of actual prediction of scores on the 16PF from the 16PF Select, particularly as it relates to the comparability of the overall model similarity score based on the data provided by the DSF, needs to be addressed. In other words how congruent are 16PF Select dimensions with the 16PF Fifth Edition dimensions in specifying the examinee's fit with the dimensions specified on the DSF? This is a critical issue because interpretation of the 16PF Select dimensions is solely based on data accumulated using the 16PF Fifth Edition.

COMMENTARY. The 16PF Select manual is well written and provides a concise overview of the use of the 16PF in personnel selection. Further, the rationale for development of the short form of the instrument is clearly presented and easy to follow. The 16PF Select has a number of potential advantages besides the shortened format and ease of interpretation. The questionnaire booklet and answer sheet are well designed to minimize coding errors. Also, the 16PF Select presumably directly addresses the personality dimensions felt to be important in a specific occupation through incorporation of the DSF and can indicate to what degree a particular candidate's profile is commensurate with the employer-specified job parameters. Further, the 16PF Select contains measures of response style that potentially allow the examiner to identify individuals who are responding to the instrument in an unusual or indiscriminate way.

At this point, data regarding the equivalence of the two instruments and the predictive validity of the 16PF Select are not yet available and need to be described in detail before the instrument can be broadly used in selection settings. For example, because scores on a shortened version of an instrument are correlated with scores on the original instrument does not necessary mean that the resulting predictions are equivalent, especially when looking at a profile or pattern of scale scores (Gass

& Luis, 2001). Indeed, the magnitude of the correlations between the 16PF Select dimensions and the 16PF Fifth Edition parent dimensions is modest and quite a bit smaller then those obtained across a number of settings between the MMPI-2 and a short form of the MMPI-2 (Gass & Luis, 2001). Even given the magnitude of the correlations between a short form of the MMPI-2 and the MMPI-2, the shortened form provides limited information and cannot be interpreted using standard MMPI-2 interpretive procedures (Gass & Luis, 2001). Consequently, extrapolating interpretive equivalence based solely on the magnitude of the correlation between two versions of an instrument should be done with great caution.

Additionally, use of the 16PF Select response style indices are problematic given the number of items lost in the shortened version and the lack of validity data associated with these indices. For example, the Impression Management scale that appears to measure social desirability lost three items from the 16PF Fifth Edition. No descriptive normative statistics are presented for any of the scales, let alone the Impression Management Scale. Normative data would be of crucial importance in interpreting the validity scales because the instrument is designed for use in personnel selection where a response bias toward social desirability would be common. In general, the guidelines for the interpretation of the response style indices are vague and the manual does not provide basic information for interpretation of those scales such as Positive Predictive Power and Negative Predictive Power across clinically relevant settings. Additionally, the distinction between the infrequency scale and "too many b responses" was unclear. Because all the infrequency scale items were keyed as b which is the "?" response on the answer form, how is this scale distinct from "too many b responses" and what would constitute "too many b responses"? More thought and effort is needed in the refinement of the response style indices and especially in the development of cut scores across relevant populations.

SUMMARY. The 16PF Select is a 107-item short version of the 16 Personality Factor Questionnaire, Fifth Edition designed to be used in selection settings. A short version of the 16PF has a number of potential advantages when used in the context of a multimethod selection evaluation given the body of data accumulated over the past 50 years on earlier versions of the 16PF. Unfortunately, as yet there is a paucity of data regarding the equivalence of the 16PF Select with the 16PF Fifth Edition. Further, there are limited validity data presented in the manual to support the use of the 16PF Select in employment selection for police and correctional officers, managers and executives, and customer service personnel. Until this information becomes available, caution must be exercised in using the 16PF Select independently in making personnel selection decisions.

REVIEWER'S REFERENCES

Carrington Rotto, P. (1995). Review of the Sixteen Personality Factor Questionnaire, Fifth Edition. In J. C. Conoley & J. C. Impara (Eds.), *The twelfth mental measurements yearbook* (pp. 948–950). Lincoln, NE: The Buros Institute of Mental Measurements.

Gass, C. S., & Luis, C. A. (2001). MMPI-2 Short Form: Psychometric characteristics in a neuropsychological setting. *Assessment, 8,* 213–219.

Review of the 16PF Select by STEPHEN E. TROTTER, Associate Professor, Department of Psychology, Tennessee State University, Nashville, TN:

DESCRIPTION. The 16PF Select is a 107-item modification of the 16PF-5th edition designed for employment settings where a match between predetermined criteria and candidate personality characteristics is desired. The candidate completes a combined questionnaire response booklet with step down format. Scoring is accomplished via mail or fax service. The use of the 16PF Select differs from other personality or personnel screening instruments in that it requires the employer's psychologist (MS or above) or like trained professional (Level 2 qualification needed for usage) to complete a Dimension Specification Form (DSF) indicating either the optimal range of sten scores on the 12 dimensions or regression weighting for the 12 dimensions. The regression weights are to be determined in the field by the purchasing psychologist. The manual states "the professional needs to have conducted a validity study and computed regression weights ... For each 16 PF Select dimension, the weight and the sign of the weight is entered onto the DSF" (p. 22). The advantage of using the regression model insofar as the report is concerned is the candidate is described as a good, moderate, or poor fit for the job. In the band method the candidate rating is restricted to good or poor. Both methods provide for feedback in the form of an "overall model similarity score" (manual, p. 35) to match candidate to predetermined 16PF scale configurations. The 16PF Select responses are scored and reported in a comprehensive fashion. The report includes the participant's primary sten scores; re-

sponse style indices; percentage of a, b, and c responses; and the number of omitted responses. The traditional 16PF scales of Reasoning and Privateness are omitted from the 16PF Select. The manual also includes a research only "performance appraisal form" (p. 67) to provide another evaluation data source.

DEVELOPMENT. The 16PF Select is a direct outgrowth of the 16PF-5th edition and as such has benefited from the recent renorming of the 16PF (Conn & Reike, 1994). The original 16PF was published in 1949 and has been the focus of many research projects and reviews. It has stood well the test of time and continues to be widely used in a variety of settings. Cattell & Krug (1986) have reported that the 16 factors identified by Raymond Cattell were replicated by over 50 studies. The 16PF Select development was based largely on what the manual calls "bare-bones" (p. 7) meta-analysis of ongoing validity studies conducted on the 16PF and solicited by IPAT from 16PF consumers. In addition, expert opinion was garnered from 10 psychologists familiar with the 16PF in regard to correlations between customer service, management, police, and sales positions vis-a-vis the 16PF Select scales. The 16PF items were also reviewed for appropriateness by 12 experts in light of the Americans with Disabilities Act (ADA). This review resulted in the dropping of six items from the Emotional Stability scale and a renaming of the scale to "Calmness."

TECHNICAL. The manual is very well written and comprehensive including chapters addressing the scoring, construction, and development. In addition, there is a very helpful section on "Best Practices in Employee Selection" (p. 49). The reported reliability coefficients ranged from .57 to .83 . Test reliability was conducted at 2- and 5-week intervals. The mean correlation at the 2-week interval was .81 and at 5 weeks .80. The manual reports evidence for 16PF construct validity but does not provide specific data for such. In the area of criterion validity the work is referenced as ongoing; however, this is supported in part by the meta-analysis used in the development of the 16PF Select. The manual also reports regression analysis for the scales not included in the 16PF Select: Reasoning, Sensitivity, and Privateness. The sample used in the development of the 16PF was a stratified random sample of 2,260 individuals selected to match the census in regard to age, gender and race. The Select uses the same normative group as a basis.

COMMENTARY. The attractiveness of this instrument resides largely in two factors: its lineage with the 16PF and the potential interactive nature of the "overall model similarity" (manual, p. 34) index. The 16PF provides a well-grounded medium of exchange between psychologists across settings. Furthermore, it appears to be less invasive than the Minnesota Multiphasic Personality Inventory–2 (MMPI-2) and technically superior to the Myers-Briggs Type Indicator (MBTI) when used for employment decisions. The manual is very well constructed and easy to follow for the trained professional. The reviewer found the chapter on "Best practices in employee selection" (p. 49) to be particularly helpful. The sensitivity to employee selection via standardized testing in light of ADA regulations was also well handled. The omission of the Reasoning scale, with the explanation the examiner might well be using a more specific measure of cognitive functioning, seems unsupported. The use of widespread intelligence testing in employment settings, other than the military is a false expectation. A gross, if somewhat limited, indicator of reasoning seems an important factor in employee selection. It was easy to respond to the scoring protocol and the stepped down format makes answering items and matching question stem to response relatively easy. The shortness of the 16PF Select and its relatively high stability is a benefit when screening large numbers of applicants. The ability to customize the desired sten score ranges in either an intuitive, expert opinion fashion or by conducting regression analysis is very helpful. The latter would appear to be far superior but far less likely to occur in the reviewer's opinion. The effort and expertise required to conduct a validity study and compute regression weights may well exceed the resources of most if not all small to medium businesses. However, large corporations or consultants might well find this an extremely attractive option when combined with IPAT's ability to customize the scoring to reflect the regression weights. The interactive nature of this process of individualizing the job criteria profiles is extremely interesting when the decision is regression based. In keeping with Paul Meehl's (1954) classic comments, the process of expert opinion in generating benchmarks is less attractive, and probably less effective but still desirable.

SUMMARY. The 16PF Select appears to be a valuable resource in making the complex decision to hire or not.

REVIEWER'S REFERENCES
Cattell, R. B., & Krug, S. E. (1986). The number of factors in the 16PF: A review of the evidence with special emphasis on methodological problems. *Educational and Psychological Measurement, 46*, 509–522.
Conn, S. R., & Reike, M. L. (Eds.). (1994). *The 16PF Fifth Edition technical manual.* Champaign, IL: Institute for Personality and Ability Testing, Inc.
Meehl, P. E. (1954). *Clinical versus statistical prediction: A theoretical analysis and review of the evidence.* Minneapolis: University of Minnesota Press.

[232]
Social Adjustment Scale—Self Report.

Purpose: Designed to assess "the ability of an individual to adapt to, and derive satisfaction from, their social roles."

Population: Age 17 and older.

Publication Date: 1999.

Acronym: SAS-SR.

Scores: 7 areas: Work, Social and Leisure Activities, Relations with Extended Family, Primary Relationship, Parenthood, Family Life, Economic.

Administration: Group.

Price Data, 2002: $102 per complete kit including 25 interview guides, 25 QuikScore™ forms, and manual; $27 per 10 question booklets; $38 per 25 QuikScore™ forms; $48 per manual; $55 per specimen set including 3 interview guides, 3 QuikScore™ forms, and manual.

Foreign Language Editions: Available in Afrikaans, Cantonese, Czech, Danish, Dutch, Finnish, French (European), French-Canadian, German, Greek, Hebrew, Hungarian, Italian, Japanese, Mandarin, Norwegian, Portuguese, Russian, Spanish (European), Spanish (South American), and Swedish.

Time: (15–20) minutes.

Author: Myrna Weissmann.

Publisher: Multi-Health Systems, Inc.

Review of the Social Adjustment Scale—Self Report by JULIE A. ALLISON, Associate Professor of Psychology, Pittsburg State University, Pittsburg, KS:

DESCRIPTION. The Social Adjustment Scale—Self Report (SAS-SR) is a 54-item assessment designed to assess an individual's ability to adapt to, and derive satisfaction from, his or her social roles. It is designed for individuals 17 years of age or older, with at least a fourth grade reading level. The scale measures six major areas of adjustment over the course of the past 2 weeks for the person completing the scale. These include Work or student functioning, Social and Leisure Activities, Relationships with Extended Family, role as marital partner, parental role, and role within family unit (which includes an economic functioning component). Relevant items are assessed using a 5-point scale, with higher scores indicating greater social adjustment problems. Within each area, both behavioral ratings (including performance at expected tasks, amount of friction with people, and finer aspects of interpersonal relations) and assessments of feelings and satisfactions are included. The results of the scale yield seven scores: one for each specific area, and an overall adjustment rating.

The SAS-SR takes from 15–20 minutes to complete, may be self administered, and is self-scored. The QuikScore' form makes standardized *T*-scores for both males and females available for interpretation by a trained professional.

The SAS-SR may be used by clinicians interested in using a complementary assessment tool for the purposes of screening, treatment planning, and/or for purposes of monitoring progress and outcomes of individuals. The SAS-SR is not intended to be used exclusively for any of these purposes. The SAS-SR may also be used for research purposes.

DEVELOPMENT. The demand for an instrument designed to assess social adjustment became clear in the 1960s, when outpatient treatment, versus inpatient hospitalization, became the treatment of choice. This demand also reflected the increased awareness of practitioners that the social context of an individual may play an important role on the treatment outcome, and hence the importance of monitoring the individual's well-being within this social context. The original version of the SAS was in interview form, and covered a period of 2 months (versus the SR 2-week format). The SAS Interview was first used in a comparison study of acutely depressed patients and a control group through the course of recovery, and found that maintenance psychotherapy improves social functioning. For practical reasons, the self-report version of the SAS was created. Since its creation, the SAS-SR has been used for a variety of different purposes, both clinical and research based. Its primary use, however, has been as an outcome assessment tool for clinical trials of pharmacological, psychological, or combination therapy.

TECHNICAL. Most research assessing the utility of the SAS-SR has been conducted using four distinct populations: community individuals, schizophrenics, alcoholics, and depressed individuals. Data on both reliability and various validity constructs are available and are generally supportive. Some evidence of the reliability and validity of the scores is limited, however, due to lack of research, or small sample sizes. Clinicians and researchers interested in specific subpopulations should carefully consider specific types of samples of previous research and their sample sizes in deciding whether this instrument is appropriate. Most of the documentation on the appropriateness of this measure comes from the research on depressed individuals. Some documentation also exists for its use in assessing the social adjustment of alcoholics and schizophrenics. Limited research is available supporting the appropriateness of the SAS-SR for individuals suffering from anxiety disorders and bulimia. The available research suggests that the SAS-SR may be a good tool for assessing individual adjustment in a social context.

Reliability data based on a sample of 92 resulted in coefficient alpha ranging from .71 to .76. Test-retest reliability (2-month interval) *r*'s range from .72 to .82.

Evidence of score validity is provided based on concurrent administration between the SAS-Interview and the SAS-SR, which resulted in significant correlation coefficients. Data that support the use of the SAS-SR as a treatment assessment tool, however, create questions. For example, the SAS-SR found significant treatment effects whereas other measures (e.g., Structured Clinical Interview for DSM-III-R, Cornell Dysthymia Rating Scale, and the GAF and HAM-D scores in some research) did not find such effects. Future research should explore whether the SAS-SR is actually a more outcomes measure of treatment sensitivity, or is more vulnerable to Type-I errors.

Evidence of the external validity of SAS-SR scores is provided by finding significant correlation coefficients between patient scores and the scores of other informants for that patient for most of the subscales.

Evidence for both convergent and discriminant score validity is provided. Specifically, significant correlations are reported between scores on the SAS-SR with responses taken from measures of depression, social support, rehabilitation status, and self-image. In addition, the SAS-SR distinguished between specific populations, including community, schizophrenic, alcoholic, and depressed individuals. The SAS-SR also distinguishes between nonpatient and patient samples, between individuals based on their work status (e.g., unemployed, underemployed, and employed), and between individuals with and without bulimia.

As predicted from the theory, the SAS-SR scores have not been related to ego development, hyperactivity, and some measures of psychoticism, demonstrating some evidence for the divergent validity of the SAS-SR scores.

COMMENTARY. The SAS-SR is based on the practical and theoretical concept that one must incorporate the social context of an individual when assessing the well-being of that individual. Certainly, work/school, friends, and family are all an important part of the overall big picture. The theoretical background is solid and parsimonious, and the SAS-SR appears to be an appropriate choice when seeking complementary assessment tools for individual clients. However, more research, with larger samples, would provide greater confidence in the reliability and validity of the scores on this measure.

The author of the SAS-SR suggests that there are three purposes for this measure for practitioners: as a screening tool, for treatment planning, and for monitoring the progress and outcomes of treatment. Less emphasis is placed on using the SAS-SR with nonclinical samples. Given the history and original intention of this tool, this is not surprising. However, utilization of this tool within the general population may be warranted. Research using the general population could also be conducted to collect additional validity and reliability data.

SUMMARY. The SAS-SR is a relatively quick and convenient method of assessing the social adjustment of individuals. Scores reflecting adjustment in six different areas (work/school, social and leisure activities, relationships with extended family, role as a marital partner, parental role, and role within the family unit) are immediately available and easily interpreted. Scores obtained from the SAS-SR should be considered in juxtaposition with other data collected when one is assessing overall well-being or treatment efficacy. This measure may be used either for research or for clinical purposes involving screening, treatment planning, or assessing treatment progress or efficacy. However, its primary use has been assessing the effectiveness of various treatment programs.

Review of the Social Adjustment Scale—Self Report by ROMEO VITELLI, Staff Psychologist, Millbrook Correctional Centre, Millbrook, Ontario, Canada:

DESCRIPTION. The Social Adjustment Scale—Self Report (SAS-SR) is the latest version of the pencil-and-paper self-report scale first developed by Dr. M. Weissman and her colleagues (Weissman & Bothwell, 1976) as a measure of level of respondent functioning in defined social roles. The test is designed for use by the respondent directly or by a relative. Areas of social functioning assessed by the SAS-SR include Work, Social and Leisure, Primary Relationship, Parental, Extended Family, and Family Unit. The category scores can be combined to yield a global score of social adjustment. It is designed to provide professionals with a concise and self-contained test of social adjustment for use in clinical settings to evaluate social functioning and therapeutic change. The test contains 54 items measuring performance in social roles, interpersonal conflict, and level of social satisfaction over the 2-week period preceding the test administration. All items are scored on a 5-point Likert scale using a Multi-Health Systems Quik-Score Form for rapid administration and scoring of the results. The test form also includes a profiling sheet for raw score and T-score conversions for each social role category and overall means scores using community-based norms broken down by gender. Test administration takes 15 to 20 minutes and requires a minimum fourth grade reading level.

The SAS-SR can be administered and scored by nonclinical staff although the manual recommends test interpretation be limited to experienced professionals familiar with professional standards of test usage to ensure appropriate use. The test manual includes guidelines and case studies to enable consistent interpretation of test results. The test authors give specific cautions concerning the use of the SAS-SR as the sole criterion for clinical decision making and recommend its use as part of an integrative assessment process including clinical interviews, collateral sources of information, and additional psychometric assessment.

DEVELOPMENT. The SAS-SR was first developed to provide a self-report equivalent to the Social Adjustment Scale-Interview (SAS-I; Weissman & Paykel, 1974), a structured interview protocol designed to assess social functioning in six role areas over a 2-month period. The interview format consisted of 54 items that could be administered as part of a semistructured interview that could be completed in 1 hour. The test manual outlines the development and validation of the SAS-I and its use as a measure of clinical change in numerous research studies that are cited in the bibliography.

The self-report version of the SAS was developed for greater ease of administration and to eliminate potential problems with interrater reliability and interviewer bias. The formats for the SAS-I and SAS-SR are identical although the reporting time frame for the Self-Report was reduced to 2 weeks and the items were changed to be less open-ended than in the interview.

TECHNICAL. Information on the normative samples and the standardization process is provided in the SAS-SR user's manual. Normative data were collected using a community sample (n = 482) from a 1967 longitudinal study sample (reinterviewed in 1978) as well as samples from different clinical populations over the years. Information on the sample demographics for the normative and clinical samples given and statistics are provided according to gender, age, social status, and religion. Analyses of the role of age, gender, and other socio-demographic factors in social adjustment are described.

Reliability data for the SAS-SR are provided with Cronbach's alpha reliability coefficients falling in the .71–.85 range for the different normative samples. Internal consistency is shown to be moderately high despite the flexible nature of the test that is tailored to the individual test-taker. Test-retest reliability coefficients are also presented; they fall into the .70–.80 range showing that social adjustment scores are reasonably stable over the 2-week test period. Standard error of measurement scores are also provided.

The manual outlines a series of validation studies of the SAS-SR examining its relationship to the SAS-I as well as established measures of depression, psychosocial functioning, and treatment sensitivity. Despite the differences between the SAS-SR and SAS-I with respect to test format and time period covered by the scales, intraclass correlation analysis across role areas fall into the .40 to .76 range with highest correspondence found for Overall Adjustment and Primary Relationship areas. Intraclass correlation analysis comparing SAS-SR ratings with ratings by family members over the sampled time period fell into the .54 to .70 range indicating strong agreement between self-report ratings and external validation measures.

Validation studies discussed in the manual indicate strong convergent and discriminant validity for the SAS-SR. Extensive correlation research has shown that measures of depression, social impairment, social support, anxiety, social satisfaction, and addiction severity were strongly correlated with the SAS-SR. Clinical research has demonstrated the value of the SAS-SR in identifying patterns of social deficits between depressed, substance abusing, and schizophrenic populations.

An important area of SAS-SR validation efforts focus on the role of the SAS-SR in measuring treatment effects. The manual provides a brief summary of some of the research that has used the SAS-SR to evaluate the impact of a broad range of treatment modalities in improving social functioning. The SAS-SR has been used in extensive medical studies testing psychiatric medication and psychotherapeutic interventions and has become one of the instruments of choice in the measurement of social impairments for treatment and research purposes.

Overall, the studies cited and the validation process meet the psychometric standards for test validation as specified in the *Standards for Educational and Psychological Testing* (AERA, APA, & NCME, 1999).

COMMENTARY. The SAS-SR is the latest version of a social functioning instrument that was first developed in 1976 and has become the focus of an impressive body of research into social impairment and is being used in research and clinical settings in countries around the world. It is a highly flexible test that was designed for ease of administration and scoring that can be used and reused to address client needs. The reliability and validity research of the SAS-SR demonstrates that it is one of the best instruments available for assessing level of social impairment in clinical populations.

The test authors acknowledged the need for further research using the SAS-SR and discussed the ongoing collection of normative data in the U.S. and in other countries. Potential avenues for development include research into the role of cultural influences in social functioning, the development of alternative forms of the SAS-SR for juvenile populations, and further examination of the role of socio-demographic factors in social functioning.

SUMMARY. The SAS-SR is a well-developed instrument based on nearly 30 years of research into social functioning. It is designed to provide professionals with a concise and self-contained test of social adjustment for use in clinical settings to evaluate social functioning and therapeutic change. The branching format provides needed flexibility to accommodate client needs and to address individual differences in social functioning across clinical populations. Guidelines and case studies are provided to enable consistent interpretation of test results. The test manual outlines the development and validation efforts for the SAS-SR and its use as a measure of social functioning and clinical change in numerous research studies that are cited in the bibliography.

REVIEWER'S REFERENCES

American Educational Research Association, American Psychological Association, & National Council on Measurement in Education. (1999). *Standards for educational and psychological testing.* Washington, DC: American Educational Research Association.
Weissman, M. M., & Bothwell, S. (1976). Assessment of social adjustment by patient self-report. *Archives of General Psychiatry, 33,* 1111-1115.
Weissman, M. M., & Paykel, E. S. (1974). *The depressed woman: A study of social relationships.* Chicago, IL: University of Chicago Press.

[233]

Social Phobia & Anxiety Inventory for Children.

Purpose: "Assesses the frequency and range of social fears and anxiety in children and adolescents."
Population: Ages 8–14.
Publication Date: 1998.
Acronym: SPAI-C.
Scores: Total score only.
Administration: Group or individual.
Price Data, 2002: $60 per complete kit; $30 per 25 QuikScore™ Forms; $37 per manual (1998, 50 pages), $38 specimen set.
Time: (20–30) minutes.
Comments: Self-report; also available as a Windows Compatible computer program with a decremented counter; "has been translated into several languages."
Authors: Deborah C. Beidel, Samuel M. Turner, and Tracy L. Morris.
Publisher: Multi-Health Systems, Inc.

Review of the Social Phobia & Anxiety Inventory for Children by SARAH J. ALLEN, Associate Professor of School Psychology, University of Cincinnati, Cincinnati, OH:

DESCRIPTION. The Social Phobia & Anxiety Inventory for Children (SPAI-C) is a brief, self-report measure designed to assess social phobia in childhood and early adolescence. Specifically, the 26-item instrument assesses somatic, cognitive, and behavioral aspects of social phobia across a broad range of settings and social situations using descriptors specifically written for children and adolescents. In either clinical or research settings, potential applications for use of the SPAI-

C range from screening, to detecting the presence of maladaptive social anxiety, to determining the effectiveness of intervention efforts.

Individual administration of the SPAI-C is recommended although group administration is possible. Using either paper-and-pencil or a computer-based format, administration and scoring of the SPAI-C is quick and easy. Respondents are asked to read a descriptive statement and then indicate the frequency with which each place or activity makes them feel nervous or scared using a 3-point Likert-type scale (*never or hardly ever, sometimes, most of the time or always*). Although many items comprising this scale require multiple responses, most children can complete the instrument in 20–30 minutes. Scoring procedures require only simple arithmetic calculations to obtain a total score. Clear directions for administration and scoring are provided in the manual, along with a sample protocol completed and scored. Additionally, a series of eight case studies are presented to illustrate clinical and research applications of the SPAI-C using several different levels of interpretation.

The SPAI-C was developed for use with children between 8 and 14 years of age who have at least a third-grade reading level. Administration procedures recommend that items be read aloud to younger children (i.e., 8-year-olds) and those who do not read at the third-grade level. Additionally, based on their clinical experience, the authors do not recommend use of this instrument with children who are younger than 8 years old, or who are not yet in the third grade, due to concern that younger children do not always respond reliably to the questions. If a client is over the age of 14 years, use of the adult version of the SPAI (Turner, Beidel, Dancu, & Stanley, 1989; T6:2317) should be considered because it samples a broader range of situations and audience characteristics.

DEVELOPMENT. Specifically intended as an inventory designed to measure social fears in children, the SPAI-C was constructed across several phases. The initial item pool was derived from a combination of clinical and structured interviews, daily rating of anxious events by children participating in those interviews and a review of the SPAI (Turner et al., 1989). Efforts also were made to ensure that a broad range of potentially relevant social situations were sampled. Consisting of 32 items, the initial item pool was reviewed by a panel of individuals with expertise in child-

and test-retest. Two studies that examined internal consistency with 154 children and 148 children reported alpha coefficients of .95 and .92, respectively, indicating a high degree of internal consistency. Test-retest reliability estimates fell within the acceptable range. A 2-week test-retest study involving 62 children produced a Pearson product-moment correlation of $r = .86$, $p < .001$. A reliability coefficient of .80 or higher is generally considered acceptable (Sattler, 2001). A second study, completed 10 months after the initial assessment with 19 children, produced a reliability coefficient $r = .63$, $p < .01$. This lower reliability coefficient may indicate the impact of treatment and interventions within the 10-month period between the two tests or could be due to maturation.

The examiner's manual reports several different types of validity. Two studies examined concurrent validity, comparing the scores on the SPAI-C with two other self-report instruments, the State-Trait Anxiety Inventory for Children (Spielberger, 1973) and the Fear Survey Schedule for Children-Revised (FSSC-R; Ollendick, 1983). Results indicated low to moderate correlations, providing evidence that these other instruments may not be measuring social phobia but rather a broad range of fears and general anxiety. Scores on the SPAI-C also were compared to parental ratings of fear and social competence as assessed by the Child Behavior Checklist (CBCL; Achenbach & Edelbrock, 1983). The SPAI-C correlated moderately with the CBCL Internalizing scale ($r = .45$, $p < .001$) but not with the Externalizing scale ($r = .18$, $p > .05$). The examiner's manual presents several studies indicating the sensitivity and specificity of the SPAI-C. These two terms are important when evaluating a screening instrument. Sensitivity refers to the instrument's ability to select children who should be referred for further assessment; whereas, specificity refers to the instrument's capacity to accurately select children who should not be identified.

COMMENTARY. The Social Phobia & Anxiety Inventory for Children provides a quick, inexpensive screening measure of social fears and anxiety in children ages 8–14. As a student self-report instrument, the Social Phobia & Anxiety Inventory for Children provides the clinician with a unique perspective from the student's viewpoint; although, like other self-report measures, the trustworthiness of the results of this instrument de-

pends on the truthfulness with which the student completes the information. Scoring the test appears to be straightforward and the examiner's manual includes several case studies to provide further information on using and interpreting the instrument.

The examiner's manual also includes chapters describing the development of the instrument and its technical aspects. Although some information is provided about the sample of children who participated in the test development, the manual does not include information regarding the geographic location(s) of the sample or whether the children were from rural or urban areas. Also, no information was provided regarding the family SES or mothers' and fathers' educational levels. During the final phase of development, African American children were overrepresented (40%) in the sample. Not included in the development samples were children who represent diverse ethnic, racial, or cultural groups such as Latinos and Asian Americans. Because these children represent a growing percent of our school population today, examiners using the Social Phobia & Anxiety Inventory for Children should exercise caution in using this instrument and interpreting results with these groups of children.

SUMMARY. The Social Phobia & Anxiety Inventory for Children fits the criteria for an effective screening instrument in that it is brief, inexpensive, technically adequate, and easy to score. The instrument is available in several languages including English, French-Canadian, and Spanish. Hispanic or Latino children and Asian American children were not included in the development sample. Examiners should use caution when using this instrument and interpreting results with these children.

REVIEWER'S REFERENCES

Sattler, J. M. (2001). *Assessment of children: Cognitive applications* (4th ed.). La Mesa, CA: Jerome M. Sattler.

Turner, S. M., Beidel, D. C., & Dancu, C. V. (1996). Social Phobia and Anxiety Inventory. Toronto: Multi-Health Systems, Inc.

[234]

The Sort-A-Sentence Test.

Purpose: Designed to assess reading comprehension.
Population: Ages 7–15.
Publication Date: 2002.
Scores: Total score only.
Administration: Group.
Forms, 2: A, B.
Price Data, 2002: £19.45 per introductory set including administrative manual (7 pages), scoring key, and 25 Form A test booklets; £3 per manual and 3.5-

inch disk scoring key; £10.45 per 25 test booklets (Form A or B); technical manual available upon request.

Time: (25) minutes.

Author: Alan Brimer.

Publisher: Educational Evaluations [England].

Review of the Sort-A-Sentence Test by JAMES K. BENISH, School Psychologist, Helena Public Schools, Adjunct Professor of Special Education, Carroll College, Helena, MT:

DESCRIPTION AND DEVELOPMENT. The Sort-A-Sentence Test (SAS), Forms A & B is described as a reading comprehension test developed in the United Kingdom for School Years 3 through 11, corresponding to ages 8 through 16. The respondee must identify two words in one sentence that have been switched, and mark two of five bubbles to indicate how the words should be assembled to formulate a correct response. There are two interchangeable forms provided for examiner use, with each containing 64 test items. Directions and examples are clearly provided on the front of each test form. The test is timed to allow 25 minutes to complete as many questions as possible.

After directing the respondee to complete identifying information on the front of the test booklet, including examples, test directions are read out loud. One is directed, "If you make a mistake, put a ring around the wrong mark and tick the correct answer." Terms familiar to those living in the United Kingdom may not bode well for students enrolled in schools in the United States.

STANDARDIZATION AND NORMS. The SAS appears to be standardized with a sample of students "from five Junior schools in the South of England" (technical manual, p. 3). This standardization was also achieved via utilizing applicants at a City Technology college who were administered the English Picture Vocabulary Test 2 (EPVT2). Norms were then established and applicants taking the EPVT2 were sorted by socioeconomic status and ethnic diversity. Various groups selected in this manner were administered the SAS, and both the means and standard deviations were calculated. The author felt that groups selected fulfilled a meaningful sample for conducting reliability and validity studies. A total of 857 boys and girls were involved in the standardization process. Various drafts were administered via reader age groups such as 8/9, 9/10, 10/11, etc. Ultimately, 64 pairs of items were selected for each of Form A and Form B.

TECHNICAL.

Reliability. SAS Kuder-Richardson reliability estimates were impressive, with both Forms A and B showing overall correlations of .93. Even performances of the 15/16-year age group maintained strong correlations of .91' and .87 for Forms A and B, respectively. No specific reliability studies were reported by gender breakout, although the author displayed tables of mean and standard deviation for age and gender.

Concomitant validity. No validity studies were reported for the SAS, although the EPVT2 results were available. The test author attempted to show a common variance between both tests. It was concluded by the test author that the SAS measures verbal comprehension, thus demonstrating itself as a valid reading test. It would appear that more data would be needed to support this premise.

COMMENTARY AND SUMMARY. The Sort-A-Sentence Test, including Forms A and B offers a way to diagnose reading comprehension by age groups ranging from 8 to 16 years. The test taker must identify which two words in a sentence have been switched, and mark the correct order to make sense of it. A fairly comprehensive study was conducted using the SAS and its companion picture vocabulary test (EPVT2). Results of the study revealed an impressive reliability coefficient of .93, although validity studies were not specifically reported.

A major drawback to the SAS in terms of applicability to U.S. populations appears to be the fact that the test was developed in the United Kingdom. Subtle cultural distinctions exist in the directions and the test items. The inclusion of terms such as "ring" instead of "circle," and "tick" instead of "check" night confuse students in the U.S. Similarly, differences in spelling "monopolised" instead of "monopolized" would probably add to the confusion.

Until validity studies are carried out, this test might be used with caution in the United Kingdom. Renorming and revising the SAS for use in the United States should be carried out before it becomes a tool in the U.S. for reading assessment. Its use is not recommended at this time.

Review of the Sort-A-Sentence Test by THANOS PATELIS, Executive Director of Psychometrics, Evaluation, & Data Reporting, The College Board, New York, NY:

DESCRIPTION. The Sort-A-Sentence Test (SAS) is a 64-item norm-referenced test with two forms, A and B, administered by paper-and-pencil in a 25-minute period. In addition, four practice questions are provided that are used during the beginning of the testing period. All items are selected-response, where the respondents are asked to select the pair of words in a sentence that should be exchanged to make the sentence meaningful. A total raw score, obtained by manually applying a scoring key, is converted to a standardized score that represents a respondent's reading comprehension.

The administrative manual indicated that educators with the ability to establish a testing situation whereby "the conditions for testing should be as conducive as possible to thoughtful work" (p. 2) could administer the test. This suggests that teachers, counselors, and any school-level educator with such an ability can administer the SAS. Scoring is performed using a scoring key. It is suggested that electronic scoring can be performed, but the manner of doing this is left to the test user. Once the total raw score is obtained, the standardized score is found using tables provided in the administration manual. Standardized scores are represented based on the school year of the examinee (i.e., School Year 3 through 11). Once the standardized score is obtained, the percentile rank is found from one table provided in the administrative manual. In the administrative manual, the test user is encouraged to use the standard error of measurement in making interpretations of the test scores. The script provided is sufficiently detailed to permit adherence to standardized conditions.

DEVELOPMENT. The administrative manual indicates that a technical supplement (i.e., technical manual) is available upon request from the publisher that provides a description of the construction of the test, development of the norms, and reliability and validity information. In the technical manual, a theoretical and historical accounting of the development of the SAS was provided. Logical arguments about the use of sentence reading as a representation of the construct of reading comprehension were provided. In addition, it was argued that the use of a multiple-choice or a modified cloze procedure did not fit the construct of measuring the reader's understanding of the meaning of the sentence. Thus, these arguments were used as justification for the use of the current item format (i.e., selection of pairs of words that need to be changed to make the sentence meaningful). It would be helpful if the author provided references to the relevant literature to support the construct on which this instrument was based.

Sets of trials were described that were undertaken in the development of the SAS. The trials provided a means of evaluating the pool of items and a process for the development of the norms. The evaluation of the quality of the items involved both a qualitative and quantitative approach. The qualitative approach involved the judgment of four content experts. Unfortunately, the specific qualifications of these experts and the operational definition of difficulty were not provided. The quantitative approach involved the examination of (a) the proportion passing each item (i.e., proportion correct called item facility in the technical manual), (b) item discrimination using point-biserial correlation coefficients, and (c) scaled item difficulties developed from an equipercentile method. The development of the norms seemed to be related to the trials, but "ten year old samples" (technical manual, p. 9) were combined to establish the norms for this age group. The reason that the reference to years is in quotes is that in the administrative manual the norms are referenced as school years, whereas in the technical manual the reference seems to be to chronological age in years. Smoothing techniques were indicated as being used before the score were converted, but the details surrounding the type of smoothing technique used were missing. Finally, the samples for the development trials and norms represented were limited to samples from Great Britain limiting the utility to other English-speaking countries including the United States.

TECHNICAL. Even though the trials involved in the development of the test are described and the use of the samples from the norms are indicated, the exact descriptive statistics of the norms are vague. As part of the development of the test, tests of speededness were examined. Empirical support during the development supported the use of a 25-minute time limit.

Reliability evidence in the form of Kuder-Richardson calculations of internal consistency using Formula 20 (i.e., KR20) was provided during the development trials. With samples of 102 of 10-year-olds, the KR20 values were .93 for both forms. With samples of 73 and 65 for Form A and

B, respectively, involving 15/16-year-olds, the KR20 values were .91 and .87, respectively. In supplementary second trials with 8–9- and 9–10-year-olds, the KR20 values were .90 in Form A for both age levels and .90 and .93 for Form B in the 8–9 and 9–10 age level samples, respectively.

Validity evidence was restricted to examining the relationship of the SAS with the English Picture Vocabulary Test (EPVT) (i.e., convergent validity). The correlation coefficients reported for both forms of the SAS and the EPVT in 10-year-olds were .62 and .61 for Forms A and B, respectively. These appeared to be uncorrected, bivariate correlation coefficients. Additionally, correlation coefficients with the 15/16-year-old examinees for each SAS form and the EPVT were .46 and .64 for Form A and B, respectively, each with 73 and 65 examinees. The rationale for using the EPVT was not provided. It was suggested that the 15/16-year-old sample was selective. A statistical correction of the correlation coefficient due to the restriction of range might have been informative. Additional evidence about the validity of the SAS was provided on the logic that older examinees would have higher scores. Conclusions to this effect were made, but direct statistical comparisons were not performed. Finally, for a test meant to measure reading comprehension, evidence related to a criterion (e.g., teacher ratings) might add to the body of evidence in support of the SAS (i.e., concurrent validity evidence).

COMMENTARY. The SAS is a promising instrument to measure reading comprehension, but due to the lack of clarity in the characteristics of the norms and the insufficient validity evidence, the SAS should be considered as an experimental instrument or used in a low-stakes environment.

Because this is a norm-referenced test, the proper interpretation of the test score is contingent on the similarity between the characteristics of the examinee and the normative samples. Even though there were descriptions of the samples during the trials and these same samples were utilized eventually as the normative samples, the exact characteristics of these normative samples were vague.

The high internal consistency of the SAS as reported provides support of the homogenous nature of the test. The validity evidence provided is promising, but insufficient. Of course, how the test is to be used should guide the extent of the validity evidence collected. Because guidance on how to use the SAS is lacking, recommendations, other than some type of concurrent validity evidence, is difficult.

SUMMARY. The author of the test argues conceptually for a reading comprehension test that is based on the nature of reading and a more authentic and pragmatic item format. Specific references to the literature would have added to the logical arguments presented. The administrative manual provided an easy-to-follow, clear script with straightforward scoring and scaling directions, although the administration of the scoring key may pose some difficulty. An accounting of the development trials was provided in the technical manual. Even though the characteristics of the samples involved in the trials were presented, there were some treatments of the samples that necessitated more salient statements about the exact characteristics of the normative samples. Internal consistency information in the form of KR20 values was impressive, supporting the homogenous nature of the test.

Finally, validity evidence in the form of correlations to performance on an apparently similar test (i.e., the EPVT) was encouraging, but insufficient. More information about the intended use of the SAS was needed, along with a similar description of the EPVT. It might be helpful to gather concurrent validity evidence with teacher ratings. The SAS seems to have some promising features, but in lieu of the need for more complete descriptions of the normative samples and additional validity evidence, use should be limited to experimental purposes and low-stakes situations.

[235]

Sources of Stress Scale [2001 Revision].

Purpose: Designed as "an instrument to identify origins of perceived and current anxiety, to quantify the intensity of such stressors, and to determine the pattern of such perceptions for predictions and subsequent interventions."

Population: High school and adults.

Publication Dates: 1986–2001.

Acronym: S.O.S.S.

Scores, 16: Personal Relationships, Finances/Money, Field Experiences, Myself, Academic Activities, Time Management, College Life, Health, Changes, Personal Life, The Future, Friends, High School, Family Issues, Children, Spouse/Partner.

Administration: Group.

Forms, 5: Graduate Students, High School Students, Family, Young Adults, Senior Citizens.

Price Data, 2002: $20 per 25 scales; $.40 per answer sheet; $20 per test manual (2001, 32 pages); $.30 per scoring scale.
Time: [5–15] minutes.
Comments: Self-rating scale.
Authors: Louise M. Soares and Anthony T. Soares.
Publisher: SOARES Associates.

Review of the Sources of Stress Scale [2001 Revision] by JOANN MURPHEY, Clinical Psychologist in Private Practice, San Antonio, TX:

DESCRIPTION AND DEVELOPMENT. As its authors claim, the Sources of Stress Scale (S.O.S.S.) is designed not so much to assess particular life events that cause stress as to examine areas in the environmental field that are perceived as causing stress. Thus the emphasis is not on quantifying and comparing one stressful event over another, but rather examining manifestations of several demands at one time as perceived across environmental fields and across time. The design of the S.O.S.S. is predicated on the authors' view that "[t]here would be a distinct advantage in focusing on the sources of stress in order to effect one's control over the level of impact of resulting stress and to re-establish normalcy" (manual, p. 4).

The S.O.S.S. consists of a manual with limited data on test development and standardization, test administration instructions, individual test forms for each of the previously mentioned groups, and forms for summarizing and profiling responses on individual test forms.

For all group forms, instructions of the S.O.S.S. are presented orally. The examinee enters one or two check marks for each of several items within each area. These are tallied and the sums transferred to a separate Profile Chart that allows a visual comparison across areas. The examiner from this can identify individuals with high cluster stressors as well as specific stressors within clusters, track changes in the profile over time, and compare individuals within groups (including families) to determine patterns and etiology of stress within the group.

TECHNICAL AND COMMENTARY. The authors claim acceptable test-retest and internal consistency reliability, as well as content and construct validity. Evaluation data supporting the authors' claim rests on "evaluation by a panel of eight experts and testing of the refined and new scales" (manual, p. 13). The test manual does not present specifics of this evaluation methodology, but does report results of a study comparing areas of stress at one time, and across time, with a group of graduate students.

The lack of more detailed validation research presented in the test manual and other supporting materials will concern the clinician who seeks confirmation before applying this measure in working with specific types of client problems, and particularly assessing the relative merits of alternative intervention methods. The authors may well be correct in assuming that the S.O.S.S. scales will be useful for counseling and clinical applications, and for purposes of individual development and organizational development. However, the test manual does not describe how the authors have related S.O.S.S. scores or profiles to particular intervention strategies, group characteristics, or organizational variables that might be of interest. The authors' claim that the S.O.S.S. measures anxiety, apart from sources of life stress, appears to have tenuous support, at best, on the basis of the materials reviewed.

SUMMARY. The concept of measuring perceived stress in various empirically supported life-experience "area" constructs conceptualizes an intriguing way of thinking about life stress that differs from the predominant event-related assessment that characterizes other life-stress scales currently in use. The S.O.S.S. may eventually provide a model with unique practical utility, once additional construct and criterion validation studies have been undertaken, across all the groups for which the test is intended.

Review of the Sources of Stress Scale [2001 Revision] by WESLEY E. SIME, Professor, Department of Health and Human Performance, University of Nebraska—Lincoln, Lincoln, NE:

DESCRIPTION. The Sources of Stress Scale (S.O.S.S.) is designed to identify origins of perceived and current anxiety, to quantify the intensity of such stressors, and to determine the pattern of such perceptions for predictions and subsequent interventions. There are 16 different potential scores covering the dimensions of Personal Relationships, Finances/Money, Field Experiences, Academic Activities, Time Management, College Life, Health, Changes, Personal Life, The Future, Friends, High School, Family Issues, Children, Spouse/Partner, and Myself.

Of the 16 possible scores, only 11 are included selectively for each of the five different population categories (high school students, graduate students, family, young adults, and senior citizens) delineated according to age and academic status. For example, in comparing the form for the high school student in contrast to the senior citizen, both forms share eight categories (Personal Relationships, Changes, Finances/Money, Time Management, The Future, Personal Life, Myself, and Health. However, the high school form includes three additional categories (Academic Activities, Friends, and High School) whereas the senior citizen form includes Children, Spouse/Partner, and Family Issues. The family version is identical to the senior citizen form except that under the heading of Children, its items deal with discipline, drugs/alcohol, academics, etc., in contrast to grandchildren, careers, and salaries for the seniors. The college student and the adult versions similarly have eight identical categories and three that are unique. In addition, each of the population categories has a special form identical in content but filled out by a close observer about the central figure in the assessment. These observer raters may be close associates such as a friend, co-worker, caretaker, teacher, colleague, sibling, partner, or supervisor. The items (eight in each) under each of the 16 categories are rated as sources of stress according three levels of response: no response = negligible, one check = major source of stress, and two checks = a very strong source of stress.

The instructions for administration are written at the top of each form with examples specifying the unusual rating format featuring one or two checks indicating severity of each item under source of stress. Semantically there would appear to be a very large difference between the lowest level (no check) and the middle level (a major source of stress). By contrast there would appear to be very little difference, semantically, between that middle level (major source) and the high level (a very strong source of stress). The scoring is accomplished simply by counting the number of checks and recording this number on the appropriate profile chart and drawing lines between each of the 11 cluster categories. The directions for circling the high points on the profile chart and the double-checked items for determining the sources of stress for any individual seem overly simplistic and contributes to self-assessment as much as or more than for group comparison or consultation. The authors also suggest the use of a profile chart shell for comparing the mean self-ratings of groups

or individuals over time. It is not entirely clear how the comparisons over time or across individuals carry any distinct level of significance.

The authors encourage converting the raw scores to T-scores for ease of comparison to other psychological assessments and for explaining the areas of high stress to the client. Finally, a composite form is offered to the consultant user in the event that a natural grouping of individuals has representation across two or three generations in a family. As such, composite scores for mother, father, grandparent, and grandchild can be charted with index scores that are labeled high, moderate, and low as sources of stress. No statistical justification is provided for the assignment of index values in this graphical representation.

The authors suggest that the advantages of the S.O.S.S. instrument for counseling purposes are: (a) identification of individual stress clusters and specific stressors, (b) tracking profile differences over time, and (c) comparison of individuals within groups, such as families, to determine etiology of stress and exacerbation factors. The instrument was developed in 1986 and was used in two research studies by the authors (1987, 1992). Apparently no other research has been conducted using this instrument in the last 16 years. The authors suggest that their instrument aids in examining the common, external, identified sources of stress as manifested across various demands at one time, across time, and in different environments. Their apparent goal in designing this instrument is to identify sources of stress in order to impart a sense of control of the level of impact. No provisions for identifying coping resources or objective outcomes on the organism are provided.

DEVELOPMENT. The S.O.S.S. was initially developed in a college setting to identify the sources of stress for three different populations of graduate students in 1987, 1988, and 1989. The authors modified some of the categories during the first few years and they also included an "other" category that they suggest can be used by the consultant to tailor an additional category for specific needs. The initial test population was tested at the beginning of graduate school and at the end of the first year. No further information is provided regarding development across other populations. No information is provided regarding theoretical foundation for the survey or how the items were developed.

The test manual furnished by the developer includes a short description of the background for stress research that is sorely outdated and incomplete. The authors cite references totally unrelated to the specific dimensions included in the instrument. For example, they note outdated research on Type A behavior, Locus of Control, and Helplessness/hopelessness that have no relationship to the dimensions in the S.O.S.S.

TECHNICAL. The information regarding norming process is nonexistent. The initial data used in the development of the instrument were obtained on graduate students. No evidence is provided for how well the instrument sample relates to the senior citizens or young adults in this survey. The authors provide one reference of their work in contrasting gender with barely marginal differences noted.

The authors offer data on reliability and validity featuring eight experts; however, no information on the credentials of the experts nor the process for validation is provided. The test-retest reliability (interval not reported) for each of the five scales ranges between .86 and .95. The internal consistency estimates ranged from .81 to .91 and the content and construct validity coefficients ranged from .49 to .59. The authors allude to the purpose of predicting intervention outcomes, but provide no evidence of differential validity needed for prediction.

The simple process of plotting the data on individual and composite profile forms is inherently user-friendly but provides questionable useful information for the stated purpose in counseling, that is, effecting some degree of control and ultimate change in the stress management skills.

COMMENTARY. The ultimate value of the S.O.S.S. is limited. Although it is very easy to conduct the survey and to explain the results to clients in families or other discrete groups, the value of the information is suspect. By focusing exclusively on sources of stress, the instrument lacks important identifiers for stress reduction resources and lifestyle variables that moderate the impact of the various stress factors that might be identified.

SUMMARY. The developers are obviously consultants who use these instruments in their professional practice. They have priced the materials and the forms at a very reasonable level for use by other clinicians or consultants. The value of the survey is that it provides a reasonable comprehensive structured format for interviewing an initial client with regard to areas of serious concern, herein referred to as sources of stress. There are many other instruments that address sources of stress with generally more statistical sophistication. This instrument may be unique in the application of five distinct population categories that lend themselves to three-generation family assessment. Furthermore, its value may lie in simplicity and the fact that no other instrument taps the kind of information on family and generational factors. Unfortunately, there is no evidence provided showing the validity of the measures to be effective in counseling or in the insight that can be garnered therein.

[236]
Space Relations (Paper Puzzles).

Purpose: Developed as an assessment of mechanical aptitude.
Population: Ages 17 and over.
Publication Dates: 1984–1996.
Scores: Total score only.
Administration: Group.
Price Data, 2002: $91 per start-up kit including 25 test booklets, score key, and interpretation and research manual; $54 per 25 tests; $28 per interpretation and research manual; $20 per score key.
Time: [9] minutes.
Authors: L. L. Thurstone and T. E. Jeffrey.
Publisher: Reid London House.

Review of Space Relations (Paper Puzzles) by PHILLIP L. ACKERMAN, Professor of Psychology, Georgia Institute of Technology, Atlanta, GA:

DESCRIPTION. The Space Relations (Paper Puzzles) test is a 30-item test, administered with paper and pencil in either individualized or group settings. Instructions for the test take about 3 minutes. The test is speeded, with a time limit of 9 minutes. Each item on the test contains a set of 4–5 polygon pieces, and a single polygon target. The respondent's task is to determine how the pieces fit together to make up the polygon, and more specifically, which remaining piece does not fit. The answer to be recorded is the single item that does not fit into the assembled polygon. The test is hand-scored, with component scores of number correct and number wrong. A correction for guessing is applied, based on the number wrong, and added to the number of correct answers for a total score. Raw scores are converted to standard scores, and placed into seven categories (from *very high* to *very low*). The publisher represents the test as measuring mechanical aptitude, and that it should be "included in mechanical aptitude test batteries" (Thurstone & Jeffrey, 1996, p. 1).

DEVELOPMENT. The Space Relations (Paper Puzzles) was originally designed by L. L. Thurstone (1951) in a study of mechanical aptitude of high school juniors (who were distinguished by high or low mechanical interest and experience). The test has much in common with other paper formboard tests (such as the Pattern Assembly Test described in the Army Air Forces Aviation Psychology Research Program Reports; Guilford & Lacey, 1947). What differentiates this test from some other paper formboard and assembly tests is that it is entirely two-dimensional (e.g., see Carroll, 1993). That is, the assembly of polygon pieces makes up a two-dimensional figure. Thurstone determined that the test loaded on two different factors, a "Space" factor and a "Closure Flexibility" factor (the latter of which shared variance with the high and low interest variables). The test has apparently not been revised since its original development.

TECHNICAL.

Norms. The only norms for this test are from the initial work by Thurstone (1951). That is, the conversion from raw to standard scores is based on a sample of 338 high school juniors. No recommendations are provided for the population of individuals to whom these norms should be relevant or useful.

Reliability/Validity. The reliability and validity data provided by the publisher only relate to the initial study by Thurstone (1951). Split-half reliability is reported to be .68 (which is probably an overestimate of other reliability estimates, given the speeded nature of the test). Two sources of validity information are provided. First, the publisher reports that the Space Relations test was one of several that significantly discriminated between the low and high mechanical interest/experience groups in the high-school junior sample. Second, it is reported that a factor analysis of the test revealed that it loaded on two factors—a spatial visualization factor and a closure flexibility factor. A much more extensive analysis of the spatial ability data from the Thurstone (1951) study, and of spatial ability tests overall, was performed by Lohman (1979), though it is not cited in the publisher's materials. Briefly, Lohman suggested that the Space Relations/Paper Puzzles test has much more in common with fluid intelligence (Gf) and with a broad spatial factor than it does with mechanical interests.

COMMENTARY. The Space Relations (Paper Puzzles) test appears to be a good test of general spatial ability. Based on other research (e.g., see Horn, 1989; Lohman, 1979 for reviews), this test is likely to share variance with tests of general intellectual ability (especially Gf), various spatial abilities (such as General Visualization [Gv], and Spatial Orientation [SO]), and with measures of mechanical abilities. The Space Relations (Paper Puzzles) test is not likely to be univocally associated with any of these major ability factors, because it requires several different component processes (rather than, for example, knowledge of specific mechanical principles). As implied by the publisher, it might be a useful part of a larger battery of tests. Possible applications might include educational selection, vocational counseling, or occupational selection. However, given the absence of any norms for adults or representative adolescents, or validity/reliability data for any particular application, it will be necessary for any application to develop local norms and local validities.

SUMMARY. For such an old test, the Space Relations (Paper Puzzles) test may be surprisingly robust. The test fits well within the extant data (Carroll, 1993; Lohman, 1979) regarding Vz and other spatial abilities. It is much less identified with other measures of mechanical aptitude or mechanical knowledge. However, without extensive development of norms and provision of reliability and validity information, this test probably is not very useful beyond laboratory research environments.

REVIEWER'S REFERENCES

Carroll, J. B. (1993). *Human cognitive abilities: A survey of factor-analytic studies.* New York: Cambridge University Press.

Guilford, J. P., & Lacey, J. I. (1947). *Army air forces aviation psychology program research reports: Printed classification tests.* Report No. 5. Washington, DC: U.S. Government Printing Office.

Horn, J. L. (1989). Cognitive diversity: A framework of learning. In P. L. Ackerman, R. J. Sternberg, & R. Glaser (Eds.), *Learning and individual differences. Advances in theory and research* (pp. 61–116). New York: W. H. Freeman.

Lohman, D. F. (1979). *Spatial ability: A review and reanalysis of the correlational literature* (Tech. Rep. No. 8). Stanford, CA: Stanford University, School of Education.

Thurstone, L. L. (1951). *An analysis of mechanical aptitude.* (Report No. 62). Chicago: The Psychometric Laboratory, The University of Chicago.

Thurstone, L. L., & Jeffrey, T. E. (1996). *Space Relations (Paper Puzzles).* Minneapolis: National Computer Systems, Inc.

Review of Space Relations (Paper Puzzles) by MARK A. ALBANESE, Professor, Population Health Sciences, Medical Sciences Center, University of Wisconsin—Madison, Madison, WI:

DESCRIPTION AND DEVELOPMENT. Space Relations (Paper Puzzles) is a very short instrument (9 minutes, or 12 minutes including instructions and practice items) that purports to assess spatial relations as related to mechanical aptitude. It is composed of 30 items, each of which presents five shapes and a composite image composed of combinations of four of the shapes. The examinee must identify which of several shapes does not contribute to making a composite shape in order to answer the item correctly. The number of shapes from which the examinee identifies the noncontributor ranges between 3 and 6.

The test is speeded and the instructions tell examinees that they are not expected to finish all of the items in the time allowed. Further, they are told not to guess because wrong answers will count against them. In the scoring, one third of the total number of wrong answers are subtracted from the number of right scores. This represents somewhat of an overcorrection for random guessing. Half of the items have four options and, therefore, would be exactly corrected for random guessing. However, 12 of the remaining 15 have five or six options, in which case they were overcorrected by subtracting one-third of the wrong responses. It is not clear what the implications might be of the overcorrection, but the directions clearly state that examinees should not guess.

TECHNICAL. The test manual suggests creating standardized score equivalents with a mean of 50 and a standard deviation of 10. A conversion chart for this purpose is provided in the examiner's manual. The data used for developing the chart are based upon 338 junior high school students used in the reliability and validity study to be described next.

The reliability and validity for the Space Relations (SR) test was originally examined for a battery of 32 group tests administered to 350 high school juniors in a study of mechanical aptitude during the 1940s. The split-half reliability is reported to be .68.

To assess what the test manual calls specific validity, the differences between scores of participants with high mechanical interest and experience and those for participants with low mechanical interest and experience were statistically tested, resulting in a p-value beyond .001. In the same study, construct validity was addressed by a factor analysis of the 32 group tests. Overall, five differ-ent independent factors were identified and the SR test loaded equally on two factors, indicating that it is not a factorially pure test. The two factors that appear to comprise the traits underlying performance on the test are: (a) the ability to visualize an image in which there is internal movement or displacement of parts and (b) the ability to keep an image in mind despite distraction (being embedded in a larger image). The manual argues that although the first factor bears the strongest relationship to mechanical aptitude, factorially pure assessments of the second factor also discriminate between high and low groups on mechanical aptitude. Therefore, the manual recommends that the SR test be included in mechanical aptitude test batteries.

COMMENTARY. Thurstone developed the SR test initially as a research instrument for use in various studies of the structure of intellect. The SR test is one of the experimental instruments that apparently has had some practical value. It was first copyrighted in 1959 and has been in use for over 40 years. The test is very efficient (total test time = 12 minutes) and provides a straightforward assessment of the ability of the examinee to rotate and combine various shapes to create a target shape. The validity studies conducted over 50 years ago indicate that those who do this well tend to have higher levels of mechanical interest and experience than those who do poorly. The SR test apparently has a long history of use to support its value for assessing mechanical aptitude.

Although it has many positive characteristics, there are issues that need to be addressed. Perhaps the most important one is the purpose of the test. The closest the manual comes to indicating a purpose is that it differentiates individuals with high mechanical interest and experience from those who are low in such qualities. Somehow, the developers think this must be good for companies, because in the examiner's manual, they state "it is generally acceptable to modify these instructions slightly based on your company's needs" (p. 3). For users, it would be helpful to further explain why it is helpful to know if a person has high mechanical interest and experience. For instance, do automobile mechanics tend to be higher on mechanical interest and experience than beauticians?

Although it is certainly a very quickly administered instrument at 12 minutes from start to finish, it is not clear whether or not one could get the same information by directly asking the examinee if they have high mechanical interest and experience, thereby saving 11.5 minutes. Clearly, demonstrating that the person has the ability to do tasks like those in the Space Relations test better than most other people would give greater confidence in the examinee's ability to do these tasks than would taking their word for it, but it is not clear if it would be a better measure of mechanical interest and experience. And if it is, it would be necessary to know what difference this information makes in interpretations of test performance.

A second issue pertains to the concept of aptitudes. In recent years, the concept of aptitudes as immutable traits that are impervious to instruction has been questioned. Even the venerable Scholastic Aptitude Test (now known as the College Board SAT I Reasoning Test; T6:580) has been attacked on this basis. Perhaps it is a misunderstanding of what aptitude means by the larger public, but using the term elicits a response from some quarters that may not be desirable. Specifically for the SR test, there are no data provided on performance of women or minorities. Without information on disparate impact, the user will have to determine for themselves if using the instrument yields results that could be considered biased in some form.

Another issue is that the test may not be aging well. The references were published between 1941 and 1951. A lot has changed in the last 50 years. Jobs that require a mechanical aptitude have changed fairly dramatically since the pervasive use of personal computers began in the late 1970s. Any data from the 1940s, if some were to exist, that suggest a relationship exists between performance on the test and aptitude for various jobs is likely to have limited utility in today's job market. Also, the normative data as well as the reliability and validity data need to be updated. Many computer games have elements that include spatial relations; Tetris and Block Solid are but two of many. These games essentially train the user how to rotate various types of randomly generated figures to make them fit into a changing landscape as the figures move toward the landscape at an increasing pace. For a new generation of students who have grown up with such computer games (as well as middle-aged computer game junkies), the norms from high school juniors a half century ago are likely to give a distorted perspective.

Users should also be aware that the test appears to have only one form. This may be problematic because there are no data that indicate whether repeatedly taking the test improves performance to any degree. The nature of the tasks contained in the tests would lend themselves easily to creating new forms. It is curious that only a single form exists, if for no other reason than it would seem likely that users would have requested additional forms to administer to applicants who repeatedly retake the examination.

A final point is that the split-half reliability for the test is only .68. It is not clear what type of split was made to arrive at this value, but for a relatively short test this is not an unreasonable reliability value. However, it is not high enough to be used to make a high stakes decision. At best the SR test should be used as a screening tool that helps inform the examinee in making a career or training decision. Maybe that is why only one form has been needed.

SUMMARY. Even though the SR test has a long history, the development and validation research is over 50 years old and aging poorly. Given changes associated with computers in the workplace and how computer games have incorporated spatial relations tasks in them, the validity of the SR for assessing mechanical aptitude and its relationship to current job categories needs to be demonstrated. At best the SR test should be used as a screening tool that helps inform the examinee in making a career or training decision, not as an instrument to make the decision for them.

[237]
Spanish/English Reading Comprehension Test [Revised].

Purpose: Designed to "determine the degrees of bilingualism."

Population: Grades 1–6.

Publication Dates: 1974–1993.

Scores: Total score and grade level equivalents.

Administration: Group or individual.

Forms, 2: English, Spanish.

Price Data, 1999: $20 per packet including manual (1993, 42 pages) and 1 English and 1 Spanish rating/answer sheet (permission to copy answer sheets is included).

Time: (30) minutes.

Comments: Spanish Reading based on Mexican curriculum materials; English Reading based on U.S.A. curriculum materials; English Reading Comprehension Test is translated from the Spanish version; pretesting and posttesting used.

Author: Steve Moreno.
Publisher: Moreno Educational Co.
Cross References: For reviews by Esteban L. Olmedo and David T. Sanchez, see 9:1161.

Review of the Spanish/English Reading Comprehension Test [Revised] by JORGE E. GONZALEZ, Research Assistant Professor, Center for At-Risk Children's Service, University of Nebraska—Lincoln, Lincoln, NE, and CRAIG S. SHWERY, Assistant Professor of Elementary Education Teaching Programs, University of Alabama, Tuscaloosa, AL:

DESCRIPTION. This informal reading test was designed for determining the reading comprehension achievement level of Spanish-speaking individuals who have entered the United States after having received all, or part, of their education in Mexico or in a Latin American Spanish-speaking country. The principal use of the Spanish/English Reading Comprehension Test (S/ERCT) is to measure learning abilities and learning potentials in the United States school systems. This determination is based upon the examinee's educational success factors in Mexico or Latin America. Although the test under review ranges from Grades 1 through 6, the manual (p. 2) states there are tests for Grades 7–12, and for adults.

Other uses cited in the manual for the S/ERCT include: (a) determining Spanish reading abilities of examinees entering a bilingual education program, (b) comparing nonnative Spanish speakers learning Spanish with native Spanish-speaking individuals from Mexico and Latin America, (c) measuring an examinee's degree of bilingual reading ability, and (d) reporting for local, district, and state purposes.

Administration of the test is restricted to "teachers, psychologists or other certified professionals" (administration manual, p. 2). The test can be administered in Spanish and/or English so an examinee's proficiency level in either or both languages can be assessed and compared. Therefore, the administrator should be proficient in Spanish and/or English. The Spanish and English examinees' test booklets are separate, although the administration test manual for S/ERCT contains Spanish and English instructions. It generally takes about 5 minutes to explain the directions to examinees and about 30 minutes to administer. The author does not recommend exceeding that time limit. The test results

may be analyzed and compared using raw scores, grade level equivalents, percentile ranking, and quartile rankings between and among each grade level in Mexico and the United States.

DEVELOPMENT. The S/ERCT was developed, standardized, and normed in Mexico using the country's curriculum reading materials. At the time the test was normed (1978), all elementary (Primaria) schools in Mexico used the same teacher workbooks, as well as the same student textbooks/workbooks for reading, math, natural sciences, and social sciences. According to the copyright date on the test booklets, the 73-item multiple-choice test has not been updated since it was first normed in 1978. Scoring is the same for both Spanish and English.

TECHNICAL. Validity evidence that centers on determining an examinee's reading comprehension achievement so that "some idea is available about the student's learning abilities and learning potential" (administration manual, p. 4) is incongruent at best. The author stated content validity was confirmed because a "test has content validity if the test items adequately cover the curricular areas that the test is supposed to evaluate. This test, therefore, has content validity" (administration manual, p. 15). Typically, it is not a simple matter to identify the universe of content. The determination of content validity usually depends considerably upon expert judgment rather than mathematical procedures. This judgment is subject to beliefs, values, and biases of individuals judging the content. Thus, an item used in a test may acquire more or different traits than it was designed to measure (Mason & Bramble, 1997).

The Kuder-Richardson Reliability formula 20 was used to establish S/ERCT odd-even split-half internal reliability coefficients consistency. There are two considerations when choosing a one-test administration procedure such as Kuder-Richardson to generate internal reliability coefficients—length of the total test and length of the subtests (Gay, 1996). Although the reliability coefficients for Grade subtest 1 through 6 of the S/ERCT are posted (administration manual, p. 16), there is no indication of the test's total reliability. Nor is the length of each subtest given.

The reason for not indicating the total test reliability may be due in part to S/ERCT being a timed test. Although the manual suggests most students will "be able to achieve the number of items correct that are expected for their grade level," most students are not expected to complete the test within the allocated 30 minutes because "the test has a high ceiling in order to measure the achievement of the high achieving students" (administration manual, p. 25). The Kuder-Richardson Reliability formula is not recommended for speeded timed tests where most examinees could not finish the entire test within the allocated time. Because S/ERÇˇ reliability coefficients estimates are used in the subtests and not for the total timed test, the use of Kuder-Richardson is acceptable. However, because total test reliability tends to be greater than the reliability of subtests, interpretations of the posted subtest reliability coefficients may be questionable.

COMMENTARY. There are several major shortcomings to the S/ERCT. The test format, test booklets, and layout are of poor quality given the importance for this assessment. There are several glaring grammatical errors. Description for the S/ERCT's purpose has inconsistent language usage (administration manual, pp. 4–5). Some of the language may be offensive to particular individuals. For instance, "Compare Spanish reading ability with friendly Mexican neighbors" (front cover) and "compared with their friendly neighbors South of the border" (pp. 4, 7).

The author makes several major assumptions about Spanish and reading comprehension. Not all Latin American Spanish-speaking countries use the same universal vocabulary to identify the same item. For instance on the first page of the examiner/examinee test booklets Example Two gives the Spanish word for avocados (los aguacates); however, this can be different for an individual coming from Peru or Chile. Such a discrepancy may cause text anxiety for the examinee. When describing that the S/ERCT could be used to compare a nonnative Spanish speaker learning Spanish with "their friendly neighbors South of the border" (p. 7), the manual states the test could "measure total growth or learning in Spanish" (p. 7). Usually the term growth refers to a maturational development, rather than a cognitive development. An indefensible statement made on the same page in the manual suggests second language acquisition has "a very close relationship between the ability to read and understand a language, and the ability to speak the language." For more than three decades, research has described the language acquisition process emerging through natural stages of development, one of which is the silent stage. An individual in this stage may have greater confidence in recognizing written words and related meanings than in pronouncing these same words in public (Krashen, 1973; O'Malley, Chamot, Stewner-Manzana-Res, Kupper, & Russo, 1985).

SUMMARY. The reviewers would not recommend the use of the S/ERCT as an evaluation tool to identify an examinee's reading comprehension proficiency. The reading process is far more complex than this test would suggest. There are better informal reading inventories available on the current market to analyze reading comprehension in Spanish and English. The S/ERCT could be better used as an assessment identifier of conversational language acquisition between native and nonnative Spanish speakers. But then, most teachers of languages already provide their own to match their curriculum.

REVIEWERS' REFERENCES

Gay, L. R. (1996). Educational research: Competencies for analysis and application (5th ed.). Upper Saddle River, NJ: Prentice-Hall, Inc.
Krashen, S. D. (1973). Lateralization, language learning, and critical period: Some new evidence. Language Learning, 23, 63–74.
O'Malley, J. M., Chamot, A. U., Stewner-Manzana-Res, G., Kupper, L., & Russo, R. P. (1985). Learning strategies used by beginning and intermediate ESL students. Language Learning, 35, 21–46.
Mason, E. J., & Bramble, W. J. (1997). Research in education and the behavioral sciences: Concepts and methods. Madison, WI: Brown and Benchmark, Publishers.

Review of the Spanish/English Reading Comprehension Test [Revised] by SALVADOR HECTOR OCHOA, Associate Professor, Department of Educational Psychology, Texas A&M University, College Station, TX:

DESCRIPTION. The Spanish Reading Comprehension Test and its translated English version, the English Reading Comprehension Test, are intended to be used with students from first to sixth grade. The manual states that these measures can be used for a variety of purposes. One use of this test is to ascertain a pupil's reading comprehension level in Spanish as compared to Mexican norms. When this measure is used for this purpose, it addresses a critical need with respect to assessing recent bilingual and/or limited English proficient (LEP) immigrant students' reading achievement. There are very few measures available that are designed for this purpose. A second purpose of these measures is to assist in instructional decisions regarding bilingual and/or LEP students. Specifically, these two measures can help provide information about where to place the child with respect to his or her achievement level in Spanish and English reading instruction in bilingual education. Moreover, these two measures can be used as pre- and postmeasures to ascertain growth while the student is in bilingual education. A third purpose is to determine and to compare a student's degree of bilingualism. A fourth purpose is to measure an English speaker's Spanish reading capabilities. A fifth purpose of these two measures is for research. The manual also states that the Spanish Reading Comprehension Test can assist psychologists to ascertain if the bilingual and/or LEP student's "learning difficulties" are a result of "a learning problem or a learning-the-language problem" (p. 12).

The Spanish Reading Comprehension Test provides the user with percentile ranks for all grades from first to sixth. Moreover, this test provides a Spanish reading comprehension grade equivalent score. The English Reading Comprehension Test also provides a percentile rank for all grades from second to sixth. The English version also provides a reading comprehension grade equivalent score.

With respect to test administration, the manual provides the examiner with sufficient information to appropriately administer the Spanish and English versions. The English and Spanish instructions that are read to the examinees are age-appropriate and clearly understandable. The manual states that the examinees are to be given only 30 minutes to take each test. The manual, however, states that "at the first grade the test should be terminated when the teacher feels that the students have reached their maximum level of understanding" (p. 25). This administration rule requires subjective judgment that might impact standardized testing procedures.

The manner in which the test is formatted is problematic. Each page of the test has two columns. Each column has reading passages. This format results in too much information being on one page. Moreover, some reading passages start at the bottom of the left-hand column and continue at the top of the right-hand column. This format can be difficult for elementary students. The test should not have been printed in the two-column format because elementary students do not use this format when they are reading. Additionally, there are several questions for each reading passage. Some questions are found on the same page as the reading passage, whereas other questions associated with the same passage are on the next page. This format can be difficult for young elementary children.

DEVELOPMENT. The Spanish Reading Comprehension Test, as well as its English counterpart, has 73 items. The stories used in the Spanish Reading Comprehension Test were taken directly from reading textbooks used in Grades 1 to 6 in Mexico.

The test author states that three item tryout administrations were conducted prior to selecting the items that were included in the final Spanish version. Only those items that obtained at least a .25 biserial coefficient with the total test score were included in the final version.

The English Reading Comprehension Test was developed by translating the Spanish version. The manual, however, fails to provide any information on the translation procedures used. There are different translation procedures that can be used and each method varies in terms of standards and rigor. Moreover, the number and qualifications of the test translators were not provided. Additionally, the test author fails to address the issue that the same word in English and Spanish can vary in terms of its difficulty level. Some words are easier in Spanish than English and vice versa. The test author fails to provide any data and information that provides assurances that the reading passages used in the English version are equivalent to the Spanish version with respect to difficulty level.

TECHNICAL.

The Spanish Reading Comprehension Test. This test was normed in Mexico in 1973. The standardization sample was composed of 3,957 students. There were a sufficient number of students across all six grade levels. The numbers in each grade level ranged from 441 in first grade to 992 in sixth grade. The standardization sample was obtained from the following Mexican states: Baja California, Sonora, Chihuaha, Coahuila, Nuevo Leon, and San Luis Potosi. The manual states the standardization sample is composed of equal numbers of children from rural and urban areas. Children from both rural and urban areas from each of the aforementioned states were included in the standardization sample. The manual fails to provide critical information about the standardization sample. There is no information about how many students were from each of the states and if this is reflective of the Mexican school-aged population. There is no information about the gender and socioeconomic characteristics of the sample. There is no information about the type of the school (public versus private) that the students attended. Although students are exposed to the same reading book regardless of the type of schooling, many individuals (including this reviewer) who have knowledge about the Mexican educational system would argue that the quality of education differs greatly between private and public schools in Mexico.

The manual has two copyright dates (1978 and 1993). It appears that the Spanish version was not renormed for the latter copyright date. Thus, the norms are 25 years old and subsequently outdated. The test author should have addressed this issue for the second copyright version.

With respect to reliability, the only type of reliability addressed in the test manual is split-half. The split-half reliability coefficients obtained for each grade level are acceptable. The split-half reliability coefficients ranged from .90 for third graders to .94 for second graders. No information regarding test-retest reliability was provided.

The test manual provides information about content and concurrent validity. Content validity evidence is based on the fact that the reading stories used were taken directly from the mandatory reading books used in the Mexico school system. Concurrent validity was examined by correlating teacher rankings of reading ability with test results. The validity coefficients obtained for each grade level are acceptable. These concurrent validity coefficients ranged from .54 to fifth graders to .67 for first graders.

The English Reading Comprehension Test. This test was normed on 1,702 American students. The manual states that the standardization sample consisted of students in "Grades 2 to 5" (p. 33). The manual, however, reports on the same page that 366 students in sixth grade were included in the standardization sample. This information is clearly contradictory. The number of students in each grade level included in the standardization sample ranged from 256 in fifth grade to 378 in fourth grade. The standardization sample was obtained from the following states: Arizona, California, Colorado, Illinois, New Mexico, and New York. The sample is not representative of the U.S. Census with respect to geographical area. Moreover, the manual fails to provide critical information about the standardization sample. There is no information about the ethnic, gender, and socio-

economic characteristics of the sample. Additionally, there is no information regarding the type of community (urban versus rural). The manual has two copyright dates (1978 and 1993). The manual fails to state when the norms were obtained.

The test manual does not provide information about reliability and validity. The manual states: "The validity and reliability coefficients were not computed with the students in the United States because time did not allow it" (p. 33).

COMMENTARY.

The Spanish Reading Comprehension Test. This test has strengths and weaknesses that merit discussion. The major strength of this test is its content validity. This test is one of a few, if not the only, commercially available measure that has reading passages that are actually from federally mandated reading texts used in Mexico. Moreover, the standardization sample used to norm this test is a strength because it used children who were from Mexico. This is rarely done. In spite of these strengths, this test has serious limitations. The standardization sample is not representative of the Mexican population in Mexico. The norms are outdated. The test manual fails to include information about test-retest reliability. Moreover, the federally required books used for reading in 1978 in Mexico might no longer be used today. This would have an impact on the test's content validity.

The English Reading Comprehension Test. This test has serious limitations. First, it should be noted that this test is a translated version of the Spanish Reading Comprehension Test. No information was provided concerning the translation procedures used to develop the English version. Moreover, the qualifications of the individuals doing the translation was not provided. This information is important to provide in order to ensure that the English version is equivalent to the Spanish version in terms of difficulty level and content. There are significant limitations to the standardization sample used for this test. It is not representative of the U.S. elementary school-age population. The manual fails to provide information regarding the ethnic, gender, socioeconomic level, geographical, and type of community (urban versus rural) characteristics of the standardization sample. Moreover, it is unclear whether the norms were obtained in 1978 or in 1993. There is no psychometric information about the reliability and validity of this test.

Moreover, one comment made by the test author raises serious concerns from a theoretical perspective. In the manual, the test author states the following concerning how test information should be used when differentiating between "a learning problem or a learning-the-language-problem" (p. 12) of bilingual and/or LEP students:

> The psychologist should then determine whether he should deal with the learning problem or the language problem. It may be best to try to teach the student sufficient functional English so that the student will be able to communicate and learn in English, and then to begin to deal with the learning problem. (p. 12)

Many experts who have expertise in providing instruction to linguistically diverse exceptional learners (Baca & Cervantes, 1998) would not support this recommendation.

SUMMARY. The test author should be commended for attempting to develop a reading comprehension test in Spanish that is reflective of the curriculum used in Mexico that was normed in the same country. The test author clearly understands the importance of obtaining reading comprehension information about bilingual and/or LEP students in this country. Given the serious aforementioned concerns noted with the Spanish Reading Comprehension Test, it should be used with extreme caution. The English Reading Comprehension Test is not recommended given the numerous aforementioned limitations.

REVIEWER'S REFERENCE

Baca, L. M., & Cervantes, H. (Eds.). (1998). *The bilingual special education interface* (3rd ed.). Upper Saddle River, NJ: Merrill Publishing Co.

[238]
Spatial Awareness Skills Program Test.

Purpose: Constructed to identify "children whose spatial awareness skills are developing more slowly than expected" and provide "information about how to remedy a deficit."

Population: Ages 4–10.

Publication Date: 1999.

Acronym: SASP Test.

Scores: Total score only.

Administration: Individual.

Price Data, 2003: $99 per complete kit including curriculum manual, instrument manual (28 pages), 25 student response booklets, and scoring transparency; $39 per 25 student response booklets.

Time: (5) minutes.

Comments: Previously titled Test of Visual Analysis Skills (T5:2721); designed to be used with the Spatial Awareness Skills Program (SASP) Curriculum; criterion-referenced.

Author: Jerome Rosner.

Publisher: PRO-ED.

Review of the Spatial Awareness Skills Program Test by CONNIE T. ENGLAND, Assistant Professor/Chair of School Counseling and Guidance, Lincoln Memorial University, Harrogate, TN:

DESCRIPTION. The Spatial Awareness Skills Program Test (SASP) is a 15-item test, administered by paper-and-pencil. All items consist of copying geometric designs and are recorded in the Student Response Booklet.

Nonclinical staff can administer, score and interpret the SASP. The test takes approximately 5 minutes to administer. According to the manual raw scores are converted to age-equivalencies by interpolation, extrapolation, and smoothing.

DEVELOPMENT. The latest version of the SASP (copyright, 1999) is a revision of two earlier tests, the Visual Analysis Test (VAT) (Rosner, 1971) and the Test of Visual Analysis Skills (TVAS) (Rosner, 1975). The original VAT was designed to collect data regarding the relative difficulty of a number of certain behaviors found to have qualities that both identified spatial awareness deficits and provided information for remediation of those deficits. The VAT was shortened in the mid-1970s and published as the Test of Visual Analysis Skills. The current version is three items shorter than the TVAS, provides improved scoring criteria, and serves as a guide to the implementation of the Spatial Awareness Skills Program Curriculum. Materials furnished by the developer (including a Spatial Awareness Skills Program Test Instrument Manual and a Spatial Awareness Skills Program Curriculum) provide information regarding initial test development. The developer describes the SASP items as test probes designed to determine a student's ability to analyze geometric designs, use mapping strategies, and organize concrete information spatially. Analyses of these distinctions are used to interpret the SASP Test results and provide information on the child's development of spatial analysis skills.

The manual defines the overarching construct of spatial awareness as "the ability to recognize that what one sees ... has definable characteristics, and that the spatial-temporal environment and the things in it ... have identifiable concrete features" (instrument manual, p. 1). Two basic assumptions are purported to provide the theoretical underpinnings for the development of the SASP: (a) Skills tested by the SASP are developmental in nature and performance should be highly correlated to chronological age, and (b) individual test items should correlate with the overall score.

TECHNICAL. The developer readily admits that only limited empirical data are available to support the statistical integrity of the SASP. He argues that given its singleness of purpose (i.e., to place students at the appropriate entry point in the curriculum), adequate data were collected and necessary psychometric analyses conducted.

The field test sample for the SASP consisted of 322 students from 21 intact classrooms, in two elementary schools in Houston, Texas. Gender and ethnicity percentages are reported, yet no evidence is provided that these variables were taken into account in the norm-setting process.

Reliability estimates for the SASP Test relative to two sources of error variance, content sampling and interscorer differences, are reported. Internal consistency for the SASP items using the scores of the entire normative sample is estimated by a single, developer-conducted study. Cronbach alphas for the normative sample are between .70 and .80 across age levels. Interrater reliability is reported as .96 for converted raw score age equivalents. To establish this correlation coefficient, two staff persons from the test developer's publication department independently scored a set of 30 randomly selected protocols. No other reliability estimates are given.

Evidence to support the validity of scores from the SASP Test is limited. Typically three sources of validity are provided: content, predictive, and construct. The manual reports content and construct validity information, but predictive validity data are absent. The developer states that given the limited purpose of the test content and construct data are sufficient to support the SASP Test's validity.

Content validity evidence ostensibly is offered in two demonstrations. The developer gives the rationale underlying the selection of formats and items used in the SASP Test as qualitative evidence of content-description validity. Quantitative evidence of content validity is presented in the form of a single study item analysis. Item discrimination coefficients and item difficulties are reported for the SASP at seven age levels.

Based on these two procedures the developer concludes that the SASP Test items are representative of the domain tested and satisfy the requirements for content validity.

Construct validity for the SASP Test is predicated on two basic constructs thought to underlie the SASP Test: (a) Spatial awareness skills are developmental in nature and test performance is strongly related to chronological age, and (b) because items on a test measure similar traits, individual test items should be highly correlated with the total test score. The manual reports an average mean/age correlation of .78 to demonstrate the relationship of age and spatial awareness skills. The manual reports analyses of the discriminating powers of the SASP Test items as evidence of the test's construct validity.

COMMENTARY. The value of the SASP as a measure of spatial awareness seems to be compromised on a number of levels. First, the test admittedly was developed for a single purpose. Although the developer alludes to the efficacy of the SASP Test to identify spatial awareness deficits and intervention strategies, clearly the test was developed for use with the SASP Curriculum Program.

Second, there are concerns—previously noted—regarding the paucity of evidence used to support the reliability and validity of the SASP Test. There is no evidence of outside research to corroborate the developer's findings of adequate interrater and internal consistency reliability. The methods used to support content and construct validity are syllogistic (i.e., item-discrimination/difficulty statistics are used to support the construct validity of the SASP Test). Predictive validity studies are absent.

Last, caution is advised when using the age-equivalency scores. The developer reports that development of age equivalents required extensive statistical manipulation of the data.

SUMMARY. The developer, to his credit, has produced a spatial awareness instrument that can be administered, scored, and interpreted in an efficient and cost-effective manner. He considered the limited purpose of the test when reporting statistics and recommends that the SASP Test be used in conjunction with his companion SASP Curriculum. He contends that the SASP Test is one of the few spatial awareness tests that assess a general ability and connects directly with a remedial training program. On the whole, however, the

SASP Test does not pass the basic requirements of test construction (i.e., adequate reliability and validity studies). Insufficient evidence exists to support that the test consistently and accurately measures its primary construct, spatial awareness. Assumptions presumed to underlie this construct are not supported by sufficient empirical evidence. Predictive validity information supporting the developer's assertion "that improvement on the SASP Test may be reliably interpreted to predict improvement on other tasks that depend on spatial awareness skills [i.e., school-based tasks]" (instrument manual, p. 3) is needed. The reader is advised to consider the SASP Test as a screening tool used to place a student in the associated SASP Curriculum. Evaluation of the curriculum's relationship to improved student performance is beyond the scope of this review; however, it should be considered before deciding on the educational utility of this test.

REVIEWER'S REFERENCES

Rosner, J. (1971). *The visual analysis test: An initial report.* Pittsburgh, PA: University of Pittsburgh, Learning Research and Development Center.

Rosner, J. (1975). Testing for teaching in an adaptive educational environment. In W. Hively & M. C. Reynolds (Eds.), *Domain-referenced testing in special education* (pp. 43–76). Reston, VA: Council for Exceptional Children.

Review of the Spatial Awareness Skills Program Test by ROBERT M. THORNDIKE, Professor of Psychology, Western Washington University, Bellingham, WA:

DESCRIPTION. The Spatial Awareness Skills Program Test (SASP Test) is a very brief (15-item) test to accompany the Spatial Awareness Skills Program, a specialized curriculum designed to develop the skill of spatial awareness, which the author claims is an essential precursor to development of various academic abilities, particularly arithmetic. "The test serves as a guide toward implementation of the remedial program … when the need is demonstrated" (instrument manual, p. v). According to the program's author:

> "Spatial awareness plays three interconnected roles for beginning school children. It enables them to identify those things that numerals and spatial words represent; this provides them a way of organizing information on the basis of some logic; and these two, in combination, make it possible for them to identify features that link one concrete fact with another, to learn by association on the basis of shared spatial characteristics" (instrument manual, p. 1).

Where a spatial skill deficit is suspected, the SASP Test can be administered to confirm the deficit and identify the level in the remedial curriculum at which instruction should start. Raw scores on the test are converted to age equivalents, and these are compared to chronological age to determine whether a deficit is present.

DEVELOPMENT. The SASP Test and its related training program constitute the latest in a series of instruments to measure spatial skills and programs for remediation produced by Jerome Rosner. The goal in the present test was to simplify administration and scoring. Test items are similar to some of the instructional activities. There are two basic item forms. The first nine items require the child to draw a design to match a sample in a grid of 5 to 25 dots where all dots are present. In the last six items, similar designs (all using 25 dots) are presented, but the child must reproduce the design in a matrix where some of the dots are missing.

Testing begins with Item 1 for all examinees and continues until the child has missed two consecutive items. A child's score is the number of the highest item passed, NOT the number of items passed. The items are quite steeply graded in difficulty and should come close to forming a Guttman scale, so this scoring procedure seems reasonable although the manual presents no data on passing rates for the items. Raw scores are converted to age equivalents using a table that is printed on the front of the test booklet. Graphical methods were used to develop the score conversions.

TECHNICAL. The author states that due to the highly restricted purpose of the test, the usual demands for norms and other technical supporting materials can be relaxed. In a sense, this is true because the test rises or falls on the validity of the assumptions underlying the curricular materials. However, it is then necessary to present empirical evidence for the validity of the curriculum, and this is not done adequately in either the test manual or the curriculum manual.

The test items were field tested, and age-equivalent norms were developed on a sample of 322 children ranging in age from 4-0 years through 10-11 years from one public elementary school and one private school in Houston, Texas. "All of the students from 22 intact classrooms were tested" (instrument manual, p. 13). Children of color were overrepresented in the sample from a national perspective, but probably not for the demographics of Houston.

The approach to reliability assessment is rather simplistic and the data are not as strong as

I would like to see. "Content sampling" reliability is assessed by internal consistency, and the coefficients (presumably computed on the entire sample of 322, but we are not told) are generally in the .70s. One potential problem with scoring, particularly for the later items, is that judgment is required. A sample of 30 protocols was scored independently by "two staff persons in PRO-ED's research department" and produced a coefficient of scorer agreement of .96. Because we have no idea how these protocols were selected, the coefficient is uninterpretable. If the 30 protocols come from 30 six-year-olds, scorer consistency is reasonably impressive. If, however, the 30 children come from the full age range, we should be much less impressed.

How much error is due to lack of spatial skill, and how much is due to lack of motor control? In view of the way the test is scored, a more informative way to assess reliability would be to fit a Guttman scalogram model or a Rasch IRT model to the data and report model fit. For example, how many students who got scores of 5 missed any of the first five items?

Validity evidence is also somewhat weak, but in this case the problem lies with the highly restricted nature of the test. The test is intended to assess whatever skill is being taught in the Spatial Analysis Skills Program itself, nothing more, nothing less. There is no independent assessment of success in the curriculum, so we must fall back on face validity. The items look like they tap the same skills the curriculum is designed to teach, therefore, they are face valid. Item analysis is also offered as evidence of validity. The discussion here reveals a lack of understanding of technical matters in item analysis and the results presented are not particularly informative. However, given the author's assertion that spatial analysis is a skill that improves with age, the pattern of item difficulties and the correlation of .78 with age suggest that test scores are functioning the way they should.

COMMENTARY. Current test theory says that the benefits and consequences of test use should be taken into account when deciding whether to use a particular test for a particular purpose. In the case of the SASP Test, using it is unlikely to result in harm to any examinee, and there may be potential benefits if the author's claims about the construct of spatial awareness and its relationship to academic success are even partially correct. The value of the test for a given potential user rests entirely on the

value one places on the SASP curriculum. If one plans to use the program, a decision that should be based on factors unrelated to the test, then one will want to use the test as well. The test looks like it probably fits well with the curriculum, and with little else in the universe. But then, it does not claim to measure anything else.

SUMMARY. The SASP Test is probably adequate for its intended (highly restricted) purpose.

[239]

Spousal Assault Risk Assessment Guide.

Purpose: "Helps criminal justice professionals predict the likelihood of domestic violence."

Population: Individuals suspected of or being treated for spousal or family-related assault.

Publication Date: 1999.

Acronym: SARA.

Scores: Total score only.

Administration: Individual.

Price Data, 2003: $55 per complete kit including 25 checklist forms, 25 assessment forms, and manual; $28 per 25 assessment forms; $15 per 25 checklist forms; $28 per manual; $30 per specimen set including 3 checklist forms, 3 assessment forms, and manual.

Time: Administration time not reported.

Comments: Completed by clinician/rater (criminal justice professional) after all available sources of information from suspect/offender, victim, etc. are gathered.

Authors: P. Randall Kropp, Stephen D. Hart, Christopher D. Webster, and Derek Eaves.

Publisher: Multi-Health Systems, Inc.

Review of the Spousal Assault Risk Assessment Guide by IRA S. KATZ, Clinical Psychologist at California Department of Corrections, Salinas Valley State Prison, Soledad, CA, and Soledad Medical Clinic, Soledad, CA, and private practice, Salinas, CA:

Family violence, especially against spouses—women in particular—is our society's "dirty little secret" that is becoming less unknown and more problematic. More and more, we are faced with situations that will not be hidden in the shadows of shame. Domestic violence involving spouses and other family members is a growing and grisly social and psychological phenomenon. The development of the Spousal Assault Risk Assessment Guide is a product of exciting research from Canada that has worldwide implications and uses.

DESCRIPTION. The Spousal Assault Risk Assessment Guide (SARA) is a very user-friendly psychometric checklist that can quickly screen risk factors of spousal assault, violence, and/or abuse.

The SARA is adaptable to be of use to many diverse clinical populations. The SARA addresses the unique similarities and differences incumbent in criminal court referrals, probation, and inmate populations. The risk factors that are assessed are very helpful in the preparation of accurate and actionable evaluations. Much information is captured in relatively short order, allowing the clinician to provide help faster and to serve more clients. Different than a pure psychometric test, the SARA has unique qualities that make it far more user-friendly and faster to administer.

Specifically, there are no cutoff scores or norms per se. In this way the SARA is similar to several other commonly used forensic assessment instruments (see Grisso, 1986). The reason the SARA should be understood as a checklist rather than a test is based on the fact that research that is addressing some of this instrument's psychometric properties is still ongoing.

The diversity and applications of the SARA impress this writer, including pretrial application, pre-sentence applications, correctional intake applications, and correctional discharge applications. Additionally, there are other immediate applications: victim safety assessment, and civil justice matters—such as separation/divorce and custody/access hearings. Warning third parties is another application that is clearly connected to mandated reporting requirements in most jurisdictions. These duties do apply to mental health professionals, counselors, and social service providers (Dickens, 1985). The SARA results can be used as an "independent check" of the professional judgment of service providers and help them support their intuitions and clinical judgments. Finally the SARA can serve as a routine quality assurance and post-critical incident review.

The SARA is also a flexible tool. It can be used in two ways by various users. First, the evaluator has the opportunity to note specific client risk factors for violence. Second, the SARA allows for factors not included in the instrument. It is hoped this will result in the utilization of more clinical judgment and wisdom as opposed to a "score."

DEVELOPMENT. In the development of the SARA there was a creation of a list of factors that would be relatively short and aimed at a moderate degree of specificity. The result was a list of 20 factors, referred to on the SARA as items, grouped into five content areas, and referred to as sections.

The SARA consists of five sections. The first section includes Criminal History. Three factors are included: Past Assault of Family Members, Past Assault of Strangers or Acquaintances, and Past Violation of Conditional Release or Community Supervision. Evaluation of these factors can help validity of the instrument as a future behavior predictor.

The next section deals with Psychosocial Adjustment. There are many items in this section that can be very helpful from a social learning intervention perspective (Widom, 1989). Other factors, such as mental disorder (Monahan, 1992), are included here. It is important to say here that the SARA does not suggest that mental illness is directly linked to the development of spousal abuse. The point of its inclusion is to make the clinician and the user aware of the fact that clients with mental disorders are more likely to make and act on poor decisions.

The next section in the SARA is that of Spousal Assault History. There are seven items in the Spousal Assault History section. The first four deal with the nature and extent of past assaults whereas the last three pertain to behaviors/attitudes related to assaultive behaviors. Here we find Past Physical Assault, Past Sexual Assault/Sexual Jealousy, Past Use of Weapons and/or Credible Threats of Death, Recent Escalation in Frequency or Severity of Assaults, Past Violations of "No Contact" Orders, Extreme Minimization or Denial of Spousal Assault History, and Attitudes that Support or Condone Spousal Assault, which covers a wide range of values and beliefs—personal, social, religious, political, and cultural—and encourages patriarchy (i.e., male prerogative), misogyny, and the use of physical violence or intimidation to resolve conflicts and enforce control.

The next section deals with Alleged/Most Recent Offense (Index Offense). There are three items in this section. These items are based on the index (alleged, current, or most recent) offense: Severe and/or Sexual Assault, Use of Weapons and/or Credible Threats of Death, and Violation of "No Contact" Order.

The final section of the SARA does not contain any specific items. It allows the evaluator to include and note risk factors not included in the SARA that are present in the particular case that may result in a decision that the individual is at high risk for violence. Risk factors might include behaviors such as a history of stalking behavior (Cooper, 1994); a history of disfiguring, torturing, or maiming intimate partners; a history of sexual sadism; and so forth.

One of the most admirable and salient features of the SARA is that, because it is not a controlled psychological test, it can be used in many contexts by many kinds of users. There is no single set of user qualifications. However, two caveats should be noted. First, when using the SARA to make decisions about an individual, the users are responsible to ensure that their evaluation conforms to relevant laws, regulations, and policies. Secondly, the users should meet the following minimal qualification: (a) expertise in individual assessment (e.g., formal training and/or work-related experience in psychological, psychiatric, social work, nursing, or correctional assessment), and (b) expertise in the area of spousal assault (e.g., formal coursework, knowledge of the relevant literature, or work-related experience).

TECHNICAL. Normative data for the SARA primarily are from Canadian offenders. However, there is much research to support utilization with United States offender populations with respect to important criminal history and psychological characteristics despite the obvious demographic differences. SARA norms for offenders in the U.S. and Sweden should be available in the near future.

There were some very interesting findings from the normative data. Probationers had lower scores than inmates. Many of the inmates had a known history of spousal assault, even though most of them were incarcerated for offenses unrelated to spousal assault (mostly robbery, drug, sex, and homicide offenses). Very few items were omitted by the norm group. About 20–35% of offenders were perceived by evaluators to be at high risk for spousal abuse. Finally, it was possible based on the data to establish descriptive cutoffs for SARA ratings that can be used.

Reliability is always an important factor in evaluating any psychometric instrument. Various forms of reliability integrity support the soundness of this instrument including Cronbach's alpha for internal consistency. Good interrater reliability values were reported.

Validity is another important psychometric property. The criterion-related validity of the SARA was examined in three ways. Concurrent validity was analyzed with respect to other measures related to risk for violence and criminality. These measures included the Hare Psychopathy Checklist: Screening Version (PCL:SV, Hart, Cox, & Hare, 1995), a rating scale of psychopathic personality disorder that is predictive of violent reoffending and other measures.

COMMENTARY AND SUMMARY. The developers of the SARA, to their credit, have produced a risk assessment instrument that can be administered, judged, and interpreted with predictive confidence in a relatively efficient and cost-effective manner. The SARA is a very valuable instrument with much social utility for doing great good; especially for the safety of potential victims. This is a well-researched instrument that has benefited from years of careful study and analysis of the relevant clinical and empirical knowledge in the criminal justice field. It is important to remember that the SARA is not a psychological test. A positive result of this is that the SARA is not limited to one particular professional group. The SARA does not replace professional judgment or responsibility.

The SARA provides guidelines to direct risk management strategies. The SARA is a powerful tool in the right hands with the right risk management strategies. This reviewer still would like to see more data with U.S. population norms, as is indicated. There may be some need to modify the questions to ensure cultural accuracy.

The SARA is a very valuable addition to the psychometric tool chests of many in the forensic and criminal justice and corrections fields. Not only is the SARA needed, but it will help keep many people potentially out of harm's way. What forensic instruments can easily make that claim?

REVIEWER'S REFERENCES

Cooper, M. (1994) *Criminal harassment and potential for treatment: Literature review and annotated bibliography.* Vancouver, BC: British Columbia Institute on Family Violence.

Dickens, B. (1985). Prediction, professionalism, and public policy. In C. D. Webster, M. H. Ben-Aron, & S. J. Hucker (Eds.), *Dangerousness: Probability and prediction, psychiatry and public policy* (pp. 177–208). New York: Cambridge University Press.

Grisso, T. (1986). *Evaluating competencies: Forensic assessments and instruments.* New York: Plenum Press.

Hart, S. D., Cox, D. N., & Hare, R. D. (1995) *Hare Psychopathy Checklist: Screening Version.* Toronto: Multi-Health Systems, Inc.

Monahan, J. (1992). Mental disorder and violent behavior: Perceptions and evidence. *American Psychologist, 47,* 511–521.

Widom, C. S. (1989). The cycle of violence. *Science, 244,* 160–166.

Review of the Spousal Assault Risk Assessment Guide by MICHAEL J. SCHEEL, Associate Professor, University of Nebraska-Lincoln, Department of Educational Psychology, Lincoln, NE:

DESCRIPTION. The Spousal Assault Risk Assessment Guide (SARA) is a paper-and-pencil

20-item checklist composed of risk factors that have been identified through a review of literature and during the Project for the Protection of Victims of Spousal Assault in British Columbia. The test manual description indicates that the instrument is a screening device to assess risk of spousal or family-related assault. The checklist is designed to be completed by mental health professionals based on information gained from interviews with victims, offenders, other pertinent individuals, police reports, and psychological tests and questionnaires. The test developers describe the SARA as "not a test or scale in the usual sense" (user's manual, p. 1). They emphasize that it should not be relied upon as "an absolute or relative measure of risk using cutoff scores or norms" (user's manual, p. 1). Instead it should be used as a "means of ensuring that pertinent information is considered and weighed by evaluators" (user's manual, p. 1).

Items appear as risk factors in five content areas, which are referred to as sections. The five sections are: (a) Criminal History (e.g., "Past assault of family members"), (b) Psychosocial Adjustment (e.g., "Recent suicidal or homicidal ideation/intent"), (c) Spousal Assault History (e.g., "Past violation of 'no contact' orders"), (d) Alleged/Most Recent Offense (e.g., "Use of weapons and/or credible threats of death"), and (e) Other Considerations. Each item in the first four sections is scored on a 3-point ordinal scale (0 = Absent, 1 = Sub-Threshold, or 2 = Present). The fifth section, Other Considerations, is not scored. The coding criteria for each category of items are specified in the manual. For example, in the "Past Assault of Family Members" section, 2 corresponds to actual or attempted assault; 1 corresponds to threatened assault; and 0 corresponds to no actual, attempted, or threatened assault. Total scores and the number of factors present are obtained through the SARA assessment form. The SARA profile form is used to convert total scores and number of factors to percentile ranks. Scores falling in the shaded zone of the profile form are labeled "high risk" and those in the unshaded area are designated as "moderate to low risk."

DEVELOPMENT. Item development of the SARA consisted of a review of literature to identify risk factors that discriminated those who were violent toward spouses from those who were not. The review revealed similar risk factors for "recidivistic violence among known spousal assaulters" (user's

manual, p. 3) and the more general risk for violence. The intent in the creation of the SARA was to produce a relatively short checklist with a moderate level of specificity. Items were written with the purpose of identifying traits, characteristics, or incidents rather than isolated or specific behavioral acts. As can be discerned from the section headings, prior criminal history, psychosocial maladjustment, spousal assault history, and recent offenses were found to be the primary risk factors for spousal or family-related assault. The fifth section, "Other Considerations" was included to allow the evaluator to include risk factors that are rare, but perhaps relevant for a specific case (e.g., history of stalking behavior; history of sexual sadism). The test developers state "to date, the primary application of the SARA has been the assessment and management of risk for spousal assault in adult male offenders who are under community supervision (probationers) or who are currently incarcerated (inmates)" (user's manual, p. 35).

TECHNICAL. Normative data were compiled in Canada, yet test developers state that "SARA users in the US should feel confident relying on the norms" (user's manual, p. 35), because Canadian and U.S. offenders appear to be similar although the demographics of ethnicity and race differ. No details are provided about the ethnic/racial makeup of the normative sample. Norms were developed on two groups of offenders, probationers ($N = 1,671$) and inmates ($N = 638$), for a total sample of 2,309. All individuals in the normative sample have a history of spousal assault. Findings from the normative sample were used to establish cutoff scores. Total scores of 20 (82nd percentile) or above and risk factors of 8 or greater (84th percentile) indicate high risk. Using these cutoffs, 23.6% of the normative sample would be classified as at risk. The test manual provides a comparison between those individuals from the normative sample that scored in the critical area, and the summary risk ratings of professionals. In 18% of the cases, the evaluation of risk by professionals did not match the evaluation of risk derived from the SARA. Tables of normative scores for each of the 20 risk factors are also provided in the test manual.

Interrater reliability estimates are somewhat questionable due to the means by which they were estimated. The paired raters of the SARA utilized differing information to form judgments about each of the risk factor items, and therefore there remains some uncertainty about whether two different raters with access to the same information would produce similar codings. Internal consistency reliability was estimated by considering the instrument to have a Part 1 (General Violence) and Part 2 (Spousal Violence). This division seems conceptually odd, because four content areas were identified during test development. Alpha levels of the two parts were modest, .66 and .73 respectively, with an overall Cronbach alpha of .78. Interitem correlations were acceptable and ranged from .16 to .43 in Part 1 and from .21 to .48 in Part 2. A factor analysis might have provided a better means of assessing the structure of the instrument.

Three different validity studies were conducted. In a known groups study, offender inmates were compared to nonoffender inmates yielding significant differences between the two groups on 17 of the 20 risk factor items. Moderate support for the concurrent validity of the SARA was gained through comparison with the Hare Psychopathy Checklist-Revised ($r = .44$; $p<.05$), the General Statistical Information on Recidivism Scale (GSIR; $r = -.07$; $p>.05$), and the Violence Risk Appraisal Guide (VRAG; $r = .29$; $p>.05$). The GSIR and the VRAG were significantly correlated with Part 1 of the SARA (General Violence) but not Part 2, and seem to indicate convergent and divergent validity evidence. In a third study, SARA scores were compared between a recidivistic and a nonrecidivistic group. Part 2 (Spousal Violence) discriminated significantly between those individuals who tended to re-offend and those who did not.

COMMENTARY. The stated purpose of the SARA is to provide a systematic method of assessing and considering risk factors, but not for use as a more typical psychological test in which individual interpretations are derived through comparisons with established normative samples. Even though the test developers do not promote the instrument as a tool for psychological practice, normative samples are provided and a means of comparing individual scores to the norm group of known offenders is also provided through the scoring sheet. Hence, some confusion exists concerning the purpose of the instrument. Despite this confusion, the psychometric properties of the SARA seem adequate, and allow the comparison of an individual score to the normative sample. Hence, this instrument is appropriate both as a means of conducting a systematic assessment, and

as a tool to evaluate risk of recidivism in comparison to other offenders. In addition, the SARA is an excellent tool for research to build predictive models of factors that are related to spousal assault and repeated assault.

SUMMARY. The SARA is an efficient instrument for the assessment of risk to re-offend through spousal assault that has benefited from a well-constructed development plan. The mental health professional completes the checklist based on information gained about the offender from other sources. Criteria for coding each item are clear and easily applied. The items represent risk factors that were derived through an extensive literature review. The SARA utilizes an extensive normative sample of past offenders who are incarcerated or on probation. The checklist would benefit from factor analysis to more clearly understand the nature of the constructs being measured. As it is, the SARA seems to be divided into two parts, spousal assault risk factors and more general risk factors for violence. The instrument possesses adequate reliability and an impressive amount of evidence supporting its predictive, concurrent, and convergent/divergent validity.

[240]
STAR Early Literacy®.

Purpose: A computer-adaptive diagnostic assessment that "can be useful for evaluating literacy development overall and in seven broad literacy domains."
Population: Prekindergarten–Grade 3.
Publication Date: 2001.
Scores, 8: Graphophonemic Knowledge, General Readiness, Phonemic Awareness, Phonics, Comprehension, Structural Analysis, Vocabulary, Scaled Score.
Administration: Group.
Price Data, 2001: $1,995 per single-computer license kit (up to 40 students) [including software manual (71 pages), installation guide (48 pages), technical manual (126 pages), CD-ROM with pre-test instructions, mouse training, practice assessment, and actual assessment questions, quick reference card, and 12-month support plan]; $2,995 per school site license (network-ready, up to 200 students, expansions available) and including same components as single-user license kit; $79 per 50-student expansion modules for school license kit..
Time: (13) minutes.
Comments: Also provides domain scores and skill scores; classifies students into one of three stages of reading development (emergent, transitional, probable reader); includes software allowing teacher to generate

reports; may be administered up to 10 times per year; uses the same database as other software from the same company. System requirements are Windows or Macintosh, CD-ROM drive, mouse, 640x480 monitor, 256 color monitor, sound card, 24 MB RAM, 310 MB hard drive, Power PC or greater and System 7.5.5 or higher (Macintosh) or 133 MHz Pentium and Windows 95 or higher (Windows).

Author: Renaissance Learning, Inc.
Publisher: Renaissance Learning, Inc.

Review of STAR Early Literacy® by THERESA GRAHAM, Adjunct Faculty, University of Nebraska—Lincoln, Lincoln, NE:

DESCRIPTION. The STAR Early Literacy assessment is a criterion-referenced computer-adaptive test intended "to measure the early literacy skills of beginning readers" (manual, p. 1). Specifically, the test assesses seven early literacy domains including General Readiness, Graphophonemic Knowledge, Phonemic Awareness, Phonics, Comprehension, Structural Analysis, and Vocabulary. In addition, 41 skills sets were identified within each domain. Although it was originally designed for children in kindergarten through Grade 2, it has been satisfactorily used with children as young as 3 through children in Grades 3 and above. The intent of the authors was to design a relatively quick test that could be repeatedly given to assess growth in reading that would allow educators to alter their instruction to promote optimal development. The test is a 25-item assessment that takes about 10 minutes to complete. Moreover, because the database of test items includes nearly 2,500 items and because the program keeps track of items previously given, it is unlikely that students receive the same item within a 30-day period. It is unique from other measures of early reading ability in that it is administered via the computer and it is adaptive to the student's responses. Practice with using the mouse and with test items are included in the computer administration through digitized audio recordings providing instruction and graphics displaying the questions. The STAR Early Literacy assessment adjusts item difficulty according to students' responses based on Adaptive Branching, a technique that shares qualities with Item Response Theory (IRT). The initial items have difficulty levels usually one or two grades below grade placement. After the first two items, STAR Early Literacy selects items such that students answer about 75% of items

correctly. On subsequent administrations, the STAR Early Literacy begins assessments at the level of the most recent score.

STAR Early Literacy provides test security to protect the content of the test and to ensure confidentiality of the test results in a number of ways. First, all of the computer information is encrypted. Second, access to information is password protected. STAR Early Literacy uses a management program that allows different levels of access. For example, unrestricted teachers have access to all test results. However, teachers with Classroom access have access to only the results for the students who are assigned to them. Test monitors and students do not have access to any student data.

STAR Early Literacy provides three types of scores: Scaled scores, domain scores, and skill scores. Scaled scores summarize overall literacy performance and are computed using procedures associated with the Rasch 1-parameter logistic response model. The scores are transformed to scores ranging from 300 to 900, roughly corresponding with the age range of children taking the test (e.g., 300s for 3-year olds, 500s for 5-year olds). The manual provides the scaled score distributions of students by grade level. Using the scaled scores, students are classified into three literacy classifications. Students with scores below 675 are classified as "Emergent Readers." Students with scores between 675–774 are classified as "Transitional Readers." Students with scores at or above 775 are classified as "Probable Readers." The selection of these scores was based on specific competencies demonstrated on the test. Domain and skill scores are proficiency scores based upon estimations of the percent of items the student would be expected to answer if all of the STAR Early Literacy items in the domain or skill were presented. Both based on the Rasch model, the domain and skill scores range from 0 to 100%. The manual provides the distribution of students by grade level and domain and skill score according to those who scored in the 10th, 50th, and 90th percentile.

DEVELOPMENT. Items were developed based on guidelines specifying design and content. Design guidelines included creating items that directly address domain or skill set, providing all instructions aurally, presenting items in a graphically recognizable fashion, and using consistent language and pronunciation throughout the test. To develop the content of the test items, a blueprint of the 41 skill sets within the seven domains was constructed. Prototype test items were written and prototype test software was developed. Over 1,500 children in prekindergarten through second grade participated. The authors provide little specific information about this prototype test except to say that the "results indicated that the prototype tryout was a success in terms of demonstrating the viability of the software prototype and of the tryout items in classrooms ranging from pre-Kindergarten through grade 2" (manual, p. 22).

To calibrate the test, nearly 1,000 items were written at each of the three grade levels, kindergarten through Grade 2. Two hundred forty-six test forms were designed using the nearly 3,000 items across the tests. The tests were administered via the computer to a sample of over 32,000 students in prekindergarten through Grade 3 in over 300 schools. The schools were chosen to roughly represent a national sample in terms of geography, socioeconomic status, and school type (Unclassified, Urban, Suburban, Rural). It is difficult to ascertain the population of students that participated in the calibration study. The authors report that 44% of their sample was "Unclassified" in terms of ethnic group affiliation.

In constructing the various test forms, items were horizontally and vertically anchored in order to get a reliable IRT scale linking. Using the Rasch IRT model analysis, items were assigned the value of a "difficulty parameter." In addition, item parameter estimation and IRT scoring were assessed using WINSTEPS. With this information, multiple reviewers evaluated each item's Rasch parameters to determine the acceptance of an item. After reviewer discrepancies were considered and independent reviewers assessed the items, 2,369 items were retained for use in the product.

TECHNICAL. To assess the reliability and validity of the STAR Early Literacy test, results from two studies were used: the calibration study outlined above and a pilot research study. The pilot research study differed from the calibration study in that it assessed the technical characteristics of an adaptive version of the STAR Early Literacy. The sample consisted of 11,000 students from 84 schools in the U.S. and Canada. Again, although the sample consisted of a broad range of students in terms of geographic region, school system, district size, and socioeconomic status, it is difficult to evaluate the ethnic group distribu-

tion. The authors report that 42.8% of their sample was "Unclassified" in terms of ethnic group affiliation. Moreover, no information is given regarding gender of the students participating.

Both test-retest reliability and generic reliability were reported. Test-retest reliability (typically at 7-day intrval between administrations) was assessed from both the calibration and pilot studies. In the calibration study, 14,000 students took two forms of the 40-item calibration tests with a test-retest correlation of .87 overall. In the pilot study, over 9,000 students took the computer-adaptive 25-item test twice with a test-retest correlation of .86 overall. Although scaled score retest and generic reliability estimates are lower by grade, they seem to be within acceptable ranges (.63–.85). In addition, Standard Errors of Measurement using both conditional and retest methods are reported for the scale scores, domain scores, and skill scores.

Content validity was based on data from the calibration and pilot studies. In both studies, scaled scores increased by age and grade level from prekindergarten to Grade 3. Moreover, grade to grade differences are greater in the earlier grades when more literacy development is occurring and less by Grade 3 when most children have mastered basic literacy skills. To assess concurrent validity, results from STAR Early Literacy tests were compared to other measures of literacy development and to a teacher rating instrument. The students in the calibration study took the STAR Reading 2.1 test, resulting in a correlation of .78. The authors note that the content and format of the two tests are not alike, suggesting that STAR Early Literacy "measures skills that are highly related to the development of reading ability in the early grades" (manual, p. 77). In the pilot study, students took a variety of different reading assessments in the different districts (e.g., Brigance K & 1 Screen for Kindergarten and First Grade, DIAL, Iowa Test of Basic Skills, Stanford Achievement Test). Average correlations between these measures and STAR Early Literacy range from .57 to .64 for the different grades. Using the corrected average correlation, the authors note that STAR Early Literacy measures similar literacy skills as do many of the other tests but also measures unique literacy skills as well.

No predictive statistics are reported. Moreover, no statistics are reported comparing results of children of different demographic characteristics (e.g., socioeconomic status, gender, ethnicity).

COMMENTARY AND SUMMARY. The authors note that this is a criterion-referenced test and not a norm-referenced test, that students are compared to a standard and not to one another. Even so, information regarding gender and an explanation of the ethnic distribution are warranted. It seems critical to examine whether there are gender or ethnic differences in performance. Given the exclusive reliance on the computer, it seems that children who have more experience with using a computer may have an advantage, thus biasing the scores. Moreover, although information is given regarding the relationship of STAR Early Literacy with other measures, no information is given regarding the specific domains or the 41 skill areas. There is no evidence provided that would support the fact that the items included in phonics, for example, indeed measure phonics knowledge. It would have been helpful if comparisons had been made between the different domains and other measures that purport to examine similar domain areas. Until this weakness is addressed in further validation studies, it is cautionary to assert that STAR Early Literacy is measuring component literacy skills. However, it is appropriate to use the STAR Early Literacy for individual readiness screening and overall early literacy assessment.

Review of STAR Early Literacy® by SANDRA B. WARD, Associate Professor of Education, The College of William and Mary, Williamsburg, VA:
DESCRIPTION. STAR Early Literacy is an individually administered, computerized test of early literacy skills of beginning readers in kindergarten through second grade. However, the publishers assert that the instrument will be suitable for teachers' use in assessing prekindergarten students and/or students in Grade 3 or beyond. The instrument assesses proficiency across seven domains: General Readiness, Graphophonemic Knowledge, Phonemic Awareness, Phonics, Comprehension, Structural Analysis, and Vocabulary. The uses of STAR Early Literacy, according to the publishers, include assessment of early literacy skills, planning instruction and intervention, and monitoring student progress. The average completion time for the test is 10 minutes with 25 multiple-choice items per administration. The computer input necessary for test completion is limited to the student's ability to move the mouse pointer to a target and to click the mouse pointer on the target. A major advantage of the STAR Early Literacy computer administration is the adaptive testing component. The program selects items of varying difficulty based on the responses of the individual. This enables the number of items to be vastly reduced and increases the efficiency of the test.

STAR Early Literacy includes a software manual and installation guide that facilitate the installation of the computer program. Directions are thorough and easy to follow. Examinees are provided with directions, mouse training, and a practice session prior to testing. Test items are multiple-choice format that requires the examinee to indicate the correct answer among three choices. This design does introduce some measurement error due to guessing. The items are clearly presented to the student; however, the latency between the item presentation and the ability of the software to accept an examinee's response seems too long for the examinee with average to above average ability and basic computer skills.

STAR Early Literacy produces three scores: scaled scores, domain scores, and skill scores. Scaled scores represent nonlinear monotonic transformations of Rasch ability estimates. The range of scaled scores is 300–900, and the scores correspond to 100 times the age range for which STAR Early Literacy was designed. Thus the scaled scores are roughly indicative of the typical age of students with similar performance. Means and standard deviations for each grade level are provided in the manual based on the calibration study sample and pilot study sample. The user is encouraged to use the values from the pilot study because the pilot study implemented the computer-adaptive procedures. Additionally, the publisher provides percentile rank values that correspond with various scores. Literacy classifications are provided based on scaled scores. Students with scores below 675 are classified as "emergent readers," those with scores between 675–774 are "transitional readers," and those with scores above 775 are "probable readers." These cut points are competency based. The distribution of literacy classification by grade is provided. Domain and skill scores are proficiency scores. The domain score is a statistical estimate of the percentage of items the student would be expected to answer correctly if all items in the domain were administered. Similarly, the skill score is an estimate of the percentage of items in a specific skill area the student would be expected to answer correctly. The distribution statistics by grade level for the seven domain scores and skills areas from the calibration study and pilot study are provided. Again the user is encouraged to use the data from the pilot study.

A detailed description of score interpretation is provided in the manual. Test users can generate a consolidated score report that aggregates each student's performance in a class over multiple test administrations. The manual also includes a helpful section of frequently asked questions. Overall, the test is user-friendly.

DEVELOPMENT. The test authors are commended for their efforts in test and item development. Items for the STAR Early Literacy were developed through careful writing, reviewing and editing and with consideration of the seven domains of proficiency assessed by the instrument. Item Response Theory (IRT) calibration was used to place every item on a continuous scale of difficulty. This was accomplished through a large calibration study in which 300 schools in the United States participated. Although data regarding the sample characteristics with respect to geographic region, SES, school size, and ethnicity were provided, there were no data on the range of student abilities at each grade/age level. A Rasch IRT model was used to calibrate items for item difficulty and item discrimination. The evaluation of these results produced a final item bank of 2,369 items available for use in adaptive testing. This probably provides a sufficient number of items for retesting without concern for previous exposure to items. The publishers supply the distribution of items by domain in the manual.

TECHNICAL. In order to collect additional psychometric data with a computer-adaptive version of the instrument, a pilot study was conducted with 11,000 students in 84 schools. This sample overrepresented the southeast region and underrepresented the northeast region of the country. Additionally, there was overrepresentation of students with average SES and underrepresentation of students with high SES in this pilot sample. Consequently, data on the technical adequacy of the instrument may not be representative of the general population.

The reliability coefficients reported in the manual are adequate for screening purposes. Test-retest reliability coefficients for the adaptive administration of STAR Early Literacy were computed on the data from the pilot study, including 9,000 students with 1 to 7 days between administrations. The average correlation was .86. The test-retest correlations ranged from .63 at the prekindergarten level to .70 at Grade 1. The authors provide a fair analysis of the test's generic reliability derived from the individual estimates of measurement error. The average reliability coefficient across all grades was .92. Taken together, the test-retest reliability coefficients and the generic reliability coefficients provide upper and lower bounds of the test's reliability.

Data are provided to support the instrument's content, construct, and concurrent validity. Support for the content validity is demonstrated in the purposeful and thorough approach to item development and selection. Construct validity is supported by the increase of scores with age/grade level as would be expected for reading ability. Although the overall correlation between STAR Early Literacy and teachers' ratings of students' skills was .69, the correlations fell dramatically at individual grade levels and ranged from .33–.50. The strongest correlation between the STAR Early Literacy and other measures of reading ability was with the STAR Reading Test (.78), a similar computer-adaptive test. However, the correlations between STAR Early Literacy and other less similar measures of reading ability were considerably lower. It should be noted that the correlations between STAR Early Literacy and other measures of reading ability are based on small sample sizes and may not be generalizable to the larger population.

COMMENTARY. STAR Early Literacy is a useful tool for teachers in screening students' early literacy skills in prekindergarten through third grade. The authors adhered to rigorous procedures and standards in the test's development. Additionally, sufficient information is provided regarding the test's reliability, and the data support the intended use of the instrument as a screener of early literacy skills. Validity data for STAR Early Literacy are generally adequate; however, the data support interpretation of the overall score. More research is needed on the domain and skill scores before they can be used confidently to plan instruction.

SUMMARY. STAR Early Literacy is a user-friendly computer-adaptive screening instrument of early literacy skills. The technical adequacy of the instrument, including item development, reliability, and validity is robust. STAR Early Literacy can be a useful tool for teachers who want to efficiently measure early literacy, monitor student progress, and plan instruction. Interpretation of the results should focus on the overall score because the validity data do not adequately support the individual interpretation of domain and skill scores for educational decision making or planning instruction.

[241]

STAR Math®.

Purpose: Designed as a computer-adaptive math test and database to place students at the appropriate math level.
Population: Grades 3–12.
Publication Dates: 1998–1999.
Scores: Total score only (grade-equivalent and percentile scores).
Administration: Individual.
Price Data, 1998: $1,499 per school license for up to 200 students, installation guide, instruction manual, 10 Quick Reference cards, technical manual (1999, 110 pages), 1-year Expert Support Plan, and Pre-Test Instruction Kit; $399 per single-computer license, Quick Install card, instruction manual, Quick Reference card; 1-year Expert Support Plan, and Pre-Test Instruction Kit.
Time: Untimed, (15) minutes.
Comments: Available for Macintosh and IBM-compatible computers; manuals are included in PDF format on CD-ROM; can be repeated at no extra cost through school year to track growth.
Author: Advantage Learning Systems, Inc.
Publisher: Renaissance Learning, Inc.

Review of the STAR Math® by JOSEPH C. CIECHALSKI, Professor of Counselor Education, East Carolina University, Greenville, NC:

DESCRIPTION. STAR Math is a computer-adaptive test and database designed to assess students' mathematical abilities in Grades 3–12 in 15 minutes or less. It is divided into two major parts, each containing 12 multiple-choice type items. The first part of the test includes two strands: Numeration Concepts and Computation Items, whereas the second part consists of six strands: Word Problems, Estimation, Statistics, Charts, and Graphs, Geometry, Measurement, and Algebra.

There are two primary purposes of the STAR Math test. First, it provides teachers with a quick estimate of their students' mathematical achievement levels based on national norms. Second, it provides a means of assessing growth over periods

of time. The authors emphasize that the STAR Math test is not intended to be used as an end-of-period performance report or for determining eligibility for promotion.

Administering the test is relatively easy using the Pre-Test Instruction Kit. It takes about 2 minutes to read the instructions to the students. Included with the instructions are overheads that show the students how the test items will look, how to respond to the test items, and how to enter their responses on the computer.

Before administering the test, there is a practice session. When the student has answered three consecutive practice items correctly, the computer program takes the student to the first item on the test. However, if the student fails to answer three items in a row by the end of the practice session, the program will stop and direct the student to ask the teacher for assistance.

The actual administration of the test begins with an item that has a difficulty level about one or two grade levels below grade placement. Subsequent items are generated according to the responses made by the student. If the previous item was answered incorrectly, the next item would be easier. Students may take the test up to five times per year. Item reuse is kept to a minimum because the item bank contains 1,434 items.

The STAR Math test yields scaled scores, percentile ranks, normal curve equivalents (NCE), and grade equivalents (GE). Percentile ranks and GE are derived from the scaled scores obtained in the STAR Math norming program.

DEVELOPMENT. The development of the STAR Math test consisted of three stages. In Stage 1, the content of the test was considered. To develop the items, the authors reviewed the content of mathematics textbooks, state curriculum guides, the Curriculum and Evaluation Standards for School Mathematics of the National Council of Teachers of Mathematics, and content specifications from the National Assessment of Educational Progress and the Third International Mathematics and Science Study. Based on their reviews, objectives were written and test specifications were organizes into eight strands, identified earlier in this review. Each of the eight strands is described in detail in the technical manual and all of the objectives are included in an appendix of the manual.

The second stage consisted of an item calibration and analysis of the 2,450 items developed in Stage 1. A national sample of over 44,000 students in Grades 3–12 were selected and stratified according to geographic region, school size, and socioeconomic status. To facilitate in the data collection, the authors constructed five levels of test booklets, consisting of 30 items in each of two sections. A description of each test booklet, grade level, item (anchor and unique items), and test form is contained in a table in the manual. Anchor items were used in equating the test forms and test levels in the analysis and the development of scale scores. The data were analyzed by level using item analyses and item response theory (IRT) methods. Of the initial 2,450 items, approximately 1,500 items were retained for additional analyses. In the final analysis, all of the test forms and levels were equated to ensure that all items could be placed on a scale covering Grades 3–12.

The third stage of development was determined by the student's performance during testing on the computer. Unlike traditional paper-and-pencil testing where students attempt to answer all of the items on the test, on the STAR Math test, a computer-adaptive test, students are tested only on items that are appropriate for their level. The level of difficulty of subsequent items will depend on how well or poorly the student is performing on the test.

TECHNICAL. Norms for the STAR Math test were developed in the spring of 1998. The norms represented the United States population according to geographic region; per-grade district enrollment, which included four groups (<200, 200–499, 500–1999, and >2000 students); and socioeconomic status. Over 400 schools agreed to participate in the initial norming process. The final norming sample consisted of approximately 25,800 students from 252 schools representing 42 states. In addition, the norming also considered data on gender and ethnic groups. The norming data were analyzed to determine scaled scores, percentile ranks, grade-equivalents, and normal curve equivalents.

The reliability of the STAR Math test was examined using the test-retest method with alternate forms and the estimation of generic reliability method. Test-retest reliability estimates were calculated using scaled scores from 1,541 students who took multiple STAR Math tests during the norming process. The authors note that little time elapsed between the first and second administration (median 5 days); however, the actual time interval is not reported. To examine test-retest reliability of the test, the STAR Math software program started both tests at the same point. The resulting reliability coefficients ranged from the mid .70s to the mid .80s.

The second method for assessing reliability was the generic estimate of reliability. This method is based on using the entire norming sample (25,795 students) utilizing the item response theory method. The resulting reliability coefficients ranged from the mid .80s to the high .80s.

Evidence of content validity is presented in an appendix of the technical manual that lists the content objectives for each of the eight strands of the test. In addition, the section on content specifications in the technical manual explains each of the eight strands in detail.

To address construct validity of the test, scores on the STAR Math test were correlated with scores on other standardized tests such as the California Achievement Test, California Test of Basic Skills, the Iowa Test of Basic Skills, the Metropolitan Achievement Test, the Stanford Achievement Test, and statewide tests. All of the tests were administered within 18 months of the spring norming of the STAR Math test. The resulting validity coefficients ranged from a low of .60 to a high of .88. It is important to note that the authors report that the validation of the STAR Math is an ongoing process.

COMMENTARY. The strengths of the STAR Math test reflect the positive characteristics of adaptive testing in general. It can be administered quickly and test items are generated based on the performance level of individual students. Students can be tested several times with the assurance that test items will not be repeated. The test scores are accurate and the results are available immediately after testing.

I was especially impressed with the quality and comprehensiveness of the accompanying documentation. The Installation Guide contains easy-to-follow instructions on installing and registering the program on either Macintosh or Windows systems. The Software Manual contains information on starting and working in the system as well as troubleshooting problems. STAR Math's Technical Manual is clearly written and conforms to the *Standards for Educational and Psychological Testing* (AERA, APA, & NCME, 1999).

I have two concerns about the STAR Math test. First, although content validity was demon-

substituted for the error variance term, and the overall scale score variance was substituted for the total test score variance. Thus, these estimates of reliability can be computed using the entire norm sample, as opposed to a subset. As expected, these estimates are higher than the alternative forms estimates of reliability and range from .81 to .88.

Some validity evidence is provided in terms of the correlation of normal curve equivalency scores obtained in STAR Math, and several other published tests. This evidence was obtained from schools that participated in the norming process and were able to provide additional student test data. However, the lack of planned validity studies is a major flaw of STAR Math. Although additional test data were collected from over 9,000 students, the multitude of grade levels and additional tests represented in these analyses result in a rather small number of students considered for any particular test and form. The largest number of students participating in any one analysis is approximately 200; however, most analyses have a much smaller number of students. Furthermore, the majority of these correlations fall below .80. This could be due to the strong emphasis on computational skills in STAR Math.

COMMENTARY. At first glance, one of the strengths of this system would appear to be its adaptive capabilities, allowing one to assess examinees of any ability by ensuring that the content is not too easy or too difficult. However, the system does not seem to be using an efficient algorithm nor fully capitalizing on the adaptive features. Upon closer inspection, it is apparent that items are primarily measuring computational skills and remembering of standard formulas. As a fictitious third grade student, I was given approximately six geometry items, all asking me to compute the area of either a triangle or a rectangle. The majority of items required the answer to some computational mathematics problem that was presented symbolically. None of the items required any higher order thinking or problem-solving skills. Furthermore, for the first half of the test the fourth response option is always "NG" for "Not Given." This was done, according to the test developers, to ensure that students do not estimate, but rather compute the answers. However, this response option seemed confusing and contradictory to the current reform movement in mathematics, which stresses estimation.

Furthermore, although I was a "very smart" third grader, obtaining the correct answers to all of the 24 items presented, I was never presented with any items that would be considered appropriate for high school students, although the test is designed for Grades 3 through 12. I never received an item that even remotely resembled anything related to high school algebra or geometry. Yet my individualized score report stated that I was ready for college preparatory mathematics curriculum! My score report also advised me to "maintain my computational skills," the obvious philosophy underlying the test specifications.

SUMMARY. The technical manual provided with this software is complete (if you can find it, that is; it is only provided in a folder on the CD-ROM, entitled "Extras") and the test developers have attempted to provide validity and reliability evidence. Furthermore, the program comes complete with user-friendly manuals to help with installation and implementation. However, the test primarily assesses computational skills and although all of the bells and whistles are nice, the hefty price of $1,499 per 200 students seems like a lot to pay to evaluate basic computational skills. Furthermore, the fact that one can prepare a multitude of individual score reports with the click of a button is a bit scary because there is no way of knowing how the diagnostic information is determined. The documentation does not describe how or from where or by whom this diagnostic information comes. Overall, this test is not very well aligned with current research in mathematics education or NCTM standards.

[242]

STAR Reading® Version 2.2.

Purpose: A computer-adaptive reading test and database "allowing teachers to … [quickly] assess students' reading abilities."

Population: Grades 1–12.

Publication Dates: 1996–2002.

Scores: Total score only.

Administration: Individual.

Price Data, 2001: $499 per single-computer license kit (up to 40 students) including Software Manual, Installation Guide, CD-ROM (which also includes technical manual), pre-test instructions, quick reference card, and 12-month support plan; $1,499 per network-wide license kit (up to 200 students, expansions available); for expansion prices contact publisher (800) 338-4204.

Time: (10) minutes.

Comments: Revision of STAR Reading® Version 1.x; provides grade equivalents, percentile scores, and instructional reading level; includes software allowing teacher to generate diagnostic reports; may be administered up to 5 times per year; version 2.x can use the same database as other software from the same company. System requirements: Windows or Macintosh, CD-ROM drive, mouse, 640x480 monitor, 256 color monitor, 8 MB RAM, 25 MB drive space, System 7.1 or higher (Macintosh) or Windows 3.1 or higher and MS-DOS version 3.3 or higher.

Authors: Renaissance Learning, Inc.

Publisher: Renaissance Learning, Inc.

Cross References: For reviews by Theresa Volpe-Johnstone and Sandra Ward of the original edition, see 14:368.

Review of the STAR Reading® Version 2.2 by LORI NEBELSICK-GULLETT, Consultant: Educational Measurement, Planning, and Accountability, Castle Rock, CO:

DESCRIPTION. STAR Reading® is a computer-adaptive test designed to assess students' reading abilities in a classroom setting. Item response theory (IRT) is used to support item calibration, ability estimation, and the Adaptive Branching™ process. The primary purposes are to provide teachers with estimates of students' instructional reading levels, to place reading level estimates relative to national norms, and to provide a metric of growth in reading ability across an academic year. The results are not indicators of eligibility for promotion or placement in special education programs.

The STAR Reading program requires an examinee to use only five keys during testing. This design feature insures simplicity, particularly for young examinees, by eliminating potential difficulties with using a mouse. Pretest instructions and practice items are easy to use and support consistency of administration. Initial item difficulty is set below grade placement for first time test takers and below the previous reading ability estimate for subsequent test sessions. Examinees complete 25 items per test session with most examinees completing a session in less than 10 minutes. An updated estimate of reading ability is computed after each item response using a proprietary Bayesian-modal IRT method until one correct and one incorrect response are obtained. The software then uses a proprietary Maximum-Likelihood IRT procedure. Justification for the 25-item termination point was not provided. All items administered in Grades 1 and 2, and the first 20 items in all other grades, are vocabulary-in-context items that present a contextualized sentence with one word missing. Students above Grade 2 answer an additional five cloze-type items embedded within longer "authentic" passages. Responses to the 20 vocabulary items set the initial difficulty level for the final five items. All items require examinees to choose the correct answer from options designed to fit semantically and/or syntactically at the appropriate vocabulary level. Time limits, varying by grade level and item type, are imposed for each item. Test administrators can override both the time limits (Version 2.2) and the estimated instructional level used to select initial items.

The software provides criterion- and norm-referenced scores. The criterion-referenced score is the Instructional Reading Level (IRL), which compares performance to vocabulary lists based on the Educational Development Laboratory's (EDL) Core vocabulary. The program uses Rasch ability scores and Rasch difficulty parameters of graded vocabulary items to estimate the IRL as the highest reading level at which an examinee can answer at least 80% of the items correctly. The norm-referenced scores include percentile ranks (PR), normal curve equivalents (NCE), and grade equivalents (GE). STAR Reading provides several reports supporting program management and several reports focused on student performance. Diagnostic, Growth, Snapshot, and/or profile information for students and groups is available through the performance reports. In addition, Zone of Proximal Development scores and diagnostic codes, both unique to STAR Reading, provide readability range information for selecting books and descriptive text to characterize readers across stages of development. Insufficient information was provided for evaluation of these indices.

DEVELOPMENT. The publishers cite the use of IRT, expansion of the item bank, standardization of test length, and the addition of passages for Grades 3–12 as program improvements in version 2.0 (technical manual, pp. 1–3). EDL's *A Revised Core Vocabulary* (1969) was cited as the most appropriate reference point for test development (technical manual, p. 2-2). Information regarding the resource selection process and a description of other potential resources were not provided.

The item bank contains 1,159 vocabulary items and 250 "authentic" passage items that extend across the difficulty range and support up to five test sessions per year with minimal re-exposure to the same items. Detailed specifications guided development of all items. Description of the item development process was adequate for the "authentic" passage items but limited for vocabulary items. Bias was addressed during item writing; a sensitivity review focused on gender and ethnicity. No statistical analyses of bias were reported.

Item validation, focused on technical and statistical quality, was referenced (March, 1995) but not described. Outcomes were used to update the EDL vocabulary lists but no explanation or examples were provided to support the validity and applicability of these changes. Item calibration was conducted using 838 vocabulary items from Version 1.x, 836 new vocabulary items, and 459 "authentic" passage items. The item calibration sample (n = 27,807) was balanced across geographic region, socioeconomic status, enrollment, and ethnicity. Item calibration was conducted using paper-and-pencil, nonadaptive forms with attention to minimizing order effects. The use of anchor items supported the equating of test forms and levels and the development of a continuous scale. Classical and item response theory statistics such as discrimination, difficulty, and fit were used by review panels to eliminate items. To maintain continuity with the Version 1.x scale, a linking study was conducted as part of the norming process. Over 4,000 students completed both test versions through a counterbalanced design. Equipercentile equating, weighted for sample size differences across grade levels, was used to link the 1.x and 2.x scales and to develop conversion tables. The resulting scaled scores, although not easily interpreted by most users, provide a continuous scale across grade levels and form the basis for the program's norm-referenced scores.

TECHNICAL. The STAR Reading computer-adaptive test was normed using a sample of 29,627 students. A portion of the norming sample was tested twice to support either test-retest reliability or the linking of Version 1.x and 2.x scales. To adjust for sample imbalance, the norming data were weighted by region and SES at all grade levels. Type and size were added for Grades 1–8. Analysis of norming data by ethnicity and gender showed slightly higher scores for females and a tendency for minority students to score .5–1 standard deviation lower than nonminority students. Although this is typical of standardized tests in many areas, the ethnicity data may not present a clear picture due to the large proportion (39.5%) of students who were unclassified. Differential performance by economic status was not evaluated but may have enhanced the results of the norming study.

A comparison of the 2.0 norms with those from Version 1.0 indicated higher median scores in Grades 1 and 2 for the newer norms. Based on these differences, the newer norms were replaced by the 1.0 norms for Grades 1 and 2. The deliberations supporting this decision were not described.

Alternate forms reliability estimates were computed for two studies. Over 2,000 students took parallel forms based on the adaptive procedure, constrained to prevent the reuse of items. Reliability estimates, corrected for score variations from the total norming sample, ranged from .79 to .91 across grade levels with an overall value of .94. Analysis of the data from the linking study produced similar estimates even though the tests differed in terms of length, item content/form, and the use of IRT. "Generic" reliability estimates were computed for each grade in the norming sample using error and score variances in the classical formula. These values ranged from .89 to .92.

Content validity of the STAR Reading test was supported through the item development process. The "authentic" passages used for Grades 3 through 12 might provide a more meaningful context, greater opportunity to apply reading strategies, and, consequently, more accurate information in terms of overall reading ability. To support construct validity, correlations between STAR Reading test performance and student scores from other standardized tests were computed for students in the norming sample. The clear majority of the reported correlations were between .60 and .90, suggesting some commonality in the underlying constructs measured. A meta-analysis of the information was not provided.

COMMENTARY. The manuals for STAR Reading are well written and easy to use. The technical manual provides a clear, useful explanation of the interpretation and use of GE scores and a valuable comparison of IRL and GE scores. Incorporating this information into the Score Definition report would support teachers and administrators who may not read the technical manual.

The usefulness of the STAR Reading test may be impacted by a number of factors. First, the EDL, although justified as a "soundly developed, validated list," may be dated in its presentation of materials relevant to a diverse examinee population. The publishers did not explain the basis of the updates to the EDL and provided no information in regard to the potential impact of culture and background experiences on understanding item context/content. Second, the decision to use 1.0 norms for Grades 1 and 2 may not be justified. The performance of these students in the 2.0 norming study could have been influenced by changes in instructional practice that support the ongoing emphasis on reading in the early grades. It was not clear that this possibility was investigated. Finally, the items used to estimate reading ability are narrow in focus and remain heavily influenced by the development of a specific vocabulary. Consequently, this test should be used as one of several indicators of student growth and/or achievement, particularly for early readers.

SUMMARY. Given the growing understanding of and attention to the development and maintenance of strong reading skills, this computer adaptive test provides teachers with a method of estimating reading ability without taking excessive time away from instruction. Although the program provides ready access to multiple indices useful for planning and decision making at the classroom, campus, and district levels, results of this test should not be used in isolation. The item format provides restricted information for Grades 1 and 2 and is expanded to only a limited degree in the upper grades. Research focused on the validity of the test results for the stated purposes should continue.

Review of STAR Reading® Version 2.2 by BETSY B. WATERMAN, Professor, Counseling and Psychological Services Department, and DAVID M. SARGENT, Associate Professor of Psychology, State University of New York at Oswego, Oswego, NY:

DESCRIPTION. The STAR Reading® computer-adaptive reading test and database is a computer-based system that includes a brief reading test and record-keeping software. The test is designed to determine the instructional reading levels of students from 1st to 12th grades, compare students' performance to national norms, and to track an individual's growth in reading across grades. It is a Renaissance Learning™ product,

and, according to the authors, the software is compatible with other Renaissance Learning programs (e.g., STAR Math®; 241) in terms of record-keeping (i.e., data-based information or student performance). The software can be used on either Macintosh or Windows platformswith relatively modest hardware requirements (i.e., Macintosh System 7.1; Windows 3.1; 8 MB RAM; 25 MB available on the Hard Drive). A CD-ROM, mouse, and VGA monitor are required. A step-by-step installation guide is provided, including diagrams with depictions of window icons primarily from the Macintosh version. Comprehensive information about using the software is presented in the manual. The program allows the tester to add and enroll students; edit records; move information about students from one grade to the next; add and delete whole classes; and generate, customize, and print reports. The purchaser of the program is entitled to toll-free technical support for a period of one year.

The testing program itself involves 25 fill-in-the-blank sentences followed by a list of three to four possible answers from which the student must select. The actual testing period cannot be initiated until the student has successfully answered 3 practice items. Difficulty levels are driven by a student's responses; that is, difficulty level rises with each correct response and reduces with each incorrect response (referred to as Adaptive Branching). Time for each question is limited to 60 seconds for first and second grades. A limit of 45 seconds is imposed for the first 20 questions and 90 seconds for the longer, final 5 questions for Grades 3 through 12. The program can be modified to extend time limits for students who require such modifications. The authors note, however, that such students are not included in the normed sample. A visual cue (a clock in the corner of the screen) warns students 15 seconds before their time runs out. Unanswered questions are counted as incorrect responses. Students select the answer of their choice by striking the numbers 1, 2, 3, or 4 and the enter/return key. They may correct or change responses at any point during the allowed time period prior to hitting the enter/return key. Scoring of the test is done automatically by the computer and can be displayed by accessing one of the many reports found within the management program. Grade equivalents, normal curve equivalents,scaled scores (ranging from 0–1,400), instructional reading level scores, and percentile ranks are all available. Instructions for the test have been standardized and cards that are designed to look similar to what the student will see on the computer are used by the examiner to acquaint the student with the program. According to the authors, a student may take the STAR Reading test up to five times during a single year because the computer program keeps track of the questions the student has previously been given.

DEVELOPMENT. The current STAR Reading test (v. 2.2) is an updated version of a previous STAR Reading test (STAR Reading 1.x). The newer version includes a much larger item pool and longer, authentic text items for Grades 3 and above. The information provided in the technical manual for the STAR Reading test included very limited information about the means used to develop the testing stimuli itself. The authors offer noncited explanations to support the use of "vocabulary-in-context" and computer-based methods for measuring reading achievement. The computer was selected, according to the authors, because of its ability to better match a student's ability level with the reading task (i.e., the computer can automatically "branch" to easier items if the student misses a question). The Educational Development Laboratory's *A Revised Core Vocabulary* provided the reference for the grade level vocabulary words used in the test items and items were reviewed for cultural, ethnic, or gender bias or language that might be considered offensive. Items were calibrated for difficulty in a study initiated in 1998 (N = 27,807) using both traditional item analysis techniques and the Rasch model. The original 2,133 items were reduced to 1,409. These items were then ordered from easiest to most difficult.

TECHNICAL. Norming of the STAR Reading test took place in the spring of 1999. The sample was large (nearly 30,000 students) and representative of the four general regions of the United States, type of school system (i.e., public vs. non-public), socioeconomic status, and racial/ethnic makeup. Test-retest reliability across an interval of 1 week resulted in adequate reliability coefficients that ranged from .79 to .91. Reliability was also estimated using the conditional standard error of measurement and the variance of the IRT-based observed variance, and resulted in an overall coefficient, across grades, of .95 and ranged from .82 to .89 within grades.

Although the means of examining content validity was not included in the manual, the authors did include an extensive report of construct validity. Construct validity, however, was examined using test scores from a variety of other reading measures that were separated in time, in certain cases, anywhere from 1 to 3 years. \ For Grades 1 through 6, validity coefficients generally ranged from .36 to .97. For Grades 7 to 9, coefficients ranged from .44 to .87 using the California Achievement Test, Comprehensive Test of Basic Skills, Explore, Gates-MacGinitie Reading Test, Iowa Test of Basic Skills, Missouri Mastery Achievement Test, and the Metropolitan Achievement Test. A comparison with the Stanford Achievement Test revealed coefficients that ranged from .25 to .90. No concurrent validity was reported.

COMMENTARY. Once the software is installed (simple menus) and set up (some hidden requirements), the STAR Reading test is quick to administer. The "branching" item feature that is available in a computer format is also a strength of this test. The graphics for the actual test are helpful in that the students can actually view the answer they have selected (i.e., it is visible on the screen following selection), can see their response in context (the answer "fills-in" the blank), and can change an answer prior to pressing the enter/return key.

A number of problems, however, exist with this measure. Despite empirical evidence to the contrary, the test stimuli appear to be difficult for the early grades and may not be appropriate for very weak readers, especially in first grade. The breadth of information obtained is restricted making diagnostic use of this test limited, which is consistent with the purpose of the assessment as a measure of reading achievement, not as a diagnostic instrument. The testing stimuli do not match day-to-day reading demands (i.e., cloze method), making generalizability questionable.

Concerns also exist about the usability of the computer software. Installing and using the STAR Reading computer program involves the use of a STAR Reading 2.2 CD-ROM disk that appears to install on Windows XP with an easy-to-use standard installation wizard. After the "Finish" screen the user is prompted to register in order to use the product, requiring a password for any operation. With the XP system, the password subroutine effectively locks up the system program. Efforts to reinstall the program or enter a new password resulted in an error window. On Windows 2000, installation was much the same as Windows XP, following the same setup screens. Again, the user could not progress beyond the password screen without information from the technical line. The toll free technical line, however, was quickly accessed and offered usable information. The detailed, extensive software manual, although well organized, was still cumbersome, but essential, to use.

Concerns related to the test construction, scoring, and norming procedures also exist. Research support for the use of the cloze method as the only testing format is simply missing in any discussion within the manuals. The scaled scores are also virtually uninterpretable. Weighted and unweighted means and standard deviations are presented in a table in the technical manual (a manual that was finally found within the "extras" folder on the CD after three calls to the publisher). Finally, no concurrent validity evidence is reported.

SUMMARY. Although the STAR Reading computer-adaptive reading test and database provides a computer format that, once it is set up, offers a quick and easy method of test administration and scoring, it also limits the type and breadth of the reading skills that can be sampled, lessening the diagnostic utility of this measure.

It appears that the STAR Reading test may have some usefulness as a prescreening tool for identifying those students who are at risk for doing poorly on end-of-year reading tests. Given the push for successful student performance on school or government mandated tests, this may be of some limited benefit as it allows for the placement of students more accurately in appropriate book levels, the identification of students who need further skill practice, and the provision of students with opportunities to practice testing skills. The length of time needed to become skilled at entering, maintaining, and interpreting data when compared with the extremely limited amount of information gained about specific reading skill performance, however, makes use of this measure questionable for any other purpose.

[243]

STAR Supplementary Tests of Achievement in Reading.

Purpose: "Designed to supplement the assessments that teachers make about their pupils' progress and achievement in reading."

Population: Ages 8–13.
Publication Date: 2001.
Administration: Group.
Levels, 2: STAR Test (4–6), STAR Test (7–9).
Forms, 2: A, B.
Price Data, 2002: NZ$38.70 per specimen set (specify level) including teacher's manual (35 pages), 1 test booklet each of Forms A and B, 1 set answer keys each of Forms A and B; NZ$9.90 per 10 test booklets (specify Form A or B, specify level); NZ$9 per photocopiable masters answer key (Level 4–6, specify Form A or B); NZ$9 per photocopiable masters marking key (Level 7–9, specify Form A or B).
Comments: Normed on children living in New Zealand.
Author: Warwick B. Elley.
Publisher: New Zealand Council for Educational Research [New Zealand].
  a) STAR TEST (4–6).
  Scores, 4: Word Recognition, Sentence Comprehension, Paragraph Comprehension, Vocabulary Range.
  Time: 20(35) minutes.
  b) STAR TEST (7–9).
  Scores, 6: Word Recognition, Sentence Comprehension, Paragraph Comprehension, Vocabulary Range, The Language of Advertising, Reading Different Genres or Styles of Writing.
  Time: 30(45) minutes.

Review of the STAR Supplementary Tests of Achievement in Reading by JOHN W. YOUNG, Associate Professor of Educational Statistics and Measurement, Rutgers University, New Brunswick, NJ:

DESCRIPTION AND DEVELOPMENT. The Supplementary Tests of Achievement in Reading (STAR), Years 4–9 (Forms A and B) are assessments of reading ability developed by the New Zealand Council for Educational Research, and are designed to supplement the other assessments of students' skills used by teachers. The STAR Reading Tests are intended to help teachers make better judgment of several aspects of their students' reading ability, as defined in the national curriculum set forth by the New Zealand Ministry of Education. The STAR Test 4–6 is designed for students in Years 4 to 6 in school and consists of four short subtests (Word Recognition, Sentence Comprehension, Paragraph Comprehension, and Vocabulary Range). The STAR Test 7–9 is designed for students in Years 7 to 9 in school and consists of six short subtests, the first four of which are the same as in the STAR Test 4–6 plus the language of advertising and reading different genres. The STAR Test 4–6 and 7–9 each have two forms, A and B. Total testing time required for STAR Test 4–6 is 35 minutes, whereas STAR Test 7–9 requires 45 minutes.

The STAR Reading Tests were developed by the author, Warwick Elley, during the 1980s and 1990s. As part of an evaluation of a teacher-training project in 1984, test sections assessing reading skills were developed by the author. Later, in 1996, the New Zealand Ministry of Education sought to develop a comprehensive reading test for an evaluation of the Duffy "Books in Homes" project. The present version of the STAR Reading Tests is a revised version of the test used in this evaluation, and is intended to fill the perceived need for a wider range of reading tests in Years 4 to 9 for use throughout New Zealand.

TECHNICAL. To obtain national norms, the STAR Test 4–6 was administered to a nationally representative sample of approximately 1,500 students in each of Years 4, 5, and 6 in 52 schools in New Zealand. One-half of the sample, randomly chosen, took Form A and the other half took Form B. The norming and standardization sample appears to be representative of the population of schools in New Zealand with respect to school size and decile level. All schools completed testing according to instructions at the end of 1999. A similar process was used with the STAR Test 7–9 with students in 68 schools in Years 7 and 8 and students in 48 schools in Year 9 used for the norming sample. The percentage of schools in the sample at each decile level and school size were almost identical to the national population. Testing for the STAR Test 7–9 took place in March and April of 2001.

The alternate forms reliability of the STAR Test 4–6 for a sample of 91 students in Year 5 was calculated to be .90. The split-half reliability of the test, based on random samples of 70 to 100 students in the norming sample, was .91 for the Total Score, .87 for the 20-item Paragraph Comprehension subtest, and from .63 to .76 for the other 10-item subtests. For the STAR Test 7–9, the alternate forms reliability based on a sample of students in Years 7 and 8 from two large schools in Auckland, tested 1 month apart, was calculated to be .92. The split-half reliability for the Total Score was reported as .91 or .92 for each year level, with the subtest reliability values clustered between .60 and .84. For both the STAR Test 4–6 and 7–9, the standard error of measurement for

the Total Score was reported to be about 3 points. Further analyses using students who took the STAR Tests twice within a 3-month period found negligible practice effects.

The content of the STAR Tests is based on reading process skills, as defined by the 1999 Literacy Task Force and the official curriculum statements on English in New Zealand schools by the Ministry of Education. In each test question, examinees are expected to read words, sentences, or paragraphs; show their ability to decode; read for meaning; respond to cues in the text; and to demonstrate their knowledge of vocabulary. It is not clear which, if any, committees reviewed the tests' specifications to ensure that it faithfully represents the national curriculum or if other content validity studies were conducted. The criterion-related validity of the STAR Tests was assessed by having samples of students take both these tests and the Progressive Achievement Tests of Reading (PAT). For students at two large schools, the correlation of STAR Total Score with PAT Reading Comprehension was .73 for students in Years 4 and 5 and .77 for Year 6 students. For three samples of students who took STAR Test Year 7–9, their scores were correlated .70, .78, and .74 with PAT Reading Comprehension. For another sample of 86 students from a school in Auckland, their STAR Test Year 7–9 scores were correlated .72 with PAT Vocabulary.

COMMENTARY. The author has made good progress in the development of an instrument for assessing the reading skills of New Zealand's students in Years 4 to 9 in school. The STAR Reading Tests appear to follow the national curriculum standards in reading as specified by the Ministry of Education. However, more evidence in the form of additional validity studies would enhance these tests. For example, the author does not clearly state whether the tests were reviewed by any professional committees with knowledge of the national reading standards. If the STAR Tests were reviewed, we do not know the qualifications of the reviewers. Furthermore, the author does not provide any evidence on the construct validity of the STAR Tests. No information on any empirical or judgmental studies regarding the construct validity of the tests was provided in the test manual. The STAR Reading Tests appear to have potential to play an important role in improving primary education in New Zealand, but additional research on the validity of the tests would greatly strengthen these instruments.

SUMMARY. Because the STAR Reading Tests are intended for use with students in New Zealand, one should not attempt to use these tests for any assessment purposes with students in the United States. Instead, the tests can provide useful information for research purposes if one is interested in the New Zealand educational system or in a cross-national or cross-cultural comparison of how reading skills in primary grade students are assessed in different countries. The curriculum and language differences between the United States and New Zealand are sufficiently great to preclude using these tests as assessment tools in classroom settings here.

REVIEWER'S REFERENCE

Literacy Task Force Report. (1999). Wellington, New Zealand: Ministry of Education.

[244]

State-Trait Anger Expression Inventory-2.

Purpose: "Designed to measure the experience, expression, and control of anger for adolescents and adults."

Population: Ages 16 and over.

Publication Dates: 1988–1999.

Acronym: STAXI-2.

Scores, 12: State Anger Scale (Feeling Angry, Feel like Expressing Anger Verbally, Feel like Expressing Anger Physically, Total), Trait Anger Scale (Angry Temperament, Angry Reaction, Total), Angry Expression and Anger Control Scales (Anger Expression—Out, Anger Expression—In, Anger Control—Out, Anger Control—In), Anger Expression Index.

Administration: Group or individual.

Price Data: Available from publisher.

Time: (12–15) minutes.

Author: Charles D. Spielberger.

Publisher: Psychological Assessment Resources, Inc.

Cross References: See T5:2496 (6 references); for reviews by David J. Pittenger and Alan J. Raphael of the Revised Research Edition, see 13:296 (52 references); see also T4:2562 (12 references); for reviews by Bruce H. Biskin and Paul Retzlaff of the STAXI-Research Edition, see 11:379 (8 references).

Review of the State-Trait Anger Expression Inventory—2 by STEPHEN J. FREEMAN, Professor, Counseling and Development, Department of Family Sciences, Texas Woman's University, Denton, TX:

DESCRIPTION. The State-Trait Anger Expression Inventory—2 (STAXI-2) is a revised and expanded version of the STAXI. Expanded from 44 to 57 items, the STAXI-2 purports to measure concisely the experience, expression, and control of anger for adolescents and adults. The inventory consists of six scales (State Anger, Trait Anger, Anger Expression—Out, Anger Expression—In, Anger Control—Out, and Anger Control—In), five subscales (State Anger/Feeling, State Anger/Verbal, State Anger/Physical, Trait Anger/Temperament, and Trait Anger/Reaction), and an Anger Expression Index. Test takers provide self-ratings in three parts of the inventory: How I feel right now (15 items), How I generally feel (10 items), and How I generally react when angry or furious (32 items). Responses are on a 4-point Likert scale.

State Anger assesses the current intensity of angry feelings, and in the STAXI-2, includes three subscales: Feeling Angry, Feeling Like Expressing Anger Verbally, and Feeling Like Expressing Anger Physically. Trait Anger reflects the general disposition of the individual to experience anger and is composed of two subscales: Anger Temperament (the disposition to experience anger without provocation) and Anger Reaction (the frequency that angry feelings are experienced with provocation). Anger Expression—Out measures how often anger is expressed outwardly. Anger Expression—In measures how often anger is experienced but not expressed (suppressed). Anger Control—Out measures the frequency of outward control exerted over anger. Anger Control—In measures how often an individual attempts to control anger by cooling off or calming down. Anger Expression Index is an overall measure of the expression and control of anger.

The STAXI-2 can be administered either individually or in group situations. Examinee responses are automatically recorded on the scoring Form HS. The manual discusses a second form, Form SP, that may be scored with an Optical Character Reader or by hand. Percentile ranks and T-scores corresponding to scale and subscale scores are provided in the Appendixes. The manual also provides a section on guidelines for interpreting high scores on both scales and subscales. Completion of the inventory requires 12 to 15 minutes. The manual recommends an experienced examiner; however, nonclinical personnel can administer and score the inventory after careful review of the manual. Interpretation, however, should be restricted to qualified professionals.

DEVELOPMENT. The development of the STAXI was the product of two decades of independent but related research programs on personality assessment by Charles D. Spielberger and his associates. The inventory was developed for two primary purposes: first, to assess components of anger for detailed evaluation of normal and abnormal personality; and second, to provide a means of measuring the contributions of various components of anger to the development of medical conditions (i.e., hypertension, coronary heart disease, and cancer). The revision and expansion of the STAXI into the STAXI-2 included three major goals: first, to develop subscales for measuring three newly identified components of State Anger; second, to revise Anger Control—Out items that more closely related to the construct; third, to construct a new scale measuring the control of suppressed anger. The manual provides excellent information on scale development and conceptual issues in defining constructs as well as a concise review of related literature associated with the STAXI and anger expression.

TECHNICAL. The normative sample consists of 1,900 individuals ranging in age from 16 to 63 years. Separate norms are provided for females and males in groups: 16 to 19 years, 20 to 29 years, and 30 years and older and further delineated by normal adult, psychiatric population, age, adolescents, and college students. Information on ethnicity and culture is conspicuously absent, and this greatly limits their usage and generalizibility. This deficiency was noted in both Pittenger's (1998) and Trotter's (2001) and Drummond's (2001) *Mental Measurements Yearbook* reviews and clearly limits the potential use of this instrument in many populations.

Evidence of internal consistency reliability is provided by alpha coefficients reported for the STAXI-2 scales ranging from .73 to .95 and from .73 to .93 for the subscales. The manual provides no information on temporal stability (test-retest reliability). These additional reliability estimates could prove helpful in addressing such issues as the ephemeral experience of and the expression of anger.

The manual presents an elaborate discussion of the scale development and validation proceedings for the STAXI-2. Construct-related validity is supported by the results of factor analysis with factor loadings being reported for the scales and subscales. Unfortunately, no information is reported on the concurrent validity of the STAXI-2. However, evidence to support the validity of the STAXI abounds. The author provides extensive data (though dated) on concurrent validity of the STAXI with comparison to such instruments as the Minnesota Multiphasic Personality Inventory (Hostility and Overt Hostility scales), Buss-Durkee Hostility Inventory, and the Eysenck Personality Questionnaire (Psychoticism and Neuroticism). Studies showing relationships between the STAXI scale and subscale scores and elevated blood pressure and hypertension are also included. The bulk of the information on validity is dated with the studies relating to medical disorders and the expression and control of anger being more recent.

COMMENTARY. The STAXI-2 is one of the few instruments currently available to measure the various aspects of anger. The inventory is simple to administer and score. It has a clear focus that results in a high degree of face validity. The manual is clearly written and provides guidelines for interpreting high scores. The section in the manual on "Conceptual Issues and Scale Development" clearly articulates the author's thinking on the concepts of anger expression that led to the development of the STAXI and the STAXI-2. The psychometric information, though not complete, is extensive. A shortcoming of the STAXI-2 is the lack of ethnic and racial information on the norming sample.

SUMMARY. The STAXI-2, like its predecessor, the STAXI, appears to offer what it purports and has much to offer the well-informed clinician. The inventory is the result of over two decades of research and continues to build on its excellent conceptual foundation by further defining and refining concepts relating to anger. Concerns center mainly on the normative sample and the lack of descriptive data concerning the ethnic and cultural make-up of the sample. Until this information is provided, interpretation of the test beyond the reported norms should be limited. Readers, although acknowledging the above cautions, will find the STAXI-2 a sound clinical instrument.

REVIEWER'S REFERENCES

Pittenger, D. J. (1998). [Review of the State-Trait Anger Expression Inventory, Revised Research Edition.] In J. C. Impara & B. S. Plake (Eds.), *The thirteenth mental measurements yearbook* (pp. 948–949). Lincoln, NE: Buros Institute of Mental Measurements.
Drummond, R. J. (2001). [Review of the State-Trait Anger Expression Inventory.] In B. S. Plake & J. C. Impara (Eds.), *The fourteenth mental measurements yearbook* (pp. 1182–1183). Lincoln, NE: Buros Institute of Mental Measurements.
Trotter, S. E. (2001). [Review of the State-Trait Anger Expression Inventory.] In B. S. Plake & J. C. Impara (Eds.), *The fourteenth mental measurements yearbook* (pp. 1183–1184). Lincoln, NE: Buros Institute of Mental Measurements.

Review of the State-Trait Anger Expression Inventory-2 by BEVERLY M. KLECKER, Assistant Professor of Education, Morehead State University, Morehead, KY:

DESCRIPTION. The State-Trait Anger Expression Inventory–2 (STAXI-2) is a revision of the State-Trait Anger Expression Inventory (STAXI). Through revision, the 44-item STAXI has become the 57-item STAXI-2 designed to measure the experience, expression, and control of anger in adolescents and adults.

The STAXI-2 rating sheet is a self-report instrument of three parts. On Part 1, the test taker rates "How I Feel Right Now," on Part 2, "How I Generally Feel," and Part 3, "How I Generally React When Angry or Furious." Each part uses 4-point (1 = *Not at all* or *Almost Never* through 4 = *Very much so* or *Almost always*) Likert-type item rating scales. Demographic data collected with the scale include: gender, age, education, marital status, and occupation. Carbonless Form HS permits immediate scoring; Form SP may be scored by hand or with an Optical Character Reader scanner. Hand scoring requires the administrator to make 12 calculations to obtain subscale scores. For example: Sum Items 27, 31, 35, 39, 43, 47, 51, 55. This is tedious, and may be a source of error. (Scoring software is available; data for the 57 items are entered by hand.)

The manual provides excellent advice on preventing missing values when the instrument is individually administered. However, the procedure suggested for inserting data for missing values is less than clear.

DEVELOPMENT. The STAXI-2 is based on the STAXI. It has six scales, five subscales, and an overall measure of anger expression and control (the Anger Expression Index). Three of the original STAXI subscales are also on the STAXI-2 (Trait Anger [T-Ang], Anger Expression—Out [AX-O], and Anger Expression—In [AX-I]), although the AX-O scale consists of only seven of the original eight STAXI Anger Control items. New scales/items on the STAXI-2 include an eight-item Anger Control—In (AC-I) Scale and five new items added to the STAXI State Anger (S-Ang) scale. These five new items are intended to assess three distinctive components of the emotional state of anger intensity. Specifically, these new items focus on Feeling Angry (S-Ang/F), Feel Like Expressing Anger Verbally (S-Ang/V), and Feel Like Expressing Anger Physically (S-Ang/P). Thus, the STAXI-2 has many of the same items and scales of the STAXI, but it has been expanded to include both new items for existing subscales and new items that represent new subscales.

TECHNICAL. The two normative samples for the STAXI-2 consisted of normal adults (N = 1,644; 977 females, 667 males) and hospitalized psychiatric patients (N = 276; 105 females, 171 males). For the psychiatric norms, "Data ... were obtained as part of routine psychological testing completed at the time of their admission into a *dual diagnosis program* [italics added] for treating psychiatric problems and addictions in a hospital facility" (professional manual, p. 9). The hospitalized psychiatric patient population "came from several different geographic areas, primarily from the east coast" (professional manual, p. 9). This reviewer is not certain whether normative comparisons are with persons presenting with psychiatric problems or with addictions. These two groups of people may have been admitted to the same facility at the same time, but it is difficult to accept them as a *single* normative group. Further, the N of this sample, 276, is far smaller than the N for the normal sample, 1,644.

The normal sample "included managerial, technical, and clerical personnel; *participants in stress management programs* [italics added]; health care managers and professionals; insurance company employees; and students enrolled in a large urban university" (professional manual, p. 9). The mean age for this sample was 27 years with a range of 16 to 63 years. The median would offer a better picture of the normal sample—was the 63-year-old an outlier?

Although the normative normal group is large, the test developer does not make a cogent argument for representativeness. Including participants in a stress management program as "normal" when one is measuring anger is puzzling. No description of the ethnic/racial make-up of either sample is given; the normal sample is predominantly female (59%). Norms are provided for three age groups: 16 to 19 years, 20 to 29 years, and 30 years and older, but there is no indication of the total n of each group. The manual stated that the normative sample for the STAXI-2 was younger than the normative group used in the original STAXI. The practitioner has no way of knowing if the norms might apply for a 49-year-old non-Caucasian adult male.

Reliability measures for the STAXI-2 subscales are reported as alpha coefficients of internal consistency. These measures are reported as being uniformly high across all scales and subscales (.84 or higher, median $r = .88$), except for the four-item T-Ang/R subscale for normal adults, which was .76 and .73 for normal females and males, respectively. However, the reliability of the Anger Expression-Out (AX-O) subscale for individuals in the 30-years-and-older category drops to .67 for females and .55 for males. Researchers using this subscale to make comparisons across age and gender should be aware of the low reliability here. No other estimates of reliability (e.g., test-retest measure of stability) are reported.

Further, the raw scores, percentiles, and T-scores are reported for individuals without reporting the standard error of measurement (*SEM*) for either the overall scales or the subscales. This could be corrected easily and would ensure ethical reporting of the individual's score(s) (National Council on Measurement in Education, 1995).

"Chapter 5: Validity Studies and Recent Research" (professional manual, pp. 31-43) presents extensive, convincing validation evidence for the STAXI, the original instrument. However, the chapter does not contain a single validation study using STAXI-2. Is there validation evidence for the new subscales? Are the 13 new items functioning as intended?

COMMENTARY. Hand calculation of the 12 subscale scores is tedious and must be done with care. The normative samples are problematic. STAXI-2 software is provided to simplify scoring. A client record sheet is provided and includes a pull-down list of options for ethnicity. The demographic information collected on the instrument does not collect ethnicity information, nor is this a descriptive characteristic found in either normative sample. A "profile" is calculated and graphed by the software; however, no indication of the standard error of measurement is reported in the individual's profile.

This reviewer considers both normative samples as less than adequate. Thus, viewing an individual's profile sheet comparing scores with no standard error of measurement with norms that are unclear yields results that are ambiguous at best. Test-retest reliability estimates for this instrument are necessary to provide evidence of the stability of the "Trait" component being measured. That is, if scores are not stable across time (a reliability established by test-retest evidence), one cannot argue that the test measures the "trait" of anger expression.

SUMMARY. The test developer does not offer cogent evidence that the normative samples are representative of either a normal population or a psychiatric population. No demographic description of ethnicity/race is presented in the normative data, nor are such data collected in the demographic section of the instrument. The age range of the "30-and-over" category should be defined clearly. Individual scores (raw, percentile, or *T*) should not be reported without the standard error of measurement (*SEM*). The necessary error bands could be calculated easily and included by the author. Validation studies should undertaken for the STAXI-2. The revised instrument is being offered to improve construct validity of the STAXI, yet no validation evidence is presented for the new instrument. The STAXI would seem to be the preferred instrument until the STAXI-2 has sufficient normative data, validation evidence, and reliability (stability) evidence supporting the trait component of anger expression.

REVIEWER'S REFERENCE

National Council on Measurement in Education. (1995). *Code of professional responsibilities in educational measurement. Educational Measurement: Issues and Practice, 14,* 17–24.

[245]

Stoelting Brief Nonverbal Intelligence Test.

Purpose: Designed as a nonverbal, nonlanguage measure of cognitive functions.
Population: Ages 6-0 to 20-11.
Publication Date: 1999.
Acronym: S-BIT.
Scores, 7: Figure Ground, Form Completion, Sequential Order, Repeated Patterns, S-BIT IQ, Visualization, Fluid Reasoning.
Administration: Individual.
Price Data, 2001: $295 per complete kit including 20 record forms, examiner's manual (1999, 191 pages), easel book, and response cards; $20 per 20 record forms; $50 per examiner's manual; $170 per easel book; $35 per carrying case; $70 per response cards.
Time: (25) minutes.
Authors: Gale H. Roid and Lucy J. Miller.
Publisher: Stoelting Co.

Review of the Stoelting Brief Nonverbal Intelligence Test by RUSSELL N. CARNEY, Professor of Psychology, Southwest Missouri State University, Springfield, MO:

DESCRIPTION. The Stoelting Brief Non-verbal Intelligence Test (S-BIT) is an individually administered test designed to measure the nonverbal cognitive abilities of children and young people ranging in age from 6 years, 0 months, to 20 years, 11 months. Derived from the Leiter International Performance Scale—Revised (Leiter-R; Roid & Miller, 1997; T6:1419), this fairly short instrument consists of four subtests: Figure Ground, Form Completion, Sequential Order, and Repeated Patterns. Further, the first two subtests can be combined to yield a composite score in Fluid Reasoning. Finally, a nonverbal intelligence quotient (IQ) based on all four subtests can be obtained.

As an alternative to traditional IQ tests, the manual suggests a variety of uses for the S-BIT. It can serve as: (a) a quick measure of cognitive abilities in non-English speakers, (b) a screening device in special education (both disabilities and giftedness), (c) an additional measure of intelligence in individuals undergoing assessment, (d) a tool in research projects, and finally (e) an aid in the testing of individuals with speech or hearing problems. The manual cautions the user, however, that "brief tests such as the S-BIT are best used for preliminary evaluations or for making tentative, reversible programmatic decisions" (manual, p. 1).

S-BIT materials come in a cloth bag, and include an examiner's manual, a large-format color easel book, a box of color response cards, and a set of record/profile forms. The examiner sits at a table with the easel in front of the examinee, allowing room for the response cards. Although cues for administration are provided on the back pages of the easel, the test should be practiced ahead of time. Directions are given using pantomime.

Generally, the four nontimed subtests are administered in a standard order. Each subtest begins with a teaching trial. Rather than a traditional ceiling based on sequential errors, for each subtest, testing ends after a specified number of *cumulative* errors (either six or seven responses, depending on the subtest). The authors deem this approach fairer for special needs students.

Responses to the test stimuli involve either (a) pointing or (b) placement of response cards on the fold-out card holder on the easel. Answers on the four subtests are scored dichotomously (either 0 or 1). The four subtest scores are normalized, and have a mean of 10 and a standard deviation of 3. Visualization, Fluid Reasoning, and nonverbal

IQ scores are also normalized, with a mean of 100 and a standard deviation of 15.

Criterion-referenced growth scores and item growth values are provided. These are analogous to the W-scale of Woodcock and Johnson (1989). In contrast to norm-referenced scores, the growth scores help to identify the skills of the individual, and his or her growth in these areas.

Finally, the back page of the record/profile form serves as an examiner rating scale to allow for clinical observations.

DEVELOPMENT. Interviews and surveys with users of the original Leiter suggested a strong need both to revise the Leiter, and to develop a briefer version (i.e., the S-BIT). Hence, the S-BIT is based on a subset of tasks from the Leiter-R (Roid & Miller, 1997)—specifically, it consists of 4 of the Leiter-R's 10 subtests. The goal was "to construct and analyze a new nonverbal brief IQ scale which would retain the strengths of the [original] Leiter and, yet, ensure the psychometric integrity of the new scale" (manual, p. 66).

Theoretically, the S-BIT is based on the fluid-crystallized theory of Horn and Cattell (1966) and on hierarchical models of intelligence developed by Gustafsson (1984) and Carroll (1993). In the Gustafsson hierarchical model, for example, general intelligence (*g*) is at the top, crystallized intelligence, fluid intelligence, and general visualization are midlevel, and finally, subabilities are positioned beneath these. The authors of the S-BIT concentrated on the fluid and visualization subabilities in developing their nonverbal instrument. A table of specifications was devised, based on a review of the literature, and with input from subject matter experts and current test users.

Extensive item and factor analyses were conducted based on a 1994 "Tryout Edition" of the revised Leiter items. This item information was then used to produce the "Standardization Edition" (1995). In this edition, four of the subtests (186 items) were designated as comprising the S-BIT. Based on this standardization, the test was further refined using statistical techniques. The result was the final version of the S-BIT (1999).

TECHNICAL.

Standardization. The S-BIT was normed as a subset of the Leiter-R (Roid & Miller, 1997). Normative data are based on a national sample of 983 young people. Following the 1993 census, the sample was stratified in terms of such variables as race, ethnicity, SES, community size, and geographic region. Age levels were 6, 7, 8, 9, 10, 11, 12–13, 14–15, 16–17, and 18–20 years, with from 92 to 102 students per level. Comparison samples were also identified (total $N = 562$). These included atypical, clinical, and exceptional samples (e.g., individual classified as mentally retarded, learning disabled, gifted, etc.).

RELIABILITY.

Internal consistency. Cronbach's (1951) alpha was used to provide conservative estimates of internal consistency. Alpha values for the different subtests across various age categories ranged from .65 to .91. Average reliabilities for Figure Ground, Form Completion, Sequential order, and Repeated Patterns were .76, .86, .76, and .75, respectively. Reliabilities were calculated for the Visualization, Fluid Reasoning, and IQ score for two age groups: ages 6 to 10 years, and ages 11 to 20 years. For the younger group, the reliability coefficients were .90, .87, and .89, respectively. For the older group, the values were .89, .84, and .89.

Test-retest. Test-retest reliability was calculated using a sample of 106 individuals, testing on two occasions approximately 2 weeks apart. These data were divided into the two age ranges used earlier: 6 to 10 years ($N = 48$), and 11 to 20 years ($N = 58$). For the younger group, test-retest correlations ranged from .77 to .83 for the four subtests, with Visualization, Fluid Reasoning, and the IQ score having values of .87, .83, and .91, respectively. Corresponding test-retest correlations for the older group subtests ranged from .88 to .90, and were .92, .92, and .96 for Visualization, Fluid Reasoning, and IQ, respectively.

Standard errors of measurement. Based on internal consistency reliability estimates, the standard errors of measurement (*SEM*s) for the subtests ranged from .95 to 1.77 across the 10 different age ranges. For the composite scores, *SEM*s are provided for two age groups, 6 to 10 years, and 11 to 21 years. For the younger group, *SEM*s for Visualization, Fluid Reasoning, and IQ were 5.41, 4.97, and 4.74, respectively. For the older group, the *SEM*s were 6.00, 4.97, and 4.97, respectively. Again, individual subtests have a mean of 10 and *SD* of 3, whereas composite scores have a mean of 100 and *SD* of 15.

VALIDITY. The test manual documents a variety of studies relating to content, criterion-related, and construct validity.

Content validity. As mentioned earlier, the S-BIT was derived from the Leiter-R, with an eye toward the cognitive theories of Horn and Cattell (1996), Gustafsson (1984), and Carroll (1993). The manual provides convincing content validity evidence based on descriptions of "a combination of careful IRT [item response theory] analysis, item selection or item development based on review of the literature, factor verification (to establish consistency with intelligence theory), expert review, and empirical studies of internal consistency" (manual, p. 91).

Criterion-related validity. While cautioning against the isolated use of the S-BIT in making classification decisions regarding giftedness or mental retardation, the authors examined classification accuracy of the S-BIT as part of their criterion-related validity evidence. The hit rate was about 97% for mentally handicapped persons (using an IQ cutoff of 70) with respect to previously identified individuals with mental retardation and a sample of typical individuals. Regarding giftedness, the hit rate was about 92% overall using a traditional IQ score cutoff of 130. However, sensitivity (i.e., the percentage of those previously classified as gifted who are correctly classified with the S-BIT) here was poor, so the manual suggests using an IQ score of 120 in order to provide for greater sensitivity.

Further, a variety of special groups were examined: severe speech/language impairment, severe hearing impairment, severe motor delay or deviation, traumatic brain injury, mental retardation, ADHD, Gifted, LD-Nonverbal Type (Performance IQ significantly below Verbal IQ), LD-Verbal Type (Verbal IQ significantly below Performance IQ), ESL-Spanish, ESL-Asian, or other. Patterns of scores were largely as expected, including near normal IQ scores for ESL students (i.e., a mean IQ of approximately 95)—supporting the argument that the S-BIT is relatively "culture-fair."

Extensive evidence for *concurrent validity* is documented in the manual by way of correlations between the S-BIT and other instruments. For example, correlations between the various scores on the S-BIT, the original Leiter, and the Leiter-R, are reported as ranging from .59 (S-BIT Visual Composite correlated with the original Leiter Mental age) to .98 (S-BIT IQ correlated with the Leiter-R Full-Scale IQ).

Children's performance on the S-BIT was correlated with their performance on the Wechsler

Intelligence Scale for Children—Third Edition (WISC-III). Correlations between the S-BIT IQ and WISC-III Full Scale IQ and Performance IQs were each .85. As one would expect, the correlation between the S-BIT IQ and WISC-III Verbal IQ was somewhat lower at .78. the manual cites a second investigation, which resulted in very similar values.

The S-BIT was also correlated with selected subtests of the Stanford-Binet Intelligence Scale—Fourth Edition (SB-IV) and the Woodcock-Johnson Psychoeducational Battery—Revised Cognitive Battery (WJ-R; Woodcock & Johnson, 1989). S-BIT IQ score correlations with the various subtests ranged from .22 to .63.

Although too detailed to mention here, the manual also cites S-BIT correlations with subtests of the Wechsler Individual Achievement Test (WIAT), the WJ-R, the Wide Range Achievement Test 3 (WRAT3), the California Achievement Test, the Comprehensive Tests of Basic Skills (CTBS), and the Stanford Achievement Test.

Construct validity. The manual documents several lines of evidence for construct validity: age trends, experimental intervention studies, various factor analytic studies, studies of the growth scales, and an analysis of culture fairness. In the first instance, during the test development process, items were chosen that followed expected growth curves. Such age trends were also found in the S-BIT composite scores. Also, two kinds of experimental interventions were conducted, which provide some construct-related evidence.

In terms of factor analytic evidence, both indirect evidence (via Tryout and Final Editions of the Leiter-R) and direct evidence (via S-BIT subtests) are described. Support was found for the notion that the S-BIT loads on a first factor (i.e., "g"), as well as for the composite scores (i.e., Reasoning and Visualization).

A cross-battery factor analysis involving subtests from the S-BIT (four), the Woodcock-Johnson-R (four), and the SB-IV (the Matrices subtest) was conducted. The first "shows strong evidence of the construct validity of the fluid-reasoning element of the S-BIT, but shows a tendency for the S-BIT to form a unified 'g' factor rather than dividing equally into fluid and visualization factors" (manual, p. 110).

Likewise, a cross-battery analysis was conducted involving the S-BIT and selected subtests

of the WISC-III. The four WISC-III subtests comprising the Perception Organization factor, the four comprising the Verbal Comprehension factor, and the four subtests of the S-BIT were subjected to a maximum likelihood factor analysis with promax rotation. This indicated that the tests share a strong first factor (i.e., "g").

The authors also found statistical validity evidence for the growth scales and the examiner rating scales, concluding that, generally, "the exploratory analyses were quite confirming of the separate subscales, particularly at ages 6–10" (manual, p. 112). The manual also provides factor analytic evidence for the examiner rating scales and their composites.

The authors also looked at the issue of cultural fairness. Studies of differential item functioning (DIF) were conducted during the development of the S-BIT. A few items were identified in this manner, and they were removed from the final version. In the end, "a high degree of uniformity and stability was found in the calibrations across subsamples, with the exception of those items deleted in the subsequent edition" (p. 113). Studies suggest relatively similar means for White, Hispanic, and Black students when grouped in terms of level of parental education.

In summary, the manual suggests that these studies show "consistent evidence of validity from content-analysis studies with extensive item analysis data, criterion-related studies with excellent results for the classification accuracy in identifying cognitive delay, and in the various construct-related studies. The S-BIT shows exceptional fairness of assessment across ethnic groups" (manual, p. 119).

COMMENTARY. The S-BIT appears to be a useful clinical instrument appropriate for exceptional and/or non-English-speaking students who require a nonverbal measure of their cognitive ability. Although the nonverbal IQ score of the S-BIT is not a direct substitute for a Wechsler or Binet IQ score, the test certainly provides useful information that may be combined with other data in order to facilitate decision making. The standardization group seems to be appropriate, and is relatively recent (1996 or thereabouts).

Great care seems to have gone into the development and standardization of the S-BIT (in conjunction with the development of the Leiter-R). Extensive reliability information is provided in the test manual. As one would expect, test-retest reliabilities for individual subtests were not as high as for composite scores. As mentioned earlier, for a younger sample (6–10 years), test-retest reliabilities were .87, .83, and .91, for Visualization, Fluid Reasoning, and the S-BIT IQ score, respectively. For an older sample (11–20 years), the corresponding reliabilities were .92, .92, and .96. Reliabilities of .90 or higher are often desired if tests are used to make high-stakes decisions, such as special education placement. At both age levels, the nonverbal IQ score meets this standard, as do both composite scores at the older age level.

Likewise, as described earlier, extensive and convincing validity evidence is provided in the test manual—as well as cautions as to the limitations of the instrument. In particular, caveats regarding the diagnosis and identification of mentally retarded, gifted, and learning-disabled students are provided. In addition, the test manual includes practical chapters with titles such as "Test Administration and Adapted Instructions" and "Interpretation and Case Studies." These may be particularly helpful to test users.

SUMMARY. The Stoelting Brief Nonverbal Intelligence Test (S-BIT) appears to be a useful test for measuring the nonverbal cognitive abilities of children and young people ranging in age from 6 to about 21 years. It is short, easy to administer/score, and has reasonable test-retest reliability—particularly in regard to the composite nonverbal IQ score. As a brief screening device, it seems valid for the limited purposes outlined in the manual regarding the assessment of special needs students, and/or those with a non-English-speaking background.

REVIEWER'S REFERENCES

Carroll, J. B. (1993). *Human cognitive abilities: A survey of factor-analytic studies.* New York: Cambridge University Press.
Cronbach, L. J. (1951). Coefficient alpha and the internal structure of tests. *Psychometrika, 16,* 297–334.
Gustafsson, J. E. (1984). A unifying model for the structure of intellectual abilities. *Intelligence, 8,* 179–203.
Horn, J. L., & Cattell, R. B. (1966). Refinement and test of the theory of fluid and crystallized general intelligences. *Journal of Educational Psychology, 57,* 253–270.
Roid, G. H., & Miller, L. J. (1997). Leiter International Performance Scale—Revised. Wood Dale, IL: Stoelting Co.
Woodcock, R. W., & Johnson, M. B. (1989). Woodcock-Johnson Psycho-Educational Battery—Revised. Chicago, IL: Riverside.

Review of the Stoelting Brief Nonverbal Intelligence Test by SUSANA URBINA, Professor of Psychology, University of North Florida, Jacksonville, FL:

DESCRIPTION. The Stoelting Brief Nonverbal Intelligence Test (S-BIT) is a short form of the Leiter International Performance Scale—Revised (Leiter-R; 14:211). It consists of 4 of the 10 subtests from the Visualization and Reasoning (VR) Battery of the Leiter-R: Figure Ground (FG) and Form Completion (FC) from the Visualization portion, as well as Sequential Order (SO) and Repeated Patterns (RP) from the Reasoning portion. In fact, the S-BIT is embedded in the Leiter-R as a "Brief IQ Screener" and was normed as part of the standardization version of the Leiter-R rather than as a separate test. The S-BIT also incorporates the Examiner Rating Scale of the Leiter-R. Psychometric data cited in the S-BIT manual are a subset of the Leiter-R data (i.e., those that pertain to the subtests and to the age range—ages 6-0 to 20-11—covered by the S-BIT).

The purpose of the S-BIT is to provide a brief screening measure of general ability suitable for individuals with communication disorders, hearing/motor impairments, and other conditions that would prevent them from either understanding or using spoken language, including individuals for whom English is not a native language. The manual makes it clear that the S-BIT is "best used for preliminary evaluations or for making tentative, reversible programmatic decisions" (p. 1).

ADMINISTRATION. The S-BIT is administered individually and entirely without the use of language. In addition to the examiner's manual, the materials include an easel book (approximately 9 x 17 x 3/4 inches), a small box of response cards, and the record/profile forms. The materials are colorful and attractive. Directions are conveyed to the test takers via pantomime and they, in turn, respond either by pointing or by placing response cards on a fold-out card holder that is part of the easel. Instructions for test administration include examples of pantomime techniques and adaptations of administrative procedures for use with exceptional populations such as culturally diverse and disabled individuals. The subtests of the S-BIT are not timed, but examiners are instructed to use a pacing rule that calls for "gentle encouragements" after 1- and 2-minute intervals and for moving on with the test if the examinee does not respond to an item after 3 minutes. Estimated time for administration is 25 minutes.

Scores. The S-BIT yields normative scores, with means of 10 and *SD*s of 3, on its four subtests, as well as an IQ and two composite scores—Visualization and Fluid Reasoning—with means of 100 and *SD*s of 15. In addition, item response theory (IRT) procedures were used to develop "growth scores" that range from approximately 400 to 550; these scores parallel the normative ones and allow for intraindividual comparisons over time on a uniform ability scale. The Examiner Rating Scale yields scores on Cognitive/Social and Emotion/Regulation composites, which are based on the examiner's ratings on eight separate dimensions, such as attention, activity level, anxiety, and sensory reactivity.

DEVELOPMENT. The idea that led to the S-BIT was simply to make a free-standing abbreviated scale from the four most reliable and widely applicable subtests of the Leiter-R. These four subtests had already been selected to make up the Brief IQ Screener of the Leiter-R. The development of the Leiter-R from Tryout to Standardization versions—detailed in Marco's (2001) review—was exemplary in many respects. To begin with, the revision of the original Leiter had a strong conceptual component and was guided by Carroll's (1993) and Gustafsson's (1984) hierarchical models; its aim was to arrive at the best possible estimate of "g" through the use of fluid reasoning and visualization tasks. Furthermore, from tryout through standardization, comparison samples of individuals with disabilities and varied ethnic and cultural backgrounds were identified and tested, in addition to the typical samples. Multiple item-level analyses, including studies of differential item functioning (DIF), were conducted during the development of the Leiter-R, thus ensuring an adequate degree of psychometric validity and fairness across ethnic groups.

The S-BIT's subtests are part of the Visualization and Reasoning Battery of the Leiter-R and do not include any subtests from the Leiter-R's Attention and Memory Battery. The two Visualization subtests, Figure Ground (FG) and Form Completion (FC), consist of 26 and 30 items, respectively. FG calls for the identification of figures or details of objects embedded within complex stimuli, whereas FC requires the recognition of an object from a randomly displayed array of its parts. Sequential Ordering (SO), with 43 items, and Repeated Patterns (RP), with 19 items, make up the Reasoning component of the S-BIT. SO calls for the test taker to select stimuli that will complete a sequence of pictorial or figural objects in a logical manner, whereas RP asks examinees to supply the missing portions of repeated patterns of pictures or objects.

TECHNICAL. The standardization group for the S-BIT consists of the 983 individuals (483 females and 500 males) who comprised the 6- to 20-year-old segment of the total standardization sample of 1,719 for the Leiter-R VR Battery. The remaining 783 participants in the Leiter-R VR sample were between the ages of 2 and 5 years and were not used for the S-BIT. Approximately 66% of the S-BIT sample was Caucasian, 16% African-American, 13% Hispanic, and the rest were Asian or Native American. The standardization sample closely reflects the demographic characteristics of the population of the United States as of the 1993 Census. Brief descriptions of the make-up of 11 special groups studied during the development of the Leiter-R, along with the means and standard deviations on all the scores yielded by the S-BIT for those groups, are included in the manual.

Reliability of the S-BIT was assessed through both classical test theory and IRT methods. The internal consistency coefficients of the S-BIT subtests across the 10 age groupings in the standardization sample range from .65 to .91, with most in the 70s and 80s. The estimated reliability coefficients for the S-BIT IQ are .90 for 6- to 10-year-olds and .89 for 11- to 20-year-olds. For the Visualization and Fluid Reasoning composites, estimated reliabilities are in the .80s; for the Examiner Rating Scales composite scores, reliabilities range from .95 to .97. Test-retest reliabilities for the subtests range from .77 to .90 and for the composite scores, including IQs, from .83 to .96; these coefficients are based on a sample of 106 children and adolescents who were tested twice with an average interval of 14 days between the testings. The test-retest reliabilities for the Examiner Rating Scales composites range from .76 to .87. IRT reliability data are presented in the form of a test information curve for the S-BIT IQ; it shows that the test provides a slightly higher degree of accuracy in the lower ability range.

Information bearing on the validity or usefulness of the S-BIT is provided in a variety of ways. Good model-data fit, using a model loosely based on Carroll's (1993) and Gustafsson's (1984) schemes, was achieved through careful development of the Leiter-R, as was fairness across gender and ethnic groups. These qualities are cited to support the content validity of the S-BIT.

Criterion-related evidence of validity is shown by the accuracy with which individuals can be classified as gifted or as cognitively delayed using various cutoff points. These studies also suggest that the S-BIT works best in screening for cognitive delays rather than for giftedness. Studies of individuals with severe language, hearing, and motor impairments, as well as a variety of other conditions—including diverse linguistic background—are also presented, as are a number of small sample studies correlating the S-BIT with other instruments that measure similar abilities. Not surprisingly, in light of the fact that the S-BIT consists of four of the "best" subtests of the Leiter-R, the correlation between the IQs derived from the two measures is extraordinarily high, .98.

Age trends, experimental intervention studies, and factor analyses are presented as construct-related evidence of the validity of S-BIT scores. The average *g* loadings of the four subtests across all age groups range from .57 to .64. Average specific variance components of the subtests range from 32% to 51%. The gist of all of these data is certainly congruent with the developers' intention to devise a test that would assess general cognitive functioning through tasks representing four distinct kinds of nonverbal abilities.

COMMENTARY. The S-BIT is an addition to the growing list of instruments for the assessment of individuals for whom language-based tests are inappropriate or unfair. As a subset of the careful and well-received revision of the Leiter International Performance Scale, it shares many of the strengths of the Leiter-R. These strengths lie principally in the sound theoretical and empirical grounding of its components, the use of IRT methods, the attractiveness of the test materials, the many helpful features of its examiner's manual, and the careful attention paid to fairness across ethnic/gender groups.

On the other hand, as a short form, the S-BIT also suffers from the limitations of that ever-expanding genre of instruments. These limitations have been cogently articulated by Kaufman and Kaufman (2001); they derive primarily from the use of part-whole correlations to support the validity of parts embedded in the whole and from the application of norms derived for a complete battery to a part of that battery. For those who do not wish to contend with such limitations, there are some alternatives. The Universal Nonverbal Intelligence Test (UNIT; T6:2636) by Bracken and McCallum (1998), applies to a slightly nar-

rower age range but provides various measures of memory, in addition to reasoning and visualization tasks. The Test of Nonverbal Intelligence, Third Edition (TONI-3; T6:2553) by Brown, Sherbenou, and Johnsen (1997), applies to a much wider age range than the S-BIT, but provides only one score. In the realm of group testing, the Beta III (T6:309; Kellogg & Morton, 1999), though more culturally loaded than the aforementioned tests, is one of several possible alternatives.

The S-BIT also shares several of the weaknesses outlined by reviewers of the Leiter-R (Marco, 2001; Stinnett, 2001). Among these are a lack of clarity in the manual concerning the precise data on which reported reliability and validity analyses are based, as well as potential difficulties caused by the use of pantomime in the administration procedures. Additional weaknesses include the fact that the norms for the Examiner Rating Scales resulted in admittedly "skewed and truncated scales" (Examiner's manual, p. 46).

SUMMARY. There is an undeniable need for brief instruments to screen individuals who require cognitive assessment through nonverbal means. However, development of the S-BIT as a separate test seems to have involved merely reducing the length of the Leiter-R VR Battery, recomputing the statistics derived during its development, and reconfiguring four of its subtests into a separate kit. Users of the Leiter-R already have the option of administering the same four subtests in the Leiter-R's Brief Screener. Others will have to decide whether to purchase a test that—although part of a fine battery—has not been normed or validated separately, or whether to use one of the existing alternatives. Because the total time saved by administering the S-BIT, as opposed to the entire VR Battery of the Leiter-R, is likely to be only about 20 minutes, the Leiter-R's VR Battery itself might prove to be the best alternative.

REVIEWER'S REFERENCES

Bracken, B. A., & McCallum, R. S. (1998). *Universal Nonverbal Intelligence Test.* Itasca, IL: Riverside.

Brown, L., Sherbenou, R. J., & Johnsen, S. K. (1997). *Test of Nonverbal Intelligence* (3rd ed.). Austin, TX: PRO-ED.

Carroll, J. B. (1993). *Human cognitive abilities: A survey of factor-analytic studies.* New York: Cambridge University Press.

Gustafsson, J. E. (1984). A unifying model for the structure of intellectual abilities. *Intelligence, 8,* 179–203.

Kaufman, J. C., & Kaufman, A. S. (2001). Time for the changing of the guard: A farewell to short forms of intelligence tests. *Journal of Psychoeducational Assessment, 19,* 245–267.

Kellogg, C. E., & Morton, N. W. (1999). *Beta III manual.* San Antonio, TX: The Psychological Corporation.

Marco, G. L. (2001). [Review of the Leiter International Performance Scale—Revised.] In B. S. Plake & J. C. Impara (Eds.), *The fourteenth mental measurements yearbook* (pp. 683–687). Lincoln, NE: Buros Institute of Mental Measurements.

Stinnett, T. A. (2001). [Review of the Leiter International Performance Scale—Revised.] In B. S. Plake & J. C. Impara (Eds.), *The fourteenth mental measurements yearbook* (pp. 687–692). Lincoln, NE: Buros Institute of Mental Measurements.

[246]
Stress in General Scale.

Purpose: Designed as a global measure of job stress.
Population: Employees.
Publication Date: 1992–2002.
Acronym: SIG.
Scores, 2: Pressure, Threat.
Administration: Individual or group.
Price Data, 2002: $20 per 100 test booklets (for commercial users); $1 per scoring key; free to nonprofit researchers and at no extra charge to purchasers of the Job Descriptive Index.
Time: Administration time not reported.
Comments: Previously listed with the Job Descriptive Index (130).
Authors: Jeffrey M. Stanton, William K. Balzer, Patricia C. Smith, Luis Fernando Parra, and Gail H. Ironson.
Publisher: Bowling Green State University, Department of Psychology.
[Editor's Note: Materials provided for reviewers were published in 1992. More current technical information became available in the October 2001 issue of *Educational and Psychological Measurement* but the first reviewer did not have access to this information.]

Review of the Stress in General Scale by C. G. BELLAH, Assistant Professor of Psychology, Northwestern State University, Natchitoches, LA:

DESCRIPTION. The Stress in General Scale (SIG) is a 15-item self-report questionnaire designed to provide a broad measure of work-related stress. The test instructions direct respondents to rate how well each item in a list of adjectives and phrases describes their work. The SIG utilizes a 3-point closed-ended item response format ranging from "No" (0 points) to "Yes" (3 points), with "?" (1.5 points) indicating the respondent "cannot decide." Scores are obtained on two summative subscales labeled "Pressure" and "Threat." High scores reflect elevated levels of job stress. The questionnaire may be individually or group administered, and a sixth grade reading level among respondents is recommended to obtain valid protocols.

DEVELOPMENT. The SIG was designed to provide a general measure of job stress that is distinctive from job satisfaction. The authors state that the theoretical development of the SIG was guided by a cognitive-phenomenological perspec-

tive, purporting that individuals are conscious of stressful encounters and are able to report the feeling tone of these experiences. Following this assumption, a preliminary list of 53 adjectives was derived from multiple sources and procedures including: a survey of the literature, dictionary and thesaurus entries, and interviews with persons employed in a variety of positions and organizations. Each item was presumed to connote a broad, affectively oriented evaluation of work-related stress. Preliminary item analyses resulted in 18 adjectives being retained for scale development.

Exploratory factor analyses (EFA) were then performed on the remaining 18 items ($N = 4,322$) using maximum likelihood factor extraction and oblique rotation to simple structure. A parallel analysis criterion was used for factor retention, resulting in two correlated subscales of general job stress subsequently labeled "Pressure" and "Threat." Examination of the factor structure revealed 1 item with an insufficient loading and 2 cross-loaded items. Consequently, these 3 items were discarded from the item pool, resulting in a 7-item composition for the Pressure subscale and an 8-item composition for the Threat subscale.

Subsequent to EFA, the authors performed a confirmatory factor analysis (CFA) on a second sample ($N = 574$) in efforts to cross-validate the factor structure derived in pilot work. Unfortunately, this second study failed to replicate previous findings, nor did the final solution provide an adequate fit to the data. Indices of the final two-factor solution revealed a significant difference between predicted and observed scores. It is noteworthy that, in efforts to maximize model fit, the authors chose to specify a measurement model that included 3 cross-loaded items. Moreover, all of the original 18 items were specified in the model, which was contra-indicated in pilot work. Thus, the final results of the 18-item CFA solution can only have limited utility in cross-validating the 15-item solution derived in exploratory analyses. Moreover, because a general factor solution provided a poor fit to the data, and given poor model parsimony for the final CFA solution, the results effectively indicate that two factors are too many and one factor is too few. Psychometrically, it is likely that these results are due to the presence of multiple items with insufficient factor loadings in the model.

sure subscales ranged from .59 to .69. With correlations in this range it appears that these two factors are measuring related but somewhat distinct constructs. Therefore, each subscale appears to be measuring somewhat unique aspects of general job stress. The authors believe the Pressure subscale probably measures typical daily job pressures, whereas the Threat scale measures a high or overwhelming degree of stress.

No normative data are currently available for this instrument. No test-retest reliability findings are reported. Across studies, the coefficient alpha reliability estimates range from .73 to .90 for the Pressure subscale and estimates range from .77 to .83 for the Threat subscale. Previous investigations using the Total score found coefficient alphas ranging from .91 to .92. These findings suggest adequate internal consistency reliability.

In the investigations of concurrent and convergent validity the test creators examined the relationship between the two subscales and other measures of stress and job satisfaction. Using a one-item measure of reported stress ("On a scale of 1 to 10, indicate the amount of stress on your job"), correlations ranged from .46 to .69 for the Total score. One study found a relationship between the one-item measure and the Pressure subscale (.70) and with the Threat subscale (.56). Compared to the Pressure subscale, larger correlations were found between the Threat subscale and both a measure of "Intent to Quit" (Threat r = .36 to .50; Pressure r = .09 to .17) and the Job in General scale (Threat r = -.47 to -.57; Pressure r = -.10 to -.17). As expected, the Time Pressure subscale of the Job Stress Index (JSI) was found to be more strongly correlated with the SIG Pressure subscale (.52) than with the Threat subscale (.34). Correlations were found between each subscale and a measure of work-family balance (Pressure: r = .43; Threat: r = .48). However, low correlations were found when the relationship between the SIG subscales and a measure of racial discrimination on the job were examined (Pressure: r = .10; Threat: r = .23).

In a further investigation of convergent validity (N = 34) blood pressure reactivity was included as a physiological measure of chronic stress. An examination of the relationship between various blood pressure readings and the two SIG subscales resulted in significant correlations, ranging from .36 to .40 for the Pressure subscale and from .12 to .21 for the Threat subscale.

The test authors have investigated divergent validity between the SIG scale and other measures of negative reactions to work, including negative affectivity in general and dissatisfaction with one's job. The correlation between negative affectivity and the Pressure subscale was .34; the correlation with the Threat subscale was .54. In three different studies examining the relationship between the JIG scale (a measure of general job satisfaction) and each SIG subscale, stronger correlations were found between the JIG scale and the Threat subscale (-.47 to -.57) than between the JIG scale and the Pressure subscale (-.10 to -.17).

Three previous studies investigated the incremental validity of the SIG scale in relation to the JIG scale. Although two studies found the Threat scale was able to explain additional variance of the Intent to Quit measure beyond that of the JIG scale, a third study failed to replicate this finding. Clearly, further research is needed to determine the incremental validity of the SIG.

COMMENTARY. The primary value of the SIG scale appears to be its use as a research instrument for the identification of employees' perceptions of their job stress. No evidence has been provided to suggest that the SIG may be effectively used on an individual basis for identification or intervention purposes. The SIG scale appears to be unique in its emphasis on general job-related stress experienced, whereas most previously published scales tend to apply only to certain occupations or to focus on specific stress factors, such as sources of stress and/or reactions to stress. However, the use of more extensive stress instruments may be warranted when attempting to identify an employee's reaction to stress more accurately, because these other instruments assess more complex characteristics of an individual's reaction to stress compared with a measure of perceived level of stress in general.

The usefulness of the SIG scale is severely limited by its lack of normative data. Without such data it is difficult to determine the meaning of individual scores. For example, how high does the score have to be to indicate a significantly elevated level of stress? Does an individual have to report high scores on both SIG subscales to denote problematic levels of stress?

There are other tests in the literature (e.g., The Occupational Stress Inventory [T6:1739] and the Occupational Stress Indicator [T6:1738]) that supply the type of data tapped by the SIG scale, but also generate additional scores concerning the test-taker and his or her experience of the stress. Both scales are significantly longer than the SIG scale, but if one takes the perspective of stress as separate from a person's ability to cope with that stress, we are not obtaining with the SIG a complete enough picture of that person's situation, his or her ability to adapt, and the possible need for intervention. The use of the two factors of the SIG scale does help somewhat in possibly predicting whether the person will quit, but it does not identify other possible important stress-related variables.

The low correlations between racial discrimination and the SIG subscales are a concern, considering that increased discrimination on the job is presumably connected to feelings of stress at work. The very small relationship here may suggest that the type of stress experienced during racial discrimination may not be the same type of job stress the SIG scale is measuring. Therefore, the type of stress being measured by the SIG scale may need to be further clarified. For example, is the "stress in general" construct, as defined here, limited to less interpersonally driven aspects of the job environment?

The SIG scale is very straightforward; the goal of the test is very obvious to the test-taker. Impression management would be quite easy should the test-taker desire to give a falsely positive or negative impression of their job stress. Also, the simplicity of the response possibilities cannot take into account changes in respondents' work situations so that, for example, they are "hectic" or "frantic" at times and at other times they are not. An example of such a situation would be a job in accounting, where one may work under extreme stress during "tax season" but under much less stress during the remainder of the year.

SUMMARY. The developers have produced a simple, straightforward, general job stress scale that is useful for research purposes. The scale requires further development before it can be useful on an individual basis. A test manual and normative data from a variety of populations would be the logical next step in the development of the SIG scale.

REVIEWERS' REFERENCES

Fisher, G., Stanton, J., Thoresen, P., Julian, A., Sinar, E., Aziz, S., Balzer, W., & Smith, P. (2000, April). *The Stress in General Scale: Exploration and validation.* Poster presented at the annual meeting of the Society for Industrial and Organizational Psychology, New Orleans, LA.

Ironson, G. H., Smith, P. C., Brannick, M. T., Gibson, W. M., & Paul, K. (1989). Construction of a job in general scale: A comparison of global, composite, and specific measures. *Journal of Applied Psychology, 74,* 193–200.

Smith, P., Balzer, W., Ironson, G., Paul, K., Hayes, B., Moore-Hirschl, S., & Parra, L. (1992, May). *Development and validation of the Stress in General (SIG) scale.* Paper presented at the annual meeting of the Society for Industrial and Organizational Psychology, Montreal, Canada.

Stanton, J., Balzer, W., Smith, P., Parra, L., & Ironson, G. (In press). *A general measure of work stress: The Stress in General (SIG) scale.* Educational and Psychological Measurement.

[247]

Stress Profile.

Purpose: Developed "to provide a brief yet comprehensive stress and health risk assessment."

Population: Adults.

Publication Date: 1999.

Scores, 16: Stress, Health Habits, Exercise, Rest/Sleep, Eating/Nutrition, Prevention, ARC Item Cluster, Social Support Network, Type A Behavior, Cognitive Hardiness, Coping Style, Positive Appraisal, Negative Appraisal, Threat Minimization, Problem Focus, Psychological Well-Being.

Administration: Group.

Price Data, 2002: $105 per kit including 25 AutoScore' forms, manual (63 pages), 1 reusable administration booklet, and a 2-use disk for on-site computer scoring and interpretation; $39.50 per 25 AutoScore' forms to be used with administration booklet; $45 per manual; $22.50 per 25 disposable administration booklets; $49.95 per 5 reusable administration booklets (quantity discounts available); prices for WPS Test Report mail-in service, disks, and FAX service available from publisher.

Time: (20–25) minutes.

Comments: Can be administered and scored by hand or by computer.

Author: Kenneth M. Nowack.

Publisher: Western Psychological Services.

Review of the Stress Profile by CARL ISENHART, Coordinator, Addictive Disorders Section, Mental Health Patient Service Line, VA Medical Center, Minneapolis, MN:

DESCRIPTION. The Stress Profile is a 123-item, self-report, paper-and-pencil, multiple choice instrument that was designed to measure two areas of health and stress risk: those circumstances that help a person withstand the effects of stress and those that make an individual vulnerable to stress. The instrument was designed to briefly assess 16 lifestyle behaviors that, based on the cognitive-transactional philosophy, have been identified as being causal to stress-related disorders. The 16 areas are: Stress, Health Habits, Exercise, Rest/Sleep, Eating/Nutrition, Prevention, an ARC Item Cluster (use of alcohol, recreational drugs, or cigarettes), Social Support Network, Type A Behavior, Cognitive Hardiness, Coping Style, Positive

tate targeted treatment interventions and lifestyle modification" (manual, p. 2).

DEVELOPMENT. The author incorporated Jackson's (1970) model of test development as a rationale for implementing the three-step validation process resulting in the development of a 300-item Health Assessment Audit. The original item pool was reduced through a process of "sorting" items into rational/theoretically appropriate categories. If a single item was sorted into the same category by "three health professionals," then the item was retained. The Health Assessment Audit was sent to 300 employees in a variety of companies, with a return rate of 64%. Subsequent retesting yielded a return rate of less than 50% of the original sample of 300 employees. These volunteer participants were primarily females (68%) working in supervisory positions, between 20–55 years of age, and were predominately college-educated individuals. Using these data, the author incorporated multiple levels of statistical analysis, resulting in a 121-item version of the Stress Profile. The author has also included a section on the theoretical basis for inclusion of retained scales (manual, pp. 20–23).

The Stress Profile standardization sample was based upon a nonclinical group of respondents, representing a number of employment fields. The mean age of this sample was 39.5 years. The sample ($n = 1,111$) was ethnically diverse, but was not the product of random or stratified random sampling techniques. The author notes that efforts were "made to achieve a diverse and representative sample" (manual, p. 22). Scores were not substantially affected by gender or ethnic background, though educational differences were observed for Health Habits and Eating/Nutrition scores. Several scales were changed during the standardization process with the author using appropriate statistical procedures to renorm the shortened scales (Prevention, Type A Behaviors, and Health Habits).

TECHNICAL. Reliability was assessed using Cronbach's alpha as a measure of internal consistency. This measure yielded a range of scores from .51 to .91 among the content scales. The overall estimate of internal consistency was .72 in the standardization sample. In terms of test-retest reliability only four scales were included in the study (Stress, Health Habits, Type A Behaviors, and Cognitive Hardiness). The test-retest reliability ranged from .76 to .86 over a 3-month elapsed period ($n = 95$). Although the publisher posits

satisfactory results in terms of reliability and internal consistency estimates, there is much work to be accomplished regarding the Threat Minimization (alpha .62), Prevention (alpha .51), and ARC Item Cluster scales (alpha .35). The author examined the construct of validity by considering the relationship of the pattern of relationships evident among scales to the underlying theoretical model. The resulting correlations are consistent with the expectation of independence. These results suggest that scales are "sufficiently independent to justify their separate interpretation" (manual, p. 25). The author undertook a principal component analysis that yielded three major factors accounting for 57% of variance. The manual also contains the results of several studies of concurrent validity that were limited to two scales (Type A Behavior and Cognitive Hardiness). The evidence supporting concurrent validity is limited and further research study is strongly encouraged. Several prospective studies were cited as measures of support of predictive validity regarding physical and psychological health. These included the prediction of burnout, prediction of health illness and absenteeism, prediction of weight loss, and prediction of performance.

COMMENTARY. The test offers a broad approach to the subject of stress. It attempts to incorporate a "brief, but comprehensive stress assessment … which can be administered and scored by hand or computer" (Stress Profile descriptive literature). The resulting assessment instrument reflects the tension between competing goals. Brief may not be consistent with comprehensive. Unfortunately, the publisher provided only the manual for review; therefore, it was not possible to evaluate the test dynamics in terms of practice or scoring procedures. Hand scoring directions are lengthy and appear to be cumbersome, though the publisher suggests that the "auto score" format facilitates the scoring process. (The publisher did not provide requested hand-scoring forms.) Much work remains to be done regarding issues of reliability and validity to increase the utility of this assessment.

SUMMARY. The Stress Profile represents a cogent conceptual framework for assessment of stress-related factors. It is a welcomed addition to the arsenal of pertinent instrumentation, though its effectiveness is limited by the need for further work regarding reliability and validity. The Stress Profile eventually may be utilized as an effective clinician's assessment instrument. Its usefulness will be enhanced through further appropriate developmental research studies.

REVIEWER'S REFERENCE

Jackson, D. N. (1970). A sequential system for personality scale development. In C. Spielberger (Ed.), *Current topics in clinical and community psychology.* New York: Academic Press.

[248]
Strong Interest Inventory® [1994].

Purpose: Designed to "identify general areas of interests as well as specific activities and occupations" for further exploration.

Population: Ages 16 and over.

Publication Dates: 1927–1994.

Acronym: Strong.

Scores, 267: 6 General Occupational Themes: Realistic, Investigative, Artistic, Social, Enterprising, Conventional; 25 Basic Interest Scales: Realistic (Agriculture, Nature, Military Activities, Athletics, Mechanical Activities), Investigative (Science, Mathematics, Medical Science), Artistic (Music/Dramatics, Art, Applied Arts, Writing, Culinary Arts), Social (Teaching, Social Service, Medical Service, Religious Activities), Enterprising (Public Speaking, Law/Politics, Merchandising, Sales, Organizational Management), Conventional (Data Management, Computer Activities, Office Services); 211 Occupational Scales: Accountant (female, male), Actuary (f, m), Advertising Executive (f, m), Agribusiness Manager (m), Architect (f, m), Artist/ Commercial (f, m), Artist/Fine (f, m), Art Teacher (f, m), Athletic Trainer (f, m), Audiologist (f, m), Auto Mechanic (f, m), Banker (f, m), Biologist (f, m), Bookkeeper (f, m), Broadcaster (f, m), Business Education Teacher (f, m), Buyer (f, m), Carpenter (f, m), Chef (f, m), Chemist (f, m), Child Care Provider (f), Chiropractor (f, m), College Professor (f, m), Community Service Organization Director (f, m), Computer Programmer/Systems Analyst (f, m), Corporate Trainer (f, m), Credit Manager (f, m), Dental Assistant (f), Dental Hygienist (f), Dentist (f, m), Dietitian (f, m), Elected Public Official (f, m), Electrician (f, m), Elementary School Teacher (f, m), Emergency Medical Technician (f, m), Engineer (f, m), English Teacher (f, m), Farmer (f, m), Flight Attendant (f, m), Florist (f, m), Food Service Manager (f, m), Foreign Language Teacher (f, m), Forester (f, m), Gardener/Groundskeeper (f, m), Geographer (f, m), Geologist (f, m), Hair Stylist (f, m), High School Counselor (f, m), Home Economics Teacher (f), Horticultural Worker (f, m), Housekeeping & Maintenance Supervisor (f, m), Human Resources Director (f, m), Interior Decorator (f, m), Investments Manager (f, m), Lawyer (f, m), Librarian (f, m), Life Insurance Agent (f, m), Marketing Executive (f, m), Mathematician (f, m), Mathematics Teacher (f, m), Medical Illustrator (f, m), Medical Records Technician (f, m), Medical Technician (f, m), Medical Technologist (f, m), Military Enlisted Personnel (f, m), Military Officer (f, m), Minister (f, m), Musician (f, m), Nurse/Licensed Practical (f, m), Nurse/Registered (f, m), Nursing Home Administrator (f, m), Occupational Therapist (f, m), Optician (f, m), Optometrist (f, m), Paralegal (f, m), Parks and Recreation Coordinator (f, m), Pharmacist (f, m), Photographer (f, m), Physical Education Teacher (f, m), Physical Therapist (f, m), Physician (f, m), Physicist (f, m), Plumber (m), Police Officer (f, m), Psychologist (f, m), Public Administrator (f, m), Public Relations Director (f, m), Purchasing Agent (f, m), Radiologic Technologist (f, m), Realtor (f, m), Reporter (f, m), Research & Development Manager (f, m), Respiratory Therapist (f, m), Restaurant Manager (f, m), School Administrator (f, m), Science Teacher (f, m), Secretary (f), Small Business Owner (f, m), Social Science Teacher (f, m), Social Worker (f, m), Sociologist (f, m), Special Education Teacher (f, m), Speech Pathologist (f, m), Store Manager (f, m), Technical Writer (f, m), Translator (f, m), Travel Agent (f, m), Veterinarian (f, m), Vocational Agriculture Teacher (f, m); 4 Personal Style Scales: Work Style, Learning Environment, Leadership Style, Risk Taking/Adventure; 27 Administrative Indexes: Total Response, Infrequent Response, Response Percentages (Like, Indifferent, Dislike) for each of 8 inventory sections (Occupations, School Subjects, Activities, Leisure Activities, Types of People, Characteristics, Preferences: Activities, Preferences: Work), Total for all parts.

Administration: Group.

Price Data, 2001: $75 per 10 prepaid profile combined item booklet/answer sheets; $235 per 10 prepaid interpretive report combined item booklet/answer sheets; $72 per Strong Applications and Technical Guide (1994, 425 pages); $18.95 per Strong Profile preview kit including prepaid profile item booklet/ answer sheet and client booklet; $23.10 per Strong interpretive report preview kit including prepaid interpretive item booklet/answer sheet and client booklet; $40 per 10 client booklets; $163 per 10 prepaid professional report combined item booklet/answer sheets; $26.50 per Strong Professional report preview kit including prepaid professional item booklet/answer sheet and booklet; $75 per 10 prepaid Strong Profile, High School Edition combined item booklet/answer sheets; $10.75 per Strong Profile, High School Edition preview kit including prepaid High School profile item booklet/answer sheet and client booklet; $75 per 10 prepaid Strong college item booklet/answer sheets; $10.75 per Strong college preview kit.

Time: (35–40) minutes.

Comments: Scoring options: Prepaid (mail-in) and CPP software system (price data available from publisher); administration also available via CPP software system and the internet: Strong Interest Inventory and Skills Confidence Inventory, Strong and MBTI Career

Report, and Strong and MBTI Entrepreneur Report also available from publisher.

Authors: Edward K. Strong, Jr. (original inventory), David P. Campbell (test and manual revision), Lenore W. Harmon (applications and technical guide), Jo-Ida C. Hansen (applications and technical guide), Fred H. Borgen (applications and technical guide), and Allen L. Hammer (applications and technical guide).

Publisher: Consulting Psychologists Press, Inc.

Cross References: See T5:1790 (19 references); for reviews by John Christian Busch and by Blaine R. Worthen and Perry Sailor of the Fourth Edition, see 12:374 (43 references); see also T4:2581 (64 references); for reviews by Wilbur L. Layton and Bert W. Westbrook, see 9:1195 (17 references); see also T3:2318 (99 references); for reviews by John O. Crites, Robert H. Dolliver, Patricia W. Lunneborg, and excerpted reviews by Richard W. Johnson, David P. Campbell, and Jean C. Steinhauer, see 8:1023 (289 references, these references are for SVIB-M, SBIV-W, and SCII). For references on the Strong Vocational Interest Blank For Men, see T2:2212 (133 references); for reviews by Martin R. Katz and Charles J. Krauskopf and excerpted reviews by David P. Campbell and John W. M. Rothney, see 7:1036 (485 references); for reviews by Alexander W. Astin and Edward J. Furst, see 6:1070 (189 references); see also 5:868 (153 references); for reviews by Edward S. Bordin and Elmer D. Hinckley, see 4:747 (98 references): see also 3:647 (102 references); for reviews by Harold D. Carter, John G. Darley, and N. W. Morton, see 2:1680 (71 references); for a review by John G. Darley, see 1:1178. For references on the Strong Vocational Interest Blank For Women, see T2:2213 (30 references); for reviews by Dorothy M. Clendenen and Barbara A. Kirk, see 7:1037 (92 references); see also 6:1071 (12 references) and 5:869 (19 references); for a review by Gwendolen Schneidler Dickson, see 3:649 (38 references); for a review by Ruth Strang, see 2:1681 (10 references); for a review by John G. Darley, see 1:1179.

Review of the Strong Interest Inventory® [1994] by KEVIN R. KELLY, Head, Department of Educational Studies, Purdue University, West Lafayette, IN:

DESCRIPTION. The Strong Interest Inventory (SII) is a 317-item interest inventory designed for use by high school and college students and adults. The reading level is between eighth- and ninth-grade levels; administration time is 35–40 minutes. Five uses are listed in the Applications and Technical Guide: (a) To aid educational and occupational decision making, (b) to structure the career assessment and counseling process, (c) to stimulate client self-exploration, (d) to assist in personnel hiring and staffing decisions, and (e) to explore reasons for job dissatisfaction.

Respondents report their preferences and perceptions in eight sections: Occupations, School Subjects, Activities, Leisure Activities, Types of People, Preferences between Two Activities, Characteristics, and World of Work Preferences. The SII yields five types of results. The six General Occupational Themes (GOTs) are homogeneous interest scales based on Holland's hexagonal model: Realistic, Investigative, Artistic, Social, Enterprising, and Conventional. The 25 Basic Interest Scales (BIS), which are also homogeneous scales, measure more specific interests than the GOTs. The 211 Occupational Scales (OSs) include separate female and male scales for 102 occupations and seven single-gender scales. The OSs are empirically derived from the response profiles of distinct occupational criterion groups. There are four Personal Style Scales (PSS): Work Style, Learning Environment, Leadership Style, and Risk Taking/Adventure. Finally, there are three Administrative Indices. The Total Response (TR) Index is a count of the number of completed items. Percentages of "like," "indifferent," and "dislike" responses in each of the eight sections are reported. The Infrequent Response (IR) Index is used to detect invalid or unusual profiles.

The Strong Profile—Standard Edition is a six-page report. The first profile page is a "Snapshot" of the rank-ordered GOTs, the top 5 BISs, and the top 10 OSs. The second profile page depicts the 6 GOTs and their corresponding BISs with box-and-whisker graphs. The boxes depict the middle 50% and the whiskers depict the middle 80% of the distribution. Results plotted beyond the whiskers represent the extreme top and bottom 10% of the distribution. The next three pages report OS results within the respective GOT interest areas. The sixth page reports the PSSs and the administrative indexes.

High School and College editions of the Strong Profile that provide links to postsecondary options and academic majors are available. Narrative Interpretive, Professional, Career Enrichment, and Career Transition reports are also available. There are three administration options. The traditional Form T317 item booklet/answer sheet is completed and mailed to a scoring center. Software is available for on-site scoring and production of profiles and reports. Finally, Internet administration is available with immediate access to the various profiles and reports.

DEVELOPMENT. The SII is unique in representing two major traditions of interest testing: Empirical and homogeneous scaling. The original Strong Vocational Interest Blank included occupational scales that empirically differentiated criterion groups from people in general. OS results are based on the likes and dislikes of the target occupation. Empirically derived interest scales are powerful because they identify specific occupational groups with which the respondent shares interests; respondents often score similar to occupational groups that had not been considered previously as career alternatives. However, respondents can be confused as to why they score "similar" to Accountants or Ministers because there are numerous ways that one can score high—or low—on any given occupational scale. This problem was addressed by introduction of the homogeneous Basic Interest Scales in 1968. Homogeneous scales are formed by grouping intercorrelated items with similar content and have the advantage of being easily understood by test takers. A respondent scoring "similar" to the Minister OS can see the link to the "very interested" results on the Religious Activities and Social Service BISs. The homogeneous GOTs were incorporated into the Strong Profile in 1974 to simplify and organize the reporting of the BIS and OS results. The Strong incorporates the immediacy of criterion-group scaling and the transparency of homogeneous scaling.

TECHNICAL.

Standardization. In 1992 and 1993 more than 55,000 people in 50 occupations were sampled to update OS criterion groups and the GOT and BIS norms. The SII was administered to respondents in 50 occupations (48 female-male paired samples, 2 single-gender samples). The median sample size for these criterion groups was 250, with fewer than 200 respondents in eight groups. The General Reference Sample (GRS) consists of random samples of 200 from 90 criterion group samples and the total sample of the 8 criterion groups that had fewer than 200 respondents. The resulting GRS consists of 18,951 (9,467 female, 9,484 male) employed adults who were: satisfied with their occupations, doing tasks typical of the occupation, successful, with at least 3 years of job incumbency. The GRS is used to calculate GOT and BIS standard scores and to identify items

differentiating occupational criterion groups for use in OS calculation.

Reliability. Cronbach alphas for the GOT, BIS, and PSS scales were calculated using the GRS. Four samples were used to demonstrate stability. The first sample included 191 employed adults who were retested following a 3- to 6-month interval. The second sample included 84 college students retested after a 1-month interval. The third (n = 79) and fourth (n = 87) samples included college students enrolled in career development classes retested after 3-month intervals.

The alpha reliability estimates for the GOTs were in the range of .90–.94. The GOT test-retest reliability coefficients were in the range of .74–.92 with median retest coefficients of .89, .86, .82, and .83 for the four samples, respectively. The alpha coefficients for the BISs were in the range of .74–.94 with a median of .87. The BIS retest reliability coefficients were in the range of .66–.94 with median retest coefficients of .86, .85, .80, and .83 for the four samples. Alpha coefficients are not reported for the OSs in the guide. The OS retest reliability coefficients were in the range of .66–.96 and median retest coefficients for the four samples were .90, .87, .85, and .84. For the PSSs, the alpha coefficients were .91 for Work Style, .86 for Learning Environment, .86 for Leadership, and .78 for Risk Taking/Adventure. The median retest reliability coefficients were .90, .86, .87, and .87 for the four samples. In general, the reliability properties of the SII scales are impressive. Stability was highest for the employed adults and was more than satisfactory for the groups of college students enrolled in career development classes.

Validity. Two forms of concurrent validity evidence are reported for the GOTs. First, the 15 highest ranking and 15 lowest ranking occupational groups were listed for each GOT. Predictable patterns were apparent. For example, auto mechanics and carpenters had the highest Realistic GOT results; childcare providers and public relations directors had the lowest scores. Second, educational majors were determined for 16,694 of the GRS respondents. The mean GOT profiles for each of the educational major groups were consistent with theoretical expectations.

The same method was used to document the concurrent validity of the 25 BISs. The highest and lowest ranking occupations on each BIS were consistent with expectations. Readers are referred to earlier versions of the Strong manual for information regarding predictive validity of the BISs. There was no direct evidence for the predictive validity of the Applied Arts, Culinary Arts, Data Management, and Computer Activities BISs that were added in 1994.

The concurrent validity of the OSs was evaluated by calculating the Tilton Overlap, which is the percentage of OS scores in an occupational criterion group that is matched by scores in the GRS distribution. A low overlap indicates that the criterion group is highly distinct from the GRS. The lowest overlap percentage was 15% for male medical illustrator, indicating that the interest profile of this occupational group was most distinct from the GRS profile. The highest overlap was 61% for female small business owner; the interest profile of this occupational group overlaps considerably with the modal GRS interest profile. The median overlap for the OSs was 36%, indicating that there was a difference of almost two standard deviations in the OS means of the criterion groups and the GRS. This evidence indicates that the OSs represent the unique interest profiles of distinct occupational groups. The mean GOT results of each OS criterion group also follow the predicted pattern. In the guide there is a detailed discussion of seven predictive validity studies of previous versions of the OSs. Overall, there is a moderate-to-excellent hit rate of approximately 65% between OSs and subsequent occupational selections. This evidence constitutes strong support for the predictive validity for the OSs.

The concurrent validity of the PSSs was addressed with the method used for the GOTs and BISs. The PSS score distributions of various occupational and educational major groups were in the predicted direction. There was no mention of predictive validity findings of the PSSs.

Differential validity. The SII developers took a multifaceted approach to dealing with the fact that women and men differ in their responses to interest inventories. First, standard scores for women and men on the GOTs and BISs are calculated using the means of the combined female and male GRS. These standard scores are graphed on the box-and-whisker graph distribution of the sex of the respondent. Even though a female respondent may have a Realistic GOT score that is lower than the male average, her score may appear higher than average on the female

distribution. Second, the box-and-whisker distributions of both genders are provided for each GOT, BIS, and PSS on the Strong profile. Each respondent is able to examine how her or his results compare to the norms of the same and other gender. Third, scores are calculated on the 102 OSs for which both female and male samples are available. Respondents can compare the similarity of their interests to those of both women and men in each of these occupations. Fourth, OSs results based on same-gender groups are graphed on the Strong Profile. The Profile provides maximal information to the respondent, but the graphic presentation is focused on same-gender results. The counselor and client are free to graph the other-gender OS results if they wish to do so. Finally, the GOT, BIS, and OS results presented in the Snapshot are compared to persons of the same gender. This approach to reporting and presenting SII results acknowledges gender difference in interest test results yet empowers the counseling dyad to choose comparison groups when interpreting test results.

Use of the Strong with racial and ethnic minorities is discussed in a separate Guide chapter. Of the 55,000 respondents in the 1992–1993 renorming of the Strong, approximately 6% were members of racial and ethnic minority groups. The test developers compared the item response distributions of the separate African American, American Indian, Asian, and Latino/Hispanic groups with those of the GRS. Using a 16% item response difference as a criterion, 31 items (10%) were found to differentiate at least one of these groups from the GRS. For example, African American respondents expressed higher interest in religious activities than the GRS. However, these item differences have little effect on the GOT or BIS scale scores. There were no differences in the mean GOT scores of these four racial/ethnic groups and the GRS means and only three BIS means were different from those of the GRS. Both female and male African Americans had higher Religious Activities scores and female African Americans had lower Nature scores than the GRS. Race and ethnicity do not appear to affect GOT, BIS, or PSS results. The effects of race and ethnicity on the OSs could not be explored because of the low distribution of minority respondents across the 211 criterion groups. Counselors have sufficient validity evidence to use the Strong with clients from these four racial and ethnic minority groups.

COMMENTARY. The SII has six notable strengths. First, it provides both empirical and homogeneous interest scale results in an attractive Profile. Second, the GOTs represent Holland's hexagonal model better than other popular interest measures (Rounds, 1995). Third, there are no significant differences in the structures of female and male GOTs (Anderson, Tracey, & Rounds, 1997). Fourth, the circular order of the six GOTs (R-I-A-S-E-C) holds for Caucasian, African American, Asian American, and Latino/Hispanic women and men (Fouad, Harmon, & Borgen, 1997). Fifth, the Administrative indices enable the counselor to assess profile validity and provide insight into conflicting or confusing results. Sixth, the guide provides extensive technical information and valuable suggestions for general interpretation of the Strong as well as for use with women, minority group members, and disabled individuals. The quality of writing and overall organization of the guide are excellent.

The SII also has four weaknesses. First, criterion group data for 62 (29%) of the 211 OSs were collected 20 or more years ago. The scores for more than a quarter of the OSs are based on old response profiles that may not adequately represent the modal interest of contemporary job incumbents. There is a pressing need for updating of the criterion groups, especially when considering that data for an additional 51 (24%) OSs were gathered in 1983 and 1984. Second, racial and ethnic group members were not adequately represented in the 1994 GRS. Of the 98 updated criterion groups, 30 had 4% or fewer minority group members; only 18 (18%) had 10% or more racial and minority group respondents. When one considers that approximately one quarter of persons in the 2000 U.S. Census were members of racial and ethnic minority groups, it is evident that the Strong GRS fails to represent the racial and ethnic diversity of the United States. To be fair, it should be acknowledged that the test developers were constrained in seeking experienced respondents who were engaged in typical work tasks and satisfied in their work. However, this constraint does not diminish the responsibility of test developers to constitute a norm group that reflects the general population. Third, the discussion of the predictive validity for the GOTs is limited. Greater efforts should have been taken to summarize the available evidence regarding the predictive power of the GOTs. Fourth, the manual does not specify

the response percentages of those comprising the occupational criterion groups. It is not clear, for example, how many potential respondents were canvassed to attain the final sample of 365 female dentists. Further, no evidence was presented to describe how typical the respondents were in comparison to all members of each occupational group. This problem is not addressed in a forthright manner in the guide.

CONCLUSIONS AND RECOMMENDATIONS. The Strong is the best interest assessment available to career counselors. It has proven reliability and validity properties. The Strong has been demonstrated to be valid for women and men as well as for various racial and ethnic groups. It provides an impressive and comprehensive profile of interests, ranging from the narrow OSs to the more general BISs to the global GOTs. The PSSs are valuable in helping respondents understand how basic personality characteristics affect their academic, leisure, and work preferences. This reviewer recommends use of the Strong without reservation.

REVIEWER'S REFERENCES

Anderson, M. Z., Tracey, T., & Rounds, J. (1997). Examining the invariance of Holland's vocational interest model across gender. *Journal of Vocational Behavior, 50,* 349–364.

Fouad, A., Harmon, L. W., & Borgen, F. H. (1997). Structure of interests in employed male and female members of U. S. racial-ethnic minority and nonminority groups. *Journal of Counseling Psychology, 44,* 339–345.

Rounds, J. (1995). Vocational interests: Evaluating structural hypotheses. In D. J. Lubinski & R. V. Dawis (Eds.), *Assessing individual differences in human behavior: New concepts, methods, and findings* (pp. 177–232). Palo Alto, CA: Davies-Black.

Review of the Strong Interest Inventory® [1994] by EUGENE P. SHEEHAN, Dean, College of Education, University of Northern Colorado, Greeley, CO:

DESCRIPTION. That the Strong Interest Inventory has been in use since 1927 is a testament to the solid psychometric foundation on which this instrument is based. The Strong requires respondents to indicate their interests in and preferences for a wide array of familiar items (e.g., occupations and occupational activities, leisure activities, types of people, and school subjects). There are 317 items and the Strong requires about 35–40 minutes to complete. Responses given on a 3-point scale are compared to the pattern of responses of people in different occupations and of different types. In general, a pattern of responses similar to the pattern gleaned from a population of, for example, corporate trainers would suggest that the respondent has interests in common with corporate trainers and that the respondent should evaluate corporate training as a potential career.

In addition to information pertaining to specific occupations, the Strong provides detailed information on respondents' occupational preferences. Scores on six General Occupational Themes describe the respondent's overall orientation to work. Scores on 25 Basic Interest Scales indicate consistency of interests or aversions in 25 specific areas including writing, science, culinary arts, and public speaking. Scores on 211 Occupational Scales portray 109 different occupations. These scores indicate how similar or dissimilar a respondent's patterns of interest are to those of women and men working in those occupations. The Personal Style Scales measure characteristics of how a person works, learns, leads, and takes risks. Finally, the three types of Administrative Indexes identify invalid or curious profiles. Clearly, this amount of information provides respondents and counselors with in-depth information to initiate a career search.

Counseling sessions are facilitated by the clear and understandable way in which profiles are presented. The graphic representations in the profiles, combined with the in-depth descriptions of the meaning of these profiles, result in a tool that is relatively easy to interpret. The presentation of data is enhanced over the 1985 version of the Strong. The information given to respondents also assists in the interpretation of seeming inconsistencies in a profile. For example, how does high interest in the Mathematics Basic Interest Scale relate with a score in the dissimilar range on the Mathematician Occupational Scale? Further, the Applications and Technical Guide provides a comprehensive explanation of the various scales and profiles and their interpretation. There are several chapters in the guide that describe the use of the Strong with different populations: adults, college students, high school students, and people with disabilities. Two other chapters discuss cross-cultural and gender issues in the development and use of the Strong. Anyone using the Strong should be thoroughly familiar with this guide. Despite all the interpretive advice, the authors caution that the Strong should be used in conjunction with other client information—aptitudes and work experience for example.

DEVELOPMENT. The 1994 edition demonstrates the test developers' continued commitment to update and improve the inventory. Items were added or deleted based on psychometric analyses. These are detailed in the technical guide.

There are 35 new items in the 1994 edition. Other items were changed to reflect current terminology (e.g., typist became word processor). Additionally, the number of Occupational Scales was revised and increased. The most intriguing development is the addition of the Personal Style Scales to replace the Special Scales in the 1985 Strong. These scales suggest environments in which respondents prefer to learn and work. The Work Style Scale, for example, attempts to assess preferences for working with people, data, ideas, or things. Other Personal Style Scales include: Learning Environment, Leadership Style, and Risk/Adventure.

TECHNICAL. The developers present important reliability evidence throughout the technical guide, in conjunction with detailed explanations of the various scales. These data reveal the Strong to provide highly reliable scores. Short-term test-retest reliabilities (in four samples over varying intervals) for the General Occupational Themes ranged from a low of .74 to a high of .92. Three-year test-retest reliabilities for these themes (on the 1985 edition) ranged from .78 to .87. In all but one case, the coefficient alphas and the test-retest reliabilities of the 1994 Strong General Occupational Themes are higher than the 1985 scale. Except for the Investigative theme, the 1994 themes contain more items than do the 1985 themes.

For the Occupational Scales, 3- to 6-month reliability coefficients are all above .81, with many above .90. Data on the number of items per Occupational Scale are provided and indicate the scales range from 23 items for male audiologist to 70 for male technical writer.

Validity data are organized much like the reliability data and are presented throughout the technical guide. These validity data support the contention that the Strong is a psychometrically sound inventory. The developers describe, for example, correlational data between the General Occupational Themes and the Vocational Preference Inventory Scales. The correlations were high (median = .77), indicating the two inventories are measuring similar interest dimensions. Additionally, construct validity evidence of the General Occupational Themes is provided through the theme intercorrelations. These intercorrelations support Holland's hexagonal model upon which the Strong is based: The highest correlations occur between the adjacent themes and the lowest occur between the opposite themes.

Concurrent and predictive validity evidence for the accuracy of the Strong in predicting the choice of college majors is also strong. In a concurrent validity study about 75% of college seniors scored above 40 on the Occupational Scales most closely related to their college major. In more predictive validity studies, the Strong accurately predicted the major of more than 55% of entering freshmen. As one might expect, given the greater difficulty in long range prediction, the predictive validity of the Basic Interest Scales is not as high as their concurrent validity. I would like to see the developers provide a summary of all validity-related studies.

COMMENTARY AND SUMMARY. The Strong is a psychometrically well-developed interest inventory. Reliability and validity data indicate the scores can be used to help make sound career decisions. Developers have continued to strive for improvements and innovations in this inventory. Complementing the solid psychometric data is the wealth of career and occupational information provided with the instrument. Career counselors, psychologists, and others using the Strong will find they have an instrument that is not only methodologically sophisticated, but also one that will provide clients with much information to ponder along with the resources with which to make reasoned career decisions.

[249]
Structured Interview for the Five-Factor Model of Personality.

Purpose: Designed "to assess personality using the Five-Factor Model."
Population: Ages 18 and above.
Publication Date: 1997.
Acronym: SIFFM.
Scores, 35: Neuroticism (Anxiety, Hostility, Depression, Self-Consciousness, Impulsiveness, Vulnerability, Total), Extraversion (Warmth, Gregariousness, Assertiveness, Activity, Excitement-Seeking, Positive Emotions, Total), Openness to Experience (Fantasy, Aesthetics, Feelings, Actions, Ideas, Values, Total), Agreeableness (Trust, Straightforwardness, Altruism, Compliance, Modesty, Tender-Mindedness, Total), Conscientiousness (Competence, Order, Dutifulness, Achievement-Striving, Self-Discipline, Deliberation, Total).
Administration: Individual.
Price Data: Available from publisher for introductory kit including 25 interview booklets and professional manual (85 pages).

Time: (60) minutes.
Authors: Timothy J. Trull and Thomas A. Widiger.
Publisher: Psychological Assessment Resources, Inc.

Review of the Structured Interview for the Five-Factor Model of Personality by PAUL M. MASTRANGELO, Associate Professor of Psychology, University of Baltimore, Baltimore, MD:

DESCRIPTION. The Structured Interview for the Five-Factor Model of Personality (SIFFM) contains 120 items designed for a one-on-one interview with a respondent. Each item potentially requires a follow-up question (e.g., Are you prone to have outbursts of anger? If yes, does your anger often feel out of your control? Give me some examples). So, use of this instrument may involve more than 120 interview questions, but the follow-up questions are all used to clarify the respondent's initial answer. Each item is scored as 0, 1, or 2 where the distinction between a 1 and a 2 is based on the follow-up question. The domain and facet scores are created by summing pertinent item scores, and the process is very straightforward. The professional manual states that formal graduate training is not required to administer the SIFFM, but "some background in psychopathology, personality, and structured interviewing is necessary" (p. 11).

The items are designed to measure the "Big Five" personality domains, which is an empirically driven, factor analytical structure of adjectives used to describe personality (see Goldberg, 1990). These continuously scored domains are Neuroticism (vs. Emotional Stability), Extroversion (vs. Introversion), Openness to Experience (vs. Closedness to Experience), Agreeableness (vs. Antagonism), and Conscientiousness (vs. Negligence). Each of these five personality domain scores also can be broken down into six facet scores. For example, the 24 Neuroticism items include 4 items for each of the following facets: Anxiety, Hostility, Depression, Self-Consciousness, Impulsiveness, and Vulnerability. Although there is little agreement among researchers regarding the number and interpretation of facets per domain, the authors chose to base their facets upon the Revised NEO Personality Inventory (NEO-PI-R) (Costa & McCrae, 1992), which is a widely recognized self-report personality instrument based on the Big Five. Despite the strong similarities between the two instruments, the SIFFM is distinct from the NEO for two reasons. First, the SIFFM was designed for an interview format rather than paper and pencil, potentially impacting the mindset of respondents. For example, someone (hypothetically) may respond more honestly when answering to an interviewer rather than an answer booklet. Second, the SIFFM was designed to measure personality within clinical as well as nonclinical populations. Thus, personality disorders can purportedly be diagnosed more easily with the SIFFM than with the NEO.

DEVELOPMENT. The SIFFM was originally developed in 1990, but has undergone four substantial changes since that time. These changes are adequately described in the professional manual, and they have made this instrument appropriate for the measure of both normal and abnormal personalities. In fact, the manual provides strong justification for using the SIFFM as a tool for diagnosing Axis II (personality) disorders from the *Diagnostic and Statistical Manual of Mental Disorders* (American Psychiatric Association, 1994). The manual provides an excellent conceptual review of each facet and its relation to the 10 DSM-IV personality disorders. For example, a client diagnosed with Schizoid personality disorder theoretically should score "low" on facets of Hostility, Self-Consciousness, Warmth, Gregariousness, Activity, Positive Emotions, and Openness to Feelings. These SIFFM profiles of personality disorders could help create clearer diagnoses, but only if there were empirical evidence supporting these hypothetical relationships. Unfortunately, the authors report no research that demonstrates accurate diagnoses using the SIFFM, and they provide no normative data that would help identify maladaptive personality traits. The SIFFM desperately needs to be researched further before it can fulfill its promise as a diagnostic tool.

TECHNICAL. The professional manual describes only five studies used to estimate psychometric properties of the SIFFM, and none of these studies was completed using the current version (even though 30% of the items are new and another 18% were modified from previous versions). The one (somewhat relevant) study on the previous version of the SIFFM used only 233 participants (187 undergraduates, 46 clinic participants). The alpha coefficients of the five domain scores were all greater than .70, but 16 of the 30 facet scores had alpha coefficients below .60, and these were predominantly in the "Agreeableness" and "Openness to Experience" domains. The interrater

reliability estimates (Pearson's *r*) were all above .91 and the test-retest reliabilities over a 2-week span ranged from .61 to .93, suggesting stable and identifiable personality profiles.

The exploratory factor analysis calculated (again on the previous SIFFM version) suggests that at least one facet in each of the five domains may be misplaced, meaning they might belong in another domain. Impulsiveness loads more highly on Conscientiousness than on Neuroticism, whereas Positive Emotions loads more highly on Neuroticism than on Extroversion, and so forth. It would be useful to have the factor loadings of individual items with a five-factor solution, but this would require more than 233 participants. Furthermore, a confirmatory factor analysis is more appropriate here because the goal is to match a particular factor structure, not explore what that structure might be.

There is evidence of construct validity in the pattern of positive correlations between SIFFM scores and corresponding NEO PI-R scores, but there is no evidence of criterion-related validity. This same study featured college students and clinic participants, so one would expect to see if these two disparate groups showed significantly different scores; however, these results were not provided. One would also expect to see a comparison between the diagnoses of the clinical participants and their SIFFM profiles to support the diagnostic accuracy of the instrument, but again these results were not provided.

Instead, SIFFM scores were correlated with "PDQ-R Personality Disorder Symptom Counts" (no psychometric properties of the PDQ-R were provided). The pattern of correlations using domain scores were purportedly consistent with previous studies, but the pattern of correlations using facet scores (Table 19, manual, p. 70) did not match the expected pattern for DSM-IV personality disorders (Table 4, manual, p. 53).

These problematic results stem from the development of the SIFFM based on the typical True Score Theory approach of building internally consistent domain scores. The manual suggests that certain personality disorders will be identified through a combination of high and low facet scores within one domain. For example, a person diagnosed with Dependent personality disorder is supposed to have high scores on the Warmth and Gregariousness facets, but low scores on the Assertiveness and Activity facets. This pattern should be unlikely because all four of these facets are positively correlated within the Extroversion domain. A person scoring highly on one facet in this domain should score highly on the other facets in this domain, too. The manual does not explain how these proposed psychometric anomalies are supposed to occur. Does a maladaptive personality have a different factor structure from a "normal" personality? If yes, then it would be impossible for the SIFFM to be applicable in both normal and clinical populations. If no, then the internal consistencies of the domain scores should actually be reduced to allow for more independence among the facet scores.

COMMENTARY. It seems unwise to publish an instrument without having conducted any research using the current version. Furthermore, it seems presumptuous to design a diagnostic psychometric instrument without examining the accuracy of the predicted diagnoses. This promising instrument needs more and better research to live up to its claims.

SUMMARY. The previous version of the SIFFM demonstrated adequate internal consistency, strong interrater reliability, and strong construct validity when assessing personality in general; however, it was not tested adequately as a measure of personality disorders. Furthermore, the professional manual reports no research on the current version of the SIFFM. The instrument should certainly be helpful for research purposes, but it is not yet ready for professional use.

REVIEWER'S REFERENCES

American Psychiatric Association. (1994). *Diagnostic and statistical manual of mental disorders* (4th ed.). Washington, DC: Author.
Costa, P. T., Jr., & McCrae, R. R. (1992). *Revised NEO Personality Inventory (NEO-PI-R) and NEO Five-Factor Inventory (NEO-FFI) professional manual.* Odessa, FL: Psychological Assessment Resources.
Goldberg, L. R. (1990). An alternative "description of personality": The Big-Five factor structure. *Journal of Personality and Social Psychology, 59,* 1216–1229.

Review of the Structured Interview for the Five-Factor Model of Personality by SUSANA URBINA, Professor of Psychology, University of North Florida, Jacksonville, FL:

DESCRIPTION. The Structured Interview for the Five-Factor Model of Personality (SIFFM) consists of 120 items designed to assess personality using the Five-Factor Model (FFM). Its scales are patterned on the version of the FFM developed by McCrae and Costa (1990) and coincide with the domains and facets embodied in the Revised NEO Personality Inventory (NEO PI-R; Costa & McCrae, 1992; T6:2110). A major difference between the NEO PI-R and the SIFFM, is the latter's semistructured interview format, which allows for follow-up questions and probes. Another difference is that the SIFFM aims to assess both normal and maladaptive aspects of the personality traits comprised within McCrae and Costa's model, whereas the NEO PI-R focuses primarily on normal aspects of personality.

In fact, the main rationale for the development of the SIFFM is Trull and Widiger's (the authors) dissatisfaction with the personality disorder categories of the *Diagnostic and Statistical Manual of Mental Disorders, Fourth Edition* (DSM-IV; American Psychiatric Association, 1994). Trull and Widiger believe that the FFM offers a more comprehensive and theoretically neutral framework for evaluating both normal and abnormal personality patterns. Furthermore, they also maintain that the FFM framework has more empirical support than the DSM-IV classification of personality disorders.

The SIFFM can be used with any individual aged 18 or older who is able to understand and respond meaningfully to verbally presented questions. Each of the dimensions in the FFM—Neuroticism, Extraversion, Openness to Experience, Agreeableness, and Conscientiousness—subsumes six facets or bipolar traits that describe more specific aspects of personality. In the SIFFM there are four questions per facet that help, along with the follow-up probes, to pinpoint the extent to which each of the 30 traits is present. If the response to a question is in the direction indicative of the presence of a trait, it may be followed by a second question aimed at establishing the strength of the trait. For example, in the Gregariousness facet of Extraversion, one question is "Do you prefer to do most activities with other people or alone?" If the answer were "With other people," the interviewer would then ask "Are you rarely by yourself?" Answers are rated on a 3-point ordinal scale (0, 1, 2), with higher scores signifying a greater degree of the trait. Thus, the maximum score on each facet is 8 (4 x 2) and the maximum score on each domain is 48 (6 x 8). Of the 120 items, 49 are reverse-scored.

DEVELOPMENT. The SIFFM was developed through a methodical multistage process. First, item writers who were familiar with the FFM and well versed in test construction generated items that would assess pathological and nonpathological levels of the traits in question.

Next, items generated by one writer were reviewed by other writers and modified as needed. Four different versions of the SIFFM, of varying lengths, were successively tried out on undergraduate students and some outpatients from a mental health clinic. These versions were evaluated and modified on the basis of their internal consistency within domains, interrater reliability, and several indices of convergent and discriminant validity of items and scales. The final version of the SIFFM has the same total number of items as Version 4. However, based on psychometric data from the earlier version, 36 of the items were replaced and are new to the final version. Twenty-two additional items also underwent minor wording changes.

In spite of the obvious care taken in developing and modifying the SIFFM items, some of them still have problems. Several are compound questions (e.g., "Do you feel that persons of different cultural, ethnic, or gender groups are asking for too much these days?") and could thus be difficult for some to answer. Other questions are loaded ("Do you tend to stick up for your rights and needs?") or have vague referents that ask interviewees to make judgments about themselves relative to other people that may be hard or impossible to make ("Are you more careful than most not to hurt others' feelings?"). Still, the majority of the questions and probes are phrased in terms of fairly unambiguous behavioral anchors and are sufficiently varied to elicit a wealth of clinically relevant material.

The largest portion of the SIFFM manual is devoted to an explanation of the domains and facets of the FFM and their relationship to psychopathology, as well as brief descriptions, mostly in terms of adjectives, of the characteristics and problematic aspects associated with individuals who are at the extreme ends of each. Although the authors of the SIFFM recognize that some domains and facets are more closely associated with psychopathology than others, they also emphasize that each domain and facet—and even each of their extreme poles—has the potential to be maladaptive within some context.

TECHNICAL. The authors of the SIFFM decided to publish this instrument without providing normative data. In support of this decision they adduce several reasons, chief among them the fact that it would have been difficult to collect data on a sufficiently large and representative normative sample. Therefore, the cutoff points for High and Low scores for each facet and domain are "rationally" rather than empirically based.

Each of the four preliminary versions of the SIFFM was evaluated for various aspects of reliability and validity on various samples. Subsequent versions were developed by dropping and adding items based on the analyses of the earlier versions. The most extensive studies were conducted on Versions 3 and 4, using a sample of 233 subjects (187 undergraduate students and 46 outpatients from a community mental health clinic). Data from the studies done on Version 4 are reported in detail in the manual.

Interrater reliability was assessed by correlating ratings of interviews done in vivo with the ratings assigned by an independent reliability checker based on audiotapes of the same interviews. Intraclass correlation coefficients, which account for between- and within-subject variance, in addition to interrater agreement, were also obtained. Both types of coefficients were high, ranging from .94 to 1.00 for domains and from .71 to 1.00 for facets, with the majority in the .90s. The stability of scores for Version 4 was assessed via test-retest (2-week interval) and intraclass correlations; coefficients ranged from .81 to .93 for domains and from .58 to .90 for facets, with most in the .70s or higher.

The validity of Version 4 of the SIFFM was investigated by means of three correlational studies and two factor analyses. In the correlational studies, patterns of convergent and discriminant validity data were examined for the SIFFM and the NEO PI-R, the SIFFM and a Personality Disorders Questionnaire (PDQ-R), and the SIFFM and a peer report version of the NEO Five-Factor Inventory (NEO-FFI; Costa & McCrae, 1992). In general, these data show good correspondence between the SIFFM and the NEO PI-R scores and between the SIFFM self-report and the NEO-FF peer report data. Intercorrelations between the SIFFM facet scores and the PDQ-R symptom counts produce interesting patterns of relationships among the facets within single domains for the different personality disorders. The factor analysis of the domain scores from the SIFFM and the NEO PI-R suggests a good deal of convergence between the two instruments. Similarly, the factor analysis of the 30 facet scores from the SIFFM, for the most part, supports the five-factor structure of the instrument.

SUMMARY. The SIFFM promises to be a useful tool for the investigation of normal and maladaptive personality patterns in both clinical and research settings. Although it joins a growing list of instruments for the assessment of personality by means of the five-factor model, its interview format makes it more attractive for clinicians, counselors, and other practitioners of individual assessment than the existing paper-and-pencil alternatives (see e.g., Widiger & Trull, 1997). However, the publication of the SIFFM at this point seems premature. Although 30% of the items in the final version of the SIFFM are new, no psychometric data are reported for that version. The potential usefulness of this innovative tool will not be fully realized until psychometric data on its final version are generated and published. Prior to that, the authors might consider some editing to reword items that are still confusing or problematic.

REVIEWER'S REFERENCES

American Psychiatric Association. (1994). *Diagnostic and statistical manual of mental disorders* (4th ed.). Washington, DC: Author.
Costa, P. T., Jr., & McCrae, R. R. (1992). Revised NEO Personality Inventory (NEO PI-R) and NEO Five-Factor Inventory (NEO-FFI) professional manual. Odessa, FL: Psychological Assessment Resources.
McCrae, R. R., & Costa, P. T., Jr. (1990). *Personality in adulthood.* New York: Guilford.
Widiger, T. A., & Trull, T. J. (1997). Assessment of the five-factor model of personality. *Journal of Personality Assessment, 68*, 228–250.

[250]

Student Behavior Survey.

Purpose: A multidimensional assessment to rate behavior and classroom performance to reflect the presence of problems in emotional and behavioral adjustment.
Population: Ages 5–18.
Publication Date: 2000.
Acronym: SBS.
Scores: 11 scales: Academic Performance, Academic Habits, Social Skills, Parent Participation, Health Concerns, Emotional Distress, Unusual Behavior, Social Problems, Verbal Aggression, Physical Aggression, Behavior Problems.
Administration: Individual.
Price Data, 2002: $78 per introductory kit including 25 AutoScore™ answer/profile forms and manual (72 pages); $29.95 per 25 AutoScore™ answer/profile forms; $52.50 per manual.
Time: Untimed.
Comments: Ratings by teachers.
Authors: David Lachar, Sabine A. Wingenfeld, Rex B. Kline, and Christian P. Gruber.
Publisher: Western Psychological Services.

Review of the Student Behavior Survey by STEPHEN N. AXFORD, *Psychologist/Assistant Director of Special Education, Pueblo School District No. Sixty, Pueblo, CO:*

DESCRIPTION AND DEVELOPMENT. The Student Behavior Survey (SBS) is a brief, multidimensional assessment for rating student (Grades K–12, ages 5–18 years) school behaviors by teachers, in identifying emotional and behavioral maladjustment. A complete distribution of exact *T*-scores is provided in the Appendix of the SBS manual for a total of 14 scales; four considering Academic Resources (Academic performance, Academic Habits, Social Skills, Parent Participation); seven considering Adjustment Problems (Health Concerns, Emotional Distress, Unusual Behavior, Social Problems, Verbal Aggression, Physical Aggression, Behavior Problems); and three considering Disruptive Behavior (Attention-Deficit/Hyperactivity, Opposition Defiant, Conduct Problems). A single-sheet (front-and-back) SBS profile form is also provided, allowing for quick conversion of raw scores corresponding to *T*-scores. Separate *T*-scores are provided for males and females. An AutoScore Form allows for efficient scoring of the SBS. The SBS materials are very well organized, user friendly, and professional in quality in terms of face validity. The SBS manual is particularly well developed, providing ample technical information and scoring/interpretation guidelines, including examples.

The SBS consists of 102 items utilizing a multipoint Likert-type scale response format. The teacher-completed SBS is a companion assessment to the parent-completed Personality Inventory for Children, Second Edition (PIC-2; Lachar & Gruber, 2000; T6:1883) and the self-report Personality Inventory for Youth (PIY; Lachar & Gruber, 1995; T6:1884). As described by the authors, the SBS is intended to be used by school psychologists, counselors, and other mental health professionals to incorporate critical information provided by educators as part of a multidimensional, comprehensive assessment. The SBS potentially has utility in making educational program decisions, as with developing an Individualized Education Plan consistent with the Individuals with Disabilities Education Act (IDEA).

TECHNICAL. Review of the psychometric properties of the SBS indicates considerable time and resources were committed to its development. Data were collected over a 6-year period (1994–1999), involving over 4,500 administrations of the instrument and over 2,300 concurrent administrations of other instruments. Standardization of the SBS involved 22 school sites across 11 states representing all four major U.S. Census regions.

The final standardization sample comprised teacher ratings on 2,612 regular education students. Approximately 200 students represented each grade level, Kindergarten through Grade 12. According to the authors, data were collected in urban, suburban, and rural areas and included a broad spectrum of socioeconomic status. This is supported by review of school sites and reported data on parents' educational levels, the latter being reasonably similar to the U.S. Census data demographic pattern. Commensurate numbers of males ($n = 1,267$, 48.5% of sample) and females ($n = 1,345$, 51.5% of sample) comprised the total regular education sample, which is comparable to U.S. Census data (respectively 49.7% and 50.3%). Ethnic background for the regular education sample was also comparable to U.S. Census data. The sample percentages for ethnicity follow: Asian American = 2.1% (U.S. Census % = 3.7), Black = 15.2 (U.S. Census % = 14.8), Hispanic = 10.1 (U.S. Census % = 13.9), White = 69.9 (U.S. Census % = 66.6), and Other = 2.7 (U.S. Census % = 1.1). Geographic region demographics were also similar to U.S. Census data: East = 15.8% (U.S. Census % = 19.3), Midwest = 27.6% (U.S. Census % = 23.3), South = 38.3% (U.S. Census = 35.1%), West = 18.4% (U.S. Census = 22.2%).

In a separate sample, 1,315 students referred for assessment related to behavioral and academic concerns were also evaluated using the SBS. The sample included individuals in special education settings, clinical settings, and juvenile justice residential centers representing 41 facilities in 17 U.S. states and one Canadian province. Although there was representation from each demographic category for this sample, greater discrepancies were observed relative to U.S. Census data (e.g., nearly twice as many males as females; male $n = 952$, female $n = 363$). However, this is understandable given the nature of referral patterns.

The authors report findings of follow-up analyses examining differences in means between the regular education sample and the sample representing clinically and educationally referred students. This addressed the power of the SBS to differentiate between students experiencing difficulties in school and those presenting as relatively

well adjusted. Additional analyses investigated the magnitude and clinical importance of the observed SBS scales mean score differences. Utilizing Cohen's d, large differences were observed for all scale means, with the exceptions of Parent Participation (Cohen's d = -.23, indicating a small difference) and Health Concerns (Cohen's d = .51, indicating a moderate difference).

The authors also examined age and gender differences, utilizing three MANOVA analyses corresponding to the SBS diagnostic groupings.

As the authors note, these analyses indicate robust findings across sets of scales. Follow-up one-way ANOVAs on the individual scales indicated pervasive gender effects. All but one scale (Emotional Distress) yielded significant F scores. Effect sizes, based on Cohen's d values, ranged from very small (d = .12) to bordering on moderate (d = .47). As is often observed in similar studies, females manifested fewer overt behavior concerns as perceived by teachers (i.e., teachers tend to rate female students more positively). These data along with the recognized need to ensure minimizing underidentification of females and overidentification of males supported development of separate norms by gender. On the other hand, age effects were observed to be considerably less pervasive, with three scales (Parent Participation, Physical Aggression, and Attention-Deficit/Hyperactivity) showing reliable age effects. In general, teachers rated problems as less severe with older students. Effect sizes ranged from very small for the Attention-Deficit/Hyperactivity scale (d = -.14) to small for the Parent Participation (d = -.24) and Physical Aggression (d = -.31) scales. Although observed age effects were modest, the authors believed they were pervasive enough to incorporate the differences into the SBS norms. As such, separate norms are provided for students ages 5–11 years and 12–18 years.

In addressing reliability, the SBS authors examined internal consistency, test-retest reliability, and interrater agreement. Standard Error of Measurement is also provide for each approach. With respect to internal consistency, Cronbach alpha values for the regular education sample and the referred sample were all in the .80s and .90s (median = .88). the Standard Error of Measurement ranged from 2.2 to 3.7 for the regular education sample, and from 2.2 to 3.9 for the referred sample.

Regarding test-retest reliability, intervals for retesting were: 1.7 weeks (ages 5–11 years, N = 52), 2.1 weeks (ages 12–17 years, N = 31), 11.4 weeks (ages 5–12 years, N = 56), and 28.5 weeks (ages 13–19 years, N = 49). As would be predicted, reliability decreased with larger intervals between testing. The median retest reliability for the two shorter interval samples was .86. the median retest reliability for the two longer interval samples was .71.

Three studies examined interrater reliability, involving a total of 60 subjects: 30 regular education, 30 special education, and a combined sample (N = 60). Raters consisted of regular classroom and special education teachers. Correlations were generally in the .70s and .80s, with a median of .73.

The authors provide detailed discussion of several studies conducted addressing SBS scale construction and validation. In general, the data reported support the validity of the SBS in terms of internal structure, scale correlates, and scale performance across contrasted groups. One study contrasting item responses of 1,173 regular education students and 601 referred or special education students showed 97% of SBS items significantly differentiated these samples. In a study involving 1,315 referred or special education students, item-to—scale correlations for the Academic Resources and Adjustment Problems scales were examined. These data provide strong support for the conceptualization of dimensions and items. The vast majority of items correlated to scales for which they were originally designed to represent. Of the 102 items examined, only 3 were strongly correlated with other scales. A similar study (N = 1,315) examined item-to-scale correlations for the Disruptive Behavior Scales (Attention-Deficit/Hyperactivity, Oppositional Defiant, and Conduct Problems). The study revealed items correlated most with scales on which they were placed. Furthermore, item placements provided support for internal consistency: Attention/Deficit Hyperactivity alpha = .94, Oppositional Defiant alpha = .95, and Conduct Problems alpha = .94.

Student Behavior Survey Scale intercorrelations, for the sample of clinically and educationally referred students (N = 1,315) indicate: (a) Academic Performance, Parent Participation, and Health Concerns are the most independent dimensions; and (b) high comorbidity between the Disruptive Behavior Scales and externalizing dimensions, as would be predicted. Factor analysis

of the SBS scales yielded a three-factor solution accounting for 71% of the common variance; the first factor relating to externalizing behaviors and noncompliance, the second factor representing internalizing symptoms and social problems, and the third factor representing academic performance.

Several studies addressed convergent and discriminate validity for the SBS. These studies involved clinician, parent, and self-report ratings. Intake evaluations and the SBS were completed for 129 subjects. The intake evaluations utilized a six-factor, 111-item symptom checklist (Clinician Symptom Rating Form) completed by clinicians. Alpha internal consistency statistics, derived from a sample of 881 referred students, follow for the six factors: Disruptive Behavior alpha = .94, Antisocial Behavior alpha = .89, Psychological Discomfort alpha = .90, Developmental Disability alpha = .85, Serious Psychopathology alpha = .71, Family Psychopathology alpha = .81. With respect to clinician rating dimensions and SBS scales having conceptual relationship, moderate to high correlations are observed. Two studies (referred N = 521, nonreferred N = 1,199) are cited, considering correlations between teacher-reported SBS and parent-reported PIC-2 scales. Again, correlations matched predictions. Similar scales across measures showed moderate to strong relations.

Two studies examined the relationship between scales of the SBS Scales and the Conners' Teacher Rating Scale, Short Form (CTRS-28; Conners, 1989) in two samples of educationally disabled and referred students (N = 226, N = 66). General findings included: (a) the SBS Oppositional Defiant scale and the CTRS-28 Conduct Problems scale were substantially correlated (r = .87); (b) the CTRS-28 Hyperactivity scale was substantially correlated with both the SBS Attention-Deficit/Hyperactivity scale (r = .81) and Behavior Problems scale (r = .77); (c) the CTRS-28 Inattentive-Passive scale was highly correlated with the SBS Attention-Deficit/Hyperactivity (r = .74) and Academic Habits (r = .69); and (d) the CTRS-28 Hyperactivity Index scale (incorporating items from the Conduct Problems, Hyperactivity, and Inattentive-Passive scales) was substantially correlated with most of the SBS scales.

The authors report findings from several studies of contrasted groups (nine student populations with N ranging from 22 to 281), in considering how effectively the SBS differentiates various clinical populations (i.e., disruptive versus nondisruptive DSM:IV diagnoses; samples defined by elevated versus nonelevated CTRS-28 Hyperactivity Index scores; and comparisons across intellectually impaired, emotionally impaired, and learning-disabled populations). In general, the data support the ability of the SBS to differentiate contrasted groups effectively.

COMMENTARY. With regard to interpretation, one limitation of the SBS is that it does not provide validity scales, in contrast with, for example, the Behavior Assessment for Children (BASC; Reynolds & Kamphaus, 1998; T6:280). However, to the authors' credit, the SBS manual gives considerable attention to this issue. This includes discussion on identifying potentially exaggerated score profiles. Three particular problematic score profiles, with specific cutoff scores, are identified. Case studies are used to further illustrate interpretive issues concerning rater bias. In addition, the authors encourage using multiple ratings employing multiple respondents whenever feasible, to minimize problems related to giving too much credence to isolated incidences of exaggerated score profiles.

SUMMARY. Critical examination of the SBS manual, scoring materials, and teacher-completed survey form indicate the instrument is psychometrically sound and thoughtfully constructed. As intended by the authors, the SBS is a useful companion to the parent-completed PIC-2 and the self-report PIY. Clinical and educational in its scope, the SBS should prove to be particularly useful for mental health professionals (e.g., school psychologists, school social workers, counselors) working in educational settings.

REVIEWER'S REFERENCES

Lachar, D., & Gruber, C. P. (1995). *Personality Inventory for Youth (PIY): Manual.* Los Angeles: Western Psychological Services.
Lachar, D., & Gruber, C. P. (2000). *Personality Inventory for Children, Second Edition (PIC-2): Manual.* Los Angeles: Western Psychological Services.
Reynolds, C. R., & Kamphaus, R. W. (1998). *Behavior Assessment System for Children: Manual.* Circle Pines, MN: American Guidance Service.

Review of the Student Behavior Survey by MICHAEL J. FURLONG, Professor, and RENEE PAVELSKI, Doctoral Candidate, University of California, Santa Barbara, Counseling/Clinical/School Psychology Program, Gevirtz Graduate School of Education, Santa Barbara, CA:

DESCRIPTION. The Student Behavior Survey (SBS) is a 102-item, multidimensional assessment that measures behavior and classroom performance of children and adolescents from Grades K through 12 (5 through 18 years of age). The teacher-completed SBS is part of a comprehensive evaluation of student adjustment when used with the parent-completed Personality Inventory for Children, Second Edition (PIC-2, Grades K through 12; Lachar & Gruber, 2000), and the self-report Personality Inventory for Youth (PIY, Grades 4 through 12; Lachar & Gruber, 1995). With the addition of the SBS, the Lachar and associates battery of instruments now can be used in a cross-informant assessment process.

For Items 1–8, teachers rate student academic behaviors using a qualitative judgment response scale: 1 = *deficient*, 2 = *below average*, 3 = *average*, 4 = *above average*, and 5 = *superior*. For the remaining items (9–102), a behavioral frequency response scale is used: 1 = *never*, 2 = *seldom*, 3 = *sometimes*, and 4 = *usually*. This four- to five-option scale, although convenient and economical, assigns equal weights for all items. For example, how often would a student need to attempt to "Destroy(s) property when angry" (Item 84) to conclude that it happens usually? Furthermore, this behavior will almost always occur more often than the behavior described by Item 87 ("Strikes or pushes school personnel"). Thus, although striking an adult at school may be a more serious offense than destroying property, it might actually receive a lower score. The authors provide no operational definition for the response scale, which may make it difficult to get a sense of the teachers' understanding of these categories in terms of their implied frequency and tolerance/intolerance of specific behaviors.

The SBS materials are organized into three major sections: Academic Resources, Adjustment Problems, and Disruptive Behavior. Each of these sections contains a number of subscales. The Academic Resources section contains four subscales: Academic Performance, Academic Habits, Social Skills, and Parent Participation. The Adjustment Problems section contains seven subscales: Health Concerns, Emotional Distress, Unusual Behavior, Social Problems, Verbal Aggression, Physical Aggression, and Behavior Problems. The third major section of the SBS, Disruptive Behavior, provides scales that illuminate three areas of clinical concern and addresses school-based behavior that reflects symptoms of the *Diagnostic and Statistical Manual-IV (DSM-IV)*: Attention Deficit/Hyperactivity, combined type, Oppositional Defiant Disorder, and Conduct Disorder. The three

Disruptive Behavior subscales each consist of 16 items taken from the adjustment problem scales. These items are presented using a mark-sensitive scoring form that facilitates easy hand scoring with raw score to *T*-score conversion tables included.

DEVELOPMENT. The SBS was developed and standardized through a multistage process spanning the years 1994 to 1999. The process through which items were developed involved identifying critical areas of school behavior and a review of trial items by classroom teachers. The manual provides limited information about how the final 102 items were selected from a presumably larger development item pool. Responses of 1,173 regular education and 601 special education students (referred for or receiving services) were used in the initial item selection process; however, no details about how this was done are provided in the manual other than that they were "based upon manifest content" (manual, p. 35). The selection of the 48 items (16 in each of the three Disruptive Behavior subscales) was based on their similarity to the DSM-IV symptoms for Attention Deficit Hyperactive Disorder, Oppositional Defiant Disorder, and Conduct Problems. All in all, the rationale for the constructs measured by the SBS is incomplete and the logical-rational process for generating items and selecting the final 102 items is insufficient for the reader to judge the adequacy of the process.

The standardization of the SBS included teacher reports on 2,612 regular education students and 1,315 clinically or educationally referred students. These samples approximated the broad 1990 U.S. Census figures for ethnicity and parental education and the nature of referral patterns for behavioral and psychological assessment and treatment in school-age children. Nonetheless, the samples include no students from the most populous states (New York and California) and 17 of the 29 participating schools and agencies were drawn from just three states (Texas, Ohio, and Arizona). Furthermore, the authors provide no data regarding the education level, age, or gender of respondents, in this instance the classroom teachers. In fact, it is unknown how many ratings each participating teacher provided on average. Thus, although the number of students who were rated is sufficient, information about the raters (those who actually provided the normative data) is lacking. Greater description of teacher demographics would aid in gaining a fuller understanding of these norms. In the future, information about the number of child ratings provided by each teacher should be provided.

An attractive aspect of the SBS is that it was co-administered with the PIC-2 and the PIY. This allowed the authors to use an actuarial method for interpretation. In addition, six clinicians completed symptom checklists for a sample of 129 referred youth. With these co-administered sources of information, correlates associated with moderate (*T*-scores between 60 and 69) and extreme (*T*-scores of 70 or higher) scores were derived and used to develop descriptive interpretation paragraphs. Interpretation is further supported by the inclusion of case studies in the manual and multiple studies involving the co-administration of the other ratings scales (e.g., the Conners Teacher Rating Scale) and administrations across special needs groups that are of interest in the context of school-based services. These special studies document that disruptive students, those with elevated scores on the Conners Hyperactivity Index, and students with emotional disturbance obtain low ratings on the Academic Resources scales (with the exception of Parent Participation) and higher ratings on the Adjustment Problem and Disruptive Behavior subscales. All in all, a strength of the SBS is the attention given to organizing information to facilitate interpretation.

TECHNICAL CHARACTERISTICS. The basic core psychometric properties of the SBS are sound. Internal consistency of the subscales is strong, with alpha values in the .80s and .90s. Reflective of the care taken in developing this instrument, four separate test-retest reliability studies were conducted. In one investigation, students were divided into groups by age of youth and the number of weeks between testing intervals (about 2 weeks, 11 weeks, and 28 weeks). The sample sizes for each group in this stability study were all under 56 youths and the number of adults who actually provided ratings was not given. Subscale retest correlations were generally strong even across an interval of approximately 28 weeks between administrations. A few low stability coefficients (between .29 and .48) were reported for Parent Participation, Health Concerns, and Unusual Behavior.

Another point of concern whenever ratings scales are developed is the degree of interrater agreement. Lachar et al. (2000) present data showing that the ratings provided by two educators

author also claims that scores can inform evaluation of classrooms and teachers. Scoring and interpretation of scores is intended to be done by qualified professionals (e.g., school psychologists) with appropriate psychometric training. Raw scores are hand calculated based on a scoring scheme provided with each copy of the assessment, and percentile ranks are determined by reference to tables provided in the professional manual. Directions for scoring missing responses are given (replace with mean item response), as well as instructions for examining response patterns for evidence of invalidity. The scores are intended to inform intervention strategies directed at school adjustment problems and to assess the effect of intervention over time. The test author suggests that the STRS is appropriate for both baseline and ongoing assessment of child-teacher relationship.

The STRS comes packaged with a plan for intervention designed to improve child-teacher relationship, along with qualitative instruments (interview protocols) intended to monitor and inform the intervention process. This review focuses only on the STRS 28-item instrument.

DEVELOPMENT. The author describes the development of the STRS as "prompted by interests in (a) teachers' own emotional and social experiences with children in their classrooms, (b) applications of attachment theory in school settings, and (c) the contribution of relationships with adults to students' academic and social competence" (professional manual, p. 1).

According to the author, an initial version of the STRS was developed in 1991 and piloted using a sample of 24 kindergarten teachers. It is assumed that the original items were developed based on the literature of child-teacher interaction and attachment theory, although the author does not make this clear.

"Based on the initial pilot study (Pianta & Nimetz, 1991) and extensive review of items by a panel of 12 elementary school teachers and administrators, several items were dropped from consideration and many items were written to assess negative aspects of the student-teacher relationship" (professional manual, p. 3). The second version of the STRS included 31 items, and was used in a number of studies related to early childcare (see professional manual, p. 3).

Through factor analysis procedures and studies of the STRS scores in relation to referral and retention to special education programs, and promotion from kindergarten to first grade, the current 28-item version of the STRS was distilled. The author reports that a three-factor solution supports the construct validity of the assessment result, and that the 28-item version is "more parsimonious and practical with respect to (a) amount of variance accounted for, (b) reliability, (c) construct validity, and (d) ease of use and interpretation" (Pianta et al., 1995; Saft & Pianta, in press; as quoted in professional manual, p. 4).

The author provides descriptions of the three constructs measured by the subscales of the STRS (Conflict, Closeness, and Dependency). Much of the test development activity seems focused on kindergarten or preschool populations, although the test is purported to be aimed at a range that includes Grade 3.

TECHNICAL. The norming process involved 275 female preschool to third grade teachers from various geographic regions of the U.S.A. who completed the STRS for from 1 to 16 students each. Of the teachers, 70% were Caucasian, 15% African American, 10% Hispanic, and 5% were of other ethnic backgrounds. The number of teachers at each grade level is not provided. The STRS was completed for a total of 1,535 students with a mean age of 5 years.

Fifty-three percent of the students were boys and 47% were girls. Sixty-three percent of the students were Caucasian, 18% African American, 10% ($n = 154$) Hispanic, 1.7% were Asian American, and 7% represented other ethnic groups or ethnicity was not reported. Socioeconomic descriptive information for the student norm group is also provided. Information about the number of students at each grade level is not provided. Norm-referenced score interpretation is based on the total student sample. Norm-referenced information is provided for total sample, boys and girls, and for Caucasian, African American, and Hispanic ethnic groups.

The statistical information provided in the professional manual concerning scale scores for norm groups does not include information about how teacher and student characteristics interact (i.e., it does not address whether teachers of particular ethnic background rate students of same or different ethnic background differently). No information is provided concerning difference in teacher ratings by teacher characteristic.

The primary weaknesses in the standardization process are the lack of information related to grade level of students and the characteristics of teachers in terms of normative scores on the STRS. Because the author claims that the STRS is appropriate for use with students and teachers from preschool to third grade, some reference to score differences by grade would be useful. In the absence of a theoretical rationale for expecting that preschool relationships are expected to be the same as third grade relationships, such evidence would provide useful normative references.

The author addresses both test-retest and internal consistency conceptions of reliability. Over a 4-week period, test-retest correlations for the total score ($r = .89$) and all subscales (Closeness, $r = .88$, Conflict, $r = .92$, and Dependency, $r = .76$) were appropriately strong. Whether the time between test and retest is appropriate within the intervention strategy tied to the STRS score is unclear.

Alpha coefficients (internal consistency) for the total sample were: .64 (Dependency scale), .86 (Closeness scale), .92 (Conflict scale), and .89 for the total scale. Alpha coefficients for norm-reference groups within the total sample (gender, ethnicity) were similar to the total sample for the subscales, but not for total score. Total scale alpha for subgroups ranged from .74 to .76. These reliability values seem marginal in terms of using the total scale score to make consequential decisions about individual students or teachers. The Dependency scale had low reliability coefficients for all norm-reference groups, with alpha ranging from .55 to .67. Based on the unreliability of its score, interpretation of the Dependency scale score as evidence for consequential decisions should be avoided.

The author presents evidence for construct validity, including results of exploratory factor analysis, coefficients of concurrence with behaviors related to the STRS (i.e., classroom adjustment), and coefficients of prediction with related behavior over time. These coefficients are high enough to provide strong validity evidence for interpreting scores from the Conflict and Closeness scales, but evidence is not persuasive for the Dependency scale. The factor analysis result does support the three factors posed by the authors, but these factors account for less than 50% of the variance for the 28 items. Evidence for the validity of score interpretation for the purpose of identifying students at risk consists of comparison between students who have classroom problems in later grades (e.g., Grades 5 and 6) and those who do not, in terms of STRS scores. Differences are in the direction expected for Conflict and Closeness, but the Dependency scale scores are not different.

The author states in chapter 7 of the professional manual that "STRS can be used to screen whole classrooms and to identify teachers who may need supportive help or consultation with individual students, with their interactive style, or to prevent teacher burnout (see Pianta & Hamre, 2001)" (p. 31). However, the author provides no evidence for the validity of interpreting STRS scores for the purpose of examining the behavior or needs of teachers.

COMMENTARY AND SUMMARY. The STRS appears to result in reliable and arguably valid total score and scale scores for Conflict and Closeness. The Dependency scale does not result in scores with sufficient reliability for use in important decisions, and reliability of total scale score for norm subgroups is marginal. The author presents convincing evidence for the validity of the STRS scores as they relate to student outcomes such as retention, assignment to special education, and future behavior, but evidence is lacking for use of the scores to make decisions about teachers. Further, the STRS is offered as part of a diagnostic and intervention program (Students, Teachers, and Relationship Support; STARS). The author does not present direct evidence for the validity of interpreting STRS scores in this context. However, this information can be found in the STARS professional manual.

Overall, the STRS can be considered an informative assessment of teacher perception of child behavior and teacher-student relationship. Resulting scores might provide useful evidence for decisions regarding the need for intervention. However, because of concerns in regard to norming and reliability, STRS scores should not be the sole determinant of intervention strategies. This reviewer concludes that use of the scores for making decisions about teachers seems inappropriate given the lack of validity evidence for this use.

Review of the Student-Teacher Relationship Scale by JORGE E. GONZALEZ, Research Assistant Professor, Center for At-Risk Children's Services, University of Nebraska—Lincoln, Lincoln, NE, and CHRIS GONZALEZ, District Title Coordinator, Weslaco Independent School District, Weslaco, TX:

DESCRIPTION. The Student-Teacher Relationship Scale (STRS) is a 28-item self-report measure that is used to examine student-teacher relationships along three dimensions, namely, Conflict, Closeness, and Dependency. The STRS is appropriate for children ages 4 through 8 years or for those preschool through third grade. Presumably, the instrument is used to assist and inform consulting personnel in developing intervention efforts aimed at fostering the teacher-child relationship. The Conflict subscale assesses the degree of negativity and conflict in the teacher-child relationship with higher scores indicative of teacher-perceived ineffectuality, student anger, and unpredictability. The Closeness subscale is a measure of teacher warmth, affection, and communication openness. High scores on Closeness are indicative of perceived effectiveness in teacher warmth, communication, and self-awareness. The Dependence subscale assesses a teacher's perception of child dependency with high scores indicative of an overly dependent child.

Administration of the STRS is rather straightforward. Teachers complete the STRS by filling out the Student-Teacher Relationship Scale response form. Items are answered along a 5-point Likert scale with 1 indicating *Definitely does not apply* and 5 indicating *Definitely applies*. Although the form is easy to administer, the manual indicates that individual charged with interpreting the scores should possess formal training in standardized testing. Administering the STRS takes approximately 5–10 minutes for individual teachers and 10–15 minutes for a group of teachers. To score the STRS, one merely has to separate the form to reveal scoring and profile sheets, add the items, and derive raw scores. The STRS yields conflict, Closeness, and Dependency scores, and a Total STRS score. Using the appropriate normative comparison group, raw scores are subsequently converted to percentile ranks. The manual also provides illustrative case studies. A major strength of the STRS is that the percentiles are stratified along gender and ethnicity thus making it possible to limit inferences and generalizations to a particular ethnic or gender group of teachers.

DEVELOPMENT. The STRS is based on a three-factor conceptual model of student-teacher relationships such that conflict and closeness are two important dimensions on which teachers vary along with their ability to foster and negotiate student autonomy (i.e., dependency). According to the author, the identified factors are also present in parent-child relationships. With the exception of Item 28, most items underlying the three dimensions appear to have adequate face validity. Item 28 appears, however, to also tap into issues of teacher efficacy rather than relationship issues. Regardless of the items or domains, the author asserts that social processes, especially relationship processes, influence student outcomes and relate to numerous important child outcomes.

Initially piloted in 1991, the STRS was subjected to an extensive item review by a panel of teachers and administrators. This process resulted in a second version of the STRS that produced 31 items and subsequently was used in numerous studies (e.g., National Institutes of Child Health and Human Development). The basis for the normative information provided in the manual was, however, obtained from a final sample that closely approximated the 1991 census along race/ethnicity and socioeconomic status dimensions. STRS reports were collected from 275 all-female teachers in classes ranging from preschool through third grade who reported on 1,535 children. Of these children, 53% were boys, and 47% were girls, with 63% being Caucasian, 18% African American, 10% Hispanic American, and 1.75 Asian American; 7% represented other ethnic backgrounds or did not report ethnicity. Overall, comparisons for gender and ethnic/racial groups revealed little or no meaningful differences on the STRS.

TECHNICAL.

Reliability. The STRS manual reports both test-retest and internal consistency reliability estimates. With regard to test-retest reliability (4-week interval), the STRS reliability coefficients were as follows: Closeness, .88; Conflict, .92; Dependence, .76; and Total, .89, thus providing adequate evidence of temporal consistency. With the exception of the Dependency subscale (.64), all other scales achieved high internal consistency estimates (i.e., Conflict, .92; Closeness, .86; Total, .89). The author asserts that the relatively low estimate of internal consistency of the Dependency subscale resulted because the scale only has five items.

Validity. The STRS manual reports evidence of construct, concurrent, and predictive validity. As evidence of construct validity, the author reports the results of a three-factor solution accounting for 48.8% of the variance, with the Conflict, Closeness, and Dependence factors accounting for 29.8%, 12.9%, and 6.2%, respectively. The author reported using Principal Components Analysis with VARIMAX rotation. Given that few if any social processes are unrelated in the world of "constructs," one would assume that the author would have used an "oblique" rotation rather than an orthogonal rotation. After all, an oblique rotation is more representative of the nature of reality. Subscale and total scale correlations yielded a moderate-to-strong level of association and in the expected direction between and among the subscales and total scale. With regard to the construct validity of scores from the STRS, with only a single version of this instrument, it is difficult to provide much evidence that the measure is actually measuring teacher-student relationships.

The manual does provide ample evidence of concurrent validity for the STRS with the STRS scales and subscales yielding moderate associations (in the expected direction) between the scores and other measures of childhood behavioral adjustment. With regard to predictive validity, the results, although intriguing, generate more speculation than answers. Although the author reports "a significant relationship between kindergarten STRS scores and selected academic outcomes" (p. 28), one has to wonder in what direction the effects occur. Does poor student achievement foster negative teacher-student relationships or perceptions? Or, does conflicted student-teacher relationships yield poor student academic outcomes? In what way does this mechanism work? Do poor student academic outcomes result from lowered teacher expectations and negative attributions? Moreover, without taking into account prior academic performance, it is somewhat difficult to interpret this finding and make inferences.

Perhaps most disturbing are data presented on the likelihood that teachers would refer or retain students as a function of the teacher-child relationship. The author reported that students who were predicted to have negative outcome who were not referred or retained had lower Conflict scores and higher Closeness scores with the converse true of students predicted to succeed. Based on these findings, one could reasonably assume that a child's academic success (or whether they get referred or not) in a regular education classroom could be a function of a teacher's perception of their interpersonal relationship with them.

COMMENTARY. One important question with regard to the STRS is why? Although the author reports the instrument is optimally used "to inform consultation and intervention efforts aimed at enhancing these relationships" (professional manual, p. 5), there is no coherent or convincing argument for its use in intervention. For example, Hispanic school-aged children represent one of the most educationally vulnerable minority groups in the United States. They often lag behind their peers in kindergarten with roughly 44% of these children one school year behind by age 13 and 40% dropping out before completing high school (Liontes, 1992). Although the relationship between the teacher and student is important, a myriad of other risk factors (e.g., poverty, parental psychopathology, low socioeconomic status) likely account for a greater part of the variance in student outcomes than a teacher's perception of their relationship with the child.

SUMMARY. Although the STRS is well constructed, has psychometric properties, and has a supportive conceptual framework to support its construction, I can think of very few applications of this instrument. Perhaps it can be used as a research instrument, but it is my opinion that the day-to-day realities of teachers and the myriad of issues they deal with precludes any useful incorporation of this instrument in interventions.

REVIEWERS' REFERENCE

Liontes, L. B. (1992). *At-risk families and schools: Becoming parents* (Eb 342 055). Eugene, OR: ERIC Clearinghouse in Education/Management.

[252]

The Substance Abuse Subtle Screening Inventory—3.

Purpose: Designed to "identify individuals who have a high probability of having a substance dependence disorder."

Population: Ages 18–73.

Publication Dates: 1983–1997.

Acronym: SASSI-3.

Scores: 10 subscales: Face Valid Alcohol, Face Valid Other Drugs, Symptoms, Obvious Attributes, Subtle Attributes, Defensiveness, Supplemental Addiction Measure, Family vs. Controls, Correctional, Random Answering Pattern.

Administration: Individual or group.

Price Data: Available from publisher.

Time: [15] minutes.

Comments: May be administered as paper-and-pencil instrument with hand scoring or scoring by optical scanning, computer administered, or via audiotape for people with special needs regarding vision or literacy.

Author: Glenn A. Miller.

Publisher: The SASSI Institute.

Cross References: See T5:2553 (6 references); for reviews by Barbara Kerr and Nicholas A. Vacc of an earlier edition, see 12:381 (1 reference); see also T4:2623 (1 reference).

Review of the Substance Abuse Subtle Screening Inventory–3 by EPHREM FERNANDEZ, Associate Professor of Clinical Psychology, Southern Methodist University, Dallas, TX:

DESCRIPTION. The Substance Abuse Subtle Screening Inventory–3 (SASSI-3) is a psychometric instrument that is designed to make inferences about substance dependence disorder. On one side, it has 14 face valid items that are quite obvious in their relationship to substance dependence; these are further divided into items related to alcohol and items related to other drugs. The other side consists of 67 items that are supposed to be indirect or nonmanifest in their relationship to substance dependence. The face valid items are to be rated on a 4-point scale of frequency, and the other items are in a true-false format. Responses can be made with reference to any one of four time frames: entire life, past 6 months, 6 months before, or 6 months since. The test is usually completed within 15 minutes and objectively scored within a minute or 2. Computerized versions are available, and so are optical scanning versions as well as an audiotaped version for those with reading difficulties.

Nine subscales are embedded in this instrument: Face Valid Alcohol, Face Valid Other Drugs, Symptoms, Obvious Attributes, Subtle Attributes, Defensiveness, Supplemental Addiction Measure, Family vs. Controls, and Correctional. In addition, there is a scale to detect random responding.

Scores are interpreted with reference to a decision rule stipulating cutoffs for each subscale. Exceeding any rule leads to an inference of high probability substance dependence disorder. Only if scores are below the cutoff on all rules is an inference of low probability made. The scores can be plotted on a profile graph. Further interpretation of individual subscale scores is possible, though (as the authors caution) such interpretations do not rest on empirical research and are best viewed as hypotheses and ideas for assessment.

DEVELOPMENT. This is a third edition of the adult form of the SASSI originally developed

by Miller (1985). An adolescent SASSI was developed in 1990, and a Spanish version emerged in 1996. The SASSI-3 was developed out of data from a sample of 2,015 respondents, most of whom were in addiction treatment facilities, general psychiatric hospitals including a dual diagnosis center, a vocational rehabilitation program, and a sex offender treatment program. A subset of 839 cases had DSM diagnoses in addition to SASSI scores, and this was randomly divided into roughly equal numbers of those diagnosed with substance use disorder and those diagnosed without it. Data from the first of these subsamples were used to formulate decision rules on SASSI scoring, and these were cross-validated in the second subsample. There were no significant differences between these two subsamples in terms of age, years of education, or other demographic variables.

TECHNICAL. Psychometric studies of the SASSI have been accumulating although many have been on the adolescent version and other previous versions of the instrument. Many of the studies also remain in the form of unpublished dissertations.

Teslak (2000) found that SASSI-3 scores correlated with scores on similar screening measures such as the Michigan Alcoholism Screening Test (MAST) and the Drug Abuse Screening Test (DAST). However, the SASSI-3 was no more accurate than either of its counterparts and did not show incremental utility. Pearson (2000) found that the SASSI-3 predicted psychiatric substance use disorder. However, the concordance rate of the SASSI-3 with psychiatric substance use disorder was .69 for true positive rate and .82 for true negative rate, and these figures are considerably lower than previously observed. Arenth, Bogner, Corrigan, and Schmidt (2001) found lower accuracy, sensitivity, and specificity for the SASSI-3 in patients with traumatic brain injury than for a sample of disabled persons in a vocational rehabilitation program. Furthermore, they found that blood alcohol level at the time of injury had higher specificity when compared to SASSI-3 test classifications. More encouraging psychometric findings have been reported by Lazowski, Miller, Boye, and Miller (1998). Working on the development sample described earlier, these authors found a 95% concordance between SASSI-3 inferences and clinical diagnoses of substance dependence. The test had a sensitivity of 96% and a specificity of 93%. Its retest reliability in a sample of 40 respondents assessed 2 weeks apart was in the range of .92 to 1.00. The authors also noted that as compared to those who were test negative on the SASSI-3, those classified as test positive had higher mean scores on the Minnesota Multiphasic Personality Inventory–2 (MMPI-2) Addiction Acknowledgment Scale, the MMPI-2 Addiction Potential Scale, the MacAndrew Alcoholism Scale-Revised, the Michigan Alcohol Screening Test, the Millon Clinical Multiaxial Inventory-II (MCMI-II) Alcohol Dependence Scale, and the MCMI-II Drug Dependence Scale. However, the absence of correlation coefficients in this context makes it difficult to conclude about the concurrent validity between the SASSI-3 and these other instruments.

The SASSI-3 is portrayed as a test of substance dependence disorder, but how this differs from other substance-related disorders is left unclear. This is compounded by the authors' references to terms such as substance use, substance abuse, and substance misuse. In an appendix to the user's guide, it is stated that the SASSI-3 can be used to flag for further evaluation of substance abuse disorder. This is misleading in that it suggests that substance dependence is a mild precursor of substance abuse when (as defined by DSM) the latter is not associated with tolerance, withdrawal, or compulsive use. Also, by way of definition, it would be useful to clarify the substances that are embodied in this category of disorders. In DSM, this extends beyond the illicit drugs (that seem to be the focus of the SASSI-3) to medications, toxins, and even items of household consumption. DSM diagnoses of substance dependence also come with specifiers such as with or without tolerance, and different types of remission. In the absence of such specifiers, a SASSI-3 diagnosis is of limited clinical utility.

An even more serious handicap of the SASSI-3 is that it permits only a dichotomous interpretation of high versus low probability of substance dependence. There are more than 80 items and nine decision rules; have the authors perhaps undersold the instrument by ignoring the possibility that the number of decision rules satisfied might be related to the confidence level in diagnosing a substance dependence disorder? At least, if statements about medium probability of

the disorder were possible, the instrument would be more clinically useful.

At a more minor level, some items in the SASSI-3 are phrased in common lingo (e.g., Item 8 on the FVOD: "Gotten really stoned or wiped out on drugs [more than just high]"). Other items use technical jargon that may not be fathomed (e.g., Item 9 on the FVA: "Had the effects of drinking recur after not drinking for a while [e.g., flashbacks, hallucinations, etc.]"). It is hard to see the purpose of a question about "weekly family take home income."

COMMENTARY. The SASSI-3 is laudable in its attempt to assess substance dependence regardless of participants' acknowledgment or denial. It does so by using a number of subtle items that may be indirectly associated with substance use. It is also convenient to administer, quick to score, and readily interpreted. However, the interpretations can only take the form of high or low likelihood of the disorder in question. This does not add much to a DSM diagnosis of substance dependence, and it also fails to shed light on the many qualifiers of such a diagnosis. No doubt, elaboration and illumination of the disorder is possible with further research in this area. Further research is also needed to quantify the psychometric features of the SASSI-3. Especially needed are factor analytic studies of the kind done on its predecessors, the SASSI-2 and the SASSI. There is reason to believe that such factorial validity as demonstrated for its predecessors will prevail in the case of the SASSI-3.

SUMMARY. As with many instruments that are driven exclusively by empirical data, the SASSI-3 is methodologically commendable but conceptually less impressive. This limits its clinical potential too. Yet, the test is widely used. With further research and revision, it can be expected to fill a significant void in the field of assessment of substance use disorders.

REVIEWER'S REFERENCES

Arenth, P. M., Bogner, J. A., Corrigan, J. D., & Schmidt, L. (2001). The utility of the Substance Abuse Subtle Screening Inventory-3 for use with individuals with brain injury. *Brain Injury, 15,* 499–510.

Lazowski, L. E., Miller, F. G., Boye, M. W., & Miller, G. A. (1998). Efficacy of the Substance Abuse Subtle Screening Inventory-3 (SASSI-3) in identifying substance dependence disorders in clinical settings. *Journal of Personality Assessment, 71,* 114–128.

Miller, G. A. (1985). The Substance Abuse Subtle Screening Inventory (SASSI): Adult SASSI-2 manual supplement. Spencer, IN: Spencer Evening World.

Pearson, B. S. (2000). Validation of the Substance Abuse Subtle Screening Inventory-3 (SASSI-3) with the adult chronically mentally ill population. *Dissertation Abstracts International: Section B: The Sciences and Engineering, 60* (12-B): 6418.

Teslak, A. G. (2000). The utility of the CAGE, MAST, DAST, and SASSI-3 in assessing substance use/misuse in a psychiatric population. *Dissertation Abstracts International: Section B: The Sciences and Engineering, 61*(5-B): 2814.

Review of the Substance Abuse Subtle Screening Inventory—3 by DAVID J. PITTENGER, Head and Associate Professor, Department of Psychology, The University of Tennessee at Chattanooga, Chattanooga, TN:

Like the proverbial better mousetrap, many clinicians and counselors will beat a path to the developer of a better indicator of substance abuse. An inexpensive instrument that readily identifies the presence of substance abuse is of considerable value for those working in a variety of venues including colleges and universities, where some students evidence the early stages of substance dependence; medical settings, where substance abuse compromises the health and treatment of the patient; and psychological treatment facilities where patients may exhibit psychiatric problems that mask significant substance abuse problems. The publishers of the third edition of the Substance Abuse Subtle Screening Inventory (SASSI-3) assure us that they have produced the better substance abuse index.

DESCRIPTION AND DEVELOPMENT. The SASSI, which was first published in 1988, is an empirically derived inventory designed to indicate the risk of substance dependence using items that are less likely to elicit suspicion and untruthful answers. Myerholtz & Rosenberg (1998) reported that the SASSI is an extremely popular instrument and used in a variety of treatment facilities as well as other settings (e.g., schools and employee assistant programs).

According to the SASSI-3 manual, the goal of the revision was to increase the ability of the SASSI to discriminate between those who are or are not substance dependent. The current version of the instrument contains most of the items used in the previous edition of the inventory and is appropriate for adults (age 18 and older). The publisher also produces an adolescent (ages 12–18) version of the SASSI.

The SASSI-3 consists of two parts that are printed on separate sides of a single paper form. The first part of the instrument represents the subtle portion of the inventory and contains 67 true-false statements. The vast majority (57) of the statements make no overt reference to drug and alcohol use, and appear to be easily under-stood by most adults. Twenty of these items were taken from the Psychological Screening Inventory (Lanyon, 1970).

Manual scoring consists of an easy-to-use transparent scoring template for the eight subscales of the first portion of the instrument. Alternatives include a computer version of the instrument and answer forms that may be machine scored. The publisher also offers an audiotape of the SASSI-3 for clients with reading problems. Scoring the first portion of the instrument yields one validity scale, five clinical scales, and two ancillary scales.

The Random Answer Pattern (RAP) is a measure of validity. It indicates whether the client answered randomly or had difficulty understanding the items.

There are three clinical scales that measure the presence of symptoms of substance abuse. The Symptoms (SYM) scale is a new scale that assesses the presence of behavioral, emotional, and social correlates of substance abuse. The Obvious Attributes (OAT) scale is an index of the social effects substance abuse (e.g., legal problems). According to the user's guide, persons diagnosed with substance abuse are likely to endorse this item when answering honestly. The Subtle Attributes (SAT) scale complements the OAT scale as it consists of statements endorsed by substance dependent patients attempting to hide their dependence as well as those who answered honestly.

The Defensiveness (DEF) scale assesses willful attempts to deny substance dependence as well as a personality trait or reaction to stressful personal circumstances. The Supplemental Addiction Measure (SAM) scale purports to differentiate between defensive clients hiding substance abuse and other defensive individuals.

The Family vs. Controls (FAM) scale identifies individuals who may live with or have a significant relationship with a substance abuser. This scale is not used in determining substance dependence, but may be used to assess the needs of those close to a substance dependent person. Similarly, the Correctional (COR) is not a clinical measure as it serves as an indication of abusers who have had a record of legal/criminal entanglements.

The second portion of the instrument consists of 12 questions that identify the extent of alcohol use and 14 questions that identify the extent of other drug use. Clients may be instructed to answer the questions within the time frame of their entire life, during the past 6 months, or 6 months before or after a critical event. Although the instrument offers these options, the manual warns that the 6-month time frames may increase the proportion of false positives. Consequently the manual encourages users to use the entire lifetime unless circumstances dictate otherwise. The scale for these questions is a Likert scale ranging from 0 (*never*) to 4 (*repeatedly*).

There are separate normative data for male and females. Interpreting the results begins by plotting each subscale score on a graph that creates a client profile and then completing a checklist for nine "decision rules." Each rule determines whether the client scored at or above a critical score for one or a combination of the scales. A positive response to any one of the rules is evidence of a high probability of substance dependence. An extensive user's guide, which is separate from the manual, provides detailed accounts of different profiles that may emerge and their clinical significance.

TECHNICAL. The promotional material and manual for the SASSI-3 make extensive reference to the predictive validity of scores from the instrument. Specifically, the claim is that the SASSI-3 has a 94% correspondence rate with clinical assessments of substance abuse. Independent research examining the utility of the SASSI-3 also suggests that the instrument is an extremely useful tool (Horrigan & Piazza, 1999; Horrigan & Katz, 2000; Horrigan, Schroeder, & Schaffer, 2000) that should be used during the initial screening for substance abuse. Although these results are encouraging, they need to be interpreted with due caution. Striking features of the manual are the data and statistical information that are not reported. Those familiar with the *Standards for Educational and Psychological Testing* (AERA, APA, & NCME, 1999) will be disappointed by the notable absence of information that would allow one to make a more informed decision regarding the utility of the instrument.

The sample used to create the norms for this version of the instrument were 848 patients drawn from addiction treatment centers, general psychiatric hospitals, dual diagnosis hospitals, vocational rehabilitation programs, and sex offender treatment programs. All participants had completed the SASSI-3 and had been independently evaluated for substance abuse using the criteria established in the *Diagnostic and Statistical Manual of Mental Disorders* (*DSM-III-R*; American Psychi-

atric Association, 1987; *DSM-IV*, American Psychiatric Association, 1994). There is no indication of the credentials of the persons rendering the diagnosis of substance abuse. Within the sample, 80% were diagnosed as substance dependent.

COMMENTARY. Although the reported accuracy rate of the SASSI-3 is high, the data should be interpreted with some caution. Using the test with populations for which there is a high proportion of substance abuse may inflate its criterion validity. Stated from a different perspective, using the instrument as a screening instrument for populations with a lower base rate of substance dependence (e.g., college students, employee assistance programs) may produce lower criterion validity estimates (Lilienfeld, Wood, & Garb, 2000). Using the data presented in the manual, I determined L_B, an asymmetric measure of association, to be $L_B = .70$. In other words, using the SASSI-3 reduces by 70% the error in predicting the criterion of substance dependence. Although this is an extremely high value, it may be substantially lower for different populations. Unfortunately, the manual provides no normative data for populations not directly associated with treatment for a psychopathology.

There are other notable absences in the supporting materials. As stated previously, the SASSI-3 contains several important clinical scales. Indeed, the user's guide describes several examples of patients who represent different clinical symptom profiles. Unfortunately, there are no data to verify the appropriateness of making these distinctions among profile patterns. Similarly, there has been no attempt to confirm the factor structure of the instrument. Indeed, Gray (2001) was unable to confirm a factor model implied by the subscales.

There is also limited information regarding the temporal stability of the instrument. The manual reports high test-retest reliability for a 2-week interval with only 40 respondents who were part of the substance abuse treatment population. Myerholtz and Rosenberg (1997, 1998) reported much lower reliabilities for the binary diagnosis of substance dependence for the 2-week interval (*phi* = .68) and the 4-week interval (*phi* = .36), and that SASSI scores are susceptible to instructions for fake good or bad.

Finally, there are no data to indicate the utility of the SASSI-3 relative to other measures of substance abuse. Myerholtz and Rosenberg (1998) reported moderate to large coefficient Kappas between the SASSI and other indicators of substance abuse, some of which are in the public domain. Given the availability of a number of alternative screening instruments, one would hope to have data that illustrate the incremental validity of using the SASSI-3 at the exclusion of other instruments.

SUMMARY. The SASSI-3 may well serve as a quick and ready triage instrument for the presence of substance abuse. Users should not be sanguine in assuming the SASSI-3 is as accurate as its publisher claims. Consequently, one hopes that the publishers of the instrument will expand their analysis of the psychometric properties of the instrument.

REVIEWER'S REFERENCES

American Educational Research Association, American Psychological Association, & National Council on Measurement in Education. (1999). *Standards for educational and psychological testing.* Washington, DC: American Educational Research Association.
American Psychiatric Association. (1987). *Diagnostic and statistical manual of mental disorders: DSM-III-R.* Washington, DC: Author.
American Psychiatric Association. (1994). *Diagnostic and statistical manual of mental disorders: DSM-IV.* Washington, DC: Author
Gray, B. T. (2001). A factor analytic study of the Substance Abuse Subtle Screening Inventory (SASSI). *Educational & Psychological Measurement, 61,* 102–118.
Horrigan, T. J., & Katz, L. (2000). Ohio's Bill 167 fails to increase prenatal referrals for substance abuse. *Journal of Substance Abuse Treatment, 18,* 283–286.
Horrigan, T. J., & Piazza, N. (1999). The Substance Abuse Subtle Screening Inventory minimizes the need for toxicology screening of prenatal patients—A post partum assessment. *Journal of Substance Abuse Treatment, 17,* 243–248.
Horrigan, T. J., Schroeder, A. V., & Schaffer, R. M. (2000). The triad of substance abuse, violence, and depression are interrelated in pregnancy—National survey findings. *Journal of Substance Abuse Treatment, 18,* 55–58.
Lanyon, R. I. (1970). Development and validation of a psychological screening inventory. *Journal of Consulting & Clinical Psychology, 35,* 24–37.
Lilienfeld, S. O., Wood, J. M., & Garb, H. N. (2000). The scientific status of projective techniques. *Psychological Science in the Public Interest, 1,* 27–67.
Myerholtz, L. E., & Rosenberg, H. (1997). Screening DUI offenders for alcohol problems: Psychometric assessment of the Substance Abuse Subtle Screening Inventory. *Psychology of Addictive Behaviors, 11,* 155–165.
Myerholtz, L., & Rosenberg, H. (1998). Screening college students for alcohol problems: Psychometric assessment of the SASSI-2. *Journal of Studies on Alcohol, 59,* 439–446.

[253]
Substance Use Disorders Diagnostic Schedule-IV.

Purpose: "Designed to elicit information related to the diagnosis of substance use disorders."
Population: Adults suspected of abusing alcohol or drugs.
Publication Dates: 1995–2001.
Acronym: SUDDS-IV.
Scores: Number of Current Dependence Symptoms in Past Year, Number of Current Dependence Categories, Number of Current Abuse Symptoms in Past Year, Number of Current Abuse Categories for 10 Substance Categories (Alcohol, Marijuana, Cocaine, Sedatives/Tranquilizers, Stimulants, Heroin/Other Opiods, Hallucinogens, PCP, Inhalants, Other/Mixed), DSM-IV Psychoactive Substance Use Disorder Diagnosis Codes (Dependence, Abuse), Ratings for Stress, Depression and Anxiety Screens.
Administration: Individual.

Price Data: Available from publisher.
Time: (30–45) minutes.
Comments: Structured diagnostic interview; also available as a computer-administered interview; designed primarily to provide comprehensive diagnostic information for substance use disorders according to DSM-IV criteria; provides information for patient placement according to American Society of Addiction Medicine criteria.
Authors: Norman G. Hoffmann and Patricia Ann Harrison.
Publisher: Evince Clinical Assessments.
Cross References: For reviews by Andres Barona and Steven I. Pfeiffer of an earlier edition, see 13:308 (2 references).

Review of the Substance Use Disorders Diagnostic Schedule-IV by TONY CELLUCCI, Associate Professor and Director of the Psychology Training Clinic, Idaho State University, Pocatello, ID:

DESCRIPTION. The Substance Use Disorders Diagnostic Schedule-IV (SUDDS-IV) is a structured clinical interview for psychoactive substance use disorders based on the DSM-IV diagnostic criteria. It is designed to be administered in approximately 50 minutes. In addition to an interview booklet and manual, a CD-ROM version adapted for correctional populations is available (Norman Hoffmann, personal communication, July 1, 2002). Counselors ask the questions as they appear on the screen and record the offender's answers on a laptop. The interview booklet begins with several initial demographic questions (e.g., ethnicity, marital status) and then asks about stressful life events in the past 12 months. Screening questions for anxiety and depressive symptoms also are included. The interviewer then inquires about smoking, alcohol use, and experiences with various drugs. There are 25 items related to the seven dependence criteria and 18 items related to the four abuse criteria. Typically, the interviewer asks about all items, and then probes those endorsed for each substance used as to the number of times it occurred in the past year and the age when it first occurred. By recording this information on a diagnostic checklist, current (last year) and lifetime diagnoses are available for alcohol, eight substance categories, and other (e.g., prescription, mixed) abuse. The manual provides very clear guidelines for administration and a sample scored interview. An interesting feature is that the respondent is asked to sign a verification statement upon completing the interview as protection against the patient not responding truthfully.

DEVELOPMENT. The SUDDS was originally developed from the earlier Substance Abuse Modified Diagnostic Interview and was revised again in 1995. The items were designed to map the intent of the DSM-IV dependence and abuse constructs that the authors argue create the face expectation of content validity. There have apparently been wording modifications (e.g., adding "hit anyone" to Item 39) based on interview experience (Norman Hoffmann, personal communication, July 1, 2002) but the manual does not provide detailed information on how items were written, selected, or reviewed. There are from two to six items for each of the dependence and abuse criteria. The anxiety/depression screens are likely to be confounded by substance effects. Smoking items might also be improved to better capture nicotine dependence (e.g., number of minutes to the first cigarette in the morning).

TECHNICAL. There is also limited technical information on the SUDDS-IV. Reliability or consistency across interviewers has not yet been demonstrated, although the interviewer makes few judgments in recording responses. Using an earlier version, the authors reported a high agreement between computer- and personal-administered versions (Davis, Hoffmann, Morse, & Luehr, 1992). Relatedly, it would be informative to examine temporal stability over a brief interval (e.g., 3 days). Data on the internal consistency of dependence and abuse item sets are available (Hoffmann & Hoffmann, 2001; Hoffmann, Gogineni, & Hoffmann, 2002) but could be presented more clearly in the manual. Based on data from the Minnesota Department of Corrections, alpha coefficients for the dependence items were .93 or above for various substances, indicating that these items tap a homogenous syndrome.

The DSM-IV criteria were meant to conceptually distinguish the dependency syndrome from social consequences of abuse (Nathan, Skinstad, & Langenbucher, 1999). However, dependent individuals also endorse the abuse criteria so that these items would constitute one factor in treatment populations. The alpha coefficients for the abuse item sets (.85–.93) are also respectable but Hoffmann et al. (2002) note that these are probably inflated due to the presence of dependent individuals in the sample. Hoffmann and Hoffmann

(2001) reported that 40% of individuals meeting alcohol abuse criteria only report problems in one category (e.g., drunk driving), which is consistent with the literature (Hasin, Paykin, Endicott, & Grant, 1999), indicating less construct validity for the DSM-IV abuse category scores.

It would be helpful to examine the SUDDS-IV items and the DSM-IV symptom criteria themselves in terms of sensitivity, specificity, and positive and negative predictive power relative to an independent but empirically determined diagnosis. The lack of published findings on the SUDDS-IV relative to other measures (e.g., Addiction Severity Index, Alcohol Use Inventory's Disrupt scale) and outcomes (e.g., course) of substance abuse disorders limits discussion of its validity.

COMMENTARY. The SUDDS-IV captures the DSM-IV dependence concept. However, insufficient information is provided regarding item selection and reliability (i.e., kappa across clinicians). Moreover, lack of evidence for criterion validity currently prohibits recommending its use beyond documenting the basis for DSM-IV diagnoses. The prior discussion of the DSM criteria themselves speaks to possible limitations in the conceptual model underlying the instrument. Criticisms of the adequacy of the criteria for detecting substance abuse in adolescents or elderly populations (Nirenberg, Lisansky-Gomberg, & Cellucci, 1998; Vik, Brown, & Myers, 1997) raise the question of the instrument's sensitivity in different populations.

The stated interview implications for several ASAM (American Society for Addiction Medicine) dimensions also merit comment. These risk indicators (e.g., any use of marijuana, limited education) appear to be largely generalizations and warrant a more empirical foundation for use in clinical practice. The reviewer's impression is that the SUDDS-IV may try to do too much by including mental health screens and ASAM implications. The author/publishers have since developed more specific tools for these purposes (e.g., the CAAPE for assessing substance abuse and comorbidity, and the LOCI-2R for justifying ASAM placement). Potential users should consider their purpose and specific needs. Similarly, not all clinicians will wish to obtain age of onset for every endorsed symptom, which would seem to add considerable interviewer time. An alternate instrument for substance abuse diagnosis, the Substance Dependence Severity Scale (SDSS) cur-

edition suggest that a window of opportunity was missed to provide users with the essential information required about important psychometric matters. The authors have made a good beginning in addressing the need for a systematic interview for alcohol, substance abuse, and dependency, but they have not made sufficient progress in helping users feel comfortable that this instrument merits the accolades they provide. Only two references are cited. One of them addresses the comparison of computer and personal administrations previously discussed, and the other suggests no evidence of supportive data.

A previous review of the SUDDS (see 13:308) indicated, "Psychometric data involving the SUDDS are not available" (Barona, 1998, p. 983). Since that review, not much more psychometric data have been added to this revision. Also, the current manual makes no mention whatsoever of a previous edition. A second review (Pfeiffer, 1998) criticized the lack of reliability information. That criticism has been addressed to a modest degree, but there is still much more work to be done before this instrument merits surety in the minds of users who care about validity and reliability.

REVIEWER'S REFERENCES

Barona, A. (1998). [Review of the Substance Use Disorder Diagnosis Schedule]. In J. C. Impara & B. S. Plake (Eds.), *The thirteenth mental measurements yearbook* (pp. 982–983). Lincoln, NE: Buros Institute of Mental Measurements.
Pfeiffer, S. I. (1998). [Review of the Substance Use Disorder Diagnosis Schedule]. In J. C. Impara & B. S. Plake (Eds.), *The thirteenth mental measurements yearbook* (p. 984). Lincoln, NE: Buros Institute of Mental Measurements.

[254]
Supervisory Behavior Description Questionnaire.

Purpose: "Designed to measure the behavior patterns of supervisory and management personnel on two major dimensions of leadership: 'Consideration' and 'Structure.'"
Population: Supervisors and prospective supervisors.
Publication Dates: 1970–1996.
Acronym: SBD.
Scores, 2: Consideration, Structure.
Administration: Group.
Price Data: Available from publisher.
Time: [20] minutes.
Comments: Paper-and-pencil or computer administration available.
Author: Edwin A. Fleishman.
Publisher: Reid London House.

*Review of the Supervisory Behavior Description Questionnaire by ALBERT M. BUGAJ, Associ-*ate Professor of Psychology, University of Wisconsin—Marinette, Marinette, WI:

As noted in its "information guide," the Supervisory Behavior Description Questionnaire (SBD) "Provides a brief measure of the leadership patterns of management personnel" (p. 2). The test can be completed by a group leader's subordinates, peers, or supervisors, or be used as a self-assessment. The test results in two scores. "Consideration" (C) is the extent to which supervisors exhibit friendship, mutual trust, and respect human relations, and similar behaviors. A high "C" score would indicate a good rapport with others. The second score, "structure" (S), indicates such things as the degree to which supervisors define their relationships with group members, between group members, schedule work activities, and set standards. The two dimensions are considered independent. Thus, an individual can be high on both, low on both, or high on one but not the other.

The information guide proposes five uses for the SBD: (a) managerial appraisal including performance evaluation, (b) counseling of managers, (c) evaluation of organizational climate, (d) as an instructional aid during managerial training, and (e) the evaluation of managerial training programs. The information guide states there is no time limit, although it mentions most people complete the test in 20 minutes. The test itself consists of 48 items; 28 measure C and the remaining 20 measure S. The test booklet contains clear, straightforward instructions for the test taker. Each item in the booklet is rated on a 5-point Likert scale. Each scale has clearly defined anchors. The booklet is well designed so that there is no possibility of confusing which scale accompanies a given item.

DEVELOPMENT. The SBD is one of four Leadership Description Questionnaires resulting from the Ohio State University Leadership Studies organized in 1945 (Fleishman, 1951). The SBD is based on a factor analysis of 140 items originally administered to industrial supervisors. Although no statistics are provided in the "information guide" submitted for purposes of this review, it does state that the 48 items selected for the test met three criteria: A high loading on the dimension in which they are included, loadings on the other factor as close to zero as possible, and the ability to "provide differentiation in the behavior of different supervisors" (p. 4). Correlations (Pearson rs) between the scales based on seven samples are provided in the guide. These range from -.33 to +.20. The mean correlation (calculated by the reviewer) is .05.

TECHNICAL.

Standardization. The information guide does not report the nature of the standardization sample. Three scores are reported in the form of percentiles, C, S, and a raw score. However, the information provides little information on the nature of the group used in the determination of norms. It is thus difficult to assess if the test is suitable for use with members of minority groups. It is important to note, however, that a 1995 study by Allen found that the factor structure for African Americans was the same as that found during the development of the test. This suggests the SBD may be valid for use in the African American population, although Allen (1995) does indicate this is only an initial study.

Reliability. Four studies of the test-retest reliability of the SBD are reported in the information guide. These range from .56 to .87 for C, and from .46 to .75 for S. The higher figures are for an interval of 11 months, the longest interval reported (other test-retest intervals are 3 weeks and 3 months). Three studies asked "employees" to rate their managers, whereas the fourth asked bank managers to rate their supervisors.

Internal consistency was measured in seven studies via the split-half method, using a wider range of test takers including ROTC candidates, paramedical personnel, and telephone company trainees. Split-half reliabilities were found to be generally in the range of .89 to .98 for C, and .68 to .93 for S.

Six studies measuring interrater reliability are also reported. These statistics range from .55 to .73 for C, and from .47 to .90 for S. This is an important measure, given that the SBD can be used to rate one's supervisor, as well as oneself.

Validity. The construct validity of the SBD has been well tested, the information booklet summarizes the results of 18 studies, the most recent dating to 1987. Most of the studies appear to have been performed in the United States, although studies from Israel, Germany, and Japan are reported. Although the vast majority of studies support the validity of the SBD, three studies indicate the need for further work in specific areas.

On the positive side, almost all the studies reported finding strong concurrent validity between SBD scores and other measures. For example, group productivity and good morale are frequently found to relate to high Consideration and Structure scores. High Consideration is also related to low rates of worker grievances. Subordinates are more satisfied with a high "structure" supervisor in work situations rated as high in ambiguity. Further, managers who score high on Consideration and Structure are also given higher proficiency ratings by their supervisors. These findings, and similar results from other studies in the information guide, point to the usefulness of the SBD for the assessment of supervisors, evaluation of organizational climate, and perhaps the counseling of managers.

Only one study in the information guide makes specific mention of separate analyses for female and male subjects. The study found that subordinates were more satisfied with their work if their supervisor was higher in Consideration. No sex difference occurred if the subordinate and superior were of the same sex. However, women who reported to men gave these supervisors the highest scores on Consideration, and the lowest on Structure. A reverse pattern occurred for male subordinates. Although only one study, it does suggest that further research on sex differences using the SBD is needed.

Two studies reported in the information guide examined the use of the SBD in conjunction with a leadership-training course. The first study indicated that the kind of supervisor one had (in terms of Consideration and Structure) was more related to the attitudes and behaviors of a subordinate than the fact they had or had not been in the leadership course. The second study found that the leadership course affected different supervisors differently in terms of their "Consideration and Structure behavior" (p. 9). The information guide points out that a conclusion of the second study was that future research was needed to find the personal and situational variables that interact with the effects of leadership training. (This conclusion is reiterated by Fleishman in a 1998 article.) The importance of these results and conclusions is that the SBD should be used with caution as an instructional aid during training, and in evaluating training programs, until the variables moderating the effects of training are uncovered.

In addition to further research on leadership training, it might be instructive to examine whether SBD scores are related to scores on other measures. Several tests of workplace climate exist, including the Work Environment Scale (Moos, 1989), and the Survey of Organizations (Rensis Likert Associates, 1988).

Still another area in which research is needed concerns the predictive validity of the SBD, an issue raised by the information guide. Most of the research using the instrument involves concurrent measures, with few studies predicting leadership behavior over time. It would be interesting to perform longitudinal research to follow individuals given the SBD at the time of promotion to leadership positions and examine their effectiveness and behavior for long periods. Such studies would also allow the variables moderating leadership training to be examined. The reliability of the SBD over extremely long periods could also be examined in longitudinal studies.

CONCLUSION. The Supervisory Behavior Description Questionnaire can be provisionally recommended for those interested in assessing workplace climate, and for counseling and evaluating group leaders. A "provisional recommendation" is given because the information provided for review purposes makes it difficult to determine if the test is suitable for use with minority group members, and whether or not sex differences in scores occur. Test users should keep these issues in mind until further research is performed in these areas. Future research should also examine personal and environmental variables related to leadership training and changes in Consideration and Structure. The test should be used with caution as an instructional aid in training programs, and in evaluating such programs, until the necessary research has been performed. It should be mentioned that although several other tests have been mentioned previously, they are not assumed by the reviewer to be superior to the SBD for evaluation and training purposes. Finally, the SBD can be highly recommended as a research tool, based on estimates of reliability and high degree of construct validity.

REVIEWER'S REFERENCES
Allen, W. (1995). Factor analytic study of interracial similarity for the Supervisory Behavior Description Questionnaire. *Educational and Psychological Measurement, 55,* 658–664.
Fleishman, E. A. (1951). *Leadership climate and supervisory behavior.* Columbus, OH: Personnel Research Board, Ohio State University.
Fleishman, E. A. (1998). Patterns of leadership behavior related to employee grievances and turnover: Some post hoc reflections. *Personnel Psychology, 51,* 825–835.
Moos, R. H. (1989). Work Environment Scale. Palo Alto, CA: Consulting Psychologists Press.
Rensis Likert Associates. (1988). Survey of Organizations. Ann Arbor, MI: Rensis Likert Associates.

Review of the Supervisory Behavior Description Questionnaire by MICHAEL J. ROSZKOWSKI, Director, Institutional Research, La Salle University, Philadelphia, PA:

DESCRIPTION. Research on leadership behaviors conducted at Ohio State University in the early 1950s identified the two basic dimensions to leadership that the Supervisory Behavior Description Questionnaire (SBD) assesses in the context of the manager/supervisor and subordinate relationship. The SBD measures subordinate perceptions of the "boss" using 48 items that produce two scores: Consideration (28 items) and Structure (20 items). Using a 5-point scale, the subordinate indicates the frequency with which the supervisor displays the behaviors defining the two dimensions. Broadly speaking, Consideration is the extent to which the supervisor engages in behaviors that indicate a concern for the well-being of the workers under his or her charge, whereas Structure reflects the degree to which the supervisor arranges the work situation to make sure that a given work task gets accomplished. Supervisors scoring high on Consideration are friendly, approachable, supportive, engage in two-way communication, show respect for the worker, give appropriate recognition, etc. Supervisors low on Consideration are apt to be more impersonal and aloof in their interactions with the work group. A supervisor with high scores on Structure plays an active role in setting expectations, planning, scheduling, and organizing the job, and actively directs the subordinates. One who is low on Structure does not give direction to the subordinates.

DEVELOPMENT. The 48 items are the ones retained on the basis of a factor analysis of 140 items administered to supervisors in an industrial setting. To be retained, the items had to show a high loading on the one dimension, a zero or near zero loading on the second dimension, and to differentiate between the behaviors of the supervisors. The researchers concluded that these two dimensions of behavior were independent of each other, allowing for four basic leadership styles: (a) high consideration and high structure, (b) high consideration and low structure, (c) low consideration and high structure, and (d) low consideration and low structure. The information guide accompanying the SBD lists seven studies supporting this contention. Indeed, the reported correlations between Consideration and Structure are quite low, ranging from +.20 to -.33, with a median of only .10. Notably, however, six of the correlations are negative in direction.

TECHNICAL. Seventeen reliability estimates are reported in the information guide: seven internal consistency reliability estimates, four test-retest coefficients, and six interrater values. For the internal consistency analyses, the split-half method was employed, corrected by the Spearman-Brown formula. The test-retest studies used the Pearson correlation procedure. The internal consistency reliabilities have a median coefficient of .92 for Consideration and .81 for Structure. The range in values is quite narrow for Consideration (.89 to .98) and somewhat broader for Structure (.68 to .93). The test-retest data are based on a variety of intervals between the two test sessions: 3 weeks (.56 Consideration, .53 Structure), 3 months (.69 Consideration, .60 Structure), and two studies based on 11-month intervals. In one 11-month test-rest analysis, the reliability coefficients were quite impressive given the length of time between the two administrations of the SBD (.87 and .75, for Consideration and Structure, respectively). In the second study using this duration between administrations, the correlations were lower, namely .58 (Consideration) and .46 (Structure). The interrater reliability indexes had a median of .65 on Consideration and .57 on Structure. All these studies point to a higher reliability for the Consideration domain, perhaps attributable in part to the larger number of items on this scale relative to the Structure scale.

The scores on the SBD do not correlate with intelligence or education, but the Structure score was found to correlate negatively (-.29) with authoritarian tendencies as measured by the F scale, which is consistent with other research reported in the information guide that found a negative relationship between leadership and authoritarian tendencies. To explain the nature of this correlation, the document cites research showing that individuals who are authoritarian find it difficult to make decisions in ambiguous situations. Although these studies are not reported in the validity section of the information guide, they can serve as evidence on the construct validity of the SBD. Under the validity section, the author of the information guide notes that the scale was constructed with the aim of maximizing construct validity through the use of factor analysis to create orthogonal dimensions.

The manual provides an annotated bibliography of 18 studies on the validity of the SBD, which are described as representative. In addition, a table in that section provides a summary of this literature, listing 25 validity coefficients for the Consideration domain and 27 for the Structure domain. The values are extremely variable. The median validity coefficient is .38 for Consideration (range: 0 to .73) and .19 for Structure (range: .02 to .71). The criteria used in these studies include proficiency ratings, turnover, absenteeism, accidents, grievances, peer ratings, ratings by superiors, length of service, and satisfaction. The samples consisted of foremen, ROTC cadets, high school teachers, social services personnel, and paramedical personnel.

The manual acknowledges that the validity data are not consistent and that most of the studies of criterion-related validity are concurrent in nature rather than predictive. Furthermore, studies are needed, states the author of the manual, to identify the moderator variables that confound the nature of some of the relationships. Organizations using the SBD are urged to conduct local validation.

COMMENTARY. In many such studies, the supervisors high on Consideration but low on Structure had employees with very high morale and member satisfaction but low productivity. Conversely, a supervisor profile of high Structure but low Consideration was associated with highly productive groups in terms of output, but grievance rates and turnover also tended to be high. It was claimed initially in the research on this topic that the most effective managers, irrespective of situation, were ones who fell into the high Consideration-high Structure quadrant. The current thinking is that there are moderating circumstances in which that particular style may not always be the single best one, as acknowledged in the SBD information guide. So, the SBD continues to be relevant, but more work still needs to be done to determine which of the four styles works best under what circumstances (Kerr & Schriesheim, 1974).

The latest validation study cited in the information guide bears a 1987 date. Of the 18 studies cited, 11% are from the 1950s, 22% have a 1960s date, 44% are from the 1970s, and 22% are from the 1980s. More recent studies are available in the literature, and the information guide needs to be updated to incorporate such studies into the discussion.

The manual (information guide) states that the SBD can be used for performance appraisal, counseling, evaluations of organizational climate, and training evaluations. The author of the information guide notes that in some situations it may be advisable to compare and contrast the subordinates' evaluation of the supervisor on Consideration and Structure behaviors and with the supervisors' own evaluation of himself or herself on these two domains. For the latter purpose, one can use the Leadership Opinion Questionnaire (LOQ; T6:1386), which examines the manager's attitudes about leadership.

In order to appreciate the appropriateness of the SBD for a particular purpose, one needs to understand the SBD and its theoretical underpinnings within the framework of the alternative theories regarding what constitutes leadership. The scales developed from the Ohio University leadership studies are based on the assumption that the primary dimensions underlying effective leadership and supervisory behavior are Consideration and Structure. These terms become widely accepted, generating numerous studies based on this model. But in recent years other models have been introduced to explain leadership (i.e., situational and contingency approaches to leadership). Some would argue that these new models supercede the two-factor model from the Ohio state studies, but there is no undisputable evidence that the new models provide a better description of the world of work. In a sense, the usefulness of the SBD depends on whether one accepts the theoretical foundations of the instrument or the more recent theories on management.

In the end, one must realize that there is no consensus regarding the definition of leadership, the number of dimensions that constitute it, nor the best way to measure it. In using any assessment device purporting to measure leadership, one needs to be aware of the theoretical model that led to the operational definitions. In using the SBD, one is implicitly accepting the behavioral leadership model proposed by the Ohio State studies about half a century ago. Clearly, the SBD has withstood the test of time. Along with the other scales created on the basis of these investigations into the nature of leadership, the SBD has had a profound impact on the academic study of this construct. Although the pace of research on the instrument itself as well as its theoretical foundations seems to have slowed down over the years as new leadership theories have been advanced, both the construct and the instrument continue to be relevant today.

SUMMARY. Few details are available about the reliability and validity studies (especially the former), which is understandable given the brevity of the information guide. Furthermore, the document(s) should be updated to discuss the more recent research dealing with the SBD. The reported reliability and validity coefficients on this instrument are not of the magnitude one would find with cognitive measures, but they are typical of what one would find with other industrial-organizational psychological tests, especially self-report measures. The SBD is more often than not used to analyze entire work groups with multiple raters, which would serve to increase reliability if the ratings are averaged. Finally, I suspect that the SBD may be a good candidate for restandardization on a more contemporary population.

REVIEWER'S REFERENCE

Kerr, S., & Schriesheim, C. A. (1974). Consideration, initiating structure and organizational criteria: An update of Korman's 1966 review. *Personnel Psychology, 27*, 555–568.

[255]

TD (Tardive Dyskinesia) Monitor.

Purpose: "Measures the presence and severity of the tardive dyskinesia movements."

Population: Patients receiving chronic neuroleptic maintenance.

Publication Date: 1992.

Acronym: TD Monitor.

Scores: Total score only.

Administration: Individual.

Price Data, 2002: $95 per complete kit including 25 Modified AIMS QuikScore™ forms, 25 Modified Webster QuikScore™ forms, 25 TD Monitor history forms, and manual; $20 per 25 QuikScore™ forms (specify Modified Webster or Modified AIMS); $30 per 25 history forms; $36 per manual; $40 per specimen set including 1 Modified AIMS QuikScore™ form, 1 Modified Webster QuikScore™ form, 1 history form, and manual.

Time: Administration time not reported.

Comments: Includes the Modified Webster Scale of Parkinsonism and centers around the Modified Abnormal Involuntary Movement Scale.

Author: William M. Glazer.

Publisher: Multi-Health Systems, Inc.

Review of the TD (Tardive Dyskinesia) Monitor by TIMOTHY J. MAKATURA, Clinical Neuropsychologist and Clinical Assistant Professor, De-

partment of Physical Medicine and Rehabilitation, University of Pittsburgh Medical Center, Pittsburgh, PA:

DESCRIPTION AND DEVELOPMENT. The TD (Tardive Dyskinesia) Monitor is a brief screening instrument designed to provide a systematic set of procedures to monitor patients receiving chronic neuroleptic medication therapy and specifically screen for symptoms of tardive diskinesia. The TD Monitor is also a structured set of clinical interview questions and clinical observations that are combined to determine the probability of the diagnosis of tardive dyskinesia. This instrument consists of three specific components: the Abnormal Involuntary Movements Scale (AIMS), a modified form of the Webster Scale for Parkinsonism, and a structured interview that probes for the presence or absence of involuntary movements. The author points out that although these components have been used individually in the past, their combined use results in heightened certainty in determining or ruling out tardive dyskinesia.

The AIMS is a 13-item instrument that was originally developed by the National Institute of Health to evaluate symptoms consistent with tardive dyskinesia (Guy, 1976). According to the manual, since its origin it has become the most widely recommended examination for dyskinesia in clinical practice. It is designed for individual administration and consists of ratings for dyskinetic movements in each of seven anatomical areas: facial, lips, tongue, jaw, upper extremities, lower extremities, and trunk. In addition, global ratings for severity, level of incapacitation, awareness, denture status, and diagnostic impression are included. Each item is scored from 0 to 4 based on presence and severity of dyskinesia. A specific format is presented in the administration section of the manual that stipulates methods for eliciting the specific behaviors and conventions for assigning severity ratings.

The Modified Webster Parkinsonism Rating is the original eight-item instrument developed by David Webster (Webster, 1968) as a rating of disability from Parkinson's disease with the addition of assessments for akathisia and dystonia as well as modification of anchor points for the existing items. It is designed for individual administration and each item is scored as 1 or 0 indicating presence or absence of a specific symptom in separate areas of the body. A specific

format in the administration section of the manual stipulates methods for eliciting the specific behaviors and conventions for assigning scores.

The Tardive Dyskinesia History Form is a structured interview that probes for historical information to generate the differential diagnoses for tardive dyskinesia. This form specifically screens for exposure to neuroleptic medication, timing of onset of abnormal movements, duration and description of movements, history of substance abuse, alternative risk factors, and other variables indicative of a differential diagnosis.

Raw scores and the sum of endorsed items are used to make all determinations on the AIMS. The criteria for probable tardive dyskinesia is endorsement of mild to severe movement symptoms in three or more of the seven anatomical areas on this measure. The Modified Webster Scale provides additional qualitative data regarding specific symptoms; however, a quantitative scoring method for this instrument is not presented. Information from the Tardive Dyskinesia History Form confirms neuroleptic medication use and screens for other possible etiological factors associated with abnormal movements.

TECHNICAL. Interrater reliabilities based on intraclass correlations of four psychiatrists' ratings for the total AIMS score were reported to be .79 (Lane, Glazer, & Hansen, 1985). In a separate study, agreement between two raters has also been reported to be .87 (Chien, Jung, Ross-Townsend, & Sterns, 1977). Instead of reporting a test-retest reliability coefficient, the author cites a study by Bergen, Griffiths, Rey, and Beumont (1984) indicating repeated measure variability is due to unreliability rather than disease fluctuations and the AIMS does not measure all aspects of tardive dyskinesia. Internal consistency is derived using nonstandard methods and unpublished data. The author concludes that reliability coefficients among all seven anatomical areas were consistently less than .5, which suggests individual item scores are not measuring the same underlying phenomenon.

Validity evidence was provided by evaluating the author's decision rule (endorsement of mild to severe movement symptoms in three or more of the seven anatomical areas) compared to more stringent criteria proposed by Schooler and Kane (1982) on a population of 238 probable TD cases (Glazer, Morgenstern, Niedzwiecki, & Hughes, 1988). The author's criteria included 28 cases that the more stringent criteria did not. Eighty-two percent of these cases were eventually considered to be "probable" TD and 46% were eventually considered to be "persistent" cases of TD. The author considers this to be evidence of the heightened sensitivity of the less restrictive criteria, but adds the cautionary note to complete the AIMS twice per visit to minimize false negatives.

Evidence of concurrent validity, as demonstrated by agreement among the AIMS and other scales, is reportedly mixed and specific correlations are not presented. In contrast, the AIMS correlated highly with instrumental measures including piezoelectric recordings of orofacial movements (Chien et al., 1977); accelometric measures associated with resting the hand, posturing, and moving the arm (Tyron & Pologe, 1987); ultrasound counts related to the orofacial areas (Bartzokis et al., 1988); and motor readiness potential (Adler, Pecevich, & Nagamoto, 1989). Construct validity evidence includes correlations between the AIMS and certain physiological measures including striatal dopamine D2 receptor density (Blin et al., 1989) and plasma HVA levels (Kirch, Hattox, Bell, Murphy, & Freedman, 1983).

COMMENTARY AND SUMMARY. Overall, the TD Monitor is not so much a new instrument as a compilation of existing instruments that are assembled to provide a comprehensive method for the identification and quantification of symptoms associated with tardive dyskinesia. Evidence for the efficacy of this instrument is presented for only a single component of the test, the Abnormal Involuntary Movement Scale (AIMS). This statistical evidence is less than compelling. Comparisons with other instruments fail to show a clear superiority of the AIMS in determining the existence of tardive dyskinesia despite some evidence that suggests a higher correlation between the AIMS and certain physiological measures. Additionally, much of the information that supports the validity and reliability of this instrument is presented in an indirect fashion. Therefore, until more conclusive evidence is presented, this instrument would be best used as a method to organize and quantify clinical evidence for the existence of tardive dyskinesia.

REVIEWER'S REFERENCES

Adler, L. E., Pecevich, M., & Nagamoto, H. (1989). Bereitschaftspotential in tardive dyskinesia. Movement Disorder, 4(2), 105–112.

Bartzokis, G., Wirshing, W. C., Hill, M. A., Cummings, J. L., Altshuler, L., & May, P. R. (1988). Comparison of electromechanical measures and observer ratings of tardive dyskinesia. Psychiatry Research, 27(2), 193–198.

Bergen, J. A., Griffiths, D. A., Rey, J. M., & Beumont, P. J. (1984). Tardive dyskinesia: Fluctuating patient or fluctuating rater. British Journal of Psychiatry, 144, 498–502.

Blin, J., Baron, J. C., Bonnet, A. M., Cambon, H., Bonner, A. M., Dubois, B., Loch, C., Baziere, B., & Agid, Y. (1989). Striatal dopamine D2 receptors in tardive dyskinesia: PET study. Neurological Psychiatry, 52(11), 1248–1282.

Chien, C. P., Jung, K., Ross-Townsend, A., & Sterns, B. (1977). The measurement of persistent dyskinesia by piezoelectric recording and clinical rating scales. Psychopharmacology Bulletin, 13(3), 34–36.

Glazer, W. M., Morgenstern, H., Niedzwiecki, D., & Hughes, J. (1988). Heterogeneity of tardive dyskinesia: A multivariate analysis. British Journal of Psychiatry, 152, 253–259.

Guy, W. (1976). ECDEU assessment manual for psychopharmacology (Publication 76-338). Washington, DC: U.S. Department of Health, Education and Welfare.

Kirch, D., Hattox, S., Bell, J., Murphy, R., & Freedman, R. (1983). Plasma homovanillic acid and tardive dyskinesia during neuroleptic maintenance and withdrawal. Psychiatry Research, 9, 217–223.

Lane, R., Glazer, W., & Hansen, T. (1985). Assessment of tardive dyskinesia using the abnormal involuntary movement scale. Journal of Nervous and Mental Disorders, 173, 353–357.

Schooler, N. R., & Kane, J. M. (1982). Research diagnoses for tardive dyskinesia. Archives of General Psychiatry, 39, 486–487.

Tyron, W. W., & Pologe, B. (1987). Accelerometric assessment of tardive dyskinesia. American Journal of Psychiatry, 144, 1584–1587.

Webster, D. D. (1968). Critical analysis of the disability in Parkinson's disease. Modern Treatment, 5, 257–282.

Review of the TD (Tardive Dyskinesia) Monitor by ANTHONY M. PAOLO, Research Associate Professor of Psychiatry and Behavioral Sciences, University of Kansas Medical Center, Kansas City, KS:

DESCRIPTION. The TD (Tardive Dyskinesia) Monitor is a set of procedures designed to screen for tardive dyskinesia. Its purpose is to provide a systematic method for monitoring patients receiving chronic neuroleptic maintenance. The components of the TD Monitor consist of the Abnormal Involuntary Movements Scale (AIMS), a modified Webster Scale for Parkinsonism, and the Tardive Dyskinesia History Form.

The AIMS is completed by examining the patient and rating the severity of movement on a 5-point scale in seven body areas including the face, lips, jaw, tongue, arm, legs, and trunk. Movements in each of the seven body areas is rated from *not present* (a rating of 0) to *severe* (a rating of 4) and a total score is computed by adding up the seven ratings. In addition, the AIMS includes global ratings of the severity of abnormal movements, incapacitation due to the abnormal movements, patient's awareness of abnormal movements, dental status, and general diagnostic impression. According to the manual, properly trained physicians or mental health professionals can administer the AIMS in 5 to 10 minutes. Videotapes are available from the test publisher to assist in training.

The Modified Webster Scale is also collected during the patient examination and is a rating of the presence or absence of common Parkinsonian signs and symptoms. The signs include bradykinesia of the hands, rigidity, posture, upper extremity swing, gait, tremor, facies, cogwheeling, and dystonia. The Modified Webster Scale also rates the severity of akathisia.

The Tardive Dyskinesia History Form is completed during the patient interview and gathers information concerning duration and description of abnormal movements, neuroleptic exposure, possible substance abuse, psychiatric history, and possible risk factors.

DEVELOPMENT. Limited information is provided in the manual concerning the development of the different components. For instance, it is mentioned that the AIMS was developed by the National Institute of Mental Health in the mid 1970s to evaluate the presence and severity of movements associated with tardive dyskinesia. Similarly, the manual states that the original Webster Scale was developed in the late 1960s to rate the disability that may result from Parkinson's Disease. Finally, the history form "was designed to permit the clinician to collect information needed for generating the differential diagnosis of tardive dyskinesia" (manual, p. 2).

Additional information concerning the development of the scales that includes samples employed, explanation for the changes made to the original Webster Scale, sensitivity, and specificity would assist clinicians in deciding whether the TD Monitor is appropriate for their purpose.

TECHNICAL. Basic psychometric characteristics are provided for only the AIMS component. Interrater reliability for the total score is good and ranged from .79 to .87. However, the sample of patients used was reported for only one of the two studies and the type of raters (i.e., psychiatrists) employed was reported for only one study. A more complete description of the sample used, the type of rater (i.e., physician, mental health worker, etc.), experience of rater with TD and/or other movement disorders, and experience of the raters with the instrument would allow clinicians to make more informed judgments concerning the adequacy of the interrater reliability.

No test-retest reliability coefficients are provided, but the authors state "that intrapatient variability of the AIMS scores with repeated measures is attributable to unreliability rather than the fluctuations in the disease" (manual, p. 39). An article is referenced to support this statement. Clearly a more complete description of the meth-

ods and results used to support this statement is necessary and should be provided in the manual.

Internal consistency reliability (alpha coefficients) estimates are inadequate and reported as less than .5 for the seven anatomical scores. A factor analysis, briefly reported in the manual, conducted with 228 patients with TD on the seven anatomical scores found three independent factors. More information concerning the factor analysis should be provided.

The poor internal consistency along with the finding of three factors suggests that the total score used for the AIMS may not always be the most appropriate score to interpret. Additional information concerning when the total score is the most appropriate and when it should not be used should be provided.

Concurrent validity evidence as reported in the manual is variable. High concurrent validity was reported between the AIMS and the Simpson Abbreviated Dyskinesia Scale, but no coefficient was provided. The correlation between the AIMS and piezoelectric recordings of orofacial movements in nine outpatients was .72. In contrast, no meaningful association between the AIMS and frequency counts of selected involuntary movements has been reported.

Several research articles are referenced that report the use of the AIMS to demonstrate treatment effects of placebo controls versus psychopharmacological interventions. In contrast, the manual provides several negative findings concerning the relationship between AIMS scores and levels of dopamine. The negative findings, as suggested by the author, may reflect the poor understanding of the neurobiology of TD rather than problems with the validity of the AIMS. However, it may be a combination of lack of understanding of the neurobiology of TD and less than optimal reliability of the AIMS.

Finally, a format for diagnosing TD from the AIMS is presented, but limited information is provided concerning its accuracy. The manual should at least provide sensitivity, specificity, and positive and negative predictive values.

COMMENTARY. The value of the TD Monitor is the bringing together of several important components to assess TD. Although the AIMS and Modified Webster Scale can be completed relatively quickly, the History Form could take some time to gather all of the proper information.

pals and university personnel were generally "congruent."

The items used in the TPA instruments are closely related, and sometimes nearly identical, to the "Indicators" defined in the Standards for Teacher Educators and the Standards for Field Experiences as published by the Association of Teacher Educators (ATE; 2000). Although not formally referenced by the TPA authors in the manual, it is apparent that many of the TPA items were derived from the ATE work that resulted in these documents.

The original set of instruments in the TPA included those for Classroom Teachers, Student Teachers, Interns, Substitute Teachers, and Classroom Aides. In 1991, the TPA scales were revised and two additional instruments were developed, one for Field Associates and one for Residents.

TECHNICAL. The reliability and validity information for the various instruments in the TPA is shown below, along with the sample size used. The criterion for predictive and concurrent validity measures is the rating by the supervisor. A total of five expert supervisors provided all the supervisor ratings that were used as the criterion for predictive and concurrent validity studies.

Based on a standardization group consisting of 140 classroom teachers, 175 student teachers, 195 interns, 55 substitute teachers, 33 classroom aides, 78 field associates, and 20 residents, the authors report internal consistency reliability for all scales that ranged from .59–.79, interrater consistence between .61–.80, construct validity from .50–.55, concurrent validity value from .46–.49, and predictive validity indices from .41–.48.

The majority of the TPA instruments have been developed and refined over a span of approximately 10 years. Unfortunately, however, their construction is weak from a number of technical perspectives. This weakness may contribute to the generally moderate to low reliability and validity figures for the TPA.

First, the instruments used for classroom teachers and student teachers indicate that up to 10 observation visits may be made. The individual completing the form is to indicate to which observation the current form refers. However, nowhere in either the directions or the manual for the TPA is any indication given as to whether the "scores" from all the forms used for the several observations should be combined to form an overall or final rating.

The instruments for substitute teacher, intern, resident, classroom aide, or field associate indicate that up to five observation visits may be made. No information is provided on whether or how to combine the data from such visits.

Second, the response scales used for the various instruments are poorly constructed. The instruments for the classroom teachers and student teachers use the three-category scale of "Strong, Good, Weak." Additionally, a rating of "Strong" on an item translates into a 5-point value, a rating of "Good" into a 3-point value, and a rating of "Weak" into a 1-point rating. Not only are the scale categories not parallel ("Strong-Weak" belongs to one scale, "Good—Bad" to another), but also the assignment of 1, 3, or 5 points to the categories promotes an inappropriate interpretation of the data as if it came from a true 5-point scale. In contrast, the remaining instruments use a 5-point scale (Low-1-2-3-4-5-High). However, other than the end points, no specific definition is provided for any other point on the scale. These problems undoubtedly contribute to the forms being less reliable than they might otherwise be.

The TPA manual indicates that the raw scores from each test fall in the following ranges: Classroom Teachers (0–75 points); Student Teachers (0–60 points); and Interns, Substitute Teachers, Classroom Aides, Field Associates, and Residents (0–80 points). Because the lowest rating on the items in each form is assigned a point value of "1," it is not clear how these raw score ranges are possible.

The raw scores obtained from the various TPA forms are converted to T-scores using tables provided in the manual. Fortunately, the conversion tables indicate the proper lowest scores of 15 or 16 (depending on the instrument) rather than the low score of zero (0) specified in the manual description of each instrument. The directions given with the form imply that the standard scores from multiple administrations of an instrument over time may be used to "show progress."

COMMENTS. The appearance of the TPA packages is that of a "home-made" set of instruments. The layout and overall organization of the TPA manual is confusing and amateurish. Although the manual has a table of contents, it provides no page numbers and no page numbers are printed on the pages themselves.

The various TPA instruments are printed on paper of differing colors. Although undoubtedly meant to make each instrument easier to identify, the result is more confusing than clarifying. In addition, no directions are printed on any form, further contributing to the possibility of inconsistency of use and its resultant impact on the reliability of the obtained data. There is little evidence of psychometric expertise or statistical sophistication in the design of the TPA and its data interpretation tables.

SUMMARY. The Teacher Performance Assessment (TPA) package consists of multiple instruments (most of them virtually identical to one another) designed to measure the instructional performance of individuals involved in teaching and provides rating data (supervisor, self, and reflected) on Classroom Teachers, Student Teachers, Substitute Teachers, Classroom Aides, Interns, Residents, and Field Associates. Although apparently based on a sound construct, the execution of the TPA package is unprofessional. The directions for the scoring and use of the various instruments are poorly written and, on occasion, clearly erroneous. The TPA may provide a moderately useful mechanism in assisting in the growth of those involved in teaching in the K–12 levels if used in a more comprehensive program of faculty development and teacher education. However, the forms, as presently constructed, do not meet the professional standards necessary for their use in the assessment of teachers for the purpose of making personnel decisions such as tenure or pay raises.

REVIEWER'S REFERENCES

ATE Standards for Field Experiences. (2000). Available from The Association of Teacher Educators (ATEK), 1900 Association Drive, Suite ATE, Reston, VA 20191.
ATE Standards for Teacher Educators. (2000). Available from The Association of Teacher Educators (ATE), 1900 Association Drive, Suite ATE, Reston, VA 20191.

Review of the Teacher Performance Assessment by SAMUEL HINTON, Professor, Educational Studies, Eastern Kentucky University, Richmond, KY:

DESCRIPTION. The Teacher Performance Assessment (TPA) consists of seven sets of performance inventories developed to provide both an assessor assessment and a self-assessment of classroom instructional activities. The rationale for developing this inventory is that there is a need for providing a more authentic assessment of classroom instruction than can be generally found when those who assess classroom instruction also create the assessment. The developers claim that there is a consistent relationship between the self-attributions of classroom and observed teaching

competencies. Because of this, they developed the TPA to provide authentic assessments in "softer" educational structures. Examples of such structures are performance portfolios and charter schools.

DEVELOPMENT. The developers provided "Standardization Data" (p. 6) in the test manual supplement. They refer to a standardization project conducted in two phases. In Phase I, 140 classroom teachers, 175 student teachers, 195 interns, 55 substitute teachers, and 33 classroom aides participated. In Phase II, 78 field associates and 20 residents were included. The developers did not present a detailed description of the "standardization" process.

Performance scales. Seven sets of performance scales were developed. They are (a) Classroom Teachers Assessments, (b) Substitute Teachers Assessments, (c) Field Associates Assessments, (d) Interns Assessments, (e) Student Teachers Assessments, (f) Classroom Aides Assessments, and (g) Residents (Leadership Apprentices Assessments). There are two levels of Internship Assessments: Internship I and Internship II. The assessment for classroom teachers contains three sets of forms. There is a Teacher Performance Assessment form to be rated by a supervisor or mentor, a self-assessment form, and a reflected self-assessment form. Level of performance is rated on two scales. One is a composite of 15 major categories in a variety of measurements found in universities and school districts across the country. The companion scale contains five specific action clusters for each item in the classroom teachers' and substitute teachers' inventories respectively. For example, on the Classroom Teacher form, Item 1 reads: "Demonstrates facility in skills of reading, writing, speaking, mathematics, and advanced technology." The first item in the supervision of Classroom Teachers form is: "My supervisor thinks that I demonstrate facility in basic skills." The clusters are listed individually as reading, writing, speaking, mathematics, and advanced technology.

The rating scale in each of the first two inventories is up to 5 points for a strong performance, up to 3 points for a good performance, and 1 point for a weak performance. The range of points possible is from 75 to 15. Refinements of broad categories in the cluster form are simply checked when applicable.

TECHNICAL. The developers stated that reliability coefficients range from .80 to .59 (inter-

supported by the magnitude and pattern of the correlations reported between the Teamwork-KSA test scores, the supervisor's ratings, and the aptitude composite score. In particular, the Teamwork-KSA test correlated .44 with the supervisors' teamwork performance, .56 with the supervisors' technical performance rating, and .52 with the supervisors' overall performance rating. The aptitude composite score correlated .33 with the supervisors' teamwork performance rating and .60 with the supervisors' technical performance rating. The correlation between the Teamwork-KSA and the supervisors' teamwork performance rating ($r = .44$) is statistically significantly greater than the correlation between the aptitude composite score and the supervisors' teamwork performance rating ($r = .33$). The correlation between the supervisors' teamwork performance rating and aptitude composite score ($r = .60$) exceeds, but is not statistically significantly greater than, the correlation between the supervisors' technical performance rating and the Teamwork-KSA Test ($r = .56$).

Hierarchical regressions were performed to evaluate whether the addition of the Teamwork-KSA test to a standard employment aptitude battery provided incremental or additional predictive power in selection decisions. The results revealed that the Teamwork-KSA Test significantly added to the explanatory variance over the aptitude test composite score.

In another study, 72 adult volunteers from a Northeastern cardboard processing plant were administered the Teamwork-KSA and the same standardized employee aptitude battery as in the first study. Peer and self-ratings enhanced the subjects' performance information. These subjects were informed that all information gathered was for research purposes only and special care was taken to assure confidentiality of employee ratings. An innovative peer nomination/rating form was utilized to prevent any negative outcomes due to employee ratings. Scores were averaged across nomination categories. The variables showed suitable variability to warrant an investigation of criterion-related validity. Convergent validity is supported by the correlation of .81 between the Teamwork-KSA test and employee aptitude composite. The Teamwork-KSA test correlated with peer ratings of teamwork (.23) and with overall peer rating of performance (.21). Supervisors' ratings of technical, overall, and teamwork ratings correlated with

the Teamwork-KSA tests scores ($r = .25$, $r = .23$, $r = .21$, respectively). These sets of correlations lend modest support for the claim of criterion-related validity. Correlations among peer ratings of technical performance and self-ratings of job performance with the Teamwork-KSA were not statistically significant. There was no statistically significant incremental addition to explained variance by the Teamwork-KSA scores over the employment aptitude tests. When data from both validity studies were combined, support was clear for the convergent and incremental validity of the Teamwork-KSA test.

COMMENTARY. The Teamwork-KSA Test is a group-administered, self-report instrument constructed after a review of the relevant literature of essential knowledge, skills, and abilities that may be predictive of effectively working in groups within an organizational setting. The basis for the content of the 35 items comprising five subscales within two dimensions of Interpersonal KSAs and Self-Management KSAs is the result of solid psychometric principles of test construction.

The two validity studies presented adequate support for the claims of convergent and incremental validity of the Teamwork-KSA. Internal consistency reliability ($r = .80$) was reported for the Overall Teamwork-KSA Test. Normative data are nonexistent. Future revisions of the Teamwork-KSA Test would benefit from the inclusion of the demographic information about the samples upon which the psychometric conclusions are based. Scoring procedures and score interpretations were not provided. Without comparative score data, meaningful normative conclusions cannot be reached.

Tests designed for the selection or the promotion of employees must be sensitive to the pressure of a candidate responding in a socially desirable manner. The high content/face validity of this test makes it particularly vulnerable to test-takers giving false impressions. An appraisal of evidence of this type of test-taking behavior and the appropriate adjustments are warranted.

SUMMARY. The Teamwork-KSA Test is designed to assess an individual's knowledge, skills, and abilities (KSAs) to work effectively within a team or group organization. The Teamwork-KSA Test is not a personality test, nor is it a test of how to optimally configure team membership, nor is it a technical assessment of skills related to work in organizations. Rather, it is designed to assess an individual's ability to work as a member of a team and whether the individual has the social and/or interpersonal skills, knowledge, and abilities to be an effective member of a team. The current, competitive, and complex organizational climate points to the need for an assessment instrument in the selection of employees who can work effectively in a group or team setting. With the addition of normative information and comparative data, the Teamwork-KSA test could make a valuable contribution to the industrial/organizational literature.

Review of the Teamwork-KSA Test by PATRICIA H. WHEELER, President and Principal Researcher, EREAPA Associates, Livermore, CA:

DESCRIPTION. The Teamwork-KSA Test was designed as a psychological instrument "to measure the essential knowledge, skills, and abilities (KSAs) that are predictive of working effectively in teams. The focus of the instrument is on (a) KSAs rather than personality traits, (b) team rather than technical KSAs, and (c) the individual rather than the team level of assessment" (Information Guide, p. 1). The directions in the test booklet say that the test measures "how you would react to situations in a team-oriented work environment" (p. 1).

The Teamwork-KSA Test consists of 35 multiple-choice items, each with four choices. The respondent marks the answers in a nonreusable test booklet next to the chosen option for each question. Using carbon paper, the answers are transferred to the back side of a page near the end of the test booklet on which the scoring information is also given. Responses are coded by subscale based on the shape of the symbol in which the correct response appears.

There are 25 items in the area of Interpersonal KSAs with subscales in Conflict Resolution (4 items), Collaborative Problem Solving (9 items), and Communication (12 items). The other 10 items are in the area of Self-Management KSAs with subscales in Goal Setting and Performance Management (5 items) and Planning and Task Coordination (5 items).

Scores are reported to authorized personnel on a confidential assessment report. For each subscale and the total score, the report lists the raw score and percentile, and displays the percentiles in horizontal bar graph format.

DEVELOPMENT. The KSAs are based on a literature review that covered organizational psychology, social psychology, industrial engineering, and socio-technical theory. For each of the identified KSA areas, several citations are listed in the Information Guide. The authors have not provided a bibliography.

TECHNICAL. The authors report that the pilot administrations showed the test to be at an eighth-grade reading level and to have an internal consistency reliability coefficient of .80.

Although the assessment report shows percentiles for each subscale score and the total score, information was not provided in the Information Guide about the sample upon which these percentiles were based nor was there a norms table. With three of the subscales having only four or five items, reporting percentile ranks derived from these subscales seems problematic and could easily lead to undue reliance on the results and the danger of excessive interpretation.

Validity is based on two studies that examined the concurrent validity of the Teamwork-KSA Test. One study was conducted in a southeastern pulp processing mill ($N = 70$ employees) and the other in a northeastern cardboard processing plant ($N = 72$ employees). No information is provided on the types of employees who participated in these two validity studies or their demographic characteristics.

In the first validity study, the Teamwork-KSA Test was correlated with a battery of nine aptitude tests and with supervisor ratings for promotion decisions. Correlation values with the aptitude measures ranged from .77 with Reading Comprehension and with Vocabulary to .52 with Visual Speed/Accuracy. Data are also shown for a series of hierarchical regression analyses that indicated incremental validity for the predictive value of the Teamwork-KSA Test in the areas of Teamwork Performance and Overall Performance.

The second validity study looked at two standardized employment aptitude tests, one in math problem solving and one in vocabulary. Regrettably, the identity of these two standardized tests was not given. This second study also looked at ratings by up to five supervisors per employee, self-ratings by the employee, and peer input, based on a listing of teammate preferences. The authors reported that the Teamwork-KSA Test scores correlated well with the aptitude composite score

(.81). Correlations with the supervisors' and peers' teamwork ratings and overall ratings were lower, but still significant at $p < .05$, ranging from .21 to .23. Correlations with self-teamwork and overall ratings were slightly negative and insignificant.

The regression analyses for the second study did not yield results supporting the predictive value of the Teamwork-KSA Test for employment decisions. The authors suggested that this might be due to the fact that in the first validity study there were immediate job consequences associated with performance on the test. This was not the case in the second study. Also, participants in the second study were volunteers (unlike the first study) and thus may have reflected a sample with less variation than that in the first study. More information on the aptitude tests, the supervisors' ratings, and the types of employees participating in the validity studies would help clarify these unresolved questions.

The Information Guide reported on analyses of three demographic factors: race, sex, and education. The first combined Black and Hispanics ($N = 80$) compared to Whites and Asians ($N = 110$). The mean score of the first group was about 2 points lower than the second group. The authors concluded that the Teamwork-KSA Test was fair. Without further information about these 190 individuals, including their English-language proficiency, it is difficult to judge the fairness of this test based on race.

The results did show a significant difference favoring females ($N = 79$) over males ($N = 212$) with the females' mean score about 2.2 points higher. No discussion was provided on this finding, however. The authors also reported finding that the Teamwork-KSA Test favored those with some education beyond high school ($N = 128$) compared to those with an educational level equal to or below a high school graduate ($N = 131$), with the first group scoring about 3.6 points higher. Based on the Ns, these apparently were not the same groups as in the two validity studies described above, but no information was provided on the samples for these three analyses by demographic variables.

COMMENTARY. The purpose of the Teamwork-KSA Test and the settings most appropriate to its use are unclear. It is not clear if the results should be used for promotions to supervisory positions, to identify employees to serve on committees, to select employees for job assignments requiring much interactive teamwork (e.g., an emergency room staff,

theatrical production actors and crew) or one where employees work as a team, but more independently of each other (e.g., classroom teachers, assembly line workers, police officers).

The packaging of the test booklet is costly. Booklets could be printed in a reusable format with a separate answer sheet. As it is currently, the answer sheet can be pulled off the back of the booklet, separating it from the test taker's name, which is entered (along with date, company, and position) on the left edge of the instructions page in a location that could be easily missed. The directions do not tell the test takers to put their names and other information on the left edge of the page. Accurate linking of answer sheet responses to the correct employee seems risky at best.

The literature review should be accompanied by a comprehensive list of references. Without the bibliography, it is difficult to ascertain the quality and comprehensiveness of the literature reviewed.

Although the assessment report shows percentile ranks, the group upon which the percentile ranks are based is not described. Moreover, giving percentile ranks of subscales with four or five items is unsound and potentially misleading. Insufficient information is provided on the nature of the supervisor ratings, and it is not clear if up to five supervisors can have enough familiarity with an employee to provide a reasonably accurate rating for that employee. Additional information on the aptitude tests, including the names of the tests, should be given. The samples should also be described in more detail and the reason(s) given as to why the individuals participated in the studies.

SUMMARY. Although working well as a member of a team can be crucial to successful job performance, it is not clear if the Teamwork-KSA Test will provide useful data for making decisions about employees and job applicants. Much depends on the nature of the other team members and on the tasks to be undertaken. Past performance of the individual provides the best indicator of future performance. The value of the Teamwork-KSA Test in making such decisions seems limited, based on the materials provided for the review.

[258]

Test for the Reception of Grammar.

Purpose: "Designed to assess understanding of grammatical contrasts in English."

Population: Ages 4–12 years and also dysphasic adults.

Publication Dates: 1983–1989.

Acronym: TROG.

Scores, 21: Noun, Verb, Adjective, Two Element Combination, Negative, Three Element Combination, Singular/Plural Personal Pronoun, Reversible Active, Masculine/Feminine Personal Pronoun, Singular/Plural Noun Inflection, Comparative/Absolute, Reversible Passive, In and On, Postmodified Subject, X But Not Y, Above and Below, Not Only X But Also Y, Relative Clause, Neither X nor Y, Embedded Sentence, Total.

Administration: Individual.

Price Data, 1998: £70 per test kit including 25 test forms, manual, stimulus book, and cards.

Time: (10–20) minutes.

Comments: An 80-item, orally administered, multiple-choice test; "suitable for American as well as British subjects."

Author: Dorothy Bishop.

Publisher: Age and Cognitive Performance Research Centre, University of Manchester [England].

Cross References: See T5:2662 (8 references).

Review of the Test for the Reception of Grammar by ROGER L. TOWNE, Associate Professor and Head, Department of Communication Disorders, Northern Michigan University, Marquette, MI:

The Test for the Reception of Grammar (TROG) was first published in 1983 as a means of assessing the understanding of grammatical concepts in children between the ages of 4 and 12 years. A second edition of the manual was published in 1989 that included additional normative data relative to normal adult performance on the test. However, only 95 adults aged 50 to 83 were tested, and the data are restricted to the percentage of these subjects who passed a certain number of question blocks. As over 2,000 British children were tested to establish the original normative data, the test is still clearly designed to be primarily given and used with children. Suggested targeted populations include individuals who have "specific language disorders, deafness, mental retardation, and cerebral palsy" and "adults with acquired dysphasia" (manual, p. 1).

Components of the test include an administration manual, test protocol, stimulus book with four colored plates on each page, and black-and-white stimulus cards to be used as a vocabulary check on younger children. The author notes that the test can be used for both a quantitative assessment and a more in-depth qualitative assessment.

The quantitative assessment of grammatical comprehension involves only administering the TROG itself and comparison of a child's performance to the normative data. The qualitative assessment additionally involves administration of the vocabulary section prior to administering the TROG and then reviewing performance to further explain the nature of an identified comprehension problem. Administration of the vocabulary section involves showing the child six plates, each with eight line drawings, and having the child name or point to the noun, verb, or adjective represented. As these 48 words are those that are later used in the TROG stimulus items, it is recommended that after the TROG is administered the examiner retest any vocabulary words to which the child did not initially respond correctly to help separate potential grammatical errors from vocabulary limitations.

Administration of the TROG itself is relatively straightforward and facilitated by the format of the test protocol. A child is shown 80 plates each with four colored pictures representing 1 of 20 grammatical concepts (e.g., noun, two element combinations, in and on, relative clause, etc.). Each concept is tested in a block of four plates. As each plate is presented, the child is asked to "point to the picture that goes with what I say. Listen carefully" (manual, p. 9). The examiner then reads the test word or sentence to the child and the child points to one of the four pictures on the plate. Verbal stimuli range from single words (e.g., shoe, eating, long) to much longer sentences (e.g., the boy is jumping over the box, the pencil is on the book that is yellow). Blocks are arranged and presented in a presumed ascending order of relative developmental level and difficulty that allows children of different ages (7 years and below, 8 and 9 years, 10 years and above) to start the test at different points. Children 8 years and older must establish a baseline of five consecutive error-free blocks, and testing is discontinued for all children after failing five consecutive blocks. Failing is defined as missing any of the four stimulus items in a block. A child's score constitutes the total number of blocks passed from which age equivalent scores, percentiles, and standard scores can be determined. The author estimates that the test should take 10 to 20 minutes to administer.

As noted above, the TROG was standardized on over 2,000 British children ranging in age between 4:0 and 12:11. The author also notes that "research by Abbeduto, Furman, and Davies (1989) has demonstrated that the test is suitable for American as well as British subjects" (manual, p. 1). Standardization testing was performed by "volunteer students who were studying for a degree or diploma to qualify as speech therapists, and who were paid on a pro rata basis for each child tested" (manual. P. 4). Each examiner tested across several age groups in a deliberate effort to spread "any bias in sample characteristics or in testing across all age groups" (manual, p. 5). Children were excluded from the sample for a variety of reasons that included receiving speech therapy, having a significant hearing or visual handicap, parents being a nonnative speaker of English, or living in a household where another language was spoken. Effort was also made to match the social class distribution of the sample to the proportions seen in the general population at that time. From these data, percentile equivalents for blocks passed, age equivalent scores for blocks passed, and standard scores for blocks passed were calculated for 13 age ranges. Other data are also presented in several appendices relative to sample error patterns, TROG scores relative to English Picture Vocabulary Test raw scores, social class effects on TROG performance, and the percent passing each block by age. Also as noted above, some normative data from a small number of normal adults are also presented.

SUMMARY. The TROG presents a rather commonly used format for testing a child's underlying receptive knowledge in some area; in this case grammatical concepts. The task is relatively simple for the child, the stimulus material is bright and colorful, and the test procedure and protocol are easy for the examiner to follow. However, there are several other factors to consider. First, only four stimulus items are used to test each of the 20 grammatical concepts, and making an error on only one will cause a child to fail the whole block. Conclusions relative to a child's actual knowledge of a grammatical concept must consider that they are based on a small sampling of performance on that concept. Second, the validity of using the TROG with American-English-speaking children has not been established. Abbeduto, Furman, and Davies (1989) noted that "we know of no evidence indicating that the culture differences between Great Britain and the United States would differentially affect the course of child language development" (p. 538), and presented data

on 60 normal American children whose mean percentile score on the TROG was 55.34. However, until the TROG is validated on American children the results should likely be used in the U.S. with some caution. Third, if one is interested in measuring a child's total language development, rather than focusing solely on grammatical development, there are other tools such as the Test of Language Development (TOLD-P:3; Newcomer & Hammill, 1997; T6:2546) and the Test of Auditory Comprehension of Language (TACL-3; Carrow-Woolfolk, 1999; T6:2513) that offer a more comprehensive language assessment using a format similar to that of the TROG.

REVIEWER'S REFERENCES

Abbeduto, L., Furman, L., & Davies, B. (1989). Relation between the receptive language and mental age of persons with mental retardation. *American Journal on Mental Retardation, 93,* 535–543.

Carrow-Woolfolk, E. (1999). Test of Auditory Comprehension of Language—Third Edition (TACL-3). Austin, TX: PRO-ED.

Newcomer, P. L., & Hammill, D. D. (1997). Test of Language Development (TOLD-P:3). Austin, TX: PRO-ED.

[259]

Test of Early Reading Ability, Third Edition.

Purpose: Designed to "assess children's mastery of early developing reading skills."

Population: Ages 3-6 to 8-6.

Publication Dates: 1981–2001.

Acronym: TERA-3.

Scores, 3: Alphabet, Conventions, Meaning.

Administration: Individual.

Forms, 2: A, B.

Price Data, 2003: $234 per complete kit including examiner's manual (2001, 127 pages), 2 picture books (Form A and Form B), 25 profile/examiner record Forms A, and 25 profile/examiner record Forms B; $81 per examiner's manual; $56 per picture book (specify Form A or Form B); $25 per 25 profile/examiner record forms (specify Form A or Form B).

Time: (30) minutes.

Authors: D. Kim Reid, Wayne P. Hresko, and Donald D. Hammill.

Publisher: PRO-ED.

Cross References: See T5:2682 (13 references) and T4:2751 (2 references); for reviews by Michael D. Beck and Robert W. Hiltonsmith of an earlier edition, see 11:429 (1 reference); for reviews by Isabel L. Beck and Janet A. Norris of the original edition, see 9:1253.

Review of the Test of Early Reading Ability, Third Edition by SHARON deFUR, Associate Professor of Special Education, College of William and Mary, Williamsburg, VA:

DESCRIPTION. The Test of Early Reading Ability, Third Edition (TERA-3) is a norm-referenced, individually administered test that assesses the mastery of emergent literacy skills in young children ages 3 years 6 months to 8 years 6 months. There are five identified purposes of the TERA-3: (a) to identify children who are below peers in reading development; (b) to identify strengths and weaknesses of individual children; (c) to document progress as a result of early reading intervention; (d) to serve as a measure in reading research; and (e) to serve as one component of a comprehensive assessment. To their credit, the authors clearly state that the TERA-3 is not to be used as a sole basis for instructional planning.

The TERA-3 has two alternate forms and the test kit includes an examiner's manual, Form A and B picture book, and examiner record booklets for Forms A and B. Three subtests comprise the TERA-3: (a) Alphabet (mastering the alphabet and its functions; (b) Conventions (understanding the arbitrary conventions of reading and writing in English); and (c) Meaning (understanding that print conveys thought and meaning). The full test can be administered typically in 30 minutes or less, but the items are not timed.

Nonclinical staff can administer the TERA-3, but the authors strongly recommend that the examiner have formal training in assessment with a basic understanding of testing statistics, and general procedures regarding test administration, scoring, and interpretation. Regardless of training, the authors recommend careful study of the examiner's manual and a minimum of three practice opportunities before using the TERA-3 in an actual testing situation.

The TERA-3 results are reported in raw scores, age and grade equivalents, percentile scores, standard scores, and confidence scores for each of the three subtests. A Reading quotient is calculated by summing scores from the three subtests and using a table to convert the sum to a Reading Quotient. The Reading Quotient is also reported as a percentile. Standard error of measurement, confidence interval, and standard score ranges are calculated for the combined subtests and for the Reading Quotient. Answers receive a score of 1 for correct or 0 for incorrect, and expected answers are clearly indicated in the examiners record booklet. Chronological age determines the start point for testing, but a basal is established when three items

are correct in a row, and a ceiling is established when three items are failed in a row. The examiner record booklet includes a profile sheet that offers a graphic comparison across the three TERA-3 subtests as well as a graph to compare the TERA-3 Reading Quotient with other comparable measures that might have been administered to the child. In addition, the examiner record booklet has space for interpretation and comments, where, in addition to diagnostic implications, the examiner can note the conditions of testing and the degree of validity obtained given the testing conditions. The authors take care to help the user interpret the scores obtained on the TERA-3. Throughout the manual, the authors emphasize that "tests do not diagnose, people do" urging the user to consider why a child responded in a certain way and not just that they did respond in a particular way.

DEVELOPMENT. The TERA-3 represents a revision of the TERA-2 with the authors taking the following actions based on the recommendations of reviewers of TERA-2. The test authors collected new normative data, addressing the need for appropriate demographic representation; conducted extensive reliability and validity studies; added items as recommended; made the test pictures in color; and re-introduced grade and age equivalents (with reluctance) because they are required by many state and local agencies. No discussion is directed at describing the specific field tests for the TERA-3; however, extensive discussion is provided in the description of the technical adequacy of the TERA-3.

The authors provide a readable review of reading literature that documents the importance of emergent literacy skills in alphabet, conventions, and meaning along with the importance of assessing reading in young children. The authors substantiate the appropriateness of addressing these three areas simultaneously, rather than sequentially, as this progression mirrors the reading development process. The theoretical framework underlying the TERA-3 is well supported in current reading research (National Reading Panel, 2000).

TECHNICAL. The TERA-3 used a relatively small norming sample ($N = 875$), but one that was well matched to the general school-age population (gender, race, ethnicity, SES, disability, and urban/rural) and representative of regions across the United States. All data were collected between February 1999 and April 2000. In re-

Valencia (1997) as providing a guiding structure for the development of the measure, with the notable exception that the TERA-3 does not include any measure of phonemic awareness. There are some questions that arise with respect to item development and placement. These relate to the numbers of item types present within each subtest across forms and the ordering of items. However, these issues are relatively minor and probably do not affect the subscores generated.

TECHNICAL.

Standardization. The norming sample included 875 children aged 3-6 to 8-6 from 22 states. This sample appears to be representative of nationwide statistics as reported in the 1999 U.S. Census, with regard to geographic region, gender, race, urban/rural residence, ethnicity, family income, educational level of parents, and disability status. The sample was also stratified by age. Participants took both forms of the TERA-3 during one testing session; no counterbalancing procedures are described.

Reliability. Evidence of reliability is presented for content sampling, time sampling, and interrater reliability. For content sampling, acceptable coefficient alpha data are given by age, form, subtest, and reading quotient score. Acceptable coefficient alpha are also given by selected subgroups: gender, ethnicity, learning disabled, language impaired, and reading disabled. However, it would have been helpful to see the data for the selected subgroups by age, as well. Correlations for the alternate forms (immediate administration) are also acceptable. Overall, for content sampling, Subtest II, Conventions, demonstrates lower reliability (.83) on both forms as compared to the other subtests (roughly .90) and the Reading Composite (.95). Test-retest reliability at a 2-week interval was investigated using $n = 30$ children aged 4–6 years from Michigan and $n = 34$ children aged 7–9 years from Texas. Though the correlations shown are acceptable, it would be difficult to generalize about stability over time given the sample characteristics. Interrater reliability on 40 randomly drawn protocols was .99.

Validity. Evidence of content validity is provided by lists of research, curriculum materials, and other tests consulted; favorable evaluations by the seven professionals (mentioned previously); and a parallel comparison of the item content on the TERA-3 to Valencia's (1997) categories of

early reading behaviors. The authors state that they selected items for the TERA-3 based on the item-total score Pearson correlation rather than the point-biserial correlation, although these are mathematically identical. A number of differential item functioning (DIF) bias studies were conducted. Although 13 items across the two forms exhibited some DIF, the amount observed was negligible. There is some concern that 7 of the 13 items demonstrating DIF were on Subtest I, Alphabet, Form B. Criterion-prediction studies were conducted using the TERA-2, the Stanford Achievement Test Series—Ninth Edition ($n = 70$), the Woodcock Reading Mastery Test—Revised-Normative Update ($n = 64$), and teacher ratings ($n = 411$). The correlations tend to be moderate to high. Evidence of construct validity was determined by correlating performance on the TERA-3 to age. Favorable correlations here are hardly surprising given the developmental nature of reading and the additional instruction received as age increases. Similarly, group differentiations comparing disability subgroups to nonclassified subgroups are what would be expected. Details of a confirmatory factor analysis need clarification.

COMMENTARY/SUMMARY. Generally, the TERA-3 accomplishes its stated purposes, especially if used in conjunction with other assessments. Its strengths lie in the ease of administration, easy to use tables for scoring, and a clearly written examiner's manual. However, claims by the authors that the TERA-3 is "a valid measure of reading" (examiner's manual, p. 76) should be viewed with caution. Tests themselves are not valid. The TERA-3 will be used with diverse types of children in a variety of settings for an assortment of reasons. As such, the validity of the TERA-3 will depend on the specific use of the test in a given situation. The authors should be commended for offering an assessment based on modern reading theory that incorporates examples from everyday life that should appeal to children.

REVIEWER'S REFERENCE

Valencia, S. W. (1997). Authentic classroom assessment of early reading: Alternatives to standardized tests. *Preventing School Failure, 41*(2), 63–70.

[260]
Test of Economic Literacy, Third Edition.

Purpose: Designed to "evaluate a student's performance and make decisions about economics instruction at the senior high school level."

Population: Grades 11–12.

Publication Dates: 1978–2001.
Acronym: TEL.
Scores: Total score only.
Administration: Group.
Forms, 2: A, B.
Price Data, 2001: $22.95 per 25 test booklets (specify Form A or B); $17.95 per examiner's manual (2001, 75 pages), which includes scoring keys and a model answer sheet (may be duplicated locally).
Time: (40-50) minutes.
Authors: William B. Walstad and Ken Rebeck.
Publisher: National Council on Economic Education.
Cross References: See T5:2686 (2 references); for reviews by Jennifer J. Fager and Dan Wright of an earlier edition, see 12:395; for a review by Anna S. Ochoa, see 9:1256; see also T2:1968 (19 references); for reviews by Edward J. Furst and Christine H. McGuire, and an excerpted review by Robert L. Ebel, see 7:901 (10 references).

Review of the Test of Economic Literacy, Third Edition by JOHN W. YOUNG, Associate Professor of Educational Statistics and Measurement, Rutgers University, New Brunswick, NJ:

DESCRIPTION AND DEVELOPMENT. The Test of Economic Literacy, Third Edition (TEL-3, Forms A and B), is a 40-item, four-option multiple-choice standardized test for measuring the achievement of high school students in economics. Eleven of the test questions are common to both forms. The questions can be answered using a machine-readable answer sheet and the test requires no more than 40 minutes of testing time. The test has a long history of use in schools across the United States for assessing what high school students know about basic economic concepts. In 1961, the National Task Force on Economic Education outlined the basic economic concepts to be taught in the nation's schools. From this outline, the Test of Economic Understanding was developed in 1964, and was then revised in 1979 and became the first edition of the Test of Economic Literacy. Since that time, the nature of economics instruction in high schools has changed, particularly due to the introduction of Advanced Placement exams in micro- and macroeconomics in 1989.

The TEL-3 was developed by the National Council on Economic Education (NCEE), and this third edition introduces significant changes in many of the old test items, adds new items to reflect changes in the content of economics, and provides better documentation of technical quality (including validity and reliability evidence). The current test is derived from two NCEE documents: A Framework for Teaching Basic Economic Concepts (Saunders & Gilliard, 1995) and the Voluntary National Content Standards in Economics (National Council on Economic Education, 1997). Work began on the third edition of the Test of Economic Literacy in the fall of 1999 and was completed about one year later.

TECHNICAL. The TEL-3 was normed at the end of the fall semester of 1999 and the end of the spring semester of 2000. A national sample of 7,243 students, mostly 12th graders, from 100 different high schools participated with Form A administered to 3,288 students and Form B administered to 3,955 students. The summary statistics for the two forms are similar with means of 23.85 for Form A (out of a maximum score of 40) and 24.50 for Form B and standard deviations of 8.33 (Form A) and 8.32 (Form B). The students in the norming sample are reported to be widely representative of high school students with regard to geographical region, type of community, size of high school, and type of courses taken. No claim is made that the group tested is exactly representative of the national high school population because it was not possible to obtain a stratified, random sample. Prior to the norming study, the TEL-3 was field tested with about 1,200 students in order to identify problems with wording of the items, test length, or administration.

The reliability of the TEL-3 was assessed using Cronbach's alpha coefficient for a measure of internal consistency. For both forms of the test, the value of alpha was .89 based on the norming sample. Also, for both test forms the standard error of measurement was 2.76. Test-retest reliability was assessed using a single sample of 37 students to whom Form A was administered twice within a short time period between which there was no economics instruction. A test-retest reliability coefficient of .94 was obtained for this sample.

The content of the TEL-3 is based on the two NCEE documents described earlier. These documents served as the guide for the development of content specification tables and the selection of test questions to be included. In addition, the test's content was reviewed by three national committees with expertise in economics education. The committees also evaluated the content of

include the slight overrepresentation of individuals living in the Northeastern and Midwestern U.S. and underrepresentation of individuals living in the West.

The average internal consistency reliability coefficient is .91. The standard error of measurement (*SEM*) for the Gross Motor Quotient is 4, for 3-, 4-, and 5-year-olds and the SEM is 5 for students ages 6 through 10. Estimates of test-retest reliability were based on testing only a total of 75 students, ages 3 through 10, based on a 2-week test interval. Test-retest reliability coefficients are reported only for very small samples of combined age groups. Thus, the test-retest coefficient for 32 children ages 3 through 5 is .88; for 13 children ages 6 through 8 the test-retest coefficient is .94; for 30 children ages 9 and 10 the coefficient is .86. Interscorer reliability is also highly suspect. Two of the publisher's employees scored 30 test records randomly selected from the standardization sample. The interscorer reliability coefficients for each of the subtests and for the Gross Motor Quotient is the same, equaling 98.

Content validity was examined by asking three content experts to determine the extent to which the skills measured were taught to preschool and school-age students and whether the skills were representative of the gross motor domain. Not surprisingly, the judges were in agreement that the test meets the content validity standard. The author examines concurrent validity by correlating performance on the TGMD-2 with the performance of 41 students in Austin, TX on the Basic Motor Generalizations subtest of the Comprehensive Scales of Student Abilities produced by the publisher of the TGMD-2 in 1994. The resulting coefficients were .63 for the Locomotor subtest, .41 for the Object Control subtest, and .63 for the Gross Motor Quotient. Construct validity evidence is similarly weak. Using evidence of differentiation of performance by age group, the author examines whether as children get older, their gross motor performance improves. The author offers additional evidence of validity by providing the results of subtest correlations and factor analysis. There are many problems with the construction of this instrument that it is difficult to evaluate construct validity.

One section of the manual discusses test interpretation. The author correctly states that the Gross Motor Quotient is the most reliable score. However, because there are concerns about the standardization sample and because the construct validity is in doubt, interpretation of this score should not be attempted. The author is correct in stating, "To make diagnostic judgments, the examiner requires information that goes far beyond that which is available from test results" (p. 20). On this point, the author is correct!

SUMMARY. The TGMD-2 is the second edition of the instrument. It was developed to assess the gross motor functioning of children ages 3 through 10 years. The test lacks technical adequacy. The manual is unnecessarily difficult to decipher. There are so many problems with this instrument that use is discouraged.

REVIEWER'S REFERENCES

American Educational Research Association, American Psychological Association, & National Council on Measurement in Education. (1985). *Standards for educational and psychological testing.* Washington, DC: American Psychological Association.

American Educational Research Association, American Psychological Association, & National Council on Measurement in Education. (1999). *Standards for educational and psychological testing.* Washington, DC: American Educational Research Association.

Review of the Test of Gross Motor Development—Second Edition by G. MICHAEL POTEAT, Associate Professor of Psychology, East Carolina University, Greenville, NC:

DESCRIPTION AND DEVELOPMENT. The Test of Gross Motor Development—Second Edition (TGMD-2) is designed to measure the gross motor growth of children from 3 years, 0 months to 10 years, 11 months of age. The TGMD-2 is a revision of the first edition published in 1985. The revision is designed to address a number of criticisms raised in the reviews published in the *Mental Measurements Yearbook* and *A Consumer's Guide to Tests in Print.* The author of the test is to be admired for both his candor in admitting the first edition's weaknesses and his willingness to try to improve the TGMD-2 to meet a higher set of standards. Improvements were made in nine different areas (e.g., new and better normative data) and these are listed in the preface of the examiner's manual.

Psychologists and special educators only infrequently assess gross motor skills, and the author (Ulrich) devotes considerable space to defining gross motor behavior and arguing for its importance. The definition used is taken from the work of Clark (1994) who defined gross motor skills as "motor skills that involve the large, force-producing muscles of the trunk, arms, and legs" (p. 245). Gross motor skills "are used to achieve a movement task or goal such as throwing a ball to a friend or jumping over a puddle" (examiner's manual, p. 1).

The TGMD-2 consists of two subtests each consisting of six direct systematic observations of behavior. The test kit consists of the examiner's manual and a packet of record forms. The items (e.g., basketball, tennis ball, traffic cones) needed to administer the TGMD-2 are described in the examiner's manual and should be readily available in most school settings or can be purchased at a sports store.

Ulrich states that the TGMD-2 has five primary uses: (a) to identify children with significant gross motor lags, (b) to help in planning remediation programs for children with delays, (c) to assess the progress of gross motor skills, (d) to assess the success of programs designed to improve gross motor development, and (e) to serve as a research instrument.

The Locomotor subtest consists of six direct measures of gross motor skill: (a) run, (b) gallop, (c) hop, (d) leap, (e) horizontal jump, and (f) slide. The Object Control subtest consists of: (a) striking a stationary ball, (b) stationary dribble, (c) catch, (d) kick, (e) overhand throw, and (f) underhand roll.

A description of each skill assessment is provided both in the examiner's manual and on the record form. The descriptions are unambiguous and an illustrated guide to administration is also provided. The directions for "Hop" are, "Tell the child to hop three times on his or her preferred foot (established before testing) and then three times on the other foot. Repeat a second trial."

Each skill has a set of performance criteria and the child's performance is assessed using a 0 or 1 for each trial. All skills have four criteria except "Leap," which has only three and "Hop," which has five performance criteria. The performance criteria for "Hop" are:

1. Nonsupport leg swings forward in pendular fashion to produce force.

2. Foot of nonsupport leg remains behind body.

3. Arms flexed and swing forward to produce force.

4. Takes off and lands three consecutive times on preferred foot.

5. Takes off and lands three consecutive times on nonpreferred foot.

The child who meets all five performance criteria on both trials would receive a raw score of 10 and the child who failed all criteria on both trials would receive a performance score of 0. The raw scores for the skills are then totaled to obtain a raw score for each of the two subtests. The raw scores can then be converted to standard scores with a mean of 10 and a standard deviation of 3. One table is provided for both boys and girls for Locomotion but separate norms for boys and girls are necessary for Object Control. Boys performed better than girls at every age on the Object Control subtest and there was a 3- to 10-point difference between the groups. The gender differences on Locomotion were much smaller and judged to be inconsequential. A separate table is provided for converting raw scores to age equivalents.

The subtest standard scores are added to obtain a Gross Motor Quotient with a mean of 100 and a standard deviation of 15. Ulrich suggests that the examiner should be cautious in interpreting the results obtained from the TGMD-2 because poor performance may be related to factors such as motivation and not skill. He points out that a diagnosis is made by the examiner and not by the test and argues for examining other sources of data related to the child's gross motor functioning. Examples of using the TGMD-2 data to assess gross motor behavior and to develop remedial programs are provided.

TECHNICAL. The normative sample for the TGMD-2 is based on a sample of 1,208 individuals from 10 states collected the fall of 1997, the spring of 1998, and the fall of 1998. The demographic characteristics of the sample match closely the demographic information from the U.S. Bureau of Census. As an example, 77% of the sample was urban compared to 75% of the school-aged population. Normative characteristics considered include geographic area, gender, race, residence (urban or rural), educational attainment of parents, and disability status. The only striking difference between the normative sample and the population is for disability status. Only 2% of the sample was identified as having a learning disability compared to 8% of the population. This difference probably reflects the age of the children in the normative sample because many children will not be identified as learning disabled until they enter middle school. Evidence is also presented to show that the match between the sample and the demographic profile was representative across the age range of children sampled.

Three aspects of reliability are addressed in the examiner's manual: content sampling (internal consistency), time sampling (temporal stability), and interscorer differences. Coefficient alphas are presented for both the Locomotor and Object Control subtests and average .85 and .88, respectively. The alpha for the Gross Motor Quotient is .91. The internal consistency measures are consistent across the age range. Temporal stability (time sampling) was examined by using a test-retest procedure across a 2-week interval with a sample of 75 children. The average reliability coefficients were .88 for the Locomotor subtest, .93 for the Object Control subtest, and .96 for the Gross Motor Quotient. The weakest evidence for reliability is provided for interscorer differences. A random sample of 30 protocols was selected from the normative sample and independently scored by two separate individuals. The resulting coefficients were, not surprisingly, very high (.98 for all three scores). However, a more meaningful measure of interscorer reliability would be to have independent observers score children's performance on the tasks and compare their scores. Comparing completed protocols measures only error due to clerical mistakes and does not examine the crucial factor of "interobserver" reliability (that is, do independent examiners assign the same or similar scores to the subject's behavior?). The objective performance criteria provided by the TGMD-2 should result in relatively high interobserver agreement but further empirical evidence is needed.

A variety of evidence is presented for the validity of the TGMD-2. Content validity is addressed by examining the rationale underlying the selection of items and through the presentation of median discrimination coefficients for the individual test items. Criterion-related or criterion-predictive validity was examined by comparing performance on the TGMD-2 with the Basic Motor Generalizations subtest on the Comprehensive Scales of Student Abilities. For a sample of 41 elementary students, the correlation between the two instruments was .63. Construct validity is examined by several methods. These methods included age differentiation (older children have higher scores on the TGMD-2), group differentiation (there is no evidence of ethnic differences on the TGMD-2 but children with Down's Syndrome do much worse), and factor analysis (a two-factor solution was obtained and a "goodness of fit" measure suggests that the two factor model is satisfactory).

Given that the TGMD-2 is a direct, systematic measure of the behavior, the key validity question is that of test content. Based on the data provided, it appears that the TGMD-2 adequately assesses most aspects of gross motor development. However, a measure of upper body strength using a dynamometer could be included as an ancillary assessment. The evidence of construct validity is adequate and the two-factor structure of the instrument appears to be a practical model for examining gross motor development. More data on the criterion-related validity of the TGMD-2 would be useful. I would be most interested in seeing if scores on the TGMD-2 correlated with physical education teachers' ratings of gross motor skills. Also, how accurate are scores obtained in preschool in the prediction of gross motor performance when children are in late childhood or early adolescence. These questions should be the subject of future investigations.

COMMENTARY AND SUMMARY. Despite these minor criticisms, the TGMD-2 is overall a well-developed instrument. I would recommend it for those professionals who need a norm-referenced measure of children's gross motor development. The TGMD has obvious applications for physical education teachers, but special education teachers and psychologists working with special education populations may also wish to consider using the TGMD-2 to obtain a reference score and as a basis for developing interventions related to gross motor development.

REVIEWER'S REFERENCE

Clark, J. E. (1994). Motor development. In V. S. Ramachandran (Ed.), *Encyclopedia of human behavior* (Vol. 3, pp. 245–255). San Diego: Academic Press.

[262]

Test of Interpersonal Competence for Employment.

Purpose: Designed to assess social interaction skills necessary for job tenure for mentally retarded adults.

Population: Mildly retarded adolescents and adults.

Publication Date: 1986.

Acronym: TICE.

Scores, 6: Handling Criticism and Correction, Requesting Assistance, Following Instructions, Cooperative Work Behavior, Handling of Teasing and Provocation, Resolving Personal Concerns.

Administration: Group.

Price Data, 2000: $99 per set including teaching guide and script (56 pages).

Time: (60) minutes.

Authors: Gilbert Foss, Doug Cheney, and Michael Bullis.
Publisher: James Stanfield Co., Inc.

Review of the Test of Interpersonal Competence for Employment (1986) by SHARON H. deFUR, Associate Professor of Special Education, College of William and Mary, Williamsburg, VA:

DESCRIPTION. The Test of Interpersonal Competence for Employment (TICE), published in 1986, is an orally administered 61-item test, designed to be given to adolescents and adults with mild mental retardation. Each item includes a scenario describing a decision-making dilemma that the examinee might encounter on a job and three possible behavioral responses to that scenario. Both the scenario and the responses are read orally; no reading is required or optional for the examinee. The examinee must circle a, b, or c on a student answer sheet to choose the behavior he or she would exhibit in response to the dilemma implied by the scenario.

The TICE can be administered to a group or to an individual. The TICE includes two sections, one entitled "Interactions with the Supervisor," the other "Interactions with Co-workers." Each section takes about 30 minutes to administer and nonclinical staff can administer, score, and interpret the TICE. Student performance is reported as a percentage of the total test score and for each of six subareas. The TICE is a criterion-referenced assessment. No validated benchmarks are provided for expectation comparisons, but the test administrator is expected to rate examinees as to whether they have a low, moderate, or high need for training or intervention in each of the six subareas. The authors hypothesize that examinees who score less than 75% have a moderate need for training, whereas a score of less than 50% indicates a high need. The authors advise that other diagnostic information (observation, ratings, etc.) be used in conjunction with the TICE to determine the level of need for training or intervention.

Test results are intended to provide special education and rehabilitation professionals with data regarding specific employability interpersonal skills of their clients that should be targeted for instruction. The TICE was intended to target instructional objectives in a companion curriculum, entitled *Interpersonal Skills Training for Employment.*

DEVELOPMENT. The TICE was developed in response to research findings that identified inappropriate social interactions in the employment setting as a major impediment to job success for youth and young adults with mild mental retardation. The authors used a Behavioral-Analytic model of test construction, which they attribute to Goldfried & D'Zurilla (1969). This four stage model included: (a) situational analysis, (b) response enumeration, (c) response evaluation, and (d) development and evaluation of the measure.

In the situational analysis stage, test developers gathered data on eight identified interpersonal behaviors. Structured interviews of competitive employers confirmed these eight behaviors as problematic. Eighteen workers with mild mental retardation and 18 supervisors of these individuals reported observations of these behaviors over a period of 1 week. These observations (collected in Oregon) were classified into one of the six subareas of the TICE. Social validation of the identified problematic interpersonal situations was then sought from 111 production supervisors in vocational training facilities in 12 western states.

In an attempt to create a response set to these identified interpersonal situations, test developers asked 64 trainees with mental retardation in vocational training facilities in Oregon and Washington to respond to the interpersonal situations. In addition, 113 vocational rehabilitation clients with mental retardation from Oregon, California, and Indiana were interviewed for response options. Only those situations that yielded a range of responses were included in the final test development. As a final review, approximately 500 employers in 12 western states were asked to evaluate the response options to each situation on a 4-point Likert scale of effectiveness. One hundred seventeen provided responses. Based on these reviews, 80 problematic situations remained in the test item pool.

The test developers chose an orally administered multiple-choice test format, asserting that other researchers had found this to be a valid format for individuals with mild mental retardation. Correct responses were determined based on the rankings of competitive employers regarding which response alternative would resolve the problematic situation. The final format for the TICE included 61 items (31 in the Interactions with Supervisor subtest and 30 in the Interactions with Coworkers subtest).

TECHNICAL. The TICE was standardized using secondary students with mild mental retardation (N = 331 from Oregon and Colorado) and adults with mild mental retardation who were working in vocational training workshops (N = 123 from Oregon, Washington, and Canada). Demographics of the high school students show an average age of 17 and average IQ of 65; 59% were male. The number of students identified as Black or Hispanic were similar, and these two racial/ethnic groups predominated the sample. The numbers provided in the technical report do not equate to the total number in the sample, so a percentage cannot be accurately determined. Students of color are overrepresented in special education classrooms for children with mild mental retardation, so it is not surprising that this pattern has a long history dating back to before the TICE was developed. Demographics of the adult population in this study reveal an average age of 27, and an average IQ of 68, with 54% of this population being male. No race or ethnicity data were obtained for this sample. (Although the gender and racial/ethnicity demographics of these standardization samples may compare to current high school and adult clients with mild mental retardation, the school and work setting have changed dramatically in the past 15 years. Increased numbers of youth and young adults with mild mental retardation have jobs within the competitive employment sector and the question must be raised as to whether this standardization sample remains comparable to the youth and young adults with mental retardation in the next decade.)

Means, standard deviations, and ranges were calculated separately for the two standardization samples. Minimal difference could be seen between these scores. Coefficient alpha internal consistency reliability estimates were computed for the two sections of the TICE. The reliability indices were similar across groups and were within accepted limits for adequate internal consistency reliability of a test. Test-retest reliability (2-week interval) scores were also obtained and fell within acceptable standards. Internal consistency coefficients for the six subareas of the TICE were not as strong; in all likelihood, these coefficients were influenced by the small number of items in each subarea.

The content validity of the TICE was examined through a systematic process of observation, interview, and validation using stakeholders (em-ployers and people with mild mental retardation) as the primary source for item and response development. The authors assert construct validity support based on research conducted prior to the publication of the TICE that found that it correlated positively to measures of role-taking ability, a construct of interpersonal competence. In addition, the TICE was used as a pre- and posttest measure of gains made in a problem-solving curriculum, and differential gains were made by those students who received the problem-solving curriculum. Criterion validity of scores from this test is supported by the strong relationship of interpersonal skills to job success for youth and young adults with mental retardation.

The developers of the TICE took care to apply careful technical measures to a test that is criterion referenced and intended to be used for curriculum planning. It is interesting to note that although the authors demonstrate careful attention to technical features, they did not establish benchmarks that would assist the user in evaluating the overall skills of interpersonal competence exhibited by the youth or young adult with mental retardation.

COMMENTARY. The primary challenge to the TICE is whether it remains viable and useful for its intended purpose 15 years after its publication. Unquestionably, social interactions and interpersonal skills remain the primary challenge for all youth in job retention, including youth with mild mental retardation. Job demands and expectations have changed dramatically in this time period. Although I would expect that following instructions, requesting assistance, handling criticism and correction, cooperative work behavior, handling teasing and provocation, and personal concerns remain important interpersonal skills, there are new scenarios that might emerge as problematic for youth and young adults. Test "credibility" and user friendliness may be compromised without a more updated review of test items and responses. Additionally, this test was specifically designed as a companion to a curriculum that, in all likelihood, would have changed in response to new curricular and social expectations.

As a stand-alone instrument, the TICE lacks any benchmarking to assist a novice user in interpretation of the findings, nor does it provide clear guidance as to how to make curricular decisions based on the findings. Although it is a criterion-referenced assessment, the explanations of how to use the information obtained on the TICE are limited.

There remains a critical need in the field of psychoeducational measurement for measures of interpersonal competence as they relate to employment success for youth and young adults with disabilities. Such measures gain credibility when there exists a comparison to youth and young adults who do not have any disabling conditions and when the social interaction problems that exist can be attributed to a lack of skill and not a lack of developmental maturity.

SUMMARY. The TICE provides a screening measure that identifies specific behaviors that may promote or inhibit job retention by youth or young adults with mental retardation. No specialized skills are required for administration, scoring, or interpretation, making it highly accessible for special educators and rehabilitation professionals who seek instruments to help guide curriculum development in employability and job retention skills. The TICE was originally published in 1986 and there have been no updates to test items or test responses since that time based on the information provided. Test item validity and test reliability may be unchanged in that time period, yet the drastic change in the employment and training options for youth and young adults with mild mental retardation may create a question about present day validity and reliability as the items and responses are currently written. Preparing youth and young adults with mental retardation to obtain and maintain employment continues to be a high priority for special educators and rehabilitation professionals; the TICE, if revised, would offer a tool that could benefit these preparation efforts.

REVIEWER'S REFERENCE

Goldfried, M. R., & D'Zurilla, R. J. (1969). A behavioral-analytic model for assessing competence. In C. D. Spielberger (Ed.), *Current topics in clinical and community psychology* (vol. 1). New York: Academic Press.

Review of the Test of Interpersonal Competence for Employment by LAWRENCE J. RYAN, California Licensed Psychologist, and Vice President and Academic Dean, St. John's Seminary College, Camarillo, CA, and Core Faculty Member, The Union Institute and University, Cincinnati, OH:

DESCRIPTION. The Test of Interpersonal Competence for Employment (TICE) is a 61-item instrument designed to assess variables pertinent to the employment tenure of mildly mentally retarded persons. The TICE is intended to be administered orally in a small group setting. The instrument is divided into two sections that address "Interactions with the Supervisor" and "Interactions with Co-Workers," respectively. Within the "Interactions with the Supervisor" section, subareas of "Following Instructions," "Requesting Assistance," and "Handling Criticism & Correction" are included. Within the "Interactions with Co-Workers," subareas of "Cooperative Work Behavior," "Handling Teasing and Provocation," and "Personal Concerns" are included. Each of the two sections of the TICE requires approximately one half hour to administer. The authors recommend that a single examiner can administer the test to a group of 10 examinees without the help of additional personnel. Scoring of the TICE is accomplished via a simple template. The TICE yields total scores for each of the sections as well as scores for each of the three variables within the two general sections. The authors indicate that the total and subarea scores have been deliberately left uninterpreted so that users may apply the resulting data in a manner appropriate to their particular context.

DEVELOPMENT. The TICE is solidly grounded in theory as well as upon systematic research conducted at the University of Oregon's Rehabilitation Research and Training Center. A four-stage instrument development schematic was utilized. The steps included situational analysis, response enumeration, response evaluation, and evaluation of the resulting measure. At two of the item development stages the responses and opinions of samples of mentally retarded individuals were obtained. Additionally, the items chosen for inclusion in the TICE were refined through presentation to approximately 500 employers in 12 western states who rated the response options of the items in terms of their effectiveness.

TECHNICAL. Although the TICE appears to be carefully developed, the instrument is without any specific normative standards. The authors justify the lack of normative data by the claim that the instrument is designed to be utilized within a rehabilitation class context yielding indicators of what areas of job tenure skills individual members of a class might need to develop further. In spite of lacking specific reported norms, the standardization sample appears to have been carefully chosen with appropriate attention to gender balance and diversity. The standardization sample of 331 students from Oregon and Colorado had an aver-

test format to assess skills that are most appropriately assessed through nontraditional means (Linder, 1990). In addition, the ToPP relies heavily on imitation and modeling, which according to Linder (1990) are not the most important elements of children's symbolic play abilities.

SUMMARY. Because play is integral to the development of language, cognition, and social skills in young children, the assessment of such activities should be part of any process that involves diagnosis or program planning; however, play is characterized by freedom from all but personally imposed rules (Linder, 1990); therefore, structuring the play activities as the ToPP attempts to do may not give a true picture of the child's cognitive and/or social development. The suggested free play observations after the formal test is administered would most likely provide more insight about the child's play interactions and skills than the contrived situations that are part of the test administration. The ToPP could be used as part of an assessment process for children in the U.K., but the language of the test would make it difficult for students elsewhere who are not accustomed to the test item descriptors.

REVIEWER'S REFERENCES

Lahey, M. (1988). *Language disorders and language development.* New York: MacMillan
Leiter, R. G. (1980). Leiter International Performance Scale. Chicago: Stoelting.
Linder, T. (1990). *Transdisciplinary play based assessment.* San Francisco: Paul H. Brookes.
Lowe, M., & Costello, A. J. (1988). Symbolic Play Test (2nd ed.). Windsor: NFER-Nelson.
Sattler, J. (2001). *Assessment of Children: Cognitive Applications* (4th ed.; pp. 116–125). San Diego, CA: Sattler Publishing
Zimmerman, I. L., Steiner, V. G., & Pond, R. E. (1991). Preschool Language Scale–3. San Antonio, TX: The Psychological Corporation.

Review of the Test of Pretend Play by LOUISE M. SOARES, Professor of Educational Psychology, University of New Haven, West Haven, CT:

DESCRIPTION. The Test of Pretend Play (ToPP) is designed to measure children's ability to play symbolically with both representational and nonrepresentational objects. Speech and language therapists, nursery and primary school teachers, and educational and clinical psychologists might find this test useful for the purpose of assessment and diagnosis of children's developmental progress. It contains two forms for structured conditions: the Nonverbal Version for children up to age 3 and older children with language difficulties or developmental problems, and the Verbal Version for children at age 3 or above.

The assessed play is the same for both versions, each occurring in four sections: (a) Self with Everyday Objects, one item; (b) Toy and Nonrepresentational Materials, graduating from one substitution to four substitutions in four items; (c) Representational Toy Alone, sequencing "reference to an absent object," "property attribution," "substitution," and "scripted play" in four items; and (d) Self Alone, with the same subsections as in Representational Toy alone but with a different order of presentation, with four items.

The procedures vary somewhat. In the Nonverbal Version, the child's ability to play symbolically is assessed by modeling what the tester does and eliciting the child's play with nonverbal gestures and short phrases. The Verbal Version employs modeling and eliciting but also instructing the child to carry out specific play actions.

A warm-up session precedes the test to help the child "feel relaxed" and to determine whether the child is "testable." Another session, "Observation of Free Play," follows in two 20-minute periods on 2 separate days for assessing spontaneous play in an unstructured condition. It contains the same four sections, and in the same order, as in the two versions of the structured conditions.

The scoring in the structured conditions is dependent upon whether the play is elicited, modeled, or instructed. In all sections, the modeled play and the instructed play receive half the points of elicited play. Each of the four sections has a maximum score—2, 8, 12, 12, respectively, with the highest possible score of 34 for each version, including the Observation of Free Play. The child is credited with the modeled response and the instructed response or the elicited response. The raw scores for the structured versions are then converted to age equivalents ranging from 16.9 months to 87.9 months.

DEVELOPMENT. The manual provides minimal information concerning initial test development, indicating only that "a thorough review of the relevant literature and extensive development work on the structured test" (p. 41) occurred in 1991. Preliminary data for 43 children were published in 1992, for 60 children in 1994, and two unpublished reports in 1993 and 1995.

The standardization project consisted of 513 children between the ages of 1 and 6 years from two sections of England. The parents provided family details and gave consent for their children's participation. Testing took place in schools, nurseries, playgroups, and homes. Sometimes the parents were present during the testing. The children were selected as a representative sample of gender, ethnic background, and the educational level of their mothers. Tables were constructed on these data to provide comparisons of each variable to numbers of children in each age group at 3-month intervals. The authors also provided the aggregated numbers of children living in rural (23%), suburban (48%), and inner-city areas (29%), as well as the numbers of children who were born first, second, third, fourth, or later born. Most of the children (56%) were first-borns. No information was provided that indicated the number of children in the standardization group of 513 who were labeled "ordinary" and those with developmental difficulties.

TECHNICAL. The manual does not delineate any differences between the performance of "ordinary young children" (p. 2) and those children with developmental difficulties or between the Nonverbal and Verbal Versions of the structured test. We must assume that the target age groups for the two versions account for the increasing total raw scores with increasing age. This point has implications for both validity and reliability.

Some of the objects are not conducive to standardized testing conditions. The doll does not readily stand or sit—necessary for several tasks. Some children may want to take off the doll's clothes for a realistic bath sequence, which is not easily accomplished. The green cloth sheds. The teddy bear cannot stand on its hind legs; it can only sit.

The manual gives few instructions or guidelines for the tester in order to ensure standard testing conditions. In the Nonverbal Version, the tester is told to gesture, point, touch, and use short phrases so that the child will copy the tester's modeling activities. There are no explanations for how the tester "encourages" a response in the eliciting parts of the test.

The administration time could be quite lengthy for some of the younger and handicapped children. If the testing situation is to be "immediately preceded" (manual, p. 10) by a warm-up session, then the testing time is expanded, affecting both the validity and the reliability of the scores. Yet, the words on page 8 of the manual contradict this arrangement. "This familiarisation session should not take place on the same day as the test."

The scoring procedures are somewhat misleading in the use of maximum scores for the four sections of each version. A child could obtain the maximum score of 8 on Section II with a 2 score on II.1a, a 2 on II.1b, and a 4 on II.2 or a score of 8 only on II.4. The manual addresses the issue of content validity sufficiently to relate the test items of object substitution, property attribution, and reference to absent objects as assessing symbolic play; but specific interpretations about developmental progress cannot be readily inferred from the test scores.

In claiming concurrent validity, the test authors used a subgroup of 40 children for testing on one other test—the Preschool Language Scale measuring verbal ability. Out of the 40 children in this group, 32 yielded scores on a second test, the Symbolic Play Test measuring functional play, and 28 children on a third test, the Leiter International Performance Test for measuring nonverbal ability. The authors did not clarify how these scales validate the criterion of symbolic play other than to note that "symbolic skills are involved in language" (manual, p. 47). The authors presented correlations between the ToPP and the other tests that were quite high (.62 to .86). When the age factor was partialled out, the coefficients dropped dramatically, ranging from -.22 to .49.

The authors clearly define symbolic play as one type of pretend play in three forms (manual, p. 1): A child (a) uses an object as if it were another object or person; (b) attributes properties to an object/person which it does not have; and (c) refers to an absent object/person/substance as if it were present. The items in the ToPP seem to support this definition of the content domain. If so, the other three tests cannot be viewed as adequately aligned with this content domain without an elaboration of that definition and without knowing the validity of those other tests.

In determining the stability of the test, the test-retest reliability coefficient for the test scores of 40 children was .87, but the interval of time between the first and second testings ranged from 7 to 64 days, with 75% of the retests occurring between 15 and 30 days. Because only one form of the test is available, recall of initial responses could be possible, and the resulting reliability coefficient could be interpreted as spuriously high.

COMMENTARY. The value of the ToPP as a measure of symbolic play is justified for determining the level of development of preschool children in any of the three forms of pretend play. It is less clear how the test measures conceptual development and the use of symbols, which the authors claim. Nor is it readily obvious how it assesses verbal ability and nonverbal ability even though the authors compared the ToPP to other tests for which stated purposes were so defined.

Because the initial group used for standardizing the instrument was based in England, the generalizability of the results to children in other countries is unknown. Reliance on the results of 40 children's scores, instead of the 513 subject-pool, raises questions about the stated reliability and validity information.

The authors do a creditable job in alerting the tester to possible differences in symbolic play scores for children with learning problems, developmental difficulties, or disabilities. They did not indicate where such children fell on the score range of the ToPP.

SUMMARY. The ToPP seems to be measuring symbolic play, as defined by the authors. The items and the sections have a logical sequence and a concise organization. Problems are evident with the scoring, the nonstandardization of the testing conditions, the objects used in the four sections, the absence of internal analyses by age group and individual development, lack of comparison of the responses on the nonverbal and verbal versions of the test, and reliance on only one form of the test.

[264]
Test of Word Finding, Second Edition.

Purpose: Designed as a diagnostic tool for the assessment of children's word finding skills.
Population: Ages 4–12.
Publication Dates: 1986–2000.
Acronyms: TWF-2.
Scores: Word Finding Quotient for Standardized Assessment (Picture Naming: Nouns, Sentence Completion Naming, Picture Naming: Verbs, Picture Naming: Categories, Comprehension Check for Picture Naming: Nouns, Comprehension Check for Sentence Completion Naming, Comprehension Check for Picture Naming: Verbs, Comprehension Check for Picture Naming: Categories); 5 scores for Informal Assessment (Delayed Response Procedure, Secondary Characteristics Tally, Phonemic Cueing Procedure, Imitation Procedure, Response Analysis for Nouns).
Administration: Individual.
Forms, 3: Preprimary, Primary, Intermediate.
Price Data, 2003: $349 per complete kit including examiner's manual (2000, 194 pages), picture books 1 and 2, 10 preprimary profile/examiner record forms, 10

primary profile/examiner record forms, and 10 intermediate profile/examiner record forms; $11 per 10 preprimary profile/examiner record forms; $18 per 10 profile/examiner record forms (specify primary or intermediate); $81 per examiner's manual; $133 per picture book 1; $97 per picture book 2.
Time: (20–30) minutes.
Author: Diane J. German.
Publisher: PRO-ED.
Cross References: See T5:2725 (10 references); for reviews by Sharon L. Weinberg and Susan Ellis Weisman of an earlier edition, see 11:443 (1 reference); for reviews by Mavis Donahue and Priscilla A. Drum of an earlier edition, see 10:373.

Review of the Test of Word Finding, Second Edition by D. JOE OLMI, Associate Professor and Clinic Director, School Psychology Program, Department of Psychology, The University of Southern Mississippi, Hattiesburg, MS:

DESCRIPTION AND DEVELOPMENT. Having been revised based on earlier critiques of previous versions of the instrument, feedback from users, and necessary changes from the author's perspective, the second edition of the Test of Word Finding (TWF-2) is designed to assess word finding and retrieval skills in children 4 years through 12 years, 11 months. The TWF-2 is an individually administered diagnostic instrument that is composed of two components and takes approximately 20–30 minutes to administer. The first portion of the TWF-2 is the formal or "standardized assessment that includes procedures for computing a Word Finding Quotient based on a student's accuracy and speed when retrieving single words" (examiner's manual, p. 17). The second is an informal procedure consisting of multiple analyses (four for students ages 4 through 6 or prekindergarten and kindergarten and five for children ages 6 through 12 or Grades 1 through 6) to assess comprehension of missed items in the first portion. The TWF-2 can be used by speech/language pathologists, teachers of children with learning disabilities, school psychologists, reading specialists, and other assessment specialists/clinicians to assess a student's word finding and retrieval abilities and/or to develop/evaluate intervention programming. Formal training in the use of the TWF-2 is not necessary, but background knowledge and experience in psychoeducational assessment and practice using the instrument are strongly recommended.

The standardized assessment is composed of four sections, all contained in the Word Finding Assessment Picture Book and designed to assess a student's word finding abilities: Picture Naming: Nouns, Sentence Completion Naming, Picture Naming: Verbs, and Picture Naming: Categories. Following the administration of the standardized assessment, the informal assessment is administered where "the examiner uses the Comprehension Check Picture Book to test the student's comprehension of the items missed during the naming accuracy testing" (examiner's manual, p. 19).

Section 1 of the standardized assessment, Picture Naming: Nouns, simply requires the student to provide the name for presented pictures or colored portions of presented pictures. Administration directions vary slightly depending on the form used. Section 2, Sentence Completion Naming, requires the examinee to provide the missing word in a sentence orally provided by the examiner. Directions are the same for all forms. Phonemic cues are used for missed items in the first two sections. Section 3, Picture Naming: Verbs, requires the examinee to provide a word that depicts what a person is doing and/or what a person just did in a presented picture, depending on the form used. Section 4, Picture Naming: Categories, requires the examinee to name individual objects contained in a presented picture and/or name a group to which all objects on a presented picture belong. Phonemic cueing is used for the Primary and Intermediate Forms. All phonemic cueing procedures are employed after the administration of each section, but before the comprehension check.

Speed of responding (less than 4 seconds) and accuracy are assessed for all four sections, and there are no basal or ceiling rules. All items in an age form are administered. For missed items in Sections 1–4, comprehension is assessed using the Comprehension Check Picture Book. This practice ensures that the examinee is not skill deficient and truly has a word finding/retrieval deficit. This procedure is required at the conclusion of administration of each section. It would seem to assist administration by including the comprehension check portion following each naming section in one book, rather than having the examiner manipulate two books during administration.

The informal assessment portion of the TWF-2 is composed of five additional analyses: Delayed Response Procedure, where a correct, but delayed response (between 4 and 8 seconds) is recorded; Secondary Characteristics Tally, where the quantity of gestures and extra verbalizations are recorded; Phonemic Cueing Procedure, where the use of phonemic cues is recorded; Imitation Procedure, where the occasions for correctly or incorrectly repeating the examiner-presented segmented target word are scored; and Response Analysis for Nouns, where errors are categorized and quantified based on type (Semantic, Phonemic, No Response, and Perceptual Substitution). All entries for this portion of the TWF-2 are also recorded on the various examiner record booklets.

Scoring procedures for this portion of the TWF-2 are straightforward, but require some practice. "The TWF-2 yields three types of scores: raw scores, quotients, and percentiles" (examiner's manual, p. 53) with the most useful and meaningful being the Word Finding Quotient, which is a standard score having a mean of 100 and standard deviation of 15. Scores falling below 90 indicate the need for further assessment or the need for word finding intervention, in that they fall "in the lowest 25% of the general population" (examiner's manual, p. 54). The author suggests that performance at this level is indicative of those who "will have difficulty finding the right words to express their thoughts. Even though they may know the answers to questions asked, they will frequently produce an incorrect answer or not respond when called on in class" (examiner's manual, p. 54). Standard scores range from <69 suggesting "very weak" performance to >130 suggesting "very strong" performance.

The kit includes the examiner's manual, the Word Finding Assessment Picture Book, the Comprehension Check Picture Book, and easy-to-use examiner record booklets for three different assessment levels including preprimary (ages 4–6 or prekindergarten and kindergarten), primary (ages 6–8 or Grades 1 and 2), and intermediate (ages 8–12 or Grades 3 through 6). Chapter 1 of the examiner's manual begins with a brief and clear explanation of the theoretical developmental model of word retrieval that underlies the TWF-2. The author follows with a logical explanation based on the previously mentioned theoretical model of why students exhibit word finding errors, indicating that they potentially fall into one of three subtypes: (a) those with retrieval problems, (b) those with comprehension problems, or (c) those with a combination of the two. The author further suggests in this chapter that children with learning disabilities, specific language impairment, reading disorders, fluency disorders, ADHD, and brain pathology of known etiology might benefit from the type of assessment provided through use of the TWF-2.

TECHNICAL. Normative data were derived from a sample of 1,836 students between 4 years and 12 years, 11 months residing in 27 states representing the four regions of the U.S. between March 1996 and May 1999. The manual was unclear as to whether the students were derived from the 27 states indicated or from the eight primary data collection sites. The author asserts that the standardization sample is representative of 1997 statistics from the U.S. Bureau of the Census for the school-age population.

Psychometric support is more than adequate with internal consistency reliability coefficients by age groupings ranging from .71 to .91, with stronger coefficients beginning with older 6-year-olds in the standardization sample. Test-retest reliability estimates from a sample of 61 average achievers with an intervening time period of 10 to 14 days was .80. Interscorer reliability across all forms of the TWF-2 was .99.

Regarding validity procedures, item selection procedures were adequate and appropriate. Care was taken to ensure that items did not adversely impact any particular group based on gender, ethnicity, and socioeconomic status. Concurrent validity when compared to the Expressive One-Word Picture Vocabulary Test—Revised was .53, .69 for the Synonyms subtest of the Word Test—Revised, and .66 for the Antonyms subtest of the Word Test—Revised. These moderate correlations are acceptable for the TWF-2. Predictive validity was unremarkable, but probably due to the lack of relationship between the TWF-2 and the comparison criterion measure. Construct validity information is less than adequate.

COMMENTARY AND SUMMARY. In conclusion, the TWF-2 is easily administered with practice, is fairly sound psychometrically, and could be a very important assessment component in a battery designed to assess memory and word retrieval skills. It could be especially useful in the assessment of children with traumatic brain injury, children with specific learning disabilities, and children with disorders/disabilities that impact acquisition of information. As part of a comprehensive battery, the TWF-2 could provide information that would contribute to the identification of deficit functioning, as well as assist in the development of intervention programming.

[265]
Test of Word Reading Efficiency.

Purpose: Constructed as a "measure of an individual's ability to pronounce printed words accurately and fluently."

Population: Ages 6-0 to 24-11.

Publication Date: 1999.

Acronym: TOWRE.

Scores, 3: Sight Word Efficiency, Phonemic Decoding Efficiency, Total Word Reading Efficiency.

Administration: Individual.

Forms, 2: A, B.

Price Data, 2003: $123 per complete kit including manual (115 pages), 25 each Forms A and B record booklets, and 1 each Forms A and B word cards; $25 per 25 record booklets (specify form); $15 per word cards (specify form); $51 per manual.

Time: (5–8) minutes.

Authors: Joseph K. Torgesen, Richard K. Wagner, and Carol A. Rashotte.

Publisher: PRO-ED.

Review of the Test of Word Reading Efficiency by GERALD TINDAL, Professor in Educational Leadership, College of Education, University of Oregon, Eugene, OR:

DESCRIPTION. "The Test of Word Reading Efficiency (TOWRE) is a measure of an individual's ability to pronounce printed words accurately and fluently" (examiner's manual, p. 1). Reading is assessed for accuracy and fluency to understand proficiency in two basic constructs of reading:

1. Phonemic Decoding Efficiency (PDE) that includes 63 pronounceable printed nonwords requiring the examinee to sound them out.

2. Sight Word Efficiency (SWE) that includes 104 words to be read as whole units.

Both lists are timed in their presentation (45 seconds) and two alternate forms are provided for each subtest. When administered together, the entire test takes about 5 minutes, with directions and practice items.

The TOWRE is recommended for monitoring growth in efficiency of phonemic decoding and sight word reading skills, diagnosing specific reading disabilities in older children and adults, and conducting research on the development of reading skills. The authors suggest using the TOWRE at regular intervals during Grades 1 and 2 as part of a general assessment and instructional program. They also note the importance of assessing rate and accuracy in any diagnosis. In a section entitled "Information to Consider before Testing" a range of issues is considered about who should use the instrument and how students should be examined. More specific information on administration is presented in the section entitled "Administering and Scoring the TOWRE" (examiner's manual, p. 19), with standardized prompts displayed for the examiner to use. In the examiner's manual, phonetic transcriptions are presented for the nonwords used in the PDE subtest. In the profile/examinee record booklet, acceptable pronunciation alternatives for vowels in the nonword list are shown within real words. Both guides are somewhat difficult to decipher and require considerable familiarity and practice to conduct a correct administration.

DEVELOPMENT. The test has a strong theoretical base that broadly views reading words from five vantages, with four of them relying on visual information in the printed words: analyzing and blending phonemes, noticing and blending familiar spelling patterns, recognizing whole words and reading them by sight, making analogies to known words, and using context clues. The authors note "the method that is of primary importance during early stages of learning to read is phonemic decoding" (examiner's manual, p. 2). This approach requires beginning readers to have phonemic awareness (know the sounds that make up the words) and then, with knowledge of the letters used to represent these phonemes, to be able to blend together the individual phonemes.

In the rationale of the TOWRE, the authors stress the importance of accurate and fluent word reading in comprehending written material. They base their instrument, in part, on the work of Gough (1996) and Gough and Hillinger (1980) in which reading is viewed as recognizing words on the page and knowing what they mean. The literature cited as context for the instrument stresses the importance of students understanding and applying phonemic skills as well as having a broad domain of sight vocabulary words that can be read fluently and automatically. The instrument is specifically designed to quantify the degree of skill a child can display in word identification processes, a goal that is different than the focus of more authentic reading tasks (which are not precise enough) or other informal tasks (which may be more instructionally oriented). Further, the authors note that the instrument is based on word reading out of context, providing a "direct assessment of children's ability to identify words solely on the basis of their visual appearance in print" (examiner's manual, p. 8).

TECHNICAL. Very thorough directions are presented in the examiner's manual for completing the record booklet, including the examinee's age. The first step in recording performance is to convert these scores to either age or grade equivalent scores. Then, the raw scores are converted to standard scores using age-based or grade-based normative tables displayed in an Appendix. Finally, a total score is recorded, representing the sum of the two subtest standard scores. All these scores are then converted to percentile ranks.

The converted scores generated from the raw score are based on a normative group of 1,500 individuals from 30 states, ages 6–24. The authors describe advantages and limitations of all possible score-reporting options. They appropriately note that raw scores are difficult to interpret given the varying difficulties of items. Age and grade equivalents are justified by reference to mandates of educational agencies though the readers are cautioned not to use them or at least to read about their limitations in suggested references. Percentiles are appropriately described as not equal in intervals. Finally, standard scores are described, with the mean set at 100 and the standard deviation at 15. The authors note two issues with respect to standard scores:

1. The grade-based norms are "not as accurate as the age-based norms" (examiner's manual, p. 35).

2. "Neither subtest is sensitive to reading difficulties at the word level during the first semester of first grade" (examiner's manual, p. 35).

A section in the examiner's manual presents detailed descriptions of the normative sample. All individuals were tested in the fall of 1997 and the spring of 1998. The sample was stratified into four geographic regions. The demographics reported in the examiner's manual generally reflect similar rates and proportions reported in the *Statistical Abstract of the United States* (U.S. Bureau of Census, 1997) for school age and adult populations.

In the examiner's manual, a very complete description is presented to help understand what the TOWRE scores mean, with four sources highlighted that may influence performance: (a) type of reading instruction, (b) amount of practice in reading, (c) influence of home and family background, and (d) intrinsic limitations in processing abilities. In the research literature cited in these four areas, the authors present a very reasoned and empirical basis for understanding performance. They highlight the need to intervene intensively, systematically, and explicitly, irrespective of the source.

In a subsequent section on instructional implications for low scores on each subtest, the authors address discrepancies in the two subtests, noting that in a relatively few cases, students may have adequate sight word skill but inadequate phonemic decoding skills. Rather, they argue that "for most children, (a) good phonemic decoding skills are necessary for the growth of a rich sight word vocabulary and (b) a rich sight word vocabulary is important for fluent reading and good reading comprehension. "Thus, we have adopted the working hypothesis that any score on the TOWRE below the 30th percentile based on current norms warrants special interventions to improve word-level reading skills" (examiner's manual, pp. 40–41). In the end, however, they argue for the primacy of low scores on the Phonemic Decoding Efficiency as the key indicator for intervening with children in early elementary school.

The final section of the examiner's manual presents a summary using the TOWRE to conduct a discrepancy analysis. Statistical significance is addressed in determining whether the difference is beyond that expected by chance. Basically, a 10–11-point difference between the two subtests is needed to achieve this level. The use of statistical significance alone identifies too many false-positive cases and, therefore, they suggest a 19–20-point difference between the two subtests. Cautions for interpreting test results are presented by focusing on reliability and external data sources for making judgments.

Four types of reliability data are reported in the examiner's manual. Content sampling is addressed first using internal consistency with alternate forms, presumably based on the entire normative sample though the authors do not describe the population explicitly. The coefficients reported across all ages range from .86 to .98 with Standard Errors of Measurement at 3–5 points. When analyzed by different subgroups of the normative

sample, alternate form coefficients are all above .95. The authors present an example using this information to report results using confidence intervals. Time sampling is addressed using test-retest stability in which 72 individuals in Florida took the test twice within 2 weeks. Coefficients range from .82 to .97. Using two scorers from PRO-ED, 30 rescored samples address interscorer differences, with extremely high agreement. Equivalence of forms is demonstrated by displaying means and standard deviations at all age levels for both forms. A .6 difference is reported between the means of the forms.

Attributing validity to be a function of purpose, the authors of the TOWRE describe three types of research: (a) content description, (b) criterion prediction, and (c) construct identification. For the first type, content description, they consider the rationale for TOWRE subtests emphasizing rate and (lack of) context. The item selection process includes sampling words according to frequency of usage as reported in the *Reading Teacher's Book of Lists* (Fry, Kress, & Fountoukidis, 1993) and various CV or CVC (and later CCVC, CVCC, and CCVCC) constructions for phonemic decoding. Conventional item analyses are conducted with item difficulties ranging from .40 to .75. Using Differential Item Functioning (DIF), a relatively small number of items appear to function because of group membership rather than ability. The Woodcock Reading Mastery Test—Revised (Woodcock, 1987) is used in a concurrent validity study with very high correlations reported. With the Gray Oral Reading Tests—Third Edition (Widerholt & Bryant, 1992), the correlations are high with the Sight Word Efficiency and moderate with Phonemic Decoding Efficiency. Finally, construct identification is demonstrated by reference to age differentiation, group differentiations, subtest interrelationships, factor analysis, item validity, and word reading efficiency of students with severe reading disabilities.

COMMENTARY. The test is a very complete and well-packaged measure of reading efficiency. The authors are to be commended on their organization of research in support of the instrument, all of which is very conceptually and theoretically anchored. The examiner's manual is well sequenced, with information easy to find and reference, and the text presents very technical issues in a straightforward manner. Cautions and caveats are presented throughout, when the technical data need to be interpreted and follow the latest guidelines (AERA, APA, & NCME, 1999). Although recommended for Grade 1, it is likely not very sensitive but would reflect a floor effect. Further, having only one alternate form, its usefulness to monitor progress is somewhat limited.

The technical data are very complete and with few exceptions support using the instrument to screen students and provide basic diagnostic information. The normative sample is minimal, with a mere 1,500 individuals across the entire country (and from ages 6–24) used to reflect a national comparison. For example, only 53 students are from the Northeast at age 6–7. Likewise, only 47 students are Black at age 6–7. Only 62 students live in rural areas at this age. The content sampling plan for both subtests could be more descriptive and the predictive validity of the measure emphasized more. With these two exceptions, the technical information is complete in most other aspects.

SUMMARY. The Test of Word Reading Efficiency is a well-developed measure of one critical aspect of reading. The authors are to be commended for their thoroughness in developing the instrument and providing user-appropriate options for interpretation. The test is extremely easy to administer and interpret. Although both age and grade bases are available for developing standard scores, users should heed the authors' recommendation to use age-based scores only. Otherwise, differences in results are likely to impede consistent interpretations. One last problem with the scoring and reporting options: Although age and grade equivalent scores are considered with caution, the record booklet has them prominently displayed as part of the conversion process.

REVIEWER'S REFERENCES

American Educational Research Association, American Psychological Association, & National Council on Measurement in Education. (1999). *Standards for Educational and Psychological Testing*. Washington, DC: American Educational Research Association.

Fry, E. B., Kress, J. E., Fountoukidis, D. L. (1993). *The reading teacher's book of lists*. Englewood Cliffs, NJ: Prentice-Hall.

Gough, P. B. (1996). How children learn to read and why they fail. *Annals of Dyslexia, 46*, 3–20.

Gough, P. B., & Hillinger, M. L. (1980). Learning to read: An unnatural act. *Bulletin of the Orton Society, 30*, 17–176.

U.S. Bureau of Census. (1997). *Statistical abstract of the United States* (117th Ed.). Washington, DC: U.S. Department of Commerce.

Wiederholt, J. L., & Bryant, B. R. (1992). Gray Oral Reading Tests—Third Edition. Austin, TX: PRO-ED.

Woodcock, R. W. (1987). Woodcock Reading Mastery Test—Revised. Circle Pines, MN: American Guidance Service.

Review of the Test of Word Reading Efficiency by JOHN J. VACCA, Assistant Professor of Indi-

vidual and Family Studies, University of Delaware, Newark, DE:

DESCRIPTION. The Test of Word Reading Efficiency (TOWRE) is an individually administered test of an individual's ability to pronounce printed words accurately and fluently. The intended use is with individuals from 6 years of age to 24 years, 11 months, inclusive. There are two subtests on the TOWRE, each of which has two alternate forms: Sight Word Efficiency and Phonemic Decoding Efficiency. Administration time is between 5 and 8 minutes.

The TOWRE can be administered by "anyone who can read and understand the test manual and has knowledge of standard assessment procedures" (examiner's manual, p. 13). There is an examiner's manual that provides practice exercises, specific directions, and scripts for what to say to the examinee.

Four types of scores are yielded on the TOWRE: raw score, age and grade equivalents, percentiles, and standard scores for each subtest and a total score (mean = 100; standard deviation = 15). There are no basal and ceiling rules on the TOWRE. Acceptable pronunciations (in the examiner's manual) accompany the instructions. The raw score for each subtest is the total number of test items read correctly in 45 seconds. Each raw score is then converted to a standard score using supplied normative tables.

Use of the TOWRE fulfills three purposes: intervention, diagnosis, and research. Additionally, the TOWRE can be used to monitor growth in efficiency of phonemic decoding and sight word reading skills, especially during the early elementary grades.

DEVELOPMENT. The development of the TOWRE was supported by grants from the National Institute of Child Health and Human Development through the Small Business Innovation Research Program. Overall, the TOWRE was developed out of a need expressed by professionals in the area of reading to quickly assess fluency and accuracy of print-based word reading strategies. Although critical issues in the development of reading skills as well as key areas where individuals have difficulty are presented, it is unclear how the words selected on the TOWRE (both real and nonsense) relate to the ample information presented in the authors' discussion of the test's rationale. Further, it is equally unclear how the

spelling intervention; (b) document and gauge progress in response to spelling intervention; and (c) provide a measure for research concerning spelling achievement of individuals with learning disabilities. The test has two parallel forms and is designed to provide normative inferences to be used with criterion-referenced measures.

DEVELOPMENT. Development of the TWS-4 can be traced through the three earlier editions. The first (the TWS, 1976) contained two subtests of 35 predictable words and 25 unpredictable words, respectively, drawn from popular spelling basal series. The normative sample included 4,544 students from 22 states. The age range was 5-0 to 13-5 years.

The Second Edition of the TWS (TWS-2) was published in 1986 with the following revisions: (a) The test was increased to 50 words per subtest; (b) the age range was expanded to 6-6 through 18-5 years; (c) standard scores supplanted earlier ratio quotients related to age; (d) the normative sample of 3,805 was aligned to census parameters; and (e) evidence of technical qualities was provided.

In 1994, the Third Edition (TWS-3) was published, retaining two subtests of 50 words each, the word-sentence-word format of administration, and the relationship of words to popular curricula. The manual was more specific about proper and improper uses of test scores, and additional psychometric evaluations were presented. The normative sample was expanded by 855 and stratified by major demographic variables keyed to the 1990 U.S. Census. Spelling ages and grade equivalents were published.

The Fourth Edition, published in 1999, has made modifications based on recent research. These modifications include: integration of predictable and unpredictable words into a single list; development of a parallel form; alignment of normative sample characteristics to the 1997 U.S. Census and the 2000 projected Census; study of item bias; estimations of reliability conditioned on gender and ethnicity; and match of the word list to six current spelling basal series. The TWS-4 examiner's manual presents two parallel forms of 50 items each, even though the TWS-3 is described as having "two subtests, each of 50 words" (p. vii), which were retained on the TWS-4. It appears that the 100 words, in total, were divided between the two forms.

Item Development. The 1976 edition was developed through review of 10 basal spelling series. The original list of 60 words appeared in each. The first revision (TWS-2) strengthened reliability at the youngest ages. The oldest age level was extended to 18 by incorporating words from the *EDL Core Vocabularies in Reading, Mathematics, Science, and Social Studies* (Taylor et al., 1989).

The resulting list of 145 words was reduced to 100 in the TWS-4 after evaluating item to whole correlations and percent correct answers (*p*-values). For each of these conventional measures, a discussion of criterion values is provided, but neither the actual decision criteria for item inclusion nor specific item values are reported. A follow-up study of the TWS-4 items using the normative sample reported median correlation values and median *p*-values for each of the 13 age groups (6 to 18) for each form. The median *p*-values ranged from .42 (age 6, Form A) to .76 (age 18, Form A), and the median item to whole correlation values ranged from .12 (age 6, Form B) to .75 (age 18, Form A). Individual item data are not reported.

TECHNICAL. The examiner's manual addresses criterion-related, construct, and content sources of validity evidence. Reliability evidence is reported from internal consistency, alternate form, test-retest, and interrater studies. Item analysis and item bias studies are also reported. Discussions about the use and interpretation of scores and available supplemental measures are informative.

Standard scores (mean = 100, standard deviation = 15) are demarcated into seven ranges that are described as Very Poor (less than 70), Poor (70–79), Below Average (80–89), Average (90–110), Above Average (111–120), Superior (121–130), and Very Superior (above 130). A standard setting study, to operationally define these ranges in terms of student skills and typical spelling errors, could help interpret these ranges in terms of the specific test items that are most likely mastered or skills that are most likely developed by students scoring within each range.

Validity. The validity discussion is organized around the nature of validity evidence. Sources of validity evidence are delineated as content description, criterion-prediction, and construct-identification. Content description evidence includes a rationale for item selection that references the appearance of items in commonly used instructional materials, conventional item analysis described above, and differential Item Functioning (DIF) analysis. The latter is better characterized as a measure of the stability of the item contribution to the construct measure across population subgroups than as evidence of content description. These analyses included delta correlations for each test form (each reported to be .99) for male/female, White/non-White, African American/non-African American, Hispanic American/non-Hispanic American, and Asian American/non-Asian American. Further analyses utilized the standardization technique described by Dorans and Holland (1993) comparing male/female, African American/non-African American, and Hispanic American/non-Hispanic American, and found none of the items to meet the rejection criterion of .01 difference between groups matched in overall ability.

Three studies of criterion-prediction evidence are presented. The first comprised TWS correlations with spelling subtests of four other instruments for 63 fourth graders. The disattenuated coefficients ranged from .78 to .97.

The second study, on 50 Texas fourth and fifth graders, yielded correlation coefficients between the TWS and two other standardized spelling measures ranging from .59 to .86. The correlations were corrected for restriction of range, presumably because the tests are designed to span the great skill differences related to the intended age ranges for the test. The third study correlated the 5-point ratings of spelling skills, from *poor* (1) to *good* (5) of 82 students by three teachers, and yielded correlations of .60 and .55 for Forms A and B, respectively.

Construct evidence of validity focused on confirming six hypotheses related to the interpretations of test scored, and demonstrated: (a) the developmentally related improvement in the measured skills of the normative sample; (b) the poorer performance of 80 students with learning disabilities; (c) the stronger relationships of the TWS-4 with measures of language and writing (convergent property) than with mathematics measured (discriminant property) for 50 subjects; (d) correlations of .56 for scores on each form of the TWS-4 for the same 50 individuals with the School Ability Index of the Otis-Lennon School Ability Test, corrected for restricted range; (e) significant pretest to posttest improvement in scores for 255 students with learning disabilities who had a 2-year intervening Alphabetic Phonics program (no control group was used); and (f) sound item to whole correlations, as described earlier. These stud-

ies might be replicated using larger samples (especially across so large an age span), integrated, and analyzed through confirmatory factor analyses or multitrait-multimethod analytical techniques.

Reliability. Coefficients alpha for each of the 13 age groups (6 years to 18 years) in the normative sample and for each of the two forms ranged from .87 for Form A for 6-year-olds to .97 for Form B for 18-year-olds. The average alphas were .94 (Form A) and .93 (Form B) over the age groups.

The alpha coefficients for five ethnic groups and for males and females were all .96 or higher. Alternate form reliabilities for the 13 age groups ranged from .86 for 6-year-olds to .98 for ages 14, 15, 16, and 18.

Test-retest reliabilities were studied for three small samples of first, third, and sixth graders, controlled for order effects, with a 2-week interadministration interval. The coefficients ranged from .94 (first grade, Form A) to .97 (sixth grade, Form B).

Finally, interrater agreement was studied correlating the scores given by two members of the publisher's research staff to 108 parochial school students in first through eighth grade. Age was partialled from the coefficients. The resulting correlations exceeded .99. The authors report that differences were only evident when student handwriting was illegible. It is not clear how many separate correlations were computed, and, therefore, the contribution of age to the agreement. In general, the publishers might consider evaluating two or more of these sources of reliability with a single regression model that estimates the contributions of variance of multiple raters, multiple forms, and items.

Use and interpretation of scores. Entry levels are recommended in terms of initial items, for 1st through 3rd, 4th through 6th, 7th through 9th, and 10th through 12th grades. A ceiling is defined as the point in which five consecutive items are answered correctly. All items below the basal are to be counted as correct and above the ceiling as incorrect. This assumes that the items are progressively more difficult. No data in support of these decision models are presented. Item Response Theory (IRT) difficulty measures or *p*-values for these four grade blocks could provide support for these models and the proposed starting items.

Considerable provision is made for recording conditions of testing and incorporating other measures. A procedure for converting scores to the

subtest scores. Factor analysis of a battery of neurolopsychological measures and aptitude assessments on the ADHD sample used for standardization provided evidence that scores on the TOL^{DX} load on a factor with other executive processing measures and not on factors with WISC-III subtests (Information, Similarities and Arithmetic). Additional research on the original TOL assessment provides evidence that the assessment strategy is sensitive to detecting patients with frontal lobe dysfunction in patients with frontal lesions, Parkinson's disease, and schizophrenia and that neurological assessments validate the relationship between increased cerebral blood flow in the frontal lobes when subjects are engaged in the TOL tasks. The improved performance of normal children ages 7 to 15 provides evidence of an age-related function in normal children and adults (up to age 60) both on the TOL and the TOL^{DX}. No construct validity evidence is provided for normal samples or mixed samples, or for various racial, ethnic, or cultural groups.

SUMMARY. The underlying rationale of the TOL^{DX} is sound and derived from evidence of the effectiveness of the Tower of London test and increasing evidence of the existence of executive functions in children and the importance of these in carrying out problem-solving activities. The test is easily administered and scored. The reliability evidence for some of the subtests of the TOL^{DX} is adequate for ADHD children, but lack of evidence of reliability with normal populations and for the rating scales makes use of the instrument with those groups questionable until further data are collected. Lack of reliability evidence and the limited evidence of validity does not justify use of the instrument alone in individual diagnosis decisions; however, the evidence provided does suggest that the TOL^{DX} may provide useful data to clinicians to pinpoint areas of deficiencies in executive planning and functioning and in identifying processing disabilities when used in conjunction with other measures of neuropsychological functioning.

REVIEWER'S REFERENCE

Shallice, T. (1982). Specific impairments of planning. *Philosophical Transactions of the Royal Society of London, B298*, 199–209.

Review of the Tower of London—Drexel University by JAMES P. VAN HANEGHAN, Associate Professor, Department of Behavioral Studies and Educational Technology, University of South Alabama, Mobile, AL:

DESCRIPTION. The Tower of London—Drexel University, (TOL^{DX}) is a neuropsychological instrument designed to measure executive function and planning in children and adults. Executive skills involve organizing behavior and sustaining attention in the pursuit of goals. The test was developed to systematize and norm Shallice's (1982) Tower of London that was used to study planning and executive function among patients with frontal lobe damage. The task, similar to other abstract measures of planning (e.g., The Tower of Hanoi), involves moving pieces into particular configurations under rule constraints in as few moves as possible. The apparatus consists of two boards with three pegs and three different colored beads. One peg holds three beads, the second two, and the third one. The examiner uses one board to illustrate the configuration the examinee will reproduce. The examinee uses the second board to move the pieces into the correct configuration. A stopwatch is needed to administer the test. Score sheets for children and adults are also supplied. The Tower of London takes about 10–15 minutes to administer. There is a maximum of 2 minutes to solve each problem. The TOL^{DX} is useful when clinicians are interested in supplemental information to investigate potential problems in executive functioning and planning. The authors noted that it should be used in conjunction with other test and interview information.

The examiner, who should be expert in neuropsychology and development, administers three sample problems, and then administers 10 increasingly complex problems of between three and seven moves. Moving the pieces directly to the goal pegs can solve the first few problems. As problems get more complex, they involve thinking ahead several moves in order to place the beads correctly in the minimum moves. Seven different scores are generated from the protocol: (a) total moves, (b) total correct, (c) total time violation, (d) total move violation, (e) total initiation time, (f) total execution time, and (g) total problem-solving time. All scores and subscores, although only some are normalized (Mean = 100, standard deviation = 15). The authors also generated percentile scores. The total move score is based on the number of moves above the minimum number to solve the problems. The total correct score involves the number of configurations solved in the minimum number of moves. The total time violation score is the number of times that the individual did not solve the problem within 1 minute. The rule violation score is the number of times the examinee violated the rules. Total initiation time is the total time to first move on each problem summed together, and the total problem-solving time is the total number of seconds to solve the problems. The scores can be interpreted quantitatively, and the patterns of scores can be qualitatively interpreted, although guidance for such interpretation could be better developed. Care must be taken in considering some of the standard scores because they are in the opposite direction of raw scores. It is also unclear whether some of the standard scores are interpretable in a linear fashion. For example, even though longer initiation time raw scores are associated with higher standard scores, it is not clear that higher initiation time indicates better performance. Examinees could score high because they are confused, or because they are planning several moves ahead. Spitz and Borys (1984) note that what goes on during planning is more important than the amount of time spent. Hence, the score interpretations can be complex because the relationship to effective planning is not a simple linear relation.

DEVELOPMENT. Versions of the "tower-like" tests have long been available. Few of these have been standardized, and some have evidenced administration and scoring problems. The original Tower of London was found to differentiate frontal lesion patients from other groups. Based on pilot testing in normally developing individuals, the authors empirically chose items that would not reach ceiling levels. Based on testing samples of adults and children, 10 three- to seven-move problems were selected. After creating the items, a standardized administration was developed and normative and clinical samples studied.

TECHNICAL.

Standardization. The standardization sample was a convenience sample. There was little geographic diversity, and minorities and low socioeconomic status individuals were underrepresented (e.g., only 1% were Hispanic). The authors also put restrictions on the achievement of the children in their sample; some were required to be average or better achievers. Hence, the child norms may be biased. The samples came from a variety of different types of settings (e.g., schools, universities, and a science center). The numbers in the sample are somewhat low for some age groups. For example, the 60- to 77-years-old age group has only 21 individuals. The 16–19- and 20–29-years-old age groups are the largest groups and may be biased towards including more university students than are in the general population. Overall, the sample is large, but it is not clearly representative. Hence, normative comparisons must be treated carefully. The authors suggest that score levels be treated as guidelines rather than absolutes. The nature of the standardization sample makes that advice important to follow.

Two groups of children with suspected attention deficit disorder (ADHD) were tested to include normative data for these children. Because there is little information in the manual on the basis for confirmation of ADHD diagnosis and little information other than the statement that they had ADHD, it is unclear what to make of this normative group as a standardization sample.

Reliability. The authors present acceptable test-retest reliability on the ADHD sample for the total move score ($r = .80$). However, there is wide-ranging variability in the intervals between testing (testing intervals ranged from 5 to 92 days), so this may be an underestimate of stability. Moderate stability is reported for time violations ($r = .67$) and weak stability for rule violations ($r = .24$). The low reliability of the rule violations may reflect the restricted range of rule violation scores (low in general) as well as decreases in rule violations after having taken the test once. No reliability data are reported for other groups. Although the test may be reliable for other groups, speculation is no substitute for data.

Validity. Data are presented that purportedly support criterion-related and construct validity. The criterion-related validity data come primarily from comparisons of the sample with ADHD to normally developing children. The authors report reasonable differentiation of the groups via classification functions. The authors report a dissertation by Kennedy (2000) that found that the test identifies whether people with mental retardation are capable of making decisions about sexual consent. Interestingly, there are no validation data examining the ability of the test to differentiate patients with frontal-lobe damage. Given that the original test was devised to differentiate that group from others, it is surprising the authors did not include such data. Developmental

exposure and greater proficiency in English would do better on the TCB than those with poor English proficiency. Comparison of college students' subtest performance with residential or mainstreamed students revealed highly significant differences favoring the college students' performance.

COMMENTARY. The value of the TCB as a measure of transition skills for "low functioning" deaf individuals seems to be compromised on a number of levels. First, the use of a signed video and written format presents logistical issues that have not been completely resolved. The novel format is at times cumbersome and slow. An alternate administration system (e.g., a computer-generated videodisc) would make the test user-friendly.

Second, the fourth subtest, Money Management, exhibited lower performance indexes and reliability coefficients than is appropriate for a screening measure. This subtest needs to be revised to have better psychometric properties.

Last, caution should be used when interpreting percentile scores. Although error bands are indicated for the 85th percentile, some test items require a 100% criterion to be acceptable. For example, failure to answer some questions correctly (e.g., the question regarding a person's Miranda rights) should be noted regardless of the overall percentile score.

SUMMARY. The developers, to their credit, have produced the first test battery of its type developed specifically for and standardized on a deaf population. They have attempted to address the challenging language demands of this population by presenting the battery in a novel testing format (i.e., written and signed video). An earnest effort was made to "allot increments of response time that would be reasonable given the heterogeneous cognitive, linguistic and intellectual abilities of each group of six to eight subjects being tested" (manual, p. 8). Unfortunately, the taped portion continues to be slow and cumbersome.

On the whole the TCB falls short of the mark. Insufficient validity evidence exists to support that results of the TCB can be used to predict performance in real life settings. It is doubtful that the test conveys any useful information in addition to simply observing an individual in an actual employment or independent living setting.

Trauma Symptom Checklist for Children.

Purpose: Designed "to measure acute and chronic posttraumatic stress and related psychological symptomatology."
Population: Ages 8–16.
Publication Date: 1996.
Acronym: TSCC.
Scores: 8 scales: Underresponse, Hyperresponse, Anxiety, Depression, Anger, Posttraumatic Stress, Dissociation, Sexual Concerns.
Administration: Group or individual.
Price Data: Available from publisher.
Time: (15–20) minutes.
Author: John Briere.
Publisher: Psychological Assessment Resources, Inc.

Review of the Trauma Symptom Checklist for Children by GREGORY J. BOYLE, Professor, Department of Psychology, Bond University, Gold Coast, Queensland, Australia, and Visiting Professor, Department of Psychiatry, University of Queensland, Royal Brisbane Hospital, Herston, Australia:

DESCRIPTION AND DEVELOPMENT. The Trauma Symptom Checklist for Children (TSCC) is a multidimensional 54-item pencil-and-paper questionnaire intended for the psychological assessment of posttraumatic symptomatology in children and adolescents who have endured trauma resulting, for example, from childhood physical and/or sexual abuse. The TSCC also purports to measure other clusters of symptoms that may occur in some traumatized children, such as dysphoric mood, and physical, sexual, and psychological sequelae that may follow child abuse. In addition, the TSCC indexes the traumatic effects of neglect, interpersonal violence (victimization by peers involving physical or sexual assault), witnessing of violence done to others, as well as trauma resulting from major accidents, and natural disasters. An alternate 44-item form devoid of items pertaining to sexual matters (TSCC-A) is also available for use in situations where sexual questions are deemed inappropriate.

The TSCC comprises two validity scales (Underresponse, Hyperresponse), six clinical scales (Anxiety, Depression, Posttraumatic Stress, Sexual Concerns, Dissociation, Anger), and four subscales (Sexual Preoccupation, Sexual Distress, Dissociation Fantasy, Overt Dissociation). Completion of the TSCC generally takes about 15–20 minutes except for the most highly traumatized children.

Scoring and completion of profiles takes approximately 10 minutes. Inclusion of the two validity scales is a good feature of the instrument, in view of the well-known problem of motivational and response distortion that is prevalent in item-transparent self-report instruments.

All items in both the TSCC and TSCC-A instruments are scored on a forced-choice 4-point Likert response scale ranging from 0 (*Never*) through 3 (*Almost all of the time*), thereby providing a quasi-interval level of measurement, and enabling application of sophisticated methods of statistical analyses such as factor analysis on the TSCC raw data. Scoring is straightforward, as demographic information and item scores are reproduced automatically on the score sheet (attached underneath the response sheet). Although the TSCC is usually administered individually, computerized scoring is also available, which is especially useful in large group testing situations. Profile sheets provide an effective summary of an individual's scores, enabling ready comparison across scales and subscales. There are separate profile sheets for children aged 8–12 years and 13–16 years (each for boys and for girls).

TECHNICAL QUALITY. Normative data stratified for gender and ethnicity were obtained on a large standardization sample of 3,008 children comprising three separate nonclinical samples. Means, standard deviations, and *T*-scores are provided for each of the four age-by-sex combinations. Also included are eight critical items (TSCC) or seven critical items (TSCC-A) (e.g., "Wanting to hurt myself" or "Wanting to hurt other people"). Although endorsement of these critical items does not necessarily suggest a child at risk, some items (e.g., "Wanting to kill myself") serve to alert responsible adults such as parents or teachers that immediate intervention may be warranted.

In regard to item homogeneity of the various TSCC scales and subscales, Cronbach alpha coefficients for the standardization sample ranged from .58 (subscale DIS-F) to .89 (Anger Full scale) (Mean alpha = .84). For samples obtained from child abuse centers, overall alpha coefficients for the clinical scales ranged from .81 to .86 (Mean alpha = .84), suggesting a somewhat narrow breadth of measurement, and possibly some item redundancy (cf. Boyle, 1991). These rather high alpha coefficients may in part be explained by the similarity of the items within each scale, wherein

the same basic item is repeated using slightly different wording (e.g., "Thinking about having sex" and "Thinking about sex when I don't want to" and "Can't stop thinking about sex").

In addition, the differing number of items allocated to the various clinical scales and subscales is somewhat problematic, unnecessarily causing discrepancies in variance, and complicating some interscale comparisons. Because no results for immediate test-retest (dependability) versus longer-term test-retest (stability) are provided in the test manual, the actual reliability of the TSCC scales and subscales remains unknown.

Moderate correlations with related instruments (such as Child Behavior Checklist, Children's Depression Inventory, Revised Children's Manifest Anxiety Scale, Children's Social Desirability Questionnaire, Children's Impact of Traumatic Events—Revised, and the Child Sexual Behavior Inventory) provide evidence of concurrent/convergent validity of the separate TSCC scales. Evidence of discriminant validity would also be useful, and should be included in future editions of the test manual. Although Briere cited in the manual several studies that have provided validity evidence, the actual construct validity of the separate TSCC scales remains uncertain. A major oversight is that no methodologically sound factor analytic evidence has been provided in the test manual to support the proposed structuring of the TSCC instrument. Despite inclusion of Underresponse and Hyperresponse scales, neither inconsistent responding nor other response sets are monitored in any way. Consequently, determination of invalid profiles remains difficult, without further psychometric development of validity scales. Furthermore, the TSCC does not appear to differentiate between state and trait measures of psychological constructs such as Depression, Anxiety, and Anger (cf. Boyle, Stankov, & Cattell, 1995), nor is any information provided in the test manual regarding item-response characteristics (cf. Boyle, 1987).

COMMENTARY. Although there is a scale (and two subscales) to measure sexual concerns, none of the items relate to circumcision-related trauma and posttraumatic stress. Because such surgery is imposed on two-thirds of American boys, there may well be long-lasting physical, sexual, and psychological sequelae (Boyle, Goldman, Svoboda, & Fernandez, in press). In

Children's Manifest Anxiety Scale (RCMAS). Convergent validity is inferred in the manual based on CDI scores correlating highest with the Depression scale of the TSCC, whereas the RCMAS correlated highest with the Anxiety and Depression scales of the TSCC.

The TSCC scores displayed a relationship with exposure to violence. Elevated TSCC scores were also found for children experiencing stressful events such as parental divorce. A study of 302 girls found that child abuse resulted in higher TSCC scores. Another study reported reduction in TSCC scores following a 6-month therapy. Discriminant validity was examined in a study of 81 sexually abused girls with 151 nonabused controls. In short, several studies are reported on the criterion-related validity of the TSCC scores.

COMMENTARY. The TSCC is a well-developed instrument for assessing trauma symptoms in children. The manual clearly presents the scale development process, samples used, psychometric data, etc. However, five concerns should be addressed in future research. First, the normative sample seems to be exclusively from the midwestern United States. The generalizability to a broader sample should be tested. Second, the manual did not report any estimates of test-retest reliability. Some measure of stability would be helpful. Third, although the six scales were developed based on theory, some confirmatory factor analytic evidence that the items cluster into the six scales as hypothesized will be helpful. Fourth, more information on the content representation of the assessments should be included in the manual. Finally, future research is needed to determine whether separate norms are needed for different cultural and racial groups.

SUMMARY. The TSCC is a short and useful instrument to assess trauma symptoms in children. The normative sample is clearly described although members of this sample appear to be primarily from the midwestern states of the United States. The administration and scoring are easy, and require no advanced training (though interpretation requires advanced graduate training, as is true for all clinical assessments). The data on internal consistency estimates, convergent and divergent validity, and criterion-related validity are impressive. Stability estimates as well as the need for different cultural and racial norms should be considered in future uses of this instrument.

[270]

Triage Assessment for Addictive Disorders.

Purpose: "Designed to cover diagnostic information for current dependence or abuse of alcohol and drugs."
Population: Adults.
Publication Dates: 1995-2000.
Acronym: TAAD.
Scores, 2: Abuse, Dependence.
Administration: Individual.
Price Data: Available from publisher.
Time: (10) minutes.
Comments: Structured interview; screens for DSM-IV diagnostic criteria, providing an estimate of the likelihood that an individual meets the criteria for abuse or dependency; covers current problems only; can be administered by paraprofessionals.
Author: Norman G. Hoffmann.
Publisher: Evince Clinical Assessments.

Review of the Triage Assessment for Addictive Disorders (TAAD) by JOANN MURPHEY, Clinical Psychologist in Private Practice, San Antonio, TX:

DESCRIPTION. The Triage Assessment for Addictive Disorders (TAAD) is a structured clinical interview to help the triage interviewer check for DSM-IV substance abuse and/or dependence diagnostic criteria in a short period of time and in an efficient format. The TAAD is a 31-item structured interview in which the examinee answers "yes" or "no" concerning whether a given event or behavior occurred within the past 12 months relative to alcohol, drugs, or both. The responses are recorded and then coded on a summary form derived from DSM-IV criteria for dependence and abuse.

DEVELOPMENT AND TECHNICAL. TAAD test items were developed from reviewing treatment data on over 35,000 cases over a 10-year period on the use of the original Substance Use Disorder Diagnostic Schedule (SUDDS). DSM-IV content and clinical input were also used in item selection. The instrument was administered to a group of 1,329 women accused of child abuse or neglect who might have a substance abuse problem. Satisfactory internal consistency was obtained from this group for items related to dependence; somewhat lower consistency was obtained for abuse items, suggesting that the instrument consistently addressed the dependence syndrome for this group. The instrument also was administered to 244 males in an after-care treatment program for offenders who had completed a boot-camp program for nonviolent drug-related offenses. Results indicated that the vast majority of diagnostically positive cases met substantially more than the minimal DSM-IV diagnostic criteria for both abuse and dependence.

COMMENTARY. The TAAD does not provide questions to cover all of the content of the DSM-IV as thoroughly as the SUDDS-IV. However, it does cover some of the content for each of the seven dependence and four abuse categories with between two to four questions. Consequently, for marginal cases where some problems are acknowledged but clear diagnostic support is lacking, the TAAD cannot insure that the individual will meet criteria for abuse or dependence. Nevertheless, for many cases the results will provide evidence of a current diagnosis, or strong indication of negative results.

Because the TAAD is designed for structuring a triage interview, it is not intended to substitute for clinical judgment on whether a diagnosis is indicated. It should be used as a tool for rapid assessment, but not in situations where a definitive or comprehensive workup is desired, or where evaluation results may be examined in a court setting. The author recommends use of the Substance Use Disorders Diagnostic Schedule-IV (SUDDS-IV; 253) in such situations. The caution always remains with interview assessment, as the author is aware, that lack of candor on the part of the examinee will distort results, and is difficult to rule out in this type of examination format.

SUMMARY. Clinicians who use the DSM-IV criteria in working with patients who may have substance abuse problems will find this brief screening inventory useful to organize the interview process to assist in ruling abuse and/or dependence diagnoses in or out, other than perhaps in the marginal cases. It helps the clinician create acceptable documentation of appropriate and comprehensive questioning for limited triage purposes. The manual provides useful information, and the author is well aware of the instrument's strengths and limitations.

Review of the Triage Assessment for Addictive Disorders by WENDY NAUMANN, Assistant Professor of School Psychology at The Ohio State University in Columbus, Columbus, OH and ROBIN RIX, Graduate Student in School Psychology at The Ohio State University in Columbus, Columbus, OH:

DESCRIPTION. The Triage Assessment of Addictive Disorders (TAAD) is a brief triage instrument that assesses current patterns of alcohol and drug use based on DSM-IV criteria. The TAAD is a structured interview with a series of multiple choice-questions. As a triage instrument, the TAAD can act as a follow-up to a screening but is not sufficient as a diagnostic instrument alone. Scales assessing abuse and dependence for both alcohol and other drugs are included; however, if only alcohol or one specific drug is of concern, the other items can be omitted.

The TAAD can be administered by a number of professionals including physicians, nurses, psychologists, social workers, technicians, and other paraprofessionals. The four-page protocol includes both the items and scoring procedures. The DSM-IV includes seven criteria for substance dependence and four criteria for substance abuse, and the TAAD has two to four items assessing each of these DSM categories for both alcohol and drugs. The items endorsed by the examinee are summed to give a total for the dependence and abuse categories for both alcohol and drugs. A decision rule is then applied to these totals to determine if dependence or abuse is a concern for the examinee. If dependence is indicated, then the abuse items do not need to be scored as a diagnosis as dependence supercedes a diagnosis of abuse. Scoring takes 3 minutes or less.

DEVELOPMENT. The TAAD is based on the DSM-IV criteria for substance abuse and dependence. Specific items were developed from treatment data of over 35,000 cases used in developing the original Substance Use Disorder Diagnostic Schedule (Harrison & Hoffman, 1985). Additionally, the literature on screening and diagnosis of substance abuse disorders and input from clinicians in the field of substance abuse were used in development and selection of test items.

TECHNICAL. Because normative scores are not included in the scoring or needed for the purposes of the test, no standardization sample was provided. Again, the items were developed based on data for 35,000 clients diagnosed with a substance abuse disorder over a 10-year period; however, the TAAD was not administered to these individuals to determine the technical qualities of the instrument.

Although a normative sample was not included in the development of the TAAD, findings

sists of scores between 0 and 100 milliseconds on Parts 1 and 2, and 0 to 350 milliseconds on Part 3, which represent very low risk. Section 5 of the manual includes numeric cut points for these categories. Section 7 of the manual includes interpretative guidelines for each of the five categories.

The UFOV is easy to install on PC computers. For example, I was able to download and calibrate the test within 5 minutes. The test program provides simple, yet flexible, data scoring and management options that make interpretation easier. Instructions for changing any of the UFOV's parameters are presented in a windows-compatible tool bar format.

The manual includes guidelines for informed consent, creating a friendly testing environment, establishing rapport with examinees, and anticipating problems. Because the UFOV is computer administered, it is possible to administer the test in a variety of institutional and private settings such as a home or assisted living environment. The manual provides clear procedures for testing, as well as information about entering and retrieving data from the UFOV's database.

DEVELOPMENT. The theoretical rationale for the UFOV is brief, yet excellent. The UFOV provides a measure of complex visual processing that is related to a number of significant behaviors such as driving. Because visual processing decreases with age, the UFOV may be an important predictor of driving and general ambulatory skill in the aged. The UFOV provides a quick measure of a person's functional visual perceptual window. The window may be impaired due to natural aging processes or disease such as stroke or glaucoma.

TECHNICAL. The manual provides somewhat limited reliability and validity information. For example, only test-retest reliability (test-retest interval ranged from 10 to 18 days) is reported on a group of 70 individuals aged 65 or older. Coefficients range from .72 to .80 for each of the three subtests, and .88 for the composite test. There is no information regarding internal consistency of responses for each of the three subtests.

Validity information focuses exclusively on the UFOV's ability to predict critical outcomes such as simulated driving skill. There is no attempt to assess the convergent and discriminant validity of the UFOV with other tests, although several other tests are used in a logistic regression analysis to compare the relative efficiency of different predictors. Gen-

erally, the predictive validity of the UFOV is good. For example, the correlation between the UFOV and on-road driving was .55.

COMMENTARY. The strengths of the UFOV include (a) quick and easy administration, (b) computerized scoring and data management, (c) a well-written manual, and (d) reasonable predictive validity with on-road driving. Weaknesses include (a) a limited standardization sample and (b) very limited reliability and validity information.

SUMMARY. Overall, the UFOV provides a quick and efficient measure of useful field of view that is correlated with simulated and on-road driving skill among people over 55 years of age. The UFOV is easy to administer, score, and interpret. It appears to be reliable after several week's delay in retesting. Although validity data are sparse, the UFOV appears to be a reasonably good predictor of reaction time and attention while driving. Given the ease with which it can be completed (i.e., 15 minutes), it provides a helpful tool in identifying individuals who may be at higher risk to experience driving problems.

Review of the Useful Field of View by JAMES P. VAN HANEGHAN, Associate Professor, Department of Behavioral Studies and Educational Technology, University of South Alabama, Mobile, AL:

DESCRIPTION. One element of safe driving is the ability to pay attention to objects in the central and peripheral part of the visual field. The Useful Field of View (UFOV) is a test that involves measuring how well elderly and other at-risk drivers are able to identify information presented to them for a brief period of time. The goal of the test is to identify drivers who are at-risk for having an accident. This computer-based test, which takes about 15 minutes to administer, has three parts. In the first part, the individual identifies whether an object presented in their central field of vision is a car or a truck. In the second part, the individual not only identifies whether the object is a car or a truck, but also has the added task of identifying where in their peripheral field a car is located. In the third part, the task is made more difficult by placing a pattern of distracting visual information on the screen as individuals make their responses. The scores generated from each part represent the amount of presentation time in milliseconds necessary to correctly identify the objects (and the location of the car in Parts 2 and 3). These quantitative scores are then transformed based on a set of decision rules to derive a risk score. There are five levels of risk, with Level 1 indicating no risk to Level 5 indicating high risk. The test comes with a counter that plugs into a parallel printer port that allows the examiner to generate score reports. The score reports are written in a straightforward manner for the examinee. The examiner can specify the amount of detail to include in the report. They have the option of simply stating risk and scores on the three parts, scores plus definitions of the constructs tested, or scores plus definitions and details of how the constructs were tested. The software was easy to install and use. This version of the test uses the computer mouse to click on the appropriate responses. The test developers found that this less expensive alternative to a touch screen worked about as well as a touch screen. The test itself included plenty of available practice trials to help elderly individuals who are not computer literate use the test. The authors also provide hints for dealing with the frustration the speeded test may create in some examinees. Finally, the manual is very readable. The authors went out of their way to provide clear definitions of commonly used terms for the examiner using the test. The only addition to the manual that would be helpful might be some case presentations to show how the test is used either by itself or in conjunction with other data to make decisions about driving competency. The authors and publishers indicate that someone with a Master's level training in psychology or related fields is the minimum level of examiner competency needed.

DEVELOPMENT. The test has its basis in research on attentional slowing in the cognitive aging literature as well as research on how to identify elderly drivers who are at-risk for accidents. The authors theorize that slowing of the processing of information leads to a less complete useful field of vision. The limitations are not because of visual system limitations, but are related to the time it takes to generate multiple samples of information to construct a representation of a situation. The slower sampling makes attention to an object in the periphery more difficult because the representation of it is not complete when it is necessary to make a decision about it. The authors developed the test by carrying out several prospective and retrospective studies of elderly drivers who have or have not had an at-fault accident. In addition, they examined driving simulation tests and on-road driving tests of elderly individuals who had taken the test. Based on those studies they empirically derived the cutoff scores for various risk levels.

TECHNICAL.

Standardization. The authors used the samples from their research to generate the standards. In general, these samples involved case-control studies where the cases were drivers identified to have had an "at-fault" accident and controls were selected from those who had not. Although the samples provide evidence that the test does differentiate, it would be helpful if a large-scale prospectively based representative sample were tested. That would help provide a more accurate indication of the validity of the test's risk levels.

Reliability. The authors provide reasonable test-retest reliability over about a 2-week time frame for the three sections of the test ($r = .72$ for Part 1, $r = .81$ for Part 2, and $r = .80$ for Part 3). There was complete agreement about risk scores for low risk drivers, and 60% of those who were at high risk on the first testing were also classified as high risk on a second. Those who moved to moderate risk were still near the cut point for high risk according to the authors. A bit more stability in the risk scores would be helpful, but given the nature of the test, some improvement in performance on a second testing would not be unexpected.

Validity. The primary validity evidence comes from case-control studies of drivers who have been involved in "at-fault" accidents versus drivers who have not. The studies involve examining individuals both retrospectively (drivers who already had accidents) and prospectively (drivers who had accidents post administration). In addition, the authors in various studies examined driving simulation and on-road driving performance among elderly individuals and found that the test was predictive of failure on the simulation and on road tests. They also found the test to differentiate among levels of dementia and predict driving skill among such individuals. Finally, they examined the UFOV in relation to other predictors of driving performance. They found that it was a better predictor than many other measures and that was as good at discriminating poorer drivers as more extensive batteries.

tween the corresponding scales were significantly larger than noncorresponding scales, supporting the convergent and discriminant validity of the VAMS scales. In another study, the VAMS test scores were found to be sensitive to a specific treatment of mood disorders (electroconvulsive therapy) among depressed patients ($N = 25$). In addition, the VAMS scales could successfully discriminate between depressed ($N = 56$) and nondepressed patients ($N = 48$). Overall, more evidence on the validity of the VAMS should be collected, especially on clinical populations that this instrument was designed to serve (e.g., most of the studies on convergent and discriminant validity were done with healthy individuals). In addition, all the studies on convergent and divergent validity used scales from the POMS as criterion variables. Future studies should use other measures of mood as criterion variables.

COMMENTARY. The VAMS is a simple instrument that could be used as a screening device to identify instances of mood-related disturbance among patients with different neurological disorders. Depressive symptoms are common in this clinical population, and the VAMS is a simple, nonlinguistically demanding instrument that could assist psychological and counseling professionals to identify patients who might need help to deal with their emotional concerns in addition to coping with their neurological impairments.

The professional manual of the VAMS was written clearly and information on administration, interpretation, and psychometrics was presented in an organized manner. The research efforts to examine the psychometric properties of the VAMS have produced some positive initial findings. There is some evidence that the VAMS scales measured mood-related constructs among healthy adults and clinical patients.

In addition to issues related to norms, reliability, and validity discussed in an earlier section, there are two additional concerns. First, it is not clear whether some or all of the VAMS scales should be used in screening for instances of mood disturbance. For example, the professional manual specifically mentioned the use of the Sad scale (a scale with low reliability) in the screening of depression, but suggested that other scales should be consulted as well. Future research efforts should look into how the scales might be used in the screening of diverse categories of mood-related

disorders. Related to this issue is the lack of a clear conceptual scheme to describe how each of the VAMS scales measures diverse mood status. Consequently, strengthening the conceptual foundation of the instrument should be an important future step in the development of the VAMS. Second, there should be evidence to show that the use of the VAMS could indeed benefit its target populations. It is imperative to collect empirical data to show that using the VAMS scales could lead to the identification and treatment of mood-related disorders among patients with neurological impairments in clinical settings.

CONCLUSION. The VAMS fills an important void in the assessment of mood-related disturbance among individuals who are not able to respond to complex and linguistically demanding instruments. The initial findings on the technical quality of the VAMS are promising. However, before the VAMS could be used in clinical settings with confidence, there should be more research efforts to strengthen the instrument both conceptually and psychometrically, especially among its target clinical populations.

REVIEWER'S REFERENCE

McNair, D. M., Lorr, M., & Droppleman, L. F. (1981). Profile of Mood Status. San Diego, CA: Educational and Industrial Testing Service.

Review of the Visual Analog Mood Scales by WILLIAM E. MARTIN, JR., *Professor of Educational Psychology, Northern Arizona University, Flagstaff, AZ:*

DESCRIPTION. The Visual Analog Mood Scales (VAMS) is used to assess symptoms of depression and anxiety among persons with neurological disorders for screening and tracking change in mood state over time. The VAMS is an eight item (scale), paper-and-pencil test that can be self-administered by the respondent or administered directly by the examiner. The test scales cover eight specific mood states (Afraid, Confused, Sad, Angry, Energetic, Tired, Happy, and Tense). Each visual analog scale is described in the *VAMS Professional Manual* as reflecting a unipolar format that includes a *"neutral* schematic face (with accompanying word) at the top of a 100 mm vertical line, and a specific *mood* face (and word) on the bottom" (p. 6). The response to each scale is scored using a clear plastic ruler that measures the distance from the neutral end of the line to the middle of the respondent's mark on the line. The respondent's raw score is derived as millimeters on the 100 mm vertical line used for each scale. For example, if the respondent marks the Sad scale line at 62 mm from the neutral face/pole, the raw score on the Sad scale is 62. The raw scores can then be converted to normative T-scores using normative tables based upon the respondent's age (18–54 or 55–94) and sex. Both scores are presented on a profile form.

DEVELOPMENT. Persons with neurological disorders such as vascular dementia, stroke, Parkinson's disease, and Huntington's disease may have difficulties in language production, understanding, attention, memory, or emotional expression that complicates assessing their symptoms of depression and anxiety. According to the author, previously developed visual analog mood scales used with these individuals lack standardization rigor and normative information. Moreover, other scales use a bipolar scale such as a happy face at the top of a vertical line and a sad face at the bottom. Respondents are asked to draw a line across the vertical line relative to their current feelings of sadness. The author believes that this format can result in misleading scores. The VAMS uses a unipolar scale that measures from neutral (top of vertical line) to the specific mood (bottom of the line). As such, the VAMS was developed to provide a standardized assessment of expanded mood states using a less ambiguous scale format placing minimal cognitive or linguistic demands on respondents who have neurological disorders.

TECHNICAL. The standardization sample for the VAMS was developed using undergraduate and graduate students from a midsize university in the Midwestern United States. Participants also included volunteers from church and other community groups in the Midwest. Two age-gender, and race-stratified samples were selected using 1990 U.S. Census figures resulting in a young adult sample consisting of 250 men and women between the ages of 18–54 and an older adult sample consisting of 175 men and women (55–94 years). The percentages of persons within ethnic groups for the younger adults and (older adults) respectively were: Caucasian—80 (93.1), African American—15.6 (2.3), Hispanic American—.8 (.0), Asian American—2.8 (1.7), Native American—.8 (2.3), and other .0 (.6). These 425 persons comprised the standardization sample of healthy, community-dwelling adults used to develop the T-score conversion tables. The test au-

thor also provides normative information relative to a sample of 290 psychiatric patients.

The VAMS has only one item for each of the eight scales so internal consistency measures were not provided. Two studies of test-retest reliability are reported. In the first study, 75 male and female undergraduate and graduate students were administered the VAMS, followed by 15 minutes of intervening tests, and then given another administration of the VAMS. The average test-retest reliability coefficient was .70 ranging from .49 (Sad) to .78 (Anxious now Tense). The second study was conducted with 27 male and female acute stroke patients and the average test-retest reliability coefficient was .66 ranging from .43 (Confused) to .84 (Afraid).

A content validity study was conducted to evaluate the VAMS scales without the associated verbal descriptors. Study participants completed the no-word VAMS and the standard form resulting in significant correlation coefficients ($p < .001$) for all scales with the exception of the Anxious scale. The Anxious scale was replaced with a more valid Tense scale.

Four convergent and discriminant validity analyses were reported. The first three studies were conducted with healthy normal adults: (a) 75 undergraduate and graduate students, (b) 140 undergraduate volunteers, and (c) 400 older men and women. The fourth study involved 41 inpatients who had experienced recent strokes. In each of the studies a multitrait-multimethod procedure was used to examine the intercorrelation matrix of the VAMS to the Profile of Mood States (POMS) scores. Convergent validity was consistently supported by the findings that the correlation coefficients between the VAMS and similar POMS scales were high. Moreover, the correlations between each of the VAMS scales and the noncorresponding POMS scales were small, as were each VAMS scale with the remaining VAMS scales providing support for discriminant validity. Similar findings related to convergent and discriminant validity were found comparing the VAMS to the Beck Depression Inventory (BDI) in two of the same studies.

A study of 25 psychiatric inpatients receiving electroconvulsive therapy (ECT) was reported as further evidence for the construct validity of the VAMS. All patients were administered the VAMS and the Hamilton Depression Rating Scale

(HDRS) prior to the beginning of ECT and again 4 days following the completion of the procedure. Both the measures showed similar significant pre-post test differences with corresponding effect sizes of VAMS Sad scale (eta^2 = .60) and HDRS total scale (eta^2 = .65). As such, the VAMS demonstrated sensitivity to treatment effects in relation to this sample.

Finally, the VAMS was shown to discriminate among psychiatric diagnostic groups. Discriminant function analysis showed that the VAMS was successful in classifying respondents into either depressed (82%) or nondepressed categories (76%).

COMMENTARY. The VAMS has clear value for professionals who need to screen or repeatedly assess the internal moods of neurologically impaired persons. However, there are aspects of the test that could be improved.

Although the eight mood states selected for the VAMS appear relevant and comprehensive, there still needs to be a discussion of how and why they were chosen. Moreover, because the VAMS used a unipolar scale format instead of the more traditional bipolar format, empirical evidence comparing the effectiveness of both scale formats would be of interest. The first two phases of test development as outlined in the *Standards for Educational and Psychological Testing* (AERA, APA, & NCME, 1999) could provide guidance for such an expanded discussion.

The standardization sample could be more clearly explained and extended. A description of the steps taken to select the standardization sample (*n* = 325) from the entire pool of available participants (*N* = 579) should be provided. A lengthy discussion of a psychiatric patient sample is presented. But guidance is lacking as to how practitioners can use this information for normative and clinical interpretations. Specific group norms also could be developed for other targeted neurologically impaired groups with accompanying interpretation guidelines.

The standardization sample is relatively small and has limited representativeness. Developmental issues influencing moods may not be captured within the two broad age ranges used for the normative data. As such, added age ranges in the *T*-score conversion tables may have interpretive benefit to practitioners. The ethnocultural group representation in the standardization sample could be improved. For example, the second largest ethnocultural group in the United States, Hispanic American, is minimally represented in the younger adults (0.8%) and older adults (0.0%) samples. Also, the standardization sample could be extended more fully to include persons from outside the Midwest.

SUMMARY. The VAMS fills a need to assess efficiently the mood states of neurological patients who may have visuospatial problems. Although the test-retest reliability coefficients are not as strong as desired, most scales were adequate for this type of instrument. There was consistent support for convergent and discriminant validity over several samples. Further work is needed to clarify test development issues. Additionally, the standardization sample needs clarification and expansion.

REVIEWER'S REFERENCE

American Educational Research Association, American Psychological Association, & National Council on Measurement in Education. (1999). *Standards for Educational and Psychological Testing.* Washington, DC: American Educational Research Association.

[273]

Vocational Interest Survey for Australia.

Purpose: Designed to "assist Australians facing career decisions by providing an assessment of their vocational interests."
Population: Job applicants.
Publication Dates: 1989–1995.
Acronym: VISA.
Scores, 8: Caring, Culture, Service, Managing, Clerical, Science, Practical, Environmental.
Administration: Group or individual.
Price Data: Available from publisher.
Time: (5–15) minutes.
Author: Robert Pryor.
Publisher: The Psychological Corporation [Australia].

Review of the Vocational Interest Survey for Australia by EUGENE V. AIDMAN, Psychology Lecturer, and NEROLI SAWYER, Statistics Instructor, University of Ballarat, Victoria, Australia:

DESCRIPTION. The Vocational Interest Survey for Australia (VISA) is a multiscale self-report instrument intended to provide a brief assessment of vocational interests for secondary school students aged 14 through adult, particularly for those, according to the test developer, with limited reading ability and from a non-English-speaking background. The VISA is an expressly Australian instrument, designed to reflect the specifics of the Australian work culture. It largely follows the logic and test format of the Strong Interest Inventory (248), but its item content is derived from the job descriptions published in the Australian Standard Classification of Occupations (ASCO; McLennan, 1997).

The instrument contains 64 items, each representing a certain work activity in a brief descriptive statement, such as "growing indoor and outdoor plants" or "writing computer programs." Response format is a 7-point Likert-type scale ranging from 1 (*extremely dislike [the activity]*) to 7 (*extremely like [it]*). The VISA subscales measure the following eight vocational interest dimensions: Caring (e.g., medical, helping, supporting, counseling), Culture (e.g., teaching, creative artistic, performing), Service (e.g., business services, tourism/hospitality), Managing (e.g., supervising, organizing, administration), Clerical (e.g., filing, typing, editing, secretarial), Science (e.g., engineering, computing, physics, chemistry), Practical (e.g., mechanical operation/repair, manual), and Environmental (e.g., outdoor, nature, agriculture, animal care). There is no cross-scale item overlap; each scale contains eight items.

The manual claims the simplicity and brevity of item content as one of the instrument's intended strengths, allowing test completion times between 5 and 15 minutes. A close inspection of item content, however, reveals a number of items with composite logic, such as items combining a statement of generic activity either with one of its possible forms (e.g., "testing scientific theories using mathematics") or with reason(s) for engaging in it (e.g., "patrolling national parks to protect the plants and animals"). Such composite logic, no matter how brief the item is, risks confounding the response required of the test taker.

SCORING AND NORMS. Manual scoring is straightforward, and self-scoring instructions are presented in the test booklet. No automated scoring service is apparently available. The VISA has been standardized on a sample of 1,079 secondary students (48% male and 52% female) aged 14–18 and representing both state and independent schools across two Australian states (New South Wales and Queensland). Normative tables convert raw scores for each subscale into percentile ranks separately for males and females, and for the combined sample. Oddly, no rationale for the separate gender norms is presented and no evidence of sex differences is discussed. Unfortu-

nately, the discussion of percentile norms is plagued with a number of technical inaccuracies. Among others, the manual questions the representativeness of its own normative sample and even the stability of the norms (p. 12).

RELIABILITY/VALIDITY. It is difficult to provide an overall appraisal of the reliability and validity of scores from the VISA. The manual reports estimates of internal consistency (alpha coefficients) ranging from .75 (Caring subscale) to .90 (Practical subscale) on the Australian standardization sample ($N = 1,079$). In a more recent study alpha coefficients ranged between .85 and .91 on a sample of 373 unemployed adults (Goddard, Patton, & Simons, 1999). The figures are comparable with levels of simultaneous reliability typical to other vocational interest inventories (e.g., Herman, 1998). Regrettably, despite the importance of evaluating the temporal stability of vocational interest scores (Murphy & Davidshofer, 2001), no test–retest reliability estimates are reported—neither in the manual, nor in subsequent literature available to date.

The VISA manual provides limited evidence for construct and concurrent validity. Construct validity is claimed to be supported by the test's factorial structure, by item homogeneity within its subscales and intercorrelations between them. Factorial structure indicates a degree of discriminant validity by generating factor loadings exceeding .50 on the intended subscale for a majority of the items after oblique rotation in an exploratory factor analysis on item responses ($N = 1,079$). The choice of oblique rotation indicates that subscale factors are substantively intercorrelated. The manual, however, does not provide any data on factor intercorrelations. The reported subscale intercorrelations are consistent with Holland's Hexagonal model (Worthen & Sailor, 1995). This consistency is presented as further supporting construct validity. Regrettably, no attempt has been made to validate VISA against constructs external to the instrument itself. This severely limits the scope of construct validation efforts and indicates that it is far from complete.

Concurrent validity is claimed to have been supported on the same normative sample against an external criterion of "occupational preference." The pattern of VISA scale scores differed significantly across the 21 groups of test takers categorized into occupational preference categories on the basis of content analysis of participants' descriptions of an "ideal job." The same pattern produced meaningful discriminant functions that were consistent with people- and object-orientation dimensions subsequently found on a sample of unemployed adults (Goddard, Patton, & Simons, 1999). Unfortunately, this interesting validation idea is difficult to evaluate: Apart from the questionable power of the statistical analyses employed, the manual does not describe the method of this unpublished study in sufficient detail to assess the reliability and validity of the criterion itself.

CONCLUSION. The VISA does not appear to be competitive with the established vocational interest inventories, such as the Strong Interest Inventory (248; Worthen & Sailor, 1995) and the Vocational Interest Inventory—Revised (Law, 1998). Although its central test construction theme of generating "genuinely local content" is intuitively appealing, its rationale is neither conceptually convincing, nor supported empirically (no evidence of its substantive differences from comparable international instruments is presented). The emphasis on simplicity and brevity makes the VISA particularly suitable for those with limited English language proficiency, such as unemployed adults (Goddard, Patton, & Simons, 1999). In its current form, however, the VISA only partially achieves its intended purpose. Evidence of its psychometric soundness is insufficient: Although internal consistency of the subscales is acceptable, their temporal stability remains unknown (no test-retest evidence reported). Validity evidence is even more limited as no comparisons between the VISA and related measurement constructs are reported. Before the test can be recommended for practical use, more specific evidence of convergent and discriminant validity is needed, along with a more detailed report on criterion validation. Until that time, it would be prudent to use more established international tests, such as the Strong Interest Inventory (248), which has been extensively examined in the context of the Australian occupational environment (cf. Naylor, Care, & Mount, 1986).

REVIEWER'S REFERENCES

Goddard, R., Patton, W., & Simons, R. (1999). The Vocational Interest Survey for Australia: Its use with unemployed individuals. *Australian Journal of Psychology, 51*(2), 104–110.
Herman, D. O. (1998). [Review of the Vocational Interest Inventory-Revised.] In J. C. Impara & B. S. Plake (Eds.), *The thirteenth mental measurements yearbook* (pp. 1119–1120). Lincoln, NE: Buros Institute of Mental Measurements.
Law, J. G., Jr. (1998). [Review of the Vocational Interest Inventory-Revised.] In J. C. Impara & B. S. Blake (Eds.), *The thirteenth mental measurements yearbook* (pp. 1120–1121). Lincoln, NE: Buros Institute of Mental Measurements.
McLennan, W. (1997). ASCO: Australian standard classification of occupations. Canberra: Australian Bureau of Statistics.
Murphy, K. R., & Davidshofer, C. O. (2001). *Psychological testing: Principles and applications* (5th ed.). Upper Saddle River, NJ: Prentice Hall.
Naylor, F. D., Care, E., & Mount, T. J. (1986). The identification of Holland categories and occupational classification by the Vocational Preference Inventory and the Strong-Campbell Interest Inventory. *Australian Journal of Psychology, 38*(2), 161–167.
Worthen, B. R., & Sailor, P. (1995). [Review of the Strong Interest Inventory, Fourth Edition.] In J. C. Conoley & J. C. Impara (Eds.), *The twelfth mental measurements yearbook* (pp. 999–1002). Lincoln, NE: Buros Institute of Mental Measurements.

Review of the Vocational Interest Survey for Australia by ROBERT FITZPATRICK, Consulting Psychologist, Cranberry Township, PA:

DESCRIPTION. To complete the Vocational Interest Survey for Australia (VISA), a respondent rates his or her degree of interest in each of 64 work-related activities on a 7-point scale. It is untimed; normally it can be completely administered to individuals or groups in about a half hour. The survey booklet provides instructions for self- or examiner-scoring: add the eight rating numbers associated with each of the eight vocational interest areas. These areas were derived from work activity descriptions in the Australian Standard Classification of Occupations (ASCO). The professional manual suggests that the VISA results may be interpreted either by reviewing the profile of these raw scores or by converting them to percentile norms based on a group of Australian high school students.

DEVELOPMENT. According to the professional manual, "vocational interests can be understood as 'work activity preference'" (p. 2). Hence, work activity descriptions in the ASCO were sampled and used as the basis for a seed set of items. A 154-item preliminary form of the VISA was administered to over 1,200 high school students. After analyses of the results and further editing, the 64-item VISA was finalized and subjected to factor analysis and other analyses. It is not clear from the professional manual, but it appears that the samples used for various purposes overlapped to some extent.

TECHNICAL. The norm group for the VISA included approximately 500 male and 540 female high school students from schools in New South Wales and Queensland. Percentile norms are tabled for the total group and for gender groups separately. The normative sample is large enough for most purposes, but it may not be adequately representative of even high-school-age respondents throughout Australia. It is on its face not representative of college students or a general adult population.

Interpretation of the VISA by reference to raw score profiles is dubious. Mean raw scores vary substantially among interest areas, especially for the females in the norm group. These means range for females from about 16 for Practical to 36 for Service (with standard deviations of about 8). This suggests that factors such as social desirability and gender stereotyping may be operating.

Based on the same sample as the norms, internal consistency was estimated by coefficient alpha (ranging from .75 for Culture to .90 for Practical) and standard errors of measurement (*SEM*s, ranging from about 3 for Practical to almost 5 for Culture). These seem generally adequate, especially in view of the fact that there are only eight items in each of the VISA scales. The author interprets the *SEM*s as indicative of expected test-retest reliability, but they are not an entirely adequate substitute for a test-retest study.

Several types of evidence suggest a degree of validity for the intended interpretations of the VISA. The most convincing is that the developmental process appears to have been carried out in a way consistent with the author's concept of vocational interests and with needed concern for technical correctness. Factor analytic data show that each of the eight scales is represented reasonably well in the patterns of factor loadings. The items appear to be placed in the interest area scales as appropriately as can be expected. In addition, a study was carried out comparing the VISA scales to a "content analysis of subject's stated 'ideal job'" (professional manual, p. 33); an analysis of variance showed consistency of the two variables. More evidence of validity for recommended applications of the VISA is needed. However, these early results are favorable.

COMMENTARY. The VISA was well conceived as a short survey of interests explicitly derived from a comprehensive set of job descriptions. For the most part, the developmental process and analyses appear to have been well carried out. More work is needed to ensure that the samples used provide sufficient information to support the inferences made by the author about norming, reliability, and validity.

SUMMARY. The VISA is a short and easily administered vocational interest survey specifically designed for Australians. It is related to the ASCO, a comprehensive description of Australian jobs. Normative data are limited to high school students in two Australian states. Reliability and validity evidence is favorable but not yet conclusive. Users are encouraged to collect and disseminate further information about the usefulness of the VISA.

[274]

Wagner Enneagram Personality Style Scales.

Purpose: Designed "to measure the nine personality styles described by Enneagram."
Population: Ages 15–85.
Publication Date: 1999.
Acronym: WEPSS.
Scores: 9 scales: The Good Person, The Loving Person, The Effective Person, The Original Person, The Wise Person, The Loyal Person, The Joyful Person, The Powerful Person, The Peaceful Person.
Administration: Group or individual.
Price Data, 2003: $148 per kit including 25 autoscore forms, manual (114 pages), 100 glossary sheets, 100 brief guides to WEPSS results, 2-use disk for on-site computer scoring and interpretation and 2 PC answer sheets; $49.50 per 25 answer forms; $52.50 per manual; $15 per glossary sheet; $15 per brief guide to WEPSS results; $15 per mail-in answer form; $235 per 25-use PC scoring disk; $15 per 100 PC answer sheets; $11 per FAX service.
Time: (20–40) minutes.
Comments: Paper-and-pencil or computer administration available.
Author: Jerome P. Wagner.
Publisher: Western Psychological Services.

Review of the Wagner Enneagram Personality Style Scales by FRANK M. BERNT, Associate Professor of Health Services, St. Joseph's University, Philadelphia, PA:

DESCRIPTION. The Wagner Enneagram Personality Style Scales (WEPSS) are designed to measure nine different personality styles or ways of "viewing, construing, and responding to people and events" (manual, p. 3). The 200 items comprising the WEPSS are rated on a 5-point scale (1 = *almost never fits me;* 5 = *almost always fits me*). In the Introduction, the author lists a variety of intended uses for the WEPSS, including understanding decision making, conflict resolution, and management styles in business settings; for identifying intrapsychic and interpersonal dynamics in clinical settings; for clarifying values in spiritual and personal growth settings; and for exploring teaching and learning styles in educational settings.

The WEPSS is administered as a paper-and-pencil test. The manual suggests using a setting that is "comfortable, private, and free from distractions," (p. 27) allowing for either group or individual administration. Tests can be scored either by hand or by computer; different response sheets are provided for each. Hand scoring of the WEPSS is somewhat involved; however, the manual provides detailed and satisfactory instructions, illustrations, and diagrams to facilitate the process. Scoring yields Total, Resourceful, and Nonresourceful percentile scores for each of the nine personality styles, as well as a style summary that identifies a core style, a "wing" (or auxiliary) style, and two "connected" styles (to which one resorts under stressful vs. relaxed conditions). A series of case studies is provided to illustrate how different types of scores and styles might be interpreted, including emotional, cognitive, and behavioral dimensions, habits of avoidance and defensive maneuvers, and childhood developmental backgrounds that pertain to each of the nine types.

DEVELOPMENT. The Enneagram, upon which the WEPSS is based, traces its historical roots to a variety of sources, including neo-Platonism, Sufi mysticism, and the Cabalistic tradition of Judaism. The Enneagram is a circle inscribed by nine points; each of the points represents a unique personality style that is related to other styles in a complex fashion.

The author's original version of the scale (the Enneagram Personality Inventory) consisted of 135 items using complete sentences and a 5-point scale (Wagner & Walker, 1983). Changes to the scale since then include replacing sentences with word- or phrase-based items; distinguishing between resourceful and nonresourceful items for each style; and an increase in the number of items to 200.

The exact process of generating and selecting items for the current version of the scale is described rather generally in the technical manual: "long" lists of items and phrases were generated based upon Enneagram theory; items were retained based upon a "rational basis" (presumably rooted in complexes of Enneagram theory), in combination with high corrected item-total correlations within each of the nine scales.

TECHNICAL. The standardization samples used for norming and for determining validity and reliability evidence were primarily participants in Enneagram workshops given in the United States over the past 20 years. The sample is described as mostly college-educated (or at least in college). The norming sample is broken down by age ranges. No other demographic characteristics are discussed, other than gender. Gender comparisons are presented to justify the use of a single set of percentile norms (i.e., gender differences for the nine scales are too small to warrant providing separate norms for males and females).

Both internal consistency and test-retest reliability are reported to be satisfactory. Median Cronbach's alpha coefficients for Total, Resourceful, and Nonresourceful scales were .85, .79, and .79, respectively (ranges .73–.88). Median test-retest correlations for the same scales over an 8-month period were .81, .75, and .77, and appear to be adequate; however, results for temporal stability should be considered preliminary, given the use of very small samples (30 subjects or less).

The author presents a factor analysis that may provide partial support for the WEPSS's construct validity; however, it is very difficult to be sure, as the details regarding what type of factor analysis was done have been omitted. It appears to have been an exploratory factor analysis that forced a nine-factor solution; there is no mention of whether any criteria for selecting the number of factors was used, nor any mention of factor rotation. A naive examination of the factor tables suggests that a solution using fewer than nine factors might have been more elegant. The manual presents results from a series of exploratory factor analyses of WEPSS Total, Resourceful, and Nonresourceful scores; results suggest that three or four second-order factors may underlie the nine scales.

Several dissertation studies have provided evidence of criterion-related validity for the WEPSS. The majority of these studies have investigated the concordance between Enneagram types and styles measured by the Myers-Briggs Type Indicator (MBTI; T6:1678). Several patterns supporting concurrent validity emerged in these studies; for example, respondents with a "Good Person" core style tend to also be "Judging Types" on the MBTI, and those with Effective, Joyful, or Powerful core styles tend to be classified as Extroverts on the MBTI; those with Loyal or Wise core styles tend to be classified as Introverts; and so on. Unfortunately, no information is provided regarding how strong these concordances are, so results are still best seen as preliminary. Another study correlating WEPSS scores to conflict styles found that Scales 2 ("Loving Person") and 8 ("Powerful Person") were moderately correlated with Accommodating and Competing subscales (respectively) of the Thomas-Kilmann Conflict Mode Instrument (T6:2599). Other correlations among subscales for the two instruments are less clear.

COMMENTARY. The WEPSS's greatest appeal and widest use seems to lie in the context of Enneagram workshops, aimed at self-understanding and growth. With this in mind, it offers an attractive alternative to more traditional instruments that have as their primary function the identification of personality and emotional disorders. The author's efforts to use quantitative psychometric tools to refine and evaluate an instrument inspired by a clearly humanistic or even mystic tradition are praiseworthy; too often, something as esoteric as Enneagram theory would be dismissed as outside the realm of such methods. At the same time, a significant amount of research needs to be done before the reliability and validity of scores from the WEPSS are well established. It is questionable whether a single set of norms is adequate for all users. In addition, the scales' temporal stability should be further studied using larger samples. Additional studies exploring the construct and criterion-related validity of the WEPSS are also needed. There is little evidence to support (and perhaps even some to contradict) the existence of nine separate scales; more careful factor analytic studies are called for. With regard to criterion-related validity, correlations with subscales on the Myers-Briggs scale help to build its concurrent validity; as the author indicates, similar studies correlating WEPSS scores to accepted measures of the prevailing five-factor model of personality characteristics is a logical next step.

Perhaps of more interest than empirically driven studies will be those studies that test particular hypotheses generated by Enneagram theory. For example, is there empirical support for the claim that wing styles coincide with core styles? That subjects actually do resort to one connected style when under stress and to the other when in a relaxed state? What the author has provided here is a valuable tool to further explore a particular model of personality for which assumptions and claims hitherto have not been directly testable. It can be imagined that having such a tool to test this intriguing theory might generate a good deal of further research.

SUMMARY. The WEPSS represents a praiseworthy effort to "cross the divide" between quantitative-based mainstream psychometric approaches and less mainstream "interpretive approaches" to personality. The appeal that the WEPSS offers is a rich, "thick description" of test results very similar in texture to that provided by the Myers-Briggs Type Indicator. The author may be forgiven if the interpretations and structure of the test (based upon Enneagram theory) are not yet adequately confirmed by empirical studies. The instrument offers a wide range of hypotheses waiting to be tested; further empirical confirmation of the WEPSS's validity and reliability will very probably draw more careful attention to it as a viable alternative to mainstream personality tests, especially among psychologists and therapists exploring such issues within a spiritual or humanistic framework.

REVIEWER'S REFERENCE

Wagner, J. P., & Walker, R. E. (1983). Reliability and validity study of a Sufi personality typology: The enneagram. *Journal of Clinical Psychology, 39,* 712–717.

Review of the Wagner Enneagram Personality Style Scales by JOHNNIE A. BROWN, Administrator, Clinician, and Adjunct Professor, University of Maryland University College, Adelphi, MD:

DESCRIPTION. The Wagner Enneagram Personality Style Scales (WEPSS) is a 200-item, self-questionnaire intended to measure nine personality styles.

The Enneagram is a conceptual model that accounts for nine personality styles. Graphically, the Enneagram paradigm is depicted by a circle with nine points, with each point representing a separate style that has its own way of viewing, construing, and responding to people and events. Each style has both adaptive and maladaptive cognitive, emotional, and behavioral features.

The 200-item inventory is composed of nine scales, measuring the characteristics of these nine personality styles. Each scale contains 11 items describing the resourceful characteristics of that style and 11 items that describe the style's nonresourceful characteristics. The remaining two items are unscored, but can be evaluated as indicants of happiness or unhappiness. Each of the

200 items is a descriptive word or phrase. The respondent determines the degree to which the description fits them personally. This is accomplished through the use of an intensity scale. The intensity scale is a 5-point Likert-type scale (Babbie, 1979). The scale is calibrated from 1 to 5, and ranges from 1 *almost never fits me* to 5 *almost always fits me.*

The results of the WEPSS are expressed as a Total score, a Resourceful Characteristic score, and a Non-Resourceful Characteristic score for each of the nine Enneagram personality styles.

The WEPSS typically can be administered in approximately 30 minutes. And it can be scored manually or by computer.

The publisher of the WEPSS, Western Psychological Services, offers a range of services that can operate on personal computer (PC) systems. The PC-based program enables one to administer the WEPSS in a paper-and-pencil format, from which the responses can be input later on a PC, or to administer the inventory online, so that the respondent reads the items from a monitor and inputs his or her responses directly. A complete interpretive report is generated whenever the WEPSS is scored by computer, regardless of which computer-scoring option is chosen. The interpretive report should be evaluated and used by a qualified professional in conjunction with other pertinent information.

The developer of the WEPSS indicates that the instrument is intended for a general audience. The developer also suggests that a glossary sheet that accompanies the instrumentation package will clear up ambiguous items, thereby making the inventory accessible to the general reader.

In this reviewer's estimation, the WEPSS should only be administered by a trained technician or higher level professional. The respondent may encounter some complexities that require interventions from the examiner so that the inventory can be reliably understood and completed.

DEVELOPMENT. The Enneagram was transported from Eastern perennial wisdom to contemporary Western psychology. There is evidence to suggest that the Enneagram was taught by George Gurdjieff, a Russian author and a contemporary of Sigmund Freud (Speeth, 1976). Ichazo, Noranjo, and others utilized, studied, or wrote about the Enneagram or comparable constructs (Ichazo, 1976; Naranjo, 1994).

The WEPSS is an outgrowth of a 1981 dissertation completed at Loyola University in Chicago, Illinois (Wagner, 1981). Since that time, Wagner has continued to expound upon his typology regarding personality types. The WEPSS was originally called the Enneagram Personality Inventory and consisted of 135 items in a complete sentence format. The instrument went through several changes to improve the reliability and validity of its scores, as well as the ease of administration, scoring, and interpretation.

TECHNICAL. The standard scores for the WEPSS were based on a normative sample of 1,122 individuals. The age of the individuals in the sample ranged from 18 to 83. The individuals in the standardization sample were college educated or were college matriculants within the United States. Approximately 63% of those individuals were females and 37% were males. The race of the individuals was not stated.

The WEPSS interpretive scores are percentile scores, which range from .1 to 99.9. The T-scores for the WEPSS are provided for researchers who wish to use scores based on group means and standard deviations to perform statistical comparisons; however, these scores should not be used to determine an individual's Enneagram style.

The most recent research findings suggest that the WEPSS will tend to produce a reliable or stable measure, and those measures, within their context, can be taken as good indicators of the Enneagram-based personality styles. The developer of the WEPSS encourages additional validity studies.

COMMENTARY. According to its developer, the WEPSS can be used in business settings, clinical settings, and in school settings to deal with interpersonal dynamics, therapeutic counseling, and to make better use of teaching and learning styles.

Havens (1995), O'Leary (1994), and Wagner (1994) conducted comparative analyses of the WEPSS to the Myers-Briggs Type Indicator (MBTI). However, the five-factor model of personality may be a better instrument for matching personalities to jobs (Barrick & Strauss, 1994).

In this reviewer's estimation, the greatest potential utility for the WEPSS lies in the clinical domain. The WEPSS is particularly well-suited as a working adjunct for the treatment of personality disorders.

This reviewer observed a significant correspondence between the 200 items in the WEPSS instrument and the descriptions of a variety of personality disorders. Once the WEPSS is administered and scored, the clinician and respondent can make use of the results. The WEPSS lends itself to the promotion of cognitive and behavioral collaboration that is sufficiently structured, standard, and appropriate.

SUMMARY. The WEPSS is a useful 200-item personality inventory. It can be used in business settings, clinical settings, and in school settings to improve interpersonal work relationships, to enhance therapeutic counseling, and to better match teaching to learning styles.

REVIEWER'S REFERENCES

Babbie, E. R. (1979). *The practice of social research* (2ⁿᵈ ed.). Belmont, CA: Wadsworth Publishing Company, Inc.
Barrick, M. R., & Strauss, J. P. (1994). Validity of observer ratings of the big five personality factors. *Journal of Applied Psychology, 79*, 272–280.
Ichazo, O. (1976). *The human process for enlightenment and freedom: A series of five lectures.* New York: Arica Institute Press.
Naranjo, C. (1994). *Character and neurosis: An integrative view.* Nevada City, CA: Gateways.
Speeth, K. (1976). *The Gurdjieff work.* Berkeley: And/Or Press.
Wagner, J. (1981). A descriptive, reliability, and validity study of the enneagram personality typology (Doctoral dissertation, Loyola University). *Dissertation Abstracts International, 41*, 11A. (University Microfilms No. GAX 81-09973)

[275]

Wechsler Individual Achievement Test— Second Edition.

Purpose: "A ... measurement tool useful for achievement skills assessment, learning disability diagnosis, special education placement, curriculum planning, and clinical appraisal for preschool children through adults."

Population: Ages 4–85 years.

Publication Dates: 1992–2001.

Acronym: WIAT-II.

Scores, 21: 9 subtests (Word Reading, Pseudowor4d Decoding, Reading Comprehension, Math Reasoning, Numerical Operations, Listening Comprehension, Oral Expression, Spelling, Written Expression), 4 composite scores (Reading Composite, Written Language Composite, Mathematics Composite, Oral Language Composite), Total Composite, 7 supplemental scores: Reading (Reading Comprehension, Target Words, Reading Speed), Written Expression (Alphabet Writing, Word Fluency, Word Count), Oral Expression (Word Fluency).

Administration: Individual.

Price Data, 2002: $321 per complete kit including stimulus book 1, stimulus book 2, 25 record forms, 25 response booklets, examiner's manual (2001, 193 pages), Scoring and Normative supplement for Grades PreK–12, Scoring and Normative Supplement for College Students and Adults, word cards, audiotape, and bag; $59 per 25 combination record forms/response booklets; $86 per stimulus book 1 or 2; $11 per word card, pseudoword card, and audiotape; $96 per examiner's

manual, Scoring and Normative Supplement for Grades PreK–12, and Scoring and Normative Supplement for College Students and Adults; $50 per administration training video (CD-ROM Windows or Videotape); $125 per WIAT-II Scoring Assistant (CD-ROM Windows); $150 per WISC-III/WIAT-II Scoring Assistant (CD-ROM Windows or Macintosh); $150 per WAIS-III/WMS-III/WIAT-11 Scoring Assistant (CD-ROM Windows); $399 per WIAT-II Kit with WIAT-II Scoring Assistant (CD-ROM Windows); $449 per WIAT-II Kit with WISC-III/WIAT-II Scoring Assistant (CD-ROM Windows); $449 per WIAT-II Kit with WAIS-III/WMS-III/WIAT-II Scoring Assistant (CD-ROM Windows); $398 per WISC-III/WIAT-II Writer or WAIS-III/WMS-III/WIAT-II Writer (CD-ROM Windows); all software also available in 3.5-inch diskettes.

Time: Comprehensive Battery: (45) minutes for Grades PreK–K; (90) minutes for Grades 1–6; (90–120) minutes for Grades 7–16.

Comments: Subtests may be given individually; includes norms for 2-year and 4-year college students; standardized with Wechsler Intelligence Scale for Children-III (T6:2694), Wechsler Preschool and Primary Scale of Intelligence—Revised (T6:2696), Wechsler Adult Intelligence Scale—Third Edition (T6:2691), and the Process Assessment of the Learner: Test Battery for Reading and Writing (T6:1986); complete battery is composed of fewer tests for Grades PreK and K; manual or computer scoring; 3 software scoring programs available; WIAT-II Scoring Assistant software generates standard scores and error analyses using raw scores; WISC-III/WIAT-II Scoring Assistant (revision of the Scoring Assistant for the Wechsler Scales) includes all capabilities of WIAT-II Scoring Assistant and computes ability-achievement discrepancy analysis using the WISC-III; WAIS-III/WMS-III/WIAT-II Scoring Assistant software (revision of the Scoring Assistant for the Wechsler Scales for Adults) includes all capabilities of WIAT-II Scoring Assistant, computes ability-achievement discrepancy analysis using the WAIS-III, and generates reports; WISC-III/WIAT-II Writer software (revision of the WISC-III Writer) summarizes results, displays results in tabular and graphic formats, generates interpretive report; WAIS-III/WMS-III/WIAT-II Writer software scores and interprets results; system requirements for all software: Windows 95/98/2000/ME/NT 4.0 Workstation, 100 MHz Pentium processor, 32 MB RAM, 2 MB video card capable of 800 x 600 resolution (256 colors), 20 MB free hard disk space, 3.5-inch floppy drive, 50 MB temporary disk space; WIAT-II PDA Pocket Norms software available, system requirements Palm OS Personal Digital Assistant.

Author: The Psychological Corporation.

Publisher: The Psychological Corporation.

Cross References: See T5:2861 (4 references); for reviews by Terry Ackerman and Steven Ferrara of a previous edition, see 13:359 (17 references).

Review of the Wechsler Individual Achievement Test—Second Edition by BETH J. DOLL, Associate Professor of Educational Psychology, University of Nebraska—Lincoln, Lincoln, NE:

DESCRIPTION. The Wechsler Individual Achievement Test—Second Edition (WIAT-II) is a comprehensive individual achievement test that is a revision of the Wechsler Individual Achievement Test (WIAT; The Psychological Corporation, 1992). It is substantially different from its predecessor in the content and format of its subtests and in the scale's administration and scoring. In most respects, changes reflect the incorporation of cutting-edge research in the acquisition and assessment of educational skills. The basic design of the test remains the same. It provides composite scores in four domains of educational achievement: reading, mathematics, written language, and oral language.

The Reading Composite incorporates subtests in Word Reading, Reading Comprehension, and Pseudoword Decoding. In addition to the word reading and passage comprehension tasks of the WIAT, the WIAT-II includes items and scores that assess phonological awareness, letter-sound awareness, automaticity of word recognition, and fluency of reading. In addition, the Reading Composite includes the only new subtest—Pseudoword Decoding—as a measure of word decoding skills. The Mathematics Composite incorporates subtests in Numerical Operations and Mathematics Reasoning. In addition to the computation, problem solving, and quantitative reasoning items of the WIAT, the WIAT-II includes items assessing counting, one-to-one correspondence, estimation, and numerical patterns. The Written Language Composite incorporates subtests in Spelling and Written Expression. The Spelling subtest is very similar to that of the WIAT. The Written Expression subtest operationalizes much of the most recent research in writing instruction, incorporating items assessing word fluency, sentence construction, writing fluency, and written responses to visual or verbal cues in addition to the WIAT's descriptive and narrative writing tasks. The Oral Language Composite incorporates subtests in Listening Comprehension and Oral Expression. These have been redesigned to include greater emphasis on fluency and expressive vocabulary and recall for contextual information, and less emphasis on literal comprehension. Scoring systems for the Reading Composite and Oral Language Composite were altered to use new scoring rules that were more consistent with instructional practices.

The WIAT-II is designed for administration to a broad range of individuals, as young as 4-year-olds and as old as 85-year-old adults. Two examiner's manuals are provided. One describes technical information for the school-aged (4 to 19 years) sample and a second, supplemental manual describes technical information for the sample of college students and adults. Administration for the entire battery ranges from approximately 45 minutes for the youngest children to 2 hours for adolescents and adults. Administration rules are generally straightforward. Start points are indicated for each subtest based upon the examinee's age, reversal rules describe when earlier basal items should be administered, and discontinue rules are described based on the examinee's missing a specified number of items in a row. The protocol guides users through the conversion of raw scores into standardized scores, using the scoring and normative supplement manual. However, administration and scoring rules for the Reading Comprehension subtest are more complex and more confusing, and these were further altered after the test's publication. Early purchasers of the kit will need ensure that they have the "updated manual" that includes these revisions.

In addition to standard scores and percentile ranks for each subtest and Composite scale, the WIAT-II yields age equivalent scores, grade equivalent scores (fall or spring), normal curve equivalents, stanines, quartile scores, and decile scores. Error analysis procedures are incorporated into the test protocol, and measures of fluency are provided by timing reading speed on the Reading Comprehension subtest and using time limits for Word Fluency. Finally, because a subset of the standardization sample was administered Wechsler intelligence scales, users can also examine the significance of achievement/intelligence discrepancies between the WIAT-II and the Wechsler Preschool and Primary Scale of Intelligence—Revised (WPPSI-R), the Wechsler Intelligence Scale for Children—Third Edition (WISC-III), or the Wechsler Adult Intelligence Scale—Third Edition (WAIS-III). The authors recommend that only professionals trained in the administration and interpretation of individually administered assessment instruments are qualified to administer the WIAT-II and translate its results into education decisions.

DEVELOPMENT. Work on the WIAT-II began in 1996, only 4 years after publication of the WIAT. Focus groups were convened with over 500 major users of individual achievement tests to design item modifications. Notes from the focus groups were organized into blueprints of the constructs that the test would assess. Next, these blueprints were compared to national and state standards and curricula such as the Principles and Standards for School Mathematics (NCTM, 2000) of the National Council of Teachers of Mathematics (NCTM), and the report of the National Reading Panel (2000). In addition, prominent researchers in each academic domain were consulted, and some were retained as advisors throughout the test development process. Revised items were piloted with 400 individuals in 1997, followed by a large scale tryout with 1,900 students. Item analysis of these data guided the selection of items for the final version of the WIAT-II. In deference to the importance of cognitive processes underlying achievement, the publishers coordinated the development of the WIAT-II with the Process Assessment of the Learner—Test Battery for Reading and Writing (Berninger, 2001).

TECHNICAL. The normative data for the WIAT-II were collected between 1999 and 2001 from 2,950 school-aged children ranging in age from 4 years 0 months to 19 years 11 months, 707 college students, and 500 adults. A stratified-random sampling procedure was used to insure that the sample would be representative of the 1998 Census of the United States on gender, race/ethnicity, geographic region, and parental education level. Students with disabilities were included in the standardization sample in proportion to their representation in public school programs, and the college sample included students from 2-year as well as 4-year campuses. Children and adults were excluded from the standardization if they did not speak English, had nerological disorders, or were taking medications that could suppress performance. A comprehensive description of the final standardization sample for school-aged children demonstrates that

it successfully approximates the demographic characteristics of the United States. To insure the integrity of the standardization data, standardization protocols were scored by the primary examiner, and then were rescored by two additional scorers trained by the test publisher.

For both samples, internal consistency reliability estimates of the WIAT-II subtests are generally high (above .85) with the exception of the Written Expression and Listening Comprehension subtests in the school-aged sample and the Written Expression and Oral Expression subtests in the college/adult sample. The reliability estimates of these subtests were only somewhat lower (above .70). Internal consistency reliability of the Composite scores was very high (above .90) in both samples with the exception of the Oral Language Composite, which was above .85. In the school-aged sample, test-retest correlations for the subtests (across intervals of approximately 10 days) were consistently above .85 and test-retest correlations for the Composite scores were above .90. Tests-retest correlations were somewhat lower in the college/adult sample, with correlations between .75 and .85 in Reading Comprehension, Written Expression, Oral Expression, and the composite scores for Written Language and Oral Language. With this level of reliability, it would be reasonable to interpret intersubtest differences for the Reading and Mathematics subtests with a moderate degree of confidence, and to interpret inter-Composite differences with good confidence for school-aged children and adults.

Limited validity information for the WIAT-II is available in the examiner's manual. Predictably, the corresponding subtests of the WIAT and the WIAT-II are strongly correlated (above .80) in the school-aged sample for those subtests with minimal content changes. However, the correlations were lower for subtests that had changed the most: Reading Comprehension ($r = .74$), Written Expression ($r = .48$), Listening Comprehension ($r = .68$), and Oral Expression ($r = .62$) subtests. Similarly, the Reading Composites and Mathematics Composites of the WIAT and WIAT-II are strongly correlated ($r \geq .85$) but the Written Language Composites and Oral Language Composites are not ($r = .66$). The examiner's manual describes very modest correlations between the school-aged WIAT-II Reading, Mathematics, and Written Language Composites and corresponding

specified scoring procedures and guidelines presented in the supplemental books; for these items, verbatim recording is required. Qualitative recording of examinee behavior also is encouraged and a checklist is provided for codifying frequency of behavioral occurrence on several dimensions. Written and Oral Expression, as well as optional Reading Comprehension, scores require conversion of raw scores to quartiles (before reporting standard scores) and are reported as unique supplemental scores. Four composite scores can be obtained on the WIAT-II by adding standard scores of individual subtests: Reading (with three subtest scores), Mathematics (with two subtest scores), Written Language (with two subtest scores), and Oral Language (with two subtest scores). Confidence intervals also can be recorded on the summary report before displaying various rank scores. Finally, the report form includes a place to report an ability-achievement discrepancy analysis and plot the results on a bell curve.

DEVELOPMENT. The most significant change in this edition is the extension of the age range from 5–19 years to 4–85 years. Development began in 1996 with a rigorous analysis of the WIAT and blueprint of content or curriculum specifications. The theoretical perspectives used to develop this edition include research reported by Berninger (2001), the National Reading Panel (2000), and the National Council of Teachers of Mathematics (NCTM, 2000) standards. Pilot testing of items was conducted in 1997 with approximately 400 individuals; the results were analyzed using traditional item analyses.

The authors note that this revision provides more complete behavior sampling in the domains, a broader range of students, closer links to instruction, improved scoring (with error analysis), and procedures for documenting ability-achievement discrepancies. In Reading, letter identification, phonological awareness, and pseudoword decoding were added along with measurement of reading rate, oral reading accuracy, fluency, and comprehension (oral and lexical) in expanded sentence and passage reading. New items were added in the Mathematics subtests to reflect both low level (patterns, counting, 1:1 correspondence, and numerical identification), as well as high-level mathematics problems (e.g., estimation, probability, and multi-step problem solving). Spelling subtests were revised to reflect morphological knowledge;

Written Expression subtests include new low measures (timed alphabet writing and fluency) in addition to the assessment of high-level skills (sentence combining and sentence generation, as well as analytic scoring on four traits). Finally, Oral Language is more anchored to real contexts as part of Reading and Writing and adds word fluency, auditory short-term recall, and story generation.

TECHNICAL. Two standardization samples were drawn (in 1999–2000 and 2000–2001): for PreK–12 (ages 4–19) and for the college/adult population. Both standardization samples were stratified on the basis of grade, age, sex, race/ethnicity, geographic region, and parent education level, using the 1998 Bureau of the Census as the basis for stratification. Over 5,000 individuals participated in the standardization process. "A stratified random sampling approach was used to select participants representative of the population" and "students who received special education services in school settings were not excluded from participation" (examiner's manual, p. 86). Sample proportions closely approximate census proportions for all stratification variables. Qualified and trained examiners, with test administration experience, were used for the standardization sample. During the standardization process, rules to start, discontinue, and stop testing were developed to conservatively allow students to avoid being tested on items deemed too easy or too difficult. A subset of the standardization participants also was administered one of the three Wechsler intelligence scales: the Wechsler Preschool and Primary Scale of Intelligence—Revised (WPPSI-R; Wechsler, 1989), the Wechsler Intelligence Scale for Children, Third Edition (WISC-III; Wechsler, 1991), or the Wechsler Adult Intelligence Scale, Third Edition (WAIS-III; Wechsler, 1997). The linking sample consisted of 1,069 participants. The information collected from this portion of the standardization process was used to develop the achievement-discrepancy statistics.

The authors report data on split-half coefficients, test-retest, and interscorer agreement. Most split-half coefficients (based on age and grade) are well above .80. Grade-based split-half coefficients are consistently lower than age-based coefficients, with coefficients falling below .80 on Numerical Reasoning, Written Expression, and Listening Comprehension in fall and spring. Age-based reliability coefficients fall below .80 for Listening

Comprehension only. The split-half coefficients for the four composites are all greater than .80. To determine test-retest reliability, a sample of 297 was drawn from three bands in the standardization sample: ages 6–9, 10–12, and 13–19. Test-retest intervals varied from 7–45 days with an average interval of 10 days. Test-retest subtest scores range between .81 and .99. Composite scores range between .91 and .92.

Two separate studies were conducted to evaluate interrater agreement. The first study examined the dichotomously scored items in the Reading Comprehension subtests for 2,180 participants. Interrater reliability coefficients ranged between .94 and .98. The second study examined the Written Expression and Oral Expression subtests for 2,180 participants. The intraclass correlations between the two sets of scores ranged from .71 to .94 across ages, with an average correlation of .85. The intraclass correlations between pairs of scores for the Oral Expression subtest ranged from .91 to .99 across ages, with an average of .96.

The WIAT-II presents evidence of content, construct, and criterion-related validity. Although curriculum objectives were referenced for item selection and experts in reading, mathematics, speech, and language arts reviewed the subtests to ascertain the degree with which items measured specific curriculum objectives, no specific information is presented (e.g., which curricula, who served as experts, and how the process was completed). Conventional and item response theory analyses are presented to document item consistency and to eliminate poorly constructed items, determine correct item order, as well as to prevent item bias. Evidence of construct validity is provided through intercorrelations of subtests, correlations with measures of ability, and group differences across grades and groups. Finally, the WIAT-II provides ample support for criterion-related validity with a number of individually administered achievement tests. Moderate correlations appear between selected WIAT-II and Process Assessment of the Learner: Test Battery for Reading and Writing (PAL-RW; Berninger, 2001; considered a companion to the WIAT-II) and WIAT subtests, the Wide Range Achievement Test—3 (WRAT3; Wilkinson, 1993), the Differential Ability Scales (DAS; Elliott, 1990), and the Peabody Picture Vocabulary Test—III (PPVT-III; Dunn & Dunn, 1997). In these stud-

ies, moderate to high correlations are presented in an extensive set of tables in the examiner's manual. Correlations with the WIAT-II and group-administered achievement tests also are presented: Results indicate moderate correlations between the WIAT-II and the Stanford Achievement Tests—Ninth Edition (Stanford 9; Harcourt Educational Measurement, 1996), and the Metropolitan Achievement Tests, Eighth Edition (MAT8; Harcourt Educational Measurement, 1999), as well as the Academic Competence Evaluation Scales (ACES; DiPerna & Elliott, 2000) and school grades. Again, the correlations are moderate to high between the WIAT-II and these tests.

Given the WIAT-II is to be used in the differential diagnosis of students with disabilities, it is important that construct validity be examined by comparing groups of students. Nine different comparisons are presented to document the performance of students participating in gifted programs (n = 123), with mental retardation (n = 39), with emotional disturbance (n = 85), with learning disabilities in reading (n = 123), with learning disabilities not specific to reading (n = 109), with attention deficit-hyperactive disorder (ADHD) (n = 179), with both ADHD and learning disabilities (n = 54), with hearing impairments (n = 31), and with speech and/or language impairments (n = 49). In all of these comparisons, the data confirm the differential performance of students with special needs.

COMMENTARY AND SUMMARY. The WIAT-II has several strong features. First, its comprehensive nature allows for a thorough examination of student strengths and weaknesses within and across several academic domains. Second, the modifications made to the most recent edition subtests reflect current trends in research and curriculum. Third, the materials are well organized and very accessible, for both administration and scoring or reporting. Finally, the link between assessment and instruction/intervention is explicit through the inclusion of an error analysis component and partial correct scoring. The examiner's manual provides a strong guiding framework for the development of interventions. However, without the thorough interpretation presented by the examiner trained in linking the data to interventions and instructional programs, the error analysis component is meaningless. The protocol alone does not lend itself to linking data to interventions.

years and involved a total of 5,586 individuals from across the U.S. Between 100 and 300 individuals participated in the standardization testing within each age or grade group. Additionally, a complete description is provided regarding the process of score derivation based upon the normative data.

TECHNICAL DATA. Measures of internal consistency and stability are presented in the manual. Split-half reliability correlations were calculated for each subtest based on the data for the 6–19-year-old group and on the data for the 17–85-year-old group. Similarly, correlations were calculated for the Spring, Fall, and College grade-based group data. The test developers reported that the split-half method was chosen to be consistent with the method used for most of the WISC-III subtests (linking data). The results indicate generally strong interitem consistency for the subtests (range = .71 to .99, with most coefficients at .90 or higher). The lowest values cluster mostly at the kindergarten through Grade 2 levels, specifically for the Numerical Operations subtest. Test-retest coefficients indicate adequate stability (corrected values .91 to .99) for three different age bands of the student sample (N = 352) and for a subgroup of the college and adult sample (N = 77). The average retest interval was reported as 10 days (range 7 to 45 days). The manual also contains the Standard Errors of Measurement values and Confidence Interval Magnitudes for the subtests. The results reveal there is generally more precision in the reading and spelling scores than the math scores at most ages. Additionally, more error in measurement appears to be present at the youngest age levels on the Numerical Operations subtest.

Content validity was addressed by a thorough process of outlining the scope of each subtest with input from many sources and utilizing item analysis techniques (conventional and item response theory methods) during the test development in order to retain the most effective items while sampling the content areas comprehensively. Item-bias studies were also conducted in order to delete problematic items.

Construct validity was examined through analysis of subtest intercorrelations that indicate that the Reading and Spelling scores are more highly correlated with each other than either is correlated with the Math scores. Correlations of the WIAT-II-A subtest scores and the Wechsler IQ scores indicate that although there is a positive

relationship between the two instruments, different skills are being measured by the instruments. Finally, changes in raw scores are associated with developmental differences in the school-age range as would be expected in an achievement test.

Criterion-related validity data for the WIAT-II-A comes from a variety of small group studies that examine the relationship among these three subtests and the subtests of other individual and group achievement tests (e.g., WIAT, WRAT-3, DAS, W-JR, PAL-RW, SAT9, MAT8). Many of the correlations reported are in the moderate range, with the highest correlations with the first edition of the WIAT (.78–.88) and lowest in Reading with the DAS (.37). The WIAT-II-A Spelling subtest consistently has the highest correlations with other group tests (.89 with the SAT9 spelling, .80 and .78 with the MAT8 Spelling), and individual tests (.78 with the WRAT-3, .76 with DAS Spelling). Data were also gathered to compare the test scores of groups of clinical and special needs individuals (e.g., gifted, emotional disturbance, learning disability, mental retardation) with matched non-special needs groups of individuals. The results revealed significant score differences consistent with the expected patterns for the groups (e.g., higher achievement scores in the gifted than nongifted group and lower scores in the learning disability group than in the matched nonlearning disability group).

SUMMARY. The WIAT-II-A is a brief achievement battery that is composed of three subtests (Word Reading, Numerical Operations, and Spelling) taken directly from the WIAT-Second Edition (WIAT-II). As part of the larger project, this instrument benefited from the publisher's investment in quality test development and standardization. The subtests are composed of items that reflect thorough sampling of the relevant academic domains and the technical data show good reliability and sound validity. The manual effectively details the administration instructions and scoring procedures. A specific strength is that the standardization sample was expanded to include older college students and adults. As a result, it may be a useful instrument for screening academic skills in adults who seek assistance in various clinical settings and in colleges. In school settings, this instrument is limited because it does not assess all of the learning disability areas as outlined by the Individuals with

Disabilities Education Act (IDEA). The comprehensive form of the WIAT-II would be a more appropriate choice for school age individuals. These subtests, as acknowledged in the manual, are not complete, comprehensive assessments (i.e., Word Reading is only one aspect of the reading domain). It also seems unlikely that this test would function as a progress monitoring device, as suggested in the manual. Although the item sampling is thorough, this norm-referenced test is not sensitive enough to measure small changes in academic skill. For progress monitoring, curriculum-based measures would be more appropriate choices.

The test developers provided a nice format for gathering qualitative observations. If this same data were collected during the standardization process, it is unfortunate that the developers stopped short by not analyzing the data for pertinent patterns, or offering methods of using the data collected. Another element that would make the WIAT-II-A more user friendly would be to spiral-bind the manual so it is easier to use during administration. Other options to address this issue could include: removing the administration pages from the manual and binding them separately or laminating those pages similar to what was done with the Spelling administration items. These are minor issues, however, because the WIAT-II-A is a well-developed, technically sound screening instrument. It will provide adequate data in specific situations that require such a norm-referenced assessment.

REVIEWER'S REFERENCES

Horn, L., & Berktold, J. (1999). *Students with disabilities in post secondary special education: A profile of preparation, participation and outcomes.* Washington, DC: U.S. Dept. of Education, National Center for Education Statistics.
Snyder, T. D., & Hoffman, C. M. (2001). *Digest of education statistics, 2000* (NCES 2001-034). Washington, DC: U.S. Dept. of Education, National Center for Education Statistics.

[277]

The Wellness Evaluation of Lifestyle.

Purpose: Designed as "an instrument for assessing and planning wellness lifestyles."
Population: Ages 18 and over.
Publication Dates: 1994–2001.
Acronym: WEL.
Scores, 20: Spirituality, Self-Regulation (Sense of Worth, Sense of Control, Realistic Beliefs, Emotional Responsiveness, Intellectual Stimulation, Sense of Humor, Nutrition, Exercise, Self-Care, Stress Management, Gender Identity, Culture Identity, Total), Work & Leisure (Work, Leisure), Friendship, Love, Perceived Wellness, Total Wellness.
Administration: Group.

Price Data, 2003: $30 per sampler set including one of each test component, question/answer sheet, manual (32 pages), and scoring directions; $120 per permission set including one copy of instrument and permission to make up to 150 copies; web-based administration yielding a profile with scale interpretations ($10 or less per report).
Time: [20–30] minutes.
Authors: Jane E. Myers, Thomas J. Sweeney, and J. Melvin Witmer.
Publisher: Mind Garden, Inc.

Review of the Wellness Evaluation of Lifestyle by ANDREW A. COX, Professor, Counseling and Psychology Troy State University, Phenix City, AL:

DESCRIPTION. The Wellness Evaluation of Lifestyle (WEL) is a 131-item paper-pencil inventory. The first 123 items use a 5-item Likert scale format in which the respondent endorses items as *strongly agree, agree, undecided or neutral, disagree,* and *strongly disagree.* On the inventory's remaining 8 items, the test taker describes demographic information to include marital status, employment and occupational status, educational level, ethnic/cultural background, and residential community size. The WEL is designed to measure the five life tasks and 14 dimensions of the wheel of wellness, a holistic model of wellness and prevention over the life span developed by Witmer and Sweeney (1992) and Myers, Sweeney, and Witmer (2000). Test items consist of a variety of positively and negatively worded items that are direct in nature and deal with life style behaviors, perceptions, thoughts, and attitudes. The inventory can be handscored using the paper-pencil answer sheet and scoring key or administered and scored via the Internet at www.mindgarden.com.

The instrument is straightforward to score with a provided scoring grid allowing the test administrator to obtain and convert raw scores into percentage scores. No information is provided within the manual for interpreting scores. However, Myers, Sweeney, and Witmer (2000) indicate that the inventory's scores are based upon a linear transformation with the highest possible score being 100. Scores are provided for each of the 17 dimensions of the wellness model that comprise the instrument's theoretical construct and three composite scores depicting self-regulation/self direction, perceived wellness, and total wellness.

DEVELOPMENT. The test manual indicates that a large pool of items were developed to assess each component of the wellness model delineated by Myers (1991), Witmer and Sweeney (1992), and Myers, Sweeney, and Witmer (2000). An initial 114-item version of the WEL was developed. Items were selected by the instrument's authors to represent the five life tasks and subtasks of the wellness model. The revised Wellness Evaluation of Lifestyle includes the original scale's 114 items and 17 additional items developed for the test revision. A version of the instrument with a seventh grade reading level is also available for use with high school students and bicultural individuals.

Little is described in the manual about item development or the mechanisms used to select the final pool of items for use in the instrument's revisions. Apparently, items were field-tested with undergraduate and graduate student convenience samples of unknown sample size at two universities. TECHNICAL. The original version of The Wellness Evaluation of Lifestyle was normed on the above-noted student convenience samples of unknown size. The revised version of The Wellness Evaluation of Lifestyle is normed on convenience samples of undergraduate and graduate students, a national sample of corporate managers, and professional counselors attending conferences and training workshops. Once again, the number or characteristics of individuals comprising this normative sample are not described. The adolescent version of the WEL has a normative sample of 121 rural North Carolina high school students, with 20% of the sample being of Native American origin. Other demographic characteristics for this adolescent normative sample are not described.

Factorial analyses for the three versions of the WEL are referenced but details describing these analyses are not provided within the test manual. Details of these analyses have been reported elsewhere (Hattie, Myers, & Sweeney, in press) but this information is not currently available in the literature. Myers, Sweeney, and Witmer (2000) report norming the instrument on more than 4,000 individuals to include adolescents, young, midlife, and older adults. However, these normative data are also not described within the manual.

Reliability estimates are reported for the instrument. Test-retest reliabilities with a 2-week interval range from .68 to .94, with an average reliability index of .81. Internal consistency alpha coefficients range from .61 to .89, with an average

coefficient of .77. Reliability estimates were obtained with a sample of 99 undergraduate students. It is unclear which university setting was used to obtain this sample. Reliability levels appear to be satisfactory for this measure but the evidence should be considered preliminary in nature.

Validation data are not described within the test manual. The authors indicate that test items are based upon a wellness model suggesting some construct validation. However, formal construct validation or other validation methods are not described within the test manual. Myers, Sweeney, and Witmer (2000) report that a factor analysis and analyses of variance have been conducted to determine the discriminatory power of the scales, citing Hattie, Myers, and Sweeney (in press) for details regarding these data. This descriptive information is not included in the test manual and the latter reference is unavailable within the literature.

COMMENTARY. The inventory has value as a counseling and intervention measure. It directly assesses dimensions associated with a specific theoretical model of wellness. If this model is used as the basis for therapeutic interventions, the instrument could be used to evaluate effectiveness of intervention programs. A workbook is available that would enhance the instrument's use in intervention processes. Several studies cite using the WEL in program evaluation (Garrett, 1999; Granello, 2000; Hermon & Hazler, 1999).

Technical characteristics for this measure are weak. Some reliability estimates are reported. Validation data are not included within the manual though this information may be available elsewhere in the literature. Information relative to score interpretation is also lacking within the manual.

SUMMARY. The Wellness Evaluation of Lifestyle is an instrument that appears to be related to a conceptual model of wellness with items having face validity relative to this model. From this perspective, the instrument may have use for practitioners working with individuals and groups on wellness and lifestyle issues. The instrument has satisfactory preliminary evidence for reliability. Formal instrument validation is not described within the manual. Additional descriptive information is necessary to insure that derived scores are useable and interpretable.

Data further supporting the WEL appear to be reported elsewhere in the literature. The test developers are encouraged to revise the test manual to include this additional information that would allow test purchasers and consumers to make informed choices regarding the instrument. The instrument shows promise for evaluating wellness interventions and research. At this time, the WEL should be used with other wellness inventories until such time that more is known about the instrument's psychometric properties. Other instruments for such use are described in Palombi (1992).

REVIEWER'S REFERENCES

Garrett, M. T. (1999). Soaring on the wings of the eagle: Wellness of Native American high school students. *Professional School Counseling, 3,* 57–64.

Granello, P. (2000). Integrating wellness work into mental health private practice. *Journal of Psychotherapy in Independent Practice, 1,* 3–16.

Hattie, J. A., Myers, J. E., & Sweeney, T. J. (in press). A multidisciplinary model of wellness: The development of the wellness evaluation of lifestyle. *Journal of Counseling and Development.*

Hermon, D. A., & Hazler, R. J. (1999). Adherence to a wellness model and perceptions of psychological well-being. *Journal of Counseling and Development, 77,* 339–343.

Myers, J. E. (1991). Wellness as the paradigm for counseling and development: The possible future. *Counselor Education and Supervision, 30,* 183–193.

Myers, J. E., Sweeney, T. J., & Witmer, J. M. (2000). The wheel of wellness counseling for wellness: A holistic model for treatment planning. *Journal of Counseling and Development, 78,* 251–266.

Palombi, B. J. (1992). Psychometric properties of wellness instruments. *Journal of Counseling and Development, 71,* 221–225.

Witmer, J. M., & Sweeney, T. J. (1992). A holistic model for wellness and prevention over the life span. *Journal of Counseling and Development, 71,* 140–148.

Review of The Wellness Evaluation of Lifestyle by ASHRAF KAGEE, Research Fellow, Department of Psychology, University of Stellenbosch, Maitland, South Africa:

DESCRIPTION. The Wellness Evaluation of Lifestyle (WEL) is a 131-item self-administered paper-and-pencil questionnaire that measures several dimensions of wellness. The first 123 items assess wellness traits and are scored on a Likert-type scale (Strongly Agree to Strongly Disagree), whereas the final 8 questions assess demographic characteristics that affect wellness and are presented in a multiple-choice format. Items on the scale appear as self-statements and fall into five interrelated and interconnected subscales, called life tasks, namely, Spirituality (10 items), Self-Regulation (64 items), Work & Leisure (14 items), Friendship (7 items), and Love (8 items). Also included are several distracter items that are not included in the scoring.

The WEL may be administered and scored by nonclinical staff with minimal training, but interpretation of the test requires an understanding of the model of wellness on which it is based. No software is required to score the test, as it is handscored. The scoring key is self-explanatory and easy to follow, and permits calculation of a raw score and "percentage score" for each of the life tasks. The Self-Regulation and Work & Leisure life tasks have 12 and 2 subscales, respectively, for which raw and "percentage" scores may be calculated. The key also permits the calculation of a Total Wellness raw and "percentage" score. The manual does not provide any information about the meaning of either the subscale or total scores, and thus, it is unclear what significance a high or low score may have.

DEVELOPMENT. The WEL is a relatively new test (copyright, 2001) and has been in development since 1998. [Editor's Note: The publisher advises in February 2003 that the WEL has been in development since 1993 and that Form S, which was provided for review, is a fourth version and has been in use since 1994. Unfortunately, none of this information was reflected in the materials provided for review.] The materials furnished by the developer do not specifically indicate the target population for which the instrument was designed. However, as it was developed, the test was administered to convenience samples of undergraduate students enrolled in career and life planning courses, graduate students in counseling, and mid-level managers and professional counselors attending training conferences and continuing education workshops. A version of the WEL was also administered to samples of high school students. Following item analyses of the first three versions of the WEL and a series of factor analyses, the final version of the WEL, the WEL-S, was developed.

The WEL is based on a theoretical model, called the Wheel of Wellness, which apparently represents a holistic model of wellness over the lifespan. The model is informed by a combination of different aspects of the theories of Adler, Jung, and Maslow, in particular their contribution to lifespan development. The definitions of the life tasks are extensive and are based on a thorough review of the relevant literature. However, it is unclear how the constructs that inform the subscales fit together and constitute a holistic model of wellness. By attempting to be all-encompassing, the model appears to define wellness rather loosely and, therefore, the subscales are conceptually distant from one another. On the other hand, some subscales such as Friendship and Love appear to overlap and it is unclear what has been done either theoretically or empirically to discriminate between these life tasks.

TECHNICAL. Information describing the norming process is vaguely presented in the manual and no details are provided about the scores obtained from the norm samples. The reference list provided in the manual also does not appear to contain published research containing norms. As such, it is difficult for a user of the WEL to interpret scores obtained from a sample of respondents. This seems to be a serious limitation of the measure as it is presented, and future versions of the manual should include data at least describing means and standard deviations obtained from the samples on which the test was normed.

Some of the items on the scale appear to be redundant such as "I believe in the existence of a power greater than myself" and "I have had an experience in which I felt a sense of oneness with nature, the universe, or a higher power." The validity of the second item rests on the assumption that the respondent has endorsed the first item in the scorable direction, thus obviating the need for it. Similar cases of redundant items may be found in other subscales of the measure. On the other hand, some items are vague and it may be difficult for a respondent to know what is being asked (e.g., "My cultural heritage enhances my quality of life" and "I have sources of support with respect to my race, color, or culture").

The alpha coefficients of the various subscales are almost all above .70. Although this is desirable, it is possible that this may be partly accounted for by the redundancy of the items. Test-retest reliability (2-week interval) is also high, ranging from .68 to .94, suggesting good stability of the measure over time. However, these data are presented in the form of an aggregate from the various norm samples. It is thus not possible for the reader to discern the data set from which they were derived. The distracter items are appropriately negatively presented to guard against a uniformly positive response set. No validity data are presented.

COMMENTARY. The value of the WEL as a measure of wellness lifestyles seems compromised on a number of levels. First, the authors do not motivate sufficiently for another measure of wellness beyond those that already exist. Second, in an attempt to assess a holistic and all-encompassing construct of wellness, the measure has conceptually disparate subscales, to the extent that the construct may be rendered too broad to be useful. Third, normative data with which to compare respondents' scores are not presented, thus limiting the utility of the scale. Finally, it would also have been useful if the authors had specified the groups for which this measure is specifically intended. That the scale may have been intended for use with all populations in all contexts is a limitation because its specificity and relevance are likely to be lost in the process.

SUMMARY. The WEL is a new measure designed to assess wellness behavior. It is apparently intended for use with diverse populations, including adolescents. The authors have not described the development of the scale in any detail, neither have they presented normative data with which to compare respondents' obtained scores. Despite the ease with which this measure may be administered and scored, these omissions constitute important limitations to its usefulness in its present form.

[278]
Who Am I?

Purpose: Assesses "a child's readiness for particular types of learning experiences and identifies the levels that children have reached in their understanding and use of conventional symbols and relevant early learning skills."

Population: Preschool–Year 2 in Australian school system.

Publication Date: 1999.

Scores, 4: Copying, Symbols, Drawing, Total.

Administration: Group or individual.

Price Data, 2002: A\$49 per specimen set including task booklet, assessment manual (36 pages), and administration instructions; A\$25 per 10 task booklets; A\$39.95 per assessment manual; A\$8 per administration instructions.

Time: (10–20) minutes.

Authors: Marion de Lemos and Brian Doig.

Publisher: Australian Council for Educational Research Ltd. [Australia].

Review of Who Am I? by G. MICHAEL POTEAT, Associate Professor of Psychology, East Carolina University, Greenville, NC:

DESCRIPTION AND DEVELOPMENT. Who Am I? is a developmental assessment scale developed by the Australian Council for Educational Research (ACER) between 1997 and 1999. The instrument is described as being intended, primarily, for the assessment of children entering school. Other suggested uses include monitoring preschool children's development and assessing the development of older children who have problems with academics. Who Am I? consists of three scales: Copying (of geometric figures), Symbols (a measure of the child's awareness of the symbols), and Drawing (the child draws a picture of himself or herself). The specimen set included an assessment manual, administrative instructions, and a test booklet. The administrative instruction booklet is very simple and easy to follow. The tasks are straightforward and the instructions for administration are adequate. The test booklet parallels the instructions booklet. Who Am I? is designed to be administered on either an individual or a group basis. The assessment is started by asking the child to write their name on the front of the test booklet. Copying tasks consist of copying a circle, a cross, a square, a triangle, and a diamond. For Symbols, children are asked to write numbers, letters, words, and a sentence. For Drawing, the child is asked to draw a picture of himself or herself. All instructions are worded in a very simple form (e.g., the examiner points to a circle in the test booklet and says, "Draw a shape just like this").

Who Am I? provides four raw scores: Drawing (0–4), Symbols (0–20), Copying (0–20), and Total (0–44). The raw scores can be transferred to an individual profile that provides normative developmental ranges. The information for scoring the child's responses is adequate and should cause no difficulties for anyone even minimally trained in developmental or educational assessment. The total score can then be converted to percentiles and stanines using either age norms or school-level (grade) norms. The tables are brief and easy to use. No tables are provided for the individual scales.

TECHNICAL. Age norms are based on 4,314 children assessed in May and June of 1998. The school-level (grade-level) norms are based on a sample of 3,984 children tested in May and June of 1998 (for older children) and November and December of 1998 (for younger children). The rationale for the different assessment periods is based on the conjecture that the November/December assessment provides a better indicator of preschool children's performance when they enter school. Children in the normative sample ranged from 4 years, 0 months to over 7 years, 1 month in age. The majority of the children assessed were more than 5 years, 6 months in age. Children from all districts in Australia were sampled with the

exception of Tasmania. No information is provided on the gender, ethnic background, or socioeconomic status of the children included in the normative sample.

Evidence for reliability (temporal stability) is presented through the examination of the scores of preschool children assessed in June with their scores in November. A correlation of .82 is reported but the number of children in the sample is not identified. Measures of internal consistency are provided for the total scale across both age and school level groups and range from .51 to .67. Evidence for validity consists of the demonstration of changes in performance related to age (i.e., older children tend to get higher scores) and the correlations between Who Am I? and other tests designed to measure academic performance (the correlations ranged from approximately .4 to .6). An argument is made for the content validity on the basis that the items on the scale are those required for children entering school.

COMMENTARY AND SUMMARY. Overall, Who Am I? can be characterized as a simple, quick, and rough guide to a child's developmental readiness for school. It provides an approximate estimate of the child's developmental readiness but is based entirely on behaviors related to "fine-motor" skills. I would recommend it only as a screening instrument and suggest that it be used only to evaluate fine motor skills. It does tap certain conceptual abilities but the expression of those conceptual skills is entirely through writing or drawing. Scores from the instrument seem to be moderately reliable and to have some evidence for predicting academic performance. However, the lack of information about the normative sample makes it difficult to assess its suitability for use with diverse populations. It would certainly be more suitable for use in Australia than in the U.S. because of differences in the structure of educational programs and the age when children enter formal public school programs. If a school system outside of Australia elected to use Who Am I?, I would suggest developing a set of local norms and examining the relationship between the scores on the instrument and academic performance. One advantage is that the instrument is inexpensive and should be relatively easy and quick to administer. Nonetheless, I would not recommend its use, outside of Australia, as a screening instrument without the development of local norms.

General IQ (GIQ). Contributing to the GIQ is Verbal$_{Crystallized}$ Intelligence represented by the *Verbal IQ* and Visual$_{Fluid}$ Intelligence, which is represented by the *Visual IQ*. Verbal$_{Crystallized}$ ability is assessed with two subtests, *Verbal Analogies* and *Vocabulary*, whereas Visual$_{Fluid}$ ability is assessed with *Matrices* and *Diamonds*. Verbal Analogies (36 items) measures verbal abstraction and generalization of meanings and is dependent on the examinee's oral expression. Vocabulary (33 items) reflects knowledge of word meanings and the ability to understand and produce oral language. Matrices (44 items) requires minimal verbalization from the examinee and is a measure of ability to visualize the relationship between complex visual patterns and matrix reasoning. Diamonds (18 items) is a nonverbal timed construction task that requires the analysis and construction of part-whole relationships of figural stimuli using manipulatives. The test materials in a start-up kit include an easel for the Diamonds and Matrices items, the diamond-shaped manipulatives, an administration-technical manual, and 25 examiner forms. The WRIT is attractive and well constructed and produced. The examiner's form is logically designed and user friendly with identifying information and score summary boxes and a profile chart on the first page.

There are seven possible scores that describe performance on the WRIT: Verbal, Visual, and General IQs and scores for each of the 4 subtests. The WRIT scores are converted to standard scores ($M = 100$, $SD = 15$). Percentile ranks and confidence intervals at the 90% or 95% confidence level can also be obtained for the IQ scores. The administration and scoring chapters in the manual are exemplary. Both contain clear, concise instructions, good examples, and unambiguous criteria. The interpretation chapter is also superb. The authors discuss diagnoses of mental retardation and giftedness, the value of g in relation to outcomes such as scholastic achievement, job training, and work performance and its relationship with variables such as educational level and social correlates such as conduct difficulties and other adjustment problems.

Descriptive labels for the standard scores are provided based on SD units from the mean (*Very Superior* to *Very Low*). There is a good explanation of the proper use of confidence limits (the WRIT uses the 90% and 95% levels), and the authors

offer suggestions for the proper use of standard scores and confidence intervals. The Standard Errors of Measurement are also presented for IQ scores and subtests by four age categories (4–5, 6–12, 13–18, and 19 years and older). The authors discuss the meaning of statistically significant differences between the Verbal IQ and the Visual IQ with concomitant illustration of the use of base rate or prevalence information to further interpret these score differences. Tables are included in the manual for users to determine the level of significance between the scores (at the .05 and .01 levels) and base rates by age group and total sample.

The authors also present a fair discussion of the pros and cons of profile analysis and interpretation of subtest strengths and weakness. They recommend the same interpretive method for subtest analysis as they do for Verbal IQ and Visual IQ discrepancies (i.e., the determination of both statistical significance and prevalence estimates). The manual provides tables for these interpretive activities.

The manual includes tables for determining ability-achievement discrepancies between WRIT IQs and Wide Range Achievement Test—3 (WRAT 3, Wilkinson, 1993) achievement scores. The WRIT and the WRAT 3 were co-normed with one another. The ability-achievement discrepancy table estimates are based on univariate regression models. The authors give clear examples and suggestions for evaluating IQ-achievement differences and offer appropriate cautions about the possibility of Type I error if multiple comparisons are made. In addition, the authors include prevalence estimates for determining differences that would be rare in the population.

DEVELOPMENT. The WRIT structure emphasizes the constructs of crystallized and fluid abilities, which are strongly related to g and have been shown repeatedly in the literature to offer the most diagnostic and treatment validity of any ability beyond g. Fluid abilities may be more important to assess when the examinee has a hearing impairment, language disorder, English as a second language, or has had inadequate opportunity for formal academic training. Crystallized abilities may be more important to assess when the examinee has visual impairments, physical limitations, or certain forms of acute brain injury. The subtests are narrow ability contributors to Fluid and Crystallized domains.

Preliminary item development resulted in twice as many items for each subtest than are in the published version of the test. Items were subjected to Rasch scaling (Wright & Stone, 1979) to derive the final subtest item sets. Item and person separation indices for each subtest are excellent. Item separation reliabilities were .98 or higher, person separation reliabilities were from .76–.97 in the individual age groups, but ranged from .94–.97 for the total sample.

TECHNICAL.

Normative characteristics. The normative sample (N = 2,285) is excellent. Participants from 4–85 years were included in a national, stratified sample based on selected characteristics of the population based on the U.S. Census (U.S. Bureau of the Census, 1997). The sampling design controlled for age, gender, ethnicity, geographic residence, and parent (for minors) or participant level of educational achievement. This is a gold standard sample with most of the sample demographic variables matching the census data within a few percentage points. The standard score tables between the ages of 4 years, 0 months and 16 years, 11 months are separated into 3-month intervals for the subtests. One table is provided for ages 17 years, 0 months to 19 years, 11 months, whereas the ages 20 years to 84 years are presented in 5-year intervals. IQs percentiles, age equivalent scores, and confidence intervals transformations are in a separate table and are not separated by age.

RELIABILITY. A variety of reliability estimates are provided in addition to the Rasch item and person statistics discussed earlier. Alpha coefficients indicate the WRIT has excellent internal consistency; the averaged IQ alphas were .95, .94, and .92 for General, Verbal, and Visual IQs, respectively. The subtest alphas were slightly lower, as would be expected, but these are comparable to reliabilities found in other instruments that measure cognitive ability.

Test-retest reliability coefficients are presented for two age groups in the standardization sample, 4–18 years (n = 68), 19–85 years (n = 32) and for the total of both groups (n = 100). The time interval between administrations averaged 30.5 days. The coefficients (corrected for attenuation) for IQs for both age groups and the total sample were in the .90s (.90 to .97), and indicate the test is stable over short time periods and that the IQs are satisfactory for diagnostic purposes. The corrected *subtest* reli-ability coefficients were somewhat lower ranging from .70 to 1.0 so users should be more cautious about individual subtest stability.

Interscorer reliability was also examined for the Vocabulary and Verbal Analogies scales. For Vocabulary the intraclass correlation coefficient was .98 and for Verbal Analogies it was .99. This suggests there was little error associated with scoring these WRIT subtests in this sample (n = 40).

Validity. The WRIT internal structure was examined and supported with a series of factor analyses. Principal components analysis of the standardization data (N = 2,285) indicated the WRIT to be a strong measure of *g*. A one-factor solution accounted for 56% of the variance in WRIT performance with the subtest component loadings of .82, .80, .72, and .64 for Verbal Analogies, Vocabulary, Matrices, and Diamonds, respectively.

Principal axis factor analysis was used to examine a forced two-factor solution to determine whether the WRIT subtests would align as theoretically expected. Results gave empirical support for the WRIT's theoretical design; Vocabulary and Verbal Analogies loaded on a verbal factor at .81 and .68 and Diamonds and Matrices loaded on a visual factor at .59 and .44. The two-factor solution accounted for a total of 74% of the variance. Further evidence of the instrument's capacity to measure *g* was garnered by examination of the factor intercorrelations. The degree of association between the two factors was high (r = .75, r^2 = .56) indicating an ample amount of shared variance suggesting some redundant measurement, which could be attributed to a single higher-order *g* factor.

The two-factor solution was replicated for gender, ethnicity/race, educational level, and age level. Coefficients for factorial congruence were computed for the scales (Verbal, Visual) across groups based on the demographic stratum in the standardization sample (gender, ethnicity, educational, and age level). The congruence coefficients for gender, ethnicity, and educational level ranged from .997 to .957. A high degree of similarity is inferred when coefficients exceed .90. This is evidence that the WRIT measured equitably across groups based on the specified demographic variables. For the age analysis (4–6 years; 7–9 years; 10–12 years; 13–15 years, 16–19 years; 25, 35, and 45 years; 55, 65, and 75 years and higher) the congruence coefficients were .900 for the Verbal

a single principal component revealed high loadings from all four subtests, providing evidence of their relation to general intelligence. Extraction and rotation of two factors revealed two clear factors, one with loadings for the two Verbal tests and one for the two Visual tests. When separate factor analyses were performed for groups defined by gender, ethnicity, education level, or age, the coefficients of congruence across groups for corresponding factors were quite acceptable (i.e., >.95) for all comparisons except for comparisons across age groups. Next, confirmatory factor analytic procedures were applied to the data. These analyses showed acceptable fit of a two-factor model for the entire norming sample, with a .83 correlation between the Verbal and Visual factors. Multiple-group models were also fit, with groups defined separately by gender, ethnicity, education level, or age. With these more refined solutions, models with factor loadings constrained to invariance across groups showed adequate fit across all comparisons. Two multi-battery confirmatory factor analyses were performed, one including the WISC-III and the WRIT on a sample of children and adolescents, and the other including the WAIS-III and the WRIT on a sample of adults. Both analyses revealed very high correlations (above .98) for the general factors from the different batteries, and very high correlations (between .98 and .99) between the subgeneral factors (e.g., WISC-III Verbal with WRIT Verbal, WISC-III Performance with WRIT Visual). These extremely high correlations must be interpreted with caution, as they are correlations corrected for unreliability, but are substantial evidence for similarity of dimensions at the latent variable level.

Developmental age changes in WRIT subtest raw scores were consistent with predictions of fluid-crystallized theory: The Visual tests showed earlier and larger declines with age than did the Verbal tests. Item bias analyses were conducted in two ways: (a) subjectively, through inspection of item content by a panel of experts; and (b) objectively, by correlations of item difficulties across groups. Both approaches revealed miniscule levels of item bias.

WRIT IQ scores were also compared to those from the WISC-III and the WAIS-III with regard to their means and cross-battery correlations. In a sample of children, the WRIT and WISC-III yielded quite comparable mean scores for all three IQ indices, and the correlations between corresponding IQ scores were fairly high: .90 for General IQ, .85 for Verbal IQ, and .78 for Visual IQ. In a sample of adults, the WRIT gave somewhat lower scores (between 3 and 5 points lower) than comparable scales from the WAIS-III, but the correlations between corresponding IQ scores were quite high: .91 for General IQ, .90 for Verbal IQ, and .85 for Visual IQ.

When assessing persons at young ages (e.g., below the age of 8 years), the WRIT may have insufficient floor and poor item gradient to allow ready use for determining mental retardation. But, at all other ages, the WRIT appears to have sufficient floors and ceilings for discrimination at both the low and high ends of the dimension of general intelligence.

COMMENTARY. The WRIT is a fairly solid battery of ability tests designed to yield Verbal, Visual, and General IQ scores that are similar in nature to the corresponding scores from the WISC and WAIS and to key constructs within hierarchical theories of the structure of mental abilities. Moreover, the relatively high correlations between corresponding scores from the WRIT and the WISC and WAIS demonstrate that the batteries provide quite similar information regarding individual differences on the major dimensions of intelligence.

The principal advantage of the WRIT over the WISC or WAIS is efficiency of administration. Because the WRIT can be administered in less than 30 minutes, obtaining scores from the WRIT consumes much less time and effort, while still yielding scores with sufficient quality for many research and applied uses.

The only major drawback of the WRIT is the restricted set of subtests and the resulting somewhat low correlations with scores from other batteries. Although correlations in the range from .78 to .90 are minimally adequate, higher levels of correlation would provide greater assurance that scores across instruments are essentially interchangeable. On the other hand, the correlations obtained with the WRIT are impressively large when one considers the relatively short nature of the test battery.

SUMMARY. The WRIT is a short ability battery that can be administered and scored in an efficient manner and that can be used across a very wide age range. The scores derived from the WRIT have strong psychometric properties and are quite highly correlated with comparable scores from the WISC and the WAIS. With some limitations, the WRIT can be used in high stakes testing situations, such as determining whether a person has mental retardation. Moreover, if one wished to obtain Verbal/Crystallized, Visual/Fluid, or General IQ scores for research or many applied uses, the WRIT is an easily administered test that yields scores that are comparable to those obtained using the WISC or WAIS. For its intended uses, the WRIT is a clear and valuable alternative to the more complex and time-consuming WISC and WAIS batteries.

[280]
Wisconsin Card Sorting Test—64 Card Version.

Purpose: "Developed as a measure of abstracted reasoning ability and ability to shift cognitive set."
Population: Ages 6.5–89.
Publication Dates: 1981–2000.
Acronym: WCST-64.
Scores, 10: Total Number Correct, Total Number of Errors, Perseverative Responses, Perseverative Errors, Nonperseverative Errors, Conceptual Level Responses, Number of Categories Completed, Trials to Complete First Category, Failure to Maintain Set, Learning to Learn.
Administration: Individual.
Price Data: Available from publisher for introductory kit including 50 record booklets, manual (2000, 246 pages), and card deck.
Time: Untimed.
Comments: Abbreviated form of the standard 128-card version of the Wisconsin Card Sorting Test (T6:2725).
Authors: Susan K. Kongs, Laetitia L. Thompson, Grant L. Iverson, and Robert K. Heaton.
Publisher: Psychological Assessment Resources, Inc.
Cross References: For information on the Wisconsin Card Sorting Test, Revised and Expanded, see T5:2892 (309 references) and T4:2967 (96 references); for reviews by Byron Egeland and Robert P. Markley of an earlier edition, see 9:1372 (11 references).

Review of the Wisconsin Card Sorting Test—64 Card Version by MICHAEL S. TREVISAN, Associate Professor, Department of Educational Leadership & Counseling Psychology, Washington State University, Pullman, WA:

DESCRIPTION. The Wisconsin Card Sorting Test—64 Card Version (WCST-64) is a shortened version of the well-regarded 128-card Wisconsin Card Sorting Test (WCST; 14:420). The task requirements for the WCST-64 are the same as those used in the WCST, and the normative and technical features of the WCST-64 are derived from the same sample as that of the WCST. Thus, the authors suggest that a good deal of what is known about the WCST can be applied to the WCST-64. In this regard, this review of the WCST-64 will also include descriptions of various features of the WCST, particularly as it bears on the appraisal of the new WCST-64.

According to the authors, the rationale for the shortened version of the WCST stems from the need for a cost effective, efficient appraisal of executive functioning. Other shorter versions of the WCST exist but none maintain the same task requirements as the original WCST. Thus, the authors are optimistic about the viability of the WCST-64. In point of fact, the major difference between the WCST-64 and the WCST is that the WCST-64 employs only one set of 64 matching cards whereas the WCST employs two sets.

DEVELOPMENT. The WCST and, therefore, the WCST-64 is designed as an assessment of executive functioning, "requiring the ability to develop and maintain an appropriate problem-solving strategy across changing stimulus conditions in order to achieve a future goal" (professional manual, p. 1). The WCST-64 employs four stimulus cards and 64 response cards with varying shapes, forms, and colors. Respondents are asked to match the 64 response cards with the stimulus cards and told only whether or not the match is correct. A unique feature of this assessment is the appraisal of perseveration. Indicators of perseveration are provided through the Percent Perseverative Response Score and the Percent Perseverative Errors Score.

Tests in Print V (Murphy, Impara, & Plake, 1999) published in 1999 by the Buros Institute of Mental Measurements, lists over 300 studies which investigated various features and applications of the WCST. Thus, there is an extensive literature base for this instrument. The WCST may, in fact, be one of the most studied mental measurements to date. There is evidence that the WCST is sensitive to patients with frontal lobe lesions, and is widely regarded as a test for this purpose (Clark, 2001). The literature also suggests a variety of other forms of brain dysfunction can be identified with the WCST across a variety of groups.

The authors of the WCST-64 acknowledge that given its recent addition to the field, few

Price Data: $601 per Tests of Cognitive Abilities Battery including Cognitive Standard and Extended test books, examiner's manual, audio cassette, 25 test records, 25 response booklets, 5 Brief Intellectual ability Test Records, CompuScore® and Profiles Program version 1.1b (Windows and Macintosh), technical manual, and scoring guides; $679.50 per Tests of Cognitive Abilities Battery with leather carrying case; $58 per 25 Cognitive test records and subject response booklets; $26.50 per 25 Brief Intellectual Ability Test Records.

Time: Approximately (5) minutes per test; (35–45) minutes per Standard Battery; (90–115) minutes per Extended Battery.

Cross References: See T5:2901 (140 references); for reviews by Jack A. Cummings and by Steven W. Lee and Elaine Flory Stefany of the 1991 edition, see 12:415 (56 references); see also T4:2973 (90 references); for reviews by Jack A. Cummings and Alan S. Kaufman of the 1977 edition, see 9:1387 (6 references); see also T3:2639 (3 references).

Review of the Woodcock-Johnson® III by GREGORY J. CIZEK, Professor of Educational Measurement and Evaluation, University of North Carolina—Chapel Hill, Chapel Hill, NC:

DESCRIPTION. The Woodcock-Johnson III (WJ III) is an updated version of its predecessor, the Woodcock-Johnson Psycho-Educational Battery—Revised (WJ-R), published in 1989. The WJ III is a comprehensive, norm-referenced, individually administered assessment of those cognitive abilities, skills, and academic knowledge most recognized as comprising human intelligence and routinely encountered in school and other settings. The WJ III tests are appropriate for administration to children as young as 2 years of age and to adults to age 90.

The WJ III actually consists of two separate batteries. One battery, the WJ III Test of Cognitive Abilities (WJ III COG) is designed to measure general and specific cognitive functions. The apparent primary purpose of the other battery, the WJ III Tests of Achievement (WJ III ACH) is "to determine and describe the present status of an individual's academic strengths and weaknesses" (Mather & Woodcock, 2001, p. 6). When administered in tandem, the batteries permit users to investigate over/underachievement and to examine patterns of intraindividual discrepancies among cognitive or achievement areas.

The batteries of the WJ III COG and WJ III ACH are further classified as standard or extended. The single form of the standard WJ III COG battery comprises 10 subtests (e.g., Verbal Comprehension, Spatial Relations, Concept Formation, Auditory Working Memory, and so on); the extended WJ III COG adds 10 additional subtests (e.g., Retrieval Fluency, Picture Recognition, Auditory Attention, Decision Speed). The standard and extended versions of the WJ III ACH are available as parallel Forms A and B. The Standard WJ III ACH comprises 12 subtests (e.g., Reading Fluency, Math Fluency, Spelling) and a Handwriting Legibility scale is also available. The extended achievement battery supplements the standard battery with 10 additional tests (e.g., Word Attack, Reading Vocabulary, Editing, Academic Knowledge). Two beneficial results of these configurations lie in the facts that the user can administer only selected subtests (which reduces unnecessary testing) or, by administering the extended batteries, users can take advantage of the additional information yielded by the greater number and breadth of cluster scores provided.

The materials for the WJ III include folding, easel-type binders that permit stimulus materials to be viewed easily by examinees, while also affording a barrier so that examinees cannot observe the examiner's recording and scoring of responses or written comments. There are separate binders for the WJ III ACH and WJ III COG. Standard and extended batteries for each test are also in separate binders. Audio tapes are included for subtests requiring standardized presentation of oral material.

In addition to raw scores, virtually any derived score that a user could want from a norm-referenced test is provided as part of the WJ III scoring system. These scores include grade and age equivalents, percentile ranks, discrepancy scores, and scores reported on various scales developed for the WJ III. In addition, the WJ III COG provides two indices of general cognitive functioning (i.e., intelligence) by means of the General Intellectual Ability (GIA) score and the Brief Intellectual Ability (BIA) score. The BIA may be especially of interest to practitioners who desire to obtain a highly reliable (median reliability of .95 across ages 5–19) measure of intelligence in very short testing time (the BIA is obtained via administration of only three of the WJ III subtests). Such contexts would include reevaluations of students with individualized educational plans, or research contexts in which the amount of time participants can devote to testing is limited.

Unlike many similar tests, the WJ III ACH includes two particularly useful scores for upper-level and post-secondary school students: the basic interpersonal communication skill (BICS) scores, and the cognitive-academic language proficiency (CALP) score. These scores are helpful for determining the ability of nonnative speakers of English to function in informal settings and academic settings (e.g., college lectures), respectively.

The WJ III tests may be hand scored, although interpretation of an examinee's performance is made easier if the WJ III software, Compuscore, is used. In addition to producing standard reports, the software allows the user to make modifications. For example, summary narratives of student performance can be printed in either English or Spanish; users can select the size of standard score confidence bands that are reported; and discrepancy cut-score criteria can be changed.

DEVELOPMENT. Several significant changes in the WJ III distinguish it from the WJ-R. Perhaps the most important developmental element is that the batteries have been renormed on a large, representative sample of participants ranging from preschoolers to adults. Of note is that the cognitive and achievement batteries were normed on the same sample. This co-norming has the potential to offer users greater confidence when interpreting discrepancies between examinees' ability and achievement scores because the inherent inaccuracies introduced by sampling variation in independently normed ability and achievement measures are eliminated.

Substantive additions to the WJ III have also been made. For example, to the WJ III COG, eight new subtests have been added and one subtest previously in the cognitive battery (Oral Language) has been moved to the achievement battery. In addition, grade norms have been extended to span graduate-level college students, and early development items have been added to some subtests. To the WJ III ACH, seven new subtests have been added; three subtests from the WJ-R (Science, Social Studies, and Humanities) have been collapsed into one subtest called Academic Knowledge; and items using an analogy format have been introduced into the Reading Vocabulary subtest. Some changes are also common to both the WJ III COG and the WJ III ACH. These include new clusterings of subtests to increase the diagnostic utility of the cluster scores

and attention to Spanish language examinees by including examples of appropriate key responses in Spanish. The computerized scoring and reporting system also permits the user to produce reports in English or Spanish.

Abundant documentation for both the cognitive and achievement batteries is provided in a single Technical manual (McGrew & Woodcock, 2001). Separate Examiner's Manual and Examiner Training Workbooks accompany the cognitive and achievement batteries. The materials also include booklets for examiners to record responses, examinee response booklets for tests requiring test takers to record written responses, and hand-scoring overlays.

Overall, the technical and examiner's manuals provide complete documentation regarding the theoretical grounding, developmental procedures, reliability and validity evidence, administration and scoring procedures, and interpretive guides and cautions. A few elements included in the documentation for the WJ III warrant special note. First, it is apparent that the *Standards for Educational and Psychological Testing* (hereafter, *Standards*, AERA/APA/NCME, 1999) actually informed the current revision of the WJ III. The *Standards* are referenced throughout the manuals at relevant junctures and, more importantly, appear to have served as foundational organizing guidelines throughout the development of the batteries, in the gathering of reliability and validity evidence, and in the content of supporting documentation. Tables sprinkled throughout the manuals illustrate specific references to the *Standards* and provide concise definitions of key technical terms.

Second, the supporting documentation for the WJ III demonstrates substantial attention to accuracy and test fairness. Qualifications for examiners are spelled out in detail; training materials, examiner checklists, and practice exercises for examiners are included to ensure that those who administer the WJ III are appropriately trained. Cautions are spelled out regarding confidentiality of test materials and examinee results. A "Test Session Observation Checklist" is provided as the cover of the examiner's recording booklet which requires, for each test administration, that the examiner evaluate the test-taker's levels of cooperation, self-confidence, attention, concentration, and so on. Examiners are also directed to respond to the question, "Do you have any reason to believe this testing session may not represent a fair sample of the subject's abilities?" (Achievement manual, p. 31) and to document any hypotheses for why the test-taker's performance may not be an accurate reflection. Finally, the manuals accompanying the WJ III devote substantial treatment (approximately 13 pages) to appropriate test accommodations, including special considerations for very young children, English language learners, special needs students, and individuals with hearing, vision, or other physical impairments.

TECHNICAL. The foundation of the WJ III rests on theoretical and empirical work on the structure of human cognitive functioning conducted over the past several decades. Specifically, the WJ III is aligned with a stratified model of intellectual abilities defined and refined by Cattell, Horn, and Carroll. This perspective is referred to as the CHC theory of cognitive abilities; support for the CHC perspective relies heavily on the scores of factor-analytic studies conducted to test and refine the theory. In essence, CHC theory posits a single general factor (General Intelligence), which subsumes eight broad categories of abilities (called Stratum II abilities, such as Fluid Intelligence, General Memory and Learning, and Processing Speed), which, in turn, are derived from 69 specific or "narrow abilities" (called Stratum I abilities, such as Lexical Knowledge, Closure Speed, Musical Discrimination, Associative Memory, and Mental-Comparison Speed). An abundance of empirical support for this structure exists—much of it is referenced or described in the technical manual—and it is clear that the CHC theoretical model suffused the conceptualization and revisions of the WJ III.

However, limited information is provided in the WJ III technical manual regarding precisely how the CHC model guided practical activities such as item development for the cognitive battery. Specific information is also skimpy regarding item development for the achievement battery, although the manual indicates that more detailed information is available in other sources. Nonetheless, the WJ III manuals do describe some of the technical aspects involved in item selection. One-parameter item response theory calibrations were used and "items retained [for the final versions of the WJ III] had to fit the Rasch model as well as other criteria" (McGrew & Woodcock, 2001, p. 14) although the precise fit statistic limits are not stated, nor is a complete list of the other

criteria provided. One important criterion mentioned in the manual is that forms of the WJ III were built to achieve a uniform average difference in item difficulty along the entire WJ III score scale. Combined with the preferential inclusion of items with similar fit statistics, this procedure helped yield fairly uniform standard errors of measurement along the score scale.

The norming of the WJ III is a centerpiece of the technical revisions. As stated previously, the fact that the norm group took both the WJ III COG and WJ III ACH provides distinct technical advantages. The cognitive and achievement components of the WJ III were co-normed using a sample of 8,818 participants consisting of 1,143 preschool-aged children, 4,783 students in kindergarten through 12th grade, and 1,843 adult participants. The norm group was obtained via a three-stage sampling procedure (communities, schools within communities, students within schools). For school-aged children, the norm group included public, private, and home-schooled students. The group also included students with disabilities "to the extent that they were included at least part-time in regular classes" (McGrew & Woodcock, 2001, p. 25). English language learners were also included if they had one year or more of experience in regular English-speaking classes. Continuous-year norming was employed; age-based norms are provided in 1-month intervals for children aged 24 months to 19 years and in 1-year intervals for adults from age 20 to 90 and above.

Overall, the descriptions of the norming sample provided in the technical manual support the conclusion that the norm group is adequately representative of the North American population. The only weakness in the sample may be in the adult age range. For example, college-aged participants were recruited via notices posted on campus bulletin boards and reduced demographic information is presented for this subgroup; the procedures for recruiting and selecting adult participants are not described in adequate detail to permit evaluation of the representativeness of the sample, although adequate demographic information on the adult sample is presented.

Internal consistency reliability estimates for the WJ III subtests and clusters were calculated in two ways. For speeded tests, reliability estimates were calculated using a Rasch approach in which estimated error scores for each examinee in the norming sample were obtained; the variance of those error scores and the total observed variance were then used to compute a reliability estimate. For tests that were not speeded, traditional split-half reliabilities were calculated. Appendices to the technical manual present all of the information that the AERA/APA/NCME (1999) *Standards* suggest is appropriate, including means, standard deviations, and sample sizes on which the reliability coefficients were computed, along with the respective reliability estimates and standard errors of measurement.

Because of the sheer number of tests, composite scores, and age groupings for which separate reliability estimates are reported, it is practical to provide only an overall evaluation of the reliability evidence for the WJ III in this review. In general, however, internal consistency reliability estimates appear to be uniformly high, most often with magnitudes in the .80s and .90s for individual tests and in the .90s for clusters. Users interested in the reliability estimate for any specific test or cluster should consult the technical manual.

Although complete information for all tests was not presented in the technical manual, stability reliability was also estimated for selected tests from the WJ III ACH and WJ III COG. In one study, test-retest reliabilities were calculated for three time intervals; less than 1 year, 1 to 2 years, and 3 to 10 years. Median reliabilities mostly ranged from the .70s to the .90s. A second stability study was conducted using a 1-year interval; the test-retest reliabilities from this study are typically in the .80s and .90s. Very high (upper .90s) interrater correlations are also reported for the three WJ III tests (Writing Sample, Writing Fluency, Handwriting) that require subjective ratings of examinees' responses according to a rubric provided. Finally, the information provided on the equivalence of the two forms available for the WJ III ACH (Form A, Form B) suggests that the forms can be used interchangeably.

The technical manual includes a section on validity evidence organized according to the framework used in the AERA/APA/NCME (1999) *Standards*. The vast majority of the information bears on the validity of the scores from the WJ III COG, with comparatively less information for the WJ III ACH. The section does argue for a linkage between WJ III ACH tests and school curricular areas, though specific evidence of content validity is not provided. A section called "Evidence-Based on Test Content" (technical manual, p. 50) contains information that demonstrates the clear attempt to build the WJ III COG so that it addresses the general and specific abilities embodied in the CHC model that provides the empirical/theoretical grounding of the test.

Support for the internal structure of the WJ III was obtained via fundamental correlational analysis and confirmatory factory analyses. The correlational evidence provides support for the validity of WJ III scores in that the expected pattern of relationships among tests was observed; that is, test hypothesized to measure more similar characteristics correlated more strongly among themselves than did tests hypothesized to measure more dissimilar constructs. One example of these patterns described in the technical manual (p. 59) is observed in the Verbal Comprehension, General Information, Picture Vocabulary, and Academic Knowledge tests, which have intercorrelations of .70 to .80. As would be hypothesized by CHC theory, those same tests yield substantially weaker correlations when compared to tests such as Spatial Relations and Picture Recognition (.20 to .40). Other validation procedures for both the WJ III COG and WJ III ACH comprised correlational studies of the relationship between scores on those tests and other measures.

Fairly extensive confirmatory factor analyses also provide validity evidence for the WJ III. The model implied by CHC theory is fully presented in graphic form (see McGrew & Woodcock, 2001, pp. 62–63). That model was compared to six alternative models, including a no-factor model, a single factor (*g*) model, and models implied by four other commonly used tests (the Wechsler Adult Intelligence Scale—Third Edition, the Stanford-Binet Intelligence Scale—Fourth Edition, the Kaufman Adolescent and Adult Intelligence Scale, and the Das-Naglieri Cognitive Assessment System). A comparison of the goodness-of-fit of each model to data from the WJ III COG revealed that the CHC model demonstrated the closest alignment to the hypothesized structure.

Finally, the technical manual indicates that "bias and sensitivity reviews were conducted" (p. 52) to identify potentially differentially functioning items for females, individuals with disabilities, and cultural and linguistic minorities. Although specific details on the bias and sensitivity procedures were not provided, the technical manual states that items identified as potentially biased were revised or eliminated during test development.

COMMENTS AND SUMMARY. Overall, the WJ III provides a model for other norm-referenced, individual ability/achievement batteries to emulate. The careful attention to relevant professional standards for development and provision of reliability and validity evidence is laudatory. As a result, the WJ III appears to be justified in making the claim that "the tests, clusters, factors, and scales of the WJ III provide more precise measures and a wider breadth of coverage of human cognitive abilities than are found in any other system of psychological and educational assessment" (McGrew & Woodcock, 2001, p. 2).

Room for improvement exists, of course. For example, the technical manual and examiner's manuals would benefit from inclusion of examples of Compuscore output and interpretive aids. Also, though the WJ III claims to be highly diagnostically useful, specific examples of diagnostic indications paired with appropriate intervention recommendations would probably be helpful for many users. Finally, as this review (and previous reviews) have noted, the comparatively skimpy treatment of content validity evidence for the WJ III ACH should be strengthened.

Previous reviews have also concluded that the strengths of the Woodcock-Johnson ability and achievement tests outweigh their weaknesses. In separate reviews of the previous version of the battery, Cummings commented that the WJ-R was "a significant contribution to norm-reference psycho-educational assessment" (1995, p. 1115); a review by Lee and Stefany observed that the "psychometric properties [of the WJ-R] are exceptional" and concluded that the battery represented "an outstanding contribution to the field of cognitive and achievement testing" (1995, p. 1117). Clearly, these conclusions are only strengthened by the revisions, renorming, and additional reliability and validity evidence gathering that has been undertaken in support of the WJ III. Of the batteries available to users such as school psychologists and others who require individual norm-referenced ability and achievement measurement, the WJ III is clearly a superior instrument.

REVIEWER'S REFERENCES

American Educational Research Association, American Psychological Association, & National Council on Measurement in Education. (1999). *Standards for educational and psychological testing.* Washington, DC: American Educational Research Association.

Cummings, J. A. (1995). [Review of the Woodcock-Johnson Psycho-Educational Battery—Revised.] In J. C. Conoley & J. C. Impara (Eds.), *The twelfth mental measurements yearbook* (pp. 1113–1116). Lincoln, NE: Buros Institute of Mental Measurements.

Lee, S. W., & Stefany, E. F. (1995). [Review of the Woodcock-Johnson Psycho-Educational Battery—Revised.] In J. C. Conoley & J. C. Impara (Eds.), *The twelfth mental measurements yearbook* (pp. 1116–1117). Lincoln, NE: Buros Institute of Mental Measurements.

Mather, N., & Woodcock, R. J. (2001). *Examiner's manual: Woodcock-Johnson III Tests of Achievement.* Itasca, IL: Riverside.

McGrew, K. S., & Woodcock, R. J. (2001). *Technical manual: Woodcock-Johnson III.* Itasca, IL: Riverside.

Review of the Woodcock-Johnson® III by JONATHAN SANDOVAL, *Professor of Education, University of California, Davis, CA:*

The Woodcock-Johnson III (WJ III) is a battery of individually administered tests for measuring intellectual abilities and academic achievement. It is the revision of what was called a Psycho-Educational Battery in previous incarnations, but this descriptor has been omitted from the third edition.

DESCRIPTION. Although normed on the same sample, this battery can be considered two separate instruments: The Woodcock-Johnson III Tests of Cognitive Abilities (WJ III COG) and the Woodcock-Johnson III Test of Achievement (WJ III ACH), containing 20 and 22 tests respectively. Further, both sets of tests can be subdivided into a Standard Battery of 10 cognitive tests and 12 achievement tests, and Extended Batteries of all the Cognitive or Achievement tests. The achievement tests have two forms available. Included with the writing sample test on the WJ III ACH, besides a holistic score, are a Handwriting Legibility Scale and a Writing Evaluation Scale. The battery was standardized on a sample from age 2 to 90; however, the test is most applicable to a school-aged population centered around age 10.

The tests in this battery are relatively easy to administer, because almost the entire battery uses an easel format. The examiner reads the directions from a stand-up booklet and flips pages containing the test items on the side facing the examinee. Ten of the tests are administered from a prerecorded tape, and the examiner must supply an appropriate cassette playback machine with headphones. Eleven tests require the use of a response booklet. Most of the tests have liberal time limits, but five of the Cognitive Tests and three Achievement tests are strictly timed, because they measure speed and fluency.

The most difficult task in administration is beginning the test to establish a "floor" or basal level of performance, and ending the test at an appropriate "ceiling" where the examinee is unlikely to correctly answer more questions. Appropriate guidance is supplied, and seasoned examiners will be familiar with this process. The authors assert that the test may be administered by those with specific training in administration and scoring, but should only be interpreted by professionals with graduate level training in relevant areas.

Scoring guidelines for each item are included in the administration easel and on the record form. On some tests, bilingual participants may have a correct response given in a language other than English scored as correct. Unfortunately, examiners may not recognize the correctness of the response, unless they, or someone else, speaks the child's dialect. Although recommended by the authors, the practicality and validity of this procedure and other recommended testing accommodations for participants with handicaps have not been established. Nevertheless, the inclusion of information on special accommodations is welcome as a start. Totals from the record form must be entered into a provided software program, which outputs a large number of norm-referenced scores, discrepancy scores, and interpretations.

DEVELOPMENT. The WJ III is the successor to the Woodcock-Johnson Psycho-Educational Battery—Revised (Woodcock & Johnson, 1989) and the original Battery (Woodcock & Johnson, 1977). Items and formats of the tests are related to other tests developed by the first author. It is appropriate to re-norm a test every decade as the authors have done.

The 20 WJ III COG tests were devised to provide measures consistent with the Cattell-Horn and Carroll (CHC) conceptualization of cognitive abilities based on the study of factor analyses of numerous mental tests (Carroll, 1993; Horn & Noll, 1997. The intent is to have a robust measure of a general factor (General Intellectual Ability or GIA), measures of the broad abilities or cognitive performance clusters (Verbal Ability, Thinking Ability, and Cognitive Efficiency), and factor cluster scores of eight more narrow abilities. In addition, the battery yields what the authors term "clinically useful clusters" (manual, p. 21), such as Phonemic Awareness and Executive Processes, which are based on empirical findings in the literature on reading development and neuropsychology. Some of these clinical clusters use information from the WJ III ACH. Also available for screening is a Brief Intellectual Ability score based on the average of three COG tests.

The 22 WJ III ACH tests were also intended to measure CHC factors or clusters as well as traditional curriculum areas of interest to schools, namely Reading, Oral Language, Writing, Mathematics, and Academic Knowledge in science, social studies, and the humanities. Special clusters are also available to assess Academic Skills in reading, mathematics, and spelling, Academic Fluency, and Academic Applications. Other clusters are Phoneme/Grapheme Knowledge and Total Achievement.

Items for the test were derived from previous versions of the battery and from research instruments. Eight new tests assessing information processing were added to the WJ III COG and seven new tests were added to the WJ III ACH. Item selection and calibration were based on the use of the Rasch single-parameter logistic test model. The use of these scaling techniques has resulted in relatively brief tests consisting of items covering a wide range of ability. The items are presented in an attractive format with simple but clear graphic style.

TECHNICAL. The battery was normed from 1996 to 1999 on a large sample of 8,818 individuals who matched the demographics of the U.S. relative to geographic region, community size, gender, race, Hispanic origin, and type of school or college. For adults, representativeness was also based on educational level, employment status, and occupational level. To the extent that the obtained sample did not match the target sample in a category, the test scores were weighted to achieve a match to the population. No weights were extreme. The data for adults are grouped by decade, and there are fewer cases for adults than for children, except for those of college age. The norms by level of college—2-year college and 4-year college/university—are unusual and useful. Scores produced by the test are based on an individual's age in months. The standardization seems very well done.

The procedure for estimating scores for the extremes of ability and age are based on a scaling procedure using linear and area transformations, rather than based on actual cases. The range of scores at extreme ages and ability levels seems large, as great as a standard score of 300 and as low as 6. These resulting standard scores will be different from those found on other cognitive tests, where the range of standard scores is narrower.

As would be expected from the Rasch scaling, the battery has good reliability. Reliability was determined by the split-half method for most of the tests, and by Rasch analysis procedures for speeded tests and for tests with multiple-point scores. Median split-half coefficients for the tests are above .80 for 38 of the tests, and above .90 for 11. The lowest reliabilities on the WJ III COG are found on Picture Recognition, Planning, and Pair Cancellation, with a few reliabilities as low as .61 for some age groups. Except for a few tests at the extreme ages, none of the WJ III ACH reliabilities fall below .70. One-day test-retest reliabilities for the speeded tests ranged from .69 to .96, with the means generally indicating improved performance with practice. Test-retest reliabilities of the nonspeeded tests over a year or more in time are similarly high, although the means for these data are not reported. Interrater reliabilities for the writing test evaluations based on correlations of scores are reported to be in the high .90s. Data are presented in the manual supporting the equivalence of Forms A and B of the WJ III ACH tests.

The reliabilities of the cluster scores are almost all in the .90s. Some exceptions are Visual-Spatial Thinking (median = .81) and Oral Expression (.85). GIA has the highest median reliability across ages (.97 Standard Battery, .98 Extended Battery) along with total achievement cluster score (.98). These reliabilities are sufficiently high to justify the creation of discrepancy scores and to make inferences about individual test takers.

The technical manual presents a considerable amount of evidence supporting the validity of scores from the test, noting that the earlier versions of the battery have also been shown to have validity. Test content on the WJ III COG has emerged from previous versions, is similar to the content found on other well-established cognitive measures, or is based on sound experimental instruments. The WJ III ACH content is similar to other achievement tests in subject areas and to established practice in schools. Growth curves of cluster scores in the technical manual illustrate expected developmental progressions, with steep growth from age 5 to 25, with a decline thereafter.

The most extensively presented data focus on validity evidence from confirmatory factor analyses of test scores from participants age 6 to adult. These analyses show that the seven-factor CHC cognitive model is more closely related to the observed internal structure than six other models derived from other commonly used cognitive batteries. The internal correlations of the entire battery are consistent with relations between areas of achievement and between areas of achievement and ability clusters. Factor studies of subjects younger than 6 are not reported. Nevertheless, the same CHC model is applied to this age group.

The authors report reasonably high correlations between cognitive scores and other popular individual tests of intellectual ability obtained from several studies. WJ III GCA correlates in the .70s with other total scores, although the clusters of Visual-Spatial Thinking, Auditory Processing, Phonemic Awareness, and Processing Speed do not correlate very highly with measures on other tests, and suggest that these are areas where the test measures different abilities than those measured by other tests. In general, scores on the WJIII COG are lower that the scores obtained on other measures such as the Wechsler Intelligence Scale for Children—Third Edition.

Scores on the WJ III ACH measures typically correlate in the range .50 to .80 with corresponding tests on the Kaufman Test of Educational Achievement and the Wechsler Individual Achievement Test. Some of the achievement tests, such as Academic Knowledge, have no counterparts on the other tests, and some correlations are surprisingly low, such as the .31 correlation between Written Expression on the WJ III and Written Expression on the Wechsler Individual Achievement Test. Nevertheless, the battery has good concurrent validity overall.

The cognitive clusters intended to predict achievement do correlate with the achievement clusters yielding correlations in the .70 range. These correlations are higher than those found between ability scores and achievement scores on many other cognitive measures suggesting excellent predictive validity.

Validity evidence also comes from the performance of known groups such as children with ADHD. The scores of these identified participants follow expected patterns. However, performances of children identified as gifted and as mentally retarded are missing from the manual. Given the way the test is used, the absence of these data is disappointing.

Data on test fairness are also reported in the technical manual. In addition to having experts review the items for sensitive and culturally biased items, differential item functioning was assessed across gender, ethnic, and racial groups. Factor analysis results suggest the same factors are being measured across groups. Politically sensitive racial group differences in mean performance have not been reported.

Scoring software produces the normative scores for the test. There is no way to score the test by hand, leaving the user to depend on the software. Norms may be obtained based on age, grade, or level of college. The software is easy to use and provides a number of options for reporting scores: Age equivalents, grade equivalents, percentiles, standard scores, Rasch ability scores (W scores). Coupled with cluster scores and discrepancy scores based on predicted ability and achievement, and on intra-ability and intra-individual differences, an enormous amount of information is available from the test. Results from the software can be exported directly to a word processing program.

COMMENTARY. The test materials, examiner manuals, training materials, and software are all state of the art. The technical manual is one of the most complete available and is largely in compliance with the latest Standards for Educational and Psychological Testing (AERA, APA, & NCME, 1999). Even more data on test validity would be welcome, however. The individual tests in the battery are efficient in identifying an ability level and the cluster scores and overall scores have good reliability. The battery yields results consistent with current factor theories of ability. The software reduces clerical errors and produces a wealth of information. Many options are open to the test user to select tests to administer and scores to analyze.

The authors compare their battery to a tool chest, and suggest that test users not use any subset of the tests routinely, but rather select tests and scores for particular diagnostic purposes. Although they have supplied an excellent tool kit, sharp or complex tools may be dangerous in the hands of those lacking the knowledge, training, and talent to use them. For the battery to be used intelligently, tests users will need advanced training. Many users will be overwhelmed with the information the battery produces, and will not be able to use the battery to the fullest extent possible. In addition, many of the cluster scores overlap in the tests they draw from, leading the unwary to draw incorrect inferences.

Although the test measures what it measures very well, it may not cover some abilities as efficiently as other cognitive measures. Research will eventually demonstrate how efficiently these tests measure narrow abilities, compared to other tests. In addition, other achievement measures may yield equally useful information in a shorter period of testing time.

One development that will need to be followed by test users is the implementation of new curriculum standards in the schools. As curriculum is shifted to earlier grades, the achievement and grade level norms may need to be interpreted with caution.

Dependence on the software makes it difficult to get a sense of the norms, particularly at the extremes. Past errors in the software have been corrected, but there remains a difficulty in the scoring of Reading Fluency, where skipped items should not be counted as errors, yet were counted as errors in the norm development process. This test should not be considered valid for those children who elect to skip items frequently.

Other cognitive measures may be used with more confidence with preschool children. The skipping problem mentioned above will be a problem for young children. The lack of validity evidence for this age group, and the result of normalizing the distribution at the young ages and extremes of ability, make inferences about the scores of young children dangerous. For these reasons, the test should be used with great caution with preschool children.

SUMMARY. The WJ III must be considered the premier battery for measuring both the cognitive abilities and school achievement of school-aged children and young adults. The test has been well standardized and thoughtfully developed. The evidence presented in the manual permits the test to be used with confidence in place of other individual measures of intellectual ability and achievement for the school-aged population, although the scores may not be always equivalent to other measures. Time will provide us with more information about the diagnostic utility of the reported discrepancy and cluster scores, but they hold good promise for educational planning, neuropsychological assessment, forensic evaluation, and other uses.

REVIEWER'S REFERENCES

American Educational Research Association, American Psychological Association, & National Council on Measurement in Education. (1999). Standards for educational and psychological testing. Washington, DC: American Educational Research Association.
Carroll, J. B. (1993). Human cognitive abilities: A survey of factor-analytic studies. New York: Cambridge University Press.
Horn, J. L., & Noll, J. (1997). Human cognitive capabilities: Gf-Gc theory. In D. P. Flanagan, J. L. Genshaft, & P. L. Harrison (Eds.), Contemporary intellectual assessment: Theories, tests and issues (pp. 53–91). New York: Guilford Press.

stricted to tertiary graduates with some under-standing of models and procedures underlying the measurement and measurementof human charac-teristics" (p. 2).

The abilities items are scored right or wrong, whereas the self-description items are condensed into two categories such as true-untrue, impor-tant-unimportant, or easy-difficult. The manual calls for a scorer to transcribe these dichotomized item responses onto a separate answer sheet, pref-erably using a highlighter pen. The answer keys are overlaid in turn on the answer sheet; keyed answers are summed to produce raw scores, which are entered on a separate individual summary form for each examinee. The 19 raw scores are trans-formed into 19 10-point scale scores and then summed and transformed into 6 10-point area scores. (Each scale or area score ranges from 0 to 10, with the number 1 omitted.) An overall sum-mary score may also be calculated. The scores are not entirely independent of one another: 18 items are used in two different scales and 3 are used in three scales. The 12-item Self-image scale in-cludes 5 items that also form part of the 13-item Need for Status scale. The number of items used in the scales ranges from 7 to 13.

A group summary form is also included for use in working with or studying a group of examinees.

The manual asserts: "The items on which the descriptive assessment of the client is based are criterion-referenced. This means that they permit the interpretation of the client's performance in relation to generally understood defined disposi-tions, competencies or behaviours" (p. 3). This is correct only in a commonsense way and not in the technical meaning of criterion-referenced as tied to some standard or criterion of performance.

Interpretation of the WPP, according to the manual, may be based on study of the profile of scores for the individual or group. As a rough guideline, it may be said that scores of 6 or higher are indicative of adequate coping or adjustment skills, whereas scores of 4 or lower may indicate the need for intervention to help prepare the person or group in seeking employment and, in-deed, for functioning in activities of everyday life. Alternatively, the scores may be interpreted in relation to the average responses of samples of employed and unemployed individuals.

The manual features several case examples, showing how the author believes the WPP should be applied in conjunction with other information about the individual or group in question.

DEVELOPMENT. The WPP items were chosen by a "professional panel" (p. 5), after litera-ture searches and "a number of interviews with employed and unemployed persons, and with psy-chologists working for employment agencies" (p. 5). Further specifics are not provided. There is no argument or evidence in the manual to justify the formulation of items, the choice of areas, the assignment of items to scales, and the combina-tion of scales into areas. Some of the choices and assignments are questionable. Three examples: (a) items relating to trust in other people appear on both Scale 2.4 (Pervasive Distrust, Delusions) and Scale 3.1 (Attitude Towards Others); (b) an item contains two negatives: How true is it that I am not bothered by X when I am not Y; and (c) some scales are justified in part because they distinguish between employed and unemployed samples at a level of statistical significance, whereas others are retained even though they do not, on the grounds that the within-group variation happens to be too large compared to between-group differences.

TECHNICAL. The manual cites no data concerning individual items. Rather, it appears, analysis has been limited to the scale and area scores. Because the content and wording of the items are fundamental to the value of the WPP, this is an unfortunate shortcoming.

The manual claims validity for the WPP scores primarily on the basis of factor analyses showing similar factor structures for samples of employed and unemployed persons. Separate analyses were carried out for the total sample of 358 Australians, for a subgroup of 275 unem-ployed individuals, for 121 of those individuals who had been unemployed for 2 years or more, for another subgroup of 83 persons employed in a variety of positions (but probably not repre-sentative of all Australian workers), and for a separate sample of 61 people in management or professional jobs.

The manual asserts that scores on the WPP are adequately reliable on the basis of two test-retest studies over a 5–7-week period with a sample of 10 employed and a sample of 11 unemployed persons (over a 9-day test interval). The sample sizes are entirely inadequate. Some form of inter-nal-consistency analysis of reliability could easily have been carried out in connection with the factor analyses, but no such analysis is described in the manual.

Normative information is limited to presentation of means and standard deviations of the scale and area scores for the 275 unemployed, 83 employed, and total sample of 358 used in the factor analytic studies. (There are minor errors in the tables displaying these data, evidenced by the fact that some of the listed means for the total sample are inconsistent with the listings for the two subgroups.) It appears from these data that the average scale or area score to be expected will in most cases be well above the midpoint of the 10-point scale. These scales are said in the manual to be standard scores, but they apparently are not, in the technical meaning of the term, because they do not have common means and standard deviations in relation to some specified norm group.

COMMENTARY. The factor analytic studies are relevant but far from conclusive in demonstrating evidence of validity for intended uses of the WPP. Information on the development of the instrument, on the functioning of the items, and on the relationships of the WPP to various other measures is needed for a balanced evaluation of validity.

The WPP is at an early stage of its development. The underlying idea seems promising and the specific application to a single country may well be appropriate because laws and customs related to employment differ substantially across jurisdictions and cultures. It is to be hoped that the author and the publisher will devote additional effort to the evaluation and improvement of the WPP.

SUMMARY. The WPP is a good idea in search of adequate implementation and evaluation. Validity and reliability information are inadequate, as are normative data. Potential users are advised to review the item content and scale construction carefully in view of the applications that are desired, and to be cautious in interpreting the scores of clients who complete the questionnaire.

[283]
Work Profile Questionnaire: Emotional Intelligence.

Purpose: "Designed to measure emotional intelligence ... and also identifies respondents' preferred [work] team role."
Population: Adults
Publication Date: 1999.

Acronym: WPQei.
Scores, 8: Self-Awareness, Empathy, Intuition, Emotions, Motivation, Innovation, Social Skills, Emotional Intelligence.
Administration: Group.
Price Data, 2001: £37.50 per technical manual; £85 per 10 self-scoring questionnaire/answer sheet/profile set; £25 per computer-based WPQei Administrator and Narrative Report Generator.
Time: Untimed.
Comments: Based on the Belbin model of work team functioning; can be administered in paper-and-pencil or personal computer format; requires IBM-compatible PC running Microsoft Windows 95/98/NT, 800x600 resolution display with 256 colors, recommends Pentium processor at 90 Mhz or more, 8 Mb RAM.
Author: Allan Cameron.
Publisher: The Test Agency Limited.

Review of the Work Profile Questionnaire: Emotional Intelligence by MARK POPE, Associate Professor, Division of Counseling & Family Therapy, College of Education, University of Missouri—St. Louis, St. Louis, MO:

DESCRIPTION. The Work Profile Questionnaire: Emotional Intelligence (WPQei) is designed to assess a person's emotional intelligence, and to measure personality, team role preferences, and the personal qualities and competencies that employees need to develop to manage emotion at work. The WPQei can be used with employees in managerial, professional, service, and clerical occupations, and can be used for personnel selection, job analysis, performance evaluation, leadership development, team building, and counseling.

The WPQei is composed of 84 items that result in eight different scales (Self-Awareness, Empathy, Intuition, Managing Emotions, Motivation, Innovation, Social Skills, and Overall Emotional Intelligence).

A user's guide (technical manual) accompanied the materials and had much to say about Emotional Intelligence in general crediting Mayer and Salovey (1993) for originating the term and Goleman (1998) for popularizing it. Although Goleman had a five-factor model for emotional intelligence, Cameron (the test author) described a seven-factor model, which he used in the development of this instrument.

A four-page folded brochure called the WPQei Emotional Intelligence Questionnaire accompanies the materials and is essentially a report

ployees. There is also no mechanism for detecting fake-good or fake-bad responses, nor is there any evidence of test-retest reliability.

SUMMARY. The WPQei is administered via a small, easy-to-use program, with a manual written in common language appropriate for use by nonspecialists. However, there is no validity or reliability information to suggest that the test measures what it claims to measure, predicts job performance, or even measures its constructs consistently. Use of the test cannot be recommended until additional evidence of its utility becomes available.

[284]

Worley's ID Profile.

Purpose: Designed to identify temperament.
Population: Ages 6 and over.
Publication Dates: 1995–2000.
Acronym: WIDP.
Scores, 8: 3 profile scores: Social, Leadership, Relationship; 5 behavior scores: Introverted Sanguine, Sanguine, Phlegmatic, Melancholy, Choleric.
Administration: Individual or group.
Forms, 2: Adult and Youth (ages 6 to 16).
Price Data: Available from publisher.
Foreign Language Editions: Available in English, Spanish, and Portuguese.
Time: (10) minutes.
Author: John W. Worley.
Publisher: Worley's Identity Discovery Profile, Inc.

Review of the Worley's ID Profile by EUGENE V. AIDMAN, Lecturer in Psychology, University of Ballarat, Victoria, Australia:

DESCRIPTION. According to the test developer, the Worley's ID Profile (WIDP) is a 60-item self-report questionnaire designed to assess "needs, desires and interpersonal behaviors" (manual, p. 1) with the purpose to "yield a quick but detailed summary of individual temperament" (manual, p. 1). Target population is never explicitly stated, but can be assumed to include general adult population (Adult form) and adolescents (Youth form). There are Spanish and Portuguese versions of both forms. The WIDP can be administered on screen, via a proprietary software, or in a paper-and-pencil format, with completion times between 7 and 10 minutes. Manual scoring is not available; responses have to be entered into the software. The WIDP software appears to be the centerpiece of the instrument, containing the bulk

of its "know-how." It produces a 16–18 page narrative report on the basis of six subscale scores.

DEVELOPMENT. The instrument's development followed an interesting distinction between the self-report on the test taker's own behavior (labelled as *demonstrated* score) and his of her preferences for behaviors/responses received from others (labelled as *desired* score). As a result of this relatively novel distinction, the WIDP yields a pair of corresponding subtest scores (demonstrated and desired) for each of the following three areas: Social, Leadership, and Relationship. This produces a total of six subscale scores for the test. Just how these scores are derived remains unclear. This reviewer could only infer (from a sample narrative report) that the scores may represent (a) the degree of extroversion/introversion in the respondent's own behavior and (b) the degree of extroversion/introversion they wish to see in people with whom they interact.

Unfortunately, test materials provide no explanation of scoring procedures, nor the interpretation of the meaning of specific subtest scores, thus leaving a degree of confusion regarding the definitions of the test's measurement constructs. This confusion is compounded by the inclusion of temperament types (Sanguine, Choleric, etc.) in the rhetoric of the instrument. How these temperament types can possibly be measured by the WIDP is entirely unclear (test materials contain no indication of the existence of relevant subscales). The introduction of the fifth, unsubstantiated "introverted-sanguine" type confuses the measurement constructs even further.

TECHNICAL. The psychometric soundness of the WIDP is very difficult to evaluate. The manual provided by the publisher contains masses of irrelevant material, such as the developer's resume and glowing customer testimonials, but fails to provide critical details of validation studies that would be sufficient for review. In particular, KR-20 estimates of internal consistency are inappropriate for a 6-point Likert scale response format used in the test. The manual claims (p. 7) that subscale items are scored dichotomously, but does not provide details of—nor any rationale for—the conversion of the 6-point Likert type response format into a dichotomous scoring. Whether any such distinction is observed remains unknown, as no description of the test's scoring procedures is provided.

Reliability. The only internal consistency figure reported is an average KR-20 of .54 across the six subscales. Leaving aside the mystery of KR-20 calculations for the test's nondichotomous scale format and the absence of any description of the sample(s) on which they were obtained, reporting average estimates is not sufficient; they should be reported for each subscale separately. Retest reliability is again reported as an average of .70 across the six subscales, over a 4-month period (*n* = 39, sample composition unknown). Why these stability coefficients were not reported for each subscale remains unclear.

Validity. Validity data are scarce and presented in a series of assertions about associations between WIDP scales and certain clinical conditions, such as depression, obsessive-compulsive disorder, and alcohol dependence. Unfortunately, no tangible evidence is provided to support these assertions: The manual reports no detail of the samples or method used in these unpublished validation studies.

Standardization. The instrument's normative data are completely missing in the documentation provided by the publisher. The manual reports that the developer "has collected a database of 585 administrations of the instrument" (p. 6). There is, however, no evidence of standardization or norms tables. The reviewer assumes that the test yields no standard scores, thus operating with raw scores only.

SUMMARY. Overall evidence of psychometric soundness of the WIDP, as currently documented, is insufficient. The manual provided by the publisher lacks critical technical detail necessary for review. Nor does it contain any reference to current research on temperament or any articulation of the developer's conceptualization of the WIDP's measurement constructs. It must, therefore, be concluded that the WIDP, in its current form, cannot be recommended for use as a proven instrument, unless more rigorous validation research is forthcoming.

Review of Worley's ID Profile (WIDP) by
FREDERICK T. L. LEONG, *Professor of Psychology, The Ohio State University at Columbus, Columbus, OH:*

DESCRIPTION. The Worley Identity Discovery Program (Worley's ID Profile; WIDP) is a 60-item measure of an individual's temperament based loosely on the personality typology of Hippocrates. Accordingly, the WIDP provides five behavioral scores related to Hippocrates's theory: (a) Introverted Sanguine, (b) Sanguine, (c) Phlegmatic, (d) Melancholy, and (e) Choleric. The measure is also divided into three profiles scores: (a) Social, (b) Leadership, and (c) Relationship. These three profile types are further divided into two dimensions each: (a) Demonstrated and (b) Desired.

TECHNICAL. In terms of the psychometric properties of the WIDP, such information was limited. The author did report some evidence of reliability and validity but the data reported in support of these dimensions were both incomplete and scanty. For example, only half a page was devoted to a description of the assessment of the reliability of the WIDP. Furthermore, no tables were presented in either of the sections on reliability or validity that would allow the reader to gauge the relative strength of the five behavioral scores or the three profile dimensions. Instead, only global estimates were presented, such as the average test-retest reliability (4 months) of the WIDP of .70 and the internal consistency estimate (KR-20) of .54. For the relative low internal consistency estimates of the WIDP scores, the author made reference to the similarly low internal consistency estimates of the Minnesota Multiphasic Personality Inventory (MMPI) clinical scales. The absence of detailed reliability estimates such as Cronbach's alpha for the individual scales made it impossible to evaluate the claims of the author that the WIDP was a reliable measure. This is especially relevant because a great deal of weight is placed on the meaning of the typologies (e.g., the Sanguine or the Phlegmatic person) when interpreting the WIDP.

The evidence for the validity of the WIDP was equally limited. The author evaluated the validity of the WIDP using two separated procedures. First, using a known-group procedure, the WIDP scores of individuals who had been diagnosed with specific psychological problems (i.e., major depression, obsessive compulsive disorder, marital problems, and alcohol dependence) by psychologists were examined. The author claimed support for the validity because certain scores on the WIDP were related to these various psychological disorders. There are several problems with this procedure. These included the fact that complete information about the correlations between specific WIDP scores and the psychological problems were never presented. Instead, the author selectively presented some of the significant relationships. Furthermore, some of the significant relationships between WIDP scores and psychological disorders were quite vague and served as distal evidence of validity at best. For example, the author claimed support for the validity of the measure when persons diagnosed with obsessive-compulsive disorder had higher scores on Desired Relationship and lower scores on Demonstrated Leadership than the average person. Even when discussing these significant relationships, no numerical data are ever presented.

The second test of the validity evaluation was the author's finding that the WIDP scores were not systematically related to Rosenberg's (1965) measure of self-esteem. Once again, no individual or specific scores were ever presented. Although it is useful to demonstrate that the WIDP was not systematically related to self-esteem, this assessment alone is not sufficient. What is needed even more is direct evidence of construct validity.

Unfortunately, many important indices of construct validity were not available for the WIDP. For example, the author needs to provide other evidence of concurrent validity such as the relationship between the WIDP and existing measures of temperament. Additionally, given the low internal consistency estimates of the five behavioral scales, the author needs to conduct a factor analysis to determine if the five temperament types are valid and distinct. At the very least, he needs to provide a table of the intercorrelations of those five behavioral scale scores. High intercorrelations would suggest that the five temperament types are neither well defined nor properly operationalized in the current measure. Finally, it needs to be demonstrated that these five behavioral scales relate differentially to a variety of measures in a theoretically consistent fashion.

COMMENTARY. The test manual that accompanied the measure was quite limited and did not even specify the five behavioral types in the section describing the test nor did it explain the relationships between the five behavioral types and the three profile categories (Social, Leadership, and Relationship). Furthermore, the author did not provide any rationale as to why Hippocrates's personality theory was chosen as the theoretical foundation for the current measure. This is addi-

tionally troubling because no attempts were made to directly validate the Hippocrates typology operationalized in the current measure. The manual also contained some exaggerated claims such as the "WIDP provides a comprehensive identification of needs, desires, and interpersonal behaviors in three fundamental areas of life" (p. 1). It is quite unlikely that a 60-item measure of temperament can really provide a "comprehensive" measure of needs, desires, and interpersonal behaviors. Each of these domains (e.g., needs) has psychometrically sound measures that consist of hundreds of items because they are such complex domains. For example, the Edwards Personal Preference Schedule (Edwards, 1959), which is a commonly used measure of needs based on Henry Murray's theory, consists of 225 items covering 16 different needs (e.g., Abasement, Deference, Order, Exhibition).

SUMMARY. In conclusion, given the problems with the psychometric properties of Worley's ID Profile identified above, it cannot be recommended as a good test of temperament or interpersonal behavior. Furthermore, the author chose to develop a measure of personality temperament based on Hippocrates's typology and yet provided no rationale for this choice nor any direct attempts to validate that Hippocrates's types had been accurately measured. Readers who are looking for measures of personality temperament would be well advised to look elsewhere and use measures such as the Emotionality Activity Sociability Impulsivity (EASI) measure developed by Buss and Plomin (1984) that has been much better researched and validated.

REVIEWER'S REFERENCES

Buss, A. H., & Plomin, R. (1984). *Temperament: Early development and personality traits.* Hillsdale, NJ: Lawrence Erlbaum Associates.
Edwards, A. L. (1959). *Edwards Personal Preference Schedule.* New York: The Psychological Corporation.
Rosenberg, M. (1965). *Society and adolescent self-image.* Princeton, NJ: Princeton University Press.

[285]

Young Children's Achievement Test.

Purpose: Designed to help determine early academic abilities.
Population: Ages 4-0 to 7-11.
Publication Date: 2000.
Acronym: YCAT.
Scores, 6: General Information, Reading, Mathematics, Writing, Spoken Language, and Early Achievement Composite.
Administration: Individual.

Price Data, 2003: $184 per complete kit including examiner's manual (154 pages), picture book (48 pages), 25 student response forms, and 25 profile/examiner record booklets; $57 per examiner's manual; $66 per picture book; $25 per 25 student response forms; $41 per 25 profile/examiner record booklets.
Time: (25–45) minutes.
Authors: Wayne P. Hresko, Pamela K. Peak, Shelley R. Herron, and Deanna L. Bridges.
Publisher: PRO-ED.

Review of the Young Children's Achievement Test by RUSSELL N. CARNEY, Professor of Psychology, Southwest Missouri State University, Springfield, MO:

DESCRIPTION. The Young Children's Achievement Test (YCAT) is an individually administered test designed to measure early academic abilities. Its central purpose is to aid in the identification of young children at risk for school failure. YCAT materials include the examiner's manual, a picture book, profile/examiner record booklets, and student response forms. Designed for English-speaking preschoolers, kindergartners, and first-graders (ages 4-0 through 7-11), the five subtests of the YCAT measure General Information, Reading, Mathematics, Writing, and Spoken Language. The five resultant scores can be combined to yield an Early Achievement Composite score. The YCAT can also be used to document educational progress.

The YCAT is nontimed, and the subtests can be administered in any order. Approximately 25 to 45 minutes are required for administration. An easel with color pictures (the picture book) allows for the presentation of many of the test items. The profile/examiner record booklet lists each question, and also provides one or more examples of the correct response as an aid to scoring. Items are scored as either correct (1) or incorrect (0). The examiner begins with the first item on each subtest, and continues until a ceiling is reached. The subtests are each about 20 items in length, except for the spoken language subtest, which is composed of 36 items.

Types of scores provided include raw scores, age equivalents, percentiles, and standard scores. In particular, standard scores are normalized and are based on a mean of 100 and a standard deviation of 15. Children with standard composite scores below 90 are considered at risk. Additionally, a table in the manual allows the user to convert the scores to normal curve equivalents (NCEs), z-scores, T-scores, and stanines.

DEVELOPMENT. The YCAT was developed to help identify young children at risk for academic failure. The test manual authors list eight reasons why such testing should take place. Central to their argument is the notion that it is best to identify academic problems early on in order to provide interventions that have the greatest likelihood of success. The authors acknowledge that early achievement is based on the interaction of several factors, such as physical/psychological well-being, the child's environmental experiences, informal and formal instruction, and finally, the child's intrinsic curiosity and motivation.

In developing this instrument, a large number of early childhood tests and curriculum materials were reviewed, which are listed in the manual. Based on this review, 183 test items were initially generated, of which 117 were eventually chosen for the YCAT.

Test developers conducted traditional item analysis by examining difficulty and item discrimination (using an item/total-score Pearson correlation index). Median percentages of item difficulty and discrimination are reported across age ranges and across the five subtests. The values provided appear to be acceptable.

Two differential item functioning (DIF) techniques were used as a screen to detect item bias: the logistic regression approach and the Delta Plot approach. Four groups were compared: male vs. female, European Americans vs. non-European Americans, African Americans vs. non-African Americans, and Hispanic Americans vs. non-Hispanic Americans. The logistic regression approach yielded a relatively small number of potentially biased items per group. These items were examined, and the authors did not feel that they were particularly biased. The Delta Plot approach suggested little if any bias in the items for the four comparison groups.

TECHNICAL.

Standardization. Normative data are based on 1,224 children sampled from 32 states (1996–1999). This sample was designed to be representative of the nation. The manual provides a table listing the demographic characteristics of the sample next to census figures for these areas: geographic region, gender, race, residence, ethnicity, family income, parents' educational attainment, and disability status. The sample percentages, and those of the census, seem quite comparable.

Reliability. Internal consistency was estimated using Cronbach's (1951) coefficient alpha. Values across the subtests, and at different ages, ranged from .74 (General Information, age 7) to .92 (Reading, age 4). The majority of the subtest values were in the mid- to high .80s. The Early Achievement Composite score yielded high internal consistency values: .95 to .97. The authors went on to calculate alphas for nine subgroups (e.g., males, females, African Americans, those classified as learning disabled, those classified as mentally retarded). Nearly all of these values were in the .90s for the various subtests, and ranged from .97 to .99 for the composite score—very high values. The authors argue that this suggests that the YCAT is "about equally reliable" (examiner's manual, p. 57) for the different subgroups examined.

Test-retest reliability (approximately 2-week interval) was calculated using a sample of 190 children from two different schools. The five subtests had high test-retest reliability, ranging from .97 to .99. The correlations were corrected for restriction of the range where appropriate. No value was reported for the composite score.

Interscorer reliability was estimated as follows. Two graduate students independently scored 100 completed protocols. The correlations between their scores on the five subtests ranged from .97 to .99, indicating a high degree of agreement. Again, no value was reported for the composite score.

VALIDITY.

Content validity. As described in the Development section, to build content validity into their test, the authors reviewed a number of early childhood tests and curriculum materials in order to produce test items.

Criterion-related validity. Concurrent validity was measured by correlating performance on the YCAT with a variety of other tests, including the Comprehensive Scales of Student Abilities (1994), the Kaufman Survey of Early Academic and Language Skills (1993), the Metropolitan Readiness Tests (1995), and the Gates-MacGinitie Reading Tests (1989). The numerous resultant correlations are listed in the manual, and for the most part, provide evidence for concurrent validity.

Construct validity. The manual discusses six premises related to construct validation: age differentiation, group differentiation, the YCAT's relationship to academic ability, the YCAT's relationship to intelligence, subtest interrelationships, and item validity. In the first instance, as expected, evidence is provided that the YCAT does indeed differentiate between students on the basis of age. Older students make higher scores than younger students on the various subtests. Second, group means for Whites, Blacks, Hispanics, and ADHD individuals were virtually identical, whereas means for those with learning disabilities and mental retardation were lower—as one would expect if the test was working correctly. Third, as described earlier under concurrent validity, the YCAT correlates with other achievement tests. Likewise, the YCAT correlates to some extent with the Slosson Intelligence Test for Children and Adults (1990). Correlations with the Slosson for the five YCAT subtests ranged from .44 to .73, and the correlation was .68 for the YCAT composite score. Fifth, the five subtests of the YCAT were intercorrelated, with values ranging from .57 to .71. This suggests that they tap into the same construct: academic abilities. Finally, the items of a subtest should correlate with the total score on that subtest. Item discrimination values were discussed in the test development section. The presence of good item discrimination is another piece of evidence supporting construct validity.

COMMENTARY. The test manual for the YCAT describes it as a "quick, reliable, and valid instrument to help determine early academic abilities" (examiner's manual, p. 3), and I am inclined to agree. Administration is relatively simple, and is facilitated by way of a colorful easel display format, as well as an easy-to-follow record booklet. Scoring instructions are clear (as evidenced by high interscorer reliability), and a variety of scores are reported, including percentiles and standard scores. Even though age-equivalent scores are provided, the authors of the manual rightly caution against their use.

Reliability appears to be a strength. Based on coefficient alpha reliabilities, the standard error of measurement (*SEM*) was only ±3 points across the board on the composite score. On the subtests, the *SEM* ranged from ±4 to 8 points, with the majority of the values being ±5 or 6 points. I was especially impressed with the test-retest reliabilities (2-week interval), which ranged from .97 to .99. It is important to note that these were corrected for restriction of the range where appropriate. It would have been interesting to have seen the values prior to the corrections. Also, I was curious as to why no test-retest reliability was calculated for the composite score.

Likewise, validity evidence was provided for content, concurrent, and construct validity. The evidence for all three types was convincing. I was particularly taken by the efforts made to reduce bias, which seem to have been successful. For example, the mean scores on the five subtests, and the composite, are nearly identical for Anglo-European Americans, African Americans, and Hispanic Americans. Eliminating potential bias was clearly a priority during the development of this test.

Because the YCAT is designed to predict school failure, it would be worthwhile to have an estimate of the instrument's predictive validity by testing a sample of young children, and then correlating their scores with their actual school performance after 1 or 2 years. Such information was probably unavailable when the manual was published. However, it could be included when the manual is next revised.

Finally, the test manual seems to be particularly well-written. Beyond the usual chapters dealing with administration, scoring, norms, reliability, and validity, the manual includes informative sections titled "Information to Consider Before Testing," "Interpreting the YCAT Results," "Controlling for Test Bias," and "Other Important Factors Relating to Testing Children's Early Development." Throughout, the manual often refers to the *Standards for Educational and Psychological Testing* (AERA, APA, & NCME, 1985)—and a variety of measurement references—providing useful information and cautionary notes where appropriate. Also very important, the manual stresses that the assessment of young children should involve information *from a variety of sources*—not just the scores from a single test. Further, the manual advises care in interpreting scores when the test has been administered to children who speak nonstandard English, or who are bilingual.

SUMMARY. The Young Children's Achievement Test (YCAT) is an individually administered test of academic abilities for English-speaking children ages 4-0 to 7-11 years. Particular attention was paid to the *Standards* (AERA, APA, & NCME, 1985) in its development, and the result appears to be a technically sound test that is easy to administer and score. It should be a useful instrument for the purposes of identifying young children at risk for school failure, and for measuring academic progress.

REVIEWER'S REFERENCE

American Educational Research Association, American Psychological Association, & National Council on Measurement in Education. (1985). *Standards for educational and psychological testing.* Washington, DC: American Psychological Association, Inc.

Review of the Young Children's Achievement Test by SUSAN J. MALLER, Associate Professor of Educational Studies, Purdue University, West Lafayette, IN:

DESCRIPTION. The Young Children's Achievement Test (YCAT) is an individually administered test that measures academic skills, including General fund of Information, Reading, Mathematics, Writing, and Spoken Language, necessary for children in preschool through first grade. The manual states that the YCAT can be used (a) to identify whether a child's academic skills are developing normally, (b) to document progress, (c) along with other measures, and (d) in research.

The test materials include the examiner's manual, picture book (in the form of an easel), 25 student response forms, and 25 profile/examiner record booklets. Other materials needed include pencils, erasers, 1 nickel, 2 dimes, and 6 pennies. The artwork for the items in the picture book is clear and attractive. It should be noted that the technical manual is written very clearly. The authors did a good job of explaining the technical aspects of the test.

The YCAT can be used for children ages 4-0 through 7-11. The manual states that the test is appropriate for children who can understand the directions and who can "read, write, and speak English" (p. 7). However, it appears that the test also is appropriate for children at the younger ages who have prereading skills.

The YCAT should be administered by a person who has had formal training in administering and interpreting results from assessments. The manual cites the guidelines suggested by Anastasi and Urbina (1997) and also recommends that the examiner have had supervised training in using the screening tests and have practiced administering the YCAT several times with colleagues.

YCAT administration requires approximately 25–45 minutes, although the test is not timed. Breaks are allowed for children who cannot sit through the entire testing period, especially younger children.

All items are scored as correct or incorrect. All subtests have no basals and have a ceiling level

tic regression method is preferred, because it controls for ability. The manual does not state whether the method of purification was used to match examinees of equal ability. A table reports the numbers of items found to exhibit DIF at the $p<.01$ level. Although the manual states that the number of DIF items was well within the level of chance, at this significance level only one item should be found to exhibit DIF in each analysis. For the groups studied, the number of DIF items ranged from 2 for Hispanics versus all others to 11 for males versus females. The manual goes on to state that no items were judged to contain "indications of overt bias" (p. 71), although it does not state how this was concluded. Admittedly, DIF investigations are expensive and often are not reported for individually administered tests. The test authors have taken notable initial steps toward investigating DIF; however, more information is needed regarding the analysis, and justification is needed for the criterion used for determining DIF. In terms of test bias investigations, no evidence is presented to demonstrate that the YCAT predicts criterion measures similarly across groups. That is, no studies of differential prediction were reported.

COMMENTARY AND SUMMARY. The YCAT is an individually administered test of academic skills necessary for preschoolers through first grade. The YCAT manual is written well and easy to follow. The test materials are attractive and clearly presented. Relevant literature is cited justifying the underlying theoretical constructs of the YCAT. Reliability coefficients are impressive. The validity evidence that is presented is fairly convincing; however, further evidence is needed (a) to determine whether the YCAT predicts meaningful criterion measures, (b) regarding the internal structure of the YCAT, and (c) regarding the lack of DIF and test bias in the YCAT. Overall, the first version of the YCAT indicates that it is likely to be a promising measure of academic abilities in young children, especially when more of the above-mentioned evidence is obtained regarding the validity of the instrument.

REVIEWER'S REFERENCES

Anastasi, A., & Urbina, S. J. (1997). *Psychological testing* (7th ed.). Upper Saddle River, NJ: Prentice Hall.
Bryk, A. (1980). [Review of *Bias in mental testing*]. *Journal of Educational Measurement, 17*, 369–374.
Camilli, G., & Shepard, L. A. (1994). *Methods for identifying biased test items.* Thousand Oaks, CA: Sage.
Linn, R. L., & Gronlund, N. E. (1995). *Measurement and assessment in teaching* (7th ed.). Englewood Cliffs, NJ: Merrill.

[286]
Youth's Inventory—4.

Purpose: Designed to determine "the extent to which the adolescent patient is aware of his or her symptoms" [of adolescent psychopathology], as determined by self-report.
Population: Ages 12–18.
Publication Date: 1999.
Acronym: YI-4.
Scores, 11: AD/HD Inattentive, Hyperactive-Impulsive, Combined, Oppositional Defiant Disorder, Conduct Disorder, Generalized Anxiety Disorder, Major Depressive Disorder, Dysthymic Disorder, Separation Anxiety Disorder, Eating Problems, Bipolar Disorder.
Administration: Individual.
Price Data, 2001: $75 per deluxe kit including 50 checklists, 50 symptom count score sheets, 50 symptom severity profile score sheets, and manual (170 pages); $52 per 50 checklists.
Time: [15] minutes.
Authors: Kenneth D. Gadow and Joyce Sprafkin.
Publisher: Checkmate Plus, Ltd.

Review of Youth's Inventory—4 by HAROLD R. KELLER, Professor and Chair, Department of Psychological and Social Foundations, University of South Florida, Tampa, FL:

DESCRIPTION. The Youth's Inventory—4 (YI-4) was designed to determine the extent to which adolescents (12–18 years) in clinic settings are aware of and/or are willing to acknowledge their symptoms, as determined previously or concurrently by teacher and parent report. Its use is recommended with the parent and teacher versions of the Adolescent Symptom Inventory—4 (ASI-4; Gadow & Sprafkin, 1997, 1998; 12). The authors indicate that the YI-4 is not intended to be a screening instrument to help identify adolescents who may have an emotional or behavioral disorder.

The YI-4 consists of 118 items that are rated on a 4-point scale that "best describes your overall behavior" (*never, sometimes, often, very often*). The items are grouped in 14 item groups, ranging from 2 to 18 items per group. For scoring purposes, items are grouped into 25 symptom categories corresponding to *DSM-IV* categories (American Psychiatric Association, 1994), plus an inconsistency score. The number of items per symptom category range from 1 (for specific phobia, panic attack, obsessions, compulsions, motor tics, vocal tics) to 18 (for attention deficit hyperactivity disorder, combined type, ADHD). The inconsistency score is based upon a pairing of the last 8 items that are identical in content, with minor word changes, to 8 items interspersed throughout the first 110 items. Some items are used in more than one symptom category.

Two scoring approaches are used, one a symptom count score and the other a symptom severity score. For the symptom count score, the weights assigned to the four response choices are: *never* and *sometimes* each 0, and *often* and *very often* each 1. The "sometimes" response alternative is weighted with a "1" for 13 items that relate to illegal activities and trouble with alcohol use. The symptom count score sheet also specifies a symptom cutoff score related to the minimum number of symptoms necessary for a diagnosis of a given disorder. The authors appropriately advise that this cutoff score merely indicates that adolescents are aware of problem behaviors that may be indicative of an emotional or behavioral disorder.

The symptom severity score is based upon a more typical item weighting system (i.e., *never* = 0, *sometimes* = 1, *often* = 2, *very often* = 3). This score is designed to determine the degree of behavioral deviance compared with a norm sample. *T*-scores are provided, with scores between one and two standard deviation units above the mean indicating moderate severity, and scores two or more standard deviations above the mean indicating high symptom severity. The authors' stated intent is that normative data are to be used primarily as an indication of symptom base rates in the general population.

DEVELOPMENT. A clinic sample and a norm sample were used to develop the YI-4. The clinic sample consisted of consecutive referrals to a child and adolescent psychiatry outpatient service. Data were obtained from 134 youths (12 to 18 years of age), of whom 99 were males and 35 were females. ADHD and oppositional defiant disorder were the two most prevalent clinical diagnoses, with mood and anxiety disorders next (either as a co-morbid disorder or as the only disorder). The norm sample was derived from a "large" (p. 42) school district in Florida with participants coming from the middle school and high school in the district. The final sample consisted of 573 students (276 males and 297 females), after eliminating five checklists for skipped items, two checklists for response bias (a single response to all items), 13 students who were receiving special education services, and 28 students with too high inconsistency scores. Descriptive information was provided for sample proportions at each grade level, in various racial/ethnic groups, in parental occupational status groups, and receiving medication for emotional and behavioral problems. No comparative information was given concerning the distributions in that community, region or national population. The authors justified this approach by restating that their intention was not to use the YI-4 as a screening device in the general population. Clearly, both the clinic and norm samples limit the generalizability of the data and usefulness of the YI-4.

TECHNICAL. The authors attempted to address validity issues in a variety of ways. They provided indices of both sensitivity (the degree to which a cutoff score identifies correctly individuals diagnosed with the disorder) and specificity (the degree to which a cutoff score identifies correctly individuals who do not have a diagnosed disorder). About 40% of the diagnostic categories had too few diagnosed clients in the clinic sample to determine sensitivity estimates. Intercorrelations among category scores were moderate to high in many instances. Such findings may relate to overlapping items across categories, to the lack of construct differentiation, to comorbidity, and/or to sample and measure characteristics. Intercorrelational data among categories generally raise questions about differential diagnosis when using categorical systems. Cross-informant agreement for the clinic sample was low and consistent with the findings of others for youth ratings in comparison to parent or teacher ratings (Achenbach & Edelbrock, 1978; Costenbader & Keller, 1990). They present some excellent clinic sample data with regard to ADHD and enhanced sensitivity when using both parent and teacher ratings. The YI-4 data did not add incrementally to sensitivity, supporting the authors' contention that the YI-4 is not to be used for screening or diagnostic purposes. It is important to recognize that, while suggesting the YI-4 be used with ASI-4 parent and teacher ratings, the norm sample data for the parent, teacher, and youth checklists are based on different norm samples. Therefore, direct cross-source comparisons are not possible with the norm sample data. The YI-4 was found to have good evidence of concurrent validity for pertinent symptom categories with the Youth Self Report (Achenbach, 1991) and the Children's Depression Inventory (Kovacs, 1992). Gender differences throughout are consistent with other measures and data, supporting the use of gender-specific norms. Discriminant validity on severity scores evidence was limited to a very few symptom categories because of the small numbers in either or both the clinic and/or norm samples for many of the symptom categories. The authors suggested that the YI-4 might be helpful with treatment decisions. Adolescents who are aware of and acknowledge symptoms reported by their parents and/or teachers might be helped and enlisted in the treatment process very differently than youth who are not aware and/or do not acknowledge their symptoms. No specific treatment validity data are presented for the YI-4.

COMMENTARY. The authors provide excellent discussion of general and specific clinical considerations in the use of the YI-4 and symptom category data. The authors frequently emphasize that the YI-4 is not to be used for diagnosis or screening, but rather to determine adolescents' awareness/recognition of their symptoms, as identified by others. The YI-4 manual, however, presents two scoring procedures that, on a superficial level, appear to provide help in the diagnostic process and in understanding the severity of problems. Critical psychometric and sampling information is missing and inadequate for either of those purposes. Presenting these scores, in spite of the lack of supportive data for categorical or dimensionality/severity decision making is problematic, even with the frequent reminders that the YI-4 is not intended for diagnosis or screening. Substantial national samples of youth in clinical and nonclinical settings are needed for these purposes. The authors are lauded for their strong cautionary statements about the use of the YI-4 and about the diagnosis of adolescents throughout the manual, and particularly in the chapter on clinical applications. The clinical applications chapter has excellent tables summarizing reasonable clinical considerations when using the YI-4 as a symptom inventory for each of the symptom clusters. Unfortunately, in many of the tables, the data are such that the authors must point out that there were "too few adolescents" with the diagnosed condition. Discrepancies between YI-4 and ASI-4 data for a given client and his or her parent or teacher might well be fruitful avenues for discussion with a youth as part of the treatment process.

Beyond that general statement, given the lack of conorming of the measures, there is little more that can be done with the cross-source data. The authors indicate that professionals may need to alter cutoff scores and criteria in their own settings based upon their professional experiences. Ignoring the issue of the problems with the adequacy of the clinical and norm samples, the authors provide no guidance for how clinicians might alter cutoffs and criteria.

SUMMARY. The YI-4 appears to be a reasonable approach to determining the extent to which adolescents in clinic settings are aware of and/or are willing to acknowledge their symptoms, as determined previously or concurrently by teacher and parent report. There are many useful discussions of how the measure might be used in a manner congruent with that intended purpose. The YI-4 manual also presents two scoring procedures (symptom counts and symptom severity) that appear to suggest that the measure can do more than the authors intended. The clinical and norm samples are grossly inadequate for diagnostic and screening purposes, and do not allow adequate determination of important psychometric considerations such as reliability and validity. No direct evidence is provided concerning the treatment validity or decision-making validity (Barnett, Lentz, & Macmann, 2000) of knowledge of adolescents' awareness/acknowledgement of the symptoms.

REVIEWER'S REFERENCES

Achenbach, T. M. (1991). *Manual for the Youth Self-Report and 1991 Profile.* Burlington, VT: Author.
Achenbach, T. M., & Edelbrock, C. S. (1978). The classification of child psychopathology: A review and analysis of empirical efforts. *Psychological Bulletin, 85,* 1275-1301.
American Psychiatric Association. (1994). *Diagnostic and statistical manual of mental disorders* (4th ed.). Washington, DC: Author.
Barnett, D. W., Lentz, F. E., Jr., & Macmann, G. (2000). Psychometric qualities of professional practice. In E. S. Shapiro & T. R. Kratochwill (Eds.), *Behavioral assessment in schools: Theory, research and clinical foundations* (2nd ed.) (pp. 355-386). New York: Guilford Press.
Costenbader, V. K., & Keller, H. R. (1990). Behavioral ratings of emotionally handicapped, learning disabled, and nonreferred children: Scale and source consistency. *Journal of Psychoeducational Assessment, 8,* 485-496.
Gadow, K. D., & Sprafkin, J. (1997). *Adolescent Symptom Inventory-4 screening manual.* Stony Brook, NY: Checkmate Plus.
Gadow, K. D., & Sprafkin, J. (1998). *Adolescent Symptom Inventory-4 norms manual.* Stony Brook, NY: Checkmate Plus.
Kovacs, M. (1992). *Children's Depression Inventory manual.* North Tonawanda, NY: Multi-Health Systems.

Review of the Youth's Inventory—4 by JOHN J. VACCA, Assistant Professor of Individual and Family Studies, University of Delaware, Newark, DE:

DESCRIPTION. The Youth's Inventory—4 (YI-4) is an individually administered symptom inventory that contains the behavioral symptoms of 17 emotional and behavioral disorders arranged in a checklist format. Use of the YI-4 is designed to determine "the extent to which the adolescent patient is aware of his or her symptoms" [of adolescent psychopathology], as "determined by parent and teacher report" (manual, p. 3). The intended age is 12 to 18 years, inclusive.

The YI-4 is to be used only by qualified, licensed clinicians in the mental health or related field. The authors indicate, further, that the professionals using the YI-4 should have a basic understanding of the principles of psychological testing, knowledge of ethics related to psychological/psychiatric assessment and treatment, and postgraduate training in child and adolescent psychology/psychiatry.

A total of 128 items are grouped together in 17 areas. There are two ways to score the responses on the YI-4: Symptom Count Score and Symptom Severity Score. Four weights are assigned to each response (Symptom Count: Never = 0, Sometimes = 0, Often = 1, Very Often = 1; Symptom Severity Score: Never = 0, Sometimes = 1, Often = 2, Very Often = 3). The Symptom Count Score is based on the criteria set forth in the Diagnostic and Statistical Manual of Mental Disorders—IV (DSM-IV; American Psychiatric Association, 1994) for each of the disorders addressed. The individual is given the YI-4, and they go through each item and indicate the presence using the four weights previously noted. The authors do not mention a specific time allotment for completion. YI-4 items have a one-to-one correspondence with items in the Adolescent Symptom Inventory-4 (ASI-4; Gadow & Sprafkin, 1997). Further, there are no clear directions for administration, although the authors mention that the YI-4 should be integrated with a clinical interview of a client.

According to the authors, individuals exhibiting the minimum number of symptoms necessary for a diagnosis as specified in the DSM-IV receive a "Yes" that indicates they are aware of their symptoms and that they may be suffering from a particular psychiatric disorder. With the Symptom Severity Score, scores received from individual administrations are compared to a norm sample to determine behavioral deviance. Scores that are between one and two standard deviations above the mean (T = 60 to 69) denote symptoms of moderate severity, and scores above two standard deviations indicate high symptom severity. The authors specify that the YI-4 "does not provide diagnoses" (manual, p. 71). Rather, the results simply indicate the individual's (possible) awareness of his or her symptoms. Professionals are encouraged to employ other assessment strategies including review of the DSM-IV before making a formal diagnosis.

DEVELOPMENT. The YI-4 is based on a series of previously developed screening instruments titled the Symptoms Inventories: the Early Childhood Inventory—4, the Child Symptom Inventory—4, and the Adolescent Symptom Inventory—4. The items on each of these screening inventories assess the behavioral, affective, and cognitive symptomatology of a variety of child and adolescent psychiatric disorders described in the DSM-IV. The primary impetus for the three scales arose from the need to ease the collection and transmission of diagnostic information about patients between the professionals serving them. As professionals began using the scales more consistently, there arose an additional need to allow the adolescent to be able to reflect on his or her own symptoms and difficulties in a self-report form. Hence, the YI-4 was developed. Unlike the Symptom Inventories, use of the YI-4 is not to screen individuals suspected of having psychiatric problems but rather is to assess an identified patient's own awareness of his or her psychiatric symptoms. The authors acknowledge the influence of levels of awareness and denial on the patient's ability to self-reflect, but they feel most youths are capable of some type of reflection despite their emotional state. Caution should still be given in interpretation of the results from the YI-4, and data from other assessment techniques (including observation) should be used in tandem with data received from the YI-4 to help determine the overall validity of the responses received.

The norming sample consisted of both a normative data sample (N = 573) and an outpatient clinic sample (N = 134 youths between the ages of 12 and 18 years; 99 males, 35 females). Participants for the norming sample were recruited from a large school district in Florida. Letters and questionnaires were randomly distributed in various classes. Responses were then grouped according to the diagnostic criteria for each of the disorders to determine the prevalence within the sample.

TECHNICAL. In terms of validity, measures of predictive validity were employed. More specifically, values of sensitivity and specificity were computed for each of the 17 diagnostic categories. Values ranged from .31 to .98. These values were enhanced when ratings from parent and teacher were jointly considered, thus supporting the need to augment results received from self-report measures. Intercorrelation values for the scores on the YI-4 in comparison to the norm and clinic samples were very low to high (.11 to .96).

In regard to concurrent validity, Product-Moment correlations between the YI-4 and the Adolescent Symptom Inventory—4 were very low to moderate. Values reflective of the comparison of the YI-4 with Achenbach's Youth Self Report Inventory also ranged from very low to moderate. There is no information about reliability of scores from the YI-4.

COMMENTARY. There are several fundamental flaws with the YI-4. First, the psychometric properties are not firmly established, especially with respect to reliability. In consideration of the intended use and the population for whom the YI-4 was designed, more data are needed to support its use. Second, there is no clear connection between the use of the YI-4 and other psychiatric procedures. Although the authors identify that the YI-4 should be used with clinical interviews, they do not specify how the responses and scores on the YI-4 can be integrated with those received from extensive mental status examinations. Third, the critical issue of treatment utility is not addressed. Fourth, the make-up of the normative and clinic sample is questionable. As a result, it is unclear what a standard score represents in terms of the larger population. Finally, more data are needed in terms of the use of self-report measures with clients with psychiatric disorders and the connection between the results received and the subsequent development of appropriate treatment programs.

The manual is not organized effectively. The tables are difficult to understand, and the manner in which the scale is described is vague.

Self-report measures can be helpful in the context of treatment, yet more guidance should be given to the professional to assist them in determining the authenticity of the responses received.

SUMMARY. Even though there are several concerns about the use of the YI-4, the authors should be commended for recognizing the client's role in the therapeutic process by allowing them to reflect on their own emotional well being. A majority of psychiatric inventories place the client in a passive role by having others provide information about the client. The client then receives interventions based on other's interpretations of that information. The question then enters the clinical situation as to when the client has a say in the type of intervention that is recommended. The use of self-report is intended to give the client more of an active role in the process and to assist the professionals in individualizing intervention plans for their clients. Although the intent is good, the results can be affected by many variables such as the client's own cognitive abilities and emotional state. Because of this, it is recommended that other measures such as parent report, observation, and teacher interviews be used to help validate the responses received on the self-report measures. Generally, information obtained in extensive clinical interviews, including the administration of projective measures, is more beneficial and informative than that received from completion of self-report measures. If such measures are desired, there are better established techniques such as the Achenbach Youth Self Report Inventory (T6:35) and the self-report form for the Behavior Assessment System for Children (T6:280). Overall, the authors of the YI-4 are urged to pursue their efforts to formally include self-report in traditional psychiatric evaluations, and they are urged to complete more research to refine the contents of the YI-4 and to clarify how the information received can assist professionals in their efforts to serve their clients.

REVIEWER'S REFERENCES
American Psychiatric Association. (1994). Diagnostic and statistical manual of mental disorders (4th ed.). Washington, DC: Author.
Gadow, K. D., & Sprafkin, J. (1997). Adolescent Symptom Inventory screening manual. Stony Brook, NY: Checkmate Plus.

APPENDIX

TESTS LACKING SUFFICIENT TECHNICAL DOCUMENTATION FOR REVIEW

Effective with The Fourteenth Mental Measurements Yearbook *(2001), an additional criterion has been added for tests reviewed in* The Mental Measurements Yearbook. *Only those tests for which at least minimal technical or test development information is provided are now reviewed. This list includes the names of new and revised tests received since publication of the* Fourteenth Mental Measurements Yearbook *that are lacking this documentation. The publishers have been advised that these tests do not meet our review criteria.*

[287]
Addiction Severity Index—Multimedia Version.
Publisher: The Psychological Corporation.

[288]
Adult Level of Care Index–2R.
Publisher: Evince Clinical Assessments.

[289]
Advanced Placement Examination in Human Geography.
Publisher: The College Board.

[290]
Advanced Placement Examination in World History.
Publisher: The College Board

[291]
The AMA DISC Survey.
Publisher: American Management Association; distributed by Human Synergistics International.

[292]
Applicant Potential Inventory.
Publisher: Reid London House.

[293]
Attention Deficit Disorder Checklist.
Publisher: Academic Consulting & Testing Service.

[294]
Birds of Different Feathers Work Style Assessment.
Publisher: Consulting Psychologists Press, Inc.

[295]
Birmingham Object Recognition Battery
Publisher: Psychology Press

[296]
Booker Profiles in Mathematics: Problem Solving.
Publisher: Australian Council for Educational Research Ltd. [Australia].

[297]
The Camden Memory Tests.
Publisher: Psychology Press.

[298]
The Category-Specific Names Test.
Publisher: Psychology Press.

[299]
Change Readiness Survey.
Publisher: Lore International Institute.

[300]
Child Well-Being Scales and Rating Form.
Publisher: Child Welfare League of America, Inc.

[301]

Client/Server Skills Test.
Publisher: Walden Personnel Performance, Inc.
[Canada].

[302]

Community-Based Social Skill Performance Assessment Tool.
Publisher: James Stanfield Co., Inc.

[303]

Comprehensive Assessment of Mathematics Strategies.
Publisher: Curriculum Associates, Inc.

[304]

Computer Literacy Skills Profile.
Publisher: Walden Personnel Performance, Inc.
[Canada].

[305]

Conference Meeting Rating Scale.
Publisher: Psychometric Affiliates.

[306]

Cultural Competence Self-Assessment Instrument.
Publisher: Child Welfare League of America, Inc.

[307]

Customer Service Applicant Inventory.
Publisher: Reid London House.

[308]

Database Analyst Staff Selector.
Publisher: Walden Personnel Performance, Inc.
[Canada].

[309]

Developmental Assessment of Life Experiences (2000 Edition).
Publisher: The Barber Center Press, Inc.

[310]

Dissemination Self-Inventory.
Publisher: Southwest Educational Development
Laboratory.

[311]

Elementary Program Implementation Profile.
Publisher: High/Scope Educational Research Foundation.

[312]

Employee Safety Inventory.
Publisher: Reid London House.

[313]

Everyday Life Activities: Photo Series.
Publisher: Psychology Press.

[314]

Executive Administrative Assistant Skills Test.
Publisher: Walden Personnel Performance, Inc.
[Canada].

[315]

Expectations Edition of the Personal Values Inventory.
Publisher: Personal Strengths Publishing.

[316]

Hare P-Scan.
Publisher: Multi-Health Systems, Inc.

[317]

Help Desk Support Staff Selector.
Publisher: Walden Personnel Performance, Inc.
[Canada].

[318]

Higher Education Learning Profile.
Publisher: Educational Resources, Inc.

[319]

The Infant-Toddler and Family Instrument.
Publisher: Paul H. Brookes Publishing Co., Inc.

[320]

IT Consultant Skills Evaluation.
Publisher: Walden Personnel Performance, Inc.

[321]
Job Readiness Skills Pre- and Post-Assessment.
Publisher: Education Associates.

[322]
Kilmanns Organizational Belief Survey.
Publisher: Consulting Psychologists Press, Inc.

[323]
Language Arts Objective Sequence.
Publisher: Research Press.

[324]
Leadership/Impact.
Publisher: Human Synergistics International.

[325]
Learning/Behavior Problems Checklist.
Publisher: Academic Consulting & Testing Service.

[326]
Learning Style Questionnaire.
Publisher: Human Resource Development Press.

[327]
The Listening for Meaning Test.
Publisher: Educational Evaluations [England].

[328]
LSI Conflict.
Publisher: Human Synergistics International.

[329]
Management Success Profile.
Publisher: Reid London House.

[330]
The Milwaukee Evaluation of Daily Living Skills.
Publisher: SLACK Incorporated.

[331]
Motor Skills Acquisition Checklist.
Publisher: Therapy Skill Builders—A Division of the Psychological Corporation.

[332]
Network Analyst Staff Selector.
Publisher: Walden Personnel Performance, Inc. [Canada].

[333]
Organizational Description Questionnaire.
Publisher: Mind Garden, Inc.

[334]
Organizational Effectiveness Inventory.
Publisher: Human Synergistics International.

[335]
Parent-Child Communication Inventory.
Publisher: Millard J. Bienvenu, Northwest Publications.

[336]
Parent/Teacher Conference Checklist.
Publisher: Academic Consulting & Testing Service.

[337]
Peacock Profile.
Publisher: Consulting Psychologists Press, Inc.

[338]
Penguin Index.
Publisher: Consulting Psychologists Press, Inc.

[339]
People Smarts: Behavioral Profiles.
Publisher: Jossey-Bass, A Wiley Company.

[340]
Personal Creativity Assessment.
Publisher: Human Resource Development Press.

[341]
Personal Effectiveness Inventory.
Publisher: Human Synergistics International.

[342]
Personality Advantage Questionnaire.
Publisher: Human Resource Development Press.

[343]
Preschool Motor Speech Evaluation & Intervention.
Publisher: Imaginart International, Inc.

[344]
Project Management Foundations Assessment.
Publisher: The Clark Wilson Group, Inc. for the exclusive use of Educational Services Institute.

[345]
Psychiatric Self-Assessment & Review.
Publisher: American Psychiatric Association.

[346]
Psycholinguistic Assessments of Language Processing in Aphasia.
Publisher: Psychology Press.

[347]
The Reading Vocabulary Tests.
Publisher: Educational Evaluations [England].

[348]
Retail Sales Skills Test.
Publisher: Walden Personnel Performance, Inc. [Canada].

[349]
Sales Professional Assessment Inventory.
Publisher: Reid London House.

[350]
Scale of Job-Related Social Skill Performance.
Publisher: James Stanfield Co., Inc.

[351]
School Readiness Checklist.
Publisher: Academic Consulting & Testing Service.

[352]
Speech Perception Instructional Curriculum and Evaluation.
Publisher: Central Institute for the Deaf.

[353]
Stress Management Questionnaire [Revised].
Publisher: The Assessment and Development Centre.

[354]
Stress Processing Report.
Publisher: Human Synergistics International.

[355]
Structured Clinical Interview for DSM-IV Dissociate Disorders—Revised.
Publisher: American Psychiatric Publishing, Inc.

[356]
Syracuse Dynamic Assessment for Birth to Three.
Publisher: Imaginart International, Inc.

[357]
Technical Support Staff Selector.
Publisher: Walden Personnel Performance, Inc. [Canada].

[358]
Telemarketing Staff Selector.
Publisher: Walden Personnel Performance, Inc. [Canada].

[359]
TQ Manager Inventory and Feedback From Others.
Publisher: Consulting Psychologists Press, Inc.

[360]
Tutor Evaluation and Self-Assessment Tool.
Publisher: The Cambridge Stratford Study Skills Institute.

[361]
VESPAR: A Verbal and Spatial Reasoning Test.
Publisher: Psychology Press.

[362]
Work Profile Questionnaire.
Publisher: The Test Agency Limited [England].

TESTS TO BE REVIEWED FOR THE SIXTEENTH MENTAL MEASUREMENTS YEARBOOK

By the time each new Mental Measurements Yearbook *reaches publication, the staff at the Buros Institute have already collected many new and revised tests destined to be reviewed in the next* Mental Measurements Yearbook. *Following is a list of tests that meet the review criteria and that will be reviewed, along with additional tests published and received in the next year, in* The Sixteenth Mental Measurements Yearbook.

Academic Competence Evaluation Scales
Accountant Staff Selector
Achenbach System of Empirically Based Assessment
Arabic Proficiency Test
Arizona Articulation Proficiency Scale, Third Revision

Basic Number Screening Test [2001 Edition]
Behavior Disorders Identification Scale—Second Edition
Beta III
Boehm Test of Basic Concepts—Third Edition
Boehm-3 Preschool
British Ability Scales: Second Edition

California Verbal Learning Test, Second Edition, Adult Version
Call Center Skills Test
Canadian Achievement Tests, Third Edition
Children's Color Trails Test
The Children's Test of Nonword Repetition
Clerical Skills Test Series [Scored by Client]
College ADHD Response Evaluation
College Student Inventory [part of the Retention Management System]
Comprehensive Mathematical Abilities Test
Computer Career Assessment Test
Conduct Disorder Scale
Customer Service Skills Test

Degrees of Reading Power—Revised
Developmental Test of Visual Perception—Adolescent and Adult
Dyslexia Adult Screening Test
Dyslexia Screening Test

Emotional and Behavior Problem Scale—Second Edition

The Five P's (Parent/Professional Preschool Performance Profile) [2002 Update]
Fox in a Box: An Adventure in Literacy

Giotto

Health Occupations Basic Entrance Test
Healthcare Customer Service Test
Home and Community Social Behavior Scales
Hopkins Verbal Learning Test—Revised

I Can Do Maths
Individual Outlook Test
InView

Job Challenge Profile

Kaplan Baycrest Neurocognitive Assessment
Kent Visual Perceptual Test
Khan-Lewis Phonological Analysis—Second Edition
Khatena-Torrance Creative Perception Inventory
Kindergarten Diagnostic Instrument—Second Edition
Kindergarten Inventory of Social-Emotional Tendencies
Knox's Cube Test

Learning Accomplishment Profile Diagnostic Edition
Listening Practices Feedback Report—360 Degrees

Martin and Pratt Nonword Reading Test
Maslach Burnout Inventory, Third Edition
Mayer-Salovey-Caruso Emotional Intelligence Test
Metropolitan Achievement Tests, Eighth Edition
Morrisby Profile
Multiple Affect Adjective Check List—Revised
Multiscale Dissociation Inventory

Neurobehavioral Functioning Inventory
Nurse Entrance Test

O*NET Interest Profiler
O*NET Work Importance Locator
Object-Oriented Programmer Analyst Staff Selector
Occupational Aptitude Survey and Interest Schedule—Third Edition

Personality Inventory for Children, Second Edition
Personalized Achievement Summary System
Personalysis®
Polish Proficiency Test
Posture and Fine Motor Assessment of Infants
Practical Adolescent Dual Diagnostic Interview
Preschool and Kindergarten Behavior Scales, Second Edition
Preschool and Primary Inventory of Phonological Awareness
The PreSchool Screening Test
Process Assessment of the Learner: Test Battery for Reading and Writing
Project Leader Skills Evaluation

Reynolds Adolescent Depression Scale—2nd Edition
Reynolds Intellectual Assessment Scales and the Reynolds Intellectual Screening Test
Rust Advanced Numerical Reasoning Appraisal

Sales Skills Test
SCAN-C: Test for Auditory Processing Disorders in Children—Revised
School Social Behavior Scales, Second Edition
Sensory Profile
Signposts Early Literacy Battery
STAR Math Version 2.0

State Trait-Depression Adjective Check Lists
Stirling Eating Disorder Scales
Structured Photographic Articulation Test II Featuring Dudsberry
Survey Ballot for Industry
Survey of Teenage Readiness and Neurodevelopment Status
Swallowing Ability and Function Evaluation

TerraNova, The Second Edition
Transition Behavior Scale—Second Edition

Utah Test of Language Development, Fourth Edition

Valpar Test of Essential Skills
Verbal Motor Production Assessment for Children
ViewPoint

Wechsler Preschool and Primary Scale of Intelligence—Third Edition
Weidner-Fensch Speech Screening Test
Wide Range Achievement Test—Expanded Edition
Word Meaning Through Listening
Work Personality Index
Working Memory Test Battery for Children
Workplace Skills Survey
World of Work Inventory

NEW TESTS REQUESTED BUT NOT RECEIVED

The staff of the Buros Institute endeavor to acquire copies of every new or revised commercially available test. Descriptions of all tests are included in Tests in Print *and reviews for all tests that meet our review criteria are included in* The Mental Measurements Yearbook. *A comprehensive search of multiple sources of test information is ongoing, and test materials are regularly requested from publishers. Many publishers routinely provide review copies of all new test publications. However, some publishers refuse to provide materials and others advertise tests long before the tests are actually published. Following is a list of test titles that have been requested and not yet provided.*

Aachen Test of Aphasia
The ABC Inventory-Extended
The Abel Assessment for Interest in Paraphilias
The Abel Assessment for Sexual Interest
Abilities Forecaster
Ability Test
Academic Profile
Accuracy Level Test
AccuRater
AccuVision
ACE Online Toolkit

Achievement Evaluation System
ACS California Chemistry Diagnostic Test
ACS Chemisty in the Community (Chem Com) Curriculum, High School Chemistry
ACS Examination in Instrumental Methods
ACT Assessment
Actions, Styles, Symbols in Kinetic Family Drawings
Adaptive Behavior Assessment System—Infant and Preschool
Admitted Student Questionnaire and Admitted Student Questionnaire Plus

The Adolescent Multiphasic Personality Inventory
Adolescent Self-Report and Projective Inventory
Adolescent/Adult Sensory Profile
Adult Child Distortion Scale
Adult Manifest Anxiety Scale
Adult Measure of Essential Skills
Adult Memory and Information Processing Battery
Adult Placement Inventory
Adult Self-Perception Profile
Adult-Adolescent Parenting Inventory
Advanced Management Tests
Advanced Placement Examination in Comparative Government and Politics
Advanced Placement Examination in Computer Science
Advanced Placement Examination in Economics
Advanced Placement Examination in Environmental Science
Advanced Placement Examination in Government and Politics
Advanced Placement Examination in International English Language
Advanced Placement Examination in Macroeconomics
Advanced Placement Examination in Microeconomics
Advanced Placement Examination in Psychology
Advanced Placement Examination in Statistics
Advanced Placement Examination in United States Government and Politics
Advanced Placement Program: Psychology
Advanced Test of Central Auditory Abilities
Advanced Work Aptitude Practice and Profile Set
AEPS Measurement for Birth to Three Years
AEPS Measurement for Three to Six Years
Ages & Stages Questionnaire: Social-Emotional
Ages & Stages Questionnaire—Second Edition
Air Conditioning Specialist
Alberta Infant Motor Scale
Alcohol Assessment and Treatment Profile
Algebra
Alleman Leadership Development Questionnaire
Alleman Mentoring Activities Questionnaire
Alleman Relationship Value Questionnaire
Allied Health Aptitude Test
American Health and Life Styles
The American Tobacco Survey
Analysis of Movement and Posture Disorganization
Analytical Reasoning
Analytical Reasoning Skills Battery
Analytical Reasoning-Apparatus
Angie/Andy Cartoon Trauma Scales
Antisocial Psychopathy Screening Device
The Aphasia Screening Test, 2nd Edition
Apperceptive Personality Test
Applicant Productivity Profile
Applicant Risk Profiler
Applied Technology Series
APTICOM
Aptitude Assessment

Aptitude Test Battery for Pupils in Standards 6 and 7
The Arabic Speaking Test
The Area Coordinator Achievement Test
Areas of Change Questionnaire
Arithmetic Test, Form A
Arizona Basic Assessment and Curriculum Utilization System for Young Handicapped Children
Armed Services Vocational Aptitude Battery
Armstrong Naming Test
Assertiveness Profile
Assess2Learn
Assessing Semantic Skills Through Everyday Themes
Assessment of Collaborative Tendencies
Assessment of Competencies and Traits
Assessment of Phonological Awareness
Assessment of Sound Awareness and Production
Assessment of Stuttering Behaviors
Associational Fluency
Associative Memory
At Risk Evaluation Surveys
Attention Battery for Children
Attention Index Survey
Attitude Survey
Attitudinal Listening Profile System
Auditory Memory Span
Auditory Perception Test for the Hearing Impaired
Auditory-Visual Single-Word Picture Vocabulary Test—Adolescent
The Austistic Continuum: An Assessment and Intervention Schedule
Authentic Assessment for the Intermediate Level in French
Authentic Assessment for the Intermediate Level in Spanish
Authentic Writing Screener
The Autistic Continuum
Auto Technician
Autobiographical Memory Interview

The Balanced Inventory of Desired Responses
Ball Aptitude Battery
The Balloons Test
BarOn Emotional Quotient 360 Assessment
BarOn Emotional Quotient-Inventory: Short Development Version
Barriers to Employment Success Inventory, 2nd Edition
Basic Academic Evaluation
Basic Academic Skills for Employment
Basic Banking Skills Battery
Basic Early Assessment of Reading
Basic English Literacy Skills Test
Basic Inventory of Natural Language
Basic Nursing Care I, II, III
Basic Proficiency in Medication Administration (First Version)
Basic Proficiency in Medication Administration (Second Version)
BDI—FastScreen for Medical Patients

Behavior Analysis Forms for Clinical Intervention
Behavior Forecaster
Behavior Rating Scale for Dementia
Behavior Style Analysis
Behavioral Intervention Plan
Behavioural Inattention Test
Benchmarking Organizational Emotional Intelligence
Bennett Mechanical Comprehension Test, Second Edition
Berlin Test of Amnesia
Bilingual Classroom Communication Profile
Bilingual Health and Developmental History Questionnaire
Bilingual Language Proficiency Questionnaire
Bilingual Vocabulary Assessment Measure
Bilingual Vocational Oral Proficiency Test
BldgTest
Bloomer Learning Test—Neurologically Enhanced
BMSI/ACCUTRACK
Body Dysmorphic Disorder Questionnaire
Body Image of Blind Children
Bogardus Scale
Boston Diagnostic Aphasia Examination, 3rd Edition
Brief Executive Assessment Battery
Brixton Spatial Anticipation Test
Building Maintenance Test
Bureau of Educational Measurements Attitude Test
Business Analyst Skills Evaluation [One-Hour]
Business English Assessment
Business Personality Indicator
B-Word Speed and Accuracy Typing Test

C, B, & A Maintenance Mechanics
CAI Study Skills Test
California Adaptive Behavior Scale
The California Critical Thinking Dispositions Inventory [Revised]
California Critical Thinking Skills Test [Revised]
The California Measure of Mental Motivation
The California Reasoning Appraisal
California Self Evaluation Scale
Caliper Inventory
Call Center Survey
The Call Centre Battery
Callier-Azusa Scale: H Edition
Cambridge-Stratford Study Skills Test
CAMDEX: The Cambridge Mental Disorders of the Elderly Examination
Campbell Leadership Index—Revised
Campbell-Hallam Team Leader Profile
Canadian Cognitive Abilities Test, Form K
Canadian Tests of Basic Skills, Forms K and L
Capability-Interest Comparisons
CAP-MOTA Motivation Assessment
CAP-SELF Self Concept Assessment
CAPSOL Style of Learning Assessment
Captain's Log

Career Ability Placement Survey
Career Assessment Battery
Career Decision Diagnostic Assessment
Career Decision Making Self-Efficacy Scale
Career Exploration Inventory: A Guide for Exploring Work, Leisure, and Learning, Second Edition
Career Finder
Career Guidance Inventory II
Career Mapper
Career Orientation Placement and Evaluation Survey
Career Portfolio Builder
Career Preference Scale
Career Selection Questionnaire
Career Suitability Profile
Caregiver-Administered Communication Inventory
Caring for Persons with AIDS
Carolina Curriculum for Infants and Toddlers with Special Needs, 2nd Edition
Carolina Developmental Profile (and kit)
Cellular Technician
Chally Assessment
Change Agent Questionnaire
Change Management Effectiveness Profile
Change Style Indicator
Chapin Social Insight Test
Chemical Abuse Scale
Chemical Dependency Assessment Profile
Chemical Reading
Chemistry Test
Child and Adolescent Diagnostic Scales
Child and Adolescent Functional Assessment Scale
Child Behavior Checklist [2001 Revisions]
Child Health Questionnaire
Children's Acquired Aphasia Screening Test
Children's Family Environment Scale
Children's Speech Intelligibility Measure
Children's Depression Inventory [Revised]
Children's Interaction Matrix
Children's Self-Report and Projective Inventory
Christenson Dietary Inventory
C.I.T.E. Academic Learning Styles
Clark-Beck Obsessive-Compulsive Inventory
Clarke Sexual History Questionnaire
Classroom Assessment of Developmental Skills
CLEP Education Assessment Series
CLEP Subject Examination in Freshman College Composition
Clerical Series Test Modules
Clerical Series Test: Dictation/Transcription Cassette
Clerical Series Test: Oral Instructions Cassette
Clerical Series Test: Oral Instructions Forms Completion
Clerical Series Test: Typing Test
Clerical Skills Series
Clerical Skills Test
The Clinical Assessment of Language Comprehension
Clock Drawing

Cloze Reading Tests 1-3, Second Edition
CNC Math (Trig. Test)
CNC Operator
Coaching Competence Questionnaire
Coaching Effectiveness Profile
Cognitive (Intelligence) Test: Nonverbal
Cognitive Abilities Test, Form 6
The Cognitive Assessment of Minnesota
Cognitive Levels Test
Cognitive Speed Battery
Cognitive Stability Index
Cognitive, Linguistic and Social-Communicative Scales
College Board Achievement Tests: French With Listening
College Board Achievement Tests: Japanese With Listening
College Board Descriptive Tests System
College Board Institutional SAT II: American History and Social Studies Subject Test
College Board Institutional SAT II: Biology E/M Subject Test
College Board Institutional SAT II: Chemistry Subject Test
College Board Institutional SAT II: Chinese with Listening Subject Test
College Board Institutional SAT II: English Language Proficiency Test
College Board Institutional SAT II: French Subject Test
College Board Institutional SAT II: French with Listening Subject Tests
College Board Institutional SAT II: German Subject Test
College Board Institutional SAT II: German with Listening Subject Test
College Board Institutional SAT II: Italian Subject Test
College Board Institutional SAT II: Japanese with Listening Subject Test
College Board Institutional SAT II: Latin Subject Test
College Board Institutional SAT II: Literature Subject Test
College Board Institutional SAT II: Mathematics Level IC Subject Tests, and SAT II: Mathematics Level II C Subject Tests
College Board Institutional SAT II: Modern Hebrew Subject Test
College Board Institutional SAT II: Physics Subject Test
College Board Institutional SAT II: Spanish Subject Test
College Board Institutional SAT II: Spanish with Listening Subject Test
College Board Institutional SAT II: World History Subject Test
College Board Institutional SAT II: Writing Subject Test
College Board SAT I Reasoning Test

College Board SAT II: American History and Social Studies Subject Test
College Board SAT II: Biology E/M Subject Test
College Board SAT II: Biology Subject Test
College Board SAT II: Chemistry Subject Test
College Board SAT II: English Language Proficiency Test
College Board SAT II: French Subject Test
College Board SAT II: French with Listening Subject Test
College Board SAT II: German Subject Test
College Board SAT II: German with Listening Subject Test
College Board SAT II: Korean with Listening Subject Test
College Board SAT II: Latin Subject Test
College Board SAT II: Literature Subject Test
College Board SAT II: Mathematics Level IC and SAT II: Mathematics Level IIC
College Board SAT II: Modern Hebrew Subject Test
College Board SAT II: Physics Subject Test
College Board SAT II: Spanish Subject Test
College Board SAT II: Spanish with Listening Subject Test
College Board SAT II: Subject Test in Chinese with Listening
College Board SAT II: Subject Test in Italian
College Board SAT II: Subject Test in Japanese with Listening
College Board SAT II: World History Subject Test
College Board SAT II: Writing Subject Test
College Board SAT Program
College Portfolio Builder
College Student Expectations Questionnaire, Second Edition
College Student Experiences Questionnaire, Fourth Edition
Collegiate Assessment of Academic Proficiency [Revised]
The Color Form Sorting Test
Color Span Test, Revised
Colorado Malingering Tests
Colorado Neuropsychology Tests
Combustion Control Technician
Commercial Refrigeration Examination
Communication and Symbolic Behavior Scales—Developmental Profile
The Communication Behaviors Inventory II
Communication Competency Assessment Instrument
Communication Effectiveness Profile
Communication Effectiveness Scale
Communication Independence Profile for Adults
Communication Skills Assessments
Communication Style Inventory
Communique
COMPASS Managerial Practices Profile
Compassion Manual

Competency-Based Position Analysis
Comprehensive Assessment of Reading Strategies II
Comprehensive English Language Test
Comprehensive Nursing Achievement Test
Comprehensive Nursing Achievement Test for Baccalaureate Nursing Students
Comprehensive Nursing Achievement Test for Practical Nursing Students
Comprehensive Occupational Exams
Comprehensive Stress Inventory
Comprehensive Test of Adaptive Behavior—Revised
Computer Optimized Multimedia Intelligence Test
Computer Programmer Ability Battery
Comrey Personality Scales—Short Form
The Concise Learning Styles Assessment
Concussion Resolution Index
Conners Adult ADHD Diagnostic Interview for DSM-IV
Conners' Continuous Performance Test for Windows: Kiddie Version
Controller Staff Selector
Copeland Symptom Checklist for Attention Deficit Disorders
Coping Operations Preference Enquiry
COPS Interest Inventory (1995 Revision)
Corporate Communication Assessment
Cortical Vision Screening Test
Creativity Questionnaire
Creativity/Innovation Effectiveness Profile
Criterion Inventory Series
Criterion Test of Basic Skills-2
Criterion Validated Written Test for Emergency Medical Practitioner
Criterion Validated Written Test for Fire Medic
Criterion Validated Written Tests for Firefighter [Revised]
Criterion-Referenced Articulation Profile
Critical Thinking Test
CRT Skills Test
Cube Construction Test
Cultural Diversity and Awareness Profile
Culture for Diversity Inventory
Customer Service Climate Survey
Customer Service Commitment Profile
Customer Service Listening Skills Exercise
Customer Service Profile
Customer Service Simulator
Customer Service Skills Assessment
Customer Service Skills Inventory
Customer Service Survey

Daily Living Questionnaire
Data Entry and Data Checking Tests
Data Rater
De Santi Cloze Reading Inventory
Dealing With Conflict Instrument
DecideX

Decision Scale for Hearing Officers
Defendant Questionnaire
Denison Leadership Development Survey
Denison Organizational Culture Survey
DEST: Dental Ethical Sensitivity Test
Detention Promotions Test—Complete Service [Revised]
Developmental Eye Movement Test
Developmental Inventory of Learned Skills
Developmental Reading Assessment
Diagnostic and Evaluative Procedure for Autogenic Training
Diagnostic Assessment Scales for Attention Deficit/Hyperactivity Disorder
Diagnostic Behavior Checklist
Diagnostic German Test
Diagnostic Prescriptive Assessment
Diagnostic Readiness Test for RN Licensure
Diagnostic Test for High School Math
Diagnostic Test for Pre-Algebra Math
DIBELS: Dynamic Indicators of Basic Early Literacy Skills, Sixth Edition
DIBELS: Oral Reading Fluency Assessment
Diet Therapy and Applied Nutrition
Dimensional Assessment of Personality Pathology—Basic Questionnaire
The Dimensions of Depression Profile for Children and Adolescents
The Discovering Diversity Profile and Facilitator's Kit
Disruptive Behavior Disorders Rating Scale
Disruptive Behavior Rating Scale
Diversity Survey
Doors and People
Draw A Person Questionnaire
Drug Abuse Screening Test
Drug Store Applicant Inventory
Drug Use Screening Inventory
Drug/Alcohol Attitude Survey
DSM-Oriented Scales [Revised]
Dynamic Assessment of Test Accommodations
Dynamic Factors Survey

Early Childhood Inventory-4 Norms Kit
Early Literacy Diagnostic Test
Early Math Diagnostic Assessment
Early Motor Control Scales
Early Reading Diagnostic Assessment—Revised
Eating Disorder Examination (Diagnostic Version), Edition 11.3
Edinburgh Reading Tests (Stages 1–4)
Edinburgh Reasoning Series
EDS Diagnostic Skill Level Inventory For Writing Skills
Education Interest Inventory II
Educational Development Series [1997-1998 Norms]
Educational Values

Educators Survey

Effective Reading Tests

Efron Visual Acuity Test

Elect. & Inst. Technician

ElecTest

Electrical Technician I

Electrical Technician II

Emo Questionnaire [Revised]

Emotional Competence Inventory

Emotional Intelligence Style Profile

Emotional or Behavior Disorder Scale [Revised]

Employability Attitudes

Employee Adjustment Survey

Employee Empowerment Survey

Employee Evaluation of Management Survey

Employee Opinion Survey

Employee Productivity Index

Employee Productivity Profile

Employment Productivity Index

Empowerment Management Inventory

English and Citizenship Test

The English Language Skills Profile

Enriching and Nurturing Relationship Issues, Communication, and Happiness

Entry Level Police Officer Examination

ERB Writing Assessment [Revised]

Erhardt Developmental Prehension Assessment (Revised)

Erhardt Developmental Vision Assessment (Revised)

Essential Skills Screener

Evaluating Movement and Posture Disorganization: A Criteria-Based Reference Format for Observing and Analyzing Motor Behavior in Children with Learning Disabilities

The Expressive Language Test

Extended DISC

Eysenck Personality Questionnaire [Revised]

Eysenck Personality Scales

Facial Expressions of Emotion: Stimulus Test

Family Crisis Oriented Personal Evaluation Scales

Family History Analysis

Family Inventories

F.A.S.T. Test (Flowers Auditory Screening Test)

Feedback Edition of the Strength Development Inventory

Feedback Portrait of Overdone Strengths

Feedback Portrait of Personal Strengths

Finger Dexterity

Fire Engineer

Fire Inspector and Senior Fire Inspector

Fire Promotion Tests—Complete Service [Revised]

Fire Service Administrator (Battalion Chief)

Fire Service Administrator (Captain) 574

Fire Service Administrator (Chief) 578

Fire Service Administrator (Deputy Chief)

Fire Service Supervisor (Sergeant, Lieutenant)

Fire Service Test: Radio Operator and Senior Radio Operator

Firefighter Examinations 275.1 and 275.2

Firefighter Test: B-3

Firefighter Test: B-4

Fleishman Job Analysis Survey

Fogel Word Processing Operator Test

Four Sigma Qualifying Test

Frames of Reference in Sentencing and Parole Inventory

Freiburger Personality Inventory, Revised Version

French Reading Comprehension Tests

The French Speaking Test

Functional Analysis of Behavior

Functional Assessment and Intervention System: Improving School Behavior

Functional Communication Profile

Fundamentals for Practical Nursing Students

Fundamentals of Drug Therapy

The Gardner Children's Projective Battery

Gardner Social (Maturity) Developmental Scale

Gates-MacGinitie Reading Test, Second Canadian Edition

Gates-MacGinitie Reading Tests, Forms S and T, Fourth Edition

General Clerical Test—Revised

General Education Performance Index

General Interests Scale

General Office Work Test, Revised Edition

The German Speaking Test

Gerontological Test of Concentration

Gesell Kindergarten Assessment—Ages 4-6

Gesell Preschool Assessment—Ages 2 1/2 to 6

Gesell School Age Assessment—Ages 5-9

Giessen Complaint Inventory for Children and Adolescents

Giessen Test

Gifted and Talented Evaluation Scales

Gifted Rating Scales

Goal/Objective Setting Profile

Graded Assessment in Mathematics

Graded Nonword Reading Test

Graduate Appraisal Questionnaire

Graduate Program Self-Assessment Service

The Graduate Record Examinations Biochemistry, Cell and Molecular Biology Test

The Graduation Exam Book

Grammatical Analysis of Elicited Language—Complex Sentence Level

Griffiths Mental Development Scales [Revised]

Group Literacy Assessment

Group Mathematics Test, Third Edition

Group Perceptions Inventory

Group Reading Test 9-14

Group Review of Algebra Topics

Group-Level Team Assessment

Job Skills Training Needs Assessment
Job Values Inventory
Job-O Enhanced
Jonico Questionnaire
Jordan Left-Right Reversal Test—Revised
The Julia Farr Services Post-Traumatic Amnesia Scale
Junior Assessment Tests
Junior High School Test of Economics
Junior Scholastic Aptitude Test Battery (Standard 5)

The Kaufman Speech Praxis Test for Children
The Kendrick Assessment Scales of Cognitive Age-
    ing
Kindergarten Readiness Checklists for Parents
Knowledge of Occupations Test (Revised)
Kuder Career Search
Kuder Skills Assessment
Kuhlmann-Anderson Tests [1997 norms/standards]

Laboratory Technician (Mfg.)
Langdon Adult Intelligence Test
Language Processing Test-Revised
Language Proficiency Measure
LARR Test of Emergent Literacy
Law Enforcement Applicant Inventory
LEAD (Leader Effectiveness and Adaptability De-
    scription) Instrument: Self/Other
Leadership Dynamics Inventory
Leadership Effectiveness Profile
Leadership Qualities Scale
Leadership Scale: Staff Member/Manager
Leadership Skills Assessment
Leadership Skills Test
Learning/Working Styles Media Kit
Legal Issues for Managers Skills Assessments
Legendary Service Leader Assessment
Leisure to Occupations Search
Leisure/Work Search Inventory
The Leisure-Occupation Connection Search
Level of Service Inventory—Case Management Inven-
    tory
Level of Service Inventory—Revised: Youth Version
Life Events Scale for Children
Life Interpersonal History Enquiry
Life Style Inventory
Lifespace Access Profile
Lifestyle Questionnaire
Light Commercial Air-Conditioning and Heating Ex-
    amination
Lights' Retention Scale [Revised Edition 1998]
Listening Effectiveness Profile
The Listening Test
Literacy Assessment Survey
Literacy Probe 7–9
Location Learning Test
Long-Term Care Nursing Assistant Test
Lore Leadership Assessment II

MacArthur Competence Assessment Tool for Treat-
    ment
The MacArthur Competence Assessment Tool—Crimi-
    nal Adjudication
Macmillan Group Reading Test 9-14
Macmillan Individual Reading Analysis
Maculaitis Assessment of Competencies II
Maintenance Electrician A or B
Major Field Tests
Making a Terrific Career Happen
Management & Leadership Skills Assessments
Management & Supervisory Skills
Management Aptitude Test
Management Behavior Assessment Test
Management Burnout Scale
Management Candidate Profile
Management Practices Inventory
Management Preference Inventory
Management Readiness Profile
Management Training Needs Analysis
Manual Dexterity Test
MAP: Mathematics Assessment Process (Grades K-8)
Marital Attitude Evaluation
Marriage Assessment Inventory
Match Check
Maternity and Child Nursing
Maternity Nursing for Practical Nursing Students (New
    Edition)
Mathematical Achievement Test
Mathematics Tests, Diagnostic, Primary Level
Matson Evaluation of Social Skills With Youngsters
Mattox Performance Appraisal Data Sheet
The Meade Movement Assessment
Measure of Individual Differences in Dominance-Sub-
    missiveness
Measures of Guidance Impact
Measures of Individual Differences in Temperament
Mechanical Technician
Medical Profile Questionnaire
Medications for Coronary Care
Meeker Structure of Intellect Screening for Learning &
    Thinking Abilities
Meeting Effectiveness Inventory Self/Other
Meeting Effectiveness Questionnaire
Member Satisfaction Survey
Mental Health Concepts for Practical Nursing Stu-
    dents
Metric Assessment of Personality
METROPOLITAN8 Writing Test
Michigan Prescriptive Program in English [1996 Revi-
    sion]
Michigan Screening Profile of Parenting
Middle Infant Screening Test
The Middlesex Elderly Assessment of Mental State
Miller Dependency Scale
Millwright Test
MindLadder: Primary Sources Inventory

Mini-Hilson Life Adjustment Profile
Mini-SCID
Minnesota Developmental Programming System Behavioral Scales
Minnesota Handwriting Assessment
Minnesota Prekindergarten Inventory
Mirror Edition of the Personal Values Inventory
Missouri Aptitude and Career Information Inventory
Missouri Comprehensive Student Needs Survey
Mobile Equipment Mechanic
Mobile Equipment Operator
Moray House Tests
Mortimer-Filkins Test for Problem Drinkers
Motivation Questionnaire
Motivational Structure Questionnaire
Motive-A Motivational Analysis
Movement ABC
Multi-CrafTest
Multi-Digit Memory Test
Multidimensional Perfectionism Scale
Multidimensional Personality Questionnaire
Multidisciplinary Cognitive Assessment System
Multifactor Leadership Questionnaire for Teams for Research
Multilingual Aphasia Examination—2nd Edition
Multiphasic Sex Inventory
Multiple Assessment Series for the Primary Grades
Multiple Intelligences Development Assessment Scales
Multistate Bar Examination
Multistate Essay Examination
Multistate Performance Test
Musical Aptitude Profile [1995 Revision]

Naglieri Nonverbal Ability Test—Individual Administration
National Assessment of Educational Progress—Released Exercises
National Curriculum Checkpoints
National Survey of Student Engagement
Naturalist Action Test
NCTE Cooperative Test of Critical Reading and Appreciation
Negotiating Style Instrument
Nelson Quickcheck Placement Tests
Network Technician Staff Selector
Networking & Relationship Building Profile
Neuropsychological Aging Inventory
New Citizens Project: The English and Citizenship Test
The New Jersey Test of Children's Reasoning
The New Jersey Test of Reasoning [Adult Version]
New Reading Analysis
New Standards Reference Examinations: English Language Arts
New Standards Reference Examinations: Mathematics
New Tower of London

The New York Longitudinal Study Adult Temperament Questionnaire
NFER-Nelson Non-Verbal Reasoning Tests
NFER-Nelson Verbal Reasoning Tests
NOCTI Experienced Worker Assessments
NOCTI Industrial Assessments
NOCTI Job Ready Assessments
The Nonspeech Test for Receptive/Expressive Language
Normative Adaptive Behavior Checklist—Revised
Norris-Ryan Argument Analysis Test
NSight Personality Questionnaire
NSight Positive IMpressions Questionnaire
NTE Specialty Area Tests: School Social Worker
Numerical Computation
Numerical Reasoning
Nurse Aide (Assistant) Program
Nursing Care in Mental Health and Mental Illness
Nursing Care of Adults in Special Care Units
Nursing Care of Adults, Parts I and II
Nursing Mobility Profile I
Nursing Mobility Profile II (New Edition 1989)
Nursing of Children
Nursing of Children for Practical Nursing Students
Nursing the Childbearing Family

Observation Ability Test for the Police Service
Occupational Clues
Occupational Interest Test II
Occupational Preference Inventory
Occupational Skills Inventory
Office Proficiency Assessment & Certification
Office Skills Assessment Battery
Office Systems Battery
Ohio Vocational Competency Assessment
O'Neill Talent Inventory
OPQ32
The Optimizer II
OQ-10.2 (mini-OQ)
OQ-45.2
Oral Communication Battery
Organic Dysfunction Survey Schedules
Organization Change & Employee Perceptions Skills Assessments
Organizational Assessment Survey
Organizational Focus Questionnaire
Organizational Survey System
Orpheus
OSHA Violations Safety Test
Outcome Questionnaire
Overseas Assignment Inventory

Pacesetter
PACS Toys Screening Assessment
Pain Assessment Questionnaire—Revised
Pair Behavioral Style Instrument
Paper Folding
Parent Success Indicator

Parent-Child Care
Parenting Stress Index—Third Edition Short Form
Parsky Inventory of Basic Math Skills
Partner Power Profile
Partnering Development Assessment
P.A.S.S. III Survey
Pathognomonic Scale
Pathways to Independence, Second Edition
PAVE (Principles, Attitudes, and Values for Employ-
    ment)
PCA Checklist for Computer Access
Pediatric Oral Skills Package
Pediatric Symptoms Checklist
Perceptual Archetypal Orientation Inventory
Performance Management Assessment System
Performance On-Line
Performance Skills Quality Teams Assessment
Performer
Personal Characteristics Inventory
Personal Competency Framework
The Personal Development Profile
Personal Directions®
Personal Dynamics Profile
Personal Interest and Values Survey
Personal Productivity Assessment
Personal Profile System 2800 Series
Personal Resource Assessment Battery
Personal Stress & Well-being Assessment
Personal Styles Inventory [PSI-120] [1999 Revision]
Personal Success Profile
The Personality Preference Profile
Personality Questionnaire
Personality Scanner
The Personalized Relationship Need Profile
Personalyis
The Personnel Assessment Form
Personnel Security Standards Psychological Questionnaire
Personnel Selection Inventory
The PETAL Speech Assessment
PFK9-14: Personality Questionnaire for Children aged
    9 to 14 Years, 3 Revised Edition
Pharmacology for Practical Nursing Students (New
    Edition)
Pharmacology in Clinical Nursing (New Edition)
Pharmacology Readiness Test
Phonics-Based Reading Test
The Phonological Awareness Profile
The Phonological Awareness Test
Pictorial Inventory of Careers
Picture Interest Exploration Survey
Picture Motivation Tests
Picture Personality Test for Indian South Africans
Picture Situation Test
Piers-Harris Children's Self-Concept Scale (The Way
    I Feel About Myself) [Revised]
Pikunas Adult Stress Inventory
PIN-POINT

PIP Developmental Charts, Second Edition
PipeTest
PLAN [Revised]
Plotkin Index
Plumber-Pipefitter Test
PM Benchmark Kit
Police Promotion Test—Complete Service [Revised]
Police Administrator (Assistant Chief) 566
Police Administrator (Captain) 565
Police Administrator (Chief) 568
Police Administrator (Lieutenant) 564
Police Corporal/Sergeant Examination 562 and 563
Police Officer Examinations 175.1 and 175.2
Police Officer: A-2
Police Radio Dispatcher
Polymath Intellectual Ability Scale
Post-Heroic Leadership
Power and Performance Measures
Power Perception Profile
Pragmatics Profile of Everyday Communication Skills
    in Adults
Pragmatics Profile of Everyday Communication Skills
    in Children
The Praxis Series: Professional Assessments for Begin-
    ning Teachers
Pre-Admission Examination-PN
Precision Handling Performance Assessment Unit
Precision Measurement
Predictive Index
The Predictive Reading Profile
Predictive Sales Survey
The Preliminary Chinese Proficiency Test
The Preliminary Hindi Proficiency Test
The Preliminary Japanese Speaking Test
Premorbid Ability Evaluator
The Pre-School Evaluation Scale
Preschool Language Scale, Fourth Edition
Preschool Reading Attitude Scale
The Press Test [Revised]
Prevention Planning Survey
The Prevue Assessment
Primary Sources Inventory
Pro Care
Probity/Honesty Inventory
Problem Situation Inventory
Problem-Solving & Decision-Making Profile
Process Flow
Production & Maintenance Technician (Metal Pro-
    cessing)
The Professional Judgment Rating Form
Professional Role Orientation Inventory
Profile of Adaptation to Life
Profile of Mood States, Bi-Polar Form
Profile of Personal Development Needs
The Profile Test
Program Evaluation Survey
Programmer Analyst Aptitude Test [One-Hour Version]

Progress in English 8-13
Project Engineer
Projective Storytelling Cards
ProQuest
Psychiatric Diagnostic Screening Questionnaire
Psychopathy Screening Device
Psychotropic Drug Administration
Pyramids and Palm Trees Test

Quality Customer Service Assessment
Quality Customer Service Test
Quality Effectiveness Profile
Quality Healthcare Employee Inventory
The Quant Q
Questionnaire on Aggressive Behavior in Real Situations
Questionnaire on Beliefs of Competency and Locus of Control
Quick Assessments for Neurogenic Communication Disorders

Radio Operator and Senior Radio Operator
Randot Stereotests
Rate Level Test
Rauding Efficiency Level Test
Rauding Scale Qualification Test
RCJS Office Arithmetic (Form CA)
RCJS Office Reading (Form G)
RCJS Reading Prints and Drawings (Form A)
Readiness Scale Self/Manager
Readiness Scale Staff Member/Manager
Readiness Style Match Staff Member/Manager
Reading (Electronics & Instrumentation)
Reading (Food Industry)
Reading Efficiency Level Battery
Reading Prints & Drawings (Decimal Version)
Reading Progress Scale
Reading Style Inventory 2000
Reading Test
Reading Test, Form A
Recent Memory Screening Test
Recruitment Consultant Questionnaire
Refrigeration Mechanic
Rehabilitation Survey of Problems and Coping
Reid Drug Scale
Reid Sales Productivity Scale
Reid Service Relations Scale
Reiss Screen for Maladaptive Behavior
Relationship Sellilng Skills Inventory
Repertory Grid Technique
RESIST
Retail Management Assessment Inventory
Retail Sales Questionnaire
Retail Store Manager Staff Selector
Revised Child Behavior Checklist
Reynell Developmental Language Scales—Second Revision (1986)
Reynolds Bully-Victimization Scales For Schools

The Right Hemisphere Language Battery, 2nd Edition
Rivermead Assessment of Somatosensory Performance
The Rivermead Behavioural Memory Test—Extended Version
Rossetti Infant-Toddler Language Scale

Safety Effectiveness Profile
Sage Vocational Assessment System
Sales Indicator
Sales Potential Inventory
Sales Skills
Sales Skills Profile
Sales Talent Assessment Review
Salford Sentence Reading Test (Revised)
SAT On-Campus Program (Institutional SAT I: Reasoning Test and SAT II: Subject Tests)
SBS Inventory
Scale of Intrinsic versus Extrinsic Orientation in the Classroom
Schedules for Clinical Assessment in Neuropsychiatry
Schematic Differential Scale
Scholastic Proficiency Test—Higher Primary Level
School and College Ability Tests, Third Edition
School Child Stress Scale
School Diversity Inventory
School Improvement Follow-Up Survey
School Leaders Licensure Assessment
School Principal Job Functions Inventory
School Readiness Tests for Blind Children
School Situations Questionnaire
School-Age Care Environment Rating Scale
School-to-Work Career Survey
Science Research Temperament Scale
Scoreboard
Screening Kit of Language Development
Screening Personality and Intellectual Impairment in the Aged
Secord Contextual Articulation Tests
Security Aptitude Fitness Evaluation—Resistance
The Self-Administered Planning Test
Self-Assessment of Counselor Competencies
Self-Directed Learning Readiness Scale [Revised]
Self-Directed Search—New Zealand Revision
Self-Directed Team Assessment
The Self-Perception Profile for Adults
Self-Perception Profile for Learning Disabled Students
Semistructured Clinical Interview for Children and Adolescents [Revised]
Senior South African Individual Scale—Revised
Sensorimotor Performance Analysis
The Sensorimotor Performance Analysis
SEPO (Serial Position) Test for the Detection of Guilty/Special Knowledge
Service Ability Inventory
Service Skills Indicator
Severe Impairment Battery
SF-12: Physical and Mental Health Summary Scales

SF-36: Physical and Mental Health Summary Scales
Shape Assembly
The Shapes Analysis Test
Shared Vision Survey
Sheffield Screening Test for Acquired Language Disorders
Side Effects Profile for Exceptional Children
Sitting Assessment for Children with Neuromotor Dysfunction
Situational Leadership II Leadership 16PF Clinical Analysis Questionnaire
Skills Assessment
Situational Leadership® [Revised]
Six Factor Automated Vocational Assessment System
SkillCheck Professional Plus
Skills Confidence Inventory
Slosson Intelligence Test—Primary
Slosson Oral Reading Test—Revised 3
Slosson Visual-Motor Performance Test
Slosson Written Expression Test
Slosson-Diagnostic Math Screener
Social Competency Rating Form
Social Problem Solving Inventory—Revised
The Social Support Scale for Children
Socially Appropriate and Inappropriate Development
Socio-Sexual Knowledge—Attitudes Assessment Tool—Revised
Somatization-Malingering Inventory
SON—R2 1/2–7
Spanish Articulation Measures
Spanish Language Assessment Procedures [Revised 1995 Edition]
Spanish Reading Inventory
Spanish Speaking Test (The)
The Spanish Structured Photographic Expressive Language Test–II
Spanish Test for Assessing Morphologic Production
Specialty Practice Tests: End-of-Course Exams
The Speed and Capacity of Language-Processing Test
Spelling: Approaches to Teaching and Assessment (includes the South Australian Spelling Test)
Sr. Maint. Tech. Pipefitter
Staff Burnout Scale for Police and Security Personnel
The Staffordshire Mathematics Test
Stages of Concern Questionnaire
Stanford-Binet Intelligence Scale, Fourth Edition—Nonverbal Short Form
Stanford-Binet Intelligence Scales, Fifth Edition
Station Employee Applicant Inventory
Station Manager Applicant Inventory
Step One Survey
Stephen's Oral Language Screening Test
Stones: The Concepts About Print Test
Story Recall Test
Stress Vector Analysis Test Series
Strong Interest and Skills Confidence Inventory
Stroop Test

Structural Analysis of Social Behavior
Structured Interview for Disorders of Extreme Stress & Traumatic Antecedents Questionnaire—Self Report
Structured Observational Test of Function
Student Instructional Report II
Student Motivation Diagnostic Questionnaire
Success Profiler
Super's Work Values Inventory—Revised
SuperSelect
Supervisory Attitude Test
Supervisory Proficiency Tests
Supervisory Simulator
Supervisory Skills Test
The Supplement to the Children's Apperception Test
The Survey of Quality Values in Practice
Syracuse Play-Based Assessment
System for Testing and Evaluation of Potential
Systematic Assessment of Voice

Tactile Abilities Test
Tangent Screen
TapDance
Teacher Rating of Academic Achievement Motivation
Teacher-Student Communication Inventory
Team Climate Inventory
Team Communication Effectiveness Assessment
Team Empowerment Practices Test
Team Leader Skills Assessment
Team Member Behavior Analysis
Team Performance Questionnaire
Team Skills
Team Skills Indicator
Teambuilding Effectiveness
Team-Building Effectiveness Profile
Team-Review Survey
Technology and Internet Assessment
Teele Inventory for Multiple Intelligences
Telemarketing Applicant Inventory
Temperament and Atypical Behavior Scale
Temperament Comparator
Test Alert (Test Preparation)
Test of Academic Achievement Skills—Revised
Test of Adult Literacy Skills
Test of Attentiveness Under Pressure
Test of Auditory Processes
Test of Auditory Reasoning and Processing Skills
Test of Auditory-Perceptual Skills, Second Edition
Test of Auditory-Perceptual Skills, Upper Level
Test of Early Learning Skills
Test of Everyday Attention
Test of Everyday Attention for Children
The Test of Everyday Reasoning
Test of Functional Cerebral Damage
Test of General Intellectual Skills
Test of Handwriting Skills
Test of Inductive Reasoning Principles
Test of Joining Numbers

Test of Linguistic Awareness in Reading Readiness
Test of Oral Reading and Comprehension Skills
Test of Pictures/Forms/Letters/Numbers Spatial Orientation and Sequencing Skills
Test of Problem Solving—Adolescent
Test of Problem Solving—Elementary, Revised
Test of Problem Solving-Revised-Elementary
Test of Relational Concepts [Norms for Deaf Children]
Test of Visual-Motor Skills, Revised
Test of Visual-Motor Skills, Upper Level
Test of Visual-Perceptual Skills (Non-Motor) Upper Level: Revised
Test of Visual-Perceptual Skills (Non-Motor): Revised
Test of Visual-Perceptual Skills, Upper Level
Test That's Not a Test
Tests of General Educational Development [The GED Tests] [1993 Revision]
Tests of Reading Comprehension—Revised
Tetreau-Trahan Visual Interest Test
The Texas Oral Proficiency Test
The ACT Evaluation/Survey Service [Revised]
Theological School Inventory
Thinking Creatively with Sounds and Words
360 Degree Assessment and Development
360 Degree Feedback Assessment
Time Management Effectiveness Profile
Time Management Inventory
Titmus Stereo Fly Test
Tobacco Use Survey
The Toglia Category Assessment
Took Knowledge & Use
Torrance Tests of Creative Thinking [with 1998 norms]
Total Quality Management Survey
TotalView
Training Needs Assessment for Modern Leaders Skills
Training Needs Assessment Test
Training Proficiency Scale
Trier Personality Inventory
Truck Driver Inventory
Trustworthiness Attitude Survey
The Two Cultures Test
Type Rater
Type Rater Plus

Undergraduate Assessment Program: Business Test
Understanding Ambiguity: An Assessment of Pragmatic Meaning
Urban District Assessment Consortium's Alternative Accountability Assessments

Verb and Sentence Test
Verbal Fluency Task
Verbal Integration Test
Vigil Continuous Performance Test
Visit-Specific Patient Satisfaction Survey for Clinics

The Visual Object and Space Perception Battery
Visual Patterns Test
Vocabulary
The Vocabulary Gradient Test
Vocational Decision-Making Interview, Revised Edition
Vocational Interest Profile Report
Vocational Interest, Experience and Skill Assessment (VIESA), 2nd Canadian Edition
Voices of Faith: A Portrait of Congregational Life

W-APT Programming Aptitude Test
Warehouse & Shipping Reading
Warehouse/Plant Worker Staff Selector
Watson-Glaser Critical Thinking Appraisal—Short Form
Ways of Coping Scale
Wechsler Test of Adult Reading
Weinbaum Schooling Attitudes Scale
Welder, Repair & Maint.
The Wessex Head Injury Matrix
What About You?
Wide Range Achievement Test—Expanded Early Reading Assessment
Wilde Intelligence Test
Wonderlic Employee Opinion Survey
Wonderlic Personnel Test: Americans With Disabilities Act Hiring Kit
Word Association
Word Identification Scale [1999 Revision]
Word Processing Aptitude Battery
Word Rater
The WORD Test-Adolescent
The WORD Test-R (Elementary)
Work Mate
Work Orientation and Values Survey
Work Preference Inventory
Work Preference Questionnaire
The Work Sampling System
Work Skills Series Manual Dexterity
Work Style Preference Inventory
Work Team Simulator
Workforce Learning Systems
Working Together: An Assessment of Collaboration
Workplace Ergonomics Profile
Workplace Skills Survey—Form E
Work-Readiness Cognitive Screen
Wright & Ayre Stuttering Self-Rating Profile
Writing Speed

Y-OQ-2.01
Y-OQ-SR 2.0
Yorkdale Test of Basic English Competence

Zurich Reading Abilities Test

CONTRIBUTING TEST REVIEWERS

SHAWN K. ACHESON, Assistant Professor, Western Carolina University, Cullowhee, NC

PHILLIP L. ACKERMAN, Professor of Psychology, Georgia Institute of Technology, Atlanta, GA

EUGENE V. AIDMAN, Lecturer in Psychology, University of Ballarat, Victoria, Australia

MARK A. ALBANESE, Professor, Population Health Sciences, Medical Sciences Center, University of Wisconsin—Madison, Madison, WI

FELITO ALDARONDO, Senior Staff Psychologist, University Counseling and Testing Center, University of Kentucky, Lexington, KY

SARAH J. ALLEN, Associate Professor of School Psychology, University of Cincinnati, Cincinnati, OH

JULIE A. ALLISON, Associate Professor of Psychology, Pittsburg State University, Pittsburg, KS

JOHN O. ANDERSON, Professor and Chair, Department of Educational Psychology, University of Victoria, Victoria, British Columbia, Canada

LUANNE ANDERSSON, Assistant Professor, Department of Speech-Language Pathology and Audiology, Ithaca College, Ithaca, NY

PAUL A. ARBISI, Staff Psychologist, Minneapolis VA Medical Center, and Assistant Professor, Departments of Psychiatry and Psychology, University of Minnesota, Minneapolis, MN

RAOUL A. ARREOLA, Professor and Director, Educational Evaluation and Development, The University of Tennessee Health Science Center, Memphis, TN

MICHELLE ATHANASIOU, Associate Professor of School Psychology, University of Northern Colorado, Greeley, CO

JAMES A. ATHANASOU, Associate Professor, Faculty of Education, University of Technology, Sydney, Australia

MARK J. ATKINSON, Adjunct Associate Professor, Department of Psychiatry, University of Calgary, Calgary, Alberta, Canada

JEFFREY A. ATLAS, Clinical Psychologist, St. Christopehr-Ottilie Services for Children and Families, Queens, NY

STEPHEN N. AXFORD, Psychologist/Assistant Director of Special Education, Pueblo School District No. Sixty, Pueblo, CO

PATRICIA A. BACHELOR, Professor of Psychology, California State University, Long Beach, CA

JOAN C. BALLARD, Clinical Neuropsychologist, Associate Professor of Psychology, State University of New York College at Geneseo, Geneseo, NY

LAURA L. B. BARNES, Associate Professor of Educational Research and Evaluation, Oklahoma State University, Tulsa, OK

SHERI BAUMAN, Assistant Professor, Department of Educational Psychology, University of Arizona, Tucson, AZ

C. G. BELLAH, Assistant Professor of Psychology, Northwestern State University, Natchitoches, LA

JAMES K. BENISH, School Psychologist, Helena Public Schools, Adjunct Professor of Special Education, Carroll College, Helena, MT

PETER MILES BERGER, Area Manager, Mental After Care Association, London, U.K.

RONALD A. BERK, Professor of Biostatistics and Measurement, The Johns Hopkins University, Baltimore, MD

FRANK M. BERNT, Associate Professor of Health Services, St. Joseph's University, Philadelphia, PA

RICKI KOREY BIRNBAUM, Adjunct Assistant Professor, Warner School of Education, University of Rochester, Rochester, NY

LISA BISCHOFF, Associate Professor, School of Education, Indiana State University, Terre Haute, IN

KIMBERLY ANN BLAIR, Assistant Professor of Education, Duquesne University, Pittsburgh, PA

BRIAN F. BOLTON, University Professor of Rehabilitation Education and Research, University of Arkansas, Fayetteville, AR

MIKE BONNER, Assistant Professor in School Psychology, University of Nebraska at Omaha, Omaha, NE

ROGER A. BOOTHROYD, Associate Professor, Department of Mental Health Law and Policy, Louis de la Parte Florida Mental Health Institute, University of South Florida, Tampa, FL

THERESA GRAHAM, Adjunct Faculty, University of Nebraska—Lincoln, Lincoln, NE

ZANDRA S. GRATZ, Associate Professor of Psychology, Kean University, Union, NJ

THOMAS E. HANCOCK, Associate Professor of Education, George Fox University, Newberg, OR

LEONARD HANDLER, Professor of Psychology, University of Tennessee, Knoxville, TN

WILLIAM E. HANSON, Assistant Professor, Department of Educational Psychology, University of Nebraska-Lincoln, Lincoln, NE

RICHARD E. HARDING, Principal and Director of Research, Kenexa Technology, Lincoln, NE

DELWYN L. HARNISCH, Professor, Department of Curriculum & Instruction, University of Nebraska—Lincoln, Lincoln, NE

PATTI L. HARRISON, Professor of School Psychology, The University of Alabama, Tuscaloosa, AL

JAN HARTING-McCHESNEY, Assistant Professor of Child Study, St. Joseph's College, Patchogue, NY

MICHAEL R. HARWELL, Professor, Program in Research Methodology, Department of Educational Psychology, University of Minnesota, Minneapolis, MN

KEITH HATTRUP, Associate Professor of Psychology, San Diego State University, San Diego, CA

THEODORE L. HAYES, Personnel Research Psychologist, U.S. Immigration & Naturalization Service, Washington, DC

SANDRA D. HAYNES, Interim Associate Dean, School of Professional Studies, Metropolitan State College of Denver, Denver, CO

CARLEN HENINGTON, Associate Professor of Educational and School Psychology, Mississippi State University, Mississippi State, MS

JAMES J. HENNESSY, Professor (Counseling Psychology), Graduate School of Education, Fordham University, New York, NY

ALLEN K. HESS, Professor, Auburn University at Montgomery, Montgomery, AL

BRIAN HESS, Director of Test Development & Research, National Commission on Certification of Physician Assistants, Norcross, GA

SAMUEL HINTON, Professor, Educational Studies, Eastern Kentucky University, Richmond, KY

KATHRYN E. HOFF, Assistant Professor, Department of Psychology, Illinois State University, Normal, IL

THOMAS P. HOGAN, Professor of Psychology, University of Scranton, Scranton, PA

ANITA M. HUBLEY, Associate Professor of Measurement, Evaluation, and Research Methodology, University of British Columbia, Vancouver, British Columbia, Canada

DAVID P. HURFORD, Director of the Center for the Assessment and Remediation of Reading Difficulties and Professor of Psychology and Counseling, Pittsburg State University, Pittsburg, KS

CARL ISENHART, Coordinator, Addictive Disorders Section, Mental Health Patient Service Line, VA Medical Center, Minneapolis, MN

MARC JANOSON, Forensic Psychologist in Independent Practice, Manhattan, NY

CHANTALE JEANRIE, Industrial/Organizational Psychologist, Associate Professor of Measurement and Evaluation, Department of Fondements et pratiques en education, Faculty of Education, Laval University, Quebec, Canada

JEFFREY A. JENKINS, Assistant Professor, Roger Williams University Bristol, RI

JILL ANN JENKINS, Consultant Child & School Psychologist, Barcelona, Spain

KAREN E. JENNINGS, Clinical Psychologist, LaMora Psychological Associates, Nashua, NH

CHRISTOPHER JOHNSON, Professor of Music Education and Music Therapy, The University of Kansas, Lawrence, KS

JACQUELINE JOHNSON, Research Scientist, New York State Office of Mental Health, Albany, NY

KATHLEEN M. JOHNSON, Psychologist, Lincoln Public Schools, Lincoln, NE

ROBERT L. JOHNSON, Associate Professor, Educational Psychology, University of South Carolina, Columbia, SC

KEVIN M. JONES, Assistant Professor, University of Cincinnati, Cincinnati, OH

ASHRAF KAGEE, Research Fellow, Department of Psychology, University of Stellenbosch, Maitland, South Africa

HARRISON D. KANE, Assistant Professor, Western Carolina University, Cullowhee, NC

IRA S. KATZ, Clinical Psychologist at California Department of Corrections—Salinas Valley State Prison, Soledad, CA, and Soledad Medical Clinic, Soledad, CA, and Private Practice, Salinas, CA

MICHAEL G. KAVAN, Associate Dean for Student Affairs and Associate Professor of Family Practice, Creighton University School of Medicine, Omaha, NE

TIMOTHY Z. KEITH, Professor of Educational Psychology, The University of Texas—Austin, Austin, TX

HAROLD R. KELLER, Professor and Chair, Department of Psychological and Social Foundations, University of South Florida, Tampa, FL

PEGGY KELLERS, Associate Professor, School of Kinesiology and Recreational Studies, James Madison University, Harrisonburg, VA

MARY LOU KELLEY, Professor of Psychology, Louisiana State University, Baton Rouge, LA

KEVIN R. KELLY, Head, Department of Educational Studies, Purdue University, West Lafayette, IN

CAROL E. KESSLER, Assistant Professor of Education, Cabrini College, Radnor, PA

JEAN POWELL KIRNAN, Associate Professor of Psychology, The College of New Jersey, Ewing, NJ

BEVERLY M. KLECKER, Assistant Professor of Education, Morehead State University, Morehead, KY

HOWARD M. KNOFF, Professor of School Psychology, University of South Florida, Tampa, FL

JODY L. KULSTAD, Assistant Professor, Professional Psychology and Family Therapy, Seton Hall University, South Orange, NJ

JOSEPH C. KUSH, Associate Professor and Coordinator, School Psychology Program, Duquesne University, Pittsburgh, PA

KWONG-LIEM KARL KWAN, Associate Professor, Department of Educational Studies, Counseling and Development Program, Purdue University, West Lafayette, IN

MATTHEW E. LAMBERT, Clinical Assistant Professor of Neuropsychiatry, Texas Tech University Health Sciences Center, Lubbock, TX

SUZANNE LANE, Professor, Research Methodology Program, University of Pittsburgh, Pittsburgh, PA

KEVIN LANNING, Associate Professor of Psychology, Wilkes Honors College of Florida Atlantic University, Jupiter, FL

JOSEPH G. LAW, JR., Professor of Behavioral Studies, University of South Alabama, Mobile, AL

ROBERT A. LEARK, Associate Professor, Pacific Christian College, Fullerton, CA

FREDERICK T. L. LEONG, Professor of Psychology, The Ohio State University at Columbus, Columbus, OH

S. ALVIN LEUNG, Professor, Department of Educational Psychology, The Chinese University of Hong Kong, Hong Kong, China

PAM LINDSEY, Associate Professor of Education, Tarleton State University, Stephenville, TX

CEDERICK O. LINDSKOG, Professor, Department of Psychology and Counseling, Pittsburg State University, Pittsburg, KS

SANDRA A. LOEW, Assistant Professor of Counselor Education, University of North Alabama, Florence, AL

STEVEN LONG, Assistant Professor, Communication Sciences, Case Western Reserve University, Cleveland, OH

ALFRED LONGO, Instructor in Education, Social Science Department, Ocean County College, Toms River, NJ

CLEBORNE D. MADDUX, Professor of Counseling and Educational Psychology, University of Nevada, Reno, NV

RONALD A. MADLE, School Psychologist, Shikellamy School District, Sunbury, PA and Adjunct Associate Professor of School Psychology, The Pennsylvania State University, University Park, PA

TIMOTHY J. MAKATURA, Clinical Neuropsychologist and Clinical Assistant Professor, Department of Physical Medicine and Rehabilitation, University of Pittsburgh Medical Center, Pittsburgh, PA

KORESSA KUTSICK MALCOLM, School Psychologist, Augusta County Public Schools, and Adjunct Faculty Member, Mary Baldwin College, Staunton, VA

SUSAN J. MALLER, Associate Professor of Educational Studies, Purdue University, West Lafayette, IN

WILLIAM E. MARTIN, JR., Professor of Educational Psychology, Northern Arizona University, Flagstaff, AZ

TREY MARTINDALE, Assistant Professor, East Carolina University, Greenville, NC

M. MASTRANGELO, Associate Professor of Psychology, University of Baltimore, Baltimore, MD

KEVIN J. McCARTHY, Clinical Assistant Professor of Psychiatry, Louisiana State University, Health Sciences Center, New Orleans, LA

REBECCA McCAULEY, Professor of Communication Sciences, University of Vermont, Burlington, VT

DAVID McCONE, Assistant Professor, Department of Behavioral Sciences and Leadership, United States Air Force Academy, USAF Academy, CO

CAROL M. McGREGOR, Associate Professor of Education and Human Development, Brenau University, Gainesville, GA

VALENTINA McINERNEY, Professor of Educational Psychology, School of Psychology, University of Western Sydney, Sydney, Australia

THOMAS McKNIGHT, Psychologist, Private Practice, Spokane, WA

SCOTT T. MEIER, Professor of Counseling Psychology, The State University of New York at Buffalo, Buffalo, NY

JOYCE MEIKAMP, Professor of Special Education, Marshall University Graduate College, South Charleston, WV

BRAD M. MERKER, Graduate Assistant, Buros Institute of Mental Measurements, University of Nebraska—Lincoln, Lincoln, NE

WILLIAM B. MICHAEL, Professor of Educational Psychology, University of Southern California, Los Angeles, CA

DANIEL C. MILLER, Professor, Texas Woman's University, Denton, TX

M. DAVID MILLER, Professor of Educational Psychology, University of Florida, Gainesville, FL

MARIE MILLER-WHITEHEAD, Director, Tennessee Valley Educators for Excellence (TVEE.ORG), Muscle Shoals, AL

PAT MIRENDA, Associate Professor, Faculty of Education, University of British Columbia, Vancouver, British Columbia, Canada

CAROLYN MITCHELL-PERSON, Associate Professor in the Special Education Department and Director of the Research Roundtable (Title III) at Southern University, Baton Rouge, LA

JUDITH A. MONSAAS, Professor of Education, North Georgia College and State University, Dahlonega, GA

JOANN MURPHEY, Clinical Psychologist in Private Practice, San Antonio, TX

WENDY NAUMANN, Assistant Professor of School Psychology at The Ohio State University in Columbus, Columbus, OH

LORI NEBELSICK-GULLETT, Consultant: Educational Measurement, Planning, and Accountability, Castle Rock, CO

LEAH M. NELLIS, Assistant Professor of Educational and Counseling Psychology, University of Kentucky, Lexington, KY

JANET NORRIS, Professor, Communication Disorders, Louisiana State University, Baton Rouge, LA

MICHELLE NUTTER, Research Associate, Behavioral Research and Teaching, College of Education, University of Oregon, Eugene, OR

SALVADOR HECTOR OCHOA, Associate Professor, Department of Educational Psychology, Texas A&M University, College Station, TX

D. JOE OLMI, Associate Professor and Clinic Director, School Psychology Program, Department of Psychology, The University of Southern Mississippi, Hattiesburg, MS

DENIZ S. ONES, Hellervik Professor of Industrial Psychology, Department of Psychology, University of Minnesota, Minneapolis, MN

DONALD OSWALD, Associate Professor, Department of Psychiatry, Virginia Commonwealth University, Richmond, VA

GRETCHEN OWENS, Professor of Child Study, St. Joseph's College, Patchoque, NY

HEIDI K. PAA, Senior Researcher, Renaissance Learning, Inc., Madison, WI

NATHANIEL J. PALLONE, University Distinguished Professor (Psychology), Center of Alcohol Studies, Rutgers University, Piscataway, NJ

ANTHONY M. PAOLO, Research Associate Professor of Psychiatry and Behavioral Sciences, University of Kansas Medical Center, Kansas City, KS

THANOS PATELIS, Executive Director of Psychometrics, Evaluation, & Data Reporting, The College Board, New York, NY

RENEE PAVELSKI, Doctoral Candidate, Counseling/Clinical/School Psychology Program, University of California at Santa Barbara, Santa Barbara, CA

L. CAROLYN PEARSON, Professor of Education, University of West Florida, Pensacola, FL

MICHAEL PERSAMPIERI, Doctoral Student, University of Nebraska—Lincoln, Lincoln, NE

STEVEN I. PFEIFFER, Research Professor of Education and Executive Director, Duke University Talent Identification Program, Durham, NC

IRIS PHILLIPS, Assistant Professor of Social Work, University of Southern Indiana, Evansville, IN

JAMES W. PINKNEY, Professor of Counselor and Adult Education, East Carolina University, Greenville, NC

DAVID J. PITTENGER, Head and Associate Professor, Department of Psychology, The University of Tennessee at Chattanooga, Chattanooga, TN

MARK POPE, Associate Professor, Division of Counseling & Family Therapy, College of Education, University of Missouri—St. Louis, St. Louis, MO

G. MICHAEL POTEAT, Associate Professor of Psychology, East Carolina University, Greenville, NC

SHAWN POWELL, Director, Cadet Counseling and Leadership Development Center, United States Air Force Academy, USAF Academy, CO

SHEILA PRATT, Assistant Professor, Department of Communication Science & Disorders, University of Pittsburgh, Pittsburgh, PA

NAMBURY S. RAJU, Distinguished Professor, Institute of Psychology, Illinois Institute of Technology, Chicago, IL

PAMILLA RAMSDEN, Senior Lecturer, Bolton Institute, Bolton, Lancashire, England

JAMES C. REED, Chief Psychologist, St. Luke's Hospital, New Bedford, MA

JUDITH A. REIN, President, Interaction Research of Arizona, Tucson, AZ

PAUL RETZLAFF, Professor of Psychology, University of Northern Colorado, Greeley, CO

CECIL R. REYNOLDS, Professor of Educational Psychology, Professor of Neuroscience, Distinguished Research Scholar, Texas A&M University, College Station, TX

WILLIAM M. REYNOLDS, Professor, Department of Psychology, Humboldt State University, Arcata, CA

ROBIN RIX, Graduate Student in School Psychology at The Ohio State University in Columbus, Columbus, OH

BRUCE G. ROGERS, Professor of Educational Psychology, University of Northern Iowa, Cedar Falls, IA

CYNTHIA A. ROHRBECK, Associate Professor of Psychology, The George Washington University, Washington, DC

MICHAEL J. ROSZKOWSKI, Director of Institutional Research, La Salle University, Philadelphia, PA

LAWRENCE J. RYAN, California Licensed Psychologist, and Vice President and Academic Dean, St. John's Seminary College, Camarillo, CA, and Core Faculty Member, The Union Institute, Cincinnati, OH

DARRELL L. SABERS, Professor of Educational Psychology, University of Arizona, Tucson, AZ

VINCENT J. SAMAR, Associate Professor, Department of Research, National Technical Institute for the Deaf, Rochester Institute of Technology, Rochester, NY

JONATHAN SANDOVAL, Professor of Education, University of California, Davis, CA

ELEANOR E. SANFORD, Vice-President for Research and Development, MetaMetrics, Inc., Durham, NC

DAVID M. SARGENT, Associate Professor of Psychology, State University of New York at Oswego, Oswego, NY

WILLIAM I. SAUSER, JR., Associate Dean and Professor, Business and Engineering Outreach, Auburn University, Auburn, AL

NEROLI SAWYER, Statistics Instructor, University of Ballarat, Victoria, Australia

MICHAEL J. SCHEEL, Associate Professor, University of Nebraska-Lincoln, Department of Educational Psychology, Lincoln, NE

GERALD R. SCHNECK, Professor of Rehabilitation Counseling, Minnesota State University, Mankato, MN

GREGORY SCHRAW, Professor, Department of Educational Psychology, University of Nevada—Las Vegas, Las Vegas, NV

GENE SCHWARTING, Associate Professor, Education Department, Fontbonne University, St. Louis, MO

STEVEN R. SHAW, Lead School Psychologist, Department of Developmental Pediatrics, The Children's Hospital, Greenville, SC, and Associate Professor of Pediatrics (Greenville), Medical University of South Carolina, Greenville, SC

EUGENE P. SHEEHAN, Dean, College of Education, University of Northern Colorado, Greeley, CO

DAVID SHUM, Senior Lecturer of Psychology, Griffith University, Brisbane, Australia

CRAIG S. SHWERY, Assistant Professor of Elementary Education Teaching Programs, University of Alabama, Tuscaloosa, AL

WESLEY E. SIME, Professor of Health and Human Performance, University of Nebraska—Lincoln, Lincoln, NE

SURENDRA P. SINGH, Clinical Neuropsychologist, Professor Learning and Behavior Disorders, College of Education, University of South Florida, Tampa, FL

JEFFREY K. SMITH, Professor and Chair, Department of Educational Psychology, Rutgers, The State University of New Jersey, New Brunswick, NJ

LARISSA SMITH, Presley Center for Crime and Justice Studies, University of California, Riverside, CA

LISA F. SMITH, Associate Professor, Psychology Department, Kean University, Union, NJ

KATHARINE A. SNYDER, Assistant Professor of Psychology, Shepherd College, Shepherdstown, WV

LOUISE M. SOARES, Professor of Educational Psychology, University of New Haven, West Haven, CT

MICHAEL SPANGLER, Dean of Business and Technology, Highland Community College, Freeport, IL

LORAINE J. SPENCINER, Professor of Special Education, University of Maine at Farmington, Farmington, ME

MARK A. STAAL, Director of Counseling Services and Associate Professor of Behavioral Sciences, Department of Behavioral Sciences and Leadership, United States Air Force Academy, CO

JAYNE E. STAKE, Professor of Psychology, University of Missouri—St. Louis, St. Louis, MO

STEPHANIE STEIN, Professor of Psychology, Central Washington University, Ellensburg, WA

WENDY J. STEINBERG, Assistant Professor of Psychology, Eastern University, St. Davids, PA

HUGH STEPHENSON, Assistant Professor of Psychology, Ithaca College, Ithaca, NY

JAY R. STEWART, Associate Professor and Director, Rehabilitation Counseling Program, Bowling Green State University, Bowling Green, OH

TERRY A. STINNETT, Professor, School of Applied Health and Educational Psychology, Oklahoma State University, Stillwater, OK

MARK H. STONE, Professor, Adler School of Professional Psychology, Chicago, IL

DONALD LEE STOVALL, Associate Professor, Department of Counseling & School Psychology, University of Wisconsin—River Falls, River Falls, WI

RICHARD B. STUART, Program Director, Respecialization in Clinical Psychology, The Fielding Graduate Institute, and Clinical Professor Emeritus, Department of Psychiatry, University of Washington, Seattle, WA

GABRIELLE STUTMAN, Adjunct Assistant Professor, CUNY/Bronx Community College, Private Practice, Westchester and New York City, NY

HOI K. SUEN, Professor of Educational Psychology, Pennsylvania State University, University Park, PA

MARK E. SWERDLIK, Professor, Department of Psychology, Illinois State University, Normal, IL

DONALD L. THOMPSON, Professor of Counseling and Psychology, Troy State University Montgomery, Montgomery, AL

NORA M. THOMPSON, Psychologist—Learning Disability Specialist, University of Washington, Seattle, WA

ROBERT M. THORNDIKE, Professor of Psychology, Western Washington University, Bellingham, WA

GERALD TINDAL, Professor in Educational Leadership, College of Education, University of Oregon, Eugene, OR

WILLIAM C. TIRRE, Senior Research Psychologist and Research Manager, Career Vision, The Ball Foundation, Glen Ellyn, IL

JOHN TIVENDELL, Professor of Psychology, Université de Moncton, Moncton, New Brunswick, Canada

ROGER L. TOWNE, Associate Professor and Head, Department of Communication Disorders, Northern Michigan University, Marquette, MI

MICHAEL S. TREVISAN, Associate Professor, Department of Educational Leadership & Counseling Psychology, Washington State University, Pullman, WA

STEPHEN E. TROTTER, Associate Professor, Department of Psychology, Tennessee State University, Nashville, TN

SUSANA URBINA, Professor of Psychology, University of North Florida, Jacksonville, FL

JOHN J. VACCA, Assistant Professor of Individual and Family Studies, University of Delaware, Newark, DE

WILFRED G. VAN GORP, Associate Professor of Psychology in Psychiatry, and Director, Neuropsychology Assessment Program, Weill Medical College of Cornell University, New York, NY

JAMES P. VAN HANEGHAN, Associate Professor, Department of Behavioral Studies and Educational Technology, University of South Alabama, Mobile, AL

CHOCKALINGAM VISWESVARAN, Associate Professor, Florida International University, Miami, FL

ROMEO VITELLI, Staff Psychologist, Millbrook Correctional Centre, Millbrook, Ontario, Canada

ROBERT J. VOLPE, Doctoral Candidate, School Psychology Program, Lehigh University, Bethlehem, PA

THERESA VOLPE-JOHNSTONE, Clinical and School Psychologist, Pleasanton, CA

DELORES D. WALCOTT, Associate Professor, Western Michigan University, University Counseling and Testing Center, Kalamazoo, MI

CINDY M. WALKER, Assistant Professor, Department of Educational Psychology—Research & Evaluation, University of Wisconsin—Milwaukee, Milwaukee, WI

ROBERT E. WALL, Graduate Professor, Department of Reading, Special Education and Instructional Technology, Towson University, Towson, MD

AIMIN WANG, Associate Professor of Educational Psychology, Miami University, Oxford, OH

ANNITA MARIE WARD, Associate Professor of Education and TESL, Salem International University, Salem, WV

SANDRA B. WARD, Associate Professor of Education, The College of William and Mary, Williamsburg, VA

BETSY B. WATERMAN, Professor, Counseling and Psychological Services Department, State University of New York at Oswego, Oswego, NY

T. STEUART WATSON, Professor of Educational Psychology, Mississippi State University, Starkville, MS

PATRICIA H. WHEELER, President and Principal Researcher, EREAPA Associates, Livermore, CA

SUSAN C. WHISTON, Professor of Counseling and Educational Psychology, Indiana University, Bloomington, IN

KEITH F. WIDAMAN, Professor of Psychology, University of California, Davis, CA

WILLIAM K. WILKINSON, Consulting Educational Psychologist, Boleybeg, Barna, County Galway, Republic of Ireland

CLAUDIA R. WRIGHT, Professor of Educational Psychology, California State University, Long Beach, CA

JOHN W. YOUNG, Associate Professor of Educational Statistics and Measurement, Rutgers University, New Brunswick, NJ

PETER ZACHAR, Associate Professor of Psychology, Auburn University Montgomery, Montgomery, AL

SHELDON ZEDECK, Professor of Psychology, University of California at Berkeley, Berkeley, CA

INDEX OF TITLES

This title index lists all the tests included in The Fifteenth Mental Measurements Yearbook. *Citations are to test entry numbers, not to pages (e.g., 54 refers to test 54 and not page 54). Test numbers along with test titles are indicated in the running heads at the top of each page, whereas page numbers, used only in the Table of Contents but not in the indexes, appear at the bottom of each page. Superseded titles are listed with cross references to current titles, and alternative titles are also cross referenced.*

Many tests in this volume were previously listed in Tests in Print VI *(2002). An (N) appearing immediately after a test number indicates that the test is a new, recently published test, and/or that it has not appeared before in any Buros Institute publication other than* Tests in Print VI. *An (R) indicates that the test has been revised or supplemented since last included in a Buros publication.*

INDEX OF ACRONYMS

This Index of Acronyms refers the reader to the appropriate test in The Fifteenth Mental Measurements Yearbook. *In some cases tests are better known by their acronyms than by their full titles, and this index can be of substantial help to the person who knows the former but not the latter. Acronyms are only listed if the author or publisher has made substantial use of the acronym in referring to the test, or if the test is widely known by the acronym. A few acronyms are registered trademarks (e.g., SAT); where this is known to us, only the test with the registered trademarks is referenced. There is some danger in the overuse of acronyms. However, this index, like all other indexes in this work, is provided to make the task of identifying a test as easy as possible. All numbers refer to test numbers, not page numbers.*

CLASSIFIED SUBJECT INDEX

The Classified Subject Index classifies all tests included in The Mental Measurements Yearbook *into 18 major categories: Achievement, Behavior Assessment, Developmental, Education, English and Language, Fine Arts, Foreign Languages, Intelligence and General Aptitude, Mathematics, Miscellaneous, Neuropsychological, Personality, Reading, Science, Sensory–Motor, Social Studies, Speech and Hearing, and Vocations. This Classified Subject Index for the tests reviewed in* The Fifteenth Mental Measurements Yearbook *includes tests in 17 of the 18 available categories. (The category of Science has no representative tests in this volume.) Each category appears in alphabetical order and tests are ordered alphabetically within each category. Each test entry includes test title, population for which the test is intended, and the test entry number in* The Fifteenth Mental Measurements Yearbook. *All numbers refer to test numbers, not to page numbers. Brief suggestions for the use of this index are presented in the introduction and definitions of the categories are provided at the beginning of this index.*

Achievement

Tests that measure acquired knowledge across school subject content areas. Included here are test batteries that measure multiple content areas and individual subject areas not having separate classification categories. (Note: Some batteries include both achievement and aptitude subtests. Such batteries may be classified under the categories of either Achievement or Intelligence and Aptitude depending upon the principal content area.)

See also Fine Arts, Intelligence and General Aptitude, Mathematics, Reading, Science, and Social Studies.

Behavior Assessment

Tests that measure general or specific behavior within educational, vocational, community, or home settings. Included here are checklists, rating scales, and surveys that measure observer's interpretations of behavior in relation to adaptive or social skills, functional skills, and appropriateness or dysfunction within settings/situations.

Developmental

Tests that are designed to assess skills or emerging skills (such as number concepts, conservation, memory, fine motor, gross motor, communication, letter recognition, social competence) of young children (0-7 years) or tests which are designed to assess such skills in severely or profoundly disabled school-aged individuals. Included here are early screeners, developmental surveys/profiles, kindergarten or school readiness tests, early learning profiles, infant development scales, tests of play behavior, social acceptance/social skills; and preschool psychoeducational batteries. Content specific screeners, such as those assessing readiness, are classified by content area (e.g., Reading).

See also Neuropsychological and Sensory-Motor.

Education

General education-related tests, including measures of instructional/school environment, effective schools/teaching, study skills and strategies, learning styles and strategies, school attitudes, educational programs/curriculae, interest inventories, and educational leadership.

Specific content area tests (i.e., science, mathematics, social studies, etc.) are listed by their content area.

English and Language

Tests that measure skills in using or understanding the English language in spoken or written form. Included here are tests of language proficiency, applied literacy, language comprehension/development/proficiency, English skills/proficiency, communication skills, listening comprehension, linguistics, and receptive/expressive vocabulary. (Tests designed to measure the mechanics of speaking or communicating are classified under the category Speech and Hearing.)

Fine Arts

Tests that measure knowledge, skills, abilities, attitudes, and interests within the various areas of fine and performing arts. Included here are tests of aptitude, achievement, creativity/talent/giftedness specific to the Fine Arts area, and tests of aesthetic judgment.

Foreign Languages

Tests that measure competencies and readiness in reading, comprehending, and speaking a language other than English.

Intelligence and General Aptitude

Tests that measure general acquired knowledge, aptitudes, or cognitive ability and those that assess specific aspects of these general categories. Included here are tests of critical thinking skills, nonverbal/verbal reasoning, cognitive abilities/processing, learning potential/aptitude/efficiency, logical reasoning, abstract thinking, creative thinking/creativity; entrance exams and academic admissions tests.

Mathematics

Tests that measure competencies and attitudes in any of the various areas of mathematics (e.g., algebra, geometry, calculus) and those related to general mathematics achievement/proficiency. (Note: Included here are tests that assess personality or affective variables related to mathematics.)

Miscellaneous

Tests that cannot be sorted into any of the current MMY categories as listed and defined above. Included here are tests of handwriting, ethics and morality, religion, driving and safety, health and physical education, environment (e.g., classroom environment, family environment), custody decisions, substance abuse, and addictions. (See also Personality.)

Neuropsychological

Tests that measure neurological functioning or brain-behavior relationships either generally or in relation to specific areas of functioning. Included here are neuropsychological test batteries, questionnaires, and screening tests. Also included are tests that measure memory impairment, various disorders or decline associated with dementia, brain/head injury, visual attention, digit recognition, finger tapping, laterality, aphasia, and behavior (associated with organic brain dysfunction or brain injury).

See also Developmental, Intelligence and General Aptitude, Sensory-Motor, and Speech and Hearing.

Personality

Tests that measure individuals' ways of thinking, behaving, and functioning within family and society. Included here are projective and apperception tests, needs inventories, anxiety/depression scales; tests assessing substance use/abuse (or propensity for abuse), risk taking behavior, general mental health, emotional intelligence, self-image/-concept/-esteem, empathy, suicidal ideation, schizophrenia, depression/hopelessness, abuse, coping skills/stress, eating disorders, grief, decision-making, racial attitudes; general motivation, attributions, perceptions; adjustment, parenting styles, and marital issues/satisfaction.

For content-specific tests, see subject area categories (e.g., math efficacy instruments are located in Mathematics). Some areas, such as substance abuse, are cross-referenced with the Personality category.

Reading

Tests that measure competencies and attitudes within the broadly defined area of reading. Included here are reading inventories, tests of reading achievement and aptitude, reading readiness/early reading ability, reading comprehension, reading decoding, and oral reading. (Note: Included here are tests that assess personality or affective variables related to reading.)

Science

Tests that measure competencies and attitudes within any of the various areas of science (e.g., biology, chemistry, physics), and those related to general science achievement/proficiency. (Note: Included here are tests that assess personality or affective variables related to science.)

Sensory-Motor

Tests that are general or specific measures of any or all of the five senses and those that assess fine or gross motor skills. Included here are tests of manual dexterity, perceptual skills, visual-motor skills, perceptual-motor skills, movement and posture, laterality preference, sensory integration, motor development, color blindness/discrimination, visual perception/organization, and visual acuity. (Note: See also the categories Neuropsychological and Speech and Hearing.)

Social Studies

Tests that measure competencies and attitudes within the broadly defined area of social studies. In cluded here are tests related to economics, sociology, history, geography, and political science, and those related to general social studies achievement/proficiency. (Note: Also included here are tests that assess personality or affective variables related to social studies.)

Speech and Hearing

Tests that measure the mechanics of speaking or hearing the spoken word. Included here are tests of articulation, voice fluency, stuttering, speech sound perception/discrimination, auditory discrimination/comprehension, audiometry, deafness, and hearing loss/impairment. (Note: See Developmental, English and Language, Neuropsychological, and Sensory-Motor.)

Vocations

Tests that measure employee skills, behaviors, attitudes, values, and perceptions relative to jobs, employment, and the work place or organizational environment. Included here are tests of management skill/style/competence, leader behavior, careers (development, exploration, attitudes); job- or work-related selection/admission/entrance tests; tests of work adjustment, team or group processes/communication/effectiveness, employability, vocational/occupational interests, employee aptitudes/competencies, and organizational climate.

See also Intelligence and General Aptitude, and Personality and also specific content area categories (e.g., Mathematics, Reading).

ACHIEVEMENT

BEHAVIOR ASSESSMENT

DEVELOPMENTAL

EDUCATION

ENGLISH AND LANGUAGE

FINE ARTS

FOREIGN LANGUAGES

INTELLIGENCE AND GENERAL APTITUDE

MATHEMATICS

MISCELLANEOUS

NEUROPSYCHOLOGICAL

PERSONALITY

READING

SENSORY MOTOR

SOCIAL STUDIES

SPEECH AND HEARING

VOCATIONS

PUBLISHERS DIRECTORY
AND INDEX

This directory and index gives the names and test entry numbers of all publishers represented in The Fifteenth Mental Measurements Yearbook. *Current addresses are listed for all publishers for which this is known. Those publishers for which a current address is not available are listed as "Address Unknown." This directory and index also provides telephone and FAX numbers and e-mail and Web addresses for those publishers who responded to our request for this information. Please note that all test numbers refer to test entry numbers, not page numbers. Publishers are an important source of information about catalogs, specimen sets, price changes, test revisions, and many other matters.*

ABackans DCP, Inc.
566 White Pond Drive
Suite C #178
Akron, OH 44320-1116
Telephone: 330-745-4450
FAX: 330-745-4450
E-mail: ABackans@abackans.com
Web: abackans.com
Tests: 5, 192

Academic Consulting & Testing Service
P.O. Box 1883
Lake Oswego, OR 97035
Telephone: 503-639-3292
FAX: 503-639-3292
E-mail: HEDSbyACTS@aol.com
Tests: 80, 293, 325, 336, 351

Academic Therapy Publications
20 Commercial Boulevard
Novato, CA 94949-6191
Telephone: 800-422-7249
FAX: 415-883-3720
E-mail: atp@aol.com
Web: www.atpub.com
Tests: 95, 194, 205

ACT, Inc.
2201 N. Dodge Street
P.O. Box 168
Iowa City, IA 52243-0168
Telephone: 319-337-1000
FAX: 319-339-3021
Web: www.act.org
Tests: 44, 94

American Association for Active Lifestyles and Fitness
1900 Association Drive
Reston, VA 22091
Telephone: 800-213-7193
FAX: 703-476-9527
E-mail: aaalf@aahperd.org
Web: www.aahperd.org
Tests: 107

American Guidance Service, Inc.
4201 Woodland Road
Circle Pines, MN 55014-1796
Telephone: 800-328-2560
FAX: 651-287-7221
E-mail: agsmail@agsnet
Web: www.agsnet.com
Tests: 58, 109, 113, 204

American Management Association
135 West 50th Street
New York, NY 10020
Tests: 291

American Psychiatric Association
1400 K Street, N.W.
Washington, DC 20005
Tests: 345

American Psychiatric Publishing, Inc.
1400 K Street, NW — Suite 1101
Washington, DC 20005-2403
Telephone: 800-368-5777
FAX: 202-682-6341
E-mail: appi@psych.org
Web: www.appi.org
Tests: 48, 355

The Assessment and Development Centre
6890 E. Sunrise Drive, #120-382
Tucson, AZ 85750
Telephone: 520-299-5501
FAX: 520-299-5348
E-mail: stressmaster@qwest.net
Web: www.stressmaster.com
Tests: 180, 353

Australian Council for Educational Research Ltd.
19 Prospect Hill Road
Private Bag 55, Camberwell,
Melbourne, Victoria 3124
Australia
Telephone: +61 3 8266 5555
FAX: +61 3 9277 5500
E-mail: sales@acer.edu.au
Web: www.acer.edu.au
Tests: 2, 3, 4, 16, 70, 78, 79, 83, 133, 144, 173, 199,
    200, 223, 278, 282, 296

The Barber Center Press, Inc.
136 East Avenue
Erie, PA 16507
Telephone: 814-453-7661
FAX: 814-455-1132
E-mail: gabcmain@drbarbercenter.org
Web: www.drbarbercenter.org
Tests: 309

Behaviordata, Inc.
2166 The Alameda
San Jose, CA 95126-1144
Tests: 91

Millard J. Bienvenu, Ph.D.
Northwest Publications
710 Watson Drive
Natchitoches, LA 71457
Tests: 335

Bigby, Havis, & Associates, Inc.
12750 Merit Drive, Suite 660
Dallas, TX 75251
Telephone: 972-233-6055
FAX: 972-233-3154
E-mail: kcapelle@bigby.com
Web: www.bigby.com
Tests: 213

Dr. Dorothy Bishop
c/o TROG Research Fund
Age and Cognitive Performance Research Centre
University of Manchester
Manchester M13 9PL
England
Web: epwww.psych.ox.ac.uk/oscci/
Tests: 258

Bowling Green State University
JDI Office
Department of Psychology
Bowling Green, OH 43403
Telephone: 419-372-8247
FAX: 419-372-6013
E-mail: JDI_RA@bgnet.bgnet.bgsu.edu
Web: www.bgsu.edu/departments/psych/JDI
Tests: 130, 246

British Columbia Institute Against Family Violence
Suite 551
409 Granville Street
Vancouver, British Columbia V6C 1T2
Canada
Tests: 228

Brookes Publishing Co., Inc.
P.O. Box 10624
Baltimore, MD 21285-0624
Telephone: 800-638-3775
FAX: 410-337-8539
E-mail: custserv@brookespublishing.com
Web: www.brookespublishing.com
Tests: 319

Brougham Press
P.O. Box 2702
Olathe, KS 66063-0702
Telephone: 800-360-6244
FAX: 913-782-1116
E-mail: CISE@BroughamPress.com
Web: www.BroughamPress.com
Tests: 50

The Cambridge Stratford Study Skills Institute
8560 Main Street
Williamsville, NY 14221
Telephone: 800-466-2232
FAX: 716-626-9076
E-mail: cambridges@aol.com
Web: www.cambridgesTraTford.com
Tests: 360

Center for Creative Leadership
One Leadership Place
P.O. Box 26300
Greensboro, NC 27438-6300
Telephone: 336-286-7210
FAX: 336-286-3999
Web: www.ccl.org
Tests: 35, 137

Central Institute for the Deaf
Publications Department
4560 Clayton Avenue
St. Louis, MO 63110
Telephone: 314-977-0133
FAX: 314-977-0016
E-mail: dgushleff@cid.wustl.edu
Web: www.cid.wustl.edu
Tests: 352

Checkmate Plus, Ltd.
P.O. Box 696
Stony Brook, NY 11790-0696
Telephone: 800-779-4292
FAX: 631-360-3432
E-mail: info@checkmateplus.com
Web: www.checkmateplus.com
Tests: 8, 12, 47, 286

Child Welfare League of America
P.O. Box 2019
Annapolis Jct., MD 20701
Tests: 300, 306

The Clark Wilson Group, Inc.
4900 Nautilus Court N., Suite 220
Boulder, CO 80301-3242
Telephone: 800-537-7249

FAX: 303-581-9326
E-mail: info@clarkwilsongroup.com
Web: www.clarkwilsongroup.com
Tests: 344

Clinical Psychometric Research, Inc.
P.O. Box 619
Riderwood, MD 21139
Telephone: 800-245-0277 or 410-321-6165
FAX: 410-321-6341
E-mail: mdero@aol.com
Web: derogatis-tests.com
Tests: 76

The College Board
45 Columbus Avenue
New York, NY 10023-6992
Tests: 289, 290

Consulting Psychologists Press, Inc.
3803 East Bayshore Road
Palo Alto, CA 94303
Telephone: 800-624-1765
FAX: 650-623-9273
E-mail: knw@cpp-db.com
Web: www.cpp-db.com
Tests: 43, 104, 172, 248, 294, 322, 337, 338, 359

CTB/McGraw-Hill
20 Ryan Ranch Road
Monterey, CA 93940-5703
Tests: 195

Curriculum Associates, Inc.
153 Rangeway Road
P.O. Box 2001
North Billerica, MA 01862-0901
Telephone: 800-225-0248
FAX: 800-366-1158
E-mail: cainfo@curriculumassociates.com
Web: www.curriculumassociates.com
Tests: 41, 303

Directional Insight International, Inc.
1111 McKinley Street
Ft. Worth, TX 76126
Telephone: 800-852-2001
FAX: 817-249-6266
E-mail: test@nsightsuccess.com
Web: www.nsightsuccess.com
Tests: 174

Education Associates
P.O. Box 23308
Louisville, KY 40223
Telephone: 800-626-2950
FAX: 502-327-5106
E-mail: stw@e-a-i.com
Web: www.educationassociates.com
Tests: 321

Educational Evaluations
Awre
Newnham, Gloucestershire GL14 1ET
England
Telephone: 01594 510503
FAX: 01594 510503
Tests: 176, 234, 327, 347

Educational Resources, Inc.
8910 West 62nd Terrace
P.O. Box 29160
Shawnee Mission, KS 66201
Telephone: 1-800-292-2273
FAX: 913-362-4627
E-mail: testing@eriworld.com
Web: www.eriworld.com
Tests: 318

Elbern Publications
P.O. Box 09497
Columbus, OH 43209
Telephone: 614-235-2643
FAX: 614-237-2637
Tests: 203

Ellsworth Krebs Associates
3615 130th Avenue, NE
Bellevue, WA 98005-1351
Telephone: 425-883-4762
FAX: 425-883-4762
Tests: 46

English Language Institute
University of Michigan
3020 North University Building
1205 North University Avenue
Ann Arbor, MI 48109-1057
Telephone: 734-764-2416
FAX: 734-763-0369
E-mail: melabelium@umich.edu
Web: www.lsa.umich.edu/eli/
Tests: 151

Evince Clinical Assessments
Attn. Dr. Norman G. Hoffmann
P.O. Box 17305
Smithfield, RI 02917
Telephone: 401-231-2993

FAX: 401-231-2055
E-mail: evinceassessment@aol.com
Tests: 34, 253, 270, 288

Guilford Publications, Inc.
72 Spring Street
New York, NY 10012
Telephone: 212-431-9800
FAX: 212-966-6708
Web: www.guilford.com
Tests: 7

Joseph Hartman Consulting Psychology, Inc.
Albanna Office Center
6015 Chester Circle, Suite 113
Jacksonville, FL 32217-2270
Telephone: 904-636-5757
E-mail: jhartman@bellsouth.net
Tests: 201

Hay Group
Hay Resources Direct
116 Huntington Avenue
Boston, MA 02116-5712
Telephone: 800-729-8074
FAX: 617-927-5008
E-mail: Haytrg@haygroup.com
Web: www.hayresourcesdirect.haygroup.com
Tests: 136

Mary J. Heppner, Ph.D.
Career Center
305 Noyes Hall
University of Missouri
Columbia, MO 65211
Tests: 45

High/Scope Educational Research Foundation
600 North River Street
Ypsilanti, MI 48198-2898
Telephone: 734-485-2000
FAX: 734-485-0704
E-mail: info@highscope.org
Web: www.highscope.org
Tests: 198, 311

Hodder & Stoughton Educational
Hodder Headline PLC
338 Euston Road
London NW1 3BH
England
Telephone: 0207 873 6000
FAX: 0207 873 6299
E-mail: chas.knight@hodder.co.uk
Web: www.hoddertests.co.uk
Tests: 27, 28, 84, 110, 124, 222

Hogrefe & Huber Publishers
P.O. Box 2487
Kirkland, WA 98083-2487
Telephone: 800-228-3749
FAX: 425-823-8324
E-mail: hh@hhpub.com
Web: www.hhpub.com
Tests: 73, 87, 98, 179, 216

Human Resource Development Press
22 Amherst Road
Amherst, MA 01002–9709
Tests: 140, 197, 326, 340, 342

Human Synergistics International
39819 Plymouth Road, C-8020
Plymouth, MI 48170-8020
Telephone: 800-622-7584
FAX: 734-459-5557
E-mail: info@humansyn.com
Web: www.humansyn.com
Tests: 324, 328, 334, 341, 354

The IDEA Center
211 South Seth Child Road
Manhattan, KS 66502-3089
Telephone: 800-255-2757
FAX: 785-532-5725
E-mail: IDEA@ksu.edu
Web: www.IDEA.ksu.edu
Tests: 121

Imaginart International, Inc.
307 Arizona Street
Bisbee, AZ 85603
Telephone: 520-432-5741
FAX: 520-432-5134
E-mail: imaginart@compuserve.com
Web: www.imaginartonline.com
Tests: 343, 356

The Institute for Matching Person & Technology, Inc.
486 Lake Road
Webster, NY 14580
Telephone: 585-671-3461
FAX: 585-671-3461
E-mail: impt97@aol.com
Web: members.aol.com/IMPT97/MPT.html
Tests: 145, 227

Institute for Personality and Ability Testing, Inc. (IPAT)
P.O. Box 1188
Champaign, IL 61824-1188
Telephone: 217-352-4739
FAX: 217-352-9674
E-mail: custserv@ipat.com
Web: www.ipat.com

Tests: 230, 231
International Forgiveness Institute
P.O. Box 6153
Madison, WI 53716-0153
Telephone: 608-231-9117
E-mail: GAYLEREED6@aol.com
Web: www.Forgiveness-institute.org
Tests: 89

James Stanfield Co., Inc.
P.O. Box 41058
Santa Barbara, CA 93140
Telephone: 800-421-6534
FAX: 805-897-1187
E-mail: maindesk@stanfield.com
Web: www.stanfield.com
Tests: 262, 268, 302, 350

Jossey-Bass, A Wiley Company
989 Market Street
San Francisco, CA 94103
Tests: 339

Kaplan Early Learning Company
1310 Lewisville-Clemmons Road
Lewisville, NC 27023
Tests: 81

Kendall/Hunt Publishing Company
4050 Westmark Drive
P.O. Box 1840
Dubuque, IA 52004-1840
Telephone: 800-228-0810
FAX: 800-772-9165
E-mail: orders@kendallhunt.com
Web: www.kendallhunt.com
Tests: 29

Lore International Institute
P.O. Box 1287
1130 Main Avenue
Durango, CO 81301
Telephone: 970-385-4955
FAX: 970-385-4998
E-mail: assessmentcenter@lorenet.com
Web: www.lorenet.com
Tests: 299

Mental Health, Law, and Policy Institute
Simon Fraser University
8888 University Drive
Burnaby, British Columbia V5A 1S6
Canada
Telephone: 604-291-4554
FAX: 604-268-6695
E-mail: mhlpi@sfu.ca
Web: www.sfu.ca/psychology/groups/mhlpi

Tests: 115
Meta Development LLC
4313 Garnet Street
Regina, Saskatchewan S4S 6J8
Canada
Tests: 152, 153, 154, 156, 157, 158, 159, 160, 161, 162, 163

MetriTech, Inc.
4106 Fieldstone Road
P.O. Box 6479
Champaign, IL 61826-6479
Telephone: 800-747-4868
FAX: 217-398-5798
E-mail: mtinfo@metritech.com
Web: www.metritech.com
Tests: 134

Mind Garden, Inc.
1690 Woodside Road, Suite #202
Redwood City, CA 94061
Telephone: 650-261-3500
FAX: 650-261-3505
E-mail: info@mindgarden.com
Web: www.mindgarden.com
Tests: 116, 277, 333

Moreno Educational Co.
P.O. Box 19329
San Diego, CA 91259-0329
Tests: 237

Multi-Health Systems, Inc.
P.O. Box 950
North Tonawanda, NY 14120-0950
Telephone: 416-424-1700
FAX: 416-424-1736
E-mail: customerservice@mhs.com
Web: www.mhs.com
Tests: 26, 52, 62, 63, 65, 66, 69, 71, 138, 183, 206, 232, 233, 239, 255, 267, 316, 218

National Council on Economic Education
1140 Avenue of the Americas
New York, NY 10036
Telephone: 212-730-7007
FAX: 212-730-1793
E-mail: econed@ncee.net
Web: www.ncee.net
Tests: 260

NCS Assessments
Sales Department
5605 Green Circle Drive
Minnetonka, MN 55343

Tests: 38, 117, 164
New Zealand Council for Educational Research
Education House West
178-182 Willis Street
Box 3237
Wellington 6000
New Zealand
Telephone: 00 64 4 384 7939
FAX: 00 64 4 384 7933
E-mail: jane.dugdale@nzcer.org.nz
Web: www.nzcer.org.nz
Tests: 90, 243

NFER-Nelson Publishing Co., Ltd.
Darville House
2 Oxford Road East
Windsor, Berkshire SL4 1DF
England
Tests: 25, 118, 189, 217

Personal Strengths Publishing
P.O. Box 2605
Carlsbad, CA 92018-2605
Telephone: 800-624-7347
FAX: 760-602-0087
E-mail: mail@PersonalStrengths.com
Web: www.PersonalStrengths.com
Tests: 315

Dr. Issy Pilowsky
University of Sydney
Department of Psychological Medicine
Camperdown, New South Wales 2006
Australia
Tests: 123

Piney Mountain Press, Inc.
P.O. Box 333
Cleveland, GA 30528
Telephone: 800-255-3127
FAX: 800-905-3127
E-mail: cyberguy@alltel.net
Web: www.pineymountain.com
Tests: 30, 171

PRO-ED
8700 Shoal Creek Blvd.
Austin, TX 78757-6897
Telephone: 800-897-3202
FAX: 512-451-8542
E-mail: proedrd2@aol.com
Web: www.proedinc.com
Tests: 15, 17, 18, 19, 36, 53, 59, 60, 61, 72, 82, 105, 108, 111, 112, 122, 165, 184, 187, 190, 191, 196, 208, 218, 219, 220, 238, 259, 261, 264, 265, 266, 285

Psych Press
Level 4 398 Lonsdale Street
Melbourne, VIC 3000
Australia
Tests: 92

Psychological Assessment Resources, Inc.
16204 N. Florida Avenue
Lutz, FL 33549-8119
Telephone: 800-331-8378
FAX: 800-727-9329
E-mail: custsupp@parinc.com
Web: www.parinc.com
Tests: 10, 11, 32, 37, 39, 40, 51, 54, 56, 67, 75, 77, 96,
    106, 126, 127, 132, 155, 166, 169, 177, 181, 207,
    209, 210, 211, 244, 249, 251, 269, 272, 280

The Psychological Corporation
19500 Bulverde Road
San Antonio, TX 78259
Telephone: 800-211-8378
FAX: 800-232-1223
E-mail: customer_care@harcourt.com
Web: www.PsychCorp.com
Tests: 6, 31, 42, 55, 64, 74, 128, 178, 271, 275, 276,
    287

The Psychological Corporation [Australia]
30–52 Smidmore Street
Marrickville, New South Wales 2204
Australia
Tests: 23, 24, 273, 85

The Psychological Corporation Europe
Harcourt Place
32 Jamestown Road
London NW1 7BY
United Kingdom
Telephone: 020 7424 4262
FAX: 020 7424 4457
Web: www.tpc-international.com
Tests: 88, 139, 167, 188, 224, 263

Psychological Services, Inc.
100 West Broadway, Suite #1100
Glendale, CA 91210
Telephone: 818-244-0033
FAX: 818-247-7223
Web: www.psionline.com
Tests: 102, 103

Psychology Press
29 West 35th Street
New York, NY 10001
Telephone: 212-216-7800

FAX: 212-643-1430
Web: www.psypress.com
Tests: 295, 297, 298, 313, 346, 361

Psychometric Affiliates
P.O. Box 807
Murfreesboro, TN 37133-0807
Telephone: 615-890-6296
FAX: 615-890-6296
E-mail: jheritage@a1.mtsu.edu
Tests: 21, 57, 97, 99, 100, 101, 114, 142, 146, 147, 148,
    149, 150, 168, 193, 225, 305

Reid London House
One North Dearborn, Suite 1600
Chicago, IL 60602
Tests: 03, 175, 185, 186, 202, 212, 236, 254, 257, 292,
    307, 312, 329, 349

Renaissance Learning, Inc.
P.O. Box 8036
2911 Peach Street
Wisconsin Rapids, WI 54495-8036
Telephone: 800-338-4204
FAX: 800-788-1272
E-mail: answers@renlearn.com
Web: www.renlearn.com
Tests: 240, 241, 242

Research Press
P.O. Box 9177
Champaign, IL 61826
Telephone: 217-352-3273
FAX: 217-352-1221
E-mail: gs@researchpress.com
Web: www.researchpress.com
Tests: 33, 119, 323

Richmond Products, Inc.
1021 S. Rogers Circle, Suite #6
Boca Raton, FL 33487-2894
Telephone: 561-994-2112
FAX: 561-994-2235
E-mail: RichmndPro@aol.com
Web: www.RichmondProducts.com
Tests: 120

Riverside Publishing
425 Spring Lake Drive
Itasca, IL 60143-2079
Telephone: 800-323-9540
FAX: 630-467-7192
Web: www.riversidepublishing.com
Tests: 281

The SASSI Institute
201 Camelot Lane
Springville, IN 47462
Telephone: 800-726-0526
FAX: 800-546-7995
E-mail: sassi@sassi.com
Web: www.sassi.com
Tests: 252

Search Institute
700 South 3rd Street, Suite 210
Minneapolis, MN 55415-1138
Telephone: 800-888-7828
FAX: 612-376-8956
E-mail: si@search-institute.org
Web: www.search-institute.org
Tests: 221

Sigma Assessment Systems, Inc.
511 Fort Street, Suite 435
P.O. Box 610984
Port Huron, MI 48061-0984
Telephone: 800-265-1285
FAX: 800-361-9411
E-mail: SIGMA@sigmaassessmentsystems.com
Web: www.sigmaassessmentsystems.com
Tests: 68, 129, 135, 170, 229, 330

SLACK Incorporated
6900 Grove Road
Thorofare, NJ 08086-9447
Tests: 330

SOARES Associates
111 Teeter Rock Road
Trumbull, CT 06611
Telephone: 203-375-5353
FAX: 203-375-2999
E-mail: atsoares@snet.net
Web: www.castleconsultants.com
Tests: 1, 226, 235, 256

Southwest Educational Development Laboratory
211 East Seventh Street, Suite 400
Austin, TX 78701-3281
Tests: 310

Stoelting Co.
620 Wheat Lane
Wood Dale, IL 60191
Telephone: 630-860-9700
FAX: 630-860-9775
E-mail: psychtests@stoeltingco.com
Web: www.stoeltingco.com/tests
Tests: 131, 245

Teachers College Press
Teachers College
Columbia University
525 W. 120th Street, Box 303
New York, NY 10027
Telephone: 800-575-6566
FAX: 802-864-7626
E-mail: tcpress@tc.columbia.edu
Web: www.teacherscollegepress.com
Tests: 20

The Test Agency Limited
Cray House
Woodlands Road
Henley-on-Thames, Oxfordshire RG9 4AE
England
Telephone: 01491 413413
FAX: 01491 572249
E-mail: info@testagency.com
Web: www.testagency.com
Tests: 141, 182, 283, 362

Therapy Skill Builders—A Division of The Psychological Corporation
19500 Bulverde Road
San Antonio, TX 78259
Tests: 331

University of Utah
Department of Psychology—SBS
390 South 1530 East
Salt Lake City, UT 84112-0251
Tests: 214

Village Publishing
73 Valley Drive
Furlong, PA 18925
Telephone: 800-553-7678
FAX: 215-794-3386
E-mail: VP@custody-vp.com
Web: www.custody-vp.com
Tests: 86

Walden Personnel Performance, Inc.
4155 Sherbrooke, W #100
Montreal, Quebec H3Z 1K9
Canada
Telephone: 514-989-9555
FAX: 514-989-9934
E-mail: tests@waldentesting.com
Web: www.waldentesting.com
Tests: 14, 301, 304, 308, 314, 317, 320, 332, 348, 357, 358

Western Psychological Services
12031 Wilshire Blvd.
Los Angeles, CA 90025-1251
Telephone: 310-478-2061
FAX: 310-478-7838
Web: www.wpspublish.com
Tests: 113, 22, 49, 125, 143, 247, 250, 274

Wide Range, Inc.
P.O. Box 3410
Wilmington, DE 19804-0250
Tests: 9, 279

Worley's Identity Discovery Profile, Inc.
44 Farmers Row
Groton, MA 01450-1802
Telephone: 978-448-2047
FAX: 978-448-3910
E-mail: WIDP@worleyid.com
Web: www.worleyid.com
Tests: 284

INDEX OF NAMES

This index indicates whether a citation refers to authorship of a test, a test review, or a reviewer's reference for a specific test. Numbers refer to test entries, not to pages. The abbreviations and numbers following the names may be interpreted as follows: "test, 73" indicates authorship of test 73; "rev, 86" indicates authorship of a review of test 86; "ref, 45" indicates a reference in one of the "Reviewer's References" sections for test 45. Reviewer names mentioned in cross references are also indexed.

Aarons, M.: test, 25; ref, 25
Abbeduto, L.: ref, 258
Abbott-Shim, M.: ref, 20
Abidin, R. R.: test, 181; ref, 181
Abrams, R. C.: ref,
Achenbach, T.: ref, 250
Achenbach, T. M.: ref, 7, 8, 12, 32, 47, 69, 201, 230, 233, 286
Acheson, S. K.: rev, 106
Ackerman, P. L.: rev, 87, 236; ref, 87
Ackerman, R. J.: test, 5, 192
Ackerman, T.: rev, 275
ACT, Inc.: test, 44, 94
Adams, E.: ref, 158
Adams, G. R.: rev, 72
Adams, W.: test, 279
Adcock, C. J.: rev, 231
Adler, L. E.: ref, 255
Adrian, M.: test, 107
Agid, Y.: ref, 255
Aidman, E. V.: rev, 273, 284
Aiken, L. R.: rev, 4, 219; ref, 206
Albanese, M. A.: rev, 166, 236
Aldarondo, F.: rev, 126, 225
Alden, L. E.: test, 128; ref 128
Aldous, C.: test, 83
Alexander, J.: ref, 72
Alexander, M.: ref, 61
Allen, C. C.: test, 210, 211; ref, 209, 211
Allen, M. J.: rev, 164
Allen, S. J.: rev, 180, 233
Allen, W.: ref, 254
Allison, J. A.: rev, 157, 232
Allison, S. N.: ref, 101
Altshuler, L.: ref, 255

American Association on Mental Retardation: ref, 6
American Bar Association: ref, 155
American Educational Research Association: ref, 9, 20, 29, 35, 36, 37, 54, 56, 62, 63, 71, 78, 86, 93, 107, 118, 120, 126, 128, 131, 136, 150, 154, 159, 166, 173, 176, 183, 186, 197, 207, 216, 225, 226, 232, 241, 261, 265, 272, 281, 285
American Psychiatric Association: ref, 7, 8, 9, 11, 12, 17, 34, 38, 47, 48, 65, 91, 96, 108, 116, 123, 127, 155, 201, 230, 249, 252, 286
American Psychological Association: ref, 9, 20, 29, 35, 36, 37, 54, 56, 62, 63, 71, 78, 86, 93, 107, 118, 120, 126, 128, 131, 136, 150, 154, 159, 166, 173, 176, 183, 186, 197, 207, 216, 225, 226, 232, 241, 261, 265, 272, 281, 285
Ammer, J. J.: test, 36
Amos, J. F.: ref, 120
Anastasi, A.: ref, 38, 87, 176, 184, 190, 285
Anastopoulos, A. D.: test, 7
Anderson, D. O.: rev, 103
Anderson, J. O.: rev, 28, 222
Anderson, M. Z.: ref, 248
Andersson, L.: rev, 59
Andreoli, A.: ref, 126
Andrews, D.: test, 138
Andrews, D.A.: ref, 138
Andrews, J. V.: rev, 29
Andrews, T. J.: ref, 46
Angoff, W. H.: ref, 5, 103
Angold, A.: ref, 52
Anthony, J. C.: ref, 166
Antoni, M.: test, 164
Antony, M. M.: ref, 179
Arbisi, P. A.: rev, 115, 231
Arenth, P. M.: ref, 252

SCORE INDEX

This Score Index lists all the scores, in alphabetical order, for all the tests included in The Fifteenth Mental Measurements Yearbook. *Because test scores can be regarded as operational definitions of the variable measured, sometimes the scores provide better leads to what a test actually measures than the test title or other available information. The Score Index is very detailed, and the reader should keep in mind that a given variable (or concept) of interest may be defined in several different ways. Thus the reader should look up these several possible alternative definitions before drawing final conclusions about whether tests measuring a particular variable of interest can be located in this volume. If the kind of score sought is located in a particular test or tests, the reader should then read the test descriptive information carefully to determine whether the test(s) in which the score is found is (are) consistent with reader purpose. Used wisely, the Score Index can be another useful resource in locating the right score in the right test. As usual, all numbers in the index are test numbers, not page numbers.*